Presented to

DORIS A. MONTMINY

By

1021 SEBASTIAN RD.
BAREFOOT BAY, FL 32976

On

FEB. 10, 2003

This Certifies that

(MARTEL)

DORIS ANNETTE MONTMINY

and

ROLAND RAYMOND MONTMINY

were united in

Holy Matrimony

on ___SAT.___ the ___30th___

day of ___AUGUST___ , ___1958___ A.D.

at ___ST. MATTHEW'S CHURCH___

in accordance with the laws of ___THE CHURCH___

Dated this _____ the _____

day of _____ , _____ A.D.

Officiating _____

Witness _____

Witness _____

Births

CHERYL ANN (11/25/59)

FAY MARIE (5/2/61)

LINDA-LEE MARIE (1/6/63)

ANNE-MARIE (8/15/64)

DAVID ROLAND (10/30/66)

Marriages

_____

_____

_____

_____

_____

_____

_____

_____

_____

Deaths

_____

_____

_____

_____

_____

_____

_____

_____

_____

_____

Family Record

_____

_____

_____

_____

_____

_____

_____

_____

_____

_____

Church Record

_____

_____

_____

_____

_____

_____

_____

_____

_____

_____

NEW INTERNATIONAL VERSION OF
The Holy Bible

The
HOLY
BIBLE

NEW INTERNATIONAL VERSION

Containing The Old Testament
and The New Testament

GRAND RAPIDS, MICHIGAN 49530

Contents

Preface to The New International Version   vii

THE BOOKS OF

The Old Testament

THE BOOKS OF

The New Testament

ABBREVIATIONS FOR THE BOOKS OF THE BIBLE

Genesis	Ge	Nahum	Na
Exodus	Ex	Habakkuk	Hab
Leviticus	Lev	Zephaniah	Zep
Numbers	Nu	Haggai	Hag
Deuteronomy	Dt	Zechariah	Zec
Joshua	Jos	Malachi	Mal
Judges	Jdg	Matthew	Mt
Ruth	Ru	Mark	Mk
1 Samuel	1Sa	Luke	Lk
2 Samuel	2Sa	John	Jn
1 Kings	1Ki	Acts	Ac
2 Kings	2Ki	Romans	Ro
1 Chronicles	1Ch	1 Corinthians	1Co
2 Chronicles	2Ch	2 Corinthians	2Co
Ezra	Ezr	Galatians	Gal
Nehemiah	Ne	Ephesians	Eph
Esther	Est	Philippians	Php
Job	Job	Colossians	Col
Psalms	Ps	1 Thessalonians	1Th
Proverbs	Pr	2 Thessalonians	2Th
Ecclesiastes	Ecc	1 Timothy	1Ti
Song of Songs	SS	2 Timothy	2Ti
Isaiah	Isa	Titus	Tit
Jeremiah	Jer	Philemon	Phm
Lamentations	La	Hebrews	Heb
Ezekiel	Eze	James	Jas
Daniel	Da	1 Peter	1Pe
Hosea	Hos	2 Peter	2Pe
Joel	Joel	1 John	1Jn
Amos	Am	2 John	2Jn
Obadiah	Ob	3 John	3Jn
Jonah	Jnh	Jude	Jude
Micah	Mic	Revelation	Rev

Preface

THE NEW INTERNATIONAL VERSION is a completely new translation of the Holy Bible made by over a hundred scholars working directly from the best available Hebrew, Aramaic and Greek texts. It had its beginning in 1965 when, after several years of exploratory study by committees from the Christian Reformed Church and the National Association of Evangelicals, a group of scholars met at Palos Heights, Illinois, and concurred in the need for a new translation of the Bible in contemporary English. This group, though not made up of official church representatives, was transdenominational. Its conclusion was endorsed by a large number of leaders from many denominations who met in Chicago in 1966.

Responsibility for the new version was delegated by the Palos Heights group to a self-governing body of fifteen, the Committee on Bible Translation, composed for the most part of biblical scholars from colleges, universities and seminaries. In 1967 the New York Bible Society (now the International Bible Society) generously undertook the financial sponsorship of the project—a sponsorship that made it possible to enlist the help of many distinguished scholars. The fact that participants from the United States, Great Britain, Canada, Australia and New Zealand worked together gave the project its international scope. That they were from many denominations—including Anglican, Assemblies of God, Baptist, Brethren, Christian Reformed, Church of Christ, Evangelical Free, Lutheran, Mennonite, Methodist, Nazarene, Presbyterian, Wesleyan and other churches—helped to safeguard the translation from sectarian bias.

How it was made helps to give the New International Version its distinctiveness. The translation of each book was assigned to a team of scholars. Next, one of the Intermediate Editorial Committees revised the initial translation, with constant reference to the Hebrew, Aramaic or Greek. Their work then went to one of the General Editorial Committees, which checked it in detail and made another thorough revision. This revision in turn was carefully reviewed by the Committee on Bible Translation, which made further changes and then released the final version for publication. In this way the entire Bible underwent three revisions, during each of which the translation was examined for its faithfulness to the original languages and for its English style.

All this involved many thousands of hours of research and discussion regarding the meaning of the texts and the precise way of putting them into English. It may well be that no other translation has been made by a more thorough process of review and revision from committee to committee than this one.

From the beginning of the project, the Committee on Bible Translation held to certain goals for the New International Version: that it would be an accurate translation and one that would have clarity and literary quality and so prove suitable for public and private reading, teaching, preaching, memorizing and liturgical use. The Committee also sought to preserve some measure of continuity with the long tradition of translating the Scriptures into English.

In working toward these goals, the translators were united in their commitment to the authority and infallibility of the Bible as God's Word in written form. They believe that it contains the divine answer to the deepest needs of humanity, that it sheds unique light on our path in a dark world, and that it sets forth the way to our eternal well-being.

The first concern of the translators has been the accuracy of the translation and its fidelity to the thought of the biblical writers. They have weighed the significance of the lexical and grammatical details of the Hebrew, Aramaic and Greek texts. At the same time, they have striven for more than a word-for-word translation. Because thought patterns and syntax differ from language to language, faithful communication of the meaning of the writers of the Bible demands frequent modifications in sentence structure and constant regard for the contextual meanings of words.

A sensitive feeling for style does not always accompany scholarship. Accordingly the Committee on Bible Translation submitted the developing version to a number of stylistic consultants. Two of them read every book of both Old and New Testaments twice—once before and once after the last major revision—and made invaluable suggestions. Samples of the translation were tested for clarity and ease of reading by various kinds of people—young and old, highly educated and less well educated, ministers and laymen.

Concern for clear and natural English—that the New International Version should be idiomatic but not idiosyncratic, contemporary but not dated—motivated the translators and consultants. At the same time, they tried to reflect the differing styles of the biblical writers. In view of the international use of English, the translators sought to avoid obvious Americanisms on the one hand and obvious Anglicisms on the other. A British edition reflects the comparatively few differences of significant idiom and of spelling.

As for the traditional pronouns "thou," "thee" and "thine" in reference to the Deity, the translators judged that to use these archaisms (along with the old verb forms such as "doest," "wouldest" and "hadst") would violate accuracy in translation. Neither Hebrew, Aramaic nor Greek uses special pronouns for the persons of the Godhead. A present-day translation is not enhanced by forms that in the time of the King James Version were used in everyday speech, whether referring to God or man.

For the Old Testament the standard Hebrew text, the Masoretic Text as published in the latest editions of *Biblia Hebraica*, was used throughout. The Dead Sea Scrolls contain material bearing on an earlier stage of the Hebrew text. They were consulted, as were the Samaritan Pentateuch and the ancient scribal traditions relating to textual changes. Sometimes a variant Hebrew reading in the margin of the Masoretic Text was followed instead of the text itself. Such instances, being variants within the Masoretic tradition, are not specified by footnotes. In rare cases, words in the consonantal text were divided differently from the way they appear in the Masoretic Text. Footnotes indicate this. The translators also consulted the more important early versions—the Septuagint; Aquila, Symmachus and Theodotion; the Vulgate; the Syriac Peshitta; the Targums; and for the Psalms the *Juxta Hebraica* of Jerome. Readings from these versions were occasionally followed where the Masoretic Text seemed doubtful and where accepted principles of textual criticism showed that one or more of these textual witnesses appeared to provide the correct reading. Such instances are footnoted. Sometimes vowel letters and vowel signs did not, in the judgment of the translators, represent the correct vowels for the original consonantal text. Accordingly some words were read with a different set of vowels. These instances are usually not indicated by footnotes.

The Greek text used in translating the New Testament was an eclectic one. No other piece of ancient literature has such an abundance of manuscript witnesses as does the New Testament. Where existing manuscripts differ, the translators made their choice of readings according to accepted principles of New Testament textual criticism. Footnotes call attention to places where there was uncertainty about what the original text was. The best current printed texts of the Greek New Testament were used.

There is a sense in which the work of translation is never wholly finished. This applies to all great literature and uniquely so to the Bible. In 1973 the New Testament in the New International Version was published. Since then, suggestions for corrections and revisions have been received from various sources. The Committee on Bible Translation carefully considered the suggestions and adopted a number of them. These were incorporated in the first printing of the entire Bible in 1978. Additional revisions were made by the Committee on Bible Translation in 1983 and appear in printings after that date.

As in other ancient documents, the precise meaning of the biblical texts is sometimes uncertain. This is more often the case with the Hebrew and Aramaic texts than with the Greek text. Although archaeological and linguistic discoveries in this century aid in understanding difficult passages, some uncertainties remain. The more significant of these have been called to the reader's attention in the footnotes.

In regard to the divine name *YHWH*, commonly referred to as the *Tetragrammaton*, the translators adopted the device used in most English versions of rendering that name as "Lord" in capital letters to distinguish it from *Adonai*, another Hebrew word rendered "Lord," for which small letters are used. Wherever the two names stand together in the Old Testament as a compound name of God, they are rendered "Sovereign Lord."

Because for most readers today the phrases "the Lord of hosts" and "God of hosts" have little meaning, this version renders them "the Lord Almighty" and "God Almighty." These renderings convey the sense of the Hebrew, namely, "he who is sovereign over all the 'hosts' (powers) in heaven and on earth, especially over the 'hosts' (armies) of Israel." For readers unacquainted with Hebrew this does not make clear the distinction between *Sabaoth* ("hosts" or "Almighty") and

Shaddai (which can also be translated "Almighty"), but the latter occurs infrequently and is always footnoted. When *Adonai* and *YHWH Sabaoth* occur together, they are rendered "the Lord, the LORD Almighty."

As for other proper nouns, the familiar spellings of the King James Version are generally retained. Names traditionally spelled with "ch," except where it is final, are usually spelled in this translation with "k" or "c," since the biblical languages do not have the sound that "ch" frequently indicates in English—for example, in *chant.* For well-known names such as Zechariah, however, the traditional spelling has been retained. Variation in the spelling of names in the original languages has usually not been indicated. Where a person or place has two or more different names in the Hebrew, Aramaic or Greek texts, the more familiar one has generally been used, with footnotes where needed.

To achieve clarity the translators sometimes supplied words not in the original texts but required by the context. If there was uncertainty about such material, it is enclosed in brackets. Also for the sake of clarity or style, nouns, including some proper nouns, are sometimes substituted for pronouns, and vice versa. And though the Hebrew writers often shifted back and forth between first, second and third personal pronouns without change of antecedent, this translation often makes them uniform, in accordance with English style and without the use of footnotes.

Poetical passages are printed as poetry, that is, with indentation of lines and with separate stanzas. These are generally designed to reflect the structure of Hebrew poetry. This poetry is normally characterized by parallelism in balanced lines. Most of the poetry in the Bible is in the Old Testament, and scholars differ regarding the scansion of Hebrew lines. The translators determined the stanza divisions for the most part by analysis of the subject matter. The stanzas therefore serve as poetic paragraphs.

As an aid to the reader, italicized sectional headings are inserted in most of the books. They are not to be regarded as part of the NIV text, are not for oral reading, and are not intended to dictate the interpretation of the sections they head.

The footnotes in this version are of several kinds, most of which need no explanation. Those giving alternative translations begin with "Or" and generally introduce the alternative with the last word preceding it in the text, except when it is a single-word alternative; in poetry quoted in a footnote a slant mark indicates a line division. Footnotes introduced by "Or" do not have uniform significance. In some cases two possible translations were considered to have about equal validity. In other cases, though the translators were convinced that the translation in the text was correct, they judged that another interpretation was possible and of sufficient importance to be represented in a footnote.

In the New Testament, footnotes that refer to uncertainty regarding the original text are introduced by "Some manuscripts" or similar expressions. In the Old Testament, evidence for the reading chosen is given first and evidence for the alternative is added after a semicolon (for example: Septuagint; Hebrew *father*). In such notes the term "Hebrew" refers to the Masoretic Text.

It should be noted that minerals, flora and fauna, architectural details, articles of clothing and jewelry, musical instruments and other articles cannot always be identified with precision. Also measures of capacity in the biblical period are particularly uncertain (see the table of weights and measures following the text).

Like all translations of the Bible, made as they are by imperfect man, this one undoubtedly falls short of its goals. Yet we are grateful to God for the extent to which he has enabled us to realize these goals and for the strength he has given us and our colleagues to complete our task. We offer this version of the Bible to him in whose name and for whose glory it has been made. We pray that it will lead many into a better understanding of the Holy Scriptures and a fuller knowledge of Jesus Christ the incarnate Word, of whom the Scriptures so faithfully testify.

The Committee on Bible Translation

June 1978
(Revised August 1983)

Names of the translators and editors may be secured
from the International Bible Society,
translation sponsors of the New International Version,
1820 Jet Stream Drive, Colorado Springs, Colorado,
80921-3696 U.S.A.

INTRODUCTION TO END OF PARAGRAPH REFERENCE SYSTEM

The New International Version has one of the most thorough, accurate and best organized cross-reference systems available. From its very comprehensive scope, only the references that are most widely used have been chosen to appear in this abridged edition.

Cross-references appear at the ends of paragraphs or following lines of poetry. The most significant references are placed first in the lists. If reference is made to a verse within the same chapter, that verse (indicated by "ver") is listed first.

In the Old Testament some references are marked with an asterisk (*), which means that the Old Testament verse or phrase is quoted in the New Testament (see, for example, Jeremiah 9:24). The corresponding information is provided in the New Testament by the NIV text note (see 1 Corinthians 1:31).

When two or more sections of Scripture are nearly identical or deal with the same event, the parallel passage is given the highest priority in the list of references. These parallel Scriptures often appear in the Gospels and in Samuel, Kings, and Chronicles.

To conserve space and avoid repetition, references that appear in the NIV text notes are not included in the reference lists.

The
Old Testament

Genesis

The Beginning

1 In the beginning God created the heavens and the earth. [2]Now the earth was[a] formless and empty, darkness was over the surface of the deep, and the Spirit of God was hovering over the waters. *Jn 1:1-2*

[3]And God said, "Let there be light," and there was light. [4]God saw that the light was good, and he separated the light from the darkness. [5]God called the light "day," and the darkness he called "night." And there was evening, and there was morning—the first day. *2Co 4:6; Ps 33:6,9; 74:16*

[6]And God said, "Let there be an expanse between the waters to separate water from water." [7]So God made the expanse and separated the water under the expanse from the water above it. And it was so. [8]God called the expanse "sky." And there was evening, and there was morning—the second day. *Ps 148:4; Jer 10:12*

[9]And God said, "Let the water under the sky be gathered to one place, and let dry ground appear." And it was so. [10]God called the dry ground "land," and the gathered waters he called "seas." And God saw that it was good. *Ps 104:6-9*

[11]Then God said, "Let the land produce vegetation: seed-bearing plants and trees on the land that bear fruit with seed in it, according to their various kinds." And it was so. [12]The land produced vegetation: plants bearing seed according to their kinds and trees bearing fruit with seed in it according to their kinds. And God saw that it was good. [13]And there was evening, and there was morning—the third day. *Ps 65:9-13*

[14]And God said, "Let there be lights in the expanse of the sky to separate the day from the night, and let them serve as signs to mark seasons and days and years, [15]and let them be lights in the expanse of the sky to give light on the earth." And it was so. [16]God made two great lights—the greater light to govern the day and the lesser light to govern the night. He also made the stars. [17]God set them in the expanse of the sky to give light on the

---

a 2 Or possibly *became*

earth, ¹⁸to govern the day and the night, and to separate light from darkness. And God saw that it was good. ¹⁹And there was evening, and there was morning—the fourth day. Ps 74:16; 104:19; 136:9

²⁰And God said, "Let the water teem with living creatures, and let birds fly above the earth across the expanse of the sky." ²¹So God created the great creatures of the sea and every living and moving thing with which the water teems, according to their kinds, and every winged bird according to its kind. And God saw that it was good. ²²God blessed them and said, "Be fruitful and increase in number and fill the water in the seas, and let the birds increase on the earth." ²³And there was evening, and there was morning—the fifth day. Ge 8:17

²⁴And God said, "Let the land produce living creatures according to their kinds: livestock, creatures that move along the ground, and wild animals, each according to its kind." And it was so. ²⁵God made the wild animals according to their kinds, the livestock according to their kinds, and all the creatures that move along the ground according to their

kinds. And God saw that it was good.

²⁶Then God said, "Let us make man in our image, in our likeness, and let them rule over the fish of the sea and the birds of the air, over the livestock, over all the earth,ᵃ and over all the creatures that move along the ground."

²⁷So God created man in his own image,   1Co 11:7
    in the image of God he
        created him;
male and female he created
    them.   Ge 5:2; Mk 10:6

²⁸God blessed them and said to them, "Be fruitful and increase in number; fill the earth and subdue it. Rule over the fish of the sea and the birds of the air and over every living creature that moves on the ground." Ge 9:1,7; Lev 26:9

²⁹Then God said, "I give you every seed-bearing plant on the face of the whole earth and every tree that has fruit with seed in it. They will be yours for food. ³⁰And to all the beasts of the earth and all the birds of the air and all the creatures that move on the ground—everything that has the breath of life in it—I give every green plant for food." And it was so. Ps 104:14,27

³¹God saw all that he had

made, and it was very good. And there was evening, and there was morning—the sixth day.   Ps 104:24

2 Thus the heavens and the earth were completed in all their vast array.   Isa 44:24

²By the seventh day God had finished the work he had been doing; so on the seventh day he rested*ᵃ* from all his work. ³And God blessed the seventh day and made it holy, because on it he rested from all the work of creating that he had done.   Ex 20:11; Heb 4:4

Adam and Eve

⁴This is the account of the heavens and the earth when they were created.

When the LORD God made the earth and the heavens— ⁵and no shrub of the field had yet appeared on the earth*ᵇ* and no plant of the field had yet sprung up, for the LORD God had not sent rain on the earth*ᵇ* and there was no man to work the ground, ⁶but streams*ᶜ* came up from the earth and watered the whole surface of the ground— ⁷the LORD God formed the man*ᵈ* from the dust of the ground and breathed into his nostrils the breath of life, and the man became a living being.   1Co 15:45

⁸Now the LORD God had planted a garden in the east, in Eden; and there he put the man he had formed. ⁹And the LORD God made all kinds of trees grow out of the ground—trees that were pleasing to the eye and good for food. In the middle of the garden were the tree of life and the tree of the knowledge of good and evil.   Ge 3:22,24

¹⁰A river watering the garden flowed from Eden; from there it was separated into four headwaters. ¹¹The name of the first is the Pishon; it winds through the entire land of Havilah, where there is gold. ¹²(The gold of that land is good; aromatic resin*ᵉ* and onyx are also there.) ¹³The name of the second river is the Gihon; it winds through the entire land of Cush.*ᶠ* ¹⁴The name of the third river is the Tigris; it runs along the east side of Asshur. And the fourth river is the Euphrates.   Da 10:4

¹⁵The LORD God took the man and put him in the Garden of Eden to work it and take care of it. ¹⁶And the LORD God commanded the man, "You are free to eat from any tree in the garden; ¹⁷but you must not eat from the tree of the knowledge of good and evil, for when you eat of it you will surely die."

¹⁸The LORD God said, "It is not good for the man to be alone. I will make a helper suitable for him."

¹⁹Now the LORD God had formed

ᵃ2 Or *ceased*; also in verse 3   *ᵇ5* Or *land*; also in verse 6   *ᶜ6* Or *mist*   *ᵈ7* The Hebrew for *man* (*adam*) sounds like and may be related to the Hebrew for *ground* (*adamah*); it is also the name *Adam* (see Gen. 2:20).   *ᵉ12* Or *good; pearls*   *ᶠ13* Possibly southeast Mesopotamia

out of the ground all the beasts of the field and all the birds of the air. He brought them to the man to see what he would name them; and whatever the man called each living creature, that was its name. ²⁰So the man gave names to all the livestock, the birds of the air and all the beasts of the field.   Ps 8:7

But for Adam*ᵃ* no suitable helper was found. ²¹So the LORD God caused the man to fall into a deep sleep; and while he was sleeping, he took one of the man's ribs*ᵇ* and closed up the place with flesh. ²²Then the LORD God made a woman from the rib*ᶜ* he had taken out of the man, and he brought her to the man.   1Co 11:8-9,12

²³The man said,

"This is now bone of my bones
    and flesh of my flesh;
she shall be called 'woman,*ᵈ*'
    for she was taken out of
    man."

²⁴For this reason a man will leave his father and mother and be united to his wife, and they will become one flesh.   Mt 19:5; Eph 5:31

²⁵The man and his wife were both naked, and they felt no shame.   Ge 3:7,10-11

The Fall of Man

3 Now the serpent was more crafty than any of the wild animals the LORD God had made. He said to the woman, "Did God really say, 'You must not eat from any tree in the garden'?"   2Co 11:3

²The woman said to the serpent, "We may eat fruit from the trees in the garden, ³but God did say, 'You must not eat fruit from the tree that is in the middle of the garden, and you must not touch it, or you will die.'"

⁴"You will not surely die," the serpent said to the woman. ⁵"For God knows that when you eat of it your eyes will be opened, and you will be like God, knowing good and evil."   Jn 8:44; Isa 14:14

⁶When the woman saw that the fruit of the tree was good for food and pleasing to the eye, and also desirable for gaining wisdom, she took some and ate it. She also gave some to her husband, who was with her, and he ate it. ⁷Then the eyes of both of them were opened, and they realized they were naked; so they sewed fig leaves together and made coverings for themselves.   1Ti 2:14; Jas 1:14-15; 1Jn 2:16

⁸Then the man and his wife heard the sound of the LORD God as he was walking in the garden in the cool of the day, and they hid from the LORD God among the trees of the garden. ⁹But the LORD God called to the man, "Where are you?"   Job 31:33

¹⁰He answered, "I heard you in

ᵃ20 Or *the man*   *ᵇ21* Or *took part of the man's side*   *ᶜ22* Or *part*   *ᵈ23* The Hebrew for *woman* sounds like the Hebrew for *man*.

the garden, and I was afraid because I was naked; so I hid."

¹¹And he said, "Who told you that you were naked? Have you eaten from the tree that I commanded you not to eat from?"

¹²The man said, "The woman you put here with me—she gave me some fruit from the tree, and I ate it."

¹³Then the Lᴏʀᴅ God said to the woman, "What is this you have done?"

The woman said, "The serpent deceived me, and I ate."   2Co 11:3

¹⁴So the Lᴏʀᴅ God said to the serpent, "Because you have done this,

"Cursed are you above all the
     livestock   Dt 28:15-20
and all the wild animals!
You will crawl on your belly
   and you will eat dust   Isa 65:25
   all the days of your life.
¹⁵And I will put enmity
   between you and the
       woman,
   and between your offspringᵃ
     and hers;   Rev 12:17; 1Jn 3:8
he will crushᵇ your head,
   and you will strike his
       heel."

¹⁶To the woman he said,

"I will greatly increase your
     pains in childbearing;
   with pain you will give birth
     to children.

Your desire will be for your
     husband,
   and he will rule over you."

¹⁷To Adam he said, "Because you listened to your wife and ate from the tree about which I commanded you, 'You must not eat of it,'

"Cursed is the ground because
     of you;   Ro 8:20-22; Ge 5:29
through painful toil you will
     eat of it
   all the days of your life.
¹⁸It will produce thorns and
     thistles for you,   Job 31:40
   and you will eat the plants
     of the field.   Ps 104:14
¹⁹By the sweat of your brow
   you will eat your food
until you return to the ground,
   since from it you were
     taken;
for dust you are
   and to dust you will return."

²⁰Adamᶜ named his wife Eve,ᵈ because she would become the mother of all the living.   1Ti 2:13

²¹The Lᴏʀᴅ God made garments of skin for Adam and his wife and clothed them. ²²And the Lᴏʀᴅ God said, "The man has now become like one of us, knowing good and evil. He must not be allowed to reach out his hand and take also from the tree of life and eat, and live forever." ²³So the Lᴏʀᴅ God banished him from the Garden of

---

ᵃ 15 Or *seed*   ᵇ 15 Or *strike*   ᶜ 20 Or *The man*   ᵈ 20 *Eve* probably means *living.*

Eden to work the ground from which he had been taken. ²⁴After he drove the man out, he placed on the east side*a* of the Garden of Eden cherubim and a flaming sword flashing back and forth to guard the way to the tree of life.

Cain and Abel

4 Adam*b* lay with his wife Eve, and she became pregnant and gave birth to Cain.*c* She said, "With the help of the LORD I have brought forth*d* a man." ²Later she gave birth to his brother Abel.

Now Abel kept flocks, and Cain worked the soil. ³In the course of time Cain brought some of the fruits of the soil as an offering to the LORD. ⁴But Abel brought fat portions from some of the first-born of his flock. The LORD looked with favor on Abel and his offering, ⁵but on Cain and his offering he did not look with favor. So Cain was very angry, and his face was downcast.   Heb 11:4; Ex 13:2,12; Nu 18:12

⁶Then the LORD said to Cain, "Why are you angry? Why is your face downcast? ⁷If you do what is right, will you not be accepted? But if you do not do what is right, sin is crouching at your door; it desires to have you, but you must master it."   Ro 6:16; Nu 32:23

⁸Now Cain said to his brother Abel, "Let's go out to the field."*e* And while they were in the field, Cain attacked his brother Abel and killed him.   Mt 23:35; 1Jn 3:12

⁹Then the LORD said to Cain, "Where is your brother Abel?"

"I don't know," he replied. "Am I my brother's keeper?"

¹⁰The LORD said, "What have you done? Listen! Your brother's blood cries out to me from the ground. ¹¹Now you are under a curse and driven from the ground, which opened its mouth to receive your brother's blood from your hand. ¹²When you work the ground, it will no longer yield its crops for you. You will be a restless wanderer on the earth."

¹³Cain said to the LORD, "My punishment is more than I can bear. ¹⁴Today you are driving me from the land, and I will be hidden from your presence; I will be a restless wanderer on the earth, and whoever finds me will kill me."   Ps 51:11; Nu 35:19,21,27,33

¹⁵But the LORD said to him, "Not so*f*; if anyone kills Cain, he will suffer vengeance seven times over." Then the LORD put a mark on Cain so that no one who found him would kill him. ¹⁶So Cain went out from the LORD's presence and lived in the land of Nod,*g* east of Eden.   Eze 9:4,6; Ge 2:8

¹⁷Cain lay with his wife, and she became pregnant and gave birth to

---

a 24 Or *placed in front*   *b 1* Or *The man*   *c 1 Cain* sounds like the Hebrew for *brought forth* or *acquired.*   *d 1* Or *have acquired*   *e 8* Samaritan Pentateuch, Septuagint, Vulgate and Syriac; Masoretic Text does not have *"Let's go out to the field."*   *f 15* Septuagint, Vulgate and Syriac; Hebrew *Very well*   *g 16 Nod* means *wandering* (see verses 12 and 14).

Enoch. Cain was then building a city, and he named it after his son Enoch. ¹⁸To Enoch was born Irad, and Irad was the father of Mehujael, and Mehujael was the father of Methushael, and Methushael was the father of Lamech. **Ps 49:11**

¹⁹Lamech married two women, one named Adah and the other Zillah. ²⁰Adah gave birth to Jabal; he was the father of those who live in tents and raise livestock. ²¹His brother's name was Jubal; he was the father of all who play the harp and flute. ²²Zillah also had a son, Tubal-Cain, who forged all kinds of tools out of*a* bronze and iron. Tubal-Cain's sister was Naamah.

²³Lamech said to his wives,

"Adah and Zillah, listen to me;
    wives of Lamech, hear my
        words.
I have killed*b* a man for
        wounding me,   **Ex 20:13**
    a young man for injuring
        me.
²⁴If Cain is avenged seven times,
    then Lamech seventy-seven
        times."   **ver 15; Mt 18:22**

²⁵Adam lay with his wife again, and she gave birth to a son and named him Seth,*c* saying, "God has granted me another child in place of Abel, since Cain killed him." ²⁶Seth also had a son, and he named him Enosh.   **Ge 5:3**

At that time men began to call on*d* the name of the LORD.   **Ge 12:8**

From Adam to Noah

5 This is the written account of Adam's line.

When God created man, he made him in the likeness of God. ²He created them male and female and blessed them. And when they were created, he called them "man.*e*"   **Ge 1:27; Eph 4:24; Col 3:10**

³When Adam had lived 130 years, he had a son in his own likeness, in his own image; and he named him Seth. ⁴After Seth was born, Adam lived 800 years and had other sons and daughters. ⁵Altogether, Adam lived 930 years, and then he died.   **Ge 3:19**

⁶When Seth had lived 105 years, he became the father*f* of Enosh. ⁷And after he became the father of Enosh, Seth lived 807 years and had other sons and daughters. ⁸Altogether, Seth lived 912 years, and then he died.   **Ge 4:26**

⁹When Enosh had lived 90 years, he became the father of Kenan. ¹⁰And after he became the father of Kenan, Enosh lived 815 years and had other sons and daughters. ¹¹Altogether, Enosh lived 905 years, and then he died.

¹²When Kenan had lived 70 years, he became the father of Mahalalel. ¹³And after he became the father of Mahalalel, Kenan lived

---

*a*22 Or *who instructed all who work in*   *b*23 Or *I will kill*   *c*25 *Seth* probably means *granted.*
*d*26 Or *to proclaim*   *e*2 Hebrew *adam*   *f*6 *Father* may mean *ancestor*; also in verses 7-26.

840 years and had other sons and daughters. ¹⁴Altogether, Kenan lived 910 years, and then he died.

¹⁵When Mahalalel had lived 65 years, he became the father of Jared. ¹⁶And after he became the father of Jared, Mahalalel lived 830 years and had other sons and daughters. ¹⁷Altogether, Mahalalel lived 895 years, and then he died.

¹⁸When Jared had lived 162 years, he became the father of Enoch. ¹⁹And after he became the father of Enoch, Jared lived 800 years and had other sons and daughters. ²⁰Altogether, Jared lived 962 years, and then he died.

²¹When Enoch had lived 65 years, he became the father of Methuselah. ²²And after he became the father of Methuselah, Enoch walked with God 300 years and had other sons and daughters. ²³Altogether, Enoch lived 365 years. ²⁴Enoch walked with God; then he was no more, because God took him away.   Ge 6:9; Mic 6:8; Heb 11:5

²⁵When Methuselah had lived 187 years, he became the father of Lamech. ²⁶And after he became the father of Lamech, Methuselah lived 782 years and had other sons and daughters. ²⁷Altogether, Methuselah lived 969 years, and then he died.

²⁸When Lamech had lived 182 years, he had a son. ²⁹He named him Noah[a] and said, "He will comfort us in the labor and painful toil of our hands caused by the ground the LORD has cursed." ³⁰After Noah was born, Lamech lived 595 years and had other sons and daughters. ³¹Altogether, Lamech lived 777 years, and then he died.   Ro 8:20

³²After Noah was 500 years old, he became the father of Shem, Ham and Japheth.   Ge 10:1

The Flood

6 When men began to increase in number on the earth and daughters were born to them, ²the sons of God saw that the daughters of men were beautiful, and they married any of them they chose. ³Then the LORD said, "My Spirit will not contend with[b] man forever, for he is mortal[c]; his days will be a hundred and twenty years."

⁴The Nephilim were on the earth in those days—and also afterward—when the sons of God went to the daughters of men and had children by them. They were the heroes of old, men of renown.

⁵The LORD saw how great man's wickedness on the earth had become, and that every inclination of the thoughts of his heart was only evil all the time. ⁶The LORD was grieved that he had made man on the earth, and his heart was filled with pain. ⁷So the LORD said, "I will wipe mankind, whom I have created, from the face of the earth—men and animals, and creatures that move along the ground, and

---

[a] 29 Noah sounds like the Hebrew for comfort.   [b] 3 Or My spirit will not remain in   [c] 3 Or corrupt

birds of the air—for I am grieved that I have made them." ⁸But Noah found favor in the eyes of the LORD.

⁹This is the account of Noah.

Noah was a righteous man, blameless among the people of his time, and he walked with God. ¹⁰Noah had three sons: Shem, Ham and Japheth.   Ge 5:22; Heb 11:7

¹¹Now the earth was corrupt in God's sight and was full of violence. ¹²God saw how corrupt the earth had become, for all the people on earth had corrupted their ways. ¹³So God said to Noah, "I am going to put an end to all people, for the earth is filled with violence because of them. I am surely going to destroy both them and the earth. ¹⁴So make yourself an ark of cypress*a* wood; make rooms in it and coat it with pitch inside and out. ¹⁵This is how you are to build it: The ark is to be 450 feet long, 75 feet wide and 45 feet high.*b* ¹⁶Make a roof for it and finish*c* the ark to within 18 inches*d* of the top. Put a door in the side of the ark and make lower, middle and upper decks. ¹⁷I am going to bring floodwaters on the earth to destroy all life under the heavens, every creature that has the breath of life in it. Everything on earth will perish. ¹⁸But I will establish my covenant with you, and you will enter the ark—you and your sons and your wife and your sons' wives with you. ¹⁹You are to bring into the ark two of all living creatures, male and female, to keep them alive with you. ²⁰Two of every kind of bird, of every kind of animal and of every kind of creature that moves along the ground will come to you to be kept alive. ²¹You are to take every kind of food that is to be eaten and store it away as food for you and for them."   Ge 9:9-16

²²Noah did everything just as God commanded him.   Ge 7:5,9,16

7 The LORD then said to Noah, "Go into the ark, you and your whole family, because I have found you righteous in this generation. ²Take with you seven*e* of every kind of clean animal, a male and its mate, and two of every kind of unclean animal, a male and its mate, ³and also seven of every kind of bird, male and female, to keep their various kinds alive throughout the earth. ⁴Seven days from now I will send rain on the earth for forty days and forty nights, and I will wipe from the face of the earth every living creature I have made."   Ge 6:9; Heb 11:7

⁵And Noah did all that the LORD commanded him.   Ge 6:22

⁶Noah was six hundred years old when the floodwaters came on the earth. ⁷And Noah and his sons

---

a 14 The meaning of the Hebrew for this word is uncertain.   *b 15* Hebrew *300 cubits long, 50 cubits wide and 30 cubits high* (about 140 meters long, 23 meters wide and 13.5 meters high)   *c 16* Or *Make an opening for light by finishing*   *d 16* Hebrew *a cubit* (about 0.5 meter)   *e 2* Or *seven pairs*; also in verse 3

and his wife and his sons' wives entered the ark to escape the waters of the flood. **8**Pairs of clean and unclean animals, of birds and of all creatures that move along the ground, **9**male and female, came to Noah and entered the ark, as God had commanded Noah. **10**And after the seven days the floodwaters came on the earth.   Ge 5:32

11In the six hundredth year of Noah's life, on the seventeenth day of the second month—on that day all the springs of the great deep burst forth, and the floodgates of the heavens were opened. **12**And rain fell on the earth forty days and forty nights.   Ge 8:2

13On that very day Noah and his sons, Shem, Ham and Japheth, together with his wife and the wives of his three sons, entered the ark. **14**They had with them every wild animal according to its kind, all livestock according to their kinds, every creature that moves along the ground according to its kind and every bird according to its kind, everything with wings. **15**Pairs of all creatures that have the breath of life in them came to Noah and entered the ark. **16**The animals going in were male and female of every living thing, as God had commanded Noah. Then the Lord shut him in.   Ge 6:19

17For forty days the flood kept coming on the earth, and as the waters increased they lifted the ark high above the earth. **18**The waters rose and increased greatly on the earth, and the ark floated on the surface of the water. **19**They rose greatly on the earth, and all the high mountains under the entire heavens were covered. **20**The waters rose and covered the mountains to a depth of more than twenty feet.*a, b* **21**Every living thing that moved on the earth perished— birds, livestock, wild animals, all the creatures that swarm over the earth, and all mankind. **22**Everything on dry land that had the breath of life in its nostrils died. **23**Every living thing on the face of the earth was wiped out; men and animals and the creatures that move along the ground and the birds of the air were wiped from the earth. Only Noah was left, and those with him in the ark.   2Pe 2:5

24The waters flooded the earth for a hundred and fifty days.

8 But God remembered Noah and all the wild animals and the livestock that were with him in the ark, and he sent a wind over the earth, and the waters receded. **2**Now the springs of the deep and the floodgates of the heavens had been closed, and the rain had stopped falling from the sky. **3**The water receded steadily from the earth. At the end of the hundred and fifty days the water had gone

---

a 20 Hebrew *fifteen cubits* (about 6.9 meters)   *b 20* Or *rose more than twenty feet, and the mountains were covered*

down, ⁴and on the seventeenth day of the seventh month the ark came to rest on the mountains of Ararat. ⁵The waters continued to recede until the tenth month, and on the first day of the tenth month the tops of the mountains became visible.   Ge 19:29; 9:15

⁶After forty days Noah opened the window he had made in the ark ⁷and sent out a raven, and it kept flying back and forth until the water had dried up from the earth. ⁸Then he sent out a dove to see if the water had receded from the surface of the ground. ⁹But the dove could find no place to set its feet because there was water over all the surface of the earth; so it returned to Noah in the ark. He reached out his hand and took the dove and brought it back to himself in the ark. ¹⁰He waited seven more days and again sent out the dove from the ark. ¹¹When the dove returned to him in the evening, there in its beak was a freshly plucked olive leaf! Then Noah knew that the water had receded from the earth. ¹²He waited seven more days and sent the dove out again, but this time it did not return to him.   Ge 7:12

¹³By the first day of the first month of Noah's six hundred and first year, the water had dried up from the earth. Noah then removed the covering from the ark and saw that the surface of the ground was dry. ¹⁴By the twenty-seventh day of the second month the earth was completely dry.

¹⁵Then God said to Noah, ¹⁶"Come out of the ark, you and your wife and your sons and their wives. ¹⁷Bring out every kind of living creature that is with you—the birds, the animals, and all the creatures that move along the ground—so they can multiply on the earth and be fruitful and increase in number upon it." Ge 1:22

¹⁸So Noah came out, together with his sons and his wife and his sons' wives. ¹⁹All the animals and all the creatures that move along the ground and all the birds—everything that moves on the earth—came out of the ark, one kind after another.

²⁰Then Noah built an altar to the LORD and, taking some of all the clean animals and clean birds, he sacrificed burnt offerings on it. ²¹The LORD smelled the pleasing aroma and said in his heart: "Never again will I curse the ground because of man, even though[a] every inclination of his heart is evil from childhood. And never again will I destroy all living creatures, as I have done.   Ge 9:11,15; 12:7-8; 22:2,13

²²"As long as the earth endures,
    seedtime and harvest,
    cold and heat,
    summer and winter,
    day and night
will never cease."   Jer 33:20,25

---

[a]21 Or man, for

God's Covenant With Noah

9 Then God blessed Noah and his sons, saying to them, "Be fruitful and increase in number and fill the earth. ²The fear and dread of you will fall upon all the beasts of the earth and all the birds of the air, upon every creature that moves along the ground, and upon all the fish of the sea; they are given into your hands. ³Everything that lives and moves will be food for you. Just as I gave you the green plants, I now give you everything.   Ge 1:22,29

⁴"But you must not eat meat that has its lifeblood still in it. ⁵And for your lifeblood I will surely demand an accounting. I will demand an accounting from every animal. And from each man, too, I will demand an accounting for the life of his fellow man.   Ge 4:10

⁶"Whoever sheds the blood of
   man,
   by man shall his blood be
      shed;   Ex 21:12,14; Mt 26:52
   for in the image of God
   has God made man.   Ge 1:26

⁷As for you, be fruitful and increase in number; multiply on the earth and increase upon it."

⁸Then God said to Noah and to his sons with him: ⁹"I now establish my covenant with you and with your descendants after you ¹⁰and with every living creature that was with you—the birds, the livestock and all the wild animals, all those that came out of the ark with you—every living creature on earth. ¹¹I establish my covenant with you: Never again will all life be cut off by the waters of a flood; never again will there be a flood to destroy the earth."   Ge 6:18; 8:21

¹²And God said, "This is the sign of the covenant I am making between me and you and every living creature with you, a covenant for all generations to come: ¹³I have set my rainbow in the clouds, and it will be the sign of the covenant between me and the earth. ¹⁴Whenever I bring clouds over the earth and the rainbow appears in the clouds, ¹⁵I will remember my covenant between me and you and all living creatures of every kind. Never again will the waters become a flood to destroy all life. ¹⁶Whenever the rainbow appears in the clouds, I will see it and remember the everlasting covenant between God and all living creatures of every kind on the earth."

¹⁷So God said to Noah, "This is the sign of the covenant I have established between me and all life on the earth."   ver 12; Ge 17:11

The Sons of Noah

¹⁸The sons of Noah who came out of the ark were Shem, Ham and Japheth. (Ham was the father of Canaan.) ¹⁹These were the three sons of Noah, and from them came the people who were scattered over the earth.   Ge 10:32

²⁰Noah, a man of the soil, pro-ceeded*a* to plant a vineyard. ²¹When he drank some of its wine, he became drunk and lay uncovered inside his tent. ²²Ham, the father of Canaan, saw his father's nakedness and told his two brothers outside. ²³But Shem and Japheth took a garment and laid it across their shoulders; then they walked in backward and covered their father's nakedness. Their faces were turned the other way so that they would not see their father's nakedness.   Hab 2:15

²⁴When Noah awoke from his wine and found out what his youngest son had done to him, ²⁵he said,

"Cursed be Canaan!   ver 18
   The lowest of slaves
   will he be to his brothers."

²⁶He also said,

"Blessed be the Lᴏʀᴅ, the God
   of Shem!
May Canaan be the slave of
   Shem.*b*   1Ki 9:21
²⁷May God extend the territory
   of Japheth*c*;   Ge 10:2-5
may Japheth live in the tents
   of Shem,   Eph 2:13-14
and may Canaan be his*d*
   slave."

²⁸After the flood Noah lived 350 years. ²⁹Altogether, Noah lived 950 years, and then he died.   Ge 2:17

The Table of Nations

10 This is the account of Shem, Ham and Japheth, Noah's sons, who themselves had sons after the flood.   Ge 2:4

The Japhethites

²The sons*e* of Japheth:
   Gomer, Magog, Madai, Javan, Tubal, Meshech and Tiras.   Eze 38:2,6; Rev 20:8
³The sons of Gomer:
   Ashkenaz, Riphath and Togarmah.   Eze 38:6; Jer 51:27
⁴The sons of Javan:
   Elishah, Tarshish, the Kittim and the Rodanim.*f*
   ⁵(From these the maritime peoples spread out into their territories by their clans within their nations, each with its own language.)   1Ch 1:5-7; Jnh 1:3

The Hamites

⁶The sons of Ham:
   Cush, Mizraim,*g* Put and Canaan.   ver 15; Ge 9:18
⁷The sons of Cush:
   Seba, Havilah, Sabtah, Raamah and Sabteca.

---

*a*20 Or *soil, was the first*   *b*26 Or *be his slave*   *c*27 *Japheth* sounds like the Hebrew for *extend.*
*d*27 Or *their*   *e*2 *Sons* may mean *descendants* or *successors* or *nations*; also in verses 3, 4, 6, 7, 20-23, 29 and 31.   *f*4 Some manuscripts of the Masoretic Text and Samaritan Pentateuch (see also Septuagint and 1 Chron. 1:7); most manuscripts of the Masoretic Text *Dodanim*   *g*6 That is, Egypt; also in verse

The sons of Raamah:
Sheba and Dedan.

8Cush was the father*a* of Nimrod, who grew to be a mighty warrior on the earth. **9**He was a mighty hunter before the LORD; that is why it is said, "Like Nimrod, a mighty hunter before the LORD." **10**The first centers of his kingdom were Babylon, Erech, Akkad and Calneh, in*b* Shinar.*c* **11**From that land he went to Assyria, where he built Nineveh, Rehoboth Ir,*d* Calah **12**and Resen, which is between Nineveh and Calah; that is the great city.　　Ge 11:9; Mic 5:6; Jnh 1:2

13Mizraim was the father of
the Ludites, Anamites, Lehabites, Naphtuhites, **14**Pathrusites, Casluhites (from whom the Philistines came) and Caphtorites.
15Canaan was the father of
Sidon his firstborn,*e* and of the Hittites, **16**Jebusites, Amorites, Girgashites, **17**Hivites, Arkites, Sinites, **18**Arvadites, Zemarites and Hamathites.　　Ge 9:18; Eze 28:21

Later the Canaanite clans scattered **19**and the borders of Canaan reached from Sidon toward Gerar as far as Gaza, and then toward Sodom, Gomorrah, Admah and Zeboiim, as far as Lasha.　　Ge 13:12
20These are the sons of Ham by their clans and languages, in their territories and nations.　　1Ch 1:8-16

The Semites

21Sons were also born to Shem, whose older brother was*f* Japheth; Shem was the ancestor of all the sons of Eber.　　Nu 24:24

22The sons of Shem:
Elam, Asshur, Arphaxad, Lud and Aram.　　Jer 49:34
23The sons of Aram:
Uz, Hul, Gether and Meshech.*g*　　Job 1:1
24Arphaxad was the father of*h* Shelah,
and Shelah the father of Eber.　　Lk 3:35
25Two sons were born to Eber:
One was named Peleg,*i* because in his time the earth was divided; his brother was named Joktan.
26Joktan was the father of
Almodad, Sheleph, Hazarmaveth, Jerah, **27**Hadoram, Uzal, Diklah, **28**Obal, Abimael, Sheba, **29**Ophir, Havilah and Jobab. All these were sons of Joktan.

30The region where they lived stretched from Mesha toward Sephar, in the eastern hill country. **31**These are the sons of Shem by

---

a 8 Father may mean *ancestor* or *predecessor* or *founder*; also in verses 13, 15, 24 and 26.　　*b 10* Or *Erech and Akkad—all of them in*　　*c 10* That is, Babylonia　　*d 11* Or *Nineveh with its city squares*　　*e 15* Or *of the Sidonians, the foremost*　　*f 21* Or *Shem, the older brother of*　　*g 23* See Septuagint and 1 Chron. 1:17; Hebrew *Mash*　　*h 24* Hebrew; Septuagint *father of Cainan, and Cainan was the father of*　　*i 25 Peleg* means *division.*

their clans and languages, in their territories and nations. Ge 11:10-27

32These are the clans of Noah's sons, according to their lines of descent, within their nations. From these the nations spread out over the earth after the flood. Ge 9:19

The Tower of Babel

11 Now the whole world had one language and a common speech. **2**As men moved eastward,*a* they found a plain in Shinar*b* and settled there. Ge 10:10
3They said to each other, "Come, let's make bricks and bake them thoroughly." They used brick instead of stone, and tar for mortar. **4**Then they said, "Come, let us build ourselves a city, with a tower that reaches to the heavens, so that we may make a name for ourselves and not be scattered over the face of the whole earth."
5But the LORD came down to see the city and the tower that the men were building. **6**The LORD said, "If as one people speaking the same language they have begun to do this, then nothing they plan to do will be impossible for them. **7**Come, let us go down and confuse their language so they will not understand each other." Ge 18:21; 42:23
8So the LORD scattered them

from there over all the earth, and they stopped building the city. **9**That is why it was called Babel*c* —because there the LORD confused the language of the whole world. From there the LORD scattered them over the face of the whole earth. Lk 1:51; Ge 10:10

From Shem to Abram

10This is the account of Shem.

Two years after the flood, when Shem was 100 years old, he became the father*d* of Arphaxad. **11**And after he became the father of Arphaxad, Shem lived 500 years and had other sons and daughters.
12When Arphaxad had lived 35 years, he became the father of Shelah. **13**And after he became the father of Shelah, Arphaxad lived 403 years and had other sons and daughters.*e* Lk 3:35
14When Shelah had lived 30 years, he became the father of Eber. **15**And after he became the father of Eber, Shelah lived 403 years and had other sons and daughters. Lk 3:35
16When Eber had lived 34 years, he became the father of Peleg. **17**And after he became the father of Peleg, Eber lived 430 years and had other sons and daughters.
18When Peleg had lived 30

---

a2 Or *from the east*; or *in the east*   *b2* That is, Babylonia   *c9* That is, Babylon; *Babel* sounds like the Hebrew for *confused.*   *d10 Father* may mean *ancestor*; also in verses 11-25.   *e12,13* Hebrew; Septuagint (see also Luke 3:35, 36 and note at Gen. 10:24) *35 years, he became the father of Cainan.* *13And after he became the father of Cainan, Arphaxad lived 430 years and had other sons and daughters, and then he died. When Cainan had lived 130 years, he became the father of Shelah. And after he became the father of Shelah, Cainan lived 330 years and had other sons and daughters*

years, he became the father of Reu. ¹⁹And after he became the father of Reu, Peleg lived 209 years and had other sons and daughters.

²⁰When Reu had lived 32 years, he became the father of Serug. ²¹And after he became the father of Serug, Reu lived 207 years and had other sons and daughters.

²²When Serug had lived 30 years, he became the father of Nahor. ²³And after he became the father of Nahor, Serug lived 200 years and had other sons and daughters.

²⁴When Nahor had lived 29 years, he became the father of Terah. ²⁵And after he became the father of Terah, Nahor lived 119 years and had other sons and daughters.   Lk 3:34

²⁶After Terah had lived 70 years, he became the father of Abram, Nahor and Haran.   Ge 10:21-31

²⁷This is the account of Terah.

Terah became the father of Abram, Nahor and Haran. And Haran became the father of Lot. ²⁸While his father Terah was still alive, Haran died in Ur of the Chaldeans, in the land of his birth. ²⁹Abram and Nahor both married. The name of Abram's wife was Sarai, and the name of Nahor's wife was Milcah; she was the daughter of Haran, the father of both Milcah and Iscah. ³⁰Now Sarai was barren; she had no children.   Ge 12:4; 16:1

³¹Terah took his son Abram, his grandson Lot son of Haran, and his daughter-in-law Sarai, the wife of his son Abram, and together they set out from Ur of the Chaldeans to go to Canaan. But when they came to Haran, they settled there.

³²Terah lived 205 years, and he died in Haran.

The Call of Abram

12 The Lord had said to Abram, "Leave your country, your people and your father's household and go to the land I will show you.   Ac 7:3; Heb 11:8

²"I will make you into a great
          nation   Ge 17:2,4; 18:18
    and I will bless you;   Ge 24:1,35
I will make your name great,
    and you will be a blessing.
³I will bless those who bless
          you,
    and whoever curses you I
          will curse;   Ge 27:29; Nu 24:9
and all peoples on earth
    will be blessed through you."

⁴So Abram left, as the Lord had told him; and Lot went with him. Abram was seventy-five years old when he set out from Haran. ⁵He took his wife Sarai, his nephew Lot, all the possessions they had accumulated and the people they had acquired in Haran, and they set out for the land of Canaan, and they arrived there.   Ge 11:31; 14:14

⁶Abram traveled through the land as far as the site of the great tree of Moreh at Shechem. At that time the Canaanites were in the land. ⁷The Lord appeared to

Abram and said, "To your off-spring[a] I will give this land." So he built an altar there to the Lord, who had appeared to him.

⁸From there he went on toward the hills east of Bethel and pitched his tent, with Bethel on the west and Ai on the east. There he built an altar to the Lord and called on the name of the Lord. ⁹Then Abram set out and continued toward the Negev.   Ge 4:26; 13:3

Abram in Egypt

¹⁰Now there was a famine in the land, and Abram went down to Egypt to live there for a while because the famine was severe. ¹¹As he was about to enter Egypt, he said to his wife Sarai, "I know what a beautiful woman you are. ¹²When the Egyptians see you, they will say, 'This is his wife.' Then they will kill me but will let you live. ¹³Say you are my sister, so that I will be treated well for your sake and my life will be spared because of you."   Ge 20:2

¹⁴When Abram came to Egypt, the Egyptians saw that she was a very beautiful woman. ¹⁵And when Pharaoh's officials saw her, they praised her to Pharaoh, and she was taken into his palace. ¹⁶He treated Abram well for her sake, and Abram acquired sheep and cattle, male and female donkeys, menservants and maidservants, and camels.   Ge 24:35; Job 1:3

¹⁷But the Lord inflicted serious diseases on Pharaoh and his household because of Abram's wife Sarai. ¹⁸So Pharaoh summoned Abram. "What have you done to me?" he said. "Why didn't you tell me she was your wife? ¹⁹Why did you say, 'She is my sister,' so that I took her to be my wife? Now then, here is your wife. Take her and go!" ²⁰Then Pharaoh gave orders about Abram to his men, and they sent him on his way, with his wife and everything he had.   Ge 20:1-18; 26:1-11; 1Ch 16:21

Abram and Lot Separate

13 So Abram went up from Egypt to the Negev, with his wife and everything he had, and Lot went with him. ²Abram had become very wealthy in livestock and in silver and gold.

³From the Negev he went from place to place until he came to Bethel, to the place between Bethel and Ai where his tent had been earlier ⁴and where he had first built an altar. There Abram called on the name of the Lord.   Ge 12:7-8

⁵Now Lot, who was moving about with Abram, also had flocks and herds and tents. ⁶But the land could not support them while they stayed together, for their possessions were so great that they were not able to stay together. ⁷And quarreling arose between Abram's herdsmen and the herdsmen of

a 7 Or seed

Lot. The Canaanites and Perizzites were also living in the land at that time.　Ge 26:20-21; 36:7; 12:6

⁸So Abram said to Lot, "Let's not have any quarreling between you and me, or between your herdsmen and mine, for we are brothers. ⁹Is not the whole land before you? Let's part company. If you go to the left, I'll go to the right; if you go to the right, I'll go to the left."

¹⁰Lot looked up and saw that the whole plain of the Jordan was well watered, like the garden of the LORD, like the land of Egypt, toward Zoar. (This was before the LORD destroyed Sodom and Gomorrah.) ¹¹So Lot chose for himself the whole plain of the Jordan and set out toward the east. The two men parted company: ¹²Abram lived in the land of Canaan, while Lot lived among the cities of the plain and pitched his tents near Sodom. ¹³Now the men of Sodom were wicked and were sinning greatly against the LORD.

¹⁴The LORD said to Abram after Lot had parted from him, "Lift up your eyes from where you are and look north and south, east and west. ¹⁵All the land that you see I will give to you and your offspring*a* forever. ¹⁶I will make your offspring like the dust of the earth, so that if anyone could count the dust, then your offspring could be counted. ¹⁷Go, walk through the length and breadth of the land, for I am giving it to you."　Ge 12:7

¹⁸So Abram moved his tents and went to live near the great trees of Mamre at Hebron, where he built an altar to the LORD.　Ge 8:20; 14:13,24

Abram Rescues Lot

14 At this time Amraphel king of Shinar,*b* Arioch king of Ellasar, Kedorlaomer king of Elam and Tidal king of Goiim ²went to war against Bera king of Sodom, Birsha king of Gomorrah, Shinab king of Admah, Shemeber king of Zeboiim, and the king of Bela (that is, Zoar). ³All these latter kings joined forces in the Valley of Siddim (the Salt Sea*c*). ⁴For twelve years they had been subject to Kedorlaomer, but in the thirteenth year they rebelled.　Nu 34:3,12; Jos 3:16

⁵In the fourteenth year, Kedorlaomer and the kings allied with him went out and defeated the Rephaites in Ashteroth Karnaim, the Zuzites in Ham, the Emites in Shaveh Kiriathaim ⁶and the Horites in the hill country of Seir, as far as El Paran near the desert. ⁷Then they turned back and went to En Mishpat (that is, Kadesh), and they conquered the whole territory of the Amalekites, as well as the Amorites who were living in Hazazon Tamar.　Dt 2:12,22; Ge 21:21

⁸Then the king of Sodom, the king of Gomorrah, the king of Admah, the king of Zeboiim and

---

a 15 Or *seed*; also in verse 16   *b* 1 That is, Babylonia; also in verse 9   *c* 3 That is, the Dead Sea

the king of Bela (that is, Zoar) marched out and drew up their battle lines in the Valley of Siddim ⁹against Kedorlaomer king of Elam, Tidal king of Goiim, Amraphel king of Shinar and Arioch king of Ellasar—four kings against five. ¹⁰Now the Valley of Siddim was full of tar pits, and when the kings of Sodom and Gomorrah fled, some of the men fell into them and the rest fled to the hills. ¹¹The four kings seized all the goods of Sodom and Gomorrah and all their food; then they went away. ¹²They also carried off Abram's nephew Lot and his possessions, since he was living in Sodom.   Ge 13:10; 19:17-29; Dt 29:23

¹³One who had escaped came and reported this to Abram the Hebrew. Now Abram was living near the great trees of Mamre the Amorite, a brother*a* of Eshcol and Aner, all of whom were allied with Abram. ¹⁴When Abram heard that his relative had been taken captive, he called out the 318 trained men born in his household and went in pursuit as far as Dan. ¹⁵During the night Abram divided his men to attack them and he routed them, pursuing them as far as Hobah, north of Damascus. ¹⁶He recovered all the goods and brought back his relative Lot and his possessions, together with the women and the other people.

¹⁷After Abram returned from defeating Kedorlaomer and the kings allied with him, the king of Sodom came out to meet him in the Valley of Shaveh (that is, the King's Valley).

¹⁸Then Melchizedek king of Salem*b* brought out bread and wine. He was priest of God Most High, ¹⁹and he blessed Abram, saying,

"Blessed be Abram by God
        Most High,
    Creator*c* of heaven and
        earth.
²⁰And blessed be*d* God Most
        High,
    who delivered your enemies
        into your hand."   Ge 24:27

Then Abram gave him a tenth of everything.   Heb 7:4

²¹The king of Sodom said to Abram, "Give me the people and keep the goods for yourself."

²²But Abram said to the king of Sodom, "I have raised my hand to the LORD, God Most High, Creator of heaven and earth, and have taken an oath ²³that I will accept nothing belonging to you, not even a thread or the thong of a sandal, so that you will never be able to say, 'I made Abram rich.' ²⁴I will accept nothing but what my men have eaten and the share that belongs to the men who went with me—to Aner, Eshcol and Mamre. Let them have their share."   Ex 6:8; Rev 10:5-6

---

a 13 Or *a relative*; or *an ally*   *b 18* That is, Jerusalem   *c 19* Or *Possessor*; also in verse 22   *d 20* Or *And praise be to*

God's Covenant With Abram

15 After this, the word of the Lord came to Abram in a vision: Nu 12:6

"Do not be afraid, Abram.
    I am your shield,[a]   Dt 33:29
    your very great reward.[b]"

²But Abram said, "O Sovereign Lord, what can you give me since I remain childless and the one who will inherit[c] my estate is Eliezer of Damascus?" ³And Abram said, "You have given me no children; so a servant in my household will be my heir."   Ac 7:5; Ge 24:2,34

⁴Then the word of the Lord came to him: "This man will not be your heir, but a son coming from your own body will be your heir." ⁵He took him outside and said, "Look up at the heavens and count the stars—if indeed you can count them." Then he said to him, "So shall your offspring be."   Gal 4:28

⁶Abram believed the Lord, and he credited it to him as righteousness.   Ro 4:3,20-24; Gal 3:6; Jas 2:23

⁷He also said to him, "I am the Lord, who brought you out of Ur of the Chaldeans to give you this land to take possession of it."   Ge 13:17

⁸But Abram said, "O Sovereign Lord, how can I know that I will gain possession of it?"   Lk 1:18

⁹So the Lord said to him, "Bring me a heifer, a goat and a ram, each three years old, along with a dove and a young pigeon."   Nu 19:2; Dt 21:3

¹⁰Abram brought all these to him, cut them in two and arranged the halves opposite each other; the birds, however, he did not cut in half. ¹¹Then birds of prey came down on the carcasses, but Abram drove them away.   Lev 1:17; Jer 34:18;

¹²As the sun was setting, Abram fell into a deep sleep, and a thick and dreadful darkness came over him. ¹³Then the Lord said to him, "Know for certain that your descendants will be strangers in a country not their own, and they will be enslaved and mistreated four hundred years. ¹⁴But I will punish the nation they serve as slaves, and afterward they will come out with great possessions. ¹⁵You, however, will go to your fathers in peace and be buried at a good old age. ¹⁶In the fourth generation your descendants will come back here, for the sin of the Amorites has not yet reached its full measure."   Ex 12:32-38,40; Ge 25:8

¹⁷When the sun had set and darkness had fallen, a smoking firepot with a blazing torch appeared and passed between the pieces. ¹⁸On that day the Lord made a covenant with Abram and said, "To your descendants I give this land, from the river[d] of Egypt to the great river, the Euphrates— ¹⁹the land of the Kenites, Keniz-

---

[a] 1 Or *sovereign*   [b] 1 Or *shield; / your reward will be very great*   [c] 2 The meaning of the Hebrew for this phrase is uncertain.   [d] 18 Or *Wadi*

zites, Kadmonites, ²⁰Hittites, Perizzites, Rephaites, ²¹Amorites, Canaanites, Girgashites and Jebusites."   Ge 17:2,4,7

Hagar and Ishmael

16 Now Sarai, Abram's wife, had borne him no children. But she had an Egyptian maidservant named Hagar; ²so she said to Abram, "The LORD has kept me from having children. Go, sleep with my maidservant; perhaps I can build a family through her."   Ge 11:30; 30:3-4,9-10; Gal 4:24-25

Abram agreed to what Sarai said. ³So after Abram had been living in Canaan ten years, Sarai his wife took her Egyptian maidservant Hagar and gave her to her husband to be his wife. ⁴He slept with Hagar, and she conceived.

When she knew she was pregnant, she began to despise her mistress. ⁵Then Sarai said to Abram, "You are responsible for the wrong I am suffering. I put my servant in your arms, and now that she knows she is pregnant, she despises me. May the LORD judge between you and me."   Ge 31:53

⁶"Your servant is in your hands," Abram said. "Do with her whatever you think best." Then Sarai mistreated Hagar; so she fled from her.   Jos 9:25

⁷The angel of the LORD found Hagar near a spring in the desert; it was the spring that is beside the road to Shur. ⁸And he said, "Hagar, servant of Sarai, where have you come from, and where are you going?"   Ge 21:17; 22:11,15

"I'm running away from my mistress Sarai," she answered.

⁹Then the angel of the LORD told her, "Go back to your mistress and submit to her." ¹⁰The angel added, "I will so increase your descendants that they will be too numerous to count."   Ge 13:16; 17:20

¹¹The angel of the LORD also said to her:

"You are now with child
   and you will have a son.
You shall name him Ishmael,ᵃ
   for the LORD has heard of
      your misery.   Ex 2:24; 3:7,9
¹²He will be a wild donkey of a
      man;
his hand will be against
      everyone
and everyone's hand against
      him,
and he will live in hostility
   towardᵇ all his brothers."

¹³She gave this name to the LORD who spoke to her: "You are the God who sees me," for she said, "I have now seenᶜ the One who sees me." ¹⁴That is why the well was called Beer Lahai Roiᵈ; it is still there, between Kadesh and Bered.

¹⁵So Hagar bore Abram a son, and Abram gave the name Ishmael

ᵃ11 Ishmael means God hears.   ᵇ12 Or live to the east / of   ᶜ13 Or seen the back of   ᵈ14 Beer Lahai Roi means well of the Living One who sees me.

to the son she had borne. ¹⁶Abram was eighty-six years old when Hagar bore him Ishmael.   Gal 4:22

The Covenant of Circumcision

17 When Abram was ninety-nine years old, the LORD appeared to him and said, "I am God Almighty*a*; walk before me and be blameless. ²I will confirm my covenant between me and you and will greatly increase your numbers."   Ge 15:18; 28:3; Dt 18:13

³Abram fell facedown, and God said to him, ⁴"As for me, this is my covenant with you: You will be the father of many nations. ⁵No longer will you be called Abram*b*; your name will be Abraham,*c* for I have made you a father of many nations. ⁶I will make you very fruitful; I will make nations of you, and kings will come from you. ⁷I will establish my covenant as an everlasting covenant between me and you and your descendants after you for the generations to come, to be your God and the God of your descendants after you. ⁸The whole land of Canaan, where you are now an alien, I will give as an everlasting possession to you and your descendants after you; and I will be their God."   Ge 12:2; 35:11; Ro 4:17

⁹Then God said to Abraham, "As for you, you must keep my covenant, you and your descendants after you for the generations to come. ¹⁰This is my covenant with you and your descendants after you, the covenant you are to keep: Every male among you shall be circumcised. ¹¹You are to undergo circumcision, and it will be the sign of the covenant between me and you. ¹²For the generations to come every male among you who is eight days old must be circumcised, including those born in your household or bought with money from a foreigner—those who are not your offspring. ¹³Whether born in your household or bought with your money, they must be circumcised. My covenant in your flesh is to be an everlasting covenant. ¹⁴Any uncircumcised male, who has not been circumcised in the flesh, will be cut off from his people; he has broken my covenant."   Ro 4:11; Lev 12:3; Ge 21:4

¹⁵God also said to Abraham, "As for Sarai your wife, you are no longer to call her Sarai; her name will be Sarah. ¹⁶I will bless her and will surely give you a son by her. I will bless her so that she will be the mother of nations; kings of peoples will come from her."

¹⁷Abraham fell facedown; he laughed and said to himself, "Will a son be born to a man a hundred years old? Will Sarah bear a child at the age of ninety?" ¹⁸And Abraham said to God, "If only Ishmael might live under your blessing!"

¹⁹Then God said, "Yes, but your wife Sarah will bear you a son, and

---

a 1 Hebrew *El-Shaddai*   *b* 5 Abram means *exalted father.*   *c* 5 Abraham means *father of many.*

you will call him Isaac.*ᵃ* I will establish my covenant with him as an everlasting covenant for his descendants after him. ²⁰And as for Ishmael, I have heard you: I will surely bless him; I will make him fruitful and will greatly increase his numbers. He will be the father of twelve rulers, and I will make him into a great nation. ²¹But my covenant I will establish with Isaac, whom Sarah will bear to you by this time next year." ²²When he had finished speaking with Abraham, God went up from him.

²³On that very day Abraham took his son Ishmael and all those born in his household or bought with his money, every male in his household, and circumcised them, as God told him. ²⁴Abraham was ninety-nine years old when he was circumcised, ²⁵and his son Ishmael was thirteen; ²⁶Abraham and his son Ishmael were both circumcised on that same day. ²⁷And every male in Abraham's household, including those born in his household or bought from a foreigner, was circumcised with him. Ro 4:11

The Three Visitors

18 The LORD appeared to Abraham near the great trees of Mamre while he was sitting at the entrance to his tent in the heat of the day. ²Abraham looked up and saw three men standing nearby. When he saw them, he hurried from the entrance of his tent to meet them and bowed low to the ground.

³He said, "If I have found favor in your eyes, my lord,*ᵇ* do not pass your servant by. ⁴Let a little water be brought, and then you may all wash your feet and rest under this tree. ⁵Let me get you something to eat, so you can be refreshed and then go on your way—now that you have come to your servant."

"Very well," they answered, "do as you say."

⁶So Abraham hurried into the tent to Sarah. "Quick," he said, "get three seahs*ᶜ* of fine flour and knead it and bake some bread."

⁷Then he ran to the herd and selected a choice, tender calf and gave it to a servant, who hurried to prepare it. ⁸He then brought some curds and milk and the calf that had been prepared, and set these before them. While they ate, he stood near them under a tree.

⁹"Where is your wife Sarah?" they asked him.

"There, in the tent," he said.

¹⁰Then the LORD*ᵈ* said, "I will surely return to you about this time next year, and Sarah your wife will have a son." Ro 9:9

Now Sarah was listening at the entrance to the tent, which was behind him. ¹¹Abraham and Sarah were already old and well ad-

ᵃ19 Isaac means *he laughs.*   *ᵇ3* Or *O Lord*   *ᶜ6* That is, probably about 20 quarts (about 22 liters)
ᵈ10 Hebrew *Then he*

vanced in years, and Sarah was past the age of childbearing. ¹²So Sarah laughed to herself as she thought, "After I am worn out and my master*ᵃ* is old, will I now have this pleasure?"   Ge 17:17; Ro 4:19; 1Pe 3:6

¹³Then the LORD said to Abraham, "Why did Sarah laugh and say, 'Will I really have a child, now that I am old?' ¹⁴Is anything too hard for the LORD? I will return to you at the appointed time next year and Sarah will have a son."

¹⁵Sarah was afraid, so she lied and said, "I did not laugh."

But he said, "Yes, you did laugh."

Abraham Pleads for Sodom

¹⁶When the men got up to leave, they looked down toward Sodom, and Abraham walked along with them to see them on their way. ¹⁷Then the LORD said, "Shall I hide from Abraham what I am about to do? ¹⁸Abraham will surely become a great and powerful nation, and all nations on earth will be blessed through him. ¹⁹For I have chosen him, so that he will direct his children and his household after him to keep the way of the LORD by doing what is right and just, so that the LORD will bring about for Abraham what he has promised him."

²⁰Then the LORD said, "The outcry against Sodom and Gomorrah is so great and their sin so grievous ²¹that I will go down and see if what they have done is as bad as the outcry that has reached me. If not, I will know."   Ge 19:13; Eze 16:46

²²The men turned away and went toward Sodom, but Abraham remained standing before the LORD.*ᵇ* ²³Then Abraham approached him and said: "Will you sweep away the righteous with the wicked? ²⁴What if there are fifty righteous people in the city? Will you really sweep it away and not spare*ᶜ* the place for the sake of the fifty righteous people in it? ²⁵Far be it from you to do such a thing— to kill the righteous with the wicked, treating the righteous and the wicked alike. Far be it from you! Will not the Judge*ᵈ* of all the earth do right?"   Nu 16:22; Ro 3:6

²⁶The LORD said, "If I find fifty righteous people in the city of Sodom, I will spare the whole place for their sake."   Jer 5:1

²⁷Then Abraham spoke up again: "Now that I have been so bold as to speak to the Lord, though I am nothing but dust and ashes, ²⁸what if the number of the righteous is five less than fifty? Will you destroy the whole city because of five people?"   Ge 2:7

"If I find forty-five there," he said, "I will not destroy it."

²⁹Once again he spoke to him, "What if only forty are found there?"

ᵃ12 Or *husband*   *ᵇ22* Masoretic Text; an ancient Hebrew scribal tradition *but the LORD remained standing before Abraham*   *ᶜ24* Or *forgive*; also in verse 26   *ᵈ25* Or *Ruler*

He said, "For the sake of forty, I will not do it."

³⁰Then he said, "May the Lord not be angry, but let me speak. What if only thirty can be found there?"

He answered, "I will not do it if I find thirty there."

³¹Abraham said, "Now that I have been so bold as to speak to the Lord, what if only twenty can be found there?"

He said, "For the sake of twenty, I will not destroy it."

³²Then he said, "May the Lord not be angry, but let me speak just once more. What if only ten can be found there?"   Jdg 6:39

He answered, "For the sake of ten, I will not destroy it."

³³When the Lord had finished speaking with Abraham, he left, and Abraham returned home.

Sodom and Gomorrah Destroyed

19 The two angels arrived at Sodom in the evening, and Lot was sitting in the gateway of the city. When he saw them, he got up to meet them and bowed down with his face to the ground. ²"My lords," he said, "please turn aside to your servant's house. You can wash your feet and spend the night and then go on your way early in the morning."   Ge 18:22

"No," they answered, "we will spend the night in the square."

³But he insisted so strongly that they did go with him and entered his house. He prepared a meal for them, baking bread without yeast, and they ate. ⁴Before they had gone to bed, all the men from every part of the city of Sodom—both young and old—surrounded the house. ⁵They called to Lot, "Where are the men who came to you tonight? Bring them out to us so that we can have sex with them."   Jdg 19:22; Ro 1:24-27

⁶Lot went outside to meet them and shut the door behind him ⁷and said, "No, my friends. Don't do this wicked thing. ⁸Look, I have two daughters who have never slept with a man. Let me bring them out to you, and you can do what you like with them. But don't do anything to these men, for they have come under the protection of my roof."   Jdg 19:24; 2Pe 2:7-8

⁹"Get out of our way," they replied. And they said, "This fellow came here as an alien, and now he wants to play the judge! We'll treat you worse than them." They kept bringing pressure on Lot and moved forward to break down the door.   Ac 7:27

¹⁰But the men inside reached out and pulled Lot back into the house and shut the door. ¹¹Then they struck the men who were at the door of the house, young and old, with blindness so that they could not find the door. Dt 28:28-29

¹²The two men said to Lot, "Do you have anyone else here—sons-in-law, sons or daughters, or any-

one else in the city who belongs to you? Get them out of here, ¹³because we are going to destroy this place. The outcry to the LORD against its people is so great that he has sent us to destroy it."

¹⁴So Lot went out and spoke to his sons-in-law, who were pledged to marry[a] his daughters. He said, "Hurry and get out of this place, because the LORD is about to destroy the city!" But his sons-in-law thought he was joking.   Nu 16:21

¹⁵With the coming of dawn, the angels urged Lot, saying, "Hurry! Take your wife and your two daughters who are here, or you will be swept away when the city is punished."   Nu 16:26; Rev 18:4

¹⁶When he hesitated, the men grasped his hand and the hands of his wife and of his two daughters and led them safely out of the city, for the LORD was merciful to them. ¹⁷As soon as they had brought them out, one of them said, "Flee for your lives! Don't look back, and don't stop anywhere in the plain! Flee to the mountains or you will be swept away!"   ver 26

¹⁸But Lot said to them, "No, my lords,[b] please! ¹⁹Your[c] servant has found favor in your[c] eyes, and you[c] have shown great kindness to me in sparing my life. But I can't flee to the mountains; this disaster will overtake me, and I'll die. ²⁰Look, here is a town near enough to run to, and it is small. Let me flee to it—it is very small, isn't it? Then my life will be spared."

²¹He said to him, "Very well, I will grant this request too; I will not overthrow the town you speak of. ²²But flee there quickly, because I cannot do anything until you reach it." (That is why the town was called Zoar.[d])   Ge 13:10

²³By the time Lot reached Zoar, the sun had risen over the land. ²⁴Then the LORD rained down burning sulfur on Sodom and Gomorrah—from the LORD out of the heavens. ²⁵Thus he overthrew those cities and the entire plain, including all those living in the cities—and also the vegetation in the land. ²⁶But Lot's wife looked back, and she became a pillar of salt.

²⁷Early the next morning Abraham got up and returned to the place where he had stood before the LORD. ²⁸He looked down toward Sodom and Gomorrah, toward all the land of the plain, and he saw dense smoke rising from the land, like smoke from a furnace.   Ge 18:22; Rev 18:9

²⁹So when God destroyed the cities of the plain, he remembered Abraham, and he brought Lot out of the catastrophe that overthrew the cities where Lot had lived.

Lot and His Daughters

³⁰Lot and his two daughters left

---

a 14 Or *were married to*   b 18 Or *No, Lord*; or *No, my lord*   c 19 The Hebrew is singular.   d 22 Zoar means *small*.

Zoar and settled in the mountains, for he was afraid to stay in Zoar. He and his two daughters lived in a cave. **31**One day the older daughter said to the younger, "Our father is old, and there is no man around here to lie with us, as is the custom all over the earth. **32**Let's get our father to drink wine and then lie with him and preserve our family line through our father." Ge 14:10

33That night they got their father to drink wine, and the older daughter went in and lay with him. He was not aware of it when she lay down or when she got up.

34The next day the older daughter said to the younger, "Last night I lay with my father. Let's get him to drink wine again tonight, and you go in and lie with him so we can preserve our family line through our father." **35**So they got their father to drink wine that night also, and the younger daughter went and lay with him. Again he was not aware of it when she lay down or when she got up.

36So both of Lot's daughters became pregnant by their father. **37**The older daughter had a son, and she named him Moab*a*; he is the father of the Moabites of today. **38**The younger daughter also had a son, and she named him Ben-Ammi*b*; he is the father of the Ammonites of today. Dt 2:9,19

Abraham and Abimelech

20 Now Abraham moved on from there into the region of the Negev and lived between Kadesh and Shur. For a while he stayed in Gerar, **2**and there Abraham said of his wife Sarah, "She is my sister." Then Abimelech king of Gerar sent for Sarah and took her. ver 12; Ge 12:13; 26:7

3But God came to Abimelech in a dream one night and said to him, "You are as good as dead because of the woman you have taken; she is a married woman." Ge 26:11

4Now Abimelech had not gone near her, so he said, "Lord, will you destroy an innocent nation? **5**Did he not say to me, 'She is my sister,' and didn't she also say, 'He is my brother'? I have done this with a clear conscience and clean hands."

6Then God said to him in the dream, "Yes, I know you did this with a clear conscience, and so I have kept you from sinning against me. That is why I did not let you touch her. **7**Now return the man's wife, for he is a prophet, and he will pray for you and you will live. But if you do not return her, you may be sure that you and all yours will die." 1Sa 7:5; 25:26,34

8Early the next morning Abimelech summoned all his officials, and when he told them all that had happened, they were very much afraid. **9**Then Abimelech called

---

a 37 Moab sounds like the Hebrew for *from father.*   *b 38* Ben-Ammi means *son of my people.*

Abraham in and said, "What have you done to us? How have I wronged you that you have brought such great guilt upon me and my kingdom? You have done things to me that should not be done." ¹⁰And Abimelech asked Abraham, "What was your reason for doing this?"   Ge 12:18

¹¹Abraham replied, "I said to myself, 'There is surely no fear of God in this place, and they will kill me because of my wife.' ¹²Besides, she really is my sister, the daughter of my father though not of my mother; and she became my wife. ¹³And when God had me wander from my father's household, I said to her, 'This is how you can show your love to me: Everywhere we go, say of me, "He is my brother." ' "   Ps 36:1; Ge 12:12; 26:7

¹⁴Then Abimelech brought sheep and cattle and male and female slaves and gave them to Abraham, and he returned Sarah his wife to him. ¹⁵And Abimelech said, "My land is before you; live wherever you like."

¹⁶To Sarah he said, "I am giving your brother a thousand shekels[a] of silver. This is to cover the offense against you before all who are with you; you are completely vindicated."   Ge 12:16; 13:9

¹⁷Then Abraham prayed to God, and God healed Abimelech, his wife and his slave girls so they could have children again, ¹⁸for the LORD had closed up every womb in Abimelech's household because of Abraham's wife Sarah.

The Birth of Isaac

21 Now the LORD was gracious to Sarah as he had said, and the LORD did for Sarah what he had promised. ²Sarah became pregnant and bore a son to Abraham in his old age, at the very time God had promised him. ³Abraham gave the name Isaac[b] to the son Sarah bore him. ⁴When his son Isaac was eight days old, Abraham circumcised him, as God commanded him. ⁵Abraham was a hundred years old when his son Isaac was born to him.

⁶Sarah said, "God has brought me laughter, and everyone who hears about this will laugh with me." ⁷And she added, "Who would have said to Abraham that Sarah would nurse children? Yet I have borne him a son in his old age."

Hagar and Ishmael Sent Away

⁸The child grew and was weaned, and on the day Isaac was weaned Abraham held a great feast. ⁹But Sarah saw that the son whom Hagar the Egyptian had borne to Abraham was mocking, ¹⁰and she said to Abraham, "Get rid of that slave woman and her son, for that slave woman's son will never share in the inheritance with my son Isaac."   Gal 4:30; Ge 16:15

---

a 16 That is, about 25 pounds (about 11.5 kilograms)   b 3 Isaac means he laughs.

11The matter distressed Abraham greatly because it concerned his son. **12**But God said to him, "Do not be so distressed about the boy and your maidservant. Listen to whatever Sarah tells you, because it is through Isaac that your offspring*a* will be reckoned. **13**I will make the son of the maidservant into a nation also, because he is your offspring." Ro 9:7; Heb 11:18

14Early the next morning Abraham took some food and a skin of water and gave them to Hagar. He set them on her shoulders and then sent her off with the boy. She went on her way and wandered in the desert of Beersheba. ver 31-32

15When the water in the skin was gone, she put the boy under one of the bushes. **16**Then she went off and sat down nearby, about a bowshot away, for she thought, "I cannot watch the boy die." And as she sat there nearby, she*b* began to sob.

17God heard the boy crying, and the angel of God called to Hagar from heaven and said to her, "What is the matter, Hagar? Do not be afraid; God has heard the boy crying as he lies there. **18**Lift the boy up and take him by the hand, for I will make him into a great nation." Ge 17:20; Ex 3:7

19Then God opened her eyes and she saw a well of water. So she went and filled the skin with water and gave the boy a drink. Nu 22:31

20God was with the boy as he grew up. He lived in the desert and became an archer. **21**While he was living in the Desert of Paran, his mother got a wife for him from Egypt. Ge 28:15; Lk 1:66; Ge 24:4,38

The Treaty at Beersheba

22At that time Abimelech and Phicol the commander of his forces said to Abraham, "God is with you in everything you do. **23**Now swear to me here before God that you will not deal falsely with me or my children or my descendants. Show to me and the country where you are living as an alien the same kindness I have shown to you." Ge 26:28; Ge 39:2,3

24Abraham said, "I swear it."

25Then Abraham complained to Abimelech about a well of water that Abimelech's servants had seized. **26**But Abimelech said, "I don't know who has done this. You did not tell me, and I heard about it only today."

27So Abraham brought sheep and cattle and gave them to Abimelech, and the two men made a treaty. **28**Abraham set apart seven ewe lambs from the flock, **29**and Abimelech asked Abraham, "What is the meaning of these seven ewe lambs you have set apart by themselves?" Ge 26:28,31

30He replied, "Accept these seven lambs from my hand as a witness that I dug this well."

---

a 12 Or *seed*   *b* 16 Hebrew; Septuagint *the child*

³¹So that place was called Beer-sheba,ᵃ because the two men swore an oath there. Ge 26:33

³²After the treaty had been made at Beersheba, Abimelech and Phicol the commander of his forces returned to the land of the Philistines. ³³Abraham planted a tamarisk tree in Beersheba, and there he called upon the name of the LORD, the Eternal God. ³⁴And Abraham stayed in the land of the Philistines for a long time. Ge 4:26

Abraham Tested

22 Some time later God tested Abraham. He said to him, "Abraham!" Dt 8:2,16; Heb 11:17

"Here I am," he replied.

²Then God said, "Take your son, your only son, Isaac, whom you love, and go to the region of Moriah. Sacrifice him there as a burnt offering on one of the mountains I will tell you about." Jn 3:16; Heb 11:17

³Early the next morning Abraham got up and saddled his donkey. He took with him two of his servants and his son Isaac. When he had cut enough wood for the burnt offering, he set out for the place God had told him about. ⁴On the third day Abraham looked up and saw the place in the distance. ⁵He said to his servants, "Stay here with the donkey while I and the boy go over there. We will worship and then we will come back to you."

⁶Abraham took the wood for the burnt offering and placed it on his son Isaac, and he himself carried the fire and the knife. As the two of them went on together, ⁷Isaac spoke up and said to his father Abraham, "Father?" Jn 19:17

"Yes, my son?" Abraham replied.

"The fire and wood are here," Isaac said, "but where is the lamb for the burnt offering?" Lev 1:10

⁸Abraham answered, "God himself will provide the lamb for the burnt offering, my son." And the two of them went on together.

⁹When they reached the place God had told him about, Abraham built an altar there and arranged the wood on it. He bound his son Isaac and laid him on the altar, on top of the wood. ¹⁰Then he reached out his hand and took the knife to slay his son. ¹¹But the angel of the LORD called out to him from heaven, "Abraham! Abraham!" Heb 11:17-19; Jas 2:21

"Here I am," he replied.

¹²"Do not lay a hand on the boy," he said. "Do not do anything to him. Now I know that you fear God, because you have not withheld from me your son, your only son." 1Sa 15:22; Jn 3:16; 1Jn 4:9

¹³Abraham looked up and there in a thicket he saw a ramᵇ caught

---

ᵃ31 Beersheba can mean well of seven or well of the oath.   ᵇ13 Many manuscripts of the Masoretic Text, Samaritan Pentateuch, Septuagint and Syriac; most manuscripts of the Masoretic Text a ram behind him.

by its horns. He went over and took the ram and sacrificed it as a burnt offering instead of his son. ¹⁴So Abraham called that place The Lord Will Provide. And to this day it is said, "On the mountain of the Lord it will be provided."

¹⁵The angel of the Lord called to Abraham from heaven a second time ¹⁶and said, "I swear by myself, declares the Lord, that because you have done this and have not withheld your son, your only son, ¹⁷I will surely bless you and make your descendants as numerous as the stars in the sky and as the sand on the seashore. Your descendants will take possession of the cities of their enemies, ¹⁸and through your offspring*a* all nations on earth will be blessed, because you have obeyed me."

¹⁹Then Abraham returned to his servants, and they set off together for Beersheba. And Abraham stayed in Beersheba.

Nahor's Sons

²⁰Some time later Abraham was told, "Milcah is also a mother; she has borne sons to your brother Nahor: ²¹Uz the firstborn, Buz his brother, Kemuel (the father of Aram), ²²Kesed, Hazo, Pildash, Jidlaph and Bethuel." ²³Bethuel became the father of Rebekah. Milcah bore these eight sons to Abraham's brother Nahor. ²⁴His concubine, whose name was Reumah, also had sons: Tebah, Gaham, Tahash and Maacah.   Ge 24:15

The Death of Sarah

23 Sarah lived to be a hundred and twenty-seven years old. ²She died at Kiriath Arba (that is, Hebron) in the land of Canaan, and Abraham went to mourn for Sarah and to weep over her.

³Then Abraham rose from beside his dead wife and spoke to the Hittites.*b* He said, ⁴"I am an alien and a stranger among you. Sell me some property for a burial site here so I can bury my dead."   Ps 105:12

⁵The Hittites replied to Abraham, ⁶"Sir, listen to us. You are a mighty prince among us. Bury your dead in the choicest of our tombs. None of us will refuse you his tomb for burying your dead."

⁷Then Abraham rose and bowed down before the people of the land, the Hittites. ⁸He said to them, "If you are willing to let me bury my dead, then listen to me and intercede with Ephron son of Zohar on my behalf ⁹so he will sell me the cave of Machpelah, which belongs to him and is at the end of his field. Ask him to sell it to me for the full price as a burial site among you."   Ge 25:9

¹⁰Ephron the Hittite was sitting among his people and he replied to Abraham in the hearing of all the Hittites who had come to the gate of his city. ¹¹"No, my lord," he

---

a 18 Or *seed*   *b 3* Or *the sons of Heth*; also in verses 5, 7, 10, 16, 18 and 20

said. "Listen to me; I give[a] you the field, and I give[a] you the cave that is in it. I give[a] it to you in the presence of my people. Bury your dead."   Ru 4:4

[12]Again Abraham bowed down before the people of the land [13]and he said to Ephron in their hearing, "Listen to me, if you will. I will pay the price of the field. Accept it from me so I can bury my dead there."

[14]Ephron answered Abraham, [15]"Listen to me, my lord; the land is worth four hundred shekels[b] of silver, but what is that between me and you? Bury your dead."

[16]Abraham agreed to Ephron's terms and weighed out for him the price he had named in the hearing of the Hittites: four hundred shekels of silver, according to the weight current among the merchants.   Jer 32:9

[17]So Ephron's field in Machpelah near Mamre—both the field and the cave in it, and all the trees within the borders of the field—was deeded [18]to Abraham as his property in the presence of all the Hittites who had come to the gate of the city. [19]Afterward Abraham buried his wife Sarah in the cave in the field of Machpelah near Mamre (which is at Hebron) in the land of Canaan. [20]So the field and the cave in it were deeded to Abraham by the Hittites as a burial site.

Isaac and Rebekah

24 Abraham was now old and well advanced in years, and the LORD had blessed him in every way. [2]He said to the chief[c] servant in his household, the one in charge of all that he had, "Put your hand under my thigh. [3]I want you to swear by the LORD, the God of heaven and the God of earth, that you will not get a wife for my son from the daughters of the Canaanites, among whom I am living, [4]but will go to my country and my own relatives and get a wife for my son Isaac."   Ge 12:1; 28:2

[5]The servant asked him, "What if the woman is unwilling to come back with me to this land? Shall I then take your son back to the country you came from?"   Heb 11:15

[6]"Make sure that you do not take my son back there," Abraham said. [7]"The LORD, the God of heaven, who brought me out of my father's household and my native land and who spoke to me and promised me on oath, saying, 'To your offspring[d] I will give this land'—he will send his angel before you so that you can get a wife for my son from there. [8]If the woman is unwilling to come back with you, then you will be released from this oath of mine. Only do not take my son back there." [9]So the servant put his hand under the thigh of his master Abraham and

---

[a]11 Or sell   [b]15 That is, about 10 pounds (about 4.5 kilograms)   [c]2 Or oldest   [d]7 Or seed

swore an oath to him concerning this matter.   Ge 12:7; 13:15; Gal 3:16

¹⁰Then the servant took ten of his master's camels and left, taking with him all kinds of good things from his master. He set out for Aram Naharaim^a and made his way to the town of Nahor. ¹¹He had the camels kneel down near the well outside the town; it was toward evening, the time the women go out to draw water.   1Sa 9:11

¹²Then he prayed, "O Lord, God of my master Abraham, give me success today, and show kindness to my master Abraham. ¹³See, I am standing beside this spring, and the daughters of the townspeople are coming out to draw water. ¹⁴May it be that when I say to a girl, 'Please let down your jar that I may have a drink,' and she says, 'Drink, and I'll water your camels too'— let her be the one you have chosen for your servant Isaac. By this I will know that you have shown kindness to my master."   Ge 26:24

¹⁵Before he had finished praying, Rebekah came out with her jar on her shoulder. She was the daughter of Bethuel son of Milcah, who was the wife of Abraham's brother Nahor. ¹⁶The girl was very beautiful, a virgin; no man had ever lain with her. She went down to the spring, filled her jar and came up again.   Ge 22:23; 26:7

¹⁷The servant hurried to meet her and said, "Please give me a little water from your jar."

¹⁸"Drink, my lord," she said, and quickly lowered the jar to her hands and gave him a drink.

¹⁹After she had given him a drink, she said, "I'll draw water for your camels too, until they have finished drinking." ²⁰So she quickly emptied her jar into the trough, ran back to the well to draw more water, and drew enough for all his camels. ²¹Without saying a word, the man watched her closely to learn whether or not the Lord had made his journey successful.

²²When the camels had finished drinking, the man took out a gold nose ring weighing a beka^b and two gold bracelets weighing ten shekels.^c ²³Then he asked, "Whose daughter are you? Please tell me, is there room in your father's house for us to spend the night?"   ver 47

²⁴She answered him, "I am the daughter of Bethuel, the son that Milcah bore to Nahor." ²⁵And she added, "We have plenty of straw and fodder, as well as room for you to spend the night."   Ge 11:29

²⁶Then the man bowed down and worshiped the Lord, ²⁷saying, "Praise be to the Lord, the God of my master Abraham, who has not abandoned his kindness and faithfulness to my master. As for me, the Lord has led me on the journey

---

^a10 That is, Northwest Mesopotamia   ^b22 That is, about 1/5 ounce (about 5.5 grams)   ^c22 That is, about 4 ounces (about 110 grams)

to the house of my master's relatives." ver 48,52; Ge 32:10

²⁸The girl ran and told her mother's household about these things. ²⁹Now Rebekah had a brother named Laban, and he hurried out to the man at the spring. ³⁰As soon as he had seen the nose ring, and the bracelets on his sister's arms, and had heard Rebekah tell what the man said to her, he went out to the man and found him standing by the camels near the spring. ³¹"Come, you who are blessed by the Lᴏʀᴅ," he said. "Why are you standing out here? I have prepared the house and a place for the camels." Ge 26:29; 29:5,12,13

³²So the man went to the house, and the camels were unloaded. Straw and fodder were brought for the camels, and water for him and his men to wash their feet. ³³Then food was set before him, but he said, "I will not eat until I have told you what I have to say." Ge 43:24

"Then tell us," Laban said.

³⁴So he said, "I am Abraham's servant. ³⁵The Lᴏʀᴅ has blessed my master abundantly, and he has become wealthy. He has given him sheep and cattle, silver and gold, menservants and maidservants, and camels and donkeys. ³⁶My master's wife Sarah has borne him a son in herᵃ old age, and he has given him everything he owns. ³⁷And my master made me swear an oath, and said, 'You must not

get a wife for my son from the daughters of the Canaanites, in whose land I live, ³⁸but go to my father's family and to my own clan, and get a wife for my son.' ³⁹"Then I asked my master, 'What if the woman will not come back with me?' ver 5

⁴⁰"He replied, 'The Lᴏʀᴅ, before whom I have walked, will send his angel with you and make your journey a success, so that you can get a wife for my son from my own clan and from my father's family. ⁴¹Then, when you go to my clan, you will be released from my oath even if they refuse to give her to you—you will be released from my oath.' ver 7-8

⁴²"When I came to the spring today, I said, 'O Lᴏʀᴅ, God of my master Abraham, if you will, please grant success to the journey on which I have come. ⁴³See, I am standing beside this spring; if a maiden comes out to draw water and I say to her, "Please let me drink a little water from your jar," ⁴⁴and if she says to me, "Drink, and I'll draw water for your camels too," let her be the one the Lᴏʀᴅ has chosen for my master's son.'

⁴⁵"Before I finished praying in my heart, Rebekah came out, with her jar on her shoulder. She went down to the spring and drew water, and I said to her, 'Please give me a drink.' 1Sa 1:13

⁴⁶"She quickly lowered her jar

from her shoulder and said, 'Drink, and I'll water your camels too.' So I drank, and she watered the camels also.   ver 18-19

⁴⁷"I asked her, 'Whose daughter are you?'   ver 23

"She said, 'The daughter of Bethuel son of Nahor, whom Milcah bore to him.'   ver 24

"Then I put the ring in her nose and the bracelets on her arms, ⁴⁸and I bowed down and worshiped the LORD. I praised the LORD, the God of my master Abraham, who had led me on the right road to get the granddaughter of my master's brother for his son. ⁴⁹Now if you will show kindness and faithfulness to my master, tell me; and if not, tell me, so I may know which way to turn."

⁵⁰Laban and Bethuel answered, "This is from the LORD; we can say nothing to you one way or the other. ⁵¹Here is Rebekah; take her and go, and let her become the wife of your master's son, as the LORD has directed."   Ps 118:23; Ge 31:7,24,29,42

⁵²When Abraham's servant heard what they said, he bowed down to the ground before the LORD. ⁵³Then the servant brought out gold and silver jewelry and articles of clothing and gave them to Rebekah; he also gave costly gifts to her brother and to her mother. ⁵⁴Then he and the men who were with him ate and drank and spent the night there.   ver 26

When they got up the next morning, he said, "Send me on my way to my master."   ver 56,59

⁵⁵But her brother and her mother replied, "Let the girl remain with us ten days or so; then you[a] may go."   Jdg 19:4

⁵⁶But he said to them, "Do not detain me, now that the LORD has granted success to my journey. Send me on my way so I may go to my master."   ver 12

⁵⁷Then they said, "Let's call the girl and ask her about it." ⁵⁸So they called Rebekah and asked her, "Will you go with this man?"

"I will go," she said.   Ru 1:16

⁵⁹So they sent their sister Rebekah on her way, along with her nurse and Abraham's servant and his men. ⁶⁰And they blessed Rebekah and said to her,   Ge 35:8

"Our sister, may you increase
    to thousands upon
        thousands;   Ge 17:16
may your offspring possess
    the gates of their enemies."

⁶¹Then Rebekah and her maids got ready and mounted their camels and went back with the man. So the servant took Rebekah and left.

⁶²Now Isaac had come from Beer Lahai Roi, for he was living in the Negev. ⁶³He went out to the field one evening to meditate,[b] and as he looked up, he saw cam-

els approaching. ⁶⁴Rebekah also looked up and saw Isaac. She got down from her camel ⁶⁵and asked the servant, "Who is that man in the field coming to meet us?"

"He is my master," the servant answered. So she took her veil and covered herself.

⁶⁶Then the servant told Isaac all he had done. ⁶⁷Isaac brought her into the tent of his mother Sarah, and he married Rebekah. So she became his wife, and he loved her; and Isaac was comforted after his mother's death.   Ge 25:20; 29:18,20

The Death of Abraham

25 Abraham took*ᵃ* another wife, whose name was Keturah. ²She bore him Zimran, Jokshan, Medan, Midian, Ishbak and Shuah. ³Jokshan was the father of Sheba and Dedan; the descendants of Dedan were the Asshurites, the Letushites and the Leummites. ⁴The sons of Midian were Ephah, Epher, Hanoch, Abida and Eldaah. All these were descendants of Keturah.   1Ch 1:32-33

⁵Abraham left everything he owned to Isaac. ⁶But while he was still living, he gave gifts to the sons of his concubines and sent them away from his son Isaac to the land of the east.   Ge 24:36; 21:10

⁷Altogether, Abraham lived a hundred and seventy-five years. ⁸Then Abraham breathed his last and died at a good old age, an old man and full of years; and he was gathered to his people. ⁹His sons Isaac and Ishmael buried him in the cave of Machpelah near Mamre, in the field of Ephron son of Zohar the Hittite, ¹⁰the field Abraham had bought from the Hittites.*ᵇ* There Abraham was buried with his wife Sarah. ¹¹After Abraham's death, God blessed his son Isaac, who then lived near Beer Lahai Roi.   Ge 15:15; 23:16; 49:29,33

Ishmael's Sons

¹²This is the account of Abraham's son Ishmael, whom Sarah's maidservant, Hagar the Egyptian, bore to Abraham.   Ge 16:15

¹³These are the names of the sons of Ishmael, listed in the order of their birth: Nebaioth the firstborn of Ishmael, Kedar, Adbeel, Mibsam, ¹⁴Mishma, Dumah, Massa, ¹⁵Hadad, Tema, Jetur, Naphish and Kedemah. ¹⁶These were the sons of Ishmael, and these are the names of the twelve tribal rulers according to their settlements and camps. ¹⁷Altogether, Ishmael lived a hundred and thirty-seven years. He breathed his last and died, and he was gathered to his people. ¹⁸His descendants settled in the area from Havilah to Shur, near the border of Egypt, as you go toward Asshur. And they lived in hostility toward*ᶜ* all their brothers.

---

*ᵃ*1 Or *had taken*   *ᵇ*10 Or *the sons of Heth*   *ᶜ*18 Or *lived to the east of*

Jacob and Esau

¹⁹This is the account of Abraham's son Isaac.

Abraham became the father of Isaac, ²⁰and Isaac was forty years old when he married Rebekah daughter of Bethuel the Aramean from Paddan Aram[a] and sister of Laban the Aramean. Ge 24:29

²¹Isaac prayed to the LORD on behalf of his wife, because she was barren. The LORD answered his prayer, and his wife Rebekah became pregnant. ²²The babies jostled each other within her, and she said, "Why is this happening to me?" So she went to inquire of the LORD. 1Ch 5:20; 1Sa 9:9

²³The LORD said to her,

"Two nations are in your
    womb, Ge 17:4
and two peoples from within
    you will be separated;
one people will be stronger
    than the other,
and the older will serve the
    younger." Ge 27:29,40

²⁴When the time came for her to give birth, there were twin boys in her womb. ²⁵The first to come out was red, and his whole body was like a hairy garment; so they named him Esau.[b] ²⁶After this, his brother came out, with his hand grasping Esau's heel; so he was named Jacob.[c] Isaac was sixty years old when Rebekah gave birth to them. Hos 12:3; Ge 27:11,36

²⁷The boys grew up, and Esau became a skillful hunter, a man of the open country, while Jacob was a quiet man, staying among the tents. ²⁸Isaac, who had a taste for wild game, loved Esau, but Rebekah loved Jacob. Ge 27:3,5

²⁹Once when Jacob was cooking some stew, Esau came in from the open country, famished. ³⁰He said to Jacob, "Quick, let me have some of that red stew! I'm famished!" (That is why he was also called Edom.[d]) Ge 32:3

³¹Jacob replied, "First sell me your birthright." Dt 21:16-17

³²"Look, I am about to die," Esau said. "What good is the birthright to me?"

³³But Jacob said, "Swear to me first." So he swore an oath to him, selling his birthright to Jacob.

³⁴Then Jacob gave Esau some bread and some lentil stew. He ate and drank, and then got up and left.

So Esau despised his birthright.

Isaac and Abimelech

26 Now there was a famine in the land—besides the earlier famine of Abraham's time—and Isaac went to Abimelech king of the Philistines in Gerar. ²The LORD appeared to Isaac and said, "Do not go down to Egypt; live in

---

a 20 That is, Northwest Mesopotamia   b 25 Esau may mean hairy; he was also called Edom, which means red.   c 26 Jacob means he grasps the heel (figuratively, he deceives).   d 30 Edom means red.

the land where I tell you to live. ³Stay in this land for a while, and I will be with you and will bless you. For to you and your descendants I will give all these lands and will confirm the oath I swore to your father Abraham. ⁴I will make your descendants as numerous as the stars in the sky and will give them all these lands, and through your offspringᵃ all nations on earth will be blessed, ⁵because Abraham obeyed me and kept my requirements, my commands, my decrees and my laws." ⁶So Isaac stayed in Gerar.   Ge 12:1,7,10

⁷When the men of that place asked him about his wife, he said, "She is my sister," because he was afraid to say, "She is my wife." He thought, "The men of this place might kill me on account of Rebekah, because she is beautiful."

⁸When Isaac had been there a long time, Abimelech king of the Philistines looked down from a window and saw Isaac caressing his wife Rebekah. ⁹So Abimelech summoned Isaac and said, "She is really your wife! Why did you say, 'She is my sister'?"

Isaac answered him, "Because I thought I might lose my life on account of her."

¹⁰Then Abimelech said, "What is this you have done to us? One of the men might well have slept with your wife, and you would have brought guilt upon us."   Ge 20:9

¹¹So Abimelech gave orders to all the people: "Anyone who molests this man or his wife shall surely be put to death."   Ge 12:10-20

¹²Isaac planted crops in that land and the same year reaped a hundredfold, because the LORD blessed him. ¹³The man became rich, and his wealth continued to grow until he became very wealthy. ¹⁴He had so many flocks and herds and servants that the Philistines envied him. ¹⁵So all the wells that his father's servants had dug in the time of his father Abraham, the Philistines stopped up, filling them with earth.   ver 3

¹⁶Then Abimelech said to Isaac, "Move away from us; you have become too powerful for us."   Ex 1:9

¹⁷So Isaac moved away from there and encamped in the Valley of Gerar and settled there. ¹⁸Isaac reopened the wells that had been dug in the time of his father Abraham, which the Philistines had stopped up after Abraham died, and he gave them the same names his father had given them.

¹⁹Isaac's servants dug in the valley and discovered a well of fresh water there. ²⁰But the herdsmen of Gerar quarreled with Isaac's herdsmen and said, "The water is ours!" So he named the well Esek,ᵇ because they disputed with him. ²¹Then they dug another well, but they quarreled over that one also; so he named it Sitnah.ᶜ ²²He

---

ᵃ4 Or seed   ᵇ20 Esek means dispute.   ᶜ21 Sitnah means opposition.

moved on from there and dug another well, and no one quarreled over it. He named it Rehoboth,[a] saying, "Now the LORD has given us room and we will flourish in the land." Ge 17:6

23From there he went up to Beersheba. 24That night the LORD appeared to him and said, "I am the God of your father Abraham. Do not be afraid, for I am with you; I will bless you and will increase the number of your descendants for the sake of my servant Abraham." 25Isaac built an altar there and called on the name of the LORD. There he pitched his tent, and there his servants dug a well.

26Meanwhile, Abimelech had come to him from Gerar, with Ahuzzath his personal adviser and Phicol the commander of his forces. 27Isaac asked them, "Why have you come to me, since you were hostile to me and sent me away?" Ge 21:22

28They answered, "We saw clearly that the LORD was with you; so we said, 'There ought to be a sworn agreement between us'— between us and you. Let us make a treaty with you 29that you will do us no harm, just as we did not molest you but always treated you well and sent you away in peace. And now you are blessed by the LORD." Ge 21:22; 24:31

30Isaac then made a feast for them, and they ate and drank. 31Early the next morning the men swore an oath to each other. Then Isaac sent them on their way, and they left him in peace. Ge 21:31

32That day Isaac's servants came and told him about the well they had dug. They said, "We've found water!" 33He called it Shibah,[b] and to this day the name of the town has been Beersheba.[c] Ge 21:14

34When Esau was forty years old, he married Judith daughter of Beeri the Hittite, and also Basemath daughter of Elon the Hittite. 35They were a source of grief to Isaac and Rebekah. Ge 27:46; 36:2

Jacob Gets Isaac's Blessing

27 When Isaac was old and his eyes were so weak that he could no longer see, he called for Esau his older son and said to him, "My son." Ge 25:25; 48:10

"Here I am," he answered.

2Isaac said, "I am now an old man and don't know the day of my death. 3Now then, get your weapons—your quiver and bow—and go out to the open country to hunt some wild game for me. 4Prepare me the kind of tasty food I like and bring it to me to eat, so that I may give you my blessing before I die."

5Now Rebekah was listening as Isaac spoke to his son Esau. When Esau left for the open country to

---

a 22 Rehoboth means room.　b 33 Shibah can mean oath or seven.　c 33 Beersheba can mean well of the oath or well of seven.

hunt game and bring it back, 6Rebekah said to her son Jacob, "Look, I overheard your father say to your brother Esau, 7'Bring me some game and prepare me some tasty food to eat, so that I may give you my blessing in the presence of the LORD before I die.' 8Now, my son, listen carefully and do what I tell you: 9Go out to the flock and bring me two choice young goats, so I can prepare some tasty food for your father, just the way he likes it. 10Then take it to your father to eat, so that he may give you his blessing before he dies."

11Jacob said to Rebekah his mother, "But my brother Esau is a hairy man, and I'm a man with smooth skin. 12What if my father touches me? I would appear to be tricking him and would bring down a curse on myself rather than a blessing."   ver 22; Ge 25:25

13His mother said to him, "My son, let the curse fall on me. Just do what I say; go and get them for me."   Mt 27:25

14So he went and got them and brought them to his mother, and she prepared some tasty food, just the way his father liked it. 15Then Rebekah took the best clothes of Esau her older son, which she had in the house, and put them on her younger son Jacob. 16She also covered his hands and the smooth part of his neck with the goatskins. 17Then she handed to her son Jacob the tasty food and the bread she had made.   ver 27

18He went to his father and said, "My father."

"Yes, my son," he answered. "Who is it?"

19Jacob said to his father, "I am Esau your firstborn. I have done as you told me. Please sit up and eat some of my game so that you may give me your blessing."   ver 4

20Isaac asked his son, "How did you find it so quickly, my son?"

"The LORD your God gave me success," he replied.   Ge 24:12

21Then Isaac said to Jacob, "Come near so I can touch you, my son, to know whether you really are my son Esau or not."   ver 12

22Jacob went close to his father Isaac, who touched him and said, "The voice is the voice of Jacob, but the hands are the hands of Esau." 23He did not recognize him, for his hands were hairy like those of his brother Esau; so he blessed him. 24"Are you really my son Esau?" he asked.   ver 16; Ge 45:4

"I am," he replied.

25Then he said, "My son, bring me some of your game to eat, so that I may give you my blessing."

Jacob brought it to him and he ate; and he brought some wine and he drank. 26Then his father Isaac said to him, "Come here, my son, and kiss me."

27So he went to him and kissed him. When Isaac caught the smell of his clothes, he blessed him and said,   Heb 11:20; SS 4:11

"Ah, the smell of my son

is like the smell of a field
that the LORD has blessed.
²⁸May God give you of heaven's
    dew   Dt 33:13
and of earth's richness—
an abundance of grain and
    new wine.   Dt 33:28
²⁹May nations serve you   Isa 49:7,23
and peoples bow down to
    you.   Ge 9:25; 25:23
Be lord over your brothers,
and may the sons of your
    mother bow down to
    you.
May those who curse you be
    cursed
and those who bless you be
    blessed."   Ge 12:3

³⁰After Isaac finished blessing him and Jacob had scarcely left his father's presence, his brother Esau came in from hunting. ³¹He too prepared some tasty food and brought it to his father. Then he said to him, "My father, sit up and eat some of my game, so that you may give me your blessing." ver 4

³²His father Isaac asked him, "Who are you?"

"I am your son," he answered, "your firstborn, Esau."

³³Isaac trembled violently and said, "Who was it, then, that hunted game and brought it to me? I ate it just before you came and I blessed him—and indeed he will be blessed!" Ge 28:3,4; Ro 11:29

³⁴When Esau heard his father's words, he burst out with a loud and bitter cry and said to his father, "Bless me—me too, my father!" Heb 12:17

³⁵But he said, "Your brother came deceitfully and took your blessing." Jer 9:4

³⁶Esau said, "Isn't he rightly named Jacob[a]? He has deceived me these two times: He took my birthright, and now he's taken my blessing!" Then he asked, "Haven't you reserved any blessing for me?" Ge 25:26,33

³⁷Isaac answered Esau, "I have made him lord over you and have made all his relatives his servants, and I have sustained him with grain and new wine. So what can I possibly do for you, my son?"

³⁸Esau said to his father, "Do you have only one blessing, my father? Bless me too, my father!" Then Esau wept aloud. Heb 12:17

³⁹His father Isaac answered him,

"Your dwelling will be
    away from the earth's
    richness,
    away from the dew of
    heaven above.   ver 28
⁴⁰You will live by the sword
and you will serve your
    brother.   Ge 25:23
But when you grow restless,
    you will throw his yoke
    from off your neck." 2Ki 8:20-22

---

[a] 36 *Jacob* means *he grasps the heel* (figuratively, *he deceives*).

Jacob Flees to Laban

41Esau held a grudge against Jacob because of the blessing his father had given him. He said to himself, "The days of mourning for my father are near; then I will kill my brother Jacob." *Ge 32:11*

42When Rebekah was told what her older son Esau had said, she sent for her younger son Jacob and said to him, "Your brother Esau is consoling himself with the thought of killing you. **43**Now then, my son, do what I say: Flee at once to my brother Laban in Haran. **44**Stay with him for a while until your brother's fury subsides. **45**When your brother is no longer angry with you and forgets what you did to him, I'll send word for you to come back from there. Why should I lose both of you in one day?" *ver 8; Ge 11:31*

46Then Rebekah said to Isaac, "I'm disgusted with living because of these Hittite women. If Jacob takes a wife from among the women of this land, from Hittite women like these, my life will not be worth living." *Ge 26:35*

28 So Isaac called for Jacob and blessed[a] him and commanded him: "Do not marry a Canaanite woman. **2**Go at once to Paddan Aram,[b] to the house of your mother's father Bethuel. Take a wife for yourself there, from among the daughters of Laban, your mother's brother. **3**May God Almighty[c] bless you and make you fruitful and increase your numbers until you become a community of peoples. **4**May he give you and your descendants the blessing given to Abraham, so that you may take possession of the land where you now live as an alien, the land God gave to Abraham." **5**Then Isaac sent Jacob on his way, and he went to Paddan Aram, to Laban son of Bethuel the Aramean, the brother of Rebekah, who was the mother of Jacob and Esau. *Ge 12:2-3; 17:8; 24:3*

6Now Esau learned that Isaac had blessed Jacob and had sent him to Paddan Aram to take a wife from there, and that when he blessed him he commanded him, "Do not marry a Canaanite woman," **7**and that Jacob had obeyed his father and mother and had gone to Paddan Aram. **8**Esau then realized how displeasing the Canaanite women were to his father Isaac; **9**so he went to Ishmael and married Mahalath, the sister of Nebaioth and daughter of Ishmael son of Abraham, in addition to the wives he already had. *Ge 26:34-35*

Jacob's Dream at Bethel

10Jacob left Beersheba and set out for Haran. **11**When he reached a certain place, he stopped for the night because the sun had set. Taking one of the stones there, he put it under his head and lay down

---

a 1 Or greeted   b 2 That is, Northwest Mesopotamia; also in verses 5, 6 and 7   c 3 Hebrew El-Shaddai

to sleep. ¹²He had a dream in which he saw a stairway*a* resting on the earth, with its top reaching to heaven, and the angels of God were ascending and descending on it. ¹³There above it*b* stood the LORD, and he said: "I am the LORD, the God of your father Abraham and the God of Isaac. I will give you and your descendants the land on which you are lying. ¹⁴Your descendants will be like the dust of the earth, and you will spread out to the west and to the east, to the north and to the south. All peoples on earth will be blessed through you and your offspring. ¹⁵I am with you and will watch over you wherever you go, and I will bring you back to this land. I will not leave you until I have done what I have promised you."   Jn 1:51; Ge 12:3

¹⁶When Jacob awoke from his sleep, he thought, "Surely the LORD is in this place, and I was not aware of it." ¹⁷He was afraid and said, "How awesome is this place! This is none other than the house of God; this is the gate of heaven."

¹⁸Early the next morning Jacob took the stone he had placed under his head and set it up as a pillar and poured oil on top of it. ¹⁹He called that place Bethel,*c* though the city used to be called Luz.

²⁰Then Jacob made a vow, saying, "If God will be with me and will watch over me on this journey I am taking and will give me food to eat and clothes to wear ²¹so that I return safely to my father's house, then the LORD*d* will be my God ²²and*e* this stone that I have set up as a pillar will be God's house, and of all that you give me I will give you a tenth."   Dt 26:17

Jacob Arrives in Paddan Aram

29 Then Jacob continued on his journey and came to the land of the eastern peoples. ²There he saw a well in the field, with three flocks of sheep lying near it because the flocks were watered from that well. The stone over the mouth of the well was large. ³When all the flocks were gathered there, the shepherds would roll the stone away from the well's mouth and water the sheep. Then they would return the stone to its place over the mouth of the well.   Jdg 6:3,33

⁴Jacob asked the shepherds, "My brothers, where are you from?"

"We're from Haran," they replied.   Ge 28:10

⁵He said to them, "Do you know Laban, Nahor's grandson?"

"Yes, we know him," they answered.   Ge 11:29

⁶Then Jacob asked them, "Is he well?"

"Yes, he is," they said, "and here

---

a 12 Or *ladder*   *b* 13 Or *There beside him*   *c* 19 *Bethel* means *house of God.*   *d* 20,21 Or *Since God ... father's house, the* LORD   *e* 21,22 Or *house, and the* LORD *will be my God,* ²²*then*

comes his daughter Rachel with the sheep."

⁷"Look," he said, "the sun is still high; it is not time for the flocks to be gathered. Water the sheep and take them back to pasture."

⁸"We can't," they replied, "until all the flocks are gathered and the stone has been rolled away from the mouth of the well. Then we will water the sheep."   Ge 24:13

⁹While he was still talking with them, Rachel came with her father's sheep, for she was a shepherdess. ¹⁰When Jacob saw Rachel daughter of Laban, his mother's brother, and Laban's sheep, he went over and rolled the stone away from the mouth of the well and watered his uncle's sheep. ¹¹Then Jacob kissed Rachel and began to weep aloud. ¹²He had told Rachel that he was a relative of her father and a son of Rebekah. So she ran and told her father.

¹³As soon as Laban heard the news about Jacob, his sister's son, he hurried to meet him. He embraced him and kissed him and brought him to his home, and there Jacob told him all these things. ¹⁴Then Laban said to him, "You are my own flesh and blood."

Jacob Marries Leah and Rachel

After Jacob had stayed with him for a whole month, ¹⁵Laban said to him, "Just because you are a relative of mine, should you work for

me for nothing? Tell me what your wages should be."   Ge 31:7,41

¹⁶Now Laban had two daughters; the name of the older was Leah, and the name of the younger was Rachel. ¹⁷Leah had weak[a] eyes, but Rachel was lovely in form, and beautiful. ¹⁸Jacob was in love with Rachel and said, "I'll work for you seven years in return for your younger daughter Rachel."   Hos 12:12

¹⁹Laban said, "It's better that I give her to you than to some other man. Stay here with me." ²⁰So Jacob served seven years to get Rachel, but they seemed like only a few days to him because of his love for her.   Ge 31:15; Hos 12:12

²¹Then Jacob said to Laban, "Give me my wife. My time is completed, and I want to lie with her."

²²So Laban brought together all the people of the place and gave a feast. ²³But when evening came, he took his daughter Leah and gave her to Jacob, and Jacob lay with her. ²⁴And Laban gave his servant girl Zilpah to his daughter as her maidservant.   Jdg 14:10; Jn 2:1-2

²⁵When morning came, there was Leah! So Jacob said to Laban, "What is this you have done to me? I served you for Rachel, didn't I? Why have you deceived me?"

²⁶Laban replied, "It is not our custom here to give the younger daughter in marriage before the older one. ²⁷Finish this daughter's

---

[a] 17 Or *delicate*

bridal week; then we will give you the younger one also, in return for another seven years of work."

28And Jacob did so. He finished the week with Leah, and then Laban gave him his daughter Rachel to be his wife. 29Laban gave his servant girl Bilhah to his daughter Rachel as her maidservant. 30Jacob lay with Rachel also, and he loved Rachel more than Leah. And he worked for Laban another seven years.   Ge 31:41

Jacob's Children

31When the LORD saw that Leah was not loved, he opened her womb, but Rachel was barren. 32Leah became pregnant and gave birth to a son. She named him Reuben,a for she said, "It is because the LORD has seen my misery. Surely my husband will love me now."   Dt 21:15-17; Ps 127:3; Ge 16:11

33She conceived again, and when she gave birth to a son she said, "Because the LORD heard that I am not loved, he gave me this one too." So she named him Simeon.b

34Again she conceived, and when she gave birth to a son she said, "Now at last my husband will become attached to me, because I have borne him three sons." So he was named Levi.c   Ge 49:5-7

35She conceived again, and when she gave birth to a son she

said, "This time I will praise the LORD." So she named him Judah.d Then she stopped having children.

30 When Rachel saw that she was not bearing Jacob any children, she became jealous of her sister. So she said to Jacob, "Give me children, or I'll die!"

2Jacob became angry with her and said, "Am I in the place of God, who has kept you from having children?"   Ge 16:2

3Then she said, "Here is Bilhah, my maidservant. Sleep with her so that she can bear children for me and that through her I too can build a family."   Ge 16:2

4So she gave him her servant Bilhah as a wife. Jacob slept with her, 5and she became pregnant and bore him a son. 6Then Rachel said, "God has vindicated me; he has listened to my plea and given me a son." Because of this she named him Dan.e   Ge 16:3-4; 49:16-17

7Rachel's servant Bilhah conceived again and bore Jacob a second son. 8Then Rachel said, "I have had a great struggle with my sister, and I have won." So she named him Naphtali.f   Ge 49:21

9When Leah saw that she had stopped having children, she took her maidservant Zilpah and gave her to Jacob as a wife. 10Leah's servant Zilpah bore Jacob a son. 11Then Leah said, "What good for-

---

a32 Reuben sounds like the Hebrew for he has seen my misery; the name means see, a son.
b33 Simeon probably means one who hears.   c34 Levi sounds like and may be derived from the Hebrew for attached.   d35 Judah sounds like and may be derived from the Hebrew for praise.
e6 Dan here means he has vindicated.   f8 Naphtali means my struggle.

tune!"ᵃ So she named him Gad.ᵇ

¹²Leah's servant Zilpah bore Jacob a second son. ¹³Then Leah said, "How happy I am! The women will call me happy." So she named him Asher.ᶜ   Lk 1:48; Ge 49:20

¹⁴During wheat harvest, Reuben went out into the fields and found some mandrake plants, which he brought to his mother Leah. Rachel said to Leah, "Please give me some of your son's mandrakes."

¹⁵But she said to her, "Wasn't it enough that you took away my husband? Will you take my son's mandrakes too?"   Nu 16:9,13

"Very well," Rachel said, "he can sleep with you tonight in return for your son's mandrakes."   Eze 16:33

¹⁶So when Jacob came in from the fields that evening, Leah went out to meet him. "You must sleep with me," she said. "I have hired you with my son's mandrakes." So he slept with her that night.

¹⁷God listened to Leah, and she became pregnant and bore Jacob a fifth son. ¹⁸Then Leah said, "God has rewarded me for giving my maidservant to my husband." So she named him Issachar.ᵈ   Ge 46:13

¹⁹Leah conceived again and bore Jacob a sixth son. ²⁰Then Leah said, "God has presented me with a precious gift. This time my husband will treat me with honor, because I have borne him six sons." So she named him Zebulun.ᵉ

²¹Some time later she gave birth to a daughter and named her Dinah.   Ge 34:1

²²Then God remembered Rachel; he listened to her and opened her womb. ²³She became pregnant and gave birth to a son and said, "God has taken away my disgrace." ²⁴She named him Joseph,ᶠ and said, "May the LORD add to me another son."   Ge 35:17; Isa 4:1; Lk 1:25

Jacob's Flocks Increase

²⁵After Rachel gave birth to Joseph, Jacob said to Laban, "Send me on my way so I can go back to my own homeland. ²⁶Give me my wives and children, for whom I have served you, and I will be on my way. You know how much work I've done for you."   Ge 24:54

²⁷But Laban said to him, "If I have found favor in your eyes, please stay. I have learned by divination thatᵍ the LORD has blessed me because of you." ²⁸He added, "Name your wages, and I will pay them."   Ge 26:24; 29:15; 39:3,5

²⁹Jacob said to him, "You know how I have worked for you and how your livestock has fared under my care. ³⁰The little you had before I came has increased greatly, and the LORD has blessed you wherever I have been. But now, when may I do something for my own household?"   Ge 31:38-40; 1Ti 5:8

ᵃ11 Or "A troop is coming!"   ᵇ11 Gad can mean good fortune or a troop.   ᶜ13 Asher means happy.
ᵈ18 Issachar sounds like the Hebrew for reward.   ᵉ20 Zebulun probably means honor.   ᶠ24 Joseph means may he add.   ᵍ27 Or possibly have become rich and

31"What shall I give you?" he asked.

"Don't give me anything," Jacob replied. "But if you will do this one thing for me, I will go on tending your flocks and watching over them: **32**Let me go through all your flocks today and remove from them every speckled or spotted sheep, every dark-colored lamb and every spotted or speckled goat. They will be my wages. **33**And my honesty will testify for me in the future, whenever you check on the wages you have paid me. Any goat in my possession that is not speckled or spotted, or any lamb that is not dark-colored, will be considered stolen."

34"Agreed," said Laban. "Let it be as you have said." **35**That same day he removed all the male goats that were streaked or spotted, and all the speckled or spotted female goats (all that had white on them) and all the dark-colored lambs, and he placed them in the care of his sons. **36**Then he put a three-day journey between himself and Jacob, while Jacob continued to tend the rest of Laban's flocks.   Ge 31:1

37Jacob, however, took fresh-cut branches from poplar, almond and plane trees and made white stripes on them by peeling the bark and exposing the white inner wood of the branches. **38**Then he placed the peeled branches in all the watering troughs, so that they would be directly in front of the flocks when they came to drink. When the flocks were in heat and came to drink, **39**they mated in front of the branches. And they bore young that were streaked or speckled or spotted. **40**Jacob set apart the young of the flock by themselves, but made the rest face the streaked and dark-colored animals that belonged to Laban. Thus he made separate flocks for himself and did not put them with Laban's animals. **41**Whenever the stronger females were in heat, Jacob would place the branches in the troughs in front of the animals so they would mate near the branches, **42**but if the animals were weak, he would not place them there. So the weak animals went to Laban and the strong ones to Jacob. **43**In this way the man grew exceedingly prosperous and came to own large flocks, and maidservants and menservants, and camels and donkeys.

Jacob Flees From Laban

31 Jacob heard that Laban's sons were saying, "Jacob has taken everything our father owned and has gained all this wealth from what belonged to our father." **2**And Jacob noticed that Laban's attitude toward him was not what it had been.   Ge 30:42

3Then the LORD said to Jacob, "Go back to the land of your fathers and to your relatives, and I will be with you."   Ge 21:22; 26:3; 32:9

4So Jacob sent word to Rachel and Leah to come out to the fields where his flocks were. **5**He said to them, "I see that your father's attitude toward me is not what it was before, but the God of my father has been with me. ⁶You know that I've worked for your father with all my strength, ⁷yet your father has cheated me by changing my wages ten times. However, God has not allowed him to harm me. ⁸If he said, 'The speckled ones will be your wages,' then all the flocks gave birth to speckled young; and if he said, 'The streaked ones will be your wages,' then all the flocks bore streaked young. ⁹So God has taken away your father's livestock and has given them to me.

¹⁰"In breeding season I once had a dream in which I looked up and saw that the male goats mating with the flock were streaked, speckled or spotted. ¹¹The angel of God said to me in the dream, 'Jacob.' I answered, 'Here I am.' ¹²And he said, 'Look up and see that all the male goats mating with the flock are streaked, speckled or spotted, for I have seen all that Laban has been doing to you. ¹³I am the God of Bethel, where you anointed a pillar and where you made a vow to me. Now leave this land at once and go back to your native land.'" Ge 28:10-22; Ex 3:7

¹⁴Then Rachel and Leah replied, "Do we still have any share in the inheritance of our father's estate? ¹⁵Does he not regard us as foreigners? Not only has he sold us, but he has used up what was paid for us. ¹⁶Surely all the wealth that God took away from our father belongs to us and our children. So do whatever God has told you." Ge 29:20

¹⁷Then Jacob put his children and his wives on camels, ¹⁸and he drove all his livestock ahead of him, along with all the goods he had accumulated in Paddan Aram,ᵃ to go to his father Isaac in the land of Canaan. Ge 35:27

¹⁹When Laban had gone to shear his sheep, Rachel stole her father's household gods. ²⁰Moreover, Jacob deceived Laban the Aramean by not telling him he was running away. ²¹So he fled with all he had, and crossing the River,ᵇ he headed for the hill country of Gilead. Ge 27:36; 35:2; Jdg 17:5

Laban Pursues Jacob

²²On the third day Laban was told that Jacob had fled. ²³Taking his relatives with him, he pursued Jacob for seven days and caught up with him in the hill country of Gilead. ²⁴Then God came to Laban the Aramean in a dream at night and said to him, "Be careful not to say anything to Jacob, either good or bad." Ge 20:3; 24:50

²⁵Jacob had pitched his tent in the hill country of Gilead when Laban overtook him, and Laban and his relatives camped there too. ²⁶Then Laban said to Jacob, "What have you done? You've deceived

---

ᵃ18 That is, Northwest Mesopotamia   ᵇ21 That is, the Euphrates

me, and you've carried off my daughters like captives in war. ²⁷Why did you run off secretly and deceive me? Why didn't you tell me, so I could send you away with joy and singing to the music of tambourines and harps? ²⁸You didn't even let me kiss my grandchildren and my daughters goodby. You have done a foolish thing. ²⁹I have the power to harm you; but last night the God of your father said to me, 'Be careful not to say anything to Jacob, either good or bad.' ³⁰Now you have gone off because you longed to return to your father's house. But why did you steal my gods?"   ver 19,55

³¹Jacob answered Laban, "I was afraid, because I thought you would take your daughters away from me by force. ³²But if you find anyone who has your gods, he shall not live. In the presence of our relatives, see for yourself whether there is anything of yours here with me; and if so, take it." Now Jacob did not know that Rachel had stolen the gods.   Ge 44:9

³³So Laban went into Jacob's tent and into Leah's tent and into the tent of the two maidservants, but he found nothing. After he came out of Leah's tent, he entered Rachel's tent. ³⁴Now Rachel had taken the household gods and put them inside her camel's saddle and was sitting on them. Laban searched through everything in the tent but found nothing.   ver 37

³⁵Rachel said to her father,

"Don't be angry, my lord, that I cannot stand up in your presence; I'm having my period." So he searched but could not find the household gods.   Lev 19:3,32

³⁶Jacob was angry and took Laban to task. "What is my crime?" he asked Laban. "What sin have I committed that you hunt me down? ³⁷Now that you have searched through all my goods, what have you found that belongs to your household? Put it here in front of your relatives and mine, and let them judge between the two of us.   ver 23

³⁸"I have been with you for twenty years now. Your sheep and goats have not miscarried, nor have I eaten rams from your flocks. ³⁹I did not bring you animals torn by wild beasts; I bore the loss myself. And you demanded payment from me for whatever was stolen by day or night. ⁴⁰This was my situation: The heat consumed me in the daytime and the cold at night, and sleep fled from my eyes. ⁴¹It was like this for the twenty years I was in your household. I worked for you fourteen years for your two daughters and six years for your flocks, and you changed my wages ten times. ⁴²If the God of my father, the God of Abraham and the Fear of Isaac, had not been with me, you would surely have sent me away empty-handed. But God has seen my hardship and the toil of my hands, and last night he rebuked you."

⁴³Laban answered Jacob, "The women are my daughters, the children are my children, and the flocks are my flocks. All you see is mine. Yet what can I do today about these daughters of mine, or about the children they have borne? ⁴⁴Come now, let's make a covenant, you and I, and let it serve as a witness between us."

⁴⁵So Jacob took a stone and set it up as a pillar. ⁴⁶He said to his relatives, "Gather some stones." So they took stones and piled them in a heap, and they ate there by the heap. ⁴⁷Laban called it Jegar Sahadutha,ᵃ and Jacob called it Galeed.ᵇ   Ge 28:18

⁴⁸Laban said, "This heap is a witness between you and me today." That is why it was called Galeed. ⁴⁹It was also called Mizpah,ᶜ because he said, "May the LORD keep watch between you and me when we are away from each other. ⁵⁰If you mistreat my daughters or if you take any wives besides my daughters, even though no one is with us, remember that God is a witness between you and me."

⁵¹Laban also said to Jacob, "Here is this heap, and here is this pillar I have set up between you and me. ⁵²This heap is a witness, and this pillar is a witness, that I will not go past this heap to your side to harm you and that you will not go past this heap and pillar to my side to harm me. ⁵³May the God of Abraham and the God of Nahor, the God of their father, judge between us."   Ge 16:5

So Jacob took an oath in the name of the Fear of his father Isaac. ⁵⁴He offered a sacrifice there in the hill country and invited his relatives to a meal. After they had eaten, they spent the night there.

⁵⁵Early the next morning Laban kissed his grandchildren and his daughters and blessed them. Then he left and returned home.

Jacob Prepares to Meet Esau

32 Jacob also went on his way, and the angels of God met him. ²When Jacob saw them, he said, "This is the camp of God!" So he named that place Mahanaim.ᵈ   Ps 34:7; 91:11

³Jacob sent messengers ahead of him to his brother Esau in the land of Seir, the country of Edom. ⁴He instructed them: "This is what you are to say to my master Esau: 'Your servant Jacob says, I have been staying with Laban and have remained there till now. ⁵I have cattle and donkeys, sheep and goats, menservants and maidservants. Now I am sending this message to my lord, that I may find favor in your eyes.' "   Ge 12:16

⁶When the messengers returned to Jacob, they said, "We went to your brother Esau, and now he is

---

ᵃ47 The Aramaic *Jegar Sahadutha* means *witness heap.*   ᵇ47 The Hebrew *Galeed* means *witness heap.*
ᶜ49 *Mizpah* means *watchtower.*   ᵈ2 *Mahanaim* means *two camps.*

coming to meet you, and four hundred men are with him." Ge 33:1

⁷In great fear and distress Jacob divided the people who were with him into two groups,ᵃ and the flocks and herds and camels as well. ⁸He thought, "If Esau comes and attacks one group,ᵇ the groupᵇ that is left may escape."

⁹Then Jacob prayed, "O God of my father Abraham, God of my father Isaac, O LORD, who said to me, 'Go back to your country and your relatives, and I will make you prosper,' ¹⁰I am unworthy of all the kindness and faithfulness you have shown your servant. I had only my staff when I crossed this Jordan, but now I have become two groups. ¹¹Save me, I pray, from the hand of my brother Esau, for I am afraid he will come and attack me, and also the mothers with their children. ¹²But you have said, 'I will surely make you prosper and will make your descendants like the sand of the sea, which cannot be counted.' "

¹³He spent the night there, and from what he had with him he selected a gift for his brother Esau: ¹⁴two hundred female goats and twenty male goats, two hundred ewes and twenty rams, ¹⁵thirty female camels with their young, forty cows and ten bulls, and twenty female donkeys and ten male donkeys. ¹⁶He put them in the care of his servants, each herd by itself,

and said to his servants, "Go ahead of me, and keep some space between the herds." Ge 43:11,15,25-26

¹⁷He instructed the one in the lead: "When my brother Esau meets you and asks, 'To whom do you belong, and where are you going, and who owns all these animals in front of you?' ¹⁸then you are to say, 'They belong to your servant Jacob. They are a gift sent to my lord Esau, and he is coming behind us.' " Ge 18:3

¹⁹He also instructed the second, the third and all the others who followed the herds: "You are to say the same thing to Esau when you meet him. ²⁰And be sure to say, 'Your servant Jacob is coming behind us.' " For he thought, "I will pacify him with these gifts I am sending on ahead; later, when I see him, perhaps he will receive me." ²¹So Jacob's gifts went on ahead of him, but he himself spent the night in the camp. Ge 33:10; Pr 21:14

Jacob Wrestles With God

²²That night Jacob got up and took his two wives, his two maidservants and his eleven sons and crossed the ford of the Jabbok. ²³After he had sent them across the stream, he sent over all his possessions. ²⁴So Jacob was left alone, and a man wrestled with him till daybreak. ²⁵When the man saw that he could not overpower him, he touched the socket of Jacob's

ᵃ7 Or camps; also in verse 10   ᵇ8 Or camp

hip so that his hip was wrenched as he wrestled with the man. **26**Then the man said, "Let me go, for it is daybreak."

But Jacob replied, "I will not let you go unless you bless me."

27The man asked him, "What is your name?"

"Jacob," he answered.

28Then the man said, "Your name will no longer be Jacob, but Israel,*a* because you have struggled with God and with men and have overcome."   Ge 17:5; 35:10

29Jacob said, "Please tell me your name."   Jdg 13:17

But he replied, "Why do you ask my name?" Then he blessed him there.   Ge 35:9

30So Jacob called the place Peniel,*b* saying, "It is because I saw God face to face, and yet my life was spared."   Ge 16:13; Ex 24:11; Jdg 6:22

31The sun rose above him as he passed Peniel,*c* and he was limping because of his hip. **32**Therefore to this day the Israelites do not eat the tendon attached to the socket of the hip, because the socket of Jacob's hip was touched near the tendon.   ver 25

Jacob Meets Esau

33 Jacob looked up and there was Esau, coming with his four hundred men; so he divided the children among Leah, Rachel and the two maidservants. **2**He put the maidservants and their children in front, Leah and her children next, and Rachel and Joseph in the rear. **3**He himself went on ahead and bowed down to the ground seven times as he approached his brother.   Ge 32:6; 42:6

4But Esau ran to meet Jacob and embraced him; he threw his arms around his neck and kissed him. And they wept. **5**Then Esau looked up and saw the women and children. "Who are these with you?" he asked.   Ge 45:14-15

Jacob answered, "They are the children God has graciously given your servant."   Ge 48:9; Ps 127:3; Isa 8:18

6Then the maidservants and their children approached and bowed down. **7**Next, Leah and her children came and bowed down. Last of all came Joseph and Rachel, and they too bowed down.

8Esau asked, "What do you mean by all these droves I met?"

"To find favor in your eyes, my lord," he said.   Ge 24:9

9But Esau said, "I already have plenty, my brother. Keep what you have for yourself."

10"No, please!" said Jacob. "If I have found favor in your eyes, accept this gift from me. For to see your face is like seeing the face of God, now that you have received me favorably. **11**Please accept the present that was brought to you, for God has been gracious to me

---

a 28 Israel means *he struggles with God.*   *b 30 Peniel* means *face of God.*   *c 31* Hebrew *Penuel,* a variant of *Peniel*

and I have all I need." And because Jacob insisted, Esau accepted it.

[12]Then Esau said, "Let us be on our way; I'll accompany you."

[13]But Jacob said to him, "My lord knows that the children are tender and that I must care for the ewes and cows that are nursing their young. If they are driven hard just one day, all the animals will die. [14]So let my lord go on ahead of his servant, while I move along slowly at the pace of the droves before me and that of the children, until I come to my lord in Seir."

[15]Esau said, "Then let me leave some of my men with you."

"But why do that?" Jacob asked. "Just let me find favor in the eyes of my lord."   Ge 34:11

[16]So that day Esau started on his way back to Seir. [17]Jacob, however, went to Succoth, where he built a place for himself and made shelters for his livestock. That is why the place is called Succoth.[a]

[18]After Jacob came from Paddan Aram,[b] he arrived safely at the[c] city of Shechem in Canaan and camped within sight of the city. [19]For a hundred pieces of silver,[d] he bought from the sons of Hamor, the father of Shechem, the plot of ground where he pitched his tent. [20]There he set up an altar and called it El Elohe Israel.[e]

Dinah and the Shechemites

34 Now Dinah, the daughter Leah had borne to Jacob, went out to visit the women of the land. [2]When Shechem son of Hamor the Hivite, the ruler of that area, saw her, he took her and violated her. [3]His heart was drawn to Dinah daughter of Jacob, and he loved the girl and spoke tenderly to her. [4]And Shechem said to his father Hamor, "Get me this girl as my wife."   Ge 30:21

[5]When Jacob heard that his daughter Dinah had been defiled, his sons were in the fields with his livestock; so he kept quiet about it until they came home.

[6]Then Shechem's father Hamor went out to talk with Jacob. [7]Now Jacob's sons had come in from the fields as soon as they heard what had happened. They were filled with grief and fury, because Shechem had done a disgraceful thing in[f] Israel by lying with Jacob's daughter—a thing that should not be done.   Dt 22:21; Jdg 20:6; 2Sa 13:12

[8]But Hamor said to them, "My son Shechem has his heart set on your daughter. Please give her to him as his wife. [9]Intermarry with us; give us your daughters and take our daughters for yourselves. [10]You can settle among us; the land is open to you. Live in it,

---

[a]17 *Succoth* means *shelters.*   [b]18 That is, Northwest Mesopotamia   [c]18 Or *arrived at Shalem, a*
[d]19 Hebrew *hundred kesitahs*; a kesitah was a unit of money of unknown weight and value.   [e]20 *El Elohe Israel* can mean *God, the God of Israel* or *mighty is the God of Israel.*   [f]7 Or *against*

trade*a* in it, and acquire property in it." Ge 13:9; 42:34; 47:6,27

¹¹Then Shechem said to Dinah's father and brothers, "Let me find favor in your eyes, and I will give you whatever you ask. ¹²Make the price for the bride and the gift I am to bring as great as you like, and I'll pay whatever you ask me. Only give me the girl as my wife."

¹³Because their sister Dinah had been defiled, Jacob's sons replied deceitfully as they spoke to Shechem and his father Hamor. ¹⁴They said to them, "We can't do such a thing; we can't give our sister to a man who is not circumcised. That would be a disgrace to us. ¹⁵We will give our consent to you on one condition only: that you become like us by circumcising all your males. ¹⁶Then we will give you our daughters and take your daughters for ourselves. We'll settle among you and become one people with you. ¹⁷But if you will not agree to be circumcised, we'll take our sister*b* and go." Ge 17:14; Ex 12:48

¹⁸Their proposal seemed good to Hamor and his son Shechem. ¹⁹The young man, who was the most honored of all his father's household, lost no time in doing what they said, because he was delighted with Jacob's daughter. ²⁰So Hamor and his son Shechem went to the gate of their city to speak to their fellow townsmen. ²¹"These men are friendly toward us," they said. "Let them live in our land and trade in it; the land has plenty of room for them. We can marry their daughters and they can marry ours. ²²But the men will consent to live with us as one people only on the condition that our males be circumcised, as they themselves are. ²³Won't their livestock, their property and all their other animals become ours? So let us give our consent to them, and they will settle among us." ver 3; Ru 4:1

²⁴All the men who went out of the city gate agreed with Hamor and his son Shechem, and every male in the city was circumcised.

²⁵Three days later, while all of them were still in pain, two of Jacob's sons, Simeon and Levi, Dinah's brothers, took their swords and attacked the unsuspecting city, killing every male. ²⁶They put Hamor and his son Shechem to the sword and took Dinah from Shechem's house and left. ²⁷The sons of Jacob came upon the dead bodies and looted the city where*c* their sister had been defiled. ²⁸They seized their flocks and herds and donkeys and everything else of theirs in the city and out in the fields. ²⁹They carried off all their wealth and all their women and children, taking as plunder everything in the houses. Ge 49:5,7

---

a 10 Or move about freely; also in verse 21   *b 17 Hebrew daughter*   *c 27 Or because*

³⁰Then Jacob said to Simeon and Levi, "You have brought trouble on me by making me a stench to the Canaanites and Perizzites, the people living in this land. We are few in number, and if they join forces against me and attack me, I and my household will be destroyed." Ex 5:21; 1Ch 16:19 ³¹But they replied, "Should he have treated our sister like a prostitute?"

Jacob Returns to Bethel

35 Then God said to Jacob, "Go up to Bethel and settle there, and build an altar there to God, who appeared to you when you were fleeing from your brother Esau." Ge 27:43; 28:19 ²So Jacob said to his household and to all who were with him, "Get rid of the foreign gods you have with you, and purify yourselves and change your clothes. ³Then come, let us go up to Bethel, where I will build an altar to God, who answered me in the day of my distress and who has been with me wherever I have gone." ⁴So they gave Jacob all the foreign gods they had and the rings in their ears, and Jacob buried them under the oak at Shechem. ⁵Then they set out, and the terror of God fell upon the towns all around them so that no one pursued them.

⁶Jacob and all the people with him came to Luz (that is, Bethel) in the land of Canaan. ⁷There he built an altar, and he called the place El Bethel,ᵃ because it was there that God revealed himself to him when he was fleeing from his brother. Ge 28:13,19

⁸Now Deborah, Rebekah's nurse, died and was buried under the oak below Bethel. So it was named Allon Bacuth.ᵇ Ge 24:59

⁹After Jacob returned from Paddan Aram,ᶜ God appeared to him again and blessed him. ¹⁰God said to him, "Your name is Jacob,ᵈ but you will no longer be called Jacob; your name will be Israel.ᵉ" So he named him Israel. Ge 17:5; 32:29

¹¹And God said to him, "I am God Almightyᶠ; be fruitful and increase in number. A nation and a community of nations will come from you, and kings will come from your body. ¹²The land I gave to Abraham and Isaac I also give to you, and I will give this land to your descendants after you." ¹³Then God went up from him at the place where he had talked with him. Ge 13:15; 17:6

¹⁴Jacob set up a stone pillar at the place where God had talked with him, and he poured out a drink offering on it; he also poured oil on it. ¹⁵Jacob called the place where God had talked with him Bethel.ᵍ Ge 28:18-19

ᵃ7 El Bethel means God of Bethel.   ᵇ8 Allon Bacuth means oak of weeping.   ᶜ9 That is, Northwest Mesopotamia; also in verse 26   ᵈ10 Jacob means he grasps the heel (figuratively, he deceives).   ᵉ10 Israel means he struggles with God.   ᶠ11 Hebrew El-Shaddai   ᵍ15 Bethel means house of God.

The Deaths of Rachel and Isaac

¹⁶Then they moved on from Bethel. While they were still some distance from Ephrath, Rachel began to give birth and had great difficulty. ¹⁷And as she was having great difficulty in childbirth, the midwife said to her, "Don't be afraid, for you have another son." ¹⁸As she breathed her last—for she was dying—she named her son Ben-Oni.^a But his father named him Benjamin.^b   Ge 30:24

¹⁹So Rachel died and was buried on the way to Ephrath (that is, Bethlehem). ²⁰Over her tomb Jacob set up a pillar, and to this day that pillar marks Rachel's tomb.

²¹Israel moved on again and pitched his tent beyond Migdal Eder. ²²While Israel was living in that region, Reuben went in and slept with his father's concubine Bilhah, and Israel heard of it.

Jacob had twelve sons:

²³The sons of Leah:

> Reuben the firstborn of Jacob,   Ge 46:8
> Simeon, Levi, Judah, Issachar and Zebulun.   Ge 29:35

²⁴The sons of Rachel:

> Joseph and Benjamin.

²⁵The sons of Rachel's maidservant Bilhah:

> Dan and Naphtali.

²⁶The sons of Leah's maidservant Zilpah:

> Gad and Asher.   Ge 30:11,13

These were the sons of Jacob, who were born to him in Paddan Aram.   1Ch 2:1-2

²⁷Jacob came home to his father Isaac in Mamre, near Kiriath Arba (that is, Hebron), where Abraham and Isaac had stayed. ²⁸Isaac lived a hundred and eighty years. ²⁹Then he breathed his last and died and was gathered to his people, old and full of years. And his sons Esau and Jacob buried him.

Esau's Descendants

36

¹This is the account of Esau (that is, Edom).

²Esau took his wives from the women of Canaan: Adah daughter of Elon the Hittite, and Oholibamah daughter of Anah and granddaughter of Zibeon the Hivite— ³also Basemath daughter of Ishmael and sister of Nebaioth.

⁴Adah bore Eliphaz to Esau, Basemath bore Reuel, ⁵and Oholibamah bore Jeush, Jalam and Korah. These were the sons of Esau, who were born to him in Canaan.

⁶Esau took his wives and sons and daughters and all the members of his household, as well as his livestock and all his other animals and all the goods he had acquired in Canaan, and moved to a

---

^a 18 Ben-Oni means son of my trouble.   ^b 18 Benjamin means son of my right hand.

land some distance from his brother Jacob. ⁷Their possessions were too great for them to remain together; the land where they were staying could not support them both because of their livestock. ⁸So Esau (that is, Edom) settled in the hill country of Seir.

⁹This is the account of Esau the father of the Edomites in the hill country of Seir.

¹⁰These are the names of Esau's sons:

Eliphaz, the son of Esau's wife Adah, and Reuel, the son of Esau's wife Basemath.

¹¹The sons of Eliphaz:

Teman, Omar, Zepho, Gatam and Kenaz.   Am 1:12

¹²Esau's son Eliphaz also had a concubine named Timna, who bore him Amalek. These were grandsons of Esau's wife Adah.   Ex 17:8,16

¹³The sons of Reuel:

Nahath, Zerah, Shammah and Mizzah. These were grandsons of Esau's wife Basemath.

¹⁴The sons of Esau's wife Oholibamah daughter of Anah and granddaughter of Zibeon, whom she bore to Esau:

Jeush, Jalam and Korah.

¹⁵These were the chiefs among Esau's descendants: Ex 15:15

The sons of Eliphaz the firstborn of Esau:

Chiefs Teman, Omar, Zepho, Kenaz, ¹⁶Korah,ᵃ Gatam and Amalek. These were the chiefs descended from Eliphaz in Edom; they were grandsons of Adah.

¹⁷The sons of Esau's son Reuel:

Chiefs Nahath, Zerah, Shammah and Mizzah. These were the chiefs descended from Reuel in Edom; they were grandsons of Esau's wife Basemath.

¹⁸The sons of Esau's wife Oholibamah:

Chiefs Jeush, Jalam and Korah. These were the chiefs descended from Esau's wife Oholibamah daughter of Anah.

¹⁹These were the sons of Esau (that is, Edom), and these were their chiefs.   Ge 25:30

²⁰These were the sons of Seir the Horite, who were living in the region: Ge 14:6; Dt 2:12,22

Lotan, Shobal, Zibeon, Anah, ²¹Dishon, Ezer and Dishan. These sons of Seir in Edom were Horite chiefs.

²²The sons of Lotan:

Hori and Homam.ᵇ Timna was Lotan's sister.

ᵃ16 Masoretic Text; Samaritan Pentateuch (see also Gen. 36:11 and 1 Chron. 1:36) does not have *Korah*.
ᵇ22 Hebrew *Hemam*, a variant of *Homam* (see 1 Chron. 1:39)

²³The sons of Shobal:

Alvan, Manahath, Ebal, Shepho and Onam.

²⁴The sons of Zibeon:

Aiah and Anah. This is the Anah who discovered the hot springs[a] in the desert while he was grazing the donkeys of his father Zibeon.

²⁵The children of Anah:

Dishon and Oholibamah daughter of Anah.

²⁶The sons of Dishon[b]:

Hemdan, Eshban, Ithran and Keran.

²⁷The sons of Ezer:

Bilhan, Zaavan and Akan.

²⁸The sons of Dishan:

Uz and Aran.   1Ch 1:38-42

²⁹These were the Horite chiefs:

Lotan, Shobal, Zibeon, Anah, ³⁰Dishon, Ezer and Dishan. These were the Horite chiefs, according to their divisions, in the land of Seir.

The Rulers of Edom

³¹These were the kings who reigned in Edom before any Israelite king reigned[c]:

³²Bela son of Beor became king of Edom. His city was named Dinhabah.   1Ch 1:43

³³When Bela died, Jobab son of Zerah from Bozrah succeeded him as king.

³⁴When Jobab died, Husham from the land of the Temanites succeeded him as king.   Eze 25:13

³⁵When Husham died, Hadad son of Bedad, who defeated Midian in the country of Moab, succeeded him as king. His city was named Avith.   Ge 19:37; Ru 1:1,6

³⁶When Hadad died, Samlah from Masrekah succeeded him as king.

³⁷When Samlah died, Shaul from Rehoboth on the river[d] succeeded him as king.

³⁸When Shaul died, Baal-Hanan son of Acbor succeeded him as king.

³⁹When Baal-Hanan son of Acbor died, Hadad[e] succeeded him as king. His city was named Pau, and his wife's name was Mehetabel daughter of Matred, the daughter of Me-Zahab.

⁴⁰These were the chiefs descended from Esau, by name, according to their clans and regions:

Timna, Alvah, Jetheth, ⁴¹Oholibamah, Elah, Pinon, ⁴²Kenaz, Teman, Mibzar, ⁴³Magdiel and Iram. These were the chiefs of Edom, according to their settle-

---

[a]24 Vulgate; Syriac *discovered water;* the meaning of the Hebrew for this word is uncertain.
[b]26 Hebrew *Dishan,* a variant of *Dishon*   [c]31 Or *before an Israelite king reigned over them*
[d]37 Possibly the Euphrates   [e]39 Many manuscripts of the Masoretic Text, Samaritan Pentateuch and Syriac (see also 1 Chron. 1:50); most manuscripts of the Masoretic Text *Hadar*

ments in the land they occupied.

This was Esau the father of the Edomites.   1Ch 1:43-54

Joseph's Dreams

37 Jacob lived in the land where his father had stayed, the land of Canaan.

²This is the account of Jacob.

Joseph, a young man of seventeen, was tending the flocks with his brothers, the sons of Bilhah and the sons of Zilpah, his father's wives, and he brought their father a bad report about them.   1Sa 2:24

³Now Israel loved Joseph more than any of his other sons, because he had been born to him in his old age; and he made a richly ornamented*ᵃ* robe for him. ⁴When his brothers saw that their father loved him more than any of them, they hated him and could not speak a kind word to him.

⁵Joseph had a dream, and when he told it to his brothers, they hated him all the more. ⁶He said to them, "Listen to this dream I had: ⁷We were binding sheaves of grain out in the field when suddenly my sheaf rose and stood upright, while your sheaves gathered around mine and bowed down to it."   Ge 42:6,9; 44:14; 50:18

⁸His brothers said to him, "Do you intend to reign over us? Will you actually rule us?" And they hated him all the more because of his dream and what he had said.

⁹Then he had another dream, and he told it to his brothers. "Listen," he said, "I had another dream, and this time the sun and moon and eleven stars were bowing down to me."   Ge 28:12

¹⁰When he told his father as well as his brothers, his father rebuked him and said, "What is this dream you had? Will your mother and I and your brothers actually come and bow down to the ground before you?" ¹¹His brothers were jealous of him, but his father kept the matter in mind.   Ge 27:29; Lk 2:19,51

Joseph Sold by His Brothers

¹²Now his brothers had gone to graze their father's flocks near Shechem, ¹³and Israel said to Joseph, "As you know, your brothers are grazing the flocks near Shechem. Come, I am going to send you to them."

"Very well," he replied.

¹⁴So he said to him, "Go and see if all is well with your brothers and with the flocks, and bring word back to me." Then he sent him off from the Valley of Hebron.

When Joseph arrived at Shechem, ¹⁵a man found him wandering around in the fields and asked him, "What are you looking for?"

¹⁶He replied, "I'm looking for

ᵃ3 The meaning of the Hebrew for *richly ornamented* is uncertain; also in verses 23 and 32.

my brothers. Can you tell me where they are grazing their flocks?"

¹⁷"They have moved on from here," the man answered. "I heard them say, 'Let's go to Dothan.' "

So Joseph went after his brothers and found them near Dothan. ¹⁸But they saw him in the distance, and before he reached them, they plotted to kill him. Mk 14:1

¹⁹"Here comes that dreamer!" they said to each other. ²⁰"Come now, let's kill him and throw him into one of these cisterns and say that a ferocious animal devoured him. Then we'll see what comes of his dreams." Ge 50:20

²¹When Reuben heard this, he tried to rescue him from their hands. "Let's not take his life," he said. ²²"Don't shed any blood. Throw him into this cistern here in the desert, but don't lay a hand on him." Reuben said this to rescue him from them and take him back to his father. Ge 42:22

²³So when Joseph came to his brothers, they stripped him of his robe—the richly ornamented robe he was wearing— ²⁴and they took him and threw him into the cistern. Now the cistern was empty; there was no water in it. Jer 41:7

²⁵As they sat down to eat their meal, they looked up and saw a caravan of Ishmaelites coming from Gilead. Their camels were loaded with spices, balm and myrrh, and they were on their way to take them down to Egypt.

²⁶Judah said to his brothers, "What will we gain if we kill our brother and cover up his blood? ²⁷Come, let's sell him to the Ishmaelites and not lay our hands on him; after all, he is our brother, our own flesh and blood." His brothers agreed. Ge 4:10; 42:21

²⁸So when the Midianite merchants came by, his brothers pulled Joseph up out of the cistern and sold him for twenty shekels^a of silver to the Ishmaelites, who took him to Egypt. Ge 45:4-5

²⁹When Reuben returned to the cistern and saw that Joseph was not there, he tore his clothes. ³⁰He went back to his brothers and said, "The boy isn't there! Where can I turn now?" ver 22; Ge 42:13,36; Job 1:20

³¹Then they got Joseph's robe, slaughtered a goat and dipped the robe in the blood. ³²They took the ornamented robe back to their father and said, "We found this. Examine it to see whether it is your son's robe." ver 3,23

³³He recognized it and said, "It is my son's robe! Some ferocious animal has devoured him. Joseph has surely been torn to pieces."

³⁴Then Jacob tore his clothes, put on sackcloth and mourned for his son many days. ³⁵All his sons and daughters came to comfort him, but he refused to be comforted. "No," he said, "in mourning

^a28 That is, about 8 ounces (about 0.2 kilogram)

will I go down to the grave[a] to my son." So his father wept for him.

[36]Meanwhile, the Midianites[b] sold Joseph in Egypt to Potiphar, one of Pharaoh's officials, the captain of the guard. Ge 39:1

Judah and Tamar

38 At that time, Judah left his brothers and went down to stay with a man of Adullam named Hirah. [2]There Judah met the daughter of a Canaanite man named Shua. He married her and lay with her; [3]she became pregnant and gave birth to a son, who was named Er. [4]She conceived again and gave birth to a son and named him Onan. [5]She gave birth to still another son and named him Shelah. It was at Kezib that she gave birth to him. 1Ch 2:3; 4:21

[6]Judah got a wife for Er, his firstborn, and her name was Tamar. [7]But Er, Judah's firstborn, was wicked in the LORD's sight; so the LORD put him to death. 1Ch 2:3

[8]Then Judah said to Onan, "Lie with your brother's wife and fulfill your duty to her as a brother-in-law to produce offspring for your brother." [9]But Onan knew that the offspring would not be his; so whenever he lay with his brother's wife, he spilled his semen on the ground to keep from producing offspring for his brother. [10]What he did was wicked in the LORD's sight; so he put him to death also.

[11]Judah then said to his daughter-in-law Tamar, "Live as a widow in your father's house until my son Shelah grows up." For he thought, "He may die too, just like his brothers." So Tamar went to live in her father's house. Ru 1:13

[12]After a long time Judah's wife, the daughter of Shua, died. When Judah had recovered from his grief, he went up to Timnah, to the men who were shearing his sheep, and his friend Hirah the Adullamite went with him. Jos 15:10,57

[13]When Tamar was told, "Your father-in-law is on his way to Timnah to shear his sheep," [14]she took off her widow's clothes, covered herself with a veil to disguise herself, and then sat down at the entrance to Enaim, which is on the road to Timnah. For she saw that, though Shelah had now grown up, she had not been given to him as his wife. Ge 31:19

[15]When Judah saw her, he thought she was a prostitute, for she had covered her face. [16]Not realizing that she was his daughter-in-law, he went over to her by the roadside and said, "Come now, let me sleep with you." Lev 18:15; 20:12

"And what will you give me to sleep with you?" she asked.

[17]"I'll send you a young goat from my flock," he said. Eze 16:33

"Will you give me something as

---

[a] 35 Hebrew *Sheol*   [b] 36 Samaritan Pentateuch, Septuagint, Vulgate and Syriac (see also verse 28); Masoretic Text *Medanites*

a pledge until you send it?" she asked.

¹⁸He said, "What pledge should I give you?"

"Your seal and its cord, and the staff in your hand," she answered. So he gave them to her and slept with her, and she became pregnant by him. ¹⁹After she left, she took off her veil and put on her widow's clothes again.

²⁰Meanwhile Judah sent the young goat by his friend the Adullamite in order to get his pledge back from the woman, but he did not find her. ²¹He asked the men who lived there, "Where is the shrine prostitute who was beside the road at Enaim?" Lev 19:29

"There hasn't been any shrine prostitute here," they said.

²²So he went back to Judah and said, "I didn't find her. Besides, the men who lived there said, 'There hasn't been any shrine prostitute here.' "

²³Then Judah said, "Let her keep what she has, or we will become a laughingstock. After all, I did send her this young goat, but you didn't find her."

²⁴About three months later Judah was told, "Your daughter-in-law Tamar is guilty of prostitution, and as a result she is now pregnant."

Judah said, "Bring her out and have her burned to death!"

²⁵As she was being brought out, she sent a message to her father-in-law. "I am pregnant by the man who owns these," she said. And she added, "See if you recognize whose seal and cord and staff these are." ver 18

²⁶Judah recognized them and said, "She is more righteous than I, since I wouldn't give her to my son Shelah." And he did not sleep with her again. 1Sa 24:17

²⁷When the time came for her to give birth, there were twin boys in her womb. ²⁸As she was giving birth, one of them put out his hand; so the midwife took a scarlet thread and tied it on his wrist and said, "This one came out first." ²⁹But when he drew back his hand, his brother came out, and she said, "So this is how you have broken out!" And he was named Perez.ᵃ ³⁰Then his brother, who had the scarlet thread on his wrist, came out and he was given the name Zerah.ᵇ Ge 46:12; Nu 26:20-21; Mt 1:3

Joseph and Potiphar's Wife

39 Now Joseph had been taken down to Egypt. Potiphar, an Egyptian who was one of Pharaoh's officials, the captain of the guard, bought him from the Ishmaelites who had taken him there. Ge 37:25,36; Ps 105:17

²The LORD was with Joseph and he prospered, and he lived in the house of his Egyptian master. ³When his master saw that the

---

ᵃ 29 Perez means breaking out.   ᵇ 30 Zerah can mean scarlet or brightness.

LORD was with him and that the LORD gave him success in everything he did, ⁴Joseph found favor in his eyes and became his attendant. Potiphar put him in charge of his household, and he entrusted to his care everything he owned. ⁵From the time he put him in charge of his household and of all that he owned, the LORD blessed the household of the Egyptian because of Joseph. The blessing of the LORD was on everything Potiphar had, both in the house and in the field. ⁶So he left in Joseph's care everything he had; with Joseph in charge, he did not concern himself with anything except the food he ate. Ge 21:22; 26:28; Ps 1:3

Now Joseph was well-built and handsome, ⁷and after a while his master's wife took notice of Joseph and said, "Come to bed with me!" Pr 7:15-18

⁸But he refused. "With me in charge," he told her, "my master does not concern himself with anything in the house; everything he owns he has entrusted to my care. ⁹No one is greater in this house than I am. My master has withheld nothing from me except you, because you are his wife. How then could I do such a wicked thing and sin against God?" ¹⁰And though she spoke to Joseph day after day, he refused to go to bed with her or even be with her.

¹¹One day he went into the house to attend to his duties, and none of the household servants was inside. ¹²She caught him by his cloak and said, "Come to bed with me!" But he left his cloak in her hand and ran out of the house.

¹³When she saw that he had left his cloak in her hand and had run out of the house, ¹⁴she called her household servants. "Look," she said to them, "this Hebrew has been brought to us to make sport of us! He came in here to sleep with me, but I screamed. ¹⁵When he heard me scream for help, he left his cloak beside me and ran out of the house." Dt 22:24,27

¹⁶She kept his cloak beside her until his master came home. ¹⁷Then she told him this story: "That Hebrew slave you brought us came to me to make sport of me. ¹⁸But as soon as I screamed for help, he left his cloak beside me and ran out of the house."

¹⁹When his master heard the story his wife told him, saying, "This is how your slave treated me," he burned with anger. ²⁰Joseph's master took him and put him in prison, the place where the king's prisoners were confined.

But while Joseph was there in the prison, ²¹the LORD was with him; he showed him kindness and granted him favor in the eyes of the prison warden. ²²So the warden put Joseph in charge of all those held in the prison, and he was made responsible for all that was done there. ²³The warden paid no attention to anything under Joseph's care, because the LORD was with Joseph and gave him success in whatever he did.   ver 3; Ex 3:21

The Cupbearer and the Baker

40 Some time later, the cupbearer and the baker of the king of Egypt offended their master, the king of Egypt. ²Pharaoh was angry with his two officials, the chief cupbearer and the chief baker, ³and put them in custody in the house of the captain of the guard, in the same prison where Joseph was confined. ⁴The captain of the guard assigned them to Joseph, and he attended them.

After they had been in custody for some time, ⁵each of the two men—the cupbearer and the baker of the king of Egypt, who were being held in prison—had a dream the same night, and each dream had a meaning of its own.

⁶When Joseph came to them the next morning, he saw that they were dejected. ⁷So he asked Pharaoh's officials who were in custody with him in his master's house, "Why are your faces so sad today?"

⁸"We both had dreams," they answered, "but there is no one to interpret them."   Ge 41:8,15

Then Joseph said to them, "Do not interpretations belong to God? Tell me your dreams."   Ge 41:16

⁹So the chief cupbearer told Joseph his dream. He said to him, "In my dream I saw a vine in front of me, ¹⁰and on the vine were three branches. As soon as it budded, it blossomed, and its clusters ripened into grapes. ¹¹Pharaoh's cup was in my hand, and I took the grapes, squeezed them into Pharaoh's cup and put the cup in his hand."

¹²"This is what it means," Joseph said to him. "The three branches are three days. ¹³Within three days Pharaoh will lift up your head and restore you to your position, and you will put Pharaoh's cup in his hand, just as you used to do when you were his cupbearer. ¹⁴But when all goes well with you, remember me and show me kindness; mention me to Pharaoh and get me out of this prison. ¹⁵For I was forcibly carried off from the land of the Hebrews, and even here I have done nothing to deserve being put in a dungeon."

¹⁶When the chief baker saw that Joseph had given a favorable interpretation, he said to Joseph, "I too had a dream: On my head were three baskets of bread.ᵃ ¹⁷In the top basket were all kinds of baked goods for Pharaoh, but the birds were eating them out of the basket on my head."

¹⁸"This is what it means," Joseph said. "The three baskets are three days. ¹⁹Within three days Pharaoh will lift off your head and hang you on a tree.ᵇ And the birds will eat away your flesh."   ver 12-13

²⁰Now the third day was Phar-

ᵃ16 Or three wicker baskets   ᵇ19 Or and impale you on a pole

aoh's birthday, and he gave a feast for all his officials. He lifted up the heads of the chief cupbearer and the chief baker in the presence of his officials: ²¹He restored the chief cupbearer to his position, so that he once again put the cup into Pharaoh's hand, ²²but he hanged*a* the chief baker, just as Joseph had said to them in his interpretation. ²³The chief cupbearer, however, did not remember Joseph; he forgot him.   Job 19:14

Pharaoh's Dreams

41 When two full years had passed, Pharaoh had a dream: He was standing by the Nile, ²when out of the river there came up seven cows, sleek and fat, and they grazed among the reeds. ³After them, seven other cows, ugly and gaunt, came up out of the Nile and stood beside those on the riverbank. ⁴And the cows that were ugly and gaunt ate up the seven sleek, fat cows. Then Pharaoh woke up.   Ge 20:3; Isa 19:6

⁵He fell asleep again and had a second dream: Seven heads of grain, healthy and good, were growing on a single stalk. ⁶After them, seven other heads of grain sprouted—thin and scorched by the east wind. ⁷The thin heads of grain swallowed up the seven healthy, full heads. Then Pharaoh woke up; it had been a dream.

⁸In the morning his mind was troubled, so he sent for all the magicians and wise men of Egypt. Pharaoh told them his dreams, but no one could interpret them for him.   Da 2:1,3; 4:5,19; Ex 7:11,22

⁹Then the chief cupbearer said to Pharaoh, "Today I am reminded of my shortcomings. ¹⁰Pharaoh was once angry with his servants, and he imprisoned me and the chief baker in the house of the captain of the guard. ¹¹Each of us had a dream the same night, and each dream had a meaning of its own. ¹²Now a young Hebrew was there with us, a servant of the captain of the guard. We told him our dreams, and he interpreted them for us, giving each man the interpretation of his dream. ¹³And things turned out exactly as he interpreted them to us: I was restored to my position, and the other man was hanged.*a*"

¹⁴So Pharaoh sent for Joseph, and he was quickly brought from the dungeon. When he had shaved and changed his clothes, he came before Pharaoh.   Ps 105:20; Da 2:25

¹⁵Pharaoh said to Joseph, "I had a dream, and no one can interpret it. But I have heard it said of you that when you hear a dream you can interpret it."   Da 5:16

¹⁶"I cannot do it," Joseph replied to Pharaoh, "but God will give Pharaoh the answer he desires."

¹⁷Then Pharaoh said to Joseph, "In my dream I was standing on

---

a 22,13 Or impaled

the bank of the Nile, [18]when out of the river there came up seven cows, fat and sleek, and they grazed among the reeds. [19]After them, seven other cows came up— scrawny and very ugly and lean. I had never seen such ugly cows in all the land of Egypt. [20]The lean, ugly cows ate up the seven fat cows that came up first. [21]But even after they ate them, no one could tell that they had done so; they looked just as ugly as before. Then I woke up.

[22]"In my dreams I also saw seven heads of grain, full and good, growing on a single stalk. [23]After them, seven other heads sprouted —withered and thin and scorched by the east wind. [24]The thin heads of grain swallowed up the seven good heads. I told this to the magicians, but none could explain it to me."   ver 8

[25]Then Joseph said to Pharaoh, "The dreams of Pharaoh are one and the same. God has revealed to Pharaoh what he is about to do. [26]The seven good cows are seven years, and the seven good heads of grain are seven years; it is one and the same dream. [27]The seven lean, ugly cows that came up afterward are seven years, and so are the seven worthless heads of grain scorched by the east wind: They are seven years of famine.   Da 2:45

[28]"It is just as I said to Pharaoh: God has shown Pharaoh what he is about to do. [29]Seven years of great abundance are coming throughout the land of Egypt, [30]but seven years of famine will follow them. Then all the abundance in Egypt will be forgotten, and the famine will ravage the land. [31]The abundance in the land will not be remembered, because the famine that follows it will be so severe. [32]The reason the dream was given to Pharaoh in two forms is that the matter has been firmly decided by God, and God will do it soon.

[33]"And now let Pharaoh look for a discerning and wise man and put him in charge of the land of Egypt. [34]Let Pharaoh appoint commissioners over the land to take a fifth of the harvest of Egypt during the seven years of abundance. [35]They should collect all the food of these good years that are coming and store up the grain under the authority of Pharaoh, to be kept in the cities for food. [36]This food should be held in reserve for the country, to be used during the seven years of famine that will come upon Egypt, so that the country may not be ruined by the famine."

[37]The plan seemed good to Pharaoh and to all his officials. [38]So Pharaoh asked them, "Can we find anyone like this man, one in whom is the spirit of God[a]?"

[39]Then Pharaoh said to Joseph, "Since God has made all this known to you, there is no one so

[a] 38 Or of the gods

discerning and wise as you. **40**You shall be in charge of my palace, and all my people are to submit to your orders. Only with respect to the throne will I be greater than you." Ps 105:21-22; Ac 7:10

Joseph in Charge of Egypt

41So Pharaoh said to Joseph, "I hereby put you in charge of the whole land of Egypt." **42**Then Pharaoh took his signet ring from his finger and put it on Joseph's finger. He dressed him in robes of fine linen and put a gold chain around his neck. **43**He had him ride in a chariot as his second-in-command,[a] and men shouted before him, "Make way[b]!" Thus he put him in charge of the whole land of Egypt. Ge 42:6; Est 3:10; Da 5:7,16,29

44Then Pharaoh said to Joseph, "I am Pharaoh, but without your word no one will lift hand or foot in all Egypt." **45**Pharaoh gave Joseph the name Zaphenath-Paneah and gave him Asenath daughter of Potiphera, priest of On,[c] to be his wife. And Joseph went throughout the land of Egypt. Ps 105:22

46Joseph was thirty years old when he entered the service of Pharaoh king of Egypt. And Joseph went out from Pharaoh's presence and traveled throughout Egypt. **47**During the seven years of abundance the land produced plentifully. **48**Joseph collected all the food produced in those seven years of abundance in Egypt and stored it in the cities. In each city he put the food grown in the fields surrounding it. **49**Joseph stored up huge quantities of grain, like the sand of the sea; it was so much that he stopped keeping records because it was beyond measure. Da 1:19

50Before the years of famine came, two sons were born to Joseph by Asenath daughter of Potiphera, priest of On. **51**Joseph named his firstborn Manasseh[d] and said, "It is because God has made me forget all my trouble and all my father's household." **52**The second son he named Ephraim[e] and said, "It is because God has made me fruitful in the land of my suffering." Ge 17:6; 49:22

53The seven years of abundance in Egypt came to an end, **54**and the seven years of famine began, just as Joseph had said. There was famine in all the other lands, but in the whole land of Egypt there was food. **55**When all Egypt began to feel the famine, the people cried to Pharaoh for food. Then Pharaoh told all the Egyptians, "Go to Joseph and do what he tells you."

56When the famine had spread over the whole country, Joseph opened the storehouses and sold grain to the Egyptians, for the famine was severe throughout Egypt. **57**And all the countries came to

---

a43 Or in the chariot of his second-in-command; or in his second chariot   b43 Or Bow down
c45 That is, Heliopolis; also in verse 50   d51 Manasseh sounds like and may be derived from the Hebrew for forget.   e52 Ephraim sounds like the Hebrew for twice fruitful.

Egypt to buy grain from Joseph, because the famine was severe in all the world. Ge 12:10; 42:5

Joseph's Brothers Go to Egypt

42 When Jacob learned that there was grain in Egypt, he said to his sons, "Why do you just keep looking at each other?" ²He continued, "I have heard that there is grain in Egypt. Go down there and buy some for us, so that we may live and not die." Ge 43:8

³Then ten of Joseph's brothers went down to buy grain from Egypt. ⁴But Jacob did not send Benjamin, Joseph's brother, with the others, because he was afraid that harm might come to him. ⁵So Israel's sons were among those who went to buy grain, for the famine was in the land of Canaan also. ver 38; Ac 7:11

⁶Now Joseph was the governor of the land, the one who sold grain to all its people. So when Joseph's brothers arrived, they bowed down to him with their faces to the ground. ⁷As soon as Joseph saw his brothers, he recognized them, but he pretended to be a stranger and spoke harshly to them. "Where do you come from?" he asked. Ge 37:7-10; 41:41

"From the land of Canaan," they replied, "to buy food."

⁸Although Joseph recognized his brothers, they did not recognize him. ⁹Then he remembered his dreams about them and said to them, "You are spies! You have come to see where our land is unprotected." Ge 37:7

¹⁰"No, my lord," they answered. "Your servants have come to buy food. ¹¹We are all the sons of one man. Your servants are honest men, not spies."

¹²"No!" he said to them. "You have come to see where our land is unprotected."

¹³But they replied, "Your servants were twelve brothers, the sons of one man, who lives in the land of Canaan. The youngest is now with our father, and one is no more." Ge 37:30,33; 44:20

¹⁴Joseph said to them, "It is just as I told you: You are spies! ¹⁵And this is how you will be tested: As surely as Pharaoh lives, you will not leave this place unless your youngest brother comes here. ¹⁶Send one of your number to get your brother; the rest of you will be kept in prison, so that your words may be tested to see if you are telling the truth. If you are not, then as surely as Pharaoh lives, you are spies!" ¹⁷And he put them all in custody for three days.

¹⁸On the third day, Joseph said to them, "Do this and you will live, for I fear God: ¹⁹If you are honest men, let one of your brothers stay here in prison, while the rest of you go and take grain back for your starving households. ²⁰But you must bring your youngest brother to me, so that your words may be verified and that you may

not die." This they proceeded to do. _{ver 15,34; Ge 43:5; Lev 25:43}

²¹They said to one another, "Surely we are being punished because of our brother. We saw how distressed he was when he pleaded with us for his life, but we would not listen; that's why this distress has come upon us."

²²Reuben replied, "Didn't I tell you not to sin against the boy? But you wouldn't listen! Now we must give an accounting for his blood." ²³They did not realize that Joseph could understand them, since he was using an interpreter. _{Ge 9:5}

²⁴He turned away from them and began to weep, but then turned back and spoke to them again. He had Simeon taken from them and bound before their eyes.

²⁵Joseph gave orders to fill their bags with grain, to put each man's silver back in his sack, and to give them provisions for their journey. After this was done for them, ²⁶they loaded their grain on their donkeys and left. _{Ro 12:17,20-21}

²⁷At the place where they stopped for the night one of them opened his sack to get feed for his donkey, and he saw his silver in the mouth of his sack. ²⁸"My silver has been returned," he said to his brothers. "Here it is in my sack."

Their hearts sank and they turned to each other trembling and said, "What is this that God has done to us?" _{Ge 43:23}

²⁹When they came to their father Jacob in the land of Canaan, they told him all that had happened to them. They said, ³⁰"The man who is lord over the land spoke harshly to us and treated us as though we were spying on the land. ³¹But we said to him, 'We are honest men; we are not spies. ³²We were twelve brothers, sons of one father. One is no more, and the youngest is now with our father in Canaan.' _{ver 7}

³³"Then the man who is lord over the land said to us, 'This is how I will know whether you are honest men: Leave one of your brothers here with me, and take food for your starving households and go. ³⁴But bring your youngest brother to me so I will know that you are not spies but honest men. Then I will give your brother back to you, and you can trade*a* in the land.' " _{Ge 34:10}

³⁵As they were emptying their sacks, there in each man's sack was his pouch of silver! When they and their father saw the money pouches, they were frightened. ³⁶Their father Jacob said to them, "You have deprived me of my children. Joseph is no more and Simeon is no more, and now you want to take Benjamin. Everything is against me!" _{Ge 43:14}

³⁷Then Reuben said to his father, "You may put both of my sons to death if I do not bring

a 34 Or move about freely

him back to you. Entrust him to my care, and I will bring him back."

38But Jacob said, "My son will not go down there with you; his brother is dead and he is the only one left. If harm comes to him on the journey you are taking, you will bring my gray head down to the grave*a* in sorrow." Ge 37:33,35

The Second Journey to Egypt

43 Now the famine was still severe in the land. **2**So when they had eaten all the grain they had brought from Egypt, their father said to them, "Go back and buy us a little more food."

3But Judah said to him, "The man warned us solemnly, 'You will not see my face again unless your brother is with you.' **4**If you will send our brother along with us, we will go down and buy food for you. **5**But if you will not send him, we will not go down, because the man said to us, 'You will not see my face again unless your brother is with you.'" Ge 42:15

6Israel asked, "Why did you bring this trouble on me by telling the man you had another brother?"

7They replied, "The man questioned us closely about ourselves and our family. 'Is your father still living?' he asked us. 'Do you have another brother?' We simply answered his questions. How were

we to know he would say, 'Bring your brother down here'?"

8Then Judah said to Israel his father, "Send the boy along with me and we will go at once, so that we and you and our children may live and not die. **9**I myself will guarantee his safety; you can hold me personally responsible for him. If I do not bring him back to you and set him here before you, I will bear the blame before you all my life. **10**As it is, if we had not delayed, we could have gone and returned twice." Ge 42:37; 44:32; Phm 1:18-19

11Then their father Israel said to them, "If it must be, then do this: Put some of the best products of the land in your bags and take them down to the man as a gift—a little balm and a little honey, some spices and myrrh, some pistachio nuts and almonds. **12**Take double the amount of silver with you, for you must return the silver that was put back into the mouths of your sacks. Perhaps it was a mistake. **13**Take your brother also and go back to the man at once. **14**And may God Almighty*b* grant you mercy before the man so that he will let your other brother and Benjamin come back with you. As for me, if I am bereaved, I am bereaved." Ge 32:20; 37:25; 42:25

15So the men took the gifts and double the amount of silver, and Benjamin also. They hurried down to Egypt and presented themselves

---

a 38 Hebrew *Sheol*   *b 14* Hebrew *El-Shaddai*

to Joseph. ¹⁶When Joseph saw Benjamin with them, he said to the steward of his house, "Take these men to my house, slaughter an animal and prepare dinner; they are to eat with me at noon."

¹⁷The man did as Joseph told him and took the men to Joseph's house. ¹⁸Now the men were frightened when they were taken to his house. They thought, "We were brought here because of the silver that was put back into our sacks the first time. He wants to attack us and overpower us and seize us as slaves and take our donkeys."

¹⁹So they went up to Joseph's steward and spoke to him at the entrance to the house. ²⁰"Please, sir," they said, "we came down here the first time to buy food. ²¹But at the place where we stopped for the night we opened our sacks and each of us found his silver—the exact weight—in the mouth of his sack. So we have brought it back with us. ²²We have also brought additional silver with us to buy food. We don't know who put our silver in our sacks."

²³"It's all right," he said. "Don't be afraid. Your God, the God of your father, has given you treasure in your sacks; I received your silver." Then he brought Simeon out to them.   Ge 42:28

²⁴The steward took the men into Joseph's house, gave them water to wash their feet and provided fodder for their donkeys. ²⁵They prepared their gifts for Joseph's arrival at noon, because they had heard that they were to eat there.

²⁶When Joseph came home, they presented to him the gifts they had brought into the house, and they bowed down before him to the ground. ²⁷He asked them how they were, and then he said, "How is your aged father you told me about? Is he still living?"

²⁸They replied, "Your servant our father is still alive and well." And they bowed low to pay him honor.   Ge 37:7

²⁹As he looked about and saw his brother Benjamin, his own mother's son, he asked, "Is this your youngest brother, the one you told me about?" And he said, "God be gracious to you, my son." ³⁰Deeply moved at the sight of his brother, Joseph hurried out and looked for a place to weep. He went into his private room and wept there.   Ge 42:13,24; 45:2,14,15

³¹After he had washed his face, he came out and, controlling himself, said, "Serve the food."

³²They served him by himself, the brothers by themselves, and the Egyptians who ate with him by themselves, because Egyptians could not eat with Hebrews, for that is detestable to Egyptians. ³³The men had been seated before him in the order of their ages, from the firstborn to the youngest; and they looked at each other in astonishment. ³⁴When portions were served to them from Joseph's table, Benjamin's portion was five

times as much as anyone else's. So they feasted and drank freely with him.   Ge 37:3; 45:22; 46:34

A Silver Cup in a Sack

44 Now Joseph gave these instructions to the steward of his house: "Fill the men's sacks with as much food as they can carry, and put each man's silver in the mouth of his sack. ²Then put my cup, the silver one, in the mouth of the youngest one's sack, along with the silver for his grain." And he did as Joseph said.   Ge 42:25

³As morning dawned, the men were sent on their way with their donkeys. ⁴They had not gone far from the city when Joseph said to his steward, "Go after those men at once, and when you catch up with them, say to them, 'Why have you repaid good with evil? ⁵Isn't this the cup my master drinks from and also uses for divination? This is a wicked thing you have done.' "

⁶When he caught up with them, he repeated these words to them. ⁷But they said to him, "Why does my lord say such things? Far be it from your servants to do anything like that! ⁸We even brought back to you from the land of Canaan the silver we found inside the mouths of our sacks. So why would we steal silver or gold from your master's house? ⁹If any of your servants is found to have it, he will die; and the rest of us will become my lord's slaves."   Ge 31:32; 42:25

¹⁰"Very well, then," he said, "let it be as you say. Whoever is found to have it will become my slave; the rest of you will be free from blame."

¹¹Each of them quickly lowered his sack to the ground and opened it. ¹²Then the steward proceeded to search, beginning with the oldest and ending with the youngest. And the cup was found in Benjamin's sack. ¹³At this, they tore their clothes. Then they all loaded their donkeys and returned to the city.   Ge 37:29; Nu 14:6

¹⁴Joseph was still in the house when Judah and his brothers came in, and they threw themselves to the ground before him. ¹⁵Joseph said to them, "What is this you have done? Don't you know that a man like me can find things out by divination?"   ver 5; Ge 37:7,10

¹⁶"What can we say to my lord?" Judah replied. "What can we say? How can we prove our innocence? God has uncovered your servants' guilt. We are now my lord's slaves —we ourselves and the one who was found to have the cup."   ver 9

¹⁷But Joseph said, "Far be it from me to do such a thing! Only the man who was found to have the cup will become my slave. The rest of you, go back to your father in peace."

¹⁸Then Judah went up to him and said: "Please, my lord, let your servant speak a word to my lord. Do not be angry with your servant, though you are equal to Pharaoh himself. ¹⁹My lord asked his ser-

vants, 'Do you have a father or a brother?' ²⁰And we answered, 'We have an aged father, and there is a young son born to him in his old age. His brother is dead, and he is the only one of his mother's sons left, and his father loves him.'

²¹"Then you said to your servants, 'Bring him down to me so I can see him for myself.' ²²And we said to my lord, 'The boy cannot leave his father; if he leaves him, his father will die.' ²³But you told your servants, 'Unless your youngest brother comes down with you, you will not see my face again.' ²⁴When we went back to your servant my father, we told him what my lord had said.

²⁵"Then our father said, 'Go back and buy a little more food.' ²⁶But we said, 'We cannot go down. Only if our youngest brother is with us will we go. We cannot see the man's face unless our youngest brother is with us.'

²⁷"Your servant my father said to us, 'You know that my wife bore me two sons. ²⁸One of them went away from me, and I said, "He has surely been torn to pieces." And I have not seen him since. ²⁹If you take this one from me too and harm comes to him, you will bring my gray head down to the grave*ᵃ* in misery.'   Ge 37:33; 42:38; 46:19

³⁰"So now, if the boy is not with us when I go back to your servant my father and if my father, whose life is closely bound up with the boy's life, ³¹sees that the boy isn't there, he will die. Your servants will bring the gray head of our father down to the grave in sorrow. ³²Your servant guaranteed the boy's safety to my father. I said, 'If I do not bring him back to you, I will bear the blame before you, my father, all my life!'   Ge 43:9; 1Sa 18:1

³³"Now then, please let your servant remain here as my lord's slave in place of the boy, and let the boy return with his brothers. ³⁴How can I go back to my father if the boy is not with me? No! Do not let me see the misery that would come upon my father."

Joseph Makes Himself Known

45 Then Joseph could no longer control himself before all his attendants, and he cried out, "Have everyone leave my presence!" So there was no one with Joseph when he made himself known to his brothers. ²And he wept so loudly that the Egyptians heard him, and Pharaoh's household heard about it.   Ge 29:11

³Joseph said to his brothers, "I am Joseph! Is my father still living?" But his brothers were not able to answer him, because they were terrified at his presence.

⁴Then Joseph said to his brothers, "Come close to me." When they had done so, he said, "I am your brother Joseph, the one you

ᵃ 29 Hebrew *Sheol*; also in verse 31

sold into Egypt! ⁵And now, do not be distressed and do not be angry with yourselves for selling me here, because it was to save lives that God sent me ahead of you. ⁶For two years now there has been famine in the land, and for the next five years there will not be plowing and reaping. ⁷But God sent me ahead of you to preserve for you a remnant on earth and to save your lives by a great deliverance.ᵃ

⁸"So then, it was not you who sent me here, but God. He made me father to Pharaoh, lord of his entire household and ruler of all Egypt. ⁹Now hurry back to my father and say to him, 'This is what your son Joseph says: God has made me lord of all Egypt. Come down to me; don't delay. ¹⁰You shall live in the region of Goshen and be near me—you, your children and grandchildren, your flocks and herds, and all you have. ¹¹I will provide for you there, because five years of famine are still to come. Otherwise you and your household and all who belong to you will become destitute.'

¹²"You can see for yourselves, and so can my brother Benjamin, that it is really I who am speaking to you. ¹³Tell my father about all the honor accorded me in Egypt and about everything you have seen. And bring my father down here quickly."   Ac 7:14

¹⁴Then he threw his arms around his brother Benjamin and wept, and Benjamin embraced him, weeping. ¹⁵And he kissed all his brothers and wept over them. Afterward his brothers talked with him.   Lk 15:20

¹⁶When the news reached Pharaoh's palace that Joseph's brothers had come, Pharaoh and all his officials were pleased. ¹⁷Pharaoh said to Joseph, "Tell your brothers, 'Do this: Load your animals and return to the land of Canaan, ¹⁸and bring your father and your families back to me. I will give you the best of the land of Egypt and you can enjoy the fat of the land.'   Ge 27:28

¹⁹"You are also directed to tell them, 'Do this: Take some carts from Egypt for your children and your wives, and get your father and come. ²⁰Never mind about your belongings, because the best of all Egypt will be yours.'"

²¹So the sons of Israel did this. Joseph gave them carts, as Pharaoh had commanded, and he also gave them provisions for their journey. ²²To each of them he gave new clothing, but to Benjamin he gave three hundred shekelsᵇ of silver and five sets of clothes. ²³And this is what he sent to his father: ten donkeys loaded with the best things of Egypt, and ten female donkeys loaded with grain and bread and other provisions for his journey. ²⁴Then he sent his brothers away, and as they were leaving

---

ᵃ7 Or *save you as a great band of survivors*   ᵇ22 That is, about 7 1/2 pounds (about 3.5 kilograms)

he said to them, "Don't quarrel on the way!"   Ge 42:21-22

²⁵So they went up out of Egypt and came to their father Jacob in the land of Canaan. ²⁶They told him, "Joseph is still alive! In fact, he is ruler of all Egypt." Jacob was stunned; he did not believe them. ²⁷But when they told him everything Joseph had said to them, and when he saw the carts Joseph had sent to carry him back, the spirit of their father Jacob revived. ²⁸And Israel said, "I'm convinced! My son Joseph is still alive. I will go and see him before I die."   ver 19

Jacob Goes to Egypt

46 So Israel set out with all that was his, and when he reached Beersheba, he offered sacrifices to the God of his father Isaac.   Ge 31:42

²And God spoke to Israel in a vision at night and said, "Jacob! Jacob!"   Ge 15:1; Job 33:14-15

"Here I am," he replied.   Ge 22:1

³"I am God, the God of your father," he said. "Do not be afraid to go down to Egypt, for I will make you into a great nation there. ⁴I will go down to Egypt with you, and I will surely bring you back again. And Joseph's own hand will close your eyes."   Ge 12:2; 50:1,24

⁵Then Jacob left Beersheba, and Israel's sons took their father Jacob and their children and their wives in the carts that Pharaoh had sent to transport him. ⁶They also took with them their livestock and the possessions they had acquired in Canaan, and Jacob and all his offspring went to Egypt. ⁷He took with him to Egypt his sons and grandsons and his daughters and granddaughters—all his offspring.

⁸These are the names of the sons of Israel (Jacob and his descendants) who went to Egypt: Ex 1:1

Reuben the firstborn of Jacob. ⁹The sons of Reuben: 1Ch 5:3
    Hanoch, Pallu, Hezron and Carmi.
¹⁰The sons of Simeon: Ge 29:33
    Jemuel, Jamin, Ohad, Jakin, Zohar and Shaul the son of a Canaanite woman.
¹¹The sons of Levi: Ge 29:34
    Gershon, Kohath and Merari.
¹²The sons of Judah: Ge 29:35
    Er, Onan, Shelah, Perez and Zerah (but Er and Onan had died in the land of Canaan). The sons of Perez: 1Ch 2:5
    Hezron and Hamul.
¹³The sons of Issachar: Ge 30:18
    Tola, Puah,ᵃ Jashubᵇ and Shimron.
¹⁴The sons of Zebulun: Ge 30:20
    Sered, Elon and Jahleel.
¹⁵These were the sons Leah bore to Jacob in Paddan Aram,ᶜ besides his daughter Dinah. These sons

---

ᵃ13 Samaritan Pentateuch and Syriac (see also 1 Chron. 7:1); Masoretic Text *Puvah*   ᵇ13 Samaritan Pentateuch and some Septuagint manuscripts (see also Num. 26:24 and 1 Chron. 7:1); Masoretic Text *Iob*   ᶜ15 That is, Northwest Mesopotamia

and daughters of his were thirty-three in all.

¹⁶The sons of Gad: Ge 30:11
Zephon,ᵃ Haggi, Shuni, Ezbon, Eri, Arodi and Areli.
¹⁷The sons of Asher: Ge 30:13
Imnah, Ishvah, Ishvi and Beriah.
Their sister was Serah.
The sons of Beriah:
Heber and Malkiel.

¹⁸These were the children born to Jacob by Zilpah, whom Laban had given to his daughter Leah—sixteen in all.

¹⁹The sons of Jacob's wife Rachel:
Joseph and Benjamin. ²⁰In Egypt, Manasseh and Ephraim were born to Joseph by Asenath daughter of Potiphera, priest of On.ᵇ
²¹The sons of Benjamin:
Bela, Beker, Ashbel, Gera, Naaman, Ehi, Rosh, Muppim, Huppim and Ard.

²²These were the sons of Rachel who were born to Jacob—fourteen in all.

²³The son of Dan:
Hushim.
²⁴The sons of Naphtali:
Jahziel, Guni, Jezer and Shillem.

²⁵These were the sons born to Jacob by Bilhah, whom Laban had given to his daughter Rachel—seven in all.   Ge 29:29; 30:8

²⁶All those who went to Egypt with Jacob—those who were his direct descendants, not counting his sons' wives—numbered sixty-six persons. ²⁷With the two sonsᶜ who had been born to Joseph in Egypt, the members of Jacob's family, which went to Egypt, were seventyᵈ in all.   Ac 7:14; Ex 1:5; Dt 10:22

²⁸Now Jacob sent Judah ahead of him to Joseph to get directions to Goshen. When they arrived in the region of Goshen, ²⁹Joseph had his chariot made ready and went to Goshen to meet his father Israel. As soon as Joseph appeared before him, he threw his arms around his fatherᵉ and wept for a long time.

³⁰Israel said to Joseph, "Now I am ready to die, since I have seen for myself that you are still alive."

³¹Then Joseph said to his brothers and to his father's household, "I will go up and speak to Pharaoh and will say to him, 'My brothers and my father's household, who were living in the land of Canaan, have come to me. ³²The men are shepherds; they tend livestock, and they have brought along their flocks and herds and everything they own.' ³³When Pharaoh calls you in and asks, 'What is your occupation?' ³⁴you should answer, 'Your servants have tended live-

ᵃ16 Samaritan Pentateuch and Septuagint (see also Num. 26:15); Masoretic Text Ziphion   ᵇ20 That is, Heliopolis   ᶜ27 Hebrew; Septuagint the nine children   ᵈ27 Hebrew (see also Exodus 1:5 and footnote); Septuagint (see also Acts 7:14) seventy-five   ᵉ29 Hebrew around him

stock from our boyhood on, just as our fathers did.' Then you will be allowed to settle in the region of Goshen, for all shepherds are detestable to the Egyptians." Ge 43:32

47 Joseph went and told Pharaoh, "My father and brothers, with their flocks and herds and everything they own, have come from the land of Canaan and are now in Goshen." ²He chose five of his brothers and presented them before Pharaoh. Ge 46:31

³Pharaoh asked the brothers, "What is your occupation?"

"Your servants are shepherds," they replied to Pharaoh, "just as our fathers were." ⁴They also said to him, "We have come to live here awhile, because the famine is severe in Canaan and your servants' flocks have no pasture. So now, please let your servants settle in Goshen." Ge 46:34

⁵Pharaoh said to Joseph, "Your father and your brothers have come to you, ⁶and the land of Egypt is before you; settle your father and your brothers in the best part of the land. Let them live in Goshen. And if you know of any among them with special ability, put them in charge of my own livestock." Ge 45:18; Ex 18:21,25

⁷Then Joseph brought his father Jacob in and presented him before Pharaoh. After Jacob blessed*ᵃ* Pharaoh, ⁸Pharaoh asked him, "How old are you?"

⁹And Jacob said to Pharaoh, "The years of my pilgrimage are a hundred and thirty. My years have been few and difficult, and they do not equal the years of the pilgrimage of my fathers." ¹⁰Then Jacob blessed*ᵇ* Pharaoh and went out from his presence. ver 7; Ge 25:7; 35:28

¹¹So Joseph settled his father and his brothers in Egypt and gave them property in the best part of the land, the district of Rameses, as Pharaoh directed. ¹²Joseph also provided his father and his brothers and all his father's household with food, according to the number of their children. Ex 1:11; 12:37

Joseph and the Famine

¹³There was no food, however, in the whole region because the famine was severe; both Egypt and Canaan wasted away because of the famine. ¹⁴Joseph collected all the money that was to be found in Egypt and Canaan in payment for the grain they were buying, and he brought it to Pharaoh's palace. ¹⁵When the money of the people of Egypt and Canaan was gone, all Egypt came to Joseph and said, "Give us food. Why should we die before your eyes? Our money is used up." Ge 41:30,56

¹⁶"Then bring your livestock," said Joseph. "I will sell you food in exchange for your livestock, since your money is gone." ¹⁷So they brought their livestock to Joseph,

a 7 Or *greeted*   *b 10* Or *said farewell to*

and he gave them food in exchange for their horses, their sheep and goats, their cattle and donkeys. And he brought them through that year with food in exchange for all their livestock.

18When that year was over, they came to him the following year and said, "We cannot hide from our lord the fact that since our money is gone and our livestock belongs to you, there is nothing left for our lord except our bodies and our land. 19Why should we perish before your eyes—we and our land as well? Buy us and our land in exchange for food, and we with our land will be in bondage to Pharaoh. Give us seed so that we may live and not die, and that the land may not become desolate."

20So Joseph bought all the land in Egypt for Pharaoh. The Egyptians, one and all, sold their fields, because the famine was too severe for them. The land became Pharaoh's, 21and Joseph reduced the people to servitude,a from one end of Egypt to the other. 22However, he did not buy the land of the priests, because they received a regular allotment from Pharaoh and had food enough from the allotment Pharaoh gave them. That is why they did not sell their land.

23Joseph said to the people, "Now that I have bought you and your land today for Pharaoh, here is seed for you so you can plant the ground. 24But when the crop comes in, give a fifth of it to Pharaoh. The other four-fifths you may keep as seed for the fields and as food for yourselves and your households and your children."

25"You have saved our lives," they said. "May we find favor in the eyes of our lord; we will be in bondage to Pharaoh." Ge 32:5

26So Joseph established it as a law concerning land in Egypt—still in force today—that a fifth of the produce belongs to Pharaoh. It was only the land of the priests that did not become Pharaoh's.

27Now the Israelites settled in Egypt in the region of Goshen. They acquired property there and were fruitful and increased greatly in number. Ge 17:6

28Jacob lived in Egypt seventeen years, and the years of his life were a hundred and forty-seven. 29When the time drew near for Israel to die, he called for his son Joseph and said to him, "If I have found favor in your eyes, put your hand under my thigh and promise that you will show me kindness and faithfulness. Do not bury me in Egypt, 30but when I rest with my fathers, carry me out of Egypt and bury me where they are buried."

"I will do as you say," he said.

31"Swear to me," he said. Then Joseph swore to him, and Israel

---

a21 Samaritan Pentateuch and Septuagint (see also Vulgate); Masoretic Text and he moved the people into the cities

worshiped as he leaned on the top of his staff.[a]   Heb 11:21

Manasseh and Ephraim

48 Some time later Joseph was told, "Your father is ill." So he took his two sons Manasseh and Ephraim along with him. [2]When Jacob was told, "Your son Joseph has come to you," Israel rallied his strength and sat up on the bed.   Ge 41:52

[3]Jacob said to Joseph, "God Almighty[b] appeared to me at Luz in the land of Canaan, and there he blessed me [4]and said to me, 'I am going to make you fruitful and will increase your numbers. I will make you a community of peoples, and I will give this land as an everlasting possession to your descendants after you.'   Ge 28:13,19

[5]"Now then, your two sons born to you in Egypt before I came to you here will be reckoned as mine; Ephraim and Manasseh will be mine, just as Reuben and Simeon are mine. [6]Any children born to you after them will be yours; in the territory they inherit they will be reckoned under the names of their brothers. [7]As I was returning from Paddan,[c] to my sorrow Rachel died in the land of Canaan while we were still on the way, a little distance from Ephrath. So I buried her there beside the road to Ephrath" (that is, Bethlehem).   Ge 35:19

[8]When Israel saw the sons of Joseph, he asked, "Who are these?"

[9]"They are the sons God has given me here," Joseph said to his father.   Ge 33:5

Then Israel said, "Bring them to me so I may bless them."   Ge 27:4

[10]Now Israel's eyes were failing because of old age, and he could hardly see. So Joseph brought his sons close to him, and his father kissed them and embraced them.

[11]Israel said to Joseph, "I never expected to see your face again, and now God has allowed me to see your children too."

[12]Then Joseph removed them from Israel's knees and bowed down with his face to the ground. [13]And Joseph took both of them, Ephraim on his right toward Israel's left hand and Manasseh on his left toward Israel's right hand, and brought them close to him. [14]But Israel reached out his right hand and put it on Ephraim's head, though he was the younger, and crossing his arms, he put his left hand on Manasseh's head, even though Manasseh was the firstborn.   Ge 41:51

[15]Then he blessed Joseph and said,   Ge 17:1

"May the God before whom
   my fathers
Abraham and Isaac walked,
the God who has been my
   shepherd   Ge 49:24

---

[a]31 Or *Israel bowed down at the head of his bed*   [b]3 Hebrew *El-Shaddai*   [c]7 That is, Northwest Mesopotamia

all my life to this day,
¹⁶the Angel who has delivered
        me from all harm
—may he bless these boys.
May they be called by my
        name
    and the names of my fathers
        Abraham and Isaac,
    and may they increase greatly
        upon the earth."

¹⁷When Joseph saw his father placing his right hand on Ephraim's head he was displeased; so he took hold of his father's hand to move it from Ephraim's head to Manasseh's head. ¹⁸Joseph said to him, "No, my father, this one is the firstborn; put your right hand on his head." ver 14; Ge 25:23
¹⁹But his father refused and said, "I know, my son, I know. He too will become a people, and he too will become great. Nevertheless, his younger brother will be greater than he, and his descendants will become a group of nations." ²⁰He blessed them that day and said,

    "In your*a* name will Israel
        pronounce this blessing:
    'May God make you like
        Ephraim and
        Manasseh.' " Nu 2:20; Ru 4:11

So he put Ephraim ahead of Manasseh.
²¹Then Israel said to Joseph, "I am about to die, but God will be with you*b* and take you*b* back to the land of your*b* fathers. ²²And to you, as one who is over your brothers, I give the ridge of land*c* I took from the Amorites with my sword and my bow." Jn 4:5; Ge 26:3

Jacob Blesses His Sons

49 Then Jacob called for his sons and said: "Gather around so I can tell you what will happen to you in days to come.

²"Assemble and listen, sons of
        Jacob;
    listen to your father Israel.

³"Reuben, you are my firstborn,
    my might, the first sign of
        my strength,   Dt 21:17
    excelling in honor, excelling
        in power.
⁴Turbulent as the waters, you
        will no longer excel,
    for you went up onto your
        father's bed,
    onto my couch and defiled
        it.   Ge 35:22; Dt 27:20

⁵"Simeon and Levi are
        brothers—
    their swords*d* are weapons
        of violence.   Ge 34:25
⁶Let me not enter their council,
    let me not join their
        assembly,   Pr 1:15; Eph 5:11
    for they have killed men in
        their anger   Ge 34:26
    and hamstrung oxen as they
        pleased.

---

a 20 The Hebrew is singular.   *b 21* The Hebrew is plural.   *c 22* Or *And to you I give one portion more than to your brothers—the portion*   *d 5* The meaning of the Hebrew for this word is uncertain.

⁷Cursed be their anger, so
    fierce,
and their fury, so cruel!
I will scatter them in Jacob
and disperse them in Israel.

⁸"Judah,ᵃ your brothers will
    praise you;
your hand will be on the
    neck of your enemies;
your father's sons will bow
    down to you.   1Ch 5:2
⁹You are a lion's cub, O Judah;
you return from the prey,
    my son.
Like a lion he crouches and
    lies down,
like a lioness—who dares to
    rouse him?
¹⁰The scepter will not depart
    from Judah,   Nu 24:17,19
nor the ruler's staff from
    between his feet,
until he comes to whom it
    belongsᵇ
and the obedience of the
    nations is his.   Ps 2:9
¹¹He will tether his donkey to a
    vine,
his colt to the choicest
    branch;
he will wash his garments in
    wine,
his robes in the blood of
    grapes.
¹²His eyes will be darker than
    wine,
his teeth whiter than milk.ᶜ

¹³"Zebulun will live by the
    seashore   Dt 33:18-19
and become a haven for
    ships;
his border will extend
    toward Sidon.

¹⁴"Issachar is a rawbonedᵈ
    donkey
lying down between two
    saddlebags.ᵉ
¹⁵When he sees how good is his
    resting place
and how pleasant is his land,
he will bend his shoulder to
    the burden
and submit to forced labor.

¹⁶"Danᶠ will provide justice for
    his people   Dt 33:22
as one of the tribes of Israel.
¹⁷Dan will be a serpent by the
    roadside,   Jdg 18:27
a viper along the path,
that bites the horse's heels
so that its rider tumbles
    backward.

¹⁸"I look for your deliverance,
    O Lᴏʀᴅ.

¹⁹"Gadᵍ will be attacked by a
    band of raiders,   Dt 33:20
but he will attack them at
    their heels.

²⁰"Asher's food will be rich;
he will provide delicacies fit
    for a king.

ᵃ8 Judah sounds like and may be derived from the Hebrew for praise.   ᵇ10 Or until Shiloh comes; or
until he comes to whom tribute belongs   ᶜ12 Or will be dull from wine, / his teeth white from milk
ᵈ14 Or strong   ᵉ14 Or campfires   ᶠ16 Dan here means he provides justice.   ᵍ19 Gad can mean
attack and band of raiders.

21"Naphtali is a doe set free
  that bears beautiful fawns.[a]

22"Joseph is a fruitful vine,
  a fruitful vine near a spring,
  whose branches climb over a
    wall.[b]
23With bitterness archers
    attacked him;
  they shot at him with
    hostility.
24But his bow remained steady,
  his strong arms stayed[c]
    limber,   Ps 18:34
  because of the hand of the
    Mighty One of Jacob,
  because of the Shepherd, the
    Rock of Israel,   Isa 28:16
25because of your father's God,
  who helps you,   Ge 28:13
  because of the Almighty,[d]
  who blesses you
  with blessings of the heavens
    above,
  blessings of the deep that
    lies below,
  blessings of the breast and
    womb.
26Your father's blessings are
    greater
  than the blessings of the
    ancient mountains,
  than[e] the bounty of the
    age-old hills.
  Let all these rest on the head
    of Joseph,
  on the brow of the prince
    among[f] his brothers.

27"Benjamin is a ravenous wolf;
  in the morning he devours
    the prey,
  in the evening he divides the
    plunder."

28All these are the twelve tribes
of Israel, and this is what their father said to them when he blessed
them, giving each the blessing appropriate to him.   Dt 33:1-29

The Death of Jacob

29Then he gave them these instructions: "I am about to be gathered to my people. Bury me with
my fathers in the cave in the field
of Ephron the Hittite, 30the cave in
the field of Machpelah, near Mamre in Canaan, which Abraham
bought as a burial place from
Ephron the Hittite, along with the
field. 31There Abraham and his
wife Sarah were buried, there Isaac
and his wife Rebekah were buried,
and there I buried Leah. 32The field
and the cave in it were bought
from the Hittites.[g]"   Ge 25:9; 35:29
33When Jacob had finished giv-
ing instructions to his sons, he
drew his feet up into the bed,
breathed his last and was gathered
to his people.   Ge 25:8

50 Joseph threw himself upon
his father and wept over
him and kissed him. 2Then Joseph
directed the physicians in his service to embalm his father Israel. So

---

[a]21 Or free; / he utters beautiful words   [b]22 Or Joseph is a wild colt, / a wild colt near a spring, / a
wild donkey on a terraced hill   [c]23,24 Or archers will attack ... will shoot ... will remain ... will stay
[d]25 Hebrew Shaddai   [e]26 Or of my progenitors, / as great as   [f]26 Or the one separated from
[g]32 Or the sons of Heth

the physicians embalmed him, ³taking a full forty days, for that was the time required for embalming. And the Egyptians mourned for him seventy days.   Ge 46:4

⁴When the days of mourning had passed, Joseph said to Pharaoh's court, "If I have found favor in your eyes, speak to Pharaoh for me. Tell him, ⁵'My father made me swear an oath and said, "I am about to die; bury me in the tomb I dug for myself in the land of Canaan." Now let me go up and bury my father; then I will return.' "

⁶Pharaoh said, "Go up and bury your father, as he made you swear to do."

⁷So Joseph went up to bury his father. All Pharaoh's officials accompanied him—the dignitaries of his court and all the dignitaries of Egypt— ⁸besides all the members of Joseph's household and his brothers and those belonging to his father's household. Only their children and their flocks and herds were left in Goshen. ⁹Chariots and horsemenᵃ also went up with him. It was a very large company.

¹⁰When they reached the threshing floor of Atad, near the Jordan, they lamented loudly and bitterly; and there Joseph observed a seven-day period of mourning for his father. ¹¹When the Canaanites who lived there saw the mourning at the threshing floor of Atad, they said, "The Egyptians are holding a solemn ceremony of mourning." That is why that place near the Jordan is called Abel Mizraim.ᵇ

¹²So Jacob's sons did as he had commanded them: ¹³They carried him to the land of Canaan and buried him in the cave in the field of Machpelah, near Mamre, which Abraham had bought as a burial place from Ephron the Hittite, along with the field. ¹⁴After burying his father, Joseph returned to Egypt, together with his brothers and all the others who had gone with him to bury his father.

Joseph Reassures His Brothers

¹⁵When Joseph's brothers saw that their father was dead, they said, "What if Joseph holds a grudge against us and pays us back for all the wrongs we did to him?" ¹⁶So they sent word to Joseph, saying, "Your father left these instructions before he died: ¹⁷'This is what you are to say to Joseph: I ask you to forgive your brothers the sins and the wrongs they committed in treating you so badly.' Now please forgive the sins of the servants of the God of your father." When their message came to him, Joseph wept.   Ge 37:28

¹⁸His brothers then came and threw themselves down before him. "We are your slaves," they said.   Ge 37:7

¹⁹But Joseph said to them, "Don't be afraid. Am I in the place

ᵃ9 Or *charioteers*   ᵇ11 *Abel Mizraim* means *mourning of the Egyptians.*

of God? ²⁰You intended to harm me, but God intended it for good to accomplish what is now being done, the saving of many lives. ²¹So then, don't be afraid. I will provide for you and your children." And he reassured them and spoke kindly to them. Ro 8:28; 12:19

The Death of Joseph

²²Joseph stayed in Egypt, along with all his father's family. He lived a hundred and ten years ²³and saw the third generation of Ephraim's children. Also the children of Makir son of Manasseh were placed at birth on Joseph's knees.^a Nu 32:39-40

²⁴Then Joseph said to his brothers, "I am about to die. But God will surely come to your aid and take you up out of this land to the land he promised on oath to Abraham, Isaac and Jacob." ²⁵And Joseph made the sons of Israel swear an oath and said, "God will surely come to your aid, and then you must carry my bones up from this place." Ge 12:7; 26:3

²⁶So Joseph died at the age of a hundred and ten. And after they embalmed him, he was placed in a coffin in Egypt.

^a 23 That is, were counted as his

Exodus

The Israelites Oppressed

1 These are the names of the
sons of Israel who went to
Egypt with Jacob, each with his
family: 2Reuben, Simeon, Levi and
Judah; 3Issachar, Zebulun and
Benjamin; 4Dan and Naphtali; Gad
and Asher. 5The descendants of Jacob numbered seventy[a] in all; Joseph was already in Egypt.

6Now Joseph and all his brothers and all that generation died,
7but the Israelites were fruitful and
multiplied greatly and became exceedingly numerous, so that the
land was filled with them. Ge 46:3

8Then a new king, who did not
know about Joseph, came to power in Egypt. 9"Look," he said to his
people, "the Israelites have become much too numerous for us.
10Come, we must deal shrewdly
with them or they will become
even more numerous and, if war
breaks out, will join our enemies,
fight against us and leave the
country." Ps 105:24-25; Ac 7:17-19

11So they put slave masters over
them to oppress them with forced
labor, and they built Pithom and
Rameses as store cities for Pharaoh. 12But the more they were oppressed, the more they multiplied
and spread; so the Egyptians came
to dread the Israelites 13and
worked them ruthlessly. 14They
made their lives bitter with hard
labor in brick and mortar and with
all kinds of work in the fields; in all
their hard labor the Egyptians
used them ruthlessly. Ex 3:7; 2:23

15The king of Egypt said to the
Hebrew midwives, whose names
were Shiphrah and Puah, 16"When
you help the Hebrew women in
childbirth and observe them on
the delivery stool, if it is a boy, kill
him; but if it is a girl, let her live."
17The midwives, however, feared
God and did not do what the king
of Egypt had told them to do; they
let the boys live. 18Then the king of
Egypt summoned the midwives
and asked them, "Why have you
done this? Why have you let the
boys live?" ver 21; Pr 16:6

19The midwives answered Pharaoh, "Hebrew women are not like
Egyptian women; they are vigorous and give birth before the midwives arrive." Jos 2:4-6

20So God was kind to the midwives and the people increased
and became even more numerous.
21And because the midwives

[a]5 Masoretic Text (see also Gen. 46:27); Dead Sea Scrolls and Septuagint (see also Acts 7:14 and note at Gen. 46:27) *seventy-five*

feared God, he gave them families of their own.   1Sa 2:35

22Then Pharaoh gave this order to all his people: "Every boy that is born*a* you must throw into the Nile, but let every girl live."

The Birth of Moses

2 Now a man of the house of Levi married a Levite woman, 2and she became pregnant and gave birth to a son. When she saw that he was a fine child, she hid him for three months. 3But when she could hide him no longer, she got a papyrus basket for him and coated it with tar and pitch. Then she placed the child in it and put it among the reeds along the bank of the Nile. 4His sister stood at a distance to see what would happen to him.   Heb 11:23; Ex 15:20; 6:20

5Then Pharaoh's daughter went down to the Nile to bathe, and her attendants were walking along the river bank. She saw the basket among the reeds and sent her slave girl to get it. 6She opened it and saw the baby. He was crying, and she felt sorry for him. "This is one of the Hebrew babies," she said.

7Then his sister asked Pharaoh's daughter, "Shall I go and get one of the Hebrew women to nurse the baby for you?"

8"Yes, go," she answered. And the girl went and got the baby's mother. 9Pharaoh's daughter said to her, "Take this baby and nurse him for me, and I will pay you." So the woman took the baby and nursed him. 10When the child grew older, she took him to Pharaoh's daughter and he became her son. She named him Moses,*b* saying, "I drew him out of the water."

Moses Flees to Midian

11One day, after Moses had grown up, he went out to where his own people were and watched them at their hard labor. He saw an Egyptian beating a Hebrew, one of his own people. 12Glancing this way and that and seeing no one, he killed the Egyptian and hid him in the sand. 13The next day he went out and saw two Hebrews fighting. He asked the one in the wrong, "Why are you hitting your fellow Hebrew?"   Ac 7:23; Heb 11:24-26

14The man said, "Who made you ruler and judge over us? Are you thinking of killing me as you killed the Egyptian?" Then Moses was afraid and thought, "What I did must have become known."

15When Pharaoh heard of this, he tried to kill Moses, but Moses fled from Pharaoh and went to live in Midian, where he sat down by a well. 16Now a priest of Midian had seven daughters, and they came to draw water and fill the troughs to water their father's flock. 17Some shepherds came along and drove

---

a 22 Masoretic Text; Samaritan Pentateuch, Septuagint and Targums *born to the Hebrews*   *b 10 Moses* sounds like the Hebrew for *draw out*.

them away, but Moses got up and came to their rescue and watered their flock.   Ex 3:1; Ge 29:10

¹⁸When the girls returned to Reuel their father, he asked them, "Why have you returned so early today?"   Nu 10:29

¹⁹They answered, "An Egyptian rescued us from the shepherds. He even drew water for us and watered the flock."

²⁰"And where is he?" he asked his daughters. "Why did you leave him? Invite him to have something to eat."   Ge 31:54

²¹Moses agreed to stay with the man, who gave his daughter Zipporah to Moses in marriage. ²²Zipporah gave birth to a son, and Moses named him Gershom,ᵃ saying, "I have become an alien in a foreign land."   Ex 18:2; Heb 11:13

²³During that long period, the king of Egypt died. The Israelites groaned in their slavery and cried out, and their cry for help because of their slavery went up to God. ²⁴God heard their groaning and he remembered his covenant with Abraham, with Isaac and with Jacob. ²⁵So God looked on the Israelites and was concerned about them.   Ex 3:7; Ps 105:10,42

Moses and the Burning Bush

3 Now Moses was tending the flock of Jethro his father-inlaw, the priest of Midian, and he led the flock to the far side of the desert and came to Horeb, the mountain of God. ²There the angel of the LORD appeared to him in flames of fire from within a bush. Moses saw that though the bush was on fire it did not burn up. ³So Moses thought, "I will go over and see this strange sight—why the bush does not burn up."   Dt 33:16

⁴When the LORD saw that he had gone over to look, God called to him from within the bush, "Moses! Moses!"

And Moses said, "Here I am."

⁵"Do not come any closer," God said. "Take off your sandals, for the place where you are standing is holy ground." ⁶Then he said, "I am the God of your father, the God of Abraham, the God of Isaac and the God of Jacob." At this, Moses hid his face, because he was afraid to look at God.   Ac 7:32-33; Mt 22:32

⁷The LORD said, "I have indeed seen the misery of my people in Egypt. I have heard them crying out because of their slave drivers, and I am concerned about their suffering. ⁸So I have come down to rescue them from the hand of the Egyptians and to bring them up out of that land into a good and spacious land, a land flowing with milk and honey—the home of the Canaanites, Hittites, Amorites, Perizzites, Hivites and Jebusites. ⁹And now the cry of the Israelites has reached me, and I have seen the way the Egyptians are oppress-

---

ᵃ22 *Gershom* sounds like the Hebrew for *an alien there.*

ing them. **¹⁰**So now, go. I am sending you to Pharaoh to bring my people the Israelites out of Egypt."

¹¹But Moses said to God, "Who am I, that I should go to Pharaoh and bring the Israelites out of Egypt?"   Ex 6:12,30; 1Sa 18:18

¹²And God said, "I will be with you. And this will be the sign to you that it is I who have sent you: When you have brought the people out of Egypt, you*ᵃ* will worship God on this mountain."   Ro 8:31

¹³Moses said to God, "Suppose I go to the Israelites and say to them, 'The God of your fathers has sent me to you,' and they ask me, 'What is his name?' Then what shall I tell them?"

¹⁴God said to Moses, "I AM WHO I AM.*ᵇ* This is what you are to say to the Israelites: 'I AM has sent me to you.' "   Ex 6:2-3; Jn 8:58; Heb 13:8

¹⁵God also said to Moses, "Say to the Israelites, 'The LORD,*ᶜ* the God of your fathers—the God of Abraham, the God of Isaac and the God of Jacob—has sent me to you.' This is my name forever, the name by which I am to be remembered from generation to generation.

¹⁶"Go, assemble the elders of Israel and say to them, 'The LORD, the God of your fathers—the God of Abraham, Isaac and Jacob—appeared to me and said: I have watched over you and have seen what has been done to you in Egypt. **¹⁷**And I have promised to bring you up out of your misery in Egypt into the land of the Canaanites, Hittites, Amorites, Perizzites, Hivites and Jebusites—a land flowing with milk and honey.'

¹⁸"The elders of Israel will listen to you. Then you and the elders are to go to the king of Egypt and say to him, 'The LORD, the God of the Hebrews, has met with us. Let us take a three-day journey into the desert to offer sacrifices to the LORD our God.' **¹⁹**But I know that the king of Egypt will not let you go unless a mighty hand compels him. **²⁰**So I will stretch out my hand and strike the Egyptians with all the wonders that I will perform among them. After that, he will let you go.   Ex 6:1,6; 12:31-33; Dt 6:22

²¹"And I will make the Egyptians favorably disposed toward this people, so that when you leave you will not go empty-handed. **²²**Every woman is to ask her neighbor and any woman living in her house for articles of silver and gold and for clothing, which you will put on your sons and daughters. And so you will plunder the Egyptians."   Ps 105:37; Ex 11:2

Signs for Moses

4 Moses answered, "What if they do not believe me or listen to me and say, 'The LORD did not appear to you'?"   Ex 3:18

ᵃ12 The Hebrew is plural.   *ᵇ14* Or *I WILL BE WHAT I WILL BE*   *ᶜ15* The Hebrew for LORD sounds like and may be derived from the Hebrew for *I AM* in verse 14.

²Then the Lord said to him, "What is that in your hand?"

"A staff," he replied.   ver 17,20

³The Lord said, "Throw it on the ground."

Moses threw it on the ground and it became a snake, and he ran from it. ⁴Then the Lord said to him, "Reach out your hand and take it by the tail." So Moses reached out and took hold of the snake and it turned back into a staff in his hand. ⁵"This," said the Lord, "is so that they may believe that the Lord, the God of their fathers—the God of Abraham, the God of Isaac and the God of Jacob—has appeared to you."   Ex 19:9

⁶Then the Lord said, "Put your hand inside your cloak." So Moses put his hand into his cloak, and when he took it out, it was leprous,ᵃ like snow.   Nu 12:10; 2Ki 5:1,27

⁷"Now put it back into your cloak," he said. So Moses put his hand back into his cloak, and when he took it out, it was restored, like the rest of his flesh.

⁸Then the Lord said, "If they do not believe you or pay attention to the first miraculous sign, they may believe the second. ⁹But if they do not believe these two signs or listen to you, take some water from the Nile and pour it on the dry ground. The water you take from the river will become blood on the ground."   Ex 7:17-21

¹⁰Moses said to the Lord, "O Lord, I have never been eloquent, neither in the past nor since you have spoken to your servant. I am slow of speech and tongue."

¹¹The Lord said to him, "Who gave man his mouth? Who makes him deaf or mute? Who gives him sight or makes him blind? Is it not I, the Lord? ¹²Now go; I will help you speak and will teach you what to say."   Isa 50:4; Jer 1:9; Lk 12:12

¹³But Moses said, "O Lord, please send someone else to do it."

¹⁴Then the Lord's anger burned against Moses and he said, "What about your brother, Aaron the Levite? I know he can speak well. He is already on his way to meet you, and his heart will be glad when he sees you. ¹⁵You shall speak to him and put words in his mouth; I will help both of you speak and will teach you what to do. ¹⁶He will speak to the people for you, and it will be as if he were your mouth and as if you were God to him. ¹⁷But take this staff in your hand so you can perform miraculous signs with it."   Ex 7:1-2,9-21

Moses Returns to Egypt

¹⁸Then Moses went back to Jethro his father-in-law and said to him, "Let me go back to my own people in Egypt to see if any of them are still alive."

Jethro said, "Go, and I wish you well."

¹⁹Now the Lord had said to Mo-

ᵃ6 The Hebrew word was used for various diseases affecting the skin—not necessarily leprosy.

ses in Midian, "Go back to Egypt, for all the men who wanted to kill you are dead." **20**So Moses took his wife and sons, put them on a donkey and started back to Egypt. And he took the staff of God in his hand.   Ex 2:15,23

21The Lord said to Moses, "When you return to Egypt, see that you perform before Pharaoh all the wonders I have given you the power to do. But I will harden his heart so that he will not let the people go. **22**Then say to Pharaoh, 'This is what the Lord says: Israel is my firstborn son, **23**and I told you, "Let my son go, so he may worship me." But you refused to let him go; so I will kill your firstborn son.' "   Ex 12:12,29; Jer 31:9

24At a lodging place on the way, the Lord met ˌMoses,ᵃ and was about to kill him. **25**But Zipporah took a flint knife, cut off her son's foreskin and touched ˌMoses'ˌ feet with it.ᵇ "Surely you are a bridegroom of blood to me," she said. **26**So the Lord let him alone. (At that time she said "bridegroom of blood," referring to circumcision.)

27The Lord said to Aaron, "Go into the desert to meet Moses." So he met Moses at the mountain of God and kissed him. **28**Then Moses told Aaron everything the Lord had sent him to say, and also about all the miraculous signs he had commanded him to perform.

29Moses and Aaron brought together all the elders of the Israelites, **30**and Aaron told them everything the Lord had said to Moses. He also performed the signs before the people, **31**and they believed. And when they heard that the Lord was concerned about them and had seen their misery, they bowed down and worshiped.

Bricks Without Straw

5 Afterward Moses and Aaron went to Pharaoh and said, "This is what the Lord, the God of Israel, says: 'Let my people go, so that they may hold a festival to me in the desert.' "   Ex 4:23

2Pharaoh said, "Who is the Lord, that I should obey him and let Israel go? I do not know the Lord and I will not let Israel go." **3**Then they said, "The God of the Hebrews has met with us. Now let us take a three-day journey into the desert to offer sacrifices to the Lord our God, or he may strike us with plagues or with the sword."

4But the king of Egypt said, "Moses and Aaron, why are you taking the people away from their labor? Get back to your work!" **5**Then Pharaoh said, "Look, the people of the land are now numerous, and you are stopping them from working."   Ex 1:11

6That same day Pharaoh gave this order to the slave drivers and foremen in charge of the people: **7**"You are no longer to supply the

---

ᵃ24 Or ˌMoses' sonˌ; Hebrew *him*   ᵇ25 Or *and drew near* ˌMoses'ˌ *feet*

people with straw for making bricks; let them go and gather their own straw. **8**But require them to make the same number of bricks as before; don't reduce the quota. They are lazy; that is why they are crying out, 'Let us go and sacrifice to our God.' **9**Make the work harder for the men so that they keep working and pay no attention to lies."   Ge 15:13

10Then the slave drivers and the foremen went out and said to the people, "This is what Pharaoh says: 'I will not give you any more straw. **11**Go and get your own straw wherever you can find it, but your work will not be reduced at all.' " **12**So the people scattered all over Egypt to gather stubble to use for straw. **13**The slave drivers kept pressing them, saying, "Complete the work required of you for each day, just as when you had straw." **14**The Israelite foremen appointed by Pharaoh's slave drivers were beaten and were asked, "Why didn't you meet your quota of bricks yesterday or today, as before?"   Isa 10:24

15Then the Israelite foremen went and appealed to Pharaoh: "Why have you treated your servants this way? **16**Your servants are given no straw, yet we are told, 'Make bricks!' Your servants are being beaten, but the fault is with your own people."

17Pharaoh said, "Lazy, that's what you are—lazy! That is why you keep saying, 'Let us go and sacrifice to the LORD.' **18**Now get to work. You will not be given any straw, yet you must produce your full quota of bricks."

19The Israelite foremen realized they were in trouble when they were told, "You are not to reduce the number of bricks required of you for each day." **20**When they left Pharaoh, they found Moses and Aaron waiting to meet them, **21**and they said, "May the LORD look upon you and judge you! You have made us a stench to Pharaoh and his officials and have put a sword in their hand to kill us."

God Promises Deliverance

22Moses returned to the LORD and said, "O Lord, why have you brought trouble upon this people? Is this why you sent me? **23**Ever since I went to Pharaoh to speak in your name, he has brought trouble upon this people, and you have not rescued your people at all."

6 Then the LORD said to Moses, "Now you will see what I will do to Pharaoh: Because of my mighty hand he will let them go; because of my mighty hand he will drive them out of his country."

2God also said to Moses, "I am the LORD. **3**I appeared to Abraham, to Isaac and to Jacob as God Almighty,*a* but by my name the LORD*b* I did not make myself

---

a 3 Hebrew *El-Shaddai*   *b 3* See note at Exodus 3:15.

known to them.[a] [4]I also established my covenant with them to give them the land of Canaan, where they lived as aliens. [5]Moreover, I have heard the groaning of the Israelites, whom the Egyptians are enslaving, and I have remembered my covenant.   Ex 2:23; 3:14

[6]"Therefore, say to the Israelites: 'I am the LORD, and I will bring you out from under the yoke of the Egyptians. I will free you from being slaves to them, and I will redeem you with an outstretched arm and with mighty acts of judgment. [7]I will take you as my own people, and I will be your God. Then you will know that I am the LORD your God, who brought you out from under the yoke of the Egyptians. [8]And I will bring you to the land I swore with uplifted hand to give to Abraham, to Isaac and to Jacob. I will give it to you as a possession. I am the LORD.' "   Ge 15:18

[9]Moses reported this to the Israelites, but they did not listen to him because of their discouragement and cruel bondage.

[10]Then the LORD said to Moses, [11]"Go, tell Pharaoh king of Egypt to let the Israelites go out of his country."

[12]But Moses said to the LORD, "If the Israelites will not listen to me, why would Pharaoh listen to me, since I speak with faltering lips[b]?"

Family Record of Moses and Aaron

[13]Now the LORD spoke to Moses and Aaron about the Israelites and Pharaoh king of Egypt, and he commanded them to bring the Israelites out of Egypt.

[14]These were the heads of their families[c]:   Ge 46:9

The sons of Reuben the firstborn son of Israel were Hanoch and Pallu, Hezron and Carmi. These were the clans of Reuben.

[15]The sons of Simeon were Jemuel, Jamin, Ohad, Jakin, Zohar and Shaul the son of a Canaanite woman. These were the clans of Simeon.

[16]These were the names of the sons of Levi according to their records: Gershon, Kohath and Merari. Levi lived 137 years.   Ge 46:11; Nu 3:17

[17]The sons of Gershon, by clans, were Libni and Shimei.

[18]The sons of Kohath were Amram, Izhar, Hebron and Uzziel. Kohath lived 133 years.   1Ch 6:2,18

[19]The sons of Merari were Mahli and Mushi.   1Ch 6:19

These were the clans of Levi according to their records.

[20]Amram married his fa-

---

[a]3 Or *Almighty, and by my name the* LORD *did I not let myself be known to them?*   [b]12 Hebrew *I am uncircumcised of lips*; also in verse 30   [c]14 The Hebrew for *families* here and in verse 25 refers to units larger than clans.

ther's sister Jochebed, who bore him Aaron and Moses. Amram lived 137 years.

²¹The sons of Izhar were Korah, Nepheg and Zicri.

²²The sons of Uzziel were Mishael, Elzaphan and Sithri.

²³Aaron married Elisheba, daughter of Amminadab and sister of Nahshon, and she bore him Nadab and Abihu, Eleazar and Ithamar.   Lev 10:1

²⁴The sons of Korah were Assir, Elkanah and Abiasaph. These were the Korahite clans.   Nu 26:11

²⁵Eleazar son of Aaron married one of the daughters of Putiel, and she bore him Phinehas.   Nu 25:7,11; Jos 24:33

These were the heads of the Levite families, clan by clan.

²⁶It was this same Aaron and Moses to whom the LORD said, "Bring the Israelites out of Egypt by their divisions." ²⁷They were the ones who spoke to Pharaoh king of Egypt about bringing the Israelites out of Egypt. It was the same Moses and Aaron.   Ex 7:4

Aaron to Speak for Moses

²⁸Now when the LORD spoke to Moses in Egypt, ²⁹he said to him, "I am the LORD. Tell Pharaoh king of Egypt everything I tell you."

³⁰But Moses said to the LORD, "Since I speak with faltering lips, why would Pharaoh listen to me?"

7 Then the LORD said to Moses, "See, I have made you like God to Pharaoh, and your brother Aaron will be your prophet. ²You are to say everything I command you, and your brother Aaron is to tell Pharaoh to let the Israelites go out of his country. ³But I will harden Pharaoh's heart, and though I multiply my miraculous signs and wonders in Egypt, ⁴he will not listen to you. Then I will lay my hand on Egypt and with mighty acts of judgment I will bring out my divisions, my people the Israelites. ⁵And the Egyptians will know that I am the LORD when I stretch out my hand against Egypt and bring the Israelites out of it."   Ex 3:20

⁶Moses and Aaron did just as the LORD commanded them. ⁷Moses was eighty years old and Aaron eighty-three when they spoke to Pharaoh.   Dt 34:7; Ac 7:23,30

Aaron's Staff Becomes a Snake

⁸The LORD said to Moses and Aaron, ⁹"When Pharaoh says to you, 'Perform a miracle,' then say to Aaron, 'Take your staff and throw it down before Pharaoh,' and it will become a snake."

¹⁰So Moses and Aaron went to Pharaoh and did just as the LORD commanded. Aaron threw his staff down in front of Pharaoh and his officials, and it became a snake. ¹¹Pharaoh then summoned wise men and sorcerers, and the Egyptian magicians also did the same things by their secret arts: ¹²Each

one threw down his staff and it became a snake. But Aaron's staff swallowed up their staffs. ¹³Yet Pharaoh's heart became hard and he would not listen to them, just as the LORD had said.   Ge 41:8; Ex 4:2-5

The Plague of Blood

¹⁴Then the LORD said to Moses, "Pharaoh's heart is unyielding; he refuses to let the people go. ¹⁵Go to Pharaoh in the morning as he goes out to the water. Wait on the bank of the Nile to meet him, and take in your hand the staff that was changed into a snake. ¹⁶Then say to him, 'The LORD, the God of the Hebrews, has sent me to say to you: Let my people go, so that they may worship me in the desert. But until now you have not listened. ¹⁷This is what the LORD says: By this you will know that I am the LORD: With the staff that is in my hand I will strike the water of the Nile, and it will be changed into blood. ¹⁸The fish in the Nile will die, and the river will stink; the Egyptians will not be able to drink its water.' "   Ex 3:18; 4:9; Rev 16:4

¹⁹The LORD said to Moses, "Tell Aaron, 'Take your staff and stretch out your hand over the waters of Egypt—over the streams and canals, over the ponds and all the reservoirs'—and they will turn to blood. Blood will be everywhere in Egypt, even in the wooden buckets and stone jars.'"   Ex 14:21

²⁰Moses and Aaron did just as the LORD had commanded. He raised his staff in the presence of Pharaoh and his officials and struck the water of the Nile, and all the water was changed into blood. ²¹The fish in the Nile died, and the river smelled so bad that the Egyptians could not drink its water. Blood was everywhere in Egypt.

²²But the Egyptian magicians did the same things by their secret arts, and Pharaoh's heart became hard; he would not listen to Moses and Aaron, just as the LORD had said. ²³Instead, he turned and went into his palace, and did not take even this to heart. ²⁴And all the Egyptians dug along the Nile to get drinking water, because they could not drink the water of the river.   ver 11

The Plague of Frogs

²⁵Seven days passed after the LORD struck the Nile. ¹Then **8** the LORD said to Moses, "Go to Pharaoh and say to him, 'This is what the LORD says: Let my people go, so that they may worship me. ²If you refuse to let them go, I will plague your whole country with frogs. ³The Nile will teem with frogs. They will come up into your palace and your bedroom and onto your bed, into the houses of your officials and on your people, and into your ovens and kneading troughs. ⁴The frogs will go up on you and your people and all your officials.' "   Ex 3:12,18; 10:6

⁵Then the LORD said to Moses, "Tell Aaron, 'Stretch out your

hand with your staff over the streams and canals and ponds, and make frogs come up on the land of Egypt.' "   Ex 7:19

[6]So Aaron stretched out his hand over the waters of Egypt, and the frogs came up and covered the land. [7]But the magicians did the same things by their secret arts; they also made frogs come up on the land of Egypt.   Ex 7:11; Ps 78:45

[8]Pharaoh summoned Moses and Aaron and said, "Pray to the LORD to take the frogs away from me and my people, and I will let your people go to offer sacrifices to the LORD."   Ex 9:28; 10:17

[9]Moses said to Pharaoh, "I leave to you the honor of setting the time for me to pray for you and your officials and your people that you and your houses may be rid of the frogs, except for those that remain in the Nile."

[10]"Tomorrow," Pharaoh said.

Moses replied, "It will be as you say, so that you may know there is no one like the LORD our God. [11]The frogs will leave you and your houses, your officials and your people; they will remain only in the Nile."   Ex 9:14; Dt 33:26

[12]After Moses and Aaron left Pharaoh, Moses cried out to the LORD about the frogs he had brought on Pharaoh. [13]And the LORD did what Moses asked. The frogs died in the houses, in the courtyards and in the fields. [14]They were piled into heaps, and the land reeked of them. [15]But

when Pharaoh saw that there was relief, he hardened his heart and would not listen to Moses and Aaron, just as the LORD had said.

The Plague of Gnats

[16]Then the LORD said to Moses, "Tell Aaron, 'Stretch out your staff and strike the dust of the ground,' and throughout the land of Egypt the dust will become gnats." [17]They did this, and when Aaron stretched out his hand with the staff and struck the dust of the ground, gnats came upon men and animals. All the dust throughout the land of Egypt became gnats. [18]But when the magicians tried to produce gnats by their secret arts, they could not. And the gnats were on men and animals.   Ex 9:11

[19]The magicians said to Pharaoh, "This is the finger of God." But Pharaoh's heart was hard and he would not listen, just as the LORD had said.   Ex 7:5; Ps 8:3; Lk 11:20

The Plague of Flies

[20]Then the LORD said to Moses, "Get up early in the morning and confront Pharaoh as he goes to the water and say to him, 'This is what the LORD says: Let my people go, so that they may worship me. [21]If you do not let my people go, I will send swarms of flies on you and your officials, on your people and into your houses. The houses of the Egyptians will be full of flies, and even the ground where they are.

[22]" 'But on that day I will deal

differently with the land of Go-shen, where my people live; no swarms of flies will be there, so that you will know that I, the LORD, am in this land. [23]I will make a distinction[a] between my people and your people. This miraculous sign will occur tomorrow.' "   Ex 7:5

[24]And the LORD did this. Dense swarms of flies poured into Pharaoh's palace and into the houses of his officials, and throughout Egypt the land was ruined by the flies.

[25]Then Pharaoh summoned Moses and Aaron and said, "Go, sacrifice to your God here in the land."

[26]But Moses said, "That would not be right. The sacrifices we offer the LORD our God would be detestable to the Egyptians. And if we offer sacrifices that are detestable in their eyes, will they not stone us? [27]We must take a three-day journey into the desert to offer sacrifices to the LORD our God, as he commands us."   Ge 43:32; Ex 3:18

[28]Pharaoh said, "I will let you go to offer sacrifices to the LORD your God in the desert, but you must not go very far. Now pray for me."

[29]Moses answered, "As soon as I leave you, I will pray to the LORD, and tomorrow the flies will leave Pharaoh and his officials and his people. Only be sure that Pharaoh does not act deceitfully again by not letting the people go to offer sacrifices to the LORD."

[30]Then Moses left Pharaoh and prayed to the LORD, [31]and the LORD did what Moses asked: The flies left Pharaoh and his officials and his people; not a fly remained. [32]But this time also Pharaoh hardened his heart and would not let the people go.   ver 12; Ex 4:21

The Plague on Livestock

9 Then the LORD said to Moses, "Go to Pharaoh and say to him, 'This is what the LORD, the God of the Hebrews, says: "Let my people go, so that they may worship me." [2]If you refuse to let them go and continue to hold them back, [3]the hand of the LORD will bring a terrible plague on your livestock in the field—on your horses and donkeys and camels and on your cattle and sheep and goats. [4]But the LORD will make a distinction between the livestock of Israel and that of Egypt, so that no animal belonging to the Israelites will die.' "   Ex 8:1,22

[5]The LORD set a time and said, "Tomorrow the LORD will do this in the land." [6]And the next day the LORD did it: All the livestock of the Egyptians died, but not one animal belonging to the Israelites died. [7]Pharaoh sent men to investigate and found that not even one of the animals of the Israelites had died. Yet his heart was unyielding and he would not let the people go.

---

[a] 23 Septuagint and Vulgate; Hebrew *will put a deliverance*

The Plague of Boils

[8]Then the LORD said to Moses and Aaron, "Take handfuls of soot from a furnace and have Moses toss it into the air in the presence of Pharaoh. [9]It will become fine dust over the whole land of Egypt, and festering boils will break out on men and animals throughout the land."   Rev 16:2

[10]So they took soot from a furnace and stood before Pharaoh. Moses tossed it into the air, and festering boils broke out on men and animals. [11]The magicians could not stand before Moses because of the boils that were on them and on all the Egyptians. [12]But the LORD hardened Pharaoh's heart and he would not listen to Moses and Aaron, just as the LORD had said to Moses.   Ex 4:21

The Plague of Hail

[13]Then the LORD said to Moses, "Get up early in the morning, confront Pharaoh and say to him, 'This is what the LORD, the God of the Hebrews, says: Let my people go, so that they may worship me, [14]or this time I will send the full force of my plagues against you and against your officials and your people, so you may know that there is no one like me in all the earth. [15]For by now I could have stretched out my hand and struck you and your people with a plague that would have wiped you off the earth. [16]But I have raised you up[a] for this very purpose, that I might show you my power and that my name might be proclaimed in all the earth. [17]You still set yourself against my people and will not let them go. [18]Therefore, at this time tomorrow I will send the worst hailstorm that has ever fallen on Egypt, from the day it was founded till now. [19]Give an order now to bring your livestock and everything you have in the field to a place of shelter, because the hail will fall on every man and animal that has not been brought in and is still out in the field, and they will die.' "   Ro 9:17; Ex 8:10

[20]Those officials of Pharaoh who feared the word of the LORD hurried to bring their slaves and their livestock inside. [21]But those who ignored the word of the LORD left their slaves and livestock in the field.   Pr 13:13

[22]Then the LORD said to Moses, "Stretch out your hand toward the sky so that hail will fall all over Egypt—on men and animals and on everything growing in the fields of Egypt." [23]When Moses stretched out his staff toward the sky, the LORD sent thunder and hail, and lightning flashed down to the ground. So the LORD rained hail on the land of Egypt; [24]hail fell and lightning flashed back and forth. It was the worst storm in all the land of Egypt since it had become a na-

[a]16 Or *have spared you*

tion. ²⁵Throughout Egypt hail struck everything in the fields—both men and animals; it beat down everything growing in the fields and stripped every tree. ²⁶The only place it did not hail was the land of Goshen, where the Israelites were.   ver 4; Ps 105:32-33; Jos 10:11

²⁷Then Pharaoh summoned Moses and Aaron. "This time I have sinned," he said to them. "The LORD is in the right, and I and my people are in the wrong. ²⁸Pray to the LORD, for we have had enough thunder and hail. I will let you go; you don't have to stay any longer."

²⁹Moses replied, "When I have gone out of the city, I will spread out my hands in prayer to the LORD. The thunder will stop and there will be no more hail, so you may know that the earth is the LORD's. ³⁰But I know that you and your officials still do not fear the LORD God."   1Ki 8:22,38; Ps 24:1

³¹(The flax and barley were destroyed, since the barley had headed and the flax was in bloom. ³²The wheat and spelt, however, were not destroyed, because they ripen later.)   Ru 1:22

³³Then Moses left Pharaoh and went out of the city. He spread out his hands toward the LORD; the thunder and hail stopped, and the rain no longer poured down on the land. ³⁴When Pharaoh saw that the rain and hail and thunder had stopped, he sinned again: He and his officials hardened their hearts. ³⁵So Pharaoh's heart was hard and he would not let the Israelites go, just as the LORD had said through Moses.   Ex 4:21

The Plague of Locusts

10 Then the LORD said to Moses, "Go to Pharaoh, for I have hardened his heart and the hearts of his officials so that I may perform these miraculous signs of mine among them ²that you may tell your children and grandchildren how I dealt harshly with the Egyptians and how I performed my signs among them, and that you may know that I am the LORD."

³So Moses and Aaron went to Pharaoh and said to him, "This is what the LORD, the God of the Hebrews, says: 'How long will you refuse to humble yourself before me? Let my people go, so that they may worship me. ⁴If you refuse to let them go, I will bring locusts into your country tomorrow. ⁵They will cover the face of the ground so that it cannot be seen. They will devour what little you have left after the hail, including every tree that is growing in your fields. ⁶They will fill your houses and those of all your officials and all the Egyptians—something neither your fathers nor your forefathers have ever seen from the day they settled in this land till now.'" Then Moses turned and left Pharaoh.   Joel 1:4

⁷Pharaoh's officials said to him, "How long will this man be a snare

to us? Let the people go, so that they may worship the LORD their God. Do you not yet realize that Egypt is ruined?"   Ex 8:19; 23:33

⁸Then Moses and Aaron were brought back to Pharaoh. "Go, worship the LORD your God," he said. "But just who will be going?"

⁹Moses answered, "We will go with our young and old, with our sons and daughters, and with our flocks and herds, because we are to celebrate a festival to the LORD."

¹⁰Pharaoh said, "The LORD be with you—if I let you go, along with your women and children! Clearly you are bent on evil.ᵃ ¹¹No! Have only the men go; and worship the LORD, since that's what you have been asking for." Then Moses and Aaron were driven out of Pharaoh's presence.

¹²And the LORD said to Moses, "Stretch out your hand over Egypt so that locusts will swarm over the land and devour everything growing in the fields, everything left by the hail."   Ex 7:19

¹³So Moses stretched out his staff over Egypt, and the LORD made an east wind blow across the land all that day and all that night. By morning the wind had brought the locusts; ¹⁴they invaded all Egypt and settled down in every area of the country in great numbers. Never before had there been such a plague of locusts, nor will there ever be again. ¹⁵They cov-

ered all the ground until it was black. They devoured all that was left after the hail—everything growing in the fields and the fruit on the trees. Nothing green remained on tree or plant in all the land of Egypt.   Joel 2:1-11,25

¹⁶Pharaoh quickly summoned Moses and Aaron and said, "I have sinned against the LORD your God and against you. ¹⁷Now forgive my sin once more and pray to the LORD your God to take this deadly plague away from me."   Ex 9:27

¹⁸Moses then left Pharaoh and prayed to the LORD. ¹⁹And the LORD changed the wind to a very strong west wind, which caught up the locusts and carried them into the Red Sea.ᵇ Not a locust was left anywhere in Egypt. ²⁰But the LORD hardened Pharaoh's heart, and he would not let the Israelites go.

The Plague of Darkness

²¹Then the LORD said to Moses, "Stretch out your hand toward the sky so that darkness will spread over Egypt—darkness that can be felt." ²²So Moses stretched out his hand toward the sky, and total darkness covered all Egypt for three days. ²³No one could see anyone else or leave his place for three days. Yet all the Israelites had light in the places where they lived.   Ps 105:28; Rev 16:10

²⁴Then Pharaoh summoned Mo-

ᵃ 10 Or Be careful, trouble is in store for you!   ᵇ 19 Hebrew Yam Suph; that is, Sea of Reeds

ses and said, "Go, worship the LORD. Even your women and children may go with you; only leave your flocks and herds behind."

25But Moses said, "You must allow us to have sacrifices and burnt offerings to present to the LORD our God. 26Our livestock too must go with us; not a hoof is to be left behind. We have to use some of them in worshiping the LORD our God, and until we get there we will not know what we are to use to worship the LORD."

27But the LORD hardened Pharaoh's heart, and he was not willing to let them go. 28Pharaoh said to Moses, "Get out of my sight! Make sure you do not appear before me again! The day you see my face you will die."

29"Just as you say," Moses replied, "I will never appear before you again."   Heb 11:27

The Plague on the Firstborn

11 Now the LORD had said to Moses, "I will bring one more plague on Pharaoh and on Egypt. After that, he will let you go from here, and when he does, he will drive you out completely. 2Tell the people that men and women alike are to ask their neighbors for articles of silver and gold." 3(The LORD made the Egyptians favorably disposed toward the people, and Moses himself was highly regarded in Egypt by Pharaoh's officials and by the people.)   Dt 34:11

4So Moses said, "This is what the LORD says: 'About midnight I will go throughout Egypt. 5Every firstborn son in Egypt will die, from the firstborn son of Pharaoh, who sits on the throne, to the firstborn son of the slave girl, who is at her hand mill, and all the firstborn of the cattle as well. 6There will be loud wailing throughout Egypt— worse than there has ever been or ever will be again. 7But among the Israelites not a dog will bark at any man or animal.' Then you will know that the LORD makes a distinction between Egypt and Israel. 8All these officials of yours will come to me, bowing down before me and saying, 'Go, you and all the people who follow you!' After that I will leave." Then Moses, hot with anger, left Pharaoh.   Ex 8:22; 12:31-33

9The LORD had said to Moses, "Pharaoh will refuse to listen to you—so that my wonders may be multiplied in Egypt." 10Moses and Aaron performed all these wonders before Pharaoh, but the LORD hardened Pharaoh's heart, and he would not let the Israelites go out of his country.   Ex 4:21; 7:4

The Passover

12 The LORD said to Moses and Aaron in Egypt, 2"This month is to be for you the first month, the first month of your year. 3Tell the whole community of Israel that on the tenth day of this month each man is to take a lamb*a* for his family, one for each household. ⁴If any household is too small for a whole lamb, they must share one with their nearest neighbor, having taken into account the number of people there are. You are to determine the amount of lamb needed in accordance with what each person will eat. ⁵The animals you choose must be year-old males without defect, and you may take them from the sheep or the goats. ⁶Take care of them until the fourteenth day of the month, when all the people of the community of Israel must slaughter them at twilight. ⁷Then they are to take some of the blood and put it on the sides and tops of the doorframes of the houses where they eat the lambs. ⁸That same night they are to eat the meat roasted over the fire, along with bitter herbs, and bread made without yeast. ⁹Do not eat the meat raw or cooked in water, but roast it over the fire—head, legs and inner parts. ¹⁰Do not leave any of it till morning; if some is left till morning, you must burn it. ¹¹This is how you are to eat it: with your cloak tucked into your belt, your sandals on your feet and your staff in your hand. Eat it in haste; it is the LORD's Passover.   Dt 16:1,3

¹²"On that same night I will pass through Egypt and strike down every firstborn—both men and animals—and I will bring judgment on all the gods of Egypt. I am the LORD. ¹³The blood will be a sign for you on the houses where you are; and when I see the blood, I will pass over you. No destructive plague will touch you when I strike Egypt.   Nu 33:4; Heb 11:28

¹⁴"This is a day you are to commemorate; for the generations to come you shall celebrate it as a festival to the LORD—a lasting ordinance. ¹⁵For seven days you are to eat bread made without yeast. On the first day remove the yeast from your houses, for whoever eats anything with yeast in it from the first day through the seventh must be cut off from Israel. ¹⁶On the first day hold a sacred assembly, and another one on the seventh day. Do no work at all on these days, except to prepare food for everyone to eat—that is all you may do.

¹⁷"Celebrate the Feast of Unleavened Bread, because it was on this very day that I brought your divisions out of Egypt. Celebrate this day as a lasting ordinance for the generations to come. ¹⁸In the first month you are to eat bread made without yeast, from the evening of the fourteenth day until the evening of the twenty-first day. ¹⁹For seven days no yeast is to be found in your houses. And whoever eats anything with yeast in it must be cut off from the community of Israel, whether he is an alien or native-born. ²⁰Eat nothing made with

a3 The Hebrew word can mean lamb or kid; also in verse 4.

yeast. Wherever you live, you must eat unleavened bread."

21Then Moses summoned all the elders of Israel and said to them, "Go at once and select the animals for your families and slaughter the Passover lamb. 22Take a bunch of hyssop, dip it into the blood in the basin and put some of the blood on the top and on both sides of the doorframe. Not one of you shall go out the door of his house until morning. 23When the Lord goes through the land to strike down the Egyptians, he will see the blood on the top and sides of the doorframe and will pass over that doorway, and he will not permit the destroyer to enter your houses and strike you down.   Mk 14:12-16

24"Obey these instructions as a lasting ordinance for you and your descendants. 25When you enter the land that the Lord will give you as he promised, observe this ceremony. 26And when your children ask you, 'What does this ceremony mean to you?' 27then tell them, 'It is the Passover sacrifice to the Lord, who passed over the houses of the Israelites in Egypt and spared our homes when he struck down the Egyptians.'" Then the people bowed down and worshiped. 28The Israelites did just what the Lord commanded Moses and Aaron.   ver 11; Jos 4:6

29At midnight the Lord struck down all the firstborn in Egypt, from the firstborn of Pharaoh, who sat on the throne, to the firstborn of the prisoner, who was in the dungeon, and the firstborn of all the livestock as well. 30Pharaoh and all his officials and all the Egyptians got up during the night, and there was loud wailing in Egypt, for there was not a house without someone dead.   Ex 4:23

The Exodus

31During the night Pharaoh summoned Moses and Aaron and said, "Up! Leave my people, you and the Israelites! Go, worship the Lord as you have requested. 32Take your flocks and herds, as you have said, and go. And also bless me."   Ex 10:9,26

33The Egyptians urged the people to hurry and leave the country. "For otherwise," they said, "we will all die!" 34So the people took their dough before the yeast was added, and carried it on their shoulders in kneading troughs wrapped in clothing. 35The Israelites did as Moses instructed and asked the Egyptians for articles of silver and gold and for clothing. 36The Lord had made the Egyptians favorably disposed toward the people, and they gave them what they asked for; so they plundered the Egyptians.   Ex 3:22

37The Israelites journeyed from Rameses to Succoth. There were about six hundred thousand men on foot, besides women and children. 38Many other people went up with them, as well as large droves of livestock, both flocks and herds.

³⁹With the dough they had brought from Egypt, they baked cakes of unleavened bread. The dough was without yeast because they had been driven out of Egypt and did not have time to prepare food for themselves.   Nu 11:13,21

⁴⁰Now the length of time the Israelite people lived in Egypt*a* was 430 years. ⁴¹At the end of the 430 years, to the very day, all the Lord's divisions left Egypt. ⁴²Because the Lord kept vigil that night to bring them out of Egypt, on this night all the Israelites are to keep vigil to honor the Lord for the generations to come.   Dt 16:1,6; Ac 7:6

Passover Restrictions

⁴³The Lord said to Moses and Aaron, "These are the regulations for the Passover: ver 11

"No foreigner is to eat of it. ⁴⁴Any slave you have bought may eat of it after you have circumcised him, ⁴⁵but a temporary resident and a hired worker may not eat of it.   Ge 17:12-13

⁴⁶"It must be eaten inside one house; take none of the meat outside the house. Do not break any of the bones. ⁴⁷The whole community of Israel must celebrate it.

⁴⁸"An alien living among you who wants to celebrate the Lord's Passover must have all the males in his household circumcised; then he may take part like one born in the land. No uncircum-

cised male may eat of it. ⁴⁹The same law applies to the native-born and to the alien living among you."   Nu 9:14; 15:15-16,29

⁵⁰All the Israelites did just what the Lord had commanded Moses and Aaron. ⁵¹And on that very day the Lord brought the Israelites out of Egypt by their divisions.   Ex 6:26

Consecration of the Firstborn

13 The Lord said to Moses, ²"Consecrate to me every firstborn male. The first offspring of every womb among the Israelites belongs to me, whether man or animal."   Lk 2:23

³Then Moses said to the people, "Commemorate this day, the day you came out of Egypt, out of the land of slavery, because the Lord brought you out of it with a mighty hand. Eat nothing containing yeast. ⁴Today, in the month of Abib, you are leaving. ⁵When the Lord brings you into the land of the Canaanites, Hittites, Amorites, Hivites and Jebusites—the land he swore to your forefathers to give you, a land flowing with milk and honey—you are to observe this ceremony in this month: ⁶For seven days eat bread made without yeast and on the seventh day hold a festival to the Lord. ⁷Eat unleavened bread during those seven days; nothing with yeast in it is to be seen among you, nor shall any

---

a40 Masoretic Text; Samaritan Pentateuch and Septuagint *Egypt and Canaan*

yeast be seen anywhere within your borders. **8**On that day tell your son, 'I do this because of what the LORD did for me when I came out of Egypt.' **9**This observance will be for you like a sign on your hand and a reminder on your forehead that the law of the LORD is to be on your lips. For the LORD brought you out of Egypt with his mighty hand. **10**You must keep this ordinance at the appointed time year after year. Ex 12:15-20; Dt 6:8

11"After the LORD brings you into the land of the Canaanites and gives it to you, as he promised on oath to you and your forefathers, **12**you are to give over to the LORD the first offspring of every womb. All the firstborn males of your livestock belong to the LORD. **13**Redeem with a lamb every firstborn donkey, but if you do not redeem it, break its neck. Redeem every firstborn among your sons.

14"In days to come, when your son asks you, 'What does this mean?' say to him, 'With a mighty hand the LORD brought us out of Egypt, out of the land of slavery. **15**When Pharaoh stubbornly refused to let us go, the LORD killed every firstborn in Egypt, both man and animal. This is why I sacrifice to the LORD the first male offspring of every womb and redeem each of my firstborn sons.' **16**And it will be like a sign on your hand and a symbol on your forehead that the LORD brought us out of Egypt with his mighty hand." Ex 12:29; Dt 6:20

Crossing the Sea

17When Pharaoh let the people go, God did not lead them on the road through the Philistine country, though that was shorter. For God said, "If they face war, they might change their minds and return to Egypt." **18**So God led the people around by the desert road toward the Red Sea.*a* The Israelites went up out of Egypt armed for battle. Ex 14:11

19Moses took the bones of Joseph with him because Joseph had made the sons of Israel swear an oath. He had said, "God will surely come to your aid, and then you must carry my bones up with you from this place."*b* Ge 50:24-25

20After leaving Succoth they camped at Etham on the edge of the desert. **21**By day the LORD went ahead of them in a pillar of cloud to guide them on their way and by night in a pillar of fire to give them light, so that they could travel by day or night. **22**Neither the pillar of cloud by day nor the pillar of fire by night left its place in front of the people. Ex 14:19,24; Ps 78:14; 1Co 10:1

14 Then the LORD said to Moses, **2**"Tell the Israelites to turn back and encamp near Pi Hahiroth, between Migdol and the sea. They are to encamp by the sea, directly opposite Baal Zephon.

---

a 18 Hebrew *Yam Suph*; that is, Sea of Reeds   *b 19* See Gen. 50:25.

³Pharaoh will think, 'The Israelites are wandering around the land in confusion, hemmed in by the desert.' ⁴And I will harden Pharaoh's heart, and he will pursue them. But I will gain glory for myself through Pharaoh and all his army, and the Egyptians will know that I am the LORD." So the Israelites did this.   Ro 9:17,22-23; Ex 4:21

⁵When the king of Egypt was told that the people had fled, Pharaoh and his officials changed their minds about them and said, "What have we done? We have let the Israelites go and have lost their services!" ⁶So he had his chariot made ready and took his army with him. ⁷He took six hundred of the best chariots, along with all the other chariots of Egypt, with officers over all of them. ⁸The LORD hardened the heart of Pharaoh king of Egypt, so that he pursued the Israelites, who were marching out boldly. ⁹The Egyptians—all Pharaoh's horses and chariots, horsemen*a* and troops—pursued the Israelites and overtook them as they camped by the sea near Pi Hahiroth, opposite Baal Zephon.

¹⁰As Pharaoh approached, the Israelites looked up, and there were the Egyptians, marching after them. They were terrified and cried out to the LORD. ¹¹They said to Moses, "Was it because there were no graves in Egypt that you brought us to the desert to die? What have you done to us by bringing us out of Egypt? ¹²Didn't we say to you in Egypt, 'Leave us alone; let us serve the Egyptians'? It would have been better for us to serve the Egyptians than to die in the desert!"   Ne 9:9; Ps 34:17

¹³Moses answered the people, "Do not be afraid. Stand firm and you will see the deliverance the LORD will bring you today. The Egyptians you see today you will never see again. ¹⁴The LORD will fight for you; you need only to be still."   Ps 46:10; Isa 30:15; Ex 15:3

¹⁵Then the LORD said to Moses, "Why are you crying out to me? Tell the Israelites to move on. ¹⁶Raise your staff and stretch out your hand over the sea to divide the water so that the Israelites can go through the sea on dry ground. ¹⁷I will harden the hearts of the Egyptians so that they will go in after them. And I will gain glory through Pharaoh and all his army, through his chariots and his horsemen. ¹⁸The Egyptians will know that I am the LORD when I gain glory through Pharaoh, his chariots and his horsemen."   Ex 4:17; Isa 10:26

¹⁹Then the angel of God, who had been traveling in front of Israel's army, withdrew and went behind them. The pillar of cloud also moved from in front and stood behind them, ²⁰coming between the armies of Egypt and Israel. Throughout the night the cloud

a9 Or charioteers; also in verses 17, 18, 23, 26 and 28

brought darkness to the one side and light to the other side; so neither went near the other all night long.   Ex 13:21

²¹Then Moses stretched out his hand over the sea, and all that night the LORD drove the sea back with a strong east wind and turned it into dry land. The waters were divided, ²²and the Israelites went through the sea on dry ground, with a wall of water on their right and on their left.   Heb 11:29; Isa 63:12

²³The Egyptians pursued them, and all Pharaoh's horses and chariots and horsemen followed them into the sea. ²⁴During the last watch of the night the LORD looked down from the pillar of fire and cloud at the Egyptian army and threw it into confusion. ²⁵He made the wheels of their chariots come off[a] so that they had difficulty driving. And the Egyptians said, "Let's get away from the Israelites! The LORD is fighting for them against Egypt."   ver 14; Ex 13:21

²⁶Then the LORD said to Moses, "Stretch out your hand over the sea so that the waters may flow back over the Egyptians and their chariots and horsemen." ²⁷Moses stretched out his hand over the sea, and at daybreak the sea went back to its place. The Egyptians were fleeing toward[b] it, and the LORD swept them into the sea. ²⁸The water flowed back and cov-

ered the chariots and horsemen— the entire army of Pharaoh that had followed the Israelites into the sea. Not one of them survived.

²⁹But the Israelites went through the sea on dry ground, with a wall of water on their right and on their left. ³⁰That day the LORD saved Israel from the hands of the Egyptians, and Israel saw the Egyptians lying dead on the shore. ³¹And when the Israelites saw the great power the LORD displayed against the Egyptians, the people feared the LORD and put their trust in him and in Moses his servant.   Jn 2:11

The Song of Moses and Miriam

15 Then Moses and the Israelites sang this song to the LORD: Rev 15:3

"I will sing to the LORD,   Ps 106:12
　for he is highly exalted.
The horse and its rider
　he has hurled into the sea.
²The LORD is my strength and
　　my song;   Ps 59:17
　he has become my salvation.
He is my God, and I will praise
　　him,
　my father's God, and I will
　　exalt him.   Ex 3:6,15-16
³The LORD is a warrior;   Rev 19:11
　the LORD is his name.
⁴Pharaoh's chariots and his
　　army
　he has hurled into the sea.

---

[a] 25 Or *He jammed the wheels of their chariots* (see Samaritan Pentateuch, Septuagint and Syriac)
[b] 27 Or *from*

The best of Pharaoh's officers
are drowned in the Red
Sea.*a*

⁵The deep waters have covered
them;
they sank to the depths like
a stone.   Ne 9:11

⁶"Your right hand, O Lᴏʀᴅ,
was majestic in power.
Your right hand, O Lᴏʀᴅ,
shattered the enemy.
⁷In the greatness of your
majesty
you threw down those who
opposed you.
You unleashed your burning
anger;
it consumed them like
stubble.
⁸By the blast of your nostrils
the waters piled up.   Ps 78:13
The surging waters stood firm
like a wall;
the deep waters congealed in
the heart of the sea.

⁹"The enemy boasted,
'I will pursue, I will overtake
them.   Ex 14:5-9
I will divide the spoils;
I will gorge myself on them.
I will draw my sword
and my hand will destroy
them.'
¹⁰But you blew with your breath,
and the sea covered them.
They sank like lead
in the mighty waters.

¹¹"Who among the gods is like
you, O Lᴏʀᴅ?   Ex 8:10
Who is like you—
majestic in holiness,   Isa 6:3
awesome in glory,   Ps 18:1
working wonders?
¹²You stretched out your right
hand
and the earth swallowed
them.

¹³"In your unfailing love you will
lead   Ne 9:12
the people you have
redeemed.
In your strength you will guide
them
to your holy dwelling. Ps 78:54
¹⁴The nations will hear and
tremble;
anguish will grip the people
of Philistia.
¹⁵The chiefs of Edom will be
terrified,
the leaders of Moab will be
seized with trembling,
the people*b* of Canaan will
melt away;
¹⁶ terror and dread will fall
upon them.
By the power of your arm
they will be as still as a
stone—
until your people pass by,
O Lᴏʀᴅ,
until the people you bought*c*
pass by.   Ps 74:2
¹⁷You will bring them in and
plant them   Ps 44:2

*a*4 Hebrew *Yam Suph*; that is, Sea of Reeds; also in verse 22   *b*15 Or *rulers*   *c*16 Or *created*

on the mountain of your
    inheritance—   Ps 78:54,68
the place, O LORD, you made
    for your dwelling,
the sanctuary, O Lord, your
    hands established.
¹⁸The LORD will reign
    for ever and ever."

¹⁹When Pharaoh's horses, chariots and horsemen[a] went into the sea, the LORD brought the waters of the sea back over them, but the Israelites walked through the sea on dry ground. ²⁰Then Miriam the prophetess, Aaron's sister, took a tambourine in her hand, and all the women followed her, with tambourines and dancing. ²¹Miriam sang to them: Ex 14:28; Nu 26:59

"Sing to the LORD,
    for he is highly exalted.
The horse and its rider
    he has hurled into the sea."

The Waters of Marah and Elim

²²Then Moses led Israel from the Red Sea and they went into the Desert of Shur. For three days they traveled in the desert without finding water. ²³When they came to Marah, they could not drink its water because it was bitter. (That is why the place is called Marah.[b]) ²⁴So the people grumbled against Moses, saying, "What are we to drink?"   Nu 33:8 ²⁵Then Moses cried out to the LORD, and the LORD showed him a

piece of wood. He threw it into the water, and the water became sweet.

There the LORD made a decree and a law for them, and there he tested them. ²⁶He said, "If you listen carefully to the voice of the LORD your God and do what is right in his eyes, if you pay attention to his commands and keep all his decrees, I will not bring on you any of the diseases I brought on the Egyptians, for I am the LORD, who heals you."   Ex 23:25-26; Dt 28:27,58-60

²⁷Then they came to Elim, where there were twelve springs and seventy palm trees, and they camped there near the water.

Manna and Quail

16 The whole Israelite community set out from Elim and came to the Desert of Sin, which is between Elim and Sinai, on the fifteenth day of the second month after they had come out of Egypt. ²In the desert the whole community grumbled against Moses and Aaron. ³The Israelites said to them, "If only we had died by the LORD's hand in Egypt! There we sat around pots of meat and ate all the food we wanted, but you have brought us out into this desert to starve this entire assembly to death."   Nu 11:4,34; 1Co 10:10

⁴Then the LORD said to Moses, "I will rain down bread from heaven for you. The people are to go out

---

[a] 19 Or charioteers   [b] 23 Marah means bitter.

each day and gather enough for that day. In this way I will test them and see whether they will follow my instructions. ⁵On the sixth day they are to prepare what they bring in, and that is to be twice as much as they gather on the other days." Dt 8:3; Jn 6:31

⁶So Moses and Aaron said to all the Israelites, "In the evening you will know that it was the Lord who brought you out of Egypt, ⁷and in the morning you will see the glory of the Lord, because he has heard your grumbling against him. Who are we, that you should grumble against us?" ⁸Moses also said, "You will know that it was the Lord when he gives you meat to eat in the evening and all the bread you want in the morning, because he has heard your grumbling against him. Who are we? You are not grumbling against us, but against the Lord." Nu 16:11; Ro 13:2

⁹Then Moses told Aaron, "Say to the entire Israelite community, 'Come before the Lord, for he has heard your grumbling.'"

¹⁰While Aaron was speaking to the whole Israelite community, they looked toward the desert, and there was the glory of the Lord appearing in the cloud. Ex 13:21

¹¹The Lord said to Moses, ¹²"I have heard the grumbling of the Israelites. Tell them, 'At twilight you will eat meat, and in the morning you will be filled with bread.

Then you will know that I am the Lord your God.'"

¹³That evening quail came and covered the camp, and in the morning there was a layer of dew around the camp. ¹⁴When the dew was gone, thin flakes like frost on the ground appeared on the desert floor. ¹⁵When the Israelites saw it, they said to each other, "What is it?" For they did not know what it was. Nu 11:7-9,31; Ps 78:27-28

Moses said to them, "It is the bread the Lord has given you to eat. ¹⁶This is what the Lord has commanded: 'Each one is to gather as much as he needs. Take an omer*a* for each person you have in your tent.'"

¹⁷The Israelites did as they were told; some gathered much, some little. ¹⁸And when they measured it by the omer, he who gathered much did not have too much, and he who gathered little did not have too little. Each one gathered as much as he needed. 2Co 8:15

¹⁹Then Moses said to them, "No one is to keep any of it until morning." Ex 12:10

²⁰However, some of them paid no attention to Moses; they kept part of it until morning, but it was full of maggots and began to smell. So Moses was angry with them.

²¹Each morning everyone gathered as much as he needed, and when the sun grew hot, it melted away. ²²On the sixth day, they

a 16 That is, probably about 2 quarts (about 2 liters); also in verses 18, 32, 33 and 36

gathered twice as much—two omers[a] for each person—and the leaders of the community came and reported this to Moses. ²³He said to them, "This is what the LORD commanded: 'Tomorrow is to be a day of rest, a holy Sabbath to the LORD. So bake what you want to bake and boil what you want to boil. Save whatever is left and keep it until morning.' "

²⁴So they saved it until morning, as Moses commanded, and it did not stink or get maggots in it. ²⁵"Eat it today," Moses said, "because today is a Sabbath to the LORD. You will not find any of it on the ground today. ²⁶Six days you are to gather it, but on the seventh day, the Sabbath, there will not be any." Ge 2:3; Ex 20:8

²⁷Nevertheless, some of the people went out on the seventh day to gather it, but they found none. ²⁸Then the LORD said to Moses, "How long will you[b] refuse to keep my commands and my instructions? ²⁹Bear in mind that the LORD has given you the Sabbath; that is why on the sixth day he gives you bread for two days. Everyone is to stay where he is on the seventh day; no one is to go out." ³⁰So the people rested on the seventh day.

³¹The people of Israel called the bread manna.[c] It was white like coriander seed and tasted like wafers made with honey. ³²Moses said, "This is what the LORD has commanded: 'Take an omer of manna and keep it for the generations to come, so they can see the bread I gave you to eat in the desert when I brought you out of Egypt.' "

³³So Moses said to Aaron, "Take a jar and put an omer of manna in it. Then place it before the LORD to be kept for the generations to come." Heb 9:4

³⁴As the LORD commanded Moses, Aaron put the manna in front of the Testimony, that it might be kept. ³⁵The Israelites ate manna forty years, until they came to a land that was settled; they ate manna until they reached the border of Canaan. Ex 25:16,21-22; Jos 5:12

³⁶(An omer is one tenth of an ephah.)

Water From the Rock

17 The whole Israelite community set out from the Desert of Sin, traveling from place to place as the LORD commanded. They camped at Rephidim, but there was no water for the people to drink. ²So they quarreled with Moses and said, "Give us water to drink." Nu 20:2

Moses replied, "Why do you quarrel with me? Why do you put the LORD to the test?" Dt 6:16

³But the people were thirsty for water there, and they grumbled

---

a22 That is, probably about 4 quarts (about 4.5 liters) means What is it? (see verse 15).   b28 The Hebrew is plural.   c31 Manna

against Moses. They said, "Why did you bring us up out of Egypt to make us and our children and livestock die of thirst?"   Ex 15:24; 16:2-3

⁴Then Moses cried out to the LORD, "What am I to do with these people? They are almost ready to stone me."   Nu 14:10

⁵The LORD answered Moses, "Walk on ahead of the people. Take with you some of the elders of Israel and take in your hand the staff with which you struck the Nile, and go. ⁶I will stand there before you by the rock at Horeb. Strike the rock, and water will come out of it for the people to drink." So Moses did this in the sight of the elders of Israel. ⁷And he called the place Massah*a* and Meribah*b* because the Israelites quarreled and because they tested the LORD saying, "Is the LORD among us or not?"   Nu 20:11; 1Co 10:4

The Amalekites Defeated

⁸The Amalekites came and attacked the Israelites at Rephidim. ⁹Moses said to Joshua, "Choose some of our men and go out to fight the Amalekites. Tomorrow I will stand on top of the hill with the staff of God in my hands."

¹⁰So Joshua fought the Amalekites as Moses had ordered, and Moses, Aaron and Hur went to the top of the hill. ¹¹As long as Moses held up his hands, the Israelites were winning, but whenever he lowered his hands, the Amalekites were winning. ¹²When Moses' hands grew tired, they took a stone and put it under him and he sat on it. Aaron and Hur held his hands up—one on one side, one on the other—so that his hands remained steady till sunset. ¹³So Joshua overcame the Amalekite army with the sword.   Jas 5:16

¹⁴Then the LORD said to Moses, "Write this on a scroll as something to be remembered and make sure that Joshua hears it, because I will completely blot out the memory of Amalek from under heaven."   Ex 34:27

¹⁵Moses built an altar and called it The LORD is my Banner. ¹⁶He said, "For hands were lifted up to the throne of the LORD. The*c* LORD will be at war against the Amalekites from generation to generation."   Ge 22:14; Nu 24:7

Jethro Visits Moses

18 Now Jethro, the priest of Midian and father-in-law of Moses, heard of everything God had done for Moses and for his people Israel, and how the LORD had brought Israel out of Egypt.

²After Moses had sent away his wife Zipporah, his father-in-law Jethro received her ³and her two sons. One son was named Gershom,*d* for Moses said, "I have be-

---

a 7 Massah means *testing.*   *b 7 Meribah* means *quarreling.*   *c 16* Or *"Because a hand was against the throne of the LORD, the*   *d 3 Gershom* sounds like the Hebrew for *an alien there.*

come an alien in a foreign land"; ⁴and the other was named Eliezer,ᵃ for he said, "My father's God was my helper; he saved me from the sword of Pharaoh." Ex 2:22; 4:25

⁵Jethro, Moses' father-in-law, together with Moses' sons and wife, came to him in the desert, where he was camped near the mountain of God. ⁶Jethro had sent word to him, "I, your father-in-law Jethro, am coming to you with your wife and her two sons."

⁷So Moses went out to meet his father-in-law and bowed down and kissed him. They greeted each other and then went into the tent. ⁸Moses told his father-in-law about everything the LORD had done to Pharaoh and the Egyptians for Israel's sake and about all the hardships they had met along the way and how the LORD had saved them. Ge 29:13; 43:28

⁹Jethro was delighted to hear about all the good things the LORD had done for Israel in rescuing them from the hand of the Egyptians. ¹⁰He said, "Praise be to the LORD, who rescued you from the hand of the Egyptians and of Pharaoh, and who rescued the people from the hand of the Egyptians. ¹¹Now I know that the LORD is greater than all other gods, for he did this to those who had treated Israel arrogantly." ¹²Then Jethro, Moses' father-in-law, brought a burnt offering and other sacrifices to God, and Aaron came with all the elders of Israel to eat bread with Moses' father-in-law in the presence of God. Lk 1:51; Ps 68:19-20

¹³The next day Moses took his seat to serve as judge for the people, and they stood around him from morning till evening. ¹⁴When his father-in-law saw all that Moses was doing for the people, he said, "What is this you are doing for the people? Why do you alone sit as judge, while all these people stand around you from morning till evening?"

¹⁵Moses answered him, "Because the people come to me to seek God's will. ¹⁶Whenever they have a dispute, it is brought to me, and I decide between the parties and inform them of God's decrees and laws." Nu 9:6,8; Dt 17:8-13

¹⁷Moses' father-in-law replied, "What you are doing is not good. ¹⁸You and these people who come to you will only wear yourselves out. The work is too heavy for you; you cannot handle it alone. ¹⁹Listen now to me and I will give you some advice, and may God be with you. You must be the people's representative before God and bring their disputes to him. ²⁰Teach them the decrees and laws, and show them the way to live and the duties they are to perform. ²¹But select capable men from all the people—men who fear God, trustworthy men who hate dishonest

---

ᵃ4 Eliezer means *my God is helper.*

gain—and appoint them as officials over thousands, hundreds, fifties and tens. ²²Have them serve as judges for the people at all times, but have them bring every difficult case to you; the simple cases they can decide themselves. That will make your load lighter, because they will share it with you. ²³If you do this and God so commands, you will be able to stand the strain, and all these people will go home satisfied."

²⁴Moses listened to his father-in-law and did everything he said. ²⁵He chose capable men from all Israel and made them leaders of the people, officials over thousands, hundreds, fifties and tens. ²⁶They served as judges for the people at all times. The difficult cases they brought to Moses, but the simple ones they decided themselves.   ver 22; Dt 1:13-15

²⁷Then Moses sent his father-in-law on his way, and Jethro returned to his own country.

At Mount Sinai

19 In the third month after the Israelites left Egypt—on the very day—they came to the Desert of Sinai. ²After they set out from Rephidim, they entered the Desert of Sinai, and Israel camped there in the desert in front of the mountain.   Ex 17:1

³Then Moses went up to God, and the Lord called to him from the mountain and said, "This is what you are to say to the house of Jacob and what you are to tell the people of Israel: ⁴'You yourselves have seen what I did to Egypt, and how I carried you on eagles' wings and brought you to myself. ⁵Now if you obey me fully and keep my covenant, then out of all nations you will be my treasured possession. Although the whole earth is mine, ⁶youᵃ will be for me a kingdom of priests and a holy nation.' These are the words you are to speak to the Israelites."   Dt 7:6

⁷So Moses went back and summoned the elders of the people and set before them all the words the Lord had commanded him to speak. ⁸The people all responded together, "We will do everything the Lord has said." So Moses brought their answer back to the Lord.   Ex 24:3,7; Dt 5:27

⁹The Lord said to Moses, "I am going to come to you in a dense cloud, so that the people will hear me speaking with you and will always put their trust in you." Then Moses told the Lord what the people had said.   ver 16; Ex 24:15-16

¹⁰And the Lord said to Moses, "Go to the people and consecrate them today and tomorrow. Have them wash their clothes ¹¹and be ready by the third day, because on that day the Lord will come down on Mount Sinai in the sight of all the people. ¹²Put limits for the peo-

ᵃ 5,6 Or *possession, for the whole earth is mine.* ⁶*You*

ple around the mountain and tell them, 'Be careful that you do not go up the mountain or touch the foot of it. Whoever touches the mountain shall surely be put to death. ¹³He shall surely be stoned or shot with arrows; not a hand is to be laid on him. Whether man or animal, he shall not be permitted to live.' Only when the ram's horn sounds a long blast may they go up to the mountain."   Lev 11:44; Heb 12:20

¹⁴After Moses had gone down the mountain to the people, he consecrated them, and they washed their clothes. ¹⁵Then he said to the people, "Prepare yourselves for the third day. Abstain from sexual relations."   Ge 35:2

¹⁶On the morning of the third day there was thunder and lightning, with a thick cloud over the mountain, and a very loud trumpet blast. Everyone in the camp trembled. ¹⁷Then Moses led the people out of the camp to meet with God, and they stood at the foot of the mountain. ¹⁸Mount Sinai was covered with smoke, because the LORD descended on it in fire. The smoke billowed up from it like smoke from a furnace, the whole mountain[a] trembled violently, ¹⁹and the sound of the trumpet grew louder and louder. Then Moses spoke and the voice of God answered him.[b]

²⁰The LORD descended to the top of Mount Sinai and called Moses to the top of the mountain. So Moses went up ²¹and the LORD said to him, "Go down and warn the people so they do not force their way through to see the LORD and many of them perish. ²²Even the priests, who approach the LORD, must consecrate themselves, or the LORD will break out against them."

²³Moses said to the LORD, "The people cannot come up Mount Sinai, because you yourself warned us, 'Put limits around the mountain and set it apart as holy.'"

²⁴The LORD replied, "Go down and bring Aaron up with you. But the priests and the people must not force their way through to come up to the LORD, or he will break out against them."   Ex 24:1,9

²⁵So Moses went down to the people and told them.

The Ten Commandments

20 And God spoke all these words:

²"I am the LORD your God, who brought you out of Egypt, out of the land of slavery.   Ex 13:3

³"You shall have no other gods before[c] me.   Dt 6:14

⁴"You shall not make for yourself an idol in the form of anything in heaven above or on the earth beneath or in the waters below. ⁵You shall not bow

---

a 18 Most Hebrew manuscripts; a few Hebrew manuscripts and Septuagint *all the people*   *b 19* Or *and God answered him with thunder*   *c 3* Or *besides*

down to them or worship them; for I, the LORD your God, am a jealous God, punishing the children for the sin of the fathers to the third and fourth generation of those who hate me, 6but showing love to a thousand ˻generations˼ of those who love me and keep my commandments. Dt 4:24

7"You shall not misuse the name of the LORD your God, for the LORD will not hold anyone guiltless who misuses his name.

8"Remember the Sabbath day by keeping it holy. 9Six days you shall labor and do all your work, 10but the seventh day is a Sabbath to the LORD your God. On it you shall not do any work, neither you, nor your son or daughter, nor your manservant or maidservant, nor your animals, nor the alien within your gates. 11For in six days the LORD made the heavens and the earth, the sea, and all that is in them, but he rested on the seventh day. Therefore the LORD blessed the Sabbath day and made it holy.

12"Honor your father and your mother, so that you may live long in the land the LORD your God is giving you. Mt 15:4; Eph 6:2

13"You shall not murder.

14"You shall not commit adultery. Mt 19:18

15"You shall not steal.

16"You shall not give false testimony against your neighbor. Ex 23:1,7

17"You shall not covet your neighbor's house. You shall not covet your neighbor's wife, or his manservant or maidservant, his ox or donkey, or anything that belongs to your neighbor." Dt 5:6-21

18When the people saw the thunder and lightning and heard the trumpet and saw the mountain in smoke, they trembled with fear. They stayed at a distance 19and said to Moses, "Speak to us yourself and we will listen. But do not have God speak to us or we will die." Dt 5:5,23-27; Ex 19:16-19

20Moses said to the people, "Do not be afraid. God has come to test you, so that the fear of God will be with you to keep you from sinning." Pr 16:6

21The people remained at a distance, while Moses approached the thick darkness where God was.

Idols and Altars

22Then the LORD said to Moses, "Tell the Israelites this: 'You have seen for yourselves that I have spoken to you from heaven: 23Do not make any gods to be alongside me; do not make for yourselves gods of silver or gods of gold. ver 3

²⁴" 'Make an altar of earth for me and sacrifice on it your burnt offerings and fellowship offerings,ᵃ your sheep and goats and your cattle. Wherever I cause my name to be honored, I will come to you and bless you. ²⁵If you make an altar of stones for me, do not build it with dressed stones, for you will defile it if you use a tool on it. ²⁶And do not go up to my altar on steps, lest your nakedness be exposed on it.'

21

"These are the laws you are to set before them:

Hebrew Servants

²"If you buy a Hebrew servant, he is to serve you for six years. But in the seventh year, he shall go free, without paying anything. ³If he comes alone, he is to go free alone; but if he has a wife when he comes, she is to go with him. ⁴If his master gives him a wife and she bears him sons or daughters, the woman and her children shall belong to her master, and only the man shall go free. Jer 34:8,14

⁵"But if the servant declares, 'I love my master and my wife and children and do not want to go free,' ⁶then his master must take him before the judges.ᵇ He shall take him to the door or the door-

post and pierce his ear with an awl. Then he will be his servant for life.

⁷"If a man sells his daughter as a servant, she is not to go free as menservants do. ⁸If she does not please the master who has selected her for himself,ᶜ he must let her be redeemed. He has no right to sell her to foreigners, because he has broken faith with her. ⁹If he selects her for his son, he must grant her the rights of a daughter. ¹⁰If he marries another woman, he must not deprive the first one of her food, clothing and marital rights. ¹¹If he does not provide her with these three things, she is to go free, without any payment of money.

Personal Injuries

¹²"Anyone who strikes a man and kills him shall surely be put to death. ¹³However, if he does not do it intentionally, but God lets it happen, he is to flee to a place I will designate. ¹⁴But if a man schemes and kills another man deliberately, take him away from my altar and put him to death.

¹⁵"Anyone who attacksᵈ his father or his mother must be put to death.

¹⁶"Anyone who kidnaps another and either sells him or still has him when he is caught must be put to death. Dt 24:7

¹⁷"Anyone who curses his father or mother must be put to death.

ᵃ24 Traditionally *peace offerings*   ᵇ6 Or *before God*   ᶜ8 Or *master so that he does not choose her*   ᵈ15 Or *kills*

18"If men quarrel and one hits the other with a stone or with his fist[a] and he does not die but is confined to bed, **19**the one who struck the blow will not be held responsible if the other gets up and walks around outside with his staff; however, he must pay the injured man for the loss of his time and see that he is completely healed.

20"If a man beats his male or female slave with a rod and the slave dies as a direct result, he must be punished, **21**but he is not to be punished if the slave gets up after a day or two, since the slave is his property.   Lev 25:44-46

22"If men who are fighting hit a pregnant woman and she gives birth prematurely[b] but there is no serious injury, the offender must be fined whatever the woman's husband demands and the court allows. **23**But if there is serious injury, you are to take life for life, **24**eye for eye, tooth for tooth, hand for hand, foot for foot, **25**burn for burn, wound for wound, bruise for bruise.   Mt 5:38

26"If a man hits a manservant or maidservant in the eye and destroys it, he must let the servant go free to compensate for the eye. **27**And if he knocks out the tooth of a manservant or maidservant, he must let the servant go free to compensate for the tooth.

28"If a bull gores a man or a woman to death, the bull must be stoned to death, and its meat must not be eaten. But the owner of the bull will not be held responsible. **29**If, however, the bull has had the habit of goring and the owner has been warned but has not kept it penned up and it kills a man or woman, the bull must be stoned and the owner also must be put to death. **30**However, if payment is demanded of him, he may redeem his life by paying whatever is demanded. **31**This law also applies if the bull gores a son or daughter. **32**If the bull gores a male or female slave, the owner must pay thirty shekels[c] of silver to the master of the slave, and the bull must be stoned.   Zec 11:12-13; Mt 26:15; Ge 9:5

33"If a man uncovers a pit or digs one and fails to cover it and an ox or a donkey falls into it, **34**the owner of the pit must pay for the loss; he must pay its owner, and the dead animal will be his.

35"If a man's bull injures the bull of another and it dies, they are to sell the live one and divide both the money and the dead animal equally. **36**However, if it was known that the bull had the habit of goring, yet the owner did not keep it penned up, the owner must pay, animal for animal, and the dead animal will be his.

[a]18 Or with a tool   [b]22 Or she has a miscarriage   [c]32 That is, about 12 ounces (about 0.3 kilogram)

Protection of Property

22 "If a man steals an ox or a sheep and slaughters it or sells it, he must pay back five head of cattle for the ox and four sheep for the sheep.   2Sa 12:6

²"If a thief is caught breaking in and is struck so that he dies, the defender is not guilty of bloodshed; ³but if it happens*ᵃ* after sunrise, he is guilty of bloodshed.

"A thief must certainly make restitution, but if he has nothing, he must be sold to pay for his theft.

⁴"If the stolen animal is found alive in his possession—whether ox or donkey or sheep—he must pay back double.   Ge 43:12

⁵"If a man grazes his livestock in a field or vineyard and lets them stray and they graze in another man's field, he must make restitution from the best of his own field or vineyard.   ver 1

⁶"If a fire breaks out and spreads into thornbushes so that it burns shocks of grain or standing grain or the whole field, the one who started the fire must make restitution.   Jdg 15:5

⁷"If a man gives his neighbor silver or goods for safekeeping and they are stolen from the neighbor's house, the thief, if he is caught, must pay back double. ⁸But if the thief is not found, the owner of the house must appear before the judges*ᵇ* to determine whether he has laid his hands on the other man's property. ⁹In all cases of illegal possession of an ox, a donkey, a sheep, a garment, or any other lost property about which somebody says, 'This is mine,' both parties are to bring their cases before the judges. The one whom the judges declare*ᶜ* guilty must pay back double to his neighbor.

¹⁰"If a man gives a donkey, an ox, a sheep or any other animal to his neighbor for safekeeping and it dies or is injured or is taken away while no one is looking, ¹¹the issue between them will be settled by the taking of an oath before the LORD that the neighbor did not lay hands on the other person's property. The owner is to accept this, and no restitution is required. ¹²But if the animal was stolen from the neighbor, he must make restitution to the owner. ¹³If it was torn to pieces by a wild animal, he shall bring in the remains as evidence and he will not be required to pay for the torn animal.   Ge 31:39; Heb 6:16

¹⁴"If a man borrows an animal from his neighbor and it is injured or dies while the owner is not present, he must make restitution. ¹⁵But if the owner is with the animal, the borrower will not have to pay. If the animal was hired, the money paid for the hire covers the loss.   Lev 19:13

Social Responsibility

¹⁶"If a man seduces a virgin who

---

*ᵃ*3 Or *if he strikes him*   *ᵇ*8 Or *before God*; also in verse 9   *ᶜ*9 Or *whom God declares* is not pledged to be married and sleeps with her, he must pay the bride-price, and she shall be his wife. ¹⁷If her father absolutely refuses to give her to him, he must still pay the bride-price for virgins.

¹⁸"Do not allow a sorceress to live. Lev 20:27; Dt 18:11

¹⁹"Anyone who has sexual relations with an animal must be put to death. Lev 18:23

²⁰"Whoever sacrifices to any god other than the LORD must be destroyed.ᵃ Dt 17:2-5

²¹"Do not mistreat an alien or oppress him, for you were aliens in Egypt. Dt 10:19

²²"Do not take advantage of a widow or an orphan. ²³If you do and they cry out to me, I will certainly hear their cry. ²⁴My anger will be aroused, and I will kill you with the sword; your wives will become widows and your children fatherless. Ps 18:6; 109:9; Lk 18:7

²⁵"If you lend money to one of my people among you who is needy, do not be like a moneylender; charge him no interest.ᵇ ²⁶If you take your neighbor's cloak as a pledge, return it to him by sunset, ²⁷because his cloak is the only covering he has for his body. What else will he sleep in? When he cries out to me, I will hear, for I am compassionate. Ex 34:6; Lev 25:35-37

²⁸"Do not blaspheme Godᶜ or curse the ruler of your people.

²⁹"Do not hold back offerings from your granaries or your vats.ᵈ

"You must give me the firstborn of your sons. ³⁰Do the same with your cattle and your sheep. Let them stay with their mothers for seven days, but give them to me on the eighth day. Ex 13:2; Lev 22:27

³¹"You are to be my holy people. So do not eat the meat of an animal torn by wild beasts; throw it to the dogs. Lev 19:2

Laws of Justice and Mercy

23 "Do not spread false reports. Do not help a wicked man by being a malicious witness.

²"Do not follow the crowd in doing wrong. When you give testimony in a lawsuit, do not pervert justice by siding with the crowd, ³and do not show favoritism to a poor man in his lawsuit. Dt 16:19

⁴"If you come across your enemy's ox or donkey wandering off, be sure to take it back to him. ⁵If you see the donkey of someone who hates you fallen down under its load, do not leave it there; be sure you help him with it. Dt 22:4

⁶"Do not deny justice to your poor people in their lawsuits. ⁷Have nothing to do with a false charge and do not put an innocent or honest person to death, for I will not acquit the guilty. Eph 4:25

⁸"Do not accept a bribe, for a bribe blinds those who see and

---

ᵃ20 The Hebrew term refers to the irrevocable giving over of things or persons to the LORD, often by totally destroying them.   ᵇ25 Or *excessive interest*   ᶜ28 Or *Do not revile the judges*   ᵈ29 The meaning of the Hebrew for this phrase is uncertain.

twists the words of the righteous.

9"Do not oppress an alien; you yourselves know how it feels to be aliens, because you were aliens in Egypt.   Ex 22:21

Sabbath Laws

10"For six years you are to sow your fields and harvest the crops, 11but during the seventh year let the land lie unplowed and unused. Then the poor among your people may get food from it, and the wild animals may eat what they leave. Do the same with your vineyard and your olive grove.

12"Six days do your work, but on the seventh day do not work, so that your ox and your donkey may rest and the slave born in your household, and the alien as well, may be refreshed.   Ex 20:9

13"Be careful to do everything I have said to you. Do not invoke the names of other gods; do not let them be heard on your lips.

The Three Annual Festivals

14"Three times a year you are to celebrate a festival to me.

15"Celebrate the Feast of Unleavened Bread; for seven days eat bread made without yeast, as I commanded you. Do this at the appointed time in the month of Abib, for in that month you came out of Egypt.   Ex 12:17

"No one is to appear before me empty-handed.   Ex 34:20

16"Celebrate the Feast of Harvest with the firstfruits of the crops you sow in your field.   Ex 34:22

"Celebrate the Feast of Ingathering at the end of the year, when you gather in your crops from the field.   Dt 16:13

17"Three times a year all the men are to appear before the Sovereign LORD.   Dt 16:16

18"Do not offer the blood of a sacrifice to me along with anything containing yeast.   Ex 34:25

"The fat of my festival offerings must not be kept until morning.

19"Bring the best of the firstfruits of your soil to the house of the LORD your God.   Dt 26:2,10

"Do not cook a young goat in its mother's milk.   Dt 14:21

God's Angel to Prepare the Way

20"See, I am sending an angel ahead of you to guard you along the way and to bring you to the place I have prepared. 21Pay attention to him and listen to what he says. Do not rebel against him; he will not forgive your rebellion, since my Name is in him. 22If you listen carefully to what he says and do all that I say, I will be an enemy to your enemies and will oppose those who oppose you. 23My angel will go ahead of you and bring you into the land of the Amorites, Hittites, Perizzites, Canaanites, Hivites and Jebusites, and I will wipe them out. 24Do not bow down before their gods or worship them or follow their practices. You must demolish them and break their sacred stones to pieces. 25Worship the LORD your God, and his blessing will be on your food and water. I will take away sickness from among you, 26and none will miscarry or be barren in your land. I will give you a full life span.

27"I will send my terror ahead of you and throw into confusion every nation you encounter. I will make all your enemies turn their backs and run. 28I will send the hornet ahead of you to drive the Hivites, Canaanites and Hittites out of your way. 29But I will not drive them out in a single year, because the land would become desolate and the wild animals too numerous for you. 30Little by little I will drive them out before you, until you have increased enough to take possession of the land.

31"I will establish your borders from the Red Sea^a to the Sea of the Philistines,^b and from the desert to the River.^c I will hand over to you the people who live in the land and you will drive them out before you. 32Do not make a covenant with them or with their gods. 33Do not let them live in your land, or they will cause you to sin against me, because the worship of their gods will certainly be a snare to you."   Dt 7:16; Jos 21:44

The Covenant Confirmed

24 Then he said to Moses, "Come up to the LORD, you and Aaron, Nadab and Abihu, and seventy of the elders of Israel. You are to worship at a distance, 2but Moses alone is to approach the LORD; the others must not come near. And the people may not come up with him."   Nu 11:16

3When Moses went and told the people all the LORD's words and laws, they responded with one voice, "Everything the LORD has said we will do." 4Moses then wrote down everything the LORD had said.   Ex 19:8; Dt 31:9

He got up early the next morning and built an altar at the foot of the mountain and set up twelve stone pillars representing the twelve tribes of Israel. 5Then he sent young Israelite men, and they offered burnt offerings and sacrificed young bulls as fellowship offerings^d to the LORD. 6Moses took half of the blood and put it in bowls, and the other half he sprinkled on the altar. 7Then he took the Book of the Covenant and read it to the people. They responded, "We will do everything the LORD has said; we will obey."   Heb 9:19

8Moses then took the blood, sprinkled it on the people and said, "This is the blood of the covenant that the LORD has made with you in accordance with all these words."

---

^a31 Hebrew *Yam Suph*; that is, Sea of Reeds   ^b31 That is, the Mediterranean   ^c31 That is, the Euphrates   ^d5 Traditionally *peace offerings*

⁹Moses and Aaron, Nadab and Abihu, and the seventy elders of Israel went up ¹⁰and saw the God of Israel. Under his feet was something like a pavement made of sapphire,ᵃ clear as the sky itself. ¹¹But God did not raise his hand against these leaders of the Israelites; they saw God, and they ate and drank.

¹²The Lord said to Moses, "Come up to me on the mountain and stay here, and I will give you the tablets of stone, with the law and commands I have written for their instruction." Ex 32:15-16

¹³Then Moses set out with Joshua his aide, and Moses went up on the mountain of God. ¹⁴He said to the elders, "Wait here for us until we come back to you. Aaron and Hur are with you, and anyone involved in a dispute can go to them." Ex 3:1; 17:9

¹⁵When Moses went up on the mountain, the cloud covered it, ¹⁶and the glory of the Lord settled on Mount Sinai. For six days the cloud covered the mountain, and on the seventh day the Lord called to Moses from within the cloud. ¹⁷To the Israelites the glory of the Lord looked like a consuming fire on top of the mountain. ¹⁸Then Moses entered the cloud as he went on up the mountain. And he stayed on the mountain forty days and forty nights. Heb 12:18,29; Ex 19:9

Offerings for the Tabernacle

25 The Lord said to Moses, ²"Tell the Israelites to bring me an offering. You are to receive the offering for me from each man whose heart prompts him to give. ³These are the offerings you are to receive from them: gold, silver and bronze; ⁴blue, purple and scarlet yarn and fine linen; goat hair; ⁵ram skins dyed red and hides of sea cowsᵇ; acacia wood; ⁶olive oil for the light; spices for the anointing oil and for the fragrant incense; ⁷and onyx stones and other gems to be mounted on the ephod and breastpiece.

⁸"Then have them make a sanctuary for me, and I will dwell among them. ⁹Make this tabernacle and all its furnishings exactly like the pattern I will show you.

The Ark

¹⁰"Have them make a chest of acacia wood—two and a half cubits long, a cubit and a half wide, and a cubit and a half high.ᶜ ¹¹Overlay it with pure gold, both inside and out, and make a gold molding around it. ¹²Cast four gold rings for it and fasten them to its four feet, with two rings on one side and two rings on the other. ¹³Then make poles of acacia wood and overlay them with gold. ¹⁴Insert the poles into the rings on the sides of the chest to carry it. ¹⁵The

---

ᵃ10 Or *lapis lazuli*   ᵇ5 That is, dugongs   ᶜ10 That is, about 3 3/4 feet (about 1.1 meters) long and 2 1/4 feet (about 0.7 meter) wide and high

poles are to remain in the rings of this ark; they are not to be removed. [16]Then put in the ark the Testimony, which I will give you.

[17]"Make an atonement cover[a] of pure gold—two and a half cubits long and a cubit and a half wide.[b] [18]And make two cherubim out of hammered gold at the ends of the cover. [19]Make one cherub on one end and the second cherub on the other; make the cherubim of one piece with the cover, at the two ends. [20]The cherubim are to have their wings spread upward, overshadowing the cover with them. The cherubim are to face each other, looking toward the cover. [21]Place the cover on top of the ark and put in the ark the Testimony, which I will give you. [22]There, above the cover between the two cherubim that are over the ark of the Testimony, I will meet with you and give you all my commands for the Israelites.   Ex 37:1-9

The Table

[23]"Make a table of acacia wood —two cubits long, a cubit wide and a cubit and a half high.[c] [24]Overlay it with pure gold and make a gold molding around it. [25]Also make around it a rim a handbreadth[d] wide and put a gold molding on the rim. [26]Make four gold rings for the table and fasten them to the four corners, where the four legs are. [27]The rings are to be close to the rim to hold the poles used in carrying the table. [28]Make the poles of acacia wood, overlay them with gold and carry the table with them. [29]And make its plates and dishes of pure gold, as well as its pitchers and bowls for the pouring out of offerings. [30]Put the bread of the Presence on this table to be before me at all times.   Ex 37:10-16; Nu 4:7

The Lampstand

[31]"Make a lampstand of pure gold and hammer it out, base and shaft; its flowerlike cups, buds and blossoms shall be of one piece with it. [32]Six branches are to extend from the sides of the lampstand—three on one side and three on the other. [33]Three cups shaped like almond flowers with buds and blossoms are to be on one branch, three on the next branch, and the same for all six branches extending from the lampstand. [34]And on the lampstand there are to be four cups shaped like almond flowers with buds and blossoms. [35]One bud shall be under the first pair of branches extending from the lampstand, a second bud under the second pair, and a third bud under the third pair—six branches in all. [36]The buds and branches shall all be of one piece with the

---

[a]17 Traditionally *a mercy seat*   [b]17 That is, about 3 3/4 feet (about 1.1 meters) long and 2 1/4 feet (about 0.7 meter) wide   [c]23 That is, about 3 feet (about 0.9 meter) long and 1 1/2 feet (about 0.5 meter) wide and 2 1/4 feet (about 0.7 meter) high   [d]25 That is, about 3 inches (about 8 centimeters)

lampstand, hammered out of pure gold.   Zec 4:2; Rev 1:12

37"Then make its seven lamps and set them up on it so that they light the space in front of it. 38Its wick trimmers and trays are to be of pure gold. 39A talent[a] of pure gold is to be used for the lamp-stand and all these accessories. 40See that you make them accord-ing to the pattern shown you on the mountain.   Ex 37:17-24; Ac 7:44

The Tabernacle

26 "Make the tabernacle with ten curtains of finely twist-ed linen and blue, purple and scar-let yarn, with cherubim worked into them by a skilled craftsman. 2All the curtains are to be the same size—twenty-eight cubits long and four cubits wide.[b] 3Join five of the curtains together, and do the same with the other five. 4Make loops of blue material along the edge of the end curtain in one set, and do the same with the end cur-tain in the other set. 5Make fifty loops on one curtain and fifty loops on the end curtain of the oth-er set, with the loops opposite each other. 6Then make fifty gold clasps and use them to fasten the curtains together so that the tabernacle is a unit.   Ex 36:8-13

7"Make curtains of goat hair for the tent over the tabernacle—elev-en altogether. 8All eleven curtains are to be the same size—thirty cu-bits long and four cubits wide.[c] 9Join five of the curtains together into one set and the other six into another set. Fold the sixth curtain double at the front of the tent. 10Make fifty loops along the edge of the end curtain in one set and also along the edge of the end cur-tain in the other set. 11Then make fifty bronze clasps and put them in the loops to fasten the tent togeth-er as a unit. 12As for the additional length of the tent curtains, the half curtain that is left over is to hang down at the rear of the tabernacle. 13The tent curtains will be a cubit[d] longer on both sides; what is left will hang over the sides of the tab-ernacle so as to cover it. 14Make for the tent a covering of ram skins dyed red, and over that a covering of hides of sea cows.[e]   Ex 36:14-19

15"Make upright frames of aca-cia wood for the tabernacle. 16Each frame is to be ten cubits long and a cubit and a half wide,[f] 17with two projections set parallel to each other. Make all the frames of the tabernacle in this way. 18Make twenty frames for the south side of the tabernacle 19and make forty silver bases to go under them— two bases for each frame, one un-der each projection. 20For the oth-er side, the north side of the taber-

---

a39 That is, about 75 pounds (about 34 kilograms) long and 6 feet (about 1.8 meters) wide   c8 That is, about 45 feet (about 13.5 meters) long and 6 feet (about 1.8 meters) wide   d13 That is, about 1 1/2 feet (about 0.5 meter)   e14 That is, dugongs   b2 That is, about 42 feet (about 12.5 meters) f16 That is, about 15 feet (about 4.5 meters) long and 2 1/4 feet (about 0.7 meter) wide

nacle, make twenty frames ²¹and forty silver bases—two under each frame. ²²Make six frames for the far end, that is, the west end of the tabernacle, ²³and make two frames for the corners at the far end. ²⁴At these two corners they must be double from the bottom all the way to the top, and fitted into a single ring; both shall be like that. ²⁵So there will be eight frames and sixteen silver bases—two under each frame.   Ex 36:20-30

²⁶"Also make crossbars of acacia wood: five for the frames on one side of the tabernacle, ²⁷five for those on the other side, and five for the frames on the west, at the far end of the tabernacle. ²⁸The center crossbar is to extend from end to end at the middle of the frames. ²⁹Overlay the frames with gold and make gold rings to hold the crossbars. Also overlay the crossbars with gold.   Ex 36:31-34

³⁰"Set up the tabernacle according to the plan shown you on the mountain.   Ex 25:9,40; Ac 7:44; Heb 8:5

³¹"Make a curtain of blue, purple and scarlet yarn and finely twisted linen, with cherubim worked into it by a skilled craftsman. ³²Hang it with gold hooks on four posts of acacia wood overlaid with gold and standing on four silver bases. ³³Hang the curtain from the clasps and place the ark of the Testimony behind the curtain. The curtain will separate the Holy Place from the Most Holy Place. ³⁴Put the atonement cover on the ark of the Testimony in the Most Holy Place. ³⁵Place the table outside the curtain on the north side of the tabernacle and put the lampstand opposite it on the south side.

³⁶"For the entrance to the tent make a curtain of blue, purple and scarlet yarn and finely twisted linen—the work of an embroiderer. ³⁷Make gold hooks for this curtain and five posts of acacia wood overlaid with gold. And cast five bronze bases for them.   Ex 36:37-38

The Altar of Burnt Offering

27 "Build an altar of acacia wood, three cubits*a* high; it is to be square, five cubits long and five cubits wide.*b* ²Make a horn at each of the four corners, so that the horns and the altar are of one piece, and overlay the altar with bronze. ³Make all its utensils of bronze—its pots to remove the ashes, and its shovels, sprinkling bowls, meat forks and firepans. ⁴Make a grating for it, a bronze network, and make a bronze ring at each of the four corners of the network. ⁵Put it under the ledge of the altar so that it is halfway up the altar. ⁶Make poles of acacia wood for the altar and overlay them with bronze. ⁷The poles are to be inserted into the rings so they will be on

---

a 1 That is, about 4 1/2 feet (about 1.3 meters)   *b* 1 That is, about 7 1/2 feet (about 2.3 meters) long and wide

two sides of the altar when it is carried. ⁸Make the altar hollow, out of boards. It is to be made just as you were shown on the mountain.   Ex 38:1-7

The Courtyard

⁹"Make a courtyard for the tabernacle. The south side shall be a hundred cubits*a* long and is to have curtains of finely twisted linen, ¹⁰with twenty posts and twenty bronze bases and with silver hooks and bands on the posts. ¹¹The north side shall also be a hundred cubits long and is to have curtains, with twenty posts and twenty bronze bases and with silver hooks and bands on the posts.

¹²"The west end of the courtyard shall be fifty cubits*b* wide and have curtains, with ten posts and ten bases. ¹³On the east end, toward the sunrise, the courtyard shall also be fifty cubits wide. ¹⁴Curtains fifteen cubits*c* long are to be on one side of the entrance, with three posts and three bases, ¹⁵and curtains fifteen cubits long are to be on the other side, with three posts and three bases.

¹⁶"For the entrance to the courtyard, provide a curtain twenty cubits*d* long, of blue, purple and scarlet yarn and finely twisted linen—the work of an embroiderer—with four posts and four bases.

¹⁷All the posts around the courtyard are to have silver bands and hooks, and bronze bases. ¹⁸The courtyard shall be a hundred cubits long and fifty cubits wide,*e* with curtains of finely twisted linen five cubits*f* high, and with bronze bases. ¹⁹All the other articles used in the service of the tabernacle, whatever their function, including all the tent pegs for it and those for the courtyard, are to be of bronze.   Ex 38:9-20

Oil for the Lampstand

²⁰"Command the Israelites to bring you clear oil of pressed olives for the light so that the lamps may be kept burning. ²¹In the Tent of Meeting, outside the curtain that is in front of the Testimony, Aaron and his sons are to keep the lamps burning before the LORD from evening till morning. This is to be a lasting ordinance among the Israelites for the generations to come.   Lev 24:1-3

The Priestly Garments

28 "Have Aaron your brother brought to you from among the Israelites, along with his sons Nadab and Abihu, Eleazar and Ithamar, so they may serve me as priests. ²Make sacred garments for your brother Aaron, to give him dignity and honor. ³Tell all the

---

a 9 That is, about 150 feet (about 46 meters); also in verse 11   *b 12* That is, about 75 feet (about 23 meters); also in verse 13   *c 14* That is, about 22 1/2 feet (about 6.9 meters); also in verse 15   *d 16* That is, about 30 feet (about 9 meters)   *e 18* That is, about 150 feet (about 46 meters) long and 75 feet (about 23 meters) wide   *f 18* That is, about 7 1/2 feet (about 2.3 meters)

skilled men to whom I have given wisdom in such matters that they are to make garments for Aaron, for his consecration, so he may serve me as priest. ⁴These are the garments they are to make: a breastpiece, an ephod, a robe, a woven tunic, a turban and a sash. They are to make these sacred garments for your brother Aaron and his sons, so they may serve me as priests. ⁵Have them use gold, and blue, purple and scarlet yarn, and fine linen.   Ex 31:3,6

The Ephod

⁶"Make the ephod of gold, and of blue, purple and scarlet yarn, and of finely twisted linen—the work of a skilled craftsman. ⁷It is to have two shoulder pieces attached to two of its corners, so it can be fastened. ⁸Its skillfully woven waistband is to be like it—of one piece with the ephod and made with gold, and with blue, purple and scarlet yarn, and with finely twisted linen.

⁹"Take two onyx stones and engrave on them the names of the sons of Israel ¹⁰in the order of their birth—six names on one stone and the remaining six on the other. ¹¹Engrave the names of the sons of Israel on the two stones the way a gem cutter engraves a seal. Then mount the stones in gold filigree settings ¹²and fasten them on the shoulder pieces of the ephod as memorial stones for the sons of Israel. Aaron is to bear the names on his shoulders as a memorial before the LORD. ¹³Make gold filigree settings ¹⁴and two braided chains of pure gold, like a rope, and attach the chains to the settings.   Ex 39:2-7

The Breastpiece

¹⁵"Fashion a breastpiece for making decisions—the work of a skilled craftsman. Make it like the ephod: of gold, and of blue, purple and scarlet yarn, and of finely twisted linen. ¹⁶It is to be square— a span*ᵃ* long and a span wide— and folded double. ¹⁷Then mount four rows of precious stones on it. In the first row there shall be a ruby, a topaz and a beryl; ¹⁸in the second row a turquoise, a sapphire*ᵇ* and an emerald; ¹⁹in the third row a jacinth, an agate and an amethyst; ²⁰in the fourth row a chrysolite, an onyx and a jasper.*ᶜ* Mount them in gold filigree settings. ²¹There are to be twelve stones, one for each of the names of the sons of Israel, each engraved like a seal with the name of one of the twelve tribes.   Rev 21:12

²²"For the breastpiece make braided chains of pure gold, like a rope. ²³Make two gold rings for it and fasten them to two corners of the breastpiece. ²⁴Fasten the two gold chains to the rings at the cor-

---

ᵃ16 That is, about 9 inches (about 22 centimeters)   *ᵇ18* Or *lapis lazuli*   *ᶜ20* The precise identification of some of these precious stones is uncertain.

ners of the breastpiece, ²⁵and the other ends of the chains to the two settings, attaching them to the shoulder pieces of the ephod at the front. ²⁶Make two gold rings and attach them to the other two corners of the breastpiece on the inside edge next to the ephod. ²⁷Make two more gold rings and attach them to the bottom of the shoulder pieces on the front of the ephod, close to the seam just above the waistband of the ephod. ²⁸The rings of the breastpiece are to be tied to the rings of the ephod with blue cord, connecting it to the waistband, so that the breastpiece will not swing out from the ephod.

²⁹"Whenever Aaron enters the Holy Place, he will bear the names of the sons of Israel over his heart on the breastpiece of decision as a continuing memorial before the Lord. ³⁰Also put the Urim and the Thummim in the breastpiece, so they may be over Aaron's heart whenever he enters the presence of the Lord. Thus Aaron will always bear the means of making decisions for the Israelites over his heart before the Lord.   Lev 8:8

Other Priestly Garments

³¹"Make the robe of the ephod entirely of blue cloth, ³²with an opening for the head in its center. There shall be a woven edge like a collar[a] around this opening, so that it will not tear. ³³Make pome-granates of blue, purple and scarlet yarn around the hem of the robe, with gold bells between them. ³⁴The gold bells and the pomegranates are to alternate around the hem of the robe. ³⁵Aaron must wear it when he ministers. The sound of the bells will be heard when he enters the Holy Place before the Lord and when he comes out, so that he will not die.

³⁶"Make a plate of pure gold and engrave on it as on a seal: HOLY TO THE LORD. ³⁷Fasten a blue cord to it to attach it to the turban; it is to be on the front of the turban. ³⁸It will be on Aaron's forehead, and he will bear the guilt involved in the sacred gifts the Israelites consecrate, whatever their gifts may be. It will be on Aaron's forehead continually so that they will be acceptable to the Lord.   Nu 18:1; Zec 14:20

³⁹"Weave the tunic of fine linen and make the turban of fine linen. The sash is to be the work of an embroiderer. ⁴⁰Make tunics, sashes and headbands for Aaron's sons, to give them dignity and honor. ⁴¹After you put these clothes on your brother Aaron and his sons, anoint and ordain them. Consecrate them so they may serve me as priests.   Ex 29:7-9

⁴²"Make linen undergarments as a covering for the body, reaching from the waist to the thigh. ⁴³Aaron and his sons must wear them whenever they enter the Tent of

---

[a] 32 The meaning of the Hebrew for this word is uncertain.

Meeting or approach the altar to minister in the Holy Place, so that they will not incur guilt and die.

"This is to be a lasting ordinance for Aaron and his descendants.

Consecration of the Priests

29 "This is what you are to do to consecrate them, so they may serve me as priests: Take a young bull and two rams without defect. ²And from fine wheat flour, without yeast, make bread, and cakes mixed with oil, and wafers spread with oil. ³Put them in a basket and present them in it—along with the bull and the two rams. ⁴Then bring Aaron and his sons to the entrance to the Tent of Meeting and wash them with water. ⁵Take the garments and dress Aaron with the tunic, the robe of the ephod, the ephod itself and the breastpiece. Fasten the ephod on him by its skillfully woven waistband. ⁶Put the turban on his head and attach the sacred diadem to the turban. ⁷Take the anointing oil and anoint him by pouring it on his head. ⁸Bring his sons and dress them in tunics ⁹and put headbands on them. Then tie sashes on Aaron and his sons.ᵃ The priesthood is theirs by a lasting ordinance. In this way you shall ordain Aaron and his sons.   Nu 18:7; Ex 30:25,30-31

¹⁰"Bring the bull to the front of the Tent of Meeting, and Aaron and his sons shall lay their hands

on its head. ¹¹Slaughter it in the Lord's presence at the entrance to the Tent of Meeting. ¹²Take some of the bull's blood and put it on the horns of the altar with your finger, and pour out the rest of it at the base of the altar. ¹³Then take all the fat around the inner parts, the covering of the liver, and both kidneys with the fat on them, and burn them on the altar. ¹⁴But burn the bull's flesh and its hide and its offal outside the camp. It is a sin offering.   Lev 1:4; Heb 13:11

¹⁵"Take one of the rams, and Aaron and his sons shall lay their hands on its head. ¹⁶Slaughter it and take the blood and sprinkle it against the altar on all sides. ¹⁷Cut the ram into pieces and wash the inner parts and the legs, putting them with the head and the other pieces. ¹⁸Then burn the entire ram on the altar. It is a burnt offering to the Lord, a pleasing aroma, an offering made to the Lord by fire.

¹⁹"Take the other ram, and Aaron and his sons shall lay their hands on its head. ²⁰Slaughter it, take some of its blood and put it on the lobes of the right ears of Aaron and his sons, on the thumbs of their right hands, and on the big toes of their right feet. Then sprinkle blood against the altar on all sides. ²¹And take some of the blood on the altar and some of the anointing oil and sprinkle it on Aaron and his garments and on his

sons and their garments. Then he and his sons and their garments will be consecrated. Heb 9:22

²²"Take from this ram the fat, the fat tail, the fat around the inner parts, the covering of the liver, both kidneys with the fat on them, and the right thigh. (This is the ram for the ordination.) ²³From the basket of bread made without yeast, which is before the LORD, take a loaf, and a cake made with oil, and a wafer. ²⁴Put all these in the hands of Aaron and his sons and wave them before the LORD as a wave offering. ²⁵Then take them from their hands and burn them on the altar along with the burnt offering for a pleasing aroma to the LORD, an offering made to the LORD by fire. ²⁶After you take the breast of the ram for Aaron's ordination, wave it before the LORD as a wave offering, and it will be your share.

²⁷"Consecrate those parts of the ordination ram that belong to Aaron and his sons: the breast that was waved and the thigh that was presented. ²⁸This is always to be the regular share from the Israelites for Aaron and his sons. It is the contribution the Israelites are to make to the LORD from their fellowship offerings.ᵃ Lev 7:31,34

²⁹"Aaron's sacred garments will belong to his descendants so that they can be anointed and ordained in them. ³⁰The son who succeeds

him as priest and comes to the Tent of Meeting to minister in the Holy Place is to wear them seven days. Nu 20:26,28

³¹"Take the ram for the ordination and cook the meat in a sacred place. ³²At the entrance to the Tent of Meeting, Aaron and his sons are to eat the meat of the ram and the bread that is in the basket. ³³They are to eat these offerings by which atonement was made for their ordination and consecration. But no one else may eat them, because they are sacred. ³⁴And if any of the meat of the ordination ram or any bread is left over till morning, burn it up. It must not be eaten, because it is sacred. Lev 22:10,13

³⁵"Do for Aaron and his sons everything I have commanded you, taking seven days to ordain them. ³⁶Sacrifice a bull each day as a sin offering to make atonement. Purify the altar by making atonement for it, and anoint it to consecrate it. ³⁷For seven days make atonement for the altar and consecrate it. Then the altar will be most holy, and whatever touches it will be holy. Lev 8:1-36

³⁸"This is what you are to offer on the altar regularly each day: two lambs a year old. ³⁹Offer one in the morning and the other at twilight. ⁴⁰With the first lamb offer a tenth of an ephahᵇ of fine flour mixed with a quarter of a hinᶜ of

---

ᵃ28 Traditionally *peace offerings*   ᵇ40 That is, probably about 2 quarts (about 2 liters)   ᶜ40 That is, probably about 1 quart (about 1 liter)

oil from pressed olives, and a quarter of a hin of wine as a drink offering. **41**Sacrifice the other lamb at twilight with the same grain offering and its drink offering as in the morning—a pleasing aroma, an offering made to the LORD by fire.

42"For the generations to come this burnt offering is to be made regularly at the entrance to the Tent of Meeting before the LORD. There I will meet you and speak to you; **43**there also I will meet with the Israelites, and the place will be consecrated by my glory.   Ex 25:22

44"So I will consecrate the Tent of Meeting and the altar and will consecrate Aaron and his sons to serve me as priests. **45**Then I will dwell among the Israelites and be their God. **46**They will know that I am the LORD their God, who brought them out of Egypt so that I might dwell among them. I am the LORD their God.   Ex 25:8; 2Co 6:16

The Altar of Incense

30 "Make an altar of acacia wood for burning incense. **2**It is to be square, a cubit long and a cubit wide, and two cubits high*a*—its horns of one piece with it. **3**Overlay the top and all the sides and the horns with pure gold, and make a gold molding around it. **4**Make two gold rings for the altar below the molding—two on opposite sides—to hold the poles used

to carry it. **5**Make the poles of acacia wood and overlay them with gold. **6**Put the altar in front of the curtain that is before the ark of the Testimony—before the atonement cover that is over the Testimony—where I will meet with you.

7"Aaron must burn fragrant incense on the altar every morning when he tends the lamps. **8**He must burn incense again when he lights the lamps at twilight so incense will burn regularly before the LORD for the generations to come. **9**Do not offer on this altar any other incense or any burnt offering or grain offering, and do not pour a drink offering on it. **10**Once a year Aaron shall make atonement on its horns. This annual atonement must be made with the blood of the atoning sin offering for the generations to come. It is most holy to the LORD."

Atonement Money

11Then the LORD said to Moses, **12**"When you take a census of the Israelites to count them, each one must pay the LORD a ransom for his life at the time he is counted. Then no plague will come on them when you number them. **13**Each one who crosses over to those already counted is to give a half shekel,*b* according to the sanctuary shekel, which weighs twenty gerahs. This half shekel is an offering to the

---

a 2 That is, about 1 1/2 feet (about 0.5 meter) long and wide and about 3 feet (about 0.9 meter) high
b 13 That is, about 1/5 ounce (about 6 grams); also in verse 15

LORD. [14]All who cross over, those twenty years old or more, are to give an offering to the LORD. [15]The rich are not to give more than a half shekel and the poor are not to give less when you make the offering to the LORD to atone for your lives. [16]Receive the atonement money from the Israelites and use it for the service of the Tent of Meeting. It will be a memorial for the Israelites before the LORD, making atonement for your lives."

Basin for Washing

[17]Then the LORD said to Moses, [18]"Make a bronze basin, with its bronze stand, for washing. Place it between the Tent of Meeting and the altar, and put water in it. [19]Aaron and his sons are to wash their hands and feet with water from it. [20]Whenever they enter the Tent of Meeting, they shall wash with water so that they will not die. Also, when they approach the altar to minister by presenting an offering made to the LORD by fire, [21]they shall wash their hands and feet so that they will not die. This is to be a lasting ordinance for Aaron and his descendants for the generations to come."   Ex 27:21; 40:31-32

Anointing Oil

[22]Then the LORD said to Moses, [23]"Take the following fine spices: 500 shekels[a] of liquid myrrh, half

as much (that is, 250 shekels) of fragrant cinnamon, 250 shekels of fragrant cane, [24]500 shekels of cassia—all according to the sanctuary shekel—and a hin[b] of olive oil. [25]Make these into a sacred anointing oil, a fragrant blend, the work of a perfumer. It will be the sacred anointing oil. [26]Then use it to anoint the Tent of Meeting, the ark of the Testimony, [27]the table and all its articles, the lampstand and its accessories, the altar of incense, [28]the altar of burnt offering and all its utensils, and the basin with its stand. [29]You shall consecrate them so they will be most holy, and whatever touches them will be holy.   Ex 37:29; Lev 8:10

[30]"Anoint Aaron and his sons and consecrate them so they may serve me as priests. [31]Say to the Israelites, 'This is to be my sacred anointing oil for the generations to come. [32]Do not pour it on men's bodies and do not make any oil with the same formula. It is sacred, and you are to consider it sacred. [33]Whoever makes perfume like it and whoever puts it on anyone other than a priest must be cut off from his people.' "   Lev 8:2,12,30

Incense

[34]Then the LORD said to Moses, "Take fragrant spices—gum resin, onycha and galbanum—and pure frankincense, all in equal

---

[a]23 That is, about 12 1/2 pounds (about 6 kilograms)   [b]24 That is, probably about 4 quarts (about 4 liters)

amounts, [35]and make a fragrant blend of incense, the work of a perfumer. It is to be salted and pure and sacred. [36]Grind some of it to powder and place it in front of the Testimony in the Tent of Meeting, where I will meet with you. It shall be most holy to you. [37]Do not make any incense with this formula for yourselves; consider it holy to the LORD. [38]Whoever makes any like it to enjoy its fragrance must be cut off from his people."

Bezalel and Oholiab

31 Then the LORD said to Moses, [2]"See, I have chosen Bezalel son of Uri, the son of Hur, of the tribe of Judah, [3]and I have filled him with the Spirit of God, with skill, ability and knowledge in all kinds of crafts— [4]to make artistic designs for work in gold, silver and bronze, [5]to cut and set stones, to work in wood, and to engage in all kinds of craftsmanship. [6]Moreover, I have appointed Oholiab son of Ahisamach, of the tribe of Dan, to help him. Also I have given skill to all the craftsmen to make everything I have commanded you: [7]the Tent of Meeting, the ark of the Testimony with the atonement cover on it, and all the other furnishings of the tent— [8]the table and its articles, the pure gold lampstand and all its accessories, the altar of incense, [9]the altar of burnt offering and all

its utensils, the basin with its stand — [10]and also the woven garments, both the sacred garments for Aaron the priest and the garments for his sons when they serve as priests, [11]and the anointing oil and fragrant incense for the Holy Place. They are to make them just as I commanded you."   Ex 35:30-35

The Sabbath

[12]Then the LORD said to Moses, [13]"Say to the Israelites, 'You must observe my Sabbaths. This will be a sign between me and you for the generations to come, so you may know that I am the LORD, who makes you holy.[a]   Eze 20:12,20

[14]"'Observe the Sabbath, because it is holy to you. Anyone who desecrates it must be put to death; whoever does any work on that day must be cut off from his people. [15]For six days, work is to be done, but the seventh day is a Sabbath of rest, holy to the LORD. Whoever does any work on the Sabbath day must be put to death. [16]The Israelites are to observe the Sabbath, celebrating it for the generations to come as a lasting covenant. [17]It will be a sign between me and the Israelites forever, for in six days the LORD made the heavens and the earth, and on the seventh day he abstained from work and rested.'"   Ex 20:8-11

[18]When the LORD finished speaking to Moses on Mount Sinai,

---

[a] 13 Or who sanctifies you; or who sets you apart as holy

he gave him the two tablets of the Testimony, the tablets of stone inscribed by the finger of God.

The Golden Calf

32 When the people saw that Moses was so long in coming down from the mountain, they gathered around Aaron and said, "Come, make us gods*a* who will go before us. As for this fellow Moses who brought us up out of Egypt, we don't know what has happened to him." Ac 7:40

²Aaron answered them, "Take off the gold earrings that your wives, your sons and your daughters are wearing, and bring them to me." ³So all the people took off their earrings and brought them to Aaron. ⁴He took what they handed him and made it into an idol cast in the shape of a calf, fashioning it with a tool. Then they said, "These are your gods,*b* O Israel, who brought you up out of Egypt."

⁵When Aaron saw this, he built an altar in front of the calf and announced, "Tomorrow there will be a festival to the LORD." ⁶So the next day the people rose early and sacrificed burnt offerings and presented fellowship offerings.*c* Afterward they sat down to eat and drink and got up to indulge in revelry. 1Co 10:7

⁷Then the LORD said to Moses, "Go down, because your people, whom you brought up out of Egypt, have become corrupt. ⁸They have been quick to turn away from what I commanded them and have made themselves an idol cast in the shape of a calf. They have bowed down to it and sacrificed to it and have said, 'These are your gods, O Israel, who brought you up out of Egypt.'

⁹"I have seen these people," the LORD said to Moses, "and they are a stiff-necked people. ¹⁰Now leave me alone so that my anger may burn against them and that I may destroy them. Then I will make you into a great nation." Ex 33:3,5

¹¹But Moses sought the favor of the LORD his God. "O LORD," he said, "why should your anger burn against your people, whom you brought out of Egypt with great power and a mighty hand? ¹²Why should the Egyptians say, 'It was with evil intent that he brought them out, to kill them in the mountains and to wipe them off the face of the earth'? Turn from your fierce anger; relent and do not bring disaster on your people. ¹³Remember your servants Abraham, Isaac and Israel, to whom you swore by your own self: 'I will make your descendants as numerous as the stars in the sky and I will give your descendants all this land I promised them, and it will be their inheritance forever.' " ¹⁴Then

---

a 1 Or *a god*; also in verses 23 and 31   *b 4* Or *This is your god*; also in verse 8   *c 6* Traditionally *peace offerings*

the LORD relented and did not bring on his people the disaster he had threatened. Nu 14:13-16; Dt 9:18

15Moses turned and went down the mountain with the two tablets of the Testimony in his hands. They were inscribed on both sides, front and back. 16The tablets were the work of God; the writing was the writing of God, engraved on the tablets. Ex 31:18; Dt 9:15

17When Joshua heard the noise of the people shouting, he said to Moses, "There is the sound of war in the camp."

18Moses replied:

"It is not the sound of victory,
    it is not the sound of defeat;
    it is the sound of singing
        that I hear."

19When Moses approached the camp and saw the calf and the dancing, his anger burned and he threw the tablets out of his hands, breaking them to pieces at the foot of the mountain. 20And he took the calf they had made and burned it in the fire; then he ground it to powder, scattered it on the water and made the Israelites drink it.

21He said to Aaron, "What did these people do to you, that you led them into such great sin?"

22"Do not be angry, my lord," Aaron answered. "You know how prone these people are to evil. 23They said to me, 'Make us gods who will go before us. As for this fellow Moses who brought us up out of Egypt, we don't know what has happened to him.' 24So I told them, 'Whoever has any gold jewelry, take it off.' Then they gave me the gold, and I threw it into the fire, and out came this calf!"

25Moses saw that the people were running wild and that Aaron had let them get out of control and so become a laughingstock to their enemies. 26So he stood at the entrance to the camp and said, "Whoever is for the LORD, come to me." And all the Levites rallied to him.

27Then he said to them, "This is what the LORD, the God of Israel, says: 'Each man strap a sword to his side. Go back and forth through the camp from one end to the other, each killing his brother and friend and neighbor.'" 28The Levites did as Moses commanded, and that day about three thousand of the people died. 29Then Moses said, "You have been set apart to the LORD today, for you were against your own sons and brothers, and he has blessed you this day." Nu 25:3,5; Dt 33:9

30The next day Moses said to the people, "You have committed a great sin. But now I will go up to the LORD; perhaps I can make atonement for your sin." Lev 1:4

31So Moses went back to the LORD and said, "Oh, what a great sin these people have committed! They have made themselves gods of gold. 32But now, please forgive their sin—but if not, then blot me out of the book you have written."

33The LORD replied to Moses, "Whoever has sinned against me I will blot out of my book. 34Now go, lead the people to the place I spoke of, and my angel will go before you. However, when the time comes for me to punish, I will punish them for their sin." Dt 29:20

35And the LORD struck the people with a plague because of what they did with the calf Aaron had made.

33 Then the LORD said to Moses, "Leave this place, you and the people you brought up out of Egypt, and go up to the land I promised on oath to Abraham, Isaac and Jacob, saying, 'I will give it to your descendants.' 2I will send an angel before you and drive out the Canaanites, Amorites, Hittites, Perizzites, Hivites and Jebusites. 3Go up to the land flowing with milk and honey. But I will not go with you, because you are a stiff-necked people and I might destroy you on the way." Ex 3:8; 32:10

4When the people heard these distressing words, they began to mourn and no one put on any ornaments. 5For the LORD had said to Moses, "Tell the Israelites, 'You are a stiff-necked people. If I were to go with you even for a moment, I might destroy you. Now take off your ornaments and I will decide what to do with you.' " 6So the Israelites stripped off their ornaments at Mount Horeb. Nu 14:39

The Tent of Meeting

7Now Moses used to take a tent and pitch it outside the camp some distance away, calling it the "tent of meeting." Anyone inquiring of the LORD would go to the tent of meeting outside the camp. 8And whenever Moses went out to the tent, all the people rose and stood at the entrances to their tents, watching Moses until he entered the tent. 9As Moses went into the tent, the pillar of cloud would come down and stay at the entrance, while the LORD spoke with Moses. 10Whenever the people saw the pillar of cloud standing at the entrance to the tent, they all stood and worshiped, each at the entrance to his tent. 11The LORD would speak to Moses face to face, as a man speaks with his friend. Then Moses would return to the camp, but his young aide Joshua son of Nun did not leave the tent.

Moses and the Glory of the LORD

12Moses said to the LORD, "You have been telling me, 'Lead these people,' but you have not let me know whom you will send with me. You have said, 'I know you by name and you have found favor with me.' 13If you are pleased with me, teach me your ways so I may know you and continue to find favor with you. Remember that this nation is your people." Dt 9:26,29

14The LORD replied, "My Presence will go with you, and I will give you rest." Jos 21:44; Isa 63:9

¹⁵Then Moses said to him, "If your Presence does not go with us, do not send us up from here. ¹⁶How will anyone know that you are pleased with me and with your people unless you go with us? What else will distinguish me and your people from all the other people on the face of the earth?"

¹⁷And the LORD said to Moses, "I will do the very thing you have asked, because I am pleased with you and I know you by name."

¹⁸Then Moses said, "Now show me your glory." Ex 16:7; Jn 1:14

¹⁹And the LORD said, "I will cause all my goodness to pass in front of you, and I will proclaim my name, the LORD, in your presence. I will have mercy on whom I will have mercy, and I will have compassion on whom I will have compassion. ²⁰But," he said, "you cannot see my face, for no one may see me and live." Ro 9:15

²¹Then the LORD said, "There is a place near me where you may stand on a rock. ²²When my glory passes by, I will put you in a cleft in the rock and cover you with my hand until I have passed by. ²³Then I will remove my hand and you will see my back; but my face must not be seen." Ps 91:4

The New Stone Tablets

34 The LORD said to Moses, "Chisel out two stone tablets like the first ones, and I will write on them the words that were on the first tablets, which you broke. ²Be ready in the morning, and then come up on Mount Sinai. Present yourself to me there on top of the mountain. ³No one is to come with you or be seen anywhere on the mountain; not even the flocks and herds may graze in front of the mountain." Ex 19:11

⁴So Moses chiseled out two stone tablets like the first ones and went up Mount Sinai early in the morning, as the LORD had commanded him; and he carried the two stone tablets in his hands. ⁵Then the LORD came down in the cloud and stood there with him and proclaimed his name, the LORD. ⁶And he passed in front of Moses, proclaiming, "The LORD, the LORD, the compassionate and gracious God, slow to anger, abounding in love and faithfulness, ⁷maintaining love to thousands, and forgiving wickedness, rebellion and sin. Yet he does not leave the guilty unpunished; he punishes the children and their children for the sin of the fathers to the third and fourth generation." Ex 20:6; Ps 103:3

⁸Moses bowed to the ground at once and worshiped. ⁹"O Lord, if I have found favor in your eyes," he said, "then let the Lord go with us. Although this is a stiff-necked people, forgive our wickedness and our sin, and take us as your inheritance." Ps 33:12

¹⁰Then the LORD said: "I am

making a covenant with you. Before all your people I will do wonders never before done in any nation in all the world. The people you live among will see how awesome is the work that I, the LORD, will do for you. ¹¹Obey what I command you today. I will drive out before you the Amorites, Canaanites, Hittites, Perizzites, Hivites and Jebusites. ¹²Be careful not to make a treaty with those who live in the land where you are going, or they will be a snare among you. ¹³Break down their altars, smash their sacred stones and cut down their Asherah poles.ᵃ ¹⁴Do not worship any other god, for the LORD, whose name is Jealous, is a jealous God.   Ex 33:2; Dt 5:2-3

¹⁵"Be careful not to make a treaty with those who live in the land; for when they prostitute themselves to their gods and sacrifice to them, they will invite you and you will eat their sacrifices. ¹⁶And when you choose some of their daughters as wives for your sons and those daughters prostitute themselves to their gods, they will lead your sons to do the same.

¹⁷"Do not make cast idols.

¹⁸"Celebrate the Feast of Unleavened Bread. For seven days eat bread made without yeast, as I commanded you. Do this at the appointed time in the month of Abib, for in that month you came out of Egypt.   Ex 12:2,15,17

¹⁹"The first offspring of every womb belongs to me, including all the firstborn males of your livestock, whether from herd or flock. ²⁰Redeem the firstborn donkey with a lamb, but if you do not redeem it, break its neck. Redeem all your firstborn sons.   Ex 13:2

"No one is to appear before me empty-handed.   Dt 16:16

²¹"Six days you shall labor, but on the seventh day you shall rest; even during the plowing season and harvest you must rest.   Ex 20:9

²²"Celebrate the Feast of Weeks with the firstfruits of the wheat harvest, and the Feast of Ingathering at the turn of the year.ᵇ ²³Three times a year all your men are to appear before the Sovereign LORD, the God of Israel. ²⁴I will drive out nations before you and enlarge your territory, and no one will covet your land when you go up three times each year to appear before the LORD your God.   Ex 23:14,16

²⁵"Do not offer the blood of a sacrifice to me along with anything containing yeast, and do not let any of the sacrifice from the Passover Feast remain until morning.   Ex 23:18

²⁶"Bring the best of the firstfruits of your soil to the house of the LORD your God.   Ex 22:29

"Do not cook a young goat in its mother's milk."   Ex 23:19

²⁷Then the LORD said to Moses, "Write down these words, for in

ᵃ13 That is, symbols of the goddess Asherah   ᵇ22 That is, in the fall

accordance with these words I have made a covenant with you and with Israel." ²⁸Moses was there with the LORD forty days and forty nights without eating bread or drinking water. And he wrote on the tablets the words of the covenant—the Ten Commandments.

The Radiant Face of Moses

²⁹When Moses came down from Mount Sinai with the two tablets of the Testimony in his hands, he was not aware that his face was radiant because he had spoken with the LORD. ³⁰When Aaron and all the Israelites saw Moses, his face was radiant, and they were afraid to come near him. ³¹But Moses called to them; so Aaron and all the leaders of the community came back to him, and he spoke to them. ³²Afterward all the Israelites came near him, and he gave them all the commands the LORD had given him on Mount Sinai. Mt 17:2

³³When Moses finished speaking to them, he put a veil over his face. ³⁴But whenever he entered the LORD's presence to speak with him, he removed the veil until he came out. And when he came out and told the Israelites what he had been commanded, ³⁵they saw that his face was radiant. Then Moses would put the veil back over his face until he went in to speak with the LORD. 2Co 3:13

Sabbath Regulations

35 Moses assembled the whole Israelite community and said to them, "These are the things the LORD has commanded you to do: ²For six days, work is to be done, but the seventh day shall be your holy day, a Sabbath of rest to the LORD. Whoever does any work on it must be put to death. ³Do not light a fire in any of your dwellings on the Sabbath day."

Materials for the Tabernacle

⁴Moses said to the whole Israelite community, "This is what the LORD has commanded: ⁵From what you have, take an offering for the LORD. Everyone who is willing is to bring to the LORD an offering of gold, silver and bronze; ⁶blue, purple and scarlet yarn and fine linen; goat hair; ⁷ram skins dyed red and hides of sea cows*a*; acacia wood; ⁸olive oil for the light; spices for the anointing oil and for the fragrant incense; ⁹and onyx stones and other gems to be mounted on the ephod and breastpiece.

¹⁰"All who are skilled among you are to come and make everything the LORD has commanded: ¹¹the tabernacle with its tent and its covering, clasps, frames, crossbars, posts and bases; ¹²the ark with its poles and the atonement cover and the curtain that shields it; ¹³the table with its poles and all its articles and the bread of the

a 7 That is, dugongs; also in verse 23

Presence; ¹⁴the lampstand that is for light with its accessories, lamps and oil for the light; ¹⁵the altar of incense with its poles, the anointing oil and the fragrant incense; the curtain for the doorway at the entrance to the tabernacle; ¹⁶the altar of burnt offering with its bronze grating, its poles and all its utensils; the bronze basin with its stand; ¹⁷the curtains of the courtyard with its posts and bases, and the curtain for the entrance to the courtyard; ¹⁸the tent pegs for the tabernacle and for the courtyard, and their ropes; ¹⁹the woven garments worn for ministering in the sanctuary—both the sacred garments for Aaron the priest and the garments for his sons when they serve as priests."   Ex 39:32-41

²⁰Then the whole Israelite community withdrew from Moses' presence, ²¹and everyone who was willing and whose heart moved him came and brought an offering to the LORD for the work on the Tent of Meeting, for all its service, and for the sacred garments. ²²All who were willing, men and women alike, came and brought gold jewelry of all kinds: brooches, earrings, rings and ornaments. They all presented their gold as a wave offering to the LORD. ²³Everyone who had blue, purple or scarlet yarn or fine linen, or goat hair, ram skins dyed red or hides of sea cows brought them. ²⁴Those presenting an offering of silver or bronze brought it as an offering to the LORD, and everyone who had acacia wood for any part of the work brought it. ²⁵Every skilled woman spun with her hands and brought what she had spun—blue, purple or scarlet yarn or fine linen. ²⁶And all the women who were willing and had the skill spun the goat hair. ²⁷The leaders brought onyx stones and other gems to be mounted on the ephod and breastpiece. ²⁸They also brought spices and olive oil for the light and for the anointing oil and for the fragrant incense. ²⁹All the Israelite men and women who were willing brought to the LORD freewill offerings for all the work the LORD through Moses had commanded them to do.   ver 4-9; Ex 25:1-7; 36:3

Bezalel and Oholiab

³⁰Then Moses said to the Israelites, "See, the LORD has chosen Bezalel son of Uri, the son of Hur, of the tribe of Judah, ³¹and he has filled him with the Spirit of God, with skill, ability and knowledge in all kinds of crafts— ³²to make artistic designs for work in gold, silver and bronze, ³³to cut and set stones, to work in wood and to engage in all kinds of artistic craftsmanship. ³⁴And he has given both him and Oholiab son of Ahisamach, of the tribe of Dan, the ability to teach others. ³⁵He has filled them with skill to do all kinds of work as craftsmen, designers, embroiderers in blue, purple and scarlet yarn and fine linen,

and weavers—all of them master craftsmen and designers.

36

¹So Bezalel, Oholiab and every skilled person to whom the LORD has given skill and ability to know how to carry out all the work of constructing the sanctuary are to do the work just as the Lord has commanded."   Ex 21:2-6

²Then Moses summoned Bezalel and Oholiab and every skilled person to whom the LORD had given ability and who was willing to come and do the work. ³They received from Moses all the offerings the Israelites had brought to carry out the work of constructing the sanctuary. And the people continued to bring freewill offerings morning after morning. ⁴So all the skilled craftsmen who were doing all the work on the sanctuary left their work ⁵and said to Moses, "The people are bringing more than enough for doing the work the LORD commanded to be done."

⁶Then Moses gave an order and they sent this word throughout the camp: "No man or woman is to make anything else as an offering for the sanctuary." And so the people were restrained from bringing more, ⁷because what they already had was more than enough to do all the work.

The Tabernacle

⁸All the skilled men among the workmen made the tabernacle with ten curtains of finely twisted linen and blue, purple and scarlet yarn, with cherubim worked into them by a skilled craftsman. ⁹All the curtains were the same size—twenty-eight cubits long and four cubits wide.ᵃ ¹⁰They joined five of the curtains together and did the same with the other five. ¹¹Then they made loops of blue material along the edge of the end curtain in one set, and the same was done with the end curtain in the other set. ¹²They also made fifty loops on one curtain and fifty loops on the end curtain of the other set, with the loops opposite each other. ¹³Then they made fifty gold clasps and used them to fasten the two sets of curtains together so that the tabernacle was a unit.

¹⁴They made curtains of goat hair for the tent over the tabernacle—eleven altogether. ¹⁵All eleven curtains were the same size—thirty cubits long and four cubits wide.ᵇ ¹⁶They joined five of the curtains into one set and the other six into another set. ¹⁷Then they made fifty loops along the edge of the end curtain in one set and also along the edge of the end curtain in the other set. ¹⁸They made fifty bronze clasps to fasten the tent together as a unit. ¹⁹Then they made for the tent a covering of ram skins

---

ᵃ9 That is, about 42 feet (about 12.5 meters) long and 6 feet (about 1.8 meters) wide   ᵇ15 That is, about 45 feet (about 13.5 meters) long and 6 feet (about 1.8 meters) wide

dyed red, and over that a covering of hides of sea cows.*

²⁰They made upright frames of acacia wood for the tabernacle. ²¹Each frame was ten cubits long and a cubit and a half wide,*^b ²²with two projections set parallel to each other. They made all the frames of the tabernacle in this way. ²³They made twenty frames for the south side of the tabernacle ²⁴and made forty silver bases to go under them—two bases for each frame, one under each projection. ²⁵For the other side, the north side of the tabernacle, they made twenty frames ²⁶and forty silver bases —two under each frame. ²⁷They made six frames for the far end, that is, the west end of the tabernacle, ²⁸and two frames were made for the corners of the tabernacle at the far end. ²⁹At these two corners the frames were double from the bottom all the way to the top and fitted into a single ring; both were made alike. ³⁰So there were eight frames and sixteen silver bases— two under each frame.

³¹They also made crossbars of acacia wood: five for the frames on one side of the tabernacle, ³²five for those on the other side, and five for the frames on the west, at the far end of the tabernacle. ³³They made the center crossbar so that it extended from end to end at the middle of the frames. ³⁴They overlaid the frames with gold and made gold rings to hold the crossbars. They also overlaid the crossbars with gold.

³⁵They made the curtain of blue, purple and scarlet yarn and finely twisted linen, with cherubim worked into it by a skilled craftsman. ³⁶They made four posts of acacia wood for it and overlaid them with gold. They made gold hooks for them and cast their four silver bases. ³⁷For the entrance to the tent they made a curtain of blue, purple and scarlet yarn and finely twisted linen—the work of an embroiderer; ³⁸and they made five posts with hooks for them. They overlaid the tops of the posts and their bands with gold and made their five bases of bronze.

The Ark

37 Bezalel made the ark of acacia wood—two and a half cubits long, a cubit and a half wide, and a cubit and a half high.^c ²He overlaid it with pure gold, both inside and out, and made a gold molding around it. ³He cast four gold rings for it and fastened them to its four feet, with two rings on one side and two rings on the other. ⁴Then he made poles of acacia wood and overlaid them with gold. ⁵And he inserted the poles into the rings on the sides of the ark to carry it.   ver 11,26; Ex 31:2

---

^a19 That is, dugongs   *^b21* That is, about 15 feet (about 4.5 meters) long and 2 1/4 feet (about 0.7 meter) wide   *^c1* That is, about 3 3/4 feet (about 1.1 meters) long and 2 1/4 feet (about 0.7 meter) wide and high

⁶He made the atonement cover of pure gold—two and a half cubits long and a cubit and a half wide.ᵃ ⁷Then he made two cherubim out of hammered gold at the ends of the cover. ⁸He made one cherub on one end and the second cherub on the other; at the two ends he made them of one piece with the cover. ⁹The cherubim had their wings spread upward, overshadowing the cover with them. The cherubim faced each other, looking toward the cover.

The Table

¹⁰Theyᵇ made the table of acacia wood—two cubits long, a cubit wide, and a cubit and a half high.ᶜ ¹¹Then they overlaid it with pure gold and made a gold molding around it. ¹²They also made around it a rim a handbreadthᵈ wide and put a gold molding on the rim. ¹³They cast four gold rings for the table and fastened them to the four corners, where the four legs were. ¹⁴The rings were put close to the rim to hold the poles used in carrying the table. ¹⁵The poles for carrying the table were made of acacia wood and were overlaid with gold. ¹⁶And they made from pure gold the articles for the table—its plates and dishes and bowls and its pitchers for the pouring out of drink offerings.

The Lampstand

¹⁷They made the lampstand of pure gold and hammered it out, base and shaft; its flowerlike cups, buds and blossoms were of one piece with it. ¹⁸Six branches extended from the sides of the lampstand—three on one side and three on the other. ¹⁹Three cups shaped like almond flowers with buds and blossoms were on one branch, three on the next branch and the same for all six branches extending from the lampstand. ²⁰And on the lampstand were four cups shaped like almond flowers with buds and blossoms. ²¹One bud was under the first pair of branches extending from the lampstand, a second bud under the second pair, and a third bud under the third pair—six branches in all. ²²The buds and the branches were all of one piece with the lampstand, hammered out of pure gold. Heb 9:2; Rev 1:12

²³They made its seven lamps, as well as its wick trimmers and trays, of pure gold. ²⁴They made the lampstand and all its accessories from one talentᵉ of pure gold.

The Altar of Incense

²⁵They made the altar of incense out of acacia wood. It was square, a cubit long and a cubit wide, and

---

ᵃ6 That is, about 3 3/4 feet (about 1.1 meters) long and 2 1/4 feet (about 0.7 meter) wide   ᵇ10 Or He; also in verses 11-29   ᶜ10 That is, about 3 feet (about 0.9 meter) long, 1 1/2 feet (about 0.5 meter) wide, and 2 1/4 feet (about 0.7 meter) high   ᵈ12 That is, about 3 inches (about 8 centimeters) ᵉ24 That is, about 75 pounds (about 34 kilograms)

two cubits high[a]—its horns of one piece with it. [26]They overlaid the top and all the sides and the horns with pure gold, and made a gold molding around it. [27]They made two gold rings below the molding —two on opposite sides—to hold the poles used to carry it. [28]They made the poles of acacia wood and overlaid them with gold.   Ex 30:1-5

[29]They also made the sacred anointing oil and the pure, fragrant incense—the work of a perfumer.

The Altar of Burnt Offering

38 They[b] built the altar of burnt offering of acacia wood, three cubits[c] high; it was square, five cubits long and five cubits wide.[d] [2]They made a horn at each of the four corners, so that the horns and the altar were of one piece, and they overlaid the altar with bronze. [3]They made all its utensils of bronze—its pots, shovels, sprinkling bowls, meat forks and firepans. [4]They made a grating for the altar, a bronze network, to be under its ledge, halfway up the altar. [5]They cast bronze rings to hold the poles for the four corners of the bronze grating. [6]They made the poles of acacia wood and overlaid them with bronze. [7]They inserted the poles into the rings so they would be on the sides of the

altar for carrying it. They made it hollow, out of boards.   Ex 27:1-8

Basin for Washing

[8]They made the bronze basin and its bronze stand from the mirrors of the women who served at the entrance to the Tent of Meeting.   Dt 23:17; 1Sa 2:22

The Courtyard

[9]Next they made the courtyard. The south side was a hundred cubits[e] long and had curtains of finely twisted linen, [10]with twenty posts and twenty bronze bases, and with silver hooks and bands on the posts. [11]The north side was also a hundred cubits long and had twenty posts and twenty bronze bases, with silver hooks and bands on the posts.

[12]The west end was fifty cubits[f] wide and had curtains, with ten posts and ten bases, with silver hooks and bands on the posts. [13]The east end, toward the sunrise, was also fifty cubits wide. [14]Curtains fifteen cubits[g] long were on one side of the entrance, with three posts and three bases, [15]and curtains fifteen cubits long were on the other side of the entrance to the courtyard, with three posts and three bases. [16]All the curtains around the courtyard were of fine-

---

[a]25 That is, about 1 1/2 feet (about 0.5 meter) long and wide, and about 3 feet (about 0.9 meter) high
[b]1 Or He; also in verses 2-9   [c]1 That is, about 4 1/2 feet (about 1.3 meters)   [d]1 That is, about
7 1/2 feet (about 2.3 meters) long and wide   [e]9 That is, about 150 feet (about 46 meters)
[f]12 That is, about 75 feet (about 23 meters)   [g]14 That is, about 22 1/2 feet (about 6.9 meters)

ly twisted linen. ¹⁷The bases for the posts were bronze. The hooks and bands on the posts were silver, and their tops were overlaid with silver; so all the posts of the courtyard had silver bands.

¹⁸The curtain for the entrance to the courtyard was of blue, purple and scarlet yarn and finely twisted linen—the work of an embroiderer. It was twenty cubits*a* long and, like the curtains of the courtyard, five cubits*b* high, ¹⁹with four posts and four bronze bases. Their hooks and bands were silver, and their tops were overlaid with silver. ²⁰All the tent pegs of the tabernacle and of the surrounding courtyard were bronze.   Ex 27:9-19

The Materials Used

²¹These are the amounts of the materials used for the tabernacle, the tabernacle of the Testimony, which were recorded at Moses' command by the Levites under the direction of Ithamar son of Aaron, the priest. ²²(Bezalel son of Uri, the son of Hur, of the tribe of Judah, made everything the LORD commanded Moses; ²³with him was Oholiab son of Ahisamach, of the tribe of Dan—a craftsman and designer, and an embroiderer in blue, purple and scarlet yarn and fine linen.) ²⁴The total amount of the gold from the wave offering used for all the work on the sanctuary was 29 talents and 730 shekels,*c* according to the sanctuary shekel.   Nu 1:50,53; 9:15

²⁵The silver obtained from those of the community who were counted in the census was 100 talents and 1,775 shekels,*d* according to the sanctuary shekel—²⁶one beka per person, that is, half a shekel,*e* according to the sanctuary shekel, from everyone who had crossed over to those counted, twenty years old or more, a total of 603,550 men. ²⁷The 100 talents*f* of silver were used to cast the bases for the sanctuary and for the curtain—100 bases from the 100 talents, one talent for each base. ²⁸They used the 1,775 shekels*g* to make the hooks for the posts, to overlay the tops of the posts, and to make their bands.   Ex 30:12-14

²⁹The bronze from the wave offering was 70 talents and 2,400 shekels.*h* ³⁰They used it to make the bases for the entrance to the Tent of Meeting, the bronze altar with its bronze grating and all its utensils, ³¹the bases for the surrounding courtyard and those for its entrance and all the tent pegs for the tabernacle and those for the surrounding courtyard.

---

a18 That is, about 30 feet (about 9 meters)   *b18* That is, about 7 1/2 feet (about 2.3 meters)
c24 The weight of the gold was a little over one ton (about 1 metric ton).   *d25* The weight of the silver was a little over 3 3/4 tons (about 3.4 metric tons).   *e26* That is, about 1/5 ounce (about 5.5 grams)   *f27* That is, about 3 3/4 tons (about 3.4 metric tons)   *g28* That is, about 45 pounds (about 20 kilograms)   *h29* The weight of the bronze was about 2 1/2 tons (about 2.4 metric tons).

The Priestly Garments

39 From the blue, purple and scarlet yarn they made woven garments for ministering in the sanctuary. They also made sacred garments for Aaron, as the LORD commanded Moses.

The Ephod

[2] They[a] made the ephod of gold, and of blue, purple and scarlet yarn, and of finely twisted linen. [3] They hammered out thin sheets of gold and cut strands to be worked into the blue, purple and scarlet yarn and fine linen—the work of a skilled craftsman. [4] They made shoulder pieces for the ephod, which were attached to two of its corners, so it could be fastened. [5] Its skillfully woven waistband was like it—of one piece with the ephod and made with gold, and with blue, purple and scarlet yarn, and with finely twisted linen, as the LORD commanded Moses.

[6] They mounted the onyx stones in gold filigree settings and engraved them like a seal with the names of the sons of Israel. [7] Then they fastened them on the shoulder pieces of the ephod as memorial stones for the sons of Israel, as the LORD commanded Moses.

The Breastpiece

[8] They fashioned the breastpiece —the work of a skilled craftsman. They made it like the ephod: of gold, and of blue, purple and scarlet yarn, and of finely twisted linen. [9] It was square—a span[b] long and a span wide—and folded double. [10] Then they mounted four rows of precious stones on it. In the first row there was a ruby, a topaz and a beryl; [11] in the second row a turquoise, a sapphire[c] and an emerald; [12] in the third row a jacinth, an agate and an amethyst; [13] in the fourth row a chrysolite, an onyx and a jasper.[d] They were mounted in gold filigree settings. [14] There were twelve stones, one for each of the names of the sons of Israel, each engraved like a seal with the name of one of the twelve tribes.

[15] For the breastpiece they made braided chains of pure gold, like a rope. [16] They made two gold filigree settings and two gold rings, and fastened the rings to two of the corners of the breastpiece. [17] They fastened the two gold chains to the rings at the corners of the breastpiece, [18] and the other ends of the chains to the two settings, attaching them to the shoulder pieces of the ephod at the front. [19] They made two gold rings and attached them to the other two corners of the breastpiece on the inside edge next to the ephod. [20] Then they made two more gold rings and at-

---

[a] 2 Or *He*; also in verses 7, 8 and 22   [b] 9 That is, about 9 inches (about 22 centimeters)   [c] 11 Or *lapis lazuli*   [d] 13 The precise identification of some of these precious stones is uncertain.

tached them to the bottom of the shoulder pieces on the front of the ephod, close to the seam just above the waistband of the ephod. [21]They tied the rings of the breastpiece to the rings of the ephod with blue cord, connecting it to the waistband so that the breastpiece would not swing out from the ephod—as the LORD commanded Moses.   Ex 28:15-28

Other Priestly Garments

[22]They made the robe of the ephod entirely of blue cloth—the work of a weaver— [23]with an opening in the center of the robe like the opening of a collar,[a] and a band around this opening, so that it would not tear. [24]They made pomegranates of blue, purple and scarlet yarn and finely twisted linen around the hem of the robe. [25]And they made bells of pure gold and attached them around the hem between the pomegranates. [26]The bells and pomegranates alternated around the hem of the robe to be worn for ministering, as the LORD commanded Moses.

[27]For Aaron and his sons, they made tunics of fine linen—the work of a weaver— [28]and the turban of fine linen, the linen headbands and the undergarments of finely twisted linen. [29]The sash was of finely twisted linen and blue, purple and scarlet yarn—the work of an embroiderer—as the LORD commanded Moses.   Ex 28:4

[30]They made the plate, the sacred diadem, out of pure gold and engraved on it, like an inscription on a seal: HOLY TO THE LORD. [31]Then they fastened a blue cord to it to attach it to the turban, as the LORD commanded Moses.   Ex 28:31-43

Moses Inspects the Tabernacle

[32]So all the work on the tabernacle, the Tent of Meeting, was completed. The Israelites did everything just as the LORD commanded Moses. [33]Then they brought the tabernacle to Moses: the tent and all its furnishings, its clasps, frames, crossbars, posts and bases; [34]the covering of ram skins dyed red, the covering of hides of sea cows[b] and the shielding curtain; [35]the ark of the Testimony with its poles and the atonement cover; [36]the table with all its articles and the bread of the Presence; [37]the pure gold lampstand with its row of lamps and all its accessories, and the oil for the light; [38]the gold altar, the anointing oil, the fragrant incense, and the curtain for the entrance to the tent; [39]the bronze altar with its bronze grating, its poles and all its utensils; the basin with its stand; [40]the curtains of the courtyard with its posts and bases, and the curtain for the entrance to the courtyard; the ropes and tent pegs for the courtyard; all the fur-

---

a 23 The meaning of the Hebrew for this word is uncertain.   b 34 That is, dugongs

nishings for the tabernacle, the Tent of Meeting; [41]and the woven garments worn for ministering in the sanctuary, both the sacred garments for Aaron the priest and the garments for his sons when serving as priests. Ex 35:10-19

[42]The Israelites had done all the work just as the Lord had commanded Moses. [43]Moses inspected the work and saw that they had done it just as the Lord had commanded. So Moses blessed them.

Setting Up the Tabernacle

40 Then the Lord said to Moses: [2]"Set up the tabernacle, the Tent of Meeting, on the first day of the first month. [3]Place the ark of the Testimony in it and shield the ark with the curtain. [4]Bring in the table and set out what belongs on it. Then bring in the lampstand and set up its lamps. [5]Place the gold altar of incense in front of the ark of the Testimony and put the curtain at the entrance to the tabernacle. Ex 26:33; Nu 1:1

[6]"Place the altar of burnt offering in front of the entrance to the tabernacle, the Tent of Meeting; [7]place the basin between the Tent of Meeting and the altar and put water in it. [8]Set up the courtyard around it and put the curtain at the entrance to the courtyard. Ex 30:18

[9]"Take the anointing oil and anoint the tabernacle and everything in it; consecrate it and all its furnishings, and it will be holy.

[10]Then anoint the altar of burnt offering and all its utensils; consecrate the altar, and it will be most holy. [11]Anoint the basin and its stand and consecrate them.

[12]"Bring Aaron and his sons to the entrance to the Tent of Meeting and wash them with water. [13]Then dress Aaron in the sacred garments, anoint him and consecrate him so he may serve me as priest. [14]Bring his sons and dress them in tunics. [15]Anoint them just as you anointed their father, so they may serve me as priests. Their anointing will be to a priesthood that will continue for all generations to come." [16]Moses did everything just as the Lord commanded him. Ex 29:9; Nu 25:13

[17]So the tabernacle was set up on the first day of the first month in the second year. [18]When Moses set up the tabernacle, he put the bases in place, erected the frames, inserted the crossbars and set up the posts. [19]Then he spread the tent over the tabernacle and put the covering over the tent, as the Lord commanded him. Nu 7:1

[20]He took the Testimony and placed it in the ark, attached the poles to the ark and put the atonement cover over it. [21]Then he brought the ark into the tabernacle and hung the shielding curtain and shielded the ark of the Testimony, as the Lord commanded him.

[22]Moses placed the table in the Tent of Meeting on the north side of the tabernacle outside the cur-

tain ²³and set out the bread on it before the Lord, as the Lord commanded him. Ex 26:35

²⁴He placed the lampstand in the Tent of Meeting opposite the table on the south side of the tabernacle ²⁵and set up the lamps before the Lord, as the Lord commanded him. Ex 26:35

²⁶Moses placed the gold altar in the Tent of Meeting in front of the curtain ²⁷and burned fragrant incense on it, as the Lord commanded him. ²⁸Then he put up the curtain at the entrance to the tabernacle. Ex 30:6

²⁹He set the altar of burnt offering near the entrance to the tabernacle, the Tent of Meeting, and offered on it burnt offerings and grain offerings, as the Lord commanded him. ver 6; Ex 29:38-42

³⁰He placed the basin between the Tent of Meeting and the altar and put water in it for washing, ³¹and Moses and Aaron and his sons used it to wash their hands and feet. ³²They washed whenever they entered the Tent of Meeting or approached the altar, as the Lord commanded Moses. Ex 30:20

³³Then Moses set up the courtyard around the tabernacle and altar and put up the curtain at the entrance to the courtyard. And so Moses finished the work. ver 8

The Glory of the Lord

³⁴Then the cloud covered the Tent of Meeting, and the glory of the Lord filled the tabernacle. ³⁵Moses could not enter the Tent of Meeting because the cloud had settled upon it, and the glory of the Lord filled the tabernacle.

³⁶In all the travels of the Israelites, whenever the cloud lifted from above the tabernacle, they would set out; ³⁷but if the cloud did not lift, they did not set out—until the day it lifted. ³⁸So the cloud of the Lord was over the tabernacle by day, and fire was in the cloud by night, in the sight of all the house of Israel during all their travels. Nu 9:17-23

Leviticus

The Burnt Offering

1 The LORD called to Moses and spoke to him from the Tent of Meeting. He said, ²"Speak to the Israelites and say to them: 'When any of you brings an offering to the LORD, bring as your offering an animal from either the herd or the flock. Lev 22:18-19

³" 'If the offering is a burnt offering from the herd, he is to offer a male without defect. He must present it at the entrance to the Tent of Meeting so that it*a* will be acceptable to the LORD. ⁴He is to lay his hand on the head of the burnt offering, and it will be accepted on his behalf to make atonement for him. ⁵He is to slaughter the young bull before the LORD, and then Aaron's sons the priests shall bring the blood and sprinkle it against the altar on all sides at the entrance to the Tent of Meeting. ⁶He is to skin the burnt offering and cut it into pieces. ⁷The sons of Aaron the priest are to put fire on the altar and arrange wood on the fire. ⁸Then Aaron's sons the priests shall arrange the pieces, including the head and the fat, on the burning wood that is on the altar. ⁹He is to wash the inner parts and the legs with water, and the priest is to burn all of it on the altar. It is a burnt offering, an offering made by fire, an aroma pleasing to the LORD. Ge 8:21; Eph 5:2

¹⁰" 'If the offering is a burnt offering from the flock, from either the sheep or the goats, he is to offer a male without defect. ¹¹He is to slaughter it at the north side of the altar before the LORD, and Aaron's sons the priests shall sprinkle its blood against the altar on all sides. ¹²He is to cut it into pieces, and the priest shall arrange them, including the head and the fat, on the burning wood that is on the altar. ¹³He is to wash the inner parts and the legs with water, and the priest is to bring all of it and burn it on the altar. It is a burnt offering, an offering made by fire, an aroma pleasing to the LORD.

¹⁴" 'If the offering to the LORD is a burnt offering of birds, he is to offer a dove or a young pigeon. ¹⁵The priest shall bring it to the altar, wring off the head and burn it on the altar; its blood shall be drained out on the side of the altar. ¹⁶He is to remove the crop with its contents*b* and throw it to the east side of the altar, where the ashes are. ¹⁷He shall tear it open by the wings, not severing it completely,

---

a 3 Or *he*   *b* 16 Or *crop and the feathers*; the meaning of the Hebrew for this word is uncertain.

and then the priest shall burn it on the wood that is on the fire on the altar. It is a burnt offering, an offering made by fire, an aroma pleasing to the LORD.   Lev 5:7; 6:10

The Grain Offering

2 " 'When someone brings a grain offering to the LORD, his offering is to be of fine flour. He is to pour oil on it, put incense on it ²and take it to Aaron's sons the priests. The priest shall take a handful of the fine flour and oil, together with all the incense, and burn this as a memorial portion on the altar, an offering made by fire, an aroma pleasing to the LORD. ³The rest of the grain offering belongs to Aaron and his sons; it is a most holy part of the offerings made to the LORD by fire.

⁴" 'If you bring a grain offering baked in an oven, it is to consist of fine flour: cakes made without yeast and mixed with oil, or*a* wafers made without yeast and spread with oil. ⁵If your grain offering is prepared on a griddle, it is to be made of fine flour mixed with oil, and without yeast. ⁶Crumble it and pour oil on it; it is a grain offering. ⁷If your grain offering is cooked in a pan, it is to be made of fine flour and oil. ⁸Bring the grain offering made of these things to the LORD; present it to the priest, who shall take it to the altar. ⁹He shall take out the memorial por-

tion from the grain offering and burn it on the altar as an offering made by fire, an aroma pleasing to the LORD. ¹⁰The rest of the grain offering belongs to Aaron and his sons; it is a most holy part of the offerings made to the LORD by fire.

¹¹" 'Every grain offering you bring to the LORD must be made without yeast, for you are not to burn any yeast or honey in an offering made to the LORD by fire. ¹²You may bring them to the LORD as an offering of the firstfruits, but they are not to be offered on the altar as a pleasing aroma. ¹³Season all your grain offerings with salt. Do not leave the salt of the covenant of your God out of your grain offerings; add salt to all your offerings.   Nu 18:19; Eze 43:24

¹⁴" 'If you bring a grain offering of firstfruits to the LORD, offer crushed heads of new grain roasted in the fire. ¹⁵Put oil and incense on it; it is a grain offering. ¹⁶The priest shall burn the memorial portion of the crushed grain and the oil, together with all the incense, as an offering made to the LORD by fire.   Lev 23:10

The Fellowship Offering

3 " 'If someone's offering is a fellowship offering,*b* and he offers an animal from the herd, whether male or female, he is to present before the LORD an animal without defect. ²He is to lay his

---

*a*4 Or *and*   *b*1 Traditionally *peace offering*; also in verses 3, 6 and 9

hand on the head of his offering and slaughter it at the entrance to the Tent of Meeting. Then Aaron's sons the priests shall sprinkle the blood against the altar on all sides. ³From the fellowship offering he is to bring a sacrifice made to the Lord by fire: all the fat that covers the inner parts or is connected to them, ⁴both kidneys with the fat on them near the loins, and the covering of the liver, which he will remove with the kidneys. ⁵Then Aaron's sons are to burn it on the altar on top of the burnt offering that is on the burning wood, as an offering made by fire, an aroma pleasing to the Lord.   Lev 7:11-34

⁶" 'If he offers an animal from the flock as a fellowship offering to the Lord, he is to offer a male or female without defect. ⁷If he offers a lamb, he is to present it before the Lord. ⁸He is to lay his hand on the head of his offering and slaughter it in front of the Tent of Meeting. Then Aaron's sons shall sprinkle its blood against the altar on all sides. ⁹From the fellowship offering he is to bring a sacrifice made to the Lord by fire: its fat, the entire fat tail cut off close to the backbone, all the fat that covers the inner parts or is connected to them, ¹⁰both kidneys with the fat on them near the loins, and the covering of the liver, which he will remove with the kidneys. ¹¹The priest shall burn them on the altar as food, an offering made to the Lord by fire.   Lev 21:6,17

¹²" 'If his offering is a goat, he is to present it before the Lord. ¹³He is to lay his hand on its head and slaughter it in front of the Tent of Meeting. Then Aaron's sons shall sprinkle its blood against the altar on all sides. ¹⁴From what he offers he is to make this offering to the Lord by fire: all the fat that covers the inner parts or is connected to them, ¹⁵both kidneys with the fat on them near the loins, and the covering of the liver, which he will remove with the kidneys. ¹⁶The priest shall burn them on the altar as food, an offering made by fire, a pleasing aroma. All the fat is the Lord's.   Lev 1:9; 1Sa 2:16

¹⁷" 'This is a lasting ordinance for the generations to come, wherever you live: You must not eat any fat or any blood.' "

The Sin Offering

4 The Lord said to Moses, ²"Say to the Israelites: 'When anyone sins unintentionally and does what is forbidden in any of the Lord's commands—   Lev 5:15-18

³" 'If the anointed priest sins, bringing guilt on the people, he must bring to the Lord a young bull without defect as a sin offering for the sin he has committed. ⁴He is to present the bull at the entrance to the Tent of Meeting before the Lord. He is to lay his hand on its head and slaughter it before the Lord. ⁵Then the anointed priest shall take some of the bull's

blood and carry it into the Tent of Meeting. ⁶He is to dip his finger into the blood and sprinkle some of it seven times before the LORD, in front of the curtain of the sanctuary. ⁷The priest shall then put some of the blood on the horns of the altar of fragrant incense that is before the LORD in the Tent of Meeting. The rest of the bull's blood he shall pour out at the base of the altar of burnt offering at the entrance to the Tent of Meeting. ⁸He shall remove all the fat from the bull of the sin offering—the fat that covers the inner parts or is connected to them, ⁹both kidneys with the fat on them near the loins, and the covering of the liver, which he will remove with the kidneys— ¹⁰just as the fat is removed from the ox*a* sacrificed as a fellowship offering.*b* Then the priest shall burn them on the altar of burnt offering. ¹¹But the hide of the bull and all its flesh, as well as the head and legs, the inner parts and offal— ¹²that is, all the rest of the bull—he must take outside the camp to a place ceremonially clean, where the ashes are thrown, and burn it in a wood fire on the ash heap.   Lev 5:9; Heb 13:11

¹³" 'If the whole Israelite community sins unintentionally and does what is forbidden in any of the LORD's commands, even though the community is unaware of the matter, they are guilty. ¹⁴When they become aware of the sin they committed, the assembly must bring a young bull as a sin offering and present it before the Tent of Meeting. ¹⁵The elders of the community are to lay their hands on the bull's head before the LORD, and the bull shall be slaughtered before the LORD. ¹⁶Then the anointed priest is to take some of the bull's blood into the Tent of Meeting. ¹⁷He shall dip his finger into the blood and sprinkle it before the LORD seven times in front of the curtain. ¹⁸He is to put some of the blood on the horns of the altar that is before the LORD in the Tent of Meeting. The rest of the blood he shall pour out at the base of the altar of burnt offering at the entrance to the Tent of Meeting. ¹⁹He shall remove all the fat from it and burn it on the altar, ²⁰and do with this bull just as he did with the bull for the sin offering. In this way the priest will make atonement for them, and they will be forgiven. ²¹Then he shall take the bull outside the camp and burn it as he burned the first bull. This is the sin offering for the community.   ver 3; Nu 15:25

²²" 'When a leader sins unintentionally and does what is forbidden in any of the commands of the LORD his God, he is guilty. ²³When he is made aware of the sin he

---

a 10 The Hebrew word can include both male and female.   *b 10* Traditionally *peace offering*; also in verses 26, 31 and 35

committed, he must bring as his offering a male goat without defect. ²⁴He is to lay his hand on the goat's head and slaughter it at the place where the burnt offering is slaughtered before the LORD. It is a sin offering. ²⁵Then the priest shall take some of the blood of the sin offering with his finger and put it on the horns of the altar of burnt offering and pour out the rest of the blood at the base of the altar. ²⁶He shall burn all the fat on the altar as he burned the fat of the fellowship offering. In this way the priest will make atonement for the man's sin, and he will be forgiven.

²⁷" 'If a member of the community sins unintentionally and does what is forbidden in any of the LORD's commands, he is guilty. ²⁸When he is made aware of the sin he committed, he must bring as his offering for the sin he committed a female goat without defect. ²⁹He is to lay his hand on the head of the sin offering and slaughter it at the place of the burnt offering. ³⁰Then the priest is to take some of the blood with his finger and put it on the horns of the altar of burnt offering and pour out the rest of the blood at the base of the altar. ³¹He shall remove all the fat, just as the fat is removed from the fellowship offering, and the priest shall burn it on the altar as an aroma pleasing to the LORD. In this way the priest will make atonement for him, and he will be forgiven.

³²" 'If he brings a lamb as his sin offering, he is to bring a female without defect. ³³He is to lay his hand on its head and slaughter it for a sin offering at the place where the burnt offering is slaughtered. ³⁴Then the priest shall take some of the blood of the sin offering with his finger and put it on the horns of the altar of burnt offering and pour out the rest of the blood at the base of the altar. ³⁵He shall remove all the fat, just as the fat is removed from the lamb of the fellowship offering, and the priest shall burn it on the altar on top of the offerings made to the LORD by fire. In this way the priest will make atonement for him for the sin he has committed, and he will be forgiven. Ex 29:38; Lev 1:4; 9:3

5 " 'If a person sins because he does not speak up when he hears a public charge to testify regarding something he has seen or learned about, he will be held responsible. Pr 29:24

²" 'Or if a person touches anything ceremonially unclean—whether the carcasses of unclean wild animals or of unclean livestock or of unclean creatures that move along the ground—even though he is unaware of it, he has become unclean and is guilty.

³" 'Or if he touches human uncleanness—anything that would make him unclean—even though he is unaware of it, when he learns of it he will be guilty. Nu 19:11-16

⁴" 'Or if a person thoughtlessly takes an oath to do anything, whether good or evil—in any matter one might carelessly swear about—even though he is unaware of it, in any case when he learns of it he will be guilty.

⁵" 'When anyone is guilty in any of these ways, he must confess in what way he has sinned ⁶and, as a penalty for the sin he has committed, he must bring to the LORD a female lamb or goat from the flock as a sin offering; and the priest shall make atonement for him for his sin.   Lev 16:21; 26:40

⁷" 'If he cannot afford a lamb, he is to bring two doves or two young pigeons to the LORD as a penalty for his sin—one for a sin offering and the other for a burnt offering. ⁸He is to bring them to the priest, who shall first offer the one for the sin offering. He is to wring its head from its neck, not severing it completely, ⁹and is to sprinkle some of the blood of the sin offering against the side of the altar; the rest of the blood must be drained out at the base of the altar. It is a sin offering. ¹⁰The priest shall then offer the other as a burnt offering in the prescribed way and make atonement for him for the sin he has committed, and he will be forgiven.   Lev 12:8; 14:21

¹¹" 'If, however, he cannot afford two doves or two young pigeons, he is to bring as an offering for his sin a tenth of an ephah ͣ of fine flour for a sin offering. He must not put oil or incense on it, because it is a sin offering. ¹²He is to bring it to the priest, who shall take a handful of it as a memorial portion and burn it on the altar on top of the offerings made to the LORD by fire. It is a sin offering. ¹³In this way the priest will make atonement for him for any of these sins he has committed, and he will be forgiven. The rest of the offering will belong to the priest, as in the case of the grain offering.' "

The Guilt Offering

¹⁴The LORD said to Moses: ¹⁵"When a person commits a violation and sins unintentionally in regard to any of the LORD's holy things, he is to bring to the LORD as a penalty a ram from the flock, one without defect and of the proper value in silver, according to the sanctuary shekel. ͩ It is a guilt offering. ¹⁶He must make restitution for what he has failed to do in regard to the holy things, add a fifth of the value to that and give it all to the priest, who will make atonement for him with the ram as a guilt offering, and he will be forgiven.   Lev 6:4; 22:14; Nu 5:7

¹⁷"If a person sins and does what is forbidden in any of the LORD's commands, even though he does

___

ͣ 11 That is, probably about 2 quarts (about 2 liters) grams)

ͩ 15 That is, about 2/5 ounce (about 11.5

not know it, he is guilty and will be held responsible. ¹⁸He is to bring to the priest as a guilt offering a ram from the flock, one without defect and of the proper value. In this way the priest will make atonement for him for the wrong he has committed unintentionally, and he will be forgiven. ¹⁹It is a guilt offering; he has been guilty of ᵃ wrongdoing against the LORD."

6 The LORD said to Moses: ²"If anyone sins and is unfaithful to the LORD by deceiving his neighbor about something entrusted to him or left in his care or stolen, or if he cheats him, ³or if he finds lost property and lies about it, or if he swears falsely, or if he commits any such sin that people may do — ⁴when he thus sins and becomes guilty, he must return what he has stolen or taken by extortion, or what was entrusted to him, or the lost property he found, ⁵or whatever it was he swore falsely about. He must make restitution in full, add a fifth of the value to it and give it all to the owner on the day he presents his guilt offering. ⁶And as a penalty he must bring to the priest, that is, to the LORD, his guilt offering, a ram from the flock, one without defect and of the proper value. ⁷In this way the priest will make atonement for him before the LORD, and he will be forgiven for any of these things he did that made him guilty."   Lev 5:15; Dt 22:1-3

The Burnt Offering

⁸The LORD said to Moses: ⁹"Give Aaron and his sons this command: 'These are the regulations for the burnt offering: The burnt offering is to remain on the altar hearth throughout the night, till morning, and the fire must be kept burning on the altar. ¹⁰The priest shall then put on his linen clothes, with linen undergarments next to his body, and shall remove the ashes of the burnt offering that the fire has consumed on the altar and place them beside the altar. ¹¹Then he is to take off these clothes and put on others, and carry the ashes outside the camp to a place that is ceremonially clean. ¹²The fire on the altar must be kept burning; it must not go out. Every morning the priest is to add firewood and arrange the burnt offering on the fire and burn the fat of the fellowship offeringsᵇ on it. ¹³The fire must be kept burning on the altar continuously; it must not go out.

The Grain Offering

¹⁴" 'These are the regulations for the grain offering: Aaron's sons are to bring it before the LORD, in front of the altar. ¹⁵The priest is to take a handful of fine flour and oil, together with all the incense on the grain offering, and burn the memorial portion on the altar as an aroma pleasing to the LORD. ¹⁶Aaron and his sons shall eat the rest of

---

ᵃ 19 Or *has made full expiation for his*   ᵇ 12 Traditionally *peace offerings*

it, but it is to be eaten without yeast in a holy place; they are to eat it in the courtyard of the Tent of Meeting. [17]It must not be baked with yeast; I have given it as their share of the offerings made to me by fire. Like the sin offering and the guilt offering, it is most holy. [18]Any male descendant of Aaron may eat it. It is his regular share of the offerings made to the LORD by fire for the generations to come. Whatever touches them will become holy.[a]' "   Lev 2:3; Eze 44:29

[19]The LORD also said to Moses, [20]"This is the offering Aaron and his sons are to bring to the LORD on the day he[b] is anointed: a tenth of an ephah[c] of fine flour as a regular grain offering, half of it in the morning and half in the evening. [21]Prepare it with oil on a griddle; bring it well-mixed and present the grain offering broken[d] in pieces as an aroma pleasing to the LORD. [22]The son who is to succeed him as anointed priest shall prepare it. It is the LORD's regular share and is to be burned completely. [23]Every grain offering of a priest shall be burned completely; it must not be eaten."   Ex 29:2; Lev 2:5

The Sin Offering

[24]The LORD said to Moses, [25]"Say to Aaron and his sons: 'These are the regulations for the sin offering: The sin offering is to be slaugh-tered before the LORD in the place the burnt offering is slaughtered; it is most holy. [26]The priest who offers it shall eat it; it is to be eaten in a holy place, in the courtyard of the Tent of Meeting. [27]Whatever touches any of the flesh will become holy, and if any of the blood is spattered on a garment, you must wash it in a holy place. [28]The clay pot the meat is cooked in must be broken; but if it is cooked in a bronze pot, the pot is to be scoured and rinsed with water. [29]Any male in a priest's family may eat it; it is most holy. [30]But any sin offering whose blood is brought into the Tent of Meeting to make atonement in the Holy Place must not be eaten; it must be burned.

The Guilt Offering

7 " 'These are the regulations for the guilt offering, which is most holy: [2]The guilt offering is to be slaughtered in the place where the burnt offering is slaughtered, and its blood is to be sprinkled against the altar on all sides. [3]All its fat shall be offered: the fat tail and the fat that covers the inner parts, [4]both kidneys with the fat on them near the loins, and the covering of the liver, which is to be removed with the kidneys. [5]The priest shall burn them on the altar as an offering made to the LORD by fire. It is a guilt offering. [6]Any male

---

[a]18 Or *Whoever touches them must be holy*; similarly in verse 27   [b]20 Or *each*   [c]20 That is, probably about 2 quarts (about 2 liters)   [d]21 The meaning of the Hebrew for this word is uncertain.

in a priest's family may eat it, but it must be eaten in a holy place; it is most holy.   Ex 29:13; Lev 6:18

⁷" 'The same law applies to both the sin offering and the guilt offering: They belong to the priest who makes atonement with them. ⁸The priest who offers a burnt offering for anyone may keep its hide for himself. ⁹Every grain offering baked in an oven or cooked in a pan or on a griddle belongs to the priest who offers it, ¹⁰and every grain offering, whether mixed with oil or dry, belongs equally to all the sons of Aaron.   Lev 2:5; 16:17,26

The Fellowship Offering

¹¹" 'These are the regulations for the fellowship offering*a* a person may present to the LORD:

¹²" 'If he offers it as an expression of thankfulness, then along with this thank offering he is to offer cakes of bread made without yeast and mixed with oil, wafers made without yeast and spread with oil, and cakes of fine flour well-kneaded and mixed with oil. ¹³Along with his fellowship offering of thanksgiving he is to present an offering with cakes of bread made with yeast. ¹⁴He is to bring one of each kind as an offering, a contribution to the LORD; it belongs to the priest who sprinkles the blood of the fellowship offerings. ¹⁵The meat of his fellowship offering of thanksgiving must be eaten on the day it is offered; he must leave none of it till morning.

¹⁶" 'If, however, his offering is the result of a vow or is a freewill offering, the sacrifice shall be eaten on the day he offers it, but anything left over may be eaten on the next day. ¹⁷Any meat of the sacrifice left over till the third day must be burned up. ¹⁸If any meat of the fellowship offering is eaten on the third day, it will not be accepted. It will not be credited to the one who offered it, for it is impure; the person who eats any of it will be held responsible.   Lev 19:5-8; Nu 18:27

¹⁹" 'Meat that touches anything ceremonially unclean must not be eaten; it must be burned up. As for other meat, anyone ceremonially clean may eat it. ²⁰But if anyone who is unclean eats any meat of the fellowship offering belonging to the LORD, that person must be cut off from his people. ²¹If anyone touches something unclean—whether human uncleanness or an unclean animal or any unclean, detestable thing—and then eats any of the meat of the fellowship offering belonging to the LORD, that person must be cut off from his people.' "   Lev 22:3-7

Eating Fat and Blood Forbidden

²²The LORD said to Moses, ²³"Say to the Israelites: 'Do not eat any of

---

a 11 Traditionally *peace offering*; also in verses 13-37

the fat of cattle, sheep or goats. [24]The fat of an animal found dead or torn by wild animals may be used for any other purpose, but you must not eat it. [25]Anyone who eats the fat of an animal from which an offering by fire may be[a] made to the LORD must be cut off from his people. [26]And wherever you live, you must not eat the blood of any bird or animal. [27]If anyone eats blood, that person must be cut off from his people.' "

The Priests' Share

[28]The LORD said to Moses, [29]"Say to the Israelites: 'Anyone who brings a fellowship offering to the LORD is to bring part of it as his sacrifice to the LORD. [30]With his own hands he is to bring the offering made to the LORD by fire; he is to bring the fat, together with the breast, and wave the breast before the LORD as a wave offering. [31]The priest shall burn the fat on the altar, but the breast belongs to Aaron and his sons. [32]You are to give the right thigh of your fellowship offerings to the priest as a contribution. [33]The son of Aaron who offers the blood and the fat of the fellowship offering shall have the right thigh as his share. [34]From the fellowship offerings of the Israelites, I have taken the breast that is waved and the thigh that is presented and have given them to Aaron the priest and his sons as

their regular share from the Israelites.' "   Ex 29:27; Nu 18:18-19

[35]This is the portion of the offerings made to the LORD by fire that were allotted to Aaron and his sons on the day they were presented to serve the LORD as priests. [36]On the day they were anointed, the LORD commanded that the Israelites give this to them as their regular share for the generations to come.   Lev 8:12,30

[37]These, then, are the regulations for the burnt offering, the grain offering, the sin offering, the guilt offering, the ordination offering and the fellowship offering, [38]which the LORD gave Moses on Mount Sinai on the day he commanded the Israelites to bring their offerings to the LORD, in the Desert of Sinai.   Lev 1:2; 6:9

The Ordination of Aaron and His Sons

8 The LORD said to Moses, [2]"Bring Aaron and his sons, their garments, the anointing oil, the bull for the sin offering, the two rams and the basket containing bread made without yeast, [3]and gather the entire assembly at the entrance to the Tent of Meeting." [4]Moses did as the LORD commanded him, and the assembly gathered at the entrance to the Tent of Meeting.   Ex 29:2-3; 30:23-25,30

[5]Moses said to the assembly,

---

[a] 25 Or fire is

"This is what the Lord has commanded to be done." ⁶Then Moses brought Aaron and his sons forward and washed them with water. ⁷He put the tunic on Aaron, tied the sash around him, clothed him with the robe and put the ephod on him. He also tied the ephod to him by its skillfully woven waistband; so it was fastened on him. ⁸He placed the breastpiece on him and put the Urim and Thummim in the breastpiece. ⁹Then he placed the turban on Aaron's head and set the gold plate, the sacred diadem, on the front of it, as the Lord commanded Moses.

¹⁰Then Moses took the anointing oil and anointed the tabernacle and everything in it, and so consecrated them. ¹¹He sprinkled some of the oil on the altar seven times, anointing the altar and all its utensils and the basin with its stand, to consecrate them. ¹²He poured some of the anointing oil on Aaron's head and anointed him to consecrate him. ¹³Then he brought Aaron's sons forward, put tunics on them, tied sashes around them and put headbands on them, as the Lord commanded Moses.

¹⁴He then presented the bull for the sin offering, and Aaron and his sons laid their hands on its head. ¹⁵Moses slaughtered the bull and took some of the blood, and with his finger he put it on all the horns of the altar to purify the altar. He poured out the rest of the blood at the base of the altar. So he consecrated it to make atonement for it. ¹⁶Moses also took all the fat around the inner parts, the covering of the liver, and both kidneys and their fat, and burned it on the altar. ¹⁷But the bull with its hide and its flesh and its offal he burned up outside the camp, as the Lord commanded Moses.   Ps 66:15; Heb 9:22

¹⁸He then presented the ram for the burnt offering, and Aaron and his sons laid their hands on its head. ¹⁹Then Moses slaughtered the ram and sprinkled the blood against the altar on all sides. ²⁰He cut the ram into pieces and burned the head, the pieces and the fat. ²¹He washed the inner parts and the legs with water and burned the whole ram on the altar as a burnt offering, a pleasing aroma, an offering made to the Lord by fire, as the Lord commanded Moses.

²²He then presented the other ram, the ram for the ordination, and Aaron and his sons laid their hands on its head. ²³Moses slaughtered the ram and took some of its blood and put it on the lobe of Aaron's right ear, on the thumb of his right hand and on the big toe of his right foot. ²⁴Moses also brought Aaron's sons forward and put some of the blood on the lobes of their right ears, on the thumbs of their right hands and on the big toes of their right feet. Then he sprinkled blood against the altar on all sides. ²⁵He took the fat, the fat tail, all the fat around the inner parts, the covering of the liver,

both kidneys and their fat and the right thigh. 26Then from the basket of bread made without yeast, which was before the LORD, he took a cake of bread, and one made with oil, and a wafer; he put these on the fat portions and on the right thigh. 27He put all these in the hands of Aaron and his sons and waved them before the LORD as a wave offering. 28Then Moses took them from their hands and burned them on the altar on top of the burnt offering as an ordination offering, a pleasing aroma, an offering made to the LORD by fire. 29He also took the breast—Moses' share of the ordination ram—and waved it before the LORD as a wave offering, as the LORD commanded Moses.   Lev 7:31-34; Heb 9:18-22

30Then Moses took some of the anointing oil and some of the blood from the altar and sprinkled them on Aaron and his garments and on his sons and their garments. So he consecrated Aaron and his garments and his sons and their garments.   Nu 3:3

31Moses then said to Aaron and his sons, "Cook the meat at the entrance to the Tent of Meeting and eat it there with the bread from the basket of ordination offerings, as I commanded, saying,a 'Aaron and his sons are to eat it.' 32Then burn up the rest of the meat and the bread. 33Do not leave the entrance

to the Tent of Meeting for seven days, until the days of your ordination are completed, for your ordination will last seven days. 34What has been done today was commanded by the LORD to make atonement for you. 35You must stay at the entrance to the Tent of Meeting day and night for seven days and do what the LORD requires, so you will not die; for that is what I have been commanded." 36So Aaron and his sons did everything the LORD commanded through Moses.   Ex 29:1-37; Dt 11:1

The Priests Begin Their Ministry

9 On the eighth day Moses summoned Aaron and his sons and the elders of Israel. 2He said to Aaron, "Take a bull calf for your sin offering and a ram for your burnt offering, both without defect, and present them before the LORD. 3Then say to the Israelites: 'Take a male goat for a sin offering, a calf and a lamb—both a year old and without defect—for a burnt offering, 4and an oxb and a ram for a fellowship offeringc to sacrifice before the LORD, together with a grain offering mixed with oil. For today the LORD will appear to you.'"   Ex 29:43; Eze 43:27

5They took the things Moses commanded to the front of the Tent of Meeting, and the entire as-

a31 Or I was commanded: b4 The Hebrew word can include both male and female; also in verses 18 and 19.   c4 Traditionally peace offering; also in verses 18 and 22

sembly came near and stood before the LORD. 6Then Moses said, "This is what the LORD has commanded you to do, so that the glory of the LORD may appear to you."

7Moses said to Aaron, "Come to the altar and sacrifice your sin offering and your burnt offering and make atonement for yourself and the people; sacrifice the offering that is for the people and make atonement for them, as the LORD has commanded." Heb 5:1,3; 7:27

8So Aaron came to the altar and slaughtered the calf as a sin offering for himself. 9His sons brought the blood to him, and he dipped his finger into the blood and put it on the horns of the altar; the rest of the blood he poured out at the base of the altar. 10On the altar he burned the fat, the kidneys and the covering of the liver from the sin offering, as the LORD commanded Moses; 11the flesh and the hide he burned up outside the camp.

12Then he slaughtered the burnt offering. His sons handed him the blood, and he sprinkled it against the altar on all sides. 13They handed him the burnt offering piece by piece, including the head, and he burned them on the altar. 14He washed the inner parts and the legs and burned them on top of the burnt offering on the altar. Lev 1:8

15Aaron then brought the offering that was for the people. He took the goat for the people's sin offering and slaughtered it and offered it for a sin offering as he did with the first one. Lev 4:27-31

16He brought the burnt offering and offered it in the prescribed way. 17He also brought the grain offering, took a handful of it and burned it on the altar in addition to the morning's burnt offering.

18He slaughtered the ox and the ram as the fellowship offering for the people. His sons handed him the blood, and he sprinkled it against the altar on all sides. 19But the fat portions of the ox and the ram—the fat tail, the layer of fat, the kidneys and the covering of the liver— 20these they laid on the breasts, and then Aaron burned the fat on the altar. 21Aaron waved the breasts and the right thigh before the LORD as a wave offering, as Moses commanded. Lev 3:1-11

22Then Aaron lifted his hands toward the people and blessed them. And having sacrificed the sin offering, the burnt offering and the fellowship offering, he stepped down. Nu 6:23; Lk 24:50

23Moses and Aaron then went into the Tent of Meeting. When they came out, they blessed the people; and the glory of the LORD appeared to all the people. 24Fire came out from the presence of the LORD and consumed the burnt offering and the fat portions on the altar. And when all the people saw it, they shouted for joy and fell facedown. 1Ki 18:39

The Death of Nadab and Abihu

10 Aaron's sons Nadab and Abihu took their censers, put fire in them and added incense; and they offered unauthorized fire before the LORD, contrary to his command. ²So fire came out from the presence of the LORD and consumed them, and they died before the LORD. ³Moses then said to Aaron, "This is what the LORD spoke of when he said: Lev 16:12

" 'Among those who approach me
    I will show myself holy;
in the sight of all the people
    I will be honored.' "   Isa 49:3

Aaron remained silent.

⁴Moses summoned Mishael and Elzaphan, sons of Aaron's uncle Uzziel, and said to them, "Come here; carry your cousins outside the camp, away from the front of the sanctuary." ⁵So they came and carried them, still in their tunics, outside the camp, as Moses ordered.   Ex 6:22

⁶Then Moses said to Aaron and his sons Eleazar and Ithamar, "Do not let your hair become unkempt,ª and do not tear your clothes, or you will die and the LORD will be angry with the whole community. But your relatives, all the house of Israel, may mourn for those the LORD has destroyed by fire. ⁷Do not leave the entrance to the Tent of Meeting or you will die, because the LORD's anointing oil is on you." So they did as Moses said.

⁸Then the LORD said to Aaron, ⁹"You and your sons are not to drink wine or other fermented drink whenever you go into the Tent of Meeting, or you will die. This is a lasting ordinance for the generations to come. ¹⁰You must distinguish between the holy and the common, between the unclean and the clean, ¹¹and you must teach the Israelites all the decrees the LORD has given them through Moses."   Lev 20:25; Eze 44:21

¹²Moses said to Aaron and his remaining sons, Eleazar and Ithamar, "Take the grain offering left over from the offerings made to the LORD by fire and eat it prepared without yeast beside the altar, for it is most holy. ¹³Eat it in a holy place, because it is your share and your sons' share of the offerings made to the LORD by fire; for so I have been commanded. ¹⁴But you and your sons and your daughters may eat the breast that was waved and the thigh that was presented. Eat them in a ceremonially clean place; they have been given to you and your children as your share of the Israelites' fellowship offerings.ᵇ ¹⁵The thigh that was presented and the breast that was waved must be brought with the fat portions of the offerings made by fire, to be waved before the

---

ª6 Or *Do not uncover your heads*   ᵇ14 Traditionally *peace offerings*

Lord as a wave offering. This will be the regular share for you and your children, as the Lord has commanded." Lev 6:14-18; 7:34

¹⁶When Moses inquired about the goat of the sin offering and found that it had been burned up, he was angry with Eleazar and Ithamar, Aaron's remaining sons, and asked, ¹⁷"Why didn't you eat the sin offering in the sanctuary area? It is most holy; it was given to you to take away the guilt of the community by making atonement for them before the Lord. ¹⁸Since its blood was not taken into the Holy Place, you should have eaten the goat in the sanctuary area, as I commanded." Lev 6:26,30; 9:3

¹⁹Aaron replied to Moses, "Today they sacrificed their sin offering and their burnt offering before the Lord, but such things as this have happened to me. Would the Lord have been pleased if I had eaten the sin offering today?" ²⁰When Moses heard this, he was satisfied. Lev 9:12

Clean and Unclean Food

11 The Lord said to Moses and Aaron, ²"Say to the Israelites: 'Of all the animals that live on land, these are the ones you may eat: ³You may eat any animal that has a split hoof completely divided and that chews the cud.

⁴"'There are some that only chew the cud or only have a split hoof, but you must not eat them. The camel, though it chews the cud, does not have a split hoof; it is ceremonially unclean for you. ⁵The coney,^a though it chews the cud, does not have a split hoof; it is unclean for you. ⁶The rabbit, though it chews the cud, does not have a split hoof; it is unclean for you. ⁷And the pig, though it has a split hoof completely divided, does not chew the cud; it is unclean for you. ⁸You must not eat their meat or touch their carcasses; they are unclean for you. Isa 65:4

⁹"'Of all the creatures living in the water of the seas and the streams, you may eat any that have fins and scales. ¹⁰But all creatures in the seas or streams that do not have fins and scales—whether among all the swarming things or among all the other living creatures in the water—you are to detest. ¹¹And since you are to detest them, you must not eat their meat and you must detest their carcasses. ¹²Anything living in the water that does not have fins and scales is to be detestable to you.

¹³"'These are the birds you are to detest and not eat because they are detestable: the eagle, the vulture, the black vulture, ¹⁴the red kite, any kind of black kite, ¹⁵any kind of raven, ¹⁶the horned owl, the screech owl, the gull, any kind of hawk, ¹⁷the little owl, the cormorant, the great owl, ¹⁸the white

---

^a 5 That is, the hyrax or rock badger

owl, the desert owl, the osprey, ¹⁹the stork, any kind of heron, the hoopoe and the bat.ᵃ

²⁰" 'All flying insects that walk on all fours are to be detestable to you. ²¹There are, however, some winged creatures that walk on all fours that you may eat: those that have jointed legs for hopping on the ground. ²²Of these you may eat any kind of locust, katydid, cricket or grasshopper. ²³But all other winged creatures that have four legs you are to detest.   Dt 14:3-20

²⁴" 'You will make yourselves unclean by these; whoever touches their carcasses will be unclean till evening. ²⁵Whoever picks up one of their carcasses must wash his clothes, and he will be unclean till evening.   Lev 14:8,47; 15:5

²⁶" 'Every animal that has a split hoof not completely divided or that does not chew the cud is unclean for you; whoever touches ˌthe carcass ofˌ any of them will be unclean. ²⁷Of all the animals that walk on all fours, those that walk on their paws are unclean for you; whoever touches their carcasses will be unclean till evening. ²⁸Anyone who picks up their carcasses must wash his clothes, and he will be unclean till evening. They are unclean for you.

²⁹" 'Of the animals that move about on the ground, these are unclean for you: the weasel, the rat, any kind of great lizard, ³⁰the gecko, the monitor lizard, the wall lizard, the skink and the chameleon. ³¹Of all those that move along the ground, these are unclean for you. Whoever touches them when they are dead will be unclean till evening. ³²When one of them dies and falls on something, that article, whatever its use, will be unclean, whether it is made of wood, cloth, hide or sackcloth. Put it in water; it will be unclean till evening, and then it will be clean. ³³If one of them falls into a clay pot, everything in it will be unclean, and you must break the pot. ³⁴Any food that could be eaten but has water on it from such a pot is unclean, and any liquid that could be drunk from it is unclean. ³⁵Anything that one of their carcasses falls on becomes unclean; an oven or cooking pot must be broken up. They are unclean, and you are to regard them as unclean. ³⁶A spring, however, or a cistern for collecting water remains clean, but anyone who touches one of these carcasses is unclean. ³⁷If a carcass falls on any seeds that are to be planted, they remain clean. ³⁸But if water has been put on the seed and a carcass falls on it, it is unclean for you.   Lev 15:12

³⁹" 'If an animal that you are allowed to eat dies, anyone who touches the carcass will be unclean till evening. ⁴⁰Anyone who eats some of the carcass must

ᵃ 19 The precise identification of some of the birds, insects and animals in this chapter is uncertain.

wash his clothes, and he will be unclean till evening. Anyone who picks up the carcass must wash his clothes, and he will be unclean till evening. Lev 17:15; 22:8

⁴¹" 'Every creature that moves about on the ground is detestable; it is not to be eaten. ⁴²You are not to eat any creature that moves about on the ground, whether it moves on its belly or walks on all fours or on many feet; it is detestable. ⁴³Do not defile yourselves by any of these creatures. Do not make yourselves unclean by means of them or be made unclean by them. ⁴⁴I am the LORD your God; consecrate yourselves and be holy, because I am holy. Do not make yourselves unclean by any creature that moves about on the ground. ⁴⁵I am the LORD who brought you up out of Egypt to be your God; therefore be holy, because I am holy. Ex 19:6; Lev 19:2

⁴⁶" 'These are the regulations concerning animals, birds, every living thing that moves in the water and every creature that moves about on the ground. ⁴⁷You must distinguish between the unclean and the clean, between living creatures that may be eaten and those that may not be eaten.' " Lev 10:10

Purification After Childbirth

12 The LORD said to Moses, ²"Say to the Israelites: 'A woman who becomes pregnant and gives birth to a son will be ceremonially unclean for seven days, just as she is unclean during her monthly period. ³On the eighth day the boy is to be circumcised. ⁴Then the woman must wait thirty-three days to be purified from her bleeding. She must not touch anything sacred or go to the sanctuary until the days of her purification are over. ⁵If she gives birth to a daughter, for two weeks the woman will be unclean, as during her period. Then she must wait sixty-six days to be purified from her bleeding. Ge 17:12; Lk 1:59

⁶" 'When the days of her purification for a son or daughter are over, she is to bring to the priest at the entrance to the Tent of Meeting a year-old lamb for a burnt offering and a young pigeon or a dove for a sin offering. ⁷He shall offer them before the LORD to make atonement for her, and then she will be ceremonially clean from her flow of blood.

" 'These are the regulations for the woman who gives birth to a boy or a girl. ⁸If she cannot afford a lamb, she is to bring two doves or two young pigeons, one for a burnt offering and the other for a sin offering. In this way the priest will make atonement for her, and she will be clean.' " Lev 4:26; 5:7

Regulations About Infectious Skin Diseases

13 The LORD said to Moses and Aaron, ²"When anyone has a swelling or a rash or a bright spot on his skin that may become an infectious skin disease,[a] he must be brought to Aaron the priest or to one of his sons[b] who is a priest. ³The priest is to examine the sore on his skin, and if the hair in the sore has turned white and the sore appears to be more than skin deep,[c] it is an infectious skin disease. When the priest examines him, he shall pronounce him ceremonially unclean. ⁴If the spot on his skin is white but does not appear to be more than skin deep and the hair in it has not turned white, the priest is to put the infected person in isolation for seven days. ⁵On the seventh day the priest is to examine him, and if he sees that the sore is unchanged and has not spread in the skin, he is to keep him in isolation another seven days. ⁶On the seventh day the priest is to examine him again, and if the sore has faded and has not spread in the skin, the priest shall pronounce him clean; it is only a rash. The man must wash his clothes, and he will be clean. ⁷But if the rash does spread in his skin after he has shown himself to the priest to be pronounced clean, he must appear before the priest again. ⁸The priest is to examine him, and if the rash has spread in the skin, he shall pronounce him unclean; it is an infectious disease.

⁹"When anyone has an infectious skin disease, he must be brought to the priest. ¹⁰The priest is to examine him, and if there is a white swelling in the skin that has turned the hair white and if there is raw flesh in the swelling, ¹¹it is a chronic skin disease and the priest shall pronounce him unclean. He is not to put him in isolation, because he is already unclean. Lev 14:8; Nu 12:10

¹²"If the disease breaks out all over his skin and, so far as the priest can see, it covers all the skin of the infected person from head to foot, ¹³the priest is to examine him, and if the disease has covered his whole body, he shall pronounce that person clean. Since it has all turned white, he is clean. ¹⁴But whenever raw flesh appears on him, he will be unclean. ¹⁵When the priest sees the raw flesh, he shall pronounce him unclean. The raw flesh is unclean; he has an infectious disease. ¹⁶Should the raw flesh change and turn white, he must go to the priest. ¹⁷The priest is to examine him, and if the sores have turned white, the priest shall pronounce the infected person clean; then he will be clean. ver 2,6

¹⁸"When someone has a boil on his skin and it heals, ¹⁹and in the place where the boil was, a white swelling or reddish-white spot appears, he must present himself to

---

a2 Traditionally *leprosy*; the Hebrew word was used for various diseases affecting the skin—not necessarily leprosy; also elsewhere in this chapter.   b2 Or *descendants*   c3 Or *be lower than the rest of the skin*; also elsewhere in this chapter

the priest. ²⁰The priest is to examine it, and if it appears to be more than skin deep and the hair in it has turned white, the priest shall pronounce him unclean. It is an infectious skin disease that has broken out where the boil was. ²¹But if, when the priest examines it, there is no white hair in it and it is not more than skin deep and has faded, then the priest is to put him in isolation for seven days. ²²If it is spreading in the skin, the priest shall pronounce him unclean; it is infectious. ²³But if the spot is unchanged and has not spread, it is only a scar from the boil, and the priest shall pronounce him clean.

²⁴"When someone has a burn on his skin and a reddish-white or white spot appears in the raw flesh of the burn, ²⁵the priest is to examine the spot, and if the hair in it has turned white, and it appears to be more than skin deep, it is an infectious disease that has broken out in the burn. The priest shall pronounce him unclean; it is an infectious skin disease. ²⁶But if the priest examines it and there is no white hair in the spot and if it is not more than skin deep and has faded, then the priest is to put him in isolation for seven days. ²⁷On the seventh day the priest is to examine him, and if it is spreading in the skin, the priest shall pronounce him unclean; it is an infectious skin disease. ²⁸If, however, the spot is unchanged and has not spread in the skin but has faded, it

is a swelling from the burn, and the priest shall pronounce him clean; it is only a scar from the burn.   ver 4-5

²⁹"If a man or woman has a sore on the head or on the chin, ³⁰the priest is to examine the sore, and if it appears to be more than skin deep and the hair in it is yellow and thin, the priest shall pronounce that person unclean; it is an itch, an infectious disease of the head or chin. ³¹But if, when the priest examines this kind of sore, it does not seem to be more than skin deep and there is no black hair in it, then the priest is to put the infected person in isolation for seven days. ³²On the seventh day the priest is to examine the sore, and if the itch has not spread and there is no yellow hair in it and it does not appear to be more than skin deep, ³³he must be shaved except for the diseased area, and the priest is to keep him in isolation another seven days. ³⁴On the seventh day the priest is to examine the itch, and if it has not spread in the skin and appears to be no more than skin deep, the priest shall pronounce him clean. He must wash his clothes, and he will be clean. ³⁵But if the itch does spread in the skin after he is pronounced clean, ³⁶the priest is to examine him, and if the itch has spread in the skin, the priest does not need to look for yellow hair; the person is unclean. ³⁷If, however, in his judgment it is unchanged and

black hair has grown in it, the itch is healed. He is clean, and the priest shall pronounce him clean.

38"When a man or woman has white spots on the skin, **39**the priest is to examine them, and if the spots are dull white, it is a harmless rash that has broken out on the skin; that person is clean.

40"When a man has lost his hair and is bald, he is clean. **41**If he has lost his hair from the front of his scalp and has a bald forehead, he is clean. **42**But if he has a reddish-white sore on his bald head or forehead, it is an infectious disease breaking out on his head or forehead. **43**The priest is to examine him, and if the swollen sore on his head or forehead is reddish-white like an infectious skin disease, **44**the man is diseased and is unclean. The priest shall pronounce him unclean because of the sore on his head.   2Ki 2:23; Eze 29:18

45"The person with such an infectious disease must wear torn clothes, let his hair be unkempt,[a] cover the lower part of his face and cry out, 'Unclean! Unclean!' **46**As long as he has the infection he remains unclean. He must live alone; he must live outside the camp.

Regulations About Mildew

47"If any clothing is contaminated with mildew—any woolen or linen clothing, **48**any woven or knitted material of linen or wool,

any leather or anything made of leather— **49**and if the contamination in the clothing, or leather, or woven or knitted material, or any leather article, is greenish or reddish, it is a spreading mildew and must be shown to the priest. **50**The priest is to examine the mildew and isolate the affected article for seven days. **51**On the seventh day he is to examine it, and if the mildew has spread in the clothing, or the woven or knitted material, or the leather, whatever its use, it is a destructive mildew; the article is unclean. **52**He must burn up the clothing, or the woven or knitted material of wool or linen, or any leather article that has the contamination in it, because the mildew is destructive; the article must be burned up.   Mk 1:44; Lev 14:44

53"But if, when the priest examines it, the mildew has not spread in the clothing, or the woven or knitted material, or the leather article, **54**he shall order that the contaminated article be washed. Then he is to isolate it for another seven days. **55**After the affected article has been washed, the priest is to examine it, and if the mildew has not changed its appearance, even though it has not spread, it is unclean. Burn it with fire, whether the mildew has affected one side or the other. **56**If, when the priest examines it, the mildew has faded after the article has been washed,

---

a 45 Or *clothes, uncover his head*

he is to tear the contaminated part out of the clothing, or the leather, or the woven or knitted material. ⁵⁷But if it reappears in the clothing, or in the woven or knitted material, or in the leather article, it is spreading, and whatever has the mildew must be burned with fire. ⁵⁸The clothing, or the woven or knitted material, or any leather article that has been washed and is rid of the mildew, must be washed again, and it will be clean."

⁵⁹These are the regulations concerning contamination by mildew in woolen or linen clothing, woven or knitted material, or any leather article, for pronouncing them clean or unclean.

Cleansing From Infectious Skin Diseases

14 The LORD said to Moses, ²"These are the regulations for the diseased person at the time of his ceremonial cleansing, when he is brought to the priest: ³The priest is to go outside the camp and examine him. If the person has been healed of his infectious skin disease,ᵃ ⁴the priest shall order that two live clean birds and some cedar wood, scarlet yarn and hyssop be brought for the one to be cleansed. ⁵Then the priest shall order that one of the birds be killed over fresh water in a clay pot. ⁶He is then to take the live bird and dip it, together with the cedar wood, the scarlet yarn and the hyssop, into the blood of the bird that was killed over the fresh water. ⁷Seven times he shall sprinkle the one to be cleansed of the infectious disease and pronounce him clean. Then he is to release the live bird in the open fields.   Mt 8:2-4; Nu 19:6

⁸"The person to be cleansed must wash his clothes, shave off all his hair and bathe with water; then he will be ceremonially clean. After this he may come into the camp, but he must stay outside his tent for seven days. ⁹On the seventh day he must shave off all his hair; he must shave his head, his beard, his eyebrows and the rest of his hair. He must wash his clothes and bathe himself with water, and he will be clean.   Lev 11:25; 13:6

¹⁰"On the eighth day he must bring two male lambs and one ewe lamb a year old, each without defect, along with three-tenths of an ephahᵇ of fine flour mixed with oil for a grain offering, and one logᶜ of oil. ¹¹The priest who pronounces him clean shall present both the one to be cleansed and his offerings before the LORD at the entrance to the Tent of Meeting.

¹²"Then the priest is to take one of the male lambs and offer it as a guilt offering, along with the log of oil; he shall wave them before the LORD as a wave offering. ¹³He is to

---

ᵃ3 Traditionally *leprosy*; the Hebrew word was used for various diseases affecting the skin—not necessarily leprosy; also elsewhere in this chapter.   ᵇ10 That is, probably about 6 quarts (about 6.5 liters)   ᶜ10 That is, probably about 2/3 pint (about 0.3 liter); also in verses 12, 15, 21 and 24

slaughter the lamb in the holy place where the sin offering and the burnt offering are slaughtered. Like the sin offering, the guilt offering belongs to the priest; it is most holy. ¹⁴The priest is to take some of the blood of the guilt offering and put it on the lobe of the right ear of the one to be cleansed, on the thumb of his right hand and on the big toe of his right foot. ¹⁵The priest shall then take some of the log of oil, pour it in the palm of his own left hand, ¹⁶dip his right forefinger into the oil in his palm, and with his finger sprinkle some of it before the Lord seven times. ¹⁷The priest is to put some of the oil remaining in his palm on the lobe of the right ear of the one to be cleansed, on the thumb of his right hand and on the big toe of his right foot, on top of the blood of the guilt offering. ¹⁸The rest of the oil in his palm the priest shall put on the head of the one to be cleansed and make atonement for him before the Lord.   Ex 29:11

¹⁹"Then the priest is to sacrifice the sin offering and make atonement for the one to be cleansed from his uncleanness. After that, the priest shall slaughter the burnt offering ²⁰and offer it on the altar, together with the grain offering, and make atonement for him, and he will be clean.

²¹"If, however, he is poor and cannot afford these, he must take one male lamb as a guilt offering to be waved to make atonement for him, together with a tenth of an ephah*ᵃ* of fine flour mixed with oil for a grain offering, a log of oil, ²²and two doves or two young pigeons, which he can afford, one for a sin offering and the other for a burnt offering.   Lev 5:7; 12:8

²³"On the eighth day he must bring them for his cleansing to the priest at the entrance to the Tent of Meeting, before the Lord. ²⁴The priest is to take the lamb for the guilt offering, together with the log of oil, and wave them before the Lord as a wave offering. ²⁵He shall slaughter the lamb for the guilt offering and take some of its blood and put it on the lobe of the right ear of the one to be cleansed, on the thumb of his right hand and on the big toe of his right foot. ²⁶The priest is to pour some of the oil into the palm of his own left hand, ²⁷and with his right forefinger sprinkle some of the oil from his palm seven times before the Lord. ²⁸Some of the oil in his palm he is to put on the same places he put the blood of the guilt offering—on the lobe of the right ear of the one to be cleansed, on the thumb of his right hand and on the big toe of his right foot. ²⁹The rest of the oil in his palm the priest shall put on the head of the one to be cleansed, to make atonement for him before the Lord. ³⁰Then he shall sacrifice

---

*ᵃ21 That is, probably about 2 quarts (about 2 liters)

the doves or the young pigeons, which the person can afford, [31]one[a] as a sin offering and the other as a burnt offering, together with the grain offering. In this way the priest will make atonement before the LORD on behalf of the one to be cleansed."

[32]These are the regulations for anyone who has an infectious skin disease and who cannot afford the regular offerings for his cleansing.

Cleansing From Mildew

[33]The LORD said to Moses and Aaron, [34]"When you enter the land of Canaan, which I am giving you as your possession, and I put a spreading mildew in a house in that land, [35]the owner of the house must go and tell the priest, 'I have seen something that looks like mildew in my house.' [36]The priest is to order the house to be emptied before he goes in to examine the mildew, so that nothing in the house will be pronounced unclean. After this the priest is to go in and inspect the house. [37]He is to examine the mildew on the walls, and if it has greenish or reddish depressions that appear to be deeper than the surface of the wall, [38]the priest shall go out the doorway of the house and close it up for seven days. [39]On the seventh day the priest shall return to inspect the house. If the mildew has spread on the walls, [40]he is to or-

der that the contaminated stones be torn out and thrown into an unclean place outside the town. [41]He must have all the inside walls of the house scraped and the material that is scraped off dumped into an unclean place outside the town. [42]Then they are to take other stones to replace these and take new clay and plaster the house.

[43]"If the mildew reappears in the house after the stones have been torn out and the house scraped and plastered, [44]the priest is to go and examine it and, if the mildew has spread in the house, it is a destructive mildew; the house is unclean. [45]It must be torn down—its stones, timbers and all the plaster—and taken out of the town to an unclean place.   Lev 13:51

[46]"Anyone who goes into the house while it is closed up will be unclean till evening. [47]Anyone who sleeps or eats in the house must wash his clothes.   Lev 11:24-25

[48]"But if the priest comes to examine it and the mildew has not spread after the house has been plastered, he shall pronounce the house clean, because the mildew is gone. [49]To purify the house he is to take two birds and some cedar wood, scarlet yarn and hyssop. [50]He shall kill one of the birds over fresh water in a clay pot. [51]Then he is to take the cedar wood, the hyssop, the scarlet yarn and the live bird, dip them into the blood of the

---

[a] 31 Septuagint and Syriac; Hebrew [31]such as the person can afford, one

dead bird and the fresh water, and sprinkle the house seven times. ⁵²He shall purify the house with the bird's blood, the fresh water, the live bird, the cedar wood, the hyssop and the scarlet yarn. ⁵³Then he is to release the live bird in the open fields outside the town. In this way he will make atonement for the house, and it will be clean." Lev 13:6; Ps 51:7

⁵⁴These are the regulations for any infectious skin disease, for an itch, ⁵⁵for mildew in clothing or in a house, ⁵⁶and for a swelling, a rash or a bright spot, ⁵⁷to determine when something is clean or unclean. Lev 13:2,47-52

These are the regulations for infectious skin diseases and mildew.

Discharges Causing Uncleanness

15 The LORD said to Moses and Aaron, ²"Speak to the Israelites and say to them: 'When any man has a bodily discharge, the discharge is unclean. ³Whether it continues flowing from his body or is blocked, it will make him unclean. This is how his discharge will bring about uncleanness:

⁴" 'Any bed the man with a discharge lies on will be unclean, and anything he sits on will be unclean. ⁵Anyone who touches his bed must wash his clothes and bathe with water, and he will be unclean till evening. ⁶Whoever sits on anything that the man with a discharge sat on must wash his clothes and bathe with water, and he will be unclean till evening.

⁷" 'Whoever touches the man who has a discharge must wash his clothes and bathe with water, and he will be unclean till evening.

⁸" 'If the man with the discharge spits on someone who is clean, that person must wash his clothes and bathe with water, and he will be unclean till evening. Nu 12:14

⁹" 'Everything the man sits on when riding will be unclean, ¹⁰and whoever touches any of the things that were under him will be unclean till evening; whoever picks up those things must wash his clothes and bathe with water, and he will be unclean till evening.

¹¹" 'Anyone the man with a discharge touches without rinsing his hands with water must wash his clothes and bathe with water, and he will be unclean till evening.

¹²" 'A clay pot that the man touches must be broken, and any wooden article is to be rinsed with water. Lev 6:28

¹³" 'When a man is cleansed from his discharge, he is to count off seven days for his ceremonial cleansing; he must wash his clothes and bathe himself with fresh water, and he will be clean. ¹⁴On the eighth day he must take two doves or two young pigeons and come before the LORD to the entrance to the Tent of Meeting and give them to the priest. ¹⁵The priest is to sacrifice them, the one

for a sin offering and the other for a burnt offering. In this way he will make atonement before the LORD for the man because of his discharge. Lev 8:33; 14:18-19

¹⁶" 'When a man has an emission of semen, he must bathe his whole body with water, and he will be unclean till evening. ¹⁷Any clothing or leather that has semen on it must be washed with water, and it will be unclean till evening. ¹⁸When a man lies with a woman and there is an emission of semen, both must bathe with water, and they will be unclean till evening.

¹⁹" 'When a woman has her regular flow of blood, the impurity of her monthly period will last seven days, and anyone who touches her will be unclean till evening.

²⁰" 'Anything she lies on during her period will be unclean, and anything she sits on will be unclean. ²¹Whoever touches her bed must wash his clothes and bathe with water, and he will be unclean till evening. ²²Whoever touches anything she sits on must wash his clothes and bathe with water, and he will be unclean till evening. ²³Whether it is the bed or anything she was sitting on, when anyone touches it, he will be unclean till evening.

²⁴" 'If a man lies with her and her monthly flow touches him, he will be unclean for seven days; any bed he lies on will be unclean.

²⁵" 'When a woman has a discharge of blood for many days at a time other than her monthly period or has a discharge that continues beyond her period, she will be unclean as long as she has the discharge, just as in the days of her period. ²⁶Any bed she lies on while her discharge continues will be unclean, as is her bed during her monthly period, and anything she sits on will be unclean, as during her period. ²⁷Whoever touches them will be unclean; he must wash his clothes and bathe with water, and he will be unclean till evening. Mt 9:20

²⁸" 'When she is cleansed from her discharge, she must count off seven days, and after that she will be ceremonially clean. ²⁹On the eighth day she must take two doves or two young pigeons and bring them to the priest at the entrance to the Tent of Meeting. ³⁰The priest is to sacrifice one for a sin offering and the other for a burnt offering. In this way he will make atonement for her before the LORD for the uncleanness of her discharge. Lev 14:22

³¹" 'You must keep the Israelites separate from things that make them unclean, so they will not die in their uncleanness for defiling my dwelling place,ᵃ which is among them.' " Nu 19:13,20; Eze 5:11

³²These are the regulations for a man with a discharge, for anyone

ᵃ31 Or my tabernacle

made unclean by an emission of semen, ³³for a woman in her monthly period, for a man or a woman with a discharge, and for a man who lies with a woman who is ceremonially unclean.   ver 2

The Day of Atonement

16 The LORD spoke to Moses after the death of the two sons of Aaron who died when they approached the LORD. ²The LORD said to Moses: "Tell your brother Aaron not to come whenever he chooses into the Most Holy Place behind the curtain in front of the atonement cover on the ark, or else he will die, because I appear in the cloud over the atonement cover.   Ex 25:22; Lev 10:1

³"This is how Aaron is to enter the sanctuary area: with a young bull for a sin offering and a ram for a burnt offering. ⁴He is to put on the sacred linen tunic, with linen undergarments next to his body; he is to tie the linen sash around him and put on the linen turban. These are sacred garments; so he must bathe himself with water before he puts them on. ⁵From the Israelite community he is to take two male goats for a sin offering and a ram for a burnt offering.

⁶"Aaron is to offer the bull for his own sin offering to make atonement for himself and his household. ⁷Then he is to take the two goats and present them before the LORD at the entrance to the Tent of Meeting. ⁸He is to cast lots for the two goats—one lot for the LORD and the other for the scapegoat.^a ⁹Aaron shall bring the goat whose lot falls to the LORD and sacrifice it for a sin offering. ¹⁰But the goat chosen by lot as the scapegoat shall be presented alive before the LORD to be used for making atonement by sending it into the desert as a scapegoat.   Lev 9:7; Heb 7:27; 9:7,12

¹¹"Aaron shall bring the bull for his own sin offering to make atonement for himself and his household, and he is to slaughter the bull for his own sin offering. ¹²He is to take a censer full of burning coals from the altar before the LORD and two handfuls of finely ground fragrant incense and take them behind the curtain. ¹³He is to put the incense on the fire before the LORD, and the smoke of the incense will conceal the atonement cover above the Testimony, so that he will not die. ¹⁴He is to take some of the bull's blood and with his finger sprinkle it on the front of the atonement cover; then he shall sprinkle some of it with his finger seven times before the atonement cover.   Lev 10:1; Heb 9:7,13,25

¹⁵"He shall then slaughter the goat for the sin offering for the people and take its blood behind the curtain and do with it as he did with the bull's blood: He shall sprinkle it on the atonement cover

---

^a8 That is, the goat of removal; Hebrew *azazel*; also in verses 10 and 26

and in front of it. ¹⁶In this way he will make atonement for the Most Holy Place because of the uncleanness and rebellion of the Israelites, whatever their sins have been. He is to do the same for the Tent of Meeting, which is among them in the midst of their uncleanness. ¹⁷No one is to be in the Tent of Meeting from the time Aaron goes in to make atonement in the Most Holy Place until he comes out, having made atonement for himself, his household and the whole community of Israel.   Ex 29:36

¹⁸"Then he shall come out to the altar that is before the LORD and make atonement for it. He shall take some of the bull's blood and some of the goat's blood and put it on all the horns of the altar. ¹⁹He shall sprinkle some of the blood on it with his finger seven times to cleanse it and to consecrate it from the uncleanness of the Israelites.

²⁰"When Aaron has finished making atonement for the Most Holy Place, the Tent of Meeting and the altar, he shall bring forward the live goat. ²¹He is to lay both hands on the head of the live goat and confess over it all the wickedness and rebellion of the Israelites—all their sins—and put them on the goat's head. He shall send the goat away into the desert in the care of a man appointed for the task. ²²The goat will carry on itself all their sins to a solitary place; and the man shall release it in the desert.   Lev 5:5; Isa 53:12

²³"Then Aaron is to go into the Tent of Meeting and take off the linen garments he put on before he entered the Most Holy Place, and he is to leave them there. ²⁴He shall bathe himself with water in a holy place and put on his regular garments. Then he shall come out and sacrifice the burnt offering for himself and the burnt offering for the people, to make atonement for himself and for the people. ²⁵He shall also burn the fat of the sin offering on the altar.   Eze 42:14; 44:19

²⁶"The man who releases the goat as a scapegoat must wash his clothes and bathe himself with water; afterward he may come into the camp. ²⁷The bull and the goat for the sin offerings, whose blood was brought into the Most Holy Place to make atonement, must be taken outside the camp; their hides, flesh and offal are to be burned up. ²⁸The man who burns them must wash his clothes and bathe himself with water; afterward he may come into the camp.

²⁹"This is to be a lasting ordinance for you: On the tenth day of the seventh month you must deny yourselves[a] and not do any work —whether native-born or an alien living among you— ³⁰because on this day atonement will be made for you, to cleanse you. Then, before the LORD, you will be clean

---

from all your sins. ³¹It is a sabbath of rest, and you must deny yourselves; it is a lasting ordinance. ³²The priest who is anointed and ordained to succeed his father as high priest is to make atonement. He is to put on the sacred linen garments ³³and make atonement for the Most Holy Place, for the Tent of Meeting and the altar, and for the priests and all the people of the community.   Nu 29:7; Eph 5:26

³⁴"This is to be a lasting ordinance for you: Atonement is to be made once a year for all the sins of the Israelites."   Heb 9:7,25

And it was done, as the LORD commanded Moses.   Lev 23:26-32

Eating Blood Forbidden

17 The LORD said to Moses, ²"Speak to Aaron and his sons and to all the Israelites and say to them: 'This is what the LORD has commanded: ³Any Israelite who sacrifices an ox,ᵃ a lamb or a goat in the camp or outside of it ⁴instead of bringing it to the entrance to the Tent of Meeting to present it as an offering to the LORD in front of the tabernacle of the LORD—that man shall be considered guilty of bloodshed; he has shed blood and must be cut off from his people. ⁵This is so the Israelites will bring to the LORD the sacrifices they are now making in the open fields. They must bring them to the priest, that is, to the LORD, at the entrance to the Tent of Meeting and sacrifice them as fellowship offerings.ᵇ ⁶The priest is to sprinkle the blood against the altar of the LORD at the entrance to the Tent of Meeting and burn the fat as an aroma pleasing to the LORD. ⁷They must no longer offer any of their sacrifices to the goat idolsᶜ to whom they prostitute themselves. This is to be a lasting ordinance for them and for the generations to come.'   Ex 34:15

⁸"Say to them: 'Any Israelite or any alien living among them who offers a burnt offering or sacrifice ⁹and does not bring it to the entrance to the Tent of Meeting to sacrifice it to the LORD—that man must be cut off from his people.

¹⁰ 'Any Israelite or any alien living among them who eats any blood—I will set my face against that person who eats blood and will cut him off from his people. ¹¹For the life of a creature is in the blood, and I have given it to you to make atonement for yourselves on the altar; it is the blood that makes atonement for one's life. ¹²Therefore I say to the Israelites, "None of you may eat blood, nor may an alien living among you eat blood."

¹³" 'Any Israelite or any alien living among you who hunts any animal or bird that may be eaten must drain out the blood and cover it

---

ᵃ3 The Hebrew word can include both male and female.   ᵇ5 Traditionally *peace offerings*   ᶜ7 Or *demons*

with earth, ¹⁴because the life of every creature is its blood. That is why I have said to the Israelites, "You must not eat the blood of any creature, because the life of every creature is its blood; anyone who eats it must be cut off."   Ge 9:4

¹⁵" 'Anyone, whether native-born or alien, who eats anything found dead or torn by wild animals must wash his clothes and bathe with water, and he will be ceremonially unclean till evening; then he will be clean. ¹⁶But if he does not wash his clothes and bathe himself, he will be held responsible.' "   Ex 22:31; Dt 14:21

Unlawful Sexual Relations

18 The LORD said to Moses, ²"Speak to the Israelites and say to them: 'I am the LORD your God. ³You must not do as they do in Egypt, where you used to live, and you must not do as they do in the land of Canaan, where I am bringing you. Do not follow their practices. ⁴You must obey my laws and be careful to follow my decrees. I am the LORD your God. ⁵Keep my decrees and laws, for the man who obeys them will live by them. I am the LORD.

⁶" 'No one is to approach any close relative to have sexual relations. I am the LORD.

⁷" 'Do not dishonor your father by having sexual relations with your mother. She is your mother; do not have relations with her.

⁸" 'Do not have sexual relations with your father's wife; that would dishonor your father.   Lev 20:11

⁹" 'Do not have sexual relations with your sister, either your father's daughter or your mother's daughter, whether she was born in the same home or elsewhere.

¹⁰" 'Do not have sexual relations with your son's daughter or your daughter's daughter; that would dishonor you.

¹¹" 'Do not have sexual relations with the daughter of your father's wife, born to your father; she is your sister.

¹²" 'Do not have sexual relations with your father's sister; she is your father's close relative.

¹³" 'Do not have sexual relations with your mother's sister, because she is your mother's close relative.

¹⁴" 'Do not dishonor your father's brother by approaching his wife to have sexual relations; she is your aunt.   Lev 20:20

¹⁵" 'Do not have sexual relations with your daughter-in-law. She is your son's wife; do not have relations with her.   Lev 20:12

¹⁶" 'Do not have sexual relations with your brother's wife; that would dishonor your brother.

¹⁷" 'Do not have sexual relations with both a woman and her daughter. Do not have sexual relations with either her son's daughter or her daughter's daughter; they are her close relatives. That is wickedness.   Lev 20:14

¹⁸" 'Do not take your wife's sis-

ter as a rival wife and have sexual relations with her while your wife is living.

¹⁹" 'Do not approach a woman to have sexual relations during the uncleanness of her monthly period.   Lev 15:24

²⁰" 'Do not have sexual relations with your neighbor's wife and defile yourself with her.   Ex 20:14

²¹" 'Do not give any of your children to be sacrificed[a] to Molech, for you must not profane the name of your God. I am the LORD.

²²" 'Do not lie with a man as one lies with a woman; that is detestable.   Lev 20:13; Ro 1:27

²³" 'Do not have sexual relations with an animal and defile yourself with it. A woman must not present herself to an animal to have sexual relations with it; that is a perversion.   Lev 20:15

²⁴" 'Do not defile yourselves in any of these ways, because this is how the nations that I am going to drive out before you became defiled. ²⁵Even the land was defiled; so I punished it for its sin, and the land vomited out its inhabitants. ²⁶But you must keep my decrees and my laws. The native-born and the aliens living among you must not do any of these detestable things, ²⁷for all these things were done by the people who lived in the land before you, and the land became defiled. ²⁸And if you defile the land, it will vomit you out as it

vomited out the nations that were before you.   Dt 18:12

²⁹" 'Everyone who does any of these detestable things—such persons must be cut off from their people. ³⁰Keep my requirements and do not follow any of the detestable customs that were practiced before you came and do not defile yourselves with them. I am the LORD your God.' "   Dt 11:1

Various Laws

19 The LORD said to Moses, ²"Speak to the entire assembly of Israel and say to them: 'Be holy because I, the LORD your God, am holy.   Lev 11:44; 1Pe 1:16

³" 'Each of you must respect his mother and father, and you must observe my Sabbaths. I am the LORD your God.   Ex 20:12

⁴" 'Do not turn to idols or make gods of cast metal for yourselves. I am the LORD your God.   Ps 96:5

⁵" 'When you sacrifice a fellowship offering[b] to the LORD, sacrifice it in such a way that it will be accepted on your behalf. ⁶It shall be eaten on the day you sacrifice it or on the next day; anything left over until the third day must be burned up. ⁷If any of it is eaten on the third day, it is impure and will not be accepted. ⁸Whoever eats it will be held responsible because he has desecrated what is holy to the LORD; that person must be cut off from his people.   Lev 7:16-17

---

a 21 Or *to be passed through the fire,*   b 5 Traditionally *peace offering*

9" 'When you reap the harvest of your land, do not reap to the very edges of your field or gather the gleanings of your harvest. 10Do not go over your vineyard a second time or pick up the grapes that have fallen. Leave them for the poor and the alien. I am the LORD your God.   Dt 24:19-22

11" 'Do not steal.   Ex 20:15

" 'Do not lie.   Eph 4:25

" 'Do not deceive one another.

12" 'Do not swear falsely by my name and so profane the name of your God. I am the LORD.   Ex 20:7

13" 'Do not defraud your neighbor or rob him.   Ex 22:15,25-27

" 'Do not hold back the wages of a hired man overnight.   Dt 24:15

14" 'Do not curse the deaf or put a stumbling block in front of the blind, but fear your God. I am the LORD.   Dt 27:18

15" 'Do not pervert justice; do not show partiality to the poor or favoritism to the great, but judge your neighbor fairly.   Ex 23:2,6

16" 'Do not go about spreading slander among your people.

" 'Do not do anything that endangers your neighbor's life. I am the LORD.   Ex 23:7

17" 'Do not hate your brother in your heart. Rebuke your neighbor frankly so you will not share in his guilt.   Jn 2:9; Mt 18:15

18" 'Do not seek revenge or bear a grudge against one of your people, but love your neighbor as yourself. I am the LORD.   Mt 5:43

19" 'Keep my decrees.

" 'Do not mate different kinds of animals.

" 'Do not plant your field with two kinds of seed.

" 'Do not wear clothing woven of two kinds of material.   Dt 22:9,11

20" 'If a man sleeps with a woman who is a slave girl promised to another man but who has not been ransomed or given her freedom, there must be due punishment. Yet they are not to be put to death, because she had not been freed. 21The man, however, must bring a ram to the entrance to the Tent of Meeting for a guilt offering to the LORD. 22With the ram of the guilt offering the priest is to make atonement for him before the LORD for the sin he has committed, and his sin will be forgiven.   Lev 5:15

23" 'When you enter the land and plant any kind of fruit tree, regard its fruit as forbidden.ᵃ For three years you are to consider it forbiddenᵃ; it must not be eaten. 24In the fourth year all its fruit will be holy, an offering of praise to the LORD. 25But in the fifth year you may eat its fruit. In this way your harvest will be increased. I am the LORD your God.   Pr 3:9

26" 'Do not eat any meat with the blood still in it.   Lev 17:10

" 'Do not practice divination or sorcery.   Dt 18:10

ᵃ23 Hebrew uncircumcised

27" 'Do not cut the hair at the sides of your head or clip off the edges of your beard.   Lev 21:5

28" 'Do not cut your bodies for the dead or put tattoo marks on yourselves. I am the LORD.

29" 'Do not degrade your daughter by making her a prostitute, or the land will turn to prostitution and be filled with wickedness.

30" 'Observe my Sabbaths and have reverence for my sanctuary. I am the LORD.   Lev 26:2

31" 'Do not turn to mediums or seek out spiritists, for you will be defiled by them. I am the LORD your God.   Lev 20:6; Isa 8:19

32" 'Rise in the presence of the aged, show respect for the elderly and revere your God. I am the LORD.   Job 32:4; 1Ti 5:1

33" 'When an alien lives with you in your land, do not mistreat him. **34**The alien living with you must be treated as one of your native-born. Love him as yourself, for you were aliens in Egypt. I am the LORD your God.   ver 18; Ex 12:48; Dt 10:19

35" 'Do not use dishonest standards when measuring length, weight or quantity. **36**Use honest scales and honest weights, an honest ephah*a* and an honest hin.*b* I am the LORD your God, who brought you out of Egypt.

37" 'Keep all my decrees and all my laws and follow them. I am the LORD.' "   2Ki 17:37

Punishments for Sin

20 The LORD said to Moses, **2**"Say to the Israelites: 'Any Israelite or any alien living in Israel who gives*c* any of his children to Molech must be put to death. The people of the community are to stone him. **3**I will set my face against that man and I will cut him off from his people; for by giving his children to Molech, he has defiled my sanctuary and profaned my holy name. **4**If the people of the community close their eyes when that man gives one of his children to Molech and they fail to put him to death, **5**I will set my face against that man and his family and will cut off from their people both him and all who follow him in prostituting themselves to Molech.

6" 'I will set my face against the person who turns to mediums and spiritists to prostitute himself by following them, and I will cut him off from his people.   Lev 19:31

7" 'Consecrate yourselves and be holy, because I am the LORD your God. **8**Keep my decrees and follow them. I am the LORD, who makes you holy.*d*   Eph 1:4; 1Pe 1:16

9" 'If anyone curses his father or mother, he must be put to death. He has cursed his father or his mother, and his blood will be on his own head.   Ex 21:17; Dt 27:16

10" 'If a man commits adultery with another man's wife—with the

---

a 36 An ephah was a dry measure.   *b 36* A hin was a liquid measure.   *c 2* Or *sacrifices*; also in verses 3 and 4   *d 8* Or *who sanctifies you*; or *who sets you apart as holy* wife of his neighbor—both the adulterer and the adulteress must be put to death. Ex 20:14

11" 'If a man sleeps with his father's wife, he has dishonored his father. Both the man and the woman must be put to death; their blood will be on their own heads.

12" 'If a man sleeps with his daughter-in-law, both of them must be put to death. What they have done is a perversion; their blood will be on their own heads.

13" 'If a man lies with a man as one lies with a woman, both of them have done what is detestable. They must be put to death; their blood will be on their own heads. Lev 18:22

14" 'If a man marries both a woman and her mother, it is wicked. Both he and they must be burned in the fire, so that no wickedness will be among you.

15" 'If a man has sexual relations with an animal, he must be put to death, and you must kill the animal. Lev 18:23

16" 'If a woman approaches an animal to have sexual relations with it, kill both the woman and the animal. They must be put to death; their blood will be on their own heads.

17" 'If a man marries his sister, the daughter of either his father or his mother, and they have sexual relations, it is a disgrace. They must be cut off before the eyes of their people. He has dishonored his sister and will be held responsible. Lev 18:9

18" 'If a man lies with a woman during her monthly period and has sexual relations with her, he has exposed the source of her flow, and she has also uncovered it. Both of them must be cut off from their people. Lev 15:24; 18:19

19" 'Do not have sexual relations with the sister of either your mother or your father, for that would dishonor a close relative; both of you would be held responsible.

20" 'If a man sleeps with his aunt, he has dishonored his uncle. They will be held responsible; they will die childless. Lev 18:14

21" 'If a man marries his brother's wife, it is an act of impurity; he has dishonored his brother. They will be childless. Lev 18:16

22" 'Keep all my decrees and laws and follow them, so that the land where I am bringing you to live may not vomit you out. 23You must not live according to the customs of the nations I am going to drive out before you. Because they did all these things, I abhorred them. 24But I said to you, "You will possess their land; I will give it to you as an inheritance, a land flowing with milk and honey." I am the LORD your God, who has set you apart from the nations. Ex 33:16

25" 'You must therefore make a distinction between clean and unclean animals and between unclean and clean birds. Do not defile yourselves by any animal or bird or anything that moves along the ground—those which I have set apart as unclean for you. 26You are to be holy to me[a] because I, the LORD, am holy, and I have set you apart from the nations to be my own.   Dt 14:3-21

27" 'A man or woman who is a medium or spiritist among you must be put to death. You are to stone them; their blood will be on their own heads.' "   Lev 19:31

Rules for Priests

21 The LORD said to Moses, "Speak to the priests, the sons of Aaron, and say to them: 'A priest must not make himself ceremonially unclean for any of his people who die, 2except for a close relative, such as his mother or father, his son or daughter, his brother, 3or an unmarried sister who is dependent on him since she has no husband—for her he may make himself unclean. 4He must not make himself unclean for people related to him by marriage,[b] and so defile himself.

5" 'Priests must not shave their heads or shave off the edges of their beards or cut their bodies. 6They must be holy to their God and must not profane the name of their God. Because they present the offerings made to the LORD by fire, the food of their God, they are to be holy.   Lev 18:21; 19:28

7" 'They must not marry women defiled by prostitution or divorced from their husbands, because priests are holy to their God. 8Regard them as holy, because they offer up the food of your God. Consider them holy, because I the LORD am holy—I who make you holy.[c]   Eze 44:22

9" 'If a priest's daughter defiles herself by becoming a prostitute, she disgraces her father; she must be burned in the fire.   Ge 38:24

10" 'The high priest, the one among his brothers who has had the anointing oil poured on his head and who has been ordained to wear the priestly garments, must not let his hair become unkempt[d] or tear his clothes. 11He must not enter a place where there is a dead body. He must not make himself unclean, even for his father or mother, 12nor leave the sanctuary of his God or desecrate it, because he has been dedicated by the anointing oil of his God. I am the LORD.   Lev 10:6-7

13" 'The woman he marries must be a virgin. 14He must not marry a widow, a divorced woman, or a woman defiled by prostitution, but only a virgin from his own people, 15so he will not defile his offspring among his people. I am the LORD, who makes him holy.[e] ' "   Eze 44:22

16The LORD said to Moses, 17"Say to Aaron: 'For the generations to

---

[a]26 Or be my holy ones who set you apart as holy   [b]4 Or unclean as a leader among his people   [c]8 Or who sanctify you; or   [d]10 Or not uncover his head   [e]15 Or who sanctifies him; or who sets him apart as holy

come none of your descendants who has a defect may come near to offer the food of his God. ¹⁸No man who has any defect may come near: no man who is blind or lame, disfigured or deformed; ¹⁹no man with a crippled foot or hand, ²⁰or who is hunchbacked or dwarfed, or who has any eye defect, or who has festering or running sores or damaged testicles. ²¹No descendant of Aaron the priest who has any defect is to come near to present the offerings made to the LORD by fire. He has a defect; he must not come near to offer the food of his God. ²²He may eat the most holy food of his God, as well as the holy food; ²³yet because of his defect, he must not go near the curtain or approach the altar, and so desecrate my sanctuary. I am the LORD, who makes them holy.ᵃ' " Lev 22:19-25; Dt 23:1

²⁴So Moses told this to Aaron and his sons and to all the Israelites.

22 The LORD said to Moses, ²"Tell Aaron and his sons to treat with respect the sacred offerings the Israelites consecrate to me, so they will not profane my holy name. I am the LORD. Lev 19:8

³"Say to them: 'For the generations to come, if any of your descendants is ceremonially unclean and yet comes near the sacred offerings that the Israelites consecrate to the LORD, that person must be cut off from my presence. I am the LORD. Lev 7:20-21

⁴" 'If a descendant of Aaron has an infectious skin diseaseᵇ or a bodily discharge, he may not eat the sacred offerings until he is cleansed. He will also be unclean if he touches something defiled by a corpse or by anyone who has an emission of semen, ⁵or if he touches any crawling thing that makes him unclean, or any person who makes him unclean, whatever the uncleanness may be. ⁶The one who touches any such thing will be unclean till evening. He must not eat any of the sacred offerings unless he has bathed himself with water. ⁷When the sun goes down, he will be clean, and after that he may eat the sacred offerings, for they are his food. ⁸He must not eat anything found dead or torn by wild animals, and so become unclean through it. I am the LORD.

⁹" 'The priests are to keep my requirements so that they do not become guilty and die for treating them with contempt. I am the LORD, who makes them holy.ᶜ

¹⁰" 'No one outside a priest's family may eat the sacred offering, nor may the guest of a priest or his hired worker eat it. ¹¹But if a priest buys a slave with money, or if a slave is born in his household, that slave may eat his food. ¹²If a

---

ᵃ23 Or who sanctifies them; or who sets them apart as holy   ᵇ4 Traditionally leprosy; the Hebrew word was used for various diseases affecting the skin—not necessarily leprosy.   ᶜ9 Or who sanctifies them; or who sets them apart as holy; also in verse 16

priest's daughter marries anyone other than a priest, she may not eat any of the sacred contributions. [13]But if a priest's daughter becomes a widow or is divorced, yet has no children, and she returns to live in her father's house as in her youth, she may eat of her father's food. No unauthorized person, however, may eat any of it.

[14]" 'If anyone eats a sacred offering by mistake, he must make restitution to the priest for the offering and add a fifth of the value to it. [15]The priests must not desecrate the sacred offerings the Israelites present to the LORD [16]by allowing them to eat the sacred offerings and so bring upon them guilt requiring payment. I am the LORD, who makes them holy.' "   Lev 5:15

Unacceptable Sacrifices

[17]The LORD said to Moses, [18]"Speak to Aaron and his sons and to all the Israelites and say to them: 'If any of you—either an Israelite or an alien living in Israel—presents a gift for a burnt offering to the LORD, either to fulfill a vow or as a freewill offering, [19]you must present a male without defect from the cattle, sheep or goats in order that it may be accepted on your behalf. [20]Do not bring anything with a defect, because it will not be accepted on your behalf. [21]When anyone brings from the herd or flock a fellowship offering[a] to the LORD to fulfill a special vow or as a freewill offering, it must be without defect or blemish to be acceptable. [22]Do not offer to the LORD the blind, the injured or the maimed, or anything with warts or festering or running sores. Do not place any of these on the altar as an offering made to the LORD by fire. [23]You may, however, present as a freewill offering an ox[b] or a sheep that is deformed or stunted, but it will not be accepted in fulfillment of a vow. [24]You must not offer to the LORD an animal whose testicles are bruised, crushed, torn or cut. You must not do this in your own land, [25]and you must not accept such animals from the hand of a foreigner and offer them as the food of your God. They will not be accepted on your behalf, because they are deformed and have defects.' "   Lev 3:6; Dt 15:21

[26]The LORD said to Moses, [27]"When a calf, a lamb or a goat is born, it is to remain with its mother for seven days. From the eighth day on, it will be acceptable as an offering made to the LORD by fire. [28]Do not slaughter a cow or a sheep and its young on the same day.   Ex 22:30; Dt 22:6-7

[29]"When you sacrifice a thank offering to the LORD, sacrifice it in such a way that it will be accepted on your behalf. [30]It must be eaten that same day; leave none of it till morning. I am the LORD.   Lev 7:12

a 21 Traditionally peace offering   b 23 The Hebrew word can include both male and female.

³¹"Keep my commands and follow them. I am the Lord. ³²Do not profane my holy name. I must be acknowledged as holy by the Israelites. I am the Lord, who makes^a you holy^b ³³and who brought you out of Egypt to be your God. I am the Lord."   Dt 4:2,40; Ps 105:45

23 The Lord said to Moses, ²"Speak to the Israelites and say to them: 'These are my appointed feasts, the appointed feasts of the Lord, which you are to proclaim as sacred assemblies.

The Sabbath

³" 'There are six days when you may work, but the seventh day is a Sabbath of rest, a day of sacred assembly. You are not to do any work; wherever you live, it is a Sabbath to the Lord.   Ex 20:9-10

The Passover and Unleavened Bread

⁴" 'These are the Lord's appointed feasts, the sacred assemblies you are to proclaim at their appointed times: ⁵The Lord's Passover begins at twilight on the fourteenth day of the first month. ⁶On the fifteenth day of that month the Lord's Feast of Unleavened Bread begins; for seven days you must eat bread made without yeast. ⁷On the first day hold a sacred assembly and do no regular work. ⁸For seven days present an offering made to the Lord by fire. And on the seventh day hold a sacred assembly and do no regular work.' "

Firstfruits

⁹The Lord said to Moses, ¹⁰"Speak to the Israelites and say to them: 'When you enter the land I am going to give you and you reap its harvest, bring to the priest a sheaf of the first grain you harvest. ¹¹He is to wave the sheaf before the Lord so it will be accepted on your behalf; the priest is to wave it on the day after the Sabbath. ¹²On the day you wave the sheaf, you must sacrifice as a burnt offering to the Lord a lamb a year old without defect, ¹³together with its grain offering of two-tenths of an ephah^c of fine flour mixed with oil—an offering made to the Lord by fire, a pleasing aroma—and its drink offering of a quarter of a hin^d of wine. ¹⁴You must not eat any bread, or roasted or new grain, until the very day you bring this offering to your God. This is to be a lasting ordinance for the generations to come, wherever you live.   Ex 23:16,19

Feast of Weeks

¹⁵" 'From the day after the Sabbath, the day you brought the sheaf of the wave offering, count off seven full weeks. ¹⁶Count off

---

^a32 Or made   ^b32 Or who sanctifies you; or who sets you apart as holy   ^c13 That is, probably about 4 quarts (about 4.5 liters); also in verse 17   ^d13 That is, probably about 1 quart (about 1 liter)

fifty days up to the day after the seventh Sabbath, and then present an offering of new grain to the LORD. [17]From wherever you live, bring two loaves made of two-tenths of an ephah of fine flour, baked with yeast, as a wave offering of firstfruits to the LORD. [18]Present with this bread seven male lambs, each a year old and without defect, one young bull and two rams. They will be a burnt offering to the LORD, together with their grain offerings and drink offerings — an offering made by fire, an aroma pleasing to the LORD. [19]Then sacrifice one male goat for a sin offering and two lambs, each a year old, for a fellowship offering.[a] [20]The priest is to wave the two lambs before the LORD as a wave offering, together with the bread of the firstfruits. They are a sacred offering to the LORD for the priest. [21]On that same day you are to proclaim a sacred assembly and do no regular work. This is to be a lasting ordinance for the generations to come, wherever you live.

[22]" 'When you reap the harvest of your land, do not reap to the very edges of your field or gather the gleanings of your harvest. Leave them for the poor and the alien. I am the LORD your God.' "

Feast of Trumpets

[23]The LORD said to Moses, [24]"Say to the Israelites: 'On the first day of the seventh month you are to have a day of rest, a sacred assembly commemorated with trumpet blasts. [25]Do no regular work, but present an offering made to the LORD by fire.' "   Nu 29:1-6

Day of Atonement

[26]The LORD said to Moses, [27]"The tenth day of this seventh month is the Day of Atonement. Hold a sacred assembly and deny yourselves,[b] and present an offering made to the LORD by fire. [28]Do no work on that day, because it is the Day of Atonement, when atonement is made for you before the LORD your God. [29]Anyone who does not deny himself on that day must be cut off from his people. [30]I will destroy from among his people anyone who does any work on that day. [31]You shall do no work at all. This is to be a lasting ordinance for the generations to come, wherever you live. [32]It is a sabbath of rest for you, and you must deny yourselves. From the evening of the ninth day of the month until the following evening you are to observe your sabbath."   Lev 16:2-34

Feast of Tabernacles

[33]The LORD said to Moses, [34]"Say to the Israelites: 'On the fifteenth day of the seventh month the LORD's Feast of Tabernacles begins, and it lasts for seven days. [35]The first day is a sacred assem-

---

[a] 19 Traditionally *peace offering*   [b] 27 Or *and fast*; also in verses 29 and 32

bly; do no regular work. **36**For seven days present offerings made to the Lord by fire, and on the eighth day hold a sacred assembly and present an offering made to the Lord by fire. It is the closing assembly; do no regular work.

37(" 'These are the Lord's appointed feasts, which you are to proclaim as sacred assemblies for bringing offerings made to the Lord by fire—the burnt offerings and grain offerings, sacrifices and drink offerings required for each day. **38**These offerings are in addition to those for the Lord's Sabbaths and*a* in addition to your gifts and whatever you have vowed and all the freewill offerings you give to the Lord.)   ver 2,4; Eze 45:17

39" 'So beginning with the fifteenth day of the seventh month, after you have gathered the crops of the land, celebrate the festival to the Lord for seven days; the first day is a day of rest, and the eighth day also is a day of rest. **40**On the first day you are to take choice fruit from the trees, and palm fronds, leafy branches and poplars, and rejoice before the Lord your God for seven days. **41**Celebrate this as a festival to the Lord for seven days each year. This is to be a lasting ordinance for the generations to come; celebrate it in the seventh month. **42**Live in booths for seven days: All native-born Is-

raelites are to live in booths **43**so your descendants will know that I had the Israelites live in booths when I brought them out of Egypt. I am the Lord your God.' "

44So Moses announced to the Israelites the appointed feasts of the Lord.

Oil and Bread Set Before the Lord

24 The Lord said to Moses, **2**"Command the Israelites to bring you clear oil of pressed olives for the light so that the lamps may be kept burning continually. **3**Outside the curtain of the Testimony in the Tent of Meeting, Aaron is to tend the lamps before the Lord from evening till morning, continually. This is to be a lasting ordinance for the generations to come. **4**The lamps on the pure gold lampstand before the Lord must be tended continually.

5"Take fine flour and bake twelve loaves of bread, using two-tenths of an ephah*b* for each loaf. **6**Set them in two rows, six in each row, on the table of pure gold before the Lord. **7**Along each row put some pure incense as a memorial portion to represent the bread and to be an offering made to the Lord by fire. **8**This bread is to be set out before the Lord regularly, Sabbath after Sabbath, on behalf of the Israelites, as a lasting covenant. **9**It be-

---

a 38 Or *These feasts are in addition to the Lord's Sabbaths, and these offerings are*   *b* 5 That is, probably about 4 quarts (about 4.5 liters)

longs to Aaron and his sons, who are to eat it in a holy place, because it is a most holy part of their regular share of the offerings made to the LORD by fire."   Mt 12:4; Nu 4:7

A Blasphemer Stoned

[10]Now the son of an Israelite mother and an Egyptian father went out among the Israelites, and a fight broke out in the camp between him and an Israelite. [11]The son of the Israelite woman blasphemed the Name with a curse; so they brought him to Moses. (His mother's name was Shelomith, the daughter of Dibri the Danite.) [12]They put him in custody until the will of the LORD should be made clear to them.   Ex 18:16

[13]Then the LORD said to Moses: [14]"Take the blasphemer outside the camp. All those who heard him are to lay their hands on his head, and the entire assembly is to stone him. [15]Say to the Israelites: 'If anyone curses his God, he will be held responsible; [16]anyone who blasphemes the name of the LORD must be put to death. The entire assembly must stone him. Whether an alien or native-born, when he blasphemes the Name, he must be put to death.   Dt 13:9; 1Ki 21:10,13

[17]" 'If anyone takes the life of a human being, he must be put to death. [18]Anyone who takes the life of someone's animal must make restitution—life for life. [19]If anyone injures his neighbor, whatever he has done must be done to him:

[20]fracture for fracture, eye for eye, tooth for tooth. As he has injured the other, so he is to be injured. [21]Whoever kills an animal must make restitution, but whoever kills a man must be put to death. [22]You are to have the same law for the alien and the native-born. I am the LORD your God.' "   Ex 21:12; Mt 5:38

[23]Then Moses spoke to the Israelites, and they took the blasphemer outside the camp and stoned him. The Israelites did as the LORD commanded Moses.

The Sabbath Year

25 The LORD said to Moses on Mount Sinai, [2]"Speak to the Israelites and say to them: 'When you enter the land I am going to give you, the land itself must observe a sabbath to the LORD. [3]For six years sow your fields, and for six years prune your vineyards and gather their crops. [4]But in the seventh year the land is to have a sabbath of rest, a sabbath to the LORD. Do not sow your fields or prune your vineyards. [5]Do not reap what grows of itself or harvest the grapes of your untended vines. The land is to have a year of rest. [6]Whatever the land yields during the sabbath year will be food for you—for yourself, your manservant and maidservant, and the hired worker and temporary resident who live among you, [7]as well as for your livestock and the wild animals in your land. Whatever the land produces may be eaten.

The Year of Jubilee

8" 'Count off seven sabbaths of years—seven times seven years—so that the seven sabbaths of years amount to a period of forty-nine years. ⁹Then have the trumpet sounded everywhere on the tenth day of the seventh month; on the Day of Atonement sound the trumpet throughout your land. ¹⁰Consecrate the fiftieth year and proclaim liberty throughout the land to all its inhabitants. It shall be a jubilee for you; each one of you is to return to his family property and each to his own clan. ¹¹The fiftieth year shall be a jubilee for you; do not sow and do not reap what grows of itself or harvest the untended vines. ¹²For it is a jubilee and is to be holy for you; eat only what is taken directly from the fields.   Jer 34:8,15,17; Lk 4:19

¹³" 'In this Year of Jubilee everyone is to return to his own property.   ver 10

¹⁴" 'If you sell land to one of your countrymen or buy any from him, do not take advantage of each other. ¹⁵You are to buy from your countryman on the basis of the number of years since the Jubilee. And he is to sell to you on the basis of the number of years left for harvesting crops. ¹⁶When the years are many, you are to increase the price, and when the years are few, you are to decrease the price, because what he is really selling you is the number of crops. ¹⁷Do not take advantage of each other, but fear your God. I am the LORD your God.   Lev 19:14,32

¹⁸" 'Follow my decrees and be careful to obey my laws, and you will live safely in the land. ¹⁹Then the land will yield its fruit, and you will eat your fill and live there in safety. ²⁰You may ask, "What will we eat in the seventh year if we do not plant or harvest our crops?" ²¹I will send you such a blessing in the sixth year that the land will yield enough for three years. ²²While you plant during the eighth year, you will eat from the old crop and will continue to eat from it until the harvest of the ninth year comes in.   Lev 26:10

²³" 'The land must not be sold permanently, because the land is mine and you are but aliens and my tenants. ²⁴Throughout the country that you hold as a possession, you must provide for the redemption of the land.   Ge 23:4

²⁵" 'If one of your countrymen becomes poor and sells some of his property, his nearest relative is to come and redeem what his countryman has sold. ²⁶If, however, a man has no one to redeem it for him but he himself prospers and acquires sufficient means to redeem it, ²⁷he is to determine the value for the years since he sold it and refund the balance to the man to whom he sold it; he can then go back to his own property. ²⁸But if he does not acquire the means to repay him, what he sold will re-

main in the possession of the buyer until the Year of Jubilee. It will be returned in the Jubilee, and he can then go back to his property.

²⁹"'If a man sells a house in a walled city, he retains the right of redemption a full year after its sale. During that time he may redeem it. ³⁰If it is not redeemed before a full year has passed, the house in the walled city shall belong permanently to the buyer and his descendants. It is not to be returned in the Jubilee. ³¹But houses in villages without walls around them are to be considered as open country. They can be redeemed, and they are to be returned in the Jubilee.

³²"'The Levites always have the right to redeem their houses in the Levitical towns, which they possess. ³³So the property of the Levites is redeemable—that is, a house sold in any town they hold —and is to be returned in the Jubilee, because the houses in the towns of the Levites are their property among the Israelites. ³⁴But the pastureland belonging to their towns must not be sold; it is their permanent possession. Nu 35:1-8

³⁵"'If one of your countrymen becomes poor and is unable to support himself among you, help him as you would an alien or a temporary resident, so he can continue to live among you. ³⁶Do not take interest of any kindᵃ from

him, but fear your God, so that your countryman may continue to live among you. ³⁷You must not lend him money at interest or sell him food at a profit. ³⁸I am the LORD your God, who brought you out of Egypt to give you the land of Canaan and to be your God.

³⁹"'If one of your countrymen becomes poor among you and sells himself to you, do not make him work as a slave. ⁴⁰He is to be treated as a hired worker or a temporary resident among you; he is to work for you until the Year of Jubilee. ⁴¹Then he and his children are to be released, and he will go back to his own clan and to the property of his forefathers. ⁴²Because the Israelites are my servants, whom I brought out of Egypt, they must not be sold as slaves. ⁴³Do not rule over them ruthlessly, but fear your God.

⁴⁴"'Your male and female slaves are to come from the nations around you; from them you may buy slaves. ⁴⁵You may also buy some of the temporary residents living among you and members of their clans born in your country, and they will become your property. ⁴⁶You can will them to your children as inherited property and can make them slaves for life, but you must not rule over your fellow Israelites ruthlessly.

⁴⁷"'If an alien or a temporary resident among you becomes rich

ᵃ 36 Or take excessive interest; similarly in verse 37

and one of your countrymen becomes poor and sells himself to the alien living among you or to a member of the alien's clan, **48**he retains the right of redemption after he has sold himself. One of his relatives may redeem him: **49**An uncle or a cousin or any blood relative in his clan may redeem him. Or if he prospers, he may redeem himself. **50**He and his buyer are to count the time from the year he sold himself up to the Year of Jubilee. The price for his release is to be based on the rate paid to a hired man for that number of years. **51**If many years remain, he must pay for his redemption a larger share of the price paid for him. **52**If only a few years remain until the Year of Jubilee, he is to compute that and pay for his redemption accordingly. **53**He is to be treated as a man hired from year to year; you must see to it that his owner does not rule over him ruthlessly. Ex 21:2-11

54" 'Even if he is not redeemed in any of these ways, he and his children are to be released in the Year of Jubilee, **55**for the Israelites belong to me as servants. They are my servants, whom I brought out of Egypt. I am the LORD your God.

Reward for Obedience

26 " 'Do not make idols or set up an image or a sacred stone for yourselves, and do not place a carved stone in your land

to bow down before it. I am the LORD your God. Ex 20:4; Dt 5:8

2" 'Observe my Sabbaths and have reverence for my sanctuary. I am the LORD. Lev 19:30

3" 'If you follow my decrees and are careful to obey my commands, **4**I will send you rain in its season, and the ground will yield its crops and the trees of the field their fruit. **5**Your threshing will continue until grape harvest and the grape harvest will continue until planting, and you will eat all the food you want and live in safety in your land. Lev 25:18; Dt 28:1,9

6" 'I will grant peace in the land, and you will lie down and no one will make you afraid. I will remove savage beasts from the land, and the sword will not pass through your country. **7**You will pursue your enemies, and they will fall by the sword before you. **8**Five of you will chase a hundred, and a hundred of you will chase ten thousand, and your enemies will fall by the sword before you. Ps 29:11

9" 'I will look on you with favor and make you fruitful and increase your numbers, and I will keep my covenant with you. **10**You will still be eating last year's harvest when you will have to move it out to make room for the new. **11**I will put my dwelling place*a* among you, and I will not abhor you. **12**I will walk among you and be your God, and you will be my people. **13**I am

---

a 11 Or my tabernacle

the LORD your God, who brought you out of Egypt so that you would no longer be slaves to the Egyptians; I broke the bars of your yoke and enabled you to walk with heads held high.   Ge 17:6; 2Co 6:16

Punishment for Disobedience

14" 'But if you will not listen to me and carry out all these commands, 15and if you reject my decrees and abhor my laws and fail to carry out all my commands and so violate my covenant, 16then I will do this to you: I will bring upon you sudden terror, wasting diseases and fever that will destroy your sight and drain away your life. You will plant seed in vain, because your enemies will eat it. 17I will set my face against you so that you will be defeated by your enemies; those who hate you will rule over you, and you will flee even when no one is pursuing you.

18" 'If after all this you will not listen to me, I will punish you for your sins seven times over. 19I will break down your stubborn pride and make the sky above you like iron and the ground beneath you like bronze. 20Your strength will be spent in vain, because your soil will not yield its crops, nor will the trees of the land yield their fruit.

21" 'If you remain hostile toward me and refuse to listen to me, I will multiply your afflictions seven times over, as your sins deserve. 22I will send wild animals against you, and they will rob you of your children, destroy your cattle and make you so few in number that your roads will be deserted.

23" 'If in spite of these things you do not accept my correction but continue to be hostile toward me, 24I myself will be hostile toward you and will afflict you for your sins seven times over. 25And I will bring the sword upon you to avenge the breaking of the covenant. When you withdraw into your cities, I will send a plague among you, and you will be given into enemy hands. 26When I cut off your supply of bread, ten women will be able to bake your bread in one oven, and they will dole out the bread by weight. You will eat, but you will not be satisfied.

27" 'If in spite of this you still do not listen to me but continue to be hostile toward me, 28then in my anger I will be hostile toward you, and I myself will punish you for your sins seven times over. 29You will eat the flesh of your sons and the flesh of your daughters. 30I will destroy your high places, cut down your incense altars and pile your dead bodies on the lifeless forms of your idols, and I will abhor you. 31I will turn your cities into ruins and lay waste your sanctuaries, and I will take no delight in the pleasing aroma of your offerings. 32I will lay waste the land, so that your enemies who live there will be appalled. 33I will scatter you among the nations and will draw out my sword and pursue you. Your land will be laid waste, and your cities will lie in ruins. **34**Then the land will enjoy its sabbath years all the time that it lies desolate and you are in the country of your enemies; then the land will rest and enjoy its sabbaths. **35**All the time that it lies desolate, the land will have the rest it did not have during the sabbaths you lived in it.   Dt 4:27; Ps 74:3-7; Jer 9:11

36" 'As for those of you who are left, I will make their hearts so fearful in the lands of their enemies that the sound of a windblown leaf will put them to flight. They will run as though fleeing from the sword, and they will fall, even though no one is pursuing them. **37**They will stumble over one another as though fleeing from the sword, even though no one is pursuing them. So you will not be able to stand before your enemies. **38**You will perish among the nations; the land of your enemies will devour you. **39**Those of you who are left will waste away in the lands of their enemies because of their sins; also because of their fathers' sins they will waste away.

40" 'But if they will confess their sins and the sins of their fathers—their treachery against me and their hostility toward me, **41**which made me hostile toward them so that I sent them into the land of their enemies—then when their uncircumcised hearts are humbled and they pay for their sin, **42**I will remember my covenant with Jacob and my covenant with Isaac and my covenant with Abraham, and I will remember the land. **43**For the land will be deserted by them and will enjoy its sabbaths while it lies desolate without them. They will pay for their sins because they rejected my laws and abhorred my decrees. **44**Yet in spite of this, when they are in the land of their enemies, I will not reject them or abhor them so as to destroy them completely, breaking my covenant with them. I am the LORD their God. **45**But for their sake I will remember the covenant with their ancestors whom I brought out of Egypt in the sight of the nations to be their God. I am the LORD.' "

46These are the decrees, the laws and the regulations that the LORD established on Mount Sinai between himself and the Israelites through Moses.   Lev 7:38; 27:34

Redeeming What Is the LORD's

27 The LORD said to Moses, **2**"Speak to the Israelites and say to them: 'If anyone makes a special vow to dedicate persons to the LORD by giving equivalent values, **3**set the value of a male between the ages of twenty and sixty at fifty shekels*a* of silver, according to the sanctuary shekel*b*; **4**and

a3 That is, about 1 1/4 pounds (about 0.6 kilogram); also in verse 16   *b3* That is, about 2/5 ounce (about 11.5 grams); also in verse 25

if it is a female, set her value at thirty shekels.*a* ⁵If it is a person between the ages of five and twenty, set the value of a male at twenty shekels*b* and of a female at ten shekels.*c* ⁶If it is a person between one month and five years, set the value of a male at five shekels*d* of silver and that of a female at three shekels*e* of silver. ⁷If it is a person sixty years old or more, set the value of a male at fifteen shekels*f* and of a female at ten shekels. ⁸If anyone making the vow is too poor to pay the specified amount, he is to present the person to the priest, who will set the value for him according to what the man making the vow can afford.   Ex 30;13; Nu 18:16

⁹" 'If what he vowed is an animal that is acceptable as an offering to the LORD, such an animal given to the LORD becomes holy. ¹⁰He must not exchange it or substitute a good one for a bad one, or a bad one for a good one; if he should substitute one animal for another, both it and the substitute become holy. ¹¹If what he vowed is a ceremonially unclean animal—one that is not acceptable as an offering to the LORD—the animal must be presented to the priest, ¹²who will judge its quality as good or bad. Whatever value the priest then sets, that is what it will be. ¹³If the owner wishes to redeem the animal, he must add a fifth to its value.   Lev 25:25; Dt 15:19

¹⁴" 'If a man dedicates his house as something holy to the LORD, the priest will judge its quality as good or bad. Whatever value the priest then sets, so it will remain. ¹⁵If the man who dedicates his house redeems it, he must add a fifth to its value, and the house will again become his.   ver 13,20

¹⁶" 'If a man dedicates to the LORD part of his family land, its value is to be set according to the amount of seed required for it—fifty shekels of silver to a homer*g* of barley seed. ¹⁷If he dedicates his field during the Year of Jubilee, the value that has been set remains. ¹⁸But if he dedicates his field after the Jubilee, the priest will determine the value according to the number of years that remain until the next Year of Jubilee, and its set value will be reduced. ¹⁹If the man who dedicates the field wishes to redeem it, he must add a fifth to its value, and the field will again become his. ²⁰If, however, he does not redeem the field, or if he has sold it to someone else, it can never be redeemed. ²¹When the field is released in the Jubilee, it will become holy, like a field devoted to the LORD; it will become the property of the priests.*h*   Nu 18:14

²²" 'If a man dedicates to the

---

a4 That is, about 12 ounces (about 0.3 kilogram)   *b5* That is, about 8 ounces (about 0.2 kilogram)
c5 That is, about 4 ounces (about 110 grams); also in verse 7   *d6* That is, about 2 ounces (about 55
grams)   *e6* That is, about 1 1/4 ounces (about 35 grams)   *f7* That is, about 6 ounces (about 170
grams)   *g16* That is, probably about 6 bushels (about 220 liters)   *h21* Or *priest*

LORD a field he has bought, which is not part of his family land, ²³the priest will determine its value up to the Year of Jubilee, and the man must pay its value on that day as something holy to the LORD. ²⁴In the Year of Jubilee the field will revert to the person from whom he bought it, the one whose land it was. ²⁵Every value is to be set according to the sanctuary shekel, twenty gerahs to the shekel.

²⁶" 'No one, however, may dedicate the firstborn of an animal, since the firstborn already belongs to the LORD; whether an ox[a] or a sheep, it is the LORD's. ²⁷If it is one of the unclean animals, he may buy it back at its set value, adding a fifth of the value to it. If he does not redeem it, it is to be sold at its set value.   Ex 13:2,12

²⁸" 'But nothing that a man owns and devotes[b] to the LORD— whether man or animal or family land—may be sold or redeemed; everything so devoted is most holy to the LORD.   Jos 6:17-19

²⁹" 'No person devoted to destruction[c] may be ransomed; he must be put to death.

³⁰" 'A tithe of everything from the land, whether grain from the soil or fruit from the trees, belongs to the LORD; it is holy to the LORD. ³¹If a man redeems any of his tithe, he must add a fifth of the value to it. ³²The entire tithe of the herd and flock—every tenth animal that passes under the shepherd's rod— will be holy to the LORD. ³³He must not pick out the good from the bad or make any substitution. If he does make a substitution, both the animal and its substitute become holy and cannot be redeemed.' "

³⁴These are the commands the LORD gave Moses on Mount Sinai for the Israelites.   Lev 26:46

---

[a] 26 The Hebrew word can include both male and female.   [b] 28 The Hebrew term refers to the irrevocable giving over of things or persons to the LORD.   [c] 29 The Hebrew term refers to the irrevocable giving over of things or persons to the LORD, often by totally destroying them.

Numbers

The Census

1 The LORD spoke to Moses in the Tent of Meeting in the Desert of Sinai on the first day of the second month of the second year after the Israelites came out of Egypt. He said: ²"Take a census of the whole Israelite community by their clans and families, listing every man by name, one by one. ³You and Aaron are to number by their divisions all the men in Israel twenty years old or more who are able to serve in the army. ⁴One man from each tribe, each the head of his family, is to help you. ⁵These are the names of the men who are to assist you: Ex 30:11-16

from Reuben, Elizur son of Shedeur;   Rev 7:5
⁶from Simeon, Shelumiel son of Zurishaddai;   Nu 25:14
⁷from Judah, Nahshon son of Amminadab;   Ge 29:35
⁸from Issachar, Nethanel son of Zuar;   Ge 30:18
⁹from Zebulun, Eliab son of Helon;   Nu 10:16
¹⁰from the sons of Joseph:
    from Ephraim, Elishama son of Ammihud;   Nu 2:18
    from Manasseh, Gamaliel son of Pedahzur;   Nu 10:23
¹¹from Benjamin, Abidan son of Gideoni;   Nu 10:24

¹²from Dan, Ahiezer son of Ammishaddai;   Nu 2:25
¹³from Asher, Pagiel son of Ocran;   Nu 2:27; 10:26
¹⁴from Gad, Eliasaph son of Deuel;   Nu 2:14; 10:20
¹⁵from Naphtali, Ahira son of Enan."   Nu 2:29; 10:27

¹⁶These were the men appointed from the community, the leaders of their ancestral tribes. They were the heads of the clans of Israel.

¹⁷Moses and Aaron took these men whose names had been given, ¹⁸and they called the whole community together on the first day of the second month. The people indicated their ancestry by their clans and families, and the men twenty years old or more were listed by name, one by one, ¹⁹as the LORD commanded Moses. And so he counted them in the Desert of Sinai: Ezr 2:59; Heb 7:3

²⁰From the descendants of Reuben the firstborn son of Israel:
    All the men twenty years old or more who were able to serve in the army were listed by name, one by one, according to the records of their clans and families. ²¹The number from the tribe of Reuben was 46,500.

²²From the descendants of Simeon:

Nu 26:12-14; Rev 7:7

All the men twenty years old or more who were able to serve in the army were counted and listed by name, one by one, according to the records of their clans and families. ²³The number from the tribe of Simeon was 59,300.

²⁴From the descendants of Gad: All the men twenty years old or more who were able to serve in the army were listed by name, according to the records of their clans and families. ²⁵The number from the tribe of Gad was 45,650.

²⁶From the descendants of Judah: All the men twenty years old or more who were able to serve in the army were listed by name, according to the records of their clans and families. ²⁷The number from the tribe of Judah was 74,600.

²⁸From the descendants of Issachar:

Nu 26:23-25; Rev 7:7

All the men twenty years old or more who were able to serve in the army were listed by name, according to the records of their clans and families. ²⁹The number from the tribe of Issachar was 54,400.

³⁰From the descendants of Zebulun:

Nu 26:26-27; Rev 7:8

All the men twenty years old or more who were able to serve in the army were listed by name, according to the records of their clans and families. ³¹The number from the tribe of Zebulun was 57,400.

³²From the sons of Joseph:
From the descendants of Ephraim: All the men twenty years old or more who were able to serve in the army were listed by name, according to the records of their clans and families. ³³The number from the tribe of Ephraim was 40,500.

³⁴From the descendants of Manasseh:

Nu 26:28-34; Rev 7:6

All the men twenty years old or more who were able to serve in the army were listed by name, according to the records of their clans and families. ³⁵The number from the tribe of Manasseh was 32,200.

³⁶From the descendants of Benjamin:

Nu 26:38-41; Rev 7:8

All the men twenty years old or more who were able to serve in the army were listed by name, according to the records of their clans and families. ³⁷The number from the tribe of Benjamin was 35,400.

38From the descendants of Dan: All the men twenty years old or more who were able to serve in the army were listed by name, according to the records of their clans and families. **39**The number from the tribe of Dan was 62,700.

40From the descendants of Asher: All the men twenty years old or more who were able to serve in the army were listed by name, according to the records of their clans and families. **41**The number from the tribe of Asher was 41,500.

42From the descendants of Naphtali: Nu 26:48-50; Rev 7:6
All the men twenty years old or more who were able to serve in the army were listed by name, according to the records of their clans and families. **43**The number from the tribe of Naphtali was 53,400.

44These were the men counted by Moses and Aaron and the twelve leaders of Israel, each one representing his family. **45**All the Israelites twenty years old or more who were able to serve in Israel's army were counted according to their families. **46**The total number was 603,550.   Nu 2:32; 26:64
47The families of the tribe of Levi, however, were not counted along with the others. **48**The Lord had said to Moses: **49**"You must not count the tribe of Levi or include them in the census of the other Israelites. **50**Instead, appoint the Levites to be in charge of the tabernacle of the Testimony—over all its furnishings and everything belonging to it. They are to carry the tabernacle and all its furnishings; they are to take care of it and encamp around it. **51**Whenever the tabernacle is to move, the Levites are to take it down, and whenever the tabernacle is to be set up, the Levites shall do it. Anyone else who goes near it shall be put to death. **52**The Israelites are to set up their tents by divisions, each man in his own camp under his own standard. **53**The Levites, however, are to set up their tents around the tabernacle of the Testimony so that wrath will not fall on the Israelite community. The Levites are to be responsible for the care of the tabernacle of the Testimony."   Nu 2:33; 18:2-4
54The Israelites did all this just as the Lord commanded Moses.

The Arrangement of the Tribal Camps

2 The Lord said to Moses and Aaron: **2**"The Israelites are to camp around the Tent of Meeting some distance from it, each man under his standard with the banners of his family."

3On the east, toward the

sunrise, the divisions of the camp of Judah are to encamp under their standard. The leader of the people of Judah is Nahshon son of Amminadab. ⁴His division numbers 74,600.   Nu 10:14

⁵The tribe of Issachar will camp next to them. The leader of the people of Issachar is Nethanel son of Zuar. ⁶His division numbers 54,400.

⁷The tribe of Zebulun will be next. The leader of the people of Zebulun is Eliab son of Helon. ⁸His division numbers 57,400.   Nu 1:9

⁹All the men assigned to the camp of Judah, according to their divisions, number 186,400. They will set out first.

¹⁰On the south will be the divisions of the camp of Reuben under their standard. The leader of the people of Reuben is Elizur son of Shedeur. ¹¹His division numbers 46,500.   Nu 1:5

¹²The tribe of Simeon will camp next to them. The leader of the people of Simeon is Shelumiel son of Zurishaddai. ¹³His division numbers 59,300.   Nu 1:6

¹⁴The tribe of Gad will be next. The leader of the people of Gad is Eliasaph son of Deuel.ᵃ ¹⁵His division numbers 45,650.   Nu 1:14

¹⁶All the men assigned to the camp of Reuben, according to their divisions, number 151,450. They will set out second.

¹⁷Then the Tent of Meeting and the camp of the Levites will set out in the middle of the camps. They will set out in the same order as they encamp, each in his own place under his standard.

¹⁸On the west will be the divisions of the camp of Ephraim under their standard. The leader of the people of Ephraim is Elishama son of Ammihud. ¹⁹His division numbers 40,500.   Ge 48:20; Nu 1:10

²⁰The tribe of Manasseh will be next to them. The leader of the people of Manasseh is Gamaliel son of Pedahzur. ²¹His division numbers 32,200.   Nu 1:10

²²The tribe of Benjamin will be next. The leader of the people of Benjamin is Abidan son of Gideoni. ²³His division numbers 35,400.   Nu 1:11

²⁴All the men assigned to the camp of Ephraim, according to their divisions, number 108,100. They will set out third.

ᵃ 14 Many manuscripts of the Masoretic Text, Samaritan Pentateuch and Vulgate (see also Num. 1:14); most manuscripts of the Masoretic Text *Reuel*

²⁵On the north will be the divisions of the camp of Dan, under their standard. The leader of the people of Dan is Ahiezer son of Ammishaddai. ²⁶His division numbers 62,700.   Nu 1:12

²⁷The tribe of Asher will camp next to them. The leader of the people of Asher is Pagiel son of Ocran. ²⁸His division numbers 41,500.

²⁹The tribe of Naphtali will be next. The leader of the people of Naphtali is Ahira son of Enan. ³⁰His division numbers 53,400.   Nu 1:15

³¹All the men assigned to the camp of Dan number 157,600. They will set out last, under their standards.

³²These are the Israelites, counted according to their families. All those in the camps, by their divisions, number 603,550. ³³The Levites, however, were not counted along with the other Israelites, as the LORD commanded Moses.

³⁴So the Israelites did everything the LORD commanded Moses; that is the way they encamped under their standards, and that is the way they set out, each with his clan and family.   Ex 38:26; Nu 1:46-47

The Levites

3 This is the account of the family of Aaron and Moses at the time the LORD talked with Moses on Mount Sinai.   Ex 6:27

²The names of the sons of Aaron were Nadab the firstborn and Abihu, Eleazar and Ithamar. ³Those were the names of Aaron's sons, the anointed priests, who were ordained to serve as priests. ⁴Nadab and Abihu, however, fell dead before the LORD when they made an offering with unauthorized fire before him in the Desert of Sinai. They had no sons; so only Eleazar and Ithamar served as priests during the lifetime of their father Aaron.   Ex 6:23; Lev 10:1-2

⁵The LORD said to Moses, ⁶"Bring the tribe of Levi and present them to Aaron the priest to assist him. ⁷They are to perform duties for him and for the whole community at the Tent of Meeting by doing the work of the tabernacle. ⁸They are to take care of all the furnishings of the Tent of Meeting, fulfilling the obligations of the Israelites by doing the work of the tabernacle. ⁹Give the Levites to Aaron and his sons; they are the Israelites who are to be given wholly to him.ᵃ ¹⁰Appoint Aaron and his sons to serve as priests; anyone else who approaches the sanctuary must be put to death."   Nu 1:51; 8:6-22; 18:1-7

ᵃ9 Most manuscripts of the Masoretic Text; some manuscripts of the Masoretic Text, Samaritan Pentateuch and Septuagint (see also Num. 8:16) *to me*

¹¹The LORD also said to Moses, ¹²"I have taken the Levites from among the Israelites in place of the first male offspring of every Israelite woman. The Levites are mine, ¹³for all the firstborn are mine. When I struck down all the firstborn in Egypt, I set apart for myself every firstborn in Israel, whether man or animal. They are to be mine. I am the LORD."   Ex 13:12

¹⁴The LORD said to Moses in the Desert of Sinai, ¹⁵"Count the Levites by their families and clans. Count every male a month old or more." ¹⁶So Moses counted them, as he was commanded by the word of the LORD.   Nu 26:62

¹⁷These were the names of the
    sons of Levi: Ge 46:11
    Gershon, Kohath and Me-
    rari.   Ex 6:16
¹⁸These were the names of the
    Gershonite clans:
    Libni and Shimei.   Ex 6:17
¹⁹The Kohathite clans:
    Amram, Izhar, Hebron and
    Uzziel.   Ex 6:18
²⁰The Merarite clans: Ge 46:11
    Mahli and Mushi.   Ex 6:19
These were the Levite clans, according to their families.

²¹To Gershon belonged the clans of the Libnites and Shimeites; these were the Gershonite clans. ²²The number of all the males a month old or more who were counted was 7,500. ²³The Gershonite clans were to camp on the west, behind the tabernacle. ²⁴The leader of the families of the Gershonites was Eliasaph son of Lael. ²⁵At the Tent of Meeting the Gershonites were responsible for the care of the tabernacle and tent, its coverings, the curtain at the entrance to the Tent of Meeting, ²⁶the curtains of the courtyard, the curtain at the entrance to the courtyard surrounding the tabernacle and altar, and the ropes—and everything related to their use.

²⁷To Kohath belonged the clans of the Amramites, Izharites, Hebronites and Uzzielites; these were the Kohathite clans. ²⁸The number of all the males a month old or more was 8,600.ᵃ The Kohathites were responsible for the care of the sanctuary. ²⁹The Kohathite clans were to camp on the south side of the tabernacle. ³⁰The leader of the families of the Kohathite clans was Elizaphan son of Uzziel. ³¹They were responsible for the care of the ark, the table, the lampstand, the altars, the articles of the sanctuary used in ministering, the curtain, and everything related to their use. ³²The chief leader of the Levites was Eleazar son of Aaron, the priest. He was appointed over those who were responsible for the care of the sanctuary.

³³To Merari belonged the clans of the Mahlites and the Mushites;

ᵃ28 Hebrew; some Septuagint manuscripts 8,300

these were the Merarite clans. ³⁴The number of all the males a month old or more who were counted was 6,200. ³⁵The leader of the families of the Merarite clans was Zuriel son of Abihail; they were to camp on the north side of the tabernacle. ³⁶The Merarites were appointed to take care of the frames of the tabernacle, its crossbars, posts, bases, all its equipment, and everything related to their use, ³⁷as well as the posts of the surrounding courtyard with their bases, tent pegs and ropes.

³⁸Moses and Aaron and his sons were to camp to the east of the tabernacle, toward the sunrise, in front of the Tent of Meeting. They were responsible for the care of the sanctuary on behalf of the Israelites. Anyone else who approached the sanctuary was to be put to death.   Nu 18:5

³⁹The total number of Levites counted at the Lord's command by Moses and Aaron according to their clans, including every male a month old or more, was 22,000.

⁴⁰The Lord said to Moses, "Count all the firstborn Israelite males who are a month old or more and make a list of their names. ⁴¹Take the Levites for me in place of all the firstborn of the Israelites, and the livestock of the Levites in place of all the firstborn of the livestock of the Israelites. I am the Lord."   ver 12,15

⁴²So Moses counted all the firstborn of the Israelites, as the Lord commanded him. ⁴³The total number of firstborn males a month old or more, listed by name, was 22,273.

⁴⁴The Lord also said to Moses, ⁴⁵"Take the Levites in place of all the firstborn of Israel, and the livestock of the Levites in place of their livestock. The Levites are to be mine. I am the Lord. ⁴⁶To redeem the 273 firstborn Israelites who exceed the number of the Levites, ⁴⁷collect five shekels[a] for each one, according to the sanctuary shekel, which weighs twenty gerahs. ⁴⁸Give the money for the redemption of the additional Israelites to Aaron and his sons."

⁴⁹So Moses collected the redemption money from those who exceeded the number redeemed by the Levites. ⁵⁰From the firstborn of the Israelites he collected silver weighing 1,365 shekels,[b] according to the sanctuary shekel. ⁵¹Moses gave the redemption money to Aaron and his sons, as he was commanded by the word of the Lord.   ver 46-48

The Kohathites

4 The Lord said to Moses and Aaron: ²"Take a census of the Kohathite branch of the Levites by

---

a47 That is, about 2 ounces (about 55 grams)   b50 That is, about 35 pounds (about 15.5 kilograms)

their clans and families. ³Count all the men from thirty to fifty years of age who come to serve in the work in the Tent of Meeting.   Ex 30:12

⁴"This is the work of the Kohathites in the Tent of Meeting: the care of the most holy things. ⁵When the camp is to move, Aaron and his sons are to go in and take down the shielding curtain and cover the ark of the Testimony with it. ⁶Then they are to cover this with hides of sea cows,ᵃ spread a cloth of solid blue over that and put the poles in place.   Ex 25:10,16

⁷"Over the table of the Presence they are to spread a blue cloth and put on it the plates, dishes and bowls, and the jars for drink offerings; the bread that is continually there is to remain on it. ⁸Over these they are to spread a scarlet cloth, cover that with hides of sea cows and put its poles in place.

⁹"They are to take a blue cloth and cover the lampstand that is for light, together with its lamps, its wick trimmers and trays, and all its jars for the oil used to supply it. ¹⁰Then they are to wrap it and all its accessories in a covering of hides of sea cows and put it on a carrying frame.   Ex 25:31,37-38

¹¹"Over the gold altar they are to spread a blue cloth and cover that with hides of sea cows and put its poles in place.   Ex 30:1

¹²"They are to take all the arti-cles used for ministering in the sanctuary, wrap them in a blue cloth, cover that with hides of sea cows and put them on a carrying frame.

¹³"They are to remove the ashes from the bronze altar and spread a purple cloth over it. ¹⁴Then they are to place on it all the utensils used for ministering at the altar, including the firepans, meat forks, shovels and sprinkling bowls. Over it they are to spread a covering of hides of sea cows and put its poles in place.   Ex 27:1-8

¹⁵"After Aaron and his sons have finished covering the holy furnishings and all the holy articles, and when the camp is ready to move, the Kohathites are to come to do the carrying. But they must not touch the holy things or they will die. The Kohathites are to carry those things that are in the Tent of Meeting.   Nu 1:51; 2Sa 6:6-7

¹⁶"Eleazar son of Aaron, the priest, is to have charge of the oil for the light, the fragrant incense, the regular grain offering and the anointing oil. He is to be in charge of the entire tabernacle and everything in it, including its holy furnishings and articles."   Ex 25:6; 29:41

¹⁷The LORD said to Moses and Aaron, ¹⁸"See that the Kohathite tribal clans are not cut off from the Levites. ¹⁹So that they may live and not die when they come near the most holy things, do this for them:

ᵃ6 That is, dugongs; also in verses 8, 10, 11, 12, 14 and 25

Aaron and his sons are to go into the sanctuary and assign to each man his work and what he is to carry. 20But the Kohathites must not go in to look at the holy things, even for a moment, or they will die." Ex 19:21; 1Sa 6:19

The Gershonites

21The LORD said to Moses, 22"Take a census also of the Gershonites by their families and clans. 23Count all the men from thirty to fifty years of age who come to serve in the work at the Tent of Meeting.

24"This is the service of the Gershonite clans as they work and carry burdens: 25They are to carry the curtains of the tabernacle, the Tent of Meeting, its covering and the outer covering of hides of sea cows, the curtains for the entrance to the Tent of Meeting, 26the curtains of the courtyard surrounding the tabernacle and altar, the curtain for the entrance, the ropes and all the equipment used in its service. The Gershonites are to do all that needs to be done with these things. 27All their service, whether carrying or doing other work, is to be done under the direction of Aaron and his sons. You shall assign to them as their responsibility all they are to carry. 28This is the service of the Gershonite clans at the Tent of Meeting. Their duties are to be under the direction of Ithamar son of Aaron, the priest.

The Merarites

29"Count the Merarites by their clans and families. 30Count all the men from thirty to fifty years of age who come to serve in the work at the Tent of Meeting. 31This is their duty as they perform service at the Tent of Meeting: to carry the frames of the tabernacle, its crossbars, posts and bases, 32as well as the posts of the surrounding courtyard with their bases, tent pegs, ropes, all their equipment and everything related to their use. Assign to each man the specific things he is to carry. 33This is the service of the Merarite clans as they work at the Tent of Meeting under the direction of Ithamar son of Aaron, the priest." Ge 46:11

The Numbering of the Levite Clans

34Moses, Aaron and the leaders of the community counted the Kohathites by their clans and families. 35All the men from thirty to fifty years of age who came to serve in the work in the Tent of Meeting, 36counted by clans, were 2,750. 37This was the total of all those in the Kohathite clans who served in the Tent of Meeting. Moses and Aaron counted them according to the LORD's command through Moses. Nu 3:27

38The Gershonites were counted by their clans and families. 39All the men from thirty to fifty years of age who came to serve in the work at the Tent of Meeting, [40]counted by their clans and families, were 2,630. [41]This was the total of those in the Gershonite clans who served at the Tent of Meeting. Moses and Aaron counted them according to the LORD's command.

[42]The Merarites were counted by their clans and families. [43]All the men from thirty to fifty years of age who came to serve in the work at the Tent of Meeting, [44]counted by their clans, were 3,200. [45]This was the total of those in the Merarite clans. Moses and Aaron counted them according to the LORD's command through Moses.   ver 29

[46]So Moses, Aaron and the leaders of Israel counted all the Levites by their clans and families. [47]All the men from thirty to fifty years of age who came to do the work of serving and carrying the Tent of Meeting [48]numbered 8,580. [49]At the LORD's command through Moses, each was assigned his work and told what to carry.   Nu 3:39

Thus they were counted, as the LORD commanded Moses.   Nu 1:47

The Purity of the Camp

5 The LORD said to Moses, [2]"Command the Israelites to send away from the camp anyone who has an infectious skin disease[a] or a discharge of any kind, or who is ceremonially unclean because of a dead body. [3]Send away male and female alike; send them outside the camp so they will not defile their camp, where I dwell among them." [4]The Israelites did this; they sent them outside the camp. They did just as the LORD had instructed Moses.   Lev 26:12

Restitution for Wrongs

[5]The LORD said to Moses, [6]"Say to the Israelites: 'When a man or woman wrongs another in any way[b] and so is unfaithful to the LORD, that person is guilty [7]and must confess the sin he has committed. He must make full restitution for his wrong, add one fifth to it and give it all to the person he has wronged. [8]But if that person has no close relative to whom restitution can be made for the wrong, the restitution belongs to the LORD and must be given to the priest, along with the ram with which atonement is made for him. [9]All the sacred contributions the Israelites bring to a priest will belong to him. [10]Each man's sacred gifts are his own, but what he gives to the priest will belong to the priest.' "   Lev 5:5; 6:2; Lk 19:8

The Test for an Unfaithful Wife

[11]Then the LORD said to Moses, [12]"Speak to the Israelites and say to them: 'If a man's wife goes astray and is unfaithful to him [13]by

---

[a]2 Traditionally *leprosy*; the Hebrew word was used for various diseases affecting the skin—not necessarily leprosy.   [b]6 Or *woman commits any wrong common to mankind*

sleeping with another man, and this is hidden from her husband and her impurity is undetected (since there is no witness against her and she has not been caught in the act), [14]and if feelings of jealousy come over her husband and he suspects his wife and she is impure—or if he is jealous and suspects her even though she is not impure— [15]then he is to take his wife to the priest. He must also take an offering of a tenth of an ephah[a] of barley flour on her behalf. He must not pour oil on it or put incense on it, because it is a grain offering for jealousy, a reminder offering to draw attention to guilt.   Eze 29:16

[16]" 'The priest shall bring her and have her stand before the Lord. [17]Then he shall take some holy water in a clay jar and put some dust from the tabernacle floor into the water. [18]After the priest has had the woman stand before the Lord, he shall loosen her hair and place in her hands the reminder offering, the grain offering for jealousy, while he himself holds the bitter water that brings a curse. [19]Then the priest shall put the woman under oath and say to her, "If no other man has slept with you and you have not gone astray and become impure while married to your husband, may this bitter water that brings a curse not

harm you. [20]But if you have gone astray while married to your husband and you have defiled yourself by sleeping with a man other than your husband"— [21]here the priest is to put the woman under this curse of the oath—"may the Lord cause your people to curse and denounce you when he causes your thigh to waste away and your abdomen to swell.[b] [22]May this water that brings a curse enter your body so that your abdomen swells and your thigh wastes away.[c]"

" 'Then the woman is to say, "Amen. So be it." '   Dt 27:15

[23]" 'The priest is to write these curses on a scroll and then wash them off into the bitter water. [24]He shall have the woman drink the bitter water that brings a curse, and this water will enter her and cause bitter suffering. [25]The priest is to take from her hands the grain offering for jealousy, wave it before the Lord and bring it to the altar. [26]The priest is then to take a handful of the grain offering as a memorial offering and burn it on the altar; after that, he is to have the woman drink the water. [27]If she has defiled herself and been unfaithful to her husband, then when she is made to drink the water that brings a curse, it will go into her and cause bitter suffering; her abdomen will swell and her thigh waste away,[d] and she will

---

[a]15 That is, probably about 2 quarts (about 2 liters)   [b]21 Or causes you to have a miscarrying womb and barrenness   [c]22 Or body and cause you to be barren and have a miscarrying womb   [d]27 Or suffering; she will have barrenness and a miscarrying womb

become accursed among her people. ²⁸If, however, the woman has not defiled herself and is free from impurity, she will be cleared of guilt and will be able to have children.   Jer 29:18; 42:18

²⁹" 'This, then, is the law of jealousy when a woman goes astray and defiles herself while married to her husband, ³⁰or when feelings of jealousy come over a man because he suspects his wife. The priest is to have her stand before the LORD and is to apply this entire law to her. ³¹The husband will be innocent of any wrongdoing, but the woman will bear the consequences of her sin.' "   Lev 5:1; 20:17

The Nazirite

6 The LORD said to Moses, ²"Speak to the Israelites and say to them: 'If a man or woman wants to make a special vow, a vow of separation to the LORD as a Nazirite, ³he must abstain from wine and other fermented drink and must not drink vinegar made from wine or from other fermented drink. He must not drink grape juice or eat grapes or raisins. ⁴As long as he is a Nazirite, he must not eat anything that comes from the grapevine, not even the seeds or skins.   Jdg 13:5; Am 2:11-12; Ac 21:23

⁵" 'During the entire period of his vow of separation no razor may be used on his head. He must be holy until the period of his separation to the LORD is over; he must let the hair of his head grow long.

⁶Throughout the period of his separation to the LORD he must not go near a dead body. ⁷Even if his own father or mother or brother or sister dies, he must not make himself ceremonially unclean on account of them, because the symbol of his separation to God is on his head. ⁸Throughout the period of his separation he is consecrated to the LORD.   Nu 9:6; 1Sa 1:11

⁹" 'If someone dies suddenly in his presence, thus defiling the hair he has dedicated, he must shave his head on the day of his cleansing—the seventh day. ¹⁰Then on the eighth day he must bring two doves or two young pigeons to the priest at the entrance to the Tent of Meeting. ¹¹The priest is to offer one as a sin offering and the other as a burnt offering to make atonement for him because he sinned by being in the presence of the dead body. That same day he is to consecrate his head. ¹²He must dedicate himself to the LORD for the period of his separation and must bring a year-old male lamb as a guilt offering. The previous days do not count, because he became defiled during his separation.

¹³" 'Now this is the law for the Nazirite when the period of his separation is over. He is to be brought to the entrance to the Tent of Meeting. ¹⁴There he is to present his offerings to the LORD: a year-old male lamb without defect for a burnt offering, a year-old ewe lamb without defect for a sin offer-

ing, a ram without defect for a fellowship offering,[a] 15together with their grain offerings and drink offerings, and a basket of bread made without yeast—cakes made of fine flour mixed with oil, and wafers spread with oil.   Lev 14:10

16" 'The priest is to present them before the Lord and make the sin offering and the burnt offering. 17He is to present the basket of unleavened bread and is to sacrifice the ram as a fellowship offering to the Lord, together with its grain offering and drink offering.   Lev 1:3

18" 'Then at the entrance to the Tent of Meeting, the Nazirite must shave off the hair that he dedicated. He is to take the hair and put it in the fire that is under the sacrifice of the fellowship offering.

19" 'After the Nazirite has shaved off the hair of his dedication, the priest is to place in his hands a boiled shoulder of the ram, and a cake and a wafer from the basket, both made without yeast. 20The priest shall then wave them before the Lord as a wave offering; they are holy and belong to the priest, together with the breast that was waved and the thigh that was presented. After that, the Nazirite may drink wine.

21" 'This is the law of the Nazirite who vows his offering to the Lord in accordance with his separation, in addition to whatever else he can afford. He must fulfill the vow he has made, according to the law of the Nazirite.' "   ver 2,13

The Priestly Blessing

22The Lord said to Moses, 23"Tell Aaron and his sons, 'This is how you are to bless the Israelites. Say to them: 1Ch 23:13

24" ' "The Lord bless you   Dt 28:3-6
    and keep you;
25the Lord make his face shine
        upon you   Ps 80:3; 119:135
    and be gracious to you;
26the Lord turn his face toward
        you   Ps 4:6; 44:3
    and give you peace." '   Ps 29:11

27"So they will put my name on the Israelites, and I will bless them."   Dt 28:10; 2Ch 7:14

Offerings at the Dedication of the Tabernacle

7 When Moses finished setting up the tabernacle, he anointed it and consecrated it and all its furnishings. He also anointed and consecrated the altar and all its utensils. 2Then the leaders of Israel, the heads of families who were the tribal leaders in charge of those who were counted, made offerings. 3They brought as their gifts before the Lord six covered carts and twelve oxen—an ox from each leader and a cart from every two. These they presented before the tabernacle.   Ex 40:9,17

---

a 14 Traditionally *peace offering*; also in verses 17 and 18

⁴The LORD said to Moses, ⁵"Accept these from them, that they may be used in the work at the Tent of Meeting. Give them to the Levites as each man's work requires."

⁶So Moses took the carts and oxen and gave them to the Levites. ⁷He gave two carts and four oxen to the Gershonites, as their work required, ⁸and he gave four carts and eight oxen to the Merarites, as their work required. They were all under the direction of Ithamar son of Aaron, the priest. ⁹But Moses did not give any to the Kohathites, because they were to carry on their shoulders the holy things, for which they were responsible.

¹⁰When the altar was anointed, the leaders brought their offerings for its dedication and presented them before the altar. ¹¹For the LORD had said to Moses, "Each day one leader is to bring his offering for the dedication of the altar."

¹²The one who brought his offering on the first day was Nahshon son of Amminadab of the tribe of Judah.

¹³His offering was one silver plate weighing a hundred and thirty shekels,ᵃ and one silver sprinkling bowl weighing seventy shekels,ᵇ both according to the sanctuary shekel, each filled with fine flour mixed

with oil as a grain offering; ¹⁴one gold dish weighing ten shekels,ᶜ filled with incense; ¹⁵one young bull, one ram and one male lamb a year old, for a burnt offering; ¹⁶one male goat for a sin offering; ¹⁷and two oxen, five rams, five male goats and five male lambs a year old, to be sacrificed as a fellowship offering.ᵈ This was the offering of Nahshon son of Amminadab.

¹⁸On the second day Nethanel son of Zuar, the leader of Issachar, brought his offering.

¹⁹The offering he brought was one silver plate weighing a hundred and thirty shekels, and one silver sprinkling bowl weighing seventy shekels, both according to the sanctuary shekel, each filled with fine flour mixed with oil as a grain offering; ²⁰one gold dish weighing ten shekels, filled with incense; ²¹one young bull, one ram and one male lamb a year old, for a burnt offering; ²²one male goat for a sin offering; ²³and two oxen, five rams, five male goats and five male lambs a year old, to be sacrificed as a fellowship offering. This was the offering of Nethanel son of Zuar.

ᵃ13 That is, about 3 1/4 pounds (about 1.5 kilograms); also elsewhere in this chapter   ᵇ13 That is, about 1 3/4 pounds (about 0.8 kilogram); also elsewhere in this chapter   ᶜ14 That is, about 4 ounces (about 110 grams); also elsewhere in this chapter   ᵈ17 Traditionally *peace offering*; also elsewhere in this chapter

²⁴On the third day, Eliab son of Helon, the leader of the people of Zebulun, brought his offering.

²⁵His offering was one silver plate weighing a hundred and thirty shekels, and one silver sprinkling bowl weighing seventy shekels, both according to the sanctuary shekel, each filled with fine flour mixed with oil as a grain offering; ²⁶one gold dish weighing ten shekels, filled with incense; ²⁷one young bull, one ram and one male lamb a year old, for a burnt offering; ²⁸one male goat for a sin offering; ²⁹and two oxen, five rams, five male goats and five male lambs a year old, to be sacrificed as a fellowship offering. This was the offering of Eliab son of Helon.

³⁰On the fourth day Elizur son of Shedeur, the leader of the people of Reuben, brought his offering.

³¹His offering was one silver plate weighing a hundred and thirty shekels, and one silver sprinkling bowl weighing seventy shekels, both according to the sanctuary shekel, each filled with fine flour mixed with oil as a grain offering; ³²one gold dish weighing ten shekels, filled with incense; ³³one young bull, one ram and one male lamb a year old, for a burnt offering; ³⁴one male goat for a sin offering;

³⁵and two oxen, five rams, five male goats and five male lambs a year old, to be sacrificed as a fellowship offering. This was the offering of Elizur son of Shedeur.

³⁶On the fifth day Shelumiel son of Zurishaddai, the leader of the people of Simeon, brought his offering.

³⁷His offering was one silver plate weighing a hundred and thirty shekels, and one silver sprinkling bowl weighing seventy shekels, both according to the sanctuary shekel, each filled with fine flour mixed with oil as a grain offering; ³⁸one gold dish weighing ten shekels, filled with incense; ³⁹one young bull, one ram and one male lamb a year old, for a burnt offering; ⁴⁰one male goat for a sin offering; ⁴¹and two oxen, five rams, five male goats and five male lambs a year old, to be sacrificed as a fellowship offering. This was the offering of Shelumiel son of Zurishaddai.

⁴²On the sixth day Eliasaph son of Deuel, the leader of the people of Gad, brought his offering.

⁴³His offering was one silver plate weighing a hundred and thirty shekels, and one silver sprinkling bowl weighing seventy shekels, both according to the sanctuary shekel, each filled with fine flour mixed

with oil as a grain offering; ⁴⁴one gold dish weighing ten shekels, filled with incense; ⁴⁵one young bull, one ram and one male lamb a year old, for a burnt offering; ⁴⁶one male goat for a sin offering; ⁴⁷and two oxen, five rams, five male goats and five male lambs a year old, to be sacrificed as a fellowship offering. This was the offering of Eliasaph son of Deuel.

⁴⁸On the seventh day Elishama son of Ammihud, the leader of the people of Ephraim, brought his offering.
    ⁴⁹His offering was one silver plate weighing a hundred and thirty shekels, and one silver sprinkling bowl weighing seventy shekels, both according to the sanctuary shekel, each filled with fine flour mixed with oil as a grain offering; ⁵⁰one gold dish weighing ten shekels, filled with incense; ⁵¹one young bull, one ram and one male lamb a year old, for a burnt offering; ⁵²one male goat for a sin offering; ⁵³and two oxen, five rams, five male goats and five male lambs a year old, to be sacrificed as a fellowship offering. This was the offering of Elishama son of Ammihud.

⁵⁴On the eighth day Gamaliel son of Pedahzur, the leader of the peo-ple of Manasseh, brought his offering.
    ⁵⁵His offering was one silver plate weighing a hundred and thirty shekels, and one silver sprinkling bowl weighing seventy shekels, both according to the sanctuary shekel, each filled with fine flour mixed with oil as a grain offering; ⁵⁶one gold dish weighing ten shekels, filled with incense; ⁵⁷one young bull, one ram and one male lamb a year old, for a burnt offering; ⁵⁸one male goat for a sin offering; ⁵⁹and two oxen, five rams, five male goats and five male lambs a year old, to be sacrificed as a fellowship offering. This was the offering of Gamaliel son of Pedahzur.

⁶⁰On the ninth day Abidan son of Gideoni, the leader of the people of Benjamin, brought his offering.
    ⁶¹His offering was one silver plate weighing a hundred and thirty shekels, and one silver sprinkling bowl weighing seventy shekels, both according to the sanctuary shekel, each filled with fine flour mixed with oil as a grain offering; ⁶²one gold dish weighing ten shekels, filled with incense; ⁶³one young bull, one ram and one male lamb a year old, for a burnt offering; ⁶⁴one male goat for a sin offering; ⁶⁵and two oxen, five rams,

five male goats and five male lambs a year old, to be sacrificed as a fellowship offering. This was the offering of Abidan son of Gideoni.

⁶⁶On the tenth day Ahiezer son of Ammishaddai, the leader of the people of Dan, brought his offering.
⁶⁷His offering was one silver plate weighing a hundred and thirty shekels, and one silver sprinkling bowl weighing seventy shekels, both according to the sanctuary shekel, each filled with fine flour mixed with oil as a grain offering; ⁶⁸one gold dish weighing ten shekels, filled with incense; ⁶⁹one young bull, one ram and one male lamb a year old, for a burnt offering; ⁷⁰one male goat for a sin offering; ⁷¹and two oxen, five rams, five male goats and five male lambs a year old, to be sacrificed as a fellowship offering. This was the offering of Ahiezer son of Ammishaddai.

⁷²On the eleventh day Pagiel son of Ocran, the leader of the people of Asher, brought his offering.
⁷³His offering was one silver plate weighing a hundred and thirty shekels, and one silver sprinkling bowl weighing seventy shekels, both according to the sanctuary shekel, each filled with fine flour mixed with oil as a grain offering;

⁷⁴one gold dish weighing ten shekels, filled with incense; ⁷⁵one young bull, one ram and one male lamb a year old, for a burnt offering; ⁷⁶one male goat for a sin offering; ⁷⁷and two oxen, five rams, five male goats and five male lambs a year old, to be sacrificed as a fellowship offering. This was the offering of Pagiel son of Ocran.

⁷⁸On the twelfth day Ahira son of Enan, the leader of the people of Naphtali, brought his offering.
⁷⁹His offering was one silver plate weighing a hundred and thirty shekels, and one silver sprinkling bowl weighing seventy shekels, both according to the sanctuary shekel, each filled with fine flour mixed with oil as a grain offering; ⁸⁰one gold dish weighing ten shekels, filled with incense; ⁸¹one young bull, one ram and one male lamb a year old, for a burnt offering; ⁸²one male goat for a sin offering; ⁸³and two oxen, five rams, five male goats and five male lambs a year old, to be sacrificed as a fellowship offering. This was the offering of Ahira son of Enan.

⁸⁴These were the offerings of the Israelite leaders for the dedication of the altar when it was anointed: twelve silver plates, twelve silver sprinkling bowls and twelve gold

dishes. 85Each silver plate weighed a hundred and thirty shekels, and each sprinkling bowl seventy shekels. Altogether, the silver dishes weighed two thousand four hundred shekels,*a* according to the sanctuary shekel. 86The twelve gold dishes filled with incense weighed ten shekels each, according to the sanctuary shekel. Altogether, the gold dishes weighed a hundred and twenty shekels.*b* 87The total number of animals for the burnt offering came to twelve young bulls, twelve rams and twelve male lambs a year old, together with their grain offering. Twelve male goats were used for the sin offering. 88The total number of animals for the sacrifice of the fellowship offering came to twenty-four oxen, sixty rams, sixty male goats and sixty male lambs a year old. These were the offerings for the dedication of the altar after it was anointed.   ver 1,10

89When Moses entered the Tent of Meeting to speak with the LORD, he heard the voice speaking to him from between the two cherubim above the atonement cover on the ark of the Testimony. And he spoke with him.   Ex 25:21-22; Ps 80:1

Setting Up the Lamps

8 The LORD said to Moses, 2"Speak to Aaron and say to him, 'When you set up the seven lamps, they are to light the area in front of the lampstand.' "

3Aaron did so; he set up the lamps so that they faced forward on the lampstand, just as the LORD commanded Moses. 4This is how the lampstand was made: It was made of hammered gold—from its base to its blossoms. The lampstand was made exactly like the pattern the LORD had shown Moses.   Ex 25:36-37

The Setting Apart of the Levites

5The LORD said to Moses: 6"Take the Levites from among the other Israelites and make them ceremonially clean. 7To purify them, do this: Sprinkle the water of cleansing on them; then have them shave their whole bodies and wash their clothes, and so purify themselves. 8Have them take a young bull with its grain offering of fine flour mixed with oil; then you are to take a second young bull for a sin offering. 9Bring the Levites to the front of the Tent of Meeting and assemble the whole Israelite community. 10You are to bring the Levites before the LORD, and the Israelites are to lay their hands on them. 11Aaron is to present the Levites before the LORD as a wave offering from the Israelites, so that they may be ready to do the work of the LORD.   Lev 8:3

---

a 85 That is, about 60 pounds (about 28 kilograms) kilograms)

b 86 That is, about 3 pounds (about 1.4

¹²"After the Levites lay their hands on the heads of the bulls, use the one for a sin offering to the LORD and the other for a burnt offering, to make atonement for the Levites. ¹³Have the Levites stand in front of Aaron and his sons and then present them as a wave offering to the LORD. ¹⁴In this way you are to set the Levites apart from the other Israelites, and the Levites will be mine.   Nu 3:12

¹⁵"After you have purified the Levites and presented them as a wave offering, they are to come to do their work at the Tent of Meeting. ¹⁶They are the Israelites who are to be given wholly to me. I have taken them as my own in place of the firstborn, the first male offspring from every Israelite woman. ¹⁷Every firstborn male in Israel, whether man or animal, is mine. When I struck down all the firstborn in Egypt, I set them apart for myself. ¹⁸And I have taken the Levites in place of all the firstborn sons in Israel. ¹⁹Of all the Israelites, I have given the Levites as gifts to Aaron and his sons to do the work at the Tent of Meeting on behalf of the Israelites and to make atonement for them so that no plague will strike the Israelites when they go near the sanctuary."

²⁰Moses, Aaron and the whole Israelite community did with the Levites just as the LORD commanded Moses. ²¹The Levites purified themselves and washed their clothes. Then Aaron presented them as a wave offering before the LORD and made atonement for them to purify them. ²²After that, the Levites came to do their work at the Tent of Meeting under the supervision of Aaron and his sons. They did with the Levites just as the LORD commanded Moses.

²³The LORD said to Moses, ²⁴"This applies to the Levites: Men twenty-five years old or more shall come to take part in the work at the Tent of Meeting, ²⁵but at the age of fifty, they must retire from their regular service and work no longer. ²⁶They may assist their brothers in performing their duties at the Tent of Meeting, but they themselves must not do the work. This, then, is how you are to assign the responsibilities of the Levites."

The Passover

9 The LORD spoke to Moses in the Desert of Sinai in the first month of the second year after they came out of Egypt. He said, ²"Have the Israelites celebrate the Passover at the appointed time. ³Celebrate it at the appointed time, at twilight on the fourteenth day of this month, in accordance with all its rules and regulations."

⁴So Moses told the Israelites to celebrate the Passover, ⁵and they did so in the Desert of Sinai at twilight on the fourteenth day of the first month. The Israelites did everything just as the LORD commanded Moses.   Ex 12:1-13; Jos 5:10

⁶But some of them could not cel-

ebrate the Passover on that day because they were ceremonially unclean on account of a dead body.
So they came to Moses and Aaron
that same day [7]and said to Moses,
"We have become unclean because of a dead body, but why
should we be kept from presenting
the LORD's offering with the other
Israelites at the appointed time?"
[8]Moses answered them, "Wait
until I find out what the LORD commands concerning you."   Nu 27:5,21
[9]Then the LORD said to Moses,
[10]"Tell the Israelites: 'When any of
you or your descendants are unclean because of a dead body or
are away on a journey, they may
still celebrate the LORD's Passover.
[11]They are to celebrate it on the
fourteenth day of the second
month at twilight. They are to eat
the lamb, together with unleavened bread and bitter herbs.
[12]They must not leave any of it till
morning or break any of its bones.
When they celebrate the Passover,
they must follow all the regulations. [13]But if a man who is ceremonially clean and not on a journey fails to celebrate the Passover, that person must be cut off
from his people because he did
not present the LORD's offering
at the appointed time. That man
will bear the consequences of his
sin.
[14]" 'An alien living among you
who wants to celebrate the LORD's
Passover must do so in accordance
with its rules and regulations. You
must have the same regulations
for the alien and the native-born.' "

The Cloud Above the Tabernacle

[15]On the day the tabernacle, the
Tent of the Testimony, was set up,
the cloud covered it. From evening
till morning the cloud above the
tabernacle looked like fire. [16]That
is how it continued to be; the cloud
covered it, and at night it looked
like fire. [17]Whenever the cloud lifted from above the Tent, the Israelites set out; wherever the cloud
settled, the Israelites encamped.
[18]At the LORD's command the Israelites set out, and at his command
they encamped. As long as the
cloud stayed over the tabernacle,
they remained in camp. [19]When
the cloud remained over the tabernacle a long time, the Israelites
obeyed the LORD's order and did
not set out. [20]Sometimes the cloud
was over the tabernacle only a few
days; at the LORD's command they
would encamp, and then at his
command they would set out.
[21]Sometimes the cloud stayed only
from evening till morning, and
when it lifted in the morning, they
set out. Whether by day or by
night, whenever the cloud lifted,
they set out. [22]Whether the cloud
stayed over the tabernacle for two
days or a month or a year, the Israelites would remain in camp and
not set out; but when it lifted, they
would set out. [23]At the LORD's command they encamped, and at the

LORD's command they set out. They obeyed the LORD's order, in accordance with his command through Moses. Ex 13:21; 40:36-38

The Silver Trumpets

10 The LORD said to Moses: ²"Make two trumpets of hammered silver, and use them for calling the community together and for having the camps set out. ³When both are sounded, the whole community is to assemble before you at the entrance to the Tent of Meeting. ⁴If only one is sounded, the leaders—the heads of the clans of Israel—are to assemble before you. ⁵When a trumpet blast is sounded, the tribes camping on the east are to set out. ⁶At the sounding of a second blast, the camps on the south are to set out. The blast will be the signal for setting out. ⁷To gather the assembly, blow the trumpets, but not with the same signal. Ps 47:5

⁸"The sons of Aaron, the priests, are to blow the trumpets. This is to be a lasting ordinance for you and the generations to come. ⁹When you go into battle in your own land against an enemy who is oppressing you, sound a blast on the trumpets. Then you will be remembered by the LORD your God and rescued from your enemies. ¹⁰Also at your times of rejoicing—your appointed feasts and New Moon festivals—you are to sound the trumpets over your burnt offerings and fellowship offerings,ᵃ and they will be a memorial for you before your God. I am the LORD your God." Lev 23:24; Ps 106:4

The Israelites Leave Sinai

¹¹On the twentieth day of the second month of the second year, the cloud lifted from above the tabernacle of the Testimony. ¹²Then the Israelites set out from the Desert of Sinai and traveled from place to place until the cloud came to rest in the Desert of Paran. ¹³They set out, this first time, at the LORD's command through Moses.

¹⁴The divisions of the camp of Judah went first, under their standard. Nahshon son of Amminadab was in command. ¹⁵Nethanel son of Zuar was over the division of the tribe of Issachar, ¹⁶and Eliab son of Helon was over the division of the tribe of Zebulun. ¹⁷Then the tabernacle was taken down, and the Gershonites and Merarites, who carried it, set out. Nu 2:3-9; 4:21-32

¹⁸The divisions of the camp of Reuben went next, under their standard. Elizur son of Shedeur was in command. ¹⁹Shelumiel son of Zurishaddai was over the division of the tribe of Simeon, ²⁰and Eliasaph son of Deuel was over the division of the tribe of Gad. ²¹Then the Kohathites set out, carrying the holy things. The tabernacle was to be set up before they arrived.

ᵃ10 Traditionally *peace offerings*

²²The divisions of the camp of Ephraim went next, under their standard. Elishama son of Ammihud was in command. ²³Gamaliel son of Pedahzur was over the division of the tribe of Manasseh, ²⁴and Abidan son of Gideoni was over the division of the tribe of Benjamin. Nu 1:10-11; 2:24

²⁵Finally, as the rear guard for all the units, the divisions of the camp of Dan set out, under their standard. Ahiezer son of Ammishaddai was in command. ²⁶Pagiel son of Ocran was over the division of the tribe of Asher, ²⁷and Ahira son of Enan was over the division of the tribe of Naphtali. ²⁸This was the order of march for the Israelite divisions as they set out. Nu 2:31

²⁹Now Moses said to Hobab son of Reuel the Midianite, Moses' father-in-law, "We are setting out for the place about which the LORD said, 'I will give it to you.' Come with us and we will treat you well, for the LORD has promised good things to Israel." Ge 12:7; Ex 2:18

³⁰He answered, "No, I will not go; I am going back to my own land and my own people."

³¹But Moses said, "Please do not leave us. You know where we should camp in the desert, and you can be our eyes. ³²If you come with us, we will share with you whatever good things the LORD gives us."

³³So they set out from the mountain of the LORD and traveled for three days. The ark of the covenant of the LORD went before them during those three days to find them a place to rest. ³⁴The cloud of the LORD was over them by day when they set out from the camp. Nu 9:15-23; Jos 3:3

³⁵Whenever the ark set out, Moses said,

"Rise up, O LORD!
May your enemies be
    scattered;   Ps 68:1
may your foes flee before
    you."   Dt 7:10; 32:41

³⁶Whenever it came to rest, he said,

"Return, O LORD,
    to the countless thousands
        of Israel."   Dt 1:10

Fire From the LORD

11 Now the people complained about their hardships in the hearing of the LORD, and when he heard them his anger was aroused. Then fire from the LORD burned among them and consumed some of the outskirts of the camp. ²When the people cried out to Moses, he prayed to the LORD and the fire died down. ³So that place was called Taberah,ᵃ because fire from the LORD had burned among them. Lev 10:2

Quail From the LORD

⁴The rabble with them began to

ᵃ3 *Taberah* means *burning*.

crave other food, and again the Israelites started wailing and said, "If only we had meat to eat! ⁵We remember the fish we ate in Egypt at no cost—also the cucumbers, melons, leeks, onions and garlic. ⁶But now we have lost our appetite; we never see anything but this manna!" Ex 16:3; Ps 78:18

⁷The manna was like coriander seed and looked like resin. ⁸The people went around gathering it, and then ground it in a handmill or crushed it in a mortar. They cooked it in a pot or made it into cakes. And it tasted like something made with olive oil. ⁹When the dew settled on the camp at night, the manna also came down.

¹⁰Moses heard the people of every family wailing, each at the entrance to his tent. The LORD became exceedingly angry, and Moses was troubled. ¹¹He asked the LORD, "Why have you brought this trouble on your servant? What have I done to displease you that you put the burden of all these people on me? ¹²Did I conceive all these people? Did I give them birth? Why do you tell me to carry them in my arms, as a nurse carries an infant, to the land you promised on oath to their forefathers? ¹³Where can I get meat for all these people? They keep wailing to me, 'Give us meat to eat!' ¹⁴I cannot carry all these people by myself; the burden is too heavy for me. ¹⁵If this is how you are going to treat me, put me to death right now—if I have found favor in your eyes—and do not let me face my own ruin." Ex 5:22; 18:18; 1Ki 19:4

¹⁶The LORD said to Moses: "Bring me seventy of Israel's elders who are known to you as leaders and officials among the people. Have them come to the Tent of Meeting, that they may stand there with you. ¹⁷I will come down and speak with you there, and I will take of the Spirit that is on you and put the Spirit on them. They will help you carry the burden of the people so that you will not have to carry it alone. Ex 18:18

¹⁸"Tell the people: 'Consecrate yourselves in preparation for tomorrow, when you will eat meat. The LORD heard you when you wailed, "If only we had meat to eat! We were better off in Egypt!" Now the LORD will give you meat, and you will eat it. ¹⁹You will not eat it for just one day, or two days, or five, ten or twenty days, ²⁰but for a whole month—until it comes out of your nostrils and you loathe it—because you have rejected the LORD, who is among you, and have wailed before him, saying, "Why did we ever leave Egypt?"'"

²¹But Moses said, "Here I am among six hundred thousand men on foot, and you say, 'I will give them meat to eat for a whole month!' ²²Would they have enough if flocks and herds were slaughtered for them? Would they have enough if all the fish in the sea were caught for them?"

²³The Lord answered Moses, "Is the Lord's arm too short? You will now see whether or not what I say will come true for you." Isa 50:2

²⁴So Moses went out and told the people what the Lord had said. He brought together seventy of their elders and had them stand around the Tent. ²⁵Then the Lord came down in the cloud and spoke with him, and he took of the Spirit that was on him and put the Spirit on the seventy elders. When the Spirit rested on them, they prophesied, but they did not do so again.ᵃ

²⁶However, two men, whose names were Eldad and Medad, had remained in the camp. They were listed among the elders, but did not go out to the Tent. Yet the Spirit also rested on them, and they prophesied in the camp. ²⁷A young man ran and told Moses, "Eldad and Medad are prophesying in the camp."

²⁸Joshua son of Nun, who had been Moses' aide since youth, spoke up and said, "Moses, my lord, stop them!" Mk 9:38-40

²⁹But Moses replied, "Are you jealous for my sake? I wish that all the Lord's people were prophets and that the Lord would put his Spirit on them!" ³⁰Then Moses and the elders of Israel returned to the camp. 1Co 14:5

³¹Now a wind went out from the Lord and drove quail in from the sea. It brought themᵇ down all around the camp to about three feetᶜ above the ground, as far as a day's walk in any direction. ³²All that day and night and all the next day the people went out and gathered quail. No one gathered less than ten homers.ᵈ Then they spread them out all around the camp. ³³But while the meat was still between their teeth and before it could be consumed, the anger of the Lord burned against the people, and he struck them with a severe plague. ³⁴Therefore the place was named Kibroth Hattaavah,ᵉ because there they buried the people who had craved other food.

³⁵From Kibroth Hattaavah the people traveled to Hazeroth and stayed there. Nu 33:17

Miriam and Aaron Oppose Moses

12 Miriam and Aaron began to talk against Moses because of his Cushite wife, for he had married a Cushite. ²"Has the Lord spoken only through Moses?" they asked. "Hasn't he also spoken through us?" And the Lord heard this. Ex 2:21; Nu 11:1

³(Now Moses was a very humble man, more humble than anyone else on the face of the earth.)

⁴At once the Lord said to Moses, Aaron and Miriam, "Come out to the Tent of Meeting, all three of

---

ᵃ25 Or *prophesied and continued to do so*   ᵇ31 Or *They flew*   ᶜ31 Hebrew *two cubits* (about 1 meter)   ᵈ32 That is, probably about 60 bushels (about 2.2 kiloliters)   ᵉ34 *Kibroth Hattaavah* means *graves of craving.*

you." So the three of them came out. [5]Then the LORD came down in a pillar of cloud; he stood at the entrance to the Tent and summoned Aaron and Miriam. When both of them stepped forward, [6]he said, "Listen to my words:

"When a prophet of the LORD
    is among you,
I reveal myself to him in
    visions,   Ge 15:1; 46:2
I speak to him in dreams.
[7]But this is not true of my
    servant Moses;   Ps 105:26
he is faithful in all my
    house.   Heb 3:2,5
[8]With him I speak face to face,
    clearly and not in riddles;
he sees the form of the LORD.
Why then were you not afraid
    to speak against my servant
    Moses?"

[9]The anger of the LORD burned against them, and he left them.

[10]When the cloud lifted from above the Tent, there stood Miriam—leprous,[a] like snow. Aaron turned toward her and saw that she had leprosy; [11]and he said to Moses, "Please, my lord, do not hold against us the sin we have so foolishly committed. [12]Do not let her be like a stillborn infant coming from its mother's womb with its flesh half eaten away."   Dt 24:9

[13]So Moses cried out to the LORD, "O God, please heal her!"

[14]The LORD replied to Moses, "If her father had spit in her face, would she not have been in disgrace for seven days? Confine her outside the camp for seven days; after that she can be brought back." [15]So Miriam was confined outside the camp for seven days, and the people did not move on till she was brought back.   Lev 13:46

[16]After that, the people left Hazeroth and encamped in the Desert of Paran.   Nu 11:35

Exploring Canaan

13 The LORD said to Moses, [2]"Send some men to explore the land of Canaan, which I am giving to the Israelites. From each ancestral tribe send one of its leaders."   Dt 1:22

[3]So at the LORD's command Moses sent them out from the Desert of Paran. All of them were leaders of the Israelites. [4]These are their names: Nu 1:16

from the tribe of Reuben,
    Shammua son of Zaccur;
[5]from the tribe of Simeon, Shaphat son of Hori;
[6]from the tribe of Judah, Caleb
    son of Jephunneh;
[7]from the tribe of Issachar, Igal
    son of Joseph;
[8]from the tribe of Ephraim, Hoshea son of Nun;   Nu 11:28
[9]from the tribe of Benjamin,
    Palti son of Raphu;

---

[a] 10 The Hebrew word was used for various diseases affecting the skin—not necessarily leprosy.

¹⁰from the tribe of Zebulun, Gaddiel son of Sodi;

¹¹from the tribe of Manasseh (a tribe of Joseph), Gaddi son of Susi;

¹²from the tribe of Dan, Ammiel son of Gemalli;

¹³from the tribe of Asher, Sethur son of Michael;

¹⁴from the tribe of Naphtali, Nahbi son of Vophsi;

¹⁵from the tribe of Gad, Geuel son of Maki.

¹⁶These are the names of the men Moses sent to explore the land. (Moses gave Hoshea son of Nun the name Joshua.)   Dt 32:44

¹⁷When Moses sent them to explore Canaan, he said, "Go up through the Negev and on into the hill country. ¹⁸See what the land is like and whether the people who live there are strong or weak, few or many. ¹⁹What kind of land do they live in? Is it good or bad? What kind of towns do they live in? Are they unwalled or fortified? ²⁰How is the soil? Is it fertile or poor? Are there trees on it or not? Do your best to bring back some of the fruit of the land." (It was the season for the first ripe grapes.)

²¹So they went up and explored the land from the Desert of Zin as far as Rehob, toward Leboᵃ Hamath. ²²They went up through the Negev and came to Hebron, where Ahiman, Sheshai and Talmai, the descendants of Anak, lived. (Hebron had been built seven years before Zoan in Egypt.) ²³When they reached the Valley of Eshcol,ᵇ they cut off a branch bearing a single cluster of grapes. Two of them carried it on a pole between them, along with some pomegranates and figs. ²⁴That place was called the Valley of Eshcol because of the cluster of grapes the Israelites cut off there. ²⁵At the end of forty days they returned from exploring the land.   Jos 15:13-14

Report on the Exploration

²⁶They came back to Moses and Aaron and the whole Israelite community at Kadesh in the Desert of Paran. There they reported to them and to the whole assembly and showed them the fruit of the land. ²⁷They gave Moses this account: "We went into the land to which you sent us, and it does flow with milk and honey! Here is its fruit. ²⁸But the people who live there are powerful, and the cities are fortified and very large. We even saw descendants of Anak there. ²⁹The Amalekites live in the Negev; the Hittites, Jebusites and Amorites live in the hill country; and the Canaanites live near the sea and along the Jordan."   Ex 3:8

³⁰Then Caleb silenced the people before Moses and said, "We should go up and take possession

---

ᵃ21 Or *toward the entrance to*   ᵇ23 *Eshcol* means *cluster*; also in verse 24.

of the land, for we can certainly do it."

31But the men who had gone up with him said, "We can't attack those people; they are stronger than we are." 32And they spread among the Israelites a bad report about the land they had explored. They said, "The land we explored devours those living in it. All the people we saw there are of great size. 33We saw the Nephilim there (the descendants of Anak come from the Nephilim). We seemed like grasshoppers in our own eyes, and we looked the same to them."

The People Rebel

14 That night all the people of the community raised their voices and wept aloud. 2All the Israelites grumbled against Moses and Aaron, and the whole assembly said to them, "If only we had died in Egypt! Or in this desert! 3Why is the LORD bringing us to this land only to let us fall by the sword? Our wives and children will be taken as plunder. Wouldn't it be better for us to go back to Egypt?" 4And they said to each other, "We should choose a leader and go back to Egypt."   Nu 11:1

5Then Moses and Aaron fell facedown in front of the whole Israelite assembly gathered there. 6Joshua son of Nun and Caleb son of Jephunneh, who were among those who had explored the land, tore their clothes 7and said to the entire Israelite assembly, "The land we passed through and explored is exceedingly good. 8If the LORD is pleased with us, he will lead us into that land, a land flowing with milk and honey, and will give it to us. 9Only do not rebel against the LORD. And do not be afraid of the people of the land, because we will swallow them up. Their protection is gone, but the LORD is with us. Do not be afraid of them."   Dt 1:21; 9:7,23,24; 10:15

10But the whole assembly talked about stoning them. Then the glory of the LORD appeared at the Tent of Meeting to all the Israelites. 11The LORD said to Moses, "How long will these people treat me with contempt? How long will they refuse to believe in me, in spite of all the miraculous signs I have performed among them? 12I will strike them down with a plague and destroy them, but I will make you into a nation greater and stronger than they."   Ex 32:10; Lev 9:23

13Moses said to the LORD, "Then the Egyptians will hear about it! By your power you brought these people up from among them. 14And they will tell the inhabitants of this land about it. They have already heard that you, O LORD, are with these people and that you, O LORD, have been seen face to face, that your cloud stays over them, and that you go before them in a pillar of cloud by day and a pillar of fire by night. 15If you put these people to death all at one time, the nations who have heard this report about you will say, [16]'The LORD was not able to bring these people into the land he promised them on oath; so he slaughtered them in the desert.'   Ex 13:21; 15:14; 32:11-14

[17]"Now may the Lord's strength be displayed, just as you have declared: [18]'The LORD is slow to anger, abounding in love and forgiving sin and rebellion. Yet he does not leave the guilty unpunished; he punishes the children for the sin of the fathers to the third and fourth generation.' [19]In accordance with your great love, forgive the sin of these people, just as you have pardoned them from the time they left Egypt until now."   Ex 20:5

[20]The LORD replied, "I have forgiven them, as you asked. [21]Nevertheless, as surely as I live and as surely as the glory of the LORD fills the whole earth, [22]not one of the men who saw my glory and the miraculous signs I performed in Egypt and in the desert but who disobeyed me and tested me ten times— [23]not one of them will ever see the land I promised on oath to their forefathers. No one who has treated me with contempt will ever see it. [24]But because my servant Caleb has a different spirit and follows me wholeheartedly, I will bring him into the land he went to, and his descendants will inherit it. [25]Since the Amalekites and Canaanites are living in the valleys, turn back tomorrow and set out to-

ward the desert along the route to the Red Sea.[a]"   Nu 32:12; Jos 14:8,14

[26]The LORD said to Moses and Aaron: [27]"How long will this wicked community grumble against me? I have heard the complaints of these grumbling Israelites. [28]So tell them, 'As surely as I live, declares the LORD, I will do to you the very things I heard you say: [29]In this desert your bodies will fall—every one of you twenty years old or more who was counted in the census and who has grumbled against me. [30]Not one of you will enter the land I swore with uplifted hand to make your home, except Caleb son of Jephunneh and Joshua son of Nun. [31]As for your children that you said would be taken as plunder, I will bring them in to enjoy the land you have rejected. [32]But you—your bodies will fall in this desert. [33]Your children will be shepherds here for forty years, suffering for your unfaithfulness, until the last of your bodies lies in the desert. [34]For forty years—one year for each of the forty days you explored the land—you will suffer for your sins and know what it is like to have me against you.' [35]I, the LORD, have spoken, and I will surely do these things to this whole wicked community, which has banded together against me. They will meet their end in this desert; here they will die."

[36]So the men Moses had sent to

---

[a]25 Hebrew *Yam Suph*; that is, Sea of Reeds

explore the land, who returned and made the whole community grumble against him by spreading a bad report about it— ³⁷these men responsible for spreading the bad report about the land were struck down and died of a plague before the Lord. ³⁸Of the men who went to explore the land, only Joshua son of Nun and Caleb son of Jephunneh survived.   Nu 13:32

³⁹When Moses reported this to all the Israelites, they mourned bitterly. ⁴⁰Early the next morning they went up toward the high hill country. "We have sinned," they said. "We will go up to the place the Lord promised."   Dt 1:41

⁴¹But Moses said, "Why are you disobeying the Lord's command? This will not succeed! ⁴²Do not go up, because the Lord is not with you. You will be defeated by your enemies, ⁴³for the Amalekites and Canaanites will face you there. Because you have turned away from the Lord, he will not be with you and you will fall by the sword."

⁴⁴Nevertheless, in their presumption they went up toward the high hill country, though neither Moses nor the ark of the Lord's covenant moved from the camp. ⁴⁵Then the Amalekites and Canaanites who lived in that hill country came down and attacked them and beat them down all the way to Hormah.   Nu 21:3; Dt 1:43-44

Supplementary Offerings

15 The Lord said to Moses, ²"Speak to the Israelites and say to them: 'After you enter the land I am giving you as a home ³and you present to the Lord offerings made by fire, from the herd or the flock, as an aroma pleasing to the Lord—whether burnt offerings or sacrifices, for special vows or freewill offerings or festival offerings— ⁴then the one who brings his offering shall present to the Lord a grain offering of a tenth of an ephah^a of fine flour mixed with a quarter of a hin^b of oil. ⁵With each lamb for the burnt offering or the sacrifice, prepare a quarter of a hin of wine as a drink offering.

⁶" 'With a ram prepare a grain offering of two-tenths of an ephah^c of fine flour mixed with a third of a hin^d of oil, ⁷and a third of a hin of wine as a drink offering. Offer it as an aroma pleasing to the Lord.   Nu 28:12

⁸" 'When you prepare a young bull as a burnt offering or sacrifice, for a special vow or a fellowship offering^e to the Lord, ⁹bring with the bull a grain offering of three-tenths of an ephah^f of fine flour mixed with half a hin^g of oil.

---

^{a}4 That is, probably about 2 quarts (about 2 liters); also in verse 5 ^{c}6 That is, probably about 4 quarts (about 4.5 liters) ^{d}6 That is, probably about 1 1/4 quarts (about 1.2 liters); also in verse 7 ^{e}8 Traditionally *peace offering* ^{f}9 That is, probably about 6 quarts (about 6.5 liters) ^{g}9 That is, probably about 2 quarts (about 2 liters); also in verse 10 ^{b}4 That is, probably about 1 quart (about 1 liter);

¹⁰Also bring half a hin of wine as a drink offering. It will be an offering made by fire, an aroma pleasing to the Lord. ¹¹Each bull or ram, each lamb or young goat, is to be prepared in this manner. ¹²Do this for each one, for as many as you prepare. Lev 1:3; 14:10

¹³" 'Everyone who is native-born must do these things in this way when he brings an offering made by fire as an aroma pleasing to the Lord. ¹⁴For the generations to come, whenever an alien or anyone else living among you presents an offering made by fire as an aroma pleasing to the Lord, he must do exactly as you do. ¹⁵The community is to have the same rules for you and for the alien living among you; this is a lasting ordinance for the generations to come. You and the alien shall be the same before the Lord: ¹⁶The same laws and regulations will apply both to you and to the alien living among you.' " ver 29

¹⁷The Lord said to Moses, ¹⁸"Speak to the Israelites and say to them: 'When you enter the land to which I am taking you ¹⁹and you eat the food of the land, present a portion as an offering to the Lord. ²⁰Present a cake from the first of your ground meal and present it as an offering from the threshing floor. ²¹Throughout the generations to come you are to give this offering to the Lord from the first of your ground meal. Jos 5:11-12

Offerings for Unintentional Sins

²²" 'Now if you unintentionally fail to keep any of these commands the Lord gave Moses— ²³any of the Lord's commands to you through him, from the day the Lord gave them and continuing through the generations to come — ²⁴and if this is done unintentionally without the community being aware of it, then the whole community is to offer a young bull for a burnt offering as an aroma pleasing to the Lord, along with its prescribed grain offering and drink offering, and a male goat for a sin offering. ²⁵The priest is to make atonement for the whole Israelite community, and they will be forgiven, for it was not intentional and they have brought to the Lord for their wrong an offering made by fire and a sin offering. ²⁶The whole Israelite community and the aliens living among them will be forgiven, because all the people were involved in the unintentional wrong. Lev 4:2,14,20

²⁷" 'But if just one person sins unintentionally, he must bring a year-old female goat for a sin offering. ²⁸The priest is to make atonement before the Lord for the one who erred by sinning unintentionally, and when atonement has been made for him, he will be forgiven. ²⁹One and the same law applies to everyone who sins unin-

tentionally, whether he is a native-born Israelite or an alien.

30 " 'But anyone who sins defiantly, whether native-born or alien, blasphemes the LORD, and that person must be cut off from his people. 31 Because he has despised the LORD's word and broken his commands, that person must surely be cut off; his guilt remains on him.' " Lev 5:1; Dt 17:13; 2Sa 12:9

The Sabbath-Breaker Put to Death

32 While the Israelites were in the desert, a man was found gathering wood on the Sabbath day. 33 Those who found him gathering wood brought him to Moses and Aaron and the whole assembly, 34 and they kept him in custody, because it was not clear what should be done to him. 35 Then the LORD said to Moses, "The man must die. The whole assembly must stone him outside the camp." 36 So the assembly took him outside the camp and stoned him to death, as the LORD commanded Moses. Ex 31:14-15

Tassels on Garments

37 The LORD said to Moses, 38 "Speak to the Israelites and say to them: 'Throughout the generations to come you are to make tassels on the corners of your garments, with a blue cord on each tassel. 39 You will have these tassels to look at and so you will remember all the commands of the LORD, that you may obey them and not prostitute yourselves by going after the lusts of your own hearts and eyes. 40 Then you will remember to obey all my commands and will be consecrated to your God. 41 I am the LORD your God, who brought you out of Egypt to be your God. I am the LORD your God.' " Lev 11:44; Ro 12:1; Col 1:22

Korah, Dathan and Abiram

16 Korah son of Izhar, the son of Kohath, the son of Levi, and certain Reubenites—Dathan and Abiram, sons of Eliab, and On son of Peleth—became insolent[a] 2 and rose up against Moses. With them were 250 Israelite men, well-known community leaders who had been appointed members of the council. 3 They came as a group to oppose Moses and Aaron and said to them, "You have gone too far! The whole community is holy, every one of them, and the LORD is with them. Why then do you set yourselves above the LORD's assembly?" Ex 19:6; Ps 106:16

4 When Moses heard this, he fell facedown. 5 Then he said to Korah and all his followers: "In the morning the LORD will show who belongs to him and who is holy, and he will have that person come near him. The man he chooses he will cause to come near him. 6 You, Ko-

---

a 1 Or Peleth—took men,

rah, and all your followers are to do this: Take censers [7]and tomorrow put fire and incense in them before the LORD. The man the LORD chooses will be the one who is holy. You Levites have gone too far!"   Nu 14:5; 17:5

[8]Moses also said to Korah, "Now listen, you Levites! [9]Isn't it enough for you that the God of Israel has separated you from the rest of the Israelite community and brought you near himself to do the work at the LORD's tabernacle and to stand before the community and minister to them? [10]He has brought you and all your fellow Levites near himself, but now you are trying to get the priesthood too. [11]It is against the LORD that you and all your followers have banded together. Who is Aaron that you should grumble against him?"

[12]Then Moses summoned Dathan and Abiram, the sons of Eliab. But they said, "We will not come! [13]Isn't it enough that you have brought us up out of a land flowing with milk and honey to kill us in the desert? And now you also want to lord it over us? [14]Moreover, you haven't brought us into a land flowing with milk and honey or given us an inheritance of fields and vineyards. Will you gouge out the eyes of[a] these men? No, we will not come!"   Lev 20:24; Ac 7:27,35

[15]Then Moses became very angry and said to the LORD, "Do not accept their offering. I have not taken so much as a donkey from them, nor have I wronged any of them."   1Sa 12:3

[16]Moses said to Korah, "You and all your followers are to appear before the LORD tomorrow—you and they and Aaron. [17]Each man is to take his censer and put incense in it—250 censers in all—and present it before the LORD. You and Aaron are to present your censers also." [18]So each man took his censer, put fire and incense in it, and stood with Moses and Aaron at the entrance to the Tent of Meeting. [19]When Korah had gathered all his followers in opposition to them at the entrance to the Tent of Meeting, the glory of the LORD appeared to the entire assembly. [20]The LORD said to Moses and Aaron, [21]"Separate yourselves from this assembly so I can put an end to them at once."   Ex 32:10; Nu 14:10

[22]But Moses and Aaron fell facedown and cried out, "O God, God of the spirits of all mankind, will you be angry with the entire assembly when only one man sins?"

[23]Then the LORD said to Moses, [24]"Say to the assembly, 'Move away from the tents of Korah, Dathan and Abiram.' "

[25]Moses got up and went to Dathan and Abiram, and the elders of Israel followed him. [26]He warned the assembly, "Move back from the tents of these wicked men! Do

---

[a] 14 Or *you make slaves of*; or *you deceive*

not touch anything belonging to them, or you will be swept away because of all their sins." **27**So they moved away from the tents of Korah, Dathan and Abiram. Dathan and Abiram had come out and were standing with their wives, children and little ones at the entrances to their tents.   Ge 19:15

28Then Moses said, "This is how you will know that the LORD has sent me to do all these things and that it was not my idea: **29**If these men die a natural death and experience only what usually happens to men, then the LORD has not sent me. **30**But if the LORD brings about something totally new, and the earth opens its mouth and swallows them, with everything that belongs to them, and they go down alive into the grave,[a] then you will know that these men have treated the LORD with contempt."   Ex 3:12

31As soon as he finished saying all this, the ground under them split apart **32**and the earth opened its mouth and swallowed them, with their households and all Korah's men and all their possessions. **33**They went down alive into the grave, with everything they owned; the earth closed over them, and they perished and were gone from the community. **34**At their cries, all the Israelites around them fled, shouting, "The earth is going to swallow us too!"   Nu 26:11

35And fire came out from the LORD and consumed the 250 men who were offering the incense.

36The LORD said to Moses, **37**"Tell Eleazar son of Aaron, the priest, to take the censers out of the smoldering remains and scatter the coals some distance away, for the censers are holy— **38**the censers of the men who sinned at the cost of their lives. Hammer the censers into sheets to overlay the altar, for they were presented before the LORD and have become holy. Let them be a sign to the Israelites."   Nu 26:10; Pr 20:2; Eze 14:8

39So Eleazar the priest collected the bronze censers brought by those who had been burned up, and he had them hammered out to overlay the altar, **40**as the LORD directed him through Moses. This was to remind the Israelites that no one except a descendant of Aaron should come to burn incense before the LORD, or he would become like Korah and his followers.

41The next day the whole Israelite community grumbled against Moses and Aaron. "You have killed the LORD's people," they said.

42But when the assembly gathered in opposition to Moses and Aaron and turned toward the Tent of Meeting, suddenly the cloud covered it and the glory of the LORD appeared. **43**Then Moses and Aaron went to the front of the Tent of Meeting, **44**and the LORD said to Moses, **45**"Get away from this as-

a 30 Hebrew Sheol; also in verse 33

sembly so I can put an end to them at once." And they fell facedown. ⁴⁶Then Moses said to Aaron, "Take your censer and put incense in it, along with fire from the altar, and hurry to the assembly to make atonement for them. Wrath has come out from the LORD; the plague has started." ⁴⁷So Aaron did as Moses said, and ran into the midst of the assembly. The plague had already started among the people, but Aaron offered the incense and made atonement for them. ⁴⁸He stood between the living and the dead, and the plague stopped. ⁴⁹But 14,700 people died from the plague, in addition to those who had died because of Korah. ⁵⁰Then Aaron returned to Moses at the entrance to the Tent of Meeting, for the plague had stopped.   Ps 106:30; Nu 8:19; 25:13

The Budding of Aaron's Staff

17 The LORD said to Moses, ²"Speak to the Israelites and get twelve staffs from them, one from the leader of each of their ancestral tribes. Write the name of each man on his staff. ³On the staff of Levi write Aaron's name, for there must be one staff for the head of each ancestral tribe. ⁴Place them in the Tent of Meeting in front of the Testimony, where I meet with you. ⁵The staff belonging to the man I choose will sprout, and I will rid myself of this constant grumbling against you by the Israelites."   Nu 16:5; Ex 16:7; 25:22

⁶So Moses spoke to the Israelites, and their leaders gave him twelve staffs, one for the leader of each of their ancestral tribes, and Aaron's staff was among them. ⁷Moses placed the staffs before the LORD in the Tent of the Testimony.

⁸The next day Moses entered the Tent of the Testimony and saw that Aaron's staff, which represented the house of Levi, had not only sprouted but had budded, blossomed and produced almonds. ⁹Then Moses brought out all the staffs from the LORD's presence to all the Israelites. They looked at them, and each man took his own staff.   Eze 17:24; Heb 9:4

¹⁰The LORD said to Moses, "Put back Aaron's staff in front of the Testimony, to be kept as a sign to the rebellious. This will put an end to their grumbling against me, so that they will not die." ¹¹Moses did just as the LORD commanded him.

¹²The Israelites said to Moses, "We will die! We are lost, we are all lost! ¹³Anyone who even comes near the tabernacle of the LORD will die. Are we all going to die?"

Duties of Priests and Levites

18 The LORD said to Aaron, "You, your sons and your father's family are to bear the responsibility for offenses against the sanctuary, and you and your sons alone are to bear the responsibility for offenses against the priesthood. ²Bring your fellow Levites from your ancestral tribe to

join you and assist you when you and your sons minister before the Tent of the Testimony. ³They are to be responsible to you and are to perform all the duties of the Tent, but they must not go near the furnishings of the sanctuary or the altar, or both they and you will die. ⁴They are to join you and be responsible for the care of the Tent of Meeting—all the work at the Tent—and no one else may come near where you are.   Nu 3:10; 4:15

⁵"You are to be responsible for the care of the sanctuary and the altar, so that wrath will not fall on the Israelites again. ⁶I myself have selected your fellow Levites from among the Israelites as a gift to you, dedicated to the LORD to do the work at the Tent of Meeting. ⁷But only you and your sons may serve as priests in connection with everything at the altar and inside the curtain. I am giving you the service of the priesthood as a gift. Anyone else who comes near the sanctuary must be put to death."

Offerings for Priests and Levites

⁸Then the LORD said to Aaron, "I myself have put you in charge of the offerings presented to me; all the holy offerings the Israelites give me I give to you and your sons as your portion and regular share. ⁹You are to have the part of the most holy offerings that is kept from the fire. From all the gifts they bring me as most holy offerings, whether grain or sin or guilt offerings, that part belongs to you and your sons. ¹⁰Eat it as something most holy; every male shall eat it. You must regard it as holy.

¹¹"This also is yours: whatever is set aside from the gifts of all the wave offerings of the Israelites. I give this to you and your sons and daughters as your regular share. Everyone in your household who is ceremonially clean may eat it.

¹²"I give you all the finest olive oil and all the finest new wine and grain they give the LORD as the firstfruits of their harvest. ¹³All the land's firstfruits that they bring to the LORD will be yours. Everyone in your household who is ceremonially clean may eat it.   Ex 23:19

¹⁴"Everything in Israel that is devoted^a to the LORD is yours. ¹⁵The first offspring of every womb, both man and animal, that is offered to the LORD is yours. But you must redeem every firstborn son and every firstborn male of unclean animals. ¹⁶When they are a month old, you must redeem them at the redemption price set at five shekels^b of silver, according to the sanctuary shekel, which weighs twenty gerahs.   Ex 13:2; Lev 27:6,28

¹⁷"But you must not redeem the firstborn of an ox, a sheep or a

---

^{a}14 The Hebrew term refers to the irrevocable giving over of things or persons to the LORD. ^{b}16 That is, about 2 ounces (about 55 grams)

goat; they are holy. Sprinkle their blood on the altar and burn their fat as an offering made by fire, an aroma pleasing to the LORD. [18]Their meat is to be yours, just as the breast of the wave offering and the right thigh are yours. [19]Whatever is set aside from the holy offerings the Israelites present to the LORD I give to you and your sons and daughters as your regular share. It is an everlasting covenant of salt before the LORD for both you and your offspring."   2Ch 13:5; Lev 3:2

[20]The LORD said to Aaron, "You will have no inheritance in their land, nor will you have any share among them; I am your share and your inheritance among the Israelites.   Dt 10:9; 18:1-2; Jos 13:33

[21]"I give to the Levites all the tithes in Israel as their inheritance in return for the work they do while serving at the Tent of Meeting. [22]From now on the Israelites must not go near the Tent of Meeting, or they will bear the consequences of their sin and will die. [23]It is the Levites who are to do the work at the Tent of Meeting and bear the responsibility for offenses against it. This is a lasting ordinance for the generations to come. They will receive no inheritance among the Israelites. [24]Instead, I give to the Levites as their inheritance the tithes that the Israelites present as an offering to the LORD. That is why I said concerning them: 'They will have no inheritance among the Israelites.' "

[25]The LORD said to Moses, [26]"Speak to the Levites and say to them: 'When you receive from the Israelites the tithe I give you as your inheritance, you must present a tenth of that tithe as the LORD's offering. [27]Your offering will be reckoned to you as grain from the threshing floor or juice from the winepress. [28]In this way you also will present an offering to the LORD from all the tithes you receive from the Israelites. From these tithes you must give the LORD's portion to Aaron the priest. [29]You must present as the LORD's portion the best and holiest part of everything given to you.'   Ne 10:38

[30]"Say to the Levites: 'When you present the best part, it will be reckoned to you as the product of the threshing floor or the winepress. [31]You and your households may eat the rest of it anywhere, for it is your wages for your work at the Tent of Meeting. [32]By presenting the best part of it you will not be guilty in this matter; then you will not defile the holy offerings of the Israelites, and you will not die.' "   Lev 19:8; 22:15

The Water of Cleansing

19 The LORD said to Moses and Aaron: [2]"This is a requirement of the law that the LORD has commanded: Tell the Israelites to bring you a red heifer without defect or blemish and that has never been under a yoke. [3]Give it to Eleazar the priest; it is to be taken outside the camp and slaughtered in his presence. ⁴Then Eleazar the priest is to take some of its blood on his finger and sprinkle it seven times toward the front of the Tent of Meeting. ⁵While he watches, the heifer is to be burned—its hide, flesh, blood and offal. ⁶The priest is to take some cedar wood, hyssop and scarlet wool and throw them onto the burning heifer. ⁷After that, the priest must wash his clothes and bathe himself with water. He may then come into the camp, but he will be ceremonially unclean till evening. ⁸The man who burns it must also wash his clothes and bathe with water, and he too will be unclean till evening.

⁹"A man who is clean shall gather up the ashes of the heifer and put them in a ceremonially clean place outside the camp. They shall be kept by the Israelite community for use in the water of cleansing; it is for purification from sin. ¹⁰The man who gathers up the ashes of the heifer must also wash his clothes, and he too will be unclean till evening. This will be a lasting ordinance both for the Israelites and for the aliens living among them.   ver 13; Nu 8:7; Heb 9:13

¹¹"Whoever touches the dead body of anyone will be unclean for seven days. ¹²He must purify himself with the water on the third day and on the seventh day; then he will be clean. But if he does not purify himself on the third and seventh days, he will not be clean.

¹³Whoever touches the dead body of anyone and fails to purify himself defiles the Lord's tabernacle. That person must be cut off from Israel. Because the water of cleansing has not been sprinkled on him, he is unclean; his uncleanness remains on him.   Lev 7:20; 21:1; Nu 31:19

¹⁴"This is the law that applies when a person dies in a tent: Anyone who enters the tent and anyone who is in it will be unclean for seven days, ¹⁵and every open container without a lid fastened on it will be unclean.

¹⁶"Anyone out in the open who touches someone who has been killed with a sword or someone who has died a natural death, or anyone who touches a human bone or a grave, will be unclean for seven days.   Nu 31:19; Mt 23:27

¹⁷"For the unclean person, put some ashes from the burned purification offering into a jar and pour fresh water over them. ¹⁸Then a man who is ceremonially clean is to take some hyssop, dip it in the water and sprinkle the tent and all the furnishings and the people who were there. He must also sprinkle anyone who has touched a human bone or a grave or someone who has been killed or someone who has died a natural death. ¹⁹The man who is clean is to sprinkle the unclean person on the third and seventh days, and on the seventh day he is to purify him. The person being cleansed must wash his clothes and bathe with water,

and that evening he will be clean. 20But if a person who is unclean does not purify himself, he must be cut off from the community, because he has defiled the sanctuary of the LORD. The water of cleansing has not been sprinkled on him, and he is unclean. 21This is a lasting ordinance for them.   Eze 36:25

"The man who sprinkles the water of cleansing must also wash his clothes, and anyone who touches the water of cleansing will be unclean till evening. 22Anything that an unclean person touches becomes unclean, and anyone who touches it becomes unclean till evening."   Lev 5:2; Hag 2:13-14

Water From the Rock

20 In the first month the whole Israelite community arrived at the Desert of Zin, and they stayed at Kadesh. There Miriam died and was buried.   Ex 15:20

2Now there was no water for the community, and the people gathered in opposition to Moses and Aaron. 3They quarreled with Moses and said, "If only we had died when our brothers fell dead before the LORD! 4Why did you bring the LORD's community into this desert, that we and our livestock should die here? 5Why did you bring us up out of Egypt to this terrible place? It has no grain or figs, grapevines or pomegranates. And there is no water to drink!"   Ex 14:11; 17:1-2

6Moses and Aaron went from the assembly to the entrance to the Tent of Meeting and fell facedown, and the glory of the LORD appeared to them. 7The LORD said to Moses, 8"Take the staff, and you and your brother Aaron gather the assembly together. Speak to that rock before their eyes and it will pour out its water. You will bring water out of the rock for the community so they and their livestock can drink."   Ex 17:6; Isa 43:20; Nu 14:5

9So Moses took the staff from the LORD's presence, just as he commanded him. 10He and Aaron gathered the assembly together in front of the rock and Moses said to them, "Listen, you rebels, must we bring you water out of this rock?" 11Then Moses raised his arm and struck the rock twice with his staff. Water gushed out, and the community and their livestock drank.

12But the LORD said to Moses and Aaron, "Because you did not trust in me enough to honor me as holy in the sight of the Israelites, you will not bring this community into the land I give them."   Nu 27:14

13These were the waters of Meribah,a where the Israelites quarreled with the LORD and where he showed himself holy among them.

Edom Denies Israel Passage

14Moses sent messengers from Kadesh to the king of Edom, saying:

---

a 13 Meribah means quarreling.

"This is what your brother Israel says: You know about all the hardships that have come upon us. [15]Our forefathers went down into Egypt, and we lived there many years. The Egyptians mistreated us and our fathers, [16]but when we cried out to the LORD, he heard our cry and sent an angel and brought us out of Egypt.   Ex 2:23; 14:19

"Now we are here at Kadesh, a town on the edge of your territory. [17]Please let us pass through your country. We will not go through any field or vineyard, or drink water from any well. We will travel along the king's highway and not turn to the right or to the left until we have passed through your territory."   Nu 21:22

[18]But Edom answered:

"You may not pass through here; if you try, we will march out and attack you with the sword."   Nu 21:23

[19]The Israelites replied:

"We will go along the main road, and if we or our livestock drink any of your water, we will pay for it. We only want to pass through on foot —nothing else."   Dt 2:6,28

[20]Again they answered:

"You may not pass through."

Then Edom came out against them with a large and powerful army. [21]Since Edom refused to let them go through their territory, Israel turned away from them.

The Death of Aaron

[22]The whole Israelite community set out from Kadesh and came to Mount Hor. [23]At Mount Hor, near the border of Edom, the LORD said to Moses and Aaron, [24]"Aaron will be gathered to his people. He will not enter the land I give the Israelites, because both of you rebelled against my command at the waters of Meribah. [25]Get Aaron and his son Eleazar and take them up Mount Hor. [26]Remove Aaron's garments and put them on his son Eleazar, for Aaron will be gathered to his people; he will die there."

[27]Moses did as the LORD commanded: They went up Mount Hor in the sight of the whole community. [28]Moses removed Aaron's garments and put them on his son Eleazar. And Aaron died there on top of the mountain. Then Moses and Eleazar came down from the mountain, [29]and when the whole community learned that Aaron had died, the entire house of Israel mourned for him thirty days.

Arad Destroyed

21 When the Canaanite king of Arad, who lived in the

Negev, heard that Israel was coming along the road to Atharim, he attacked the Israelites and captured some of them. ²Then Israel made this vow to the LORD: "If you will deliver these people into our hands, we will totally destroy[a] their cities." ³The LORD listened to Israel's plea and gave the Canaanites over to them. They completely destroyed them and their towns; so the place was named Hormah.[b]

The Bronze Snake

⁴They traveled from Mount Hor along the route to the Red Sea,[c] to go around Edom. But the people grew impatient on the way; ⁵they spoke against God and against Moses, and said, "Why have you brought us up out of Egypt to die in the desert? There is no bread! There is no water! And we detest this miserable food!"   Ps 78:19

⁶Then the LORD sent venomous snakes among them; they bit the people and many Israelites died. ⁷The people came to Moses and said, "We sinned when we spoke against the LORD and against you. Pray that the LORD will take the snakes away from us." So Moses prayed for the people.   Dt 8:15

⁸The LORD said to Moses, "Make a snake and put it up on a pole; anyone who is bitten can look at it and live." ⁹So Moses made a bronze snake and put it up on a pole. Then when anyone was bitten by a snake and looked at the bronze snake, he lived.   Jn 3:14-15

The Journey to Moab

¹⁰The Israelites moved on and camped at Oboth. ¹¹Then they set out from Oboth and camped in Iye Abarim, in the desert that faces Moab toward the sunrise. ¹²From there they moved on and camped in the Zered Valley. ¹³They set out from there and camped alongside the Arnon, which is in the desert extending into Amorite territory. The Arnon is the border of Moab, between Moab and the Amorites. ¹⁴That is why the Book of the Wars of the LORD says: Nu 33:44; Dt 2:13-14

"... Waheb in Suphah[d] and
     the ravines,
   the Arnon ¹⁵and[e] the slopes
     of the ravines
that lead to the site of Ar
   and lie along the border of
     Moab."

¹⁶From there they continued on to Beer, the well where the LORD said to Moses, "Gather the people together and I will give them water."
¹⁷Then Israel sang this song:

"Spring up, O well!
   Sing about it,
¹⁸about the well that the princes
     dug,

---

[a]2 The Hebrew term refers to the irrevocable giving over of things or persons to the LORD, often by totally destroying them; also in verse 3.   [b]3 Hormah means destruction.   [c]4 Hebrew Yam Suph; that is, Sea of Reeds   [d]14 The meaning of the Hebrew for this phrase is uncertain.   [e]14,15 Or "I have been given from Suphah and the ravines / of the Arnon ¹⁵to

that the nobles of the people
    sank—
the nobles with scepters and
    staffs."

Then they went from the desert to Mattanah, ¹⁹from Mattanah to Nahaliel, from Nahaliel to Bamoth, ²⁰and from Bamoth to the valley in Moab where the top of Pisgah overlooks the wasteland.

Defeat of Sihon and Og

²¹Israel sent messengers to say to Sihon king of the Amorites:

²²"Let us pass through your country. We will not turn aside into any field or vineyard, or drink water from any well. We will travel along the king's highway until we have passed through your territory."   Nu 20:17

²³But Sihon would not let Israel pass through his territory. He mustered his entire army and marched out into the desert against Israel. When he reached Jahaz, he fought with Israel. ²⁴Israel, however, put him to the sword and took over his land from the Arnon to the Jabbok, but only as far as the Ammonites, because their border was fortified. ²⁵Israel captured all the cities of the Amorites and occupied them, including Heshbon and all its surrounding settlements. ²⁶Heshbon was the city of Sihon king of the Amorites, who had fought against the former king of Moab and had taken from him all his land as far as the Arnon.   Dt 2:32; 29:7; Ps 135:10-11
²⁷That is why the poets say:

"Come to Heshbon and let it
    be rebuilt;
let Sihon's city be restored.

²⁸"Fire went out from Heshbon,
a blaze from the city of
    Sihon.   Jer 48:45
It consumed Ar of Moab,
the citizens of Arnon's
    heights.   Isa 15:2
²⁹Woe to you, O Moab!
You are destroyed, O people
    of Chemosh!   Jdg 11:24
He has given up his sons as
    fugitives
and his daughters as captives
to Sihon king of the
    Amorites.

³⁰"But we have overthrown
    them;
Heshbon is destroyed all the
    way to Dibon.   Nu 32:3
We have demolished them as
    far as Nophah,
which extends to Medeba."

³¹So Israel settled in the land of the Amorites.

³²After Moses had sent spies to Jazer, the Israelites captured its surrounding settlements and drove out the Amorites who were there. ³³Then they turned and went up along the road toward Bashan, and Og king of Bashan and his whole army marched out to meet them in battle at Edrei.

³⁴The LORD said to Moses, "Do

not be afraid of him, for I have handed him over to you, with his whole army and his land. Do to him what you did to Sihon king of the Amorites, who reigned in Heshbon."   Dt 3:2

³⁵So they struck him down, together with his sons and his whole army, leaving them no survivors. And they took possession of his land.

Balak Summons Balaam

22 Then the Israelites traveled to the plains of Moab and camped along the Jordan across from Jericho.ᵃ   Nu 33:48

²Now Balak son of Zippor saw all that Israel had done to the Amorites, ³and Moab was terrified because there were so many people. Indeed, Moab was filled with dread because of the Israelites.

⁴The Moabites said to the elders of Midian, "This horde is going to lick up everything around us, as an ox licks up the grass of the field."

So Balak son of Zippor, who was king of Moab at that time, ⁵sent messengers to summon Balaam son of Beor, who was at Pethor, near the River,ᵇ in his native land. Balak said:

"A people has come out of Egypt; they cover the face of the land and have settled next to me. ⁶Now come and put a curse on these people, because they are too powerful for me. Perhaps then I will be able to defeat them and drive them out of the country. For I know that those you bless are blessed, and those you curse are cursed."   Nu 23:7,11,13

⁷The elders of Moab and Midian left, taking with them the fee for divination. When they came to Balaam, they told him what Balak had said.   Ge 30:27

⁸"Spend the night here," Balaam said to them, "and I will bring you back the answer the LORD gives me." So the Moabite princes stayed with him.

⁹God came to Balaam and asked, "Who are these men with you?"

¹⁰Balaam said to God, "Balak son of Zippor, king of Moab, sent me this message: ¹¹'A people that has come out of Egypt covers the face of the land. Now come and put a curse on them for me. Perhaps then I will be able to fight them and drive them away.' "

¹²But God said to Balaam, "Do not go with them. You must not put a curse on those people, because they are blessed."   Ge 12:2

¹³The next morning Balaam got up and said to Balak's princes, "Go back to your own country, for the LORD has refused to let me go with you."

¹⁴So the Moabite princes re-

ᵃ1 Hebrew *Jordan of Jericho*; possibly an ancient name for the Jordan River   ᵇ5 That is, the Euphrates

turned to Balak and said, "Balaam refused to come with us."

¹⁵Then Balak sent other princes, more numerous and more distinguished than the first. ¹⁶They came to Balaam and said:

"This is what Balak son of Zippor says: Do not let anything keep you from coming to me, ¹⁷because I will reward you handsomely and do whatever you say. Come and put a curse on these people for me."

¹⁸But Balaam answered them, "Even if Balak gave me his palace filled with silver and gold, I could not do anything great or small to go beyond the command of the LORD my God. ¹⁹Now stay here tonight as the others did, and I will find out what else the LORD will tell me."   Nu 24:13; 1Ki 22:14; 2Ch 18:13

²⁰That night God came to Balaam and said, "Since these men have come to summon you, go with them, but do only what I tell you."   Nu 23:5,12,16,26

Balaam's Donkey

²¹Balaam got up in the morning, saddled his donkey and went with the princes of Moab. ²²But God was very angry when he went, and the angel of the LORD stood in the road to oppose him. Balaam was riding on his donkey, and his two servants were with him. ²³When the donkey saw the angel of the LORD standing in the road with a drawn sword in his hand, she turned off the road into a field. Balaam beat her to get her back on the road.   Ex 23:20

²⁴Then the angel of the LORD stood in a narrow path between two vineyards, with walls on both sides. ²⁵When the donkey saw the angel of the LORD, she pressed close to the wall, crushing Balaam's foot against it. So he beat her again.

²⁶Then the angel of the LORD moved on ahead and stood in a narrow place where there was no room to turn, either to the right or to the left. ²⁷When the donkey saw the angel of the LORD, she lay down under Balaam, and he was angry and beat her with his staff. ²⁸Then the LORD opened the donkey's mouth, and she said to Balaam, "What have I done to you to make you beat me these three times?"

²⁹Balaam answered the donkey, "You have made a fool of me! If I had a sword in my hand, I would kill you right now."   Pr 12:10; Mt 15:19

³⁰The donkey said to Balaam, "Am I not your own donkey, which you have always ridden, to this day? Have I been in the habit of doing this to you?"

"No," he said.

³¹Then the LORD opened Balaam's eyes, and he saw the angel of the LORD standing in the road with his sword drawn. So he bowed low and fell facedown.

³²The angel of the LORD asked him, "Why have you beaten your

donkey these three times? I have come here to oppose you because your path is a reckless one before me.[a] ³³The donkey saw me and turned away from me these three times. If she had not turned away, I would certainly have killed you by now, but I would have spared her."

³⁴Balaam said to the angel of the LORD, "I have sinned. I did not realize you were standing in the road to oppose me. Now if you are displeased, I will go back." Nu 14:40

³⁵The angel of the LORD said to Balaam, "Go with the men, but speak only what I tell you." So Balaam went with the princes of Balak.

³⁶When Balak heard that Balaam was coming, he went out to meet him at the Moabite town on the Arnon border, at the edge of his territory. ³⁷Balak said to Balaam, "Did I not send you an urgent summons? Why didn't you come to me? Am I really not able to reward you?" Nu 21:13

³⁸"Well, I have come to you now," Balaam replied. "But can I say just anything? I must speak only what God puts in my mouth."

³⁹Then Balaam went with Balak to Kiriath Huzoth. ⁴⁰Balak sacrificed cattle and sheep, and gave some to Balaam and the princes who were with him. ⁴¹The next morning Balak took Balaam up to Bamoth Baal, and from there he saw part of the people. Nu 21:28

Balaam's First Oracle

23 Balaam said, "Build me seven altars here, and prepare seven bulls and seven rams for me." ²Balak did as Balaam said, and the two of them offered a bull and a ram on each altar. ver 14,30

³Then Balaam said to Balak, "Stay here beside your offering while I go aside. Perhaps the LORD will come to meet with me. Whatever he reveals to me I will tell you." Then he went off to a barren height. ver 15

⁴God met with him, and Balaam said, "I have prepared seven altars, and on each altar I have offered a bull and a ram."

⁵The LORD put a message in Balaam's mouth and said, "Go back to Balak and give him this message." Dt 18:18; Jer 1:9

⁶So he went back to him and found him standing beside his offering, with all the princes of Moab. ⁷Then Balaam uttered his oracle: ver 18; Nu 24:3,21

"Balak brought me from
        Aram,
    the king of Moab from the
        eastern mountains.
'Come,' he said, 'curse Jacob
        for me;
    come, denounce Israel.'

[8]How can I curse
    those whom God has not
    cursed?   Nu 22:12
  How can I denounce
    those whom the LORD has
    not denounced?
[9]From the rocky peaks I see
    them,
  from the heights I view
    them.
  I see a people who live
    apart
  and do not consider
    themselves one of the
    nations.   Dt 32:8; 33:28
[10]Who can count the dust of
    Jacob
  or number the fourth part of
    Israel?
  Let me die the death of the
    righteous,
  and may my end be like
    theirs!"   Ps 37:37

[11]Balak said to Balaam, "What
have you done to me? I brought
you to curse my enemies, but you
have done nothing but bless
them!"   Nu 24:10; Ne 13:2

[12]He answered, "Must I not
speak what the LORD puts in my
mouth?"   Nu 22:20,38

Balaam's Second Oracle

[13]Then Balak said to him, "Come
with me to another place where
you can see them; you will see
only a part but not all of them. And
from there, curse them for me."

[14]So he took him to the field of Zo-
phim on the top of Pisgah, and
there he built seven altars and offered a bull and a ram on each altar.

[15]Balaam said to Balak, "Stay
here beside your offering while I
meet with him over there."

[16]The LORD met with Balaam
and put a message in his mouth
and said, "Go back to Balak and
give him this message."   Nu 22:38

[17]So he went to him and found
him standing beside his offering,
with the princes of Moab. Balak
asked him, "What did the LORD
say?"

[18]Then he uttered his oracle:

  "Arise, Balak, and listen;
    hear me, son of Zippor.
[19]God is not a man, that he
    should lie,   Isa 55:9; Hos 11:9
  nor a son of man, that he
    should change his mind.
  Does he speak and then not
    act?
  Does he promise and not
    fulfill?
[20]I have received a command to
    bless;
  he has blessed, and I cannot
    change it.   Ge 22:17; Nu 22:12
[21]"No misfortune is seen in
    Jacob,   Ps 32:2,5; Ro 4:7-8
  no misery observed in
    Israel.[a]
  The LORD their God is with
    them;

a21 Or He has not looked on Jacob's offenses / or on the wrongs found in Israel.

the shout of the King is
among them. Ps 89:15-18
22God brought them out of
Egypt;
they have the strength of a
wild ox. Nu 24:8; Dt 33:17
23There is no sorcery against
Jacob,
no divination against Israel.
It will now be said of Jacob
and of Israel, 'See what God
has done!'
24The people rise like a lioness;
they rouse themselves like a
lion Ge 49:9
that does not rest till he
devours his prey
and drinks the blood of his
victims."

25Then Balak said to Balaam,
"Neither curse them at all nor
bless them at all!"
26Balaam answered, "Did I not
tell you I must do whatever the
LORD says?"

Balaam's Third Oracle

27Then Balak said to Balaam,
"Come, let me take you to another
place. Perhaps it will please God to
let you curse them for me from
there." 28And Balak took Balaam to
the top of Peor, overlooking the
wasteland. Ps 106:28
29Balaam said, "Build me seven
altars here, and prepare seven
bulls and seven rams for me."
30Balak did as Balaam had said,

and offered a bull and a ram on
each altar.

24 Now when Balaam saw
that it pleased the LORD to
bless Israel, he did not resort to
sorcery as at other times, but
turned his face toward the desert.
2When Balaam looked out and saw
Israel encamped tribe by tribe, the
Spirit of God came upon him 3and
he uttered his oracle: Nu 11:25-26

"The oracle of Balaam son of
Beor,
the oracle of one whose eye
sees clearly,
4the oracle of one who hears
the words of God,
who sees a vision from the
Almighty,a Ge 15:1
who falls prostrate, and
whose eyes are opened:

5"How beautiful are your tents,
O Jacob,
your dwelling places,
O Israel!

6"Like valleys they spread out,
like gardens beside a river,
like aloes planted by the LORD,
like cedars beside the waters.
7Water will flow from their
buckets;
their seed will have
abundant water.

"Their king will be greater than
Agag;
their kingdom will be
exalted. 2Sa 5:12; 1Ch 14:2

a 4 Hebrew Shaddai; also in verse 16

8"God brought them out of
  Egypt;
they have the strength of a
  wild ox.
They devour hostile nations
and break their bones in
  pieces;   Ps 2:9; Jer 50:17
with their arrows they pierce
  them.   Ps 45:5
9Like a lion they crouch and lie
  down,
like a lioness—who dares to
  rouse them?

"May those who bless you be
  blessed
and those who curse you be
  cursed!"   Ge 12:3

10Then Balak's anger burned
against Balaam. He struck his
hands together and said to him, "I
summoned you to curse my enemies, but you have blessed them
these three times. 11Now leave at
once and go home! I said I would
reward you handsomely, but the
LORD has kept you from being rewarded."   Nu 22:17; 23:11
12Balaam answered Balak, "Did I
not tell the messengers you sent
me, 13'Even if Balak gave me his
palace filled with silver and gold, I
could not do anything of my own
accord, good or bad, to go beyond
the command of the LORD—and I
must say only what the LORD says'?
14Now I am going back to my people, but come, let me warn you of
what this people will do to your
people in days to come."

Balaam's Fourth Oracle

15Then he uttered his oracle:

"The oracle of Balaam son of
  Beor,
the oracle of one whose eye
  sees clearly,
16the oracle of one who hears
  the words of God,
who has knowledge from the
  Most High,
who sees a vision from the
  Almighty,
who falls prostrate, and
  whose eyes are opened:

17"I see him, but not now;
I behold him, but not near.
A star will come out of Jacob;
a scepter will rise out of
  Israel.   Ge 49:10
He will crush the foreheads of
  Moab,
  the skulls*a* of*b* all the sons
    of Sheth.*c*
18Edom will be conquered;
Seir, his enemy, will be
  conquered,
but Israel will grow strong.
19A ruler will come out of Jacob
  and destroy the survivors of
    the city."   Ge 49:10; Mic 5:2

Balaam's Final Oracles

20Then Balaam saw Amalek and
uttered his oracle:

a 17 Samaritan Pentateuch (see also Jer. 48:45); the meaning of the word in the Masoretic Text is
uncertain.   *b* 17 Or possibly *Moab, / batter*   *c* 17 Or *all the noisy boasters*

"Amalek was first among the
        nations,
    but he will come to ruin at
        last."   Dt 25:19

21Then he saw the Kenites and
uttered his oracle:

"Your dwelling place is
        secure,
    your nest is set in a
        rock;
22yet you Kenites will be
        destroyed
    when Asshur takes you
        captive."   Ge 10:22

23Then he uttered his oracle:

"Ah, who can live when God
        does this?a
24   Ships will come from the
        shores of Kittim;
    they will subdue Asshur and
        Eber,
    but they too will come to
        ruin."   Ge 10:4,21

25Then Balaam got up and returned home and Balak went his
own way.   Nu 31:8

Moab Seduces Israel

25 While Israel was staying in
        Shittim, the men began to
indulge in sexual immorality with
Moabite women, 2who invited
them to the sacrifices to their gods.
The people ate and bowed down
before these gods. 3So Israel joined
in worshiping the Baal of Peor.

And the LORD's anger burned
against them.   Ex 20:5; Nu 31:16; Ps 106:28
4The LORD said to Moses, "Take
all the leaders of these people, kill
them and expose them in broad
daylight before the LORD, so that
the LORD's fierce anger may turn
away from Israel."   Dt 4:3; 13:17
5So Moses said to Israel's
judges, "Each of you must put to
death those of your men who have
joined in worshiping the Baal of
Peor."

6Then an Israelite man brought
to his family a Midianite woman
right before the eyes of Moses and
the whole assembly of Israel while
they were weeping at the entrance
to the Tent of Meeting. 7When
Phinehas son of Eleazar, the son of
Aaron, the priest, saw this, he left
the assembly, took a spear in his
hand 8and followed the Israelite
into the tent. He drove the spear
through both of them—through
the Israelite and into the woman's
body. Then the plague against the
Israelites was stopped; 9but those
who died in the plague numbered
24,000.   Nu 14:37; 1Co 10:8
10The LORD said to Moses,
11"Phinehas son of Eleazar, the son
of Aaron, the priest, has turned my
anger away from the Israelites; for
he was as zealous as I am for my
honor among them, so that in my
zeal I did not put an end to
them. 12Therefore tell him I am
making my covenant of peace

---

a23 Masoretic Text; with a different word division of the Hebrew A people will gather from the north.

with him. ¹³He and his descendants will have a covenant of a lasting priesthood, because he was zealous for the honor of his God and made atonement for the Israelites."   Isa 54:10

¹⁴The name of the Israelite who was killed with the Midianite woman was Zimri son of Salu, the leader of a Simeonite family. ¹⁵And the name of the Midianite woman who was put to death was Cozbi daughter of Zur, a tribal chief of a Midianite family.   Nu 31:8; Jos 13:21

¹⁶The Lord said to Moses, ¹⁷"Treat the Midianites as enemies and kill them, ¹⁸because they treated you as enemies when they deceived you in the affair of Peor and their sister Cozbi, the daughter of a Midianite leader, the woman who was killed when the plague came as a result of Peor."

The Second Census

26 After the plague the Lord said to Moses and Eleazar son of Aaron, the priest, ²"Take a census of the whole Israelite community by families—all those twenty years old or more who are able to serve in the army of Israel." ³So on the plains of Moab by the Jordan across from Jericho,^a Moses and Eleazar the priest spoke with them and said, ⁴"Take a census of the men twenty years old or more, as the Lord commanded Moses."   Ex 30:11-16; Nu 22:1

These were the Israelites who came out of Egypt:

⁵The descendants of Reuben, the firstborn son of Israel, were:
through Hanoch, the Hanochite clan;
through Pallu, the Palluite clan;
⁶through Hezron, the Hezronite clan;
through Carmi, the Carmite clan.   Nu 1:20; 1Ch 5:3
⁷These were the clans of Reuben; those numbered were 43,730.

⁸The son of Pallu was Eliab, ⁹and the sons of Eliab were Nemuel, Dathan and Abiram. The same Dathan and Abiram were the community officials who rebelled against Moses and Aaron and were among Korah's followers when they rebelled against the Lord. ¹⁰The earth opened its mouth and swallowed them along with Korah, whose followers died when the fire devoured the 250 men. And they served as a warning sign. ¹¹The line of Korah, however, did not die out.   Ex 6:24; Nu 16:2; Dt 24:16

¹²The descendants of Simeon by their clans were:
through Nemuel, the Nemuelite clan;
through Jamin, the Jaminite clan;   1Ch 4:24
through Jakin, the Jakinite clan;
¹³through Zerah, the Zerahite clan;   Ge 46:10

---

^a3 Hebrew *Jordan of Jericho*; possibly an ancient name for the Jordan River; also in verse 63

through Shaul, the Shaulite clan.

¹⁴These were the clans of Simeon; there were 22,200 men.

¹⁵The descendants of Gad by their clans were:

through Zephon, the Zephonite clan;   Ge 46:16

through Haggi, the Haggite clan;

through Shuni, the Shunite clan;

¹⁶through Ozni, the Oznite clan;

through Eri, the Erite clan;

¹⁷through Arodi,ᵃ the Arodite clan;

through Areli, the Arelite clan.

¹⁸These were the clans of Gad; those numbered were 40,500.

¹⁹Er and Onan were sons of Judah, but they died in Canaan. Ge 38:2-10

²⁰The descendants of Judah by their clans were:

through Shelah, the Shelanite clan;   1Ch 2:3

through Perez, the Perezite clan;

through Zerah, the Zerahite clan.

²¹The descendants of Perez were:

through Hezron, the Hezronite clan;

through Hamul, the Hamulite clan.

²²These were the clans of Judah; those numbered were 76,500.

²³The descendants of Issachar by their clans were:

through Tola, the Tolaite clan;   Ge 46:13

through Puah, the Puiteᵇ clan;

²⁴through Jashub, the Jashubite clan;

through Shimron, the Shimronite clan.

²⁵These were the clans of Issachar; those numbered were 64,300.

²⁶The descendants of Zebulun by their clans were:

through Sered, the Seredite clan;

through Elon, the Elonite clan;

through Jahleel, the Jahleelite clan.

²⁷These were the clans of Zebulun; those numbered were 60,500.

²⁸The descendants of Joseph by their clans through Manasseh and Ephraim were:

²⁹The descendants of Manasseh:

through Makir, the Makirite clan (Makir was the father of Gilead);   Jos 17:1

through Gilead, the Gileadite clan.

³⁰These were the descendants of Gilead:

ᵃ 17 Samaritan Pentateuch and Syriac (see also Gen. 46:16); Masoretic Text *Arod*   ᵇ 23 Samaritan Pentateuch, Septuagint, Vulgate and Syriac (see also 1 Chron. 7:1); Masoretic Text *through Puvah, the Punite*

through Iezer, the Iezerite
clan;   Jos 17:2; Jdg 6:11

through Helek, the Helekite
clan;

31through Asriel, the Asrielite
clan;

through Shechem, the She-
chemite clan;

32through Shemida, the She-
midaite clan;

through Hepher, the He-
pherite clan.

33(Zelophehad son of Hepher
had no sons; he had only
daughters, whose names
were Mahlah, Noah, Hog-
lah, Milcah and Tirzah.)

34These were the clans of Manasseh; those numbered were 52,700.

35These were the descendants of
Ephraim by their clans:

through Shuthelah, the Shu-
thelahite clan;

through Beker, the Bekerite
clan;

through Tahan, the Tahanite
clan.

36These were the descendants
of Shuthelah:

through Eran, the Eranite
clan.

37These were the clans of Ephraim;
those numbered were 32,500.

These were the descendants of Joseph by their clans.

38The descendants of Benjamin by
their clans were: Ge 46:21

through Bela, the Belaite clan;

through Ashbel, the Ashbelite
clan;

through Ahiram, the Ahiram-
ite clan;

39through Shupham,a the Shu-
phamite clan;

through Hupham, the Hu-
phamite clan.

40The descendants of Bela
through Ard and Naaman
were:

through Ard,b the Ardite
clan;

through Naaman, the Naa-
mite clan.

41These were the clans of Benjamin; those numbered were 45,600.

42These were the descendants of
Dan by their clans:

through Shuham, the Shu-
hamite clan.   Ge 46:23

These were the clans of Dan: 43All
of them were Shuhamite clans;
and those numbered were 64,400.

44The descendants of Asher by
their clans were:

through Imnah, the Imnite
clan;

through Ishvi, the Ishvite
clan;

through Beriah, the Beriite
clan;

45and through the descendants
of Beriah:

---

a 39 A few manuscripts of the Masoretic Text, Samaritan Pentateuch, Vulgate and Syriac (see also
Septuagint); most manuscripts of the Masoretic Text Shephupham   b 40 Samaritan Pentateuch and
Vulgate (see also Septuagint); Masoretic Text does not have through Ard.

through Heber, the Heberite clan;

through Malkiel, the Malkielite clan.

⁴⁶(Asher had a daughter named Serah.)

⁴⁷These were the clans of Asher; those numbered were 53,400.

⁴⁸The descendants of Naphtali by their clans were:

through Jahzeel, the Jahzeelite clan;

through Guni, the Gunite clan;

⁴⁹through Jezer, the Jezerite clan;

through Shillem, the Shillemite clan.

⁵⁰These were the clans of Naphtali; those numbered were 45,400.

⁵¹The total number of the men of Israel was 601,730.   Ex 12:37; 38:26

⁵²The LORD said to Moses, ⁵³"The land is to be allotted to them as an inheritance based on the number of names. ⁵⁴To a larger group give a larger inheritance, and to a smaller group a smaller one; each is to receive its inheritance according to the number of those listed. ⁵⁵Be sure that the land is distributed by lot. What each group inherits will be according to the names for its ancestral tribe. ⁵⁶Each inheritance is to be distributed by lot among the larger and smaller groups."   Nu 33:54; 34:14

⁵⁷These were the Levites who were counted by their clans: Ge 46:11

through Gershon, the Gershonite clan;

through Kohath, the Kohathite clan;

through Merari, the Merarite clan.

⁵⁸These also were Levite clans:
the Libnite clan,
the Hebronite clan,
the Mahlite clan,
the Mushite clan,
the Korahite clan.
(Kohath was the forefather of Amram; ⁵⁹the name of Amram's wife was Jochebed, a descendant of Levi, who was born to the Levites*a* in Egypt. To Amram she bore Aaron, Moses and their sister Miriam. ⁶⁰Aaron was the father of Nadab and Abihu, Eleazar and Ithamar. ⁶¹But Nadab and Abihu died when they made an offering before the LORD with unauthorized fire.)

⁶²All the male Levites a month old or more numbered 23,000. They were not counted along with the other Israelites because they received no inheritance among them.   Nu 1:47; 18:23

⁶³These are the ones counted by Moses and Eleazar the priest when

a 59 Or Jochebed, a daughter of Levi, who was born to Levi

they counted the Israelites on the plains of Moab by the Jordan across from Jericho. ⁶⁴Not one of them was among those counted by Moses and Aaron the priest when they counted the Israelites in the Desert of Sinai. ⁶⁵For the LORD had told those Israelites they would surely die in the desert, and not one of them was left except Caleb son of Jephunneh and Joshua son of Nun. Nu 14:28; Dt 2:14-15; Heb 3:17

Zelophehad's Daughters

27 The daughters of Zelophehad son of Hepher, the son of Gilead, the son of Makir, the son of Manasseh, belonged to the clans of Manasseh son of Joseph. The names of the daughters were Mahlah, Noah, Hoglah, Milcah and Tirzah. They approached ²the entrance to the Tent of Meeting and stood before Moses, Eleazar the priest, the leaders and the whole assembly, and said, ³"Our father died in the desert. He was not among Korah's followers, who banded together against the LORD, but he died for his own sin and left no sons. ⁴Why should our father's name disappear from his clan because he had no son? Give us property among our father's relatives."

⁵So Moses brought their case before the LORD ⁶and the LORD said to him, ⁷"What Zelophehad's daughters are saying is right. You must certainly give them property as an inheritance among their father's relatives and turn their father's inheritance over to them. Nu 9:8

⁸"Say to the Israelites, 'If a man dies and leaves no son, turn his inheritance over to his daughter. ⁹If he has no daughter, give his inheritance to his brothers. ¹⁰If he has no brothers, give his inheritance to his father's brothers. ¹¹If his father had no brothers, give his inheritance to the nearest relative in his clan, that he may possess it. This is to be a legal requirement for the Israelites, as the LORD commanded Moses.' " Nu 36:1-12

Joshua to Succeed Moses

¹²Then the LORD said to Moses, "Go up this mountain in the Abarim range and see the land I have given the Israelites. ¹³After you have seen it, you too will be gathered to your people, as your brother Aaron was, ¹⁴for when the community rebelled at the waters in the Desert of Zin, both of you disobeyed my command to honor me as holy before their eyes." (These were the waters of Meribah Kadesh, in the Desert of Zin.)

¹⁵Moses said to the LORD, ¹⁶"May the LORD, the God of the spirits of all mankind, appoint a man over this community ¹⁷to go out and come in before them, one who will lead them out and bring them in, so the LORD's people will not be like sheep without a shepherd."

¹⁸So the LORD said to Moses, "Take Joshua son of Nun, a man in

whom is the spirit,[a] and lay your hand on him. [19]Have him stand before Eleazar the priest and the entire assembly and commission him in their presence. [20]Give him some of your authority so the whole Israelite community will obey him. [21]He is to stand before Eleazar the priest, who will obtain decisions for him by inquiring of the Urim before the LORD. At his command he and the entire community of the Israelites will go out, and at his command they will come in."

[22]Moses did as the LORD commanded him. He took Joshua and had him stand before Eleazar the priest and the whole assembly. [23]Then he laid his hands on him and commissioned him, as the LORD instructed through Moses.

Daily Offerings

28 The LORD said to Moses, [2]"Give this command to the Israelites and say to them: 'See that you present to me at the appointed time the food for my offerings made by fire, as an aroma pleasing to me.' [3]Say to them: 'This is the offering made by fire that you are to present to the LORD: two lambs a year old without defect, as a regular burnt offering each day. [4]Prepare one lamb in the morning and the other at twilight, [5]together with a grain offering of a tenth of an ephah[b] of fine flour mixed with a quarter of a hin[c] of oil from pressed olives. [6]This is the regular burnt offering instituted at Mount Sinai as a pleasing aroma, an offering made to the LORD by fire. [7]The accompanying drink offering is to be a quarter of a hin of fermented drink with each lamb. Pour out the drink offering to the LORD at the sanctuary. [8]Prepare the second lamb at twilight, along with the same kind of grain offering and drink offering that you prepare in the morning. This is an offering made by fire, an aroma pleasing to the LORD.   Ex 29:38; Lev 2:1

Sabbath Offerings

[9]" 'On the Sabbath day, make an offering of two lambs a year old without defect, together with its drink offering and a grain offering of two-tenths of an ephah[d] of fine flour mixed with oil. [10]This is the burnt offering for every Sabbath, in addition to the regular burnt offering and its drink offering.

Monthly Offerings

[11]" 'On the first of every month, present to the LORD a burnt offering of two young bulls, one ram and seven male lambs a year old, all without defect. [12]With each bull there is to be a grain offering of three-tenths of an ephah[e] of fine

---

[a]18 Or *Spirit*   [b]5 That is, probably about 2 quarts (about 2 liters); also in verses 13, 21 and 29   [c]5 That is, probably about 1 quart (about 1 liter); also in verses 7 and 14   [d]9 That is, probably about 4 quarts (about 4.5 liters); also in verses 12, 20 and 28   [e]12 That is, probably about 6 quarts (about 6.5 liters); also in verses 20 and 28

flour mixed with oil; with the ram, a grain offering of two-tenths of an ephah of fine flour mixed with oil; ¹³and with each lamb, a grain offering of a tenth of an ephah of fine flour mixed with oil. This is for a burnt offering, a pleasing aroma, an offering made to the LORD by fire. ¹⁴With each bull there is to be a drink offering of half a hin*a* of wine; with the ram, a third of a hin*b*; and with each lamb, a quarter of a hin. This is the monthly burnt offering to be made at each new moon during the year. ¹⁵Besides the regular burnt offering with its drink offering, one male goat is to be presented to the LORD as a sin offering.   Lev 4:3; Nu 10:10

The Passover

¹⁶" 'On the fourteenth day of the first month the LORD's Passover is to be held. ¹⁷On the fifteenth day of this month there is to be a festival; for seven days eat bread made without yeast. ¹⁸On the first day hold a sacred assembly and do no regular work. ¹⁹Present to the LORD an offering made by fire, a burnt offering of two young bulls, one ram and seven male lambs a year old, all without defect. ²⁰With each bull prepare a grain offering of three-tenths of an ephah of fine flour mixed with oil; with the ram, two-tenths; ²¹and with each of the seven lambs, one-tenth. ²²Include

one male goat as a sin offering to make atonement for you. ²³Prepare these in addition to the regular morning burnt offering. ²⁴In this way prepare the food for the offering made by fire every day for seven days as an aroma pleasing to the LORD; it is to be prepared in addition to the regular burnt offering and its drink offering. ²⁵On the seventh day hold a sacred assembly and do no regular work.

Feast of Weeks

²⁶" 'On the day of firstfruits, when you present to the LORD an offering of new grain during the Feast of Weeks, hold a sacred assembly and do no regular work. ²⁷Present a burnt offering of two young bulls, one ram and seven male lambs a year old as an aroma pleasing to the LORD. ²⁸With each bull there is to be a grain offering of three-tenths of an ephah of fine flour mixed with oil; with the ram, two-tenths; ²⁹and with each of the seven lambs, one-tenth. ³⁰Include one male goat to make atonement for you. ³¹Prepare these together with their drink offerings, in addition to the regular burnt offering and its grain offering. Be sure the animals are without defect.

Feast of Trumpets

29 " 'On the first day of the seventh month hold a sa-

---

a 14 That is, probably about 2 quarts (about 2 liters)   *b 14* That is, probably about 1 1/4 quarts (about 1.2 liters) cred assembly and do no regular work. It is a day for you to sound the trumpets. ²As an aroma pleasing to the LORD, prepare a burnt offering of one young bull, one ram and seven male lambs a year old, all without defect. ³With the bull prepare a grain offering of three-tenths of an ephah*a* of fine flour mixed with oil; with the ram, two-tenths*b*; ⁴and with each of the seven lambs, one-tenth.*c* ⁵Include one male goat as a sin offering to make atonement for you. ⁶These are in addition to the monthly and daily burnt offerings with their grain offerings and drink offerings as specified. They are offerings made to the LORD by fire—a pleasing aroma.   Lev 23:23-25

Day of Atonement

⁷" 'On the tenth day of this seventh month hold a sacred assembly. You must deny yourselves*d* and do no work. ⁸Present as an aroma pleasing to the LORD a burnt offering of one young bull, one ram and seven male lambs a year old, all without defect. ⁹With the bull prepare a grain offering of three-tenths of an ephah of fine flour mixed with oil; with the ram, two-tenths; ¹⁰and with each of the seven lambs, one-tenth. ¹¹Include one male goat as a sin offering, in addition to the sin offering for atonement and the regular burnt

offering with its grain offering, and their drink offerings.   Lev 16:2-34

Feast of Tabernacles

¹²" 'On the fifteenth day of the seventh month, hold a sacred assembly and do no regular work. Celebrate a festival to the LORD for seven days. ¹³Present an offering made by fire as an aroma pleasing to the LORD, a burnt offering of thirteen young bulls, two rams and fourteen male lambs a year old, all without defect. ¹⁴With each of the thirteen bulls prepare a grain offering of three-tenths of an ephah of fine flour mixed with oil; with each of the two rams, two-tenths; ¹⁵and with each of the fourteen lambs, one-tenth. ¹⁶Include one male goat as a sin offering, in addition to the regular burnt offering with its grain offering and drink offering.

¹⁷" 'On the second day prepare twelve young bulls, two rams and fourteen male lambs a year old, all without defect. ¹⁸With the bulls, rams and lambs, prepare their grain offerings and drink offerings according to the number specified. ¹⁹Include one male goat as a sin offering, in addition to the regular burnt offering with its grain offering, and their drink offerings.

²⁰" 'On the third day prepare eleven bulls, two rams and fourteen male lambs a year old, all

---

a3 That is, probably about 6 quarts (about 6.5 liters); also in verses 9 and 14   *b3* That is, probably about 4 quarts (about 4.5 liters); also in verses 9 and 14   *c4* That is, probably about 2 quarts (about 2 liters); also in verses 10 and 15   *d7* Or *must fast* without defect. [21]With the bulls, rams and lambs, prepare their grain offerings and drink offerings according to the number specified. [22]Include one male goat as a sin offering, in addition to the regular burnt offering with its grain offering and drink offering.

[23]" 'On the fourth day prepare ten bulls, two rams and fourteen male lambs a year old, all without defect. [24]With the bulls, rams and lambs, prepare their grain offerings and drink offerings according to the number specified. [25]Include one male goat as a sin offering, in addition to the regular burnt offering with its grain offering and drink offering.

[26]" 'On the fifth day prepare nine bulls, two rams and fourteen male lambs a year old, all without defect. [27]With the bulls, rams and lambs, prepare their grain offerings and drink offerings according to the number specified. [28]Include one male goat as a sin offering, in addition to the regular burnt offering with its grain offering and drink offering.

[29]" 'On the sixth day prepare eight bulls, two rams and fourteen male lambs a year old, all without defect. [30]With the bulls, rams and lambs, prepare their grain offerings and drink offerings according to the number specified. [31]Include one male goat as a sin offering, in addition to the regular burnt offer-

ing with its grain offering and drink offering.

[32]" 'On the seventh day prepare seven bulls, two rams and fourteen male lambs a year old, all without defect. [33]With the bulls, rams and lambs, prepare their grain offerings and drink offerings according to the number specified. [34]Include one male goat as a sin offering, in addition to the regular burnt offering with its grain offering and drink offering.

[35]" 'On the eighth day hold an assembly and do no regular work. [36]Present an offering made by fire as an aroma pleasing to the LORD, a burnt offering of one bull, one ram and seven male lambs a year old, all without defect. [37]With the bull, the ram and the lambs, prepare their grain offerings and drink offerings according to the number specified. [38]Include one male goat as a sin offering, in addition to the regular burnt offering with its grain offering and drink offering.

[39]" 'In addition to what you vow and your freewill offerings, prepare these for the LORD at your appointed feasts: your burnt offerings, grain offerings, drink offerings and fellowship offerings.[a]' "

[40]Moses told the Israelites all that the LORD commanded him.

Vows

30
Moses said to the heads of the tribes of Israel: "This is

what the LORD commands: ²When a man makes a vow to the LORD or takes an oath to obligate himself by a pledge, he must not break his word but must do everything he said.   Dt 23:21-23; Ps 50:14; Pr 20:25

³"When a young woman still living in her father's house makes a vow to the LORD or obligates herself by a pledge ⁴and her father hears about her vow or pledge but says nothing to her, then all her vows and every pledge by which she obligated herself will stand. ⁵But if her father forbids her when he hears about it, none of her vows or the pledges by which she obligated herself will stand; the LORD will release her because her father has forbidden her.

⁶"If she marries after she makes a vow or after her lips utter a rash promise by which she obligates herself ⁷and her husband hears about it but says nothing to her, then her vows or the pledges by which she obligated herself will stand. ⁸But if her husband forbids her when he hears about it, he nullifies the vow that obligates her or the rash promise by which she obligates herself, and the LORD will release her.   Ge 3:16; Lev 5:4

⁹"Any vow or obligation taken by a widow or divorced woman will be binding on her.

¹⁰"If a woman living with her husband makes a vow or obligates herself by a pledge under oath ¹¹and her husband hears about it but says nothing to her and does not forbid her, then all her vows or the pledges by which she obligated herself will stand. ¹²But if her husband nullifies them when he hears about them, then none of the vows or pledges that came from her lips will stand. Her husband has nullified them, and the LORD will release her. ¹³Her husband may confirm or nullify any vow she makes or any sworn pledge to deny herself. ¹⁴But if her husband says nothing to her about it from day to day, then he confirms all her vows or the pledges binding on her. He confirms them by saying nothing to her when he hears about them. ¹⁵If, however, he nullifies them some time after he hears about them, then he is responsible for her guilt."   Eph 5:22; Col 3:18

¹⁶These are the regulations the LORD gave Moses concerning relationships between a man and his wife, and between a father and his young daughter still living in his house.

Vengeance on the Midianites

31 The LORD said to Moses, ²"Take vengeance on the Midianites for the Israelites. After that, you will be gathered to your people."   Nu 20:26; 27:13

³So Moses said to the people, "Arm some of your men to go to war against the Midianites and to carry out the LORD's vengeance on them. ⁴Send into battle a thousand men from each of the tribes of Israel." ⁵So twelve thousand men

armed for battle, a thousand from each tribe, were supplied from the clans of Israel. ⁶Moses sent them into battle, a thousand from each tribe, along with Phinehas son of Eleazar, the priest, who took with him articles from the sanctuary and the trumpets for signaling.

⁷They fought against Midian, as the LORD commanded Moses, and killed every man. ⁸Among their victims were Evi, Rekem, Zur, Hur and Reba—the five kings of Midian. They also killed Balaam son of Beor with the sword. ⁹The Israelites captured the Midianite women and children and took all the Midianite herds, flocks and goods as plunder. ¹⁰They burned all the towns where the Midianites had settled, as well as all their camps. ¹¹They took all the plunder and spoils, including the people and animals, ¹²and brought the captives, spoils and plunder to Moses and Eleazar the priest and the Israelite assembly at their camp on the plains of Moab, by the Jordan across from Jericho.ᵃ   Dt 20:13

¹³Moses, Eleazar the priest and all the leaders of the community went to meet them outside the camp. ¹⁴Moses was angry with the officers of the army—the commanders of thousands and commanders of hundreds—who returned from the battle.   Ex 18:21

¹⁵"Have you allowed all the women to live?" he asked them.

¹⁶"They were the ones who followed Balaam's advice and were the means of turning the Israelites away from the LORD in what happened at Peor, so that a plague struck the LORD's people. ¹⁷Now kill all the boys. And kill every woman who has slept with a man, ¹⁸but save for yourselves every girl who has never slept with a man.

¹⁹"All of you who have killed anyone or touched anyone who was killed must stay outside the camp seven days. On the third and seventh days you must purify yourselves and your captives. ²⁰Purify every garment as well as everything made of leather, goat hair or wood."   Nu 19:12,16

²¹Then Eleazar the priest said to the soldiers who had gone into battle, "This is the requirement of the law that the LORD gave Moses: ²²Gold, silver, bronze, iron, tin, lead ²³and anything else that can withstand fire must be put through the fire, and then it will be clean. But it must also be purified with the water of cleansing. And whatever cannot withstand fire must be put through that water. ²⁴On the seventh day wash your clothes and you will be clean. Then you may come into the camp."   1Co 3:13

Dividing the Spoils

²⁵The LORD said to Moses, ²⁶"You and Eleazar the priest and

ᵃ 12 Hebrew *Jordan of Jericho*; possibly an ancient name for the Jordan River

the family heads of the community are to count all the people and animals that were captured. **27**Divide the spoils between the soldiers who took part in the battle and the rest of the community. **28**From the soldiers who fought in the battle, set apart as tribute for the LORD one out of every five hundred, whether persons, cattle, donkeys, sheep or goats. **29**Take this tribute from their half share and give it to Eleazar the priest as the LORD's part. **30**From the Israelites' half, select one out of every fifty, whether persons, cattle, donkeys, sheep, goats or other animals. Give them to the Levites, who are responsible for the care of the LORD's tabernacle." **31**So Moses and Eleazar the priest did as the LORD commanded Moses.   Nu 3:7; 18:21; Jos 22:8

32The plunder remaining from the spoils that the soldiers took was 675,000 sheep, **33**72,000 cattle, **34**61,000 donkeys **35**and 32,000 women who had never slept with a man.

36The half share of those who fought in the battle was:

> 337,500 sheep, **37**of which the tribute for the LORD was 675;
> **38**36,000 cattle, of which the tribute for the LORD was 72;
> **39**30,500 donkeys, of which the tribute for the LORD was 61;

4016,000 people, of which the tribute for the LORD was 32.

41Moses gave the tribute to Eleazar the priest as the LORD's part, as the LORD commanded Moses.

42The half belonging to the Israelites, which Moses set apart from that of the fighting men— **43**the community's half—was 337,500 sheep, **44**36,000 cattle, **45**30,500 donkeys **46**and 16,000 people. **47**From the Israelites' half, Moses selected one out of every fifty persons and animals, as the LORD commanded him, and gave them to the Levites, who were responsible for the care of the LORD's tabernacle.

48Then the officers who were over the units of the army—the commanders of thousands and commanders of hundreds—went to Moses **49**and said to him, "Your servants have counted the soldiers under our command, and not one is missing. **50**So we have brought as an offering to the LORD the gold articles each of us acquired—armlets, bracelets, signet rings, earrings and necklaces—to make atonement for ourselves before the LORD."   Ex 30:16; Jer 23:4

51Moses and Eleazar the priest accepted from them the gold—all the crafted articles. **52**All the gold from the commanders of thousands and commanders of hundreds that Moses and Eleazar presented as a gift to the LORD weighed 16,750 shekels.*a* 53Each soldier had taken plunder for himself. 54Moses and Eleazar the priest accepted the gold from the commanders of thousands and commanders of hundreds and brought it into the Tent of Meeting as a memorial for the Israelites before the LORD.   Ex 28:12; Dt 20:14

The Transjordan Tribes

32 The Reubenites and Gadites, who had very large herds and flocks, saw that the lands of Jazer and Gilead were suitable for livestock. 2So they came to Moses and Eleazar the priest and to the leaders of the community, and said, 3"Ataroth, Dibon, Jazer, Nimrah, Heshbon, Elealeh, Sebam, Nebo and Beon— 4the land the LORD subdued before the people of Israel—are suitable for livestock, and your servants have livestock. 5If we have found favor in your eyes," they said, "let this land be given to your servants as our possession. Do not make us cross the Jordan."   Ex 12:38

6Moses said to the Gadites and Reubenites, "Shall your countrymen go to war while you sit here? 7Why do you discourage the Israelites from going over into the land the LORD has given them? 8This is what your fathers did when I sent them from Kadesh Barnea to look over the land. 9After they went up to the Valley of Eshcol and viewed the land, they discouraged the Israelites from entering the land the LORD had given them. 10The LORD's anger was aroused that day and he swore this oath: 11'Because they have not followed me wholeheartedly, not one of the men twenty years old or more who came up out of Egypt will see the land I promised on oath to Abraham, Isaac and Jacob— 12not one except Caleb son of Jephunneh the Kenizzite and Joshua son of Nun, for they followed the LORD wholeheartedly.' 13The LORD's anger burned against Israel and he made them wander in the desert forty years, until the whole generation of those who had done evil in his sight was gone.   Nu 13:27-14:4

14"And here you are, a brood of sinners, standing in the place of your fathers and making the LORD even more angry with Israel. 15If you turn away from following him, he will again leave all this people in the desert, and you will be the cause of their destruction."

16Then they came up to him and said, "We would like to build pens here for our livestock and cities for our women and children. 17But we are ready to arm ourselves and go ahead of the Israelites until we have brought them to their place. Meanwhile our women and children will live in fortified cities, for protection from the inhabitants of the land. 18We will not return to

---

a52 That is, about 420 pounds (about 190 kilograms)

our homes until every Israelite has received his inheritance. ¹⁹We will not receive any inheritance with them on the other side of the Jordan, because our inheritance has come to us on the east side of the Jordan." Jos 4:12-13; 12:1; 22:1-4

²⁰Then Moses said to them, "If you will do this—if you will arm yourselves before the LORD for battle, ²¹and if all of you will go armed over the Jordan before the LORD until he has driven his enemies out before him— ²²then when the land is subdued before the LORD, you may return and be free from your obligation to the LORD and to Israel. And this land will be your possession before the LORD. Dt 3:18-20

²³"But if you fail to do this, you will be sinning against the LORD; and you may be sure that your sin will find you out. ²⁴Build cities for your women and children, and pens for your flocks, but do what you have promised." Ge 4:7

²⁵The Gadites and Reubenites said to Moses, "We your servants will do as our lord commands. ²⁶Our children and wives, our flocks and herds will remain here in the cities of Gilead. ²⁷But your servants, every man armed for battle, will cross over to fight before the LORD, just as our lord says."

²⁸Then Moses gave orders about them to Eleazar the priest and Joshua son of Nun and to the family heads of the Israelite tribes. ²⁹He said to them, "If the Gadites and Reubenites, every man armed for battle, cross over the Jordan with you before the LORD, then when the land is subdued before you, give them the land of Gilead as their possession. ³⁰But if they do not cross over with you armed, they must accept their possession with you in Canaan." Dt 3:18-20

³¹The Gadites and Reubenites answered, "Your servants will do what the LORD has said. ³²We will cross over before the LORD into Canaan armed, but the property we inherit will be on this side of the Jordan."

³³Then Moses gave to the Gadites, the Reubenites and the half-tribe of Manasseh son of Joseph the kingdom of Sihon king of the Amorites and the kingdom of Og king of Bashan—the whole land with its cities and the territory around them. Nu 21:24; Jos 12:6

³⁴The Gadites built up Dibon, Ataroth, Aroer, ³⁵Atroth Shophan, Jazer, Jogbehah, ³⁶Beth Nimrah and Beth Haran as fortified cities, and built pens for their flocks. ³⁷And the Reubenites rebuilt Heshbon, Elealeh and Kiriathaim, ³⁸as well as Nebo and Baal Meon (these names were changed) and Sibmah. They gave names to the cities they rebuilt. ver 3; Dt 2:36

³⁹The descendants of Makir son of Manasseh went to Gilead, captured it and drove out the Amorites who were there. ⁴⁰So Moses gave Gilead to the Makirites, the descendants of Manasseh, and they settled there. ⁴¹Jair, a descen-

dant of Manasseh, captured their settlements and called them Hav-voth Jair.*ᵃ* **⁴²**And Nobah captured Kenath and its surrounding settle-ments and called it Nobah after himself.   Ge 50:23; Dt 3:14; 2Sa 18:18

Stages in Israel's Journey

33 Here are the stages in the journey of the Israelites when they came out of Egypt by divisions under the leadership of Moses and Aaron. **²**At the LORD's command Moses recorded the stages in their journey. This is their journey by stages:

³The Israelites set out from Rameses on the fifteenth day of the first month, the day af-ter the Passover. They marched out boldly in full view of all the Egyptians, **⁴**who were burying all their firstborn, whom the LORD had struck down among them; for the LORD had brought judg-ment on their gods.   Ex 12:12

⁵The Israelites left Rameses and camped at Succoth.

⁶They left Succoth and camped at Etham, on the edge of the desert.   Ex 13:20

⁷They left Etham, turned back to Pi Hahiroth, to the east of Baal Zephon, and camped near Migdol.   Ex 14:2

⁸They left Pi Hahiroth *ᵇ* and passed through the sea into the desert, and when they had traveled for three days in the Desert of Etham, they camped at Marah.   Ex 14:22

⁹They left Marah and went to Elim, where there were twelve springs and seventy palm trees, and they camped there.   Ex 15:27

¹⁰They left Elim and camped by the Red Sea.*ᶜ*

¹¹They left the Red Sea and camped in the Desert of Sin.

¹²They left the Desert of Sin and camped at Dophkah.

¹³They left Dophkah and camped at Alush.

¹⁴They left Alush and camped at Rephidim, where there was no water for the people to drink.

¹⁵They left Rephidim and camped in the Desert of Sinai.

¹⁶They left the Desert of Si-nai and camped at Kibroth Hattaavah.   Nu 11:34

¹⁷They left Kibroth Hattaa-vah and camped at Hazeroth.

¹⁸They left Hazeroth and camped at Rithmah.

¹⁹They left Rithmah and camped at Rimmon Perez.

²⁰They left Rimmon Perez and camped at Libnah.

²¹They left Libnah and camped at Rissah.

---

*ᵃ*41 Or *them the settlements of Jair*   *ᵇ*8 Many manuscripts of the Masoretic Text, Samaritan Pentateuch and Vulgate; most manuscripts of the Masoretic Text *left from before Hahiroth* *ᶜ*10 Hebrew *Yam Suph*; that is, Sea of Reeds; also in verse 11

²²They left Rissah and camped at Kehelathah.

²³They left Kehelathah and camped at Mount Shepher.

²⁴They left Mount Shepher and camped at Haradah.

²⁵They left Haradah and camped at Makheloth.

²⁶They left Makheloth and camped at Tahath.

²⁷They left Tahath and camped at Terah.

²⁸They left Terah and camped at Mithcah.

²⁹They left Mithcah and camped at Hashmonah.

³⁰They left Hashmonah and camped at Moseroth.   Dt 10:6

³¹They left Moseroth and camped at Bene Jaakan.

³²They left Bene Jaakan and camped at Hor Haggidgad.

³³They left Hor Haggidgad and camped at Jotbathah.

³⁴They left Jotbathah and camped at Abronah.

³⁵They left Abronah and camped at Ezion Geber.

³⁶They left Ezion Geber and camped at Kadesh, in the Desert of Zin.   Nu 20:1

³⁷They left Kadesh and camped at Mount Hor, on the border of Edom. ³⁸At the Lord's command Aaron the priest went up Mount Hor, where he died on the first day of the fifth month of the forti-eth year after the Israelites came out of Egypt. ³⁹Aaron was a hundred and twenty-three years old when he died on Mount Hor.   Nu 20:22,25-28

⁴⁰The Canaanite king of Arad, who lived in the Negev of Canaan, heard that the Israelites were coming.   Nu 21:1

⁴¹They left Mount Hor and camped at Zalmonah.

⁴²They left Zalmonah and camped at Punon.

⁴³They left Punon and camped at Oboth.   Nu 21:10

⁴⁴They left Oboth and camped at Iye Abarim, on the border of Moab.

⁴⁵They left Iyim*ᵃ* and camped at Dibon Gad.

⁴⁶They left Dibon Gad and camped at Almon Diblathaim.

⁴⁷They left Almon Diblatha-im and camped in the mountains of Abarim, near Nebo.

⁴⁸They left the mountains of Abarim and camped on the plains of Moab by the Jordan across from Jericho.ᵇ ⁴⁹There on the plains of Moab they camped along the Jordan from Beth Jeshimoth to Abel Shittim.   Nu 22:1; 25:1

⁵⁰On the plains of Moab by the Jordan across from Jericho the Lord said to Moses, ⁵¹"Speak to the Israelites and say to them: 'When you cross the Jordan into Canaan,

---

ᵃ45 That is, Iye Abarim   ᵇ48 Hebrew Jordan of Jericho; possibly an ancient name for the Jordan River; also in verse 50

[52]drive out all the inhabitants of the land before you. Destroy all their carved images and their cast idols, and demolish all their high places. [53]Take possession of the land and settle in it, for I have given you the land to possess. [54]Distribute the land by lot, according to your clans. To a larger group give a larger inheritance, and to a smaller group a smaller one. Whatever falls to them by lot will be theirs. Distribute it according to your ancestral tribes.   Ex 23:24

[55]" 'But if you do not drive out the inhabitants of the land, those you allow to remain will become barbs in your eyes and thorns in your sides. They will give you trouble in the land where you will live. [56]And then I will do to you what I plan to do to them.' "

Boundaries of Canaan

34 The LORD said to Moses, [2]"Command the Israelites and say to them: 'When you enter Canaan, the land that will be allotted to you as an inheritance will have these boundaries: Ge 17:8

[3]" 'Your southern side will include some of the Desert of Zin along the border of Edom. On the east, your southern boundary will start from the end of the Salt Sea,[a] [4]cross south of Scorpion[b] Pass, continue on to Zin and go south of Kadesh Barnea. Then it will go to Hazar Addar and over to Azmon, [5]where it will turn, join the Wadi of Egypt and end at the Sea.[c]

[6]" 'Your western boundary will be the coast of the Great Sea. This will be your boundary on the west.

[7]" 'For your northern boundary, run a line from the Great Sea to Mount Hor [8]and from Mount Hor to Lebo[d] Hamath. Then the boundary will go to Zedad, [9]continue to Ziphron and end at Hazar Enan. This will be your boundary on the north.   Eze 47:15-17; Nu 13:21

[10]" 'For your eastern boundary, run a line from Hazar Enan to Shepham. [11]The boundary will go down from Shepham to Riblah on the east side of Ain and continue along the slopes east of the Sea of Kinnereth.[e] [12]Then the boundary will go down along the Jordan and end at the Salt Sea.   Dt 3:17; 2Ki 23:33

" 'This will be your land, with its boundaries on every side.' "

[13]Moses commanded the Israelites: "Assign this land by lot as an inheritance. The LORD has ordered that it be given to the nine and a half tribes, [14]because the families of the tribe of Reuben, the tribe of Gad and the half-tribe of Manasseh have received their inheritance. [15]These two and a half tribes have received their inheritance on the east side of the Jordan of Jericho,[f] toward the sunrise."   Nu 32:33

---

[a]3 That is, the Dead Sea; also in verse 12   [b]4 Hebrew *Akrabbim*   [c]5 That is, the Mediterranean; also in verses 6 and 7   [d]8 Or *to the entrance to*   [e]11 That is, Galilee   [f]15 *Jordan of Jericho* was possibly an ancient name for the Jordan River.

¹⁶The LORD said to Moses, ¹⁷"These are the names of the men who are to assign the land for you as an inheritance: Eleazar the priest and Joshua son of Nun. ¹⁸And appoint one leader from each tribe to help assign the land. ¹⁹These are their names: Nu 1:4,16

Caleb son of Jephunneh,
     from the tribe of Judah;
²⁰Shemuel son of Ammihud,
     from the tribe of Simeon;
²¹Elidad son of Kislon,
     from the tribe of Benjamin;
²²Bukki son of Jogli,
     the leader from the tribe of
     Dan;
²³Hanniel son of Ephod,
     the leader from the tribe of
     Manasseh son of Joseph;
²⁴Kemuel son of Shiphtan,
     the leader from the tribe of
     Ephraim son of Joseph;
²⁵Elizaphan son of Parnach,
     the leader from the tribe of
     Zebulun;
²⁶Paltiel son of Azzan,
     the leader from the tribe of
     Issachar;
²⁷Ahihud son of Shelomi,
     the leader from the tribe of
     Asher;   Nu 1:40
²⁸Pedahel son of Ammihud,
     the leader from the tribe of
     Naphtali."

²⁹These are the men the LORD commanded to assign the inheri- tance to the Israelites in the land of Canaan.

Towns for the Levites

35 On the plains of Moab by the Jordan across from Jer- icho,ᵃ the LORD said to Moses, ²"Command the Israelites to give the Levites towns to live in from the inheritance the Israelites will possess. And give them pasture- lands around the towns. ³Then they will have towns to live in and pasturelands for their cattle, flocks and all their other livestock.

⁴"The pasturelands around the towns that you give the Levites will extend out fifteen hundred feetᵇ from the town wall. ⁵Outside the town, measure three thousand feetᶜ on the east side, three thou- sand on the south side, three thou- sand on the west and three thou- sand on the north, with the town in the center. They will have this area as pastureland for the towns.

Cities of Refuge

⁶"Six of the towns you give the Levites will be cities of refuge, to which a person who has killed someone may flee. In addition, give them forty-two other towns. ⁷In all you must give the Levites forty-eight towns, together with their pasturelands. ⁸The towns you give the Levites from the land the Israelites possess are to be giv-

---

ᵃ1 Hebrew *Jordan of Jericho*; possibly an ancient name for the Jordan River   ᵇ4 Hebrew *a thousand cubits* (about 450 meters)   ᶜ5 Hebrew *two thousand cubits* (about 900 meters)

en in proportion to the inheritance of each tribe: Take many towns from a tribe that has many, but few from one that has few." Nu 26:54

⁹Then the LORD said to Moses: ¹⁰"Speak to the Israelites and say to them: 'When you cross the Jordan into Canaan, ¹¹select some towns to be your cities of refuge, to which a person who has killed someone accidentally may flee. ¹²They will be places of refuge from the avenger, so that a person accused of murder may not die before he stands trial before the assembly. ¹³These six towns you give will be your cities of refuge. ¹⁴Give three on this side of the Jordan and three in Canaan as cities of refuge. ¹⁵These six towns will be a place of refuge for Israelites, aliens and any other people living among them, so that anyone who has killed another accidentally can flee there. Ex 21:13; Jos 20:3

¹⁶" 'If a man strikes someone with an iron object so that he dies, he is a murderer; the murderer shall be put to death. ¹⁷Or if anyone has a stone in his hand that could kill, and he strikes someone so that he dies, he is a murderer; the murderer shall be put to death. ¹⁸Or if anyone has a wooden object in his hand that could kill, and he hits someone so that he dies, he is a murderer; the murderer shall be put to death. ¹⁹The avenger of blood shall put the murderer to death; when he meets him, he shall put him to death. ²⁰If anyone with malice aforethought shoves another or throws something at him intentionally so that he dies ²¹or if in hostility he hits him with his fist so that he dies, that person shall be put to death; he is a murderer. The avenger of blood shall put the murderer to death when he meets him. Ex 21:12,14; Lev 24:17

²²" 'But if without hostility someone suddenly shoves another or throws something at him unintentionally ²³or, without seeing him, drops a stone on him that could kill him, and he dies, then since he was not his enemy and he did not intend to harm him, ²⁴the assembly must judge between him and the avenger of blood according to these regulations. ²⁵The assembly must protect the one accused of murder from the avenger of blood and send him back to the city of refuge to which he fled. He must stay there until the death of the high priest, who was anointed with the holy oil. Ex 21:13; 29:7

²⁶" 'But if the accused ever goes outside the limits of the city of refuge to which he has fled ²⁷and the avenger of blood finds him outside the city, the avenger of blood may kill the accused without being guilty of murder. ²⁸The accused must stay in his city of refuge until the death of the high priest; only after the death of the high priest may he return to his own property.

²⁹" 'These are to be legal requirements for you throughout the

generations to come, wherever you live.

30" 'Anyone who kills a person is to be put to death as a murderer only on the testimony of witnesses. But no one is to be put to death on the testimony of only one witness.   Dt 17:6; Mt 18:16; 2Co 13:1

31" 'Do not accept a ransom for the life of a murderer, who deserves to die. He must surely be put to death.

32" 'Do not accept a ransom for anyone who has fled to a city of refuge and so allow him to go back and live on his own land before the death of the high priest.

33" 'Do not pollute the land where you are. Bloodshed pollutes the land, and atonement cannot be made for the land on which blood has been shed, except by the blood of the one who shed it. 34Do not defile the land where you live and where I dwell, for I, the LORD, dwell among the Israelites.' "   Dt 4:41-43

Inheritance of Zelophehad's Daughters

36 The family heads of the clan of Gilead son of Makir, the son of Manasseh, who were from the clans of the descendants of Joseph, came and spoke before Moses and the leaders, the heads of the Israelite families. 2They said, "When the LORD commanded my lord to give the land as an inheritance to the Israelites by lot, he ordered you to give the inheritance of our brother Zelophehad to his daughters. 3Now suppose they marry men from other Israelite tribes; then their inheritance will be taken from our ancestral inheritance and added to that of the tribe they marry into. And so part of the inheritance allotted to us will be taken away. 4When the Year of Jubilee for the Israelites comes, their inheritance will be added to that of the tribe into which they marry, and their property will be taken from the tribal inheritance of our forefathers."

5Then at the LORD's command Moses gave this order to the Israelites: "What the tribe of the descendants of Joseph is saying is right. 6This is what the LORD commands for Zelophehad's daughters: They may marry anyone they please as long as they marry within the tribal clan of their father. 7No inheritance in Israel is to pass from tribe to tribe, for every Israelite shall keep the tribal land inherited from his forefathers. 8Every daughter who inherits land in any Israelite tribe must marry someone in her father's tribal clan, so that every Israelite will possess the inheritance of his fathers. 9No inheritance may pass from tribe to tribe, for each Israelite tribe is to keep the land it inherits."   1Ki 21:3

10So Zelophehad's daughters did as the LORD commanded Moses. 11Zelophehad's daughters— Mahlah, Tirzah, Hoglah, Milcah and Noah—married their cousins on their father's side. ¹²They married within the clans of the descendants of Manasseh son of Joseph, and their inheritance remained in their father's clan and tribe.

¹³These are the commands and regulations the Lord gave through Moses to the Israelites on the plains of Moab by the Jordan across from Jericho.^a   Lev 26:46

---

^a 13 Hebrew *Jordan of Jericho*; possibly an ancient name for the Jordan River

on their father's side. ¹²They married within the clan of the descendants of Manasseh son of Joseph, and their inheritance remained in their father's clan and tribe.

¹³These are the commands and regulations the LORD gave through Moses to the Israelites on the plains of Moab by the Jordan across from Jericho.   Lev 26:46

Deuteronomy

The Command to Leave Horeb

1 These are the words Moses spoke to all Israel in the desert east of the Jordan—that is, in the Arabah—opposite Suph, between Paran and Tophel, Laban, Hazeroth and Dizahab. ²(It takes eleven days to go from Horeb to Kadesh Barnea by the Mount Seir road.)

³In the fortieth year, on the first day of the eleventh month, Moses proclaimed to the Israelites all that the LORD had commanded him concerning them. ⁴This was after he had defeated Sihon king of the Amorites, who reigned in Heshbon, and at Edrei had defeated Og king of Bashan, who reigned in Ashtaroth.   Nu 21:33-35; 33:38; Jos 13:12

⁵East of the Jordan in the territory of Moab, Moses began to expound this law, saying:

⁶The LORD our God said to us at Horeb, "You have stayed long enough at this mountain. ⁷Break camp and advance into the hill country of the Amorites; go to all the neighboring peoples in the Arabah, in the mountains, in the western foothills, in the Negev and along the coast, to the land of the Canaanites and to Lebanon, as far as the great river, the Euphrates. ⁸See, I have given you this land. Go in and take possession of the land that the LORD swore he would give to your fathers—to Abraham, Isaac and Jacob—and to their descendants after them."   Ge 12:7

The Appointment of Leaders

⁹At that time I said to you, "You are too heavy a burden for me to carry alone. ¹⁰The LORD your God has increased your numbers so that today you are as many as the stars in the sky. ¹¹May the LORD, the God of your fathers, increase you a thousand times and bless you as he has promised! ¹²But how can I bear your problems and your burdens and your disputes all by myself? ¹³Choose some wise, understanding and respected men from each of your tribes, and I will set them over you."   Ex 18:18; Ge 15:5

¹⁴You answered me, "What you propose to do is good."

¹⁵So I took the leading men of your tribes, wise and respected men, and appointed them to have authority over you—as commanders of thousands, of hundreds, of fifties and of tens and as tribal officials. ¹⁶And I charged your judges at that time: Hear the disputes between your brothers and judge fairly, whether the case is between brother Israelites or between one of them and an alien. ¹⁷Do not show partiality in judging; hear

both small and great alike. Do not be afraid of any man, for judgment belongs to God. Bring me any case too hard for you, and I will hear it. ¹⁸And at that time I told you everything you were to do.   Ex 18:25

Spies Sent Out

¹⁹Then, as the Lord our God commanded us, we set out from Horeb and went toward the hill country of the Amorites through all that vast and dreadful desert that you have seen, and so we reached Kadesh Barnea. ²⁰Then I said to you, "You have reached the hill country of the Amorites, which the Lord our God is giving us. ²¹See, the Lord your God has given you the land. Go up and take possession of it as the Lord, the God of your fathers, told you. Do not be afraid; do not be discouraged."

²²Then all of you came to me and said, "Let us send men ahead to spy out the land for us and bring back a report about the route we are to take and the towns we will come to."   Nu 13:1-3

²³The idea seemed good to me; so I selected twelve of you, one man from each tribe. ²⁴They left and went up into the hill country, and came to the Valley of Eshcol and explored it. ²⁵Taking with them some of the fruit of the land, they brought it down to us and reported, "It is a good land that the Lord our God is giving us."

Rebellion Against the Lord

²⁶But you were unwilling to go up; you rebelled against the command of the Lord your God. ²⁷You grumbled in your tents and said, "The Lord hates us; so he brought us out of Egypt to deliver us into the hands of the Amorites to destroy us. ²⁸Where can we go? Our brothers have made us lose heart. They say, 'The people are stronger and taller than we are; the cities are large, with walls up to the sky. We even saw the Anakites there.' "

²⁹Then I said to you, "Do not be terrified; do not be afraid of them. ³⁰The Lord your God, who is going before you, will fight for you, as he did for you in Egypt, before your very eyes, ³¹and in the desert. There you saw how the Lord your God carried you, as a father carries his son, all the way you went until you reached this place."   Dt 32:10-12

³²In spite of this, you did not trust in the Lord your God, ³³who went ahead of you on your journey, in fire by night and in a cloud by day, to search out places for you to camp and to show you the way you should go.   Ps 106:24

³⁴When the Lord heard what you said, he was angry and solemnly swore: ³⁵"Not a man of this evil generation shall see the good land I swore to give your forefathers, ³⁶except Caleb son of Jephunneh. He will see it, and I will give him and his descendants the land he set his feet on, because

he followed the Lord wholeheart-
edly."   Nu 14:23,28-30

37Because of you the Lord became angry with me also and said,
"You shall not enter it, either.
38But your assistant, Joshua son of
Nun, will enter it. Encourage him,
because he will lead Israel to inherit it. **39**And the little ones that
you said would be taken captive,
your children who do not yet
know good from bad—they will
enter the land. I will give it to them
and they will take possession of it.
40But as for you, turn around and
set out toward the desert along the
route to the Red Sea.*ª*"   Nu 20:12

41Then you replied, "We have
sinned against the Lord. We will
go up and fight, as the Lord our
God commanded us." So every one
of you put on his weapons, thinking it easy to go up into the hill
country.

42But the Lord said to me, "Tell
them, 'Do not go up and fight, because I will not be with you. You
will be defeated by your ene-
mies.'"   Nu 14:41-43

43So I told you, but you would
not listen. You rebelled against the
Lord's command and in your arrogance you marched up into the hill
country. **44**The Amorites who lived
in those hills came out against
you; they chased you like a swarm
of bees and beat you down from
Seir all the way to Hormah. **45**You
came back and wept before the

Lord, but he paid no attention to
your weeping and turned a deaf
ear to you. **46**And so you stayed in
Kadesh many days—all the time
you spent there.   Job 27:9; Ps 118:12

Wanderings in the Desert

2 Then we turned back and set
out toward the desert along
the route to the Red Sea,*ª* as the
Lord had directed me. For a long
time we made our way around the
hill country of Seir.

2Then the Lord said to me,
3"You have made your way around
this hill country long enough; now
turn north. **4**Give the people these
orders: 'You are about to pass
through the territory of your
brothers the descendants of Esau,
who live in Seir. They will be afraid
of you, but be very careful. **5**Do not
provoke them to war, for I will not
give you any of their land, not even
enough to put your foot on. I have
given Esau the hill country of Seir
as his own. **6**You are to pay them
in silver for the food you eat and
the water you drink.'"   Jos 24:4

7The Lord your God has blessed
you in all the work of your hands.
He has watched over your journey
through this vast desert. These forty years the Lord your God has
been with you, and you have not
lacked anything.   Dt 8:2-4

8So we went on past our brothers the descendants of Esau, who
live in Seir. We turned from the

ª 40,1 Hebrew Yam Suph; that is, Sea of Reeds

Arabah road, which comes up from Elath and Ezion Geber, and traveled along the desert road of Moab. 1Ki 9:26; Dt 1:1

⁹Then the LORD said to me, "Do not harass the Moabites or provoke them to war, for I will not give you any part of their land. I have given Ar to the descendants of Lot as a possession." Ge 19:36-38

¹⁰(The Emites used to live there —a people strong and numerous, and as tall as the Anakites. ¹¹Like the Anakites, they too were considered Rephaites, but the Moabites called them Emites. ¹²Horites used to live in Seir, but the descendants of Esau drove them out. They destroyed the Horites from before them and settled in their place, just as Israel did in the land the LORD gave them as their possession.) ver 22; Ge 14:5

¹³And the LORD said, "Now get up and cross the Zered Valley." So we crossed the valley.

¹⁴Thirty-eight years passed from the time we left Kadesh Barnea until we crossed the Zered Valley. By then, that entire generation of fighting men had perished from the camp, as the LORD had sworn to them. ¹⁵The LORD's hand was against them until he had completely eliminated them from the camp. Nu 14:29-35; Dt 1:34-35; Ps 106:26

¹⁶Now when the last of these fighting men among the people had died, ¹⁷the LORD said to me,

¹⁸"Today you are to pass by the region of Moab at Ar. ¹⁹When you come to the Ammonites, do not harass them or provoke them to war, for I will not give you possession of any land belonging to the Ammonites. I have given it as a possession to the descendants of Lot." ver 9; Ge 19:38

²⁰(That too was considered a land of the Rephaites, who used to live there; but the Ammonites called them Zamzummites. ²¹They were a people strong and numerous, and as tall as the Anakites. The LORD destroyed them from before the Ammonites, who drove them out and settled in their place. ²²The LORD had done the same for the descendants of Esau, who lived in Seir, when he destroyed the Horites from before them. They drove them out and have lived in their place to this day. ²³And as for the Avvites who lived in villages as far as Gaza, the Caphtorites coming out from Caphtor[a] destroyed them and settled in their place.)

Defeat of Sihon King of Heshbon

²⁴"Set out now and cross the Arnon Gorge. See, I have given into your hand Sihon the Amorite, king of Heshbon, and his country. Begin to take possession of it and engage him in battle. ²⁵This very day I will begin to put the terror and fear of you on all the nations under

---

a23 That is, Crete

heaven. They will hear reports of you and will tremble and be in anguish because of you." Ex 15:14-16

²⁶From the desert of Kedemoth I sent messengers to Sihon king of Heshbon offering peace and saying, ²⁷"Let us pass through your country. We will stay on the main road; we will not turn aside to the right or to the left. ²⁸Sell us food to eat and water to drink for their price in silver. Only let us pass through on foot— ²⁹as the descendants of Esau, who live in Seir, and the Moabites, who live in Ar, did for us—until we cross the Jordan into the land the LORD our God is giving us." ³⁰But Sihon king of Heshbon refused to let us pass through. For the LORD your God had made his spirit stubborn and his heart obstinate in order to give him into your hands, as he has now done. Ex 4:21; Nu 21:21-22

³¹The LORD said to me, "See, I have begun to deliver Sihon and his country over to you. Now begin to conquer and possess his land." Dt 1:8

³²When Sihon and all his army came out to meet us in battle at Jahaz, ³³the LORD our God delivered him over to us and we struck him down, together with his sons and his whole army. ³⁴At that time we took all his towns and completely destroyed[a] them—men, women and children. We left no survivors. ³⁵But the livestock and the plunder from the towns we had captured we carried off for ourselves. ³⁶From Aroer on the rim of the Arnon Gorge, and from the town in the gorge, even as far as Gilead, not one town was too strong for us. The LORD our God gave us all of them. ³⁷But in accordance with the command of the LORD our God, you did not encroach on any of the land of the Ammonites, neither the land along the course of the Jabbok nor that around the towns in the hills.

Defeat of Og King of Bashan

3 Next we turned and went up along the road toward Bashan, and Og king of Bashan with his whole army marched out to meet us in battle at Edrei. ²The LORD said to me, "Do not be afraid of him, for I have handed him over to you with his whole army and his land. Do to him what you did to Sihon king of the Amorites, who reigned in Heshbon." Nu 21:33

³So the LORD our God also gave into our hands Og king of Bashan and all his army. We struck them down, leaving no survivors. ⁴At that time we took all his cities. There was not one of the sixty cities that we did not take from them —the whole region of Argob, Og's kingdom in Bashan. ⁵All these cities were fortified with high walls

---

[a] 34 The Hebrew term refers to the irrevocable giving over of things or persons to the LORD, often by totally destroying them.

and with gates and bars, and there were also a great many unwalled villages. ⁶We completely destroyed*a* them, as we had done with Sihon king of Heshbon, destroying*a* every city—men, women and children. ⁷But all the livestock and the plunder from their cities we carried off for ourselves.

⁸So at that time we took from these two kings of the Amorites the territory east of the Jordan, from the Arnon Gorge as far as Mount Hermon. ⁹(Hermon is called Sirion by the Sidonians; the Amorites call it Senir.) ¹⁰We took all the towns on the plateau, and all Gilead, and all Bashan as far as Salecah and Edrei, towns of Og's kingdom in Bashan. ¹¹(Only Og king of Bashan was left of the remnant of the Rephaites. His bed*b* was made of iron and was more than thirteen feet long and six feet wide.*c* It is still in Rabbah of the Ammonites.)   Ge 14:5; 2Sa 12:26; Ps 29:6

Division of the Land

¹²Of the land that we took over at that time, I gave the Reubenites and the Gadites the territory north of Aroer by the Arnon Gorge, including half the hill country of Gilead, together with its towns. ¹³The rest of Gilead and also all of Bashan, the kingdom of Og, I gave to the half tribe of Manasseh. (The whole region of Argob in Bashan used to be known as a land of the Rephaites. ¹⁴Jair, a descendant of Manasseh, took the whole region of Argob as far as the border of the Geshurites and the Maacathites; it was named after him, so that to this day Bashan is called Havvoth Jair.*d*) ¹⁵And I gave Gilead to Makir. ¹⁶But to the Reubenites and the Gadites I gave the territory extending from Gilead down to the Arnon Gorge (the middle of the gorge being the border) and out to the Jabbok River, which is the border of the Ammonites. ¹⁷Its western border was the Jordan in the Arabah, from Kinnereth to the Sea of the Arabah (the Salt Sea*e*), below the slopes of Pisgah.

¹⁸I commanded you at that time: "The LORD your God has given you this land to take possession of it. But all your able-bodied men, armed for battle, must cross over ahead of your brother Israelites. ¹⁹However, your wives, your children and your livestock (I know you have much livestock) may stay in the towns I have given you, ²⁰until the LORD gives rest to your brothers as he has to you, and they too have taken over the land that the LORD your God is giving them, across the Jordan. After that, each of you may go back to the possession I have given you."   Nu 32:17

---

*a*6 The Hebrew term refers to the irrevocable giving over of things or persons to the LORD, often by totally destroying them.   *b*11 Or *sarcophagus*   *c*11 Hebrew *nine cubits long and four cubits wide* (about 4 meters long and 1.8 meters wide)   *d*14 Or *called the settlements of Jair*   *e*17 That is, the Dead Sea

Moses Forbidden to Cross the Jordan

²¹At that time I commanded Joshua: "You have seen with your own eyes all that the LORD your God has done to these two kings. The LORD will do the same to all the kingdoms over there where you are going. ²²Do not be afraid of them; the LORD your God himself will fight for you." Ex 14:14; Dt 1:29

²³At that time I pleaded with the LORD: ²⁴"O Sovereign LORD, you have begun to show to your servant your greatness and your strong hand. For what god is there in heaven or on earth who can do the deeds and mighty works you do? ²⁵Let me go over and see the good land beyond the Jordan—that fine hill country and Lebanon." Dt 4:22; Ex 15:11; Dt 11:2

²⁶But because of you the LORD was angry with me and would not listen to me. "That is enough," the LORD said. "Do not speak to me anymore about this matter. ²⁷Go up to the top of Pisgah and look west and north and south and east. Look at the land with your own eyes, since you are not going to cross this Jordan. ²⁸But commission Joshua, and encourage and strengthen him, for he will lead this people across and will cause them to inherit the land that you will see." ²⁹So we stayed in the valley near Beth Peor. Dt 1:37; Nu 27:12

Obedience Commanded

4 Hear now, O Israel, the decrees and laws I am about to teach you. Follow them so that you may live and may go in and take possession of the land that the LORD, the God of your fathers, is giving you. ²Do not add to what I command you and do not subtract from it, but keep the commands of the LORD your God that I give you.

³You saw with your own eyes what the LORD did at Baal Peor. The LORD your God destroyed from among you everyone who followed the Baal of Peor, ⁴but all of you who held fast to the LORD your God are still alive today.

⁵See, I have taught you decrees and laws as the LORD my God commanded me, so that you may follow them in the land you are entering to take possession of it. ⁶Observe them carefully, for this will show your wisdom and understanding to the nations, who will hear about all these decrees and say, "Surely this great nation is a wise and understanding people." ⁷What other nation is so great as to have their gods near them the way the LORD our God is near us whenever we pray to him? ⁸And what other nation is so great as to have such righteous decrees and laws as this body of laws I am setting before you today? 2Sa 7:23; Isa 55:6

⁹Only be careful, and watch yourselves closely so that you do not forget the things your eyes

have seen or let them slip from your heart as long as you live. Teach them to your children and to their children after them. [10]Remember the day you stood before the LORD your God at Horeb, when he said to me, "Assemble the people before me to hear my words so that they may learn to revere me as long as they live in the land and may teach them to their children." [11]You came near and stood at the foot of the mountain while it blazed with fire to the very heavens, with black clouds and deep darkness. [12]Then the LORD spoke to you out of the fire. You heard the sound of words but saw no form; there was only a voice. [13]He declared to you his covenant, the Ten Commandments, which he commanded you to follow and then wrote them on two stone tablets. [14]And the LORD directed me at that time to teach you the decrees and laws you are to follow in the land that you are crossing the Jordan to possess.   Pr 4:23; Eph 6:4; Ex 34:28

Idolatry Forbidden

[15]You saw no form of any kind the day the LORD spoke to you at Horeb out of the fire. Therefore watch yourselves very carefully, [16]so that you do not become corrupt and make for yourselves an idol, an image of any shape, whether formed like a man or a woman, [17]or like any animal on earth or any bird that flies in the air, [18]or like any creature that moves along the ground or any fish in the waters below. [19]And when you look up to the sky and see the sun, the moon and the stars —all the heavenly array—do not be enticed into bowing down to them and worshiping things the LORD your God has apportioned to all the nations under heaven. [20]But as for you, the LORD took you and brought you out of the iron-smelting furnace, out of Egypt, to be the people of his inheritance, as you now are.   Ex 20:4-5; Dt 5:8; 1Ki 8:51

[21]The LORD was angry with me because of you, and he solemnly swore that I would not cross the Jordan and enter the good land the LORD your God is giving you as your inheritance. [22]I will die in this land; I will not cross the Jordan; but you are about to cross over and take possession of that good land. [23]Be careful not to forget the covenant of the LORD your God that he made with you; do not make for yourselves an idol in the form of anything the LORD your God has forbidden. [24]For the LORD your God is a consuming fire, a jealous God.   Heb 12:29; Dt 1:37; 3:25

[25]After you have had children and grandchildren and have lived in the land a long time—if you then become corrupt and make any kind of idol, doing evil in the eyes of the LORD your God and provoking him to anger, [26]I call heaven and earth as witnesses against you this day that you will quickly perish from the land that you are

crossing the Jordan to possess. You will not live there long but will certainly be destroyed. ²⁷The Lord will scatter you among the peoples, and only a few of you will survive among the nations to which the Lord will drive you. ²⁸There you will worship man-made gods of wood and stone, which cannot see or hear or eat or smell. ²⁹But if from there you seek the Lord your God, you will find him if you look for him with all your heart and with all your soul. ³⁰When you are in distress and all these things have happened to you, then in later days you will return to the Lord your God and obey him. ³¹For the Lord your God is a merciful God; he will not abandon or destroy you or forget the covenant with your forefathers, which he confirmed to them by oath.   Dt 30:18-19; 2Ki 17:2,17; 2Ch 15:4

The Lord Is God

³²Ask now about the former days, long before your time, from the day God created man on the earth; ask from one end of the heavens to the other. Has anything so great as this ever happened, or has anything like it ever been heard of? ³³Has any other people heard the voice of Godᵃ speaking out of fire, as you have, and lived? ³⁴Has any god ever tried to take for himself one nation out of another nation, by testings, by miraculous signs and wonders, by war, by a mighty hand and an outstretched arm, or by great and awesome deeds, like all the things the Lord your God did for you in Egypt before your very eyes?   Dt 5:24-26; 7:19

³⁵You were shown these things so that you might know that the Lord is God; besides him there is no other. ³⁶From heaven he made you hear his voice to discipline you. On earth he showed you his great fire, and you heard his words from out of the fire. ³⁷Because he loved your forefathers and chose their descendants after them, he brought you out of Egypt by his Presence and his great strength, ³⁸to drive out before you nations greater and stronger than you and to bring you into their land to give it to you for your inheritance, as it is today.   Ex 19:9,19; Dt 10:15; 1Sa 2:2

³⁹Acknowledge and take to heart this day that the Lord is God in heaven above and on the earth below. There is no other. ⁴⁰Keep his decrees and commands, which I am giving you today, so that it may go well with you and your children after you and that you may live long in the land the Lord your God gives you for all time.

Cities of Refuge

⁴¹Then Moses set aside three cities east of the Jordan, ⁴²to which anyone who had killed a person could flee if he had unintention-

---

ᵃ 33 Or of a god

ally killed his neighbor without malice aforethought. He could flee into one of these cities and save his life. **43**The cities were these: Bezer in the desert plateau, for the Reubenites; Ramoth in Gilead, for the Gadites; and Golan in Bashan, for the Manassites.   Nu 35:6-34; Dt 19:1-14

Introduction to the Law

44This is the law Moses set before the Israelites. **45**These are the stipulations, decrees and laws Moses gave them when they came out of Egypt **46**and were in the valley near Beth Peor east of the Jordan, in the land of Sihon king of the Amorites, who reigned in Heshbon and was defeated by Moses and the Israelites as they came out of Egypt. **47**They took possession of his land and the land of Og king of Bashan, the two Amorite kings east of the Jordan. **48**This land extended from Aroer on the rim of the Arnon Gorge to Mount Siyon*a* (that is, Hermon), **49**and included all the Arabah east of the Jordan, as far as the Sea of the Arabah,*b* below the slopes of Pisgah.

The Ten Commandments

5 Moses summoned all Israel and said:
Hear, O Israel, the decrees and laws I declare in your hearing today. Learn them and be sure to follow them. **2**The LORD our God

made a covenant with us at Horeb. **3**It was not with our fathers that the LORD made this covenant, but with us, with all of us who are alive here today. **4**The LORD spoke to you face to face out of the fire on the mountain. **5**(At that time I stood between the LORD and you to declare to you the word of the LORD, because you were afraid of the fire and did not go up the mountain.) And he said: Ex 19:5

6"I am the LORD your God,
who brought you out of
Egypt, out of the land of
slavery.   Lev 26:1
7"You shall have no other gods
before*c* me.
8"You shall not make for yourself an idol in the form of anything in heaven above or on the earth beneath or in the waters below. **9**You shall not bow down to them or worship them; for I, the LORD your God, am a jealous God, punishing the children for the sin of the fathers to the third and fourth generation of those who hate me, **10**but showing love to a thousand ᴸgenerationsⱼ of those who love me and keep my commandments.   Ex 34:7
11"You shall not misuse the name of the LORD your God, for the LORD will not

---

*a*48 Hebrew; Syriac (see also Deut. 3:9) *Sirion*   *b*49 That is, the Dead Sea   *c*7 Or *besides*

hold anyone guiltless who misuses his name. ¹²"Observe the Sabbath day by keeping it holy, as the LORD your God has commanded you. ¹³Six days you shall labor and do all your work, ¹⁴but the seventh day is a Sabbath to the LORD your God. On it you shall not do any work, neither you, nor your son or daughter, nor your manservant or maidservant, nor your ox, your donkey or any of your animals, nor the alien within your gates, so that your manservant and maidservant may rest, as you do. ¹⁵Remember that you were slaves in Egypt and that the LORD your God brought you out of there with a mighty hand and an outstretched arm. Therefore the LORD your God has commanded you to observe the Sabbath day.   Ge 2:2; Heb 4:4

¹⁶"Honor your father and your mother, as the LORD your God has commanded you, so that you may live long and that it may go well with you in the land the LORD your God is giving you.   Lev 19:3; Eph 6:2-3

¹⁷"You shall not murder.   Ge 9:6

¹⁸"You shall not commit adultery.   Mt 5:27-30; Jas 2:11

¹⁹"You shall not steal.   Lev 19:11

²⁰"You shall not give false testimony against your neighbor.   Mk 10:19

²¹"You shall not covet your neighbor's wife. You shall not set your desire on your neighbor's house or land, his manservant or maidservant, his ox or donkey, or anything that belongs to your neighbor."   Ex 20:1-17

²²These are the commandments the LORD proclaimed in a loud voice to your whole assembly there on the mountain from out of the fire, the cloud and the deep darkness; and he added nothing more. Then he wrote them on two stone tablets and gave them to me. ²³When you heard the voice out of the darkness, while the mountain was ablaze with fire, all the leading men of your tribes and your elders came to me. ²⁴And you said, "The LORD our God has shown us his glory and his majesty, and we have heard his voice from the fire. Today we have seen that a man can live even if God speaks with him. ²⁵But now, why should we die? This great fire will consume us, and we will die if we hear the voice of the LORD our God any longer. ²⁶For what mortal man has ever heard the voice of the living God speaking out of fire, as we

have, and survived? ²⁷Go near and listen to all that the Lord our God says. Then tell us whatever the Lord our God tells you. We will listen and obey." Dt 4:33; 18:16

²⁸The Lord heard you when you spoke to me and the Lord said to me, "I have heard what this people said to you. Everything they said was good. ²⁹Oh, that their hearts would be inclined to fear me and keep all my commands always, so that it might go well with them and their children forever! Ps 81:8,13

³⁰"Go, tell them to return to their tents. ³¹But you stay here with me so that I may give you all the commands, decrees and laws you are to teach them to follow in the land I am giving them to possess."

³²So be careful to do what the Lord your God has commanded you; do not turn aside to the right or to the left. ³³Walk in all the way that the Lord your God has commanded you, so that you may live and prosper and prolong your days in the land that you will possess. Dt 17:11,20; Jos 1:7; Jer 7:23

Love the Lord Your God

6 These are the commands, decrees and laws the Lord your God directed me to teach you to observe in the land that you are crossing the Jordan to possess, ²so that you, your children and their children after them may fear the Lord your God as long as you live by keeping all his decrees and commands that I give you, and so that you may enjoy long life. ³Hear, O Israel, and be careful to obey so that it may go well with you and that you may increase greatly in a land flowing with milk and honey, just as the Lord, the God of your fathers, promised you.

⁴Hear, O Israel: The Lord our God, the Lord is one.^a ⁵Love the Lord your God with all your heart and with all your soul and with all your strength. ⁶These commandments that I give you today are to be upon your hearts. ⁷Impress them on your children. Talk about them when you sit at home and when you walk along the road, when you lie down and when you get up. ⁸Tie them as symbols on your hands and bind them on your foreheads. ⁹Write them on the doorframes of your houses and on your gates. Mt 22:37; Dt 11:18; Eph 6:4

¹⁰When the Lord your God brings you into the land he swore to your fathers, to Abraham, Isaac and Jacob, to give you—a land with large, flourishing cities you did not build, ¹¹houses filled with all kinds of good things you did not provide, wells you did not dig, and vineyards and olive groves you did not plant—then when you eat and are satisfied, ¹²be careful that you do not forget the Lord,

---

^a4 Or The Lord our God is one Lord; or The Lord is our God, the Lord is one; or The Lord is our God, the Lord alone

who brought you out of Egypt, out of the land of slavery. Dt 8:10

¹³Fear the LORD your God, serve him only and take your oaths in his name. ¹⁴Do not follow other gods, the gods of the peoples around you; ¹⁵for the LORD your God, who is among you, is a jealous God and his anger will burn against you, and he will destroy you from the face of the land. ¹⁶Do not test the LORD your God as you did at Massah. ¹⁷Be sure to keep the commands of the LORD your God and the stipulations and decrees he has given you. ¹⁸Do what is right and good in the LORD's sight, so that it may go well with you and you may go in and take over the good land that the LORD promised on oath to your forefathers, ¹⁹thrusting out all your enemies before you, as the LORD said.

²⁰In the future, when your son asks you, "What is the meaning of the stipulations, decrees and laws the LORD our God has commanded you?" ²¹tell him: "We were slaves of Pharaoh in Egypt, but the LORD brought us out of Egypt with a mighty hand. ²²Before our eyes the LORD sent miraculous signs and wonders—great and terrible—upon Egypt and Pharaoh and his whole household. ²³But he brought us out from there to bring us in and give us the land that he promised on oath to our forefa-

thers. ²⁴The LORD commanded us to obey all these decrees and to fear the LORD our God, so that we might always prosper and be kept alive, as is the case today. ²⁵And if we are careful to obey all this law before the LORD our God, as he has commanded us, that will be our righteousness." Ex 13:14; Jer 32:39

Driving Out the Nations

7 When the LORD your God brings you into the land you are entering to possess and drives out before you many nations—the Hittites, Girgashites, Amorites, Canaanites, Perizzites, Hivites and Jebusites, seven nations larger and stronger than you— ²and when the LORD your God has delivered them over to you and you have defeated them, then you must destroy them totally.ᵃ Make no treaty with them, and show them no mercy. ³Do not intermarry with them. Do not give your daughters to their sons or take their daughters for your sons, ⁴for they will turn your sons away from following me to serve other gods, and the LORD's anger will burn against you and will quickly destroy you. ⁵This is what you are to do to them: Break down their altars, smash their sacred stones, cut down their Asherah polesᵇ and burn their idols in the fire. ⁶For you are a people holy to the LORD your God. The

---

ᵃ2 The Hebrew term refers to the irrevocable giving over of things or persons to the LORD, often by totally destroying them; also in verse 26.   ᵇ5 That is, symbols of the goddess Asherah; here and elsewhere in Deuteronomy

LORD your God has chosen you out of all the peoples on the face of the earth to be his people, his treasured possession. Ex 23:32; Dt 14:2; 31:3

⁷The LORD did not set his affection on you and choose you because you were more numerous than other peoples, for you were the fewest of all peoples. ⁸But it was because the LORD loved you and kept the oath he swore to your forefathers that he brought you out with a mighty hand and redeemed you from the land of slavery, from the power of Pharaoh king of Egypt. ⁹Know therefore that the LORD your God is God; he is the faithful God, keeping his covenant of love to a thousand generations of those who love him and keep his commands. ¹⁰But

those who hate him he will
      repay to their face by
      destruction;
he will not be slow to repay
      to their face those who
      hate him.

¹¹Therefore, take care to follow the commands, decrees and laws I give you today.

¹²If you pay attention to these laws and are careful to follow them, then the LORD your God will keep his covenant of love with you, as he swore to your forefathers. ¹³He will love you and bless you and increase your numbers. He will bless the fruit of your womb, the crops of your land—your grain, new wine and oil—the calves of your herds and the lambs of your flocks in the land that he swore to your forefathers to give you. ¹⁴You will be blessed more than any other people; none of your men or women will be childless, nor any of your livestock without young. ¹⁵The LORD will keep you free from every disease. He will not inflict on you the horrible diseases you knew in Egypt, but he will inflict them on all who hate you. ¹⁶You must destroy all the peoples the LORD your God gives over to you. Do not look on them with pity and do not serve their gods, for that will be a snare to you. Dt 28:1-14; Ex 23:26; 15:26

¹⁷You may say to yourselves, "These nations are stronger than we are. How can we drive them out?" ¹⁸But do not be afraid of them; remember well what the LORD your God did to Pharaoh and to all Egypt. ¹⁹You saw with your own eyes the great trials, the miraculous signs and wonders, the mighty hand and outstretched arm, with which the LORD your God brought you out. The LORD your God will do the same to all the peoples you now fear. ²⁰Moreover, the LORD your God will send the hornet among them until even the survivors who hide from you have perished. ²¹Do not be terrified by them, for the LORD your God, who is among you, is a great and awesome God. ²²The LORD your God will drive out those nations before you, little by little.

You will not be allowed to eliminate them all at once, or the wild animals will multiply around you. ²³But the LORD your God will deliver them over to you, throwing them into great confusion until they are destroyed. ²⁴He will give their kings into your hand, and you will wipe out their names from under heaven. No one will be able to stand up against you; you will destroy them. ²⁵The images of their gods you are to burn in the fire. Do not covet the silver and gold on them, and do not take it for yourselves, or you will be ensnared by it, for it is detestable to the LORD your God. ²⁶Do not bring a detestable thing into your house or you, like it, will be set apart for destruction. Utterly abhor and detest it, for it is set apart for destruction. Dt 4:34; Ex 23:28-30; Ps 105:5

Do Not Forget the LORD

8 Be careful to follow every command I am giving you today, so that you may live and increase and may enter and possess the land that the LORD promised on oath to your forefathers. ²Remember how the LORD your God led you all the way in the desert these forty years, to humble you and to test you in order to know what was in your heart, whether or not you would keep his commands. ³He humbled you, causing you to hunger and then feeding you with manna, which neither you nor your fathers had known, to teach you that man does not live on bread alone but on every word that comes from the mouth of the LORD. ⁴Your clothes did not wear out and your feet did not swell during these forty years. ⁵Know then in your heart that as a man disciplines his son, so the LORD your God disciplines you. Dt 4:1; Mt 4:4

⁶Observe the commands of the LORD your God, walking in his ways and revering him. ⁷For the LORD your God is bringing you into a good land—a land with streams and pools of water, with springs flowing in the valleys and hills; ⁸a land with wheat and barley, vines and fig trees, pomegranates, olive oil and honey; ⁹a land where bread will not be scarce and you will lack nothing; a land where the rocks are iron and you can dig copper out of the hills. Dt 11:9-12; Jer 2:7

¹⁰When you have eaten and are satisfied, praise the LORD your God for the good land he has given you. ¹¹Be careful that you do not forget the LORD your God, failing to observe his commands, his laws and his decrees that I am giving you this day. ¹²Otherwise, when you eat and are satisfied, when you build fine houses and settle down, ¹³and when your herds and flocks grow large and your silver and gold increase and all you have is multiplied, ¹⁴then your heart will become proud and you will forget the LORD your God, who brought you out of Egypt, out of the land of slavery. ¹⁵He led you through the

vast and dreadful desert, that thirsty and waterless land, with its venomous snakes and scorpions. He brought you water out of hard rock. ¹⁶He gave you manna to eat in the desert, something your fathers had never known, to humble and to test you so that in the end it might go well with you. ¹⁷You may say to yourself, "My power and the strength of my hands have produced this wealth for me." ¹⁸But remember the LORD your God, for it is he who gives you the ability to produce wealth, and so confirms his covenant, which he swore to your forefathers, as it is today.   Dt 6:10-12; Pr 10:22; Hos 2:8

¹⁹If you ever forget the LORD your God and follow other gods and worship and bow down to them, I testify against you today that you will surely be destroyed. ²⁰Like the nations the LORD destroyed before you, so you will be destroyed for not obeying the LORD your God.   Dt 4:26; 30:18

Not Because of Israel's Righteousness

9 Hear, O Israel. You are now about to cross the Jordan to go in and dispossess nations greater and stronger than you, with large cities that have walls up to the sky. ²The people are strong and tall— Anakites! You know about them and have heard it said: "Who can stand up against the Anakites?" ³But be assured today that the LORD your God is the one who goes

across ahead of you like a devouring fire. He will destroy them; he will subdue them before you. And you will drive them out and annihilate them quickly, as the LORD has promised you.   Nu 13:22,28,32-33

⁴After the LORD your God has driven them out before you, do not say to yourself, "The LORD has brought me here to take possession of this land because of my righteousness." No, it is on account of the wickedness of these nations that the LORD is going to drive them out before you. ⁵It is not because of your righteousness or your integrity that you are going in to take possession of their land; but on account of the wickedness of these nations, the LORD your God will drive them out before you, to accomplish what he swore to your fathers, to Abraham, Isaac and Jacob. ⁶Understand, then, that it is not because of your righteousness that the LORD your God is giving you this good land to possess, for you are a stiff-necked people.

The Golden Calf

⁷Remember this and never forget how you provoked the LORD your God to anger in the desert. From the day you left Egypt until you arrived here, you have been rebellious against the LORD. ⁸At Horeb you aroused the LORD's wrath so that he was angry enough to destroy you. ⁹When I went up on the mountain to receive the tab-

lets of stone, the tablets of the covenant that the LORD had made with you, I stayed on the mountain forty days and forty nights; I ate no bread and drank no water. ¹⁰The LORD gave me two stone tablets inscribed by the finger of God. On them were all the commandments the LORD proclaimed to you on the mountain out of the fire, on the day of the assembly.   Ps 106:19

¹¹At the end of the forty days and forty nights, the LORD gave me the two stone tablets, the tablets of the covenant. ¹²Then the LORD told me, "Go down from here at once, because your people whom you brought out of Egypt have become corrupt. They have turned away quickly from what I commanded them and have made a cast idol for themselves."   Ex 32:7-8; Jdg 2:17

¹³And the LORD said to me, "I have seen this people, and they are a stiff-necked people indeed! ¹⁴Let me alone, so that I may destroy them and blot out their name from under heaven. And I will make you into a nation stronger and more numerous than they."   Ex 32:10

¹⁵So I turned and went down from the mountain while it was ablaze with fire. And the two tablets of the covenant were in my hands.ᵃ ¹⁶When I looked, I saw that you had sinned against the LORD your God; you had made for yourselves an idol cast in the shape of a calf. You had turned

aside quickly from the way that the LORD had commanded you. ¹⁷So I took the two tablets and threw them out of my hands, breaking them to pieces before your eyes.   Ex 32:15

¹⁸Then once again I fell prostrate before the LORD for forty days and forty nights; I ate no bread and drank no water, because of all the sin you had committed, doing what was evil in the LORD's sight and so provoking him to anger. ¹⁹I feared the anger and wrath of the LORD, for he was angry enough with you to destroy you. But again the LORD listened to me. ²⁰And the LORD was angry enough with Aaron to destroy him, but at that time I prayed for Aaron too. ²¹Also I took that sinful thing of yours, the calf you had made, and burned it in the fire. Then I crushed it and ground it to powder as fine as dust and threw the dust into a stream that flowed down the mountain.

²²You also made the LORD angry at Taberah, at Massah and at Kibroth Hattaavah.   Nu 11:3; Ex 17:7

²³And when the LORD sent you out from Kadesh Barnea, he said, "Go up and take possession of the land I have given you." But you rebelled against the command of the LORD your God. You did not trust him or obey him. ²⁴You have been rebellious against the LORD ever since I have known you.

²⁵I lay prostrate before the LORD

ᵃ15 Or And I had the two tablets of the covenant with me, one in each hand

those forty days and forty nights because the LORD had said he would destroy you. ²⁶I prayed to the LORD and said, "O Sovereign LORD, do not destroy your people, your own inheritance that you redeemed by your great power and brought out of Egypt with a mighty hand. ²⁷Remember your servants Abraham, Isaac and Jacob. Overlook the stubbornness of this people, their wickedness and their sin. ²⁸Otherwise, the country from which you brought us will say, 'Because the LORD was not able to take them into the land he had promised them, and because he hated them, he brought them out to put them to death in the desert.' ²⁹But they are your people, your inheritance that you brought out by your great power and your outstretched arm." Ex 32:11; Dt 4:20; 1Ki 8:51

Tablets Like the First Ones

10 At that time the LORD said to me, "Chisel out two stone tablets like the first ones and come up to me on the mountain. Also make a wooden chest.ᵃ ²I will write on the tablets the words that were on the first tablets, which you broke. Then you are to put them in the chest." Ex 25:16,21; 34:1-2

³So I made the ark out of acacia wood and chiseled out two stone tablets like the first ones, and I went up on the mountain with the two tablets in my hands. ⁴The LORD wrote on these tablets what he had written before, the Ten Commandments he had proclaimed to you on the mountain, out of the fire, on the day of the assembly. And the LORD gave them to me. ⁵Then I came back down the mountain and put the tablets in the ark I had made, as the LORD commanded me, and they are there now. Ex 20:1; 40:20

⁶(The Israelites traveled from the wells of the Jaakanites to Moserah. There Aaron died and was buried, and Eleazar his son succeeded him as priest. ⁷From there they traveled to Gudgodah and on to Jotbathah, a land with streams of water. ⁸At that time the LORD set apart the tribe of Levi to carry the ark of the covenant of the LORD, to stand before the LORD to minister and to pronounce blessings in his name, as they still do today. ⁹That is why the Levites have no share or inheritance among their brothers; the LORD is their inheritance, as the LORD your God told them.)

¹⁰Now I had stayed on the mountain forty days and nights, as I did the first time, and the LORD listened to me at this time also. It was not his will to destroy you. ¹¹"Go," the LORD said to me, "and lead the people on their way, so that they may enter and possess the land that I swore to their fathers to give them." Ex 34:28

ᵃ1 That is, an ark

Fear the LORD

[12]And now, O Israel, what does the LORD your God ask of you but to fear the LORD your God, to walk in all his ways, to love him, to serve the LORD your God with all your heart and with all your soul, [13]and to observe the LORD's commands and decrees that I am giving you today for your own good?

[14]To the LORD your God belong the heavens, even the highest heavens, the earth and everything in it. [15]Yet the LORD set his affection on your forefathers and loved them, and he chose you, their descendants, above all the nations, as it is today. [16]Circumcise your hearts, therefore, and do not be stiff-necked any longer. [17]For the LORD your God is God of gods and Lord of lords, the great God, mighty and awesome, who shows no partiality and accepts no bribes. [18]He defends the cause of the fatherless and the widow, and loves the alien, giving him food and clothing. [19]And you are to love those who are aliens, for you yourselves were aliens in Egypt. [20]Fear the LORD your God and serve him. Hold fast to him and take your oaths in his name. [21]He is your praise; he is your God, who performed for you those great and awesome wonders you saw with your own eyes. [22]Your forefathers who went down into Egypt were seventy in all, and now the LORD your God has made you as numerous as the stars in the sky.

Love and Obey the LORD

11 Love the LORD your God and keep his requirements, his decrees, his laws and his commands always. [2]Remember today that your children were not the ones who saw and experienced the discipline of the LORD your God: his majesty, his mighty hand, his outstretched arm; [3]the signs he performed and the things he did in the heart of Egypt, both to Pharaoh king of Egypt and to his whole country; [4]what he did to the Egyptian army, to its horses and chariots, how he overwhelmed them with the waters of the Red Sea[a] as they were pursuing you, and how the LORD brought lasting ruin on them. [5]It was not your children who saw what he did for you in the desert until you arrived at this place, [6]and what he did to Dathan and Abiram, sons of Eliab the Reubenite, when the earth opened its mouth right in the middle of all Israel and swallowed them up with their households, their tents and every living thing that belonged to them. [7]But it was your own eyes that saw all these great things the LORD has done.   Nu 16:1-35; Dt 5:24

[8]Observe therefore all the commands I am giving you today, so that you may have the strength to go in and take over the land that

---

[a]4 Hebrew *Yam Suph*; that is, Sea of Reeds

you are crossing the Jordan to possess, ⁹and so that you may live long in the land that the LORD swore to your forefathers to give to them and their descendants, a land flowing with milk and honey. ¹⁰The land you are entering to take over is not like the land of Egypt, from which you have come, where you planted your seed and irrigated it by foot as in a vegetable garden. ¹¹But the land you are crossing the Jordan to take possession of is a land of mountains and valleys that drinks rain from heaven. ¹²It is a land the LORD your God cares for; the eyes of the LORD your God are continually on it from the beginning of the year to its end.

¹³So if you faithfully obey the commands I am giving you today—to love the LORD your God and to serve him with all your heart and with all your soul— ¹⁴then I will send rain on your land in its season, both autumn and spring rains, so that you may gather in your grain, new wine and oil. ¹⁵I will provide grass in the fields for your cattle, and you will eat and be satisfied.   Dt 4:29; Joel 2:23; Ps 104:14

¹⁶Be careful, or you will be enticed to turn away and worship other gods and bow down to them. ¹⁷Then the LORD's anger will burn against you, and he will shut the heavens so that it will not rain and the ground will yield no produce, and you will soon perish from the good land the LORD is giving you. ¹⁸Fix these words of mine in your hearts and minds; tie them as symbols on your hands and bind them on your foreheads. ¹⁹Teach them to your children, talking about them when you sit at home and when you walk along the road, when you lie down and when you get up. ²⁰Write them on the doorframes of your houses and on your gates, ²¹so that your days and the days of your children may be many in the land that the LORD swore to give your forefathers, as many as the days that the heavens are above the earth.   Dt 4:9-10; 6:6-8

²²If you carefully observe all these commands I am giving you to follow—to love the LORD your God, to walk in all his ways and to hold fast to him— ²³then the LORD will drive out all these nations before you, and you will dispossess nations larger and stronger than you. ²⁴Every place where you set your foot will be yours: Your territory will extend from the desert to Lebanon, and from the Euphrates River to the western sea.ᵃ ²⁵No man will be able to stand against you. The LORD your God, as he promised you, will put the terror and fear of you on the whole land, wherever you go.   Ge 15:18; Dt 7:24; 9:1

²⁶See, I am setting before you today a blessing and a curse— ²⁷the blessing if you obey the commands of the LORD your God that

ᵃ24 That is, the Mediterranean

I am giving you today; 28the curse if you disobey the commands of the LORD your God and turn from the way that I command you today by following other gods, which you have not known. 29When the LORD your God has brought you into the land you are entering to possess, you are to proclaim on Mount Gerizim the blessings, and on Mount Ebal the curses. 30As you know, these mountains are across the Jordan, west of the road,*a* toward the setting sun, near the great trees of Moreh, in the territory of those Canaanites living in the Arabah in the vicinity of Gilgal. 31You are about to cross the Jordan to enter and take possession of the land the LORD your God is giving you. When you have taken it over and are living there, 32be sure that you obey all the decrees and laws I am setting before you today.

The One Place of Worship

12 These are the decrees and laws you must be careful to follow in the land that the LORD, the God of your fathers, has given you to possess—as long as you live in the land. 2Destroy completely all the places on the high mountains and on the hills and under every spreading tree where the nations you are dispossessing worship their gods. 3Break down their altars, smash their sacred stones and burn their Asherah poles in the fire; cut down the idols of their gods and wipe out their names from those places.   Dt 4:9-10; Nu 33:52

4You must not worship the LORD your God in their way. 5But you are to seek the place the LORD your God will choose from among all your tribes to put his Name there for his dwelling. To that place you must go; 6there bring your burnt offerings and sacrifices, your tithes and special gifts, what you have vowed to give and your free-will offerings, and the firstborn of your herds and flocks. 7There, in the presence of the LORD your God, you and your families shall eat and shall rejoice in everything you have put your hand to, because the LORD your God has blessed you.

8You are not to do as we do here today, everyone as he sees fit, 9since you have not yet reached the resting place and the inheritance the LORD your God is giving you. 10But you will cross the Jordan and settle in the land the LORD your God is giving you as an inheritance, and he will give you rest from all your enemies around you so that you will live in safety. 11Then to the place the LORD your God will choose as a dwelling for his Name—there you are to bring everything I command you: your burnt offerings and sacrifices, your tithes and special gifts, and all the choice possessions you have vowed to the LORD. 12And

a 30 Or *Jordan, westward*

there rejoice before the LORD your God, you, your sons and daughters, your menservants and maidservants, and the Levites from your towns, who have no allotment or inheritance of their own. ¹³Be careful not to sacrifice your burnt offerings anywhere you please. ¹⁴Offer them only at the place the LORD will choose in one of your tribes, and there observe everything I command you.

¹⁵Nevertheless, you may slaughter your animals in any of your towns and eat as much of the meat as you want, as if it were gazelle or deer, according to the blessing the LORD your God gives you. Both the ceremonially unclean and the clean may eat it. ¹⁶But you must not eat the blood; pour it out on the ground like water. ¹⁷You must not eat in your own towns the tithe of your grain and new wine and oil, or the firstborn of your herds and flocks, or whatever you have vowed to give, or your freewill offerings or special gifts. ¹⁸Instead, you are to eat them in the presence of the LORD your God at the place the LORD your God will choose—you, your sons and daughters, your menservants and maidservants, and the Levites from your towns—and you are to rejoice before the LORD your God in everything you put your hand to. ¹⁹Be careful not to neglect the Levites as long as you live in your land.

²⁰When the LORD your God has enlarged your territory as he promised you, and you crave meat and say, "I would like some meat," then you may eat as much of it as you want. ²¹If the place where the LORD your God chooses to put his Name is too far away from you, you may slaughter animals from the herds and flocks the LORD has given you, as I have commanded you, and in your own towns you may eat as much of them as you want. ²²Eat them as you would gazelle or deer. Both the ceremonially unclean and the clean may eat. ²³But be sure you do not eat the blood, because the blood is the life, and you must not eat the life with the meat. ²⁴You must not eat the blood; pour it out on the ground like water. ²⁵Do not eat it, so that it may go well with you and your children after you, because you will be doing what is right in the eyes of the LORD. Ge 15:18

²⁶But take your consecrated things and whatever you have vowed to give, and go to the place the LORD will choose. ²⁷Present your burnt offerings on the altar of the LORD your God, both the meat and the blood. The blood of your sacrifices must be poured beside the altar of the LORD your God, but you may eat the meat. ²⁸Be careful to obey all these regulations I am giving you, so that it may always go well with you and your children after you, because you will be doing what is good and right in the eyes of the LORD your God.

²⁹The LORD your God will cut off

before you the nations you are about to invade and dispossess. But when you have driven them out and settled in their land, ³⁰and after they have been destroyed before you, be careful not to be ensnared by inquiring about their gods, saying, "How do these nations serve their gods? We will do the same." ³¹You must not worship the LORD your God in their way, because in worshiping their gods, they do all kinds of detestable things the LORD hates. They even burn their sons and daughters in the fire as sacrifices to their gods.

³²See that you do all I command you; do not add to it or take away from it.   Dt 4:2

Worshiping Other Gods

13 If a prophet, or one who foretells by dreams, appears among you and announces to you a miraculous sign or wonder, ²and if the sign or wonder of which he has spoken takes place, and he says, "Let us follow other gods" (gods you have not known) "and let us worship them," ³you must not listen to the words of that prophet or dreamer. The LORD your God is testing you to find out whether you love him with all your heart and with all your soul. ⁴It is the LORD your God you must follow, and him you must revere. Keep his commands and obey him; serve him and hold fast to him. ⁵That prophet or dreamer must be put to death, because he preached rebellion against the LORD your God, who brought you out of Egypt and redeemed you from the land of slavery; he has tried to turn you from the way the LORD your God commanded you to follow. You must purge the evil from among you.   Dt 8:2,16; 2Ki 23:3

⁶If your very own brother, or your son or daughter, or the wife you love, or your closest friend secretly entices you, saying, "Let us go and worship other gods" (gods that neither you nor your fathers have known, ⁷gods of the peoples around you, whether near or far, from one end of the land to the other), ⁸do not yield to him or listen to him. Show him no pity. Do not spare him or shield him. ⁹You must certainly put him to death. Your hand must be the first in putting him to death, and then the hands of all the people. ¹⁰Stone him to death, because he tried to turn you away from the LORD your God, who brought you out of Egypt, out of the land of slavery. ¹¹Then all Israel will hear and be afraid, and no one among you will do such an evil thing again.

¹²If you hear it said about one of the towns the LORD your God is giving you to live in ¹³that wicked men have arisen among you and have led the people of their town astray, saying, "Let us go and worship other gods" (gods you have not known), ¹⁴then you must inquire, probe and investigate it thoroughly. And if it is true and it

has been proved that this detestable thing has been done among you, [15]you must certainly put to the sword all who live in that town. Destroy it completely,[a] both its people and its livestock. [16]Gather all the plunder of the town into the middle of the public square and completely burn the town and all its plunder as a whole burnt offering to the LORD your God. It is to remain a ruin forever, never to be rebuilt. [17]None of those condemned things[a] shall be found in your hands, so that the LORD will turn from his fierce anger; he will show you mercy, have compassion on you, and increase your numbers, as he promised on oath to your forefathers, [18]because you obey the LORD your God, keeping all his commands that I am giving you today and doing what is right in his eyes.   Jos 8:28; Nu 25:4; Dt 7:25-26

Clean and Unclean Food

14 You are the children of the LORD your God. Do not cut yourselves or shave the front of your heads for the dead, [2]for you are a people holy to the LORD your God. Out of all the peoples on the face of the earth, the LORD has chosen you to be his treasured possession.   Lev 21:5; Ro 8:14; Dt 7:6

[3]Do not eat any detestable thing. [4]These are the animals you may eat: the ox, the sheep, the goat, [5]the deer, the gazelle, the roe deer, the wild goat, the ibex, the antelope and the mountain sheep.[b] [6]You may eat any animal that has a split hoof divided in two and that chews the cud. [7]However, of those that chew the cud or that have a split hoof completely divided you may not eat the camel, the rabbit or the coney.[c] Although they chew the cud, they do not have a split hoof; they are ceremonially unclean for you. [8]The pig is also unclean; although it has a split hoof, it does not chew the cud. You are not to eat their meat or touch their carcasses.   Lev 11:2-45; Eze 4:14

[9]Of all the creatures living in the water, you may eat any that has fins and scales. [10]But anything that does not have fins and scales you may not eat; for you it is unclean.

[11]You may eat any clean bird. [12]But these you may not eat: the eagle, the vulture, the black vulture, [13]the red kite, the black kite, any kind of falcon, [14]any kind of raven, [15]the horned owl, the screech owl, the gull, any kind of hawk, [16]the little owl, the great owl, the white owl, [17]the desert owl, the osprey, the cormorant, [18]the stork, any kind of heron, the hoopoe and the bat.

[19]All flying insects that swarm are unclean to you; do not eat them. [20]But any winged creature that is clean you may eat.

---

[a]15,17 The Hebrew term refers to the irrevocable giving over of things or persons to the LORD, often by totally destroying them.   [b]5 The precise identification of some of the birds and animals in this chapter is uncertain.   [c]7 That is, the hyrax or rock badger

²¹Do not eat anything you find already dead. You may give it to an alien living in any of your towns, and he may eat it, or you may sell it to a foreigner. But you are a people holy to the LORD your God.

Do not cook a young goat in its mother's milk.   Ex 34:26

Tithes

²²Be sure to set aside a tenth of all that your fields produce each year. ²³Eat the tithe of your grain, new wine and oil, and the firstborn of your herds and flocks in the presence of the LORD your God at the place he will choose as a dwelling for his Name, so that you may learn to revere the LORD your God always. ²⁴But if that place is too distant and you have been blessed by the LORD your God and cannot carry your tithe (because the place where the LORD will choose to put his Name is so far away), ²⁵then exchange your tithe for silver, and take the silver with you and go to the place the LORD your God will choose. ²⁶Use the silver to buy whatever you like: cattle, sheep, wine or other fermented drink, or anything you wish. Then you and your household shall eat there in the presence of the LORD your God and rejoice. ²⁷And do not neglect the Levites living in your towns, for they have no allotment or inheritance of their own.   Lev 27:30

²⁸At the end of every three years, bring all the tithes of that year's produce and store it in your towns,

²⁹so that the Levites (who have no allotment or inheritance of their own) and the aliens, the fatherless and the widows who live in your towns may come and eat and be satisfied, and so that the LORD your God may bless you in all the work of your hands.   Dt 15:10; 26:12

The Year for Canceling Debts

15 At the end of every seven years you must cancel debts. ²This is how it is to be done: Every creditor shall cancel the loan he has made to his fellow Israelite. He shall not require payment from his fellow Israelite or brother, because the LORD's time for canceling debts has been proclaimed. ³You may require payment from a foreigner, but you must cancel any debt your brother owes you. ⁴However, there should be no poor among you, for in the land the LORD your God is giving you to possess as your inheritance, he will richly bless you, ⁵if only you fully obey the LORD your God and are careful to follow all these commands I am giving you today. ⁶For the LORD your God will bless you as he has promised, and you will lend to many nations but will borrow from none. You will rule over many nations but none will rule over you.   Dt 31:10; 23:20; 28:12-13,44

⁷If there is a poor man among your brothers in any of the towns of the land that the LORD your God is giving you, do not be hardhearted or tightfisted toward your poor

brother. [8]Rather be openhanded and freely lend him whatever he needs. [9]Be careful not to harbor this wicked thought: "The seventh year, the year for canceling debts, is near," so that you do not show ill will toward your needy brother and give him nothing. He may then appeal to the LORD against you, and you will be found guilty of sin. [10]Give generously to him and do so without a grudging heart; then because of this the LORD your God will bless you in all your work and in everything you put your hand to. [11]There will always be poor people in the land. Therefore I command you to be openhanded toward your brothers and toward the poor and needy in your land.   Lev 25:8-38; Mt 26:11; 1Jn 3:17

Freeing Servants

[12]If a fellow Hebrew, a man or a woman, sells himself to you and serves you six years, in the seventh year you must let him go free. [13]And when you release him, do not send him away empty-handed. [14]Supply him liberally from your flock, your threshing floor and your winepress. Give to him as the LORD your God has blessed you. [15]Remember that you were slaves in Egypt and the LORD your God redeemed you. That is why I give you this command today.   Ex 21:2-6

[16]But if your servant says to you, "I do not want to leave you," because he loves you and your family and is well off with you, [17]then take an awl and push it through his ear lobe into the door, and he will become your servant for life. Do the same for your maidservant.

[18]Do not consider it a hardship to set your servant free, because his service to you these six years has been worth twice as much as that of a hired hand. And the LORD your God will bless you in everything you do.

The Firstborn Animals

[19]Set apart for the LORD your God every firstborn male of your herds and flocks. Do not put the firstborn of your oxen to work, and do not shear the firstborn of your sheep. [20]Each year you and your family are to eat them in the presence of the LORD your God at the place he will choose. [21]If an animal has a defect, is lame or blind, or has any serious flaw, you must not sacrifice it to the LORD your God. [22]You are to eat it in your own towns. Both the ceremonially unclean and the clean may eat it, as if it were gazelle or deer. [23]But you must not eat the blood; pour it out on the ground like water.   Ex 13:2

Passover

16 Observe the month of Abib and celebrate the Passover of the LORD your God, because in the month of Abib he brought you out of Egypt by night. [2]Sacrifice as the Passover to the LORD your God an animal from your flock or herd at the place the LORD will choose as a dwelling for his Name. ³Do not eat it with bread made with yeast, but for seven days eat unleavened bread, the bread of affliction, because you left Egypt in haste—so that all the days of your life you may remember the time of your departure from Egypt. ⁴Let no yeast be found in your possession in all your land for seven days. Do not let any of the meat you sacrifice on the evening of the first day remain until morning.   Ex 12:2; 34:25

⁵You must not sacrifice the Passover in any town the LORD your God gives you ⁶except in the place he will choose as a dwelling for his Name. There you must sacrifice the Passover in the evening, when the sun goes down, on the anniversary[a] of your departure from Egypt. ⁷Roast it and eat it at the place the LORD your God will choose. Then in the morning return to your tents. ⁸For six days eat unleavened bread and on the seventh day hold an assembly to the LORD your God and do no work.

Feast of Weeks

⁹Count off seven weeks from the time you begin to put the sickle to the standing grain. ¹⁰Then celebrate the Feast of Weeks to the LORD your God by giving a freewill offering in proportion to the blessings the LORD your God has given you. ¹¹And rejoice before the LORD your God at the place he will choose as a dwelling for his Name —you, your sons and daughters, your menservants and maidservants, the Levites in your towns, and the aliens, the fatherless and the widows living among you. ¹²Remember that you were slaves in Egypt, and follow carefully these decrees.   Lev 23:15-22; Nu 28:26-31

Feast of Tabernacles

¹³Celebrate the Feast of Tabernacles for seven days after you have gathered the produce of your threshing floor and your winepress. ¹⁴Be joyful at your Feast— you, your sons and daughters, your menservants and maidservants, and the Levites, the aliens, the fatherless and the widows who live in your towns. ¹⁵For seven days celebrate the Feast to the LORD your God at the place the LORD will choose. For the LORD your God will bless you in all your harvest and in all the work of your hands, and your joy will be complete.   Lev 23:34

¹⁶Three times a year all your men must appear before the LORD your God at the place he will choose: at the Feast of Unleavened Bread, the Feast of Weeks and the Feast of Tabernacles. No man should appear before the LORD empty-handed: ¹⁷Each of you must bring a gift in proportion to the way the LORD your God has blessed you.   Lev 23:33-43; Nu 29:12-39

---

a6 Or down, at the time of day

Judges

¹⁸Appoint judges and officials for each of your tribes in every town the LORD your God is giving you, and they shall judge the people fairly. ¹⁹Do not pervert justice or show partiality. Do not accept a bribe, for a bribe blinds the eyes of the wise and twists the words of the righteous. ²⁰Follow justice and justice alone, so that you may live and possess the land the LORD your God is giving you.   Ex 23:2,8; Dt 1:17

Worshiping Other Gods

²¹Do not set up any wooden Asherah pole^a beside the altar you build to the LORD your God, ²²and do not erect a sacred stone, for these the LORD your God hates.

17 Do not sacrifice to the LORD your God an ox or a sheep that has any defect or flaw in it, for that would be detestable to him.

²If a man or woman living among you in one of the towns the LORD gives you is found doing evil in the eyes of the LORD your God in violation of his covenant, ³and contrary to my command has worshiped other gods, bowing down to them or to the sun or the moon or the stars of the sky, ⁴and this has been brought to your attention, then you must investigate it thoroughly. If it is true and it has been proved that this detestable thing has been done in Israel, ⁵take the man or woman who has done this evil deed to your city gate and stone that person to death. ⁶On the testimony of two or three witnesses a man shall be put to death, but no one shall be put to death on the testimony of only one witness. ⁷The hands of the witnesses must be the first in putting him to death, and then the hands of all the people. You must purge the evil from among you.   Nu 35:30; Dt 13:6-11; Mt 18:16

Law Courts

⁸If cases come before your courts that are too difficult for you to judge—whether bloodshed, lawsuits or assaults—take them to the place the LORD your God will choose. ⁹Go to the priests, who are Levites, and to the judge who is in office at that time. Inquire of them and they will give you the verdict. ¹⁰You must act according to the decisions they give you at the place the LORD will choose. Be careful to do everything they direct you to do. ¹¹Act according to the law they teach you and the decisions they give you. Do not turn aside from what they tell you, to the right or to the left. ¹²The man who shows contempt for the judge or for the priest who stands ministering there to the LORD your God must be put to death. You must purge the evil from Israel. ¹³All the peo-

---

^a21 Or Do not plant any tree dedicated to Asherah

ple will hear and be afraid, and will not be contemptuous again.

The King

¹⁴When you enter the land the LORD your God is giving you and have taken possession of it and settled in it, and you say, "Let us set a king over us like all the nations around us," ¹⁵be sure to appoint over you the king the LORD your God chooses. He must be from among your own brothers. Do not place a foreigner over you, one who is not a brother Israelite. ¹⁶The king, moreover, must not acquire great numbers of horses for himself or make the people return to Egypt to get more of them, for the LORD has told you, "You are not to go back that way again." ¹⁷He must not take many wives, or his heart will be led astray. He must not accumulate large amounts of silver and gold.   1Sa 8:5,19-20; 1Ki 10:26

¹⁸When he takes the throne of his kingdom, he is to write for himself on a scroll a copy of this law, taken from that of the priests, who are Levites. ¹⁹It is to be with him, and he is to read it all the days of his life so that he may learn to revere the LORD his God and follow carefully all the words of this law and these decrees ²⁰and not consider himself better than his brothers and turn from the law to the right or to the left. Then he and his descendants will reign a long time over his kingdom in Israel.   Jos 1:8

Offerings for Priests and Levites

18 The priests, who are Levites—indeed the whole tribe of Levi—are to have no allotment or inheritance with Israel. They shall live on the offerings made to the LORD by fire, for that is their inheritance. ²They shall have no inheritance among their brothers; the LORD is their inheritance, as he promised them.

³This is the share due the priests from the people who sacrifice a bull or a sheep: the shoulder, the jowls and the inner parts. ⁴You are to give them the firstfruits of your grain, new wine and oil, and the first wool from the shearing of your sheep, ⁵for the LORD your God has chosen them and their descendants out of all your tribes to stand and minister in the LORD's name always.   Lev 7:28-34; Nu 18:12; Dt 10:8

⁶If a Levite moves from one of your towns anywhere in Israel where he is living, and comes in all earnestness to the place the LORD will choose, ⁷he may minister in the name of the LORD his God like all his fellow Levites who serve there in the presence of the LORD. ⁸He is to share equally in their benefits, even though he has received money from the sale of family possessions.   Ne 12:44,47

Detestable Practices

⁹When you enter the land the LORD your God is giving you, do

not learn to imitate the detestable ways of the nations there. [10]Let no one be found among you who sacrifices his son or daughter in[a] the fire, who practices divination or sorcery, interprets omens, engages in witchcraft, [11]or casts spells, or who is a medium or spiritist or who consults the dead. [12]Anyone who does these things is detestable to the LORD, and because of these detestable practices the LORD your God will drive out those nations before you. [13]You must be blameless before the LORD your God. Dt 12:31; Lev 18:24

The Prophet

[14]The nations you will dispossess listen to those who practice sorcery or divination. But as for you, the LORD your God has not permitted you to do so. [15]The LORD your God will raise up for you a prophet like me from among your own brothers. You must listen to him. [16]For this is what you asked of the LORD your God at Horeb on the day of the assembly when you said, "Let us not hear the voice of the LORD our God nor see this great fire anymore, or we will die."

[17]The LORD said to me: "What they say is good. [18]I will raise up for them a prophet like you from among their brothers; I will put my words in his mouth, and he will tell them everything I command him. [19]If anyone does not listen to my words that the prophet speaks in my name, I myself will call him to account. [20]But a prophet who presumes to speak in my name anything I have not commanded him to say, or a prophet who speaks in the name of other gods, must be put to death." Isa 51:16

[21]You may say to yourselves, "How can we know when a message has not been spoken by the LORD?" [22]If what a prophet proclaims in the name of the LORD does not take place or come true, that is a message the LORD has not spoken. That prophet has spoken presumptuously. Do not be afraid of him. Jer 28:9

Cities of Refuge

19 When the LORD your God has destroyed the nations whose land he is giving you, and when you have driven them out and settled in their towns and houses, [2]then set aside for yourselves three cities centrally located in the land the LORD your God is giving you to possess. [3]Build roads to them and divide into three parts the land the LORD your God is giving you as an inheritance, so that anyone who kills a man may flee there. Dt 12:29

[4]This is the rule concerning the man who kills another and flees there to save his life—one who kills his neighbor unintentionally, without malice aforethought. [5]For

---

a 10 Or who makes his son or daughter pass through

instance, a man may go into the forest with his neighbor to cut wood, and as he swings his ax to fell a tree, the head may fly off and hit his neighbor and kill him. That man may flee to one of these cities and save his life. ⁶Otherwise, the avenger of blood might pursue him in a rage, overtake him if the distance is too great, and kill him even though he is not deserving of death, since he did it to his neighbor without malice aforethought. ⁷This is why I command you to set aside for yourselves three cities.

⁸If the Lord your God enlarges your territory, as he promised on oath to your forefathers, and gives you the whole land he promised them, ⁹because you carefully follow all these laws I command you today—to love the Lord your God and to walk always in his ways—then you are to set aside three more cities. ¹⁰Do this so that innocent blood will not be shed in your land, which the Lord your God is giving you as your inheritance, and so that you will not be guilty of bloodshed.   Dt 21:1-9

¹¹But if a man hates his neighbor and lies in wait for him, assaults and kills him, and then flees to one of these cities, ¹²the elders of his town shall send for him, bring him back from the city, and hand him over to the avenger of blood to die. ¹³Show him no pity. You must purge from Israel the guilt of shedding innocent blood, so that it may go well with you.

¹⁴Do not move your neighbor's boundary stone set up by your predecessors in the inheritance you receive in the land the Lord your God is giving you to possess.

Witnesses

¹⁵One witness is not enough to convict a man accused of any crime or offense he may have committed. A matter must be established by the testimony of two or three witnesses.

¹⁶If a malicious witness takes the stand to accuse a man of a crime, ¹⁷the two men involved in the dispute must stand in the presence of the Lord before the priests and the judges who are in office at the time. ¹⁸The judges must make a thorough investigation, and if the witness proves to be a liar, giving false testimony against his brother, ¹⁹then do to him as he intended to do to his brother. You must purge the evil from among you. ²⁰The rest of the people will hear of this and be afraid, and never again will such an evil thing be done among you. ²¹Show no pity: life for life, eye for eye, tooth for tooth, hand for hand, foot for foot.

Going to War

20 When you go to war against your enemies and see horses and chariots and an army greater than yours, do not be afraid of them, because the Lord your God, who brought you up out of Egypt, will be with you. ²When

you are about to go into battle, the priest shall come forward and address the army. ³He shall say: "Hear, O Israel, today you are going into battle against your enemies. Do not be fainthearted or afraid; do not be terrified or give way to panic before them. ⁴For the LORD your God is the one who goes with you to fight for you against your enemies to give you victory."

⁵The officers shall say to the army: "Has anyone built a new house and not dedicated it? Let him go home, or he may die in battle and someone else may dedicate it. ⁶Has anyone planted a vineyard and not begun to enjoy it? Let him go home, or he may die in battle and someone else enjoy it. ⁷Has anyone become pledged to a woman and not married her? Let him go home, or he may die in battle and someone else marry her." ⁸Then the officers shall add, "Is any man afraid or fainthearted? Let him go home so that his brothers will not become disheartened too." ⁹When the officers have finished speaking to the army, they shall appoint commanders over it.   Dt 24:5; Jdg 7:3

¹⁰When you march up to attack a city, make its people an offer of peace. ¹¹If they accept and open their gates, all the people in it shall be subject to forced labor and shall work for you. ¹²If they refuse to make peace and they engage you in battle, lay siege to that city. ¹³When the LORD your God delivers it into your hand, put to the sword all the men in it. ¹⁴As for the women, the children, the livestock and everything else in the city, you may take these as plunder for yourselves. And you may use the plunder the LORD your God gives you from your enemies. ¹⁵This is how you are to treat all the cities that are at a distance from you and do not belong to the nations nearby.   Nu 31:7; Jos 8:2; 1Ki 9:21

¹⁶However, in the cities of the nations the LORD your God is giving you as an inheritance, do not leave alive anything that breathes. ¹⁷Completely destroy[a] them—the Hittites, Amorites, Canaanites, Perizzites, Hivites and Jebusites—as the LORD your God has commanded you. ¹⁸Otherwise, they will teach you to follow all the detestable things they do in worshiping their gods, and you will sin against the LORD your God.

¹⁹When you lay siege to a city for a long time, fighting against it to capture it, do not destroy its trees by putting an ax to them, because you can eat their fruit. Do not cut them down. Are the trees of the field people, that you should besiege them?[b] ²⁰However, you may cut down trees that you know are not fruit trees and use them to

---

a 17 The Hebrew term refers to the irrevocable giving over of things or persons to the LORD, often by totally destroying them.   b 19 Or down to use in the siege, for the fruit trees are for the benefit of man.

build siege works until the city at war with you falls.

Atonement for an Unsolved Murder

21 If a man is found slain, lying in a field in the land the LORD your God is giving you to possess, and it is not known who killed him, ²your elders and judges shall go out and measure the distance from the body to the neighboring towns. ³Then the elders of the town nearest the body shall take a heifer that has never been worked and has never worn a yoke ⁴and lead her down to a valley that has not been plowed or planted and where there is a flowing stream. There in the valley they are to break the heifer's neck. ⁵The priests, the sons of Levi, shall step forward, for the LORD your God has chosen them to minister and to pronounce blessings in the name of the LORD and to decide all cases of dispute and assault. ⁶Then all the elders of the town nearest the body shall wash their hands over the heifer whose neck was broken in the valley, ⁷and they shall declare: "Our hands did not shed this blood, nor did our eyes see it done. ⁸Accept this atonement for your people Israel, whom you have redeemed, O LORD, and do not hold your people guilty of the blood of an innocent man." And the bloodshed will be atoned for. ⁹So you will purge from yourselves the guilt of shedding innocent blood, since you have done what is right in the eyes of the LORD.   Dt 17:8-11

Marrying a Captive Woman

¹⁰When you go to war against your enemies and the LORD your God delivers them into your hands and you take captives, ¹¹if you notice among the captives a beautiful woman and are attracted to her, you may take her as your wife. ¹²Bring her into your home and have her shave her head, trim her nails ¹³and put aside the clothes she was wearing when captured. After she has lived in your house and mourned her father and mother for a full month, then you may go to her and be her husband and she shall be your wife. ¹⁴If you are not pleased with her, let her go wherever she wishes. You must not sell her or treat her as a slave, since you have dishonored her.

The Right of the Firstborn

¹⁵If a man has two wives, and he loves one but not the other, and both bear him sons but the firstborn is the son of the wife he does not love, ¹⁶when he wills his property to his sons, he must not give the rights of the firstborn to the son of the wife he loves in preference to his actual firstborn, the son of the wife he does not love. ¹⁷He must acknowledge the son of his unloved wife as the firstborn by giving him a double share of all he has. That son is the first sign of his

father's strength. The right of the firstborn belongs to him.   Ge 29:33

A Rebellious Son

¹⁸If a man has a stubborn and rebellious son who does not obey his father and mother and will not listen to them when they discipline him, ¹⁹his father and mother shall take hold of him and bring him to the elders at the gate of his town. ²⁰They shall say to the elders, "This son of ours is stubborn and rebellious. He will not obey us. He is a profligate and a drunkard." ²¹Then all the men of his town shall stone him to death. You must purge the evil from among you. All Israel will hear of it and be afraid.   Dt 13:11; Eph 6:1-3

Various Laws

²²If a man guilty of a capital offense is put to death and his body is hung on a tree, ²³you must not leave his body on the tree overnight. Be sure to bury him that same day, because anyone who is hung on a tree is under God's curse. You must not desecrate the land the LORD your God is giving you as an inheritance.   Gal 3:13

22 If you see your brother's ox or sheep straying, do not ignore it but be sure to take it back to him. ²If the brother does not live near you or if you do not know who he is, take it home with you and keep it until he comes looking for it. Then give it back to him. ³Do the same if you find your brother's donkey or his cloak or anything he loses. Do not ignore it.

⁴If you see your brother's donkey or his ox fallen on the road, do not ignore it. Help him get it to its feet.

⁵A woman must not wear men's clothing, nor a man wear women's clothing, for the LORD your God detests anyone who does this.

⁶If you come across a bird's nest beside the road, either in a tree or on the ground, and the mother is sitting on the young or on the eggs, do not take the mother with the young. ⁷You may take the young, but be sure to let the mother go, so that it may go well with you and you may have a long life.   Lev 22:28

⁸When you build a new house, make a parapet around your roof so that you may not bring the guilt of bloodshed on your house if someone falls from the roof.

⁹Do not plant two kinds of seed in your vineyard; if you do, not only the crops you plant but also the fruit of the vineyard will be defiled.ᵃ   Lev 19:19

¹⁰Do not plow with an ox and a donkey yoked together.   2Co 6:14

¹¹Do not wear clothes of wool and linen woven together.

¹²Make tassels on the four corners of the cloak you wear.

ᵃ9 Or be forfeited to the sanctuary

Marriage Violations

¹³If a man takes a wife and, after lying with her, dislikes her ¹⁴and slanders her and gives her a bad name, saying, "I married this woman, but when I approached her, I did not find proof of her virginity," ¹⁵then the girl's father and mother shall bring proof that she was a virgin to the town elders at the gate. ¹⁶The girl's father will say to the elders, "I gave my daughter in marriage to this man, but he dislikes her. ¹⁷Now he has slandered her and said, 'I did not find your daughter to be a virgin.' But here is the proof of my daughter's virginity." Then her parents shall display the cloth before the elders of the town, ¹⁸and the elders shall take the man and punish him. ¹⁹They shall fine him a hundred shekels of silver[a] and give them to the girl's father, because this man has given an Israelite virgin a bad name. She shall continue to be his wife; he must not divorce her as long as he lives. Ex 18:21; Dt 1:9-18

²⁰If, however, the charge is true and no proof of the girl's virginity can be found, ²¹she shall be brought to the door of her father's house and there the men of her town shall stone her to death. She has done a disgraceful thing in Israel by being promiscuous while still in her father's house. You must purge the evil from among you. Ge 34:7; Dt 13:5

²²If a man is found sleeping with another man's wife, both the man who slept with her and the woman must die. You must purge the evil from Israel. Lev 20:10; Jn 8:5

²³If a man happens to meet in a town a virgin pledged to be married and he sleeps with her, ²⁴you shall take both of them to the gate of that town and stone them to death—the girl because she was in a town and did not scream for help, and the man because he violated another man's wife. You must purge the evil from among you.

²⁵But if out in the country a man happens to meet a girl pledged to be married and rapes her, only the man who has done this shall die. ²⁶Do nothing to the girl; she has committed no sin deserving death. This case is like that of someone who attacks and murders his neighbor, ²⁷for the man found the girl out in the country, and though the betrothed girl screamed, there was no one to rescue her.

²⁸If a man happens to meet a virgin who is not pledged to be married and rapes her and they are discovered, ²⁹he shall pay the girl's father fifty shekels of silver.[b] He must marry the girl, for he has violated her. He can never divorce her as long as he lives. Ex 22:16

---

a 19 That is, about 2 1/2 pounds (about 1 kilogram) kilogram)

b 29 That is, about 1 1/4 pounds (about 0.6

³⁰A man is not to marry his father's wife; he must not dishonor his father's bed.   Lev 18:8; Dt 27:20

Exclusion From the Assembly

23 No one who has been emasculated by crushing or cutting may enter the assembly of the Lord.

²No one born of a forbidden marriage[a] nor any of his descendants may enter the assembly of the Lord, even down to the tenth generation.

³No Ammonite or Moabite or any of his descendants may enter the assembly of the Lord, even down to the tenth generation. ⁴For they did not come to meet you with bread and water on your way when you came out of Egypt, and they hired Balaam son of Beor from Pethor in Aram Naharaim[b] to pronounce a curse on you. ⁵However, the Lord your God would not listen to Balaam but turned the curse into a blessing for you, because the Lord your God loves you. ⁶Do not seek a treaty of friendship with them as long as you live.   Nu 22:5-6; Ezr 9:12; Ne 13:2

⁷Do not abhor an Edomite, for he is your brother. Do not abhor an Egyptian, because you lived as an alien in his country. ⁸The third generation of children born to them may enter the assembly of the Lord.   Ge 25:26; Ex 22:21

Uncleanness in the Camp

⁹When you are encamped against your enemies, keep away from everything impure. ¹⁰If one of your men is unclean because of a nocturnal emission, he is to go outside the camp and stay there. ¹¹But as evening approaches he is to wash himself, and at sunset he may return to the camp.   Lev 15:16

¹²Designate a place outside the camp where you can go to relieve yourself. ¹³As part of your equipment have something to dig with, and when you relieve yourself, dig a hole and cover up your excrement. ¹⁴For the Lord your God moves about in your camp to protect you and to deliver your enemies to you. Your camp must be holy, so that he will not see among you anything indecent and turn away from you.   Lev 26:12

Miscellaneous Laws

¹⁵If a slave has taken refuge with you, do not hand him over to his master. ¹⁶Let him live among you wherever he likes and in whatever town he chooses. Do not oppress him.   1Sa 30:15

¹⁷No Israelite man or woman is to become a shrine prostitute. ¹⁸You must not bring the earnings of a female prostitute or of a male prostitute[c] into the house of the Lord your God to pay any vow, because the Lord your God detests them both.   Lev 19:29; 20:13

---

a2 Or one of illegitimate birth   b4 That is, Northwest Mesopotamia   c18 Hebrew of a dog

¹⁹Do not charge your brother interest, whether on money or food or anything else that may earn interest. ²⁰You may charge a foreigner interest, but not a brother Israelite, so that the LORD your God may bless you in everything you put your hand to in the land you are entering to possess.   Ex 22:25

²¹If you make a vow to the LORD your God, do not be slow to pay it, for the LORD your God will certainly demand it of you and you will be guilty of sin. ²²But if you refrain from making a vow, you will not be guilty. ²³Whatever your lips utter you must be sure to do, because you made your vow freely to the LORD your God with your own mouth.   Nu 30:1-2; Mt 5:33

²⁴If you enter your neighbor's vineyard, you may eat all the grapes you want, but do not put any in your basket. ²⁵If you enter your neighbor's grainfield, you may pick kernels with your hands, but you must not put a sickle to his standing grain.   Mt 12:1; Mk 2:23

24 If a man marries a woman who becomes displeasing to him because he finds something indecent about her, and he writes her a certificate of divorce, gives it to her and sends her from his house, ²and if after she leaves his house she becomes the wife of another man, ³and her second husband dislikes her and writes her a certificate of divorce, gives it to her and sends her from his house, or if he dies, ⁴then her first husband, who divorced her, is not allowed to marry her again after she has been defiled. That would be detestable in the eyes of the LORD. Do not bring sin upon the land the LORD your God is giving you as an inheritance.   Jer 3:1; Mt 5:31; 19:7-9

⁵If a man has recently married, he must not be sent to war or have any other duty laid on him. For one year he is to be free to stay at home and bring happiness to the wife he has married.   Dt 20:7

⁶Do not take a pair of millstones —not even the upper one—as security for a debt, because that would be taking a man's livelihood as security.

⁷If a man is caught kidnapping one of his brother Israelites and treats him as a slave or sells him, the kidnapper must die. You must purge the evil from among you.

⁸In cases of leprous ᵃ diseases be very careful to do exactly as the priests, who are Levites, instruct you. You must follow carefully what I have commanded them. ⁹Remember what the LORD your God did to Miriam along the way after you came out of Egypt.

¹⁰When you make a loan of any kind to your neighbor, do not go into his house to get what he is offering as a pledge. ¹¹Stay outside and let the man to whom you are making the loan bring the pledge

---

ᵃ8 The Hebrew word was used for various diseases affecting the skin—not necessarily leprosy.

out to you. ¹²If the man is poor, do not go to sleep with his pledge in your possession. ¹³Return his cloak to him by sunset so that he may sleep in it. Then he will thank you, and it will be regarded as a righteous act in the sight of the LORD your God.   Ex 22:26; Dt 6:25

¹⁴Do not take advantage of a hired man who is poor and needy, whether he is a brother Israelite or an alien living in one of your towns. ¹⁵Pay him his wages each day before sunset, because he is poor and is counting on it. Otherwise he may cry to the LORD against you, and you will be guilty of sin.   Lev 19:13; Jas 5:4

¹⁶Fathers shall not be put to death for their children, nor children put to death for their fathers; each is to die for his own sin.

¹⁷Do not deprive the alien or the fatherless of justice, or take the cloak of the widow as a pledge. ¹⁸Remember that you were slaves in Egypt and the LORD your God redeemed you from there. That is why I command you to do this.

¹⁹When you are harvesting in your field and you overlook a sheaf, do not go back to get it. Leave it for the alien, the fatherless and the widow, so that the LORD your God may bless you in all the work of your hands. ²⁰When you beat the olives from your trees, do not go over the branches a second time. Leave what remains for the alien, the fatherless and the widow. ²¹When you harvest the grapes in your vineyard, do not go over the vines again. Leave what remains for the alien, the fatherless and the widow. ²²Remember that you were slaves in Egypt. That is why I command you to do this.

25 When men have a dispute, they are to take it to court and the judges will decide the case, acquitting the innocent and condemning the guilty. ²If the guilty man deserves to be beaten, the judge shall make him lie down and have him flogged in his presence with the number of lashes his crime deserves, ³but he must not give him more than forty lashes. If he is flogged more than that, your brother will be degraded in your eyes.   Dt 17:8-13; 19:17; 2Co 11:24

⁴Do not muzzle an ox while it is treading out the grain.   1Ti 5:18

⁵If brothers are living together and one of them dies without a son, his widow must not marry outside the family. Her husband's brother shall take her and marry her and fulfill the duty of a brother-in-law to her. ⁶The first son she bears shall carry on the name of the dead brother so that his name will not be blotted out from Israel.

⁷However, if a man does not want to marry his brother's wife, she shall go to the elders at the town gate and say, "My husband's brother refuses to carry on his brother's name in Israel. He will not fulfill the duty of a brother-in-law to me." ⁸Then the elders of his town shall summon him and talk

to him. If he persists in saying, "I do not want to marry her," ⁹his brother's widow shall go up to him in the presence of the elders, take off one of his sandals, spit in his face and say, "This is what is done to the man who will not build up his brother's family line." ¹⁰That man's line shall be known in Israel as The Family of the Unsandaled.

¹¹If two men are fighting and the wife of one of them comes to rescue her husband from his assailant, and she reaches out and seizes him by his private parts, ¹²you shall cut off her hand. Show her no pity.

¹³Do not have two differing weights in your bag—one heavy, one light. ¹⁴Do not have two differing measures in your house—one large, one small. ¹⁵You must have accurate and honest weights and measures, so that you may live long in the land the Lᴏʀᴅ your God is giving you. ¹⁶For the Lᴏʀᴅ your God detests anyone who does these things, anyone who deals dishonestly.   Lev 19:35-37; Pr 11:1

¹⁷Remember what the Amalekites did to you along the way when you came out of Egypt. ¹⁸When you were weary and worn out, they met you on your journey and cut off all who were lagging behind; they had no fear of God. ¹⁹When the Lᴏʀᴅ your God gives you rest from all the enemies around you in the land he is giving you to possess as an inheritance, you shall blot out the memory of Amalek from under heaven. Do not forget!   Ex 17:8; Ps 36:1; 1Sa 15:2-3

Firstfruits and Tithes

26 When you have entered the land the Lᴏʀᴅ your God is giving you as an inheritance and have taken possession of it and settled in it, ²take some of the firstfruits of all that you produce from the soil of the land the Lᴏʀᴅ your God is giving you and put them in a basket. Then go to the place the Lᴏʀᴅ your God will choose as a dwelling for his Name ³and say to the priest in office at the time, "I declare today to the Lᴏʀᴅ your God that I have come to the land the Lᴏʀᴅ swore to our forefathers to give us." ⁴The priest shall take the basket from your hands and set it down in front of the altar of the Lᴏʀᴅ your God. ⁵Then you shall declare before the Lᴏʀᴅ your God: "My father was a wandering Aramean, and he went down into Egypt with a few people and lived there and became a great nation, powerful and numerous. ⁶But the Egyptians mistreated us and made us suffer, putting us to hard labor. ⁷Then we cried out to the Lᴏʀᴅ, the God of our fathers, and the Lᴏʀᴅ heard our voice and saw our misery, toil and oppression. ⁸So the Lᴏʀᴅ brought us out of Egypt with a mighty hand and an outstretched arm, with great terror and with miraculous signs and wonders. ⁹He brought us to this place and gave us this land, a land flowing with

milk and honey; [10]and now I bring the firstfruits of the soil that you, O Lord, have given me." Place the basket before the Lord your God and bow down before him. [11]And you and the Levites and the aliens among you shall rejoice in all the good things the Lord your God has given to you and your household.

[12]When you have finished setting aside a tenth of all your produce in the third year, the year of the tithe, you shall give it to the Levite, the alien, the fatherless and the widow, so that they may eat in your towns and be satisfied. [13]Then say to the Lord your God: "I have removed from my house the sacred portion and have given it to the Levite, the alien, the fatherless and the widow, according to all you commanded. I have not turned aside from your commands nor have I forgotten any of them. [14]I have not eaten any of the sacred portion while I was in mourning, nor have I removed any of it while I was unclean, nor have I offered any of it to the dead. I have obeyed the Lord my God; I have done everything you commanded me. [15]Look down from heaven, your holy dwelling place, and bless your people Israel and the land you have given us as you promised on oath to our forefathers, a land flowing with milk and honey."

Follow the Lord's Commands

[16]The Lord your God commands you this day to follow these decrees and laws; carefully observe them with all your heart and with all your soul. [17]You have declared this day that the Lord is your God and that you will walk in his ways, that you will keep his decrees, commands and laws, and that you will obey him. [18]And the Lord has declared this day that you are his people, his treasured possession as he promised, and that you are to keep all his commands. [19]He has declared that he will set you in praise, fame and honor high above all the nations he has made and that you will be a people holy to the Lord your God, as he promised.   Dt 7:6; 28:1,13,44; 4:7-8

The Altar on Mount Ebal

27 Moses and the elders of Israel commanded the people: "Keep all these commands that I give you today. [2]When you have crossed the Jordan into the land the Lord your God is giving you, set up some large stones and coat them with plaster. [3]Write on them all the words of this law when you have crossed over to enter the land the Lord your God is giving you, a land flowing with milk and honey, just as the Lord, the God of your fathers, promised you. [4]And when you have crossed the Jordan, set up these stones on Mount Ebal, as I command you today, and coat them with plaster. [5]Build there an altar to the Lord your God, an altar of stones. Do not use any iron tool upon them.

⁶Build the altar of the LORD your God with fieldstones and offer burnt offerings on it to the LORD your God. ⁷Sacrifice fellowship offerings*a* there, eating them and rejoicing in the presence of the LORD your God. ⁸And you shall write very clearly all the words of this law on these stones you have set up." Ex 20:25; Dt 26:9; Jos 8:31

Curses From Mount Ebal

⁹Then Moses and the priests, who are Levites, said to all Israel, "Be silent, O Israel, and listen! You have now become the people of the LORD your God. ¹⁰Obey the LORD your God and follow his commands and decrees that I give you today."

¹¹On the same day Moses commanded the people:

¹²When you have crossed the Jordan, these tribes shall stand on Mount Gerizim to bless the people: Simeon, Levi, Judah, Issachar, Joseph and Benjamin. ¹³And these tribes shall stand on Mount Ebal to pronounce curses: Reuben, Gad, Asher, Zebulun, Dan and Naphtali.

¹⁴The Levites shall recite to all the people of Israel in a loud voice:

¹⁵"Cursed is the man who carves an image or casts an idol—a thing detestable to the LORD, the work of the craftsman's hands—and sets it up in secret." Ex 20:4; 34:17

Then all the people shall say, "Amen!"

¹⁶"Cursed is the man who dishonors his father or his mother." Ex 21:17

Then all the people shall say, "Amen!"

¹⁷"Cursed is the man who moves his neighbor's boundary stone." Pr 22:28

Then all the people shall say, "Amen!"

¹⁸"Cursed is the man who leads the blind astray on the road." Lev 19:14

Then all the people shall say, "Amen!"

¹⁹"Cursed is the man who withholds justice from the alien, the fatherless or the widow." Dt 10:18; 24:19

Then all the people shall say, "Amen!"

²⁰"Cursed is the man who sleeps with his father's wife, for he dishonors his father's bed." Lev 18:7; Dt 22:30

Then all the people shall say, "Amen!"

²¹"Cursed is the man who has sexual relations with any animal." Lev 18:23

Then all the people shall say, "Amen!"

²²"Cursed is the man who sleeps with his sister, the daughter of his father or the daughter of his mother."

---

a 7 Traditionally *peace offerings*

Then all the people shall say, "Amen!"

23"Cursed is the man who sleeps with his mother-in-law."

Then all the people shall say, "Amen!"

24"Cursed is the man who kills his neighbor secretly."

Then all the people shall say, "Amen!"

25"Cursed is the man who accepts a bribe to kill an innocent person."   Ex 23:7-8

Then all the people shall say, "Amen!"

26"Cursed is the man who does not uphold the words of this law by carrying them out."   Gal 3:10

Then all the people shall say, "Amen!"

Blessings for Obedience

28 If you fully obey the Lord your God and carefully follow all his commands I give you today, the Lord your God will set you high above all the nations on earth. 2All these blessings will come upon you and accompany you if you obey the Lord your God:

3You will be blessed in the city and blessed in the country.   Ge 39:5

4The fruit of your womb will be blessed, and the crops of your land and the young of your livestock—the calves of your herds and the lambs of your flocks.   Ge 49:25

5Your basket and your kneading trough will be blessed.

6You will be blessed when you come in and blessed when you go out.   Ps 121:8

7The Lord will grant that the enemies who rise up against you will be defeated before you. They will come at you from one direction but flee from you in seven.

8The Lord will send a blessing on your barns and on everything you put your hand to. The Lord your God will bless you in the land he is giving you.

9The Lord will establish you as his holy people, as he promised you on oath, if you keep the commands of the Lord your God and walk in his ways. 10Then all the peoples on earth will see that you are called by the name of the Lord, and they will fear you. 11The Lord will grant you abundant prosperity—in the fruit of your womb, the young of your livestock and the crops of your ground—in the land he swore to your forefathers to give you.   Ex 19:6; 2Ch 7:14

12The Lord will open the heavens, the storehouse of his bounty, to send rain on your land in season and to bless all the work of your hands. You will lend to many nations but will borrow from none. 13The Lord will make you the head, not the tail. If you pay attention to the commands of the Lord your God that I give you this day and carefully follow them, you will always be at the top, never at the bottom. ¹⁴Do not turn aside from any of the commands I give you today, to the right or to the left, following other gods and serving them. Lev 26:4; Dt 5:32; 15:3,6

Curses for Disobedience

¹⁵However, if you do not obey the LORD your God and do not carefully follow all his commands and decrees I am giving you today, all these curses will come upon you and overtake you:

¹⁶You will be cursed in the city and cursed in the country.

¹⁷Your basket and your kneading trough will be cursed.

¹⁸The fruit of your womb will be cursed, and the crops of your land, and the calves of your herds and the lambs of your flocks.

¹⁹You will be cursed when you come in and cursed when you go out.

²⁰The LORD will send on you curses, confusion and rebuke in everything you put your hand to, until you are destroyed and come to sudden ruin because of the evil you have done in forsaking him.ᵃ ²¹The LORD will plague you with diseases until he has destroyed you from the land you are entering

to possess. ²²The LORD will strike you with wasting disease, with fever and inflammation, with scorching heat and drought, with blight and mildew, which will plague you until you perish. ²³The sky over your head will be bronze, the ground beneath you iron. ²⁴The LORD will turn the rain of your country into dust and powder; it will come down from the skies until you are destroyed.

²⁵The LORD will cause you to be defeated before your enemies. You will come at them from one direction but flee from them in seven, and you will become a thing of horror to all the kingdoms on earth. ²⁶Your carcasses will be food for all the birds of the air and the beasts of the earth, and there will be no one to frighten them away. ²⁷The LORD will afflict you with the boils of Egypt and with tumors, festering sores and the itch, from which you cannot be cured. ²⁸The LORD will afflict you with madness, blindness and confusion of mind. ²⁹At midday you will grope about like a blind man in the dark. You will be unsuccessful in everything you do; day after day you will be oppressed and robbed, with no one to rescue you.

³⁰You will be pledged to be married to a woman, but another will take her and ravish her. You will build a house, but you will not live in it. You will plant a vineyard, but

ᵃ 20 Hebrew me

you will not even begin to enjoy its fruit. ³¹Your ox will be slaughtered before your eyes, but you will eat none of it. Your donkey will be forcibly taken from you and will not be returned. Your sheep will be given to your enemies, and no one will rescue them. ³²Your sons and daughters will be given to another nation, and you will wear out your eyes watching for them day after day, powerless to lift a hand. ³³A people that you do not know will eat what your land and labor produce, and you will have nothing but cruel oppression all your days. ³⁴The sights you see will drive you mad. ³⁵The LORD will afflict your knees and legs with painful boils that cannot be cured, spreading from the soles of your feet to the top of your head.

³⁶The LORD will drive you and the king you set over you to a nation unknown to you or your fathers. There you will worship other gods, gods of wood and stone. ³⁷You will become a thing of horror and an object of scorn and ridicule to all the nations where the LORD will drive you. Dt 4:28; Jer 16:13

³⁸You will sow much seed in the field but you will harvest little, because locusts will devour it. ³⁹You will plant vineyards and cultivate them but you will not drink the wine or gather the grapes, because worms will eat them. ⁴⁰You will have olive trees throughout your country but you will not use the oil, because the olives will drop off. ⁴¹You will have sons and daughters but you will not keep them, because they will go into captivity. ⁴²Swarms of locusts will take over all your trees and the crops of your land. Joel 1:4; Mic 6:15

⁴³The alien who lives among you will rise above you higher and higher, but you will sink lower and lower. ⁴⁴He will lend to you, but you will not lend to him. He will be the head, but you will be the tail.

⁴⁵All these curses will come upon you. They will pursue you and overtake you until you are destroyed, because you did not obey the LORD your God and observe the commands and decrees he gave you. ⁴⁶They will be a sign and a wonder to you and your descendants forever. ⁴⁷Because you did not serve the LORD your God joyfully and gladly in the time of prosperity, ⁴⁸therefore in hunger and thirst, in nakedness and dire poverty, you will serve the enemies the LORD sends against you. He will put an iron yoke on your neck until he has destroyed you.

⁴⁹The LORD will bring a nation against you from far away, from the ends of the earth, like an eagle swooping down, a nation whose language you will not understand, ⁵⁰a fierce-looking nation without respect for the old or pity for the young. ⁵¹They will devour the young of your livestock and the crops of your land until you are destroyed. They will leave you no grain, new wine or oil, nor any

calves of your herds or lambs of your flocks until you are ruined. ⁵²They will lay siege to all the cities throughout your land until the high fortified walls in which you trust fall down. They will besiege all the cities throughout the land the LORD your God is giving you.

⁵³Because of the suffering that your enemy will inflict on you during the siege, you will eat the fruit of the womb, the flesh of the sons and daughters the LORD your God has given you. ⁵⁴Even the most gentle and sensitive man among you will have no compassion on his own brother or the wife he loves or his surviving children, ⁵⁵and he will not give to one of them any of the flesh of his children that he is eating. It will be all he has left because of the suffering your enemy will inflict on you during the siege of all your cities. ⁵⁶The most gentle and sensitive woman among you—so sensitive and gentle that she would not venture to touch the ground with the sole of her foot—will begrudge the husband she loves and her own son or daughter ⁵⁷the afterbirth from her womb and the children she bears. For she intends to eat them secretly during the siege and in the distress that your enemy will inflict on you in your cities.

⁵⁸If you do not carefully follow all the words of this law, which are written in this book, and do not revere this glorious and awesome name—the LORD your God— ⁵⁹the LORD will send fearful plagues on you and your descendants, harsh and prolonged disasters, and severe and lingering illnesses. ⁶⁰He will bring upon you all the diseases of Egypt that you dreaded, and they will cling to you. ⁶¹The LORD will also bring on you every kind of sickness and disaster not recorded in this Book of the Law, until you are destroyed. ⁶²You who were as numerous as the stars in the sky will be left but few in number, because you did not obey the LORD your God. ⁶³Just as it pleased the LORD to make you prosper and increase in number, so it will please him to ruin and destroy you. You will be uprooted from the land you are entering to possess.

⁶⁴Then the LORD will scatter you among all nations, from one end of the earth to the other. There you will worship other gods—gods of wood and stone, which neither you nor your fathers have known. ⁶⁵Among those nations you will find no repose, no resting place for the sole of your foot. There the LORD will give you an anxious mind, eyes weary with longing, and a despairing heart. ⁶⁶You will live in constant suspense, filled with dread both night and day, never sure of your life. ⁶⁷In the morning you will say, "If only it were evening!" and in the evening, "If only it were morning!"—because of the terror that will fill your hearts and the sights that your eyes will see. ⁶⁸The LORD will

send you back in ships to Egypt on a journey I said you should never make again. There you will offer yourselves for sale to your enemies as male and female slaves, but no one will buy you.   Dt 4:27

Renewal of the Covenant

29 These are the terms of the covenant the LORD commanded Moses to make with the Israelites in Moab, in addition to the covenant he had made with them at Horeb.   Dt 5:2-3

²Moses summoned all the Israelites and said to them:

Your eyes have seen all that the LORD did in Egypt to Pharaoh, to all his officials and to all his land. ³With your own eyes you saw those great trials, those miraculous signs and great wonders. ⁴But to this day the LORD has not given you a mind that understands or eyes that see or ears that hear. ⁵During the forty years that I led you through the desert, your clothes did not wear out, nor did the sandals on your feet. ⁶You ate no bread and drank no wine or other fermented drink. I did this so that you might know that I am the LORD your God.   Dt 8:4; Isa 6:10; Ro 11:8

⁷When you reached this place, Sihon king of Heshbon and Og king of Bashan came out to fight against us, but we defeated them. ⁸We took their land and gave it as an inheritance to the Reubenites,

the Gadites and the half-tribe of Manasseh.   Nu 21:21-24,33-35; 32:33

⁹Carefully follow the terms of this covenant, so that you may prosper in everything you do. ¹⁰All of you are standing today in the presence of the LORD your God—your leaders and chief men, your elders and officials, and all the other men of Israel, ¹¹together with your children and your wives, and the aliens living in your camps who chop your wood and carry your water. ¹²You are standing here in order to enter into a covenant with the LORD your God, a covenant the LORD is making with you this day and sealing with an oath, ¹³to confirm you this day as his people, that he may be your God as he promised you and as he swore to your fathers, Abraham, Isaac and Jacob. ¹⁴I am making this covenant, with its oath, not only with you ¹⁵who are standing here with us today in the presence of the LORD our God but also with those who are not here today.

¹⁶You yourselves know how we lived in Egypt and how we passed through the countries on the way here. ¹⁷You saw among them their detestable images and idols of wood and stone, of silver and gold. ¹⁸Make sure there is no man or woman, clan or tribe among you today whose heart turns away from the LORD our God to go and worship the gods of those nations; make sure there is no root among

you that produces such bitter poison.   Dt 28:36; Heb 12:15

[19]When such a person hears the words of this oath, he invokes a blessing on himself and therefore thinks, "I will be safe, even though I persist in going my own way." This will bring disaster on the watered land as well as the dry.[a] [20]The LORD will never be willing to forgive him; his wrath and zeal will burn against that man. All the curses written in this book will fall upon him, and the LORD will blot out his name from under heaven. [21]The LORD will single him out from all the tribes of Israel for disaster, according to all the curses of the covenant written in this Book of the Law.   Dt 9:14; Ps 74:1; 79:5

[22]Your children who follow you in later generations and foreigners who come from distant lands will see the calamities that have fallen on the land and the diseases with which the LORD has afflicted it. [23]The whole land will be a burning waste of salt and sulfur—nothing planted, nothing sprouting, no vegetation growing on it. It will be like the destruction of Sodom and Gomorrah, Admah and Zeboiim, which the LORD overthrew in fierce anger. [24]All the nations will ask: "Why has the LORD done this to this land? Why this fierce, burning anger?"   Jer 19:8; 22:8-9; Zep 2:9

[25]And the answer will be: "It is because this people abandoned the covenant of the LORD, the God of their fathers, the covenant he made with them when he brought them out of Egypt. [26]They went off and worshiped other gods and bowed down to them, gods they did not know, gods he had not given them. [27]Therefore the LORD's anger burned against this land, so that he brought on it all the curses written in this book. [28]In furious anger and in great wrath the LORD uprooted them from their land and thrust them into another land, as it is now."   1Ki 14:15; 2Ki 17:23; Da 9:11,13-14

[29]The secret things belong to the LORD our God, but the things revealed belong to us and to our children forever, that we may follow all the words of this law.   2Ti 3:16

Prosperity After Turning to the LORD

30 When all these blessings and curses I have set before you come upon you and you take them to heart wherever the LORD your God disperses you among the nations, [2]and when you and your children return to the LORD your God and obey him with all your heart and with all your soul according to everything I command you today, [3]then the LORD your God will restore your fortunes[b] and have compassion on you and gather you again from all the nations where he scattered you. [4]Even if you have been ban-

---

[a] 19 Or way, in order to add drunkenness to thirst."   [b] 3 Or will bring you back from captivity

ished to the most distant land under the heavens, from there the LORD your God will gather you and bring you back. ⁵He will bring you to the land that belonged to your fathers, and you will take possession of it. He will make you more prosperous and numerous than your fathers. ⁶The LORD your God will circumcise your hearts and the hearts of your descendants, so that you may love him with all your heart and with all your soul, and live. ⁷The LORD your God will put all these curses on your enemies who hate and persecute you. ⁸You will again obey the LORD and follow all his commands I am giving you today. ⁹Then the LORD your God will make you most prosperous in all the work of your hands and in the fruit of your womb, the young of your livestock and the crops of your land. The LORD will again delight in you and make you prosperous, just as he delighted in your fathers, ¹⁰if you obey the LORD your God and keep his commands and decrees that are written in this Book of the Law and turn to the LORD your God with all your heart and with all your soul.   Dt 11:26; Ps 126:4; Jer 32:39

The Offer of Life or Death

¹¹Now what I am commanding you today is not too difficult for you or beyond your reach. ¹²It is not up in heaven, so that you have to ask, "Who will ascend into heaven to get it and proclaim it to us so we may obey it?" ¹³Nor is it beyond the sea, so that you have to ask, "Who will cross the sea to get it and proclaim it to us so we may obey it?" ¹⁴No, the word is very near you; it is in your mouth and in your heart so you may obey it.

¹⁵See, I set before you today life and prosperity, death and destruction. ¹⁶For I command you today to love the LORD your God, to walk in his ways, and to keep his commands, decrees and laws; then you will live and increase, and the LORD your God will bless you in the land you are entering to possess.   Dt 4:1

¹⁷But if your heart turns away and you are not obedient, and if you are drawn away to bow down to other gods and worship them, ¹⁸I declare to you this day that you will certainly be destroyed. You will not live long in the land you are crossing the Jordan to enter and possess.   Dt 8:19

¹⁹This day I call heaven and earth as witnesses against you that I have set before you life and death, blessings and curses. Now choose life, so that you and your children may live ²⁰and that you may love the LORD your God, listen to his voice, and hold fast to him. For the LORD is your life, and he will give you many years in the land he swore to give to your fathers, Abraham, Isaac and Jacob.

Joshua to Succeed Moses

31 Then Moses went out and spoke these words to all Israel: ²"I am now a hundred and twenty years old and I am no longer able to lead you. The Lord has said to me, 'You shall not cross the Jordan.' ³The Lord your God himself will cross over ahead of you. He will destroy these nations before you, and you will take possession of their land. Joshua also will cross over ahead of you, as the Lord said. ⁴And the Lord will do to them what he did to Sihon and Og, the kings of the Amorites, whom he destroyed along with their land. ⁵The Lord will deliver them to you, and you must do to them all that I have commanded you. ⁶Be strong and courageous. Do not be afraid or terrified because of them, for the Lord your God goes with you; he will never leave you nor forsake you."   Dt 3:23,26; 7:2; Jos 10:25

⁷Then Moses summoned Joshua and said to him in the presence of all Israel, "Be strong and courageous, for you must go with this people into the land that the Lord swore to their forefathers to give them, and you must divide it among them as their inheritance. ⁸The Lord himself goes before you and will be with you; he will never leave you nor forsake you. Do not be afraid; do not be discouraged."

The Reading of the Law

⁹So Moses wrote down this law and gave it to the priests, the sons of Levi, who carried the ark of the covenant of the Lord, and to all the elders of Israel. ¹⁰Then Moses commanded them: "At the end of every seven years, in the year for canceling debts, during the Feast of Tabernacles, ¹¹when all Israel comes to appear before the Lord your God at the place he will choose, you shall read this law before them in their hearing. ¹²Assemble the people—men, women and children, and the aliens living in your towns—so they can listen and learn to fear the Lord your God and follow carefully all the words of this law. ¹³Their children, who do not know this law, must hear it and learn to fear the Lord your God as long as you live in the land you are crossing the Jordan to possess."   Nu 4:15; Dt 15:1; Jos 8:34-35

Israel's Rebellion Predicted

¹⁴The Lord said to Moses, "Now the day of your death is near. Call Joshua and present yourselves at the Tent of Meeting, where I will commission him." So Moses and Joshua came and presented themselves at the Tent of Meeting.

¹⁵Then the Lord appeared at the Tent in a pillar of cloud, and the cloud stood over the entrance to the Tent. ¹⁶And the Lord said to Moses: "You are going to rest with your fathers, and these people will soon prostitute themselves to the foreign gods of the land they are entering. They will forsake me and break the covenant I made with them. ¹⁷On that day I will become angry with them and forsake them; I will hide my face from

them, and they will be destroyed. Many disasters and difficulties will come upon them, and on that day they will ask, 'Have not these disasters come upon us because our God is not with us?' ¹⁸And I will certainly hide my face on that day because of all their wickedness in turning to other gods.   Ex 33:9

¹⁹"Now write down for yourselves this song and teach it to the Israelites and have them sing it, so that it may be a witness for me against them. ²⁰When I have brought them into the land flowing with milk and honey, the land I promised on oath to their forefathers, and when they eat their fill and thrive, they will turn to other gods and worship them, rejecting me and breaking my covenant. ²¹And when many disasters and difficulties come upon them, this song will testify against them, because it will not be forgotten by their descendants. I know what they are disposed to do, even before I bring them into the land I promised them on oath." ²²So Moses wrote down this song that day and taught it to the Israelites.

²³The LORD gave this command to Joshua son of Nun: "Be strong and courageous, for you will bring the Israelites into the land I promised them on oath, and I myself will be with you."   Jos 1:6

²⁴After Moses finished writing in a book the words of this law from beginning to end, ²⁵he gave this command to the Levites who carried the ark of the covenant of the LORD: ²⁶"Take this Book of the Law and place it beside the ark of the covenant of the LORD your God. There it will remain as a witness against you. ²⁷For I know how rebellious and stiff-necked you are. If you have been rebellious against the LORD while I am still alive and with you, how much more will you rebel after I die! ²⁸Assemble before me all the elders of your tribes and all your officials, so that I can speak these words in their hearing and call heaven and earth to testify against them. ²⁹For I know that after my death you are sure to become utterly corrupt and to turn from the way I have commanded you. In days to come, disaster will fall upon you because you will do evil in the sight of the LORD and provoke him to anger by what your hands have made."   Dt 4:26

The Song of Moses

³⁰And Moses recited the words of this song from beginning to end in the hearing of the whole assembly of Israel:

32 Listen, O heavens, and I
will speak;
hear, O earth, the words of
my mouth.   Dt 4:26; Isa 1:2
²Let my teaching fall like rain
and my words descend like
dew,
like showers on new grass,
like abundant rain on tender
plants.   Isa 55:11

[3]I will proclaim the name of the
    LORD.   Ex 33:19
  Oh, praise the greatness of
    our God!   Dt 3:24
[4]He is the Rock, his works are
    perfect,   2Sa 22:31
  and all his ways are just.
  A faithful God who does no
    wrong,
  upright and just is he.   Dt 7:9

[5]They have acted corruptly
    toward him;
  to their shame they are no
    longer his children,
  but a warped and crooked
    generation.[a]   Dt 31:29
[6]Is this the way you repay the
    LORD,
  O foolish and unwise
    people?   Ps 74:2; 116:12
  Is he not your Father, your
    Creator,[b]
  who made you and formed
    you?   Dt 1:31; Isa 63:16

[7]Remember the days of old;
  consider the generations
    long past.   Ps 44:1; Job 8:8
  Ask your father and he will tell
    you,
  your elders, and they will
    explain to you.   Ex 13:14
[8]When the Most High gave the
    nations their
    inheritance,
  when he divided all
    mankind,
  he set up boundaries for the
    peoples

according to the number of
    the sons of Israel.[c]
[9]For the LORD's portion is his
    people,
  Jacob his allotted
    inheritance.   Jer 10:16

[10]In a desert land he found
    him,
  in a barren and howling
    waste.   Jer 2:6
  He shielded him and cared for
    him;
  he guarded him as the apple
    of his eye,   Ps 17:8; Zec 2:8
[11]like an eagle that stirs up its
    nest
  and hovers over its young,
  that spreads its wings to catch
    them
  and carries them on its
    pinions.   Ex 19:4
[12]The LORD alone led him;
  no foreign god was with
    him.   Dt 4:35; Isa 43:12

[13]He made him ride on the
    heights of the land
  and fed him with the fruit of
    the fields.
  He nourished him with honey
    from the rock,
  and with oil from the flinty
    crag,   Dt 8:8; Job 29:6
[14]with curds and milk from herd
    and flock
  and with fattened lambs and
    goats,
  with choice rams of Bashan

---

[a]5 Or *Corrupt are they and not his children, / a generation warped and twisted to their shame*   [b]6 Or
Father, who bought you   [c]8 Masoretic Text; Dead Sea Scrolls (see also Septuagint) *sons of God*

and the finest kernels of
    wheat.
You drank the foaming blood
    of the grape.   Ps 81:16

¹⁵Jeshurun*ᵃ* grew fat and
    kicked;
    filled with food, he became
        heavy and sleek.   Dt 31:20
He abandoned the God who
        made him
    and rejected the Rock his
        Savior.   Isa 1:4,28
¹⁶They made him jealous with
        their foreign gods
    and angered him with their
        detestable idols.   1Co 10:22
¹⁷They sacrificed to demons,
        which are not God—
    gods they had not known,
    gods that recently appeared,
    gods your fathers did not
        fear.   Dt 28:64; Jdg 5:8
¹⁸You deserted the Rock, who
        fathered you;
    you forgot the God who gave
        you birth.   Ps 106:21; Isa 17:10

¹⁹The Lᴏʀᴅ saw this and rejected
        them   Jer 44:21-23
    because he was angered by
        his sons and daughters.
²⁰"I will hide my face from
        them," he said,   Dt 31:17,29
    "and see what their end will
        be;
    for they are a perverse
        generation,
    children who are unfaithful.

²¹They made me jealous by what
        is no god
    and angered me with their
        worthless idols.
I will make them envious by
        those who are not a
        people;
    I will make them angry by a
        nation that has no
        understanding.   Ro 10:19
²²For a fire has been kindled by
        my wrath,
    one that burns to the realm
        of death*ᵇ* below.
It will devour the earth and its
        harvests
    and set afire the foundations
        of the mountains.
²³"I will heap calamities upon
        them
    and spend my arrows against
        them.   Dt 29:21; Ps 18:14
²⁴I will send wasting famine
        against them,
    consuming pestilence and
        deadly plague;   Dt 28:22
I will send against them the
        fangs of wild beasts,
    the venom of vipers that
        glide in the dust.
²⁵In the street the sword will
        make them childless;
    in their homes terror will
        reign.
Young men and young women
        will perish,
    infants and gray-haired men.
²⁶I said I would scatter them

ᵃ 15 Jeshurun means *the upright one,* that is, Israel.   *ᵇ 22* Hebrew *to Sheol*

and blot out their memory
from mankind, Dt 4:27
²⁷but I dreaded the taunt of the
enemy,
lest the adversary
misunderstand
and say, 'Our hand has
triumphed;
the LORD has not done all
this.'" Isa 10:13
²⁸They are a nation without
sense,
there is no discernment in
them. Isa 1:3; 27:11
²⁹If only they were wise and
would understand this
and discern what their end
will be! Ps 81:13
³⁰How could one man chase a
thousand,
or two put ten thousand to
flight,
unless their Rock had sold
them,
unless the LORD had given
them up? Lev 26:8; Ps 44:12
³¹For their rock is not like our
Rock,
as even our enemies
concede. Ge 49:24
³²Their vine comes from the vine
of Sodom
and from the fields of
Gomorrah.
Their grapes are filled with
poison,
and their clusters with
bitterness. Dt 29:18
³³Their wine is the venom of
serpents,

the deadly poison of cobras.
³⁴"Have I not kept this in reserve
and sealed it in my vaults?
³⁵It is mine to avenge; I will
repay.
In due time their foot will
slip;
their day of disaster is near
and their doom rushes upon
them." Ro 12:19; Heb 10:30
³⁶The LORD will judge his people
and have compassion on his
servants
when he sees their strength is
gone
and no one is left, slave or
free. Ps 135:14; Joel 2:14
³⁷He will say: "Now where are
their gods,
the rock they took refuge in,
³⁸the gods who ate the fat of
their sacrifices
and drank the wine of their
drink offerings?
Let them rise up to help you!
Let them give you shelter!

³⁹"See now that I myself am He!
There is no god besides me.
I put to death and I bring to
life,
I have wounded and I will
heal,
and no one can deliver out
of my hand. Ps 50:22
⁴⁰I lift my hand to heaven and
declare:
As surely as I live forever,
⁴¹when I sharpen my flashing
sword

and my hand grasps it in
judgment, Isa 66:16
I will take vengeance on my
adversaries
and repay those who hate
me. Jer 50:29
42I will make my arrows drunk
with blood,
while my sword devours
flesh:
the blood of the slain and the
captives,
the heads of the enemy
leaders." Jer 12:12; 46:10,14

43Rejoice, O nations, with his
people,*a, b* Ro 15:10
for he will avenge the blood
of his servants;
he will take vengeance on his
enemies
and make atonement for his
land and people. Ps 85:1

44Moses came with Joshua*c* son
of Nun and spoke all the words of
this song in the hearing of the people. 45When Moses finished recit-
ing all these words to all Israel,
46he said to them, "Take to heart
all the words I have solemnly declared to you this day, so that you
may command your children to
obey carefully all the words of this
law. 47They are not just idle words
for you—they are your life. By
them you will live long in the land
you are crossing the Jordan to possess." Eze 40:4; Dt 30:20

Moses to Die on Mount Nebo

48On that same day the LORD told
Moses, 49"Go up into the Abarim
Range to Mount Nebo in Moab,
across from Jericho, and view Canaan, the land I am giving the Israelites as their own possession.
50There on the mountain that you
have climbed you will die and be
gathered to your people, just as
your brother Aaron died on Mount
Hor and was gathered to his people. 51This is because both of you
broke faith with me in the presence of the Israelites at the waters
of Meribah Kadesh in the Desert of
Zin and because you did not uphold my holiness among the Israelites. 52Therefore, you will see the
land only from a distance; you will
not enter the land I am giving to
the people of Israel." Ge 25:8

Moses Blesses the Tribes

33 This is the blessing that
Moses the man of God pro-
nounced on the Israelites before
his death. 2He said: Jos 14:6

"The LORD came from Sinai
and dawned over them from
Seir;
he shone forth from Mount
Paran. Ps 50:2; 68:8; Hab 3:3
He came with*d* myriads of holy
ones
from the south, from his
mountain slopes.*e*

a43 Or Make his people rejoice, O nations *b43 Masoretic Text; Dead Sea Scrolls (see also Septuagint)*
people, / and let all the angels worship him / *c44 Hebrew Hoshea, a variant of Joshua* *d2 Or from*
e2 The meaning of the Hebrew for this phrase is uncertain.

³Surely it is you who love the
    people;
all the holy ones are in your
    hand.
At your feet they all bow
    down,
and from you receive
    instruction,   Lk 10:39
⁴the law that Moses gave us,
    the possession of the
    assembly of Jacob.
⁵He was king over Jeshurunᵃ
when the leaders of the
    people assembled,
along with the tribes of
    Israel.   Nu 23:21

⁶"Let Reuben live and not die,
    norᵇ his men be few."

⁷And this he said about Judah:

"Hear, O Lᴏʀᴅ, the cry of
    Judah;
bring him to his people.
With his own hands he
    defends his cause.
Oh, be his help against his
    foes!"   Ge 49:10

⁸About Levi he said:

"Your Thummim and Urim
    belong
to the man you favored.
You tested him at Massah;
    you contended with him at
    the waters of Meribah.
⁹He said of his father and
    mother,

'I have no regard for them.'
He did not recognize his
    brothers
or acknowledge his own
    children,
but he watched over your word
    and guarded your covenant.
¹⁰He teaches your precepts to
    Jacob
and your law to Israel.
He offers incense before you
    and whole burnt offerings on
    your altar.   Ps 51:19; Lev 10:11
¹¹Bless all his skills, O Lᴏʀᴅ,
    and be pleased with the
    work of his hands.
Smite the loins of those who
    rise up against him;
strike his foes till they rise
    no more."

¹²About Benjamin he said:

"Let the beloved of the Lᴏʀᴅ
    rest secure in him,
for he shields him all day
    long,
and the one the Lᴏʀᴅ loves
    rests between his
    shoulders."   Ex 28:12; Dt 12:10

¹³About Joseph he said:

"May the Lᴏʀᴅ bless his land
    with the precious dew from
    heaven above
and with the deep waters
    that lie below;   Ge 27:28
¹⁴with the best the sun brings
    forth

ᵃ5 *Jeshurun* means *the upright one,* that is, Israel; also in verse 26.   ᵇ6 Or *but let*

and the finest the moon can
yield;
¹⁵with the choicest gifts of the
ancient mountains
and the fruitfulness of the
everlasting hills;　Hab 3:6
¹⁶with the best gifts of the earth
and its fullness
and the favor of him who
dwelt in the burning
bush.
Let all these rest on the head
of Joseph,
on the brow of the prince
among*a* his brothers.
¹⁷In majesty he is like a firstborn
bull;
his horns are the horns of a
wild ox.
With them he will gore the
nations,
even those at the ends of the
earth.　Nu 23:22; 1Ki 22:11
Such are the ten thousands of
Ephraim;
such are the thousands of
Manasseh."

¹⁸About Zebulun he said:

"Rejoice, Zebulun, in your
going out,
and you, Issachar, in your
tents.　Ge 49:13-15
¹⁹They will summon peoples to
the mountain
and there offer sacrifices of
righteousness;　Ps 4:5; Isa 2:3
they will feast on the
abundance of the seas,

on the treasures hidden in
the sand."　Isa 60:5,11

²⁰About Gad he said:

"Blessed is he who enlarges
Gad's domain!
Gad lives there like a lion,
tearing at arm or head.
²¹He chose the best land for
himself;
the leader's portion was kept
for him.　Nu 32:1-5,31-32
When the heads of the people
assembled,
he carried out the LORD's
righteous will,
and his judgments
concerning Israel."

²²About Dan he said:

"Dan is a lion's cub,
springing out of Bashan."

²³About Naphtali he said:

"Naphtali is abounding with
the favor of the LORD
and is full of his blessing;
he will inherit southward to
the lake."　Ge 30:8

²⁴About Asher he said:

"Most blessed of sons is Asher;
let him be favored by his
brothers,
and let him bathe his feet in
oil.　Ge 49:21; Job 29:6

a 16 Or *of the one separated from*

²⁵The bolts of your gates will be
　　iron and bronze,　Ne 3:3
　and your strength will equal
　　your days.　Dt 4:40
²⁶"There is no one like the God
　　of Jeshurun,
　who rides on the heavens to
　　help you
　and on the clouds in his
　　majesty.　Ex 15:11; 2Sa 22:10
²⁷The eternal God is your refuge,
　and underneath are the
　　everlasting arms.　Ps 90:1
He will drive out your enemy
　before you,
　saying, 'Destroy him!'　Dt 7:2
²⁸So Israel will live in safety
　　alone;
　Jacob's spring is secure
in a land of grain and new
　　wine,
　where the heavens drop
　　dew.　Ge 27:28; Jer 23:6
²⁹Blessed are you, O Israel!
　Who is like you,
　a people saved by the LORD?
He is your shield and helper
　and your glorious sword.
Your enemies will cower
　　before you,
　and you will trample down
　　their high places.^a"

The Death of Moses

34 Then Moses climbed
Mount Nebo from the
plains of Moab to the top of Pisgah,
across from Jericho. There the
LORD showed him the whole land
—from Gilead to Dan, ²all of Naphtali, the territory of Ephraim and
Manasseh, all the land of Judah as
far as the western sea,^b ³the Negev
and the whole region from the Val-
ley of Jericho, the City of Palms, as
far as Zoar. ⁴Then the LORD said to
him, "This is the land I promised
on oath to Abraham, Isaac and Jacob when I said, 'I will give it to
your descendants.' I have let you
see it with your eyes, but you will
not cross over into it."　Ge 12:7

⁵And Moses the servant of the
LORD died there in Moab, as the
LORD had said. ⁶He buried him^c in
Moab, in the valley opposite Beth
Peor, but to this day no one knows
where his grave is. ⁷Moses was a
hundred and twenty years old
when he died, yet his eyes were
not weak nor his strength gone.
⁸The Israelites grieved for Moses
in the plains of Moab thirty days,
until the time of weeping and
mourning was over.　Jos 1:1-2

⁹Now Joshua son of Nun was
filled with the spirit^d of wisdom
because Moses had laid his hands
on him. So the Israelites listened to
him and did what the LORD had
commanded Moses.　Nu 27:18,23

¹⁰Since then, no prophet has ris-
en in Israel like Moses, whom the
LORD knew face to face, ¹¹who did
all those miraculous signs and
wonders the LORD sent him to do in

---

^a29 Or *will tread upon their bodies*　　^b2 That is, the Mediterranean　　^c6 Or *He was buried*　　^d9 Or
Spirit

Egypt—to Pharaoh and to all his officials and to his whole land. ¹²For no one has ever shown the mighty power or performed the awesome deeds that Moses did in the sight of all Israel. Dt 18:15,18

Egypt—to Pharaoh and to all his
officials and to his whole [land].
[14]For no one has ever [...] deeds that Moses did in
[the sight of all Israel.]

Joshua

The Lord Commands Joshua

1 After the death of Moses the servant of the Lord, the Lord said to Joshua son of Nun, Moses' aide: [2]"Moses my servant is dead. Now then, you and all these people, get ready to cross the Jordan River into the land I am about to give to them—to the Israelites. [3]I will give you every place where you set your foot, as I promised Moses. [4]Your territory will extend from the desert to Lebanon, and from the great river, the Euphrates —all the Hittite country—to the Great Sea[a] on the west. [5]No one will be able to stand up against you all the days of your life. As I was with Moses, so I will be with you; I will never leave you nor forsake you. Dt 7:24; 11:24; 31:6-8

[6]"Be strong and courageous, because you will lead these people to inherit the land I swore to their forefathers to give them. [7]Be strong and very courageous. Be careful to obey all the law my servant Moses gave you; do not turn from it to the right or to the left, that you may be successful wherever you go. [8]Do not let this Book of the Law depart from your mouth; meditate on it day and night, so that you may be careful to do everything written in it. Then you will be prosperous and successful. [9]Have I not commanded you? Be strong and courageous. Do not be terrified; do not be discouraged, for the Lord your God will be with you wherever you go."

[10]So Joshua ordered the officers of the people: [11]"Go through the camp and tell the people, 'Get your supplies ready. Three days from now you will cross the Jordan here to go in and take possession of the land the Lord your God is giving you for your own.' " Jos 3:2; Joel 3:2

[12]But to the Reubenites, the Gadites and the half-tribe of Manasseh, Joshua said, [13]"Remember the command that Moses the servant of the Lord gave you: 'The Lord your God is giving you rest and has granted you this land.' [14]Your wives, your children and your livestock may stay in the land that Moses gave you east of the Jordan, but all your fighting men, fully armed, must cross over ahead of your brothers. You are to help your brothers [15]until the Lord gives them rest, as he has done for you, and until they too have taken possession of the land that the Lord your God is giving them. After that, you may go back and oc-

---

a 4 That is, the Mediterranean

cupy your own land, which Moses the servant of the Lord gave you east of the Jordan toward the sunrise." Nu 32:20-22; Jos 22:1-4; Dt 3:18-20

16Then they answered Joshua, "Whatever you have commanded us we will do, and wherever you send us we will go. 17Just as we fully obeyed Moses, so we will obey you. Only may the Lord your God be with you as he was with Moses. 18Whoever rebels against your word and does not obey your words, whatever you may command them, will be put to death. Only be strong and courageous!"

Rahab and the Spies

2 Then Joshua son of Nun secretly sent two spies from Shittim. "Go, look over the land," he said, "especially Jericho." So they went and entered the house of a prostitute[a] named Rahab and stayed there. Heb 11:31; Jas 2:25

2The king of Jericho was told, "Look! Some of the Israelites have come here tonight to spy out the land." 3So the king of Jericho sent this message to Rahab: "Bring out the men who came to you and entered your house, because they have come to spy out the whole land."

4But the woman had taken the two men and hidden them. She said, "Yes, the men came to me, but I did not know where they had come from. 5At dusk, when it was time to close the city gate, the men left. I don't know which way they went. Go after them quickly. You may catch up with them." 6(But she had taken them up to the roof and hidden them under the stalks of flax she had laid out on the roof.) 7So the men set out in pursuit of the spies on the road that leads to the fords of the Jordan, and as soon as the pursuers had gone out, the gate was shut.

8Before the spies lay down for the night, she went up on the roof 9and said to them, "I know that the Lord has given this land to you and that a great fear of you has fallen on us, so that all who live in this country are melting in fear because of you. 10We have heard how the Lord dried up the water of the Red Sea[b] for you when you came out of Egypt, and what you did to Sihon and Og, the two kings of the Amorites east of the Jordan, whom you completely destroyed.[c] 11When we heard of it, our hearts melted and everyone's courage failed because of you, for the Lord your God is God in heaven above and on the earth below. 12Now then, please swear to me by the Lord that you will show kindness to my family, because I have shown kindness to you. Give me a sure sign 13that you will spare the lives of my father and mother, my

---

a 1 Or possibly an innkeeper   b 10 Hebrew Yam Suph; that is, Sea of Reeds   c 10 The Hebrew term refers to the irrevocable giving over of things or persons to the Lord, often by totally destroying them.

brothers and sisters, and all who belong to them, and that you will save us from death." Ex 14:21; 23:27

14"Our lives for your lives!" the men assured her. "If you don't tell what we are doing, we will treat you kindly and faithfully when the LORD gives us the land."   Jdg 1:24

15So she let them down by a rope through the window, for the house she lived in was part of the city wall. 16Now she had said to them, "Go to the hills so the pursuers will not find you. Hide yourselves there three days until they return, and then go on your way."

17The men said to her, "This oath you made us swear will not be binding on us 18unless, when we enter the land, you have tied this scarlet cord in the window through which you let us down, and unless you have brought your father and mother, your brothers and all your family into your house. 19If anyone goes outside your house into the street, his blood will be on his own head; we will not be responsible. As for anyone who is in the house with you, his blood will be on our head if a hand is laid on him. 20But if you tell what we are doing, we will be released from the oath you made us swear."   Ge 24:8; Mt 27:25; Eze 33:4

21"Agreed," she replied. "Let it be as you say." So she sent them away and they departed. And she tied the scarlet cord in the window.

22When they left, they went into the hills and stayed there three days, until the pursuers had searched all along the road and returned without finding them. 23Then the two men started back. They went down out of the hills, forded the river and came to Joshua son of Nun and told him everything that had happened to them. 24They said to Joshua, "The LORD has surely given the whole land into our hands; all the people are melting in fear because of us."

Crossing the Jordan

3 Early in the morning Joshua and all the Israelites set out from Shittim and went to the Jordan, where they camped before crossing over. 2After three days the officers went throughout the camp, 3giving orders to the people: "When you see the ark of the covenant of the LORD your God, and the priests, who are Levites, carrying it, you are to move out from your positions and follow it. 4Then you will know which way to go, since you have never been this way before. But keep a distance of about a thousand yards[a] between you and the ark; do not go near it."

5Joshua told the people, "Consecrate yourselves, for tomorrow the LORD will do amazing things among you."   Ex 19:10,14; Jos 7:13

---

[a] 4 Hebrew about two thousand cubits (about 900 meters)

6Joshua said to the priests, "Take up the ark of the covenant and pass on ahead of the people." So they took it up and went ahead of them.

7And the LORD said to Joshua, "Today I will begin to exalt you in the eyes of all Israel, so they may know that I am with you as I was with Moses. 8Tell the priests who carry the ark of the covenant: 'When you reach the edge of the Jordan's waters, go and stand in the river.'"   Jos 1:5; 1Ch 29:25

9Joshua said to the Israelites, "Come here and listen to the words of the LORD your God. 10This is how you will know that the living God is among you and that he will certainly drive out before you the Canaanites, Hittites, Hivites, Perizzites, Girgashites, Amorites and Jebusites. 11See, the ark of the covenant of the Lord of all the earth will go into the Jordan ahead of you. 12Now then, choose twelve men from the tribes of Israel, one from each tribe. 13And as soon as the priests who carry the ark of the LORD—the Lord of all the earth—set foot in the Jordan, its waters flowing downstream will be cut off and stand up in a heap."   Dt 5:26

14So when the people broke camp to cross the Jordan, the priests carrying the ark of the covenant went ahead of them. 15Now the Jordan is at flood stage all during harvest. Yet as soon as the priests who carried the ark reached the Jordan and their feet touched the water's edge, 16the water from upstream stopped flowing. It piled up in a heap a great distance away, at a town called Adam in the vicinity of Zarethan, while the water flowing down to the Sea of the Arabah (the Salt Sea a) was completely cut off. So the people crossed over opposite Jericho. 17The priests who carried the ark of the covenant of the LORD stood firm on dry ground in the middle of the Jordan, while all Israel passed by until the whole nation had completed the crossing on dry ground.   Ex 14:22,29; Jos 4:18

4 When the whole nation had finished crossing the Jordan, the LORD said to Joshua, 2"Choose twelve men from among the people, one from each tribe, 3and tell them to take up twelve stones from the middle of the Jordan from right where the priests stood and to carry them over with you and put them down at the place where you stay tonight."   Dt 27:2

4So Joshua called together the twelve men he had appointed from the Israelites, one from each tribe, 5and said to them, "Go over before the ark of the LORD your God into the middle of the Jordan. Each of you is to take up a stone on his shoulder, according to the number of the tribes of the Israelites, 6to serve as a sign among you. In the

a 16 That is, the Dead Sea

future, when your children ask you, 'What do these stones mean?' [7]tell them that the flow of the Jordan was cut off before the ark of the covenant of the LORD. When it crossed the Jordan, the waters of the Jordan were cut off. These stones are to be a memorial to the people of Israel forever."   Ex 12:26

[8]So the Israelites did as Joshua commanded them. They took twelve stones from the middle of the Jordan, according to the number of the tribes of the Israelites, as the LORD had told Joshua; and they carried them over with them to their camp, where they put them down. [9]Joshua set up the twelve stones that had been[a] in the middle of the Jordan at the spot where the priests who carried the ark of the covenant had stood. And they are there to this day.   Ex 28:21

[10]Now the priests who carried the ark remained standing in the middle of the Jordan until everything the LORD had commanded Joshua was done by the people, just as Moses had directed Joshua. The people hurried over, [11]and as soon as all of them had crossed, the ark of the LORD and the priests came to the other side while the people watched. [12]The men of Reuben, Gad and the half-tribe of Manasseh crossed over, armed, in front of the Israelites, as Moses had directed them. [13]About forty thousand armed for battle crossed over before the LORD to the plains of Jericho for war.   Ex 13:18; Nu 32:27

[14]That day the LORD exalted Joshua in the sight of all Israel; and they revered him all the days of his life, just as they had revered Moses.   Jos 3:7

[15]Then the LORD said to Joshua, [16]"Command the priests carrying the ark of the Testimony to come up out of the Jordan."   Ex 25:22

[17]So Joshua commanded the priests, "Come up out of the Jordan."

[18]And the priests came up out of the river carrying the ark of the covenant of the LORD. No sooner had they set their feet on the dry ground than the waters of the Jordan returned to their place and ran at flood stage as before.   Jos 3:15

[19]On the tenth day of the first month the people went up from the Jordan and camped at Gilgal on the eastern border of Jericho. [20]And Joshua set up at Gilgal the twelve stones they had taken out of the Jordan. [21]He said to the Israelites, "In the future when your descendants ask their fathers, 'What do these stones mean?' [22]tell them, 'Israel crossed the Jordan on dry ground.' [23]For the LORD your God dried up the Jordan before you until you had crossed over. The LORD your God did to the Jordan just what he had done to the Red Sea[b] when he dried it up before us until we had crossed over.

---

[a]9 Or Joshua also set up twelve stones   [b]23 Hebrew Yam Suph; that is, Sea of Reeds

²⁴He did this so that all the peoples of the earth might know that the hand of the LORD is powerful and so that you might always fear the LORD your God."   Ex 15:16; 1Ki 8:42-43

Circumcision at Gilgal

5 Now when all the Amorite kings west of the Jordan and all the Canaanite kings along the coast heard how the LORD had dried up the Jordan before the Israelites until we had crossed over, their hearts melted and they no longer had the courage to face the Israelites.   Nu 13:29; Jos 2:9-11

²At that time the LORD said to Joshua, "Make flint knives and circumcise the Israelites again." ³So Joshua made flint knives and circumcised the Israelites at Gibeath Haaraloth.ᵃ   Ex 4:25

⁴Now this is why he did so: All those who came out of Egypt—all the men of military age—died in the desert on the way after leaving Egypt. ⁵All the people that came out had been circumcised, but all the people born in the desert during the journey from Egypt had not. ⁶The Israelites had moved about in the desert forty years until all the men who were of military age when they left Egypt had died, since they had not obeyed the LORD. For the LORD had sworn to them that they would not see the land that he had solemnly prom-

ised their fathers to give us, a land flowing with milk and honey. ⁷So he raised up their sons in their place, and these were the ones Joshua circumcised. They were still uncircumcised because they had not been circumcised on the way. ⁸And after the whole nation had been circumcised, they remained where they were in camp until they were healed.   Dt 2:7,14

⁹Then the LORD said to Joshua, "Today I have rolled away the reproach of Egypt from you." So the place has been called Gilgalᵇ to this day.

¹⁰On the evening of the fourteenth day of the month, while camped at Gilgal on the plains of Jericho, the Israelites celebrated the Passover. ¹¹The day after the Passover, that very day, they ate some of the produce of the land: unleavened bread and roasted grain. ¹²The manna stopped the day afterᶜ they ate this food from the land; there was no longer any manna for the Israelites, but that year they ate of the produce of Canaan.   Ex 12:6; 16:35; Nu 15:19

The Fall of Jericho

¹³Now when Joshua was near Jericho, he looked up and saw a man standing in front of him with a drawn sword in his hand. Joshua went up to him and asked, "Are you for us or for our enemies?"

ᵃ3 Gibeath Haaraloth means hill of foreskins.   ᵇ9 Gilgal sounds like the Hebrew for roll.   ᶜ12 Or the day

¹⁴"Neither," he replied, "but as commander of the army of the LORD I have now come." Then Joshua fell facedown to the ground in reverence, and asked him, "What message does my Lord^a have for his servant?"

¹⁵The commander of the LORD's army replied, "Take off your sandals, for the place where you are standing is holy." And Joshua did so.   Ex 3:5; Ac 7:33

6 Now Jericho was tightly shut up because of the Israelites. No one went out and no one came in.   Jos 24:11

²Then the LORD said to Joshua, "See, I have delivered Jericho into your hands, along with its king and its fighting men. ³March around the city once with all the armed men. Do this for six days. ⁴Have seven priests carry trumpets of rams' horns in front of the ark. On the seventh day, march around the city seven times, with the priests blowing the trumpets. ⁵When you hear them sound a long blast on the trumpets, have all the people give a loud shout; then the wall of the city will collapse and the people will go up, every man straight in."   Dt 7:24; Lev 25:9

⁶So Joshua son of Nun called the priests and said to them, "Take up the ark of the covenant of the LORD and have seven priests carry trumpets in front of it." ⁷And he ordered the people, "Advance! March

around the city, with the armed guard going ahead of the ark of the LORD."   Ex 14:15; 1Sa 4:3

⁸When Joshua had spoken to the people, the seven priests carrying the seven trumpets before the LORD went forward, blowing their trumpets, and the ark of the LORD's covenant followed them. ⁹The armed guard marched ahead of the priests who blew the trumpets, and the rear guard followed the ark. All this time the trumpets were sounding. ¹⁰But Joshua had commanded the people, "Do not give a war cry, do not raise your voices, do not say a word until the day I tell you to shout. Then shout!" ¹¹So he had the ark of the LORD carried around the city, circling it once. Then the people returned to camp and spent the night there.   Isa 52:12

¹²Joshua got up early the next morning and the priests took up the ark of the LORD. ¹³The seven priests carrying the seven trumpets went forward, marching before the ark of the LORD and blowing the trumpets. The armed men went ahead of them and the rear guard followed the ark of the LORD, while the trumpets kept sounding. ¹⁴So on the second day they marched around the city once and returned to the camp. They did this for six days.

¹⁵On the seventh day, they got up at daybreak and marched

around the city seven times in the same manner, except that on that day they circled the city seven times. [16]The seventh time around, when the priests sounded the trumpet blast, Joshua commanded the people, "Shout! For the Lord has given you the city! [17]The city and all that is in it are to be devoted[a] to the Lord. Only Rahab the prostitute[b] and all who are with her in her house shall be spared, because she hid the spies we sent. [18]But keep away from the devoted things, so that you will not bring about your own destruction by taking any of them. Otherwise you will make the camp of Israel liable to destruction and bring trouble on it. [19]All the silver and gold and the articles of bronze and iron are sacred to the Lord and must go into his treasury."   Lev 27:28; Jos 2:4

[20]When the trumpets sounded, the people shouted, and at the sound of the trumpet, when the people gave a loud shout, the wall collapsed; so every man charged straight in, and they took the city. [21]They devoted the city to the Lord and destroyed with the sword every living thing in it—men and women, young and old, cattle, sheep and donkeys.   Dt 20:16; Am 2:2

[22]Joshua said to the two men who had spied out the land, "Go into the prostitute's house and bring her out and all who belong to her, in accordance with your oath to her." [23]So the young men who had done the spying went in and brought out Rahab, her father and mother and brothers and all who belonged to her. They brought out her entire family and put them in a place outside the camp of Israel.

[24]Then they burned the whole city and everything in it, but they put the silver and gold and the articles of bronze and iron into the treasury of the Lord's house. [25]But Joshua spared Rahab the prostitute, with her family and all who belonged to her, because she hid the men Joshua had sent as spies to Jericho—and she lives among the Israelites to this day.   Jdg 1:25

[26]At that time Joshua pronounced this solemn oath: "Cursed before the Lord is the man who undertakes to rebuild this city, Jericho:

"At the cost of his firstborn
        son
    will he lay its foundations;
at the cost of his youngest
    will he set up its gates."

[27]So the Lord was with Joshua, and his fame spread throughout the land.   Jos 1:5; 9:1

Achan's Sin

7 But the Israelites acted unfaithfully in regard to the de-

---

[a]17 The Hebrew term refers to the irrevocable giving over of things or persons to the Lord, often by totally destroying them; also in verses 18 and 21.   [b]17 Or possibly *innkeeper*; also in verses 22 and 25

voted things[a]; Achan son of Carmi, the son of Zimri,[b] the son of Zerah, of the tribe of Judah, took some of them. So the LORD's anger burned against Israel.   Jos 6:18

[2]Now Joshua sent men from Jericho to Ai, which is near Beth Aven to the east of Bethel, and told them, "Go up and spy out the region." So the men went up and spied out Ai.   Jos 18:12

[3]When they returned to Joshua, they said, "Not all the people will have to go up against Ai. Send two or three thousand men to take it and do not weary all the people, for only a few men are there." [4]So about three thousand men went up; but they were routed by the men of Ai, [5]who killed about thirty-six of them. They chased the Israelites from the city gate as far as the stone quarries[c] and struck them down on the slopes. At this the hearts of the people melted and became like water.   Lev 26:17

[6]Then Joshua tore his clothes and fell facedown to the ground before the ark of the LORD, remaining there till evening. The elders of Israel did the same, and sprinkled dust on their heads. [7]And Joshua said, "Ah, Sovereign LORD, why did you ever bring this people across the Jordan to deliver us into the hands of the Amorites to destroy us? If only we had been content to stay on the other side of the Jor-

dan! [8]O Lord, what can I say, now that Israel has been routed by its enemies? [9]The Canaanites and the other people of the country will hear about this and they will surround us and wipe out our name from the earth. What then will you do for your own great name?"

[10]The LORD said to Joshua, "Stand up! What are you doing down on your face? [11]Israel has sinned; they have violated my covenant, which I commanded them to keep. They have taken some of the devoted things; they have stolen, they have lied, they have put them with their own possessions. [12]That is why the Israelites cannot stand against their enemies; they turn their backs and run because they have been made liable to destruction. I will not be with you anymore unless you destroy whatever among you is devoted to destruction.   Jos 6:17-19; Ac 5:1-2; Dt 29:27

[13]"Go, consecrate the people. Tell them, 'Consecrate yourselves in preparation for tomorrow; for this is what the LORD, the God of Israel, says: That which is devoted is among you, O Israel. You cannot stand against your enemies until you remove it.   Jos 3:5; 6:18

[14]" 'In the morning, present yourselves tribe by tribe. The tribe that the LORD takes shall come forward clan by clan; the clan that the LORD takes shall come forward

[a] 1 The Hebrew term refers to the irrevocable giving over of things or persons to the LORD, often by totally destroying them; also in verses 11, 12, 13 and 15.   [b] 1 See Septuagint and 1 Chron. 2:6; Hebrew Zabdi; also in verses 17 and 18.   [c] 5 Or as far as Shebarim

family by family; and the family that the LORD takes shall come forward man by man. ¹⁵He who is caught with the devoted things shall be destroyed by fire, along with all that belongs to him. He has violated the covenant of the LORD and has done a disgraceful thing in Israel!' "   Ge 34:7; 1Sa 14:39

¹⁶Early the next morning Joshua had Israel come forward by tribes, and Judah was taken. ¹⁷The clans of Judah came forward, and he took the Zerahites. He had the clan of the Zerahites come forward by families, and Zimri was taken. ¹⁸Joshua had his family come forward man by man, and Achan son of Carmi, the son of Zimri, the son of Zerah, of the tribe of Judah, was taken.   Nu 26:20

¹⁹Then Joshua said to Achan, "My son, give glory to the LORD,ᵃ the God of Israel, and give him the praise.ᵇ Tell me what you have done; do not hide it from me."

²⁰Achan replied, "It is true! I have sinned against the LORD, the God of Israel. This is what I have done: ²¹When I saw in the plunder a beautiful robe from Babylonia,ᶜ two hundred shekelsᵈ of silver and a wedge of gold weighing fifty shekels,ᵉ I coveted them and took them. They are hidden in the ground inside my tent, with the silver underneath."   Eph 5:5; 1Ti 6:10

²²So Joshua sent messengers, and they ran to the tent, and there it was, hidden in his tent, with the silver underneath. ²³They took the things from the tent, brought them to Joshua and all the Israelites and spread them out before the LORD.

²⁴Then Joshua, together with all Israel, took Achan son of Zerah, the silver, the robe, the gold wedge, his sons and daughters, his cattle, donkeys and sheep, his tent and all that he had, to the Valley of Achor. ²⁵Joshua said, "Why have you brought this trouble on us? The LORD will bring trouble on you today."   Jos 6:18; 15:7

Then all Israel stoned him, and after they had stoned the rest, they burned them. ²⁶Over Achan they heaped up a large pile of rocks, which remains to this day. Then the LORD turned from his fierce anger. Therefore that place has been called the Valley of Achorᶠ ever since.   Dt 13:17; 17:5

Ai Destroyed

8 Then the LORD said to Joshua, "Do not be afraid; do not be discouraged. Take the whole army with you, and go up and attack Ai. For I have delivered into your hands the king of Ai, his people, his city and his land. ²You shall do to Ai and its king as you did to Jericho and its king, except that you may carry off their plunder

---

ᵃ19 A solemn charge to tell the truth   ᵇ19 Or and confess to him   ᶜ21 Hebrew Shinar   ᵈ21 That is, about 5 pounds (about 2.3 kilograms)   ᵉ21 That is, about 1 1/4 pounds (about 0.6 kilogram)   ᶠ26 Achor means trouble.

and livestock for yourselves. Set an ambush behind the city."

³So Joshua and the whole army moved out to attack Ai. He chose thirty thousand of his best fighting men and sent them out at night ⁴with these orders: "Listen carefully. You are to set an ambush behind the city. Don't go very far from it. All of you be on the alert. ⁵I and all those with me will advance on the city, and when the men come out against us, as they did before, we will flee from them. ⁶They will pursue us until we have lured them away from the city, for they will say, 'They are running away from us as they did before.' So when we flee from them, ⁷you are to rise up from ambush and take the city. The LORD your God will give it into your hand. ⁸When you have taken the city, set it on fire. Do what the LORD has commanded. See to it; you have my orders." Jdg 7:7; 20:29-38

⁹Then Joshua sent them off, and they went to the place of ambush and lay in wait between Bethel and Ai, to the west of Ai—but Joshua spent that night with the people.

¹⁰Early the next morning Joshua mustered his men, and he and the leaders of Israel marched before them to Ai. ¹¹The entire force that was with him marched up and approached the city and arrived in front of it. They set up camp north of Ai, with the valley between them and the city. ¹²Joshua had taken about five thousand men

and set them in ambush between Bethel and Ai, to the west of the city. ¹³They had the soldiers take up their positions—all those in the camp to the north of the city and the ambush to the west of it. That night Joshua went into the valley.

¹⁴When the king of Ai saw this, he and all the men of the city hurried out early in the morning to meet Israel in battle at a certain place overlooking the Arabah. But he did not know that an ambush had been set against him behind the city. ¹⁵Joshua and all Israel let themselves be driven back before them, and they fled toward the desert. ¹⁶All the men of Ai were called to pursue them, and they pursued Joshua and were lured away from the city. ¹⁷Not a man remained in Ai or Bethel who did not go after Israel. They left the city open and went in pursuit of Israel. Jos 15:61; 18:12; Jdg 20:34

¹⁸Then the LORD said to Joshua, "Hold out toward Ai the javelin that is in your hand, for into your hand I will deliver the city." So Joshua held out his javelin toward Ai. ¹⁹As soon as he did this, the men in the ambush rose quickly from their position and rushed forward. They entered the city and captured it and quickly set it on fire. Ex 14:16; 17:9-12

²⁰The men of Ai looked back and saw the smoke of the city rising against the sky, but they had no chance to escape in any direction, for the Israelites who had

been fleeing toward the desert had turned back against their pursuers. 21For when Joshua and all Israel saw that the ambush had taken the city and that smoke was going up from the city, they turned around and attacked the men of Ai. 22The men of the ambush also came out of the city against them, so that they were caught in the middle, with Israelites on both sides. Israel cut them down, leaving them neither survivors nor fugitives. 23But they took the king of Ai alive and brought him to Joshua.   Dt 7:2

24When Israel had finished killing all the men of Ai in the fields and in the desert where they had chased them, and when every one of them had been put to the sword, all the Israelites returned to Ai and killed those who were in it. 25Twelve thousand men and women fell that day—all the people of Ai. 26For Joshua did not draw back the hand that held out his javelin until he had destroyeda all who lived in Ai. 27But Israel did carry off for themselves the livestock and plunder of this city, as the Lord had instructed Joshua.

28So Joshua burned Ai and made it a permanent heap of ruins, a desolate place to this day. 29He hung the king of Ai on a tree and left him there until evening. At sunset, Joshua ordered them to take his body from the tree and throw it down at the entrance of the city gate. And they raised a large pile of rocks over it, which remains to this day.   Dt 13:16; 21:23; Jn 19:31

The Covenant Renewed at Mount Ebal

30Then Joshua built on Mount Ebal an altar to the Lord, the God of Israel, 31as Moses the servant of the Lord had commanded the Israelites. He built it according to what is written in the Book of the Law of Moses—an altar of uncut stones, on which no iron tool had been used. On it they offered to the Lord burnt offerings and sacrificed fellowship offerings.b 32There, in the presence of the Israelites, Joshua copied on stones the law of Moses, which he had written. 33All Israel, aliens and citizens alike, with their elders, officials and judges, were standing on both sides of the ark of the covenant of the Lord, facing those who carried it—the priests, who were Levites. Half of the people stood in front of Mount Gerizim and half of them in front of Mount Ebal, as Moses the servant of the Lord had formerly commanded when he gave instructions to bless the people of Israel.

34Afterward, Joshua read all the words of the law—the blessings and the curses—just as it is written in the Book of the Law. 35There was not a word of all that Moses

---

a26 The Hebrew term refers to the irrevocable giving over of things or persons to the Lord, often by totally destroying them.   b31 Traditionally peace offerings

had commanded that Joshua did not read to the whole assembly of Israel, including the women and children, and the aliens who lived among them.   Dt 31:12; Jos 1:8

The Gibeonite Deception

9 Now when all the kings west of the Jordan heard about these things—those in the hill country, in the western foothills, and along the entire coast of the Great Sea*a* as far as Lebanon (the kings of the Hittites, Amorites, Canaanites, Perizzites, Hivites and Jebusites)— ²they came together to make war against Joshua and Israel.   Nu 34:6; Ex 3:17

³However, when the people of Gibeon heard what Joshua had done to Jericho and Ai, ⁴they resorted to a ruse: They went as a delegation whose donkeys were loaded*b* with worn-out sacks and old wineskins, cracked and mended. ⁵The men put worn and patched sandals on their feet and wore old clothes. All the bread of their food supply was dry and moldy. ⁶Then they went to Joshua in the camp at Gilgal and said to him and the men of Israel, "We have come from a distant country; make a treaty with us."   Jos 5:10

⁷The men of Israel said to the Hivites, "But perhaps you live near us. How then can we make a treaty with you?"   Ex 23:32; Jos 11:19

⁸"We are your servants," they said to Joshua.

But Joshua asked, "Who are you and where do you come from?" ⁹They answered: "Your servants have come from a very distant country because of the fame of the LORD your God. For we have heard reports of him: all that he did in Egypt, ¹⁰and all that he did to the two kings of the Amorites east of the Jordan—Sihon king of Heshbon, and Og king of Bashan, who reigned in Ashtaroth. ¹¹And our elders and all those living in our country said to us, 'Take provisions for your journey; go and meet them and say to them, "We are your servants; make a treaty with us." ' ¹²This bread of ours was warm when we packed it at home on the day we left to come to you. But now see how dry and moldy it is. ¹³And these wineskins that we filled were new, but see how cracked they are. And our clothes and sandals are worn out by the very long journey."   Dt 20:15; Jos 2:9

¹⁴The men of Israel sampled their provisions but did not inquire of the LORD. ¹⁵Then Joshua made a treaty of peace with them to let them live, and the leaders of the assembly ratified it by oath.

¹⁶Three days after they made the treaty with the Gibeonites, the Israelites heard that they were neighbors, living near them. ¹⁷So

---

*a*1 That is, the Mediterranean   *b*4 Most Hebrew manuscripts; some Hebrew manuscripts, Vulgate and Syriac (see also Septuagint) *They prepared provisions and loaded their donkeys* the Israelites set out and on the third day came to their cities: Gibeon, Kephirah, Beeroth and Kiriath Jearim. [18]But the Israelites did not attack them, because the leaders of the assembly had sworn an oath to them by the LORD, the God of Israel.   Jos 18:25; Ps 15:4

The whole assembly grumbled against the leaders, [19]but all the leaders answered, "We have given them our oath by the LORD, the God of Israel, and we cannot touch them now. [20]This is what we will do to them: We will let them live, so that wrath will not fall on us for breaking the oath we swore to them." [21]They continued, "Let them live, but let them be woodcutters and water carriers for the entire community." So the leaders' promise to them was kept.

[22]Then Joshua summoned the Gibeonites and said, "Why did you deceive us by saying, 'We live a long way from you,' while actually you live near us? [23]You are now under a curse: You will never cease to serve as woodcutters and water carriers for the house of my God."   Ge 9:25

[24]They answered Joshua, "Your servants were clearly told how the LORD your God had commanded his servant Moses to give you the whole land and to wipe out all its inhabitants from before you. So we feared for our lives because of

you, and that is why we did this. [25]We are now in your hands. Do to us whatever seems good and right to you."   Ge 16:6; Jer 26:14

[26]So Joshua saved them from the Israelites, and they did not kill them. [27]That day he made the Gibeonites woodcutters and water carriers for the community and for the altar of the LORD at the place the LORD would choose. And that is what they are to this day.   Dt 12:5

The Sun Stands Still

10 Now Adoni-Zedek king of Jerusalem heard that Joshua had taken Ai and totally destroyed[a] it, doing to Ai and its king as he had done to Jericho and its king, and that the people of Gibeon had made a treaty of peace with Israel and were living near them. [2]He and his people were very much alarmed at this, because Gibeon was an important city, like one of the royal cities; it was larger than Ai, and all its men were good fighters. [3]So Adoni-Zedek king of Jerusalem appealed to Hoham king of Hebron, Piram king of Jarmuth, Japhia king of Lachish and Debir king of Eglon. [4]"Come up and help me attack Gibeon," he said, "because it has made peace with Joshua and the Israelites."

[5]Then the five kings of the Amorites—the kings of Jerusalem, He-

---

[a]1 The Hebrew term refers to the irrevocable giving over of things or persons to the LORD, often by totally destroying them; also in verses 28, 35, 37, 39 and 40.

bron, Jarmuth, Lachish and Eglon —joined forces. They moved up with all their troops and took up positions against Gibeon and attacked it.   Nu 13:29

⁶The Gibeonites then sent word to Joshua in the camp at Gilgal: "Do not abandon your servants. Come up to us quickly and save us! Help us, because all the Amorite kings from the hill country have joined forces against us."

⁷So Joshua marched up from Gilgal with his entire army, including all the best fighting men. ⁸The LORD said to Joshua, "Do not be afraid of them; I have given them into your hand. Not one of them will be able to withstand you."

⁹After an all-night march from Gilgal, Joshua took them by surprise. ¹⁰The LORD threw them into confusion before Israel, who defeated them in a great victory at Gibeon. Israel pursued them along the road going up to Beth Horon and cut them down all the way to Azekah and Makkedah. ¹¹As they fled before Israel on the road down from Beth Horon to Azekah, the LORD hurled large hailstones down on them from the sky, and more of them died from the hailstones than were killed by the swords of the Israelites.   Dt 7:23; Jdg 5:20; Ps 18:12

¹²On the day the LORD gave the Amorites over to Israel, Joshua said to the LORD in the presence of Israel:

"O sun, stand still over Gibeon,
    O moon, over the Valley of
        Aijalon."   Am 2:9
¹³So the sun stood still,
    and the moon stopped,
    till the nation avenged itself
        on[a] its enemies,

as it is written in the Book of Jashar.   2Sa 1:18; Hab 3:11

The sun stopped in the middle of the sky and delayed going down about a full day. ¹⁴There has never been a day like it before or since, a day when the LORD listened to a man. Surely the LORD was fighting for Israel!   Ex 14:14; Isa 38:8

¹⁵Then Joshua returned with all Israel to the camp at Gilgal.   ver 43

Five Amorite Kings Killed

¹⁶Now the five kings had fled and hidden in the cave at Makkedah. ¹⁷When Joshua was told that the five kings had been found hiding in the cave at Makkedah, ¹⁸he said, "Roll large rocks up to the mouth of the cave, and post some men there to guard it. ¹⁹But don't stop! Pursue your enemies, attack them from the rear and don't let them reach their cities, for the LORD your God has given them into your hand."

²⁰So Joshua and the Israelites destroyed them completely—almost to a man—but the few who were left reached their fortified cities. ²¹The whole army then re-

---

a 13 Or nation triumphed over

turned safely to Joshua in the camp at Makkedah, and no one uttered a word against the Israelites.

²²Joshua said, "Open the mouth of the cave and bring those five kings out to me." ²³So they brought the five kings out of the cave—the kings of Jerusalem, Hebron, Jarmuth, Lachish and Eglon. ²⁴When they had brought these kings to Joshua, he summoned all the men of Israel and said to the army commanders who had come with him, "Come here and put your feet on the necks of these kings." So they came forward and placed their feet on their necks.

²⁵Joshua said to them, "Do not be afraid; do not be discouraged. Be strong and courageous. This is what the LORD will do to all the enemies you are going to fight." ²⁶Then Joshua struck and killed the kings and hung them on five trees, and they were left hanging on the trees until evening.

²⁷At sunset Joshua gave the order and they took them down from the trees and threw them into the cave where they had been hiding. At the mouth of the cave they placed large rocks, which are there to this day.   Dt 21:23

²⁸That day Joshua took Makkedah. He put the city and its king to the sword and totally destroyed everyone in it. He left no survivors. And he did to the king of Makkedah as he had done to the king of Jericho.   Dt 20:16; Jos 6:21

Southern Cities Conquered

²⁹Then Joshua and all Israel with him moved on from Makkedah to Libnah and attacked it. ³⁰The LORD also gave that city and its king into Israel's hand. The city and everyone in it Joshua put to the sword. He left no survivors there. And he did to its king as he had done to the king of Jericho.

³¹Then Joshua and all Israel with him moved on from Libnah to Lachish; he took up positions against it and attacked it. ³²The LORD handed Lachish over to Israel, and Joshua took it on the second day. The city and everyone in it he put to the sword, just as he had done to Libnah. ³³Meanwhile, Horam king of Gezer had come up to help Lachish, but Joshua defeated him and his army—until no survivors were left.

³⁴Then Joshua and all Israel with him moved on from Lachish to Eglon; they took up positions against it and attacked it. ³⁵They captured it that same day and put it to the sword and totally destroyed everyone in it, just as they had done to Lachish.

³⁶Then Joshua and all Israel with him went up from Eglon to Hebron and attacked it. ³⁷They took the city and put it to the sword, together with its king, its villages and everyone in it. They left no survivors. Just as at Eglon, they totally destroyed it and everyone in it.   Jos 14:13; 15:13; Jdg 1:10

38Then Joshua and all Israel with him turned around and attacked Debir. 39They took the city, its king and its villages, and put them to the sword. Everyone in it they totally destroyed. They left no survivors. They did to Debir and its king as they had done to Libnah and its king and to Hebron.

40So Joshua subdued the whole region, including the hill country, the Negev, the western foothills and the mountain slopes, together with all their kings. He left no survivors. He totally destroyed all who breathed, just as the LORD, the God of Israel, had commanded. 41Joshua subdued them from Kadesh Barnea to Gaza and from the whole region of Goshen to Gibeon. 42All these kings and their lands Joshua conquered in one campaign, because the LORD, the God of Israel, fought for Israel.   Dt 7:24

43Then Joshua returned with all Israel to the camp at Gilgal.

Northern Kings Defeated

11 When Jabin king of Hazor heard of this, he sent word to Jobab king of Madon, to the kings of Shimron and Acshaph, 2and to the northern kings who were in the mountains, in the Arabah south of Kinnereth, in the western foothills and in Naphoth Dor[a] on the west; 3to the Canaan-ites in the east and west; to the Amorites, Hittites, Perizzites and Jebusites in the hill country; and to the Hivites below Hermon in the region of Mizpah. 4They came out with all their troops and a large number of horses and chariots—a huge army, as numerous as the sand on the seashore. 5All these kings joined forces and made camp together at the Waters of Merom, to fight against Israel.

6The LORD said to Joshua, "Do not be afraid of them, because by this time tomorrow I will hand all of them over to Israel, slain. You are to hamstring their horses and burn their chariots."   Jos 10:8; 2Sa 8:4

7So Joshua and his whole army came against them suddenly at the Waters of Merom and attacked them, 8and the LORD gave them into the hand of Israel. They defeated them and pursued them all the way to Greater Sidon, to Misrephoth Maim, and to the Valley of Mizpah on the east, until no survivors were left. 9Joshua did to them as the LORD had directed: He hamstrung their horses and burned their chariots.   Jos 13:6

10At that time Joshua turned back and captured Hazor and put its king to the sword. (Hazor had been the head of all these kingdoms.) 11Everyone in it they put to the sword. They totally destroyed[b] them, not sparing anything that

---

a2 Or in the heights of Dor   b11 The Hebrew term refers to the irrevocable giving over of things or persons to the LORD, often by totally destroying them; also in verses 12, 20 and 21.

breathed, and he burned up Hazor itself. Dt 20:16-17

¹²Joshua took all these royal cities and their kings and put them to the sword. He totally destroyed them, as Moses the servant of the LORD had commanded. ¹³Yet Israel did not burn any of the cities built on their mounds—except Hazor, which Joshua burned. ¹⁴The Israelites carried off for themselves all the plunder and livestock of these cities, but all the people they put to the sword until they completely destroyed them, not sparing anyone that breathed. ¹⁵As the LORD commanded his servant Moses, so Moses commanded Joshua, and Joshua did it; he left nothing undone of all that the LORD commanded Moses. Ex 34:11; Nu 33:50-52

¹⁶So Joshua took this entire land: the hill country, all the Negev, the whole region of Goshen, the western foothills, the Arabah and the mountains of Israel with their foothills, ¹⁷from Mount Halak, which rises toward Seir, to Baal Gad in the Valley of Lebanon below Mount Hermon. He captured all their kings and struck them down, putting them to death. ¹⁸Joshua waged war against all these kings for a long time. ¹⁹Except for the Hivites living in Gibeon, not one city made a treaty of peace with the Israelites, who took them all in battle. ²⁰For it was the LORD himself who hardened their hearts to wage war against Israel, so that he might destroy them totally, exterminating them without mercy, as the LORD had commanded Moses. Ex 14:17; Jos 9:3; 10:41

²¹At that time Joshua went and destroyed the Anakites from the hill country: from Hebron, Debir and Anab, from all the hill country of Judah, and from all the hill country of Israel. Joshua totally destroyed them and their towns. ²²No Anakites were left in Israelite territory; only in Gaza, Gath and Ashdod did any survive. ²³So Joshua took the entire land, just as the LORD had directed Moses, and he gave it as an inheritance to Israel according to their tribal divisions.

Then the land had rest from war.

List of Defeated Kings

12 These are the kings of the land whom the Israelites had defeated and whose territory they took over east of the Jordan, from the Arnon Gorge to Mount Hermon, including all the eastern side of the Arabah: Dt 3:8

²Sihon king of the Amorites, who reigned in Heshbon. He ruled from Aroer on the rim of the Arnon Gorge—from the middle of the gorge—to the Jabbok River, which is the border of the Ammonites. This included half of Gilead. ³He also ruled over the eastern Arabah from the Sea of

Kinnereth[a] to the Sea of the Arabah (the Salt Sea[b]), to Beth Jeshimoth, and then southward below the slopes of Pisgah.   Jos 11:2; 13:20; Jdg 11:19

[4]And the territory of Og king of Bashan,

one of the last of the Rephaites, who reigned in Ashtaroth and Edrei. [5]He ruled over Mount Hermon, Salecah, all of Bashan to the border of the people of Geshur and Maacah, and half of Gilead to the border of Sihon king of Heshbon.   Nu 21:21,33; Dt 1:4; 3:10

[6]Moses, the servant of the LORD, and the Israelites conquered them. And Moses the servant of the LORD gave their land to the Reubenites, the Gadites and the half-tribe of Manasseh to be their possession.

[7]These are the kings of the land that Joshua and the Israelites conquered on the west side of the Jordan, from Baal Gad in the Valley of Lebanon to Mount Halak, which rises toward Seir (their lands Joshua gave as an inheritance to the tribes of Israel according to their tribal divisions— [8]the hill country, the western foothills, the Arabah, the mountain slopes, the desert and the Negev—the lands of the Hittites, Amorites, Canaanites, Perizzites, Hivites and Jebusites):

[9]the king of Jericho	one
the king of Ai (near Bethel)	one
[10]the king of Jerusalem	one
the king of Hebron	one
[11]the king of Jarmuth	one
the king of Lachish	one
[12]the king of Eglon	one
the king of Gezer	one
[13]the king of Debir	one
the king of Geder	one
[14]the king of Hormah	one
the king of Arad	one
[15]the king of Libnah	one
the king of Adullam	one
[16]the king of Makkedah	one
the king of Bethel	one
[17]the king of Tappuah	one
the king of Hepher	one
[18]the king of Aphek	one
the king of Lasharon	one
[19]the king of Madon	one
the king of Hazor	one
[20]the king of Shimron Meron	one
the king of Acshaph	one
[21]the king of Taanach	one
the king of Megiddo	one
[22]the king of Kedesh	one
the king of Jokneam in Carmel	one
[23]the king of Dor (in Naphoth Dor[c])	one
the king of Goyim in Gilgal	one
[24]the king of Tirzah	one
thirty-one kings in all. Jos 6:2; 10:33	

---

[a]3 That is, Galilee   [b]3 That is, the Dead Sea   [c]23 Or *in the heights of Dor*

Land Still to Be Taken

13 When Joshua was old and well advanced in years, the LORD said to him, "You are very old, and there are still very large areas of land to be taken over.

2"This is the land that remains: all the regions of the Philistines and Geshurites: 3from the Shihor River on the east of Egypt to the territory of Ekron on the north, all of it counted as Canaanite (the territory of the five Philistine rulers in Gaza, Ashdod, Ashkelon, Gath and Ekron—that of the Avvites); 4from the south, all the land of the Canaanites, from Arah of the Sidonians as far as Aphek, the region of the Amorites, 5the area of the Gebalites[a]; and all Lebanon to the east, from Baal Gad below Mount Hermon to Lebo[b] Hamath.   Dt 2:23; Jdg 3:3; Am 2:10

6"As for all the inhabitants of the mountain regions from Lebanon to Misrephoth Maim, that is, all the Sidonians, I myself will drive them out before the Israelites. Be sure to allocate this land to Israel for an inheritance, as I have instructed you, 7and divide it as an inheritance among the nine tribes and half of the tribe of Manasseh."

Division of the Land East of the Jordan

8The other half of Manasseh,[c] the Reubenites and the Gadites had received the inheritance that Moses had given them east of the Jordan, as he, the servant of the LORD, had assigned it to them.

9It extended from Aroer on the rim of the Arnon Gorge, and from the town in the middle of the gorge, and included the whole plateau of Medeba as far as Dibon, 10and all the towns of Sihon king of the Amorites, who ruled in Heshbon, out to the border of the Ammonites. 11It also included Gilead, the territory of the people of Geshur and Maacah, all of Mount Hermon and all Bashan as far as Salecah— 12that is, the whole kingdom of Og in Bashan, who had reigned in Ashtaroth and Edrei and had survived as one of the last of the Rephaites. Moses had defeated them and taken over their land. 13But the Israelites did not drive out the people of Geshur and Maacah, so they continue to live among the Israelites to this day.   Dt 2:36; 3:11; Jos 12:4

14But to the tribe of Levi he gave

---

a5 That is, the area of Byblos   b5 Or to the entrance to   c8 Hebrew With it (that is, with the other half of Manasseh) no inheritance, since the offerings made by fire to the Lord, the God of Israel, are their inheritance, as he promised them.   Dt 18:1-2

15This is what Moses had given to the tribe of Reuben, clan by clan:

16The territory from Aroer on the rim of the Arnon Gorge, and from the town in the middle of the gorge, and the whole plateau past Medeba 17to Heshbon and all its towns on the plateau, including Dibon, Bamoth Baal, Beth Baal Meon, 18Jahaz, Kedemoth, Mephaath, 19Kiriathaim, Sibmah, Zereth Shahar on the hill in the valley, 20Beth Peor, the slopes of Pisgah, and Beth Jeshimoth 21—all the towns on the plateau and the entire realm of Sihon king of the Amorites, who ruled at Heshbon. Moses had defeated him and the Midianite chiefs, Evi, Rekem, Zur, Hur and Reba—princes allied with Sihon—who lived in that country. 22In addition to those slain in battle, the Israelites had put to the sword Balaam son of Beor, who practiced divination. 23The boundary of the Reubenites was the bank of the Jordan. These towns and their villages were the inheritance of the Reubenites, clan by clan.   Nu 21:23; 31:8; 32:37

24This is what Moses had given to the tribe of Gad, clan by clan:

25The territory of Jazer, all the towns of Gilead and half the Ammonite country as far as Aroer, near Rabbah; 26and from Heshbon to Ramath Mizpah and Betonim, and from Mahanaim to the territory of Debir; 27and in the valley, Beth Haram, Beth Nimrah, Succoth and Zaphon with the rest of the realm of Sihon king of Heshbon (the east side of the Jordan, the territory up to the end of the Sea of Kinnereth[a]). 28These towns and their villages were the inheritance of the Gadites, clan by clan.   Nu 21:32; 34:11

29This is what Moses had given to the half-tribe of Manasseh, that is, to half the family of the descendants of Manasseh, clan by clan:

30The territory extending from Mahanaim and including all of Bashan, the entire realm of Og king of Bashan—all the settlements of Jair in Bashan, sixty towns, 31half of Gilead, and Ashtaroth and Edrei (the royal cities of Og in Bashan). This was for the descendants of Makir son of Manasseh—for half of the sons of Makir, clan by clan.

32This is the inheritance Moses

---

had given when he was in the plains of Moab across the Jordan east of Jericho. ³³But to the tribe of Levi, Moses had given no inheritance; the LORD, the God of Israel, is their inheritance, as he promised them.   Nu 18:20

Division of the Land West of the Jordan

14 Now these are the areas the Israelites received as an inheritance in the land of Canaan, which Eleazar the priest, Joshua son of Nun and the heads of the tribal clans of Israel allotted to them. ²Their inheritances were assigned by lot to the nine-and-a-half tribes, as the LORD had commanded through Moses. ³Moses had granted the two-and-a-half tribes their inheritance east of the Jordan but had not granted the Levites an inheritance among the rest, ⁴for the sons of Joseph had become two tribes—Manasseh and Ephraim. The Levites received no share of the land but only towns to live in, with pasturelands for their flocks and herds. ⁵So the Israelites divided the land, just as the LORD had commanded Moses.

Hebron Given to Caleb

⁶Now the men of Judah approached Joshua at Gilgal, and Caleb son of Jephunneh the Kenizzite said to him, "You know what the LORD said to Moses the man of God at Kadesh Barnea about you and me. ⁷I was forty years old when Moses the servant of the LORD sent me from Kadesh Barnea to explore the land. And I brought him back a report according to my convictions, ⁸but my brothers who went up with me made the hearts of the people melt with fear. I, however, followed the LORD my God wholeheartedly. ⁹So on that day Moses swore to me, 'The land on which your feet have walked will be your inheritance and that of your children forever, because you have followed the LORD my God wholeheartedly.'^a   Nu 13:30

¹⁰"Now then, just as the LORD promised, he has kept me alive for forty-five years since the time he said this to Moses, while Israel moved about in the desert. So here I am today, eighty-five years old! ¹¹I am still as strong today as the day Moses sent me out; I'm just as vigorous to go out to battle now as I was then. ¹²Now give me this hill country that the LORD promised me that day. You yourself heard then that the Anakites were there and their cities were large and fortified, but, the LORD helping me, I will drive them out just as he said."

¹³Then Joshua blessed Caleb son of Jephunneh and gave him Hebron as his inheritance. ¹⁴So Hebron has belonged to Caleb son of Jephunneh the Kenizzite ever since, because he followed the

^a9 Deut. 1:36

LORD, the God of Israel, whole-heartedly. ¹⁵(Hebron used to be called Kiriath Arba after Arba, who was the greatest man among the Anakites.)   Jos 22:6-7; Jdg 1:20

Then the land had rest from war.

Allotment for Judah

15 The allotment for the tribe of Judah, clan by clan, extended down to the territory of Edom, to the Desert of Zin in the extreme south.

²Their southern boundary started from the bay at the southern end of the Salt Sea,*ᵃ* ³crossed south of Scorpion*ᵇ* Pass, continued on to Zin and went over to the south of Kadesh Barnea. Then it ran past Hezron up to Addar and curved around to Karka. ⁴It then passed along to Azmon and joined the Wadi of Egypt, ending at the sea. This is their*ᶜ* southern boundary.

⁵The eastern boundary is the Salt Sea as far as the mouth of the Jordan.   Ge 14:3

The northern boundary started from the bay of the sea at the mouth of the Jordan, ⁶went up to Beth Hoglah and continued north of Beth Arabah to the Stone of Bohan son of Reuben. ⁷The boundary then went up to Debir from the Valley of Achor and turned north to Gilgal, which faces the Pass of Adummim south of the gorge. It continued along to the waters of En Shemesh and came out at En Rogel. ⁸Then it ran up the Valley of Ben Hinnom along the southern slope of the Jebusite city (that is, Jerusalem). From there it climbed to the top of the hill west of the Hinnom Valley at the northern end of the Valley of Rephaim. ⁹From the hilltop the boundary headed toward the spring of the waters of Nephtoah, came out at the towns of Mount Ephron and went down toward Baalah (that is, Kiriath Jearim). ¹⁰Then it curved westward from Baalah to Mount Seir, ran along the northern slope of Mount Jearim (that is, Kesalon), continued down to Beth Shemesh and crossed to Timnah. ¹¹It went to the northern slope of Ekron, turned toward Shikkeron, passed along to Mount Baalah and reached Jabneel. The boundary ended at the sea.   Jos 7:24; 18:17; 1Ch 13:6

¹²The western boundary is the coastline of the Great Sea.*ᵈ*   Nu 34:6

These are the boundaries around the people of Judah by their clans.

¹³In accordance with the LORD's

ᵃ2 That is, the Dead Sea; also in verse 5   *ᵇ3* Hebrew *Akrabbim*   *ᶜ4* Hebrew *your*   *ᵈ12* That is, the Mediterranean; also in verse 47

command to him, Joshua gave to Caleb son of Jephunneh a portion in Judah—Kiriath Arba, that is, Hebron. (Arba was the forefather of Anak.) ¹⁴From Hebron Caleb drove out the three Anakites— Sheshai, Ahiman and Talmai— descendants of Anak. ¹⁵From there he marched against the people living in Debir (formerly called Kiriath Sepher). ¹⁶And Caleb said, "I will give my daughter Acsah in marriage to the man who attacks and captures Kiriath Sepher." ¹⁷Othniel son of Kenaz, Caleb's brother, took it; so Caleb gave his daughter Acsah to him in marriage.

¹⁸One day when she came to Othniel, she urged him*a* to ask her father for a field. When she got off her donkey, Caleb asked her, "What can I do for you?"

¹⁹She replied, "Do me a special favor. Since you have given me land in the Negev, give me also springs of water." So Caleb gave her the upper and lower springs.

²⁰This is the inheritance of the tribe of Judah, clan by clan:

²¹The southernmost towns of the tribe of Judah in the Negev toward the boundary of Edom were:

Kabzeel, Eder, Jagur, ²²Kinah, Dimonah, Adadah, ²³Kedesh, Hazor, Ithnan, ²⁴Ziph, Telem, Bealoth, ²⁵Hazor Ha-dattah, Kerioth Hezron (that is, Hazor), ²⁶Amam, Shema, Moladah, ²⁷Hazar Gaddah, Heshmon, Beth Pelet, ²⁸Hazar Shual, Beersheba, Biziothiah, ²⁹Baalah, Iim, Ezem, ³⁰Eltolad, Kesil, Hormah, ³¹Ziklag, Madmannah, Sansannah, ³²Lebaoth, Shilhim, Ain and Rimmon—a total of twenty-nine towns and their villages.

³³In the western foothills:

Eshtaol, Zorah, Ashnah, ³⁴Zanoah, En Gannim, Tappuah, Enam, ³⁵Jarmuth, Adullam, Socoh, Azekah, ³⁶Shaaraim, Adithaim and Gederah (or Gederothaim)*b*—fourteen towns and their villages.

³⁷Zenan, Hadashah, Migdal Gad, ³⁸Dilean, Mizpah, Joktheel, ³⁹Lachish, Bozkath, Eglon, ⁴⁰Cabbon, Lahmas, Kitlish, ⁴¹Gederoth, Beth Dagon, Naamah and Makkedah—sixteen towns and their villages.

⁴²Libnah, Ether, Ashan, ⁴³Iphtah, Ashnah, Nezib, ⁴⁴Keilah, Aczib and Mareshah —nine towns and their villages.   1Ch 6:59

⁴⁵Ekron, with its surrounding settlements and villages; ⁴⁶west of Ekron, all that were in the vicinity of Ashdod, together with their villages; ⁴⁷Ashdod, its surrounding settlements and villages; and

---

a 18 Hebrew and some Septuagint manuscripts; other Septuagint manuscripts (see also note at Judges 1:14) *Othniel, he urged her*   *b 36* Or *Gederah and Gederothaim*

Gaza, its settlements and villages, as far as the Wadi of Egypt and the coastline of the Great Sea. Nu 34:6

48In the hill country:

Shamir, Jattir, Socoh, 49Dannah, Kiriath Sannah (that is, Debir), 50Anab, Eshtemoh, Anim, 51Goshen, Holon and Giloh—eleven towns and their villages. Jos 10:41; Jdg 10:1

52Arab, Dumah, Eshan, 53Janim, Beth Tappuah, Aphekah, 54Humtah, Kiriath Arba (that is, Hebron) and Zior—nine towns and their villages. Ge 25:14

55Maon, Carmel, Ziph, Juttah, 56Jezreel, Jokdeam, Zanoah, 57Kain, Gibeah and Timnah—ten towns and their villages. Jdg 10:12; 1Ch 11:31

58Halhul, Beth Zur, Gedor, 59Maarath, Beth Anoth and Eltekon—six towns and their villages.

60Kiriath Baal (that is, Kiriath Jearim) and Rabbah—two towns and their villages.

61In the desert:

Beth Arabah, Middin, Secacah, 62Nibshan, the City of Salt and En Gedi—six towns and their villages. Jos 8:15

63Judah could not dislodge the Jebusites, who were living in Jerusalem; to this day the Jebusites live there with the people of Judah.

Allotment for Ephraim and Manasseh

16 The allotment for Joseph began at the Jordan of Jericho,[a] east of the waters of Jericho, and went up from there through the desert into the hill country of Bethel. 2It went on from Bethel (that is, Luz),[b] crossed over to the territory of the Arkites in Ataroth, 3descended westward to the territory of the Japhletites as far as the region of Lower Beth Horon and on to Gezer, ending at the sea.

4So Manasseh and Ephraim, the descendants of Joseph, received their inheritance. Jos 18:5

5This was the territory of Ephraim, clan by clan:

The boundary of their inheritance went from Ataroth Addar in the east to Upper Beth Horon 6and continued to the sea. From Micmethath on the north it curved eastward to Taanath Shiloh, passing by it to Janoah on the east. 7Then it went down from Janoah to Ataroth and Naarah, touched Jericho and came out at the Jordan. 8From Tappuah the

---

a 1 Jordan of Jericho was possibly an ancient name for the Jordan River.   b 2 Septuagint; Hebrew Bethel to Luz

border went west to the Kanah Ravine and ended at the sea. This was the inheritance of the tribe of the Ephraimites, clan by clan. ⁹It also included all the towns and their villages that were set aside for the Ephraimites within the inheritance of the Manassites.

¹⁰They did not dislodge the Canaanites living in Gezer; to this day the Canaanites live among the people of Ephraim but are required to do forced labor.

17 This was the allotment for the tribe of Manasseh as Joseph's firstborn, that is, for Makir, Manasseh's firstborn. Makir was the ancestor of the Gileadites, who had received Gilead and Bashan because the Makirites were great soldiers. ²So this allotment was for the rest of the people of Manasseh—the clans of Abiezer, Helek, Asriel, Shechem, Hepher and Shemida. These are the other male descendants of Manasseh son of Joseph by their clans.

³Now Zelophehad son of Hepher, the son of Gilead, the son of Makir, the son of Manasseh, had no sons but only daughters, whose names were Mahlah, Noah, Hoglah, Milcah and Tirzah. ⁴They went to Eleazar the priest, Joshua son of Nun, and the leaders and said, "The LORD commanded Moses to give us an inheritance among our brothers." So Joshua gave them an inheritance along with the brothers of their father, according to the LORD's command. ⁵Manasseh's share consisted of ten tracts of land besides Gilead and Bashan east of the Jordan, ⁶because the daughters of the tribe of Manasseh received an inheritance among the sons. The land of Gilead belonged to the rest of the descendants of Manasseh.

⁷The territory of Manasseh extended from Asher to Micmethath east of Shechem. The boundary ran southward from there to include the people living at En Tappuah. ⁸(Manasseh had the land of Tappuah, but Tappuah itself, on the boundary of Manasseh, belonged to the Ephraimites.) ⁹Then the boundary continued south to the Kanah Ravine. There were towns belonging to Ephraim lying among the towns of Manasseh, but the boundary of Manasseh was the northern side of the ravine and ended at the sea. ¹⁰On the south the land belonged to Ephraim, on the north to Manasseh. The territory of Manasseh reached the sea and bordered Asher on the north and Issachar on the east.   Jos 16:8; Eze 48:5

¹¹Within Issachar and Asher, Manasseh also had Beth Shan, Ibleam and the people of Dor, Endor, Taanach and Megiddo, together with their surrounding settlements (the

third in the list is Naphoth[a]).

¹²Yet the Manassites were not able to occupy these towns, for the Canaanites were determined to live in that region. ¹³However, when the Israelites grew stronger, they subjected the Canaanites to forced labor but did not drive them out completely.   Jos 16:10; Jdg 1:27

¹⁴The people of Joseph said to Joshua, "Why have you given us only one allotment and one portion for an inheritance? We are a numerous people and the LORD has blessed us abundantly."   Nu 26:28-37

¹⁵"If you are so numerous," Joshua answered, "and if the hill country of Ephraim is too small for you, go up into the forest and clear land for yourselves there in the land of the Perizzites and Rephaites."

¹⁶The people of Joseph replied, "The hill country is not enough for us, and all the Canaanites who live in the plain have iron chariots, both those in Beth Shan and its settlements and those in the Valley of Jezreel."   Jdg 1:19; 1Sa 29:1

¹⁷But Joshua said to the house of Joseph—to Ephraim and Manasseh— "You are numerous and very powerful. You will have not only one allotment ¹⁸but the forested hill country as well. Clear it, and its farthest limits will be yours; though the Canaanites have iron chariots and though they are strong, you can drive them out."

Division of the Rest of the Land

18 The whole assembly of the Israelites gathered at Shiloh and set up the Tent of Meeting there. The country was brought under their control, ²but there were still seven Israelite tribes who had not yet received their inheritance.   Jos 19:51; Jer 7:12

³So Joshua said to the Israelites: "How long will you wait before you begin to take possession of the land that the LORD, the God of your fathers, has given you? ⁴Appoint three men from each tribe. I will send them out to make a survey of the land and to write a description of it, according to the inheritance of each. Then they will return to me. ⁵You are to divide the land into seven parts. Judah is to remain in its territory on the south and the house of Joseph in its territory on the north. ⁶After you have written descriptions of the seven parts of the land, bring them here to me and I will cast lots for you in the presence of the LORD our God. ⁷The Levites, however, do not get a portion among you, because the priestly service of the LORD is their inheritance. And Gad, Reuben and the half-tribe of Manasseh have already received their inheritance on the east side of the Jordan. Moses the servant of the LORD gave it to them."   Jos 13:33; 15:1; 16:1-4

---

a 11 That is, Naphoth Dor

[8]As the men started on their way to map out the land, Joshua instructed them, "Go and make a survey of the land and write a description of it. Then return to me, and I will cast lots for you here at Shiloh in the presence of the LORD." [9]So the men left and went through the land. They wrote its description on a scroll, town by town, in seven parts, and returned to Joshua in the camp at Shiloh. [10]Joshua then cast lots for them in Shiloh in the presence of the LORD, and there he distributed the land to the Israelites according to their tribal divisions.   Jos 19:51; Jer 7:12

Allotment for Benjamin

[11]The lot came up for the tribe of Benjamin, clan by clan. Their allotted territory lay between the tribes of Judah and Joseph:

[12]On the north side their boundary began at the Jordan, passed the northern slope of Jericho and headed west into the hill country, coming out at the desert of Beth Aven. [13]From there it crossed to the south slope of Luz (that is, Bethel) and went down to Ataroth Addar on the hill south of Lower Beth Horon.   Ge 28:19; Jos 16:1; Jdg 1:23

[14]From the hill facing Beth Horon on the south the boundary turned south along the western side and came out at Kiriath Baal (that is, Kiriath Jearim), a town of the people of Judah. This was the western side.

[15]The southern side began at the outskirts of Kiriath Jearim on the west, and the boundary came out at the spring of the waters of Nephtoah. [16]The boundary went down to the foot of the hill facing the Valley of Ben Hinnom, north of the Valley of Rephaim. It continued down the Hinnom Valley along the southern slope of the Jebusite city and so to En Rogel. [17]It then curved north, went to En Shemesh, continued to Geliloth, which faces the Pass of Adummim, and ran down to the Stone of Bohan son of Reuben. [18]It continued to the northern slope of Beth Arabah[a] and on down into the Arabah. [19]It then went to the northern slope of Beth Hoglah and came out at the northern bay of the Salt Sea,[b] at the mouth of the Jordan in the south. This was the southern boundary.   Ge 14:3; Jos 15:9

[20]The Jordan formed the boundary on the eastern side. These were the boundaries that marked out the inheritance of the clans of Benjamin on all sides.

---

[a]18 Septuagint; Hebrew *slope facing the Arabah*   [b]19 That is, the Dead Sea

21The tribe of Benjamin, clan by clan, had the following cities:

Jericho, Beth Hoglah, Emek Keziz, **22**Beth Arabah, Zemaraim, Bethel, **23**Avvim, Parah, Ophrah, **24**Kephar Ammoni, Ophni and Geba—twelve towns and their villages.

25Gibeon, Ramah, Beeroth, **26**Mizpah, Kephirah, Mozah, **27**Rekem, Irpeel, Taralah, **28**Zelah, Haeleph, the Jebusite city (that is, Jerusalem), Gibeah and Kiriath—fourteen towns and their villages.

This was the inheritance of Benjamin for its clans.   Eze 48:23

Allotment for Simeon

19 The second lot came out for the tribe of Simeon, clan by clan. Their inheritance lay within the territory of Judah. **2**It included:

Beersheba (or Sheba),*a* Moladah, **3**Hazar Shual, Balah, Ezem, **4**Eltolad, Bethul, Hormah, **5**Ziklag, Beth Marcaboth, Hazar Susah, **6**Beth Lebaoth and Sharuhen—thirteen towns and their villages;

7Ain, Rimmon, Ether and Ashan—four towns and their villages— **8**and all the villages around these towns as far as Baalath Beer (Ramah in the Negev).   Jos 15:32

This was the inheritance of the tribe of the Simeonites, clan by clan. **9**The inheritance of the Simeonites was taken from the share of Judah, because Judah's portion was more than they needed. So the Simeonites received their inheritance within the territory of Judah.

Allotment for Zebulun

10The third lot came up for Zebulun, clan by clan:

The boundary of their inheritance went as far as Sarid. **11**Going west it ran to Maralah, touched Dabbesheth, and extended to the ravine near Jokneam. **12**It turned east from Sarid toward the sunrise to the territory of Kisloth Tabor and went on to Daberath and up to Japhia. **13**Then it continued eastward to Gath Hepher and Eth Kazin; it came out at Rimmon and turned toward Neah. **14**There the boundary went around on the north to Hannathon and ended at the Valley of Iphtah El. **15**Included were Kattath, Nahalal, Shimron, Idalah and Bethlehem. There were twelve towns and their villages.   Ge 35:19; Jos 12:22; 1Ch 6:72

16These towns and their villages were the inheritance of Zebulun, clan by clan.   Eze 48:26

Allotment for Issachar

17The fourth lot came out for Issa-

---

a 2 Or *Beersheba, Sheba;* 1 Chron. 4:28 does not have *Sheba.*

char, clan by clan. ¹⁸Their territory included:

Jezreel, Kesulloth, Shunem, ¹⁹Hapharaim, Shion, Anaharath, ²⁰Rabbith, Kishion, Ebez, ²¹Remeth, En Gannim, En Haddah and Beth Pazzez. ²²The boundary touched Tabor, Shahazumah and Beth Shemesh, and ended at the Jordan. There were sixteen towns and their villages. ²³These towns and their villages were the inheritance of the tribe of Issachar, clan by clan.

Allotment for Asher

²⁴The fifth lot came out for the tribe of Asher, clan by clan. ²⁵Their territory included:

Helkath, Hali, Beten, Acshaph, ²⁶Allammelech, Amad and Mishal. On the west the boundary touched Carmel and Shihor Libnath. ²⁷It then turned east toward Beth Dagon, touched Zebulun and the Valley of Iphtah El, and went north to Beth Emek and Neiel, passing Cabul on the left. ²⁸It went to Abdon,ᵃ Rehob, Hammon and Kanah, as far as Greater Sidon. ²⁹The boundary then turned back toward Ramah and went to the fortified city of Tyre, turned toward Hosah and came out at the sea in the region of Aczib, ³⁰Ummah, Aphek and Rehob.

There were twenty-two towns and their villages.   Ge 10:19

³¹These towns and their villages were the inheritance of the tribe of Asher, clan by clan.   Ge 30:13

Allotment for Naphtali

³²The sixth lot came out for Naphtali, clan by clan:

³³Their boundary went from Heleph and the large tree in Zaanannim, passing Adami Nekeb and Jabneel to Lakkum and ending at the Jordan. ³⁴The boundary ran west through Aznoth Tabor and came out at Hukkok. It touched Zebulun on the south, Asher on the west and the Jordanᵇ on the east. ³⁵The fortified cities were Ziddim, Zer, Hammath, Rakkath, Kinnereth, ³⁶Adamah, Ramah, Hazor, ³⁷Kedesh, Edrei, En Hazor, ³⁸Iron, Migdal El, Horem, Beth Anath and Beth Shemesh. There were nineteen towns and their villages.

³⁹These towns and their villages were the inheritance of the tribe of Naphtali, clan by clan.   Dt 33:23

Allotment for Dan

⁴⁰The seventh lot came out for the tribe of Dan, clan by clan. ⁴¹The territory of their inheritance included:

ᵃ 28 Some Hebrew manuscripts (see also Joshua 21:30); most Hebrew manuscripts *Ebron*
ᵇ 34 Septuagint; Hebrew *west, and Judah, the Jordan,*

Zorah, Eshtaol, Ir Shemesh,
⁴²Shaalabbin, Aijalon, Ithlah,
⁴³Elon, Timnah, Ekron, ⁴⁴Elte-
keh, Gibbethon, Baalath, ⁴⁵Je-
hud, Bene Berak, Gath Rimmon, ⁴⁶Me Jarkon and Rak-
kon, with the area facing
Joppa.   Jdg 1:35; Jnh 1:3

⁴⁷(But the Danites had difficulty
taking possession of their territory, so they went up and attacked
Leshem, took it, put it to the sword
and occupied it. They settled in Leshem and named it Dan after their
forefather.)   Jdg 18:1,27,29

⁴⁸These towns and their villages
were the inheritance of the tribe of
Dan, clan by clan.

Allotment for Joshua

⁴⁹When they had finished dividing the land into its allotted portions, the Israelites gave Joshua
son of Nun an inheritance among
them, ⁵⁰as the LORD had commanded. They gave him the town he
asked for—Timnath Serahᵃ in
the hill country of Ephraim. And
he built up the town and settled
there.

⁵¹These are the territories that
Eleazar the priest, Joshua son of
Nun and the heads of the tribal
clans of Israel assigned by lot at
Shiloh in the presence of the LORD
at the entrance to the Tent of Meeting. And so they finished dividing
the land.   Jos 14:1; 18:10

Cities of Refuge

20 Then the LORD said to Joshua: ²"Tell the Israelites to
designate the cities of refuge, as I
instructed you through Moses, ³so
that anyone who kills a person accidentally and unintentionally
may flee there and find protection
from the avenger of blood. Lev 4:2

⁴"When he flees to one of these
cities, he is to stand in the entrance
of the city gate and state his case
before the elders of that city. Then
they are to admit him into their
city and give him a place to live
with them. ⁵If the avenger of blood
pursues him, they must not surrender the one accused, because
he killed his neighbor unintentionally and without malice aforethought. ⁶He is to stay in that city
until he has stood trial before the
assembly and until the death of the
high priest who is serving at that
time. Then he may go back to his
own home in the town from which
he fled."   Nu 35:12; Ru 4:1

⁷So they set apart Kedesh in Galilee in the hill country of Naphtali,
Shechem in the hill country of
Ephraim, and Kiriath Arba (that is,
Hebron) in the hill country of Judah. ⁸On the east side of the Jordan of Jerichoᵇ they designated
Bezer in the desert on the plateau
in the tribe of Reuben, Ramoth in
Gilead in the tribe of Gad, and Golan in Bashan in the tribe of Ma-

---

ᵃ50 Also known as *Timnath Heres* (see Judges 2:9)
name for the Jordan River.

ᵇ8 *Jordan of Jericho* was possibly an ancient

nasseh. [9]Any of the Israelites or any alien living among them who killed someone accidentally could flee to these designated cities and not be killed by the avenger of blood prior to standing trial before the assembly.   Nu 35:9-34; Dt 4:41-43

Towns for the Levites

21 Now the family heads of the Levites approached Eleazar the priest, Joshua son of Nun, and the heads of the other tribal families of Israel [2]at Shiloh in Canaan and said to them, "The LORD commanded through Moses that you give us towns to live in, with pasturelands for our livestock." [3]So, as the LORD had commanded, the Israelites gave the Levites the following towns and pasturelands out of their own inheritance: Nu 35:2-3; Jos 14:1; Lev 25:32

[4]The first lot came out for the Kohathites, clan by clan. The Levites who were descendants of Aaron the priest were allotted thirteen towns from the tribes of Judah, Simeon and Benjamin. [5]The rest of Kohath's descendants were allotted ten towns from the clans of the tribes of Ephraim, Dan and half of Manasseh.   Nu 3:17

[6]The descendants of Gershon were allotted thirteen towns from the clans of the tribes of Issachar, Asher, Naphtali and the half-tribe of Manasseh in Bashan.   Ge 30:18

[7]The descendants of Merari, clan by clan, received twelve towns from the tribes of Reuben, Gad and Zebulun.   Ex 6:16

[8]So the Israelites allotted to the Levites these towns and their pasturelands, as the LORD had commanded through Moses.

[9]From the tribes of Judah and Simeon they allotted the following towns by name [10](these towns were assigned to the descendants of Aaron who were from the Kohathite clans of the Levites, because the first lot fell to them):

[11]They gave them Kiriath Arba (that is, Hebron), with its surrounding pastureland, in the hill country of Judah. (Arba was the forefather of Anak.) [12]But the fields and villages around the city they had given to Caleb son of Jephunneh as his possession.

[13]So to the descendants of Aaron the priest they gave Hebron (a city of refuge for one accused of murder), Libnah, [14]Jattir, Eshtemoa, [15]Holon, Debir, [16]Ain, Juttah and Beth Shemesh, together with their pasturelands—nine towns from these two tribes.

[17]And from the tribe of Benjamin they gave them Gibeon, Geba, [18]Anathoth and Almon, together with their pasturelands—four towns.   Jos 18:24

[19]All the towns for the priests, the descendants of Aaron, were thirteen, together with their pasturelands.   2Ch 31:15

²⁰The rest of the Kohathite clans of the Levites were allotted towns from the tribe of Ephraim:

²¹In the hill country of Ephraim they were given Shechem (a city of refuge for one accused of murder) and Gezer, ²²Kibzaim and Beth Horon, together with their pasturelands—four towns.

²³Also from the tribe of Dan they received Eltekeh, Gibbethon, ²⁴Aijalon and Gath Rimmon, together with their pasturelands—four towns.

²⁵From half the tribe of Manasseh they received Taanach and Gath Rimmon, together with their pasturelands—two towns.

²⁶All these ten towns and their pasturelands were given to the rest of the Kohathite clans.

²⁷The Levite clans of the Gershonites were given:

from the half-tribe of Manasseh, Golan in Bashan (a city of refuge for one accused of murder) and Be Eshtarah, together with their pasturelands—two towns;   Nu 35:6; Jos 12:5
²⁸from the tribe of Issachar, Kishion, Daberath, ²⁹Jarmuth and En Gannim, together with their pasturelands — four towns;   Ge 30:18
³⁰from the tribe of Asher, Mishal, Abdon, ³¹Helkath and Rehob, together with their pasturelands—four towns;

³²from the tribe of Naphtali, Kedesh in Galilee (a city of refuge for one accused of murder), Hammoth Dor and Kartan, together with their pasturelands—three towns.

³³All the towns of the Gershonite clans were thirteen, together with their pasturelands.

³⁴The Merarite clans (the rest of the Levites) were given:

from the tribe of Zebulun, Jokneam, Kartah, ³⁵Dimnah and Nahalal, together with their   pasturelands — four towns;   1Ch 6:77; Jos 12:22
³⁶from the tribe of Reuben, Bezer, Jahaz, ³⁷Kedemoth and Mephaath, together with their pasturelands—four towns;
³⁸from the tribe of Gad, Ramoth in Gilead (a city of refuge for one accused of murder), Mahanaim, ³⁹Heshbon and Jazer, together with their   pasturelands — four towns in all.   1Ch 6:54-80; Dt 4:43

⁴⁰All the towns allotted to the Merarite clans, who were the rest of the Levites, were twelve.

⁴¹The towns of the Levites in the territory held by the Israelites were forty-eight in all, together with their pasturelands. ⁴²Each of these towns had pasturelands surrounding it; this was true for all these towns.   Nu 35:7

⁴³So the LORD gave Israel all the land he had sworn to give their forefathers, and they took posses-

sion of it and settled there. **44**The Lord gave them rest on every side, just as he had sworn to their forefathers. Not one of their enemies withstood them; the Lord handed all their enemies over to them. **45**Not one of all the Lord's good promises to the house of Israel failed; every one was fulfilled.

Eastern Tribes Return Home

22 Then Joshua summoned the Reubenites, the Gadites and the half-tribe of Manasseh **2**and said to them, "You have done all that Moses the servant of the Lord commanded, and you have obeyed me in everything I commanded. **3**For a long time now—to this very day—you have not deserted your brothers but have carried out the mission the Lord your God gave you. **4**Now that the Lord your God has given your brothers rest as he promised, return to your homes in the land that Moses the servant of the Lord gave you on the other side of the Jordan. **5**But be very careful to keep the commandment and the law that Moses the servant of the Lord gave you: to love the Lord your God, to walk in all his ways, to obey his commands, to hold fast to him and to serve him with all your heart and all your soul."   Dt 3:20; 5:29; Nu 32:18

6Then Joshua blessed them and sent them away, and they went to their homes. **7**(To the half-tribe of Manasseh Moses had given land in Bashan, and to the other half of the tribe Joshua gave land on the west side of the Jordan with their brothers.) When Joshua sent them home, he blessed them, **8**saying, "Return to your homes with your great wealth—with large herds of livestock, with silver, gold, bronze and iron, and a great quantity of clothing—and divide with your brothers the plunder from your enemies."   Ex 39:43; Nu 31:27; 1Sa 30:16

9So the Reubenites, the Gadites and the half-tribe of Manasseh left the Israelites at Shiloh in Canaan to return to Gilead, their own land, which they had acquired in accordance with the command of the Lord through Moses.   Nu 32:26,29

10When they came to Geliloth near the Jordan in the land of Canaan, the Reubenites, the Gadites and the half-tribe of Manasseh built an imposing altar there by the Jordan. **11**And when the Israelites heard that they had built the altar on the border of Canaan at Geliloth near the Jordan on the Israelite side, **12**the whole assembly of Israel gathered at Shiloh to go to war against them.   Jos 18:1

13So the Israelites sent Phinehas son of Eleazar, the priest, to the land of Gilead—to Reuben, Gad and the half-tribe of Manasseh. **14**With him they sent ten of the chief men, one for each of the tribes of Israel, each the head of a family division among the Israelite clans.   Nu 1:4; 25:7

15When they went to Gilead—to Reuben, Gad and the half-tribe of

Manasseh—they said to them: [16]"The whole assembly of the LORD says: 'How could you break faith with the God of Israel like this? How could you turn away from the LORD and build yourselves an altar in rebellion against him now? [17]Was not the sin of Peor enough for us? Up to this very day we have not cleansed ourselves from that sin, even though a plague fell on the community of the LORD! [18]And are you now turning away from the LORD? Nu 25:1-9; Dt 12:13-14

" 'If you rebel against the LORD today, tomorrow he will be angry with the whole community of Israel. [19]If the land you possess is defiled, come over to the LORD's land, where the LORD's tabernacle stands, and share the land with us. But do not rebel against the LORD or against us by building an altar for yourselves, other than the altar of the LORD our God. [20]When Achan son of Zerah acted unfaithfully regarding the devoted things,[a] did not wrath come upon the whole community of Israel? He was not the only one who died for his sin.' " Nu 16:22; Jos 7:1

[21]Then Reuben, Gad and the half-tribe of Manasseh replied to the heads of the clans of Israel: [22]"The Mighty One, God, the LORD! The Mighty One, God, the LORD! He knows! And let Israel know! If this has been in rebellion or disobedience to the LORD, do not spare us this day. [23]If we have built our own altar to turn away from the LORD and to offer burnt offerings and grain offerings, or to sacrifice fellowship offerings[b] on it, may the LORD himself call us to account. Dt 10:17; 18:19; 1Ki 8:39

[24]"No! We did it for fear that some day your descendants might say to ours, 'What do you have to do with the LORD, the God of Israel? [25]The LORD has made the Jordan a boundary between us and you—you Reubenites and Gadites! You have no share in the LORD.' So your descendants might cause ours to stop fearing the LORD.

[26]"That is why we said, 'Let us get ready and build an altar—but not for burnt offerings or sacrifices.' [27]On the contrary, it is to be a witness between us and you and the generations that follow, that we will worship the LORD at his sanctuary with our burnt offerings, sacrifices and fellowship offerings. Then in the future your descendants will not be able to say to ours, 'You have no share in the LORD.' Dt 12:6; Jos 24:27

[28]"And we said, 'If they ever say this to us, or to our descendants, we will answer: Look at the replica of the LORD's altar, which our fathers built, not for burnt offerings

---

[a]20 The Hebrew term refers to the irrevocable giving over of things or persons to the LORD, often by totally destroying them.   [b]23 Traditionally *peace offerings*; also in verse 27

and sacrifices, but as a witness between us and you.'

29"Far be it from us to rebel against the Lord and turn away from him today by building an altar for burnt offerings, grain offerings and sacrifices, other than the altar of the Lord our God that stands before his tabernacle."

30When Phinehas the priest and the leaders of the community—the heads of the clans of the Israelites—heard what Reuben, Gad and Manasseh had to say, they were pleased. 31And Phinehas son of Eleazar, the priest, said to Reuben, Gad and Manasseh, "Today we know that the Lord is with us, because you have not acted unfaithfully toward the Lord in this matter. Now you have rescued the Israelites from the Lord's hand."

32Then Phinehas son of Eleazar, the priest, and the leaders returned to Canaan from their meeting with the Reubenites and Gadites in Gilead and reported to the Israelites. 33They were glad to hear the report and praised God. And they talked no more about going to war against them to devastate the country where the Reubenites and the Gadites lived. 1Ch 29:20; Da 2:19

34And the Reubenites and the Gadites gave the altar this name: A Witness Between Us that the Lord is God. Ge 21:30

Joshua's Farewell to the Leaders

23 After a long time had passed and the Lord had given Israel rest from all their enemies around them, Joshua, by then old and well advanced in years, 2summoned all Israel—their elders, leaders, judges and officials—and said to them: "I am old and well advanced in years. 3You yourselves have seen everything the Lord your God has done to all these nations for your sake; it was the Lord your God who fought for you. 4Remember how I have allotted as an inheritance for your tribes all the land of the nations that remain—the nations I conquered—between the Jordan and the Great Sea[a] in the west. 5The Lord your God himself will drive them out of your way. He will push them out before you, and you will take possession of their land, as the Lord your God promised you.

6"Be very strong; be careful to obey all that is written in the Book of the Law of Moses, without turning aside to the right or to the left. 7Do not associate with these nations that remain among you; do not invoke the names of their gods or swear by them. You must not serve them or bow down to them. 8But you are to hold fast to the Lord your God, as you have until now. Ex 23:13; Dt 10:20; Jos 1:7

a4 That is, the Mediterranean

⁹"The Lord has driven out before you great and powerful nations; to this day no one has been able to withstand you. ¹⁰One of you routs a thousand, because the Lord your God fights for you, just as he promised. ¹¹So be very careful to love the Lord your God.

¹²"But if you turn away and ally yourselves with the survivors of these nations that remain among you and if you intermarry with them and associate with them, ¹³then you may be sure that the Lord your God will no longer drive out these nations before you. Instead, they will become snares and traps for you, whips on your backs and thorns in your eyes, until you perish from this good land, which the Lord your God has given you.

¹⁴"Now I am about to go the way of all the earth. You know with all your heart and soul that not one of all the good promises the Lord your God gave you has failed. Every promise has been fulfilled; not one has failed. ¹⁵But just as every good promise of the Lord your God has come true, so the Lord will bring on you all the evil he has threatened, until he has destroyed you from this good land he has given you. ¹⁶If you violate the covenant of the Lord your God, which he commanded you, and go and serve other gods and bow down to them, the Lord's anger will burn against you, and you will quickly perish from the good land he has given you."   Dt 28:15; Jos 21:45; 1Ki 2:2

The Covenant Renewed at Shechem

24 Then Joshua assembled all the tribes of Israel at Shechem. He summoned the elders, leaders, judges and officials of Israel, and they presented themselves before God.   Jos 23:2

²Joshua said to all the people, "This is what the Lord, the God of Israel, says: 'Long ago your forefathers, including Terah the father of Abraham and Nahor, lived beyond the River*ᵃ* and worshiped other gods. ³But I took your father Abraham from the land beyond the River and led him throughout Canaan and gave him many descendants. I gave him Isaac, ⁴and to Isaac I gave Jacob and Esau. I assigned the hill country of Seir to Esau, but Jacob and his sons went down to Egypt.

⁵" 'Then I sent Moses and Aaron, and I afflicted the Egyptians by what I did there, and I brought you out. ⁶When I brought your fathers out of Egypt, you came to the sea, and the Egyptians pursued them with chariots and horsemen*ᵇ* as far as the Red Sea.*ᶜ* ⁷But they cried to the Lord for help, and he put darkness between you and the Egyptians; he brought the sea over them and covered them. You saw

---

ᵃ2 That is, the Euphrates; also in verses 3, 14 and 15   *ᵇ6* Or *charioteers*   *ᶜ6* Hebrew *Yam Suph;* that is, Sea of Reeds

with your own eyes what I did to the Egyptians. Then you lived in the desert for a long time. Ex 3:10

⁸" 'I brought you to the land of the Amorites who lived east of the Jordan. They fought against you, but I gave them into your hands. I destroyed them from before you, and you took possession of their land. ⁹When Balak son of Zippor, the king of Moab, prepared to fight against Israel, he sent for Balaam son of Beor to put a curse on you. ¹⁰But I would not listen to Balaam, so he blessed you again and again, and I delivered you out of his hand. Ex 23:23; Nu 22:2; Dt 23:5

¹¹" 'Then you crossed the Jordan and came to Jericho. The citizens of Jericho fought against you, as did also the Amorites, Perizzites, Canaanites, Hittites, Girgashites, Hivites and Jebusites, but I gave them into your hands. ¹²I sent the hornet ahead of you, which drove them out before you—also the two Amorite kings. You did not do it with your own sword and bow. ¹³So I gave you a land on which you did not toil and cities you did not build; and you live in them and eat from vineyards and olive groves that you did not plant.' Dt 6:10-11; Jos 3:16-17; Ps 44:3,6-7

¹⁴"Now fear the LORD and serve him with all faithfulness. Throw away the gods your forefathers worshiped beyond the River and in Egypt, and serve the LORD. ¹⁵But if serving the LORD seems undesirable to you, then choose for yourselves this day whom you will serve, whether the gods your forefathers served beyond the River, or the gods of the Amorites, in whose land you are living. But as for me and my household, we will serve the LORD." Dt 10:12; Ru 1:16; 1Sa 12:24

¹⁶Then the people answered, "Far be it from us to forsake the LORD to serve other gods! ¹⁷It was the LORD our God himself who brought us and our fathers up out of Egypt, from that land of slavery, and performed those great signs before our eyes. He protected us on our entire journey and among all the nations through which we traveled. ¹⁸And the LORD drove out before us all the nations, including the Amorites, who lived in the land. We too will serve the LORD, because he is our God."

¹⁹Joshua said to the people, "You are not able to serve the LORD. He is a holy God; he is a jealous God. He will not forgive your rebellion and your sins. ²⁰If you forsake the LORD and serve foreign gods, he will turn and bring disaster on you and make an end of you, after he has been good to you."

²¹But the people said to Joshua, "No! We will serve the LORD."

²²Then Joshua said, "You are witnesses against yourselves that you have chosen to serve the LORD." Ru 4:10; Ps 119:30,173

"Yes, we are witnesses," they replied. Dt 25:9

²³"Now then," said Joshua, "throw away the foreign gods that

are among you and yield your hearts to the LORD, the God of Israel." 1Ki 8:58

²⁴And the people said to Joshua, "We will serve the LORD our God and obey him." Ex 19:8; 24:3,7

²⁵On that day Joshua made a covenant for the people, and there at Shechem he drew up for them decrees and laws. ²⁶And Joshua recorded these things in the Book of the Law of God. Then he took a large stone and set it up there under the oak near the holy place of the LORD. Ex 24:8; Dt 31:24

²⁷"See!" he said to all the people. "This stone will be a witness against us. It has heard all the words the LORD has said to us. It will be a witness against you if you are untrue to your God." Jos 22:27

Buried in the Promised Land

²⁸Then Joshua sent the people away, each to his own inheritance.

²⁹After these things, Joshua son of Nun, the servant of the LORD, died at the age of a hundred and ten. ³⁰And they buried him in the land of his inheritance, at Timnath Serah[a] in the hill country of Ephraim, north of Mount Gaash.

³¹Israel served the LORD throughout the lifetime of Joshua and of the elders who outlived him and who had experienced everything the LORD had done for Israel.

³²And Joseph's bones, which the Israelites had brought up from Egypt, were buried at Shechem in the tract of land that Jacob bought for a hundred pieces of silver[b] from the sons of Hamor, the father of Shechem. This became the inheritance of Joseph's descendants.

³³And Eleazar son of Aaron died and was buried at Gibeah, which had been allotted to his son Phinehas in the hill country of Ephraim.

---

[a] 30 Also known as *Timnath Heres* (see Judges 2:9)
unit of money of unknown weight and value.

[b] 32 Hebrew *hundred kesitahs*; a kesitah was a

Judges

¹⁶The descendants of Moses' father-in-law, the Kenite, went
from the City of Palms with the

Israel Fights the Remaining Canaanites

1 After the death of Joshua, the Israelites asked the LORD, "Who will be the first to go up and fight for us against the Canaanites?" Nu 27:21; Jos 24:29; Jdg 3:1-6

²The LORD answered, "Judah is to go; I have given the land into their hands." Ge 49:8

³Then the men of Judah said to the Simeonites their brothers, "Come up with us into the territory allotted to us, to fight against the Canaanites. We in turn will go with you into yours." So the Simeonites went with them.

⁴When Judah attacked, the LORD gave the Canaanites and Perizzites into their hands and they struck down ten thousand men at Bezek. ⁵It was there that they found Adoni-Bezek and fought against him, putting to rout the Canaanites and Perizzites. ⁶Adoni-Bezek fled, but they chased him and caught him, and cut off his thumbs and big toes. Ge 13:7; Jos 3:10

⁷Then Adoni-Bezek said, "Seventy kings with their thumbs and big toes cut off have picked up scraps under my table. Now God has paid me back for what I did to

them." They brought him to Jerusalem, and he died there. Lev 24:19

⁸The men of Judah attacked Jerusalem also and took it. They put the city to the sword and set it on fire. Jos 15:63

⁹After that, the men of Judah went down to fight against the Canaanites living in the hill country, the Negev and the western foothills. ¹⁰They advanced against the Canaanites living in Hebron (formerly called Kiriath Arba) and defeated Sheshai, Ahiman and Talmai. Nu 13:17; Jos 15:14

¹¹From there they advanced against the people living in Debir (formerly called Kiriath Sepher). ¹²And Caleb said, "I will give my daughter Acsah in marriage to the man who attacks and captures Kiriath Sepher." ¹³Othniel son of Kenaz, Caleb's younger brother, took it; so Caleb gave his daughter Acsah to him in marriage.

¹⁴One day when she came to Othniel, she urged him[a] to ask her father for a field. When she got off her donkey, Caleb asked her, "What can I do for you?"

¹⁵She replied, "Do me a special favor. Since you have given me land in the Negev, give me also springs of water." Then Caleb gave

[a] 14 Hebrew; Septuagint and Vulgate *Othniel, he urged her*

her the upper and lower springs.

¹⁶The descendants of Moses' father-in-law, the Kenite, went up from the City of Palms*a* with the men of Judah to live among the people of the Desert of Judah in the Negev near Arad.   Nu 10:29

¹⁷Then the men of Judah went with the Simeonites their brothers and attacked the Canaanites living in Zephath, and they totally destroyed*b* the city. Therefore it was called Hormah.*c* ¹⁸The men of Judah also took*d* Gaza, Ashkelon and Ekron—each city with its territory.   Nu 21:3; Jos 11:22

¹⁹The LORD was with the men of Judah. They took possession of the hill country, but they were unable to drive the people from the plains, because they had iron chariots. ²⁰As Moses had promised, Hebron was given to Caleb, who drove from it the three sons of Anak. ²¹The Benjamites, however, failed to dislodge the Jebusites, who were living in Jerusalem; to this day the Jebusites live there with the Benjamites.   Jos 14:9; 15:63

²²Now the house of Joseph attacked Bethel, and the LORD was with them. ²³When they sent men to spy out Bethel (formerly called Luz), ²⁴the spies saw a man coming out of the city and they said to him, "Show us how to get into the city and we will see that you are treated well." ²⁵So he showed them, and they put the city to the sword but spared the man and his whole family. ²⁶He then went to the land of the Hittites, where he built a city and called it Luz, which is its name to this day.   Ge 28:19

²⁷But Manasseh did not drive out the people of Beth Shan or Taanach or Dor or Ibleam or Megiddo and their surrounding settlements, for the Canaanites were determined to live in that land. ²⁸When Israel became strong, they pressed the Canaanites into forced labor but never drove them out completely. ²⁹Nor did Ephraim drive out the Canaanites living in Gezer, but the Canaanites continued to live there among them. ³⁰Neither did Zebulun drive out the Canaanites living in Kitron or Nahalol, who remained among them; but they did subject them to forced labor. ³¹Nor did Asher drive out those living in Acco or Sidon or Ahlab or Aczib or Helbah or Aphek or Rehob, ³²and because of this the people of Asher lived among the Canaanite inhabitants of the land. ³³Neither did Naphtali drive out those living in Beth Shemesh or Beth Anath; but the Naphtalites too lived among the Canaanite inhabitants of the land, and those living in Beth Shemesh and Beth Anath became forced laborers for them. ³⁴The Amorites confined the Danites to the hill country, not al-

---

a 16 That is, Jericho   *b 17* The Hebrew term refers to the irrevocable giving over of things or persons to the LORD, often by totally destroying them.   *c 17* Hormah means *destruction.*   *d 18* Hebrew; Septuagint *Judah did not take*

lowing them to come down into the plain. ³⁵And the Amorites were determined also to hold out in Mount Heres, Aijalon and Shaalbim, but when the power of the house of Joseph increased, they too were pressed into forced labor. ³⁶The boundary of the Amorites was from Scorpion^a Pass to Sela and beyond.   Jos 15:3; 16:10; 17:11

The Angel of the LORD at Bokim

2 The angel of the LORD went up from Gilgal to Bokim and said, "I brought you up out of Egypt and led you into the land that I swore to give to your forefathers. I said, 'I will never break my covenant with you, ²and you shall not make a covenant with the people of this land, but you shall break down their altars.' Yet you have disobeyed me. Why have you done this? ³Now therefore I tell you that I will not drive them out before you; they will be ₜthorns₎ in your sides and their gods will be a snare to you."   Ex 20:2; Jos 23:13; Ps 106:36

⁴When the angel of the LORD had spoken these things to all the Israelites, the people wept aloud, ⁵and they called that place Bokim.^{b} There they offered sacrifices to the LORD.

Disobedience and Defeat

⁶After Joshua had dismissed the Israelites, they went to take possession of the land, each to his own inheritance. ⁷The people served the LORD throughout the lifetime of Joshua and of the elders who outlived him and who had seen all the great things the LORD had done for Israel.

⁸Joshua son of Nun, the servant of the LORD, died at the age of a hundred and ten. ⁹And they buried him in the land of his inheritance, at Timnath Heres^c in the hill country of Ephraim, north of Mount Gaash.   Jos 24:29-31; 19:50

¹⁰After that whole generation had been gathered to their fathers, another generation grew up, who knew neither the LORD nor what he had done for Israel. ¹¹Then the Israelites did evil in the eyes of the LORD and served the Baals. ¹²They forsook the LORD, the God of their fathers, who had brought them out of Egypt. They followed and worshiped various gods of the peoples around them. They provoked the LORD to anger ¹³because they forsook him and served Baal and the Ashtoreths. ¹⁴In his anger against Israel the LORD handed them over to raiders who plundered them. He sold them to their enemies all around, whom they were no longer able to resist. ¹⁵Whenever Israel went out to fight, the hand of the LORD was against them to defeat them, just as he had sworn to

---

^{a}36 Hebrew *Akrabbim* ^{b}5 *Bokim* means *weepers.* ^{c}9 Also known as *Timnath Serah* (see Joshua 19:50 and 24:30)

them. They were in great distress. ¹⁶Then the LORD raised up judges,ᵃ who saved them out of the hands of these raiders. ¹⁷Yet they would not listen to their judges but prostituted themselves to other gods and worshiped them. Unlike their fathers, they quickly turned from the way in which their fathers had walked, the way of obedience to the LORD's commands. ¹⁸Whenever the LORD raised up a judge for them, he was with the judge and saved them out of the hands of their enemies as long as the judge lived; for the LORD had compassion on them as they groaned under those who oppressed and afflicted them. ¹⁹But when the judge died, the people returned to ways even more corrupt than those of their fathers, following other gods and serving and worshiping them. They refused to give up their evil practices and stubborn ways.   Jos 1:5; Jdg 3:12

²⁰Therefore the LORD was very angry with Israel and said, "Because this nation has violated the covenant that I laid down for their forefathers and has not listened to me, ²¹I will no longer drive out before them any of the nations Joshua left when he died. ²²I will use them to test Israel and see whether they will keep the way of the LORD and walk in it as their forefathers did." ²³The LORD had allowed those nations to remain; he did not drive them out at once by giving them into the hands of Joshua.

3 These are the nations the LORD left to test all those Israelites who had not experienced any of the wars in Canaan ²(he did this only to teach warfare to the descendants of the Israelites who had not had previous battle experience): ³the five rulers of the Philistines, all the Canaanites, the Sidonians, and the Hivites living in the Lebanon mountains from Mount Baal Hermon to Leboᵇ Hamath. ⁴They were left to test the Israelites to see whether they would obey the LORD's commands, which he had given their forefathers through Moses.   Ex 15:25; Jos 13:3

⁵The Israelites lived among the Canaanites, Hittites, Amorites, Perizzites, Hivites and Jebusites. ⁶They took their daughters in marriage and gave their own daughters to their sons, and served their gods.   Ex 34:16; Dt 7:3-4; Ps 106:35

Othniel

⁷The Israelites did evil in the eyes of the LORD; they forgot the LORD their God and served the Baals and the Asherahs. ⁸The anger of the LORD burned against Israel so that he sold them into the hands of Cushan-Rishathaim king of Aram Naharaim,ᶜ to whom the Israelites were subject for eight

---

ᵃ 16 Or *leaders*; similarly in verses 17-19   ᵇ 3 Or *to the entrance to*   ᶜ 8 That is, Northwest Mesopotamia

years. [9]But when they cried out to the LORD, he raised up for them a deliverer, Othniel son of Kenaz, Caleb's younger brother, who saved them. [10]The Spirit of the LORD came upon him, so that he became Israel's judge[a] and went to war. The LORD gave Cushan-Rishathaim king of Aram into the hands of Othniel, who overpowered him. [11]So the land had peace for forty years, until Othniel son of Kenaz died.   Nu 11:25,29; Dt 4:9; Jdg 6:34

Ehud

[12]Once again the Israelites did evil in the eyes of the LORD, and because they did this evil the LORD gave Eglon king of Moab power over Israel. [13]Getting the Ammonites and Amalekites to join him, Eglon came and attacked Israel, and they took possession of the City of Palms.[b] [14]The Israelites were subject to Eglon king of Moab for eighteen years.   Jdg 1:16

[15]Again the Israelites cried out to the LORD, and he gave them a deliverer—Ehud, a left-handed man, the son of Gera the Benjamite. The Israelites sent him with tribute to Eglon king of Moab. [16]Now Ehud had made a double-edged sword about a foot and a half[c] long, which he strapped to his right thigh under his clothing. [17]He presented the tribute to Eglon king of Moab, who was a very fat man. [18]After Ehud had presented the tribute, he sent on their way the men who had carried it. [19]At the idols[d] near Gilgal he himself turned back and said, "I have a secret message for you, O king."

The king said, "Quiet!" And all his attendants left him.

[20]Ehud then approached him while he was sitting alone in the upper room of his summer palace[e] and said, "I have a message from God for you." As the king rose from his seat, [21]Ehud reached with his left hand, drew the sword from his right thigh and plunged it into the king's belly. [22]Even the handle sank in after the blade, which came out his back. Ehud did not pull the sword out, and the fat closed in over it. [23]Then Ehud went out to the porch[f]; he shut the doors of the upper room behind him and locked them.   Am 3:15

[24]After he had gone, the servants came and found the doors of the upper room locked. They said, "He must be relieving himself in the inner room of the house." [25]They waited to the point of embarrassment, but when he did not open the doors of the room, they took a key and unlocked them. There they saw their lord fallen to the floor, dead.   1Sa 24:3; 2Ki 2:17

[26]While they waited, Ehud got away. He passed by the idols and escaped to Seirah. [27]When he ar-

---

[a]10 Or leader   [b]13 That is, Jericho   [c]16 Hebrew a cubit (about 0.5 meter)   [d]19 Or the stone quarries; also in verse 26   [e]20 The meaning of the Hebrew for this phrase is uncertain.   [f]23 The meaning of the Hebrew for this word is uncertain.

rived there, he blew a trumpet in the hill country of Ephraim, and the Israelites went down with him from the hills, with him leading them.   Jdg 6:34

²⁸"Follow me," he ordered, "for the Lord has given Moab, your enemy, into your hands." So they followed him down and, taking possession of the fords of the Jordan that led to Moab, they allowed no one to cross over. ²⁹At that time they struck down about ten thousand Moabites, all vigorous and strong; not a man escaped. ³⁰That day Moab was made subject to Israel, and the land had peace for eighty years.   Jdg 7:9,15,24; 12:5

Shamgar

³¹After Ehud came Shamgar son of Anath, who struck down six hundred Philistines with an oxgoad. He too saved Israel.   Jdg 5:6

Deborah

4 After Ehud died, the Israelites once again did evil in the eyes of the Lord. ²So the Lord sold them into the hands of Jabin, a king of Canaan, who reigned in Hazor. The commander of his army was Sisera, who lived in Harosheth Haggoyim. ³Because he had nine hundred iron chariots and had cruelly oppressed the Israelites for twenty years, they cried to the Lord for help.   Jdg 1:19; 2:19

⁴Deborah, a prophetess, the wife of Lappidoth, was leading[a] Israel at that time. ⁵She held court under the Palm of Deborah between Ramah and Bethel in the hill country of Ephraim, and the Israelites came to her to have their disputes decided. ⁶She sent for Barak son of Abinoam from Kedesh in Naphtali and said to him, "The Lord, the God of Israel, commands you: 'Go, take with you ten thousand men of Naphtali and Zebulun and lead the way to Mount Tabor. ⁷I will lure Sisera, the commander of Jabin's army, with his chariots and his troops to the Kishon River and give him into your hands.' "   Heb 11:32

⁸Barak said to her, "If you go with me, I will go; but if you don't go with me, I won't go."

⁹"Very well," Deborah said, "I will go with you. But because of the way you are going about this,[b] the honor will not be yours, for the Lord will hand Sisera over to a woman." So Deborah went with Barak to Kedesh, ¹⁰where he summoned Zebulun and Naphtali. Ten thousand men followed him, and Deborah also went with him.

¹¹Now Heber the Kenite had left the other Kenites, the descendants of Hobab, Moses' brother-in-law,[c] and pitched his tent by the great tree in Zaanannim near Kedesh.

¹²When they told Sisera that Barak son of Abinoam had gone up to Mount Tabor, ¹³Sisera gathered together his nine hundred iron

---

[a]4 Traditionally judging   [b]9 Or But on the expedition you are undertaking   [c]11 Or father-in-law

chariots and all the men with him, from Harosheth Haggoyim to the Kishon River.

¹⁴Then Deborah said to Barak, "Go! This is the day the LORD has given Sisera into your hands. Has not the LORD gone ahead of you?" So Barak went down Mount Tabor, followed by ten thousand men. ¹⁵At Barak's advance, the LORD routed Sisera and all his chariots and army by the sword, and Sisera abandoned his chariot and fled on foot. ¹⁶But Barak pursued the chariots and army as far as Harosheth Haggoyim. All the troops of Sisera fell by the sword; not a man was left.   Dt 9:3; Jos 10:10; 2Sa 5:24

¹⁷Sisera, however, fled on foot to the tent of Jael, the wife of Heber the Kenite, because there were friendly relations between Jabin king of Hazor and the clan of Heber the Kenite.

¹⁸Jael went out to meet Sisera and said to him, "Come, my lord, come right in. Don't be afraid." So he entered her tent, and she put a covering over him.

¹⁹"I'm thirsty," he said. "Please give me some water." She opened a skin of milk, gave him a drink, and covered him up.

²⁰"Stand in the doorway of the tent," he told her. "If someone comes by and asks you, 'Is anyone here?' say 'No.'"

²¹But Jael, Heber's wife, picked up a tent peg and a hammer and went quietly to him while he lay fast asleep, exhausted. She drove the peg through his temple into the ground, and he died.

²²Barak came by in pursuit of Sisera, and Jael went out to meet him. "Come," she said, "I will show you the man you're looking for." So he went in with her, and there lay Sisera with the tent peg through his temple—dead.

²³On that day God subdued Jabin, the Canaanite king, before the Israelites. ²⁴And the hand of the Israelites grew stronger and stronger against Jabin, the Canaanite king, until they destroyed him.   Ne 9:24

The Song of Deborah

5 On that day Deborah and Barak son of Abinoam sang this song: Ex 15:1

²"When the princes in Israel
	take the lead,
when the people willingly
	offer themselves—
praise the LORD!

³"Hear this, you kings! Listen,
	you rulers!
I will sing to*a* the LORD, I
	will sing;
I will make music to*b* the
	LORD, the God of Israel.

⁴"O LORD, when you went out
	from Seir,
when you marched from the
	land of Edom, Dt 33:2

---

*a*3 Or *of*   *b*3 Or / *with song I will praise*

the earth shook, the heavens
    poured,
the clouds poured down
    water.   Ps 68:8
[5]The mountains quaked before
    the LORD, the One of
    Sinai,
before the LORD, the God of
    Israel.   Ex 19:18

[6]"In the days of Shamgar son of
    Anath,   Jdg 3:31
in the days of Jael, the roads
    were abandoned;   Jdg 4:17
travelers took to winding
    paths.
[7]Village life[a] in Israel ceased,
    ceased until I,[b] Deborah,
    arose,
arose a mother in Israel.
[8]When they chose new gods,
    war came to the city gates,
and not a shield or spear was
    seen
    among forty thousand in
    Israel.
[9]My heart is with Israel's
    princes,
with the willing volunteers
    among the people.
Praise the LORD!

[10]"You who ride on white
    donkeys,   Jdg 10:4
sitting on your saddle
    blankets,
and you who walk along the
    road,
consider [11]the voice of the

singers[c] at the watering
    places.
They recite the righteous
    acts of the LORD,   1Sa 12:7
the righteous acts of his
    warriors[d] in Israel.

"Then the people of the LORD
    went down to the city gates.
[12]'Wake up, wake up, Deborah!
    Wake up, wake up, break
    out in song!
Arise, O Barak!
    Take captive your captives,
    O son of Abinoam.'

[13]"Then the men who were left
    came down to the nobles;
the people of the LORD
    came to me with the mighty.
[14]Some came from Ephraim,
    whose roots were in
    Amalek;
Benjamin was with the
    people who followed
    you.
From Makir captains came
    down,
from Zebulun those who
    bear a commander's
    staff.
[15]The princes of Issachar were
    with Deborah;   Jdg 4:10
yes, Issachar was with Barak,
    rushing after him into the
    valley.
In the districts of Reuben
    there was much searching of
    heart.

---

a 7 Or Warriors   b 7 Or you   c 11 Or archers; the meaning of the Hebrew for this word is uncertain.
d 11 Or villagers

¹⁶Why did you stay among the
    campfires*
  to hear the whistling for the
    flocks?   Nu 32:1
In the districts of Reuben
  there was much searching of
    heart.
¹⁷Gilead stayed beyond the
    Jordan.
  And Dan, why did he linger
    by the ships?
Asher remained on the coast
  and stayed in his coves.
¹⁸The people of Zebulun risked
    their very lives;
  so did Naphtali on the
    heights of the field.
¹⁹"Kings came, they fought;
  the kings of Canaan
    fought
  at Taanach by the waters of
    Megiddo,   Jdg 1:27
  but they carried off no silver,
    no plunder.
²⁰From the heavens the stars
    fought,
  from their courses they
    fought against Sisera.
²¹The river Kishon swept them
    away,
  the age-old river, the river
    Kishon.
  March on, my soul; be
    strong!
²²Then thundered the horses'
    hoofs—
  galloping, galloping go his
    mighty steeds.

²³'Curse Meroz,' said the angel
    of the LORD.
  'Curse its people bitterly,
  because they did not come to
    help the LORD,
  to help the LORD against the
    mighty.'
²⁴"Most blessed of women be
    Jael,   Jdg 4:17
  the wife of Heber the
    Kenite,
  most blessed of tent-dwelling
    women.
²⁵He asked for water, and she
    gave him milk;
  in a bowl fit for nobles she
    brought him curdled
    milk.
²⁶Her hand reached for the tent
    peg,
  her right hand for the
    workman's hammer.
She struck Sisera, she crushed
    his head,
  she shattered and pierced his
    temple.
²⁷At her feet he sank,
  he fell; there he lay.
At her feet he sank, he fell;
  where he sank, there he
    fell—dead.
²⁸"Through the window peered
    Sisera's mother;
  behind the lattice she cried
    out,   Pr 7:6
  'Why is his chariot so long in
    coming?

---

a 16 Or *saddlebags*

Why is the clatter of his
    chariots delayed?'
²⁹The wisest of her ladies answer
    her;
    indeed, she keeps saying to
      herself,
³⁰'Are they not finding and
    dividing the spoils:
    a girl or two for each man,
    colorful garments as plunder
      for Sisera,
    colorful garments
      embroidered,
    highly embroidered garments
      for my neck—
all this as plunder?'

³¹"So may all your enemies
    perish, O Lord!
    But may they who love you
      be like the sun   Ps 19:4
    when it rises in its strength."

Then the land had peace forty
years.   Jdg 3:11

Gideon

6 Again the Israelites did evil in the eyes of the Lord, and for seven years he gave them into the hands of the Midianites. ²Because the power of Midian was so oppressive, the Israelites prepared shelters for themselves in mountain clefts, caves and strongholds. ³Whenever the Israelites planted their crops, the Midianites, Amalekites and other eastern peoples invaded the country. ⁴They camped on the land and ruined the crops all the way to Gaza and did not spare a living thing for Israel, neither sheep nor cattle nor donkeys. ⁵They came up with their livestock and their tents like swarms of locusts. It was impossible to count the men and their camels; they invaded the land to ravage it. ⁶Midian so impoverished the Israelites that they cried out to the Lord for help.   Lev 26:16; Jdg 7:12

⁷When the Israelites cried to the Lord because of Midian, ⁸he sent them a prophet, who said, "This is what the Lord, the God of Israel, says: I brought you up out of Egypt, out of the land of slavery. ⁹I snatched you from the power of Egypt and from the hand of all your oppressors. I drove them from before you and gave you their land. ¹⁰I said to you, 'I am the Lord your God; do not worship the gods of the Amorites, in whose land you live.' But you have not listened to me."   Jdg 2:1; Ps 44:2

¹¹The angel of the Lord came and sat down under the oak in Ophrah that belonged to Joash the Abiezrite, where his son Gideon was threshing wheat in a winepress to keep it from the Midianites. ¹²When the angel of the Lord appeared to Gideon, he said, "The Lord is with you, mighty warrior."

¹³"But sir," Gideon replied, "if the Lord is with us, why has all this happened to us? Where are all his wonders that our fathers told us about when they said, 'Did not the Lord bring us up out of Egypt?' But now the Lord has abandoned

us and put us into the hand of Midian." Ps 44:1

¹⁴The LORD turned to him and said, "Go in the strength you have and save Israel out of Midian's hand. Am I not sending you?"

¹⁵"But Lord,ᵃ" Gideon asked, "how can I save Israel? My clan is the weakest in Manasseh, and I am the least in my family." 1Sa 9:21

¹⁶The LORD answered, "I will be with you, and you will strike down all the Midianites together."

¹⁷Gideon replied, "If now I have found favor in your eyes, give me a sign that it is really you talking to me. ¹⁸Please do not go away until I come back and bring my offering and set it before you." Ge 24:14

And the LORD said, "I will wait until you return."

¹⁹Gideon went in, prepared a young goat, and from an ephahᵇ of flour he made bread without yeast. Putting the meat in a basket and its broth in a pot, he brought them out and offered them to him under the oak. Ge 18:7-8

²⁰The angel of God said to him, "Take the meat and the unleavened bread, place them on this rock, and pour out the broth." And Gideon did so. ²¹With the tip of the staff that was in his hand, the angel of the LORD touched the meat and the unleavened bread. Fire flared from the rock, consuming the meat and the bread. And the angel

of the LORD disappeared. ²²When Gideon realized that it was the angel of the LORD, he exclaimed, "Ah, Sovereign LORD! I have seen the angel of the LORD face to face!"

²³But the LORD said to him, "Peace! Do not be afraid. You are not going to die." Da 10:19

²⁴So Gideon built an altar to the LORD there and called it The LORD is Peace. To this day it stands in Ophrah of the Abiezrites. Jdg 8:32

²⁵That same night the LORD said to him, "Take the second bull from your father's herd, the one seven years old.ᶜ Tear down your father's altar to Baal and cut down the Asherah poleᵈ beside it. ²⁶Then build a proper kind ofᵉ altar to the LORD your God on the top of this height. Using the wood of the Asherah pole that you cut down, offer the secondᶠ bull as a burnt offering." Ex 34:13

²⁷So Gideon took ten of his servants and did as the LORD told him. But because he was afraid of his family and the men of the town, he did it at night rather than in the daytime.

²⁸In the morning when the men of the town got up, there was Baal's altar, demolished, with the Asherah pole beside it cut down and the second bull sacrificed on the newly built altar! 1Ki 16:32

²⁹They asked each other, "Who did this?"

ᵃ15 Or sir   ᵇ19 That is, probably about 3/5 bushel (about 22 liters)   ᶜ25 Or Take a full-grown, mature bull from your father's herd   ᵈ25 That is, a symbol of the goddess Asherah; here and elsewhere in Judges   ᵉ26 Or build with layers of stone an   ᶠ26 Or full-grown; also in verse 28

When they carefully investigated, they were told, "Gideon son of Joash did it."

30The men of the town demanded of Joash, "Bring out your son. He must die, because he has broken down Baal's altar and cut down the Asherah pole beside it."

31But Joash replied to the hostile crowd around him, "Are you going to plead Baal's cause? Are you trying to save him? Whoever fights for him shall be put to death by morning! If Baal really is a god, he can defend himself when someone breaks down his altar." **32**So that day they called Gideon "Jerub-Baal,*a*" saying, "Let Baal contend with him," because he broke down Baal's altar.

Jdg 7:1; 1Sa 12:11

33Now all the Midianites, Amalekites and other eastern peoples joined forces and crossed over the Jordan and camped in the Valley of Jezreel. **34**Then the Spirit of the LORD came upon Gideon, and he blew a trumpet, summoning the Abiezrites to follow him. **35**He sent messengers throughout Manasseh, calling them to arms, and also into Asher, Zebulun and Naphtali, so that they too went up to meet them.

Jos 17:16; Jdg 3:10,27; 4:6

36Gideon said to God, "If you will save Israel by my hand as you have promised— **37**look, I will place a wool fleece on the threshing floor. If there is dew only on the fleece and all the ground is dry, then I will know that you will save Israel by my hand, as you said." **38**And that is what happened. Gideon rose early the next day; he squeezed the fleece and wrung out the dew—a bowlful of water.

39Then Gideon said to God, "Do not be angry with me. Let me make just one more request. Allow me one more test with the fleece. This time make the fleece dry and the ground covered with dew." **40**That night God did so. Only the fleece was dry; all the ground was covered with dew.

Ge 18:32

Gideon Defeats the Midianites

7 Early in the morning, Jerub-Baal (that is, Gideon) and all his men camped at the spring of Harod. The camp of Midian was north of them in the valley near the hill of Moreh. **2**The LORD said to Gideon, "You have too many men for me to deliver Midian into their hands. In order that Israel may not boast against me that her own strength has saved her, **3**announce now to the people, 'Anyone who trembles with fear may turn back and leave Mount Gilead.'" So twenty-two thousand men left, while ten thousand remained.

4But the LORD said to Gideon, "There are still too many men. Take them down to the water, and I will sift them for you there. If I say, 'This one shall go with you,' he shall go; but if I say, 'This one

---

a 32 *Jerub-Baal* means *let Baal contend.*

shall not go with you,' he shall not go." 1Sa 14:6

⁵So Gideon took the men down to the water. There the LORD told him, "Separate those who lap the water with their tongues like a dog from those who kneel down to drink." ⁶Three hundred men lapped with their hands to their mouths. All the rest got down on their knees to drink.

⁷The LORD said to Gideon, "With the three hundred men that lapped I will save you and give the Midianites into your hands. Let all the other men go, each to his own place." ⁸So Gideon sent the rest of the Israelites to their tents but kept the three hundred, who took over the provisions and trumpets of the others. Jos 8:7

Now the camp of Midian lay below him in the valley. ⁹During that night the LORD said to Gideon, "Get up, go down against the camp, because I am going to give it into your hands. ¹⁰If you are afraid to attack, go down to the camp with your servant Purah ¹¹and listen to what they are saying. Afterward, you will be encouraged to attack the camp." So he and Purah his servant went down to the outposts of the camp. ¹²The Midianites, the Amalekites and all the other eastern peoples had settled in the valley, thick as locusts. Their camels could no more be counted than the sand on the seashore. Jos 2:24; 11:4

¹³Gideon arrived just as a man was telling a friend his dream. "I had a dream," he was saying. "A round loaf of barley bread came tumbling into the Midianite camp. It struck the tent with such force that the tent overturned and collapsed."

¹⁴His friend responded, "This can be nothing other than the sword of Gideon son of Joash, the Israelite. God has given the Midianites and the whole camp into his hands."

¹⁵When Gideon heard the dream and its interpretation, he worshiped God. He returned to the camp of Israel and called out, "Get up! The LORD has given the Midianite camp into your hands." ¹⁶Dividing the three hundred men into three companies, he placed trumpets and empty jars in the hands of all of them, with torches inside.

¹⁷"Watch me," he told them. "Follow my lead. When I get to the edge of the camp, do exactly as I do. ¹⁸When I and all who are with me blow our trumpets, then from all around the camp blow yours and shout, 'For the LORD and for Gideon.'" Jdg 3:27

¹⁹Gideon and the hundred men with him reached the edge of the camp at the beginning of the middle watch, just after they had changed the guard. They blew their trumpets and broke the jars that were in their hands. ²⁰The three companies blew the trumpets and smashed the jars. Grasping the torches in their left hands and holding in their right hands

the trumpets they were to blow, they shouted, "A sword for the Lord and for Gideon!" ²¹While each man held his position around the camp, all the Midianites ran, crying out as they fled.   2Ki 7:7

²²When the three hundred trumpets sounded, the Lord caused the men throughout the camp to turn on each other with their swords. The army fled to Beth Shittah toward Zererah as far as the border of Abel Meholah near Tabbath. ²³Israelites from Naphtali, Asher and all Manasseh were called out, and they pursued the Midianites. ²⁴Gideon sent messengers throughout the hill country of Ephraim, saying, "Come down against the Midianites and seize the waters of the Jordan ahead of them as far as Beth Barah."

So all the men of Ephraim were called out and they took the waters of the Jordan as far as Beth Barah. ²⁵They also captured two of the Midianite leaders, Oreb and Zeeb. They killed Oreb at the rock of Oreb, and Zeeb at the winepress of Zeeb. They pursued the Midianites and brought the heads of Oreb and Zeeb to Gideon, who was by the Jordan.   Jdg 8:4; Ps 83:11; Isa 10:26

Zebah and Zalmunna

8 Now the Ephraimites asked Gideon, "Why have you treated us like this? Why didn't you call us when you went to fight Midian?" And they criticized him sharply.   Jdg 12:1

²But he answered them, "What have I accomplished compared to you? Aren't the gleanings of Ephraim's grapes better than the full grape harvest of Abiezer? ³God gave Oreb and Zeeb, the Midianite leaders, into your hands. What was I able to do compared to you?" At this, their resentment against him subsided.   Jdg 7:25; Pr 15:1

⁴Gideon and his three hundred men, exhausted yet keeping up the pursuit, came to the Jordan and crossed it. ⁵He said to the men of Succoth, "Give my troops some bread; they are worn out, and I am still pursuing Zebah and Zalmunna, the kings of Midian."   Ge 33:17

⁶But the officials of Succoth said, "Do you already have the hands of Zebah and Zalmunna in your possession? Why should we give bread to your troops?"

⁷Then Gideon replied, "Just for that, when the Lord has given Zebah and Zalmunna into my hand, I will tear your flesh with desert thorns and briers."   Jdg 7:15

⁸From there he went up to Peniel*a* and made the same request of them, but they answered as the men of Succoth had. ⁹So he said to the men of Peniel, "When I return in triumph, I will tear down this tower."   Ge 32:30; 1Ki 12:25

---

a8 Hebrew *Penuel,* a variant of *Peniel*; also in verses 9 and 17

¹⁰Now Zebah and Zalmunna were in Karkor with a force of about fifteen thousand men, all that were left of the armies of the eastern peoples; a hundred and twenty thousand swordsmen had fallen. ¹¹Gideon went up by the route of the nomads east of Nobah and Jogbehah and fell upon the unsuspecting army. ¹²Zebah and Zalmunna, the two kings of Midian, fled, but he pursued them and captured them, routing their entire army.   Jdg 7:12; Nu 32:42; Isa 9:4

¹³Gideon son of Joash then returned from the battle by the Pass of Heres. ¹⁴He caught a young man of Succoth and questioned him, and the young man wrote down for him the names of the seventy-seven officials of Succoth, the elders of the town. ¹⁵Then Gideon came and said to the men of Succoth, "Here are Zebah and Zalmunna, about whom you taunted me by saying, 'Do you already have the hands of Zebah and Zalmunna in your possession? Why should we give bread to your exhausted men?' " ¹⁶He took the elders of the town and taught the men of Succoth a lesson by punishing them with desert thorns and briers. ¹⁷He also pulled down the tower of Peniel and killed the men of the town.   Jdg 6:11

¹⁸Then he asked Zebah and Zalmunna, "What kind of men did you kill at Tabor?"   Jdg 4:6

"Men like you," they answered, "each one with the bearing of a prince."

¹⁹Gideon replied, "Those were my brothers, the sons of my own mother. As surely as the LORD lives, if you had spared their lives, I would not kill you." ²⁰Turning to Jether, his oldest son, he said, "Kill them!" But Jether did not draw his sword, because he was only a boy and was afraid.

²¹Zebah and Zalmunna said, "Come, do it yourself. 'As is the man, so is his strength.' " So Gideon stepped forward and killed them, and took the ornaments off their camels' necks.   Ps 83:11

Gideon's Ephod

²²The Israelites said to Gideon, "Rule over us — you, your son and your grandson — because you have saved us out of the hand of Midian."

²³But Gideon told them, "I will not rule over you, nor will my son rule over you. The LORD will rule over you." ²⁴And he said, "I do have one request, that each of you give me an earring from your share of the plunder." (It was the custom of the Ishmaelites to wear gold earrings.)   1Sa 8:7; 12:12; Ge 25:13

²⁵They answered, "We'll be glad to give them." So they spread out a garment, and each man threw a ring from his plunder onto it. ²⁶The weight of the gold rings he asked for came to seventeen hun-

dred shekels,ᵃ not counting the ornaments, the pendants and the purple garments worn by the kings of Midian or the chains that were on their camels' necks. ²⁷Gideon made the gold into an ephod, which he placed in Ophrah, his town. All Israel prostituted themselves by worshiping it there, and it became a snare to Gideon and his family.   Jdg 17:5; Dt 7:16; Ps 106:39

Gideon's Death

²⁸Thus Midian was subdued before the Israelites and did not raise its head again. During Gideon's lifetime, the land enjoyed peace forty years.   Jdg 5:31

²⁹Jerub-Baal son of Joash went back home to live. ³⁰He had seventy sons of his own, for he had many wives. ³¹His concubine, who lived in Shechem, also bore him a son, whom he named Abimelech. ³²Gideon son of Joash died at a good old age and was buried in the tomb of his father Joash in Ophrah of the Abiezrites.   Jdg 7:1; 9:2,5,18,24

³³No sooner had Gideon died than the Israelites again prostituted themselves to the Baals. They set up Baal-Berith as their god and ³⁴did not remember the LORD their God, who had rescued them from the hands of all their enemies on every side. ³⁵They also failed to show kindness to the family of Jerub-Baal (that is, Gideon) for all the good things he had done for them.

Abimelech

9 Abimelech son of Jerub-Baal went to his mother's brothers in Shechem and said to them and to all his mother's clan, ²"Ask all the citizens of Shechem, 'Which is better for you: to have all seventy of Jerub-Baal's sons rule over you, or just one man?' Remember, I am your flesh and blood."   Ge 29:14

³When the brothers repeated all this to the citizens of Shechem, they were inclined to follow Abimelech, for they said, "He is our brother." ⁴They gave him seventy shekelsᵇ of silver from the temple of Baal-Berith, and Abimelech used it to hire reckless adventurers, who became his followers. ⁵He went to his father's home in Ophrah and on one stone murdered his seventy brothers, the sons of Jerub-Baal. But Jotham, the youngest son of Jerub-Baal, escaped by hiding. ⁶Then all the citizens of Shechem and Beth Millo gathered beside the great tree at the pillar in Shechem to crown Abimelech king.   Jdg 8:33; 2Ki 11:2

⁷When Jotham was told about this, he climbed up on the top of Mount Gerizim and shouted to them, "Listen to me, citizens of Shechem, so that God may listen to you. ⁸One day the trees went out to anoint a king for themselves.

ᵃ26 That is, about 43 pounds (about 19.5 kilograms)   ᵇ4 That is, about 1 3/4 pounds (about 0.8 kilogram)

They said to the olive tree, 'Be our king.'   Dt 11:29; Jn 4:20

9"But the olive tree answered, 'Should I give up my oil, by which both gods and men are honored, to hold sway over the trees?'

10"Next, the trees said to the fig tree, 'Come and be our king.'

11"But the fig tree replied, 'Should I give up my fruit, so good and sweet, to hold sway over the trees?'

12"Then the trees said to the vine, 'Come and be our king.'

13"But the vine answered, 'Should I give up my wine, which cheers both gods and men, to hold sway over the trees?'   Ecc 2:3

14"Finally all the trees said to the thornbush, 'Come and be our king.'

15"The thornbush said to the trees, 'If you really want to anoint me king over you, come and take refuge in my shade; but if not, then let fire come out of the thornbush and consume the cedars of Lebanon!'   Isa 30:2

16"Now if you have acted honorably and in good faith when you made Abimelech king, and if you have been fair to Jerub-Baal and his family, and if you have treated him as he deserves— 17and to think that my father fought for you, risked his life to rescue you from the hand of Midian 18(but today you have revolted against my father's family, murdered his seventy sons on a single stone, and made Abimelech, the son of his slave girl, king over the citizens of Shechem because he is your brother) — 19if then you have acted honorably and in good faith toward Jerub-Baal and his family today, may Abimelech be your joy, and may you be his, too! 20But if you have not, let fire come out from Abimelech and consume you, citizens of Shechem and Beth Millo, and let fire come out from you, citizens of Shechem and Beth Millo, and consume Abimelech!"   Jdg 8:30

21Then Jotham fled, escaping to Beer, and he lived there because he was afraid of his brother Abimelech.

22After Abimelech had governed Israel three years, 23God sent an evil spirit between Abimelech and the citizens of Shechem, who acted treacherously against Abimelech. 24God did this in order that the crime against Jerub-Baal's seventy sons, the shedding of their blood, might be avenged on their brother Abimelech and on the citizens of Shechem, who had helped him murder his brothers. 25In opposition to him these citizens of Shechem set men on the hilltops to ambush and rob everyone who passed by, and this was reported to Abimelech.   Nu 35:33; Dt 27:25

26Now Gaal son of Ebed moved with his brothers into Shechem, and its citizens put their confidence in him. 27After they had gone out into the fields and gathered the grapes and trodden them, they held a festival in the temple of their god. While they were eating and drinking, they cursed Abimelech. ²⁸Then Gaal son of Ebed said, "Who is Abimelech, and who is Shechem, that we should be subject to him? Isn't he Jerub-Baal's son, and isn't Zebul his deputy? Serve the men of Hamor, Shechem's father! Why should we serve Abimelech? ²⁹If only this people were under my command! Then I would get rid of him. I would say to Abimelech, 'Call out your whole army!' "ᵃ   2Sa 15:4

³⁰When Zebul the governor of the city heard what Gaal son of Ebed said, he was very angry. ³¹Under cover he sent messengers to Abimelech, saying, "Gaal son of Ebed and his brothers have come to Shechem and are stirring up the city against you. ³²Now then, during the night you and your men should come and lie in wait in the fields. ³³In the morning at sunrise, advance against the city. When Gaal and his men come out against you, do whatever your hand finds to do."   1Sa 10:7

³⁴So Abimelech and all his troops set out by night and took up concealed positions near Shechem in four companies. ³⁵Now Gaal son of Ebed had gone out and was standing at the entrance to the city gate just as Abimelech and his soldiers came out from their hiding place.   Ps 32:7; Jer 49:10

³⁶When Gaal saw them, he said to Zebul, "Look, people are coming down from the tops of the mountains!"

Zebul replied, "You mistake the shadows of the mountains for men."

³⁷But Gaal spoke up again: "Look, people are coming down from the center of the land, and a company is coming from the direction of the soothsayers' tree."

³⁸Then Zebul said to him, "Where is your big talk now, you who said, 'Who is Abimelech that we should be subject to him?' Aren't these the men you ridiculed? Go out and fight them!"

³⁹So Gaal led outᵇ the citizens of Shechem and fought Abimelech. ⁴⁰Abimelech chased him, and many fell wounded in the flight—all the way to the entrance to the gate. ⁴¹Abimelech stayed in Arumah, and Zebul drove Gaal and his brothers out of Shechem.

⁴²The next day the people of Shechem went out to the fields, and this was reported to Abimelech. ⁴³So he took his men, divided them into three companies and set an ambush in the fields. When he saw the people coming out of the city, he rose to attack them. ⁴⁴Abimelech and the companies with him rushed forward to a position at the entrance to the city gate. Then two companies rushed upon

---

ᵃ 29 Septuagint; Hebrew him." Then he said to Abimelech, "Call out your whole army!"   ᵇ 39 Or Gaal went out in the sight of

those in the fields and struck them down. ⁴⁵All that day Abimelech pressed his attack against the city until he had captured it and killed its people. Then he destroyed the city and scattered salt over it.

⁴⁶On hearing this, the citizens in the tower of Shechem went into the stronghold of the temple of El-Berith. ⁴⁷When Abimelech heard that they had assembled there, ⁴⁸he and all his men went up Mount Zalmon. He took an ax and cut off some branches, which he lifted to his shoulders. He ordered the men with him, "Quick! Do what you have seen me do!" ⁴⁹So all the men cut branches and followed Abimelech. They piled them against the stronghold and set it on fire over the people inside. So all the people in the tower of Shechem, about a thousand men and women, also died.   Ps 68:14

⁵⁰Next Abimelech went to Thebez and besieged it and captured it. ⁵¹Inside the city, however, was a strong tower, to which all the men and women—all the people of the city—fled. They locked themselves in and climbed up on the tower roof. ⁵²Abimelech went to the tower and stormed it. But as he approached the entrance to the tower to set it on fire, ⁵³a woman dropped an upper millstone on his head and cracked his skull.

⁵⁴Hurriedly he called to his armor-bearer, "Draw your sword and kill me, so that they can't say, 'A woman killed him.'" So his servant ran him through, and he died. ⁵⁵When the Israelites saw that Abimelech was dead, they went home.   1Sa 31:4

⁵⁶Thus God repaid the wickedness that Abimelech had done to his father by murdering his seventy brothers. ⁵⁷God also made the men of Shechem pay for all their wickedness. The curse of Jotham son of Jerub-Baal came on them.

Tola

10 After the time of Abimelech a man of Issachar, Tola son of Puah, the son of Dodo, rose to save Israel. He lived in Shamir, in the hill country of Ephraim. ²He led ᵃ Israel twenty-three years; then he died, and was buried in Shamir.   Jdg 2:16; Ge 46:13

Jair

³He was followed by Jair of Gilead, who led Israel twenty-two years. ⁴He had thirty sons, who rode thirty donkeys. They controlled thirty towns in Gilead, which to this day are called Havvoth Jair.ᵇ ⁵When Jair died, he was buried in Kamon.   Nu 32:41

Jephthah

⁶Again the Israelites did evil in the eyes of the LORD. They served the Baals and the Ashtoreths, and

---

ᵃ2 Traditionally *judged*; also in verse 3   ᵇ4 Or *called the settlements of Jair* the gods of Aram, the gods of Sidon, the gods of Moab, the gods of the Ammonites and the gods of the Philistines. And because the Israelites forsook the Lord and no longer served him, [7]he became angry with them. He sold them into the hands of the Philistines and the Ammonites, [8]who that year shattered and crushed them. For eighteen years they oppressed all the Israelites on the east side of the Jordan in Gilead, the land of the Amorites. [9]The Ammonites also crossed the Jordan to fight against Judah, Benjamin and the house of Ephraim; and Israel was in great distress. [10]Then the Israelites cried out to the Lord, "We have sinned against you, forsaking our God and serving the Baals." Jdg 2:13; Dt 31:17

[11]The Lord replied, "When the Egyptians, the Amorites, the Ammonites, the Philistines, [12]the Sidonians, the Amalekites and the Maonites[a] oppressed you and you cried to me for help, did I not save you from their hands? [13]But you have forsaken me and served other gods, so I will no longer save you. [14]Go and cry out to the gods you have chosen. Let them save you when you are in trouble!" Dt 32:37

[15]But the Israelites said to the Lord, "We have sinned. Do with us whatever you think best, but please rescue us now." [16]Then they got rid of the foreign gods among them and served the Lord.

And he could bear Israel's misery no longer. Jos 24:23; 1Sa 3:18; Isa 63:9

[17]When the Ammonites were called to arms and camped in Gilead, the Israelites assembled and camped at Mizpah. [18]The leaders of the people of Gilead said to each other, "Whoever will launch the attack against the Ammonites will be the head of all those living in Gilead." Jdg 11:8,9,29

11 Jephthah the Gileadite was a mighty warrior. His father was Gilead; his mother was a prostitute. [2]Gilead's wife also bore him sons, and when they were grown up, they drove Jephthah away. "You are not going to get any inheritance in our family," they said, "because you are the son of another woman." [3]So Jephthah fled from his brothers and settled in the land of Tob, where a group of adventurers gathered around him and followed him. Heb 11:32

[4]Some time later, when the Ammonites made war on Israel, [5]the elders of Gilead went to get Jephthah from the land of Tob. [6]"Come," they said, "be our commander, so we can fight the Ammonites." Jdg 10:9

[7]Jephthah said to them, "Didn't you hate me and drive me from my father's house? Why do you come to me now, when you're in trouble?" Ge 26:27

[8]The elders of Gilead said to him, "Nevertheless, we are turning

---

a 12 Hebrew; some Septuagint manuscripts *Midianites*

to you now; come with us to fight the Ammonites, and you will be our head over all who live in Gilead." `Jdg 10:18`

⁹Jephthah answered, "Suppose you take me back to fight the Ammonites and the LORD gives them to me—will I really be your head?"

¹⁰The elders of Gilead replied, "The LORD is our witness; we will certainly do as you say." ¹¹So Jephthah went with the elders of Gilead, and the people made him head and commander over them. And he repeated all his words before the LORD in Mizpah. `Jer 42:5`

¹²Then Jephthah sent messengers to the Ammonite king with the question: "What do you have against us that you have attacked our country?"

¹³The king of the Ammonites answered Jephthah's messengers, "When Israel came up out of Egypt, they took away my land from the Arnon to the Jabbok, all the way to the Jordan. Now give it back peaceably." `Nu 21:24`

¹⁴Jephthah sent back messengers to the Ammonite king, ¹⁵saying:

"This is what Jephthah says: Israel did not take the land of Moab or the land of the Ammonites. ¹⁶But when they came up out of Egypt, Israel went through the desert to the Red Sea*a* and on to Kadesh.

¹⁷Then Israel sent messengers to the king of Edom, saying, 'Give us permission to go through your country,' but the king of Edom would not listen. They sent also to the king of Moab, and he refused. So Israel stayed at Kadesh.

¹⁸"Next they traveled through the desert, skirted the lands of Edom and Moab, passed along the eastern side of the country of Moab, and camped on the other side of the Arnon. They did not enter the territory of Moab, for the Arnon was its border. `Nu 21:4`

¹⁹"Then Israel sent messengers to Sihon king of the Amorites, who ruled in Heshbon, and said to him, 'Let us pass through your country to our own place.' ²⁰Sihon, however, did not trust Israel*b* to pass through his territory. He mustered all his men and encamped at Jahaz and fought with Israel. `Nu 21:21-22; Dt 2:32`

²¹"Then the LORD, the God of Israel, gave Sihon and all his men into Israel's hands, and they defeated them. Israel took over all the land of the Amorites who lived in that country, ²²capturing all of it from the Arnon to the Jabbok and from the desert to the Jordan. `Dt 2:36`

a 16 Hebrew *Yam Suph*; that is, Sea of Reeds   *b 20* Or *however, would not make an agreement for Israel*

²³"Now since the LORD, the God of Israel, has driven the Amorites out before his people Israel, what right have you to take it over? ²⁴Will you not take what your god Chemosh gives you? Likewise, whatever the LORD our God has given us, we will possess. ²⁵Are you better than Balak son of Zippor, king of Moab? Did he ever quarrel with Israel or fight with them? ²⁶For three hundred years Israel occupied Heshbon, Aroer, the surrounding settlements and all the towns along the Arnon. Why didn't you retake them during that time? ²⁷I have not wronged you, but you are doing me wrong by waging war against me. Let the LORD, the Judge,ᵃ decide the dispute this day between the Israelites and the Ammonites."   Ge 16:5

²⁸The king of Ammon, however, paid no attention to the message Jephthah sent him.

²⁹Then the Spirit of the LORD came upon Jephthah. He crossed Gilead and Manasseh, passed through Mizpah of Gilead, and from there he advanced against the Ammonites. ³⁰And Jephthah made a vow to the LORD: "If you give the Ammonites into my hands, ³¹whatever comes out of the door of my house to meet me when I return in triumph from the Ammonites will be the LORD's, and I will sacrifice it as a burnt offering."   Jdg 3:10; Ge 28:20; Lev 1:3

³²Then Jephthah went over to fight the Ammonites, and the LORD gave them into his hands. ³³He devastated twenty towns from Aroer to the vicinity of Minnith, as far as Abel Keramim. Thus Israel subdued Ammon.   Eze 27:17

³⁴When Jephthah returned to his home in Mizpah, who should come out to meet him but his daughter, dancing to the sound of tambourines! She was an only child. Except for her he had neither son nor daughter. ³⁵When he saw her, he tore his clothes and cried, "Oh! My daughter! You have made me miserable and wretched, because I have made a vow to the LORD that I cannot break."   Nu 30:2

³⁶"My father," she replied, "you have given your word to the LORD. Do to me just as you promised, now that the LORD has avenged you of your enemies, the Ammonites. ³⁷But grant me this one request," she said. "Give me two months to roam the hills and weep with my friends, because I will never marry."

³⁸"You may go," he said. And he let her go for two months. She and the girls went into the hills and wept because she would never marry. ³⁹After the two months, she returned to her father and he did to

ᵃ27 Or *Ruler*

her as he had vowed. And she was a virgin.

From this comes the Israelite custom ⁴⁰that each year the young women of Israel go out for four days to commemorate the daughter of Jephthah the Gileadite.

Jephthah and Ephraim

12 The men of Ephraim called out their forces, crossed over to Zaphon and said to Jephthah, "Why did you go to fight the Ammonites without calling us to go with you? We're going to burn down your house over your head."

²Jephthah answered, "I and my people were engaged in a great struggle with the Ammonites, and although I called, you didn't save me out of their hands. ³When I saw that you wouldn't help, I took my life in my hands and crossed over to fight the Ammonites, and the Lord gave me the victory over them. Now why have you come up today to fight me?"   1Sa 19:5

⁴Jephthah then called together the men of Gilead and fought against Ephraim. The Gileadites struck them down because the Ephraimites had said, "You Gileadites are renegades from Ephraim and Manasseh." ⁵The Gileadites captured the fords of the Jordan leading to Ephraim, and whenever a survivor of Ephraim said, "Let me cross over," the men of Gilead

asked him, "Are you an Ephraimite?" If he replied, "No," ⁶they said, "All right, say 'Shibboleth.'" If he said, "Sibboleth," because he could not pronounce the word correctly, they seized him and killed him at the fords of the Jordan. Forty-two thousand Ephraimites were killed at that time.   Jdg 3:28

⁷Jephthah led ᵃ Israel six years. Then Jephthah the Gileadite died, and was buried in a town in Gilead.

Ibzan, Elon and Abdon

⁸After him, Ibzan of Bethlehem led Israel. ⁹He had thirty sons and thirty daughters. He gave his daughters away in marriage to those outside his clan, and for his sons he brought in thirty young women as wives from outside his clan. Ibzan led Israel seven years. ¹⁰Then Ibzan died, and was buried in Bethlehem.   Ge 35:19

¹¹After him, Elon the Zebulunite led Israel ten years. ¹²Then Elon died, and was buried in Aijalon in the land of Zebulun.   Jos 10:12

¹³After him, Abdon son of Hillel, from Pirathon, led Israel. ¹⁴He had forty sons and thirty grandsons, who rode on seventy donkeys. He led Israel eight years. ¹⁵Then Abdon son of Hillel died, and was buried at Pirathon in Ephraim, in the hill country of the Amalekites.

ᵃ 7 Traditionally *judged*; also in verses 8-14

The Birth of Samson

13 Again the Israelites did evil in the eyes of the Lord, so the Lord delivered them into the hands of the Philistines for forty years.   Jdg 2:11; 14:4

²A certain man of Zorah, named Manoah, from the clan of the Danites, had a wife who was sterile and remained childless. ³The angel of the Lord appeared to her and said, "You are sterile and childless, but you are going to conceive and have a son. ⁴Now see to it that you drink no wine or other fermented drink and that you do not eat anything unclean, ⁵because you will conceive and give birth to a son. No razor may be used on his head, because the boy is to be a Nazirite, set apart to God from birth, and he will begin the deliverance of Israel from the hands of the Philistines."

⁶Then the woman went to her husband and told him, "A man of God came to me. He looked like an angel of God, very awesome. I didn't ask him where he came from, and he didn't tell me his name. ⁷But he said to me, 'You will conceive and give birth to a son. Now then, drink no wine or other fermented drink and do not eat anything unclean, because the boy will be a Nazirite of God from birth until the day of his death.' "

⁸Then Manoah prayed to the Lord: "O Lord, I beg you, let the man of God you sent to us come again to teach us how to bring up the boy who is to be born."

⁹God heard Manoah, and the angel of God came again to the woman while she was out in the field; but her husband Manoah was not with her. ¹⁰The woman hurried to tell her husband, "He's here! The man who appeared to me the other day!"

¹¹Manoah got up and followed his wife. When he came to the man, he said, "Are you the one who talked to my wife?"

"I am," he said.

¹²So Manoah asked him, "When your words are fulfilled, what is to be the rule for the boy's life and work?"

¹³The angel of the Lord answered, "Your wife must do all that I have told her. ¹⁴She must not eat anything that comes from the grapevine, nor drink any wine or other fermented drink nor eat anything unclean. She must do everything I have commanded her."

¹⁵Manoah said to the angel of the Lord, "We would like you to stay until we prepare a young goat for you."   Jdg 6:19

¹⁶The angel of the Lord replied, "Even though you detain me, I will not eat any of your food. But if you prepare a burnt offering, offer it to the Lord." (Manoah did not realize that it was the angel of the Lord.)

¹⁷Then Manoah inquired of the angel of the Lord, "What is your name, so that we may honor you when your word comes true?"

[18]He replied, "Why do you ask my name? It is beyond understanding.[a]" [19]Then Manoah took a young goat, together with the grain offering, and sacrificed it on a rock to the LORD. And the LORD did an amazing thing while Manoah and his wife watched: [20]As the flame blazed up from the altar toward heaven, the angel of the LORD ascended in the flame. Seeing this, Manoah and his wife fell with their faces to the ground. [21]When the angel of the LORD did not show himself again to Manoah and his wife, Manoah realized that it was the angel of the LORD. Lev 9:24

[22]"We are doomed to die!" he said to his wife. "We have seen God!" Dt 5:26

[23]But his wife answered, "If the LORD had meant to kill us, he would not have accepted a burnt offering and grain offering from our hands, nor shown us all these things or now told us this."

[24]The woman gave birth to a boy and named him Samson. He grew and the LORD blessed him, [25]and the Spirit of the LORD began to stir him while he was in Mahaneh Dan, between Zorah and Eshtaol.

Samson's Marriage

14 Samson went down to Timnah and saw there a young Philistine woman. [2]When he returned, he said to his father and mother, "I have seen a Philistine woman in Timnah; now get her for me as my wife." Ge 21:21

[3]His father and mother replied, "Isn't there an acceptable woman among your relatives or among all our people? Must you go to the uncircumcised Philistines to get a wife?" Ge 24:4; Ex 34:16

But Samson said to his father, "Get her for me. She's the right one for me." [4](His parents did not know that this was from the LORD, who was seeking an occasion to confront the Philistines; for at that time they were ruling over Israel.) [5]Samson went down to Timnah together with his father and mother. As they approached the vineyards of Timnah, suddenly a young lion came roaring toward him. [6]The Spirit of the LORD came upon him in power so that he tore the lion apart with his bare hands as he might have torn a young goat. But he told neither his father nor his mother what he had done. [7]Then he went down and talked with the woman, and he liked her.

[8]Some time later, when he went back to marry her, he turned aside to look at the lion's carcass. In it was a swarm of bees and some honey, [9]which he scooped out with his hands and ate as he went along. When he rejoined his parents, he gave them some, and they too ate it. But he did not tell them that he had taken the honey from the lion's carcass.

a 18 Or is wonderful

¹⁰Now his father went down to see the woman. And Samson made a feast there, as was customary for bridegrooms. ¹¹When he appeared, he was given thirty companions.

¹²"Let me tell you a riddle," Samson said to them. "If you can give me the answer within the seven days of the feast, I will give you thirty linen garments and thirty sets of clothes. ¹³If you can't tell me the answer, you must give me thirty linen garments and thirty sets of clothes." Eze 17:2; Ge 29:27

"Tell us your riddle," they said. "Let's hear it."

¹⁴He replied,

"Out of the eater, something to eat;
    out of the strong, something sweet."

For three days they could not give the answer.

¹⁵On the fourthᵃ day, they said to Samson's wife, "Coax your husband into explaining the riddle for us, or we will burn you and your father's household to death. Did you invite us here to rob us?"

¹⁶Then Samson's wife threw herself on him, sobbing, "You hate me! You don't really love me. You've given my people a riddle, but you haven't told me the answer." Jdg 16:15

"I haven't even explained it to my father or mother," he replied,

"so why should I explain it to you?" ¹⁷She cried the whole seven days of the feast. So on the seventh day he finally told her, because she continued to press him. She in turn explained the riddle to her people.

¹⁸Before sunset on the seventh day the men of the town said to him,

"What is sweeter than honey?
    What is stronger than a lion?"

Samson said to them,

"If you had not plowed with my heifer,
    you would not have solved my riddle."

¹⁹Then the Spirit of the LORD came upon him in power. He went down to Ashkelon, struck down thirty of their men, stripped them of their belongings and gave their clothes to those who had explained the riddle. Burning with anger, he went up to his father's house. ²⁰And Samson's wife was given to the friend who had attended him at his wedding. Jdg 6:34

Samson's Vengeance on the Philistines

15 Later on, at the time of wheat harvest, Samson took a young goat and went to visit his wife. He said, "I'm going to my

---

ᵃ15 Some Septuagint manuscripts and Syriac; Hebrew seventh

wife's room." But her father would not let him go in.   Ge 38:17

2"I was so sure you thoroughly hated her," he said, "that I gave her to your friend. Isn't her younger sister more attractive? Take her instead."   Jdg 14:20

3Samson said to them, "This time I have a right to get even with the Philistines; I will really harm them." 4So he went out and caught three hundred foxes and tied them tail to tail in pairs. He then fastened a torch to every pair of tails, 5lit the torches and let the foxes loose in the standing grain of the Philistines. He burned up the shocks and standing grain, together with the vineyards and olive groves.

6When the Philistines asked, "Who did this?" they were told, "Samson, the Timnite's son-in-law, because his wife was given to his friend."

So the Philistines went up and burned her and her father to death. 7Samson said to them, "Since you've acted like this, I won't stop until I get my revenge on you." 8He attacked them viciously and slaughtered many of them. Then he went down and stayed in a cave in the rock of Etam.   Jdg 14:15

9The Philistines went up and camped in Judah, spreading out near Lehi. 10The men of Judah asked, "Why have you come to fight us?"

"We have come to take Samson prisoner," they answered, "to do to him as he did to us."

11Then three thousand men from Judah went down to the cave in the rock of Etam and said to Samson, "Don't you realize that the Philistines are rulers over us? What have you done to us?"

He answered, "I merely did to them what they did to me."

12They said to him, "We've come to tie you up and hand you over to the Philistines."

Samson said, "Swear to me that you won't kill me yourselves."

13"Agreed," they answered. "We will only tie you up and hand you over to them. We will not kill you." So they bound him with two new ropes and led him up from the rock. 14As he approached Lehi, the Philistines came toward him shouting. The Spirit of the LORD came upon him in power. The ropes on his arms became like charred flax, and the bindings dropped from his hands. 15Finding a fresh jawbone of a donkey, he grabbed it and struck down a thousand men.   Lev 26:8; Jos 23:10; Jdg 14:19

16Then Samson said,

"With a donkey's jawbone
    I have made donkeys of
        them.ᵃ
With a donkey's jawbone
    I have killed a thousand
        men."

ᵃ 16 Or made a heap or two; the Hebrew for donkey sounds like the Hebrew for heap.

¹⁷When he finished speaking, he threw away the jawbone; and the place was called Ramath Lehi.ᵃ

¹⁸Because he was very thirsty, he cried out to the LORD, "You have given your servant this great victory. Must I now die of thirst and fall into the hands of the uncircumcised?" ¹⁹Then God opened up the hollow place in Lehi, and water came out of it. When Samson drank, his strength returned and he revived. So the spring was called En Hakkore,ᵇ and it is still there in Lehi.   Ge 45:27; Jdg 16:28

²⁰Samson ledᶜ Israel for twenty years in the days of the Philistines.

Samson and Delilah

16 One day Samson went to Gaza, where he saw a prostitute. He went in to spend the night with her. ²The people of Gaza were told, "Samson is here!" So they surrounded the place and lay in wait for him all night at the city gate. They made no move during the night, saying, "At dawn we'll kill him."   1Sa 19:11; Ps 118:10-12

³But Samson lay there only until the middle of the night. Then he got up and took hold of the doors of the city gate, together with the two posts, and tore them loose, bar and all. He lifted them to his shoulders and carried them to the top of the hill that faces Hebron.

⁴Some time later, he fell in love with a woman in the Valley of Sorek whose name was Delilah. ⁵The rulers of the Philistines went to her and said, "See if you can lure him into showing you the secret of his great strength and how we can overpower him so we may tie him up and subdue him. Each one of us will give you eleven hundred shekelsᵈ of silver."   Ge 24:67; Jos 13:3

⁶So Delilah said to Samson, "Tell me the secret of your great strength and how you can be tied up and subdued."

⁷Samson answered her, "If anyone ties me with seven fresh thongsᵉ that have not been dried, I'll become as weak as any other man."

⁸Then the rulers of the Philistines brought her seven fresh thongs that had not been dried, and she tied him with them. ⁹With men hidden in the room, she called to him, "Samson, the Philistines are upon you!" But he snapped the thongs as easily as a piece of string snaps when it comes close to a flame. So the secret of his strength was not discovered.

¹⁰Then Delilah said to Samson, "You have made a fool of me; you lied to me. Come now, tell me how you can be tied."

¹¹He said, "If anyone ties me securely with new ropes that have

---

ᵃ17 Ramath Lehi means jawbone hill.   ᵇ19 En Hakkore means caller's spring.   ᶜ20 Traditionally judged   ᵈ5 That is, about 28 pounds (about 13 kilograms)   ᵉ7 Or bowstrings; also in verses 8 and 9

never been used, I'll become as weak as any other man." Jdg 15:13

12So Delilah took new ropes and tied him with them. Then, with men hidden in the room, she called to him, "Samson, the Philistines are upon you!" But he snapped the ropes off his arms as if they were threads.

13Delilah then said to Samson, "Until now, you have been making a fool of me and lying to me. Tell me how you can be tied."

He replied, "If you weave the seven braids of my head into the fabric ⸤on the loom⸥ and tighten it with the pin, I'll become as weak as any other man." So while he was sleeping, Delilah took the seven braids of his head, wove them into the fabric **14**and*a* tightened it with the pin.

Again she called to him, "Samson, the Philistines are upon you!" He awoke from his sleep and pulled up the pin and the loom, with the fabric.

15Then she said to him, "How can you say, 'I love you,' when you won't confide in me? This is the third time you have made a fool of me and haven't told me the secret of your great strength." **16**With such nagging she prodded him day after day until he was tired to death. Jdg 14:16

17So he told her everything. "No razor has ever been used on my head," he said, "because I have been a Nazirite set apart to God since birth. If my head were shaved, my strength would leave me, and I would become as weak as any other man." Nu 6:2,5; Mic 7:5

18When Delilah saw that he had told her everything, she sent word to the rulers of the Philistines, "Come back once more; he has told me everything." So the rulers of the Philistines returned with the silver in their hands. **19**Having put him to sleep on her lap, she called a man to shave off the seven braids of his hair, and so began to subdue him.*b* And his strength left him.

20Then she called, "Samson, the Philistines are upon you!"

He awoke from his sleep and thought, "I'll go out as before and shake myself free." But he did not know that the LORD had left him.

21Then the Philistines seized him, gouged out his eyes and took him down to Gaza. Binding him with bronze shackles, they set him to grinding in the prison. **22**But the hair on his head began to grow again after it had been shaved.

The Death of Samson

23Now the rulers of the Philistines assembled to offer a great sacrifice to Dagon their god and to celebrate, saying, "Our god has delivered Samson, our enemy, into our hands." 1Sa 5:2

---

a 13,14 Some Septuagint manuscripts; Hebrew *"J can, if you weave the seven braids of my head into the fabric ⸤on the loom⸥." 14So she*   *b* 19 Hebrew; some Septuagint manuscripts *and he began to weaken*

²⁴When the people saw him, they praised their god, saying,

"Our god has delivered our
    enemy
into our hands,   1Sa 31:9; 1Ch 10:9
the one who laid waste our
    land
and multiplied our slain."

²⁵While they were in high spirits, they shouted, "Bring out Samson to entertain us." So they called Samson out of the prison, and he performed for them.   Jdg 9:27; Ru 3:7

When they stood him among the pillars, ²⁶Samson said to the servant who held his hand, "Put me where I can feel the pillars that support the temple, so that I may lean against them." ²⁷Now the temple was crowded with men and women; all the rulers of the Philistines were there, and on the roof were about three thousand men and women watching Samson perform. ²⁸Then Samson prayed to the Lord, "O Sovereign Lord, remember me. O God, please strengthen me just once more, and let me with one blow get revenge on the Philistines for my two eyes." ²⁹Then Samson reached toward the two central pillars on which the temple stood. Bracing himself against them, his right hand on the one and his left hand on the other, ³⁰Samson said, "Let me die with the Philistines!" Then

he pushed with all his might, and down came the temple on the rulers and all the people in it. Thus he killed many more when he died than while he lived.   Jdg 15:18

³¹Then his brothers and his father's whole family went down to get him. They brought him back and buried him between Zorah and Eshtaol in the tomb of Manoah his father. He had led*a* Israel twenty years.   Jdg 13:2; Ru 1:1

Micah's Idols

17 Now a man named Micah from the hill country of Ephraim ²said to his mother, "The eleven hundred shekels*b* of silver that were taken from you and about which I heard you utter a curse—I have that silver with me; I took it."

Then his mother said, "The Lord bless you, my son!"   Ru 2:20

³When he returned the eleven hundred shekels of silver to his mother, she said, "I solemnly consecrate my silver to the Lord for my son to make a carved image and a cast idol. I will give it back to you."   Ex 20:4,23

⁴So he returned the silver to his mother, and she took two hundred shekels*c* of silver and gave them to a silversmith, who made them into the image and the idol. And they were put in Micah's house.

⁵Now this man Micah had a

---

a31 Traditionally *judged*   *b2* That is, about 28 pounds (about 13 kilograms)   *c4* That is, about 5 pounds (about 2.3 kilograms)

shrine, and he made an ephod and some idols and installed one of his sons as his priest. ⁶In those days Israel had no king; everyone did as he saw fit.   Dt 12:8; Jdg 8:27; 19:1

⁷A young Levite from Bethlehem in Judah, who had been living within the clan of Judah, ⁸left that town in search of some other place to stay. On his way[a] he came to Micah's house in the hill country of Ephraim.   Jdg 19:1; Mic 5:2; Mt 2:1

⁹Micah asked him, "Where are you from?"

"I'm a Levite from Bethlehem in Judah," he said, "and I'm looking for a place to stay."

¹⁰Then Micah said to him, "Live with me and be my father and priest, and I'll give you ten shekels[b] of silver a year, your clothes and your food." ¹¹So the Levite agreed to live with him, and the young man was to him like one of his sons. ¹²Then Micah installed the Levite, and the young man became his priest and lived in his house. ¹³And Micah said, "Now I know that the LORD will be good to me, since this Levite has become my priest."   Nu 18:7; Jdg 18:19

Danites Settle in Laish

18 In those days Israel had no king.   Jdg 17:6

And in those days the tribe of the Danites was seeking a place of their own where they might settle, because they had not yet come into an inheritance among the tribes of Israel. ²So the Danites sent five warriors from Zorah and Eshtaol to spy out the land and explore it. These men represented all their clans. They told them, "Go, explore the land."   Jos 2:1; 19:47

The men entered the hill country of Ephraim and came to the house of Micah, where they spent the night. ³When they were near Micah's house, they recognized the voice of the young Levite; so they turned in there and asked him, "Who brought you here? What are you doing in this place? Why are you here?"   Jdg 17:1

⁴He told them what Micah had done for him, and said, "He has hired me and I am his priest."

⁵Then they said to him, "Please inquire of God to learn whether our journey will be successful."

⁶The priest answered them, "Go in peace. Your journey has the LORD's approval."

⁷So the five men left and came to Laish, where they saw that the people were living in safety, like the Sidonians, unsuspecting and secure. And since their land lacked nothing, they were prosperous.[c] Also, they lived a long way from the Sidonians and had no relationship with anyone else.[d]   Ge 34:25

⁸When they returned to Zorah

a8 Or To carry on his profession   b10 That is, about 4 ounces (about 110 grams)   c7 The meaning of the Hebrew for this clause is uncertain.   d7 Hebrew; some Septuagint manuscripts with the Arameans

and Eshtaol, their brothers asked them, "How did you find things?"

⁹They answered, "Come on, let's attack them! We have seen that the land is very good. Aren't you going to do something? Don't hesitate to go there and take it over. ¹⁰When you get there, you will find an unsuspecting people and a spacious land that God has put into your hands, a land that lacks nothing whatever." Nu 13:30; Dt 8:9

¹¹Then six hundred men from the clan of the Danites, armed for battle, set out from Zorah and Eshtaol. ¹²On their way they set up camp near Kiriath Jearim in Judah. This is why the place west of Kiriath Jearim is called Mahaneh Dan[a] to this day. ¹³From there they went on to the hill country of Ephraim and came to Micah's house.

¹⁴Then the five men who had spied out the land of Laish said to their brothers, "Do you know that one of these houses has an ephod, other household gods, a carved image and a cast idol? Now you know what to do." ¹⁵So they turned in there and went to the house of the young Levite at Micah's place and greeted him. ¹⁶The six hundred Danites, armed for battle, stood at the entrance to the gate. ¹⁷The five men who had spied out the land went inside and took the carved image, the ephod, the other household gods and the cast idol while the priest and the

six hundred armed men stood at the entrance to the gate. Ge 31:19

¹⁸When these men went into Micah's house and took the carved image, the ephod, the other household gods and the cast idol, the priest said to them, "What are you doing?"

¹⁹They answered him, "Be quiet! Don't say a word. Come with us, and be our father and priest. Isn't it better that you serve a tribe and clan in Israel as priest rather than just one man's household?" ²⁰Then the priest was glad. He took the ephod, the other household gods and the carved image and went along with the people. ²¹Putting their little children, their livestock and their possessions in front of them, they turned away and left. Jdg 17:10; Job 21:5; 29:9

²²When they had gone some distance from Micah's house, the men who lived near Micah were called together and overtook the Danites. ²³As they shouted after them, the Danites turned and said to Micah, "What's the matter with you that you called out your men to fight?"

²⁴He replied, "You took the gods I made, and my priest, and went away. What else do I have? How can you ask, 'What's the matter with you?' "

²⁵The Danites answered, "Don't argue with us, or some hot-tempered men will attack you, and

---

[a] 12 *Mahaneh Dan* means *Dan's camp*.

you and your family will lose your lives." [26]So the Danites went their way, and Micah, seeing that they were too strong for him, turned around and went back home.

[27]Then they took what Micah had made, and his priest, and went on to Laish, against a peaceful and unsuspecting people. They attacked them with the sword and burned down their city. [28]There was no one to rescue them because they lived a long way from Sidon and had no relationship with anyone else. The city was in a valley near Beth Rehob.

The Danites rebuilt the city and settled there. [29]They named it Dan after their forefather Dan, who was born to Israel—though the city used to be called Laish. [30]There the Danites set up for themselves the idols, and Jonathan son of Gershom, the son of Moses,[a] and his sons were priests for the tribe of Dan until the time of the captivity of the land. [31]They continued to use the idols Micah had made, all the time the house of God was in Shiloh.   Ex 2:22; Jos 19:47; 18:1

A Levite and His Concubine

19 In those days Israel had no king.

Now a Levite who lived in a remote area in the hill country of Ephraim took a concubine from Bethlehem in Judah. [2]But she was unfaithful to him. She left him and went back to her father's house in Bethlehem, Judah. After she had been there four months, [3]her husband went to her to persuade her to return. He had with him his servant and two donkeys. She took him into her father's house, and when her father saw him, he gladly welcomed him. [4]His father-in-law, the girl's father, prevailed upon him to stay; so he remained with him three days, eating and drinking, and sleeping there.   Ex 32:6

[5]On the fourth day they got up early and he prepared to leave, but the girl's father said to his son-in-law, "Refresh yourself with something to eat; then you can go." [6]So the two of them sat down to eat and drink together. Afterward the girl's father said, "Please stay tonight and enjoy yourself." [7]And when the man got up to go, his father-in-law persuaded him, so he stayed there that night. [8]On the morning of the fifth day, when he rose to go, the girl's father said, "Refresh yourself. Wait till afternoon!" So the two of them ate together.

[9]Then when the man, with his concubine and his servant, got up to leave, his father-in-law, the girl's father, said, "Now look, it's almost evening. Spend the night here; the day is nearly over. Stay and enjoy yourself. Early tomor-

---

[a]30 An ancient Hebrew scribal tradition, some Septuagint manuscripts and Vulgate; Masoretic Text *Manasseh*

row morning you can get up and be on your way home." ¹⁰But, unwilling to stay another night, the man left and went toward Jebus (that is, Jerusalem), with his two saddled donkeys and his concubine.   1Ch 11:4-5

¹¹When they were near Jebus and the day was almost gone, the servant said to his master, "Come, let's stop at this city of the Jebusites and spend the night."

¹²His master replied, "No. We won't go into an alien city, whose people are not Israelites. We will go on to Gibeah." ¹³He added, "Come, let's try to reach Gibeah or Ramah and spend the night in one of those places." ¹⁴So they went on, and the sun set as they neared Gibeah in Benjamin. ¹⁵There they stopped to spend the night. They went and sat in the city square, but no one took them into his home for the night.   Ge 19:2; 1Sa 10:26

¹⁶That evening an old man from the hill country of Ephraim, who was living in Gibeah (the men of the place were Benjamites), came in from his work in the fields. ¹⁷When he looked and saw the traveler in the city square, the old man asked, "Where are you going? Where did you come from?"

¹⁸He answered, "We are on our way from Bethlehem in Judah to a remote area in the hill country of Ephraim where I live. I have been to Bethlehem in Judah and now I am going to the house of the LORD. No one has taken me into his house. ¹⁹We have both straw and fodder for our donkeys and bread and wine for ourselves your servants—me, your maidservant, and the young man with us. We don't need anything."   Jdg 18:31

²⁰"You are welcome at my house," the old man said. "Let me supply whatever you need. Only don't spend the night in the square." ²¹So he took him into his house and fed his donkeys. After they had washed their feet, they had something to eat and drink.

²²While they were enjoying themselves, some of the wicked men of the city surrounded the house. Pounding on the door, they shouted to the old man who owned the house, "Bring out the man who came to your house so we can have sex with him."

²³The owner of the house went outside and said to them, "No, my friends, don't be so vile. Since this man is my guest, don't do this disgraceful thing. ²⁴Look, here is my virgin daughter, and his concubine. I will bring them out to you now, and you can use them and do to them whatever you wish. But to this man, don't do such a disgraceful thing."   Ge 34:7; Dt 22:21; 2Sa 13:12

²⁵But the men would not listen to him. So the man took his concubine and sent her outside to them, and they raped her and abused her throughout the night, and at dawn they let her go. ²⁶At daybreak the woman went back to the house where her master was staying, fell

down at the door and lay there until daylight. *Jdg 20:5; 1Sa 31:4*

²⁷When her master got up in the morning and opened the door of the house and stepped out to continue on his way, there lay his concubine, fallen in the doorway of the house, with her hands on the threshold. ²⁸He said to her, "Get up; let's go." But there was no answer. Then the man put her on his donkey and set out for home.

²⁹When he reached home, he took a knife and cut up his concubine, limb by limb, into twelve parts and sent them into all the areas of Israel. ³⁰Everyone who saw it said, "Such a thing has never been seen or done, not since the day the Israelites came up out of Egypt. Think about it! Consider it! Tell us what to do!" *Jdg 20:7*

Israelites Fight the Benjamites

20 Then all the Israelites from Dan to Beersheba and from the land of Gilead came out as one man and assembled before the Lᴏʀᴅ in Mizpah. ²The leaders of all the people of the tribes of Israel took their places in the assembly of the people of God, four hundred thousand soldiers armed with swords. ³(The Benjamites heard that the Israelites had gone up to Mizpah.) Then the Israelites said, "Tell us how this awful thing happened." *Jdg 8:10; 21:5; 1Sa 7:5*

⁴So the Levite, the husband of the murdered woman, said, "I and my concubine came to Gibeah in Benjamin to spend the night. ⁵During the night the men of Gibeah came after me and surrounded the house, intending to kill me. They raped my concubine, and she died. ⁶I took my concubine, cut her into pieces and sent one piece to each region of Israel's inheritance, because they committed this lewd and disgraceful act in Israel. ⁷Now, all you Israelites, speak up and give your verdict." *Jos 7:15*

⁸All the people rose as one man, saying, "None of us will go home. No, not one of us will return to his house. ⁹But now this is what we'll do to Gibeah: We'll go up against it as the lot directs. ¹⁰We'll take ten men out of every hundred from all the tribes of Israel, and a hundred from a thousand, and a thousand from ten thousand, to get provisions for the army. Then, when the army arrives at Gibeah* in Benjamin, it can give them what they deserve for all this vileness done in Israel." ¹¹So all the men of Israel got together and united as one man against the city.

¹²The tribes of Israel sent men throughout the tribe of Benjamin, saying, "What about this awful crime that was committed among you? ¹³Now surrender those wicked men of Gibeah so that we may put them to death and purge the evil from Israel." *Dt 13:13*

ᵃ 10 One Hebrew manuscript; most Hebrew manuscripts Geba, a variant of Gibeah

But the Benjamites would not listen to their fellow Israelites. ¹⁴From their towns they came together at Gibeah to fight against the Israelites. ¹⁵At once the Benjamites mobilized twenty-six thousand swordsmen from their towns, in addition to seven hundred chosen men from those living in Gibeah. ¹⁶Among all these soldiers there were seven hundred chosen men who were left-handed, each of whom could sling a stone at a hair and not miss. Jdg 3:15; 1Ch 12:2

¹⁷Israel, apart from Benjamin, mustered four hundred thousand swordsmen, all of them fighting men.

¹⁸The Israelites went up to Bethel[a] and inquired of God. They said, "Who of us shall go first to fight against the Benjamites?" Jos 12:9

The LORD replied, "Judah shall go first."

¹⁹The next morning the Israelites got up and pitched camp near Gibeah. ²⁰The men of Israel went out to fight the Benjamites and took up battle positions against them at Gibeah. ²¹The Benjamites came out of Gibeah and cut down twenty-two thousand Israelites on the battlefield that day. ²²But the men of Israel encouraged one another and again took up their positions where they had stationed themselves the first day. ²³The Israelites went up and wept before the LORD until evening, and they inquired of the LORD. They said, "Shall we go up again to battle against the Benjamites, our brothers?" Nu 14:1; Jos 7:6

The LORD answered, "Go up against them."

²⁴Then the Israelites drew near to Benjamin the second day. ²⁵This time, when the Benjamites came out from Gibeah to oppose them, they cut down another eighteen thousand Israelites, all of them armed with swords.

²⁶Then the Israelites, all the people, went up to Bethel, and there they sat weeping before the LORD. They fasted that day until evening and presented burnt offerings and fellowship offerings[b] to the LORD. ²⁷And the Israelites inquired of the LORD. (In those days the ark of the covenant of God was there, ²⁸with Phinehas son of Eleazar, the son of Aaron, ministering before it.) They asked, "Shall we go up again to battle with Benjamin our brother, or not?" Dt 18:5; Jdg 21:4

The LORD responded, "Go, for tomorrow I will give them into your hands." Jdg 7:9

²⁹Then Israel set an ambush around Gibeah. ³⁰They went up against the Benjamites on the third day and took up positions against Gibeah as they had done before. ³¹The Benjamites came out to meet them and were drawn away from the city. They began to inflict casualties on the Israelites as be-

---

a 18 Or *to the house of God*; also in verse 26   b 26 Traditionally *peace offerings*

fore, so that about thirty men fell in the open field and on the roads —the one leading to Bethel and the other to Gibeah. Jos 8:2,4

³²While the Benjamites were saying, "We are defeating them as before," the Israelites were saying, "Let's retreat and draw them away from the city to the roads."

³³All the men of Israel moved from their places and took up positions at Baal Tamar, and the Israelite ambush charged out of its place on the west[a] of Gibeah.[b] ³⁴Then ten thousand of Israel's finest men made a frontal attack on Gibeah. The fighting was so heavy that the Benjamites did not realize how near disaster was. ³⁵The LORD defeated Benjamin before Israel, and on that day the Israelites struck down 25,100 Benjamites, all armed with swords. ³⁶Then the Benjamites saw that they were beaten. Jos 8:19; 1Sa 9:21

Now the men of Israel had given way before Benjamin, because they relied on the ambush they had set near Gibeah. ³⁷The men who had been in ambush made a sudden dash into Gibeah, spread out and put the whole city to the sword. ³⁸The men of Israel had arranged with the ambush that they should send up a great cloud of smoke from the city, ³⁹and then the men of Israel would turn in the battle. Jos 8:15

The Benjamites had begun to inflict casualties on the men of Israel (about thirty), and they said, "We are defeating them as in the first battle." ⁴⁰But when the column of smoke began to rise from the city, the Benjamites turned and saw the smoke of the whole city going up into the sky. ⁴¹Then the men of Israel turned on them, and the men of Benjamin were terrified, because they realized that disaster had come upon them. ⁴²So they fled before the Israelites in the direction of the desert, but they could not escape the battle. And the men of Israel who came out of the towns cut them down there. ⁴³They surrounded the Benjamites, chased them and easily[c] overran them in the vicinity of Gibeah on the east. ⁴⁴Eighteen thousand Benjamites fell, all of them valiant fighters. ⁴⁵As they turned and fled toward the desert to the rock of Rimmon, the Israelites cut down five thousand men along the roads. They kept pressing after the Benjamites as far as Gidom and struck down two thousand more.

⁴⁶On that day twenty-five thousand Benjamite swordsmen fell, all of them valiant fighters. ⁴⁷But six hundred men turned and fled into the desert to the rock of Rimmon, where they stayed four months. ⁴⁸The men of Israel went back to Benjamin and put all the towns to

---

a 33 Some Septuagint manuscripts and Vulgate; the meaning of the Hebrew for this word is uncertain.
b 33 Hebrew Geba, a variant of Gibeah   c 43 The meaning of the Hebrew for this word is uncertain.

the sword, including the animals and everything else they found. All the towns they came across they set on fire.   1Sa 9:21

Wives for the Benjamites

21 The men of Israel had taken an oath at Mizpah: "Not one of us will give his daughter in marriage to a Benjamite."   Jos 9:18

²The people went to Bethel,ᵃ where they sat before God until evening, raising their voices and weeping bitterly. ³"O LORD, the God of Israel," they cried, "why has this happened to Israel? Why should one tribe be missing from Israel today?"

⁴Early the next day the people built an altar and presented burnt offerings and fellowship offerings.ᵇ   Jdg 20:26; 2Sa 24:25

⁵Then the Israelites asked, "Who from all the tribes of Israel has failed to assemble before the LORD?" For they had taken a solemn oath that anyone who failed to assemble before the LORD at Mizpah should certainly be put to death.   Jdg 5:23

⁶Now the Israelites grieved for their brothers, the Benjamites. "Today one tribe is cut off from Israel," they said. ⁷"How can we provide wives for those who are left, since we have taken an oath by the LORD not to give them any of our daughters in marriage?"

⁸Then they asked, "Which one of the tribes of Israel failed to assemble before the LORD at Mizpah?" They discovered that no one from Jabesh Gilead had come to the camp for the assembly. ⁹For when they counted the people, they found that none of the people of Jabesh Gilead were there.   1Sa 11:1

¹⁰So the assembly sent twelve thousand fighting men with instructions to go to Jabesh Gilead and put to the sword those living there, including the women and children. ¹¹"This is what you are to do," they said. "Kill every male and every woman who is not a virgin." ¹²They found among the people living in Jabesh Gilead four hundred young women who had never slept with a man, and they took them to the camp at Shiloh in Canaan.   Nu 31:17-18; Jos 18:1

¹³Then the whole assembly sent an offer of peace to the Benjamites at the rock of Rimmon. ¹⁴So the Benjamites returned at that time and were given the women of Jabesh Gilead who had been spared. But there were not enough for all of them.   Jdg 20:47

¹⁵The people grieved for Benjamin, because the LORD had made a gap in the tribes of Israel. ¹⁶And the elders of the assembly said, "With the women of Benjamin destroyed, how shall we provide wives for the men who are left? ¹⁷The Benjamite survivors must

---

ᵃ2 Or to the house of God   ᵇ4 Traditionally peace offerings

have heirs," they said, "so that a tribe of Israel will not be wiped out. [18]We can't give them our daughters as wives, since we Israelites have taken this oath: 'Cursed be anyone who gives a wife to a Benjamite.' [19]But look, there is the annual festival of the LORD in Shiloh, to the north of Bethel, and east of the road that goes from Bethel to Shechem, and to the south of Lebonah."   Jos 16:1; 1Sa 1:3

[20]So they instructed the Benjamites, saying, "Go and hide in the vineyards [21]and watch. When the girls of Shiloh come out to join in the dancing, then rush from the vineyards and each of you seize a wife from the girls of Shiloh and go to the land of Benjamin. [22]When their fathers or brothers complain to us, we will say to them, 'Do us a kindness by helping them, because we did not get wives for them during the war, and you are innocent, since you did not give your daughters to them.' "   Ex 15:20

[23]So that is what the Benjamites did. While the girls were dancing, each man caught one and carried her off to be his wife. Then they returned to their inheritance and rebuilt the towns and settled in them.   Jdg 20:48

[24]At that time the Israelites left that place and went home to their tribes and clans, each to his own inheritance.

[25]In those days Israel had no king; everyone did as he saw fit.

Ruth

Naomi and Ruth

1 In the days when the judges ruled,[a] there was a famine in the land, and a man from Bethlehem in Judah, together with his wife and two sons, went to live for a while in the country of Moab. ²The man's name was Elimelech, his wife's name Naomi, and the names of his two sons were Mahlon and Kilion. They were Ephrathites from Bethlehem, Judah. And they went to Moab and lived there.   Ge 35:19; Jdg 2:16-18; 3:30

³Now Elimelech, Naomi's husband, died, and she was left with her two sons. ⁴They married Moabite women, one named Orpah and the other Ruth. After they had lived there about ten years, ⁵both Mahlon and Kilion also died, and Naomi was left without her two sons and her husband.   Mt 1:5

⁶When she heard in Moab that the LORD had come to the aid of his people by providing food for them, Naomi and her daughters-in-law prepared to return home from there. ⁷With her two daughters-in-law she left the place where she had been living and set out on the road that would take them back to the land of Judah.   Ex 4:31; Mt 6:11

⁸Then Naomi said to her two daughters-in-law, "Go back, each of you, to your mother's home. May the LORD show kindness to you, as you have shown to your dead and to me. ⁹May the LORD grant that each of you will find rest in the home of another husband."

Then she kissed them and they wept aloud ¹⁰and said to her, "We will go back with you to your people."

¹¹But Naomi said, "Return home, my daughters. Why would you come with me? Am I going to have any more sons, who could become your husbands? ¹²Return home, my daughters; I am too old to have another husband. Even if I thought there was still hope for me —even if I had a husband tonight and then gave birth to sons— ¹³would you wait until they grew up? Would you remain unmarried for them? No, my daughters. It is more bitter for me than for you, because the LORD's hand has gone out against me!"   Ge 38:11; Jdg 2:15

¹⁴At this they wept again. Then Orpah kissed her mother-in-law good-by, but Ruth clung to her.

¹⁵"Look," said Naomi, "your sister-in-law is going back to her people and her gods. Go back with her."   Jos 24:14; Jdg 11:24

---

a 1 Traditionally judged

¹⁶But Ruth replied, "Don't urge me to leave you or to turn back from you. Where you go I will go, and where you stay I will stay. Your people will be my people and your God my God. ¹⁷Where you die I will die, and there I will be buried. May the LORD deal with me, be it ever so severely, if anything but death separates you and me." ¹⁸When Naomi realized that Ruth was determined to go with her, she stopped urging her.

¹⁹So the two women went on until they came to Bethlehem. When they arrived in Bethlehem, the whole town was stirred because of them, and the women exclaimed, "Can this be Naomi?"   Mt 21:10

²⁰"Don't call me Naomi,ᵃ" she told them. "Call me Mara,ᵇ because the Almightyᶜ has made my life very bitter. ²¹I went away full, but the LORD has brought me back empty. Why call me Naomi? The LORD has afflictedᵈ me; the Almighty has brought misfortune upon me."   Job 1:21

²²So Naomi returned from Moab accompanied by Ruth the Moabitess, her daughter-in-law, arriving in Bethlehem as the barley harvest was beginning.   Ex 9:31

Ruth Meets Boaz

2 Now Naomi had a relative on her husband's side, from the clan of Elimelech, a man of standing, whose name was Boaz.

²And Ruth the Moabitess said to Naomi, "Let me go to the fields and pick up the leftover grain behind anyone in whose eyes I find favor."

Naomi said to her, "Go ahead, my daughter." ³So she went out and began to glean in the fields behind the harvesters. As it turned out, she found herself working in a field belonging to Boaz, who was from the clan of Elimelech.

⁴Just then Boaz arrived from Bethlehem and greeted the harvesters, "The LORD be with you!"

"The LORD bless you!" they called back.   Ps 129:7-8

⁵Boaz asked the foreman of his harvesters, "Whose young woman is that?"

⁶The foreman replied, "She is the Moabitess who came back from Moab with Naomi. ⁷She said, 'Please let me glean and gather among the sheaves behind the harvesters.' She went into the field and has worked steadily from morning till now, except for a short rest in the shelter."   Ru 1:22

⁸So Boaz said to Ruth, "My daughter, listen to me. Don't go and glean in another field and don't go away from here. Stay here with my servant girls. ⁹Watch the field where the men are harvesting, and follow along after the girls. I have told the men not to

---

ᵃ20 *Naomi* means *pleasant*; also in verse 21.   ᵇ20 *Mara* means *bitter*.   ᶜ20 Hebrew *Shaddai*; also in verse 21   ᵈ21 Or *has testified against*

touch you. And whenever you are thirsty, go and get a drink from the water jars the men have filled."

[10]At this, she bowed down with her face to the ground. She exclaimed, "Why have I found such favor in your eyes that you notice me—a foreigner?"   1Sa 25:23

[11]Boaz replied, "I've been told all about what you have done for your mother-in-law since the death of your husband—how you left your father and mother and your homeland and came to live with a people you did not know before. [12]May the LORD repay you for what you have done. May you be richly rewarded by the LORD, the God of Israel, under whose wings you have come to take refuge."   Ru 1:14; 1Sa 24:19; Ps 17:8

[13]"May I continue to find favor in your eyes, my lord," she said. "You have given me comfort and have spoken kindly to your servant—though I do not have the standing of one of your servant girls."   Ge 18:3

[14]At mealtime Boaz said to her, "Come over here. Have some bread and dip it in the wine vinegar."

When she sat down with the harvesters, he offered her some roasted grain. She ate all she wanted and had some left over. [15]As she got up to glean, Boaz gave orders to his men, "Even if she gathers among the sheaves, don't embarrass her. [16]Rather, pull out some stalks for her from the bundles and leave them for her to pick up, and don't rebuke her."

[17]So Ruth gleaned in the field until evening. Then she threshed the barley she had gathered, and it amounted to about an ephah.[a] [18]She carried it back to town, and her mother-in-law saw how much she had gathered. Ruth also brought out and gave her what she had left over after she had eaten enough.

[19]Her mother-in-law asked her, "Where did you glean today? Where did you work? Blessed be the man who took notice of you!"

Then Ruth told her mother-in-law about the one at whose place she had been working. "The name of the man I worked with today is Boaz," she said.

[20]"The LORD bless him!" Naomi said to her daughter-in-law. "He has not stopped showing his kindness to the living and the dead." She added, "That man is our close relative; he is one of our kinsman-redeemers."   Ru 3:10

[21]Then Ruth the Moabitess said, "He even said to me, 'Stay with my workers until they finish harvesting all my grain.'"

[22]Naomi said to Ruth her daughter-in-law, "It will be good for you, my daughter, to go with his girls, because in someone else's field you might be harmed."

---

[a] 17 That is, probably about 3/5 bushel (about 22 liters)

²³So Ruth stayed close to the servant girls of Boaz to glean until the barley and wheat harvests were finished. And she lived with her mother-in-law.   Dt 16:9

Ruth and Boaz at the Threshing Floor

3 One day Naomi her mother-in-law said to her, "My daughter, should I not try to find a home*a* for you, where you will be well provided for? ²Is not Boaz, with whose servant girls you have been, a kinsman of ours? Tonight he will be winnowing barley on the threshing floor. ³Wash and perfume yourself, and put on your best clothes. Then go down to the threshing floor, but don't let him know you are there until he has finished eating and drinking. ⁴When he lies down, note the place where he is lying. Then go and uncover his feet and lie down. He will tell you what to do."

⁵"I will do whatever you say," Ruth answered. ⁶So she went down to the threshing floor and did everything her mother-in-law told her to do.   Eph 6:1; Col 3:20

⁷When Boaz had finished eating and drinking and was in good spirits, he went over to lie down at the far end of the grain pile. Ruth approached quietly, uncovered his feet and lay down. ⁸In the middle of the night something startled the man, and he turned and discovered a woman lying at his feet.

⁹"Who are you?" he asked.

"I am your servant Ruth," she said. "Spread the corner of your garment over me, since you are a kinsman-redeemer."   Ru 2:20

¹⁰"The LORD bless you, my daughter," he replied. "This kindness is greater than that which you showed earlier: You have not run after the younger men, whether rich or poor. ¹¹And now, my daughter, don't be afraid. I will do for you all you ask. All my fellow townsmen know that you are a woman of noble character. ¹²Although it is true that I am near of kin, there is a kinsman-redeemer nearer than I. ¹³Stay here for the night, and in the morning if he wants to redeem, good; let him redeem. But if he is not willing, as surely as the LORD lives I will do it. Lie here until morning."   Dt 25:5

¹⁴So she lay at his feet until morning, but got up before anyone could be recognized; and he said, "Don't let it be known that a woman came to the threshing floor."

¹⁵He also said, "Bring me the shawl you are wearing and hold it out." When she did so, he poured into it six measures of barley and put it on her. Then he*b* went back to town.

¹⁶When Ruth came to her moth-

---

a 1 Hebrew *find rest* (see Ruth 1:9)   *b* 15 Most Hebrew manuscripts; many Hebrew manuscripts, Vulgate and Syriac *she* er-in-law, Naomi asked, "How did it go, my daughter?"

Then she told her everything Boaz had done for her [17]and added, "He gave me these six measures of barley, saying, 'Don't go back to your mother-in-law empty-handed.' "

[18]Then Naomi said, "Wait, my daughter, until you find out what happens. For the man will not rest until the matter is settled today."

Boaz Marries Ruth

4 Meanwhile Boaz went up to the town gate and sat there. When the kinsman-redeemer he had mentioned came along, Boaz said, "Come over here, my friend, and sit down." So he went over and sat down.							Ru 3:12

[2]Boaz took ten of the elders of the town and said, "Sit here," and they did so. [3]Then he said to the kinsman-redeemer, "Naomi, who has come back from Moab, is selling the piece of land that belonged to our brother Elimelech. [4]I thought I should bring the matter to your attention and suggest that you buy it in the presence of these seated here and in the presence of the elders of my people. If you will redeem it, do so. But if you[a] will not, tell me, so I will know. For no one has the right to do it except you, and I am next in line."

"I will redeem it," he said.

[5]Then Boaz said, "On the day you buy the land from Naomi and from Ruth the Moabitess, you acquire[b] the dead man's widow, in order to maintain the name of the dead with his property."				Ge 38:8

[6]At this, the kinsman-redeemer said, "Then I cannot redeem it because I might endanger my own estate. You redeem it yourself. I cannot do it."						Ru 3:13

[7](Now in earlier times in Israel, for the redemption and transfer of property to become final, one party took off his sandal and gave it to the other. This was the method of legalizing transactions in Israel.)

[8]So the kinsman-redeemer said to Boaz, "Buy it yourself." And he removed his sandal.

[9]Then Boaz announced to the elders and all the people, "Today you are witnesses that I have bought from Naomi all the property of Elimelech, Kilion and Mahlon. [10]I have also acquired Ruth the Moabitess, Mahlon's widow, as my wife, in order to maintain the name of the dead with his property, so that his name will not disappear from among his family or from the town records. Today you are witnesses!"

[11]Then the elders and all those at the gate said, "We are witnesses. May the LORD make the woman who is coming into your home like Rachel and Leah, who together

---

[a]4 Many Hebrew manuscripts, Septuagint, Vulgate and Syriac; most Hebrew manuscripts *he*
[b]5 Hebrew; Vulgate and Syriac *Naomi, you acquire Ruth the Moabitess,*

built up the house of Israel. May you have standing in Ephrathah and be famous in Bethlehem. 12Through the offspring the LORD gives you by this young woman, may your family be like that of Perez, whom Tamar bore to Judah."

The Genealogy of David

13So Boaz took Ruth and she became his wife. Then he went to her, and the LORD enabled her to conceive, and she gave birth to a son. 14The women said to Naomi: "Praise be to the LORD, who this day has not left you without a kinsman-redeemer. May he become famous throughout Israel! 15He will renew your life and sustain you in your old age. For your daughter-in-law, who loves you and who is better to you than seven sons, has given him birth." Ge 29:31; Ru 1:16-17

16Then Naomi took the child, laid him in her lap and cared for him. 17The women living there said, "Naomi has a son." And they named him Obed. He was the father of Jesse, the father of David.

18This, then, is the family line of Perez: Mt 1:3-6

Perez was the father of Hezron,
19Hezron the father of Ram,
Ram the father of Amminadab,
20Amminadab the father of Nahshon,
Nahshon the father of Salmon,a
21Salmon the father of Boaz,
Boaz the father of Obed,
22Obed the father of Jesse,
and Jesse the father of David.

---

a20 A few Hebrew manuscripts, some Septuagint manuscripts and Vulgate (see also verse 21 and Septuagint of 1 Chron. 2:11); most Hebrew manuscripts Salma

1 Samuel

The Birth of Samuel

1 There was a certain man from Ramathaim, a Zuphite[a] from the hill country of Ephraim, whose name was Elkanah son of Jeroham, the son of Elihu, the son of Tohu, the son of Zuph, an Ephraimite. ²He had two wives; one was called Hannah and the other Peninnah. Peninnah had children, but Hannah had none. 1Ch 6:27,34

³Year after year this man went up from his town to worship and sacrifice to the LORD Almighty at Shiloh, where Hophni and Phinehas, the two sons of Eli, were priests of the LORD. ⁴Whenever the day came for Elkanah to sacrifice, he would give portions of the meat to his wife Peninnah and to all her sons and daughters. ⁵But to Hannah he gave a double portion because he loved her, and the LORD had closed her womb. ⁶And because the LORD had closed her womb, her rival kept provoking her in order to irritate her. ⁷This went on year after year. Whenever Hannah went up to the house of the LORD, her rival provoked her till she wept and would not eat. ⁸Elkanah her husband would say to her, "Hannah, why are you weeping? Why don't you eat? Why are you downhearted? Don't I mean more to you than ten sons?"

⁹Once when they had finished eating and drinking in Shiloh, Hannah stood up. Now Eli the priest was sitting on a chair by the doorpost of the LORD's temple.[b] ¹⁰In bitterness of soul Hannah wept much and prayed to the LORD. ¹¹And she made a vow, saying, "O LORD Almighty, if you will only look upon your servant's misery and remember me, and not forget your servant but give her a son, then I will give him to the LORD for all the days of his life, and no razor will ever be used on his head."

¹²As she kept on praying to the LORD, Eli observed her mouth. ¹³Hannah was praying in her heart, and her lips were moving but her voice was not heard. Eli thought she was drunk ¹⁴and said to her, "How long will you keep on getting drunk? Get rid of your wine."

¹⁵"Not so, my lord," Hannah replied, "I am a woman who is deeply troubled. I have not been drinking wine or beer; I was pouring out my soul to the LORD. ¹⁶Do not take your servant for a wicked woman; I have been praying here out of my great anguish and grief." Ps 42:4

¹⁷Eli answered, "Go in peace,

---

and may the God of Israel grant you what you have asked of him."

¹⁸She said, "May your servant find favor in your eyes." Then she went her way and ate something, and her face was no longer downcast.   Ru 2:13; Ro 15:13

¹⁹Early the next morning they arose and worshiped before the LORD and then went back to their home at Ramah. Elkanah lay with Hannah his wife, and the LORD remembered her. ²⁰So in the course of time Hannah conceived and gave birth to a son. She named him Samuel,ᵃ saying, "Because I asked the LORD for him."   Ge 30:22; Ex 2:10,22

Hannah Dedicates Samuel

²¹When the man Elkanah went up with all his family to offer the annual sacrifice to the LORD and to fulfill his vow, ²²Hannah did not go. She said to her husband, "After the boy is weaned, I will take him and present him before the LORD, and he will live there always."

²³"Do what seems best to you," Elkanah her husband told her. "Stay here until you have weaned him; only may the LORD make good hisᵇ word." So the woman stayed at home and nursed her son until she had weaned him.   Nu 30:7

²⁴After he was weaned, she took the boy with her, young as he was, along with a three-year-old bull,ᶜ

an ephahᵈ of flour and a skin of wine, and brought him to the house of the LORD at Shiloh. ²⁵When they had slaughtered the bull, they brought the boy to Eli, ²⁶and she said to him, "As surely as you live, my lord, I am the woman who stood here beside you praying to the LORD. ²⁷I prayed for this child, and the LORD has granted me what I asked of him. ²⁸So now I give him to the LORD. For his whole life he will be given over to the LORD." And he worshiped the LORD there.   Nu 15:8-10; Dt 12:5; Ge 24:26,52

Hannah's Prayer

2 Then Hannah prayed and said: Lk 1:46-55

"My heart rejoices in the LORD;
  in the LORD my hornᵉ is
    lifted high.   Isa 12:2-3
My mouth boasts over my
    enemies,
  for I delight in your
    deliverance.

²"There is no one holyᶠ like the
    LORD;   Ex 15:11
  there is no one besides you;
  there is no Rock like our
    God.   Dt 32:30-31

³"Do not keep talking so
    proudly
  or let your mouth speak
    such arrogance,   Pr 8:13

ᵃ 20 Samuel sounds like the Hebrew for heard of God.   ᵇ 23 Masoretic Text; Dead Sea Scrolls, Septuagint and Syriac your   ᶜ 24 Dead Sea Scrolls, Septuagint and Syriac; Masoretic Text with three bulls   ᵈ 24 That is, probably about 3/5 bushel (about 22 liters)   ᵉ 1 Horn here symbolizes strength; also in verse 10.   ᶠ 2 Or no Holy One

for the Lord is a God who
    knows,
and by him deeds are
    weighed.   1Sa 16:7; 1Ki 8:39

⁴"The bows of the warriors are
    broken,   Ps 37:15
but those who stumbled are
    armed with strength.
⁵Those who were full hire
    themselves out for food,
but those who were hungry
    hunger no more.
She who was barren has borne
    seven children,
but she who has had many
    sons pines away.   Ps 113:9

⁶"The Lord brings death and
    makes alive;   Dt 32:39
he brings down to the
    grave[a] and raises up.
⁷The Lord sends poverty and
    wealth;
he humbles and he exalts.
⁸He raises the poor from the
    dust
and lifts the needy from the
    ash heap;
he seats them with princes
and has them inherit a
    throne of honor.   Job 36:7

"For the foundations of the
    earth are the Lord's;
upon them he has set the
    world.   Job 38:4
⁹He will guard the feet of his
    saints,   Ps 91:12

but the wicked will be
    silenced in darkness.

"It is not by strength that one
    prevails;
¹⁰   those who oppose the Lord
    will be shattered.   Ex 15:6
He will thunder against them
    from heaven;   2Sa 22:14
the Lord will judge the ends
    of the earth.   Ps 96:13

"He will give strength to his
    king
and exalt the horn of his
    anointed."   Ps 89:24

¹¹Then Elkanah went home to Ramah, but the boy ministered before the Lord under Eli the priest.

Eli's Wicked Sons

¹²Eli's sons were wicked men; they had no regard for the Lord. ¹³Now it was the practice of the priests with the people that whenever anyone offered a sacrifice and while the meat was being boiled, the servant of the priest would come with a three-pronged fork in his hand. ¹⁴He would plunge it into the pan or kettle or caldron or pot, and the priest would take for himself whatever the fork brought up. This is how they treated all the Israelites who came to Shiloh. ¹⁵But even before the fat was burned, the servant of the priest would come and say to the man who was sacrificing, "Give the priest some

[a] 6 Hebrew *Sheol*

meat to roast; he won't accept boiled meat from you, but only raw." _{Lev 7:29-34; Jer 2:8}

¹⁶If the man said to him, "Let the fat be burned up first, and then take whatever you want," the servant would then answer, "No, hand it over now; if you don't, I'll take it by force."

¹⁷This sin of the young men was very great in the LORD's sight, for they^a were treating the LORD's offering with contempt. _{Mal 2:7-9}

¹⁸But Samuel was ministering before the LORD—a boy wearing a linen ephod. ¹⁹Each year his mother made him a little robe and took it to him when she went up with her husband to offer the annual sacrifice. ²⁰Eli would bless Elkanah and his wife, saying, "May the LORD give you children by this woman to take the place of the one she prayed for and gave to the LORD." Then they would go home. ²¹And the LORD was gracious to Hannah; she conceived and gave birth to three sons and two daughters. Meanwhile, the boy Samuel grew up in the presence of the LORD. _{Ge 21:1; Jdg 13:24; 1Sa 1:3}

²²Now Eli, who was very old, heard about everything his sons were doing to all Israel and how they slept with the women who served at the entrance to the Tent of Meeting. ²³So he said to them, "Why do you do such things? I hear from all the people about these wicked deeds of yours. ²⁴No, my sons; it is not a good report that I hear spreading among the LORD's people. ²⁵If a man sins against another man, God^b may mediate for him; but if a man sins against the LORD, who will intercede for him?" His sons, however, did not listen to their father's rebuke, for it was the LORD's will to put them to death.

²⁶And the boy Samuel continued to grow in stature and in favor with the LORD and with men.

Prophecy Against the House of Eli

²⁷Now a man of God came to Eli and said to him, "This is what the LORD says: 'Did I not clearly reveal myself to your father's house when they were in Egypt under Pharaoh? ²⁸I chose your father out of all the tribes of Israel to be my priest, to go up to my altar, to burn incense, and to wear an ephod in my presence. I also gave your father's house all the offerings made with fire by the Israelites. ²⁹Why do you^c scorn my sacrifice and offering that I prescribed for my dwelling? Why do you honor your sons more than me by fattening yourselves on the choice parts of every offering made by my people Israel?' _{Ex 4:14-16; 28:1; Dt 12:5}

³⁰"Therefore the LORD, the God of Israel, declares: 'I promised that your house and your father's house would minister before me

---

^a17 Or *men*　^b25 Or *the judges*　^c29 The Hebrew is plural.

forever.' But now the LORD declares: 'Far be it from me! Those who honor me I will honor, but those who despise me will be disdained. **31**The time is coming when I will cut short your strength and the strength of your father's house, so that there will not be an old man in your family line **32**and you will see distress in my dwelling. Although good will be done to Israel, in your family line there will never be an old man. **33**Every one of you that I do not cut off from my altar will be spared only to blind your eyes with tears and to grieve your heart, and all your descendants will die in the prime of life.

34" 'And what happens to your two sons, Hophni and Phinehas, will be a sign to you—they will both die on the same day. **35**I will raise up for myself a faithful priest, who will do according to what is in my heart and mind. I will firmly establish his house, and he will minister before my anointed one always. **36**Then everyone left in your family line will come and bow down before him for a piece of silver and a crust of bread and plead, "Appoint me to some priestly office so I can have food to eat." ' "   1Sa 4:11; 2Sa 7:11,27; 1Ki 11:38

The LORD Calls Samuel

3 The boy Samuel ministered before the LORD under Eli. In those days the word of the LORD was rare; there were not many visions.   Ps 74:9; Am 8:11; 1Sa 2:11

2One night Eli, whose eyes were becoming so weak that he could barely see, was lying down in his usual place. **3**The lamp of God had not yet gone out, and Samuel was lying down in the temple[a] of the LORD, where the ark of God was. **4**Then the LORD called Samuel.

Samuel answered, "Here I am." **5**And he ran to Eli and said, "Here I am; you called me."   Isa 6:8

But Eli said, "I did not call; go back and lie down." So he went and lay down.

6Again the LORD called, "Samuel!" And Samuel got up and went to Eli and said, "Here I am; you called me."

"My son," Eli said, "I did not call; go back and lie down."

7Now Samuel did not yet know the LORD: The word of the LORD had not yet been revealed to him.

8The LORD called Samuel a third time, and Samuel got up and went to Eli and said, "Here I am; you called me."

Then Eli realized that the LORD was calling the boy. **9**So Eli told Samuel, "Go and lie down, and if he calls you, say, 'Speak, LORD, for your servant is listening.' " So Samuel went and lay down in his place.

10The LORD came and stood there, calling as at the other times, "Samuel! Samuel!"

---

a 3 That is, tabernacle

Then Samuel said, "Speak, for your servant is listening."

[11]And the Lord said to Samuel: "See, I am about to do something in Israel that will make the ears of everyone who hears of it tingle. [12]At that time I will carry out against Eli everything I spoke against his family—from beginning to end. [13]For I told him that I would judge his family forever because of the sin he knew about; his sons made themselves contemptible,[a] and he failed to restrain them. [14]Therefore, I swore to the house of Eli, 'The guilt of Eli's house will never be atoned for by sacrifice or offering.' "   1Sa 2:27-36

[15]Samuel lay down until morning and then opened the doors of the house of the Lord. He was afraid to tell Eli the vision, [16]but Eli called him and said, "Samuel, my son."

Samuel answered, "Here I am."

[17]"What was it he said to you?" Eli asked. "Do not hide it from me. May God deal with you, be it ever so severely, if you hide from me anything he told you." [18]So Samuel told him everything, hiding nothing from him. Then Eli said, "He is the Lord; let him do what is good in his eyes."   2Sa 3:35; Isa 39:8

[19]The Lord was with Samuel as he grew up, and he let none of his words fall to the ground. [20]And all Israel from Dan to Beersheba rec-ognized that Samuel was attested as a prophet of the Lord. [21]The Lord continued to appear at Shiloh, and there he revealed himself to Samuel through his word.

4

And Samuel's word came to all Israel.

The Philistines Capture the Ark

Now the Israelites went out to fight against the Philistines. The Israelites camped at Ebenezer, and the Philistines at Aphek. [2]The Philistines deployed their forces to meet Israel, and as the battle spread, Israel was defeated by the Philistines, who killed about four thousand of them on the battlefield. [3]When the soldiers returned to camp, the elders of Israel asked, "Why did the Lord bring defeat upon us today before the Philistines? Let us bring the ark of the Lord's covenant from Shiloh, so that it[b] may go with us and save us from the hand of our enemies."

[4]So the people sent men to Shiloh, and they brought back the ark of the covenant of the Lord Almighty, who is enthroned between the cherubim. And Eli's two sons, Hophni and Phinehas, were there with the ark of the covenant of God.   2Sa 6:2

[5]When the ark of the Lord's covenant came into the camp, all Israel raised such a great shout that the ground shook. [6]Hearing the

---

[a]13 Masoretic Text; an ancient Hebrew scribal tradition and Septuagint *sons blasphemed God*
[b]3 Or *he*

uproar, the Philistines asked, "What's all this shouting in the Hebrew camp?" Jos 6:5,10

When they learned that the ark of the LORD had come into the camp, [7]the Philistines were afraid. "A god has come into the camp," they said. "We're in trouble! Nothing like this has happened before. [8]Woe to us! Who will deliver us from the hand of these mighty gods? They are the gods who struck the Egyptians with all kinds of plagues in the desert. [9]Be strong, Philistines! Be men, or you will be subject to the Hebrews, as they have been to you. Be men, and fight!" Ex 15:14; Jdg 13:1; 1Co 16:13

[10]So the Philistines fought, and the Israelites were defeated and every man fled to his tent. The slaughter was very great; Israel lost thirty thousand foot soldiers. [11]The ark of God was captured, and Eli's two sons, Hophni and Phinehas, died. Dt 28:25; 1Sa 2:34

Death of Eli

[12]That same day a Benjamite ran from the battle line and went to Shiloh, his clothes torn and dust on his head. [13]When he arrived, there was Eli sitting on his chair by the side of the road, watching, because his heart feared for the ark of God. When the man entered the town and told what had happened, the whole town sent up a cry. [14]Eli heard the outcry and asked,

"What is the meaning of this uproar?"

The man hurried over to Eli, [15]who was ninety-eight years old and whose eyes were set so that he could not see. [16]He told Eli, "I have just come from the battle line; I fled from it this very day." 1Sa 3:2

Eli asked, "What happened, my son?"

[17]The man who brought the news replied, "Israel fled before the Philistines, and the army has suffered heavy losses. Also your two sons, Hophni and Phinehas, are dead, and the ark of God has been captured."

[18]When he mentioned the ark of God, Eli fell backward off his chair by the side of the gate. His neck was broken and he died, for he was an old man and heavy. He had led[a] Israel forty years. Jdg 2:16

[19]His daughter-in-law, the wife of Phinehas, was pregnant and near the time of delivery. When she heard the news that the ark of God had been captured and that her father-in-law and her husband were dead, she went into labor and gave birth, but was overcome by her labor pains. [20]As she was dying, the women attending her said, "Don't despair; you have given birth to a son." But she did not respond or pay any attention.

[21]She named the boy Ichabod,[b] saying, "The glory has departed from Israel"—because of the cap-

---

[a] 18 Traditionally *judged*   [b] 21 *Ichabod* means *no glory*.

ture of the ark of God and the deaths of her father-in-law and her husband. [22]She said, "The glory has departed from Israel, for the ark of God has been captured."

The Ark in Ashdod and Ekron

5 After the Philistines had captured the ark of God, they took it from Ebenezer to Ashdod. [2]Then they carried the ark into Dagon's temple and set it beside Dagon. [3]When the people of Ashdod rose early the next day, there was Dagon, fallen on his face on the ground before the ark of the LORD! They took Dagon and put him back in his place. [4]But the following morning when they rose, there was Dagon, fallen on his face on the ground before the ark of the LORD! His head and hands had been broken off and were lying on the threshold; only his body remained. [5]That is why to this day neither the priests of Dagon nor any others who enter Dagon's temple at Ashdod step on the threshold.   Jdg 16:23; Isa 46:7; Eze 6:6

[6]The LORD's hand was heavy upon the people of Ashdod and its vicinity; he brought devastation upon them and afflicted them with tumors.[a] [7]When the men of Ashdod saw what was happening, they said, "The ark of the god of Israel must not stay here with us, because his hand is heavy upon us

and upon Dagon our god." [8]So they called together all the rulers of the Philistines and asked them, "What shall we do with the ark of the god of Israel?"   Ex 9:3; Ps 78:66

They answered, "Have the ark of the god of Israel moved to Gath." So they moved the ark of the God of Israel.

[9]But after they had moved it, the LORD's hand was against that city, throwing it into a great panic. He afflicted the people of the city, both young and old, with an outbreak of tumors.[b] [10]So they sent the ark of God to Ekron.   1Sa 7:13

As the ark of God was entering Ekron, the people of Ekron cried out, "They have brought the ark of the god of Israel around to us to kill us and our people." [11]So they called together all the rulers of the Philistines and said, "Send the ark of the god of Israel away; let it go back to its own place, or it[c] will kill us and our people." For death had filled the city with panic; God's hand was very heavy upon it. [12]Those who did not die were afflicted with tumors, and the outcry of the city went up to heaven.

The Ark Returned to Israel

6 When the ark of the LORD had been in Philistine territory seven months, [2]the Philistines called for the priests and the diviners and said, "What shall we do

---

[a]6 Hebrew; Septuagint and Vulgate *tumors. And rats appeared in their land, and death and destruction were throughout the city*   [b]9 Or *with tumors in the groin* (see Septuagint)   [c]11 Or *he*

with the ark of the LORD? Tell us how we should send it back to its place." _{Ge 41:8; Ex 7:11}

³They answered, "If you return the ark of the god of Israel, do not send it away empty, but by all means send a guilt offering to him. Then you will be healed, and you will know why his hand has not been lifted from you." _{Ex 23:15}

⁴The Philistines asked, "What guilt offering should we send to him?"

They replied, "Five gold tumors and five gold rats, according to the number of the Philistine rulers, because the same plague has struck both you and your rulers. ⁵Make models of the tumors and of the rats that are destroying the country, and pay honor to Israel's god. Perhaps he will lift his hand from you and your gods and your land. ⁶Why do you harden your hearts as the Egyptians and Pharaoh did? When he[a] treated them harshly, did they not send the Israelites out so they could go on their way?

⁷"Now then, get a new cart ready, with two cows that have calved and have never been yoked. Hitch the cows to the cart, but take their calves away and pen them up. ⁸Take the ark of the LORD and put it on the cart, and in a chest beside it put the gold objects you are sending back to him as a guilt offering. Send it on its way, ⁹but keep watching it. If it goes up to its own territory, toward Beth Shemesh, then the LORD has brought this great disaster on us. But if it does not, then we will know that it was not his hand that struck us and that it happened to us by chance." _{2Sa 6:3; Nu 19:2; Jos 15:10}

¹⁰So they did this. They took two such cows and hitched them to the cart and penned up their calves. ¹¹They placed the ark of the LORD on the cart and along with it the chest containing the gold rats and the models of the tumors. ¹²Then the cows went straight up toward Beth Shemesh, keeping on the road and lowing all the way; they did not turn to the right or to the left. The rulers of the Philistines followed them as far as the border of Beth Shemesh.

¹³Now the people of Beth Shemesh were harvesting their wheat in the valley, and when they looked up and saw the ark, they rejoiced at the sight. ¹⁴The cart came to the field of Joshua of Beth Shemesh, and there it stopped beside a large rock. The people chopped up the wood of the cart and sacrificed the cows as a burnt offering to the LORD. ¹⁵The Levites took down the ark of the LORD, together with the chest containing the gold objects, and placed them on the large rock. On that day the people of Beth Shemesh offered burnt offerings and made sacrifices to the LORD. ¹⁶The five rulers

---

[a] 6 That is, God

of the Philistines saw all this and then returned that same day to Ekron.   2Sa 24:22; 1Ki 19:21

17These are the gold tumors the Philistines sent as a guilt offering to the LORD—one each for Ashdod, Gaza, Ashkelon, Gath and Ekron. 18And the number of the gold rats was according to the number of Philistine towns belonging to the five rulers—the fortified towns with their country villages. The large rock, on which*a* they set the ark of the LORD, is a witness to this day in the field of Joshua of Beth Shemesh.

19But God struck down some of the men of Beth Shemesh, putting seventy*b* of them to death because they had looked into the ark of the LORD. The people mourned because of the heavy blow the LORD had dealt them, 20and the men of Beth Shemesh asked, "Who can stand in the presence of the LORD, this holy God? To whom will the ark go up from here?"   Ex 19:21

21Then they sent messengers to the people of Kiriath Jearim, saying, "The Philistines have returned the ark of the LORD. Come down and take it up to your place."

7 1So the men of Kiriath Jearim came and took up the ark of the LORD. They took it to Abinadab's house on the hill and consecrated Eleazar his son to guard the ark of the LORD.   2Sa 6:3

Samuel Subdues the Philistines at Mizpah

2It was a long time, twenty years in all, that the ark remained at Kiriath Jearim, and all the people of Israel mourned and sought after the LORD. 3And Samuel said to the whole house of Israel, "If you are returning to the LORD with all your hearts, then rid yourselves of the foreign gods and the Ashtoreths and commit yourselves to the LORD and serve him only, and he will deliver you out of the hand of the Philistines." 4So the Israelites put away their Baals and Ashtoreths, and served the LORD only.

5Then Samuel said, "Assemble all Israel at Mizpah and I will intercede with the LORD for you." 6When they had assembled at Mizpah, they drew water and poured it out before the LORD. On that day they fasted and there they confessed, "We have sinned against the LORD." And Samuel was leader*c* of Israel at Mizpah.   Jdg 10:10

7When the Philistines heard that Israel had assembled at Mizpah, the rulers of the Philistines came up to attack them. And when the Israelites heard of it, they were afraid because of the Philistines. 8They said to Samuel, "Do not stop crying out to the LORD our God for us, that he may rescue us from the hand of the Philistines." 9Then

---

a 18 A few Hebrew manuscripts (see also Septuagint); most Hebrew manuscripts *villages as far as Greater Abel, where*   *b* 19 A few Hebrew manuscripts; most Hebrew manuscripts and Septuagint *50,070*
c 6 Traditionally *judge*

Samuel took a suckling lamb and offered it up as a whole burnt offering to the LORD. He cried out to the LORD on Israel's behalf, and the LORD answered him.   1Sa 17:11

¹⁰While Samuel was sacrificing the burnt offering, the Philistines drew near to engage Israel in battle. But that day the LORD thundered with loud thunder against the Philistines and threw them into such a panic that they were routed before the Israelites. ¹¹The men of Israel rushed out of Mizpah and pursued the Philistines, slaughtering them along the way to a point below Beth Car.

¹²Then Samuel took a stone and set it up between Mizpah and Shen. He named it Ebenezer,ᵃ saying, "Thus far has the LORD helped us." ¹³So the Philistines were subdued and did not invade Israelite territory again.   Jos 4:9; Jdg 13:1,5

Throughout Samuel's lifetime, the hand of the LORD was against the Philistines. ¹⁴The towns from Ekron to Gath that the Philistines had captured from Israel were restored to her, and Israel delivered the neighboring territory from the power of the Philistines. And there was peace between Israel and the Amorites.

¹⁵Samuel continued as judge over Israel all the days of his life. ¹⁶From year to year he went on a circuit from Bethel to Gilgal to Mizpah, judging Israel in all those

places. ¹⁷But he always went back to Ramah, where his home was, and there he also judged Israel. And he built an altar there to the LORD.   1Sa 12:11; Jdg 21:4

Israel Asks for a King

8 When Samuel grew old, he appointed his sons as judges for Israel. ²The name of his firstborn was Joel and the name of his second was Abijah, and they served at Beersheba. ³But his sons did not walk in his ways. They turned aside after dishonest gain and accepted bribes and perverted justice.   Dt 16:18-19; Ps 15:5

⁴So all the elders of Israel gathered together and came to Samuel at Ramah. ⁵They said to him, "You are old, and your sons do not walk in your ways; now appoint a king to leadᵇ us, such as all the other nations have."   Dt 17:14-20; 1Sa 7:17

⁶But when they said, "Give us a king to lead us," this displeased Samuel; so he prayed to the LORD. ⁷And the LORD told him: "Listen to all that the people are saying to you; it is not you they have rejected, but they have rejected me as their king. ⁸As they have done from the day I brought them up out of Egypt until this day, forsaking me and serving other gods, so they are doing to you. ⁹Now listen to them; but warn them solemnly and let them know what the king

---

ᵃ 12 Ebenezer means stone of help.   ᵇ 5 Traditionally judge; also in verses 6 and 20

who will reign over them will do."

¹⁰Samuel told all the words of the LORD to the people who were asking him for a king. ¹¹He said, "This is what the king who will reign over you will do: He will take your sons and make them serve with his chariots and horses, and they will run in front of his chariots. ¹²Some he will assign to be commanders of thousands and commanders of fifties, and others to plow his ground and reap his harvest, and still others to make weapons of war and equipment for his chariots. ¹³He will take your daughters to be perfumers and cooks and bakers. ¹⁴He will take the best of your fields and vineyards and olive groves and give them to his attendants. ¹⁵He will take a tenth of your grain and of your vintage and give it to his officials and attendants. ¹⁶Your menservants and maidservants and the best of your cattle*a* and donkeys he will take for his own use. ¹⁷He will take a tenth of your flocks, and you yourselves will become his slaves. ¹⁸When that day comes, you will cry out for relief from the king you have chosen, and the LORD will not answer you in that day."   1Sa 14:52; 1Ki 21:7,15; Mic 3:4

¹⁹But the people refused to listen to Samuel. "No!" they said. "We want a king over us. ²⁰Then we will be like all the other nations, with a king to lead us and to go out before us and fight our battles."   Isa 66:4; Jer 44:16

²¹When Samuel heard all that the people said, he repeated it before the LORD. ²²The LORD answered, "Listen to them and give them a king."   Jdg 11:11

Then Samuel said to the men of Israel, "Everyone go back to his town."

Samuel Anoints Saul

9 There was a Benjamite, a man of standing, whose name was Kish son of Abiel, the son of Zeror, the son of Becorath, the son of Aphiah of Benjamin. ²He had a son named Saul, an impressive young man without equal among the Israelites—a head taller than any of the others.   1Sa 10:23; 14:51; 1Ch 9:39

³Now the donkeys belonging to Saul's father Kish were lost, and Kish said to his son Saul, "Take one of the servants with you and go and look for the donkeys." ⁴So he passed through the hill country of Ephraim and through the area around Shalisha, but they did not find them. They went on into the district of Shaalim, but the donkeys were not there. Then he passed through the territory of Benjamin, but they did not find them.   Jos 24:33; 2Ki 4:42

⁵When they reached the district of Zuph, Saul said to the servant who was with him, "Come, let's go back, or my father will stop think-

---

a 16 Septuagint; Hebrew *young men*

ing about the donkeys and start worrying about us." 1Sa 10:2

⁶But the servant replied, "Look, in this town there is a man of God; he is highly respected, and everything he says comes true. Let's go there now. Perhaps he will tell us what way to take." Dt 33:1; 1Sa 3:19

⁷Saul said to his servant, "If we go, what can we give the man? The food in our sacks is gone. We have no gift to take to the man of God. What do we have?" 1Ki 14:3; 2Ki 8:8

⁸The servant answered him again. "Look," he said, "I have a quarter of a shekelᵃ of silver. I will give it to the man of God so that he will tell us what way to take." ⁹(Formerly in Israel, if a man went to inquire of God, he would say, "Come, let us go to the seer," because the prophet of today used to be called a seer.) 2Sa 24:11; 1Ch 26:28

¹⁰"Good," Saul said to his servant. "Come, let's go." So they set out for the town where the man of God was.

¹¹As they were going up the hill to the town, they met some girls coming out to draw water, and they asked them, "Is the seer here?"

¹²"He is," they answered. "He's ahead of you. Hurry now; he has just come to our town today, for the people have a sacrifice at the high place. ¹³As soon as you enter the town, you will find him before he goes up to the high place to eat.

The people will not begin eating until he comes, because he must bless the sacrifice; afterward, those who are invited will eat. Go up now; you should find him about this time." Ge 31:54; Nu 28:11-15

¹⁴They went up to the town, and as they were entering it, there was Samuel, coming toward them on his way up to the high place.

¹⁵Now the day before Saul came, the LORD had revealed this to Samuel: ¹⁶"About this time tomorrow I will send you a man from the land of Benjamin. Anoint him leader over my people Israel; he will deliver my people from the hand of the Philistines. I have looked upon my people, for their cry has reached me." Ex 3:7-9; 1Sa 10:1

¹⁷When Samuel caught sight of Saul, the LORD said to him, "This is the man I spoke to you about; he will govern my people." 1Sa 16:12

¹⁸Saul approached Samuel in the gateway and asked, "Would you please tell me where the seer's house is?"

¹⁹"I am the seer," Samuel replied. "Go up ahead of me to the high place, for today you are to eat with me, and in the morning I will let you go and will tell you all that is in your heart. ²⁰As for the donkeys you lost three days ago, do not worry about them; they have been found. And to whom is all the desire of Israel turned, if not to you and all your father's family?"

ᵃ 8 That is, about 1/10 ounce (about 3 grams)

²¹Saul answered, "But am I not a Benjamite, from the smallest tribe of Israel, and is not my clan the least of all the clans of the tribe of Benjamin? Why do you say such a thing to me?" Jdg 20:35,46; 1Sa 15:17

²²Then Samuel brought Saul and his servant into the hall and seated them at the head of those who were invited—about thirty in number. ²³Samuel said to the cook, "Bring the piece of meat I gave you, the one I told you to lay aside."

²⁴So the cook took up the leg with what was on it and set it in front of Saul. Samuel said, "Here is what has been kept for you. Eat, because it was set aside for you for this occasion, from the time I said, 'I have invited guests.'" And Saul dined with Samuel that day.

²⁵After they came down from the high place to the town, Samuel talked with Saul on the roof of his house. ²⁶They rose about daybreak and Samuel called to Saul on the roof, "Get ready, and I will send you on your way." When Saul got ready, he and Samuel went outside together. ²⁷As they were going down to the edge of the town, Samuel said to Saul, "Tell the servant to go on ahead of us"—and the servant did so—"but you stay here awhile, so that I may give you a message from God." Dt 22:8

10 Then Samuel took a flask of oil and poured it on Saul's head and kissed him, saying, "Has not the Lᴏʀᴅ anointed you leader over his inheritance?ᵃ ²When you leave me today, you will meet two men near Rachel's tomb, at Zelzah on the border of Benjamin. They will say to you, 'The donkeys you set out to look for have been found. And now your father has stopped thinking about them and is worried about you. He is asking, "What shall I do about my son?"' 2Ki 9:1,3,6; Dt 32:9

³"Then you will go on from there until you reach the great tree of Tabor. Three men going up to God at Bethel will meet you there. One will be carrying three young goats, another three loaves of bread, and another a skin of wine. ⁴They will greet you and offer you two loaves of bread, which you will accept from them. Ge 35:7-8

⁵"After that you will go to Gibeah of God, where there is a Philistine outpost. As you approach the town, you will meet a procession of prophets coming down from the high place with lyres, tambourines, flutes and harps being played before them, and they will be prophesying. ⁶The Spirit of the Lᴏʀᴅ will come upon you in power, and you will prophesy with them; and you will be changed into a different person. ⁷Once

ᵃ 1 Hebrew; Septuagint and Vulgate *over his people Israel? You will reign over the Lᴏʀᴅ's people and save them from the power of their enemies round about. And this will be a sign to you that the Lᴏʀᴅ has anointed you leader over his inheritance:*

these signs are fulfilled, do whatever your hand finds to do, for God is with you. Nu 11:25; 1Sa 19:23-24

8"Go down ahead of me to Gilgal. I will surely come down to you to sacrifice burnt offerings and fellowship offerings,ᵃ but you must wait seven days until I come to you and tell you what you are to do."

Saul Made King

9As Saul turned to leave Samuel, God changed Saul's heart, and all these signs were fulfilled that day. 10When they arrived at Gibeah, a procession of prophets met him; the Spirit of God came upon him in power, and he joined in their prophesying. 11When all those who had formerly known him saw him prophesying with the prophets, they asked each other, "What is this that has happened to the son of Kish? Is Saul also among the prophets?" 1Sa 19:20,24; Mt 13:54

12A man who lived there answered, "And who is their father?" So it became a saying: "Is Saul also among the prophets?" 13After Saul stopped prophesying, he went to the high place.

14Now Saul's uncle asked him and his servant, "Where have you been?" 1Sa 14:50

"Looking for the donkeys," he said. "But when we saw they were not to be found, we went to Samuel."

15Saul's uncle said, "Tell me what Samuel said to you."

16Saul replied, "He assured us that the donkeys had been found." But he did not tell his uncle what Samuel had said about the kingship. 1Sa 9:20

17Samuel summoned the people of Israel to the LORD at Mizpah 18and said to them, "This is what the LORD, the God of Israel, says: 'I brought Israel up out of Egypt, and I delivered you from the power of Egypt and all the kingdoms that oppressed you.' 19But you have now rejected your God, who saves you out of all your calamities and distresses. And you have said, 'No, set a king over us.' So now present yourselves before the LORD by your tribes and clans." Jdg 6:8-9

20When Samuel brought all the tribes of Israel near, the tribe of Benjamin was chosen. 21Then he brought forward the tribe of Benjamin, clan by clan, and Matri's clan was chosen. Finally Saul son of Kish was chosen. But when they looked for him, he was not to be found. 22So they inquired further of the LORD, "Has the man come here yet?" 1Sa 23:2,4,9-11

And the LORD said, "Yes, he has hidden himself among the baggage."

23They ran and brought him out, and as he stood among the people he was a head taller than any of the others. 24Samuel said to all the

ᵃ 8 Traditionally peace offerings

people, "Do you see the man the LORD has chosen? There is no one like him among all the people."

Then the people shouted, "Long live the king!"   1Ki 1:25,34,39

25Samuel explained to the people the regulations of the kingship. He wrote them down on a scroll and deposited it before the LORD. Then Samuel dismissed the people, each to his own home.

26Saul also went to his home in Gibeah, accompanied by valiant men whose hearts God had touched. 27But some troublemakers said, "How can this fellow save us?" They despised him and brought him no gifts. But Saul kept silent.   1Sa 11:4; 1Ki 10:25; 2Ch 17:5

Saul Rescues the City of Jabesh

11 Nahash the Ammonite went up and besieged Jabesh Gilead. And all the men of Jabesh said to him, "Make a treaty with us, and we will be subject to you."   Jdg 21:8; 1Sa 12:12

2But Nahash the Ammonite replied, "I will make a treaty with you only on the condition that I gouge out the right eye of every one of you and so bring disgrace on all Israel."   Nu 16:14; 1Sa 17:26

3The elders of Jabesh said to him, "Give us seven days so we can send messengers throughout Israel; if no one comes to rescue us, we will surrender to you."

4When the messengers came to Gibeah of Saul and reported these terms to the people, they all wept aloud. 5Just then Saul was returning from the fields, behind his oxen, and he asked, "What is wrong with the people? Why are they weeping?" Then they repeated to him what the men of Jabesh had said.   1Sa 10:5,26; Jdg 2:4; 1Sa 30:4

6When Saul heard their words, the Spirit of God came upon him in power, and he burned with anger. 7He took a pair of oxen, cut them into pieces, and sent the pieces by messengers throughout Israel, proclaiming, "This is what will be done to the oxen of anyone who does not follow Saul and Samuel." Then the terror of the LORD fell on the people, and they turned out as one man. 8When Saul mustered them at Bezek, the men of Israel numbered three hundred thousand and the men of Judah thirty thousand.   Jdg 3:10; 19:29; 21:5

9They told the messengers who had come, "Say to the men of Jabesh Gilead, 'By the time the sun is hot tomorrow, you will be delivered.'" When the messengers went and reported this to the men of Jabesh, they were elated. 10They said to the Ammonites, "Tomorrow we will surrender to you, and you can do to us whatever seems good to you."

11The next day Saul separated his men into three divisions; during the last watch of the night they broke into the camp of the Ammonites and slaughtered them until the heat of the day. Those who survived were scattered, so that no two of them were left together.

Saul Confirmed as King

¹²The people then said to Samuel, "Who was it that asked, 'Shall Saul reign over us?' Bring these men to us and we will put them to death." 1Sa 10:27; Lk 19:27 ¹³But Saul said, "No one shall be put to death today, for this day the LORD has rescued Israel." 1Sa 19:5 ¹⁴Then Samuel said to the people, "Come, let us go to Gilgal and there reaffirm the kingship." ¹⁵So all the people went to Gilgal and confirmed Saul as king in the presence of the LORD. There they sacrificed fellowship offerings[a] before the LORD, and Saul and all the Israelites held a great celebration.

Samuel's Farewell Speech

12 Samuel said to all Israel, "I have listened to everything you said to me and have set a king over you. ²Now you have a king as your leader. As for me, I am old and gray, and my sons are here with you. I have been your leader from my youth until this day. ³Here I stand. Testify against me in the presence of the LORD and his anointed. Whose ox have I taken? Whose donkey have I taken? Whom have I cheated? Whom have I oppressed? From whose hand have I accepted a bribe to make me shut my eyes? If I have

done any of these, I will make it right." 1Sa 8:7; 24:6; 2Sa 1:14 ⁴"You have not cheated or oppressed us," they replied. "You have not taken anything from anyone's hand." Ex 22:4; Ac 23:9 ⁵Samuel said to them, "The LORD is witness against you, and also his anointed is witness this day, that you have not found anything in my hand."

"He is witness," they said.

⁶Then Samuel said to the people, "It is the LORD who appointed Moses and Aaron and brought your forefathers up out of Egypt. ⁷Now then, stand here, because I am going to confront you with evidence before the LORD as to all the righteous acts performed by the LORD for you and your fathers.

⁸"After Jacob entered Egypt, they cried to the LORD for help, and the LORD sent Moses and Aaron, who brought your forefathers out of Egypt and settled them in this place. Ex 2:23; 3:10; 4:16 ⁹"But they forgot the LORD their God; so he sold them into the hand of Sisera, the commander of the army of Hazor, and into the hands of the Philistines and the king of Moab, who fought against them. ¹⁰They cried out to the LORD and said, 'We have sinned; we have forsaken the LORD and served the Baals and the Ashtoreths. But now deliver us from the hands of our enemies, and we will serve you.'

[a] 15 Traditionally *peace offerings*

[11]Then the LORD sent Jerub-Baal,[a] Barak,[b] Jephthah and Samuel,[c] and he delivered you from the hands of your enemies on every side, so that you lived securely.

[12]"But when you saw that Nahash king of the Ammonites was moving against you, you said to me, 'No, we want a king to rule over us'—even though the LORD your God was your king. [13]Now here is the king you have chosen, the one you asked for; see, the LORD has set a king over you. [14]If you fear the LORD and serve and obey him and do not rebel against his commands, and if both you and the king who reigns over you follow the LORD your God—good! [15]But if you do not obey the LORD, and if you rebel against his commands, his hand will be against you, as it was against your fathers.

[16]"Now then, stand still and see this great thing the LORD is about to do before your eyes! [17]Is it not wheat harvest now? I will call upon the LORD to send thunder and rain. And you will realize what an evil thing you did in the eyes of the LORD when you asked for a king."

[18]Then Samuel called upon the LORD, and that same day the LORD sent thunder and rain. So all the people stood in awe of the LORD and of Samuel. Ex 14:31

[19]The people all said to Samuel, "Pray to the LORD your God for your servants so that we will not die, for we have added to all our other sins the evil of asking for a king." Ex 9:28

[20]"Do not be afraid," Samuel replied. "You have done all this evil; yet do not turn away from the LORD, but serve the LORD with all your heart. [21]Do not turn away after useless idols. They can do you no good, nor can they rescue you, because they are useless. [22]For the sake of his great name the LORD will not reject his people, because the LORD was pleased to make you his own. [23]As for me, far be it from me that I should sin against the LORD by failing to pray for you. And I will teach you the way that is good and right. [24]But be sure to fear the LORD and serve him faithfully with all your heart; consider what great things he has done for you. [25]Yet if you persist in doing evil, both you and your king will be swept away." Dt 31:6; Hab 2:18

Samuel Rebukes Saul

13 Saul was ⌜thirty⌝[d] years old when he became king, and he reigned over Israel ⌜forty-⌝[e] two years.

[2]Saul[f] chose three thousand men from Israel; two thousand were with him at Micmash and in the hill country of Bethel, and a

---

[a]11 Also called *Gideon*   [b]11 Some Septuagint manuscripts and Syriac; Hebrew *Bedan*   [c]11 Hebrew; some Septuagint manuscripts and Syriac *Samson*   [d]1 A few late manuscripts of the Septuagint; Hebrew does not have *thirty*.   [e]1 See the round number in Acts 13:21; Hebrew does not have *forty-*. [f]1,2 Or *and when he had reigned over Israel two years,* [2]*he*

thousand were with Jonathan at Gibeah in Benjamin. The rest of the men he sent back to their homes.

³Jonathan attacked the Philistine outpost at Geba, and the Philistines heard about it. Then Saul had the trumpet blown throughout the land and said, "Let the Hebrews hear!" ⁴So all Israel heard the news: "Saul has attacked the Philistine outpost, and now Israel has become a stench to the Philistines." And the people were summoned to join Saul at Gilgal.

⁵The Philistines assembled to fight Israel, with three thousand*a* chariots, six thousand charioteers, and soldiers as numerous as the sand on the seashore. They went up and camped at Micmash, east of Beth Aven. ⁶When the men of Israel saw that their situation was critical and that their army was hard pressed, they hid in caves and thickets, among the rocks, and in pits and cisterns. ⁷Some Hebrews even crossed the Jordan to the land of Gad and Gilead.   Jos 11:4

Saul remained at Gilgal, and all the troops with him were quaking with fear. ⁸He waited seven days, the time set by Samuel; but Samuel did not come to Gilgal, and Saul's men began to scatter. ⁹So he said, "Bring me the burnt offering and the fellowship offerings.*b*"

And Saul offered up the burnt offering. ¹⁰Just as he finished making the offering, Samuel arrived, and Saul went out to greet him.

¹¹"What have you done?" asked Samuel.

Saul replied, "When I saw that the men were scattering, and that you did not come at the set time, and that the Philistines were assembling at Micmash, ¹²I thought, 'Now the Philistines will come down against me at Gilgal, and I have not sought the Lord's favor.' So I felt compelled to offer the burnt offering."

¹³"You acted foolishly," Samuel said. "You have not kept the command the Lord your God gave you; if you had, he would have established your kingdom over Israel for all time. ¹⁴But now your kingdom will not endure; the Lord has sought out a man after his own heart and appointed him leader of his people, because you have not kept the Lord's command."

¹⁵Then Samuel left Gilgal*c* and went up to Gibeah in Benjamin, and Saul counted the men who were with him. They numbered about six hundred.   1Sa 14:2

Israel Without Weapons

¹⁶Saul and his son Jonathan and the men with them were staying in Gibeah*d* in Benjamin, while the

---

*a*5 Some Septuagint manuscripts and Syriac; Hebrew *thirty thousand*   *b*9 Traditionally *peace offerings*
*c*15 Hebrew; Septuagint *Gilgal and went his way; the rest of the people went after Saul to meet the army, and they went out of Gilgal*   *d*16 Two Hebrew manuscripts; most Hebrew manuscripts *Geba*, a variant of *Gibeah*

Philistines camped at Micmash. [17]Raiding parties went out from the Philistine camp in three detachments. One turned toward Ophrah in the vicinity of Shual, [18]another toward Beth Horon, and the third toward the borderland overlooking the Valley of Zeboim facing the desert. Jos 18:23; Ne 11:34

[19]Not a blacksmith could be found in the whole land of Israel, because the Philistines had said, "Otherwise the Hebrews will make swords or spears!" [20]So all Israel went down to the Philistines to have their plowshares, mattocks, axes and sickles[a] sharpened. [21]The price was two thirds of a shekel[b] for sharpening plowshares and mattocks, and a third of a shekel[c] for sharpening forks and axes and for repointing goads.

[22]So on the day of the battle not a soldier with Saul and Jonathan had a sword or spear in his hand; only Saul and his son Jonathan had them. Jdg 5:8

Jonathan Attacks the Philistines

[23]Now a detachment of Philistines had gone out to the pass at Micmash. **14** [1]One day Jonathan son of Saul said to the young man bearing his armor, "Come, let's go over to the Philistine outpost on the other side." But he did not tell his father.

[2]Saul was staying on the outskirts of Gibeah under a pomegranate tree in Migron. With him were about six hundred men, [3]among whom was Ahijah, who was wearing an ephod. He was a son of Ichabod's brother Ahitub son of Phinehas, the son of Eli, the LORD's priest in Shiloh. No one was aware that Jonathan had left.

[4]On each side of the pass that Jonathan intended to cross to reach the Philistine outpost was a cliff; one was called Bozez, and the other Seneh. [5]One cliff stood to the north toward Micmash, the other to the south toward Geba.

[6]Jonathan said to his young armor-bearer, "Come, let's go over to the outpost of those uncircumcised fellows. Perhaps the LORD will act in our behalf. Nothing can hinder the LORD from saving, whether by many or by few."

[7]"Do all that you have in mind," his armor-bearer said. "Go ahead; I am with you heart and soul."

[8]Jonathan said, "Come, then; we will cross over toward the men and let them see us. [9]If they say to us, 'Wait there until we come to you,' we will stay where we are and not go up to them. [10]But if they say, 'Come up to us,' we will climb up, because that will be our sign that the LORD has given them into our hands." Ge 24:14; Jdg 6:36-37

[11]So both of them showed them-

---

a 20 Septuagint; Hebrew *plowshares*   b 21 Hebrew *pim*; that is, about 1/4 ounce (about 8 grams)
c 21 That is, about 1/8 ounce (about 4 grams)

selves to the Philistine outpost. "Look!" said the Philistines. "The Hebrews are crawling out of the holes they were hiding in." [12]The men of the outpost shouted to Jonathan and his armor-bearer, "Come up to us and we'll teach you a lesson." 1Sa 13:6; 17:43-44

So Jonathan said to his armor-bearer, "Climb up after me; the LORD has given them into the hand of Israel." 2Sa 5:24

[13]Jonathan climbed up, using his hands and feet, with his armor-bearer right behind him. The Philistines fell before Jonathan, and his armor-bearer followed and killed behind him. [14]In that first attack Jonathan and his armor-bearer killed some twenty men in an area of about half an acre.[a]

Israel Routs the Philistines

[15]Then panic struck the whole army—those in the camp and field, and those in the outposts and raiding parties—and the ground shook. It was a panic sent by God.[b]

[16]Saul's lookouts at Gibeah in Benjamin saw the army melting away in all directions. [17]Then Saul said to the men who were with him, "Muster the forces and see who has left us." When they did, it was Jonathan and his armor-bearer who were not there.

[18]Saul said to Ahijah, "Bring the ark of God." (At that time it was with the Israelites.)[c] [19]While Saul was talking to the priest, the tumult in the Philistine camp increased more and more. So Saul said to the priest, "Withdraw your hand." Nu 27:21; 1Sa 30:7

[20]Then Saul and all his men assembled and went to the battle. They found the Philistines in total confusion, striking each other with their swords. [21]Those Hebrews who had previously been with the Philistines and had gone up with them to their camp went over to the Israelites who were with Saul and Jonathan. [22]When all the Israelites who had hidden in the hill country of Ephraim heard that the Philistines were on the run, they joined the battle in hot pursuit. [23]So the LORD rescued Israel that day, and the battle moved on beyond Beth Aven. Ex 14:30; Jdg 7:22

Jonathan Eats Honey

[24]Now the men of Israel were in distress that day, because Saul had bound the people under an oath, saying, "Cursed be any man who eats food before evening comes, before I have avenged myself on my enemies!" So none of the troops tasted food. Jos 6:26

[25]The entire army[d] entered the woods, and there was honey on the ground. [26]When they went into the woods, they saw the honey oozing out, yet no one put his

---

[a]14 Hebrew *half a yoke*; a "yoke" was the land plowed by a yoke of oxen in one day.   [b]15 Or *a terrible panic*   [c]18 Hebrew; Septuagint *"Bring the ephod."* (At that time he wore the ephod before the Israelites.)   [d]25 Or *Now all the people of the land*

hand to his mouth, because they feared the oath. ²⁷But Jonathan had not heard that his father had bound the people with the oath, so he reached out the end of the staff that was in his hand and dipped it into the honeycomb. He raised his hand to his mouth, and his eyes brightened.ᵃ ²⁸Then one of the soldiers told him, "Your father bound the army under a strict oath, saying, 'Cursed be any man who eats food today!' That is why the men are faint."   1Sa 30:12; Ps 19:10; Pr 16:24

²⁹Jonathan said, "My father has made trouble for the country. See how my eyes brightenedᵇ when I tasted a little of this honey. ³⁰How much better it would have been if the men had eaten today some of the plunder they took from their enemies. Would not the slaughter of the Philistines have been even greater?"   1Ki 18:18

³¹That day, after the Israelites had struck down the Philistines from Micmash to Aijalon, they were exhausted. ³²They pounced on the plunder and, taking sheep, cattle and calves, they butchered them on the ground and ate them, together with the blood. ³³Then someone said to Saul, "Look, the men are sinning against the LORD by eating meat that has blood in it."   Ge 9:4; Lev 17:10-14; 1Sa 15:19

"You have broken faith," he said. "Roll a large stone over here at once." ³⁴Then he said, "Go out among the men and tell them, 'Each of you bring me your cattle and sheep, and slaughter them here and eat them. Do not sin against the LORD by eating meat with blood still in it.' "

So everyone brought his ox that night and slaughtered it there. ³⁵Then Saul built an altar to the LORD; it was the first time he had done this.   1Sa 7:17

³⁶Saul said, "Let us go down after the Philistines by night and plunder them till dawn, and let us not leave one of them alive."

"Do whatever seems best to you," they replied.

But the priest said, "Let us inquire of God here."

³⁷So Saul asked God, "Shall I go down after the Philistines? Will you give them into Israel's hand?" But God did not answer him that day.   1Sa 10:22; 28:6,15

³⁸Saul therefore said, "Come here, all you who are leaders of the army, and let us find out what sin has been committed today. ³⁹As surely as the LORD who rescues Israel lives, even if it lies with my son Jonathan, he must die." But not one of the men said a word.

⁴⁰Saul then said to all the Israelites, "You stand over there; I and Jonathan my son will stand over here."

"Do what seems best to you," the men replied.

ᵃ27 Or his strength was renewed   ᵇ29 Or my strength was renewed

⁴¹Then Saul prayed to the LORD, the God of Israel, "Give me the right answer."ᵃ And Jonathan and Saul were taken by lot, and the men were cleared. ⁴²Saul said, "Cast the lot between me and Jonathan my son." And Jonathan was taken.   Ac 1:24; Pr 16:33

⁴³Then Saul said to Jonathan, "Tell me what you have done."

So Jonathan told him, "I merely tasted a little honey with the end of my staff. And now must I die?"

⁴⁴Saul said, "May God deal with me, be it ever so severely, if you do not die, Jonathan."   Ru 1:17

⁴⁵But the men said to Saul, "Should Jonathan die—he who has brought about this great deliverance in Israel? Never! As surely as the LORD lives, not a hair of his head will fall to the ground, for he did this today with God's help." So the men rescued Jonathan, and he was not put to death.   2Sa 14:11

⁴⁶Then Saul stopped pursuing the Philistines, and they withdrew to their own land.

⁴⁷After Saul had assumed rule over Israel, he fought against their enemies on every side: Moab, the Ammonites, Edom, the kingsᵇ of Zobah, and the Philistines. Wherever he turned, he inflicted punishment on them.ᶜ ⁴⁸He fought valiantly and defeated the Amalek-ites, delivering Israel from the hands of those who had plundered them.   1Sa 11:1-13; 15:2,7

Saul's Family

⁴⁹Saul's sons were Jonathan, Ishvi and Malki-Shua. The name of his older daughter was Merab, and that of the younger was Michal. ⁵⁰His wife's name was Ahinoam daughter of Ahimaaz. The name of the commander of Saul's army was Abner son of Ner, and Ner was Saul's uncle. ⁵¹Saul's father Kish and Abner's father Ner were sons of Abiel.   1Sa 9:1; 18:17-20; 31:2

⁵²All the days of Saul there was bitter war with the Philistines, and whenever Saul saw a mighty or brave man, he took him into his service.   1Sa 8:11

The LORD Rejects Saul as King

15 Samuel said to Saul, "I am the one the LORD sent to anoint you king over his people Israel; so listen now to the message from the LORD. ²This is what the LORD Almighty says: 'I will punish the Amalekites for what they did to Israel when they waylaid them as they came up from Egypt. ³Now go, attack the Amalekites and totally destroyᵈ everything that belongs to them. Do not spare them; put to death men and women, chil-

ᵃ41 Hebrew; Septuagint "Why have you not answered your servant today? If the fault is in me or my son Jonathan, respond with Urim, but if the men of Israel are at fault, respond with Thummim."
ᵇ47 Masoretic Text; Dead Sea Scrolls and Septuagint king   ᶜ47 Hebrew; Septuagint he was victorious
ᵈ3 The Hebrew term refers to the irrevocable giving over of things or persons to the LORD, often by totally destroying them; also in verses 8, 9, 15, 18, 20 and 21.

dren and infants, cattle and sheep, camels and donkeys.' "　Ex 17:8-14

[4]So Saul summoned the men and mustered them at Telaim— two hundred thousand foot soldiers and ten thousand men from Judah. [5]Saul went to the city of Amalek and set an ambush in the ravine. [6]Then he said to the Kenites, "Go away, leave the Amalekites so that I do not destroy you along with them; for you showed kindness to all the Israelites when they came up out of Egypt." So the Kenites moved away from the Amalekites.　Ex 18:10,19; Nu 10:29-32; Jdg 1:16

[7]Then Saul attacked the Amalekites all the way from Havilah to Shur, to the east of Egypt. [8]He took Agag king of the Amalekites alive, and all his people he totally destroyed with the sword. [9]But Saul and the army spared Agag and the best of the sheep and cattle, the fat calves[a] and lambs—everything that was good. These they were unwilling to destroy completely, but everything that was despised and weak they totally destroyed.

[10]Then the word of the LORD came to Samuel: [11]"I am grieved that I have made Saul king, because he has turned away from me and has not carried out my instructions." Samuel was troubled, and he cried out to the LORD all that night.　Ge 6:6; Jos 22:16; 1Ki 9:6-7

[12]Early in the morning Samuel got up and went to meet Saul, but he was told, "Saul has gone to Carmel. There he has set up a monument in his own honor and has turned and gone on down to Gilgal."　Jos 15:55

[13]When Samuel reached him, Saul said, "The LORD bless you! I have carried out the LORD's instructions."

[14]But Samuel said, "What then is this bleating of sheep in my ears? What is this lowing of cattle that I hear?"

[15]Saul answered, "The soldiers brought them from the Amalekites; they spared the best of the sheep and cattle to sacrifice to the LORD your God, but we totally destroyed the rest."

[16]"Stop!" Samuel said to Saul. "Let me tell you what the LORD said to me last night."

"Tell me," Saul replied.

[17]Samuel said, "Although you were once small in your own eyes, did you not become the head of the tribes of Israel? The LORD anointed you king over Israel. [18]And he sent you on a mission, saying, 'Go and completely destroy those wicked people, the Amalekites; make war on them until you have wiped them out.' [19]Why did you not obey the LORD? Why did you pounce on the plunder and do evil in the eyes of the LORD?"　1Sa 9:21; 14:32

[20]"But I did obey the LORD," Saul said. "I went on the mission the

a 9 Or the grown bulls; the meaning of the Hebrew for this phrase is uncertain.

LORD assigned me. I completely destroyed the Amalekites and brought back Agag their king. ²¹The soldiers took sheep and cattle from the plunder, the best of what was devoted to God, in order to sacrifice them to the LORD your God at Gilgal."

²²But Samuel replied:

"Does the LORD delight in
  burnt offerings and
  sacrifices
as much as in obeying the
  voice of the LORD?
To obey is better than sacrifice,
  and to heed is better than
  the fat of rams.   Isa 1:11-15
²³For rebellion is like the sin of
  divination,
  and arrogance like the evil of
  idolatry.
Because you have rejected the
  word of the LORD,
  he has rejected you as king."

²⁴Then Saul said to Samuel, "I have sinned. I violated the LORD's command and your instructions. I was afraid of the people and so I gave in to them. ²⁵Now I beg you, forgive my sin and come back with me, so that I may worship the LORD." Ex 10:17; 2Sa 12:13; Isa 51:12-13

²⁶But Samuel said to him, "I will not go back with you. You have rejected the word of the LORD, and the LORD has rejected you as king over Israel!" 1Sa 13:14

²⁷As Samuel turned to leave, Saul caught hold of the hem of his robe, and it tore. ²⁸Samuel said to him, "The LORD has torn the kingdom of Israel from you today and has given it to one of your neighbors—to one better than you. ²⁹He who is the Glory of Israel does not lie or change his mind; for he is not a man, that he should change his mind."   Eze 24:14; 1Sa 28:17; 1Ki 11:11,31

³⁰Saul replied, "I have sinned. But please honor me before the elders of my people and before Israel; come back with me, so that I may worship the LORD your God." ³¹So Samuel went back with Saul, and Saul worshiped the LORD.

³²Then Samuel said, "Bring me Agag king of the Amalekites."

Agag came to him confidently,^a thinking, "Surely the bitterness of death is past."

³³But Samuel said,

"As your sword has made
  women childless,
so will your mother be
  childless among
  women."   Ge 9:6; Jdg 1:7

And Samuel put Agag to death before the LORD at Gilgal.

³⁴Then Samuel left for Ramah, but Saul went up to his home in Gibeah of Saul. ³⁵Until the day Samuel died, he did not go to see Saul again, though Samuel mourned for him. And the LORD was grieved that he had made Saul king over Israel.   1Sa 11:4; 16:1; 19:24

---

a 32 Or him trembling, yet

Samuel Anoints David

16 The LORD said to Samuel, "How long will you mourn for Saul, since I have rejected him as king over Israel? Fill your horn with oil and be on your way; I am sending you to Jesse of Bethlehem. I have chosen one of his sons to be king." Ac 13:22; Ru 4:17; 1Sa 15:23

²But Samuel said, "How can I go? Saul will hear about it and kill me."

The LORD said, "Take a heifer with you and say, 'I have come to sacrifice to the LORD.' ³Invite Jesse to the sacrifice, and I will show you what to do. You are to anoint for me the one I indicate." Ex 4:15

⁴Samuel did what the LORD said. When he arrived at Bethlehem, the elders of the town trembled when they met him. They asked, "Do you come in peace?" 1Ki 2:13

⁵Samuel replied, "Yes, in peace; I have come to sacrifice to the LORD. Consecrate yourselves and come to the sacrifice with me." Then he consecrated Jesse and his sons and invited them to the sacrifice. Ex 19:10,22

⁶When they arrived, Samuel saw Eliab and thought, "Surely the LORD's anointed stands here before the LORD." 1Sa 17:13

⁷But the LORD said to Samuel, "Do not consider his appearance or his height, for I have rejected him. The LORD does not look at the things man looks at. Man looks at the outward appearance, but the LORD looks at the heart." 1Ki 8:39

⁸Then Jesse called Abinadab and had him pass in front of Samuel. But Samuel said, "The LORD has not chosen this one either." ⁹Jesse then had Shammah pass by, but Samuel said, "Nor has the LORD chosen this one." ¹⁰Jesse had seven of his sons pass before Samuel, but Samuel said to him, "The LORD has not chosen these." ¹¹So he asked Jesse, "Are these all the sons you have?" 1Sa 17:12

"There is still the youngest," Jesse answered, "but he is tending the sheep."

Samuel said, "Send for him; we will not sit down*a* until he arrives."

¹²So he sent and had him brought in. He was ruddy, with a fine appearance and handsome features. Ge 39:6; 1Sa 9:17

Then the LORD said, "Rise and anoint him; he is the one."

¹³So Samuel took the horn of oil and anointed him in the presence of his brothers, and from that day on the Spirit of the LORD came upon David in power. Samuel then went to Ramah. 1Sa 10:1,6,9-10

David in Saul's Service

¹⁴Now the Spirit of the LORD had departed from Saul, and an evil*b*

---

a 11 Some Septuagint manuscripts; Hebrew *not gather around*   *b* 14 Or *injurious*; also in verses 15, 16 and 23 spirit from the LORD tormented him. Jdg 16:20; 9:23

15Saul's attendants said to him, "See, an evil spirit from God is tormenting you. 16Let our lord command his servants here to search for someone who can play the harp. He will play when the evil spirit from God comes upon you, and you will feel better." 1Sa 18:10

17So Saul said to his attendants, "Find someone who plays well and bring him to me."

18One of the servants answered, "I have seen a son of Jesse of Bethlehem who knows how to play the harp. He is a brave man and a warrior. He speaks well and is a fine-looking man. And the LORD is with him." 1Sa 3:19; 17:32-37

19Then Saul sent messengers to Jesse and said, "Send me your son David, who is with the sheep." 20So Jesse took a donkey loaded with bread, a skin of wine and a young goat and sent them with his son David to Saul. 1Sa 10:27; Pr 18:16

21David came to Saul and entered his service. Saul liked him very much, and David became one of his armor-bearers. 22Then Saul sent word to Jesse, saying, "Allow David to remain in my service, for I am pleased with him." Ge 41:46

23Whenever the spirit from God came upon Saul, David would take his harp and play. Then relief would come to Saul; he would feel better, and the evil spirit would leave him. Jdg 9:23

David and Goliath

17 Now the Philistines gathered their forces for war and assembled at Socoh in Judah. They pitched camp at Ephes Dammim, between Socoh and Azekah. 2Saul and the Israelites assembled and camped in the Valley of Elah and drew up their battle line to meet the Philistines. 3The Philistines occupied one hill and the Israelites another, with the valley between them. 1Sa 13:5; Jos 15:35

4A champion named Goliath, who was from Gath, came out of the Philistine camp. He was over nine feet*a* tall. 5He had a bronze helmet on his head and wore a coat of scale armor of bronze weighing five thousand shekels*b*; 6on his legs he wore bronze greaves, and a bronze javelin was slung on his back. 7His spear shaft was like a weaver's rod, and its iron point weighed six hundred shekels.*c* His shield bearer went ahead of him. Jos 11:21-22; 2Sa 21:19

8Goliath stood and shouted to the ranks of Israel, "Why do you come out and line up for battle? Am I not a Philistine, and are you not the servants of Saul? Choose a man and have him come down to me. 9If he is able to fight and kill me, we will become your subjects;

---

a4 Hebrew *was six cubits and a span* (about 3 meters)   *b5* That is, about 125 pounds (about 57 kilograms)   *c7* That is, about 15 pounds (about 7 kilograms)

but if I overcome him and kill him, you will become our subjects and serve us." ¹⁰Then the Philistine said, "This day I defy the ranks of Israel! Give me a man and let us fight each other." ¹¹On hearing the Philistine's words, Saul and all the Israelites were dismayed and terrified.   1Sa 8:17

¹²Now David was the son of an Ephrathite named Jesse, who was from Bethlehem in Judah. Jesse had eight sons, and in Saul's time he was old and well advanced in years. ¹³Jesse's three oldest sons had followed Saul to the war: The firstborn was Eliab; the second, Abinadab; and the third, Shammah. ¹⁴David was the youngest. The three oldest followed Saul, ¹⁵but David went back and forth from Saul to tend his father's sheep at Bethlehem.   1Ch 2:13-15

¹⁶For forty days the Philistine came forward every morning and evening and took his stand.

¹⁷Now Jesse said to his son David, "Take this ephah[a] of roasted grain and these ten loaves of bread for your brothers and hurry to their camp. ¹⁸Take along these ten cheeses to the commander of their unit.[b] See how your brothers are and bring back some assurance[c] from them. ¹⁹They are with Saul and all the men of Israel in the Valley of Elah, fighting against the Philistines."   Ge 37:14; 1Sa 25:18

²⁰Early in the morning David left the flock with a shepherd, loaded up and set out, as Jesse had directed. He reached the camp as the army was going out to its battle positions, shouting the war cry. ²¹Israel and the Philistines were drawing up their lines facing each other. ²²David left his things with the keeper of supplies, ran to the battle lines and greeted his brothers. ²³As he was talking with them, Goliath, the Philistine champion from Gath, stepped out from his lines and shouted his usual defiance, and David heard it. ²⁴When the Israelites saw the man, they all ran from him in great fear.

²⁵Now the Israelites had been saying, "Do you see how this man keeps coming out? He comes out to defy Israel. The king will give great wealth to the man who kills him. He will also give him his daughter in marriage and will exempt his father's family from taxes in Israel."   Jos 15:16; 1Sa 18:17

²⁶David asked the men standing near him, "What will be done for the man who kills this Philistine and removes this disgrace from Israel? Who is this uncircumcised Philistine that he should defy the armies of the living God?"   1Sa 11:2

²⁷They repeated to him what they had been saying and told him, "This is what will be done for the man who kills him."

---

a 17 That is, probably about 3/5 bushel (about 22 liters)   b 18 Hebrew *thousand*   c 18 Or *some token*; or *some pledge of spoils*

²⁸When Eliab, David's oldest brother, heard him speaking with the men, he burned with anger at him and asked, "Why have you come down here? And with whom did you leave those few sheep in the desert? I know how conceited you are and how wicked your heart is; you came down only to watch the battle." Ge 37:4,8,11

²⁹"Now what have I done?" said David. "Can't I even speak?" ³⁰He then turned away to someone else and brought up the same matter, and the men answered him as before. ³¹What David said was overheard and reported to Saul, and Saul sent for him.

³²David said to Saul, "Let no one lose heart on account of this Philistine; your servant will go and fight him." Dt 20:3; 1Sa 16:18

³³Saul replied, "You are not able to go out against this Philistine and fight him; you are only a boy, and he has been a fighting man from his youth." Nu 13:31

³⁴But David said to Saul, "Your servant has been keeping his father's sheep. When a lion or a bear came and carried off a sheep from the flock, ³⁵I went after it, struck it and rescued the sheep from its mouth. When it turned on me, I seized it by its hair, struck it and killed it. ³⁶Your servant has killed both the lion and the bear; this uncircumcised Philistine will be like one of them, because he has defied the armies of the living God. ³⁷The Lord who delivered me from the paw of the lion and the paw of the bear will deliver me from the hand of this Philistine." Jer 49:19; 2Co 1:10

Saul said to David, "Go, and the Lord be with you." 1Sa 20:13

³⁸Then Saul dressed David in his own tunic. He put a coat of armor on him and a bronze helmet on his head. ³⁹David fastened on his sword over the tunic and tried walking around, because he was not used to them. Ge 41:42

"I cannot go in these," he said to Saul, "because I am not used to them." So he took them off. ⁴⁰Then he took his staff in his hand, chose five smooth stones from the stream, put them in the pouch of his shepherd's bag and, with his sling in his hand, approached the Philistine.

⁴¹Meanwhile, the Philistine, with his shield bearer in front of him, kept coming closer to David. ⁴²He looked David over and saw that he was only a boy, ruddy and handsome, and he despised him. ⁴³He said to David, "Am I a dog, that you come at me with sticks?" And the Philistine cursed David by his gods. ⁴⁴"Come here," he said, "and I'll give your flesh to the birds of the air and the beasts of the field!" 1Sa 24:14; 1Ki 20:10-11; Pr 16:18

⁴⁵David said to the Philistine, "You come against me with sword and spear and javelin, but I come against you in the name of the Lord Almighty, the God of the armies of Israel, whom you have defied. ⁴⁶This day the Lord will hand

you over to me, and I'll strike you down and cut off your head. Today I will give the carcasses of the Philistine army to the birds of the air and the beasts of the earth, and the whole world will know that there is a God in Israel. ⁴⁷All those gathered here will know that it is not by sword or spear that the Lᴏʀᴅ saves; for the battle is the Lᴏʀᴅ's, and he will give all of you into our hands."

⁴⁸As the Philistine moved closer to attack him, David ran quickly toward the battle line to meet him. ⁴⁹Reaching into his bag and taking out a stone, he slung it and struck the Philistine on the forehead. The stone sank into his forehead, and he fell facedown on the ground.

⁵⁰So David triumphed over the Philistine with a sling and a stone; without a sword in his hand he struck down the Philistine and killed him.

⁵¹David ran and stood over him. He took hold of the Philistine's sword and drew it from the scabbard. After he killed him, he cut off his head with the sword.   Heb 11:34

When the Philistines saw that their hero was dead, they turned and ran. ⁵²Then the men of Israel and Judah surged forward with a shout and pursued the Philistines to the entrance of Gathᵃ and to the gates of Ekron. Their dead were strewn along the Shaaraim road to Gath and Ekron. ⁵³When the Israelites returned from chasing the Philistines, they plundered their camp. ⁵⁴David took the Philistine's head and brought it to Jerusalem, and he put the Philistine's weapons in his own tent.   Jos 15:36

⁵⁵As Saul watched David going out to meet the Philistine, he said to Abner, commander of the army, "Abner, whose son is that young man?"   1Sa 16:21

Abner replied, "As surely as you live, O king, I don't know."

⁵⁶The king said, "Find out whose son this young man is."

⁵⁷As soon as David returned from killing the Philistine, Abner took him and brought him before Saul, with David still holding the Philistine's head.

⁵⁸"Whose son are you, young man?" Saul asked him.

David said, "I am the son of your servant Jesse of Bethlehem."

Saul's Jealousy of David

18 After David had finished talking with Saul, Jonathan became one in spirit with David, and he loved him as himself. ²From that day Saul kept David with him and did not let him return to his father's house. ³And Jonathan made a covenant with David because he loved him as himself. ⁴Jonathan took off the robe he was wearing and gave it to David, along with his tunic, and even his sword, his bow and his belt.   Ge 41:42; 44:30; 2Sa 1:26

ᵃ 52 Some Septuagint manuscripts; Hebrew *a valley*

[5]Whatever Saul sent him to do, David did it so successfully[a] that Saul gave him a high rank in the army. This pleased all the people, and Saul's officers as well.

[6]When the men were returning home after David had killed the Philistine, the women came out from all the towns of Israel to meet King Saul with singing and dancing, with joyful songs and with tambourines and lutes. [7]As they danced, they sang: Ex 15:20; Jdg 11:34

"Saul has slain his thousands,
   and David his tens of
       thousands."   1Sa 21:11

[8]Saul was very angry; this refrain galled him. "They have credited David with tens of thousands," he thought, "but me with only thousands. What more can he get but the kingdom?" [9]And from that time on Saul kept a jealous eye on David.   1Sa 15:8

[10]The next day an evil[b] spirit from God came forcefully upon Saul. He was prophesying in his house, while David was playing the harp, as he usually did. Saul had a spear in his hand [11]and he hurled it, saying to himself, "I'll pin David to the wall." But David eluded him twice.   1Sa 16:14; 19:7

[12]Saul was afraid of David, because the LORD was with David but had left Saul. [13]So he sent David away from him and gave him command over a thousand men, and David led the troops in their campaigns. [14]In everything he did he had great success,[c] because the LORD was with him. [15]When Saul saw how successful[d] he was, he was afraid of him. [16]But all Israel and Judah loved David, because he led them in their campaigns.

[17]Saul said to David, "Here is my older daughter Merab. I will give her to you in marriage; only serve me bravely and fight the battles of the LORD." For Saul said to himself, "I will not raise a hand against him. Let the Philistines do that!"

[18]But David said to Saul, "Who am I, and what is my family or my father's clan in Israel, that I should become the king's son-in-law?" [19]So[e] when the time came for Merab, Saul's daughter, to be given to David, she was given in marriage to Adriel of Meholah.   2Sa 7:18; 21 3

[20]Now Saul's daughter Michal was in love with David, and when they told Saul about it, he was pleased. [21]"I will give her to him," he thought, "so that she may be a snare to him and so that the hand of the Philistines may be against him." So Saul said to David, "Now you have a second opportunity to become my son-in-law."

[22]Then Saul ordered his attendants: "Speak to David privately and say, 'Look, the king is pleased with you, and his attendants all

---

[a]5 Or wisely   [b]10 Or injurious   [c]14 Or he was very wise   [d]15 Or wise   [e]19 Or However,

like you; now become his son-in-law.' "

²³They repeated these words to David. But David said, "Do you think it is a small matter to become the king's son-in-law? I'm only a poor man and little known."

²⁴When Saul's servants told him what David had said, ²⁵Saul replied, "Say to David, 'The king wants no other price for the bride than a hundred Philistine foreskins, to take revenge on his enemies.' " Saul's plan was to have David fall by the hands of the Philistines.   Ex 22:17; Jer 20:10

²⁶When the attendants told David these things, he was pleased to become the king's son-in-law. So before the allotted time elapsed, ²⁷David and his men went out and killed two hundred Philistines. He brought their foreskins and presented the full number to the king so that he might become the king's son-in-law. Then Saul gave him his daughter Michal in marriage.

²⁸When Saul realized that the LORD was with David and that his daughter Michal loved David, ²⁹Saul became still more afraid of him, and he remained his enemy the rest of his days.

³⁰The Philistine commanders continued to go out to battle, and as often as they did, David met with more success[a] than the rest of Saul's officers, and his name became well known.

Saul Tries to Kill David

19 Saul told his son Jonathan and all the attendants to kill David. But Jonathan was very fond of David ²and warned him, "My father Saul is looking for a chance to kill you. Be on your guard tomorrow morning; go into hiding and stay there. ³I will go out and stand with my father in the field where you are. I'll speak to him about you and will tell you what I find out."   1Sa 18:9; 20:12

⁴Jonathan spoke well of David to Saul his father and said to him, "Let not the king do wrong to his servant David; he has not wronged you, and what he has done has benefited you greatly. ⁵He took his life in his hands when he killed the Philistine. The LORD won a great victory for all Israel, and you saw it and were glad. Why then would you do wrong to an innocent man like David by killing him for no reason?"   Ge 42:22; 1Sa 11:13; Mt 27:4

⁶Saul listened to Jonathan and took this oath: "As surely as the LORD lives, David will not be put to death."

⁷So Jonathan called David and told him the whole conversation. He brought him to Saul, and David was with Saul as before.   1Sa 16:21

⁸Once more war broke out, and David went out and fought the Philistines. He struck them with such force that they fled before him.

---

[a] 30 Or *David acted more wisely*

⁹But an evil*ᵃ* spirit from the Lᴏʀᴅ came upon Saul as he was sitting in his house with his spear in his hand. While David was playing the harp, ¹⁰Saul tried to pin him to the wall with his spear, but David eluded him as Saul drove the spear into the wall. That night David made good his escape.

¹¹Saul sent men to David's house to watch it and to kill him in the morning. But Michal, David's wife, warned him, "If you don't run for your life tonight, tomorrow you'll be killed." ¹²So Michal let David down through a window, and he fled and escaped. ¹³Then Michal took an idol*ᵇ* and laid it on the bed, covering it with a garment and putting some goats' hair at the head. Jos 2:15; Ac 9:25

¹⁴When Saul sent the men to capture David, Michal said, "He is ill." Jos 2:4

¹⁵Then Saul sent the men back to see David and told them, "Bring him up to me in his bed so that I may kill him." ¹⁶But when the men entered, there was the idol in the bed, and at the head was some goats' hair.

¹⁷Saul said to Michal, "Why did you deceive me like this and send my enemy away so that he escaped?"

Michal told him, "He said to me, 'Let me get away. Why should I kill you?'"

¹⁸When David had fled and made his escape, he went to Samuel at Ramah and told him all that Saul had done to him. Then he and Samuel went to Naioth and stayed there. ¹⁹Word came to Saul: "David is in Naioth at Ramah"; ²⁰so he sent men to capture him. But when they saw a group of prophets prophesying, with Samuel standing there as their leader, the Spirit of God came upon Saul's men and they also prophesied. ²¹Saul was told about it, and he sent more men, and they prophesied too. Saul sent men a third time, and they also prophesied. ²²Finally, he himself left for Ramah and went to the great cistern at Secu. And he asked, "Where are Samuel and David?"

Nu 11:25; 1Sa 10:5

"Over in Naioth at Ramah," they said.

²³So Saul went to Naioth at Ramah. But the Spirit of God came even upon him, and he walked along prophesying until he came to Naioth. ²⁴He stripped off his robes and also prophesied in Samuel's presence. He lay that way all that day and night. This is why people say, "Is Saul also among the prophets?" 1Sa 15:35; Isa 20:2; Mic 1:8

David and Jonathan

20 Then David fled from Naioth at Ramah and went to Jonathan and asked, "What have I done? What is my crime? How

---

*ᵃ*9 Or *injurious*   *ᵇ*13 Hebrew *teraphim*; also in verse 16

have I wronged your father, that he is trying to take my life?"

²"Never!" Jonathan replied. "You are not going to die! Look, my father doesn't do anything, great or small, without confiding in me. Why would he hide this from me? It's not so!"

³But David took an oath and said, "Your father knows very well that I have found favor in your eyes, and he has said to himself, 'Jonathan must not know this or he will be grieved.' Yet as surely as the LORD lives and as you live, there is only a step between me and death."   Dt 6:13

⁴Jonathan said to David, "Whatever you want me to do, I'll do for you."

⁵So David said, "Look, tomorrow is the New Moon festival, and I am supposed to dine with the king; but let me go and hide in the field until the evening of the day after tomorrow. ⁶If your father misses me at all, tell him, 'David earnestly asked my permission to hurry to Bethlehem, his hometown, because an annual sacrifice is being made there for his whole clan.' ⁷If he says, 'Very well,' then your servant is safe. But if he loses his temper, you can be sure that he is determined to harm me. ⁸As for you, show kindness to your servant, for you have brought him into a covenant with you before the LORD. If I am guilty, then kill me yourself! Why hand me over to your father?"   1Sa 18:3; 2Sa 14:32

⁹"Never!" Jonathan said. "If I had the least inkling that my father was determined to harm you, wouldn't I tell you?"

¹⁰David asked, "Who will tell me if your father answers you harshly?"

¹¹"Come," Jonathan said, "let's go out into the field." So they went there together.

¹²Then Jonathan said to David: "By the LORD, the God of Israel, I will surely sound out my father by this time the day after tomorrow! If he is favorably disposed toward you, will I not send you word and let you know? ¹³But if my father is inclined to harm you, may the LORD deal with me, be it ever so severely, if I do not let you know and send you away safely. May the LORD be with you as he has been with my father. ¹⁴But show me unfailing kindness like that of the LORD as long as I live, so that I may not be killed, ¹⁵and do not ever cut off your kindness from my family —not even when the LORD has cut off every one of David's enemies from the face of the earth."

¹⁶So Jonathan made a covenant with the house of David, saying, "May the LORD call David's enemies to account." ¹⁷And Jonathan had David reaffirm his oath out of love for him, because he loved him as he loved himself.   1Sa 25:22

¹⁸Then Jonathan said to David: "Tomorrow is the New Moon festival. You will be missed, because your seat will be empty. ¹⁹The day

after tomorrow, toward evening, go to the place where you hid when this trouble began, and wait by the stone Ezel. ²⁰I will shoot three arrows to the side of it, as though I were shooting at a target. ²¹Then I will send a boy and say, 'Go, find the arrows.' If I say to him, 'Look, the arrows are on this side of you; bring them here,' then come, because, as surely as the LORD lives, you are safe; there is no danger. ²²But if I say to the boy, 'Look, the arrows are beyond you,' then you must go, because the LORD has sent you away. ²³And about the matter you and I discussed—remember, the LORD is witness between you and me forever." Ge 31:50; 1Sa 19:2

²⁴So David hid in the field, and when the New Moon festival came, the king sat down to eat. ²⁵He sat in his customary place by the wall, opposite Jonathan,^a and Abner sat next to Saul, but David's place was empty. ²⁶Saul said nothing that day, for he thought, "Something must have happened to David to make him ceremonially unclean—surely he is unclean." ²⁷But the next day, the second day of the month, David's place was empty again. Then Saul said to his son Jonathan, "Why hasn't the son of Jesse come to the meal, either yesterday or today?" Lev 7:20-21; 15:5

²⁸Jonathan answered, "David earnestly asked me for permission to go to Bethlehem. ²⁹He said, 'Let me go, because our family is observing a sacrifice in the town and my brother has ordered me to be there. If I have found favor in your eyes, let me get away to see my brothers.' That is why he has not come to the king's table."

³⁰Saul's anger flared up at Jonathan and he said to him, "You son of a perverse and rebellious woman! Don't I know that you have sided with the son of Jesse to your own shame and to the shame of the mother who bore you? ³¹As long as the son of Jesse lives on this earth, neither you nor your kingdom will be established. Now send and bring him to me, for he must die!"

³²"Why should he be put to death? What has he done?" Jonathan asked his father. ³³But Saul hurled his spear at him to kill him. Then Jonathan knew that his father intended to kill David.

³⁴Jonathan got up from the table in fierce anger; on that second day of the month he did not eat, because he was grieved at his father's shameful treatment of David.

³⁵In the morning Jonathan went out to the field for his meeting with David. He had a small boy with him, ³⁶and he said to the boy, "Run and find the arrows I shoot." As the boy ran, he shot an arrow beyond him. ³⁷When the boy came to the place where Jonathan's arrow

^a 25 Septuagint; Hebrew wall. Jonathan arose

had fallen, Jonathan called out after him, "Isn't the arrow beyond you?" **38**Then he shouted, "Hurry! Go quickly! Don't stop!" The boy picked up the arrow and returned to his master. **39**(The boy knew nothing of all this; only Jonathan and David knew.) **40**Then Jonathan gave his weapons to the boy and said, "Go, carry them back to town."

41After the boy had gone, David got up from the south side ˌof the stoneˌ and bowed down before Jonathan three times, with his face to the ground. Then they kissed each other and wept together — but David wept the most.

42Jonathan said to David, "Go in peace, for we have sworn friendship with each other in the name of the LORD, saying, 'The LORD is witness between you and me, and between your descendants and my descendants forever.'" Then David left, and Jonathan went back to the town.　　1Sa 1:17; 2Sa 1:26; Pr 18:24

David at Nob

21 David went to Nob, to Ahimelech the priest. Ahimelech trembled when he met him, and asked, "Why are you alone? Why is no one with you?"

2David answered Ahimelech the priest, "The king charged me with a certain matter and said to me, 'No one is to know anything about your mission and your instruc-

tions.' As for my men, I have told them to meet me at a certain place. **3**Now then, what do you have on hand? Give me five loaves of bread, or whatever you can find."

4But the priest answered David, "I don't have any ordinary bread on hand; however, there is some consecrated bread here — provided the men have kept themselves from women."　　Mt 12:4; Lev 24:8-9

5David replied, "Indeed women have been kept from us, as usual whenever*a* I set out. The men's things*b* are holy even on missions that are not holy. How much more so today!" **6**So the priest gave him the consecrated bread, since there was no bread there except the bread of the Presence that had been removed from before the LORD and replaced by hot bread on the day it was taken away.

7Now one of Saul's servants was there that day, detained before the LORD; he was Doeg the Edomite, Saul's head shepherd.　　1Sa 22:9,22

8David asked Ahimelech, "Don't you have a spear or a sword here? I haven't brought my sword or any other weapon, because the king's business was urgent."

9The priest replied, "The sword of Goliath the Philistine, whom you killed in the Valley of Elah, is here; it is wrapped in a cloth behind the ephod. If you want it, take it; there is no sword here but that one."　　1Sa 17:51

---

a 5 Or *from us in the past few days since*　　*b* 5 Or *bodies*

David said, "There is none like it; give it to me."

David at Gath

[10] That day David fled from Saul and went to Achish king of Gath. [11] But the servants of Achish said to him, "Isn't this David, the king of the land? Isn't he the one they sing about in their dances:

" 'Saul has slain his thousands,
    and David his tens of
        thousands'?"   1Sa 18:7; 29:5

[12] David took these words to heart and was very much afraid of Achish king of Gath. [13] So he pretended to be insane in their presence; and while he was in their hands he acted like a madman, making marks on the doors of the gate and letting saliva run down his beard.

[14] Achish said to his servants, "Look at the man! He is insane! Why bring him to me? [15] Am I so short of madmen that you have to bring this fellow here to carry on like this in front of me? Must this man come into my house?"

David at Adullam and Mizpah

22 David left Gath and escaped to the cave of Adullam. When his brothers and his father's household heard about it, they went down to him there. [2] All those who were in distress or in debt or discontented gathered around him, and he became their leader. About four hundred men were with him.   1Sa 25:13; 2Sa 23:13

[3] From there David went to Mizpah in Moab and said to the king of Moab, "Would you let my father and mother come and stay with you until I learn what God will do for me?" [4] So he left them with the king of Moab, and they stayed with him as long as David was in the stronghold.

[5] But the prophet Gad said to David, "Do not stay in the stronghold. Go into the land of Judah." So David left and went to the forest of Hereth.   2Sa 24:11; 1Ch 21:9; 2Ch 29:25

Saul Kills the Priests of Nob

[6] Now Saul heard that David and his men had been discovered. And Saul, spear in hand, was seated under the tamarisk tree on the hill at Gibeah, with all his officials standing around him. [7] Saul said to them, "Listen, men of Benjamin! Will the son of Jesse give all of you fields and vineyards? Will he make all of you commanders of thousands and commanders of hundreds? [8] Is that why you have all conspired against me? No one tells me when my son makes a covenant with the son of Jesse. None of you is concerned about me or tells me that my son has incited my servant to lie in wait for me, as he does today."   1Sa 8:14; 18:3; Jdg 4:5

[9] But Doeg the Edomite, who was standing with Saul's officials, said, "I saw the son of Jesse come to Ahimelech son of Ahitub at

Nob. [10]Ahimelech inquired of the LORD for him; he also gave him provisions and the sword of Goliath the Philistine." 1Sa 17:51; 21:7

[11]Then the king sent for the priest Ahimelech son of Ahitub and his father's whole family, who were the priests at Nob, and they all came to the king. [12]Saul said, "Listen now, son of Ahitub."

"Yes, my lord," he answered.

[13]Saul said to him, "Why have you conspired against me, you and the son of Jesse, giving him bread and a sword and inquiring of God for him, so that he has rebelled against me and lies in wait for me, as he does today?"

[14]Ahimelech answered the king, "Who of all your servants is as loyal as David, the king's son-in-law, captain of your bodyguard and highly respected in your household? [15]Was that day the first time I inquired of God for him? Of course not! Let not the king accuse your servant or any of his father's family, for your servant knows nothing at all about this whole affair."

[16]But the king said, "You will surely die, Ahimelech, you and your father's whole family."

[17]Then the king ordered the guards at his side: "Turn and kill the priests of the LORD, because they too have sided with David. They knew he was fleeing, yet they did not tell me."

But the king's officials were not willing to raise a hand to strike the priests of the LORD.   Ex 1:17

[18]The king then ordered Doeg, "You turn and strike down the priests." So Doeg the Edomite turned and struck them down. That day he killed eighty-five men who wore the linen ephod. [19]He also put to the sword Nob, the town of the priests, with its men and women, its children and infants, and its cattle, donkeys and sheep.   1Sa 2:18,31; 15:3

[20]But Abiathar, a son of Ahimelech son of Ahitub, escaped and fled to join David. [21]He told David that Saul had killed the priests of the LORD. [22]Then David said to Abiathar: "That day, when Doeg the Edomite was there, I knew he would be sure to tell Saul. I am responsible for the death of your father's whole family. [23]Stay with me; don't be afraid; the man who is seeking your life is seeking mine also. You will be safe with me."

David Saves Keilah

23 When David was told, "Look, the Philistines are fighting against Keilah and are looting the threshing floors," [2]he inquired of the LORD, saying, "Shall I go and attack these Philistines?"

The LORD answered him, "Go, attack the Philistines and save Keilah."

[3]But David's men said to him, "Here in Judah we are afraid. How much more, then, if we go to Keilah against the Philistine forces!"

4Once again David inquired of the LORD, and the LORD answered him, "Go down to Keilah, for I am going to give the Philistines into your hand." 5So David and his men went to Keilah, fought the Philistines and carried off their livestock. He inflicted heavy losses on the Philistines and saved the people of Keilah. 6(Now Abiathar son of Ahimelech had brought the ephod down with him when he fled to David at Keilah.)   Jos 8:7

Saul Pursues David

7Saul was told that David had gone to Keilah, and he said, "God has handed him over to me, for David has imprisoned himself by entering a town with gates and bars." 8And Saul called up all his forces for battle, to go down to Keilah to besiege David and his men.

9When David learned that Saul was plotting against him, he said to Abiathar the priest, "Bring the ephod." 10David said, "O LORD, God of Israel, your servant has heard definitely that Saul plans to come to Keilah and destroy the town on account of me. 11Will the citizens of Keilah surrender me to him? Will Saul come down, as your servant has heard? O LORD, God of Israel, tell your servant."

And the LORD said, "He will."

12Again David asked, "Will the citizens of Keilah surrender me and my men to Saul?"

And the LORD said, "They will."

13So David and his men, about six hundred in number, left Keilah and kept moving from place to place. When Saul was told that David had escaped from Keilah, he did not go there.   1Sa 22:2; 25:13

14David stayed in the desert strongholds and in the hills of the Desert of Ziph. Day after day Saul searched for him, but God did not give David into his hands.   Ps 32:7

15While David was at Horesh in the Desert of Ziph, he learned that Saul had come out to take his life. 16And Saul's son Jonathan went to David at Horesh and helped him find strength in God. 17"Don't be afraid," he said. "My father Saul will not lay a hand on you. You will be king over Israel, and I will be second to you. Even my father Saul knows this." 18The two of them made a covenant before the LORD. Then Jonathan went home, but David remained at Horesh.

19The Ziphites went up to Saul at Gibeah and said, "Is not David hiding among us in the strongholds at Horesh, on the hill of Hakilah, south of Jeshimon? 20Now, O king, come down whenever it pleases you to do so, and we will be responsible for handing him over to the king."   1Sa 26:1

21Saul replied, "The LORD bless you for your concern for me. 22Go and make further preparation. Find out where David usually goes and who has seen him there. They tell me he is very crafty. 23Find out about all the hiding places he uses and come back to me with definite information.[a] Then I will go with you; if he is in the area, I will track him down among all the clans of Judah." 1Sa 22:8

²⁴So they set out and went to Ziph ahead of Saul. Now David and his men were in the Desert of Maon, in the Arabah south of Jeshimon. ²⁵Saul and his men began the search, and when David was told about it, he went down to the rock and stayed in the Desert of Maon. When Saul heard this, he went into the Desert of Maon in pursuit of David.   Jos 15:55; 1Sa 25:2

²⁶Saul was going along one side of the mountain, and David and his men were on the other side, hurrying to get away from Saul. As Saul and his forces were closing in on David and his men to capture them, ²⁷a messenger came to Saul, saying, "Come quickly! The Philistines are raiding the land." ²⁸Then Saul broke off his pursuit of David and went to meet the Philistines. That is why they call this place Sela Hammahlekoth.[b] ²⁹And David went up from there and lived in the strongholds of En Gedi.

David Spares Saul's Life

24 After Saul returned from pursuing the Philistines, he was told, "David is in the Desert of En Gedi." ²So Saul took three thousand chosen men from all Israel and set out to look for David and his men near the Crags of the Wild Goats.   1Sa 23:28-29; 26:2

³He came to the sheep pens along the way; a cave was there, and Saul went in to relieve himself. David and his men were far back in the cave. ⁴The men said, "This is the day the LORD spoke of when he said[c] to you, 'I will give your enemy into your hands for you to deal with as you wish.'" Then David crept up unnoticed and cut off a corner of Saul's robe.   1Sa 25:28-30

⁵Afterward, David was conscience-stricken for having cut off a corner of his robe. ⁶He said to his men, "The LORD forbid that I should do such a thing to my master, the LORD's anointed, or lift my hand against him; for he is the anointed of the LORD." ⁷With these words David rebuked his men and did not allow them to attack Saul. And Saul left the cave and went his way.   1Sa 26:11; 2Sa 24:10

⁸Then David went out of the cave and called out to Saul, "My lord the king!" When Saul looked behind him, David bowed down and prostrated himself with his face to the ground. ⁹He said to Saul, "Why do you listen when men say, 'David is bent on harming you'? ¹⁰This day you have seen with your own eyes how the LORD delivered you into my hands in the cave. Some urged me to kill you, but I spared you; I said, 'I will not

---

[a] 23 Or *me at Nacon*   [b] 28 *Sela Hammahlekoth* means *rock of parting.*   [c] 4 Or *"Today the* LORD *is saying*

lift my hand against my master, because he is the LORD's anointed.' [11]See, my father, look at this piece of your robe in my hand! I cut off the corner of your robe but did not kill you. Now understand and recognize that I am not guilty of wrongdoing or rebellion. I have not wronged you, but you are hunting me down to take my life. [12]May the LORD judge between you and me. And may the LORD avenge the wrongs you have done to me, but my hand will not touch you. [13]As the old saying goes, 'From evildoers come evil deeds,' so my hand will not touch you.   Ge 16:5

[14]"Against whom has the king of Israel come out? Whom are you pursuing? A dead dog? A flea? [15]May the LORD be our judge and decide between us. May he consider my cause and uphold it; may he vindicate me by delivering me from your hand."   1Sa 17:43; Ps 35:1,23

[16]When David finished saying this, Saul asked, "Is that your voice, David my son?" And he wept aloud. [17]"You are more righteous than I," he said. "You have treated me well, but I have treated you badly. [18]You have just now told me of the good you did to me; the LORD delivered me into your hands, but you did not kill me. [19]When a man finds his enemy, does he let him get away unharmed? May the LORD reward you well for the way you treated me

today. [20]I know that you will surely be king and that the kingdom of Israel will be established in your hands. [21]Now swear to me by the LORD that you will not cut off my descendants or wipe out my name from my father's family."   Ge 38:26

[22]So David gave his oath to Saul. Then Saul returned home, but David and his men went up to the stronghold.   1Sa 23:29

David, Nabal and Abigail

25 Now Samuel died, and all Israel assembled and mourned for him; and they buried him at his home in Ramah.

Then David moved down into the Desert of Maon.[a] [2]A certain man in Maon, who had property there at Carmel, was very wealthy. He had a thousand goats and three thousand sheep, which he was shearing in Carmel. [3]His name was Nabal and his wife's name was Abigail. She was an intelligent and beautiful woman, but her husband, a Calebite, was surly and mean in his dealings.   Jos 15:55

[4]While David was in the desert, he heard that Nabal was shearing sheep. [5]So he sent ten young men and said to them, "Go up to Nabal at Carmel and greet him in my name. [6]Say to him: 'Long life to you! Good health to you and your household! And good health to all that is yours!   1Ch 12:18; Ps 122:7; Lk 10:5

[7]" 'Now I hear that it is sheep-

shearing time. When your shepherds were with us, we did not mistreat them, and the whole time they were at Carmel nothing of theirs was missing. [8]Ask your own servants and they will tell you. Therefore be favorable toward my young men, since we come at a festive time. Please give your servants and your son David whatever you can find for them.' "

[9]When David's men arrived, they gave Nabal this message in David's name. Then they waited.

[10]Nabal answered David's servants, "Who is this David? Who is this son of Jesse? Many servants are breaking away from their masters these days. [11]Why should I take my bread and water, and the meat I have slaughtered for my shearers, and give it to men coming from who knows where?"

[12]David's men turned around and went back. When they arrived, they reported every word. [13]David said to his men, "Put on your swords!" So they put on their swords, and David put on his. About four hundred men went up with David, while two hundred stayed with the supplies. 1Sa 23:13

[14]One of the servants told Nabal's wife Abigail: "David sent messengers from the desert to give our master his greetings, but he hurled insults at them. [15]Yet these men were very good to us. They did not mistreat us, and the whole time we were out in the fields near them nothing was missing. [16]Night and day they were a wall around us all the time we were herding our sheep near them. [17]Now think it over and see what you can do, because disaster is hanging over our master and his whole household. He is such a wicked man that no one can talk to him." Ex 14:22

[18]Abigail lost no time. She took two hundred loaves of bread, two skins of wine, five dressed sheep, five seahs[a] of roasted grain, a hundred cakes of raisins and two hundred cakes of pressed figs, and loaded them on donkeys. [19]Then she told her servants, "Go on ahead; I'll follow you." But she did not tell her husband Nabal.

[20]As she came riding her donkey into a mountain ravine, there were David and his men descending toward her, and she met them. [21]David had just said, "It's been useless —all my watching over this fellow's property in the desert so that nothing of his was missing. He has paid me back evil for good. [22]May God deal with David,[b] be it ever so severely, if by morning I leave alive one male of all who belong to him!" 1Sa 3:17; 1Ki 14:10; Ps 109:5

[23]When Abigail saw David, she quickly got off her donkey and bowed down before David with her face to the ground. [24]She fell at

---

[a]18 That is, probably about a bushel (about 37 liters)   [b]22 Some Septuagint manuscripts; Hebrew with David's enemies

his feet and said: "My lord, let the blame be on me alone. Please let your servant speak to you; hear what your servant has to say. ²⁵May my lord pay no attention to that wicked man Nabal. He is just like his name—his name is Fool, and folly goes with him. But as for me, your servant, I did not see the men my master sent.   1Sa 20:41

²⁶"Now since the LORD has kept you, my master, from bloodshed and from avenging yourself with your own hands, as surely as the LORD lives and as you live, may your enemies and all who intend to harm my master be like Nabal. ²⁷And let this gift, which your servant has brought to my master, be given to the men who follow you. ²⁸Please forgive your servant's offense, for the LORD will certainly make a lasting dynasty for my master, because he fights the LORD's battles. Let no wrongdoing be found in you as long as you live. ²⁹Even though someone is pursuing you to take your life, the life of my master will be bound securely in the bundle of the living by the LORD your God. But the lives of your enemies he will hurl away as from the pocket of a sling. ³⁰When the LORD has done for my master every good thing he promised concerning him and has appointed him leader over Israel, ³¹my master will not have on his conscience the staggering burden of needless bloodshed or of having avenged himself. And when the LORD has

brought my master success, remember your servant."   2Sa 7:11,26

³²David said to Abigail, "Praise be to the LORD, the God of Israel, who has sent you today to meet me. ³³May you be blessed for your good judgment and for keeping me from bloodshed this day and from avenging myself with my own hands. ³⁴Otherwise, as surely as the LORD, the God of Israel, lives, who has kept me from harming you, if you had not come quickly to meet me, not one male belonging to Nabal would have been left alive by daybreak."   Ge 24:27; Ex 18:10

³⁵Then David accepted from her hand what she had brought him and said, "Go home in peace. I have heard your words and granted your request."   Ge 19:21; 1Sa 20:42

³⁶When Abigail went to Nabal, he was in the house holding a banquet like that of a king. He was in high spirits and very drunk. So she told him nothing until daybreak. ³⁷Then in the morning, when Nabal was sober, his wife told him all these things, and his heart failed him and he became like a stone. ³⁸About ten days later, the LORD struck Nabal and he died.   Pr 20:1

³⁹When David heard that Nabal was dead, he said, "Praise be to the LORD, who has upheld my cause against Nabal for treating me with contempt. He has kept his servant from doing wrong and has brought Nabal's wrongdoing down on his own head."

Then David sent word to Abi-

gail, asking her to become his wife.
40His servants went to Carmel and
said to Abigail, "David has sent us
to you to take you to become his
wife."

41She bowed down with her face
to the ground and said, "Here is
your maidservant, ready to serve
you and wash the feet of my master's servants." **42**Abigail quickly
got on a donkey and, attended by
her five maids, went with David's
messengers and became his wife.
43David had also married Ahinoam
of Jezreel, and they both were his
wives. **44**But Saul had given his
daughter Michal, David's wife, to
Paltiel*a* son of Laish, who was
from Gallim.　　　Ge 24:61-67; Jos 15:56

David Again Spares Saul's Life

26 The Ziphites went to Saul
at Gibeah and said, "Is not
David hiding on the hill of Hakilah,
which faces Jeshimon?"　　1Sa 23:19
2So Saul went down to the
Desert of Ziph, with his three thousand chosen men of Israel, to
search there for David. **3**Saul made
his camp beside the road on the
hill of Hakilah facing Jeshimon,
but David stayed in the desert.
When he saw that Saul had followed him there, **4**he sent out
scouts and learned that Saul had
definitely arrived.*b*　　　1Sa 24:2
5Then David set out and went to
the place where Saul had camped.
He saw where Saul and Abner son

of Ner, the commander of the
army, had lain down. Saul was lying inside the camp, with the army
encamped around him.　　1Sa 17:55
6David then asked Ahimelech
the Hittite and Abishai son of Zeruiah, Joab's brother, "Who will go
down into the camp with me to
Saul?"　　2Sa 10:10; Jdg 7:10-11; 1Ch 2:16
"I'll go with you," said Abishai.
7So David and Abishai went to
the army by night, and there was
Saul, lying asleep inside the camp
with his spear stuck in the ground
near his head. Abner and the soldiers were lying around him.

8Abishai said to David, "Today
God has delivered your enemy
into your hands. Now let me pin
him to the ground with one thrust
of my spear; I won't strike him
twice."

9But David said to Abishai,
"Don't destroy him! Who can lay a
hand on the LORD's anointed and
be guiltless? **10**As surely as the
LORD lives," he said, "the LORD
himself will strike him; either his
time will come and he will die, or
he will go into battle and perish.
11But the LORD forbid that I should
lay a hand on the LORD's anointed.
Now get the spear and water jug
that are near his head, and let's
go."　　　1Sa 31:6; 2Sa 1:14; Dt 31:14
12So David took the spear and
water jug near Saul's head, and
they left. No one saw or knew
about it, nor did anyone wake up.

---

a 44 Hebrew *Palti,* a variant of *Paltiel*　　*b 4* Or *had come to Nacon*

They were all sleeping, because the Lord had put them into a deep sleep.   Ge 2:21; 15:12

¹³Then David crossed over to the other side and stood on top of the hill some distance away; there was a wide space between them. ¹⁴He called out to the army and to Abner son of Ner, "Aren't you going to answer me, Abner?"

Abner replied, "Who are you who calls to the king?"

¹⁵David said, "You're a man, aren't you? And who is like you in Israel? Why didn't you guard your lord the king? Someone came to destroy your lord the king. ¹⁶What you have done is not good. As surely as the Lord lives, you and your men deserve to die, because you did not guard your master, the Lord's anointed. Look around you. Where are the king's spear and water jug that were near his head?"

¹⁷Saul recognized David's voice and said, "Is that your voice, David my son?"   1Sa 24:16

David replied, "Yes it is, my lord the king." ¹⁸And he added, "Why is my lord pursuing his servant? What have I done, and what wrong am I guilty of? ¹⁹Now let my lord the king listen to his servant's words. If the Lord has incited you against me, then may he accept an offering. If, however, men have done it, may they be cursed before the Lord! They have now driven me from my share in the Lord's inheritance and have said, 'Go, serve other gods.' ²⁰Now do not let my blood fall to the ground far from the presence of the Lord. The king of Israel has come out to look for a flea—as one hunts a partridge in the mountains."   1Sa 24:9,11-14

²¹Then Saul said, "I have sinned. Come back, David my son. Because you considered my life precious today, I will not try to harm you again. Surely I have acted like a fool and have erred greatly."

²²"Here is the king's spear," David answered. "Let one of your young men come over and get it. ²³The Lord rewards every man for his righteousness and faithfulness. The Lord delivered you into my hands today, but I would not lay a hand on the Lord's anointed. ²⁴As surely as I valued your life today, so may the Lord value my life and deliver me from all trouble."

²⁵Then Saul said to David, "May you be blessed, my son David; you will do great things and surely triumph."

So David went on his way, and Saul returned home.

David Among the Philistines

27 But David thought to himself, "One of these days I will be destroyed by the hand of Saul. The best thing I can do is to escape to the land of the Philistines. Then Saul will give up searching for me anywhere in Israel, and I will slip out of his hand." ²So David and the six hundred men with him left and went over to Achish son of Maoch king of Gath.

³David and his men settled in Gath with Achish. Each man had his family with him, and David had his two wives: Ahinoam of Jezreel and Abigail of Carmel, the widow of Nabal. ⁴When Saul was told that David had fled to Gath, he no longer searched for him. 1Sa 25:13; 21:10

⁵Then David said to Achish, "If I have found favor in your eyes, let a place be assigned to me in one of the country towns, that I may live there. Why should your servant live in the royal city with you?"

⁶So on that day Achish gave him Ziklag, and it has belonged to the kings of Judah ever since. ⁷David lived in Philistine territory a year and four months. Jos 15:31; 19:5

⁸Now David and his men went up and raided the Geshurites, the Girzites and the Amalekites. (From ancient times these peoples had lived in the land extending to Shur and Egypt.) ⁹Whenever David attacked an area, he did not leave a man or woman alive, but took sheep and cattle, donkeys and camels, and clothes. Then he returned to Achish. Jos 13:2,13

¹⁰When Achish asked, "Where did you go raiding today?" David would say, "Against the Negev of Judah" or "Against the Negev of Jerahmeel" or "Against the Negev of the Kenites." ¹¹He did not leave a man or woman alive to be brought to Gath, for he thought, "They might inform on us and say, 'This is what David did.'" And such was his practice as long as he lived in Philistine territory. ¹²Achish trusted David and said to himself, "He has become so odious to his people, the Israelites, that he will be my servant forever."

Saul and the Witch of Endor

28 In those days the Philistines gathered their forces to fight against Israel. Achish said to David, "You must understand that you and your men will accompany me in the army." 1Sa 29:1

²David said, "Then you will see for yourself what your servant can do."

Achish replied, "Very well, I will make you my bodyguard for life."

³Now Samuel was dead, and all Israel had mourned for him and buried him in his own town of Ramah. Saul had expelled the mediums and spiritists from the land.

⁴The Philistines assembled and came and set up camp at Shunem, while Saul gathered all the Israelites and set up camp at Gilboa. ⁵When Saul saw the Philistine army, he was afraid; terror filled his heart. ⁶He inquired of the LORD, but the LORD did not answer him by dreams or Urim or prophets. ⁷Saul then said to his attendants, "Find me a woman who is a medium, so I may go and inquire of her." Ex 28:30; 1Ch 10:13-14; 2Ki 4:8

"There is one in Endor," they said. Jos 17:11

⁸So Saul disguised himself, putting on other clothes, and at night he and two men went to the wom-

an. "Consult a spirit for me," he said, "and bring up for me the one I name." Dt 18:10-11; 2Ch 18:29; Isa 8:19 ⁹But the woman said to him, "Surely you know what Saul has done. He has cut off the mediums and spiritists from the land. Why have you set a trap for my life to bring about my death?"

¹⁰Saul swore to her by the LORD, "As surely as the LORD lives, you will not be punished for this."

¹¹Then the woman asked, "Whom shall I bring up for you?"

"Bring up Samuel," he said.

¹²When the woman saw Samuel, she cried out at the top of her voice and said to Saul, "Why have you deceived me? You are Saul!"

¹³The king said to her, "Don't be afraid. What do you see?"

The woman said, "I see a spirit*a* coming up out of the ground."

¹⁴"What does he look like?" he asked.

"An old man wearing a robe is coming up," she said. 1Sa 15:27

Then Saul knew it was Samuel, and he bowed down and prostrated himself with his face to the ground.

¹⁵Samuel said to Saul, "Why have you disturbed me by bringing me up?"

"I am in great distress," Saul said. "The Philistines are fighting against me, and God has turned away from me. He no longer answers me, either by prophets or by dreams. So I have called on you to tell me what to do." 1Sa 18:12

¹⁶Samuel said, "Why do you consult me, now that the LORD has turned away from you and become your enemy? ¹⁷The LORD has done what he predicted through me. The LORD has torn the kingdom out of your hands and given it to one of your neighbors—to David. ¹⁸Because you did not obey the LORD or carry out his fierce wrath against the Amalekites, the LORD has done this to you today. ¹⁹The LORD will hand over both Israel and you to the Philistines, and tomorrow you and your sons will be with me. The LORD will also hand over the army of Israel to the Philistines." 1Sa 15:28; 31:2; 1Ki 20:42

²⁰Immediately Saul fell full length on the ground, filled with fear because of Samuel's words. His strength was gone, for he had eaten nothing all that day and night.

²¹When the woman came to Saul and saw that he was greatly shaken, she said, "Look, your maidservant has obeyed you. I took my life in my hands and did what you told me to do. ²²Now please listen to your servant and let me give you some food so you may eat and have the strength to go on your way." Jdg 12:3; 1Sa 19:5

²³He refused and said, "I will not eat."

But his men joined the woman

---

a 13 Or *see spirits*; or *see gods*

in urging him, and he listened to them. He got up from the ground and sat on the couch.   2Ki 5:13

²⁴The woman had a fattened calf at the house, which she butchered at once. She took some flour, kneaded it and baked bread without yeast. ²⁵Then she set it before Saul and his men, and they ate. That same night they got up and left.

Achish Sends David Back to Ziklag

29 The Philistines gathered all their forces at Aphek, and Israel camped by the spring in Jezreel. ²As the Philistine rulers marched with their units of hundreds and thousands, David and his men were marching at the rear with Achish. ³The commanders of the Philistines asked, "What about these Hebrews?"   1Sa 4:1; 28:1; 2Ki 9:30

Achish replied, "Is this not David, who was an officer of Saul king of Israel? He has already been with me for over a year, and from the day he left Saul until now, I have found no fault in him."

⁴But the Philistine commanders were angry with him and said, "Send the man back, that he may return to the place you assigned him. He must not go with us into battle, or he will turn against us during the fighting. How better could he regain his master's favor than by taking the heads of our own men? ⁵Isn't this the David

they sang about in their dances:

" 'Saul has slain his thousands,
   and David his tens of
      thousands'?"   1Sa 18:7; 21:11

⁶So Achish called David and said to him, "As surely as the Lord lives, you have been reliable, and I would be pleased to have you serve with me in the army. From the day you came to me until now, I have found no fault in you, but the rulers don't approve of you. ⁷Turn back and go in peace; do nothing to displease the Philistine rulers."   1Sa 27:8-12

⁸"But what have I done?" asked David. "What have you found against your servant from the day I came to you until now? Why can't I go and fight against the enemies of my lord the king?"

⁹Achish answered, "I know that you have been as pleasing in my eyes as an angel of God; nevertheless, the Philistine commanders have said, 'He must not go up with us into battle.' ¹⁰Now get up early, along with your master's servants who have come with you, and leave in the morning as soon as it is light."   2Sa 14:17,20; 19:27; 1Ch 12:19

¹¹So David and his men got up early in the morning to go back to the land of the Philistines, and the Philistines went up to Jezreel.

David Destroys the Amalekites

30 David and his men reached Ziklag on the third day. Now the Amalekites had raided the Negev and Ziklag. They had attacked Ziklag and burned it, ²and had taken captive the women and all who were in it, both young and old. They killed none of them, but carried them off as they went on their way.   1Sa 15:7; 27:8

³When David and his men came to Ziklag, they found it destroyed by fire and their wives and sons and daughters taken captive. ⁴So David and his men wept aloud until they had no strength left to weep. ⁵David's two wives had been captured—Ahinoam of Jezreel and Abigail, the widow of Nabal of Carmel. ⁶David was greatly distressed because the men were talking of stoning him; each one was bitter in spirit because of his sons and daughters. But David found strength in the LORD his God.   Ex 17:4; Ps 56:3-4,11

⁷Then David said to Abiathar the priest, the son of Ahimelech, "Bring me the ephod." Abiathar brought it to him, ⁸and David inquired of the LORD, "Shall I pursue this raiding party? Will I overtake them?"   1Sa 22:20; 23:2

"Pursue them," he answered. "You will certainly overtake them and succeed in the rescue."

⁹David and the six hundred men with him came to the Besor Ravine, where some stayed behind, ¹⁰for two hundred men were too exhausted to cross the ravine. But David and four hundred men continued the pursuit.   1Sa 27:2

¹¹They found an Egyptian in a field and brought him to David. They gave him water to drink and food to eat— ¹²part of a cake of pressed figs and two cakes of raisins. He ate and was revived, for he had not eaten any food or drunk any water for three days and three nights.   Jdg 15:19

¹³David asked him, "To whom do you belong, and where do you come from?"

He said, "I am an Egyptian, the slave of an Amalekite. My master abandoned me when I became ill three days ago. ¹⁴We raided the Negev of the Kerethites and the territory belonging to Judah and the Negev of Caleb. And we burned Ziklag."   Jos 14:13; 2Sa 8:18

¹⁵David asked him, "Can you lead me down to this raiding party?"

He answered, "Swear to me before God that you will not kill me or hand me over to my master, and I will take you down to them."

¹⁶He led David down, and there they were, scattered over the countryside, eating, drinking and reveling because of the great amount of plunder they had taken from the land of the Philistines and from Judah. ¹⁷David fought them from dusk until the evening of the next day, and none of them got away, except four hundred young men who rode off on camels and fled. ¹⁸David recovered everything the Amalekites had taken, including his two wives. ¹⁹Nothing was missing: young or old, boy or girl, plun-

der or anything else they had taken. David brought everything back. 20He took all the flocks and herds, and his men drove them ahead of the other livestock, saying, "This is David's plunder."

21Then David came to the two hundred men who had been too exhausted to follow him and who were left behind at the Besor Ravine. They came out to meet David and the people with him. As David and his men approached, he greeted them. 22But all the evil men and troublemakers among David's followers said, "Because they did not go out with us, we will not share with them the plunder we recovered. However, each man may take his wife and children and go."

23David replied, "No, my brothers, you must not do that with what the LORD has given us. He has protected us and handed over to us the forces that came against us. 24Who will listen to what you say? The share of the man who stayed with the supplies is to be the same as that of him who went down to the battle. All will share alike." 25David made this a statute and ordinance for Israel from that day to this.   Nu 31:27; Jos 22:8

26When David arrived in Ziklag, he sent some of the plunder to the elders of Judah, who were his friends, saying, "Here is a present for you from the plunder of the LORD's enemies."   Ge 33:11

27He sent it to those who were in Bethel, Ramoth Negev and Jattir; 28to those in Aroer, Siphmoth, Eshtemoa 29and Racal; to those in the towns of the Jerahmeelites and the Kenites; 30to those in Hormah, Bor Ashan, Athach 31and Hebron; and to those in all the other places where David and his men had roamed.   Jos 13:16; 14:13; Jdg 1:17

Saul Takes His Life

31 Now the Philistines fought against Israel; the Israelites fled before them, and many fell slain on Mount Gilboa. 2The Philistines pressed hard after Saul and his sons, and they killed his sons Jonathan, Abinadab and Malki-Shua. 3The fighting grew fierce around Saul, and when the archers overtook him, they wounded him critically.   1Sa 28:4; 2Sa 1:6; 1Ch 10:1-12

4Saul said to his armor-bearer, "Draw your sword and run me through, or these uncircumcised fellows will come and run me through and abuse me."   Jdg 9:54

But his armor-bearer was terrified and would not do it; so Saul took his own sword and fell on it. 5When the armor-bearer saw that Saul was dead, he too fell on his sword and died with him. 6So Saul and his three sons and his armor-bearer and all his men died together that same day.

7When the Israelites along the valley and those across the Jordan saw that the Israelite army had fled and that Saul and his sons had died, they abandoned their towns and fled. And the Philistines came and occupied them.

⁸The next day, when the Philistines came to strip the dead, they found Saul and his three sons fallen on Mount Gilboa. ⁹They cut off his head and stripped off his armor, and they sent messengers throughout the land of the Philistines to proclaim the news in the temple of their idols and among their people. ¹⁰They put his armor in the temple of the Ashtoreths and fastened his body to the wall of Beth Shan. Jos 17:11; Jdg 2:12-13

¹¹When the people of Jabesh Gilead heard of what the Philistines had done to Saul, ¹²all their valiant men journeyed through the night to Beth Shan. They took down the bodies of Saul and his sons from the wall of Beth Shan and went to Jabesh, where they burned them. ¹³Then they took their bones and buried them under a tamarisk tree at Jabesh, and they fasted seven days. 1Ch 10:1-12

2 Samuel

David Hears of Saul's Death

1 After the death of Saul, David returned from defeating the Amalekites and stayed in Ziklag two days. ²On the third day a man arrived from Saul's camp, with his clothes torn and with dust on his head. When he came to David, he fell to the ground to pay him honor. 1Sa 4:12; 30:17; 31:6

³"Where have you come from?" David asked him.

He answered, "I have escaped from the Israelite camp."

⁴"What happened?" David asked. "Tell me."

He said, "The men fled from the battle. Many of them fell and died. And Saul and his son Jonathan are dead."

⁵Then David said to the young man who brought him the report, "How do you know that Saul and his son Jonathan are dead?"

⁶"I happened to be on Mount Gilboa," the young man said, "and there was Saul, leaning on his spear, with the chariots and riders almost upon him. ⁷When he turned around and saw me, he called out to me, and I said, 'What can I do?' 1Sa 31:2-4

⁸"He asked me, 'Who are you?'

" 'An Amalekite,' I answered.

⁹"Then he said to me, 'Stand over me and kill me! I am in the throes of death, but I'm still alive.'

¹⁰"So I stood over him and killed him, because I knew that after he had fallen he could not survive. And I took the crown that was on his head and the band on his arm and have brought them here to my lord." Jdg 9:54; 2Ki 11:12

¹¹Then David and all the men with him took hold of their clothes and tore them. ¹²They mourned and wept and fasted till evening for Saul and his son Jonathan, and for the army of the LORD and the house of Israel, because they had fallen by the sword. 1Sa 31:1-13

¹³David said to the young man who brought him the report, "Where are you from?"

"I am the son of an alien, an Amalekite," he answered.

¹⁴David asked him, "Why were you not afraid to lift your hand to destroy the LORD's anointed?"

¹⁵Then David called one of his men and said, "Go, strike him down!" So he struck him down, and he died. ¹⁶For David had said to him, "Your blood be on your own head. Your own mouth testified against you when you said, 'I killed the LORD's anointed.' "

David's Lament for Saul and Jonathan

¹⁷David took up this lament concerning Saul and his son Jonathan, ¹⁸and ordered that the men of Judah be taught this lament of the bow (it is written in the Book of Jashar):   Jos 10:13; 2Ch 35:25

¹⁹"Your glory, O Israel, lies slain
      on your heights.
  How the mighty have fallen!

²⁰"Tell it not in Gath,   Mic 1:10
    proclaim it not in the streets
      of Ashkelon,
  lest the daughters of the
      Philistines be glad,
  lest the daughters of the
      uncircumcised rejoice.

²¹"O mountains of Gilboa,   1Sa 31:1
    may you have neither dew
      nor rain,
    nor fields that yield offerings
      ⌊of grain⌋.   Eze 31:15
  For there the shield of the
      mighty was defiled,
    the shield of Saul—no longer
      rubbed with oil.   Isa 21:5
²²From the blood of the slain,
    from the flesh of the mighty,
  the bow of Jonathan did not
      turn back,
    the sword of Saul did not
      return unsatisfied.

²³"Saul and Jonathan—
    in life they were loved and
      gracious,
    and in death they were not
      parted.

They were swifter than eagles,
    they were stronger than
      lions.   Jdg 14:18

²⁴"O daughters of Israel,
    weep for Saul,
  who clothed you in scarlet and
      finery,
  who adorned your garments
      with ornaments of gold.

²⁵"How the mighty have fallen in
      battle!
  Jonathan lies slain on your
      heights.
²⁶I grieve for you, Jonathan my
      brother;   1Sa 20:42
  you were very dear to me.
  Your love for me was
      wonderful,
    more wonderful than that of
      women.   1Sa 18:1

²⁷"How the mighty have fallen!
    The weapons of war have
      perished!"

David Anointed King Over Judah

2 In the course of time, David inquired of the LORD. "Shall I go up to one of the towns of Judah?" he asked.   1Sa 23:2,11-12
  The LORD said, "Go up."
  David asked, "Where shall I go?"
  "To Hebron," the LORD answered.   Ge 13:18; 1Sa 30:31
  ²So David went up there with his two wives, Ahinoam of Jezreel and Abigail, the widow of Nabal of Carmel. ³David also took the men who were with him, each with his fami-

ly, and they settled in Hebron and its towns. **4**Then the men of Judah came to Hebron and there they anointed David king over the house of Judah.   1Sa 25:42; 27:2

When David was told that it was the men of Jabesh Gilead who had buried Saul, **5**he sent messengers to the men of Jabesh Gilead to say to them, "The LORD bless you for showing this kindness to Saul your master by burying him. **6**May the LORD now show you kindness and faithfulness, and I too will show you the same favor because you have done this. **7**Now then, be strong and brave, for Saul your master is dead, and the house of Judah has anointed me king over them."   Ex 34:6; 1Sa 23:21; 1Ti 1:16

War Between the Houses of David and Saul

8Meanwhile, Abner son of Ner, the commander of Saul's army, had taken Ish-Bosheth son of Saul and brought him over to Mahanaim. **9**He made him king over Gilead, Ashuri[a] and Jezreel, and also over Ephraim, Benjamin and all Israel.   Jdg 1:32; 1Sa 14:50; 1Ch 12:29

10Ish-Bosheth son of Saul was forty years old when he became king over Israel, and he reigned two years. The house of Judah, however, followed David. **11**The length of time David was king in Hebron over the house of Judah was seven years and six months.

12Abner son of Ner, together with the men of Ish-Bosheth son of Saul, left Mahanaim and went to Gibeon. **13**Joab son of Zeruiah and David's men went out and met them at the pool of Gibeon. One group sat down on one side of the pool and one group on the other side.   Jos 18:25; 2Sa 8:16; 1Ch 2:16

14Then Abner said to Joab, "Let's have some of the young men get up and fight hand to hand in front of us."

"All right, let them do it," Joab said.

15So they stood up and were counted off—twelve men for Benjamin and Ish-Bosheth son of Saul, and twelve for David. **16**Then each man grabbed his opponent by the head and thrust his dagger into his opponent's side, and they fell down together. So that place in Gibeon was called Helkath Hazzurim.[b]

17The battle that day was very fierce, and Abner and the men of Israel were defeated by David's men.   2Sa 3:1

18The three sons of Zeruiah were there: Joab, Abishai and Asahel. Now Asahel was as fleet-footed as a wild gazelle. **19**He chased Abner, turning neither to the right nor to the left as he pursued him. **20**Abner looked behind him and asked, "Is that you, Asahel?"

"It is," he answered.

21Then Abner said to him, "Turn

---

a 9 Or *Asher*   *b* 16 *Helkath Hazzurim* means *field of daggers* or *field of hostilities*.

aside to the right or to the left; take on one of the young men and strip him of his weapons." But Asahel would not stop chasing him.

²²Again Abner warned Asahel, "Stop chasing me! Why should I strike you down? How could I look your brother Joab in the face?"

²³But Asahel refused to give up the pursuit; so Abner thrust the butt of his spear into Asahel's stomach, and the spear came out through his back. He fell there and died on the spot. And every man stopped when he came to the place where Asahel had fallen and died.

²⁴But Joab and Abishai pursued Abner, and as the sun was setting, they came to the hill of Ammah, near Giah on the way to the wasteland of Gibeon. ²⁵Then the men of Benjamin rallied behind Abner. They formed themselves into a group and took their stand on top of a hill.

²⁶Abner called out to Joab, "Must the sword devour forever? Don't you realize that this will end in bitterness? How long before you order your men to stop pursuing their brothers?" Dt 32:42

²⁷Joab answered, "As surely as God lives, if you had not spoken, the men would have continued the pursuit of their brothers until morning.ᵃ"

²⁸So Joab blew the trumpet, and all the men came to a halt; they no longer pursued Israel, nor did they fight anymore. 2Sa 18:16; Jdg 3:27

²⁹All that night Abner and his men marched through the Arabah. They crossed the Jordan, continued through the whole Bithronᵇ and came to Mahanaim.

³⁰Then Joab returned from pursuing Abner and assembled all his men. Besides Asahel, nineteen of David's men were found missing. ³¹But David's men had killed three hundred and sixty Benjamites who were with Abner. ³²They took Asahel and buried him in his father's tomb at Bethlehem. Then Joab and his men marched all night and arrived at Hebron by daybreak.

3 The war between the house of Saul and the house of David lasted a long time. David grew stronger and stronger, while the house of Saul grew weaker and weaker. 2Sa 2:17; 5:10; 1Ki 14:30

²Sons were born to David in Hebron:

His firstborn was Amnon the son of Ahinoam of Jezreel; 1Sa 25:43; 1Ch 3:1-3

³his second, Kileab the son of Abigail the widow of Nabal of Carmel; 1Sa 25:42

the third, Absalom the son of Maacah daughter of Talmai king of Geshur;

⁴the fourth, Adonijah the son of Haggith; 1Ki 1:5,11

ᵃ27 Or *spoken this morning, the men would not have taken up the pursuit of their brothers*; or *spoken, the men would have given up the pursuit of their brothers by morning*   ᵇ29 Or *morning*; or *ravine*; the meaning of the Hebrew for this word is uncertain.

the fifth, Shephatiah the son of Abital;

⁵and the sixth, Ithream the son of David's wife Eglah. These were born to David in Hebron.

Abner Goes Over to David

⁶During the war between the house of Saul and the house of David, Abner had been strengthening his own position in the house of Saul. ⁷Now Saul had had a concubine named Rizpah daughter of Aiah. And Ish-Bosheth said to Abner, "Why did you sleep with my father's concubine?"   2Sa 16:21-22

⁸Abner was very angry because of what Ish-Bosheth said and he answered, "Am I a dog's head—on Judah's side? This very day I am loyal to the house of your father Saul and to his family and friends. I haven't handed you over to David. Yet now you accuse me of an offense involving this woman! ⁹May God deal with Abner, be it ever so severely, if I do not do for David what the LORD promised him on oath ¹⁰and transfer the kingdom from the house of Saul and establish David's throne over Israel and Judah from Dan to Beersheba." ¹¹Ish-Bosheth did not dare to say another word to Abner, because he was afraid of him.

¹²Then Abner sent messengers on his behalf to say to David, "Whose land is it? Make an agreement with me, and I will help you bring all Israel over to you."

¹³"Good," said David. "I will make an agreement with you. But I demand one thing of you: Do not come into my presence unless you bring Michal daughter of Saul when you come to see me." ¹⁴Then David sent messengers to Ish-Bosheth son of Saul, demanding, "Give me my wife Michal, whom I betrothed to myself for the price of a hundred Philistine foreskins."

¹⁵So Ish-Bosheth gave orders and had her taken away from her husband Paltiel son of Laish. ¹⁶Her husband, however, went with her, weeping behind her all the way to Bahurim. Then Abner said to him, "Go back home!" So he went back.

¹⁷Abner conferred with the elders of Israel and said, "For some time you have wanted to make David your king. ¹⁸Now do it! For the LORD promised David, 'By my servant David I will rescue my people Israel from the hand of the Philistines and from the hand of all their enemies.' "   Jdg 11:11; 1Sa 9:16; 15:28

¹⁹Abner also spoke to the Benjamites in person. Then he went to Hebron to tell David everything that Israel and the whole house of Benjamin wanted to do. ²⁰When Abner, who had twenty men with him, came to David at Hebron, David prepared a feast for him and his men. ²¹Then Abner said to David, "Let me go at once and assemble all Israel for my lord the king, so that they may make a compact with you, and that you may rule over all that your heart desires." So

David sent Abner away, and he went in peace. 1Sa 10:20-21; 1Ki 11:37

Joab Murders Abner

22Just then David's men and Joab returned from a raid and brought with them a great deal of plunder. But Abner was no longer with David in Hebron, because David had sent him away, and he had gone in peace. **23**When Joab and all the soldiers with him arrived, he was told that Abner son of Ner had come to the king and that the king had sent him away and that he had gone in peace.

24So Joab went to the king and said, "What have you done? Look, Abner came to you. Why did you let him go? Now he is gone! **25**You know Abner son of Ner; he came to deceive you and observe your movements and find out everything you are doing."

26Joab then left David and sent messengers after Abner, and they brought him back from the well of Sirah. But David did not know it. **27**Now when Abner returned to Hebron, Joab took him aside into the gateway, as though to speak with him privately. And there, to avenge the blood of his brother Asahel, Joab stabbed him in the stomach, and he died. 2Sa 2:22

28Later, when David heard about this, he said, "I and my kingdom are forever innocent before the LORD concerning the blood of Abner son of Ner. **29**May his blood fall upon the head of Joab and upon all his father's house! May Joab's house never be without someone who has a running sore or leprosy[a] or who leans on a crutch or who falls by the sword or who lacks food." Dt 21:9; Lev 15:2; 1Ki 2:31-33

30(Joab and his brother Abishai murdered Abner because he had killed their brother Asahel in the battle at Gibeon.)

31Then David said to Joab and all the people with him, "Tear your clothes and put on sackcloth and walk in mourning in front of Abner." King David himself walked behind the bier. **32**They buried Abner in Hebron, and the king wept aloud at Abner's tomb. All the people wept also. Ge 37:34; Pr 24:17; Isa 20:2

33The king sang this lament for Abner: 2Sa 1:17

"Should Abner have died as
    the lawless die?
34 Your hands were not bound,
    your feet were not fettered.
You fell as one falls before
    wicked men."

And all the people wept over him again.

35Then they all came and urged David to eat something while it was still day; but David took an oath, saying, "May God deal with me, be it ever so severely, if I taste bread or anything else before the sun sets!" Ru 1:17; 2Sa 1:12; 12:17

---

[a] **29** The Hebrew word was used for various diseases affecting the skin—not necessarily leprosy.

³⁶All the people took note and were pleased; indeed, everything the king did pleased them. ³⁷So on that day all the people and all Israel knew that the king had no part in the murder of Abner son of Ner. ³⁸Then the king said to his men, "Do you not realize that a prince and a great man has fallen in Israel this day? ³⁹And today, though I am the anointed king, I am weak, and these sons of Zeruiah are too strong for me. May the Lord repay the evildoer according to his evil deeds!"   2Sa 19:5-7; 1Ki 2:5-6,33-34; Ps 41:10

Ish-Bosheth Murdered

4 When Ish-Bosheth son of Saul heard that Abner had died in Hebron, he lost courage, and all Israel became alarmed. ²Now Saul's son had two men who were leaders of raiding bands. One was named Baanah and the other Recab; they were sons of Rimmon the Beerothite from the tribe of Benjamin—Beeroth is considered part of Benjamin, ³because the people of Beeroth fled to Gittaim and have lived there as aliens to this day.   2Sa 3:27; Jos 9:17; Ne 11:33

⁴(Jonathan son of Saul had a son who was lame in both feet. He was five years old when the news about Saul and Jonathan came from Jezreel. His nurse picked him up and fled, but as she hurried to leave, he fell and became crippled. His name was Mephibosheth.)

⁵Now Recab and Baanah, the sons of Rimmon the Beerothite, set out for the house of Ish-Bosheth, and they arrived there in the heat of the day while he was taking his noonday rest. ⁶They went into the inner part of the house as if to get some wheat, and they stabbed him in the stomach. Then Recab and his brother Baanah slipped away.

⁷They had gone into the house while he was lying on the bed in his bedroom. After they stabbed and killed him, they cut off his head. Taking it with them, they traveled all night by way of the Arabah. ⁸They brought the head of Ish-Bosheth to David at Hebron and said to the king, "Here is the head of Ish-Bosheth son of Saul, your enemy, who tried to take your life. This day the Lord has avenged my lord the king against Saul and his offspring."   1Sa 24:4

⁹David answered Recab and his brother Baanah, the sons of Rimmon the Beerothite, "As surely as the Lord lives, who has delivered me out of all trouble, ¹⁰when a man told me, 'Saul is dead,' and thought he was bringing good news, I seized him and put him to death in Ziklag. That was the reward I gave him for his news! ¹¹How much more—when wicked men have killed an innocent man in his own house and on his own bed—should I not now demand his blood from your hand and rid the earth of you!"   1Ki 1:29; 2Sa 1:2-16

¹²So David gave an order to his men, and they killed them. They cut off their hands and feet and

hung the bodies by the pool in Hebron. But they took the head of Ish-Bosheth and buried it in Abner's tomb at Hebron. 2Sa 1:15

David Becomes King Over Israel

5 All the tribes of Israel came to David at Hebron and said, "We are your own flesh and blood. 2In the past, while Saul was king over us, you were the one who led Israel on their military campaigns. And the LORD said to you, 'You will shepherd my people Israel, and you will become their ruler.' "

3When all the elders of Israel had come to King David at Hebron, the king made a compact with them at Hebron before the LORD, and they anointed David king over Israel. 1Ch 11:1-3; 2Sa 2:4; 3:21

4David was thirty years old when he became king, and he reigned forty years. 5In Hebron he reigned over Judah seven years and six months, and in Jerusalem he reigned over all Israel and Judah thirty-three years. Lk 3:23

David Conquers Jerusalem

6The king and his men marched to Jerusalem to attack the Jebusites, who lived there. The Jebusites said to David, "You will not get in here; even the blind and the lame can ward you off." They thought, "David cannot get in here." 7Nevertheless, David cap-

tured the fortress of Zion, the City of David. Jos 15:8; Jdg 1:8; 1Ki 2:10

8On that day, David said, "Anyone who conquers the Jebusites will have to use the water shaft[a] to reach those 'lame and blind' who are David's enemies.[b]" That is why they say, "The 'blind and lame' will not enter the palace."

9David then took up residence in the fortress and called it the City of David. He built up the area around it, from the supporting terraces[c] inward. 10And he became more and more powerful, because the LORD God Almighty was with him. 1Ch 11:4-9; 2Sa 3:1; 1Ki 9:15,24

11Now Hiram king of Tyre sent messengers to David, along with cedar logs and carpenters and stonemasons, and they built a palace for David. 12And David knew that the LORD had established him as king over Israel and had exalted his kingdom for the sake of his people Israel. 1Ki 5:1,18; 1Ch 14:1

13After he left Hebron, David took more concubines and wives in Jerusalem, and more sons and daughters were born to him. 14These are the names of the children born to him there: Shammua, Shobab, Nathan, Solomon, 15Ibhar, Elishua, Nepheg, Japhia, 16Elishama, Eliada and Eliphelet.

David Defeats the Philistines

17When the Philistines heard that David had been anointed king

---

a8 Or use scaling hooks   b8 Or are hated by David   c9 Or the Millo

over Israel, they went up in full force to search for him, but David heard about it and went down to the stronghold. [18]Now the Philistines had come and spread out in the Valley of Rephaim; [19]so David inquired of the LORD, "Shall I go and attack the Philistines? Will you hand them over to me?"

The LORD answered him, "Go, for I will surely hand the Philistines over to you."

[20]So David went to Baal Perazim, and there he defeated them. He said, "As waters break out, the LORD has broken out against my enemies before me." So that place was called Baal Perazim.[a] [21]The Philistines abandoned their idols there, and David and his men carried them off.   1Ch 14:12; Isa 28:21; 46:2

[22]Once more the Philistines came up and spread out in the Valley of Rephaim; [23]so David inquired of the LORD, and he answered, "Do not go straight up, but circle around behind them and attack them in front of the balsam trees. [24]As soon as you hear the sound of marching in the tops of the balsam trees, move quickly, because that will mean the LORD has gone out in front of you to strike the Philistine army." [25]So David did as the LORD commanded him, and he struck down the Philistines all the way from Gibeon[b] to Gezer.   1Ch 14:8-17; Jdg 4:14; 2Ki 7:6

The Ark Brought to Jerusalem

6 David again brought together out of Israel chosen men, thirty thousand in all. [2]He and all his men set out from Baalah of Judah[c] to bring up from there the ark of God, which is called by the Name,[d] the name of the LORD Almighty, who is enthroned between the cherubim that are on the ark. [3]They set the ark of God on a new cart and brought it from the house of Abinadab, which was on the hill. Uzzah and Ahio, sons of Abinadab, were guiding the new cart [4]with the ark of God on it,[e] and Ahio was walking in front of it. [5]David and the whole house of Israel were celebrating with all their might before the LORD, with songs[f] and with harps, lyres, tambourines, sistrums and cymbals.

[6]When they came to the threshing floor of Nacon, Uzzah reached out and took hold of the ark of God, because the oxen stumbled. [7]The LORD's anger burned against Uzzah because of his irreverent act; therefore God struck him down and he died there beside the ark of God.   Ex 19:22; Nu 4:15,19-20

---

[a]20 *Baal Perazim* means *the lord who breaks out.*   [b]25 Septuagint (see also 1 Chron. 14:16); Hebrew *Geba*   [c]2 That is, Kiriath Jearim; Hebrew *Baale Judah,* a variant of *Baalah of Judah*   [d]2 Hebrew; Septuagint and Vulgate do not have *the Name.*   [e]3,4 Dead Sea Scrolls and some Septuagint manuscripts; Masoretic Text *cart* [4]*and they brought it with the ark of God from the house of Abinadab, which was on the hill*   [f]5 See Dead Sea Scrolls, Septuagint and 1 Chronicles 13:8; Masoretic Text *celebrating before the LORD with all kinds of instruments made of pine.*

⁸Then David was angry because the LORD's wrath had broken out against Uzzah, and to this day that place is called Perez Uzzah.ᵃ

⁹David was afraid of the LORD that day and said, "How can the ark of the LORD ever come to me?" ¹⁰He was not willing to take the ark of the LORD to be with him in the City of David. Instead, he took it aside to the house of Obed-Edom the Gittite. ¹¹The ark of the LORD remained in the house of Obed-Edom the Gittite for three months, and the LORD blessed him and his entire household.   1Ch 13:1-14; Ge 39:5

¹²Now King David was told, "The LORD has blessed the household of Obed-Edom and everything he has, because of the ark of God." So David went down and brought up the ark of God from the house of Obed-Edom to the City of David with rejoicing. ¹³When those who were carrying the ark of the LORD had taken six steps, he sacrificed a bull and a fattened calf. ¹⁴David, wearing a linen ephod, danced before the LORD with all his might, ¹⁵while he and the entire house of Israel brought up the ark of the LORD with shouts and the sound of trumpets.

¹⁶As the ark of the LORD was entering the City of David, Michal daughter of Saul watched from a window. And when she saw King David leaping and dancing before the LORD, she despised him in her heart.

¹⁷They brought the ark of the LORD and set it in its place inside the tent that David had pitched for it, and David sacrificed burnt offerings and fellowship offeringsᵇ before the LORD. ¹⁸After he had finished sacrificing the burnt offerings and fellowship offerings, he blessed the people in the name of the LORD Almighty. ¹⁹Then he gave a loaf of bread, a cake of dates and a cake of raisins to each person in the whole crowd of Israelites, both men and women. And all the people went to their homes.

²⁰When David returned home to bless his household, Michal daughter of Saul came out to meet him and said, "How the king of Israel has distinguished himself today, disrobing in the sight of the slave girls of his servants as any vulgar fellow would!"

²¹David said to Michal, "It was before the LORD, who chose me rather than your father or anyone from his house when he appointed me ruler over the LORD's people Israel—I will celebrate before the LORD. ²²I will become even more undignified than this, and I will be humiliated in my own eyes. But by these slave girls you spoke of, I will be held in honor."   1Sa 13:14

²³And Michal daughter of Saul had no children to the day of her death.

ᵃ8 Perez Uzzah means outbreak against Uzzah.   ᵇ17 Traditionally peace offerings; also in verse 18

God's Promise to David

7 After the king was settled in his palace and the Lord had given him rest from all his enemies around him, ²he said to Nathan the prophet, "Here I am, living in a palace of cedar, while the ark of God remains in a tent."   Ex 26:1; 2Sa 5:11

³Nathan replied to the king, "Whatever you have in mind, go ahead and do it, for the Lord is with you."

⁴That night the word of the Lord came to Nathan, saying:

⁵"Go and tell my servant David, 'This is what the Lord says: Are you the one to build me a house to dwell in? ⁶I have not dwelt in a house from the day I brought the Israelites up out of Egypt to this day. I have been moving from place to place with a tent as my dwelling. ⁷Wherever I have moved with all the Israelites, did I ever say to any of their rulers whom I commanded to shepherd my people Israel, "Why have you not built me a house of cedar?"'

⁸"Now then, tell my servant David, 'This is what the Lord Almighty says: I took you from the pasture and from following the flock to be ruler over my people Israel. ⁹I have been with you wherever you have gone, and I have cut off all your enemies from before you. Now I will make your name great, like the names of the greatest men of the earth. ¹⁰And I will provide a place for my people Israel and will plant them so that they can have a home of their own and no longer be disturbed. Wicked people will not oppress them anymore, as they did at the beginning ¹¹and have done ever since the time I appointed leaders[a] over my people Israel. I will also give you rest from all your enemies.   1Sa 16:11; Ps 18:37-42; Isa 5:1-7

" 'The Lord declares to you that the Lord himself will establish a house for you: ¹²When your days are over and you rest with your fathers, I will raise up your offspring to succeed you, who will come from your own body, and I will establish his kingdom. ¹³He is the one who will build a house for my Name, and I will establish the throne of his kingdom forever. ¹⁴I will be his father, and he will be my son. When he does wrong, I will punish him with the rod of men, with floggings inflicted by men. ¹⁵But my love will never be taken away from him, as I took it away from Saul, whom I removed from before you.

---

a 11 Traditionally *judges*

¹⁶Your house and your kingdom will endure forever before me^a; your throne will be established forever.' "

¹⁷Nathan reported to David all the words of this entire revelation.

David's Prayer

¹⁸Then King David went in and sat before the LORD, and he said:

"Who am I, O Sovereign LORD, and what is my family, that you have brought me this far? ¹⁹And as if this were not enough in your sight, O Sovereign LORD, you have also spoken about the future of the house of your servant. Is this your usual way of dealing with man, O Sovereign LORD?

²⁰"What more can David say to you? For you know your servant, O Sovereign LORD. ²¹For the sake of your word and according to your will, you have done this great thing and made it known to your servant.   1Sa 16:7; Jn 21:17

²²"How great you are, O Sovereign LORD! There is no one like you, and there is no God but you, as we have heard with our own ears. ²³And who is like your people Israel—the one nation on earth that God went out to redeem as a people for himself, and to make a name for himself, and to perform great and awesome wonders by driving out nations and their gods from before your people, whom you redeemed from Egypt?^b ²⁴You have established your people Israel as your very own forever, and you, O LORD, have become their God.   Dt 3:24; 4:32-38; 26:18

²⁵"And now, LORD God, keep forever the promise you have made concerning your servant and his house. Do as you promised, ²⁶so that your name will be great forever. Then men will say, 'The LORD Almighty is God over Israel!' And the house of your servant David will be established before you.

²⁷"O LORD Almighty, God of Israel, you have revealed this to your servant, saying, 'I will build a house for you.' So your servant has found courage to offer you this prayer. ²⁸O Sovereign LORD, you are God! Your words are trustworthy, and you have promised these good things to your servant. ²⁹Now be pleased to bless the house of your servant, that it may continue forever in your sight; for you, O

---

^a16 Some Hebrew manuscripts and Septuagint; most Hebrew manuscripts *you*   ^b23 See Septuagint and 1 Chron. 17:21; Hebrew *wonders for y ur land and before your people, whom you redeemed from Egypt, from the nations and their gods.*

Sovereign Lord, have spoken, and with your blessing the house of your servant will be blessed forever."   1Ch 17:16-27

David's Victories

8 In the course of time, David defeated the Philistines and subdued them, and he took Metheg Ammah from the control of the Philistines.

²David also defeated the Moabites. He made them lie down on the ground and measured them off with a length of cord. Every two lengths of them were put to death, and the third length was allowed to live. So the Moabites became subject to David and brought tribute.   Nu 24:17

³Moreover, David fought Hadadezer son of Rehob, king of Zobah, when he went to restore his control along the Euphrates River. ⁴David captured a thousand of his chariots, seven thousand charioteers[a] and twenty thousand foot soldiers. He hamstrung all but a hundred of the chariot horses.

⁵When the Arameans of Damascus came to help Hadadezer king of Zobah, David struck down twenty-two thousand of them. ⁶He put garrisons in the Aramean kingdom of Damascus, and the Arameans became subject to him and brought tribute. The Lord gave David victory wherever he went.

⁷David took the gold shields that belonged to the officers of Hadadezer and brought them to Jerusalem. ⁸From Tebah[b] and Berothai, towns that belonged to Hadadezer, King David took a great quantity of bronze.   1Ki 10:16; Eze 47:16

⁹When Tou[c] king of Hamath heard that David had defeated the entire army of Hadadezer, ¹⁰he sent his son Joram[d] to King David to greet him and congratulate him on his victory in battle over Hadadezer, who had been at war with Tou. Joram brought with him articles of silver and gold and bronze.

¹¹King David dedicated these articles to the Lord, as he had done with the silver and gold from all the nations he had subdued: ¹²Edom[e] and Moab, the Ammonites and the Philistines, and Amalek. He also dedicated the plunder taken from Hadadezer son of Rehob, king of Zobah.   1Ki 7:51

¹³And David became famous after he returned from striking down eighteen thousand Edomites[f] in the Valley of Salt.   2Ki 14:7

¹⁴He put garrisons throughout Edom, and all the Edomites became subject to David. The Lord gave David victory wherever he went.   1Ch 18:1-13; Ge 27:29,37-40

---

[a]4 Septuagint (see also Dead Sea Scrolls and 1 Chron. 18:4); Masoretic Text *captured seventeen hundred of his charioteers*   [b]8 See some Septuagint manuscripts (see also 1 Chron. 18:8); Hebrew *Betah*.   [c]9 Hebrew *Toi*, a variant of *Tou*; also in verse 10   [d]10 A variant of *Hadoram*   [e]12 Some Hebrew manuscripts, Septuagint and Syriac (see also 1 Chron. 18:11); most Hebrew manuscripts *Aram*   [f]13 A few Hebrew manuscripts, Septuagint and Syriac (see also 1 Chron. 18:12); most Hebrew manuscripts *Aram* (that is, Arameans)

David's Officials

[15]David reigned over all Israel, doing what was just and right for all his people. [16]Joab son of Zeruiah was over the army; Jehoshaphat son of Ahilud was recorder; [17]Zadok son of Ahitub and Ahimelech son of Abiathar were priests; Seraiah was secretary; [18]Benaiah son of Jehoiada was over the Kerethites and Pelethites; and David's sons were royal advisers.[a]

David and Mephibosheth

9 David asked, "Is there anyone still left of the house of Saul to whom I can show kindness for Jonathan's sake?"   1Sa 20:14-17,42

[2]Now there was a servant of Saul's household named Ziba. They called him to appear before David, and the king said to him, "Are you Ziba?"   2Sa 16:1-4; 19:17,26,29

"Your servant," he replied.

[3]The king asked, "Is there no one still left of the house of Saul to whom I can show God's kindness?"

Ziba answered the king, "There is still a son of Jonathan; he is crippled in both feet."   2Sa 4:4

[4]"Where is he?" the king asked.

Ziba answered, "He is at the house of Makir son of Ammiel in Lo Debar."   2Sa 17:27-29

[5]So King David had him brought from Lo Debar, from the house of Makir son of Ammiel.

[6]When Mephibosheth son of Jonathan, the son of Saul, came to David, he bowed down to pay him honor.

David said, "Mephibosheth!"

"Your servant," he replied.

[7]"Don't be afraid," David said to him, "for I will surely show you kindness for the sake of your father Jonathan. I will restore to you all the land that belonged to your grandfather Saul, and you will always eat at my table."   1Ki 2:7

[8]Mephibosheth bowed down and said, "What is your servant, that you should notice a dead dog like me?"   2Sa 16:9

[9]Then the king summoned Ziba, Saul's servant, and said to him, "I have given your master's grandson everything that belonged to Saul and his family. [10]You and your sons and your servants are to farm the land for him and bring in the crops, so that your master's grandson may be provided for. And Mephibosheth, grandson of your master, will always eat at my table." (Now Ziba had fifteen sons and twenty servants.)

[11]Then Ziba said to the king, "Your servant will do whatever my lord the king commands his servant to do." So Mephibosheth ate at David's[b] table like one of the king's sons.

[12]Mephibosheth had a young son named Mica, and all the members of Ziba's household were servants of Mephibosheth. [13]And Me-

---

[a] 18 Or *were priests*   [b] 11 Septuagint; Hebrew *my*

phibosheth lived in Jerusalem, because he always ate at the king's table, and he was crippled in both feet.   1Ch 8:34

David Defeats the Ammonites

10 In the course of time, the king of the Ammonites died, and his son Hanun succeeded him as king. ²David thought, "I will show kindness to Hanun son of Nahash, just as his father showed kindness to me." So David sent a delegation to express his sympathy to Hanun concerning his father.   1Sa 11:1

When David's men came to the land of the Ammonites, ³the Ammonite nobles said to Hanun their lord, "Do you think David is honoring your father by sending men to you to express sympathy? Hasn't David sent them to you to explore the city and spy it out and overthrow it?" ⁴So Hanun seized David's men, shaved off half of each man's beard, cut off their garments in the middle at the buttocks, and sent them away.

⁵When David was told about this, he sent messengers to meet the men, for they were greatly humiliated. The king said, "Stay at Jericho till your beards have grown, and then come back."

⁶When the Ammonites realized that they had become a stench in David's nostrils, they hired twenty thousand Aramean foot soldiers from Beth Rehob and Zobah, as well as the king of Maacah with a thousand men, and also twelve thousand men from Tob.   Ge 34:30

⁷On hearing this, David sent Joab out with the entire army of fighting men. ⁸The Ammonites came out and drew up in battle formation at the entrance to their city gate, while the Arameans of Zobah and Rehob and the men of Tob and Maacah were by themselves in the open country.

⁹Joab saw that there were battle lines in front of him and behind him; so he selected some of the best troops in Israel and deployed them against the Arameans. ¹⁰He put the rest of the men under the command of Abishai his brother and deployed them against the Ammonites. ¹¹Joab said, "If the Arameans are too strong for me, then you are to come to my rescue; but if the Ammonites are too strong for you, then I will come to rescue you. ¹²Be strong and let us fight bravely for our people and the cities of our God. The Lᴏʀᴅ will do what is good in his sight."   Dt 31:6

¹³Then Joab and the troops with him advanced to fight the Arameans, and they fled before him. ¹⁴When the Ammonites saw that the Arameans were fleeing, they fled before Abishai and went inside the city. So Joab returned from fighting the Ammonites and came to Jerusalem.

¹⁵After the Arameans saw that they had been routed by Israel, they regrouped. ¹⁶Hadadezer had Arameans brought from beyond

the River[a]; they went to Helam, with Shobach the commander of Hadadezer's army leading them.

[17]When David was told of this, he gathered all Israel, crossed the Jordan and went to Helam. The Arameans formed their battle lines to meet David and fought against him. [18]But they fled before Israel, and David killed seven hundred of their charioteers and forty thousand of their foot soldiers.[b] He also struck down Shobach the commander of their army, and he died there. [19]When all the kings who were vassals of Hadadezer saw that they had been defeated by Israel, they made peace with the Israelites and became subject to them.   2Sa 8:6

So the Arameans were afraid to help the Ammonites anymore.

David and Bathsheba

11 In the spring, at the time when kings go off to war, David sent Joab out with the king's men and the whole Israelite army. They destroyed the Ammonites and besieged Rabbah. But David remained in Jerusalem.   1Ki 20:22,26

[2]One evening David got up from his bed and walked around on the roof of the palace. From the roof he saw a woman bathing. The woman was very beautiful, [3]and David sent someone to find out about her. The man said, "Isn't this Bathsheba, the daughter of Eliam and the wife of Uriah the Hittite?" [4]Then David sent messengers to get her. She came to him, and he slept with her. (She had purified herself from her uncleanness.) Then[c] she went back home. [5]The woman conceived and sent word to David, saying, "I am pregnant."

[6]So David sent this word to Joab: "Send me Uriah the Hittite." And Joab sent him to David. [7]When Uriah came to him, David asked him how Joab was, how the soldiers were and how the war was going. [8]Then David said to Uriah, "Go down to your house and wash your feet." So Uriah left the palace, and a gift from the king was sent after him. [9]But Uriah slept at the entrance to the palace with all his master's servants and did not go down to his house.   1Ch 11:41

[10]When David was told, "Uriah did not go home," he asked him, "Haven't you just come from a distance? Why didn't you go home?"

[11]Uriah said to David, "The ark and Israel and Judah are staying in tents, and my master Joab and my lord's men are camped in the open fields. How could I go to my house to eat and drink and lie with my wife? As surely as you live, I will not do such a thing!"   2Sa 7:2

[12]Then David said to him, "Stay here one more day, and tomorrow I will send you back." So Uriah re-

---

[a]16 That is, the Euphrates   [b]18 Some Septuagint manuscripts (see also 1 Chron. 19:18); Hebrew *horsemen*   [c]4 Or *with her. When she purified herself from her uncleanness,*

mained in Jerusalem that day and the next. ¹³At David's invitation, he ate and drank with him, and David made him drunk. But in the evening Uriah went out to sleep on his mat among his master's servants; he did not go home.

¹⁴In the morning David wrote a letter to Joab and sent it with Uriah. ¹⁵In it he wrote, "Put Uriah in the front line where the fighting is fiercest. Then withdraw from him so he will be struck down and die."

¹⁶So while Joab had the city under siege, he put Uriah at a place where he knew the strongest defenders were. ¹⁷When the men of the city came out and fought against Joab, some of the men in David's army fell; moreover, Uriah the Hittite died.

¹⁸Joab sent David a full account of the battle. ¹⁹He instructed the messenger: "When you have finished giving the king this account of the battle, ²⁰the king's anger may flare up, and he may ask you, 'Why did you get so close to the city to fight? Didn't you know they would shoot arrows from the wall? ²¹Who killed Abimelech son of Jerub-Besheth ᵃ? Didn't a woman throw an upper millstone on him from the wall, so that he died in Thebez? Why did you get so close to the wall?' If he asks you this, then say to him, 'Also, your servant Uriah the Hittite is dead.' "

²²The messenger set out, and when he arrived he told David everything Joab had sent him to say. ²³The messenger said to David, "The men overpowered us and came out against us in the open, but we drove them back to the entrance to the city gate. ²⁴Then the archers shot arrows at your servants from the wall, and some of the king's men died. Moreover, your servant Uriah the Hittite is dead."

²⁵David told the messenger, "Say this to Joab: 'Don't let this upset you; the sword devours one as well as another. Press the attack against the city and destroy it.' Say this to encourage Joab."

²⁶When Uriah's wife heard that her husband was dead, she mourned for him. ²⁷After the time of mourning was over, David had her brought to his house, and she became his wife and bore him a son. But the thing David had done displeased the LORD.   2Sa 12:9

Nathan Rebukes David

12 The LORD sent Nathan to David. When he came to him, he said, "There were two men in a certain town, one rich and the other poor. ²The rich man had a very large number of sheep and cattle, ³but the poor man had nothing except one little ewe lamb he had bought. He raised it, and it grew up with him and his children.

ᵃ21 Also known as Jerub-Baal (that is, Gideon)

It shared his food, drank from his cup and even slept in his arms. It was like a daughter to him.

⁴"Now a traveler came to the rich man, but the rich man refrained from taking one of his own sheep or cattle to prepare a meal for the traveler who had come to him. Instead, he took the ewe lamb that belonged to the poor man and prepared it for the one who had come to him."

⁵David burned with anger against the man and said to Nathan, "As surely as the Lord lives, the man who did this deserves to die! ⁶He must pay for that lamb four times over, because he did such a thing and had no pity."

⁷Then Nathan said to David, "You are the man! This is what the Lord, the God of Israel, says: 'I anointed you king over Israel, and I delivered you from the hand of Saul. ⁸I gave your master's house to you, and your master's wives into your arms. I gave you the house of Israel and Judah. And if all this had been too little, I would have given you even more. ⁹Why did you despise the word of the Lord by doing what is evil in his eyes? You struck down Uriah the Hittite with the sword and took his wife to be your own. You killed him with the sword of the Ammonites. ¹⁰Now, therefore, the sword will never depart from your house, because you despised me and took the wife of Uriah the Hittite to be your own.'   2Sa 11:15; 13:28; 1Ki 20:42

¹¹"This is what the Lord says: 'Out of your own household I am going to bring calamity upon you. Before your very eyes I will take your wives and give them to one who is close to you, and he will lie with your wives in broad daylight. ¹²You did it in secret, but I will do this thing in broad daylight before all Israel.' "   Dt 28:30; 2Sa 11:4-15; 16:21-22

¹³Then David said to Nathan, "I have sinned against the Lord."

Nathan replied, "The Lord has taken away your sin. You are not going to die. ¹⁴But because by doing this you have made the enemies of the Lord show utter contempt,ᵃ the son born to you will die."   Pr 28:13; Isa 52:5; Mic 7:18-19

¹⁵After Nathan had gone home, the Lord struck the child that Uriah's wife had borne to David, and he became ill. ¹⁶David pleaded with God for the child. He fasted and went into his house and spent the nights lying on the ground. ¹⁷The elders of his household stood beside him to get him up from the ground, but he refused, and he would not eat any food with them.   1Sa 25:38; 2Sa 13:31; Ps 5:7

¹⁸On the seventh day the child died. David's servants were afraid to tell him that the child was dead, for they thought, "While the child was still living, we spoke to David but he would not listen to us. How

---

ᵃ 14 Masoretic Text; an ancient Hebrew scribal tradition *this you have shown utter contempt for the Lord*

can we tell him the child is dead? He may do something desperate."

¹⁹David noticed that his servants were whispering among themselves and he realized the child was dead. "Is the child dead?" he asked.

"Yes," they replied, "he is dead."

²⁰Then David got up from the ground. After he had washed, put on lotions and changed his clothes, he went into the house of the LORD and worshiped. Then he went to his own house, and at his request they served him food, and he ate.   Job 1:20

²¹His servants asked him, "Why are you acting this way? While the child was alive, you fasted and wept, but now that the child is dead, you get up and eat!"

²²He answered, "While the child was still alive, I fasted and wept. I thought, 'Who knows? The LORD may be gracious to me and let the child live.' ²³But now that he is dead, why should I fast? Can I bring him back again? I will go to him, but he will not return to me."

²⁴Then David comforted his wife Bathsheba, and he went to her and lay with her. She gave birth to a son, and they named him Solomon. The LORD loved him; ²⁵and because the LORD loved him, he sent word through Nathan the prophet to name him Jedidiah.ᵃ

²⁶Meanwhile Joab fought against Rabbah of the Ammonites and captured the royal citadel. ²⁷Joab then sent messengers to David, saying, "I have fought against Rabbah and taken its water supply. ²⁸Now muster the rest of the troops and besiege the city and capture it. Otherwise I will take the city, and it will be named after me."   Dt 3:11

²⁹So David mustered the entire army and went to Rabbah, and attacked and captured it. ³⁰He took the crown from the head of their kingᵇ—its weight was a talentᶜ of gold, and it was set with precious stones—and it was placed on David's head. He took a great quantity of plunder from the city ³¹and brought out the people who were there, consigning them to labor with saws and with iron picks and axes, and he made them work at brickmaking.ᵈ He did this to all the Ammonite towns. Then David and his entire army returned to Jerusalem.   1Ch 20:1-3; 1Sa 14:47

Amnon and Tamar

13 In the course of time, Amnon son of David fell in love with Tamar, the beautiful sister of Absalom son of David.

²Amnon became frustrated to the point of illness on account of his sister Tamar, for she was a virgin, and it seemed impossible for him to do anything to her.

ᵃ25 Jedidiah means loved by the LORD.   ᵇ30 Or of Milcom (that is, Molech)   ᶜ30 That is, about 75 pounds (about 34 kilograms)   ᵈ31 The meaning of the Hebrew for this clause is uncertain.

³Now Amnon had a friend named Jonadab son of Shimeah, David's brother. Jonadab was a very shrewd man. ⁴He asked Amnon, "Why do you, the king's son, look so haggard morning after morning? Won't you tell me?"

Amnon said to him, "I'm in love with Tamar, my brother Absalom's sister."

⁵"Go to bed and pretend to be ill," Jonadab said. "When your father comes to see you, say to him, 'I would like my sister Tamar to come and give me something to eat. Let her prepare the food in my sight so I may watch her and then eat it from her hand.'"

⁶So Amnon lay down and pretended to be ill. When the king came to see him, Amnon said to him, "I would like my sister Tamar to come and make some special bread in my sight, so I may eat from her hand."

⁷David sent word to Tamar at the palace: "Go to the house of your brother Amnon and prepare some food for him." ⁸So Tamar went to the house of her brother Amnon, who was lying down. She took some dough, kneaded it, made the bread in his sight and baked it. ⁹Then she took the pan and served him the bread, but he refused to eat.

"Send everyone out of here," Amnon said. So everyone left him. ¹⁰Then Amnon said to Tamar, "Bring the food here into my bedroom so I may eat from your hand." And Tamar took the bread she had prepared and brought it to her brother Amnon in his bedroom. ¹¹But when she took it to him to eat, he grabbed her and said, "Come to bed with me, my sister." ^{Ge 39:12; 45:1}

¹²"Don't, my brother!" she said to him. "Don't force me. Such a thing should not be done in Israel! Don't do this wicked thing. ¹³What about me? Where could I get rid of my disgrace? And what about you? You would be like one of the wicked fools in Israel. Please speak to the king; he will not keep me from being married to you." ¹⁴But he refused to listen to her, and since he was stronger than she, he raped her. ^{Lev 18:9; Dt 22:25; Jdg 19:23}

¹⁵Then Amnon hated her with intense hatred. In fact, he hated her more than he had loved her. Amnon said to her, "Get up and get out!"

¹⁶"No!" she said to him. "Sending me away would be a greater wrong than what you have already done to me."

But he refused to listen to her. ¹⁷He called his personal servant and said, "Get this woman out of here and bolt the door after her." ¹⁸So his servant put her out and bolted the door after her. She was wearing a richly ornamented[a] robe, for this was the kind of gar-

---

[a] 18 The meaning of the Hebrew for this phrase is uncertain.

ment the virgin daughters of the king wore. [19]Tamar put ashes on her head and tore the ornamented[a] robe she was wearing. She put her hand on her head and went away, weeping aloud as she went.

[20]Her brother Absalom said to her, "Has that Amnon, your brother, been with you? Be quiet now, my sister; he is your brother. Don't take this thing to heart." And Tamar lived in her brother Absalom's house, a desolate woman.

[21]When King David heard all this, he was furious. [22]Absalom never said a word to Amnon, either good or bad; he hated Amnon because he had disgraced his sister Tamar.   Ge 31:24; Lev 19:17-18; 1Jn 2:9-11

Absalom Kills Amnon

[23]Two years later, when Absalom's sheepshearers were at Baal Hazor near the border of Ephraim, he invited all the king's sons to come there. [24]Absalom went to the king and said, "Your servant has had shearers come. Will the king and his officials please join me?"

[25]"No, my son," the king replied. "All of us should not go; we would only be a burden to you." Although Absalom urged him, he still refused to go, but gave him his blessing.

[26]Then Absalom said, "If not, please let my brother Amnon come with us."

The king asked him, "Why should he go with you?" [27]But Absalom urged him, so he sent with him Amnon and the rest of the king's sons.

[28]Absalom ordered his men, "Listen! When Amnon is in high spirits from drinking wine and I say to you, 'Strike Amnon down,' then kill him. Don't be afraid. Have not I given you this order? Be strong and brave." [29]So Absalom's men did to Amnon what Absalom had ordered. Then all the king's sons got up, mounted their mules and fled.   Jdg 19:6,9,22; 1Sa 25:36

[30]While they were on their way, the report came to David: "Absalom has struck down all the king's sons; not one of them is left." [31]The king stood up, tore his clothes and lay down on the ground; and all his servants stood by with their clothes torn.   Nu 14:6

[32]But Jonadab son of Shimeah, David's brother, said, "My lord should not think that they killed all the princes; only Amnon is dead. This has been Absalom's expressed intention ever since the day Amnon raped his sister Tamar. [33]My lord the king should not be concerned about the report that all the king's sons are dead. Only Amnon is dead."

[34]Meanwhile, Absalom had fled. Now the man standing watch looked up and saw many people on the road west of him, coming down the side of the hill. The

---

[a] 19 The meaning of the Hebrew for this word is uncertain.

watchman went and told the king, "I see men in the direction of Horonaim, on the side of the hill."[a]

35Jonadab said to the king, "See, the king's sons are here; it has happened just as your servant said."

36As he finished speaking, the king's sons came in, wailing loudly. The king, too, and all his servants wept very bitterly.

37Absalom fled and went to Talmai son of Ammihud, the king of Geshur. But King David mourned for his son every day.   2Sa 3:3

38After Absalom fled and went to Geshur, he stayed there three years. 39And the spirit of the king[b] longed to go to Absalom, for he was consoled concerning Amnon's death.   2Sa 12:19-23

Absalom Returns to Jerusalem

14 Joab son of Zeruiah knew that the king's heart longed for Absalom. 2So Joab sent someone to Tekoa and had a wise woman brought from there. He said to her, "Pretend you are in mourning. Dress in mourning clothes, and don't use any cosmetic lotions. Act like a woman who has spent many days grieving for the dead. 3Then go to the king and speak these words to him." And Joab put the words in her mouth.

4When the woman from Tekoa went[c] to the king, she fell with her face to the ground to pay him honor, and she said, "Help me, O king!"

5The king asked her, "What is troubling you?"

She said, "I am indeed a widow; my husband is dead. 6I your servant had two sons. They got into a fight with each other in the field, and no one was there to separate them. One struck the other and killed him. 7Now the whole clan has risen up against your servant; they say, 'Hand over the one who struck his brother down, so that we may put him to death for the life of his brother whom he killed; then we will get rid of the heir as well.' They would put out the only burning coal I have left, leaving my husband neither name nor descendant on the face of the earth."

8The king said to the woman, "Go home, and I will issue an order in your behalf."   1Sa 25:35

9But the woman from Tekoa said to him, "My lord the king, let the blame rest on me and on my father's family, and let the king and his throne be without guilt."

10The king replied, "If anyone says anything to you, bring him to me, and he will not bother you again."

11She said, "Then let the king invoke the LORD his God to prevent the avenger of blood from adding to the destruction, so that my son will not be destroyed."   Nu 35:12,21

[a]34 Septuagint; Hebrew does not have this sentence.   [b]39 Dead Sea Scrolls and some Septuagint manuscripts; Masoretic Text But the spirit of, David the king   [c]4 Many Hebrew manuscripts, Septuagint, Vulgate and Syriac; most Hebrew manuscripts spoke

"As surely as the Lord lives," he said, "not one hair of your son's head will fall to the ground."

¹²Then the woman said, "Let your servant speak a word to my lord the king."

"Speak," he replied.

¹³The woman said, "Why then have you devised a thing like this against the people of God? When the king says this, does he not convict himself, for the king has not brought back his banished son? ¹⁴Like water spilled on the ground, which cannot be recovered, so we must die. But God does not take away life; instead, he devises ways so that a banished person may not remain estranged from him.

¹⁵"And now I have come to say this to my lord the king because the people have made me afraid. Your servant thought, 'I will speak to the king; perhaps he will do what his servant asks. ¹⁶Perhaps the king will agree to deliver his servant from the hand of the man who is trying to cut off both me and my son from the inheritance God gave us.'

¹⁷"And now your servant says, 'May the word of my lord the king bring me rest, for my lord the king is like an angel of God in discerning good and evil. May the Lord your God be with you.'" 2Sa 19:27

¹⁸Then the king said to the woman, "Do not keep from me the answer to what I am going to ask you."

"Let my lord the king speak," the woman said.

¹⁹The king asked, "Isn't the hand of Joab with you in all this?"

The woman answered, "As surely as you live, my lord the king, no one can turn to the right or to the left from anything my lord the king says. Yes, it was your servant Joab who instructed me to do this and who put all these words into the mouth of your servant. ²⁰Your servant Joab did this to change the present situation. My lord has wisdom like that of an angel of God— he knows everything that happens in the land." 2Sa 18:13; Isa 28:6

²¹The king said to Joab, "Very well, I will do it. Go, bring back the young man Absalom."

²²Joab fell with his face to the ground to pay him honor, and he blessed the king. Joab said, "Today your servant knows that he has found favor in your eyes, my lord the king, because the king has granted his servant's request."

²³Then Joab went to Geshur and brought Absalom back to Jerusalem. ²⁴But the king said, "He must go to his own house; he must not see my face." So Absalom went to his own house and did not see the face of the king.

²⁵In all Israel there was not a man so highly praised for his handsome appearance as Absalom. From the top of his head to the sole of his foot there was no blemish in him. ²⁶Whenever he cut the hair of his head—he used to

cut his hair from time to time when it became too heavy for him —he would weigh it, and its weight was two hundred shekels[a] by the royal standard.   Eze 44:20

27Three sons and a daughter were born to Absalom. The daughter's name was Tamar, and she became a beautiful woman.   2Sa 13:1

28Absalom lived two years in Jerusalem without seeing the king's face. **29**Then Absalom sent for Joab in order to send him to the king, but Joab refused to come to him. So he sent a second time, but he refused to come. **30**Then he said to his servants, "Look, Joab's field is next to mine, and he has barley there. Go and set it on fire." So Absalom's servants set the field on fire.

31Then Joab did go to Absalom's house and he said to him, "Why have your servants set my field on fire?"   Jdg 15:5

32Absalom said to Joab, "Look, I sent word to you and said, 'Come here so I can send you to the king to ask, "Why have I come from Geshur? It would be better for me if I were still there!" ' Now then, I want to see the king's face, and if I am guilty of anything, let him put me to death."   1Sa 20:8; 2Sa 3:3

33So Joab went to the king and told him this. Then the king summoned Absalom, and he came in and bowed down with his face to the ground before the king. And the king kissed Absalom.   Ge 33:4

Absalom's Conspiracy

15 In the course of time, Absalom provided himself with a chariot and horses and with fifty men to run ahead of him. **2**He would get up early and stand by the side of the road leading to the city gate. Whenever anyone came with a complaint to be placed before the king for a decision, Absalom would call out to him, "What town are you from?" He would answer, "Your servant is from one of the tribes of Israel." **3**Then Absalom would say to him, "Look, your claims are valid and proper, but there is no representative of the king to hear you." **4**And Absalom would add, "If only I were appointed judge in the land! Then everyone who has a complaint or case could come to me and I would see that he gets justice."   Jdg 9:29

5Also, whenever anyone approached him to bow down before him, Absalom would reach out his hand, take hold of him and kiss him. **6**Absalom behaved in this way toward all the Israelites who came to the king asking for justice, and so he stole the hearts of the men of Israel.   Ro 16:18

7At the end of four[b] years, Absalom said to the king, "Let me go to Hebron and fulfill a vow I made to

---

[a] 26 That is, about 5 pounds (about 2.3 kilograms) Josephus; Hebrew *forty*

[b] 7 Some Septuagint manuscripts, Syriac and

the LORD. **8**While your servant was living at Geshur in Aram, I made this vow: 'If the LORD takes me back to Jerusalem, I will worship the LORD in Hebron.*a*' "   Ge 28:20

9The king said to him, "Go in peace." So he went to Hebron.

10Then Absalom sent secret messengers throughout the tribes of Israel to say, "As soon as you hear the sound of the trumpets, then say, 'Absalom is king in Hebron.' " **11**Two hundred men from Jerusalem had accompanied Absalom. They had been invited as guests and went quite innocently, knowing nothing about the matter. **12**While Absalom was offering sacrifices, he also sent for Ahithophel the Gilonite, David's counselor, to come from Giloh, his hometown. And so the conspiracy gained strength, and Absalom's following kept on increasing.   2Sa 16:15,23

David Flees

13A messenger came and told David, "The hearts of the men of Israel are with Absalom."

14Then David said to all his officials who were with him in Jerusalem, "Come! We must flee, or none of us will escape from Absalom. We must leave immediately, or he will move quickly to overtake us and bring ruin upon us and put the city to the sword."   2Sa 19:9; 1Ki 2:26

15The king's officials answered him, "Your servants are ready to do whatever our lord the king chooses."

16The king set out, with his entire household following him; but he left ten concubines to take care of the palace. **17**So the king set out, with all the people following him, and they halted at a place some distance away. **18**All his men marched past him, along with all the Kerethites and Pelethites; and all the six hundred Gittites who had accompanied him from Gath marched before the king.   2Sa 8:18

19The king said to Ittai the Gittite, "Why should you come along with us? Go back and stay with King Absalom. You are a foreigner, an exile from your homeland. **20**You came only yesterday. And today shall I make you wander about with us, when I do not know where I am going? Go back, and take your countrymen. May kindness and faithfulness be with you."

21But Ittai replied to the king, "As surely as the LORD lives, and as my lord the king lives, wherever my lord the king may be, whether it means life or death, there will your servant be."   Ru 1:16-17; Pr 17:17

22David said to Ittai, "Go ahead, march on." So Ittai the Gittite marched on with all his men and the families that were with him.

23The whole countryside wept aloud as all the people passed by. The king also crossed the Kidron

a 8 Some Septuagint manuscripts; Hebrew does not have in Hebron.

Valley, and all the people moved on toward the desert.   1Sa 11:4

24Zadok was there, too, and all the Levites who were with him were carrying the ark of the covenant of God. They set down the ark of God, and Abiathar offered sacrifices*a* until all the people had finished leaving the city.   Nu 4:15

25Then the king said to Zadok, "Take the ark of God back into the city. If I find favor in the LORD's eyes, he will bring me back and let me see it and his dwelling place again. 26But if he says, 'I am not pleased with you,' then I am ready; let him do to me whatever seems good to him."   Ex 15:13; 1Sa 3:18; Ps 43:3

27The king also said to Zadok the priest, "Aren't you a seer? Go back to the city in peace, with your son Ahimaaz and Jonathan son of Abiathar. You and Abiathar take your two sons with you. 28I will wait at the fords in the desert until word comes from you to inform me." 29So Zadok and Abiathar took the ark of God back to Jerusalem and stayed there.   1Sa 9:9; 2Sa 17:17

30But David continued up the Mount of Olives, weeping as he went; his head was covered and he was barefoot. All the people with him covered their heads too and were weeping as they went up. 31Now David had been told, "Ahithophel is among the conspirators with Absalom." So David

prayed, "O LORD, turn Ahithophel's counsel into foolishness."

32When David arrived at the summit, where people used to worship God, Hushai the Arkite was there to meet him, his robe torn and dust on his head. 33David said to him, "If you go with me, you will be a burden to me. 34But if you return to the city and say to Absalom, 'I will be your servant, O king; I was your father's servant in the past, but now I will be your servant,' then you can help me by frustrating Ahithophel's advice. 35Won't the priests Zadok and Abiathar be there with you? Tell them anything you hear in the king's palace. 36Their two sons, Ahimaaz son of Zadok and Jonathan son of Abiathar, are there with them. Send them to me with anything you hear."   2Sa 17:15-16; 19:35

37So David's friend Hushai arrived at Jerusalem as Absalom was entering the city.   1Ch 27:33

David and Ziba

16 When David had gone a short distance beyond the summit, there was Ziba, the steward of Mephibosheth, waiting to meet him. He had a string of donkeys saddled and loaded with two hundred loaves of bread, a hundred cakes of raisins, a hundred cakes of figs and a skin of wine. 2The king asked Ziba, "Why have you brought these?"

a 24 Or Abiathar went up

Ziba answered, "The donkeys are for the king's household to ride on, the bread and fruit are for the men to eat, and the wine is to refresh those who become exhausted in the desert."   2Sa 17:27-29

³The king then asked, "Where is your master's grandson?"

Ziba said to him, "He is staying in Jerusalem, because he thinks, 'Today the house of Israel will give me back my grandfather's kingdom.'"

⁴Then the king said to Ziba, "All that belonged to Mephibosheth is now yours."

"I humbly bow," Ziba said. "May I find favor in your eyes, my lord the king."

Shimei Curses David

⁵As King David approached Bahurim, a man from the same clan as Saul's family came out from there. His name was Shimei son of Gera, and he cursed as he came out. ⁶He pelted David and all the king's officials with stones, though all the troops and the special guard were on David's right and left. ⁷As he cursed, Shimei said, "Get out, get out, you man of blood, you scoundrel! ⁸The LORD has repaid you for all the blood you shed in the household of Saul, in whose place you have reigned. The LORD has handed the kingdom over to your son Absalom. You have come to ruin because you are a man of blood!"   2Sa 19:16-23; 1Ki 2:8-9,36,44

⁹Then Abishai son of Zeruiah said to the king, "Why should this dead dog curse my lord the king? Let me go over and cut off his head."   Ex 22:28; 2Sa 9:8

¹⁰But the king said, "What do you and I have in common, you sons of Zeruiah? If he is cursing because the LORD said to him, 'Curse David,' who can ask, 'Why do you do this?'"   2Sa 19:22; Ro 9:20

¹¹David then said to Abishai and all his officials, "My son, who is of my own flesh, is trying to take my life. How much more, then, this Benjamite! Leave him alone; let him curse, for the LORD has told him to. ¹²It may be that the LORD will see my distress and repay me with good for the cursing I am receiving today."   Dt 23:5; 2Sa 12:11

¹³So David and his men continued along the road while Shimei was going along the hillside opposite him, cursing as he went and throwing stones at him and showering him with dirt. ¹⁴The king and all the people with him arrived at their destination exhausted. And there he refreshed himself.

The Advice of Hushai and Ahithophel

¹⁵Meanwhile, Absalom and all the men of Israel came to Jerusalem, and Ahithophel was with him. ¹⁶Then Hushai the Arkite, David's friend, went to Absalom and said to him, "Long live the king! Long live the king!"   2Sa 15:37

¹⁷Absalom asked Hushai, "Is

this the love you show your friend? Why didn't you go with your friend?"   2Sa 19:25

[18]Hushai said to Absalom, "No, the one chosen by the LORD, by these people, and by all the men of Israel—his I will be, and I will remain with him. [19]Furthermore, whom should I serve? Should I not serve the son? Just as I served your father, so I will serve you."

[20]Absalom said to Ahithophel, "Give us your advice. What should we do?"

[21]Ahithophel answered, "Lie with your father's concubines whom he left to take care of the palace. Then all Israel will hear that you have made yourself a stench in your father's nostrils, and the hands of everyone with you will be strengthened." [22]So they pitched a tent for Absalom on the roof, and he lay with his father's concubines in the sight of all Israel.   2Sa 12:11-12

[23]Now in those days the advice Ahithophel gave was like that of one who inquires of God. That was how both David and Absalom regarded all of Ahithophel's advice.

17

Ahithophel said to Absalom, "I would[a] choose twelve thousand men and set out tonight in pursuit of David. [2]I would[b] attack him while he is weary and weak. I would[b] strike him with terror, and then all the people with him will flee. I would[b]

strike down only the king [3]and bring all the people back to you. The death of the man you seek will mean the return of all; all the people will be unharmed." [4]This plan seemed good to Absalom and to all the elders of Israel.   2Sa 16:14

[5]But Absalom said, "Summon also Hushai the Arkite, so we can hear what he has to say." [6]When Hushai came to him, Absalom said, "Ahithophel has given this advice. Should we do what he says? If not, give us your opinion."

[7]Hushai replied to Absalom, "The advice Ahithophel has given is not good this time. [8]You know your father and his men; they are fighters, and as fierce as a wild bear robbed of her cubs. Besides, your father is an experienced fighter; he will not spend the night with the troops. [9]Even now, he is hidden in a cave or some other place. If he should attack your troops first,[c] whoever hears about it will say, 'There has been a slaughter among the troops who follow Absalom.' [10]Then even the bravest soldier, whose heart is like the heart of a lion, will melt with fear, for all Israel knows that your father is a fighter and that those with him are brave.   Jos 2:9,11; 1Sa 16:18

[11]"So I advise you: Let all Israel, from Dan to Beersheba—as numerous as the sand on the seashore—be gathered to you, with you yourself leading them into

---

[a]1 Or Let me   [b]2 Or will   [c]9 Or When some of the men fall at the first attack

battle. ¹²Then we will attack him wherever he may be found, and we will fall on him as dew settles on the ground. Neither he nor any of his men will be left alive. ¹³If he withdraws into a city, then all Israel will bring ropes to that city, and we will drag it down to the valley until not even a piece of it can be found." Ge 12:2; 22:17; Mic 1:6

¹⁴Absalom and all the men of Israel said, "The advice of Hushai the Arkite is better than that of Ahithophel." For the LORD had determined to frustrate the good advice of Ahithophel in order to bring disaster on Absalom.

¹⁵Hushai told Zadok and Abiathar, the priests, "Ahithophel has advised Absalom and the elders of Israel to do such and such, but I have advised them to do so and so. ¹⁶Now send a message immediately and tell David, 'Do not spend the night at the fords in the desert; cross over without fail, or the king and all the people with him will be swallowed up.' "

¹⁷Jonathan and Ahimaaz were staying at En Rogel. A servant girl was to go and inform them, and they were to go and tell King David, for they could not risk being seen entering the city. ¹⁸But a young man saw them and told Absalom. So the two of them left quickly and went to the house of a man in Bahurim. He had a well in his courtyard, and they climbed down into it. ¹⁹His wife took a covering and spread it out over the opening of the well and scattered grain over it. No one knew anything about it. Jos 2:6; 15:7; 2Sa 3:16

²⁰When Absalom's men came to the woman at the house, they asked, "Where are Ahimaaz and Jonathan?"

The woman answered them, "They crossed over the brook."ᵃ The men searched but found no one, so they returned to Jerusalem. Ex 1:19; Jos 2:3-5; 1Sa 19:12-17

²¹After the men had gone, the two climbed out of the well and went to inform King David. They said to him, "Set out and cross the river at once; Ahithophel has advised such and such against you." ²²So David and all the people with him set out and crossed the Jordan. By daybreak, no one was left who had not crossed the Jordan.

²³When Ahithophel saw that his advice had not been followed, he saddled his donkey and set out for his house in his hometown. He put his house in order and then hanged himself. So he died and was buried in his father's tomb.

²⁴David went to Mahanaim, and Absalom crossed the Jordan with all the men of Israel. ²⁵Absalom had appointed Amasa over the army in place of Joab. Amasa was the son of a man named Jether,ᵇ

ᵃ20 Or "They passed by the sheep pen toward the water."　　ᵇ25 Hebrew Ithra, a variant of Jether

an Israelite[a] who had married Abigail,[b] the daughter of Nahash and sister of Zeruiah the mother of Joab. **26**The Israelites and Absalom camped in the land of Gilead.

27When David came to Mahanaim, Shobi son of Nahash from Rabbah of the Ammonites, and Makir son of Ammiel from Lo Debar, and Barzillai the Gileadite from Rogelim **28**brought bedding and bowls and articles of pottery. They also brought wheat and barley, flour and roasted grain, beans and lentils,[c] **29**honey and curds, sheep, and cheese from cows' milk for David and his people to eat. For they said, "The people have become hungry and tired and thirsty in the desert."   2Sa 10:1-2; 16:2; 19:31-39

Absalom's Death

18 David mustered the men who were with him and appointed over them commanders of thousands and commanders of hundreds. **2**David sent the troops out—a third under the command of Joab, a third under Joab's brother Abishai son of Zeruiah, and a third under Ittai the Gittite. The king told the troops, "I myself will surely march out with you."

3But the men said, "You must not go out; if we are forced to flee, they won't care about us. Even if half of us die, they won't care; but

you are worth ten thousand of us.[d] It would be better now for you to give us support from the city."

4The king answered, "I will do whatever seems best to you."

So the king stood beside the gate while all the men marched out in units of hundreds and of thousands. **5**The king commanded Joab, Abishai and Ittai, "Be gentle with the young man Absalom for my sake." And all the troops heard the king giving orders concerning Absalom to each of the commanders.

6The army marched into the field to fight Israel, and the battle took place in the forest of Ephraim. **7**There the army of Israel was defeated by David's men, and the casualties that day were great— twenty thousand men. **8**The battle spread out over the whole countryside, and the forest claimed more lives that day than the sword.

9Now Absalom happened to meet David's men. He was riding his mule, and as the mule went under the thick branches of a large oak, Absalom's head got caught in the tree. He was left hanging in midair, while the mule he was riding kept on going.   2Sa 14:26

10When one of the men saw this, he told Joab, "I just saw Absalom hanging in an oak tree."

11Joab said to the man who had

---

a 25 Hebrew and some Septuagint manuscripts; other Septuagint manuscripts (see also 1 Chron. 2:17) *Ishmaelite* or *Jezreelite*   *b 25* Hebrew *Abigal,* a variant of *Abigail*   *c 28* Most Septuagint manuscripts and Syriac; Hebrew *lentils, and roasted grain*   *d 3* Two Hebrew manuscripts, some Septuagint manuscripts and Vulgate; most Hebrew manuscripts *care; for now there are ten thousand like us*

told him this, "What! You saw him? Why didn't you strike him to the ground right there? Then I would have had to give you ten shekels[a] of silver and a warrior's belt."

¹²But the man replied, "Even if a thousand shekels[b] were weighed out into my hands, I would not lift my hand against the king's son. In our hearing the king commanded you and Abishai and Ittai, 'Protect the young man Absalom for my sake.[c]' ¹³And if I had put my life in jeopardy[d]—and nothing is hidden from the king—you would have kept your distance from me."

¹⁴Joab said, "I'm not going to wait like this for you." So he took three javelins in his hand and plunged them into Absalom's heart while Absalom was still alive in the oak tree. ¹⁵And ten of Joab's armor-bearers surrounded Absalom, struck him and killed him.

¹⁶Then Joab sounded the trumpet, and the troops stopped pursuing Israel, for Joab halted them. ¹⁷They took Absalom, threw him into a big pit in the forest and piled up a large heap of rocks over him. Meanwhile, all the Israelites fled to their homes.   2Sa 2:28; 20:22; Jos 7:26

¹⁸During his lifetime Absalom had taken a pillar and erected it in the King's Valley as a monument to himself, for he thought, "I have no son to carry on the memory of my name." He named the pillar after himself, and it is called Absalom's Monument to this day.

David Mourns

¹⁹Now Ahimaaz son of Zadok said, "Let me run and take the news to the king that the LORD has delivered him from the hand of his enemies."   Jdg 11:36; 2Sa 15:36

²⁰"You are not the one to take the news today," Joab told him. "You may take the news another time, but you must not do so today, because the king's son is dead."

²¹Then Joab said to a Cushite, "Go, tell the king what you have seen." The Cushite bowed down before Joab and ran off.

²²Ahimaaz son of Zadok again said to Joab, "Come what may, please let me run behind the Cushite."

But Joab replied, "My son, why do you want to go? You don't have any news that will bring you a reward."

²³He said, "Come what may, I want to run."

So Joab said, "Run!" Then Ahimaaz ran by way of the plain[e] and outran the Cushite.

²⁴While David was sitting between the inner and outer gates, the watchman went up to the roof

---

a11 That is, about 4 ounces (about 115 grams)   b12 That is, about 25 pounds (about 11 kilograms)
c12 A few Hebrew manuscripts, Septuagint, Vulgate and Syriac; most Hebrew manuscripts may be translated *Absalom, whoever you may be.*   d13 Or *Otherwise, if I had acted treacherously toward him*
e23 That is, the plain of the Jordan

of the gateway by the wall. As he looked out, he saw a man running alone. ²⁵The watchman called out to the king and reported it.

The king said, "If he is alone, he must have good news." And the man came closer and closer.

²⁶Then the watchman saw another man running, and he called down to the gatekeeper, "Look, another man running alone!"

The king said, "He must be bringing good news, too."   1Ki 1:42

²⁷The watchman said, "It seems to me that the first one runs like Ahimaaz son of Zadok."

"He's a good man," the king said. "He comes with good news."

²⁸Then Ahimaaz called out to the king, "All is well!" He bowed down before the king with his face to the ground and said, "Praise be to the LORD your God! He has delivered up the men who lifted their hands against my lord the king."

²⁹The king asked, "Is the young man Absalom safe?"

Ahimaaz answered, "I saw great confusion just as Joab was about to send the king's servant and me, your servant, but I don't know what it was."

³⁰The king said, "Stand aside and wait here." So he stepped aside and stood there.

³¹Then the Cushite arrived and said, "My lord the king, hear the good news! The LORD has delivered you today from all who rose up against you."

³²The king asked the Cushite, "Is the young man Absalom safe?"

The Cushite replied, "May the enemies of my lord the king and all who rise up to harm you be like that young man."   Jdg 5:31; 1Sa 25:26

³³The king was shaken. He went up to the room over the gateway and wept. As he went, he said: "O my son Absalom! My son, my son Absalom! If only I had died instead of you—O Absalom, my son, my son!"   Ex 32:32; Ro 9:3

19 Joab was told, "The king is weeping and mourning for Absalom." ²And for the whole army the victory that day was turned into mourning, because on that day the troops heard it said, "The king is grieving for his son." ³The men stole into the city that day as men steal in who are ashamed when they flee from battle. ⁴The king covered his face and cried aloud, "O my son Absalom! O Absalom, my son, my son!"

⁵Then Joab went into the house to the king and said, "Today you have humiliated all your men, who have just saved your life and the lives of your sons and daughters and the lives of your wives and concubines. ⁶You love those who hate you and hate those who love you. You have made it clear today that the commanders and their men mean nothing to you. I see that you would be pleased if Absalom were alive today and all of us were dead. ⁷Now go out and encourage your men. I swear by the

LORD that if you don't go out, not a man will be left with you by nightfall. This will be worse for you than all the calamities that have come upon you from your youth till now." Pr 14:28

⁸So the king got up and took his seat in the gateway. When the men were told, "The king is sitting in the gateway," they all came before him. 2Sa 15:2

David Returns to Jerusalem

Meanwhile, the Israelites had fled to their homes. ⁹Throughout the tribes of Israel, the people were all arguing with each other, saying, "The king delivered us from the hand of our enemies; he is the one who rescued us from the hand of the Philistines. But now he has fled the country because of Absalom; ¹⁰and Absalom, whom we anointed to rule over us, has died in battle. So why do you say nothing about bringing the king back?"

¹¹King David sent this message to Zadok and Abiathar, the priests: "Ask the elders of Judah, 'Why should you be the last to bring the king back to his palace, since what is being said throughout Israel has reached the king at his quarters? ¹²You are my brothers, my own flesh and blood. So why should you be the last to bring back the king?' ¹³And say to Amasa, 'Are you not my own flesh and blood? May God deal with me, be it ever so severely, if from now on you are

not the commander of my army in place of Joab.'" Ge 29:14; 2Sa 2:13

¹⁴He won over the hearts of all the men of Judah as though they were one man. They sent word to the king, "Return, you and all your men." ¹⁵Then the king returned and went as far as the Jordan.

Now the men of Judah had come to Gilgal to go out and meet the king and bring him across the Jordan. ¹⁶Shimei son of Gera, the Benjamite from Bahurim, hurried down with the men of Judah to meet King David. ¹⁷With him were a thousand Benjamites, along with Ziba, the steward of Saul's household, and his fifteen sons and twenty servants. They rushed to the Jordan, where the king was. ¹⁸They crossed at the ford to take the king's household over and to do whatever he wished. Jos 5:9

When Shimei son of Gera crossed the Jordan, he fell prostrate before the king ¹⁹and said to him, "May my lord not hold me guilty. Do not remember how your servant did wrong on the day my lord the king left Jerusalem. May the king put it out of his mind. ²⁰For I your servant know that I have sinned, but today I have come here as the first of the whole house of Joseph to come down and meet my lord the king." 1Sa 22:15

²¹Then Abishai son of Zeruiah said, "Shouldn't Shimei be put to death for this? He cursed the LORD's anointed." Ex 22:28

²²David replied, "What do you

and I have in common, you sons of Zeruiah? This day you have become my adversaries! Should anyone be put to death in Israel today? Do I not know that today I am king over Israel?" ²³So the king said to Shimei, "You shall not die." And the king promised him on oath.

²⁴Mephibosheth, Saul's grandson, also went down to meet the king. He had not taken care of his feet or trimmed his mustache or washed his clothes from the day the king left until the day he returned safely. ²⁵When he came from Jerusalem to meet the king, the king asked him, "Why didn't you go with me, Mephibosheth?"

²⁶He said, "My lord the king, since I your servant am lame, I said, 'I will have my donkey saddled and will ride on it, so I can go with the king.' But Ziba my servant betrayed me. ²⁷And he has slandered your servant to my lord the king. My lord the king is like an angel of God; so do whatever pleases you. ²⁸All my grandfather's descendants deserved nothing but death from my lord the king, but you gave your servant a place among those who eat at your table. So what right do I have to make any more appeals to the king?"   2Sa 14:17,20; 2Sa 21:6-9

²⁹The king said to him, "Why say more? I order you and Ziba to divide the fields."

³⁰Mephibosheth said to the king, "Let him take everything, now that my lord the king has arrived home safely."

³¹Barzillai the Gileadite also came down from Rogelim to cross the Jordan with the king and to send him on his way from there. ³²Now Barzillai was a very old man, eighty years of age. He had provided for the king during his stay in Mahanaim, for he was a very wealthy man. ³³The king said to Barzillai, "Cross over with me and stay with me in Jerusalem, and I will provide for you."

³⁴But Barzillai answered the king, "How many more years will I live, that I should go up to Jerusalem with the king? ³⁵I am now eighty years old. Can I tell the difference between what is good and what is not? Can your servant taste what he eats and drinks? Can I still hear the voices of men and women singers? Why should your servant be an added burden to my lord the king? ³⁶Your servant will cross over the Jordan with the king for a short distance, but why should the king reward me in this way? ³⁷Let your servant return, that I may die in my own town near the tomb of my father and mother. But here is your servant Kimham. Let him cross over with my lord the king. Do for him whatever pleases you."

³⁸The king said, "Kimham shall cross over with me, and I will do for him whatever pleases you. And anything you desire from me I will do for you."

³⁹So all the people crossed the

Jordan, and then the king crossed over. The king kissed Barzillai and gave him his blessing, and Barzillai returned to his home. Ge 31:55

⁴⁰When the king crossed over to Gilgal, Kimham crossed with him. All the troops of Judah and half the troops of Israel had taken the king over.

⁴¹Soon all the men of Israel were coming to the king and saying to him, "Why did our brothers, the men of Judah, steal the king away and bring him and his household across the Jordan, together with all his men?" Jdg 8:1; 12:1

⁴²All the men of Judah answered the men of Israel, "We did this because the king is closely related to us. Why are you angry about it? Have we eaten any of the king's provisions? Have we taken anything for ourselves?"

⁴³Then the men of Israel answered the men of Judah, "We have ten shares in the king; and besides, we have a greater claim on David than you have. So why do you treat us with contempt? Were we not the first to speak of bringing back our king?"

But the men of Judah responded even more harshly than the men of Israel.

Sheba Rebels Against David

20 Now a troublemaker named Sheba son of Bicri, a Benjamite, happened to be there. He sounded the trumpet and shouted,

"We have no share in David,
  no part in Jesse's son!
Every man to his tent,
  O Israel!"

²So all the men of Israel deserted David to follow Sheba son of Bicri. But the men of Judah stayed by their king all the way from the Jordan to Jerusalem.

³When David returned to his palace in Jerusalem, he took the ten concubines he had left to take care of the palace and put them in a house under guard. He provided for them, but did not lie with them. They were kept in confinement till the day of their death, living as widows. 2Sa 15:16; 16:21-22

⁴Then the king said to Amasa, "Summon the men of Judah to come to me within three days, and be here yourself." ⁵But when Amasa went to summon Judah, he took longer than the time the king had set for him. 2Sa 19:13

⁶David said to Abishai, "Now Sheba son of Bicri will do us more harm than Absalom did. Take your master's men and pursue him, or he will find fortified cities and escape from us." ⁷So Joab's men and the Kerethites and Pelethites and all the mighty warriors went out under the command of Abishai. They marched out from Jerusalem to pursue Sheba son of Bicri.

⁸While they were at the great rock in Gibeon, Amasa came to meet them. Joab was wearing his military tunic, and strapped over it

at his waist was a belt with a dagger in its sheath. As he stepped forward, it dropped out of its sheath.

⁹Joab said to Amasa, "How are you, my brother?" Then Joab took Amasa by the beard with his right hand to kiss him. ¹⁰Amasa was not on his guard against the dagger in Joab's hand, and Joab plunged it into his belly, and his intestines spilled out on the ground. Without being stabbed again, Amasa died. Then Joab and his brother Abishai pursued Sheba son of Bicri.

¹¹One of Joab's men stood beside Amasa and said, "Whoever favors Joab, and whoever is for David, let him follow Joab!" ¹²Amasa lay wallowing in his blood in the middle of the road, and the man saw that all the troops came to a halt there. When he realized that everyone who came up to Amasa stopped, he dragged him from the road into a field and threw a garment over him. ¹³After Amasa had been removed from the road, all the men went on with Joab to pursue Sheba son of Bicri.   2Sa 2:23

¹⁴Sheba passed through all the tribes of Israel to Abel Beth Maacah*ᵃ* and through the entire region of the Berites, who gathered together and followed him. ¹⁵All the troops with Joab came and besieged Sheba in Abel Beth Maacah. They built a siege ramp up to the city, and it stood against the outer fortifications. While they were battering the wall to bring it down, ¹⁶a wise woman called from the city, "Listen! Listen! Tell Joab to come here so I can speak to him." ¹⁷He went toward her, and she asked, "Are you Joab?"   2Sa 14:2; 2Ki 19:32

"I am," he answered.

She said, "Listen to what your servant has to say."

"I'm listening," he said.

¹⁸She continued, "Long ago they used to say, 'Get your answer at Abel,' and that settled it. ¹⁹We are the peaceful and faithful in Israel. You are trying to destroy a city that is a mother in Israel. Why do you want to swallow up the Lord's inheritance?"   Dt 2:26; 1Sa 26:19; 2Sa 21:3

²⁰"Far be it from me!" Joab replied, "Far be it from me to swallow up or destroy! ²¹That is not the case. A man named Sheba son of Bicri, from the hill country of Ephraim, has lifted up his hand against the king, against David. Hand over this one man, and I'll withdraw from the city."

The woman said to Joab, "His head will be thrown to you from the wall."   2Sa 4:8

²²Then the woman went to all the people with her wise advice, and they cut off the head of Sheba son of Bicri and threw it to Joab. So he sounded the trumpet, and his men dispersed from the city, each returning to his home. And Joab went back to the king in Jerusalem.   Ecc 9:13

ᵃ 14 Or *Abel, even Beth Maacah*; also in verse 15

²³Joab was over Israel's entire army; Benaiah son of Jehoiada was over the Kerethites and Pelethites; ²⁴Adoniram*a* was in charge of forced labor; Jehoshaphat son of Ahilud was recorder; ²⁵Sheva was secretary; Zadok and Abiathar were priests; ²⁶and Ira the Jairite was David's priest.   2Sa 8:16-18

The Gibeonites Avenged

21 During the reign of David, there was a famine for three successive years; so David sought the face of the LORD. The LORD said, "It is on account of Saul and his blood-stained house; it is because he put the Gibeonites to death."   Ge 12:10; Ex 32:11

²The king summoned the Gibeonites and spoke to them. (Now the Gibeonites were not a part of Israel but were survivors of the Amorites; the Israelites had sworn to ,spare, them, but Saul in his zeal for Israel and Judah had tried to annihilate them.) ³David asked the Gibeonites, "What shall I do for you? How shall I make amends so that you will bless the LORD's inheritance?"   Jos 9:15; 1Sa 26:19; 2Sa 20:19

⁴The Gibeonites answered him, "We have no right to demand silver or gold from Saul or his family, nor do we have the right to put anyone in Israel to death."

"What do you want me to do for you?" David asked.

⁵They answered the king, "As for the man who destroyed us and plotted against us so that we have been decimated and have no place anywhere in Israel, ⁶let seven of his male descendants be given to us to be killed and exposed before the LORD at Gibeah of Saul—the LORD's chosen one."   Nu 25:4

So the king said, "I will give them to you."

⁷The king spared Mephibosheth son of Jonathan, the son of Saul, because of the oath before the LORD between David and Jonathan son of Saul. ⁸But the king took Armoni and Mephibosheth, the two sons of Aiah's daughter Rizpah, whom she had borne to Saul, together with the five sons of Saul's daughter Merab,*b* whom she had borne to Adriel son of Barzillai the Meholathite. ⁹He handed them over to the Gibeonites, who killed and exposed them on a hill before the LORD. All seven of them fell together; they were put to death during the first days of the harvest, just as the barley harvest was beginning.   1Sa 20:8,15; 2Sa 3:7; 4:4

¹⁰Rizpah daughter of Aiah took sackcloth and spread it out for herself on a rock. From the beginning of the harvest till the rain poured down from the heavens on the bodies, she did not let the birds of the air touch them by day or the wild animals by night. ¹¹When Da-

---

a 24 Some Septuagint manuscripts (see also 1 Kings 4:6 and 5:14); Hebrew *Adoram*   *b 8* Two Hebrew manuscripts, some Septuagint manuscripts and Syriac (see also 1 Samuel 18:19); most Hebrew and Septuagint manuscripts *Michal*

vid was told what Aiah's daughter Rizpah, Saul's concubine, had done, [12]he went and took the bones of Saul and his son Jonathan from the citizens of Jabesh Gilead. (They had taken them secretly from the public square at Beth Shan, where the Philistines had hung them after they struck Saul down on Gilboa.) [13]David brought the bones of Saul and his son Jonathan from there, and the bones of those who had been killed and exposed were gathered up.   Dt 21:23

[14]They buried the bones of Saul and his son Jonathan in the tomb of Saul's father Kish, at Zela in Benjamin, and did everything the king commanded. After that, God answered prayer in behalf of the land.   Jos 7:26; 18:28; 2Sa 24:25

Wars Against the Philistines

[15]Once again there was a battle between the Philistines and Israel. David went down with his men to fight against the Philistines, and he became exhausted. [16]And Ishbi-Benob, one of the descendants of Rapha, whose bronze spearhead weighed three hundred shekels[a] and who was armed with a new ˌswordˌ, said he would kill David. [17]But Abishai son of Zeruiah came to David's rescue; he struck the Philistine down and killed him. Then David's men swore to him, saying, "Never again will you go out with us to battle, so that the lamp of Israel will not be extinguished."   2Sa 18:3; 20:6; 1Ki 11:36

[18]In the course of time, there was another battle with the Philistines, at Gob. At that time Sibbecai the Hushathite killed Saph, one of the descendants of Rapha.

[19]In another battle with the Philistines at Gob, Elhanan son of Jaare-Oregim[b] the Bethlehemite killed Goliath[c] the Gittite, who had a spear with a shaft like a weaver's rod.   1Sa 17:7

[20]In still another battle, which took place at Gath, there was a huge man with six fingers on each hand and six toes on each foot—twenty-four in all. He also was descended from Rapha. [21]When he taunted Israel, Jonathan son of Shimeah, David's brother, killed him.   1Ch 20:4-8; 1Sa 16:9

[22]These four were descendants of Rapha in Gath, and they fell at the hands of David and his men.

David's Song of Praise

22 David sang to the LORD the words of this song when the LORD delivered him from the hand of all his enemies and from the hand of Saul. [2]He said: Ex 15:1

"The LORD is my rock, my fortress and my deliverer;   Dt 32:4; Ps 31:3

---

[a]16 That is, about 7 1/2 pounds (about 3.5 kilograms)   [b]19 Or son of Jair the weaver   [c]19 Hebrew and Septuagint; 1 Chron. 20:5 son of Jair killed Lahmi the brother of Goliath

³ my God is my rock, in
    whom I take refuge,
my shield and the horn^a of
    my salvation.   Ge 15:1
He is my stronghold, my
    refuge and my savior—
from violent men you save
    me.
⁴I call to the Lord, who is
    worthy of praise,   Ps 48:1
and I am saved from my
    enemies.

⁵"The waves of death swirled
    about me;   Ps 69:14-15; 93:4
the torrents of destruction
    overwhelmed me.
⁶The cords of the grave^b coiled
    around me;   Ps 116:3
the snares of death
    confronted me.
⁷In my distress I called to the
    Lord;
I called out to my God.
From his temple he heard my
    voice;
my cry came to his ears.

⁸"The earth trembled and
    quaked,   Jdg 5:4; Ps 77:18
the foundations of the
    heavens^c shook;   Job 26:11
they trembled because he
    was angry.
⁹Smoke rose from his nostrils;
consuming fire came from
    his mouth,   Ps 97:3; Heb 12:29
burning coals blazed out of
    it.

¹⁰He parted the heavens and
    came down;
dark clouds were under his
    feet.   1Ki 8:12; Na 1:3
¹¹He mounted the cherubim and
    flew;
he soared^d on the wings of
    the wind.   Ps 104:3
¹²He made darkness his canopy
    around him—
the dark^e rain clouds of the
    sky.
¹³Out of the brightness of his
    presence
bolts of lightning blazed
    forth.   ver 9
¹⁴The Lord thundered from
    heaven;   1Sa 2:10
the voice of the Most High
    resounded.
¹⁵He shot arrows and scattered
    the enemies,   Dt 32:23
bolts of lightning and routed
    them.
¹⁶The valleys of the sea were
    exposed
and the foundations of the
    earth laid bare
at the rebuke of the Lord,
at the blast of breath from
    his nostrils.

¹⁷"He reached down from on
    high and took hold of
    me;   Ps 144:7
he drew me out of deep
    waters.   Ex 2:10
¹⁸He rescued me from my
    powerful enemy,

---

^a3 *Horn* here symbolizes strength.   ^b6 Hebrew *Sheol*   ^c8 Hebrew; Vulgate and Syriac (see also Psalm 18:7) *mountains*   ^d11 Many Hebrew manuscripts (see also Psalm 18:10); most Hebrew manuscripts *appeared*   ^e12 Septuagint and Vulgate (see also Psalm 18:11); Hebrew *massed*

from my foes, who were too
   strong for me.
¹⁹They confronted me in the day
   of my disaster,
but the LORD was my
   support.   Ps 23:4
²⁰He brought me out into a
   spacious place;   Ps 31:8
he rescued me because he
   delighted in me.   2Sa 15:26

²¹"The LORD has dealt with me
   according to my
   righteousness;   1Sa 26:23
according to the cleanness of
   my hands he has
   rewarded me.   Ps 24:4
²²For I have kept the ways of the
   LORD; Ge 18:19; Ps 128:1; Pr 8:32
I have not done evil by
   turning from my God.
²³All his laws are before me;
I have not turned away from
   his decrees.   Ps 119:102
²⁴I have been blameless before
   him   Ge 6:9; Eph 1:4
and have kept myself from
   sin.
²⁵The LORD has rewarded me
   according to my
   righteousness,   ver 21
according to my cleanness[a]
   in his sight.

²⁶"To the faithful you show
   yourself faithful,
to the blameless you show
   yourself blameless,

²⁷to the pure you show yourself
   pure,   Mt 5:8
but to the crooked you show
   yourself shrewd.
²⁸You save the humble, Ps 72:12-13
but your eyes are on the
   haughty to bring them
   low.   Isa 2:12,17; 5:15
²⁹You are my lamp, O LORD;
   the LORD turns my darkness
   into light.
³⁰With your help I can advance
   against a troop[b];
with my God I can scale a
   wall.

³¹"As for God, his way is perfect;
   the word of the LORD is
   flawless.   Ps 12:6; 119:140
He is a shield   Ge 15:1
   for all who take refuge in
   him.
³²For who is God besides the
   LORD?
   And who is the Rock except
   our God?   1Sa 2:2
³³It is God who arms me with
   strength[c]
and makes my way perfect.
³⁴He makes my feet like the feet
   of a deer;   Hab 3:19
he enables me to stand on
   the heights.   Dt 32:13
³⁵He trains my hands for battle;
   my arms can bend a bow of
   bronze.
³⁶You give me your shield of
   victory;   Eph 6:16

---

[a]25 Hebrew; Septuagint and Vulgate (see also Psalm 18:24) *to the cleanness of my hands*   [b]30 Or *can run through a barricade*   [c]33 Dead Sea Scrolls, some Septuagint manuscripts, Vulgate and Syriac (see also Psalm 18:32); Masoretic Text *who is my strong refuge*

you stoop down to make me
    great.
[37]You broaden the path beneath
    me,   Pr 4:11
  so that my ankles do not
    turn.

[38]"I pursued my enemies and
    crushed them;
  I did not turn back till they
    were destroyed.
[39]I crushed them completely,
    and they could not rise;
  they fell beneath my feet.
[40]You armed me with strength
    for battle;
  you made my adversaries
    bow at my feet.   Ps 44:5
[41]You made my enemies turn
    their backs in flight,
  and I destroyed my foes.
[42]They cried for help, but there
    was no one to save
    them—   Ps 50:22; Isa 1:15
  to the LORD, but he did not
    answer.
[43]I beat them as fine as the dust
    of the earth;
  I pounded and trampled
    them like mud in the
    streets.   Isa 10:6; Mic 7:10

[44]"You have delivered me from
    the attacks of my
    people;   2Sa 3:1
  you have preserved me as
    the head of nations.
  People I did not know are
    subject to me,   Isa 55:3-5

[45]and foreigners come cringing
    to me;   Ps 66:3; 81:15
  as soon as they hear me,
    they obey me.
[46]They all lose heart;
  they come trembling[a] from
    their strongholds.   Mic 7:17

[47]"The LORD lives! Praise be to
    my Rock!
  Exalted be God, the Rock,
    my Savior!   Ps 89:26
[48]He is the God who avenges
    me,
  who puts the nations under
    me,   Ps 144:2
[49] who sets me free from my
    enemies.   Ps 140:1,4
  You exalted me above my foes;
  from violent men you
    rescued me.
[50]Therefore I will praise you,
    O LORD, among the
    nations;
  I will sing praises to your
    name.   Ro 15:9
[51]He gives his king great
    victories;   Ps 144:9-10
  he shows unfailing kindness
    to his anointed,   Ps 89:20
  to David and his descendants
    forever."   Ps 18:1-50; 89:24,29

The Last Words of David

23 These are the last words of
David:

"The oracle of David son of
    Jesse,

---

[a]46 Some Septuagint manuscripts and Vulgate (see also Psalm 18:45); Masoretic Text *they arm themselves.*

the oracle of the man exalted
by the Most High,
the man anointed by the God
of Jacob,   1Sa 16:12-13
Israel's singer of songs[a]:

2"The Spirit of the LORD spoke
through me;   Mt 22:43
his word was on my tongue.
3The God of Israel spoke,
the Rock of Israel said to
me: Dt 32:4; 2Sa 22:2,32
'When one rules over men in
righteousness,   Ps 72:2
when he rules in the fear of
God,   2Ch 19:7,9; Isa 11:1-5
4he is like the light of morning
at sunrise   Jdg 5:31; Ps 89:36
on a cloudless morning,
like the brightness after rain
that brings the grass from
the earth.'

5"Is not my house right with
God?
Has he not made with me an
everlasting covenant,
arranged and secured in
every part?
Will he not bring to fruition
my salvation
and grant me my every
desire?
6But evil men are all to be cast
aside like thorns,
which are not gathered with
the hand.

7Whoever touches thorns
uses a tool of iron or the
shaft of a spear;
they are burned up where
they lie."

David's Mighty Men

8These are the names of David's
mighty men: 2Sa 17:10
Joseb-Basshebeth,[b] a Tahke-
monite,[c] was chief of the Three;
he raised his spear against eight
hundred men, whom he killed[d] in
one encounter.   1Ch 27:2
9Next to him was Eleazar son of
Dodai the Ahohite. As one of the
three mighty men, he was with David when they taunted the Philistines gathered at Pas Dammim,[e]
for battle. Then the men of Israel
retreated, 10but he stood his
ground and struck down the Philistines till his hand grew tired and
froze to the sword. The LORD
brought about a great victory
that day. The troops returned to
Eleazar, but only to strip the
dead.
11Next to him was Shammah
son of Agee the Hararite. When the
Philistines banded together at a
place where there was a field full
of lentils, Israel's troops fled from
them. 12But Shammah took his
stand in the middle of the field. He
defended it and struck the Philis-

---

[a]1 Or *Israel's beloved singer*   [b]8 Hebrew; some Septuagint manuscripts suggest *Ish-Bosheth,* that is, *Esh-Baal* (see also 1 Chron. 11:11 *Jashobeam*).   [c]8 Probably a variant of *Hacmonite* (see 1 Chron. 11:11)   [d]8 Some Septuagint manuscripts (see also 1 Chron. 11:11); Hebrew and other Septuagint manuscripts *Three; it was Adino the Eznite who killed eight hundred men*   [e]9 See 1 Chron. 11:13; Hebrew *gathered there.*

tines down, and the Lord brought about a great victory.

13During harvest time, three of the thirty chief men came down to David at the cave of Adullam, while a band of Philistines was encamped in the Valley of Rephaim. **14**At that time David was in the stronghold, and the Philistine garrison was at Bethlehem. **15**David longed for water and said, "Oh, that someone would get me a drink of water from the well near the gate of Bethlehem!" **16**So the three mighty men broke through the Philistine lines, drew water from the well near the gate of Bethlehem and carried it back to David. But he refused to drink it; instead, he poured it out before the Lord. **17**"Far be it from me, O Lord, to do this!" he said. "Is it not the blood of men who went at the risk of their lives?" And David would not drink it.   1Sa 22:4-5; 2Sa 5:18; Ge 35:14

Such were the exploits of the three mighty men.

18Abishai the brother of Joab son of Zeruiah was chief of the Three.[a] He raised his spear against three hundred men, whom he killed, and so he became as famous as the Three. **19**Was he not held in greater honor than the Three? He became their commander, even though he was not included among them.   2Sa 10:10,14

20Benaiah son of Jehoiada was a valiant fighter from Kabzeel, who performed great exploits. He struck down two of Moab's best men. He also went down into a pit on a snowy day and killed a lion. **21**And he struck down a huge Egyptian. Although the Egyptian had a spear in his hand, Benaiah went against him with a club. He snatched the spear from the Egyptian's hand and killed him with his own spear. **22**Such were the exploits of Benaiah son of Jehoiada; he too was as famous as the three mighty men. **23**He was held in greater honor than any of the Thirty, but he was not included among the Three. And David put him in charge of his bodyguard.   2Sa 8:18

24Among the Thirty were:
Asahel the brother of Joab,
Elhanan son of Dodo from Bethlehem,
25Shammah the Harodite,
Elika the Harodite,
26Helez the Paltite,   1Ch 27:10
Ira son of Ikkesh from Tekoa,
27Abiezer from Anathoth,
Mebunnai[b] the Hushathite,
28Zalmon the Ahohite,
Maharai the Netophathite,
29Heled[c] son of Baanah the Netophathite,
Ithai son of Ribai from Gibeah in Benjamin,
30Benaiah the Pirathonite,

a 18 Most Hebrew manuscripts (see also 1 Chron. 11:20); two Hebrew manuscripts and Syriac *Thirty*
b 27 Hebrew; some Septuagint manuscripts (see also 1 Chron. 11:29) *Sibbecai*   *c 29* Some Hebrew manuscripts and Vulgate (see also 1 Chron. 11:30); most Hebrew manuscripts *Heleb*

Hiddai[a] from the ravines of
Gaash,   Jos 24:30
[31]Abi-Albon the Arbathite,
Azmaveth the Barhumite,
[32]Eliahba the Shaalbonite,
the sons of Jashen,
Jonathan [33]son of[b] Shammah the Hararite,
Ahiam son of Sharar[c] the
Hararite,
[34]Eliphelet son of Ahasbai
the Maacathite,   Dt 3:14
Eliam son of Ahithophel
the Gilonite,   2Sa 11:3; 15:12
[35]Hezro the Carmelite,
Paarai the Arbite,
[36]Igal son of Nathan from Zo-
bah,   1Sa 14:47
the son of Hagri,[d]
[37]Zelek the Ammonite,
Naharai the Beerothite, the
armor-bearer of Joab son
of Zeruiah,
[38]Ira the Ithrite,   1Ch 2:53
Gareb the Ithrite
[39]and Uriah the Hittite.
There were thirty-seven in all.

David Counts the Fighting Men

24 Again the anger of the
LORD burned against Israel,
and he incited David against them,
saying, "Go and take a census of
Israel and Judah."   Jos 9:15; 1Ch 27:23
[2]So the king said to Joab and the
army commanders[e] with him, "Go
throughout the tribes of Israel
from Dan to Beersheba and enroll
the fighting men, so that I may
know how many there are."

[3]But Joab replied to the king,
"May the LORD your God multiply
the troops a hundred times over,
and may the eyes of my lord the
king see it. But why does my lord
the king want to do such a thing?"

[4]The king's word, however,
overruled Joab and the army commanders; so they left the presence
of the king to enroll the fighting
men of Israel.

[5]After crossing the Jordan, they
camped near Aroer, south of the
town in the gorge, and then went
through Gad and on to Jazer.
[6]They went to Gilead and the region of Tahtim Hodshi, and on to
Dan Jaan and around toward Sidon. [7]Then they went toward the
fortress of Tyre and all the towns
of the Hivites and Canaanites. Finally, they went on to Beersheba
in the Negev of Judah.   Jos 13:9

[8]After they had gone through
the entire land, they came back to
Jerusalem at the end of nine
months and twenty days.

[9]Joab reported the number of
the fighting men to the king: In Israel there were eight hundred
thousand able-bodied men who

---

[a]30 Hebrew; some Septuagint manuscripts (see also 1 Chron. 11:32) *Hurai*   [b]33 Some Septuagint
manuscripts (see also 1 Chron. 11:34); Hebrew does not have *son of.*   [c]33 Hebrew; some Septuagint
manuscripts (see also 1 Chron. 11:35) *Sacar*   [d]36 Some Septuagint manuscripts (see also 1 Chron.
11:38); Hebrew *Haggadi*   [e]2 Septuagint (see also verse 4 and 1 Chron. 21:2); Hebrew *Joab the army
commander*

could handle a sword, and in Judah five hundred thousand.

¹⁰David was conscience-stricken after he had counted the fighting men, and he said to the LORD, "I have sinned greatly in what I have done. Now, O LORD, I beg you, take away the guilt of your servant. I have done a very foolish thing."

¹¹Before David got up the next morning, the word of the LORD had come to Gad the prophet, David's seer: ¹²"Go and tell David, 'This is what the LORD says: I am giving you three options. Choose one of them for me to carry out against you.' "   1Sa 9:9; 22:5; 1Ch 29:29

¹³So Gad went to David and said to him, "Shall there come upon you three*a* years of famine in your land? Or three months of fleeing from your enemies while they pursue you? Or three days of plague in your land? Now then, think it over and decide how I should answer the one who sent me."   Eze 14:21

¹⁴David said to Gad, "I am in deep distress. Let us fall into the hands of the LORD, for his mercy is great; but do not let me fall into the hands of men."   Ps 51:1; 103:8,13

¹⁵So the LORD sent a plague on Israel from that morning until the end of the time designated, and seventy thousand of the people from Dan to Beersheba died. ¹⁶When the angel stretched out his hand to destroy Jerusalem, the LORD was grieved because of the calamity and said to the angel who was afflicting the people, "Enough! Withdraw your hand." The angel of the LORD was then at the threshing floor of Araunah the Jebusite.   Ge 6:6; Ex 12:23; 1Ch 27:24

¹⁷When David saw the angel who was striking down the people, he said to the LORD, "I am the one who has sinned and done wrong. These are but sheep. What have they done? Let your hand fall upon me and my family."   1Ch 21:1-17

David Builds an Altar

¹⁸On that day Gad went to David and said to him, "Go up and build an altar to the LORD on the threshing floor of Araunah the Jebusite." ¹⁹So David went up, as the LORD had commanded through Gad. ²⁰When Araunah looked and saw the king and his men coming toward him, he went out and bowed down before the king with his face to the ground.

²¹Araunah said, "Why has my lord the king come to his servant?"

"To buy your threshing floor," David answered, "so I can build an altar to the LORD, that the plague on the people may be stopped."

²²Araunah said to David, "Let my lord the king take whatever pleases him and offer it up. Here are oxen for the burnt offering, and here are threshing sledges and ox yokes for the wood. ²³O king, Araunah gives all this to the king."

---

a 13 Septuagint (see also 1 Chron. 21:12); Hebrew *seven*

Araunah also said to him, "May the LORD your God accept you."

24But the king replied to Araunah, "No, I insist on paying you for it. I will not sacrifice to the LORD my God burnt offerings that cost me nothing." Mal 1:13-14

So David bought the threshing floor and the oxen and paid fifty shekels[a] of silver for them. 25David built an altar to the LORD there and sacrificed burnt offerings and fellowship offerings.[b] Then the LORD answered prayer in behalf of the land, and the plague on Israel was stopped. 1Ch 21:18-26; 2Sa 21:14

---

[a]24 That is, about 1 1/4 pounds (about 0.6 kilogram)   [b]25 Traditionally *peace offerings*

1 Kings

Adonijah Sets Himself Up as King

1 When King David was old and well advanced in years, he could not keep warm even when they put covers over him. ²So his servants said to him, "Let us look for a young virgin to attend the king and take care of him. She can lie beside him so that our lord the king may keep warm."

³Then they searched throughout Israel for a beautiful girl and found Abishag, a Shunammite, and brought her to the king. ⁴The girl was very beautiful; she took care of the king and waited on him, but the king had no intimate relations with her.

⁵Now Adonijah, whose mother was Haggith, put himself forward and said, "I will be king." So he got chariots and horsesᵃ ready, with fifty men to run ahead of him. ⁶(His father had never interfered with him by asking, "Why do you behave as you do?" He was also very handsome and was born next after Absalom.)   2Sa 3:4; 15:1

⁷Adonijah conferred with Joab son of Zeruiah and with Abiathar the priest, and they gave him their support. ⁸But Zadok the priest, Benaiah son of Jehoiada, Nathan the prophet, Shimei and Reiᵇ and David's special guard did not join Adonijah.   2Sa 20:25; 23:8; 1Ki 2:22,28

⁹Adonijah then sacrificed sheep, cattle and fattened calves at the Stone of Zoheleth near En Rogel. He invited all his brothers, the king's sons, and all the men of Judah who were royal officials, ¹⁰but he did not invite Nathan the prophet or Benaiah or the special guard or his brother Solomon.

¹¹Then Nathan asked Bathsheba, Solomon's mother, "Have you not heard that Adonijah, the son of Haggith, has become king without our lord David's knowing it? ¹²Now then, let me advise you how you can save your own life and the life of your son Solomon. ¹³Go in to King David and say to him, 'My lord the king, did you not swear to me your servant: "Surely Solomon your son shall be king after me, and he will sit on my throne"? Why then has Adonijah become king?' ¹⁴While you are still there talking to the king, I will come in and confirm what you have said."

¹⁵So Bathsheba went to see the aged king in his room, where Abishag the Shunammite was attend-

---

ᵃ 5 Or charioteers   ᵇ 8 Or and his friends

ing him. [16]Bathsheba bowed low and knelt before the king.   ver 1

"What is it you want?" the king asked.

[17]She said to him, "My lord, you yourself swore to me your servant by the LORD your God: 'Solomon your son shall be king after me, and he will sit on my throne.' [18]But now Adonijah has become king, and you, my lord the king, do not know about it. [19]He has sacrificed great numbers of cattle, fattened calves, and sheep, and has invited all the king's sons, Abiathar the priest and Joab the commander of the army, but he has not invited Solomon your servant. [20]My lord the king, the eyes of all Israel are on you, to learn from you who will sit on the throne of my lord the king after him. [21]Otherwise, as soon as my lord the king is laid to rest with his fathers, I and my son Solomon will be treated as criminals."   ver 13,30; Dt 31:16; 1Ki 2:10

[22]While she was still speaking with the king, Nathan the prophet arrived. [23]And they told the king, "Nathan the prophet is here." So he went before the king and bowed with his face to the ground.

[24]Nathan said, "Have you, my lord the king, declared that Adonijah shall be king after you, and that he will sit on your throne? [25]Today he has gone down and sacrificed great numbers of cattle, fattened calves, and sheep. He has invited all the king's sons, the commanders of the army and Abiathar the priest. Right now they are eating and drinking with him and saying, 'Long live King Adonijah!' [26]But me your servant, and Zadok the priest, and Benaiah son of Jehoiada, and your servant Solomon he did not invite. [27]Is this something my lord the king has done without letting his servants know who should sit on the throne of my lord the king after him?"

David Makes Solomon King

[28]Then King David said, "Call in Bathsheba." So she came into the king's presence and stood before him.

[29]The king then took an oath: "As surely as the LORD lives, who has delivered me out of every trouble, [30]I will surely carry out today what I swore to you by the LORD, the God of Israel: Solomon your son shall be king after me, and he will sit on my throne in my place."

[31]Then Bathsheba bowed low with her face to the ground and, kneeling before the king, said, "May my lord King David live forever!"

[32]King David said, "Call in Zadok the priest, Nathan the prophet and Benaiah son of Jehoiada." When they came before the king, [33]he said to them: "Take your lord's servants with you and set Solomon my son on my own mule and take him down to Gihon. [34]There have Zadok the priest and Nathan the prophet anoint him king over Israel. Blow the trumpet

and shout, 'Long live King Solomon!' ³⁵Then you are to go up with him, and he is to come and sit on my throne and reign in my place. I have appointed him ruler over Israel and Judah." 1Sa 10:1; 2Sa 15:10

³⁶Benaiah son of Jehoiada answered the king, "Amen! May the LORD, the God of my lord the king, so declare it. ³⁷As the LORD was with my lord the king, so may he be with Solomon to make his throne even greater than the throne of my lord King David!"

³⁸So Zadok the priest, Nathan the prophet, Benaiah son of Jehoiada, the Kerethites and the Pelethites went down and put Solomon on King David's mule and escorted him to Gihon. ³⁹Zadok the priest took the horn of oil from the sacred tent and anointed Solomon. Then they sounded the trumpet and all the people shouted, "Long live King Solomon!" ⁴⁰And all the people went up after him, playing flutes and rejoicing greatly, so that the ground shook with the sound.

⁴¹Adonijah and all the guests who were with him heard it as they were finishing their feast. On hearing the sound of the trumpet, Joab asked, "What's the meaning of all the noise in the city?"

⁴²Even as he was speaking, Jonathan son of Abiathar the priest arrived. Adonijah said, "Come in. A worthy man like you must be bringing good news." 2Sa 18:26

⁴³"Not at all!" Jonathan answered. "Our lord King David has made Solomon king. ⁴⁴The king has sent with him Zadok the priest, Nathan the prophet, Benaiah son of Jehoiada, the Kerethites and the Pelethites, and they have put him on the king's mule, ⁴⁵and Zadok the priest and Nathan the prophet have anointed him king at Gihon. From there they have gone up cheering, and the city resounds with it. That's the noise you hear. ⁴⁶Moreover, Solomon has taken his seat on the royal throne. ⁴⁷Also, the royal officials have come to congratulate our lord King David, saying, 'May your God make Solomon's name more famous than yours and his throne greater than yours!' And the king bowed in worship on his bed ⁴⁸and said, 'Praise be to the LORD, the God of Israel, who has allowed my eyes to see a successor on my throne today.' " ver 37; 1Ki 3:6

⁴⁹At this, all Adonijah's guests rose in alarm and dispersed. ⁵⁰But Adonijah, in fear of Solomon, went and took hold of the horns of the altar. ⁵¹Then Solomon was told, "Adonijah is afraid of King Solomon and is clinging to the horns of the altar. He says, 'Let King Solomon swear to me today that he will not put his servant to death with the sword.' " 1Ki 2:28

⁵²Solomon replied, "If he shows himself to be a worthy man, not a hair of his head will fall to the ground; but if evil is found in him, he will die." ⁵³Then King Solomon sent men, and they brought him

down from the altar. And Adonijah came and bowed down to King Solomon, and Solomon said, "Go to your home."   1Ch 29:21-25; 1Sa 14:45

David's Charge to Solomon

2 When the time drew near for David to die, he gave a charge to Solomon his son.

[2]"I am about to go the way of all the earth," he said. "So be strong, show yourself a man, [3]and observe what the Lord your God requires: Walk in his ways, and keep his decrees and commands, his laws and requirements, as written in the Law of Moses, so that you may prosper in all you do and wherever you go, [4]and that the Lord may keep his promise to me: 'If your descendants watch how they live, and if they walk faithfully before me with all their heart and soul, you will never fail to have a man on the throne of Israel.'   2Sa 7:13,25

[5]"Now you yourself know what Joab son of Zeruiah did to me—what he did to the two commanders of Israel's armies, Abner son of Ner and Amasa son of Jether. He killed them, shedding their blood in peacetime as if in battle, and with that blood stained the belt around his waist and the sandals on his feet. [6]Deal with him according to your wisdom, but do not let his gray head go down to the grave[a] in peace.   2Sa 2:18; 20:10

[7]"But show kindness to the sons of Barzillai of Gilead and let them be among those who eat at your table. They stood by me when I fled from your brother Absalom.

[8]"And remember, you have with you Shimei son of Gera, the Benjamite from Bahurim, who called down bitter curses on me the day I went to Mahanaim. When he came down to meet me at the Jordan, I swore to him by the Lord: 'I will not put you to death by the sword.' [9]But now, do not consider him innocent. You are a man of wisdom; you will know what to do to him. Bring his gray head down to the grave in blood."   2Sa 16:5-13

[10]Then David rested with his fathers and was buried in the City of David. [11]He had reigned forty years over Israel—seven years in Hebron and thirty-three in Jerusalem. [12]So Solomon sat on the throne of his father David, and his rule was firmly established.

Solomon's Throne Established

[13]Now Adonijah, the son of Haggith, went to Bathsheba, Solomon's mother. Bathsheba asked him, "Do you come peacefully?"

He answered, "Yes, peacefully." [14]Then he added, "I have something to say to you."

"You may say it," she replied.

[15]"As you know," he said, "the kingdom was mine. All Israel looked to me as their king. But things changed, and the kingdom

---

[a]6 Hebrew *Sheol*; also in verse 9

has gone to my brother; for it has come to him from the LORD. ¹⁶Now I have one request to make of you. Do not refuse me."

"You may make it," she said.

¹⁷So he continued, "Please ask King Solomon—he will not refuse you—to give me Abishag the Shunammite as my wife."   1Ki 1:3

¹⁸"Very well," Bathsheba replied, "I will speak to the king for you."

¹⁹When Bathsheba went to King Solomon to speak to him for Adonijah, the king stood up to meet her, bowed down to her and sat down on his throne. He had a throne brought for the king's mother, and she sat down at his right hand.   Ps 45:9; 1Ki 15:13

²⁰"I have one small request to make of you," she said. "Do not refuse me."

The king replied, "Make it, my mother; I will not refuse you."

²¹So she said, "Let Abishag the Shunammite be given in marriage to your brother Adonijah."   1Ki 1:3

²²King Solomon answered his mother, "Why do you request Abishag the Shunammite for Adonijah? You might as well request the kingdom for him—after all, he is my older brother—yes, for him and for Abiathar the priest and Joab son of Zeruiah!"   2Sa 12:8

²³Then King Solomon swore by the LORD: "May God deal with me, be it ever so severely, if Adonijah does not pay with his life for this request! ²⁴And now, as surely as

the LORD lives—he who has established me securely on the throne of my father David and has founded a dynasty for me as he promised—Adonijah shall be put to death today!" ²⁵So King Solomon gave orders to Benaiah son of Jehoiada, and he struck down Adonijah and he died.   2Sa 7:11; 8:18

²⁶To Abiathar the priest the king said, "Go back to your fields in Anathoth. You deserve to die, but I will not put you to death now, because you carried the ark of the Sovereign LORD before my father David and shared all my father's hardships." ²⁷So Solomon removed Abiathar from the priesthood of the LORD, fulfilling the word the LORD had spoken at Shiloh about the house of Eli.

²⁸When the news reached Joab, who had conspired with Adonijah though not with Absalom, he fled to the tent of the LORD and took hold of the horns of the altar. ²⁹King Solomon was told that Joab had fled to the tent of the LORD and was beside the altar. Then Solomon ordered Benaiah son of Jehoiada, "Go, strike him down!"

³⁰So Benaiah entered the tent of the LORD and said to Joab, "The king says, 'Come out!'"   Ex 21:14

But he answered, "No, I will die here."

Benaiah reported to the king, "This is how Joab answered me."

³¹Then the king commanded Benaiah, "Do as he says. Strike him

down and bury him, and so clear me and my father's house of the guilt of the innocent blood that Joab shed. ³²The LORD will repay him for the blood he shed, because without the knowledge of my father David he attacked two men and killed them with the sword. Both of them—Abner son of Ner, commander of Israel's army, and Amasa son of Jether, commander of Judah's army—were better men and more upright than he. ³³May the guilt of their blood rest on the head of Joab and his descendants forever. But on David and his descendants, his house and his throne, may there be the LORD's peace forever." Dt 19:13; Jdg 9:24

³⁴So Benaiah son of Jehoiada went up and struck down Joab and killed him, and he was buried on his own land*a* in the desert. ³⁵The king put Benaiah son of Jehoiada over the army in Joab's position and replaced Abiathar with Zadok the priest. 1Ki 4:4; 1Ch 29:22

³⁶Then the king sent for Shimei and said to him, "Build yourself a house in Jerusalem and live there, but do not go anywhere else. ³⁷The day you leave and cross the Kidron Valley, you can be sure you will die; your blood will be on your own head." 2Sa 1:16; 15:23

³⁸Shimei answered the king, "What you say is good. Your servant will do as my lord the king has said." And Shimei stayed in Jerusalem for a long time.

³⁹But three years later, two of Shimei's slaves ran off to Achish son of Maacah, king of Gath, and Shimei was told, "Your slaves are in Gath." ⁴⁰At this, he saddled his donkey and went to Achish at Gath in search of his slaves. So Shimei went away and brought the slaves back from Gath. 1Sa 27:2

⁴¹When Solomon was told that Shimei had gone from Jerusalem to Gath and had returned, ⁴²the king summoned Shimei and said to him, "Did I not make you swear by the LORD and warn you, 'On the day you leave to go anywhere else, you can be sure you will die'? At that time you said to me, 'What you say is good. I will obey.' ⁴³Why then did you not keep your oath to the LORD and obey the command I gave you?"

⁴⁴The king also said to Shimei, "You know in your heart all the wrong you did to my father David. Now the LORD will repay you for your wrongdoing. ⁴⁵But King Solomon will be blessed, and David's throne will remain secure before the LORD forever." 2Sa 7:13; 16:5-13

⁴⁶Then the king gave the order to Benaiah son of Jehoiada, and he went out and struck Shimei down and killed him.

The kingdom was now firmly established in Solomon's hands.

---

a 34 Or *buried in his tomb*

Solomon Asks for Wisdom

3 Solomon made an alliance with Pharaoh king of Egypt and married his daughter. He brought her to the City of David until he finished building his palace and the temple of the Lord, and the wall around Jerusalem. ²The people, however, were still sacrificing at the high places, because a temple had not yet been built for the Name of the Lord. ³Solomon showed his love for the Lord by walking according to the statutes of his father David, except that he offered sacrifices and burned incense on the high places.

⁴The king went to Gibeon to offer sacrifices, for that was the most important high place, and Solomon offered a thousand burnt offerings on that altar. ⁵At Gibeon the Lord appeared to Solomon during the night in a dream, and God said, "Ask for whatever you want me to give you."   Nu 12:6

⁶Solomon answered, "You have shown great kindness to your servant, my father David, because he was faithful to you and righteous and upright in heart. You have continued this great kindness to him and have given him a son to sit on his throne this very day.

⁷"Now, O Lord my God, you have made your servant king in place of my father David. But I am only a little child and do not know how to carry out my duties. ⁸Your servant is here among the people you have chosen, a great people, too numerous to count or number. ⁹So give your servant a discerning heart to govern your people and to distinguish between right and wrong. For who is able to govern this great people of yours?"

¹⁰The Lord was pleased that Solomon had asked for this. ¹¹So God said to him, "Since you have asked for this and not for long life or wealth for yourself, nor have asked for the death of your enemies but for discernment in administering justice, ¹²I will do what you have asked. I will give you a wise and discerning heart, so that there will never have been anyone like you, nor will there ever be. ¹³Moreover, I will give you what you have not asked for—both riches and honor—so that in your lifetime you will have no equal among kings. ¹⁴And if you walk in my ways and obey my statutes and commands as David your father did, I will give you a long life." ¹⁵Then Solomon awoke—and he realized it had been a dream.   1Ki 4:20-34; Pr 3:1-2,16; Jas 4:3

He returned to Jerusalem, stood before the ark of the Lord's covenant and sacrificed burnt offerings and fellowship offerings.ᵃ Then he gave a feast for all his court.   2Ch 1:2-13; 1Ki 8:65

ᵃ 15 Traditionally *peace offerings*

A Wise Ruling

[16] Now two prostitutes came to the king and stood before him. [17] One of them said, "My lord, this woman and I live in the same house. I had a baby while she was there with me. [18] The third day after my child was born, this woman also had a baby. We were alone; there was no one in the house but the two of us.

[19] "During the night this woman's son died because she lay on him. [20] So she got up in the middle of the night and took my son from my side while I your servant was asleep. She put him by her breast and put her dead son by my breast. [21] The next morning, I got up to nurse my son—and he was dead! But when I looked at him closely in the morning light, I saw that it wasn't the son I had borne."

[22] The other woman said, "No! The living one is my son; the dead one is yours."

But the first one insisted, "No! The dead one is yours; the living one is mine." And so they argued before the king.

[23] The king said, "This one says, 'My son is alive and your son is dead,' while that one says, 'No! Your son is dead and mine is alive.' "

[24] Then the king said, "Bring me a sword." So they brought a sword for the king. [25] He then gave an order: "Cut the living child in two and give half to one and half to the other."

[26] The woman whose son was alive was filled with compassion for her son and said to the king, "Please, my lord, give her the living baby! Don't kill him!" Ge 43:30

But the other said, "Neither I nor you shall have him. Cut him in two!"

[27] Then the king gave his ruling: "Give the living baby to the first woman. Do not kill him; she is his mother."

[28] When all Israel heard the verdict the king had given, they held the king in awe, because they saw that he had wisdom from God to administer justice. ver 9,11-12; Col 2:3

Solomon's Officials and Governors

4 So King Solomon ruled over all Israel. [2] And these were his chief officials:

Azariah son of Zadok—the
   priest;   1Ch 6:10
[3] Elihoreph and Ahijah, sons of
   Shisha—secretaries;
Jehoshaphat son of Ahilud—
   recorder;   2Sa 8:16
[4] Benaiah son of Jehoiada—
   commander in chief;
Zadok and Abiathar—priests;
[5] Azariah son of Nathan—in
   charge of the district officers;
Zabud son of Nathan—a
   priest and personal adviser
   to the king;

⁶Ahishar—in charge of the palace;

Adoniram son of Abda—in charge of forced labor.

⁷Solomon also had twelve district governors over all Israel, who supplied provisions for the king and the royal household. Each one had to provide supplies for one month in the year. ⁸These are their names:

Ben-Hur—in the hill country of Ephraim;   Jos 24:33

⁹Ben-Deker—in Makaz, Shaalbim, Beth Shemesh and Elon Bethhanan;   Jdg 1:35

¹⁰Ben-Hesed—in   Arubboth (Socoh and all the land of Hepher were his);   Jos 12:17

¹¹Ben-Abinadab—in Naphoth Dorᵃ (he was married to Taphath daughter of Solomon);   Jos 11:2

¹²Baana son of Ahilud—in Taanach and Megiddo, and in all of Beth Shan next to Zarethan below Jezreel, from Beth Shan to Abel Meholah across to Jokmeam;

¹³Ben-Geber—in Ramoth Gilead (the settlements of Jair son of Manasseh in Gilead were his, as well as the district of Argob in Bashan and its sixty large walled cities with bronze gate bars);

¹⁴Ahinadab son of Iddo—in Mahanaim;   Jos 13:26

¹⁵Ahimaaz—in Naphtali (he had married Basemath daughter of Solomon);

¹⁶Baana son of Hushai—in Asher and in Aloth;   2Sa 15:32

¹⁷Jehoshaphat son of Paruah—in Issachar;

¹⁸Shimei son of Ela—in Benjamin;   1Ki 1:8

¹⁹Geber son of Uri—in Gilead (the country of Sihon king of the Amorites and the country of Og king of Bashan). He was the only governor over the district.

Solomon's Daily Provisions

²⁰The people of Judah and Israel were as numerous as the sand on the seashore; they ate, they drank and they were happy. ²¹And Solomon ruled over all the kingdoms from the Riverᵇ to the land of the Philistines, as far as the border of Egypt. These countries brought tribute and were Solomon's subjects all his life.   2Ch 9:26; Ps 72:8

²²Solomon's daily provisions were thirty corsᶜ of fine flour and sixty corsᵈ of meal, ²³ten head of stall-fed cattle, twenty of pasture-fed cattle and a hundred sheep and goats, as well as deer, gazelles, roebucks and choice fowl. ²⁴For he ruled over all the kingdoms west of the River, from Tiphsah to Gaza,

---

ᵃ11 Or *in the heights of Dor*   ᵇ21 That is, the Euphrates; also in verse 24   ᶜ22 That is, probably about 185 bushels (about 6.6 kiloliters)   ᵈ22 That is, probably about 375 bushels (about 13.2 kiloliters)

and had peace on all sides. **25**During Solomon's lifetime Judah and Israel, from Dan to Beersheba, lived in safety, each man under his own vine and fig tree.   Jer 23:6

26Solomon had four[a] thousand stalls for chariot horses, and twelve thousand horses.[b]   1Ki 10:26

27The district officers, each in his month, supplied provisions for King Solomon and all who came to the king's table. They saw to it that nothing was lacking. **28**They also brought to the proper place their quotas of barley and straw for the chariot horses and the other horses.

Solomon's Wisdom

29God gave Solomon wisdom and very great insight, and a breadth of understanding as measureless as the sand on the seashore. **30**Solomon's wisdom was greater than the wisdom of all the men of the East, and greater than all the wisdom of Egypt. **31**He was wiser than any other man, including Ethan the Ezrahite—wiser than Heman, Calcol and Darda, the sons of Mahol. And his fame spread to all the surrounding nations. **32**He spoke three thousand proverbs and his songs numbered a thousand and five. **33**He described plant life, from the cedar of Lebanon to the hyssop that grows out of walls. He also taught about animals and birds, reptiles and fish. **34**Men of all nations came to listen to Solomon's wisdom, sent by all the kings of the world, who had heard of his wisdom.   1Ki 3:12

Preparations for Building the Temple

5 When Hiram king of Tyre heard that Solomon had been anointed king to succeed his father David, he sent his envoys to Solomon, because he had always been on friendly terms with David. **2**Solomon sent back this message to Hiram:

3"You know that because of the wars waged against my father David from all sides, he could not build a temple for the Name of the LORD his God until the LORD put his enemies under his feet. **4**But now the LORD my God has given me rest on every side, and there is no adversary or disaster. **5**I intend, therefore, to build a temple for the Name of the LORD my God, as the LORD told my father David, when he said, 'Your son whom I will put on the throne in your place will build the temple for my Name.'   2Sa 7:13; 1Ch 17:12; 22:9

6"So give orders that cedars of Lebanon be cut for me. My men will work with yours, and I will pay you for your men whatever wages you set.

---

a 26 Some Septuagint manuscripts (see also 2 Chron. 9:25); Hebrew *forty*   *b 26* Or *charioteers*

You know that we have no one so skilled in felling timber as the Sidonians."

⁷When Hiram heard Solomon's message, he was greatly pleased and said, "Praise be to the LORD today, for he has given David a wise son to rule over this great nation."

⁸So Hiram sent word to Solomon:

"I have received the message you sent me and will do all you want in providing the cedar and pine logs. ⁹My men will haul them down from Lebanon to the sea, and I will float them in rafts by sea to the place you specify. There I will separate them and you can take them away. And you are to grant my wish by providing food for my royal household."   Ezr 3:7; Eze 27:17

¹⁰In this way Hiram kept Solomon supplied with all the cedar and pine logs he wanted, ¹¹and Solomon gave Hiram twenty thousand corsᵃ of wheat as food for his household, in addition to twenty thousand bathsᵇ,ᶜ of pressed olive oil. Solomon continued to do this for Hiram year after year. ¹²The LORD gave Solomon wisdom, just as he had promised him. There

were peaceful relations between Hiram and Solomon, and the two of them made a treaty.   1Ki 3:12

¹³King Solomon conscripted laborers from all Israel—thirty thousand men. ¹⁴He sent them off to Lebanon in shifts of ten thousand a month, so that they spent one month in Lebanon and two months at home. Adoniram was in charge of the forced labor. ¹⁵Solomon had seventy thousand carriers and eighty thousand stonecutters in the hills, ¹⁶as well as thirty-three hundredᵈ foremen who supervised the project and directed the workmen. ¹⁷At the king's command they removed from the quarry large blocks of quality stone to provide a foundation of dressed stone for the temple. ¹⁸The craftsmen of Solomon and Hiram and the men of Gebalᵉ cut and prepared the timber and stone for the building of the temple.   1Ki 4:6

Solomon Builds the Temple

6 In the four hundred and eight-iethᶠ year after the Israelites had come out of Egypt, in the fourth year of Solomon's reign over Israel, in the month of Ziv, the second month, he began to build the temple of the LORD.   Ac 7:47

²The temple that King Solomon built for the LORD was sixty cubits long, twenty wide and thirty

---

ᵃ 11 That is, probably about 125,000 bushels (about 4,400 kiloliters)   ᵇ 11 Septuagint (see also 2 Chron. 2:10); Hebrew twenty cors   ᶜ 11 That is, about 115,000 gallons (about 440 kiloliters)   ᵈ 16 Hebrew; some Septuagint manuscripts (see also 2 Chron. 2:2, 18) thirty-six hundred   ᵉ 18 That is, Byblos   ᶠ 1 Hebrew; Septuagint four hundred and fortieth

high.[a] [3]The portico at the front of the main hall of the temple extended the width of the temple, that is twenty cubits,[b] and projected ten cubits[c] from the front of the temple. [4]He made narrow clerestory windows in the temple. [5]Against the walls of the main hall and inner sanctuary he built a structure around the building, in which there were side rooms. [6]The lowest floor was five cubits[d] wide, the middle floor six cubits[e] and the third floor seven.[f] He made offset ledges around the outside of the temple so that nothing would be inserted into the temple walls.

[7]In building the temple, only blocks dressed at the quarry were used, and no hammer, chisel or any other iron tool was heard at the temple site while it was being built.   Ex 20:25; Dt 27:5

[8]The entrance to the lowest[g] floor was on the south side of the temple; a stairway led up to the middle level and from there to the third. [9]So he built the temple and completed it, roofing it with beams and cedar planks. [10]And he built the side rooms all along the temple. The height of each was five cubits, and they were attached to the temple by beams of cedar.

[11]The word of the Lord came to Solomon: [12]"As for this temple you are building, if you follow my decrees, carry out my regulations and keep all my commands and obey them, I will fulfill through you the promise I gave to David your father. [13]And I will live among the Israelites and will not abandon my people Israel."

[14]So Solomon built the temple and completed it. [15]He lined its interior walls with cedar boards, paneling them from the floor of the temple to the ceiling, and covered the floor of the temple with planks of pine. [16]He partitioned off twenty cubits[b] at the rear of the temple with cedar boards from floor to ceiling to form within the temple an inner sanctuary, the Most Holy Place. [17]The main hall in front of this room was forty cubits[h] long. [18]The inside of the temple was cedar, carved with gourds and open flowers. Everything was cedar; no stone was to be seen.   Ex 26:33

[19]He prepared the inner sanctuary within the temple to set the ark of the covenant of the Lord there. [20]The inner sanctuary was twenty cubits long, twenty wide and twenty high.[i] He overlaid the inside with pure gold, and he also overlaid the altar of cedar. [21]Solomon covered the inside of the temple with pure gold, and he extended gold chains across the front of the

---

[a]2 That is, about 90 feet (about 27 meters) long and 30 feet (about 9 meters) wide and 45 feet (about 13.5 meters) high   [b]3,16 That is, about 30 feet (about 9 meters)   [c]3 That is, about 15 feet (about 4.5 meters)   [d]6 That is, about 7 1/2 feet (about 2.3 meters); also in verses 10 and 24   [e]6 That is, about 9 feet (about 2.7 meters)   [f]6 That is, about 10 1/2 feet (about 3.1 meters)   [g]8 Septuagint; Hebrew middle   [h]17 That is, about 60 feet (about 18 meters)   [i]20 That is, about 30 feet (about 9 meters) long, wide and high

inner sanctuary, which was overlaid with gold. ²²So he overlaid the whole interior with gold. He also overlaid with gold the altar that belonged to the inner sanctuary.

²³In the inner sanctuary he made a pair of cherubim of olive wood, each ten cubits*a* high. ²⁴One wing of the first cherub was five cubits long, and the other wing five cubits—ten cubits from wing tip to wing tip. ²⁵The second cherub also measured ten cubits, for the two cherubim were identical in size and shape. ²⁶The height of each cherub was ten cubits. ²⁷He placed the cherubim inside the innermost room of the temple, with their wings spread out. The wing of one cherub touched one wall, while the wing of the other touched the other wall, and their wings touched each other in the middle of the room. ²⁸He overlaid the cherubim with gold.   Ex 25:20

²⁹On the walls all around the temple, in both the inner and outer rooms, he carved cherubim, palm trees and open flowers. ³⁰He also covered the floors of both the inner and outer rooms of the temple with gold.   2Ch 3:1-14

³¹For the entrance of the inner sanctuary he made doors of olive wood with five-sided jambs. ³²And on the two olive wood doors he carved cherubim, palm trees and open flowers, and overlaid the cherubim and palm trees with beaten gold. ³³In the same way he made four-sided jambs of olive wood for the entrance to the main hall. ³⁴He also made two pine doors, each having two leaves that turned in sockets. ³⁵He carved cherubim, palm trees and open flowers on them and overlaid them with gold hammered evenly over the carvings.

³⁶And he built the inner courtyard of three courses of dressed stone and one course of trimmed cedar beams.   1Ki 7:12; Ezr 6:4

³⁷The foundation of the temple of the LORD was laid in the fourth year, in the month of Ziv. ³⁸In the eleventh year in the month of Bul, the eighth month, the temple was finished in all its details according to its specifications. He had spent seven years building it.   Heb 8:5

Solomon Builds His Palace

7 It took Solomon thirteen years, however, to complete the construction of his palace. ²He built the Palace of the Forest of Lebanon a hundred cubits long, fifty wide and thirty high,*b* with four rows of cedar columns supporting trimmed cedar beams. ³It was roofed with cedar above the beams that rested on the columns —forty-five beams, fifteen to a row. ⁴Its windows were placed high in sets of three, facing each

a 23 That is, about 15 feet (about 4.5 meters)   *b 2* That is, about 150 feet (about 46 meters) long, 75 feet (about 23 meters) wide and 45 feet (about 13.5 meters) high

other. **5**All the doorways had rectangular frames; they were in the front part in sets of three, facing each other.*a*   1Ki 9:10; 10:17; 2Ch 8:1

6He made a colonnade fifty cubits long and thirty wide.*b* In front of it was a portico, and in front of that were pillars and an overhanging roof.

7He built the throne hall, the Hall of Justice, where he was to judge, and he covered it with cedar from floor to ceiling.*c* **8**And the palace in which he was to live, set farther back, was similar in design. Solomon also made a palace like this hall for Pharaoh's daughter, whom he had married.   1Ki 3:1; 6:15

9All these structures, from the outside to the great courtyard and from foundation to eaves, were made of blocks of high-grade stone cut to size and trimmed with a saw on their inner and outer faces. **10**The foundations were laid with large stones of good quality, some measuring ten cubits*d* and some eight.*e* **11**Above were high-grade stones, cut to size, and cedar beams. **12**The great courtyard was surrounded by a wall of three courses of dressed stone and one course of trimmed cedar beams, as was the inner courtyard of the temple of the LORD with its portico.

The Temple's Furnishings

13King Solomon sent to Tyre and brought Huram,*f* **14**whose mother was a widow from the tribe of Naphtali and whose father was a man of Tyre and a craftsman in bronze. Huram was highly skilled and experienced in all kinds of bronze work. He came to King Solomon and did all the work assigned to him.   Ex 31:2-5; 2Ch 2:14

15He cast two bronze pillars, each eighteen cubits high and twelve cubits around,*g* by line. **16**He also made two capitals of cast bronze to set on the tops of the pillars; each capital was five cubits*h* high. **17**A network of interwoven chains festooned the capitals on top of the pillars, seven for each capital. **18**He made pomegranates in two rows*i* encircling each network to decorate the capitals on top of the pillars.*j* He did the same for each capital. **19**The capitals on top of the pillars in the portico were in the shape of lilies, four cubits*k* high. **20**On the capitals of both pillars, above the bowl-shaped part next to the network, were the two hundred pomegranates in rows all around. **21**He erected the pillars at the portico of the temple. The pillar to the south he

---

a5 The meaning of the Hebrew for this verse is uncertain.   *b6* That is, about 75 feet (about 23 meters) long and 45 feet (about 13.5 meters) wide   *c7* Vulgate and Syriac; Hebrew *floor*   *d10* That is, about 15 feet (about 4.5 meters)   *e10* That is, about 12 feet (about 3.6 meters)   *f13* Hebrew *Hiram*, a variant of *Huram*; also in verses 40 and 45   *g15* That is, about 27 feet (about 8.1 meters) high and 18 feet (about 5.4 meters) around   *h16* That is, about 7 1/2 feet (about 2.3 meters); also in verse 23   *i18* Two Hebrew manuscripts and Septuagint; most Hebrew manuscripts *made the pillars, and there were two rows*   *j18* Many Hebrew manuscripts and Syriac; most Hebrew manuscripts *pomegranates*   *k19* That is, about 6 feet (about 1.8 meters); also in verse 38

named Jakin[a] and the one to the north Boaz.[b] [22]The capitals on top were in the shape of lilies. And so the work on the pillars was completed. 2Ki 25:17; 2Ch 3:16-17; 4:13

[23]He made the Sea of cast metal, circular in shape, measuring ten cubits[c] from rim to rim and five cubits high. It took a line of thirty cubits[d] to measure around it. [24]Below the rim, gourds encircled it — ten to a cubit. The gourds were cast in two rows in one piece with the Sea. 2Ki 25:13; 1Ch 18:8; Jer 52:17

[25]The Sea stood on twelve bulls, three facing north, three facing west, three facing south and three facing east. The Sea rested on top of them, and their hindquarters were toward the center. [26]It was a handbreadth[e] in thickness, and its rim was like the rim of a cup, like a lily blossom. It held two thousand baths.[f] 2Ch 4:2-5; Jer 52:20

[27]He also made ten movable stands of bronze; each was four cubits long, four wide and three high.[g] [28]This is how the stands were made: They had side panels attached to uprights. [29]On the panels between the uprights were lions, bulls and cherubim — and on the uprights as well. Above and below the lions and bulls were wreaths of hammered work.

[30]Each stand had four bronze wheels with bronze axles, and each had a basin resting on four supports, cast with wreaths on each side. [31]On the inside of the stand there was an opening that had a circular frame one cubit[h] deep. This opening was round, and with its basework it measured a cubit and a half.[i] Around its opening there was engraving. The panels of the stands were square, not round. [32]The four wheels were under the panels, and the axles of the wheels were attached to the stand. The diameter of each wheel was a cubit and a half. [33]The wheels were made like chariot wheels; the axles, rims, spokes and hubs were all of cast metal.

[34]Each stand had four handles, one on each corner, projecting from the stand. [35]At the top of the stand there was a circular band half a cubit[j] deep. The supports and panels were attached to the top of the stand. [36]He engraved cherubim, lions and palm trees on the surfaces of the supports and on the panels, in every available space, with wreaths all around. [37]This is the way he made the ten stands. They were all cast in the same molds and were identical in size and shape.

---

a21 Jakin probably means he establishes.   b21 Boaz probably means in him is strength.   c23 That is, about 15 feet (about 4.5 meters)   d23 That is, about 45 feet (about 13.5 meters)   e26 That is, about 3 inches (about 8 centimeters)   f26 That is, probably about 11,500 gallons (about 44 kiloliters); the Septuagint does not have this sentence.   g27 That is, about 6 feet (about 1.8 meters) long and wide and about 4 1/2 feet (about 1.3 meters) high   h31 That is, about 1 1/2 feet (about 0.5 meter)   i31 That is, about 2 1/4 feet (about 0.7 meter); also in verse 32   j35 That is, about 3/4 foot (about 0.2 meter)

38He then made ten bronze basins, each holding forty baths*a* and measuring four cubits across, one basin to go on each of the ten stands. **39**He placed five of the stands on the south side of the temple and five on the north. He placed the Sea on the south side, at the southeast corner of the temple. **40**He also made the basins and shovels and sprinkling bowls.

So Huram finished all the work he had undertaken for King Solomon in the temple of the LORD:

41the two pillars;

the two bowl-shaped capitals on top of the pillars;

the two sets of network decorating the two bowl-shaped capitals on top of the pillars;

42the four hundred pomegranates for the two sets of network (two rows of pomegranates for each network, decorating the bowl-shaped capitals on top of the pillars); ver 20

43the ten stands with their ten basins;

44the Sea and the twelve bulls under it;

45the pots, shovels and sprinkling bowls. Ex 27:3

All these objects that Huram made for King Solomon for the temple of the LORD were of burnished bronze. **46**The king had them cast in clay molds in the plain of the Jordan between Succoth and Zarethan. **47**Solomon left all these things unweighed, because there were so many; the weight of the bronze was not determined. 1Ch 22:3

48Solomon also made all the furnishings that were in the LORD's temple:

the golden altar;

the golden table on which was the bread of the Presence;

49the lampstands of pure gold (five on the right and five on the left, in front of the inner sanctuary); Ex 25:31-38

the gold floral work and lamps and tongs;

50the pure gold basins, wick trimmers, sprinkling bowls, dishes and censers;

and the gold sockets for the doors of the innermost room, the Most Holy Place, and also for the doors of the main hall of the temple.

51When all the work King Solomon had done for the temple of the LORD was finished, he brought in the things his father David had dedicated—the silver and gold and the furnishings—and he placed them in the treasuries of the LORD's temple. 2Ch 4:6, 10-5:1; 2Sa 8:11

---

a 38 That is, about 230 gallons (about 880 liters)

The Ark Brought to the Temple

8 Then King Solomon summoned into his presence at Jerusalem the elders of Israel, all the heads of the tribes and the chiefs of the Israelite families, to bring up the ark of the LORD's covenant from Zion, the City of David. ²All the men of Israel came together to King Solomon at the time of the festival in the month of Ethanim, the seventh month.   Lev 23:34; 2Sa 5:7

³When all the elders of Israel had arrived, the priests took up the ark, ⁴and they brought up the ark of the LORD and the Tent of Meeting and all the sacred furnishings in it. The priests and Levites carried them up, ⁵and King Solomon and the entire assembly of Israel that had gathered about him were before the ark, sacrificing so many sheep and cattle that they could not be recorded or counted.

⁶The priests then brought the ark of the LORD's covenant to its place in the inner sanctuary of the temple, the Most Holy Place, and put it beneath the wings of the cherubim. ⁷The cherubim spread their wings over the place of the ark and overshadowed the ark and its carrying poles. ⁸These poles were so long that their ends could be seen from the Holy Place in front of the inner sanctuary, but not from outside the Holy Place; and they are still there today. ⁹There was nothing in the ark except the two stone tablets that Moses had placed in it at Horeb, where the LORD made a covenant with the Israelites after they came out of Egypt.   Ex 25:13-15,21; Dt 10:2-5

¹⁰When the priests withdrew from the Holy Place, the cloud filled the temple of the LORD. ¹¹And the priests could not perform their service because of the cloud, for the glory of the LORD filled his temple.   Ex 40:34-35

¹²Then Solomon said, "The LORD has said that he would dwell in a dark cloud; ¹³I have indeed built a magnificent temple for you, a place for you to dwell forever."

¹⁴While the whole assembly of Israel was standing there, the king turned around and blessed them. ¹⁵Then he said:

"Praise be to the LORD, the God of Israel, who with his own hand has fulfilled what he promised with his own mouth to my father David. For he said, ¹⁶'Since the day I brought my people Israel out of Egypt, I have not chosen a city in any tribe of Israel to have a temple built for my Name to be there, but I have chosen David to rule my people Israel.'   1Sa 16:1; Lk 1:68

¹⁷"My father David had it in his heart to build a temple for the Name of the LORD, the God of Israel. ¹⁸But the LORD said to my father David, 'Because it was in your heart to build a temple for my Name, you did

well to have this in your heart. ¹⁹Nevertheless, you are not the one to build the temple, but your son, who is your own flesh and blood—he is the one who will build the temple for my Name.'

²⁰"The LORD has kept the promise he made: I have succeeded David my father and now I sit on the throne of Israel, just as the LORD promised, and I have built the temple for the Name of the LORD, the God of Israel. ²¹I have provided a place there for the ark, in which is the covenant of the LORD that he made with our fathers when he brought them out of Egypt." 1Ch 28:6

Solomon's Prayer of Dedication

²²Then Solomon stood before the altar of the LORD in front of the whole assembly of Israel, spread out his hands toward heaven ²³and said:

"O LORD, God of Israel, there is no God like you in heaven above or on earth below—you who keep your covenant of love with your servants who continue wholeheartedly in your way. ²⁴You have kept your promise to your servant David my father; with your mouth you have promised and with your hand

you have fulfilled it—as it is today. Dt 7:9,12; Ne 1:5; 9:32

²⁵"Now LORD, God of Israel, keep for your servant David my father the promises you made to him when you said, 'You shall never fail to have a man to sit before me on the throne of Israel, if only your sons are careful in all they do to walk before me as you have done.' ²⁶And now, O God of Israel, let your word that you promised your servant David my father come true. 2Sa 7:25

²⁷"But will God really dwell on earth? The heavens, even the highest heaven, cannot contain you. How much less this temple I have built! ²⁸Yet give attention to your servant's prayer and his plea for mercy, O LORD my God. Hear the cry and the prayer that your servant is praying in your presence this day. ²⁹May your eyes be open toward this temple night and day, this place of which you said, 'My Name shall be there,' so that you will hear the prayer your servant prays toward this place. ³⁰Hear the supplication of your servant and of your people Israel when they pray toward this place. Hear from heaven, your dwelling place, and when you hear, forgive.

³¹"When a man wrongs his neighbor and is required to take an oath and he comes

and swears the oath before your altar in this temple, [32]then hear from heaven and act. Judge between your servants, condemning the guilty and bringing down on his own head what he has done. Declare the innocent not guilty, and so establish his innocence.   Ex 22:11; Dt 25:1

[33]"When your people Israel have been defeated by an enemy because they have sinned against you, and when they turn back to you and confess your name, praying and making supplication to you in this temple, [34]then hear from heaven and forgive the sin of your people Israel and bring them back to the land you gave to their fathers.   Lev 26:17

[35]"When the heavens are shut up and there is no rain because your people have sinned against you, and when they pray toward this place and confess your name and turn from their sin because you have afflicted them, [36]then hear from heaven and forgive the sin of your servants, your people Israel. Teach them the right way to live, and send rain on the land you gave your people for an inheritance.   Lev 26:19; 1Sa 12:23

[37]"When famine or plague comes to the land, or blight or mildew, locusts or grasshoppers, or when an enemy besieges them in any of their cities, whatever disaster or disease may come, [38]and when a prayer or plea is made by any of your people Israel—each one aware of the afflictions of his own heart, and spreading out his hands toward this temple— [39]then hear from heaven, your dwelling place. Forgive and act; deal with each man according to all he does, since you know his heart (for you alone know the hearts of all men), [40]so that they will fear you all the time they live in the land you gave our fathers.   1Sa 16:7; 1Ch 28:9

[41]"As for the foreigner who does not belong to your people Israel but has come from a distant land because of your name— [42]for men will hear of your great name and your mighty hand and your outstretched arm—when he comes and prays toward this temple, [43]then hear from heaven, your dwelling place, and do whatever the foreigner asks of you, so that all the peoples of the earth may know your name and fear you, as do your own people Israel, and may know that this house I have built bears your Name.   Dt 3:24; 1Sa 17:46; Ps 102:15

[44]"When your people go to war against their enemies, wherever you send them, and when they pray to the LORD

toward the city you have chosen and the temple I have built for your Name, ⁴⁵then hear from heaven their prayer and their plea, and uphold their cause. Ps 9:4; 140:12

⁴⁶"When they sin against you—for there is no one who does not sin—and you become angry with them and give them over to the enemy, who takes them captive to his own land, far away or near; ⁴⁷and if they have a change of heart in the land where they are held captive, and repent and plead with you in the land of their conquerors and say, 'We have sinned, we have done wrong, we have acted wickedly'; ⁴⁸and if they turn back to you with all their heart and soul in the land of their enemies who took them captive, and pray to you toward the land you gave their fathers, toward the city you have chosen and the temple I have built for your Name; ⁴⁹then from heaven, your dwelling place, hear their prayer and their plea, and uphold their cause. ⁵⁰And forgive your people, who have sinned against you; forgive all the offenses they have committed against you, and cause their conquerors to show them mercy; ⁵¹for they are your people and your inheritance, whom you brought out of Egypt, out of that iron-smelting furnace. Dt 9:29

⁵²"May your eyes be open to your servant's plea and to the plea of your people Israel, and may you listen to them whenever they cry out to you. ⁵³For you singled them out from all the nations of the world to be your own inheritance, just as you declared through your servant Moses when you, O Sovereign Lord, brought our fathers out of Egypt." 2Ch 6:12-40; Ex 19:5

⁵⁴When Solomon had finished all these prayers and supplications to the Lord, he rose from before the altar of the Lord, where he had been kneeling with his hands spread out toward heaven. ⁵⁵He stood and blessed the whole assembly of Israel in a loud voice, saying:

⁵⁶"Praise be to the Lord, who has given rest to his people Israel just as he promised. Not one word has failed of all the good promises he gave through his servant Moses. ⁵⁷May the Lord our God be with us as he was with our fathers; may he never leave us nor forsake us. ⁵⁸May he turn our hearts to him, to walk in all his ways and to keep the commands, decrees and regulations he gave our fathers. ⁵⁹And may these words of mine, which I have prayed be-

fore the Lord, be near to the Lord our God day and night, that he may uphold the cause of his servant and the cause of his people Israel according to each day's need, **60**so that all the peoples of the earth may know that the Lord is God and that there is no other. **61**But your hearts must be fully committed to the Lord our God, to live by his decrees and obey his commands, as at this time." 1Ki 11:4; Ps 119:36; Heb 13:5

The Dedication of the Temple

62Then the king and all Israel with him offered sacrifices before the Lord. **63**Solomon offered a sacrifice of fellowship offerings*a* to the Lord: twenty-two thousand cattle and a hundred and twenty thousand sheep and goats. So the king and all the Israelites dedicated the temple of the Lord.

64On that same day the king consecrated the middle part of the courtyard in front of the temple of the Lord, and there he offered burnt offerings, grain offerings and the fat of the fellowship offerings, because the bronze altar before the Lord was too small to hold the burnt offerings, the grain offerings and the fat of the fellowship offerings. 2Ch 4:1

65So Solomon observed the festival at that time, and all Israel with him—a vast assembly, people from Lebo*b* Hamath to the Wadi of Egypt. They celebrated it before the Lord our God for seven days and seven days more, fourteen days in all. **66**On the following day he sent the people away. They blessed the king and then went home, joyful and glad in heart for all the good things the Lord had done for his servant David and his people Israel. 2Ch 7:1-10; Ge 15:18

The Lord Appears to Solomon

9 When Solomon had finished building the temple of the Lord and the royal palace, and had achieved all he had desired to do, **2**the Lord appeared to him a second time, as he had appeared to him at Gibeon. **3**The Lord said to him:

"I have heard the prayer and plea you have made before me; I have consecrated this temple, which you have built, by putting my Name there forever. My eyes and my heart will always be there.

4"As for you, if you walk before me in integrity of heart and uprightness, as David your father did, and do all I command and observe my decrees and laws, **5**I will establish your royal throne over Israel forever, as I promised David your father when I said, 'You shall never fail to have

a63 Traditionally *peace offerings*; also in verse 64   *b65* Or *from the entrance to*

a man on the throne of Israel.'

6"But if you[a] or your sons turn away from me and do not observe the commands and decrees I have given you[a] and go off to serve other gods and worship them, 7then I will cut off Israel from the land I have given them and will reject this temple I have consecrated for my Name. Israel will then become a byword and an object of ridicule among all peoples. 8And though this temple is now imposing, all who pass by will be appalled and will scoff and say, 'Why has the LORD done such a thing to this land and to this temple?' 9People will answer, 'Because they have forsaken the LORD their God, who brought their fathers out of Egypt, and have embraced other gods, worshiping and serving them—that is why the LORD brought all this disaster on them.' "

Solomon's Other Activities

10At the end of twenty years, during which Solomon built these two buildings—the temple of the LORD and the royal palace— 11King Solomon gave twenty towns in Galilee to Hiram king of Tyre, because Hiram had supplied him with all the cedar and pine and gold he wanted. 12But when Hiram went from Tyre to see the towns that Solomon had given him, he was not pleased with them. 13"What kind of towns are these you have given me, my brother?" he asked. And he called them the Land of Cabul,[b] a name they have to this day. 14Now Hiram had sent to the king 120 talents[c] of gold.

15Here is the account of the forced labor King Solomon conscripted to build the LORD's temple, his own palace, the supporting terraces,[d] the wall of Jerusalem, and Hazor, Megiddo and Gezer. 16(Pharaoh king of Egypt had attacked and captured Gezer. He had set it on fire. He killed its Canaanite inhabitants and then gave it as a wedding gift to his daughter, Solomon's wife. 17And Solomon rebuilt Gezer.) He built up Lower Beth Horon, 18Baalath, and Tadmor[e] in the desert, within his land, 19as well as all his store cities and the towns for his chariots and for his horses[f]—whatever he desired to build in Jerusalem, in Lebanon and throughout all the territory he ruled.   2Sa 5:9; 1Ki 4:26; 5:13

20All the people left from the Amorites, Hittites, Perizzites, Hivites and Jebusites (these peoples were not Israelites), 21that is, their

---

[a]6 The Hebrew is plural.   [b]13 Cabul sounds like the Hebrew for good-for-nothing.   [c]14 That is, about 4 1/2 tons (about 4 metric tons)   [d]15 Or the Millo; also in verse 24   [e]18 The Hebrew may also be read Tamar.   [f]19 Or charioteers

descendants remaining in the land, whom the Israelites could not exterminate[a]—these Solomon conscripted for his slave labor force, as it is to this day. 22But Solomon did not make slaves of any of the Israelites; they were his fighting men, his government officials, his officers, his captains, and the commanders of his chariots and charioteers. 23They were also the chief officials in charge of Solomon's projects—550 officials supervising the men who did the work.   Lev 25:39; Jos 15:63; Ezr 2:55,58

24After Pharaoh's daughter had come up from the City of David to the palace Solomon had built for her, he constructed the supporting terraces.   1Ki 3:1; 11:27; 2Ch 32:5

25Three times a year Solomon sacrificed burnt offerings and fellowship offerings[b] on the altar he had built for the Lord, burning incense before the Lord along with them, and so fulfilled the temple obligations.   Ex 23:14; 2Ch 8:12-13,16

26King Solomon also built ships at Ezion Geber, which is near Elath in Edom, on the shore of the Red Sea.[c] 27And Hiram sent his men—sailors who knew the sea—to serve in the fleet with Solomon's men. 28They sailed to Ophir and brought back 420 talents[d] of gold, which they delivered to King Solomon.   Nu 33:35; 1Ki 10:11; 22:48

The Queen of Sheba Visits Solomon

10 When the queen of Sheba heard about the fame of Solomon and his relation to the name of the Lord, she came to test him with hard questions. 2Arriving at Jerusalem with a very great caravan—with camels carrying spices, large quantities of gold, and precious stones—she came to Solomon and talked with him about all that she had on her mind. 3Solomon answered all her questions; nothing was too hard for the king to explain to her. 4When the queen of Sheba saw all the wisdom of Solomon and the palace he had built, 5the food on his table, the seating of his officials, the attending servants in their robes, his cupbearers, and the burnt offerings he made at[e] the temple of the Lord, she was overwhelmed.   Mt 12:42

6She said to the king, "The report I heard in my own country about your achievements and your wisdom is true. 7But I did not believe these things until I came and saw with my own eyes. Indeed, not even half was told me; in wisdom and wealth you have far exceeded the report I heard. 8How happy your men must be! How happy your officials, who continually stand before you and hear your wisdom! 9Praise be to the Lord

---

[a]21 The Hebrew term refers to the irrevocable giving over of things or persons to the Lord, often by totally destroying them.   [b]25 Traditionally *peace offerings*   [c]26 Hebrew *Yam Suph*; that is, Sea of Reeds   [d]28 That is, about 16 tons (about 14.5 metric tons)   [e]5 Or *the ascent by which he went up to*

your God, who has delighted in you and placed you on the throne of Israel. Because of the LORD's eternal love for Israel, he has made you king, to maintain justice and righteousness." 2Sa 8:15; Ps 72:2; Pr 8:34

¹⁰And she gave the king 120 talents[a] of gold, large quantities of spices, and precious stones. Never again were so many spices brought in as those the queen of Sheba gave to King Solomon.

¹¹(Hiram's ships brought gold from Ophir; and from there they brought great cargoes of almugwood[b] and precious stones. ¹²The king used the almugwood to make supports for the temple of the LORD and for the royal palace, and to make harps and lyres for the musicians. So much almugwood has never been imported or seen since that day.) 1Ki 9:27-28

¹³King Solomon gave the queen of Sheba all she desired and asked for, besides what he had given her out of his royal bounty. Then she left and returned with her retinue to her own country. 2Ch 9:1-12

Solomon's Splendor

¹⁴The weight of the gold that Solomon received yearly was 666 talents,[c] ¹⁵not including the revenues from merchants and traders and from all the Arabian kings and the governors of the land. 1Ki 9:28

¹⁶King Solomon made two hundred large shields of hammered gold; six hundred bekas[d] of gold went into each shield. ¹⁷He also made three hundred small shields of hammered gold, with three minas[e] of gold in each shield. The king put them in the Palace of the Forest of Lebanon. 1Ki 7:2; 14:26-28

¹⁸Then the king made a great throne inlaid with ivory and overlaid with fine gold. ¹⁹The throne had six steps, and its back had a rounded top. On both sides of the seat were armrests, with a lion standing beside each of them. ²⁰Twelve lions stood on the six steps, one at either end of each step. Nothing like it had ever been made for any other kingdom. ²¹All King Solomon's goblets were gold, and all the household articles in the Palace of the Forest of Lebanon were pure gold. Nothing was made of silver, because silver was considered of little value in Solomon's days. ²²The king had a fleet of trading ships[f] at sea along with the ships of Hiram. Once every three years it returned, carrying gold, silver and ivory, and apes and baboons. 1Ki 9:26; Isa 60:17

²³King Solomon was greater in riches and wisdom than all the other kings of the earth. ²⁴The whole world sought audience with Solomon to hear the wisdom God

---

a 10 That is, about 4 1/2 tons (about 4 metric tons)   b 11 Probably a variant of algumwood; also in verse 12   c 14 That is, about 25 tons (about 23 metric tons)   d 16 That is, about 7 1/2 pounds (about 3.5 kilograms)   e 17 That is, about 3 3/4 pounds (about 1.7 kilograms)   f 22 Hebrew of ships of Tarshish

had put in his heart. 25Year after year, everyone who came brought a gift—articles of silver and gold, robes, weapons and spices, and horses and mules.   1Ki 3:13; 4:30

26Solomon accumulated chariots and horses; he had fourteen hundred chariots and twelve thousand horses,ᵃ which he kept in the chariot cities and also with him in Jerusalem. 27The king made silver as common in Jerusalem as stones, and cedar as plentiful as sycamore-fig trees in the foothills. 28Solomon's horses were imported from Egyptᵇ and from Kueᶜ—the royal merchants purchased them from Kue. 29They imported a chariot from Egypt for six hundred shekelsᵈ of silver, and a horse for a hundred and fifty.ᵉ They also exported them to all the kings of the Hittites and of the Arameans.

Solomon's Wives

11 King Solomon, however, loved many foreign women besides Pharaoh's daughter—Moabites, Ammonites, Edomites, Sidonians and Hittites. 2They were from nations about which the Lord had told the Israelites, "You must not intermarry with them, because they will surely turn your hearts after their gods." Nevertheless, Solomon held fast to them in love. 3He had seven hundred wives of royal birth and three hundred concubines, and his wives led him astray. 4As Solomon grew old, his wives turned his heart after other gods, and his heart was not fully devoted to the Lord his God, as the heart of David his father had been. 5He followed Ashtoreth the goddess of the Sidonians, and Molechᶠ the detestable god of the Ammonites. 6So Solomon did evil in the eyes of the Lord; he did not follow the Lord completely, as David his father had done.   Ne 13:26

7On a hill east of Jerusalem, Solomon built a high place for Chemosh the detestable god of Moab, and for Molech the detestable god of the Ammonites. 8He did the same for all his foreign wives, who burned incense and offered sacrifices to their gods.   Nu 21:29; Jdg 11:24

9The Lord became angry with Solomon because his heart had turned away from the Lord, the God of Israel, who had appeared to him twice. 10Although he had forbidden Solomon to follow other gods, Solomon did not keep the Lord's command. 11So the Lord said to Solomon, "Since this is your attitude and you have not kept my covenant and my decrees, which I commanded you, I will most certainly tear the kingdom away from you and give it to one of your subordinates. 12Nevertheless, for the sake of David your father, I will not do it during your

ᵃ26 Or charioteers   ᵇ28 Or possibly Muzur, a region in Cilicia; also in verse 29   ᶜ28 Probably Cilicia
ᵈ29 That is, about 15 pounds (about 7 kilograms)   ᵉ29 That is, about 3 3/4 pounds (about 1.7 kilograms)   ᶠ5 Hebrew Milcom; also in verse 33

lifetime. I will tear it out of the hand of your son. **13**Yet I will not tear the whole kingdom from him, but will give him one tribe for the sake of David my servant and for the sake of Jerusalem, which I have chosen." 2Sa 7:15; 1Ki 12:15-16

Solomon's Adversaries

14Then the LORD raised up against Solomon an adversary, Hadad the Edomite, from the royal line of Edom. **15**Earlier when David was fighting with Edom, Joab the commander of the army, who had gone up to bury the dead, had struck down all the men in Edom. **16**Joab and all the Israelites stayed there for six months, until they had destroyed all the men in Edom. **17**But Hadad, still only a boy, fled to Egypt with some Edomite officials who had served his father. **18**They set out from Midian and went to Paran. Then taking men from Paran with them, they went to Egypt, to Pharaoh king of Egypt, who gave Hadad a house and land and provided him with food. 2Sa 8:14; 1Ch 18:12

19Pharaoh was so pleased with Hadad that he gave him a sister of his own wife, Queen Tahpenes, in marriage. **20**The sister of Tahpenes bore him a son named Genubath, whom Tahpenes brought up in the royal palace. There Genubath lived with Pharaoh's own children.

21While he was in Egypt, Hadad heard that David rested with his fathers and that Joab the commander of the army was also dead. Then Hadad said to Pharaoh, "Let me go, that I may return to my own country."

22"What have you lacked here that you want to go back to your own country?" Pharaoh asked.

"Nothing," Hadad replied, "but do let me go!"

23And God raised up against Solomon another adversary, Rezon son of Eliada, who had fled from his master, Hadadezer king of Zobah. **24**He gathered men around him and became the leader of a band of rebels when David destroyed the forces[a] ˌof Zobahˌ; the rebels went to Damascus, where they settled and took control. **25**Rezon was Israel's adversary as long as Solomon lived, adding to the trouble caused by Hadad. So Rezon ruled in Aram and was hostile toward Israel. 2Sa 8:3; 10:8,18-19

Jeroboam Rebels Against Solomon

26Also, Jeroboam son of Nebat rebelled against the king. He was one of Solomon's officials, an Ephraimite from Zeredah, and his mother was a widow named Zeruah. 2Sa 20:21; 1Ki 12:2; 2Ch 13:6

27Here is the account of how he rebelled against the king: Solomon had built the supporting terraces[b] and had filled in the gap in the wall

---

a24 Hebrew *destroyed them*   b27 Or *the Millo*

of the city of David his father. ²⁸Now Jeroboam was a man of standing, and when Solomon saw how well the young man did his work, he put him in charge of the whole labor force of the house of Joseph. Ru 2:1; 1Ki 9:24; Pr 22:29

²⁹About that time Jeroboam was going out of Jerusalem, and Ahijah the prophet of Shiloh met him on the way, wearing a new cloak. The two of them were alone out in the country, ³⁰and Ahijah took hold of the new cloak he was wearing and tore it into twelve pieces. ³¹Then he said to Jeroboam, "Take ten pieces for yourself, for this is what the Lᴏʀᴅ, the God of Israel, says: 'See, I am going to tear the kingdom out of Solomon's hand and give you ten tribes. ³²But for the sake of my servant David and the city of Jerusalem, which I have chosen out of all the tribes of Israel, he will have one tribe. ³³I will do this because they have*ᵃ* forsaken me and worshiped Ashtoreth the goddess of the Sidonians, Chemosh the god of the Moabites, and Molech the god of the Ammonites, and have not walked in my ways, nor done what is right in my eyes, nor kept my statutes and laws as David, Solomon's father, did.

³⁴" 'But I will not take the whole kingdom out of Solomon's hand; I have made him ruler all the days of his life for the sake of David my servant, whom I chose and who observed my commands and statutes. ³⁵I will take the kingdom from his son's hands and give you ten tribes. ³⁶I will give one tribe to his son so that David my servant may always have a lamp before me in Jerusalem, the city where I chose to put my Name. ³⁷However, as for you, I will take you, and you will rule over all that your heart desires; you will be king over Israel. ³⁸If you do whatever I command you and walk in my ways and do what is right in my eyes by keeping my statutes and commands, as David my servant did, I will be with you. I will build you a dynasty as enduring as the one I built for David and will give Israel to you. ³⁹I will humble David's descendants because of this, but not forever.' " Jos 1:5; 2Sa 7:11,27

⁴⁰Solomon tried to kill Jeroboam, but Jeroboam fled to Egypt, to Shishak the king, and stayed there until Solomon's death. 2Ch 12:2

Solomon's Death

⁴¹As for the other events of Solomon's reign—all he did and the wisdom he displayed—are they not written in the book of the annals of Solomon? ⁴²Solomon reigned in Jerusalem over all Israel forty years. ⁴³Then he rested with his fathers and was buried in the city of David his father. And Rehoboam his son succeeded him as king. 2Ch 9:29-31; Mt 1:7

ᵃ33 Hebrew; Septuagint, Vulgate and Syriac *because he has*

Israel Rebels Against Rehoboam

12 Rehoboam went to Shechem, for all the Israelites had gone there to make him king. ²When Jeroboam son of Nebat heard this (he was still in Egypt, where he had fled from King Solomon), he returned from*a* Egypt. ³So they sent for Jeroboam, and he and the whole assembly of Israel went to Rehoboam and said to him: ⁴"Your father put a heavy yoke on us, but now lighten the harsh labor and the heavy yoke he put on us, and we will serve you."

⁵Rehoboam answered, "Go away for three days and then come back to me." So the people went away.

⁶Then King Rehoboam consulted the elders who had served his father Solomon during his lifetime. "How would you advise me to answer these people?" he asked.

⁷They replied, "If today you will be a servant to these people and serve them and give them a favorable answer, they will always be your servants." **Pr 15:1**

⁸But Rehoboam rejected the advice the elders gave him and consulted the young men who had grown up with him and were serving him. ⁹He asked them, "What is your advice? How should we answer these people who say to me, 'Lighten the yoke your father put on us'?"

¹⁰The young men who had grown up with him replied, "Tell these people who have said to you, 'Your father put a heavy yoke on us, but make our yoke lighter'— tell them, 'My little finger is thicker than my father's waist. ¹¹My father laid on you a heavy yoke; I will make it even heavier. My father scourged you with whips; I will scourge you with scorpions.'"

¹²Three days later Jeroboam and all the people returned to Rehoboam, as the king had said, "Come back to me in three days." ¹³The king answered the people harshly. Rejecting the advice given him by the elders, ¹⁴he followed the advice of the young men and said, "My father made your yoke heavy; I will make it even heavier. My father scourged you with whips; I will scourge you with scorpions." ¹⁵So the king did not listen to the people, for this turn of events was from the LORD, to fulfill the word the LORD had spoken to Jeroboam son of Nebat through Ahijah the Shilonite. **Dt 2:30; 1Ki 11:29; 2Ch 25:20**

¹⁶When all Israel saw that the king refused to listen to them, they answered the king:

"What share do we have in
    David,
what part in Jesse's son?
To your tents, O Israel! **2Sa 20:1**

---

a2 Or he remained in

Look after your own house,
     O David!"

So the Israelites went home. ¹⁷But as for the Israelites who were living in the towns of Judah, Rehoboam still ruled over them.

¹⁸King Rehoboam sent out Adoniram,ᵃ who was in charge of forced labor, but all Israel stoned him to death. King Rehoboam, however, managed to get into his chariot and escape to Jerusalem. ¹⁹So Israel has been in rebellion against the house of David to this day.   1Ki 4:6; 5:14; 2Ki 17:21

²⁰When all the Israelites heard that Jeroboam had returned, they sent and called him to the assembly and made him king over all Israel. Only the tribe of Judah remained loyal to the house of David.   1Ki 11:13,32

²¹When Rehoboam arrived in Jerusalem, he mustered the whole house of Judah and the tribe of Benjamin—a hundred and eighty thousand fighting men—to make war against the house of Israel and to regain the kingdom for Rehoboam son of Solomon.   2Ch 11:1

²²But this word of God came to Shemaiah the man of God: ²³"Say to Rehoboam son of Solomon king of Judah, to the whole house of Judah and Benjamin, and to the rest of the people, ²⁴'This is what the LORD says: Do not go up to fight against your brothers, the Israel-ites. Go home, every one of you, for this is my doing.'" So they obeyed the word of the LORD and went home again, as the LORD had ordered.   2Ch 10:1-11:4

Golden Calves at Bethel and Dan

²⁵Then Jeroboam fortified Shechem in the hill country of Ephraim and lived there. From there he went out and built up Peniel.ᵇ

²⁶Jeroboam thought to himself, "The kingdom will now likely revert to the house of David. ²⁷If these people go up to offer sacrifices at the temple of the LORD in Jerusalem, they will again give their allegiance to their lord, Rehoboam king of Judah. They will kill me and return to King Rehoboam."

²⁸After seeking advice, the king made two golden calves. He said to the people, "It is too much for you to go up to Jerusalem. Here are your gods, O Israel, who brought you up out of Egypt." ²⁹One he set up in Bethel, and the other in Dan. ³⁰And this thing became a sin; the people went even as far as Dan to worship the one there.   1Ki 13:34

³¹Jeroboam built shrines on high places and appointed priests from all sorts of people, even though they were not Levites. ³²He instituted a festival on the fifteenth day of the eighth month, like the

---

ᵃ18 Some Septuagint manuscripts and Syriac (see also 1 Kings 4:6 and 5:14); Hebrew *Adoram*
ᵇ25 Hebrew *Penuel,* a variant of *Peniel*

festival held in Judah, and offered sacrifices on the altar. This he did in Bethel, sacrificing to the calves he had made. And at Bethel he also installed priests at the high places he had made. ³³On the fifteenth day of the eighth month, a month of his own choosing, he offered sacrifices on the altar he had built at Bethel. So he instituted the festival for the Israelites and went up to the altar to make offerings.

The Man of God From Judah

13 By the word of the LORD a man of God came from Judah to Bethel, as Jeroboam was standing by the altar to make an offering. ²He cried out against the altar by the word of the LORD: "O altar, altar! This is what the LORD says: 'A son named Josiah will be born to the house of David. On you he will sacrifice the priests of the high places who now make offerings here, and human bones will be burned on you.'" ³That same day the man of God gave a sign: "This is the sign the LORD has declared: The altar will be split apart and the ashes on it will be poured out." 2Ki 23:15-16,20; Jn 2:11

⁴When King Jeroboam heard what the man of God cried out against the altar at Bethel, he stretched out his hand from the altar and said, "Seize him!" But the hand he stretched out toward the man shriveled up, so that he could not pull it back. ⁵Also, the altar was split apart and its ashes

poured out according to the sign given by the man of God by the word of the LORD.

⁶Then the king said to the man of God, "Intercede with the LORD your God and pray for me that my hand may be restored." So the man of God interceded with the LORD, and the king's hand was restored and became as it was before.

⁷The king said to the man of God, "Come home with me and have something to eat, and I will give you a gift." 1Sa 9:7; 2Ki 5:15

⁸But the man of God answered the king, "Even if you were to give me half your possessions, I would not go with you, nor would I eat bread or drink water here. ⁹For I was commanded by the word of the LORD: 'You must not eat bread or drink water or return by the way you came.'" ¹⁰So he took another road and did not return by the way he had come to Bethel. Nu 22:18

¹¹Now there was a certain old prophet living in Bethel, whose sons came and told him all that the man of God had done there that day. They also told their father what he had said to the king. ¹²Their father asked them, "Which way did he go?" And his sons showed him which road the man of God from Judah had taken. ¹³So he said to his sons, "Saddle the donkey for me." And when they had saddled the donkey for him, he mounted it ¹⁴and rode after the man of God. He found him sitting under an oak tree and asked, "Are

you the man of God who came from Judah?"

"I am," he replied.

¹⁵So the prophet said to him, "Come home with me and eat."

¹⁶The man of God said, "I cannot turn back and go with you, nor can I eat bread or drink water with you in this place. ¹⁷I have been told by the word of the LORD: 'You must not eat bread or drink water there or return by the way you came.'"

¹⁸The old prophet answered, "I too am a prophet, as you are. And an angel said to me by the word of the LORD: 'Bring him back with you to your house so that he may eat bread and drink water.'" (But he was lying to him.) ¹⁹So the man of God returned with him and ate and drank in his house.   Dt 13:3

²⁰While they were sitting at the table, the word of the LORD came to the old prophet who had brought him back. ²¹He cried out to the man of God who had come from Judah, "This is what the LORD says: 'You have defied the word of the LORD and have not kept the command the LORD your God gave you. ²²You came back and ate bread and drank water in the place where he told you not to eat or drink. Therefore your body will not be buried in the tomb of your fathers.'"   ver 26; 1Ki 20:35

²³When the man of God had finished eating and drinking, the prophet who had brought him back saddled his donkey for him. ²⁴As he went on his way, a lion met him on the road and killed him, and his body was thrown down on the road, with both the donkey and the lion standing beside it. ²⁵Some people who passed by saw the body thrown down there, with the lion standing beside the body, and they went and reported it in the city where the old prophet lived.   1Ki 20:36

²⁶When the prophet who had brought him back from his journey heard of it, he said, "It is the man of God who defied the word of the LORD. The LORD has given him over to the lion, which has mauled him and killed him, as the word of the LORD had warned him."

²⁷The prophet said to his sons, "Saddle the donkey for me," and they did so. ²⁸Then he went out and found the body thrown down on the road, with the donkey and the lion standing beside it. The lion had neither eaten the body nor mauled the donkey. ²⁹So the prophet picked up the body of the man of God, laid it on the donkey, and brought it back to his own city to mourn for him and bury him. ³⁰Then he laid the body in his own tomb, and they mourned over him and said, "Oh, my brother!"

³¹After burying him, he said to his sons, "When I die, bury me in the grave where the man of God is buried; lay my bones beside his bones. ³²For the message he declared by the word of the LORD against the altar in Bethel and

against all the shrines on the high places in the towns of Samaria will certainly come true." Lev 26:30

³³Even after this, Jeroboam did not change his evil ways, but once more appointed priests for the high places from all sorts of people. Anyone who wanted to become a priest he consecrated for the high places. ³⁴This was the sin of the house of Jeroboam that led to its downfall and to its destruction from the face of the earth.

Ahijah's Prophecy Against Jeroboam

14 At that time Abijah son of Jeroboam became ill, ²and Jeroboam said to his wife, "Go, disguise yourself, so you won't be recognized as the wife of Jeroboam. Then go to Shiloh. Ahijah the prophet is there—the one who told me I would be king over this people. ³Take ten loaves of bread with you, some cakes and a jar of honey, and go to him. He will tell you what will happen to the boy." ⁴So Jeroboam's wife did what he said and went to Ahijah's house in Shiloh. 1Sa 9:7; 1Ki 11:29

Now Ahijah could not see; his sight was gone because of his age. ⁵But the LORD had told Ahijah, "Jeroboam's wife is coming to ask you about her son, for he is ill, and you are to give her such and such an answer. When she arrives, she will pretend to be someone else."

⁶So when Ahijah heard the sound of her footsteps at the door, he said, "Come in, wife of Jeroboam. Why this pretense? I have been sent to you with bad news. ⁷Go, tell Jeroboam that this is what the LORD, the God of Israel, says: 'I raised you up from among the people and made you a leader over my people Israel. ⁸I tore the kingdom away from the house of David and gave it to you, but you have not been like my servant David, who kept my commands and followed me with all his heart, doing only what was right in my eyes. ⁹You have done more evil than all who lived before you. You have made for yourself other gods, idols made of metal; you have provoked me to anger and thrust me behind your back. 1Ki 11:31,33,38; 2Ch 11:15; Ps 50:17

¹⁰" 'Because of this, I am going to bring disaster on the house of Jeroboam. I will cut off from Jeroboam every last male in Israel—slave or free. I will burn up the house of Jeroboam as one burns dung, until it is all gone. ¹¹Dogs will eat those belonging to Jeroboam who die in the city, and the birds of the air will feed on those who die in the country. The LORD has spoken!' 1Ki 15:29; 16:4; 21:24

¹²"As for you, go back home. When you set foot in your city, the boy will die. ¹³All Israel will mourn for him and bury him. He is the only one belonging to Jeroboam who will be buried, because he is the only one in the house of Jeroboam in whom the LORD, the God

of Israel, has found anything good.
¹⁴"The Lᴏʀᴅ will raise up for himself a king over Israel who will cut off the family of Jeroboam. This is the day! What? Yes, even now.ᵃ ¹⁵And the Lᴏʀᴅ will strike Israel, so that it will be like a reed swaying in the water. He will uproot Israel from this good land that he gave to their forefathers and scatter them beyond the River,ᵇ because they provoked the Lᴏʀᴅ to anger by making Asherah poles.ᶜ ¹⁶And he will give Israel up because of the sins Jeroboam has committed and has caused Israel to commit."   Dt 12:3; Jos 23:15-16

¹⁷Then Jeroboam's wife got up and left and went to Tirzah. As soon as she stepped over the threshold of the house, the boy died. ¹⁸They buried him, and all Israel mourned for him, as the Lᴏʀᴅ had said through his servant the prophet Ahijah.   1Ki 16:6-9

¹⁹The other events of Jeroboam's reign, his wars and how he ruled, are written in the book of the annals of the kings of Israel. ²⁰He reigned for twenty-two years and then rested with his fathers. And Nadab his son succeeded him as king.

Rehoboam King of Judah

²¹Rehoboam son of Solomon was king in Judah. He was forty-one years old when he became king, and he reigned seventeen years in Jerusalem, the city the Lᴏʀᴅ had chosen out of all the tribes of Israel in which to put his Name. His mother's name was Naamah; she was an Ammonite.

²²Judah did evil in the eyes of the Lᴏʀᴅ. By the sins they committed they stirred up his jealous anger more than their fathers had done. ²³They also set up for themselves high places, sacred stones and Asherah poles on every high hill and under every spreading tree. ²⁴There were even male shrine prostitutes in the land; the people engaged in all the detestable practices of the nations the Lᴏʀᴅ had driven out before the Israelites.   Dt 23:17; 32:21; 2Ch 12:1

²⁵In the fifth year of King Rehoboam, Shishak king of Egypt attacked Jerusalem. ²⁶He carried off the treasures of the temple of the Lᴏʀᴅ and the treasures of the royal palace. He took everything, including all the gold shields Solomon had made. ²⁷So King Rehoboam made bronze shields to replace them and assigned these to the commanders of the guard on duty at the entrance to the royal palace. ²⁸Whenever the king went to the Lᴏʀᴅ's temple, the guards bore the shields, and afterward they returned them to the guardroom.

²⁹As for the other events of Rehoboam's reign, and all he did, are

---

ᵃ14 The meaning of the Hebrew for this sentence is uncertain.   ᵇ15 That is, the Euphrates
ᶜ15 That is, symbols of the goddess Asherah; here and elsewhere in 1 Kings

they not written in the book of the annals of the kings of Judah? ³⁰There was continual warfare between Rehoboam and Jeroboam. ³¹And Rehoboam rested with his fathers and was buried with them in the City of David. His mother's name was Naamah; she was an Ammonite. And Abijah[a] his son succeeded him as king.   2Ch 12:9-16

Abijah King of Judah

15 In the eighteenth year of the reign of Jeroboam son of Nebat, Abijah[b] became king of Judah, ²and he reigned in Jerusalem three years. His mother's name was Maacah daughter of Abishalom.[c]   2Ch 11:20; 13:2

³He committed all the sins his father had done before him; his heart was not fully devoted to the LORD his God, as the heart of David his forefather had been. ⁴Nevertheless, for David's sake the LORD his God gave him a lamp in Jerusalem by raising up a son to succeed him and by making Jerusalem strong. ⁵For David had done what was right in the eyes of the LORD and had not failed to keep any of the LORD's commands all the days of his life—except in the case of Uriah the Hittite.   2Sa 11:2-27; 12:9

⁶There was war between Rehoboam[d] and Jeroboam throughout Abijah's lifetime. ⁷As for the other events of Abijah's reign, and all he did, are they not written in the book of the annals of the kings of Judah? There was war between Abijah and Jeroboam. ⁸And Abijah rested with his fathers and was buried in the City of David. And Asa his son succeeded him as king.

Asa King of Judah

⁹In the twentieth year of Jeroboam king of Israel, Asa became king of Judah, ¹⁰and he reigned in Jerusalem forty-one years. His grandmother's name was Maacah daughter of Abishalom.   ver 2

¹¹Asa did what was right in the eyes of the LORD, as his father David had done. ¹²He expelled the male shrine prostitutes from the land and got rid of all the idols his fathers had made. ¹³He even deposed his grandmother Maacah from her position as queen mother, because she had made a repulsive Asherah pole. Asa cut the pole down and burned it in the Kidron Valley. ¹⁴Although he did not remove the high places, Asa's heart was fully committed to the LORD all his life. ¹⁵He brought into the temple of the LORD the silver and gold and the articles that he and his father had dedicated.   1Ki 7:51; 14:24

¹⁶There was war between Asa and Baasha king of Israel throughout their reigns. ¹⁷Baasha king of

---

a 31 Some Hebrew manuscripts and Septuagint (see also 2 Chron. 12:16); most Hebrew manuscripts *Abijam*   *b 1* Some Hebrew manuscripts and Septuagint (see also 2 Chron. 12:16); most Hebrew manuscripts *Abijam*; also in verses 7 and 8   *c 2* A variant of *Absalom*; also in verse 10   *d 6* Most Hebrew manuscripts; some Hebrew manuscripts and Syriac *Abijam* (that is, Abijah)

Israel went up against Judah and fortified Ramah to prevent anyone from leaving or entering the territory of Asa king of Judah.

[18]Asa then took all the silver and gold that was left in the treasuries of the LORD's temple and of his own palace. He entrusted it to his officials and sent them to Ben-Hadad son of Tabrimmon, the son of Hezion, the king of Aram, who was ruling in Damascus. [19]"Let there be a treaty between me and you," he said, "as there was between my father and your father. See, I am sending you a gift of silver and gold. Now break your treaty with Baasha king of Israel so he will withdraw from me." 1Ki 11:23-24

[20]Ben-Hadad agreed with King Asa and sent the commanders of his forces against the towns of Israel. He conquered Ijon, Dan, Abel Beth Maacah and all Kinnereth in addition to Naphtali. [21]When Baasha heard this, he stopped building Ramah and withdrew to Tirzah. [22]Then King Asa issued an order to all Judah—no one was exempt—and they carried away from Ramah the stones and timber Baasha had been using there. With them King Asa built up Geba in Benjamin, and also Mizpah.

[23]As for all the other events of Asa's reign, all his achievements, all he did and the cities he built, are they not written in the book of the annals of the kings of Judah? In his old age, however, his feet became diseased. [24]Then Asa rested with his fathers and was buried with them in the city of his father David. And Jehoshaphat his son succeeded him as king.   Mt 1:8

Nadab King of Israel

[25]Nadab son of Jeroboam became king of Israel in the second year of Asa king of Judah, and he reigned over Israel two years. [26]He did evil in the eyes of the LORD, walking in the ways of his father and in his sin, which he had caused Israel to commit.   1Ki 12:30

[27]Baasha son of Ahijah of the house of Issachar plotted against him, and he struck him down at Gibbethon, a Philistine town, while Nadab and all Israel were besieging it. [28]Baasha killed Nadab in the third year of Asa king of Judah and succeeded him as king.

[29]As soon as he began to reign, he killed Jeroboam's whole family. He did not leave Jeroboam anyone that breathed, but destroyed them all, according to the word of the LORD given through his servant Ahijah the Shilonite— [30]because of the sins Jeroboam had committed and had caused Israel to commit, and because he provoked the LORD, the God of Israel, to anger.

[31]As for the other events of Nadab's reign, and all he did, are they not written in the book of the annals of the kings of Israel? [32]There was war between Asa and Baasha king of Israel throughout their reigns.   ver 16

Baasha King of Israel

33In the third year of Asa king of Judah, Baasha son of Ahijah became king of all Israel in Tirzah, and he reigned twenty-four years. **34**He did evil in the eyes of the LORD, walking in the ways of Jeroboam and in his sin, which he had caused Israel to commit.

16 Then the word of the LORD came to Jehu son of Hanani against Baasha: **2**"I lifted you up from the dust and made you leader of my people Israel, but you walked in the ways of Jeroboam and caused my people Israel to sin and to provoke me to anger by their sins. **3**So I am about to consume Baasha and his house, and I will make your house like that of Jeroboam son of Nebat. **4**Dogs will eat those belonging to Baasha who die in the city, and the birds of the air will feed on those who die in the country."   *1Ki 14:7-11*

5As for the other events of Baasha's reign, what he did and his achievements, are they not written in the book of the annals of the kings of Israel? **6**Baasha rested with his fathers and was buried in Tirzah. And Elah his son succeeded him as king.   *1Ki 15:31,33*

7Moreover, the word of the LORD came through the prophet Jehu son of Hanani to Baasha and his house, because of all the evil he had done in the eyes of the LORD, provoking him to anger by the things he did, and becoming like the house of Jeroboam—and also because he destroyed it.

Elah King of Israel

8In the twenty-sixth year of Asa king of Judah, Elah son of Baasha became king of Israel, and he reigned in Tirzah two years.

9Zimri, one of his officials, who had command of half his chariots, plotted against him. Elah was in Tirzah at the time, getting drunk in the home of Arza, the man in charge of the palace at Tirzah. **10**Zimri came in, struck him down and killed him in the twenty-seventh year of Asa king of Judah. Then he succeeded him as king.

11As soon as he began to reign and was seated on the throne, he killed off Baasha's whole family. He did not spare a single male, whether relative or friend. **12**So Zimri destroyed the whole family of Baasha, in accordance with the word of the LORD spoken against Baasha through the prophet Jehu — **13**because of all the sins Baasha and his son Elah had committed and had caused Israel to commit, so that they provoked the LORD, the God of Israel, to anger by their worthless idols.   *Dt 32:21; 1Sa 12:21*

14As for the other events of Elah's reign, and all he did, are they not written in the book of the annals of the kings of Israel?

Zimri King of Israel

15In the twenty-seventh year of Asa king of Judah, Zimri reigned in

Tirzah seven days. The army was encamped near Gibbethon, a Philistine town. ¹⁶When the Israelites in the camp heard that Zimri had plotted against the king and murdered him, they proclaimed Omri, the commander of the army, king over Israel that very day there in the camp. ¹⁷Then Omri and all the Israelites with him withdrew from Gibbethon and laid siege to Tirzah. ¹⁸When Zimri saw that the city was taken, he went into the citadel of the royal palace and set the palace on fire around him. So he died, ¹⁹because of the sins he had committed, doing evil in the eyes of the LORD and walking in the ways of Jeroboam and in the sin he had committed and had caused Israel to commit.   Jos 19:44; 1Ki 15:27

²⁰As for the other events of Zimri's reign, and the rebellion he carried out, are they not written in the book of the annals of the kings of Israel?

Omri King of Israel

²¹Then the people of Israel were split into two factions; half supported Tibni son of Ginath for king, and the other half supported Omri. ²²But Omri's followers proved stronger than those of Tibni son of Ginath. So Tibni died and Omri became king.

²³In the thirty-first year of Asa king of Judah, Omri became king of Israel, and he reigned twelve years, six of them in Tirzah. ²⁴He bought the hill of Samaria from Shemer for two talents*a* of silver and built a city on the hill, calling it Samaria, after Shemer, the name of the former owner of the hill.

²⁵But Omri did evil in the eyes of the LORD and sinned more than all those before him. ²⁶He walked in all the ways of Jeroboam son of Nebat and in his sin, which he had caused Israel to commit, so that they provoked the LORD, the God of Israel, to anger by their worthless idols.   Dt 4:25; 32:21; Mic 6:16

²⁷As for the other events of Omri's reign, what he did and the things he achieved, are they not written in the book of the annals of the kings of Israel? ²⁸Omri rested with his fathers and was buried in Samaria. And Ahab his son succeeded him as king.

Ahab Becomes King of Israel

²⁹In the thirty-eighth year of Asa king of Judah, Ahab son of Omri became king of Israel, and he reigned in Samaria over Israel twenty-two years. ³⁰Ahab son of Omri did more evil in the eyes of the LORD than any of those before him. ³¹He not only considered it trivial to commit the sins of Jeroboam son of Nebat, but he also married Jezebel daughter of Ethbaal king of the Sidonians, and began to serve Baal and worship him.

a 24 That is, about 150 pounds (about 70 kilograms)

32He set up an altar for Baal in the temple of Baal that he built in Samaria. **33**Ahab also made an Asherah pole and did more to provoke the Lord, the God of Israel, to anger than did all the kings of Israel before him. 1Ki 14:9; 21:25

34In Ahab's time, Hiel of Bethel rebuilt Jericho. He laid its foundations at the cost of his firstborn son Abiram, and he set up its gates at the cost of his youngest son Segub, in accordance with the word of the Lord spoken by Joshua son of Nun. Jos 6:26

Elijah Fed by Ravens

17 Now Elijah the Tishbite, from Tishbe[a] in Gilead, said to Ahab, "As the Lord, the God of Israel, lives, whom I serve, there will be neither dew nor rain in the next few years except at my word." 2Ki 3:14; Lk 4:25; Jas 5:17

2Then the word of the Lord came to Elijah: **3**"Leave here, turn eastward and hide in the Kerith Ravine, east of the Jordan. **4**You will drink from the brook, and I have ordered the ravens to feed you there." Ge 8:7

5So he did what the Lord had told him. He went to the Kerith Ravine, east of the Jordan, and stayed there. **6**The ravens brought him bread and meat in the morning and bread and meat in the evening, and he drank from the brook.

The Widow at Zarephath

7Some time later the brook dried up because there had been no rain in the land. **8**Then the word of the Lord came to him: **9**"Go at once to Zarephath of Sidon and stay there. I have commanded a widow in that place to supply you with food." **10**So he went to Zarephath. When he came to the town gate, a widow was there gathering sticks. He called to her and asked, "Would you bring me a little water in a jar so I may have a drink?" **11**As she was going to get it, he called, "And bring me, please, a piece of bread."

12"As surely as the Lord your God lives," she replied, "I don't have any bread—only a handful of flour in a jar and a little oil in a jug. I am gathering a few sticks to take home and make a meal for myself and my son, that we may eat it—and die." 2Ki 4:2

13Elijah said to her, "Don't be afraid. Go home and do as you have said. But first make a small cake of bread for me from what you have and bring it to me, and then make something for yourself and your son. **14**For this is what the Lord, the God of Israel, says: 'The jar of flour will not be used up and the jug of oil will not run dry until the day the Lord gives rain on the land.' " **15**She went away and did as Elijah had told her. So there was food every day for Elijah and for the woman and her family. ¹⁶For the jar of flour was not used up and the jug of oil did not run dry, in keeping with the word of the LORD spoken by Elijah.

¹⁷Some time later the son of the woman who owned the house became ill. He grew worse and worse, and finally stopped breathing. ¹⁸She said to Elijah, "What do you have against me, man of God? Did you come to remind me of my sin and kill my son?"   2Ki 3:13; Lk 5:8

¹⁹"Give me your son," Elijah replied. He took him from her arms, carried him to the upper room where he was staying, and laid him on his bed. ²⁰Then he cried out to the LORD, "O LORD my God, have you brought tragedy also upon this widow I am staying with, by causing her son to die?" ²¹Then he stretched himself out on the boy three times and cried to the LORD, "O LORD my God, let this boy's life return to him!"   2Ki 4:34; Ac 20:10

²²The LORD heard Elijah's cry, and the boy's life returned to him, and he lived. ²³Elijah picked up the child and carried him down from the room into the house. He gave him to his mother and said, "Look, your son is alive!"

²⁴Then the woman said to Elijah, "Now I know that you are a man of God and that the word of the LORD from your mouth is the truth."   Jn 3:2; 16:30; Ps 119:43

Elijah and Obadiah

18 After a long time, in the third year, the word of the LORD came to Elijah: "Go and present yourself to Ahab, and I will send rain on the land." ²So Elijah went to present himself to Ahab.

Now the famine was severe in Samaria, ³and Ahab had summoned Obadiah, who was in charge of his palace. (Obadiah was a devout believer in the LORD. ⁴While Jezebel was killing off the LORD's prophets, Obadiah had taken a hundred prophets and hidden them in two caves, fifty in each, and had supplied them with food and water.) ⁵Ahab had said to Obadiah, "Go through the land to all the springs and valleys. Maybe we can find some grass to keep the horses and mules alive so we will not have to kill any of our animals." ⁶So they divided the land they were to cover, Ahab going in one direction and Obadiah in another.   2Ki 9:7; Ne 7:2; Isa 16:3

⁷As Obadiah was walking along, Elijah met him. Obadiah recognized him, bowed down to the ground, and said, "Is it really you, my lord Elijah?"   2Ki 1:8

⁸"Yes," he replied. "Go tell your master, 'Elijah is here.'"

⁹"What have I done wrong," asked Obadiah, "that you are handing your servant over to Ahab to be put to death? ¹⁰As surely as the LORD your God lives, there is not a nation or kingdom where my

master has not sent someone to look for you. And whenever a nation or kingdom claimed you were not there, he made them swear they could not find you. [11]But now you tell me to go to my master and say, 'Elijah is here.' [12]I don't know where the Spirit of the LORD may carry you when I leave you. If I go and tell Ahab and he doesn't find you, he will kill me. Yet I your servant have worshiped the LORD since my youth. [13]Haven't you heard, my lord, what I did while Jezebel was killing the prophets of the LORD? I hid a hundred of the LORD's prophets in two caves, fifty in each, and supplied them with food and water. [14]And now you tell me to go to my master and say, 'Elijah is here.' He will kill me!"

[15]Elijah said, "As the LORD Almighty lives, whom I serve, I will surely present myself to Ahab today."   1Ki 17:1

Elijah on Mount Carmel

[16]So Obadiah went to meet Ahab and told him, and Ahab went to meet Elijah. [17]When he saw Elijah, he said to him, "Is that you, you troubler of Israel?"   Jos 7:25; 1Ki 21:20

[18]"I have not made trouble for Israel," Elijah replied. "But you and your father's family have. You have abandoned the LORD's commands and have followed the Baals. [19]Now summon the people from all over Israel to meet me on Mount Carmel. And bring the four hundred and fifty prophets of Baal

and the four hundred prophets of Asherah, who eat at Jezebel's table."   Jos 19:26; 1Ki 16:31,33

[20]So Ahab sent word throughout all Israel and assembled the prophets on Mount Carmel. [21]Elijah went before the people and said, "How long will you waver between two opinions? If the LORD is God, follow him; but if Baal is God, follow him."   Jos 24:15; 2Ki 17:41; Mt 6:24

But the people said nothing.

[22]Then Elijah said to them, "I am the only one of the LORD's prophets left, but Baal has four hundred and fifty prophets. [23]Get two bulls for us. Let them choose one for themselves, and let them cut it into pieces and put it on the wood but not set fire to it. I will prepare the other bull and put it on the wood but not set fire to it. [24]Then you call on the name of your god, and I will call on the name of the LORD. The god who answers by fire—he is God."   1Ki 19:10; 1Ch 21:26

Then all the people said, "What you say is good."

[25]Elijah said to the prophets of Baal, "Choose one of the bulls and prepare it first, since there are so many of you. Call on the name of your god, but do not light the fire." [26]So they took the bull given them and prepared it.

Then they called on the name of Baal from morning till noon. "O Baal, answer us!" they shouted. But there was no response; no one answered. And they danced around the altar they had made.

²⁷At noon Elijah began to taunt them. "Shout louder!" he said. "Surely he is a god! Perhaps he is deep in thought, or busy, or traveling. Maybe he is sleeping and must be awakened." ²⁸So they shouted louder and slashed themselves with swords and spears, as was their custom, until their blood flowed. ²⁹Midday passed, and they continued their frantic prophesying until the time for the evening sacrifice. But there was no response, no one answered, no one paid attention.   Lev 19:28; Hab 2:19

³⁰Then Elijah said to all the people, "Come here to me." They came to him, and he repaired the altar of the LORD, which was in ruins. ³¹Elijah took twelve stones, one for each of the tribes descended from Jacob, to whom the word of the LORD had come, saying, "Your name shall be Israel." ³²With the stones he built an altar in the name of the LORD, and he dug a trench around it large enough to hold two seahs*a* of seed. ³³He arranged the wood, cut the bull into pieces and laid it on the wood. Then he said to them, "Fill four large jars with water and pour it on the offering and on the wood."   1Ki 19:10; 2Ki 17:34; Col 3:17

³⁴"Do it again," he said, and they did it again.

"Do it a third time," he ordered, and they did it the third time.

³⁵The water ran down around the altar and even filled the trench.

³⁶At the time of sacrifice, the prophet Elijah stepped forward and prayed: "O LORD, God of Abraham, Isaac and Israel, let it be known today that you are God in Israel and that I am your servant and have done all these things at your command. ³⁷Answer me, O LORD, answer me, so these people will know that you, O LORD, are God, and that you are turning their hearts back again."   Nu 16:28; Jos 4:24

³⁸Then the fire of the LORD fell and burned up the sacrifice, the wood, the stones and the soil, and also licked up the water in the trench.   Lev 9:24; 1Ch 21:26; 2Ch 7:1

³⁹When all the people saw this, they fell prostrate and cried, "The LORD—he is God! The LORD—he is God!"   ver 24; Ps 46:10

⁴⁰Then Elijah commanded them, "Seize the prophets of Baal. Don't let anyone get away!" They seized them, and Elijah had them brought down to the Kishon Valley and slaughtered there.   Dt 13:5; 18:20

⁴¹And Elijah said to Ahab, "Go, eat and drink, for there is the sound of a heavy rain." ⁴²So Ahab went off to eat and drink, but Elijah climbed to the top of Carmel, bent down to the ground and put his face between his knees.

⁴³"Go and look toward the sea," he told his servant. And he went up and looked.

---

a 32 That is, probably about 13 quarts (about 15 liters)

"There is nothing there," he said.

Seven times Elijah said, "Go back."

44The seventh time the servant reported, "A cloud as small as a man's hand is rising from the sea."

So Elijah said, "Go and tell Ahab, 'Hitch up your chariot and go down before the rain stops you.'"

45Meanwhile, the sky grew black with clouds, the wind rose, a heavy rain came on and Ahab rode off to Jezreel. **46**The power of the LORD came upon Elijah and, tucking his cloak into his belt, he ran ahead of Ahab all the way to Jezreel.   2Ki 3:15; 4:29

Elijah Flees to Horeb

19 Now Ahab told Jezebel everything Elijah had done and how he had killed all the prophets with the sword. **2**So Jezebel sent a messenger to Elijah to say, "May the gods deal with me, be it ever so severely, if by this time tomorrow I do not make your life like that of one of them."

3Elijah was afraid[a] and ran for his life. When he came to Beersheba in Judah, he left his servant there, **4**while he himself went a day's journey into the desert. He came to a broom tree, sat down under it and prayed that he might die. "I have had enough, LORD," he said. "Take my life; I am no better

than my ancestors." **5**Then he lay down under the tree and fell asleep.   Nu 11:15; Jnh 4:8; Ge 31:21

All at once an angel touched him and said, "Get up and eat." **6**He looked around, and there by his head was a cake of bread baked over hot coals, and a jar of water. He ate and drank and then lay down again.   Ge 16:7

7The angel of the LORD came back a second time and touched him and said, "Get up and eat, for the journey is too much for you." **8**So he got up and ate and drank. Strengthened by that food, he traveled forty days and forty nights until he reached Horeb, the mountain of God. **9**There he went into a cave and spent the night.   Ex 3:1; 34:28

The LORD Appears to Elijah

And the word of the LORD came to him: "What are you doing here, Elijah?"

10He replied, "I have been very zealous for the LORD God Almighty. The Israelites have rejected your covenant, broken down your altars, and put your prophets to death with the sword. I am the only one left, and now they are trying to kill me too."   1Ki 18:4,22

11The LORD said, "Go out and stand on the mountain in the presence of the LORD, for the LORD is about to pass by."   Ex 24:12

Then a great and powerful wind tore the mountains apart and shat-

a 3 Or *Elijah saw*

tered the rocks before the LORD, but the LORD was not in the wind. After the wind there was an earthquake, but the LORD was not in the earthquake. [12]After the earthquake came a fire, but the LORD was not in the fire. And after the fire came a gentle whisper. [13]When Elijah heard it, he pulled his cloak over his face and went out and stood at the mouth of the cave.   Zec 4:6

Then a voice said to him, "What are you doing here, Elijah?"

[14]He replied, "I have been very zealous for the LORD God Almighty. The Israelites have rejected your covenant, broken down your altars, and put your prophets to death with the sword. I am the only one left, and now they are trying to kill me too."   Ro 11:3

[15]The LORD said to him, "Go back the way you came, and go to the Desert of Damascus. When you get there, anoint Hazael king over Aram. [16]Also, anoint Jehu son of Nimshi king over Israel, and anoint Elisha son of Shaphat from Abel Meholah to succeed you as prophet. [17]Jehu will put to death any who escape the sword of Hazael, and Elisha will put to death any who escape the sword of Jehu. [18]Yet I reserve seven thousand in Israel—all whose knees have not bowed down to Baal and all whose mouths have not kissed him."

The Call of Elisha

[19]So Elijah went from there and found Elisha son of Shaphat. He was plowing with twelve yoke of oxen, and he himself was driving the twelfth pair. Elijah went up to him and threw his cloak around him. [20]Elisha then left his oxen and ran after Elijah. "Let me kiss my father and mother good-by," he said, "and then I will come with you."   2Ki 2:8,14; Mt 8:21-22; Lk 9:61

"Go back," Elijah replied. "What have I done to you?"

[21]So Elisha left him and went back. He took his yoke of oxen and slaughtered them. He burned the plowing equipment to cook the meat and gave it to the people, and they ate. Then he set out to follow Elijah and became his attendant.

Ben-Hadad Attacks Samaria

20 Now Ben-Hadad king of Aram mustered his entire army. Accompanied by thirty-two kings with their horses and chariots, he went up and besieged Samaria and attacked it. [2]He sent messengers into the city to Ahab king of Israel, saying, "This is what Ben-Hadad says: [3]'Your silver and gold are mine, and the best of your wives and children are mine.'"

[4]The king of Israel answered, "Just as you say, my lord the king. I and all I have are yours."

[5]The messengers came again and said, "This is what Ben-Hadad says: 'I sent to demand your silver and gold, your wives and your children. [6]But about this time tomorrow I am going to send my officials to search your palace and the

houses of your officials. They will seize everything you value and carry it away.' "

⁷The king of Israel summoned all the elders of the land and said to them, "See how this man is looking for trouble! When he sent for my wives and my children, my silver and my gold, I did not refuse him." 2Ki 5:7

⁸The elders and the people all answered, "Don't listen to him or agree to his demands."

⁹So he replied to Ben-Hadad's messengers, "Tell my lord the king, 'Your servant will do all you demanded the first time, but this demand I cannot meet.' " They left and took the answer back to Ben-Hadad.

¹⁰Then Ben-Hadad sent another message to Ahab: "May the gods deal with me, be it ever so severely, if enough dust remains in Samaria to give each of my men a handful." 1Ki 19:2

¹¹The king of Israel answered, "Tell him: 'One who puts on his armor should not boast like one who takes it off.' " Pr 27:1

¹²Ben-Hadad heard this message while he and the kings were drinking in their tents,ᵃ and he ordered his men: "Prepare to attack." So they prepared to attack the city.

Ahab Defeats Ben-Hadad

¹³Meanwhile a prophet came to Ahab king of Israel and an-nounced, "This is what the LORD says: 'Do you see this vast army? I will give it into your hand today, and then you will know that I am the LORD.' " ver 28; Ex 6:7

¹⁴"But who will do this?" asked Ahab.

The prophet replied, "This is what the LORD says: 'The young officers of the provincial commanders will do it.' "

"And who will start the battle?" he asked. Jdg 1:1

The prophet answered, "You will."

¹⁵So Ahab summoned the young officers of the provincial commanders, 232 men. Then he assembled the rest of the Israelites, 7,000 in all. ¹⁶They set out at noon while Ben-Hadad and the 32 kings allied with him were in their tents getting drunk. ¹⁷The young officers of the provincial commanders went out first. ver 12

Now Ben-Hadad had dispatched scouts, who reported, "Men are advancing from Samaria."

¹⁸He said, "If they have come out for peace, take them alive; if they have come out for war, take them alive."

¹⁹The young officers of the provincial commanders marched out of the city with the army behind them ²⁰and each one struck down his opponent. At that, the Arameans fled, with the Israelites in pursuit. But Ben-Hadad king of Aram

ᵃ12 Or in Succoth; also in verse 16

escaped on horseback with some of his horsemen. ²¹The king of Israel advanced and overpowered the horses and chariots and inflicted heavy losses on the Arameans.

²²Afterward, the prophet came to the king of Israel and said, "Strengthen your position and see what must be done, because next spring the king of Aram will attack you again."   2Sa 11:1

²³Meanwhile, the officials of the king of Aram advised him, "Their gods are gods of the hills. That is why they were too strong for us. But if we fight them on the plains, surely we will be stronger than they. ²⁴Do this: Remove all the kings from their commands and replace them with other officers. ²⁵You must also raise an army like the one you lost—horse for horse and chariot for chariot—so we can fight Israel on the plains. Then surely we will be stronger than they." He agreed with them and acted accordingly.   1Ki 14:23; Ro 1:21-23

²⁶The next spring Ben-Hadad mustered the Arameans and went up to Aphek to fight against Israel. ²⁷When the Israelites were also mustered and given provisions, they marched out to meet them. The Israelites camped opposite them like two small flocks of goats, while the Arameans covered the countryside.   Jdg 6:6; 1Sa 13:6; 2Ki 13:17

²⁸The man of God came up and told the king of Israel, "This is what the LORD says: 'Because the Arameans think the LORD is a god of the hills and not a god of the valleys, I will deliver this vast army into your hands, and you will know that I am the LORD.' "   ver 13

²⁹For seven days they camped opposite each other, and on the seventh day the battle was joined. The Israelites inflicted a hundred thousand casualties on the Aramean foot soldiers in one day. ³⁰The rest of them escaped to the city of Aphek, where the wall collapsed on twenty-seven thousand of them. And Ben-Hadad fled to the city and hid in an inner room.

³¹His officials said to him, "Look, we have heard that the kings of the house of Israel are merciful. Let us go to the king of Israel with sackcloth around our waists and ropes around our heads. Perhaps he will spare your life."   Ge 37:34

³²Wearing sackcloth around their waists and ropes around their heads, they went to the king of Israel and said, "Your servant Ben-Hadad says: 'Please let me live.' "

The king answered, "Is he still alive? He is my brother."

³³The men took this as a good sign and were quick to pick up his word. "Yes, your brother Ben-Hadad!" they said.

"Go and get him," the king said. When Ben-Hadad came out, Ahab had him come up into his chariot.

³⁴"I will return the cities my father took from your father," Ben-Hadad offered. "You may set up your own market areas in Damas-

cus, as my father did in Samaria."
Ahab said, "On the basis of a treaty I will set you free." So he made a treaty with him, and let him go.   Ex 23:32

A Prophet Condemns Ahab

35By the word of the LORD one of the sons of the prophets said to his companion, "Strike me with your weapon," but the man refused. 36So the prophet said, "Because you have not obeyed the LORD, as soon as you leave me a lion will kill you." And after the man went away, a lion found him and killed him.   1Ki 13:24

37The prophet found another man and said, "Strike me, please." So the man struck him and wounded him. 38Then the prophet went and stood by the road waiting for the king. He disguised himself with his headband down over his eyes. 39As the king passed by, the prophet called out to him, "Your servant went into the thick of the battle, and someone came to me with a captive and said, 'Guard this man. If he is missing, it will be your life for his life, or you must pay a talent[a] of silver.' 40While your servant was busy here and there, the man disappeared."

"That is your sentence," the king of Israel said. "You have pronounced it yourself."

41Then the prophet quickly removed the headband from his eyes, and the king of Israel recognized him as one of the prophets. 42He said to the king, "This is what the LORD says: 'You have set free a man I had determined should die.[b] Therefore it is your life for his life, your people for his people.'" 43Sullen and angry, the king of Israel went to his palace in Samaria.

Naboth's Vineyard

21 Some time later there was an incident involving a vineyard belonging to Naboth the Jezreelite. The vineyard was in Jezreel, close to the palace of Ahab king of Samaria. 2Ahab said to Naboth, "Let me have your vineyard to use for a vegetable garden, since it is close to my palace. In exchange I will give you a better vineyard or, if you prefer, I will pay you whatever it is worth."

3But Naboth replied, "The LORD forbid that I should give you the inheritance of my fathers."

4So Ahab went home, sullen and angry because Naboth the Jezreelite had said, "I will not give you the inheritance of my fathers." He lay on his bed sulking and refused to eat.   1Ki 20:43

5His wife Jezebel came in and asked him, "Why are you so sullen? Why won't you eat?"

---

a39 That is, about 75 pounds (about 34 kilograms)   b42 The Hebrew term refers to the irrevocable giving over of things or persons to the LORD, often by totally destroying them.

⁶He answered her, "Because I said to Naboth the Jezreelite, 'Sell me your vineyard; or if you prefer, I will give you another vineyard in its place.' But he said, 'I will not give you my vineyard.'"

⁷Jezebel his wife said, "Is this how you act as king over Israel? Get up and eat! Cheer up. I'll get you the vineyard of Naboth the Jezreelite." 1Sa 8:14

⁸So she wrote letters in Ahab's name, placed his seal on them, and sent them to the elders and nobles who lived in Naboth's city with him. ⁹In those letters she wrote:

"Proclaim a day of fasting and seat Naboth in a prominent place among the people. ¹⁰But seat two scoundrels opposite him and have them testify that he has cursed both God and the king. Then take him out and stone him to death." Ac 6:11; Ex 22:28; Lev 24:15-16

¹¹So the elders and nobles who lived in Naboth's city did as Jezebel directed in the letters she had written to them. ¹²They proclaimed a fast and seated Naboth in a prominent place among the people. ¹³Then two scoundrels came and sat opposite him and brought charges against Naboth before the people, saying, "Naboth has cursed both God and the king." So they took him outside the city and stoned him to death. ¹⁴Then they sent word to Jezebel:

"Naboth has been stoned and is dead." 2Ki 9:26; Isa 58:4

¹⁵As soon as Jezebel heard that Naboth had been stoned to death, she said to Ahab, "Get up and take possession of the vineyard of Naboth the Jezreelite that he refused to sell you. He is no longer alive, but dead." ¹⁶When Ahab heard that Naboth was dead, he got up and went down to take possession of Naboth's vineyard. 1Sa 8:14

¹⁷Then the word of the Lord came to Elijah the Tishbite: ¹⁸"Go down to meet Ahab king of Israel, who rules in Samaria. He is now in Naboth's vineyard, where he has gone to take possession of it. ¹⁹Say to him, 'This is what the Lord says: Have you not murdered a man and seized his property?' Then say to him, 'This is what the Lord says: In the place where dogs licked up Naboth's blood, dogs will lick up your blood—yes, yours!'"

²⁰Ahab said to Elijah, "So you have found me, my enemy!"

"I have found you," he answered, "because you have sold yourself to do evil in the eyes of the Lord. ²¹I am going to bring disaster on you. I will consume your descendants and cut off from Ahab every last male in Israel—slave or free. ²²I will make your house like that of Jeroboam son of Nebat and that of Baasha son of Ahijah, because you have provoked me to anger and have caused Israel to sin.' 1Ki 12:30; 14:10; 15:29

²³"And also concerning Jezebel

the LORD says: 'Dogs will devour Jezebel by the wall of[a] Jezreel.'

24"Dogs will eat those belonging to Ahab who die in the city, and the birds of the air will feed on those who die in the country."

25(There was never a man like Ahab, who sold himself to do evil in the eyes of the LORD, urged on by Jezebel his wife. 26He behaved in the vilest manner by going after idols, like the Amorites the LORD drove out before Israel.)   Ge 15:16

27When Ahab heard these words, he tore his clothes, put on sackcloth and fasted. He lay in sackcloth and went around meekly.   Ge 37:34; 2Sa 3:31; 2Ki 6:30

28Then the word of the LORD came to Elijah the Tishbite: 29"Have you noticed how Ahab has humbled himself before me? Because he has humbled himself, I will not bring this disaster in his day, but I will bring it on his house in the days of his son."   2Ki 9:26

Micaiah Prophesies Against Ahab

22 For three years there was no war between Aram and Israel. 2But in the third year Jehoshaphat king of Judah went down to see the king of Israel. 3The king of Israel had said to his officials, "Don't you know that Ramoth Gilead belongs to us and yet we are doing nothing to retake it from the king of Aram?"   Dt 4:43

4So he asked Jehoshaphat, "Will you go with me to fight against Ramoth Gilead?"   2Ki 3:7

Jehoshaphat replied to the king of Israel, "I am as you are, my people as your people, my horses as your horses." 5But Jehoshaphat also said to the king of Israel, "First seek the counsel of the LORD."

6So the king of Israel brought together the prophets—about four hundred men—and asked them, "Shall I go to war against Ramoth Gilead, or shall I refrain?"

"Go," they answered, "for the Lord will give it into the king's hand."   1Ki 18:19

7But Jehoshaphat asked, "Is there not a prophet of the LORD here whom we can inquire of?"

8The king of Israel answered Jehoshaphat, "There is still one man through whom we can inquire of the LORD, but I hate him because he never prophesies anything good about me, but always bad. He is Micaiah son of Imlah."   Isa 5:20

"The king should not say that," Jehoshaphat replied.

9So the king of Israel called one of his officials and said, "Bring Micaiah son of Imlah at once."

10Dressed in their royal robes, the king of Israel and Jehoshaphat king of Judah were sitting on their thrones at the threshing floor by

a23 Most Hebrew manuscripts; a few Hebrew manuscripts, Vulgate and Syriac (see also 2 Kings 9:26) the plot of ground at the entrance of the gate of Samaria, with all the prophets prophesying before them. [11]Now Zedekiah son of Kenaanah had made iron horns and he declared, "This is what the LORD says: 'With these you will gore the Arameans until they are destroyed.'"   Dt 33:17

[12]All the other prophets were prophesying the same thing. "Attack Ramoth Gilead and be victorious," they said, "for the LORD will give it into the king's hand."

[13]The messenger who had gone to summon Micaiah said to him, "Look, as one man the other prophets are predicting success for the king. Let your word agree with theirs, and speak favorably."

[14]But Micaiah said, "As surely as the LORD lives, I can tell him only what the LORD tells me."   Nu 22:18

[15]When he arrived, the king asked him, "Micaiah, shall we go to war against Ramoth Gilead, or shall I refrain?"

"Attack and be victorious," he answered, "for the LORD will give it into the king's hand."

[16]The king said to him, "How many times must I make you swear to tell me nothing but the truth in the name of the LORD?"

[17]Then Micaiah answered, "I saw all Israel scattered on the hills like sheep without a shepherd, and the LORD said, 'These people have no master. Let each one go home in peace.'"   Nu 27:17; Mt 9:36

[18]The king of Israel said to Jehoshaphat, "Didn't I tell you that he never prophesies anything good about me, but only bad?"

[19]Micaiah continued, "Therefore hear the word of the LORD: I saw the LORD sitting on his throne with all the host of heaven standing around him on his right and on his left. [20]And the LORD said, 'Who will entice Ahab into attacking Ramoth Gilead and going to his death there?'   Job 1:6; Isa 6:1; Da 7:9

"One suggested this, and another that. [21]Finally, a spirit came forward, stood before the LORD and said, 'I will entice him.'

[22]"'By what means?' the LORD asked.

"'I will go out and be a lying spirit in the mouths of all his prophets,' he said.   Jdg 9:23; 2Th 2:11

"'You will succeed in enticing him,' said the LORD. 'Go and do it.'

[23]"So now the LORD has put a lying spirit in the mouths of all these prophets of yours. The LORD has decreed disaster for you."   Eze 14:9

[24]Then Zedekiah son of Kenaanah went up and slapped Micaiah in the face. "Which way did the spirit from[a] the LORD go when he went from me to speak to you?" he asked.   ver 11; Ac 23:2

[25]Micaiah replied, "You will find out on the day you go to hide in an inner room."   1Ki 20:30

[26]The king of Israel then ordered, "Take Micaiah and send

[a] 24 Or Spirit of

him back to Amon the ruler of the city and to Joash the king's son [27]and say, 'This is what the king says: Put this fellow in prison and give him nothing but bread and water until I return safely.' "

[28]Micaiah declared, "If you ever return safely, the Lord has not spoken through me." Then he added, "Mark my words, all you people!"

Ahab Killed at Ramoth Gilead

[29]So the king of Israel and Jehoshaphat king of Judah went up to Ramoth Gilead. [30]The king of Israel said to Jehoshaphat, "I will enter the battle in disguise, but you wear your royal robes." So the king of Israel disguised himself and went into battle.   2Ch 35:32

[31]Now the king of Aram had ordered his thirty-two chariot commanders, "Do not fight with anyone, small or great, except the king of Israel." [32]When the chariot commanders saw Jehoshaphat, they thought, "Surely this is the king of Israel." So they turned to attack him, but when Jehoshaphat cried out, [33]the chariot commanders saw that he was not the king of Israel and stopped pursuing him.

[34]But someone drew his bow at random and hit the king of Israel between the sections of his armor. The king told his chariot driver, "Wheel around and get me out of the fighting. I've been wounded."

[35]All day long the battle raged, and the king was propped up in his chariot facing the Arameans. The blood from his wound ran onto the floor of the chariot, and that evening he died. [36]As the sun was setting, a cry spread through the army: "Every man to his town; everyone to his land!"   2Ki 14:12

[37]So the king died and was brought to Samaria, and they buried him there. [38]They washed the chariot at a pool in Samaria (where the prostitutes bathed),[a] and the dogs licked up his blood, as the word of the Lord had declared.

[39]As for the other events of Ahab's reign, including all he did, the palace he built and inlaid with ivory, and the cities he fortified, are they not written in the book of the annals of the kings of Israel? [40]Ahab rested with his fathers. And Ahaziah his son succeeded him as king.   2Ch 9:17; Am 3:15

Jehoshaphat King of Judah

[41]Jehoshaphat son of Asa became king of Judah in the fourth year of Ahab king of Israel. [42]Jehoshaphat was thirty-five years old when he became king, and he reigned in Jerusalem twenty-five years. His mother's name was Azubah daughter of Shilhi. [43]In everything he walked in the ways of his father Asa and did not stray from them; he did what was right

---

[a]38 Or Samaria and cleaned the weapons

in the eyes of the LORD. The high places, however, were not removed, and the people continued to offer sacrifices and burn incense there. 44Jehoshaphat was also at peace with the king of Israel.

45As for the other events of Jehoshaphat's reign, the things he achieved and his military exploits, are they not written in the book of the annals of the kings of Judah? 46He rid the land of the rest of the male shrine prostitutes who remained there even after the reign of his father Asa. 47There was then no king in Edom; a deputy ruled.

48Now Jehoshaphat built a fleet of trading ships*a* to go to Ophir for gold, but they never set sail—they were wrecked at Ezion Geber. 49At that time Ahaziah son of Ahab said to Jehoshaphat, "Let my men sail with your men," but Jehoshaphat refused.   1Ki 9:26

50Then Jehoshaphat rested with his fathers and was buried with them in the city of David his father. And Jehoram his son succeeded him.   2Ch 20:31-21:1

Ahaziah King of Israel

51Ahaziah son of Ahab became king of Israel in Samaria in the seventeenth year of Jehoshaphat king of Judah, and he reigned over Israel two years. 52He did evil in the eyes of the LORD, because he walked in the ways of his father and mother and in the ways of Jeroboam son of Nebat, who caused Israel to sin. 53He served and worshiped Baal and provoked the LORD, the God of Israel, to anger, just as his father had done.

---

a 48 Hebrew *of ships of Tarshish*

2 Kings

The Lord's Judgment on Ahaziah

1 After Ahab's death, Moab rebelled against Israel. ²Now Ahaziah had fallen through the lattice of his upper room in Samaria and injured himself. So he sent messengers, saying to them, "Go and consult Baal-Zebub, the god of Ekron, to see if I will recover from this injury." *2Sa 8:2; 2Ki 3:5; Mk 3:22*

³But the angel of the Lord said to Elijah the Tishbite, "Go up and meet the messengers of the king of Samaria and ask them, 'Is it because there is no God in Israel that you are going off to consult Baal-Zebub, the god of Ekron?' ⁴Therefore this is what the Lord says: 'You will not leave the bed you are lying on. You will certainly die!' " So Elijah went. *Ge 16:7; 1Ki 17:1*

⁵When the messengers returned to the king, he asked them, "Why have you come back?"

⁶"A man came to meet us," they replied. "And he said to us, 'Go back to the king who sent you and tell him, "This is what the Lord says: Is it because there is no God in Israel that you are sending men to consult Baal-Zebub, the god of Ekron? Therefore you will not leave the bed you are lying on. You will certainly die!" ' "

⁷The king asked them, "What kind of man was it who came to meet you and told you this?"

⁸They replied, "He was a man with a garment of hair and with a leather belt around his waist."

The king said, "That was Elijah the Tishbite."

⁹Then he sent to Elijah a captain with his company of fifty men. The captain went up to Elijah, who was sitting on the top of a hill, and said to him, "Man of God, the king says, 'Come down!' " *Ex 18:25; 2Ki 6:14*

¹⁰Elijah answered the captain, "If I am a man of God, may fire come down from heaven and consume you and your fifty men!" Then fire fell from heaven and consumed the captain and his men. *1Ki 18:38; Lk 9:54*

¹¹At this the king sent to Elijah another captain with his fifty men. The captain said to him, "Man of God, this is what the king says, 'Come down at once!' "

¹²"If I am a man of God," Elijah replied, "may fire come down from heaven and consume you and your fifty men!" Then the fire of God fell from heaven and consumed him and his fifty men.

¹³So the king sent a third captain with his fifty men. This third captain went up and fell on his knees before Elijah. "Man of God," he

begged, "please have respect for my life and the lives of these fifty men, your servants! [14]See, fire has fallen from heaven and consumed the first two captains and all their men. But now have respect for my life!"   1Sa 26:21; Ps 72:14

[15]The angel of the LORD said to Elijah, "Go down with him; do not be afraid of him." So Elijah got up and went down with him to the king.   Isa 51:12; Jer 1:17; Eze 2:6

[16]He told the king, "This is what the LORD says: Is it because there is no God in Israel for you to consult that you have sent messengers to consult Baal-Zebub, the god of Ekron? Because you have done this, you will never leave the bed you are lying on. You will certainly die!" [17]So he died, according to the word of the LORD that Elijah had spoken.   2Ki 8:15; Jer 20:6; 28:17

Because Ahaziah had no son, Joram[a] succeeded him as king in the second year of Jehoram son of Jehoshaphat king of Judah. [18]As for all the other events of Ahaziah's reign, and what he did, are they not written in the book of the annals of the kings of Israel?   2Ki 3:1

Elijah Taken Up to Heaven

2 When the LORD was about to take Elijah up to heaven in a whirlwind, Elijah and Elisha were on their way from Gilgal. [2]Elijah said to Elisha, "Stay here; the LORD has sent me to Bethel."   Ge 5:24

But Elisha said, "As surely as the LORD lives and as you live, I will not leave you." So they went down to Bethel.   Ru 1:16; 1Sa 1:26

[3]The company of the prophets at Bethel came out to Elisha and asked, "Do you know that the LORD is going to take your master from you today?"   1Sa 10:5; 2Ki 4:1,38

"Yes, I know," Elisha replied, "but do not speak of it."

[4]Then Elijah said to him, "Stay here, Elisha; the LORD has sent me to Jericho."   Jos 3:16; 6:26

And he replied, "As surely as the LORD lives and as you live, I will not leave you." So they went to Jericho.

[5]The company of the prophets at Jericho went up to Elisha and asked him, "Do you know that the LORD is going to take your master from you today?"

"Yes, I know," he replied, "but do not speak of it."

[6]Then Elijah said to him, "Stay here; the LORD has sent me to the Jordan."   Jos 3:15

And he replied, "As surely as the LORD lives and as you live, I will not leave you." So the two of them walked on.   Ru 1:16

[7]Fifty men of the company of the prophets went and stood at a distance, facing the place where Elijah and Elisha had stopped at the Jordan. [8]Elijah took his cloak, rolled it up and struck the water with it. The water divided to the

---

a 17 Hebrew Jehoram, a variant of Joram

right and to the left, and the two of them crossed over on dry ground.

⁹When they had crossed, Elijah said to Elisha, "Tell me, what can I do for you before I am taken from you?"

"Let me inherit a double portion of your spirit," Elisha replied.

¹⁰"You have asked a difficult thing," Elijah said, "yet if you see me when I am taken from you, it will be yours—otherwise not."

¹¹As they were walking along and talking together, suddenly a chariot of fire and horses of fire appeared and separated the two of them, and Elijah went up to heaven in a whirlwind. ¹²Elisha saw this and cried out, "My father! My father! The chariots and horsemen of Israel!" And Elisha saw him no more. Then he took hold of his own clothes and tore them apart.

¹³He picked up the cloak that had fallen from Elijah and went back and stood on the bank of the Jordan. ¹⁴Then he took the cloak that had fallen from him and struck the water with it. "Where now is the LORD, the God of Elijah?" he asked. When he struck the water, it divided to the right and to the left, and he crossed over.

¹⁵The company of the prophets from Jericho, who were watching, said, "The spirit of Elijah is resting on Elisha." And they went to meet him and bowed to the ground before him. ¹⁶"Look," they said, "we your servants have fifty able men. Let them go and look for your master. Perhaps the Spirit of the LORD has picked him up and set him down on some mountain or in some valley." 1Ki 18:12; Ac 8:39; 1Sa 10:5

"No," Elisha replied, "do not send them."

¹⁷But they persisted until he was too ashamed to refuse. So he said, "Send them." And they sent fifty men, who searched for three days but did not find him. ¹⁸When they returned to Elisha, who was staying in Jericho, he said to them, "Didn't I tell you not to go?"

Healing of the Water

¹⁹The men of the city said to Elisha, "Look, our lord, this town is well situated, as you can see, but the water is bad and the land is unproductive."

²⁰"Bring me a new bowl," he said, "and put salt in it." So they brought it to him.

²¹Then he went out to the spring and threw the salt into it, saying, "This is what the LORD says: 'I have healed this water. Never again will it cause death or make the land unproductive.'" ²²And the water has remained wholesome to this day, according to the word Elisha had spoken. Ex 15:25; 2Ki 4:41; 6:6

Elisha Is Jeered

²³From there Elisha went up to Bethel. As he was walking along the road, some youths came out of the town and jeered at him. "Go on

up, you baldhead!" they said. "Go on up, you baldhead!" 24He turned around, looked at them and called down a curse on them in the name of the LORD. Then two bears came out of the woods and mauled forty-two of the youths. 25And he went on to Mount Carmel and from there returned to Samaria.

Moab Revolts

3 Joram[a] son of Ahab became king of Israel in Samaria in the eighteenth year of Jehoshaphat king of Judah, and he reigned twelve years. 2He did evil in the eyes of the LORD, but not as his father and mother had done. He got rid of the sacred stone of Baal that his father had made. 3Nevertheless he clung to the sins of Jeroboam son of Nebat, which he had caused Israel to commit; he did not turn away from them.   1Ki 12:28-32

4Now Mesha king of Moab raised sheep, and he had to supply the king of Israel with a hundred thousand lambs and with the wool of a hundred thousand rams. 5But after Ahab died, the king of Moab rebelled against the king of Israel. 6So at that time King Joram set out from Samaria and mobilized all Israel. 7He also sent this message to Jehoshaphat king of Judah: "The king of Moab has rebelled against me. Will you go with me to fight against Moab?"   1Ki 22:4; 2Ki 1:1; Isa 16:1

"I will go with you," he replied.

"I am as you are, my people as your people, my horses as your horses."

8"By what route shall we attack?" he asked.

"Through the Desert of Edom," he answered.

9So the king of Israel set out with the king of Judah and the king of Edom. After a roundabout march of seven days, the army had no more water for themselves or for the animals with them.   1Ki 22:47

10"What!" exclaimed the king of Israel. "Has the LORD called us three kings together only to hand us over to Moab?"

11But Jehoshaphat asked, "Is there no prophet of the LORD here, that we may inquire of the LORD through him?"   1Ki 22:7

An officer of the king of Israel answered, "Elisha son of Shaphat is here. He used to pour water on the hands of Elijah.[b]"   Ge 20:7

12Jehoshaphat said, "The word of the LORD is with him." So the king of Israel and Jehoshaphat and the king of Edom went down to him.   Nu 11:17

13Elisha said to the king of Israel, "What do we have to do with each other? Go to the prophets of your father and the prophets of your mother."

"No," the king of Israel answered, "because it was the LORD who called us three kings together to hand us over to Moab."

---

a 1 Hebrew Jehoram, a variant of Joram; also in verse 6   b 11 That is, he was Elijah's personal servant.

¹⁴Elisha said, "As surely as the LORD Almighty lives, whom I serve, if I did not have respect for the presence of Jehoshaphat king of Judah, I would not look at you or even notice you. ¹⁵But now bring me a harpist."   1Sa 16:23

While the harpist was playing, the hand of the LORD came upon Elisha ¹⁶and he said, "This is what the LORD says: Make this valley full of ditches. ¹⁷For this is what the LORD says: You will see neither wind nor rain, yet this valley will be filled with water, and you, your cattle and your other animals will drink. ¹⁸This is an easy thing in the eyes of the LORD; he will also hand Moab over to you. ¹⁹You will overthrow every fortified city and every major town. You will cut down every good tree, stop up all the springs, and ruin every good field with stones."   Ge 18:14; Jer 32:17,27

²⁰The next morning, about the time for offering the sacrifice, there it was—water flowing from the direction of Edom! And the land was filled with water.

²¹Now all the Moabites had heard that the kings had come to fight against them; so every man, young and old, who could bear arms was called up and stationed on the border. ²²When they got up early in the morning, the sun was shining on the water. To the Moabites across the way, the water looked red—like blood. ²³"That's blood!" they said. "Those kings must have fought and slaughtered each other. Now to the plunder, Moab!"

²⁴But when the Moabites came to the camp of Israel, the Israelites rose up and fought them until they fled. And the Israelites invaded the land and slaughtered the Moabites. ²⁵They destroyed the towns, and each man threw a stone on every good field until it was covered. They stopped up all the springs and cut down every good tree. Only Kir Hareseth was left with its stones in place, but men armed with slings surrounded it and attacked it as well.   Isa 16:7; Jer 48:31,36

²⁶When the king of Moab saw that the battle had gone against him, he took with him seven hundred swordsmen to break through to the king of Edom, but they failed. ²⁷Then he took his firstborn son, who was to succeed him as king, and offered him as a sacrifice on the city wall. The fury against Israel was great; they withdrew and returned to their own land.

The Widow's Oil

4 The wife of a man from the company of the prophets cried out to Elisha, "Your servant my husband is dead, and you know that he revered the LORD. But now his creditor is coming to take my two boys as his slaves."

²Elisha replied to her, "How can I help you? Tell me, what do you have in your house?"

"Your servant has nothing there at all," she said, "except a little oil."

³Elisha said, "Go around and ask all your neighbors for empty jars. Don't ask for just a few. ⁴Then go inside and shut the door behind you and your sons. Pour oil into all the jars, and as each is filled, put it to one side."

⁵She left him and afterward shut the door behind her and her sons. They brought the jars to her and she kept pouring. ⁶When all the jars were full, she said to her son, "Bring me another one."

But he replied, "There is not a jar left." Then the oil stopped flowing.

⁷She went and told the man of God, and he said, "Go, sell the oil and pay your debts. You and your sons can live on what is left."

The Shunammite's Son Restored to Life

⁸One day Elisha went to Shunem. And a well-to-do woman was there, who urged him to stay for a meal. So whenever he came by, he stopped there to eat. ⁹She said to her husband, "I know that this man who often comes our way is a holy man of God. ¹⁰Let's make a small room on the roof and put in it a bed and a table, a chair and a lamp for him. Then he can stay there whenever he comes to us."

¹¹One day when Elisha came, he went up to his room and lay down there. ¹²He said to his servant Gehazi, "Call the Shunammite." So he called her, and she stood before him. ¹³Elisha said to him, "Tell her, 'You have gone to all this trouble for us. Now what can be done for you? Can we speak on your behalf to the king or the commander of the army?' " *2Ki 8:1*

She replied, "I have a home among my own people."

¹⁴"What can be done for her?" Elisha asked.

Gehazi said, "Well, she has no son and her husband is old."

¹⁵Then Elisha said, "Call her." So he called her, and she stood in the doorway. ¹⁶"About this time next year," Elisha said, "you will hold a son in your arms." *Ge 18:10*

"No, my lord," she objected. "Don't mislead your servant, O man of God!"

¹⁷But the woman became pregnant, and the next year about that same time she gave birth to a son, just as Elisha had told her.

¹⁸The child grew, and one day he went out to his father, who was with the reapers. ¹⁹"My head! My head!" he said to his father.

His father told a servant, "Carry him to his mother." ²⁰After the servant had lifted him up and carried him to his mother, the boy sat on her lap until noon, and then he died. ²¹She went up and laid him on the bed of the man of God, then shut the door and went out.

²²She called her husband and said, "Please send me one of the servants and a donkey so I can go to the man of God quickly and return."

²³"Why go to him today?" he asked. "It's not the New Moon or the Sabbath." Nu 10:10; 1Ch 23:31; Ps 81:3

"It's all right," she said.

²⁴She saddled the donkey and said to her servant, "Lead on; don't slow down for me unless I tell you." ²⁵So she set out and came to the man of God at Mount Carmel.

When he saw her in the distance, the man of God said to his servant Gehazi, "Look! There's the Shunammite! ²⁶Run to meet her and ask her, 'Are you all right? Is your husband all right? Is your child all right?'"

"Everything is all right," she said.

²⁷When she reached the man of God at the mountain, she took hold of his feet. Gehazi came over to push her away, but the man of God said, "Leave her alone! She is in bitter distress, but the LORD has hidden it from me and has not told me why." 1Sa 1:15

²⁸"Did I ask you for a son, my lord?" she said. "Didn't I tell you, 'Don't raise my hopes'?"

²⁹Elisha said to Gehazi, "Tuck your cloak into your belt, take my staff in your hand and run. If you meet anyone, do not greet him, and if anyone greets you, do not answer. Lay my staff on the boy's face." Ex 7:19; 1Ki 18:46

³⁰But the child's mother said, "As surely as the LORD lives and as you live, I will not leave you." So he got up and followed her.

³¹Gehazi went on ahead and laid the staff on the boy's face, but there was no sound or response. So Gehazi went back to meet Elisha and told him, "The boy has not awakened."

³²When Elisha reached the house, there was the boy lying dead on his couch. ³³He went in, shut the door on the two of them and prayed to the LORD. ³⁴Then he got on the bed and lay upon the boy, mouth to mouth, eyes to eyes, hands to hands. As he stretched himself out upon him, the boy's body grew warm. ³⁵Elisha turned away and walked back and forth in the room and then got on the bed and stretched out upon him once more. The boy sneezed seven times and opened his eyes.

³⁶Elisha summoned Gehazi and said, "Call the Shunammite." And he did. When she came, he said, "Take your son." ³⁷She came in, fell at his feet and bowed to the ground. Then she took her son and went out. Heb 11:35

Death in the Pot

³⁸Elisha returned to Gilgal and there was a famine in that region. While the company of the prophets was meeting with him, he said to his servant, "Put on the large pot and cook some stew for these men." 2Ki 2:1; 8:1

³⁹One of them went out into the fields to gather herbs and found a wild vine. He gathered some of its gourds and filled the fold of his cloak. When he returned, he cut

them up into the pot of stew, though no one knew what they were. **40**The stew was poured out for the men, but as they began to eat it, they cried out, "O man of God, there is death in the pot!" And they could not eat it.

41Elisha said, "Get some flour." He put it into the pot and said, "Serve it to the people to eat." And there was nothing harmful in the pot.   Ex 15:25; 2Ki 2:21

Feeding of a Hundred

42A man came from Baal Shalishah, bringing the man of God twenty loaves of barley bread baked from the first ripe grain, along with some heads of new grain. "Give it to the people to eat," Elisha said.   1Sa 9:4,7; Mt 14:17; 15:36

43"How can I set this before a hundred men?" his servant asked.

But Elisha answered, "Give it to the people to eat. For this is what the LORD says: 'They will eat and have some left over.'" **44**Then he set it before them, and they ate and had some left over, according to the word of the LORD.   Lk 9:13; Jn 6:12

Naaman Healed of Leprosy

5 Now Naaman was commander of the army of the king of Aram. He was a great man in the sight of his master and highly regarded, because through him the LORD had given victory to Aram.

He was a valiant soldier, but he had leprosy.*a*   Lk 4:27; 2Sa 10:19

2Now bands from Aram had gone out and had taken captive a young girl from Israel, and she served Naaman's wife. **3**She said to her mistress, "If only my master would see the prophet who is in Samaria! He would cure him of his leprosy."   Ge 20:7; 2Ki 6:23; 13:20

4Naaman went to his master and told him what the girl from Israel had said. **5**"By all means, go," the king of Aram replied. "I will send a letter to the king of Israel." So Naaman left, taking with him ten talents*b* of silver, six thousand shekels*c* of gold and ten sets of clothing. **6**The letter that he took to the king of Israel read: "With this letter I am sending my servant Naaman to you so that you may cure him of his leprosy."   1Sa 9:7

7As soon as the king of Israel read the letter, he tore his robes and said, "Am I God? Can I kill and bring back to life? Why does this fellow send someone to me to be cured of his leprosy? See how he is trying to pick a quarrel with me!"

8When Elisha the man of God heard that the king of Israel had torn his robes, he sent him this message: "Why have you torn your robes? Have the man come to me and he will know that there is a prophet in Israel." **9**So Naaman went with his horses and chariots

---

a 1 The Hebrew word was used for various diseases affecting the skin—not necessarily leprosy; also in verses 3, 6, 7, 11 and 27.   *b* 5 That is, about 750 pounds (about 340 kilograms)   *c* 5 That is, about 150 pounds (about 70 kilograms)

and stopped at the door of Elisha's house. [10]Elisha sent a messenger to say to him, "Go, wash yourself seven times in the Jordan, and your flesh will be restored and you will be cleansed." Jn 9:7; Lev 14:7

[11]But Naaman went away angry and said, "I thought that he would surely come out to me and stand and call on the name of the LORD his God, wave his hand over the spot and cure me of my leprosy. [12]Are not Abana and Pharpar, the rivers of Damascus, better than any of the waters of Israel? Couldn't I wash in them and be cleansed?" So he turned and went off in a rage. Pr 14:17,29; 19:11; 29:11

[13]Naaman's servants went to him and said, "My father, if the prophet had told you to do some great thing, would you not have done it? How much more, then, when he tells you, 'Wash and be cleansed'!" [14]So he went down and dipped himself in the Jordan seven times, as the man of God had told him, and his flesh was restored and became clean like that of a young boy. Jos 6:15; Job 33:25; Lk 4:27

[15]Then Naaman and all his attendants went back to the man of God. He stood before him and said, "Now I know that there is no God in all the world except in Israel. Please accept now a gift from your servant." Jos 4:24; 1Sa 17:46

[16]The prophet answered, "As surely as the LORD lives, whom I serve, I will not accept a thing." And even though Naaman urged him, he refused. ver 20,26; Ge 14:23

[17]"If you will not," said Naaman, "please let me, your servant, be given as much earth as a pair of mules can carry, for your servant will never again make burnt offerings and sacrifices to any other god but the LORD. [18]But may the LORD forgive your servant for this one thing: When my master enters the temple of Rimmon to bow down and he is leaning on my arm and I bow there also—when I bow down in the temple of Rimmon, may the LORD forgive your servant for this." Ex 20:24; 2Ki 7:2

[19]"Go in peace," Elisha said.

After Naaman had traveled some distance, [20]Gehazi, the servant of Elisha the man of God, said to himself, "My master was too easy on Naaman, this Aramean, by not accepting from him what he brought. As surely as the LORD lives, I will run after him and get something from him." Ex 20:7

[21]So Gehazi hurried after Naaman. When Naaman saw him running toward him, he got down from the chariot to meet him. "Is everything all right?" he asked.

[22]"Everything is all right," Gehazi answered. "My master sent me to say, 'Two young men from the company of the prophets have just come to me from the hill country of Ephraim. Please give them a tal-

ent[a] of silver and two sets of clothing.' "   ver 5; Ge 45:22
²³"By all means, take two tal-
ents," said Naaman. He urged Gehazi to accept them, and then tied
up the two talents of silver in two
bags, with two sets of clothing. He
gave them to two of his servants,
and they carried them ahead of Gehazi. ²⁴When Gehazi came to the
hill, he took the things from the
servants and put them away in the
house. He sent the men away and
they left. ²⁵Then he went in and
stood before his master Elisha.

"Where have you been, Gehazi?" Elisha asked.

"Your servant didn't go anywhere," Gehazi answered.

²⁶But Elisha said to him, "Was
not my spirit with you when the
man got down from his chariot to
meet you? Is this the time to take
money, or to accept clothes, olive
groves, vineyards, flocks, herds, or
menservants and maidservants?
²⁷Naaman's leprosy will cling to
you and to your descendants forever." Then Gehazi went from Elisha's presence and he was leprous,
as white as snow.   ver 16; Ex 4:6

An Axhead Floats

6 The company of the prophets
said to Elisha, "Look, the place
where we meet with you is too
small for us. ²Let us go to the Jordan, where each of us can get a

pole; and let us build a place there
for us to live."   1Sa 10:5; 2Ki 4:38
And he said, "Go."
³Then one of them said, "Won't
you please come with your servants?"

"I will," Elisha replied. ⁴And he
went with them.

They went to the Jordan and began to cut down trees. ⁵As one of
them was cutting down a tree, the
iron axhead fell into the water.
"Oh, my lord," he cried out, "it was
borrowed!"

⁶The man of God asked, "Where
did it fall?" When he showed him
the place, Elisha cut a stick and
threw it there, and made the iron
float. ⁷"Lift it out," he said. Then
the man reached out his hand and
took it.   Ex 15:25; 2Ki 2:21

Elisha Traps Blinded Arameans

⁸Now the king of Aram was at
war with Israel. After conferring
with his officers, he said, "I will set
up my camp in such and such a
place."

⁹The man of God sent word to
the king of Israel: "Beware of passing that place, because the Arameans are going down there." ¹⁰So
the king of Israel checked on the
place indicated by the man of God.
Time and again Elisha warned the
king, so that he was on his guard
in such places.   ver 12; Jer 11:18
¹¹This enraged the king of Aram.

a22 That is, about 75 pounds (about 34 kilograms)

He summoned his officers and demanded of them, "Will you not tell me which of us is on the side of the king of Israel?"

¹²"None of us, my lord the king," said one of his officers, "but Elisha, the prophet who is in Israel, tells the king of Israel the very words you speak in your bedroom."

¹³"Go, find out where he is," the king ordered, "so I can send men and capture him." The report came back: "He is in Dothan." ¹⁴Then he sent horses and chariots and a strong force there. They went by night and surrounded the city.

¹⁵When the servant of the man of God got up and went out early the next morning, an army with horses and chariots had surrounded the city. "Oh, my lord, what shall we do?" the servant asked.

¹⁶"Don't be afraid," the prophet answered. "Those who are with us are more than those who are with them." 2Ch 32:7; Ps 55:18; 1Jn 4:4

¹⁷And Elisha prayed, "O LORD, open his eyes so he may see." Then the LORD opened the servant's eyes, and he looked and saw the hills full of horses and chariots of fire all around Elisha. 2Ki 2:11-12

¹⁸As the enemy came down toward him, Elisha prayed to the LORD, "Strike these people with blindness." So he struck them with blindness, as Elisha had asked.

¹⁹Elisha told them, "This is not the road and this is not the city. Follow me, and I will lead you to the man you are looking for." And he led them to Samaria.

²⁰After they entered the city, Elisha said, "LORD, open the eyes of these men so they can see." Then the LORD opened their eyes and they looked, and there they were, inside Samaria.

²¹When the king of Israel saw them, he asked Elisha, "Shall I kill them, my father? Shall I kill them?"

²²"Do not kill them," he answered. "Would you kill men you have captured with your own sword or bow? Set food and water before them so that they may eat and drink and then go back to their master." ²³So he prepared a great feast for them, and after they had finished eating and drinking, he sent them away, and they returned to their master. So the bands from Aram stopped raiding Israel's territory. Dt 20:11; 2Ki 5:2; Ro 12:20

Famine in Besieged Samaria

²⁴Some time later, Ben-Hadad king of Aram mobilized his entire army and marched up and laid siege to Samaria. ²⁵There was a great famine in the city; the siege lasted so long that a donkey's head sold for eighty shekels*a* of silver, and a quarter of a cab*b* of seed pods*c* for five shekels.*d* Lev 26:26

²⁶As the king of Israel was pass-

---

*a*25 That is, about 2 pounds (about 1 kilogram)   *b*25 That is, probably about 1/2 pint (about 0.3 liter)
*c*25 Or *of doves' dung*   *d*25 That is, about 2 ounces (about 55 grams)

ing by on the wall, a woman cried to him, "Help me, my lord the king!"

27The king replied, "If the LORD does not help you, where can I get help for you? From the threshing floor? From the winepress?" 28Then he asked her, "What's the matter?"

She answered, "This woman said to me, 'Give up your son so we may eat him today, and tomorrow we'll eat my son.' 29So we cooked my son and ate him. The next day I said to her, 'Give up your son so we may eat him,' but she had hidden him." Lev 26:29; Dt 28:53-55

30When the king heard the woman's words, he tore his robes. As he went along the wall, the people looked, and there, underneath, he had sackcloth on his body. 31He said, "May God deal with me, be it ever so severely, if the head of Elisha son of Shaphat remains on his shoulders today!" Ge 37:34; 1Ki 21:27

32Now Elisha was sitting in his house, and the elders were sitting with him. The king sent a messenger ahead, but before he arrived, Elisha said to the elders, "Don't you see how this murderer is sending someone to cut off my head? Look, when the messenger comes, shut the door and hold it shut against him. Is not the sound of his master's footsteps behind him?"

33While he was still talking to them, the messenger came down to him. And the king said, "This disaster is from the LORD. Why should I wait for the LORD any longer?" Job 2:9; 14:14; Isa 40:31

7 Elisha said, "Hear the word of the LORD. This is what the LORD says: About this time tomorrow, a seah*a* of flour will sell for a shekel*b* and two seahs*c* of barley for a shekel at the gate of Samaria."

2The officer on whose arm the king was leaning said to the man of God, "Look, even if the LORD should open the floodgates of the heavens, could this happen?"

"You will see it with your own eyes," answered Elisha, "but you will not eat any of it!" ver 17

The Siege Lifted

3Now there were four men with leprosy*d* at the entrance of the city gate. They said to each other, "Why stay here until we die? 4If we say, 'We'll go into the city'—the famine is there, and we will die. And if we stay here, we will die. So let's go over to the camp of the Arameans and surrender. If they spare us, we live; if they kill us, then we die." Lev 13:45-46; Nu 5:1-4

5At dusk they got up and went to the camp of the Arameans. When they reached the edge of the camp, not a man was there, 6for the Lord

---

*a*1 That is, probably about 7 quarts (about 7.3 liters); also in verses 16 and 18 *b*1 That is, about 2/5 ounce (about 11 grams); also in verses 16 and 18 *c*1 That is, probably about 13 quarts (about 15 liters); also in verses 16 and 18 *d*3 The Hebrew word is used for various diseases affecting the skin—not necessarily leprosy; also in verse 8.

had caused the Arameans to hear the sound of chariots and horses and a great army, so that they said to one another, "Look, the king of Israel has hired the Hittite and Egyptian kings to attack us!" ⁷So they got up and fled in the dusk and abandoned their tents and their horses and donkeys. They left the camp as it was and ran for their lives.   2Sa 5:24; Ps 48:4-6; Pr 28:1

⁸The men who had leprosy reached the edge of the camp and entered one of the tents. They ate and drank, and carried away silver, gold and clothes, and went off and hid them. They returned and entered another tent and took some things from it and hid them also.

⁹Then they said to each other, "We're not doing right. This is a day of good news and we are keeping it to ourselves. If we wait until daylight, punishment will overtake us. Let's go at once and report this to the royal palace."

¹⁰So they went and called out to the city gatekeepers and told them, "We went into the Aramean camp and not a man was there—not a sound of anyone—only tethered horses and donkeys, and the tents left just as they were." ¹¹The gatekeepers shouted the news, and it was reported within the palace.

¹²The king got up in the night and said to his officers, "I will tell you what the Arameans have done to us. They know we are starving; so they have left the camp to hide in the countryside, thinking, 'They will surely come out, and then we will take them alive and get into the city.' "   Jos 8:4; 2Ki 6:25-29

¹³One of his officers answered, "Have some men take five of the horses that are left in the city. Their plight will be like that of all the Israelites left here—yes, they will only be like all these Israelites who are doomed. So let us send them to find out what happened."

¹⁴So they selected two chariots with their horses, and the king sent them after the Aramean army. He commanded the drivers, "Go and find out what has happened." ¹⁵They followed them as far as the Jordan, and they found the whole road strewn with the clothing and equipment the Arameans had thrown away in their headlong flight. So the messengers returned and reported to the king. ¹⁶Then the people went out and plundered the camp of the Arameans. So a seah of flour sold for a shekel, and two seahs of barley sold for a shekel, as the Lord had said.

¹⁷Now the king had put the officer on whose arm he leaned in charge of the gate, and the people trampled him in the gateway, and he died, just as the man of God had foretold when the king came down to his house. ¹⁸It happened as the man of God had said to the king: "About this time tomorrow, a seah of flour will sell for a shekel and two seahs of barley for a shekel at the gate of Samaria."   ver 2; 2Ki 6:32

¹⁹The officer had said to the man

of God, "Look, even if the LORD should open the floodgates of the heavens, could this happen?" The man of God had replied, "You will see it with your own eyes, but you will not eat any of it!" 20And that is exactly what happened to him, for the people trampled him in the gateway, and he died.   ver 2

The Shunammite's Land Restored

8 Now Elisha had said to the woman whose son he had restored to life, "Go away with your family and stay for a while wherever you can, because the LORD has decreed a famine in the land that will last seven years." 2The woman proceeded to do as the man of God said. She and her family went away and stayed in the land of the Philistines seven years.   2Ki 4:8-37

3At the end of the seven years she came back from the land of the Philistines and went to the king to beg for her house and land. 4The king was talking to Gehazi, the servant of the man of God, and had said, "Tell me about all the great things Elisha has done." 5Just as Gehazi was telling the king how Elisha had restored the dead to life, the woman whose son Elisha had brought back to life came to beg the king for her house and land.   2Ki 4:35

Gehazi said, "This is the woman, my lord the king, and this is her son whom Elisha restored to life." 6The king asked the woman about it, and she told him.

Then he assigned an official to her case and said to him, "Give back everything that belonged to her, including all the income from her land from the day she left the country until now."

Hazael Murders Ben-Hadad

7Elisha went to Damascus, and Ben-Hadad king of Aram was ill. When the king was told, "The man of God has come all the way up here," 8he said to Hazael, "Take a gift with you and go to meet the man of God. Consult the LORD through him; ask him, 'Will I recover from this illness?'"   1Sa 9:7

9Hazael went to meet Elisha, taking with him as a gift forty camel-loads of all the finest wares of Damascus. He went in and stood before him, and said, "Your son Ben-Hadad king of Aram has sent me to ask, 'Will I recover from this illness?'"

10Elisha answered, "Go and say to him, 'You will certainly recover'; buta the LORD has revealed to me that he will in fact die." 11He stared at him with a fixed gaze until Hazael felt ashamed. Then the man of God began to weep.

12"Why is my lord weeping?" asked Hazael.

"Because I know the harm you will do to the Israelites," he an-

---

a 10 The Hebrew may also be read Go and say, 'You will certainly not recover,' for.

swered. "You will set fire to their fortified places, kill their young men with the sword, dash their little children to the ground, and rip open their pregnant women."

¹³Hazael said, "How could your servant, a mere dog, accomplish such a feat?"   1Sa 17:43; 2Sa 3:8

"The LORD has shown me that you will become king of Aram," answered Elisha.   1Ki 19:15

¹⁴Then Hazael left Elisha and returned to his master. When Ben-Hadad asked, "What did Elisha say to you?" Hazael replied, "He told me that you would certainly recover." ¹⁵But the next day he took a thick cloth, soaked it in water and spread it over the king's face, so that he died. Then Hazael succeeded him as king.   2Ki 1:17

Jehoram King of Judah

¹⁶In the fifth year of Joram son of Ahab king of Israel, when Jehoshaphat was king of Judah, Jehoram son of Jehoshaphat began his reign as king of Judah. ¹⁷He was thirty-two years old when he became king, and he reigned in Jerusalem eight years. ¹⁸He walked in the ways of the kings of Israel, as the house of Ahab had done, for he married a daughter of Ahab. He did evil in the eyes of the LORD. ¹⁹Nevertheless, for the sake of his servant David, the LORD was not willing to destroy Judah. He had promised to maintain a lamp for David and his descendants forever.   2Sa 7:13; 2Ki 1:17; 2Ch 21:1-4

²⁰In the time of Jehoram, Edom rebelled against Judah and set up its own king. ²¹So Jehoram[a] went to Zair with all his chariots. The Edomites surrounded him and his chariot commanders, but he rose up and broke through by night; his army, however, fled back home. ²²To this day Edom has been in rebellion against Judah. Libnah revolted at the same time.   Ge 27:40

²³As for the other events of Jehoram's reign, and all he did, are they not written in the book of the annals of the kings of Judah? ²⁴Jehoram rested with his fathers and was buried with them in the City of David. And Ahaziah his son succeeded him as king.   2Ch 21:5-10,20

Ahaziah King of Judah

²⁵In the twelfth year of Joram son of Ahab king of Israel, Ahaziah son of Jehoram king of Judah began to reign. ²⁶Ahaziah was twenty-two years old when he became king, and he reigned in Jerusalem one year. His mother's name was Athaliah, a granddaughter of Omri king of Israel. ²⁷He walked in the ways of the house of Ahab and did evil in the eyes of the LORD, as the house of Ahab had done, for he was related by marriage to Ahab's family.   1Ki 15:26; 16:23,30

²⁸Ahaziah went with Joram son of Ahab to war against Hazael king

---

a 21 Hebrew *Joram*, a variant of *Jehoram*; also in verses 23 and 24 of Aram at Ramoth Gilead. The Arameans wounded Joram; ²⁹so King Joram returned to Jezreel to recover from the wounds the Arameans had inflicted on him at Ramoth*a* in his battle with Hazael king of Aram.   1Ki 19:15,17; 22:3,29; 2Ki 9:15

Then Ahaziah son of Jehoram king of Judah went down to Jezreel to see Joram son of Ahab, because he had been wounded.

Jehu Anointed King of Israel

9 The prophet Elisha summoned a man from the company of the prophets and said to him, "Tuck your cloak into your belt, take this flask of oil with you and go to Ramoth Gilead. ²When you get there, look for Jehu son of Jehoshaphat, the son of Nimshi. Go to him, get him away from his companions and take him into an inner room. ³Then take the flask and pour the oil on his head and declare, 'This is what the Lord says: I anoint you king over Israel.' Then open the door and run; don't delay!"   1Ki 19:16; 2Ki 4:29; 8:28

⁴So the young man, the prophet, went to Ramoth Gilead. ⁵When he arrived, he found the army officers sitting together. "I have a message for you, commander," he said.

"For which of us?" asked Jehu.

"For you, commander," he replied.

⁶Jehu got up and went into the house. Then the prophet poured the oil on Jehu's head and declared, "This is what the Lord, the God of Israel, says: 'I anoint you king over the Lord's people Israel. ⁷You are to destroy the house of Ahab your master, and I will avenge the blood of my servants the prophets and the blood of all the Lord's servants shed by Jezebel. ⁸The whole house of Ahab will perish. I will cut off from Ahab every last male in Israel—slave or free. ⁹I will make the house of Ahab like the house of Jeroboam son of Nebat and like the house of Baasha son of Ahijah. ¹⁰As for Jezebel, dogs will devour her on the plot of ground at Jezreel, and no one will bury her.'" Then he opened the door and ran.   1Ki 14:10

¹¹When Jehu went out to his fellow officers, one of them asked him, "Is everything all right? Why did this madman come to you?"

"You know the man and the sort of things he says," Jehu replied.

¹²"That's not true!" they said. "Tell us."

Jehu said, "Here is what he told me: 'This is what the Lord says: I anoint you king over Israel.'"

¹³They hurried and took their cloaks and spread them under him on the bare steps. Then they blew the trumpet and shouted, "Jehu is king!"   Mt 21:8; 2Sa 15:10

Jehu Kills Joram and Ahaziah

¹⁴So Jehu son of Jehoshaphat,

---

a 29 Hebrew *Ramah,* a variant of *Ramoth*

the son of Nimshi, conspired against Joram. (Now Joram and all Israel had been defending Ramoth Gilead against Hazael king of Aram, [15]but King Joram[a] had returned to Jezreel to recover from the wounds the Arameans had inflicted on him in the battle with Hazael king of Aram.) Jehu said, "If this is the way you feel, don't let anyone slip out of the city to go and tell the news in Jezreel." [16]Then he got into his chariot and rode to Jezreel, because Joram was resting there and Ahaziah king of Judah had gone down to see him.

[17]When the lookout standing on the tower in Jezreel saw Jehu's troops approaching, he called out, "I see some troops coming."

"Get a horseman," Joram ordered. "Send him to meet them and ask, 'Do you come in peace?' "

[18]The horseman rode off to meet Jehu and said, "This is what the king says: 'Do you come in peace?' "

"What do you have to do with peace?" Jehu replied. "Fall in behind me."

The lookout reported, "The messenger has reached them, but he isn't coming back."

[19]So the king sent out a second horseman. When he came to them he said, "This is what the king says: 'Do you come in peace?' "

Jehu replied, "What do you have to do with peace? Fall in behind me."

[20]The lookout reported, "He has reached them, but he isn't coming back either. The driving is like that of Jehu son of Nimshi—he drives like a madman."   2Sa 18:27

[21]"Hitch up my chariot," Joram ordered. And when it was hitched up, Joram king of Israel and Ahaziah king of Judah rode out, each in his own chariot, to meet Jehu. They met him at the plot of ground that had belonged to Naboth the Jezreelite. [22]When Joram saw Jehu he asked, "Have you come in peace, Jehu?"   1Ki 21:1-7,15-19

"How can there be peace," Jehu replied, "as long as all the idolatry and witchcraft of your mother Jezebel abound?"   1Ki 18:19; 2Ch 21:13

[23]Joram turned about and fled, calling out to Ahaziah, "Treachery, Ahaziah!"   2Ki 11:14

[24]Then Jehu drew his bow and shot Joram between the shoulders. The arrow pierced his heart and he slumped down in his chariot. [25]Jehu said to Bidkar, his chariot officer, "Pick him up and throw him on the field that belonged to Naboth the Jezreelite. Remember how you and I were riding together in chariots behind Ahab his father when the LORD made this prophecy about him: [26]'Yesterday I saw the blood of Naboth and the blood of his sons, declares the LORD, and I will surely make you pay for it on

---

[a] 15 Hebrew Jehoram, a variant of Joram; also in verses 17 and 21-24

this plot of ground, declares the LORD.'ᵃ Now then, pick him up and throw him on that plot, in accordance with the word of the LORD." 1Ki 21:19-22,24-29; 22:34

²⁷When Ahaziah king of Judah saw what had happened, he fled up the road to Beth Haggan.ᵇ Jehu chased him, shouting, "Kill him too!" They wounded him in his chariot on the way up to Gur near Ibleam, but he escaped to Megiddo and died there. ²⁸His servants took him by chariot to Jerusalem and buried him with his fathers in his tomb in the City of David. ²⁹(In the eleventh year of Joram son of Ahab, Ahaziah had become king of Judah.) 2Ch 22:7-9; 2Ki 23:30; 8:25

Jezebel Killed

³⁰Then Jehu went to Jezreel. When Jezebel heard about it, she painted her eyes, arranged her hair and looked out of a window. ³¹As Jehu entered the gate, she asked, "Have you come in peace, Zimri, you murderer of your master?"ᶜ

³²He looked up at the window and called out, "Who is on my side? Who?" Two or three eunuchs looked down at him. ³³"Throw her down!" Jehu said. So they threw her down, and some of her blood spattered the wall and the horses as they trampled her underfoot.

³⁴Jehu went in and ate and drank. "Take care of that cursed woman," he said, "and bury her, for she was a king's daughter." ³⁵But when they went out to bury her, they found nothing except her skull, her feet and her hands. ³⁶They went back and told Jehu, who said, "This is the word of the LORD that he spoke through his servant Elijah the Tishbite: On the plot of ground at Jezreel dogs will devour Jezebel's flesh.ᵈ ³⁷Jezebel's body will be like refuse on the ground in the plot at Jezreel, so that no one will be able to say, 'This is Jezebel.' " 1Ki 21:23; Ps 83:10

Ahab's Family Killed

10 Now there were in Samaria seventy sons of the house of Ahab. So Jehu wrote letters and sent them to Samaria: to the officials of Jezreel,ᵉ to the elders and to the guardians of Ahab's children. He said, ²"As soon as this letter reaches you, since your master's sons are with you and you have chariots and horses, a fortified city and weapons, ³choose the best and most worthy of your master's sons and set him on his father's throne. Then fight for your master's house." 1Ki 13:32; 21:1

⁴But they were terrified and said, "If two kings could not resist him, how can we?"

⁵So the palace administrator, the city governor, the elders and guardians sent this message to

---

ᵃ26 See 1 Kings 21:19.   ᵇ27 Or *fled by way of the garden house*   ᶜ31 Or *"Did Zimri have peace, who murdered his master?"*   ᵈ36 See 1 Kings 21:23.   ᵉ1 Hebrew; some Septuagint manuscripts and Vulgate *of the city*

Jehu: "We are your servants and we will do anything you say. We will not appoint anyone as king; you do whatever you think best."

⁶Then Jehu wrote them a second letter, saying, "If you are on my side and will obey me, take the heads of your master's sons and come to me in Jezreel by this time tomorrow."

Now the royal princes, seventy of them, were with the leading men of the city, who were rearing them. ⁷When the letter arrived, these men took the princes and slaughtered all seventy of them. They put their heads in baskets and sent them to Jehu in Jezreel. ⁸When the messenger arrived, he told Jehu, "They have brought the heads of the princes."   2Sa 4:8

Then Jehu ordered, "Put them in two piles at the entrance of the city gate until morning."

⁹The next morning Jehu went out. He stood before all the people and said, "You are innocent. It was I who conspired against my master and killed him, but who killed all these? ¹⁰Know then, that not a word the LORD has spoken against the house of Ahab will fail. The LORD has done what he promised through his servant Elijah." ¹¹So Jehu killed everyone in Jezreel who remained of the house of Ahab, as well as all his chief men, his close friends and his priests, leaving him no survivor.   1Ki 21:29

¹²Jehu then set out and went toward Samaria. At Beth Eked of the Shepherds, ¹³he met some relatives of Ahaziah king of Judah and asked, "Who are you?"

They said, "We are relatives of Ahaziah, and we have come down to greet the families of the king and of the queen mother."

¹⁴"Take them alive!" he ordered. So they took them alive and slaughtered them by the well of Beth Eked—forty-two men. He left no survivor.

¹⁵After he left there, he came upon Jehonadab son of Recab, who was on his way to meet him. Jehu greeted him and said, "Are you in accord with me, as I am with you?"   1Ch 2:55; Jer 35:6,14-19

"I am," Jehonadab answered.

"If so," said Jehu, "give me your hand." So he did, and Jehu helped him up into the chariot. ¹⁶Jehu said, "Come with me and see my zeal for the LORD." Then he had him ride along in his chariot.

¹⁷When Jehu came to Samaria, he killed all who were left there of Ahab's family; he destroyed them, according to the word of the LORD spoken to Elijah.   2Ki 9:8

Ministers of Baal Killed

¹⁸Then Jehu brought all the people together and said to them, "Ahab served Baal a little; Jehu will serve him much. ¹⁹Now summon all the prophets of Baal, all his ministers and all his priests. See that no one is missing, because I am going to hold a great sacrifice for Baal. Anyone who fails to come

will no longer live." But Jehu was acting deceptively in order to destroy the ministers of Baal.

²⁰Jehu said, "Call an assembly in honor of Baal." So they proclaimed it. ²¹Then he sent word throughout Israel, and all the ministers of Baal came; not one stayed away. They crowded into the temple of Baal until it was full from one end to the other. ²²And Jehu said to the keeper of the wardrobe, "Bring robes for all the ministers of Baal." So he brought out robes for them.

²³Then Jehu and Jehonadab son of Recab went into the temple of Baal. Jehu said to the ministers of Baal, "Look around and see that no servants of the LORD are here with you—only ministers of Baal." ²⁴So they went in to make sacrifices and burnt offerings. Now Jehu had posted eighty men outside with this warning: "If one of you lets any of the men I am placing in your hands escape, it will be your life for his life." 1Ki 20:39

²⁵As soon as Jehu had finished making the burnt offering, he ordered the guards and officers: "Go in and kill them; let no one escape." So they cut them down with the sword. The guards and officers threw the bodies out and then entered the inner shrine of the temple of Baal. ²⁶They brought the sacred stone out of the temple of Baal and burned it. ²⁷They demolished the sacred stone of Baal and tore down the temple of Baal, and

people have used it for a latrine to this day. 1Ki 14:23; 18:40; 2Ki 11:18

²⁸So Jehu destroyed Baal worship in Israel. ²⁹However, he did not turn away from the sins of Jeroboam son of Nebat, which he had caused Israel to commit—the worship of the golden calves at Bethel and Dan. 1Ki 12:28-29; 19:17

³⁰The LORD said to Jehu, "Because you have done well in accomplishing what is right in my eyes and have done to the house of Ahab all I had in mind to do, your descendants will sit on the throne of Israel to the fourth generation." ³¹Yet Jehu was not careful to keep the law of the LORD, the God of Israel, with all his heart. He did not turn away from the sins of Jeroboam, which he had caused Israel to commit. 2Ki 15:12; Pr 4:23

³²In those days the LORD began to reduce the size of Israel. Hazael overpowered the Israelites throughout their territory ³³east of the Jordan in all the land of Gilead (the region of Gad, Reuben and Manasseh), from Aroer by the Arnon Gorge through Gilead to Bashan. 2Ki 8:12; 13:25

³⁴As for the other events of Jehu's reign, all he did, and all his achievements, are they not written in the book of the annals of the kings of Israel? 1Ki 15:31

³⁵Jehu rested with his fathers and was buried in Samaria. And Jehoahaz his son succeeded him as king. ³⁶The time that Jehu

reigned over Israel in Samaria was twenty-eight years.

Athaliah and Joash

11 When Athaliah the mother of Ahaziah saw that her son was dead, she proceeded to destroy the whole royal family. ²But Jehosheba, the daughter of King Jehoram*a* and sister of Ahaziah, took Joash son of Ahaziah and stole him away from among the royal princes, who were about to be murdered. She put him and his nurse in a bedroom to hide him from Athaliah; so he was not killed. ³He remained hidden with his nurse at the temple of the LORD for six years while Athaliah ruled the land.   2Ki 12:1; Jdg 9:5

⁴In the seventh year Jehoiada sent for the commanders of units of a hundred, the Carites and the guards and had them brought to him at the temple of the LORD. He made a covenant with them and put them under oath at the temple of the LORD. Then he showed them the king's son. ⁵He commanded them, saying, "This is what you are to do: You who are in the three companies that are going on duty on the Sabbath—a third of you guarding the royal palace, ⁶a third at the Sur Gate, and a third at the gate behind the guard, who take turns guarding the temple— ⁷and you who are in the other two companies that normally go off Sab-

bath duty are all to guard the temple for the king. ⁸Station yourselves around the king, each man with his weapon in his hand. Anyone who approaches your ranks*b* must be put to death. Stay close to the king wherever he goes."

⁹The commanders of units of a hundred did just as Jehoiada the priest ordered. Each one took his men—those who were going on duty on the Sabbath and those who were going off duty—and came to Jehoiada the priest. ¹⁰Then he gave the commanders the spears and shields that had belonged to King David and that were in the temple of the LORD. ¹¹The guards, each with his weapon in his hand, stationed themselves around the king—near the altar and the temple, from the south side to the north side of the temple.   2Sa 8:7; 1Ch 18:7

¹²Jehoiada brought out the king's son and put the crown on him; he presented him with a copy of the covenant and proclaimed him king. They anointed him, and the people clapped their hands and shouted, "Long live the king!" ¹³When Athaliah heard the noise made by the guards and the people, she went to the people at the temple of the LORD. ¹⁴She looked and there was the king, standing by the pillar, as the custom was. The officers and the trumpeters were beside the king,

---

a2 Hebrew *Joram*, a variant of *Jehoram*   *b8* Or *approaches the precincts*

and all the people of the land were rejoicing and blowing trumpets. Then Athaliah tore her robes and called out, "Treason! Treason!"

¹⁵Jehoiada the priest ordered the commanders of units of a hundred, who were in charge of the troops: "Bring her out between the ranks*a* and put to the sword anyone who follows her." For the priest had said, "She must not be put to death in the temple of the Lord." ¹⁶So they seized her as she reached the place where the horses enter the palace grounds, and there she was put to death.

¹⁷Jehoiada then made a covenant between the Lord and the king and people that they would be the Lord's people. He also made a covenant between the king and the people. ¹⁸All the people of the land went to the temple of Baal and tore it down. They smashed the altars and idols to pieces and killed Mattan the priest of Baal in front of the altars.   1Ki 18:40; 2Ki 10:25

Then Jehoiada the priest posted guards at the temple of the Lord. ¹⁹He took with him the commanders of hundreds, the Carites, the guards and all the people of the land, and together they brought the king down from the temple of the Lord and went into the palace, entering by way of the gate of the guards. The king then took his place on the royal throne, ²⁰and all

the people of the land rejoiced. And the city was quiet, because Athaliah had been slain with the sword at the palace.   Pr 11:10; 28:12

²¹Joash*b* was seven years old when he began to reign.

Joash Repairs the Temple

12 In the seventh year of Jehu, Joash*c* became king, and he reigned in Jerusalem forty years. His mother's name was Zibiah; she was from Beersheba. ²Joash did what was right in the eyes of the Lord all the years Jehoiada the priest instructed him. ³The high places, however, were not removed; the people continued to offer sacrifices and burn incense there.   2Ki 14:4; 15:35; 18:4

⁴Joash said to the priests, "Collect all the money that is brought as sacred offerings to the temple of the Lord—the money collected in the census, the money received from personal vows and the money brought voluntarily to the temple. ⁵Let every priest receive the money from one of the treasurers, and let it be used to repair whatever damage is found in the temple."

⁶But by the twenty-third year of King Joash the priests still had not repaired the temple. ⁷Therefore King Joash summoned Jehoiada the priest and the other priests and asked them, "Why aren't you repairing the damage done to the

---

a 15 Or *out from the precincts*   *b* 21 Hebrew *Jehoash*, a variant of *Joash*   *c* 1 Hebrew *Jehoash*, a variant of *Joash*; also in verses 2, 4, 6, 7 and 18

temple? Take no more money from your treasurers, but hand it over for repairing the temple." ⁸The priests agreed that they would not collect any more money from the people and that they would not repair the temple themselves.

⁹Jehoiada the priest took a chest and bored a hole in its lid. He placed it beside the altar, on the right side as one enters the temple of the Lord. The priests who guarded the entrance put into the chest all the money that was brought to the temple of the Lord. ¹⁰Whenever they saw that there was a large amount of money in the chest, the royal secretary and the high priest came, counted the money that had been brought into the temple of the Lord and put it into bags. ¹¹When the amount had been determined, they gave the money to the men appointed to supervise the work on the temple. With it they paid those who worked on the temple of the Lord —the carpenters and builders, ¹²the masons and stonecutters. They purchased timber and dressed stone for the repair of the temple of the Lord, and met all the other expenses of restoring the temple.   Mk 12:41; Lk 21:1

¹³The money brought into the temple was not spent for making silver basins, wick trimmers, sprinkling bowls, trumpets or any other articles of gold or silver for the temple of the Lord; ¹⁴it was paid to the workmen, who used it to repair the temple. ¹⁵They did not require an accounting from those to whom they gave the money to pay the workers, because they acted with complete honesty. ¹⁶The money from the guilt offerings and sin offerings was not brought into the temple of the Lord; it belonged to the priests.

¹⁷About this time Hazael king of Aram went up and attacked Gath and captured it. Then he turned to attack Jerusalem. ¹⁸But Joash king of Judah took all the sacred objects dedicated by his fathers—Jehoshaphat, Jehoram and Ahaziah, the kings of Judah—and the gifts he himself had dedicated and all the gold found in the treasuries of the temple of the Lord and of the royal palace, and he sent them to Hazael king of Aram, who then withdrew from Jerusalem.   1Ki 15:18; 2Ki 8:12

¹⁹As for the other events of the reign of Joash, and all he did, are they not written in the book of the annals of the kings of Judah? ²⁰His officials conspired against him and assassinated him at Beth Millo, on the road down to Silla. ²¹The officials who murdered him were Jozabad son of Shimeath and Jehozabad son of Shomer. He died and was buried with his fathers in the City of David. And Amaziah his son succeeded him as king.

Jehoahaz King of Israel

13 In the twenty-third year of Joash son of Ahaziah king

of Judah, Jehoahaz son of Jehu became king of Israel in Samaria, and he reigned seventeen years. ²He did evil in the eyes of the LORD by following the sins of Jeroboam son of Nebat, which he had caused Israel to commit, and he did not turn away from them. ³So the LORD's anger burned against Israel, and for a long time he kept them under the power of Hazael king of Aram and Ben-Hadad his son.   Jdg 2:14

⁴Then Jehoahaz sought the LORD's favor, and the LORD listened to him, for he saw how severely the king of Aram was oppressing Israel. ⁵The LORD provided a deliverer for Israel, and they escaped from the power of Aram. So the Israelites lived in their own homes as they had before. ⁶But they did not turn away from the sins of the house of Jeroboam, which he had caused Israel to commit; they continued in them. Also, the Asherah pole*a* remained standing in Samaria.   1Ki 16:33; 2Ki 14:26

⁷Nothing had been left of the army of Jehoahaz except fifty horsemen, ten chariots and ten thousand foot soldiers, for the king of Aram had destroyed the rest and made them like the dust at threshing time.   2Ki 10:32-33

⁸As for the other events of the reign of Jehoahaz, all he did and his achievements, are they not written in the book of the annals of the kings of Israel? ⁹Jehoahaz rested with his fathers and was buried in Samaria. And Jehoash*b* his son succeeded him as king.

Jehoash King of Israel

¹⁰In the thirty-seventh year of Joash king of Judah, Jehoash son of Jehoahaz became king of Israel in Samaria, and he reigned sixteen years. ¹¹He did evil in the eyes of the LORD and did not turn away from any of the sins of Jeroboam son of Nebat, which he had caused Israel to commit; he continued in them.

¹²As for the other events of the reign of Jehoash, all he did and his achievements, including his war against Amaziah king of Judah, are they not written in the book of the annals of the kings of Israel? ¹³Jehoash rested with his fathers, and Jeroboam succeeded him on the throne. Jehoash was buried in Samaria with the kings of Israel.

¹⁴Now Elisha was suffering from the illness from which he died. Jehoash king of Israel went down to see him and wept over him. "My father! My father!" he cried. "The chariots and horsemen of Israel!"

¹⁵Elisha said, "Get a bow and some arrows," and he did so. ¹⁶"Take the bow in your hands," he said to the king of Israel. When he had taken it, Elisha put his hands on the king's hands.

*a*6 That is, a symbol of the goddess Asherah; here and elsewhere in 2 Kings   *b*9 Hebrew *Joash,* a variant of *Jehoash;* also in verses 12-14 and 25

17"Open the east window," he said, and he opened it. "Shoot!" Elisha said, and he shot. "The LORD's arrow of victory, the arrow of victory over Aram!" Elisha declared. "You will completely destroy the Arameans at Aphek."

18Then he said, "Take the arrows," and the king took them. Elisha told him, "Strike the ground." He struck it three times and stopped. **19**The man of God was angry with him and said, "You should have struck the ground five or six times; then you would have defeated Aram and completely destroyed it. But now you will defeat it only three times." *ver 25*

20Elisha died and was buried.

Now Moabite raiders used to enter the country every spring. **21**Once while some Israelites were burying a man, suddenly they saw a band of raiders; so they threw the man's body into Elisha's tomb. When the body touched Elisha's bones, the man came to life and stood up on his feet. *Mt 27:52; 2Ki 3:7*

22Hazael king of Aram oppressed Israel throughout the reign of Jehoahaz. **23**But the LORD was gracious to them and had compassion and showed concern for them because of his covenant with Abraham, Isaac and Jacob. To this day he has been unwilling to destroy them or banish them from his presence. *Ex 2:24; 1Ki 19:17; 2Ki 8:12*

24Hazael king of Aram died, and Ben-Hadad his son succeeded him as king. **25**Then Jehoash son of Jehoahaz recaptured from Ben-Hadad son of Hazael the towns he had taken in battle from his father Jehoahaz. Three times Jehoash defeated him, and so he recovered the Israelite towns. *ver 18-19; 2Ki 10:32*

Amaziah King of Judah

14 In the second year of Jehoash[a] son of Jehoahaz king of Israel, Amaziah son of Joash king of Judah began to reign. **2**He was twenty-five years old when he became king, and he reigned in Jerusalem twenty-nine years. His mother's name was Jehoaddin; she was from Jerusalem. **3**He did what was right in the eyes of the LORD, but not as his father David had done. In everything he followed the example of his father Joash. **4**The high places, however, were not removed; the people continued to offer sacrifices and burn incense there.

5After the kingdom was firmly in his grasp, he executed the officials who had murdered his father the king. **6**Yet he did not put the sons of the assassins to death, in accordance with what is written in the Book of the Law of Moses where the LORD commanded: "Fathers shall not be put to death for their children, nor children put to death for their fathers; each is to die for his own sins."[b] *Jer 31:30*

---

a 1 Hebrew Joash, a variant of Jehoash; also in verses 13, 23 and 27   *b 6 Deut. 24:16*

[7]He was the one who defeated ten thousand Edomites in the Valley of Salt and captured Sela in battle, calling it Joktheel, the name it has to this day.   2Ch 25:1-4,11-12

[8]Then Amaziah sent messengers to Jehoash son of Jehoahaz, the son of Jehu, king of Israel, with the challenge: "Come, meet me face to face."

[9]But Jehoash king of Israel replied to Amaziah king of Judah: "A thistle in Lebanon sent a message to a cedar in Lebanon, 'Give your daughter to my son in marriage.' Then a wild beast in Lebanon came along and trampled the thistle underfoot. [10]You have indeed defeated Edom and now you are arrogant. Glory in your victory, but stay at home! Why ask for trouble and cause your own downfall and that of Judah also?"   Dt 8:14

[11]Amaziah, however, would not listen, so Jehoash king of Israel attacked. He and Amaziah king of Judah faced each other at Beth Shemesh in Judah. [12]Judah was routed by Israel, and every man fled to his home. [13]Jehoash king of Israel captured Amaziah king of Judah, the son of Joash, the son of Ahaziah, at Beth Shemesh. Then Jehoash went to Jerusalem and broke down the wall of Jerusalem from the Ephraim Gate to the Corner Gate—a section about six hundred feet long.[a] [14]He took all the gold and silver and all the articles found in the temple of the LORD and in the treasuries of the royal palace. He also took hostages and returned to Samaria.   Jos 15:10

[15]As for the other events of the reign of Jehoash, what he did and his achievements, including his war against Amaziah king of Judah, are they not written in the book of the annals of the kings of Israel? [16]Jehoash rested with his fathers and was buried in Samaria with the kings of Israel. And Jeroboam his son succeeded him as king.   2Ki 13:12

[17]Amaziah son of Joash king of Judah lived for fifteen years after the death of Jehoash son of Jehoahaz king of Israel. [18]As for the other events of Amaziah's reign, are they not written in the book of the annals of the kings of Judah?

[19]They conspired against him in Jerusalem, and he fled to Lachish, but they sent men after him to Lachish and killed him there. [20]He was brought back by horse and was buried in Jerusalem with his fathers, in the City of David.

[21]Then all the people of Judah took Azariah,[b] who was sixteen years old, and made him king in place of his father Amaziah. [22]He was the one who rebuilt Elath and restored it to Judah after Amaziah rested with his fathers.

Jeroboam II King of Israel

[23]In the fifteenth year of Amazi-

---

[a]13 Hebrew *four hundred cubits* (about 180 meters)   [b]21 Also called *Uzziah*

ah son of Joash king of Judah, Jeroboam son of Jehoash king of Israel became king in Samaria, and he reigned forty-one years. ²⁴He did evil in the eyes of the LORD and did not turn away from any of the sins of Jeroboam son of Nebat, which he had caused Israel to commit. ²⁵He was the one who restored the boundaries of Israel from Lebo*a* Hamath to the Sea of the Arabah,*b* in accordance with the word of the LORD, the God of Israel, spoken through his servant Jonah son of Amittai, the prophet from Gath Hepher.   Jnh 1:1; Mt 12:39; Dt 3:17

²⁶The LORD had seen how bitterly everyone in Israel, whether slave or free, was suffering; there was no one to help them. ²⁷And since the LORD had not said he would blot out the name of Israel from under heaven, he saved them by the hand of Jeroboam son of Jehoash.   2Ki 13:4; Ps 18:41; Dt 32:36

²⁸As for the other events of Jeroboam's reign, all he did, and his military achievements, including how he recovered for Israel both Damascus and Hamath, which had belonged to Yaudi,*c* are they not written in the book of the annals of the kings of Israel? ²⁹Jeroboam rested with his fathers, the kings of Israel. And Zechariah his son succeeded him as king.   2Sa 8:5; 1Ki 11:24

Azariah King of Judah

15 In the twenty-seventh year of Jeroboam king of Israel, Azariah son of Amaziah king of Judah began to reign. ²He was sixteen years old when he became king, and he reigned in Jerusalem fifty-two years. His mother's name was Jecoliah; she was from Jerusalem. ³He did what was right in the eyes of the LORD, just as his father Amaziah had done. ⁴The high places, however, were not removed; the people continued to offer sacrifices and burn incense there.

⁵The LORD afflicted the king with leprosy*d* until the day he died, and he lived in a separate house.*e* Jotham the king's son had charge of the palace and governed the people of the land.   Lev 13:46; 2Ch 27:1

⁶As for the other events of Azariah's reign, and all he did, are they not written in the book of the annals of the kings of Judah? ⁷Azariah rested with his fathers and was buried near them in the City of David. And Jotham his son succeeded him as king.   2Ch 26:3-4,21-23

Zechariah King of Israel

⁸In the thirty-eighth year of Azariah king of Judah, Zechariah son of Jeroboam became king of Israel in Samaria, and he reigned six months. ⁹He did evil in the eyes of

---

*a*25 Or *from the entrance to*   *b*25 That is, the Dead Sea   *c*28 Or *Judah*   *d*5 The Hebrew word was used for various diseases affecting the skin—not necessarily leprosy.   *e*5 Or *in a house where he was relieved of responsibility*

the LORD, as his fathers had done. He did not turn away from the sins of Jeroboam son of Nebat, which he had caused Israel to commit.

¹⁰Shallum son of Jabesh conspired against Zechariah. He attacked him in front of the people,ᵃ assassinated him and succeeded him as king. ¹¹The other events of Zechariah's reign are written in the book of the annals of the kings of Israel. ¹²So the word of the LORD spoken to Jehu was fulfilled: "Your descendants will sit on the throne of Israel to the fourth generation."ᵇ   1Ki 15:31; 2Ki 10:30

Shallum King of Israel

¹³Shallum son of Jabesh became king in the thirty-ninth year of Uzziah king of Judah, and he reigned in Samaria one month. ¹⁴Then Menahem son of Gadi went from Tirzah up to Samaria. He attacked Shallum son of Jabesh in Samaria, assassinated him and succeeded him as king.   1Ki 14:17; 2Ki 12:20

¹⁵The other events of Shallum's reign, and the conspiracy he led, are written in the book of the annals of the kings of Israel.

¹⁶At that time Menahem, starting out from Tirzah, attacked Tiphsah and everyone in the city and its vicinity, because they refused to open their gates. He sacked Tiphsah and ripped open all the pregnant women.   1Ki 4:24

Menahem King of Israel

¹⁷In the thirty-ninth year of Azariah king of Judah, Menahem son of Gadi became king of Israel, and he reigned in Samaria ten years. ¹⁸He did evil in the eyes of the LORD. During his entire reign he did not turn away from the sins of Jeroboam son of Nebat, which he had caused Israel to commit.

¹⁹Then Pulᶜ king of Assyria invaded the land, and Menahem gave him a thousand talentsᵈ of silver to gain his support and strengthen his own hold on the kingdom. ²⁰Menahem exacted this money from Israel. Every wealthy man had to contribute fifty shekelsᵉ of silver to be given to the king of Assyria. So the king of Assyria withdrew and stayed in the land no longer.   2Ki 12:18; 1Ch 5:6,26

²¹As for the other events of Menahem's reign, and all he did, are they not written in the book of the annals of the kings of Israel? ²²Menahem rested with his fathers. And Pekahiah his son succeeded him as king.

Pekahiah King of Israel

²³In the fiftieth year of Azariah king of Judah, Pekahiah son of Menahem became king of Israel in Samaria, and he reigned two years. ²⁴Pekahiah did evil in the eyes of the LORD. He did not turn away

---

ᵃ10 Hebrew; some Septuagint manuscripts *in Ibleam*   ᵇ12 2 Kings 10:30   ᶜ19 Also called *Tiglath-Pileser*   ᵈ19 That is, about 37 tons (about 34 metric tons)   ᵉ20 That is, about 1 1/4 pounds (about 0.6 kilogram)

from the sins of Jeroboam son of Nebat, which he had caused Israel to commit. ²⁵One of his chief officers, Pekah son of Remaliah, conspired against him. Taking fifty men of Gilead with him, he assassinated Pekahiah, along with Argob and Arieh, in the citadel of the royal palace at Samaria. So Pekah killed Pekahiah and succeeded him as king.   2Ki 12:20; 2Ch 28:6; Isa 7:1,4

²⁶The other events of Pekahiah's reign, and all he did, are written in the book of the annals of the kings of Israel.

Pekah King of Israel

²⁷In the fifty-second year of Azariah king of Judah, Pekah son of Remaliah became king of Israel in Samaria, and he reigned twenty years. ²⁸He did evil in the eyes of the LORD. He did not turn away from the sins of Jeroboam son of Nebat, which he had caused Israel to commit.   2Ch 28:6; Isa 7:1,4

²⁹In the time of Pekah king of Israel, Tiglath-Pileser king of Assyria came and took Ijon, Abel Beth Maacah, Janoah, Kedesh and Hazor. He took Gilead and Galilee, including all the land of Naphtali, and deported the people to Assyria. ³⁰Then Hoshea son of Elah conspired against Pekah son of Remaliah. He attacked and assassinated him, and then succeeded him as king in the twentieth year of Jotham son of Uzziah.   2Ki 16:9; 17:1,6

³¹As for the other events of Pekah's reign, and all he did, are they not written in the book of the annals of the kings of Israel?

Jotham King of Judah

³²In the second year of Pekah son of Remaliah king of Israel, Jotham son of Uzziah king of Judah began to reign. ³³He was twenty-five years old when he became king, and he reigned in Jerusalem sixteen years. His mother's name was Jerusha daughter of Zadok. ³⁴He did what was right in the eyes of the LORD, just as his father Uzziah had done. ³⁵The high places, however, were not removed; the people continued to offer sacrifices and burn incense there. Jotham rebuilt the Upper Gate of the temple of the LORD.   ver 3; 2Ch 26:4-5

³⁶As for the other events of Jotham's reign, and what he did, are they not written in the book of the annals of the kings of Judah? ³⁷(In those days the LORD began to send Rezin king of Aram and Pekah son of Remaliah against Judah.) ³⁸Jotham rested with his fathers and was buried with them in the City of David, the city of his father. And Ahaz his son succeeded him as king.   2Ch 27:1-4,7-9

Ahaz King of Judah

16 In the seventeenth year of Pekah son of Remaliah, Ahaz son of Jotham king of Judah began to reign. ²Ahaz was twenty years old when he became king, and he reigned in Jerusalem sixteen years. Unlike David his father, he did not do what was right in the eyes of the LORD his God. ³He walked in the ways of the kings of Israel and even sacrificed his son in*a* the fire, following the detestable ways of the nations the LORD had driven out before the Israelites. ⁴He offered sacrifices and burned incense at the high places, on the hilltops and under every spreading tree.   Lev 18:21; Dt 12:2,31

⁵Then Rezin king of Aram and Pekah son of Remaliah king of Israel marched up to fight against Jerusalem and besieged Ahaz, but they could not overpower him. ⁶At that time, Rezin king of Aram recovered Elath for Aram by driving out the men of Judah. Edomites then moved into Elath and have lived there to this day.   2Ki 14:22

⁷Ahaz sent messengers to say to Tiglath-Pileser king of Assyria, "I am your servant and vassal. Come up and save me out of the hand of the king of Aram and of the king of Israel, who are attacking me." ⁸And Ahaz took the silver and gold found in the temple of the LORD and in the treasuries of the royal palace and sent it as a gift to the king of Assyria. ⁹The king of Assyria complied by attacking Damascus and capturing it. He deported its inhabitants to Kir and put Rezin to death.   2Ki 12:18; 15:29; Am 1:5

¹⁰Then King Ahaz went to Damascus to meet Tiglath-Pileser king of Assyria. He saw an altar in Damascus and sent to Uriah the priest a sketch of the altar, with detailed plans for its construction. ¹¹So Uriah the priest built an altar in accordance with all the plans that King Ahaz had sent from Damascus and finished it before King Ahaz returned. ¹²When the king came back from Damascus and saw the altar, he approached it and presented offerings*b* on it. ¹³He offered up his burnt offering and grain offering, poured out his drink offering, and sprinkled the blood of his fellowship offerings*c* on the altar. ¹⁴The bronze altar that stood before the LORD he brought from the front of the temple—from between the new altar and the temple of the LORD—and put it on the north side of the new altar.   2Ch 4:1; 26:16; Isa 8:2

¹⁵King Ahaz then gave these orders to Uriah the priest: "On the large new altar, offer the morning burnt offering and the evening grain offering, the king's burnt offering and his grain offering, and the burnt offering of all the people of the land, and their grain offering and their drink offering. Sprinkle on the altar all the blood of the burnt offerings and sacrifices. But I will use the bronze altar for seeking guidance." ¹⁶And Uriah the priest did just as King Ahaz had ordered.   Ex 29:38-41; 1Sa 9:9

¹⁷King Ahaz took away the side panels and removed the basins

---

a 3 Or *even made his son pass through*   *b* 12 Or *and went up*   *c* 13 Traditionally *peace offerings*

from the movable stands. He removed the Sea from the bronze bulls that supported it and set it on a stone base. [18]He took away the Sabbath canopy[a] that had been built at the temple and removed the royal entryway outside the temple of the Lord, in deference to the king of Assyria. 1Ki 7:27; Eze 16:28

[19]As for the other events of the reign of Ahaz, and what he did, are they not written in the book of the annals of the kings of Judah? [20]Ahaz rested with his fathers and was buried with them in the City of David. And Hezekiah his son succeeded him as king. 2Ch 28:1-27

Hoshea Last King of Israel

17 In the twelfth year of Ahaz king of Judah, Hoshea son of Elah became king of Israel in Samaria, and he reigned nine years. [2]He did evil in the eyes of the Lord, but not like the kings of Israel who preceded him.

[3]Shalmaneser king of Assyria came up to attack Hoshea, who had been Shalmaneser's vassal and had paid him tribute. [4]But the king of Assyria discovered that Hoshea was a traitor, for he had sent envoys to So[b] king of Egypt, and he no longer paid tribute to the king of Assyria, as he had done year by year. Therefore Shalmaneser seized him and put him in prison. [5]The king of Assyria invaded the entire land, marched against Samaria and laid siege to it for three years. [6]In the ninth year of Hoshea, the king of Assyria captured Samaria and deported the Israelites to Assyria. He settled them in Halah, in Gozan on the Habor River and in the towns of the Medes. 2Ki 18:9-12; Hos 10:14

Israel Exiled Because of Sin

[7]All this took place because the Israelites had sinned against the Lord their God, who had brought them up out of Egypt from under the power of Pharaoh king of Egypt. They worshiped other gods [8]and followed the practices of the nations the Lord had driven out before them, as well as the practices that the kings of Israel had introduced. [9]The Israelites secretly did things against the Lord their God that were not right. From watchtower to fortified city they built themselves high places in all their towns. [10]They set up sacred stones and Asherah poles on every high hill and under every spreading tree. [11]At every high place they burned incense, as the nations whom the Lord had driven out before them had done. They did wicked things that provoked the Lord to anger. [12]They worshiped idols, though the Lord had said, "You shall not do this."[c] [13]The Lord warned Israel and Judah

---

[a]18 Or the dais of his throne (see Septuagint)   [b]4 Or to Sais, to the; So is possibly an abbreviation for Osorkon.   [c]12 Exodus 20:4, 5

through all his prophets and seers: "Turn from your evil ways. Observe my commands and decrees, in accordance with the entire Law that I commanded your fathers to obey and that I delivered to you through my servants the prophets." 1Sa 9:9; Jer 18:11

14But they would not listen and were as stiff-necked as their fathers, who did not trust in the LORD their God. **15**They rejected his decrees and the covenant he had made with their fathers and the warnings he had given them. They followed worthless idols and themselves became worthless. They imitated the nations around them although the LORD had ordered them, "Do not do as they do," and they did the things the LORD had forbidden them to do.

16They forsook all the commands of the LORD their God and made for themselves two idols cast in the shape of calves, and an Asherah pole. They bowed down to all the starry hosts, and they worshiped Baal. **17**They sacrificed their sons and daughters in[a] the fire. They practiced divination and sorcery and sold themselves to do evil in the eyes of the LORD, provoking him to anger. 1Ki 21:20

18So the LORD was very angry with Israel and removed them from his presence. Only the tribe of Judah was left, **19**and even Judah did not keep the commands of the LORD their God. They followed the practices Israel had introduced. **20**Therefore the LORD rejected all the people of Israel; he afflicted them and gave them into the hands of plunderers, until he thrust them from his presence.

21When he tore Israel away from the house of David, they made Jeroboam son of Nebat their king. Jeroboam enticed Israel away from following the LORD and caused them to commit a great sin. **22**The Israelites persisted in all the sins of Jeroboam and did not turn away from them **23**until the LORD removed them from his presence, as he had warned through all his servants the prophets. So the people of Israel were taken from their homeland into exile in Assyria, and they are still there. 1Ki 11:11

Samaria Resettled

24The king of Assyria brought people from Babylon, Cuthah, Avva, Hamath and Sepharvaim and settled them in the towns of Samaria to replace the Israelites. They took over Samaria and lived in its towns. **25**When they first lived there, they did not worship the LORD; so he sent lions among them and they killed some of the people. **26**It was reported to the king of Assyria: "The people you deported and resettled in the towns of Samaria do not know what the god of that country re-

---

a 17 Or They made their sons and daughters pass through

quires. He has sent lions among them, which are killing them off, because the people do not know what he requires." Ge 37:20; 2Ki 18:34

²⁷Then the king of Assyria gave this order: "Have one of the priests you took captive from Samaria go back to live there and teach the people what the god of the land requires." ²⁸So one of the priests who had been exiled from Samaria came to live in Bethel and taught them how to worship the LORD.

²⁹Nevertheless, each national group made its own gods in the several towns where they settled, and set them up in the shrines the people of Samaria had made at the high places. ³⁰The men from Babylon made Succoth Benoth, the men from Cuthah made Nergal, and the men from Hamath made Ashima; ³¹the Avvites made Nibhaz and Tartak, and the Sepharvites burned their children in the fire as sacrifices to Adrammelech and Anammelech, the gods of Sepharvaim. ³²They worshiped the LORD, but they also appointed all sorts of their own people to officiate for them as priests in the shrines at the high places. ³³They worshiped the LORD, but they also served their own gods in accordance with the customs of the nations from which they had been brought. ver 24; 1Ki 12:31

³⁴To this day they persist in their former practices. They neither worship the LORD nor adhere to the decrees and ordinances, the laws

and commands that the LORD gave the descendants of Jacob, whom he named Israel. ³⁵When the LORD made a covenant with the Israelites, he commanded them: "Do not worship any other gods or bow down to them, serve them or sacrifice to them. ³⁶But the LORD, who brought you up out of Egypt with mighty power and outstretched arm, is the one you must worship. To him you shall bow down and to him offer sacrifices. ³⁷You must always be careful to keep the decrees and ordinances, the laws and commands he wrote for you. Do not worship other gods. ³⁸Do not forget the covenant I have made with you, and do not worship other gods. ³⁹Rather, worship the LORD your God; it is he who will deliver you from the hand of all your enemies." Dt 44:23; 5:32

⁴⁰They would not listen, however, but persisted in their former practices. ⁴¹Even while these people were worshiping the LORD, they were serving their idols. To this day their children and grandchildren continue to do as their fathers did. 1Ki 18:21; Mt 6:24

Hezekiah King of Judah

18 In the third year of Hoshea son of Elah king of Israel, Hezekiah son of Ahaz king of Judah began to reign. ²He was twenty-five years old when he became king, and he reigned in Jerusalem twenty-nine years. His mother's

name was Abijah*a* daughter of Zechariah. ³He did what was right in the eyes of the LORD, just as his father David had done. ⁴He removed the high places, smashed the sacred stones and cut down the Asherah poles. He broke into pieces the bronze snake Moses had made, for up to that time the Israelites had been burning incense to it. (It was called*b* Nehushtan.*c*)   2Ch 29:1-2; 31:1

⁵Hezekiah trusted in the LORD, the God of Israel. There was no one like him among all the kings of Judah, either before him or after him. ⁶He held fast to the LORD and did not cease to follow him; he kept the commands the LORD had given Moses. ⁷And the LORD was with him; he was successful in whatever he undertook. He rebelled against the king of Assyria and did not serve him. ⁸From watchtower to fortified city, he defeated the Philistines, as far as Gaza and its territory.   2Ch 31:20-21

⁹In King Hezekiah's fourth year, which was the seventh year of Hoshea son of Elah king of Israel, Shalmaneser king of Assyria marched against Samaria and laid siege to it. ¹⁰At the end of three years the Assyrians took it. So Samaria was captured in Hezekiah's sixth year, which was the ninth year of Hoshea king of Israel. ¹¹The king of Assyria deported Israel to Assyria and settled them in Halah, in Gozan on the Habor River and in towns of the Medes. ¹²This happened because they had not obeyed the LORD their God, but had violated his covenant—all that Moses the servant of the LORD commanded. They neither listened to the commands nor carried them out.   2Ki 17:3-7; Da 9:6,10

¹³In the fourteenth year of King Hezekiah's reign, Sennacherib king of Assyria attacked all the fortified cities of Judah and captured them. ¹⁴So Hezekiah king of Judah sent this message to the king of Assyria at Lachish: "I have done wrong. Withdraw from me, and I will pay whatever you demand of me." The king of Assyria exacted from Hezekiah king of Judah three hundred talents*d* of silver and thirty talents*e* of gold. ¹⁵So Hezekiah gave him all the silver that was found in the temple of the LORD and in the treasuries of the royal palace.   1Ki 15:18; 2Ki 16:8

¹⁶At this time Hezekiah king of Judah stripped off the gold with which he had covered the doors and doorposts of the temple of the LORD, and gave it to the king of Assyria.

Sennacherib Threatens Jerusalem

¹⁷The king of Assyria sent his supreme commander, his chief of-

---

a 2 Hebrew *Abi*, a variant of *Abijah*   *b* 4 Or *He called it*   *c* 4 *Nehushtan* sounds like the Hebrew for *bronze* and *snake* and *unclean thing.*   *d* 14 That is, about 11 tons (about 10 metric tons)   *e* 14 That is, about 1 ton (about 1 metric ton)

ficer and his field commander with a large army, from Lachish to King Hezekiah at Jerusalem. They came up to Jerusalem and stopped at the aqueduct of the Upper Pool, on the road to the Washerman's Field. **18**They called for the king; and Eliakim son of Hilkiah the palace administrator, Shebna the secretary, and Joah son of Asaph the recorder went out to them.   2Ki 19:2; Isa 20:1

19The field commander said to them, "Tell Hezekiah:

" 'This is what the great king, the king of Assyria, says: On what are you basing this confidence of yours? **20**You say you have strategy and military strength—but you speak only empty words. On whom are you depending, that you rebel against me? **21**Look now, you are depending on Egypt, that splintered reed of a staff, which pierces a man's hand and wounds him if he leans on it! Such is Pharaoh king of Egypt to all who depend on him. **22**And if you say to me, "We are depending on the LORD our God"—isn't he the one whose high places and altars Hezekiah removed, saying to Judah and Jerusalem, "You must worship before this altar in Jerusalem"?

23" 'Come now, make a bargain with my master, the king of Assyria: I will give you two thousand horses—if you can put riders on them! **24**How can you repulse one officer of the least of my master's officials, even though you are depending on Egypt for chariots and horsemen*a*? **25**Furthermore, have I come to attack and destroy this place without word from the LORD? The LORD himself told me to march against this country and destroy it.' "   2Ki 19:6,22

26Then Eliakim son of Hilkiah, and Shebna and Joah said to the field commander, "Please speak to your servants in Aramaic, since we understand it. Don't speak to us in Hebrew in the hearing of the people on the wall."   Ezr 4:7

27But the commander replied, "Was it only to your master and you that my master sent me to say these things, and not to the men sitting on the wall—who, like you, will have to eat their own filth and drink their own urine?"

28Then the commander stood and called out in Hebrew: "Hear the word of the great king, the king of Assyria! **29**This is what the king says: Do not let Hezekiah deceive you. He cannot deliver you from my hand. **30**Do not let Hezekiah persuade you to trust in the LORD when he says, 'The LORD will surely deliver us; this city will not be

---

a 24 Or *charioteers*

given into the hand of the king of Assyria.'

³¹"Do not listen to Hezekiah. This is what the king of Assyria says: Make peace with me and come out to me. Then every one of you will eat from his own vine and fig tree and drink water from his own cistern, ³²until I come and take you to a land like your own, a land of grain and new wine, a land of bread and vineyards, a land of olive trees and honey. Choose life and not death!

"Do not listen to Hezekiah, for he is misleading you when he says, 'The LORD will deliver us.' ³³Has the god of any nation ever delivered his land from the hand of the king of Assyria? ³⁴Where are the gods of Hamath and Arpad? Where are the gods of Sepharvaim, Hena and Ivvah? Have they rescued Samaria from my hand? ³⁵Who of all the gods of these countries has been able to save his land from me? How then can the LORD deliver Jerusalem from my hand?"

³⁶But the people remained silent and said nothing in reply, because the king had commanded, "Do not answer him."

³⁷Then Eliakim son of Hilkiah the palace administrator, Shebna the secretary and Joah son of Asaph the recorder went to Hezekiah, with their clothes torn, and told him what the field commander had said.   Isa 36:1-22

Jerusalem's Deliverance Foretold

19 When King Hezekiah heard this, he tore his clothes and put on sackcloth and went into the temple of the LORD. ²He sent Eliakim the palace administrator, Shebna the secretary and the leading priests, all wearing sackcloth, to the prophet Isaiah son of Amoz. ³They told him, "This is what Hezekiah says: This day is a day of distress and rebuke and disgrace, as when children come to the point of birth and there is no strength to deliver them. ⁴It may be that the LORD your God will hear all the words of the field commander, whom his master, the king of Assyria, has sent to ridicule the living God, and that he will rebuke him for the words the LORD your God has heard. Therefore pray for the remnant that still survives."   2Sa 16:12

⁵When King Hezekiah's officials came to Isaiah, ⁶Isaiah said to them, "Tell your master, 'This is what the LORD says: Do not be afraid of what you have heard—those words with which the underlings of the king of Assyria have blasphemed me. ⁷Listen! I am going to put such a spirit in him that when he hears a certain report, he will return to his own country, and there I will have him cut down with the sword.' "   ver 37; 2Ki 18:25

⁸When the field commander heard that the king of Assyria had

left Lachish, he withdrew and found the king fighting against Libnah.   2Ki 18:14

⁹Now Sennacherib received a report that Tirhakah, the Cushite*a* king ˹of Egypt˺, was marching out to fight against him. So he again sent messengers to Hezekiah with this word: ¹⁰"Say to Hezekiah king of Judah: Do not let the god you depend on deceive you when he says, 'Jerusalem will not be handed over to the king of Assyria.' ¹¹Surely you have heard what the kings of Assyria have done to all the countries, destroying them completely. And will you be delivered? ¹²Did the gods of the nations that were destroyed by my forefathers deliver them: the gods of Gozan, Haran, Rezeph and the people of Eden who were in Tel Assar? ¹³Where is the king of Hamath, the king of Arpad, the king of the city of Sepharvaim, or of Hena or Ivvah?"   Isa 37:1-13

Hezekiah's Prayer

¹⁴Hezekiah received the letter from the messengers and read it. Then he went up to the temple of the Lord and spread it out before the Lord. ¹⁵And Hezekiah prayed to the Lord: "O Lord, God of Israel, enthroned between the cherubim, you alone are God over all the kingdoms of the earth. You have made heaven and earth. ¹⁶Give ear, O Lord, and hear; open your eyes,

O Lord, and see; listen to the words Sennacherib has sent to insult the living God.

¹⁷"It is true, O Lord, that the Assyrian kings have laid waste these nations and their lands. ¹⁸They have thrown their gods into the fire and destroyed them, for they were not gods but only wood and stone, fashioned by men's hands. ¹⁹Now, O Lord our God, deliver us from his hand, so that all kingdoms on earth may know that you alone, O Lord, are God."

Isaiah Prophesies Sennacherib's Fall

²⁰Then Isaiah son of Amoz sent a message to Hezekiah: "This is what the Lord, the God of Israel, says: I have heard your prayer concerning Sennacherib king of Assyria. ²¹This is the word that the Lord has spoken against him:

" 'The Virgin Daughter of Zion
    despises you and mocks you.
The Daughter of Jerusalem
    tosses her head as you flee.
²²Who is it you have insulted
    and blasphemed?
Against whom have you
    raised your voice
and lifted your eyes in pride?
Against the Holy One of
    Israel!   Ps 71:22; Isa 5:24
²³By your messengers
    you have heaped insults on
    the Lord.

---

a9 That is, from the upper Nile region

And you have said,   Isa 10:18
"With my many chariots
I have ascended the heights of
    the mountains,
    the utmost heights of
    Lebanon.
I have cut down its tallest
    cedars,   Isa 10:34
    the choicest of its pines.
I have reached its remotest
    parts,
    the finest of its forests.
²⁴I have dug wells in foreign
    lands
    and drunk the water there.
With the soles of my feet
    I have dried up all the
    streams of Egypt."

²⁵" 'Have you not heard?
    Long ago I ordained it.
In days of old I planned it;
    now I have brought it to
    pass,
that you have turned fortified
    cities
    into piles of stone.   Mic 1:6
²⁶Their people, drained of power,
    are dismayed and put to
    shame.   Ps 6:10
They are like plants in the
    field,
    like tender green shoots,
like grass sprouting on the
    roof,
    scorched before it grows up.

²⁷" 'But I know where you stay
    and when you come and go
    and how you rage against
    me.
²⁸Because you rage against me

and your insolence has
    reached my ears,
I will put my hook in your
    nose   Eze 29:4
    and my bit in your mouth,
    and I will make you return
    by the way you came.'

²⁹"This will be the sign for you,
O Hezekiah: Lk 2:12

"This year you will eat what
    grows by itself,   Lev 25:5
    and the second year what
    springs from that.
But in the third year sow and
    reap,
    plant vineyards and eat their
    fruit.   Ps 107:37
³⁰Once more a remnant of the
    house of Judah
    will take root below and
    bear fruit above.
³¹For out of Jerusalem will come
    a remnant,   Ge 45:7
    and out of Mount Zion a
    band of survivors.

The zeal of the LORD Almighty will
accomplish this.   Isa 9:7

³²"Therefore this is what the
LORD says concerning the king of
Assyria:

"He will not enter this city
    or shoot an arrow here.
He will not come before it with
    shield
    or build a siege ramp against
    it.
³³By the way that he came he
    will return;   ver 28

he will not enter this city,
    declares the LORD.
³⁴I will defend this city and save
    it,   2Ki 20:6
for my sake and for the sake
    of David my servant."

³⁵That night the angel of the LORD went out and put to death a hundred and eighty-five thousand men in the Assyrian camp. When the people got up the next morning—there were all the dead bodies! ³⁶So Sennacherib king of Assyria broke camp and withdrew. He returned to Nineveh and stayed there.   Ex 12:23; Job 24:24; Jnh 1:2

³⁷One day, while he was worshiping in the temple of his god Nisroch, his sons Adrammelech and Sharezer cut him down with the sword, and they escaped to the land of Ararat. And Esarhaddon his son succeeded him as king.

Hezekiah's Illness

20 In those days Hezekiah became ill and was at the point of death. The prophet Isaiah son of Amoz went to him and said, "This is what the LORD says: Put your house in order, because you are going to die; you will not recover."

²Hezekiah turned his face to the wall and prayed to the LORD, ³"Remember, O LORD, how I have walked before you faithfully and with wholehearted devotion and have done what is good in your eyes." And Hezekiah wept bitterly.

⁴Before Isaiah had left the middle court, the word of the LORD came to him: ⁵"Go back and tell Hezekiah, the leader of my people, 'This is what the LORD, the God of your father David, says: I have heard your prayer and seen your tears; I will heal you. On the third day from now you will go up to the temple of the LORD. ⁶I will add fifteen years to your life. And I will deliver you and this city from the hand of the king of Assyria. I will defend this city for my sake and for the sake of my servant David.' "

⁷Then Isaiah said, "Prepare a poultice of figs." They did so and applied it to the boil, and he recovered.   Isa 38:21

⁸Hezekiah had asked Isaiah, "What will be the sign that the LORD will heal me and that I will go up to the temple of the LORD on the third day from now?"

⁹Isaiah answered, "This is the LORD's sign to you that the LORD will do what he has promised: Shall the shadow go forward ten steps, or shall it go back ten steps?"

¹⁰"It is a simple matter for the shadow to go forward ten steps," said Hezekiah. "Rather, have it go back ten steps."

¹¹Then the prophet Isaiah called upon the LORD, and the LORD made the shadow go back the ten steps it had gone down on the stairway of Ahaz.   2Ch 32:24-26; Isa 38:1-8

Envoys From Babylon

¹²At that time Merodach-Bala-

dan son of Baladan king of Babylon sent Hezekiah letters and a gift, because he had heard of Hezekiah's illness. [13]Hezekiah received the messengers and showed them all that was in his storehouses — the silver, the gold, the spices and the fine oil — his armory and everything found among his treasures. There was nothing in his palace or in all his kingdom that Hezekiah did not show them.

[14]Then Isaiah the prophet went to King Hezekiah and asked, "What did those men say, and where did they come from?"

"From a distant land," Hezekiah replied. "They came from Babylon."

[15]The prophet asked, "What did they see in your palace?"

"They saw everything in my palace," Hezekiah said. "There is nothing among my treasures that I did not show them."

[16]Then Isaiah said to Hezekiah, "Hear the word of the LORD: [17]The time will surely come when everything in your palace, and all that your fathers have stored up until this day, will be carried off to Babylon. Nothing will be left, says the LORD. [18]And some of your descendants, your own flesh and blood, that will be born to you, will be taken away, and they will become eunuchs in the palace of the king of Babylon."   2Ki 24:15; 2Ch 33:11

[19]"The word of the LORD you have spoken is good," Hezekiah replied. For he thought, "Will there not be peace and security in my lifetime?"   Isa 39:1-8

[20]As for the other events of Hezekiah's reign, all his achievements and how he made the pool and the tunnel by which he brought water into the city, are they not written in the book of the annals of the kings of Judah? [21]Hezekiah rested with his fathers. And Manasseh his son succeeded him as king.

Manasseh King of Judah

21 Manasseh was twelve years old when he became king, and he reigned in Jerusalem fifty-five years. His mother's name was Hephzibah. [2]He did evil in the eyes of the LORD, following the detestable practices of the nations the LORD had driven out before the Israelites. [3]He rebuilt the high places his father Hezekiah had destroyed; he also erected altars to Baal and made an Asherah pole, as Ahab king of Israel had done. He bowed down to all the starry hosts and worshiped them. [4]He built altars in the temple of the LORD, of which the LORD had said, "In Jerusalem I will put my Name." [5]In both courts of the temple of the LORD, he built altars to all the starry hosts. [6]He sacrificed his own son in[a] the fire, practiced sorcery and divination, and consulted mediums and spiritists. He did much

---

[a] 6 Or *He made his own son pass through*

evil in the eyes of the LORD, provoking him to anger.   Jer 15:4

7He took the carved Asherah pole he had made and put it in the temple, of which the LORD had said to David and to his son Solomon, "In this temple and in Jerusalem, which I have chosen out of all the tribes of Israel, I will put my Name forever. 8I will not again make the feet of the Israelites wander from the land I gave their forefathers, if only they will be careful to do everything I commanded them and will keep the whole Law that my servant Moses gave them." 9But the people did not listen. Manasseh led them astray, so that they did more evil than the nations the LORD had destroyed before the Israelites.   2Ch 33:1-10

10The LORD said through his servants the prophets: 11"Manasseh king of Judah has committed these detestable sins. He has done more evil than the Amorites who preceded him and has led Judah into sin with his idols. 12Therefore this is what the LORD, the God of Israel, says: I am going to bring such disaster on Jerusalem and Judah that the ears of everyone who hears of it will tingle. 13I will stretch out over Jerusalem the measuring line used against Samaria and the plumb line used against the house of Ahab. I will wipe out Jerusalem as one wipes a dish, wiping it and turning it upside down. 14I will forsake the remnant of my inheritance and hand

them over to their enemies. They will be looted and plundered by all their foes, 15because they have done evil in my eyes and have provoked me to anger from the day their forefathers came out of Egypt until this day."   2Ki 19:4; Ps 78:58-60

16Moreover, Manasseh also shed so much innocent blood that he filled Jerusalem from end to end— besides the sin that he had caused Judah to commit, so that they did evil in the eyes of the LORD.

17As for the other events of Manasseh's reign, and all he did, including the sin he committed, are they not written in the book of the annals of the kings of Judah? 18Manasseh rested with his fathers and was buried in his palace garden, the garden of Uzza. And Amon his son succeeded him as king.

Amon King of Judah

19Amon was twenty-two years old when he became king, and he reigned in Jerusalem two years. His mother's name was Meshullemeth daughter of Haruz; she was from Jotbah. 20He did evil in the eyes of the LORD, as his father Manasseh had done. 21He walked in all the ways of his father; he worshiped the idols his father had worshiped, and bowed down to them. 22He forsook the LORD, the God of his fathers, and did not walk in the way of the LORD.

23Amon's officials conspired against him and assassinated the king in his palace. 24Then the people of the land killed all who had plotted against King Amon, and they made Josiah his son king in his place.   2Ch 33:21-25

²⁵As for the other events of Amon's reign, and what he did, are they not written in the book of the annals of the kings of Judah? ²⁶He was buried in his grave in the garden of Uzza. And Josiah his son succeeded him as king.

The Book of the Law Found

22 Josiah was eight years old when he became king, and he reigned in Jerusalem thirty-one years. His mother's name was Jedidah daughter of Adaiah; she was from Bozkath. ²He did what was right in the eyes of the LORD and walked in all the ways of his father David, not turning aside to the right or to the left.   Dt 5:32; 17:19

³In the eighteenth year of his reign, King Josiah sent the secretary, Shaphan son of Azaliah, the son of Meshullam, to the temple of the LORD. He said: ⁴"Go up to Hilkiah the high priest and have him get ready the money that has been brought into the temple of the LORD, which the doorkeepers have collected from the people. ⁵Have them entrust it to the men appointed to supervise the work on the temple. And have these men pay the workers who repair the temple of the LORD — ⁶the carpenters, the builders and the masons. Also have them purchase timber

and dressed stone to repair the temple. ⁷But they need not account for the money entrusted to them, because they are acting faithfully."

⁸Hilkiah the high priest said to Shaphan the secretary, "I have found the Book of the Law in the temple of the LORD." He gave it to Shaphan, who read it. ⁹Then Shaphan the secretary went to the king and reported to him: "Your officials have paid out the money that was in the temple of the LORD and have entrusted it to the workers and supervisors at the temple." ¹⁰Then Shaphan the secretary informed the king, "Hilkiah the priest has given me a book." And Shaphan read from it in the presence of the king.   Dt 31:24; Jer 36:21

¹¹When the king heard the words of the Book of the Law, he tore his robes. ¹²He gave these orders to Hilkiah the priest, Ahikam son of Shaphan, Acbor son of Micaiah, Shaphan the secretary and Asaiah the king's attendant: ¹³"Go and inquire of the LORD for me and for the people and for all Judah about what is written in this book that has been found. Great is the LORD's anger that burns against us because our fathers have not obeyed the words of this book; they have not acted in accordance with all that is written there concerning us."   Dt 29:24-28; 2Ki 25:22

¹⁴Hilkiah the priest, Ahikam, Acbor, Shaphan and Asaiah went to speak to the prophetess Hul-

dah, who was the wife of Shallum son of Tikvah, the son of Harhas, keeper of the wardrobe. She lived in Jerusalem, in the Second District.

[15]She said to them, "This is what the LORD, the God of Israel, says: Tell the man who sent you to me, [16]'This is what the LORD says: I am going to bring disaster on this place and its people, according to everything written in the book the king of Judah has read. [17]Because they have forsaken me and burned incense to other gods and provoked me to anger by all the idols their hands have made,[a] my anger will burn against this place and will not be quenched.' [18]Tell the king of Judah, who sent you to inquire of the LORD, 'This is what the LORD, the God of Israel, says concerning the words you heard: [19]Because your heart was responsive and you humbled yourself before the LORD when you heard what I have spoken against this place and its people, that they would become accursed and laid waste, and because you tore your robes and wept in my presence, I have heard you, declares the LORD. [20]Therefore I will gather you to your fathers, and you will be buried in peace. Your eyes will not see all the disaster I am going to bring on this place.' "   2Ch 34:1-2,8-28

So they took her answer back to the king.

Josiah Renews the Covenant

23 Then the king called together all the elders of Judah and Jerusalem. [2]He went up to the temple of the LORD with the men of Judah, the people of Jerusalem, the priests and the prophets —all the people from the least to the greatest. He read in their hearing all the words of the Book of the Covenant, which had been found in the temple of the LORD. [3]The king stood by the pillar and renewed the covenant in the presence of the LORD—to follow the LORD and keep his commands, regulations and decrees with all his heart and all his soul, thus confirming the words of the covenant written in this book. Then all the people pledged themselves to the covenant.   2Ch 34:29-32; 2Ki 22:8

[4]The king ordered Hilkiah the high priest, the priests next in rank and the doorkeepers to remove from the temple of the LORD all the articles made for Baal and Asherah and all the starry hosts. He burned them outside Jerusalem in the fields of the Kidron Valley and took the ashes to Bethel. [5]He did away with the pagan priests appointed by the kings of Judah to burn incense on the high places of the towns of Judah and on those around Jerusalem—those who burned incense to Baal, to the sun and moon, to the constellations and to all the starry hosts. [6]He took

---

[a]17 Or by everything they have done

the Asherah pole from the temple of the LORD to the Kidron Valley outside Jerusalem and burned it there. He ground it to powder and scattered the dust over the graves of the common people. ⁷He also tore down the quarters of the male shrine prostitutes, which were in the temple of the LORD and where women did weaving for Asherah.

⁸Josiah brought all the priests from the towns of Judah and desecrated the high places, from Geba to Beersheba, where the priests had burned incense. He broke down the shrines*a* at the gates — at the entrance to the Gate of Joshua, the city governor, which is on the left of the city gate. ⁹Although the priests of the high places did not serve at the altar of the LORD in Jerusalem, they ate unleavened bread with their fellow priests.

¹⁰He desecrated Topheth, which was in the Valley of Ben Hinnom, so no one could use it to sacrifice his son or daughter in*b* the fire to Molech. ¹¹He removed from the entrance to the temple of the LORD the horses that the kings of Judah had dedicated to the sun. They were in the court near the room of an official named Nathan-Melech. Josiah then burned the chariots dedicated to the sun.   Isa 30:33

¹²He pulled down the altars the kings of Judah had erected on the roof near the upper room of Ahaz, and the altars Manasseh had built in the two courts of the temple of the LORD. He removed them from there, smashed them to pieces and threw the rubble into the Kidron Valley. ¹³The king also desecrated the high places that were east of Jerusalem on the south of the Hill of Corruption — the ones Solomon king of Israel had built for Ashtoreth the vile goddess of the Sidonians, for Chemosh the vile god of Moab, and for Molech*c* the detestable god of the people of Ammon. ¹⁴Josiah smashed the sacred stones and cut down the Asherah poles and covered the sites with human bones.   Dt 7:5,25; 1Ki 11:7

¹⁵Even the altar at Bethel, the high place made by Jeroboam son of Nebat, who had caused Israel to sin — even that altar and high place he demolished. He burned the high place and ground it to powder, and burned the Asherah pole also. ¹⁶Then Josiah looked around, and when he saw the tombs that were there on the hillside, he had the bones removed from them and burned on the altar to defile it, in accordance with the word of the LORD proclaimed by the man of God who foretold these things.

¹⁷The king asked, "What is that tombstone I see?"

The men of the city said, "It marks the tomb of the man of God who came from Judah and pronounced against the altar of Bethel

---

a 8 Or *high places*   *b* 10 Or *to make his son or daughter pass through*   *c* 13 Hebrew *Milcom*

the very things you have done to it."

18"Leave it alone," he said. "Don't let anyone disturb his bones." So they spared his bones and those of the prophet who had come from Samaria.   1Ki 13:31

19Just as he had done at Bethel, Josiah removed and defiled all the shrines at the high places that the kings of Israel had built in the towns of Samaria that had provoked the LORD to anger. 20Josiah slaughtered all the priests of those high places on the altars and burned human bones on them. Then he went back to Jerusalem.

21The king gave this order to all the people: "Celebrate the Passover to the LORD your God, as it is written in this Book of the Covenant." 22Not since the days of the judges who led Israel, nor throughout the days of the kings of Israel and the kings of Judah, had any such Passover been observed. 23But in the eighteenth year of King Josiah, this Passover was celebrated to the LORD in Jerusalem.

24Furthermore, Josiah got rid of the mediums and spiritists, the household gods, the idols and all the other detestable things seen in Judah and Jerusalem. This he did to fulfill the requirements of the law written in the book that Hilkiah the priest had discovered in the temple of the LORD. 25Neither before nor after Josiah was there a king like him who turned to the LORD as he did — with all his heart and with all his soul and with all his strength, in accordance with all the Law of Moses.   Dt 18:11; 2Ki 18:5

26Nevertheless, the LORD did not turn away from the heat of his fierce anger, which burned against Judah because of all that Manasseh had done to provoke him to anger. 27So the LORD said, "I will remove Judah also from my presence as I removed Israel, and I will reject Jerusalem, the city I chose, and this temple, about which I said, 'There shall my Name be.'a"

28As for the other events of Josiah's reign, and all he did, are they not written in the book of the annals of the kings of Judah?

29While Josiah was king, Pharaoh Neco king of Egypt went up to the Euphrates River to help the king of Assyria. King Josiah marched out to meet him in battle, but Neco faced him and killed him at Megiddo. 30Josiah's servants brought his body in a chariot from Megiddo to Jerusalem and buried him in his own tomb. And the people of the land took Jehoahaz son of Josiah and anointed him and made him king in place of his father.   2Ch 35:20-36:1

Jehoahaz King of Judah

31Jehoahaz was twenty-three years old when he became king, and he reigned in Jerusalem three

---

a27 1 Kings 8:29

months. His mother's name was Hamutal daughter of Jeremiah; she was from Libnah. ³²He did evil in the eyes of the LORD, just as his fathers had done. ³³Pharaoh Neco put him in chains at Riblah in the land of Hamath*ᵃ* so that he might not reign in Jerusalem, and he imposed on Judah a levy of a hundred talents*ᵇ* of silver and a talent*ᶜ* of gold. ³⁴Pharaoh Neco made Eliakim son of Josiah king in place of his father Josiah and changed Eliakim's name to Jehoiakim. But he took Jehoahaz and carried him off to Egypt, and there he died. ³⁵Jehoiakim paid Pharaoh Neco the silver and gold he demanded. In order to do so, he taxed the land and exacted the silver and gold from the people of the land according to their assessments.   2Ch 36:2-4

Jehoiakim King of Judah

³⁶Jehoiakim was twenty-five years old when he became king, and he reigned in Jerusalem eleven years. His mother's name was Zebidah daughter of Pedaiah; she was from Rumah. ³⁷And he did evil in the eyes of the LORD, just as his fathers had done.   Jer 26:1

24 During Jehoiakim's reign, Nebuchadnezzar king of Babylon invaded the land, and Jehoiakim became his vassal for three years. But then he changed his mind and rebelled against Neb-

uchadnezzar. ²The LORD sent Babylonian,*ᵈ* Aramean, Moabite and Ammonite raiders against him. He sent them to destroy Judah, in accordance with the word of the LORD proclaimed by his servants the prophets. ³Surely these things happened to Judah according to the LORD's command, in order to remove them from his presence because of the sins of Manasseh and all he had done, ⁴including the shedding of innocent blood. For he had filled Jerusalem with innocent blood, and the LORD was not willing to forgive.   2Ki 21:16; 23:26

⁵As for the other events of Jehoiakim's reign, and all he did, are they not written in the book of the annals of the kings of Judah? ⁶Jehoiakim rested with his fathers. And Jehoiachin his son succeeded him as king.   2Ch 36:5-8; Jer 22:19

⁷The king of Egypt did not march out from his own country again, because the king of Babylon had taken all his territory, from the Wadi of Egypt to the Euphrates River.   Jer 37:5-7; 46:2

Jehoiachin King of Judah

⁸Jehoiachin was eighteen years old when he became king, and he reigned in Jerusalem three months. His mother's name was Nehushta daughter of Elnathan; she was from Jerusalem. ⁹He did

ᵃ33 Hebrew; Septuagint (see also 2 Chron. 36:3) *Neco at Riblah in Hamath removed him*   *ᵇ33* That is, about 3 3/4 tons (about 3.4 metric tons)   *ᶜ33* That is, about 75 pounds (about 34 kilograms)   *ᵈ2* Or *Chaldean*

evil in the eyes of the LORD, just as his father had done.   1Ch 3:16

¹⁰At that time the officers of Nebuchadnezzar king of Babylon advanced on Jerusalem and laid siege to it, ¹¹and Nebuchadnezzar himself came up to the city while his officers were besieging it. ¹²Jehoiachin king of Judah, his mother, his attendants, his nobles and his officials all surrendered to him.

In the eighth year of the reign of the king of Babylon, he took Jehoiachin prisoner. ¹³As the LORD had declared, Nebuchadnezzar removed all the treasures from the temple of the LORD and from the royal palace, and took away all the gold articles that Solomon king of Israel had made for the temple of the LORD. ¹⁴He carried into exile all Jerusalem: all the officers and fighting men, and all the craftsmen and artisans—a total of ten thousand. Only the poorest people of the land were left.   2Ki 25:12; Jer 40:7

¹⁵Nebuchadnezzar took Jehoiachin captive to Babylon. He also took from Jerusalem to Babylon the king's mother, his wives, his officials and the leading men of the land. ¹⁶The king of Babylon also deported to Babylon the entire force of seven thousand fighting men, strong and fit for war, and a thousand craftsmen and artisans. ¹⁷He made Mattaniah, Jehoiachin's uncle, king in his place and changed his name to Zedekiah.

Zedekiah King of Judah

¹⁸Zedekiah was twenty-one years old when he became king, and he reigned in Jerusalem eleven years. His mother's name was Hamutal daughter of Jeremiah; she was from Libnah. ¹⁹He did evil in the eyes of the LORD, just as Jehoiakim had done. ²⁰It was because of the LORD's anger that all this happened to Jerusalem and Judah, and in the end he thrust them from his presence.

The Fall of Jerusalem

Now Zedekiah rebelled against the king of Babylon.

25 So in the ninth year of Zedekiah's reign, on the tenth day of the tenth month, Nebuchadnezzar king of Babylon marched against Jerusalem with his whole army. He encamped outside the city and built siege works all around it. ²The city was kept under siege until the eleventh year of King Zedekiah. ³By the ninth day of the ⌊fourth⌋ ͣ month the famine in the city had become so severe that there was no food for the people to eat. ⁴Then the city wall was broken through, and the whole army fled at night through the gate between the two walls near the king's garden, though the Babylonians ᵇ were surrounding the city. They fled toward the Ara-

---

ͣ 3 See Jer. 52:6.   ᵇ 4 Or *Chaldeans*; also in verses 13, 25 and 26 bah,[a] [5]but the Babylonian[b] army pursued the king and overtook him in the plains of Jericho. All his soldiers were separated from him and scattered, [6]and he was captured. He was taken to the king of Babylon at Riblah, where sentence was pronounced on him. [7]They killed the sons of Zedekiah before his eyes. Then they put out his eyes, bound him with bronze shackles and took him to Babylon.

[8]On the seventh day of the fifth month, in the nineteenth year of Nebuchadnezzar king of Babylon, Nebuzaradan commander of the imperial guard, an official of the king of Babylon, came to Jerusalem. [9]He set fire to the temple of the LORD, the royal palace and all the houses of Jerusalem. Every important building he burned down. [10]The whole Babylonian army, under the commander of the imperial guard, broke down the walls around Jerusalem. [11]Nebuzaradan the commander of the guard carried into exile the people who remained in the city, along with the rest of the populace and those who had gone over to the king of Babylon. [12]But the commander left behind some of the poorest people of the land to work the vineyards and fields.   Jer 39:1-10; 2Ki 24:14

[13]The Babylonians broke up the bronze pillars, the movable stands and the bronze Sea that were at the temple of the LORD and they carried the bronze to Babylon. [14]They also took away the pots, shovels, wick trimmers, dishes and all the bronze articles used in the temple service. [15]The commander of the imperial guard took away the censers and sprinkling bowls—all that were made of pure gold or silver.

[16]The bronze from the two pillars, the Sea and the movable stands, which Solomon had made for the temple of the LORD, was more than could be weighed. [17]Each pillar was twenty-seven feet[c] high. The bronze capital on top of one pillar was four and a half feet[d] high and was decorated with a network and pomegranates of bronze all around. The other pillar, with its network, was similar.

[18]The commander of the guard took as prisoners Seraiah the chief priest, Zephaniah the priest next in rank and the three doorkeepers. [19]Of those still in the city, he took the officer in charge of the fighting men and five royal advisers. He also took the secretary who was chief officer in charge of conscripting the people of the land and sixty of his men who were found in the city. [20]Nebuzaradan the commander took them all and brought them to the king of Babylon at Riblah. [21]There at Riblah, in the land of Hamath, the king had them executed.   Jer 21:1; 29:25

---

[a]4 Or *the Jordan Valley*   [b]5 Or *Chaldean*; also in verses 10 and 24   [c]17 Hebrew *eighteen cubits* (about 8.1 meters)   [d]17 Hebrew *three cubits* (about 1.3 meters)

So Judah went into captivity, away from her land. 2Ch 36:17-20

²²Nebuchadnezzar king of Babylon appointed Gedaliah son of Ahikam, the son of Shaphan, to be over the people he had left behind in Judah. ²³When all the army officers and their men heard that the king of Babylon had appointed Gedaliah as governor, they came to Gedaliah at Mizpah—Ishmael son of Nethaniah, Johanan son of Kareah, Seraiah son of Tanhumeth the Netophathite, Jaazaniah the son of the Maacathite, and their men. ²⁴Gedaliah took an oath to reassure them and their men. "Do not be afraid of the Babylonian officials," he said. "Settle down in the land and serve the king of Babylon, and it will go well with you."

²⁵In the seventh month, however, Ishmael son of Nethaniah, the son of Elishama, who was of royal blood, came with ten men and as-sassinated Gedaliah and also the men of Judah and the Babylonians who were with him at Mizpah. ²⁶At this, all the people from the least to the greatest, together with the army officers, fled to Egypt for fear of the Babylonians. Jer 40:7-9

Jehoiachin Released

²⁷In the thirty-seventh year of the exile of Jehoiachin king of Judah, in the year Evil-Merodach[a] became king of Babylon, he released Jehoiachin from prison on the twenty-seventh day of the twelfth month. ²⁸He spoke kindly to him and gave him a seat of honor higher than those of the other kings who were with him in Babylon. ²⁹So Jehoiachin put aside his prison clothes and for the rest of his life ate regularly at the king's table. ³⁰Day by day the king gave Jehoiachin a regular allowance as long as he lived. Jer 52:31-34

a 27 Also called Amel-Marduk

1 Chronicles

Historical Records From Adam to Abraham

To Noah's Sons

1 Adam, Seth, Enosh, ²Kenan, Mahalalel, Jared, ³Enoch, Methuselah, Lamech, Noah. Ge 5:1-32

⁴The sons of Noah:ᵃ
Shem, Ham and Japheth.

The Japhethites

⁵The sonsᵇ of Japheth:
Gomer, Magog, Madai, Javan, Tubal, Meshech and Tiras.
⁶The sons of Gomer:
Ashkenaz, Riphathᶜ and Togarmah.
⁷The sons of Javan:
Elishah, Tarshish, the Kittim and the Rodanim.

The Hamites

⁸The sons of Ham:
Cush, Mizraim,ᵈ Put and Canaan.
⁹The sons of Cush:
Seba, Havilah, Sabta, Raamah and Sabteca.
The sons of Raamah:
Sheba and Dedan.
¹⁰Cush was the fatherᵉ of Nimrod, who grew to be a mighty warrior on earth.
¹¹Mizraim was the father of the Ludites, Anamites, Lehabites, Naphtuhites, ¹²Pathrusites, Casluhites (from whom the Philistines came) and Caphtorites.
¹³Canaan was the father of Sidon his firstborn,ᶠ and of the Hittites, ¹⁴Jebusites, Amorites, Girgashites, ¹⁵Hivites, Arkites, Sinites, ¹⁶Arvadites, Zemarites and Hamathites. Ge 10:6-20

The Semites

¹⁷The sons of Shem:
Elam, Asshur, Arphaxad, Lud and Aram.
The sons of Aramᵍ:
Uz, Hul, Gether and Meshech.
¹⁸Arphaxad was the father of Shelah,
and Shelah the father of Eber.
¹⁹Two sons were born to Eber:
One was named Peleg,ʰ be-

ᵃ4 Septuagint; Hebrew does not have *The sons of Noah:* ᵇ5 *Sons* may mean *descendants* or *successors* or *nations*; also in verses 6-10, 17 and 20. ᶜ6 Many Hebrew manuscripts and Vulgate (see also Septuagint and Gen. 10:3); most Hebrew manuscripts *Diphath* ᵈ8 That is, Egypt; also in verse 11 ᵉ10 *Father* may mean *ancestor* or *predecessor* or *founder*; also in verses 11, 13, 18 and 20. ᶠ13 Or *of the Sidonians, the foremost* ᵍ17 One Hebrew manuscript and some Septuagint manuscripts (see also Gen. 10:23); most Hebrew manuscripts do not have this line. ʰ19 *Peleg* means *division*.

cause in his time the earth was divided; his brother was named Joktan.

²⁰Joktan was the father of Almodad, Sheleph, Hazarmaveth, Jerah, ²¹Hadoram, Uzal, Diklah, ²²Obal,ᵃ Abimael, Sheba, ²³Ophir, Havilah and Jobab. All these were sons of Joktan.

²⁴Shem, Arphaxad,ᵇ Shelah, ²⁵Eber, Peleg, Reu, ²⁶Serug, Nahor, Terah ²⁷and Abram (that is, Abraham).

The Family of Abraham

²⁸The sons of Abraham:
Isaac and Ishmael.

Descendants of Hagar

²⁹These were their descendants:
Nebaioth the firstborn of Ishmael, Kedar, Adbeel, Mibsam, ³⁰Mishma, Dumah, Massa, Hadad, Tema, ³¹Jetur, Naphish and Kedemah. These were the sons of Ishmael.   Ge 25:12-16

Descendants of Keturah

³²The sons born to Keturah, Abraham's concubine:
Zimran, Jokshan, Medan, Midian, Ishbak and Shuah.

The sons of Jokshan:
Sheba and Dedan.   Ge 10:7

³³The sons of Midian:
Ephah, Epher, Hanoch, Abida and Eldaah.

All these were descendants of Keturah.   Ge 25:1-4

Descendants of Sarah

³⁴Abraham was the father of Isaac.   Ge 21:2-3; Mt 1:2; Ac 7:8

The sons of Isaac:
Esau and Israel.   Ge 17:5

Esau's Sons

³⁵The sons of Esau: Ge 36:19
Eliphaz, Reuel, Jeush, Jalam and Korah.   Ge 36:4

³⁶The sons of Eliphaz:
Teman, Omar, Zepho,ᶜ Gatam and Kenaz;
by Timna: Amalek.ᵈ

³⁷The sons of Reuel: Ge 36:17
Nahath, Zerah, Shammah and Mizzah.   Ge 36:10-14

The People of Seir in Edom

³⁸The sons of Seir:
Lotan, Shobal, Zibeon, Anah, Dishon, Ezer and Dishan.

³⁹The sons of Lotan:
Hori and Homam. Timna was Lotan's sister.

⁴⁰The sons of Shobal:

ᵃ22 Some Hebrew manuscripts and Syriac (see also Gen. 10:28); most Hebrew manuscripts Ebal   ᵇ24 Hebrew; some Septuagint manuscripts Arphaxad, Cainan (see also note at Gen. 11:10)   ᶜ36 Many Hebrew manuscripts, some Septuagint manuscripts and Syriac (see also Gen. 36:11); most Hebrew manuscripts Zephi   ᵈ36 Some Septuagint manuscripts (see also Gen. 36:12); Hebrew Gatam, Kenaz, Timna and Amalek

Alvan,[a] Manahath, Ebal, Shepho and Onam.

The sons of Zibeon:
Aiah and Anah.   Ge 36:2

⁴¹The son of Anah:
Dishon.

The sons of Dishon:
Hemdan,[b] Eshban, Ithran and Keran.

⁴²The sons of Ezer:
Bilhan, Zaavan and Akan.[c]

The sons of Dishan[d]:
Uz and Aran.   Ge 36:20-28

The Rulers of Edom

⁴³These were the kings who reigned in Edom before any Israelite king reigned[e]:
Bela son of Beor, whose city was named Dinhabah.

⁴⁴When Bela died, Jobab son of Zerah from Bozrah succeeded him as king.

⁴⁵When Jobab died, Husham from the land of the Temanites succeeded him as king.   Ge 36:11

⁴⁶When Husham died, Hadad son of Bedad, who defeated Midian in the country of Moab, succeeded him as king. His city was named Avith.

⁴⁷When Hadad died, Samlah from Masrekah succeeded him as king.

⁴⁸When Samlah died, Shaul from Rehoboth on the river[f] succeeded him as king.

⁴⁹When Shaul died, Baal-Hanan son of Acbor succeeded him as king.

⁵⁰When Baal-Hanan died, Hadad succeeded him as king. His city was named Pau,[g] and his wife's name was Mehetabel daughter of Matred, the daughter of Me-Zahab. ⁵¹Hadad also died.

The chiefs of Edom were:
Timna, Alvah, Jetheth, ⁵²Oholibamah, Elah, Pinon, ⁵³Kenaz, Teman, Mibzar, ⁵⁴Magdiel and Iram. These were the chiefs of Edom.

Israel's Sons

2 These were the sons of Israel: Reuben, Simeon, Levi, Judah, Issachar, Zebulun, ²Dan, Joseph, Benjamin, Naphtali, Gad and Asher.

Judah

To Hezron's Sons

³The sons of Judah: Ge 38:2-10
Er, Onan and Shelah. These three were born to him by a

---

a40 Many Hebrew manuscripts and some Septuagint manuscripts (see also Gen. 36:23); most Hebrew manuscripts *Alian*   b41 Many Hebrew manuscripts and some Septuagint manuscripts (see also Gen. 36:26); most Hebrew manuscripts *Hamran*   c42 Many Hebrew and Septuagint manuscripts (see also Gen. 36:27); most Hebrew manuscripts *Zaavan, Jaakan*   d42 Hebrew *Dishon*, a variant of *Dishan*   e43 Or *before an Israelite king reigned over them*   f48 Possibly the Euphrates   g50 Many Hebrew manuscripts, some Septuagint manuscripts, Vulgate and Syriac (see also Gen. 36:39); most Hebrew manuscripts *Pai*

Canaanite woman, the daughter of Shua. Er, Judah's firstborn, was wicked in the LORD's sight; so the LORD put him to death. ⁴Tamar, Judah's daughter-in-law, bore him Perez and Zerah. Judah had five sons in all.   Ge 38:11-30

⁵The sons of Perez: Ge 46:12
Hezron and Hamul.
⁶The sons of Zerah:
Zimri, Ethan, Heman, Calcol and Darda*ᵃ*—five in all.
⁷The son of Carmi:
Achar,*ᵇ* who brought trouble on Israel by violating the ban on taking devoted things.*ᶜ*   Jos 6:18; 7:1
⁸The son of Ethan:
Azariah.
⁹The sons born to Hezron were:
Jerahmeel, Ram and Caleb.*ᵈ*   Nu 26:21

From Ram Son of Hezron

¹⁰Ram was the father of Amminadab, and Amminadab the father of Nahshon, the leader of the people of Judah. ¹¹Nahshon was the father of Salmon,*ᵉ* Salmon the father of Boaz, ¹²Boaz the father of Obed and Obed the father of Jesse.

¹³Jesse was the father of Eliab his firstborn; the second son was Abinadab, the third Shimea, ¹⁴the fourth Nethanel, the fifth Raddai, ¹⁵the sixth Ozem and the seventh David. ¹⁶Their sisters were Zeruiah and Abigail. Zeruiah's three sons were Abishai, Joab and Asahel. ¹⁷Abigail was the mother of Amasa, whose father was Jether the Ishmaelite.   Ru 4:18-22; Mt 1:3-6

Caleb Son of Hezron

¹⁸Caleb son of Hezron had children by his wife Azubah (and by Jerioth). These were her sons: Jesher, Shobab and Ardon. ¹⁹When Azubah died, Caleb married Ephrath, who bore him Hur. ²⁰Hur was the father of Uri, and Uri the father of Bezalel.   ver 42,50; Ex 31:2
²¹Later, Hezron lay with the daughter of Makir the father of Gilead (he had married her when he was sixty years old), and she bore him Segub. ²²Segub was the father of Jair, who controlled twenty-three towns in Gilead. ²³(But Geshur and Aram captured Hav-

---

*ᵃ*6 Many Hebrew manuscripts, some Septuagint manuscripts and Syriac (see also 1 Kings 4:31); most Hebrew manuscripts *Dara*   *ᵇ*7 *Achar* means *trouble*; *Achar* is called *Achan* in Joshua.   *ᶜ*7 The Hebrew term refers to the irrevocable giving over of things or persons to the LORD, often by totally destroying them.   *ᵈ*9 Hebrew *Kelubai,* a variant of *Caleb*   *ᵉ*11 Septuagint (see also Ruth 4:21); Hebrew *Salma*

voth Jair,^{a} as well as Kenath with its surrounding settlements—sixty towns.) All these were descendants of Makir the father of Gilead.   Nu 32:41; Dt 3:14; Jos 13:30

²⁴After Hezron died in Caleb Ephrathah, Abijah the wife of Hezron bore him Ashhur the father^b of Tekoa.

Jerahmeel Son of Hezron

²⁵The sons of Jerahmeel the firstborn of Hezron:
Ram his firstborn, Bunah, Oren, Ozem and^c Ahijah.
²⁶Jerahmeel had another wife, whose name was Atarah; she was the mother of Onam.
²⁷The sons of Ram the firstborn of Jerahmeel:
Maaz, Jamin and Eker.
²⁸The sons of Onam:
Shammai and Jada.
The sons of Shammai:
Nadab and Abishur.
²⁹Abishur's wife was named Abihail, who bore him Ahban and Molid.
³⁰The sons of Nadab:
Seled and Appaim. Seled died without children.
³¹The son of Appaim:
Ishi, who was the father of Sheshan.
Sheshan was the father of Ahlai.

³²The sons of Jada, Shammai's brother:
Jether and Jonathan. Jether died without children.
³³The sons of Jonathan:
Peleth and Zaza.
These were the descendants of Jerahmeel.
³⁴Sheshan had no sons—only daughters.
He had an Egyptian servant named Jarha. ³⁵Sheshan gave his daughter in marriage to his servant Jarha, and she bore him Attai.
³⁶Attai was the father of Nathan,
Nathan the father of Zabad,
³⁷Zabad the father of Ephlal,
Ephlal the father of Obed,
³⁸Obed the father of Jehu,
Jehu the father of Azariah,
³⁹Azariah the father of Helez,
Helez the father of Eleasah,
⁴⁰Eleasah the father of Sismai,
Sismai the father of Shallum,
⁴¹Shallum the father of Jekamiah,
and Jekamiah the father of Elishama.

The Clans of Caleb

⁴²The sons of Caleb the brother of Jerahmeel: ver 19
Mesha his firstborn, who was the father of Ziph, and

---

^{a}23 Or *captured the settlements of Jair* ^{b}24 *Father* may mean *civic leader* or *military leader*; also in verses 42, 45, 49-52 and possibly elsewhere. ^{c}25 Or *Oren and Ozem, by* his son Mareshah,[a] who was the father of Hebron.

[43]The sons of Hebron:

Korah, Tappuah, Rekem and Shema. [44]Shema was the father of Raham, and Raham the father of Jorke-am. Rekem was the father of Shammai. [45]The son of Shammai was Maon, and Maon was the father of Beth Zur. Jos 15:55,58

[46]Caleb's concubine Ephah was the mother of Haran, Moza and Gazez. Haran was the father of Gazez.

[47]The sons of Jahdai:

Regem, Jotham, Geshan, Pelet, Ephah and Shaaph.

[48]Caleb's concubine Maacah was the mother of Sheber and Tirhanah. [49]She also gave birth to Shaaph the father of Madmannah and to Sheva the father of Mac-benah and Gibea. Caleb's daughter was Acsah. [50]These were the descendants of Caleb. Jos 15:16,31

The sons of Hur the firstborn of Ephrathah: 1Ch 4:4

Shobal the father of Kiriath Jearim, [51]Salma the father of Bethlehem, and Hareph the father of Beth Gader.

[52]The descendants of Shobal the father of Kiriath Jearim were:

Haroeh, half the Manahath-ites, [53]and the clans of Kiri-ath Jearim: the Ithrites, Pu-thites, Shumathites and Mishraites. From these de-scended the Zorathites and Eshtaolites. 2Sa 23:38

[54]The descendants of Salma:

Bethlehem, the Netopha-thites, Atroth Beth Joab, half the Manahathites, the Zorites, [55]and the clans of scribes[b] who lived at Jabez: the Tirathites, Shimeathites and Sucathites. These are the Kenites who came from Hammath, the father of the house of Recab.[c] Jdg 1:16

The Sons of David

3 These were the sons of David born to him in Hebron:

The firstborn was Amnon the son of Ahinoam of Jez-reel; Jos 15:56

the second, Daniel the son of Abigail of Carmel;

[2]the third, Absalom the son of Maacah daughter of Tal-mai king of Geshur;

the fourth, Adonijah the son of Haggith; 1Ki 2:22

[3]the fifth, Shephatiah the son of Abital;

and the sixth, Ithream, by his wife Eglah.

[4]These six were born to Da-vid in Hebron, where he

---

[a]42 The meaning of the Hebrew for this phrase is uncertain.   [b]55 Or of the Sopherites   [c]55 Or father of Beth Recab

reigned seven years and six
months.   2Sa 3:2-5
David reigned in Jerusalem thirty-
three years, **5**and these were the
children born to him there:
Shammua,*a* Shobab, Na-
than and Solomon. These
four were by Bathsheba*b*
daughter of Ammiel.
6There were also Ibhar, Elishua,*c* Eliphelet, **7**Nogah,
Nepheg, Japhia, **8**Elishama,
Eliada and Eliphelet—nine
in all. **9**All these were the
sons of David, besides his
sons by his concubines.
And Tamar was their sister.

The Kings of Judah

10Solomon's son was Rehobo-
am,   1Ki 11:43; 14:21-31
　　Abijah his son,
　　Asa his son,
　　Jehoshaphat his son,
11Jehoram*d* his son,
　　Ahaziah his son,   2Ch 22:1-10
　　Joash his son,   2Ki 11:1-12:21
12Amaziah his son,   2Ki 14:1-22
　　Azariah his son,
　　Jotham his son,   Isa 1:1
13Ahaz his son,   Isa 7:1
　　Hezekiah his son,   Jer 26:19
　　Manasseh his son,   2Ch 33:1
14Amon his son,   2Ki 21:19-26
　　Josiah his son.   Jer 1:2; 25:3
15The sons of Josiah:
　　Johanan the firstborn,

　　Jehoiakim the second son,
　　Zedekiah the third,   Jer 37:1
　　Shallum the fourth.
16The successors of Jehoiakim:
　　Jehoiachin*e* his son,
　　and Zedekiah.   2Ki 24:18

The Royal Line After the Exile

17The descendants of Jehoia-
chin the captive:
　　Shealtiel his son, **18**Malki-
ram, Pedaiah, Shenazzar,
Jekamiah, Hoshama and
Nedabiah.   Ezr 1:8; 5:14; Jer 22:30
19The sons of Pedaiah:
　　Zerubbabel and Shimei.
　　The sons of Zerubbabel:
　　Meshullam and Hananiah.
　　Shelomith was their sister.
20There were also five others:
　　Hashubah, Ohel, Berekiah,
Hasadiah and Jushab-He-
sed.
21The descendants of Hananiah:
　　Pelatiah and Jeshaiah, and
the sons of Rephaiah, of Ar-
nan, of Obadiah and of
Shecaniah.
22The descendants of Shecaniah:
　　Shemaiah and his sons:
　　Hattush, Igal, Bariah, Neariah and Shaphat—six in all.
23The sons of Neariah:
　　Elioenai, Hizkiah and Azrikam—three in all.

---

a 5 Hebrew *Shimea,* a variant of *Shammua*   *b 5* One Hebrew manuscript and Vulgate (see also
Septuagint and 2 Samuel 11:3); most Hebrew manuscripts *Bathshua*   *c 6* Two Hebrew manuscripts (see
also 2 Samuel 5:15 and 1 Chron. 14:5); most Hebrew manuscripts *Elishama*   *d 11* Hebrew *Joram,* a
variant of *Jehoram*   *e 16* Hebrew *Jeconiah,* a variant of *Jehoiachin;* also in verse 17

²⁴The sons of Elioenai:
Hodaviah, Eliashib, Pela-
iah, Akkub, Johanan, Delaiah and Anani—seven in
all.

Other Clans of Judah

4 The descendants of Judah:
Perez, Hezron, Carmi, Hur
and Shobal. Nu 26:21
²Reaiah son of Shobal was the
father of Jahath, and Jahath
the father of Ahumai and
Lahad. These were the
clans of the Zorathites.
³These were the sonsᵃ of
Etam:
Jezreel, Ishma and Idbash.
Their sister was named
Hazzelelponi. ⁴Penuel was
the father of Gedor, and
Ezer the father of Hushah.
These were the descendants
of Hur, the firstborn of Ephrathah and fatherᵇ of Bethlehem. Ru 1:19; 1Ch 2:50
⁵Ashhur the father of Tekoa
had two wives, Helah and
Naarah. 1Ch 2:24
⁶Naarah bore him Ahuzzam,
Hepher, Temeni and Haa-
hashtari. These were the
descendants of Naarah.
⁷The sons of Helah:
Zereth, Zohar, Ethnan,
⁸and Koz, who was the fa-
ther of Anub and Hazzobe-
bah and of the clans of
Aharhel son of Harum.

⁹Jabez was more honorable
than his brothers. His mother had
named him Jabez,ᶜ saying, "I gave
birth to him in pain." ¹⁰Jabez cried
out to the God of Israel, "Oh, that
you would bless me and enlarge
my territory! Let your hand be
with me, and keep me from harm
so that I will be free from pain."
And God granted his request.

¹¹Kelub, Shuhah's brother, was
the father of Mehir, who
was the father of Eshton.
¹²Eshton was the father of
Beth Rapha, Paseah and Te-
hinnah the father of Ir Na-
hash.ᵈ These were the men
of Recah.

¹³The sons of Kenaz:
Othniel and Seraiah.
The sons of Othniel:
Hathath and Meonothai.ᵉ
¹⁴Meonothai was the father
of Ophrah.
Seraiah was the father of
Joab,
the father of Ge Harashim.ᶠ
It was called this because
its people were craftsmen.
¹⁵The sons of Caleb son of Je-
phunneh:
Iru, Elah and Naam.
The son of Elah:
Kenaz.

ᵃ3 Some Septuagint manuscripts (see also Vulgate); Hebrew *father*   ᵇ4 *Father* may mean *civic leader*
or *military leader*; also in verses 12, 14, 17, 18 and possibly elsewhere.   ᶜ9 *Jabez* sounds like the
Hebrew for *pain*.   ᵈ12 Or *of the city of Nahash*   ᵉ13 Some Septuagint manuscripts and Vulgate;
Hebrew does not have *and Meonothai*.   ᶠ14 *Ge Harashim* means *valley of craftsmen*.

¹⁶The sons of Jehallelel:
Ziph, Ziphah, Tiria and As-
arel.
¹⁷The sons of Ezrah:
Jether, Mered, Epher and
Jalon. One of Mered's
wives gave birth to Miriam,
Shammai and Ishbah the
father of Eshtemoa. ¹⁸(His
Judean wife gave birth to
Jered the father of Gedor,
Heber the father of Soco,
and Jekuthiel the father
of Zanoah.) These were
the children of Pharaoh's
daughter Bithiah, whom
Mered had married.
¹⁹The sons of Hodiah's wife, the
sister of Naham:
the father of Keilah the Gar-
mite, and Eshtemoa the
Maacathite.   Dt 3:14; Jos 15:44
²⁰The sons of Shimon:
Amnon, Rinnah, Ben-Ha-
nan and Tilon.
The descendants of Ishi:
Zoheth and Ben-Zoheth.
²¹The sons of Shelah son of Judah:
Er the father of Lecah, Laa-
dah the father of Mareshah
and the clans of the linen
workers at Beth Ashbea,
²²Jokim, the men of Coze-
ba, and Joash and Saraph,
who ruled in Moab and Ja-
shubi Lehem. (These
records are from ancient
times.) ²³They were the

potters who lived at Netaim
and Gederah; they stayed
there and worked for the
king.   Ge 38:5

Simeon

²⁴The descendants of Simeon:
Nemuel, Jamin, Jarib, Ze-
rah and Shaul;   Nu 26:12
²⁵Shallum was Shaul's son,
Mibsam his son and Mish-
ma his son.
²⁶The descendants of Mishma:
Hammuel his son, Zaccur
his son and Shimei his son.
²⁷Shimei had sixteen sons and
six daughters, but his brothers did
not have many children; so their
entire clan did not become as numerous as the people of Judah.
²⁸They lived in Beersheba, Moladah, Hazar Shual, ²⁹Bilhah, Ezem,
Tolad, ³⁰Bethuel, Hormah, Ziklag,
³¹Beth Marcaboth, Hazar Susim,
Beth Biri and Shaaraim. These
were their towns until the reign of
David. ³²Their surrounding villages were Etam, Ain, Rimmon,
Token and Ashan—five towns—
³³and all the villages around these
towns as far as Baalath.ᵃ These
were their settlements. And they
kept a genealogical record.

³⁴Meshobab, Jamlech, Joshah
son of Amaziah, ³⁵Joel, Jehu
son of Joshibiah, the son of
Seraiah, the son of Asiel,
³⁶also Elioenai, Jaakobah,

ᵃ 33 Some Septuagint manuscripts (see also Joshua 19:8); Hebrew *Baal*

Jeshohaiah, Asaiah, Adiel, Jesimiel, Benaiah, [37]and Ziza son of Shiphi, the son of Allon, the son of Jedaiah, the son of Shimri, the son of Shemaiah.

[38]The men listed above by name were leaders of their clans. Their families increased greatly, [39]and they went to the outskirts of Gedor to the east of the valley in search of pasture for their flocks. [40]They found rich, good pasture, and the land was spacious, peaceful and quiet. Some Hamites had lived there formerly.   Jdg 18:7-10

[41]The men whose names were listed came in the days of Hezekiah king of Judah. They attacked the Hamites in their dwellings and also the Meunites who were there and completely destroyed[a] them, as is evident to this day. Then they settled in their place, because there was pasture for their flocks. [42]And five hundred of these Simeonites, led by Pelatiah, Neariah, Rephaiah and Uzziel, the sons of Ishi, invaded the hill country of Seir. [43]They killed the remaining Amalekites who had escaped, and they have lived there to this day.

Reuben

5 The sons of Reuben the firstborn of Israel (he was the firstborn, but when he defiled his father's marriage bed, his rights as firstborn were given to the sons of Joseph son of Israel; so he could not be listed in the genealogical record in accordance with his birthright, [2]and though Judah was the strongest of his brothers and a ruler came from him, the rights of the firstborn belonged to Joseph) — [3]the sons of Reuben the firstborn of Israel: Ps 60:7; Mic 5:2

Hanoch, Pallu, Hezron and Carmi.   Nu 26:5

[4]The descendants of Joel:

Shemaiah his son, Gog his son,

Shimei his son, [5]Micah his son,

Reaiah his son, Baal his son,

[6]and Beerah his son, whom Tiglath-Pileser[b] king of Assyria took into exile. Beerah was a leader of the Reubenites.   2Ki 15:19; 16:10; 2Ch 28:20

[7]Their relatives by clans, listed according to their genealogical records: ver 17

Jeiel the chief, Zechariah, [8]and Bela son of Azaz, the son of Shema, the son of Joel. They settled in the area from Aroer to Nebo and Baal Meon. [9]To the east they occupied the land up to the edge of the desert that extends to the Euphrates River, because their

---

[a]41 The Hebrew term refers to the irrevocable giving over of things or persons to the LORD, often by totally destroying them.   [b]6 Hebrew Tilgath-Pilneser, a variant of Tiglath-Pileser; also in verse 26

livestock had increased in Gilead.   Nu 32:26; Jos 22:9

¹⁰During Saul's reign they waged war against the Hagrites, who were defeated at their hands; they occupied the dwellings of the Hagrites throughout the entire region east of Gilead.   ver 18-21

Gad

¹¹The Gadites lived next to them in Bashan, as far as Salecah: Jos 13:11,24-28
¹²Joel was the chief, Shapham the second, then Janai and Shaphat, in Bashan.
¹³Their relatives, by families, were:

Michael, Meshullam, Sheba, Jorai, Jacan, Zia and Eber—seven in all.

¹⁴These were the sons of Abihail son of Huri, the son of Jaroah, the son of Gilead, the son of Michael, the son of Jeshishai, the son of Jahdo, the son of Buz.
¹⁵Ahi son of Abdiel, the son of Guni, was head of their family.
¹⁶The Gadites lived in Gilead, in Bashan and its outlying villages, and on all the pasturelands of Sharon as far as they extended.
¹⁷All these were entered in the genealogical records during the reigns of Jotham king of Judah and Jeroboam king of Israel.

¹⁸The Reubenites, the Gadites and the half-tribe of Manasseh had 44,760 men ready for military service—able-bodied men who could handle shield and sword, who could use a bow, and who were trained for battle. ¹⁹They waged war against the Hagrites, Jetur, Naphish and Nodab. ²⁰They were helped in fighting them, and God handed the Hagrites and all their allies over to them, because they cried out to him during the battle. He answered their prayers, because they trusted in him. ²¹They seized the livestock of the Hagrites—fifty thousand camels, two hundred fifty thousand sheep and two thousand donkeys. They also took one hundred thousand people captive, ²²and many others fell slain, because the battle was God's. And they occupied the land until the exile.   2Ki 15:29; 17:6; Da 6:23

The Half-Tribe of Manasseh

²³The people of the half-tribe of Manasseh were numerous; they settled in the land from Bashan to Baal Hermon, that is, to Senir (Mount Hermon).   Dt 3:8-9; SS 4:8
²⁴These were the heads of their families: Epher, Ishi, Eliel, Azriel, Jeremiah, Hodaviah and Jahdiel. They were brave warriors, famous men, and heads of their families. ²⁵But they were unfaithful to the God of their fathers and prostituted themselves to the gods of the peoples of the land, whom God had destroyed before them. ²⁶So

the God of Israel stirred up the spirit of Pul king of Assyria (that is, Tiglath-Pileser king of Assyria), who took the Reubenites, the Gadites and the half-tribe of Manasseh into exile. He took them to Halah, Habor, Hara and the river of Gozan, where they are to this day.

Levi

6 The sons of Levi: Ge 46:11
Gershon, Kohath and Merari.

²The sons of Kohath:
Amram, Izhar, Hebron and Uzziel.

³The children of Amram:
Aaron, Moses and Miriam.
The sons of Aaron:
Nadab, Abihu, Eleazar and Ithamar.   Lev 10:1

⁴Eleazar was the father of Phinehas,
Phinehas the father of Abishua,

⁵Abishua the father of Bukki,
Bukki the father of Uzzi,

⁶Uzzi the father of Zerahiah,
Zerahiah the father of Meraioth,

⁷Meraioth the father of Amariah,
Amariah the father of Ahitub,

⁸Ahitub the father of Zadok,
Zadok the father of Ahimaaz,

⁹Ahimaaz the father of Azariah,
Azariah the father of Johanan,

¹⁰Johanan the father of Azariah (it was he who served as priest in the temple Solomon built in Jerusalem),

¹¹Azariah the father of Amariah,
Amariah the father of Ahitub,

¹²Ahitub the father of Zadok,
Zadok the father of Shallum,

¹³Shallum the father of Hilkiah,   2Ki 22:1-20; 2Ch 34:9; 35:8
Hilkiah the father of Azariah,

¹⁴Azariah the father of Seraiah,
and Seraiah the father of Jehozadak.   Ezr 2:2; Ne 11:11

¹⁵Jehozadak was deported when the LORD sent Judah and Jerusalem into exile by the hand of Nebuchadnezzar.

¹⁶The sons of Levi: Ge 29:34
Gershon,ᵃ Kohath and Merari.   Nu 26:57

¹⁷These are the names of the sons of Gershon:
Libni and Shimei.

¹⁸The sons of Kohath:
Amram, Izhar, Hebron and Uzziel.

¹⁹The sons of Merari: 1Ch 23:21
Mahli and Mushi.

ᵃ 16 Hebrew *Gershom*, a variant of *Gershon*; also in verses 17, 20, 43, 62 and 71

These are the clans of the Levites listed according to their fathers:

²⁰Of Gershon:
Libni his son, Jehath his son,
Zimmah his son, ²¹Joah his son,
Iddo his son, Zerah his son and Jeatherai his son.

²²The descendants of Kohath:
Amminadab his son, Korah his son,   Ex 6:24
Assir his son, ²³Elkanah his son,
Ebiasaph his son, Assir his son,
²⁴Tahath his son, Uriel his son,   1Ch 15:5
Uzziah his son and Shaul his son.

²⁵The descendants of Elkanah:
Amasai, Ahimoth,
²⁶Elkanah his son,ᵃ Zophai his son,
Nahath his son, ²⁷Eliab his son,
Jeroham his son, Elkanah his son   1Sa 1:1
and Samuel his son.ᵇ

²⁸The sons of Samuel:
Joelᶜ the firstborn   ver 33
and Abijah the second son.

²⁹The descendants of Merari:
Mahli, Libni his son,
Shimei his son, Uzzah his son,

³⁰Shimea his son, Haggiah his son
and Asaiah his son.

The Temple Musicians

³¹These are the men David put in charge of the music in the house of the LORD after the ark came to rest there. ³²They ministered with music before the tabernacle, the Tent of Meeting, until Solomon built the temple of the LORD in Jerusalem. They performed their duties according to the regulations laid down for them.   1Ch 15:19

³³Here are the men who served, together with their sons:
From the Kohathites:
Heman, the musician,
the son of Joel, the son of Samuel,
³⁴the son of Elkanah, the son of Jeroham,   1Sa 1:1
the son of Eliel, the son of Toah,
³⁵the son of Zuph, the son of Elkanah,
the son of Mahath, the son of Amasai,
³⁶the son of Elkanah, the son of Joel,
the son of Azariah, the son of Zephaniah,
³⁷the son of Tahath, the son of Assir,
the son of Ebiasaph, the son of Korah,   Ex 6:24

ᵃ26 Some Hebrew manuscripts, Septuagint and Syriac; most Hebrew manuscripts *Ahimoth* ²⁶*and Elkanah. The sons of Elkanah:*   ᵇ27 Some Septuagint manuscripts (see also 1 Samuel 1:19,20 and 1 Chron. 6:33,34); Hebrew does not have *and Samuel his son.*   ᶜ28 Some Septuagint manuscripts and Syriac (see also 1 Samuel 8:2 and 1 Chron. 6:33); Hebrew does not have *Joel.*

38the son of Izhar, the son of Kohath,   Ex 6:21
the son of Levi, the son of Israel;

39and Heman's associate Asaph, who served at his right hand: 1Ch 25:1,9
Asaph son of Berekiah, the son of Shimea,   1Ch 15:17

40the son of Michael, the son of Baaseiah,[a]
the son of Malkijah, **41**the son of Ethni,
the son of Zerah, the son of Adaiah,

42the son of Ethan, the son of Zimmah,
the son of Shimei, **43**the son of Jahath,
the son of Gershon, the son of Levi;

44and from their associates, the Merarites, at his left hand:
Ethan son of Kishi, the son of Abdi,
the son of Malluch, **45**the son of Hashabiah,
the son of Amaziah, the son of Hilkiah,

46the son of Amzi, the son of Bani,
the son of Shemer, **47**the son of Mahli,
the son of Mushi, the son of Merari,
the son of Levi.

48Their fellow Levites were assigned to all the other duties of the tabernacle, the house of God. **49**But Aaron and his descendants were the ones who presented offerings on the altar of burnt offering and on the altar of incense in connection with all that was done in the Most Holy Place, making atonement for Israel, in accordance with all that Moses the servant of God had commanded.   Ex 27:1-8; 30:1-7,10

50These were the descendants of Aaron:
Eleazar his son, Phinehas his son,
Abishua his son, **51**Bukki his son,
Uzzi his son, Zerahiah his son,
52Meraioth his son, Amariah his son,
Ahitub his son, **53**Zadok his son   2Sa 8:17
and Ahimaaz his son.

54These were the locations of their settlements allotted as their territory (they were assigned to the descendants of Aaron who were from the Kohathite clan, because the first lot was for them): **55**They were given Hebron in Judah with its surrounding pasturelands. **56**But the fields and villages around the city were given to Caleb son of Jephunneh.   Jos 14:13; 15:13
57So the descendants of Aaron were given Hebron (a

---

[a] 40 Most Hebrew manuscripts; some Hebrew manuscripts, one Septuagint manuscript and Syriac *Maaseiah*

city of refuge), and Libnah,^a Jattir, Eshtemoa, ⁵⁸Hilen, Debir, ⁵⁹Ashan, Juttah^b and Beth Shemesh, together with their pasturelands. ⁶⁰And from the tribe of Benjamin they were given Gibeon,^c Geba, Alemeth and Anathoth, together with their pasturelands.

These towns, which were distributed among the Kohathite clans, were thirteen in all.

⁶¹The rest of Kohath's descendants were allotted ten towns from the clans of half the tribe of Manasseh.

⁶²The descendants of Gershon, clan by clan, were allotted thirteen towns from the tribes of Issachar, Asher and Naphtali, and from the part of the tribe of Manasseh that is in Bashan.

⁶³The descendants of Merari, clan by clan, were allotted twelve towns from the tribes of Reuben, Gad and Zebulun.

⁶⁴So the Israelites gave the Levites these towns and their pasturelands. ⁶⁵From the tribes of Judah, Simeon and Benjamin they allotted the previously named towns.   Nu 35:1-8; Jos 21:3,41-42

⁶⁶Some of the Kohathite clans were given as their territory towns from the tribe of Ephraim.

⁶⁷In the hill country of Ephraim they were given She-

chem (a city of refuge), and Gezer,^d ⁶⁸Jokmeam, Beth Horon, ⁶⁹Aijalon and Gath Rimmon, together with their pasturelands.   Jos 10:10,12; 19:45

⁷⁰And from half the tribe of Manasseh the Israelites gave Aner and Bileam, together with their pasturelands, to the rest of the Kohathite clans.

⁷¹The Gershonites received the following: 1Ch 23:7
From the clan of the half-tribe of Manasseh
they received Golan in Bashan and also Ashtaroth, together with their pasturelands;   Jos 20:8
⁷²from the tribe of Issachar
they received Kedesh, Daberath, ⁷³Ramoth and Anem, together with their pasturelands;   Jos 19:12
⁷⁴from the tribe of Asher
they received Mashal, Abdon, ⁷⁵Hukok and Rehob, together with their pasturelands;   Nu 13:21; Jos 19:28,34
⁷⁶and from the tribe of Naphtali
they received Kedesh in Galilee, Hammon and Kiriathaim, together with their pasturelands.   Nu 32:37

⁷⁷The Merarites (the rest of the Levites) received the following:
From the tribe of Zebulun

---

^a57 See Joshua 21:13; Hebrew *given the cities of refuge: Hebron, Libnah.*   ^b59 Syriac (see also Septuagint and Joshua 21:16); Hebrew does not have *Juttah.*   ^c60 See Joshua 21:17; Hebrew does not have *Gibeon.*   ^d67 See Joshua 21:21; Hebrew *given the cities of refuge: Shechem, Gezer.*

they received Jokneam, Kartah,ᵃ Rimmono and Tabor, together with their pasturelands;

⁷⁸from the tribe of Reuben across the Jordan east of Jericho

they received Bezer in the desert, Jahzah, ⁷⁹Kedemoth and Mephaath, together with their pasturelands;

⁸⁰and from the tribe of Gad

they received Ramoth in Gilead, Mahanaim, ⁸¹Heshbon and Jazer, together with their pasturelands.

Issachar

7 The sons of Issachar: Nu 26:23
Tola, Puah, Jashub and Shimron—four in all.

²The sons of Tola:

Uzzi, Rephaiah, Jeriel, Jahmai, Ibsam and Samuel—heads of their families. During the reign of David, the descendants of Tola listed as fighting men in their genealogy numbered 22,600.

³The son of Uzzi:

Izrahiah.

The sons of Izrahiah:

Michael, Obadiah, Joel and Isshiah. All five of them were chiefs. ⁴According to their family genealogy, they had 36,000 men ready for battle, for they had many wives and children.

⁵The relatives who were fighting men belonging to all the clans of Issachar, as listed in their genealogy, were 87,000 in all.

Benjamin

⁶Three sons of Benjamin:

Bela, Beker and Jediael.

⁷The sons of Bela:

Ezbon, Uzzi, Uzziel, Jerimoth and Iri, heads of families—five in all. Their genealogical record listed 22,034 fighting men.

⁸The sons of Beker:

Zemirah, Joash, Eliezer, Elioenai, Omri, Jeremoth, Abijah, Anathoth and Alemeth. All these were the sons of Beker. ⁹Their genealogical record listed the heads of families and 20,200 fighting men.

¹⁰The son of Jediael:

Bilhan.

The sons of Bilhan:

Jeush, Benjamin, Ehud, Kenaanah, Zethan, Tarshish and Ahishahar. ¹¹All these sons of Jediael were heads of families. There were 17,200 fighting men ready to go out to war.

¹²The Shuppites and Huppites were the descendants of Ir, and the Hushites the descendants of Aher.

ᵃ77 See Septuagint and Joshua 21:34; Hebrew does not have Jokneam, Kartah.

Naphtali

13The sons of Naphtali: Ge 30:8
Jahziel, Guni, Jezer and Shillem[a]—the descendants of Bilhah.

Manasseh

14The descendants of Manasseh: Ge 41:51; Jos 17:1; 1Ch 5:23

Asriel was his descendant through his Aramean concubine. She gave birth to Makir the father of Gilead. **15**Makir took a wife from among the Huppites and Shuppites. His sister's name was Maacah.

Another descendant was named Zelophehad, who had only daughters.   Nu 36:1-12

16Makir's wife Maacah gave birth to a son and named him Peresh. His brother was named Sheresh, and his sons were Ulam and Rakem.

17The son of Ulam:
Bedan.

These were the sons of Gilead son of Makir, the son of Manasseh. **18**His sister Hammoleketh gave birth to Ishhod, Abiezer and Mahlah.

19The sons of Shemida were:
Ahian, Shechem, Likhi and Aniam.

Ephraim

20The descendants of Ephraim:

Shuthelah, Bered his son, Tahath his son, Eleadah his son, Tahath his son, **21**Zabad his son and Shuthelah his son.

Ezer and Elead were killed by the native-born men of Gath, when they went down to seize their livestock. **22**Their father Ephraim mourned for them many days, and his relatives came to comfort him. **23**Then he lay with his wife again, and she became pregnant and gave birth to a son. He named him Beriah,[b] because there had been misfortune in his family. **24**His daughter was Sheerah, who built Lower and Upper Beth Horon as well as Uzzen Sheerah.   Jos 16:3,5

25Rephah was his son, Resheph his son,[c] Telah his son, Tahan his son, **26**Ladan his son, Ammihud his son, Elishama his son, **27**Nun his son and Joshua his son.

28Their lands and settlements included Bethel and its surrounding villages, Naaran to the east, Gezer and its villages to the west, and Shechem and its villages all the way to Ayyah and its villages.

---

[a] 13 Some Hebrew and Septuagint manuscripts (see also Gen. 46:24 and Num. 26:49); most Hebrew manuscripts *Shallum*   [b] 23 *Beriah* sounds like the Hebrew for *misfortune*.   [c] 25 Some Septuagint manuscripts; Hebrew does not have *his son*.

²⁹Along the borders of Manasseh were Beth Shan, Taanach, Megiddo and Dor, together with their villages. The descendants of Joseph son of Israel lived in these towns.

Asher

³⁰The sons of Asher: Ge 46:17
Imnah, Ishvah, Ishvi and Beriah. Their sister was Serah.
³¹The sons of Beriah:
Heber and Malkiel, who was the father of Birzaith.
³²Heber was the father of Japhlet, Shomer and Hotham and of their sister Shua.
³³The sons of Japhlet:
Pasach, Bimhal and Ashvath.
These were Japhlet's sons.
³⁴The sons of Shomer:
Ahi, Rohgah,ᵃ Hubbah and Aram.
³⁵The sons of his brother Helem:
Zophah, Imna, Shelesh and Amal.
³⁶The sons of Zophah:
Suah, Harnepher, Shual, Beri, Imrah, ³⁷Bezer, Hod, Shamma, Shilshah, Ithranᵇ and Beera.
³⁸The sons of Jether:
Jephunneh, Pispah and Ara.
³⁹The sons of Ulla:
Arah, Hanniel and Rizia.

⁴⁰All these were descendants of Asher—heads of families, choice men, brave warriors and outstanding leaders. The number of men ready for battle, as listed in their genealogy, was 26,000.

The Genealogy of Saul the Benjamite

8 Benjamin was the father of Bela his firstborn,   Ge 46:21
Ashbel the second son, Aharah the third,
²Nohah the fourth and Rapha the fifth.
³The sons of Bela were:
Addar, Gera, Abihud,ᶜ ⁴Abishua, Naaman, Ahoah, ⁵Gera, Shephuphan and Huram.   2Sa 23:9
⁶These were the descendants of Ehud, who were heads of families of those living in Geba and were deported to Manahath: 1Ch 2:52
⁷Naaman, Ahijah, and Gera, who deported them and who was the father of Uzza and Ahihud.
⁸Sons were born to Shaharaim in Moab after he had divorced his wives Hushim and Baara. ⁹By his wife Hodesh he had Jobab, Zibia, Mesha, Malcam, ¹⁰Jeuz, Sakia and Mirmah. These were his sons, heads of

ᵃ 34 Or of his brother Shomer: Rohgah   ᵇ 37 Possibly a variant of Jether   ᶜ 3 Or Gera the father of Ehud

families. ¹¹By Hushim he had Abitub and Elpaal.

¹²The sons of Elpaal:

Eber, Misham, Shemed (who built Ono and Lod with its surrounding villages), ¹³and Beriah and Shema, who were heads of families of those living in Aijalon and who drove out the inhabitants of Gath.

¹⁴Ahio, Shashak, Jeremoth, ¹⁵Zebadiah, Arad, Eder, ¹⁶Michael, Ishpah and Joha were the sons of Beriah.

¹⁷Zebadiah, Meshullam, Hizki, Heber, ¹⁸Ishmerai, Izliah and Jobab were the sons of Elpaal.

¹⁹Jakim, Zicri, Zabdi, ²⁰Elienai, Zillethai, Eliel, ²¹Adaiah, Beraiah and Shimrath were the sons of Shimei.

²²Ishpan, Eber, Eliel, ²³Abdon, Zicri, Hanan, ²⁴Hananiah, Elam, Anthothijah, ²⁵Iphdeiah and Penuel were the sons of Shashak.

²⁶Shamsherai, Shehariah, Athaliah, ²⁷Jaareshiah, Elijah and Zicri were the sons of Jeroham.

²⁸All these were heads of families, chiefs as listed in their genealogy, and they lived in Jerusalem.

²⁹Jeiel^a the father^b of Gibeon lived in Gibeon.   Jos 9:3

His wife's name was Maacah, ³⁰and his firstborn son was Abdon, followed by Zur, Kish, Baal, Ner,^c Nadab, ³¹Gedor, Ahio, Zeker ³²and Mikloth, who was the father of Shimeah. They too lived near their relatives in Jerusalem.

³³Ner was the father of Kish, Kish the father of Saul, and Saul the father of Jonathan, Malki-Shua, Abinadab and Esh-Baal.^d   1Sa 9:1; 2Sa 2:8

³⁴The son of Jonathan: 2Sa 9:12

Merib-Baal,^e who was the father of Micah.   2Sa 4:4

³⁵The sons of Micah:

Pithon, Melech, Tarea and Ahaz.

³⁶Ahaz was the father of Jehoaddah, Jehoaddah was the father of Alemeth, Azmaveth and Zimri, and Zimri was the father of Moza. ³⁷Moza was the father of Binea; Raphah was his son, Eleasah his son and Azel his son.

³⁸Azel had six sons, and these were their names:

Azrikam, Bokeru, Ishmael, Sheariah, Obadiah and Hanan. All these were the sons of Azel.   1Ch 9:34-44

³⁹The sons of his brother Eshek: Ulam his firstborn, Jeush the second son and Eliphe-

---

^a29 Some Septuagint manuscripts (see also 1 Chron. 9:35); Hebrew does not have *Jeiel*.   ^b29 *Father* may mean *civic leader* or *military leader*.   ^c30 Some Septuagint manuscripts (see also 1 Chron. 9:36); Hebrew does not have *Ner*.   ^d33 Also known as *Ish-Bosheth*   ^e34 Also known as *Mephibosheth*

let the third. [40]The sons of Ulam were brave warriors who could handle the bow. They had many sons and grandsons—150 in all.

All these were the descendants of Benjamin.   Nu 26:38

9 All Israel was listed in the genealogies recorded in the book of the kings of Israel.

The People in Jerusalem

The people of Judah were taken captive to Babylon because of their unfaithfulness. [2]Now the first to resettle on their own property in their own towns were some Israelites, priests, Levites and temple servants.   1Ch 5:25; Ezr 2:43,58,70

[3]Those from Judah, from Benjamin, and from Ephraim and Manasseh who lived in Jerusalem were:

[4]Uthai son of Ammihud, the son of Omri, the son of Imri, the son of Bani, a descendant of Perez son of Judah.   Ge 46:12

[5]Of the Shilonites:

Asaiah the firstborn and his sons.

[6]Of the Zerahites:

Jeuel.

The people from Judah numbered 690.

[7]Of the Benjamites:

Sallu son of Meshullam, the son of Hodaviah, the son of Hassenuah;

[8]Ibneiah son of Jeroham;

Elah son of Uzzi, the son of Micri; and Meshullam son of Shephatiah, the son of Reuel, the son of Ibnijah.

[9]The people from Benjamin, as listed in their genealogy, numbered 956. All these men were heads of their families.

[10]Of the priests:

Jedaiah; Jehoiarib; Jakin;

[11]Azariah son of Hilkiah, the son of Meshullam, the son of Zadok, the son of Meraioth, the son of Ahitub, the official in charge of the house of God;

[12]Adaiah son of Jeroham, the son of Pashhur, the son of Malkijah; and Maasai son of Adiel, the son of Jahzerah, the son of Meshullam, the son of Meshillemith, the son of Immer.   Ezr 2:38

[13]The priests, who were heads of families, numbered 1,760. They were able men, responsible for ministering in the house of God.

[14]Of the Levites:

Shemaiah son of Hasshub, the son of Azrikam, the son of Hashabiah, a Merarite;

[15]Bakbakkar, Heresh, Galal and Mattaniah son of Mica, the son of Zicri, the son of Asaph; [16]Obadiah son of Shemaiah, the son of Galal, the son of Jeduthun; and Berekiah son of Asa, the

son of Elkanah, who lived in the villages of the Netophathites. 2Ch 20:14; Ne 11:22

[17]The gatekeepers: ver 22; 1Ch 26:1 Shallum, Akkub, Talmon, Ahiman and their brothers, Shallum their chief [18]being stationed at the King's Gate on the east, up to the present time. These were the gatekeepers belonging to the camp of the Levites. [19]Shallum son of Kore, the son of Ebiasaph, the son of Korah, and his fellow gatekeepers from his family (the Korahites) were responsible for guarding the thresholds of the Tent[a] just as their fathers had been responsible for guarding the entrance to the dwelling of the LORD. [20]In earlier times Phinehas son of Eleazar was in charge of the gatekeepers, and the LORD was with him. [21]Zechariah son of Meshelemiah was the gatekeeper at the entrance to the Tent of Meeting.

[22]Altogether, those chosen to be gatekeepers at the thresholds numbered 212. They were registered by genealogy in their villages. The gatekeepers had been assigned to their positions of trust by David and Samuel the seer. [23]They and their descendants were in charge of guarding the gates of the house of the LORD—the house called the Tent. [24]The gatekeepers were on the four sides: east, west, north and south. [25]Their brothers in their villages had to come from time to time and share their duties for seven-day periods. [26]But the four principal gatekeepers, who were Levites, were entrusted with the responsibility for the rooms and treasuries in the house of God. [27]They would spend the night stationed around the house of God, because they had to guard it; and they had charge of the key for opening it each morning.

[28]Some of them were in charge of the articles used in the temple service; they counted them when they were brought in and when they were taken out. [29]Others were assigned to take care of the furnishings and all the other articles of the sanctuary, as well as the flour and wine, and the oil, incense and spices. [30]But some of the priests took care of mixing the spices. [31]A Levite named Mattithiah, the firstborn son of Shallum the Korahite, was entrusted with the responsibility for baking the offering bread. [32]Some of their Kohathite brothers were in charge of preparing for every Sabbath the bread set out on the table.

[33]Those who were musicians, heads of Levite families, stayed in the rooms of the temple and were exempt from other duties because

---

[a] 19 That is, the temple; also in verses 21 and 23

they were responsible for the work day and night. 1Ch 6:31; Ps 134:1

34All these were heads of Levite families, chiefs as listed in their genealogy, and they lived in Jerusalem.

The Genealogy of Saul

35Jeiel the father[a] of Gibeon lived in Gibeon. 1Ch 8:29

His wife's name was Maacah, 36and his firstborn son was Abdon, followed by Zur, Kish, Baal, Ner, Nadab, 37Gedor, Ahio, Zechariah and Mikloth. 38Mikloth was the father of Shimeam. They too lived near their relatives in Jerusalem.

39Ner was the father of Kish, Kish the father of Saul, and Saul the father of Jonathan, Malki-Shua, Abinadab and Esh-Baal.[b] 1Sa 9:1; 13:22

40The son of Jonathan:

Merib-Baal,[c] who was the father of Micah. 2Sa 4:4

41The sons of Micah:

Pithon, Melech, Tahrea and Ahaz.[d]

42Ahaz was the father of Jadah, Jadah[e] was the father of Alemeth, Azmaveth and Zimri, and Zimri was the father of Moza. 43Moza was the father of Binea; Repha-

iah was his son, Eleasah his son and Azel his son.

44Azel had six sons, and these were their names:

Azrikam, Bokeru, Ishmael, Sheariah, Obadiah and Hanan. These were the sons of Azel. 1Ch 8:28-38

Saul Takes His Life

10 Now the Philistines fought against Israel; the Israelites fled before them, and many fell slain on Mount Gilboa. 2The Philistines pressed hard after Saul and his sons, and they killed his sons Jonathan, Abinadab and Malki-Shua. 3The fighting grew fierce around Saul, and when the archers overtook him, they wounded him.

4Saul said to his armor-bearer, "Draw your sword and run me through, or these uncircumcised fellows will come and abuse me."

But his armor-bearer was terrified and would not do it; so Saul took his own sword and fell on it. 5When the armor-bearer saw that Saul was dead, he too fell on his sword and died. 6So Saul and his three sons died, and all his house died together.

7When all the Israelites in the valley saw that the army had fled and that Saul and his sons had died, they abandoned their towns

---

a35 *Father* may mean *civic leader* or *military leader*.   b39 Also known as *Ish-Bosheth*   c40 Also known as *Mephibosheth*   d41 Vulgate and Syriac (see also Septuagint and 1 Chron. 8:35); Hebrew does not have *and Ahaz*.   e42 Some Hebrew manuscripts and Septuagint (see also 1 Chron. 8:36); most Hebrew manuscripts *Jarah, Jarah*

and fled. And the Philistines came and occupied them.

⁸The next day, when the Philistines came to strip the dead, they found Saul and his sons fallen on Mount Gilboa. ⁹They stripped him and took his head and his armor, and sent messengers throughout the land of the Philistines to proclaim the news among their idols and their people. ¹⁰They put his armor in the temple of their gods and hung up his head in the temple of Dagon.   Jdg 16:23

¹¹When all the inhabitants of Jabesh Gilead heard of everything the Philistines had done to Saul, ¹²all their valiant men went and took the bodies of Saul and his sons and brought them to Jabesh. Then they buried their bones under the great tree in Jabesh, and they fasted seven days.   1Sa 31:1-13

¹³Saul died because he was unfaithful to the Lord; he did not keep the word of the Lord and even consulted a medium for guidance, ¹⁴and did not inquire of the Lord. So the Lord put him to death and turned the kingdom over to David son of Jesse.   1Sa 15:28; 2Sa 1:1

David Becomes King Over Israel

11 All Israel came together to David at Hebron and said, "We are your own flesh and blood. ²In the past, even while Saul was king, you were the one who led Israel on their military campaigns. And the Lord your God said to you, 'You will shepherd my people Israel, and you will become their ruler.'"   1Sa 18:5,16; 1Ch 5:2; Mt 2:6

³When all the elders of Israel had come to King David at Hebron, he made a compact with them at Hebron before the Lord, and they anointed David king over Israel, as the Lord had promised through Samuel.   2Sa 5:1-3; 1Sa 16:1-13

David Conquers Jerusalem

⁴David and all the Israelites marched to Jerusalem (that is, Jebus). The Jebusites who lived there ⁵said to David, "You will not get in here." Nevertheless, David captured the fortress of Zion, the City of David.   Jdg 1:21; 19:10

⁶David had said, "Whoever leads the attack on the Jebusites will become commander-in-chief." Joab son of Zeruiah went up first, and so he received the command.

⁷David then took up residence in the fortress, and so it was called the City of David. ⁸He built up the city around it, from the supporting terraces*a* to the surrounding wall, while Joab restored the rest of the city. ⁹And David became more and more powerful, because the Lord Almighty was with him.   2Sa 3:1

David's Mighty Men

¹⁰These were the chiefs of David's mighty men—they, together

a 8 Or the Millo

with all Israel, gave his kingship strong support to extend it over the whole land, as the Lord had promised— [11]this is the list of David's mighty men: ver 3; 2Sa 17:10

Jashobeam,[a] a Hacmonite, was chief of the officers[b]; he raised his spear against three hundred men, whom he killed in one encounter. [12]Next to him was Eleazar son of Dodai the Ahohite, one of the three mighty men. [13]He was with David at Pas Dammim when the Philistines gathered there for battle. At a place where there was a field full of barley, the troops fled from the Philistines. [14]But they took their stand in the middle of the field. They defended it and struck the Philistines down, and the Lord brought about a great victory.

[15]Three of the thirty chiefs came down to David to the rock at the cave of Adullam, while a band of Philistines was encamped in the Valley of Rephaim. [16]At that time David was in the stronghold, and the Philistine garrison was at Bethlehem. [17]David longed for water and said, "Oh, that someone would get me a drink of water from the well near the gate of Bethlehem!" [18]So the Three broke through the Philistine lines, drew water from the well near the gate of Bethlehem and carried it back to David. But he refused to drink it; instead, he poured it out before the Lord. [19]"God forbid that I should do this!" he said. "Should I drink the blood of these men who went at the risk of their lives?" Because they risked their lives to bring it back, David would not drink it.

Such were the exploits of the three mighty men.

[20]Abishai the brother of Joab was chief of the Three. He raised his spear against three hundred men, whom he killed, and so he became as famous as the Three. [21]He was doubly honored above the Three and became their commander, even though he was not included among them. 1Sa 26:6

[22]Benaiah son of Jehoiada was a valiant fighter from Kabzeel, who performed great exploits. He struck down two of Moab's best men. He also went down into a pit on a snowy day and killed a lion. [23]And he struck down an Egyptian who was seven and a half feet[c] tall. Although the Egyptian had a spear like a weaver's rod in his hand, Benaiah went against him with a club. He snatched the spear from the Egyptian's hand and killed him with his own spear. [24]Such were the exploits of Benaiah son of Jehoiada; he too was as famous as the three mighty men. [25]He was held in greater honor than any of the Thirty, but he was not included among the Three.

---

[a] 11 Possibly a variant of *Jashob-Baal* [b] 11 Or *Thirty*; some Septuagint manuscripts *Three* (see also 2 Samuel 23:8) [c] 23 Hebrew *five cubits* (about 2.3 meters)

And David put him in charge of his bodyguard.   1Sa 17:7,36; Jos 15:21

26The mighty men were:

Asahel the brother of Joab,
Elhanan son of Dodo from Bethlehem,
27Shammoth the Harorite,
Helez the Pelonite,
28Ira son of Ikkesh from Tekoa,
Abiezer from Anathoth,
29Sibbecai the Hushathite,
Ilai the Ahohite,
30Maharai the Netophathite,
Heled son of Baanah the Netophathite,
31Ithai son of Ribai from Gibeah in Benjamin,
Benaiah the Pirathonite,
32Hurai from the ravines of Gaash,
Abiel the Arbathite,
33Azmaveth the Baharumite,
Eliahba the Shaalbonite,
34the sons of Hashem the Gizonite,
Jonathan son of Shagee the Hararite,
35Ahiam son of Sacar the Hararite,
Eliphal son of Ur,
36Hepher the Mekerathite,
Ahijah the Pelonite,
37Hezro the Carmelite,
Naarai son of Ezbai,
38Joel the brother of Nathan,
Mibhar son of Hagri,
39Zelek the Ammonite,
Naharai the Berothite, the

armor-bearer of Joab son of Zeruiah,
40Ira the Ithrite,
Gareb the Ithrite,
41Uriah the Hittite,   2Sa 11:6
Zabad son of Ahlai,
42Adina son of Shiza the Reubenite, who was chief of the Reubenites, and the thirty with him,
43Hanan son of Maacah,
Joshaphat the Mithnite,
44Uzzia the Ashterathite,
Shama and Jeiel the sons of Hotham the Aroerite,
45Jediael son of Shimri,
his brother Joha the Tizite,
46Eliel the Mahavite,
Jeribai and Joshaviah the sons of Elnaam,
Ithmah the Moabite,
47Eliel, Obed and Jaasiel the Mezobaite.

Warriors Join David

12 These were the men who came to David at Ziklag, while he was banished from the presence of Saul son of Kish (they were among the warriors who helped him in battle; 2they were armed with bows and were able to shoot arrows or to sling stones right-handed or left-handed; they were kinsmen of Saul from the tribe of Benjamin):

3Ahiezer their chief and Joash the sons of Shemaah the Gibeathite; Jeziel and Pelet the sons of Azmaveth; Beracah,

Jehu the Anathothite, [4]and Ishmaiah the Gibeonite, a mighty man among the Thirty, who was a leader of the Thirty; Jeremiah, Jahaziel, Johanan, Jozabad the Gederathite, [5]Eluzai, Jerimoth, Bealiah, Shemariah and Shephatiah the Haruphite; [6]Elkanah, Isshiah, Azarel, Joezer and Jashobeam the Korahites; [7]and Joelah and Zebadiah the sons of Jeroham from Gedor.

[8]Some Gadites defected to David at his stronghold in the desert. They were brave warriors, ready for battle and able to handle the shield and spear. Their faces were the faces of lions, and they were as swift as gazelles in the mountains.

[9]Ezer was the chief,
Obadiah the second in command, Eliab the third,
[10]Mishmannah the fourth, Jeremiah the fifth,
[11]Attai the sixth, Eliel the seventh,
[12]Johanan the eighth, Elzabad the ninth,
[13]Jeremiah the tenth and Macbannai the eleventh.

[14]These Gadites were army commanders; the least was a match for a hundred, and the greatest for a thousand. [15]It was they who crossed the Jordan in the first month when it was overflowing all its banks, and they put to flight everyone living in the valleys, to the east and to the west.   Dt 32:30

[16]Other Benjamites and some men from Judah also came to David in his stronghold. [17]David went out to meet them and said to them, "If you have come to me in peace, to help me, I am ready to have you unite with me. But if you have come to betray me to my enemies when my hands are free from violence, may the God of our fathers see it and judge you."   2Sa 3:19

[18]Then the Spirit came upon Amasai, chief of the Thirty, and he said: Jdg 6:34; 2Sa 17:25

"We are yours, O David!
We are with you, O son of Jesse!
Success, success to you,
and success to those who help you,
for your God will help you."

So David received them and made them leaders of his raiding bands.

[19]Some of the men of Manasseh defected to David when he went with the Philistines to fight against Saul. (He and his men did not help the Philistines because, after consultation, their rulers sent him away. They said, "It will cost us our heads if he deserts to his master Saul.") [20]When David went to Ziklag, these were the men of Manasseh who defected to him: Adnah, Jozabad, Jediael, Michael, Jozabad, Elihu and Zillethai, leaders of units of a thousand in Manasseh. [21]They helped David

against raiding bands, for all of them were brave warriors, and they were commanders in his army. [22]Day after day men came to help David, until he had a great army, like the army of God.[a]

Others Join David at Hebron

[23]These are the numbers of the men armed for battle who came to David at Hebron to turn Saul's kingdom over to him, as the LORD had said: 1Sa 16:1; 2Sa 2:3-4; 1Ch 10:14

[24]men of Judah, carrying shield and spear— 6,800 armed for battle;

[25]men of Simeon, warriors ready for battle— 7,100;

[26]men of Levi— 4,600, [27]including Jehoiada, leader of the family of Aaron, with 3,700 men, [28]and Zadok, a brave young warrior, with 22 officers from his family;   2Sa 8:17; 1Ch 6:8

[29]men of Benjamin, Saul's kinsmen— 3,000, most of whom had remained loyal to Saul's house until then;

[30]men of Ephraim, brave warriors, famous in their own clans— 20,800;

[31]men of half the tribe of Manasseh, designated by name to come and make David king— 18,000;

[32]men of Issachar, who understood the times and knew what Israel should do— 200 chiefs, with all their relatives under their command;

[33]men of Zebulun, experienced soldiers prepared for battle with every type of weapon, to help David with undivided loyalty— 50,000;

[34]men of Naphtali— 1,000 officers, together with 37,000 men carrying shields and spears;

[35]men of Dan, ready for battle — 28,600;

[36]men of Asher, experienced soldiers prepared for battle —40,000;

[37]and from east of the Jordan, men of Reuben, Gad and the half-tribe of Manasseh, armed with every type of weapon— 120,000.

[38]All these were fighting men who volunteered to serve in the ranks. They came to Hebron fully determined to make David king over all Israel. All the rest of the Israelites were also of one mind to make David king. [39]The men spent three days there with David, eating and drinking, for their families had supplied provisions for them. [40]Also, their neighbors from as far away as Issachar, Zebulun and Naphtali came bringing food on donkeys, camels, mules and oxen. There were plentiful supplies of flour, fig cakes, raisin cakes, wine, oil, cattle and sheep, for there was joy in Israel.   1Sa 25:18; 2Sa 5:1-3

a 22 Or a great and mighty army

Bringing Back the Ark

13 David conferred with each of his officers, the commanders of thousands and commanders of hundreds. ²He then said to the whole assembly of Israel, "If it seems good to you and if it is the will of the Lord our God, let us send word far and wide to the rest of our brothers throughout the territories of Israel, and also to the priests and Levites who are with them in their towns and pasturelands, to come and join us. ³Let us bring the ark of our God back to us, for we did not inquire of*a* it*b* during the reign of Saul." ⁴The whole assembly agreed to do this, because it seemed right to all the people.   1Sa 7:1-2; 2Ch 1:5

⁵So David assembled all the Israelites, from the Shihor River in Egypt to Lebo*c* Hamath, to bring the ark of God from Kiriath Jearim. ⁶David and all the Israelites with him went to Baalah of Judah (Kiriath Jearim) to bring up from there the ark of God the Lord, who is enthroned between the cherubim —the ark that is called by the Name.   Jos 15:9; 2Ki 19:15; 1Ch 15:3

⁷They moved the ark of God from Abinadab's house on a new cart, with Uzzah and Ahio guiding it. ⁸David and all the Israelites were celebrating with all their might before God, with songs and with harps, lyres, tambourines, cymbals and trumpets.   Nu 4:15

⁹When they came to the threshing floor of Kidon, Uzzah reached out his hand to steady the ark, because the oxen stumbled. ¹⁰The Lord's anger burned against Uzzah, and he struck him down because he had put his hand on the ark. So he died there before God.

¹¹Then David was angry because the Lord's wrath had broken out against Uzzah, and to this day that place is called Perez Uzzah.*d*

¹²David was afraid of God that day and asked, "How can I ever bring the ark of God to me?" ¹³He did not take the ark to be with him in the City of David. Instead, he took it aside to the house of Obed-Edom the Gittite. ¹⁴The ark of God remained with the family of Obed-Edom in his house for three months, and the Lord blessed his household and everything he had.

David's House and Family

14 Now Hiram king of Tyre sent messengers to David, along with cedar logs, stonemasons and carpenters to build a palace for him. ²And David knew that the Lord had established him as king over Israel and that his kingdom had been highly exalted for the sake of his people Israel.

³In Jerusalem David took more wives and became the father of

---

a3 Or *we neglected against Uzzah.*   *b3* Or *him*   *c5* Or *to the entrance to*   *d11* *Perez Uzzah* means *outbreak*

more sons and daughters. **⁴**These are the names of the children born to him there: Shammua, Shobab, Nathan, Solomon, **⁵**Ibhar, Elishua, Elpelet, **⁶**Nogah, Nepheg, Japhia, **⁷**Elishama, Beeliada*ᵃ* and Eliphelet.   2Sa 5:11-16; 1Ch 3:5-8

David Defeats the Philistines

⁸When the Philistines heard that David had been anointed king over all Israel, they went up in full force to search for him, but David heard about it and went out to meet them. **⁹**Now the Philistines had come and raided the Valley of Rephaim; **¹⁰**so David inquired of God: "Shall I go and attack the Philistines? Will you hand them over to me?"   1Ch 11:1,15

The Lord answered him, "Go, I will hand them over to you."

¹¹So David and his men went up to Baal Perazim, and there he defeated them. He said, "As waters break out, God has broken out against my enemies by my hand." So that place was called Baal Perazim.*ᵇ* **¹²**The Philistines had abandoned their gods there, and David gave orders to burn them in the fire.   Ex 32:20; Jos 7:15; Isa 28:21

¹³Once more the Philistines raided the valley; **¹⁴**so David inquired of God again, and God answered him, "Do not go straight up, but circle around them and attack them in front of the balsam trees. **¹⁵**As soon as you hear the sound of marching in the tops of the balsam trees, move out to battle, because that will mean God has gone out in front of you to strike the Philistine army." **¹⁶**So David did as God commanded him, and they struck down the Philistine army, all the way from Gibeon to Gezer.   ver 9

¹⁷So David's fame spread throughout every land, and the Lord made all the nations fear him.   2Sa 5:17-25

The Ark Brought to Jerusalem

15 After David had constructed buildings for himself in the City of David, he prepared a place for the ark of God and pitched a tent for it. **²**Then David said, "No one but the Levites may carry the ark of God, because the Lord chose them to carry the ark of the Lord and to minister before him forever."   Nu 4:15; Dt 10:8; 1Ch 16:1

³David assembled all Israel in Jerusalem to bring up the ark of the Lord to the place he had prepared for it. **⁴**He called together the descendants of Aaron and the Levites: 1Ki 8:1; 1Ch 13:5

⁵From the descendants of Kohath,
Uriel the leader and 120 relatives;
⁶from the descendants of Merari,
Asaiah the leader and 220 relatives;

ᵃ 7 A variant of *Eliada*   *ᵇ 11* Baal Perazim means *the lord who breaks out.*

⁷from the descendants of Gershon,ᵃ

Joel the leader and 130 relatives;

⁸from the descendants of Elizaphan,   Ex 6:22

Shemaiah the leader and 200 relatives;

⁹from the descendants of Hebron,   Ex 6:18

Eliel the leader and 80 relatives;

¹⁰from the descendants of Uzziel,

Amminadab the leader and 112 relatives.

¹¹Then David summoned Zadok and Abiathar the priests, and Uriel, Asaiah, Joel, Shemaiah, Eliel and Amminadab the Levites. ¹²He said to them, "You are the heads of the Levitical families; you and your fellow Levites are to consecrate yourselves and bring up the ark of the Lord, the God of Israel, to the place I have prepared for it. ¹³It was because you, the Levites, did not bring it up the first time that the Lord our God broke out in anger against us. We did not inquire of him about how to do it in the prescribed way." ¹⁴So the priests and Levites consecrated themselves in order to bring up the ark of the Lord, the God of Israel. ¹⁵And the Levites carried the ark of God with the poles on their shoulders, as Moses had commanded in accordance with the word of the Lord.   Ex 25:14; 2Sa 6:3; 1Ch 13:7-10

¹⁶David told the leaders of the Levites to appoint their brothers as singers to sing joyful songs, accompanied by musical instruments: lyres, harps and cymbals.

¹⁷So the Levites appointed Heman son of Joel; from his brothers, Asaph son of Berekiah; and from their brothers the Merarites, Ethan son of Kushaiah; ¹⁸and with them their brothers next in rank: Zechariah,ᵇ Jaaziel, Shemiramoth, Jehiel, Unni, Eliab, Benaiah, Maaseiah, Mattithiah, Eliphelehu, Mikneiah, Obed-Edom and Jeiel,ᶜ the gatekeepers.   1Ch 6:33,39,44; 26:4-5

¹⁹The musicians Heman, Asaph and Ethan were to sound the bronze cymbals; ²⁰Zechariah, Aziel, Shemiramoth, Jehiel, Unni, Eliab, Maaseiah and Benaiah were to play the lyres according to *alamoth,ᵈ* ²¹and Mattithiah, Eliphelehu, Mikneiah, Obed-Edom, Jeiel and Azaziah were to play the harps, directing according to *sheminith.ᵈ* ²²Kenaniah the head Levite was in charge of the singing; that was his responsibility because he was skillful at it.   1Ch 25:6

²³Berekiah and Elkanah were to be doorkeepers for the ark. ²⁴Shebaniah, Joshaphat, Nethanel, Amasai, Zechariah, Benaiah and Eliezer

---

ᵃ7 Hebrew *Gershom*, a variant of *Gershon*   ᵇ18 Three Hebrew manuscripts and most Septuagint manuscripts (see also verse 20 and 1 Chron. 16:5); most Hebrew manuscripts *Zechariah son and* or *Zechariah, Ben and*   ᶜ18 Hebrew; Septuagint (see also verse 21) *Jeiel and Azaziah*   ᵈ20,21 Probably a musical term

the priests were to blow trumpets before the ark of God. Obed-Edom and Jehiah were also to be door-keepers for the ark.   ver 28; 1Ch 16:6

²⁵So David and the elders of Israel and the commanders of units of a thousand went to bring up the ark of the covenant of the LORD from the house of Obed-Edom, with rejoicing. ²⁶Because God had helped the Levites who were carrying the ark of the covenant of the LORD, seven bulls and seven rams were sacrificed. ²⁷Now David was clothed in a robe of fine linen, as were all the Levites who were carrying the ark, and as were the singers, and Kenaniah, who was in charge of the singing of the choirs. David also wore a linen ephod. ²⁸So all Israel brought up the ark of the covenant of the LORD with shouts, with the sounding of rams' horns and trumpets, and of cymbals, and the playing of lyres and harps.   1Ch 13:8,13; 2Ch 1:4

²⁹As the ark of the covenant of the LORD was entering the City of David, Michal daughter of Saul watched from a window. And when she saw King David dancing and celebrating, she despised him in her heart.

16 They brought the ark of God and set it inside the tent that David had pitched for it, and they presented burnt offerings and fellowship offerings[a] before God. ²After David had finished sac-

rificing the burnt offerings and fellowship offerings, he blessed the people in the name of the LORD. ³Then he gave a loaf of bread, a cake of dates and a cake of raisins to each Israelite man and woman.

⁴He appointed some of the Levites to minister before the ark of the LORD, to make petition, to give thanks, and to praise the LORD, the God of Israel: ⁵Asaph was the chief, Zechariah second, then Jeiel, Shemiramoth, Jehiel, Mattithiah, Eliab, Benaiah, Obed-Edom and Jeiel. They were to play the lyres and harps, Asaph was to sound the cymbals, ⁶and Benaiah and Jahaziel the priests were to blow the trumpets regularly before the ark of the covenant of God.

David's Psalm of Thanks

⁷That day David first committed to Asaph and his associates this psalm of thanks to the LORD:

⁸Give thanks to the LORD, call
        on his name;   ver 34; Ps 136:1
    make known among the
        nations what he has
        done.   2Ki 19:19
⁹Sing to him, sing praise to him;
    tell of all his wonderful acts.
¹⁰Glory in his holy name;
    let the hearts of those who
        seek the LORD rejoice.
¹¹Look to the LORD and his
        strength;

---

a 1 Traditionally *peace offerings*; also in verse 2

seek his face always. Ps 24:6

[12] Remember the wonders he has
    done, Ps 77:11
  his miracles, and the
    judgments he
    pronounced, Ps 78:43
[13] O descendants of Israel his
    servant,
  O sons of Jacob, his chosen
    ones.

[14] He is the LORD our God;
  his judgments are in all the
    earth. Isa 26:9
[15] He remembers[a] his covenant
    forever,
  the word he commanded, for
    a thousand generations,
[16] the covenant he made with
    Abraham, Ge 17:2; 26:3
  the oath he swore to Isaac.
[17] He confirmed it to Jacob as a
    decree, Ge 35:9-12
  to Israel as an everlasting
    covenant:
[18] "To you I will give the land of
    Canaan Ge 13:14-17
  as the portion you will
    inherit."

[19] When they were but few in
    number, Ge 34:30; Dt 7:7
  few indeed, and strangers in
    it,
[20] they[b] wandered from nation to
    nation,
  from one kingdom to
    another.

[21] He allowed no man to oppress
    them;
  for their sake he rebuked
    kings: Ge 12:17; 20:3; Ex 7:15-18
[22] "Do not touch my anointed
    ones;
  do my prophets no harm."

[23] Sing to the LORD, all the earth;
  proclaim his salvation day
    after day.
[24] Declare his glory among the
    nations,
  his marvelous deeds among
    all peoples.
[25] For great is the LORD and most
    worthy of praise; Ps 48:1
  he is to be feared above all
    gods. Ps 89:7
[26] For all the gods of the nations
    are idols,
  but the LORD made the
    heavens. Lev 19:4; Ps 102:25
[27] Splendor and majesty are
    before him;
  strength and joy in his
    dwelling place.
[28] Ascribe to the LORD, O families
    of nations,
  ascribe to the LORD glory and
    strength, Ps 29:1-2
[29]   ascribe to the LORD the glory
    due his name.
  Bring an offering and come
    before him;
  worship the LORD in the
    splendor of his[c]
    holiness.

---

[a] 15 Some Septuagint manuscripts (see also Psalm 105:8); Hebrew *Remember*   [b] 18-20 One Hebrew
manuscript, Septuagint and Vulgate (see also Psalm 105:12); most Hebrew manuscripts *inherit,* /
[19]*though you are but few in number,* / *few indeed, and strangers in it."* / [20]*They*   [c] 29 Or LORD *with the
splendor of*

30Tremble before him, all the
earth!   Ps 114:7
The world is firmly
established; it cannot be
moved.
31Let the heavens rejoice, let the
earth be glad;   Isa 49:13
let them say among the
nations, "The LORD
reigns!"   Ps 93:1
32Let the sea resound, and all
that is in it;   Ps 98:7
let the fields be jubilant, and
everything in them!
33Then the trees of the forest
will sing,
they will sing for joy before
the LORD,
for he comes to judge the
earth.   Ps 96:1-13
34Give thanks to the LORD, for he
is good;
his love endures forever.
35Cry out, "Save us, O God our
Savior;   Mic 7:7
gather us and deliver us
from the nations,
that we may give thanks to
your holy name,
that we may glory in your
praise."
36Praise be to the LORD, the God
of Israel,
from everlasting to
everlasting.

Then all the people said "Amen"
and "Praise the LORD."

37David left Asaph and his associates before the ark of the covenant of the LORD to minister there
regularly, according to each day's
requirements. 38He also left Obed-
Edom and his sixty-eight associates to minister with them. Obed-
Edom son of Jeduthun, and also
Hosah, were gatekeepers. 1Ch 13:13

39David left Zadok the priest and
his fellow priests before the tabernacle of the LORD at the high place
in Gibeon 40to present burnt offerings to the LORD on the altar of
burnt offering regularly, morning
and evening, in accordance with
everything written in the Law of
the LORD, which he had given Israel. 41With them were Heman and
Jeduthun and the rest of those
chosen and designated by name to
give thanks to the LORD, "for his
love endures forever." 42Heman
and Jeduthun were responsible for
the sounding of the trumpets and
cymbals and for the playing of the
other instruments for sacred song.
The sons of Jeduthun were stationed at the gate.   Ex 29:38; 2Ch 5:13

43Then all the people left, each
for his own home, and David returned home to bless his family.

God's Promise to David

17 After David was settled in
his palace, he said to Nathan the prophet, "Here I am, living in a palace of cedar, while the
ark of the covenant of the LORD is
under a tent."   1Ch 15:1

2Nathan replied to David,
"Whatever you have in mind, do it,
for God is with you."   2Ch 6:7

³That night the word of God came to Nathan, saying:

⁴"Go and tell my servant David, 'This is what the Lord says: You are not the one to build me a house to dwell in. ⁵I have not dwelt in a house from the day I brought Israel up out of Egypt to this day. I have moved from one tent site to another, from one dwelling place to another. ⁶Wherever I have moved with all the Israelites, did I ever say to any of their leaders*a* whom I commanded to shepherd my people, "Why have you not built me a house of cedar?"'

⁷"Now then, tell my servant David, 'This is what the Lord Almighty says: I took you from the pasture and from following the flock, to be ruler over my people Israel. ⁸I have been with you wherever you have gone, and I have cut off all your enemies from before you. Now I will make your name like the names of the greatest men of the earth. ⁹And I will provide a place for my people Israel and will plant them so that they can have a home of their own and no longer be disturbed. Wicked people will not oppress them anymore, as they did at the beginning ¹⁰and have

done ever since the time I appointed leaders over my people Israel. I will also subdue all your enemies. *Jdg 2:16*

" 'I declare to you that the Lord will build a house for you: ¹¹When your days are over and you go to be with your fathers, I will raise up your offspring to succeed you, one of your own sons, and I will establish his kingdom. ¹²He is the one who will build a house for me, and I will establish his throne forever. ¹³I will be his father, and he will be my son. I will never take my love away from him, as I took it away from your predecessor. ¹⁴I will set him over my house and my kingdom forever; his throne will be established forever.' "

¹⁵Nathan reported to David all the words of this entire revelation.

David's Prayer

¹⁶Then King David went in and sat before the Lord, and he said:

"Who am I, O Lord God, and what is my family, that you have brought me this far? ¹⁷And as if this were not enough in your sight, O God, you have spoken about the future of the house of your servant. You have looked on me

---

a 6 Traditionally *judges;* also in verse 10

as though I were the most exalted of men, O LORD God.

18"What more can David say to you for honoring your servant? For you know your servant, 19O LORD. For the sake of your servant and according to your will, you have done this great thing and made known all these great promises.

20"There is no one like you, O LORD, and there is no God but you, as we have heard with our own ears. 21And who is like your people Israel—the one nation on earth whose God went out to redeem a people for himself, and to make a name for yourself, and to perform great and awesome wonders by driving out nations from before your people, whom you redeemed from Egypt? 22You made your people Israel your very own forever, and you, O LORD, have become their God.

23"And now, LORD, let the promise you have made concerning your servant and his house be established forever. Do as you promised, 24so that it will be established and that your name will be great forever. Then men will say, 'The LORD Almighty, the God over Israel, is Israel's God!' And the house of your servant David will be established before you.   1Ki 8:25

25"You, my God, have revealed to your servant that you will build a house for him. So your servant has found courage to pray to you. 26O LORD, you are God! You have promised these good things to your servant. 27Now you have been pleased to bless the house of your servant, that it may continue forever in your sight; for you, O LORD, have blessed it, and it will be blessed forever."

David's Victories

18 In the course of time, David defeated the Philistines and subdued them, and he took Gath and its surrounding villages from the control of the Philistines.

2David also defeated the Moabites, and they became subject to him and brought tribute.   Nu 21:29

3Moreover, David fought Hadadezer king of Zobah, as far as Hamath, when he went to establish his control along the Euphrates River. 4David captured a thousand of his chariots, seven thousand charioteers and twenty thousand foot soldiers. He hamstrung all but a hundred of the chariot horses.

5When the Arameans of Damascus came to help Hadadezer king of Zobah, David struck down twenty-two thousand of them. 6He put garrisons in the Aramean kingdom of Damascus, and the Arameans became subject to him and brought tribute. The LORD gave David victory everywhere he went.

⁷David took the gold shields carried by the officers of Hadadezer and brought them to Jerusalem. ⁸From Tebahᵃ and Cun, towns that belonged to Hadadezer, David took a great quantity of bronze, which Solomon used to make the bronze Sea, the pillars and various bronze articles.   1Ki 7:23; 2Ch 4:12,15-16

⁹When Tou king of Hamath heard that David had defeated the entire army of Hadadezer king of Zobah, ¹⁰he sent his son Hadoram to King David to greet him and congratulate him on his victory in battle over Hadadezer, who had been at war with Tou. Hadoram brought all kinds of articles of gold and silver and bronze.

¹¹King David dedicated these articles to the LORD, as he had done with the silver and gold he had taken from all these nations: Edom and Moab, the Ammonites and the Philistines, and Amalek.   Nu 24:18,20

¹²Abishai son of Zeruiah struck down eighteen thousand Edomites in the Valley of Salt. ¹³He put garrisons in Edom, and all the Edomites became subject to David. The LORD gave David victory everywhere he went.   2Sa 8:1-14; 1Ki 11:15

David's Officials

¹⁴David reigned over all Israel, doing what was just and right for all his people. ¹⁵Joab son of Zeruiah was over the army; Jehoshaphat son of Ahilud was recorder; ¹⁶Zadok son of Ahitub and Ahimelechᵇ son of Abiathar were priests; Shavsha was secretary; ¹⁷Benaiah son of Jehoiada was over the Kerethites and Pelethites; and David's sons were chief officials at the king's side.   2Sa 8:15-18; 1Ch 29:26

The Battle Against the Ammonites

19 In the course of time, Nahash king of the Ammonites died, and his son succeeded him as king. ²David thought, "I will show kindness to Hanun son of Nahash, because his father showed kindness to me." So David sent a delegation to express his sympathy to Hanun concerning his father.   Ge 19:38; Jdg 10:17-11:33

When David's men came to Hanun in the land of the Ammonites to express sympathy to him, ³the Ammonite nobles said to Hanun, "Do you think David is honoring your father by sending men to you to express sympathy? Haven't his men come to you to explore and spy out the country and overthrow it?" ⁴So Hanun seized David's men, shaved them, cut off their garments in the middle at the buttocks, and sent them away.

⁵When someone came and told David about the men, he sent mes-

---

ᵃ 8 Hebrew *Tibhath*, a variant of *Tebah*   ᵇ 16 Some Hebrew manuscripts, Vulgate and Syriac (see also 2 Samuel 8:17); most Hebrew manuscripts *Abimelech*

sengers to meet them, for they were greatly humiliated. The king said, "Stay at Jericho till your beards have grown, and then come back."

[6]When the Ammonites realized that they had become a stench in David's nostrils, Hanun and the Ammonites sent a thousand talents[a] of silver to hire chariots and charioteers from Aram Naharaim,[b] Aram Maacah and Zobah. [7]They hired thirty-two thousand chariots and charioteers, as well as the king of Maacah with his troops, who came and camped near Medeba, while the Ammonites were mustered from their towns and moved out for battle.

[8]On hearing this, David sent Joab out with the entire army of fighting men. [9]The Ammonites came out and drew up in battle formation at the entrance to their city, while the kings who had come were by themselves in the open country.

[10]Joab saw that there were battle lines in front of him and behind him; so he selected some of the best troops in Israel and deployed them against the Arameans. [11]He put the rest of the men under the command of Abishai his brother, and they were deployed against the Ammonites. [12]Joab said, "If the Arameans are too strong for me, then you are to rescue me; but if the Ammonites are too strong for you, then I will rescue you. [13]Be strong and let us fight bravely for our people and the cities of our God. The LORD will do what is good in his sight."   1Sa 26:6

[14]Then Joab and the troops with him advanced to fight the Arameans, and they fled before him. [15]When the Ammonites saw that the Arameans were fleeing, they too fled before his brother Abishai and went inside the city. So Joab went back to Jerusalem.

[16]After the Arameans saw that they had been routed by Israel, they sent messengers and had Arameans brought from beyond the River,[c] with Shophach the commander of Hadadezer's army leading them.

[17]When David was told of this, he gathered all Israel and crossed the Jordan; he advanced against them and formed his battle lines opposite them. David formed his lines to meet the Arameans in battle, and they fought against him. [18]But they fled before Israel, and David killed seven thousand of their charioteers and forty thousand of their foot soldiers. He also killed Shophach the commander of their army.

[19]When the vassals of Hadadezer saw that they had been defeated by Israel, they made peace with David and became subject to him.

---

[a]6 That is, about 37 tons (about 34 metric tons)   [b]6 That is, Northwest Mesopotamia   [c]16 That is, the Euphrates

So the Arameans were not willing to help the Ammonites anymore.

2Sa 10:1-19

The Capture of Rabbah

20 In the spring, at the time when kings go off to war, Joab led out the armed forces. He laid waste the land of the Ammonites and went to Rabbah and besieged it, but David remained in Jerusalem. Joab attacked Rabbah and left it in ruins. ²David took the crown from the head of their king[a] —its weight was found to be a talent[b] of gold, and it was set with precious stones—and it was placed on David's head. He took a great quantity of plunder from the city ³and brought out the people who were there, consigning them to labor with saws and with iron picks and axes. David did this to all the Ammonite towns. Then David and his entire army returned to Jerusalem.

2Sa 11:1; 12:29-31

War With the Philistines

⁴In the course of time, war broke out with the Philistines, at Gezer. At that time Sibbecai the Hushathite killed Sippai, one of the descendants of the Rephaites, and the Philistines were subjugated.

⁵In another battle with the Philistines, Elhanan son of Jair killed Lahmi the brother of Goliath the Gittite, who had a spear with a shaft like a weaver's rod.

⁶In still another battle, which took place at Gath, there was a huge man with six fingers on each hand and six toes on each foot—twenty-four in all. He also was descended from Rapha. ⁷When he taunted Israel, Jonathan son of Shimea, David's brother, killed him.

⁸These were descendants of Rapha in Gath, and they fell at the hands of David and his men.

David Numbers the Fighting Men

21 Satan rose up against Israel and incited David to take a census of Israel. ²So David said to Joab and the commanders of the troops, "Go and count the Israelites from Beersheba to Dan. Then report back to me so that I may know how many there are."

³But Joab replied, "May the LORD multiply his troops a hundred times over. My lord the king, are they not all my lord's subjects? Why does my lord want to do this? Why should he bring guilt on Israel?"

Dt 1:11

⁴The king's word, however, overruled Joab; so Joab left and went throughout Israel and then came back to Jerusalem. ⁵Joab reported the number of the fighting men to David: In all Israel there were one million one hundred thousand men who could handle a

---

a2 Or *of Milcom*, that is, Molech   b2 That is, about 75 pounds (about 34 kilograms)

sword, including four hundred and seventy thousand in Judah.

6But Joab did not include Levi and Benjamin in the numbering, because the king's command was repulsive to him. **7**This command was also evil in the sight of God; so he punished Israel.

8Then David said to God, "I have sinned greatly by doing this. Now, I beg you, take away the guilt of your servant. I have done a very foolish thing."

9The LORD said to Gad, David's seer, **10**"Go and tell David, 'This is what the LORD says: I am giving you three options. Choose one of them for me to carry out against you.'"   1Sa 9:9; 22:5

11So Gad went to David and said to him, "This is what the LORD says: 'Take your choice: **12**three years of famine, three months of being swept away[a] before your enemies, with their swords overtaking you, or three days of the sword of the LORD—days of plague in the land, with the angel of the LORD ravaging every part of Israel.' Now then, decide how I should answer the one who sent me."   Dt 32:24

13David said to Gad, "I am in deep distress. Let me fall into the hands of the LORD, for his mercy is very great; but do not let me fall into the hands of men."   Ps 130:4,7

14So the LORD sent a plague on Israel, and seventy thousand men of Israel fell dead. **15**And God sent an angel to destroy Jerusalem. But as the angel was doing so, the LORD saw it and was grieved because of the calamity and said to the angel who was destroying the people, "Enough! Withdraw your hand." The angel of the LORD was then standing at the threshing floor of Araunah[b] the Jebusite.   Ge 6:6

16David looked up and saw the angel of the LORD standing between heaven and earth, with a drawn sword in his hand extended over Jerusalem. Then David and the elders, clothed in sackcloth, fell facedown.   Nu 14:5; Jos 7:6

17David said to God, "Was it not I who ordered the fighting men to be counted? I am the one who has sinned and done wrong. These are but sheep. What have they done? O LORD my God, let your hand fall upon me and my family, but do not let this plague remain on your people."   2Sa 7:8; Ps 74:1

18Then the angel of the LORD ordered Gad to tell David to go up and build an altar to the LORD on the threshing floor of Araunah the Jebusite. **19**So David went up in obedience to the word that Gad had spoken in the name of the LORD.   2Ch 3:1

20While Araunah was threshing wheat, he turned and saw the angel; his four sons who were with him hid themselves. **21**Then David

---

a 12 Hebrew; Septuagint and Vulgate (see also 2 Samuel 24:13) *of fleeing*   *b* 15 Hebrew *Ornan,* a variant of *Araunah;* also in verses 18-28

approached, and when Araunah looked and saw him, he left the threshing floor and bowed down before David with his face to the ground.   Jdg 6:11

22David said to him, "Let me have the site of your threshing floor so I can build an altar to the Lord, that the plague on the people may be stopped. Sell it to me at the full price."

23Araunah said to David, "Take it! Let my lord the king do whatever pleases him. Look, I will give the oxen for the burnt offerings, the threshing sledges for the wood, and the wheat for the grain offering. I will give all this."

24But King David replied to Araunah, "No, I insist on paying the full price. I will not take for the Lord what is yours, or sacrifice a burnt offering that costs me nothing."

25So David paid Araunah six hundred shekels*a* of gold for the site. **26**David built an altar to the Lord there and sacrificed burnt offerings and fellowship offerings.*b* He called on the Lord, and the Lord answered him with fire from heaven on the altar of burnt offering.   2Sa 24:1-25

27Then the Lord spoke to the angel, and he put his sword back into its sheath. **28**At that time, when David saw that the Lord had answered him on the threshing floor of Araunah the Jebusite, he offered sacrifices there. **29**The tabernacle of the Lord, which Moses had made in the desert, and the altar of burnt offering were at that time on the high place at Gibeon. **30**But David could not go before it to inquire of God, because he was afraid of the sword of the angel of the Lord.   1Ki 3:4; 1Ch 16:39

22 Then David said, "The house of the Lord God is to be here, and also the altar of burnt offering for Israel."   1Ch 21:18-29

Preparations for the Temple

2So David gave orders to assemble the aliens living in Israel, and from among them he appointed stonecutters to prepare dressed stone for building the house of God. **3**He provided a large amount of iron to make nails for the doors of the gateways and for the fittings, and more bronze than could be weighed. **4**He also provided more cedar logs than could be counted, for the Sidonians and Tyrians had brought large numbers of them to David.   1Ki 5:6; 9:21

5David said, "My son Solomon is young and inexperienced, and the house to be built for the Lord should be of great magnificence and fame and splendor in the sight of all the nations. Therefore I will make preparations for it." So David made extensive preparations before his death.   1Ch 29:1

6Then he called for his son Solo-

---

a 25 That is, about 15 pounds (about 7 kilograms)   *b 26* Traditionally *peace offerings*

mon and charged him to build a house for the LORD, the God of Israel. ⁷David said to Solomon: "My son, I had it in my heart to build a house for the Name of the LORD my God. ⁸But this word of the LORD came to me: 'You have shed much blood and have fought many wars. You are not to build a house for my Name, because you have shed much blood on the earth in my sight. ⁹But you will have a son who will be a man of peace and rest, and I will give him rest from all his enemies on every side. His name will be Solomon,ᵃ and I will grant Israel peace and quiet during his reign. ¹⁰He is the one who will build a house for my Name. He will be my son, and I will be his father. And I will establish the throne of his kingdom over Israel forever.'   2Sa 7:13; 1Ch 17:12

¹¹"Now, my son, the LORD be with you, and may you have success and build the house of the LORD your God, as he said you would. ¹²May the LORD give you discretion and understanding when he puts you in command over Israel, so that you may keep the law of the LORD your God. ¹³Then you will have success if you are careful to observe the decrees and laws that the LORD gave Moses for Israel. Be strong and courageous. Do not be afraid or discouraged.   Jos 1:6-9; 1Ki 3:9-12

¹⁴"I have taken great pains to provide for the temple of the LORD a hundred thousand talentsᵇ of gold, a million talentsᶜ of silver, quantities of bronze and iron too great to be weighed, and wood and stone. And you may add to them. ¹⁵You have many workmen: stonecutters, masons and carpenters, as well as men skilled in every kind of work ¹⁶in gold and silver, bronze and iron—craftsmen beyond number. Now begin the work, and the LORD be with you."   ver 11; 2Ch 2:7

¹⁷Then David ordered all the leaders of Israel to help his son Solomon. ¹⁸He said to them, "Is not the LORD your God with you? And has he not granted you rest on every side? For he has handed the inhabitants of the land over to me, and the land is subject to the LORD and to his people. ¹⁹Now devote your heart and soul to seeking the LORD your God. Begin to build the sanctuary of the LORD God, so that you may bring the ark of the covenant of the LORD and the sacred articles belonging to God into the temple that will be built for the Name of the LORD."   2Ch 5:7; 1Ch 23:25

The Levites

23 When David was old and full of years, he made his son Solomon king over Israel.

²He also gathered together all the leaders of Israel, as well as the

---

ᵃ9 *Solomon* sounds like and may be derived from the Hebrew for *peace*.   ᵇ14 That is, about 3,750 tons (about 3,450 metric tons)   ᶜ14 That is, about 37,500 tons (about 34,500 metric tons)

priests and Levites. ³The Levites thirty years old or more were counted, and the total number of men was thirty-eight thousand. ⁴David said, "Of these, twenty-four thousand are to supervise the work of the temple of the LORD and six thousand are to be officials and judges. ⁵Four thousand are to be gatekeepers and four thousand are to praise the LORD with the musical instruments I have provided for that purpose." 1Ch 15:16; 2Ch 19:8

⁶David divided the Levites into groups corresponding to the sons of Levi: Gershon, Kohath and Merari. 2Ch 8:14; 29:25

Gershonites

⁷Belonging to the Gershonites:
Ladan and Shimei.

⁸The sons of Ladan:
Jehiel the first, Zetham and Joel—three in all.

⁹The sons of Shimei:
Shelomoth, Haziel and Haran—three in all.
These were the heads of the families of Ladan.

¹⁰And the sons of Shimei:
Jahath, Ziza,ᵃ Jeush and Beriah.
These were the sons of Shimei—four in all.

¹¹Jahath was the first and Ziza the second, but Jeush and Beriah did not have many sons; so they were counted as one family with one assignment.

Kohathites

¹²The sons of Kohath:
Amram, Izhar, Hebron and Uzziel—four in all. Ex 6:18

¹³The sons of Amram: Ex 6:20
Aaron and Moses.
Aaron was set apart, he and his descendants forever, to consecrate the most holy things, to offer sacrifices before the LORD, to minister before him and to pronounce blessings in his name forever. ¹⁴The sons of Moses the man of God were counted as part of the tribe of Levi. Ex 30:7-10; Dt 33:1

¹⁵The sons of Moses:
Gershom and Eliezer.

¹⁶The descendants of Gershom:
Shubael was the first.

¹⁷The descendants of Eliezer:
Rehabiah was the first.
Eliezer had no other sons, but the sons of Rehabiah were very numerous.

¹⁸The sons of Izhar:
Shelomith was the first.

¹⁹The sons of Hebron: 1Ch 24:23
Jeriah the first, Amariah the second, Jahaziel the third and Jekameam the fourth.

²⁰The sons of Uzziel:
Micah the first and Isshiah the second.

ᵃ 10 One Hebrew manuscript, Septuagint and Vulgate (see also verse 11); most Hebrew manuscripts Zina

Merarites

²¹The sons of Merari: 1Ch 24:26
   Mahli and Mushi.
   The sons of Mahli:
   Eleazar and Kish.
²²Eleazar died without having sons: he had only
   daughters. Their cousins,
   the sons of Kish, married
   them.
²³The sons of Mushi:
   Mahli, Eder and Jerimoth —
   three in all.

²⁴These were the descendants of
Levi by their families — the heads
of families as they were registered
under their names and counted in-
dividually, that is, the workers
twenty years old or more who
served in the temple of the LORD.
²⁵For David had said, "Since the
LORD, the God of Israel, has granted rest to his people and has come
to dwell in Jerusalem forever, ²⁶the
Levites no longer need to carry the
tabernacle or any of the articles
used in its service." ²⁷According to
the last instructions of David, the
Levites were counted from those
twenty years old or more.

²⁸The duty of the Levites was to
help Aaron's descendants in the
service of the temple of the LORD:
to be in charge of the courtyards,
the side rooms, the purification of
all sacred things and the perfor-
mance of other duties at the house
of God. ²⁹They were in charge of
the bread set out on the table, the
flour for the grain offerings, the
unleavened wafers, the baking and
the mixing, and all measurements
of quantity and size. ³⁰They were
also to stand every morning to
thank and praise the LORD. They
were to do the same in the evening
³¹and whenever burnt offerings
were presented to the LORD on Sabbaths and at New Moon festivals
and at appointed feasts. They were
to serve before the LORD regularly
in the proper number and in the
way prescribed for them.   Ex 25:30

³²And so the Levites carried out
their responsibilities for the Tent
of Meeting, for the Holy Place and,
under their brothers the descendants of Aaron, for the service of
the temple of the LORD.   Nu 1:53

The Divisions of Priests

24 These were the divisions of
   the sons of Aaron: Nu 3:2-4
   The sons of Aaron were Nadab,
Abihu, Eleazar and Ithamar. ²But
Nadab and Abihu died before their
father did, and they had no sons;
so Eleazar and Ithamar served as
the priests. ³With the help of Zadok a descendant of Eleazar and
Ahimelech a descendant of Ithamar, David separated them into divisions for their appointed order of
ministering. ⁴A larger number of
leaders were found among Eleazar's descendants than among Ithamar's, and they were divided accordingly: sixteen heads of families from Eleazar's descendants
and eight heads of families from
Ithamar's descendants. ⁵They di-

vided them impartially by drawing lots, for there were officials of the sanctuary and officials of God among the descendants of both Eleazar and Ithamar.   Ex 6:23; Lev 10:1-2

⁶The scribe Shemaiah son of Nethanel, a Levite, recorded their names in the presence of the king and of the officials: Zadok the priest, Ahimelech son of Abiathar and the heads of families of the priests and of the Levites—one family being taken from Eleazar and then one from Ithamar.

⁷The first lot fell to Jehoiarib,
  the second to Jedaiah,
⁸the third to Harim,   Ezr 2:39
  the fourth to Seorim,
⁹the fifth to Malkijah,
  the sixth to Mijamin,
¹⁰the seventh to Hakkoz,
  the eighth to Abijah,
¹¹the ninth to Jeshua,
  the tenth to Shecaniah,
¹²the eleventh to Eliashib,
  the twelfth to Jakim,
¹³the thirteenth to Huppah,
  the fourteenth to Jeshebeab,
¹⁴the fifteenth to Bilgah,
  the sixteenth to Immer,
¹⁵the seventeenth to Hezir,
  the eighteenth to Happizzez,
¹⁶the nineteenth to Pethahiah,
  the twentieth to Jehezkel,
¹⁷the twenty-first to Jakin,
  the twenty-second to Gamul,
¹⁸the twenty-third to Delaiah

and the twenty-fourth to Maaziah.

¹⁹This was their appointed order of ministering when they entered the temple of the LORD, according to the regulations prescribed for them by their forefather Aaron, as the LORD, the God of Israel, had commanded him.

The Rest of the Levites

²⁰As for the rest of the descendants of Levi: 1Ch 23:6
  from the sons of Amram: Shubael;
  from the sons of Shubael: Jehdeiah.
²¹As for Rehabiah, from his sons: 1Ch 23:17
  Isshiah was the first.
²²From the Izharites: Shelomoth;
  from the sons of Shelomoth: Jahath.
²³The sons of Hebron: Jeriah the first,ᵃ Amariah the second, Jahaziel the third and Jekameam the fourth.
²⁴The son of Uzziel: Micah;
  from the sons of Micah: Shamir.
²⁵The brother of Micah: Isshiah;
  from the sons of Isshiah: Zechariah.
²⁶The sons of Merari: Mahli and Mushi.   1Ch 6:19; 23:21
  The son of Jaaziah: Beno.

ᵃ 23 Two Hebrew manuscripts and some Septuagint manuscripts (see also 1 Chron. 23:19); most Hebrew manuscripts *The sons of Jeriah:*

27The sons of Merari:
> from Jaaziah: Beno, Sho-
> ham, Zaccur and Ibri.

28From Mahli: Eleazar, who had
> no sons.

29From Kish: the son of Kish:
> Jerahmeel.

30And the sons of Mushi: Mahli,
> Eder and Jerimoth.

These were the Levites, according to their families. 31They also
cast lots, just as their brothers the
descendants of Aaron did, in the
presence of King David and of Zadok, Ahimelech, and the heads of
families of the priests and of the
Levites. The families of the oldest
brother were treated the same as
those of the youngest.

The Singers

25 David, together with the
commanders of the army,
set apart some of the sons of
Asaph, Heman and Jeduthun for
the ministry of prophesying, accompanied by harps, lyres and
cymbals. Here is the list of the men
who performed this service:

2From the sons of Asaph:
> Zaccur, Joseph, Nethaniah
> and Asarelah. The sons of
> Asaph were under the super-
> vision of Asaph, who prophe-
> sied under the king's supervi-
> sion.

3As for Jeduthun, from his sons:
Gedaliah, Zeri, Jeshaiah,
Shimei,[a] Hashabiah and Mattithiah, six in all, under the
supervision of their father Jeduthun, who prophesied, using the harp in thanking and
praising the LORD.   Ge 4:21

4As for Heman, from his sons:
Bukkiah, Mattaniah, Uzziel,
Shubael and Jerimoth; Hananiah, Hanani, Eliathah, Giddalti and Romamti-Ezer; Joshbekashah, Mallothi, Hothir
and Mahazioth. 5All these
were sons of Heman the
king's seer. They were given
him through the promises of
God to exalt him.[b] God gave
Heman fourteen sons and
three daughters.

6All these men were under the
supervision of their fathers for the
music of the temple of the LORD,
with cymbals, lyres and harps, for
the ministry at the house of God.
Asaph, Jeduthun and Heman were
under the supervision of the king.
7Along with their relatives—all of
them trained and skilled in music
for the LORD—they numbered 288.
8Young and old alike, teacher as
well as student, cast lots for their
duties.   1Ch 15:16,19; 26:13

9The first lot, which was
> for Asaph, fell to Jo-
> seph, his sons and rela-
> tives,[c]   12[d]

---

a3 One Hebrew manuscript and some Septuagint manuscripts (see also verse 17); most Hebrew
manuscripts do not have *Shimei*.   b5 Hebrew *exalt the horn*   c9 See Septuagint; Hebrew does not
have *his sons and relatives*.   d9 See the total in verse 7; Hebrew does not have *twelve*.

the second to Gedaliah,
he and his relatives and
sons,   12
[10]the third to Zaccur,
his sons and relatives,   12
[11]the fourth to Izri,[a]
his sons and relatives,   12
[12]the fifth to Nethaniah,
his sons and relatives,   12
[13]the sixth to Bukkiah,
his sons and relatives,   12
[14]the seventh to Jesarelah,[b]
his sons and relatives,   12
[15]the eighth to Jeshaiah,
his sons and relatives,   12
[16]the ninth to Mattaniah,
his sons and relatives,   12
[17]the tenth to Shimei,
his sons and relatives,   12
[18]the eleventh to Azarel,[c]
his sons and relatives,   12
[19]the twelfth to Hashabiah,
his sons and relatives,   12
[20]the thirteenth to Shubael,
his sons and relatives,   12
[21]the fourteenth to Mattithiah,
his sons and relatives,   12
[22]the fifteenth to Jerimoth,
his sons and relatives,   12
[23]the sixteenth to Hananiah,
his sons and relatives,   12
[24]the seventeenth to
Joshbekashah,
his sons and relatives,   12
[25]the eighteenth to Hanani,
his sons and relatives,   12
[26]the nineteenth to Mallothi,
his sons and relatives,   12
[27]the twentieth to Eliathah,

his sons and relatives,   12
[28]the twenty-first to Hothir,
his sons and relatives,   12
[29]the twenty-second to
Giddalti,
his sons and relatives,   12
[30]the twenty-third to
Mahazioth,
his sons and relatives,   12
[31]the twenty-fourth to
Romamti-Ezer,
his sons and relatives,   12

The Gatekeepers

26 The divisions of the gatekeepers: 1Ch 9:17

From the Korahites: Meshele-
miah son of Kore, one of
the sons of Asaph.
[2]Meshelemiah had sons:
Zechariah the firstborn,
Jediael the second,
Zebadiah the third,
Jathniel the fourth,
[3]Elam the fifth,
Jehohanan the sixth
and Eliehoenai the seventh.
[4]Obed-Edom also had sons:
Shemaiah the firstborn,
Jehozabad the second,
Joah the third,
Sacar the fourth,
Nethanel the fifth,
[5]Ammiel the sixth,
Issachar the seventh
and Peullethai the eighth.
(For God had blessed Obed-
Edom.)   2Sa 6:10; 1Ch 13:13

---

[a] 11 A variant of Zeri   [b] 14 A variant of Asarelah   [c] 18 A variant of Uzziel

[6]His son Shemaiah also had sons, who were leaders in their father's family because they were very capable men. [7]The sons of Shemaiah: Othni, Rephael, Obed and Elzabad; his relatives Elihu and Semakiah were also able men. [8]All these were descendants of Obed-Edom; they and their sons and their relatives were capable men with the strength to do the work— descendants of Obed-Edom, 62 in all.

[9]Meshelemiah had sons and relatives, who were able men—18 in all.

[10]Hosah the Merarite had sons: Shimri the first (although he was not the firstborn, his father had appointed him the first), [11]Hilkiah the second, Tabaliah the third and Zechariah the fourth. The sons and relatives of Hosah were 13 in all.   Dt 21:16

[12]These divisions of the gatekeepers, through their chief men, had duties for ministering in the temple of the LORD, just as their relatives had. [13]Lots were cast for each gate, according to their families, young and old alike.

[14]The lot for the East Gate fell to Shelemiah.[a] Then lots were cast for his son Zechariah, a wise counselor, and the lot for the North Gate fell to him. [15]The lot for the South Gate fell to Obed-Edom, and the lot for the storehouse fell to his sons. [16]The lots for the West Gate and the Shalleketh Gate on the upper road fell to Shuppim and Hosah.   1Ch 9:18,21; 13:13

Guard was alongside of guard: [17]There were six Levites a day on the east, four a day on the north, four a day on the south and two at a time at the storehouse. [18]As for the court to the west, there were four at the road and two at the court itself.

[19]These were the divisions of the gatekeepers who were descendants of Korah and Merari.

The Treasurers and Other Officials

[20]Their fellow Levites were[b] in charge of the treasuries of the house of God and the treasuries for the dedicated things.   1Ch 28:12

[21]The descendants of Ladan, who were Gershonites through Ladan and who were heads of families belonging to Ladan the Gershonite, were Jehieli, [22]the sons of Jehieli, Zetham and his brother Joel. They were in charge of the treasuries of the temple of the LORD.   1Ch 23:7; 29:8

[23]From the Amramites, the Izharites, the Hebronites and the Uzzielites: Nu 3:27

---

[a]14 A variant of *Meshelemiah*   [b]20 Septuagint; Hebrew *As for the Levites, Ahijah was*

²⁴Shubael, a descendant of Gershom son of Moses, was the officer in charge of the treasuries. ²⁵His relatives through Eliezer: Rehabiah his son, Jeshaiah his son, Joram his son, Zicri his son and Shelomith his son. ²⁶Shelomith and his relatives were in charge of all the treasuries for the things dedicated by King David, by the heads of families who were the commanders of thousands and commanders of hundreds, and by the other army commanders. ²⁷Some of the plunder taken in battle they dedicated for the repair of the temple of the Lᴏʀᴅ. ²⁸And everything dedicated by Samuel the seer and by Saul son of Kish, Abner son of Ner and Joab son of Zeruiah, and all the other dedicated things were in the care of Shelomith and his relatives. 1Sa 9:9; 2Sa 8:11

²⁹From the Izharites: Kenaniah and his sons were assigned duties away from the temple, as officials and judges over Israel. 1Ch 23:4; Ne 11:16

³⁰From the Hebronites: Hashabiah and his relatives — seventeen hundred able men — were responsible in Israel west of the Jordan for all the work of the Lᴏʀᴅ and for the king's service. ³¹As for the Hebronites, Jeriah was their chief according to the genealogical records of their families. In the fortieth year of David's reign a search was made in the records, and capable men among the Hebronites were found at Jazer in Gilead. ³²Jeriah had twenty-seven hundred relatives, who were able men and heads of families, and King David put them in charge of the Reubenites, the Gadites and the half-tribe of Manasseh for every matter pertaining to God and for the affairs of the king. 1Ch 23:19

Army Divisions

27 This is the list of the Israelites — heads of families, commanders of thousands and commanders of hundreds, and their officers, who served the king in all that concerned the army divisions that were on duty month by month throughout the year. Each division consisted of 24,000 men.

²In charge of the first division, for the first month, was Jashobeam son of Zabdiel. There were 24,000 men in his division. ³He was a descendant of Perez and chief of all the army officers for the first month. ⁴In charge of the division for the second month was Dodai the Ahohite; Mikloth was the

leader of his division. There were 24,000 men in his division.   2Sa 23:9

⁵The third army commander, for the third month, was Benaiah son of Jehoiada the priest. He was chief and there were 24,000 men in his division. ⁶This was the Benaiah who was a mighty man among the Thirty and was over the Thirty. His son Ammizabad was in charge of his division.

⁷The fourth, for the fourth month, was Asahel the brother of Joab; his son Zebadiah was his successor. There were 24,000 men in his division.

⁸The fifth, for the fifth month, was the commander Shamhuth the Izrahite. There were 24,000 men in his division.

⁹The sixth, for the sixth month, was Ira the son of Ikkesh the Tekoite. There were 24,000 men in his division.   2Sa 23:26

¹⁰The seventh, for the seventh month, was Helez the Pelonite, an Ephraimite. There were 24,000 men in his division.   2Sa 23:26; 1Ch 11:27

¹¹The eighth, for the eighth month, was Sibbecai the Hushathite, a Zerahite. There were 24,000 men in his division.   2Sa 21:18

¹²The ninth, for the ninth month, was Abiezer the Anathothite, a Benjamite. There were 24,000 men in his division.

¹³The tenth, for the tenth month, was Maharai the Netophathite, a Zerahite. There were 24,000 men in his division.

¹⁴The eleventh, for the eleventh month, was Benaiah the Pirathonite, an Ephraimite. There were 24,000 men in his division.   1Ch 11:31

¹⁵The twelfth, for the twelfth month, was Heldai the Netophathite, from the family of Othniel. There were 24,000 men in his division.   Jos 15:17

Officers of the Tribes

¹⁶The officers over the tribes of Israel:

over the Reubenites: Eliezer son of Zicri;

over the Simeonites: Shephatiah son of Maacah;

¹⁷over Levi: Hashabiah son of Kemuel;   1Ch 26:30

over Aaron: Zadok;   1Ch 12:28

¹⁸over Judah: Elihu, a brother of David;

over Issachar: Omri son of Michael;

¹⁹over Zebulun: Ishmaiah son of Obadiah;

over Naphtali: Jerimoth son of Azriel;

²⁰over the Ephraimites: Hoshea son of Azaziah;

over half the tribe of Manasseh: Joel son of Pedaiah;

²¹over the half-tribe of Manasseh in Gilead: Iddo son of Zechariah;

over Benjamin: Jaasiel son of Abner;

²²over Dan: Azarel son of Jeroham.

These were the officers over the tribes of Israel.

²³David did not take the number of the men twenty years old or less, because the LORD had promised to make Israel as numerous as the stars in the sky. ²⁴Joab son of Zeruiah began to count the men but did not finish. Wrath came on Israel on account of this numbering, and the number was not entered in the book*a* of the annals of King David.   Ge 15:5; 2Sa 24:15

The King's Overseers

²⁵Azmaveth son of Adiel was in charge of the royal storehouses.

Jonathan son of Uzziah was in charge of the storehouses in the outlying districts, in the towns, the villages and the watchtowers.

²⁶Ezri son of Kelub was in charge of the field workers who farmed the land.

²⁷Shimei the Ramathite was in charge of the vineyards.

Zabdi the Shiphmite was in charge of the produce of the vineyards for the wine vats.

²⁸Baal-Hanan the Gederite was in charge of the olive and sycamore-fig trees in the western foothills.   1Ki 10:27

Joash was in charge of the supplies of olive oil.

²⁹Shitrai the Sharonite was in charge of the herds grazing in Sharon.

Shaphat son of Adlai was in charge of the herds in the valleys.

³⁰Obil the Ishmaelite was in charge of the camels.

Jehdeiah the Meronothite was in charge of the donkeys.

³¹Jaziz the Hagrite was in charge of the flocks.   1Ch 5:10

All these were the officials in charge of King David's property.

³²Jonathan, David's uncle, was a counselor, a man of insight and a scribe. Jehiel son of Hacmoni took care of the king's sons.

³³Ahithophel was the king's counselor.   2Sa 15:12

Hushai the Arkite was the king's friend. ³⁴Ahithophel was succeeded by Jehoiada son of Benaiah and by Abiathar.   2Sa 15:37; 1Ki 1:7

Joab was the commander of the royal army.   1Ch 11:6

David's Plans for the Temple

28 David summoned all the officials of Israel to assemble at Jerusalem: the officers over the tribes, the commanders of the divisions in the service of the king, the commanders of thousands and commanders of hundreds, and the officials in charge of all the property and livestock belonging to the

a 24 Septuagint; Hebrew number

king and his sons, together with the palace officials, the mighty men and all the brave warriors.

²King David rose to his feet and said: "Listen to me, my brothers and my people. I had it in my heart to build a house as a place of rest for the ark of the covenant of the LORD, for the footstool of our God, and I made plans to build it. ³But God said to me, 'You are not to build a house for my Name, because you are a warrior and have shed blood.'　1Ch 22:8; Ps 132:7

⁴"Yet the LORD, the God of Israel, chose me from my whole family to be king over Israel forever. He chose Judah as leader, and from the house of Judah he chose my family, and from my father's sons he was pleased to make me king over all Israel. ⁵Of all my sons— and the LORD has given me many —he has chosen my son Solomon to sit on the throne of the kingdom of the LORD over Israel. ⁶He said to me: 'Solomon your son is the one who will build my house and my courts, for I have chosen him to be my son, and I will be his father. ⁷I will establish his kingdom forever if he is unswerving in carrying out my commands and laws, as is being done at this time.'　2Sa 7:13

⁸"So now I charge you in the sight of all Israel and of the assembly of the LORD, and in the hearing of our God: Be careful to follow all the commands of the LORD your God, that you may possess this good land and pass it on as an in-heritance to your descendants forever.　Dt 4:1; 6:1

⁹"And you, my son Solomon, acknowledge the God of your father, and serve him with wholehearted devotion and with a willing mind, for the LORD searches every heart and understands every motive behind the thoughts. If you seek him, he will be found by you; but if you forsake him, he will reject you forever. ¹⁰Consider now, for the LORD has chosen you to build a temple as a sanctuary. Be strong and do the work."　1Sa 16:7; 2Ch 15:2

¹¹Then David gave his son Solomon the plans for the portico of the temple, its buildings, its storerooms, its upper parts, its inner rooms and the place of atonement. ¹²He gave him the plans of all that the Spirit had put in his mind for the courts of the temple of the LORD and all the surrounding rooms, for the treasuries of the temple of God and for the treasuries for the dedicated things. ¹³He gave him instructions for the divisions of the priests and Levites, and for all the work of serving in the temple of the LORD, as well as for all the articles to be used in its service. ¹⁴He designated the weight of gold for all the gold articles to be used in various kinds of service, and the weight of silver for all the silver articles to be used in various kinds of service: ¹⁵the weight of gold for the gold lampstands and their lamps, with the weight for each lampstand and its

lamps; and the weight of silver for each silver lampstand and its lamps, according to the use of each lampstand; ¹⁶the weight of gold for each table for consecrated bread; the weight of silver for the silver tables; ¹⁷the weight of pure gold for the forks, sprinkling bowls and pitchers; the weight of gold for each gold dish; the weight of silver for each silver dish; ¹⁸and the weight of the refined gold for the altar of incense. He also gave him the plan for the chariot, that is, the cherubim of gold that spread their wings and shelter the ark of the covenant of the LORD.   Ex 25:18-22

¹⁹"All this," David said, "I have in writing from the hand of the LORD upon me, and he gave me understanding in all the details of the plan."   Ex 25:9; 1Ki 6:38

²⁰David also said to Solomon his son, "Be strong and courageous, and do the work. Do not be afraid or discouraged, for the LORD God, my God, is with you. He will not fail you or forsake you until all the work for the service of the temple of the LORD is finished. ²¹The divisions of the priests and Levites are ready for all the work on the temple of God, and every willing man skilled in any craft will help you in all the work. The officials and all the people will obey your every command."   Ex 35:25-36:5; Dt 31:6

Gifts for Building the Temple

29 Then King David said to the whole assembly: "My son Solomon, the one whom God has chosen, is young and inexperienced. The task is great, because this palatial structure is not for man but for the LORD God. ²With all my resources I have provided for the temple of my God—gold for the gold work, silver for the silver, bronze for the bronze, iron for the iron and wood for the wood, as well as onyx for the settings, turquoise,ᵃ stones of various colors, and all kinds of fine stone and marble—all of these in large quantities. ³Besides, in my devotion to the temple of my God I now give my personal treasures of gold and silver for the temple of my God, over and above everything I have provided for this holy temple: ⁴three thousand talentsᵇ of gold (gold of Ophir) and seven thousand talentsᶜ of refined silver, for the overlaying of the walls of the buildings, ⁵for the gold work and the silver work, and for all the work to be done by the craftsmen. Now, who is willing to consecrate himself today to the LORD?"

⁶Then the leaders of families, the officers of the tribes of Israel, the commanders of thousands and commanders of hundreds, and the officials in charge of the king's

---

ᵃ2 The meaning of the Hebrew for this word is uncertain.   ᵇ4 That is, about 110 tons (about 100 metric tons)   ᶜ4 That is, about 260 tons (about 240 metric tons)

work gave willingly. 7They gave toward the work on the temple of God five thousand talents*a* and ten thousand darics*b* of gold, ten thousand talents*c* of silver, eighteen thousand talents*d* of bronze and a hundred thousand talents*e* of iron. 8Any who had precious stones gave them to the treasury of the temple of the LORD in the custody of Jehiel the Gershonite. 9The people rejoiced at the willing response of their leaders, for they had given freely and wholeheartedly to the LORD. David the king also rejoiced greatly.   1Ki 8:61; 1Ch 26:21; 2Co 9:7

David's Prayer

10David praised the LORD in the presence of the whole assembly, saying,

"Praise be to you, O LORD,
   God of our father Israel,
   from everlasting to
      everlasting.
11Yours, O LORD, is the greatness
      and the power   Ps 24:8
   and the glory and the
      majesty and the
      splendor,
   for everything in heaven and
      earth is yours.   Ps 89:11
Yours, O LORD, is the kingdom;
   you are exalted as head over
      all.   Rev 5:12-13
12Wealth and honor come from
      you;   2Ch 1:12

you are the ruler of all
      things.   2Ch 20:6; Ro 11:36
In your hands are strength and
      power
   to exalt and give strength to
      all.
13Now, our God, we give you
      thanks,
   and praise your glorious
      name.

14"But who am I, and who are my people, that we should be able to give as generously as this? Everything comes from you, and we have given you only what comes from your hand. 15We are aliens and strangers in your sight, as were all our forefathers. Our days on earth are like a shadow, without hope. 16O LORD our God, as for all this abundance that we have provided for building you a temple for your Holy Name, it comes from your hand, and all of it belongs to you. 17I know, my God, that you test the heart and are pleased with integrity. All these things have I given willingly and with honest intent. And now I have seen with joy how willingly your people who are here have given to you. 18O LORD, God of our fathers Abraham, Isaac and Israel, keep this desire in the hearts of your people forever, and keep their hearts loyal to you. 19And give my son Solomon the wholehearted devotion to keep

---

a7 That is, about 190 tons (about 170 metric tons)   *b7* That is, about 185 pounds (about 84 kilograms)   *c7* That is, about 375 tons (about 345 metric tons)   *d7* That is, about 675 tons (about 610 metric tons)   *e7* That is, about 3,750 tons (about 3,450 metric tons)

your commands, requirements and decrees and to do everything to build the palatial structure for which I have provided." 1Ch 22:14

²⁰Then David said to the whole assembly, "Praise the LORD your God." So they all praised the LORD, the God of their fathers; they bowed low and fell prostrate before the LORD and the king.

Solomon Acknowledged as King

²¹The next day they made sacrifices to the LORD and presented burnt offerings to him: a thousand bulls, a thousand rams and a thousand male lambs, together with their drink offerings, and other sacrifices in abundance for all Israel. ²²They ate and drank with great joy in the presence of the LORD that day. 1Ki 8:62; 1Ch 23:1

Then they acknowledged Solomon son of David as king a second time, anointing him before the LORD to be ruler and Zadok to be priest. ²³So Solomon sat on the throne of the LORD as king in place of his father David. He prospered and all Israel obeyed him. ²⁴All the officers and mighty men, as well as all of King David's sons, pledged their submission to King Solomon.

²⁵The LORD highly exalted Solomon in the sight of all Israel and bestowed on him royal splendor such as no king over Israel ever had before. 1Ki 1:28-53; 3:13

The Death of David

²⁶David son of Jesse was king over all Israel. ²⁷He ruled over Israel forty years—seven in Hebron and thirty-three in Jerusalem. ²⁸He died at a good old age, having enjoyed long life, wealth and honor. His son Solomon succeeded him as king. Ge 15:15; 1Ki 2:10-12; 1Ch 23:1

²⁹As for the events of King David's reign, from beginning to end, they are written in the records of Samuel the seer, the records of Nathan the prophet and the records of Gad the seer, ³⁰together with the details of his reign and power, and the circumstances that surrounded him and Israel and the kingdoms of all the other lands.

2 Chronicles

Solomon Asks for Wisdom

1 Solomon son of David established himself firmly over his kingdom, for the LORD his God was with him and made him exceedingly great. Ge 39:2; 1Ki 2:12,26; 1Ch 29:25

2 Then Solomon spoke to all Israel—to the commanders of thousands and commanders of hundreds, to the judges and to all the leaders in Israel, the heads of families— 3 and Solomon and the whole assembly went to the high place at Gibeon, for God's Tent of Meeting was there, which Moses the LORD's servant had made in the desert. 4 Now David had brought up the ark of God from Kiriath Jearim to the place he had prepared for it, because he had pitched a tent for it in Jerusalem. 5 But the bronze altar that Bezalel son of Uri, the son of Hur, had made was in Gibeon in front of the tabernacle of the LORD; so Solomon and the assembly inquired of him there. 6 Solomon went up to the bronze altar before the LORD in the Tent of Meeting and offered a thousand burnt offerings on it. Ex 36:8; 38:2

7 That night God appeared to Solomon and said to him, "Ask for whatever you want me to give you." 2Ch 7:12

8 Solomon answered God, "You have shown great kindness to David my father and have made me king in his place. 9 Now, LORD God, let your promise to my father David be confirmed, for you have made me king over a people who are as numerous as the dust of the earth. 10 Give me wisdom and knowledge, that I may lead this people, for who is able to govern this great people of yours?"

11 God said to Solomon, "Since this is your heart's desire and you have not asked for wealth, riches or honor, nor for the death of your enemies, and since you have not asked for a long life but for wisdom and knowledge to govern my people over whom I have made you king, 12 therefore wisdom and knowledge will be given you. And I will also give you wealth, riches and honor, such as no king who was before you ever had and none after you will have." 1Ch 29:25

13 Then Solomon went to Jerusalem from the high place at Gibeon, from before the Tent of Meeting. And he reigned over Israel.

14 Solomon accumulated chariots and horses; he had fourteen hundred chariots and twelve thousand horses,[a] which he kept in the

---

chariot cities and also with him in Jerusalem. [15]The king made silver and gold as common in Jerusalem as stones, and cedar as plentiful as sycamore-fig trees in the foothills. [16]Solomon's horses were imported from Egypt[a] and from Kue[b]—the royal merchants purchased them from Kue. [17]They imported a chariot from Egypt for six hundred shekels[c] of silver, and a horse for a hundred and fifty.[d] They also exported them to all the kings of the Hittites and of the Arameans.

Preparations for Building the Temple

2 Solomon gave orders to build a temple for the Name of the Lord and a royal palace for himself. [2]He conscripted seventy thousand men as carriers and eighty thousand as stonecutters in the hills and thirty-six hundred as foremen over them.　　ver 18; 2Ch 10:4

[3]Solomon sent this message to Hiram[e] king of Tyre:

"Send me cedar logs as you did for my father David when you sent him cedar to build a palace to live in. [4]Now I am about to build a temple for the Name of the Lord my God and to dedicate it to him for burning fragrant incense before him, for setting out the conse-

crated bread regularly, and for making burnt offerings every morning and evening and on Sabbaths and New Moons and at the appointed feasts of the Lord our God. This is a lasting ordinance for Israel.

[5]"The temple I am going to build will be great, because our God is greater than all other gods. [6]But who is able to build a temple for him, since the heavens, even the highest heavens, cannot contain him? Who then am I to build a temple for him, except as a place to burn sacrifices before him?

[7]"Send me, therefore, a man skilled to work in gold and silver, bronze and iron, and in purple, crimson and blue yarn, and experienced in the art of engraving, to work in Judah and Jerusalem with my skilled craftsmen, whom my father David provided.

[8]"Send me also cedar, pine and algum[f] logs from Lebanon, for I know that your men are skilled in cutting timber there. My men will work with yours [9]to provide me with plenty of lumber, because the temple I build must be large and magnificent. [10]I will give your servants, the woodsmen who cut the timber, twenty

---

[a]16 Or possibly *Muzur*, a region in Cilicia; also in verse 17　　[b]16 Probably Cilicia　　[c]17 That is, about 15 pounds (about 7 kilograms)　　[d]17 That is, about 3 3/4 pounds (about 1.7 kilograms)　　[e]3 Hebrew *Huram*, a variant of *Hiram*; also in verses 11 and 12　　[f]8 Probably a variant of *almug*; possibly juniper

thousand cors*a* of ground wheat, twenty thousand cors of barley, twenty thousand baths*b* of wine and twenty thousand baths of olive oil."

¹¹Hiram king of Tyre replied by letter to Solomon:

"Because the LORD loves his people, he has made you their king."　1Ki 10:9; 2Ch 9:8

¹²And Hiram added:

"Praise be to the LORD, the God of Israel, who made heaven and earth! He has given King David a wise son, endowed with intelligence and discernment, who will build a temple for the LORD and a palace for himself.　Ps 33:6; 102:25
¹³"I am sending you Huram-Abi, a man of great skill, ¹⁴whose mother was from Dan and whose father was from Tyre. He is trained to work in gold and silver, bronze and iron, stone and wood, and with purple and blue and crimson yarn and fine linen. He is experienced in all kinds of engraving and can execute any design given to him. He will work with your craftsmen and with those of my lord, David your father.　Ex 31:6; 1Ki 7:13

¹⁵"Now let my lord send his servants the wheat and barley and the olive oil and wine he promised, ¹⁶and we will cut all the logs from Lebanon that you need and will float them in rafts by sea down to Joppa. You can then take them up to Jerusalem."　Jos 19:46; Jnh 1:3

¹⁷Solomon took a census of all the aliens who were in Israel, after the census his father David had taken; and they were found to be 153,600. ¹⁸He assigned 70,000 of them to be carriers and 80,000 to be stonecutters in the hills, with 3,600 foremen over them to keep the people working.　1Ki 5:1-16

Solomon Builds the Temple

3 Then Solomon began to build the temple of the LORD in Jerusalem on Mount Moriah, where the LORD had appeared to his father David. It was on the threshing floor of Araunah*c* the Jebusite, the place provided by David. ²He began building on the second day of the second month in the fourth year of his reign.　1Ch 21:18; Ac 7:47

³The foundation Solomon laid for building the temple of God was sixty cubits long and twenty cubits wide*d* (using the cubit of the old standard). ⁴The portico at the front of the temple was twenty cubits*e*

---

a 10 That is, probably about 125,000 bushels (about 4,400 kiloliters)　*b 10* That is, probably about 115,000 gallons (about 440 kiloliters)　*c 1* Hebrew *Ornan*, a variant of *Araunah*　*d 3* That is, about 90 feet (about 27 meters) long and 30 feet (about 9 meters) wide　*e 4* That is, about 30 feet (about 9 meters); also in verses 8, 11 and 13

long across the width of the building and twenty cubits[a] high.

He overlaid the inside with pure gold. [5]He paneled the main hall with pine and covered it with fine gold and decorated it with palm tree and chain designs. [6]He adorned the temple with precious stones. And the gold he used was gold of Parvaim. [7]He overlaid the ceiling beams, doorframes, walls and doors of the temple with gold, and he carved cherubim on the walls. Ge 3:24; 1Ki 6:29-35; Eze 40:16

[8]He built the Most Holy Place, its length corresponding to the width of the temple—twenty cubits long and twenty cubits wide. He overlaid the inside with six hundred talents[b] of fine gold. [9]The gold nails weighed fifty shekels.[c] He also overlaid the upper parts with gold. Ex 26:32-33

[10]In the Most Holy Place he made a pair of sculptured cherubim and overlaid them with gold. [11]The total wingspan of the cherubim was twenty cubits. One wing of the first cherub was five cubits[d] long and touched the temple wall, while its other wing, also five cubits long, touched the wing of the other cherub. [12]Similarly one wing of the second cherub was five cubits long and touched the other temple wall, and its other wing, also five cubits long, touched the wing of the first cherub. [13]The wings of these cherubim extended twenty cubits. They stood on their feet, facing the main hall.[e]

[14]He made the curtain of blue, purple and crimson yarn and fine linen, with cherubim worked into it. 1Ki 6:1-29

[15]In the front of the temple he made two pillars, which together, were thirty-five cubits[f] long, each with a capital on top measuring five cubits. [16]He made interwoven chains[g] and put them on top of the pillars. He also made a hundred pomegranates and attached them to the chains. [17]He erected the pillars in the front of the temple, one to the south and one to the north. The one to the south he named Jakin[h] and the one to the north Boaz.[i] 1Ki 7:15,17,20

The Temple's Furnishings

4 He made a bronze altar twenty cubits long, twenty cubits wide and ten cubits high.[j] [2]He made the Sea of cast metal, circular in shape, measuring ten cubits from rim to rim and five cubits[k] high. It took a line of thirty cubits[l] to measure around it. [3]Below the rim, figures of bulls encircled it—

---

[a]4 Some Septuagint and Syriac manuscripts; Hebrew *and a hundred and twenty*   [b]8 That is, about 23 tons (about 21 metric tons)   [c]9 That is, about 1 1/4 pounds (about 0.6 kilogram)   [d]11 That is, about 7 1/2 feet (about 2.3 meters); also in verse 15   [e]13 Or *facing inward*   [f]15 That is, about 52 feet (about 16 meters)   [g]16 Or possibly *made chains in the inner sanctuary*; the meaning of the Hebrew for this phrase is uncertain.   [h]17 *Jakin* probably means *he establishes.*   [i]17 *Boaz* probably means *in him is strength.*   [j]1 That is, about 30 feet (about 9 meters) long and wide, and about 15 feet (about 4.5 meters) high   [k]2 That is, about 7 1/2 feet (about 2.3 meters)   [l]2 That is, about 45 feet (about 13.5 meters)

ten to a cubit.*ᵃ* The bulls were cast in two rows in one piece with the Sea.   Ex 27:1-2; 2Ki 16:14

⁴The Sea stood on twelve bulls, three facing north, three facing west, three facing south and three facing east. The Sea rested on top of them, and their hindquarters were toward the center. ⁵It was a handbreadth*ᵇ* in thickness, and its rim was like the rim of a cup, like a lily blossom. It held three thousand baths.*ᶜ*

⁶He then made ten basins for washing and placed five on the south side and five on the north. In them the things to be used for the burnt offerings were rinsed, but the Sea was to be used by the priests for washing.   1Ki 7:23-26,38-51

⁷He made ten gold lampstands according to the specifications for them and placed them in the temple, five on the south side and five on the north.   Ex 25:31,40

⁸He made ten tables and placed them in the temple, five on the south side and five on the north. He also made a hundred gold sprinkling bowls.   Ex 25:23; Nu 4:14

⁹He made the courtyard of the priests, and the large court and the doors for the court, and overlaid the doors with bronze. ¹⁰He placed the Sea on the south side, at the southeast corner.   1Ki 6:36; 2Ki 21:5

¹¹He also made the pots and shovels and sprinkling bowls.

So Huram finished the work he had undertaken for King Solomon in the temple of God: 1Ki 7:14

¹²the two pillars;
  the two bowl-shaped capitals on top of the pillars;
  the two sets of network decorating the two bowl-shaped capitals on top of the pillars;
¹³the four hundred pomegranates for the two sets of network (two rows of pomegranates for each network, decorating the bowl-shaped capitals on top of the pillars);
¹⁴the stands with their basins;
¹⁵the Sea and the twelve bulls under it;
¹⁶the pots, shovels, meat forks and all related articles.

All the objects that Huram-Abi made for King Solomon for the temple of the Lᴏʀᴅ were of polished bronze. ¹⁷The king had them cast in clay molds in the plain of the Jordan between Succoth and Zarethan.*ᵈ* ¹⁸All these things that Solomon made amounted to so much that the weight of the bronze was not determined.

¹⁹Solomon also made all the furnishings that were in God's temple:

  the golden altar;

---

*ᵃ*3 That is, about 1 1/2 feet (about 0.5 meter)   *ᵇ*5 That is, about 3 inches (about 8 centimeters)
*ᶜ*5 That is, about 17,500 gallons (about 66 kiloliters)   *ᵈ*17 Hebrew *Zeredatha*, a variant of *Zarethan*

the tables on which was the bread of the Presence;

²⁰the lampstands of pure gold with their lamps, to burn in front of the inner sanctuary as prescribed;   Ex 25:31

²¹the gold floral work and lamps and tongs (they were solid gold);

²²the pure gold wick trimmers, sprinkling bowls, dishes and censers; and the gold doors of the temple: the inner doors to the Most Holy Place and the doors of the main hall.   Lev 10:1; Nu 7:14

5 When all the work Solomon had done for the temple of the LORD was finished, he brought in the things his father David had dedicated—the silver and gold and all the furnishings—and he placed them in the treasuries of God's temple.   2Sa 8:11; 1Ki 6:14

The Ark Brought to the Temple

²Then Solomon summoned to Jerusalem the elders of Israel, all the heads of the tribes and the chiefs of the Israelite families, to bring up the ark of the LORD's covenant from Zion, the City of David. ³And all the men of Israel came together to the king at the time of the festival in the seventh month.

⁴When all the elders of Israel had arrived, the Levites took up the ark, ⁵and they brought up the ark and the Tent of Meeting and all the sacred furnishings in it. The priests, who were Levites, carried them up; ⁶and King Solomon and the entire assembly of Israel that had gathered about him were before the ark, sacrificing so many sheep and cattle that they could not be recorded or counted.

⁷The priests then brought the ark of the LORD's covenant to its place in the inner sanctuary of the temple, the Most Holy Place, and put it beneath the wings of the cherubim. ⁸The cherubim spread their wings over the place of the ark and covered the ark and its carrying poles. ⁹These poles were so long that their ends, extending from the ark, could be seen from in front of the inner sanctuary, but not from outside the Holy Place; and they are still there today. ¹⁰There was nothing in the ark except the two tablets that Moses had placed in it at Horeb, where the LORD made a covenant with the Israelites after they came out of Egypt.   Dt 10:2; Ge 3:24; Rev 11:19

¹¹The priests then withdrew from the Holy Place. All the priests who were there had consecrated themselves, regardless of their divisions. ¹²All the Levites who were musicians—Asaph, Heman, Jeduthun and their sons and relatives—stood on the east side of the altar, dressed in fine linen and playing cymbals, harps and lyres. They were accompanied by 120 priests sounding trumpets. ¹³The trumpeters and singers joined in unison, as with one voice, to give

praise and thanks to the LORD. Accompanied by trumpets, cymbals and other instruments, they raised their voices in praise to the LORD and sang: 1Ch 15:24; 25:1

"He is good;
　his love endures forever."

Then the temple of the LORD was filled with a cloud, ¹⁴and the priests could not perform their service because of the cloud, for the glory of the LORD filled the temple of God. Ex 29:43; 2Ch 7:2

6 Then Solomon said, "The LORD has said that he would dwell in a dark cloud; ²I have built a magnificent temple for you, a place for you to dwell forever."

³While the whole assembly of Israel was standing there, the king turned around and blessed them. ⁴Then he said:

"Praise be to the LORD, the God of Israel, who with his hands has fulfilled what he promised with his mouth to my father David. For he said, ⁵'Since the day I brought my people out of Egypt, I have not chosen a city in any tribe of Israel to have a temple built for my Name to be there, nor have I chosen anyone to be the leader over my people Israel. ⁶But now I have chosen Jerusalem for my Name to be there, and I have chosen Da-

vid to rule my people Israel.'
⁷"My father David had it in his heart to build a temple for the Name of the LORD, the God of Israel. ⁸But the LORD said to my father David, 'Because it was in your heart to build a temple for my Name, you did well to have this in your heart. ⁹Nevertheless, you are not the one to build the temple, but your son, who is your own flesh and blood—he is the one who will build the temple for my Name.' 1Sa 10:7; Ac 7:46

¹⁰"The LORD has kept the promise he made. I have succeeded David my father and now I sit on the throne of Israel, just as the LORD promised, and I have built the temple for the Name of the LORD, the God of Israel. ¹¹There I have placed the ark, in which is the covenant of the LORD that he made with the people of Israel."

Solomon's Prayer of Dedication

¹²Then Solomon stood before the altar of the LORD in front of the whole assembly of Israel and spread out his hands. ¹³Now he had made a bronze platform, five cubits*a* long, five cubits wide and three cubits*b* high, and had placed it in the center of the outer court. He stood on the platform and then

a 13 That is, about 7 1/2 feet (about 2.3 meters)　*b 13 That is, about 4 1/2 feet (about 1.3 meters)*

knelt down before the whole assembly of Israel and spread out his hands toward heaven. [14]He said:

"O Lord, God of Israel, there is no God like you in heaven or on earth—you who keep your covenant of love with your servants who continue wholeheartedly in your way. [15]You have kept your promise to your servant David my father; with your mouth you have promised and with your hand you have fulfilled it—as it is today. *Dt 7:9*

[16]"Now Lord, God of Israel, keep for your servant David my father the promises you made to him when you said, 'You shall never fail to have a man to sit before me on the throne of Israel, if only your sons are careful in all they do to walk before me according to my law, as you have done.' [17]And now, O Lord, God of Israel, let your word that you promised your servant David come true. *2Sa 7:13,15; 1Ki 2:4*

[18]"But will God really dwell on earth with men? The heavens, even the highest heavens, cannot contain you. How much less this temple I have built! [19]Yet give attention to your servant's prayer and his plea for mercy, O Lord my God. Hear the cry and the prayer that your servant is praying in your presence.

[20]May your eyes be open toward this temple day and night, this place of which you said you would put your Name there. May you hear the prayer your servant prays toward this place. [21]Hear the supplications of your servant and of your people Israel when they pray toward this place. Hear from heaven, your dwelling place; and when you hear, forgive. *Isa 43:25; Mic 7:18*

[22]"When a man wrongs his neighbor and is required to take an oath and he comes and swears the oath before your altar in this temple, [23]then hear from heaven and act. Judge between your servants, repaying the guilty by bringing down on his own head what he has done. Declare the innocent not guilty and so establish his innocence. *Ex 22:11; Isa 3:11*

[24]"When your people Israel have been defeated by an enemy because they have sinned against you and when they turn back and confess your name, praying and making supplication before you in this temple, [25]then hear from heaven and forgive the sin of your people Israel and bring them back to the land you gave to them and their fathers. *Lev 26:17*

[26]"When the heavens are shut up and there is no rain

because your people have sinned against you, and when they pray toward this place and confess your name and turn from their sin because you have afflicted them, ²⁷then hear from heaven and forgive the sin of your servants, your people Israel. Teach them the right way to live, and send rain on the land you gave your people for an inheritance.   1Ki 17:1

²⁸"When famine or plague comes to the land, or blight or mildew, locusts or grasshoppers, or when enemies besiege them in any of their cities, whatever disaster or disease may come, ²⁹and when a prayer or plea is made by any of your people Israel—each one aware of his afflictions and pains, and spreading out his hands toward this temple — ³⁰then hear from heaven, your dwelling place. Forgive, and deal with each man according to all he does, since you know his heart (for you alone know the hearts of men), ³¹so that they will fear you and walk in your ways all the time they live in the land you gave our fathers.   1Sa 16:7

³²"As for the foreigner who does not belong to your people Israel but has come from a distant land because of your great name and your mighty hand and your outstretched arm—when he comes and prays toward this temple, ³³then hear from heaven, your dwelling place, and do whatever the foreigner asks of you, so that all the peoples of the earth may know your name and fear you, as do your own people Israel, and may know that this house I have built bears your Name.   2Ch 7:14

³⁴"When your people go to war against their enemies, wherever you send them, and when they pray to you toward this city you have chosen and the temple I have built for your Name, ³⁵then hear from heaven their prayer and their plea, and uphold their cause.

³⁶"When they sin against you—for there is no one who does not sin—and you become angry with them and give them over to the enemy, who takes them captive to a land far away or near; ³⁷and if they have a change of heart in the land where they are held captive, and repent and plead with you in the land of their captivity and say, 'We have sinned, we have done wrong and acted wickedly'; ³⁸and if they turn back to you with all their heart and soul in the land of their captivity where they were taken, and pray toward the land you gave their fathers, toward the city you have chosen and toward the

temple I have built for your Name; **39**then from heaven, your dwelling place, hear their prayer and their pleas, and uphold their cause. And forgive your people, who have sinned against you.

40"Now, my God, may your eyes be open and your ears attentive to the prayers offered in this place. 1Ki 8:22-53

41"Now arise, O Lord God,
    and come to your
    resting place,
    you and the ark of your
    might.
May your priests, O Lord
    God, be clothed
    with salvation,
may your saints rejoice
    in your goodness.
42O Lord God, do not reject
    your anointed one.
Remember the great
    love promised to
    David your
    servant." Ps 132:8-10

The Dedication of the Temple

7 When Solomon finished praying, fire came down from heaven and consumed the burnt offering and the sacrifices, and the glory of the Lord filled the temple. **2**The priests could not enter the temple of the Lord because the glory of the Lord filled it. **3**When all the Israelites saw the fire coming down and the glory of the Lord above the temple, they knelt on the pavement with their faces to the ground, and they worshiped and gave thanks to the Lord, saying, Ex 29:43; 40:35; 2Ch 5:14

"He is good;
    his love endures forever."

4Then the king and all the people offered sacrifices before the Lord. **5**And King Solomon offered a sacrifice of twenty-two thousand head of cattle and a hundred and twenty thousand sheep and goats. So the king and all the people dedicated the temple of God. **6**The priests took their positions, as did the Levites with the Lord's musical instruments, which King David had made for praising the Lord and which were used when he gave thanks, saying, "His love endures forever." Opposite the Levites, the priests blew their trumpets, and all the Israelites were standing. 1Ch 15:16; 2Ch 5:12-13

7Solomon consecrated the middle part of the courtyard in front of the temple of the Lord, and there he offered burnt offerings and the fat of the fellowship offerings,[a] because the bronze altar he had made could not hold the burnt offerings, the grain offerings and the fat portions.

8So Solomon observed the festival at that time for seven days, and all Israel with him—a vast assembly, people from Lebo*a* Hamath to the Wadi of Egypt. ⁹On the eighth day they held an assembly, for they had celebrated the dedication of the altar for seven days and the festival for seven days more. ¹⁰On the twenty-third day of the seventh month he sent the people to their homes, joyful and glad in heart for the good things the LORD had done for David and Solomon and for his people Israel.   Lev 23:36

The LORD Appears to Solomon

¹¹When Solomon had finished the temple of the LORD and the royal palace, and had succeeded in carrying out all he had in mind to do in the temple of the LORD and in his own palace, ¹²the LORD appeared to him at night and said:

"I have heard your prayer and have chosen this place for myself as a temple for sacrifices.   Dt 12:5

¹³"When I shut up the heavens so that there is no rain, or command locusts to devour the land or send a plague among my people, ¹⁴if my people, who are called by my name, will humble themselves and pray and seek my face and turn from their wicked ways, then will I hear from heaven and will forgive their sin and will heal their land. ¹⁵Now my eyes will be open

and my ears attentive to the prayers offered in this place. ¹⁶I have chosen and consecrated this temple so that my Name may be there forever. My eyes and my heart will always be there.   2Ch 6:27,37,40

¹⁷"As for you, if you walk before me as David your father did, and do all I command, and observe my decrees and laws, ¹⁸I will establish your royal throne, as I covenanted with David your father when I said, 'You shall never fail to have a man to rule over Israel.'   1Ki 9:4; 2Ch 6:16

¹⁹"But if you*b* turn away and forsake the decrees and commands I have given you*b* and go off to serve other gods and worship them, ²⁰then I will uproot Israel from my land, which I have given them, and will reject this temple I have consecrated for my Name. I will make it a byword and an object of ridicule among all peoples. ²¹And though this temple is now so imposing, all who pass by will be appalled and say, 'Why has the LORD done such a thing to this land and to this temple?' ²²People will answer, 'Because they have forsaken the LORD, the God of their fathers, who brought them out of Egypt, and have embraced

a8 Or *from the entrance to*   *b19* The Hebrew is plural.

other gods, worshiping and serving them—that is why he brought all this disaster on them.' "

Solomon's Other Activities

8 At the end of twenty years, during which Solomon built the temple of the Lord and his own palace, ²Solomon rebuilt the villages that Hiram*a* had given him, and settled Israelites in them. ³Solomon then went to Hamath Zobah and captured it. ⁴He also built up Tadmor in the desert and all the store cities he had built in Hamath. ⁵He rebuilt Upper Beth Horon and Lower Beth Horon as fortified cities, with walls and with gates and bars, ⁶as well as Baalath and all his store cities, and all the cities for his chariots and for his horses*b*—whatever he desired to build in Jerusalem, in Lebanon and throughout all the territory he ruled.

⁷All the people left from the Hittites, Amorites, Perizzites, Hivites and Jebusites (these peoples were not Israelites), ⁸that is, their descendants remaining in the land, whom the Israelites had not destroyed—these Solomon conscripted for his slave labor force, as it is to this day. ⁹But Solomon did not make slaves of the Israelites for his work; they were his fighting men, commanders of his captains, and commanders of his chariots and charioteers. ¹⁰They

were also King Solomon's chief officials—two hundred and fifty officials supervising the men. Ge 10:16

¹¹Solomon brought Pharaoh's daughter up from the City of David to the palace he had built for her, for he said, "My wife must not live in the palace of David king of Israel, because the places the ark of the Lord has entered are holy."

¹²On the altar of the Lord that he had built in front of the portico, Solomon sacrificed burnt offerings to the Lord, ¹³according to the daily requirement for offerings commanded by Moses for Sabbaths, New Moons and the three annual feasts—the Feast of Unleavened Bread, the Feast of Weeks and the Feast of Tabernacles. ¹⁴In keeping with the ordinance of his father David, he appointed the divisions of the priests for their duties, and the Levites to lead the praise and to assist the priests according to each day's requirement. He also appointed the gatekeepers by divisions for the various gates, because this was what David the man of God had ordered. ¹⁵They did not deviate from the king's commands to the priests or to the Levites in any matter, including that of the treasuries. Nu 28:3; 1Ch 25:1; Ne 12:24,36

¹⁶All Solomon's work was carried out, from the day the foundation of the temple of the Lord was laid until its completion. So the temple of the Lord was finished.

---

*a*2 Hebrew *Huram*, a variant of *Hiram*; also in verse 18   *b*6 Or *charioteers*

17Then Solomon went to Ezion Geber and Elath on the coast of Edom. **18**And Hiram sent him ships commanded by his own officers, men who knew the sea. These, with Solomon's men, sailed to Ophir and brought back four hundred and fifty talents[a] of gold, which they delivered to King Solomon. 1Ki 9:10-28; 2Ch 9:9

The Queen of Sheba Visits Solomon

9 When the queen of Sheba heard of Solomon's fame, she came to Jerusalem to test him with hard questions. Arriving with a very great caravan—with camels carrying spices, large quantities of gold, and precious stones—she came to Solomon and talked with him about all she had on her mind. **2**Solomon answered all her questions; nothing was too hard for him to explain to her. **3**When the queen of Sheba saw the wisdom of Solomon, as well as the palace he had built, **4**the food on his table, the seating of his officials, the attending servants in their robes, the cupbearers in their robes and the burnt offerings he made at[b] the temple of the LORD, she was overwhelmed. 1Ki 5:12; Mt 12:42; Lk 11:31

5She said to the king, "The report I heard in my own country about your achievements and your wisdom is true. **6**But I did not believe what they said until I came and saw with my own eyes. Indeed, not even half the greatness of your wisdom was told me; you have far exceeded the report I heard. **7**How happy your men must be! How happy your officials, who continually stand before you and hear your wisdom! **8**Praise be to the LORD your God, who has delighted in you and placed you on his throne as king to rule for the LORD your God. Because of the love of your God for Israel and his desire to uphold them forever, he has made you king over them, to maintain justice and righteousness." 1Ch 28:5; 29:23

9Then she gave the king 120 talents[c] of gold, large quantities of spices, and precious stones. There had never been such spices as those the queen of Sheba gave to King Solomon. 2Ch 8:18

10(The men of Hiram and the men of Solomon brought gold from Ophir; they also brought algumwood[d] and precious stones. **11**The king used the algumwood to make steps for the temple of the LORD and for the royal palace, and to make harps and lyres for the musicians. Nothing like them had ever been seen in Judah.) 2Ch 8:18

12King Solomon gave the queen of Sheba all she desired and asked for; he gave her more than she had brought to him. Then she left and

---

a 18 That is, about 17 tons (about 16 metric tons)   *b 4* Or *the ascent by which he went up to*
c 9 That is, about 4 1/2 tons (about 4 metric tons)   *d 10* Probably a variant of *almugwood*

returned with her retinue to her own country.   1Ki 10:1-13

Solomon's Splendor

13The weight of the gold that Solomon received yearly was 666 talents,[a] 14not including the revenues brought in by merchants and traders. Also all the kings of Arabia and the governors of the land brought gold and silver to Solomon.   2Ch 17:11; Isa 21:13; Jer 25:24

15King Solomon made two hundred large shields of hammered gold; six hundred bekas[b] of hammered gold went into each shield. 16He also made three hundred small shields of hammered gold, with three hundred bekas[c] of gold in each shield. The king put them in the Palace of the Forest of Lebanon.   1Ki 7:2; 2Ch 12:9

17Then the king made a great throne inlaid with ivory and overlaid with pure gold. 18The throne had six steps, and a footstool of gold was attached to it. On both sides of the seat were armrests, with a lion standing beside each of them. 19Twelve lions stood on the six steps, one at either end of each step. Nothing like it had ever been made for any other kingdom. 20All King Solomon's goblets were gold, and all the household articles in the Palace of the Forest of Lebanon were pure gold. Nothing was made of silver, because silver was considered of little value in Solomon's day. 21The king had a fleet of trading ships[d] manned by Hiram's[e] men. Once every three years it returned, carrying gold, silver and ivory, and apes and baboons.

22King Solomon was greater in riches and wisdom than all the other kings of the earth. 23All the kings of the earth sought audience with Solomon to hear the wisdom God had put in his heart. 24Year after year, everyone who came brought a gift—articles of silver and gold, and robes, weapons and spices, and horses and mules.

25Solomon had four thousand stalls for horses and chariots, and twelve thousand horses,[f] which he kept in the chariot cities and also with him in Jerusalem. 26He ruled over all the kings from the River[g] to the land of the Philistines, as far as the border of Egypt. 27The king made silver as common in Jerusalem as stones, and cedar as plentiful as sycamore-fig trees in the foothills. 28Solomon's horses were imported from Egypt[h] and from all other countries.

Solomon's Death

29As for the other events of Solomon's reign, from beginning to

---

a 13 That is, about 25 tons (about 23 metric tons) b 15 That is, about 7 1/2 pounds (about 3.5 kilograms) c 16 That is, about 3 3/4 pounds (about 1.7 kilograms) d 21 Hebrew of ships that could go to Tarshish e 21 Hebrew Huram, a variant of Hiram f 25 Or charioteers g 26 That is, the Euphrates h 28 Or possibly Muzur, a region in Cilicia

end, are they not written in the records of Nathan the prophet, in the prophecy of Ahijah the Shilonite and in the visions of Iddo the seer concerning Jeroboam son of Nebat? ³⁰Solomon reigned in Jerusalem over all Israel forty years. ³¹Then he rested with his fathers and was buried in the city of David his father. And Rehoboam his son succeeded him as king.   1Ki 2:10

Israel Rebels Against Rehoboam

10 Rehoboam went to Shechem, for all the Israelites had gone there to make him king. ²When Jeroboam son of Nebat heard this (he was in Egypt, where he had fled from King Solomon), he returned from Egypt. ³So they sent for Jeroboam, and he and all Israel went to Rehoboam and said to him: ⁴"Your father put a heavy yoke on us, but now lighten the harsh labor and the heavy yoke he put on us, and we will serve you."

⁵Rehoboam answered, "Come back to me in three days." So the people went away.

⁶Then King Rehoboam consulted the elders who had served his father Solomon during his lifetime. "How would you advise me to answer these people?" he asked.

⁷They replied, "If you will be kind to these people and please them and give them a favorable answer, they will always be your servants."   Pr 15:1

⁸But Rehoboam rejected the advice the elders gave him and consulted the young men who had grown up with him and were serving him. ⁹He asked them, "What is your advice? How should we answer these people who say to me, 'Lighten the yoke your father put on us'?"   2Sa 17:14; Pr 13:20

¹⁰The young men who had grown up with him replied, "Tell the people who have said to you, 'Your father put a heavy yoke on us, but make our yoke lighter'— tell them, 'My little finger is thicker than my father's waist. ¹¹My father laid on you a heavy yoke; I will make it even heavier. My father scourged you with whips; I will scourge you with scorpions.' "

¹²Three days later Jeroboam and all the people returned to Rehoboam, as the king had said, "Come back to me in three days." ¹³The king answered them harshly. Rejecting the advice of the elders, ¹⁴he followed the advice of the young men and said, "My father made your yoke heavy; I will make it even heavier. My father scourged you with whips; I will scourge you with scorpions." ¹⁵So the king did not listen to the people, for this turn of events was from God, to fulfill the word the LORD had spoken to Jeroboam son of Nebat through Ahijah the Shilonite.   1Ki 11:29; 2Ch 25:16-20

¹⁶When all Israel saw that the king refused to listen to them, they answered the king: 1Ch 9:1

"What share do we have in
     David,   2Sa 20:1
   what part in Jesse's
     son?
To your tents, O Israel!
   Look after your own house,
     O David!"

So all the Israelites went home.
¹⁷But as for the Israelites who were
living in the towns of Judah, Rehoboam still ruled over them.

¹⁸King Rehoboam sent out Adoniram,ᵃ who was in charge of
forced labor, but the Israelites
stoned him to death. King Rehoboam, however, managed to get into
his chariot and escape to Jerusalem. ¹⁹So Israel has been in rebellion against the house of David to
this day.   1Ki 5:14

11 When Rehoboam arrived
in Jerusalem, he mustered
the house of Judah and Benjamin
—a hundred and eighty thousand
fighting men—to make war
against Israel and to regain the
kingdom for Rehoboam.   1Ki 12:21
²But this word of the LORD came
to Shemaiah the man of God: ³"Say
to Rehoboam son of Solomon king
of Judah and to all the Israelites in
Judah and Benjamin, ⁴"This is
what the LORD says: Do not go up
to fight against your brothers. Go
home, every one of you, for this
is my doing.'" So they obeyed
the words of the LORD and turned
back from marching against Jeroboam.

Rehoboam Fortifies Judah

⁵Rehoboam lived in Jerusalem
and built up towns for defense in
Judah: ⁶Bethlehem, Etam, Tekoa,
⁷Beth Zur, Soco, Adullam, ⁸Gath,
Mareshah, Ziph, ⁹Adoraim, Lachish, Azekah, ¹⁰Zorah, Aijalon
and Hebron. These were fortified
cities in Judah and Benjamin. ¹¹He
strengthened their defenses and
put commanders in them, with
supplies of food, olive oil and
wine. ¹²He put shields and spears
in all the cities, and made them
very strong. So Judah and Benjamin were his.

¹³The priests and Levites from
all their districts throughout Israel
sided with him. ¹⁴The Levites even
abandoned their pasturelands and
property, and came to Judah and
Jerusalem because Jeroboam and
his sons had rejected them as
priests of the LORD. ¹⁵And he appointed his own priests for the
high places and for the goat and
calf idols he had made. ¹⁶Those
from every tribe of Israel who set
their hearts on seeking the LORD,
the God of Israel, followed the Levites to Jerusalem to offer sacrifices to the LORD, the God of their
fathers. ¹⁷They strengthened the
kingdom of Judah and supported
Rehoboam son of Solomon three
years, walking in the ways of
David and Solomon during this
time.

ᵃ 18 Hebrew *Hadoram*, a variant of *Adoniram*

Rehoboam's Family

18Rehoboam married Mahalath, who was the daughter of David's son Jerimoth and of Abihail, the daughter of Jesse's son Eliab. **19**She bore him sons: Jeush, Shemariah and Zaham. **20**Then he married Maacah daughter of Absalom, who bore him Abijah, Attai, Ziza and Shelomith. **21**Rehoboam loved Maacah daughter of Absalom more than any of his other wives and concubines. In all, he had eighteen wives and sixty concubines, twenty-eight sons and sixty daughters.   Dt 17:17; 1Ki 15:2

22Rehoboam appointed Abijah son of Maacah to be the chief prince among his brothers, in order to make him king. **23**He acted wisely, dispersing some of his sons throughout the districts of Judah and Benjamin, and to all the fortified cities. He gave them abundant provisions and took many wives for them.   Dt 21:15-17

Shishak Attacks Jerusalem

12 After Rehoboam's position as king was established and he had become strong, he and all Israel[a] with him abandoned the law of the LORD. **2**Because they had been unfaithful to the LORD, Shishak king of Egypt attacked Jerusalem in the fifth year of King Rehoboam. **3**With twelve hundred chariots and sixty thousand horsemen and the innumerable troops of Libyans, Sukkites and Cushites[b] that came with him from Egypt, **4**he captured the fortified cities of Judah and came as far as Jerusalem.   2Ch 11:10; 16:8

5Then the prophet Shemaiah came to Rehoboam and to the leaders of Judah who had assembled in Jerusalem for fear of Shishak, and he said to them, "This is what the LORD says, 'You have abandoned me; therefore, I now abandon you to Shishak.' "

6The leaders of Israel and the king humbled themselves and said, "The LORD is just."   Ex 9:27

7When the LORD saw that they humbled themselves, this word of the LORD came to Shemaiah: "Since they have humbled themselves, I will not destroy them but will soon give them deliverance. My wrath will not be poured out on Jerusalem through Shishak. **8**They will, however, become subject to him, so that they may learn the difference between serving me and serving the kings of other lands."   Dt 28:48; 1Ki 21:29; Ps 78:38

9When Shishak king of Egypt attacked Jerusalem, he carried off the treasures of the temple of the LORD and the treasures of the royal palace. He took everything, including the gold shields Solomon had made. **10**So King Rehoboam made bronze shields to replace them and assigned these to the commanders of the guard on duty at the en-

---

a 1 That is, Judah, as frequently in 2 Chronicles   *b 3* That is, people from the upper Nile region

trance to the royal palace. [11]Whenever the king went to the LORD's temple, the guards went with him, bearing the shields, and afterward they returned them to the guardroom.   2Ch 9:16

[12]Because Rehoboam humbled himself, the LORD's anger turned from him, and he was not totally destroyed. Indeed, there was some good in Judah.   2Ch 19:3

[13]King Rehoboam established himself firmly in Jerusalem and continued as king. He was forty-one years old when he became king, and he reigned seventeen years in Jerusalem, the city the LORD had chosen out of all the tribes of Israel in which to put his Name. His mother's name was Naamah; she was an Ammonite. [14]He did evil because he had not set his heart on seeking the LORD.   Dt 12:5

[15]As for the events of Rehoboam's reign, from beginning to end, are they not written in the records of Shemaiah the prophet and of Iddo the seer that deal with genealogies? There was continual warfare between Rehoboam and Jeroboam. [16]Rehoboam rested with his fathers and was buried in the City of David. And Abijah his son succeeded him as king.   1Ki 14:21,25-31

Abijah King of Judah

13 In the eighteenth year of the reign of Jeroboam, Abijah became king of Judah, [2]and he reigned in Jerusalem three years. His mother's name was Maacah,[a] a daughter[b] of Uriel of Gibeah.

There was war between Abijah and Jeroboam. [3]Abijah went into battle with a force of four hundred thousand able fighting men, and Jeroboam drew up a battle line against him with eight hundred thousand able troops.   1Ki 15:6

[4]Abijah stood on Mount Zemaraim, in the hill country of Ephraim, and said, "Jeroboam and all Israel, listen to me! [5]Don't you know that the LORD, the God of Israel, has given the kingship of Israel to David and his descendants forever by a covenant of salt? [6]Yet Jeroboam son of Nebat, an official of Solomon son of David, rebelled against his master. [7]Some worthless scoundrels gathered around him and opposed Rehoboam son of Solomon when he was young and indecisive and not strong enough to resist them.   Nu 18:19

[8]"And now you plan to resist the kingdom of the LORD, which is in the hands of David's descendants. You are indeed a vast army and have with you the golden calves that Jeroboam made to be your gods. [9]But didn't you drive out the priests of the LORD, the sons of Aaron, and the Levites, and make priests of your own as the peoples of other lands do? Whoever comes

---

[a]2 Most Septuagint manuscripts and Syriac (see also 2 Chron. 11:20 and 1 Kings 15:2); Hebrew *Micaiah*
[b]2 Or *granddaughter*

to consecrate himself with a young bull and seven rams may become a priest of what are not gods.

10"As for us, the Lord is our God, and we have not forsaken him. The priests who serve the Lord are sons of Aaron, and the Levites assist them. 11Every morning and evening they present burnt offerings and fragrant incense to the Lord. They set out the bread on the ceremonially clean table and light the lamps on the gold lampstand every evening. We are observing the requirements of the Lord our God. But you have forsaken him. 12God is with us; he is our leader. His priests with their trumpets will sound the battle cry against you. Men of Israel, do not fight against the Lord, the God of your fathers, for you will not succeed." Nu 10:8-9; Ac 5:39

13Now Jeroboam had sent troops around to the rear, so that while he was in front of Judah the ambush was behind them. 14Judah turned and saw that they were being attacked at both front and rear. Then they cried out to the Lord. The priests blew their trumpets 15and the men of Judah raised the battle cry. At the sound of their battle cry, God routed Jeroboam and all Israel before Abijah and Judah. 16The Israelites fled before Judah, and God delivered them into their hands. 17Abijah and his men inflicted heavy losses on them, so that there were five hundred thousand casualties among Israel's able men. 18The men of Israel were subdued on that occasion, and the men of Judah were victorious because they relied on the Lord, the God of their fathers. 2Ch 14:11; 16:8

19Abijah pursued Jeroboam and took from him the towns of Bethel, Jeshanah and Ephron, with their surrounding villages. 20Jeroboam did not regain power during the time of Abijah. And the Lord struck him down and he died.

21But Abijah grew in strength. He married fourteen wives and had twenty-two sons and sixteen daughters.

22The other events of Abijah's reign, what he did and what he said, are written in the annotations of the prophet Iddo.

14 And Abijah rested with his fathers and was buried in the City of David. Asa his son succeeded him as king, and in his days the country was at peace for ten years. 1Ki 15:1-2,6-8

Asa King of Judah

2Asa did what was good and right in the eyes of the Lord his God. 3He removed the foreign altars and the high places, smashed the sacred stones and cut down the Asherah poles.*a* 4He commanded Judah to seek the Lord, the God of their fathers, and to obey his laws and commands. 5He

a 3 That is, symbols of the goddess Asherah; here and elsewhere in 2 Chronicles removed the high places and incense altars in every town in Judah, and the kingdom was at peace under him. ⁶He built up the fortified cities of Judah, since the land was at peace. No one was at war with him during those years, for the LORD gave him rest.   1Ki 15:11-12

⁷"Let us build up these towns," he said to Judah, "and put walls around them, with towers, gates and bars. The land is still ours, because we have sought the LORD our God; we sought him and he has given us rest on every side." So they built and prospered.

⁸Asa had an army of three hundred thousand men from Judah, equipped with large shields and with spears, and two hundred and eighty thousand from Benjamin, armed with small shields and with bows. All these were brave fighting men.

⁹Zerah the Cushite marched out against them with a vast army*a* and three hundred chariots, and came as far as Mareshah. ¹⁰Asa went out to meet him, and they took up battle positions in the Valley of Zephathah near Mareshah.

¹¹Then Asa called to the LORD his God and said, "LORD, there is no one like you to help the powerless against the mighty. Help us, O LORD our God, for we rely on you, and in your name we have come against this vast army. O LORD, you

are our God; do not let man prevail against you."   1Sa 17:45; 2Ch 13:14

¹²The LORD struck down the Cushites before Asa and Judah. The Cushites fled, ¹³and Asa and his army pursued them as far as Gerar. Such a great number of Cushites fell that they could not recover; they were crushed before the LORD and his forces. The men of Judah carried off a large amount of plunder. ¹⁴They destroyed all the villages around Gerar, for the terror of the LORD had fallen upon them. They plundered all these villages, since there was much booty there. ¹⁵They also attacked the camps of the herdsmen and carried off droves of sheep and goats and camels. Then they returned to Jerusalem.   Ge 10:19; 35:5; 2Ch 13:15

Asa's Reform

15 The Spirit of God came upon Azariah son of Oded. ²He went out to meet Asa and said to him, "Listen to me, Asa and all Judah and Benjamin. The LORD is with you when you are with him. If you seek him, he will be found by you, but if you forsake him, he will forsake you. ³For a long time Israel was without the true God, without a priest to teach and without the law. ⁴But in their distress they turned to the LORD, the God of Israel, and sought him, and he was found by them. ⁵In those days it was not safe to travel about, for all

---

a 9 Hebrew with an army of a thousand thousands or with an army of thousands upon thousands

the inhabitants of the lands were in great turmoil. ⁶One nation was being crushed by another and one city by another, because God was troubling them with every kind of distress. ⁷But as for you, be strong and do not give up, for your work will be rewarded."   Jos 1:7,9; Jas 4:8

⁸When Asa heard these words and the prophecy of Azariah son of*ᵃ* Oded the prophet, he took courage. He removed the detestable idols from the whole land of Judah and Benjamin and from the towns he had captured in the hills of Ephraim. He repaired the altar of the Lᴏʀᴅ that was in front of the portico of the Lᴏʀᴅ's temple.

⁹Then he assembled all Judah and Benjamin and the people from Ephraim, Manasseh and Simeon who had settled among them, for large numbers had come over to him from Israel when they saw that the Lᴏʀᴅ his God was with him.   2Ch 11:16-17

¹⁰They assembled at Jerusalem in the third month of the fifteenth year of Asa's reign. ¹¹At that time they sacrificed to the Lᴏʀᴅ seven hundred head of cattle and seven thousand sheep and goats from the plunder they had brought back. ¹²They entered into a covenant to seek the Lᴏʀᴅ, the God of their fathers, with all their heart and soul. ¹³All who would not seek the Lᴏʀᴅ, the God of Israel, were to be put to death, whether small or great, man or woman. ¹⁴They took an oath to the Lᴏʀᴅ with loud acclamation, with shouting and with trumpets and horns. ¹⁵All Judah rejoiced about the oath because they had sworn it wholeheartedly. They sought God eagerly, and he was found by them. So the Lᴏʀᴅ gave them rest on every side.

¹⁶King Asa also deposed his grandmother Maacah from her position as queen mother, because she had made a repulsive Asherah pole. Asa cut the pole down, broke it up and burned it in the Kidron Valley. ¹⁷Although he did not remove the high places from Israel, Asa's heart was fully committed ₗto the Lᴏʀᴅ⌋ all his life. ¹⁸He brought into the temple of God the silver and gold and the articles that he and his father had dedicated.

¹⁹There was no more war until the thirty-fifth year of Asa's reign.

Asa's Last Years

16 In the thirty-sixth year of Asa's reign Baasha king of Israel went up against Judah and fortified Ramah to prevent anyone from leaving or entering the territory of Asa king of Judah.   Jer 41:9

²Asa then took the silver and gold out of the treasuries of the Lᴏʀᴅ's temple and of his own palace and sent it to Ben-Hadad king of Aram, who was ruling in Damascus. ³"Let there be a treaty between me and you," he said, "as

---

ᵃ 8 Vulgate and Syriac (see also Septuagint and verse 1); Hebrew does not have *Azariah son of.*

there was between my father and your father. See, I am sending you silver and gold. Now break your treaty with Baasha king of Israel so he will withdraw from me."

⁴Ben-Hadad agreed with King Asa and sent the commanders of his forces against the towns of Israel. They conquered Ijon, Dan, Abel Maim*a* and all the store cities of Naphtali. ⁵When Baasha heard this, he stopped building Ramah and abandoned his work. ⁶Then King Asa brought all the men of Judah, and they carried away from Ramah the stones and timber Baasha had been using. With them he built up Geba and Mizpah.

⁷At that time Hanani the seer came to Asa king of Judah and said to him: "Because you relied on the king of Aram and not on the Lord your God, the army of the king of Aram has escaped from your hand. ⁸Were not the Cushites*b* and Libyans a mighty army with great numbers of chariots and horsemen*c*? Yet when you relied on the Lord, he delivered them into your hand. ⁹For the eyes of the Lord range throughout the earth to strengthen those whose hearts are fully committed to him. You have done a foolish thing, and from now on you will be at war." 1Sa 13:13; Pr 15:3

¹⁰Asa was angry with the seer because of this; he was so enraged that he put him in prison. At the same time Asa brutally oppressed some of the people.

¹¹The events of Asa's reign, from beginning to end, are written in the book of the kings of Judah and Israel. ¹²In the thirty-ninth year of his reign Asa was afflicted with a disease in his feet. Though his disease was severe, even in his illness he did not seek help from the Lord, but only from the physicians. ¹³Then in the forty-first year of his reign Asa died and rested with his fathers. ¹⁴They buried him in the tomb that he had cut out for himself in the City of David. They laid him on a bier covered with spices and various blended perfumes, and they made a huge fire in his honor. Ge 50:2; 2Ch 21:19

Jehoshaphat King of Judah

17 Jehoshaphat his son succeeded him as king and strengthened himself against Israel. ²He stationed troops in all the fortified cities of Judah and put garrisons in Judah and in the towns of Ephraim that his father Asa had captured. 1Ki 15:23-24

³The Lord was with Jehoshaphat because in his early years he walked in the ways his father David had followed. He did not consult the Baals ⁴but sought the God of his father and followed his commands rather than the practices of Israel. ⁵The Lord established the

---

*a*4 Also known as *Abel Beth Maacah*   *b*8 That is, people from the upper Nile region   *c*8 Or *charioteers*

kingdom under his control; and all Judah brought gifts to Jehoshaphat, so that he had great wealth and honor. ⁶His heart was devoted to the ways of the LORD; furthermore, he removed the high places and the Asherah poles from Judah.

⁷In the third year of his reign he sent his officials Ben-Hail, Obadiah, Zechariah, Nethanel and Micaiah to teach in the towns of Judah. ⁸With them were certain Levites— Shemaiah, Nethaniah, Zebadiah, Asahel, Shemiramoth, Jehonathan, Adonijah, Tobijah and Tob-Adonijah—and the priests Elishama and Jehoram. ⁹They taught throughout Judah, taking with them the Book of the Law of the LORD; they went around to all the towns of Judah and taught the people.   Dt 6:4-9; 2Ch 15:3; 19:8

¹⁰The fear of the LORD fell on all the kingdoms of the lands surrounding Judah, so that they did not make war with Jehoshaphat. ¹¹Some Philistines brought Jehoshaphat gifts and silver as tribute, and the Arabs brought him flocks: seven thousand seven hundred rams and seven thousand seven hundred goats.   Ge 35:5

¹²Jehoshaphat became more and more powerful; he built forts and store cities in Judah ¹³and had large supplies in the towns of Judah. He also kept experienced fighting men in Jerusalem. ¹⁴Their enrollment by families was as follows: 2Sa 24:2

From Judah, commanders of units of 1,000:
Adnah the commander, with 300,000 fighting men;
¹⁵next, Jehohanan the commander, with 280,000;
¹⁶next, Amasiah son of Zicri, who volunteered himself for the service of the LORD, with 200,000.
¹⁷From Benjamin: Nu 1:36
Eliada, a valiant soldier, with 200,000 men armed with bows and shields;
¹⁸next, Jehozabad, with 180,000 men armed for battle.

¹⁹These were the men who served the king, besides those he stationed in the fortified cities throughout Judah.   2Ch 11:10; 25:5

Micaiah Prophesies Against Ahab

18 Now Jehoshaphat had great wealth and honor, and he allied himself with Ahab by marriage. ²Some years later he went down to visit Ahab in Samaria. Ahab slaughtered many sheep and cattle for him and the people with him and urged him to attack Ramoth Gilead. ³Ahab king of Israel asked Jehoshaphat king of Judah, "Will you go with me against Ramoth Gilead?"   2Ch 17:5; 21:6

Jehoshaphat replied, "I am as you are, and my people as your people; we will join you in the war." ⁴But Jehoshaphat also said to the king of Israel, "First seek the counsel of the LORD."

⁵So the king of Israel brought together the prophets—four hundred men—and asked them, "Shall we go to war against Ramoth Gilead, or shall I refrain?"

"Go," they answered, "for God will give it into the king's hand."

⁶But Jehoshaphat asked, "Is there not a prophet of the LORD here whom we can inquire of?"

⁷The king of Israel answered Jehoshaphat, "There is still one man through whom we can inquire of the LORD, but I hate him because he never prophesies anything good about me, but always bad. He is Micaiah son of Imlah."

"The king should not say that," Jehoshaphat replied.

⁸So the king of Israel called one of his officials and said, "Bring Micaiah son of Imlah at once."

⁹Dressed in their royal robes, the king of Israel and Jehoshaphat king of Judah were sitting on their thrones at the threshing floor by the entrance to the gate of Samaria, with all the prophets prophesying before them. ¹⁰Now Zedekiah son of Kenaanah had made iron horns, and he declared, "This is what the LORD says: 'With these you will gore the Arameans until they are destroyed.' "

¹¹All the other prophets were prophesying the same thing. "Attack Ramoth Gilead and be victori-

ous," they said, "for the LORD will give it into the king's hand."

¹²The messenger who had gone to summon Micaiah said to him, "Look, as one man the other prophets are predicting success for the king. Let your word agree with theirs, and speak favorably."

¹³But Micaiah said, "As surely as the LORD lives, I can tell him only what my God says."   Nu 22:18,20,35

¹⁴When he arrived, the king asked him, "Micaiah, shall we go to war against Ramoth Gilead, or shall I refrain?"

"Attack and be victorious," he answered, "for they will be given into your hand."

¹⁵The king said to him, "How many times must I make you swear to tell me nothing but the truth in the name of the LORD?"

¹⁶Then Micaiah answered, "I saw all Israel scattered on the hills like sheep without a shepherd, and the LORD said, 'These people have no master. Let each one go home in peace.' "   Nu 27:17; Eze 34:5-8

¹⁷The king of Israel said to Jehoshaphat, "Didn't I tell you that he never prophesies anything good about me, but only bad?"

¹⁸Micaiah continued, "Therefore hear the word of the LORD: I saw the LORD sitting on his throne with all the host of heaven standing on his right and on his left. ¹⁹And the LORD said, 'Who will entice Ahab king of Israel into attacking Ramoth Gilead and going to his death there?'   Da 7:9

"One suggested this, and another that. ²⁰Finally, a spirit came forward, stood before the Lord and said, 'I will entice him.'

" 'By what means?' the Lord asked.

²¹" 'I will go and be a lying spirit in the mouths of all his prophets,' he said.   Job 1:6; Jn 8:44

" 'You will succeed in enticing him,' said the Lord. 'Go and do it.'

²²"So now the Lord has put a lying spirit in the mouths of these prophets of yours. The Lord has decreed disaster for you."

²³Then Zedekiah son of Kenaanah went up and slapped Micaiah in the face. "Which way did the spirit from*ᵃ* the Lord go when he went from me to speak to you?" he asked.   Jer 20:2; Mk 14:65; Ac 23:2

²⁴Micaiah replied, "You will find out on the day you go to hide in an inner room."

²⁵The king of Israel then ordered, "Take Micaiah and send him back to Amon the ruler of the city and to Joash the king's son, ²⁶and say, 'This is what the king says: Put this fellow in prison and give him nothing but bread and water until I return safely.' "

²⁷Micaiah declared, "If you ever return safely, the Lord has not spoken through me." Then he added, "Mark my words, all you people!"

Ahab Killed at Ramoth Gilead

²⁸So the king of Israel and Jehoshaphat king of Judah went up to Ramoth Gilead. ²⁹The king of Israel said to Jehoshaphat, "I will enter the battle in disguise, but you wear your royal robes." So the king of Israel disguised himself and went into battle.

³⁰Now the king of Aram had ordered his chariot commanders, "Do not fight with anyone, small or great, except the king of Israel." ³¹When the chariot commanders saw Jehoshaphat, they thought, "This is the king of Israel." So they turned to attack him, but Jehoshaphat cried out, and the Lord helped him. God drew them away from him, ³²for when the chariot commanders saw that he was not the king of Israel, they stopped pursuing him.

³³But someone drew his bow at random and hit the king of Israel between the sections of his armor. The king told the chariot driver, "Wheel around and get me out of the fighting. I've been wounded." ³⁴All day long the battle raged, and the king of Israel propped himself up in his chariot facing the Arameans until evening. Then at sunset he died.   1Ki 22:29-36; 2Ch 13:14

19 When Jehoshaphat king of Judah returned safely to his palace in Jerusalem, ²Jehu the seer, the son of Hanani, went out to meet him and said to the king, "Should you help the wicked and love*ᵇ* those who hate the Lord? Be-

ᵃ 23 Or Spirit of   *ᵇ 2 Or and make alliances with*

cause of this, the wrath of the Lord is upon you. ³There is, however, some good in you, for you have rid the land of the Asherah poles and have set your heart on seeking God."   2Ch 17:6; 32:25; Ps 139:21-22

Jehoshaphat Appoints Judges

⁴Jehoshaphat lived in Jerusalem, and he went out again among the people from Beersheba to the hill country of Ephraim and turned them back to the Lord, the God of their fathers. ⁵He appointed judges in the land, in each of the fortified cities of Judah. ⁶He told them, "Consider carefully what you do, because you are not judging for man but for the Lord, who is with you whenever you give a verdict. ⁷Now let the fear of the Lord be upon you. Judge carefully, for with the Lord our God there is no injustice or partiality or bribery."

⁸In Jerusalem also, Jehoshaphat appointed some of the Levites, priests and heads of Israelite families to administer the law of the Lord and to settle disputes. And they lived in Jerusalem. ⁹He gave them these orders: "You must serve faithfully and wholeheartedly in the fear of the Lord. ¹⁰In every case that comes before you from your fellow countrymen who live in the cities—whether bloodshed or other concerns of the law, com-

mands, decrees or ordinances—you are to warn them not to sin against the Lord; otherwise his wrath will come on you and your brothers. Do this, and you will not sin.   Dt 17:8-13; 2Ch 17:8-9

¹¹"Amariah the chief priest will be over you in any matter concerning the Lord, and Zebadiah son of Ishmael, the leader of the tribe of Judah, will be over you in any matter concerning the king, and the Levites will serve as officials before you. Act with courage, and may the Lord be with those who do well."   1Ch 28:20

Jehoshaphat Defeats Moab and Ammon

20 After this, the Moabites and Ammonites with some of the Meunites[a] came to make war on Jehoshaphat.   1Ch 4:41

²Some men came and told Jehoshaphat, "A vast army is coming against you from Edom,[b] from the other side of the Sea.[c] It is already in Hazazon Tamar" (that is, En Gedi). ³Alarmed, Jehoshaphat resolved to inquire of the Lord, and he proclaimed a fast for all Judah. ⁴The people of Judah came together to seek help from the Lord; indeed, they came from every town in Judah to seek him.   Ge 14:7

⁵Then Jehoshaphat stood up in the assembly of Judah and Jerusalem at the temple of the Lord in the

---

[a]1 Some Septuagint manuscripts; Hebrew *Ammonites*   [b]2 One Hebrew manuscript; most Hebrew manuscripts, Septuagint and Vulgate *Aram*   [c]2 That is, the Dead Sea

front of the new courtyard ⁶and said:

"O LORD, God of our fathers, are you not the God who is in heaven? You rule over all the kingdoms of the nations. Power and might are in your hand, and no one can withstand you. ⁷O our God, did you not drive out the inhabitants of this land before your people Israel and give it forever to the descendants of Abraham your friend? ⁸They have lived in it and have built in it a sanctuary for your Name, saying, ⁹'If calamity comes upon us, whether the sword of judgment, or plague or famine, we will stand in your presence before this temple that bears your Name and will cry out to you in our distress, and you will hear us and save us.' Dt 4:39; 1Ch 29:11-12; Isa 41:8

¹⁰"But now here are men from Ammon, Moab and Mount Seir, whose territory you would not allow Israel to invade when they came from Egypt; so they turned away from them and did not destroy them. ¹¹See how they are repaying us by coming to drive us out of the possession you gave us as an inheritance. ¹²O our God, will you not judge them? For we have no power to face this vast army that is attacking us. We do not know what to do, but our eyes are upon you." Ps 25:15; 83:1-12

¹³All the men of Judah, with their wives and children and little ones, stood there before the LORD.

¹⁴Then the Spirit of the LORD came upon Jahaziel son of Zechariah, the son of Benaiah, the son of Jeiel, the son of Mattaniah, a Levite and descendant of Asaph, as he stood in the assembly. 2Ch 15:1

¹⁵He said: "Listen, King Jehoshaphat and all who live in Judah and Jerusalem! This is what the LORD says to you: 'Do not be afraid or discouraged because of this vast army. For the battle is not yours, but God's. ¹⁶Tomorrow march down against them. They will be climbing up by the Pass of Ziz, and you will find them at the end of the gorge in the Desert of Jeruel. ¹⁷You will not have to fight this battle. Take up your positions; stand firm and see the deliverance the LORD will give you, O Judah and Jerusalem. Do not be afraid; do not be discouraged. Go out to face them tomorrow, and the LORD will be with you.'" Ex 14:13; 1Sa 17:47; 2Ch 32:7

¹⁸Jehoshaphat bowed with his face to the ground, and all the people of Judah and Jerusalem fell down in worship before the LORD. ¹⁹Then some Levites from the Kohathites and Korahites stood up and praised the LORD, the God of Israel, with very loud voice.

²⁰Early in the morning they left for the Desert of Tekoa. As they set

out, Jehoshaphat stood and said, "Listen to me, Judah and people of Jerusalem! Have faith in the LORD your God and you will be upheld; have faith in his prophets and you will be successful." [21]After consulting the people, Jehoshaphat appointed men to sing to the LORD and to praise him for the splendor of his[a] holiness as they went out at the head of the army, saying:

"Give thanks to the LORD,
    for his love endures forever."

[22]As they began to sing and praise, the LORD set ambushes against the men of Ammon and Moab and Mount Seir who were invading Judah, and they were defeated. [23]The men of Ammon and Moab rose up against the men from Mount Seir to destroy and annihilate them. After they finished slaughtering the men from Seir, they helped to destroy one another.   Jdg 7:22; 1Sa 14:20; 2Ch 23:13

[24]When the men of Judah came to the place that overlooks the desert and looked toward the vast army, they saw only dead bodies lying on the ground; no one had escaped. [25]So Jehoshaphat and his men went to carry off their plunder, and they found among them a great amount of equipment and clothing[b] and also articles of value —more than they could take away.

There was so much plunder that it took three days to collect it. [26]On the fourth day they assembled in the Valley of Beracah, where they praised the LORD. This is why it is called the Valley of Beracah[c] to this day.

[27]Then, led by Jehoshaphat, all the men of Judah and Jerusalem returned joyfully to Jerusalem, for the LORD had given them cause to rejoice over their enemies. [28]They entered Jerusalem and went to the temple of the LORD with harps and lutes and trumpets.

[29]The fear of God came upon all the kingdoms of the countries when they heard how the LORD had fought against the enemies of Israel. [30]And the kingdom of Jehoshaphat was at peace, for his God had given him rest on every side.   2Ch 15:15; 17:10

The End of Jehoshaphat's Reign

[31]So Jehoshaphat reigned over Judah. He was thirty-five years old when he became king of Judah, and he reigned in Jerusalem twenty-five years. His mother's name was Azubah daughter of Shilhi. [32]He walked in the ways of his father Asa and did not stray from them; he did what was right in the eyes of the LORD. [33]The high places, however, were not removed, and the people still had

---

[a] 21 Or *him with the splendor of*   [b] 25 Some Hebrew manuscripts and Vulgate; most Hebrew manuscripts *corpses*   [c] 26 *Beracah* means *praise.*

not set their hearts on the God of their fathers. 2Ch 17:6; 19:3

³⁴The other events of Jehoshaphat's reign, from beginning to end, are written in the annals of Jehu son of Hanani, which are recorded in the book of the kings of Israel. 1Ki 16:1

³⁵Later, Jehoshaphat king of Judah made an alliance with Ahaziah king of Israel, who was guilty of wickedness. ³⁶He agreed with him to construct a fleet of trading ships.ᵃ After these were built at Ezion Geber, ³⁷Eliezer son of Dodavahu of Mareshah prophesied against Jehoshaphat, saying, "Because you have made an alliance with Ahaziah, the LORD will destroy what you have made." The ships were wrecked and were not able to set sail to trade.ᵇ

21 Then Jehoshaphat rested with his fathers and was buried with them in the City of David. And Jehoram his son succeeded him as king. ²Jehoram's brothers, the sons of Jehoshaphat, were Azariah, Jehiel, Zechariah, Azariahu, Michael and Shephatiah. All these were sons of Jehoshaphat king of Israel.ᶜ ³Their father had given them many gifts of silver and gold and articles of value, as well as fortified cities in Judah, but he had given the kingdom to Jehoram because he was his firstborn son.

Jehoram King of Judah

⁴When Jehoram established himself firmly over his father's kingdom, he put all his brothers to the sword along with some of the princes of Israel. ⁵Jehoram was thirty-two years old when he became king, and he reigned in Jerusalem eight years. ⁶He walked in the ways of the kings of Israel, as the house of Ahab had done, for he married a daughter of Ahab. He did evil in the eyes of the LORD. ⁷Nevertheless, because of the covenant the LORD had made with David, the LORD was not willing to destroy the house of David. He had promised to maintain a lamp for him and his descendants forever.

⁸In the time of Jehoram, Edom rebelled against Judah and set up its own king. ⁹So Jehoram went there with his officers and all his chariots. The Edomites surrounded him and his chariot commanders, but he rose up and broke through by night. ¹⁰To this day Edom has been in rebellion against Judah.

Libnah revolted at the same time, because Jehoram had forsaken the LORD, the God of his fathers. ¹¹He had also built high places on the hills of Judah and had caused the people of Jerusalem to prostitute themselves and had led Judah astray.

ᵃ 36 Hebrew *of ships that could go to Tarshish*   ᵇ 37 Hebrew *sail for Tarshish*   ᶜ 2 That is, Judah, as frequently in 2 Chronicles

¹²Jehoram received a letter from Elijah the prophet, which said:

"This is what the LORD, the God of your father David, says: 'You have not walked in the ways of your father Jehoshaphat or of Asa king of Judah. ¹³But you have walked in the ways of the kings of Israel, and you have led Judah and the people of Jerusalem to prostitute themselves, just as the house of Ahab did. You have also murdered your own brothers, members of your father's house, men who were better than you. ¹⁴So now the LORD is about to strike your people, your sons, your wives and everything that is yours, with a heavy blow. ¹⁵You yourself will be very ill with a lingering disease of the bowels, until the disease causes your bowels to come out.' "

¹⁶The LORD aroused against Jehoram the hostility of the Philistines and of the Arabs who lived near the Cushites. ¹⁷They attacked Judah, invaded it and carried off all the goods found in the king's palace, together with his sons and wives. Not a son was left to him except Ahaziah,ᵃ the youngest.

¹⁸After all this, the LORD afflicted Jehoram with an incurable disease of the bowels. ¹⁹In the course of time, at the end of the second year, his bowels came out because of the disease, and he died in great pain. His people made no fire in his honor, as they had for his fathers.   2Ch 16:14

²⁰Jehoram was thirty-two years old when he became king, and he reigned in Jerusalem eight years. He passed away, to no one's regret, and was buried in the City of David, but not in the tombs of the kings.   2Ki 8:16-24; 2Ch 24:25

Ahaziah King of Judah

22 The people of Jerusalem made Ahaziah, Jehoram's youngest son, king in his place, since the raiders, who came with the Arabs into the camp, had killed all the older sons. So Ahaziah son of Jehoram king of Judah began to reign.

²Ahaziah was twenty-twoᵇ years old when he became king, and he reigned in Jerusalem one year. His mother's name was Athaliah, a granddaughter of Omri.

³He too walked in the ways of the house of Ahab, for his mother encouraged him in doing wrong. ⁴He did evil in the eyes of the LORD, as the house of Ahab had done, for after his father's death they became his advisers, to his undoing. ⁵He also followed their counsel when he went with Joramᶜ son of Ahab king of Israel to war against

---

ᵃ17 Hebrew *Jehoahaz*, a variant of *Ahaziah*   ᵇ2 Some Septuagint manuscripts and Syriac (see also 2 Kings 8:26); Hebrew *forty-two*   ᶜ5 Hebrew *Jehoram*, a variant of *Joram*; also in verses 6 and 7

Hazael king of Aram at Ramoth Gilead. The Arameans wounded Joram; [6]so he returned to Jezreel to recover from the wounds they had inflicted on him at Ramoth[a] in his battle with Hazael king of Aram.
2Ch 18:1; 21:6

Then Ahaziah[b] son of Jehoram king of Judah went down to Jezreel to see Joram son of Ahab because he had been wounded.

[7]Through Ahaziah's visit to Joram, God brought about Ahaziah's downfall. When Ahaziah arrived, he went out with Joram to meet Jehu son of Nimshi, whom the Lord had anointed to destroy the house of Ahab. [8]While Jehu was executing judgment on the house of Ahab, he found the princes of Judah and the sons of Ahaziah's relatives, who had been attending Ahaziah, and he killed them. [9]He then went in search of Ahaziah, and his men captured him while he was hiding in Samaria. He was brought to Jehu and put to death. They buried him, for they said, "He was a son of Jehoshaphat, who sought the Lord with all his heart." So there was no one in the house of Ahaziah powerful enough to retain the kingdom.

Athaliah and Joash

[10]When Athaliah the mother of Ahaziah saw that her son was dead, she proceeded to destroy the whole royal family of the house of Judah. [11]But Jehosheba,[c] the daughter of King Jehoram, took Joash son of Ahaziah and stole him away from among the royal princes who were about to be murdered and put him and his nurse in a bedroom. Because Jehosheba,[c] the daughter of King Jehoram and wife of the priest Jehoiada, was Ahaziah's sister, she hid the child from Athaliah so she could not kill him. [12]He remained hidden with them at the temple of God for six years while Athaliah ruled the land.

23 In the seventh year Jehoiada showed his strength. He made a covenant with the commanders of units of a hundred: Azariah son of Jeroham, Ishmael son of Jehohanan, Azariah son of Obed, Maaseiah son of Adaiah, and Elishaphat son of Zicri. [2]They went throughout Judah and gathered the Levites and the heads of Israelite families from all the towns. When they came to Jerusalem, [3]the whole assembly made a covenant with the king at the temple of God.
Nu 35:2-5; 2Ki 11:17

Jehoiada said to them, "The king's son shall reign, as the Lord promised concerning the descendants of David. [4]Now this is what you are to do: A third of you priests and Levites who are going on duty on the Sabbath are to keep watch

[a]6 Hebrew *Ramah*, a variant of *Ramoth*   [b]6 Some Hebrew manuscripts, Septuagint, Vulgate and Syriac (see also 2 Kings 8:29); most Hebrew manuscripts *Azariah*   [c]11 Hebrew *Jehoshabeath*, a variant of *Jehosheba*

at the doors, **5**a third of you at the royal palace and a third at the Foundation Gate, and all the other men are to be in the courtyards of the temple of the LORD. **6**No one is to enter the temple of the LORD except the priests and Levites on duty; they may enter because they are consecrated, but all the other men are to guard what the LORD has assigned to them.*a* **7**The Levites are to station themselves around the king, each man with his weapons in his hand. Anyone who enters the temple must be put to death. Stay close to the king wherever he goes." 2Sa 7:12; 1Ki 2:4

8The Levites and all the men of Judah did just as Jehoiada the priest ordered. Each one took his men—those who were going on duty on the Sabbath and those who were going off duty—for Jehoiada the priest had not released any of the divisions. **9**Then he gave the commanders of units of a hundred the spears and the large and small shields that had belonged to King David and that were in the temple of God. **10**He stationed all the men, each with his weapon in his hand, around the king—near the altar and the temple, from the south side to the north side of the temple. 2Ki 11:9; 1Ch 24:1

11Jehoiada and his sons brought out the king's son and put the crown on him; they presented him with a copy of the covenant and proclaimed him king. They anointed him and shouted, "Long live the king!" Dt 17:18; 1Sa 10:24

12When Athaliah heard the noise of the people running and cheering the king, she went to them at the temple of the LORD. **13**She looked, and there was the king, standing by his pillar at the entrance. The officers and the trumpeters were beside the king, and all the people of the land were rejoicing and blowing trumpets, and singers with musical instruments were leading the praises. Then Athaliah tore her robes and shouted, "Treason! Treason!"

14Jehoiada the priest sent out the commanders of units of a hundred, who were in charge of the troops, and said to them: "Bring her out between the ranks*b* and put to the sword anyone who follows her." For the priest had said, "Do not put her to death at the temple of the LORD." **15**So they seized her as she reached the entrance of the Horse Gate on the palace grounds, and there they put her to death. Ne 3:28; Jer 31:40

16Jehoiada then made a covenant that he and the people and the king*c* would be the LORD's people. **17**All the people went to the temple of Baal and tore it down. They smashed the altars and idols

---

a 6 Or *to observe the LORD's command not to enter*   *b 14* Or *out from the precincts*   *c 16* Or *covenant between the LORD, and the people and the king that they* (see 2 Kings 11:17)

and killed Mattan the priest of Baal in front of the altars.   Dt 13:6-9
¹⁸Then Jehoiada placed the oversight of the temple of the LORD in the hands of the priests, who were Levites, to whom David had made assignments in the temple, to present the burnt offerings of the LORD as written in the Law of Moses, with rejoicing and singing, as David had ordered. ¹⁹He also stationed doorkeepers at the gates of the LORD's temple so that no one who was in any way unclean might enter.   1Ch 9:22; 23:6,28-32
²⁰He took with him the commanders of hundreds, the nobles, the rulers of the people and all the people of the land and brought the king down from the temple of the LORD. They went into the palace through the Upper Gate and seated the king on the royal throne, ²¹and all the people of the land rejoiced. And the city was quiet, because Athaliah had been slain with the sword.   2Ki 11:1-21; 15:35

Joash Repairs the Temple

24 Joash was seven years old when he became king, and he reigned in Jerusalem forty years. His mother's name was Zibiah; she was from Beersheba. ²Joash did what was right in the eyes of the LORD all the years of Jehoiada the priest. ³Jehoiada chose two wives for him, and he had sons and daughters.   2Ch 26:5
⁴Some time later Joash decided to restore the temple of the LORD.

⁵He called together the priests and Levites and said to them, "Go to the towns of Judah and collect the money due annually from all Israel, to repair the temple of your God. Do it now." But the Levites did not act at once.   Ex 30:16; 1Ch 11:1
⁶Therefore the king summoned Jehoiada the chief priest and said to him, "Why haven't you required the Levites to bring in from Judah and Jerusalem the tax imposed by Moses the servant of the LORD and by the assembly of Israel for the Tent of the Testimony?"   Ex 30:12-16
⁷Now the sons of that wicked woman Athaliah had broken into the temple of God and had used even its sacred objects for the Baals.
⁸At the king's command, a chest was made and placed outside, at the gate of the temple of the LORD. ⁹A proclamation was then issued in Judah and Jerusalem that they should bring to the LORD the tax that Moses the servant of God had required of Israel in the desert. ¹⁰All the officials and all the people brought their contributions gladly, dropping them into the chest until it was full. ¹¹Whenever the chest was brought in by the Levites to the king's officials and they saw that there was a large amount of money, the royal secretary and the officer of the chief priest would come and empty the chest and carry it back to its place. They did this regularly and collected a great amount of money. ¹²The king and

Jehoiada gave it to the men who carried out the work required for the temple of the LORD. They hired masons and carpenters to restore the LORD's temple, and also workers in iron and bronze to repair the temple.

13The men in charge of the work were diligent, and the repairs progressed under them. They rebuilt the temple of God according to its original design and reinforced it. 14When they had finished, they brought the rest of the money to the king and Jehoiada, and with it were made articles for the LORD's temple: articles for the service and for the burnt offerings, and also dishes and other objects of gold and silver. As long as Jehoiada lived, burnt offerings were presented continually in the temple of the LORD.   2Ki 12:1-16; 1Ch 29:3,6,9

15Now Jehoiada was old and full of years, and he died at the age of a hundred and thirty. 16He was buried with the kings in the City of David, because of the good he had done in Israel for God and his temple.

The Wickedness of Joash

17After the death of Jehoiada, the officials of Judah came and paid homage to the king, and he listened to them. 18They abandoned the temple of the LORD, the God of their fathers, and worshiped Asherah poles and idols.

Because of their guilt, God's anger came upon Judah and Jerusalem. 19Although the LORD sent prophets to the people to bring them back to him, and though they testified against them, they would not listen.   Ex 34:13; 2Ch 19:2; Jer 7:25

20Then the Spirit of God came upon Zechariah son of Jehoiada the priest. He stood before the people and said, "This is what God says: 'Why do you disobey the LORD's commands? You will not prosper. Because you have forsaken the LORD, he has forsaken you.' "   Nu 14:41; 2Ch 15:2; 20:14

21But they plotted against him, and by order of the king they stoned him to death in the courtyard of the LORD's temple. 22King Joash did not remember the kindness Zechariah's father Jehoiada had shown him but killed his son, who said as he lay dying, "May the LORD see this and call you to account."   Ge 9:5; Ne 9:26; Ac 7:58-59

23At the turn of the year,a the army of Aram marched against Joash; it invaded Judah and Jerusalem and killed all the leaders of the people. They sent all the plunder to their king in Damascus. 24Although the Aramean army had come with only a few men, the LORD delivered into their hands a much larger army. Because Judah had forsaken the LORD, the God of their fathers, judgment was executed on Joash. 25When the Ara-

a23 Probably in the spring

means withdrew, they left Joash severely wounded. His officials conspired against him for murdering the son of Jehoiada the priest, and they killed him in his bed. So he died and was buried in the City of David, but not in the tombs of the kings.   Lev 26:23-25; 2Ki 12:17-18

²⁶Those who conspired against him were Zabad,ᵃ son of Shimeath an Ammonite woman, and Jehozabad, son of Shimrithᵇ a Moabite woman. ²⁷The account of his sons, the many prophecies about him, and the record of the restoration of the temple of God are written in the annotations on the book of the kings. And Amaziah his son succeeded him as king.   2Ki 12:17-21

Amaziah King of Judah

25 Amaziah was twenty-five years old when he became king, and he reigned in Jerusalem twenty-nine years. His mother's name was Jehoaddinᶜ; she was from Jerusalem. ²He did what was right in the eyes of the LORD, but not wholeheartedly. ³After the kingdom was firmly in his control, he executed the officials who had murdered his father the king. ⁴Yet he did not put their sons to death, but acted in accordance with what is written in the Law, in the Book of Moses, where the LORD commanded: "Fathers shall not be put to death for their children, nor children put to death for their fathers; each is to die for his own sins."ᵈ   2Ki 14:1-6; Dt 24:16; 28:61

⁵Amaziah called the people of Judah together and assigned them according to their families to commanders of thousands and commanders of hundreds for all Judah and Benjamin. He then mustered those twenty years old or more and found that there were three hundred thousand men ready for military service, able to handle the spear and shield. ⁶He also hired a hundred thousand fighting men from Israel for a hundred talentsᵉ of silver.   Nu 1:3; 1Ch 21:1

⁷But a man of God came to him and said, "O king, these troops from Israel must not march with you, for the LORD is not with Israel —not with any of the people of Ephraim. ⁸Even if you go and fight courageously in battle, God will overthrow you before the enemy, for God has the power to help or to overthrow."   2Ch 14:11; 20:6

⁹Amaziah asked the man of God, "But what about the hundred talents I paid for these Israelite troops?"

The man of God replied, "The LORD can give you much more than that."   Dt 8:18; Pr 10:22

¹⁰So Amaziah dismissed the troops who had come to him from Ephraim and sent them home.

ᵃ26 A variant of *Jozabad*   ᵇ26 A variant of *Shomer*   ᶜ1 Hebrew *Jehoaddan,* a variant of *Jehoaddin*
ᵈ4 Deut. 24:16   ᵉ6 That is, about 3 3/4 tons (about 3.4 metric tons); also in verse 9

They were furious with Judah and left for home in a great rage.

[11] Amaziah then marshaled his strength and led his army to the Valley of Salt, where he killed ten thousand men of Seir. [12] The army of Judah also captured ten thousand men alive, took them to the top of a cliff and threw them down so that all were dashed to pieces.

[13] Meanwhile the troops that Amaziah had sent back and had not allowed to take part in the war raided Judean towns from Samaria to Beth Horon. They killed three thousand people and carried off great quantities of plunder.

[14] When Amaziah returned from slaughtering the Edomites, he brought back the gods of the people of Seir. He set them up as his own gods, bowed down to them and burned sacrifices to them. [15] The anger of the LORD burned against Amaziah, and he sent a prophet to him, who said, "Why do you consult this people's gods, which could not save their own people from your hand?"   Ex 20:3

[16] While he was still speaking, the king said to him, "Have we appointed you an adviser to the king? Stop! Why be struck down?"

So the prophet stopped but said, "I know that God has determined to destroy you, because you have done this and have not listened to my counsel."

[17] After Amaziah king of Judah consulted his advisers, he sent this challenge to Jehoash[a] son of Jehoahaz, the son of Jehu, king of Israel: "Come, meet me face to face."

[18] But Jehoash king of Israel replied to Amaziah king of Judah: "A thistle in Lebanon sent a message to a cedar in Lebanon, 'Give your daughter to my son in marriage.' Then a wild beast in Lebanon came along and trampled the thistle underfoot. [19] You say to yourself that you have defeated Edom, and now you are arrogant and proud. But stay at home! Why ask for trouble and cause your own downfall and that of Judah also?"

[20] Amaziah, however, would not listen, for God so worked that he might hand them over to ˻Jehoash˼, because they sought the gods of Edom. [21] So Jehoash king of Israel attacked. He and Amaziah king of Judah faced each other at Beth Shemesh in Judah. [22] Judah was routed by Israel, and every man fled to his home. [23] Jehoash king of Israel captured Amaziah king of Judah, the son of Joash, the son of Ahaziah,[b] at Beth Shemesh. Then Jehoash brought him to Jerusalem and broke down the wall of Jerusalem from the Ephraim Gate to the Corner Gate—a section about six hundred feet[c] long. [24] He took all the gold and silver and all the articles found in the temple of God

---

[a] 17 Hebrew Joash, a variant of Jehoash; also in verses 18, 21, 23 and 25   [b] 23 Hebrew Jehoahaz, a variant of Ahaziah   [c] 23 Hebrew four hundred cubits (about 180 meters)

that had been in the care of Obed-Edom, together with the palace treasures and the hostages, and returned to Samaria.   1Ki 12:15; 2Ch 22:7

²⁵Amaziah son of Joash king of Judah lived for fifteen years after the death of Jehoash son of Jehoahaz king of Israel. ²⁶As for the other events of Amaziah's reign, from beginning to end, are they not written in the book of the kings of Judah and Israel? ²⁷From the time that Amaziah turned away from following the LORD, they conspired against him in Jerusalem and he fled to Lachish, but they sent men after him to Lachish and killed him there. ²⁸He was brought back by horse and was buried with his fathers in the City of Judah.

Uzziah King of Judah

26 Then all the people of Judah took Uzziah,ᵃ who was sixteen years old, and made him king in place of his father Amaziah. ²He was the one who rebuilt Elath and restored it to Judah after Amaziah rested with his fathers.

³Uzziah was sixteen years old when he became king, and he reigned in Jerusalem fifty-two years. His mother's name was Jecoliah; she was from Jerusalem. ⁴He did what was right in the eyes of the LORD, just as his father Amaziah had done. ⁵He sought God during the days of Zechariah, who instructed him in the fearᵇ of God. As long as he sought the LORD, God gave him success.   2Ki 14:21-22; 15:1-3

⁶He went to war against the Philistines and broke down the walls of Gath, Jabneh and Ashdod. He then rebuilt towns near Ashdod and elsewhere among the Philistines. ⁷God helped him against the Philistines and against the Arabs who lived in Gur Baal and against the Meunites. ⁸The Ammonites brought tribute to Uzziah, and his fame spread as far as the border of Egypt, because he had become very powerful.   2Ch 17:11; 21:16; Isa 14:29

⁹Uzziah built towers in Jerusalem at the Corner Gate, at the Valley Gate and at the angle of the wall, and he fortified them. ¹⁰He also built towers in the desert and dug many cisterns, because he had much livestock in the foothills and in the plain. He had people working his fields and vineyards in the hills and in the fertile lands, for he loved the soil.   2Ch 25:23; Ne 3:13

¹¹Uzziah had a well-trained army, ready to go out by divisions according to their numbers as mustered by Jeiel the secretary and Maaseiah the officer under the direction of Hananiah, one of the royal officials. ¹²The total number of family leaders over the fighting men was 2,600. ¹³Under their command was an army of 307,500 men trained for war, a powerful

ᵃ 1 Also called *Azariah*   ᵇ 5 Many Hebrew manuscripts, Septuagint and Syriac; other Hebrew manuscripts *vision* force to support the king against his enemies. [14]Uzziah provided shields, spears, helmets, coats of armor, bows and slingstones for the entire army. [15]In Jerusalem he made machines designed by skillful men for use on the towers and on the corner defenses to shoot arrows and hurl large stones. His fame spread far and wide, for he was greatly helped until he became powerful.　　　　Jer 46:4

[16]But after Uzziah became powerful, his pride led to his downfall. He was unfaithful to the LORD his God, and entered the temple of the LORD to burn incense on the altar of incense. [17]Azariah the priest with eighty other courageous priests of the LORD followed him in. [18]They confronted him and said, "It is not right for you, Uzziah, to burn incense to the LORD. That is for the priests, the descendants of Aaron, who have been consecrated to burn incense. Leave the sanctuary, for you have been unfaithful; and you will not be honored by the LORD God."

[19]Uzziah, who had a censer in his hand ready to burn incense, became angry. While he was raging at the priests in their presence before the incense altar in the LORD's temple, leprosy[a] broke out on his forehead. [20]When Azariah the chief priest and all the other priests looked at him, they saw

that he had leprosy on his forehead, so they hurried him out. Indeed, he himself was eager to leave, because the LORD had afflicted him.　　　　2Ki 5:25-27

[21]King Uzziah had leprosy until the day he died. He lived in a separate house[b] —leprous, and excluded from the temple of the LORD. Jotham his son had charge of the palace and governed the people of the land.

[22]The other events of Uzziah's reign, from beginning to end, are recorded by the prophet Isaiah son of Amoz. [23]Uzziah rested with his fathers and was buried near them in a field for burial that belonged to the kings, for people said, "He had leprosy." And Jotham his son succeeded him as king.　　2Ki 15:5-7

Jotham King of Judah

27 Jotham was twenty-five years old when he became king, and he reigned in Jerusalem sixteen years. His mother's name was Jerusha daughter of Zadok. [2]He did what was right in the eyes of the LORD, just as his father Uzziah had done, but unlike him he did not enter the temple of the LORD. The people, however, continued their corrupt practices. [3]Jotham rebuilt the Upper Gate of the temple of the LORD and did extensive work on the wall at the hill of Ophel. [4]He built towns in the Judean hills and

---

[a]19 The Hebrew word was used for various diseases affecting the skin—not necessarily leprosy; also in verses 20, 21 and 23.　　[b]21 Or *in a house where he was relieved of responsibilities*

forts and towers in the wooded areas. 2Ch 33:14; Ne 3:26; 1Ch 3:12

⁵Jotham made war on the king of the Ammonites and conquered them. That year the Ammonites paid him a hundred talents*ᵃ* of silver, ten thousand cors*ᵇ* of wheat and ten thousand cors of barley. The Ammonites brought him the same amount also in the second and third years. Ge 19:38

⁶Jotham grew powerful because he walked steadfastly before the LORD his God. 2Ch 26:5

⁷The other events in Jotham's reign, including all his wars and the other things he did, are written in the book of the kings of Israel and Judah. ⁸He was twenty-five years old when he became king, and he reigned in Jerusalem sixteen years. ⁹Jotham rested with his fathers and was buried in the City of David. And Ahaz his son succeeded him as king. 2Ki 15:33-38

Ahaz King of Judah

28 Ahaz was twenty years old when he became king, and he reigned in Jerusalem sixteen years. Unlike David his father, he did not do what was right in the eyes of the LORD. ²He walked in the ways of the kings of Israel and also made cast idols for worshiping the Baals. ³He burned sacrifices in the Valley of Ben Hinnom and sacrificed his sons in the fire, following the detestable ways of the nations the LORD had driven out before the Israelites. ⁴He offered sacrifices and burned incense at the high places, on the hilltops and under every spreading tree. Lev 18:21

⁵Therefore the LORD his God handed him over to the king of Aram. The Arameans defeated him and took many of his people as prisoners and brought them to Damascus. Isa 7:1

He was also given into the hands of the king of Israel, who inflicted heavy casualties on him. ⁶In one day Pekah son of Remaliah killed a hundred and twenty thousand soldiers in Judah—because Judah had forsaken the LORD, the God of their fathers. ⁷Zicri, an Ephraimite warrior, killed Maaseiah the king's son, Azrikam the officer in charge of the palace, and Elkanah, second to the king. ⁸The Israelites took captive from their kinsmen two hundred thousand wives, sons and daughters. They also took a great deal of plunder, which they carried back to Samaria. 2Ki 15:25,27; 2Ch 11:4

⁹But a prophet of the LORD named Oded was there, and he went out to meet the army when it returned to Samaria. He said to them, "Because the LORD, the God of your fathers, was angry with Judah, he gave them into your hand. But you have slaughtered them in a rage that reaches to heaven.

---

*ᵃ5 That is, about 3 3/4 tons (about 3.4 metric tons) (about 2,200 kiloliters)   *ᵇ5 That is, probably about 62,000 bushels

¹⁰And now you intend to make the men and women of Judah and Jerusalem your slaves. But aren't you also guilty of sins against the LORD your God? ¹¹Now listen to me! Send back your fellow countrymen you have taken as prisoners, for the LORD's fierce anger rests on you." Lev 25:39-46; Ezr 9:6

¹²Then some of the leaders in Ephraim—Azariah son of Jehohanan, Berekiah son of Meshillemoth, Jehizkiah son of Shallum, and Amasa son of Hadlai—confronted those who were arriving from the war. ¹³"You must not bring those prisoners here," they said, "or we will be guilty before the LORD. Do you intend to add to our sin and guilt? For our guilt is already great, and his fierce anger rests on Israel."

¹⁴So the soldiers gave up the prisoners and plunder in the presence of the officials and all the assembly. ¹⁵The men designated by name took the prisoners, and from the plunder they clothed all who were naked. They provided them with clothes and sandals, food and drink, and healing balm. All those who were weak they put on donkeys. So they took them back to their fellow countrymen at Jericho, the City of Palms, and returned to Samaria. Jdg 1:16; 2Ki 6:22

¹⁶At that time King Ahaz sent to the king[a] of Assyria for help. ¹⁷The Edomites had again come and attacked Judah and carried away prisoners, ¹⁸while the Philistines had raided towns in the foothills and in the Negev of Judah. They captured and occupied Beth Shemesh, Aijalon and Gederoth, as well as Soco, Timnah and Gimzo, with their surrounding villages. ¹⁹The LORD had humbled Judah because of Ahaz king of Israel,[b] for he had promoted wickedness in Judah and had been most unfaithful to the LORD. ²⁰Tiglath-Pileser[c] king of Assyria came to him, but he gave him trouble instead of help. ²¹Ahaz took some of the things from the temple of the LORD and from the royal palace and from the princes and presented them to the king of Assyria, but that did not help him. 2Ki 16:7

²²In his time of trouble King Ahaz became even more unfaithful to the LORD. ²³He offered sacrifices to the gods of Damascus, who had defeated him; for he thought, "Since the gods of the kings of Aram have helped them, I will sacrifice to them so they will help me." But they were his downfall and the downfall of all Israel.

²⁴Ahaz gathered together the furnishings from the temple of God and took them away.[d] He shut the doors of the LORD's temple and set up altars at every street corner in Jerusalem. ²⁵In every

---

a 16 One Hebrew manuscript, Septuagint and Vulgate (see also 2 Kings 16:7); most Hebrew manuscripts kings b 19 That is, Judah, as frequently in 2 Chronicles c 20 Hebrew Tilgath-Pilneser, a variant of Tiglath-Pileser d 24 Or and cut them up

town in Judah he built high places to burn sacrifices to other gods and provoked the LORD, the God of his fathers, to anger.   2Ki 16:18

²⁶The other events of his reign and all his ways, from beginning to end, are written in the book of the kings of Judah and Israel. ²⁷Ahaz rested with his fathers and was buried in the city of Jerusalem, but he was not placed in the tombs of the kings of Israel. And Hezekiah his son succeeded him as king.

Hezekiah Purifies the Temple

29 Hezekiah was twenty-five years old when he became king, and he reigned in Jerusalem twenty-nine years. His mother's name was Abijah daughter of Zechariah. ²He did what was right in the eyes of the LORD, just as his father David had done.   2Ki 18:1-3

³In the first month of the first year of his reign, he opened the doors of the temple of the LORD and repaired them. ⁴He brought in the priests and the Levites, assembled them in the square on the east side ⁵and said: "Listen to me, Levites! Consecrate yourselves now and consecrate the temple of the LORD, the God of your fathers. Remove all defilement from the sanctuary. ⁶Our fathers were unfaithful; they did evil in the eyes of the LORD our God and forsook him. They turned their faces away from the LORD's dwelling place and turned their backs on him. ⁷They also shut the doors of the portico and put out the lamps. They did not burn incense or present any burnt offerings at the sanctuary to the God of Israel. ⁸Therefore, the anger of the LORD has fallen on Judah and Jerusalem; he has made them an object of dread and horror and scorn, as you can see with your own eyes. ⁹This is why our fathers have fallen by the sword and why our sons and daughters and our wives are in captivity. ¹⁰Now I intend to make a covenant with the LORD, the God of Israel, so that his fierce anger will turn away from us. ¹¹My sons, do not be negligent now, for the LORD has chosen you to stand before him and serve him, to minister before him and to burn incense."   Nu 3:6

¹²Then these Levites set to work: Nu 3:17-20
from the Kohathites,
    Mahath son of Amasai and
        Joel son of Azariah;
from the Merarites,
    Kish son of Abdi and Azariah son of Jehallelel;
from the Gershonites,
    Joah son of Zimmah and
        Eden son of Joah;
¹³from the descendants of Elizaphan,
    Shimri and Jeiel;
from the descendants of Asaph,   1Ch 6:39
    Zechariah and Mattaniah;
¹⁴from the descendants of Heman,
    Jehiel and Shimei;

from the descendants of Jeduthun,
Shemaiah and Uzziel.

¹⁵When they had assembled
their brothers and consecrated
themselves, they went in to purify
the temple of the LORD, as the king
had ordered, following the word of
the LORD. ¹⁶The priests went into
the sanctuary of the LORD to purify
it. They brought out to the courtyard of the LORD's temple everything unclean that they found in
the temple of the LORD. The Levites
took it and carried it out to the Kidron Valley. ¹⁷They began the consecration on the first day of the
first month, and by the eighth day
of the month they reached the portico of the LORD. For eight more
days they consecrated the temple
of the LORD itself, finishing on the
sixteenth day of the first month.
¹⁸Then they went in to King
Hezekiah and reported: "We have
purified the entire temple of the
LORD, the altar of burnt offering
with all its utensils, and the table
for setting out the consecrated
bread, with all its articles. ¹⁹We
have prepared and consecrated all
the articles that King Ahaz removed in his unfaithfulness while
he was king. They are now in front
of the LORD's altar." 2Ch 28:24
²⁰Early the next morning King
Hezekiah gathered the city officials together and went up to the
temple of the LORD. ²¹They
brought seven bulls, seven rams,
seven male lambs and seven male
goats as a sin offering for the kingdom, for the sanctuary and for Judah. The king commanded the
priests, the descendants of Aaron,
to offer these on the altar of the
LORD. ²²So they slaughtered the
bulls, and the priests took the
blood and sprinkled it on the altar;
next they slaughtered the rams
and sprinkled their blood on the
altar; then they slaughtered the
lambs and sprinkled their blood
on the altar. ²³The goats for the sin
offering were brought before the
king and the assembly, and they
laid their hands on them. ²⁴The
priests then slaughtered the goats
and presented their blood on the
altar for a sin offering to atone for
all Israel, because the king had ordered the burnt offering and the
sin offering for all Israel.

²⁵He stationed the Levites in the
temple of the LORD with cymbals,
harps and lyres in the way prescribed by David and Gad the
king's seer and Nathan the prophet; this was commanded by the
LORD through his prophets. ²⁶So
the Levites stood ready with David's instruments, and the priests
with their trumpets. 1Ch 15:24; 23:5
²⁷Hezekiah gave the order to
sacrifice the burnt offering on the
altar. As the offering began, singing to the LORD began also, accompanied by trumpets and the instruments of David king of Israel.
²⁸The whole assembly bowed in
worship, while the singers sang
and the trumpeters played. All this

continued until the sacrifice of the burnt offering was completed.

²⁹When the offerings were finished, the king and everyone present with him knelt down and worshiped. ³⁰King Hezekiah and his officials ordered the Levites to praise the Lord with the words of David and of Asaph the seer. So they sang praises with gladness and bowed their heads and worshiped.   2Ch 20:18

³¹Then Hezekiah said, "You have now dedicated yourselves to the Lord. Come and bring sacrifices and thank offerings to the temple of the Lord." So the assembly brought sacrifices and thank offerings, and all whose hearts were willing brought burnt offerings.   Ex 35:22; Heb 13:15-16

³²The number of burnt offerings the assembly brought was seventy bulls, a hundred rams and two hundred male lambs—all of them for burnt offerings to the Lord. ³³The animals consecrated as sacrifices amounted to six hundred bulls and three thousand sheep and goats. ³⁴The priests, however, were too few to skin all the burnt offerings; so their kinsmen the Levites helped them until the task was finished and until other priests had been consecrated, for the Levites had been more conscientious in consecrating themselves than the priests had been. ³⁵There were burnt offerings in abundance, together with the fat of the fellowship offerings[a] and the drink offerings that accompanied the burnt offerings.   Lev 3:16

So the service of the temple of the Lord was reestablished. ³⁶Hezekiah and all the people rejoiced at what God had brought about for his people, because it was done so quickly.

Hezekiah Celebrates the Passover

30 Hezekiah sent word to all Israel and Judah and also wrote letters to Ephraim and Manasseh, inviting them to come to the temple of the Lord in Jerusalem and celebrate the Passover to the Lord, the God of Israel. ²The king and his officials and the whole assembly in Jerusalem decided to celebrate the Passover in the second month. ³They had not been able to celebrate it at the regular time because not enough priests had consecrated themselves and the people had not assembled in Jerusalem. ⁴The plan seemed right both to the king and to the whole assembly. ⁵They decided to send a proclamation throughout Israel, from Beersheba to Dan, calling the people to come to Jerusalem and celebrate the Passover to the Lord, the God of Israel. It had not been celebrated in large numbers according to what was written.   Jdg 20:1; Nu 9:10

ᵃ 35 Traditionally *peace offerings*

⁶At the king's command, couriers went throughout Israel and Judah with letters from the king and from his officials, which read:

"People of Israel, return to the LORD, the God of Abraham, Isaac and Israel, that he may return to you who are left, who have escaped from the hand of the kings of Assyria. ⁷Do not be like your fathers and brothers, who were unfaithful to the LORD, the God of their fathers, so that he made them an object of horror, as you see. ⁸Do not be stiff-necked, as your fathers were; submit to the LORD. Come to the sanctuary, which he has consecrated forever. Serve the LORD your God, so that his fierce anger will turn away from you. ⁹If you return to the LORD, then your brothers and your children will be shown compassion by their captors and will come back to this land, for the LORD your God is gracious and compassionate. He will not turn his face from you if you return to him." Dt 30:2-5; Mic 7:18

¹⁰The couriers went from town to town in Ephraim and Manasseh, as far as Zebulun, but the people scorned and ridiculed them. ¹¹Nevertheless, some men of Asher, Manasseh and Zebulun humbled themselves and went to Jerusalem. ¹²Also in Judah the hand of God was on the people to give them unity of mind to carry out what the king and his officials had ordered, following the word of the LORD. 2Ch 36:16; Jer 32:39

¹³A very large crowd of people assembled in Jerusalem to celebrate the Feast of Unleavened Bread in the second month. ¹⁴They removed the altars in Jerusalem and cleared away the incense altars and threw them into the Kidron Valley. Nu 28:16; 2Ch 28:24

¹⁵They slaughtered the Passover lamb on the fourteenth day of the second month. The priests and the Levites were ashamed and consecrated themselves and brought burnt offerings to the temple of the LORD. ¹⁶Then they took up their regular positions as prescribed in the Law of Moses the man of God. The priests sprinkled the blood handed to them by the Levites. ¹⁷Since many in the crowd had not consecrated themselves, the Levites had to kill the Passover lambs for all those who were not ceremonially clean and could not consecrate their lambs to the LORD. ¹⁸Although most of the many people who came from Ephraim, Manasseh, Issachar and Zebulun had not purified themselves, yet they ate the Passover, contrary to what was written. But Hezekiah prayed for them, saying, "May the LORD, who is good, pardon everyone ¹⁹who sets his heart on seeking God—the LORD, the God of his fathers—even if he is not clean ac-

cording to the rules of the sanctuary." 20And the LORD heard Hezekiah and healed the people.   2Ch 7:14

21The Israelites who were present in Jerusalem celebrated the Feast of Unleavened Bread for seven days with great rejoicing, while the Levites and priests sang to the LORD every day, accompanied by the LORD's instruments of praise.*a*

22Hezekiah spoke encouragingly to all the Levites, who showed good understanding of the service of the LORD. For the seven days they ate their assigned portion and offered fellowship offerings*b* and praised the LORD, the God of their fathers.   Ex 12:15,17; 13:6

23The whole assembly then agreed to celebrate the festival seven more days; so for another seven days they celebrated joyfully. 24Hezekiah king of Judah provided a thousand bulls and seven thousand sheep and goats for the assembly, and the officials provided them with a thousand bulls and ten thousand sheep and goats. A great number of priests consecrated themselves. 25The entire assembly of Judah rejoiced, along with the priests and Levites and all who had assembled from Israel, including the aliens who had come from Israel and those who lived in Judah. 26There was great joy in Jerusalem, for since the days of Solomon son of David king of Israel there had been nothing like this in Jerusalem. 27The priests and the Levites stood to bless the people, and God heard them, for their prayer reached heaven, his holy dwelling place.   Nu 6:23; Dt 26:15

31 When all this had ended, the Israelites who were there went out to the towns of Judah, smashed the sacred stones and cut down the Asherah poles. They destroyed the high places and the altars throughout Judah and Benjamin and in Ephraim and Manasseh. After they had destroyed all of them, the Israelites returned to their own towns and to their own property.   2Ki 18:4; 2Ch 32:12

Contributions for Worship

2Hezekiah assigned the priests and Levites to divisions—each of them according to their duties as priests or Levites—to offer burnt offerings and fellowship offerings,*b* to minister, to give thanks and to sing praises at the gates of the LORD's dwelling. 3The king contributed from his own possessions for the morning and evening burnt offerings and for the burnt offerings on the Sabbaths, New Moons and appointed feasts as written in the Law of the LORD. 4He ordered the people living in Jerusalem to give the portion due the priests and Levites so they could

a 21 Or priests praised the LORD every day with resounding instruments belonging to the LORD
b 22,2 Traditionally peace offerings

devote themselves to the Law of the LORD. ⁵As soon as the order went out, the Israelites generously gave the firstfruits of their grain, new wine, oil and honey and all that the fields produced. They brought a great amount, a tithe of everything. ⁶The men of Israel and Judah who lived in the towns of Judah also brought a tithe of their herds and flocks and a tithe of the holy things dedicated to the LORD their God, and they piled them in heaps. ⁷They began doing this in the third month and finished in the seventh month. ⁸When Hezekiah and his officials came and saw the heaps, they praised the LORD and blessed his people Israel.   Dt 14:28

⁹Hezekiah asked the priests and Levites about the heaps; ¹⁰and Azariah the chief priest, from the family of Zadok, answered, "Since the people began to bring their contributions to the temple of the LORD, we have had enough to eat and plenty to spare, because the LORD has blessed his people, and this great amount is left over."

¹¹Hezekiah gave orders to prepare storerooms in the temple of the LORD, and this was done. ¹²Then they faithfully brought in the contributions, tithes and dedicated gifts. Conaniah, a Levite, was in charge of these things, and his brother Shimei was next in rank. ¹³Jehiel, Azaziah, Nahath, Asahel, Jerimoth, Jozabad, Eliel, Ismakiah, Mahath and Benaiah were supervisors under Conaniah and Shimei his brother, by appointment of King Hezekiah and Azariah the official in charge of the temple of God.   2Ch 35:9

¹⁴Kore son of Imnah the Levite, keeper of the East Gate, was in charge of the freewill offerings given to God, distributing the contributions made to the LORD and also the consecrated gifts. ¹⁵Eden, Miniamin, Jeshua, Shemaiah, Amariah and Shecaniah assisted him faithfully in the towns of the priests, distributing to their fellow priests according to their divisions, old and young alike.   Jos 21:9-19; 2Ch 29:12

¹⁶In addition, they distributed to the males three years old or more whose names were in the genealogical records—all who would enter the temple of the LORD to perform the daily duties of their various tasks, according to their responsibilities and their divisions. ¹⁷And they distributed to the priests enrolled by their families in the genealogical records and likewise to the Levites twenty years old or more, according to their responsibilities and their divisions. ¹⁸They included all the little ones, the wives, and the sons and daughters of the whole community listed in these genealogical records. For they were faithful in consecrating themselves.   1Ch 23:3; Ezr 3:4

¹⁹As for the priests, the descendants of Aaron, who lived on the farm lands around their towns or in any other towns, men were designated by name to distribute por-

tions to every male among them and to all who were recorded in the genealogies of the Levites. ²⁰This is what Hezekiah did throughout Judah, doing what was good and right and faithful before the LORD his God. ²¹In everything that he undertook in the service of God's temple and in obedience to the law and the commands, he sought his God and worked whole-heartedly. And so he prospered.

Sennacherib Threatens Jerusalem

32 After all that Hezekiah had so faithfully done, Sennacherib king of Assyria came and invaded Judah. He laid siege to the fortified cities, thinking to conquer them for himself. ²When Hezekiah saw that Sennacherib had come and that he intended to make war on Jerusalem, ³he consulted with his officials and military staff about blocking off the water from the springs outside the city, and they helped him. ⁴A large force of men assembled, and they blocked all the springs and the stream that flowed through the land. "Why should the kings*a* of Assyria come and find plenty of water?" they said. ⁵Then he worked hard repairing all the broken sections of the wall and building towers on it. He built another wall outside that one and reinforced the supporting ter-races*b* of the City of David. He also

made large numbers of weapons and shields. 1Ki 9:24; 1Ch 11:8; Isa 22:8

⁶He appointed military officers over the people and assembled them before him in the square at the city gate and encouraged them with these words: ⁷"Be strong and courageous. Do not be afraid or discouraged because of the king of Assyria and the vast army with him, for there is a greater power with us than with him. ⁸With him is only the arm of flesh, but with us is the LORD our God to help us and to fight our battles." And the people gained confidence from what Hezekiah the king of Judah said.

⁹Later, when Sennacherib king of Assyria and all his forces were laying siege to Lachish, he sent his officers to Jerusalem with this message for Hezekiah king of Judah and for all the people of Judah who were there:

¹⁰"This is what Sennacherib king of Assyria says: On what are you basing your confidence, that you remain in Jerusalem under siege? ¹¹When Hezekiah says, 'The LORD our God will save us from the hand of the king of Assyria,' he is misleading you, to let you die of hunger and thirst. ¹²Did not Hezekiah himself remove this god's high places and altars, saying to Judah

a4 Hebrew; Septuagint and Syriac *king* *b5* Or *the Millo* and Jerusalem, 'You must worship before one altar and burn sacrifices on it'? 2Ch 31:1

¹³"Do you not know what I and my fathers have done to all the peoples of the other lands? Were the gods of those nations ever able to deliver their land from my hand? ¹⁴Who of all the gods of these nations that my fathers destroyed has been able to save his people from me? How then can your god deliver you from my hand? ¹⁵Now do not let Hezekiah deceive you and mislead you like this. Do not believe him, for no god of any nation or kingdom has been able to deliver his people from my hand or the hand of my fathers. How much less will your god deliver you from my hand!" Ex 5:2; Da 3:15

¹⁶Sennacherib's officers spoke further against the LORD God and against his servant Hezekiah. ¹⁷The king also wrote letters insulting the LORD, the God of Israel, and saying this against him: "Just as the gods of the peoples of the other lands did not rescue their people from my hand, so the god of Hezekiah will not rescue his people from my hand." ¹⁸Then they called out in Hebrew to the people of Jerusalem who were on the wall, to terrify them and make them afraid in order to capture the city. ¹⁹They spoke about the God of Jerusalem as they did about the gods of the other peoples of the world—the work of men's hands.

²⁰King Hezekiah and the prophet Isaiah son of Amoz cried out in prayer to heaven about this. ²¹And the LORD sent an angel, who annihilated all the fighting men and the leaders and officers in the camp of the Assyrian king. So he withdrew to his own land in disgrace. And when he went into the temple of his god, some of his sons cut him down with the sword. 2Ki 19:35-37

²²So the LORD saved Hezekiah and the people of Jerusalem from the hand of Sennacherib king of Assyria and from the hand of all others. He took care of them[a] on every side. ²³Many brought offerings to Jerusalem for the LORD and valuable gifts for Hezekiah king of Judah. From then on he was highly regarded by all the nations.

Hezekiah's Pride, Success and Death

²⁴In those days Hezekiah became ill and was at the point of death. He prayed to the LORD, who answered him and gave him a miraculous sign. ²⁵But Hezekiah's heart was proud and he did not respond to the kindness shown him; therefore the LORD's wrath was on him and on Judah and Jerusalem. ²⁶Then Hezekiah repented of the

---

ᵃ 22 Hebrew; Septuagint and Vulgate He gave them rest

pride of his heart, as did the people of Jerusalem; therefore the LORD's wrath did not come upon them during the days of Hezekiah.

27Hezekiah had very great riches and honor, and he made treasuries for his silver and gold and for his precious stones, spices, shields and all kinds of valuables. 28He also made buildings to store the harvest of grain, new wine and oil; and he made stalls for various kinds of cattle, and pens for the flocks. 29He built villages and acquired great numbers of flocks and herds, for God had given him very great riches.   1Ch 29:12

30It was Hezekiah who blocked the upper outlet of the Gihon spring and channeled the water down to the west side of the City of David. He succeeded in everything he undertook. 31But when envoys were sent by the rulers of Babylon to ask him about the miraculous sign that had occurred in the land, God left him to test him and to know everything that was in his heart.   Dt 8:16; Isa 39:1

32The other events of Hezekiah's reign and his acts of devotion are written in the vision of the prophet Isaiah son of Amoz in the book of the kings of Judah and Israel. 33Hezekiah rested with his fathers and was buried on the hill where the tombs of David's descendants are. All Judah and the people of Jerusalem honored him when he died. And Manasseh his son succeeded him as king.

Manasseh King of Judah

33 Manasseh was twelve years old when he became king, and he reigned in Jerusalem fifty-five years. 2He did evil in the eyes of the LORD, following the detestable practices of the nations the LORD had driven out before the Israelites. 3He rebuilt the high places his father Hezekiah had demolished; he also erected altars to the Baals and made Asherah poles. He bowed down to all the starry hosts and worshiped them. 4He built altars in the temple of the LORD, of which the LORD had said, "My Name will remain in Jerusalem forever." 5In both courts of the temple of the LORD, he built altars to all the starry hosts. 6He sacrificed his sons in[a] the fire in the Valley of Ben Hinnom, practiced sorcery, divination and witchcraft, and consulted mediums and spiritists. He did much evil in the eyes of the LORD, provoking him to anger.   Lev 18:21; 19:31; 1Sa 28:13

7He took the carved image he had made and put it in God's temple, of which God had said to David and to his son Solomon, "In this temple and in Jerusalem, which I have chosen out of all the tribes of Israel, I will put my Name forever. 8I will not again make the feet of the Israelites leave the land

a6 Or He made his sons pass through

I assigned to your forefathers, if only they will be careful to do everything I commanded them concerning all the laws, decrees and ordinances given through Moses." [9]But Manasseh led Judah and the people of Jerusalem astray, so that they did more evil than the nations the LORD had destroyed before the Israelites.   2Ki 21:1-10; Jer 15:4

[10]The LORD spoke to Manasseh and his people, but they paid no attention. [11]So the LORD brought against them the army commanders of the king of Assyria, who took Manasseh prisoner, put a hook in his nose, bound him with bronze shackles and took him to Babylon. [12]In his distress he sought the favor of the LORD his God and humbled himself greatly before the God of his fathers. [13]And when he prayed to him, the LORD was moved by his entreaty and listened to his plea; so he brought him back to Jerusalem and to his kingdom. Then Manasseh knew that the LORD is God.   2Ch 32:26; 1Pe 5:6

[14]Afterward he rebuilt the outer wall of the City of David, west of the Gihon spring in the valley, as far as the entrance of the Fish Gate and encircling the hill of Ophel; he also made it much higher. He stationed military commanders in all the fortified cities in Judah.

[15]He got rid of the foreign gods and removed the image from the temple of the LORD, as well as all the altars he had built on the temple hill and in Jerusalem; and he threw them out of the city. [16]Then he restored the altar of the LORD and sacrificed fellowship offerings[a] and thank offerings on it, and told Judah to serve the LORD, the God of Israel. [17]The people, however, continued to sacrifice at the high places, but only to the LORD their God.   ver 3-7; Lev 7:11-18

[18]The other events of Manasseh's reign, including his prayer to his God and the words the seers spoke to him in the name of the LORD, the God of Israel, are written in the annals of the kings of Israel.[b] [19]His prayer and how God was moved by his entreaty, as well as all his sins and unfaithfulness, and the sites where he built high places and set up Asherah poles and idols before he humbled himself—all are written in the records of the seers.[c] [20]Manasseh rested with his fathers and was buried in his palace. And Amon his son succeeded him as king.   2Ki 21:17-18

Amon King of Judah

[21]Amon was twenty-two years old when he became king, and he reigned in Jerusalem two years. [22]He did evil in the eyes of the LORD, as his father Manasseh had done. Amon worshiped and offered sacrifices to all the idols Ma-

---

[a] 16 Traditionally *peace offerings*   [b] 18 That is, Judah, as frequently in 2 Chronicles   [c] 19 One Hebrew manuscript and Septuagint; most Hebrew manuscripts *of Hozai*

nasseh had made. ²³But unlike his father Manasseh, he did not humble himself before the Lord; Amon increased his guilt.

²⁴Amon's officials conspired against him and assassinated him in his palace. ²⁵Then the people of the land killed all who had plotted against King Amon, and they made Josiah his son king in his place.

Josiah's Reforms

34 Josiah was eight years old when he became king, and he reigned in Jerusalem thirty-one years. ²He did what was right in the eyes of the Lord and walked in the ways of his father David, not turning aside to the right or to the left.   2Ki 22:1-2; 1Ch 3:14; 2Ch 29:2

³In the eighth year of his reign, while he was still young, he began to seek the God of his father David. In his twelfth year he began to purge Judah and Jerusalem of high places, Asherah poles, carved idols and cast images. ⁴Under his direction the altars of the Baals were torn down; he cut to pieces the incense altars that were above them, and smashed the Asherah poles, the idols and the images. These he broke to pieces and scattered over the graves of those who had sacrificed to them. ⁵He burned the bones of the priests on their altars, and so he purged Judah and Jerusalem. ⁶In the towns of Manasseh, Ephraim and Simeon, as far as Naphtali, and in the ruins around them, ⁷he tore down the altars and the Asherah poles and crushed the idols to powder and cut to pieces all the incense altars throughout Israel. Then he went back to Jerusalem.   Lev 26:30; 1Ki 13:2; 2Ch 31:1

⁸In the eighteenth year of Josiah's reign, to purify the land and the temple, he sent Shaphan son of Azaliah and Maaseiah the ruler of the city, with Joah son of Joahaz, the recorder, to repair the temple of the Lord his God.

⁹They went to Hilkiah the high priest and gave him the money that had been brought into the temple of God, which the Levites who were the doorkeepers had collected from the people of Manasseh, Ephraim and the entire remnant of Israel and from all the people of Judah and Benjamin and the inhabitants of Jerusalem. ¹⁰Then they entrusted it to the men appointed to supervise the work on the Lord's temple. These men paid the workers who repaired and restored the temple. ¹¹They also gave money to the carpenters and builders to purchase dressed stone, and timber for joists and beams for the buildings that the kings of Judah had allowed to fall into ruin.   2Ch 33:4-7; 35:8

¹²The men did the work faithfully. Over them to direct them were Jahath and Obadiah, Levites descended from Merari, and Zechariah and Meshullam, descended from Kohath. The Levites—all who were skilled in playing musical instruments— ¹³had charge of

the laborers and supervised all the workers from job to job. Some of the Levites were secretaries, scribes and doorkeepers. 2Ki 12:15

The Book of the Law Found

14While they were bringing out the money that had been taken into the temple of the LORD, Hilkiah the priest found the Book of the Law of the LORD that had been given through Moses. 15Hilkiah said to Shaphan the secretary, "I have found the Book of the Law in the temple of the LORD." He gave it to Shaphan. 2Ki 22:8; Ezr 7:6; Ne 8:1

16Then Shaphan took the book to the king and reported to him: "Your officials are doing everything that has been committed to them. 17They have paid out the money that was in the temple of the LORD and have entrusted it to the supervisors and workers." 18Then Shaphan the secretary informed the king, "Hilkiah the priest has given me a book." And Shaphan read from it in the presence of the king.

19When the king heard the words of the Law, he tore his robes. 20He gave these orders to Hilkiah, Ahikam son of Shaphan, Abdon son of Micah,a Shaphan the secretary and Asaiah the king's attendant: 21"Go and inquire of the LORD for me and for the remnant in Israel and Judah about what is written in this book that has been found. Great is the LORD's anger that is poured out on us because our fathers have not kept the word of the LORD; they have not acted in accordance with all that is written in this book." 2Ch 29:8; La 2:4; Eze 36:18

22Hilkiah and those the king had sent with himb went to speak to the prophetess Huldah, who was the wife of Shallum son of Tokhath,c the son of Hasrah,d keeper of the wardrobe. She lived in Jerusalem, in the Second District.

23She said to them, "This is what the LORD, the God of Israel, says: Tell the man who sent you to me, 24'This is what the LORD says: I am going to bring disaster on this place and its people—all the curses written in the book that has been read in the presence of the king of Judah. 25Because they have forsaken me and burned incense to other gods and provoked me to anger by all that their hands have made,e my anger will be poured out on this place and will not be quenched.' 26Tell the king of Judah, who sent you to inquire of the LORD, 'This is what the LORD, the God of Israel, says concerning the words you heard: 27Because your heart was responsive and you humbled yourself before God when you heard what he spoke against this place and its people, and because you humbled your-

---

a20 Also called Acbor son of Micaiah   b22 One Hebrew manuscript, Vulgate and Syriac; most Hebrew manuscripts do not have had sent with him.   c22 Also called Tikvah   d22 Also called Harhas
e25 Or by everything they have done

self before me and tore your robes and wept in my presence, I have heard you, declares the Lord. **28**Now I will gather you to your fathers, and you will be buried in peace. Your eyes will not see all the disaster I am going to bring on this place and on those who live here.'" 2Ch 12:7; 32:26; 35:20-25

So they took her answer back to the king. 2Ki 22:8-20

29Then the king called together all the elders of Judah and Jerusalem. **30**He went up to the temple of the Lord with the men of Judah, the people of Jerusalem, the priests and the Levites—all the people from the least to the greatest. He read in their hearing all the words of the Book of the Covenant, which had been found in the temple of the Lord. **31**The king stood by his pillar and renewed the covenant in the presence of the Lord—to follow the Lord and keep his commands, regulations and decrees with all his heart and all his soul, and to obey the words of the covenant written in this book. **32**Then he had everyone in Jerusalem and Benjamin pledge themselves to it; the people of Jerusalem did this in accordance with the covenant of God, the God of their fathers. 2Ki 23:1-3; 2Ch 23:16

33Josiah removed all the detestable idols from all the territory belonging to the Israelites, and he had all who were present in Israel serve the Lord their God. As long as he lived, they did not fail to fol-low the Lord, the God of their fathers. ver 3-7; Dt 18:9

Josiah Celebrates the Passover

35 Josiah celebrated the Passover to the Lord in Jerusalem, and the Passover lamb was slaughtered on the fourteenth day of the first month. **2**He appointed the priests to their duties and encouraged them in the service of the Lord's temple. **3**He said to the Levites, who instructed all Israel and who had been consecrated to the Lord: "Put the sacred ark in the temple that Solomon son of David king of Israel built. It is not to be carried about on your shoulders. Now serve the Lord your God and his people Israel. **4**Prepare yourselves by families in your divisions, according to the directions written by David king of Israel and by his son Solomon. Ex 12:1-30

5"Stand in the holy place with a group of Levites for each subdivision of the families of your fellow countrymen, the lay people. **6**Slaughter the Passover lambs, consecrate yourselves and prepare the lambs for your fellow countrymen, doing what the Lord commanded through Moses." Lev 11:44

7Josiah provided for all the lay people who were there a total of thirty thousand sheep and goats for the Passover offerings, and also three thousand cattle—all from the king's own possessions. **8**His officials also contributed voluntarily to the people and the priests and Levites. Hilkiah, Zechariah and Jehiel, the administrators of God's temple, gave the priests twenty-six hundred Passover offerings and three hundred cattle. ⁹Also Conaniah along with Shemaiah and Nethanel, his brothers, and Hashabiah, Jeiel and Jozabad, the leaders of the Levites, provided five thousand Passover offerings and five hundred head of cattle for the Levites. 2Ch 31:12-13

¹⁰The service was arranged and the priests stood in their places with the Levites in their divisions as the king had ordered. ¹¹The Passover lambs were slaughtered, and the priests sprinkled the blood handed to them, while the Levites skinned the animals. ¹²They set aside the burnt offerings to give them to the subdivisions of the families of the people to offer to the LORD, as is written in the Book of Moses. They did the same with the cattle. ¹³They roasted the Passover animals over the fire as prescribed, and boiled the holy offerings in pots, caldrons and pans and served them quickly to all the people. ¹⁴After this, they made preparations for themselves and for the priests, because the priests, the descendants of Aaron, were sacrificing the burnt offerings and the fat portions until nightfall. So the Levites made preparations for themselves and for the Aaronic priests. Ex 12:2-11; 29:13; 2Ch 29:22,34

¹⁵The musicians, the descendants of Asaph, were in the places prescribed by David, Asaph, Heman and Jeduthun the king's seer. The gatekeepers at each gate did not need to leave their posts, because their fellow Levites made the preparations for them. 1Ch 25:1

¹⁶So at that time the entire service of the LORD was carried out for the celebration of the Passover and the offering of burnt offerings on the altar of the LORD, as King Josiah had ordered. ¹⁷The Israelites who were present celebrated the Passover at that time and observed the Feast of Unleavened Bread for seven days. ¹⁸The Passover had not been observed like this in Israel since the days of the prophet Samuel; and none of the kings of Israel had ever celebrated such a Passover as did Josiah, with the priests, the Levites and all Judah and Israel who were there with the people of Jerusalem. ¹⁹This Passover was celebrated in the eighteenth year of Josiah's reign.

The Death of Josiah

²⁰After all this, when Josiah had set the temple in order, Neco king of Egypt went up to fight at Carchemish on the Euphrates, and Josiah marched out to meet him in battle. ²¹But Neco sent messengers to him, saying, "What quarrel is there between you and me, O king of Judah? It is not you I am attacking at this time, but the house with

which I am at war. God has told me to hurry; so stop opposing God, who is with me, or he will destroy you." 1Ki 13:18; Isa 10:9

²²Josiah, however, would not turn away from him, but disguised himself to engage him in battle. He would not listen to what Neco had said at God's command but went to fight him on the plain of Megiddo. 1Sa 28:8; 2Ch 18:29

²³Archers shot King Josiah, and he told his officers, "Take me away; I am badly wounded." ²⁴So they took him out of his chariot, put him in the other chariot he had and brought him to Jerusalem, where he died. He was buried in the tombs of his fathers, and all Judah and Jerusalem mourned for him. 1Ki 22:34

²⁵Jeremiah composed laments for Josiah, and to this day all the men and women singers commemorate Josiah in the laments. These became a tradition in Israel and are written in the Laments.

²⁶The other events of Josiah's reign and his acts of devotion, according to what is written in the Law of the LORD— ²⁷all the events, from beginning to end, are written in the book of the kings of Israel and Judah. ¹And the people of the land took Jehoahaz son of Josiah and made him king in Jerusalem in place of his father. 2Ki 23:28-30

Jehoahaz King of Judah

²Jehoahaz[a] was twenty-three years old when he became king, and he reigned in Jerusalem three months. ³The king of Egypt dethroned him in Jerusalem and imposed on Judah a levy of a hundred talents[b] of silver and a talent[c] of gold. ⁴The king of Egypt made Eliakim, a brother of Jehoahaz, king over Judah and Jerusalem and changed Eliakim's name to Jehoiakim. But Neco took Eliakim's brother Jehoahaz and carried him off to Egypt. 2Ki 23:31-34

Jehoiakim King of Judah

⁵Jehoiakim was twenty-five years old when he became king, and he reigned in Jerusalem eleven years. He did evil in the eyes of the LORD his God. ⁶Nebuchadnezzar king of Babylon attacked him and bound him with bronze shackles to take him to Babylon. ⁷Nebuchadnezzar also took to Babylon articles from the temple of the LORD and put them in his temple[d] there. 2Ki 24:13; Jer 26:1; 35:1

⁸The other events of Jehoiakim's reign, the detestable things he did and all that was found against him, are written in the book of the kings of Israel and Judah. And Jehoiachin his son succeeded him as king. 2Ki 23:36–24:6

---

a2 Hebrew *Joahaz,* a variant of *Jehoahaz*; also in verse 4   *b3* That is, about 3 3/4 tons (about 3.4 metric tons)   *c3* That is, about 75 pounds (about 34 kilograms)   *d7* Or *palace*

Jehoiachin King of Judah

⁹Jehoiachin was eighteen[a] years old when he became king, and he reigned in Jerusalem three months and ten days. He did evil in the eyes of the Lord. ¹⁰In the spring, King Nebuchadnezzar sent for him and brought him to Babylon, together with articles of value from the temple of the Lord, and he made Jehoiachin's uncle,[b] Zedekiah, king over Judah and Jerusalem.   Jer 22:25; 37:1; Eze 17:12

Zedekiah King of Judah

¹¹Zedekiah was twenty-one years old when he became king, and he reigned in Jerusalem eleven years. ¹²He did evil in the eyes of the Lord his God and did not humble himself before Jeremiah the prophet, who spoke the word of the Lord. ¹³He also rebelled against King Nebuchadnezzar, who had made him take an oath in God's name. He became stiffnecked and hardened his heart and would not turn to the Lord, the God of Israel. ¹⁴Furthermore, all the leaders of the priests and the people became more and more unfaithful, following all the detestable practices of the nations and defiling the temple of the Lord, which he had consecrated in Jerusalem.   2Ki 24:18-20; Jer 52:1-3

The Fall of Jerusalem

¹⁵The Lord, the God of their fathers, sent word to them through his messengers again and again, because he had pity on his people and on his dwelling place. ¹⁶But they mocked God's messengers, despised his words and scoffed at his prophets until the wrath of the Lord was aroused against his people and there was no remedy. ¹⁷He brought up against them the king of the Babylonians,[c] who killed their young men with the sword in the sanctuary, and spared neither young man nor young woman, old man or aged. God handed all of them over to Nebuchadnezzar. ¹⁸He carried to Babylon all the articles from the temple of God, both large and small, and the treasures of the Lord's temple and the treasures of the king and his officials. ¹⁹They set fire to God's temple and broke down the wall of Jerusalem; they burned all the palaces and destroyed everything of value there.

²⁰He carried into exile to Babylon the remnant, who escaped from the sword, and they became servants to him and his sons until the kingdom of Persia came to power. ²¹The land enjoyed its sabbath rests; all the time of its deso-

---

[a]9 One Hebrew manuscript, some Septuagint manuscripts and Syriac (see also 2 Kings 24:8); most Hebrew manuscripts *eight*   [b]10 Hebrew *brother*, that is, relative (see 2 Kings 24:17)   [c]17 Or *Chaldeans*

lation it rested, until the seventy years were completed in fulfillment of the word of the LORD spoken by Jeremiah.   Ezr 1:1-3; Jer 25:11

22In the first year of Cyrus king of Persia, in order to fulfill the word of the LORD spoken by Jeremiah, the LORD moved the heart of Cyrus king of Persia to make a proclamation throughout his realm and to put it in writing:

23"This is what Cyrus king of Persia says:

"'The LORD, the God of heaven, has given me all the kingdoms of the earth and he has appointed me to build a temple for him at Jerusalem in Judah. Anyone of his people among you—may the LORD his God be with him, and let him go up.'"   Jdg 4:10

Ezra

Cyrus Helps the Exiles to Return

1 In the first year of Cyrus king of Persia, in order to fulfill the word of the LORD spoken by Jeremiah, the LORD moved the heart of Cyrus king of Persia to make a proclamation throughout his realm and to put it in writing:

²"This is what Cyrus king of Persia says: 2Ch 36:22-23

" 'The LORD, the God of heaven, has given me all the kingdoms of the earth and he has appointed me to build a temple for him at Jerusalem in Judah. ³Anyone of his people among you—may his God be with him, and let him go up to Jerusalem in Judah and build the temple of the LORD, the God of Israel, the God who is in Jerusalem. ⁴And the people of any place where survivors may now be living are to provide him with silver and gold, with goods and livestock, and with freewill offerings for the temple of God in Jerusalem.' "   Ezr 4:3; 5:13; 6:3,14

⁵Then the family heads of Judah and Benjamin, and the priests and Levites—everyone whose heart God had moved—prepared to go up and build the house of the LORD in Jerusalem. ⁶All their neighbors assisted them with articles of silver and gold, with goods and livestock, and with valuable gifts, in addition to all the freewill offerings. ⁷Moreover, King Cyrus brought out the articles belonging to the temple of the LORD, which Nebuchadnezzar had carried away from Jerusalem and had placed in the temple of his god.*a* ⁸Cyrus king of Persia had them brought by Mithredath the treasurer, who counted them out to Sheshbazzar the prince of Judah.   2Ki 24:13

⁹This was the inventory:

gold dishes	30
silver dishes	1,000
silver pans*b*	29
¹⁰gold bowls	30
matching silver bowls	410
other articles	1,000

¹¹In all, there were 5,400 articles of gold and of silver. Sheshbazzar brought all these along when the exiles came up from Babylon to Jerusalem.

---

*a*7 Or *gods*   *b*9 The meaning of the Hebrew for this word is uncertain.

The List of the Exiles Who Returned

2 Now these are the people of the province who came up from the captivity of the exiles, whom Nebuchadnezzar king of Babylon had taken captive to Babylon (they returned to Jerusalem and Judah, each to his own town, ²in company with Zerubbabel, Jeshua, Nehemiah, Seraiah, Reelaiah, Mordecai, Bilshan, Mispar, Bigvai, Rehum and Baanah):

The list of the men of the people of Israel:

³the descendants of Parosh 2,172
⁴of Shephatiah 372
⁵of Arah 775
⁶of Pahath-Moab (through the line of Jeshua and Joab) 2,812
⁷of Elam 1,254
⁸of Zattu 945
⁹of Zaccai 760
¹⁰of Bani 642
¹¹of Bebai 623
¹²of Azgad 1,222
¹³of Adonikam 666
¹⁴of Bigvai 2,056
¹⁵of Adin 454
¹⁶of Ater (through Hezekiah) 98
¹⁷of Bezai 323
¹⁸of Jorah 112
¹⁹of Hashum 223
²⁰of Gibbar 95

²¹the men of Bethlehem 123
²²of Netophah 56
²³of Anathoth 128
²⁴of Azmaveth 42
²⁵of Kiriath Jearim,ᵃ Kephirah and Beeroth 743
²⁶of Ramah and Geba 621
²⁷of Micmash 122
²⁸of Bethel and Ai 223
²⁹of Nebo 52
³⁰of Magbish 156
³¹of the other Elam 1,254
³²of Harim 320
³³of Lod, Hadid and Ono 725
³⁴of Jericho 345
³⁵of Senaah 3,630

³⁶The priests:

the descendants of Jedaiah (through the family of Jeshua) 973
³⁷of Immer 1,052
³⁸of Pashhur 1,247
³⁹of Harim 1,017

⁴⁰The Levites: Ge 29:34; Nu 3:9

the descendants of Jeshua and Kadmiel (through the line of Hodaviah) 74

⁴¹The singers: 1Ch 15:16

the descendants of Asaph 128

⁴²The gatekeepers of the temple: 1Sa 3:15; 1Ch 9:17

ᵃ25 See Septuagint (see also Neh. 7:29); Hebrew *Kiriath Arim.*

the descendants of
    Shallum, Ater, Talmon,
    Akkub, Hatita and
    Shobai   139

⁴³The temple servants: 1Ch 9:2

the descendants of
    Ziha, Hasupha, Tabbaoth,
⁴⁴Keros, Siaha, Padon,
⁴⁵Lebanah, Hagabah,
    Akkub,
⁴⁶Hagab, Shalmai, Hanan,
⁴⁷Giddel, Gahar, Reaiah,
⁴⁸Rezin, Nekoda, Gazzam,
⁴⁹Uzza, Paseah, Besai,
⁵⁰Asnah, Meunim,
    Nephussim,
⁵¹Bakbuk, Hakupha,
    Harhur,
⁵²Bazluth, Mehida, Harsha,
⁵³Barkos, Sisera, Temah,
⁵⁴Neziah and Hatipha

⁵⁵The descendants of the servants of Solomon:

the descendants of
    Sotai, Hassophereth,
    Peruda,
⁵⁶Jaala, Darkon, Giddel,
⁵⁷Shephatiah, Hattil,
    Pokereth-Hazzebaim and
    Ami

⁵⁸The temple servants and the
    descendants of the
    servants of Solomon   392

⁵⁹The following came up
from the towns of Tel Melah,
Tel Harsha, Kerub, Addon
and Immer, but they could
not show that their families
were descended from Israel:

⁶⁰The descendants of
    Delaiah, Tobiah and
    Nekoda   652

⁶¹And from among the
priests:

The descendants of
    Hobaiah, Hakkoz and
    Barzillai (a man who had
    married a daughter of
    Barzillai the Gileadite and
    was called by that name).
⁶²These searched for their
family records, but they could
not find them and so were excluded from the priesthood as
unclean. ⁶³The governor ordered them not to eat any of
the most sacred food until
there was a priest ministering
with the Urim and Thummim.

⁶⁴The whole company
numbered 42,360, ⁶⁵besides
their 7,337 menservants and
maidservants; and they also
had 200 men and women
singers. ⁶⁶They had 736
horses, 245 mules, ⁶⁷435 camels and 6,720 donkeys.

⁶⁸When they arrived at the
house of the LORD in Jerusalem,
some of the heads of the families
gave freewill offerings toward the
rebuilding of the house of God on
its site. ⁶⁹According to their ability
they gave to the treasury for this

work 61,000 drachmas*a* of gold, 5,000 minas*b* of silver and 100 priestly garments.   Ex 25:2

70The priests, the Levites, the singers, the gatekeepers and the temple servants settled in their own towns, along with some of the other people, and the rest of the Israelites settled in their towns.

Rebuilding the Altar

3 When the seventh month came and the Israelites had settled in their towns, the people assembled as one man in Jerusalem. **2**Then Jeshua son of Jozadak and his fellow priests and Zerubbabel son of Shealtiel and his associates began to build the altar of the God of Israel to sacrifice burnt offerings on it, in accordance with what is written in the Law of Moses the man of God. **3**Despite their fear of the peoples around them, they built the altar on its foundation and sacrificed burnt offerings on it to the LORD, both the morning and evening sacrifices. **4**Then in accordance with what is written, they celebrated the Feast of Tabernacles with the required number of burnt offerings prescribed for each day. **5**After that, they presented the regular burnt offerings, the New Moon sacrifices and the sacrifices for all the appointed sacred feasts of the LORD, as well as those brought as freewill offerings to the

LORD. **6**On the first day of the seventh month they began to offer burnt offerings to the LORD, though the foundation of the LORD's temple had not yet been laid.   Ex 23:16

Rebuilding the Temple

7Then they gave money to the masons and carpenters, and gave food and drink and oil to the people of Sidon and Tyre, so that they would bring cedar logs by sea from Lebanon to Joppa, as authorized by Cyrus king of Persia.   Ezr 1:2-4

8In the second month of the second year after their arrival at the house of God in Jerusalem, Zerubbabel son of Shealtiel, Jeshua son of Jozadak and the rest of their brothers (the priests and the Levites and all who had returned from the captivity to Jerusalem) began the work, appointing Levites twenty years of age and older to supervise the building of the house of the LORD. **9**Jeshua and his sons and brothers and Kadmiel and his sons (descendants of Hodaviah*c*) and the sons of Henadad and their sons and brothers—all Levites—joined together in supervising those working on the house of God.   1Ch 23:24; Ezr 2:40

10When the builders laid the foundation of the temple of the LORD, the priests in their vestments and with trumpets, and the Levites (the sons of Asaph) with cymbals,

---

*a*69 That is, about 1,100 pounds (about 500 kilograms)   *b*69 That is, about 3 tons (about 2.9 metric tons)   *c*9 Hebrew *Yehudah*, probably a variant of *Hodaviah*

took their places to praise the Lord, as prescribed by David king of Israel. ¹¹With praise and thanksgiving they sang to the Lord:

"He is good;
> his love to Israel endures
> forever."   1Ch 16:34,41; 2Ch 7:3

And all the people gave a great shout of praise to the Lord, because the foundation of the house of the Lord was laid. ¹²But many of the older priests and Levites and family heads, who had seen the former temple, wept aloud when they saw the foundation of this temple being laid, while many others shouted for joy. ¹³No one could distinguish the sound of the shouts of joy from the sound of weeping, because the people made so much noise. And the sound was heard far away.   Ne 12:24; Isa 16:9

Opposition to the Rebuilding

4 When the enemies of Judah and Benjamin heard that the exiles were building a temple for the Lord, the God of Israel, ²they came to Zerubbabel and to the heads of the families and said, "Let us help you build because, like you, we seek your God and have been sacrificing to him since the time of Esarhaddon king of Assyria, who brought us here." ³But Zerubbabel, Jeshua and the rest of the heads of the families of Israel answered, "You have no part with us in building a temple to our God. We alone will build it for the Lord, the God of Israel, as King Cyrus, the king of Persia, commanded us."   Ezr 1:1-4; Ne 2:20

⁴Then the peoples around them set out to discourage the people of Judah and make them afraid to go on building.ᵃ ⁵They hired counselors to work against them and frustrate their plans during the entire reign of Cyrus king of Persia and down to the reign of Darius king of Persia.   Ezr 3:3

Later Opposition Under Xerxes and Artaxerxes

⁶At the beginning of the reign of Xerxes,ᵇ they lodged an accusation against the people of Judah and Jerusalem.   Est 1:1; Da 9:1

⁷And in the days of Artaxerxes king of Persia, Bishlam, Mithredath, Tabeel and the rest of his associates wrote a letter to Artaxerxes. The letter was written in Aramaic script and in the Aramaic language.ᶜ,ᵈ   2Ki 18:26; Da 2:4

⁸Rehum the commanding officer and Shimshai the secretary wrote a letter against Jerusalem to Artaxerxes the king as follows:

⁹Rehum the commanding officer and Shimshai the secretary, together with the rest of their associates—the judges and officials over the men

---

ᵃ4 Or and troubled them as they built   ᵇ6 Hebrew Ahasuerus, a variant of Xerxes' Persian name
ᶜ7 Or written in Aramaic and translated   ᵈ7 The text of Ezra 4:8—6:18 is in Aramaic.

from Tripolis, Persia,*a* Erech and Babylon, the Elamites of Susa, ¹⁰and the other people whom the great and honorable Ashurbanipal*b* deported and settled in the city of Samaria and elsewhere in Trans-Euphrates.   Ezr 5:6; Ne 4:2

¹¹(This is a copy of the letter they sent him.)

To King Artaxerxes,

From your servants, the men of Trans-Euphrates:

¹²The king should know that the Jews who came up to us from you have gone to Jerusalem and are rebuilding that rebellious and wicked city. They are restoring the walls and repairing the foundations.   Ezr 5:3,9

¹³Furthermore, the king should know that if this city is built and its walls are restored, no more taxes, tribute or duty will be paid, and the royal revenues will suffer. ¹⁴Now since we are under obligation to the palace and it is not proper for us to see the king dishonored, we are sending this message to inform the king, ¹⁵so that a search may be made in the archives of your predecessors. In these records you will find that this city is a rebellious city, troublesome to kings and provinces, a place of rebellion from ancient times. That is why this city was destroyed. ¹⁶We inform the king that if this city is built and its walls are restored, you will be left with nothing in Trans-Euphrates.   Ezr 7:24; Ne 5:4; Est 3:8

¹⁷The king sent this reply:

To Rehum the commanding officer, Shimshai the secretary and the rest of their associates living in Samaria and elsewhere in Trans-Euphrates:

Greetings.

¹⁸The letter you sent us has been read and translated in my presence. ¹⁹I issued an order and a search was made, and it was found that this city has a long history of revolt against kings and has been a place of rebellion and sedition. ²⁰Jerusalem has had powerful kings ruling over the whole of Trans-Euphrates, and taxes, tribute and duty were paid to them. ²¹Now issue an order to these men to stop work, so that this city will not be rebuilt until I so order. ²²Be careful not to neglect this matter. Why let this

---

a9 Or *officials, magistrates and governors over the men from Ashurbanipal*   *b10* Aramaic *Osnappar,* a variant of

threat grow, to the detriment of the royal interests? 1Ki 4:21

²³As soon as the copy of the letter of King Artaxerxes was read to Rehum and Shimshai the secretary and their associates, they went immediately to the Jews in Jerusalem and compelled them by force to stop.

²⁴Thus the work on the house of God in Jerusalem came to a standstill until the second year of the reign of Darius king of Persia.

Tattenai's Letter to Darius

5 Now Haggai the prophet and Zechariah the prophet, a descendant of Iddo, prophesied to the Jews in Judah and Jerusalem in the name of the God of Israel, who was over them. ²Then Zerubbabel son of Shealtiel and Jeshua son of Jozadak set to work to rebuild the house of God in Jerusalem. And the prophets of God were with them, helping them. Ezr 3:2

³At that time Tattenai, governor of Trans-Euphrates, and Shethar-Bozenai and their associates went to them and asked, "Who authorized you to rebuild this temple and restore this structure?" ⁴They also asked, "What are the names of the men constructing this building?"ᵃ ⁵But the eye of their God was watching over the elders of the Jews, and they were not stopped until a report could go to Darius and his written reply be received. Ezr 1:3; 6:6; Ps 33:18

⁶This is a copy of the letter that Tattenai, governor of Trans-Euphrates, and Shethar-Bozenai and their associates, the officials of Trans-Euphrates, sent to King Darius. ⁷The report they sent him read as follows:

To King Darius:

Cordial greetings.

⁸The king should know that we went to the district of Judah, to the temple of the great God. The people are building it with large stones and placing the timbers in the walls. The work is being carried on with diligence and is making rapid progress under their direction.

⁹We questioned the elders and asked them, "Who authorized you to rebuild this temple and restore this structure?" ¹⁰We also asked them their names, so that we could write down the names of their leaders for your information.

¹¹This is the answer they gave us:

"We are the servants of the God of heaven and earth, and we are rebuilding the temple that was built many years ago, one that a great king of Israel

---

ᵃ4 See Septuagint; Aramaic ⁴We told them the names of the men constructing this building.

built and finished. ¹²But be-cause our fathers angered the God of heaven, he handed them over to Nebuchadnez-zar the Chaldean, king of Bab-ylon, who destroyed this tem-ple and deported the people to Babylon.   2Ki 24:1; 25:8-9,11

¹³"However, in the first year of Cyrus king of Babylon, King Cyrus issued a decree to rebuild this house of God. ¹⁴He even removed from the temple^a of Babylon the gold and silver articles of the house of God, which Nebu-chadnezzar had taken from the temple in Jerusalem and brought to the temple^a in Babylon.   Ezr 1:7; 6:5

"Then King Cyrus gave them to a man named Shesh-bazzar, whom he had ap-pointed governor, ¹⁵and he told him, 'Take these articles and go and deposit them in the temple in Jerusalem. And rebuild the house of God on its site.' ¹⁶So this Sheshbazzar came and laid the foundations of the house of God in Jerusa-lem. From that day to the present it has been under con-struction but is not yet fin-ished."   Ezr 3:10; 6:15

¹⁷Now if it pleases the king, let a search be made in the royal archives of Babylon to see if King Cyrus did in fact issue a decree to rebuild this house of God in Jerusalem. Then let the king send us his decision in this matter.

The Decree of Darius

6 King Darius then issued an or-der, and they searched in the archives stored in the treasury at Babylon. ²A scroll was found in the citadel of Ecbatana in the province of Media, and this was written on it: Ezr 5:17

Memorandum:

³In the first year of King Cy-rus, the king issued a decree concerning the temple of God in Jerusalem:

Let the temple be rebuilt as a place to present sacrifices, and let its foundations be laid. It is to be ninety feet^b high and ninety feet wide, ⁴with three courses of large stones and one of timbers. The costs are to be paid by the royal treasury. ⁵Also, the gold and silver articles of the house of God, which Nebuchadnezzar took from the temple in Jeru-salem and brought to Bab-ylon, are to be returned to their places in the temple in Jerusalem; they are to be de-posited in the house of God.

^{a}14 Or *palace* ^{b}3 Aramaic *sixty cubits* (about 27 meters)

⁶Now then, Tattenai, governor of Trans-Euphrates, and Shethar-Bozenai and you, their fellow officials of that province, stay away from there. ⁷Do not interfere with the work on this temple of God. Let the governor of the Jews and the Jewish elders rebuild this house of God on its site.   Ezr 5:3

⁸Moreover, I hereby decree what you are to do for these elders of the Jews in the construction of this house of God:

The expenses of these men are to be fully paid out of the royal treasury, from the revenues of Trans-Euphrates, so that the work will not stop. ⁹Whatever is needed—young bulls, rams, male lambs for burnt offerings to the God of heaven, and wheat, salt, wine and oil, as requested by the priests in Jerusalem—must be given them daily without fail, ¹⁰so that they may offer sacrifices pleasing to the God of heaven and pray for the well-being of the king and his sons.   Ezr 7:23; 1Ti 2:1-2

¹¹Furthermore, I decree that if anyone changes this edict, a beam is to be pulled from his house and he is to be lifted up and impaled on it. And for this crime his house is to be made a pile of rubble. ¹²May God, who has caused his Name to dwell there, over-throw any king or people who lifts a hand to change this decree or to destroy this temple in Jerusalem.   Dt 12:5; Ezr 7:26

I Darius have decreed it. Let it be carried out with diligence.

Completion and Dedication of the Temple

¹³Then, because of the decree King Darius had sent, Tattenai, governor of Trans-Euphrates, and Shethar-Bozenai and their associates carried it out with diligence. ¹⁴So the elders of the Jews continued to build and prosper under the preaching of Haggai the prophet and Zechariah, a descendant of Iddo. They finished building the temple according to the command of the God of Israel and the decrees of Cyrus, Darius and Artaxerxes, kings of Persia. ¹⁵The temple was completed on the third day of the month Adar, in the sixth year of the reign of King Darius.   Ezr 5:1

¹⁶Then the people of Israel—the priests, the Levites and the rest of the exiles—celebrated the dedication of the house of God with joy. ¹⁷For the dedication of this house of God they offered a hundred bulls, two hundred rams, four hundred male lambs and, as a sin offering for all Israel, twelve male goats, one for each of the tribes of Israel. ¹⁸And they installed the priests in their divisions and the Levites in their groups for the ser-

vice of God at Jerusalem, according to what is written in the Book of Moses.   1Ki 8:63; 2Ch 7:5; 35:4

The Passover

¹⁹On the fourteenth day of the first month, the exiles celebrated the Passover. ²⁰The priests and Levites had purified themselves and were all ceremonially clean. The Levites slaughtered the Passover lamb for all the exiles, for their brothers the priests and for themselves. ²¹So the Israelites who had returned from the exile ate it, together with all who had separated themselves from the unclean practices of their Gentile neighbors in order to seek the LORD, the God of Israel. ²²For seven days they celebrated with joy the Feast of Unleavened Bread, because the LORD had filled them with joy by changing the attitude of the king of Assyria, so that he assisted them in the work on the house of God, the God of Israel.   Ex 12:11; Ezr 1:1

Ezra Comes to Jerusalem

7 After these things, during the reign of Artaxerxes king of Persia, Ezra son of Seraiah, the son of Azariah, the son of Hilkiah, ²the son of Shallum, the son of Zadok, the son of Ahitub, ³the son of Amariah, the son of Azariah, the son of Meraioth, ⁴the son of Zerahiah, the son of Uzzi, the son of Bukki, ⁵the son of Abishua, the son of Phine-

has, the son of Eleazar, the son of Aaron the chief priest— ⁶this Ezra came up from Babylon. He was a teacher well versed in the Law of Moses, which the LORD, the God of Israel, had given. The king had granted him everything he asked, for the hand of the LORD his God was on him. ⁷Some of the Israelites, including priests, Levites, singers, gatekeepers and temple servants, also came up to Jerusalem in the seventh year of King Artaxerxes.   Ezr 8:1; Ne 12:36; Isa 41:20

⁸Ezra arrived in Jerusalem in the fifth month of the seventh year of the king. ⁹He had begun his journey from Babylon on the first day of the first month, and he arrived in Jerusalem on the first day of the fifth month, for the gracious hand of his God was on him. ¹⁰For Ezra had devoted himself to the study and observance of the Law of the LORD, and to teaching its decrees and laws in Israel.   Dt 33:10; Ne 8:1-8

King Artaxerxes' Letter to Ezra

¹¹This is a copy of the letter King Artaxerxes had given to Ezra the priest and teacher, a man learned in matters concerning the commands and decrees of the LORD for Israel:

¹²ᵃArtaxerxes, king of kings,

To Ezra the priest, a teacher of the Law of the God of heaven:

ᵃ12 The text of Ezra 7:12-26 is in Aramaic.

Greetings.

¹³Now I decree that any of the Israelites in my kingdom, including priests and Levites, who wish to go to Jerusalem with you, may go. ¹⁴You are sent by the king and his seven advisers to inquire about Judah and Jerusalem with regard to the Law of your God, which is in your hand. ¹⁵Moreover, you are to take with you the silver and gold that the king and his advisers have freely given to the God of Israel, whose dwelling is in Jerusalem, ¹⁶together with all the silver and gold you may obtain from the province of Babylon, as well as the freewill offerings of the people and priests for the temple of their God in Jerusalem. ¹⁷With this money be sure to buy bulls, rams and male lambs, together with their grain offerings and drink offerings, and sacrifice them on the altar of the temple of your God in Jerusalem.   2Ch 6:2

¹⁸You and your brother Jews may then do whatever seems best with the rest of the silver and gold, in accordance with the will of your God. ¹⁹Deliver to the God of Jerusalem all the articles entrusted to you for worship in the temple of your God. ²⁰And anything else needed for the temple of your God that you may have occasion to supply, you may provide from the royal treasury.   Ezr 6:4; Jer 27:22

²¹Now I, King Artaxerxes, order all the treasurers of Trans-Euphrates to provide with diligence whatever Ezra the priest, a teacher of the Law of the God of heaven, may ask of you— ²²up to a hundred talentsᵃ of silver, a hundred corsᵇ of wheat, a hundred bathsᶜ of wine, a hundred bathsᶜ of olive oil, and salt without limit. ²³Whatever the God of heaven has prescribed, let it be done with diligence for the temple of the God of heaven. Why should there be wrath against the realm of the king and of his sons? ²⁴You are also to know that you have no authority to impose taxes, tribute or duty on any of the priests, Levites, singers, gatekeepers, temple servants or other workers at this house of God.   Ezr 6:10; 8:36

²⁵And you, Ezra, in accordance with the wisdom of your God, which you possess, appoint magistrates and judges to administer justice to all the people of Trans-Eu-

---

ᵃ 22 That is, about 3 3/4 tons (about 3.4 metric tons)   ᵇ 22 That is, probably about 600 bushels (about 22 kiloliters)   ᶜ 22 That is, probably about 600 gallons (about 2.2 kiloliters)

phrates—all who know the laws of your God. And you are to teach any who do not know them. ²⁶Whoever does not obey the law of your God and the law of the king must surely be punished by death, banishment, confiscation of property, or imprisonment.

²⁷Praise be to the LORD, the God of our fathers, who has put it into the king's heart to bring honor to the house of the LORD in Jerusalem in this way ²⁸and who has extended his good favor to me before the king and his advisers and all the king's powerful officials. Because the hand of the LORD my God was on me, I took courage and gathered leading men from Israel to go up with me.   Ezr 5:5; 9:9

List of the Family Heads Returning With Ezra

8 These are the family heads and those registered with them who came up with me from Babylon during the reign of King Artaxerxes: Ezr 7:7

²of the descendants of Phinehas, Gershom;
of the descendants of Ithamar, Daniel;
of the descendants of David, Hattush ³of the descendants of Shecaniah;
of the descendants of Parosh,

Zechariah, and with him were registered 150 men;
⁴of the descendants of Pahath-Moab, Eliehoenai son of Zerahiah, and with him 200 men;   Ezr 2:6
⁵of the descendants of Zattu,ᵃ Shecaniah son of Jahaziel, and with him 300 men;
⁶of the descendants of Adin, Ebed son of Jonathan, and with him 50 men;   Ezr 2:15
⁷of the descendants of Elam, Jeshaiah son of Athaliah, and with him 70 men;
⁸of the descendants of Shephatiah, Zebadiah son of Michael, and with him 80 men;
⁹of the descendants of Joab, Obadiah son of Jehiel, and with him 218 men;
¹⁰of the descendants of Bani,ᵇ Shelomith son of Josiphiah, and with him 160 men;
¹¹of the descendants of Bebai, Zechariah son of Bebai, and with him 28 men;
¹²of the descendants of Azgad, Johanan son of Hakkatan, and with him 110 men;
¹³of the descendants of Adonikam, the last ones, whose names were Eliphelet, Jeuel and Shemaiah, and with them 60 men;   Ezr 2:13
¹⁴of the descendants of Bigvai,

ᵃ5 Some Septuagint manuscripts (also 1 Esdras 8:32); Hebrew does not have *Zattu*.   ᵇ10 Some Septuagint manuscripts (also 1 Esdras 8:36); Hebrew does not have *Bani*.

Uthai and Zaccur, and with them 70 men.

The Return to Jerusalem

¹⁵I assembled them at the canal that flows toward Ahava, and we camped there three days. When I checked among the people and the priests, I found no Levites there. ¹⁶So I summoned Eliezer, Ariel, Shemaiah, Elnathan, Jarib, Elnathan, Nathan, Zechariah and Meshullam, who were leaders, and Joiarib and Elnathan, who were men of learning, ¹⁷and I sent them to Iddo, the leader in Casiphia. I told them what to say to Iddo and his kinsmen, the temple servants in Casiphia, so that they might bring attendants to us for the house of our God. ¹⁸Because the gracious hand of our God was on us, they brought us Sherebiah, a capable man, from the descendants of Mahli son of Levi, the son of Israel, and Sherebiah's sons and brothers, 18 men; ¹⁹and Hashabiah, together with Jeshaiah from the descendants of Merari, and his brothers and nephews, 20 men. ²⁰They also brought 220 of the temple servants—a body that David and the officials had established to assist the Levites. All were registered by name.   Ezr 2:43

²¹There, by the Ahava Canal, I proclaimed a fast, so that we might humble ourselves before our God and ask him for a safe journey for us and our children, with all our possessions. ²²I was ashamed to ask the king for soldiers and horsemen to protect us from enemies on the road, because we had told the king, "The gracious hand of our God is on everyone who looks to him, but his great anger is against all who forsake him." ²³So we fasted and petitioned our God about this, and he answered our prayer.

²⁴Then I set apart twelve of the leading priests, together with Sherebiah, Hashabiah and ten of their brothers, ²⁵and I weighed out to them the offering of silver and gold and the articles that the king, his advisers, his officials and all Israel present there had donated for the house of our God. ²⁶I weighed out to them 650 talents[a] of silver, silver articles weighing 100 talents,[b] 100 talents[b] of gold, ²⁷20 bowls of gold valued at 1,000 darics,[c] and two fine articles of polished bronze, as precious as gold.

²⁸I said to them, "You as well as these articles are consecrated to the LORD. The silver and gold are a freewill offering to the LORD, the God of your fathers. ²⁹Guard them carefully until you weigh them out in the chambers of the house of the LORD in Jerusalem before the lead-

---

a26 That is, about 25 tons (about 22 metric tons)   *b26* That is, about 3 3/4 tons (about 3.4 metric tons)   *c27* That is, about 19 pounds (about 8.5 kilograms)

ing priests and the Levites and the family heads of Israel." **30**Then the priests and Levites received the silver and gold and sacred articles that had been weighed out to be taken to the house of our God in Jerusalem.   Lev 21:6; 22:2-3

31On the twelfth day of the first month we set out from the Ahava Canal to go to Jerusalem. The hand of our God was on us, and he protected us from enemies and bandits along the way. **32**So we arrived in Jerusalem, where we rested three days.   Ge 40:13; Ne 2:11

33On the fourth day, in the house of our God, we weighed out the silver and gold and the sacred articles into the hands of Meremoth son of Uriah, the priest. Eleazar son of Phinehas was with him, and so were the Levites Jozabad son of Jeshua and Noadiah son of Binnui. **34**Everything was accounted for by number and weight, and the entire weight was recorded at that time.   Ne 3:4,21,24

35Then the exiles who had returned from captivity sacrificed burnt offerings to the God of Israel: twelve bulls for all Israel, ninety-six rams, seventy-seven male lambs and, as a sin offering, twelve male goats. All this was a burnt offering to the LORD. **36**They also delivered the king's orders to the royal satraps and to the governors of Trans-Euphrates, who then gave assistance to the people and to the house of God.   Ezr 7:21-24; Est 9:3

Ezra's Prayer About Intermarriage

9 After these things had been done, the leaders came to me and said, "The people of Israel, including the priests and the Levites, have not kept themselves separate from the neighboring peoples with their detestable practices, like those of the Canaanites, Hittites, Perizzites, Jebusites, Ammonites, Moabites, Egyptians and Amorites. **2**They have taken some of their daughters as wives for themselves and their sons, and have mingled the holy race with the peoples around them. And the leaders and officials have led the way in this unfaithfulness."

3When I heard this, I tore my tunic and cloak, pulled hair from my head and beard and sat down appalled. **4**Then everyone who trembled at the words of the God of Israel gathered around me because of this unfaithfulness of the exiles. And I sat there appalled until the evening sacrifice.   Ezr 10:3

5Then, at the evening sacrifice, I rose from my self-abasement, with my tunic and cloak torn, and fell on my knees with my hands spread out to the LORD my God **6**and prayed:

"O my God, I am too ashamed and disgraced to lift up my face to you, my God, because our sins are higher than our heads and our guilt has reached to the heavens.

⁷From the days of our forefathers until now, our guilt has been great. Because of our sins, we and our kings and our priests have been subjected to the sword and captivity, to pillage and humiliation at the hand of foreign kings, as it is today.   Dt 28:37; 2Ch 28:9; Rev 18:5

⁸"But now, for a brief moment, the Lᴏʀᴅ our God has been gracious in leaving us a remnant and giving us a firm place in his sanctuary, and so our God gives light to our eyes and a little relief in our bondage. ⁹Though we are slaves, our God has not deserted us in our bondage. He has shown us kindness in the sight of the kings of Persia: He has granted us new life to rebuild the house of our God and repair its ruins, and he has given us a wall of protection in Judah and Jerusalem.   Ne 9:36; Ps 13:3

¹⁰"But now, O our God, what can we say after this? For we have disregarded the commands ¹¹you gave through your servants the prophets when you said: 'The land you are entering to possess is a land polluted by the corruption of its peoples. By their detestable practices they have filled it with their impurity from one end to the other. ¹²Therefore, do not give your daughters in marriage to their sons or take their daughters for your sons. Do not seek a treaty of friendship with them at any time, that you may be strong and eat the good things of the land and leave it to your children as an everlasting inheritance.'   Dt 7:3; 23:6

¹³"What has happened to us is a result of our evil deeds and our great guilt, and yet, our God, you have punished us less than our sins have deserved and have given us a remnant like this. ¹⁴Shall we again break your commands and intermarry with the peoples who commit such detestable practices? Would you not be angry enough with us to destroy us, leaving us no remnant or survivor? ¹⁵O Lᴏʀᴅ, God of Israel, you are righteous! We are left this day as a remnant. Here we are before you in our guilt, though because of it not one of us can stand in your presence."

The People's Confession of Sin

10 While Ezra was praying and confessing, weeping and throwing himself down before the house of God, a large crowd of Israelites—men, women and children—gathered around him. They too wept bitterly. ²Then Shecaniah son of Jehiel, one of the descendants of Elam, said to Ezra, "We have been unfaithful to our God by marrying foreign women from the peoples around us. But in spite of

this, there is still hope for Israel. ³Now let us make a covenant before our God to send away all these women and their children, in accordance with the counsel of my lord and of those who fear the commands of our God. Let it be done according to the Law. ⁴Rise up; this matter is in your hands. We will support you, so take courage and do it." Dt 7:2-3; Ezr 9:4

⁵So Ezra rose up and put the leading priests and Levites and all Israel under oath to do what had been suggested. And they took the oath. ⁶Then Ezra withdrew from before the house of God and went to the room of Jehohanan son of Eliashib. While he was there, he ate no food and drank no water, because he continued to mourn over the unfaithfulness of the exiles. Dt 9:18; Ne 5:12; 13:25

⁷A proclamation was then issued throughout Judah and Jerusalem for all the exiles to assemble in Jerusalem. ⁸Anyone who failed to appear within three days would forfeit all his property, in accordance with the decision of the officials and elders, and would himself be expelled from the assembly of the exiles.

⁹Within the three days, all the men of Judah and Benjamin had gathered in Jerusalem. And on the twentieth day of the ninth month, all the people were sitting in the square before the house of God, greatly distressed by the occasion and because of the rain. ¹⁰Then Ezra the priest stood up and said to them, "You have been unfaithful; you have married foreign women, adding to Israel's guilt. ¹¹Now make confession to the LORD, the God of your fathers, and do his will. Separate yourselves from the peoples around you and from your foreign wives." Dt 24:1; Mal 2:10-16

¹²The whole assembly responded with a loud voice: "You are right! We must do as you say. ¹³But there are many people here and it is the rainy season; so we cannot stand outside. Besides, this matter cannot be taken care of in a day or two, because we have sinned greatly in this thing. ¹⁴Let our officials act for the whole assembly. Then let everyone in our towns who has married a foreign woman come at a set time, along with the elders and judges of each town, until the fierce anger of our God in this matter is turned away from us." ¹⁵Only Jonathan son of Asahel and Jahzeiah son of Tikvah, supported by Meshullam and Shabbethai the Levite, opposed this. 2Ch 29:10; 30:8; Ne 11:16

¹⁶So the exiles did as was proposed. Ezra the priest selected men who were family heads, one from each family division, and all of them designated by name. On the first day of the tenth month they sat down to investigate the cases, ¹⁷and by the first day of the first month they finished dealing

with all the men who had married foreign women.

Those Guilty of Intermarriage

18Among the descendants of the priests, the following had married foreign women: Jdg 3:6

From the descendants of Jeshua son of Jozadak, and his brothers: Maaseiah, Eliezer, Jarib and Gedaliah. **19**(They all gave their hands in pledge to put away their wives, and for their guilt they each presented a ram from the flock as a guilt offering.) Lev 5:15; 2Ki 10:15; Ezr 2:2

20From the descendants of Immer: 1Ch 24:14
Hanani and Zebadiah.

21From the descendants of Harim: 1Ch 24:8
Maaseiah, Elijah, Shemaiah, Jehiel and Uzziah.

22From the descendants of Pashhur: 1Ch 9:12
Elioenai, Maaseiah, Ishmael, Nethanel, Jozabad and Elasah.

23Among the Levites: Ne 8:7; 9:4

Jozabad, Shimei, Kelaiah (that is, Kelita), Pethahiah, Judah and Eliezer.

24From the singers:
Eliashib. Ne 3:1; 12:10; 13:7,28
From the gatekeepers:
Shallum, Telem and Uri.

25And among the other Israelites:

From the descendants of Parosh: Ezr 2:3
Ramiah, Izziah, Malkijah, Mijamin, Eleazar, Malkijah and Benaiah.

26From the descendants of Elam:
Mattaniah, Zechariah, Jehiel, Abdi, Jeremoth and Elijah.

27From the descendants of Zattu:
Elioenai, Eliashib, Mattaniah, Jeremoth, Zabad and Aziza.

28From the descendants of Bebai:
Jehohanan, Hananiah, Zabbai and Athlai.

29From the descendants of Bani:
Meshullam, Malluch, Adaiah, Jashub, Sheal and Jeremoth.

30From the descendants of Pahath-Moab:
Adna, Kelal, Benaiah, Maaseiah, Mattaniah, Bezalel, Binnui and Manasseh.

31From the descendants of Harim:
Eliezer, Ishijah, Malkijah, Shemaiah, Shimeon, **32**Benjamin, Malluch and Shemariah.

33From the descendants of Hashum:
Mattenai, Mattattah, Zabad,

Eliphelet, Jeremai, Manasseh and Shimei.

³⁴From the descendants of Bani:

Maadai, Amram, Uel, ³⁵Benaiah, Bedeiah, Keluhi, ³⁶Vaniah, Meremoth, Eliashib, ³⁷Mattaniah, Mattenai and Jaasu.

³⁸From the descendants of Binnui:^a

Shimei, ³⁹Shelemiah, Nathan, Adaiah, ⁴⁰Macnadebai, Shashai, Sharai, ⁴¹Azarel, Shelemiah, Shemariah, ⁴²Shallum, Amariah and Joseph.

⁴³From the descendants of Nebo:

Jeiel, Mattithiah, Zabad, Zebina, Jaddai, Joel and Benaiah.

⁴⁴All these had married foreign women, and some of them had children by these wives.^b

^a37,38 See Septuagint (also 1 Esdras 9:34); Hebrew *Jaasu* ³⁸*and Bani and Binnui,*   ^b44 Or *and they sent them away with their children*

Nehemiah

bai, Shashai, Sharai, ⁴¹Aza-
seh and Shimei, Shemariah,
⁴²From the descendants of Amariah and Joseph.
⁴³From the descendants of
Nebo:
Jeiel, Mattithiah, Zabad,
Zebina, Jaddai, Joel and Benaiah.

Eliphelet, Jeremai, Manasseh and Shimei.
³⁴From the descendants of
Bani:
Maadai, Amram, Uel, ³⁵Be-

Nehemiah's Prayer

1 The words of Nehemiah son of Hacaliah:

In the month of Kislev in the twentieth year, while I was in the citadel of Susa, ²Hanani, one of my brothers, came from Judah with some other men, and I questioned them about the Jewish remnant that survived the exile, and also about Jerusalem.   Ne 10:1; Zec 7:1

³They said to me, "Those who survived the exile and are back in the province are in great trouble and disgrace. The wall of Jerusalem is broken down, and its gates have been burned with fire."

⁴When I heard these things, I sat down and wept. For some days I mourned and fasted and prayed before the God of heaven. ⁵Then I said:

"O Lord, God of heaven, the great and awesome God, who keeps his covenant of love with those who love him and obey his commands, ⁶let your ear be attentive and your eyes open to hear the prayer your servant is praying before you day and night for your servants, the people of Israel. I confess the sins we Israelites, including myself and my father's house, have committed against you. ⁷We have acted very wickedly toward you. We have not obeyed the commands, decrees and laws you gave your servant Moses.

⁸"Remember the instruction you gave your servant Moses, saying, 'If you are unfaithful, I will scatter you among the nations, ⁹but if you return to me and obey my commands, then even if your exiled people are at the farthest horizon, I will gather them from there and bring them to the place I have chosen as a dwelling for my Name.'   Lev 26:33; Dt 30:4

¹⁰"They are your servants and your people, whom you redeemed by your great strength and your mighty hand. ¹¹O Lord, let your ear be attentive to the prayer of this your servant and to the prayer of your servants who delight in revering your name. Give your servant success today by granting him favor in the presence of this man."   Dt 9:29

I was cupbearer to the king.

Artaxerxes Sends Nehemiah to Jerusalem

2 In the month of Nisan in the twentieth year of King Artaxerxes, when wine was brought for him, I took the wine and gave it to the king. I had not been sad in his presence before; ²so the king asked me, "Why does your face look so sad when you are not ill? This can be nothing but sadness of heart." Ezr 7:1

I was very much afraid, ³but I said to the king, "May the king live forever! Why should my face not look sad when the city where my fathers are buried lies in ruins, and its gates have been destroyed by fire?" Ne 1:3; Da 2:4

⁴The king said to me, "What is it you want?"

Then I prayed to the God of heaven, ⁵and I answered the king, "If it pleases the king and if your servant has found favor in his sight, let him send me to the city in Judah where my fathers are buried so that I can rebuild it."

⁶Then the king, with the queen sitting beside him, asked me, "How long will your journey take, and when will you get back?" It pleased the king to send me; so I set a time. Ne 5:14; 13:6

⁷I also said to him, "If it pleases the king, may I have letters to the governors of Trans-Euphrates, so that they will provide me safe-conduct until I arrive in Judah? ⁸And may I have a letter to Asaph, keeper of the king's forest, so he will give me timber to make beams for the gates of the citadel by the temple and for the city wall and for the residence I will occupy?" And because the gracious hand of my God was upon me, the king granted my requests. ⁹So I went to the governors of Trans-Euphrates and gave them the king's letters. The king had also sent army officers and cavalry with me. Ezr 7:6; 8:22,36

¹⁰When Sanballat the Horonite and Tobiah the Ammonite official heard about this, they were very much disturbed that someone had come to promote the welfare of the Israelites. Ne 4:3; 13:4-7; Est 10:3

Nehemiah Inspects Jerusalem's Walls

¹¹I went to Jerusalem, and after staying there three days ¹²I set out during the night with a few men. I had not told anyone what my God had put in my heart to do for Jerusalem. There were no mounts with me except the one I was riding on. ¹³By night I went out through the Valley Gate toward the Jackal[a] Well and the Dung Gate, examining the walls of Jerusalem, which had been broken down, and its gates, which had been destroyed by fire. ¹⁴Then I moved on toward

---

ᵃ13 Or *Serpent* or *Fig*

the Fountain Gate and the King's Pool, but there was not enough room for my mount to get through; [15]so I went up the valley by night, examining the wall. Finally, I turned back and reentered through the Valley Gate. [16]The officials did not know where I had gone or what I was doing, because as yet I had said nothing to the Jews or the priests or nobles or officials or any others who would be doing the work.   Ne 1:3; 3:13,15

[17]Then I said to them, "You see the trouble we are in: Jerusalem lies in ruins, and its gates have been burned with fire. Come, let us rebuild the wall of Jerusalem, and we will no longer be in disgrace." [18]I also told them about the gracious hand of my God upon me and what the king had said to me.

They replied, "Let us start rebuilding." So they began this good work.

[19]But when Sanballat the Horonite, Tobiah the Ammonite official and Geshem the Arab heard about it, they mocked and ridiculed us. "What is this you are doing?" they asked. "Are you rebelling against the king?"   Ps 44:13-16

[20]I answered them by saying, "The God of heaven will give us success. We his servants will start rebuilding, but as for you, you have no share in Jerusalem or any claim or historic right to it."

Builders of the Wall

3 Eliashib the high priest and his fellow priests went to work and rebuilt the Sheep Gate. They dedicated it and set its doors in place, building as far as the Tower of the Hundred, which they dedicated, and as far as the Tower of Hananel. [2]The men of Jericho built the adjoining section, and Zaccur son of Imri built next to them.

[3]The Fish Gate was rebuilt by the sons of Hassenaah. They laid its beams and put its doors and bolts and bars in place. [4]Meremoth son of Uriah, the son of Hakkoz, repaired the next section. Next to him Meshullam son of Berekiah, the son of Meshezabel, made repairs, and next to him Zadok son of Baana also made repairs. [5]The next section was repaired by the men of Tekoa, but their nobles would not put their shoulders to the work under their supervisors.[a]

[6]The Jeshanah[b] Gate was repaired by Joiada son of Paseah and Meshullam son of Besodeiah. They laid its beams and put its doors and bolts and bars in place. [7]Next to them, repairs were made by men from Gibeon and Mizpah —Melatiah of Gibeon and Jadon of Meronoth—places under the authority of the governor of Trans-Euphrates. [8]Uzziel son of Harhaiah, one of the goldsmiths, repaired the next section; and

---

a5 Or *their Lord* or *the governor*   b6 Or *Old*

Hananiah, one of the perfume-makers, made repairs next to that. They restored[a] Jerusalem as far as the Broad Wall. [9]Rephaiah son of Hur, ruler of a half-district of Jerusalem, repaired the next section. [10]Adjoining this, Jedaiah son of Harumaph made repairs opposite his house, and Hattush son of Hashabneiah made repairs next to him. [11]Malkijah son of Harim and Hasshub son of Pahath-Moab repaired another section and the Tower of the Ovens. [12]Shallum son of Hallohesh, ruler of a half-district of Jerusalem, repaired the next section with the help of his daughters.   Ne 2:7; 12:38-39

[13]The Valley Gate was repaired by Hanun and the residents of Zanoah. They rebuilt it and put its doors and bolts and bars in place. They also repaired five hundred yards[b] of the wall as far as the Dung Gate.   Ne 2:13; 2Ch 26:9

[14]The Dung Gate was repaired by Malkijah son of Recab, ruler of the district of Beth Hakkerem. He rebuilt it and put its doors and bolts and bars in place.   Jer 6:1

[15]The Fountain Gate was repaired by Shallun son of Col-Hozeh, ruler of the district of Mizpah. He rebuilt it, roofing it over and putting its doors and bolts and bars in place. He also repaired the wall of the Pool of Siloam,[c] by the King's Garden, as far as the steps going down from the City of David. [16]Beyond him, Nehemiah son of Azbuk, ruler of a half-district of Beth Zur, made repairs up to a point opposite the tombs[d] of David, as far as the artificial pool and the House of the Heroes.   Jos 15:58

[17]Next to him, the repairs were made by the Levites under Rehum son of Bani. Beside him, Hashabiah, ruler of half the district of Keilah, carried out repairs for his district. [18]Next to him, the repairs were made by their countrymen under Binnui[e] son of Henadad, ruler of the other half-district of Keilah. [19]Next to him, Ezer son of Jeshua, ruler of Mizpah, repaired another section, from a point facing the ascent to the armory as far as the angle. [20]Next to him, Baruch son of Zabbai zealously repaired another section, from the angle to the entrance of the house of Eliashib the high priest. [21]Next to him, Meremoth son of Uriah, the son of Hakkoz, repaired another section, from the entrance of Eliashib's house to the end of it.   Jos 15:44

[22]The repairs next to him were made by the priests from the surrounding region. [23]Beyond them, Benjamin and Hasshub made repairs in front of their house; and next to them, Azariah son of Maa-

---

[a]8 Or *They left out part of*   [b]13 Hebrew *a thousand cubits* (about 450 meters)   [c]15 Hebrew *Shelah*, a variant of *Shiloah*, that is, Siloam   [d]16 Hebrew; Septuagint, some Vulgate manuscripts and Syriac *tomb*   [e]18 Two Hebrew manuscripts and Syriac (see also Septuagint and verse 24); most Hebrew manuscripts *Bavvai*

seiah, the son of Ananiah, made repairs beside his house. ²⁴Next to him, Binnui son of Henadad repaired another section, from Azariah's house to the angle and the corner, ²⁵and Palal son of Uzai worked opposite the angle and the tower projecting from the upper palace near the court of the guard. Next to him, Pedaiah son of Parosh ²⁶and the temple servants living on the hill of Ophel made repairs up to a point opposite the Water Gate toward the east and the projecting tower. ²⁷Next to them, the men of Tekoa repaired another section, from the great projecting tower to the wall of Ophel.   Ne 8:1,3,16; Jer 32:2

²⁸Above the Horse Gate, the priests made repairs, each in front of his own house. ²⁹Next to them, Zadok son of Immer made repairs opposite his house. Next to him, Shemaiah son of Shecaniah, the guard at the East Gate, made repairs. ³⁰Next to him, Hananiah son of Shelemiah, and Hanun, the sixth son of Zalaph, repaired another section. Next to them, Meshullam son of Berekiah made repairs opposite his living quarters. ³¹Next to him, Malkijah, one of the goldsmiths, made repairs as far as the house of the temple servants and the merchants, opposite the Inspection Gate, and as far as the room above the corner; ³²and between the room above the corner

and the Sheep Gate the goldsmiths and merchants made repairs.

Opposition to the Rebuilding

4 When Sanballat heard that we were rebuilding the wall, he became angry and was greatly incensed. He ridiculed the Jews, ²and in the presence of his associates and the army of Samaria, he said, "What are those feeble Jews doing? Will they restore their wall? Will they offer sacrifices? Will they finish in a day? Can they bring the stones back to life from those heaps of rubble—burned as they are?"   Ne 2:10; Ps 79:1

³Tobiah the Ammonite, who was at his side, said, "What they are building—if even a fox climbed up on it, he would break down their wall of stones!"

⁴Hear us, O our God, for we are despised. Turn their insults back on their own heads. Give them over as plunder in a land of captivity. ⁵Do not cover up their guilt or blot out their sins from your sight, for they have thrown insults in the face ofᵃ the builders.   Ps 69:27-28

⁶So we rebuilt the wall till all of it reached half its height, for the people worked with all their heart. ⁷But when Sanballat, Tobiah, the Arabs, the Ammonites and the men of Ashdod heard that the repairs to Jerusalem's walls had gone ahead and that the gaps were

ᵃ5 Or *have provoked you to anger before*

being closed, they were very angry. ⁸They all plotted together to come and fight against Jerusalem and stir up trouble against it. ⁹But we prayed to our God and posted a guard day and night to meet this threat.   Ps 2:2; 83:1-18

¹⁰Meanwhile, the people in Judah said, "The strength of the laborers is giving out, and there is so much rubble that we cannot rebuild the wall."   1Ch 23:4

¹¹Also our enemies said, "Before they know it or see us, we will be right there among them and will kill them and put an end to the work."

¹²Then the Jews who lived near them came and told us ten times over, "Wherever you turn, they will attack us."

¹³Therefore I stationed some of the people behind the lowest points of the wall at the exposed places, posting them by families, with their swords, spears and bows. ¹⁴After I looked things over, I stood up and said to the nobles, the officials and the rest of the people, "Don't be afraid of them. Remember the Lord, who is great and awesome, and fight for your brothers, your sons and your daughters, your wives and your homes."

¹⁵When our enemies heard that we were aware of their plot and that God had frustrated it, we all returned to the wall, each to his own work.   2Sa 17:14; Job 5:12

¹⁶From that day on, half of my men did the work, while the other half were equipped with spears, shields, bows and armor. The officers posted themselves behind all the people of Judah ¹⁷who were building the wall. Those who carried materials did their work with one hand and held a weapon in the other, ¹⁸and each of the builders wore his sword at his side as he worked. But the man who sounded the trumpet stayed with me.

¹⁹Then I said to the nobles, the officials and the rest of the people, "The work is extensive and spread out, and we are widely separated from each other along the wall. ²⁰Wherever you hear the sound of the trumpet, join us there. Our God will fight for us!"   Ex 14:14

²¹So we continued the work with half the men holding spears, from the first light of dawn till the stars came out. ²²At that time I also said to the people, "Have every man and his helper stay inside Jerusalem at night, so they can serve us as guards by night and workmen by day." ²³Neither I nor my brothers nor my men nor the guards with me took off our clothes; each had his weapon, even when he went for water.^a

Nehemiah Helps the Poor

5 Now the men and their wives raised a great outcry against their Jewish brothers. ²Some were

^a23 The meaning of the Hebrew for this clause is uncertain.

saying, "We and our sons and daughters are numerous; in order for us to eat and stay alive, we must get grain."

³Others were saying, "We are mortgaging our fields, our vineyards and our homes to get grain during the famine." Ge 47:23

⁴Still others were saying, "We have had to borrow money to pay the king's tax on our fields and vineyards. ⁵Although we are of the same flesh and blood as our countrymen and though our sons are as good as theirs, yet we have to subject our sons and daughters to slavery. Some of our daughters have already been enslaved, but we are powerless, because our fields and our vineyards belong to others." Lev 25:39-43,47; Ezr 4:13

⁶When I heard their outcry and these charges, I was very angry. ⁷I pondered them in my mind and then accused the nobles and officials. I told them, "You are exacting usury from your own countrymen!" So I called together a large meeting to deal with them ⁸and said: "As far as possible, we have bought back our Jewish brothers who were sold to the Gentiles. Now you are selling your brothers, only for them to be sold back to us!" They kept quiet, because they could find nothing to say.

⁹So I continued, "What you are doing is not right. Shouldn't you walk in the fear of our God to avoid the reproach of our Gentile ene-

mies? ¹⁰I and my brothers and my men are also lending the people money and grain. But let the exacting of usury stop! ¹¹Give back to them immediately their fields, vineyards, olive groves and houses, and also the usury you are charging them—the hundredth part of the money, grain, new wine and oil." Ex 22:25; Isa 52:5; 58:6

¹²"We will give it back," they said. "And we will not demand anything more from them. We will do as you say."

Then I summoned the priests and made the nobles and officials take an oath to do what they had promised. ¹³I also shook out the folds of my robe and said, "In this way may God shake out of his house and possessions every man who does not keep this promise. So may such a man be shaken out and emptied!"

At this the whole assembly said, "Amen," and praised the LORD. And the people did as they had promised. Ezr 10:5; Mt 10:14; Ac 18:6

¹⁴Moreover, from the twentieth year of King Artaxerxes, when I was appointed to be their governor in the land of Judah, until his thirty-second year—twelve years—neither I nor my brothers ate the food allotted to the governor. ¹⁵But the earlier governors—those preceding me—placed a heavy burden on the people and took forty shekels[a] of silver from them in addition to food and wine. Their as-

a15 That is, about 1 pound (about 0.5 kilogram)

sistants also lorded it over the people. But out of reverence for God I did not act like that. [16]Instead, I devoted myself to the work on this wall. All my men were assembled there for the work; we[a] did not acquire any land.   Ne 13:6; Jer 40:7

[17]Furthermore, a hundred and fifty Jews and officials ate at my table, as well as those who came to us from the surrounding nations. [18]Each day one ox, six choice sheep and some poultry were prepared for me, and every ten days an abundant supply of wine of all kinds. In spite of all this, I never demanded the food allotted to the governor, because the demands were heavy on these people.

[19]Remember me with favor, O my God, for all I have done for these people.   Ge 8:1; Ne 1:8; 13:14,22,31

Further Opposition to the Rebuilding

6 When word came to Sanballat, Tobiah, Geshem the Arab and the rest of our enemies that I had rebuilt the wall and not a gap was left in it—though up to that time I had not set the doors in the gates — [2]Sanballat and Geshem sent me this message: "Come, let us meet together in one of the villages[b] on the plain of Ono."   1Ch 8:12; Ne 2:10,19

But they were scheming to harm me; [3]so I sent messengers to them with this reply: "I am carrying on a great project and cannot go down. Why should the work stop while I leave it and go down to you?" [4]Four times they sent me the same message, and each time I gave them the same answer.

[5]Then, the fifth time, Sanballat sent his aide to me with the same message, and in his hand was an unsealed letter [6]in which was written:

"It is reported among the nations—and Geshem[c] says it is true—that you and the Jews are plotting to revolt, and therefore you are building the wall. Moreover, according to these reports you are about to become their king [7]and have even appointed prophets to make this proclamation about you in Jerusalem: 'There is a king in Judah!' Now this report will get back to the king; so come, let us confer together."

[8]I sent him this reply: "Nothing like what you are saying is happening; you are just making it up out of your head."

[9]They were all trying to frighten us, thinking, "Their hands will get too weak for the work, and it will not be completed."

But I prayed, "Now strengthen my hands."

---

[a]16 Most Hebrew manuscripts; some Hebrew manuscripts, Septuagint, Vulgate and Syriac I
[b]2 Or in Kephirim   [c]6 Hebrew Gashmu, a variant of Geshem

¹⁰One day I went to the house of Shemaiah son of Delaiah, the son of Mehetabel, who was shut in at his home. He said, "Let us meet in the house of God, inside the temple, and let us close the temple doors, because men are coming to kill you—by night they are coming to kill you." _{Nu 18:7}

¹¹But I said, "Should a man like me run away? Or should one like me go into the temple to save his life? I will not go!" ¹²I realized that God had not sent him, but that he had prophesied against me because Tobiah and Sanballat had hired him. ¹³He had been hired to intimidate me so that I would commit a sin by doing this, and then they would give me a bad name to discredit me. _{Ne 2:10; Eze 13:22-23}

¹⁴Remember Tobiah and Sanballat, O my God, because of what they have done; remember also the prophetess Noadiah and the rest of the prophets who have been trying to intimidate me. _{Ne 13:29}

The Completion of the Wall

¹⁵So the wall was completed on the twenty-fifth of Elul, in fifty-two days. ¹⁶When all our enemies heard about this, all the surrounding nations were afraid and lost their self-confidence, because they realized that this work had been done with the help of our God.

¹⁷Also, in those days the nobles of Judah were sending many letters to Tobiah, and replies from Tobiah kept coming to them. ¹⁸For many in Judah were under oath to him, since he was son-in-law to Shecaniah son of Arah, and his son Jehohanan had married the daughter of Meshullam son of Berekiah. ¹⁹Moreover, they kept reporting to me his good deeds and then telling him what I said. And Tobiah sent letters to intimidate me.

7 After the wall had been rebuilt and I had set the doors in place, the gatekeepers and the singers and the Levites were appointed. ²I put in charge of Jerusalem my brother Hanani, along with*ª* Hananiah the commander of the citadel, because he was a man of integrity and feared God more than most men do. ³I said to them, "The gates of Jerusalem are not to be opened until the sun is hot. While the gatekeepers are still on duty, have them shut the doors and bar them. Also appoint residents of Jerusalem as guards, some at their posts and some near their own houses." _{Ne 1:2; 8:9}

The List of the Exiles Who Returned

⁴Now the city was large and spacious, but there were few people in it, and the houses had not yet been rebuilt. ⁵So my God put it into my heart to assemble the nobles, the

ª2 Or *Hanani, that is,*

officials and the common people for registration by families. I found the genealogical record of those who had been the first to return. This is what I found written there:

6These are the people of the province who came up from the captivity of the exiles whom Nebuchadnezzar king of Babylon had taken captive (they returned to Jerusalem and Judah, each to his own town, 7in company with Zerubbabel, Jeshua, Nehemiah, Azariah, Raamiah, Nahamani, Mordecai, Bilshan, Mispereth, Bigvai, Nehum and Baanah):

The list of the men of Israel:

8the descendants of	
Parosh	2,172
9of Shephatiah	372
10of Arah	652
11of Pahath-Moab (through the line of Jeshua and Joab)	2,818
12of Elam	1,254
13of Zattu	845
14of Zaccai	760
15of Binnui	648
16of Bebai	628
17of Azgad	2,322
18of Adonikam	667
19of Bigvai	2,067
20of Adin	655
21of Ater (through Hezekiah)	98
22of Hashum	328
23of Bezai	324
24of Hariph	112
25of Gibeon	95
26the men of Bethlehem and Netophah	188
27of Anathoth	128
28of Beth Azmaveth	42
29of Kiriath Jearim, Kephirah and Beeroth	743
30of Ramah and Geba	621
31of Micmash	122
32of Bethel and Ai	123
33of the other Nebo	52
34of the other Elam	1,254
35of Harim	320
36of Jericho	345
37of Lod, Hadid and Ono	721
38of Senaah	3,930

39The priests:

the descendants of Jedaiah (through the family of Jeshua)	973
40of Immer	1,052
41of Pashhur	1,247
42of Harim	1,017

43The Levites:

the descendants of Jeshua (through Kadmiel through the line of Hodaviah)	74

44The singers: Ne 11:23

the descendants of Asaph	148

45The gatekeepers: 1Ch 9:17

the descendants of
Shallum, Ater, Talmon,
Akkub, Hatita and
Shobai   138

46The temple servants: Ne 3:26

the descendants of
Ziha, Hasupha, Tabbaoth,
47Keros, Sia, Padon,
48Lebana, Hagaba, Shalmai,
49Hanan, Giddel, Gahar,
50Reaiah, Rezin, Nekoda,
51Gazzam, Uzza, Paseah,
52Besai, Meunim,
Nephussim,
53Bakbuk, Hakupha,
Harhur,
54Bazluth, Mehida, Harsha,
55Barkos, Sisera, Temah,
56Neziah and Hatipha

57The descendants of the servants of Solomon:

the descendants of
Sotai, Sophereth, Perida,
58Jaala, Darkon, Giddel,
59Shephatiah, Hattil,
Pokereth-Hazzebaim and
Amon

60The temple servants and the
descendants of the
servants of Solomon   392

61The following came up
from the towns of Tel Melah,
Tel Harsha, Kerub, Addon
and Immer, but they could

not show that their families
were descended from Israel:

62the descendants of
Delaiah, Tobiah and
Nekoda   642

63And from among the priests:

the descendants of
Hobaiah, Hakkoz and
Barzillai (a man who had
married a daughter of
Barzillai the Gileadite and
was called by that name).

64These searched for their
family records, but they could
not find them and so were excluded from the priesthood
as unclean. 65The governor,
therefore, ordered them not
to eat any of the most sacred
food until there should be a
priest ministering with the
Urim and Thummim.

66The whole company
numbered 42,360, 67besides
their 7,337 menservants and
maidservants; and they also
had 245 men and women
singers. 68There were 736
horses, 245 mules,a 69435
camels and 6,720 donkeys.

70Some of the heads of the
families contributed to the
work. The governor gave to
the treasury 1,000 drachmasb
of gold, 50 bowls and 530 garments for priests. 71Some of

---

a68 Some Hebrew manuscripts (see also Ezra 2:66); most Hebrew manuscripts do not have this verse.
b70 That is, about 19 pounds (about 8.5 kilograms)

the heads of the families gave to the treasury for the work 20,000 drachmas[a] of gold and 2,200 minas[b] of silver. [72]The total given by the rest of the people was 20,000 drachmas of gold, 2,000 minas[c] of silver and 67 garments for priests.   Ex 25:2; 1Ch 29:7

[73]The priests, the Levites, the gatekeepers, the singers and the temple servants, along with certain of the people and the rest of the Israelites, settled in their own towns.

Ezra Reads the Law

When the seventh month came and the Israelites had settled in their towns, [1]all the people assembled as one man in the square before the Water Gate. They told Ezra the scribe to bring out the Book of the Law of Moses, which the Lord had commanded for Israel.   Dt 28:61; Ne 3:26; Ezr 7:6

[2]So on the first day of the seventh month Ezra the priest brought the Law before the assembly, which was made up of men and women and all who were able to understand. [3]He read it aloud from daybreak till noon as he faced the square before the Water Gate in the presence of the men, women and others who could understand. And all the people listened attentively to the Book of the Law.   Lev 23:23-25; Dt 31:11; Ne 3:26

[4]Ezra the scribe stood on a high wooden platform built for the occasion. Beside him on his right stood Mattithiah, Shema, Anaiah, Uriah, Hilkiah and Maaseiah; and on his left were Pedaiah, Mishael, Malkijah, Hashum, Hashbaddanah, Zechariah and Meshullam.

[5]Ezra opened the book. All the people could see him because he was standing above them; and as he opened it, the people all stood up. [6]Ezra praised the Lord, the great God; and all the people lifted their hands and responded, "Amen! Amen!" Then they bowed down and worshiped the Lord with their faces to the ground.

[7]The Levites—Jeshua, Bani, Sherebiah, Jamin, Akkub, Shabbethai, Hodiah, Maaseiah, Kelita, Azariah, Jozabad, Hanan and Pelaiah —instructed the people in the Law while the people were standing there. [8]They read from the Book of the Law of God, making it clear[d] and giving the meaning so that the people could understand what was being read.   Lev 10:11; 2Ch 17:7

[9]Then Nehemiah the governor, Ezra the priest and scribe, and the Levites who were instructing the people said to them all, "This day is sacred to the Lord your God. Do not mourn or weep." For all the people had been weeping as they

[a]71 That is, about 375 pounds (about 170 kilograms); also in verse 72   [b]71 That is, about 1 1/3 tons (about 1.2 metric tons)   [c]72 That is, about 1 1/4 tons (about 1.1 metric tons)   [d]8 Or God, translating it

listened to the words of the Law. [10]Nehemiah said, "Go and enjoy choice food and sweet drinks, and send some to those who have nothing prepared. This day is sacred to our Lord. Do not grieve, for the joy of the LORD is your strength." Lev 23:40; Dt 12:18; Lk 14:12-14

[11]The Levites calmed all the people, saying, "Be still, for this is a sacred day. Do not grieve."

[12]Then all the people went away to eat and drink, to send portions of food and to celebrate with great joy, because they now understood the words that had been made known to them. Est 9:22

[13]On the second day of the month, the heads of all the families, along with the priests and the Levites, gathered around Ezra the scribe to give attention to the words of the Law. [14]They found written in the Law, which the LORD had commanded through Moses, that the Israelites were to live in booths during the feast of the seventh month [15]and that they should proclaim this word and spread it throughout their towns and in Jerusalem: "Go out into the hill country and bring back branches from olive and wild olive trees, and from myrtles, palms and shade trees, to make booths"—as it is written.[a]

[16]So the people went out and brought back branches and built themselves booths on their own roofs, in their courtyards, in the courts of the house of God and in the square by the Water Gate and the one by the Gate of Ephraim. [17]The whole company that had returned from exile built booths and lived in them. From the days of Joshua son of Nun until that day, the Israelites had not celebrated it like this. And their joy was very great. 2Ch 30:21; Ne 12:39

[18]Day after day, from the first day to the last, Ezra read from the Book of the Law of God. They celebrated the feast for seven days, and on the eighth day, in accordance with the regulation, there was an assembly. Nu 29:35; Dt 31:11

The Israelites Confess Their Sins

9 On the twenty-fourth day of the same month, the Israelites gathered together, fasting and wearing sackcloth and having dust on their heads. [2]Those of Israelite descent had separated themselves from all foreigners. They stood in their places and confessed their sins and the wickedness of their fathers. [3]They stood where they were and read from the Book of the Law of the LORD their God for a quarter of the day, and spent another quarter in confession and in worshiping the LORD their God. [4]Standing on the stairs were the Levites—Jeshua, Bani, Kadmiel, Shebaniah, Bunni, Sherebiah, Bani

[a] 15 See Lev. 23:37-40.

and Kenani—who called with loud voices to the LORD their God. ⁵And the Levites—Jeshua, Kadmiel, Bani, Hashabneiah, Sherebiah, Hodiah, Shebaniah and Pethahiah—said: "Stand up and praise the LORD your God, who is from everlasting to everlasting.ᵃ"

"Blessed be your glorious name, and may it be exalted above all blessing and praise. ⁶You alone are the LORD. You made the heavens, even the highest heavens, and all their starry host, the earth and all that is on it, the seas and all that is in them. You give life to everything, and the multitudes of heaven worship you. ⁷"You are the LORD God, who chose Abram and brought him out of Ur of the Chaldeans and named him Abraham. ⁸You found his heart faithful to you, and you made a covenant with him to give to his descendants the land of the Canaanites, Hittites, Amorites, Perizzites, Jebusites and Girgashites. You have kept your promise because you are righteous.

⁹"You saw the suffering of our forefathers in Egypt; you heard their cry at the Red Sea.ᵇ ¹⁰You sent miraculous signs and wonders against Pharaoh, against all his officials and all the people of his land, for you knew how arrogantly the Egyptians treated them. You made a name for yourself, which remains to this day. ¹¹You divided the sea before them, so that they passed through it on dry ground, but you hurled their pursuers into the depths, like a stone into mighty waters. ¹²By day you led them with a pillar of cloud, and by night with a pillar of fire to give them light on the way they were to take.   Ex 13:21; 14:21

¹³"You came down on Mount Sinai; you spoke to them from heaven. You gave them regulations and laws that are just and right, and decrees and commands that are good. ¹⁴You made known to them your holy Sabbath and gave them commands, decrees and laws through your servant Moses. ¹⁵In their hunger you gave them bread from heaven and in their thirst you brought them water from the rock; you told them to go in and take possession of the land you had sworn with uplifted hand to give them.

¹⁶"But they, our forefathers, became arrogant and stiff-necked, and did not obey your commands. ¹⁷They refused to listen and failed to re-

---

ᵃ5 Or *God for ever and ever*   ᵇ9 Hebrew *Yam Suph*; that is, Sea of Reeds

member the miracles you performed among them. They became stiff-necked and in their rebellion appointed a leader in order to return to their slavery. But you are a forgiving God, gracious and compassionate, slow to anger and abounding in love. Therefore you did not desert them, ¹⁸even when they cast for themselves an image of a calf and said, 'This is your god, who brought you up out of Egypt,' or when they committed awful blasphemies.

¹⁹"Because of your great compassion you did not abandon them in the desert. By day the pillar of cloud did not cease to guide them on their path, nor the pillar of fire by night to shine on the way they were to take. ²⁰You gave your good Spirit to instruct them. You did not withhold your manna from their mouths, and you gave them water for their thirst. ²¹For forty years you sustained them in the desert; they lacked nothing, their clothes did not wear out nor did their feet become swollen. Nu 11:17; Dt 2:7; Isa 63:11,14

²²"You gave them kingdoms and nations, allotting to them even the remotest frontiers. They took over the country of Sihon*a* king of Heshbon and the country of Og king of Bashan. ²³You made their sons as numerous as the stars in the sky, and you brought them into the land that you told their fathers to enter and possess. ²⁴Their sons went in and took possession of the land. You subdued before them the Canaanites, who lived in the land; you handed the Canaanites over to them, along with their kings and the peoples of the land, to deal with them as they pleased. ²⁵They captured fortified cities and fertile land; they took possession of houses filled with all kinds of good things, wells already dug, vineyards, olive groves and fruit trees in abundance. They ate to the full and were well-nourished; they reveled in your great goodness.

²⁶"But they were disobedient and rebelled against you; they put your law behind their backs. They killed your prophets, who had admonished them in order to turn them back to you; they committed awful blasphemies. ²⁷So you handed them over to their enemies, who oppressed them. But when they were oppressed they cried out to you. From heaven you heard them, and in your great compassion

---

*a*22 One Hebrew manuscript and Septuagint; most Hebrew manuscripts *Sihon, that is, the country of the*

you gave them deliverers, who rescued them from the hand of their enemies.

28"But as soon as they were at rest, they again did what was evil in your sight. Then you abandoned them to the hand of their enemies so that they ruled over them. And when they cried out to you again, you heard from heaven, and in your compassion you delivered them time after time.   Ps 106:43

29"You warned them to return to your law, but they became arrogant and disobeyed your commands. They sinned against your ordinances, by which a man will live if he obeys them. Stubbornly they turned their backs on you, became stiff-necked and refused to listen. 30For many years you were patient with them. By your Spirit you admonished them through your prophets. Yet they paid no attention, so you handed them over to the neighboring peoples. 31But in your great mercy you did not put an end to them or abandon them, for you are a gracious and merciful God.   Dt 30:16; 2Ki 17:13-18

32"Now therefore, O our God, the great, mighty and awesome God, who keeps his covenant of love, do not let all this hardship seem trifling in your eyes—the hardship that

has come upon us, upon our kings and leaders, upon our priests and prophets, upon our fathers and all your people, from the days of the kings of Assyria until today. 33In all that has happened to us, you have been just; you have acted faithfully, while we did wrong. 34Our kings, our leaders, our priests and our fathers did not follow your law; they did not pay attention to your commands or the warnings you gave them. 35Even while they were in their kingdom, enjoying your great goodness to them in the spacious and fertile land you gave them, they did not serve you or turn from their evil ways.   Ge 18:25; Dt 28:45-48

36"But see, we are slaves today, slaves in the land you gave our forefathers so they could eat its fruit and the other good things it produces. 37Because of our sins, its abundant harvest goes to the kings you have placed over us. They rule over our bodies and our cattle as they please. We are in great distress.

The Agreement of the People

38"In view of all this, we are making a binding agreement, putting it in writing, and our leaders, our Levites and our priests are affixing their seals to it."   2Ch 23:16

10

Those who sealed it were:

Nehemiah the governor, the son of Hacaliah.

Zedekiah, ²Seraiah, Azariah, Jeremiah,   Ezr 2:2
³Pashhur, Amariah, Malkijah,
⁴Hattush, Shebaniah, Malluch,
⁵Harim, Meremoth, Obadiah,
⁶Daniel, Ginnethon, Baruch,
⁷Meshullam, Abijah, Mijamin,
⁸Maaziah, Bilgai and Shemaiah.
These were the priests.

⁹The Levites: Ne 12:1

Jeshua son of Azaniah, Binnui of the sons of Henadad, Kadmiel,
¹⁰and their associates: Shebaniah,
Hodiah, Kelita, Pelaiah, Hanan,
¹¹Mica, Rehob, Hashabiah,
¹²Zaccur, Sherebiah, Shebaniah,
¹³Hodiah, Bani and Beninu.

¹⁴The leaders of the people:

Parosh, Pahath-Moab, Elam, Zattu, Bani,
¹⁵Bunni, Azgad, Bebai,
¹⁶Adonijah, Bigvai, Adin,   Ezr 8:6
¹⁷Ater, Hezekiah, Azzur,
¹⁸Hodiah, Hashum, Bezai,
¹⁹Hariph, Anathoth, Nebai,
²⁰Magpiash, Meshullam, Hezir,
²¹Meshezabel, Zadok, Jaddua,
²²Pelatiah, Hanan, Anaiah,

²³Hoshea, Hananiah, Hasshub,
²⁴Hallohesh, Pilha, Shobek,
²⁵Rehum, Hashabnah, Maaseiah,
²⁶Ahiah, Hanan, Anan,
²⁷Malluch, Harim and Baanah.

²⁸"The rest of the people—priests, Levites, gatekeepers, singers, temple servants and all who separated themselves from the neighboring peoples for the sake of the Law of God, together with their wives and all their sons and daughters who are able to understand—²⁹all these now join their brothers the nobles, and bind themselves with a curse and an oath to follow the Law of God given through Moses the servant of God and to obey carefully all the commands, regulations and decrees of the LORD our Lord.   Ne 9:2; Ps 119:106

³⁰"We promise not to give our daughters in marriage to the peoples around us or take their daughters for our sons.

³¹"When the neighboring peoples bring merchandise or grain to sell on the Sabbath, we will not buy from them on the Sabbath or on any holy day. Every seventh year we will forgo working the land and will cancel all debts.

³²"We assume the responsibility for carrying out the commands to give a third of a

shekel[a] each year for the service of the house of our God: [33]for the bread set out on the table; for the regular grain offerings and burnt offerings; for the offerings on the Sabbaths, New Moon festivals and appointed feasts; for the holy offerings; for sin offerings to make atonement for Israel; and for all the duties of the house of our God.

[34]"We—the priests, the Levites and the people—have cast lots to determine when each of our families is to bring to the house of our God at set times each year a contribution of wood to burn on the altar of the LORD our God, as it is written in the Law.

[35]"We also assume responsibility for bringing to the house of the LORD each year the firstfruits of our crops and of every fruit tree.   Ex 23:19

[36]"As it is also written in the Law, we will bring the firstborn of our sons and of our cattle, of our herds and of our flocks to the house of our God, to the priests ministering there.   Ex 13:2; Nu 18:14-16

[37]"Moreover, we will bring to the storerooms of the house of our God, to the priests, the first of our ground meal, of our grain, offerings, of the fruit of all our trees and of our new wine and oil. And we will bring a tithe of our crops to the Levites, for it is the Levites who collect the tithes in all the towns where we work. [38]A priest descended from Aaron is to accompany the Levites when they receive the tithes, and the Levites are to bring a tenth of the tithes up to the house of our God, to the storerooms of the treasury. [39]The people of Israel, including the Levites, are to bring their contributions of grain, new wine and oil to the storerooms where the articles for the sanctuary are kept and where the ministering priests, the gatekeepers and the singers stay.   Lev 23:17; Nu 18:21,26

"We will not neglect the house of our God."

The New Residents of Jerusalem

11 Now the leaders of the people settled in Jerusalem, and the rest of the people cast lots to bring one out of every ten to live in Jerusalem, the holy city, while the remaining nine were to stay in their own towns. [2]The people commended all the men who volunteered to live in Jerusalem.

[3]These are the provincial leaders who settled in Jerusalem (now some Israelites, priests, Levites, temple servants and descendants

[a] 32 That is, about 1/8 ounce (about 4 grams)

of Solomon's servants lived in the towns of Judah, each on his own property in the various towns, [4]while other people from both Judah and Benjamin lived in Jerusalem): 1Ch 9:2-3; Ezr 2:1

From the descendants of Judah:

Athaiah son of Uzziah, the son of Zechariah, the son of Amariah, the son of Shephatiah, the son of Mahalalel, a descendant of Perez; [5]and Maaseiah son of Baruch, the son of Col-Hozeh, the son of Hazaiah, the son of Adaiah, the son of Joiarib, the son of Zechariah, a descendant of Shelah. [6]The descendants of Perez who lived in Jerusalem totaled 468 able men.

[7]From the descendants of Benjamin:

Sallu son of Meshullam, the son of Joed, the son of Pedaiah, the son of Kolaiah, the son of Maaseiah, the son of Ithiel, the son of Jeshaiah, [8]and his followers, Gabbai and Sallai—928 men. [9]Joel son of Zicri was their chief officer, and Judah son of Hassenuah was over the Second District of the city.

[10]From the priests:

Jedaiah; the son of Joiarib; Jakin; [11]Seraiah son of Hilkiah, the son of Meshullam, the son of Zadok, the son of Meraioth, the son of Ahitub, supervisor in the house of God, [12]and their associates, who carried on work for the temple—822 men; Adaiah son of Jeroham, the son of Pelaliah, the son of Amzi, the son of Zechariah, the son of Pashhur, the son of Malkijah, [13]and his associates, who were heads of families—242 men; Amashsai son of Azarel, the son of Ahzai, the son of Meshillemoth, the son of Immer, [14]and his[a] associates, who were able men—128. Their chief officer was Zabdiel son of Haggedolim.

[15]From the Levites:

Shemaiah son of Hasshub, the son of Azrikam, the son of Hashabiah, the son of Bunni; [16]Shabbethai and Jozabad, two of the heads of the Levites, who had charge of the outside work of the house of God; [17]Mattaniah son of Mica, the son of Zabdi, the son of Asaph, the director who led in thanksgiving and prayer; Bakbukiah, second among his associates; and Abda son of Shammua, the son of Galal, the son of Jeduthun. [18]The Levites in the holy city totaled 284. 1Ch 9:15; 25:1; Rev 21:2

---

[a] 14 Most Septuagint manuscripts; Hebrew *their*

¹⁹The gatekeepers:

Akkub, Talmon and their associates, who kept watch at the gates—172 men.

²⁰The rest of the Israelites, with the priests and Levites, were in all the towns of Judah, each on his ancestral property.

²¹The temple servants lived on the hill of Ophel, and Ziha and Gishpa were in charge of them.

²²The chief officer of the Levites in Jerusalem was Uzzi son of Bani, the son of Hashabiah, the son of Mattaniah, the son of Mica. Uzzi was one of Asaph's descendants, who were the singers responsible for the service of the house of God. ²³The singers were under the king's orders, which regulated their daily activity. 1Ch 9:15; Ne 7:44

²⁴Pethahiah son of Meshezabel, one of the descendants of Zerah son of Judah, was the king's agent in all affairs relating to the people.

²⁵As for the villages with their fields, some of the people of Judah lived in Kiriath Arba and its surrounding settlements, in Dibon and its settlements, in Jekabzeel and its villages, ²⁶in Jeshua, in Moladah, in Beth Pelet, ²⁷in Hazar Shual, in Beersheba and its settlements, ²⁸in Ziklag, in Meconah and its settlements, ²⁹in En Rimmon, in Zorah, in Jarmuth, ³⁰Zanoah, Adullam and their villages, in Lachish and its fields, and in Azekah and its settlements. So they were living all the way from Beersheba to the Valley of Hinnom.

³¹The descendants of the Benjamites from Geba lived in Micmash, Aija, Bethel and its settlements, ³²in Anathoth, Nob and Ananiah, ³³in Hazor, Ramah and Gittaim, ³⁴in Hadid, Zeboim and Neballat, ³⁵in Lod and Ono, and in the Valley of the Craftsmen. Jos 11:1; 21:17

³⁶Some of the divisions of the Levites of Judah settled in Benjamin.

Priests and Levites

12 These were the priests and Levites who returned with Zerubbabel son of Shealtiel and with Jeshua: 1Ch 3:19; Ezr 2:2
Seraiah, Jeremiah, Ezra,
²Amariah, Malluch, Hattush,
³Shecaniah, Rehum, Meremoth,
⁴Iddo, Ginnethon,ᵃ Abijah,
⁵Mijamin,ᵇ Moadiah, Bilgah,
⁶Shemaiah, Joiarib, Jedaiah,
⁷Sallu, Amok, Hilkiah and Jedaiah.
These were the leaders of the priests and their associates in the days of Jeshua.

⁸The Levites were Jeshua, Binnui, Kadmiel, Sherebiah, Judah, and also Mattaniah, who, together with his associates, was in charge of the songs of thanksgiving. ⁹Bak-

ᵃ4 Many Hebrew manuscripts and Vulgate (see also Neh. 12:16); most Hebrew manuscripts *Ginnethoi*
ᵇ5 A variant of *Miniamin*

bukiah and Unni, their associates, stood opposite them in the services. _{Ne 11:17}

[10]Jeshua was the father of Joiakim, Joiakim the father of Eliashib, Eliashib the father of Joiada, [11]Joiada the father of Jonathan, and Jonathan the father of Jaddua.

[12]In the days of Joiakim, these were the heads of the priestly families:

of Seraiah's family, Meraiah;

of Jeremiah's, Hananiah;

[13]of Ezra's, Meshullam;

of Amariah's, Jehohanan;

[14]of Malluch's, Jonathan;

of Shecaniah's,[a] Joseph;

[15]of Harim's, Adna;

of Meremoth's,[b] Helkai;

[16]of Iddo's, Zechariah;

of Ginnethon's, Meshullam;

[17]of Abijah's, Zicri;

of Miniamin's and of Moadiah's, Piltai;

[18]of Bilgah's, Shammua;

of Shemaiah's, Jehonathan;

[19]of Joiarib's, Mattenai;

of Jedaiah's, Uzzi;

[20]of Sallu's, Kallai;

of Amok's, Eber;

[21]of Hilkiah's, Hashabiah;

of Jedaiah's, Nethanel.

[22]The family heads of the Levites in the days of Eliashib, Joiada, Johanan and Jaddua, as well as those of the priests, were recorded in the reign of Darius the Persian. [23]The family heads among the descendants of Levi up to the time of Johanan son of Eliashib were recorded in the book of the annals. [24]And the leaders of the Levites were Hashabiah, Sherebiah, Jeshua son of Kadmiel, and their associates, who stood opposite them to give praise and thanksgiving, one section responding to the other, as prescribed by David the man of God. _{Ezr 2:40}

[25]Mattaniah, Bakbukiah, Obadiah, Meshullam, Talmon and Akkub were gatekeepers who guarded the storerooms at the gates. [26]They served in the days of Joiakim son of Jeshua, the son of Jozadak, and in the days of Nehemiah the governor and of Ezra the priest and scribe.

Dedication of the Wall of Jerusalem

[27]At the dedication of the wall of Jerusalem, the Levites were sought out from where they lived and were brought to Jerusalem to celebrate joyfully the dedication with songs of thanksgiving and with the music of cymbals, harps and lyres. [28]The singers also were brought together from the region around Jerusalem—from the villages of the Netophathites, [29]from Beth Gilgal, and from the area of Geba and Azmaveth, for the singers had built villages for themselves around Jerusalem. [30]When

---

a 14 Very many Hebrew manuscripts, some Septuagint manuscripts and Syriac (see also Neh. 12:3); most Hebrew manuscripts *Shebaniah's* *b 15* Some Septuagint manuscripts (see also Neh. 12:3); Hebrew *Meraioth's*

the priests and Levites had purified themselves ceremonially, they purified the people, the gates and the wall.   1Ch 25:6; Ps 92:3

³¹I had the leaders of Judah go up on top^a of the wall. I also assigned two large choirs to give thanks. One was to proceed on top^b of the wall to the right, toward the Dung Gate. ³²Hoshaiah and half the leaders of Judah followed them, ³³along with Azariah, Ezra, Meshullam, ³⁴Judah, Benjamin, Shemaiah, Jeremiah, ³⁵as well as some priests with trumpets, and also Zechariah son of Jonathan, the son of Shemaiah, the son of Mattaniah, the son of Micaiah, the son of Zaccur, the son of Asaph, ³⁶and his associates—Shemaiah, Azarel, Milalai, Gilalai, Maai, Nethanel, Judah and Hanani—with musical instruments ˻prescribed by˼ David the man of God. Ezra the scribe led the procession. ³⁷At the Fountain Gate they continued directly up the steps of the City of David on the ascent to the wall and passed above the house of David to the Water Gate on the east.   Ne 2:13-14; 3:15,26

³⁸The second choir proceeded in the opposite direction. I followed them on top^c of the wall, together with half the people—past the Tower of the Ovens to the Broad Wall, ³⁹over the Gate of Ephraim, the Jeshanah^d Gate, the Fish Gate, the Tower of Hananel and the Tower of the Hundred, as far as the Sheep Gate. At the Gate of the Guard they stopped.   Ne 3:1,3,8,11

⁴⁰The two choirs that gave thanks then took their places in the house of God; so did I, together with half the officials, ⁴¹as well as the priests—Eliakim, Maaseiah, Miniamin, Micaiah, Elioenai, Zechariah and Hananiah with their trumpets— ⁴²and also Maaseiah, Shemaiah, Eleazar, Uzzi, Jehohanan, Malkijah, Elam and Ezer. The choirs sang under the direction of Jezrahiah. ⁴³And on that day they offered great sacrifices, rejoicing because God had given them great joy. The women and children also rejoiced. The sound of rejoicing in Jerusalem could be heard far away.

⁴⁴At that time men were appointed to be in charge of the storerooms for the contributions, firstfruits and tithes. From the fields around the towns they were to bring into the storerooms the portions required by the Law for the priests and the Levites, for Judah was pleased with the ministering priests and Levites. ⁴⁵They performed the service of their God and the service of purification, as did also the singers and gatekeepers, according to the commands of David and his son Solomon. ⁴⁶For long ago, in the days of David and Asaph, there had been directors for the singers and for the songs of

praise and thanksgiving to God. ⁴⁷So in the days of Zerubbabel and of Nehemiah, all Israel contributed the daily portions for the singers and gatekeepers. They also set aside the portion for the other Levites, and the Levites set aside the portion for the descendants of Aaron. Nu 18:21; Dt 18:8; 1Ch 25:1

Nehemiah's Final Reforms

13 On that day the Book of Moses was read aloud in the hearing of the people and there it was found written that no Ammonite or Moabite should ever be admitted into the assembly of God, ²because they had not met the Israelites with food and water but had hired Balaam to call a curse down on them. (Our God, however, turned the curse into a blessing.) ³When the people heard this law, they excluded from Israel all who were of foreign descent.

⁴Before this, Eliashib the priest had been put in charge of the storerooms of the house of our God. He was closely associated with Tobiah, ⁵and he had provided him with a large room formerly used to store the grain offerings and incense and temple articles, and also the tithes of grain, new wine and oil prescribed for the Levites, singers and gatekeepers, as well as the contributions for the priests. Nu 18:21; Ne 2:10; 12:44

⁶But while all this was going on, I was not in Jerusalem, for in the thirty-second year of Artaxerxes king of Babylon I had returned to the king. Some time later I asked his permission ⁷and came back to Jerusalem. Here I learned about the evil thing Eliashib had done in providing Tobiah a room in the courts of the house of God. ⁸I was greatly displeased and threw all Tobiah's household goods out of the room. ⁹I gave orders to purify the rooms, and then I put back into them the equipment of the house of God, with the grain offerings and the incense. 2Ch 29:5; Ne 5:14

¹⁰I also learned that the portions assigned to the Levites had not been given to them, and that all the Levites and singers responsible for the service had gone back to their own fields. ¹¹So I rebuked the officials and asked them, "Why is the house of God neglected?" Then I called them together and stationed them at their posts. Ne 10:37-39

¹²All Judah brought the tithes of grain, new wine and oil into the storerooms. ¹³I put Shelemiah the priest, Zadok the scribe, and a Levite named Pedaiah in charge of the storerooms and made Hanan son of Zaccur, the son of Mattaniah, their assistant, because these men were considered trustworthy. They were made responsible for distributing the supplies to their brothers. Ne 10:37-39; 12:44; Ac 6:1-5

¹⁴Remember me for this, O my God, and do not blot out what I have so faithfully done for the house of my God and its services.

¹⁵In those days I saw men in Judah treading winepresses on the Sabbath and bringing in grain and loading it on donkeys, together with wine, grapes, figs and all other kinds of loads. And they were bringing all this into Jerusalem on the Sabbath. Therefore I warned them against selling food on that day. ¹⁶Men from Tyre who lived in Jerusalem were bringing in fish and all kinds of merchandise and selling them in Jerusalem on the Sabbath to the people of Judah. ¹⁷I rebuked the nobles of Judah and said to them, "What is this wicked thing you are doing—desecrating the Sabbath day? ¹⁸Didn't your forefathers do the same things, so that our God brought all this calamity upon us and upon this city? Now you are stirring up more wrath against Israel by desecrating the Sabbath." Ex 20:8-11; Ne 10:31

¹⁹When evening shadows fell on the gates of Jerusalem before the Sabbath, I ordered the doors to be shut and not opened until the Sabbath was over. I stationed some of my own men at the gates so that no load could be brought in on the Sabbath day. ²⁰Once or twice the merchants and sellers of all kinds of goods spent the night outside Jerusalem. ²¹But I warned them and said, "Why do you spend the night by the wall? If you do this again, I will lay hands on you." From that time on they no longer came on the Sabbath. ²²Then I commanded the Levites to purify themselves and go and guard the gates in order to keep the Sabbath day holy. Lev 23:32; Ne 12:30

Remember me for this also, O my God, and show mercy to me according to your great love.

²³Moreover, in those days I saw men of Judah who had married women from Ashdod, Ammon and Moab. ²⁴Half of their children spoke the language of Ashdod or the language of one of the other peoples, and did not know how to speak the language of Judah. ²⁵I rebuked them and called curses down on them. I beat some of the men and pulled out their hair. I made them take an oath in God's name and said: "You are not to give your daughters in marriage to their sons, nor are you to take their daughters in marriage for your sons or for yourselves. ²⁶Was it not because of marriages like these that Solomon king of Israel sinned? Among the many nations there was no king like him. He was loved by his God, and God made him king over all Israel, but even he was led into sin by foreign women. ²⁷Must we hear now that you too are doing all this terrible wickedness and are being unfaithful to our God by marrying foreign women?" 1Ki 11:3; 2Ch 1:12; Ezr 10:2

²⁸One of the sons of Joiada son of Eliashib the high priest was son-

in-law to Sanballat the Horonite. And I drove him away from me.

²⁹Remember them, O my God, because they defiled the priestly office and the covenant of the priesthood and of the Levites.

³⁰So I purified the priests and the Levites of everything foreign, and assigned them duties, each to his own task. ³¹I also made provision for contributions of wood at designated times, and for the first-fruits.

Ne 10:30,34-36

Remember me with favor, O my God.

ver 14,22; Ge 8:1

Esther

Queen Vashti Deposed

1 This is what happened during the time of Xerxes,[a] the Xerxes who ruled over 127 provinces stretching from India to Cush[b]: 2At that time King Xerxes reigned from his royal throne in the citadel of Susa, 3and in the third year of his reign he gave a banquet for all his nobles and officials. The military leaders of Persia and Media, the princes, and the nobles of the provinces were present. Est 8:9; 9:30

4For a full 180 days he displayed the vast wealth of his kingdom and the splendor and glory of his majesty. 5When these days were over, the king gave a banquet, lasting seven days, in the enclosed garden of the king's palace, for all the people from the least to the greatest, who were in the citadel of Susa. 6The garden had hangings of white and blue linen, fastened with cords of white linen and purple material to silver rings on marble pillars. There were couches of gold and silver on a mosaic pavement of porphyry, marble, mother-of-pearl and other costly stones. 7Wine was served in goblets of gold, each one different from the other, and the royal wine was abundant, in keeping with the king's liberality. 8By the king's command each guest was allowed to drink in his own way, for the king instructed all the wine stewards to serve each man what he wished. Est 2:18; 7:7-8; Eze 23:41

9Queen Vashti also gave a banquet for the women in the royal palace of King Xerxes. 1Ki 3:15

10On the seventh day, when King Xerxes was in high spirits from wine, he commanded the seven eunuchs who served him—Mehuman, Biztha, Harbona, Bigtha, Abagtha, Zethar and Carcas—11to bring before him Queen Vashti, wearing her royal crown, in order to display her beauty to the people and nobles, for she was lovely to look at. 12But when the attendants delivered the king's command, Queen Vashti refused to come. Then the king became furious and burned with anger.

13Since it was customary for the king to consult experts in matters of law and justice, he spoke with the wise men who understood the times 14and were closest to the king—Carshena, Shethar, Admatha, Tarshish, Meres, Marsena and

---

a 1 Hebrew *Ahasuerus*, a variant of Xerxes' Persian name; here and throughout Esther   b 1 That is, the upper Nile region

Memucan, the seven nobles of Persia and Media who had special access to the king and were highest in the kingdom.   2Ki 25:19; 1Ch 12:32

15"According to law, what must be done to Queen Vashti?" he asked. "She has not obeyed the command of King Xerxes that the eunuchs have taken to her."

16Then Memucan replied in the presence of the king and the nobles, "Queen Vashti has done wrong, not only against the king but also against all the nobles and the peoples of all the provinces of King Xerxes. 17For the queen's conduct will become known to all the women, and so they will despise their husbands and say, 'King Xerxes commanded Queen Vashti to be brought before him, but she would not come.' 18This very day the Persian and Median women of the nobility who have heard about the queen's conduct will respond to all the king's nobles in the same way. There will be no end of disrespect and discord.

19"Therefore, if it pleases the king, let him issue a royal decree and let it be written in the laws of Persia and Media, which cannot be repealed, that Vashti is never again to enter the presence of King Xerxes. Also let the king give her royal position to someone else who is better than she. 20Then when the king's edict is proclaimed throughout all his vast realm, all the women will respect their husbands, from the least to the greatest."

21The king and his nobles were pleased with this advice, so the king did as Memucan proposed. 22He sent dispatches to all parts of the kingdom, to each province in its own script and to each people in its own language, proclaiming in each people's tongue that every man should be ruler over his own household.   Ne 13:24; Eph 5:22-24

Esther Made Queen

2 Later when the anger of King Xerxes had subsided, he remembered Vashti and what she had done and what he had decreed about her. 2Then the king's personal attendants proposed, "Let a search be made for beautiful young virgins for the king. 3Let the king appoint commissioners in every province of his realm to bring all these beautiful girls into the harem at the citadel of Susa. Let them be placed under the care of Hegai, the king's eunuch, who is in charge of the women; and let beauty treatments be given to them. 4Then let the girl who pleases the king be queen instead of Vashti." This advice appealed to the king, and he followed it.   Est 1:19-20; 7:10

5Now there was in the citadel of Susa a Jew of the tribe of Benjamin, named Mordecai son of Jair, the son of Shimei, the son of Kish, 6who had been carried into exile from Jerusalem by Nebuchadnezzar king of Babylon, among those

...aken captive with Jehoiachin[a] king of Judah. [7]Mordecai had a cousin named Hadassah, whom he had brought up because she had neither father nor mother. This girl, who was also known as Esther, was lovely in form and features, and Mordecai had taken her as his own daughter when her father and mother died.   2Ki 24:6,15

[8]When the king's order and edict had been proclaimed, many girls were brought to the citadel of Susa and put under the care of Hegai. Esther also was taken to the king's palace and entrusted to Hegai, who had charge of the harem. [9]The girl pleased him and won his favor. Immediately he provided her with her beauty treatments and special food. He assigned to her seven maids selected from the king's palace and moved her and her maids into the best place in the harem.   2Ki 25:30; Est 1:2

[10]Esther had not revealed her nationality and family background, because Mordecai had forbidden her to do so. [11]Every day he walked back and forth near the courtyard of the harem to find out how Esther was and what was happening to her.   ver 20

[12]Before a girl's turn came to go in to King Xerxes, she had to complete twelve months of beauty treatments prescribed for the women, six months with oil of myrrh and six with perfumes and cosmetics. [13]And this is how she would go to the king: Anything she wanted was given her to take with her from the harem to the king's palace. [14]In the evening she would go there and in the morning return to another part of the harem to the care of Shaashgaz, the king's eunuch who was in charge of the concubines. She would not return to the king unless he was pleased with her and summoned her by name.   1Ki 11:3; Est 4:11; Pr 27:9

[15]When the turn came for Esther (the girl Mordecai had adopted, the daughter of his uncle Abihail) to go to the king, she asked for nothing other than what Hegai, the king's eunuch who was in charge of the harem, suggested. And Esther won the favor of everyone who saw her. [16]She was taken to King Xerxes in the royal residence in the tenth month, the month of Tebeth, in the seventh year of his reign.   Est 9:29; Ps 45:14

[17]Now the king was attracted to Esther more than to any of the other women, and she won his favor and approval more than any of the other virgins. So he set a royal crown on her head and made her queen instead of Vashti. [18]And the king gave a great banquet, Esther's banquet, for all his nobles and officials. He proclaimed a holiday throughout the provinces and distributed gifts with royal liberality.

Mordecai Uncovers a Conspiracy

¹⁹When the virgins were assembled a second time, Mordecai was sitting at the king's gate. ²⁰But Esther had kept secret her family background and nationality just as Mordecai had told her to do, for she continued to follow Mordecai's instructions as she had done when he was bringing her up.

²¹During the time Mordecai was sitting at the king's gate, Bigthana*a* and Teresh, two of the king's officers who guarded the doorway, became angry and conspired to assassinate King Xerxes. ²²But Mordecai found out about the plot and told Queen Esther, who in turn reported it to the king, giving credit to Mordecai. ²³And when the report was investigated and found to be true, the two officials were hanged on a gallows.*b* All this was recorded in the book of the annals in the presence of the king.

Haman's Plot to Destroy the Jews

3 After these events, King Xerxes honored Haman son of Hammedatha, the Agagite, elevating him and giving him a seat of honor higher than that of all the other nobles. ²All the royal officials at the king's gate knelt down and paid honor to Haman, for the king had commanded this con-

cerning him. But Mordecai would not kneel down or pay him honor.

³Then the royal officials at the king's gate asked Mordecai, "Why do you disobey the king's command?" ⁴Day after day they spoke to him but he refused to comply. Therefore they told Haman about it to see whether Mordecai's behavior would be tolerated, for he had told them he was a Jew.

⁵When Haman saw that Mordecai would not kneel down or pay him honor, he was enraged. ⁶Yet having learned who Mordecai's people were, he scorned the idea of killing only Mordecai. Instead Haman looked for a way to destroy all Mordecai's people, the Jews, throughout the whole kingdom of Xerxes.   Est 5:9; Ps 83:4

⁷In the twelfth year of King Xerxes, in the first month, the month of Nisan, they cast the *pur* (that is, the lot) in the presence of Haman to select a day and month. And the lot fell on*c* the twelfth month, the month of Adar.   Est 9:24,26

⁸Then Haman said to King Xerxes, "There is a certain people dispersed and scattered among the peoples in all the provinces of your kingdom whose customs are different from those of all other people and who do not obey the king's laws; it is not in the king's best interest to tolerate them. ⁹If it pleases the king, let a decree be

---

*a*21 Hebrew *Bigthan,* a variant of *Bigthana*   *b*23 Or *were hung* (or *impaled*) *on poles;* similarly elsewhere in Esther   *c*7 Septuagint; Hebrew does not have *And the lot fell on.*

issued to destroy them, and I will put ten thousand talents[a] of silver into the royal treasury for the men who carry out this business."

¹⁰So the king took his signet ring from his finger and gave it to Haman son of Hammedatha, the Agagite, the enemy of the Jews. ¹¹"Keep the money," the king said to Haman, "and do with the people as you please."　　Ge 41:42; Est 7:6; 8:2

¹²Then on the thirteenth day of the first month the royal secretaries were summoned. They wrote out in the script of each province and in the language of each people all Haman's orders to the king's satraps, the governors of the various provinces and the nobles of the various peoples. These were written in the name of King Xerxes himself and sealed with his own ring. ¹³Dispatches were sent by couriers to all the king's provinces with the order to destroy, kill and annihilate all the Jews—young and old, women and little children —on a single day, the thirteenth day of the twelfth month, the month of Adar, and to plunder their goods. ¹⁴A copy of the text of the edict was to be issued as law in every province and made known to the people of every nationality so they would be ready for that day.　　　1Ki 21:8; Est 8:10-14; 9:10

¹⁵Spurred on by the king's command, the couriers went out, and the edict was issued in the citadel of Susa. The king and Haman sat down to drink, but the city of Susa was bewildered.　　Est 1:10; 8:15

Mordecai Persuades Esther to Help

4 When Mordecai learned of all that had been done, he tore his clothes, put on sackcloth and ashes, and went out into the city, wailing loudly and bitterly. ²But he went only as far as the king's gate, because no one clothed in sackcloth was allowed to enter it. ³In every province to which the edict and order of the king came, there was great mourning among the Jews, with fasting, weeping and wailing. Many lay in sackcloth and ashes.　　Nu 14:6; Est 2:19; Eze 27:30-31

⁴When Esther's maids and eunuchs came and told her about Mordecai, she was in great distress. She sent clothes for him to put on instead of his sackcloth, but he would not accept them. ⁵Then Esther summoned Hathach, one of the king's eunuchs assigned to attend her, and ordered him to find out what was troubling Mordecai and why.

⁶So Hathach went out to Mordecai in the open square of the city in front of the king's gate. ⁷Mordecai told him everything that had happened to him, including the exact amount of money Haman had promised to pay into the royal treasury for the destruction of the

---

[a]9 That is, about 375 tons (about 345 metric tons)

Jews. [8]He also gave him a copy of the text of the edict for their annihilation, which had been published in Susa, to show to Esther and explain it to her, and he told him to urge her to go into the king's presence to beg for mercy and plead with him for her people.

[9]Hathach went back and reported to Esther what Mordecai had said. [10]Then she instructed him to say to Mordecai, [11]"All the king's officials and the people of the royal provinces know that for any man or woman who approaches the king in the inner court without being summoned the king has but one law: that he be put to death. The only exception to this is for the king to extend the gold scepter to him and spare his life. But thirty days have passed since I was called to go to the king."   Da 2:9

[12]When Esther's words were reported to Mordecai, [13]he sent back this answer: "Do not think that because you are in the king's house you alone of all the Jews will escape. [14]For if you remain silent at this time, relief and deliverance for the Jews will arise from another place, but you and your father's family will perish. And who knows but that you have come to royal position for such a time as this?"

[15]Then Esther sent this reply to Mordecai: [16]"Go, gather together all the Jews who are in Susa, and fast for me. Do not eat or drink for three days, night or day. I and my maids will fast as you do. When this is done, I will go to the king, even though it is against the law. And if I perish, I perish."   Ge 43:14

[17]So Mordecai went away and carried out all of Esther's instructions.

Esther's Request to the King

5 On the third day Esther put on her royal robes and stood in the inner court of the palace, in front of the king's hall. The king was sitting on his royal throne in the hall, facing the entrance. [2]When he saw Queen Esther standing in the court, he was pleased with her and held out to her the gold scepter that was in his hand. So Esther approached and touched the tip of the scepter.

[3]Then the king asked, "What is it, Queen Esther? What is your request? Even up to half the kingdom, it will be given you."   Est 7:2

[4]"If it pleases the king," replied Esther, "let the king, together with Haman, come today to a banquet I have prepared for him."

[5]"Bring Haman at once," the king said, "so that we may do what Esther asks."

So the king and Haman went to the banquet Esther had prepared. [6]As they were drinking wine, the king again asked Esther, "Now what is your petition? It will be given you. And what is your request? Even up to half the kingdom, it will be granted."   Est 7:2; 9:12

[7]Esther replied, "My petition and my request is this: [8]If the king

regards me with favor and if it pleases the king to grant my petition and fulfill my request, let the king and Haman come tomorrow to the banquet I will prepare for them. Then I will answer the king's question." Est 2:15; 6:14

Haman's Rage Against Mordecai

⁹Haman went out that day happy and in high spirits. But when he saw Mordecai at the king's gate and observed that he neither rose nor showed fear in his presence, he was filled with rage against Mordecai. ¹⁰Nevertheless, Haman restrained himself and went home.

Calling together his friends and Zeresh, his wife, ¹¹Haman boasted to them about his vast wealth, his many sons, and all the ways the king had honored him and how he had elevated him above the other nobles and officials. ¹²"And that's not all," Haman added. "I'm the only person Queen Esther invited to accompany the king to the banquet she gave. And she has invited me along with the king tomorrow. ¹³But all this gives me no satisfaction as long as I see that Jew Mordecai sitting at the king's gate."

¹⁴His wife Zeresh and all his friends said to him, "Have a gallows built, seventy-five feet[a] high, and ask the king in the morning to have Mordecai hanged on it. Then go with the king to the dinner and be happy." This suggestion delighted Haman, and he had the gallows built. Est 6:4; 7:9

Mordecai Honored

6 That night the king could not sleep; so he ordered the book of the chronicles, the record of his reign, to be brought in and read to him. ²It was found recorded there that Mordecai had exposed Bigthana and Teresh, two of the king's officers who guarded the doorway, who had conspired to assassinate King Xerxes. Est 2:23; Da 6:18

³"What honor and recognition has Mordecai received for this?" the king asked.

"Nothing has been done for him," his attendants answered.

⁴The king said, "Who is in the court?" Now Haman had just entered the outer court of the palace to speak to the king about hanging Mordecai on the gallows he had erected for him.

⁵His attendants answered, "Haman is standing in the court."

"Bring him in," the king ordered.

⁶When Haman entered, the king asked him, "What should be done for the man the king delights to honor?"

Now Haman thought to himself, "Who is there that the king would rather honor than me?" ⁷So he answered the king, "For the man the king delights to honor, ⁸have them

---

a 14 Hebrew *fifty cubits* (about 23 meters)

bring a royal robe the king has worn and a horse the king has ridden, one with a royal crest placed on its head. [9]Then let the robe and horse be entrusted to one of the king's most noble princes. Let them robe the man the king delights to honor, and lead him on the horse through the city streets, proclaiming before him, 'This is what is done for the man the king delights to honor!' " Ge 41:43; 1Ki 1:33

[10]"Go at once," the king commanded Haman. "Get the robe and the horse and do just as you have suggested for Mordecai the Jew, who sits at the king's gate. Do not neglect anything you have recommended."

[11]So Haman got the robe and the horse. He robed Mordecai, and led him on horseback through the city streets, proclaiming before him, "This is what is done for the man the king delights to honor!"

[12]Afterward Mordecai returned to the king's gate. But Haman rushed home, with his head covered in grief, [13]and told Zeresh his wife and all his friends everything that had happened to him.

His advisers and his wife Zeresh said to him, "Since Mordecai, before whom your downfall has started, is of Jewish origin, you cannot stand against him—you will surely come to ruin!" [14]While they were still talking with him,

the king's eunuchs arrived and hurried Haman away to the banquet Esther had prepared. 1Ki 3:15

Haman Hanged

7 So the king and Haman went to dine with Queen Esther, [2]and as they were drinking wine on that second day, the king again asked, "Queen Esther, what is your petition? It will be given you. What is your request? Even up to half the kingdom, it will be granted."

[3]Then Queen Esther answered, "If I have found favor with you, O king, and if it pleases your majesty, grant me my life—this is my petition. And spare my people—this is my request. [4]For I and my people have been sold for destruction and slaughter and annihilation. If we had merely been sold as male and female slaves, I would have kept quiet, because no such distress would justify disturbing the king.[a]" Est 2:15; 3:9

[5]King Xerxes asked Queen Esther, "Who is he? Where is the man who has dared to do such a thing?"

[6]Esther said, "The adversary and enemy is this vile Haman."

Then Haman was terrified before the king and queen. [7]The king got up in a rage, left his wine and went out into the palace garden. But Haman, realizing that the king had already decided his fate,

---

[a]4 Or quiet, but the compensation our adversary offers cannot be compared with the loss the king would suffer

stayed behind to beg Queen Esther for his life.   2Ki 21:18; Est 1:12; 6:13

8Just as the king returned from the palace garden to the banquet hall, Haman was falling on the couch where Esther was reclining. The king exclaimed, "Will he even molest the queen while she is with me in the house?"   Ge 34:7

As soon as the word left the king's mouth, they covered Haman's face. 9Then Harbona, one of the eunuchs attending the king, said, "A gallows seventy-five feet[a] high stands by Haman's house. He had it made for Mordecai, who spoke up to help the king."

The king said, "Hang him on it!" 10So they hanged Haman on the gallows he had prepared for Mordecai. Then the king's fury subsided.   Ps 7:14-16; Pr 11:5-6

The King's Edict in Behalf of the Jews

8 That same day King Xerxes gave Queen Esther the estate of Haman, the enemy of the Jews. And Mordecai came into the presence of the king, for Esther had told how he was related to her. 2The king took off his signet ring, which he had reclaimed from Haman, and presented it to Mordecai. And Esther appointed him over Haman's estate.   Est 2:7; 3:10; Pr 13:22

3Esther again pleaded with the king, falling at his feet and weeping. She begged him to put an end

to the evil plan of Haman the Agagite, which he had devised against the Jews. 4Then the king extended the gold scepter to Esther and she arose and stood before him.

5"If it pleases the king," she said, "and if he regards me with favor and thinks it the right thing to do, and if he is pleased with me, let an order be written overruling the dispatches that Haman son of Hammedatha, the Agagite, devised and wrote to destroy the Jews in all the king's provinces. 6For how can I bear to see disaster fall on my people? How can I bear to see the destruction of my family?"   Est 7:4; 9:1

7King Xerxes replied to Queen Esther and to Mordecai the Jew, "Because Haman attacked the Jews, I have given his estate to Esther, and they have hanged him on the gallows. 8Now write another decree in the king's name in behalf of the Jews as seems best to you, and seal it with the king's signet ring—for no document written in the king's name and sealed with his ring can be revoked."   Est 1:19

9At once the royal secretaries were summoned—on the twenty-third day of the third month, the month of Sivan. They wrote out all Mordecai's orders to the Jews, and to the satraps, governors and nobles of the 127 provinces stretching from India to Cush.[b] These orders were written in the script of each province and the language of

---

[a]9 Hebrew *fifty cubits* (about 23 meters)   [b]9 That is, the upper Nile region

each people and also to the Jews in their own script and language. ¹⁰Mordecai wrote in the name of King Xerxes, sealed the dispatches with the king's signet ring, and sent them by mounted couriers, who rode fast horses especially bred for the king.   Est 1:1,22

¹¹The king's edict granted the Jews in every city the right to assemble and protect themselves; to destroy, kill and annihilate any armed force of any nationality or province that might attack them and their women and children; and to plunder the property of their enemies. ¹²The day appointed for the Jews to do this in all the provinces of King Xerxes was the thirteenth day of the twelfth month, the month of Adar. ¹³A copy of the text of the edict was to be issued as law in every province and made known to the people of every nationality so that the Jews would be ready on that day to avenge themselves on their enemies.   Est 3:14; 9:10,15,16

¹⁴The couriers, riding the royal horses, raced out, spurred on by the king's command. And the edict was also issued in the citadel of Susa.

¹⁵Mordecai left the king's presence wearing royal garments of blue and white, a large crown of gold and a purple robe of fine linen. And the city of Susa held a joyous celebration. ¹⁶For the Jews it was a time of happiness and joy, gladness and honor. ¹⁷In every province and in every city, wherever the edict of the king went, there was joy and gladness among the Jews, with feasting and celebrating. And many people of other nationalities became Jews because fear of the Jews had seized them.

Triumph of the Jews

9 On the thirteenth day of the twelfth month, the month of Adar, the edict commanded by the king was to be carried out. On this day the enemies of the Jews had hoped to overpower them, but now the tables were turned and the Jews got the upper hand over those who hated them. ²The Jews assembled in their cities in all the provinces of King Xerxes to attack those seeking their destruction. No one could stand against them, because the people of all the other nationalities were afraid of them. ³And all the nobles of the provinces, the satraps, the governors and the king's administrators helped the Jews, because fear of Mordecai had seized them. ⁴Mordecai was prominent in the palace; his reputation spread throughout the provinces, and he became more and more powerful.   2Sa 3:1

⁵The Jews struck down all their enemies with the sword, killing and destroying them, and they did what they pleased to those who hated them. ⁶In the citadel of Susa, the Jews killed and destroyed five hundred men. ⁷They also killed Parshandatha, Dalphon, Aspatha,

⁸Poratha, Adalia, Aridatha, ⁹Parmashta, Arisai, Aridai and Vaizatha, ¹⁰the ten sons of Haman son of Hammedatha, the enemy of the Jews. But they did not lay their hands on the plunder.   Est 5:11; 8:11

¹¹The number of those slain in the citadel of Susa was reported to the king that same day. ¹²The king said to Queen Esther, "The Jews have killed and destroyed five hundred men and the ten sons of Haman in the citadel of Susa. What have they done in the rest of the king's provinces? Now what is your petition? It will be given you. What is your request? It will also be granted."   Est 5:6; 7:2

¹³"If it pleases the king," Esther answered, "give the Jews in Susa permission to carry out this day's edict tomorrow also, and let Haman's ten sons be hanged on gallows."   Dt 21:22-23; Est 5:11

¹⁴So the king commanded that this be done. An edict was issued in Susa, and they hanged the ten sons of Haman. ¹⁵The Jews in Susa came together on the fourteenth day of the month of Adar, and they put to death in Susa three hundred men, but they did not lay their hands on the plunder.   Ge 14:23

¹⁶Meanwhile, the remainder of the Jews who were in the king's provinces also assembled to protect themselves and get relief from their enemies. They killed seventy-five thousand of them but did not lay their hands on the plunder. ¹⁷This happened on the thirteenth day of the month of Adar, and on the fourteenth they rested and made it a day of feasting and joy.

Purim Celebrated

¹⁸The Jews in Susa, however, had assembled on the thirteenth and fourteenth, and then on the fifteenth they rested and made it a day of feasting and joy.

¹⁹That is why rural Jews—those living in villages—observe the fourteenth of the month of Adar as a day of joy and feasting, a day for giving presents to each other.

²⁰Mordecai recorded these events, and he sent letters to all the Jews throughout the provinces of King Xerxes, near and far, ²¹to have them celebrate annually the fourteenth and fifteenth days of the month of Adar ²²as the time when the Jews got relief from their enemies, and as the month when their sorrow was turned into joy and their mourning into a day of celebration. He wrote them to observe the days as days of feasting and joy and giving presents of food to one another and gifts to the poor.   Ne 8:12; Ps 30:11-12

²³So the Jews agreed to continue the celebration they had begun, doing what Mordecai had written to them. ²⁴For Haman son of Hammedatha, the Agagite, the enemy of all the Jews, had plotted against the Jews to destroy them and had cast the *pur* (that is, the lot) for their ruin and destruction. ²⁵But when the plot came to the king's

attention,[a] he issued written orders that the evil scheme Haman had devised against the Jews should come back onto his own head, and that he and his sons should be hanged on the gallows. [26](Therefore these days were called Purim, from the word *pur*.) Because of everything written in this letter and because of what they had seen and what had happened to them, [27]the Jews took it upon themselves to establish the custom that they and their descendants and all who join them should without fail observe these two days every year, in the way prescribed and at the time appointed. [28]These days should be remembered and observed in every generation by every family, and in every province and in every city. And these days of Purim should never cease to be celebrated by the Jews, nor should the memory of them die out among their descendants. Est 3:7; 7:10; Ps 7:16

[29]So Queen Esther, daughter of Abihail, along with Mordecai the Jew, wrote with full authority to confirm this second letter concerning Purim. [30]And Mordecai sent letters to all the Jews in the 127 provinces of the kingdom of Xerxes—words of goodwill and assurance— [31]to establish these days of Purim at their designated times, as Mordecai the Jew and Queen Esther had decreed for them, and as they had established for themselves and their descendants in regard to their times of fasting and lamentation. [32]Esther's decree confirmed these regulations about Purim, and it was written down in the records. Est 4:1-3,16

The Greatness of Mordecai

10 King Xerxes imposed tribute throughout the empire, to its distant shores. [2]And all his acts of power and might, together with a full account of the greatness of Mordecai to which the king had raised him, are they not written in the book of the annals of the kings of Media and Persia? [3]Mordecai the Jew was second in rank to King Xerxes, preeminent among the Jews, and held in high esteem by his many fellow Jews, because he worked for the good of his people and spoke up for the welfare of all the Jews. Ne 2:10; Jer 29:4-7; Da 6:3

[a]25 Or *when Esther came before the king*

Job

Prologue

1 In the land of Uz there lived a man whose name was Job. This man was blameless and upright; he feared God and shunned evil. ²He had seven sons and three daughters, ³and he owned seven thousand sheep, three thousand camels, five hundred yoke of oxen and five hundred donkeys, and had a large number of servants. He was the greatest man among all the people of the East. Ge 6:9; 17:1

⁴His sons used to take turns holding feasts in their homes, and they would invite their three sisters to eat and drink with them. ⁵When a period of feasting had run its course, Job would send and have them purified. Early in the morning he would sacrifice a burnt offering for each of them, thinking, "Perhaps my children have sinned and cursed God in their hearts." This was Job's regular custom. Ge 8:20; 1Ki 21:10,13

Job's First Test

⁶One day the angels*a* came to present themselves before the LORD, and Satan*b* also came with them. ⁷The LORD said to Satan, "Where have you come from?"

Satan answered the LORD, "From roaming through the earth and going back and forth in it." 1Pe 5:8

⁸Then the LORD said to Satan, "Have you considered my servant Job? There is no one on earth like him; he is blameless and upright, a man who fears God and shuns evil." Jos 7:1; Job 42:7-8

⁹"Does Job fear God for nothing?" Satan replied. ¹⁰"Have you not put a hedge around him and his household and everything he has? You have blessed the work of his hands, so that his flocks and herds are spread throughout the land. ¹¹But stretch out your hand and strike everything he has, and he will surely curse you to your face." Job 2:5; 29:6; Ps 34:7

¹²The LORD said to Satan, "Very well, then, everything he has is in your hands, but on the man himself do not lay a finger."

Then Satan went out from the presence of the LORD.

¹³One day when Job's sons and daughters were feasting and drinking wine at the oldest brother's house, ¹⁴a messenger came to Job and said, "The oxen were plowing and the donkeys were grazing nearby, ¹⁵and the Sabeans attacked and carried them off. They put the servants to the sword, and

---

a 6 Hebrew *the sons of God*   *b* 6 *Satan* means *accuser.*

I am the only one who has escaped to tell you!" Ge 10:7; Job 6:19

¹⁶While he was still speaking, another messenger came and said, "The fire of God fell from the sky and burned up the sheep and the servants, and I am the only one who has escaped to tell you!"

¹⁷While he was still speaking, another messenger came and said, "The Chaldeans formed three raiding parties and swept down on your camels and carried them off. They put the servants to the sword, and I am the only one who has escaped to tell you!"

¹⁸While he was still speaking, yet another messenger came and said, "Your sons and daughters were feasting and drinking wine at the oldest brother's house, ¹⁹when suddenly a mighty wind swept in from the desert and struck the four corners of the house. It collapsed on them and they are dead, and I am the only one who has escaped to tell you!" Jer 4:11; 13:24

²⁰At this, Job got up and tore his robe and shaved his head. Then he fell to the ground in worship ²¹and said: Ge 37:29; 1Pe 5:6

"Naked I came from my
    mother's womb,
  and naked I will depart.ᵃ
The Lord gave and the Lord
    has taken away;
  may the name of the Lord
    be praised." Job 2:10

²²In all this, Job did not sin by charging God with wrongdoing.

Job's Second Test

2 On another day the angelsᵇ came to present themselves before the Lord, and Satan also came with them to present himself before him. ²And the Lord said to Satan, "Where have you come from?" Job 1:6

Satan answered the Lord, "From roaming through the earth and going back and forth in it."

³Then the Lord said to Satan, "Have you considered my servant Job? There is no one on earth like him; he is blameless and upright, a man who fears God and shuns evil. And he still maintains his integrity, though you incited me against him to ruin him without any reason." Job 9:17; 27:6

⁴"Skin for skin!" Satan replied. "A man will give all he has for his own life. ⁵But stretch out your hand and strike his flesh and bones, and he will surely curse you to your face." Job 1:11; 19:20

⁶The Lord said to Satan, "Very well, then, he is in your hands; but you must spare his life."

⁷So Satan went out from the presence of the Lord and afflicted Job with painful sores from the soles of his feet to the top of his head. ⁸Then Job took a piece of broken pottery and scraped him-

ᵃ21 Or will return there   ᵇ1 Hebrew the sons of God

self with it as he sat among the ashes. Job 42:6; Eze 27:30; Mt 11:21

⁹His wife said to him, "Are you still holding on to your integrity? Curse God and die!"

¹⁰He replied, "You are talking like a foolish*ᵃ* woman. Shall we accept good from God, and not trouble?" Job 1:21

In all this, Job did not sin in what he said. Jas 1:12; 5:11

Job's Three Friends

¹¹When Job's three friends, Eliphaz the Temanite, Bildad the Shuhite and Zophar the Naamathite, heard about all the troubles that had come upon him, they set out from their homes and met together by agreement to go and sympathize with him and comfort him. ¹²When they saw him from a distance, they could hardly recognize him; they began to weep aloud, and they tore their robes and sprinkled dust on their heads. ¹³Then they sat on the ground with him for seven days and seven nights. No one said a word to him, because they saw how great his suffering was. Ge 50:10; Pr 17:28

Job Speaks

3 After this, Job opened his mouth and cursed the day of his birth. ²He said:

³"May the day of my birth
    perish,

and the night it was said, 'A
    boy is born!' Jer 20:14-18
⁴That day—may it turn to
    darkness;
may God above not care
    about it;
may no light shine upon it.
⁵May darkness and deep
    shadow*ᵇ* claim it once
    more; Job 10:21-22; Jer 2:6
may a cloud settle over it;
may blackness overwhelm its
    light.
⁶That night—may thick
    darkness seize it;
may it not be included
    among the days of the
    year
nor be entered in any of the
    months.
⁷May that night be barren;
may no shout of joy be
    heard in it.
⁸May those who curse days*ᶜ*
    curse that day,
those who are ready to rouse
    Leviathan. Job 41:1,8,10,25
⁹May its morning stars become
    dark;
may it wait for daylight in
    vain
and not see the first rays of
    dawn, Job 41:18
¹⁰for it did not shut the doors of
    the womb on me
to hide trouble from my
    eyes.

¹¹"Why did I not perish at birth,

---

*ᵃ*10 The Hebrew word rendered *foolish* denotes moral deficiency.   *ᵇ*5 Or *and the shadow of death*
*ᶜ*8 Or *the sea*

and die as I came from the
    womb?   Job 10:18
¹²Why were there knees to
    receive me   Ge 30:3; Isa 66:12
and breasts that I might be
    nursed?
¹³For now I would be lying
    down in peace;   Job 17:13
I would be asleep and at rest
¹⁴with kings and counselors of
    the earth,   Job 12:17
who built for themselves
    places now lying in
    ruins,   Job 15:28
¹⁵with rulers who had gold,
who filled their houses with
    silver.   Job 27:17
¹⁶Or why was I not hidden in
    the ground like a
    stillborn child,   Ps 58:8
like an infant who never saw
    the light of day?
¹⁷There the wicked cease from
    turmoil,
and there the weary are at
    rest.   Job 17:16
¹⁸Captives also enjoy their ease;
they no longer hear the slave
    driver's shout.   Job 39:7
¹⁹The small and the great are
    there,
and the slave is freed from
    his master.

²⁰"Why is light given to those in
    misery,
and life to the bitter of soul,
²¹to those who long for death
    that does not come,
who search for it more than
    for hidden treasure,

²²who are filled with gladness
    and rejoice when they reach
    the grave?
²³Why is life given to a man
    whose way is hidden,
    whom God has hedged in?
²⁴For sighing comes to me
    instead of food;   Job 6:7
my groans pour out like
    water.   Ps 42:3-4
²⁵What I feared has come upon
    me;
what I dreaded has
    happened to me.   Job 30:15
²⁶I have no peace, no quietness;
I have no rest, but only
    turmoil."   Job 7:4,14

Eliphaz

4 Then Eliphaz the Temanite re-
    plied:

²"If someone ventures a word
    with you, will you be
    impatient?
But who can keep from
    speaking?   Job 32:20
³Think how you have instructed
    many,
how you have strengthened
    feeble hands.   Isa 35:3
⁴Your words have supported
    those who stumbled;
you have strengthened
    faltering knees.   Isa 35:3
⁵But now trouble comes to you,
    and you are
    discouraged;
it strikes you, and you are
    dismayed.   Job 6:14; 19:21

⁶Should not your piety be your
　　confidence　　　　　　　Pr 3:26
　and your blameless ways
　　your hope?　　　　　　　Job 1:1
⁷"Consider now: Who, being
　　innocent, has ever
　　perished?　　　　　　　Job 36:7
　Where were the upright ever
　　destroyed?　　Job 8:20; Ps 37:25
⁸As I have observed, those who
　　plow evil　　　　　　　Job 15:35
　and those who sow trouble
　　reap it.　　　　Pr 22:8; Hos 10:13
⁹At the breath of God they are
　　destroyed;　　　Isa 30:33; 2Th 2:8
　at the blast of his anger they
　　perish.　　　　　　　　Job 40:13
¹⁰The lions may roar and growl,
　　yet the teeth of the great
　　lions are broken.　　Job 5:15
¹¹The lion perishes for lack of
　　prey,　　　　　　　　Ps 34:10
　and the cubs of the lioness
　　are scattered.
¹²"A word was secretly brought
　　to me,
　my ears caught a whisper of
　　it.　　　　　Job 26:14; 33:14
¹³Amid disquieting dreams in the
　　night,
　when deep sleep falls on
　　men,　　　　　　　　Job 33:15
¹⁴fear and trembling seized me
　and made all my bones
　　shake.　　　　Jer 23:9; Hab 3:16
¹⁵A spirit glided past my face,
　and the hair on my body
　　stood on end.

¹⁶It stopped,
　but I could not tell what it
　　was.
　A form stood before my
　　eyes,
　and I heard a hushed
　　voice:
¹⁷'Can a mortal be more
　　righteous than God?
　Can a man be more pure
　　than his Maker?　　Job 35:10
¹⁸If God places no trust in his
　　servants,
　if he charges his angels with
　　error,　　　　　　　Job 15:15
¹⁹how much more those who
　　live in houses of clay,
　whose foundations are in the
　　dust,　　　　Ge 2:7; Job 22:16
　who are crushed more
　　readily than a moth!
²⁰Between dawn and dusk they
　　are broken to pieces;
　unnoticed, they perish
　　forever.　　　　　　Job 20:7;
²¹Are not the cords of their tent
　　pulled up,
　so that they die without
　　wisdom?'ᵃ　　　　　Job 36:12

5 "Call if you will, but who
　　will answer you?
　To which of the holy ones
　　will you turn?　　Job 15:15
²Resentment kills a fool,
　and envy slays the simple.
³I myself have seen a fool
　　taking root,　　　　Jer 12:2
　but suddenly his house was
　　cursed.　　　　　　Job 24:18

ᵃ21 Some interpreters end the quotation after verse 17.

⁴His children are far from
    safety,   Job 4:11
  crushed in court without a
    defender.   Am 5:12
⁵The hungry consume his
    harvest,   Job 18:8-10
  taking it even from among
    thorns,
  and the thirsty pant after his
    wealth.
⁶For hardship does not spring
    from the soil,
  nor does trouble sprout from
    the ground.
⁷Yet man is born to trouble
  as surely as sparks fly
    upward.

⁸"But if it were I, I would
    appeal to God;
  I would lay my cause before
    him.   Ps 35:23; 50:15
⁹He performs wonders that
    cannot be fathomed,
  miracles that cannot be
    counted.
¹⁰He bestows rain on the
    earth;
  he sends water upon the
    countryside.   Job 36:28
¹¹The lowly he sets on high,
  and those who mourn are
    lifted to safety.
¹²He thwarts the plans of the
    crafty,   Ne 4:15; Ps 33:10
  so that their hands achieve
    no success.
¹³He catches the wise in their
    craftiness,   1Co 3:19

and the schemes of the wily
    are swept away.
¹⁴Darkness comes upon them in
    the daytime;   Job 12:25
  at noon they grope as in the
    night.   Dt 28:29
¹⁵He saves the needy from the
    sword in their mouth;
  he saves them from the
    clutches of the powerful.
¹⁶So the poor have hope,
  and injustice shuts its
    mouth.   Ps 107:42

¹⁷"Blessed is the man whom God
    corrects;   Jas 1:12
  so do not despise the
    discipline of the
    Almighty.ᵃ   Ps 94:12; Pr 3:11
¹⁸For he wounds, but he also
    binds up;   Isa 30:26
  he injures, but his hands
    also heal.   1Sa 2:6
¹⁹From six calamities he will
    rescue you;
  in seven no harm will befall
    you.   Ps 34:19; 91:10
²⁰In famine he will ransom you
    from death,   Ps 33:19
  and in battle from the stroke
    of the sword.   Ps 144:10
²¹You will be protected from the
    lash of the tongue,
  and need not fear when
    destruction comes.
²²You will laugh at destruction
    and famine,
  and need not fear the beasts
    of the earth.   Ps 91:13

ᵃ 17 Hebrew Shaddai; here and throughout Job

23For you will have a covenant
    with the stones of the
    field,   Ps 91:12
and the wild animals will be
    at peace with you.
24You will know that your tent is
    secure;
you will take stock of your
    property and find
    nothing missing.   Job 8:6
25You will know that your
    children will be many,
and your descendants like
    the grass of the earth.
26You will come to the grave in
    full vigor,   Ge 15:15
like sheaves gathered in
    season.

27"We have examined this, and it
    is true.
So hear it and apply it to
    yourself."   Job 8:5; 32:10,17

Job

6 Then Job replied:
2"If only my anguish could
    be weighed
and all my misery be placed
    on the scales!   Job 31:6
3It would surely outweigh the
    sand of the seas—   Pr 27:3
no wonder my words have
    been impetuous.   Job 23:2
4The arrows of the Almighty are
    in me,   Job 16:12-13; Ps 38:2
my spirit drinks in their
    poison;   Job 21:20

God's terrors are marshaled
    against me.   Ps 88:15-18
5Does a wild donkey bray when
    it has grass,
or an ox bellow when it has
    fodder?
6Is tasteless food eaten without
    salt,
or is there flavor in the
    white of an egg*a*?
7I refuse to touch it;
such food makes me ill.

8"Oh, that I might have my
    request,
that God would grant what I
    hope for,   Job 14:13
9that God would be willing to
    crush me,
to let loose his hand and cut
    me off!   Nu 11:15; 1Ki 19:4
10Then I would still have this
    consolation—
my joy in unrelenting pain—
that I had not denied the
    words of the Holy One.

11"What strength do I have, that
    I should still hope?
What prospects, that I
    should be patient?
12Do I have the strength of
    stone?
Is my flesh bronze?
13Do I have any power to help
    myself,   Job 26:2
now that success has been
    driven from me?

14"A despairing man should have

_____
a 6 The meaning of the Hebrew for this phrase is uncertain.

the devotion of his
friends,   Job 4:5; 15:4
even though he forsakes the
fear of the Almighty.
¹⁵But my brothers are as
undependable as
intermittent streams,
as the streams that overflow
¹⁶when darkened by thawing ice
and swollen with melting
snow,
¹⁷but that cease to flow in the
dry season,
and in the heat vanish from
their channels.   Job 24:19
¹⁸Caravans turn aside from their
routes;
they go up into the
wasteland and perish.
¹⁹The caravans of Tema look for
water,   Ge 25:15; Isa 21:14
the traveling merchants of
Sheba look in hope.
²⁰They are distressed, because
they had been
confident;
they arrive there, only to be
disappointed.   Jer 14:3
²¹Now you too have proved to
be of no help;
you see something dreadful
and are afraid.   Ps 38:11
²²Have I ever said, 'Give
something on my
behalf,
pay a ransom for me from
your wealth,
²³deliver me from the hand of
the enemy,

ransom me from the clutches
of the ruthless'?
²⁴"Teach me, and I will be quiet;
show me where I have been
wrong.
²⁵How painful are honest words!
But what do your arguments
prove?
²⁶Do you mean to correct what I
say,
and treat the words of a
despairing man as wind?
²⁷You would even cast lots for
the fatherless   Joel 3:3
and barter away your friend.
²⁸"But now be so kind as to look
at me.
Would I lie to your face?
²⁹Relent, do not be unjust;
reconsider, for my integrity
is at stake.ᵃ   Job 23:7,10
³⁰Is there any wickedness on my
lips?   Job 27:4
Can my mouth not discern
malice?   Job 12:11

7 "Does not man have hard
service on earth?   Job 14:14
Are not his days like those
of a hired man?   Job 14:6
²Like a slave longing for the
evening shadows,
or a hired man waiting
eagerly for his wages,
³so I have been allotted months
of futility,
and nights of misery have
been assigned to me.

ᵃ29 Or my righteousness still stands

4When I lie down I think, 'How
  long before I get up?'
The night drags on, and I
  toss till dawn.
5My body is clothed with
  worms and scabs,
my skin is broken and
  festering.

6"My days are swifter than a
  weaver's shuttle,   Job 9:25
and they come to an end
  without hope.   Job 13:15
7Remember, O God, that my life
  is but a breath;   Ps 78:39
my eyes will never see
  happiness again.   Job 9:25
8The eye that now sees me will
  see me no longer;
you will look for me, but I
  will be no more.
9As a cloud vanishes and is
  gone,
so he who goes down to the
  grave*a* does not return.
10He will never come to his
  house again;
his place will know him no
  more.   Job 8:18; 27:21,23

11"Therefore I will not keep
  silent;   Ps 40:9
I will speak out in the
  anguish of my spirit,
I will complain in the
  bitterness of my soul.
12Am I the sea, or the monster of
  the deep,   Eze 32:2-3
that you put me under
  guard?

13When I think my bed will
  comfort me
and my couch will ease my
  complaint,   Job 9:27
14even then you frighten me
  with dreams
and terrify me with visions,
15so that I prefer strangling and
  death,   1Ki 19:4
rather than this body of
  mine.
16I despise my life; I would not
  live forever.   Job 10:1
Let me alone; my days have
  no meaning.

17"What is man that you make
  so much of him,
that you give him so much
  attention,   Ps 8:4; 144:3
18that you examine him every
  morning
and test him every moment?
19Will you never look away from
  me,
or let me alone even for an
  instant?   Job 9:18
20If I have sinned, what have I
  done to you,   Job 35:6
O watcher of men?
Why have you made me your
  target?   Job 16:12
Have I become a burden to
  you?*b*
21Why do you not pardon my
  offenses
and forgive my sins?   Job 10:14
For I will soon lie down in the
  dust;   Ps 104:29

---

*a*9 Hebrew *Sheol*   *b*20 A few manuscripts of the Masoretic Text, an ancient Hebrew scribal tradition
and Septuagint; most manuscripts of the Masoretic Text *I have become a burden to myself.*

you will search for me, but I
will be no more."

Bildad

8 Then Bildad the Shuhite replied:

2"How long will you say such
things?
Your words are a blustering
wind.   Job 6:26
3Does God pervert justice?   Dt 32:4
Does the Almighty pervert
what is right?   Ge 18:25
4When your children sinned
against him,
he gave them over to the
penalty of their sin.
5But if you will look to God
and plead with the
Almighty,
6if you are pure and upright,
even now he will rouse
himself on your behalf
and restore you to your
rightful place.   Job 5:24
7Your beginnings will seem
humble,
so prosperous will your
future be.   Job 42:12

8"Ask the former generations
and find out what their
fathers learned,
9for we were born only
yesterday and know
nothing,   Ge 47:9
and our days on earth are
but a shadow.   1Ch 29:15

10Will they not instruct you and
tell you?
Will they not bring forth
words from their
understanding?   Pr 4:1
11Can papyrus grow tall where
there is no marsh?
Can reeds thrive without
water?
12While still growing and uncut,
they wither more quickly
than grass.   Ps 129:6; Jer 17:6
13Such is the destiny of all who
forget God;   Ps 9:17
so perishes the hope of the
godless.   Job 11:20; Pr 10:28
14What he trusts in is fragile[a];
what he relies on is a
spider's web.   Isa 59:5
15He leans on his web, but it
gives way;   Job 27:18
he clings to it, but it does
not hold.   Ps 49:11
16He is like a well-watered plant
in the sunshine,
spreading its shoots over the
garden;   Ps 37:35; 80:11
17it entwines its roots around a
pile of rocks
and looks for a place among
the stones.
18But when it is torn from its
spot,
that place disowns it and
says, 'I never saw
you.'
19Surely its life withers away,
and[b] from the soil other
plants grow.   Ecc 1:4

---

[a] 14 The meaning of the Hebrew for this word is uncertain.   [b] 19 Or Surely all the joy it has / is that

²⁰"Surely God does not reject a
       blameless man   Job 1:1
   or strengthen the hands of
       evildoers.   Job 21:30
²¹He will yet fill your mouth
       with laughter   Job 5:22
   and your lips with shouts of
       joy.   Ps 126:2
²²Your enemies will be clothed
       in shame,   Ps 35:26; 109:29
   and the tents of the wicked
       will be no more."

Job

9 Then Job replied:
   ²"Indeed, I know that this is
       true.
   But how can a mortal be
       righteous before God?
³Though one wished to dispute
       with him,
   he could not answer him
       one time out of a
       thousand.   Job 10:2
⁴His wisdom is profound, his
       power is vast.   Job 11:6; 36:5
   Who has resisted him and
       come out unscathed?
⁵He moves mountains without
       their knowing it
   and overturns them in his
       anger.   Mic 1:4
⁶He shakes the earth from its
       place   Isa 2:21; Heb 12:26
   and makes its pillars
       tremble.   Job 26:11
⁷He speaks to the sun and it
       does not shine;
   he seals off the light of the
       stars.   Isa 13:10; Eze 32:8

⁸He alone stretches out the
       heavens   Ge 1:6; Ps 104:2-3
   and treads on the waves of
       the sea.   Job 38:16; Ps 77:19
⁹He is the Maker of the Bear
       and Orion,
   the Pleiades and the
       constellations of the
       south.   Ge 1:16; Job 38:31
¹⁰He performs wonders that
       cannot be fathomed,
   miracles that cannot be
       counted.   Job 5:9
¹¹When he passes me, I cannot
       see him;
   when he goes by, I cannot
       perceive him.   Job 23:8-9
¹²If he snatches away, who can
       stop him?   Job 11:10
   Who can say to him, 'What
       are you doing?'   Isa 45:9
¹³God does not restrain his
       anger;
   even the cohorts of Rahab
       cowered at his feet.
¹⁴"How then can I dispute with
       him?
   How can I find words to
       argue with him?
¹⁵Though I were innocent, I
       could not answer him;
   I could only plead with my
       Judge for mercy.   Job 8:5
¹⁶Even if I summoned him and
       he responded,
   I do not believe he would
       give me a hearing.
¹⁷He would crush me with a
       storm   Job 16:12; 30:22

and multiply my wounds for
　　no reason. Job 2:3; 16:14
[18]He would not let me regain my
　　breath
　but would overwhelm me
　　with misery. Job 7:19
[19]If it is a matter of strength, he
　　is mighty! Ne 9:32
　And if it is a matter of
　　justice, who will
　　summon him[a]?
[20]Even if I were innocent, my
　　mouth would condemn
　　me;
　if I were blameless, it would
　　pronounce me guilty.

[21]"Although I am blameless,
　I have no concern for
　　myself;
　I despise my own life. Job 7:16
[22]It is all the same; that is why I
　　say,
　'He destroys both the
　　blameless and the
　　wicked.' Ecc 9:2-3; Eze 21:3
[23]When a scourge brings sudden
　　death, Heb 11:36
　he mocks the despair of the
　　innocent. Job 24:1,12
[24]When a land falls into the
　　hands of the wicked,
　he blindfolds its judges.
　If it is not he, then who is it?

[25]"My days are swifter than a
　　runner; Job 7:6
　they fly away without a
　　glimpse of joy.

[26]They skim past like boats of
　　papyrus, Isa 18:2
　like eagles swooping down
　　on their prey. Hab 1:8
[27]If I say, 'I will forget my
　　complaint, Job 7:11
　I will change my expression,
　　and smile,'
[28]I still dread all my sufferings,
　for I know you will not hold
　　me innocent. Job 7:21
[29]Since I am already found
　　guilty,
　why should I struggle in
　　vain? Ps 37:33
[30]Even if I washed myself with
　　soap[b]
　and my hands with washing
　　soda, Jer 2:22
[31]you would plunge me into a
　　slime pit
　so that even my clothes
　　would detest me.

[32]"He is not a man like me that I
　　might answer him,
　that we might confront each
　　other in court. Ecc 6:10
[33]If only there were someone to
　　arbitrate between us,
　to lay his hand upon us
　　both,
[34]someone to remove God's rod
　　from me, Ps 39:10
　so that his terror would
　　frighten me no more.
[35]Then I would speak up without
　　fear of him,

a 19 See Septuagint; Hebrew me.　b 30 Or snow

but as it now stands with
me, I cannot.   Job 13:21

10 "I loathe my very life;
therefore I will give free
rein to my complaint
and speak out in the
bitterness of my soul.
²I will say to God: Do not
condemn me,
but tell me what charges you
have against me.   Job 9:29
³Does it please you to oppress
me,   Job 9:22
to spurn the work of your
hands,   Job 14:15; Ps 138:8
while you smile on the
schemes of the wicked?
⁴Do you have eyes of flesh?
Do you see as a mortal sees?
⁵Are your days like those of a
mortal
or your years like those of a
man,   Ps 90:2,4; 2Pe 3:8
⁶that you must search out my
faults
and probe after my sin—
⁷though you know that I am not
guilty
and that no one can rescue
me from your hand?

⁸"Your hands shaped me and
made me.   Ps 119:73
Will you now turn and
destroy me?
⁹Remember that you molded
me like clay.   Isa 64:8
Will you now turn me to
dust again?   Ge 2:7

¹⁰Did you not pour me out like
milk
and curdle me like cheese,
¹¹clothe me with skin and
flesh
and knit me together with
bones and sinews?
¹²You gave me life and showed
me kindness,   Job 33:4
and in your providence
watched over my spirit.

¹³"But this is what you
concealed in your heart,
and I know that this was in
your mind: Job 23:13
¹⁴If I sinned, you would be
watching me
and would not let my
offense go unpunished.
¹⁵If I am guilty—woe to me!
Even if I am innocent, I
cannot lift my head,
for I am full of shame
and drowned in*ᵃ* my
affliction.
¹⁶If I hold my head high, you
stalk me like a lion
and again display your
awesome power against
me.
¹⁷You bring new witnesses
against me   Job 16:8
and increase your anger
toward me;   Ru 1:21
your forces come against me
wave upon wave.

¹⁸"Why then did you bring me
out of the womb?   Job 3:11

ᵃ 15 Or and aware of

I wish I had died before any
　　eye saw me.
¹⁹If only I had never come into
　　being,
　　or had been carried straight
　　　from the womb to the
　　　grave!
²⁰Are not my few days almost
　　over?   Job 7:19; 14:1
　　Turn away from me so I can
　　　have a moment's joy
²¹before I go to the place of no
　　return,   Job 3:13; 16:22
　　to the land of gloom and
　　　deep shadow,ᵃ   Ps 23:4
²²to the land of deepest night,
　　of deep shadow and
　　　disorder,
　　where even the light is like
　　　darkness."

Zophar

11 Then Zophar the Naama-
　　thite replied:

²"Are all these words to go
　　unanswered?   Job 8:2
　　Is this talker to be
　　　vindicated?
³Will your idle talk reduce men
　　to silence?
　　Will no one rebuke you
　　　when you mock?   Job 17:2
⁴You say to God, 'My beliefs are
　　flawless   Job 6:10
　　and I am pure in your sight.'
⁵Oh, how I wish that God
　　would speak,

that he would open his lips
　　against you
⁶and disclose to you the secrets
　　of wisdom,   Job 9:4
　　for true wisdom has two
　　　sides.
　　Know this: God has even
　　　forgotten some of your
　　　sin.   Ezr 9:13; Job 15:5
⁷"Can you fathom the mysteries
　　of God?   Ecc 3:11; Ro 11:33
　　Can you probe the limits of
　　　the Almighty?
⁸They are higher than the
　　heavens—what can you
　　do?   Job 22:12
　　They are deeper than the
　　　depths of the
　　　graveᵇ—what can you
　　　know?   Ps 139:8
⁹Their measure is longer than
　　the earth
　　and wider than the sea.

¹⁰"If he comes along and
　　confines you in prison
　　and convenes a court, who
　　can oppose him?   Job 9:12
¹¹Surely he recognizes deceitful
　　men;
　　and when he sees evil, does
　　　he not take note?
¹²But a witless man can no more
　　become wise
　　than a wild donkey's colt
　　　can be born a man.ᶜ
¹³"Yet if you devote your heart
　　to him   1Sa 7:3; Ps 78:8

ᵃ21 Or *and the shadow of death*; also in verse 22　　ᵇ8 Hebrew *than Sheol*　　ᶜ12 Or *wild donkey can
be born tame*

and stretch out your hands
to him,   Ps 88:9
¹⁴if you put away the sin that is
in your hand
and allow no evil to dwell in
your tent,   Job 22:23; Ps 101:4
¹⁵then you will lift up your face
without shame;   Jn 3:21
you will stand firm and
without fear.
¹⁶You will surely forget your
trouble,   Isa 65:16
recalling it only as waters
gone by.   Job 22:11
¹⁷Life will be brighter than
noonday,   Ps 37:6; Isa 58:8,10
and darkness will become
like morning.
¹⁸You will be secure, because
there is hope;
you will look about you and
take your rest in safety.
¹⁹You will lie down, with no one
to make you afraid,
and many will court your
favor.   Isa 45:14
²⁰But the eyes of the wicked will
fail,   Dt 28:65; Job 17:5
and escape will elude them;
their hope will become a
dying gasp.”   Job 8:13

Job

12 Then Job replied:
²“Doubtless you are the
people,
and wisdom will die with
you!   Job 17:10

³But I have a mind as well as
you;
I am not inferior to you.
Who does not know all these
things?   Job 13:2
⁴“I have become a
laughingstock to my
friends,   Job 21:3
though I called upon God
and he answered—
a mere laughingstock,
though righteous and
blameless!   Job 6:29
⁵Men at ease have contempt for
misfortune
as the fate of those whose
feet are slipping.
⁶The tents of marauders are
undisturbed,   Job 22:18
and those who provoke God
are secure—   Job 9:24; 21:9
those who carry their god in
their hands.ᵃ
⁷“But ask the animals, and they
will teach you,
or the birds of the air, and
they will tell you;   Mt 6:26
⁸or speak to the earth, and it
will teach you,
or let the fish of the sea
inform you.
⁹Which of all these does not
know
that the hand of the Lord
has done this?   Isa 41:20
¹⁰In his hand is the life of every
creature

ᵃ6 Or *secure / in what God's hand brings them*

and the breath of all
       mankind.   Job 27:3; 33:4
[11]Does not the ear test words
       as the tongue tastes food?
[12]Is not wisdom found among
       the aged?   Job 15:10
   Does not long life bring
       understanding?   Job 32:7,9

[13]"To God belong wisdom and
       power;   Job 9:4
   counsel and understanding
       are his.   Job 32:8
[14]What he tears down cannot be
       rebuilt;   Job 19:10; 37:7; Isa 25:2
   the man he imprisons cannot
       be released.
[15]If he holds back the waters,
       there is drought;   1Ki 8:35
   if he lets them loose, they
       devastate the land.
[16]To him belong strength and
       victory;
   both deceived and deceiver
       are his.   Job 13:7,9
[17]He leads counselors away
       stripped   Job 19:9
   and makes fools of judges.
[18]He takes off the shackles put
       on by kings   Ps 116:16
   and ties a loincloth[a] around
       their waist.
[19]He leads priests away stripped
   and overthrows men long
       established.   Job 24:12,22
[20]He silences the lips of trusted
       advisers
   and takes away the
       discernment of elders.

[21]He pours contempt on nobles
   and disarms the mighty.
[22]He reveals the deep things of
       darkness   1Co 4:5
   and brings deep shadows
       into the light.   Job 3:5
[23]He makes nations great, and
       destroys them;   Jer 25:9
   he enlarges nations, and
       disperses them.   Ps 107:38
[24]He deprives the leaders of the
       earth of their reason;
   he sends them wandering
       through a trackless
       waste.
[25]They grope in darkness with
       no light;   Job 5:14
   he makes them stagger like
       drunkards.   Ps 107:27

13 "My eyes have seen all
       this,
   my ears have heard and
       understood it.
[2]What you know, I also know;
   I am not inferior to you.
[3]But I desire to speak to the
       Almighty
   and to argue my case with
       God.   Job 23:3-4
[4]You, however, smear me with
       lies;   Ps 119:69; Jer 23:32
   you are worthless
       physicians, all of you!
[5]If only you would be altogether
       silent!
   For you, that would be
       wisdom.   Pr 17:28
[6]Hear now my argument;

---

a 18 Or *shackles of kings / and ties a belt*

listen to the plea of my lips.
⁷Will you speak wickedly on
  God's behalf?
Will you speak deceitfully
  for him?   Job 36:4
⁸Will you show him partiality?
Will you argue the case for
  God?
⁹Would it turn out well if he
  examined you?
Could you deceive him as
  you might deceive men?
¹⁰He would surely rebuke you
  if you secretly showed
  partiality.
¹¹Would not his splendor terrify
  you?   Job 31:23
Would not the dread of him
  fall on you?
¹²Your maxims are proverbs of
  ashes;
your defenses are defenses
  of clay.

¹³"Keep silent and let me speak;
  then let come to me what
  may.   Job 9:21
¹⁴Why do I put myself in
  jeopardy
and take my life in my
  hands?
¹⁵Though he slay me, yet will I
  hope in him;   Job 7:6; Ps 23:4
I will surely^a defend my
  ways to his face.   Job 27:5
¹⁶Indeed, this will turn out for
  my deliverance,   Isa 12:1
for no godless man would
  dare come before him!

¹⁷Listen carefully to my words;
  let your ears take in what I
  say.
¹⁸Now that I have prepared my
  case,   Job 23:4
I know I will be vindicated.
¹⁹Can anyone bring charges
  against me?   Isa 50:8
If so, I will be silent and
  die.

²⁰"Only grant me these two
  things, O God,
and then I will not hide from
  you:
²¹Withdraw your hand far from
  me,   Ps 39:10
and stop frightening me with
  your terrors.
²²Then summon me and I will
  answer,   Job 14:15
or let me speak, and you
  reply.   Job 9:16
²³How many wrongs and sins
  have I committed?
Show me my offense and my
  sin.
²⁴Why do you hide your face
  and consider me your
  enemy?   Job 19:11; La 2:5
²⁵Will you torment a windblown
  leaf?
Will you chase after dry
  chaff?   Job 21:18; Isa 42:3
²⁶For you write down bitter
  things against me
and make me inherit the sins
  of my youth.   Ps 25:7
²⁷You fasten my feet in shackles;

---

^a 15 Or *He will surely slay me; I have no hope* — / *yet I will*

you keep close watch on all
   my paths
by putting marks on the
   soles of my feet.

28"So man wastes away like
   something rotten,
like a garment eaten by
   moths.   Isa 50:9; Jas 5:2

14 "Man born of woman
is of few days and full of
   trouble.   Job 5:7; Ecc 2:23
2He springs up like a flower and
   withers away;   Ps 90:5-6
like a fleeting shadow, he
   does not endure.   Job 8:9
3Do you fix your eye on such a
   one?   Ps 144:3
Will you bring him*a* before
   you for judgment?
4Who can bring what is pure
   from the impure? Ps 51:10
No one!   Jn 3:6; Ro 5:12
5Man's days are determined;
you have decreed the
   number of his months
and have set limits he
   cannot exceed.
6So look away from him and let
   him alone,   Job 7:19
till he has put in his time
   like a hired man. Job 7:1-2

7"At least there is hope for a
   tree:
If it is cut down, it will
   sprout again,
and its new shoots will not
   fail.

8Its roots may grow old in the
   ground
and its stump die in the
   soil,
9yet at the scent of water it will
   bud
and put forth shoots like a
   plant.   Lev 26:4
10But man dies and is laid low;
he breathes his last and is
   no more.   Job 13:19
11As water disappears from the
   sea
or a riverbed becomes
   parched and dry, Isa 19:5
12so man lies down and does not
   rise;
till the heavens are no more,
   men will not awake
or be roused from their
   sleep.   Ac 3:21

13"If only you would hide me in
   the grave*b*
and conceal me till your
   anger has passed!
If only you would set me a
   time
and then remember me!
14If a man dies, will he live
   again?
All the days of my hard
   service
I will wait for my renewal*c*
   to come.
15You will call and I will answer
   you;   Job 13:22
you will long for the creature
   your hands have made.

---

a 3 Septuagint, Vulgate and Syriac; Hebrew *me* *b* 13 Hebrew *Sheol* *c* 14 Or *release*

¹⁶Surely then you will count my
    steps   Pr 5:21; Jer 32:19
but not keep track of my sin.
¹⁷My offenses will be sealed up
    in a bag;   Dt 32:34
you will cover over my sin.

¹⁸"But as a mountain erodes and
    crumbles
and as a rock is moved from
    its place,   Job 18:4
¹⁹as water wears away stones
and torrents wash away the
    soil,   Job 7:6
so you destroy man's hope.
²⁰You overpower him once for
    all, and he is gone;
you change his countenance
    and send him away.
²¹If his sons are honored, he
    does not know it;
if they are brought low, he
    does not see it.   Ecc 9:5
²²He feels but the pain of his
    own body
and mourns only for
    himself."   Job 21:21

Eliphaz

15 Then Eliphaz the Temanite
replied:

²"Would a wise man answer
    with empty notions
or fill his belly with the hot
    east wind?   Job 6:26
³Would he argue with useless
    words,
with speeches that have no
    value?
⁴But you even undermine piety
and hinder devotion to God.

⁵Your sin prompts your mouth;
you adopt the tongue of the
    crafty.   Job 5:13
⁶Your own mouth condemns
    you, not mine;
your own lips testify against
    you.   Lk 19:22

⁷"Are you the first man ever
    born?   Job 38:21
Were you brought forth
    before the hills?   Ps 90:2
⁸Do you listen in on God's
    council?   Ro 11:34; 1Co 2:11
Do you limit wisdom to
    yourself?
⁹What do you know that we do
    not know?
What insights do you have
    that we do not have?
¹⁰The gray-haired and the aged
    are on our side,   Job 32:6-7
men even older than your
    father.
¹¹Are God's consolations not
    enough for you,   2Co 1:3-4
words spoken gently to you?
¹²Why has your heart carried
    you away,   Job 11:13
and why do your eyes flash,
¹³so that you vent your rage
    against God   Pr 29:11
and pour out such words
    from your mouth?

¹⁴"What is man, that he could be
    pure,
or one born of woman, that
    he could be righteous?
¹⁵If God places no trust in his
    holy ones,

if even the heavens are not
    pure in his eyes,   Job 25:5
¹⁶how much less man, who is
    vile and corrupt,   Ps 14:1
who drinks up evil like
    water!   Job 34:7; Pr 19:28
¹⁷"Listen to me and I will
    explain to you;
let me tell you what I have
    seen,
¹⁸what wise men have declared,
    hiding nothing received from
    their fathers   Job 8:8
¹⁹(to whom alone the land was
    given
when no alien passed among
    them):
²⁰All his days the wicked man
    suffers torment,
the ruthless through all the
    years stored up for him.
²¹Terrifying sounds fill his
    ears;
when all seems well,
    marauders attack him.
²²He despairs of escaping the
    darkness;
he is marked for the
    sword.
²³He wanders about—food for
    vultures^a;   Ps 109:10
he knows the day of
    darkness is at hand.
²⁴Distress and anguish fill him
    with terror;
they overwhelm him, like a
    king poised to attack,
²⁵because he shakes his fist at
    God

and vaunts himself against
    the Almighty,   Job 36:9
²⁶defiantly charging against
    him
with a thick, strong shield.
²⁷"Though his face is covered
    with fat
and his waist bulges with
    flesh,   Ps 17:10
²⁸he will inhabit ruined towns
and houses where no one
    lives,   Isa 5:9
houses crumbling to
    rubble.
²⁹He will no longer be rich and
    his wealth will not
    endure,   Job 27:16-17
nor will his possessions
    spread over the land.
³⁰He will not escape the
    darkness;   Job 5:14
a flame will wither his
    shoots,   Job 22:20
and the breath of God's
    mouth will carry him
    away.   Job 4:9
³¹Let him not deceive himself by
    trusting what is
    worthless,   Isa 59:4
for he will get nothing in
    return.
³²Before his time he will be paid
    in full,   Job 22:16; Ps 55:23
and his branches will not
    flourish.   Job 18:16
³³He will be like a vine stripped
    of its unripe grapes,
like an olive tree shedding
    its blossoms.

^a 23 Or about, looking for food

34For the company of the godless
will be barren,
and fire will consume the
tents of those who love
bribes.   Job 8:22
35They conceive trouble and give
birth to evil;   Ps 7:14; Isa 59:4
their womb fashions deceit."

Job

16

Then Job replied:
2"I have heard many
things like these;
miserable comforters are you
all!   Job 13:4
3Will your long-winded
speeches never end?
What ails you that you keep
on arguing?   Job 6:26
4I also could speak like you,
if you were in my place;
I could make fine speeches
against you
and shake my head at you.
5But my mouth would
encourage you;
comfort from my lips would
bring you relief.

6"Yet if I speak, my pain is not
relieved;
and if I refrain, it does not
go away.
7Surely, O God, you have worn
me out;   Job 7:3
you have devastated my
entire household.
8You have bound me—and it
has become a witness;
my gauntness rises up and
testifies against me.

9God assails me and tears me in
his anger   Hos 6:1
and gnashes his teeth at me;
my opponent fastens on me
his piercing eyes.
10Men open their mouths to jeer
at me;   Ps 22:13
they strike my cheek in
scorn   La 3:30; Mic 5:1; Ac 23:2
and unite together against
me.   Ps 35:15
11God has turned me over to evil
men
and thrown me into the
clutches of the wicked.
12All was well with me, but he
shattered me;
he seized me by the neck
and crushed me.   Job 9:17
He has made me his target;
13 his archers surround me.
Without pity, he pierces my
kidneys   Job 20:24
and spills my gall on the
ground.
14Again and again he bursts
upon me;   Job 9:17
he rushes at me like a
warrior.   Joel 2:7

15"I have sewed sackcloth over
my skin   Ge 37:34
and buried my brow in the
dust.
16My face is red with weeping,
deep shadows ring my eyes;
17yet my hands have been free
of violence   Isa 59:6; Jnh 3:8
and my prayer is pure.

18"O earth, do not cover my
blood;   Isa 26:21

may my cry never be laid to
  rest!   Ps 66:18-19
¹⁹Even now my witness is in
  heaven;   Ro 1:9; 1Th 2:5
  my advocate is on high.
²⁰My intercessor is my friend^a
  as my eyes pour out tears to
  God;   La 2:19
²¹on behalf of a man he pleads
  with God   Ps 9:4
  as a man pleads for his
  friend.

²²"Only a few years will pass
  before I go on the journey of
  no return.   Ecc 12:5

17 ¹My spirit is broken,
  my days are cut short,
  the grave awaits me.   Ps 88:3-4
²Surely mockers surround me;
  my eyes must dwell on their
  hostility.

³"Give me, O God, the pledge
  you demand.   Ps 119:122
  Who else will put up
  security for me?   Isa 38:14
⁴You have closed their minds to
  understanding;
  therefore you will not let
  them triumph.
⁵If a man denounces his friends
  for reward,
  the eyes of his children will
  fail.   Job 11:20

⁶"God has made me a byword
  to everyone,   Job 30:9
  a man in whose face people
  spit.

⁷My eyes have grown dim with
  grief;   Job 16:8
  my whole frame is but a
  shadow.
⁸Upright men are appalled at
  this;
  the innocent are aroused
  against the ungodly.
⁹Nevertheless, the righteous will
  hold to their ways,
  and those with clean hands
  will grow stronger.

¹⁰"But come on, all of you, try
  again!
  I will not find a wise man
  among you.   Job 12:2
¹¹My days have passed, my
  plans are shattered,
  and so are the desires of my
  heart.   Job 7:6
¹²These men turn night into day;
  in the face of darkness they
  say, 'Light is near.'
¹³If the only home I hope for is
  the grave,^b   Job 3:13
  if I spread out my bed in
  darkness,
¹⁴if I say to corruption, 'You are
  my father,'   Job 13:28
  and to the worm, 'My
  mother' or 'My sister,'
¹⁵where then is my hope?   Job 7:6
  Who can see any hope for
  me?
¹⁶Will it go down to the gates of
  death^b?   Job 3:17-19; Jnh 2:6
  Will we descend together
  into the dust?"

---

^a20 Or *My friends treat me with scorn*   ^b13,16 Hebrew *Sheol*

Bildad

18

Then Bildad the Shuhite replied:

²"When will you end these
      speeches?   Job 16:3
  Be sensible, and then we can
      talk.
³Why are we regarded as cattle
  and considered stupid in
      your sight?   Ps 73:22
⁴You who tear yourself to
      pieces in your anger,
  is the earth to be abandoned
      for your sake?
  Or must the rocks be moved
      from their place?

⁵"The lamp of the wicked is
      snuffed out;   Pr 13:9; 20:20
  the flame of his fire stops
      burning.
⁶The light in his tent becomes
      dark;
  the lamp beside him goes
      out.   Job 11:17
⁷The vigor of his step is
      weakened;   Pr 4:12
  his own schemes throw him
      down.   Job 5:13; 15:6
⁸His feet thrust him into a net
  and he wanders into its
      mesh.
⁹A trap seizes him by the heel;
  a snare holds him fast.
¹⁰A noose is hidden for him on
      the ground;
  a trap lies in his path.
¹¹Terrors startle him on every
      side   Job 15:21

and dog his every step.
¹²Calamity is hungry for him;
  disaster is ready for him
      when he falls.
¹³It eats away parts of his
      skin;
  death's firstborn devours his
      limbs.   Zec 14:12
¹⁴He is torn from the security of
      his tent   Job 8:22
  and marched off to the king
      of terrors.
¹⁵Fire resides[a] in his tent;
  burning sulfur is scattered
      over his dwelling.   Ps 11:6
¹⁶His roots dry up below   Isa 5:24
  and his branches wither
      above.   Mal 4:1
¹⁷The memory of him perishes
      from the earth;
  he has no name in the
      land.
¹⁸He is driven from light into
      darkness   Job 5:14
  and is banished from the
      world.
¹⁹He has no offspring or
      descendants among his
      people,   Isa 14:22; Jer 22:30
  no survivor where once he
      lived.
²⁰Men of the west are appalled
      at his fate;   Ps 37:13; Jer 50:27
  men of the east are seized
      with horror.
²¹Surely such is the dwelling of
      an evil man;
  such is the place of one who
      knows not God."   1Th 4:5

---

a 15 Or *Nothing he had remains*

Job

19

Then Job replied:

²"How long will you
    torment me   Job 13:25
and crush me with words?
³Ten times now you have
    reproached me;
shamelessly you attack me.
⁴If it is true that I have gone
    astray,
my error remains my
    concern alone.   Job 6:24
⁵If indeed you would exalt
    yourselves above me
and use my humiliation
    against me,
⁶then know that God has
    wronged me   Job 27:2
and drawn his net around
    me.   Job 18:8

⁷"Though I cry, 'I've been
    wronged!' I get no
    response;   Job 30:20
though I call for help, there
    is no justice.   Job 9:24
⁸He has blocked my way so I
    cannot pass;   Job 3:23; La 3:7
he has shrouded my paths in
    darkness.   Job 30:26
⁹He has stripped me of my
    honor   Job 12:17
and removed the crown from
    my head.   Ps 89:39,44; La 5:16
¹⁰He tears me down on every
    side till I am gone;
he uproots my hope like a
    tree.   Job 7:6; 24:20
¹¹His anger burns against me;

he counts me among his
    enemies.   Job 13:24
¹²His troops advance in force;
they build a siege ramp
    against me   Job 30:12
and encamp around my
    tent.

¹³"He has alienated my brothers
    from me;   Ps 69:8
my acquaintances are
    completely estranged
    from me.   Job 16:7; Ps 88:8
¹⁴My kinsmen have gone away;
my friends have forgotten
    me.   Ps 88:18
¹⁵My guests and my
    maidservants count me
    a stranger;
they look upon me as an
    alien.
¹⁶I summon my servant, but he
    does not answer,
though I beg him with my
    own mouth.
¹⁷My breath is offensive to my
    wife;
I am loathsome to my own
    brothers.
¹⁸Even the little boys scorn me;
when I appear, they ridicule
    me.
¹⁹All my intimate friends detest
    me;   Ps 38:11; 55:12-13
those I love have turned
    against me.   Jn 13:18
²⁰I am nothing but skin and
    bones;   Job 33:21; Ps 102:5
I have escaped with only the
    skin of my teeth.ᵃ

ᵃ20 Or *only my gums*

²¹"Have pity on me, my friends,
      have pity,   Job 6:14
   for the hand of God has
      struck me.
²²Why do you pursue me as God
      does?   Job 13:25; 16:11
   Will you never get enough of
      my flesh?   Ps 69:26

²³"Oh, that my words were
      recorded,
   that they were written on a
      scroll,   Isa 30:8
²⁴that they were inscribed with
      an iron tool on[a] lead,
   or engraved in rock forever!
²⁵I know that my Redeemer[b]
      lives,   Job 16:19; Ps 78:35
   and that in the end he will
      stand upon the earth.[c]
²⁶And after my skin has been
      destroyed,
   yet[d] in[e] my flesh I will see
      God;   Mt 5:8; 1Co 13:12; 1Jn 3:2
²⁷I myself will see him
   with my own eyes—I, and
      not another.
   How my heart yearns within
      me!   Ps 73:26

²⁸"If you say, 'How we will
      hound him,   Job 13:25
   since the root of the trouble
      lies in him,[f]'
²⁹you should fear the sword
      yourselves;

for wrath will bring
      punishment by the
      sword,   Job 15:22
   and then you will know that
      there is judgment.[g]"

Zophar

20 Then Zophar the Naama-
         thite replied: Job 2:11
²"My troubled thoughts prompt
      me to answer
   because I am greatly
      disturbed.   Ps 42:5
³I hear a rebuke that dishonors
      me,   Job 19:3
   and my understanding
      inspires me to reply.

⁴"Surely you know how it has
      been from of old,   Dt 4:32
   ever since man[h] was placed
      on the earth,
⁵that the mirth of the wicked is
      brief,
   the joy of the godless lasts
      but a moment.   Ps 37:35-36
⁶Though his pride reaches to
      the heavens
   and his head touches the
      clouds,   Isa 14:13-14; Ob 1:3-4
⁷he will perish forever, like his
      own dung;   Job 4:20
   those who have seen him
      will say, 'Where is he?'
⁸Like a dream he flies away, no
      more to be found,
   banished like a vision of the
      night.   Ps 90:5

---

⁹The eye that saw him will not
    see him again;
his place will look on him
    no more.   Job 7:8
¹⁰His children must make
    amends to the poor;
his own hands must give
    back his wealth.
¹¹The youthful vigor that fills his
    bones   Job 13:26
will lie with him in the
    dust.

¹²"Though evil is sweet in his
    mouth
and he hides it under his
    tongue,
¹³though he cannot bear to let it
    go
and keeps it in his mouth,
¹⁴yet his food will turn sour in
    his stomach;
it will become the venom of
    serpents within him.
¹⁵He will spit out the riches he
    swallowed;
God will make his stomach
    vomit them up.
¹⁶He will suck the poison of
    serpents;   Dt 32:32
the fangs of an adder will
    kill him.
¹⁷He will not enjoy the streams,
the rivers flowing with
    honey and cream.
¹⁸What he toiled for he must
    give back uneaten;
he will not enjoy the profit
    from his trading.
¹⁹For he has oppressed the poor
    and left them destitute;

he has seized houses he did
    not build.

²⁰"Surely he will have no respite
    from his craving;
he cannot save himself by
    his treasure.
²¹Nothing is left for him to
    devour;
his prosperity will not
    endure.   Job 15:29
²²In the midst of his plenty,
    distress will overtake
    him;
the full force of misery will
    come upon him.
²³When he has filled his belly,
    God will vent his burning
    anger against him
and rain down his blows
    upon him.   Ps 78:30-31
²⁴Though he flees from an iron
    weapon,   Isa 24:18; Am 5:19
a bronze-tipped arrow
    pierces him.
²⁵He pulls it out of his back,
the gleaming point out of his
    liver.
Terrors will come over him;
²⁶   total darkness lies in wait for
    his treasures.   Job 18:18
A fire unfanned will consume
    him   Ps 21:9
and devour what is left in
    his tent.
²⁷The heavens will expose his
    guilt;
the earth will rise up against
    him.
²⁸A flood will carry off his
    house,   Dt 28:31

rushing waters[a] on the day
of God's wrath.
²⁹Such is the fate God allots the
wicked,
the heritage appointed for
them by God."   Job 27:13

Job

21 Then Job replied:

²"Listen carefully to my
words;   Job 13:17
let this be the consolation
you give me.
³Bear with me while I speak,
and after I have spoken,
mock on.   Job 16:10

⁴"Is my complaint directed to
man?
Why should I not be
impatient?   Job 6:11
⁵Look at me and be astonished;
clap your hand over your
mouth.   Jdg 18:19; Job 40:4
⁶When I think about this, I am
terrified;
trembling seizes my body.
⁷Why do the wicked live
on,
growing old and increasing
in power?   Ps 73:3; Jer 12:1
⁸They see their children
established around
them,
their offspring before their
eyes.   Ps 17:14
⁹Their homes are safe and free
from fear;   Ps 73:5

the rod of God is not upon
them.
¹⁰Their bulls never fail to breed;
their cows calve and do not
miscarry.   Ex 23:26
¹¹They send forth their children
as a flock;
their little ones dance about.
¹²They sing to the music of
tambourine and harp;
they make merry to the
sound of the flute.   Ps 81:2
¹³They spend their years in
prosperity   Job 36:11
and go down to the grave[b]
in peace.[c]
¹⁴Yet they say to God, 'Leave us
alone!   Job 22:17
We have no desire to know
your ways.   Pr 1:29
¹⁵Who is the Almighty, that we
should serve him?
What would we gain by
praying to him?'   Job 34:9
¹⁶But their prosperity is not in
their own hands,
so I stand aloof from the
counsel of the wicked.

¹⁷"Yet how often is the lamp of
the wicked snuffed out?
How often does calamity
come upon them,
the fate God allots in his
anger?
¹⁸How often are they like straw
before the wind,
like chaff swept away by a
gale?   Ps 1:4

---

[a]28 Or *The possessions in his house will be carried off, / washed away*   [b]13 Hebrew *Sheol*   [c]13 Or
in an instant

¹⁹It is said, 'God stores up a
man's punishment for
his sons.'   Ex 20:5
Let him repay the man
himself, so that he will
know it!
²⁰Let his own eyes see his
destruction;
let him drink of the wrath of
the Almighty.ᵃ   Isa 51:17
²¹For what does he care about
the family he leaves
behind
when his allotted months
come to an end?

²²"Can anyone teach knowledge
to God,   Isa 40:13-14; Ro 11:34
since he judges even the
highest?   Ps 82:1
²³One man dies in full vigor,
completely secure and at
ease,
²⁴his bodyᵇ well nourished,
his bones rich with marrow.
²⁵Another man dies in bitterness
of soul,
never having enjoyed
anything good.
²⁶Side by side they lie in the
dust,
and worms cover them both.

²⁷"I know full well what you are
thinking,
the schemes by which you
would wrong me.
²⁸You say, 'Where now is the
great man's house,

the tents where wicked men
lived?'   Job 8:22
²⁹Have you never questioned
those who travel?
Have you paid no regard to
their accounts—
³⁰that the evil man is spared
from the day of
calamity,   Pr 16:4
that he is delivered fromᶜ
the day of wrath?
³¹Who denounces his conduct to
his face?
Who repays him for what he
has done?
³²He is carried to the grave,
and watch is kept over his
tomb.
³³The soil in the valley is sweet
to him;   Job 3:22; 17:16; 24:24
all men follow after him,
and a countless throng goesᵈ
before him.   Job 3:19

³⁴"So how can you console me
with your nonsense?
Nothing is left of your
answers but falsehood!"

Eliphaz

22 Then Eliphaz the Temanite
replied:

²"Can a man be of benefit to
God?   Lk 17:10
Can even a wise man benefit
him?

ᵃ17-20 Verses 17 and 18 may be taken as exclamations and 19 and 20 as declarations.   ᵇ24 The
meaning of the Hebrew for this word is uncertain.   ᶜ30 Or *man is reserved for the day of calamity, /
that he is brought forth to*   ᵈ33 Or */ as a countless throng went*

³What pleasure would it give
   the Almighty if you
   were righteous?   Isa 1:11
What would he gain if your
   ways were blameless?

⁴"Is it for your piety that he
   rebukes you
and brings charges against
   you?   Job 14:3; 19:29
⁵Is not your wickedness great?
   Are not your sins endless?
⁶You demanded security from
   your brothers for no
   reason;   Ex 22:26
   you stripped men of their
   clothing, leaving them
   naked.
⁷You gave no water to the
   weary
   and you withheld food from
   the hungry,   Job 31:17,21,31
⁸though you were a powerful
   man, owning land —
   an honored man, living on it.
⁹And you sent widows away
   empty-handed   Job 24:3,21
   and broke the strength of the
   fatherless.
¹⁰That is why snares are all
   around you,
   why sudden peril terrifies
   you,
¹¹why it is so dark you cannot
   see,   Job 5:14
   and why a flood of water
   covers you. Ps 69:1-2; 124:4-5
¹²"Is not God in the heights of
   heaven?   Job 11:8
   And see how lofty are the
   highest stars!

¹³Yet you say, 'What does God
   know?   Ps 10:11
Does he judge through such
   darkness?   Eze 8:12
¹⁴Thick clouds veil him, so he
   does not see us   Job 26:9
   as he goes about in the
   vaulted heavens.'
¹⁵Will you keep to the old path
   that evil men have trod?
¹⁶They were carried off before
   their time,   Job 15:32
   their foundations washed
   away by a flood.
¹⁷They said to God, 'Leave us
   alone!
   What can the Almighty do to
   us?'
¹⁸Yet it was he who filled their
   houses with good
   things,   Job 12:6
   so I stand aloof from the
   counsel of the wicked.

¹⁹"The righteous see their ruin
   and rejoice;   Ps 58:10; 107:42
   the innocent mock them,
   saying,   Ps 52:6
²⁰'Surely our foes are destroyed,
   and fire devours their
   wealth.'   Job 15:30

²¹"Submit to God and be at
   peace with him;
   in this way prosperity will
   come to you.   Ps 34:8-10
²²Accept instruction from his
   mouth
   and lay up his words in your
   heart.
²³If you return to the Almighty,
   you will be restored:

If you remove wickedness
far from your tent
²⁴and assign your nuggets to the
dust,
your gold of Ophir to the
rocks in the ravines,
²⁵then the Almighty will be your
gold,
the choicest silver for you.
²⁶Surely then you will find
delight in the Almighty
and will lift up your face to
God.
²⁷You will pray to him, and he
will hear you,   Isa 58:9
and you will fulfill your
vows.
²⁸What you decide on will be
done,
and light will shine on your
ways.
²⁹When men are brought low
and you say, 'Lift them
up!'
then he will save the
downcast.   Mt 23:12; 1Pe 5:5
³⁰He will deliver even one who
is not innocent,
who will be delivered
through the cleanness of
your hands."   Job 42:7-8

Job

23

Then Job replied:

²"Even today my
complaint is bitter;
his hand*a* is heavy in spite
of*b* my groaning.   Ps 6:6

³If only I knew where to find
him;
if only I could go to his
dwelling!
⁴I would state my case before
him   Job 13:18
and fill my mouth with
arguments.
⁵I would find out what he
would answer me,
and consider what he would
say.
⁶Would he oppose me with
great power?   Job 9:4
No, he would not press
charges against me.
⁷There an upright man could
present his case before
him,   Job 13:3
and I would be delivered
forever from my judge.
⁸"But if I go to the east, he is
not there;
if I go to the west, I do not
find him.
⁹When he is at work in the
north, I do not see him;
when he turns to the south,
I catch no glimpse of
him.   Job 9:11
¹⁰But he knows the way that I
take;
when he has tested me, I
will come forth as gold.
¹¹My feet have closely followed
his steps;
I have kept to his way
without turning aside.

a 2 Septuagint and Syriac; Hebrew / *the hand on me*   *b 2* Or *heavy on me in*

¹²I have not departed from the
  commands of his lips;
I have treasured the words
  of his mouth more than
  my daily bread.   Jn 4:32,34

¹³"But he stands alone, and who
  can oppose him?
He does whatever he
  pleases.   Ps 115:3
¹⁴He carries out his decree
  against me,
and many such plans he still
  has in store.   1Th 3:3
¹⁵That is why I am terrified
  before him;
when I think of all this, I
  fear him.
¹⁶God has made my heart faint;
  the Almighty has terrified
  me.
¹⁷Yet I am not silenced by the
  darkness,   Job 19:8
by the thick darkness that
  covers my face.

24 "Why does the Almighty
  not set times for
  judgment?   Jer 46:10
Why must those who know
  him look in vain for
  such days?   Ac 1:7
²Men move boundary stones;
  they pasture flocks they have
  stolen.
³They drive away the orphan's
  donkey
and take the widow's ox in
  pledge.   Job 22:6

⁴They thrust the needy from the
  path
and force all the poor of the
  land into hiding.   Pr 28:28
⁵Like wild donkeys in the
  desert,
the poor go about their labor
  of foraging food;   Ps 104:23
the wasteland provides food
  for their children.
⁶They gather fodder in the
  fields
and glean in the vineyards of
  the wicked.   Ru 2:22
⁷Lacking clothes, they spend the
  night naked;
they have nothing to cover
  themselves in the cold.
⁸They are drenched by
  mountain rains
and hug the rocks for lack of
  shelter.   La 4:5
⁹The fatherless child is snatched
  from the breast;   Dt 24:17
the infant of the poor is
  seized for a debt.
¹⁰Lacking clothes, they go about
  naked;
they carry the sheaves, but
  still go hungry.   Lev 19:9
¹¹They crush olives among the
  terraces*ᵃ*;
they tread the winepresses,
  yet suffer thirst.
¹²The groans of the dying rise
  from the city,
and the souls of the
  wounded cry out for
  help.   Eze 26:15

ᵃ 11 Or olives between the millstones; the meaning of the Hebrew for this word is uncertain.

But God charges no one with
wrongdoing.   Job 9:23

¹³"There are those who rebel
against the light,
who do not know its
ways
or stay in its paths.   Isa 5:20
¹⁴When daylight is gone, the
murderer rises up
and kills the poor and
needy;
in the night he steals forth
like a thief.   Ps 10:9
¹⁵The eye of the adulterer
watches for dusk;   Pr 7:8-9
he thinks, 'No eye will see
me,'   Ps 10:11
and he keeps his face
concealed.
¹⁶In the dark, men break into
houses,   Ex 22:2
but by day they shut
themselves in;
they want nothing to do with
the light.   Jn 3:20
¹⁷For all of them, deep darkness
is their morning[a];
they make friends with the
terrors of darkness.[b]

¹⁸"Yet they are foam on the
surface of the water;
their portion of the land is
cursed,
so that no one goes to the
vineyards.
¹⁹As heat and drought snatch
away the melted snow,

so the grave[c] snatches away
those who have sinned.
²⁰The womb forgets them,
the worm feasts on them;
evil men are no longer
remembered   Pr 10:7
but are broken like a
tree.
²¹They prey on the barren and
childless woman,
and to the widow show no
kindness.   Job 22:9
²²But God drags away the
mighty by his power;
though they become
established, they have
no assurance of life.
²³He may let them rest in a
feeling of security,
but his eyes are on their
ways.   Job 12:6
²⁴For a little while they are
exalted, and then they
are gone;   Ps 37:10
they are brought low and
gathered up like all
others;
they are cut off like heads of
grain.   Isa 17:5
²⁵"If this is not so, who can
prove me false
and reduce my words to
nothing?"   Job 6:28; 27:4

Bildad

25

Then Bildad the Shuhite
replied:

---

[a]17 Or *them, their morning is like the shadow of death*   [b]17 Or *of the shadow of death*
[c]19 Hebrew *Sheol*

²"Dominion and awe belong to
    God;   Job 9:4; Rev 1:6
he establishes order in the
    heights of heaven.
³Can his forces be numbered?
Upon whom does his light
    not rise?   Jas 1:17
⁴How then can a man be
    righteous before God?
How can one born of woman
    be pure?   Job 4:17
⁵If even the moon is not bright
and the stars are not pure in
    his eyes,   Job 15:15
⁶how much less man, who is
    but a maggot—
a son of man, who is only a
    worm!"   Ps 22:6

Job

26

Then Job replied:
²"How you have helped
    the powerless!   Job 6:12
How you have saved the arm
    that is feeble!   Ps 71:9
³What advice you have offered
    to one without wisdom!
And what great insight you
    have displayed!   Job 34:35
⁴Who has helped you utter
    these words?
And whose spirit spoke from
    your mouth?

⁵"The dead are in deep anguish,
those beneath the waters
    and all that live in them.
⁶Death*ᵃ* is naked before God;
    Destruction*ᵇ* lies uncovered.

⁷He spreads out the northern
    ˌskiesˌ over empty space;
he suspends the earth over
    nothing.
⁸He wraps up the waters in his
    clouds,   Pr 30:4
yet the clouds do not burst
    under their weight.
⁹He covers the face of the full
    moon,
spreading his clouds over
    it.
¹⁰He marks out the horizon on
    the face of the waters
for a boundary between light
    and darkness.   Job 38:8-11
¹¹The pillars of the heavens
    quake,
aghast at his rebuke.
¹²By his power he churned up
    the sea;   Isa 51:15; Jer 31:35
by his wisdom he cut Rahab
    to pieces.
¹³By his breath the skies became
    fair;
his hand pierced the gliding
    serpent.   Isa 27:1
¹⁴And these are but the outer
    fringe of his works;
how faint the whisper we
    hear of him!
Who then can understand
    the thunder of his
    power?"   Job 36:29

27

And Job continued his discourse:
²"As surely as God lives, who
    has denied me justice,

ᵃ6 Hebrew *Sheol*   *ᵇ6* Hebrew *Abaddon*

the Almighty, who has made
me taste bitterness of
soul,　　　　　　　Job 9:18
³as long as I have life within
me,
the breath of God in my
nostrils,　　Job 32:8; 33:4
⁴my lips will not speak
wickedness,
and my tongue will utter no
deceit.　　　　　Job 6:28
⁵I will never admit you are in
the right;
till I die, I will not deny my
integrity.　　Job 2:9; 13:15
⁶I will maintain my
righteousness and never
let go of it;
my conscience will not
reproach me as long as I
live.　　　　　　Job 2:3

⁷"May my enemies be like the
wicked,
my adversaries like the
unjust!
⁸For what hope has the godless
when he is cut off,
when God takes away his
life?　　Job 11:20; Lk 12:20
⁹Does God listen to his cry
when distress comes upon
him?　　Job 35:12; Pr 1:28; Isa 1:15
¹⁰Will he find delight in the
Almighty?　　　Job 22:26
Will he call upon God at all
times?

¹¹"I will teach you about the
power of God;
the ways of the Almighty I
will not conceal.　　Job 36:23

¹²You have all seen this
yourselves.
Why then this meaningless
talk?

¹³"Here is the fate God allots to
the wicked,
the heritage a ruthless man
receives from the
Almighty:　　　Job 20:29
¹⁴However many his children,
their fate is the sword;
his offspring will never have
enough to eat.　　Job 20:10
¹⁵The plague will bury those
who survive him,
and their widows will not
weep for them.　　Ps 78:64
¹⁶Though he heaps up silver like
dust
and clothes like piles of clay,
¹⁷what he lays up the righteous
will wear,　　Pr 28:8; Ecc 2:26
and the innocent will divide
his silver.
¹⁸The house he builds is like a
moth's cocoon,　　Job 8:14
like a hut made by a
watchman.　　　Isa 1:8
¹⁹He lies down wealthy, but will
do so no more;　　Job 7:8
when he opens his eyes, all
is gone.
²⁰Terrors overtake him like a
flood;　　　　　Job 15:21
a tempest snatches him away
in the night.　　Job 20:8
²¹The east wind carries him off,
and he is gone;
it sweeps him out of his
place.　　　　　Job 7:10

²²It hurls itself against him
without mercy   Jer 13:14
as he flees headlong from its
power.
²³It claps its hands in derision
and hisses him out of his
place.   Job 18:18

28 "There is a mine for
silver
and a place where gold is
refined.   Ps 12:6
²Iron is taken from the earth,
and copper is smelted from
ore.   Dt 8:9
³Man puts an end to the
darkness;   Ecc 1:13
he searches the farthest
recesses
for ore in the blackest
darkness.   Job 26:10
⁴Far from where people dwell
he cuts a shaft,   2Sa 5:8
in places forgotten by the
foot of man;
far from men he dangles and
sways.
⁵The earth, from which food
comes,   Ps 104:14
is transformed below as by
fire;
⁶sapphiresᵃ come from its
rocks,   Isa 54:11
and its dust contains nuggets
of gold.   Job 22:24
⁷No bird of prey knows that
hidden path,
no falcon's eye has seen
it.

⁸Proud beasts do not set foot on
it,   Job 41:34
and no lion prowls
there.
⁹Man's hand assaults the flinty
rock   Dt 8:15
and lays bare the roots of
the mountains.   Jnh 2:6
¹⁰He tunnels through the rock;
his eyes see all its treasures.
¹¹He searchesᵇ the sources of
the rivers   Ge 7:11
and brings hidden things to
light.   Isa 48:6
¹²"But where can wisdom be
found?   Pr 1:20; 8:1; Ecc 7:24
Where does understanding
dwell?
¹³Man does not comprehend its
worth;   Pr 3:15; Mt 13:44-46
it cannot be found in the
land of the living.   Dt 29:29
¹⁴The deep says, 'It is not in
me';   Ps 42:7
the sea says, 'It is not with
me.'   Dt 30:13
¹⁵It cannot be bought with the
finest gold,
nor can its price be weighed
in silver.   Pr 3:13-14; 8:10-11
¹⁶It cannot be bought with the
gold of Ophir,   Ge 10:29
with precious onyx or
sapphires.   Ex 24:10
¹⁷Neither gold nor crystal can
compare with it,   Ps 119:72
nor can it be had for jewels
of gold.   Pr 16:16

ᵃ6 Or lapis lazuli; also in verse 16   ᵇ11 Septuagint, Aquila and Vulgate; Hebrew He dams up

¹⁸Coral and jasper are not
    worthy of mention;
  the price of wisdom is
    beyond rubies.   Pr 3:15
¹⁹The topaz of Cush cannot
    compare with it;   Ex 28:17
  it cannot be bought with
    pure gold.   Pr 8:19

²⁰"Where then does wisdom
    come from?
  Where does understanding
    dwell?   ver 23,28
²¹It is hidden from the eyes of
    every living thing,
  concealed even from the
    birds of the air.
²²Destructionᵃ and Death say,
  'Only a rumor of it has
    reached our ears.'
²³God understands the way to it
  and he alone knows where it
    dwells,   Pr 8:22-31
²⁴for he views the ends of the
    earth   Ps 33:13-14
  and sees everything under
    the heavens.   Pr 15:3
²⁵When he established the force
    of the wind
  and measured out the
    waters,   Job 12:15; Ps 135:7
²⁶when he made a decree for the
    rain
  and a path for the
    thunderstorm,   Job 37:3,8,11
²⁷then he looked at wisdom and
    appraised it;
  he confirmed it and tested
    it.
²⁸And he said to man,

'The fear of the Lord—that
    is wisdom,
  and to shun evil is
    understanding.' "   Dt 4:6

29 Job continued his dis-
    course: Job 13:12

²"How I long for the months
    gone by,
  for the days when God
    watched over me,
³when his lamp shone upon my
    head
  and by his light I walked
    through darkness!
⁴Oh, for the days when I was in
    my prime,
  when God's intimate
    friendship blessed my
    house,   Ps 25:14
⁵when the Almighty was still
    with me
  and my children were
    around me,
⁶when my path was drenched
    with cream   Job 20:17
  and the rock poured out for
    me streams of olive oil.

⁷"When I went to the gate of
    the city   Job 31:21
  and took my seat in the
    public square,
⁸the young men saw me and
    stepped aside
  and the old men rose to
    their feet;
⁹the chief men refrained from
    speaking

ᵃ22 Hebrew *Abaddon*

and covered their mouths
   with their hands;   Job 21:5
¹⁰the voices of the nobles were
   hushed,
and their tongues stuck to
   the roof of their mouths.
¹¹Whoever heard me spoke well
   of me,
and those who saw me
   commended me,
¹²because I rescued the poor
   who cried for help,
and the fatherless who had
   none to assist him.
¹³The man who was dying
   blessed me;
I made the widow's heart
   sing.   Job 22:9
¹⁴I put on righteousness as my
   clothing;   Isa 59:17; 61:10
justice was my robe and my
   turban.
¹⁵I was eyes to the blind   Nu 10:31
and feet to the lame.
¹⁶I was a father to the needy;
I took up the case of the
   stranger.
¹⁷I broke the fangs of the wicked
and snatched the victims
   from their teeth.   Ps 3:7

¹⁸"I thought, 'I will die in my
   own house,
my days as numerous as the
   grains of sand.   Ps 30:6
¹⁹My roots will reach to the
   water,   Jer 17:8
and the dew will lie all night
   on my branches.

²⁰My glory will remain fresh in
   me,
the bow ever new in my
   hand.'   Ge 49:24; Ps 18:34
²¹"Men listened to me
   expectantly,
waiting in silence for my
   counsel.
²²After I had spoken, they spoke
   no more;
my words fell gently on their
   ears.   Dt 32:2
²³They waited for me as for
   showers
and drank in my words as
   the spring rain.
²⁴When I smiled at them, they
   scarcely believed it;
the light of my face was
   precious to them.^a
²⁵I chose the way for them and
   sat as their chief;
I dwelt as a king among his
   troops;   Job 1:3
I was like one who comforts
   mourners.   Job 4:4

30

"But now they mock me,
   men younger than I,
whose fathers I would have
   disdained
to put with my sheep
   dogs.
²Of what use was the strength
   of their hands to me,
since their vigor had gone
   from them?
³Haggard from want and
   hunger,

^a24 The meaning of the Hebrew for this clause is uncertain.

they roamed[a] the parched
  land   Isa 8:21
in desolate wastelands at
  night.   Job 24:5
[4]In the brush they gathered salt
  herbs,   Job 39:6
and their food[b] was the root
  of the broom tree.
[5]They were banished from their
  fellow men,
shouted at as if they were
  thieves.
[6]They were forced to live in the
  dry stream beds,
among the rocks and in
  holes in the ground.
[7]They brayed among the bushes
and huddled in the
  undergrowth.
[8]A base and nameless brood,
they were driven out of the
  land.   Job 18:18

[9]"And now their sons mock me
  in song;   Job 12:4; Ps 69:11
I have become a byword
  among them.   Job 17:6
[10]They detest me and keep their
  distance;
they do not hesitate to spit
  in my face.   Nu 12:14; Dt 25:9
[11]Now that God has unstrung
  my bow and afflicted
  me,   Ru 1:21
they throw off restraint in
  my presence.   Ps 32:9
[12]On my right the tribe[c] attacks;
they lay snares for my feet,

they build their siege ramps
  against me.   Job 19:12
[13]They break up my road; Isa 3:12
they succeed in destroying
  me—
without anyone's helping
  them.[d]
[14]They advance as through a
  gaping breach;
amid the ruins they come
  rolling in.
[15]Terrors overwhelm me;   Ps 55:4-5
my dignity is driven away as
  by the wind,
my safety vanishes like a
  cloud.   Job 3:25; Hos 13:3

[16]"And now my life ebbs away;
days of suffering grip
  me.
[17]Night pierces my bones;
my gnawing pains never
  rest.
[18]In his great power ˻God˼
  becomes like clothing to
  me[e];
he binds me like the neck of
  my garment.
[19]He throws me into the mud,
and I am reduced to dust
  and ashes.
[20]"I cry out to you, O God, but
  you do not answer;
I stand up, but you merely
  look at me.
[21]You turn on me ruthlessly;
with the might of your hand
  you attack me.

---

[a]3 Or gnawed   [b]4 Or fuel   [c]12 The meaning of the Hebrew for this word is uncertain.   [d]13 Or
me. / 'No one can help him,' ˻they say˼.   [e]18 Hebrew; Septuagint ˻God˼ grasps my clothing

²²You snatch me up and drive
    me before the wind;
you toss me about in the
    storm.   Job 9:17
²³I know you will bring me
    down to death,   Job 9:22
to the place appointed for all
    the living.

²⁴"Surely no one lays a hand on
    a broken man
when he cries for help in his
    distress.   Job 19:7
²⁵Have I not wept for those in
    trouble?
Has not my soul grieved for
    the poor? Job 24:4; Ps 35:13-14
²⁶Yet when I hoped for good,
    evil came;
when I looked for light, then
    came darkness.   Jer 8:15
²⁷The churning inside me never
    stops;   La 2:11
days of suffering confront
    me.
²⁸I go about blackened, but not
    by the sun;   Ps 42:9
I stand up in the assembly
    and cry for help. Job 19:7
²⁹I have become a brother of
    jackals,   Ps 44:19
a companion of owls. Mic 1:8
³⁰My skin grows black and
    peels;
my body burns with fever.
³¹My harp is tuned to mourning,
    and my flute to the sound of
    wailing.

31 "I made a covenant with
    my eyes

not to look lustfully at a girl.
²For what is man's lot from God
    above,
his heritage from the
    Almighty on high?
³Is it not ruin for the wicked,
    disaster for those who do
    wrong?   Job 34:22
⁴Does he not see my ways
    and count my every
    step?

⁵"If I have walked in falsehood
    or my foot has hurried after
    deceit—   Mic 2:11
⁶let God weigh me in honest
    scales   Job 6:2
and he will know that I am
    blameless—
⁷if my steps have turned from
    the path,   Job 23:11
if my heart has been led by
    my eyes,
or if my hands have been
    defiled,   Job 9:30
⁸then may others eat what I
    have sown,   Lev 26:16
and may my crops be
    uprooted.   Mic 6:15

⁹"If my heart has been enticed
    by a woman,   Job 24:15
or if I have lurked at my
    neighbor's door,
¹⁰then may my wife grind
    another man's grain,
and may other men sleep
    with her.   Jer 8:10
¹¹For that would have been
    shameful,
a sin to be judged. Ge 38:24

¹²It is a fire that burns to
    Destruction*ᵃ*;   Job 15:30
  it would have uprooted my
    harvest.   Job 20:28
¹³"If I have denied justice to my
    menservants and
    maidservants
  when they had a grievance
    against me,   Dt 24:14-15
¹⁴what will I do when God
    confronts me?
  What will I answer when
    called to account?
¹⁵Did not he who made me in
    the womb make them?
  Did not the same one form
    us both within our
    mothers?   Job 10:3
¹⁶"If I have denied the desires of
    the poor   Job 5:16
  or let the eyes of the widow
    grow weary,   Job 22:9
¹⁷if I have kept my bread to
    myself,
  not sharing it with the
    fatherless—   Job 22:7
¹⁸but from my youth I reared
    him as would a father,
  and from my birth I guided
    the widow—
¹⁹if I have seen anyone perishing
    for lack of clothing,
  or a needy man without a
    garment,   Job 24:4
²⁰and his heart did not bless
    me
  for warming him with the
    fleece from my sheep,

²¹if I have raised my hand
    against the fatherless,
  knowing that I had influence
    in court,
²²then let my arm fall from the
    shoulder,
  let it be broken off at the
    joint.   Job 38:15
²³For I dreaded destruction from
    God,
  and for fear of his splendor I
    could not do such
    things.   Job 13:11
²⁴"If I have put my trust in
    gold
  or said to pure gold, 'You
    are my security,'   Mt 6:24
²⁵if I have rejoiced over my great
    wealth,   Ps 62:10
  the fortune my hands had
    gained,
²⁶if I have regarded the sun in
    its radiance   Eze 8:16
  or the moon moving in
    splendor,
²⁷so that my heart was secretly
    enticed
  and my hand offered them a
    kiss of homage,
²⁸then these also would be sins
    to be judged,   Dt 17:2-7
  for I would have been
    unfaithful to God on
    high.
²⁹"If I have rejoiced at my
    enemy's misfortune
  or gloated over the trouble
    that came to him—

ᵃ12 Hebrew *Abaddon*

³⁰I have not allowed my mouth
to sin
by invoking a curse against
his life—
³¹if the men of my household
have never said,
'Who has not had his fill of
Job's meat?'—   Job 22:7
³²but no stranger had to spend
the night in the street,
for my door was always
open to the traveler—
³³if I have concealed my sin as
men do,ᵃ   Pr 28:13
by hiding my guilt in my
heart   Ge 3:8
³⁴because I so feared the crowd
and so dreaded the contempt
of the clans
that I kept silent and would
not go outside

³⁵("Oh, that I had someone to
hear me!   Job 19:7; 30:28
I sign now my defense—let
the Almighty answer
me;
let my accuser put his
indictment in writing.
³⁶Surely I would wear it on my
shoulder,
I would put it on like a
crown.
³⁷I would give him an account of
my every step;
like a prince I would
approach him.)—   Job 1:3
³⁸"if my land cries out against
me   Ge 4:10

and all its furrows are wet
with tears,
³⁹if I have devoured its yield
without payment   1Ki 21:19
or broken the spirit of its
tenants,   Jas 5:4
⁴⁰then let briers come up instead
of wheat   Ge 3:18
and weeds instead of
barley."

The words of Job are ended.

Elihu

32

So these three men
stopped answering Job,
because he was righteous in his
own eyes. ²But Elihu son of Barakel the Buzite, of the family of
Ram, became very angry with
Job for justifying himself rather
than God. ³He was also angry with
the three friends, because they had
found no way to refute Job, and
yet had condemned him.ᵇ ⁴Now
Elihu had waited before speaking
to Job because they were older
than he. ⁵But when he saw that the
three men had nothing more to
say, his anger was aroused.
⁶So Elihu son of Barakel the Buzite said:

"I am young in years,
and you are old;   Job 15:10
that is why I was fearful,
not daring to tell you what I
know.

ᵃ 33 Or *as Adam did*   ᵇ 3 Masoretic Text; an ancient Hebrew scribal tradition *Job, and so had condemned God*

[7]I thought, 'Age should speak;
　　advanced years should teach
　　　wisdom.'
[8]But it is the spirit[a] in a man,
　　the breath of the Almighty,
　　　that gives him
　　　understanding.　　Job 27:3
[9]It is not only the old[b] who are
　　wise,　　1Co 1:26
　　not only the aged who
　　　understand what is
　　　right.　　Job 12:12,20; Lk 2:47

[10]"Therefore I say: Listen to
　　me;
　　I too will tell you what I
　　　know.　　Job 5:27
[11]I waited while you spoke,
　　I listened to your reasoning;
　　while you were searching for
　　　words,
[12]　I gave you my full attention.
　　But not one of you has proved
　　　Job wrong;
　　none of you has answered
　　　his arguments.
[13]Do not say, 'We have found
　　wisdom;　　Jer 9:23
　　let God refute him, not
　　　man.'
[14]But Job has not marshaled his
　　words against me,
　　and I will not answer him
　　　with your arguments.

[15]"They are dismayed and have
　　no more to say;
　　words have failed them.
[16]Must I wait, now that they are
　　silent,

now that they stand there
　　with no reply?
[17]I too will have my say;
　　I too will tell what I know.
[18]For I am full of words,
　　and the spirit within me
　　　compels me;　　Ac 4:20
[19]inside I am like bottled-up
　　wine,
　　like new wineskins ready to
　　　burst.
[20]I must speak and find relief;
　　I must open my lips and
　　　reply.
[21]I will show partiality to no one,
　　nor will I flatter any man;
[22]for if I were skilled in flattery,
　　my Maker would soon take
　　　me away.　　Ps 12:2-4

33 "But now, Job, listen to
　　　my words;
　　pay attention to everything I
　　　say.　　Job 13:6
[2]I am about to open my mouth;
　　my words are on the tip of
　　　my tongue.
[3]My words come from an
　　upright heart;
　　my lips sincerely speak what
　　　I know.　　Job 6:28; 27:4; 36:4
[4]The Spirit of God has made
　　me;　　Ge 2:7
　　the breath of the Almighty
　　　gives me life.　　Job 27:3
[5]Answer me then, if you can;
　　prepare yourself and
　　　confront me.　　Job 13:18
[6]I am just like you before
　　God;

---

[a]8 Or *Spirit*; also in verse 18　　[b]9 Or *many*; or *great*

I too have been taken from
   clay.   Job 4:19
[7]No fear of me should alarm
   you,
nor should my hand be
   heavy upon you.   Job 9:34

[8]"But you have said in my
   hearing—
I heard the very words—
[9]'I am pure and without sin;
I am clean and free from
   guilt.
[10]Yet God has found fault with
   me;
he considers me his enemy.
[11]He fastens my feet in shackles;
he keeps close watch on all
   my paths.'   Job 14:16

[12]"But I tell you, in this you are
   not right,
for God is greater than man.
[13]Why do you complain to him
that he answers none of
   man's words[a]?
[14]For God does speak—now one
   way, now another—
though man may not
   perceive it.
[15]In a dream, in a vision of the
   night,   Job 4:13
when deep sleep falls on
   men
as they slumber in their
   beds,
[16]he may speak in their ears
and terrify them with
   warnings,

[17]to turn man from wrongdoing
and keep him from
   pride,
[18]to preserve his soul from the
   pit,[b]
his life from perishing by the
   sword.[c]   Job 15:22
[19]Or a man may be chastened on
   a bed of pain
with constant distress in his
   bones,
[20]so that his very being finds
   food repulsive   Ps 107:18
and his soul loathes the
   choicest meal.   Job 3:24
[21]His flesh wastes away to
   nothing,
and his bones, once hidden,
   now stick out.   Job 16:8
[22]His soul draws near to the
   pit,[d]
and his life to the
   messengers of death.[e]
[23]"Yet if there is an angel on his
   side
as a mediator, one out of a
   thousand,
to tell a man what is right
   for him,   Mic 6:8
[24]to be gracious to him and say,
'Spare him from going down
   to the pit[f];   Isa 38:17
I have found a ransom for
   him'—
[25]then his flesh is renewed like a
   child's;
it is restored as in the days
   of his youth.   2Ki 5:14

---

[a]13 Or *that he does not answer for any of his actions*   [b]18 Or *preserve him from the grave*   [c]18 Or *from crossing the River*   [d]22 Or *He draws near to the grave*   [e]22 Or *to the dead*   [f]24 Or *grave*

²⁶He prays to God and finds
    favor with him,   Job 34:28
he sees God's face and
    shouts for joy;   Job 22:26
he is restored by God to his
    righteous state.   Ps 50:15
²⁷Then he comes to men and
    says,
'I sinned, and perverted what
    was right,   2Sa 12:13; Lk 15:21
but I did not get what I
    deserved.   Ro 6:21
²⁸He redeemed my soul from
    going down to the pit,ᵃ
and I will live to enjoy the
    light.'   Job 22:28

²⁹"God does all these things to a
    man —   Eph 1:11; Php 2:13
twice, even three times —
³⁰to turn back his soul from the
    pit,ᵇ
that the light of life may
    shine on him.   Ps 56:13

³¹"Pay attention, Job, and listen
    to me;
be silent, and I will speak.
³²If you have anything to say,
    answer me;
speak up, for I want you to
    be cleared.
³³But if not, then listen to me;
be silent, and I will teach
    you wisdom."   Ps 34:11

34 Then Elihu said:
²"Hear my words, you
    wise men;

listen to me, you men of
    learning.
³For the ear tests words
    as the tongue tastes food.
⁴Let us discern for ourselves
    what is right;
let us learn together what is
    good.   1Th 5:21

⁵"Job says, 'I am innocent,
    but God denies me justice.
⁶Although I am right,
    I am considered a liar;
although I am guiltless,
    his arrow inflicts an
    incurable wound.'   Job 6:4
⁷What man is like Job,
    who drinks scorn like water?
⁸He keeps company with
    evildoers;
he associates with wicked
    men.   Ps 50:18
⁹For he says, 'It profits a man
    nothing
when he tries to please God.'

¹⁰"So listen to me, you men of
    understanding.
Far be it from God to do
    evil,   Ge 18:25
from the Almighty to do
    wrong.   Dt 32:4; Job 8:3
¹¹He repays a man for what he
    has done;   Ps 62:12; Mt 16:27
he brings upon him what his
    conduct deserves.
¹²It is unthinkable that God
    would do wrong,
that the Almighty would
    pervert justice.   Job 8:3

ᵃ28 Or *redeemed me from going down to the grave*   ᵇ30 Or *turn him back from the grave*

¹³Who appointed him over the
earth?
Who put him in charge of
the whole world?
¹⁴If it were his intention
and he withdrew his spirit*ᵃ*
and breath,   Ps 104:29
¹⁵all mankind would perish
together
and man would return to the
dust.   Ge 3:19; Job 9:22

¹⁶"If you have understanding,
hear this;
listen to what I say.
¹⁷Can he who hates justice
govern?   2Sa 23:3-4
Will you condemn the just
and mighty One?   Job 40:8
¹⁸Is he not the One who says to
kings, 'You are
worthless,'
and to nobles, 'You are
wicked,'   Ex 22:28
¹⁹who shows no partiality to
princes   Dt 10:17; Ac 10:34
and does not favor the rich
over the poor,
for they are all the work of
his hands?   Job 10:3
²⁰They die in an instant, in the
middle of the night;
the people are shaken and
they pass away;   Job 12:19
the mighty are removed
without human hand.

²¹"His eyes are on the ways of
men;
he sees their every step.

²²There is no dark place, no
deep shadow,   Ps 139:12
where evildoers can hide.
²³God has no need to examine
men further,
that they should come before
him for judgment.
²⁴Without inquiry he shatters the
mighty   Job 12:19
and sets up others in their
place.   Da 2:21
²⁵Because he takes note of their
deeds,
he overthrows them in the
night and they are
crushed.   Pr 5:21-23
²⁶He punishes them for their
wickedness
where everyone can see
them,
²⁷because they turned from
following him   Ps 28:5
and had no regard for any of
his ways.   1Sa 15:11
²⁸They caused the cry of the
poor to come before
him,
so that he heard the cry of
the needy.   Ex 22:23; Jas 5:4
²⁹But if he remains silent, who
can condemn him?
If he hides his face, who can
see him?
Yet he is over man and nation
alike,
³⁰ to keep a godless man from
ruling,
from laying snares for the
people.   Pr 29:2-12

ᵃ 14 Or *Spirit*

³¹"Suppose a man says to God,
    'I am guilty but will offend
        no more.
³²Teach me what I cannot see;
    if I have done wrong, I will
        not do so again.' Job 33:27
³³Should God then reward you
        on your terms,
    when you refuse to repent?
You must decide, not I;
    so tell me what you know.

³⁴"Men of understanding declare,
    wise men who hear me say
        to me,
³⁵'Job speaks without
        knowledge;   Job 35:16
    his words lack insight.'
³⁶Oh, that Job might be tested to
        the utmost
    for answering like a wicked
        man!   Job 22:15
³⁷To his sin he adds rebellion;
    scornfully he claps his hands
        among us   Job 27:23
    and multiplies his words
        against God."   Job 23:2

35 Then Elihu said:
    ²"Do you think this is
        just?
    You say, 'I will be cleared by
        God.ᵃ'   Job 32:2
³Yet you ask him, 'What profit
    is it to me,ᵇ
    and what do I gain by not
        sinning?'   Job 9:29-31; 34:9

⁴"I would like to reply to you

and to your friends with
    you.
⁵Look up at the heavens and
    see;   Ge 15:5
    gaze at the clouds so high
        above you.   Job 22:12
⁶If you sin, how does that affect
    him?
    If your sins are many, what
        does that do to him?
⁷If you are righteous, what do
        you give to him,   Ro 11:35
    or what does he receive from
        your hand?   Job 22:2-3; Pr 9:12
⁸Your wickedness affects only a
    man like yourself,
    and your righteousness only
        the sons of men.

⁹"Men cry out under a load of
    oppression;   Ex 2:23
    they plead for relief from the
        arm of the powerful.
¹⁰But no one says, 'Where is
    God my Maker,
    who gives songs in the night,
¹¹who teaches more to us than
        toᶜ the beasts of the
        earth   Ps 94:12
    and makes us wiser thanᵈ
        the birds of the air?'
¹²He does not answer when men
    cry out   Pr 1:28
    because of the arrogance of
        the wicked.
¹³Indeed, God does not listen to
        their empty plea;
    the Almighty pays no
        attention to it.   Isa 1:15

ᵃ2 Or *My righteousness is more than God's*   ᵇ3 Or *you*   ᶜ11 Or *teaches us by*   ᵈ11 Or *us wise by*

¹⁴How much less, then, will he
    listen
  when you say that you do
    not see him,   Job 9:11
  that your case is before him
  and you must wait for him,
¹⁵and further, that his anger
    never punishes
  and he does not take the
    least notice of
    wickedness.ᵃ   Ps 10:11
¹⁶So Job opens his mouth with
    empty talk;
  without knowledge he
    multiplies words."

36 Elihu continued:
  ²"Bear with me a little
    longer and I will show
    you
  that there is more to be said
    in God's behalf.
³I get my knowledge from afar;
  I will ascribe justice to my
    Maker.   Job 8:3
⁴Be assured that my words are
    not false;   Job 33:3
  one perfect in knowledge is
    with you.   Job 37:5,16,23

⁵"God is mighty, but does not
    despise men;   Ps 22:24
  he is mighty, and firm in his
    purpose.   Job 12:13
⁶He does not keep the wicked
    alive   Job 8:22
  but gives the afflicted their
    rights.   Job 5:15

⁷He does not take his eyes off
    the righteous;   Ps 33:18
  he enthrones them with
    kings   Ps 113:8
  and exalts them forever.
⁸But if men are bound in
    chains,   Ps 107:10,14
  held fast by cords of
    affliction,
⁹he tells them what they have
    done—
  that they have sinned
    arrogantly.   Job 15:25
¹⁰He makes them listen to
    correction   Job 33:16
  and commands them to
    repent of their evil.
¹¹If they obey and serve him,
  they will spend the rest of
    their days in prosperity
  and their years in
    contentment.
¹²But if they do not listen,
  they will perish by the
    swordᵇ   Job 15:22
  and die without knowledge.

¹³"The godless in heart harbor
    resentment;   Ro 2:5
  even when he fetters them,
    they do not cry for help.
¹⁴They die in their youth,
  among male prostitutes of
    the shrines.   Dt 23:17
¹⁵But those who suffer he
    delivers in their
    suffering;
  he speaks to them in their
    affliction.

ᵃ15 Symmachus, Theodotion and Vulgate; the meaning of the Hebrew for this word is uncertain.
ᵇ12 Or will cross the River

16"He is wooing you from the
        jaws of distress   Hos 2:14
    to a spacious place free from
        restriction,
    to the comfort of your table
        laden with choice food.
17But now you are laden with
        the judgment due the
        wicked;
    judgment and justice have
        taken hold of you.
18Be careful that no one entices
        you by riches;
    do not let a large bribe turn
        you aside.   Job 34:33
19Would your wealth
    or even all your mighty
        efforts
    sustain you so you would
        not be in distress?
20Do not long for the night,
    to drag people away from
        their homes.ᵃ
21Beware of turning to evil,
    which you seem to prefer to
        affliction.   Heb 11:25

22"God is exalted in his power.
    Who is a teacher like
        him?
23Who has prescribed his ways
        for him,   Job 34:13
    or said to him, 'You have
        done wrong'?
24Remember to extol his work,
    which men have praised in
        song.   Rev 15:3
25All mankind has seen it;
    men gaze on it from afar.

26How great is God—beyond our
        understanding!   1Co 13:12
    The number of his years is
        past finding out.   Heb 1:12
27"He draws up the drops of
        water,
    which distill as rain to the
        streamsᵇ;   Job 38:28; Ps 147:8
28the clouds pour down their
        moisture
    and abundant showers fall
        on mankind.   Job 5:10
29Who can understand how he
        spreads out the clouds,
    how he thunders from his
        pavilion?   Job 37:16
30See how he scatters his
        lightning about him,
    bathing the depths of the
        sea.
31This is the way he governsᶜ
        the nations   Job 37:13
    and provides food in
        abundance.   Ac 14:17
32He fills his hands with
        lightning
    and commands it to strike its
        mark.   Job 37:12,15
33His thunder announces the
        coming storm;
    even the cattle make known
        its approach.ᵈ   Job 28:26

37 "At this my heart pounds
        and leaps from its place.
2Listen! Listen to the roar of his
        voice,   Job 32:10

ᵃ20 The meaning of the Hebrew for verses 18-20 is uncertain.   ᵇ27 Or distill from the mist as rain
ᶜ31 Or nourishes   ᵈ33 Or announces his coming— / the One zealous against evil

to the rumbling that comes
from his mouth. Ps 29:3-9
³He unleashes his lightning
beneath the whole
heaven
and sends it to the ends of
the earth. Job 36:32
⁴After that comes the sound of
his roar;
he thunders with his
majestic voice. Ex 20:19
When his voice resounds,
he holds nothing back.
⁵God's voice thunders in
marvelous ways;
he does great things beyond
our understanding.
⁶He says to the snow, 'Fall on
the earth,' Job 38:22
and to the rain shower, 'Be a
mighty downpour.'
⁷So that all men he has made
may know his work,
he stops every man from his
labor.ᵃ Job 12:14
⁸The animals take cover;
they remain in their dens.
⁹The tempest comes out from
its chamber,
the cold from the driving
winds.
¹⁰The breath of God produces
ice,
and the broad waters
become frozen.
¹¹He loads the clouds with
moisture;
he scatters his lightning
through them. Job 36:27,29

¹²At his direction they swirl
around
over the face of the whole
earth
to do whatever he
commands them. Ps 148:8
¹³He brings the clouds to punish
men, 1Sa 12:17
or to water his earthᵇ and
show his love. Ex 9:18
¹⁴"Listen to this, Job; Job 32:10
stop and consider God's
wonders. Job 5:9
¹⁵Do you know how God
controls the clouds
and makes his lightning
flash? Job 36:30,32
¹⁶Do you know how the clouds
hang poised,
those wonders of him who is
perfect in knowledge?
¹⁷You who swelter in your
clothes
when the land lies hushed
under the south wind,
¹⁸can you join him in spreading
out the skies, Isa 44:24
hard as a mirror of cast
bronze? Dt 28:23

¹⁹"Tell us what we should say to
him; Ro 8:26
we cannot draw up our case
because of our darkness.
²⁰Should he be told that I want
to speak?
Would any man ask to be
swallowed up?

ᵃ7 Or / he fills all men with fear by his power   ᵇ13 Or to favor them

²¹Now no one can look at the
        sun,   Jdg 5:31
    bright as it is in the skies
    after the wind has swept
        them clean.
²²Out of the north he comes in
        golden splendor;   Ps 19:5
    God comes in awesome
        majesty.
²³The Almighty is beyond our
        reach and exalted in
        power;   Job 9:4; 1Ti 6:16
    in his justice and great
        righteousness, he does
        not oppress.   Isa 63:9
²⁴Therefore, men revere him,
    for does he not have regard
        for all the wise in
        heart?^a"   Mt 11:25

The LORD Speaks

38 Then the LORD answered
        Job out of the storm. He
said: Job 40:6

²"Who is this that darkens my
        counsel
    with words without
        knowledge?   1Ti 1:7
³Brace yourself like a man;
    I will question you,
    and you shall answer me.

⁴"Where were you when I laid
        the earth's foundation?
    Tell me, if you understand.
⁵Who marked off its
        dimensions? Surely you
        know!   Pr 8:29; Isa 40:12

Who stretched a measuring
        line across it?
⁶On what were its footings set,
    or who laid its cornerstone—
⁷while the morning stars sang
        together
    and all the angels^b shouted
        for joy?

⁸"Who shut up the sea behind
        doors   Jer 5:22
    when it burst forth from the
        womb,   Ge 1:9-10
⁹when I made the clouds its
        garment
    and wrapped it in thick
        darkness,
¹⁰when I fixed limits for it   Ps 33:7
    and set its doors and bars in
        place,   Job 26:10
¹¹when I said, 'This far you may
        come and no farther;
    here is where your proud
        waves halt'?   Ps 89:9

¹²"Have you ever given orders to
        the morning,
    or shown the dawn its place,
¹³that it might take the earth by
        the edges
    and shake the wicked out of
        it?   Ps 104:35
¹⁴The earth takes shape like clay
        under a seal;
    its features stand out like
        those of a garment.
¹⁵The wicked are denied their
        light,   Job 18:5
    and their upraised arm is
        broken.   Ps 10:15

---

^a24 Or *for he does not have regard for any who think they are wise.*   ^b7 Hebrew *the sons of God*

16"Have you journeyed to the
      springs of the sea
  or walked in the recesses of
      the deep?   Ps 77:19
17Have the gates of death been
      shown to you?   Ps 9:13
  Have you seen the gates of
      the shadow of death*a*?
18Have you comprehended the
      vast expanses of the
      earth?   Job 28:24
  Tell me, if you know all this.

19"What is the way to the abode
      of light?
  And where does darkness
      reside?
20Can you take them to their
      places?
  Do you know the paths to
      their dwellings?   Job 26:10
21Surely you know, for you were
      already born!   Job 15:7
  You have lived so many
      years!

22"Have you entered the
      storehouses of the snow
  or seen the storehouses of
      the hail,
23which I reserve for times of
      trouble,   Isa 30:30; Eze 13:11
  for days of war and battle?
24What is the way to the place
      where the lightning is
      dispersed,
  or the place where the east
      winds are scattered over
      the earth?

25Who cuts a channel for the
      torrents of rain,
  and a path for the
      thunderstorm,   Job 28:26
26to water a land where no man
      lives,   Job 36:27
  a desert with no one in it,
27to satisfy a desolate wasteland
  and make it sprout with
      grass?   Ps 104:14
28Does the rain have a father?
  Who fathers the drops of
      dew?
29From whose womb comes the
      ice?
  Who gives birth to the frost
      from the heavens
30when the waters become hard
      as stone,
  when the surface of the deep
      is frozen?   Job 37:10

31"Can you bind the beautiful*b*
      Pleiades?
  Can you loose the cords of
      Orion?   Job 9:9; Am 5:8
32Can you bring forth the
      constellations in their
      seasons*c*
  or lead out the Bear*d* with
      its cubs?
33Do you know the laws of the
      heavens?   Ps 148:6; Jer 31:36
  Can you set up ͺGod's*e*ͺ
      dominion over the
      earth?

34"Can you raise your voice to
      the clouds

---

*a*17 Or *gates of deep shadows*   *b*31 Or *the twinkling;* or *the chains of the*   *c*32 Or *the morning star*
in its season   *d*32 Or *out Leo*   *e*33 Or *his;* or *their*

and cover yourself with a
flood of water?   Job 22:11
³⁵Do you send the lightning
bolts on their way?
Do they report to you, 'Here
we are'?
³⁶Who endowed the heart^a with
wisdom   Job 9:4
or gave understanding to the
mind^a?   Job 32:8; Ps 51:6
³⁷Who has the wisdom to count
the clouds?
Who can tip over the water
jars of the heavens
³⁸when the dust becomes hard
and the clods of earth stick
together?   1Ki 18:45
³⁹"Do you hunt the prey for the
lioness
and satisfy the hunger of the
lions   Ps 104:21
⁴⁰when they crouch in their dens
or lie in wait in a thicket?
⁴¹Who provides food for the
raven   Lk 12:24
when its young cry out to
God
and wander about for lack of
food?   Ps 147:9; Mt 6:26

39 "Do you know when the
mountain goats give
birth?   Dt 14:5
Do you watch when the doe
bears her fawn?
²Do you count the months till
they bear?
Do you know the time they
give birth?

³They crouch down and bring
forth their young;
their labor pains are
ended.
⁴Their young thrive and grow
strong in the wilds;
they leave and do not
return.
⁵"Who let the wild donkey go
free?   Job 6:5
Who untied his ropes?
⁶I gave him the wasteland as his
home,   Job 24:5; Jer 2:24
the salt flats as his habitat.
⁷He laughs at the commotion in
the town;
he does not hear a driver's
shout.   Job 3:18
⁸He ranges the hills for his
pasture
and searches for any green
thing.
⁹"Will the wild ox consent to
serve you?   Nu 23:22; Dt 33:17
Will he stay by your manger
at night?
¹⁰Can you hold him to the
furrow with a harness?
Will he till the valleys
behind you?
¹¹Will you rely on him for his
great strength?   Ps 147:10
Will you leave your heavy
work to him?
¹²Can you trust him to bring in
your grain
and gather it to your
threshing floor?

^a 36 The meaning of the Hebrew for this word is uncertain.

13"The wings of the ostrich flap
    joyfully,
  but they cannot compare
      with the pinions and
      feathers of the stork.
14She lays her eggs on the
    ground
  and lets them warm in the
    sand,
15unmindful that a foot may
    crush them,
  that some wild animal may
    trample them.
16She treats her young harshly,
    as if they were not hers;
  she cares not that her labor
    was in vain,
17for God did not endow her
    with wisdom
  or give her a share of good
    sense.   Job 35:11
18Yet when she spreads her
    feathers to run,
  she laughs at horse and
    rider.

19"Do you give the horse his
    strength
  or clothe his neck with a
    flowing mane?
20Do you make him leap like a
    locust,   Joel 2:4-5
  striking terror with his proud
    snorting?   Jer 8:16
21He paws fiercely, rejoicing in
    his strength,
  and charges into the fray.
22He laughs at fear, afraid of
    nothing;
  he does not shy away from
    the sword.

23The quiver rattles against his
    side,
  along with the flashing spear
    and lance.
24In frenzied excitement he eats
    up the ground;
  he cannot stand still when
    the trumpet sounds.
25At the blast of the trumpet he
    snorts, 'Aha!'   Jos 6:5
  He catches the scent of
    battle from afar,
  the shout of commanders
    and the battle cry.

26"Does the hawk take flight by
    your wisdom
  and spread his wings toward
    the south?
27Does the eagle soar at your
    command
  and build his nest on high?
28He dwells on a cliff and stays
    there at night;
  a rocky crag is his
    stronghold.
29From there he seeks out his
    food;   Job 9:26
  his eyes detect it from afar.
30His young ones feast on blood,
  and where the slain are,
    there is he."   Mt 24:28

40 The Lord said to Job:
  2"Will the one who
    contends with the
    Almighty correct him?
  Let him who accuses God
    answer him!"   Job 9:3

3Then Job answered the Lord:

⁴"I am unworthy—how can I
	reply to you?	Job 42:6
I put my hand over my
	mouth.	Job 29:9
⁵I spoke once, but I have no
	answer—	Job 9:3
twice, but I will say no
	more."

⁶Then the LORD spoke to Job out
of the storm:	Job 38:1

⁷"Brace yourself like a man;
	I will question you,
	and you shall answer me.

⁸"Would you discredit my
	justice?	Ro 3:3
Would you condemn me to
	justify yourself?
⁹Do you have an arm like
	God's,	2Ch 32:8
and can your voice thunder
	like his?	Job 37:5; Ps 29:3-4
¹⁰Then adorn yourself with glory
	and splendor,
	and clothe yourself in honor
	and majesty.	Ps 93:1; 104:1
¹¹Unleash the fury of your
	wrath,	Isa 42:25; Na 1:6
look at every proud man and
	bring him low,
¹²look at every proud man and
	humble him,	1Sa 2:7
crush the wicked where they
	stand.	Isa 13:11; 63:2-3,6
¹³Bury them all in the dust
	together;
	shroud their faces in the
	grave.

¹⁴Then I myself will admit to
	you
	that your own right hand
	can save you.	Ps 20:6

¹⁵"Look at the behemoth,ᵃ
	which I made along with
	you	Job 9:9
and which feeds on grass
	like an ox.	Isa 11:7
¹⁶What strength he has in his
	loins,	Job 39:11
what power in the muscles
	of his belly!	Job 41:9
¹⁷His tailᵇ sways like a cedar;
	the sinews of his thighs are
	close-knit.
¹⁸His bones are tubes of bronze,
	his limbs like rods of
	iron.
¹⁹He ranks first among the works
	of God,	Job 41:33
yet his Maker can approach
	him with his sword.
²⁰The hills bring him their
	produce,	Ps 104:14
and all the wild animals play
	nearby.	Ps 104:26
²¹Under the lotus plants he lies,
	hidden among the reeds in
	the marsh.
²²The lotuses conceal him in
	their shadow;
	the poplars by the stream
	surround him.	Isa 44:4
²³When the river rages, he is not
	alarmed;	Isa 8:7
he is secure, though the
	Jordan should surge
	against his mouth.	Jos 3:1

ᵃ 15 Possibly the hippopotamus or the elephant	ᵇ 17 Possibly trunk

²⁴Can anyone capture him by the
  eyes,ᵃ
    or trap him and pierce his
      nose?   Job 41:2,7,26

41 "Can you pull in the
      leviathanᵇ with a
      fishhook   Ps 104:26; Isa 27:1
    or tie down his tongue with
      a rope?
²Can you put a cord through his
    nose
    or pierce his jaw with a
      hook?   Isa 37:29
³Will he keep begging you for
    mercy?
    Will he speak to you with
      gentle words?
⁴Will he make an agreement
    with you
    for you to take him as your
      slave for life?   Ex 21:6
⁵Can you make a pet of him
    like a bird
    or put him on a leash for
      your girls?
⁶Will traders barter for him?
    Will they divide him up
      among the merchants?
⁷Can you fill his hide with
    harpoons
    or his head with fishing
      spears?   Job 40:24
⁸If you lay a hand on him,
    you will remember the
      struggle and never do it
        again!   Job 3:8
⁹Any hope of subduing him is
    false;

the mere sight of him is
    overpowering.   Job 40:16
¹⁰No one is fierce enough to
    rouse him.   Job 3:8
    Who then is able to stand
      against me?   Jer 50:44
¹¹Who has a claim against me
    that I must pay?   Ro 11:35
    Everything under heaven
      belongs to me.   Ex 19:5

¹²"I will not fail to speak of his
    limbs,   Job 40:18
    his strength and his graceful
      form.   Job 39:11
¹³Who can strip off his outer
    coat?
    Who would approach him
      with a bridle?   Job 30:11
¹⁴Who dares open the doors of
    his mouth,   Ps 22:13
    ringed about with his
      fearsome teeth?
¹⁵His back hasᶜ rows of shields
    tightly sealed together;
¹⁶each is so close to the next
    that no air can pass between.
¹⁷They are joined fast to one
    another;
    they cling together and
      cannot be parted.
¹⁸His snorting throws out flashes
    of light;
    his eyes are like the rays of
      dawn.   Job 3:9
¹⁹Firebrands stream from his
    mouth;   Da 10:6
    sparks of fire shoot out.
²⁰Smoke pours from his nostrils

ᵃ24 Or by a water hole   ᵇ1 Possibly the crocodile   ᶜ15 Or His pride is his

as from a boiling pot over a
  fire of reeds.
²¹His breath sets coals ablaze,
  and flames dart from his
  mouth.   Ps 18:8
²²Strength resides in his neck;
  dismay goes before him.
²³The folds of his flesh are
  tightly joined;
  they are firm and
  immovable.
²⁴His chest is hard as rock,
  hard as a lower millstone.
²⁵When he rises up, the mighty
  are terrified;   Job 39:20
  they retreat before his
  thrashing.   Job 3:8
²⁶The sword that reaches him
  has no effect,
  nor does the spear or the
  dart or the javelin.
²⁷Iron he treats like straw
  and bronze like rotten wood.
²⁸Arrows do not make him
  flee;
  slingstones are like chaff to
  him.
²⁹A club seems to him but a
  piece of straw;
  he laughs at the rattling of
  the lance.   Job 5:22
³⁰His undersides are jagged
  potsherds,
  leaving a trail in the mud
  like a threshing sledge.
³¹He makes the depths churn
  like a boiling caldron
  and stirs up the sea like a
  pot of ointment.   Eze 32:2
³²Behind him he leaves a
  glistening wake;

one would think the deep
  had white hair.
³³Nothing on earth is his
  equal—   Job 40:19
  a creature without fear.
³⁴He looks down on all that are
  haughty;
  he is king over all that are
  proud."   Job 28:8

Job

42 Then Job replied to the
       Lord:
²"I know that you can do all
  things;   Ge 18:14; Mt 19:26
  no plan of yours can be
  thwarted.   2Ch 20:6
³ You asked, 'Who is this that
  obscures my counsel
  without knowledge?'
  Surely I spoke of things I did
  not understand,
  things too wonderful for me
  to know.   Ps 40:5

⁴ "You said, 'Listen now, and I
  will speak;
  I will question you,
  and you shall answer me.'
⁵My ears had heard of you
  but now my eyes have seen
  you.   Jdg 13:22; Isa 6:5
⁶Therefore I despise myself
  and repent in dust and
  ashes."   Job 40:4; Ro 12:3

Epilogue

⁷After the Lord had said these
things to Job, he said to Eliphaz
the Temanite, "I am angry with

you and your two friends, because you have not spoken of me what is right, as my servant Job has. 8So now take seven bulls and seven rams and go to my servant Job and sacrifice a burnt offering for yourselves. My servant Job will pray for you, and I will accept his prayer and not deal with you according to your folly. You have not spoken of me what is right, as my servant Job has." 9So Eliphaz the Temanite, Bildad the Shuhite and Zophar the Naamathite did what the Lord told them; and the Lord accepted Job's prayer.   Job 22:30; Jas 5:15-16

10After Job had prayed for his friends, the Lord made him prosperous again and gave him twice as much as he had before. 11All his brothers and sisters and everyone who had known him before came and ate with him in his house. They comforted and consoled him over all the trouble the Lord had brought upon him, and each one gave him a piece of silver[a] and a gold ring.   Dt 30:3; Ps 14:7

12The Lord blessed the latter part of Job's life more than the first. He had fourteen thousand sheep, six thousand camels, a thousand yoke of oxen and a thousand donkeys. 13And he also had seven sons and three daughters. 14The first daughter he named Jemimah, the second Keziah and the third Keren-Happuch. 15Nowhere in all the land were there found women as beautiful as Job's daughters, and their father granted them an inheritance along with their brothers.

16After this, Job lived a hundred and forty years; he saw his children and their children to the fourth generation. 17And so he died, old and full of years.   Ge 25:8

a 11 Hebrew *him a kesitah*; a kesitah was a unit of money of unknown weight and value.

Psalms

BOOK I

Psalms 1–41

Psalm 1

¹Blessed is the man
　who does not walk in the
　　counsel of the wicked
or stand in the way of sinners
　or sit in the seat of mockers.
²But his delight is in the law of
　the LORD,　　　　　Ps 119:16,35
　and on his law he meditates
　　day and night.　　　Jos 1:8
³He is like a tree planted by
　streams of water,　　Jer 17:8
which yields its fruit in
　　season
and whose leaf does not
　　wither.
Whatever he does prospers.

⁴Not so the wicked!
　They are like chaff
　that the wind blows away.
⁵Therefore the wicked will not
　stand in the judgment,
　nor sinners in the assembly
　　of the righteous.

⁶For the LORD watches over the
　way of the righteous,
　but the way of the wicked
　will perish.

Psalm 2

¹Why do the nations conspire[a]
　and the peoples plot in vain?
²The kings of the earth take
　　their stand
　and the rulers gather
　　together
against the LORD
　and against his Anointed
　　One.[b]　　　Jn 1:41; Ac 4:25-26*
³"Let us break their chains,"
　　they say,
　"and throw off their fetters."

⁴The One enthroned in heaven
　　laughs;
　the Lord scoffs at them.
⁵Then he rebukes them in his
　　anger
　and terrifies them in his
　　wrath, saying,
⁶"I have installed my King[c]
　on Zion, my holy hill."

⁷I will proclaim the decree of the
LORD:

He said to me, "You are my
　　Son[d];
　today I have become your
　　Father.[e]　　　Ac 13:33*
⁸Ask of me,
　and I will make the nations
　　your inheritance,

a 1 Hebrew; Septuagint *rage*　*b* 2 Or *anointed one*　*c* 6 Or *king*　*d* 7 Or *son*; also in verse 12
e 7 Or *have begotten you*

the ends of the earth your
 possession.   Ps 22:27
⁹You will rule them with an
 iron scepter*a*;
 you will dash them to pieces
 like pottery."   Ps 89:23
¹⁰Therefore, you kings, be wise;
 be warned, you rulers of the
 earth.
¹¹Serve the Lᴏʀᴅ with fear
 and rejoice with trembling.
¹²Kiss the Son, lest he be angry
 and you be destroyed in
 your way,
 for his wrath can flare up in a
 moment.   Rev 6:16
 Blessed are all who take
 refuge in him.   Ps 34:8

Psalm 3

A psalm of David. When he fled
from his son Absalom.

¹O Lᴏʀᴅ, how many are my
 foes!
 How many rise up against
 me!
²Many are saying of me,
 "God will not deliver him."
     *Selah*b

³But you are a shield around
 me, O Lᴏʀᴅ;   Ge 15:1; Ps 28:7
 you bestow glory on me and
 lift*c* up my head.   Ps 27:6
⁴To the Lᴏʀᴅ I cry aloud,
 and he answers me from his
 holy hill.   *Selah*

⁵I lie down and sleep;   Lev 26:6
 I wake again, because the
 Lᴏʀᴅ sustains me.
⁶I will not fear the tens of
 thousands
 drawn up against me on
 every side.   Ps 27:3

⁷Arise, O Lᴏʀᴅ!
 Deliver me, O my God!
 Strike all my enemies on the
 jaw;
 break the teeth of the
 wicked.   Job 16:10

⁸From the Lᴏʀᴅ comes
 deliverance.   Isa 43:3,11
 May your blessing be on
 your people.   *Selah*

Psalm 4

For the director of music. With
stringed instruments. A psalm
of David.

¹Answer me when I call to
 you,
 O my righteous God.
 Give me relief from my
 distress;
 be merciful to me and hear
 my prayer.   Ps 17:6

²How long, O men, will you
 turn my glory into
 shame*d*?
 How long will you love
 delusions and seek false
 gods*e*?   *Selah*

a9 Or will break them with a rod of iron   *b2 A word of uncertain meaning, occurring frequently in
the Psalms; possibly a musical term*   *c3 Or Lᴏʀᴅ, / my Glorious One, who lifts*   *d2 Or you dishonor
my Glorious One*   *e2 Or seek lies*

³Know that the LORD has set
   apart the godly for
   himself;   Ps 31:23
the LORD will hear when I
   call to him.   Ps 6:8

⁴In your anger do not sin;
when you are on your beds,
   search your hearts and be
   silent.   *Selah*
⁵Offer right sacrifices
   and trust in the LORD.   Dt 33:19

⁶Many are asking, "Who can
   show us any good?"
Let the light of your face
   shine upon us, O LORD.
⁷You have filled my heart with
   greater joy   Isa 9:3
than when their grain and
   new wine abound.
⁸I will lie down and sleep in
   peace,   Ps 3:5
for you alone, O LORD,
make me dwell in safety.

Psalm 5

For the director of music. For flutes.
A psalm of David.

¹Give ear to my words, O LORD,
   consider my sighing.
²Listen to my cry for help,   Ps 3:4
   my King and my God,   Ps 84:3
   for to you I pray.
³In the morning, O LORD, you
   hear my voice;
in the morning I lay my
   requests before you
   and wait in expectation.

⁴You are not a God who takes
   pleasure in evil;

with you the wicked cannot
   dwell.   Ps 11:5; 92:1
⁵The arrogant cannot stand in
   your presence;   Ps 1:5; 73:
you hate all who do wrong.
⁶You destroy those who tell lies;
   bloodthirsty and deceitful
   men
   the LORD abhors.

⁷But I, by your great mercy,
   will come into your house;
in reverence will I bow down
   toward your holy temple.
⁸Lead me, O LORD, in your
   righteousness   Ps 31:
because of my enemies—
make straight your way
   before me.   Ps 27:1

⁹Not a word from their mouth
   can be trusted;
their heart is filled with
   destruction.
Their throat is an open grave;
with their tongue they speak
   deceit.   Ro 3:13*
¹⁰Declare them guilty, O God!
   Let their intrigues be their
   downfall.
Banish them for their many
   sins,   Ps 9:16
for they have rebelled
   against you.   Ps 107:11

¹¹But let all who take refuge in
   you be glad;
let them ever sing for joy.
Spread your protection over
   them,

that those who love your
    name may rejoice in
    you.   Ps 69:36; Isa 65:13
¹²For surely, O Lᴏʀᴅ, you bless
    the righteous;
    you surround them with
    your favor as with a
    shield.   Ps 32:7

Psalm 6

For the director of music. With
stringed instruments. According to
sheminith.[a] A psalm of David.

¹O Lᴏʀᴅ, do not rebuke me in
    your anger   Ps 38:1
    or discipline me in your
    wrath.
²Be merciful to me, Lᴏʀᴅ, for I
    am faint;
    O Lᴏʀᴅ, heal me, for my
    bones are in agony.
³My soul is in anguish.   Jn 12:27
    How long, O Lᴏʀᴅ, how
    long?

⁴Turn, O Lᴏʀᴅ, and deliver me;
    save me because of your
    unfailing love.   Ps 17:13
⁵No one remembers you when
    he is dead.
    Who praises you from the
    grave[b]?   Ps 30:9; Isa 38:18

⁶I am worn out from groaning;
    all night long I flood my bed
    with weeping
    and drench my couch with
    tears.   Ps 42:3
⁷My eyes grow weak with
    sorrow;   Ps 31:9

they fail because of all my
    foes.

⁸Away from me, all you who do
    evil,   Ps 119:115
    for the Lᴏʀᴅ has heard my
    weeping.
⁹The Lᴏʀᴅ has heard my cry for
    mercy;   Ps 116:1
    the Lᴏʀᴅ accepts my prayer.
¹⁰All my enemies will be
    ashamed and dismayed;
    they will turn back in
    sudden disgrace.   Ps 71:24

Psalm 7

A *shiggaion*[c] of David, which he
sang to the Lᴏʀᴅ concerning Cush,
a Benjamite.

¹O Lᴏʀᴅ my God, I take refuge
    in you;
    save and deliver me from all
    who pursue me,   Ps 31:15
²or they will tear me like a lion
    and rip me to pieces with no
    one to rescue me.

³O Lᴏʀᴅ my God, if I have done
    this
    and there is guilt on my
    hands—   1Sa 24:11; Isa 59:3
⁴if I have done evil to him who
    is at peace with me
    or without cause have
    robbed my foe—
⁵then let my enemy pursue and
    overtake me;
    let him trample my life to
    the ground

---

[a] Title: Probably a musical term   [b] 5 Hebrew *Sheol*   [c] Title: Probably a literary or musical term

and make me sleep in the
   dust.   *Selah*

6Arise, O LORD, in your anger;
   rise up against the rage of
   my enemies.
  Awake, my God; decree
   justice.   Ps 44:23
7Let the assembled peoples
   gather around you.
  Rule over them from on
   high;
8 let the LORD judge the
   peoples.
  Judge me, O LORD, according to
   my righteousness,
  according to my integrity,
   O Most High.
9O righteous God,   Jer 11:20
  who searches minds and
   hearts,   Rev 2:23
  bring to an end the violence of
   the wicked
  and make the righteous
   secure.

10My shield*a* is God Most
   High,
  who saves the upright in
   heart.   Ps 125:4
11God is a righteous judge,
   a God who expresses his
   wrath every day.
12If he does not relent,
   he*b* will sharpen his sword;
  he will bend and string his
   bow.
13He has prepared his deadly
   weapons;

he makes ready his flaming
   arrows.

14He who is pregnant with evil
   and conceives trouble gives
   birth to disillusionment.
15He who digs a hole and scoops
   it out
  falls into the pit he has
   made.   Job 4:8
16The trouble he causes recoils
   on himself;
  his violence comes down on
   his own head.

17I will give thanks to the LORD
   because of his
   righteousness   Ps 71:15-16
  and will sing praise to the
   name of the LORD Most
   High.

Psalm 8

For the director of music. According
to gittith.c A psalm of David.

1O LORD, our Lord,
  how majestic is your name
   in all the earth!   1Ch 16:10

You have set your glory
  above the heavens.   Ps 113:4
2From the lips of children and
   infants
  you have ordained praise*d*
because of your enemies,
  to silence the foe and the
   avenger.   Ps 44:16

3When I consider your heavens,
  the work of your fingers,

---

a 10 Or sovereign   *b 12 Or If a man does not repent, / God*   *cTitle: Probably a musical term*   *d2 Or*
strength

the moon and the stars,
which you have set in place,
[4]what is man that you are
mindful of him,
the son of man that you care
for him?   Job 7:17
[5]You made him a little lower
than the heavenly
beings[a]
and crowned him with glory
and honor.   Ps 21:5; 103:4

[6]You made him ruler over the
works of your hands;
you put everything under his
feet: Heb 2:6-8*
[7]all flocks and herds,
and the beasts of the field,
[8]the birds of the air,
and the fish of the sea,
all that swim the paths of
the seas.   Ge 1:26

[9]O LORD, our Lord,
how majestic is your name
in all the earth!   ver 1

Psalm 9[b]

For the director of music. To the
tune of, "The Death of the Son."
A psalm of David.

[1]I will praise you, O LORD, with
all my heart;   Ps 86:12
I will tell of all your
wonders.
[2]I will be glad and rejoice in
you;   Ps 5:11

I will sing praise to your
name, O Most High.

[3]My enemies turn back;
they stumble and perish
before you.
[4]For you have upheld my right
and my cause;   Ps 140:12
you have sat on your throne,
judging righteously.
[5]You have rebuked the nations
and destroyed the
wicked;
you have blotted out their
name for ever and ever.
[6]Endless ruin has overtaken the
enemy,
you have uprooted their
cities;
even the memory of them
has perished.   Ps 34:16

[7]The LORD reigns forever;
he has established his throne
for judgment.
[8]He will judge the world in
righteousness;   Ps 96:13
he will govern the peoples
with justice.
[9]The LORD is a refuge for the
oppressed,
a stronghold in times of
trouble.   Ps 32:7
[10]Those who know your name
will trust in you,   Ps 91:14
for you, LORD, have never
forsaken those who seek
you.

---

[a]5 Or than God   [b]Psalms 9 and 10 may have been originally a single acrostic poem, the stanzas of
which begin with the successive letters of the Hebrew alphabet. In the Septuagint they constitute one
psalm.

¹¹Sing praises to the LORD,
      enthroned in Zion;
   proclaim among the nations
      what he has done.
¹²For he who avenges blood
      remembers;   Ge 9:5
   he does not ignore the cry of
      the afflicted.

¹³O LORD, see how my enemies
      persecute me!   Ps 38:19
   Have mercy and lift me up
      from the gates of death,
¹⁴that I may declare your praises
      in the gates of the Daughter
         of Zion
   and there rejoice in your
      salvation.   Ps 13:5
¹⁵The nations have fallen into
      the pit they have dug;
   their feet are caught in the
      net they have hidden.
¹⁶The LORD is known by his
      justice;
   the wicked are ensnared by
      the work of their hands.
                  *Higgaion.*ᵃ *Selah*
¹⁷The wicked return to the
      grave,ᵇ
   all the nations that forget
      God.   Job 8:13
¹⁸But the needy will not always
      be forgotten,
   nor the hope of the afflicted
      ever perish.   Pr 23:18

¹⁹Arise, O LORD, let not man
      triumph;

   let the nations be judged in
      your presence.   Ps 110:6
²⁰Strike them with terror,
      O LORD;
   let the nations know they
      are but men.   *Selah*

Psalm 10ᶜ

¹Why, O LORD, do you stand far
      off?   Ps 22:1,11
   Why do you hide yourself in
      times of trouble?   Ps 13:1

²In his arrogance the wicked
      man hunts down the
         weak,
   who are caught in the
      schemes he devises.
³He boasts of the cravings of his
      heart;   Ps 94:4
   he blesses the greedy and
      reviles the LORD.
⁴In his pride the wicked does
      not seek him;
   in all his thoughts there is
      no room for God.   Ps 14:1
⁵His ways are always
      prosperous;
   he is haughty and your laws
      are far from him;
   he sneers at all his enemies.
⁶He says to himself, "Nothing
      will shake me;
   I'll always be happy and
      never have trouble."
⁷His mouth is full of curses and
      lies and threats;   Ro 3:14*

ᵃ16 Or *Meditation*; possibly a musical notation   ᵇ17 Hebrew *Sheol*   ᶜPsalms 9 and 10 may have been originally a single acrostic poem, the stanzas of which begin with the successive letters of the Hebrew alphabet. In the Septuagint they constitute one psalm.

trouble and evil are under
  his tongue.
[8]He lies in wait near the
  villages;
from ambush he murders the
  innocent,   Ps 94:6
watching in secret for his
  victims.
[9]He lies in wait like a lion in
  cover;
he lies in wait to catch the
  helpless;   Ps 17:12
he catches the helpless and
  drags them off in his
  net.
[10]His victims are crushed, they
  collapse;
they fall under his strength.
[11]He says to himself, "God has
  forgotten;   Job 22:13
he covers his face and never
  sees."

[12]Arise, Lord! Lift up your hand,
  O God.   Mic 5:9
Do not forget the helpless.
[13]Why does the wicked man
  revile God?
Why does he say to himself,
  "He won't call me to
  account"?
[14]But you, O God, do see trouble
  and grief;   Ps 22:11
you consider it to take it in
  hand.
The victim commits himself to
  you;
you are the helper of the
  fatherless.   Ps 68:5

[15]Break the arm of the wicked
  and evil man;   Ps 37:17
call him to account for his
  wickedness
that would not be found out.
[16]The Lord is King for ever and
  ever;   Ps 29:10
the nations will perish from
  his land.   Dt 8:20
[17]You hear, O Lord, the desire of
  the afflicted;
you encourage them, and
  you listen to their cry,
[18]defending the fatherless and
  the oppressed, Ps 9:9; 82:3
in order that man, who is of
  the earth, may terrify no
  more.

Psalm 11

For the director of music. Of David.

[1]In the Lord I take refuge.
  How then can you say to
  me:
"Flee like a bird to your
  mountain.
[2]For look, the wicked bend their
  bows;
they set their arrows against
  the strings   Ps 7:13
to shoot from the shadows
  at the upright in heart.
[3]When the foundations are
  being destroyed, Ps 82:5
what can the righteous do[a]?"

[4]The Lord is in his holy temple;

[a]3 Or *what is the Righteous One doing*

the Lord is on his heavenly
    throne.
He observes the sons of men;
    his eyes examine them.
⁵The Lord examines the
    righteous,   Ge 22:1
but the wicked*a* and those
    who love violence
    his soul hates.   Ps 5:5
⁶On the wicked he will rain
    fiery coals and burning
    sulfur;   Eze 38:22
a scorching wind will be
    their lot.   Jer 4:11-12

⁷For the Lord is righteous,
    he loves justice;
upright men will see his
    face.   Ps 17:15

Psalm 12

For the director of music. According
to *sheminith.*ᵇ A psalm of David.

¹Help, Lord, for the godly are
    no more;   Isa 57:1
the faithful have vanished
    from among men.
²Everyone lies to his neighbor;
    their flattering lips speak
    with deception.   Ps 10:7

³May the Lord cut off all
    flattering lips
and every boastful tongue
⁴that says, "We will triumph
    with our tongues;
we own our lips*c*—who is
    our master?"

⁵"Because of the oppression of
    the weak
and the groaning of the
    needy,
I will now arise," says the
    Lord.
"I will protect them from
    those who malign
    them."   Ps 10:18; 34:6
⁶And the words of the Lord are
    flawless,   2Sa 22:31; Ps 18:30
like silver refined in a
    furnace of clay,
    purified seven times.

⁷O Lord, you will keep us safe
    and protect us from such
    people forever.   Ps 37:28
⁸The wicked freely strut about
    when what is vile is honored
    among men.   Ps 55:10-11

Psalm 13

For the director of music. A psalm
of David.

¹How long, O Lord? Will you
    forget me forever?
How long will you hide your
    face from me?   Job 13:24
²How long must I wrestle with
    my thoughts   Ps 42:4
and every day have sorrow
    in my heart?
How long will my enemy
    triumph over me?   Ps 42:9

³Look on me and answer,
    O Lord my God.

---

a 5 Or *The Lord, the Righteous One, examines the wicked, /
/ our lips are our plowshares*   *b* Title: Probably a musical term   *c* 4 Or

Give light to my eyes, or I
will sleep in death;
⁴my enemy will say, "I have
overcome him,"   Ps 25:2
and my foes will rejoice
when I fall.

⁵But I trust in your unfailing
love;
my heart rejoices in your
salvation.   Ps 9:14
⁶I will sing to the LORD,
for he has been good to me.

Psalm 14

For the director of music. Of David.

¹The fool[a] says in his heart,
"There is no God."   Ps 10:4
They are corrupt, their deeds
are vile;
there is no one who does
good.

²The LORD looks down from
heaven   Ps 33:13
on the sons of men
to see if there are any who
understand,   Ps 92:6
any who seek God.
³All have turned aside,
they have together become
corrupt;   Ps 58:3
there is no one who does good,
not even one.   Ro 3:10-12*

⁴Will evildoers never learn—
those who devour my people
as men eat bread
and who do not call on the
LORD?   Isa 64:7

⁵There they are, overwhelmed
with dread,
for God is present in the
company of the
righteous.
⁶You evildoers frustrate the
plans of the poor,
but the LORD is their refuge.

⁷Oh, that salvation for Israel
would come out of
Zion!
When the LORD restores the
fortunes of his people,
let Jacob rejoice and Israel
be glad!

Psalm 15

A psalm of David.

¹LORD, who may dwell in your
sanctuary?   Ps 27:5-6
Who may live on your holy
hill?   Ps 24:3-5

²He whose walk is blameless
and who does what is
righteous,
who speaks the truth from his
heart   Eph 4:25
³ and has no slander on his
tongue,   Ex 23:1
who does his neighbor no
wrong
and casts no slur on his
fellowman,
⁴who despises a vile man
but honors those who fear
the LORD,   Ac 28:10
who keeps his oath

---

a 1 The Hebrew words rendered *fool* in Psalms denote one who is morally deficient.

even when it hurts,
⁵who lends his money without
    usury   Ex 22:25
and does not accept a bribe
    against the innocent.

He who does these things
    will never be shaken.   2Pe 1:10

Psalm 16

A *miktam*ᵃ of David.

¹Keep me safe, O God,
    for in you I take refuge.

²I said to the LORD, "You are my
    Lord;
apart from you I have no
    good thing."   Ps 73:25
³As for the saints who are in
    the land,
they are the glorious ones in
    whom is all my
    delight.ᵇ   Ps 101:6
⁴The sorrows of those will
    increase
who run after other gods.
I will not pour out their
    libations of blood
or take up their names on
    my lips.   Ex 23:13

⁵LORD, you have assigned me
    my portion and my cup;
you have made my lot
    secure.
⁶The boundary lines have fallen
    for me in pleasant
    places;

surely I have a delightful
    inheritance.   Ps 78:55

⁷I will praise the LORD, who
    counsels me;   Ps 73:24
even at night my heart
    instructs me.
⁸I have set the LORD always
    before me.
Because he is at my right
    hand,   Ps 73:23
I will not be shaken.

⁹Therefore my heart is glad and
    my tongue rejoices;
my body also will rest
    secure,
¹⁰because you will not abandon
    me to the grave,ᶜ
nor will you let your Holy
    Oneᵈ see decay.   Ac 13:35*
¹¹You have madeᵉ known to me
    the path of life;   Mt 7:14
you will fill me with joy in
    your presence,   Ac 2:25-28*
with eternal pleasures at
    your right hand.

Psalm 17

A prayer of David.

¹Hear, O LORD, my righteous
    plea;
listen to my cry.   Ps 61:1
Give ear to my prayer—
    it does not rise from
    deceitful lips.   Isa 29:13
²May my vindication come from
    you;

ᵃTitle: Probably a literary or musical term   ᵇ3 Or *As for the pagan priests who are in the land / and the nobles in whom all delight, I said:*   ᶜ10 Hebrew *Sheol*   ᵈ10 Or *your faithful one*   ᵉ11 Or *You will make*

may your eyes see what is
    right.

³Though you probe my heart
    and examine me at
    night,
    though you test me, you will
    find nothing;   Job 23:10
I have resolved that my
    mouth will not sin.
⁴As for the deeds of men—
    by the word of your lips
I have kept myself
    from the ways of the
    violent.
⁵My steps have held to your
    paths;   Ps 44:18
    my feet have not slipped.

⁶I call on you, O God, for you
    will answer me;   Ps 86:7
    give ear to me and hear my
    prayer.   Ps 116:2
⁷Show the wonder of your great
    love,   Ps 31:21
    you who save by your right
    hand
    those who take refuge in you
    from their foes.
⁸Keep me as the apple of your
    eye;   Dt 32:10
    hide me in the shadow of
    your wings
⁹from the wicked who assail
    me,
    from my mortal enemies
    who surround me.

¹⁰They close up their callous
    hearts,   Ps 73:7

and their mouths speak with
    arrogance.   1Sa 2:3
¹¹They have tracked me down,
    they now surround me,
    with eyes alert, to throw me
    to the ground.
¹²They are like a lion hungry for
    prey,   Ps 7:2
    like a great lion crouching in
    cover.

¹³Rise up, O LORD, confront
    them, bring them down;
    rescue me from the wicked
    by your sword.
¹⁴O LORD, by your hand save me
    from such men,
    from men of this world
    whose reward is in this
    life.   Lk 16:8

You still the hunger of those
    you cherish;
    their sons have plenty,
    and they store up wealth for
    their children.   Ps 73:3-7
¹⁵And I—in righteousness I will
    see your face;
    when I awake, I will be
    satisfied with seeing
    your likeness.   Ps 4:6-7

Psalm 18

For the director of music. Of David
the servant of the LORD. He sang to
the LORD the words of this song
when the LORD delivered him from
the hand of all his enemies and
from the hand of Saul. He said:

¹I love you, O LORD, my
    strength.   Ex 15:2

²The Lord is my rock, my
 fortress and my
 deliverer; Ps 19:14
my God is my rock, in
 whom I take refuge.
He is my shield and the
 horn[a] of my salvation,
 my stronghold. Ps 59:11
³I call to the Lord, who is
 worthy of praise, Ps 48:1
and I am saved from my
 enemies.

⁴The cords of death entangled
 me; Ps 116:3
the torrents of destruction
 overwhelmed me. Ps 124:4
⁵The cords of the grave[b] coiled
 around me;
the snares of death
 confronted me. Ps 116:3
⁶In my distress I called to the
 Lord;
I cried to my God for
 help.
From his temple he heard my
 voice; Ps 34:15
my cry came before him,
 into his ears.

⁷The earth trembled and
 quaked, Jdg 5:4
and the foundations of the
 mountains shook;
they trembled because he
 was angry. Ps 68:7-8
⁸Smoke rose from his nostrils;
consuming fire came from
 his mouth, Ps 50:3

burning coals blazed out of
 it.
⁹He parted the heavens and
 came down; Ps 144:5
dark clouds were under his
 feet.
¹⁰He mounted the cherubim and
 flew;
he soared on the wings of
 the wind. Ps 104:3
¹¹He made darkness his
 covering, his canopy
 around him—
the dark rain clouds of the
 sky. Ps 97:2
¹²Out of the brightness of his
 presence clouds
 advanced, Ps 104:2
with hailstones and bolts of
 lightning.
¹³The Lord thundered from
 heaven;
the voice of the Most High
 resounded.[c] Ps 29:3
¹⁴He shot his arrows and
 scattered ͺthe enemiesͺͺ,
great bolts of lightning and
 routed them. Ps 144:6
¹⁵The valleys of the sea were
 exposed
and the foundations of the
 earth laid bare
at your rebuke, O Lord, Ps 76:6
at the blast of breath from
 your nostrils.

¹⁶He reached down from on high
 and took hold of me;

---

[a] 2 *Horn* here symbolizes strength. [b] 5 Hebrew *Sheol* [c] 13 Some Hebrew manuscripts and
Septuagint (see also 2 Samuel 22:14); most Hebrew manuscripts *resounded, / amid hailstones and bolts
of lightning*

he drew me out of deep
  waters.   Ps 144:7
[17]He rescued me from my
  powerful enemy,
from my foes, who were too
  strong for me.   Ps 35:10
[18]They confronted me in the day
  of my disaster,
but the Lord was my
  support.   Ps 59:16
[19]He brought me out into a
  spacious place;   Ps 31:8
he rescued me because he
  delighted in me.   Ps 118:5

[20]The Lord has dealt with me
  according to my
  righteousness;
according to the cleanness of
  my hands he has
  rewarded me.   Ps 24:4
[21]For I have kept the ways of the
  Lord;   2Ch 34:33
I have not done evil by
  turning from my God.
[22]All his laws are before me;
I have not turned away from
  his decrees.   Ps 119:30
[23]I have been blameless before
  him
and have kept myself from
  sin.
[24]The Lord has rewarded me
  according to my
  righteousness,   1Sa 26:23
according to the cleanness of
  my hands in his sight.

[25]To the faithful you show
  yourself faithful,   1Ki 8:32

to the blameless you show
  yourself blameless,
[26]to the pure you show yourself
  pure,   Mt 5:8
but to the crooked you show
  yourself shrewd.   Pr 3:34
[27]You save the humble
but bring low those whose
  eyes are haughty.   Pr 6:17
[28]You, O Lord, keep my lamp
  burning;
my God turns my darkness
  into light.   Job 18:6
[29]With your help I can advance
  against a troop[a];   Heb 11:34
with my God I can scale a
  wall.

[30]As for God, his way is perfect;
the word of the Lord is
  flawless.   Ps 12:6
He is a shield
for all who take refuge in
  him.
[31]For who is God besides the
  Lord?   Dt 32:39; Ps 86:8
And who is the Rock except
  our God?   Dt 32:31
[32]It is God who arms me with
  strength
and makes my way perfect.
[33]He makes my feet like the feet
  of a deer;   Hab 3:19
he enables me to stand on
  the heights.   Dt 32:13
[34]He trains my hands for battle;
my arms can bend a bow of
  bronze.
[35]You give me your shield of
  victory,

[a] 29 Or can run through a barricade

and your right hand sustains
    me;   Ps 119:116
you stoop down to make me
    great.
³⁶You broaden the path beneath
    me,
  so that my ankles do not
    turn.
³⁷I pursued my enemies and
    overtook them;   Ps 37:20
  I did not turn back till they
    were destroyed.
³⁸I crushed them so that they
    could not rise;   Ps 36:12
  they fell beneath my feet.
³⁹You armed me with strength
    for battle;
  you made my adversaries
    bow at my feet.
⁴⁰You made my enemies turn
    their backs in flight,
  and I destroyed my foes.
⁴¹They cried for help, but there
    was no one to save
    them—   Ps 50:22
  to the LORD, but he did not
    answer.   Pr 1:28
⁴²I beat them as fine as dust
    borne on the wind;
  I poured them out like mud
    in the streets.
⁴³You have delivered me from
    the attacks of the
    people;
  you have made me the head
    of nations;
  people I did not know are
    subject to me.   Isa 52:15
⁴⁴As soon as they hear me, they
    obey me;

foreigners cringe before
    me.
⁴⁵They all lose heart;
  they come trembling from
    their strongholds.   Mic 7:17
⁴⁶The LORD lives! Praise be to
    my Rock!
  Exalted be God my Savior!
⁴⁷He is the God who avenges
    me,
  who subdues nations under
    me,   Ps 47:3
⁴⁸ who saves me from my
    enemies.   Ps 59:1
  You exalted me above my foes;
  from violent men you
    rescued me.
⁴⁹Therefore I will praise you
    among the nations,
    O LORD;
  I will sing praises to your
    name.   Ps 108:1; Ro 15:9*
⁵⁰He gives his king great
    victories;
  he shows unfailing kindness
    to his anointed,
  to David and his descendants
    forever.   Ps 144:10

Psalm 19

For the director of music. A psalm
of David.

¹The heavens declare the glory
    of God;   Isa 40:22; Ro 1:19
  the skies proclaim the work
    of his hands.
²Day after day they pour forth
    speech;

night after night they display
  knowledge.   Ps 74:16
³There is no speech or language
  where their voice is not
    heard.ᵃ
⁴Their voiceᵇ goes out into all
    the earth,
  their words to the ends of
    the world.   Ro 10:18*

In the heavens he has pitched
    a tent for the sun,
5   which is like a bridegroom
      coming forth from his
      pavilion,
  like a champion rejoicing to
    run his course.
⁶It rises at one end of the
    heavens
  and makes its circuit to the
    other;   Ps 113:3
  nothing is hidden from its
    heat.

⁷The law of the Lord is perfect,
  reviving the soul.   Ps 23:3
The statutes of the Lord are
    trustworthy,   Ps 93:5; 111:7
  making wise the simple.
⁸The precepts of the Lord are
    right,   Ps 119:128
  giving joy to the heart.
The commands of the Lord are
    radiant,
  giving light to the eyes.
⁹The fear of the Lord is pure,
  enduring forever.
The ordinances of the Lord are
    sure
  and altogether righteous.

¹⁰They are more precious than
    gold,   Pr 8:10
  than much pure gold;
  they are sweeter than honey,
    than honey from the comb.
¹¹By them is your servant
    warned;
  in keeping them there is
    great reward.

¹²Who can discern his errors?
  Forgive my hidden faults.
¹³Keep your servant also from
    willful sins;
  may they not rule over me.
Then will I be blameless,
  innocent of great
    transgression.

¹⁴May the words of my mouth
    and the meditation of
    my heart
  be pleasing in your sight,
  O Lord, my Rock and my
    Redeemer.   Ps 18:2; Isa 47:4

Psalm 20

For the director of music. A psalm
of David.

¹May the Lord answer you
  when you are in
    distress;
  may the name of the God of
    Jacob protect you.
²May he send you help from
    the sanctuary
  and grant you support from
    Zion.

ᵃ3 Or *They have no speech, there are no words; / no sound is heard from them*   ᵇ4 Septuagint,
Jerome and Syriac; Hebrew *line*

³May he remember all your
sacrifices   Ac 10:4
and accept your burnt
offerings.   *Selah*
⁴May he give you the desire of
your heart   Ps 21:2; 145:16,19
and make all your plans
succeed.
⁵We will shout for joy when
you are victorious
and will lift up our banners
in the name of our God.
May the LORD grant all your
requests.   1Sa 1:17

⁶Now I know that the LORD
saves his anointed;
he answers him from his
holy heaven
with the saving power of his
right hand.
⁷Some trust in chariots and
some in horses,
but we trust in the name of
the LORD our God.
⁸They are brought to their
knees and fall,
but we rise up and stand
firm.   Ps 37:23

⁹O LORD, save the king!
Answer*ᵃ* us when we call!

Psalm 21

For the director of music. A psalm
of David.

¹O LORD, the king rejoices in
your strength.

How great is his joy in the
victories you give!
²You have granted him the
desire of his heart   Ps 37:4
and have not withheld the
request of his lips. *Selah*
³You welcomed him with rich
blessings
and placed a crown of pure
gold on his head.
⁴He asked you for life, and you
gave it to him—
length of days, for ever and
ever.   Ps 133:3
⁵Through the victories you
gave, his glory is great;
you have bestowed on him
splendor and majesty.
⁶Surely you have granted him
eternal blessings
and made him glad with the
joy of your presence.
⁷For the king trusts in the
LORD;
through the unfailing love of
the Most High
he will not be shaken.   Ps 15:5

⁸Your hand will lay hold on all
your enemies;
your right hand will seize
your foes.   Isa 10:10
⁹At the time of your appearing
you will make them like a
fiery furnace.   Ps 50:3; La 2:2
In his wrath the LORD will
swallow them up,
and his fire will consume
them.

ᵃ9 Or save! / O King, answer

[10]You will destroy their
      descendants from the
      earth,
   their posterity from
      mankind.   Dt 28:18
[11]Though they plot evil against
      you   Ps 2:1
   and devise wicked schemes,
      they cannot succeed;
[12]for you will make them turn
      their backs   Ps 7:12-13; 18:40
   when you aim at them with
      drawn bow.

[13]Be exalted, O LORD, in your
      strength;   Ps 18:46
   we will sing and praise your
      might.

Psalm 22

For the director of music. To the
tune of, "The Doe of the Morning."
A psalm of David.

[1]My God, my God, why have
      you forsaken me?
   Why are you so far from
      saving me,
   so far from the words of my
      groaning?
[2]O my God, I cry out by day,
      but you do not answer,
   by night, and am not silent.

[3]Yet you are enthroned as the
      Holy One;   Ps 99:9
   you are the praise of Israel.[a]
[4]In you our fathers put their
      trust;
   they trusted and you
      delivered them.

[5]They cried to you and were
      saved;
   in you they trusted and were
      not disappointed.   Isa 49:23

[6]But I am a worm and not a
      man,   Job 25:6
   scorned by men and
      despised by the people.
[7]All who see me mock me;
   they hurl insults, shaking
      their heads: Mt 27:39,44
[8]"He trusts in the LORD;
   let the LORD rescue him.
   Let him deliver him,
   since he delights in him."

[9]Yet you brought me out of the
      womb;   Ps 71:6
   you made me trust in you
      even at my mother's breast.
[10]From birth I was cast upon
      you;   Isa 46:3
   from my mother's womb you
      have been my God.
[11]Do not be far from me,
   for trouble is near
   and there is no one to help.

[12]Many bulls surround me;
   strong bulls of Bashan
      encircle me.
[13]Roaring lions tearing their prey
   open their mouths wide
      against me.
[14]I am poured out like water,
   and all my bones are out of
      joint.
   My heart has turned to wax;

---

[a]3 Or Yet you are holy, / enthroned on the praises of Israel

it has melted away within
  me.   Da 5:6
[15]My strength is dried up like a
  potsherd,
and my tongue sticks to the
  roof of my mouth;
you lay me[a] in the dust of
  death.   Ps 104:29
[16]Dogs have surrounded me;
a band of evil men has
  encircled me,
they have pierced[b] my
  hands and my feet.
[17]I can count all my bones;
people stare and gloat over
  me.   Lk 23:35
[18]They divide my garments
  among them
and cast lots for my clothing.

[19]But you, O LORD, be not far off;
O my Strength, come quickly
  to help me.   Ps 70:5
[20]Deliver my life from the sword,
my precious life from the
  power of the dogs.
[21]Rescue me from the mouth of
  the lions;
save[c] me from the horns of
  the wild oxen.

[22]I will declare your name to my
  brothers;
in the congregation I will
  praise you.   Heb 2:12*
[23]You who fear the LORD, praise
  him!   Ps 135:19
All you descendants of
  Jacob, honor him!

Revere him, all you
  descendants of Israel!
[24]For he has not despised or
  disdained
the suffering of the afflicted
  one;
he has not hidden his face
  from him   Ps 69:17
but has listened to his cry
  for help.   Heb 5:7

[25]From you comes the theme of
  my praise in the great
  assembly;   Ps 35:18
before those who fear you[d]
  will I fulfill my vows.
[26]The poor will eat and be
  satisfied;   Ps 107:9
they who seek the LORD will
  praise him—   Ps 40:16
may your hearts live forever!
[27]All the ends of the earth   Ps 2:8
will remember and turn to
  the LORD,
and all the families of the
  nations
will bow down before him,
[28]for dominion belongs to the
  LORD
and he rules over the
  nations.   Ps 47:7-8

[29]All the rich of the earth will
  feast and worship;
all who go down to the dust
  will kneel before him—
those who cannot keep
  themselves alive.
[30]Posterity will serve him;

---

[a] 15 Or / I am laid   [b] 16 Some Hebrew manuscripts, Septuagint and Syriac; most Hebrew manuscripts
/ like the lion,   [c] 21 Or / you have heard   [d] 25 Hebrew him

future generations will be
    told about the Lord.
³¹They will proclaim his
    righteousness
to a people yet unborn—
    for he has done it.

Psalm 23

A psalm of David.

¹The LORD is my shepherd, I
    shall not be in want.
² He makes me lie down in
    green pastures,
he leads me beside quiet
    waters,   Eze 34:14; Rev 7:17
³ he restores my soul.
He guides me in paths of
    righteousness   Ps 5:8
for his name's sake.
⁴Even though I walk
    through the valley of the
    shadow of death,ᵃ
I will fear no evil,   Ps 3:6; 27:1
for you are with me;   Isa 43:2
your rod and your staff,
    they comfort me.

⁵You prepare a table before me
    in the presence of my
    enemies.
You anoint my head with oil;
    my cup overflows.   Ps 16:5
⁶Surely goodness and love will
    follow me
all the days of my life,
and I will dwell in the house of
    the LORD
    forever.

Psalm 24

Of David. A psalm.

¹The earth is the LORD's, and
    everything in it,   Ps 89:11
the world, and all who live
    in it;   1Co 10:26
²for he founded it upon the seas
    and established it upon the
    waters.

³Who may ascend the hill of
    the LORD?
Who may stand in his holy
    place?   Ps 15:1
⁴He who has clean hands and a
    pure heart,   Job 17:9; Mt 5:8
who does not lift up his soul
    to an idol
or swear by what is false.ᵇ
⁵He will receive blessing from
    the LORD
and vindication from God his
    Savior.   Ps 17:2
⁶Such is the generation of those
    who seek him,
who seek your face, O God
    of Jacob.ᶜ   Selah

⁷Lift up your heads, O you
    gates;   Isa 26:2
be lifted up, you ancient
    doors,
that the King of glory may
    come in.   Ps 97:6; 1Co 2:8
⁸Who is this King of glory?
The LORD strong and mighty,
    the LORD mighty in battle.
⁹Lift up your heads, O you
    gates;

ᵃ4 Or through the darkest valley   ᵇ4 Or swear falsely   ᶜ6 Two Hebrew manuscripts and Syriac (see
also Septuagint); most Hebrew manuscripts face, Jacob

lift them up, you ancient
    doors,
that the King of glory may
    come in.
¹⁰Who is he, this King of glory?
    The LORD Almighty—   1Sa 1:11
    he is the King of glory. *Selah*

Psalm 25 *ᵃ*

Of David.

¹To you, O LORD, I lift up my
    soul;   Ps 86:4
² in you I trust, O my God.
Do not let me be put to shame,
    nor let my enemies triumph
    over me.
³No one whose hope is in you
    will ever be put to shame,
but they will be put to shame
    who are treacherous without
    excuse.

⁴Show me your ways, O LORD,
    teach me your paths;   Ex 33:13
⁵guide me in your truth and
    teach me,
    for you are God my Savior,
    and my hope is in you all
    day long.
⁶Remember, O LORD, your great
    mercy and love,   Ps 103:17
for they are from of old.
⁷Remember not the sins of my
    youth   Job 13:26; Jer 3:25
    and my rebellious ways;
according to your love
    remember me,   Ps 51:1
for you are good, O LORD.

⁸Good and upright is the LORD;
    therefore he instructs sinners
    in his ways.   Ps 32:8
⁹He guides the humble in what
    is right   Ps 23:3
    and teaches them his way.
¹⁰All the ways of the LORD are
    loving and faithful
    for those who keep the
    demands of his
    covenant.   Ps 103:18
¹¹For the sake of your name,
    O LORD,   Ps 31:3; 79:9
    forgive my iniquity, though
    it is great.
¹²Who, then, is the man that
    fears the LORD?
He will instruct him in the
    way chosen for him.
¹³He will spend his days in
    prosperity,   Pr 19:23
    and his descendants will
    inherit the land.
¹⁴The LORD confides in those
    who fear him;   Pr 3:32
    he makes his covenant
    known to them.
¹⁵My eyes are ever on the LORD,
    for only he will release my
    feet from the snare.

¹⁶Turn to me and be gracious to
    me,   Ps 69:16
    for I am lonely and afflicted.
¹⁷The troubles of my heart have
    multiplied;
    free me from my anguish.
¹⁸Look upon my affliction and
    my distress   2Sa 16:12

---

*ᵃ*This psalm is an acrostic poem, the verses of which begin with the successive letters of the Hebrew alphabet.

and take away all my sins.
¹⁹See how my enemies have
    increased   Ps 3:1
and how fiercely they hate
    me!
²⁰Guard my life and rescue me;
    let me not be put to shame,
    for I take refuge in you.
²¹May integrity and uprightness
    protect me,   Ps 41:12
    because my hope is in you.

²²Redeem Israel, O God,
    from all their troubles!

Psalm 26

Of David.

¹Vindicate me, O LORD,
    for I have led a blameless
    life;   Ps 7:8
I have trusted in the LORD
    without wavering.   2Ki 20:3
²Test me, O LORD, and try me,
    examine my heart and my
    mind;   Ps 7:9
³for your love is ever before me,
    and I walk continually in
    your truth.   2Ki 20:3
⁴I do not sit with deceitful men,
    nor do I consort with
    hypocrites;
⁵I abhor the assembly of
    evildoers   Ps 139:21
and refuse to sit with the
    wicked.
⁶I wash my hands in innocence,
    and go about your altar,
    O LORD,
⁷proclaiming aloud your praise

and telling of all your
    wonderful deeds.   Ps 9:1
⁸I love the house where you
    live, O LORD,   Ps 27:4
the place where your glory
    dwells.

⁹Do not take away my soul
    along with sinners,
    my life with bloodthirsty
    men,   Ps 28:3
¹⁰in whose hands are wicked
    schemes,
    whose right hands are full of
    bribes.   1Sa 8:3
¹¹But I lead a blameless life;
    redeem me and be merciful
    to me.   Ps 69:18
¹²My feet stand on level ground;
    in the great assembly I will
    praise the LORD.

Psalm 27

Of David.

¹The LORD is my light and my
    salvation—   Ex 15:2; Isa 60:19
whom shall I fear?
The LORD is the stronghold of
    my life—
of whom shall I be afraid?
²When evil men advance
    against me
to devour my flesh,^a
when my enemies and my foes
    attack me,
    they will stumble and fall.
³Though an army besiege me,
    my heart will not fear;   Ps 3:6

---

^a2 Or to slander me

though war break out against
me,
even then will I be
confident.

4One thing I ask of the LORD,
this is what I seek:
that I may dwell in the house
of the LORD
all the days of my life,   Ps 26:8
to gaze upon the beauty of the
LORD
and to seek him in his
temple.
5For in the day of trouble
he will keep me safe in his
dwelling;
he will hide me in the shelter
of his tabernacle   Ps 17:8
and set me high upon a
rock.   Ps 40:2
6Then my head will be exalted
above the enemies who
surround me;
at his tabernacle will I sacrifice
with shouts of joy;
I will sing and make music
to the LORD.

7Hear my voice when I call,
O LORD;
be merciful to me and
answer me.   Ps 13:3
8My heart says of you, "Seek
his*a* face!"
Your face, LORD, I will seek.
9Do not hide your face from
me,   Ps 69:17
do not turn your servant
away in anger;

you have been my helper.
Do not reject me or forsake
me,
O God my Savior.
10Though my father and mother
forsake me,
the LORD will receive me.
11Teach me your way, O LORD;
lead me in a straight path
because of my oppressors.
12Do not turn me over to the
desire of my foes,
for false witnesses rise up
against me,   Mt 26:60; Ac 9:1
breathing out violence.

13I am still confident of this:
I will see the goodness of
the LORD   Ps 31:19
in the land of the living.
14Wait for the LORD;
be strong and take heart
and wait for the LORD.   Ps 40:1

Psalm 28

Of David.

1To you I call, O LORD my Rock;
do not turn a deaf ear to
me.
For if you remain silent,   Ps 83:1
I will be like those who have
gone down to the pit.
2Hear my cry for mercy   Ps 138:2
as I call to you for help,
as I lift up my hands
toward your Most Holy
Place.   Ps 5:7

a8 Or *To you, O my heart, he has said, "Seek my*

3Do not drag me away with the
   wicked,
 with those who do evil,
who speak cordially with their
   neighbors
 but harbor malice in their
   hearts.   Ps 12:2
4Repay them for their deeds
   and for their evil work;
repay them for what their
   hands have done   2Ti 4:14
 and bring back upon them
   what they deserve.
5Since they show no regard for
   the works of the LORD
 and what his hands have
   done,   Isa 5:12
he will tear them down
 and never build them up
   again.

6Praise be to the LORD,
 for he has heard my cry for
   mercy.
7The LORD is my strength and
   my shield;   Ps 18:1
 my heart trusts in him, and I
   am helped.   Ps 13:5
 My heart leaps for joy
 and I will give thanks to him
   in song.   Ps 40:3; 69:30

8The LORD is the strength of his
   people,
 a fortress of salvation for his
   anointed one.   Ps 20:6
9Save your people and bless
   your inheritance;   Dt 9:29
 be their shepherd and carry
   them forever.   Dt 1:31

Psalm 29

A psalm of David.

1Ascribe to the LORD, O mighty
   ones,
                                   1Ch 16:28
 ascribe to the LORD glory and
   strength.   Ps 96:7-9
2Ascribe to the LORD the glory
   due his name;
 worship the LORD in the
   splendor of his[a]
   holiness.   2Ch 20:21

3The voice of the LORD is over
   the waters;   Job 37:5
 the God of glory thunders,
 the LORD thunders over the
   mighty waters.
4The voice of the LORD is
   powerful;   Ps 68:33
 the voice of the LORD is
   majestic.
5The voice of the LORD breaks
   the cedars;
 the LORD breaks in pieces the
   cedars of Lebanon.
6He makes Lebanon skip like a
   calf,   Ps 114:4
 Sirion[b] like a young wild ox.
7The voice of the LORD strikes
   with flashes of lightning.
8The voice of the LORD shakes
   the desert;
 the LORD shakes the Desert
   of Kadesh.   Nu 13:26
9The voice of the LORD twists
   the oaks[c]
 and strips the forests bare.
 And in his temple all cry,
   "Glory!"   Ps 26:8

---

a2 Or LORD with the splendor of   b6 That is, Mount Hermon   c9 Or LORD makes the deer give birth

¹⁰The Lord sits^a enthroned over
    the flood;
  the Lord is enthroned as
    King forever.   Ps 10:16
¹¹The Lord gives strength to his
    people;   Ps 28:8
  the Lord blesses his people
    with peace.   Ps 37:11

Psalm 30

A psalm. A song. For the dedication
of the temple.^b Of David.

¹I will exalt you, O Lord,
  for you lifted me out of the
    depths
  and did not let my enemies
    gloat over me.   Ps 25:2
²O Lord my God, I called to you
    for help
  and you healed me.   Ps 6:2
³O Lord, you brought me up
    from the grave^c;
  you spared me from going
    down into the pit.

⁴Sing to the Lord, you saints of
    his;   Ps 149:1
  praise his holy name.
⁵For his anger lasts only a
    moment,   Ps 103:9
  but his favor lasts a lifetime;
  weeping may remain for a
    night,
  but rejoicing comes in the
    morning.   2Co 4:17

⁶When I felt secure, I said,
  "I will never be shaken."
⁷O Lord, when you favored me,

  you made my mountain^d
    stand firm;
  but when you hid your face,
    I was dismayed.   Ps 104:29

⁸To you, O Lord, I called;
  to the Lord I cried for mercy:
⁹"What gain is there in my
    destruction,^e
  in my going down into the
    pit?
  Will the dust praise you?
  Will it proclaim your
    faithfulness?   Ps 6:5
¹⁰Hear, O Lord, and be merciful
    to me;   Ps 4:1
  O Lord, be my help."

¹¹You turned my wailing into
    dancing;
  you removed my sackcloth
    and clothed me with
    joy,   Ps 4:7; Jer 31:4,13
¹²that my heart may sing to you
    and not be silent.
  O Lord my God, I will give
    you thanks forever.

Psalm 31

For the director of music. A psalm
of David.

¹In you, O Lord, I have taken
    refuge;   Ps 7:1
  let me never be put to
    shame;
  deliver me in your
    righteousness.
²Turn your ear to me,
  come quickly to my rescue;

^a10 Or sat   ^bTitle: Or palace   ^c3 Hebrew Sheol   ^d7 Or hill country   ^e9 Or there if I am silenced

be my rock of refuge,
  a strong fortress to save me.
³Since you are my rock and my
    fortress,   Ps 18:2
  for the sake of your name
    lead and guide me.
⁴Free me from the trap that is
    set for me,
  for you are my refuge.
⁵Into your hands I commit my
    spirit;   Lk 23:46
  redeem me, O Lᴏʀᴅ, the God
    of truth.

⁶I hate those who cling to
    worthless idols;
  I trust in the Lᴏʀᴅ.   Jnh 2:8
⁷I will be glad and rejoice in
    your love,
  for you saw my affliction
  and knew the anguish of my
    soul.   Ps 10:14; Jn 10:27
⁸You have not handed me over
    to the enemy   Dt 32:30
  but have set my feet in a
    spacious place.

⁹Be merciful to me, O Lᴏʀᴅ, for
    I am in distress;
  my eyes grow weak with
    sorrow,   Ps 6:7
  my soul and my body with
    grief.
¹⁰My life is consumed by
    anguish
  and my years by groaning;
  my strength fails because of
    my affliction,ᵃ
  and my bones grow weak.
¹¹Because of all my enemies,

I am the utter contempt of
    my neighbors;   Ps 38:11
I am a dread to my friends—
  those who see me on the
    street flee from me.
¹²I am forgotten by them as
    though I were dead;
  I have become like broken
    pottery.
¹³For I hear the slander of many;
  there is terror on every side;
  they conspire against me
  and plot to take my life.

¹⁴But I trust in you, O Lᴏʀᴅ;
  I say, "You are my God."
¹⁵My times are in your hands;
  deliver me from my enemies
  and from those who pursue
    me.
¹⁶Let your face shine on your
    servant;   Ps 4:6
  save me in your unfailing
    love.
¹⁷Let me not be put to shame,
    O Lᴏʀᴅ,   Ps 25:2-3
  for I have cried out to you;
  but let the wicked be put to
    shame
  and lie silent in the grave.ᵇ
¹⁸Let their lying lips be silenced,
  for with pride and contempt
  they speak arrogantly against
    the righteous.   Ps 94:4

¹⁹How great is your goodness,
  which you have stored up
    for those who fear you,
  which you bestow in the sight
    of men   Isa 64:4

ᵃ10 Or guilt   ᵇ17 Hebrew Sheol

on those who take refuge in
    you.
20In the shelter of your presence
        you hide them   Ps 27:5
    from the intrigues of men;
    in your dwelling you keep
        them safe
    from accusing tongues.

21Praise be to the LORD,
    for he showed his wonderful
        love to me   Ps 17:7
    when I was in a besieged
        city.   1Sa 23:7
22In my alarm I said,   Ps 116:11
    "I am cut off from your
        sight!"
    Yet you heard my cry for
        mercy
    when I called to you for
        help.   Ps 145:19

23Love the LORD, all his saints!
    The LORD preserves the
        faithful,
    but the proud he pays back
        in full.   Ps 94:2
24Be strong and take heart,
    all you who hope in the
        LORD.

Psalm 32

Of David. A *maskil.*[a]

1Blessed is he
    whose transgressions are
        forgiven,
    whose sins are covered.
2Blessed is the man

whose sin the LORD does not
    count against him
    and in whose spirit is no
        deceit.   Jn 1:47

3When I kept silent,
    my bones wasted away
    through my groaning all day
        long.
4For day and night
    your hand was heavy upon
        me;   Job 33:7
    my strength was sapped
    as in the heat of summer.
        Selah
5Then I acknowledged my sin
        to you
    and did not cover up my
        iniquity.
    I said, "I will confess   Pr 28:13
        my transgressions to the
        LORD"—
    and you forgave
        the guilt of my sin.   *Selah*

6Therefore let everyone who is
        godly pray to you
    while you may be found;
    surely when the mighty waters
        rise,
    they will not reach him.
7You are my hiding place;
    you will protect me from
        trouble   Ps 9:9
    and surround me with songs
        of deliverance.   *Selah*

8I will instruct you and teach
    you in the way you
        should go;

---

a Title: Probably a literary or musical term

I will counsel you and watch
    over you.   Ps 33:18
⁹Do not be like the horse or the
    mule,
which have no
    understanding
but must be controlled by bit
    and bridle
or they will not come to you.
¹⁰Many are the woes of the
    wicked,   Ro 2:9
but the Lord's unfailing love
    surrounds the man who
    trusts in him.   Pr 16:20

¹¹Rejoice in the Lord and be
    glad, you righteous;
sing, all you who are upright
    in heart!

Psalm 33

¹Sing joyfully to the Lord, you
    righteous;
it is fitting for the upright to
    praise him.   Ps 32:11; 147:1
²Praise the Lord with the harp;
make music to him on the
    ten-stringed lyre.
³Sing to him a new song;   Ps 96:1
play skillfully, and shout for
    joy.

⁴For the word of the Lord is
    right and true;   Ps 19:8
he is faithful in all he does.
⁵The Lord loves righteousness
    and justice;   Ps 11:7
the earth is full of his
    unfailing love.   Ps 119:64

⁶By the word of the Lord were
    the heavens made,
their starry host by the
    breath of his mouth.
⁷He gathers the waters of the
    sea into jars*a*;
he puts the deep into
    storehouses.
⁸Let all the earth fear the Lord;
let all the people of the
    world revere him.   Ps 67:7
⁹For he spoke, and it came to
    be;
he commanded, and it stood
    firm.   Ge 1:3
¹⁰The Lord foils the plans of the
    nations;   Isa 8:10
he thwarts the purposes of
    the peoples.
¹¹But the plans of the Lord stand
    firm forever,
the purposes of his heart
    through all generations.

¹²Blessed is the nation whose
    God is the Lord,
the people he chose for his
    inheritance.   Ex 19:5; Dt 7:6
¹³From heaven the Lord looks
    down
and sees all mankind;
¹⁴from his dwelling place he
    watches
all who live on earth—
¹⁵he who forms the hearts of
    all,
who considers everything
    they do.   Jer 32:19
¹⁶No king is saved by the size of
    his army;

---

a 7 Or sea as into a heap

no warrior escapes by his
   great strength.
¹⁷A horse is a vain hope for
   deliverance;   Ps 20:7
despite all its great strength
   it cannot save.
¹⁸But the eyes of the LORD are on
   those who fear him,
on those whose hope is in
   his unfailing love,
¹⁹to deliver them from death
and keep them alive in
   famine.   Job 5:20

²⁰We wait in hope for the LORD;
   he is our help and our
   shield.
²¹In him our hearts rejoice,
   for we trust in his holy
   name.
²²May your unfailing love rest
   upon us, O LORD,
even as we put our hope in
   you.   Ps 6:4

Psalm 34^a

Of David. When he pretended to be
insane before Abimelech, who drove
him away, and he left.

¹I will extol the LORD at all
   times;
his praise will always be on
   my lips.   Ps 71:6; Eph 5:20
²My soul will boast in the LORD;
   let the afflicted hear and
   rejoice.
³Glorify the LORD with me;

let us exalt his name
   together.   Lk 1:46
⁴I sought the LORD, and he
   answered me;   Mt 7:7
he delivered me from all my
   fears.
⁵Those who look to him are
   radiant;   Ps 36:9
their faces are never covered
   with shame.
⁶This poor man called, and the
   LORD heard him;
he saved him out of all his
   troubles.   Ps 25:17
⁷The angel of the LORD encamps
   around those who fear
   him,   Da 6:22
and he delivers them.

⁸Taste and see that the LORD is
   good;   1Pe 2:3
blessed is the man who
   takes refuge in him.
⁹Fear the LORD, you his saints,
   for those who fear him lack
   nothing.   Ps 23:1
¹⁰The lions may grow weak and
   hungry,
but those who seek the LORD
   lack no good thing.

¹¹Come, my children, listen to
   me;
I will teach you the fear of
   the LORD.
¹²Whoever of you loves life
   and desires to see many
   good days,

---

^aThis psalm is an acrostic poem, the verses of which begin with the successive letters of the Hebrew
alphabet.

¹³keep your tongue from evil
and your lips from speaking
lies.
¹⁴Turn from evil and do good;
seek peace and pursue it.

¹⁵The eyes of the Lord are on
the righteous   Job 36:7
and his ears are attentive to
their cry;
¹⁶the face of the Lord is against
those who do evil,
to cut off the memory of
them from the earth.

¹⁷The righteous cry out, and the
Lord hears them;
he delivers them from all
their troubles.
¹⁸The Lord is close to the
brokenhearted   Isa 57:15
and saves those who are
crushed in spirit.

¹⁹A righteous man may have
many troubles,
but the Lord delivers him
from them all;   Pr 24:16
²⁰he protects all his bones,
not one of them will be
broken.   Jn 19:36

²¹Evil will slay the wicked;
the foes of the righteous will
be condemned.
²²The Lord redeems his servants;
no one will be condemned
who takes refuge in
him.

Psalm 35

Of David.

¹Contend, O Lord, with those
who contend with me;
fight against those who fight
against me.   Ps 43:1
²Take up shield and buckler;
arise and come to my aid.
³Brandish spear and javelin^a
against those who pursue
me.
Say to my soul,
"I am your salvation."

⁴May those who seek my
life
be disgraced and put to
shame;   Ps 70:2
may those who plot my ruin
be turned back in dismay.
⁵May they be like chaff before
the wind,   Job 21:18
with the angel of the Lord
driving them away;
⁶may their path be dark and
slippery,
with the angel of the Lord
pursuing them.
⁷Since they hid their net for me
without cause
and without cause dug a pit
for me,   Ps 7:4
⁸may ruin overtake them by
surprise—   1Th 5:3
may the net they hid
entangle them,
may they fall into the pit, to
their ruin.

^a 3 Or and block the way

⁹Then my soul will rejoice in
the Lᴏʀᴅ   Lk 1:47
and delight in his salvation.
¹⁰My whole being will exclaim,
"Who is like you, O Lᴏʀᴅ?
You rescue the poor from
those too strong for
them,
the poor and needy from
those who rob them."

¹¹Ruthless witnesses come
forward;
they question me on things I
know nothing about.
¹²They repay me evil for good
and leave my soul forlorn.
¹³Yet when they were ill, I put
on sackcloth
and humbled myself with
fasting.   Job 30:25
When my prayers returned to
me unanswered,
¹⁴   I went about mourning
as though for my friend or
brother.
I bowed my head in grief
as though weeping for my
mother.
¹⁵But when I stumbled, they
gathered in glee;
attackers gathered against
me when I was
unaware.
They slandered me without
ceasing.   Job 30:1,8
¹⁶Like the ungodly they
maliciously mockedᵃ;
they gnashed their teeth at
me.   La 2:16

¹⁷O Lord, how long will you look
on?   Hab 1:13
Rescue my life from their
ravages,
my precious life from these
lions.   Ps 22:20
¹⁸I will give you thanks in the
great assembly;
among throngs of people I
will praise you.   Ps 22:22

¹⁹Let not those gloat over me
who are my enemies without
cause;
let not those who hate me
without reason   Ps 38:19
maliciously wink the eye.
²⁰They do not speak peaceably,
but devise false accusations
against those who live
quietly in the land.
²¹They gape at me and say,
"Aha! Aha!   Ps 22:13; 40:15
With our own eyes we have
seen it."

²²O Lᴏʀᴅ, you have seen this; be
not silent.   Ex 3:7
Do not be far from me,
O Lord.   Ps 10:1
²³Awake, and rise to my defense!
Contend for me, my God and
Lord.
²⁴Vindicate me in your
righteousness, O Lᴏʀᴅ
my God;
do not let them gloat over
me.   Ps 22:17
²⁵Do not let them think, "Aha,
just what we wanted!"

ᵃ 16 Septuagint; Hebrew may mean *ungodly circle of mockers*.

or say, "We have swallowed
   him up."   La 2:16

²⁶May all who gloat over my
   distress
be put to shame and
   confusion;   Ps 40:14; 109:29
may all who exalt themselves
   over me
be clothed with shame and
   disgrace.
²⁷May those who delight in my
   vindication   Ps 9:4
shout for joy and gladness;
may they always say, "The
   LORD be exalted,
who delights in the
   well-being of his
   servant."   Ps 147:11
²⁸My tongue will speak of your
   righteousness   Ps 51:14
and of your praises all day
   long.

Psalm 36

For the director of music. Of David
the servant of the LORD.

¹An oracle is within my heart
   concerning the sinfulness of
   the wicked:ᵃ
There is no fear of God
   before his eyes.   Ro 3:18*
²For in his own eyes he flatters
   himself
too much to detect or hate
   his sin.
³The words of his mouth are
   wicked and deceitful;

he has ceased to be wise and
   to do good.   Jer 4:22
⁴Even on his bed he plots evil;
he commits himself to a
   sinful course   Isa 65:2
and does not reject what is
   wrong.

⁵Your love, O LORD, reaches to
   the heavens,
your faithfulness to the
   skies.   Ps 57:10
⁶Your righteousness is like the
   mighty mountains,
your justice like the great
   deep.   Ro 11:33
O LORD, you preserve both man
   and beast.
⁷ How priceless is your
   unfailing love!
Both high and low among men
findᵇ refuge in the shadow
   of your wings.   Ru 2:12
⁸They feast on the abundance
   of your house;   Ps 65:4
you give them drink from
   your river of delights.
⁹For with you is the fountain of
   life;   Jer 2:13
in your light we see light.

¹⁰Continue your love to those
   who know you,
your righteousness to the
   upright in heart.   Ps 7:10
¹¹May the foot of the proud not
   come against me,
nor the hand of the wicked
   drive me away.   Ps 71:4

ᵃ1 Or heart: / Sin proceeds from the wicked.   ᵇ7 Or love, O God! / Men find; or love! / Both heavenly
beings and men / find

¹²See how the evildoers lie
    fallen—
thrown down, not able to
    rise!   Ps 140:10

Psalm 37ᵃ

Of David.

¹Do not fret because of evil
    men
or be envious of those who
    do wrong;   Ps 73:3; Pr 23:17-18
²for like the grass they will
    soon wither,
like green plants they will
    soon die away.   Ps 90:6

³Trust in the Lord and do good;
    dwell in the land and enjoy
    safe pasture.
⁴Delight yourself in the Lord
    and he will give you the
    desires of your heart.

⁵Commit your way to the Lord;
    trust in him and he will do
    this: Ps 55:22
⁶He will make your
    righteousness shine like
    the dawn,   Job 11:17
the justice of your cause like
    the noonday sun.

⁷Be still before the Lord and
    wait patiently for him;
do not fret when men
    succeed in their ways,
when they carry out their
    wicked schemes.   Ps 40:1

⁸Refrain from anger and turn
    from wrath;   Eph 4:31; Col 3:8
do not fret—it leads only to
    evil.
⁹For evil men will be cut off,
    but those who hope in the
    Lord will inherit the
    land.   Isa 57:13; 60:21

¹⁰A little while, and the wicked
    will be no more;   Job 7:10
though you look for them,
    they will not be found.
¹¹But the meek will inherit the
    land   Mt 5:5
and enjoy great peace.

¹²The wicked plot against the
    righteous
and gnash their teeth at
    them;   Ps 35:16
¹³but the Lord laughs at the
    wicked,
for he knows their day is
    coming.   1Sa 26:10; Ps 2:4

¹⁴The wicked draw the sword
    and bend the bow   Ps 11:2
to bring down the poor and
    needy,   Ps 35:10
to slay those whose ways are
    upright.
¹⁵But their swords will pierce
    their own hearts,   Ps 9:16
and their bows will be
    broken.

¹⁶Better the little that the
    righteous have

ᵃThis psalm is an acrostic poem, the stanzas of which begin with the successive letters of the Hebrew alphabet.

than the wealth of many
   wicked;   Pr 15:16
¹⁷for the power of the wicked
   will be broken,   Ps 10:15
   but the LORD upholds the
   righteous.

¹⁸The days of the blameless are
   known to the LORD,
   and their inheritance will
   endure forever.
¹⁹In times of disaster they will
   not wither;
   in days of famine they will
   enjoy plenty.

²⁰But the wicked will perish:
   The LORD's enemies will be
   like the beauty of the
   fields,
   they will vanish—vanish like
   smoke.   Ps 102:3

²¹The wicked borrow and do not
   repay,
   but the righteous give
   generously;   Ps 112:5
²²those the LORD blesses will
   inherit the land,
   but those he curses will be
   cut off.   Pr 3:33

²³If the LORD delights in a man's
   way,
   he makes his steps firm;
²⁴though he stumble, he will not
   fall,   Pr 24:16
   for the LORD upholds him
   with his hand.

²⁵I was young and now I am old,
   yet I have never seen the
   righteous forsaken

or their children begging
   bread.
²⁶They are always generous and
   lend freely;
   their children will be
   blessed.   Ps 147:13

²⁷Turn from evil and do good;
   then you will dwell in the
   land forever.
²⁸For the LORD loves the just
   and will not forsake his
   faithful ones.   Ps 21:10

They will be protected forever,
   but the offspring of the
   wicked will be cut off;
²⁹the righteous will inherit the
   land
   and dwell in it forever.

³⁰The mouth of the righteous
   man utters wisdom,
   and his tongue speaks what
   is just.
³¹The law of his God is in his
   heart;   Dt 6:6; Ps 40:8
   his feet do not slip.

³²The wicked lie in wait for the
   righteous,   Ps 10:8
   seeking their very lives;
³³but the LORD will not leave
   them in their power
   or let them be condemned
   when brought to trial.

³⁴Wait for the LORD   Ps 27:14
   and keep his way.
   He will exalt you to inherit the
   land;
   when the wicked are cut off,
   you will see it.   Ps 52:6

³⁵I have seen a wicked and
  ruthless man
flourishing like a green tree
  in its native soil,   Job 5:3
³⁶but he soon passed away and
  was no more;
though I looked for him, he
  could not be found.

³⁷Consider the blameless,
  observe the upright;
there is a future^a for the
  man of peace.   Isa 57:1-2
³⁸But all sinners will be
  destroyed;
the future^b of the wicked
  will be cut off.   Ps 1:4

³⁹The salvation of the righteous
  comes from the LORD;
he is their stronghold in time
  of trouble.   Ps 9:9
⁴⁰The LORD helps them and
  delivers them;   1Ch 5:20
he delivers them from the
  wicked and saves them,
because they take refuge in
  him.

Psalm 38

A psalm of David. A petition.

¹O LORD, do not rebuke me in
  your anger
or discipline me in your
  wrath.   Ps 6:1
²For your arrows have pierced
  me,   Job 6:4; Ps 32:4
and your hand has come
  down upon me.

³Because of your wrath there is
  no health in my body;
my bones have no
  soundness because of
  my sin.   Ps 6:2; Isa 1:6
⁴My guilt has overwhelmed
  me
like a burden too heavy to
  bear.   Ezr 9:6

⁵My wounds fester and are
  loathsome
because of my sinful folly.
⁶I am bowed down and brought
  very low;
all day long I go about
  mourning.   Ps 35:14
⁷My back is filled with searing
  pain;
there is no health in my
  body.
⁸I am feeble and utterly
  crushed;
I groan in anguish of
  heart.

⁹All my longings lie open before
  you, O Lord;
my sighing is not hidden
  from you.   Job 3:24
¹⁰My heart pounds, my strength
  fails me;
even the light has gone from
  my eyes.   Ps 6:7
¹¹My friends and companions
  avoid me because of my
  wounds;
my neighbors stay far
  away.

^a37 Or *there will be posterity*   ^b38 Or *posterity*

¹²Those who seek my life set
  their traps,   Ps 140:5
those who would harm me
  talk of my ruin;
all day long they plot
  deception.   Ps 35:20

¹³I am like a deaf man, who
  cannot hear,
like a mute, who cannot
  open his mouth;
¹⁴I have become like a man who
  does not hear,
whose mouth can offer no
  reply.
¹⁵I wait for you, O LORD;   Ps 39:7
you will answer, O Lord my
  God.
¹⁶For I said, "Do not let them
  gloat   Ps 35:26
or exalt themselves over me
  when my foot slips."

¹⁷For I am about to fall,
and my pain is ever with
  me.
¹⁸I confess my iniquity;   Ps 32:5
I am troubled by my sin.
¹⁹Many are those who are my
  vigorous enemies;
those who hate me without
  reason are numerous.
²⁰Those who repay my good
  with evil   Ps 35:12
slander me when I pursue
  what is good.

²¹O LORD, do not forsake me;
be not far from me, O my
  God.   Ps 35:22
²²Come quickly to help me,
O Lord my Savior.   Ps 27:1

Psalm 39

For the director of music. For
Jeduthun. A psalm of David.

¹I said, "I will watch my ways
  and keep my tongue from
    sin;
I will put a muzzle on my
    mouth
  as long as the wicked are in
    my presence."
²But when I was silent and still,
  not even saying anything
    good,
  my anguish increased.
³My heart grew hot within me,
  and as I meditated, the fire
    burned;   Jer 20:9
  then I spoke with my
    tongue:

⁴"Show me, O LORD, my life's
    end
  and the number of my days;
  let me know how fleeting is
    my life.   Ps 103:14
⁵You have made my days a
    mere handbreadth;
  the span of my years is as
    nothing before you.
  Each man's life is but a
    breath.   *Selah*
⁶Man is a mere phantom as he
    goes to and fro: 1Pe 1:24
  He bustles about, but only in
    vain;   Ps 127:2
  he heaps up wealth, not
    knowing who will get it.

⁷"But now, Lord, what do I look
    for?
  My hope is in you.

⁸Save me from all my
    transgressions;   Ps 44:13
do not make me the scorn of
    fools.
⁹I was silent; I would not open
    my mouth,   Job 2:10
for you are the one who has
    done this.
¹⁰Remove your scourge from me;
    I am overcome by the blow
        of your hand.   Job 9:34
¹¹You rebuke and discipline men
    for their sin;
you consume their wealth
    like a moth—   Job 13:28
each man is but a breath.
                            Selah

¹²"Hear my prayer, O Lord,
    listen to my cry for help;
be not deaf to my weeping.
For I dwell with you as an
    alien,   1Pe 2:11
a stranger, as all my fathers
    were.   Heb 11:13
¹³Look away from me, that I
    may rejoice again
before I depart and am no
    more."   Job 10:21

Psalm 40

For the director of music. Of David.
A psalm.

¹I waited patiently for the Lord;
    he turned to me and heard
        my cry.
²He lifted me out of the slimy
    pit,

out of the mud and mire;
he set my feet on a rock   Ps 27:5
    and gave me a firm place to
        stand.
³He put a new song in my
    mouth,   Ps 33:3
a hymn of praise to our God.
Many will see and fear
    and put their trust in the
        Lord.

⁴Blessed is the man
    who makes the Lord his
        trust,   Ps 84:12
who does not look to the
    proud,
to those who turn aside to
    false gods.ᵃ
⁵Many, O Lord my God,
    are the wonders you have
        done.   Ps 136:4
The things you planned for us
    no one can recount to you;
were I to speak and tell of
    them,
they would be too many to
    declare.

⁶Sacrifice and offering you did
    not desire,   1Sa 15:22
but my ears you have
    piercedᵇ,ᶜ;
burnt offerings and sin
    offerings
you did not require.   Isa 1:11
⁷Then I said, "Here I am, I have
    come—
it is written about me in the
    scroll.ᵈ

ᵃ4 Or *to falsehood*   ᵇ6 Hebrew; Septuagint *but a body you have prepared for me* (see also
Symmachus and Theodotion)   ᶜ6 Or *opened*   ᵈ7 Or *come / with the scroll written for me*

⁸I desire to do your will, O my
        God;   Jn 4:34
    your law is within my
        heart."   Ps 37:31

⁹I proclaim righteousness in the
        great assembly;   Ps 22:25
    I do not seal my lips,
    as you know, O Lᴏʀᴅ.
¹⁰I do not hide your
        righteousness in my
        heart;
    I speak of your faithfulness
        and salvation.   Ps 89:1
    I do not conceal your love and
        your truth
    from the great assembly.

¹¹Do not withhold your mercy
        from me, O Lᴏʀᴅ;
    may your love and your
        truth always protect me.
¹²For troubles without number
        surround me;
    my sins have overtaken me,
        and I cannot see.   Ps 38:4
    They are more than the hairs
        of my head,
    and my heart fails within
        me.   Ps 73:26

¹³Be pleased, O Lᴏʀᴅ, to save
        me;
    O Lᴏʀᴅ, come quickly to
        help me.   Ps 70:1
¹⁴May all who seek to take my
        life
    be put to shame and
        confusion;
    may all who desire my ruin
    be turned back in disgrace.

¹⁵May those who say to me,
        "Aha! Aha!"
    be appalled at their own
        shame.
¹⁶But may all who seek you
    rejoice and be glad in you;
    may those who love your
        salvation always say,
    "The Lᴏʀᴅ be exalted!"

¹⁷Yet I am poor and needy;
    may the Lord think of
        me.
    You are my help and my
        deliverer;
    O my God, do not delay.

Psalm 41
For the director of music. A psalm
of David.

¹Blessed is he who has regard
        for the weak;   Ps 82:3-4
    the Lᴏʀᴅ delivers him in
        times of trouble.
²The Lᴏʀᴅ will protect him and
        preserve his life;
    he will bless him in the
        land
    and not surrender him to the
        desire of his foes.   Ps 27:12
³The Lᴏʀᴅ will sustain him on
        his sickbed
    and restore him from his bed
        of illness.

⁴I said, "O Lᴏʀᴅ, have mercy on
        me;   Ps 6:2
    heal me, for I have sinned
        against you."   Ps 51:4
⁵My enemies say of me in
        malice,

"When will he die and his
  name perish?"   Ps 38:12
⁶Whenever one comes to see
  me,
he speaks falsely, while his
  heart gathers slander;
then he goes out and
  spreads it abroad.

⁷All my enemies whisper
  together against me;
they imagine the worst for
  me, saying,
⁸"A vile disease has beset him;
  he will never get up from
  the place where he lies."
⁹Even my close friend, whom I
  trusted,   Ps 55:12
he who shared my bread,
  has lifted up his heel against
  me.   Job 19:19; Jn 13:18*

¹⁰But you, O Lᴏʀᴅ, have mercy
  on me;
raise me up, that I may
  repay them.   Ps 3:3
¹¹I know that you are pleased
  with me,   Ps 147:11
for my enemy does not
  triumph over me.
¹²In my integrity you uphold me
  and set me in your presence
  forever.   Job 36:7

¹³Praise be to the Lᴏʀᴅ, the God
  of Israel,
from everlasting to
  everlasting.
  Amen and Amen.

BOOK II

Psalms 42–72

Psalm 42ᵃ

For the director of music.
A *maskil*ᵇ of the
Sons of Korah.

¹As the deer pants for streams
  of water,
so my soul pants for you,
  O God.   Ps 119:131
²My soul thirsts for God, for the
  living God.   Ps 63:1
When can I go and meet
  with God?
³My tears have been my food
  day and night,   Ps 80:5
while men say to me all day
  long,
  "Where is your God?"
⁴These things I remember
  as I pour out my soul:
how I used to go with the
  multitude,
leading the procession to the
  house of God,   Isa 30:29
with shouts of joy and
  thanksgiving   Ps 100:4
among the festive throng.

⁵Why are you downcast, O my
  soul?   Ps 38:6; 77:3
Why so disturbed within
  me?
Put your hope in God,   La 3:24
for I will yet praise him,
  my Savior and ⁶my God.

ᵃIn many Hebrew manuscripts Psalms 42 and 43 constitute one psalm.   ᵇTitle: Probably a literary or musical term

My[a] soul is downcast within
      me;
   therefore I will remember
      you
from the land of the Jordan,
   the heights of
      Hermon—from Mount
      Mizar.
7Deep calls to deep
   in the roar of your
      waterfalls;
all your waves and breakers
   have swept over me.   Ps 88:7

8By day the LORD directs his
      love,
   at night his song is with
      me—   Job 35:10
a prayer to the God of my
      life.

9I say to God my Rock,
   "Why have you forgotten
      me?
Why must I go about
      mourning,   Ps 38:6
   oppressed by the enemy?"
10My bones suffer mortal
      agony
   as my foes taunt me,
saying to me all day
      long,
   "Where is your God?"

11Why are you downcast, O my
      soul?
   Why so disturbed within
      me?

Put your hope in God,
   for I will yet praise him,
   my Savior and my God.

Psalm 43[b]

1Vindicate me, O God,
   and plead my cause against
      an ungodly nation;
   rescue me from deceitful and
      wicked men.
2You are God my stronghold.
   Why have you rejected
      me?
Why must I go about
      mourning,
   oppressed by the enemy?
3Send forth your light and your
      truth,   Ps 36:9
   let them guide me;
   let them bring me to your holy
      mountain,   Ps 42:4
   to the place where you
      dwell.   Ps 84:1
4Then will I go to the altar of
      God,   Ps 26:6
   to God, my joy and my
      delight.
   I will praise you with the
      harp,
   O God, my God.   Ps 33:2

5Why are you downcast, O my
      soul?
   Why so disturbed within
      me?
Put your hope in God,
   for I will yet praise him,
   my Savior and my God.

---

[a] 5,6 A few Hebrew manuscripts, Septuagint and Syriac; most Hebrew manuscripts *praise him for his
saving help.* / 6O my God, my   [b] In many Hebrew manuscripts Psalms 42 and 43 constitute one psalm.

Psalm 44

For the director of music. Of the
Sons of Korah. A *maskil.*[a]

[1]We have heard with our ears,
    O God;
  our fathers have told us
what you did in their days,
  in days long ago.
[2]With your hand you drove out
    the nations
  and planted our fathers;
you crushed the peoples
  and made our fathers
    flourish.   Ps 80:9
[3]It was not by their sword that
    they won the land,
  nor did their arm bring them
    victory;
it was your right hand, your
    arm,
  and the light of your face,
    for you loved them.

[4]You are my King and my
    God,
  who decrees[b] victories for
    Jacob.
[5]Through you we push back
    our enemies;
  through your name we
    trample our foes.
[6]I do not trust in my bow,
  my sword does not bring me
    victory;
[7]but you give us victory over
    our enemies,   Ps 136:24
  you put our adversaries to
    shame.   Ps 53:5

[8]In God we make our boast all
    day long,   Ps 34:2
  and we will praise your
    name forever.   *Selah*
[9]But now you have rejected and
    humbled us;   Ps 60:1,10
  you no longer go out with
    our armies.
[10]You made us retreat before the
    enemy,   Lev 26:17
  and our adversaries have
    plundered us.
[11]You gave us up to be devoured
    like sheep   Ro 8:36
  and have scattered us among
    the nations.   Dt 28:64
[12]You sold your people for a
    pittance,   Isa 52:3; Jer 15:13
  gaining nothing from their
    sale.

[13]You have made us a reproach
    to our neighbors,
  the scorn and derision of
    those around us.   Dt 28:37
[14]You have made us a byword
    among the nations;
  the peoples shake their
    heads at us.   Jer 24:9
[15]My disgrace is before me all
    day long,
  and my face is covered with
    shame
[16]at the taunts of those who
    reproach and revile
    me,
  because of the enemy, who
    is bent on revenge.

---

[a]Title: Probably a literary or musical term   [b]4 Septuagint, Aquila and Syriac; Hebrew *King, O God;* /
command

17All this happened to us,
  though we had not forgotten
    you   Ps 78:7,57
  or been false to your
    covenant.
18Our hearts had not turned
    back;   Job 23:11
  our feet had not strayed
    from your path.
19But you crushed us and made
    us a haunt for jackals
  and covered us over with
    deep darkness.

20If we had forgotten the name
    of our God   Ps 78:11
  or spread out our hands to a
    foreign god,   Dt 6:14; Ps 81:9
21would not God have discovered
    it,
  since he knows the secrets
    of the heart?   Ps 139:1-2
22Yet for your sake we face
    death all day long;
  we are considered as sheep
    to be slaughtered.

23Awake, O Lord! Why do you
    sleep?   Ps 7:6
  Rouse yourself! Do not reject
    us forever.
24Why do you hide your face
  and forget our misery and
    oppression?

25We are brought down to the
    dust;   Ps 119:25
  our bodies cling to the
    ground.

26Rise up and help us;
  redeem us because of your
    unfailing love.   Ps 25:22

Psalm 45

For the director of music. To the
tune of, "Lilies." Of the Sons of
Korah. A *maskil.*[a] A wedding song.

1My heart is stirred by a noble
    theme
  as I recite my verses for the
    king;
  my tongue is the pen of a
    skillful writer.

2You are the most excellent of
    men
  and your lips have been
    anointed with grace,
  since God has blessed you
    forever.
3Gird your sword upon your
    side, O mighty one;
  clothe yourself with splendor
    and majesty.
4In your majesty ride forth
    victoriously   Rev 6:2
  in behalf of truth, humility
    and righteousness;
  let your right hand display
    awesome deeds.   Dt 4:34
5Let your sharp arrows pierce
    the hearts of the king's
    enemies;
  let the nations fall beneath
    your feet.
6Your throne, O God, will last
    for ever and ever;   Ps 93:2

a Title: Probably a literary or musical term

a scepter of justice will be
  the scepter of your
  kingdom.
⁷You love righteousness and
  hate wickedness;   Ps 33:5
  therefore God, your God, has
  set you above your
  companions
  by anointing you with the oil
  of joy.   Heb 1:8-9*
⁸All your robes are fragrant
  with myrrh and aloes
  and cassia;   SS 1:3
  from palaces adorned with
  ivory
  the music of the strings
  makes you glad.
⁹Daughters of kings are among
  your honored women;
  at your right hand is the
  royal bride in gold of
  Ophir.   1Ki 2:19

¹⁰Listen, O daughter, consider
  and give ear:
  Forget your people and your
  father's house.   Dt 21:13
¹¹The king is enthralled by your
  beauty;
  honor him, for he is your
  lord.   Ps 95:6; Isa 54:5
¹²The Daughter of Tyre will
  come with a gift,ᵃ
  men of wealth will seek your
  favor.   Ps 22:29

¹³All glorious is the princess
  within ⸤her chamber⸥;
  her gown is interwoven with
  gold.

¹⁴In embroidered garments she is
  led to the king;   SS 1:4
  her virgin companions follow
  her
  and are brought to you.
¹⁵They are led in with joy and
  gladness;
  they enter the palace of the
  king.
¹⁶Your sons will take the place
  of your fathers;
  you will make them princes
  throughout the land.
¹⁷I will perpetuate your memory
  through all generations;
  therefore the nations will
  praise you for ever and
  ever.   Ps 138:4

Psalm 46

For the director of music. Of the
Sons of Korah. According to
alamoth.ᵇ A song.

¹God is our refuge and strength,
  an ever-present help in
  trouble.   Dt 4:7
²Therefore we will not fear,
  though the earth give
  way   Ps 23:4; 82:5
  and the mountains fall into
  the heart of the sea,
³though its waters roar and
  foam   Ps 93:3
  and the mountains quake
  with their surging. *Selah*

⁴There is a river whose streams
  make glad the city of
  God,   Ps 48:1,8; Isa 60:14

ᵃ 12 Or *A Tyrian robe is among the gifts*   ᵇ Title: Probably a musical term

the holy place where the
　　Most High dwells.
⁵God is within her, she will not
　　fall;　　　　　　　　　Isa 12:6
God will help her at break of
　　day.
⁶Nations are in uproar,
　　kingdoms fall;　　　Ps 2:1
he lifts his voice, the earth
　　melts.

⁷The Lᴏʀᴅ Almighty is with
　　us;
the God of Jacob is our
　　fortress.　　　　　　*Selah*

⁸Come and see the works of the
　　Lᴏʀᴅ,　　　　　　　Ps 66:5
the desolations he has
　　brought on the
　　earth.
⁹He makes wars cease to the
　　ends of the earth;　Isa 2:4
he breaks the bow and
　　shatters the spear,　Ps 76:3
he burns the shields*ᵃ* with
　　fire.　　　　　　　Eze 39:9
¹⁰"Be still, and know that I am
　　God;　　　　　　　Ps 100:3
I will be exalted among the
　　nations,
I will be exalted in the
　　earth."　　　　　　Isa 2:11

¹¹The Lᴏʀᴅ Almighty is with
　　us;
the God of Jacob is our
　　fortress.　　　　　　*Selah*

Psalm 47

For the director of music. Of the
Sons of Korah. A psalm.

¹Clap your hands, all you
　　nations;　　　Ps 98:8; Isa 55:12
shout to God with cries of
　　joy.
²How awesome is the Lᴏʀᴅ
　　Most High,　　　　Dt 7:21
the great King over all the
　　earth!
³He subdued nations under
　　us,
peoples under our feet.
⁴He chose our inheritance for
　　us,　　　　　　　　1Pe 1:4
the pride of Jacob, whom he
　　loved.　　　　　　*Selah*

⁵God has ascended amid shouts
　　of joy,
the Lᴏʀᴅ amid the sounding
　　of trumpets.　Ps 68:33; 98:6
⁶Sing praises to God, sing
　　praises;
sing praises to our King, sing
　　praises.　　　　　Ps 68:4

⁷For God is the King of all the
　　earth;
sing to him a psalm*ᵇ* of
　　praise.　　　　　　Col 3:16
⁸God reigns over the nations;
　　God is seated on his holy
　　throne.
⁹The nobles of the nations
　　assemble
as the people of the God of
　　Abraham,

---

*ᵃ*9 Or *chariots*　　*ᵇ*7 Or *a maskil* (probably a literary or musical term)

for the kings[a] of the earth
  belong to God;   Ps 89:18
he is greatly exalted.

Psalm 48

A song. A psalm of the Sons of
Korah.

[1]Great is the LORD, and most
  worthy of praise,   Ps 96:4
in the city of our God, his
  holy mountain.   Mic 4:1
[2]It is beautiful in its loftiness,
  the joy of the whole earth.
Like the utmost heights of
  Zaphon[b] is Mount Zion,
the[c] city of the Great King.
[3]God is in her citadels;
  he has shown himself to be
  her fortress.   Ps 46:7

[4]When the kings joined forces,
  when they advanced
  together,   2Sa 10:1-19
[5]they saw her, and were
  astounded;
  they fled in terror.   Ex 15:16
[6]Trembling seized them there,
  pain like that of a woman in
  labor.
[7]You destroyed them like ships
  of Tarshish
shattered by an east wind.

[8]As we have heard,
  so have we seen
in the city of the LORD
  Almighty,
in the city of our God:

God makes her secure
  forever.   *Selah*

[9]Within your temple, O God,
  we meditate on your
  unfailing love.   Ps 26:3
[10]Like your name, O God,   Jos 7:9
  your praise reaches to the
  ends of the earth;
your right hand is filled with
  righteousness.
[11]Mount Zion rejoices,
  the villages of Judah are glad
because of your judgments.

[12]Walk about Zion, go around
  her,
count her towers,
[13]consider well her ramparts,
  view her citadels,   Ps 122:7
that you may tell of them to
  the next generation.
[14]For this God is our God for
  ever and ever;
he will be our guide even to
  the end.   Ps 23:4

Psalm 49

For the director of music. Of the
Sons of Korah. A psalm.

[1]Hear this, all you peoples;
  listen, all who live in this
  world,   Ps 33:8
[2]both low and high,
  rich and poor alike:
[3]My mouth will speak words of
  wisdom;   Ps 37:30
the utterance from my heart
  will give understanding.

---

[a]9 Or *shields*   [b]2 *Zaphon* can refer to a sacred mountain or the direction north.   [c]2 Or *earth,* /
Mount Zion, on the northern side / *of the*

4I will turn my ear to a proverb;
  with the harp I will expound
     my riddle:

5Why should I fear when evil
     days come,   Ps 23:4
  when wicked deceivers
     surround me—
6those who trust in their
     wealth
  and boast of their great
     riches?
7No man can redeem the life of
     another
  or give to God a ransom for
     him—
8the ransom for a life is costly,
  no payment is ever
     enough—   Mt 16:26
9that he should live on forever
  and not see decay.   Ps 89:48

10For all can see that wise men
     die;   Ecc 2:16
  the foolish and the senseless
     alike perish
  and leave their wealth to
     others.   Ecc 2:18,21
11Their tombs will remain their
     houses*a* forever,
  their dwellings for endless
     generations,
  though they had*b* named
     lands after themselves.

12But man, despite his riches,
  does not endure;

he is*c* like the beasts that
     perish.
13This is the fate of those who
     trust in themselves,
  and of their followers, who
     approve their sayings.
                                   Selah
14Like sheep they are destined
     for the grave,*d*   Job 24:19
  and death will feed on them.
  The upright will rule over them
     in the morning;   Da 7:18
  their forms will decay in the
     grave,*d*
  far from their princely
     mansions.
15But God will redeem my life*e*
     from the grave;   Hos 13:14
  he will surely take me to
     himself.   *Selah*

16Do not be overawed when a
     man grows rich,
  when the splendor of his
     house increases;
17for he will take nothing with
     him when he dies,
  his splendor will not
     descend with him.
18Though while he lived he
     counted himself
     blessed—   Lk 12:19
  and men praise you when
     you prosper—
19he will join the generation of
     his fathers,
  who will never see the light
     ˻of life˼.   Job 33:30

---

a 11 Septuagint and Syriac; Hebrew *In their thoughts their houses will remain*   *b 11* Or / *for they have*
c 12 Hebrew; Septuagint and Syriac read verse 12 the same as verse 20.   *d 14* Hebrew *Sheol*; also in
verse 15   *e 15* Or *soul*

²⁰A man who has riches without
    understanding
is like the beasts that perish.

Psalm 50

A psalm of Asaph.

¹The Mighty One, God, the
    LORD,
speaks and summons the
    earth
from the rising of the sun to
    the place where it sets.
²From Zion, perfect in beauty,
God shines forth.   Dt 33:2; Ps 80:1
³Our God comes and will not be
    silent;
a fire devours before him,
and around him a tempest
    rages.
⁴He summons the heavens
    above,
and the earth, that he may
    judge his people: Dt 4:26
⁵"Gather to me my consecrated
    ones,
who made a covenant with
    me by sacrifice."   Ex 24:7
⁶And the heavens proclaim his
    righteousness,
for God himself is judge.
                                        Selah

⁷"Hear, O my people, and I will
    speak,
O Israel, and I will testify
    against you:
I am God, your God.   Ex 20:2
⁸I do not rebuke you for your
    sacrifices

or your burnt offerings,
    which are ever before
    me.   Hos 6:6
⁹I have no need of a bull from
    your stall
or of goats from your pens,
¹⁰for every animal of the forest is
    mine,
and the cattle on a thousand
    hills.   Ps 104:24
¹¹I know every bird in the
    mountains,   Mt 6:26
and the creatures of the field
    are mine.
¹²If I were hungry I would not
    tell you,
for the world is mine, and all
    that is in it.   Ex 19:5
¹³Do I eat the flesh of bulls
or drink the blood of goats?
¹⁴Sacrifice thank offerings to
    God,   Heb 13:15
fulfill your vows to the Most
    High,   Dt 23:21
¹⁵and call upon me in the day of
    trouble;
I will deliver you, and you
    will honor me."   Ps 22:23

¹⁶But to the wicked, God says:

"What right have you to recite
    my laws
or take my covenant on your
    lips?   Isa 29:13
¹⁷You hate my instruction
and cast my words behind
    you.   Ne 9:26; Ro 2:21-22
¹⁸When you see a thief, you join
    with him;   Ro 1:32; 1Ti 5:22
you throw in your lot with
    adulterers.

19You use your mouth for evil
and harness your tongue to
deceit.   Ps 52:2
20You speak continually against
your brother
and slander your own
mother's son.
21These things you have done
and I kept silent;   Ecc 8:11
you thought I was
altogether[a] like you.
But I will rebuke you
and accuse you to your face.

22"Consider this, you who forget
God,   Job 8:13; Ps 9:17
or I will tear you to pieces,
with none to rescue:
23He who sacrifices thank
offerings honors me,
and he prepares the way
so that I may show him[b] the
salvation of God."

Psalm 51

For the director of music. A psalm
of David. When the prophet Nathan
came to him after David had
committed adultery with Bathsheba.

1Have mercy on me, O God,
according to your unfailing
love;
according to your great
compassion
blot out my transgressions.
2Wash away all my iniquity
and cleanse me from my
sin.

3For I know my transgressions,
and my sin is always before
me.   Isa 59:12
4Against you, you only, have I
sinned
and done what is evil in
your sight,   Ge 20:6; Lk 15:21
so that you are proved right
when you speak
and justified when you
judge.   Ro 3:4
5Surely I was sinful at birth,
sinful from the time my
mother conceived
me.
6Surely you desire truth in the
inner parts[c];
you teach[d] me wisdom in
the inmost place.   Ps 15:2

7Cleanse me with hyssop, and I
will be clean;   Lev 14:4
wash me, and I will be
whiter than snow.   Isa 1:18
8Let me hear joy and gladness;
let the bones you have
crushed rejoice.
9Hide your face from my sins
and blot out all my iniquity.

10Create in me a pure heart,
O God,   Ac 15:9
and renew a steadfast spirit
within me.   Eze 18:31
11Do not cast me from your
presence
or take your Holy Spirit from
me.   Eph 4:30

---

a 21 Or thought the 'I AM' was   b 23 Or and to him who considers his way / I will show   c 6 The
meaning of the Hebrew for this phrase is uncertain.   *d 6 Or you desired . . . ; / you taught*

12Restore to me the joy of your
        salvation   Ps 13:5
    and grant me a willing spirit,
        to sustain me.

13Then I will teach transgressors
        your ways,   Ac 9:21-22
    and sinners will turn back to
        you.
14Save me from bloodguilt,
        O God,   2Sa 12:9
    the God who saves
        me,
    and my tongue will sing of
        your righteousness.
15O Lord, open my lips,   Ps 9:14
    and my mouth will declare
        your praise.
16You do not delight in sacrifice,
        or I would bring it;
    you do not take pleasure in
        burnt offerings.
17The sacrifices of God are*a* a
        broken spirit;
    a broken and contrite
        heart,
    O God, you will not
        despise.

18In your good pleasure make
        Zion prosper;   Ps 102:16
    build up the walls of
        Jerusalem.
19Then there will be righteous
        sacrifices,   Ps 4:5
    whole burnt offerings to
        delight you;
    then bulls will be offered on
        your altar.   Ps 66:15

Psalm 52

For the director of music. A *maskil*b
of David. When Doeg the Edomite
had gone to Saul and told him:
"David has gone to the house of
Ahimelech."

1Why do you boast of evil, you
        mighty man?
    Why do you boast all day
        long,   Ps 94:4
    you who are a disgrace in
        the eyes of God?
2Your tongue plots destruction;
    it is like a sharpened
        razor,
    you who practice deceit.
3You love evil rather than good,
    falsehood rather than
        speaking the truth. *Selah*
4You love every harmful word,
    O you deceitful tongue!

5Surely God will bring you
        down to everlasting
        ruin:
    He will snatch you up and
        tear you from your tent;
    he will uproot you from the
        land of the living. *Selah*
6The righteous will see and fear;
    they will laugh at him,
        saying,   Job 22:19; Ps 37:34
7"Here now is the man
    who did not make God his
        stronghold
    but trusted in his great wealth
    and grew strong by
        destroying others!"

---

a 17 Or *My sacrifice, O God, is*   b Title: Probably a literary or musical term

8But I am like an olive tree
   flourishing in the house of
      God;
I trust in God's unfailing love
   for ever and ever.
9I will praise you forever for
      what you have done;
   in your name I will hope, for
      your name is good.
   I will praise you in the
      presence of your saints.

Psalm 53

For the director of music. According
to *mahalath.*[a] A *maskil*[b] of David.

1The fool says in his heart,
   "There is no God."   Ps 10:4
They are corrupt, and their
      ways are vile;
   there is no one who does
      good.

2God looks down from heaven
      on the sons of men
   to see if there are any who
      understand,
   any who seek God.   2Ch 15:2
3Everyone has turned away,
   they have together become
      corrupt;
   there is no one who does good,
      not even one.   Ro 3:10-12*

4Will the evildoers never
      learn—
   those who devour my people
      as men eat bread
   and who do not call on God?
5There they were, overwhelmed
      with dread,

where there was nothing to
      dread.   Lev 26:17
God scattered the bones of
      those who attacked you;
   you put them to shame, for
      God despised them.

6Oh, that salvation for Israel
      would come out of
      Zion!
   When God restores the
      fortunes of his people,
   let Jacob rejoice and Israel
      be glad!

Psalm 54

For the director of music. With
stringed instruments. A *maskil*[b] of
David. When the Ziphites had gone
to Saul and said, "Is not David
hiding among us?"

1Save me, O God, by your
      name;   Ps 20:1
   vindicate me by your might.
2Hear my prayer, O God;
   listen to the words of my
      mouth.   Ps 5:1; 55:1

3Strangers are attacking me;
   ruthless men seek my life—
   men without regard for God.
                              Selah

4Surely God is my help;   Ps 118:7
   the Lord is the one who
      sustains me.   Ps 41:12

5Let evil recoil on those who
      slander me;
   in your faithfulness destroy
      them.   Ps 89:49

---

a Title: Probably a musical term   b Title: Probably a literary or musical term

⁶I will sacrifice a freewill
        offering to you;
    I will praise your name,
        O Lᴏʀᴅ,
    for it is good.   Ps 52:9
⁷For he has delivered me from
        all my troubles,
    and my eyes have looked in
        triumph on my foes.

Psalm 55

For the director of music. With
stringed instruments. A *maskil*ᵃ
of David.

¹Listen to my prayer, O God,
    do not ignore my plea;   Ps 27:9
²   hear me and answer me.
    My thoughts trouble me and I
        am distraught   Isa 38:14
³   at the voice of the enemy,
        at the stares of the wicked;
    for they bring down suffering
        upon me   2Sa 16:6-8
    and revile me in their anger.

⁴My heart is in anguish within
        me;
    the terrors of death assail
        me.   Ps 116:3
⁵Fear and trembling have beset
        me;   Job 21:6; Ps 119:120
    horror has overwhelmed
        me.
⁶I said, "Oh, that I had the
        wings of a dove!
    I would fly away and be at
        rest—

⁷I would flee far away
    and stay in the desert; *Selah*
⁸I would hurry to my place of
        shelter,
    far from the tempest and
        storm."   Isa 4:6

⁹Confuse the wicked, O Lord,
    confound their speech,
    for I see violence and strife
        in the city.   Jer 6:7
¹⁰Day and night they prowl
        about on its walls;
    malice and abuse are within
        it.
¹¹Destructive forces are at work
        in the city;   Ps 5:9
    threats and lies never leave
        its streets.   Ps 10:7

¹²If an enemy were insulting
        me,
    I could endure it;
    if a foe were raising himself
        against me,
    I could hide from him.
¹³But it is you, a man like
        myself,
    my companion, my close
        friend,   Ps 41:9
¹⁴with whom I once enjoyed
        sweet fellowship
    as we walked with the
        throng at the house of
        God.   Ps 42:4

¹⁵Let death take my enemies by
        surprise;
    let them go down alive to
        the grave,ᵇ   Nu 16:30,33

ᵃTitle: Probably a literary or musical term   ᵇ15 Hebrew *Sheol*

for evil finds lodging among
them.

¹⁶But I call to God,
and the Lord saves me.
¹⁷Evening, morning and noon
I cry out in distress,
and he hears my voice.
¹⁸He ransoms me unharmed
from the battle waged
against me,
even though many oppose
me.
¹⁹God, who is enthroned forever,
will hear them and afflict
them—   *Selah*
men who never change their
ways
and have no fear of God.

²⁰My companion attacks his
friends;   Ps 7:4
he violates his covenant.
²¹His speech is smooth as butter,
yet war is in his heart;
his words are more soothing
than oil,
yet they are drawn swords.

²²Cast your cares on the Lord
and he will sustain you;
he will never let the
righteous fall.   Ps 37:24
²³But you, O God, will bring
down the wicked
into the pit of corruption;
bloodthirsty and deceitful men
will not live out half their
days.   Job 15:32; Pr 10:27

But as for me, I trust in you.

Psalm 56

For the director of music. To the
tune of, "A Dove on Distant Oaks."
Of David. A *miktam.* ª When the
Philistines had seized him in Gath.

¹Be merciful to me, O God, for
men hotly pursue me;
all day long they press their
attack.
²My slanderers pursue me all
day long;   Ps 57:3
many are attacking me in
their pride.

³When I am afraid,   Ps 55:4-5
I will trust in you.
⁴In God, whose word I praise,
in God I trust; I will not be
afraid.
What can mortal man do to
me?   Ps 118:6; Heb 13:6

⁵All day long they twist my
words;   Ps 41:7
they are always plotting to
harm me.
⁶They conspire, they lurk,   Ps 59:3
they watch my steps,
eager to take my life.

⁷On no account let them
escape;
in your anger, O God, bring
down the nations.
⁸Record my lament;
list my tears on your
scrollᵇ—
are they not in your record?

⁹Then my enemies will turn
back   Ps 9:3

ª Title: Probably a literary or musical term   ᵇ 8 Or / *put my tears in your wineskin*

when I call for help.   Ps 102:2
By this I will know that God
    is for me.   Ro 8:31
¹⁰In God, whose word I praise,
    in the LORD, whose word I
    praise—
¹¹in God I trust; I will not be
    afraid.
    What can man do to me?

¹²I am under vows to you,
    O God;   Ps 50:14
    I will present my thank
    offerings to you.
¹³For you have delivered me*a*
    from death   Ps 116:8
    and my feet from stumbling,
that I may walk before God
    in the light of life.*b*   Job 33:30

Psalm 57

For the director of music. To the
tune of, "Do Not Destroy." Of David.
A *miktam.*c When he had fled from
Saul into the cave.

¹Have mercy on me, O God,
    have mercy on me,
    for in you my soul takes
    refuge.   Ps 2:12
    I will take refuge in the
    shadow of your wings
until the disaster has passed.

²I cry out to God Most High,
    to God, who fulfills his
    purpose for me.   Ps 138:8
³He sends from heaven and
    saves me,   Ps 18:9,16
    rebuking those who hotly
    pursue me;   Selah

God sends his love and his
    faithfulness.

⁴I am in the midst of lions;
    I lie among ravenous
    beasts—
men whose teeth are spears
    and arrows,
    whose tongues are sharp
    swords.   Pr 30:14

⁵Be exalted, O God, above the
    heavens;
    let your glory be over all the
    earth.   Ps 108:5
⁶They spread a net for my
    feet—
    I was bowed down in
    distress.   Ps 145:14
They dug a pit in my path—
    but they have fallen into it
    themselves.   Selah

⁷My heart is steadfast, O God,
    my heart is steadfast;   Ps 108:1
    I will sing and make music.
⁸Awake, my soul!
    Awake, harp and lyre!   Ps 16:9
    I will awaken the dawn.

⁹I will praise you, O Lord,
    among the nations;
    I will sing of you among the
    peoples.
¹⁰For great is your love, reaching
    to the heavens;
    your faithfulness reaches to
    the skies.   Ps 36:5

¹¹Be exalted, O God, above the
    heavens;

---

a 13 Or *my soul*   *b* 13 Or *the land of the living*   *c* Title: Probably a literary or musical term

let your glory be over all the
  earth.   ver 5

Psalm 58

For the director of music. To the
tune of "Do Not Destroy." Of David.
A *miktam.*ᵃ

¹Do you rulers indeed speak
    justly?   Ps 82:2
  Do you judge uprightly
    among men?
²No, in your heart you devise
    injustice,
  and your hands mete out
    violence on the earth.
³Even from birth the wicked go
    astray;
  from the womb they are
    wayward and speak lies.
⁴Their venom is like the venom
    of a snake,   Ps 140:3
  like that of a cobra that has
    stopped its ears,
⁵that will not heed the tune of
    the charmer,
  however skillful the
    enchanter may be.

⁶Break the teeth in their
    mouths, O God;
  tear out, O LORD, the fangs
    of the lions!   Job 4:10
⁷Let them vanish like water that
    flows away;   Jos 7:5
  when they draw the bow, let
    their arrows be blunted.
⁸Like a slug melting away as it
    moves along,

like a stillborn child, may
    they not see the sun.

⁹Before your pots can feel the
    heat of the thorns—
  whether they be green or
    dry—the wicked will be
    swept away.ᵇ   Pr 10:25
¹⁰The righteous will be glad
    when they are avenged,
  when they bathe their feet in
    the blood of the wicked.
¹¹Then men will say,
  "Surely the righteous still are
    rewarded;
  surely there is a God who
    judges the earth."   Ps 9:8

Psalm 59

For the director of music. To the
tune of "Do Not Destroy." Of David.
A *miktam.*ᵃ When Saul had sent
men to watch David's house in
order to kill him.

¹Deliver me from my enemies,
    O God;   Ps 143:9
  protect me from those who
    rise up against me.
²Deliver me from evildoers
  and save me from
    bloodthirsty men.

³See how they lie in wait for
    me!
  Fierce men conspire against
    me   Ps 56:6
  for no offense or sin of
    mine, O LORD.
⁴I have done no wrong, yet they
    are ready to attack me.

ᵃTitle: Probably a literary or musical term   ᵇ9 The meaning of the Hebrew for this verse is uncertain.

Arise to help me; look on
   my plight!
⁵O LORD God Almighty, the God
   of Israel,
   rouse yourself to punish all
      the nations;
   show no mercy to wicked
      traitors.   *Selah*

⁶They return at evening,
   snarling like dogs,   ver 14
   and prowl about the city.
⁷See what they spew from their
      mouths—
   they spew out swords from
      their lips,   Ps 57:4
   and they say, "Who can hear
      us?"   Ps 10:11
⁸But you, O LORD, laugh at
      them;   Ps 37:13
   you scoff at all those
      nations.   Ps 2:4

⁹O my Strength, I watch for
      you;
   you, O God, are my fortress,
      ¹⁰my loving God.   Ps 62:2

God will go before me
   and will let me gloat over
      those who slander me.
¹¹But do not kill them, O Lord
   our shield,ᵃ   Ps 84:9
   or my people will forget.
In your might make them
      wander about,
   and bring them down.
¹²For the sins of their mouths,
   for the words of their lips,

let them be caught in their
   pride.
For the curses and lies they
   utter,
¹³ consume them in wrath,
   consume them till they are
      no more.   Ps 104:35
Then it will be known to the
   ends of the earth
   that God rules over Jacob.
      Selah

¹⁴They return at evening,
   snarling like dogs,
   and prowl about the city.
¹⁵They wander about for food
   and howl if not satisfied.
¹⁶But I will sing of your strength,
   in the morning I will sing of
      your love;   Ps 101:1
for you are my fortress,
   my refuge in times of
      trouble.   Ps 46:1

¹⁷O my Strength, I sing praise to
      you;
   you, O God, are my fortress,
      my loving God.   ver 10

Psalm 60

For the director of music. To the
tune of "The Lily of the Covenant."
A *miktam*ᵇ of David. For teaching.
When he fought Aram Naharaimᶜ
and Aram Zobah,ᵈ and when Joab
returned and struck down twelve
thousand Edomites in the
Valley of Salt.

¹You have rejected us, O God,
   and burst forth upon us;

ᵃ 11 Or *sovereign*   ᵇ Title: Probably a literary or musical term   ᶜ Title: That is, Arameans of Northwest
Mesopotamia   ᵈ Title: That is, Arameans of central Syria

you have been angry—now
  restore us!   Ps 79:5; 80:3
²You have shaken the land and
  torn it open;   Ps 18:7
mend its fractures, for it is
  quaking.   2Ch 7:14
³You have shown your people
  desperate times;   Ps 71:20
you have given us wine that
  makes us stagger.

⁴But for those who fear you,
  you have raised a
  banner   Isa 11:10,12
to be unfurled against the
  bow.   *Selah*

⁵Save us and help us with your
  right hand,   Ps 108:6
that those you love may be
  delivered.
⁶God has spoken from his
  sanctuary:
"In triumph I will parcel out
  Shechem   Ge 12:6
and measure off the Valley
  of Succoth.
⁷Gilead is mine, and Manasseh
  is mine;   Jos 13:31
Ephraim is my helmet,
Judah my scepter.   Ge 49:10
⁸Moab is my washbasin,
  upon Edom I toss my sandal;
over Philistia I shout in
  triumph."   2Sa 8:1

⁹Who will bring me to the
  fortified city?
Who will lead me to Edom?
¹⁰Is it not you, O God, you who
  have rejected us

and no longer go out with
  our armies?   Jos 7:12
¹¹Give us aid against the enemy,
  for the help of man is
  worthless.   Ps 146:3
¹²With God we will gain the
  victory,
and he will trample down
  our enemies.   Nu 24:18

Psalm 61

For the director of music. With
stringed instruments. Of David.

¹Hear my cry, O God;   Ps 64:1
  listen to my prayer.

²From the ends of the earth I
  call to you,
I call as my heart grows
  faint;   Ps 77:3
lead me to the rock that is
  higher than I.   Ps 18:2
³For you have been my refuge,
  a strong tower against the
  foe.   Pr 18:10

⁴I long to dwell in your tent
  forever
and take refuge in the
  shelter of your wings.
                            Selah
⁵For you have heard my vows,
  O God;   Ps 56:12
you have given me the
  heritage of those who
  fear your name.   Ps 86:11

⁶Increase the days of the king's
  life,
his years for many
  generations.   Ps 21:4

⁷May he be enthroned in God's
    presence forever;   Ps 41:12
appoint your love and
    faithfulness to protect
    him.

⁸Then will I ever sing praise to
    your name   Ps 65:1
and fulfill my vows day after
    day.

Psalm 62

For the director of music. For
Jeduthun. A psalm of David.

¹My soul finds rest in God
    alone;   Dt 23:21
my salvation comes from
    him.
²He alone is my rock and my
    salvation;   Ps 89:26
he is my fortress, I will
    never be shaken.   Ps 59:9

³How long will you assault a
    man?
Would all of you throw him
    down—
this leaning wall, this
    tottering fence?   Isa 30:13
⁴They fully intend to topple
    him
from his lofty place;
they take delight in lies.
With their mouths they bless,
but in their hearts they
    curse.   *Selah*

⁵Find rest, O my soul, in God
    alone;
my hope comes from him.
⁶He alone is my rock and my
    salvation;
he is my fortress, I will not
    be shaken.
⁷My salvation and my honor
    depend on God*ᵃ*;
he is my mighty rock, my
    refuge.   Ps 46:1; 85:9
⁸Trust in him at all times,
    O people;
pour out your hearts to
    him,
for God is our refuge.   *Selah*

⁹Lowborn men are but a breath,
    the highborn are but a
    lie;
if weighed on a balance, they
    are nothing;   Isa 40:15
together they are only a
    breath.
¹⁰Do not trust in extortion
or take pride in stolen
    goods;
though your riches increase,
do not set your heart on
    them.   Job 31:25; 1Ti 6:6-10

¹¹One thing God has spoken,
    two things have I heard:
that you, O God, are strong,
¹² and that you, O Lord, are
    loving.   Ps 86:5
Surely you will reward each
    person
according to what he has
    done.   Mt 16:27

ᵃ7 Or / God Most High is my salvation and my honor

Psalm 63

A psalm of David. When he was in
the Desert of Judah.

[1]O God, you are my God,
   earnestly I seek you;
my soul thirsts for you,   Ps 42:2
   my body longs for you,
in a dry and weary land
   where there is no water.

[2]I have seen you in the
     sanctuary   Ps 27:4
   and beheld your power and
     your glory.
[3]Because your love is better
     than life,   Ps 69:16
   my lips will glorify you.
[4]I will praise you as long as I
     live,   Ps 104:33
   and in your name I will lift
     up my hands.
[5]My soul will be satisfied as
     with the richest of
     foods;   Ps 36:8
   with singing lips my mouth
     will praise you.

[6]On my bed I remember you;
   I think of you through the
     watches of the night.
[7]Because you are my help,
   I sing in the shadow of your
     wings.
[8]My soul clings to you;
   your right hand upholds me.

[9]They who seek my life will be
     destroyed;   Ps 40:14
   they will go down to the
     depths of the earth.

[10]They will be given over to the
     sword
   and become food for jackals.

[11]But the king will rejoice in
     God;
   all who swear by God's
     name will praise him,
   while the mouths of liars
     will be silenced.

Psalm 64

For the director of music. A psalm
of David.

[1]Hear me, O God, as I voice my
     complaint;   Ps 55:2
   protect my life from the
     threat of the enemy.
[2]Hide me from the conspiracy
     of the wicked,   Ps 56:6; 59:2
   from that noisy crowd of
     evildoers.

[3]They sharpen their tongues
     like swords
   and aim their words like
     deadly arrows.   Ps 58:7
[4]They shoot from ambush at
     the innocent man;   Ps 11:2
   they shoot at him suddenly,
     without fear.   Ps 55:19

[5]They encourage each other in
     evil plans,
   they talk about hiding their
     snares;
   they say, "Who will see
     them[a]?"   Ps 10:11
[6]They plot injustice and say,

a5 Or us

"We have devised a perfect
plan!"
Surely the mind and heart of
man are cunning.

7But God will shoot them with
arrows;
suddenly they will be struck
down.
8He will turn their own tongues
against them   Pr 18:7
and bring them to ruin;
all who see them will shake
their heads in scorn.

9All mankind will fear;
they will proclaim the works
of God
and ponder what he has
done.   Jer 51:10
10Let the righteous rejoice in the
LORD
and take refuge in him;
let all the upright in heart
praise him!   Ps 32:11

Psalm 65

For the director of music. A psalm
of David. A song.

1Praise awaits[a] you, O God, in
Zion;
to you our vows will be
fulfilled.   Ps 116:18
2O you who hear prayer,
to you all men will come.
3When we were overwhelmed
by sins,   Ps 38:4
you forgave[b] our
transgressions.   Heb 9:14

4Blessed are those you choose
and bring near to live in
your courts!
We are filled with the good
things of your house,
of your holy temple.

5You answer us with awesome
deeds of righteousness,
O God our Savior,   Ps 85:4
the hope of all the ends of the
earth
and of the farthest seas,
6who formed the mountains by
your power,
having armed yourself with
strength,   Ps 93:1
7who stilled the roaring of the
seas,   Mt 8:26
the roaring of their waves,
and the turmoil of the
nations.   Isa 17:12-13
8Those living far away fear your
wonders;
where morning dawns and
evening fades
you call forth songs of joy.

9You care for the land and
water it;   Ps 68:9-10
you enrich it abundantly.
The streams of God are filled
with water
to provide the people with
grain,   Ps 46:4; 104:14
for so you have ordained it.[c]
10You drench its furrows
and level its ridges;
you soften it with showers

---

[a]1 Or befits; the meaning of the Hebrew for this word is uncertain.   [b]3 Or made atonement for
[c]9 Or for that is how you prepare the land

and bless its crops.
¹¹You crown the year with your
    bounty,
  and your carts overflow with
    abundance.
¹²The grasslands of the desert
    overflow;   Job 28:26
  the hills are clothed with
    gladness.
¹³The meadows are covered with
    flocks   Ps 144:13
  and the valleys are mantled
    with grain;   Ps 72:16
  they shout for joy and sing.

Psalm 66

For the director of music. A song.
A psalm.

¹Shout with joy to God, all the
    earth!   Ps 100:1
²   Sing the glory of his name;
  make his praise glorious!
³Say to God, "How awesome are
    your deeds!   Ps 65:5
  So great is your power
  that your enemies cringe
    before you.   Ps 18:44
⁴All the earth bows down to
    you;
  they sing praise to you,
  they sing praise to your
    name."   Selah

⁵Come and see what God has
    done,
  how awesome his works in
    man's behalf!
⁶He turned the sea into dry
    land,   Ex 14:22

they passed through the
    waters on foot—
  come, let us rejoice in him.
⁷He rules forever by his power,
  his eyes watch the nations—
  let not the rebellious rise up
    against him.   Selah

⁸Praise our God, O peoples,
  let the sound of his praise be
    heard;
⁹he has preserved our lives
  and kept our feet from
    slipping.   Ps 121:3
¹⁰For you, O God, tested us;
  you refined us like silver.
¹¹You brought us into prison
  and laid burdens on our
    backs.   La 1:13
¹²You let men ride over our
    heads;   Isa 51:23
  we went through fire and
    water,
  but you brought us to a
    place of abundance.

¹³I will come to your temple
    with burnt offerings
  and fulfill my vows to you—
¹⁴vows my lips promised and my
    mouth spoke
  when I was in trouble.
¹⁵I will sacrifice fat animals to
    you
  and an offering of rams;
  I will offer bulls and goats.
                                   Selah

¹⁶Come and listen, all you who
    fear God;
  let me tell you what he has
    done for me.   Ps 71:15,24

17I cried out to him with my
    mouth;
his praise was on my
    tongue.
18If I had cherished sin in my
    heart,
the Lord would not have
    listened;   Jas 4:3
19but God has surely listened
and heard my voice in
    prayer.   Ps 116:1-2
20Praise be to God,
who has not rejected my
    prayer   Ps 22:24; 68:35
or withheld his love from
    me!

Psalm 67

For the director of music. With
stringed instruments. A psalm.
        A song.

1May God be gracious to us and
    bless us
and make his face shine
    upon us,   Selah
2that your ways may be known
    on earth,
your salvation among all
    nations.   Tit 2:11

3May the peoples praise you,
    O God;
may all the peoples praise
    you.
4May the nations be glad and
    sing for joy,   Ps 100:1-2
for you rule the peoples
    justly   Ps 96:10-13

and guide the nations of the
    earth.   Selah
5May the peoples praise you,
    O God;
may all the peoples praise
    you.
6Then the land will yield its
    harvest,   Lev 26:4; Eze 34:27
and God, our God, will bless
    us.
7God will bless us,
and all the ends of the earth
    will fear him.   Ps 33:8

Psalm 68

For the director of music. Of David.
    A psalm. A song.

1May God arise, may his
    enemies be scattered;
may his foes flee before
    him.
2As smoke is blown away by
    the wind,   Hos 13:3
may you blow them away;
as wax melts before the fire,
    may the wicked perish
    before God.
3But may the righteous be glad
and rejoice before God;
may they be happy and
    joyful.

4Sing to God, sing praise to his
    name,   Ps 66:2
extol him who rides on the
    cloudsa—   Dt 33:26

a4 Or / prepare the way for him who rides through the deserts

his name is the Lord —   Ex 6:3
    and rejoice before him.
⁵A father to the fatherless, a
        defender of widows,
    is God in his holy dwelling.
⁶God sets the lonely in
        families,ᵃ   Ps 113:9
    he leads forth the prisoners
        with singing;   Ac 12:6
    but the rebellious live in a
        sun-scorched land.

⁷When you went out before
        your people, O God,
    when you marched through
        the wasteland,   *Selah*
⁸the earth shook,
    the heavens poured down
        rain,
    before God, the One of Sinai,
    before God, the God of
        Israel.
⁹You gave abundant showers,
        O God;   Dt 11:11
    you refreshed your weary
        inheritance.
¹⁰Your people settled in it,
    and from your bounty,
        O God, you provided for
        the poor.   Ps 74:19

¹¹The Lord announced the word,
    and great was the company
        of those who proclaimed
        it:
¹²"Kings and armies flee in
        haste;   Jos 10:16
    in the camps men divide the
        plunder.

¹³Even while you sleep among
        the campfires,ᵇ   Ge 49:14
    the wings of ˎmyˎ dove are
        sheathed with silver,
    its feathers with shining
        gold."
¹⁴When the Almightyᶜ scattered
        the kings in the land,
    it was like snow fallen on
        Zalmon.
¹⁵The mountains of Bashan are
        majestic mountains;
    rugged are the mountains of
        Bashan.
¹⁶Why gaze in envy, O rugged
        mountains,
    at the mountain where God
        chooses to reign,   Dt 12:5
    where the Lord himself will
        dwell forever?
¹⁷The chariots of God are tens of
        thousands
    and thousands of thousands;
    the Lord ˎhas comeˎ from
        Sinai into his sanctuary.
¹⁸When you ascended on
        high,
    you led captives in your
        train;   Jdg 5:12
    you received gifts from
        men,
    even fromᵈ the rebellious —
    that you,ᵉ O Lord God,
        might dwell there.

¹⁹Praise be to the Lord, to God
        our Savior,   Ps 65:5
    who daily bears our burdens.
                              Selah

ᵃ6 Or *the desolate in a homeland*   ᵇ13 Or *saddlebags*   ᶜ14 Hebrew *Shaddai*   ᵈ18 Or *gifts for*
men, / even   ᵉ18 Or *they*

²⁰Our God is a God who
　　saves;
　　from the Sovereign LORD
　　comes escape from
　　death.   Ps 56:13

²¹Surely God will crush the
　　heads of his enemies,
　　the hairy crowns of those
　　who go on in their sins.
²²The Lord says, "I will bring
　　them from Bashan;
　　I will bring them from the
　　depths of the sea,
²³that you may plunge your feet
　　in the blood of your
　　foes,   Ps 58:10
　　while the tongues of your
　　dogs have their share."

²⁴Your procession has come into
　　view, O God,
　　the procession of my God
　　and King into the
　　sanctuary.   Ps 63:2
²⁵In front are the singers, after
　　them the musicians;
　　with them are the maidens
　　playing tambourines.
²⁶Praise God in the great
　　congregation;
　　praise the LORD in the
　　assembly of Israel.
²⁷There is the little tribe of
　　Benjamin, leading them,
　　there the great throng of
　　Judah's princes,
　　and there the princes of
　　Zebulun and of
　　Naphtali.   Jdg 5:18

²⁸Summon your power, O God[a];
　　show us your strength,
　　O God, as you have
　　done before.
²⁹Because of your temple at
　　Jerusalem
　　kings will bring you gifts.
³⁰Rebuke the beast among the
　　reeds,
　　the herd of bulls among the
　　calves of the nations.
　　Humbled, may it bring bars of
　　silver.
　　Scatter the nations who
　　delight in war.
³¹Envoys will come from
　　Egypt;
　　Cush[b] will submit herself to
　　God.

³²Sing to God, O kingdoms of
　　the earth,
　　sing praise to the Lord, *Selah*
³³to him who rides the ancient
　　skies above,   Ps 18:10
　　who thunders with mighty
　　voice.
³⁴Proclaim the power of God,
　　whose majesty is over
　　Israel,
　　whose power is in the
　　skies.
³⁵You are awesome, O God, in
　　your sanctuary;
　　the God of Israel gives power
　　and strength to his
　　people.   Ps 29:11

Praise be to God!   Ps 66:20

---

a 28 Many Hebrew manuscripts, Septuagint and Syriac; most Hebrew manuscripts Your God has summoned power for you   b 31 That is, the upper Nile region

Psalm 69

For the director of music. To the tune of, "Lilies." Of David.

¹Save me, O God,
　for the waters have come up
　　to my neck.　　　　Jnh 2:5
²I sink in the miry depths,
　where there is no foothold.
I have come into the deep
　　waters;
　the floods engulf me.
³I am worn out calling for help;
　my throat is parched.
My eyes fail,　　　Ps 119:82; Isa 38:14
　looking for my God.
⁴Those who hate me without
　　reason　　　　　Jn 15:25*
　outnumber the hairs of my
　　head;
many are my enemies without
　　cause,　　　　　Ps 35:19
　those who seek to destroy
　　me.
I am forced to restore
　what I did not steal.

⁵You know my folly, O God;
　my guilt is not hidden from
　　you.　　　　　Ps 44:21

⁶May those who hope in you
　not be disgraced because of
　　me,
　O Lord, the Lᴏʀᴅ Almighty;
may those who seek you
　not be put to shame because
　　of me,
　O God of Israel.
⁷For I endure scorn for your
　　sake,　　　　　Jer 15:15
　and shame covers my face.

⁸I am a stranger to my brothers,
　an alien to my own mother's
　　sons;　　　　Ps 31:11; Isa 53:3
⁹for zeal for your house
　　consumes me,　　Jn 2:17
　and the insults of those who
　　insult you fall on me.
¹⁰When I weep and fast,　　Ps 35:13
　I must endure scorn;
¹¹when I put on sackcloth,
　people make sport of me.
¹²Those who sit at the gate mock
　　me,
　and I am the song of the
　　drunkards.　　　Job 30:9

¹³But I pray to you, O Lᴏʀᴅ,
　in the time of your favor;
in your great love, O God,
　answer me with your sure
　　salvation.
¹⁴Rescue me from the mire,
　do not let me sink;
deliver me from those who
　　hate me,
　from the deep waters.　　Ps 144:7
¹⁵Do not let the floodwaters
　　engulf me
　or the depths swallow me
　　up
　or the pit close its mouth
　　over me.
¹⁶Answer me, O Lᴏʀᴅ, out of the
　　goodness of your love;
　in your great mercy turn to
　　me.
¹⁷Do not hide your face from
　　your servant;　　Ps 27:9
　answer me quickly, for I am
　　in trouble.
¹⁸Come near and rescue me;

redeem me because of my
    foes.

¹⁹You know how I am scorned,
        disgraced and shamed;
    all my enemies are before
        you.
²⁰Scorn has broken my heart
        and has left me helpless;
    I looked for sympathy, but
        there was none,
    for comforters, but I found
        none.   Job 16:2; Isa 63:5
²¹They put gall in my food
    and gave me vinegar for my
        thirst.   Jn 19:28-30

²²May the table set before them
        become a snare;
    may it become retribution
        andᵃ a trap.
²³May their eyes be darkened so
        they cannot see,
    and their backs be bent
        forever.   Ro 11:9-10*
²⁴Pour out your wrath on
        them;
    let your fierce anger overtake
        them.
²⁵May their place be deserted;
    let there be no one to dwell
        in their tents.
²⁶For they persecute those you
        wound
    and talk about the pain of
        those you hurt.   Isa 53:4
²⁷Charge them with crime upon
        crime;
    do not let them share in
        your salvation.

²⁸May they be blotted out of the
        book of life   Ex 32:32-33
    and not be listed with the
        righteous.

²⁹I am in pain and distress;
    may your salvation, O God,
        protect me.   Ps 59:1; 70:5

³⁰I will praise God's name in
        song   Ps 28:7
    and glorify him with
        thanksgiving.
³¹This will please the LORD more
        than an ox,
    more than a bull with its
        horns and hoofs.
³²The poor will see and be
        glad—   Ps 34:2
    you who seek God, may
        your hearts live!   Ps 22:26
³³The LORD hears the needy
    and does not despise his
        captive people.

³⁴Let heaven and earth praise
        him,
    the seas and all that move in
        them,   Ps 96:11; Isa 44:23
³⁵for God will save Zion
    and rebuild the cities of
        Judah.   Ps 51:18; Isa 44:26
    Then people will settle there
        and possess it;
³⁶   the children of his servants
        will inherit it,
    and those who love his
        name will dwell there.

ᵃ 22 Or snare / and their fellowship become

Psalm 70

For the director of music. Of David.
A petition.

¹Hasten, O God, to save me;
O Lᴏʀᴅ, come quickly to
help me.   Ps 40:13
²May those who seek my life
be put to shame and
confusion;
may all who desire my ruin
be turned back in disgrace.
³May those who say to me,
"Aha! Aha!"
turn back because of their
shame.
⁴But may all who seek you
rejoice and be glad in you;
may those who love your
salvation always say,
"Let God be exalted!"   Ps 35:27

⁵Yet I am poor and needy;
come quickly to me, O God.
You are my help and my
deliverer;   Ps 18:2
O Lᴏʀᴅ, do not delay.

Psalm 71

¹In you, O Lᴏʀᴅ, I have taken
refuge;
let me never be put to
shame.   Ps 25:2-3; 31:1
²Rescue me and deliver me in
your righteousness;
turn your ear to me and save
me.   Ps 17:6
³Be my rock of refuge,
to which I can always go;
give the command to save me

for you are my rock and my
fortress.   Ps 18:2; 31:2-3
⁴Deliver me, O my God, from
the hand of the wicked,
from the grasp of evil and
cruel men.

⁵For you have been my hope,
O Sovereign Lᴏʀᴅ,
my confidence since my
youth.   Jer 17:7
⁶From birth I have relied on
you;   Ps 22:10
you brought me forth from
my mother's womb.
I will ever praise you.   Ps 34:1
⁷I have become like a portent to
many,   Isa 8:18; 1Co 4:9
but you are my strong
refuge.   Ps 61:3
⁸My mouth is filled with your
praise,
declaring your splendor all
day long.   Ps 35:28

⁹Do not cast me away when I
am old;   ver 18
do not forsake me when my
strength is gone.
¹⁰For my enemies speak against
me;
those who wait to kill me
conspire together.   Ps 10:8
¹¹They say, God has forsaken
him;
pursue him and seize him,
for no one will rescue him."
¹²Be not far from me, O God;
come quickly, O my God, to
help me.   Ps 70:1
¹³May my accusers perish in
shame;

may those who want to
harm me
be covered with scorn and
disgrace. ver 24

¹⁴But as for me, I will always
have hope; Ps 130:7
I will praise you more and
more.
¹⁵My mouth will tell of your
righteousness, Ps 35:28; 40:5
of your salvation all day
long,
though I know not its
measure.
¹⁶I will come and proclaim your
mighty acts, O Sovereign
LORD; Ps 106:2
I will proclaim your
righteousness, yours
alone.
¹⁷Since my youth, O God, you
have taught me,
and to this day I declare
your marvelous deeds.
¹⁸Even when I am old and gray,
do not forsake me, O God,
till I declare your power to the
next generation,
your might to all who are to
come. Ps 22:30,31; 78:4

¹⁹Your righteousness reaches to
the skies, O God, Ps 57:10
you who have done great
things.
Who, O God, is like you?
²⁰Though you have made me see
troubles, many and
bitter,

you will restore my life
again; Hos 6:2
from the depths of the earth
you will again bring me up.
²¹You will increase my honor
and comfort me once again.

²²I will praise you with the harp
for your faithfulness, O my
God;
I will sing praise to you with
the lyre,
O Holy One of Israel. 2Ki 19:22
²³My lips will shout for joy
when I sing praise to you—
I, whom you have redeemed.
²⁴My tongue will tell of your
righteous acts
all day long, Ps 35:28
for those who wanted to harm
me
have been put to shame and
confusion.

Psalm 72

Of Solomon.

¹Endow the king with your
justice, O God,
the royal son with your
righteousness.
²He willᵃ judge your people in
righteousness, Isa 9:7
your afflicted ones with
justice.
³The mountains will bring
prosperity to the people,
the hills the fruit of
righteousness.

ᵃ2 Or May he; similarly in verses 3-11 and 17

⁴He will defend the afflicted
      among the people
   and save the children of the
      needy;   Isa 11:4
   he will crush the oppressor.

⁵He will endure[a] as long as the
      sun,
   as long as the moon,
      through all generations.
⁶He will be like rain falling on a
      mown field,   Hos 6:3
   like showers watering the
      earth.
⁷In his days the righteous will
      flourish;   Ps 92:12; Isa 2:4
   prosperity will abound till
      the moon is no more.

⁸He will rule from sea to sea
   and from the River[b] to the
      ends of the earth.[c]
⁹The desert tribes will bow
      before him
   and his enemies will lick the
      dust.
¹⁰The kings of Tarshish and of
      distant shores
   will bring tribute to him;
   the kings of Sheba and Seba
   will present him gifts.   2Ch 9:24
¹¹All kings will bow down to
      him
   and all nations will serve
      him.

¹²For he will deliver the needy
      who cry out,
   the afflicted who have no
      one to help.

¹³He will take pity on the weak
      and the needy
   and save the needy from
      death.
¹⁴He will rescue them from
      oppression and violence,
   for precious is their blood in
      his sight.   Ps 116:15

¹⁵Long may he live!
   May gold from Sheba be
      given him.   Isa 60:6
   May people ever pray for him
   and bless him all day long.
¹⁶Let grain abound throughout
      the land;
   on the tops of the hills may
      it sway.
   Let its fruit flourish like
      Lebanon;   Ps 104:16
   let it thrive like the grass of
      the field.
¹⁷May his name endure forever;
   may it continue as long as
      the sun.   Ps 89:36

   All nations will be blessed
      through him,
   and they will call him
      blessed.   Ge 12:3; Lk 1:48

¹⁸Praise be to the Lord God, the
      God of Israel,   1Ch 29:10
   who alone does marvelous
      deeds.
¹⁹Praise be to his glorious name
      forever;
   may the whole earth be
      filled with his glory.
   Amen and Amen.

---

[a]5 Septuagint; Hebrew *You will be feared*   [b]8 That is, the Euphrates   [c]8 Or *the end of the land*

²⁰This concludes the prayers of
David son of Jesse.

BOOK III
Psalms 73–89

Psalm 73

A psalm of Asaph.

¹Surely God is good to Israel,
to those who are pure in
heart.   Mt 5:8

²But as for me, my feet had
almost slipped;
I had nearly lost my
foothold.
³For I envied the arrogant   Ps 37:1
when I saw the prosperity of
the wicked.   Job 21:7

⁴They have no struggles;
their bodies are healthy and
strong.ᵃ
⁵They are free from the burdens
common to man;   Job 21:9
they are not plagued by
human ills.
⁶Therefore pride is their
necklace;
they clothe themselves with
violence.   Ps 109:18
⁷From their callous hearts
comes iniquityᵇ;   Ps 17:10
the evil conceits of their
minds know no limits.

⁸They scoff, and speak with
malice;
in their arrogance they
threaten oppression.
⁹Their mouths lay claim to
heaven,
and their tongues take
possession of the earth.
¹⁰Therefore their people turn to
them
and drink up waters in
abundance.ᶜ
¹¹They say, "How can God
know?
Does the Most High have
knowledge?"

¹²This is what the wicked are
like—
always carefree, they
increase in wealth.

¹³Surely in vain have I kept my
heart pure;   Job 34:9
in vain have I washed my
hands in innocence.
¹⁴All day long I have been
plagued;
I have been punished every
morning.

¹⁵If I had said, "I will speak
thus,"
I would have betrayed your
children.
¹⁶When I tried to understand all
this,
it was oppressive to me

ᵃ4 With a different word division of the Hebrew; Masoretic Text *struggles at their death; / their bodies
are healthy*   ᵇ7 Syriac (see also Septuagint); Hebrew *Their eyes bulge with fat*   ᶜ10 The meaning of
the Hebrew for this verse is uncertain.

¹⁷till I entered the sanctuary of
   God;   Ps 77:13
   then I understood their final
   destiny.   Ps 37:38

¹⁸Surely you place them on
   slippery ground;   Ps 35:6
   you cast them down to
   ruin.
¹⁹How suddenly are they
   destroyed,   Isa 47:11
   completely swept away by
   terrors!
²⁰As a dream when one
   awakes,
   so when you arise, O Lord,
   you will despise them as
   fantasies.

²¹When my heart was grieved
   and my spirit embittered,
²²I was senseless and ignorant;
   I was a brute beast before
   you.   Ecc 3:18

²³Yet I am always with you;
   you hold me by my right
   hand.
²⁴You guide me with your
   counsel,   Ps 32:8; 48:14
   and afterward you will take
   me into glory.
²⁵Whom have I in heaven but
   you?
   And earth has nothing I
   desire besides you.
²⁶My flesh and my heart may
   fail,   Ps 84:2
   but God is the strength of
   my heart

ᵃTitle: Probably a literary or musical term

and my portion forever.

²⁷Those who are far from you
   will perish;   Ps 119:155
   you destroy all who are
   unfaithful to you.
²⁸But as for me, it is good to be
   near God.   Heb 10:22; Jas 4:8
   I have made the Sovereign
   LORD my refuge;
   I will tell of all your deeds.

Psalm 74

A *maskil*ᵃ of Asaph.

¹Why have you rejected us
   forever, O God?   Dt 29:20
   Why does your anger
   smolder against the
   sheep of your pasture?
²Remember the people you
   purchased of old,   Ex 15:16
   the tribe of your inheritance,
   whom you redeemed—
   Mount Zion, where you
   dwelt.   Ps 68:16
³Turn your steps toward these
   everlasting ruins,
   all this destruction the
   enemy has brought on
   the sanctuary.

⁴Your foes roared in the place
   where you met with
   us;
   they set up their standards
   as signs.
⁵They behaved like men
   wielding axes

to cut through a thicket of
trees.   Jer 46:22
[6]They smashed all the carved
paneling
with their axes and hatchets.
[7]They burned your sanctuary to
the ground;
they defiled the dwelling
place of your Name.
[8]They said in their hearts, "We
will crush them
completely!"   Ps 83:4
They burned every place
where God was
worshiped in the land.
[9]We are given no miraculous
signs;
no prophets are left,   1Sa 3:1
and none of us knows how
long this will be.

[10]How long will the enemy mock
you, O God?
Will the foe revile your
name forever?   Ps 44:16
[11]Why do you hold back your
hand, your right hand?
Take it from the folds of
your garment and
destroy them!

[12]But you, O God, are my king
from of old;   Ps 44:4
you bring salvation upon the
earth.
[13]It was you who split open the
sea by your power;
you broke the heads of the
monster in the waters.
[14]It was you who crushed the
heads of Leviathan

and gave him as food to the
creatures of the desert.
[15]It was you who opened up
springs and streams;
you dried up the ever
flowing rivers.   Jos 43:13
[16]The day is yours, and yours
also the night;
you established the sun and
moon.   Ge 1:16; Ps 136:7-9
[17]It was you who set all the
boundaries of the earth;
you made both summer and
winter.   Ge 8:22

[18]Remember how the enemy has
mocked you, O LORD,
how foolish people have
reviled your name.
[19]Do not hand over the life of
your dove to wild
beasts;
do not forget the lives of
your afflicted people
forever.   Ps 9:18
[20]Have regard for your covenant,
because haunts of violence
fill the dark places of
the land.
[21]Do not let the oppressed
retreat in disgrace;
may the poor and needy
praise your name.

[22]Rise up, O God, and defend
your cause;
remember how fools mock
you all day long.   Ps 53:1
[23]Do not ignore the clamor of
your adversaries,   Ps 65:7
the uproar of your enemies,
which rises continually.

Psalm 75

For the director of music. To the
tune of "Do Not Destroy." A psalm
of Asaph. A song.

¹We give thanks to you, O God,
    we give thanks, for your
        Name is near;   Ps 145:18
    men tell of your wonderful
        deeds.   Ps 44:1; 71:16

²You say, "I choose the
        appointed time;
    it is I who judge uprightly.
³When the earth and all its
        people quake,   Isa 24:19
    it is I who hold its pillars
        firm.   *Selah*
⁴To the arrogant I say, 'Boast no
        more,'
    and to the wicked, 'Do not
        lift up your horns.
⁵Do not lift your horns against
        heaven;
    do not speak with
        outstretched neck.' "

⁶No one from the east or the
        west
    or from the desert can exalt
        a man.
⁷But it is God who judges:
    He brings one down, he
        exalts another.   1Sa 2:7
⁸In the hand of the LORD is a
        cup
    full of foaming wine mixed
        with spices;   Pr 23:30
    he pours it out, and all the
        wicked of the earth
    drink it down to its very
        dregs.   Jer 25:15

⁹As for me, I will declare this
        forever;   Ps 40:10
    I will sing praise to the God
        of Jacob.
¹⁰I will cut off the horns of all
        the wicked,
    but the horns of the
        righteous will be lifted
        up.   Ps 89:17; 148:14

Psalm 76

For the director of music. With
stringed instruments. A psalm of
Asaph. A song.

¹In Judah God is known;
    his name is great in Israel.
²His tent is in Salem,   Ge 14:18
    his dwelling place in Zion.
³There he broke the flashing
        arrows,
    the shields and the swords,
        the weapons of war.
        Selah

⁴You are resplendent with light,
    more majestic than
        mountains rich with
        game.
⁵Valiant men lie plundered,
    they sleep their last sleep;
    not one of the warriors
        can lift his hands.
⁶At your rebuke, O God of
        Jacob,
    both horse and chariot lie
        still.   Ex 15:1
⁷You alone are to be feared.
    Who can stand before you
        when you are angry?
⁸From heaven you pronounced
        judgment,

and the land feared and was
quiet— 2Ch 20:29-30
⁹when you, O God, rose up to
judge, Ps 9:8
to save all the afflicted of the
land. *Selah*
¹⁰Surely your wrath against men
brings you praise, Ex 9:16
and the survivors of your
wrath are restrained.ᵃ

¹¹Make vows to the Lᴏʀᴅ your
God and fulfill them;
let all the neighboring lands
bring gifts to the One to be
feared. Ps 68:29
¹²He breaks the spirit of rulers;
he is feared by the kings of
the earth.

Psalm 77

For the director of music. For
Jeduthun. Of Asaph. A psalm.

¹I cried out to God for help;
I cried out to God to hear
me.
²When I was in distress, I
sought the Lord; Ps 50:15
at night I stretched out
untiring hands Job 11:13
and my soul refused to be
comforted. Ge 37:35

³I remembered you, O God, and
I groaned;
I mused, and my spirit grew
faint. *Selah*
⁴You kept my eyes from
closing;

I was too troubled to speak.
⁵I thought about the former
days, Dt 32:7; Ps 143:5; Isa 51:9
the years of long ago;
⁶I remembered my songs in the
night.
My heart mused and my
spirit inquired:

⁷"Will the Lord reject forever?
Will he never show his favor
again? Ps 85:1
⁸Has his unfailing love vanished
forever?
Has his promise failed for all
time? 2Pe 3:9
⁹Has God forgotten to be
merciful?
Has he in anger withheld his
compassion?" *Selah*

¹⁰Then I thought, "To this I will
appeal:
the years of the right hand
of the Most High."
¹¹I will remember the deeds of
the Lᴏʀᴅ;
yes, I will remember your
miracles of long ago.
¹²I will meditate on all your
works
and consider all your mighty
deeds.

¹³Your ways, O God, are holy.
What god is so great as our
God? Ex 15:11
¹⁴You are the God who performs
miracles;

ᵃ10 Or *Surely the wrath of men brings you praise, / and with the remainder of wrath you arm yourself*

you display your power
among the peoples.
¹⁵With your mighty arm you
redeemed your people,
the descendants of Jacob
and Joseph.   *Selah*

¹⁶The waters saw you, O God,
the waters saw you and
writhed;   Ps 114:4
the very depths were
convulsed.
¹⁷The clouds poured down
water,   Jdg 5:4
the skies resounded with
thunder;
your arrows flashed back
and forth.
¹⁸Your thunder was heard in the
whirlwind,
your lightning lit up the
world;
the earth trembled and
quaked.   Jdg 5:4
¹⁹Your path led through the sea,
your way through the
mighty waters,
though your footprints were
not seen.

²⁰You led your people like a
flock   Ex 13:21; Isa 63:11
by the hand of Moses and
Aaron.

Psalm 78

A *maskil*[a] of Asaph.

¹O my people, hear my
teaching;   Isa 51:4

listen to the words of my
mouth.
²I will open my mouth in
parables,   Mt 13:35*
I will utter hidden things,
things from of old—
³what we have heard and
known,
what our fathers have told
us.   Ps 44:1
⁴We will not hide them from
their children;   Dt 11:19
we will tell the next
generation
the praiseworthy deeds of the
LORD,   Ps 26:7; 71:17
his power, and the wonders
he has done.
⁵He decreed statutes for
Jacob
and established the law in
Israel,
which he commanded our
forefathers
to teach their children,
⁶so the next generation would
know them,
even the children yet to be
born,   Ps 102:18
and they in turn would tell
their children.
⁷Then they would put their
trust in God
and would not forget his
deeds
but would keep his
commands.
⁸They would not be like their
forefathers—

---

[a] Title: Probably a literary or musical term

a stubborn and rebellious
   generation,   Ex 32:9
whose hearts were not loyal to
   God,
   whose spirits were not
      faithful to him.

⁹The men of Ephraim, though
   armed with bows,
   turned back on the day of
      battle;   Jdg 20:39
¹⁰they did not keep God's
   covenant   2Ki 17:15
   and refused to live by his
      law.
¹¹They forgot what he had done,
   the wonders he had shown
      them.
¹²He did miracles in the sight of
   their fathers
   in the land of Egypt, in the
      region of Zoan.   Nu 13:22
¹³He divided the sea and led
   them through;   Ex 14:21
   he made the water stand
      firm like a wall.   Ex 15:8
¹⁴He guided them with the cloud
   by day
   and with light from the fire
      all night.   Ex 13:21
¹⁵He split the rocks in the desert
   and gave them water as
      abundant as the seas;
¹⁶he brought streams out of a
   rocky crag
   and made water flow down
      like rivers.

¹⁷But they continued to sin
   against him,   Heb 3:16
   rebelling in the desert
      against the Most High.

¹⁸They willfully put God to the
   test   1Co 10:9
   by demanding the food they
      craved.   Nu 11:4
¹⁹They spoke against God,
   saying,   Nu 21:5
   "Can God spread a table in
      the desert?
²⁰When he struck the rock,
   water gushed out,
   and streams flowed
      abundantly.
   But can he also give us food?
   Can he supply meat for his
      people?"   Nu 11:18
²¹When the LORD heard them, he
   was very angry;
   his fire broke out against
      Jacob,   Nu 11:1
   and his wrath rose against
      Israel,
²²for they did not believe in
   God
   or trust in his deliverance.
²³Yet he gave a command to the
   skies above
   and opened the doors of the
      heavens;   Ge 7:11; Mal 3:10
²⁴he rained down manna for the
   people to eat,   Jn 6:31*
   he gave them the grain of
      heaven.
²⁵Men ate the bread of angels;
   he sent them all the food
      they could eat.
²⁶He let loose the east wind from
   the heavens   Nu 11:31
   and led forth the south wind
      by his power.
²⁷He rained meat down on them
      like dust,

flying birds like sand on the
  seashore.
28He made them come down
  inside their camp,
all around their tents.
29They ate till they had more
  than enough,   Nu 11:20
for he had given them what
  they craved.
30But before they turned from
  the food they craved,
even while it was still in
  their mouths,   Nu 11:33
31God's anger rose against
  them;
he put to death the sturdiest
  among them,   Isa 10:16
cutting down the young men
  of Israel.

32In spite of all this, they kept
  on sinning;
in spite of his wonders, they
  did not believe.   ver 11,22
33So he ended their days in
  futility   Nu 14:29,35
and their years in terror.
34Whenever God slew them, they
  would seek him;   Hos 5:15
they eagerly turned to him
  again.
35They remembered that God
  was their Rock,   Dt 32:4
that God Most High was
  their Redeemer.   Dt 9:26
36But then they would flatter
  him with their mouths,
lying to him with their
  tongues;
37their hearts were not loyal to
  him,

they were not faithful to his
  covenant.   Ac 8:21
38Yet he was merciful;   Ex 34:6
he forgave their iniquities
and did not destroy them.
Time after time he restrained
  his anger
and did not stir up his full
  wrath.
39He remembered that they were
  but flesh,   Ps 103:14
a passing breeze that does
  not return.   Job 7:7

40How often they rebelled
  against him in the
  desert
and grieved him in the
  wasteland!   Ps 95:8
41Again and again they put God
  to the test;   Nu 14:22
they vexed the Holy One of
  Israel.   Ps 89:18
42They did not remember his
  power—
the day he redeemed them
  from the oppressor,
43the day he displayed his
  miraculous signs in
  Egypt,
his wonders in the region of
  Zoan.
44He turned their rivers to blood;
they could not drink from
  their streams.
45He sent swarms of flies that
  devoured them,   Ex 8:24
and frogs that devastated
  them.   Ex 8:2,6
46He gave their crops to the
  grasshopper,

their produce to the locust.
⁴⁷He destroyed their vines with
hail   Ex 9:23
and their sycamore-figs with
sleet.
⁴⁸He gave over their cattle to the
hail,
their livestock to bolts of
lightning.
⁴⁹He unleashed against them his
hot anger,   Ex 15:7
his wrath, indignation and
hostility—
a band of destroying
angels.
⁵⁰He prepared a path for his
anger;
he did not spare them from
death
but gave them over to the
plague.
⁵¹He struck down all the
firstborn of Egypt,
the firstfruits of manhood in
the tents of Ham.
⁵²But he brought his people out
like a flock;   Ps 77:20
he led them like sheep
through the desert.
⁵³He guided them safely, so they
were unafraid;
but the sea engulfed their
enemies.   Ex 14:28
⁵⁴Thus he brought them to the
border of his holy land,
to the hill country his right
hand had taken.   Ps 44:3
⁵⁵He drove out nations before
them   Ps 44:2
and allotted their lands to
them as an inheritance;

he settled the tribes of Israel
in their homes.
⁵⁶But they put God to the test
and rebelled against the
Most High;
they did not keep his
statutes.
⁵⁷Like their fathers they were
disloyal and faithless,
as unreliable as a faulty bow.
⁵⁸They angered him with their
high places;   Lev 26:30
they aroused his jealousy
with their idols.   Dt 32:21
⁵⁹When God heard them, he was
very angry;
he rejected Israel completely.
⁶⁰He abandoned the tabernacle
of Shiloh,   Jos 18:1
the tent he had set up
among men.
⁶¹He sent ˌthe ark ofˌ his might
into captivity,   Ps 132:8
his splendor into the hands
of the enemy.
⁶²He gave his people over to the
sword;
he was very angry with his
inheritance.
⁶³Fire consumed their young
men,   Nu 11:1
and their maidens had no
wedding songs;   Jer 7:34
⁶⁴their priests were put to the
sword,   1Sa 22:18
and their widows could not
weep.

⁶⁵Then the Lord awoke as from
sleep,

as a man wakes from the
   stupor of wine.
⁶⁶He beat back his enemies;
   he put them to everlasting
      shame.   1Sa 5:6
⁶⁷Then he rejected the tents of
   Joseph,
   he did not choose the tribe
      of Ephraim;
⁶⁸but he chose the tribe of
   Judah,
   Mount Zion, which he loved.
⁶⁹He built his sanctuary like the
   heights,
   like the earth that he
      established forever.
⁷⁰He chose David his servant
   and took him from the sheep
      pens;
⁷¹from tending the sheep he
   brought him
   to be the shepherd of his
      people Jacob,   2Sa 5:2
   of Israel his inheritance.
⁷²And David shepherded them
   with integrity of heart;
   with skillful hands he led
      them.

Psalm 79

A psalm of Asaph.

¹O God, the nations have
   invaded your
      inheritance;   Ps 74:2
   they have defiled your holy
      temple,
   they have reduced Jerusalem
      to rubble.   2Ki 25:9
²They have given the dead
   bodies of your servants

as food to the birds of the
   air,
   the flesh of your saints to
      the beasts of the earth.
³They have poured out blood
   like water
   all around Jerusalem,
   and there is no one to bury
      the dead.   Jer 16:4
⁴We are objects of reproach to
   our neighbors,
   of scorn and derision to
      those around us.   Ps 44:13
⁵How long, O LORD? Will you be
   angry forever?   Ps 74:1,10
   How long will your jealousy
      burn like fire?   Zep 3:8
⁶Pour out your wrath on the
   nations
   that do not acknowledge
      you,   Jer 10:25; 2Th 1:8
 on the kingdoms
   that do not call on your
      name;   Ps 14:4
⁷for they have devoured Jacob
   and destroyed his homeland.
⁸Do not hold against us the sins
   of the fathers;   Isa 64:9
   may your mercy come
      quickly to meet us,
   for we are in desperate
      need.
⁹Help us, O God our Savior,
   for the glory of your name;
 deliver us and forgive our sins
   for your name's sake.   Jer 14:7
¹⁰Why should the nations say,
   "Where is their God?"   Ps 42:10
 Before our eyes, make known
   among the nations

that you avenge the
outpoured blood of your
servants.   Ps 94:1
11May the groans of the
prisoners come before
you;
by the strength of your arm
preserve those condemned to
die.
12Pay back into the laps of our
neighbors seven times
the reproach they have
hurled at you, O Lord.
13Then we your people, the
sheep of your pasture,
will praise you forever;
from generation to generation
we will recount your praise.

Psalm 80

For the director of music. To the
tune of, "The Lilies of the
Covenant." Of Asaph. A psalm.

1Hear us, O Shepherd of Israel,
you who lead Joseph like a
flock;   Ps 77:20
you who sit enthroned
between the cherubim,
shine forth   Ex 25:22
2   before Ephraim, Benjamin
and Manasseh.   Nu 2:18-24
Awaken your might;
come and save us.

3Restore us, O God;   Nu 6:25; La 5:21
make your face shine upon
us,
that we may be saved.

4O Lord God Almighty,
how long will your anger
smolder   Dt 29:20
against the prayers of your
people?
5You have fed them with the
bread of tears;
you have made them drink
tears by the bowlful.
6You have made us a source of
contention to our
neighbors,
and our enemies mock us.

7Restore us, O God Almighty;
make your face shine upon
us,
that we may be saved.

8You brought a vine out of
Egypt;   Isa 5:1-2
you drove out the nations
and planted it.   Jos 13:6
9You cleared the ground for it,
and it took root and filled
the land.
10The mountains were covered
with its shade,
the mighty cedars with its
branches.
11It sent out its boughs to the
Sea,a
its shoots as far as the
River.b   Ps 72:8
12Why have you broken down its
walls
so that all who pass by pick
its grapes?
13Boars from the forest ravage it

a 11 Probably the Mediterranean   b 11 That is, the Euphrates

and the creatures of the field
   feed on it.
¹⁴Return to us, O God Almighty!
   Look down from heaven and
      see!   Isa 63:15
Watch over this vine,
¹⁵   the root your right hand has
         planted,
      the son*a* you have raised up
         for yourself.

¹⁶Your vine is cut down, it is
      burned with fire;
   at your rebuke your people
         perish.   Ps 39:11; 76:6
¹⁷Let your hand rest on the man
      at your right hand,
   the son of man you have
      raised up for yourself.
¹⁸Then we will not turn away
      from you;
   revive us, and we will call
      on your name.   Ps 5:6

¹⁹Restore us, O LORD God
      Almighty;
   make your face shine upon
      us,
   that we may be saved.

Psalm 81

For the director of music. According
   to *gittith.*ᵇ Of Asaph.

¹Sing for joy to God our
      strength;
   shout aloud to the God of
      Jacob!   Ps 66:1
²Begin the music, strike the
      tambourine,

play the melodious harp and
   lyre.   Ps 92:3

³Sound the ram's horn at the
      New Moon,
   and when the moon is full,
      on the day of our Feast;
⁴this is a decree for Israel,
   an ordinance of the God of
      Jacob.
⁵He established it as a statute
      for Joseph
   when he went out against
      Egypt,   Ex 11:4
   where we heard a language
      we did not understand.ᶜ

⁶He says, "I removed the
      burden from their
      shoulders;   Isa 9:4
   their hands were set free
      from the basket.
⁷In your distress you called and
      I rescued you,   Ex 2:23
   I answered you out of a
      thundercloud;   Ex 19:19
   I tested you at the waters of
      Meribah.   *Selah*

⁸"Hear, O my people, and I will
      warn you—   Ps 50:7
   if you would but listen to
      me, O Israel!
⁹You shall have no foreign god
      among you;   Ex 20:3; Dt 32:12
   you shall not bow down to
      an alien god.
¹⁰I am the LORD your God,
   who brought you up out of
      Egypt.   Ex 20:2

---

a 15 Or *branch*   *b* Title: Probably a musical term   *c 5* Or / *and we heard a voice we had not known*

Open wide your mouth and I
    will fill it.   Ps 107:9

11"But my people would not
    listen to me;
Israel would not submit to
    me.
12So I gave them over to their
    stubborn hearts   Ac 7:42
to follow their own devices.

13"If my people would but listen
    to me,   Dt 5:29; Isa 48:18
if Israel would follow my
    ways,
14how quickly would I subdue
    their enemies   Ps 47:3
and turn my hand against
    their foes!   Am 1:8
15Those who hate the LORD
    would cringe before
    him,
and their punishment would
    last forever.
16But you would be fed with the
    finest of wheat;   Dt 32:14
with honey from the rock I
    would satisfy you."

Psalm 82

A psalm of Asaph.

1God presides in the great
    assembly;
he gives judgment among
    the "gods":   Ps 58:11; Isa 3:13

2"How long will you*a* defend
    the unjust
and show partiality to the
    wicked?   *Selah*

3Defend the cause of the weak
    and fatherless;   Dt 24:17
maintain the rights of the
    poor and oppressed.
4Rescue the weak and needy;
    deliver them from the hand
    of the wicked.

5"They know nothing, they
    understand nothing.
They walk about in
    darkness;
all the foundations of the
    earth are shaken.   Ps 11:3

6"I said, 'You are "gods";
    you are all sons of the Most
    High.'
7But you will die like mere
    men;   Ps 49:12
you will fall like every other
    ruler."

8Rise up, O God, judge the
    earth,
for all the nations are your
    inheritance.   Ps 2:8; Rev 11:15

Psalm 83

A song. A psalm of Asaph.

1O God, do not keep silent;
    be not quiet, O God, be not
    still.
2See how your enemies are
    astir,   Ps 2:1
how your foes rear their
    heads.   Ps 81:15
3With cunning they conspire
    against your people;

*a*2 The Hebrew is plural.

they plot against those you
cherish.
⁴"Come," they say, "let us
destroy them as a
nation,   Est 3:6
that the name of Israel be
remembered no more."

⁵With one mind they plot
together;   Ps 2:2
they form an alliance against
you—
⁶the tents of Edom and the
Ishmaelites,
of Moab and the Hagrites,
⁷Gebal,ᵃ Ammon and Amalek,
Philistia, with the people of
Tyre.
⁸Even Assyria has joined
them
to lend strength to the
descendants of Lot.
                           Selah

⁹Do to them as you did to
Midian,   Jdg 7:1-23
as you did to Sisera and
Jabin at the river
Kishon,   Jdg 4:23-24
¹⁰who perished at Endor
and became like refuse on
the ground.   Zep 1:17
¹¹Make their nobles like Oreb
and Zeeb,
all their princes like Zebah
and Zalmunna,   Jdg 8:12,21
¹²who said, "Let us take
possession
of the pasturelands of
God."

¹³Make them like tumbleweed,
O my God,
like chaff before the wind.
¹⁴As fire consumes the forest
or a flame sets the
mountains ablaze,
¹⁵so pursue them with your
tempest
and terrify them with your
storm.
¹⁶Cover their faces with shame
so that men will seek your
name, O LORD.

¹⁷May they ever be ashamed and
dismayed;
may they perish in disgrace.
¹⁸Let them know that you,
whose name is the
LORD—
that you alone are the Most
High over all the earth.

Psalm 84

For the director of music. According
to *gittith.* ᵇ Of the Sons of Korah.
A psalm.

¹How lovely is your dwelling
place,   Ps 27:4
O LORD Almighty!
²My soul yearns, even faints,
for the courts of the LORD;
my heart and my flesh cry out
for the living God.   Jos 3:10

³Even the sparrow has found a
home,
and the swallow a nest for
herself,

ᵃ 7 That is, Byblos   ᵇ Title: Probably a musical term

where she may have her
young—
a place near your altar,   Ps 43:4
O Lord Almighty, my King
and my God.   Ps 5:2
⁴Blessed are those who dwell in
your house;
they are ever praising you.
Selah

⁵Blessed are those whose
strength is in you,   Ps 81:1
who have set their hearts on
pilgrimage.   Jer 31:6
⁶As they pass through the
Valley of Baca,
they make it a place of
springs;
the autumn rains also cover
it with pools.ᵃ   Joel 2:23
⁷They go from strength to
strength,   Pr 4:18
till each appears before God
in Zion.   Dt 16:16

⁸Hear my prayer, O Lord God
Almighty;
listen to me, O God of Jacob.
Selah
⁹Look upon our shield,ᵇ O God;
look with favor on your
anointed one.   1Sa 16:6

¹⁰Better is one day in your
courts
than a thousand elsewhere;
I would rather be a doorkeeper
in the house of my God
than dwell in the tents of the
wicked.

¹¹For the Lord God is a sun and
shield;   Isa 60:19
the Lord bestows favor and
honor;
no good thing does he
withhold   Ps 34:10
from those whose walk is
blameless.

¹²O Lord Almighty,
blessed is the man who
trusts in you.   Ps 2:12

Psalm 85

For the director of music. Of the
Sons of Korah. A psalm.

¹You showed favor to your
land, O Lord;
you restored the fortunes of
Jacob.   Jer 30:18; Eze 39:25
²You forgave the iniquity of
your people   Nu 14:19
and covered all their sins.
Selah
³You set aside all your wrath
and turned from your fierce
anger.   Dt 13:17

⁴Restore us again, O God our
Savior,   Ps 80:3,7
and put away your
displeasure toward us.
⁵Will you be angry with us
forever?   Ps 79:5
Will you prolong your anger
through all generations?
⁶Will you not revive us again,
that your people may rejoice
in you?

ᵃ6 Or *blessings*   ᵇ9 Or *sovereign*

⁷Show us your unfailing love,
  O Lᴏʀᴅ,
  and grant us your salvation.

⁸I will listen to what God the
  Lᴏʀᴅ will say;
  he promises peace to his
    people, his saints—
  but let them not return to
    folly.
⁹Surely his salvation is near
    those who fear him,
  that his glory may dwell in
    our land.   Zec 2:5

¹⁰Love and faithfulness meet
    together;
  righteousness and peace kiss
    each other.   Ps 72:2-3
¹¹Faithfulness springs forth from
    the earth,
  and righteousness looks
    down from heaven.
¹²The Lᴏʀᴅ will indeed give what
    is good,   Ps 84:11; Jas 1:17
  and our land will yield its
    harvest.   Ps 67:6; Zec 8:12
¹³Righteousness goes before him
  and prepares the way for his
    steps.

Psalm 86

A prayer of David.

¹Hear, O Lᴏʀᴅ, and answer me,
  for I am poor and needy.
²Guard my life, for I am
    devoted to you.
  You are my God; save your
    servant
  who trusts in you.

³Have mercy on me, O Lord,
  for I call to you all day
    long.
⁴Bring joy to your servant,
  for to you, O Lord,
  I lift up my soul.   Ps 143:8

⁵You are forgiving and good,
  O Lord,
  abounding in love to all who
    call to you.   Ps 145:8; Joel 2:13
⁶Hear my prayer, O Lᴏʀᴅ;
  listen to my cry for mercy.
⁷In the day of my trouble I will
    call to you,   Ps 50:15
  for you will answer me.

⁸Among the gods there is none
    like you, O Lord;   Ex 15:11
  no deeds can compare with
    yours.
⁹All the nations you have made
  will come and worship
    before you, O Lord;
  they will bring glory to your
    name.
¹⁰For you are great and do
    marvelous deeds;   Ps 72:18
  you alone are God.   Dt 6:4

¹¹Teach me your way, O Lᴏʀᴅ,
  and I will walk in your
    truth;
  give me an undivided heart,
    that I may fear your name.
¹²I will praise you, O Lord my
    God, with all my heart;
  I will glorify your name
    forever.
¹³For great is your love toward
    me;

you have delivered me from
the depths of the
grave.^a   Ps 16:10

¹⁴The arrogant are attacking me,
O God;
a band of ruthless men seeks
my life—
men without regard for you.
¹⁵But you, O Lord, are a
compassionate and
gracious God,   Ps 103:8
slow to anger, abounding in
love and faithfulness.
¹⁶Turn to me and have mercy on
me;
grant your strength to your
servant
and save the son of your
maidservant.^b   Ps 116:16
¹⁷Give me a sign of your
goodness,
that my enemies may see it
and be put to shame,
for you, O LORD, have helped
me and comforted me.

Psalm 87

Of the Sons of Korah. A psalm.
A song.

¹He has set his foundation on
the holy mountain;
² the LORD loves the gates of
Zion   Ps 78:68
more than all the dwellings
of Jacob.
³Glorious things are said of you,
O city of God: Selah

⁴"I will record Rahab^c and
Babylon   Job 9:13
among those who
acknowledge me—
Philistia too, and Tyre, along
with Cush^d—
and will say, 'This^e one was
born in Zion.' "   Isa 19:25

⁵Indeed, of Zion it will be said,
"This one and that one were
born in her,
and the Most High himself
will establish her."
⁶The LORD will write in the
register of the peoples:
"This one was born in Zion."
    Selah
⁷As they make music they will
sing,
"All my fountains are in
you."   Ps 36:9

Psalm 88

A song. A psalm of the Sons of
Korah. For the director of music.
According to *mahalath leannoth*.^f A
maskil^g of Heman the Ezrahite.

¹O LORD, the God who saves
me,   Ps 51:14
day and night I cry out
before you.   Ps 22:2
²May my prayer come before
you;
turn your ear to my cry.

³For my soul is full of trouble

---

^a13 Hebrew *Sheol*   ^b16 Or *save your faithful son*   ^c4 A poetic name for Egypt   ^d4 That is, the
upper Nile region   ^e4 Or "O Rahab and Babylon, / Philistia, Tyre and Cush, / I will record concerning
those who acknowledge me: / 'This   ^fTitle: Possibly a tune, "The Suffering of Affliction"   ^gTitle:
Probably a literary or musical term

and my life draws near the
grave.[a]   Ps 107:18,26
[4]I am counted among those
who go down to the pit;
I am like a man without
strength.
[5]I am set apart with the dead,
like the slain who lie in the
grave,
whom you remember no more,
who are cut off from your
care.   Isa 53:8

[6]You have put me in the lowest
pit,
in the darkest depths.   Ps 69:15
[7]Your wrath lies heavily upon
me;
you have overwhelmed me
with all your waves.
                    Selah
[8]You have taken from me my
closest friends   Job 19:13
and have made me repulsive
to them.
I am confined and cannot
escape;
[9]   my eyes are dim with grief.

I call to you, O LORD, every
day;   Ps 86:3
I spread out my hands to
you.   Ps 143:6
[10]Do you show your wonders to
the dead?
Do those who are dead rise
up and praise you?
                    Selah
[11]Is your love declared in the
grave,

your faithfulness in
Destruction[b]?   Ps 30:9
[12]Are your wonders known in
the place of darkness,
or your righteous deeds in
the land of oblivion?

[13]But I cry to you for help,
O LORD;   Ps 30:2
in the morning my prayer
comes before you.   Ps 5:3
[14]Why, O LORD, do you reject me
and hide your face from me?

[15]From my youth I have been
afflicted and close to
death;
I have suffered your terrors
and am in despair.
[16]Your wrath has swept over me;
your terrors have destroyed
me.
[17]All day long they surround me
like a flood;   Ps 22:16
they have completely
engulfed me.
[18]You have taken my
companions and loved
ones from me;   Job 19:13
the darkness is my closest
friend.

Psalm 89

A *maskil*[c] of Ethan the Ezrahite.

[1]I will sing of the LORD's great
love forever;   Ps 101:1
with my mouth I will make
your faithfulness known
through all generations.

---

[a]3 Hebrew *Sheol*   [b]11 Hebrew *Abaddon*   [c]Title: Probably a literary or musical term

²I will declare that your love
	stands firm forever,
that you established your
	faithfulness in heaven
	itself. Ps 36:5

³You said, "I have made a
	covenant with my
	chosen one,
I have sworn to David my
	servant,
⁴'I will establish your line
	forever
and make your throne firm
	through all
	generations.'" *Selah*

⁵The heavens praise your
	wonders, O LORD, Ps 19:1
your faithfulness too, in the
	assembly of the holy
	ones.
⁶For who in the skies above can
	compare with the LORD?
Who is like the LORD among
	the heavenly beings?
⁷In the council of the holy ones
	God is greatly feared;
he is more awesome than all
	who surround him.
⁸O LORD God Almighty, who is
	like you? Ps 71:19
You are mighty, O LORD, and
	your faithfulness
	surrounds you.

⁹You rule over the surging sea;
when its waves mount up,
	you still them. Ps 65:7

¹⁰You crushed Rahab like one of
	the slain; Ps 87:4
with your strong arm you
	scattered your enemies.
¹¹The heavens are yours, and
	yours also the earth;
you founded the world and
	all that is in it. Ge 1:1
¹²You created the north and the
	south;
Tabor and Hermon sing for
	joy at your name. Jos 12:1
¹³Your arm is endued with
	power;
your hand is strong, your
	right hand exalted.

¹⁴Righteousness and justice are
	the foundation of your
	throne;
love and faithfulness go
	before you. Ps 97:2
¹⁵Blessed are those who have
	learned to acclaim you,
who walk in the light of
	your presence, O LORD.
¹⁶They rejoice in your name all
	day long;
they exult in your
	righteousness.
¹⁷For you are their glory and
	strength,
and by your favor you exalt
	our horn.ᵃ Ps 75:10; 148:14
¹⁸Indeed, our shieldᵇ belongs to
	the LORD,
our king to the Holy One of
	Israel. Ps 47:9
¹⁹Once you spoke in a vision,

ᵃ17 *Horn* here symbolizes strong one.   ᵇ18 Or *sovereign*

to your faithful people you
    said:
"I have bestowed strength on a
    warrior;
I have exalted a young man
    from among the people.
²⁰I have found David my servant;
    with my sacred oil I have
    anointed him.   1Sa 16:1,12
²¹My hand will sustain him;
    surely my arm will
    strengthen him.   Ps 18:35
²²No enemy will subject him to
    tribute;
    no wicked man will oppress
    him.   2Sa 7:10
²³I will crush his foes before him
    and strike down his
    adversaries.   2Sa 7:9
²⁴My faithful love will be with
    him,
    and through my name his
    horn^a will be exalted.
²⁵I will set his hand over the sea,
    his right hand over the
    rivers.   Ps 72:8
²⁶He will call out to me, 'You are
    my Father,
    my God, the Rock my
    Savior.'   2Sa 22:47
²⁷I will also appoint him my
    firstborn,
    the most exalted of the kings
    of the earth.   Nu 24:7
²⁸I will maintain my love to him
    forever,
    and my covenant with him
    will never fail.   ver 33-34
²⁹I will establish his line forever,

his throne as long as the
    heavens endure.   Dt 11:21
³⁰"If his sons forsake my law
    and do not follow my
    statutes,
³¹if they violate my decrees
    and fail to keep my
    commands,
³²I will punish their sin with the
    rod,
    their iniquity with flogging;
³³but I will not take my love
    from him,   2Sa 7:15
    nor will I ever betray my
    faithfulness.
³⁴I will not violate my covenant
    or alter what my lips have
    uttered.   Nu 23:19
³⁵Once for all, I have sworn by
    my holiness—
    and I will not lie to David—
³⁶that his line will continue
    forever
    and his throne endure before
    me like the sun;
³⁷it will be established forever
    like the moon,
    the faithful witness in the
    sky."   *Selah*

³⁸But you have rejected, you
    have spurned,   Dt 32:19
    you have been very angry
    with your anointed one.
³⁹You have renounced the
    covenant with your
    servant
    and have defiled his crown
    in the dust.   La 5:16

^a24 *Horn* here symbolizes strength.

40You have broken through all
his walls
and reduced his strongholds
to ruins.   La 2:2
41All who pass by have
plundered him;
he has become the scorn of
his neighbors.   Ps 44:13
42You have exalted the right
hand of his foes;
you have made all his
enemies rejoice.   Ps 13:2
43You have turned back the edge
of his sword
and have not supported him
in battle.   Ps 44:10
44You have put an end to his
splendor
and cast his throne to the
ground.
45You have cut short the days of
his youth;
you have covered him with a
mantle of shame. *Selah*
46How long, O LORD? Will you
hide yourself forever?
How long will your wrath
burn like fire?   Ps 79:5
47Remember how fleeting is my
life.   Job 7:7
For what futility you have
created all men!
48What man can live and not see
death,
or save himself from the
power of the grave*a*?
                              Selah
49O Lord, where is your former
great love,

which in your faithfulness
you swore to David?
50Remember, Lord, how your
servant has*b* been
mocked,   Ps 69:19
how I bear in my heart the
taunts of all the nations,
51the taunts with which your
enemies have mocked,
O LORD,
with which they have
mocked every step of
your anointed one.

52Praise be to the LORD forever!
Amen and Amen.

BOOK IV
Psalms 90–106

Psalm 90

A prayer of Moses the man of God.

1Lord, you have been our
dwelling place   Eze 11:16
throughout all generations.
2Before the mountains were
born   Pr 8:25
or you brought forth the
earth and the world,
from everlasting to
everlasting you are God.

3You turn men back to dust,
saying, "Return to dust,
O sons of men."   Ge 3:19

---

a 48 Hebrew *Sheol*   *b 50* Or *your servants have*

⁴For a thousand years in your
    sight
are like a day that has just
    gone by,
or like a watch in the
    night.
⁵You sweep men away in the
    sleep of death;   Isa 40:6
they are like the new grass
    of the morning—
⁶though in the morning it
    springs up new,
by evening it is dry and
    withered.   Mt 6:30; Jas 1:10

⁷We are consumed by your
    anger
and terrified by your
    indignation.
⁸You have set our iniquities
    before you,
our secret sins in the light of
    your presence.   Ps 19:12
⁹All our days pass away under
    your wrath;
we finish our years with a
    moan.   Ps 78:33
¹⁰The length of our days is
    seventy years—
or eighty, if we have the
    strength;
yet their span[a] is but trouble
    and sorrow,
for they quickly pass, and
    we fly away.   Job 20:8

¹¹Who knows the power of your
    anger?
For your wrath is as great as
    the fear that is due you.

¹²Teach us to number our days
    aright,   Ps 39:4
that we may gain a heart of
    wisdom.

¹³Relent, O Lord! How long will
    it be?
Have compassion on your
    servants.   Dt 32:36
¹⁴Satisfy us in the morning with
    your unfailing love,
that we may sing for joy and
    be glad all our days.
¹⁵Make us glad for as many days
    as you have afflicted us,
for as many years as we
    have seen trouble.
¹⁶May your deeds be shown to
    your servants,
your splendor to their
    children.   Hab 3:2

¹⁷May the favor[b] of the Lord our
    God rest upon us;
establish the work of our
    hands for us—
yes, establish the work of
    our hands.

Psalm 91

¹He who dwells in the shelter of
    the Most High   Ps 31:20
will rest in the shadow of
    the Almighty.[c]   Ps 17:8
²I will say[d] of the Lord, "He is
    my refuge and my
    fortress,   Ps 142:5
my God, in whom I trust."

a 10 Or yet the best of them   *b 17 Or beauty*   *c 1 Hebrew Shaddai*   *d 2 Or He says*

³Surely he will save you from
    the fowler's snare   Ps 124:7
and from the deadly
    pestilence.   1Ki 8:37
⁴He will cover you with his
    feathers,
and under his wings you will
    find refuge;   Ps 17:8
his faithfulness will be your
    shield and rampart.
⁵You will not fear the terror of
    night,   Job 5:21
nor the arrow that flies by
    day,
⁶nor the pestilence that stalks in
    the darkness,
nor the plague that destroys
    at midday.
⁷A thousand may fall at your
    side,
ten thousand at your right
    hand,
but it will not come near
    you.
⁸You will only observe with
    your eyes
and see the punishment of
    the wicked.   Mal 1:5

⁹If you make the Most High
    your dwelling—
even the LORD, who is my
    refuge—
¹⁰then no harm will befall
    you,
no disaster will come near
    your tent.
¹¹For he will command his
    angels concerning you
to guard you in all your
    ways;   Ps 34:7

¹²they will lift you up in their
    hands,
so that you will not strike
    your foot against a
    stone.   Mt 4:6*; Lk 4:10-11*
¹³You will tread upon the lion
    and the cobra;
you will trample the great
    lion and the serpent.

¹⁴"Because he loves me," says
    the LORD, "I will rescue
    him;
I will protect him, for he
    acknowledges my name.
¹⁵He will call upon me, and I
    will answer him;
I will be with him in trouble,
I will deliver him and honor
    him.   1Sa 2:30; Ps 50:15
¹⁶With long life will I satisfy him
    and show him my salvation."

Psalm 92

A psalm. A song. For the Sabbath
day.

¹It is good to praise the LORD
    and make music to your
    name, O Most High,
²to proclaim your love in the
    morning
and your faithfulness at
    night,   Ps 89:1
³to the music of the ten-stringed
    lyre
and the melody of the harp.

⁴For you make me glad by your
    deeds, O LORD;
I sing for joy at the works of
    your hands.   Ps 8:6; 143:5

⁵How great are your works,
　O LORD,
how profound your
　thoughts!　　Ps 40:5; Ro 11:33
⁶The senseless man does not
　know,　　　　　Ps 73:22
fools do not understand,
⁷that though the wicked spring
　up like grass
and all evildoers flourish,
they will be forever destroyed.

⁸But you, O LORD, are exalted
　forever.

⁹For surely your enemies,
　O LORD,
surely your enemies will
　perish;
all evildoers will be
　scattered.　　　　Ps 68:1
¹⁰You have exalted my horn*a*
　like that of a wild ox;
fine oils have been poured
　upon me.　　　Ps 23:5
¹¹My eyes have seen the defeat
　of my adversaries;
my ears have heard the rout
　of my wicked foes.

¹²The righteous will flourish like
　a palm tree,
they will grow like a cedar
　of Lebanon;　　Ps 52:8; Hos 14:6
¹³planted in the house of the
　LORD,
they will flourish in the
　courts of our God.
¹⁴They will still bear fruit in old
　age,　　　　　Jn 15:2

they will stay fresh and
　green,
¹⁵proclaiming, "The LORD is
　upright;
he is my Rock, and there is
　no wickedness in him."

Psalm 93

¹The LORD reigns, he is robed in
　majesty;　　　Ps 97:1; 104:1
the LORD is robed in majesty
and is armed with strength.
The world is firmly
　established;
it cannot be moved.　　Ps 96:10
²Your throne was established
　long ago;
you are from all eternity.

³The seas have lifted up,
　O LORD,　　　　Ps 96:11
the seas have lifted up their
　voice;
the seas have lifted up their
　pounding waves.
⁴Mightier than the thunder of
　the great waters,　　Ps 65:7
mightier than the breakers of
　the sea—
the LORD on high is mighty.

⁵Your statutes stand firm;
holiness adorns your house
　for endless days, O LORD.

Psalm 94

¹O LORD, the God who avenges,
　O God who avenges, shine
　forth.

a 10 Horn here symbolizes strength.

²Rise up, O Judge of the earth;
    pay back to the proud what
        they deserve.   Ps 31:23
³How long will the wicked,
        O Lord,
    how long will the wicked be
        jubilant?   Ps 13:2

⁴They pour out arrogant words;
    all the evildoers are full of
        boasting.
⁵They crush your people,
        O Lord;   Isa 3:15
    they oppress your
        inheritance.
⁶They slay the widow and the
        alien;
    they murder the fatherless.
⁷They say, "The Lord does not
        see;   Ps 10:11
    the God of Jacob pays no
        heed."

⁸Take heed, you senseless ones
    among the people;   Ps 92:6
    you fools, when will you
        become wise?
⁹Does he who implanted the ear
    not hear?
    Does he who formed the eye
        not see?   Ex 4:11
¹⁰Does he who disciplines
    nations not punish?
    Does he who teaches man
        lack knowledge?   Job 35:11
¹¹The Lord knows the thoughts
    of man;
    he knows that they are
        futile.   1Co 3:20*

¹²Blessed is the man you
    discipline, O Lord,

the man you teach from
    your law;
¹³you grant him relief from days
    of trouble,
    till a pit is dug for the
        wicked.   Ps 55:23
¹⁴For the Lord will not reject his
    people;   1Sa 12:22; Ro 11:2
    he will never forsake his
        inheritance.
¹⁵Judgment will again be
    founded on
    righteousness,   Ps 97:2
    and all the upright in heart
        will follow it.

¹⁶Who will rise up for me
    against the wicked?
    Who will take a stand for me
        against evildoers?   Ps 59:2
¹⁷Unless the Lord had given me
    help,   Ps 124:2
    I would soon have dwelt in
        the silence of death.
¹⁸When I said, "My foot is
    slipping,"   Ps 38:16
    your love, O Lord, supported
        me.
¹⁹When anxiety was great within
    me,   Ecc 11:10
    your consolation brought joy
        to my soul.

²⁰Can a corrupt throne be allied
    with you—
    one that brings on misery by
        its decrees?   Ps 58:2
²¹They band together against the
    righteous   Ps 56:6
    and condemn the innocent
        to death.   Pr 17:15,26

²²But the LORD has become my
    fortress,
and my God the rock in
    whom I take refuge.
²³He will repay them for their
    sins   Ps 7:16
and destroy them for their
    wickedness;
the LORD our God will
    destroy them.

Psalm 95

¹Come, let us sing for joy to the
    LORD;   Ps 5:11
let us shout aloud to the
    Rock of our salvation.
²Let us come before him with
    thanksgiving   Mic 6:6
and extol him with music
    and song.   Ps 81:2; Eph 5:19

³For the LORD is the great God,
    the great King above all
    gods.   Ps 96:4
⁴In his hand are the depths of
    the earth,
and the mountain peaks
    belong to him.
⁵The sea is his, for he made it,
and his hands formed the
    dry land.   Ge 1:9; Ps 146:6

⁶Come, let us bow down in
    worship,   Php 2:10
let us kneel before the LORD
    our Maker;   Ps 100:3; 149:2
⁷for he is our God
and we are the people of his
    pasture,   Ps 79:13

the flock under his care.

Today, if you hear his voice,
8   do not harden your hearts as
        you did at Meribah,ᵃ
    as you did that day at
        Massahᵇ in the desert,
⁹where your fathers tested and
        tried me,   Ps 78:18; 1Co 10:9
    though they had seen what I
        did.
¹⁰For forty years I was angry
        with that generation;
    I said, "They are a people
        whose hearts go astray,
    and they have not known
        my ways."   Dt 8:6
¹¹So I declared on oath in my
        anger,
    "They shall never enter my
        rest."   Heb 4:3*

Psalm 96

¹Sing to the LORD a new song;
    sing to the LORD, all the
        earth.
²Sing to the LORD, praise his
        name;
    proclaim his salvation day
        after day.   Ps 71:15
³Declare his glory among the
        nations,   Ps 8:1
    his marvelous deeds among
        all peoples.   Ps 71:17

⁴For great is the LORD and most
        worthy of praise;   Ps 18:3
    he is to be feared above all
        gods.   Ps 95:3

ᵃ8 Meribah means quarreling.   ᵇ8 Massah means testing.

⁵For all the gods of the nations
 are idols,
 but the Lord made the
  heavens.   Ps 115:15
⁶Splendor and majesty are
 before him;
 strength and glory are in his
  sanctuary.   Ps 29:1

⁷Ascribe to the Lord, O families
 of nations,   Ps 29:1
 ascribe to the Lord glory and
  strength.
⁸Ascribe to the Lord the glory
 due his name;
 bring an offering and come
  into his courts.   Ps 45:12
⁹Worship the Lord in the
 splendor of his[a]
 holiness;   Ps 29:2
 tremble before him, all the
  earth.

¹⁰Say among the nations, "The
 Lord reigns."   Ps 97:1
 The world is firmly
  established, it cannot be
  moved;   Ps 93:1
 he will judge the peoples
  with equity.   Ps 67:4
¹¹Let the heavens rejoice, let the
 earth be glad;
 let the sea resound, and all
  that is in it;
¹² let the fields be jubilant, and
  everything in them.
 Then all the trees of the forest
  will sing for joy;   Ps 65:13
¹³ they will sing before the
  Lord, for he comes,

he comes to judge the earth.
He will judge the world in
 righteousness
and the peoples in his truth.

Psalm 97

¹The Lord reigns, let the earth
 be glad;   Ps 96:10
 let the distant shores rejoice.

²Clouds and thick darkness
 surround him;   Ps 18:11
 righteousness and justice are
  the foundation of his
  throne.   Ps 89:14
³Fire goes before him
 and consumes his foes on
  every side.   Ps 18:8
⁴His lightning lights up the
 world;
 the earth sees and trembles.
⁵The mountains melt like wax
 before the Lord,   Mic 1:4
 before the Lord of all the
  earth.
⁶The heavens proclaim his
 righteousness,   Ps 50:6
 and all the peoples see his
  glory.   Ps 19:1

⁷All who worship images are
 put to shame,
 those who boast in idols—
 worship him, all you gods!

⁸Zion hears and rejoices
 and the villages of Judah are
  glad
 because of your judgments,
  O Lord.   Ps 48:11

[a] 9 Or Lord with the splendor of

[9] For you, O L ORD, are the Most
        High over all the earth;
    you are exalted far above all
        gods.   Ex 18:11

[10] Let those who love the L ORD
        hate evil,   Ps 34:14; Am 5:15
    for he guards the lives of his
        faithful ones
    and delivers them from the
        hand of the wicked.
[11] Light is shed upon the
        righteous   Job 22:28
    and joy on the upright in
        heart.
[12] Rejoice in the L ORD, you who
        are righteous,
    and praise his holy name.

Psalm 98

A psalm.

[1] Sing to the L ORD a new song,
    for he has done marvelous
        things;
    his right hand and his holy
        arm   Ex 15:6; Isa 52:10
    have worked salvation for
        him.
[2] The L ORD has made his
        salvation known   Isa 52:10
    and revealed his
        righteousness to the
        nations.
[3] He has remembered his love
    and his faithfulness to the
        house of Israel;
    all the ends of the earth have
        seen
    the salvation of our
        God.

[4] Shout for joy to the L ORD, all
        the earth,   Isa 44:23
    burst into jubilant song with
        music;
[5] make music to the L ORD with
        the harp,   Ps 92:3
    with the harp and the sound
        of singing,
[6] with trumpets and the blast of
        the ram's horn—   Nu 10:10
    shout for joy before the
        L ORD, the King.   Ps 47:7
[7] Let the sea resound, and
        everything in it,
    the world, and all who live
        in it.   Ps 24:1
[8] Let the rivers clap their hands,
    let the mountains sing
        together for joy;   Isa 55:12
[9] let them sing before the
        L ORD,
    for he comes to judge the
        earth.
    He will judge the world in
        righteousness
    and the peoples with equity.

Psalm 99

[1] The L ORD reigns,   Ps 97:1
    let the nations tremble;
    he sits enthroned between the
        cherubim,   Ex 25:22
    let the earth shake.
[2] Great is the L ORD in Zion;
    he is exalted over all the
        nations.   Ps 97:9
[3] Let them praise your great and
        awesome name—   Ps 76:1
    he is holy.

⁴The King is mighty, he loves
        justice—   Ps 11:7
you have established equity;
in Jacob you have done
what is just and right.
⁵Exalt the LORD our God   Ps 132:7
    and worship at his footstool;
he is holy.

⁶Moses and Aaron were among
        his priests,
    Samuel was among those
        who called on his name;
they called on the LORD
    and he answered them.
⁷He spoke to them from the
        pillar of cloud;   Ex 33:9
    they kept his statutes and
        the decrees he gave
        them.

⁸O LORD our God,
    you answered them;
you were to Israel*a* a forgiving
        God,   Nu 14:20
    though you punished their
        misdeeds.*b*
⁹Exalt the LORD our God
    and worship at his holy
        mountain,
    for the LORD our God is holy.

Psalm 100

A psalm. For giving thanks.

¹Shout for joy to the LORD, all
        the earth.   Ps 98:4
² Worship the LORD with
        gladness;

come before him with joyful
        songs.   Ps 95:2
³Know that the LORD is God.
    It is he who made us, and
        we are his*c*;
    we are his people, the sheep
        of his pasture.   Ps 74:1
⁴Enter his gates with
        thanksgiving
    and his courts with praise;
    give thanks to him and
        praise his name.   Ps 116:17
⁵For the LORD is good and his
        love endures forever;
    his faithfulness continues
        through all generations.

Psalm 101

Of David. A psalm.

¹I will sing of your love and
        justice;   Ps 89:1
    to you, O LORD, I will sing
        praise.
²I will be careful to lead a
        blameless life—   Ge 17:1
    when will you come to me?

I will walk in my house
    with blameless heart.
³I will set before my eyes
    no vile thing.   Dt 15:9

The deeds of faithless men I
        hate;   Ps 40:4
    they will not cling to me.
⁴Men of perverse heart shall be
        far from me;   Pr 11:20
    I will have nothing to do
        with evil.

---

*a*8 Hebrew *them*   *b*8 Or / *an avenger of the wrongs done to them*   *c*3 Or *and not we ourselves*

⁵Whoever slanders his neighbor
      in secret,   Ps 50:20
   him will I put to silence;
   whoever has haughty eyes and
      a proud heart,   Pr 6:17
   him will I not endure.

⁶My eyes will be on the faithful
      in the land,
   that they may dwell with
      me;
   he whose walk is blameless
      will minister to me.

⁷No one who practices deceit
      will dwell in my house;
   no one who speaks falsely
      will stand in my presence.

⁸Every morning I will put to
      silence   Jer 21:12
   all the wicked in the land;
   I will cut off every evildoer
      from the city of the LORD.

Psalm 102

A prayer of an afflicted man. When
he is faint and pours out his lament
before the LORD.

¹Hear my prayer, O LORD;
   let my cry for help come to
      you.   Ex 2:23
²Do not hide your face from me
   when I am in distress.
   Turn your ear to me;   2Ki 19:16
   when I call, answer me
      quickly.

³For my days vanish like
      smoke;   Jas 4:14
   my bones burn like glowing
      embers.

⁴My heart is blighted and
      withered like grass;
   I forget to eat my food.
⁵Because of my loud groaning
   I am reduced to skin and
      bones.
⁶I am like a desert owl,   Isa 34:11
   like an owl among the
      ruins.
⁷I lie awake; I have become
   like a bird alone on a roof.
⁸All day long my enemies taunt
      me;   Ps 42:10
   those who rail against me
      use my name as a curse.
⁹For I eat ashes as my food
   and mingle my drink with
      tears   Ps 42:3
¹⁰because of your great wrath,
   for you have taken me up
      and thrown me aside.
¹¹My days are like the evening
      shadow;   Job 14:2
   I wither away like grass.

¹²But you, O LORD, sit enthroned
      forever;   Ps 9:7
   your renown endures
      through all generations.
¹³You will arise and have
      compassion on Zion,
   for it is time to show favor
      to her;
   the appointed time has
      come.   Ex 13:10
¹⁴For her stones are dear to your
      servants;
   her very dust moves them to
      pity.
¹⁵The nations will fear the name
      of the LORD,   1Ki 8:43

all the kings of the earth will
  revere your glory.
¹⁶For the LORD will rebuild Zion
  and appear in his glory.
¹⁷He will respond to the prayer
  of the destitute;
  he will not despise their
  plea.

¹⁸Let this be written for a future
  generation,   Ro 15:4
  that a people not yet created
  may praise the LORD:
¹⁹"The LORD looked down from
  his sanctuary on high,
  from heaven he viewed the
  earth,
²⁰to hear the groans of the
  prisoners
  and release those
  condemned to death."
²¹So the name of the LORD will
  be declared in Zion
  and his praise in Jerusalem
²²when the peoples and the
  kingdoms
  assemble to worship the
  LORD.   Ps 22:27

²³In the course of my life[a] he
  broke my strength;
  he cut short my days.   Ps 39:5
²⁴So I said:
  "Do not take me away, O my
  God, in the midst of my
  days;
  your years go on through all
  generations.   Ps 90:2
²⁵In the beginning you laid the
  foundations of the earth,

and the heavens are the
  work of your hands.
²⁶They will perish, but you
  remain;   Isa 34:4
  they will all wear out like a
  garment.
  Like clothing you will change
  them
  and they will be discarded.
²⁷But you remain the same,
  and your years will never
  end.
²⁸The children of your servants
  will live in your
  presence;   Ps 69:36
  their descendants will be
  established before you."

Psalm 103

Of David.

¹Praise the LORD, O my soul;
  all my inmost being, praise
  his holy name.   Ps 30:4
²Praise the LORD, O my soul,
  and forget not all his
  benefits—
³who forgives all your sins
  and heals all your diseases,
⁴who redeems your life from
  the pit   Ps 34:22
  and crowns you with love
  and compassion,   Ps 8:5
⁵who satisfies your desires with
  good things   Ps 90:14
  so that your youth is
  renewed like the eagle's.

^a 23 Or By his power

⁶The LORD works righteousness
and justice for all the
oppressed.   Ps 74:21

⁷He made known his ways to
Moses,   Ex 33:13
his deeds to the people of
Israel: Ps 106:22
⁸The LORD is compassionate and
gracious,   Ex 34:6; Ps 86:15
slow to anger, abounding in
love.
⁹He will not always accuse,
nor will he harbor his anger
forever;   Ps 30:5
¹⁰he does not treat us as our sins
deserve   Ezr 9:13
or repay us according to our
iniquities.
¹¹For as high as the heavens are
above the earth,
so great is his love for those
who fear him;   Ps 57:10
¹²as far as the east is from the
west,
so far has he removed our
transgressions from us.
¹³As a father has compassion on
his children,   Mal 3:17
so the LORD has compassion
on those who fear him;
¹⁴for he knows how we are
formed,   Isa 29:16
he remembers that we are
dust.
¹⁵As for man, his days are like
grass,
he flourishes like a flower of
the field;   Job 14:2; 1Pe 1:24
¹⁶the wind blows over it and it is
gone,   Isa 40:7

and its place remembers it
no more.   Job 7:10
¹⁷But from everlasting to
everlasting
the LORD's love is with those
who fear him,
and his righteousness with
their children's
children—   Ge 48:11
¹⁸with those who keep his
covenant   Dt 29:9
and remember to obey his
precepts.   Dt 7:9

¹⁹The LORD has established his
throne in heaven,
and his kingdom rules over
all.   Ps 47:2
²⁰Praise the LORD, you his angels,
you mighty ones who do his
bidding,
who obey his word.
²¹Praise the LORD, all his
heavenly hosts,   1Ki 22:19
you his servants who do his
will.
²²Praise the LORD, all his works
everywhere in his dominion.

Praise the LORD, O my soul.

Psalm 104

¹Praise the LORD, O my soul.

O LORD my God, you are very
great;
you are clothed with
splendor and majesty.
²He wraps himself in light as
with a garment;   Da 7:9

he stretches out the heavens
  like a tent   Isa 40:22
3 and lays the beams of his
  upper chambers on their
  waters.   Am 9:6
He makes the clouds his
  chariot   Isa 19:1
and rides on the wings of
  the wind.   Ps 18:10
⁴He makes winds his
  messengers,ª   Heb 1:7*
flames of fire his servants.

⁵He set the earth on its
  foundations;   Job 26:7
it can never be moved.
⁶You covered it with the deep
  as with a garment; Ge 1:2
the waters stood above the
  mountains.
⁷But at your rebuke the waters
  fled,   Ps 18:15
at the sound of your thunder
  they took to flight;
⁸they flowed over the
  mountains,
they went down into the
  valleys,
to the place you assigned for
  them.   Ps 33:7
⁹You set a boundary they
  cannot cross;
never again will they cover
  the earth.

¹⁰He makes springs pour water
  into the ravines;   Ps 107:33
it flows between the
  mountains.

¹¹They give water to all the
  beasts of the field;
the wild donkeys quench
  their thirst.   Ge 16:12
¹²The birds of the air nest by the
  waters;   Mt 8:20
they sing among the
  branches.
¹³He waters the mountains from
  his upper chambers;
the earth is satisfied by the
  fruit of his work.
¹⁴He makes grass grow for the
  cattle,   Job 38:27; Ps 147:8
and plants for man to
  cultivate—
bringing forth food from the
  earth: Ge 1:30; Job 28:5
¹⁵wine that gladdens the heart of
  man,   Jdg 9:13
oil to make his face shine,
and bread that sustains his
  heart.
¹⁶The trees of the Lord are well
  watered,
the cedars of Lebanon that
  he planted.   Ps 72:16
¹⁷There the birds make their
  nests;   ver 12
the stork has its home in the
  pine trees.
¹⁸The high mountains belong to
  the wild goats;
the crags are a refuge for the
  coneys.ᵇ   Pr 30:26

¹⁹The moon marks off the
  seasons,   Ge 1:14

ª4 Or *angels*   ᵇ18 That is, the hyrax or rock badger

and the sun knows when to
go down.
²⁰You bring darkness, it becomes
night,   Isa 45:7
and all the beasts of the
forest prowl.
²¹The lions roar for their
prey
and seek their food from
God.   Job 38:39
²²The sun rises, and they steal
away;
they return and lie down in
their dens.
²³Then man goes out to his
work,   Ge 3:19
to his labor until evening.

²⁴How many are your works,
O LORD!
In wisdom you made them
all;   Pr 3:19
the earth is full of your
creatures.
²⁵There is the sea, vast and
spacious,   Ps 69:34
teeming with creatures
beyond number—
living things both large and
small.
²⁶There the ships go to and fro,
and the leviathan, which you
formed to frolic there.

²⁷These all look to you
to give them their food at
the proper time.   Ps 136:25
²⁸When you give it to them,
they gather it up;
when you open your hand,

they are satisfied with good
things.   Ps 145:16
²⁹When you hide your face,
they are terrified;   Dt 31:17
when you take away their
breath,
they die and return to the
dust.   Job 34:14; Ecc 12:7
³⁰When you send your Spirit,
they are created,
and you renew the face of
the earth.

³¹May the glory of the LORD
endure forever;
may the LORD rejoice in his
works—   Ge 1:31
³²he who looks at the earth, and
it trembles,
who touches the mountains,
and they smoke.   Ps 144:5
³³I will sing to the LORD all my
life;   Ps 63:4
I will sing praise to my God
as long as I live.
³⁴May my meditation be pleasing
to him,   Ps 9:2
as I rejoice in the LORD.
³⁵But may sinners vanish from
the earth   Ps 37:38
and the wicked be no more.

Praise the LORD, O my soul.

Praise the LORD.ᵃ   Ps 105:45; 106:48

Psalm 105

¹Give thanks to the LORD, call
on his name;   1Ch 16:34

ᵃ35 Hebrew *Hallelu Yah*; in the Septuagint this line stands at the beginning of Psalm 105.

make known among the
    nations what he has
    done.
²Sing to him, sing praise to
    him;
  tell of all his wonderful
    acts.
³Glory in his holy name;
  let the hearts of those who
    seek the LORD rejoice.
⁴Look to the LORD and his
    strength;
  seek his face always.   Ps 27:8
⁵Remember the wonders he has
    done,   Ps 40:5
  his miracles, and the
    judgments he
    pronounced,   Ps 77:11
⁶O descendants of Abraham his
    servant,
  O sons of Jacob, his chosen
    ones.   Ps 106:5
⁷He is the LORD our God;
  his judgments are in all the
    earth.
⁸He remembers his covenant
    forever,   Lk 1:72
  the word he commanded, for
    a thousand generations,
⁹the covenant he made with
    Abraham,   Ge 17:2; 22:16-18
  the oath he swore to Isaac.
¹⁰He confirmed it to Jacob as a
    decree,   Ge 28:13-15
  to Israel as an everlasting
    covenant:
¹¹"To you I will give the land of
    Canaan   Ge 13:15; 15:18
  as the portion you will
    inherit."   Nu 34:2

¹²When they were but few in
    number,   Ge 34:30; Dt 7:7
  few indeed, and strangers in
    it,   Heb 11:9
¹³they wandered from nation to
    nation,
  from one kingdom to
    another.
¹⁴He allowed no one to oppress
    them;   Ge 35:5
  for their sake he rebuked
    kings: Ge 12:17-20
¹⁵"Do not touch my anointed
    ones;
  do my prophets no harm."
¹⁶He called down famine on the
    land   Lev 26:26; Isa 3:1
  and destroyed all their
    supplies of food;
¹⁷and he sent a man before
    them—
  Joseph, sold as a slave.
¹⁸They bruised his feet with
    shackles,
  his neck was put in irons,
¹⁹till what he foretold came to
    pass,   Ge 40:20-22
  till the word of the LORD
    proved him true.
²⁰The king sent and released
    him,
  the ruler of peoples set him
    free.   Ge 41:14
²¹He made him master of his
    household,
  ruler over all he possessed,
²²to instruct his princes as he
    pleased   Ge 41:43-44
  and teach his elders
    wisdom.

²³Then Israel entered Egypt;
    Jacob lived as an alien in the
    land of Ham.
²⁴The Lord made his people very
    fruitful;
    he made them too numerous
    for their foes,   Ex 1:7,9
²⁵whose hearts he turned to hate
    his people,
    to conspire against his
    servants.
²⁶He sent Moses his servant,
    and Aaron, whom he had
    chosen.
²⁷They performed his miraculous
    signs among them,
    his wonders in the land of
    Ham.
²⁸He sent darkness and made the
    land dark—   Ex 10:22
    for had they not rebelled
    against his words?
²⁹He turned their waters into
    blood,
    causing their fish to die.
³⁰Their land teemed with frogs,
    which went up into the
    bedrooms of their rulers.
³¹He spoke, and there came
    swarms of flies,
    and gnats throughout their
    country.   Ex 8:16-18
³²He turned their rain into hail,
    with lightning throughout
    their land;
³³he struck down their vines and
    fig trees   Ps 78:47
    and shattered the trees of
    their country.
³⁴He spoke, and the locusts
    came,   Ex 10:4,12-15

grasshoppers without
    number;
³⁵they ate up every green thing
    in their land,
    ate up the produce of their
    soil.
³⁶Then he struck down all the
    firstborn in their land,
    the firstfruits of all their
    manhood.

³⁷He brought out Israel, laden
    with silver and gold,
    and from among their tribes
    no one faltered.
³⁸Egypt was glad when they left,
    because dread of Israel had
    fallen on them.   Ex 15:16
³⁹He spread out a cloud as a
    covering,   Ex 13:21
    and a fire to give light at
    night.
⁴⁰They asked, and he brought
    them quail   Ex 16:13
    and satisfied them with the
    bread of heaven.
⁴¹He opened the rock, and water
    gushed out;   1Co 10:4
    like a river it flowed in the
    desert.

⁴²For he remembered his holy
    promise   Ge 15:13-16
    given to his servant
    Abraham.
⁴³He brought out his people with
    rejoicing,   Ex 15:1-18; Ps 106:12
    his chosen ones with shouts
    of joy;
⁴⁴he gave them the lands of the
    nations,   Jos 13:6-7

and they fell heir to what
   others had toiled for—
45that they might keep his
   precepts
and observe his laws.   Dt 4:40

Praise the LORD.[a]   Ps 104:35

Psalm 106

1Praise the LORD.[b]   Ps 22:23

Give thanks to the LORD, for he
   is good;   Ps 100:5; 105:1
his love endures forever.
2Who can proclaim the mighty
   acts of the LORD
or fully declare his praise?
3Blessed are they who maintain
   justice,
who constantly do what is
   right.   Ps 15:2
4Remember me, O LORD, when
   you show favor to your
   people,   Ps 119:132
come to my aid when you
   save them,
5that I may enjoy the prosperity
   of your chosen ones,
that I may share in the joy
   of your nation   Ps 118:15
and join your inheritance in
   giving praise.

6We have sinned, even as our
   fathers did;   Da 9:5
we have done wrong and
   acted wickedly.
7When our fathers were in
   Egypt,

they gave no thought to your
   miracles;
they did not remember your
   many kindnesses,
and they rebelled by the sea,
   the Red Sea.[c]   Ex 14:11-12
8Yet he saved them for his
   name's sake,   Ex 9:16
to make his mighty power
   known.
9He rebuked the Red Sea, and it
   dried up;   Ex 14:21; Ps 18:15
he led them through the
   depths as through a
   desert.   Isa 63:11-14
10He saved them from the hand
   of the foe;   Ex 14:30
from the hand of the enemy
   he redeemed them.
11The waters covered their
   adversaries;   Ex 14:28; 15:5
not one of them survived.
12Then they believed his
   promises
and sang his praise.

13But they soon forgot what he
   had done   Ex 15:24
and did not wait for his
   counsel.
14In the desert they gave in to
   their craving;
in the wasteland they put
   God to the test.   1Co 10:9
15So he gave them what they
   asked for,   Nu 11:31
but sent a wasting disease
   upon them.   Isa 10:16

---

a45 Hebrew *Hallelu Yah*   b1 Hebrew *Hallelu Yah*; also in verse 48   c7 Hebrew *Yam Suph*; that is,
Sea of Reeds; also in verses 9 and 22

¹⁶In the camp they grew envious
    of Moses   Nu 16:1-3
  and of Aaron, who was
    consecrated to the Lord.
¹⁷The earth opened up and
    swallowed Dathan;
  it buried the company of
    Abiram.
¹⁸Fire blazed among their
    followers;
  a flame consumed the
    wicked.   Nu 16:35

¹⁹At Horeb they made a calf
  and worshiped an idol cast
    from metal.
²⁰They exchanged their Glory
  for an image of a bull, which
    eats grass.
²¹They forgot the God who saved
    them,   Ps 78:11
  who had done great things
    in Egypt,
²²miracles in the land of Ham
  and awesome deeds by the
    Red Sea.
²³So he said he would destroy
    them—   Ex 32:10
  had not Moses, his chosen
    one,
  stood in the breach before him
  to keep his wrath from
    destroying them.

²⁴Then they despised the
    pleasant land;   Dt 8:7
  they did not believe his
    promise.   Heb 3:18-19
²⁵They grumbled in their tents
  and did not obey the Lord.

²⁶So he swore to them with
    uplifted hand   Eze 20:15
  that he would make them
    fall in the desert,
²⁷make their descendants fall
    among the nations
  and scatter them throughout
    the lands.   Ps 44:11

²⁸They yoked themselves to the
    Baal of Peor   Nu 25:2-3
  and ate sacrifices offered to
    lifeless gods;
²⁹they provoked the Lord to
    anger by their wicked
    deeds,
  and a plague broke out
    among them.
³⁰But Phinehas stood up and
    intervened,
  and the plague was checked.
³¹This was credited to him as
    righteousness   Nu 25:11-13
  for endless generations to
    come.

³²By the waters of Meribah they
    angered the Lord,
  and trouble came to Moses
    because of them;
³³for they rebelled against the
    Spirit of God,   Ex 23:21
  and rash words came from
    Moses' lips.^a   Nu 20:8-12

³⁴They did not destroy the
    peoples   Jdg 1:21
  as the Lord had commanded
    them,   Dt 7:16

^a 33 Or *against his spirit, / and rash words came from his lips*

35but they mingled with the
    nations   Jdg 3:5-6
and adopted their customs.
36They worshiped their idols,
    which became a snare to
    them.
37They sacrificed their sons
    and their daughters to
    demons.
38They shed innocent blood,
    the blood of their sons and
    daughters,   Nu 35:33
whom they sacrificed to the
    idols of Canaan,
and the land was desecrated
    by their blood.
39They defiled themselves by
    what they did;   Eze 20:18
by their deeds they
    prostituted themselves.

40Therefore the LORD was angry
    with his people
and abhorred his inheritance.
41He handed them over to the
    nations,   Jdg 2:14; Ne 9:27
and their foes ruled over
    them.
42Their enemies oppressed them
    and subjected them to their
    power.
43Many times he delivered them,
    but they were bent on
    rebellion   Jdg 2:16-19
and they wasted away in
    their sin.

44But he took note of their
    distress
when he heard their cry;

45for their sake he remembered
    his covenant   Lev 26:42
and out of his great love he
    relented.   Jdg 2:18
46He caused them to be pitied
    by all who held them
    captive.

47Save us, O LORD our God,
    and gather us from the
    nations,   Ps 147:2
that we may give thanks to
    your holy name
and glory in your praise.

48Praise be to the LORD, the God
    of Israel,
    from everlasting to
    everlasting.
Let all the people say, "Amen!"

Praise the LORD.

BOOK V

Psalms 107–150

Psalm 107

1Give thanks to the LORD, for he
    is good;   Ps 106:1
his love endures forever.
2Let the redeemed of the LORD
    say this—   Ps 106:10
those he redeemed from the
    hand of the foe,
3those he gathered from the
    lands,   Ps 106:47
from east and west, from
    north and south.*ᵃ*

---

a 3 Hebrew *north and the sea*

⁴Some wandered in desert
    wastelands,   Nu 14:33; 32:13
finding no way to a city
    where they could settle.
⁵They were hungry and thirsty,
    and their lives ebbed away.
⁶Then they cried out to the
    LORD in their trouble,
and he delivered them from
    their distress.
⁷He led them by a straight way
    to a city where they could
    settle.
⁸Let them give thanks to the
    LORD for his unfailing
    love   Ps 6:4
and his wonderful deeds for
    men,   Ps 75:1
⁹for he satisfies the thirsty
    and fills the hungry with
    good things.   Ps 34:10

¹⁰Some sat in darkness and the
    deepest gloom,   Lk 1:79
    prisoners suffering in iron
    chains,   Job 36:8
¹¹for they had rebelled against
    the words of God
    and despised the counsel of
    the Most High.   2Ch 36:16
¹²So he subjected them to bitter
    labor;
    they stumbled, and there
    was no one to help.
¹³Then they cried to the LORD in
    their trouble,
    and he saved them from
    their distress.
¹⁴He brought them out of
    darkness and the
    deepest gloom

and broke away their chains.
¹⁵Let them give thanks to the
    LORD for his unfailing
    love   Ps 105:1
and his wonderful deeds for
    men,   Ps 75:1
¹⁶for he breaks down gates of
    bronze
    and cuts through bars of
    iron.
¹⁷Some became fools through
    their rebellious ways
    and suffered affliction
    because of their
    iniquities.   Isa 65:6-7; La 3:39
¹⁸They loathed all food
    and drew near the gates of
    death.   Ps 9:13
¹⁹Then they cried to the LORD in
    their trouble,
    and he saved them from
    their distress.
²⁰He sent forth his word and
    healed them;   Ps 103:3
    he rescued them from the
    grave.   Ps 30:3
²¹Let them give thanks to the
    LORD for his unfailing
    love
and his wonderful deeds for
    men.
²²Let them sacrifice thank
    offerings   Lev 7:12
    and tell of his works with
    songs of joy.   Ps 9:11; 73:28

²³Others went out on the sea in
    ships;
    they were merchants on the
    mighty waters.

²⁴They saw the works of the
  LORD,   Ps 64:9
his wonderful deeds in the
  deep.
²⁵For he spoke and stirred up a
  tempest   Jnh 1:4
that lifted high the waves.
²⁶They mounted up to the
  heavens and went down
  to the depths;
in their peril their courage
  melted away.   Ps 22:14
²⁷They reeled and staggered like
  drunken men;
they were at their wits'
  end.
²⁸Then they cried out to the
  LORD in their trouble,
and he brought them out of
  their distress.   Jnh 1:6
²⁹He stilled the storm to a
  whisper;   Mt 8:26
the waves of the sea were
  hushed.   Ps 89:9
³⁰They were glad when it grew
  calm,
and he guided them to their
  desired haven.
³¹Let them give thanks to the
  LORD for his unfailing
  love   Ps 6:4
and his wonderful deeds for
  men.
³²Let them exalt him in the
  assembly of the people
and praise him in the
  council of the elders.

³³He turned rivers into a desert,
  flowing springs into thirsty
  ground,

³⁴and fruitful land into a salt
  waste,   Ge 13:10
because of the wickedness of
  those who lived there.
³⁵He turned the desert into pools
  of water   Ps 114:8; Isa 41:18
and the parched ground into
  flowing springs;
³⁶there he brought the hungry to
  live,
and they founded a city
  where they could settle.
³⁷They sowed fields and planted
  vineyards   Isa 65:21
that yielded a fruitful
  harvest;
³⁸he blessed them, and their
  numbers greatly
  increased,   Ge 12:2
and he did not let their
  herds diminish.

³⁹Then their numbers decreased,
  and they were humbled
by oppression, calamity and
  sorrow;
⁴⁰he who pours contempt on
  nobles   Job 12:21
made them wander in a
  trackless waste.   Job 12:24
⁴¹But he lifted the needy out of
  their affliction   1Sa 2:8
and increased their families
  like flocks.
⁴²The upright see and rejoice,
  but all the wicked shut their
  mouths.   Job 5:16; Ro 3:19

⁴³Whoever is wise, let him heed
  these things   Jer 9:12
and consider the great love
  of the LORD.   Ps 64:9

Psalm 108

A song. A psalm of David.

¹My heart is steadfast, O God;
  I will sing and make music
    with all my soul.   Ps 18:49
²Awake, harp and lyre!   Job 21:12
  I will awaken the dawn.
³I will praise you, O Lᴏʀᴅ,
    among the nations;
  I will sing of you among the
    peoples.
⁴For great is your love, higher
    than the heavens;
  your faithfulness reaches to
    the skies.   Ps 36:5
⁵Be exalted, O God, above the
    heavens,   Ps 8:1
  and let your glory be over all
    the earth.   Ps 57:5

⁶Save us and help us with your
    right hand,   Job 40:14
  that those you love may be
    delivered.
⁷God has spoken from his
    sanctuary: Ps 68:35
  "In triumph I will parcel out
    Shechem   Ge 12:6
  and measure off the Valley
    of Succoth.   Ge 33:17
⁸Gilead is mine, Manasseh is
    mine;
  Ephraim is my helmet,
  Judah my scepter.   Ge 49:10
⁹Moab is my washbasin,
  upon Edom I toss my
    sandal;
  over Philistia I shout in
    triumph."   2Sa 8:1

¹⁰Who will bring me to the
    fortified city?
  Who will lead me to Edom?
¹¹Is it not you, O God, you who
    have rejected us
  and no longer go out with
    our armies?   Ps 44:9
¹²Give us aid against the enemy,
  for the help of man is
    worthless.   Ps 118:8
¹³With God we will gain the
    victory,
  and he will trample down
    our enemies.   Ps 44:5

Psalm 109

For the director of music. Of David.
A psalm.

¹O God, whom I praise,
  do not remain silent,   Ps 83:1
²for wicked and deceitful men
  have opened their mouths
    against me;
  they have spoken against me
    with lying tongues.
³With words of hatred they
    surround me;   Ps 69:4
  they attack me without
    cause.
⁴In return for my friendship
    they accuse me,
  but I am a man of prayer.
⁵They repay me evil for good,
  and hatred for my
    friendship.

⁶Appoint ᵃ an evil man ᵇ to
    oppose him;

ᵃ6 Or ˌThey say:ˌ "Appoint (with quotation marks at the end of verse 19)   ᵇ6 Or the Evil One

let an accuser[a] stand at his
  right hand.   Zec 3:1
[7]When he is tried, let him be
  found guilty,
  and may his prayers
    condemn him.   Pr 28:9
[8]May his days be few;
  may another take his place
    of leadership.   Ac 1:20*
[9]May his children be fatherless
  and his wife a widow. Ex 22:24
[10]May his children be wandering
    beggars;
  may they be driven[b] from
    their ruined homes.
[11]May a creditor seize all he has;
  may strangers plunder the
    fruits of his labor.   Job 5:5
[12]May no one extend kindness to
    him
  or take pity on his fatherless
    children.
[13]May his descendants be cut
    off,
                              Ps 37:28
  their names blotted out from
    the next generation.
[14]May the iniquity of his fathers
    be remembered before
    the Lord;   Ex 20:5; Ne 4:5
  may the sin of his mother
    never be blotted out.
[15]May their sins always remain
    before the Lord,
  that he may cut off the
    memory of them from
    the earth.   Ps 34:16

[16]For he never thought of doing
    a kindness,

but hounded to death the
  poor
and the needy and the
    brokenhearted.   Ps 34:18
[17]He loved to pronounce a
    curse—
  may it[c] come on him;   Pr 14:14
  he found no pleasure in
    blessing—
  may it be[d] far from him.
[18]He wore cursing as his
    garment;
  it entered into his body like
    water,   Nu 5:22
  into his bones like oil.
[19]May it be like a cloak wrapped
    about him,
  like a belt tied forever
    around him.
[20]May this be the Lord's
    payment to my accusers,
  to those who speak evil of
    me.   Ps 71:10

[21]But you, O Sovereign Lord,
  deal well with me for your
    name's sake;   Ps 79:9
  out of the goodness of your
    love, deliver me.   Ps 69:16
[22]For I am poor and needy,
  and my heart is wounded
    within me.
[23]I fade away like an evening
    shadow;   Ps 102:11
  I am shaken off like a
    locust.
[24]My knees give way from
    fasting;   Heb 12:12
  my body is thin and gaunt.

---

[a]6 Or *let Satan*   [b]10 Septuagint; Hebrew *sought*   [c]17 Or *curse, / and it has*   [d]17 Or *blessing, /*
and it is

²⁵I am an object of scorn to my
	accusers; Ps 22:6
when they see me, they
	shake their heads.

²⁶Help me, O LORD my God;
	save me in accordance with
	your love.
²⁷Let them know that it is your
	hand, Job 37:7
	that you, O LORD, have done
	it.
²⁸They may curse, but you will
	bless; 2Sa 16:12
	when they attack they will
	be put to shame,
	but your servant will rejoice.
²⁹My accusers will be clothed
	with disgrace
	and wrapped in shame as in
	a cloak. Ps 35:26

³⁰With my mouth I will greatly
	extol the LORD;
	in the great throng I will
	praise him.
³¹For he stands at the right hand
	of the needy one, Ps 16:8
	to save his life from those
	who condemn him.

Psalm 110

Of David. A psalm.

¹The LORD says to my Lord:
	"Sit at my right hand
until I make your enemies
	a footstool for your feet."

²The LORD will extend your
	mighty scepter from
	Zion; Ps 45:6
you will rule in the midst of
	your enemies.
³Your troops will be willing
	on your day of battle.
Arrayed in holy majesty,   Jdg 5:2
	from the womb of the dawn
	you will receive the dew of
	your youth.ᵃ Mic 5:7

⁴The LORD has sworn
	and will not change his
	mind: Nu 23:19
"You are a priest forever,
	in the order of Melchizedek."

⁵The Lord is at your right
	hand;
	he will crush kings on the
	day of his wrath. Ps 2:5,12
⁶He will judge the nations,
	heaping up the dead
and crushing the rulers of
	the whole earth. Ps 68:21
⁷He will drink from a brook
	beside the wayᵇ;
	therefore he will lift up his
	head. Ps 27:6

Psalm 111ᶜ

¹Praise the LORD.ᵈ

I will extol the LORD with all
	my heart Ps 34:1
	in the council of the upright
	and in the assembly.

ᵃ3 Or / your young men will come to you like the dew   ᵇ7 Or / The One who grants succession will
set him in authority   ᶜThis psalm is an acrostic poem, the lines of which begin with the successive
letters of the Hebrew alphabet.   ᵈ1 Hebrew Hallelu Yah

²Great are the works of the
  LORD;   Ps 92:5
  they are pondered by all
    who delight in them.
³Glorious and majestic are his
    deeds,
  and his righteousness
    endures forever.   Ps 112:3,9
⁴He has caused his wonders to
    be remembered;
  the LORD is gracious and
    compassionate.   Ps 103:8
⁵He provides food for those
    who fear him;   Mt 6:26,31-33
  he remembers his covenant
    forever.
⁶He has shown his people the
    power of his works,
  giving them the lands of
    other nations.   Ps 105:44
⁷The works of his hands are
    faithful and just;
  all his precepts are
    trustworthy.   Ps 19:7
⁸They are steadfast for ever and
    ever,
  done in faithfulness and
    uprightness.
⁹He provided redemption for his
    people;   Lk 1:68
  he ordained his covenant
    forever—
  holy and awesome is his
    name.   Ps 99:3

¹⁰The fear of the LORD is the
    beginning of wisdom;

all who follow his precepts
  have good
    understanding.   Ecc 12:13
To him belongs eternal
    praise.   Ps 145:2

Psalm 112ᵃ

¹Praise the LORD.ᵇ   Ps 33:2
Blessed is the man who fears
    the LORD,   Ps 128:1
  who finds great delight in
    his commands.

²His children will be mighty in
    the land;   Ps 25:13
  the generation of the upright
    will be blessed.
³Wealth and riches are in his
    house,   Dt 8:18
  and his righteousness
    endures forever.   Ps 37:6
⁴Even in darkness light dawns
    for the upright,   Job 11:17
  for the gracious and
    compassionate and
    righteous man.ᶜ   Ps 97:11
⁵Good will come to him who is
    generous and lends
    freely,   Ps 37:21,26
  who conducts his affairs
    with justice.
⁶Surely he will never be shaken;
  a righteous man will be
    remembered forever.
⁷He will have no fear of bad
    news;
  his heart is steadfast,
    trusting in the LORD.

ᵃThis psalm is an acrostic poem, the lines of which begin with the successive letters of the Hebrew
alphabet.   ᵇ1 Hebrew *Hallelu Yah*   ᶜ4 Or / *for the LORD, is gracious and compassionate and*
righteous

8His heart is secure, he will
    have no fear;
in the end he will look in
    triumph on his foes.
9He has scattered abroad his
    gifts to the poor,   2Co 9:9
his righteousness endures
    forever;
his horn*a* will be lifted high
    in honor.   Ps 75:10

10The wicked man will see and
    be vexed,
he will gnash his teeth and
    waste away;   Ps 37:12
the longings of the wicked
    will come to nothing.

Psalm 113

1Praise the LORD.*b*

Praise, O servants of the LORD,
    praise the name of the LORD.
2Let the name of the LORD be
    praised,
both now and forevermore.
3From the rising of the sun to
    the place where it sets,
the name of the LORD is to
    be praised.

4The LORD is exalted over all the
    nations,   Ps 99:2
his glory above the heavens.
5Who is like the LORD our God,
    the One who sits enthroned
    on high,
6who stoops down to look
    on the heavens and the
    earth?

7He raises the poor from the
    dust   1Sa 2:8
and lifts the needy from the
    ash heap;   Ps 107:41
8he seats them with princes,
    with the princes of their
    people.
9He settles the barren woman in
    her home   1Sa 2:5
as a happy mother of
    children.

Praise the LORD.

Psalm 114

1When Israel came out of Egypt,
    the house of Jacob from a
    people of foreign
    tongue,
2Judah became God's sanctuary,
    Israel his dominion.

3The sea looked and fled,
    the Jordan turned back;
4the mountains skipped like
    rams,
    the hills like lambs.

5Why was it, O sea, that you
    fled,   Ex 14:21
O Jordan, that you turned
    back,
6you mountains, that you
    skipped like rams,
you hills, like lambs?

7Tremble, O earth, at the
    presence of the Lord,
at the presence of the God of
    Jacob,

---

*a*9 *Horn* here symbolizes dignity.   *b*1 Hebrew *Hallelu Yah*; also in verse 9

8who turned the rock into a
    pool,
    the hard rock into springs of
    water.   Ex 17:6; Nu 20:11

Psalm 115

1Not to us, O LORD, not to us
    but to your name be the
        glory,   Ps 96:8
    because of your love and
        faithfulness.   Ex 34:6

2Why do the nations say,
    "Where is their God?"   Ps 42:3
3Our God is in heaven;   Ps 103:19
    he does whatever pleases
        him.   Ps 135:6
4But their idols are silver and
        gold,
    made by the hands of men.
5They have mouths, but cannot
        speak,   Jer 10:5
    eyes, but they cannot see;
6they have ears, but cannot
        hear,
    noses, but they cannot
        smell;
7they have hands, but cannot
        feel,
    feet, but they cannot walk;
    nor can they utter a sound
        with their throats.
8Those who make them will be
        like them,
    and so will all who trust in
        them.

9O house of Israel, trust in the
    LORD—   Ps 37:3

    he is their help and shield.
10O house of Aaron, trust in the
    LORD—   Ps 118:3
    he is their help and shield.
11You who fear him, trust in the
    LORD—   Ps 22:23
    he is their help and shield.

12The LORD remembers us and
        will bless us:
    He will bless the house of
        Israel,
    he will bless the house of
        Aaron,
13he will bless those who fear
        the LORD—   Ps 128:1,4
    small and great alike.

14May the LORD make you
        increase,
    both you and your
        children.
15May you be blessed by the
        LORD,
    the Maker of heaven and
        earth.   Ps 96:5

16The highest heavens belong to
        the LORD,   Ps 89:11
    but the earth he has given to
        man.
17It is not the dead who praise
        the LORD,   Ps 6:5
    those who go down to
        silence;
18it is we who extol the LORD,
    both now and forevermore.

Praise the LORD.a   Ps 28:6

a 18 Hebrew Hallelu Yah

Psalm 116

[1]I love the LORD, for he heard
    my voice;   *Ps 18:1*
he heard my cry for mercy.
[2]Because he turned his ear to
    me,   *Ps 40:1*
I will call on him as long as
    I live.

[3]The cords of death entangled
    me,   *Ps 18:4-5*
the anguish of the grave[a]
    came upon me;
I was overcome by trouble
    and sorrow.
[4]Then I called on the name of
    the LORD: *Ps 118:5*
"O LORD, save me!"   *Ps 22:20*

[5]The LORD is gracious and
    righteous;   *Ezr 9:15; Ps 103:8*
our God is full of
    compassion.
[6]The LORD protects the
    simplehearted;
when I was in great need, he
    saved me.   *Ps 19:7; 79:8*

[7]Be at rest once more, O my
    soul,   *Mt 11:29*
for the LORD has been good
    to you.   *Ps 13:6*

[8]For you, O LORD, have
    delivered my soul from
    death,   *Ps 56:13*
my eyes from tears,
my feet from stumbling,
[9]that I may walk before the
    LORD

in the land of the living.
[10]I believed; therefore[b] I said,
    "I am greatly afflicted."
[11]And in my dismay I said,
    "All men are liars."   *Ro 3:4*

[12]How can I repay the LORD
    for all his goodness to me?
[13]I will lift up the cup of
    salvation
and call on the name of the
    LORD.
[14]I will fulfill my vows to the
    LORD   *Ps 22:25*
in the presence of all his
    people.

[15]Precious in the sight of the
    LORD   *Ps 72:14*
is the death of his saints.
[16]O LORD, truly I am your
    servant;   *Ps 119:125; 143:12*
I am your servant, the son of
    your maidservant[c];
you have freed me from my
    chains.

[17]I will sacrifice a thank offering
    to you   *Ps 50:14*
and call on the name of the
    LORD.
[18]I will fulfill my vows to the
    LORD
in the presence of all his
    people,
[19]in the courts of the house of
    the LORD —   *Ps 96:8*
in your midst, O Jerusalem.

Praise the LORD.[d]

---

[a]3 Hebrew *Sheol*   [b]10 Or *believed even when*   [c]16 Or *servant, your faithful son*   [d]19 Hebrew *Hallelu Yah*

Psalm 117

[1]Praise the LORD, all you
    nations;   Ro 15:11*
extol him, all you peoples.
[2]For great is his love toward us,
    and the faithfulness of the
    LORD endures forever.

Praise the LORD.[a]

Psalm 118

[1]Give thanks to the LORD, for he
    is good;   1Ch 16:8
his love endures forever.

[2]Let Israel say: Ps 115:9
    "His love endures forever."
[3]Let the house of Aaron say:
    "His love endures forever."
[4]Let those who fear the LORD
    say: Ps 115:11
    "His love endures forever."

[5]In my anguish I cried to the
    LORD,   Ps 120:1
    and he answered by setting
    me free.
[6]The LORD is with me; I will not
    be afraid.   Heb 13:6*
    What can man do to me?
[7]The LORD is with me; he is my
    helper.
    I will look in triumph on my
    enemies.   Ps 59:10

[8]It is better to take refuge in the
    LORD
    than to trust in man.   Ps 40:4
[9]It is better to take refuge in the
    LORD
    than to trust in princes.

[10]All the nations surrounded me,
    but in the name of the LORD
    I cut them off.
[11]They surrounded me on every
    side,   Ps 3:6; 88:17
    but in the name of the LORD
    I cut them off.
[12]They swarmed around me like
    bees,   Dt 1:44
    but they died out as quickly
    as burning thorns;
    in the name of the LORD I
    cut them off.

[13]I was pushed back and about
    to fall,
    but the LORD helped me.
[14]The LORD is my strength and
    my song;   Ex 15:2
    he has become my salvation.

[15]Shouts of joy and victory
    resound in the tents of the
    righteous:
    "The LORD's right hand has
    done mighty things!
[16]   The LORD's right hand is
    lifted high;
    the LORD's right hand has
    done mighty things!"

[17]I will not die but live,   Hab 1:12
    and will proclaim what the
    LORD has done.   Ps 73:28
[18]The LORD has chastened me
    severely,
    but he has not given me
    over to death.   2Co 6:9

¹⁹Open for me the gates of
    righteousness;   Isa 26:2
  I will enter and give thanks
    to the Lord.
²⁰This is the gate of the Lord
    through which the righteous
    may enter.   Rev 22:14
²¹I will give you thanks, for you
    answered me;   Ps 116:1
  you have become my
    salvation.

²²The stone the builders rejected
    has become the capstone;
²³the Lord has done this,
    and it is marvelous in our
    eyes.   Mt 21:42*
²⁴This is the day the Lord has
    made;
  let us rejoice and be glad in
    it.   Ps 70:4

²⁵O Lord, save us;
  O Lord, grant us success.
²⁶Blessed is he who comes in the
    name of the Lord.
  From the house of the Lord
    we bless you.^a
²⁷The Lord is God,
    and he has made his light
    shine upon us.   1Pe 2:9
  With boughs in hand, join in
    the festal procession
  up^b to the horns of the altar.

²⁸You are my God, and I will
    give you thanks;
  you are my God, and I will
    exalt you.   Ex 15:2; Isa 25:1

²⁹Give thanks to the Lord, for he
    is good;
  his love endures forever.

Psalm 119^c

א Aleph

¹Blessed are they whose ways
    are blameless,   Ge 17:1
  who walk according to the
    law of the Lord.   Ps 128:1
²Blessed are they who keep his
    statutes
  and seek him with all their
    heart.   Dt 6:5
³They do nothing wrong;   Jn 3:9
  they walk in his ways.
⁴You have laid down precepts
    that are to be fully obeyed.
⁵Oh, that my ways were
    steadfast
  in obeying your decrees!
⁶Then I would not be put to
    shame
  when I consider all your
    commands.   ver 117
⁷I will praise you with an
    upright heart
  as I learn your righteous
    laws.   Dt 4:8
⁸I will obey your decrees;
  do not utterly forsake me.

ב Beth

⁹How can a young man keep
    his way pure?   Ps 39:1
  By living according to your
    word.   2Ch 6:16

---

^a26 The Hebrew is plural.   ^b27 Or *Bind the festal sacrifice with ropes / and take it*   ^cThis psalm is
an acrostic poem; the verses of each stanza begin with the same letter of the Hebrew alphabet.

¹⁰I seek you with all my heart;
    do not let me stray from
        your commands.
¹¹I have hidden your word in my
    heart   Ps 37:31; Lk 2:19,51
    that I might not sin against
        you.
¹²Praise be to you, O LORD;
    teach me your decrees.
¹³With my lips I recount
    all the laws that come from
        your mouth.   Ps 40:9
¹⁴I rejoice in following your
    statutes
    as one rejoices in great
        riches.
¹⁵I meditate on your precepts
    and consider your ways.
¹⁶I delight in your decrees;   Ps 1:2
    I will not neglect your word.

ג   Gimel

¹⁷Do good to your servant, and I
    will live;   Ps 13:6; 116:7
    I will obey your word.
¹⁸Open my eyes that I may see
    wonderful things in your
        law.
¹⁹I am a stranger on earth;
    do not hide your commands
        from me.
²⁰My soul is consumed with
    longing   Ps 42:2; 84:2
    for your laws at all times.
²¹You rebuke the arrogant, who
    are cursed   Job 30:1; Ps 5:5
    and who stray from your
        commands.   ver 10
²²Remove from me scorn and
    contempt,   Ps 39:8
    for I keep your statutes.

²³Though rulers sit together and
    slander me,
    your servant will meditate
        on your decrees.
²⁴Your statutes are my delight;
    they are my counselors.

ד   Daleth

²⁵I am laid low in the dust;
    preserve my life according to
        your word.   Ps 143:11
²⁶I recounted my ways and you
    answered me;
    teach me your decrees.
²⁷Let me understand the
    teaching of your
        precepts;
    then I will meditate on your
        wonders.   Ps 145:5
²⁸My soul is weary with sorrow;
    strengthen me according to
        your word.   Ps 20:2; 1Pe 5:10
²⁹Keep me from deceitful ways;
    be gracious to me through
        your law.   Nu 6:25
³⁰I have chosen the way of truth;
    I have set my heart on your
        laws.   Ps 108:1
³¹I hold fast to your statutes,
        O LORD;   Dt 10:20; 11:22
    do not let me be put to
        shame.
³²I run in the path of your
    commands,
    for you have set my heart
        free.

ה   He

³³Teach me, O LORD, to follow
    your decrees;   ver 12

then I will keep them to the
    end.
³⁴Give me understanding, and I
    will keep your law   Dt 6:25
and obey it with all my
    heart.
³⁵Direct me in the path of your
    commands,
for there I find delight.   Ps 1:2
³⁶Turn my heart toward your
    statutes
and not toward selfish gain.
³⁷Turn my eyes away from
    worthless things;
preserve my life according to
    your word.ᵃ   Ps 71:20
³⁸Fulfill your promise to your
    servant,   2Sa 7:25
so that you may be feared.
³⁹Take away the disgrace I
    dread,   Ps 69:9
for your laws are good.
⁴⁰How I long for your precepts!
Preserve my life in your
    righteousness.

ו   Waw

⁴¹May your unfailing love come
    to me, O LORD,   Ps 6:4
your salvation according to
    your promise;
⁴²then I will answer the one who
    taunts me,   Pr 27:11
for I trust in your word.
⁴³Do not snatch the word of
    truth from my mouth,
for I have put my hope in
    your laws.   ver 74,81,114,147

⁴⁴I will always obey your law,
    for ever and ever.
⁴⁵I will walk about in freedom,
    for I have sought out your
    precepts.   ver 94,155
⁴⁶I will speak of your statutes
    before kings   Mt 10:18
and will not be put to
    shame,
⁴⁷for I delight in your commands
    because I love them.
⁴⁸I lift up my hands toᵇ your
    commands, which I
    love,
and I meditate on your
    decrees.   Ge 24:63

ז   Zayin

⁴⁹Remember your word to your
    servant,
for you have given me hope.
⁵⁰My comfort in my suffering is
    this:
Your promise preserves my
    life.   Ro 15:4
⁵¹The arrogant mock me without
    restraint,   Jer 20:7
but I do not turn from your
    law.   Job 23:11
⁵²I remember your ancient laws,
    O LORD,   Ps 103:18
and I find comfort in them.
⁵³Indignation grips me because
    of the wicked,   Ezr 9:3
who have forsaken your law.
⁵⁴Your decrees are the theme of
    my song
wherever I lodge.

ᵃ37 Two manuscripts of the Masoretic Text and Dead Sea Scrolls; most manuscripts of the Masoretic
Text *life in your way*   ᵇ48 Or *for*

⁵⁵In the night I remember your
      name, O LORD,   Ps 63:6
   and I will keep your law.
⁵⁶This has been my practice:
   I obey your precepts.   Nu 15:40

ח Heth

⁵⁷You are my portion, O LORD;
   I have promised to obey
      your words.
⁵⁸I have sought your face with
      all my heart;
   be gracious to me according
      to your promise.   1Ki 13:6
⁵⁹I have considered my ways
   and have turned my steps to
      your statutes.
⁶⁰I will hasten and not delay
   to obey your commands.
⁶¹Though the wicked bind me
      with ropes,
   I will not forget your law.
⁶²At midnight I rise to give you
      thanks   Ac 16:25
   for your righteous laws.
⁶³I am a friend to all who fear
      you,   Ps 101:6-7
   to all who follow your
      precepts.
⁶⁴The earth is filled with your
      love, O LORD;   Ps 33:5
   teach me your decrees.

ט Teth

⁶⁵Do good to your servant
   according to your word,
      O LORD.   Ps 125:4; Mic 2:7
⁶⁶Teach me knowledge and good
      judgment,   Ps 51:6
   for I believe in your
      commands.

⁶⁷Before I was afflicted I went
      astray,   Jer 31:18-19; Heb 12:11
   but now I obey your word.
⁶⁸You are good, and what you
      do is good;   Ps 106:1; 107:1
   teach me your decrees.
⁶⁹Though the arrogant have
      smeared me with lies,
   I keep your precepts with all
      my heart.
⁷⁰Their hearts are callous and
      unfeeling,   Ps 17:10; Ac 28:27
   but I delight in your law.
⁷¹It was good for me to be
      afflicted   ver 67,75
   so that I might learn your
      decrees.
⁷²The law from your mouth is
      more precious to me
   than thousands of pieces of
      silver and gold.   Ps 19:10

י Yodh

⁷³Your hands made me and
      formed me;   Job 10:8; Ps 138:8
   give me understanding to
      learn your commands.
⁷⁴May those who fear you rejoice
      when they see me,
   for I have put my hope in
      your word.
⁷⁵I know, O LORD, that your laws
      are righteous,
   and in faithfulness you have
      afflicted me.   Heb 12:5-11
⁷⁶May your unfailing love be my
      comfort,
   according to your promise to
      your servant.   ver 41
⁷⁷Let your compassion come to
      me that I may live,   ver 41

for your law is my delight.
⁷⁸May the arrogant be put to
shame for wronging me
without cause; ver 86,161
but I will meditate on your
precepts.
⁷⁹May those who fear you turn
to me,
those who understand your
statutes. ver 27,125
⁸⁰May my heart be blameless
toward your decrees,
that I may not be put to
shame.

ⴽ Kaph

⁸¹My soul faints with longing for
your salvation, Ps 84:2
but I have put my hope in
your word.
⁸²My eyes fail, looking for your
promise; Ps 69:3; La 2:11
I say, "When will you
comfort me?"
⁸³Though I am like a wineskin in
the smoke,
I do not forget your decrees.
⁸⁴How long must your servant
wait? Ps 39:4; Rev 6:10
When will you punish my
persecutors?
⁸⁵The arrogant dig pitfalls for
me, Ps 35:7; Jer 18:20,22
contrary to your law.
⁸⁶All your commands are
trustworthy; Ps 35:19
help me, for men persecute
me without cause.
⁸⁷They almost wiped me from
the earth,

but I have not forsaken your
precepts. Isa 58:2
⁸⁸Preserve my life according to
your love,
and I will obey the statutes
of your mouth.

ⵍ Lamedh

⁸⁹Your word, O LORD, is eternal;
it stands firm in the heavens.
⁹⁰Your faithfulness continues
through all generations;
you established the earth,
and it endures. Ps 148:6
⁹¹Your laws endure to this day,
for all things serve you.
⁹²If your law had not been my
delight, Ps 37:4
I would have perished in my
affliction.
⁹³I will never forget your
precepts,
for by them you have
preserved my life.
⁹⁴Save me, for I am yours;
I have sought out your
precepts.
⁹⁵The wicked are waiting to
destroy me, Ps 69:4
but I will ponder your
statutes.
⁹⁶To all perfection I see a limit;
but your commands are
boundless. Ps 19:7

ⵎ Mem

⁹⁷Oh, how I love your law!
I meditate on it all day long.
⁹⁸Your commands make me
wiser than my enemies,
for they are ever with me.

⁹⁹I have more insight than all
my teachers,
for I meditate on your
statutes.   ver 15
¹⁰⁰I have more understanding
than the elders,
for I obey your precepts.
¹⁰¹I have kept my feet from
every evil path   Pr 1:15
so that I might obey your
word.
¹⁰²I have not departed from your
laws,
for you yourself have taught
me.
¹⁰³How sweet are your words to
my taste,
sweeter than honey to my
mouth!   Ps 19:10; Pr 8:11
¹⁰⁴I gain understanding from
your precepts;
therefore I hate every wrong
path.   ver 128

נ   Nun

¹⁰⁵Your word is a lamp to my
feet
and a light for my path.
¹⁰⁶I have taken an oath and
confirmed it,   Ne 10:29
that I will follow your
righteous laws.
¹⁰⁷I have suffered much;
preserve my life, O LORD,
according to your word.
¹⁰⁸Accept, O LORD, the willing
praise of my mouth,
and teach me your laws.
¹⁰⁹Though I constantly take my
life in my hands,   Jdg 12:3
I will not forget your law.

¹¹⁰The wicked have set a snare
for me,   Ps 140:5; 141:9
but I have not strayed from
your precepts.
¹¹¹Your statutes are my heritage
forever;
they are the joy of my heart.
¹¹²My heart is set on keeping
your decrees   Ps 108:1
to the very end.

ס   Samekh

¹¹³I hate double-minded men,
but I love your law.
¹¹⁴You are my refuge and my
shield;   Ps 32:7; 91:1
I have put my hope in your
word.
¹¹⁵Away from me, you evildoers,
that I may keep the
commands of my God!
¹¹⁶Sustain me according to your
promise, and I will live;
do not let my hopes be
dashed.   Ps 25:2; Ro 5:5
¹¹⁷Uphold me, and I will be
delivered;   Isa 41:10
I will always have regard for
your decrees.
¹¹⁸You reject all who stray from
your decrees,
for their deceitfulness is in
vain.
¹¹⁹All the wicked of the earth
you discard like dross;
therefore I love your
statutes.
¹²⁰My flesh trembles in fear of
you;   Hab 3:16
I stand in awe of your
laws.

ע Ayin

¹²¹I have done what is righteous
     and just;   2Sa 8:15
  do not leave me to my
     oppressors.
¹²²Ensure your servant's
     well-being;   Job 17:3
  let not the arrogant oppress
     me.
¹²³My eyes fail, looking for your
     salvation,
  looking for your righteous
     promise.   ver 82
¹²⁴Deal with your servant
     according to your love
  and teach me your decrees.
¹²⁵I am your servant; give me
     discernment   Ps 116:16
  that I may understand your
     statutes.
¹²⁶It is time for you to act,
     O Lord;
  your law is being broken.
¹²⁷Because I love your
     commands
  more than gold, more than
     pure gold,   Ps 19:10
¹²⁸and because I consider all
     your precepts right,
  I hate every wrong path.

פ Pe

¹²⁹Your statutes are wonderful;
  therefore I obey them.
¹³⁰The unfolding of your words
     gives light;   Pr 6:23
  it gives understanding to the
     simple.   Ps 19:7
¹³¹I open my mouth and pant,
  longing for your commands.

¹³²Turn to me and have mercy
     on me,   Ps 25:16; 106:4
  as you always do to those
     who love your name.
¹³³Direct my footsteps according
     to your word;   Ps 17:5
  let no sin rule over me.
¹³⁴Redeem me from the
     oppression of men,
  that I may obey your
     precepts.
¹³⁵Make your face shine upon
     your servant   Ps 4:6
  and teach me your decrees.
¹³⁶Streams of tears flow from my
     eyes,   Jer 9:1,18
  for your law is not obeyed.

צ Tsadhe

¹³⁷Righteous are you, O Lord,
  and your laws are right.
¹³⁸The statutes you have laid
     down are righteous;
  they are fully trustworthy.
¹³⁹My zeal wears me out,   Ps 69:9
  for my enemies ignore your
     words.
¹⁴⁰Your promises have been
     thoroughly tested,   Ps 12:6
  and your servant loves them.
¹⁴¹Though I am lowly and
     despised,   Ps 22:6
  I do not forget your
     precepts.
¹⁴²Your righteousness is
     everlasting
  and your law is true.   Ps 19:7
¹⁴³Trouble and distress have
     come upon me,
  but your commands are my
     delight.

144Your statutes are forever right;
  give me understanding that I
    may live.   Ps 19:9

ק   Qoph

145I call with all my heart;
    answer me, O Lord,
  and I will obey your decrees.
146I call out to you; save me
  and I will keep your statutes.
147I rise before dawn and cry for
    help;   Ps 5:3; 57:8; 108:2
  I have put my hope in your
    word.
148My eyes stay open through
    the watches of the night,
  that I may meditate on your
    promises.
149Hear my voice in accordance
    with your love;   Ps 27:7
  preserve my life, O Lord,
    according to your laws.
150Those who devise wicked
    schemes are near,
  but they are far from your
    law.
151Yet you are near, O Lord,
  and all your commands are
    true.   ver 142
152Long ago I learned from your
    statutes
  that you established them to
    last forever.   Lk 21:33

ר   Resh

153Look upon my suffering and
    deliver me,   La 5:1
  for I have not forgotten your
    law.   Pr 3:1
154Defend my cause and redeem
    me;   1Sa 24:15

preserve my life according to
  your promise.
155Salvation is far from the
    wicked,
  for they do not seek out
    your decrees.   Job 5:4
156Your compassion is great,
    O Lord;
  preserve my life according to
    your laws.   2Sa 24:14
157Many are the foes who
    persecute me,   Ps 7:1
  but I have not turned from
    your statutes.
158I look on the faithless with
    loathing,   Ps 139:21
  for they do not obey your
    word.
159See how I love your precepts;
  preserve my life, O Lord,
    according to your love.
160All your words are true;
  all your righteous laws are
    eternal.   ver 89; Ps 111:8

ש   Sin and Shin

161Rulers persecute me without
    cause,   1Sa 24:11
  but my heart trembles at
    your word.
162I rejoice in your promise
  like one who finds great
    spoil.   1Sa 30:16
163I hate and abhor falsehood
  but I love your law.   ver 47
164Seven times a day I praise you
  for your righteous laws.
165Great peace have they who
    love your law,   Pr 3:2
  and nothing can make them
    stumble.

166I wait for your salvation,
    O LORD,   Ge 49:18
and I follow your
    commands.
167I obey your statutes,
    for I love them greatly.
168I obey your precepts and your
    statutes,
for all my ways are known
    to you.   Pr 5:21

ת Taw

169May my cry come before you,
    O LORD;   Ps 18:6
give me understanding
    according to your word.
170May my supplication come
    before you;   Ps 28:2
deliver me according to your
    promise.   Ps 31:2
171May my lips overflow with
    praise,   Ps 51:15
for you teach me your
    decrees.
172May my tongue sing of your
    word,
for all your commands are
    righteous.
173May your hand be ready to
    help me,   Ps 37:24
for I have chosen your
    precepts.   Jos 24:22
174I long for your salvation,
    O LORD,
and your law is my delight.
175Let me live that I may praise
    you,   Isa 55:3
and may your laws sustain
    me.
176I have strayed like a lost
    sheep.   Isa 53:6

Seek your servant,
for I have not forgotten your
    commands.   Ps 44:17

Psalm 120

A song of ascents.

1I call on the LORD in my
    distress,   Jnh 2:2
and he answers me.
2Save me, O LORD, from lying
    lips   Pr 12:22
and from deceitful tongues.

3What will he do to you,
    and what more besides,
        O deceitful tongue?
4He will punish you with a
    warrior's sharp arrows,
with burning coals of the
    broom tree.

5Woe to me that I dwell in
    Meshech,
that I live among the tents of
    Kedar!   Ge 25:13; Jer 49:28
6Too long have I lived
among those who hate
    peace.
7I am a man of peace;
but when I speak, they are
    for war.

Psalm 121

A song of ascents.

1I lift up my eyes to the hills—
where does my help come
    from?
2My help comes from the LORD,
the Maker of heaven and
    earth.   Ps 124:8

³He will not let your foot slip—
  he who watches over you
    will not slumber;
⁴indeed, he who watches over
    Israel   Ps 127:1
  will neither slumber nor
    sleep.

⁵The LORD watches over you—
  the LORD is your shade at
    your right hand;
⁶the sun will not harm you by
    day,   Ps 91:5; Isa 49:10
  nor the moon by night.

⁷The LORD will keep you from
    all harm—   Ps 41:2; 91:10-12
  he will watch over your life;
⁸the LORD will watch over your
    coming and going
  both now and forevermore.

Psalm 122

A song of ascents. Of David.

¹I rejoiced with those who said
    to me,
  "Let us go to the house of
    the LORD."
²Our feet are standing
  in your gates, O Jerusalem.

³Jerusalem is built like a city
  that is closely compacted
    together.
⁴That is where the tribes go up,
  the tribes of the LORD,
to praise the name of the LORD
  according to the statute
    given to Israel.
⁵There the thrones for judgment
    stand,

the thrones of the house of
    David.

⁶Pray for the peace of
    Jerusalem:
  "May those who love you be
    secure.   Ps 51:18
⁷May there be peace within
    your walls   1Sa 25:6
  and security within your
    citadels."   Ps 48:3
⁸For the sake of my brothers
    and friends,
  I will say, "Peace be within
    you."
⁹For the sake of the house of
    the LORD our God,
  I will seek your prosperity.

Psalm 123

A song of ascents.

¹I lift up my eyes to you,
  to you whose throne is in
    heaven.   Ps 11:4; 121:1; 141:8
²As the eyes of slaves look to
    the hand of their
    master,
  as the eyes of a maid look to
    the hand of her
    mistress,
so our eyes look to the LORD
    our God,   Ps 25:15
  till he shows us his mercy.

³Have mercy on us, O LORD,
    have mercy on us,
  for we have endured much
    contempt.
⁴We have endured much
    ridicule from the proud,

much contempt from the
arrogant.

Psalm 124

A song of ascents. Of David.

¹If the LORD had not been on
    our side—
let Israel say—   Ps 129:1
²if the LORD had not been on
    our side
when men attacked us,
³when their anger flared against
    us,
they would have swallowed
    us alive;
⁴the flood would have engulfed
    us,
the torrent would have
    swept over us,
⁵the raging waters
would have swept us away.

⁶Praise be to the LORD,
who has not let us be torn
    by their teeth.
⁷We have escaped like a bird
out of the fowler's snare;
the snare has been broken,
and we have escaped.
⁸Our help is in the name of the
    LORD,
the Maker of heaven and
    earth.   Ge 1:1; Ps 121:2

Psalm 125

A song of ascents.

¹Those who trust in the LORD
are like Mount Zion,

which cannot be shaken but
    endures forever.
²As the mountains surround
    Jerusalem,
so the LORD surrounds his
    people   Ps 121:8; Zec 2:4-5
both now and forevermore.

³The scepter of the wicked will
    not remain   Pr 22:8; Isa 14:5
over the land allotted to the
    righteous,
for then the righteous might
    use
their hands to do evil.

⁴Do good, O LORD, to those who
    are good,   Ps 119:68
to those who are upright in
    heart.   Ps 7:10; 94:15
⁵But those who turn to crooked
    ways   Pr 2:15; Isa 59:8
the LORD will banish with the
    evildoers.

Peace be upon Israel.   Ps 128:6

Psalm 126

A song of ascents.

¹When the LORD brought back
    the captives toᵃ Zion,
we were like men who
    dreamed.ᵇ
²Our mouths were filled with
    laughter,
our tongues with songs of
    joy.   Ps 51:14
Then it was said among the
    nations,

ᵃ1 Or LORD restored the fortunes of   ᵇ1 Or men restored to health

"The LORD has done great
    things for them." Ps 71:19
³The LORD has done great things
    for us,
and we are filled with joy.

⁴Restore our fortunes,ᵃ O LORD,
    like streams in the Negev.
⁵Those who sow in tears
    will reap with songs of joy.
⁶He who goes out weeping,
    carrying seed to sow,
will return with songs of joy,
    carrying sheaves with him.

Psalm 127

A song of ascents. Of Solomon.

¹Unless the LORD builds the
    house,   Ps 78:69
    its builders labor in vain.
Unless the LORD watches over
    the city,   Ps 121:4
the watchmen stand guard in
    vain.
²In vain you rise early
    and stay up late,
toiling for food to eat—   Ge 3:17
for he grants sleep toᵇ those
    he loves.   Job 11:18

³Sons are a heritage from the
    LORD,
    children a reward from him.
⁴Like arrows in the hands of a
    warrior,   Ps 112:2
are sons born in one's youth.
⁵Blessed is the man
    whose quiver is full of them.
They will not be put to shame

when they contend with
    their enemies in the
    gate.   Pr 27:11

Psalm 128

A song of ascents.

¹Blessed are all who fear the
    LORD,   Ps 112:1
who walk in his ways.
²You will eat the fruit of your
    labor;   Isa 3:10
blessings and prosperity will
    be yours.   Ecc 8:12
³Your wife will be like a fruitful
    vine
within your house;   Eze 19:10
your sons will be like olive
    shoots
around your table.   Ps 52:8
⁴Thus is the man blessed
    who fears the LORD.

⁵May the LORD bless you from
    Zion   Ps 134:3
all the days of your life;
may you see the prosperity of
    Jerusalem,
⁶ and may you live to see your
    children's children.

Peace be upon Israel.   Ps 125:5

Psalm 129

A song of ascents.

¹They have greatly oppressed
    me from my youth—
let Israel say—   Ps 124:1

ᵃ4 Or *Bring back our captives*   ᵇ2 Or *eat— / for while they sleep he provides for*

²they have greatly oppressed me
　　from my youth,
　but they have not gained the
　　victory over me.　　Mt 16:18
³Plowmen have plowed my
　　back
　and made their furrows long.
⁴But the LORD is righteous;
　he has cut me free from the
　　cords of the wicked.

⁵May all who hate Zion　　Mic 4:11
　be turned back in shame.
⁶May they be like grass on the
　　roof,
　which withers before it can
　　grow;　　Ps 37:2
⁷with it the reaper cannot fill
　　his hands,　　Dt 28:38
　nor the one who gathers fill
　　his arms.
⁸May those who pass by not
　　say,
　"The blessing of the LORD be
　　upon you;
　we bless you in the name of
　　the LORD."　　Ru 2:4; Ps 118:26

Psalm 130

A song of ascents.

¹Out of the depths I cry to you,
　　O LORD;　　Ps 42:7; 69:2; La 3:55
²　O Lord, hear my voice.　　Ps 28:2
Let your ears be attentive
　to my cry for mercy.

³If you, O LORD, kept a record
　　of sins,
　O Lord, who could stand?
⁴But with you there is
　　forgiveness;　　Ex 34:7; Jer 33:8

therefore you are feared.

⁵I wait for the LORD, my soul
　　waits,　　Ps 27:14; 33:20; Isa 8:17
　and in his word I put my
　　hope.　　Ps 119:81
⁶My soul waits for the Lord
　more than watchmen wait
　　for the morning,
　more than watchmen wait
　　for the morning.

⁷O Israel, put your hope in the
　　LORD,　　Ps 131:3
　for with the LORD is unfailing
　　love
　and with him is full
　　redemption.
⁸He himself will redeem Israel
　from all their sins.

Psalm 131

A song of ascents. Of David.

¹My heart is not proud, O LORD,
　my eyes are not haughty;
I do not concern myself with
　　great matters　　Jer 45:5
　or things too wonderful for
　　me.
²But I have stilled and quieted
　　my soul;　　Ps 116:7
　like a weaned child with its
　　mother,
　like a weaned child is my
　　soul within me.　　Mt 18:3

³O Israel, put your hope in the
　　LORD　　Ps 130:7
　both now and forevermore.

Psalm 132

A song of ascents.

¹O LORD, remember David
  and all the hardships he
    endured.   1Sa 18:11

²He swore an oath to the LORD
  and made a vow to the
    Mighty One of Jacob:
³"I will not enter my house
  or go to my bed—
⁴I will allow no sleep to my
    eyes,
  no slumber to my eyelids,
⁵till I find a place for the
    LORD,
  a dwelling for the Mighty
    One of Jacob."

⁶We heard it in Ephrathah,
  we came upon it in the
    fields of Jaar*:*ᵇ   1Sa 7:2
⁷"Let us go to his dwelling
    place;   Ps 5:7
  let us worship at his
    footstool—   Ps 99:5
⁸arise, O LORD, and come to
    your resting place,
  you and the ark of your
    might.
⁹May your priests be clothed
    with righteousness;
  may your saints sing for
    joy."

¹⁰For the sake of David your
    servant,

do not reject your anointed
  one.
¹¹The LORD swore an oath to
    David,   Ps 89:3-4,35
  a sure oath that he will not
    revoke:
"One of your own descendants
  I will place on your throne—
¹²if your sons keep my covenant
  and the statutes I teach
    them,
then their sons will sit
  on your throne for ever and
    ever."
¹³For the LORD has chosen Zion,
  he has desired it for his
    dwelling:
¹⁴"This is my resting place for
    ever and ever;   Ps 68:16
  here I will sit enthroned, for
    I have desired it—
¹⁵I will bless her with abundant
    provisions;
  her poor will I satisfy with
    food.   Ps 147:14
¹⁶I will clothe her priests with
    salvation,
  and her saints will ever sing
    for joy.
¹⁷"Here I will make a hornᶜ
  grow for David   Eze 29:21
  and set up a lamp for my
    anointed one.
¹⁸I will clothe his enemies with
    shame,   Ps 35:26; 109:29
  but the crown on his head
    will be resplendent."

ᵃ6 That is, Kiriath Jearim   ᵇ6 Or heard of it in Ephrathah, / we found it in the fields of Jaar. (And no
quotes around verses 7-9)   ᶜ17 Horn here symbolizes strong one, that is, king.

Psalm 133

A song of ascents. Of David.

¹How good and pleasant it is
    when brothers live together
        in unity!   Ge 13:8
²It is like precious oil poured on
        the head,   Ex 30:25
    running down on the beard,
    running down on Aaron's
        beard,
    down upon the collar of his
        robes.
³It is as if the dew of Hermon
    were falling on Mount Zion.
For there the LORD bestows his
        blessing,   Lev 25:21
    even life forevermore.   Ps 42:8

Psalm 134

A song of ascents.

¹Praise the LORD, all you
        servants of the LORD
    who minister by night in the
        house of the LORD.
²Lift up your hands in the
        sanctuary   1Ti 2:8
    and praise the LORD.

³May the LORD, the Maker of
        heaven and earth,
    bless you from Zion.   Ps 128:5

Psalm 135

¹Praise the LORD.ᵃ

Praise the name of the LORD;
    praise him, you servants of
        the LORD,   Ps 113:1; 134:1

ᵃ1 Hebrew *Hallelu Yah*; also in verses 3 and 21

²you who minister in the house
    of the LORD,   Lk 2:37
    in the courts of the house of
        our God.   Ps 116:19
³Praise the LORD, for the LORD is
        good;   Ps 119:68
    sing praise to his name, for
        that is pleasant.   Ps 147:1
⁴For the LORD has chosen Jacob
    to be his own,   1Pe 2:9
    Israel to be his treasured
        possession.   Ex 19:5; Dt 7:6

⁵I know that the LORD is great,
    that our Lord is greater than
        all gods.
⁶The LORD does whatever
        pleases him,   Ps 115:3
    in the heavens and on the
        earth,
    in the seas and all their
        depths.
⁷He makes clouds rise from the
        ends of the earth;
    he sends lightning with the
        rain   Jer 10:13; Zec 10:1
    and brings out the wind
        from his storehouses.

⁸He struck down the firstborn
    of Egypt,   Ex 12:12
    the firstborn of men and
        animals.
⁹He sent his signs and wonders
        into your midst,
    O Egypt,
    against Pharaoh and all his
        servants.   Ps 136:10-15
¹⁰He struck down many nations

and killed mighty kings—
¹¹Sihon king of the Amorites,
  Og king of Bashan
and all the kings of
  Canaan—   Jos 12:7-24
¹²and he gave their land as an
  inheritance,
  an inheritance to his people
  Israel.

¹³Your name, O Lord, endures
  forever,   Ex 3:15
your renown, O Lord,
  through all generations.
¹⁴For the Lord will vindicate his
  people   Heb 10:30
and have compassion on his
  servants.   Dt 32:36

¹⁵The idols of the nations are
  silver and gold,   Ps 96:5
made by the hands of men.
¹⁶They have mouths, but cannot
  speak,   1Ki 18:26
eyes, but they cannot see;
¹⁷they have ears, but cannot
  hear,
nor is there breath in their
  mouths.   Jer 10:14
¹⁸Those who make them will be
  like them,
and so will all who trust in
  them.

¹⁹O house of Israel, praise the
  Lord;   Ps 22:23
O house of Aaron, praise the
  Lord;
²⁰O house of Levi, praise the
  Lord;
you who fear him, praise the
  Lord.

²¹Praise be to the Lord from
  Zion,   Ps 134:3
to him who dwells in
  Jerusalem.

Praise the Lord.

Psalm 136

¹Give thanks to the Lord, for he
  is good.   Ps 106:1
  His love endures forever.
²Give thanks to the God of
  gods.   Dt 10:17
  His love endures forever.
³Give thanks to the Lord of
  lords:
  His love endures forever.

⁴to him who alone does great
  wonders,   Ps 72:18
  His love endures forever.
⁵who by his understanding
  made the heavens,   Ge 1:1
  His love endures forever.
⁶who spread out the earth upon
  the waters,   Jer 10:12
  His love endures forever.
⁷who made the great lights—
  His love endures forever.
⁸the sun to govern the day,
  His love endures forever.
⁹the moon and stars to govern
  the night;
  His love endures forever.

¹⁰to him who struck down the
  firstborn of Egypt   Ex 12:29
  His love endures forever.
¹¹and brought Israel out from
  among them   Ex 6:6; 12:51
  His love endures forever.

¹²with a mighty hand and
   outstretched arm;   Dt 4:34
   His love endures forever.

¹³to him who divided the Red
   Sea*ᵃ* asunder   Ex 14:21
   His love endures forever.
¹⁴and brought Israel through the
   midst of it,
   His love endures forever.
¹⁵but swept Pharaoh and his
   army into the Red Sea;
   His love endures forever.

¹⁶to him who led his people
   through the desert,
   His love endures forever.
¹⁷who struck down great kings,
   His love endures forever.
¹⁸and killed mighty kings—
   His love endures forever.
¹⁹Sihon king of the Amorites
   His love endures forever.
²⁰and Og king of Bashan—
   His love endures forever.
²¹and gave their land as an
   inheritance,   Jos 12:1
   His love endures forever.
²²an inheritance to his servant
   Israel;
   His love endures forever.

²³to the One who remembered
   us in our low estate
   His love endures forever.
²⁴and freed us from our enemies,
   His love endures forever.
²⁵and who gives food to every
   creature.   Ps 104:27; 145:15
   His love endures forever.

²⁶Give thanks to the God of
   heaven.   Ps 115:3
   His love endures forever.

Psalm 137

¹By the rivers of Babylon we sat
   and wept   Eze 1:1,3; Ne 1:4
when we remembered Zion.
²There on the poplars
   we hung our harps,   Job 30:31
³for there our captors asked us
   for songs,
   our tormentors demanded
   songs of joy;   Ps 80:6
they said, "Sing us one of
   the songs of Zion!"

⁴How can we sing the songs of
   the LORD   Ne 12:46
while in a foreign land?
⁵If I forget you, O Jerusalem,
   may my right hand forget ₄its
   skill₎.
⁶May my tongue cling to the
   roof of my mouth   Eze 3:26
if I do not remember you,
if I do not consider Jerusalem
   my highest joy.

⁷Remember, O LORD, what the
   Edomites did   Jer 49:7
on the day Jerusalem fell.
"Tear it down," they cried,
   "tear it down to its
   foundations!"

⁸O Daughter of Babylon,
   doomed to destruction,
happy is he who repays you

ᵃ13 Hebrew *Yam Suph*; that is, Sea of Reeds; also in verse 15

for what you have done to
 us—
⁹he who seizes your infants
 and dashes them against the
 rocks. 2Ki 8:12; Isa 13:16

Psalm 138

Of David.

¹I will praise you, O Lᴏʀᴅ, with
 all my heart;
 before the "gods" I will sing
 your praise. Ps 95:3; 96:4
²I will bow down toward your
 holy temple 1Ki 8:29; Ps 5:7
and will praise your name
for your love and your
 faithfulness,
for you have exalted above all
 things
 your name and your word.
³When I called, you answered
 me;
 you made me bold and
 stouthearted. Ps 28:7

⁴May all the kings of the earth
 praise you, O Lᴏʀᴅ,
 when they hear the words of
 your mouth.
⁵May they sing of the ways of
 the Lᴏʀᴅ,
 for the glory of the Lᴏʀᴅ is
 great.

⁶Though the Lᴏʀᴅ is on high, he
 looks upon the lowly,
 but the proud he knows
 from afar. Pr 3:34; Jas 4:6
⁷Though I walk in the midst of
 trouble, Ps 23:4
 you preserve my life;

you stretch out your hand
 against the anger of my
 foes, Jer 51:25
with your right hand you
 save me. Ps 71:20
⁸The Lᴏʀᴅ will fulfill ⸤his
 purpose⸥ for me; Ps 57:2
your love, O Lᴏʀᴅ, endures
 forever—
do not abandon the works of
 your hands. Job 10:3,8

Psalm 139

For the director of music. Of David. A psalm.

¹O Lᴏʀᴅ, you have searched me
 and you know me. Jer 12:3
²You know when I sit and when
 I rise; 2Ki 19:27
 you perceive my thoughts
 from afar. Mt 9:4; Jn 2:24
³You discern my going out and
 my lying down;
 you are familiar with all my
 ways. Job 31:4
⁴Before a word is on my tongue
 you know it completely,
 O Lᴏʀᴅ. Heb 4:13

⁵You hem me in—behind and
 before; Ps 34:7
 you have laid your hand
 upon me.
⁶Such knowledge is too
 wonderful for me,
 too lofty for me to attain.

⁷Where can I go from your
 Spirit?
 Where can I flee from your
 presence? Jer 23:24; Jnh 1:3

8If I go up to the heavens, you
    are there;   Am 9:2-3
if I make my bed in the
    depths,*a* you are there.
9If I rise on the wings of the
    dawn,
if I settle on the far side of
    the sea,
10even there your hand will
    guide me,   Ps 23:3
your right hand will hold me
    fast.

11If I say, "Surely the darkness
    will hide me
and the light become night
    around me,"
12even the darkness will not be
    dark to you;   Job 34:22
the night will shine like the
    day,
for darkness is as light to
    you.

13For you created my inmost
    being;   Ps 119:73
you knit me together in my
    mother's womb.   Job 10:11
14I praise you because I am
    fearfully and
    wonderfully made;
your works are wonderful,
I know that full well.
15My frame was not hidden from
    you
when I was made in the
    secret place.
When I was woven together in
    the depths of the earth,

16 your eyes saw my unformed
    body.
All the days ordained for me
    were written in your book
    before one of them came to
    be.

17How precious to*b* me are your
    thoughts, O God!   Ps 40:5
How vast is the sum of
    them!
18Were I to count them,
    they would outnumber the
    grains of sand.
When I awake,
    I am still with you.   Ps 3:5

19If only you would slay the
    wicked, O God!   Isa 11:4
Away from me, you
    bloodthirsty men!
20They speak of you with evil
    intent;
your adversaries misuse your
    name.   Jude 15
21Do I not hate those who hate
    you, O LORD,   Ps 119:158
and abhor those who rise up
    against you?
22I have nothing but hatred for
    them;
I count them my enemies.

23Search me, O God, and know
    my heart;   Job 31:6; Ps 26:2
test me and know my
    anxious thoughts.
24See if there is any offensive
    way in me,

a 8 Hebrew *Sheol*   *b 17* Or *concerning*

and lead me in the way
   everlasting.   Ps 5:8; 143:10

Psalm 140

For the director of music. A psalm
of David.

¹Rescue me, O LORD, from evil
   men;   Ps 17:13
protect me from men of
   violence,   Ps 18:48
²who devise evil plans in their
   hearts   Ps 56:6
and stir up war every day.
³They make their tongues as
   sharp as a serpent's;
the poison of vipers is on
   their lips.   Selah

⁴Keep me, O LORD, from the
   hands of the wicked;
protect me from men of
   violence
who plan to trip my feet.
⁵Proud men have hidden a
   snare for me;   Job 34:30
they have spread out the
   cords of their net   Job 18:8
and have set traps for me
   along my path.   Selah

⁶O LORD, I say to you, "You are
   my God."   Ps 16:2
Hear, O LORD, my cry for
   mercy.   Ps 116:1; 143:1
⁷O Sovereign LORD, my strong
   deliverer,   Ps 28:8
who shields my head in the
   day of battle—
⁸do not grant the wicked their
   desires, O LORD;   Ps 10:2-3

do not let their plans
   succeed,
or they will become proud.
                      Selah
⁹Let the heads of those who
   surround me
be covered with the trouble
   their lips have caused.
¹⁰Let burning coals fall upon
   them;
may they be thrown into the
   fire,   Ps 11:6; 21:9
into miry pits, never to rise.
¹¹Let slanderers not be
   established in the land;
may disaster hunt down men
   of violence.   Ps 34:21

¹²I know that the LORD secures
   justice for the poor
and upholds the cause of the
   needy.   Ps 9:4; 35:10
¹³Surely the righteous will praise
   your name   Ps 97:12
and the upright will live
   before you.   Ps 11:7

Psalm 141

A psalm of David.

¹O LORD, I call to you; come
   quickly to me.   Ps 70:5
Hear my voice when I call to
   you.   Ps 143:1
²May my prayer be set before
   you like incense;   Rev 5:8
may the lifting up of my
   hands be like the
   evening sacrifice.

³Set a guard over my mouth,
    O LORD;   Ps 34:13
  keep watch over the door of
    my lips.   Ps 12:2
⁴Let not my heart be drawn to
    what is evil,   Jos 24:23
  to take part in wicked deeds
with men who are evildoers;
  let me not eat of their
    delicacies.   Pr 23:6

⁵Let a righteous man*a* strike
    me—it is a kindness;
  let him rebuke me—it is oil
    on my head.   Ps 23:5; Pr 9:8
  My head will not refuse it.

  Yet my prayer is ever against
    the deeds of evildoers;
⁶ their rulers will be thrown
    down from the cliffs,
  and the wicked will learn
    that my words were well
    spoken.
⁷They will say, "As one plows
    and breaks up the earth,
  so our bones have been
    scattered at the mouth
    of the grave.*b*"   Ps 53:5

⁸But my eyes are fixed on you,
    O Sovereign LORD;
  in you I take refuge—do not
    give me over to death.
⁹Keep me from the snares they
    have laid for me,   Ps 140:4
  from the traps set by
    evildoers.   Ps 38:12
¹⁰Let the wicked fall into their
    own nets,   Ps 35:8
  while I pass by in safety.

Psalm 142

A *maskil*ᶜ of David. When he was
in the cave. A prayer.

¹I cry aloud to the LORD;
  I lift up my voice to the
    LORD for mercy.   Ps 30:8
²I pour out my complaint before
    him;   Isa 26:16
  before him I tell my trouble.

³When my spirit grows faint
    within me,   Ps 140:5; 143:4,7
  it is you who know my
    way.
  In the path where I walk
    men have hidden a snare for
    me.
⁴Look to my right and see;
  no one is concerned for
    me.
  I have no refuge;
  no one cares for my life.

⁵I cry to you, O LORD;
  I say, "You are my refuge,
  my portion in the land of the
    living."   Ps 27:13
⁶Listen to my cry,   Ps 17:1
  for I am in desperate need;
  rescue me from those who
    pursue me,   Ps 25:20
  for they are too strong for
    me.
⁷Set me free from my prison,
  that I may praise your name.

  Then the righteous will gather
    about me
  because of your goodness to
    me.   Ps 13:6

---

a 5 Or *Let the Righteous One*   *b 7* Hebrew *Sheol*   ᶜTitle: Probably a literary or musical term

Psalm 143

A psalm of David.

¹O LORD, hear my prayer,
    listen to my cry for mercy;
in your faithfulness and
        righteousness   Ps 71:2; 89:1-2
    come to my relief.
²Do not bring your servant into
        judgment,
    for no one living is righteous
        before you.   Ps 14:3; Ecc 7:20

³The enemy pursues me,
    he crushes me to the
        ground;
he makes me dwell in darkness
    like those long dead.
⁴So my spirit grows faint within
        me;
    my heart within me is
        dismayed.   Ps 142:3

⁵I remember the days of long
        ago;   Ps 77:6
    I meditate on all your works
    and consider what your
        hands have done.
⁶I spread out my hands to you;
    my soul thirsts for you like a
        parched land.   *Selah*

⁷Answer me quickly, O LORD;
    my spirit fails.
Do not hide your face from me
    or I will be like those who
        go down to the pit.
⁸Let the morning bring me word
    of your unfailing love,

for I have put my trust in
        you.   Ps 34:13
Show me the way I should go,
    for to you I lift up my soul.
⁹Rescue me from my enemies,
        O LORD,   Ps 31:15
    for I hide myself in you.
¹⁰Teach me to do your will,
    for you are my God;
may your good Spirit
    lead me on level ground.

¹¹For your name's sake, O LORD,
        preserve my life;   Ps 119:25
    in your righteousness, bring
        me out of trouble.   Ps 31:1
¹²In your unfailing love, silence
        my enemies;
    destroy all my foes,   Ps 54:5
    for I am your servant.

Psalm 144

Of David.

¹Praise be to the LORD my Rock,
    who trains my hands for
        war,
    my fingers for battle.
²He is my loving God and my
        fortress,   Ps 59:9; 91:2
    my stronghold and my
        deliverer,
my shield, in whom I take
        refuge,   Ps 84:9
    who subdues peoples[a] under
        me.

³O LORD, what is man that you
        care for him,   Ps 8:4; Heb 2:6

---

[a]2 Many manuscripts of the Masoretic Text, Dead Sea Scrolls, Aquila, Jerome and Syriac; most
manuscripts of the Masoretic Text *subdues my people*

the son of man that you
think of him?
⁴Man is like a breath;
his days are like a fleeting
shadow. Ps 102:11
⁵Part your heavens, O LORD, and
come down; Ps 18:9; Isa 64:1
touch the mountains, so that
they smoke. Ps 104:32
⁶Send forth lightning and scatter
the enemies,;
shoot your arrows and rout
them. Ps 18:14
⁷Reach down your hand from
on high;
deliver me and rescue me
from the mighty waters,
from the hands of foreigners
⁸whose mouths are full of lies,
whose right hands are
deceitful.

⁹I will sing a new song to you,
O God;
on the ten-stringed lyre I will
make music to you,
¹⁰to the One who gives victory to
kings,
who delivers his servant
David from the deadly
sword. Ps 18:50

¹¹Deliver me and rescue me
from the hands of foreigners
whose mouths are full of lies,
whose right hands are
deceitful. Ps 12:2; Isa 44:20

¹²Then our sons in their youth
will be like well-nurtured
plants, Ps 128:3
and our daughters will be like
pillars SS 4:4
carved to adorn a palace.
¹³Our barns will be filled Pr 3:10
with every kind of provision.
Our sheep will increase by
thousands,
by tens of thousands in our
fields;
¹⁴ our oxen will draw heavy
loads.ᵃ Pr 14:4
There will be no breaching of
walls, 2Ki 25:11
no going into captivity,
no cry of distress in our
streets. Isa 24:11

¹⁵Blessed are the people of
whom this is true;
blessed are the people whose
God is the LORD.

Psalm 145ᵇ

A psalm of praise. Of David.

¹I will exalt you, my God the
King; Ps 30:1; 34:1
I will praise your name for
ever and ever.
²Every day I will praise you
and extol your name for ever
and ever.

³Great is the LORD and most
worthy of praise;
his greatness no one can
fathom. Job 5:9; Ro 11:33

ᵃ 14 Or *our chieftains will be firmly established*   ᵇ This psalm is an acrostic poem, the verses of which
(including verse 13b) begin with the successive letters of the Hebrew alphabet.

⁴One generation will commend
    your works to another;
they will tell of your mighty
    acts.
⁵They will speak of the glorious
    splendor of your
    majesty,
and I will meditate on your
    wonderful works.ᵃ
⁶They will tell of the power of
    your awesome works,
and I will proclaim your
    great deeds.   Dt 32:3
⁷They will celebrate your
    abundant goodness
and joyfully sing of your
    righteousness.   Ps 51:14

⁸The LORD is gracious and
    compassionate,   Ps 86:15
slow to anger and rich in
    love.
⁹The LORD is good to all;   Ps 100:5
he has compassion on all he
    has made.
¹⁰All you have made will praise
    you, O LORD;   Ps 19:1
your saints will extol you.
¹¹They will tell of the glory of
    your kingdom
and speak of your might,
¹²so that all men may know of
    your mighty acts   Ps 105:1
and the glorious splendor of
    your kingdom.
¹³Your kingdom is an everlasting
    kingdom,   1Ti 1:17; 2Pe 1:11

and your dominion endures
    through all generations.

The LORD is faithful to all his
    promises   Dt 7:9
and loving toward all he has
    made.ᵇ
¹⁴The LORD upholds all those
    who fall   Ps 37:24
and lifts up all who are
    bowed down.   Ps 146:8
¹⁵The eyes of all look to you,
and you give them their food
    at the proper time.
¹⁶You open your hand
and satisfy the desires of
    every living thing.

¹⁷The LORD is righteous in all his
    ways
and loving toward all he has
    made.
¹⁸The LORD is near to all who
    call on him,   Dt 4:7; Jn 4:24
to all who call on him in
    truth.
¹⁹He fulfills the desires of those
    who fear him;   Ps 37:4
he hears their cry and saves
    them.   Pr 15:29
²⁰The LORD watches over all who
    love him,   Ps 31:23; 97:10
but all the wicked he will
    destroy.   Ps 9:5
²¹My mouth will speak in praise
    of the LORD.   Ps 71:8

ᵃ5 Dead Sea Scrolls and Syriac (see also Septuagint); Masoretic Text *On the glorious splendor of your majesty / and on your wonderful works I will meditate*   ᵇ13 One manuscript of the Masoretic Text, Dead Sea Scrolls and Syriac (see also Septuagint); most manuscripts of the Masoretic Text do not have the last two lines of verse 13.

Let every creature praise his
  holy name
for ever and ever.

Psalm 146

¹Praise the LORD.ᵃ

Praise the LORD, O my soul.
² I will praise the LORD all my
    life;   Ps 104:33
  I will sing praise to my God
    as long as I live.

³Do not put your trust in
    princes,   Ps 118:9
  in mortal men, who cannot
    save.   Isa 2:22
⁴When their spirit departs, they
    return to the ground;
  on that very day their plans
    come to nothing.   Ps 33:10

⁵Blessed is he whose help is the
    God of Jacob,   Ps 144:15
  whose hope is in the LORD
    his God,
⁶the Maker of heaven and earth,
    the sea, and everything in
      them—
  the LORD, who remains
    faithful forever.   Ps 117:2
⁷He upholds the cause of the
    oppressed   Ps 103:6
  and gives food to the
    hungry.   Ps 107:9
The LORD sets prisoners free,
⁸ the LORD gives sight to the
    blind,   Mt 9:30

the LORD lifts up those who are
    bowed down,
  the LORD loves the righteous.
⁹The LORD watches over the
    alien
  and sustains the fatherless
    and the widow,   Dt 10:18
  but he frustrates the ways of
    the wicked.

¹⁰The LORD reigns forever,   Ex 15:18
  your God, O Zion, for all
    generations.

Praise the LORD.

Psalm 147

¹Praise the LORD.ᵇ

How good it is to sing praises
    to our God,
  how pleasant and fitting to
    praise him!   Ps 33:1; 135:3

²The LORD builds up Jerusalem;
  he gathers the exiles of
    Israel.   Dt 30:3
³He heals the brokenhearted
  and binds up their wounds.

⁴He determines the number of
    the stars   Isa 40:26
  and calls them each by
    name.
⁵Great is our Lord and mighty
    in power;   Ps 48:1
  his understanding has no
    limit.   Isa 40:28
⁶The LORD sustains the humble

ᵃ1 Hebrew *Hallelu Yah*; also in verse 10   ᵇ1 Hebrew *Hallelu Yah*; also in verse 20

but casts the wicked to the
    ground.

⁷Sing to the LORD with
    thanksgiving;   Ps 33:3
make music to our God on
    the harp.
⁸He covers the sky with clouds;
he supplies the earth with
    rain   Job 38:26
and makes grass grow on the
    hills.   Ps 104:14
⁹He provides food for the cattle
and for the young ravens
    when they call.   Job 38:41

¹⁰His pleasure is not in the
    strength of the horse,
nor his delight in the legs of
    a man;
¹¹the LORD delights in those who
    fear him,   Ps 33:18
who put their hope in his
    unfailing love.   Ps 119:43

¹²Extol the LORD, O Jerusalem;
    praise your God, O Zion,
¹³for he strengthens the bars of
    your gates   Dt 33:25
and blesses your people
    within you.   Lev 25:21
¹⁴He grants peace to your
    borders   Isa 60:17-18
and satisfies you with the
    finest of wheat.   Ps 132:15

¹⁵He sends his command to the
    earth;
his word runs swiftly.
¹⁶He spreads the snow like wool

and scatters the frost like
    ashes.
¹⁷He hurls down his hail like
    pebbles.
Who can withstand his icy
    blast?
¹⁸He sends his word and melts
    them;   Ps 33:9
he stirs up his breezes, and
    the waters flow.

¹⁹He has revealed his word to
    Jacob,
his laws and decrees to
    Israel.   Mal 4:4
²⁰He has done this for no other
    nation;   Dt 4:7-8,32-34
they do not know his laws.

Praise the LORD.

Psalm 148

¹Praise the LORD.ᵃ   Ps 33:2; 103:1

Praise the LORD from the
    heavens,
praise him in the heights
    above.
²Praise him, all his angels,
praise him, all his heavenly
    hosts.
³Praise him, sun and moon,
praise him, all you shining
    stars.
⁴Praise him, you highest
    heavens
and you waters above the
    skies.   Ge 1:7
⁵Let them praise the name of
    the LORD,

ᵃ 1 Hebrew *Hallelu Yah*; also in verse 14

for he commanded and they
 were created. Ge 1:1,6
⁶He set them in place for ever
 and ever;
he gave a decree that will
 never pass away. Ps 89:37

⁷Praise the Lord from the earth,
 you great sea creatures and
 all ocean depths,
⁸lightning and hail, snow and
 clouds,
stormy winds that do his
 bidding, Ps 147:15-18
⁹you mountains and all hills,
 fruit trees and all cedars,
¹⁰wild animals and all cattle,
 small creatures and flying
 birds,
¹¹kings of the earth and all
 nations,
you princes and all rulers on
 earth,
¹²young men and maidens,
 old men and children.

¹³Let them praise the name of
 the Lord, Isa 12:4
for his name alone is
 exalted;
his splendor is above the
 earth and the heavens.
¹⁴He has raised up for his people
 a horn,ᵃ Ps 75:10
the praise of all his saints,
of Israel, the people close to
 his heart. Dt 26:19

Praise the Lord.

Psalm 149

¹Praise the Lord.ᵇ Ps 33:2

Sing to the Lord a new song,
 his praise in the assembly of
 the saints. Ps 35:18
²Let Israel rejoice in their
 Maker; Ps 95:6
let the people of Zion be
 glad in their King. Ps 47:6
³Let them praise his name with
 dancing
and make music to him with
 tambourine and harp.
⁴For the Lord takes delight in
 his people; Ps 35:27
he crowns the humble with
 salvation. Ps 132:16
⁵Let the saints rejoice in this
 honor
and sing for joy on their
 beds. Job 35:10

⁶May the praise of God be in
 their mouths
and a double-edged sword in
 their hands, Heb 4:12
⁷to inflict vengeance on the
 nations Nu 31:3
and punishment on the
 peoples, Ps 81:15
⁸to bind their kings with fetters,
 their nobles with shackles of
 iron, 2Ch 33:11
⁹to carry out the sentence
 written against them.
This is the glory of all his
 saints. Ps 148:14

Praise the Lord.

ᵃ14 *Horn* here symbolizes strong one, that is, king. ᵇ1 Hebrew *Hallelu Yah*; also in verse 9

Psalm 150

¹Praise the LORD.ᵃ

Praise God in his sanctuary;
    praise him in his mighty
        heavens.
²Praise him for his acts of
        power;   Dt 3:24
    praise him for his surpassing
        greatness.   Ps 145:5-6
³Praise him with the sounding
        of the trumpet,
    praise him with the harp and
        lyre,   Ps 149:3

⁴praise him with tambourine
        and dancing,   Ex 15:20
    praise him with the strings
        and flute,   Isa 38:20
⁵praise him with the clash of
        cymbals,   1Ch 15:16
    praise him with resounding
        cymbals.

⁶Let everything that has breath
        praise the LORD.   Ps 145:21

Praise the LORD.

ᵃ1 Hebrew *Hallelu Yah*; also in verse 6

Proverbs

Prologue: Purpose and Theme

1 The proverbs of Solomon son of David, king of Israel:

²for attaining wisdom and discipline;
  for understanding words of insight;
³for acquiring a disciplined and prudent life,
  doing what is right and just and fair;
⁴for giving prudence to the simple,   Pr 8:5
  knowledge and discretion to the young—   Pr 8:12
⁵let the wise listen and add to their learning,   Pr 9:9
  and let the discerning get guidance—
⁶for understanding proverbs and parables,   Ps 78:2
  the sayings and riddles of the wise.

⁷The fear of the LORD is the beginning of knowledge,
  but fools[a] despise wisdom and discipline.   Pr 8:33-36

Exhortations to Embrace Wisdom

Warning Against Enticement

⁸Listen, my son, to your father's instruction   Pr 4:1
  and do not forsake your mother's teaching.   Pr 6:20
⁹They will be a garland to grace your head
  and a chain to adorn your neck.   Pr 4:1-9

¹⁰My son, if sinners entice you,
  do not give in to them.   Dt 13:8
¹¹If they say, "Come along with us;
  let's lie in wait for someone's blood,
  let's waylay some harmless soul;
¹²let's swallow them alive, like the grave,[b]
  and whole, like those who go down to the pit;
¹³we will get all sorts of valuable things
  and fill our houses with plunder;
¹⁴throw in your lot with us,
  and we will share a common purse"—

---

[a]7 The Hebrew words rendered *fool* in Proverbs, and often elsewhere in the Old Testament, denote one who is morally deficient.   [b]12 Hebrew *Sheol*

¹⁵my son, do not go along with
them,
do not set foot on their
paths;   Ps 1:1; 119:101
¹⁶for their feet rush into sin,
they are swift to shed blood.
¹⁷How useless to spread a net
in full view of all the birds!
¹⁸These men lie in wait for their
own blood;   Ps 71:10
they waylay only
themselves!
¹⁹Such is the end of all who go
after ill-gotten gain;
it takes away the lives of
those who get it.   Pr 15:27

Warning Against Rejecting Wisdom

²⁰Wisdom calls aloud in the
street,   Pr 8:1
she raises her voice in the
public squares;
²¹at the head of the noisy
streetsᵃ she cries out,
in the gateways of the city
she makes her speech:

²²"How long will you simple
onesᵇ love your simple
ways?   Pr 8:5
How long will mockers
delight in mockery
and fools hate knowledge?
²³If you had responded to my
rebuke,
I would have poured out my
heart to you

and made my thoughts
known to you.
²⁴But since you rejected me
when I called   Isa 65:12; 66:4
and no one gave heed when
I stretched out my hand,
²⁵since you ignored all my
advice
and would not accept my
rebuke,
²⁶I in turn will laugh at your
disaster;   Ps 2:4
I will mock when calamity
overtakes you—   Pr 10:24
²⁷when calamity overtakes you
like a storm,
when disaster sweeps over
you like a whirlwind,
when distress and trouble
overwhelm you.

²⁸"Then they will call to me but
I will not answer;   Isa 1:15
they will look for me but
will not find me.   Eze 8:18
²⁹Since they hated knowledge
and did not choose to fear
the LORD,   Job 21:14
³⁰since they would not accept
my advice
and spurned my rebuke,
³¹they will eat the fruit of their
ways
and be filled with the fruit of
their schemes.   Isa 3:11
³²For the waywardness of the
simple will kill them,
and the complacency of fools
will destroy them;

ᵃ21 Hebrew; Septuagint / on the tops of the walls   ᵇ22 The Hebrew word rendered simple in Proverbs
generally denotes one without moral direction and inclined to evil.

33but whoever listens to me will
    live in safety   Ps 25:12
    and be at ease, without fear
      of harm."   Ps 112:8

Moral Benefits of Wisdom

2 My son, if you accept my
     words
    and store up my commands
      within you,
2turning your ear to wisdom
    and applying your heart to
      understanding,   Pr 22:17
3and if you call out for insight
    and cry aloud for
      understanding,
4and if you look for it as for
     silver
    and search for it as for
      hidden treasure,   Pr 3:14
5then you will understand the
     fear of the LORD
    and find the knowledge of
      God.   Pr 1:7
6For the LORD gives wisdom,
    and from his mouth come
      knowledge and
      understanding.
7He holds victory in store for
     the upright,
    he is a shield to those whose
      walk is blameless,
8for he guards the course of the
     just
    and protects the way of his
      faithful ones.   1Sa 2:9
9Then you will understand what
     is right and just   Dt 1:16

and fair—every good path.
10For wisdom will enter your
     heart,   Pr 14:33
    and knowledge will be
      pleasant to your soul.
11Discretion will protect you,
    and understanding will guard
      you.   Pr 6:22

12Wisdom will save you from the
     ways of wicked men,
    from men whose words are
      perverse,
13who leave the straight paths
    to walk in dark ways,   Jn 3:19
14who delight in doing wrong
    and rejoice in the
      perverseness of evil,
15whose paths are crooked
    and who are devious in their
      ways.   Pr 21:8

16It will save you also from the
     adulteress,
    from the wayward wife with
      her seductive words,
17who has left the partner of her
     youth
    and ignored the covenant
      she made before God.*a*
18For her house leads down to
     death
    and her paths to the spirits
      of the dead.   Pr 7:27
19None who go to her return
    or attain the paths of life.

20Thus you will walk in the ways
     of good men

a 17 Or covenant of her God

and keep to the paths of the
    righteous.
²¹For the upright will live in the
    land,   Ps 37:29
and the blameless will
    remain in it;
²²but the wicked will be cut off
    from the land,   Job 18:17
and the unfaithful will be
    torn from it.   Dt 28:63

Further Benefits of Wisdom

3 My son, do not forget my
    teaching,   Pr 4:5
but keep my commands in
    your heart,
²for they will prolong your life
    many years   Pr 4:10
and bring you prosperity.

³Let love and faithfulness never
    leave you;
bind them around your neck,
write them on the tablet of
    your heart.   Pr 6:21; 2Co 3:3
⁴Then you will win favor and a
    good name
in the sight of God and man.

⁵Trust in the Lord with all your
    heart   Ps 37:3,5
and lean not on your own
    understanding;
⁶in all your ways acknowledge
    him,
and he will make your paths
    straight.ᵃ   1Ch 28:9; Pr 16:3

⁷Do not be wise in your own
    eyes;   Ro 12:16

    fear the Lord and shun evil.
⁸This will bring health to your
    body,   Pr 4:22
and nourishment to your
    bones.   Job 21:24
⁹Honor the Lord with your
    wealth,
with the firstfruits of all your
    crops;   Ex 22:29; Dt 26:1-15
¹⁰then your barns will be filled
    to overflowing,   Dt 28:8
and your vats will brim over
    with new wine.   Joel 2:24
¹¹My son, do not despise the
    Lord's discipline   Job 5:17
and do not resent his
    rebuke,
¹²because the Lord disciplines
    those he loves,   Pr 13:24
as a fatherᵇ the son he
    delights in.   Dt 8:5
¹³Blessed is the man who finds
    wisdom,
the man who gains
    understanding,
¹⁴for she is more profitable than
    silver
and yields better returns
    than gold.   Job 28:15; Pr 8:19
¹⁵She is more precious than
    rubies;   Job 28:18
nothing you desire can
    compare with her.   Pr 8:11
¹⁶Long life is in her right hand;
in her left hand are riches
    and honor.   Pr 8:18
¹⁷Her ways are pleasant ways,

ᵃ6 Or *will direct your paths*   ᵇ12 Hebrew; Septuagint / *and he punishes*

and all her paths are peace.
¹⁸She is a tree of life to those
who embrace her;   Ge 2:9
those who lay hold of her
will be blessed.

¹⁹By wisdom the Lᴏʀᴅ laid the
earth's foundations,
by understanding he set the
heavens in place;
²⁰by his knowledge the deeps
were divided,
and the clouds let drop the
dew.

²¹My son, preserve sound
judgment and
discernment,
do not let them out of your
sight;   Pr 4:20-22
²²they will be life for you,
an ornament to grace your
neck.   Pr 1:8-9
²³Then you will go on your way
in safety,
and your foot will not
stumble;   Pr 4:12
²⁴when you lie down, you will
not be afraid;   Ps 3:5
when you lie down, your
sleep will be sweet.
²⁵Have no fear of sudden
disaster
or of the ruin that overtakes
the wicked,
²⁶for the Lᴏʀᴅ will be your
confidence
and will keep your foot from
being snared.   1Sa 2:9

²⁷Do not withhold good from
those who deserve it,

when it is in your power to
act.
²⁸Do not say to your neighbor,
"Come back later; I'll give it
tomorrow"—
when you now have it with
you.   Lev 19:13
²⁹Do not plot harm against your
neighbor,
who lives trustfully near
you.
³⁰Do not accuse a man for no
reason—
when he has done you no
harm.

³¹Do not envy a violent man
or choose any of his ways,
³²for the Lᴏʀᴅ detests a perverse
man   Pr 11:20
but takes the upright into his
confidence.   Ps 25:14

³³The Lᴏʀᴅ's curse is on the
house of the wicked,
but he blesses the home of
the righteous.   Ps 1:3
³⁴He mocks proud mockers
but gives grace to the
humble.   Jas 4:6*; 1Pe 5:5*
³⁵The wise inherit honor,
but fools he holds up to
shame.

Wisdom Is Supreme

4 Listen, my sons, to a father's
instruction;   Pr 1:8
pay attention and gain
understanding.
²I give you sound learning,

so do not forsake my
teaching.
³When I was a boy in my
father's house,
still tender, and an only
child of my mother,
⁴he taught me and said,
"Lay hold of my words with
all your heart;
keep my commands and you
will live.   Pr 7:2
⁵Get wisdom, get
understanding;   Pr 16:16
do not forget my words or
swerve from them.
⁶Do not forsake wisdom, and
she will protect you;
love her, and she will watch
over you.
⁷Wisdom is supreme; therefore
get wisdom.
Though it cost all you have,ᵃ
get understanding.
⁸Esteem her, and she will exalt
you;
embrace her, and she will
honor you.   1Sa 2:30; Pr 3:18
⁹She will set a garland of grace
on your head
and present you with a
crown of splendor."
¹⁰Listen, my son, accept what I
say,
and the years of your life
will be many.   Pr 3:2
¹¹I guide you in the way of
wisdom   1Sa 12:23
and lead you along straight
paths.

¹²When you walk, your steps
will not be hampered;
when you run, you will not
stumble.   Job 18:7; Pr 3:23
¹³Hold on to instruction, do not
let it go;
guard it well, for it is your
life.   Pr 3:22
¹⁴Do not set foot on the path of
the wicked
or walk in the way of evil
men.   Ps 1:1; Pr 1:15
¹⁵Avoid it, do not travel on it;
turn from it and go on your
way.
¹⁶For they cannot sleep till they
do evil;   Ps 36:4; Mic 2:1
they are robbed of slumber
till they make someone
fall.
¹⁷They eat the bread of
wickedness
and drink the wine of
violence.   Pr 1:10-19

¹⁸The path of the righteous is
like the first gleam of
dawn,   Isa 26:7
shining ever brighter till the
full light of day.   2Sa 23:4
¹⁹But the way of the wicked is
like deep darkness;
they do not know what
makes them stumble.

²⁰My son, pay attention to what
I say;
listen closely to my words.
²¹Do not let them out of your
sight,   Pr 3:21

ᵃ 7 Or *Whatever else you get*

keep them within your heart;
²²for they are life to those who
    find them
    and health to a man's whole
    body.   Pr 3:8; 12:18
²³Above all else, guard your
    heart,
    for it is the wellspring of life.
²⁴Put away perversity from your
    mouth;
    keep corrupt talk far from
    your lips.
²⁵Let your eyes look straight
    ahead,
    fix your gaze directly before
    you.
²⁶Make level*ᵃ* paths for your
    feet
    and take only ways that are
    firm.
²⁷Do not swerve to the right or
    the left;   Dt 5:32; 28:14
    keep your foot from evil.

Warning Against Adultery

5 My son, pay attention to my
    wisdom,
    listen well to my words of
    insight,   Pr 4:20
²that you may maintain
    discretion
    and your lips may preserve
    knowledge.
³For the lips of an adulteress
    drip honey,
    and her speech is smoother
    than oil;   Ps 55:21; Pr 2:16
⁴but in the end she is bitter as
    gall,   Ecc 7:26

sharp as a double-edged
    sword.
⁵Her feet go down to death;
    her steps lead straight to the
    grave.*ᵇ*   Pr 7:26-27
⁶She gives no thought to the
    way of life;
    her paths are crooked, but
    she knows it not.   Pr 30:20

⁷Now then, my sons, listen to
    me;   Pr 7:24
    do not turn aside from what
    I say.
⁸Keep to a path far from her,
    do not go near the door of
    her house,
⁹lest you give your best strength
    to others
    and your years to one who
    is cruel,
¹⁰lest strangers feast on your
    wealth
    and your toil enrich another
    man's house.   Pr 29:3
¹¹At the end of your life you will
    groan,
    when your flesh and body
    are spent.
¹²You will say, "How I hated
    discipline!
    How my heart spurned
    correction!   Pr 1:29; 12:1
¹³I would not obey my
    teachers
    or listen to my instructors.
¹⁴I have come to the brink of
    utter ruin   Pr 1:24-27
    in the midst of the whole
    assembly."

ᵃ 26 Or *Consider the*   ᵇ 5 Hebrew *Sheol*

¹⁵Drink water from your own
cistern,
running water from your
own well.
¹⁶Should your springs overflow
in the streets,
your streams of water in the
public squares?
¹⁷Let them be yours alone,
never to be shared with
strangers.
¹⁸May your fountain be blessed,
and may you rejoice in the
wife of your youth.
¹⁹A loving doe, a graceful deer—
may her breasts satisfy you
always,
may you ever be captivated
by her love.
²⁰Why be captivated, my son, by
an adulteress?
Why embrace the bosom of
another man's wife?

²¹For a man's ways are in full
view of the LORD,   Hos 7:2
and he examines all his
paths.   Job 31:4; 34:21; Pr 15:3
²²The evil deeds of a wicked
man ensnare him;   Ps 9:16
the cords of his sin hold him
fast.   Nu 32:23; Ps 7:15-16
²³He will die for lack of
discipline,   Job 4:21; 36:12
led astray by his own great
folly.

Warnings Against Folly

6 My son, if you have put up
security for your
neighbor,   Pr 17:18

if you have struck hands in
pledge for another,
²if you have been trapped by
what you said,
ensnared by the words of
your mouth,
³then do this, my son, to free
yourself,
since you have fallen into
your neighbor's hands:
Go and humble yourself;
press your plea with your
neighbor!
⁴Allow no sleep to your
eyes,
no slumber to your eyelids.
⁵Free yourself, like a gazelle
from the hand of the
hunter,
like a bird from the snare of
the fowler.   Ps 91:3

⁶Go to the ant, you sluggard;
consider its ways and be
wise!
⁷It has no commander,
no overseer or ruler,
⁸yet it stores its provisions in
summer
and gathers its food at
harvest.   Pr 10:4

⁹How long will you lie there,
you sluggard?   Pr 24:30-34
When will you get up from
your sleep?
¹⁰A little sleep, a little slumber,
a little folding of the hands
to rest—   Pr 24:33
¹¹and poverty will come on you
like a bandit   Pr 24:30-34

and scarcity like an armed
    man.^a

¹²A scoundrel and villain,
    who goes about with a
        corrupt mouth,
¹³ who winks with his eye,
    signals with his feet
    and motions with his fingers,
¹⁴ who plots evil with deceit in
    his heart—   Mic 2:1
    he always stirs up
        dissension.   ver 16-19
¹⁵Therefore disaster will overtake
    him in an instant;
    he will suddenly be
        destroyed—without
        remedy.   2Ch 36:16
¹⁶There are six things the LORD
    hates,
    seven that are detestable to
        him:
¹⁷ haughty eyes,
    a lying tongue,   Ps 120:2
    hands that shed innocent
        blood,   Isa 1:15
¹⁸ a heart that devises
        wicked schemes,
    feet that are quick to rush
        into evil,   Ge 6:5
¹⁹ a false witness who pours
    out lies   Ps 27:12
    and a man who stirs up
        dissension among
        brothers.   ver 12-15

Warning Against Adultery

²⁰My son, keep your father's
    commands

    and do not forsake your
        mother's teaching.   Pr 1:8
²¹Bind them upon your heart
        forever;
    fasten them around your
        neck.   Pr 3:3; 7:1-3
²²When you walk, they will
        guide you;
    when you sleep, they will
        watch over you;
    when you awake, they will
        speak to you.
²³For these commands are a
        lamp,
    this teaching is a light,   Ps 19:8
  and the corrections of
        discipline
    are the way to life,
²⁴keeping you from the immoral
        woman,
    from the smooth tongue of
        the wayward wife.   Pr 2:16
²⁵Do not lust in your heart after
        her beauty
    or let her captivate you with
        her eyes,
²⁶for the prostitute reduces you
        to a loaf of bread,
    and the adulteress preys
        upon your very life.
²⁷Can a man scoop fire into his
        lap
    without his clothes being
        burned?
²⁸Can a man walk on hot coals
    without his feet being
        scorched?
²⁹So is he who sleeps with
        another man's wife;

^a 11 Or *like a vagrant / and scarcity like a beggar*

no one who touches her will
   go unpunished.

³⁰Men do not despise a thief if
   he steals
to satisfy his hunger when
   he is starving.
³¹Yet if he is caught, he must
   pay sevenfold,   Ex 22:1-14
though it costs him all the
   wealth of his house.
³²But a man who commits
   adultery lacks judgment;
whoever does so destroys
   himself.
³³Blows and disgrace are his
   lot,
and his shame will never be
   wiped away;   Pr 5:9-14
³⁴for jealousy arouses a
   husband's fury,   Ge 34:7
and he will show no mercy
   when he takes revenge.
³⁵He will not accept any
   compensation;
he will refuse the bribe,
   however great it is.

Warning Against the Adulteress

7 My son, keep my words
   and store up my commands
   within you.
²Keep my commands and you
   will live;   Pr 4:4
guard my teachings as the
   apple of your eye.
³Bind them on your fingers;
   write them on the tablet of
   your heart.   Dt 6:8; Pr 3:3

⁴Say to wisdom, "You are my
   sister,"
and call understanding your
   kinsman;
⁵they will keep you from the
   adulteress,
from the wayward wife with
   her seductive words.

⁶At the window of my house
   I looked out through the
   lattice.
⁷I saw among the simple,
   I noticed among the young
   men,
a youth who lacked
   judgment.   Pr 6:32
⁸He was going down the street
   near her corner,
walking along in the
   direction of her house
⁹at twilight, as the day was
   fading,   Job 24:15
as the dark of night set
   in.

¹⁰Then out came a woman to
   meet him,
dressed like a prostitute and
   with crafty intent.
¹¹(She is loud and defiant,   Pr 9:13
   her feet never stay at
   home;
¹²now in the street, now in the
   squares,
at every corner she lurks.)
¹³She took hold of him and
   kissed him   Ge 39:12
and with a brazen face she
   said:

¹⁴"I have fellowship offerings^a at
    home;   Lev 7:11-18
  today I fulfilled my vows.
¹⁵So I came out to meet you;
  I looked for you and have
    found you!
¹⁶I have covered my bed
  with colored linens from
    Egypt.
¹⁷I have perfumed my bed   Est 1:6
  with myrrh, aloes and
    cinnamon.   Ge 37:25
¹⁸Come, let's drink deep of love
    till morning;
  let's enjoy ourselves with
    love!   Ge 39:7
¹⁹My husband is not at home;
  he has gone on a long
    journey.
²⁰He took his purse filled with
    money
  and will not be home till full
    moon."

²¹With persuasive words she led
    him astray;
  she seduced him with her
    smooth talk.   Pr 5:3
²²All at once he followed her
  like an ox going to the
    slaughter,
  like a deer^b stepping into a
    noose^c   Job 18:10
²³ till an arrow pierces his
    liver,
  like a bird darting into a
    snare,
  little knowing it will cost
    him his life.   Ecc 9:12

²⁴Now then, my sons, listen to
    me;   Pr 1:8-9
  pay attention to what I say.
²⁵Do not let your heart turn to
    her ways
  or stray into her paths.
²⁶Many are the victims she has
    brought down;
  her slain are a mighty
    throng.
²⁷Her house is a highway to the
    grave,^d
  leading down to the
    chambers of death.

Wisdom's Call

8 Does not wisdom call out?
  Does not understanding raise
    her voice?
²On the heights along the way,
  where the paths meet, she
    takes her stand;
³beside the gates leading into
    the city,
  at the entrances, she cries
    aloud: Job 29:7
⁴"To you, O men, I call out;
  I raise my voice to all
    mankind.
⁵You who are simple, gain
    prudence;   Pr 1:4,22
  you who are foolish, gain
    understanding.
⁶Listen, for I have worthy things
    to say;
  I open my lips to speak what
    is right.
⁷My mouth speaks what is true,

---

^a14 Traditionally *peace offerings*   ^b22 Syriac (see also Septuagint); Hebrew *fool*   ^c22 The meaning
of the Hebrew for this line is uncertain.   ^d27 Hebrew *Sheol*

for my lips detest
wickedness.
⁸All the words of my mouth are
just;
none of them is crooked or
perverse.
⁹To the discerning all of them
are right;
they are faultless to those
who have knowledge.
¹⁰Choose my instruction instead
of silver,
knowledge rather than
choice gold,   Pr 3:14-15
¹¹for wisdom is more precious
than rubies,   Job 28:17-19
and nothing you desire can
compare with her.

¹²"I, wisdom, dwell together with
prudence;
I possess knowledge and
discretion.   Pr 1:4
¹³To fear the LORD is to hate
evil;
I hate pride and arrogance,
evil behavior and perverse
speech.
¹⁴Counsel and sound judgment
are mine;
I have understanding and
power.   Ecc 7:19
¹⁵By me kings reign
and rulers make laws that
are just;   Da 2:21; Ro 13:1
¹⁶by me princes govern,
and all nobles who rule on
earth.ᵃ

¹⁷I love those who love me,
and those who seek me find
me.   Pr 1:28; Jas 1:5
¹⁸With me are riches and
honor,
enduring wealth and
prosperity.   Mt 6:33
¹⁹My fruit is better than fine
gold;
what I yield surpasses choice
silver.   Pr 3:13-14; 10:20
²⁰I walk in the way of
righteousness,
along the paths of justice,
²¹bestowing wealth on those
who love me
and making their treasuries
full.   Pr 15:6; 24:4

²²"The LORD brought me forth as
the first of his works,ᵇ,ᶜ
before his deeds of old;
²³I was appointedᵈ from eternity,
from the beginning, before
the world began.
²⁴When there were no oceans, I
was given birth,
when there were no springs
abounding with water;
²⁵before the mountains were
settled in place,
before the hills, I was given
birth,   Job 15:7
²⁶before he made the earth or its
fields
or any of the dust of the
world.   Ps 90:2

ᵃ 16 Many Hebrew manuscripts and Septuagint; most Hebrew manuscripts *and nobles—all righteous
rulers*   ᵇ 22 Or *way*; or *dominion*   ᶜ 22 Or *The LORD possessed me at the beginning of his work*; or
The LORD brought me forth at the beginning of his work   ᵈ 23 Or *fashioned*

²⁷I was there when he set the
　　heavens in place,　　Pr 3:19
　when he marked out the
　　horizon on the face of
　　the deep,
²⁸when he established the clouds
　　above
　and fixed securely the
　　fountains of the deep,
²⁹when he gave the sea its
　　boundary　　Ge 1:9; Job 38:10
　so the waters would not
　　overstep his command,
　and when he marked out the
　　foundations of the earth.
³⁰　Then I was the craftsman at
　　his side.　　Jn 1:1-3
　I was filled with delight day
　　after day,
　rejoicing always in his
　　presence,
³¹rejoicing in his whole world
　　and delighting in mankind.

³²"Now then, my sons, listen to
　　me;
　blessed are those who keep
　　my ways.　　Ps 119:1-2; Lk 11:28
³³Listen to my instruction and be
　　wise;
　do not ignore it.
³⁴Blessed is the man who listens
　　to me,　　Pr 3:13,18
　watching daily at my doors,
　waiting at my doorway.
³⁵For whoever finds me finds life
　and receives favor from the
　　LORD.　　Pr 12:2
³⁶But whoever fails to find me
　　harms himself;　　Pr 15:32
　all who hate me love death."

Invitations of Wisdom and of Folly

9 Wisdom has built her house;
　　she has hewn out its seven
　　pillars.
²She has prepared her meat and
　　mixed her wine;
　she has also set her table.
³She has sent out her maids,
　　and she calls　　Pr 8:1-3
　from the highest point of the
　　city.
⁴"Let all who are simple come
　　in here!"
　she says to those who lack
　　judgment.　　Pr 6:32
⁵"Come, eat my food
　and drink the wine I have
　　mixed.　　Isa 55:1
⁶Leave your simple ways and
　　you will live;　　Pr 8:35
　walk in the way of
　　understanding.

⁷"Whoever corrects a mocker
　　invites insult;
　whoever rebukes a wicked
　　man incurs abuse.　　Pr 23:9
⁸Do not rebuke a mocker or he
　　will hate you;
　rebuke a wise man and he
　　will love you.　　Ps 141:5
⁹Instruct a wise man and he
　　will be wiser still;
　teach a righteous man and
　　he will add to his
　　learning.　　Pr 1:5,7

¹⁰"The fear of the LORD is the
　　beginning of wisdom,

and knowledge of the Holy
One is understanding.
[11]For through me your days will
be many,
and years will be added to
your life.   Pr 3:16
[12]If you are wise, your wisdom
will reward you;
if you are a mocker, you
alone will suffer."

[13]The woman Folly is loud;
she is undisciplined and
without knowledge.
[14]She sits at the door of her
house,
on a seat at the highest point
of the city,   ver 3
[15]calling out to those who pass
by,
who go straight on their
way.
[16]"Let all who are simple come
in here!"
she says to those who lack
judgment.   Pr 1:22
[17]"Stolen water is sweet;
food eaten in secret is
delicious!"   Pr 20:17
[18]But little do they know that the
dead are there,
that her guests are in the
depths of the grave.[a]

Proverbs of Solomon

10

The proverbs of Solomon:
A wise son brings joy to
his father,   Pr 15:20

but a foolish son grief to his
mother.

[2]Ill-gotten treasures are of no
value,   Pr 21:6
but righteousness delivers
from death.

[3]The LORD does not let the
righteous go hungry
but he thwarts the craving of
the wicked.

[4]Lazy hands make a man poor,
but diligent hands bring
wealth.   Pr 13:4

[5]He who gathers crops in
summer is a wise son,
but he who sleeps during
harvest is a disgraceful
son.

[6]Blessings crown the head of
the righteous,
but violence overwhelms the
mouth of the wicked.[b]

[7]The memory of the righteous
will be a blessing,
but the name of the wicked
will rot.   Ps 109:13

[8]The wise in heart accept
commands,
but a chattering fool comes
to ruin.   Mt 7:24-27

[9]The man of integrity walks
securely,   Ps 23:4; Isa 33:15
but he who takes crooked
paths will be found out.

---

[a] 18 Hebrew *Sheol*   [b] 6 Or *but the mouth of the wicked conceals violence*; also in verse 11

¹⁰He who winks maliciously
        causes grief,
    and a chattering fool comes
        to ruin.

¹¹The mouth of the righteous is
        a fountain of life,   Ps 37:30
    but violence overwhelms the
        mouth of the wicked.

¹²Hatred stirs up dissension,
    but love covers over all
        wrongs.   1Pe 4:8

¹³Wisdom is found on the lips of
        the discerning,
    but a rod is for the back of
        him who lacks
        judgment.   Pr 26:3

¹⁴Wise men store up knowledge,
    but the mouth of a fool
        invites ruin.   Pr 18:6-7

¹⁵The wealth of the rich is their
        fortified city,   Pr 18:11
    but poverty is the ruin of the
        poor.   Pr 19:7

¹⁶The wages of the righteous
        bring them life,
    but the income of the
        wicked brings them
        punishment.   Pr 11:18-19

¹⁷He who heeds discipline shows
        the way to life,   Pr 6:23
    but whoever ignores
        correction leads others
        astray.

¹⁸He who conceals his hatred
        has lying lips,   Ps 31:18
    and whoever spreads slander
        is a fool.

¹⁹When words are many, sin is
        not absent,
    but he who holds his tongue
        is wise.   Pr 17:28; Ecc 5:3

²⁰The tongue of the righteous is
        choice silver,
    but the heart of the wicked
        is of little value.

²¹The lips of the righteous
        nourish many,
    but fools die for lack of
        judgment.   Hos 4:1,6,14

²²The blessing of the LORD brings
        wealth,   Ge 24:35
    and he adds no trouble to it.

²³A fool finds pleasure in evil
        conduct,   Pr 15:21
    but a man of understanding
        delights in wisdom.

²⁴What the wicked dreads will
        overtake him;   Isa 66:4
    what the righteous desire
        will be granted.

²⁵When the storm has swept by,
        the wicked are gone,
    but the righteous stand firm
        forever.   Ps 15:5

²⁶As vinegar to the teeth and
        smoke to the eyes,
    so is a sluggard to those who
        send him.   Pr 26:6

²⁷The fear of the LORD adds
        length to life,   Pr 9:10-11
    but the years of the wicked
        are cut short.   Job 15:32

28The prospect of the righteous
    is joy,
but the hopes of the wicked
    come to nothing.   Job 8:13

29The way of the Lord is a
    refuge for the righteous,
but it is the ruin of those
    who do evil.   Pr 21:15

30The righteous will never be
    uprooted,
but the wicked will not
    remain in the land.

31The mouth of the righteous
    brings forth wisdom,
but a perverse tongue will be
    cut out.

32The lips of the righteous know
    what is fitting,   Ecc 10:12
but the mouth of the wicked
    only what is perverse.

11 The Lord abhors
    dishonest scales,   Lev 19:36
but accurate weights are his
    delight.   Pr 16:11

2When pride comes, then comes
    disgrace,   Pr 16:18
but with humility comes
    wisdom.   Pr 18:12

3The integrity of the upright
    guides them,
but the unfaithful are
    destroyed by their
    duplicity.   Pr 13:6

4Wealth is worthless in the day
    of wrath,   Eze 7:19; Zep 1:18
but righteousness delivers
    from death.   Ge 7:1

5The righteousness of the
    blameless makes a
    straight way for them,
but the wicked are brought
    down by their own
    wickedness.   Pr 5:21-23

6The righteousness of the
    upright delivers them,
but the unfaithful are
    trapped by evil desires.

7When a wicked man dies, his
    hope perishes;
all he expected from his
    power comes to nothing.

8The righteous man is rescued
    from trouble,
and it comes on the wicked
    instead.   Pr 21:18

9With his mouth the godless
    destroys his neighbor,
but through knowledge the
    righteous escape.   Jer 45:5

10When the righteous prosper,
    the city rejoices;   Pr 28:12
when the wicked perish,
    there are shouts of joy.

11Through the blessing of the
    upright a city is exalted,
but by the mouth of the
    wicked it is destroyed.

12A man who lacks judgment
    derides his neighbor,
but a man of understanding
    holds his tongue.

13A gossip betrays a confidence,
but a trustworthy man keeps
    a secret.

¹⁴For lack of guidance a nation
     falls,
  but many advisers make
     victory sure.   Pr 15:22; 24:6

¹⁵He who puts up security for
     another will surely
     suffer,   Pr 6:1
  but whoever refuses to strike
     hands in pledge is safe.

¹⁶A kindhearted woman gains
     respect,   Pr 31:31
  but ruthless men gain only
     wealth.

¹⁷A kind man benefits himself,
  but a cruel man brings
     trouble on himself.

¹⁸The wicked man earns
     deceptive wages,
  but he who sows
     righteousness reaps a
     sure reward.   Hos 10:12-13

¹⁹The truly righteous man attains
     life,   Dt 30:15
  but he who pursues evil
     goes to his death.

²⁰The Lord detests men of
     perverse heart
  but he delights in those
     whose ways are
     blameless. Ps 119:1; Pr 12:2,22

²¹Be sure of this: The wicked
     will not go unpunished,
  but those who are righteous
     will go free.   Pr 16:5

²²Like a gold ring in a pig's
     snout

is a beautiful woman who
     shows no discretion.

²³The desire of the righteous
     ends only in good,
  but the hope of the wicked
     only in wrath.

²⁴One man gives freely, yet gains
     even more;
  another withholds unduly,
     but comes to poverty.

²⁵A generous man will prosper;
  he who refreshes others will
     himself be refreshed.

²⁶People curse the man who
     hoards grain,
  but blessing crowns him
     who is willing to sell.

²⁷He who seeks good finds
     goodwill,
  but evil comes to him who
     searches for it.   Est 7:10

²⁸Whoever trusts in his riches
     will fall,   Mk 10:25; 1Ti 6:17
  but the righteous will thrive
     like a green leaf. Ps 1:3

²⁹He who brings trouble on his
     family will inherit only
     wind,
  and the fool will be servant
     to the wise.   Pr 14:19

³⁰The fruit of the righteous is a
     tree of life,   Jas 5:20
  and he who wins souls is
     wise.

³¹If the righteous receive their
     due on earth,   Pr 13:21

12 Whoever loves discipline
loves knowledge,
but he who hates correction
is stupid.   Pr 9:7-9

²A good man obtains favor from
the LORD,   Ps 84:11
but the LORD condemns a
crafty man.

³A man cannot be established
through wickedness,
but the righteous cannot be
uprooted.   Pr 10:25

⁴A wife of noble character is
her husband's crown,
but a disgraceful wife is like
decay in his bones.

⁵The plans of the righteous are
just,
but the advice of the wicked
is deceitful.

⁶The words of the wicked lie in
wait for blood,
but the speech of the upright
rescues them.   Pr 14:3

⁷Wicked men are overthrown
and are no more,   Ps 37:36
but the house of the
righteous stands firm.

⁸A man is praised according to
his wisdom,
but men with warped minds
are despised.

⁹Better to be a nobody and yet
have a servant

than pretend to be
somebody and have no
food.

¹⁰A righteous man cares for the
needs of his animal,
but the kindest acts of the
wicked are cruel.

¹¹He who works his land will
have abundant food,
but he who chases fantasies
lacks judgment.   Pr 28:19

¹²The wicked desire the plunder
of evil men,
but the root of the righteous
flourishes.

¹³An evil man is trapped by his
sinful talk,   Pr 18:7
but a righteous man escapes
trouble.   2Pe 2:9

¹⁴From the fruit of his lips a
man is filled with good
things   Pr 13:2
as surely as the work of his
hands rewards him.

¹⁵The way of a fool seems right
to him,   Pr 14:12; 16:2,25
but a wise man listens to
advice.

¹⁶A fool shows his annoyance at
once,
but a prudent man overlooks
an insult.   Pr 29:11

¹⁷A truthful witness gives honest
testimony,
but a false witness tells lies.

¹⁸Reckless words pierce like a
    sword,   Ps 57:4
but the tongue of the wise
    brings healing.   Pr 15:4

¹⁹Truthful lips endure forever,
but a lying tongue lasts only
    a moment.

²⁰There is deceit in the hearts of
    those who plot evil,
but joy for those who
    promote peace.

²¹No harm befalls the righteous,
but the wicked have their fill
    of trouble.

²²The LORD detests lying lips,
but he delights in men who
    are truthful.   Pr 11:20

²³A prudent man keeps his
    knowledge to himself,
but the heart of fools blurts
    out folly.

²⁴Diligent hands will rule,
but laziness ends in slave
    labor.   Pr 10:4

²⁵An anxious heart weighs a
    man down,   Pr 15:13; Isa 50:4
but a kind word cheers him
    up.

²⁶A righteous man is cautious in
    friendship,ᵃ
but the way of the wicked
    leads them astray.

²⁷The lazy man does not roastᵇ
    his game,

but the diligent man prizes
    his possessions.

²⁸In the way of righteousness
    there is life;   Dt 30:15
along that path is
    immortality.

13 A wise son heeds his
father's instruction,
but a mocker does not listen
    to rebuke.   Pr 10:1

²From the fruit of his lips a
    man enjoys good things,
but the unfaithful have a
    craving for violence.

³He who guards his lips guards
    his life,   Pr 21:23; Jas 3:2
but he who speaks rashly
    will come to ruin.

⁴The sluggard craves and gets
    nothing,   Pr 21:25-26
but the desires of the
    diligent are fully
    satisfied.

⁵The righteous hate what is
    false,   Ps 119:128
but the wicked bring shame
    and disgrace.

⁶Righteousness guards the man
    of integrity,
but wickedness overthrows
    the sinner.   Pr 11:3,5

⁷One man pretends to be rich,
    yet has nothing;
another pretends to be poor,
    yet has great wealth.

ᵃ26 Or *man is a guide to his neighbor*   ᵇ27 The meaning of the Hebrew for this word is uncertain.

⁸A man's riches may ransom his
life,
but a poor man hears no
threat.

⁹The light of the righteous
shines brightly,
but the lamp of the wicked
is snuffed out.   Job 18:5

¹⁰Pride only breeds quarrels,
but wisdom is found in
those who take advice.

¹¹Dishonest money dwindles
away,   Pr 10:2
but he who gathers money
little by little makes it
grow.

¹²Hope deferred makes the heart
sick,
but a longing fulfilled is a
tree of life.

¹³He who scorns instruction will
pay for it,   Nu 15:31; 2Ch 36:16
but he who respects a
command is rewarded.

¹⁴The teaching of the wise is a
fountain of life,   Pr 10:11
turning a man from the
snares of death.   Pr 14:27

¹⁵Good understanding wins
favor,
but the way of the unfaithful
is hard.ᵃ

¹⁶Every prudent man acts out of
knowledge,
but a fool exposes his folly.

¹⁷A wicked messenger falls into
trouble,
but a trustworthy envoy
brings healing.   Pr 25:13

¹⁸He who ignores discipline
comes to poverty and
shame,
but whoever heeds
correction is honored.

¹⁹A longing fulfilled is sweet to
the soul,
but fools detest turning from
evil.

²⁰He who walks with the wise
grows wise,
but a companion of fools
suffers harm.   Pr 15:31

²¹Misfortune pursues the sinner,
but prosperity is the reward
of the righteous.   Ps 32:10

²²A good man leaves an
inheritance for his
children's children,
but a sinner's wealth is
stored up for the
righteous.   Job 27:17; Ecc 2:26

²³A poor man's field may
produce abundant food,
but injustice sweeps it away.

²⁴He who spares the rod hates
his son,
but he who loves him is
careful to discipline him.

²⁵The righteous eat to their
hearts' content,

ᵃ 15 Or unfaithful does not endure

but the stomach of the
wicked goes hungry.

14 The wise woman builds
her house,   Pr 24:3
but with her own hands the
foolish one tears hers
down.

²He whose walk is upright fears
the LORD,
but he whose ways are
devious despises him.

³A fool's talk brings a rod to his
back,   Pr 10:14; Ecc 10:12
but the lips of the wise
protect them.   Pr 12:6

⁴Where there are no oxen, the
manger is empty,
but from the strength of an
ox comes an abundant
harvest.

⁵A truthful witness does not
deceive,
but a false witness pours out
lies.   Pr 6:19; 12:17

⁶The mocker seeks wisdom and
finds none,
but knowledge comes easily
to the discerning.   Pr 9:9

⁷Stay away from a foolish man,
for you will not find
knowledge on his lips.

⁸The wisdom of the prudent is
to give thought to their
ways,   Pr 15:28
but the folly of fools is
deception.   ver 24

⁹Fools mock at making amends
for sin,
but goodwill is found among
the upright.

¹⁰Each heart knows its own
bitterness,
and no one else can share its
joy.

¹¹The house of the wicked will
be destroyed,
but the tent of the upright
will flourish.   Pr 3:33; 12:7

¹²There is a way that seems right
to a man,   Pr 12:15
but in the end it leads to
death.   Pr 16:25

¹³Even in laughter the heart may
ache,   Ecc 2:2
and joy may end in grief.

¹⁴The faithless will be fully
repaid for their ways,
and the good man rewarded
for his.   Pr 12:14

¹⁵A simple man believes
anything,
but a prudent man gives
thought to his steps.

¹⁶A wise man fears the LORD and
shuns evil,   Pr 22:3
but a fool is hotheaded and
reckless.   1Sa 25:25

¹⁷A quick-tempered man does
foolish things,   ver 29
and a crafty man is hated.

¹⁸The simple inherit folly,

but the prudent are crowned
with knowledge.

¹⁹Evil men will bow down in the
presence of the good,
and the wicked at the gates
of the righteous.   Pr 11:29

²⁰The poor are shunned even by
their neighbors,
but the rich have many
friends.   Pr 19:4,7

²¹He who despises his neighbor
sins,   Pr 11:12
but blessed is he who is
kind to the needy.   Ps 41:1

²²Do not those who plot evil go
astray?   Pr 4:16-17
But those who plan what is
good find*ᵃ love and
faithfulness.

²³All hard work brings a profit,
but mere talk leads only to
poverty.

²⁴The wealth of the wise is their
crown,
but the folly of fools yields
folly.   ver 8

²⁵A truthful witness saves lives,
but a false witness is
deceitful.   ver 5

²⁶He who fears the LORD has a
secure fortress,   Pr 18:10
and for his children it will
be a refuge.

²⁷The fear of the LORD is a
fountain of life,   Pr 10:11

turning a man from the
snares of death.   Pr 13:14

²⁸A large population is a king's
glory,
but without subjects a prince
is ruined.   2Sa 19:7

²⁹A patient man has great
understanding,   Pr 17:27
but a quick-tempered man
displays folly.   Ecc 7:8-9

³⁰A heart at peace gives life to
the body,
but envy rots the bones.

³¹He who oppresses the poor
shows contempt for
their Maker,   Pr 17:5
but whoever is kind to the
needy honors God.

³²When calamity comes, the
wicked are brought
down,   Pr 6:15
but even in death the
righteous have a refuge.

³³Wisdom reposes in the heart of
the discerning   Pr 2:6-10
and even among fools she
lets herself be known.ᵇ

³⁴Righteousness exalts a nation,
but sin is a disgrace to any
people.

³⁵A king delights in a wise
servant,
but a shameful servant
incurs his wrath.

ᵃ22 Or show   ᵇ33 Hebrew; Septuagint and Syriac / but in the heart of fools she is not known

15

A gentle answer turns
away wrath,   Pr 25:15
but a harsh word stirs up
anger.

²The tongue of the wise
commends knowledge,
but the mouth of the fool
gushes folly.   Pr 12:23

³The eyes of the LORD are
everywhere,   2Ch 16:9
keeping watch on the wicked
and the good.   Jer 16:17

⁴The tongue that brings healing
is a tree of life,   Ps 5:9
but a deceitful tongue
crushes the spirit.   Pr 12:18

⁵A fool spurns his father's
discipline,
but whoever heeds
correction shows
prudence.   Pr 13:1

⁶The house of the righteous
contains great treasure,
but the income of the
wicked brings them
trouble.   Pr 10:16

⁷The lips of the wise spread
knowledge;   Pr 10:13
not so the hearts of fools.

⁸The LORD detests the sacrifice
of the wicked,   Pr 21:27
but the prayer of the upright
pleases him.   ver 29

⁹The LORD detests the way of
the wicked   Pr 6:16

but he loves those who
pursue righteousness.

¹⁰Stern discipline awaits him
who leaves the path;
he who hates correction will
die.   Pr 1:31-32

¹¹Death and Destruction*a* lie
open before the LORD —
how much more the hearts
of men!   2Ch 6:30; Ps 44:21

¹²A mocker resents correction;
he will not consult the wise.

¹³A happy heart makes the face
cheerful,
but heartache crushes the
spirit.   Pr 12:25; 17:22

¹⁴The discerning heart seeks
knowledge,   Pr 18:15
but the mouth of a fool
feeds on folly.

¹⁵All the days of the oppressed
are wretched,
but the cheerful heart has a
continual feast.   ver 13

¹⁶Better a little with the fear of
the LORD
than great wealth with
turmoil.   Ps 37:16-17; 1Ti 6:6

¹⁷Better a meal of vegetables
where there is love
than a fattened calf with
hatred.   Pr 17:1

¹⁸A hot-tempered man stirs up
dissension,   Pr 26:21

---

a 11 Hebrew *Sheol and Abaddon*

but a patient man calms a
   quarrel.   Ge 13:8

19The way of the sluggard is
   blocked with thorns,
but the path of the upright is
   a highway.

20A wise son brings joy to his
   father,   Pr 10:1
but a foolish man despises
   his mother.

21Folly delights a man who lacks
   judgment,   Pr 10:23
but a man of understanding
   keeps a straight course.

22Plans fail for lack of counsel,
but with many advisers they
   succeed.   Pr 11:14

23A man finds joy in giving an
   apt reply—   Pr 12:14
and how good is a timely
   word!   Pr 25:11

24The path of life leads upward
   for the wise
to keep him from going
   down to the grave.a

25The LORD tears down the proud
   man's house   Pr 12:7
but he keeps the widow's
   boundaries intact.

26The LORD detests the thoughts
   of the wicked, Pr 6:16
but those of the pure are
   pleasing to him.

27A greedy man brings trouble to
   his family,

but he who hates bribes will
   live.   Ex 23:8; Isa 33:15

28The heart of the righteous
   weighs its answers,
but the mouth of the wicked
   gushes evil.

29The LORD is far from the
   wicked
but he hears the prayer of
   the righteous. Ps 145:18-19

30A cheerful look brings joy to
   the heart,
and good news gives health
   to the bones.   Pr 25:25

31He who listens to a life-giving
   rebuke
will be at home among the
   wise.   ver 5

32He who ignores discipline
   despises himself, Pr 1:7
but whoever heeds
   correction gains
   understanding. Pr 9:7-9

33The fear of the LORD teaches a
   man wisdom,b Pr 1:7
and humility comes before
   honor.   Pr 18:12

16 To man belong the plans
   of the heart,
but from the LORD comes the
   reply of the tongue.

2All a man's ways seem
   innocent to him, Pr 12:15
but motives are weighed by
   the LORD.   Pr 21:2

a24 Hebrew *Sheol*   b33 Or *Wisdom teaches the fear of the* LORD

³Commit to the LORD whatever
  you do,
  and your plans will succeed.

⁴The LORD works out everything
  for his own ends—
  even the wicked for a day of
  disaster.   Ro 9:22

⁵The LORD detests all the proud
  of heart.   Pr 6:16
  Be sure of this: They will not
  go unpunished.   Pr 11:20-21

⁶Through love and faithfulness
  sin is atoned for;
  through the fear of the LORD
  a man avoids evil.

⁷When a man's ways are
  pleasing to the LORD,
  he makes even his enemies
  live at peace with him.

⁸Better a little with
  righteousness
  than much gain with
  injustice.   Ps 37:16

⁹In his heart a man plans his
  course,
  but the LORD determines his
  steps.   Jer 10:23

¹⁰The lips of a king speak as an
  oracle,
  and his mouth should not
  betray justice.   Pr 17:7

¹¹Honest scales and balances are
  from the LORD;
  all the weights in the bag are
  of his making.   Pr 11:1

¹²Kings detest wrongdoing,

for a throne is established
  through righteousness.

¹³Kings take pleasure in honest
  lips;
  they value a man who
  speaks the truth.   Pr 14:35

¹⁴A king's wrath is a messenger
  of death,   Pr 19:12
  but a wise man will appease
  it.   Ecc 10:4

¹⁵When a king's face brightens,
  it means life;   Job 29:24
  his favor is like a rain cloud
  in spring.   Pr 19:12

¹⁶How much better to get
  wisdom than gold,
  to choose understanding
  rather than silver!

¹⁷The highway of the upright
  avoids evil;
  he who guards his way
  guards his life.   Pr 19:16

¹⁸Pride goes before destruction,
  a haughty spirit before a fall.

¹⁹Better to be lowly in spirit and
  among the oppressed
  than to share plunder with
  the proud.

²⁰Whoever gives heed to
  instruction prospers,
  and blessed is he who trusts
  in the LORD.   Ps 34:8; Jer 17:7

²¹The wise in heart are called
  discerning,

and pleasant words promote
instruction.*a* ver 23

22Understanding is a fountain of
life to those who have
it, Pr 13:14
but folly brings punishment
to fools.

23A wise man's heart guides his
mouth, Job 15:5
and his lips promote
instruction.*b* ver 21

24Pleasant words are a
honeycomb, 1Sa 14:27
sweet to the soul and
healing to the bones.

25There is a way that seems right
to a man, Pr 12:15
but in the end it leads to
death. Pr 14:12

26The laborer's appetite works
for him;
his hunger drives him on.

27A scoundrel plots evil, Ps 140:2
and his speech is like a
scorching fire. Jas 3:6

28A perverse man stirs up
dissension, Pr 15:18
and a gossip separates close
friends. Pr 17:9

29A violent man entices his
neighbor
and leads him down a path
that is not good. Pr 1:10

30He who winks with his eye is
plotting perversity;
he who purses his lips is
bent on evil.

31Gray hair is a crown of
splendor; Pr 20:29
it is attained by a righteous
life.

32Better a patient man than a
warrior,
a man who controls his
temper than one who
takes a city.

33The lot is cast into the lap,
but its every decision is from
the LORD. Pr 18:18

17 Better a dry crust with
peace and quiet
than a house full of
feasting,*c* with strife.

2A wise servant will rule over a
disgraceful son,
and will share the
inheritance as one of the
brothers.

3The crucible for silver and the
furnace for gold, Pr 27:21
but the LORD tests the heart.

4A wicked man listens to evil
lips;
a liar pays attention to a
malicious tongue.

a 21 Or words make a man persuasive   *b 23 Or mouth / and makes his lips persuasive*   *c 1 Hebrew sacrifices*

⁵He who mocks the poor shows
    contempt for their
    Maker;   Pr 14:31
  whoever gloats over disaster
    will not go unpunished.

⁶Children's children are a crown
    to the aged,   Pr 13:22
  and parents are the pride of
    their children.

⁷Arrogant*ᵃ* lips are unsuited to
    a fool—
  how much worse lying lips
    to a ruler!   Pr 16:10

⁸A bribe is a charm to the one
    who gives it;
  wherever he turns, he
    succeeds.   Ex 23:8

⁹He who covers over an offense
    promotes love,   Pr 10:12
  but whoever repeats the
    matter separates close
    friends.   Pr 16:28

¹⁰A rebuke impresses a man of
    discernment
  more than a hundred lashes
    a fool.

¹¹An evil man is bent only on
    rebellion;
  a merciless official will be
    sent against him.

¹²Better to meet a bear robbed of
    her cubs
  than a fool in his folly.

¹³If a man pays back evil for
    good,   Ps 109:4-5; Jer 18:20

evil will never leave his
    house.

¹⁴Starting a quarrel is like
    breaching a dam;
  so drop the matter before a
    dispute breaks out.

¹⁵Acquitting the guilty and
    condemning the
    innocent—   Pr 18:5
  the LORD detests them both.

¹⁶Of what use is money in the
    hand of a fool,
  since he has no desire to get
    wisdom?   Pr 23:23

¹⁷A friend loves at all times,
  and a brother is born for
    adversity.   Pr 27:10

¹⁸A man lacking in judgment
    strikes hands in pledge
  and puts up security for his
    neighbor.   Pr 6:1-5; 11:15

¹⁹He who loves a quarrel loves
    sin;
  he who builds a high gate
    invites destruction.

²⁰A man of perverse heart does
    not prosper;
  he whose tongue is deceitful
    falls into trouble.

²¹To have a fool for a son brings
    grief;
  there is no joy for the father
    of a fool.   Pr 10:1

²²A cheerful heart is good
    medicine,

ᵃ7 Or Eloquent

but a crushed spirit dries up
the bones.   Ps 22:15; Pr 15:13

²³A wicked man accepts a bribe
in secret   Ex 23:8
to pervert the course of
justice.   Job 34:33

²⁴A discerning man keeps
wisdom in view,
but a fool's eyes wander to
the ends of the earth.

²⁵A foolish son brings grief to
his father
and bitterness to the one
who bore him.   Pr 10:1

²⁶It is not good to punish an
innocent man,   Pr 18:5
or to flog officials for their
integrity.

²⁷A man of knowledge uses
words with restraint,
and a man of understanding
is even-tempered.   Pr 14:29

²⁸Even a fool is thought wise if
he keeps silent,
and discerning if he holds
his tongue.   Job 13:5

18 An unfriendly man
pursues selfish ends;
he defies all sound
judgment.

²A fool finds no pleasure in
understanding
but delights in airing his
own opinions.   Pr 12:23

³When wickedness comes, so
does contempt,

and with shame comes
disgrace.

⁴The words of a man's mouth
are deep waters,   Ps 18:16
but the fountain of wisdom
is a bubbling brook.

⁵It is not good to be partial to
the wicked   Lev 19:15
or to deprive the innocent of
justice.   Pr 17:15

⁶A fool's lips bring him strife,
and his mouth invites a
beating.

⁷A fool's mouth is his undoing,
and his lips are a snare to
his soul.   Ps 140:9; Pr 10:14

⁸The words of a gossip are like
choice morsels;
they go down to a man's
inmost parts.   Pr 26:22

⁹One who is slack in his work
is brother to one who
destroys.   Pr 28:24

¹⁰The name of the Lord is a
strong tower;   2Sa 22:3
the righteous run to it and
are safe.   Pr 14:26

¹¹The wealth of the rich is their
fortified city;   Pr 10:15
they imagine it an unscalable
wall.

¹²Before his downfall a man's
heart is proud,
but humility comes before
honor.   Pr 11:2; 16:18

¹³He who answers before
    listening—
that is his folly and his
    shame.   Pr 20:25; Jn 7:51

¹⁴A man's spirit sustains him in
    sickness,
but a crushed spirit who can
    bear?   Pr 15:13; 17:22

¹⁵The heart of the discerning
    acquires knowledge;
the ears of the wise seek it
    out.

¹⁶A gift opens the way for the
    giver   Ge 32:20
and ushers him into the
    presence of the great.

¹⁷The first to present his case
    seems right,
till another comes forward
    and questions him.

¹⁸Casting the lot settles disputes
    and keeps strong opponents
    apart.

¹⁹An offended brother is more
    unyielding than a
    fortified city,   1Sa 17:28
and disputes are like the
    barred gates of a citadel.

²⁰From the fruit of his mouth a
    man's stomach is filled;
with the harvest from his
    lips he is satisfied.

²¹The tongue has the power of
    life and death,   Ps 12:4
and those who love it will
    eat its fruit.   Mt 12:37

²²He who finds a wife finds what
    is good   Pr 12:4
and receives favor from the
    Lord.   Pr 19:14

²³A poor man pleads for mercy,
but a rich man answers
    harshly.

²⁴A man of many companions
    may come to ruin,
but there is a friend who
    sticks closer than a
    brother.   Pr 17:17; Jn 15:13-15

19 Better a poor man whose
    walk is blameless
than a fool whose lips are
    perverse.   Pr 28:6

²It is not good to have zeal
    without knowledge,
nor to be hasty and miss the
    way.   Pr 29:20

³A man's own folly ruins his
    life,   Ps 14:1
yet his heart rages against
    the Lord.   Jas 1:13-15

⁴Wealth brings many friends,
but a poor man's friend
    deserts him.   Pr 14:20

⁵A false witness will not go
    unpunished,   Ex 23:1
and he who pours out lies
    will not go free.   Dt 19:19

⁶Many curry favor with a ruler,
and everyone is the friend of
    a man who gives gifts.

⁷A poor man is shunned by all
    his relatives—

how much more do his
friends avoid him!
Though he pursues them with
pleading,
they are nowhere to be
found.^{a} Ps 38:11

^{8}He who gets wisdom loves his
own soul;
he who cherishes
understanding prospers.

^{9}A false witness will not go
unpunished,
and he who pours out lies
will perish.   ver 5

^{10}It is not fitting for a fool to live
in luxury—   Pr 26:1
how much worse for a slave
to rule over princes!

^{11}A man's wisdom gives him
patience;   Pr 16:32
it is to his glory to overlook
an offense.

^{12}A king's rage is like the roar of
a lion,   Pr 20:2
but his favor is like dew on
the grass.   Pr 16:14-15

^{13}A foolish son is his father's
ruin,   Pr 10:1
and a quarrelsome wife is
like a constant dripping.

^{14}Houses and wealth are
inherited from parents,
but a prudent wife is from
the Lord.   Pr 18:22

^{15}Laziness brings on deep sleep,

and the shiftless man goes
hungry.   Pr 6:9; 10:4

^{16}He who obeys instructions
guards his life,
but he who is contemptuous
of his ways will die.

^{17}He who is kind to the poor
lends to the Lord,
and he will reward him for
what he has done.

^{18}Discipline your son, for in that
there is hope;
do not be a willing party to
his death.   Pr 13:24

^{19}A hot-tempered man must pay
the penalty;
if you rescue him, you will
have to do it again.

^{20}Listen to advice and accept
instruction,   Pr 4:1
and in the end you will be
wise.   Pr 12:15

^{21}Many are the plans in a man's
heart,
but it is the Lord's purpose
that prevails.   Ps 33:11

^{22}What a man desires is
unfailing love^b;
better to be poor than a liar.

^{23}The fear of the Lord leads to
life:
Then one rests content,
untouched by trouble.

^{24}The sluggard buries his hand
in the dish;

---

^{a}7 The meaning of the Hebrew for this sentence is uncertain. ^{b}22 Or *A man's greed is his shame*

he will not even bring it
    back to his mouth!

²⁵Flog a mocker, and the simple
    will learn prudence;
rebuke a discerning man,
    and he will gain
    knowledge.   Pr 9:9

²⁶He who robs his father and
    drives out his mother
is a son who brings shame
    and disgrace.

²⁷Stop listening to instruction,
    my son,   Pr 1:8
and you will stray from the
    words of knowledge.

²⁸A corrupt witness mocks at
    justice,
and the mouth of the wicked
    gulps down evil.   Job 15:16

²⁹Penalties are prepared for
    mockers,
and beatings for the backs of
    fools.   Pr 26:3

20 Wine is a mocker and
    beer a brawler;   1Sa 25:36
whoever is led astray by
    them is not wise.   Pr 31:4

²A king's wrath is like the roar
    of a lion;   Pr 19:12
he who angers him forfeits
    his life.   Pr 8:36

³It is to a man's honor to avoid
    strife,
but every fool is quick to
    quarrel.   Pr 17:14

⁴A sluggard does not plow in
    season;   Pr 6:6
so at harvest time he looks
    but finds nothing.

⁵The purposes of a man's heart
    are deep waters,   Ps 18:16
but a man of understanding
    draws them out.

⁶Many a man claims to have
    unfailing love,
but a faithful man who can
    find?   Ps 12:1

⁷The righteous man leads a
    blameless life;   Ps 26:1
blessed are his children after
    him.   Ps 37:25-26

⁸When a king sits on his throne
    to judge,   1Ki 7:7
he winnows out all evil with
    his eyes.   ver 26; Pr 25:4-5

⁹Who can say, "I have kept my
    heart pure;   Job 15:14
I am clean and without sin"?

¹⁰Differing weights and differing
    measures—
the LORD detests them both.

¹¹Even a child is known by his
    actions,
by whether his conduct is
    pure and right.   Mt 7:16

¹²Ears that hear and eyes that
    see—
the LORD has made them
    both.   Ps 94:9

¹³Do not love sleep or you will
    grow poor;   Pr 6:11; 19:15

stay awake and you will
    have food to spare.

¹⁴"It's no good, it's no good!"
    says the buyer;
then off he goes and boasts
    about his purchase.

¹⁵Gold there is, and rubies in
    abundance,
but lips that speak
    knowledge are a rare
    jewel.

¹⁶Take the garment of one who
    puts up security for a
    stranger;
hold it in pledge if he does it
    for a wayward woman.

¹⁷Food gained by fraud tastes
    sweet to a man,   Pr 9:17
but he ends up with a
    mouth full of gravel.

¹⁸Make plans by seeking advice;
if you wage war, obtain
    guidance.   Pr 24:6

¹⁹A gossip betrays a confidence;
so avoid a man who talks
    too much.

²⁰If a man curses his father or
    mother,   Pr 30:11
his lamp will be snuffed out
    in pitch darkness.   Job 18:5

²¹An inheritance quickly gained
    at the beginning
will not be blessed at the
    end.

²²Do not say, "I'll pay you back
    for this wrong!"   Pr 24:29
Wait for the LORD, and he
    will deliver you.   Ro 12:19

²³The LORD detests differing
    weights,
and dishonest scales do not
    please him.   ver 10

²⁴A man's steps are directed by
    the LORD.   Ps 90:12
How then can anyone
    understand his own
    way?   Jer 10:23

²⁵It is a trap for a man to
    dedicate something
    rashly
and only later to consider
    his vows.   Ecc 5:2,4-5

²⁶A wise king winnows out the
    wicked;
he drives the threshing
    wheel over them.   ver 8

²⁷The lamp of the LORD searches
    the spirit of a manª;
it searches out his inmost
    being.   Pr 16:2

²⁸Love and faithfulness keep a
    king safe;
through love his throne is
    made secure.   Pr 29:14

²⁹The glory of young men is
    their strength,
gray hair the splendor of the
    old.   Pr 16:31

ª27 Or The spirit of man is the LORD's lamp

³⁰Blows and wounds cleanse
　　away evil,   Pr 22:15
and beatings purge the
　　inmost being.   Isa 1:5

21 The king's heart is in the
　　hand of the LORD;
he directs it like a
　　watercourse wherever
　　he pleases.   Est 5:1

²All a man's ways seem right to
　　him,
but the LORD weighs the
　　heart.   Pr 16:2; 24:12; Lk 16:15

³To do what is right and just
is more acceptable to the
　　LORD than sacrifice.

⁴Haughty eyes and a proud
　　heart,   Pr 6:17
the lamp of the wicked, are
　　sin!

⁵The plans of the diligent lead
　　to profit   Pr 10:4
as surely as haste leads to
　　poverty.

⁶A fortune made by a lying
　　tongue
is a fleeting vapor and a
　　deadly snare.ᵃ   2Pe 2:3

⁷The violence of the wicked will
　　drag them away,   Pr 11:5
for they refuse to do what is
　　right.

⁸The way of the guilty is
　　devious,   Pr 2:15

but the conduct of the
　　innocent is upright.

⁹Better to live on a corner of
　　the roof
than share a house with a
　　quarrelsome wife.   Pr 25:24

¹⁰The wicked man craves evil;
his neighbor gets no mercy
　　from him.

¹¹When a mocker is punished,
　　the simple gain wisdom;
when a wise man is
　　instructed, he gets
　　knowledge.   Pr 19:25

¹²The Righteous Oneᵇ takes note
　　of the house of the
　　wicked
and brings the wicked to
　　ruin.   Pr 14:11

¹³If a man shuts his ears to the
　　cry of the poor,
he too will cry out and not
　　be answered.   Mt 18:30-34

¹⁴A gift given in secret soothes
　　anger,
and a bribe concealed in the
　　cloak pacifies great
　　wrath.   Pr 18:16; 19:6

¹⁵When justice is done, it brings
　　joy to the righteous
but terror to evildoers.

¹⁶A man who strays from the
　　path of understanding

ᵃ6 Some Hebrew manuscripts, Septuagint and Vulgate; most Hebrew manuscripts *vapor for those who seek death*　　ᵇ12 Or *The righteous man*

comes to rest in the
   company of the dead.

17He who loves pleasure will
   become poor;
   whoever loves wine and oil
     will never be rich.

18The wicked become a ransom
   for the righteous,   Pr 11:8
   and the unfaithful for the
     upright.

19Better to live in a desert
   than with a quarrelsome and
     ill-tempered wife.   ver 9

20In the house of the wise are
   stores of choice food
   and oil,
   but a foolish man devours
     all he has.

21He who pursues righteousness
   and love
   finds life, prosperity*a* and
     honor.   Mt 5:6

22A wise man attacks the city of
   the mighty   Ecc 9:15-16
   and pulls down the
     stronghold in which
     they trust.

23He who guards his mouth and
   his tongue   Jas 3:2
   keeps himself from calamity.

24The proud and arrogant
   man—"Mocker" is his
     name;   Ps 1:1
   he behaves with
     overweening pride.

25The sluggard's craving will be
   the death of him,   Pr 13:4
   because his hands refuse to
     work.
26All day long he craves for
   more,
   but the righteous give
     without sparing.   Ps 37:26

27The sacrifice of the wicked is
   detestable—   Jer 6:20
   how much more so when
     brought with evil intent!

28A false witness will perish,
   and whoever listens to him
     will be destroyed
     forever.*b*

29A wicked man puts up a bold
   front,
   but an upright man gives
     thought to his ways.

30There is no wisdom, no
   insight, no plan   Jer 9:23
   that can succeed against the
     Lord.   Isa 8:10; Ac 5:39

31The horse is made ready for
   the day of battle,
   but victory rests with the
     Lord.   Ps 3:8

22 A good name is more
   desirable than great
     riches;
   to be esteemed is better than
     silver or gold.   Ecc 7:1

2Rich and poor have this in
   common:

---

a21 Or *righteousness*   *b28* Or / *but the words of an obedient man will live on*

The L<small>ORD</small> is the Maker of
  them all.   Job 31:15

³A prudent man sees danger
    and takes refuge,   Pr 14:16
  but the simple keep going
    and suffer for it.   Pr 27:12

⁴Humility and the fear of the
    L<small>ORD</small>
  bring wealth and honor and
    life.   Pr 10:27; 15:33

⁵In the paths of the wicked lie
    thorns and snares,
  but he who guards his soul
    stays far from them.

⁶Train^a a child in the way he
    should go,   Eph 6:4
  and when he is old he will
    not turn from it.   Dt 6:7

⁷The rich rule over the poor,
    and the borrower is servant
    to the lender.

⁸He who sows wickedness reaps
    trouble,   Job 4:8
  and the rod of his fury will
    be destroyed.   Ps 125:3

⁹A generous man will himself
    be blessed,   2Co 9:6
  for he shares his food with
    the poor.   Pr 19:17

¹⁰Drive out the mocker, and out
    goes strife;
  quarrels and insults are
    ended.   Pr 26:20

¹¹He who loves a pure heart and
    whose speech is
    gracious
  will have the king for his
    friend.   Mt 5:8

¹²The eyes of the L<small>ORD</small> keep
    watch over knowledge,
  but he frustrates the words
    of the unfaithful.

¹³The sluggard says, "There is a
    lion outside!"   Pr 26:13
  or, "I will be murdered in
    the streets!"

¹⁴The mouth of an adulteress is
    a deep pit;   Pr 2:16; 5:3-5
  he who is under the L<small>ORD</small>'s
    wrath will fall into it.

¹⁵Folly is bound up in the heart
    of a child,
  but the rod of discipline will
    drive it far from him.

¹⁶He who oppresses the poor to
    increase his wealth
  and he who gives gifts to the
    rich—both come to
    poverty.

Sayings of the Wise

¹⁷Pay attention and listen to the
    sayings of the wise;
  apply your heart to what I
    teach,   Pr 2:2
¹⁸for it is pleasing when you
    keep them in your heart
  and have all of them ready
    on your lips.

^a6 Or Start

¹⁹So that your trust may be in
    the Lᴏʀᴅ,
  I teach you today, even you.
²⁰Have I not written thirty*ᵃ*
    sayings for you,
  sayings of counsel and
    knowledge,
²¹teaching you true and reliable
    words,   Lk 1:3-4; 1Pe 3:15
  so that you can give sound
    answers
  to him who sent you?

²²Do not exploit the poor
    because they are poor
  and do not crush the needy
    in court,   Ex 23:6; Mal 3:5
²³for the Lᴏʀᴅ will take up their
    case   Ps 12:5
  and will plunder those who
    plunder them.   Pr 23:10-11

²⁴Do not make friends with a
    hot-tempered man,
  do not associate with one
    easily angered,
²⁵or you may learn his ways
    and get yourself ensnared.

²⁶Do not be a man who strikes
    hands in pledge   Pr 11:15
  or puts up security for debts;
²⁷if you lack the means to pay,
    your very bed will be
    snatched from under
    you.   Pr 17:18

²⁸Do not move an ancient
    boundary stone   Dt 19:14
  set up by your forefathers.

²⁹Do you see a man skilled in
    his work?
  He will serve before kings;
  he will not serve before
    obscure men.

23 When you sit to dine
    with a ruler,
  note well what*ᵇ* is before
    you,
²and put a knife to your throat
    if you are given to gluttony.
³Do not crave his delicacies,
    for that food is deceptive.

⁴Do not wear yourself out to get
    rich;
  have the wisdom to show
    restraint.
⁵Cast but a glance at riches, and
    they are gone,   Mt 6:19
  for they will surely sprout
    wings
  and fly off to the sky like an
    eagle.   Pr 27:24

⁶Do not eat the food of a stingy
    man,
  do not crave his delicacies;
⁷for he is the kind of man
  who is always thinking
    about the cost.*ᶜ*
  "Eat and drink," he says to
    you,
  but his heart is not with you.
⁸You will vomit up the little you
    have eaten
  and will have wasted your
    compliments.

ᵃ20 Or *not formerly written; or not written excellent*   *ᵇ1* Or *who*   *ᶜ7* Or *for as he thinks within himself, / so he is;* or *for as he puts on a feast, / so he is*

⁹Do not speak to a fool,
    for he will scorn the wisdom
        of your words. Pr 9:7; Mt 7:6

¹⁰Do not move an ancient
    boundary stone   Dt 19:14
    or encroach on the fields of
        the fatherless,
¹¹for their Defender is strong;
    he will take up their case
        against you.   Pr 22:22-23

¹²Apply your heart to instruction
    and your ears to words of
        knowledge.

¹³Do not withhold discipline
    from a child;
    if you punish him with the
        rod, he will not die.
¹⁴Punish him with the rod
    and save his soul from
        death.ᵃ   Pr 13:24

¹⁵My son, if your heart is wise,
    then my heart will be glad;
¹⁶my inmost being will rejoice
    when your lips speak what is
        right.   ver 24; Pr 27:11

¹⁷Do not let your heart envy
    sinners,   Ps 37:1; Pr 28:14
    but always be zealous for
        the fear of the Lord.
¹⁸There is surely a future hope
    for you,
    and your hope will not be
        cut off.   Pr 24:14,19-20

¹⁹Listen, my son, and be wise,
    and keep your heart on the
        right path.

²⁰Do not join those who drink
    too much wine   Isa 5:11,22
    or gorge themselves on
        meat,
²¹for drunkards and gluttons
    become poor,   Pr 21:17
    and drowsiness clothes them
        in rags.

²²Listen to your father, who gave
    you life,
    and do not despise your
        mother when she is old.
²³Buy the truth and do not sell
    it;
    get wisdom, discipline and
        understanding.   Pr 4:7
²⁴The father of a righteous man
    has great joy;
    he who has a wise son
        delights in him.   ver 15-16
²⁵May your father and mother be
    glad;
    may she who gave you birth
        rejoice!   Pr 10:1

²⁶My son, give me your heart
    and let your eyes keep to my
        ways,   Ps 18:21
²⁷for a prostitute is a deep pit
    and a wayward wife is a
        narrow well.
²⁸Like a bandit she lies in wait,
    and multiplies the unfaithful
        among men.

²⁹Who has woe? Who has
    sorrow?
    Who has strife? Who has
        complaints?

ᵃ 14 Hebrew *Sheol*

Who has needless bruises?
Who has bloodshot
eyes?
30Those who linger over wine,
who go to sample bowls of
mixed wine.
31Do not gaze at wine when it is
red,
when it sparkles in the cup,
when it goes down
smoothly!
32In the end it bites like a snake
and poisons like a viper.
33Your eyes will see strange
sights
and your mind imagine
confusing things.
34You will be like one sleeping
on the high seas,
lying on top of the rigging.
35"They hit me," you will say,
"but I'm not hurt!
They beat me, but I don't
feel it!
When will I wake up
so I can find another drink?"

24 Do not envy wicked men,
do not desire their
company;
2for their hearts plot violence,
and their lips talk about
making trouble.   Ps 10:7

3By wisdom a house is built,
and through understanding it
is established;
4through knowledge its rooms
are filled
with rare and beautiful
treasures.   Pr 8:21

5A wise man has great power,
and a man of knowledge
increases strength;
6for waging war you need
guidance,
and for victory many
advisers.   Pr 11:14

7Wisdom is too high for a fool;
in the assembly at the gate
he has nothing to say.

8He who plots evil
will be known as a schemer.
9The schemes of folly are sin,
and men detest a mocker.

10If you falter in times of
trouble,
how small is your strength!

11Rescue those being led away to
death;
hold back those staggering
toward slaughter.   Ps 82:4
12If you say, "But we knew
nothing about this,"
does not he who weighs the
heart perceive it?   Pr 21:2
Does not he who guards your
life know it?
Will he not repay each
person according to
what he has done?   Ro 2:6

13Eat honey, my son, for it is
good;
honey from the comb is
sweet to your taste.
14Know also that wisdom is
sweet to your soul;

if you find it, there is a
future hope for you,
and your hope will not be
cut off.   Ps 119:103; Pr 16:24

¹⁵Do not lie in wait like an
outlaw against a
righteous man's house,
do not raid his dwelling
place;
¹⁶for though a righteous man
falls seven times, he
rises again,
but the wicked are brought
down by calamity.   Mic 7:8

¹⁷Do not gloat when your enemy
falls;   Ob 1:12
when he stumbles, do not let
your heart rejoice,
¹⁸or the Lord will see and
disapprove
and turn his wrath away
from him.   Job 31:29

¹⁹Do not fret because of evil
men   Ps 37:1
or be envious of the
wicked,
²⁰for the evil man has no future
hope,
and the lamp of the wicked
will be snuffed out.

²¹Fear the Lord and the king, my
son,   Ro 13:1-5; 1Pe 2:17
and do not join with the
rebellious,
²²for those two will send sudden
destruction upon them,
and who knows what
calamities they can
bring?

Further Sayings of the Wise

²³These also are sayings of the
wise: Pr 1:6

To show partiality in judging is
not good: Lev 19:15; Pr 28:21
²⁴Whoever says to the guilty,
"You are innocent"—
peoples will curse him and
nations denounce him.
²⁵But it will go well with those
who convict the guilty,
and rich blessing will come
upon them.

²⁶An honest answer
is like a kiss on the lips.

²⁷Finish your outdoor work
and get your fields ready;
after that, build your house.

²⁸Do not testify against your
neighbor without cause,
or use your lips to deceive.
²⁹Do not say, "I'll do to him as
he has done to me;
I'll pay that man back for
what he did."   Pr 20:22

³⁰I went past the field of the
sluggard,   Pr 6:6-11
past the vineyard of the man
who lacks judgment;
³¹thorns had come up
everywhere,
the ground was covered with
weeds,
and the stone wall was in
ruins.
³²I applied my heart to what I
observed

and learned a lesson from
   what I saw:
³³A little sleep, a little slumber,
   a little folding of the hands
     to rest —   Pr 6:10
³⁴and poverty will come on you
   like a bandit
   and scarcity like an armed
     man.ᵃ   Pr 10:4; Ecc 10:18

More Proverbs of Solomon

25 These are more proverbs
of Solomon, copied by the
men of Hezekiah king of Judah:

²It is the glory of God to
   conceal a matter;
   to search out a matter is the
     glory of kings.   Pr 16:10-15

³As the heavens are high and
   the earth is deep,
   so the hearts of kings are
     unsearchable.

⁴Remove the dross from the
   silver,
   and out comes material forᵇ
     the silversmith;
⁵remove the wicked from the
   king's presence,   Pr 20:8
   and his throne will be
     established through
     righteousness.   Pr 16:12

⁶Do not exalt yourself in the
   king's presence,
   and do not claim a place
     among great men;

⁷it is better for him to say to
   you, "Come up here,"
   than for him to humiliate
     you before a nobleman.

What you have seen with your
   eyes
⁸ do not bringᶜ hastily to
     court,
   for what will you do in the end
   if your neighbor puts you to
     shame?   Mt 5:25-26

⁹If you argue your case with a
   neighbor,
   do not betray another man's
     confidence,
¹⁰or he who hears it may shame
   you
   and you will never lose your
     bad reputation.

¹¹A word aptly spoken
   is like apples of gold in
     settings of silver.   Pr 15:23

¹²Like an earring of gold or an
   ornament of fine gold
   is a wise man's rebuke to a
     listening ear.   Pr 15:31

¹³Like the coolness of snow at
   harvest time
   is a trustworthy messenger
     to those who send him;
   he refreshes the spirit of his
     masters.   Pr 13:17

¹⁴Like clouds and wind without
   rain

ᵃ 34 Or *like a vagrant / and scarcity like a beggar
on whom you had set your eyes. / ⁸Do not go*   ᵇ 4 Or *comes a vessel from*   ᶜ 7,8 Or *nobleman /*

is a man who boasts of gifts
he does not give.

¹⁵Through patience a ruler can
be persuaded,   Ecc 10:4
and a gentle tongue can
break a bone.   Pr 15:1

¹⁶If you find honey, eat just
enough—
too much of it, and you will
vomit.   ver 27

¹⁷Seldom set foot in your
neighbor's house—
too much of you, and he will
hate you.

¹⁸Like a club or a sword or a
sharp arrow
is the man who gives false
testimony against his
neighbor.   Pr 12:18

¹⁹Like a bad tooth or a lame foot
is reliance on the unfaithful
in times of trouble.

²⁰Like one who takes away a
garment on a cold day,
or like vinegar poured on
soda,
is one who sings songs to a
heavy heart.

²¹If your enemy is hungry, give
him food to eat;
if he is thirsty, give him
water to drink.
²²In doing this, you will heap
burning coals on his
head,   Ps 18:8
and the LORD will reward
you.   2Sa 16:12; Ro 12:20

²³As a north wind brings rain,
so a sly tongue brings angry
looks.

²⁴Better to live on a corner of
the roof
than share a house with a
quarrelsome wife.   Pr 21:9

²⁵Like cold water to a weary soul
is good news from a distant
land.   Pr 15:30

²⁶Like a muddied spring or a
polluted well
is a righteous man who gives
way to the wicked.

²⁷It is not good to eat too much
honey,   ver 16
nor is it honorable to seek
one's own honor.   Pr 27:2

²⁸Like a city whose walls are
broken down
is a man who lacks
self-control.

26 Like snow in summer or
rain in harvest,   1Sa 12:17
honor is not fitting for a
fool.   Pr 19:10

²Like a fluttering sparrow or a
darting swallow,
an undeserved curse does
not come to rest.   Dt 23:5

³A whip for the horse, a halter
for the donkey,   Ps 32:9
and a rod for the backs of
fools!   Pr 10:13

⁴Do not answer a fool according
to his folly,

or you will be like him
   yourself.   ver 5; Isa 36:21

⁵Answer a fool according to his
   folly,
   or he will be wise in his own
     eyes.   ver 4; Pr 3:7

⁶Like cutting off one's feet or
   drinking violence
  is the sending of a message
   by the hand of a fool.

⁷Like a lame man's legs that
   hang limp
  is a proverb in the mouth of
   a fool.   ver 9

⁸Like tying a stone in a sling
  is the giving of honor to a
   fool.   ver 1

⁹Like a thornbush in a
   drunkard's hand
  is a proverb in the mouth of
   a fool.   ver 7

¹⁰Like an archer who wounds at
   random
  is he who hires a fool or any
   passer-by.

¹¹As a dog returns to its vomit,
  so a fool repeats his folly.

¹²Do you see a man wise in his
   own eyes?   Pr 3:7
  There is more hope for a
   fool than for him.   Pr 29:20

¹³The sluggard says, "There is a
   lion in the road,   Pr 6:6-11
  a fierce lion roaming the
   streets!"   Pr 22:13

¹⁴As a door turns on its hinges,
  so a sluggard turns on his
   bed.   Pr 6:9

¹⁵The sluggard buries his hand
   in the dish;
  he is too lazy to bring it
   back to his mouth.

¹⁶The sluggard is wiser in his
   own eyes
  than seven men who answer
   discreetly.

¹⁷Like one who seizes a dog by
   the ears
  is a passer-by who meddles
   in a quarrel not his
   own.

¹⁸Like a madman shooting
   firebrands or deadly arrows
¹⁹is a man who deceives his
   neighbor
  and says, "I was only
   joking!"

²⁰Without wood a fire goes out;
  without gossip a quarrel dies
   down.   Pr 22:10

²¹As charcoal to embers and as
   wood to fire,
  so is a quarrelsome man for
   kindling strife.   Pr 15:18

²²The words of a gossip are like
   choice morsels;
  they go down to a man's
   inmost parts.   Pr 18:8

²³Like a coating of glaze*a* over
   earthenware

---

a 23 With a different word division of the Hebrew; Masoretic Text *of silver dross*

are fervent lips with an evil
    heart.

24A malicious man disguises
    himself with his lips,
  but in his heart he harbors
    deceit.   Ps 41:6
25Though his speech is
    charming, do not believe
    him,   Ps 28:3
  for seven abominations fill
    his heart.   Jer 9:4-8
26His malice may be concealed
    by deception,
  but his wickedness will be
    exposed in the
    assembly.

27If a man digs a pit, he will fall
    into it;   Ps 7:15; Est 6:13
  if a man rolls a stone, it will
    roll back on him.   Pr 28:10

28A lying tongue hates those it
    hurts,
  and a flattering mouth works
    ruin.   Pr 29:5

27 Do not boast about
    tomorrow,   1Ki 20:11
  for you do not know what a
    day may bring forth.

2Let another praise you, and not
    your own mouth;
  someone else, and not your
    own lips.   Pr 25:27

3Stone is heavy and sand a
    burden,   Job 6:3
  but provocation by a fool is
    heavier than both.

4Anger is cruel and fury
    overwhelming,
  but who can stand before
    jealousy?   Nu 5:14
5Better is open rebuke
    than hidden love.
6Wounds from a friend can be
    trusted,
  but an enemy multiplies
    kisses.   Ps 141:5

7He who is full loathes honey,
  but to the hungry even what
    is bitter tastes sweet.
8Like a bird that strays from its
    nest   Isa 16:2
  is a man who strays from his
    home.

9Perfume and incense bring joy
    to the heart,   Est 2:12; Ps 45:8
  and the pleasantness of
    one's friend springs
    from his earnest
    counsel.

10Do not forsake your friend and
    the friend of your father,
  and do not go to your
    brother's house when
    disaster strikes you—
  better a neighbor nearby
    than a brother far away.
11Be wise, my son, and bring joy
    to my heart;   Pr 10:1
  then I can answer anyone
    who treats me with
    contempt.   Ge 24:60
12The prudent see danger and
    take refuge,

but the simple keep going
and suffer for it.   Pr 22:3

13Take the garment of one who
puts up security for a
stranger;
hold it in pledge if he does it
for a wayward woman.

14If a man loudly blesses his
neighbor early in the
morning,
it will be taken as a curse.

15A quarrelsome wife is like
a constant dripping on a
rainy day;   Pr 19:13
16restraining her is like
restraining the wind
or grasping oil with the
hand.

17As iron sharpens iron,
so one man sharpens
another.

18He who tends a fig tree will eat
its fruit,   1Co 9:7
and he who looks after his
master will be honored.

19As water reflects a face,
so a man's heart reflects the
man.

20Death and Destructiona are
never satisfied,   Hab 2:5
and neither are the eyes of
man.   Ecc 1:8

21The crucible for silver and the
furnace for gold,   Pr 17:3

but man is tested by the
praise he receives.

22Though you grind a fool in a
mortar,
grinding him like grain with
a pestle,
you will not remove his folly
from him.

23Be sure you know the
condition of your flocks,
give careful attention to your
herds;
24for riches do not endure
forever,   Pr 23:5
and a crown is not secure
for all generations.
25When the hay is removed and
new growth appears
and the grass from the hills
is gathered in,
26the lambs will provide you
with clothing,
and the goats with the price
of a field.
27You will have plenty of goats'
milk
to feed you and your family
and to nourish your servant
girls.

28 The wicked man flees
though no one pursues,
but the righteous are as bold
as a lion.   Ps 138:3

2When a country is rebellious, it
has many rulers,

a20 Hebrew Sheol and Abaddon

but a man of understanding
and knowledge
maintains order.

³A ruler[a] who oppresses the
poor
is like a driving rain that
leaves no crops.

⁴Those who forsake the law
praise the wicked,
but those who keep the law
resist them.

⁵Evil men do not understand
justice,
but those who seek the LORD
understand it fully.

⁶Better a poor man whose walk
is blameless
than a rich man whose ways
are perverse.   Pr 19:1

⁷He who keeps the law is a
discerning son,
but a companion of gluttons
disgraces his father.

⁸He who increases his wealth
by exorbitant interest
amasses it for another, who
will be kind to the poor.

⁹If anyone turns a deaf ear to
the law,
even his prayers are
detestable.   Ps 66:18; 109:7

¹⁰He who leads the upright along
an evil path
will fall into his own trap,

but the blameless will
receive a good
inheritance.

¹¹A rich man may be wise in his
own eyes,
but a poor man who has
discernment sees
through him.

¹²When the righteous triumph,
there is great elation;
but when the wicked rise to
power, men go into
hiding.   Pr 11:10

¹³He who conceals his sins does
not prosper,   Job 31:33
but whoever confesses and
renounces them finds
mercy.   Ps 32:1-5; 1Jn 1:9

¹⁴Blessed is the man who always
fears the LORD,
but he who hardens his
heart falls into trouble.

¹⁵Like a roaring lion or a
charging bear
is a wicked man ruling over
a helpless people.

¹⁶A tyrannical ruler lacks
judgment,
but he who hates ill-gotten
gain will enjoy a long
life.

¹⁷A man tormented by the guilt
of murder
will be a fugitive till death;
let no one support him.

a3 Or A poor man

18He whose walk is blameless is
    kept safe,   Jer 39:18
but he whose ways are
    perverse will suddenly
    fall.   Pr 10:9

19He who works his land will
    have abundant food,
but the one who chases
    fantasies will have his
    fill of poverty.   Pr 12:11

20A faithful man will be richly
    blessed,
but one eager to get rich will
    not go unpunished.

21To show partiality is not
    good—   Pr 18:5
yet a man will do wrong for
    a piece of bread.   Eze 13:19

22A stingy man is eager to get
    rich
and is unaware that poverty
    awaits him.   Pr 23:6

23He who rebukes a man will in
    the end gain more favor
than he who has a flattering
    tongue.   Pr 27:5-6

24He who robs his father or
    mother   Pr 19:26
and says, "It's not wrong"—
he is partner to him who
    destroys.   Pr 18:9

25A greedy man stirs up
    dissension,   Pr 14:17
but he who trusts in the
    LORD will prosper.

26He who trusts in himself is a
    fool,   Ps 4:5

but he who walks in wisdom
    is kept safe.   1Co 3:18

27He who gives to the poor will
    lack nothing,   Dt 24:19
but he who closes his eyes
    to them receives many
    curses.   Ps 109:17

28When the wicked rise to
    power, people go into
    hiding;   ver 12
but when the wicked perish,
    the righteous thrive.

29 A man who remains
    stiff-necked after many
    rebukes   Ex 32:9
will suddenly be
    destroyed—without
    remedy.   2Ch 36:16; Pr 6:15

2When the righteous thrive, the
    people rejoice;   Est 8:15
when the wicked rule, the
    people groan.   Pr 28:12

3A man who loves wisdom
    brings joy to his father,
but a companion of
    prostitutes squanders
    his wealth.   Pr 5:8-10

4By justice a king gives a
    country stability,
but one who is greedy for
    bribes tears it down.

5Whoever flatters his neighbor
    is spreading a net for his
    feet.   Pr 26:28

6An evil man is snared by his
    own sin,   Ecc 9:12

but a righteous one can sing
and be glad.

7The righteous care about
justice for the poor,
but the wicked have no such
concern.

8Mockers stir up a city,
but wise men turn away
anger.   Pr 11:11; 16:14

9If a wise man goes to court
with a fool,
the fool rages and scoffs,
and there is no peace.

10Bloodthirsty men hate a man
of integrity
and seek to kill the upright.

11A fool gives full vent to his
anger,   Job 15:13
but a wise man keeps
himself under control.

12If a ruler listens to lies,   2Ki 21:9
all his officials become
wicked.   Job 34:30

13The poor man and the
oppressor have this in
common:
The Lord gives sight to the
eyes of both.   Pr 22:2; Mt 5:45

14If a king judges the poor with
fairness,
his throne will always be
secure.   Ps 72:1-5; Pr 16:12

15The rod of correction imparts
wisdom,

but a child left to himself
disgraces his mother.

16When the wicked thrive, so
does sin,
but the righteous will see
their downfall.   Ps 37:35-36

17Discipline your son, and he
will give you peace;
he will bring delight to your
soul.   Pr 10:1

18Where there is no revelation,
the people cast off
restraint;
but blessed is he who keeps
the law.   Ps 1:1-2; 119:1-2

19A servant cannot be corrected
by mere words;
though he understands, he
will not respond.

20Do you see a man who speaks
in haste?
There is more hope for a
fool than for him.   Pr 26:12

21If a man pampers his servant
from youth,
he will bring grief a in the
end.

22An angry man stirs up
dissension,
and a hot-tempered one
commits many sins.

23A man's pride brings him low,
but a man of lowly spirit
gains honor.   Pr 11:2; Isa 66:2

a21 The meaning of the Hebrew for this word is uncertain.

²⁴The accomplice of a thief is his
own enemy;
he is put under oath and
dare not testify.   Lev 5:1

²⁵Fear of man will prove to be a
snare,   1Sa 15:24
but whoever trusts in the
LORD is kept safe.   Pr 28:25

²⁶Many seek an audience with a
ruler,   Pr 19:6
but it is from the LORD that
man gets justice.   Pr 16:33

²⁷The righteous detest the
dishonest;
the wicked detest the
upright.   ver 10

Sayings of Agur

30 The sayings of Agur son of
Jakeh—an oracle^a: Pr 22:17

This man declared to Ithiel,
to Ithiel and to Ucal:^b

²"I am the most ignorant of
men;
I do not have a man's
understanding.

³I have not learned wisdom,
nor have I knowledge of the
Holy One.   Pr 9:10

⁴Who has gone up to heaven
and come down?   Ps 24:1-2
Who has gathered up the
wind in the hollow of
his hands?   Isa 40:12
Who has wrapped up the
waters in his cloak?

Who has established all the
ends of the earth?
What is his name, and the
name of his son?
Tell me if you know!

⁵"Every word of God is flawless;
he is a shield to those who
take refuge in him.

⁶Do not add to his words,   Dt 4:2
or he will rebuke you and
prove you a liar.

⁷"Two things I ask of you,
O LORD;
do not refuse me before I
die:

⁸Keep falsehood and lies far
from me;
give me neither poverty nor
riches,
but give me only my daily
bread.   Mt 6:11

⁹Otherwise, I may have too
much and disown you
and say, 'Who is the LORD?'
Or I may become poor and
steal,
and so dishonor the name of
my God.   Dt 8:12

¹⁰"Do not slander a servant to
his master,
or he will curse you, and
you will pay for it.

¹¹"There are those who curse
their fathers
and do not bless their
mothers;   Pr 20:20

^a1 Or *Jakeh of Massa*   ^b1 Masoretic Text; with a different word division of the Hebrew *declared,* "I
am weary, O God; / I am weary, O God, and faint.

¹²those who are pure in their
       own eyes   Lk 18:11
   and yet are not cleansed of
       their filth;   Jer 2:23,35
¹³those whose eyes are ever so
       haughty,   Pr 6:17
   whose glances are so
       disdainful;
¹⁴those whose teeth are swords
   and whose jaws are set with
       knives   Ps 57:4
   to devour the poor from the
       earth,   Ps 14:4; Am 8:4
   the needy from among
       mankind.   Job 19:22

¹⁵"The leech has two daughters.
   'Give! Give!' they cry.

   "There are three things that are
       never satisfied,   Pr 27:20
   four that never say,
       'Enough!':
¹⁶the grave,ᵃ the barren womb,
   land, which is never satisfied
       with water,
   and fire, which never says,
       'Enough!'

¹⁷"The eye that mocks a father,
   that scorns obedience to a
       mother,
   will be pecked out by the
       ravens of the valley,
   will be eaten by the vultures.

¹⁸"There are three things that are
       too amazing for me,
   four that I do not
       understand:
¹⁹the way of an eagle in the sky,

the way of a snake on a
       rock,
   the way of a ship on the high
       seas,
   and the way of a man with a
       maiden.

²⁰"This is the way of an
       adulteress:
   She eats and wipes her
       mouth
   and says, 'I've done nothing
       wrong.'   Pr 5:6

²¹"Under three things the earth
       trembles,
   under four it cannot bear up:
²²a servant who becomes king,
   a fool who is full of food,
²³an unloved woman who is
       married,
   and a maidservant who
       displaces her mistress.

²⁴"Four things on earth are
       small,
   yet they are extremely wise:
²⁵Ants are creatures of little
       strength,
   yet they store up their food
       in the summer;   Pr 6:6-8
²⁶coneysᵇ are creatures of little
       power,   Ps 104:18
   yet they make their home in
       the crags;
²⁷locusts have no king,   Ex 10:4
   yet they advance together in
       ranks;
²⁸a lizard can be caught with the
       hand,

ᵃ16 Hebrew Sheol   ᵇ26 That is, the hyrax or rock badger

yet it is found in kings'
        palaces.
29"There are three things that are
        stately in their stride,
    four that move with stately
        bearing:
30a lion, mighty among beasts,
    who retreats before nothing;
31a strutting rooster, a he-goat,
    and a king with his army
        around him.[a]

32"If you have played the fool
        and exalted yourself,
    or if you have planned evil,
    clap your hand over your
        mouth!   Job 21:5
33For as churning the milk
        produces butter,
    and as twisting the nose
        produces blood,
    so stirring up anger produces
        strife."

Sayings of King Lemuel

31 The sayings of King Lemuel—an oracle[b] his mother
taught him: Pr 22:17

2"O my son, O son of my
        womb,
    O son of my vows,[c]   Isa 49:15
3do not spend your strength on
        women,
    your vigor on those who
        ruin kings.   Dt 17:17; Ne 13:26
4"It is not for kings,
    O Lemuel—

not for kings to drink wine,
    not for rulers to crave beer,
5lest they drink and forget what
        the law decrees,   1Ki 16:9
    and deprive all the
        oppressed of their
        rights.
6Give beer to those who are
        perishing,
    wine to those who are in
        anguish;   Ge 14:18
7let them drink and forget their
        poverty   Est 1:10
    and remember their misery
        no more.

8"Speak up for those who
        cannot speak for
        themselves,   Job 29:12-17
    for the rights of all who are
        destitute.
9Speak up and judge fairly;
    defend the rights of the poor
        and needy."   Lev 19:15

Epilogue: The Wife of Noble Character

10[d]A wife of noble character who
        can find?   Ru 3:11; Pr 19:14
    She is worth far more than
        rubies.
11Her husband has full
        confidence in her   Ge 2:18
    and lacks nothing of value.
12She brings him good, not
        harm,
    all the days of her life.

---

[a]31 Or king secure against revolt   [b]1 Or of Lemuel king of Massa, which   [c]2 Or / the answer to my
prayers   [d]10 Verses 10-31 are an acrostic, each verse beginning with a successive letter of the Hebrew
alphabet.

¹³She selects wool and flax
  and works with eager hands.
¹⁴She is like the merchant ships,
  bringing her food from afar.
¹⁵She gets up while it is still
    dark;
  she provides food for her
    family
  and portions for her servant
    girls.
¹⁶She considers a field and buys
    it;
  out of her earnings she
    plants a vineyard.
¹⁷She sets about her work
    vigorously;
  her arms are strong for her
    tasks.
¹⁸She sees that her trading is
    profitable,
  and her lamp does not go
    out at night.
¹⁹In her hand she holds the
    distaff
  and grasps the spindle with
    her fingers.
²⁰She opens her arms to the
    poor
  and extends her hands to the
    needy.   Dt 15:11; Eph 4:28
²¹When it snows, she has no fear
    for her household;
  for all of them are clothed in
    scarlet.
²²She makes coverings for her
    bed;

she is clothed in fine linen
  and purple.
²³Her husband is respected at
    the city gate,
  where he takes his seat
    among the elders of the
    land.   Ru 4:1,11; Pr 12:4
²⁴She makes linen garments and
    sells them,
  and supplies the merchants
    with sashes.
²⁵She is clothed with strength
    and dignity;
  she can laugh at the days to
    come.
²⁶She speaks with wisdom,
  and faithful instruction is on
    her tongue.   Pr 10:31
²⁷She watches over the affairs of
    her household
  and does not eat the bread
    of idleness.
²⁸Her children arise and call her
    blessed;
  her husband also, and he
    praises her:
²⁹"Many women do noble things,
  but you surpass them all."
³⁰Charm is deceptive, and beauty
    is fleeting;
  but a woman who fears the
    LORD is to be praised.
³¹Give her the reward she has
    earned,
  and let her works bring her
    praise at the city gate.

Ecclesiastes

Everything Is Meaningless

1 The words of the Teacher,[a] son of David, king in Jerusalem: Pr 1:1; Ecc 7:27

[2] "Meaningless! Meaningless!"
    says the Teacher.
"Utterly meaningless!
    Everything is meaningless."

[3] What does man gain from all
        his labor
    at which he toils under the
        sun? Ecc 2:11,22
[4] Generations come and
        generations go,
    but the earth remains
        forever. Ps 104:5; 119:90
[5] The sun rises and the sun sets,
    and hurries back to where it
        rises. Ps 19:5-6
[6] The wind blows to the south
    and turns to the north;
round and round it goes,
    ever returning on its course.
[7] All streams flow into the sea,
    yet the sea is never full.
To the place the streams come
        from,
    there they return again.
[8] All things are wearisome,
    more than one can say.
The eye never has enough of
        seeing, Pr 27:20
    nor the ear its fill of hearing.

[9] What has been will be again,
    what has been done will be
        done again; Ecc 3:15
there is nothing new under
        the sun.
[10] Is there anything of which one
        can say,
    "Look! This is something
        new"?
It was here already, long ago;
    it was here before our time.
[11] There is no remembrance of
        men of old,
    and even those who are yet
        to come
will not be remembered
    by those who follow. Ecc 2:16

Wisdom Is Meaningless

[12] I, the Teacher, was king over Israel in Jerusalem. [13] I devoted myself to study and to explore by wisdom all that is done under heaven. What a heavy burden God has laid on men! [14] I have seen all the things that are done under the sun; all of them are meaningless, a chasing after the wind. Ecc 3:10; 4:4

[15] What is twisted cannot be
        straightened; Ecc 7:13
    what is lacking cannot be
        counted.

[16] I thought to myself, "Look, I

---

a 1 Or *leader of the assembly*; also in verses 2 and 12

have grown and increased in wisdom more than anyone who has ruled over Jerusalem before me; I have experienced much of wisdom and knowledge." [17]Then I applied myself to the understanding of wisdom, and also of madness and folly, but I learned that this, too, is a chasing after the wind. 1Ki 3:12

[18]For with much wisdom comes
    much sorrow;
  the more knowledge, the
    more grief. Ecc 12:12

Pleasures Are Meaningless

2 I thought in my heart, "Come now, I will test you with pleasure to find out what is good." But that also proved to be meaningless. [2]"Laughter," I said, "is foolish. And what does pleasure accomplish?" [3]I tried cheering myself with wine, and embracing folly—my mind still guiding me with wisdom. I wanted to see what was worthwhile for men to do under heaven during the few days of their lives. Ecc 1:17; 7:6; Lk 12:19

[4]I undertook great projects: I built houses for myself and planted vineyards. [5]I made gardens and parks and planted all kinds of fruit trees in them. [6]I made reservoirs to water groves of flourishing trees. [7]I bought male and female slaves and had other slaves who were born in my house. I also owned more herds and flocks than any-

one in Jerusalem before me. [8]I amassed silver and gold for myself, and the treasure of kings and provinces. I acquired men and women singers, and a harem[a] as well—the delights of the heart of man. [9]I became greater by far than anyone in Jerusalem before me. In all this my wisdom stayed with me. 1Ki 9:28; 10:10,14,21

[10]I denied myself nothing my
    eyes desired;
  I refused my heart no
    pleasure.
  My heart took delight in all my
    work,
  and this was the reward for
    all my labor.
[11]Yet when I surveyed all that
    my hands had done
  and what I had toiled to
    achieve,
  everything was meaningless, a
    chasing after the wind;
  nothing was gained under
    the sun. Ecc 1:3

Wisdom and Folly Are Meaningless

[12]Then I turned my thoughts to
    consider wisdom,
  and also madness and folly.
  What more can the king's
    successor do
  than what has already been
    done? Ecc 1:9
[13]I saw that wisdom is better
    than folly, Ecc 7:11-12

---

[a]8 The meaning of the Hebrew for this phrase is uncertain.

just as light is better than
    darkness.
¹⁴The wise man has eyes in his
    head,
    while the fool walks in the
      darkness;
but I came to realize
    that the same fate overtakes
      them both.   Ps 49:10

¹⁵Then I thought in my heart,

"The fate of the fool will
    overtake me also.
What then do I gain by
    being wise?"   Ecc 6:8
I said in my heart,
"This too is meaningless."
¹⁶For the wise man, like the fool,
    will not be long
      remembered;
in days to come both will be
    forgotten.   Ecc 1:11
Like the fool, the wise man too
    must die!   Ps 49:10

Toil Is Meaningless

¹⁷So I hated life, because the
work that is done under the sun
was grievous to me. All of it is
meaningless, a chasing after the
wind. ¹⁸I hated all the things I had
toiled for under the sun, because I
must leave them to the one who
comes after me. ¹⁹And who knows
whether he will be a wise man or
a fool? Yet he will have control
over all the work into which I have
poured my effort and skill under
the sun. This too is meaningless.
²⁰So my heart began to despair
over all my toilsome labor under
the sun. ²¹For a man may do his
work with wisdom, knowledge
and skill, and then he must leave
all he owns to someone who has
not worked for it. This too is meaningless and a great misfortune.
²²What does a man get for all the
toil and anxious striving with
which he labors under the sun?
²³All his days his work is pain and
grief; even at night his mind does
not rest. This too is meaningless.

²⁴A man can do nothing better
than to eat and drink and find satisfaction in his work. This too, I
see, is from the hand of God, ²⁵for
without him, who can eat or find
enjoyment? ²⁶To the man who
pleases him, God gives wisdom,
knowledge and happiness, but to
the sinner he gives the task of gathering and storing up wealth to
hand it over to the one who
pleases God. This too is meaningless, a chasing after the wind.

A Time for Everything

3 There is a time for
    everything,   ver 11,17; Ecc 8:6
    and a season for every
      activity under heaven:

²   a time to be born and a time
      to die,
    a time to plant and a time to
      uproot,   Isa 28:24
³   a time to kill and a time to
      heal,   Dt 5:17
    a time to tear down and a
      time to build,

4   a time to weep and a time to
     laugh,
     a time to mourn and a time
     to dance,
5   a time to scatter stones and
     a time to gather them,
     a time to embrace and a
     time to refrain,
6   a time to search and a time
     to give up,
     a time to keep and a time to
     throw away,
7   a time to tear and a time to
     mend,
     a time to be silent and a
     time to speak,   Am 5:13
8   a time to love and a time to
     hate,
     a time for war and a time for
     peace.

⁹What does the worker gain from his toil? ¹⁰I have seen the burden God has laid on men. ¹¹He has made everything beautiful in its time. He has also set eternity in the hearts of men; yet they cannot fathom what God has done from beginning to end. ¹²I know that there is nothing better for men than to be happy and do good while they live. ¹³That everyone may eat and drink, and find satisfaction in all his toil—this is the gift of God. ¹⁴I know that everything God does will endure forever; nothing can be added to it and nothing taken from it. God does it so that men will revere him.

¹⁵Whatever is has already been,
     and what will be has been
     before;   Ecc 1:9
     and God will call the past to
     account.ᵃ

¹⁶And I saw something else under the sun:

In the place of
          judgment—wickedness
          was there,
     in the place of
          justice—wickedness was
          there.

¹⁷I thought in my heart,

"God will bring to judgment
     both the righteous and the
     wicked,
for there will be a time for
     every activity,
     a time for every deed."   ver 1

¹⁸I also thought, "As for men, God tests them so that they may see that they are like the animals. ¹⁹Man's fate is like that of the animals; the same fate awaits them both: As one dies, so dies the other. All have the same breathᵇ; man has no advantage over the animal. Everything is meaningless. ²⁰All go to the same place; all come from dust, and to dust all return. ²¹Who knows if the spirit of man rises upward and if the spirit of the animalᶜ goes down into the earth?" ²²So I saw that there is nothing better for a man than to enjoy his

---

ᵃ15 Or God calls back the past   ᵇ19 Or spirit   ᶜ21 Or Who knows the spirit of man, which rises upward, or the spirit of the animal, which

work, because that is his lot. For who can bring him to see what will happen after him?   Job 31:2; Ecc 2:24

Oppression, Toil, Friendlessness

4 Again I looked and saw all the oppression that was taking place under the sun: Ps 12:5; Ecc 3:16

I saw the tears of the
    oppressed—
and they have no comforter;
power was on the side of their
    oppressors—
and they have no comforter.
[2]And I declared that the dead,
    who had already died,
are happier than the living,
    who are still alive.   Job 3:17
[3]But better than both
    is he who has not yet been,
who has not seen the evil
    that is done under the sun.

[4]And I saw that all labor and all achievement spring from man's envy of his neighbor. This too is meaningless, a chasing after the wind.   Ecc 1:14

[5]The fool folds his hands   Pr 6:10
    and ruins himself.
[6]Better one handful with
    tranquillity
    than two handfuls with toil
    and chasing after the wind.

[7]Again I saw something meaningless under the sun:

[8]There was a man all alone;

he had neither son nor
    brother.
There was no end to his toil,
    yet his eyes were not
        content with his wealth.
"For whom am I toiling," he
    asked,
    "and why am I depriving
        myself of enjoyment?"
This too is meaningless—
    a miserable business!

[9]Two are better than one,
    because they have a good
        return for their work:
[10]If one falls down,
    his friend can help him up.
But pity the man who falls
    and has no one to help him
        up!
[11]Also, if two lie down together,
    they will keep warm.
    But how can one keep warm
        alone?
[12]Though one may be
    overpowered,
    two can defend themselves.
A cord of three strands is not
    quickly broken.

Advancement Is Meaningless

[13]Better a poor but wise youth than an old but foolish king who no longer knows how to take warning. [14]The youth may have come from prison to the kingship, or he may have been born in poverty within his kingdom. [15]I saw that all who lived and walked under the sun followed the youth, the king's successor. [16]There was no

end to all the people who were before them. But those who came later were not pleased with the successor. This too is meaningless, a chasing after the wind.

Stand in Awe of God

5 Guard your steps when you go to the house of God. Go near to listen rather than to offer the sacrifice of fools, who do not know that they do wrong.

²Do not be quick with your
    mouth,
  do not be hasty in your
    heart
  to utter anything before God.
God is in heaven
  and you are on earth,
  so let your words be few.
³As a dream comes when there
    are many cares,   Job 20:8
  so the speech of a fool when
    there are many words.

⁴When you make a vow to God, do not delay in fulfilling it. He has no pleasure in fools; fulfill your vow. ⁵It is better not to vow than to make a vow and not fulfill it. ⁶Do not let your mouth lead you into sin. And do not protest to the ˌtempleˌ messenger, "My vow was a mistake." Why should God be angry at what you say and destroy the work of your hands? ⁷Much dreaming and many words are meaningless. Therefore stand in awe of God.   Pr 20:25; Ac 5:4

Riches Are Meaningless

⁸If you see the poor oppressed in a district, and justice and rights denied, do not be surprised at such things; for one official is eyed by a higher one, and over them both are others higher still. ⁹The increase from the land is taken by all; the king himself profits from the fields.   Ps 12:5; Ecc 4:1

¹⁰Whoever loves money never
    has money enough;
  whoever loves wealth is
    never satisfied with his
    income.
  This too is meaningless.

¹¹As goods increase,
  so do those who consume
    them.
And what benefit are they to
    the owner
  except to feast his eyes on
    them?

¹²The sleep of a laborer is sweet,
  whether he eats little or
    much,
  but the abundance of a rich
    man
  permits him no sleep.

¹³I have seen a grievous evil under the sun: Ecc 6:1-2

  wealth hoarded to the harm of
    its owner,
¹⁴ or wealth lost through some
    misfortune,
  so that when he has a son
    there is nothing left for him.

15Naked a man comes from his
    mother's womb,
  and as he comes, so he
    departs.   Job 1:21
He takes nothing from his
    labor   Ps 49:17; 1Ti 6:7
  that he can carry in his
    hand.   Ecc 1:3

16This too is a grievous evil:

As a man comes, so he
    departs,
  and what does he gain,
    since he toils for the wind?
17All his days he eats in
    darkness,
  with great frustration,
    affliction and anger.

18Then I realized that it is good and proper for a man to eat and drink, and to find satisfaction in his toilsome labor under the sun during the few days of life God has given him—for this is his lot. **19**Moreover, when God gives any man wealth and possessions, and enables him to enjoy them, to accept his lot and be happy in his work—this is a gift of God. **20**He seldom reflects on the days of his life, because God keeps him occupied with gladness of heart.

6 I have seen another evil under the sun, and it weighs heavily on men: **2**God gives a man wealth, possessions and honor, so that he lacks nothing his heart desires, but God does not enable him to enjoy them, and a stranger enjoys them instead. This is meaningless, a grievous evil.   Ps 17:14; Ecc 5:13,19

3A man may have a hundred children and live many years; yet no matter how long he lives, if he cannot enjoy his prosperity and does not receive proper burial, I say that a stillborn child is better off than he. **4**It comes without meaning, it departs in darkness, and in darkness its name is shrouded. **5**Though it never saw the sun or knew anything, it has more rest than does that man— **6**even if he lives a thousand years twice over but fails to enjoy his prosperity. Do not all go to the same place?   Job 3:16; Ecc 4:3

7All man's efforts are for his
    mouth,
  yet his appetite is never
    satisfied.   Pr 16:26; 27:20
8What advantage has a wise
    man
  over a fool?   Ecc 2:15
What does a poor man gain
  by knowing how to conduct
    himself before others?
9Better what the eye sees
  than the roving of the
    appetite.
This too is meaningless,
  a chasing after the wind.

10Whatever exists has already
    been named,   Ecc 3:15
  and what man is has been
    known;
no man can contend
  with one who is stronger
    than he.

¹¹The more the words,
 the less the meaning,
 and how does that profit
  anyone?

¹²For who knows what is good
for a man in life, during the few
and meaningless days he passes
through like a shadow? Who can
tell him what will happen under
the sun after he is gone? Ps 39:6

Wisdom

7 A good name is better than
  fine perfume, Ps 22:1; SS 1:3
 and the day of death better
  than the day of birth.
²It is better to go to a house of
  mourning
 than to go to a house of
  feasting,
 for death is the destiny of
  every man; Ps 90:12; Pr 11:19
 the living should take this to
  heart.
³Sorrow is better than laughter,
 because a sad face is good
  for the heart.
⁴The heart of the wise is in the
  house of mourning,
 but the heart of fools is in
  the house of pleasure.
⁵It is better to heed a wise
  man's rebuke Ps 141:5
 than to listen to the song of
  fools.
⁶Like the crackling of thorns
  under the pot, Ps 58:9
 so is the laughter of fools.
 This too is meaningless.

⁷Extortion turns a wise man
  into a fool,
 and a bribe corrupts the
  heart. Ex 23:8; Dt 16:19
⁸The end of a matter is better
  than its beginning,
 and patience is better than
  pride. Pr 14:29; Gal 5:22; Eph 4:2
⁹Do not be quickly provoked in
  your spirit, Pr 14:17; Jas 1:19
 for anger resides in the lap
  of fools. Pr 14:29
¹⁰Do not say, "Why were the old
  days better than these?"
 For it is not wise to ask such
  questions.

¹¹Wisdom, like an inheritance, is
  a good thing Pr 8:10-11
 and benefits those who see
  the sun. Ecc 11:7
¹²Wisdom is a shelter
 as money is a shelter,
 but the advantage of
  knowledge is this:
 that wisdom preserves the
  life of its possessor.

¹³Consider what God has done:

Who can straighten
 what he has made crooked?
¹⁴When times are good, be
  happy;
 but when times are bad,
  consider:
God has made the one
 as well as the other. Job 1:21
Therefore, a man cannot
  discover
 anything about his future.

¹⁵In this meaningless life of
mine I have seen both of these:

a righteous man perishing in
    his righteousness,
and a wicked man living
    long in his wickedness.
¹⁶Do not be overrighteous,
    neither be overwise—
    why destroy yourself?
¹⁷Do not be overwicked,
    and do not be a fool—
    why die before your time?
¹⁸It is good to grasp the one
    and not let go of the other.
    The man who fears God will
        avoid all ˻extremes˼.^a

¹⁹Wisdom makes one wise man
        more powerful   Ecc 9:13-18
    than ten rulers in a city.

²⁰There is not a righteous man
        on earth   Ps 14:3
    who does what is right and
        never sins.   1Ki 8:46; 2Ch 6:36

²¹Do not pay attention to every
        word people say,
    or you may hear your
        servant cursing you—
²²for you know in your heart
    that many times you yourself
        have cursed others.

²³All this I tested by wisdom and
I said,

"I am determined to be
    wise"—   Ecc 1:17; Ro 1:22
but this was beyond me.
²⁴Whatever wisdom may be,

it is far off and most
    profound—
who can discover it?   Job 28:12
²⁵So I turned my mind to
    understand,
to investigate and to search
    out wisdom and the
    scheme of things   Job 28:3
and to understand the stupidity
    of wickedness
    and the madness of folly.

²⁶I find more bitter than death
    the woman who is a snare,
whose heart is a trap
    and whose hands are chains.
The man who pleases God will
    escape her,
    but the sinner she will
        ensnare.   Pr 5:3-5; 7:23; 22:14

²⁷"Look," says the Teacher,^b
"this is what I have discovered:

"Adding one thing to another
        to discover the scheme
        of things—
²⁸   while I was still searching
    but not finding—
I found one ˻upright˼ man
        among a thousand,
    but not one ˻upright˼ woman
        among them all.   1Ki 11:3
²⁹This only have I found:
    God made mankind upright,
    but men have gone in search
        of many schemes."

8 Who is like the wise man?
    Who knows the explanation
        of things?

---

^a 18 Or *will follow them both*   ^b 27 Or *leader of the assembly*

Wisdom brightens a man's face
and changes its hard
appearance.

Obey the King

²Obey the king's command, I
say, because you took an oath before God. ³Do not be in a hurry to
leave the king's presence. Do not
stand up for a bad cause, for he
will do whatever he pleases. ⁴Since
a king's word is supreme, who can
say to him, "What are you doing?"

⁵Whoever obeys his command
    will come to no harm,
    and the wise heart will know
        the proper time and
        procedure.
⁶For there is a proper time and
    procedure for every
    matter,   Ecc 3:1
    though a man's misery
        weighs heavily upon
        him.

⁷Since no man knows the
    future,
    who can tell him what is to
        come?
⁸No man has power over the
    wind to contain it ᵃ;
    so no one has power over
        the day of his death.
As no one is discharged in
    time of war,
    so wickedness will not
        release those who
        practice it.

⁹All this I saw, as I applied my
mind to everything done under the
sun. There is a time when a man
lords it over others to his own ᵇ
hurt. ¹⁰Then too, I saw the wicked
buried—those who used to come
and go from the holy place and receive praise ᶜ in the city where
they did this. This too is meaningless.   Ecc 1:11

¹¹When the sentence for a crime
is not quickly carried out, the
hearts of the people are filled with
schemes to do wrong. ¹²Although
a wicked man commits a hundred
crimes and still lives a long time, I
know that it will go better with
God-fearing men, who are reverent
before God. ¹³Yet because the
wicked do not fear God, it will not
go well with them, and their days
will not lengthen like a shadow.

¹⁴There is something else meaningless that occurs on earth: righteous men who get what the wicked deserve, and wicked men who
get what the righteous deserve.
This too, I say, is meaningless. ¹⁵So
I commend the enjoyment of life,
because nothing is better for a man
under the sun than to eat and
drink and be glad. Then joy will
accompany him in his work all the
days of the life God has given him
under the sun.   Ecc 2:24; 3:12-13; 5:18

¹⁶When I applied my mind to
know wisdom and to observe
man's labor on earth—his eyes not

ᵃ8 Or *over his spirit to retain it*   ᵇ9 Or *to their*   ᶜ10 Some Hebrew manuscripts and Septuagint
(Aquila); most Hebrew manuscripts *and are forgotten*

seeing sleep day or night— [17]then I saw all that God has done. No one can comprehend what goes on under the sun. Despite all his efforts to search it out, man cannot discover its meaning. Even if a wise man claims he knows, he cannot really comprehend it.   Ecc 3:11

A Common Destiny for All

9 So I reflected on all this and concluded that the righteous and the wise and what they do are in God's hands, but no man knows whether love or hate awaits him. [2]All share a common destiny—the righteous and the wicked, the good and the bad,[a] the clean and the unclean, those who offer sacrifices and those who do not.

As it is with the good man,
    so with the sinner;
as it is with those who take
        oaths,
    so with those who are afraid
        to take them.   Job 9:22

[3]This is the evil in everything that happens under the sun: The same destiny overtakes all. The hearts of men, moreover, are full of evil and there is madness in their hearts while they live, and afterward they join the dead. [4]Anyone who is among the living has hope[b]—even a live dog is better off than a dead lion!   Job 21:26

[5]For the living know that they
        will die,
    but the dead know nothing;
they have no further reward,
    and even the memory of
        them is forgotten.   Ps 9:6
[6]Their love, their hate
    and their jealousy have long
            since vanished;
never again will they have a
        part
    in anything that happens
        under the sun.   Job 21:21

[7]Go, eat your food with gladness, and drink your wine with a joyful heart, for it is now that God favors what you do. [8]Always be clothed in white, and always anoint your head with oil. [9]Enjoy life with your wife, whom you love, all the days of this meaningless life that God has given you under the sun— all your meaningless days. For this is your lot in life and in your toilsome labor under the sun. [10]Whatever your hand finds to do, do it with all your might, for in the grave,[c] where you are going, there is neither working nor planning nor knowledge nor wisdom.

[11]I have seen something else under the sun:

The race is not to the swift
    or the battle to the strong,
nor does food come to the
        wise   Job 32:13; Jer 9:23
    or wealth to the brilliant

---

[a]2 Septuagint (Aquila), Vulgate and Syriac; Hebrew does not have and the bad.   [b]4 Or What then is to be chosen? With all who live, there is hope   [c]10 Hebrew Sheol

or favor to the learned;
but time and chance happen to
    them all.   Dt 8:18; Ecc 2:14

12Moreover, no man knows
when his hour will come:

As fish are caught in a cruel
    net,
or birds are taken in a snare,
so men are trapped by evil
    times   Pr 29:6
that fall unexpectedly upon
    them.   Ps 73:22; Ecc 8:7

Wisdom Better Than Folly

13I also saw under the sun this
example of wisdom that greatly
impressed me: 14There was once a
small city with only a few people
in it. And a powerful king came
against it, surrounded it and built
huge siegeworks against it. 15Now
there lived in that city a man poor
but wise, and he saved the city by
his wisdom. But nobody remembered that poor man. 16So I said,
"Wisdom is better than strength."
But the poor man's wisdom is despised, and his words are no longer heeded.   Pr 21:22; Ecc 7:19

17The quiet words of the wise
    are more to be heeded
than the shouts of a ruler of
    fools.
18Wisdom is better than weapons
    of war,   ver 16; Ecc 2:13
but one sinner destroys
    much good.

10 As dead flies give
    perfume a bad smell,

so a little folly outweighs
    wisdom and honor.
2The heart of the wise inclines
    to the right,
but the heart of the fool to
    the left.
3Even as he walks along the
    road,
the fool lacks sense
and shows everyone how
    stupid he is.   Pr 13:16; 18:2
4If a ruler's anger rises against
    you,
do not leave your post;   Ecc 8:3
calmness can lay great errors
    to rest.   Pr 25:15

5There is an evil I have seen
    under the sun,
the sort of error that arises
    from a ruler:
6Fools are put in many high
    positions,   Pr 29:2
while the rich occupy the
    low ones.
7I have seen slaves on
    horseback,
while princes go on foot like
    slaves.   Pr 19:10
8Whoever digs a pit may fall
    into it;   Ps 7:15; Pr 26:27
whoever breaks through a
    wall may be bitten by a
    snake.   Est 2:23; Ps 9:16; Am 5:19
9Whoever quarries stones may
    be injured by them;
whoever splits logs may be
    endangered by them.
10If the ax is dull
    and its edge unsharpened,

more strength is needed
but skill will bring success.

¹¹If a snake bites before it is
    charmed,
  there is no profit for the
    charmer.   Ps 58:5; Isa 3:3

¹²Words from a wise man's
    mouth are gracious,
  but a fool is consumed by
    his own lips.   Pr 10:14; 14:3
¹³At the beginning his words are
    folly;
  at the end they are wicked
    madness—
¹⁴   and the fool multiplies
    words.   Pr 15:2; Ecc 5:3; 8:7

  No one knows what is
    coming—
  who can tell him what will
    happen after him?   Ecc 9:1

¹⁵A fool's work wearies him;
  he does not know the way to
    town.

¹⁶Woe to you, O land whose
    king was a servantᵃ
  and whose princes feast in
    the morning.
¹⁷Blessed are you, O land whose
    king is of noble birth
  and whose princes eat at a
    proper time—
  for strength and not for
    drunkenness.   1Sa 25:36

¹⁸If a man is lazy, the rafters
    sag;

if his hands are idle, the
    house leaks.   Pr 20:4

¹⁹A feast is made for laughter,
  and wine makes life merry,
  but money is the answer for
    everything.

²⁰Do not revile the king even in
    your thoughts,   Ex 22:28
  or curse the rich in your
    bedroom,
  because a bird of the air may
    carry your words,
  and a bird on the wing may
    report what you say.

Bread Upon the Waters

11 Cast your bread upon the
    waters,   ver 6; Isa 32:20
  for after many days you will
    find it again.   Pr 19:17
²Give portions to seven, yes to
    eight,
  for you do not know what
    disaster may come upon
    the land.

³If clouds are full of water,
  they pour rain upon the
    earth.
  Whether a tree falls to the
    south or to the north,
  in the place where it falls,
    there will it lie.
⁴Whoever watches the wind will
    not plant;
  whoever looks at the clouds
    will not reap.

ᵃ 16 Or king is a child

⁵As you do not know the path
    of the wind,   Jn 3:8-10
  or how the body is formed*ᵃ*
    in a mother's womb,
  so you cannot understand the
    work of God,
    the Maker of all things.

⁶Sow your seed in the morning,
  and at evening let not your
    hands be idle,   Ecc 9:10
for you do not know which
    will succeed,
  whether this or that,
  or whether both will do
    equally well.

Remember Your Creator While Young

⁷Light is sweet,
  and it pleases the eyes to see
    the sun.   Ecc 7:11
⁸However many years a man
    may live,
  let him enjoy them all.
But let him remember the days
    of darkness,   Ecc 12:1
  for they will be many.
Everything to come is
    meaningless.

⁹Be happy, young man, while
    you are young,
  and let your heart give you
    joy in the days of your
    youth.
Follow the ways of your heart
  and whatever your eyes see,
but know that for all these
    things

God will bring you to
    judgment.   Ecc 12:14; Ro 14:10
¹⁰So then, banish anxiety from
    your heart   Ps 94:19
  and cast off the troubles of
    your body,
  for youth and vigor are
    meaningless.   Ecc 2:24

12 Remember your Creator
    in the days of your
    youth,
before the days of trouble
    come   2Sa 19:35
  and the years approach
    when you will say,
  "I find no pleasure in
    them" —
²before the sun and the light
  and the moon and the stars
    grow dark,
  and the clouds return after
    the rain;
³when the keepers of the house
    tremble,
  and the strong men stoop,
when the grinders cease
    because they are few,
  and those looking through
    the windows grow dim;
⁴when the doors to the street
    are closed
  and the sound of grinding
    fades;
when men rise up at the sound
    of birds,
  but all their songs grow
    faint;   Jer 25:10

ᵃ5 Or *know how life* (or *the spirit*) / *enters the body being formed*

⁵when men are afraid of heights
and of dangers in the streets;
when the almond tree
blossoms
and the grasshopper drags
himself along
and desire no longer is
stirred.
Then man goes to his eternal
home   Job 17:13; 10:21
and mourners go about the
streets.   Jer 9:17; Am 5:16

⁶Remember him—before the
silver cord is severed,
or the golden bowl is
broken;
before the pitcher is shattered
at the spring,
or the wheel broken at the
well,
⁷and the dust returns to the
ground it came from,
and the spirit returns to God
who gave it.   Ecc 3:21

⁸"Meaningless! Meaningless!"
says the Teacher.ᵃ
"Everything is meaningless!"

The Conclusion of the Matter

⁹Not only was the Teacher wise,
but also he imparted knowledge to
the people. He pondered and
searched out and set in order
many proverbs. ¹⁰The Teacher
searched to find just the right
words, and what he wrote was up-
right and true.   1Ki 4:32; Pr 22:20-21
¹¹The words of the wise are like
goads, their collected sayings like
firmly embedded nails—given by
one Shepherd. ¹²Be warned, my
son, of anything in addition to
them.   Ezr 9:8
Of making many books there is
no end, and much study wearies
the body.   Ecc 1:18

¹³Now all has been heard;
here is the conclusion of the
matter:
Fear God and keep his
commandments,   Dt 4:2
for this is the whole ˌdutyˌ of
man.   Mic 6:8
¹⁴For God will bring every deed
into judgment,   Ecc 3:17
including every hidden thing,
whether it is good or evil.

ᵃ8 Or *the leader of the assembly*; also in verses 9 and 10

Song of Songs

1 Solomon's Song of Songs.

Beloved[a]

[2]Let him kiss me with the
    kisses of his mouth—
for your love is more
    delightful than wine.
[3]Pleasing is the fragrance of
    your perfumes;   SS 4:10
your name is like perfume
    poured out.   Ecc 7:1
No wonder the maidens love
    you!   Ps 45:14
[4]Take me away with you—let
    us hurry!
Let the king bring me into
    his chambers.   Ps 45:15

Friends

We rejoice and delight in you[b];
    we will praise your love
        more than wine.   ver 2

Beloved

How right they are to adore
    you!

[5]Dark am I, yet lovely,   SS 2:14; 4:3
O daughters of Jerusalem,
dark like the tents of Kedar,
like the tent curtains of
    Solomon.[c]

[6]Do not stare at me because I
    am dark,
because I am darkened by
    the sun.
My mother's sons were angry
    with me
and made me take care of
    the vineyards;   Ps 69:8
my own vineyard I have
    neglected.
[7]Tell me, you whom I love,
    where you graze your
        flock
and where you rest your
    sheep at midday.   SS 3:1-4
Why should I be like a veiled
    woman   Ge 24:65
beside the flocks of your
    friends?

Friends

[8]If you do not know, most
    beautiful of women,
follow the tracks of the
    sheep
and graze your young goats
    by the tents of the
        shepherds.

Lover

[9]I liken you, my darling, to a
    mare

---

[a]Primarily on the basis of the gender of the Hebrew pronouns used, male and female speakers are indicated in the margins by the captions *Lover* and *Beloved* respectively. The words of others are marked *Friends*. In some instances the divisions and their captions are debatable.   [b]4 The Hebrew is masculine singular.   [c]5 Or *Salma*

harnessed to one of the
chariots of Pharaoh.
¹⁰Your cheeks are beautiful with
earrings,   SS 5:13
your neck with strings of
jewels.   Isa 61:10
¹¹We will make you earrings of
gold,
studded with silver.

Beloved

¹²While the king was at his
table,
my perfume spread its
fragrance.   SS 4:11-14
¹³My lover is to me a sachet of
myrrh   Ge 37:25
resting between my breasts.
¹⁴My lover is to me a cluster of
henna blossoms   SS 2:3,17
from the vineyards of En
Gedi.   1Sa 23:29

Lover

¹⁵How beautiful you are, my
darling!   SS 4:7; 7:6
Oh, how beautiful!
Your eyes are doves.   SS 14:1

Beloved

¹⁶How handsome you are, my
lover!
Oh, how charming!
And our bed is verdant.

Lover

¹⁷The beams of our house are
cedars;   1Ki 6:9
our rafters are firs.

*Beloved*ᵃ

2 I am a roseᵇ of Sharon,
a lily of the valleys.   SS 5:13

Lover

²Like a lily among thorns
is my darling among the
maidens.

Beloved

³Like an apple tree among the
trees of the forest
is my lover among the
young men.   SS 1:14
I delight to sit in his shade,
and his fruit is sweet to my
taste.   SS 4:16
⁴He has taken me to the
banquet hall,   Est 1:11
and his banner over me is
love.   Nu 1:52
⁵Strengthen me with raisins,
refresh me with apples,   SS 7:8
for I am faint with love.
⁶His left arm is under my
head,
and his right arm embraces
me.   SS 8:3
⁷Daughters of Jerusalem, I
charge you   SS 5:8
by the gazelles and by the
does of the field:
Do not arouse or awaken love
until it so desires.   SS 3:5; 8:4
⁸Listen! My lover!
Look! Here he comes,
leaping across the mountains,

ᵃ1 Or *Lover*   ᵇ1 Possibly a member of the crocus family

bounding over the hills. ver 17
⁹My lover is like a gazelle or a
    young stag. ver 17; SS 8:14
Look! There he stands
    behind our wall,
gazing through the windows,
    peering through the lattice.
¹⁰My lover spoke and said to
    me,
    "Arise, my darling,
my beautiful one, and come
    with me.
¹¹See! The winter is past;
    the rains are over and gone.
¹²Flowers appear on the earth;
    the season of singing has
        come,
    the cooing of doves
        is heard in our land.
¹³The fig tree forms its early
        fruit; Isa 28:4; Jer 24:2
    the blossoming vines spread
        their fragrance. SS 7:12
    Arise, come, my darling;
    my beautiful one, come with
        me."

Lover

¹⁴My dove in the clefts of the
        rock, Ge 8:8; SS 1:15
    in the hiding places on the
        mountainside,
    show me your face,
        let me hear your voice;
    for your voice is sweet,
        and your face is lovely. SS 1:5
¹⁵Catch for us the foxes, Jdg 15:4
    the little foxes
    that ruin the vineyards, SS 1:6

our vineyards that are in
    bloom. SS 7:12

Beloved

¹⁶My lover is mine and I am
        his;
    he browses among the lilies.
¹⁷Until the day breaks
    and the shadows flee, SS 4:6
turn, my lover, SS 1:14
    and be like a gazelle
    or like a young stag ver 9
        on the rugged hills.ᵃ ver 8

3 All night long on my bed
    I looked for the one my
        heart loves; SS 5:6; Isa 26:9
    I looked for him but did not
        find him.
²I will get up now and go about
        the city,
    through its streets and
        squares;
    I will search for the one my
        heart loves.
    So I looked for him but did
        not find him.
³The watchmen found me
    as they made their rounds in
        the city. SS 5:7
    "Have you seen the one my
        heart loves?"
⁴Scarcely had I passed them
    when I found the one my
        heart loves.
    I held him and would not let
        him go
    till I had brought him to my
        mother's house, SS 8:2

ᵃ 17 Or *the hills of Bether*

to the room of the one who
  conceived me.   SS 6:9
⁵Daughters of Jerusalem, I
  charge you   SS 2:7
by the gazelles and by the
  does of the field:
Do not arouse or awaken
  love
until it so desires.   SS 8:4

⁶Who is this coming up from
  the desert   SS 8:5
like a column of smoke,
perfumed with myrrh and
  incense   SS 1:13; 4:6,14
made from all the spices of
  the merchant?   Ex 30:34
⁷Look! It is Solomon's carriage,
  escorted by sixty warriors,
  the noblest of Israel,
⁸all of them wearing the sword,
  all experienced in battle,
each with his sword at his
  side,
  prepared for the terrors of
  the night.   Job 15:22; Ps 91:5
⁹King Solomon made for
  himself the carriage;
he made it of wood from
  Lebanon.
¹⁰Its posts he made of silver,
  its base of gold.
Its seat was upholstered with
  purple,
  its interior lovingly inlaid
by*a* the daughters of
  Jerusalem.
¹¹Come out, you daughters of
  Zion,   Isa 4:4

and look at King Solomon
  wearing the crown,
the crown with which his
  mother crowned him
on the day of his wedding,
  the day his heart rejoiced.

Lover

4 How beautiful you are, my
  darling!
Oh, how beautiful!
Your eyes behind your veil
  are doves.   SS 1:15; 5:12
Your hair is like a flock of
  goats
descending from Mount
  Gilead.   Mic 7:14
²Your teeth are like a flock of
  sheep just shorn,
coming up from the
  washing.
Each has its twin;
  not one of them is alone.
³Your lips are like a scarlet
  ribbon;
your mouth is lovely.   SS 5:16
Your temples behind your veil
  are like the halves of a
  pomegranate.   SS 6:7
⁴Your neck is like the tower of
  David,   SS 7:4
built with elegance*b*;
on it hang a thousand shields,
  all of them shields of
  warriors.
⁵Your two breasts are like two
  fawns,   SS 7:3
like twin fawns of a gazelle

*a 10 Or its inlaid interior a gift of love / from
uncertain.*   *b 4 The meaning of the Hebrew for this word is*

that browse among the
lilies.
⁶Until the day breaks
and the shadows flee,   SS 2:17
I will go to the mountain of
myrrh
and to the hill of incense.
⁷All beautiful you are, my
darling;   SS 1:15
there is no flaw in you.

⁸Come with me from Lebanon,
my bride,   SS 5:1
come with me from
Lebanon.
Descend from the crest of
Amana,
from the top of Senir, the
summit of Hermon,
from the lions' dens
and the mountain haunts of
the leopards.
⁹You have stolen my heart, my
sister, my bride;
you have stolen my heart
with one glance of your eyes,
with one jewel of your
necklace.   Ge 41:42
¹⁰How delightful is your love,
my sister, my bride!
How much more pleasing is
your love than wine,
and the fragrance of your
perfume than any
spice!
¹¹Your lips drop sweetness as
the honeycomb, my
bride;
milk and honey are under
your tongue.   Ps 19:10; SS 5:1

The fragrance of your
garments is like that of
Lebanon.   Hos 14:6
¹²You are a garden locked up,
my sister, my bride;
you are a spring enclosed, a
sealed fountain.   Pr 5:15-18
¹³Your plants are an orchard of
pomegranates   SS 6:11; 7:12
with choice fruits,
with henna and nard,   SS 1:14
¹⁴ nard and saffron,
calamus and cinnamon,
with every kind of incense
tree,
with myrrh and aloes   SS 3:6
and all the finest spices.
¹⁵You areᵃ a garden fountain,
a well of flowing water
streaming down from
Lebanon.

Beloved

¹⁶Awake, north wind,
and come, south wind!
Blow on my garden,
that its fragrance may spread
abroad.
Let my lover come into his
garden
and taste its choice fruits.

Lover

5 I have come into my garden,
my sister, my bride;
I have gathered my myrrh
with my spice.

ᵃ15 Or *I am* (spoken by the *Beloved*)

I have eaten my honeycomb
and my honey;
I have drunk my wine and
my milk. SS 4:11; Isa 55:1

Friends

Eat, O friends, and drink;
drink your fill, O lovers.

Beloved

²I slept but my heart was
awake.
Listen! My lover is knocking:
"Open to me, my sister, my
darling,
my dove, my flawless one.
My head is drenched with dew,
my hair with the dampness
of the night."
³I have taken off my robe—
must I put it on again?
I have washed my feet—
must I soil them again?
⁴My lover thrust his hand
through the
latch-opening;
my heart began to pound for
him.
⁵I arose to open for my lover,
and my hands dripped with
myrrh,
my fingers with flowing myrrh,
on the handles of the lock.
⁶I opened for my lover, SS 6:1
but my lover had left; he
was gone. SS 6:2
My heart sank at his
departure.ᵃ

I looked for him but did not
find him. SS 3:1
I called him but he did not
answer.
⁷The watchmen found me
as they made their rounds in
the city. SS 3:3
They beat me, they bruised
me;
they took away my cloak,
those watchmen of the
walls!
⁸O daughters of Jerusalem, I
charge you— SS 2:7; 3:5
if you find my lover,
what will you tell him?
Tell him I am faint with
love. SS 2:5

Friends

⁹How is your beloved better
than others,
most beautiful of women?
How is your beloved better
than others,
that you charge us so?

Beloved

¹⁰My lover is radiant and ruddy,
outstanding among ten
thousand. Ps 45:2
¹¹His head is purest gold;
his hair is wavy
and black as a raven.
¹²His eyes are like doves SS 1:15
by the water streams,
washed in milk, Ge 49:12
mounted like jewels.

ᵃ6 Or *heart had gone out to him when he spoke*

¹³His cheeks are like beds of
    spice   SS 1:10; 6:2
    yielding perfume.
His lips are like lilies   SS 2:1
    dripping with myrrh.
¹⁴His arms are rods of gold
    set with chrysolite.
His body is like polished
    ivory
    decorated with sapphires.ᵃ
¹⁵His legs are pillars of marble
    set on bases of pure gold.
His appearance is like
    Lebanon,   1Ki 4:33; SS 7:4
    choice as its cedars.
¹⁶His mouth is sweetness itself;
    he is altogether lovely.
This is my lover, this my
    friend,   SS 7:9
    O daughters of Jerusalem.

Friends

6 Where has your lover gone,
    most beautiful of women?
Which way did your lover
    turn,
    that we may look for him
    with you?

Beloved

²My lover has gone down to his
    garden,   SS 4:12; 5:6
    to the beds of spices,   SS 5:13
to browse in the gardens
    and to gather lilies.
³I am my lover's and my lover
    is mine;   SS 7:10
    he browses among the lilies.

Lover

⁴You are beautiful, my darling,
    as Tirzah,   Jos 12:24
lovely as Jerusalem,   Ps 48:2
majestic as troops with
    banners.   ver 10
⁵Turn your eyes from me;
    they overwhelm me.
Your hair is like a flock of
    goats
    descending from Gilead.
⁶Your teeth are like a flock of
    sheep
    coming up from the
    washing.
Each has its twin,
    not one of them is alone.
⁷Your temples behind your
    veil
    are like the halves of a
    pomegranate.   SS 4:3
⁸Sixty queens there may be,
    and eighty concubines,
    and virgins beyond number;
⁹but my dove, my perfect one,
    is unique,   SS 1:15; 5:2
the only daughter of her
    mother,
the favorite of the one who
    bore her.   SS 3:4
The maidens saw her and
    called her blessed;
the queens and concubines
    praised her.

Friends

¹⁰Who is this that appears like
    the dawn,

ᵃ 14 Or *lapis lazuli*

fair as the moon, bright as
the sun,
majestic as the stars in
procession?

Lover

[11]I went down to the grove of
nut trees
to look at the new growth in
the valley,
to see if the vines had budded
or the pomegranates were in
bloom. SS 7:12
[12]Before I realized it,
my desire set me among the
royal chariots of my
people.[a]

Friends

[13]Come back, come back,
O Shulammite;
come back, come back, that
we may gaze on you!

Lover

Why would you gaze on the
Shulammite
as on the dance of
Mahanaim? Ex 15:20

7 How beautiful your sandaled
feet,
O prince's daughter! Ps 45:13
Your graceful legs are like
jewels,
the work of a craftsman's
hands.

[2]Your navel is a rounded goblet
that never lacks blended
wine.
Your waist is a mound of
wheat
encircled by lilies.
[3]Your breasts are like two
fawns, SS 4:5
twins of a gazelle.
[4]Your neck is like an ivory
tower. Ps 144:12; SS 4:4
Your eyes are the pools of
Heshbon Nu 21:26
by the gate of Bath Rabbim.
Your nose is like the tower of
Lebanon SS 5:15
looking toward Damascus.
[5]Your head crowns you like
Mount Carmel. Isa 35:2
Your hair is like royal
tapestry;
the king is held captive by
its tresses.
[6]How beautiful you are and
how pleasing, SS 1:15
O love, with your delights!
[7]Your stature is like that of the
palm,
and your breasts like clusters
of fruit. SS 4:5
[8]I said, "I will climb the palm
tree;
I will take hold of its fruit."
May your breasts be like the
clusters of the vine,
the fragrance of your breath
like apples, SS 2:5
[9] and your mouth like the best
wine.

---

[a]12 Or *among the chariots of Amminadab*; or *among the chariots of the people of the prince*

Beloved

May the wine go straight to my
      lover,   SS 5:16
   flowing gently over lips and
      teeth.ᵃ
¹⁰I belong to my lover,
   and his desire is for me.
¹¹Come, my lover, let us go to
      the countryside,
   let us spend the night in the
      villages.ᵇ
¹²Let us go early to the
      vineyards   SS 1:6
   to see if the vines have
      budded,   SS 2:15
   if their blossoms have
      opened,
   and if the pomegranates are
      in bloom —   SS 4:13; 6:11
   there I will give you my
      love.
¹³The mandrakes send out their
      fragrance,   Ge 30:14
   and at our door is every
      delicacy,
   both new and old,
      that I have stored up for
      you, my lover.   SS 4:16

8 If only you were to me like
      a brother,
   who was nursed at my
      mother's breasts!
   Then, if I found you outside,
      I would kiss you,
   and no one would despise
      me.
²I would lead you

and bring you to my
      mother's house —   SS 3:4
   she who has taught me.
   I would give you spiced wine
      to drink,
   the nectar of my
      pomegranates.
³His left arm is under my
      head
   and his right arm embraces
      me.
⁴Daughters of Jerusalem, I
      charge you:
   Do not arouse or awaken
      love
   until it so desires.   SS 2:7; 3:5

Friends

⁵Who is this coming up from
      the desert   SS 3:6
   leaning on her lover?

Beloved

Under the apple tree I roused
      you;
   there your mother conceived
      you,   SS 3:4
   there she who was in labor
      gave you birth.
⁶Place me like a seal over your
      heart,
   like a seal on your arm;
   for love is as strong as death,
      its jealousyᶜ unyielding as
      the grave.ᵈ
   It burns like blazing fire,
      like a mighty flame.ᵉ   Nu 5:14

ᵃ9 Septuagint, Aquila, Vulgate and Syriac; Hebrew *lips of sleepers*   ᵇ11 Or *henna bushes*   ᶜ6 Or
ardor   ᵈ6 Hebrew *Sheol*   ᵉ6 Or / *like the very flame of the* Lᴏʀᴅ

⁷Many waters cannot quench
love;
rivers cannot wash it away.
If one were to give
all the wealth of his house
for love,
it^a would be utterly scorned.

Friends

⁸We have a young sister,
and her breasts are not yet
grown.
What shall we do for our sister
for the day she is spoken
for?
⁹If she is a wall,
we will build towers of silver
on her.
If she is a door,
we will enclose her with
panels of cedar.

Beloved

¹⁰I am a wall,
and my breasts are like
towers.
Thus I have become in his
eyes

like one bringing
contentment.
¹¹Solomon had a vineyard in
Baal Hamon;   Ecc 2:4
he let out his vineyard to
tenants.
Each was to bring for its fruit
a thousand shekels^b of
silver.   Isa 7:23
¹²But my own vineyard is mine
to give;   SS 1:6
the thousand shekels are for
you, O Solomon,
and two hundred^c are for
those who tend its fruit.

Lover

¹³You who dwell in the gardens
with friends in attendance,
let me hear your voice!

Beloved

¹⁴Come away, my lover,
and be like a gazelle   Pr 5:19
or like a young stag   SS 2:9
on the spice-laden
mountains.   SS 2:8,17

---

^a7 Or he   ^b11 That is, about 25 pounds (about 11.5 kilograms); also in verse 12   ^c12 That is, about
5 pounds (about 2.3 kilograms)

Isaiah

1 The vision concerning Judah and Jerusalem that Isaiah son of Amoz saw during the reigns of Uzziah, Jotham, Ahaz and Hezekiah, kings of Judah.   Isa 2:1; 2Ki 16:1

A Rebellious Nation

²Hear, O heavens! Listen,
    O earth!
For the LORD has spoken:
"I reared children and brought
    them up,
but they have rebelled
    against me.   Isa 30:1,9; 65:2
³The ox knows his master,
    the donkey his owner's
    manger,
but Israel does not know,
    my people do not
    understand."   Dt 32:28

⁴Ah, sinful nation,
    a people loaded with guilt,
a brood of evildoers,   Isa 14:20
    children given to corruption!
They have forsaken the LORD;
    they have spurned the Holy
    One of Israel   Isa 5:19,24
and turned their backs on
    him.   Pr 30:9

⁵Why should you be beaten
    anymore?   Pr 20:30
Why do you persist in
    rebellion?   Isa 31:6; Heb 3:16
Your whole head is injured,
    your whole heart afflicted.
⁶From the sole of your foot to
    the top of your head
there is no soundness—
only wounds and welts
    and open sores,
not cleansed or bandaged
    or soothed with oil.   Lk 10:34

⁷Your country is desolate,
    your cities burned with fire;
your fields are being stripped
    by foreigners   Lev 26:16
    right before you,
laid waste as when
    overthrown by strangers.
⁸The Daughter of Zion is left
    like a shelter in a vineyard,
like a hut in a field of melons,
    like a city under siege.
⁹Unless the LORD Almighty
    had left us some survivors,
we would have become like
    Sodom,
we would have been like
    Gomorrah.   Ge 19:24; Ro 9:29*

¹⁰Hear the word of the LORD,
    you rulers of Sodom;   Eze 16:49
listen to the law of our God,
    you people of Gomorrah!
¹¹"The multitude of your
    sacrifices—
what are they to me?" says
    the LORD.
"I have more than enough of
    burnt offerings,

of rams and the fat of
fattened animals; Ps 50:8
I have no pleasure
in the blood of bulls and
lambs and goats. 1Sa 15:22
¹²When you come to appear
before me,
who has asked this of
you,
this trampling of my courts?
¹³Stop bringing meaningless
offerings! Isa 66:3
Your incense is detestable to
me. Jer 7:9
New Moons, Sabbaths and
convocations— 1Ch 23:31
I cannot bear your evil
assemblies.
¹⁴Your New Moon festivals and
your appointed feasts
my soul hates. Ps 11:5
They have become a burden to
me;
I am weary of bearing them.
¹⁵When you spread out your
hands in prayer,
I will hide my eyes from
you; Isa 8:17; 59:2; Mic 3:4
even if you offer many prayers,
I will not listen. Isa 59:3; Jer 2:34
Your hands are full of blood;
¹⁶ wash and make yourselves
clean. Mt 27:24; Jas 4:8
Take your evil deeds
out of my sight! Isa 52:11
Stop doing wrong, Isa 55:7; Jer 25:5
¹⁷ learn to do right! Ps 34:14
Seek justice, Zep 2:3
encourage the oppressed.ᵃ

Defend the cause of the
fatherless, Ps 82:3; 94:6
plead the case of the widow.

¹⁸"Come now, let us reason
together," Isa 41:1; 43:9,26
says the LORD.
"Though your sins are like
scarlet,
they shall be as white as
snow; Ps 51:7; Rev 7:14
though they are red as
crimson,
they shall be like wool.
¹⁹If you are willing and obedient,
you will eat the best from
the land; Dt 30:15-16; Isa 55:2
²⁰but if you resist and rebel,
you will be devoured by the
sword." Isa 3:25; 65:12
For the mouth of the
LORD has spoken.

²¹See how the faithful city
has become a harlot! Jer 2:20
She once was full of justice;
righteousness used to dwell
in her— Isa 5:7; 46:13
but now murderers! Pr 6:17
²²Your silver has become dross,
your choice wine is diluted
with water.
²³Your rulers are rebels,
companions of thieves;
they all love bribes Ex 23:8; Am 5:12
and chase after gifts.
They do not defend the cause
of the fatherless;
the widow's case does not
come before them.

ᵃ17 Or / rebuke the oppressor

²⁴Therefore the Lord, the Lᴏʀᴅ
    Almighty,
  the Mighty One of Israel,
    declares: Ge 49:24
  "Ah, I will get relief from my
    foes
  and avenge myself on my
    enemies.   Isa 35:4; 59:17; 61:2
²⁵I will turn my hand against
    you;   Dt 28:63
  I will thoroughly purge away
    your dross
  and remove all your
    impurities.   Eze 22:22; Mal 3:3
²⁶I will restore your judges as in
    days of old,   Jer 33:7,11
  your counselors as at the
    beginning.
Afterward you will be called
  the City of Righteousness,
  the Faithful City."   Isa 60:14; 62:2

²⁷Zion will be redeemed with
    justice,
  her penitent ones with
    righteousness.   Isa 35:10
²⁸But rebels and sinners will
    both be broken,
  and those who forsake the
    Lᴏʀᴅ will perish.   Ps 9:5

²⁹"You will be ashamed because
    of the sacred oaks Isa 57:5
  in which you have delighted;
you will be disgraced because
    of the gardens   Isa 65:3
  that you have chosen.
³⁰You will be like an oak with
    fading leaves,
  like a garden without water.
³¹The mighty man will become
    tinder

and his work a spark;
both will burn together,
  with no one to quench the
    fire."   Isa 5:24; 9:18-19; 26:11

The Mountain of the Lᴏʀᴅ

2 This is what Isaiah son of
Amoz saw concerning Judah
and Jerusalem: Isa 1:1

²In the last days

the mountain of the Lᴏʀᴅ's
  temple will be
  established   Mic 4:7
  as chief among the
    mountains;
it will be raised above the hills,
and all nations will stream to
    it.   Ps 102:15

³Many peoples will come and
say,

"Come, let us go up to the
    mountain of the Lᴏʀᴅ,
  to the house of the God of
    Jacob.
He will teach us his ways,
  so that we may walk in his
    paths."
The law will go out from Zion,
  the word of the Lᴏʀᴅ from
    Jerusalem.   Lk 24:47
⁴He will judge between the
    nations   Isa 1:27; Joel 3:14
  and will settle disputes for
    many peoples.   Ge 49:10
They will beat their swords
    into plowshares
  and their spears into pruning
    hooks.   Joel 3:10

Nation will not take up sword
    against nation,   Isa 32:18
nor will they train for war
    anymore.   Mic 4:1-3

⁵Come, O house of Jacob,   Isa 58:1
    let us walk in the light of the
    LORD.   Isa 60:1,19-20; 1Jn 1:5,7

The Day of the LORD

⁶You have abandoned your
    people,   Dt 31:17
    the house of Jacob.
They are full of superstitions
    from the East;
they practice divination like
    the Philistines   2Ki 1:2
and clasp hands with
    pagans.   2Ki 16:7; Pr 6:1
⁷Their land is full of silver and
    gold;   Dt 17:17
    there is no end to their
    treasures.   Ps 17:14
Their land is full of horses;
    there is no end to their
    chariots.   Isa 31:1; Mic 5:10
⁸Their land is full of idols;
    they bow down to the work
    of their hands,   Ps 135:15
to what their fingers have
    made.   Isa 17:8
⁹So man will be brought low
    and mankind humbled —
    do not forgive them.ᵃ   Ne 4:5

¹⁰Go into the rocks,
    hide in the ground
from dread of the LORD
    and the splendor of his
    majesty!   2Th 1:9; Rev 6:15-16

¹¹The eyes of the arrogant man
    will be humbled   Ne 9:29
and the pride of men
    brought low;   Isa 5:15; 37:23
the LORD alone will be exalted
    in that day.   Ps 46:10

¹²The LORD Almighty has a day
    in store   Am 5:18; Zep 1:14
for all the proud and lofty,
for all that is exalted
(and they will be humbled),
¹³for all the cedars of Lebanon,
    tall and lofty,
    and all the oaks of Bashan,
¹⁴for all the towering mountains
    and all the high hills,   Isa 30:25
¹⁵for every lofty tower   Isa 30:25
    and every fortified wall,
¹⁶for every trading shipᵇ   1Ki 10:22
    and every stately vessel.
¹⁷The arrogance of man will be
    brought low
and the pride of men
    humbled;   ver 9
the LORD alone will be exalted
    in that day,   ver 11
¹⁸   and the idols will totally
    disappear.   Isa 21:9
¹⁹Men will flee to caves in the
    rocks   Isa 7:19
and to holes in the ground
from dread of the LORD   Dt 2:25
    and the splendor of his
    majesty,   Ps 145:12
when he rises to shake the
    earth.   Heb 12:26
²⁰In that day men will throw
    away

ᵃ9 Or *not raise them up*   ᵇ16 Hebrew *every ship of Tarshish*

to the rodents and bats
their idols of silver and idols of
　　gold,　　Rev 9:20
which they made to worship.
²¹They will flee to caverns in the
　　rocks
and to the overhanging crags
from dread of the Lᴏʀᴅ
and the splendor of his
　　majesty,　　Ps 145:12
when he rises to shake the
　　earth.　　ver 19; Isa 33:10

²²Stop trusting in man,　　Ps 146:3
who has but a breath in his
　　nostrils.
Of what account is he?　　Ps 8:4

*Judgment on Jerusalem and
Judah*

3 See now, the Lord,
　　the Lᴏʀᴅ Almighty,
is about to take from
　　　　Jerusalem and Judah
both supply and support:
all supplies of food and all
　　　　supplies of water,
² 　the hero and warrior,　　Eze 17:13
the judge and prophet,
　　the soothsayer and elder,
³the captain of fifty and man of
　　rank,
the counselor, skilled
　　craftsman and clever
　　enchanter.　　2Ki 24:14 Ecc 10:11

⁴I will make boys their officials;
mere children will govern
　　them.　　Ecc 10:16 *fn*
⁵People will oppress each
　　other—

man against man, neighbor
　　against neighbor.　　Mic 7:2,6
The young will rise up against
　　the old,
the base against the
　　honorable.

⁶A man will seize one of his
　　brothers
at his father's home, and
　　say,
"You have a cloak, you be our
　　leader;
take charge of this heap of
　　ruins!"
⁷But in that day he will cry out,
"I have no remedy.　　Eze 34:4
I have no food or clothing in
　　my house;
do not make me the leader
　　of the people."　　Isa 24:2

⁸Jerusalem staggers,
Judah is falling;　　Isa 1:7
their words and deeds are
　　against the Lᴏʀᴅ,
defying his glorious
　　presence.　　Ps 73:9,11
⁹The look on their faces testifies
　　against them;
they parade their sin like
　　Sodom;　　Ge 13:13
they do not hide it.
Woe to them!
They have brought disaster
　　upon themselves.　　Pr 8:36

¹⁰Tell the righteous it will be
　　well with them,　　Dt 28:1-14
for they will enjoy the fruit
　　of their deeds.　　Ps 128:2

¹¹Woe to the wicked! Disaster is
        upon them!   Dt 28:15-68
They will be paid back for
        what their hands have
        done.   2Ch 6:23

¹²Youths oppress my people,
        women rule over them.
O my people, your guides lead
        you astray;   Isa 9:16
        they turn you from the path.

¹³The LORD takes his place in
        court;
        he rises to judge the people.
¹⁴The LORD enters into judgment
        against the elders and
        leaders of his people:
"It is you who have ruined my
        vineyard;
        the plunder from the poor is
        in your houses.   Jas 2:6
¹⁵What do you mean by
        crushing my people
and grinding the faces of the
        poor?"   Isa 10:6; 11:4
        declares the Lord, the
        LORD Almighty.

¹⁶The LORD says,
"The women of Zion are
        haughty,   SS 3:11
walking along with
        outstretched necks,
        flirting with their eyes,
tripping along with mincing
        steps,
        with ornaments jingling on
        their ankles.
¹⁷Therefore the Lord will bring
        sores on the heads of
        the women of Zion;

the LORD will make their
        scalps bald."

¹⁸In that day the Lord will
snatch away their finery: the
bangles and headbands and cres-
cent necklaces, ¹⁹the earrings
and bracelets and veils, ²⁰the
headdresses and ankle chains
and sashes, the perfume bottles and
charms, ²¹the signet rings and
nose rings, ²²the fine robes and the
capes and cloaks, the purses ²³and
mirrors, and the linen garments
and tiaras and shawls.   Isa 2:11

²⁴Instead of fragrance there will
        be a stench;   Est 2:12
instead of a sash, a rope;
instead of well-dressed hair,
        baldness;   Isa 22:12
instead of fine clothing,
        sackcloth;   La 2:10
instead of beauty, branding.
²⁵Your men will fall by the
        sword,   Isa 1:20
        your warriors in battle.
²⁶The gates of Zion will lament
        and mourn;   Jer 14:2
destitute, she will sit on the
        ground.   La 2:10
4 In that day seven women
        will take hold of one man
and say, "We will eat our own
        food   2Th 3:12
and provide our own clothes;
only let us be called by your
        name.
Take away our disgrace!"

The Branch of the LORD

²In that day the Branch of the

LORD will be beautiful and glorious, and the fruit of the land will be the pride and glory of the survivors in Israel. ³Those who are left in Zion, who remain in Jerusalem, will be called holy, all who are recorded among the living in Jerusalem. ⁴The Lord will wash away the filth of the women of Zion; he will cleanse the bloodstains from Jerusalem by a spirit*a* of judgment and a spirit*a* of fire. ⁵Then the LORD will create over all of Mount Zion and over those who assemble there a cloud of smoke by day and a glow of flaming fire by night; over all the glory will be a canopy. ⁶It will be a shelter and shade from the heat of the day, and a refuge and hiding place from the storm and rain.

The Song of the Vineyard

5 I will sing for the one I love
   a song about his vineyard:
My loved one had a vineyard
      on a fertile hillside.
²He dug it up and cleared it of
      stones
   and planted it with the
      choicest vines.   Jer 2:21
He built a watchtower in
      it
   and cut out a winepress as
      well.
Then he looked for a crop of
      good grapes,
   but it yielded only bad
      fruit.

³"Now you dwellers in
      Jerusalem and men of
      Judah,
   judge between me and my
      vineyard.   Mt 21:40
⁴What more could have been
      done for my vineyard
   than I have done for it?
When I looked for good
      grapes,
   why did it yield only bad?
⁵Now I will tell you
   what I am going to do to my
      vineyard:
I will take away its hedge,
   and it will be destroyed;
I will break down its wall,
   and it will be trampled.
⁶I will make it a wasteland,
   neither pruned nor
      cultivated,
   and briers and thorns will
      grow there.   Isa 7:23-24
I will command the clouds
   not to rain on it."

⁷The vineyard of the LORD
      Almighty
   is the house of Israel,   Ps 80:8
and the men of Judah
   are the garden of his delight.
And he looked for justice, but
      saw bloodshed;   Isa 59:15
for righteousness, but heard
      cries of distress.

Woes and Judgments

⁸Woe to you who add house to
      house   Jer 22:13

---

a 4 Or the Spirit

and join field to field   Mic 2:2
till no space is left
and you live alone in the
    land.

⁹The LORD Almighty has declared in my hearing: Isa 22:14

"Surely the great houses will
    become desolate,
the fine mansions left
    without occupants.
¹⁰A ten-acre*a* vineyard will
    produce only a bath*b* of
    wine,
a homer*c* of seed only an
    ephah*d* of grain."

¹¹Woe to those who rise early in
    the morning
to run after their drinks,
who stay up late at night
    till they are inflamed with
    wine.   Pr 23:29-30
¹²They have harps and lyres at
    their banquets,
tambourines and flutes and
    wine,
but they have no regard for the
    deeds of the LORD,
no respect for the work of
    his hands.   Ps 28:5; Am 6:5-6
¹³Therefore my people will go
    into exile
for lack of understanding;
their men of rank will die of
    hunger
and their masses will be
    parched with thirst.

¹⁴Therefore the grave*e* enlarges
    its appetite   Pr 30:16
and opens its mouth without
    limit;   Nu 16:30
into it will descend their
    nobles and masses
with all their brawlers and
    revelers.
¹⁵So man will be brought low
and mankind humbled,   Isa 2:9
the eyes of the arrogant
    humbled.   Isa 2:11
¹⁶But the LORD Almighty will be
    exalted by his justice,
and the holy God will show
    himself holy by his
    righteousness.   Isa 29:23
¹⁷Then sheep will graze as in
    their own pasture;
lambs will feed*f* among the
    ruins of the rich.

¹⁸Woe to those who draw sin
    along with cords of
    deceit,
and wickedness as with cart
    ropes,   Isa 59:4-8; Jer 23:14
¹⁹to those who say, "Let God
    hurry,
let him hasten his work
    so we may see it.
Let it approach,
let the plan of the Holy One
    of Israel come,
so we may know it."   Jer 17:15

²⁰Woe to those who call evil
    good

---

a 10 Hebrew *ten-yoke,* that is, the land plowed by 10 yoke of oxen in one day   *b 10* That is, probably
about 6 gallons (about 22 liters)   *c 10* That is, probably about 6 bushels (about 220 liters)   *d 10* That
is, probably about 3/5 bushel (about 22 liters)   *e 14* Hebrew *Sheol*   *f 17* Septuagint; Hebrew /
strangers will eat

and good evil,
who put darkness for light
 and light for darkness,
who put bitter for sweet
 and sweet for bitter.   Am 5:7

21Woe to those who are wise in
   their own eyes   Ro 12:16
 and clever in their own
   sight.

22Woe to those who are heroes
   at drinking wine   Pr 23:20
 and champions at mixing
   drinks,
23who acquit the guilty for a
   bribe,   Ex 23:8
 but deny justice to the
   innocent.   Ps 94:21; Jas 5:6
24Therefore, as tongues of fire
   lick up straw
 and as dry grass sinks down
   in the flames,
 so their roots will decay
 and their flowers blow away
   like dust;
 for they have rejected the law
   of the LORD Almighty
 and spurned the word of the
   Holy One of Israel.   Isa 8:6
25Therefore the LORD's anger
   burns against his
   people;   2Ki 22:13
 his hand is raised and he
   strikes them down.
 The mountains shake,
 and the dead bodies are like
   refuse in the streets.

 Yet for all this, his anger is not
   turned away,   Jer 4:8; Da 9:16
 his hand is still upraised.

26He lifts up a banner for the
   distant nations,
 he whistles for those at the
   ends of the earth.   Isa 7:18
 Here they come,
   swiftly and speedily!
27Not one of them grows tired or
   stumbles,
 not one slumbers or sleeps;
 not a belt is loosened at the
   waist,   Job 12:18
 not a sandal thong is broken.
28Their arrows are sharp,   Ps 45:5
 all their bows are strung;
 their horses' hoofs seem like
   flint,
 their chariot wheels like a
   whirlwind.
29Their roar is like that of the
   lion,   Jer 51:38; Zep 3:3
 they roar like young lions;
 they growl as they seize their
   prey   Isa 10:6; 49:24-25
 and carry it off with no one
   to rescue.   Isa 42:22; Mic 5:8
30In that day they will roar over
   it
 like the roaring of the sea.
 And if one looks at the land,
 he will see darkness and
   distress;   Isa 8:22; Jer 4:23-28
 even the light will be
   darkened by the clouds.

Isaiah's Commission

6 In the year that King Uzziah
  died, I saw the Lord seated on
a throne, high and exalted, and the
train of his robe filled the temple.
2Above him were seraphs, each
with six wings: With two wings

they covered their faces, with two they covered their feet, and with two they were flying. ³And they were calling to one another:

"Holy, holy, holy is the Lord Almighty;   Ex 15:11; Ps 89:8
the whole earth is full of his glory."   Ps 72:19; Rev 4:8

⁴At the sound of their voices the doorposts and thresholds shook and the temple was filled with smoke.

⁵"Woe to me!" I cried. "I am ruined! For I am a man of unclean lips, and I live among a people of unclean lips, and my eyes have seen the King, the Lord Almighty."

⁶Then one of the seraphs flew to me with a live coal in his hand, which he had taken with tongs from the altar. ⁷With it he touched my mouth and said, "See, this has touched your lips; your guilt is taken away and your sin atoned for."

⁸Then I heard the voice of the Lord saying, "Whom shall I send? And who will go for us?"   Ac 9:4

And I said, "Here am I. Send me!"   Ge 22:1; Ex 3:4

⁹He said, "Go and tell this people: Eze 3:11

" 'Be ever hearing, but never understanding;
be ever seeing, but never perceiving.'   Mt 13:15*

¹⁰Make the heart of this people calloused;   Ps 119:70
make their ears dull
and close their eyes.ᵃ
Otherwise they might see with their eyes,
hear with their ears,   Jer 5:21
understand with their hearts,
and turn and be healed."

¹¹Then I said, "For how long, O Lord?"   Ps 79:5

And he answered:

"Until the cities lie ruined
and without inhabitant,
until the houses are left deserted
and the fields ruined and ravaged,   Ps 79:1; 109:11
¹²until the Lord has sent everyone far away
and the land is utterly forsaken.   Jer 4:29; 30:17
¹³And though a tenth remains in the land,   Isa 1:9
it will again be laid waste.
But as the terebinth and oak leave stumps when they are cut down,
so the holy seed will be the stump in the land."

The Sign of Immanuel

7 When Ahaz son of Jotham, the son of Uzziah, was king of Judah, King Rezin of Aram and Pekah son of Remaliah king of Israel marched up to fight against Jerusa-

ᵃ9,10 Hebrew; Septuagint 'You will be ever hearing, but never understanding; / you will be ever seeing, but never perceiving.' / ¹⁰This people's heart has become calloused; / they hardly hear with their ears, / and they have closed their eyes

lem, but they could not over-power it. 2Ki 15:25,37; 2Ch 28:5

²Now the house of David was told, "Aram has allied itself with[a] Ephraim"; so the hearts of Ahaz and his people were shaken, as the trees of the forest are shaken by the wind. ver 13; Isa 9:9; 22:22

³Then the LORD said to Isaiah, "Go out, you and your son Shear-Jashub,[b] to meet Ahaz at the end of the aqueduct of the Upper Pool, on the road to the Washerman's Field. ⁴Say to him, 'Be careful, keep calm and don't be afraid. Do not lose heart because of these two smoldering stubs of firewood—because of the fierce anger of Rezin and Aram and of the son of Remaliah. ⁵Aram, Ephraim and Remaliah's son have plotted your ruin, saying, ⁶"Let us invade Judah; let us tear it apart and divide it among ourselves, and make the son of Tabeel king over it." ⁷Yet this is what the Sovereign LORD says: Isa 10:24

" 'It will not take place,
    it will not happen, Isa 8:10
⁸for the head of Aram is
    Damascus, Ge 14:15
    and the head of Damascus is
        only Rezin.
Within sixty-five years
    Ephraim will be too
        shattered to be a people.
⁹The head of Ephraim is
    Samaria,

and the head of Samaria is
    only Remaliah's son.
If you do not stand firm in
    your faith, 2Ch 20:20
    you will not stand at all.' "

¹⁰Again the LORD spoke to Ahaz, ¹¹"Ask the LORD your God for a sign, whether in the deepest depths or in the highest heights."

¹²But Ahaz said, "I will not ask; I will not put the LORD to the test."

¹³Then Isaiah said, "Hear now, you house of David! Is it not enough to try the patience of men? Will you try the patience of my God also? ¹⁴Therefore the Lord himself will give you[c] a sign: The virgin will be with child and will give birth to a son, and[d] will call him Immanuel.[e] ¹⁵He will eat curds and honey when he knows enough to reject the wrong and choose the right. ¹⁶But before the boy knows enough to reject the wrong and choose the right, the land of the two kings you dread will be laid waste. ¹⁷The LORD will bring on you and on your people and on the house of your father a time unlike any since Ephraim broke away from Judah—he will bring the king of Assyria."

¹⁸In that day the LORD will whistle for flies from the distant streams of Egypt and for bees from the land of Assyria. ¹⁹They will all come and settle in the steep ra-

---

[a]2 Or has set up camp in   [b]3 Shear-Jashub means a remnant will return.   [c]14 The Hebrew is plural.   [d]14 Masoretic Text; Dead Sea Scrolls and he or and they   [e]14 Immanuel means God with us.

vines and in the crevices in the rocks, on all the thornbushes and at all the water holes. ²⁰In that day the Lord will use a razor hired from beyond the River^a—the king of Assyria—to shave your head and the hair of your legs, and to take off your beards also. ²¹In that day, a man will keep alive a young cow and two goats. ²²And because of the abundance of the milk they give, he will have curds to eat. All who remain in the land will eat curds and honey. ²³In that day, in every place where there were a thousand vines worth a thousand silver shekels,^b there will be only briers and thorns. ²⁴Men will go there with bow and arrow, for the land will be covered with briers and thorns. ²⁵As for all the hills once cultivated by the hoe, you will no longer go there for fear of the briers and thorns; they will become places where cattle are turned loose and where sheep run.

Assyria, the Lord's Instrument

8 The Lord said to me, "Take a large scroll and write on it with an ordinary pen: Maher-Shal-al-Hash-Baz.^c ²And I will call in Uriah the priest and Zechariah son of Jeberekiah as reliable witnesses for me." Isa 30:8; Hab 2:2

³Then I went to the prophetess, and she conceived and gave birth to a son. And the Lord said to me,

"Name him Maher-Shalal-Hash-Baz. ⁴Before the boy knows how to say 'My father' or 'My mother,' the wealth of Damascus and the plunder of Samaria will be carried off by the king of Assyria." Isa 7:8,16

⁵The Lord spoke to me again:

⁶"Because this people has
    rejected   Isa 5:24
  the gently flowing waters of
    Shiloah   Jn 9:7
and rejoices over Rezin
  and the son of Remaliah,
⁷therefore the Lord is about to
    bring against them
  the mighty floodwaters of
    the River^a—   Isa 17:12-13
  the king of Assyria with all
    his pomp.   Isa 7:20
It will overflow all its channels,
  run over all its banks
⁸and sweep on into Judah,
    swirling over it,
  passing through it and
    reaching up to the neck.
Its outspread wings will cover
  the breadth of your
    land,
  O Immanuel^d!"   Isa 7:14

⁹Raise the war cry,^e you
    nations, and be
  shattered!   Isa 17:12-13
Listen, all you distant lands.
Prepare for battle, and be
    shattered!   Joel 3:9
Prepare for battle, and be
    shattered!

---

^a20,7 That is, the Euphrates   ^b23 That is, about 25 pounds (about 11.5 kilograms)
^c1 *Maher-Shalal-Hash-Baz* means *quick to the plunder, swift to the spoil*; also in verse 3.
^d8 *Immanuel* means *God with us.*   ^e9 Or *Do your worst*

¹⁰Devise your strategy, but it will
   be thwarted;   Job 5:12
propose your plan, but it will
   not stand,   Isa 7:7
for God is with us.ᵃ   Ro 8:31

Fear God

¹¹The LORD spoke to me with his
strong hand upon me, warning me
not to follow the way of this people. He said: Eze 2:8; 3:14

¹²"Do not call conspiracy   Isa 7:2
   everything that these people
   call conspiracyᵇ;
do not fear what they fear,
   and do not dread it.   1Pe 3:14*
¹³The LORD Almighty is the one
   you are to regard as
   holy,   Nu 20:12
he is the one you are to fear,
he is the one you are to
   dread,   Isa 29:23
¹⁴and he will be a sanctuary;
   but for both houses of Israel
   he will be
a stone that causes men to
   stumble   Lk 2:34; Ro 9:33*
and a rock that makes them
   fall.   Isa 24:17-18
And for the people of
   Jerusalem he will be
a trap and a snare.
¹⁵Many of them will stumble;
   they will fall and be broken,
   they will be snared and
   captured."

¹⁶Bind up the testimony

and seal up the law among
   my disciples.   Isa 29:11-12
¹⁷I will wait for the LORD,   Hab 2:3
   who is hiding his face from
   the house of Jacob.
I will put my trust in him.

¹⁸Here am I, and the children the
LORD has given me. We are signs
and symbols in Israel from the
LORD Almighty, who dwells on
Mount Zion.   Heb 2:13*; Ps 9:11
¹⁹When men tell you to consult
mediums and spiritists, who whisper and mutter, should not a people inquire of their God? Why consult the dead on behalf of the
living? ²⁰To the law and to the
testimony! If they do not speak according to this word, they have no
light of dawn. ²¹Distressed and
hungry, they will roam through
the land; when they are famished, they will become enraged
and, looking upward, will curse
their king and their God. ²²Then
they will look toward the earth
and see only distress and darkness and fearful gloom, and
they will be thrust into utter darkness.   Mic 3:6

To Us a Child Is Born

9 Nevertheless, there will be no
more gloom for those who
were in distress. In the past he
humbled the land of Zebulun and
the land of Naphtali, but in the future he will honor Galilee of the

---

ᵃ10 Hebrew Immanuel   ᵇ12 Or Do not call for a treaty / every time these people call for a treaty

Gentiles, by the way of the sea,
along the Jordan —   2Ki 15:29

²The people walking in
        darkness   Isa 8:20
have seen a great light;
on those living in the land of
        the shadow of death*a*
        a light has dawned.   Mt 4:15-16*
³You have enlarged the
        nation
and increased their joy;
they rejoice before you
        as people rejoice at the
        harvest,
as men rejoice
        when dividing the plunder.
⁴For as in the day of Midian's
        defeat,   Jdg 7:25
        you have shattered   Job 34:24
the yoke that burdens them,
        the bar across their
        shoulders,   Isa 10:27
        the rod of their oppressor.
⁵Every warrior's boot used in
        battle
and every garment rolled in
        blood
will be destined for burning,
        will be fuel for the fire.
⁶For to us a child is born,   Lk 2:11
        to us a son is given,   Jn 3:16
and the government will be
        on his shoulders.   Mt 28:18
And he will be called
        Wonderful Counselor,*b*
        Mighty God,   Isa 10:21; 11:2
Everlasting Father, Prince of
        Peace.   Lk 2:14; Jn 14:9-10

⁷Of the increase of his
        government and peace
        there will be no end.   Da 2:44
He will reign on David's
        throne
and over his kingdom,
establishing and upholding it
        with justice and
        righteousness   Isa 11:4; 16:5
from that time on and
        forever.
The zeal of the Lord Almighty
        will accomplish this.   Isa 37:32

The Lord's Anger Against Israel

⁸The Lord has sent a message
        against Jacob;
        it will fall on Israel.
⁹All the people will know it —
        Ephraim and the inhabitants
        of Samaria —   Isa 7:9
who say with pride
        and arrogance of heart,
¹⁰"The bricks have fallen down,
        but we will rebuild with
        dressed stone;
the fig trees have been felled,
        but we will replace them
        with cedars."   1Ki 7:2-3
¹¹But the Lord has strengthened
        Rezin's foes against
        them   Isa 7:8
and has spurred their
        enemies on.
¹²Arameans from the east and
        Philistines from the west
have devoured Israel with
        open mouth.   Ps 79:7

---

a 2 Or *land of darkness*   *b* 6 Or *Wonderful, Counselor*

Yet for all this, his anger is not
　turned away,
　his hand is still upraised.

¹³But the people have not
　returned to him who
　struck them,　　　Jer 5:3
　nor have they sought the
　LORD Almighty.　　　Isa 31:1
¹⁴So the LORD will cut off from
　Israel both head and
　tail,
　both palm branch and reed
　in a single day;　　Isa 19:15
¹⁵the elders and prominent men
　are the head,　　Isa 3:2-3
　the prophets who teach lies
　are the tail.　　Eze 13:22
¹⁶Those who guide this people
　mislead them,　　Mt 15:14
　and those who are guided
　are led astray.　　Isa 3:12
¹⁷Therefore the Lord will take no
　pleasure in the young
　men,　　　Jer 18:21
　nor will he pity the
　fatherless and widows,
　for everyone is ungodly and
　wicked,　　Isa 1:4; 10:6
　every mouth speaks vileness.

Yet for all this, his anger is not
　turned away,
　his hand is still upraised.

¹⁸Surely wickedness burns like a
　fire;　　Mal 4:1
　it consumes briers and
　thorns,

it sets the forest thickets
　ablaze,　　Ps 83:14
　so that it rolls upward in a
　column of smoke.
¹⁹By the wrath of the LORD
　Almighty　　Isa 13:9,13
　the land will be scorched
　and the people will be fuel for
　the fire;　　Isa 1:31
　no one will spare his
　brother.　　Mic 7:2,6
²⁰On the right they will devour,
　but still be hungry;　　Lev 26:26
　on the left they will
　eat,　　Isa 49:26
　but not be satisfied.
　Each will feed on the flesh of
　his own offspring*ᵃ*:
²¹　Manasseh will feed on
　Ephraim, and Ephraim
　on Manasseh;
　together they will turn
　against Judah.　　2Ch 28:6

Yet for all this, his anger is not
　turned away,
　his hand is still upraised.

10 Woe to those who make
　unjust laws,
　to those who issue
　oppressive decrees,
²to deprive the poor of their
　rights
　and withhold justice from
　the oppressed of my
　people,　　Isa 5:23
　making widows their prey
　and robbing the fatherless.

ᵃ20 Or arm

³What will you do on the day of
    reckoning,   Job 31:14; Hos 9:7
when disaster comes from
    afar?   Lk 19:44
To whom will you run for
    help?   Isa 20:6
Where will you leave your
    riches?
⁴Nothing will remain but to
    cringe among the
    captives   Isa 24:22
or fall among the slain.

Yet for all this, his anger is not
    turned away,   Isa 5:25
his hand is still upraised.

God's Judgment on Assyria

⁵"Woe to the Assyrian, the rod
    of my anger,   Isa 14:25
in whose hand is the club of
    my wrath!   Isa 30:30; 66:14
⁶I send him against a godless
    nation,   Isa 9:17
I dispatch him against a
    people who anger me,
to seize loot and snatch
    plunder,   Isa 5:29
and to trample them down
    like mud in the streets.
⁷But this is not what he intends,
    this is not what he has in
    mind;
his purpose is to destroy,
to put an end to many
    nations.
⁸'Are not my commanders all
    kings?' he says.   2Ki 18:24

⁹ 'Has not Calno fared like
    Carchemish?   2Ch 35:20
Is not Hamath like Arpad,
    and Samaria like Damascus?
¹⁰As my hand seized the
    kingdoms of the idols,
    kingdoms whose images
    excelled those of
    Jerusalem and
    Samaria—
¹¹shall I not deal with Jerusalem
    and her images
as I dealt with Samaria and
    her idols?' "   2Ki 19:13; Isa 2:8

¹²When the Lord has finished all
his work against Mount Zion and
Jerusalem, he will say, "I will punish the king of Assyria for the willful pride of his heart and the
haughty look in his eyes. ¹³For he
says: 2Ki 19:31; Jer 50:18

" 'By the strength of my hand I
    have done this,   Isa 37:24
and by my wisdom, because
    I have understanding.
I removed the boundaries of
    nations,
I plundered their treasures;
like a mighty one I
    subdued*ᵃ* their kings.
¹⁴As one reaches into a nest,
    so my hand reached for the
    wealth of the nations;
as men gather abandoned eggs,
    so I gathered all the
    countries;
not one flapped a wing,

ᵃ13 Or / I subdued the mighty,

or opened its mouth to
    chirp.'"

15Does the ax raise itself above
    him who swings it,
    or the saw boast against him
        who uses it?   Ro 9:20-21
As if a rod were to wield him
    who lifts it up,
    or a club brandish him who
        is not wood!   ver 5
16Therefore, the Lord, the Lord
    Almighty,
    will send a wasting disease
        upon his sturdy
        warriors;   ver 18; Isa 17:4
    under his pomp a fire will be
        kindled   Isa 8:7
    like a blazing flame.
17The Light of Israel will become
    a fire,   Isa 31:9
    their Holy One a flame;
    in a single day it will burn and
        consume
    his thorns and his briers.
18The splendor of his forests and
    fertile fields   2Ki 19:23
    it will completely destroy,
    as when a sick man wastes
        away.
19And the remaining trees of
    his forests will be so
        few
    that a child could write them
        down.

The Remnant of Israel

20In that day the remnant of
    Israel,   Isa 11:10-11

the survivors of the house of
    Jacob,
    will no longer rely on him
    who struck them down
    but will truly rely on the
        Lord,
    the Holy One of Israel.
21A remnant will return,[a] a
        remnant of Jacob   Isa 6:13
    will return to the Mighty
        God.   Isa 9:6
22Though your people, O Israel,
        be like the sand by the
        sea,   Ge 12:2; Isa 48:19
    only a remnant will return.
Destruction has been decreed,
    overwhelming and righteous.
23The Lord, the Lord Almighty,
        will carry out
    the destruction decreed upon
        the whole land.   Isa 28:22

24Therefore, this is what the
Lord, the Lord Almighty, says:

"O my people who live in Zion,
    do not be afraid of the
        Assyrians,
    who beat you with a rod   Ex 5:14
    and lift up a club against
        you, as Egypt did.
25Very soon my anger against
        you will end   Isa 17:14
    and my wrath will be
        directed to their
        destruction."   Da 11:36

26The Lord Almighty will lash
    them with a whip,

a21 Hebrew *shear-jashub*; also in verse 22

as when he struck down
    Midian at the rock of
    Oreb;   Isa 9:4
and he will raise his staff over
    the waters,   Ex 14:16
as he did in Egypt.
²⁷In that day their burden will be
    lifted from your
    shoulders,
    their yoke from your neck;
the yoke will be broken
    because you have grown so
    fat.ᵃ

²⁸They enter Aiath;
    they pass through Migron;
    they store supplies at
    Micmash.   1Sa 13:2
²⁹They go over the pass, and
    say,
    "We will camp overnight at
    Geba."
Ramah trembles;   Jos 18:25
    Gibeah of Saul flees.   Jdg 19:14
³⁰Cry out, O Daughter of Gallim!
    Listen, O Laishah!
    Poor Anathoth!   Ne 11:32
³¹Madmenah is in flight;
    the people of Gebim take
    cover.
³²This day they will halt at Nob;
    they will shake their fist
at the mount of the Daughter
    of Zion,   Jer 6:23
    at the hill of Jerusalem.

³³See, the Lord, the Lord
    Almighty,
    will lop off the boughs with
    great power.

The lofty trees will be felled,
    the tall ones will be brought
    low.   Am 2:9
³⁴He will cut down the forest
    thickets with an ax;
    Lebanon will fall before the
    Mighty One.   2Ki 19:23

The Branch From Jesse

11 A shoot will come up
    from the stump of Jesse;
from his roots a Branch will
    bear fruit.   Isa 4:2
²The Spirit of the Lord will rest
    on him—   Mt 3:16; Jn 1:32-33
the Spirit of wisdom and of
    understanding,   Eph 1:17
the Spirit of counsel and of
    power,   2Ti 1:7
the Spirit of knowledge and
    of the fear of the Lord—
³and he will delight in the fear
    of the Lord.

He will not judge by what he
    sees with his eyes,
or decide by what he hears
    with his ears;   Jn 2:25
⁴but with righteousness he will
    judge the needy,   Ps 72:2
with justice he will give
    decisions for the poor of
    the earth.   Isa 3:14; 9:7
He will strike the earth with
    the rod of his mouth;
with the breath of his lips he
    will slay the wicked.
⁵Righteousness will be his belt

ᵃ 27 Hebrew; Septuagint broken / from your shoulders

and faithfulness the sash
    around his waist.   Isa 25:1
⁶The wolf will live with the
    lamb,   Isa 65:25
the leopard will lie down
    with the goat,
the calf and the lion and the
    yearling*ᵃ* together;
and a little child will lead
    them.
⁷The cow will feed with the
    bear,
their young will lie down
    together,
and the lion will eat straw
    like the ox.
⁸The infant will play near the
    hole of the cobra,
and the young child put his
    hand into the viper's
    nest.   Isa 14:29
⁹They will neither harm nor
    destroy   Job 5:23
on all my holy mountain,
for the earth will be full of the
    knowledge of the LORD
as the waters cover the sea.

¹⁰In that day the Root of Jesse
will stand as a banner for the peoples; the nations will rally to him, and his place of rest will be glorious. ¹¹In that day the Lord will reach out his hand a second time to reclaim the remnant that is left of his people from Assyria, from Lower Egypt, from Upper Egypt,ᵇ from Cush,ᶜ from Elam, from Bab-

ylonia,ᵈ from Hamath and from
the islands of the sea.   Ro 15:12*

¹²He will raise a banner for the
    nations   Ps 20:5
and gather the exiles of
    Israel;   Ps 106:47; Isa 14:1
he will assemble the scattered
    people of Judah   Zep 3:10
from the four quarters of the
    earth.   Ps 48:10; Rev 7:1
¹³Ephraim's jealousy will vanish,
    and Judah's enemiesᵉ will
    be cut off;
Ephraim will not be jealous of
    Judah,
nor Judah hostile toward
    Ephraim.   Jer 3:18
¹⁴They will swoop down on the
    slopes of Philistia to the
    west;
together they will plunder
    the people to the east.
They will lay hands on Edom
    and Moab,   Da 11:41; Joel 3:19
and the Ammonites will be
    subject to them.
¹⁵The LORD will dry up
    the gulf of the Egyptian sea;
with a scorching wind he will
    sweep his hand   Isa 19:16
over the Euphrates River.ᶠ
He will break it up into seven
    streams
so that men can cross over
    in sandals.
¹⁶There will be a highway for
    the remnant of his
    people   Isa 19:23; 62:10

---

*ᵃ*6 Hebrew; Septuagint *lion will feed*   ᵇ11 Hebrew *from Pathros*   ᶜ11 That is, the upper Nile region
ᵈ11 Hebrew *Shinar*   ᵉ13 Or *hostility*   ᶠ15 Hebrew *the River*

that is left from Assyria,
as there was for Israel
  when they came up from
    Egypt.   Ex 14:26-31

Songs of Praise

12 In that day you will say:

"I will praise you,
  O LORD.   Isa 25:1
Although you were angry
  with me,
your anger has turned away
  and you have comforted
    me.
²Surely God is my salvation;
  I will trust and not be afraid.
The LORD, the LORD, is my
    strength and my song;
  he has become my
    salvation."   Ex 15:2; Ps 118:14
³With joy you will draw water
  from the wells of salvation.

⁴In that day you will say:

"Give thanks to the LORD, call
  on his name;   Ps 105:1
  make known among the
    nations what he has
    done,   Isa 54:5; 60:3
and proclaim that his name
  is exalted.   Ps 113:2
⁵Sing to the LORD, for he has
  done glorious things;
  let this be known to all the
    world.
⁶Shout aloud and sing for joy,
  people of Zion,
  for great is the Holy One of
    Israel among you."

A Prophecy Against Babylon

13 An oracle concerning Babylon that Isaiah son of
Amoz saw: Ge 10:10; Isa 14:4; 20:2

²Raise a banner on a bare
  hilltop,   Jer 50:2; 51:27
  shout to them;
beckon to them
  to enter the gates of the
    nobles.
³I have commanded my holy
    ones;
  I have summoned my
    warriors to carry out my
    wrath—   Joel 3:11
those who rejoice in my
    triumph.   Ps 149:2

⁴Listen, a noise on the
    mountains,
  like that of a great
    multitude!   Joel 3:14
Listen, an uproar among the
    kingdoms,   Ps 46:6
  like nations massing
    together!
The LORD Almighty is
    mustering
  an army for war.   Isa 47:4
⁵They come from faraway lands,
  from the ends of the
    heavens—   Isa 5:26
the LORD and the weapons of
  his wrath—   Isa 10:25
  to destroy the whole
    country.   Isa 24:1

⁶Wail, for the day of the LORD is
  near;   Eze 30:2; Joel 1:15

it will come like destruction
    from the Almighty.[a]
[7]Because of this, all hands will
    go limp,   2Ki 19:26
every man's heart will
    melt.
[8]Terror will seize them,   Isa 21:4
pain and anguish will grip
    them;   Ex 15:14
they will writhe like a
    woman in labor.   Jn 16:21
They will look aghast at each
    other,
their faces aflame.   Na 2:10
[9]See, the day of the LORD is
    coming   Isa 2:12; Jer 51:2
—a cruel day, with wrath
    and fierce anger—
to make the land desolate
and destroy the sinners
    within it.
[10]The stars of heaven and their
    constellations
will not show their light.
The rising sun will be
    darkened   Isa 5:30; Rev 8:12
and the moon will not give
    its light.   Eze 32:7; Mt 24:29*
[11]I will punish the world for its
    evil,   Isa 3:11
the wicked for their sins.
I will put an end to the
    arrogance of the
    haughty   Ps 10:5; Pr 16:18
and will humble the pride of
    the ruthless.   Isa 25:3,5
[12]I will make man scarcer than
    pure gold,   Isa 4:1

more rare than the gold of
    Ophir.   Ge 10:29
[13]Therefore I will make the
    heavens tremble;   Isa 34:4
and the earth will shake
    from its place   Isa 14:16
at the wrath of the LORD
    Almighty,   Isa 9:19
in the day of his burning
    anger.   Job 9:5

[14]Like a hunted gazelle,
like sheep without a
    shepherd,   1Ki 22:17
each will return to his own
    people,
each will flee to his native
    land.   Jer 50:16
[15]Whoever is captured will be
    thrust through;
all who are caught will fall
    by the sword.   Isa 14:19
[16]Their infants will be dashed to
    pieces before their eyes;
their houses will be looted
    and their wives
    ravished.   Ge 34:29; Hos 13:16

[17]See, I will stir up against them
    the Medes,   Jer 51:1
who do not care for silver
and have no delight in
    gold.
[18]Their bows will strike down
    the young men;   Ps 7:12
they will have no mercy on
    infants   Isa 47:6
nor will they look with
    compassion on children.

[a]6 Hebrew Shaddai

¹⁹Babylon, the jewel of
    kingdoms,
  the glory of the
    Babylonians'ᵃ pride,
will be overthrown by God
  like Sodom and Gomorrah.
²⁰She will never be inhabited
  or lived in through all
    generations;
  no Arab will pitch his tent
    there,   2Ch 17:11
  no shepherd will rest his
    flocks there.
²¹But desert creatures will lie
    there,   Rev 18:2
  jackals will fill her houses;
there the owls will dwell,
  and there the wild goats will
    leap about.
²²Hyenas will howl in her
    strongholds,   Isa 25:2
  jackals in her luxurious
    palaces.   Isa 34:13
Her time is at hand,   Jer 51:33
  and her days will not be
    prolonged.

14 The LORD will have
    compassion on Jacob;
  once again he will choose
    Israel   Zec 1:17; 2:12
  and will settle them in their
    own land.
  Aliens will join them   Eph 2:12-19
  and unite with the house of
    Jacob.
²Nations will take them
  and bring them to their own
    place.   Isa 60:9

And the house of Israel will
    possess the nations
  as menservants and
    maidservants in the
    LORD's land.
They will make captives of
    their captors   Isa 45:14
  and rule over their
    oppressors.   Isa 60:14

³On the day the LORD gives you
relief from suffering and turmoil
and cruel bondage, ⁴you will take
up this taunt against the king of
Babylon: Hab 2:6; Isa 11:10

How the oppressor has come
    to an end!   Isa 9:4
  How his furyᵇ has ended!
⁵The LORD has broken the rod
    of the wicked,   Ps 125:3
  the scepter of the rulers,
⁶which in anger struck down
    peoples   Isa 10:14
  with unceasing blows,
  and in fury subdued nations
    with relentless aggression.
⁷All the lands are at rest and at
    peace;   Ps 98:1; 126:1-3
  they break into singing.
⁸Even the pine trees and the
    cedars of Lebanon
  exult over you and say,
  "Now that you have been laid
    low,
  no woodsman comes to cut
    us down."

⁹The graveᶜ below is all astir
  to meet you at your coming;

ᵃ19 Or Chaldeans'   ᵇ4 Dead Sea Scrolls, Septuagint and Syriac; the meaning of the word in the
Masoretic Text is uncertain.   ᶜ9 Hebrew Sheol; also in verses 11 and 15

it rouses the spirits of the
　　　departed to greet you—
all those who were leaders
　　　in the world;　　Zec 10:3
it makes them rise from their
　　　thrones—
all those who were kings
　　　over the nations.　Job 3:14
¹⁰They will all respond,
　　　they will say to you,
"You also have become weak,
　　　as we are;
you have become like
　　　us."
¹¹All your pomp has been
　　　brought down to the
　　　grave,
along with the noise of your
　　　harps;
maggots are spread out
　　　beneath you
and worms cover you.　Isa 51:8

¹²How you have fallen from
　　　heaven,　　Isa 34:4; Lk 10:18
O morning star, son of the
　　　dawn!　2Pe 1:19; Rev 2:28; 8:10
You have been cast down to
　　　the earth,
you who once laid low the
　　　nations!
¹³You said in your heart,
　　"I will ascend to heaven;
I will raise my throne　Eze 28:2
　　　above the stars of God;
I will sit enthroned on the
　　　mount of assembly,
on the utmost heights of the
　　　sacred mountain.ᵃ

ᵃ13 Or the north; Hebrew Zaphon

¹⁴I will ascend above the tops of
　　　the clouds;
I will make myself like the
　　　Most High."　Isa 47:8; 2Th 2:4
¹⁵But you are brought down to
　　　the grave,
to the depths of the pit.

¹⁶Those who see you stare at
　　　you,
they ponder your fate:
"Is this the man who shook the
　　　earth
and made kingdoms tremble,
¹⁷the man who made the world a
　　　desert,　　Joel 2:3
who overthrew its cities
and would not let his
　　　captives go home?"

¹⁸All the kings of the nations lie
　　　in state,
each in his own tomb.
¹⁹But you are cast out of your
　　　tomb　　Isa 22:16-18
like a rejected branch;
you are covered with the slain,
　　　with those pierced by the
　　　sword,
those who descend to the
　　　stones of the pit.　Jer 41:7-9
Like a corpse trampled
　　　underfoot,
²⁰　you will not join them in
　　　burial,
for you have destroyed your
　　　land
and killed your people.

The offspring of the wicked

will never be mentioned
    again.   Ps 21:10
²¹Prepare a place to slaughter his
    sons
for the sins of their
    forefathers;   Ex 20:5; Lev 26:39
they are not to rise to inherit
    the land
and cover the earth with
    their cities.

²²"I will rise up against them,"
    declares the Lᴏʀᴅ Almighty.
"I will cut off from Babylon
    her name and survivors,
her offspring and
    descendants,"   1Ki 14:10
    declares the Lᴏʀᴅ.
²³"I will turn her into a place for
    owls   Isa 34:11-15; Zep 2:14
and into swampland;
I will sweep her with the
    broom of destruction,"
declares the Lᴏʀᴅ Almighty.

A Prophecy Against Assyria

²⁴The Lᴏʀᴅ Almighty has sworn,

"Surely, as I have planned, so
    it will be,
and as I have purposed, so it
    will stand.   Ac 4:28
²⁵I will crush the Assyrian in my
    land;   Isa 10:5,12
on my mountains I will
    trample him down.
His yoke will be taken from
    my people,   Isa 9:4
and his burden removed
    from their shoulders."

²⁶This is the plan determined for
    the whole world;   Isa 23:9
this is the hand stretched
    out over all nations.
²⁷For the Lᴏʀᴅ Almighty has
    purposed, and who can
    thwart him?
His hand is stretched out,
    and who can turn it
    back?   2Ch 20:6; Isa 43:13

A Prophecy Against the Philistines

²⁸This oracle came in the year
King Ahaz died: 2Ki 16:20; Isa 13:1

²⁹Do not rejoice, all you
    Philistines,   2Ch 26:6
that the rod that struck you
    is broken;
from the root of that snake will
    spring up a viper,   Isa 11:8
its fruit will be a darting,
    venomous serpent.
³⁰The poorest of the poor will
    find pasture,
and the needy will lie down
    in safety.   Isa 3:15; 7:21-22
But your root I will destroy by
    famine;   Isa 8:21; 9:20
it will slay your survivors.

³¹Wail, O gate! Howl, O city!
    Melt away, all you
    Philistines!
A cloud of smoke comes from
    the north,   Jer 1:14
and there is not a straggler
    in its ranks.
³²What answer shall be given
    to the envoys of that nation?

"The LORD has established
    Zion,   Ps 87:2,5; Isa 44:28
and in her his afflicted
    people will find refuge."

A Prophecy Against Moab

15 An oracle concerning
    Moab: Isa 11:14

Ar in Moab is ruined,   Jer 48:24,41
    destroyed in a night!
Kir in Moab is ruined,   2Ki 3:25
    destroyed in a night!
²Dibon goes up to its temple,
    to its high places to weep;
Moab wails over Nebo and
    Medeba.
Every head is shaved   Lev 21:5
    and every beard cut off.
³In the streets they wear
    sackcloth;
on the roofs and in the
    public squares   Jer 48:38
they all wail,
    prostrate with weeping.
⁴Heshbon and Elealeh cry out,
    their voices are heard all the
    way to Jahaz.
Therefore the armed men of
    Moab cry out,
    and their hearts are faint.

⁵My heart cries out over Moab;
    her fugitives flee as far as
    Zoar,
    as far as Eglath Shelishiyah.
They go up the way to Luhith,
    weeping as they go;

on the road to Horonaim
    they lament their
    destruction.   Jer 48:5
⁶The waters of Nimrim are
    dried up   Isa 19:5-7; Jer 48:34
and the grass is withered;
    the vegetation is gone
    and nothing green is left.
⁷So the wealth they have
    acquired and stored up
    they carry away over the
    Ravine of the Poplars.
⁸Their outcry echoes along the
    border of Moab;
their wailing reaches as far
    as Eglaim,
their lamentation as far as
    Beer Elim.   Nu 21:16
⁹Dimon's*a* waters are full of
    blood,
but I will bring still more
    upon Dimon*a*—
a lion upon the fugitives of
    Moab   2Ki 17:25
and upon those who remain
    in the land.

16 Send lambs as tribute
    to the ruler of the land,
from Sela, across the desert,
    to the mount of the
    Daughter of Zion.
²Like fluttering birds
    pushed from the nest,   Pr 27:8
so are the women of Moab
    at the fords of the Arnon.

³"Give us counsel,
    render a decision.

a 9 Masoretic Text; Dead Sea Scrolls, some Septuagint manuscripts and Vulgate Dibon

Make your shadow like night—
    at high noon.
Hide the fugitives,   1Ki 18:4
    do not betray the refugees.
⁴Let the Moabite fugitives stay
        with you;
    be their shelter from the
        destroyer."

The oppressor will come to an
        end,   Isa 9:4
    and destruction will cease;
    the aggressor will vanish
        from the land.
⁵In love a throne will be
        established;   Da 7:14; Mic 4:7
    in faithfulness a man will sit
        on it—
    one from the house*ᵃ* of
        David—   Lk 1:32
    one who in judging seeks
        justice   Isa 9:7
    and speeds the cause of
        righteousness.

⁶We have heard of Moab's
        pride—   Am 2:1; Ob 1:3
    her overweening pride and
        conceit,
    her pride and her insolence—
    but her boasts are empty.
⁷Therefore the Moabites wail,
    they wail together for Moab.
Lament and grieve
    for the men*ᵇ* of Kir
        Ha. reseth.   2Ki 3:25; 1Ch 16:3
⁸The fields of Heshbon wither,
    the vines of Sibmah also.
The rulers of the nations

have trampled down the
    choicest vines,   Isa 5:2
which once reached Jazer
    and spread toward the
        desert.
Their shoots spread out   Job 8:16
    and went as far as the sea.
⁹So I weep, as Jazer weeps,
    for the vines of Sibmah.
O Heshbon, O Elealeh,
    I drench you with tears!
The shouts of joy over your
        ripened fruit
    and over your harvests have
        been stilled.   Jer 40:12
¹⁰Joy and gladness are taken
        away from the orchards;
    no one sings or shouts in the
        vineyards;
    no one treads out wine at the
        presses,   Jdg 9:27; Job 24:11
    for I have put an end to the
        shouting.
¹¹My heart laments for Moab
        like a harp,   Isa 15:5
    my inmost being for Kir
        Ha. reseth.   Isa 63:15; Hos 11:8
¹²When Moab appears at her
        high place,
    she only wears herself out;
when she goes to her shrine to
        pray,   Isa 15:2
    it is to no avail.   Jer 48:29-36

¹³This is the word the Lᴏʀᴅ has
already spoken concerning Moab.
¹⁴But now the Lᴏʀᴅ says: "Within
three years, as a servant bound
by contract would count them,
Moab's splendor and all her many

ᵃ 5 Hebrew *tent*   *ᵇ 7* Or *"raisin cakes,"* a wordplay

people will be despised, and her
survivors will be very few and fee-
ble."   Isa 21:17; 25:10; Jer 48:42

An Oracle Against Damascus

17 An oracle concerning Damascus: Jer 49:23; Ac 9:2

"See, Damascus will no longer
be a city
but will become a heap of
ruins.   Am 1:3; Zec 9:1
²The cities of Aroer will be
deserted
and left to flocks, which will
lie down,   Isa 7:21; Eze 25:5
with no one to make them
afraid.   Jer 7:33; Mic 4:4
³The fortified city will disappear
from Ephraim,
and royal power from
Damascus;
the remnant of Aram will be
like the glory of the
Israelites,"   ver 4; Isa 7:8,16
declares the LORD
Almighty.

⁴"In that day the glory of Jacob
will fade;
the fat of his body will waste
away.   Isa 10:16
⁵It will be as when a reaper
gathers the standing
grain
and harvests the grain with
his arm —   Jer 51:33; Joel 3:13
as when a man gleans heads of
grain

in the Valley of Rephaim.
⁶Yet some gleanings will
remain,   Isa 24:13
as when an olive tree is
beaten,   Isa 27:12
leaving two or three olives on
the topmost branches,
four or five on the fruitful
boughs,"
declares the LORD,
the God of Israel.

⁷In that day men will look to
their Maker   Isa 10:20
and turn their eyes to the
Holy One of Israel.
⁸They will not look to the
altars,
the work of their hands,
and they will have no regard
for the Asherah poles[a]
and the incense altars their
fingers have made.   Isa 2:8

⁹In that day their strong cities,
which they left because of the Israelites, will be like places abandoned to thickets and undergrowth. And all will be desolation.

¹⁰You have forgotten God your
Savior;   Ps 68:19; Isa 12:2
you have not remembered
the Rock, your fortress.
Therefore, though you set out
the finest plants
and plant imported vines,
¹¹though on the day you set
them out, you make
them grow,

---

a 8 That is, symbols of the goddess Asherah

and on the morning when
   you plant them, you
   bring them to bud,
yet the harvest will be as
   nothing   Hos 8:7
in the day of disease and
   incurable pain.   Job 4:8

¹²Oh, the raging of many
   nations—
   they rage like the raging sea!
Oh, the uproar of the
   peoples—
   they roar like the roaring of
   great waters!
¹³Although the peoples roar like
   the roar of surging
   waters,
   when he rebukes them they
   flee far away,   Ps 9:5
driven before the wind like
   chaff on the hills,
   like tumbleweed before a
   gale.   Job 21:18
¹⁴In the evening, sudden terror!
Before the morning, they are
   gone!   2Ki 19:35
This is the portion of those
   who loot us,
   the lot of those who plunder
   us.

A Prophecy Against Cush

18 Woe to the land of
   whirring wings*ᵃ*
along the rivers of Cush,*ᵇ*
²which sends envoys by sea
   in papyrus boats over the
   water.   Ex 2:3

Go, swift messengers,
to a people tall and
   smooth-skinned,
to a people feared far and
   wide,
an aggressive nation of strange
   speech,   Ge 10:8-9; 2Ch 12:3
whose land is divided by
   rivers.   ver 7
³All you people of the world,
   you who live on the earth,
when a banner is raised on the
   mountains,   Isa 5:26
   you will see it,
and when a trumpet sounds,
   you will hear it.
⁴This is what the Lᴏʀᴅ says to
   me:
"I will remain quiet and will
   look on from my
   dwelling place,   Isa 26:21
like shimmering heat in the
   sunshine,
like a cloud of dew in the
   heat of harvest."   Isa 26:19
⁵For, before the harvest, when
   the blossom is gone
and the flower becomes a
   ripening grape,
he will cut off the shoots with
   pruning knives,
and cut down and take away
   the spreading branches.
⁶They will all be left to the
   mountain birds of prey
and to the wild animals;
the birds will feed on them all
   summer,
the wild animals all winter.

ᵃ 1 Or *of locusts*   *ᵇ 1* That is, the upper Nile region

7At that time gifts will be brought to the LORD Almighty

from a people tall and
    smooth-skinned,   Ge 41:14
from a people feared far and
    wide,   Hab 1:7
an aggressive nation of strange
    speech,
whose land is divided by
    rivers —

the gifts will be brought to Mount Zion, the place of the Name of the LORD Almighty.   Ps 68:31

A Prophecy About Egypt

19 An oracle concerning
Egypt: Ex 12:12; Jer 43:12

See, the LORD rides on a swift
    cloud   Ps 18:10; 104:3; Rev 1:7
and is coming to Egypt.
The idols of Egypt tremble
    before him,
and the hearts of the
    Egyptians melt within
    them.   Jos 2:11

2"I will stir up Egyptian against
    Egyptian —
brother will fight against
    brother,   Jdg 7:22; Mt 10:21,36
neighbor against neighbor,
city against city,
kingdom against kingdom.
3The Egyptians will lose heart,
and I will bring their plans
    to nothing;   1Ch 10:13
they will consult the idols and
    the spirits of the dead,
the mediums and the
    spiritists.   Isa 8:19; 47:13

4I will hand the Egyptians over
    to the power of a cruel
    master,
and a fierce king will rule over
    them,"   Isa 20:4; Jer 46:26
declares the Lord, the LORD
    Almighty.

5The waters of the river will dry
    up,   Jer 51:36
and the riverbed will be
    parched and dry.
6The canals will stink;   Ex 7:18
the streams of Egypt will
    dwindle and dry up.
The reeds and rushes will
    wither,   Isa 15:6
7 also the plants along the
    Nile,   Isa 23:3
at the mouth of the river.
Every sown field along the Nile
will become parched, will
    blow away and be no
    more.
8The fishermen will groan and
    lament,   Eze 47:10
all who cast hooks into the
    Nile;   Hab 1:15
those who throw nets on the
    water
will pine away.
9Those who work with combed
    flax will despair,
the weavers of fine linen will
    lose hope.   Pr 7:16; Eze 27:7
10The workers in cloth will be
    dejected,
and all the wage earners will
    be sick at heart.

11The officials of Zoan are
    nothing but fools;

the wise counselors of
    Pharaoh give senseless
    advice.   Ge 41:37
How can you say to Pharaoh,
"I am one of the wise men,
    a disciple of the ancient
    kings"?

¹²Where are your wise men
    now?   1Co 1:20
Let them show you and
    make known
what the LORD Almighty
    has planned against Egypt.
¹³The officials of Zoan have
    become fools,
    the leaders of Memphis[a] are
        deceived;   Jer 2:16; Eze 30:13,16
the cornerstones of her peoples
    have led Egypt astray.
¹⁴The LORD has poured into them
    a spirit of dizziness;   Mt 17:17
they make Egypt stagger in all
    that she does,
    as a drunkard staggers
        around in his vomit.
¹⁵There is nothing Egypt can
    do—
    head or tail, palm branch or
        reed.   Isa 9:14

¹⁶In that day the Egyptians will
be like women. They will shudder
with fear at the uplifted hand that
the LORD Almighty raises against
them. ¹⁷And the land of Judah will
bring terror to the Egyptians; everyone to whom Judah is mentioned will be terrified, because of
what the LORD Almighty is planning against them.   Isa 11:15; 14:24
¹⁸In that day five cities in Egypt
will speak the language of Canaan
and swear allegiance to the LORD
Almighty. One of them will be
called the City of Destruction.[b]

¹⁹In that day there will be an altar to the LORD in the heart of
Egypt, and a monument to the
LORD at its border. ²⁰It will be a sign
and witness to the LORD Almighty
in the land of Egypt. When they
cry out to the LORD because of their
oppressors, he will send them a
savior and defender, and he will
rescue them. ²¹So the LORD will
make himself known to the Egyptians, and in that day they will acknowledge the LORD. They will
worship with sacrifices and grain
offerings; they will make vows to
the LORD and keep them. ²²The
LORD will strike Egypt with a
plague; he will strike them and
heal them. They will turn to the
LORD, and he will respond to their
pleas and heal them.   Isa 45:14

²³In that day there will be a highway from Egypt to Assyria. The Assyrians will go to Egypt and the
Egyptians to Assyria. The Egyptians and Assyrians will worship
together. ²⁴In that day Israel will
be the third, along with Egypt and
Assyria, a blessing on the earth.
²⁵The LORD Almighty will bless
them, saying, "Blessed be Egypt

---

a 13 Hebrew Noph   b 18 Most manuscripts of the Masoretic Text; some manuscripts of the Masoretic
Text, Dead Sea Scrolls and Vulgate City of the Sun (that is, Heliopolis)

my people, Assyria my handiwork, and Israel my inheritance."

A Prophecy Against Egypt and Cush

20 In the year that the supreme commander, sent by Sargon king of Assyria, came to Ashdod and attacked and captured it— ²at that time the LORD spoke through Isaiah son of Amoz. He said to him, "Take off the sackcloth from your body and the sandals from your feet." And he did so, going around stripped and barefoot.   1Sa 19:24; Mic 1:8; Zec 13:4

³Then the LORD said, "Just as my servant Isaiah has gone stripped and barefoot for three years, as a sign and portent against Egypt and Cush,ᵃ ⁴so the king of Assyria will lead away stripped and barefoot the Egyptian captives and Cushite exiles, young and old, with buttocks bared—to Egypt's shame. ⁵Those who trusted in Cush and boasted in Egypt will be afraid and put to shame. ⁶In that day the people who live on this coast will say, 'See what has happened to those we relied on, those we fled to for help and deliverance from the king of Assyria! How then can we escape?' "   2Ki 18:21; Jer 30:15-17; Mt 23:33

A Prophecy Against Babylon

21 An oracle concerning the Desert by the Sea: Isa 13:21

Like whirlwinds sweeping
        through the southland,
    an invader comes from the
        desert,
    from a land of terror.

²A dire vision has been shown
        to me: Ps 60:3
    The traitor betrays, the
        looter takes loot.   Isa 33:1
Elam, attack! Media, lay siege!
    I will bring to an end all the
        groaning she caused.

³At this my body is racked with
        pain,
    pangs seize me, like those of
        a woman in labor;   Ps 48:6
I am staggered by what I hear,
    I am bewildered by what I
        see.
⁴My heart falters,
    fear makes me tremble;
the twilight I longed for
    has become a horror to
        me.

⁵They set the tables,
    they spread the rugs,
    they eat, they drink!
Get up, you officers,
    oil the shields!   2Sa 1:21

⁶This is what the Lord says to me:

"Go, post a lookout   2Ki 9:17
    and have him report what he
        sees.
⁷When he sees chariots   ver 9
    with teams of horses,

ᵃ3 That is, the upper Nile region; also in verse 5

riders on donkeys
    or riders on camels,
let him be alert,
    fully alert."

[8]And the lookout[a] shouted,

"Day after day, my lord, I
    stand on the
    watchtower;
every night I stay at my
    post.
[9]Look, here comes a man in a
    chariot
with a team of horses.
And he gives back the answer:
'Babylon has fallen, has
    fallen!   Jer 51:8; Rev 14:8; 18:2
All the images of its gods
lie shattered on the
    ground!' "

[10]O my people, crushed on the
    threshing floor,   Jer 51:33
I tell you what I have heard
from the Lord Almighty,
    from the God of Israel.

A Prophecy Against Edom

[11]An oracle concerning Dumah[b]:   Ge 25:14

Someone calls to me from Seir,
"Watchman, what is left of
    the night?
Watchman, what is left of
    the night?"
[12]The watchman replies,
    "Morning is coming, but also
    the night.

If you would ask, then ask;
    and come back yet again."

A Prophecy Against Arabia

[13]An oracle concerning Arabia:

You caravans of Dedanites,
    who camp in the thickets of
        Arabia,
[14]   bring water for the thirsty;
you who live in Tema,   Ge 25:15
    bring food for the fugitives.
[15]They flee from the sword,
    from the drawn sword,
from the bent bow
    and from the heat of battle.

[16]This is what the Lord says to
me: "Within one year, as a servant
bound by contract would count it,
all the pomp of Kedar will come to
an end. [17]The survivors of the
bowmen, the warriors of Kedar,
will be few." The Lord, the God of
Israel, has spoken.   Ps 120:5; Isa 16:14

A Prophecy About Jerusalem

22 An oracle concerning the
    Valley of Vision: Isa 13:1

What troubles you now,
    that you have all gone up on
        the roofs,
[2]O town full of commotion,
    O city of tumult and revelry?
Your slain were not killed by
    the sword,   2Ki 25:3; Isa 10:4
    nor did they die in battle.
[3]All your leaders have fled
    together;

---

[a]8 Dead Sea Scrolls and Syriac; Masoretic Text *A lion* wordplay on *Edom*.   [b]11 *Dumah* means *silence* or *stillness*, a

they have been captured
    without using the bow.
All you who were caught were
    taken prisoner together,
having fled while the enemy
    was still far away.
⁴Therefore I said, "Turn away
    from me;
let me weep bitterly.   Isa 15:3
Do not try to console me
    over the destruction of my
    people."   Jer 9:1

⁵The Lord, the Lᴏʀᴅ Almighty,
    has a day   Isa 2:12
of tumult and trampling and
    terror   La 1:5; Zep 1:15
in the Valley of Vision,
a day of battering down walls
and of crying out to the
    mountains.
⁶Elam takes up the quiver,
    with her charioteers and
    horses;
Kir uncovers the shield.
⁷Your choicest valleys are full of
    chariots,
and horsemen are posted at
    the city gates;   2Ch 32:1-2
⁸ the defenses of Judah are
    stripped away.

And you looked in that day
    to the weapons in the Palace
    of the Forest;   1Ki 7:2
⁹you saw that the City of David
    had many breaches in its
    defenses;
you stored up water
    in the Lower Pool.   2Ch 32:4
¹⁰You counted the buildings in
    Jerusalem

and tore down houses to
    strengthen the wall.
¹¹You built a reservoir between
    the two walls   2Ki 25:4
for the water of the Old
    Pool,   2Ch 32:4
but you did not look to the
    One who made it,
or have regard for the One
    who planned it long
    ago.   2Ki 19:25
¹²The Lord, the Lᴏʀᴅ Almighty,
    called you on that day
to weep and to wail,   Joel 2:17
    to tear out your hair and put
    on sackcloth.   Joel 1:13
¹³But see, there is joy and
    revelry,
slaughtering of cattle and
    killing of sheep,
eating of meat and drinking
    of wine!   Isa 56:12; Lk 17:26-29
"Let us eat and drink," you
    say,
    "for tomorrow we die!"

¹⁴The Lᴏʀᴅ Almighty has revealed this in my hearing: "Till
your dying day this sin will not be
atoned for," says the Lord, the
Lᴏʀᴅ Almighty.   Isa 5:9; 13:11; 26:21

¹⁵This is what the Lord, the Lᴏʀᴅ
Almighty, says:

"Go, say to this steward,
    to Shebna, who is in charge
    of the palace: 2Ki 18:18
¹⁶What are you doing here and
    who gave you
    permission

to cut out a grave for
    yourself here,   *Mt 27:60*
hewing your grave on the
    height
and chiseling your resting
    place in the rock?

[17]"Beware, the LORD is about to
    take firm hold of you
and hurl you away, O you
    mighty man.
[18]He will roll you up tightly like
    a ball
and throw you into a large
    country.   *Isa 17:13*
There you will die
and there your splendid
    chariots will remain—
you disgrace to your
    master's house!
[19]I will depose you from your
    office,
and you will be ousted from
    your position.   *1Sa 2:7*

[20]"In that day I will summon my
servant, Eliakim son of Hilkiah. [21]I
will clothe him with your robe and
fasten your sash around him and
hand your authority over to him.
He will be a father to those who
live in Jerusalem and to the house
of Judah. [22]I will place on his
shoulder the key to the house of
David; what he opens no one can
shut, and what he shuts no one
can open. [23]I will drive him like a
peg into a firm place; he will be a
seat[a] of honor for the house of his

father. [24]All the glory of his family
will hang on him: its offspring and
offshoots—all its lesser vessels,
from the bowls to all the jars.

[25]"In that day," declares the
LORD Almighty, "the peg driven
into the firm place will give way; it
will be sheared off and will fall,
and the load hanging on it will be
cut down." The LORD has spoken.

A Prophecy About Tyre

23 An oracle concerning Tyre:

Wail, O ships of
    Tarshish!   *Ge 10:4; 1Ki 10:22*
For Tyre is destroyed
and left without house or
    harbor.
From the land of Cyprus[b]
word has come to them.

[2]Be silent, you people of the
    island
and you merchants of Sidon,
    whom the seafarers have
    enriched.
[3]On the great waters
    came the grain of the Shihor;
the harvest of the Nile[c] was
      the revenue of Tyre,
and she became the
      marketplace of the
      nations.

[4]Be ashamed, O Sidon, and you,
    O fortress of the sea,
for the sea has spoken:

---

*a 23 Or throne   b 1,12 Hebrew Kittim   c 2,3 Masoretic Text; one Dead Sea Scroll Sidon, / who cross
over the sea; / your envoys 3are on the great waters. / The grain of the Shihor, / the harvest of the Nile,*

"I have neither been in labor
　　nor given birth;
I have neither reared sons
　　nor brought up
　　daughters."
⁵When word comes to Egypt,
　　they will be in anguish at
　　the report from Tyre.

⁶Cross over to Tarshish;
　　wail, you people of the
　　island.
⁷Is this your city of revelry,
　　the old, old city,
whose feet have taken her
　　to settle in far-off lands?
⁸Who planned this against
　　Tyre,
　　the bestower of crowns,
whose merchants are princes,
　　whose traders are renowned
　　in the earth?   Eze 28:5
⁹The LORD Almighty planned it,
　　to bring low the pride of all
　　glory   Job 40:11
and to humble all who are
　　renowned on the earth.

¹⁰Till*a* your land as along the
　　Nile,
　　O Daughter of Tarshish,
for you no longer have a
　　harbor.
¹¹The LORD has stretched out his
　　hand over the sea
and made its kingdoms
　　tremble.   Ps 46:6
He has given an order
　　concerning Phoenicia*b*

that her fortresses be
　　destroyed.   Isa 25:2; Zec 9:3-4
¹²He said, "No more of your
　　reveling,   Rev 18:22
O Virgin Daughter of Sidon,
　　now crushed!   Isa 47:1

"Up, cross over to Cyprus*c*;
　　even there you will find no
　　rest."
¹³Look at the land of the
　　Babylonians,*d*
this people that is now of no
　　account!
The Assyrians have made it
　　a place for desert creatures;
they raised up their siege
　　towers,
　　they stripped its fortresses
　　bare
and turned it into a ruin.

¹⁴Wail, you ships of Tarshish;
　　your fortress is destroyed!

¹⁵At that time Tyre will be forgotten for seventy years, the span
of a king's life. But at the end of
these seventy years, it will happen
to Tyre as in the song of the prostitute: Jer 25:22

¹⁶"Take up a harp, walk through
　　the city,
O prostitute forgotten;
play the harp well, sing many
　　a song,
so that you will be
　　remembered."

¹⁷At the end of seventy years,

---

a 10 Dead Sea Scrolls and some Septuagint manuscripts; Masoretic Text *Go through*   *b 11* Hebrew
Canaan   *c 1,12* Hebrew *Kittim*   *d 13* Or *Chaldeans*

the Lord will deal with Tyre. She will return to her hire as a prostitute and will ply her trade with all the kingdoms on the face of the earth. [18]Yet her profit and her earnings will be set apart for the Lord; they will not be stored up or hoarded. Her profits will go to those who live before the Lord, for abundant food and fine clothes.

The Lord's Devastation of the Earth

24 See, the Lord is going to
       lay waste the earth
   and devastate it;
   he will ruin its face
       and scatter its inhabitants —
[2]it will be the same
       for priest as for people,
   for master as for servant,
   for mistress as for maid,
   for seller as for buyer,   Eze 7:12
   for borrower as for lender,
   for debtor as for creditor.
[3]The earth will be completely
       laid waste
   and totally plundered.
           The Lord has spoken
               this word.

[4]The earth dries up and withers,
   the world languishes and
       withers,
   the exalted of the earth
       languish.   Isa 2:12
[5]The earth is defiled by its
       people;   Ge 3:17; Nu 35:33
   they have disobeyed the
       laws,   Isa 10:6; 59:12

violated the statutes
   and broken the everlasting
       covenant.
[6]Therefore a curse consumes
       the earth;
   its people must bear their
       guilt.
   Therefore earth's inhabitants
       are burned up,   Isa 1:31
   and very few are left.
[7]The new wine dries up and the
       vine withers;   Joel 1:10-12
   all the merrymakers groan.
[8]The gaiety of the tambourines
       is stilled,   Isa 5:12
   the noise of the revelers has
       stopped,   Hos 2:11
   the joyful harp is silent.
[9]No longer do they drink wine
       with a song;   Isa 5:11,22
   the beer is bitter to its
       drinkers.   Isa 5:20
[10]The ruined city lies desolate;
   the entrance to every house
       is barred.
[11]In the streets they cry out for
       wine;
   all joy turns to gloom,
   all gaiety is banished from
       the earth.
[12]The city is left in ruins,   Isa 19:18
   its gate is battered to pieces.
[13]So will it be on the earth
   and among the nations,
   as when an olive tree is
       beaten,   Isa 17:6
   or as when gleanings are left
       after the grape harvest.

[14]They raise their voices, they
       shout for joy;   Isa 12:6

from the west they acclaim
    the LORD's majesty.
15Therefore in the east give glory
    to the LORD;   Isa 66:19
exalt the name of the LORD,
    the God of Israel,   Mal 1:11
in the islands of the sea.
16From the ends of the earth we
    hear singing: Ps 48:10; 65:8
    "Glory to the Righteous
    One."   Isa 28:5

But I said, "I waste away, I
    waste away!
Woe to me!
The treacherous betray!
With treachery the
    treacherous betray!"
17Terror and pit and snare await
    you,   Jer 48:43
    O people of the earth.   Lk 21:35
18Whoever flees at the sound of
    terror   Job 20:24
will fall into a pit;
whoever climbs out of the pit
will be caught in a snare.

The floodgates of the heavens
    are opened,   Ge 7:11
    the foundations of the earth
    shake.   Ps 18:7
19The earth is broken up,
    the earth is split asunder,
    the earth is thoroughly
    shaken.
20The earth reels like a
    drunkard,   Isa 19:14
    it sways like a hut in the
    wind;

so heavy upon it is the guilt of
    its rebellion   Isa 1:2,28; 43:27
that it falls—never to rise
    again.   Ps 46:2
21In that day the LORD will
    punish   Isa 10:12
    the powers in the heavens
    above
    and the kings on the earth
    below.   Isa 2:12
22They will be herded together
    like prisoners bound in a
    dungeon;   Isa 10:4; 42:7,22
    they will be shut up in prison
    and be punished[a] after many
    days.   Eze 38:8
23The moon will be abashed, the
    sun ashamed;   Isa 13:10
    for the LORD Almighty will
    reign   Rev 22:5
on Mount Zion and in
    Jerusalem,   Heb 12:22
and before its elders,
    gloriously.   Isa 60:19

Praise to the LORD

25 O LORD, you are my God;
    I will exalt you and
    praise your name,
for in perfect faithfulness
you have done marvelous
    things,   Ps 98:1
things planned long ago.
2You have made the city a heap
    of rubble,   Isa 17:1
the fortified town a ruin,
the foreigners' stronghold a
    city no more;   Isa 13:22

a22 Or released

it will never be rebuilt.

³Therefore strong peoples will
      honor you;   Ex 6:2; Ps 22:23
   cities of ruthless nations will
      revere you.   Isa 13:11
⁴You have been a refuge for the
      poor,   Isa 4:6; 17:10
   a refuge for the needy in his
      distress,   Isa 14:30
   a shelter from the storm   Ps 55:8
   and a shade from the
      heat.
For the breath of the ruthless
   is like a storm driving
      against a wall
⁵   and like the heat of the
      desert.
You silence the uproar of
      foreigners;   Jer 51:55
   as heat is reduced by the
      shadow of a cloud,
   so the song of the ruthless is
      stilled.

⁶On this mountain the LORD
      Almighty will prepare
   a feast of rich food for all
      peoples,   Mt 8:11; 22:4
   a banquet of aged wine—
   the best of meats and the
      finest of wines.   Pr 9:2
⁷On this mountain he will
      destroy
   the shroud that enfolds all
      peoples,   2Co 3:15-16; Eph 4:18
   the sheet that covers all
      nations;
⁸   he will swallow up death
      forever.   Hos 13:14

The Sovereign LORD will wipe
      away the tears   Rev 7:17
   from all faces;
   he will remove the disgrace of
      his people   Mt 5:11; 1Pe 4:14
   from all the earth.
      The LORD has spoken.
⁹In that day they will say,

"Surely this is our God;   Isa 40:9
   we trusted in him, and he
      saved us.   Ps 20:5; Isa 33:22
This is the LORD, we trusted in
      him;
   let us rejoice and be glad in
      his salvation."   Isa 35:2,10

¹⁰The hand of the LORD will rest
      on this mountain;   Isa 2:2
   but Moab will be trampled
      under him   Am 2:1-3
   as straw is trampled down in
      the manure.
¹¹They will spread out their
      hands in it,
   as a swimmer spreads out
      his hands to swim.
God will bring down their
      pride   Job 40:12; Isa 5:25
   despite the cleverness[a] of
      their hands.
¹²He will bring down your high
      fortified walls
   and lay them low;   Isa 15:1
   he will bring them down to the
      ground,
   to the very dust.

a11 The meaning of the Hebrew for this word is uncertain.

A Song of Praise

26 In that day this song will be sung in the land of Judah:

We have a strong city; Isa 14:32
  God makes salvation
  its walls and ramparts.
²Open the gates
  that the righteous nation
    may enter, Isa 54:14; 58:8
  the nation that keeps faith.
³You will keep in perfect peace
  him whose mind is steadfast,
  because he trusts in you.
⁴Trust in the LORD forever,
  for the LORD, the LORD, is the
    Rock eternal. Ge 49:24
⁵He humbles those who dwell
    on high,
  he lays the lofty city low;
  he levels it to the ground
    and casts it down to the
      dust.
⁶Feet trample it down—
  the feet of the oppressed,
  the footsteps of the poor.

⁷The path of the righteous is
    level;
  O upright One, you make the
    way of the righteous
    smooth. Isa 42:16
⁸Yes, LORD, walking in the way
    of your laws,ᵃ Isa 56:1
  we wait for you; Ps 37:9
  your name and renown Isa 12:4
  are the desire of our hearts.
⁹My soul yearns for you in the
    night;

in the morning my spirit
    longs for you. Ps 63:1; 78:34
When your judgments come
    upon the earth,
  the people of the world learn
    righteousness. Mt 6:33
¹⁰Though grace is shown to the
    wicked,
  they do not learn
    righteousness;
  even in a land of uprightness
    they go on doing evil
  and regard not the majesty
    of the LORD. Isa 22:12-13
¹¹O LORD, your hand is lifted
    high,
  but they do not see it.
Let them see your zeal for
    your people and be put
    to shame;
  let the fire reserved for your
    enemies consume them.

¹²LORD, you establish peace for
    us; Ps 119:165; Isa 9:6
  all that we have
    accomplished you have
    done for us. Ps 68:28
¹³O LORD, our God, other lords
    besides you have ruled
    over us, Isa 2:8; 10:5,11
  but your name alone do we
    honor. Isa 63:7
¹⁴They are now dead, they live
    no more; Dt 4:28
  those departed spirits do not
    rise.
You punished them and
    brought them to ruin;

ᵃ8 Or *judgments*

you wiped out all memory of
  them.
¹⁵You have enlarged the nation,
  O LORD;
you have enlarged the
  nation.   Isa 14:2
You have gained glory for
  yourself;
you have extended all the
  borders of the land.

¹⁶LORD, they came to you in their
  distress;   Hos 5:15
when you disciplined them,
they could barely whisper a
  prayer.ᵃ
¹⁷As a woman with child and
  about to give birth
writhes and cries out in her
  pain,
so were we in your presence,
  O LORD.
¹⁸We were with child, we
  writhed in pain,
but we gave birth to wind.
We have not brought salvation
  to the earth;   Ps 17:14
we have not given birth to
  people of the world.

¹⁹But your dead will live;   Isa 25:8
  their bodies will rise.
You who dwell in the dust,
  wake up and shout for
  joy.
Your dew is like the dew of
  the morning;
the earth will give birth to
  her dead.   Eze 37:1-14; Da 12:2

²⁰Go, my people, enter your
  rooms
and shut the doors behind
  you;   Ex 12:23
hide yourselves for a little
  while   Ps 91:1,4
until his wrath has passed
  by.   Ps 30:5; Isa 54:7-8
²¹See, the LORD is coming out of
  his dwelling   Mic 1:3
to punish the people of the
  earth for their sins.
The earth will disclose the
  blood shed upon her;
she will conceal her slain no
  longer.

Deliverance of Israel

27 In that day,
  the LORD will punish with
  his sword,   Isa 34:6; 66:16
his fierce, great and powerful
  sword,
Leviathan the gliding serpent,
Leviathan the coiling
  serpent;
he will slay the monster of the
  sea.   Ps 74:13; Rev 12:9

²In that day—

"Sing about a fruitful vineyard:
³ I, the LORD, watch over it;
I water it continually.   Isa 58:11
I guard it day and night   Ps 91:4
  so that no one may harm it.
⁴ I am not angry.
If only there were briers and
  thorns confronting me!

ᵃ16 The meaning of the Hebrew for this clause is uncertain.

I would march against them
  in battle;
I would set them all on fire.
⁵Or else let them come to me
  for refuge;   Isa 25:4
let them make peace with
  me,   Job 22:21; Ro 5:1; 2Co 5:20
yes, let them make peace
  with me."

⁶In days to come Jacob will
  take root,   Isa 11:10
Israel will bud and blossom
and fill all the world with
  fruit.   Isa 37:31

⁷Has the Lᴏʀᴅ struck her
  as he struck down those
  who struck her?
Has she been killed
  as those were killed who
  killed her?
⁸By warfare* and exile you
  contend with her—
with his fierce blast he
  drives her out,
as on a day the east wind
  blows.
⁹By this, then, will Jacob's guilt
  be atoned for,   Ps 78:38
and this will be the full
  fruitage of the removal
  of his sin: Ro 11:27*
When he makes all the altar
  stones
  to be like chalk stones
  crushed to pieces,
no Asherah poles* or incense
  altars   Ex 34:13

will be left standing.
¹⁰The fortified city stands
  desolate,   Isa 32:14; Jer 26:6
an abandoned settlement,
  forsaken like the desert;
there the calves graze,
  there they lie down;   Isa 17:2
they strip its branches bare.
¹¹When its twigs are dry, they
  are broken off
and women come and make
  fires with them.
For this is a people without
  understanding;   Dt 32:28
so their Maker has no
  compassion on them,
and their Creator shows
  them no favor.   Dt 32:18

¹²In that day the Lᴏʀᴅ will thresh
from the flowing Euphrates* to the
Wadi of Egypt, and you, O Israelites, will be gathered up one by
one. ¹³And in that day a great
trumpet will sound. Those who
were perishing in Assyria and
those who were exiled in Egypt
will come and worship the Lᴏʀᴅ on
the holy mountain in Jerusalem.

Woe to Ephraim

28 Woe to that wreath, the
      pride of Ephraim's
      drunkards,   ver 3; Isa 9:9
to the fading flower, his
  glorious beauty,
set on the head of a fertile
  valley—   ver 4

---

a 8 See Septuagint; the meaning of the Hebrew for this word is uncertain.   *b 9* That is, symbols of the
goddess Asherah   *c 12* Hebrew *River*

to that city, the pride of
 those laid low by wine!
²See, the Lord has one who is
 powerful and strong.
Like a hailstorm and a
 destructive wind,   Isa 29:6
like a driving rain and a
 flooding downpour,
he will throw it forcefully to
 the ground.
³That wreath, the pride of
 Ephraim's drunkards,
will be trampled underfoot.
⁴That fading flower, his glorious
 beauty,
set on the head of a fertile
 valley,
will be like a fig ripe before
 harvest —   Hos 9:10; Na 3:12
as soon as someone sees it
 and takes it in his hand,
he swallows it.

⁵In that day the Lord Almighty
 will be a glorious crown,
a beautiful wreath
 for the remnant of his
 people.   Isa 1:9
⁶He will be a spirit of justice
to him who sits in judgment,
a source of strength
 to those who turn back the
 battle at the gate.   2Ch 32:8

⁷And these also stagger from
 wine   Isa 22:13
and reel from beer: Isa 56:10-12
Priests and prophets stagger
 from beer   Isa 9:15; 24:2
and are befuddled with wine;
they reel from beer,
 they stagger when seeing
 visions,   Isa 29:11; Hos 4:11
they stumble when rendering
 decisions.
⁸All the tables are covered with
 vomit   Jer 48:26
and there is not a spot
 without filth.

⁹"Who is it he is trying to
 teach?   ver 26; Isa 30:20
To whom is he explaining
 his message?   Isa 53:1
To children weaned from their
 milk,   Ps 131:2; Heb 5:12-13
to those just taken from the
 breast?
¹⁰For it is:
Do and do, do and do,
rule on rule, rule on rule[a];
a little here, a little there."

¹¹Very well then, with foreign
 lips and strange tongues
God will speak to this
 people,   1Co 14:21*
¹²to whom he said,
"This is the resting place, let
 the weary rest";
and, "This is the place of
 repose" —
but they would not listen.
¹³So then, the word of the Lord
 to them will become:
Do and do, do and do,
rule on rule, rule on rule;
a little here, a little there —

---

a 10 Hebrew / sav lasav sav lasav / kav lakav kav lakav (possibly meaningless sounds; perhaps a mimicking of the prophet's words); also in verse 13

so that they will go and fall
    backward,
    be injured and snared and
    captured.   Mt 21:44; Isa 8:15

¹⁴Therefore hear the word of the
    LORD, you scoffers   Isa 1:10
    who rule this people in
    Jerusalem.
¹⁵You boast, "We have entered
    into a covenant with
    death,
    with the grave^a we have
    made an agreement.
When an overwhelming
    scourge sweeps by,
    it cannot touch us,
for we have made a lie our
    refuge   Isa 9:15
    and falsehood^b our hiding
    place."   Isa 29:15

¹⁶So this is what the Sovereign
LORD says:

"See, I lay a stone in Zion,
    a tested stone,   Ps 118:22; Ac 4:11
a precious cornerstone for a
    sure foundation;   Jer 51:26
    the one who trusts will
    never be dismayed.
¹⁷I will make justice the
    measuring line   Isa 5:16
    and righteousness the plumb
    line;   2Ki 21:13
hail will sweep away your
    refuge, the lie,
    and water will overflow your
    hiding place.

¹⁸Your covenant with death will
    be annulled;
    your agreement with the
    grave will not stand.
When the overwhelming
    scourge sweeps by,   ver 15
    you will be beaten down by
    it.   Da 8:13
¹⁹As often as it comes it will
    carry you away;   2Ki 24:2
    morning after morning, by
    day and by night,
    it will sweep through."

The understanding of this
    message
    will bring sheer terror.
²⁰The bed is too short to stretch
    out on,
    the blanket too narrow to
    wrap around you.   Isa 59:6
²¹The LORD will rise up as he did
    at Mount Perazim,
    he will rouse himself as in
    the Valley of Gibeon—
to do his work, his strange
    work,   Isa 10:12; Lk 19:41-44
    and perform his task, his
    alien task.
²²Now stop your mocking,
    or your chains will become
    heavier;
    the Lord, the LORD Almighty,
    has told me
    of the destruction decreed
    against the whole land.

²³Listen and hear my voice;
    pay attention and hear what
    I say.

^a 15 Hebrew *Sheol*; also in verse 18   ^b 15 Or *false gods*

24When a farmer plows for
    planting, does he plow
    continually?   Ecc 3:2
Does he keep on breaking
    up and harrowing the
    soil?
25When he has leveled the
    surface,
does he not sow caraway
    and scatter cummin?
Does he not plant wheat in its
    place,[a]
barley in its plot,[a]
and spelt in its field?   Ex 9:32
26His God instructs him
    and teaches him the right
    way.   Ps 94:10

27Caraway is not threshed with a
    sledge,   Job 41:30
nor is a cartwheel rolled
    over cummin;
caraway is beaten out with a
    rod,   Isa 10:5
and cummin with a stick.
28Grain must be ground to make
    bread;
so one does not go on
    threshing it forever.
Though he drives the wheels
    of his threshing cart
    over it,   Isa 21:10
his horses do not grind
    it.
29All this also comes from the
    LORD Almighty,
wonderful in counsel and
    magnificent in wisdom.

Woe to David's City

29 Woe to you, Ariel, Ariel,
    the city where David
    settled!   2Sa 5:7
Add year to year
    and let your cycle of festivals
    go on.   Isa 1:14
2Yet I will besiege Ariel;
    she will mourn and lament,
    she will be to me like an
    altar hearth.[b]
3I will encamp against you all
    around;
I will encircle you with
    towers   Lk 19:43-44
and set up my siege works
    against you.   2Ki 25:1
4Brought low, you will speak
    from the ground;
your speech will mumble out
    of the dust.   Isa 8:19
Your voice will come ghostlike
    from the earth;
out of the dust your speech
    will whisper.   Isa 26:16

5But your many enemies will
    become like fine dust,
the ruthless hordes like
    blown chaff.   Isa 17:13
Suddenly, in an instant,
6   the LORD Almighty will come
with thunder and earthquake
    and great noise,   Mt 24:7
with windstorm and tempest
    and flames of a
    devouring fire.   Ps 83:13-15

---

[a] 25 The meaning of the Hebrew for this word is uncertain.   [b] 2 The Hebrew for *altar hearth* sounds like the Hebrew for *Ariel*.

⁷Then the hordes of all the
    nations that fight against
    Ariel,   Mic 4:11-12; Zec 12:9
    that attack her and her
      fortress and besiege her,
will be as it is with a
    dream,
with a vision in the
    night—
⁸as when a hungry man dreams
    that he is eating,
    but he awakens, and his
      hunger remains;   Ps 73:20
as when a thirsty man dreams
    that he is drinking,
    but he awakens faint, with
      his thirst unquenched.
So will it be with the hordes of
    all the nations
    that fight against Mount
      Zion.   Isa 17:12-14; 54:17

⁹Be stunned and amazed,   Jer 4:9
    blind yourselves and be
      sightless;   Isa 6:10
be drunk, but not from wine,
    stagger, but not from beer.
¹⁰The Lᴏʀᴅ has brought over you
    a deep sleep:
He has sealed your eyes (the
    prophets);   Ps 69:23; Isa 6:9-10
he has covered your heads
    (the seers).   1Sa 9:9

¹¹For you this whole vision is
nothing but words sealed in a
scroll. And if you give the scroll to
someone who can read, and say to
him, "Read this, please," he will
answer, "I can't; it is sealed." ¹²Or
if you give the scroll to someone
who cannot read, and say, "Read
this, please," he will answer, "I
don't know how to read."   Isa 8:16

¹³The Lord says:

"These people come near to
    me with their mouth
and honor me with their
    lips,   Ps 50:16
but their hearts are far from
    me.   Eze 33:31
Their worship of me
    is made up only of rules
      taught by men.ᵃ
¹⁴Therefore once more I will
    astound these people
    with wonder upon wonder;
the wisdom of the wise will
    perish,   Jer 49:7
    the intelligence of the
      intelligent will vanish."
¹⁵Woe to those who go to great
    depths
    to hide their plans from the
      Lᴏʀᴅ,   Isa 28:15
who do their work in darkness
    and think,
    "Who sees us? Who will
      know?"   Job 22:13; Ps 94:7
¹⁶You turn things upside down,
    as if the potter were thought
      to be like the clay!
Shall what is formed say to
    him who formed it,
    "He did not make me"?
Can the pot say of the potter,
    "He knows nothing"?   Job 9:12

ᵃ 13 Hebrew; Septuagint *They worship me in vain; / their teachings are but rules taught by men*

¹⁷In a very short time, will not
        Lebanon be turned into
        a fertile field   Ps 84:6
    and the fertile field seem like
        a forest?   Isa 32:15
¹⁸In that day the deaf will hear
        the words of the scroll,
    and out of gloom and
        darkness
    the eyes of the blind will see.
¹⁹Once more the humble will
        rejoice in the LORD;
    the needy will rejoice in the
        Holy One of Israel.
²⁰The ruthless will vanish,
    the mockers will disappear,
    and all who have an eye for
        evil will be cut down—
²¹those who with a word make a
        man out to be guilty,
    who ensnare the defender in
        court   Am 5:10,15
    and with false testimony
        deprive the innocent of
        justice.   Isa 32:7

²²Therefore this is what the
LORD, who redeemed Abraham,
says to the house of Jacob:

"No longer will Jacob be
        ashamed;   Isa 49:23
    no longer will their faces
        grow pale.   Jer 30:6,10
²³When they see among them
        their children,   Isa 49:20-26
    the work of my hands,
    they will keep my name holy;
    they will acknowledge the
        holiness of the Holy
        One of Jacob,   Isa 5:19

    and will stand in awe of the
        God of Israel.
²⁴Those who are wayward in
        spirit will gain
        understanding;   Isa 28:7
    those who complain will
        accept instruction."

Woe to the Obstinate Nation

30 "Woe to the obstinate
        children,"   Isa 29:15
    declares the LORD,
    "to those who carry out plans
        that are not mine,
    forming an alliance, but not
        by my Spirit,   Isa 8:12
    heaping sin upon sin;
²who go down to Egypt   Isa 31:1
    without consulting me;
    who look for help to Pharaoh's
        protection,   Isa 36:9
    to Egypt's shade for refuge.
³But Pharaoh's protection will
        be to your shame,
    Egypt's shade will bring you
        disgrace.   Isa 20:4-5; 36:6
⁴Though they have officials in
        Zoan   Isa 19:11
    and their envoys have
        arrived in Hanes,
⁵everyone will be put to shame
    because of a people useless
        to them,   ver 7; 2Ki 18:21
    who bring neither help nor
        advantage,   Jer 37:3-5
    but only shame and
        disgrace."   2Ki 18:21

⁶An oracle concerning the animals of the Negev: Isa 13:1

Through a land of hardship
    and distress,   Ex 5:10,21
    of lions and lionesses,
    of adders and darting snakes,
the envoys carry their riches
    on donkeys' backs,
    their treasures on the humps
    of camels,   Isa 15:7
to that unprofitable nation,
⁷ to Egypt, whose help is
    utterly useless.   2Ki 18:21
Therefore I call her
    Rahab the Do-Nothing.

⁸Go now, write it on a tablet for
    them,   Dt 27:8
    inscribe it on a scroll,   Isa 8:1
that for the days to come
    it may be an everlasting
    witness.   Jos 24:26-27
⁹These are rebellious people,
    deceitful children,
    children unwilling to listen
    to the LORD's
    instruction.   Isa 1:10
¹⁰They say to the seers,
    "See no more visions!"
and to the prophets,
    "Give us no more visions of
    what is right!
Tell us pleasant things,   1Ki 22:8
    prophesy illusions.   Eze 13:7
¹¹Leave this way,   ver 21; Pr 3:6
    get off this path,
and stop confronting us
    with the Holy One of Israel!"

¹²Therefore, this is what the
Holy One of Israel says: Isa 5:19

"Because you have rejected
    this message,   Isa 5:24

relied on oppression   Isa 5:7
    and depended on deceit,
¹³this sin will become for
    you
like a high wall, cracked and
    bulging,   Ps 62:3
that collapses suddenly, in
    an instant.   1Ki 20:30; Isa 29:5
¹⁴It will break in pieces like
    pottery,   Ps 2:9; Jer 19:10-11
    shattered so mercilessly
that among its pieces not a
    fragment will be found
for taking coals from a
    hearth
or scooping water out of a
    cistern."

¹⁵This is what the Sovereign
LORD, the Holy One of Israel, says:

"In repentance and rest is your
    salvation,   Ex 14:14; Jos 1:13
in quietness and trust is
    your strength,   Isa 32:17
but you would have none of
    it.   Isa 8:6; 42:24
¹⁶You said, 'No, we will flee on
    horses.'   Isa 31:1,3
Therefore you will flee!
You said, 'We will ride off on
    swift horses.'
Therefore your pursuers will
    be swift!
¹⁷A thousand will flee
    at the threat of one;
at the threat of five   Lev 26:8
    you will all flee away,   Dt 28:25
till you are left   Isa 1:8
    like a flagstaff on a
    mountaintop,

like a banner on a hill."
¹⁸Yet the LORD longs to be
    gracious to you;   Isa 42:14
he rises to show you
    compassion.   Ps 78:38
For the LORD is a God of
    justice.   Isa 5:16
Blessed are all who wait for
    him!   Isa 25:9; La 3:25

¹⁹O people of Zion, who live in
Jerusalem, you will weep no more.
How gracious he will be when you
cry for help! As soon as he hears,
he will answer you. ²⁰Although the
Lord gives you the bread of adver-
sity and the water of affliction,
your teachers will be hidden no
more; with your own eyes you will
see them. ²¹Whether you turn to
the right or to the left, your ears
will hear a voice behind you, saying, "This is the way; walk in it."
²²Then you will defile your idols
overlaid with silver and your images covered with gold; you will
throw them away like a menstrual
cloth and say to them, "Away with
you!"   Ps 74:9; Isa 29:24; Am 8:11

²³He will also send you rain for
the seed you sow in the ground,
and the food that comes from the
land will be rich and plentiful. In
that day your cattle will graze in
broad meadows. ²⁴The oxen and
donkeys that work the soil will eat
fodder and mash, spread out with
fork and shovel. ²⁵In the day of
great slaughter, when the towers
fall, streams of water will flow on
every high mountain and every

lofty hill. ²⁶The moon will shine
like the sun, and the sunlight will
be seven times brighter, like the
light of seven full days, when the
LORD binds up the bruises of his
people and heals the wounds he
inflicted.   Isa 1:5; 60:19-20; Rev 21:23

²⁷See, the Name of the LORD
    comes from afar,   Isa 59:19
with burning anger and
    dense clouds of smoke;
his lips are full of wrath,   Isa 10:5
and his tongue is a
    consuming fire.   Job 41:21
²⁸His breath is like a rushing
    torrent,   Isa 11:4
    rising up to the neck.   Isa 8:8
He shakes the nations in the
    sieve of destruction;
he places in the jaws of the
    peoples
    a bit that leads them astray.
²⁹And you will sing
    as on the night you celebrate
        a holy festival;   Isa 25:6
your hearts will rejoice   Isa 12:1
    as when people go up with
        flutes
to the mountain of the LORD,
    to the Rock of Israel.   Ge 49:24
³⁰The LORD will cause men to
    hear his majestic voice
    and will make them see his
        arm coming down   Isa 9:12
with raging anger and
    consuming fire,   Isa 10:25
with cloudburst,
    thunderstorm and hail.
³¹The voice of the LORD will
    shatter Assyria;   Isa 10:5,12

with his scepter he will
  strike them down.   Isa 11:4
32Every stroke the LORD lays on
    them
  with his punishing rod
will be to the music of
    tambourines and harps,
  as he fights them in battle
    with the blows of his
    arm.   Isa 11:15; Eze 32:10
33Topheth has long been
    prepared;
  it has been made ready for
    the king.
Its fire pit has been made deep
    and wide,
  with an abundance of fire
    and wood;
the breath of the LORD,
  like a stream of burning
    sulfur,   Ge 19:24; Rev 9:17
  sets it ablaze.   Isa 1:31

*Woe to Those Who Rely
on Egypt*

31 Woe to those who go
    down to Egypt for help,
  who rely on horses,
who trust in the multitude of
    their chariots   Isa 2:7
  and in the great strength of
    their horsemen,
but do not look to the Holy
    One of Israel,
  or seek help from the
    LORD.
2Yet he too is wise and can
    bring disaster;   Isa 45:7
  he does not take back his
    words.   Nu 23:19

He will rise up against the
    house of the wicked,
  against those who help
    evildoers.
3But the Egyptians are men and
    not God;   Eze 28:9
  their horses are flesh and
    not spirit.   Isa 30:16
When the LORD stretches out
    his hand,   Isa 9:17,21
  he who helps will stumble,
  he who is helped will fall;
    both will perish together.

4This is what the LORD says to
me:

"As a lion growls,   Am 3:8
    a great lion over his prey—
  and though a whole band of
    shepherds
  is called together against
    him,
  he is not frightened by their
    shouts
    or disturbed by their
    clamor—
so the LORD Almighty will
    come down   Isa 42:13
  to do battle on Mount Zion
    and on its heights.
5Like birds hovering overhead,
  the LORD Almighty will
    shield Jerusalem;   Ps 91:4
  he will shield it and deliver it,
  he will 'pass over' it and will
    rescue it."   Ex 12:23

6Return to him you have so
greatly revolted against, O Israelites. 7For in that day every one of
you will reject the idols of silver

and gold your sinful hands have
made.   Isa 2:20; 30:22

⁸"Assyria will fall by a sword
    that is not of man;
a sword, not of mortals, will
    devour them.   Isa 14:25; 37:7
They will flee before the sword
    and their young men will be
    put to forced labor.
⁹Their stronghold will fall
    because of terror;
  at sight of the battle
    standard their
    commanders will panic,"
declares the LORD,
    whose fire is in Zion,   Isa 10:17
    whose furnace is in
    Jerusalem.   Mal 4:1

The Kingdom of Righteousness

32 See, a king will reign in
    righteousness   Eze 37:24
and rulers will rule with
    justice.   Isa 9:7
²Each man will be like a shelter
    from the wind   Isa 4:6
and a refuge from the storm,
like streams of water in the
    desert   Ps 23:2; 107:35; Jer 31:9
and the shadow of a great
    rock in a thirsty land.

³Then the eyes of those who
    see will no longer be
    closed,   Isa 29:18
and the ears of those who
    hear will listen.   Dt 29:4
⁴The mind of the rash will
    know and understand,

and the stammering tongue
    will be fluent and clear.
⁵No longer will the fool be
    called noble   1Sa 25:25
nor the scoundrel be highly
    respected.
⁶For the fool speaks folly,   Pr 19:3
    his mind is busy with evil:
He practices ungodliness   Isa 9:17
  and spreads error concerning
    the LORD;   Isa 9:16
the hungry he leaves empty
  and from the thirsty he
    withholds water.
⁷The scoundrel's methods are
    wicked,   Jer 5:26-28
he makes up evil schemes
to destroy the poor with lies,
  even when the plea of the
    needy is just.   Isa 61:1
⁸But the noble man makes
    noble plans,
and by noble deeds he
    stands.   Pr 11:25

The Women of Jerusalem

⁹You women who are so
    complacent,
  rise up and listen to me;
you daughters who feel
    secure,
  hear what I have to say!
¹⁰In little more than a year
  you who feel secure will
    tremble;
the grape harvest will fail,
  and the harvest of fruit will
    not come.
¹¹Tremble, you complacent
    women;

shudder, you daughters who
    feel secure!
Strip off your clothes,   Isa 47:2
    put sackcloth around your
        waists.   Isa 3:24
¹²Beat your breasts for the
        pleasant fields,   Na 2:7
    for the fruitful vines   Isa 16:9
¹³and for the land of my people,
    a land overgrown with
        thorns and briers—
    yes, mourn for all houses of
        merriment
    and for this city of revelry.
¹⁴The fortress will be abandoned,
    the noisy city deserted;
    citadel and watchtower will
        become a wasteland
        forever,   Isa 34:13
    the delight of donkeys, a
        pasture for flocks,
¹⁵till the Spirit is poured upon us
        from on high,   Joel 2:28
    and the desert becomes a
        fertile field,   Ps 107:35
    and the fertile field seems
        like a forest.   Isa 29:17
¹⁶Justice will dwell in the desert
    and righteousness live in the
        fertile field.   Ps 48:1
¹⁷The fruit of righteousness will
        be peace;   Ps 119:165; Jas 3:18
    the effect of righteousness
        will be quietness and
        confidence forever.
¹⁸My people will live in peaceful
        dwelling places,   Isa 2:4
    in secure homes,   Isa 26:1
    in undisturbed places of
        rest.
¹⁹Though hail flattens the forest

and the city is leveled
        completely,   Isa 24:10; 27:10
²⁰how blessed you will be,
    sowing your seed by every
        stream,   Ecc 11:1
    and letting your cattle and
        donkeys range free.

Distress and Help

33 Woe to you, O destroyer,
    you who have not been
        destroyed!
Woe to you, O traitor,
    you who have not been
        betrayed!
When you stop destroying,
    you will be destroyed;   Hab 2:8
when you stop betraying,
    you will be betrayed.   Isa 21:2

²O Lord, be gracious to us;
    we long for you.
Be our strength every morning,
    our salvation in time of
        distress.   Isa 5:30; 25:9
³At the thunder of your voice,
    the peoples flee;   Ps 68:1
    when you rise up, the
        nations scatter.   Isa 59:16-18
⁴Your plunder, O nations, is
    harvested as by young
        locusts;   Joel 1:4
    like a swarm of locusts men
        pounce on it.

⁵The Lord is exalted, for he
        dwells on high;   Ps 97:9
    he will fill Zion with justice
        and righteousness.
⁶He will be the sure foundation
    for your times,

a rich store of salvation and
　　wisdom and knowledge;
the fear of the LORD is the
　　key to this treasure.*a*

7Look, their brave men cry
　　aloud in the streets;
the envoys of peace weep
　　bitterly.　　　　　　　2Ki 18:37
8The highways are deserted,
　　no travelers are on the
　　　roads.　　　Jdg 5:6; Isa 35:8
The treaty is broken,
　　its witnesses*b* are despised,
　　no one is respected.
9The land mourns*c* and wastes
　　away,　　　　　　　　Isa 3:26
Lebanon is ashamed and
　　withers;　　　　Isa 2:13; 24:4
Sharon is like the Arabah,
　　and Bashan and Carmel drop
　　　their leaves.　1Ki 18:19; Na 1:4

10"Now will I arise," says the
　　LORD.　　　　　Ps 12:5; Isa 2:21
"Now will I be exalted;
　　now will I be lifted up.
11You conceive chaff,　Ps 7:14; Isa 59:4
　　you give birth to straw;
your breath is a fire that
　　consumes you.　　　　Isa 1:31
12The peoples will be burned as
　　if to lime;
like cut thornbushes they
　　will be set ablaze."

13You who are far away, hear
　　what I have done;　　Ps 49:1
you who are near,
　　acknowledge my power!

14The sinners in Zion are
　　terrified;
trembling grips the godless:
"Who of us can dwell with the
　　consuming fire?　　Isa 30:30
Who of us can dwell with
　　everlasting burning?"
15He who walks righteously
　　and speaks what is right,
who rejects gain from extortion
　　and keeps his hand from
　　　accepting bribes,　Pr 15:27
who stops his ears against
　　plots of murder
and shuts his eyes against
　　contemplating evil—
16this is the man who will dwell
　　on the heights,
whose refuge will be the
　　mountain fortress.　Isa 25:4
His bread will be supplied,
　　and water will not fail him.

17Your eyes will see the king in
　　his beauty　　　　　Isa 6:5
and view a land that
　　stretches afar.　　Isa 26:15
18In your thoughts you will
　　ponder the former
　　terror:　　　　　　Isa 17:14
"Where is that chief officer?
Where is the one who took
　　the revenue?
Where is the officer in
　　charge of the towers?"
19You will see those arrogant
　　people no more,
those people of an obscure
　　speech,

---

*a*6 Or *is a treasure from him*　　*b*8 Dead Sea Scrolls; Masoretic Text / *the cities*　　*c*9 Or *dries up*

with their strange,
   incomprehensible
   tongue.   Isa 28:11; Jer 5:15

20Look upon Zion, the city of
   our festivals;
   your eyes will see Jerusalem,
   a peaceful abode, a tent that
   will not be moved;
   its stakes will never be pulled
   up,
   nor any of its ropes broken.
21There the LORD will be our
   Mighty One.
   It will be like a place of
   broad rivers and
   streams.   Isa 41:18; 48:18
No galley with oars will ride
   them,
   no mighty ship will sail
   them.
22For the LORD is our judge,
   the LORD is our lawgiver,
   the LORD is our king;   Ps 89:18
   it is he who will save us.

23Your rigging hangs loose:
   The mast is not held
   secure,
   the sail is not spread.
Then an abundance of spoils
   will be divided
   and even the lame will carry
   off plunder.   2Ki 7:8,16
24No one living in Zion will say,
   "I am ill";   Isa 30:26
   and the sins of those who
   dwell there will be
   forgiven.   Jer 50:20; 1Jn 1:7-9

Judgment Against the Nations

34 Come near, you nations,
      and listen;
   pay attention, you peoples!
Let the earth hear, and all that
   is in it,   Ps 49:1
   the world, and all that comes
   out of it!   Dt 32:1
2The LORD is angry with all
   nations;
   his wrath is upon all their
   armies.
He will totally destroya them,
   he will give them over to
   slaughter.   Isa 30:25
3Their slain will be thrown out,
   their dead bodies will send
   up a stench;   Joel 2:20
   the mountains will be
   soaked with their blood.
4All the stars of the heavens
   will be dissolved   Isa 13:13
   and the sky rolled up like a
   scroll;   Eze 32:7-8
   all the starry host will fall
   like withered leaves from the
   vine,   Isa 15:6; Mt 21:19
   like shriveled figs from the
   fig tree.

5My sword has drunk its fill in
   the heavens;   Jer 46:10
   see, it descends in judgment
   on Edom,   Am 1:11-12
   the people I have totally
   destroyed.   Mal 1:4; Isa 24:6
6The sword of the LORD is
   bathed in blood,   Dt 32:41

a2 The Hebrew term refers to the irrevocable giving over of things or persons to the LORD, often by totally destroying them; also in verse 5.

it is covered with fat—
the blood of lambs and goats,
fat from the kidneys of
rams.
For the LORD has a sacrifice in
Bozrah   Ge 36:33
and a great slaughter in
Edom.   Isa 30:25
⁷And the wild oxen will fall
with them,
the bull calves and the great
bulls.   Ps 68:30
Their land will be drenched
with blood,
and the dust will be soaked
with fat.

⁸For the LORD has a day of
vengeance,   Isa 63:4
a year of retribution, to
uphold Zion's cause.
⁹Edom's streams will be turned
into pitch,
her dust into burning sulfur;
her land will become blazing
pitch!
¹⁰It will not be quenched night
and day;
its smoke will rise forever.
From generation to generation
it will lie desolate;
no one will ever pass
through it again.
¹¹The desert owlᵃ and screech
owlᵃ will possess it;
the great owlᵃ and the raven
will nest there.
God will stretch out over Edom
the measuring line of chaos

and the plumb line of
desolation.   2Ki 21:13; La 2:8
¹²Her nobles will have nothing
there to be called a
kingdom,
all her princes will vanish
away.   Isa 41:11-12; Jer 27:20
¹³Thorns will overrun her
citadels,
nettles and brambles her
strongholds.   Isa 13:22; 32:13
She will become a haunt for
jackals,   Ps 44:19; Jer 9:11
a home for owls.
¹⁴Desert creatures will meet with
hyenas,   Isa 13:22
and wild goats will bleat to
each other;
there the night creatures will
also repose   Rev 18:2
and find for themselves
places of rest.
¹⁵The owl will nest there and lay
eggs,
she will hatch them, and
care for her young
under the shadow of her
wings;
there also the falcons will
gather,   Dt 14:13
each with its mate.

¹⁶Look in the scroll of the LORD
and read: Isa 30:8

None of these will be
missing,
not one will lack her mate.
For it is his mouth that has
given the order,   Isa 1:20

ᵃ11 The precise identification of these birds is uncertain.

and his Spirit will gather
      them together.
[17]He allots their portions;   Isa 17:14
      his hand distributes them by
      measure.
They will possess it forever
      and dwell there from
      generation to generation.

Joy of the Redeemed

35 The desert and the
         parched land will be
         glad;   Isa 27:10; 41:18-19
   the wilderness will rejoice
      and blossom.   Isa 51:3
Like the crocus, [2]it will burst
      into bloom;   SS 2:1
   it will rejoice greatly and
      shout for joy.   Isa 25:9; 55:12
The glory of Lebanon will be
      given to it,   Isa 32:15
   the splendor of Carmel and
      Sharon;   SS 7:5
   they will see the glory of the
      Lord,   Ex 16:7; Isa 4:5
   the splendor of our God.

[3]Strengthen the feeble hands,
   steady the knees that give
      way;   Job 4:4; Heb 12:12
[4]say to those with fearful
      hearts,   Isa 40:2; Zec 1:13
   "Be strong, do not fear;   Isa 7:4
your God will come,   Isa 62:11
   he will come with
      vengeance;   Isa 1:24
   with divine retribution
      he will come to save you."

[5]Then will the eyes of the blind
      be opened   Mt 11:5; Jn 9:6-7
   and the ears of the deaf
      unstopped.   Isa 29:18
[6]Then will the lame leap like a
      deer,   Mt 15:30; Jn 5:8-9
   and the mute tongue shout
      for joy.   Mt 9:32-33
Water will gush forth in the
      wilderness
   and streams in the desert.
[7]The burning sand will become
      a pool,
   the thirsty ground bubbling
      springs.   Isa 49:10
In the haunts where jackals
      once lay,   Isa 13:22
   grass and reeds and papyrus
      will grow.   Job 8:11

[8]And a highway will be there;
   it will be called the Way of
      Holiness.   Isa 4:3; 1Pe 1:15
The unclean will not journey
      on it;   Isa 52:1
   it will be for those who walk
      in that Way;
   wicked fools will not go
      about on it.[a]
[9]No lion will be there,   Isa 30:6
   nor will any ferocious beast
      get up on it;   Isa 34:14
   they will not be found there.
But only the redeemed will
      walk there,   Isa 51:11; 62:12
[10] and the ransomed of the
      Lord will return.   Isa 1:27
They will enter Zion with
      singing;

---

[a]8 Or / the simple will not stray from it

everlasting joy will crown
their heads.   Isa 25:9
Gladness and joy will overtake
them,   Ps 51:8; Isa 51:3
and sorrow and sighing will
flee away.   Isa 51:11; Rev 7:17

Sennacherib Threatens Jerusalem

36 In the fourteenth year of King Hezekiah's reign, Sennacherib king of Assyria attacked all the fortified cities of Judah and captured them. ²Then the king of Assyria sent his field commander with a large army from Lachish to King Hezekiah at Jerusalem. When the commander stopped at the aqueduct of the Upper Pool, on the road to the Washerman's Field, ³Eliakim son of Hilkiah the palace administrator, Shebna the secretary, and Joah son of Asaph the recorder went out to him.   2Ch 32:1; Isa 22:20-21

⁴The field commander said to them, "Tell Hezekiah,

" 'This is what the great king, the king of Assyria, says: On what are you basing this confidence of yours? ⁵You say you have strategy and military strength—but you speak only empty words. On whom are you depending, that you rebel against me? ⁶Look now, you are depending on Egypt, that splintered reed of a staff, which pierces a man's hand and wounds him if he leans

on it! Such is Pharaoh king of Egypt to all who depend on him. ⁷And if you say to me, "We are depending on the LORD our God"—isn't he the one whose high places and altars Hezekiah removed, saying to Judah and Jerusalem, "You must worship before this altar"?   2Ki 18:4; Isa 30:2,5

⁸" 'Come now, make a bargain with my master, the king of Assyria: I will give you two thousand horses—if you can put riders on them! ⁹How then can you repulse one officer of the least of my master's officials, even though you are depending on Egypt for chariots and horsemen? ¹⁰Furthermore, have I come to attack and destroy this land without the LORD? The LORD himself told me to march against this country and destroy it.' "

¹¹Then Eliakim, Shebna and Joah said to the field commander, "Please speak to your servants in Aramaic, since we understand it. Don't speak to us in Hebrew in the hearing of the people on the wall."

¹²But the commander replied, "Was it only to your master and you that my master sent me to say these things, and not to the men sitting on the wall—who, like you, will have to eat their own filth and drink their own urine?"

¹³Then the commander stood and called out in Hebrew, "Hear

the words of the great king, the king of Assyria! **14**This is what the king says: Do not let Hezekiah deceive you. He cannot deliver you! **15**Do not let Hezekiah persuade you to trust in the LORD when he says, 'The LORD will surely deliver us; this city will not be given into the hand of the king of Assyria.'

16"Do not listen to Hezekiah. This is what the king of Assyria says: Make peace with me and come out to me. Then every one of you will eat from his own vine and fig tree and drink water from his own cistern, **17**until I come and take you to a land like your own — a land of grain and new wine, a land of bread and vineyards.

18"Do not let Hezekiah mislead you when he says, 'The LORD will deliver us.' Has the god of any nation ever delivered his land from the hand of the king of Assyria? **19**Where are the gods of Hamath and Arpad? Where are the gods of Sepharvaim? Have they rescued Samaria from my hand? **20**Who of all the gods of these countries has been able to save his land from me? How then can the LORD deliver Jerusalem from my hand?"

21But the people remained silent and said nothing in reply, because the king had commanded, "Do not answer him."   Pr 9:7-8

22Then Eliakim son of Hilkiah the palace administrator, Shebna the secretary, and Joah son of Asaph the recorder went to Heze-kiah, with their clothes torn, and told him what the field commander had said.   2Ki 18:17-37; 2Ch 32:9-19

Jerusalem's Deliverance Foretold

37 When King Hezekiah heard this, he tore his clothes and put on sackcloth and went into the temple of the LORD. **2**He sent Eliakim the palace administrator, Shebna the secretary, and the leading priests, all wearing sackcloth, to the prophet Isaiah son of Amoz. **3**They told him, "This is what Hezekiah says: This day is a day of distress and rebuke and disgrace, as when children come to the point of birth and there is no strength to deliver them. **4**It may be that the LORD your God will hear the words of the field commander, whom his master, the king of Assyria, has sent to ridicule the living God, and that he will rebuke him for the words the LORD your God has heard. Therefore pray for the remnant that still survives."   1Sa 7:8

5When King Hezekiah's officials came to Isaiah, **6**Isaiah said to them, "Tell your master, 'This is what the LORD says: Do not be afraid of what you have heard — those words with which the underlings of the king of Assyria have blasphemed me. **7**Listen! I am going to put a spirit in him so that when he hears a certain report, he will return to his own country, and there I will have him cut down with the sword.'" Isa 7:4

⁸When the field commander heard that the king of Assyria had left Lachish, he withdrew and found the king fighting against Libnah. Nu 33:20

⁹Now Sennacherib received a report that Tirhakah, the Cushite*a* king ˻of Egypt˼, was marching out to fight against him. When he heard it, he sent messengers to Hezekiah with this word: ¹⁰"Say to Hezekiah king of Judah: Do not let the god you depend on deceive you when he says, 'Jerusalem will not be handed over to the king of Assyria.' ¹¹Surely you have heard what the kings of Assyria have done to all the countries, destroying them completely. And will you be delivered? ¹²Did the gods of the nations that were destroyed by my forefathers deliver them—the gods of Gozan, Haran, Rezeph and the people of Eden who were in Tel Assar? ¹³Where is the king of Hamath, the king of Arpad, the king of the city of Sepharvaim, or of Hena or Ivvah?" 2Ki 19:1-13

Hezekiah's Prayer

¹⁴Hezekiah received the letter from the messengers and read it. Then he went up to the temple of the LORD and spread it out before the LORD. ¹⁵And Hezekiah prayed to the LORD: ¹⁶"O LORD Almighty, God of Israel, enthroned between the cherubim, you alone are God over all the kingdoms of the earth. You have made heaven and earth. ¹⁷Give ear, O LORD, and hear; open your eyes, O LORD, and see; listen to all the words Sennacherib has sent to insult the living God.

¹⁸"It is true, O LORD, that the Assyrian kings have laid waste all these peoples and their lands. ¹⁹They have thrown their gods into the fire and destroyed them, for they were not gods but only wood and stone, fashioned by human hands. ²⁰Now, O LORD our God, deliver us from his hand, so that all kingdoms on earth may know that you alone, O LORD, are God.*b*"

Sennacherib's Fall

²¹Then Isaiah son of Amoz sent a message to Hezekiah: "This is what the LORD, the God of Israel, says: Because you have prayed to me concerning Sennacherib king of Assyria, ²²this is the word the LORD has spoken against him:

"The Virgin Daughter of Zion
   despises and mocks you.
The Daughter of Jerusalem
   tosses her head as you flee.
²³Who is it you have insulted
   and blasphemed?
Against whom have you
   raised your voice
and lifted your eyes in pride?

---

a9 That is, from the upper Nile region   *b20* Dead Sea Scrolls (see also 2 Kings 19:19); Masoretic Text *alone are the LORD*

Against the Holy One of
    Israel!   Isa 1:4; 12:6
24By your messengers
    you have heaped insults on
        the Lord.
And you have said,
    'With my many chariots
I have ascended the heights of
    the mountains,
    the utmost heights of
        Lebanon.   Isa 14:8
I have cut down its tallest
    cedars,
    the choicest of its pines.
I have reached its remotest
    heights,
    the finest of its forests.
25I have dug wells in foreign
    lands*a*
    and drunk the water there.
With the soles of my feet
    I have dried up all the
        streams of Egypt.' Dt 11:10

26"Have you not heard?
    Long ago I ordained it. Ac 2:23
In days of old I planned it;
    now I have brought it to
        pass,
    that you have turned fortified
        cities
    into piles of stone.   Isa 25:2
27Their people, drained of power,
    are dismayed and put to
        shame.
They are like plants in the
    field,
    like tender green shoots,

like grass sprouting on the
    roof,   Ps 129:6
    scorched*b* before it grows
        up.
28"But I know where you stay
    and when you come and go
    and how you rage against
        me.   Ps 2:1
29Because you rage against me
    and because your insolence
        has reached my ears,
I will put my hook in your
    nose   Isa 30:28; Eze 38:4
    and my bit in your mouth,
and I will make you return
    by the way you came.   ver 34

30"This will be the sign for you,
O Hezekiah:
                              Isa 20:3

"This year you will eat what
    grows by itself,
    and the second year what
        springs from that.
But in the third year sow and
    reap,   Isa 16:14
    plant vineyards and eat their
        fruit.   Ps 107:37; Isa 30:23
31Once more a remnant of the
    house of Judah
    will take root below and
        bear fruit above.   Isa 27:6
32For out of Jerusalem will come
    a remnant,
    and out of Mount Zion a
        band of survivors.
The zeal of the LORD Almighty
    will accomplish this.   Isa 9:7

---

*a*25 Dead Sea Scrolls (see also 2 Kings 19:24); Masoretic Text does not have *in foreign lands.*
*b*27 Some manuscripts of the Masoretic Text, Dead Sea Scrolls and some Septuagint manuscripts (see also 2 Kings 19:26); most manuscripts of the Masoretic Text *roof / and terraced fields*

³³"Therefore this is what the LORD says concerning the king of Assyria:

"He will not enter this city
    or shoot an arrow here.
He will not come before it with shield
    or build a siege ramp against it.
³⁴By the way that he came he
    will return;   ver 29
he will not enter this city,"
            declares the LORD.
³⁵"I will defend this city and
    save it,   Isa 38:6
for my sake and for the sake
    of David my servant!"

³⁶Then the angel of the LORD went out and put to death a hundred and eighty-five thousand men in the Assyrian camp. When the people got up the next morning—there were all the dead bodies! ³⁷So Sennacherib king of Assyria broke camp and withdrew. He returned to Nineveh and stayed there.   Ge 10:11; Isa 10:12

³⁸One day, while he was worshiping in the temple of his god Nisroch, his sons Adrammelech and Sharezer cut him down with the sword, and they escaped to the land of Ararat. And Esarhaddon his son succeeded him as king.

Hezekiah's Illness

38 In those days Hezekiah became ill and was at the point of death. The prophet Isaiah son of Amoz went to him and said, "This is what the LORD says: Put your house in order, because you are going to die; you will not recover."   2Sa 17:23; 2Ki 8:10; Isa 37:2

²Hezekiah turned his face to the wall and prayed to the LORD, ³"Remember, O LORD, how I have walked before you faithfully and with wholehearted devotion and have done what is good in your eyes." And Hezekiah wept bitterly.

⁴Then the word of the LORD came to Isaiah: ⁵"Go and tell Hezekiah, 'This is what the LORD, the God of your father David, says: I have heard your prayer and seen your tears; I will add fifteen years to your life. ⁶And I will deliver you and this city from the hand of the king of Assyria. I will defend this city.   2Ki 18:2; Isa 37:35

⁷" 'This is the LORD's sign to you that the LORD will do what he has promised: ⁸I will make the shadow cast by the sun go back the ten steps it has gone down on the stairway of Ahaz.' " So the sunlight went back the ten steps it had gone down.   2Ki 20:1-11; 2Ch 32:24-26

⁹A writing of Hezekiah king of Judah after his illness and recovery:

¹⁰I said, "In the prime of my life
    must I go through the gates
        of death\a   Ps 107:18; 2Co 1:9

\a 10 Hebrew *Sheol*

and be robbed of the rest of
my years?"   Job 17:11

[11]I said, "I will not again see the
LORD,
the LORD, in the land of the
living;   Ps 27:13; 116:9
no longer will I look on
mankind,
or be with those who now
dwell in this world.[a]

[12]Like a shepherd's tent my
house   2Co 5:1,4; 2Pe 1:13-14
has been pulled down and
taken from me.   Job 4:21
Like a weaver I have rolled up
my life,   Heb 1:12
and he has cut me off from
the loom;   Job 7:6
day and night you made an
end of me.   Ps 73:14

[13]I waited patiently till dawn,
but like a lion he broke all
my bones;   Job 10:16; Ps 51:8
day and night you made an
end of me.

[14]I cried like a swift or thrush,
I moaned like a mourning
dove.   Isa 59:11
My eyes grew weak as I looked
to the heavens.   Ps 6:7
I am troubled; O Lord, come
to my aid!"   Job 17:3

[15]But what can I say?
He has spoken to me, and
he himself has done
this.   Ps 39:9
I will walk humbly all my
years   1Ki 21:27

because of this anguish of
my soul.   Job 7:11

[16]Lord, by such things men
live;
and my spirit finds life in
them too.
You restored me to health
and let me live.   Ps 119:25

[17]Surely it was for my benefit
that I suffered such anguish.
In your love you kept me
from the pit of destruction;
you have put all my sins
behind your back.   Isa 43:25

[18]For the grave[b] cannot praise
you,   Ecc 9:10
death cannot sing your
praise;   Ps 6:5; 88:10-11
those who go down to the pit
cannot hope for your
faithfulness.

[19]The living, the living—they
praise you,   Dt 6:7; Ps 118:17
as I am doing today;
fathers tell their children
about your faithfulness.

[20]The LORD will save me,
and we will sing with
stringed instruments
all the days of our lives   Ps 116:2
in the temple of the LORD.

[21]Isaiah had said, "Prepare a
poultice of figs and apply it to the
boil, and he will recover."

[22]Hezekiah had asked, "What
will be the sign that I will go up to
the temple of the LORD?"   2Ch 32:31

---

[a]11 A few Hebrew manuscripts; most Hebrew manuscripts *in the place of cessation*   [b]18 Hebrew
Sheol

Envoys From Babylon

39 At that time Merodach-Baladan son of Baladan king of Babylon sent Hezekiah letters and a gift, because he had heard of his illness and recovery. ²Hezekiah received the envoys gladly and showed them what was in his storehouses—the silver, the gold, the spices, the fine oil, his entire armory and everything found among his treasures. There was nothing in his palace or in all his kingdom that Hezekiah did not show them.   2Ki 18:15; 2Ch 32:31

³Then Isaiah the prophet went to King Hezekiah and asked, "What did those men say, and where did they come from?"

"From a distant land," Hezekiah replied. "They came to me from Babylon."   Dt 28:49

⁴The prophet asked, "What did they see in your palace?"

"They saw everything in my palace," Hezekiah said. "There is nothing among my treasures that I did not show them."

⁵Then Isaiah said to Hezekiah, "Hear the word of the LORD Almighty: ⁶The time will surely come when everything in your palace, and all that your fathers have stored up until this day, will be carried off to Babylon. Nothing will be left, says the LORD. ⁷And some of your descendants, your own flesh and blood who will be born to you, will be taken away, and they will become eunuchs in the palace of the king of Babylon."

⁸"The word of the LORD you have spoken is good," Hezekiah replied. For he thought, "There will be peace and security in my lifetime."   2Ki 20:12-19; 2Ch 32:26

Comfort for God's People

40 Comfort, comfort my
    people,   Isa 12:1; 49:13
   says your God.
²Speak tenderly to Jerusalem,
   and proclaim to her
that her hard service has been
     completed,   Isa 41:11-13
   that her sin has been paid
     for,
that she has received from the
     LORD's hand
   double for all her sins.   Isa 61:7

³A voice of one calling:
"In the desert prepare
   the way for the LORD*a*;   Mal 3:1
make straight in the wilderness
   a highway for our God.*b*
⁴Every valley shall be raised up,
   every mountain and hill
     made low;
the rough ground shall become
     level,   Isa 45:2,13
   the rugged places a plain.
⁵And the glory of the LORD will
     be revealed,

---

a 3 Or *A voice of one calling in the desert: / "Prepare the way for the* LORD   *b* 3 Hebrew; Septuagint
make straight the paths of our God

and all mankind together
will see it.
    For the mouth of the
    LORD has spoken."

⁶A voice says, "Cry out."
And I said, "What shall I
cry?"

"All men are like grass,   Job 14:2
and all their glory is like the
flowers of the field.
⁷The grass withers and the
flowers fall,   Isa 15:6
because the breath of the
LORD blows on them.
Surely the people are grass.
⁸The grass withers and the
flowers fall,
but the word of our God
stands forever."   Isa 55:11

⁹You who bring good tidings to
Zion,   Isa 52:7-10; Ro 10:15
go up on a high mountain.
You who bring good tidings to
Jerusalem,ᵃ
lift up your voice with a
shout,
lift it up, do not be afraid;
say to the towns of Judah,
"Here is your God!"   Isa 25:9
¹⁰See, the Sovereign LORD comes
with power,   Rev 22:7
and his arm rules for him.
See, his reward is with him,
and his recompense
accompanies him.
¹¹He tends his flock like a
shepherd: Eze 34:23; Mic 5:4

He gathers the lambs in his
arms   Nu 11:12
and carries them close to his
heart;   Dt 26:19
he gently leads those that
have young.   Ge 33:13
¹²Who has measured the waters
in the hollow of his
hand,   Job 38:10; Pr 30:4
or with the breadth of his
hand marked off the
heavens?   Heb 1:10-12
Who has held the dust of the
earth in a basket,
or weighed the mountains
on the scales
and the hills in a balance?
¹³Who has understood the
mindᵇ of the LORD,
or instructed him as his
counselor?   Ro 11:34*
¹⁴Whom did the LORD consult to
enlighten him,
and who taught him the
right way?
Who was it that taught him
knowledge   Job 21:22; Col 2:3
or showed him the path of
understanding?   Job 12:13
¹⁵Surely the nations are like a
drop in a bucket;
they are regarded as dust on
the scales;   Ps 62:9
he weighs the islands as
though they were fine
dust.   Dt 9:21
¹⁶Lebanon is not sufficient for
altar fires,

ᵃ9 Or O Zion, bringer of good tidings, / go up on a high mountain. / O Jerusalem, bringer of good
tidings   ᵇ13 Or Spirit; or spirit

nor its animals enough for
    burnt offerings.   Ps 50:9-11
¹⁷Before him all the nations are
    as nothing;   Isa 29:7; 30:28
they are regarded by him as
    worthless
and less than nothing.   Da 4:35

¹⁸To whom, then, will you
    compare God?   Ex 8:10
What image will you
    compare him to?   Ac 17:29
¹⁹As for an idol, a craftsman
    casts it,   Ps 115:4
and a goldsmith overlays it
    with gold   Isa 2:20; 41:7
and fashions silver chains for
    it.
²⁰A man too poor to present
    such an offering
selects wood that will not
    rot.
He looks for a skilled
    craftsman
to set up an idol that will
    not topple.   1Sa 5:3

²¹Do you not know?
    Have you not heard?
Has it not been told you from
    the beginning?   Ps 19:1
Have you not understood
    since the earth was
    founded?   Ro 1:19; Isa 48:13
²²He sits enthroned above the
    circle of the earth,
and its people are like
    grasshoppers.   Ps 104:2
He stretches out the heavens
    like a canopy,   Job 22:14
and spreads them out like a
    tent to live in.   Job 36:29

²³He brings princes to naught
and reduces the rulers of
    this world to nothing.
²⁴No sooner are they planted,
no sooner are they sown,
no sooner do they take root
    in the ground,
than he blows on them and
    they wither,   Isa 41:16
and a whirlwind sweeps
    them away like chaff.

²⁵"To whom will you compare
    me?   ver 18; 1Ch 16:25
Or who is my equal?" says
    the Holy One.   Isa 1:4
²⁶Lift your eyes and look to the
    heavens: Isa 51:6
Who created all these?
He who brings out the starry
    host one by one,   Ps 147:4
and calls them each by
    name.
Because of his great power and
    mighty strength,   Isa 45:24
not one of them is missing.

²⁷Why do you say, O Jacob,
and complain, O Israel,
"My way is hidden from the
    LORD;
my cause is disregarded by
    my God"?   Job 27:2; Lk 18:7-8
²⁸Do you not know?
    Have you not heard?
The LORD is the everlasting
    God,   Ps 90:2
the Creator of the ends of
    the earth.   Isa 37:16
He will not grow tired or
    weary,   Isa 44:12

and his understanding no
    one can fathom.   Ps 147:5
²⁹He gives strength to the
    weary
    and increases the power of
      the weak.
³⁰Even youths grow tired and
    weary,
    and young men stumble and
      fall;   Isa 9:17; Jer 6:11; 9:21
³¹but those who hope in the
    Lᴏʀᴅ   Lk 18:1
  will renew their strength.
They will soar on wings like
    eagles;   Ps 103:5
  they will run and not grow
    weary,
  they will walk and not be
    faint.   2Co 4:1; Heb 12:1-3

The Helper of Israel

41 "Be silent before me, you
    islands!   Zec 2:13
Let the nations renew their
    strength!
Let them come forward and
    speak;   Isa 48:16
  let us meet together at the
    place of judgment.

²"Who has stirred up one from
    the east,   Ezr 1:2; Isa 45:1,13
  calling him in righteousness
    to his service*a*?
He hands nations over to him
  and subdues kings before
    him.
He turns them to dust with his
    sword,   2Sa 22:43

to windblown chaff with his
    bow.   Isa 40:24
³He pursues them and moves
    on unscathed,
  by a path his feet have not
    traveled before.
⁴Who has done this and carried
    it through,
  calling forth the generations
    from the beginning?
I, the Lᴏʀᴅ—with the first of
    them
  and with the last—I am he."

⁵The islands have seen it and
    fear;   Eze 26:17-18
  the ends of the earth
    tremble.   Isa 11:12
They approach and come
    forward;
⁶ each helps the other
  and says to his brother, "Be
    strong!"   Jos 1:6
⁷The craftsman encourages the
    goldsmith,   Isa 40:19
  and he who smooths with
    the hammer
  spurs on him who strikes the
    anvil.
He says of the welding, "It is
    good."
He nails down the idol so it
    will not topple.   1Sa 5:3

⁸"But you, O Israel, my servant,
Jacob, whom I have chosen,
  you descendants of Abraham
    my friend,   2Ch 20:7; Jas 2:23
⁹I took you from the ends of
    the earth,   Isa 11:12

---

a2 Or / whom victory meets at every step

from its farthest corners I
    called you.
I said, 'You are my servant';
    I have chosen you and have
        not rejected you.   Dt 7:6
¹⁰So do not fear, for I am with
        you;   Isa 43:2,5; Ro 8:31
    do not be dismayed, for I am
        your God.
I will strengthen you and help
        you;   ver 13-14; Isa 44:2
    I will uphold you with my
        righteous right hand.

¹¹"All who rage against you
    will surely be ashamed and
        disgraced;   Isa 45:24
those who oppose you   Ex 23:22
    will be as nothing and
        perish.   Isa 29:8
¹²Though you search for your
        enemies,
    you will not find them.
Those who wage war against
        you
    will be as nothing at all.
¹³For I am the LORD, your God,
    who takes hold of your right
        hand   Isa 42:6; 45:1
and says to you, Do not
        fear;
    I will help you.   ver 10
¹⁴Do not be afraid, O worm
        Jacob,   Ge 15:1; Job 4:19
    O little Israel,
for I myself will help you,"
        declares the LORD,
    your Redeemer, the Holy
        One of Israel.   Ex 15:13
¹⁵"See, I will make you into a
        threshing sledge,   Mic 4:13

new and sharp, with many
    teeth.
You will thresh the mountains
    and crush them,   Ex 19:18
and reduce the hills to
    chaff.
¹⁶You will winnow them, the
    wind will pick them up,
and a gale will blow them
    away.   Isa 40:24
But you will rejoice in the
    LORD   Isa 25:9
and glory in the Holy One of
    Israel.   Isa 45:25; Mi 1:24

¹⁷"The poor and needy search
    for water,   Isa 43:20
but there is none;
    their tongues are parched
        with thirst.
But I the LORD will answer
    them;   Isa 30:19
I, the God of Israel, will not
    forsake them.   Dt 31:6
¹⁸I will make rivers flow on
    barren heights,   Isa 30:25
and springs within the
    valleys.
I will turn the desert into pools
    of water,   Isa 43:19
and the parched ground into
    springs.   Isa 35:7
¹⁹I will put in the desert   Isa 35:1
    the cedar and the acacia, the
        myrtle and the olive.
I will set pines in the
    wasteland,
    the fir and the cypress
        together,   Isa 60:13
²⁰so that people may see and
    know,   Ex 6:7

may consider and
    understand,   Isa 29:24
that the hand of the Lord has
    done this,   Ezr 7:6; 8:31
that the Holy One of Israel
    has created it.   Job 12:9

²¹"Present your case," says the
    Lord.
"Set forth your arguments,"
    says Jacob's King.
²²"Bring in ⌐your idols⌐ to tell us
    what is going to happen.
Tell us what the former things
    were,
so that we may consider
    them
and know their final
    outcome.
Or declare to us the things to
    come,   Isa 46:10; Jn 13:19
²³   tell us what the future holds,
so we may know that you
    are gods.   Isa 42:9; 44:7-8; 45:3
Do something, whether good
    or bad,   Jer 10:5
so that we will be dismayed
    and filled with fear.
²⁴But you are less than nothing
    and your works are utterly
    worthless;
he who chooses you is
    detestable.   Ps 115:8

²⁵"I have stirred up one from the
    north, and he comes—
one from the rising sun who
    calls on my name.
He treads on rulers as if they
    were mortar,   2Sa 22:43
as if he were a potter
    treading the clay.

²⁶Who told of this from the
    beginning, so we could
    know,
or beforehand, so we could
    say, 'He was right'?
No one told of this,
    no one foretold it,
no one heard any words
    from you.   Hab 2:18-19
²⁷I was the first to tell Zion,
    'Look, here they are!'
I gave to Jerusalem a
    messenger of good
    tidings.   Isa 40:9
²⁸I look but there is no one—
    no one among them to give
    counsel,   Isa 40:13-14
no one to give answer when
    I ask them.
²⁹See, they are all false!
    Their deeds amount to
    nothing;   ver 24
their images are but wind
    and confusion.   Jer 5:13

The Servant of the Lord

42 "Here is my servant,
    whom I uphold,   Isa 20:3
my chosen one in whom I
    delight;   Isa 43:10; 1Pe 2:4,6
I will put my Spirit on him
    and he will bring justice to
    the nations.   Ge 49:10; Isa 9:7
²He will not shout or cry out,
    or raise his voice in the
    streets.
³A bruised reed he will not
    break,   Isa 36:6
and a smoldering wick he
    will not snuff out.

In faithfulness he will bring
forth justice;   Ps 72:2; 96:13
⁴ he will not falter or be
discouraged
till he establishes justice on
earth.   Isa 2:4
In his law the islands will
put their hope."

⁵This is what God the Lord
says—
he who created the heavens
and stretched them out,
who spread out the earth
and all that comes out
of it,   Ps 24:2
who gives breath to its people,
and life to those who walk
on it:
⁶"I, the Lord, have called you in
righteousness;   Isa 43:1
I will take hold of your
hand.
I will keep you and will make
you   Isa 26:3
to be a covenant for the
people   Isa 49:8
and a light for the Gentiles,
⁷to open eyes that are blind,
to free captives from prison
and to release from the
dungeon those who sit
in darkness.   Ps 107:10,14

⁸"I am the Lord; that is my
name!   Ex 3:15
I will not give my glory to
another   Isa 48:11
or my praise to idols.   Ex 8:10
⁹See, the former things have
taken place,   Isa 41:22
and new things I declare;

before they spring into being
I announce them to you."

Song of Praise to the Lord

¹⁰Sing to the Lord a new song,
his praise from the ends of
the earth,   Isa 49:6
you who go down to the sea,
and all that is in it,
you islands, and all who live
in them.   Isa 11:11
¹¹Let the desert and its towns
raise their voices;   Isa 32:16
let the settlements where
Kedar lives rejoice.
Let the people of Sela sing for
joy;
let them shout from the
mountaintops.   Isa 52:7
¹²Let them give glory to the Lord
and proclaim his praise in
the islands.   Ps 26:7; 66:2
¹³The Lord will march out like a
mighty man,   Isa 9:6
like a warrior he will stir up
his zeal;   Isa 26:11
with a shout he will raise the
battle cry   Hos 11:10
and will triumph over his
enemies.   Isa 66:14

¹⁴"For a long time I have kept
silent,   Ps 50:21
I have been quiet and held
myself back.   Ge 43:31
But now, like a woman in
childbirth,
I cry out, I gasp and pant.
¹⁵I will lay waste the mountains
and hills   Eze 38:20

and dry up all their
  vegetation;
I will turn rivers into islands
  and dry up the pools.   Isa 50:2
¹⁶I will lead the blind by ways
    they have not known,
  along unfamiliar paths I will
    guide them;
I will turn the darkness into
    light before them
  and make the rough places
    smooth.   Lk 3:5
These are the things I will do;
  I will not forsake them.
¹⁷But those who trust in idols,
  who say to images, 'You are
    our gods,'
  will be turned back in utter
    shame.   Ps 97:7; Isa 1:29; 44:11

Israel Blind and Deaf

¹⁸"Hear, you deaf;   Isa 35:5
  look, you blind, and see!
¹⁹Who is blind but my servant,
  and deaf like the messenger
    I send?   Isa 44:26
Who is blind like the one
    committed to me,   Isa 26:3
  blind like the servant of the
    LORD?
²⁰You have seen many things,
    but have paid no
    attention;
  your ears are open, but you
    hear nothing."   Jer 6:10
²¹It pleased the LORD
  for the sake of his
    righteousness
  to make his law great and
    glorious.   ver 4; 2Co 3:7

²²But this is a people plundered
    and looted,   2Ki 24:13
  all of them trapped in pits
    or hidden away in prisons.
They have become plunder,
    with no one to rescue them;
  they have been made loot,
    with no one to say, "Send
      them back."
²³Which of you will listen to this
    or pay close attention in
      time to come?   Isa 48:18
²⁴Who handed Jacob over to
      become loot,
  and Israel to the plunderers?
Was it not the LORD,
  against whom we have
    sinned?
For they would not follow his
    ways;   Isa 30:15
  they did not obey his law.
²⁵So he poured out on them his
    burning anger,   2Ki 22:13
  the violence of war.
It enveloped them in flames,
    yet they did not
    understand;   2Ki 25:9
  it consumed them, but they
    did not take it to heart.

Israel's Only Savior

43 But now, this is what the
     LORD says—
  he who created you,
    O Jacob,
  he who formed you,
    O Israel: Isa 44:21
"Fear not, for I have redeemed
    you;   Isa 44:2,6

I have summoned you by
name; you are mine.
²When you pass through the
waters,   Isa 8:7
I will be with you;   Dt 31:6,8
and when you pass through
the rivers,
they will not sweep over
you.
When you walk through the
fire,   Isa 29:6; 30:27
you will not be burned;
the flames will not set you
ablaze.   Ps 66:12; Da 3:25-27
³For I am the LORD, your
God,
the Holy One of Israel, your
Savior;   Ps 3:8; Isa 41:20
I give Egypt for your ransom,
Cush*a* and Seba in your
stead.   Pr 21:18; Isa 20:3
⁴Since you are precious and
honored in my sight,
and because I love you,
I will give men in exchange for
you,
and people in exchange for
your life.
⁵Do not be afraid, for I am with
you;   Isa 44:2; Jer 30:10-11
I will bring your children
from the east   Isa 41:8
and gather you from the
west.   Isa 24:14; Zec 8:7
⁶I will say to the north, 'Give
them up!'
and to the south, 'Do not
hold them back.'   Ps 107:3
Bring my sons from afar

and my daughters from the
ends of the earth—
⁷everyone who is called by my
name,   Isa 56:5; Jas 2:7
whom I created for my glory,
whom I formed and made."

⁸Lead out those who have eyes
but are blind,   Isa 6:9-10
who have ears but are
deaf.
⁹All the nations gather together
and the peoples assemble.
Which of them foretold this
and proclaimed to us the
former things?   Isa 41:26
Let them bring in their
witnesses to prove they
were right,
so that others may hear and
say, "It is true."
¹⁰"You are my witnesses,"
declares the LORD,
"and my servant whom I
have chosen,   Isa 41:8-9
so that you may know and
believe me   Ex 6:7
and understand that I am
he.
Before me no god was formed,
nor will there be one after
me.   Dt 4:35; Jer 14:22
¹¹I, even I, am the LORD,
and apart from me there is
no savior.   Isa 45:21
¹²I have revealed and saved and
proclaimed—
I, and not some foreign god
among you.   Dt 32:12; Ps 81:9

a 3 That is, the upper Nile region

You are my witnesses,"
     declares the LORD, "that
     I am God.   Isa 44:8
¹³ Yes, and from ancient days I
     am he.   Ps 90:2
No one can deliver out of my
     hand.
     When I act, who can reverse
     it?"   Isa 14:27

God's Mercy and Israel's Unfaithfulness

¹⁴This is what the LORD says—
     your Redeemer, the Holy
       One of Israel: Ex 15:13
"For your sake I will send to
     Babylon
and bring down as fugitives
     all the Babylonians,ª
in the ships in which they
     took pride.
¹⁵I am the LORD, your Holy One,
     Israel's Creator, your King."

¹⁶This is what the LORD says—
     he who made a way through
       the sea,
     a path through the mighty
       waters,   Isa 51:10
¹⁷who drew out the chariots and
     horses,   Ps 118:12; Isa 1:31
     the army and reinforcements
       together,   Ex 14:9
and they lay there, never to
     rise again,
     extinguished, snuffed out
       like a wick: Job 13:25
¹⁸"Forget the former things;
     do not dwell on the past.

¹⁹See, I am doing a new thing!
     Now it springs up; do you
       not perceive it?
I am making a way in the
       desert   Ex 17:6; Nu 20:11
and streams in the
       wasteland.   Ps 126:4
²⁰The wild animals honor me,
     the jackals and the owls,
because I provide water in the
       desert;   Isa 48:21
and streams in the
       wasteland,
to give drink to my people, my
       chosen,
²¹ the people I formed for
       myself   Mal 3:17
that they may proclaim my
       praise.   Ps 102:18; 1Pe 2:9
²²"Yet you have not called upon
       me, O Jacob,
you have not wearied
       yourselves for me,
       O Israel.   Isa 30:11
²³You have not brought me
       sheep for burnt
       offerings,
     nor honored me with your
       sacrifices.   Am 5:25; Zec 7:5-6
I have not burdened you with
       grain offerings
nor wearied you with
       demands for incense.
²⁴You have not bought any
       fragrant calamus for me,
or lavished on me the fat of
       your sacrifices.
But you have burdened me
       with your sins

ª 14 Or Chaldeans

and wearied me with your
offenses.   Isa 1:14; Mal 2:17

25"I, even I, am he who blots out
your transgressions, for my
own sake,   Ac 3:19; Eze 36:22
and remembers your sins no
more.   Jer 31:34
26Review the past for me,
let us argue the matter
together;   Isa 1:18
state the case for your
innocence.   Isa 41:1; 50:8
27Your first father sinned;
your spokesmen rebelled
against me.   Isa 9:15; 28:7
28So I will disgrace the
dignitaries of your
temple,
and I will consign Jacob to
destruction[a]
and Israel to scorn.   Jer 24:9

Israel the Chosen

44 "But now listen, O Jacob,
my servant,   Jer 30:10
Israel, whom I have chosen.
2This is what the LORD says—
he who made you, who
formed you in the
womb,   Ps 139:13; 149:2
and who will help you:
Do not be afraid, O Jacob, my
servant,
Jeshurun, whom I have
chosen.   Dt 32:15
3For I will pour water on the
thirsty land,   Joel 3:18

and streams on the dry
ground;   Isa 32:2
I will pour out my Spirit on
your offspring,   Joel 2:28
and my blessing on your
descendants.   Isa 61:9; 65:23
4They will spring up like grass
in a meadow,
like poplar trees by flowing
streams.   Lev 23:40; Job 40:22
5One will say, 'I belong to the
LORD';   Ps 116:16
another will call himself by
the name of Jacob;
still another will write on his
hand, 'The LORD's,'
and will take the name
Israel.

The LORD, Not Idols

6"This is what the LORD says—
Israel's King and Redeemer,
the LORD Almighty:
I am the first and I am the last;
apart from me there is no
God.   Dt 6:4; 1Ch 17:20
7Who then is like me? Let him
proclaim it.
Let him declare and lay out
before me
what has happened since I
established my ancient
people,
and what is yet to come—
yes, let him foretell what will
come.   Isa 41:22,26
8Do not tremble, do not be
afraid.

---

[a]28 The Hebrew term refers to the irrevocable giving over of things or persons to the LORD, often by
totally destroying them.

Did I not proclaim this and
  foretell it long ago?
You are my witnesses. Is there
  any God besides me?
No, there is no other Rock; I
  know not one."   Dt 4:35

⁹All who make idols are
  nothing,
  and the things they treasure
    are worthless.   Isa 41:24
Those who would speak up for
  them are blind;
  they are ignorant, to their
    own shame.   Isa 1:29
¹⁰Who shapes a god and casts an
  idol,
  which can profit him
    nothing?   Isa 41:29; Jer 10:5
¹¹He and his kind will be put to
  shame;   Isa 1:29
  craftsmen are nothing but
    men.
Let them all come together and
  take their stand;
  they will be brought down to
    terror and infamy.

¹²The blacksmith takes a tool
  and works with it in the
    coals;
  he shapes an idol with
    hammers,
  he forges it with the might
    of his arm.   Ac 17:29
He gets hungry and loses his
  strength;
  he drinks no water and
    grows faint.   Isa 40:28
¹³The carpenter measures with a
  line   Isa 41:7

and makes an outline with a
  marker;
he roughs it out with chisels
  and marks it with
    compasses.
He shapes it in the form of
  man,   Ps 115:4-7
  of man in all his glory,
  that it may dwell in a shrine.
¹⁴He cut down cedars,
  or perhaps took a cypress or
    oak.
He let it grow among the trees
  of the forest,
  or planted a pine, and the
    rain made it grow.
¹⁵It is man's fuel for burning;
  some of it he takes and
    warms himself,
  he kindles a fire and bakes
    bread.
But he also fashions a god and
  worships it;
  he makes an idol and bows
    down to it.   2Ch 25:14
¹⁶Half of the wood he burns in
  the fire;
  over it he prepares his meal,
  he roasts his meat and eats
    his fill.
He also warms himself and
  says,
  "Ah! I am warm; I see the
    fire."
¹⁷From the rest he makes a god,
  his idol;
  he bows down to it and
    worships.
He prays to it and says,   1Ki 18:26
  "Save me; you are my
    god."

18They know nothing, they
understand nothing;
their eyes are plastered over
so they cannot see,
and their minds closed so
they cannot understand.
19No one stops to think,
no one has the knowledge or
understanding to say,
"Half of it I used for fuel;
I even baked bread over its
coals,
I roasted meat and I ate.
Shall I make a detestable thing
from what is left?   Dt 27:15
Shall I bow down to a block
of wood?"
20He feeds on ashes, a deluded
heart misleads him;
he cannot save himself, or
say,
"Is not this thing in my right
hand a lie?"   Isa 59:3-4,13

21"Remember these things,
O Jacob,   Isa 46:8; Zec 10:9
for you are my servant,
O Israel.
I have made you, you are my
servant;   ver 1-2
O Israel, I will not forget
you.   Isa 49:15
22I have swept away your
offenses like a cloud,
your sins like the morning
mist.
Return to me,   Isa 55:7
for I have redeemed you."

23Sing for joy, O heavens, for the
LORD has done this;
shout aloud, O earth
beneath.   Ps 148:7
Burst into song, you
mountains,   Ps 98:8
you forests and all your
trees,
for the LORD has redeemed
Jacob,
he displays his glory in
Israel.   Isa 61:3

Jerusalem to Be Inhabited

24"This is what the LORD says—
your Redeemer, who formed
you in the womb:
I am the LORD,
who has made all things,
who alone stretched out the
heavens,   Isa 42:5
who spread out the earth by
myself,

25who foils the signs of false
prophets   Ps 33:10
and makes fools of diviners,
who overthrows the learning of
the wise   1Co 1:27
and turns it into nonsense,
26who carries out the words of
his servants   Zec 1:6
and fulfills the predictions of
his messengers,   Isa 55:11

who says of Jerusalem, 'It shall
be inhabited,'
of the towns of Judah, 'They
shall be built,'
and of their ruins, 'I will
restore them,'   Isa 49:8-21
27who says to the watery deep,
'Be dry,

and I will dry up your
   streams,'   Isa 11:15
²⁸who says of Cyrus, 'He is my
   shepherd   2Ch 36:22
   and will accomplish all that I
     please;
he will say of Jerusalem,
   "Let it be rebuilt,"
   and of the temple, "Let its
     foundations be laid." '

45 "This is what the LORD
    says to his anointed,
   to Cyrus, whose right hand I
     take hold of   Ps 73:23
to subdue nations before him
   and to strip kings of their
     armor,
to open doors before him
   so that gates will not be
     shut:
²I will go before you   Ex 23:20
   and will level the
     mountains ͣ;   Isa 40:4
I will break down gates of
     bronze
   and cut through bars of iron.
³I will give you the treasures of
     darkness,   Jer 50:37
   riches stored in secret
     places,   Jer 41:8
so that you may know that I
     am the LORD,   Isa 41:23
the God of Israel, who
     summons you by name.
⁴For the sake of Jacob my
     servant,   Isa 41:8-9
   of Israel my chosen,
I summon you by name

and bestow on you a title of
   honor,
though you do not
   acknowledge me.   Ac 17:23
⁵I am the LORD, and there is no
     other;   Isa 44:8
   apart from me there is no
     God.   Ps 18:31
I will strengthen you,   Ps 18:39
   though you have not
     acknowledge me,
⁶so that from the rising of the
     sun
   to the place of its setting
men may know there is none
     besides me.   Isa 11:9
I am the LORD, and there is
     no other.
⁷I form the light and create
     darkness,
   I bring prosperity and create
     disaster;   Isa 31:2; Am 3:6
I, the LORD, do all these
     things.

⁸"You heavens above, rain
     down righteousness;
   let the clouds shower it
     down.
Let the earth open wide,
   let salvation spring up,
let righteousness grow with it;
   I, the LORD, have created it.

⁹"Woe to him who quarrels
     with his Maker,   Job 15:25
   to him who is but a potsherd
     among the potsherds on
     the ground.
Does the clay say to the potter,

ͣ2 Dead Sea Scrolls and Septuagint; the meaning of the word in the Masoretic Text is uncertain.

'What are you making?'
Does your work say,
    'He has no hands'?
[10]Woe to him who says to his
        father,
    'What have you begotten?'
or to his mother,
    'What have you brought to
        birth?'

[11]"This is what the LORD says—
    the Holy One of Israel, and
        its Maker: Isa 1:4; 51:13
Concerning things to come,
    do you question me about
        my children,
    or give me orders about the
        work of my hands?
[12]It is I who made the earth
    and created mankind upon
        it.
My own hands stretched out
        the heavens;   Ge 2:1; Isa 42:5
    I marshaled their starry
        hosts.   Ne 9:6
[13]I will raise up Cyrus[a] in my
        righteousness: Isa 41:2
    I will make all his ways
        straight.   Ps 26:12; Isa 40:4
He will rebuild my city
    and set my exiles free,
but not for a price or reward,
    says the LORD Almighty."

[14]This is what the LORD says:

"The products of Egypt and the
        merchandise of Cush,[b]
    and those tall Sabeans—
they will come over to you

and will be yours;
they will trudge behind you,
    coming over to you in
        chains.   Isa 14:1-2
They will bow down before
        you
    and plead with you, saying,
'Surely God is with you, and
        there is no other;
    there is no other god.' "

[15]Truly you are a God who hides
        himself,   Ps 44:24
    O God and Savior of Israel.
[16]All the makers of idols will be
        put to shame and
        disgraced;   Isa 44:9,11
    they will go off into disgrace
        together.
[17]But Israel will be saved by the
        LORD   Ro 11:26
    with an everlasting salvation;
you will never be put to shame
        or disgraced,   Ge 30:23
    to ages everlasting.

[18]For this is what the LORD
        says—
    he who created the heavens,
        he is God;
    he who fashioned and made
        the earth,
        he founded it;
    he did not create it to be
        empty,   Ge 1:2
    but formed it to be
        inhabited—   Ge 1:26; Isa 42:5
he says:
"I am the LORD,
    and there is no other.   ver 5

<hr>

[a]13 Hebrew *him*   [b]14 That is, the upper Nile region

¹⁹I have not spoken in secret,
   from somewhere in a land of
      darkness;
I have not said to Jacob's
   descendants,   Isa 41:8
'Seek me in vain.'   2Ch 15:2
I, the LORD, speak the truth;
   I declare what is right.

²⁰"Gather together and come;
   assemble, you fugitives from
      the nations.
Ignorant are those who carry
   about idols of wood,
who pray to gods that
   cannot save.   Isa 46:6-7
²¹Declare what is to be, present
      it—
let them take counsel
      together.
Who foretold this long ago,
   who declared it from the
      distant past?
Was it not I, the LORD?
   And there is no God apart
      from me,   ver 5; Ps 46:10
a righteous God and a Savior;
   there is none but me.

²²"Turn to me and be saved,
   all you ends of the earth;
for I am God, and there is
      no other.   Hos 13:4
²³By myself I have sworn,   Ge 22:16
   my mouth has uttered in all
      integrity   Heb 6:13
a word that will not be
      revoked: Isa 55:11
Before me every knee will
      bow;

by me every tongue will
      swear.   Ro 14:11*; Php 2:10-11
²⁴They will say of me, 'In the
   LORD alone
are righteousness and
      strength.' "   Jer 33:16
All who have raged against
      him
   will come to him and be put
      to shame.   Isa 41:11
²⁵But in the LORD all the
      descendants of Israel
   will be found righteous and
      will exult.   Isa 41:16

Gods of Babylon

46 Bel bows down, Nebo
   stoops low;   Isa 21:9; Jer 50:2
their idols are borne by
   beasts of burden.ᵃ   1Sa 5:2
The images that are carried
      about are burdensome,
   a burden for the weary.
²They stoop and bow down
      together;
unable to rescue the burden,
they themselves go off into
      captivity.   Jdg 18:17-18

³"Listen to me, O house of
      Jacob,   ver 12; Isa 48:12
all you who remain of the
      house of Israel,   Isa 1:9
you whom I have upheld since
      you were conceived,
and have carried since your
      birth.   Ps 22:10
⁴Even to your old age and gray
      hairs   Ps 71:18

ᵃ 1 Or *are but beasts and cattle*

I am he, I am he who will
  sustain you.   Isa 43:13
I have made you and I will
  carry you;
I will sustain you and I will
  rescue you.   Ps 18:35

5"To whom will you compare
  me or count me equal?
To whom will you liken me
  that we may be
  compared?   Isa 40:18,25
6Some pour out gold from their
  bags
and weigh out silver on the
  scales;
they hire a goldsmith to make
  it into a god,   Isa 40:19
and they bow down and
  worship it.   Isa 44:17
7They lift it to their shoulders
  and carry it;   ver 1
they set it up in its place,
  and there it stands.
From that spot it cannot
  move.
Though one cries out to it, it
  does not answer;   1Ki 18:26
it cannot save him from his
  troubles.   Isa 44:17; 45:20

8"Remember this, fix it in
  mind,
take it to heart, you rebels.
9Remember the former things,
  those of long ago;   Dt 32:7
I am God, and there is no
  other;
I am God, and there is none
  like me.   Isa 45:5,21

10I make known the end from
  the beginning,
from ancient times, what is
  still to come.   Isa 45:21
I say: My purpose will stand,
  and I will do all that I
  please.
11From the east I summon a bird
  of prey;
from a far-off land, a man to
  fulfill my purpose.
What I have said, that will I
  bring about;
what I have planned, that
  will I do.   Isa 25:1; Jer 44:28
12Listen to me, you
  stubborn-hearted,   ver 3
you who are far from
  righteousness.   Jer 2:5
13I am bringing my
  righteousness near,
it is not far away;
and my salvation will not be
  delayed.   Ps 85:9
I will grant salvation to Zion,
  my splendor to Israel.   Isa 44:23

The Fall of Babylon

47 "Go down, sit in the dust,
  Virgin Daughter of
  Babylon;   Isa 23:12
sit on the ground without a
  throne,
Daughter of the
  Babylonians.*a*   Jer 51:33
No more will you be called
  tender or delicate.   Dt 28:56
2Take millstones and grind
  flour;   Ex 11:5; Mt 24:41

a 1 Or *Chaldeans*; also in verse 5

take off your veil.   Ge 24:65
Lift up your skirts, bare your
        legs,   Isa 32:11
and wade through the
        streams.
³Your nakedness will be
        exposed   Eze 16:37; Na 3:5
and your shame uncovered.
I will take vengeance;   Isa 34:8
I will spare no one.”

⁴Our Redeemer—the Lord
        Almighty is his name—
        is the Holy One of Israel.

⁵“Sit in silence, go into
        darkness,   Isa 13:10
        Daughter of the Babylonians;
no more will you be called
        queen of kingdoms.   Isa 13:19
⁶I was angry with my people
        and desecrated my
        inheritance;   Dt 13:15
I gave them into your hand,
        and you showed them no
        mercy.   Isa 14:6
Even on the aged
        you laid a very heavy yoke.
⁷You said, ‘I will continue
        forever—
        the eternal queen!’   ver 5
But you did not consider these
        things
or reflect on what might
        happen.   Dt 32:29; Isa 42:23,25

⁸“Now then, listen, you wanton
        creature,
        lounging in your security
and saying to yourself,
        ‘I am, and there is none
        besides me.   Isa 45:6; Zep 2:15

I will never be a widow   Rev 18:7
        or suffer the loss of
        children.’
⁹Both of these will overtake
        you
        in a moment, on a single
        day: 1Th 5:3; Rev 18:8-10
        loss of children and
        widowhood.   Isa 13:18
They will come upon you in
        full measure,
        in spite of your many
        sorceries   Na 3:4
        and all your potent spells.
¹⁰You have trusted in your
        wickedness   Ps 52:7; 62:10
        and have said, ‘No one sees
        me.’   Isa 29:15
Your wisdom and knowledge
        mislead you   Isa 5:21; 44:20
        when you say to yourself,
        ‘I am, and there is none
        besides me.’
¹¹Disaster will come upon you,
        and you will not know how
        to conjure it away.
A calamity will fall upon you
        that you cannot ward off
        with a ransom;
a catastrophe you cannot
        foresee
will suddenly come upon
        you.   1Th 5:3

¹²“Keep on, then, with your
        magic spells
        and with your many
        sorceries,   ver 9; Ex 7:11
        which you have labored at
        since childhood.
Perhaps you will succeed,

perhaps you will cause
terror.

¹³All the counsel you have
received has only worn
you out!   Isa 57:10; Jer 51:58
Let your astrologers come
forward,   Isa 44:25
those stargazers who make
predictions month by
month,
let them save you from what
is coming upon you.

¹⁴Surely they are like stubble;
the fire will burn them up.
They cannot even save
themselves
from the power of the flame.
Here are no coals to warm
anyone;
here is no fire to sit by.

¹⁵That is all they can do for
you—
these you have labored
with
and trafficked with since
childhood.   Rev 18:11
Each of them goes on in his
error;
there is not one that can
save you.   ver 13; Isa 44:17

Stubborn Israel

48 "Listen to this, O house
of Jacob,
you who are called by the
name of Israel   Ge 17:5
and come from the line of
Judah,
you who take oaths in the
name of the LORD

and invoke the God of
Israel—   Isa 58:2
but not in truth or
righteousness—   Jer 4:2

²you who call yourselves
citizens of the holy city
and rely on the God of
Israel—   Mic 3:11; Ro 2:17
the LORD Almighty is his
name: Isa 47:4

³I foretold the former things
long ago,   Isa 41:22
my mouth announced them
and I made them
known;   Isa 45:21
then suddenly I acted, and
they came to pass.

⁴For I knew how stubborn you
were;   Dt 31:27
the sinews of your neck
were iron,   Ex 32:9; Ac 7:51
your forehead was bronze.

⁵Therefore I told you these
things long ago;
before they happened I
announced them to
you
so that you could not say,
'My idols did them;   Jer 44:15-18
my wooden image and metal
god ordained them.'

⁶You have heard these things;
look at them all.
Will you not admit them?

"From now on I will tell you of
new things,   Isa 41:22
of hidden things unknown to
you.

⁷They are created now, and not
long ago;   Isa 45:21

you have not heard of them
before today.
So you cannot say,
'Yes, I knew of them.'   Ex 6:7
⁸You have neither heard nor
understood;   Isa 1:3
from of old your ear has not
been open.   Dt 29:4
Well do I know how
treacherous you are;
you were called a rebel from
birth.   Dt 9:7,24; Ps 58:3
⁹For my own name's sake I
delay my wrath;   Ps 78:38
for the sake of my praise I
hold it back from you,
so as not to cut you off.
¹⁰See, I have refined you, though
not as silver;
I have tested you in the
furnace of affliction.
¹¹For my own sake, for my own
sake, I do this.   1Sa 12:22
How can I let myself be
defamed?   Dt 32:27
I will not yield my glory to
another.   Isa 42:8

Israel Freed

¹²"Listen to me, O Jacob,   Isa 46:3
Israel, whom I have called:
I am he;   Isa 43:13
I am the first and I am the
last.   Isa 41:4; Rev 1:17; 22:13
¹³My own hand laid the
foundations of the earth,
and my right hand spread
out the heavens;   Ex 20:11
when I summon them,

they all stand up together.
¹⁴"Come together, all of you, and
listen: Isa 43:9
Which of ₜthe idolsₗ has
foretold these things?
The LORD's chosen ally
will carry out his purpose
against Babylon;
his arm will be against the
Babylonians.ᵃ
¹⁵I, even I, have spoken;
yes, I have called him.   Isa 45:1
I will bring him,
and he will succeed in his
mission.

¹⁶"Come near me and listen to
this: Isa 41:1

"From the first announcement I
have not spoken in
secret;   Isa 45:19
at the time it happens, I am
there."

And now the Sovereign LORD
has sent me,   Zec 2:9,11
with his Spirit.   Isa 11:2

¹⁷This is what the LORD says—
your Redeemer, the Holy
One of Israel: Isa 43:14; 49:7
"I am the LORD your God,
who teaches you what is
best for you,   Isa 28:9
who directs you in the way
you should go.   Ps 32:8
¹⁸If only you had paid attention
to my commands,

ᵃ *14* Or *Chaldeans*; also in verse 20

your peace would have been
   like a river,   Ps 119:165
your righteousness like the
   waves of the sea.   Isa 45:8
¹⁹Your descendants would have
   been like the sand,
your children like its
   numberless grains;
their name would never be cut
   off   Isa 56:5; 66:22
nor destroyed from before
   me."

²⁰Leave Babylon,
   flee from the Babylonians!
Announce this with shouts of
   joy   Isa 49:13
   and proclaim it.
Send it out to the ends of the
   earth;
   say, "The Lord has
   redeemed his servant
   Jacob."   Isa 52:9; 63:9
²¹They did not thirst when he
   led them through the
   deserts;   Isa 41:17
he made water flow for them
   from the rock;   Isa 30:25
he split the rock
   and water gushed out.   Ex 17:6

²²"There is no peace," says the
   Lord, "for the wicked."

The Servant of the Lord

49 Listen to me, you islands;
   hear this, you distant
   nations:
Before I was born the Lord
   called me;   Isa 44:24; 46:3
from my birth he has made
   mention of my name.
²He made my mouth like a
   sharpened sword,   Isa 11:4
in the shadow of his hand
   he hid me;   Ps 91:1
he made me into a polished
   arrow   Dt 32:23; Zec 9:13
and concealed me in his
   quiver.
³He said to me, "You are my
   servant,   Zec 3:8
Israel, in whom I will display
   my splendor."   Isa 44:23
⁴But I said, "I have labored to
   no purpose;
I have spent my strength in
   vain and for nothing.
Yet what is due me is in the
   Lord's hand,
and my reward is with my
   God."   Isa 35:4

⁵And now the Lord says—
he who formed me in the
   womb to be his servant
to bring Jacob back to him
   and gather Israel to himself,
for I am honored in the eyes of
   the Lord   Isa 43:4
and my God has been my
   strength—   Ps 18:1
⁶he says:
"It is too small a thing for you
   to be my servant
to restore the tribes of
   Jacob
and bring back those of
   Israel I have kept.   Isa 1:9
I will also make you a light for
   the Gentiles,   Lk 2:32; Jn 1:9

that you may bring my
   salvation to the ends of
   the earth."   Jn 11:52; Ac 13:47*

⁷This is what the LORD says—
   the Redeemer and Holy One
   of Israel—   Isa 48:17
to him who was despised and
   abhorred by the nation,
to the servant of rulers:
"Kings will see you and rise
   up,   Isa 52:15
   princes will see and bow
   down,
because of the LORD, who is
   faithful,   1Co 1:9
the Holy One of Israel, who
   has chosen you."   Isa 14:1

Restoration of Israel

⁸This is what the LORD says:

"In the time of my favor I will
   answer you,   Ps 69:13
and in the day of salvation I
   will help you;   2Co 6:2*
I will keep you and will make
   you   Isa 26:3
to be a covenant for the
   people,   Isa 42:6
to restore the land   Isa 44:26
and to reassign its desolate
   inheritances,   Isa 60:21
⁹to say to the captives, 'Come
   out,'   Isa 42:7; Lk 4:19
and to those in darkness, 'Be
   free!'

"They will feed beside the
   roads

and find pasture on every
   barren hill.   Isa 41:18
¹⁰They will neither hunger nor
   thirst,   Isa 33:16
nor will the desert heat or
   the sun beat upon them.
He who has compassion on
   them will guide them
and lead them beside springs
   of water.   Isa 35:7
¹¹I will turn all my mountains
   into roads,
and my highways will be
   raised up.   Isa 11:16; 40:4
¹²See, they will come from
   afar—   Isa 43:5-6
some from the north, some
   from the west,
some from the region of
   Aswan.ᵃ"

¹³Shout for joy, O heavens;
   rejoice, O earth;
   burst into song,
   O mountains!   Isa 44:23
For the LORD comforts his
   people   Isa 40:1; 2Co 1:4
and will have compassion on
   his afflicted ones.   Ps 9:12

¹⁴But Zion said, "The LORD has
   forsaken me,   Ps 9:10; 71:11
the Lord has forgotten me."

¹⁵"Can a mother forget the baby
   at her breast
and have no compassion on
   the child she has borne?
Though she may forget,
   I will not forget you!   Isa 44:21

────────────────
ᵃ 12 Dead Sea Scrolls; Masoretic Text *Sinim*

¹⁶See, I have engraved you on
    the palms of my hands;
your walls are ever before
    me.   Ps 48:12-13; Isa 62:6
¹⁷Your sons hasten back,
and those who laid you
    waste depart from you.
¹⁸Lift up your eyes and look
    around;
all your sons gather and
    come to you.   Isa 60:4; 43:5
As surely as I live," declares
    the Lord,   Ro 14:11*
"you will wear them all as
    ornaments;   Isa 52:1
you will put them on, like a
    bride.

¹⁹"Though you were ruined and
    made desolate   Isa 54:1,3
and your land laid waste,
now you will be too small for
    your people,   Zec 10:10
and those who devoured you
    will be far away.   Isa 1:20
²⁰The children born during your
    bereavement
will yet say in your hearing,
'This place is too small for
    us;
give us more space to live
    in.'   Isa 54:1-3
²¹Then you will say in your
    heart,
'Who bore me these?
I was bereaved and barren;
    I was exiled and rejected.
Who brought these up?
I was left all alone,   Isa 1:8

but these—where have they
    come from?' "

²²This is what the Sovereign
Lord says: Ge 15:2

"See, I will beckon to the
    Gentiles,
I will lift up my banner to
    the peoples;   Isa 11:10
they will bring your sons in
    their arms   Isa 11:12
and carry your daughters on
    their shoulders.   Isa 60:4
²³Kings will be your foster
    fathers,   Isa 60:3,10-11
and their queens your
    nursing mothers.   Isa 60:16
They will bow down before
    you with their faces to
    the ground;
they will lick the dust at
    your feet.   Ps 72:9
Then you will know that I am
    the Lord;   Mic 7:17
those who hope in me will
    not be disappointed."

²⁴Can plunder be taken from
    warriors,   Mt 12:29; Lk 11:21
or captives rescued from the
    fierce[a]?

²⁵But this is what the Lord says:

"Yes, captives will be taken
    from warriors,   Isa 14:2
and plunder retrieved from
    the fierce;
I will contend with those who
    contend with you,

[a] 24 Dead Sea Scrolls, Vulgate and Syriac (see also Septuagint and verse 25); Masoretic Text *righteous*

and your children I will
save.
26I will make your oppressors eat
their own flesh;   Isa 9:4,20
they will be drunk on their
own blood, as with
wine.   Rev 16:6
Then all mankind will know
that I, the LORD, am your
Savior,   Isa 25:9
your Redeemer, the Mighty
One of Jacob."   Isa 48:17

Israel's Sin and the Servant's Obedience

50 This is what the LORD says:
"Where is your mother's
certificate of divorce
with which I sent her away?
Or to which of my creditors
did I sell you?   Ne 5:5; Mt 18:25
Because of your sins you were
sold;   Dt 32:30; Isa 52:3
because of your
transgressions your
mother was sent away.
2When I came, why was there
no one?
When I called, why was
there no one to answer?
Was my arm too short to
ransom you?   Nu 11:23
Do I lack the strength to
rescue you?   Ge 18:14
By a mere rebuke I dry up the
sea,   Ex 14:22; Jos 3:16
I turn rivers into a desert;
their fish rot for lack of water
and die of thirst.
3I clothe the sky with darkness

and make sackcloth its
covering."   Rev 6:12
4The Sovereign LORD has given
me an instructed
tongue,   Ex 4:12
to know the word that
sustains the weary.
He wakens me morning by
morning,   Ps 5:3; 119:147
wakens my ear to listen like
one being taught.   Isa 28:9
5The Sovereign LORD has
opened my ears,   Isa 35:5
and I have not been
rebellious;   Mt 26:39; Jn 14:31
I have not drawn back.
6I offered my back to those who
beat me,   Isa 53:5; Mt 27:30
my cheeks to those who
pulled out my beard;
I did not hide my face
from mocking and spitting.
7Because the Sovereign LORD
helps me,   Isa 42:1
I will not be disgraced.
Therefore have I set my face
like flint,   Eze 3:8-9
and I know I will not be put
to shame.   Isa 28:16
8He who vindicates me is
near.
Who then will bring charges
against me?   Isa 43:26
Let us face each other!
Who is my accuser?
Let him confront me!
9It is the Sovereign LORD who
helps me.   Isa 41:10
Who is he that will condemn
me?   Ro 8:1,34

They will all wear out like a
    garment;
  the moths will eat them up.

[10]Who among you fears the Lord
  and obeys the word of his
    servant?   Isa 49:3
Let him who walks in the dark,
  who has no light,   Ps 107:14
trust in the name of the Lord
  and rely on his God.
[11]But now, all you who light
    fires
  and provide yourselves with
    flaming torches,   Pr 26:18
go, walk in the light of your
    fires   Jas 3:6
and of the torches you have
    set ablaze.
This is what you shall receive
    from my hand: Pr 26:27
You will lie down in
    torment.   Isa 65:13-15

Everlasting Salvation for Zion

51 "Listen to me, you who
    pursue righteousness
and who seek the Lord:
Look to the rock from which
  you were cut   Isa 17:10
and to the quarry from
    which you were hewn;
[2]look to Abraham, your father,
  and to Sarah, who gave you
    birth.
When I called him he was but
    one,
  and I blessed him and made
    him many.   Ge 12:2
[3]The Lord will surely comfort
    Zion   Isa 40:1

and will look with
  compassion on all her
    ruins;   Isa 52:9
he will make her deserts like
    Eden,   Ge 2:8
her wastelands like the
    garden of the Lord.
Joy and gladness will be found
    in her, Isa 25:9; 66:10
thanksgiving and the sound
    of singing.   Jer 17:26

[4]"Listen to me, my people;
  hear me, my nation:
The law will go out from me;
  my justice will become a
    light to the nations.
[5]My righteousness draws near
    speedily,
  my salvation is on the way,
  and my arm will bring
    justice to the nations.
The islands will look to me
  and wait in hope for my
    arm.   Ge 49:10; Ps 37:9
[6]Lift up your eyes to the
    heavens,
  look at the earth beneath;
the heavens will vanish like
    smoke,   Mt 24:35; 2Pe 3:10
the earth will wear out like a
    garment   Ps 102:25-26
and its inhabitants die like
    flies.
But my salvation will last
    forever,   Ps 119:89
  my righteousness will never
    fail.   Ps 89:33

[7]"Hear me, you who know what
  is right,

you people who have my
  law in your hearts:
Do not fear the reproach of
  men
or be terrified by their
  insults.   Mt 5:11; Ac 5:41
⁸For the moth will eat them up
  like a garment;   Isa 50:9
the worm will devour them
  like wool.   Isa 14:11
But my righteousness will last
  forever,   ver 6
my salvation through all
  generations."

⁹Awake, awake! Clothe yourself
  with strength,   Isa 52:1
O arm of the Lord;
awake, as in days gone by,
  as in generations of old.
Was it not you who cut Rahab
  to pieces,   Job 9:13
who pierced that monster
  through?   Ps 74:13
¹⁰Was it not you who dried up
  the sea,   Ex 14:22
the waters of the great
  deep,
who made a road in the depths
  of the sea   Job 36:30
so that the redeemed might
  cross over?   Ex 15:13
¹¹The ransomed of the Lord will
  return.   Isa 35:9
They will enter Zion with
  singing;   Ps 109:28
everlasting joy will crown
  their heads.
Gladness and joy will overtake
  them,   Jer 33:11

and sorrow and sighing will
  flee away.   Rev 7:17
¹²"I, even I, am he who comforts
  you.   2Co 1:4
Who are you that you fear
  mortal men,   Ps 118:6
the sons of men, who are
  but grass,   1Pe 1:24
¹³that you forget the Lord your
  Maker,   Isa 17:10; 45:11
who stretched out the
  heavens   Ps 104:2; Isa 48:13
and laid the foundations of
  the earth,
that you live in constant terror
  every day   Isa 7:4
because of the wrath of the
  oppressor,
who is bent on destruction?
For where is the wrath of the
  oppressor?   Isa 9:4
¹⁴   The cowering prisoners will
  soon be set free;
they will not die in their
  dungeon,
  nor will they lack bread.
¹⁵For I am the Lord your God,
  who churns up the sea so
    that its waves roar—
  the Lord Almighty is his
    name.   Isa 13:4
¹⁶I have put my words in your
  mouth   Dt 18:18; Isa 59:21
and covered you with the
  shadow of my hand—
I who set the heavens in place,
  who laid the foundations of
    the earth,   Isa 48:13
and who say to Zion, 'You
  are my people.' "   Jer 7:23

The Cup of the LORD's Wrath

17Awake, awake!   Isa 52:1
   Rise up, O Jerusalem,
you who have drunk from the
      hand of the LORD
   the cup of his wrath,   Job 21:20
you who have drained to its
      dregs   Ps 75:8
   the goblet that makes men
      stagger.   Ps 60:3
18Of all the sons she bore   Ps 88:18
   there was none to guide her;
of all the sons she reared
   there was none to take her
      by the hand.
19These double calamities have
      come upon you —   Isa 47:9
   who can comfort you? —
ruin and destruction, famine
      and sword —   Isa 14:30
   who can*a* console you?
20Your sons have fainted;
   they lie at the head of every
      street,   Isa 5:25; Jer 14:16
   like antelope caught in a net.
They are filled with the wrath
      of the LORD   Job 40:11
   and the rebuke of your God.

21Therefore hear this, you
      afflicted one,   Isa 14:32
   made drunk, but not with
      wine.   Isa 29:9
22This is what your Sovereign
      LORD says,
   your God, who defends his
      people: Isa 49:25
"See, I have taken out of your
      hand

the cup that made you
      stagger;   ver 17; Jer 25:15
from that cup, the goblet of my
      wrath,
   you will never drink again.
23I will put it into the hands of
      your tormentors,
   who said to you,
'Fall prostrate that we may
   walk over you.'   Zec 12:2
And you made your back like
      the ground,
   like a street to be walked
      over."   Ps 66:12

52 Awake, awake, O Zion,
      clothe yourself with
         strength.   Isa 51:9
Put on your garments of
      splendor,   Ps 110:3
   O Jerusalem, the holy city.
The uncircumcised and defiled
   will not enter you again.
2Shake off your dust;   Isa 29:4
   rise up, sit enthroned,
      O Jerusalem.
Free yourself from the chains
      on your neck,   Ps 81:6
   O captive Daughter of Zion.

3For this is what the LORD says:

"You were sold for nothing,
   and without money you will
      be redeemed."   Isa 45:13

4For this is what the Sovereign
LORD says:

"At first my people went down
   to Egypt to live;   Ge 46:6

---

a 19 Dead Sea Scrolls, Septuagint, Vulgate and Syriac; Masoretic Text / *how can I*

lately, Assyria has oppressed
        them.

5"And now what do I have
here?" declares the LORD.

"For my people have been
        taken away for nothing,
and those who rule them
        mock,[a]"
                declares the LORD.
"And all day long
        my name is constantly
        blasphemed.   Eze 36:20
6Therefore my people will know
        my name;   Isa 49:23
therefore in that day they
        will know   Isa 10:20
that it is I who foretold it.
        Yes, it is I."

7How beautiful on the
        mountains
are the feet of those who
        bring good news,
who proclaim peace,   Eph 6:15
who bring good tidings,
who proclaim salvation,
who say to Zion,
        "Your God reigns!"   Ps 93:1
8Listen! Your watchmen lift up
        their voices;   Isa 62:6
together they shout for joy.
When the LORD returns to
        Zion,   Isa 59:20
they will see it with their
        own eyes.
9Burst into songs of joy
        together,   Ps 98:4
you ruins of Jerusalem,

for the LORD has comforted his
        people,   Lk 2:25
he has redeemed Jerusalem.
10The LORD will lay bare his holy
        arm   Ps 44:3
in the sight of all the
        nations,   Isa 66:18
and all the ends of the earth
        will see   Isa 11:9
the salvation of our God.

11Depart, depart, go out from
        there!   Isa 48:20
Touch no unclean thing!
Come out from it and be pure,
        you who carry the vessels of
        the LORD.   2Ch 36:10
12But you will not leave in haste
        or go in flight;
for the LORD will go before
        you,   Mic 2:13
the God of Israel will be
        your rear guard.   Ex 14:19

The Suffering and Glory of the Servant

13See, my servant will act
        wisely[b];   Isa 42:1
he will be raised and lifted
        up and highly exalted.
14Just as there were many who
        were appalled at him[c]—
his appearance was so
        disfigured beyond that
        of any man   2Sa 10:4
and his form marred beyond
        human likeness—
15so will he sprinkle many
        nations,[d]   Lev 14:7; 16:14-15

---

a5 Dead Sea Scrolls and Vulgate; Masoretic Text *wail*   b13 Or *will prosper*   c14 Hebrew *you*
d15 Hebrew; Septuagint *so will many nations marvel at him*

and kings will shut their
mouths because of him.
For what they were not told,
they will see,
and what they have not
heard, they will
understand.   Ro 15:21*

53 Who has believed our
message   Ro 10:16*
and to whom has the arm of
the LORD been revealed?
²He grew up before him like a
tender shoot,   2Ki 19:26
and like a root out of dry
ground.   Isa 11:10
He had no beauty or majesty
to attract us to him,
nothing in his appearance
that we should desire
him.   Isa 52:14
³He was despised and rejected
by men,
a man of sorrows, and
familiar with suffering.
Like one from whom men hide
their faces   Dt 31:17
he was despised, and we
esteemed him not.   Ps 22:6

⁴Surely he took up our
infirmities
and carried our sorrows,
yet we considered him stricken
by God,   Jn 19:7
smitten by him, and
afflicted.   Ge 12:17; Ru 1:21
⁵But he was pierced for our
transgressions,   Ro 4:25

he was crushed for our
iniquities;   Ps 34:18
the punishment that brought
us peace was upon him,
and by his wounds we are
healed.   1Pe 2:24-25
⁶We all, like sheep, have gone
astray,   Ps 95:10; 1Pe 2:24-25
each of us has turned to his
own way;   1Sa 8:3
and the LORD has laid on him
the iniquity of us all.   Ex 28:38

⁷He was oppressed and
afflicted,   Isa 49:26
yet he did not open his
mouth;   Mk 14:61
he was led like a lamb to the
slaughter,   Ps 44:22
and as a sheep before her
shearers is silent,
so he did not open his
mouth.
⁸By oppression[a] and judgment
he was taken away.
And who can speak of his
descendants?
For he was cut off from the
land of the living;   Da 9:26
for the transgression of my
people he was stricken.[b]
⁹He was assigned a grave with
the wicked,
and with the rich in his
death,   Mt 27:57-60
though he had done no
violence,   Isa 42:1-3
nor was any deceit in his
mouth.   1Pe 2:22*

---

[a]8 Or From arrest   [b]8 Or away. / Yet who of his generation considered / that he was cut off from the
land of the living / for the transgression of my people, / to whom the blow was due?

¹⁰Yet it was the LORD's will to
crush him and cause
him to suffer,   Isa 46:10
and though the LORD makes*ᵃ*
his life a guilt offering,
he will see his offspring and
prolong his days,   Ps 22:30
and the will of the LORD will
prosper in his hand.
¹¹After the suffering of his soul,
he will see the light ⌊of life⌋*ᵇ*
and be satisfied*ᶜ*;
by his knowledge*ᵈ* my
righteous servant will
justify many,   Ro 5:18-19
and he will bear their
iniquities.   Ex 28:38
¹²Therefore I will give him a
portion among the
great,*ᵉ*   Php 2:9
and he will divide the spoils
with the strong,*ᶠ*   Lk 11:22
because he poured out his life
unto death,   Mt 26:28,38-39,42
and was numbered with the
transgressors.   Lk 22:37*
For he bore the sin of many,
and made intercession for
the transgressors.   Ro 8:34

The Future Glory of Zion

54 "Sing, O barren woman,
you who never bore a
child;
burst into song, shout for joy,
you who were never in
labor;   Isa 66:7

because more are the children
of the desolate woman
than of her who has a
husband,"   Gal 4:27*
   says the LORD.
²"Enlarge the place of your
tent,
stretch your tent curtains
wide,
do not hold back;
lengthen your cords,
strengthen your stakes.
³For you will spread out to the
right and to the left;
your descendants will
dispossess nations
and settle in their desolate
cities.   Isa 49:19

⁴"Do not be afraid; you will not
suffer shame.   Isa 28:16
Do not fear disgrace; you
will not be humiliated.
You will forget the shame of
your youth   Jer 2:2
and remember no more the
reproach of your
widowhood.   Isa 51:7
⁵For your Maker is your
husband—   Jer 3:14
the LORD Almighty is his
name—
the Holy One of Israel is your
Redeemer;   Isa 48:17
he is called the God of all
the earth.   Isa 6:3
⁶The LORD will call you back

ᵃ 10 Hebrew *though you make*   *ᵇ* 11 Dead Sea Scrolls (see also Septuagint); Masoretic Text does not
have *the light ⌊of life⌋.*   *ᶜ* 11 Or (with Masoretic Text) *¹¹He will see the result of the suffering of his soul
/ and be satisfied*   *ᵈ* 11 Or *by knowledge of him*   *ᵉ* 12 Or *many*   *ᶠ* 12 Or *numerous*

as if you were a wife
   deserted and distressed
   in spirit—   *Isa 62:4,12*
a wife who married young,
   only to be rejected," says
   your God.
⁷"For a brief moment I
   abandoned you,   *Isa 26:20*
but with deep compassion I
   will bring you back.
⁸In a surge of anger   *Isa 60:10*
I hid my face from you for a
   moment,   *Isa 1:15*
but with everlasting kindness
I will have compassion on
   you,"   *Ps 102:13; Isa 14:1*
says the LORD your
   Redeemer.   *Isa 48:17*

⁹"To me this is like the days of
   Noah,
when I swore that the waters
   of Noah would never
   again cover the earth.
So now I have sworn not to be
   angry with you,   *Isa 12:1*
   never to rebuke you again.
¹⁰Though the mountains be
   shaken   *Ps 46:2; Rev 6:14*
and the hills be removed,
yet my unfailing love for you
   will not be shaken
nor my covenant of peace be
   removed,"   *Ps 89:34; Isa 42:6*
says the LORD, who has
   compassion on you.   *ver 8*
¹¹"O afflicted city, lashed by
   storms and not
   comforted,   *Isa 14:32; 28:2*

I will build you with stones
   of turquoise,ᵃ   *1Ch 29:2*
your foundations with
   sapphires.ᵇ   *Isa 28:16*
¹²I will make your battlements of
   rubies,
your gates of sparkling
   jewels,
and all your walls of
   precious stones.
¹³All your sons will be taught by
   the LORD,   *Jn 6:45*; Heb 8:11*
and great will be your
   children's peace.   *Isa 48:18*
¹⁴In righteousness you will be
   established: *Isa 26:2*
Tyranny will be far from you;
   you will have nothing to
   fear.   *Zep 3:15*
Terror will be far removed;
   it will not come near you.
¹⁵If anyone does attack you, it
   will not be my doing;
whoever attacks you will
   surrender to you.

¹⁶"See, it is I who created the
   blacksmith   *Isa 44:12*
who fans the coals into
   flame
and forges a weapon fit for
   its work.   *Isa 10:5*
And it is I who have created
   the destroyer to work
   havoc;   *Isa 13:5*
¹⁷ no weapon forged against
   you will prevail,   *Isa 29:8*
and you will refute every
   tongue that accuses you.

ᵃ 11 The meaning of the Hebrew for this word is uncertain.   ᵇ 11 Or *lapis lazuli*

This is the heritage of the
　　servants of the Lord,
and this is their vindication
　　from me,"　　　　Ps 17:2
　　　　declares the Lord.

Invitation to the Thirsty

55 "Come, all you who are
　　thirsty,　　　Jn 4:14; 7:37
come to the waters;　　Jer 2:13
and you who have no money,
　　come, buy and eat!　　Rev 3:18
Come, buy wine and milk
　　without money and without
　　cost.　　　Hos 14:4; Mt 10:8
²Why spend money on what is
　　not bread,
and your labor on what does
　　not satisfy?　　Ps 22:26; Hos 8:7
Listen, listen to me, and eat
　　what is good,　　　Isa 1:19
and your soul will delight in
　　the richest of fare.
³Give ear and come to me;
　　hear me, that your soul may
　　live.　　　Lev 18:5; Ro 10:5
I will make an everlasting
　　covenant with you,
　　my faithful love promised to
　　David.　　　Ac 13:34*; Isa 54:8
⁴See, I have made him a
　　witness to the peoples,
　　a leader and commander of
　　the peoples.
⁵Surely you will summon
　　nations you know not,
　　and nations that do not
　　know you will hasten to
　　you,　　　Isa 2:3
because of the Lord your God,

the Holy One of Israel,　Isa 12:6
for he has endowed you
　　with splendor."　　Isa 60:9
⁶Seek the Lord while he may be
　　found;　　　Ps 32:6; 2Co 6:1-2
call on him while he is near.
⁷Let the wicked forsake his way
　　and the evil man his
　　thoughts.　　　Isa 32:7; 59:7
Let him turn to the Lord, and
　　he will have mercy on
　　him,　　　Isa 44:22; 54:10
and to our God, for he will
　　freely pardon.　　Isa 1:18; 40:2
⁸"For my thoughts are not your
　　thoughts,　　　Php 2:5; 4:8
neither are your ways my
　　ways,"　　　Isa 53:6; Mic 4:12
　　　declares the Lord.
⁹"As the heavens are higher
　　than the earth,　　Ps 103:11
so are my ways higher than
　　your ways
and my thoughts than your
　　thoughts.　　　Isa 40:13-14
¹⁰As the rain and the snow
　　come down from heaven,
and do not return to it
　　without watering the earth
and making it bud and
　　flourish,　　　Ps 67:6
so that it yields seed for the
　　sower and bread for the
　　eater,　　　2Co 9:10
¹¹so is my word that goes out
　　from my mouth:　　Dt 32:2
It will not return to me
　　empty,　　　Isa 45:23
but will accomplish what I
　　desire

and achieve the purpose for
  which I sent it. Isa 44:26
[12]You will go out in joy Ps 98:4
  and be led forth in peace;
  the mountains and hills
  will burst into song before
    you, Ps 65:12-13
  and all the trees of the field
  will clap their hands. Ps 98:8
[13]Instead of the thornbush will
  grow the pine tree,
  and instead of briers the
    myrtle will grow. Isa 5:6
This will be for the LORD's
  renown, Isa 63:12
  for an everlasting sign,
  which will not be
    destroyed."

Salvation for Others

56 This is what the LORD says:
  "Maintain justice Isa 1:17
  and do what is right, Isa 26:8
  for my salvation is close at
    hand Ps 85:9
  and my righteousness will
    soon be revealed. Jer 23:6
[2]Blessed is the man who does
    this, Ps 119:2
  the man who holds it fast,
  who keeps the Sabbath without
    desecrating it, Ex 20:8,10
  and keeps his hand from
    doing any evil."

[3]Let no foreigner who has
    bound himself to the
    LORD say, Ex 12:43
  "The LORD will surely
    exclude me from his
    people." Dt 23:3

And let not any eunuch
    complain, Ac 8:27
  "I am only a dry tree."

[4]For this is what the LORD says:

"To the eunuchs who keep my
    Sabbaths,
  who choose what pleases me
  and hold fast to my
    covenant— Ex 31:13
[5]to them I will give within my
    temple and its walls
  a memorial and a name
  better than sons and
    daughters;
  I will give them an everlasting
    name
  that will not be cut off.
[6]And foreigners who bind
    themselves to the LORD
  to serve him, Isa 60:7,10; 61:5
  to love the name of the LORD,
  and to worship him,
  all who keep the Sabbath
    without desecrating it
  and who hold fast to my
    covenant—
[7]these I will bring to my holy
    mountain Isa 2:2
  and give them joy in my
    house of prayer.
  Their burnt offerings and
    sacrifices Ro 12:1; Heb 13:15
  will be accepted on my altar;
  for my house will be called
  a house of prayer for all
    nations." Mt 21:13*; Mk 11:17*
[8]The Sovereign LORD declares—
  he who gathers the exiles of
    Israel:

"I will gather still others to
    them   Isa 11:12; Jn 10:16
besides those already
    gathered."

God's Accusation Against the Wicked

⁹Come, all you beasts of the
    field,   Jer 12:9
come and devour, all you
    beasts of the forest!
¹⁰Israel's watchmen are blind,
    they all lack knowledge;
they are all mute dogs,
    they cannot bark;
they lie around and dream,
    they love to sleep.   Na 3:18
¹¹They are dogs with mighty
    appetites;
    they never have enough.
They are shepherds who lack
    understanding;   Isa 1:3
they all turn to their own
    way,   Isa 53:6
    each seeks his own gain.
¹²"Come," each one cries, "let
    me get wine!   Lev 10:9
Let us drink our fill of beer!
And tomorrow will be like
    today,
    or even far better."   Lk 12:18-19

57 The righteous perish,
    and no one ponders it in
    his heart;   Isa 42:25
devout men are taken away,
    and no one understands
that the righteous are taken
    away
    to be spared from evil.

²Those who walk uprightly
    enter into peace;
they find rest as they lie in
    death.   Da 12:13

³"But you—come here, you
    sons of a sorceress,
you offspring of adulterers
    and prostitutes!   Isa 1:21
⁴Whom are you mocking?
    At whom do you sneer
    and stick out your tongue?
Are you not a brood of rebels,
    the offspring of liars?
⁵You burn with lust among the
    oaks
    and under every spreading
    tree;   2Ki 16:4
you sacrifice your children in
    the ravines   Lev 18:21
    and under the overhanging
    crags.
⁶The idols among the smooth
    stones of the ravines are
    your portion;   Jer 3:9
    they, they are your lot.
Yes, to them you have poured
    out drink offerings
    and offered grain offerings.
In the light of these things,
    should I relent?   Jer 5:9,29
⁷You have made your bed on a
    high and lofty hill;   Jer 3:6
there you went up to offer
    your sacrifices.   Jer 13:27
⁸Behind your doors and your
    doorposts
you have put your pagan
    symbols.
Forsaking me, you uncovered
    your bed,

you climbed into it and
    opened it wide;
you made a pact with those
    whose beds you love,
and you looked on their
    nakedness.   Eze 23:18
⁹You went to Molech[a] with
    olive oil   1Ki 11:5
and increased your
    perfumes.
You sent your ambassadors[b]
    far away;   Eze 23:16,40
you descended to the grave[c]
    itself!   Isa 8:19
¹⁰You were wearied by all your
    ways,
but you would not say, 'It is
    hopeless.'   Jer 2:25; 18:12
You found renewal of your
    strength,
and so you did not faint.

¹¹"Whom have you so dreaded
    and feared   Pr 29:25
that you have been false to
    me,
and have neither remembered
    me   Jer 2:32; 3:21
nor pondered this in your
    hearts?   Isa 42:23
Is it not because I have long
    been silent   Ps 50:21
that you do not fear me?
¹²I will expose your
    righteousness and your
    works,   Isa 29:15; Mic 3:2-4,8
and they will not benefit
    you.
¹³When you cry out for help,

let your collection ˌof idolsˌ
    save you!
The wind will carry all of them
    off,
a mere breath will blow
    them away.   Is 40:7,24
But the man who makes me
    his refuge   Ps 118:8
will inherit the land   Ps 37:9
and possess my holy
    mountain."   Isa 65:9-11

Comfort for the Contrite

¹⁴And it will be said:

"Build up, build up, prepare
    the road!
Remove the obstacles out of
    the way of my people."
¹⁵For this is what the high and
    lofty One says—   Isa 52:13
he who lives forever, whose
    name is holy: Dt 33:27
"I live in a high and holy
    place,   Job 16:19
but also with him who is
    contrite and lowly in
    spirit,   Ps 34:18; 51:17; 147:3
to revive the spirit of the lowly
and to revive the heart of the
    contrite.   Isa 61:1
¹⁶I will not accuse forever,
    nor will I always be angry,
for then the spirit of man
    would grow faint before
    me—
the breath of man that I
    have created.   Ge 2:7

─────────────────────

ᵃ9 Or *to the king*   ᵇ9 Or *idols*   ᶜ9 Hebrew *Sheol*

17I was enraged by his sinful
        greed;   Isa 56:11
I punished him, and hid my
        face in anger,   Isa 1:15
yet he kept on in his willful
        ways.   Isa 1:4
18I have seen his ways, but I will
        heal him;   Isa 30:26
I will guide him and restore
        comfort to him,   Isa 61:1-3
19 creating praise on the lips of
        the mourners in Israel.
Peace, peace, to those far and
        near,"   Ac 2:39; Eph 2:17
says the LORD. "And I will
        heal them."
20But the wicked are like the
        tossing sea,   Job 18:5-21
which cannot rest,
whose waves cast up mire
        and mud.   Ps 69:14
21"There is no peace," says my
        God, "for the wicked."

True Fasting

58 "Shout it aloud, do not
        hold back.   Isa 40:6
Raise your voice like a
        trumpet.   Ex 20:18
Declare to my people their
        rebellion   Isa 48:8
and to the house of Jacob
        their sins.   Isa 57:12
2For day after day they seek me
        out;   Isa 48:1; Tit 1:16; Jas 4:8
they seem eager to know my
        ways,
as if they were a nation that
        does what is right

and has not forsaken the
        commands of its God.
They ask me for just decisions
and seem eager for God to
        come near them.   Isa 29:13
3'Why have we fasted,' they
        say,   Lev 16:29
'and you have not seen
        it?
Why have we humbled
        ourselves,   Ex 10:3
and you have not noticed?'

"Yet on the day of your fasting,
        you do as you please
and exploit all your workers.
4Your fasting ends in quarreling
        and strife,   1Ki 21:9-13; Isa 59:6
and in striking each other
        with wicked fists.
You cannot fast as you do
        today
and expect your voice to be
        heard on high.   Isa 59:2
5Is this the kind of fast I have
        chosen,   Zec 7:5
only a day for a man to
        humble himself?   1Ki 21:27
Is it only for bowing one's
        head like a reed
and for lying on sackcloth
        and ashes?   Job 2:8
Is that what you call a fast,
a day acceptable to the
        LORD?
6"Is not this the kind of fasting
        I have chosen: Joel 2:12-14
to loose the chains of
        injustice
and untie the cords of the
        yoke,

to set the oppressed free   Jer 34:9
   and break every yoke?   Isa 9:4
⁷Is it not to share your food
   with the hungry   Eze 18:16
and to provide the poor
   wanderer with shelter—
when you see the naked, to
   clothe him,   Job 31:19-20
and not to turn away from
   your own flesh and
   blood?   Ge 29:14; Lk 10:31-32
⁸Then your light will break
   forth like the dawn,
   and your healing will quickly
   appear;   Isa 30:26
then your righteousness[a] will
   go before you,   Isa 26:2
and the glory of the Lord
   will be your rear guard.
⁹Then you will call, and the
   Lord will answer;   Ps 50:15
you will cry for help, and he
   will say: Here am I.

"If you do away with the yoke
   of oppression,
with the pointing finger and
   malicious talk,   Ps 12:2
¹⁰and if you spend yourselves in
   behalf of the hungry
and satisfy the needs of the
   oppressed,   Dt 15:7-8
then your light will rise in the
   darkness,   Isa 42:16
and your night will become
   like the noonday.
¹¹The Lord will guide you
   always;   Ps 48:14
he will satisfy your needs in

a sun-scorched land
   and will strengthen your
   frame.   Ps 72:16
You will be like a well-watered
   garden,   SS 4:15
like a spring whose waters
   never fail.   Jn 4:14
¹²Your people will rebuild the
   ancient ruins   Isa 49:8
and will raise up the age-old
   foundations;   Isa 44:28
you will be called Repairer of
   Broken Walls,   Ne 2:17
Restorer of Streets with
   Dwellings.

¹³"If you keep your feet from
   breaking the Sabbath
and from doing as you
   please on my holy
   day,
if you call the Sabbath a
   delight   Ps 84:2,10
and the Lord's holy day
   honorable,
and if you honor it by not
   going your own way
and not doing as you please
   or speaking idle words,
¹⁴then you will find your joy in
   the Lord,   Job 22:26
and I will cause you to ride
   on the heights of the
   land   Dt 32:13
and to feast on the
   inheritance of your
   father Jacob."   Ps 105:10-11
   The mouth of the Lord
   has spoken.

---

a 8 Or your righteous One

Sin, Confession and Redemption

59 Surely the arm of the LORD is not too short to save,   Nu 11:23; Isa 50:2
nor his ear too dull to hear.
²But your iniquities have separated
you from your God;
your sins have hidden his face from you,
so that he will not hear.
³For your hands are stained with blood,   Isa 1:15
your fingers with guilt.   Ps 7:3
Your lips have spoken lies,
and your tongue mutters wicked things.
⁴No one calls for justice;   Isa 5:23
no one pleads his case with integrity.
They rely on empty arguments and speak lies;   Isa 44:20
they conceive trouble and give birth to evil.
⁵They hatch the eggs of vipers
and spin a spider's web.
Whoever eats their eggs will die,
and when one is broken, an adder is hatched.
⁶Their cobwebs are useless for clothing;
they cannot cover themselves with what they make.   Isa 28:20
Their deeds are evil deeds,
and acts of violence are in their hands.   Isa 58:4
⁷Their feet rush into sin;

they are swift to shed innocent blood.   Pr 6:17
Their thoughts are evil thoughts;   Mk 7:21-22
ruin and destruction mark their ways.   Ro 3:15-17*
⁸The way of peace they do not know;   Ro 3:15-17*
there is no justice in their paths.
They have turned them into crooked roads;
no one who walks in them will know peace.   Isa 57:21

⁹So justice is far from us,
and righteousness does not reach us.
We look for light, but all is darkness;   Isa 5:30
for brightness, but we walk in deep shadows.
¹⁰Like the blind we grope along the wall,   Dt 28:29
feeling our way like men without eyes.
At midday we stumble as if it were twilight;   Isa 8:15
among the strong, we are like the dead.   La 3:6
¹¹We all growl like bears;
we moan mournfully like doves.   Isa 38:14; Eze 7:16
We look for justice, but find none;
for deliverance, but it is far away.

¹²For our offenses are many in your sight,   Ezr 9:6
and our sins testify against us.   Isa 3:9

Our offenses are ever with us,
  and we acknowledge our
    iniquities: Ps 51:3
¹³rebellion and treachery against
    the Lord,   Isa 46:8
  turning our backs on our
    God,   Tit 1:16
  fomenting oppression and
    revolt,   Isa 5:7
  uttering lies our hearts have
    conceived.   Mk 7:21-22
¹⁴So justice is driven back,
  and righteousness stands at
    a distance;   Isa 1:21
  truth has stumbled in the
    streets,   Isa 48:1
  honesty cannot enter.
¹⁵Truth is nowhere to be found,
  and whoever shuns evil
    becomes a prey.

The Lord looked and was
    displeased
  that there was no justice.
¹⁶He saw that there was no one,
  he was appalled that there
    was no one to intervene;
  so his own arm worked
    salvation for him,   Ps 98:1
  and his own righteousness
    sustained him.   Isa 45:8,13
¹⁷He put on righteousness as his
    breastplate,   Eph 6:14
  and the helmet of salvation
    on his head;   1Th 5:8
  he put on the garments of
    vengeance   Isa 63:3
  and wrapped himself in zeal
    as in a cloak.   Isa 9:7

¹⁸According to what they have
    done,
  so will he repay   Mt 16:27
  wrath to his enemies
    and retribution to his foes;
  he will repay the islands
    their due.
¹⁹From the west, men will fear
    the name of the Lord,
  and from the rising of the
    sun, they will revere his
    glory.   Ps 113:3
For he will come like a pent-up
    flood
  that the breath of the Lord
    drives along.ᵃ   Isa 11:4

²⁰"The Redeemer will come to
    Zion,   Job 19:25; Isa 52:8
  to those in Jacob who repent
    of their sins,"   Ro 11:26-27*
  declares the Lord.

²¹"As for me, this is my covenant
with them," says the Lord. "My
Spirit, who is on you, and my
words that I have put in your
mouth will not depart from your
mouth, or from the mouths of your
children, or from the mouths of
their descendants from this time
on and forever," says the Lord.

The Glory of Zion

60 "Arise, shine, for your
    light has come,   Eph 5:14
  and the glory of the Lord
    rises upon you.   Isa 4:5

ᵃ19 Or When the enemy comes in like a flood, / the Spirit of the Lord will put him to flight

²See, darkness covers the earth
  and thick darkness is over
    the peoples,   Col 1:13
but the LORD rises upon you
  and his glory appears over
    you.
³Nations will come to your
    light,   Isa 45:14; Rev 21:24
  and kings to the brightness
    of your dawn.   Isa 49:23

⁴"Lift up your eyes and look
    about you:
  All assemble and come to
    you;   Isa 11:12
your sons come from afar,
  and your daughters are
    carried on the arm.
⁵Then you will look and be
    radiant,   Ex 34:29
  your heart will throb and
    swell with joy;   Isa 35:2
the wealth on the seas will be
    brought to you,   Dt 33:19
  to you the riches of the
    nations will come.
⁶Herds of camels will cover
    your land,
  young camels of Midian and
    Ephah.   Ge 25:2,4
And all from Sheba will come,
  bearing gold and incense
  and proclaiming the praise of
    the LORD.   Isa 42:10
⁷All Kedar's flocks will be
    gathered to you,   Ge 25:13
  the rams of Nebaioth will
    serve you;
they will be accepted as
  offerings on my altar,

and I will adorn my glorious
    temple.   Hag 2:3,7,9

⁸"Who are these that fly along
    like clouds,   Isa 49:21
  like doves to their nests?
⁹Surely the islands look to me;
  in the lead are the ships of
    Tarshish,ᵃ   Isa 2:16
bringing your sons from afar,
  with their silver and gold,
to the honor of the LORD your
    God,   Ps 22:23
  the Holy One of Israel,
  for he has endowed you
    with splendor.   Isa 55:5

¹⁰"Foreigners will rebuild your
    walls,   Isa 14:1-2
  and their kings will serve
    you.   Isa 49:23; Rev 21:24
Though in anger I struck you,
  in favor I will show you
    compassion.   Isa 54:8
¹¹Your gates will always stand
    open,   Isa 62:10; Rev 21:25
  they will never be shut, day
    or night,
so that men may bring you the
    wealth of the nations—
  their kings led in triumphal
    procession.   Ps 149:8
¹²For the nation or kingdom that
    will not serve you will
    perish;   Isa 14:2
  it will be utterly ruined.

¹³"The glory of Lebanon will
    come to you,   Isa 35:2

the pine, the fir and the
　　cypress together,　Isa 41:19
to adorn the place of my
　　sanctuary;
and I will glorify the place of
　　my feet.　1Ch 28:2; Ps 132:7
¹⁴The sons of your oppressors
　　will come bowing before
　　you;　Isa 14:2
all who despise you will bow
　　down at your feet
and will call you the City of
　　the Lord,　Isa 1:26
Zion of the Holy One of
　　Israel.　Heb 12:22

¹⁵"Although you have been
　　forsaken and hated,
with no one traveling
　　through,　Isa 33:8
I will make you the everlasting
　　pride　Isa 4:2
　　and the joy of all
　　generations.　Isa 65:18
¹⁶You will drink the milk of
　　nations
and be nursed at royal
　　breasts.　Isa 49:23; 66:11-12
Then you will know that I, the
　　Lord, am your Savior,
　　your Redeemer, the Mighty
　　One of Jacob.　Isa 59:20
¹⁷Instead of bronze I will bring
　　you gold,
　　and silver in place of
　　iron.
Instead of wood I will bring
　　you bronze,
　　and iron in place of stones.
I will make peace your
　　governor　Ps 85:8; Isa 66:12

and righteousness your
　　ruler.
¹⁸No longer will violence be
　　heard in your land,
nor ruin or destruction
　　within your borders,
but you will call your walls
　　Salvation　Isa 26:1
and your gates Praise.　Isa 61:11
¹⁹The sun will no more be your
　　light by day,
nor will the brightness of the
　　moon shine on you,
for the Lord will be your
　　everlasting light,　Rev 22:5
and your God will be your
　　glory.　Zec 2:5; Rev 21:23
²⁰Your sun will never set
　　again,
　　and your moon will wane no
　　more;
the Lord will be your
　　everlasting light,
and your days of sorrow will
　　end.　Isa 35:10
²¹Then will all your people be
　　righteous　Rev 21:27
and they will possess the
　　land forever.　Ps 37:11,22
They are the shoot I have
　　planted,　Mt 15:13
the work of my hands,
for the display of my
　　splendor.　Isa 52:1
²²The least of you will become a
　　thousand,
　　the smallest a mighty
　　nation.
I am the Lord;
　　in its time I will do this
　　swiftly."　Isa 5:19

The Year of the LORD's Favor

61 The Spirit of the
Sovereign LORD is on
me,   Isa 11:2
because the LORD has
anointed me   Ps 45:7
to preach good news to the
poor.   Mt 11:5; Lk 7:22
He has sent me to bind up the
brokenhearted,   Isa 57:15
to proclaim freedom for the
captives   Isa 42:7; 49:9
and release from darkness
for the prisoners,[a]
²to proclaim the year of the
LORD's favor   Lk 4:18-19*
and the day of vengeance of
our God,   Isa 34:8
to comfort all who mourn,
³   and provide for those who
grieve in Zion—
to bestow on them a crown of
beauty   Isa 3:23
instead of ashes,
the oil of gladness   Isa 1:6
instead of mourning,
and a garment of praise
instead of a spirit of
despair.
They will be called oaks of
righteousness,
a planting of the LORD   Ps 1:3
for the display of his
splendor.   Isa 60:20-21

⁴They will rebuild the ancient
ruins   Isa 49:8; Eze 36:33; Am 9:14
and restore the places long
devastated;

they will renew the ruined
cities
that have been devastated
for generations.
⁵Aliens will shepherd your
flocks;   Isa 14:1-2
foreigners will work your
fields and vineyards.
⁶And you will be called priests
of the LORD,   Ex 19:6; 1Pe 2:5
you will be named ministers
of our God.
You will feed on the wealth of
nations,   Isa 60:11
and in their riches you will
boast.

⁷Instead of their shame
my people will receive a
double portion,   Isa 40:2
and instead of disgrace
they will rejoice in their
inheritance;
and so they will inherit a
double portion in their
land,   Isa 60:21
and everlasting joy will be
theirs.   Isa 25:9

⁸"For I, the LORD, love justice;
I hate robbery and
iniquity.
In my faithfulness I will reward
them
and make an everlasting
covenant with them.
⁹Their descendants will be
known among the
nations   Isa 43:5

---

a 1 Hebrew; Septuagint *the blind*

and their offspring among
the peoples.
All who see them will
acknowledge
that they are a people the
LORD has blessed."

¹⁰I delight greatly in the
LORD;
my soul rejoices in my
God.
For he has clothed me with
garments of salvation
and arrayed me in a robe of
righteousness,   Ps 132:9
as a bridegroom adorns his
head like a priest,
and as a bride adorns herself
with her jewels.   Isa 49:18
¹¹For as the soil makes the
sprout come up
and a garden causes seeds to
grow,
so the Sovereign LORD will
make righteousness and
praise   Ps 85:11
spring up before all nations.

Zion's New Name

62 For Zion's sake I will not
keep silent,   Ps 50:21
for Jerusalem's sake I will
not remain quiet,
till her righteousness shines
out like the dawn,   Isa 1:26
her salvation like a blazing
torch.   Ps 67:2
²The nations will see your
righteousness,   Isa 52:10

and all kings your glory;
you will be called by a new
name   ver 4,12; Isa 1:26
that the mouth of the LORD
will bestow.
³You will be a crown of
splendor in the LORD's
hand,   Zec 9:16; 1Th 2:19
a royal diadem in the hand
of your God.
⁴No longer will they call you
Deserted,   Isa 54:6
or name your land Desolate.
But you will be called
Hephzibah,ᵃ
and your land Beulahᵇ;
for the LORD will take delight
in you,   Jer 32:41; Zep 3:17
and your land will be
married.   Jer 3:14; Hos 2:19
⁵As a young man marries a
maiden,
so will your sonsᶜ marry
you;
as a bridegroom rejoices over
his bride,
so will your God rejoice over
you.   Isa 65:19; Zep 3:17
⁶I have posted watchmen on
your walls, O Jerusalem;
they will never be silent day
or night.
You who call on the LORD,
give yourselves no rest,
⁷and give him no rest till he
establishes Jerusalem
and makes her the praise of
the earth.   Dt 26:19

ᵃ4 *Hephzibah* means *my delight is in her.*   ᵇ4 *Beulah* means *married.*   ᶜ5 Or *Builder*

8The Lord has sworn by his
      right hand
and by his mighty arm:
"Never again will I give your
      grain
      as food for your enemies,
and never again will foreigners
      drink the new wine
      for which you have toiled;
9but those who harvest it will
      eat it   Isa 1:19
      and praise the Lord,   Dt 12:7
and those who gather the
      grapes will drink it
      in the courts of my
      sanctuary."   Lev 23:39

10Pass through, pass through the
      gates!   Isa 60:11
      Prepare the way for the
      people.
Build up, build up the
      highway!   Isa 11:16; 57:14
      Remove the stones.
Raise a banner for the nations.

11The Lord has made
      proclamation
      to the ends of the earth:
"Say to the Daughter of
      Zion,
      'See, your Savior comes!
See, his reward is with him,
      and his recompense
      accompanies him.' "
12They will be called the Holy
      People,   ver 4; Ge 32:28; 1Pe 2:9
      the Redeemed of the Lord;
and you will be called Sought
      After,
      the City No Longer Deserted.

God's Day of Vengeance and Redemption

63 Who is this coming from
      Edom,   2Ch 28:17
from Bozrah, with his
      garments stained
      crimson?   Am 1:12
Who is this, robed in splendor,
      striding forward in the
      greatness of his
      strength?   Isa 45:24

"It is I, speaking in
      righteousness,
mighty to save."   Isa 46:13

2Why are your garments red,
      like those of one treading
      the winepress?   Ge 49:11

3"I have trodden the winepress
      alone;   Rev 14:20; 19:15
from the nations no one was
      with me.
I trampled them in my anger
      and trod them down in my
      wrath;   Isa 22:5
their blood spattered my
      garments,   Rev 19:13
      and I stained all my clothing.
4For the day of vengeance was
      in my heart,   Jer 50:15
      and the year of my
      redemption has come.
5I looked, but there was no one
      to help,   Isa 41:28
I was appalled that no one
      gave support;
so my own arm worked
      salvation for me,   Ps 44:3

and my own wrath sustained
    me.   Isa 59:16
6I trampled the nations in my
    anger;   Ps 108:13
in my wrath I made them
    drunk   Isa 29:9
and poured their blood on
    the ground."   Isa 34:3

Praise and Prayer

7I will tell of the kindnesses of
    the LORD,   Isa 54:8
the deeds for which he is to
    be praised,
according to all the LORD has
    done for us—
yes, the many good things he
    has done   Ex 18:9
for the house of Israel,
according to his compassion
    and many kindnesses.
8He said, "Surely they are my
    people,   Isa 51:4
sons who will not be false to
    me";
and so he became their
    Savior.   Isa 25:9
9In all their distress he too was
    distressed,
and the angel of his
    presence saved them.
In his love and mercy he
    redeemed them;   Dt 7:7-8
he lifted them up and carried
    them   Dt 1:31
all the days of old.   Dt 32:7
10Yet they rebelled   Ps 78:40
and grieved his Holy Spirit.

So he turned and became their
    enemy   Ps 106:40
and he himself fought
    against them.   Jos 10:14
11Then his people recalled*a* the
    days of old,
the days of Moses and his
    people—
where is he who brought them
    through the sea,
with the shepherd of his
    flock?
Where is he who set
    his Holy Spirit among
    them,
12who sent his glorious arm of
    power
to be at Moses' right hand,
who divided the waters before
    them,   Ex 14:21-22; Isa 11:15
to gain for himself
    everlasting renown,
13who led them through the
    depths?   Dt 32:12
Like a horse in open country,
    they did not stumble; Jer 31:9
14like cattle that go down to the
    plain,
they were given rest by the
    Spirit of the LORD.   Dt 12:9
This is how you guided your
    people
to make for yourself a
    glorious name.

15Look down from heaven and
    see   Dt 26:15; Ps 80:14
from your lofty throne, holy
    and glorious.   Ps 123:1

---

a 11 Or *But may he recall*

Where are your zeal and your
    might?   Isa 9:7
Your tenderness and
    compassion are withheld
    from us.   Jer 31:20; Hos 11:8
¹⁶But you are our Father,   Ex 4:22
    though Abraham does not
    know us
    or Israel acknowledge us;
    you, O LORD, are our Father,
    our Redeemer from of old is
    your name.   Isa 41:14; 44:6
¹⁷Why, O LORD, do you make us
    wander from your ways
    and harden our hearts so we
    do not revere you?
Return for the sake of your
    servants,   Nu 10:36
    the tribes that are your
    inheritance.   Ex 34:9
¹⁸For a little while your people
    possessed your holy
    place,   Dt 4:26; 11:17
    but now our enemies have
    trampled down your
    sanctuary.   Ps 74:3-8
¹⁹We are yours from of old;
    but you have not ruled over
    them,
    they have not been called by
    your name.ᵃ   Isa 43:7

64 Oh, that you would rend
    the heavens and come
    down,   Ps 144:5; Mic 1:3
    that the mountains would
    tremble before you!
²As when fire sets twigs ablaze
    and causes water to boil,
come down to make your
    name known to your
    enemies
    and cause the nations to
    quake before you!   Ps 99:1
³For when you did awesome
    things that we did not
    expect,   Ps 65:5
    you came down, and the
    mountains trembled
    before you.
⁴Since ancient times no one has
    heard,
    no ear has perceived,
    no eye has seen any God
    besides you,   Isa 43:10-11
    who acts on behalf of those
    who wait for him.
⁵You come to the help of those
    who gladly do right,
    who remember your ways.
But when we continued to sin
    against them,
    you were angry.   Isa 10:4
    How then can we be saved?
⁶All of us have become like one
    who is unclean,   Lev 5:2
    and all our righteous acts are
    like filthy rags;   Isa 46:12
    we all shrivel up like a leaf,
    and like the wind our sins
    sweep us away.   Jer 4:12
⁷No one calls on your name
    or strives to lay hold of
    you;
    for you have hidden your face
    from us   Dt 31:18; Isa 1:15; 54:8
    and made us waste away
    because of our sins.

ᵃ 19 Or *We are like those you have never ruled, / like those never called by your name*

⁸Yet, O Lᴏʀᴅ, you are our
    Father.   Isa 63:16
We are the clay, you are the
    potter;   Isa 29:16
we are all the work of your
    hand.   Isa 19:25
⁹Do not be angry beyond
    measure, O Lᴏʀᴅ; Isa 57:17
do not remember our sins
    forever.   Isa 43:25
Oh, look upon us, we pray,
    for we are all your people.
¹⁰Your sacred cities have become
    a desert;   Isa 1:26
even Zion is a desert,
    Jerusalem a desolation.
¹¹Our holy and glorious temple,
    where our fathers
    praised you,   Ps 74:3-7
has been burned with fire,
and all that we treasured lies
    in ruins.   La 1:7,10
¹²After all this, O Lᴏʀᴅ, will you
    hold yourself back?
Will you keep silent and
    punish us beyond
    measure?   Ps 83:1

Judgment and Salvation

65 "I revealed myself to
those who did not ask
for me;
I was found by those who
    did not seek me. Ro 10:20*
To a nation that did not call on
    my name,   Eph 2:12
I said, 'Here am I, here am
    I.'
²All day long I have held out
    my hands

to an obstinate people,
who walk in ways not good,
    pursuing their own
      imaginations— Ps 81:11-12
³a people who continually
    provoke me
to my very face,   Job 1:11
offering sacrifices in gardens
and burning incense on
    altars of brick;
⁴who sit among the graves
and spend their nights
    keeping secret vigil;
who eat the flesh of pigs,
and whose pots hold broth
    of unclean meat;
⁵who say, 'Keep away; don't
    come near me,
for I am too sacred for you!'
Such people are smoke in my
    nostrils,
    a fire that keeps burning all
    day.

⁶"See, it stands written before
    me:
I will not keep silent but will
    pay back in full; Ps 50:3
I will pay it back into their
    laps—   Ps 79:12
⁷both your sins and the sins of
    your fathers," Ex 20:5
says the Lᴏʀᴅ.
"Because they burned sacrifices
    on the mountains
and defied me on the hills,
I will measure into their laps
    the full payment for their
    former deeds." Pr 10:24

⁸This is what the Lᴏʀᴅ says:

"As when juice is still found in
　　a cluster of grapes
　and men say, 'Don't destroy
　　it,
　there is yet some good in it,'
so will I do in behalf of my
　　servants;　　　　　Isa 54:17
I will not destroy them all.
⁹I will bring forth descendants
　　from Jacob,　　　Isa 45:19
　and from Judah those who
　　will possess my
　　mountains;　　　Am 9:11-15
my chosen people will inherit
　　them,　　　　　　Isa 14:1
　and there will my servants
　　live.　　　　　　Isa 32:18
¹⁰Sharon will become a pasture
　　for flocks,　　　Isa 35:2
　and the Valley of Achor a
　　resting place for herds,
　for my people who seek me.

¹¹"But as for you who forsake
　　the Lord　　Dt 29:24-25; Isa 1:28
　and forget my holy
　　mountain,　　　Ps 137:5
who spread a table for Fortune
　and fill bowls of mixed wine
　　for Destiny,　　　Isa 5:22
¹²I will destine you for the
　　sword,　　　　　Isa 27:1
　and you will all bend down
　　for the slaughter;
for I called but you did not
　　answer,　　Pr 1:24-25; Isa 41:28
　I spoke but you did not
　　listen.　　2Ch 36:15-16; Jer 7:13
You did evil in my sight
　and chose what displeases
　　me."　　　　　Isa 1:24; 66:4

¹³Therefore this is what the Sovereign Lord says:

"My servants will eat,　　Isa 1:19
　but you will go hungry;
my servants will drink,　　Isa 33:16
　but you will go thirsty;
my servants will rejoice,　　Isa 60:5
　but you will be put to
　　shame.　　　　　Isa 44:9
¹⁴My servants will sing
　out of the joy of their hearts,
but you will cry out　　Mt 8:12
　from anguish of heart
　and wail in brokenness of
　　spirit.
¹⁵You will leave your name
　to my chosen ones as a
　　curse;　　　　　Zec 8:13
the Sovereign Lord will put
　　you to death,
　but to his servants he will
　　give another name.
¹⁶Whoever invokes a blessing in
　　the land　　　　Dt 29:19
　will do so by the God of
　　truth;　　　　　Ps 31:5
he who takes an oath in the
　　land
　will swear by the God of
　　truth.　　　　　Isa 19:18
For the past troubles will be
　　forgotten　　　Job 11:16
　and hidden from my eyes.

New Heavens and a New Earth

¹⁷"Behold, I will create
　new heavens and a new
　　earth.　　　Isa 66:22; 2Pe 3:13
The former things will not be
　　remembered,　　Isa 43:18

nor will they come to mind.

¹⁸But be glad and rejoice forever
  in what I will create,
for I will create Jerusalem to
    be a delight
  and its people a joy.
¹⁹I will rejoice over Jerusalem
  and take delight in my
      people;
the sound of weeping and of
    crying   Isa 25:8; Rev 7:17
  will be heard in it no more.

²⁰"Never again will there be in it
  an infant who lives but a
      few days,
or an old man who does not
    live out his years;   Ecc 8:13
he who dies at a hundred
  will be thought a mere
      youth;
he who fails to reach a
    hundred
  will be considered accursed.
²¹They will build houses and
    dwell in them;   Isa 32:18
  they will plant vineyards and
      eat their fruit.   Isa 37:30
²²No longer will they build
    houses and others live
    in them,   Dt 28:30
  or plant and others eat.
For as the days of a tree,
  so will be the days of my
      people;   Ps 21:4; 91:16
my chosen ones will long
    enjoy   Isa 14:1
  the works of their hands.
²³They will not toil in vain   Isa 49:4

or bear children doomed to
    misfortune;   Jer 16:3-4
for they will be a people
    blessed by the Lord,
  they and their descendants
      with them.   Ac 2:39
²⁴Before they call I will answer;
  while they are still speaking
      I will hear.   Da 9:20-23; 10:12
²⁵The wolf and the lamb will
    feed together,   Isa 11:6
  and the lion will eat straw
    like the ox,
but dust will be the serpent's
    food.   Ge 3:14; Mic 7:17
They will neither harm nor
    destroy
  on all my holy mountain,"
                        says the Lord.

Judgment and Hope

66 This is what the Lord says:
  "Heaven is my throne,
  and the earth is my
      footstool.   1Ki 8:27; Mt 5:34-35
Where is the house you will
    build for me?   2Sa 7:7
  Where will my resting place
    be?
²Has not my hand made all
    these things,   Ac 7:50*
  and so they came into
      being?"
                      declares the Lord.

"This is the one I esteem:
  he who is humble and
    contrite in spirit,   Isa 57:15
  and trembles at my word.

---

a 20 Or / the sinner who reaches

³But whoever sacrifices a bull
   is like one who kills a man,
and whoever offers a lamb,
   like one who breaks a dog's
     neck;
whoever makes a grain offering
   is like one who presents
     pig's blood,
and whoever burns memorial
   incense,   Lev 2:2
   like one who worships an
     idol.
They have chosen their own
   ways,   Isa 57:17
and their souls delight in
   their abominations;
⁴so I also will choose harsh
   treatment for them
   and will bring upon them
   what they dread.   Pr 10:24
For when I called, no one
   answered,   Pr 1:24; Jer 7:13
when I spoke, no one
   listened.
They did evil in my sight
   and chose what displeases
     me."   Isa 65:12

⁵Hear the word of the Lord,
   you who tremble at his
     word:
"Your brothers who hate you,
   and exclude you because of
     my name, have said,
'Let the Lord be glorified,
   that we may see your joy!'
Yet they will be put to
     shame.   Lk 13:17
⁶Hear that uproar from the city,
   hear that noise from the
     temple!

It is the sound of the Lord
   repaying his enemies all they
     deserve.   Isa 65:6; Joel 3:7

⁷"Before she goes into labor,
   she gives birth;
before the pains come upon
     her,
   she delivers a son.   Rev 12:5
⁸Who has ever heard of such a
     thing?
Who has ever seen such
     things?   Isa 64:4
Can a country be born in a day
   or a nation be brought forth
     in a moment?
Yet no sooner is Zion in labor
   than she gives birth to her
     children.   Isa 49:21
⁹Do I bring to the moment of
     birth   Isa 37:3
   and not give delivery?" says
     the Lord.
"Do I close up the womb
   when I bring to delivery?"
     says your God.
¹⁰"Rejoice with Jerusalem and be
   glad for her,   Dt 32:43
   all you who love her; Ps 26:8
rejoice greatly with her,
   all you who mourn over her.
¹¹For you will nurse and be
     satisfied   Isa 60:16
   at her comforting breasts;
you will drink deeply
   and delight in her
     overflowing abundance."

¹²For this is what the Lord says:

"I will extend peace to her like
   a river,   Isa 48:18

and the wealth of nations
  like a flooding stream;
you will nurse and be carried
  on her arm   Isa 60:4
and dandled on her
  knees.
¹³As a mother comforts her
  child,
so will I comfort you;   Isa 40:1
and you will be comforted
  over Jerusalem."

¹⁴When you see this, your heart
  will rejoice   Joel 2:23
and you will flourish like
  grass;
the hand of the LORD will be
  made known to his
  servants,   Isa 54:17
but his fury will be shown to
  his foes.   Isa 10:5
¹⁵See, the LORD is coming with
  fire,   Isa 1:31
and his chariots are like a
  whirlwind;   Ps 68:17
he will bring down his anger
  with fury,
and his rebuke with flames
  of fire.   Ps 9:5
¹⁶For with fire and with his
  sword   Isa 27:1; 30:30
the LORD will execute
  judgment upon all men,
and many will be those slain
  by the LORD.   Isa 10:4

¹⁷"Those who consecrate and
purify themselves to go into the
gardens, following the one in the
midst ofᵃ those who eat the flesh
of pigs and rats and other abominable things—they will meet
their end together," declares the
LORD.

¹⁸"And I, because of their actions and their imaginations, am
about to comeᵇ and gather all nations and tongues, and they will
come and see my glory.   Isa 59:19

¹⁹"I will set a sign among them,
and I will send some of those who
survive to the nations—to Tarshish, to the Libyansᶜ and Lydians
(famous as archers), to Tubal and
Greece, and to the distant islands
that have not heard of my fame or
seen my glory. They will proclaim
my glory among the nations.
²⁰And they will bring all your
brothers, from all the nations, to
my holy mountain in Jerusalem as
an offering to the LORD—on
horses, in chariots and wagons,
and on mules and camels," says
the LORD. "They will bring them, as
the Israelites bring their grain offerings, to the temple of the LORD
in ceremonially clean vessels.
²¹And I will select some of them
also to be priests and Levites," says
the LORD.   Ex 19:6; Isa 61:6; 1Pe 2:5,9

²²"As the new heavens and the
new earth that I make will endure
before me," declares the LORD, "so
will your name and descendants

ᵃ17 Or *gardens behind one of your temples, and*   ᵇ18 The meaning of the Hebrew for this clause is
uncertain.   ᶜ19 Some Septuagint manuscripts *Put* (Libyans); Hebrew *Pul*

endure. [23]From one New Moon to another and from one Sabbath to another, all mankind will come and bow down before me," says the LORD. [24]"And they will go out and look upon the dead bodies of those who rebelled against me; their worm will not die, nor will their fire be quenched, and they will be loathsome to all mankind."

Jeremiah

1 The words of Jeremiah son of Hilkiah, one of the priests at Anathoth in the territory of Benjamin. ²The word of the LORD came to him in the thirteenth year of the reign of Josiah son of Amon king of Judah, ³and through the reign of Jehoiakim son of Josiah king of Judah, down to the fifth month of the eleventh year of Zedekiah son of Josiah king of Judah, when the people of Jerusalem went into exile.   Jos 21:18; 1Ch 6:60; Jer 52:15

The Call of Jeremiah

⁴The word of the LORD came to me, saying,

⁵"Before I formed you in the
    womb I knew*ª* you,
before you were born I set
    you apart;   Isa 49:1
I appointed you as a prophet
    to the nations."   ver 10

⁶"Ah, Sovereign LORD," I said, "I do not know how to speak; I am only a child."   Ex 4:10; 1Ki 3:7
⁷But the LORD said to me, "Do not say, 'I am only a child.' You must go to everyone I send you to and say whatever I command you. ⁸Do not be afraid of them, for I am with you and will rescue you," declares the LORD.   Jer 15:20; Eze 2:6

⁹Then the LORD reached out his hand and touched my mouth and said to me, "Now, I have put my words in your mouth. ¹⁰See, today I appoint you over nations and kingdoms to uproot and tear down, to destroy and overthrow, to build and to plant."   Jer 18:7-10
¹¹The word of the LORD came to me: "What do you see, Jeremiah?"

"I see the branch of an almond tree," I replied.

¹²The LORD said to me, "You have seen correctly, for I am watching*ᵇ* to see that my word is fulfilled."   Jer 44:27
¹³The word of the LORD came to me again: "What do you see?"

"I see a boiling pot, tilting away from the north," I answered.

¹⁴The LORD said to me, "From the north disaster will be poured out on all who live in the land. ¹⁵I am about to summon all the peoples of the northern kingdoms," declares the LORD.   Isa 14:31

"Their kings will come and set
    up their thrones
in the entrance of the gates
    of Jerusalem;
they will come against all her
    surrounding walls
and against all the towns of
    Judah.   Jer 4:16; 9:11

ª 5 Or *chose*   *ᵇ 12* The Hebrew for *watching* sounds like the Hebrew for *almond tree.*

16I will pronounce my judgments
    on my people   Jer 4:12
because of their wickedness
    in forsaking me,   Dt 28:20
in burning incense to other
    gods   Jer 7:9
and in worshiping what their
    hands have made.

17"Get yourself ready! Stand up
and say to them whatever I command you. Do not be terrified by
them, or I will terrify you before
them. **18**Today I have made you a
fortified city, an iron pillar and a
bronze wall to stand against the
whole land—against the kings of
Judah, its officials, its priests and
the people of the land. **19**They will
fight against you but will not overcome you, for I am with you and
will rescue you," declares the
LORD.   Isa 50:7; Jer 20:11; Eze 2:6

Israel Forsakes God

2 The word of the LORD came to
me: **2**"Go and proclaim in the
hearing of Jerusalem: Isa 38:4

" 'I remember the devotion of
    your youth,   Eze 16:8-14,60
how as a bride you loved
    me
and followed me through the
    desert,   Dt 2:7
through a land not sown.
3Israel was holy to the LORD,
    the firstfruits of his harvest;

all who devoured her were
    held guilty,   Isa 41:11; Jer 50:7
and disaster overtook
    them,' "
        declares the LORD.

4Hear the word of the LORD,
    O house of Jacob,
all you clans of the house of
    Israel.

5This is what the LORD says:

"What fault did your fathers
    find in me,
that they strayed so far from
    me?
They followed worthless idols
and became worthless
    themselves.   2Ki 17:15
6They did not ask, 'Where is
    the LORD,
who brought us up out of
    Egypt   Hos 13:4
and led us through the barren
    wilderness,
through a land of deserts
    and rifts,   Dt 8:15; 32:10
a land of drought and
    darkness,*a*
a land where no one travels
    and no one lives?'
7I brought you into a fertile
    land
to eat its fruit and rich
    produce.   Nu 13:27; Dt 8:7-9
But you came and defiled my
    land
and made my inheritance
    detestable.   Ps 106:34-39

a6 Or *and the shadow of death*

⁸The priests did not ask,
    'Where is the LORD?'
Those who deal with the law
    did not know me;   Jer 4:22
the leaders rebelled against
    me.
The prophets prophesied by
    Baal,   Jer 23:13
following worthless idols.

⁹"Therefore I bring charges
    against you again,"
            declares the LORD.
"And I will bring charges
    against your children's
    children.
¹⁰Cross over to the coasts of
    Kittimᵃ and look,   Ge 10:4
send to Kedarᵇ and observe
    closely;   Ge 25:13
see if there has ever been
    anything like this:
¹¹Has a nation ever changed its
    gods?
(Yet they are not gods at
    all.)   Isa 37:19; Jer 16:20
But my people have exchanged
    theirᶜ Glory   Ps 106:20
for worthless idols.
¹²Be appalled at this, O heavens,
    and shudder with great
    horror,"
            declares the LORD.
¹³"My people have committed
    two sins:
They have forsaken me,
    the spring of living water,

and have dug their own
    cisterns,
broken cisterns that cannot
    hold water.
¹⁴Is Israel a servant, a slave by
    birth?   Ex 4:22
Why then has he become
    plunder?
¹⁵Lions have roared;   Jer 4:7; 50:17
    they have growled at him.
They have laid waste his land;
    his towns are burned and
    deserted.   2Ki 25:9
¹⁶Also, the men of Memphisᵈ
    and Tahpanhes   Isa 19:13
have shaved the crown of
    your head.ᵉ
¹⁷Have you not brought this on
    yourselves   Jer 4:18
by forsaking the LORD your
    God   Isa 1:28; Jer 17:13
when he led you in the way?
¹⁸Now why go to Egypt   Isa 30:2
    to drink water from the
    Shihorᶠ?   Jos 13:3
And why go to Assyria   Hos 5:13
    to drink water from the
    Riverᵍ?   Isa 7:20
¹⁹Your wickedness will punish
    you;
your backsliding will rebuke
    you.   Jer 3:11,22; Hos 5:5
Consider then and realize
    how evil and bitter it is for
    you   Job 20:14
when you forsake the LORD
    your God   Jer 19:4

ᵃ 10 That is, Cyprus and western coastlands   ᵇ 10 The home of Bedouin tribes in the Syro-Arabian desert   ᶜ 11 Masoretic Text; an ancient Hebrew scribal tradition *my*   ᵈ 16 Hebrew *Noph*   ᵉ 16 Or *have cracked your skull*   ᶠ 18 That is, a branch of the Nile   ᵍ 18 That is, the Euphrates

and have no awe of me,"
    declares the Lord,
    the Lᴏʀᴅ Almighty.

²⁰"Long ago you broke off your
    yoke   Lev 26:13
and tore off your bonds;
you said, 'I will not serve
    you!'
Indeed, on every high hill
and under every spreading
    tree   Dt 12:2
you lay down as a prostitute.
²¹I had planted you like a choice
    vine   Ex 15:17; Ps 80:8
of sound and reliable stock.
How then did you turn against
    me
into a corrupt, wild vine?
²²Although you wash yourself
    with soda   Ps 51:2
and use an abundance of
    soap,
the stain of your guilt is still
    before me,"
        declares the Sovereign
            Lᴏʀᴅ.
²³"How can you say, 'I am not
    defiled;   Pr 30:12
I have not run after the
    Baals'?   Jer 9:14
See how you behaved in the
    valley;   Jer 7:31
consider what you have
    done.
You are a swift she-camel
    running here and there,
²⁴a wild donkey accustomed to
    the desert,   Jer 14:6
sniffing the wind in her
    craving—

in her heat who can restrain
    her?
Any males that pursue her
    need not tire
    themselves;
at mating time they will find
    her.
²⁵Do not run until your feet are
    bare
and your throat is dry.
But you said, 'It's no use!
I love foreign gods,   Dt 32:16
and I must go after them.'

²⁶"As a thief is disgraced when
    he is caught,   Jer 48:27
so the house of Israel is
    disgraced—
they, their kings and their
    officials,
their priests and their
    prophets.   Jer 32:32
²⁷They say to wood, 'You are my
    father,'
and to stone, 'You gave me
    birth.'   Jer 3:9
They have turned their backs
    to me   Ps 14:3
and not their faces;   Jer 18:17
yet when they are in trouble,
    they say,   Isa 26:16
'Come and save us!'   Hos 5:15
²⁸Where then are the gods you
    made for yourselves?
Let them come if they can
    save you
when you are in trouble!
For you have as many gods
    as you have towns, O Judah.
²⁹"Why do you bring charges
    against me?

You have all rebelled against
    me,"   Jer 5:1; 6:13; Da 9:11
        declares the LORD.
[30]"In vain I punished your
        people;
    they did not respond to
        correction.
Your sword has devoured your
        prophets   Ac 7:52; 1Th 2:15
    like a ravening lion.

[31]"You of this generation, consider the word of the LORD:

"Have I been a desert to Israel
    or a land of great darkness?
Why do my people say, 'We
        are free to roam;
    we will come to you no
        more'?
[32]Does a maiden forget her
        jewelry,
    a bride her wedding
        ornaments?
Yet my people have forgotten
        me,   Isa 57:11
    days without number.
[33]How skilled you are at
        pursuing love!
    Even the worst of women
        can learn from your
        ways.
[34]On your clothes men find
    the lifeblood of the innocent
        poor,   2Ki 21:16
    though you did not catch
        them breaking in.   Ex 22:2
Yet in spite of all this
[35]   you say, 'I am innocent;
    he is not angry with me.'

But I will pass judgment on
    you   Jer 25:31
    because you say, 'I have not
        sinned.'   1Jn 1:8,10
[36]Why do you go about so
        much,
    changing your ways?   Jer 31:22
You will be disappointed by
        Egypt   Isa 30:2-3,7
    as you were by Assyria.
[37]You will also leave that place
    with your hands on your
        head,   2Sa 13:19
    for the LORD has rejected those
        you trust;
    you will not be helped by
        them.   Jer 37:7

3 "If a man divorces his wife
    and she leaves him and
        marries another man,
    should he return to her again?
Would not the land be
        completely defiled?
But you have lived as a
        prostitute with many
        lovers—   Jer 2:20,25
    would you now return to
        me?"   Hos 2:7
        declares the LORD.
[2]"Look up to the barren heights
        and see.
    Is there any place where you
        have not been ravished?
By the roadside you sat waiting
        for lovers,   Ge 38:14
    sat like a nomad[a] in the
        desert.
You have defiled the land   Jer 2:7

___
a 2 Or an Arab

with your prostitution and
　　wickedness.　　　　　Isa 1:21
³Therefore the showers have
　　been withheld,　　　Lev 26:19
and no spring rains have
　　fallen.　　　　　　　Jer 14:4
Yet you have the brazen look
　　of a prostitute;
you refuse to blush with
　　shame.　　　　Jer 6:15; 8:12
⁴Have you not just called to me:
'My Father, my friend from
　　my youth,　　ver 19; Jer 2:2
⁵will you always be angry?
　　Will your wrath continue
　　forever?'
This is how you talk,
　　but you do all the evil you
　　can."

Unfaithful Israel

⁶During the reign of King Josiah,
the LORD said to me, "Have you
seen what faithless Israel has
done? She has gone up on every
high hill and under every spreading tree and has committed adultery there. ⁷I thought that after she
had done all this she would return
to me but she did not, and her unfaithful sister Judah saw it. ⁸I gave
faithless Israel her certificate of divorce and sent her away because
of all her adulteries. Yet I saw that
her unfaithful sister Judah had no
fear; she also went out and committed adultery. ⁹Because Israel's
immorality mattered so little to
her, she defiled the land and committed adultery with stone and
wood. ¹⁰In spite of all this, her un-

faithful sister Judah did not return
to me with all her heart, but only
in pretense," declares the LORD.

¹¹The LORD said to me, "Faithless Israel is more righteous than
unfaithful Judah. ¹²Go, proclaim
this message toward the north:

" 'Return, faithless Israel,'
　　declares the LORD,
'I will frown on you no
　　longer,
for I am merciful,' declares the
　　LORD,　　　　　　　　Ps 6:2
'I will not be angry forever.
¹³Only acknowledge your guilt—
　　you have rebelled against the
　　LORD your God,
you have scattered your favors
　　to foreign gods　　　Jer 2:25
under every spreading tree,
and have not obeyed me,' "
　　　　　　　declares the LORD.

¹⁴"Return, faithless people," declares the LORD, "for I am your husband. I will choose you—one from
a town and two from a clan—and
bring you to Zion. ¹⁵Then I will
give you shepherds after my own
heart, who will lead you with
knowledge and understanding.
¹⁶In those days, when your numbers have increased greatly in the
land," declares the LORD, "men will
no longer say, 'The ark of the covenant of the LORD.' It will never enter their minds or be remembered;
it will not be missed, nor will another one be made. ¹⁷At that time
they will call Jerusalem The
Throne of the LORD, and all nations

will gather in Jerusalem to honor the name of the LORD. No longer will they follow the stubbornness of their evil hearts. [18]In those days the house of Judah will join the house of Israel, and together they will come from a northern land to the land I gave your forefathers as an inheritance.   Hos 2:19; Jer 11:8

[19]"I myself said,

" 'How gladly would I treat you
      like sons
   and give you a desirable
      land,
   the most beautiful
      inheritance of any
      nation.'
I thought you would call me
   'Father'   Isa 63:16
   and not turn away from
      following me.
[20]But like a woman unfaithful to
      her husband,
   so you have been unfaithful
      to me, O house of
      Israel,"
                     declares the LORD.
[21]A cry is heard on the barren
      heights,
   the weeping and pleading of
      the people of Israel,
   because they have perverted
      their ways
   and have forgotten the LORD
      their God.   Isa 57:11

[22]"Return, faithless people;
   I will cure you of
      backsliding."   Hos 6:1

"Yes, we will come to you,

   for you are the LORD our
      God.
[23]Surely the idolatrous
      commotion on the hills
   and mountains is a
      deception;
   surely in the LORD our God
   is the salvation of Israel.
[24]From our youth shameful gods
      have consumed   Hos 9:10
   the fruits of our fathers'
      labor—
   their flocks and herds,
      their sons and daughters.
[25]Let us lie down in our shame,
   and let our disgrace cover
      us.
We have sinned against the
   LORD our God,   Jdg 10:10
   both we and our fathers;
from our youth till this day
   we have not obeyed the
   LORD our God."   Eze 2:3

4 "If you will return, O Israel,
   return to me,"
                     declares the LORD.
"If you put your detestable
      idols out of my sight
   and no longer go astray,
[2]and if in a truthful, just and
      righteous way
   you swear, 'As surely as the
      LORD lives,'   Dt 10:20; Isa 65:16
   then the nations will be
      blessed by him   Ge 22:18
   and in him they will glory."

[3]This is what the LORD says to the men of Judah and to Jerusalem:

"Break up your unplowed
    ground   Hos 10:12
and do not sow among
    thorns.   Mk 4:18
⁴Circumcise yourselves to the
    LORD,
    circumcise your hearts,
    you men of Judah and
      people of Jerusalem,
or my wrath will break out and
    burn like fire   Zep 2:2
because of the evil you have
    done—   Ex 32:22
burn with no one to quench
    it.   Am 5:6

Disaster From the North

⁵"Announce in Judah and
      proclaim in Jerusalem
      and say: Jer 5:20
    'Sound the trumpet
      throughout the land!'
Cry aloud and say:
    'Gather together!
    Let us flee to the fortified
      cities!'   Jos 10:20; Jer 8:14
⁶Raise the signal to go to Zion!
    Flee for safety without delay!
For I am bringing disaster from
      the north,   Jer 1:13-15; 50:3
    even terrible destruction."

⁷A lion has come out of his lair;
    a destroyer of nations has
      set out.   Jer 6:26
He has left his place
    to lay waste your land.   Isa 1:7
Your towns will lie in ruins
    without inhabitant.

⁸So put on sackcloth,   Isa 22:12
    lament and wail,   Jer 7:29
for the fierce anger of the LORD
    has not turned away from
    us.   Jer 30:24

⁹"In that day," declares the
    LORD,
    "the king and the officials
      will lose heart,   1Sa 17:32
the priests will be horrified,
    and the prophets will be
      appalled."   Isa 29:9

¹⁰Then I said, "Ah, Sovereign
LORD, how completely you have
deceived this people and Jerusalem by saying, 'You will have
peace,' when the sword is at our
throats."   2Th 2:11; Jer 14:13

¹¹At that time this people and Jerusalem will be told, "A scorching
wind from the barren heights in
the desert blows toward my people, but not to winnow or cleanse;
¹²a wind too strong for that comes
from me.ᵃ Now I pronounce my
judgments against them."   Jer 1:16

¹³Look! He advances like the
      clouds,   Isa 19:1
    his chariots come like a
      whirlwind,   Isa 5:28
his horses are swifter than
      eagles.   Dt 28:49; Hab 1:8
Woe to us! We are ruined!
¹⁴O Jerusalem, wash the evil
    from your heart and be
      saved.   Jas 4:8

ᵃ 12 Or *comes at my command*

How long will you harbor
    wicked thoughts?   Ps 6:3
¹⁵A voice is announcing from
    Dan,   Jer 8:16
    proclaiming disaster from the
      hills of Ephraim.   Jer 31:6
¹⁶"Tell this to the nations,
    proclaim it to Jerusalem:
'A besieging army is coming
    from a distant land,
    raising a war cry against the
      cities of Judah.   Eze 21:22
¹⁷They surround her like men
      guarding a field,   2Ki 25:1,4
because she has rebelled
      against me,' "   Jer 5:23
          declares the LORD.
¹⁸"Your own conduct and actions
    have brought this upon you.
This is your punishment.
    How bitter it is!   Jer 2:19
    How it pierces to the heart!"

¹⁹Oh, my anguish, my anguish!
    I writhe in pain.
Oh, the agony of my heart!
    My heart pounds within me,
    I cannot keep silent.   Jer 20:9
For I have heard the sound of
    the trumpet;   Nu 10:2
    I have heard the battle cry.
²⁰Disaster follows disaster;   Ps 42:7
    the whole land lies in ruins.
In an instant my tents are
    destroyed,   Jer 10:20
    my shelter in a moment.
²¹How long must I see the battle
    standard   Nu 2:2
and hear the sound of the
    trumpet?   Jos 6:20; Jer 6:1

²²"My people are fools;   Jer 10:8
    they do not know me.   Jer 2:8
They are senseless children;
    they have no understanding.
They are skilled in doing evil;
    they know not how to do
      good."   Ro 16:19

²³I looked at the earth,
    and it was formless and
      empty;   Ge 1:2
and at the heavens,
    and their light was gone.
²⁴I looked at the mountains,
    and they were quaking;
    all the hills were swaying.
²⁵I looked, and there were no
    people;
    every bird in the sky had
      flown away.   Jer 9:10; Zep 1:3
²⁶I looked, and the fruitful land
      was a desert;   Jer 12:4
    all its towns lay in ruins
    before the LORD, before his
      fierce anger.   Jer 12:13

²⁷This is what the LORD says:

"The whole land will be
    ruined,
    though I will not destroy it
      completely.   Jer 5:10,18; 30:11
²⁸Therefore the earth will mourn
    and the heavens above grow
      dark,   Isa 5:30; 50:3
because I have spoken and will
    not relent,   Nu 23:19
I have decided and will not
    turn back."   Jer 23:20; 30:24

²⁹At the sound of horsemen and
    archers   Jer 6:23
    every town takes to flight.
Some go into the thickets;

some climb up among the
    rocks.   1Sa 26:20
All the towns are deserted;
    no one lives in them.

30What are you doing,
    O devastated one?
Why dress yourself in scarlet
    and put on jewels of gold?
Why shade your eyes with
    paint?   2Ki 9:30
You adorn yourself in vain.
Your lovers despise you;   La 1:2
    they seek your life.   Ps 35:4

31I hear a cry as of a woman in
    labor,   Jer 13:21
a groan as of one bearing
    her first child—
the cry of the Daughter of Zion
    gasping for breath,
stretching out her hands and
    saying,   Isa 1:15; La 1:17
"Alas! I am fainting;
    my life is given over to
    murderers."   La 2:21

Not One Is Upright

5 "Go up and down the streets
    of Jerusalem,   Eze 22:30
look around and consider,
    search through her squares.
If you can find but one person
    who deals honestly and
    seeks the truth,   Jer 14:14
    I will forgive this city.   Ge 18:24
2Although they say, 'As surely
    as the LORD lives,'   Jer 4:2
    still they are swearing
    falsely."   Lev 19:12

3O LORD, do not your eyes look
    for truth?   2Ch 16:9
You struck them, but they
    felt no pain;   Isa 9:13
you crushed them, but they
    refused correction.
They made their faces harder
    than stone   Jer 7:26; 19:15
    and refused to repent.
4I thought, "These are only the
    poor;
they are foolish,   Jer 4:22
for they do not know the way
    of the LORD,   Pr 10:21; Jer 8:7
the requirements of their
    God.
5So I will go to the leaders
    and speak to them;
surely they know the way of
    the LORD,
the requirements of their
    God."
But with one accord they too
    had broken off the yoke
    and torn off the bonds.   Ps 2:3
6Therefore a lion from the
    forest will attack them,
a wolf from the desert will
    ravage them,
a leopard will lie in wait near
    their towns   Hos 13:7
to tear to pieces any who
    venture out,
for their rebellion is great
    and their backslidings many.

7"Why should I forgive you?
Your children have forsaken
    me
and sworn by gods that are
    not gods.   Dt 32:21; Jos 23:7

I supplied all their needs,
  yet they committed adultery
and thronged to the houses
    of prostitutes.   Jer 13:27
⁸They are well-fed, lusty
    stallions,
  each neighing for another
    man's wife.   Eze 22:11
⁹Should I not punish them for
    this?"   Jer 9:9
  declares the LORD.
"Should I not avenge myself
  on such a nation as this?

¹⁰"Go through her vineyards and
    ravage them,
  but do not destroy them
    completely.   Jer 4:27; Am 9:8
Strip off her branches,
  for these people do not
    belong to the LORD.
¹¹The house of Israel and the
    house of Judah
  have been utterly unfaithful
    to me,"   Jer 3:20
        declares the LORD.

¹²They have lied about the LORD;
  they said, "He will do
    nothing!
No harm will come to us;
  we will never see sword or
    famine.   Jer 14:13
¹³The prophets are but wind
  and the word is not in them;
    so let what they say be done
    to them."

¹⁴Therefore this is what the LORD
God Almighty says:

"Because the people have
  spoken these words,

I will make my words in
    your mouth a fire   Jer 1:9
and these people the wood it
    consumes.
¹⁵O house of Israel," declares the
    LORD,
"I am bringing a distant
    nation against you—
an ancient and enduring
    nation,
a people whose language
    you do not know,
  whose speech you do not
    understand.
¹⁶Their quivers are like an open
    grave;
  all of them are mighty
    warriors.
¹⁷They will devour your harvests
    and food,   Lev 26:16; Jer 8:16
  devour your sons and
    daughters;   Dt 28:32
they will devour your flocks
    and herds,   Dt 28:31
  devour your vines and fig
    trees.   Nu 16:14
With the sword they will
    destroy   Lev 26:25
  the fortified cities in which
    you trust.   Dt 28:33

¹⁸"Yet even in those days," declares the LORD, "I will not destroy you completely. ¹⁹And when the people ask, 'Why has the LORD our God done all this to us?' you will tell them, 'As you have forsaken me and served foreign gods in your own land, so now you will serve foreigners in a land not your own.'   Dt 28:48; Jer 4:27

20"Announce this to the house of
    Jacob
and proclaim it in Judah:
21Hear this, you foolish and
    senseless people,   Jer 4:22
who have eyes but do not
    see,   Isa 6:10; Eze 12:2
who have ears but do not
    hear: Mt 13:15; Mk 8:18
22Should you not fear me?"
    declares the LORD.
"Should you not tremble in
    my presence?   Isa 64:2
I made the sand a boundary
    for the sea,   Ge 1:9
an everlasting barrier it
    cannot cross.
The waves may roll, but they
    cannot prevail;
they may roar, but they
    cannot cross it.   Ps 46:3
23But these people have
    stubborn and rebellious
    hearts;   Dt 21:18
they have turned aside and
    gone away.   Ps 14:3
24They do not say to themselves,
    'Let us fear the LORD our
    God,
who gives autumn and spring
    rains in season,   Ps 147:8
who assures us of the
    regular weeks of
    harvest.'   Ge 8:22; Ac 14:17
25Your wrongdoings have kept
    these away;
your sins have deprived you
    of good.

26"Among my people are wicked
    men

who lie in wait like men
    who snare birds   Ps 10:8
and like those who set traps
    to catch men.   Mic 7:2
27Like cages full of birds,
    their houses are full of
    deceit;   Jer 9:6
they have become rich and
    powerful   Jer 12:1
28 and have grown fat and
    sleek.   Dt 32:15
Their evil deeds have no limit;
they do not plead the case of
    the fatherless to win it,
they do not defend the rights
    of the poor.   Isa 1:23; Jer 7:6
29Should I not punish them for
    this?"
    declares the LORD.
"Should I not avenge myself
    on such a nation as this?

30"A horrible and shocking thing
    has happened in the land:
31The prophets prophesy lies,
    the priests rule by their own
    authority,   La 4:13
and my people love it this way.
But what will you do in the
    end?

Jerusalem Under Siege

6 "Flee for safety, people of
    Benjamin!
Flee from Jerusalem!
Sound the trumpet in Tekoa!
Raise the signal over Beth
    Hakkerem!   Ne 3:14
For disaster looms out of the
    north,   Jer 4:6
even terrible destruction.

²I will destroy the Daughter of
    Zion,   Ps 9:14
  so beautiful and delicate.
³Shepherds with their flocks
    will come against her;
  they will pitch their tents
    around her,   2Ki 25:4; Lk 19:43
  each tending his own
    portion."

⁴"Prepare for battle against her!
  Arise, let us attack at noon!
  But, alas, the daylight is fading,
  and the shadows of evening
    grow long.
⁵So arise, let us attack at night
  and destroy her fortresses!"

⁶This is what the LORD Almighty
says:

"Cut down the trees   Dt 20:19-20
  and build siege ramps
    against Jerusalem.
This city must be punished;
  it is filled with oppression.
⁷As a well pours out its water,
  so she pours out her
    wickedness.
Violence and destruction
    resound in her;   Ps 55:9
  her sickness and wounds are
    ever before me.
⁸Take warning, O Jerusalem,
  or I will turn away from you
and make your land desolate
  so no one can live in it."

⁹This is what the LORD Almighty
says:

"Let them glean the remnant of
    Israel
  as thoroughly as a vine;
pass your hand over the
    branches again,
  like one gathering grapes."

¹⁰To whom can I speak and give
    warning?
  Who will listen to me?
Their ears are closed*ᵃ*   Ac 7:51
  so they cannot hear.   Isa 42:20
The word of the LORD is
    offensive to them;   Jer 20:8
  they find no pleasure
    in it.
¹¹But I am full of the wrath of
    the LORD,   Jer 7:20
  and I cannot hold it in.

"Pour it out on the children in
    the street
  and on the young men
    gathered together;   Jer 9:21
both husband and wife will be
    caught in it,
  and the old, those weighed
    down with years.   La 2:21
¹²Their houses will be turned
    over to others,   Dt 28:30
  together with their fields and
    their wives,   Jer 8:10; 38:22
when I stretch out my hand
  against those who live in the
    land,"
        declares the LORD.
¹³"From the least to the greatest,
  all are greedy for gain;
prophets and priests alike,
  all practice deceit.   Jer 8:10

ᵃ10 Hebrew *uncircumcised*

¹⁴They dress the wound of my
   people
   as though it were not
      serious.
'Peace, peace,' they say,
   when there is no peace.
¹⁵Are they ashamed of their
      loathsome conduct?
No, they have no shame at
      all;
   they do not even know how
      to blush.   Jer 3:3; 8:10-12
So they will fall among the
      fallen;
   they will be brought down
      when I punish them,"
                        says the LORD.

¹⁶This is what the LORD says:

"Stand at the crossroads and
      look;
   ask for the ancient paths,
ask where the good way is,
      and walk in it,   Ps 119:3
   and you will find rest for
      your souls.   Mt 11:29
But you said, 'We will not
      walk in it.'
¹⁷I appointed watchmen over
      you and said,   Eze 3:17
   'Listen to the sound of the
      trumpet!'
But you said, 'We will not
      listen.'   Jer 11:7-8; 25:4
¹⁸Therefore hear, O nations;
   observe, O witnesses,
   what will happen to them.
¹⁹Hear, O earth: Isa 1:2; Jer 22:29
   I am bringing disaster on this
      people,   Jos 23:15
   the fruit of their schemes,

because they have not listened
      to my words
   and have rejected my law.
²⁰What do I care about incense
      from Sheba
   or sweet calamus from a
      distant land?   Ex 30:23
Your burnt offerings are not
      acceptable;   Am 5:22
   your sacrifices do not please
      me."   Isa 1:11; Mic 6:7-8

²¹Therefore this is what the LORD
says:

"I will put obstacles before this
      people.
   Fathers and sons alike will
      stumble over them;
   neighbors and friends will
      perish."

²²This is what the LORD says:

"Look, an army is coming
   from the land of the north;
a great nation is being stirred
      up
   from the ends of the earth.
²³They are armed with bow and
      spear;
   they are cruel and show no
      mercy.   Isa 13:18
They sound like the roaring
      sea
   as they ride on their horses;
they come like men in battle
      formation
   to attack you, O Daughter of
      Zion."

²⁴We have heard reports about
      them,

and our hands hang limp.
Anguish has gripped us,   Jer 4:19
  pain like that of a woman in
    labor.   Jer 4:31; 50:41-43
²⁵Do not go out to the fields
  or walk on the roads,
for the enemy has a sword,
  and there is terror on every
    side.   Jer 49:29
²⁶O my people, put on sackcloth
  and roll in ashes;   Jer 25:34
mourn with bitter wailing
  as for an only son,   Zec 12:10
for suddenly the destroyer
  will come upon us.

²⁷"I have made you a tester of
    metals   Jer 9:7
  and my people the ore,
that you may observe
  and test their ways.
²⁸They are all hardened rebels,
  going about to slander.   Jer 9:4
They are bronze and iron;
  they all act corruptly.
²⁹The bellows blow fiercely
  to burn away the lead with
    fire,
but the refining goes on in
    vain;
  the wicked are not purged
    out.
³⁰They are called rejected silver,
  because the Lord has
    rejected them."   Ps 119:119

False Religion Worthless

7 This is the word that came to
Jeremiah from the Lord:

²"Stand at the gate of the Lord's
house and there proclaim this
message: Jer 17:19

" 'Hear the word of the Lord, all
you people of Judah who come
through these gates to worship the
Lord. ³This is what the Lord Almighty, the God of Israel, says: Reform your ways and your actions,
and I will let you live in this place.
⁴Do not trust in deceptive words
and say, "This is the temple of the
Lord, the temple of the Lord, the
temple of the Lord!" ⁵If you really
change your ways and your actions and deal with each other justly, ⁶if you do not oppress the alien,
the fatherless or the widow and do
not shed innocent blood in this
place, and if you do not follow other gods to your own harm, ⁷then I
will let you live in this place, in the
land I gave your forefathers for
ever and ever. ⁸But look, you are
trusting in deceptive words that
are worthless.   Jer 18:11; 26:13; Mic 3:11

⁹" 'Will you steal and murder,
commit adultery and perjury,ᵃ
burn incense to Baal and follow
other gods you have not known,
¹⁰and then come and stand before
me in this house, which bears my
Name, and say, "We are safe"—
safe to do all these detestable
things? ¹¹Has this house, which
bears my Name, become a den of
robbers to you? But I have been
watching! declares the Lord.
¹²" 'Go now to the place in Shi-

ᵃ9 Or and swear by false gods

loh where I first made a dwelling for my Name, and see what I did to it because of the wickedness of my people Israel. [13]While you were doing all these things, declares the LORD, I spoke to you again and again, but you did not listen; I called you, but you did not answer. [14]Therefore, what I did to Shiloh I will now do to the house that bears my Name, the temple you trust in, the place I gave to you and your fathers. [15]I will thrust you from my presence, just as I did all your brothers, the people of Ephraim.'   Ps 78:67; Isa 65:12

[16]"So do not pray for this people nor offer any plea or petition for them; do not plead with me, for I will not listen to you. [17]Do you not see what they are doing in the towns of Judah and in the streets of Jerusalem? [18]The children gather wood, the fathers light the fire, and the women knead the dough and make cakes of bread for the Queen of Heaven. They pour out drink offerings to other gods to provoke me to anger. [19]But am I the one they are provoking? declares the LORD. Are they not rather harming themselves, to their own shame?   Ex 32:10; Jer 9:19

[20]" 'Therefore this is what the Sovereign LORD says: My anger and my wrath will be poured out on this place, on man and beast, on the trees of the field and on the fruit of the ground, and it will burn and not be quenched.   Jer 42:18

[21]" 'This is what the LORD Almighty, the God of Israel, says: Go ahead, add your burnt offerings to your other sacrifices and eat the meat yourselves! [22]For when I brought your forefathers out of Egypt and spoke to them, I did not just give them commands about burnt offerings and sacrifices, [23]but I gave them this command: Obey me, and I will be your God and you will be my people. Walk in all the ways I command you, that it may go well with you. [24]But they did not listen or pay attention; instead, they followed the stubborn inclinations of their evil hearts. They went backward and not forward. [25]From the time your forefathers left Egypt until now, day after day, again and again I sent you my servants the prophets. [26]But they did not listen to me or pay attention. They were stiffnecked and did more evil than their forefathers.'   Ex 19:5; Jer 16:12

[27]"When you tell them all this, they will not listen to you; when you call to them, they will not answer. [28]Therefore say to them, 'This is the nation that has not obeyed the LORD its God or responded to correction. Truth has perished; it has vanished from their lips. [29]Cut off your hair and throw it away; take up a lament on the barren heights, for the LORD has rejected and abandoned this generation that is under his wrath.

The Valley of Slaughter

[30]" 'The people of Judah have

done evil in my eyes, declares the LORD. They have set up their detestable idols in the house that bears my Name and have defiled it. ³¹They have built the high places of Topheth in the Valley of Ben Hinnom to burn their sons and daughters in the fire—something I did not command, nor did it enter my mind. ³²So beware, the days are coming, declares the LORD, when people will no longer call it Topheth or the Valley of Ben Hinnom, but the Valley of Slaughter, for they will bury the dead in Topheth until there is no more room. ³³Then the carcasses of this people will become food for the birds of the air and the beasts of the earth, and there will be no one to frighten them away. ³⁴I will bring an end to the sounds of joy and gladness and to the voices of bride and bridegroom in the towns of Judah and the streets of Jerusalem, for the land will become desolate.   Isa 24:8; Rev 18:23

8 " 'At that time, declares the LORD, the bones of the kings and officials of Judah, the bones of the priests and prophets, and the bones of the people of Jerusalem will be removed from their graves. ²They will be exposed to the sun and the moon and all the stars of the heavens, which they have loved and served and which they have followed and consulted and worshiped. They will not be gathered up or buried, but will be like refuse lying on the ground. ³Wher-

ever I banish them, all the survivors of this evil nation will prefer death to life, declares the LORD Almighty.'   Job 3:22; Rev 9:6

Sin and Punishment

⁴"Say to them, 'This is what the LORD says:

" 'When men fall down, do
     they not get up?   Pr 24:16
When a man turns away,
     does he not return?
⁵Why then have these people
     turned away?
Why does Jerusalem always
     turn away?
They cling to deceit;   Jer 5:27
they refuse to return.   Jer 7:24
⁶I have listened attentively,
but they do not say what is
     right.
No one repents of his
     wickedness,   Rev 9:20
saying, "What have I done?"
Each pursues his own course
like a horse charging into
     battle.
⁷Even the stork in the sky
knows her appointed
     seasons,
and the dove, the swift and the
     thrush
observe the time of their
     migration.
But my people do not know
the requirements of the
     LORD.
⁸" 'How can you say, "We are
     wise,

for we have the law of the
LORD,"   Ro 2:17
when actually the lying pen of
the scribes
has handled it falsely?
⁹The wise will be put to
shame;
they will be dismayed and
trapped.   Job 5:13
Since they have rejected the
word of the LORD,   Jer 6:19
what kind of wisdom do
they have?   Pr 1:7
¹⁰Therefore I will give their
wives to other men
and their fields to new
owners.   Jer 6:12
From the least to the
greatest,
all are greedy for gain;
prophets and priests alike,
all practice deceit.   Jer 23:11,15
¹¹They dress the wound of my
people
as though it were not
serious.
"Peace, peace," they say,
when there is no peace.
¹²Are they ashamed of their
loathsome conduct?
No, they have no shame at
all;   Jer 3:3
they do not even know how
to blush.
So they will fall among the
fallen;
they will be brought down
when they are punished,
says the LORD.

¹³" 'I will take away their
harvest,
declares the LORD.
There will be no grapes on
the vine.   Joel 1:7
There will be no figs on the
tree,   Lk 13:6
and their leaves will wither.
What I have given them
will be taken from them.ᵃ' "

¹⁴"Why are we sitting here?
Gather together!
Let us flee to the fortified cities
and perish there!
For the LORD our God has
doomed us to perish
and given us poisoned water
to drink,   Jer 9:15; 23:15
because we have sinned
against him.   Jer 14:7,20
¹⁵We hoped for peace   ver 11
but no good has come,
for a time of healing
but there was only terror.
¹⁶The snorting of the enemy's
horses
is heard from Dan;   Jer 4:15
at the neighing of their
stallions
the whole land trembles.
They have come to devour
the land and everything in it,
the city and all who live
there."

¹⁷"See, I will send venomous
snakes among you,
vipers that cannot be
charmed,   Ps 58:5

ᵃ13 The meaning of the Hebrew for this sentence is uncertain.

and they will bite you,"
    declares the LORD.

[18]O my Comforter[a] in sorrow,
  my heart is faint within me.
[19]Listen to the cry of my people
  from a land far away: Jer 9:16
"Is the LORD not in Zion?
  Is her King no longer
    there?"

"Why have they provoked me
  to anger with their
    images,   Jer 44:3
  with their worthless foreign
    idols?"   Dt 32:21

[20]"The harvest is past,
  the summer has ended,
  and we are not saved."

[21]Since my people are crushed, I
    am crushed;   Ps 94:5
  I mourn, and horror grips
    me.   Jer 14:17
[22]Is there no balm in Gilead?
  Is there no physician there?
Why then is there no healing
  for the wound of my people?

9 [1]Oh, that my head were a
    spring of water
  and my eyes a fountain of
    tears!   Ps 119:136
I would weep day and night
  for the slain of my people.
[2]Oh, that I had in the desert
  a lodging place for travelers,
so that I might leave my
    people
  and go away from them;

for they are all adulterers,
  a crowd of unfaithful people.

[3]"They make ready their tongue
  like a bow, to shoot lies;
it is not by truth
  that they triumph[b] in the
    land.
They go from one sin to
    another;
  they do not acknowledge
    me,"   Isa 1:3
    declares the LORD.
[4]"Beware of your friends;
  do not trust your brothers.
For every brother is a
    deceiver,[c]   Ge 27:35
  and every friend a slanderer.
[5]Friend deceives friend,   Lev 6:2
  and no one speaks the truth.
They have taught their tongues
    to lie;   Ps 52:3
  they weary themselves with
    sinning.
[6]You[d] live in the midst of
    deception;   Jer 5:27
  in their deceit they refuse to
    acknowledge me,"
    declares the LORD.

[7]Therefore this is what the LORD
Almighty says:

"See, I will refine and test
    them,   Isa 1:25; Jer 6:27
  for what else can I do
because of the sin of my
    people?
[8]Their tongue is a deadly arrow;
  it speaks with deceit.

---

[a] 18 The meaning of the Hebrew for this word is uncertain.   [b] 3 Or *lies; / they are not valiant for truth*
[c] 4 Or *a deceiving Jacob*   [d] 6 That is, Jeremiah (the Hebrew is singular)

With his mouth each speaks
　　cordially to his
　　neighbor,　　　　　　Isa 3:5
but in his heart he sets a
　　trap for him.　　　　Jer 5:26
⁹Should I not punish them for
　　this?”
　　declares the LORD.
“Should I not avenge myself
　　on such a nation as this?”

¹⁰I will weep and wail for the
　　mountains
　　and take up a lament
　　concerning the desert
　　pastures.
They are desolate and
　　untraveled,
　　and the lowing of cattle is
　　not heard.
The birds of the air have fled
　　and the animals are gone.

¹¹“I will make Jerusalem a heap
　　of ruins,
　　a haunt of jackals;　　Isa 34:13
and I will lay waste the towns
　　of Judah　　　　　　Jer 1:15
　　so no one can live there.”

¹²What man is wise enough to
understand this? Who has been instructed by the LORD and can explain it? Why has the land been
ruined and laid waste like a desert
that no one can cross?　　Ps 107:43
¹³The LORD said, “It is because
they have forsaken my law, which
I set before them; they have not
obeyed me or followed my law.
¹⁴Instead, they have followed the
stubbornness of their hearts; they

have followed the Baals, as their
fathers taught them.” ¹⁵Therefore,
this is what the LORD Almighty, the
God of Israel, says: “See, I will
make this people eat bitter food
and drink poisoned water. ¹⁶I will
scatter them among nations that
neither they nor their fathers have
known, and I will pursue them
with the sword until I have destroyed them.”　　Lev 26:33; Dt 28:64

¹⁷This is what the LORD Almighty says:

“Consider now! Call for the
　　wailing women to come;
　　send for the most skillful of
　　them.
¹⁸Let them come quickly
　　and wail over us
　　till our eyes overflow with
　　tears
　　and water streams from our
　　eyelids.　　　　　　Jer 14:17
¹⁹The sound of wailing is heard
　　from Zion:
　　‘How ruined we are!　　Jer 4:13
　　How great is our shame!
We must leave our land
　　because our houses are in
　　ruins.’ ”

²⁰Now, O women, hear the word
　　of the LORD;
　　open your ears to the words
　　of his mouth.
Teach your daughters how to
　　wail;
　　teach one another a lament.
²¹Death has climbed in through
　　our windows

and has entered our
   fortresses;
it has cut off the children from
   the streets
and the young men from the
   public squares.   2Ch 36:17

²²Say, "This is what the LORD declares:

" 'The dead bodies of men will
   lie
like refuse on the open field,
like cut grain behind the
   reaper,
with no one to gather
   them.' "

²³This is what the LORD says:

"Let not the wise man boast of
   his wisdom   Ecc 9:11
or the strong man boast of
   his strength   1Ki 20:11
or the rich man boast of his
   riches,   Eze 28:4-5
²⁴but let him who boasts boast
   about this: 1Co 1:31*; Gal 6:14
that he understands and
   knows me,   Ps 36:10
that I am the LORD, who
   exercises kindness,
justice and righteousness on
   earth,   Ps 36:6
for in these I delight,"
   declares the LORD.

²⁵"The days are coming," declares the LORD, "when I will punish all who are circumcised only in
the flesh— ²⁶Egypt, Judah, Edom,

Ammon, Moab and all who live in
the desert in distant places.ᵃ For
all these nations are really uncircumcised, and even the whole
house of Israel is uncircumcised in
heart."   Lev 26:41; Ro 2:8-9,28

God and Idols

10 Hear what the LORD says to
you, O house of Israel.
²This is what the LORD says:

"Do not learn the ways of the
   nations   Lev 20:23
or be terrified by signs in the
   sky,
though the nations are
   terrified by them.
³For the customs of the peoples
   are worthless;
they cut a tree out of the
   forest,
and a craftsman shapes it
   with his chisel.   Isa 40:19
⁴They adorn it with silver and
   gold;   Hos 13:2
they fasten it with hammer
   and nails
so it will not totter.   Isa 41:7
⁵Like a scarecrow in a melon
   patch,
their idols cannot speak;
they must be carried
   because they cannot walk.
Do not fear them;
   they can do no harm
nor can they do any good."

⁶No one is like you, O LORD;
   you are great,   Ps 48:1

ᵃ 26 Or *desert and who clip the hair by their foreheads*

and your name is mighty in
   power.
7Who should not revere
   you,
   O King of the nations?
   This is your due.
Among all the wise men of the
   nations
   and in all their kingdoms,
   there is no one like you.
8They are all senseless and
   foolish;   Isa 40:19; Jer 4:22
   they are taught by worthless
   wooden idols.   Dt 32:21
9Hammered silver is brought
   from Tarshish
   and gold from Uphaz.
What the craftsman and
   goldsmith have made
   is then dressed in blue and
   purple—
   all made by skilled workers.
10But the LORD is the true God;
   he is the living God, the
   eternal King.   Ge 21:33
When he is angry, the earth
   trembles;   Ps 29:8
   the nations cannot endure
   his wrath.   Ps 76:7

11"Tell them this: 'These gods,
who did not make the heavens and
the earth, will perish from the
earth and from under the heavens.' "[a]   Ps 96:5; Isa 2:18

12But God made the earth by his
   power;
   he founded the world by his
   wisdom

and stretched out the
   heavens by his
   understanding.   Ge 1:1,8
13When he thunders, the waters
   in the heavens roar;
   he makes clouds rise from
   the ends of the earth.
He sends lightning with the
   rain   Ps 135:7
   and brings out the wind
   from his storehouses.
14Everyone is senseless and
   without knowledge;
   every goldsmith is shamed
   by his idols.   Isa 1:29
His images are a fraud;   Isa 44:20
   they have no breath in them.
15They are worthless, the objects
   of mockery;   Isa 41:24
   when their judgment comes,
   they will perish.
16He who is the Portion of Jacob
   is not like these,   Dt 32:9
   for he is the Maker of all
   things,   ver 12; Jer 32:17
including Israel, the tribe of his
   inheritance—   Ps 74:2
   the LORD Almighty is his
   name.   Jer 51:15-19

Coming Destruction

17Gather up your belongings to
   leave the land,   Eze 12:3-12
   you who live under siege.
18For this is what the LORD says:
   "At this time I will hurl out
   those who live in this land;
   I will bring distress on them

a 11 The text of this verse is in Aramaic.

so that they may be
captured."

19Woe to me because of my
injury!
My wound is incurable!
Yet I said to myself,
"This is my sickness, and I
must endure it."   Mic 7:9
20My tent is destroyed;   Jer 4:20
all its ropes are snapped.
My sons are gone from me and
are no more;   Jer 31:15
no one is left now to pitch
my tent
or to set up my shelter.
21The shepherds are senseless
and do not inquire of the
LORD;   Isa 56:10
so they do not prosper
and all their flock is
scattered.   Jer 23:2
22Listen! The report is coming—
a great commotion from the
land of the north!
It will make the towns of
Judah desolate,
a haunt of jackals.   Jer 9:11

Jeremiah's Prayer

23I know, O LORD, that a man's
life is not his own;
it is not for man to direct his
steps.   Pr 20:24
24Correct me, LORD, but only
with justice—
not in your anger,   Ps 6:1; 38:1
lest you reduce me to
nothing.   Jer 30:11
25Pour out your wrath on the
nations   Zep 3:8

that do not acknowledge
you,
on the peoples who do not
call on your name.
For they have devoured Jacob;
they have devoured him
completely
and destroyed his homeland.

The Covenant Is Broken

11 This is the word that came
to Jeremiah from the LORD:
2"Listen to the terms of this covenant and tell them to the people
of Judah and to those who live in
Jerusalem. 3Tell them that this is
what the LORD, the God of Israel,
says: 'Cursed is the man who does
not obey the terms of this covenant— 4the terms I commanded
your forefathers when I brought
them out of Egypt, out of the iron-
smelting furnace.' I said, 'Obey me
and do everything I command you,
and you will be my people, and I
will be your God. 5Then I will fulfill the oath I swore to your forefathers, to give them a land flowing
with milk and honey'—the land
you possess today."   Ex 24:8; Jer 7:23
I answered, "Amen, LORD."
6The LORD said to me, "Proclaim
all these words in the towns of Judah and in the streets of Jerusalem: 'Listen to the terms of this
covenant and follow them. 7From
the time I brought your forefathers
up from Egypt until today, I
warned them again and again, saying, "Obey me." 8But they did not
listen or pay attention; instead,

they followed the stubbornness of their evil hearts. So I brought on them all the curses of the covenant I had commanded them to follow but that they did not keep.' "

⁹Then the LORD said to me, "There is a conspiracy among the people of Judah and those who live in Jerusalem. ¹⁰They have returned to the sins of their forefathers, who refused to listen to my words. They have followed other gods to serve them. Both the house of Israel and the house of Judah have broken the covenant I made with their forefathers. ¹¹Therefore this is what the LORD says: 'I will bring on them a disaster they cannot escape. Although they cry out to me, I will not listen to them. ¹²The towns of Judah and the people of Jerusalem will go and cry out to the gods to whom they burn incense, but they will not help them at all when disaster strikes. ¹³You have as many gods as you have towns, O Judah; and the altars you have set up to burn incense to that shameful god Baal are as many as the streets of Jerusalem.'   Eze 22:25; Jdg 2:12-13

¹⁴"Do not pray for this people nor offer any plea or petition for them, because I will not listen when they call to me in the time of their distress.   Ex 32:10

¹⁵"What is my beloved doing in
   my temple

as she works out her evil
   schemes with many?
Can consecrated meat avert
   ˻your punishment˼?
When you engage in your
   wickedness,
then you rejoice.ᵃ"   Jer 7:9-10

¹⁶The LORD called you a thriving
   olive tree   Ps 1:3
with fruit beautiful in form.
But with the roar of a mighty
   storm
he will set it on fire,   Jer 21:14
and its branches will be
   broken.   Isa 27:11; Ro 11:17-24

¹⁷The LORD Almighty, who planted you, has decreed disaster for you, because the house of Israel and the house of Judah have done evil and provoked me to anger by burning incense to Baal.   Isa 5:2; Jer 12:2

Plot Against Jeremiah

¹⁸Because the LORD revealed their plot to me, I knew it, for at that time he showed me what they were doing. ¹⁹I had been like a gentle lamb led to the slaughter; I did not realize that they had plotted against me, saying,   Jer 18:18; 20:10

"Let us destroy the tree and its
   fruit;
let us cut him off from the
   land of the living,   Isa 53:8
that his name be
   remembered no more."

ᵃ 15 Or *Could consecrated meat avert your punishment? / Then you would rejoice*

²⁰But, O Lᴏʀᴅ Almighty, you
     who judge righteously
and test the heart and mind,
let me see your vengeance
     upon them,   Ps 58:10
for to you I have committed
     my cause.

²¹"Therefore this is what the Lᴏʀᴅ says about the men of Anathoth who are seeking your life and saying, 'Do not prophesy in the name of the Lᴏʀᴅ or you will die by our hands'— ²²therefore this is what the Lᴏʀᴅ Almighty says: 'I will punish them. Their young men will die by the sword, their sons and daughters by famine. ²³Not even a remnant will be left to them, because I will bring disaster on the men of Anathoth in the year of their punishment.' "

Jeremiah's Complaint

12 You are always righteous,
     O Lᴏʀᴅ,   Ezr 9:15
when I bring a case before
     you.
Yet I would speak with you
     about your justice:
Why does the way of the
     wicked prosper?   Jer 5:27-28
Why do all the faithless live
     at ease?
²You have planted them, and
     they have taken root;
they grow and bear fruit.
You are always on their lips
     but far from their hearts.

³Yet you know me, O Lᴏʀᴅ;
     you see me and test my
     thoughts about you.
Drag them off like sheep to be
     butchered!
Set them apart for the day of
     slaughter!   Jer 17:18
⁴How long will the land lie
     parchedᵃ   Jer 4:28
and the grass in every field
     be withered?   Joel 1:10-12
Because those who live in it
     are wicked,
the animals and birds have
     perished.   Jer 4:25
Moreover, the people are
     saying,
"He will not see what
     happens to us."

God's Answer

⁵"If you have raced with men
     on foot
and they have worn you out,
how can you compete with
     horses?
If you stumble in safe
     country,ᵇ
how will you manage in the
     thickets byᶜ the Jordan?
⁶Your brothers, your own
     family—
even they have betrayed
     you;
they have raised a loud cry
     against you.   Pr 26:24-25
Do not trust them,
     though they speak well of
     you.   Ps 12:2

ᵃ4 Or *land mourn*   ᵇ5 Or *If you put your trust in a land of safety*   ᶜ5 Or *the flooding of*

7"I will forsake my house,
abandon my inheritance;
I will give the one I love   Isa 5:1
into the hands of her
enemies.   Jer 17:4
8My inheritance has become to
me
like a lion in the forest.
She roars at me;
therefore I hate her.   Hos 9:15
9Has not my inheritance
become to me
like a speckled bird of
prey
that other birds of prey
surround and attack?
Go and gather all the wild
beasts;
bring them to devour.   Isa 56:9
10Many shepherds will ruin my
vineyard   Jer 23:1
and trample down my field;
they will turn my pleasant field
into a desolate wasteland.
11It will be made a wasteland,
parched and desolate before
me;   Isa 42:25; Jer 23:10
the whole land will be laid
waste
because there is no one who
cares.
12Over all the barren heights in
the desert
destroyers will swarm,
for the sword of the LORD will
devour   Jer 47:6
from one end of the land to
the other;   Jer 3:2
no one will be safe.   Jer 7:10
13They will sow wheat but reap
thorns;

they will wear themselves
out but gain nothing.
So bear the shame of your
harvest
because of the LORD's fierce
anger."   Jer 4:26

14This is what the LORD says: "As
for all my wicked neighbors who
seize the inheritance I gave my
people Israel, I will uproot them
from their lands and I will uproot
the house of Judah from among
them. **15**But after I uproot them, I
will again have compassion and
will bring each of them back to his
own inheritance and his own
country. **16**And if they learn well
the ways of my people and swear
by my name, saying, 'As surely as
the LORD lives'—even as they once
taught my people to swear by Baal
—then they will be established
among my people. **17**But if any nation does not listen, I will completely uproot and destroy it," declares the LORD.   Isa 60:12; Jer 4:2

A Linen Belt

13 This is what the LORD said
to me: "Go and buy a linen
belt and put it around your waist,
but do not let it touch water."
2So I bought a belt, as the LORD directed, and put it around my
waist.

3Then the word of the LORD
came to me a second time: **4**"Take
the belt you bought and are wearing around your waist, and go now

to Perath[a] and hide it there in a crevice in the rocks." ⁵So I went and hid it at Perath, as the LORD told me.   Ex 40:16

⁶Many days later the LORD said to me, "Go now to Perath and get the belt I told you to hide there." ⁷So I went to Perath and dug up the belt and took it from the place where I had hidden it, but now it was ruined and completely useless.

⁸Then the word of the LORD came to me: ⁹"This is what the LORD says: 'In the same way I will ruin the pride of Judah and the great pride of Jerusalem. ¹⁰These wicked people, who refuse to listen to my words, who follow the stubbornness of their hearts and go after other gods to serve and worship them, will be like this belt —completely useless! ¹¹For as a belt is bound around a man's waist, so I bound the whole house of Israel and the whole house of Judah to me,' declares the LORD, 'to be my people for my renown and praise and honor. But they have not listened.'   Lev 26:19; Jer 7:26

Wineskins

¹²"Say to them: 'This is what the LORD, the God of Israel, says: Every wineskin should be filled with wine.' And if they say to you, 'Don't we know that every wineskin should be filled with wine?' ¹³then tell them, 'This is what the LORD says: I am going to fill with drunkenness all who live in this land, including the kings who sit on David's throne, the priests, the prophets and all those living in Jerusalem. ¹⁴I will smash them one against the other, fathers and sons alike, declares the LORD. I will allow no pity or mercy or compassion to keep me from destroying them.' "   Isa 51:17; Jer 16:5; Eze 5:10

Threat of Captivity

¹⁵Hear and pay attention,
  do not be arrogant,
  for the LORD has spoken.
¹⁶Give glory to the LORD your
      God   Jos 7:19
  before he brings the
      darkness,
before your feet stumble
  on the darkening hills.
You hope for light,
  but he will turn it to thick
      darkness
  and change it to deep gloom.
¹⁷But if you do not listen,   Mal 2:2
  I will weep in secret
  because of your pride;
my eyes will weep bitterly,
  overflowing with tears,   Jer 9:1
  because the LORD's flock will
      be taken captive.   Jer 14:18

¹⁸Say to the king and to the
      queen mother,   Isa 22:17
  "Come down from your
      thrones,
for your glorious crowns

will fall from your heads."
¹⁹The cities in the Negev will be
    shut up,
and there will be no one to
    open them.
All Judah will be carried into
    exile,   Jer 20:4; 52:30
    carried completely away.

²⁰Lift up your eyes and see
    those who are coming from
    the north.   Jer 6:22; Hab 1:6
Where is the flock that was
    entrusted to you,   Jer 23:2
the sheep of which you
    boasted?
²¹What will you say when ˌthe
    LORDˌ sets over you
those you cultivated as your
    special allies?   Jer 38:22
Will not pain grip you
    like that of a woman in
    labor?   Jer 4:31
²²And if you ask yourself,
    "Why has this happened to
    me?"—
it is because of your many sins
    that your skirts have been
    torn off   Isa 20:4
    and your body mistreated.
²³Can the Ethiopian[a] change his
    skin
or the leopard its spots?
Neither can you do good
    who are accustomed to
    doing evil.   2Ch 6:36

²⁴"I will scatter you like chaff
    driven by the desert wind.
²⁵This is your lot,

the portion I have decreed
    for you,"   Job 20:29; Mt 24:51
        declares the LORD,
"because you have forgotten
    me   Isa 17:10
and trusted in false gods.
²⁶I will pull up your skirts over
    your face
that your shame may be
    seen—   La 1:8; Eze 16:37
²⁷your adulteries and lustful
    neighings,
your shameless prostitution!
I have seen your detestable
    acts
on the hills and in the fields.
Woe to you, O Jerusalem!
    How long will you be
    unclean?"   Hos 8:5

Drought, Famine, Sword

14 This is the word of the
LORD to Jeremiah concern-
ing the drought: Isa 5:6

²"Judah mourns,   Isa 3:26; Jer 8:21
    her cities languish;
they wail for the land,
    and a cry goes up from
    Jerusalem.
³The nobles send their servants
    for water;
they go to the cisterns
    but find no water.   2Ki 18:31
They return with their jars
    unfilled;
dismayed and despairing,
    they cover their heads.
⁴The ground is cracked

---

a23 Hebrew Cushite (probably a person from the upper Nile region)

because there is no rain in
   the land;   Jer 3:3
the farmers are dismayed
   and cover their heads.
⁵Even the doe in the field
   deserts her newborn fawn
because there is no grass.
⁶Wild donkeys stand on the
    barren heights   Job 39:5-6
and pant like jackals;
   their eyesight fails
for lack of pasture."

⁷Although our sins testify
    against us,   Hos 5:5
O LORD, do something for
    the sake of your name.
For our backsliding is great;
   we have sinned against you.
⁸O Hope of Israel,   Jer 17:13
   its Savior in times of
    distress,   Ps 46:1
why are you like a stranger in
    the land,
like a traveler who stays
    only a night?
⁹Why are you like a man taken
    by surprise,
like a warrior powerless to
    save?   Isa 50:2
You are among us, O LORD,
   and we bear your name;
   do not forsake us!   Ps 27:9

¹⁰This is what the LORD says
about this people:

"They greatly love to wander;
   they do not restrain their
    feet.   Ps 119:101; Jer 2:25

So the LORD does not accept
   them;   Jer 6:20; Am 5:22
he will now remember their
   wickedness   Hos 9:9
and punish them for their
   sins."   Hos 8:13

¹¹Then the LORD said to me, "Do not pray for the well-being of this people. ¹²Although they fast, I will not listen to their cry; though they offer burnt offerings and grain offerings, I will not accept them. Instead, I will destroy them with the sword, famine and plague."

¹³But I said, "Ah, Sovereign LORD, the prophets keep telling them, 'You will not see the sword or suffer famine. Indeed, I will give you lasting peace in this place.'"

¹⁴Then the LORD said to me, "The prophets are prophesying lies in my name. I have not sent them or appointed them or spoken to them. They are prophesying to you false visions, divinations, idolatries[a] and the delusions of their own minds. ¹⁵Therefore, this is what the LORD says about the prophets who are prophesying in my name: I did not send them, yet they are saying, 'No sword or famine will touch this land.' Those same prophets will perish by sword and famine. ¹⁶And the people they are prophesying to will be thrown out into the streets of Jerusalem because of the famine and sword. There will be no one to

―――――――
[a] 14 Or visions, worthless divinations

bury them or their wives, their sons or their daughters. I will pour out on them the calamity they deserve.   Jer 5:12-13; 27:14

¹⁷"Speak this word to them:

" 'Let my eyes overflow with
        tears   Jer 9:1
    night and day without
        ceasing;
for my virgin daughter — my
        people—   2Ki 19:21
    has suffered a grievous
        wound,
    a crushing blow.   Jer 8:21
¹⁸If I go into the country,
    I see those slain by the
        sword;
if I go into the city,
    I see the ravages of famine.
Both prophet and priest
    have gone to a land they
        know not.' "   2Ch 36:10

¹⁹Have you rejected Judah
        completely?   Jer 7:29
    Do you despise Zion?
Why have you afflicted us
    so that we cannot be healed?
We hoped for peace
    but no good has come,
for a time of healing
    but there is only terror.
²⁰O Lord, we acknowledge our
        wickedness   Jer 3:13
    and the guilt of our fathers;
    we have indeed sinned
        against you.   Da 9:7-8
²¹For the sake of your name do
        not despise us;   Jos 7:9

do not dishonor your
        glorious throne.   Jer 3:17
Remember your covenant with
        us
    and do not break it.   Ex 2:24
²²Do any of the worthless idols
        of the nations bring
        rain?   Ps 135:7
Do the skies themselves
        send down showers?
No, it is you, O Lord our God.
Therefore our hope is in
        you,
    for you are the one who
        does all this.   Isa 43:10

15 Then the Lord said to me: "Even if Moses and Samuel were to stand before me, my heart would not go out to this people. Send them away from my presence! Let them go! ²And if they ask you, 'Where shall we go?' tell them, 'This is what the Lord says:

" 'Those destined for death, to
        death;
those for the sword, to the
        sword;   Jer 43:11
those for starvation, to
        starvation;   Jer 14:12
those for captivity, to captivity.'

³"I will send four kinds of destroyers against them," declares the Lord, "the sword to kill and the dogs to drag away and the birds of the air and the beasts of the earth to devour and destroy. ⁴I will make them abhorrent to all the kingdoms of the earth because of what

Manasseh son of Hezekiah king of
Judah did in Jerusalem.   Dt 28:25

5"Who will have pity on you,
   O Jerusalem?   Isa 51:19
Who will mourn for you?
Who will stop to ask how
   you are?
6You have rejected me,"
   declares the LORD.   Jer 6:19
"You keep on backsliding.
So I will lay hands on you and
   destroy you;   Zep 1:4
I can no longer show
   compassion.   Jer 7:20; Am 7:8
7I will winnow them with a
   winnowing fork
   at the city gates of the
   land.
I will bring bereavement and
   destruction on my
   people,   Jer 18:21
for they have not changed
   their ways.   2Ch 28:22
8I will make their widows more
   numerous   Isa 47:9
   than the sand of the sea.
At midday I will bring a
   destroyer   Jer 6:4
against the mothers of their
   young men;
suddenly I will bring down on
   them
   anguish and terror.   Job 18:11
9The mother of seven will grow
   faint   1Sa 2:5
   and breathe her last.
Her sun will set while it is still
   day;

she will be disgraced and
   humiliated.   Jer 7:19
I will put the survivors to the
   sword   Jer 21:7
before their enemies,"   2Ki 25:7
   declares the LORD.

10Alas, my mother, that you gave
   me birth,   Job 3:1
a man with whom the whole
   land strives and
   contends!   Jer 1:19
I have neither lent nor
   borrowed,   Lev 25:36
yet everyone curses me.

11The LORD said,

"Surely I will deliver you for a
   good purpose;   Jer 40:4
surely I will make your
   enemies plead with you
in times of disaster and
   times of distress.

12"Can a man break iron—
   iron from the north—or
   bronze?   Jer 28:14
13Your wealth and your treasures
I will give as plunder,
   without charge,   Ps 44:12
because of all your sins
   throughout your country.
14I will enslave you to your
   enemies
in*a* a land you do not know,
for my anger will kindle a fire
   that will burn against you."

15You understand, O LORD;

---

a 14 Some Hebrew manuscripts, Septuagint and Syriac (see also Jer. 17:4); most Hebrew manuscripts *I
will cause your enemies to bring you / into*

remember me and care for me.
Avenge me on my
　　persecutors.　　　Jer 12:3
You are long-suffering—do not
　　take me away;　　Ex 34:6
think of how I suffer
　　reproach for your sake.
16When your words came, I ate
　　them;　　Eze 3:3; Rev 10:10
they were my joy and my
　　heart's delight,
for I bear your name,　Jer 14:9
O Lord God Almighty.
17I never sat in the company of
　　revelers,　Ps 1:1; 26:4-5; Jer 16:8
never made merry with
　　them;
I sat alone because your hand
　　was on me　　　2Ki 3:15
and you had filled me with
　　indignation.
18Why is my pain unending
and my wound grievous and
　　incurable?　　Jer 30:15; Mic 1:9
Will you be to me like a
　　deceptive brook,
like a spring that fails?

19Therefore this is what the Lord
says:

"If you repent, I will restore
　　you
that you may serve me;
if you utter worthy, not
　　worthless, words,
you will be my spokesman.
Let this people turn to you,
but you must not turn to
　　them.

20I will make you a wall to this
　　people,
a fortified wall of bronze;
they will fight against you
but will not overcome you,
for I am with you
to rescue and save you,"
　　declares the Lord.
21"I will save you from the
　　hands of the wicked
and redeem you from the
　　grasp of the cruel."

Day of Disaster

16 Then the word of the Lord came to me: 2"You must not marry and have sons or daughters in this place." 3For this is what the Lord says about the sons and daughters born in this land and about the women who are their mothers and the men who are their fathers: 4"They will die of deadly diseases. They will not be mourned or buried but will be like refuse lying on the ground. They will perish by sword and famine, and their dead bodies will become food for the birds of the air and the beasts of the earth."　　Ps 83:10

5For this is what the Lord says: "Do not enter a house where there is a funeral meal; do not go to mourn or show sympathy, because I have withdrawn my blessing, my love and my pity from this people," declares the Lord. 6"Both high and low will die in this land. They will not be buried or mourned, and no one will cut himself or shave his head for them.

⁷No one will offer food to comfort those who mourn for the dead—not even for a father or a mother—nor will anyone give them a drink to console them. Jer 15:5; Eze 9:5-6

⁸"And do not enter a house where there is feasting and sit down to eat and drink. ⁹For this is what the Lord Almighty, the God of Israel, says: Before your eyes and in your days I will bring an end to the sounds of joy and gladness and to the voices of bride and bridegroom in this place. Rev 18:23

¹⁰"When you tell these people all this and they ask you, 'Why has the Lord decreed such a great disaster against us? What wrong have we done? What sin have we committed against the Lord our God?' ¹¹then say to them, 'It is because your fathers forsook me,' declares the Lord, 'and followed other gods and served and worshiped them. They forsook me and did not keep my law. ¹²But you have behaved more wickedly than your fathers. See how each of you is following the stubbornness of his evil heart instead of obeying me. ¹³So I will throw you out of this land into a land neither you nor your fathers have known, and there you will serve other gods day and night, for I will show you no favor.' Dt 29:24

¹⁴"However, the days are coming," declares the Lord, "when men will no longer say, 'As surely as the Lord lives, who brought the Israelites up out of Egypt,' ¹⁵but they will say, 'As surely as the Lord lives, who brought the Israelites up out of the land of the north and out of all the countries where he had banished them.' For I will restore them to the land I gave their forefathers. Jer 23:7-8; 24:6

¹⁶"But now I will send for many fishermen," declares the Lord, "and they will catch them. After that I will send for many hunters, and they will hunt them down on every mountain and hill and from the crevices of the rocks. ¹⁷My eyes are on all their ways; they are not hidden from me, nor is their sin concealed from my eyes. ¹⁸I will repay them double for their wickedness and their sin, because they have defiled my land with the lifeless forms of their vile images and have filled my inheritance with their detestable idols."

¹⁹O Lord, my strength and my
      fortress,
   my refuge in time of
      distress,   Ps 46:1
to you the nations will come
   from the ends of the earth
      and say,
"Our fathers possessed nothing
      but false gods,   Ps 4:2
   worthless idols that did them
      no good.   Isa 40:19
²⁰Do men make their own gods?
   Yes, but they are not gods!"

²¹"Therefore I will teach them—
   this time I will teach them
      my power and might.
Then they will know
   that my name is the Lord.

17

17 "Judah's sin is engraved
　　　with an iron tool,
　inscribed with a flint point,
on the tablets of their hearts
and on the horns of their
　　altars.　　　　　　　*Ex 27:2*
²Even their children remember
　their altars and Asherah
　　poles*a*　　　　　*2Ch 24:18*
beside the spreading trees
　and on the high hills.　*Jer 2:20*
³My mountain in the land
　and your*b* wealth and all
　　your treasures
I will give away as plunder,
　together with your high
　　places,　　*Jer 26:18; Mic 3:12*
because of sin throughout
　your country.　　　*Jer 15:13*
⁴Through your own fault you
　will lose
　the inheritance I gave you.
I will enslave you to your
　enemies　　*Dt 28:48; Jer 12:7*
　in a land you do not know,
for you have kindled my anger,
　and it will burn forever."

⁵This is what the LORD says:

"Cursed is the one who trusts
　in man,　　*Isa 2:22; 30:1-3*
who depends on flesh for his
　strength
　and whose heart turns away
　　from the LORD.　　*2Co 1:9*
⁶He will be like a bush in the
　wastelands;
　he will not see prosperity
　　when it comes.

He will dwell in the parched
　places of the desert,
　in a salt land where no one
　　lives.　　*Dt 29:23; Job 39:6*
⁷"But blessed is the man who
　trusts in the LORD,　*Ps 34:8*
　whose confidence is in him.
⁸He will be like a tree planted
　by the water
　that sends out its roots by
　　the stream.
It does not fear when heat
　comes;
　its leaves are always green.
It has no worries in a year of
　drought　　　　　*Jer 14:1-6*
　and never fails to bear fruit."

⁹The heart is deceitful above all
　things　　　*Ecc 9:3; Mt 13:15*
　and beyond cure.
Who can understand it?

¹⁰"I the LORD search the heart
　and examine the mind,
to reward a man according to
　his conduct,　　　*Jer 32:19*
according to what his deeds
　deserve."　　　　　*Ro 2:6*

¹¹Like a partridge that hatches
　eggs it did not lay
　is the man who gains riches
　　by unjust means.
When his life is half gone, they
　will desert him,
　and in the end he will prove
　　to be a fool.　　　*Lk 12:20*

---

a2 That is, symbols of the goddess Asherah　　*b2,3* Or *hills / ³and the mountains of the land. / Your*

¹²A glorious throne, exalted from
  the beginning,   Jer 3:17
  is the place of our sanctuary.
¹³O Lord, the hope of Israel,
  all who forsake you will be
    put to shame.   Isa 1:28
  Those who turn away from
    you will be written in
    the dust   Ps 69:28
  because they have forsaken
    the Lord,
  the spring of living water.

¹⁴Heal me, O Lord, and I will be
    healed;   Isa 30:26
  save me and I will be
    saved,
  for you are the one I
    praise.
¹⁵They keep saying to me,
  "Where is the word of the
    Lord?
  Let it now be fulfilled!"
¹⁶I have not run away from
    being your shepherd;
  you know I have not desired
    the day of despair.
  What passes my lips is open
    before you.
¹⁷Do not be a terror to me;
  you are my refuge in the day
    of disaster.   Jer 16:19; Na 1:7
¹⁸Let my persecutors be put to
    shame,
  but keep me from shame;
  let them be terrified,
  but keep me from terror.
  Bring on them the day of
    disaster;
  destroy them with double
    destruction.   Ps 35:1-8

Keeping the Sabbath Holy

¹⁹This is what the Lord said to
me: "Go and stand at the gate of
the people, through which the
kings of Judah go in and out; stand
also at all the other gates of Jerusalem. ²⁰Say to them, 'Hear the word
of the Lord, O kings of Judah and
all people of Judah and everyone
living in Jerusalem who come
through these gates. ²¹This is what
the Lord says: Be careful not to
carry a load on the Sabbath day or
bring it through the gates of Jerusalem. ²²Do not bring a load out of
your houses or do any work on the
Sabbath, but keep the Sabbath day
holy, as I commanded your forefathers. ²³Yet they did not listen or
pay attention; they were stiff-
necked and would not listen or respond to discipline. ²⁴But if you
are careful to obey me, declares
the Lord, and bring no load
through the gates of this city on
the Sabbath, but keep the Sabbath
day holy by not doing any work on
it, ²⁵then kings who sit on David's
throne will come through the gates
of this city with their officials.
They and their officials will come
riding in chariots and on horses,
accompanied by the men of Judah
and those living in Jerusalem, and
this city will be inhabited forever.
²⁶People will come from the towns
of Judah and the villages around
Jerusalem, from the territory of
Benjamin and the western foothills, from the hill country and the

Negev, bringing burnt offerings and sacrifices, grain offerings, incense and thank offerings to the house of the LORD. ²⁷But if you do not obey me to keep the Sabbath day holy by not carrying any load as you come through the gates of Jerusalem on the Sabbath day, then I will kindle an unquenchable fire in the gates of Jerusalem that will consume her fortresses.' "

At the Potter's House

18 This is the word that came to Jeremiah from the LORD: ²"Go down to the potter's house, and there I will give you my message." ³So I went down to the potter's house, and I saw him working at the wheel. ⁴But the pot he was shaping from the clay was marred in his hands; so the potter formed it into another pot, shaping it as seemed best to him.

⁵Then the word of the LORD came to me: ⁶"O house of Israel, can I not do with you as this potter does?" declares the LORD. "Like clay in the hand of the potter, so are you in my hand, O house of Israel. ⁷If at any time I announce that a nation or kingdom is to be uprooted, torn down and destroyed, ⁸and if that nation I warned repents of its evil, then I will relent and not inflict on it the disaster I had planned. ⁹And if at another time I announce that a nation or kingdom is to be built up

and planted, ¹⁰and if it does evil in my sight and does not obey me, then I will reconsider the good I had intended to do for it.   Isa 45:9

¹¹"Now therefore say to the people of Judah and those living in Jerusalem, 'This is what the LORD says: Look! I am preparing a disaster for you and devising a plan against you. So turn from your evil ways, each one of you, and reform your ways and your actions.' ¹²But they will reply, 'It's no use. We will continue with our own plans; each of us will follow the stubbornness of his evil heart.' "   2Ki 17:13; Isa 57:10

¹³Therefore this is what the LORD says:

"Inquire among the nations:
    Who has ever heard
        anything like this?
A most horrible thing has been
        done   Jer 5:30
    by Virgin Israel.   2Ki 19:21
¹⁴Does the snow of Lebanon
    ever vanish from its rocky
        slopes?
Do its cool waters from distant
        sources
    ever cease to flow?^a
¹⁵Yet my people have forgotten
        me;   Isa 17:10
    they burn incense to
        worthless idols,   Jer 10:15
which made them stumble in
        their ways
    and in the ancient paths.

---

^a14 The meaning of the Hebrew for this sentence is uncertain.

They made them walk in
bypaths
and on roads not built up.
16Their land will be laid waste,
an object of lasting scorn;
all who pass by will be
appalled
and will shake their heads.
17Like a wind from the east,
I will scatter them before
their enemies;
I will show them my back and
not my face   Jer 2:27
in the day of their disaster."

18They said, "Come, let's make
plans against Jeremiah; for the
teaching of the law by the priest
will not be lost, nor will counsel
from the wise, nor the word from
the prophets. So come, let's attack
him with our tongues and pay no
attention to anything he says."

19Listen to me, O LORD;
hear what my accusers are
saying!   Ps 71:13
20Should good be repaid with
evil?   Ge 44:4
Yet they have dug a pit for
me.   Ps 35:7; 57:6
Remember that I stood before
you   Jer 15:1
and spoke in their behalf
to turn your wrath away
from them.
21So give their children over to
famine;   Jer 11:22
hand them over to the power
of the sword.   Ps 63:10
Let their wives be made
childless and widows;

let their men be put to
death,
their young men slain by the
sword in battle.   Isa 9:17
22Let a cry be heard from their
houses   Jer 6:26
when you suddenly bring
invaders against them,
for they have dug a pit to
capture me
and have hidden snares for
my feet.   Ps 140:5
23But you know, O LORD,
all their plots to kill me.
Do not forgive their crimes
or blot out their sins from
your sight.
Let them be overthrown before
you;
deal with them in the time
of your anger.   Jer 10:24

19 This is what the LORD says:
"Go and buy a clay jar from
a potter. Take along some of the
elders of the people and of the
priests 2and go out to the Valley of
Ben Hinnom, near the entrance of
the Potsherd Gate. There proclaim
the words I tell you, 3and say,
'Hear the word of the LORD, O
kings of Judah and people of Jerusalem. This is what the LORD Almighty, the God of Israel, says: Listen! I am going to bring a disaster
on this place that will make the
ears of everyone who hears of it
tingle. 4For they have forsaken me
and made this a place of foreign
gods; they have burned sacrifices
in it to gods that neither they nor

their fathers nor the kings of Judah ever knew, and they have filled this place with the blood of the innocent. **⁵**They have built the high places of Baal to burn their sons in the fire as offerings to Baal—something I did not command or mention, nor did it enter my mind. **⁶**So beware, the days are coming, declares the LORD, when people will no longer call this place Topheth or the Valley of Ben Hinnom, but the Valley of Slaughter.

⁷" 'In this place I will ruin*ᵃ* the plans of Judah and Jerusalem. I will make them fall by the sword before their enemies, at the hands of those who seek their lives, and I will give their carcasses as food to the birds of the air and the beasts of the earth. **⁸**I will devastate this city and make it an object of scorn; all who pass by will be appalled and will scoff because of all its wounds. **⁹**I will make them eat the flesh of their sons and daughters, and they will eat one another's flesh during the stress of the siege imposed on them by the enemies who seek their lives.' Dt 28:49-57

¹⁰"Then break the jar while those who go with you are watching, **¹¹**and say to them, 'This is what the LORD Almighty says: I will smash this nation and this city just as this potter's jar is smashed and cannot be repaired. They will bury the dead in Topheth until there is no more room. **¹²**This is what I will do to this place and to those who live here, declares the LORD. I will make this city like Topheth. **¹³**The houses in Jerusalem and those of the kings of Judah will be defiled like this place, Topheth—all the houses where they burned incense on the roofs to all the starry hosts and poured out drink offerings to other gods.' " Ps 2:9; Jer 7:32

¹⁴Jeremiah then returned from Topheth, where the LORD had sent him to prophesy, and stood in the court of the LORD's temple and said to all the people, **¹⁵**"This is what the LORD Almighty, the God of Israel, says: 'Listen! I am going to bring on this city and the villages around it every disaster I pronounced against them, because they were stiff-necked and would not listen to my words.' " Jer 7:26

Jeremiah and Pashhur

20 When the priest Pashhur son of Immer, the chief officer in the temple of the LORD, heard Jeremiah prophesying these things, **²**he had Jeremiah the prophet beaten and put in the stocks at the Upper Gate of Benjamin at the LORD's temple. **³**The next day, when Pashhur released him from the stocks, Jeremiah said to him, "The LORD's name for you is not Pashhur, but Magor-Missabib.*ᵇ* **⁴**For this is what the LORD

ᵃ 7 The Hebrew for *ruin* sounds like the Hebrew for *jar* (see verses 1 and 10).　　*ᵇ 3* *Magor-Missabib* means *terror on every side*.

says: 'I will make you a terror to yourself and to all your friends; with your own eyes you will see them fall by the sword of their enemies. I will hand all Judah over to the king of Babylon, who will carry them away to Babylon or put them to the sword. ⁵I will hand over to their enemies all the wealth of this city—all its products, all its valuables and all the treasures of the kings of Judah. They will take it away as plunder and carry it off to Babylon. ⁶And you, Pashhur, and all who live in your house will go into exile to Babylon. There you will die and be buried, you and all your friends to whom you have prophesied lies.'" 2Ki 20:17; Jer 52:27

Jeremiah's Complaint

⁷O Lord, you deceivedᵃ me, and
  I was deceivedᵃ;   Ex 5:23
  you overpowered me and
    prevailed.   Isa 8:11
  I am ridiculed all day
    long;
  everyone mocks me.   Job 17:2
⁸Whenever I speak, I cry out
  proclaiming violence and
    destruction.   Jer 6:7
  So the word of the Lord has
    brought me
  insult and reproach all day
    long.   2Ch 36:16; Jer 6:10
⁹But if I say, "I will not mention
    him
  or speak any more in his
    name,"

his word is in my heart like a
    fire,   Ps 39:3
  a fire shut up in my bones.
  I am weary of holding it in;
    indeed, I cannot.
¹⁰I hear many whispering,
  "Terror on every side!   Jer 6:25
  Report him! Let's report
    him!"   Isa 29:21
  All my friends   Ps 41:9
  are waiting for me to slip,
    saying,   Lk 11:53-54
  "Perhaps he will be deceived;
    then we will prevail over
      him   1Ki 19:2
  and take our revenge on
    him."   Jer 11:19
¹¹But the Lord is with me like a
    mighty warrior;   Jer 1:8
  so my persecutors will
    stumble and not prevail.
  They will fail and be
    thoroughly disgraced;
  their dishonor will never be
    forgotten.
¹²O Lord Almighty, you who
    examine the righteous
  and probe the heart and
    mind,   Jer 17:10
  let me see your vengeance
    upon them,   Ps 54:7; 59:10
  for to you I have committed
    my cause.   Jer 11:20

¹³Sing to the Lord!   Isa 12:6
  Give praise to the Lord!
  He rescues the life of the
    needy   Ps 35:10

ᵃ7 Or persuaded

from the hands of the
wicked.   Ps 97:10

¹⁴Cursed be the day I was born!
    May the day my mother bore
      me not be blessed!
¹⁵Cursed be the man who
    brought my father the
      news,
    who made him very glad,
      saying,
    "A child is born to you—a
      son!"
¹⁶May that man be like the
    towns   Ge 19:25
    the Lord overthrew without
      pity.
    May he hear wailing in the
      morning,
    a battle cry at noon.
¹⁷For he did not kill me in the
    womb,   Job 10:18-19
    with my mother as my
      grave,
    her womb enlarged forever.
¹⁸Why did I ever come out of
    the womb   Job 3:10-11
    to see trouble and sorrow
    and to end my days in
      shame?   Ps 90:9

God Rejects Zedekiah's Request

21 The word came to Jeremiah from the Lord when King Zedekiah sent to him Pashhur son of Malkijah and the priest Zephaniah son of Maaseiah. They said: ²"Inquire now of the Lord for us because Nebuchadnezzar^a

king of Babylon is attacking us. Perhaps the Lord will perform wonders for us as in times past so that he will withdraw from us."

³But Jeremiah answered them, "Tell Zedekiah, ⁴'This is what the Lord, the God of Israel, says: I am about to turn against you the weapons of war that are in your hands, which you are using to fight the king of Babylon and the Babylonians^b who are outside the wall besieging you. And I will gather them inside this city. ⁵I myself will fight against you with an outstretched hand and a mighty arm in anger and fury and great wrath. ⁶I will strike down those who live in this city—both men and animals—and they will die of a terrible plague. ⁷After that, declares the Lord, I will hand over Zedekiah king of Judah, his officials and the people in this city who survive the plague, sword and famine, to Nebuchadnezzar king of Babylon and to their enemies who seek their lives. He will put them to the sword; he will show them no mercy or pity or compassion.'

⁸"Furthermore, tell the people, 'This is what the Lord says: See, I am setting before you the way of life and the way of death. ⁹Whoever stays in this city will die by the sword, famine or plague. But whoever goes out and surrenders to

^a2 Hebrew *Nebuchadrezzar,* of which *Nebuchadnezzar* is a variant; here and often in Jeremiah and Ezekiel   ^b4 Or *Chaldeans;* also in verse 9

the Babylonians who are besieging you will live; he will escape with his life. [10]I have determined to do this city harm and not good, declares the LORD. It will be given into the hands of the king of Babylon, and he will destroy it with fire.'   Jer 44:11,27; 52:13

[11]"Moreover, say to the royal house of Judah, 'Hear the word of the LORD; [12]O house of David, this is what the LORD says: Jer 13:18

" 'Administer justice every
          morning;   Jer 22:3
rescue from the hand of his
          oppressor   Ps 27:11
the one who has been
          robbed,
or my wrath will break out and
          burn like fire   Jer 10:10
because of the evil you have
          done—   Jer 23:2
burn with no one to quench
          it.   Isa 1:31
[13]I am against you, ⌊Jerusalem,⌋
          you who live above this
          valley   Ps 125:2
on the rocky plateau,
          declares the LORD—
you who say, "Who can come
          against us?
Who can enter our refuge?"
[14]I will punish you as your
          deeds deserve,   Isa 3:10-11
          declares the LORD.
I will kindle a fire in your
          forests   2Ch 36:19; Eze 20:47
that will consume everything
          around you.' "

Judgment Against Evil Kings

22 This is what the LORD says: "Go down to the palace of the king of Judah and proclaim this message there: [2]'Hear the word of the LORD, O king of Judah, you who sit on David's throne—you, your officials and your people who come through these gates. [3]This is what the LORD says: Do what is just and right. Rescue from the hand of his oppressor the one who has been robbed. Do no wrong or violence to the alien, the fatherless or the widow, and do not shed innocent blood in this place. [4]For if you are careful to carry out these commands, then kings who sit on David's throne will come through the gates of this palace, riding in chariots and on horses, accompanied by their officials and their people. [5]But if you do not obey these commands, declares the LORD, I swear by myself that this palace will become a ruin.' "   Jer 17:27; Mic 6:8; Heb 6:13

[6]For this is what the LORD says about the palace of the king of Judah:

"Though you are like Gilead to
          me,   Ge 31:21
like the summit of Lebanon,
I will surely make you like a
          desert,   Mic 3:12
like towns not inhabited.
[7]I will send destroyers against
          you,   Jer 4:7
each man with his weapons,

and they will cut up your fine
 cedar beams   Isa 10:34
and throw them into the fire.

⁸"People from many nations will pass by this city and will ask one another, 'Why has the LORD done such a thing to this great city?' ⁹And the answer will be: 'Because they have forsaken the covenant of the LORD their God and have worshiped and served other gods.' "

¹⁰Do not weep for the dead
 ⌊king⌋, or mourn his loss;
rather, weep bitterly for him
 who is exiled,
because he will never return
 nor see his native land again.

¹¹For this is what the LORD says about Shallumᵃ son of Josiah, who succeeded his father as king of Judah but has gone from this place: "He will never return. ¹²He will die in the place where they have led him captive; he will not see this land again."   2Ki 23:31,34

¹³"Woe to him who builds his
 palace by
  unrighteousness,   Mic 3:10
his upper rooms by injustice,
making his countrymen work
 for nothing,
not paying them for their
 labor.   Jas 5:4
¹⁴He says, 'I will build myself a
 great palace   Isa 5:8-9
with spacious upper rooms.'

So he makes large windows in
 it,
panels it with cedar   2Sa 7:2
and decorates it in red.

¹⁵"Does it make you a king
 to have more and more
  cedar?
Did not your father have food
 and drink?
He did what was right and
 just,   2Ki 23:25
 so all went well with him.
¹⁶He defended the cause of the
 poor and needy,
and so all went well.
Is that not what it means to
 know me?"   Ps 36:10
declares the LORD.
¹⁷"But your eyes and your heart
 are set only on dishonest
  gain,   Isa 56:11
on shedding innocent blood
and on oppression and
  extortion."   Dt 28:33

¹⁸Therefore this is what the LORD says about Jehoiakim son of Josiah king of Judah:

"They will not mourn for him:
 'Alas, my brother! Alas, my
  sister!'
They will not mourn for him:
 'Alas, my master! Alas, his
  splendor!'
¹⁹He will have the burial of a
 donkey—
dragged away and thrown

outside the gates of
Jerusalem."

²⁰"Go up to Lebanon and cry
    out,
  let your voice be heard in
    Bashan,   Ps 68:15
  cry out from Abarim,   Nu 27:12
  for all your allies are
    crushed.   Jer 30:14
²¹I warned you when you felt
    secure,
  but you said, 'I will not
    listen!'
  This has been your way from
    your youth;   Jer 3:25; 32:30
  you have not obeyed me.
²²The wind will drive all your
    shepherds away,   Dt 28:64
  and your allies will go into
    exile.   ver 20
  Then you will be ashamed and
    disgraced   Jer 7:19
  because of all your
    wickedness.
²³You who live in 'Lebanon,'ᵃ
  who are nestled in cedar
    buildings,
  how you will groan when
    pangs come upon you,
  pain like that of a woman in
    labor!   Jer 4:31

²⁴"As surely as I live," declares
the Lord, "even if you, Jehoia-
chinᵇ son of Jehoiakim king of Judah, were a signet ring on my right
hand, I would still pull you off. ²⁵I
will hand you over to those who

seek your life, those you fear—to
Nebuchadnezzar king of Babylon
and to the Babylonians.ᶜ ²⁶I will
hurl you and the mother who gave
you birth into another country,
where neither of you was born,
and there you both will die. ²⁷You
will never come back to the land
you long to return to."   2Ki 24:8

²⁸Is this man Jehoiachin a
    despised, broken pot,
  an object no one wants?
  Why will he and his children
    be hurled out,   Jer 15:1
  cast into a land they do not
    know?   Jer 17:4
²⁹O land, land, land,   Jer 6:19; Mic 1:2
  hear the word of the
    Lord!
³⁰This is what the Lord says:
  "Record this man as if
    childless,   1Ch 3:18; Mt 1:12
  a man who will not prosper
    in his lifetime,   Jer 10:21
  for none of his offspring will
    prosper,   Job 18:19
  none will sit on the throne
    of David   Ps 94:20
  or rule anymore in Judah."

The Righteous Branch

23 "Woe to the shepherds
who are destroying and
scattering the sheep of my pasture!" declares the Lord. ²Therefore this is what the Lord, the God
of Israel, says to the shepherds
who tend my people: "Because

ᵃ23 That is, the palace in Jerusalem (see 1 Kings 7:2)
also in verse 28   ᶜ25 Or Chaldeans   ᵇ24 Hebrew Coniah, a variant of Jehoiachin;

you have scattered my flock and driven them away and have not bestowed care on them, I will bestow punishment on you for the evil you have done," declares the Lord. ³"I myself will gather the remnant of my flock out of all the countries where I have driven them and will bring them back to their pasture, where they will be fruitful and increase in number. ⁴I will place shepherds over them who will tend them, and they will no longer be afraid or terrified, nor will any be missing," declares the Lord.

⁵"The days are coming," declares the Lord,
"when I will raise up to David[a] a righteous Branch,   Isa 4:2
a King who will reign wisely and do what is just and right in the land.   Isa 11:1; Zec 6:12
⁶In his days Judah will be saved and Israel will live in safety.
This is the name by which he will be called: Jer 33:16
The Lord Our Righteousness.

⁷"So then, the days are coming," declares the Lord, "when people will no longer say, 'As surely as the Lord lives, who brought the Israelites up out of Egypt,' ⁸but they will say, 'As surely as the Lord lives, who brought the descendants of Israel up out of the land of the north and out of all the countries where he had banished them.'

Then they will live in their own land."   Isa 43:5-6; Am 9:14-15

Lying Prophets

⁹Concerning the prophets:

My heart is broken within me;
all my bones tremble.
I am like a drunken man,
like a man overcome by wine,
because of the Lord
and his holy words.   Jer 20:8-9
¹⁰The land is full of adulterers;
because of the curse[b] the land lies parched[c]
and the pastures in the desert are withered.
The ⌊prophets⌋ follow an evil course
and use their power unjustly.

¹¹"Both prophet and priest are godless;   Jer 6:13; Zep 3:4
even in my temple I find their wickedness,"
declares the Lord.
¹²"Therefore their path will become slippery;   Jer 13:16
they will be banished to darkness
and there they will fall.
I will bring disaster on them
in the year they are punished,"   Jer 11:23
declares the Lord.

¹³"Among the prophets of Samaria

I saw this repulsive thing:
They prophesied by Baal   Jer 2:8
and led my people Israel
        astray.   Eze 13:10
¹⁴And among the prophets of
        Jerusalem
I have seen something
        horrible: Jer 5:30
They commit adultery and
        live a lie.   Jer 29:23
They strengthen the hands of
        evildoers,   Eze 13:22
so that no one turns from
        his wickedness.
They are all like Sodom to me;
        the people of Jerusalem are
        like Gomorrah."   Jer 20:16

¹⁵Therefore, this is what the
LORD Almighty says concerning
the prophets:

"I will make them eat bitter
        food
and drink poisoned water,
because from the prophets of
        Jerusalem
ungodliness has spread
        throughout the land."

¹⁶This is what the LORD Almighty says:

"Do not listen to what the
        prophets are
        prophesying to you;
they fill you with false
        hopes.
They speak visions from their
        own minds,   Jer 14:14
not from the mouth of the
        LORD.   Jer 9:20

¹⁷They keep saying to those who
        despise me,
'The LORD says: You will
        have peace.'   Jer 8:11
And to all who follow the
        stubbornness of their
        hearts   Jer 13:10
they say, 'No harm will
        come to you.'   Jer 5:12
¹⁸But which of them has stood
        in the council of the
        LORD   Ro 11:34
to see or to hear his word?
Who has listened and heard
        his word?
¹⁹See, the storm of the LORD
        will burst out in wrath,
a whirlwind swirling down
        on the heads of the wicked.
²⁰The anger of the LORD will not
        turn back   2Ki 23:26; Jer 30:24
until he fully accomplishes
        the purposes of his heart.
In days to come
        you will understand it
        clearly.
²¹I did not send these prophets,
        yet they have run with their
        message;
I did not speak to them,
        yet they have prophesied.
²²But if they had stood in my
        council,   1Ki 22:19
they would have proclaimed
        my words to my people
and would have turned them
        from their evil ways
        and from their evil deeds.
²³"Am I only a God nearby,"
        declares the LORD,

"and not a God far away?
²⁴Can anyone hide in secret
    places   Job 22:12-14
so that I cannot see him?"
                declares the Lord.
"Do not I fill heaven and
    earth?"   1Ki 8:27
                declares the Lord.

²⁵"I have heard what the prophets say who prophesy lies in my name. They say, 'I had a dream! I had a dream!' ²⁶How long will this continue in the hearts of these lying prophets, who prophesy the delusions of their own minds? ²⁷They think the dreams they tell one another will make my people forget my name, just as their fathers forgot my name through Baal worship. ²⁸Let the prophet who has a dream tell his dream, but let the one who has my word speak it faithfully. For what has straw to do with grain?" declares the Lord. ²⁹"Is not my word like fire," declares the Lord, "and like a hammer that breaks a rock in pieces?

³⁰"Therefore," declares the Lord, "I am against the prophets who steal from one another words supposedly from me. ³¹Yes," declares the Lord, "I am against the prophets who wag their own tongues and yet declare, 'The Lord declares.' ³²Indeed, I am against those who prophesy false dreams," declares the Lord. "They tell them and lead my people astray with their reckless lies, yet I did not send or appoint them. They do not benefit these people in the least," declares the Lord.

False Oracles and False Prophets

³³"When these people, or a prophet or a priest, ask you, 'What is the oracle[a] of the Lord?' say to them, 'What oracle?[b] I will forsake you, declares the Lord.' ³⁴If a prophet or a priest or anyone else claims, 'This is the oracle of the Lord,' I will punish that man and his household. ³⁵This is what each of you keeps on saying to his friend or relative: 'What is the Lord's answer?' or 'What has the Lord spoken?' ³⁶But you must not mention 'the oracle of the Lord' again, because every man's own word becomes his oracle and so you distort the words of the living God, the Lord Almighty, our God. ³⁷This is what you keep saying to a prophet: 'What is the Lord's answer to you?' or 'What has the Lord spoken?' ³⁸Although you claim, 'This is the oracle of the Lord,' this is what the Lord says: You used the words, 'This is the oracle of the Lord,' even though I told you that you must not claim, 'This is the oracle of the Lord.' ³⁹Therefore, I will surely forget you and cast you out of my presence along with the city I gave to

---

ᵃ33 Or burden (see Septuagint and Vulgate)   ᵇ33 Hebrew; Septuagint and Vulgate 'You are the burden. (The Hebrew for oracle and burden is the same.)

you and your fathers. ⁴⁰I will bring upon you everlasting disgrace—everlasting shame that will not be forgotten." Jer 20:11; Eze 5:14-15

Two Baskets of Figs

24 After Jehoiachin[a] son of Jehoiakim king of Judah and the officials, the craftsmen and the artisans of Judah were carried into exile from Jerusalem to Babylon by Nebuchadnezzar king of Babylon, the LORD showed me two baskets of figs placed in front of the temple of the LORD. ²One basket had very good figs, like those that ripen early; the other basket had very poor figs, so bad they could not be eaten. Isa 5:4

³Then the LORD asked me, "What do you see, Jeremiah?"

"Figs," I answered. "The good ones are very good, but the poor ones are so bad they cannot be eaten."

⁴Then the word of the LORD came to me: ⁵"This is what the LORD, the God of Israel, says: 'Like these good figs, I regard as good the exiles from Judah, whom I sent away from this place to the land of the Babylonians.[b] ⁶My eyes will watch over them for their good, and I will bring them back to this land. I will build them up and not tear them down; I will plant them and not uproot them. ⁷I will give them a heart to know me, that I am the LORD. They will be my people,

and I will be their God, for they will return to me with all their heart. Jer 31:33; 32:40

⁸" 'But like the poor figs, which are so bad they cannot be eaten,' says the LORD, 'so will I deal with Zedekiah king of Judah, his officials and the survivors from Jerusalem, whether they remain in this land or live in Egypt. ⁹I will make them abhorrent and an offense to all the kingdoms of the earth, a reproach and a byword, an object of ridicule and cursing, wherever I banish them. ¹⁰I will send the sword, famine and plague against them until they are destroyed from the land I gave to them and their fathers.' " Jer 15:4; 32:4-5

Seventy Years of Captivity

25 The word came to Jeremiah concerning all the people of Judah in the fourth year of Jehoiakim son of Josiah king of Judah, which was the first year of Nebuchadnezzar king of Babylon. ²So Jeremiah the prophet said to all the people of Judah and to all those living in Jerusalem: ³For twenty-three years—from the thirteenth year of Josiah son of Amon king of Judah until this very day—the word of the LORD has come to me and I have spoken to you again and again, but you have not listened. Jer 1:2; 7:26; 36:1

⁴And though the LORD has sent all his servants the prophets to you

---

ᵃ 1 Hebrew *Jeconiah,* a variant of *Jehoiachin*   ᵇ 5 Or *Chaldeans*

again and again, you have not listened or paid any attention. [5]They said, "Turn now, each of you, from your evil ways and your evil practices, and you can stay in the land the LORD gave to you and your fathers for ever and ever. [6]Do not follow other gods to serve and worship them; do not provoke me to anger with what your hands have made. Then I will not harm you."

[7]"But you did not listen to me," declares the LORD, "and you have provoked me with what your hands have made, and you have brought harm to yourselves."

[8]Therefore the LORD Almighty says this: "Because you have not listened to my words, [9]I will summon all the peoples of the north and my servant Nebuchadnezzar king of Babylon," declares the LORD, "and I will bring them against this land and its inhabitants and against all the surrounding nations. I will completely destroy[a] them and make them an object of horror and scorn, and an everlasting ruin. [10]I will banish from them the sounds of joy and gladness, the voices of bride and bridegroom, the sound of millstones and the light of the lamp. [11]This whole country will become a desolate wasteland, and these nations will serve the king of Babylon seventy years.   Jer 18:16; 27:6

[12]"But when the seventy years are fulfilled, I will punish the king of Babylon and his nation, the land of the Babylonians,[b] for their guilt," declares the LORD, "and will make it desolate forever. [13]I will bring upon that land all the things I have spoken against it, all that are written in this book and prophesied by Jeremiah against all the nations. [14]They themselves will be enslaved by many nations and great kings; I will repay them according to their deeds and the work of their hands."   Jer 50:9; 51:6

The Cup of God's Wrath

[15]This is what the LORD, the God of Israel, said to me: "Take from my hand this cup filled with the wine of my wrath and make all the nations to whom I send you drink it. [16]When they drink it, they will stagger and go mad because of the sword I will send among them."

[17]So I took the cup from the LORD's hand and made all the nations to whom he sent me drink it: [18]Jerusalem and the towns of Judah, its kings and officials, to make them a ruin and an object of horror and scorn and cursing, as they are today; [19]Pharaoh king of Egypt, his attendants, his officials and all his people, [20]and all the foreign people there; all the kings of Uz; all the kings of the Philistines (those of Ashkelon, Gaza, Ekron, and the

---

[a]9 The Hebrew term refers to the irrevocable giving over of things or persons to the LORD, often by totally destroying them.   [b]12 Or *Chaldeans*

people left at Ashdod); ²¹Edom, Moab and Ammon; ²²all the kings of Tyre and Sidon; the kings of the coastlands across the sea; ²³Dedan, Tema, Buz and all who are in distant places*a*; ²⁴all the kings of Arabia and all the kings of the foreign people who live in the desert; ²⁵all the kings of Zimri, Elam and Media; ²⁶and all the kings of the north, near and far, one after the other—all the kingdoms on the face of the earth. And after all of them, the king of Sheshach*b* will drink it too.   Jer 1:10; 44:22

²⁷"Then tell them, 'This is what the Lord Almighty, the God of Israel, says: Drink, get drunk and vomit, and fall to rise no more because of the sword I will send among you.' ²⁸But if they refuse to take the cup from your hand and drink, tell them, 'This is what the Lord Almighty says: You must drink it! ²⁹See, I am beginning to bring disaster on the city that bears my Name, and will you indeed go unpunished? You will not go unpunished, for I am calling down a sword upon all who live on the earth, declares the Lord Almighty.'

³⁰"Now prophesy all these words against them and say to them:

" 'The Lord will roar from on
        high;   Isa 16:10; 42:13
he will thunder from his
        holy dwelling   Joel 3:16

and roar mightily against his
        land.
He will shout like those who
        tread the grapes,
shout against all who live on
        the earth.
³¹The tumult will resound to the
        ends of the earth,
for the Lord will bring
        charges against the
        nations;   Hos 4:1; Joel 3:2
he will bring judgment on all
        mankind   Jer 2:35
and put the wicked to the
        sword,' "   Jer 15:9
        declares the Lord.

³²This is what the Lord Almighty says:

"Look! Disaster is spreading
        from nation to nation;   Isa 34:2
a mighty storm is rising   Jer 23:19
        from the ends of the
        earth."

³³At that time those slain by the Lord will be everywhere—from one end of the earth to the other. They will not be mourned or gathered up or buried, but will be like refuse lying on the ground.

³⁴Weep and wail, you shepherds;
        roll in the dust, you leaders
        of the flock.   Jer 6:26
For your time to be
        slaughtered has come;
you will fall and be shattered
        like fine pottery.   Jer 22:28

---

a 23 Or *who clip the hair by their foreheads*   *b* 26 *Sheshach* is a cryptogram for Babylon.

³⁵The shepherds will have
    nowhere to flee,
  the leaders of the flock no
    place to escape.   Job 11:20
³⁶Hear the cry of the shepherds,
  the wailing of the leaders of
    the flock,
  for the Lᴏʀᴅ is destroying
    their pasture.
³⁷The peaceful meadows will be
    laid waste
  because of the fierce anger
    of the Lᴏʀᴅ.
³⁸Like a lion he will leave his
    lair,   Jer 4:7
  and their land will become
    desolate   Jer 44:22
  because of the swordᵃ of the
    oppressor   Jer 46:16
  and because of the Lᴏʀᴅ's
    fierce anger.   Ex 15:7

Jeremiah Threatened With Death

26 Early in the reign of Jehoia-kim son of Josiah king of Judah, this word came from the Lᴏʀᴅ: ²"This is what the Lᴏʀᴅ says: Stand in the courtyard of the Lᴏʀᴅ's house and speak to all the people of the towns of Judah who come to worship in the house of the Lᴏʀᴅ. Tell them everything I command you; do not omit a word. ³Perhaps they will listen and each will turn from his evil way. Then I will relent and not bring on them the disaster I was planning

because of the evil they have done. ⁴Say to them, 'This is what the Lᴏʀᴅ says: If you do not listen to me and follow my law, which I have set before you, ⁵and if you do not listen to the words of my servants the prophets, whom I have sent to you again and again (though you have not listened), ⁶then I will make this house like Shiloh and this city an object of cursing among all the nations of the earth.' "   Lev 26:14; Jer 25:4

⁷The priests, the prophets and all the people heard Jeremiah speak these words in the house of the Lᴏʀᴅ. ⁸But as soon as Jeremiah finished telling all the people everything the Lᴏʀᴅ had commanded him to say, the priests, the prophets and all the people seized him and said, "You must die! ⁹Why do you prophesy in the Lᴏʀᴅ's name that this house will be like Shiloh and this city will be desolate and deserted?" And all the people crowded around Jeremiah in the house of the Lᴏʀᴅ.

¹⁰When the officials of Judah heard about these things, they went up from the royal palace to the house of the Lᴏʀᴅ and took their places at the entrance of the New Gate of the Lᴏʀᴅ's house. ¹¹Then the priests and the prophets said to the officials and all the people, "This man should be

---

ᵃ38 Some Hebrew manuscripts and Septuagint (see also Jer. 46:16 and 50:16); most Hebrew manuscripts *anger*

sentenced to death because he has prophesied against this city. You have heard it with your own ears!"

¹²Then Jeremiah said to all the officials and all the people: "The Lord sent me to prophesy against this house and this city all the things you have heard. ¹³Now reform your ways and your actions and obey the Lord your God. Then the Lord will relent and not bring the disaster he has pronounced against you. ¹⁴As for me, I am in your hands; do with me whatever you think is good and right. ¹⁵Be assured, however, that if you put me to death, you will bring the guilt of innocent blood on yourselves and on this city and on those who live in it, for in truth the Lord has sent me to you to speak all these words in your hearing."

¹⁶Then the officials and all the people said to the priests and the prophets, "This man should not be sentenced to death! He has spoken to us in the name of the Lord our God." Ac 5:34-39; 23:9,29

¹⁷Some of the elders of the land stepped forward and said to the entire assembly of people, ¹⁸"Micah of Moresheth prophesied in the days of Hezekiah king of Judah. He told all the people of Judah, 'This is what the Lord Almighty says: Mic 1:1

" 'Zion will be plowed like a
    field,   Isa 2:3
Jerusalem will become a
    heap of rubble,   Ne 4:2
the temple hill a mound
    overgrown with
    thickets.'ᵃ   Jer 17:3; Zec 8:3

¹⁹"Did Hezekiah king of Judah or anyone else in Judah put him to death? Did not Hezekiah fear the Lord and seek his favor? And did not the Lord relent, so that he did not bring the disaster he pronounced against them? We are about to bring a terrible disaster on ourselves!"   2Sa 24:16; 2Ch 32:24-26

²⁰(Now Uriah son of Shemaiah from Kiriath Jearim was another man who prophesied in the name of the Lord; he prophesied the same things against this city and this land as Jeremiah did. ²¹When King Jehoiakim and all his officers and officials heard his words, the king sought to put him to death. But Uriah heard of it and fled in fear to Egypt. ²²King Jehoiakim, however, sent Elnathan son of Acbor to Egypt, along with some other men. ²³They brought Uriah out of Egypt and took him to King Jehoiakim, who had him struck down with a sword and his body thrown into the burial place of the common people.)   Jer 36:12,25

²⁴Furthermore, Ahikam son of Shaphan supported Jeremiah, and so he was not handed over to the people to be put to death.

ᵃ18 Micah 3:12

Judah to Serve Nebuchadnezzar

27 Early in the reign of Zedekiah[a] son of Josiah king of Judah, this word came to Jeremiah from the LORD: **2**This is what the LORD said to me: "Make a yoke out of straps and crossbars and put it on your neck. **3**Then send word to the kings of Edom, Moab, Ammon, Tyre and Sidon through the envoys who have come to Jerusalem to Zedekiah king of Judah. **4**Give them a message for their masters and say, 'This is what the LORD Almighty, the God of Israel, says: "Tell this to your masters: **5**With my great power and outstretched arm I made the earth and its people and the animals that are on it, and I give it to anyone I please. **6**Now I will hand all your countries over to my servant Nebuchadnezzar king of Babylon; I will make even the wild animals subject to him. **7**All nations will serve him and his son and his grandson until the time for his land comes; then many nations and great kings will subjugate him.   Jer 25:12,14; 28:10,13

8" ' "If, however, any nation or kingdom will not serve Nebuchadnezzar king of Babylon or bow its neck under his yoke, I will punish that nation with the sword, famine and plague, declares the LORD, until I destroy it by his hand. **9**So do not listen to your prophets, your diviners, your interpreters of dreams, your mediums or your sorcerers who tell you, 'You will not serve the king of Babylon.' **10**They prophesy lies to you that will only serve to remove you far from your lands; I will banish you and you will perish. **11**But if any nation will bow its neck under the yoke of the king of Babylon and serve him, I will let that nation remain in its own land to till it and to live there, declares the LORD." ' "

12I gave the same message to Zedekiah king of Judah. I said, "Bow your neck under the yoke of the king of Babylon; serve him and his people, and you will live. **13**Why will you and your people die by the sword, famine and plague with which the LORD has threatened any nation that will not serve the king of Babylon? **14**Do not listen to the words of the prophets who say to you, 'You will not serve the king of Babylon,' for they are prophesying lies to you. **15**'I have not sent them,' declares the LORD. 'They are prophesying lies in my name. Therefore, I will banish you and you will perish, both you and the prophets who prophesy to you.' "   Jer 6:15; 14:14

16Then I said to the priests and all these people, "This is what the LORD says: Do not listen to the prophets who say, 'Very soon now the articles from the LORD's house

---

a 1 A few Hebrew manuscripts and Syriac (see also Jer. 27:3, 12 and 28:1); most Hebrew manuscripts *Jehoiakim* (Most Septuagint manuscripts do not have this verse.)

will be brought back from Babylon.' They are prophesying lies to you. [17]Do not listen to them. Serve the king of Babylon, and you will live. Why should this city become a ruin? [18]If they are prophets and have the word of the LORD, let them plead with the LORD Almighty that the furnishings remaining in the house of the LORD and in the palace of the king of Judah and in Jerusalem not be taken to Babylon. [19]For this is what the LORD Almighty says about the pillars, the Sea, the movable stands and the other furnishings that are left in this city, [20]which Nebuchadnezzar king of Babylon did not take away when he carried Jehoiachin[a] son of Jehoiakim king of Judah into exile from Jerusalem to Babylon, along with all the nobles of Judah and Jerusalem — [21]yes, this is what the LORD Almighty, the God of Israel, says about the things that are left in the house of the LORD and in the palace of the king of Judah and in Jerusalem: [22]'They will be taken to Babylon and there they will remain until the day I come for them,' declares the LORD. 'Then I will bring them back and restore them to this place.' "   Ezr 1:7; 7:19

The False Prophet Hananiah

28 In the fifth month of that same year, the fourth year, early in the reign of Zedekiah king of Judah, the prophet Hananiah son of Azzur, who was from Gibeon, said to me in the house of the LORD in the presence of the priests and all the people: [2]"This is what the LORD Almighty, the God of Israel, says: 'I will break the yoke of the king of Babylon. [3]Within two years I will bring back to this place all the articles of the LORD's house that Nebuchadnezzar king of Babylon removed from here and took to Babylon. [4]I will also bring back to this place Jehoiachin[a] son of Jehoiakim king of Judah and all the other exiles from Judah who went to Babylon,' declares the LORD, 'for I will break the yoke of the king of Babylon.' "   2Ki 24:13; Jer 22:24-27

[5]Then the prophet Jeremiah replied to the prophet Hananiah before the priests and all the people who were standing in the house of the LORD. [6]He said, "Amen! May the LORD do so! May the LORD fulfill the words you have prophesied by bringing the articles of the LORD's house and all the exiles back to this place from Babylon. [7]Nevertheless, listen to what I have to say in your hearing and in the hearing of all the people: [8]From early times the prophets who preceded you and me have prophesied war, disaster and plague against many countries and great kingdoms. [9]But the prophet who prophesies peace will be recognized as one truly sent by the

---

a 20,4 Hebrew *Jeconiah*, a variant of *Jehoiachin*

LORD only if his prediction comes true." _{Lev 26:14-17; Dt 18:22}

¹⁰Then the prophet Hananiah took the yoke off the neck of the prophet Jeremiah and broke it, ¹¹and he said before all the people, "This is what the LORD says: 'In the same way will I break the yoke of Nebuchadnezzar king of Babylon off the neck of all the nations within two years.' " At this, the prophet Jeremiah went on his way.

¹²Shortly after the prophet Hananiah had broken the yoke off the neck of the prophet Jeremiah, the word of the LORD came to Jeremiah: ¹³"Go and tell Hananiah, 'This is what the LORD says: You have broken a wooden yoke, but in its place you will get a yoke of iron. ¹⁴This is what the LORD Almighty, the God of Israel, says: I will put an iron yoke on the necks of all these nations to make them serve Nebuchadnezzar king of Babylon, and they will serve him. I will even give him control over the wild animals.' " _{Dt 28:48; Jer 27:6}

¹⁵Then the prophet Jeremiah said to Hananiah the prophet, "Listen, Hananiah! The LORD has not sent you, yet you have persuaded this nation to trust in lies. ¹⁶Therefore, this is what the LORD says: 'I am about to remove you from the face of the earth. This very year you are going to die, because you have preached rebellion against the LORD.' " _{Dt 13:5; Jer 29:32; Eze 13:6}

¹⁷In the seventh month of that same year, Hananiah the prophet died. _{2Ki 1:17}

A Letter to the Exiles

29 This is the text of the letter that the prophet Jeremiah sent from Jerusalem to the surviving elders among the exiles and to the priests, the prophets and all the other people Nebuchadnezzar had carried into exile from Jerusalem to Babylon. ²(This was after King Jehoiachin*ᵃ* and the queen mother, the court officials and the leaders of Judah and Jerusalem, the craftsmen and the artisans had gone into exile from Jerusalem.) ³He entrusted the letter to Elasah son of Shaphan and to Gemariah son of Hilkiah, whom Zedekiah king of Judah sent to King Nebuchadnezzar in Babylon. It said:

⁴This is what the LORD Almighty, the God of Israel, says to all those I carried into exile from Jerusalem to Babylon: ⁵"Build houses and settle down; plant gardens and eat what they produce. ⁶Marry and have sons and daughters; find wives for your sons and give your daughters in marriage, so that they too may have sons and daughters. Increase in number there; do not decrease. ⁷Also, seek the peace and prosperity of the

---

*ᵃ*2 Hebrew *Jeconiah,* a variant of *Jehoiachin*

city to which I have carried you into exile. Pray to the LORD for it, because if it prospers, you too will prosper." ⁸Yes, this is what the LORD Almighty, the God of Israel, says: "Do not let the prophets and diviners among you deceive you. Do not listen to the dreams you encourage them to have. ⁹They are prophesying lies to you in my name. I have not sent them," declares the LORD.   Jer 14:14; 1Ti 2:1-2

¹⁰This is what the LORD says: "When seventy years are completed for Babylon, I will come to you and fulfill my gracious promise to bring you back to this place. ¹¹For I know the plans I have for you," declares the LORD, "plans to prosper you and not to harm you, plans to give you hope and a future. ¹²Then you will call upon me and come and pray to me, and I will listen to you. ¹³You will seek me and find me when you seek me with all your heart. ¹⁴I will be found by you," declares the LORD, "and will bring you back from captivity.ᵃ I will gather you from all the nations and places where I have banished you," declares the LORD, "and will bring you back to the place from which I carried you into exile."

¹⁵You may say, "The LORD has raised up prophets for us in Babylon," ¹⁶but this is what the LORD says about the king who sits on David's throne and all the people who remain in this city, your countrymen who did not go with you into exile— ¹⁷yes, this is what the LORD Almighty says: "I will send the sword, famine and plague against them and I will make them like poor figs that are so bad they cannot be eaten. ¹⁸I will pursue them with the sword, famine and plague and will make them abhorrent to all the kingdoms of the earth and an object of cursing and horror, of scorn and reproach, among all the nations where I drive them. ¹⁹For they have not listened to my words," declares the LORD, "words that I sent to them again and again by my servants the prophets. And you exiles have not listened either," declares the LORD.

²⁰Therefore, hear the word of the LORD, all you exiles whom I have sent away from Jerusalem to Babylon. ²¹This is what the LORD Almighty, the God of Israel, says about Ahab son of Kolaiah and Zedekiah son of Maaseiah, who are prophesying lies to you in my name: "I will hand them

---

ᵃ14 Or *will restore your fortunes*

over to Nebuchadnezzar king of Babylon, and he will put them to death before your very eyes. ²²Because of them, all the exiles from Judah who are in Babylon will use this curse: 'The LORD treat you like Zedekiah and Ahab, whom the king of Babylon burned in the fire.' ²³For they have done outrageous things in Israel; they have committed adultery with their neighbors' wives and in my name have spoken lies, which I did not tell them to do. I know it and am a witness to it," declares the LORD.

Message to Shemaiah

²⁴Tell Shemaiah the Nehelamite, ²⁵"This is what the LORD Almighty, the God of Israel, says: You sent letters in your own name to all the people in Jerusalem, to Zephaniah son of Maaseiah the priest, and to all the other priests. You said to Zephaniah, ²⁶'The LORD has appointed you priest in place of Jehoiada to be in charge of the house of the LORD; you should put any madman who acts like a prophet into the stocks and neck-irons. ²⁷So why have you not reprimanded Jeremiah from Anathoth, who poses as a prophet among you? ²⁸He has sent this message to us in Babylon: It will be a long time. Therefore build houses and settle down; plant gardens and eat what they produce.' " 2Ki 25:18

²⁹Zephaniah the priest, however, read the letter to Jeremiah the prophet. ³⁰Then the word of the LORD came to Jeremiah: ³¹"Send this message to all the exiles: 'This is what the LORD says about Shemaiah the Nehelamite: Because Shemaiah has prophesied to you, even though I did not send him, and has led you to believe a lie, ³²this is what the LORD says: I will surely punish Shemaiah the Nehelamite and his descendants. He will have no one left among this people, nor will he see the good things I will do for my people, declares the LORD, because he has preached rebellion against me.' "

Restoration of Israel

30 This is the word that came to Jeremiah from the LORD: ²"This is what the LORD, the God of Israel, says: 'Write in a book all the words I have spoken to you. ³The days are coming,' declares the LORD, 'when I will bring my people Israel and Judah back from captivity*a* and restore them to the land I gave their forefathers to possess,' says the LORD." Isa 30:8; Jer 16:15; 29:14

⁴These are the words the LORD spoke concerning Israel and Judah: ⁵"This is what the LORD says:

" 'Cries of fear are heard—
    terror, not peace.

a 3 Or will restore the fortunes of my people Israel and Judah

⁶Ask and see:
　　Can a man bear children?
　Then why do I see every
　　　strong man
　　with his hands on his
　　　stomach like a woman
　　　in labor,　　　Jer 4:31
　　every face turned deathly
　　　pale?　　　Isa 29:22
⁷How awful that day will be!
　　None will be like it.
　It will be a time of trouble for
　　　Jacob,　　　Zep 1:15
　　but he will be saved out of
　　　it.　　　Jer 23:3
⁸" ' In that day,' declares the
　　　LORD Almighty,
　'I will break the yoke off
　　　their necks　　　Isa 9:4
　　and will tear off their bonds;
　　no longer will foreigners
　　　enslave them.　　　Eze 34:27
⁹Instead, they will serve the
　　　LORD their God
　　and David their king,
　　whom I will raise up for
　　　them.
¹⁰" 'So do not fear, O Jacob my
　　　servant;　　　Isa 43:5; 44:2
　　do not be dismayed,
　　　O Israel,'
　　　　declares the LORD.
　'I will surely save you out of a
　　　distant place,　　　Jer 29:14
　　your descendants from the
　　　land of their exile.
　Jacob will again have peace
　　　and security,　　　Isa 35:9
　　and no one will make him
　　　afraid.

¹¹I am with you and will save
　　　you,'
　　declares the LORD.
　'Though I completely destroy
　　　all the nations
　　among which I scatter you,
　　I will not completely destroy
　　　you.　　　Jer 4:27; 46:28
　I will discipline you but only
　　　with justice;　　　Jer 10:24
　I will not let you go entirely
　　　unpunished.'　　　Am 9:8

¹²"This is what the LORD says:

" 'Your wound is incurable,
　　your injury beyond healing.
¹³There is no one to plead your
　　　cause,
　　no remedy for your sore,
　　no healing for you.　　　Jer 8:22
¹⁴All your allies have forgotten
　　　you;　　　La 1:2
　　they care nothing for you.
　I have struck you as an enemy
　　　would　　　Job 13:24
　　and punished you as would
　　　the cruel,　　　Job 30:21
　because your guilt is so great
　　and your sins so many.　　　Jer 5:6
¹⁵Why do you cry out over your
　　　wound,
　　your pain that has no cure?
　Because of your great guilt and
　　　many sins
　I have done these things to
　　　you.　　　Pr 1:31
¹⁶" 'But all who devour you will
　　　be devoured;　　　Isa 33:1
　　all your enemies will go into
　　　exile.　　　Isa 14:2; Joel 3:4-8

Those who plunder you will be
  plundered;   Jer 50:10
all who make spoil of you I
  will despoil.
¹⁷But I will restore you to health
  and heal your wounds,'
              declares the LORD,
'because you are called an
  outcast,   Jer 33:24
Zion for whom no one
  cares.'   Ps 142:4

¹⁸"This is what the LORD says:

" 'I will restore the fortunes of
  Jacob's tents   Jer 31:23
and have compassion on his
  dwellings;   Ps 102:13
the city will be rebuilt on her
  ruins,   Jer 31:4,24,38
and the palace will stand in
  its proper place.
¹⁹From them will come songs of
  thanksgiving   Isa 35:10; 51:3
and the sound of rejoicing.
I will add to their numbers,
  and they will not be
  decreased;
I will bring them honor,   Isa 60:9
  and they will not be
  disdained.
²⁰Their children will be as in
  days of old,   Isa 54:13
and their community will be
  established before me;
I will punish all who oppress
  them.   Ex 23:22
²¹Their leader will be one of
  their own;   Jer 23:5-6

their ruler will arise from
  among them.   Dt 17:15
I will bring him near and he
  will come close to me,
for who is he who will
  devote himself
to be close to me?'
            declares the LORD.
²²" 'So you will be my people,
  and I will be your God.' "

²³See, the storm of the LORD
  will burst out in wrath,
a driving wind swirling down
  on the heads of the wicked.
²⁴The fierce anger of the LORD
  will not turn back
until he fully accomplishes
  the purposes of his heart.
In days to come
  you will understand this.

31 "At that time," declares the
    LORD, "I will be the God of
all the clans of Israel, and they will
be my people."   Jer 30:22
²This is what the LORD says:

"The people who survive the
  sword
will find favor in the desert;
I will come to give rest to
  Israel."   Ex 33:14

³The LORD appeared to us in the
past,ᵃ saying:

"I have loved you with an
  everlasting love;   Dt 4:37
I have drawn you with
  loving-kindness.   Hos 11:4

ᵃ 3 Or LORD has appeared to us from afar

⁴I will build you up again
   and you will be rebuilt,
      O Virgin Israel.   2Ki 19:21
Again you will take up your
      tambourines   Ge 31:27
and go out to dance with the
      joyful.   Jer 30:19
⁵Again you will plant vineyards
   on the hills of Samaria;
the farmers will plant them
and enjoy their fruit.   Isa 65:21
⁶There will be a day when
      watchmen cry out
on the hills of Ephraim,
'Come, let us go up to Zion,
   to the LORD our God.' "   Isa 2:3

⁷This is what the LORD says:

"Sing with joy for Jacob;
   shout for the foremost of the
      nations.   Dt 28:13; Isa 61:9
Make your praises heard, and
      say,
   'O LORD, save your people,
   the remnant of Israel.'
⁸See, I will bring them from the
      land of the north   Jer 3:18
and gather them from the
      ends of the earth.   Dt 30:4
Among them will be the blind
      and the lame,   Isa 42:16
expectant mothers and
      women in labor;
a great throng will return.
⁹They will come with weeping;
   they will pray as I bring
      them back.
I will lead them beside streams
      of water   Isa 63:13
on a level path where they
      will not stumble,   Isa 49:11

because I am Israel's father,
   and Ephraim is my firstborn
      son.

¹⁰"Hear the word of the LORD,
      O nations;
   proclaim it in distant
      coastlands: Isa 66:19
'He who scattered Israel will
      gather them   Jer 50:19
and will watch over his flock
      like a shepherd.'   Isa 40:11
¹¹For the LORD will ransom Jacob
   and redeem them from the
      hand of those stronger
      than they.   Ps 142:6; Isa 44:23
¹²They will come and shout for
      joy on the heights of
      Zion;   Eze 17:23; Mic 4:1
they will rejoice in the
      bounty of the LORD—
the grain, the new wine and
      the oil,   Hos 2:21-22
the young of the flocks and
      herds.
They will be like a
      well-watered garden,
and they will sorrow no
      more.   Isa 65:19; Jn 16:22
¹³Then maidens will dance and
      be glad,
young men and old as well.
I will turn their mourning into
      gladness;   Isa 61:3
I will give them comfort and
      joy instead of sorrow.
¹⁴I will satisfy the priests with
      abundance,   Lev 7:35-36
and my people will be filled
      with my bounty,"
      declares the LORD.

15This is what the Lord says:

"A voice is heard in Ramah,
  mourning and great weeping,
Rachel weeping for her
    children
  and refusing to be
    comforted,   Ge 37:35
because her children are no
    more."   Mt 2:17-18*

16This is what the Lord says:

"Restrain your voice from
    weeping
  and your eyes from tears,
for your work will be
    rewarded,"   Ru 2:12
        declares the Lord.
"They will return from the
    land of the enemy.
17So there is hope for your
    future,"   Job 8:7; La 3:29
        declares the Lord.
"Your children will return to
    their own land.   Jer 30:20

18"I have surely heard Ephraim's
    moaning:
'You disciplined me like an
    unruly calf,   Job 5:17; Hos 4:16
and I have been disciplined.
Restore me, and I will return,
  because you are the Lord
    my God.
19After I strayed,   Eze 36:31
  I repented;
after I came to understand,
  I beat my breast.   Eze 21:12
I was ashamed and humiliated

because I bore the disgrace
  of my youth.'   Jer 22:21
20Is not Ephraim my dear son,
  the child in whom I delight?
Though I often speak against
    him,
  I still remember him.   Hos 4:4
Therefore my heart yearns for
    him;
  I have great compassion for
    him,"   Isa 63:15; Mic 7:18
        declares the Lord.

21"Set up road signs;
  put up guideposts.
Take note of the highway,
  the road that you take.
Return, O Virgin Israel,   Isa 52:11
  return to your towns.
22How long will you wander,
  O unfaithful daughter?   Jer 3:6
The Lord will create a new
    thing on earth—   Isa 43:19
  a woman will surround^a a
    man."   Dt 32:10

23This is what the Lord Almighty, the God of Israel, says: "When I bring them back from captivity,^b the people in the land of Judah and in its towns will once again use these words: 'The Lord bless you, O righteous dwelling, O sacred mountain.' **24**People will live together in Judah and all its towns—farmers and those who move about with their flocks. **25**I will refresh the weary and satisfy the faint."   Jn 4:14; Isa 1:26; Zec 8:4-8

26At this I awoke and looked

---

^a22 Or *will go about ,seeking,*; or *will protect*   ^b23 Or *I restore their fortunes*

around. My sleep had been pleasant to me. Zec 4:1

27"The days are coming," declares the LORD, "when I will plant the house of Israel and the house of Judah with the offspring of men and of animals. 28Just as I watched over them to uproot and tear down, and to overthrow, destroy and bring disaster, so I will watch over them to build and to plant," declares the LORD. 29"In those days people will no longer say, Jer 1:10

'The fathers have eaten sour
    grapes, La 5:7
and the children's teeth are
    set on edge.' Eze 18:2

30Instead, everyone will die for his own sin; whoever eats sour grapes —his own teeth will be set on edge. Isa 3:11; Gal 6:7

31"The time is coming," declares
    the LORD,
"when I will make a new
    covenant Heb 8:8-12*; 10:16-17
with the house of Israel
and with the house of
    Judah.
32It will not be like the covenant
    I made with their forefathers
when I took them by the hand
    to lead them out of Egypt,
because they broke my
    covenant,
though I was a husband to^a
    them,^{b}" Isa 54:5
        declares the LORD.

33"This is the covenant I will
    make with the house of
    Israel
after that time," declares the
    LORD.
"I will put my law in their
    minds
and write it on their hearts.
I will be their God,
and they will be my people.
34No longer will a man teach his
    neighbor, 1Jn 2:27
or a man his brother, saying,
    'Know the LORD,'
because they will all know me,
from the least of them to the
    greatest,"
        declares the LORD.
"For I will forgive their
    wickedness Isa 54:13; Jer 33:8
and will remember their sins
    no more." Mic 7:19

35This is what the LORD says,
he who appoints the sun
    to shine by day,
who decrees the moon and
    stars
    to shine by night, Ge 1:16
who stirs up the sea Ex 14:21
    so that its waves roar—
the LORD Almighty is his
    name: Jer 10:16
36"Only if these decrees vanish
    from my sight,"
    declares the LORD,
"will the descendants of Israel
    ever cease Ps 89:36-37
to be a nation before me."

^{a}32 Hebrew; Septuagint and Syriac / and I turned away from ^{b}32 Or was their master

37This is what the LORD says:

"Only if the heavens above can
    be measured   Jer 33:22
and the foundations of the
    earth below be searched
    out
will I reject all the descendants
    of Israel   Jer 33:24-26; Ro 11:1-5
because of all they have
    done,"
                declares the LORD.

38"The days are coming," declares the LORD, "when this city will be rebuilt for me from the Tower of Hananel to the Corner Gate. **39**The measuring line will stretch from there straight to the hill of Gareb and then turn to Goah. **40**The whole valley where dead bodies and ashes are thrown, and all the terraces out to the Kidron Valley on the east as far as the corner of the Horse Gate, will be holy to the LORD. The city will never again be uprooted or demolished."   Joel 3:17; Zec 14:21

Jeremiah Buys a Field

32 This is the word that came to Jeremiah from the LORD in the tenth year of Zedekiah king of Judah, which was the eighteenth year of Nebuchadnezzar. **2**The army of the king of Babylon was then besieging Jerusalem, and Jeremiah the prophet was con-fined in the courtyard of the guard in the royal palace of Judah.

3Now Zedekiah king of Judah had imprisoned him there, saying, "Why do you prophesy as you do? You say, 'This is what the LORD says: I am about to hand this city over to the king of Babylon, and he will capture it. **4**Zedekiah king of Judah will not escape out of the hands of the Babylonians[a] but will certainly be handed over to the king of Babylon, and will speak with him face to face and see him with his own eyes. **5**He will take Zedekiah to Babylon, where he will remain until I deal with him, declares the LORD. If you fight against the Babylonians, you will not succeed.' "   Jer 34:2-3; 38:18,23

6Jeremiah said, "The word of the LORD came to me: **7**Hanamel son of Shallum your uncle is going to come to you and say, 'Buy my field at Anathoth, because as nearest relative it is your right and duty to buy it.'   Lev 25:24-25; Ru 4:3-4; Mt 27:10*

8"Then, just as the LORD had said, my cousin Hanamel came to me in the courtyard of the guard and said, 'Buy my field at Anathoth in the territory of Benjamin. Since it is your right to redeem it and possess it, buy it for yourself.'

"I knew that this was the word of the LORD; **9**so I bought the field at Anathoth from my cousin Hanamel and weighed out for him sev-

---

a4 Or *Chaldeans*; also in verses 5, 24, 25, 28, 29 and 43

enteen shekels*a* of silver. [10]I signed and sealed the deed, had it witnessed, and weighed out the silver on the scales. [11]I took the deed of purchase—the sealed copy containing the terms and conditions, as well as the unsealed copy— [12]and I gave this deed to Baruch son of Neriah, the son of Mahseiah, in the presence of my cousin Hanamel and of the witnesses who had signed the deed and of all the Jews sitting in the courtyard of the guard. Jer 36:4

[13]"In their presence I gave Baruch these instructions: [14]'This is what the LORD Almighty, the God of Israel, says: Take these documents, both the sealed and unsealed copies of the deed of purchase, and put them in a clay jar so they will last a long time. [15]For this is what the LORD Almighty, the God of Israel, says: Houses, fields and vineyards will again be bought in this land.' Jer 30:18; Am 9:14-15

[16]"After I had given the deed of purchase to Baruch son of Neriah, I prayed to the LORD:

[17]"Ah, Sovereign LORD, you have made the heavens and the earth by your great power and outstretched arm. Nothing is too hard for you. [18]You show love to thousands but bring the punishment for the fathers' sins into the laps of their children after them.

O great and powerful God, whose name is the LORD Almighty, [19]great are your purposes and mighty are your deeds. Your eyes are open to all the ways of men; you reward everyone according to his conduct and as his deeds deserve. [20]You performed miraculous signs and wonders in Egypt and have continued them to this day, both in Israel and among all mankind, and have gained the renown that is still yours. [21]You brought your people Israel out of Egypt with signs and wonders, by a mighty hand and an outstretched arm and with great terror. [22]You gave them this land you had sworn to give their forefathers, a land flowing with milk and honey. [23]They came in and took possession of it, but they did not obey you or follow your law; they did not do what you commanded them to do. So you brought all this disaster upon them. Ps 44:2

[24]"See how the siege ramps are built up to take the city. Because of the sword, famine and plague, the city will be handed over to the Babylonians who are attacking it. What you said has happened, as you now see. [25]And though the city will be handed over to

a9 That is, about 7 ounces (about 200 grams)

the Babylonians, you, O Sovereign LORD, say to me, 'Buy the field with silver and have the transaction witnessed.' "

26Then the word of the LORD came to Jeremiah: 27"I am the LORD, the God of all mankind. Is anything too hard for me? 28Therefore, this is what the LORD says: I am about to hand this city over to the Babylonians and to Nebuchadnezzar king of Babylon, who will capture it. 29The Babylonians who are attacking this city will come in and set it on fire; they will burn it down, along with the houses where the people provoked me to anger by burning incense on the roofs to Baal and by pouring out drink offerings to other gods.

30"The people of Israel and Judah have done nothing but evil in my sight from their youth; indeed, the people of Israel have done nothing but provoke me with what their hands have made, declares the LORD. 31From the day it was built until now, this city has so aroused my anger and wrath that I must remove it from my sight. 32The people of Israel and Judah have provoked me by all the evil they have done—they, their kings and officials, their priests and prophets, the men of Judah and the people of Jerusalem. 33They turned their backs to me and not their faces; though I taught them

again and again, they would not listen or respond to discipline. 34They set up their abominable idols in the house that bears my Name and defiled it. 35They built high places for Baal in the Valley of Ben Hinnom to sacrifice their sons and daughters[a] to Molech, though I never commanded, nor did it enter my mind, that they should do such a detestable thing and so make Judah sin.   Lev 18:21; Jer 19:5

36"You are saying about this city, 'By the sword, famine and plague it will be handed over to the king of Babylon'; but this is what the LORD, the God of Israel, says: 37I will surely gather them from all the lands where I banish them in my furious anger and great wrath; I will bring them back to this place and let them live in safety. 38They will be my people, and I will be their God. 39I will give them singleness of heart and action, so that they will always fear me for their own good and the good of their children after them. 40I will make an everlasting covenant with them: I will never stop doing good to them, and I will inspire them to fear me, so that they will never turn away from me. 41I will rejoice in doing them good and will assuredly plant them in this land with all my heart and soul.   Dt 30:9

42"This is what the LORD says: As I have brought all this great calamity on this people, so I will give

a35 Or to make their sons and daughters pass through the fire.

them all the prosperity I have promised them. ⁴³Once more fields will be bought in this land of which you say, 'It is a desolate waste, without men or animals, for it has been handed over to the Babylonians.' ⁴⁴Fields will be bought for silver, and deeds will be signed, sealed and witnessed in the territory of Benjamin, in the villages around Jerusalem, in the towns of Judah and in the towns of the hill country, of the western foothills and of the Negev, because I will restore their fortunes,ᵃ declares the LORD."   Jer 17:26; 33:7,11,26

Promise of Restoration

33 While Jeremiah was still confined in the courtyard of the guard, the word of the LORD came to him a second time: ²"This is what the LORD says, he who made the earth, the LORD who formed it and established it—the LORD is his name: ³'Call to me and I will answer you and tell you great and unsearchable things you do not know.' ⁴For this is what the LORD, the God of Israel, says about the houses in this city and the royal palaces of Judah that have been torn down to be used against the siege ramps and the sword ⁵in the fight with the Babyloniansᵇ: 'They will be filled with the dead bodies of the men I will slay in my anger and wrath. I will hide my face from this city because of all its wickedness.   Isa 55:6; Jer 29:12

⁶" 'Nevertheless, I will bring health and healing to it; I will heal my people and will let them enjoy abundant peace and security. ⁷I will bring Judah and Israel back from captivityᶜ and will rebuild them as they were before. ⁸I will cleanse them from all the sin they have committed against me and will forgive all their sins of rebellion against me. ⁹Then this city will bring me renown, joy, praise and honor before all nations on earth that hear of all the good things I do for it; and they will be in awe and will tremble at the abundant prosperity and peace I provide for it.'   Heb 9:13-14; Jer 3:17

¹⁰"This is what the LORD says: 'You say about this place, "It is a desolate waste, without men or animals." Yet in the towns of Judah and the streets of Jerusalem that are deserted, inhabited by neither men nor animals, there will be heard once more ¹¹the sounds of joy and gladness, the voices of bride and bridegroom, and the voices of those who bring thank offerings to the house of the LORD, saying,   Lev 7:12; Jer 32:43

"Give thanks to the LORD
    Almighty,
  for the LORD is good;   Ps 136:1
    his love endures forever."

ᵃ44 Or *will bring them back from captivity*   ᵇ5 Or *Chaldeans*   ᶜ7 Or *will restore the fortunes of Judah and Israel*

For I will restore the fortunes of the land as they were before,' says the LORD.   Ps 14:7; Isa 1:26

¹²"This is what the LORD Almighty says: 'In this place, desolate and without men or animals—in all its towns there will again be pastures for shepherds to rest their flocks. ¹³In the towns of the hill country, of the western foothills and of the Negev, in the territory of Benjamin, in the villages around Jerusalem and in the towns of Judah, flocks will again pass under the hand of the one who counts them,' says the LORD.   Lev 27:32

¹⁴" 'The days are coming,' declares the LORD, 'when I will fulfill the gracious promise I made to the house of Israel and to the house of Judah.   Jer 29:10

¹⁵" 'In those days and at that
        time
    I will make a righteous
        Branch sprout from
        David's line;   Ps 72:2; Isa 4:2
    he will do what is just and
        right in the land.
¹⁶In those days Judah will be
        saved   Isa 45:17
    and Jerusalem will live in
        safety.
    This is the name by which it[a]
        will be called: Isa 59:14
        The LORD Our
            Righteousness.'   1Co 1:30

¹⁷For this is what the LORD says: 'David will never fail to have a man to sit on the throne of the house of Israel, ¹⁸nor will the priests, who are Levites, ever fail to have a man to stand before me continually to offer burnt offerings, to burn grain offerings and to present sacrifices.' "   2Sa 7:13; 1Ki 2:4; Lk 1:33

¹⁹The word of the LORD came to Jeremiah: ²⁰"This is what the LORD says: 'If you can break my covenant with the day and my covenant with the night, so that day and night no longer come at their appointed time, ²¹then my covenant with David my servant—and my covenant with the Levites who are priests ministering before me—can be broken and David will no longer have a descendant to reign on his throne. ²²I will make the descendants of David my servant and the Levites who minister before me as countless as the stars of the sky and as measureless as the sand on the seashore.' "

²³The word of the LORD came to Jeremiah: ²⁴"Have you not noticed that these people are saying, 'The LORD has rejected the two kingdoms[b] he chose'? So they despise my people and no longer regard them as a nation. ²⁵This is what the LORD says: 'If I have not established my covenant with day and night and the fixed laws of heaven and earth, ²⁶then I will reject the descendants of Jacob and David my servant and will not choose one of his sons to rule over the

descendants of Abraham, Isaac and Jacob. For I will restore their fortunes[a] and have compassion on them.' " Ps 74:16-17; Jer 31:35-37

Warning to Zedekiah

34 While Nebuchadnezzar king of Babylon and all his army and all the kingdoms and peoples in the empire he ruled were fighting against Jerusalem and all its surrounding towns, this word came to Jeremiah from the LORD: ²"This is what the LORD, the God of Israel, says: Go to Zedekiah king of Judah and tell him, 'This is what the LORD says: I am about to hand this city over to the king of Babylon, and he will burn it down. ³You will not escape from his grasp but will surely be captured and handed over to him. You will see the king of Babylon with your own eyes, and he will speak with you face to face. And you will go to Babylon. 2Ki 25:1; Jer 32:4,29

⁴" 'Yet hear the promise of the LORD, O Zedekiah king of Judah. This is what the LORD says concerning you: You will not die by the sword; ⁵you will die peacefully. As people made a funeral fire in honor of your fathers, the former kings who preceded you, so they will make a fire in your honor and lament, "Alas, O master!" I myself make this promise, declares the LORD.' " 2Ch 16:14; Jer 22:18

⁶Then Jeremiah the prophet told all this to Zedekiah king of Judah, in Jerusalem, ⁷while the army of the king of Babylon was fighting against Jerusalem and the other cities of Judah that were still holding out—Lachish and Azekah. These were the only fortified cities left in Judah. Jos 10:3; 2Ch 11:9

Freedom for Slaves

⁸The word came to Jeremiah from the LORD after King Zedekiah had made a covenant with all the people in Jerusalem to proclaim freedom for the slaves. ⁹Everyone was to free his Hebrew slaves, both male and female; no one was to hold a fellow Jew in bondage. ¹⁰So all the officials and people who entered into this covenant agreed that they would free their male and female slaves and no longer hold them in bondage. They agreed, and set them free. ¹¹But afterward they changed their minds and took back the slaves they had freed and enslaved them again. Ex 21:2

¹²Then the word of the LORD came to Jeremiah: ¹³"This is what the LORD, the God of Israel, says: I made a covenant with your forefathers when I brought them out of Egypt, out of the land of slavery. I said, ¹⁴'Every seventh year each of you must free any fellow Hebrew who has sold himself to you. After he has served you six years, you must let him go free.'[b] Your fathers, however, did not listen to

---

[a] 26 Or *will bring them back from captivity*   [b] 14 Deut. 15:12

me or pay attention to me. [15]Recently you repented and did what is right in my sight: Each of you proclaimed freedom to his countrymen. You even made a covenant before me in the house that bears my Name. [16]But now you have turned around and profaned my name; each of you has taken back the male and female slaves you had set free to go where they wished. You have forced them to become your slaves again. Ex 20:7

[17]"Therefore, this is what the LORD says: You have not obeyed me; you have not proclaimed freedom for your fellow countrymen. So I now proclaim 'freedom' for you, declares the LORD — 'freedom' to fall by the sword, plague and famine. I will make you abhorrent to all the kingdoms of the earth. [18]The men who have violated my covenant and have not fulfilled the terms of the covenant they made before me, I will treat like the calf they cut in two and then walked between its pieces. [19]The leaders of Judah and Jerusalem, the court officials, the priests and all the people of the land who walked between the pieces of the calf, [20]I will hand over to their enemies who seek their lives. Their dead bodies will become food for the birds of the air and the beasts of the earth.

[21]"I will hand Zedekiah king of Judah and his officials over to their enemies who seek their lives, to the army of the king of Babylon, which has withdrawn from you. [22]I

am going to give the order, declares the LORD, and I will bring them back to this city. They will fight against it, take it and burn it down. And I will lay waste the towns of Judah so no one can live there." Jer 37:5; 39:1-2

The Recabites

35 This is the word that came to Jeremiah from the LORD during the reign of Jehoiakim son of Josiah king of Judah: [2]"Go to the Recabite family and invite them to come to one of the side rooms of the house of the LORD and give them wine to drink." 1Ki 6:5

[3]So I went to get Jaazaniah son of Jeremiah, the son of Habazziniah, and his brothers and all his sons — the whole family of the Recabites. [4]I brought them into the house of the LORD, into the room of the sons of Hanan son of Igdaliah the man of God. It was next to the room of the officials, which was over that of Maaseiah son of Shallum the doorkeeper. [5]Then I set bowls full of wine and some cups before the men of the Recabite family and said to them, "Drink some wine." Dt 33:1; 1Ch 9:19

[6]But they replied, "We do not drink wine, because our forefather Jonadab son of Recab gave us this command: 'Neither you nor your descendants must ever drink wine. [7]Also you must never build houses, sow seed or plant vineyards; you must never have any of these things, but must always live

in tents. Then you will live a long time in the land where you are nomads.' **8**We have obeyed everything our forefather Jonadab son of Recab commanded us. Neither we nor our wives nor our sons and daughters have ever drunk wine **9**or built houses to live in or had vineyards, fields or crops. **10**We have lived in tents and have fully obeyed everything our forefather Jonadab commanded us. **11**But when Nebuchadnezzar king of Babylon invaded this land, we said, 'Come, we must go to Jerusalem to escape the Babylonian*a* and Aramean armies.' So we have remained in Jerusalem."   2Ki 10:15

12Then the word of the LORD came to Jeremiah, saying: **13**"This is what the LORD Almighty, the God of Israel, says: Go and tell the men of Judah and the people of Jerusalem, 'Will you not learn a lesson and obey my words?' declares the LORD. **14**'Jonadab son of Recab ordered his sons not to drink wine and this command has been kept. To this day they do not drink wine, because they obey their forefather's command. But I have spoken to you again and again, yet you have not obeyed me. **15**Again and again I sent all my servants the prophets to you. They said, "Each of you must turn from your wicked ways and reform your actions; do not follow other gods to serve them. Then you will live in

the land I have given to you and your fathers." But you have not paid attention or listened to me. **16**The descendants of Jonadab son of Recab have carried out the command their forefather gave them, but these people have not obeyed me.'   Jer 7:13; 18:11; 32:33

17"Therefore, this is what the LORD God Almighty, the God of Israel, says: 'Listen! I am going to bring on Judah and on everyone living in Jerusalem every disaster I pronounced against them. I spoke to them, but they did not listen; I called to them, but they did not answer.' "   Isa 65:12; Jer 7:13; Pr 1:24

18Then Jeremiah said to the family of the Recabites, "This is what the LORD Almighty, the God of Israel, says: 'You have obeyed the command of your forefather Jonadab and have followed all his instructions and have done everything he ordered.' **19**Therefore, this is what the LORD Almighty, the God of Israel, says: 'Jonadab son of Recab will never fail to have a man to serve me.' "   Jer 15:19; 33:17

Jehoiakim Burns Jeremiah's Scroll

36 In the fourth year of Jehoiakim son of Josiah king of Judah, this word came to Jeremiah from the LORD: **2**"Take a scroll and write on it all the words I have spoken to you concerning Israel, Judah and all the other nations from

a 11 Or Chaldean

the time I began speaking to you in the reign of Josiah till now. **3**Perhaps when the people of Judah hear about every disaster I plan to inflict on them, each of them will turn from his wicked way; then I will forgive their wickedness and their sin." Jer 18:8; 26:3; Jnh 3:8

4So Jeremiah called Baruch son of Neriah, and while Jeremiah dictated all the words the LORD had spoken to him, Baruch wrote them on the scroll. **5**Then Jeremiah told Baruch, "I am restricted; I cannot go to the LORD's temple. **6**So you go to the house of the LORD on a day of fasting and read to the people from the scroll the words of the LORD that you wrote as I dictated. Read them to all the people of Judah who come in from their towns. **7**Perhaps they will bring their petition before the LORD, and each will turn from his wicked ways, for the anger and wrath pronounced against this people by the LORD are great." Jer 32:12; Eze 2:9

8Baruch son of Neriah did everything Jeremiah the prophet told him to do; at the LORD's temple he read the words of the LORD from the scroll. **9**In the ninth month of the fifth year of Jehoiakim son of Josiah king of Judah, a time of fasting before the LORD was proclaimed for all the people in Jerusalem and those who had come from the towns of Judah. **10**From the room of Gemariah son of Shaphan the secretary, which was in the upper courtyard at the entrance of the New Gate of the temple, Baruch read to all the people at the LORD's temple the words of Jeremiah from the scroll. 2Ch 20:3

11When Micaiah son of Gemariah, the son of Shaphan, heard all the words of the LORD from the scroll, **12**he went down to the secretary's room in the royal palace, where all the officials were sitting: Elishama the secretary, Delaiah son of Shemaiah, Elnathan son of Acbor, Gemariah son of Shaphan, Zedekiah son of Hananiah, and all the other officials. **13**After Micaiah told them everything he had heard Baruch read to the people from the scroll, **14**all the officials sent Jehudi son of Nethaniah, the son of Shelemiah, the son of Cushi, to say to Baruch, "Bring the scroll from which you have read to the people and come." So Baruch son of Neriah went to them with the scroll in his hand. **15**They said to him, "Sit down, please, and read it to us."

So Baruch read it to them. **16**When they heard all these words, they looked at each other in fear and said to Baruch, "We must report all these words to the king." **17**Then they asked Baruch, "Tell us, how did you come to write all this? Did Jeremiah dictate it?"

18"Yes," Baruch replied, "he dictated all these words to me, and I wrote them in ink on the scroll."

19Then the officials said to Baruch, "You and Jeremiah, go and hide. Don't let anyone know where you are." 1Ki 17:3

²⁰After they put the scroll in the room of Elishama the secretary, they went to the king in the courtyard and reported everything to him. ²¹The king sent Jehudi to get the scroll, and Jehudi brought it from the room of Elishama the secretary and read it to the king and all the officials standing beside him. ²²It was the ninth month and the king was sitting in the winter apartment, with a fire burning in the firepot in front of him. ²³Whenever Jehudi had read three or four columns of the scroll, the king cut them off with a scribe's knife and threw them into the firepot, until the entire scroll was burned in the fire. ²⁴The king and all his attendants who heard all these words showed no fear, nor did they tear their clothes. ²⁵Even though Elnathan, Delaiah and Gemariah urged the king not to burn the scroll, he would not listen to them. ²⁶Instead, the king commanded Jerahmeel, a son of the king, Seraiah son of Azriel and Shelemiah son of Abdeel to arrest Baruch the scribe and Jeremiah the prophet. But the LORD had hidden them.   1Ki 22:8

²⁷After the king burned the scroll containing the words that Baruch had written at Jeremiah's dictation, the word of the LORD came to Jeremiah: ²⁸"Take another scroll and write on it all the words that were on the first scroll, which Jehoiakim king of Judah burned up. ²⁹Also tell Jehoiakim king of Judah, 'This is what the LORD says: You burned that scroll and said, "Why did you write on it that the king of Babylon would certainly come and destroy this land and cut off both men and animals from it?" ³⁰Therefore, this is what the LORD says about Jehoiakim king of Judah: He will have no one to sit on the throne of David; his body will be thrown out and exposed to the heat by day and the frost by night. ³¹I will punish him and his children and his attendants for their wickedness; I will bring on them and those living in Jerusalem and the people of Judah every disaster I pronounced against them, because they have not listened.' "

³²So Jeremiah took another scroll and gave it to the scribe Baruch son of Neriah, and as Jeremiah dictated, Baruch wrote on it all the words of the scroll that Jehoiakim king of Judah had burned in the fire. And many similar words were added to them.   ver 4; Ex 34:1

Jeremiah in Prison

37 Zedekiah son of Josiah was made king of Judah by Nebuchadnezzar king of Babylon; he reigned in place of Jehoiachin[a] son of Jehoiakim. ²Neither he nor his attendants nor the people of the land paid any attention to the words the LORD had spoken through Jeremiah the prophet.

---

a 1 Hebrew *Coniah*, a variant of *Jehoiachin*

³King Zedekiah, however, sent Jehucal son of Shelemiah with the priest Zephaniah son of Maaseiah to Jeremiah the prophet with this message: "Please pray to the Lord our God for us."   Jer 21:1-2; 42:2

⁴Now Jeremiah was free to come and go among the people, for he had not yet been put in prison. ⁵Pharaoh's army had marched out of Egypt, and when the Babylonians*a* who were besieging Jerusalem heard the report about them, they withdrew from Jerusalem.

⁶Then the word of the Lord came to Jeremiah the prophet: ⁷"This is what the Lord, the God of Israel, says: Tell the king of Judah, who sent you to inquire of me, 'Pharaoh's army, which has marched out to support you, will go back to its own land, to Egypt. ⁸Then the Babylonians will return and attack this city; they will capture it and burn it down.'

⁹"This is what the Lord says: Do not deceive yourselves, thinking, 'The Babylonians will surely leave us.' They will not! ¹⁰Even if you were to defeat the entire Babylonian*b* army that is attacking you and only wounded men were left in their tents, they would come out and burn this city down."   Jer 34:22

¹¹After the Babylonian army had withdrawn from Jerusalem because of Pharaoh's army, ¹²Jeremiah started to leave the city to go to the territory of Benjamin to get his share of the property among the people there. ¹³But when he reached the Benjamin Gate, the captain of the guard, whose name was Irijah son of Shelemiah, the son of Hananiah, arrested him and said, "You are deserting to the Babylonians!"   Jer 32:9

¹⁴"That's not true!" Jeremiah said. "I am not deserting to the Babylonians." But Irijah would not listen to him; instead, he arrested Jeremiah and brought him to the officials. ¹⁵They were angry with Jeremiah and had him beaten and imprisoned in the house of Jonathan the secretary, which they had made into a prison.   Jer 38:26; 40:4

¹⁶Jeremiah was put into a vaulted cell in a dungeon, where he remained a long time. ¹⁷Then King Zedekiah sent for him and had him brought to the palace, where he asked him privately, "Is there any word from the Lord?"   Jer 15:11

"Yes," Jeremiah replied, "you will be handed over to the king of Babylon."   Jer 21:7

¹⁸Then Jeremiah said to King Zedekiah, "What crime have I committed against you or your officials or this people, that you have put me in prison? ¹⁹Where are your prophets who prophesied to you, 'The king of Babylon will not attack you or this land'? ²⁰But now, my lord the king, please listen. Let me bring my petition before you: Do not send me back to the house

---

a 5 Or *Chaldeans*; also in verses 8, 9, 13 and 14   *b* 10 Or *Chaldean*; also in verse 11

of Jonathan the secretary, or I will die there." 1Sa 26:18; Jn 10:32

²¹King Zedekiah then gave orders for Jeremiah to be placed in the courtyard of the guard and given bread from the street of the bakers each day until all the bread in the city was gone. So Jeremiah remained in the courtyard of the guard. Jer 32:2; 38:6,13,28; 52:6

Jeremiah Thrown Into a Cistern

38 Shephatiah son of Mattan, Gedaliah son of Pashhur, Jehucal*ᵃ* son of Shelemiah, and Pashhur son of Malkijah heard what Jeremiah was telling all the people when he said, ²"This is what the LORD says: 'Whoever stays in this city will die by the sword, famine or plague, but whoever goes over to the Babylonians*ᵇ* will live. He will escape with his life; he will live.' ³And this is what the LORD says: 'This city will certainly be handed over to the army of the king of Babylon, who will capture it.' " Jer 21:4,10; 32:3; 37:3

⁴Then the officials said to the king, "This man should be put to death. He is discouraging the soldiers who are left in this city, as well as all the people, by the things he is saying to them. This man is not seeking the good of these people but their ruin." Jer 26:11; 36:12

⁵"He is in your hands," King Zedekiah answered. "The king can do nothing to oppose you."

⁶So they took Jeremiah and put him into the cistern of Malkijah, the king's son, which was in the courtyard of the guard. They lowered Jeremiah by ropes into the cistern; it had no water in it, only mud, and Jeremiah sank down into the mud. Jer 37:21; La 3:53

⁷But Ebed-Melech, a Cushite,*ᶜ* an official*ᵈ* in the royal palace, heard that they had put Jeremiah into the cistern. While the king was sitting in the Benjamin Gate, ⁸Ebed-Melech went out of the palace and said to him, ⁹"My lord the king, these men have acted wickedly in all they have done to Jeremiah the prophet. They have thrown him into a cistern, where he will starve to death when there is no longer any bread in the city."

¹⁰Then the king commanded Ebed-Melech the Cushite, "Take thirty men from here with you and lift Jeremiah the prophet out of the cistern before he dies."

¹¹So Ebed-Melech took the men with him and went to a room under the treasury in the palace. He took some old rags and worn-out clothes from there and let them down with ropes to Jeremiah in the cistern. ¹²Ebed-Melech the Cushite said to Jeremiah, "Put these old rags and worn-out clothes under your arms to pad the

---

ᵃ 1 Hebrew *Jucal*, a variant of *Jehucal*   *ᵇ 2* Or *Chaldeans*; also in verses 18, 19 and 23   *ᶜ 7* Probably from the upper Nile region   *ᵈ 7* Or *a eunuch*

ropes." Jeremiah did so, [13]and they pulled him up with the ropes and lifted him out of the cistern. And Jeremiah remained in the courtyard of the guard.   Jer 37:21

Zedekiah Questions Jeremiah Again

[14]Then King Zedekiah sent for Jeremiah the prophet and had him brought to the third entrance to the temple of the LORD. "I am going to ask you something," the king said to Jeremiah. "Do not hide anything from me."   1Sa 3:17; Jer 37:3

[15]Jeremiah said to Zedekiah, "If I give you an answer, will you not kill me? Even if I did give you counsel, you would not listen to me."

[16]But King Zedekiah swore this oath secretly to Jeremiah: "As surely as the LORD lives, who has given us breath, I will neither kill you nor hand you over to those who are seeking your life."

[17]Then Jeremiah said to Zedekiah, "This is what the LORD God Almighty, the God of Israel, says: 'If you surrender to the officers of the king of Babylon, your life will be spared and this city will not be burned down; you and your family will live. [18]But if you will not surrender to the officers of the king of Babylon, this city will be handed over to the Babylonians and they will burn it down; you yourself will not escape from their hands.' "

[19]King Zedekiah said to Jeremiah, "I am afraid of the Jews who have gone over to the Babylonians, for the Babylonians may hand me over to them and they will mistreat me."   Isa 51:12; Jn 12:42

[20]"They will not hand you over," Jeremiah replied. "Obey the LORD by doing what I tell you. Then it will go well with you, and your life will be spared. [21]But if you refuse to surrender, this is what the LORD has revealed to me: [22]All the women left in the palace of the king of Judah will be brought out to the officials of the king of Babylon. Those women will say to you:

" 'They misled you and
      overcame you—
   those trusted friends of
      yours.   Jer 13:21
Your feet are sunk in the mud;
   your friends have deserted
      you.'

[23]"All your wives and children will be brought out to the Babylonians. You yourself will not escape from their hands but will be captured by the king of Babylon; and this city will[a] be burned down."

[24]Then Zedekiah said to Jeremiah, "Do not let anyone know about this conversation, or you may die. [25]If the officials hear that I talked with you, and they come to you and say, 'Tell us what you said to the king and what the king said to

---

[a] 23 Or and you will cause this city to

you; do not hide it from us or we will kill you,' ²⁶then tell them, 'I was pleading with the king not to send me back to Jonathan's house to die there.' "   Jer 37:15

²⁷All the officials did come to Jeremiah and question him, and he told them everything the king had ordered him to say. So they said no more to him, for no one had heard his conversation with the king.

²⁸And Jeremiah remained in the courtyard of the guard until the day Jerusalem was captured.

The Fall of Jerusalem

39 This is how Jerusalem was taken: ¹In the ninth year of Zedekiah king of Judah, in the tenth month, Nebuchadnezzar king of Babylon marched against Jerusalem with his whole army and laid siege to it. ²And on the ninth day of the fourth month of Zedekiah's eleventh year, the city wall was broken through. ³Then all the officials of the king of Babylon came and took seats in the Middle Gate: Nergal-Sharezer of Samgar, Nebo-Sarsekim^a a chief officer, Nergal-Sharezer a high official and all the other officials of the king of Babylon. ⁴When Zedekiah king of Judah and all the soldiers saw them, they fled; they left the city at night by way of the king's garden, through the gate be-

tween the two walls, and headed toward the Arabah.^b   Jer 25:29

⁵But the Babylonian^c army pursued them and overtook Zedekiah in the plains of Jericho. They captured him and took him to Nebuchadnezzar king of Babylon at Riblah in the land of Hamath, where he pronounced sentence on him. ⁶There at Riblah the king of Babylon slaughtered the sons of Zedekiah before his eyes and also killed all the nobles of Judah. ⁷Then he put out Zedekiah's eyes and bound him with bronze shackles to take him to Babylon.   2Ki 23:33

⁸The Babylonians^d set fire to the royal palace and the houses of the people and broke down the walls of Jerusalem. ⁹Nebuzaradan commander of the imperial guard carried into exile to Babylon the people who remained in the city, along with those who had gone over to him, and the rest of the people. ¹⁰But Nebuzaradan the commander of the guard left behind in the land of Judah some of the poor people, who owned nothing; and at that time he gave them vineyards and fields.   2Ki 25:1-12

¹¹Now Nebuchadnezzar king of Babylon had given these orders about Jeremiah through Nebuzaradan commander of the imperial guard: ¹²"Take him and look after him; don't harm him but do for him whatever he asks." ¹³So Nebu-

---

^a3 Or *Nergal-Sharezer, Samgar-Nebo, Sarsekim*   ^b4 Or *the Jordan Valley*   ^c5 Or *Chaldean*   ^d8 Or *Chaldeans* zaradan the commander of the guard, Nebushazban a chief officer, Nergal-Sharezer a high official and all the other officers of the king of Babylon [14]sent and had Jeremiah taken out of the courtyard of the guard. They turned him over to Gedaliah son of Ahikam, the son of Shaphan, to take him back to his home. So he remained among his own people.   Jer 38:28; 1Pe 3:13

[15]While Jeremiah had been confined in the courtyard of the guard, the word of the LORD came to him: [16]"Go and tell Ebed-Melech the Cushite, 'This is what the LORD Almighty, the God of Israel, says: I am about to fulfill my words against this city through disaster, not prosperity. At that time they will be fulfilled before your eyes. [17]But I will rescue you on that day, declares the LORD; you will not be handed over to those you fear. [18]I will save you; you will not fall by the sword but will escape with your life, because you trust in me, declares the LORD.' "   Jer 21:9; 45:5

Jeremiah Freed

40 The word came to Jeremiah from the LORD after Nebuzaradan commander of the imperial guard had released him at Ramah. He had found Jeremiah bound in chains among all the captives from Jerusalem and Judah who were being carried into exile to Babylon. [2]When the command-er of the guard found Jeremiah, he said to him, "The LORD your God decreed this disaster for this place. [3]And now the LORD has brought it about; he has done just as he said he would. All this happened because you people sinned against the LORD and did not obey him. [4]But today I am freeing you from the chains on your wrists. Come with me to Babylon, if you like, and I will look after you; but if you do not want to, then don't come. Look, the whole country lies before you; go wherever you please." [5]However, before Jeremiah turned to go,[a] Nebuzaradan added, "Go back to Gedaliah son of Ahikam, the son of Shaphan, whom the king of Babylon has appointed over the towns of Judah, and live with him among the people, or go anywhere else you please."

Then the commander gave him provisions and a present and let him go. [6]So Jeremiah went to Gedaliah son of Ahikam at Mizpah and stayed with him among the people who were left behind in the land.

Gedaliah Assassinated

[7]When all the army officers and their men who were still in the open country heard that the king of Babylon had appointed Gedaliah son of Ahikam as governor over the land and had put him in charge of the men, women and children who were the poorest in the land

---

[a] 5 Or *Jeremiah answered*

and who had not been carried into exile to Babylon, ⁸they came to Gedaliah at Mizpah—Ishmael son of Nethaniah, Johanan and Jonathan the sons of Kareah, Seraiah son of Tanhumeth, the sons of Ephai the Netophathite, and Jaazaniah*ᵃ* the son of the Maacathite, and their men. ⁹Gedaliah son of Ahikam, the son of Shaphan, took an oath to reassure them and their men. "Do not be afraid to serve the Babylonians,*ᵇ*" he said. "Settle down in the land and serve the king of Babylon, and it will go well with you. ¹⁰I myself will stay at Mizpah to represent you before the Babylonians who come to us, but you are to harvest the wine, summer fruit and oil, and put them in your storage jars, and live in the towns you have taken over."

¹¹When all the Jews in Moab, Ammon, Edom and all the other countries heard that the king of Babylon had left a remnant in Judah and had appointed Gedaliah son of Ahikam, the son of Shaphan, as governor over them, ¹²they all came back to the land of Judah, to Gedaliah at Mizpah, from all the countries where they had been scattered. And they harvested an abundance of wine and summer fruit.

Jer 43:5

¹³Johanan son of Kareah and all the army officers still in the open country came to Gedaliah at Mizpah ¹⁴and said to him, "Don't you know that Baalis king of the Ammonites has sent Ishmael son of Nethaniah to take your life?" But Gedaliah son of Ahikam did not believe them.

Jer 41:10

¹⁵Then Johanan son of Kareah said privately to Gedaliah in Mizpah, "Let me go and kill Ishmael son of Nethaniah, and no one will know it. Why should he take your life and cause all the Jews who are gathered around you to be scattered and the remnant of Judah to perish?"

2Ki 21:14; Isa 1:9; Ro 11:5

¹⁶But Gedaliah son of Ahikam said to Johanan son of Kareah, "Don't do such a thing! What you are saying about Ishmael is not true."

41 In the seventh month Ishmael son of Nethaniah, the son of Elishama, who was of royal blood and had been one of the king's officers, came with ten men to Gedaliah son of Ahikam at Mizpah. While they were eating together there, ²Ishmael son of Nethaniah and the ten men who were with him got up and struck down Gedaliah son of Ahikam, the son of Shaphan, with the sword, killing the one whom the king of Babylon had appointed as governor over the land. ³Ishmael also killed all the Jews who were with Gedaliah at Mizpah, as well as the Babylonian*ᶜ* soldiers who were there.

⁴The day after Gedaliah's assassination, before anyone knew

---

*ᵃ*8 Hebrew *Jezaniah*, a variant of *Jaazaniah*   *ᵇ*9 Or *Chaldeans*; also in verse 10   *ᶜ*3 Or *Chaldean* about it, [5]eighty men who had shaved off their beards, torn their clothes and cut themselves came from Shechem, Shiloh and Samaria, bringing grain offerings and incense with them to the house of the LORD. [6]Ishmael son of Nethaniah went out from Mizpah to meet them, weeping as he went. When he met them, he said, "Come to Gedaliah son of Ahikam." [7]When they went into the city, Ishmael son of Nethaniah and the men who were with him slaughtered them and threw them into a cistern. [8]But ten of them said to Ishmael, "Don't kill us! We have wheat and barley, oil and honey, hidden in a field." So he let them alone and did not kill them with the others. [9]Now the cistern where he threw all the bodies of the men he had killed along with Gedaliah was the one King Asa had made as part of his defense against Baasha king of Israel. Ishmael son of Nethaniah filled it with the dead.   1Ki 15:22; 2Ch 16:1,6

[10]Ishmael made captives of all the rest of the people who were in Mizpah—the king's daughters along with all the others who were left there, over whom Nebuzaradan commander of the imperial guard had appointed Gedaliah son of Ahikam. Ishmael son of Nethaniah took them captive and set out to cross over to the Ammonites. [11]When Johanan son of Kareah and all the army officers who were with him heard about all the crimes Ishmael son of Nethaniah had committed, [12]they took all their men and went to fight Ishmael son of Nethaniah. They caught up with him near the great pool in Gibeon. [13]When all the people Ishmael had with him saw Johanan son of Kareah and the army officers who were with him, they were glad. [14]All the people Ishmael had taken captive at Mizpah turned and went over to Johanan son of Kareah. [15]But Ishmael son of Nethaniah and eight of his men escaped from Johanan and fled to the Ammonites.   2Sa 2:13; Pr 28:17

Flight to Egypt

[16]Then Johanan son of Kareah and all the army officers who were with him led away all the survivors from Mizpah whom he had recovered from Ishmael son of Nethaniah after he had assassinated Gedaliah son of Ahikam: the soldiers, women, children and court officials he had brought from Gibeon. [17]And they went on, stopping at Geruth Kimham near Bethlehem on their way to Egypt [18]to escape the Babylonians.[a] They were afraid of them because Ishmael son of Nethaniah had killed Gedaliah son of Ahikam, whom the king of Babylon had appointed as governor over the land.

42 Then all the army officers, including Johanan son of

---

[a] 18 Or *Chaldeans*

Kareah and Jezaniah[a] son of Hoshaiah, and all the people from the least to the greatest approached ²Jeremiah the prophet and said to him, "Please hear our petition and pray to the LORD your God for this entire remnant. For as you now see, though we were once many, now only a few are left. ³Pray that the LORD your God will tell us where we should go and what we should do."   Ps 86:11; Pr 3:6

⁴"I have heard you," replied Jeremiah the prophet. "I will certainly pray to the LORD your God as you have requested; I will tell you everything the LORD says and will keep nothing back from you."

⁵Then they said to Jeremiah, "May the LORD be a true and faithful witness against us if we do not act in accordance with everything the LORD your God sends you to tell us. ⁶Whether it is favorable or unfavorable, we will obey the LORD our God, to whom we are sending you, so that it will go well with us, for we will obey the LORD our God."   Dt 6:3; Jer 7:23

⁷Ten days later the word of the LORD came to Jeremiah. ⁸So he called together Johanan son of Kareah and all the army officers who were with him and all the people from the least to the greatest. ⁹He said to them, "This is what the LORD, the God of Israel, to whom you sent me to present your petition, says: ¹⁰'If you stay in this

land, I will build you up and not tear you down; I will plant you and not uproot you, for I am grieved over the disaster I have inflicted on you. ¹¹Do not be afraid of the king of Babylon, whom you now fear. Do not be afraid of him, declares the LORD, for I am with you and will save you and deliver you from his hands. ¹²I will show you compassion so that he will have compassion on you and restore you to your land.'   Ps 106:44-46; Ro 8:31

¹³"However, if you say, 'We will not stay in this land,' and so disobey the LORD your God, ¹⁴and if you say, 'No, we will go and live in Egypt, where we will not see war or hear the trumpet or be hungry for bread,' ¹⁵then hear the word of the LORD, O remnant of Judah. This is what the LORD Almighty, the God of Israel, says: 'If you are determined to go to Egypt and you do go to settle there, ¹⁶then the sword you fear will overtake you there, and the famine you dread will follow you into Egypt, and there you will die. ¹⁷Indeed, all who are determined to go to Egypt to settle there will die by the sword, famine and plague; not one of them will survive or escape the disaster I will bring on them.' ¹⁸This is what the LORD Almighty, the God of Israel, says: 'As my anger and wrath have been poured out on those who lived in Jerusalem, so will my wrath be poured

---

[a] 1 Hebrew; Septuagint (see also 43:2) *Azariah*

out on you when you go to Egypt. You will be an object of cursing and horror, of condemnation and reproach; you will never see this place again.'   Jer 7:20; 29:18; 44:13

¹⁹"O remnant of Judah, the LORD has told you, 'Do not go to Egypt.' Be sure of this: I warn you today ²⁰that you made a fatal mistake[a] when you sent me to the LORD your God and said, 'Pray to the LORD our God for us; tell us everything he says and we will do it.' ²¹I have told you today, but you still have not obeyed the LORD your God in all he sent me to tell you. ²²So now, be sure of this: You will die by the sword, famine and plague in the place where you want to go to settle."   Eze 6:11; Hos 9:6

43 When Jeremiah finished telling the people all the words of the LORD their God—everything the LORD had sent him to tell them— ²Azariah son of Hoshaiah and Johanan son of Kareah and all the arrogant men said to Jeremiah, "You are lying! The LORD our God has not sent you to say, 'You must not go to Egypt to settle there.' ³But Baruch son of Neriah is inciting you against us to hand us over to the Babylonians,[b] so they may kill us or carry us into exile to Babylon."   Jer 26:8; 42:1

⁴So Johanan son of Kareah and all the army officers and all the people disobeyed the LORD's command to stay in the land of Judah.

⁵Instead, Johanan son of Kareah and all the army officers led away all the remnant of Judah who had come back to live in the land of Judah from all the nations where they had been scattered. ⁶They also led away all the men, women and children and the king's daughters whom Nebuzaradan commander of the imperial guard had left with Gedaliah son of Ahikam, the son of Shaphan, and Jeremiah the prophet and Baruch son of Neriah. ⁷So they entered Egypt in disobedience to the LORD and went as far as Tahpanhes.   Jer 40:12; 44:1

⁸In Tahpanhes the word of the LORD came to Jeremiah: ⁹"While the Jews are watching, take some large stones with you and bury them in clay in the brick pavement at the entrance to Pharaoh's palace in Tahpanhes. ¹⁰Then say to them, 'This is what the LORD Almighty, the God of Israel, says: I will send for my servant Nebuchadnezzar king of Babylon, and I will set his throne over these stones I have buried here; he will spread his royal canopy above them. ¹¹He will come and attack Egypt, bringing death to those destined for death, captivity to those destined for captivity, and the sword to those destined for the sword. ¹²He[c] will set fire to the temples of the gods of Egypt; he will burn their temples and take their gods captive. As a shepherd wraps his garment

---

[a] 20 Or *you erred in your hearts*   [b] 3 Or *Chaldeans*   [c] 12 Or *I*

around him, so will he wrap Egypt around himself and depart from there unscathed. ¹³There in the temple of the sun*a* in Egypt he will demolish the sacred pillars and will burn down the temples of the gods of Egypt.'"   Jer 15:2; 44:13

Disaster Because of Idolatry

44 This word came to Jeremiah concerning all the Jews living in Lower Egypt—in Migdol, Tahpanhes and Memphis*b*—and in Upper Egypt*c*: ²"This is what the Lord Almighty, the God of Israel, says: You saw the great disaster I brought on Jerusalem and on all the towns of Judah. Today they lie deserted and in ruins ³because of the evil they have done. They provoked me to anger by burning incense and by worshiping other gods that neither they nor you nor your fathers ever knew. ⁴Again and again I sent my servants the prophets, who said, 'Do not do this detestable thing that I hate!' ⁵But they did not listen or pay attention; they did not turn from their wickedness or stop burning incense to other gods. ⁶Therefore, my fierce anger was poured out; it raged against the towns of Judah and the streets of Jerusalem and made them the desolate ruins they are today.   Jer 7:25; 25:4; 26:5

⁷"Now this is what the Lord God Almighty, the God of Israel, says: Why bring such great disaster on yourselves by cutting off from Judah the men and women, the children and infants, and so leave yourselves without a remnant? ⁸Why provoke me to anger with what your hands have made, burning incense to other gods in Egypt, where you have come to live? You will destroy yourselves and make yourselves an object of cursing and reproach among all the nations on earth. ⁹Have you forgotten the wickedness committed by your fathers and by the kings and queens of Judah and the wickedness committed by you and your wives in the land of Judah and the streets of Jerusalem? ¹⁰To this day they have not humbled themselves or shown reverence, nor have they followed my law and the decrees I set before you and your fathers.   1Ki 9:6-9

¹¹"Therefore, this is what the Lord Almighty, the God of Israel, says: I am determined to bring disaster on you and to destroy all Judah. ¹²I will take away the remnant of Judah who were determined to go to Egypt to settle there. They will all perish in Egypt; they will fall by the sword or die from famine. From the least to the greatest, they will die by sword or famine. They will become an object of cursing and horror, of condemnation and reproach. ¹³I will punish those who live in Egypt with the sword, famine and plague, as I

---

a 13 Or *in Heliopolis*   *b* 1 Hebrew *Noph*   *c* 1 Hebrew *in Pathros*

punished Jerusalem. [14]None of the remnant of Judah who have gone to live in Egypt will escape or survive to return to the land of Judah, to which they long to return and live; none will return except a few fugitives." Jer 21:10; 22:24-27; Am 9:4

[15]Then all the men who knew that their wives were burning incense to other gods, along with all the women who were present—a large assembly—and all the people living in Lower and Upper Egypt,[a] said to Jeremiah, [16]"We will not listen to the message you have spoken to us in the name of the LORD! [17]We will certainly do everything we said we would: We will burn incense to the Queen of Heaven and will pour out drink offerings to her just as we and our fathers, our kings and our officials did in the towns of Judah and in the streets of Jerusalem. At that time we had plenty of food and were well off and suffered no harm. [18]But ever since we stopped burning incense to the Queen of Heaven and pouring out drink offerings to her, we have had nothing and have been perishing by sword and famine." Dt 23:23; Jer 7:18

[19]The women added, "When we burned incense to the Queen of Heaven and poured out drink offerings to her, did not our husbands know that we were making cakes like her image and pouring out drink offerings to her?"

[20]Then Jeremiah said to all the people, both men and women, who were answering him, [21]"Did not the LORD remember and think about the incense burned in the towns of Judah and the streets of Jerusalem by you and your fathers, your kings and your officials and the people of the land? [22]When the LORD could no longer endure your wicked actions and the detestable things you did, your land became an object of cursing and a desolate waste without inhabitants, as it is today. [23]Because you have burned incense and have sinned against the LORD and have not obeyed him or followed his law or his decrees or his stipulations, this disaster has come upon you, as you now see." 1Ki 9:9

[24]Then Jeremiah said to all the people, including the women, "Hear the word of the LORD, all you people of Judah in Egypt. [25]This is what the LORD Almighty, the God of Israel, says: You and your wives have shown by your actions what you promised when you said, 'We will certainly carry out the vows we made to burn incense and pour out drink offerings to the Queen of Heaven.' Jer 43:7

"Go ahead then, do what you promised! Keep your vows! [26]But hear the word of the LORD, all Jews living in Egypt: 'I swear by my great name,' says the LORD, 'that no one from Judah living anywhere in Egypt will ever again invoke my name or swear, "As surely as the Sovereign LORD lives." ²⁷For I am watching over them for harm, not for good; the Jews in Egypt will perish by sword and famine until they are all destroyed. ²⁸Those who escape the sword and return to the land of Judah from Egypt will be very few. Then the whole remnant of Judah who came to live in Egypt will know whose word will stand—mine or theirs.   Jer 31:28; Eze 20:39

²⁹" 'This will be the sign to you that I will punish you in this place,' declares the LORD, 'so that you will know that my threats of harm against you will surely stand.' ³⁰This is what the LORD says: 'I am going to hand Pharaoh Hophra king of Egypt over to his enemies who seek his life, just as I handed Zedekiah king of Judah over to Nebuchadnezzar king of Babylon, the enemy who was seeking his life.' "   Jer 39:5; 46:26

A Message to Baruch

45 This is what Jeremiah the prophet told Baruch son of Neriah in the fourth year of Jehoiakim son of Josiah king of Judah, after Baruch had written on a scroll the words Jeremiah was then dictating: ²"This is what the LORD, the God of Israel, says to you, Baruch: ³You said, 'Woe to me! The LORD has added sorrow to my pain; I am worn out with groaning and find no rest.' "

⁴The LORD said, "Say this to him: 'This is what the LORD says: I will overthrow what I have built and uproot what I have planted, throughout the land. ⁵Should you then seek great things for yourself? Seek them not. For I will bring disaster on all people, declares the LORD, but wherever you go I will let you escape with your life.' "

A Message About Egypt

46 This is the word of the LORD that came to Jeremiah the prophet concerning the nations: Jer 25:15-38

²Concerning Egypt:

This is the message against the army of Pharaoh Neco king of Egypt, which was defeated at Carchemish on the Euphrates River by Nebuchadnezzar king of Babylon in the fourth year of Jehoiakim son of Josiah king of Judah: 2Ki 23:29

³"Prepare your shields, both
     large and small,   Isa 21:5
   and march out for battle!
⁴Harness the horses,
   mount the steeds!
Take your positions
   with helmets on!
Polish your spears,   Eze 21:9-11
   put on your armor!   1Sa 17:5,38
⁵What do I see?
   They are terrified,
they are retreating,
   their warriors are defeated.
They flee in haste   Jer 48:44
   without looking back,

and there is terror on every
  side,"   Jer 49:29
        declares the LORD.
⁶"The swift cannot flee   Isa 30:16
  nor the strong escape.
In the north by the River
    Euphrates
  they stumble and fall.   Da 11:19
⁷"Who is this that rises like the
    Nile,
  like rivers of surging
    waters?
⁸Egypt rises like the Nile,
  like rivers of surging
    waters.
She says, 'I will rise and cover
    the earth;
  I will destroy cities and their
    people.'   Da 11:10
⁹Charge, O horses!
  Drive furiously,
        O charioteers!   Jer 47:3
  March on, O warriors—
  men of Cush*a* and Put who
    carry shields,
  men of Lydia who draw the
    bow.   Isa 66:19
¹⁰But that day belongs to the
    Lord, the LORD
    Almighty—   Joel 1:15
  a day of vengeance, for
    vengeance on his foes.
The sword will devour till it is
    satisfied,   Dt 32:42
  till it has quenched its thirst
    with blood.   Dt 32:42
For the Lord, the LORD
    Almighty, will offer
    sacrifice   Zep 1:7

in the land of the north by
    the River Euphrates.
¹¹"Go up to Gilead and get balm,
  O Virgin Daughter of Egypt.
But you multiply remedies in
    vain;
  there is no healing for you.
¹²The nations will hear of your
    shame;
  your cries will fill the earth.
One warrior will stumble over
    another;
  both will fall down
    together."   Isa 19:4; Na 3:8-10

¹³This is the message the LORD
spoke to Jeremiah the prophet
about the coming of Nebuchadnezzar king of Babylon to attack
Egypt: Isa 19:1

¹⁴"Announce this in Egypt, and
    proclaim it in Migdol;
  proclaim it also in Memphis*b*
    and Tahpanhes: Jer 43:8
  'Take your positions and get
    ready,
  for the sword devours those
    around you.'   Jer 24:8
¹⁵Why will your warriors be laid
    low?
  They cannot stand, for the
    LORD will push them
    down.   Isa 66:15-16
¹⁶They will stumble repeatedly;
  they will fall over each
    other.
They will say, 'Get up, let us
    go back

---

a9 That is, the upper Nile region   *b14* Hebrew *Noph*; also in verse 19

to our own people and our
   native lands,   Isa 13:14
away from the sword of the
   oppressor.'   Jer 25:38
¹⁷There they will exclaim,
   'Pharaoh king of Egypt is
      only a loud noise;
   he has missed his
      opportunity.'   Isa 19:11-16

¹⁸"As surely as I live," declares
      the King,   Jer 48:15
   whose name is the LORD
      Almighty,
"one will come who is like
      Tabor among the
      mountains,   Jos 19:22
   like Carmel by the sea.
¹⁹Pack your belongings for exile,
   you who live in Egypt,
   for Memphis will be laid
      waste
   and lie in ruins without
      inhabitant.

²⁰"Egypt is a beautiful heifer,
   but a gadfly is coming
      against her from the north.
²¹The mercenaries in her ranks
   are like fattened calves.
They too will turn and flee
      together,
   they will not stand their
      ground,
   for the day of disaster is
      coming upon them,
   the time for them to be
      punished.   Job 18:20
²²Egypt will hiss like a fleeing
      serpent

as the enemy advances in
      force;
they will come against her with
      axes,
   like men who cut down
      trees.
²³They will chop down her
      forest,"
                  declares the LORD,
   "dense though it be.
They are more numerous than
      locusts,   Jdg 7:12
   they cannot be counted.
²⁴The Daughter of Egypt will be
      put to shame,
   handed over to the people of
      the north."   Jer 1:15

²⁵The LORD Almighty, the God of
Israel, says: "I am about to bring
punishment on Amon god of
Thebes,^a on Pharaoh, on Egypt
and her gods and her kings, and on
those who rely on Pharaoh. ²⁶I will
hand them over to those who seek
their lives, to Nebuchadnezzar
king of Babylon and his officers.
Later, however, Egypt will be inhabited as in times past," declares
the LORD.   Eze 29:11-16; 32:11

²⁷"Do not fear, O Jacob my
      servant;   Isa 41:13; 43:5
   do not be dismayed,
      O Israel.
I will surely save you out of a
      distant place,
   your descendants from the
      land of their exile.

^a25 Hebrew *No*

Jacob will again have peace
    and security,
and no one will make him
    afraid.
²⁸Do not fear, O Jacob my
    servant,
for I am with you," declares
    the LORD.   Isa 8:9-10
"Though I completely destroy
    all the nations   Jer 4:27
among which I scatter
    you,
I will not completely destroy
    you.
I will discipline you but only
    with justice;
I will not let you go entirely
    unpunished."

A Message About the Philistines

47 This is the word of the LORD that came to Jeremiah the prophet concerning the Philistines before Pharaoh attacked Gaza: Am 1:6; Zec 9:5-7

²This is what the LORD says:

"See how the waters are rising
    in the north;   Isa 8:7; 14:31
they will become an
    overflowing torrent.
They will overflow the land
    and everything in it,
    the towns and those who
    live in them.
The people will cry out;

all who dwell in the land
    will wail   Isa 15:3
³at the sound of the hoofs of
    galloping steeds,
at the noise of enemy
    chariots   Jer 46:9; Eze 23:24
and the rumble of their
    wheels.
Fathers will not turn to help
    their children;
their hands will hang
    limp.
⁴For the day has come
    to destroy all the
    Philistines
and to cut off all survivors
    who could help Tyre and
    Sidon.   Am 1:9-10; Zec 9:2-4
The LORD is about to destroy
    the Philistines,
the remnant from the coasts
    of Caphtor.ᵃ   Dt 2:23
⁵Gaza will shave her head in
    mourning;   Jer 41:5; Mic 1:16
Ashkelon will be silenced.
O remnant on the plain,
    how long will you cut
    yourselves?

⁶" 'Ah, sword of the LORD,' ⌐you
    cry,⌐   Jer 12:12
'how long till you rest?
Return to your scabbard;
    cease and be still.'   Eze 21:30
⁷But how can it rest
    when the LORD has
    commanded it,
when he has ordered it
    to attack Ashkelon and the
    coast?"   Eze 25:15-17

ᵃ4 That is, Crete

A Message About Moab

48

Concerning Moab: Ge 19:37

This is what the LORD Almighty, the God of Israel, says:

"Woe to Nebo, for it will be
      ruined.   Nu 32:38
Kiriathaim will be disgraced
      and captured;   Nu 32:37
the stronghold*a* will be
      disgraced and shattered.
²Moab will be praised no more;
in Heshbon*b* men will plot
      her downfall: Nu 21:25
'Come, let us put an end to
      that nation.'
You too, O Madmen,*c* will be
      silenced;
the sword will pursue you.
³Listen to the cries from
      Horonaim,   Isa 15:5
cries of great havoc and
      destruction.
⁴Moab will be broken;
her little ones will cry out.*d*
⁵They go up the way to Luhith,
      weeping bitterly as they go;
on the road down to Horonaim
anguished cries over the
      destruction are heard.
⁶Flee! Run for your lives;
become like a bush*e* in the
      desert.   Jer 17:6
⁷Since you trust in your deeds
      and riches,   Ps 49:6
you too will be taken
      captive,

and Chemosh will go into
      exile,   Nu 21:29; Isa 46:1-2
together with his priests and
      officials.   Am 2:3
⁸The destroyer will come
      against every town,
and not a town will escape.
The valley will be ruined
and the plateau destroyed,
because the LORD has
      spoken.
⁹Put salt on Moab,   Jdg 9:45
for she will be laid waste*f*;
her towns will become
      desolate,
with no one to live in them.

¹⁰"A curse on him who is lax in
      doing the LORD's work!
A curse on him who keeps
      his sword from
      bloodshed!   1Ki 20:42

¹¹"Moab has been at rest from
      youth,   Zec 1:15
like wine left on its dregs,
not poured from one jar to
      another—
she has not gone into exile.
So she tastes as she did,
and her aroma is unchanged.
¹²But days are coming,"
      declares the LORD,
"when I will send men who
      pour from jars,
and they will pour her out;
they will empty her jars
and smash her jugs.

---

a1 Or */ Misgab*   *b2* The Hebrew for *Heshbon* sounds like the Hebrew for *plot.*   *c2* The name of the
Moabite town Madmen sounds like the Hebrew for *be silenced.*   *d4* Hebrew; Septuagint */ proclaim it
to Zoar*   *e6* Or *like Aroer*   *f9* Or *Give wings to Moab, / for she will fly away*

¹³Then Moab will be ashamed of
    Chemosh,   Hos 10:6
as the house of Israel was
    ashamed
when they trusted in
    Bethel.

¹⁴"How can you say, 'We are
    warriors,   Ps 33:16
men valiant in battle'?
¹⁵Moab will be destroyed and
    her towns invaded;
her finest young men will go
    down in the slaughter,"
declares the King, whose
    name is the LORD
    Almighty.   Jer 46:18; 51:57
¹⁶"The fall of Moab is at hand;
    her calamity will come
    quickly.
¹⁷Mourn for her, all who live
    around her,
all who know her fame;
say, 'How broken is the mighty
    scepter,   Ps 110:2
how broken the glorious
    staff!'

¹⁸"Come down from your glory
    and sit on the parched
    ground,   Isa 47:1
O inhabitants of the
    Daughter of Dibon,
for he who destroys Moab
    will come up against you
and ruin your fortified cities.
¹⁹Stand by the road and watch,
    you who live in Aroer.   Dt 2:36
Ask the man fleeing and the
    woman escaping,

ask them, 'What has
    happened?'
²⁰Moab is disgraced, for she is
    shattered.
Wail and cry out!   Isa 16:7
Announce by the Arnon   Nu 21:13
    that Moab is destroyed.
²¹Judgment has come to the
    plateau—
to Holon, Jahzah and
    Mephaath,   Nu 21:23; Jos 13:18
²²   to Dibon, Nebo and Beth
    Diblathaim,   Jos 13:9,17
²³   to Kiriathaim, Beth Gamul
    and Beth Meon,   Jos 13:17
²⁴   to Kerioth and Bozrah—
to all the towns of Moab, far
    and near.   Isa 15:1
²⁵Moab's hornᵃ is cut off;   Ps 75:10
    her arm is broken,"   Ps 10:15
            declares the LORD.

²⁶"Make her drunk,   Jer 25:16,27
    for she has defied the
    LORD.
Let Moab wallow in her
    vomit;
let her be an object of
    ridicule.
²⁷Was not Israel the object of
    your ridicule?   Jer 2:26
Was she caught among
    thieves,   2Ki 17:3-6
that you shake your head in
    scorn   Jer 18:16; Mic 7:8-10
whenever you speak of her?
²⁸Abandon your towns and dwell
    among the rocks,
you who live in Moab.

ᵃ25 *Horn* here symbolizes strength.

Be like a dove that makes its
　　nest　　　　　　　　Ps 55:6-7
at the mouth of a cave.

29"We have heard of Moab's
　　pride—　　　　　　　Isa 16:6
her overweening pride and
　　conceit,
her pride and arrogance
　　and the haughtiness of her
　　heart.　　　　　　　　Pr 16:18
30I know her insolence but it is
　　futile,"
　　　　　　　declares the LORD,
"and her boasts accomplish
　　nothing.　　　　　　　Ps 10:3
31Therefore I wail over Moab,
　　for all Moab I cry out,
I moan for the men of Kir
　　Hareseth.　　　　　　2Ki 3:25
32I weep for you, as Jazer weeps,
　　O vines of Sibmah.　　Isa 16:8-9
Your branches spread as far as
　　the sea;
they reached as far as the
　　sea of Jazer.
The destroyer has fallen
　　on your ripened fruit and
　　grapes.
33Joy and gladness are gone
　　from the orchards and fields
　　of Moab.
I have stopped the flow of
　　wine from the presses;
no one treads them with
　　shouts of joy.　　　　Joel 1:12
Although there are shouts,
　　they are not shouts of joy.

34"The sound of their cry rises
　　from Heshbon to Elealeh and
　　Jahaz,　　　　　　　　Isa 15:4

from Zoar as far as Horonaim
　　and Eglath Shelishiyah,
for even the waters of
　　Nimrim are dried up.
35In Moab I will put an end
　　to those who make offerings
　　on the high places
and burn incense to their
　　gods,"　　　　　　　　Jer 11:13
　　　　　　declares the LORD.
36"So my heart laments for Moab
　　like a flute;　　　　　Isa 16:11
it laments like a flute for the
　　men of Kir Hareseth.
The wealth they acquired is
　　gone.　　　　　　　　Isa 16:6-12
37Every head is shaved　　Isa 15:2
　　and every beard cut off;
every hand is slashed
　　and every waist is covered
　　with sackcloth.　　　Ge 37:34
38On all the roofs in Moab
　　and in the public squares
there is nothing but mourning,
　　for I have broken Moab
like a jar that no one wants,"
　　　　　　declares the LORD.
39"How shattered she is! How
　　they wail!
How Moab turns her back in
　　shame!
Moab has become an object of
　　ridicule,
an object of horror to all
　　those around her."

40This is what the LORD says:

"Look! An eagle is swooping
　　down,　　　　　　Dt 28:49; Hab 1:8
spreading its wings over
　　Moab.　　　　　　　　Isa 8:8

41Kerioth[a] will be captured
    and the strongholds taken.
In that day the hearts of
    Moab's warriors
    will be like the heart of a
    woman in labor.   Isa 21:3
42Moab will be destroyed as a
    nation   Ps 83:4; Isa 16:14
    because she defied the LORD.
43Terror and pit and snare await
    you,   Isa 24:17
    O people of Moab,"
        declares the LORD.
44"Whoever flees from the terror
    will fall into a pit,
    whoever climbs out of the
    pit
    will be caught in a snare;
for I will bring upon Moab
    the year of her punishment,"
        declares the LORD.

45"In the shadow of Heshbon
    the fugitives stand helpless,
for a fire has gone out from
    Heshbon,
    a blaze from the midst of
    Sihon;   Nu 21:21,26-28
it burns the foreheads of Moab,
    the skulls of the noisy
    boasters.   Nu 24:17
46Woe to you, O Moab!   Nu 21:29
    The people of Chemosh are
    destroyed;
your sons are taken into exile
    and your daughters into
    captivity.

47"Yet I will restore the fortunes
    of Moab   Jer 49:6,39

    in days to come,"
        declares the LORD.

Here ends the judgment on
Moab.

A Message About Ammon

49 Concerning the Ammon-
    ites: Am 1:13; Zep 2:8-9

This is what the LORD says:

"Has Israel no sons?
    Has she no heirs?
Why then has Molech[b] taken
    possession of Gad?
    Why do his people live in its
    towns?
2But the days are coming,"
    declares the LORD,
"when I will sound the battle
    cry   Jer 4:19
    against Rabbah of the
    Ammonites;   Dt 3:11
it will become a mound of
    ruins,   Dt 13:16
    and its surrounding villages
    will be set on fire.
Then Israel will drive out
    those who drove her out,"
        says the LORD.
3"Wail, O Heshbon, for Ai is
    destroyed!   Jos 8:28
    Cry out, O inhabitants of
    Rabbah!
Put on sackcloth and mourn;
    rush here and there inside
    the walls,
for Molech will go into exile,

---

*a*41 Or *The cities*   *b*1 Or *their king*; Hebrew *malcam*; also in verse 3

together with his priests and
officials.
⁴Why do you boast of your
    valleys,
  boast of your valleys so
    fruitful?
O unfaithful daughter,   Jer 3:6
  you trust in your riches and
    say,   Jer 9:23; 1Ti 6:17
  'Who will attack me?'   Jer 21:13
⁵I will bring terror on you
  from all those around you,"
        declares the Lord,
        the Lord Almighty.
"Every one of you will be
    driven away,
  and no one will gather the
    fugitives.

⁶"Yet afterward, I will restore
    the fortunes of the
    Ammonites,"   ver 39
        declares the Lord.

A Message About Edom

⁷Concerning Edom: Eze 25:12

This is what the Lord Almighty
says:

"Is there no longer wisdom in
    Teman?   Ge 36:11,15,34
  Has counsel perished from
    the prudent?
  Has their wisdom decayed?
⁸Turn and flee, hide in deep
    caves,
  you who live in Dedan,
  for I will bring disaster on
    Esau
  at the time I punish him.
⁹If grape pickers came to you,

would they not leave a few
    grapes?
If thieves came during the
    night,
  would they not steal only as
    much as they wanted?
¹⁰But I will strip Esau bare;
  I will uncover his hiding
    places,
  so that he cannot conceal
    himself.
His children, relatives and
    neighbors will perish,
  and he will be no more.
¹¹Leave your orphans; I will
    protect their lives.
  Your widows too can trust in
    me."   Dt 10:18; Jas 1:27

¹²This is what the Lord says: "If
those who do not deserve to drink
the cup must drink it, why should
you go unpunished? You will not
go unpunished, but must drink it.
¹³I swear by myself," declares the
Lord, "that Bozrah will become a
ruin and an object of horror, of reproach and of cursing; and all its
towns will be in ruins forever."

¹⁴I have heard a message from
    the Lord:
  An envoy was sent to the
    nations to say,
  "Assemble yourselves to attack
    it!
  Rise up for battle!"

¹⁵"Now I will make you small
    among the nations,
  despised among men.
¹⁶The terror you inspire

and the pride of your heart
  have deceived you,
you who live in the clefts of
  the rocks,
who occupy the heights of
  the hill.
Though you build your nest as
  high as the eagle's,
from there I will bring you
  down,"
          declares the LORD.
17"Edom will become an object
  of horror;
all who pass by will be
  appalled and will scoff
  because of all its wounds.
18As Sodom and Gomorrah were
  overthrown,   Ge 19:24
along with their neighboring
  towns,"
          says the LORD,
"so no one will live there;
  no man will dwell in
  it.
19"Like a lion coming up from
  Jordan's thickets   Jer 12:5
to a rich pastureland,
I will chase Edom from its land
  in an instant.
Who is the chosen one I will
  appoint for this?
Who is like me and who can
  challenge me?   Jer 50:44
And what shepherd can
  stand against me?"
20Therefore, hear what the LORD
  has planned against
  Edom,   Isa 34:5

what he has purposed
  against those who live
  in Teman: Isa 14:27
The young of the flock will be
  dragged away;   Jer 50:45
he will completely destroy
  their pasture because of
  them.   Mal 1:3-4
21At the sound of their fall the
  earth will tremble;
their cry will resound to the
  Red Sea.a   Jer 50:46; Eze 26:18
22Look! An eagle will soar and
  swoop down,   Hos 8:1
spreading its wings over
  Bozrah.   Ge 36:33
In that day the hearts of
  Edom's warriors   Jer 50:36
will be like the heart of a
  woman in labor.   Isa 13:8

A Message About Damascus

23Concerning Damascus:

"Hamath and Arpad are
  dismayed,   Isa 10:9
for they have heard bad
  news.
They are disheartened,
  troubled likeb the restless
  sea.   Isa 57:20
24Damascus has become feeble,
  she has turned to flee
  and panic has gripped her;
anguish and pain have seized
  her,
pain like that of a woman in
  labor.

---

a21 Hebrew *Yam Suph*; that is, Sea of Reeds   b23 Hebrew *on* or *by*

²⁵Why has the city of renown
　　not been abandoned,
　the town in which I delight?
²⁶Surely, her young men will fall
　　in the streets;
　all her soldiers will be
　　silenced in that day,"
　　　　　　declares the LORD
　　　　　　　　Almighty.
²⁷"I will set fire to the walls of
　　Damascus;　　　Am 1:4
　it will consume the
　　fortresses of
　　Ben-Hadad."　　1Ki 15:18

A Message About Kedar and Hazor

²⁸Concerning Kedar and the kingdoms of Hazor, which Nebuchadnezzar king of Babylon attacked:　　　　　　　Ge 25:13

This is what the LORD says:

"Arise, and attack Kedar
　and destroy the people of
　　the East.　　　Jdg 6:3
²⁹Their tents and their flocks will
　　be taken;
　their shelters will be carried
　　off
　with all their goods and
　　camels.
Men will shout to them,
　'Terror on every side!'　Jer 6:25
³⁰"Flee quickly away!
　Stay in deep caves, you who
　　live in Hazor,"　　Jdg 6:2
　　　　　　declares the LORD.

"Nebuchadnezzar king of
　Babylon has plotted
　against you;　　Jer 10:22
he has devised a plan against
　you.

³¹"Arise and attack a nation at
　ease,
　which lives in confidence,"
　　　　　declares the LORD,
"a nation that has neither gates
　　nor bars;　　Eze 38:11
　its people live alone.
³²Their camels will become
　　plunder,　　Jdg 6:5
　and their large herds will be
　　booty.
I will scatter to the winds
　　those who are in distant
　　places[a]　　Jer 9:26
　and will bring disaster on
　　them from every side,"
　　　　　declares the LORD.
³³"Hazor will become a haunt of
　　jackals,　　Isa 13:22
　a desolate place forever.
No one will live there;
　no man will dwell in it."

A Message About Elam

³⁴This is the word of the LORD that came to Jeremiah the prophet concerning Elam, early in the reign of Zedekiah king of Judah:

³⁵This is what the LORD Almighty says:

"See, I will break the bow of
　Elam,　　Isa 22:6

---

a 32 Or who clip the hair by their foreheads

the mainstay of their might.
36 I will bring against Elam the
      four winds   ver 32
   from the four quarters of the
      heavens;   Da 11:4
   I will scatter them to the four
      winds,
   and there will not be a
      nation
   where Elam's exiles do not
      go.
37 I will shatter Elam before their
      foes,
   before those who seek their
      lives;
   I will bring disaster upon
      them,
   even my fierce anger,"
                  declares the LORD.
   "I will pursue them with the
      sword   Jer 9:16
   until I have made an end of
      them.
38 I will set my throne in
      Elam
   and destroy her king and
      officials,"
               declares the LORD.

39 "Yet I will restore the fortunes
      of Elam   Jer 48:47
   in days to come,"
               declares the LORD.

A Message About Babylon

50 This is the word the LORD
spoke through Jeremiah
the prophet concerning Babylon
and the land of the Babylonians[a]:

2 "Announce and proclaim
      among the nations,
   lift up a banner and
      proclaim it;   Ps 20:5
   keep nothing back, but
      say,
   'Babylon will be captured;
   Bel will be put to shame,
   Marduk filled with terror.
   Her images will be put to
      shame
   and her idols filled with
      terror.'   Lev 26:30
3 A nation from the north will
      attack her   Isa 41:25
   and lay waste her land.
   No one will live in it;   Isa 14:22-23
   both men and animals will
      flee away.   Zep 1:3

4 "In those days, at that time,"
      declares the LORD,
   "the people of Israel and the
      people of Judah together
   will go in tears to seek the
      LORD their God.   Ezr 3:12
5 They will ask the way to Zion
   and turn their faces toward
      it.
   They will come and bind
      themselves to the LORD
   in an everlasting covenant
   that will not be forgotten.

6 "My people have been lost
      sheep;   Isa 53:6; Mt 9:36; 10:6
   their shepherds have led
      them astray   Jer 23:32
   and caused them to roam on
      the mountains.

---

[a] 1 Or *Chaldeans*; also in verses 8, 25, 35 and 45

They wandered over mountain
and hill   Jer 3:6; Eze 34:6
and forgot their own resting
place.
⁷Whoever found them devoured
them;
their enemies said, 'We are
not guilty,   Jer 2:3
for they sinned against the
LORD, their true pasture,
the LORD, the hope of their
fathers.'   Jer 14:8
⁸"Flee out of Babylon;   Isa 48:20
leave the land of the
Babylonians,
and be like the goats that
lead the flock.
⁹For I will stir up and bring
against Babylon   Isa 13:17
an alliance of great nations
from the land of the
north.   Isa 41:25; Jer 25:26
They will take up their
positions against her,
and from the north she will
be captured.
Their arrows will be like
skilled warriors   Isa 13:18
who do not return
empty-handed.
¹⁰So Babylonia*a* will be
plundered;   Jer 30:16
all who plunder her will
have their fill,"
declares the LORD.
¹¹"Because you rejoice and are
glad,
you who pillage my
inheritance,   Isa 47:6

because you frolic like a heifer
threshing grain   Jer 31:18
and neigh like stallions,
¹²your mother will be greatly
ashamed;
she who gave you birth will
be disgraced.
She will be the least of the
nations—
a wilderness, a dry land, a
desert.   Isa 21:1; Jer 25:12
¹³Because of the LORD's anger
she will not be
inhabited
but will be completely
desolate.   Jer 9:11
All who pass Babylon will be
horrified and scoff
because of all her wounds.
¹⁴"Take up your positions
around Babylon,
all you who draw the
bow.
Shoot at her! Spare no
arrows,
for she has sinned against
the LORD.
¹⁵Shout against her on every
side!   Jer 51:14
She surrenders, her towers
fall,
her walls are torn down.
Since this is the vengeance of
the LORD,   Jer 51:6
take vengeance on her;
do to her as she has done to
others.   Ps 137:8; Rev 18:6
¹⁶Cut off from Babylon the
sower,

a 10 Or Chaldea

and the reaper with his
   sickle at harvest.
Because of the sword of the
   oppressor   Jer 25:38
let everyone return to his
   own people,   Isa 13:14
let everyone flee to his own
   land.   Jer 51:9

[17]"Israel is a scattered flock
   that lions have chased away.
The first to devour him
   was the king of Assyria;
the last to crush his bones
   was Nebuchadnezzar king of
   Babylon."   2Ki 24:10,14; 25:7

[18]Therefore this is what the LORD
Almighty, the God of Israel, says:

"I will punish the king of
   Babylon and his land
as I punished the king of
   Assyria.   Isa 10:12; Eze 31:3
[19]But I will bring Israel back to
   his own pasture   Jer 31:10
and he will graze on Carmel
   and Bashan;
his appetite will be satisfied
   on the hills of Ephraim and
   Gilead.   Jer 10:12-16; 33:12
[20]In those days, at that time,"
   declares the LORD,
"search will be made for
   Israel's guilt,
but there will be none,
and for the sins of Judah,
   but none will be found,
for I will forgive the remnant
   I spare.   Isa 1:9; Jer 31:34

[21]"Attack the land of Merathaim
   and those who live in Pekod.
Pursue, kill and completely
   destroy[a] them,"
       declares the LORD.
"Do everything I have
   commanded you.
[22]The noise of battle is in the
   land,   Jer 4:19-21; 51:54
the noise of great
   destruction!
[23]How broken and shattered
   is the hammer of the whole
   earth!   Isa 10:5
How desolate is Babylon
   among the nations!
[24]I set a trap for you, O Babylon,
   and you were caught before
   you knew it;
you were found and captured
   because you opposed the
   LORD.   Job 9:4
[25]The LORD has opened his
   arsenal
and brought out the
   weapons of his wrath,
for the Sovereign LORD
   Almighty has work to
   do
in the land of the
   Babylonians.   Jer 51:25,55
[26]Come against her from afar.
   Break open her granaries;
pile her up like heaps of
   grain.
Completely destroy her
   and leave her no remnant.
[27]Kill all her young bulls;   Ps 68:30

[a]21 The Hebrew term refers to the irrevocable giving over of things or persons to the LORD, often by totally destroying them; also in verse 26.

let them go down to the
    slaughter!   Isa 30:25
Woe to them! For their day
    has come,   Job 18:20
the time for them to be
    punished.   Jer 51:6
28Listen to the fugitives and
    refugees from Babylon
declaring in Zion   Isa 48:20
how the LORD our God has
    taken vengeance,   ver 15
vengeance for his temple.

29"Summon archers against
    Babylon,
all those who draw the bow.
Encamp all around her;
    let no one escape;   Isa 13:18
Repay her for her deeds;
    do to her as she has done.
For she has defied the LORD,
    the Holy One of Israel.
30Therefore, her young men will
    fall in the streets;   Isa 13:18
all her soldiers will be
    silenced in that day,"
           declares the LORD.
31"See, I am against you,
    O arrogant one,"   Jer 21:13
declares the Lord, the LORD
    Almighty,
"for your day has come,
    the time for you to be
    punished.
32The arrogant one will stumble
    and fall   Ps 119:21
and no one will help her
    up;
I will kindle a fire in her towns
    that will consume all who
    are around her."

33This is what the LORD Almighty says:

"The people of Israel are
    oppressed,   Isa 58:6
and the people of Judah as
    well.
All their captors hold them
    fast,
refusing to let them go.
34Yet their Redeemer is
    strong;
the LORD Almighty is his
    name.   Jer 51:19
He will vigorously defend their
    cause   Jer 15:21; 51:36
so that he may bring rest to
    their land,   Isa 14:7
but unrest to those who live
    in Babylon.

35"A sword against the
    Babylonians!"   Jer 47:6
    declares the LORD—
"against those who live in
    Babylon
and against her officials and
    wise men!   Da 5:7
36A sword against her false
    prophets!
They will become fools.
A sword against her warriors!
They will be filled with
    terror.
37A sword against her horses and
    chariots   Jer 51:21
and all the foreigners in her
    ranks!
They will become women.
A sword against her treasures!
They will be plundered.

38A drought on[a] her waters!
They will dry up.   Ps 137:1
For it is a land of idols,   Jer 51:36
idols that will go mad with
terror.

39"So desert creatures and
hyenas will live there,
and there the owl will dwell.
It will never again be inhabited
or lived in from generation
to generation.   Isa 13:19-22
40As God overthrew Sodom and
Gomorrah   Ge 19:24; Mt 10:15
along with their neighboring
towns,"
declares the LORD,
"so no one will live there;
no man will dwell in it.

41"Look! An army is coming
from the north;   Jer 6:22
a great nation and many
kings
are being stirred up from the
ends of the earth.   Isa 13:4
42They are armed with bows and
spears;
they are cruel and without
mercy.   Isa 13:18
They sound like the roaring
sea   Isa 5:30
as they ride on their horses;
they come like men in battle
formation
to attack you, O Daughter of
Babylon.   Jer 6:23
43The king of Babylon has heard
reports about them,
and his hands hang limp.

Anguish has gripped him,
pain like that of a woman in
labor.   Jer 6:22-24
44Like a lion coming up from
Jordan's thickets
to a rich pastureland,
I will chase Babylon from its
land in an instant.
Who is the chosen one I will
appoint for this?   Nu 16:5
Who is like me and who can
challenge me?   Job 41:10
And what shepherd can
stand against me?"
45Therefore, hear what the LORD
has planned against
Babylon,
what he has purposed
against the land of the
Babylonians: Isa 14:24
The young of the flock will be
dragged away;
he will completely destroy
their pasture because of
them.
46At the sound of Babylon's
capture the earth will
tremble;   Jer 49:21
its cry will resound among
the nations.   Rev 18:9-10

51 This is what the LORD says:
"See, I will stir up the
spirit of a destroyer
against Babylon and the
people of Leb Kamai.[b]
2I will send foreigners to
Babylon

---

a 38 Or *A sword against*   b 1 *Leb Kamai* is a cryptogram for Chaldea, that is, Babylonia.

to winnow her and to
  devastate her land;
they will oppose her on every
  side
in the day of her disaster.
[3]Let not the archer string his
  bow,   Jer 50:29
  nor let him put on his
  armor.   Jer 46:4
Do not spare her young
  men;
  completely destroy[a] her
  army.
[4]They will fall down slain in
  Babylon,[b]   Isa 13:15
  fatally wounded in her
  streets.   Jer 49:26; 50:30
[5]For Israel and Judah have not
  been forsaken   Isa 54:6-8
  by their God, the LORD
  Almighty,
though their land[c] is full of
  guilt
  before the Holy One of   Hos 4:1
  Israel.

[6]"Flee from Babylon!   Jer 50:8
  Run for your lives!
Do not be destroyed because
  of her sins.   Rev 18:4
It is time for the LORD's
  vengeance;   Jer 50:15
  he will pay her what she
  deserves.   Jer 25:14
[7]Babylon was a gold cup in the
  LORD's hand;   Jer 25:15-16
  she made the whole earth
  drunk.
The nations drank her wine;

therefore they have now
  gone mad.
[8]Babylon will suddenly fall and
  be broken.   Isa 21:9; Rev 14:8
Wail over her!
Get balm for her pain;   Jer 46:11
  perhaps she can be healed.

[9]" 'We would have healed
  Babylon,
  but she cannot be healed;
let us leave her and each go to
  his own land,   Isa 13:14
for her judgment reaches to
  the skies,   Rev 18:4-5
  it rises as high as the
  clouds.'

[10]" 'The LORD has vindicated us;
  come, let us tell in Zion
  what the LORD our God has
  done.'   Jer 50:28

[11]"Sharpen the arrows,   Jer 50:9
  take up the shields!   Jer 46:4
The LORD has stirred up the
  kings of the Medes,
because his purpose is to
  destroy Babylon.   Jer 50:45
The LORD will take vengeance,
  vengeance for his temple.
[12]Lift up a banner against the
  walls of Babylon!   Ps 20:5
Reinforce the guard,
  station the watchmen,   2Sa 18:24
  prepare an ambush!   Jer 50:24
The LORD will carry out his
  purpose,   Ps 33:11
  his decree against the people
  of Babylon.

---

[a]3 The Hebrew term refers to the irrevocable giving over of things or persons to the LORD, often by totally destroying them.   [b]4 Or Chaldea   [c]5 Or / and the land of the Babylonians,

¹³You who live by many waters
    and are rich in treasures,
your end has come,
    the time for you to be cut
        off.   Jer 50:3
¹⁴The Lord Almighty has sworn
        by himself: Am 6:8
    I will surely fill you with
        men, as with a swarm of
        locusts,   Na 3:15
    and they will shout in
        triumph over you.

¹⁵"He made the earth by his
        power;
    he founded the world by his
        wisdom
    and stretched out the
        heavens by his
        understanding.   Ge 1:1
¹⁶When he thunders, the waters
        in the heavens roar;
    he makes clouds rise from
        the ends of the earth.
He sends lightning with the
        rain
    and brings out the wind
        from his storehouses.

¹⁷"Every man is senseless and
        without knowledge;
    every goldsmith is shamed
        by his idols.
His images are a fraud;   Isa 44:20
    they have no breath in
        them.
¹⁸They are worthless, the objects
        of mockery;   Jer 18:15
    when their judgment comes,
        they will perish.

¹⁹He who is the Portion of Jacob
        is not like these,   Ps 119:57
    for he is the Maker of all
        things,
    including the tribe of his
        inheritance—   Ex 34:9
    the Lord Almighty is his
        name.

²⁰"You are my war club,   Isa 10:5
    my weapon for battle—
    with you I shatter nations,
    with you I destroy kingdoms,
²¹with you I shatter horse and
        rider,   Ex 15:1
    with you I shatter chariot
        and driver,   Jer 50:37
²²with you I shatter man and
        woman,
    with you I shatter old man
        and youth,
    with you I shatter young
        man and maiden,
²³with you I shatter shepherd
        and flock,
    with you I shatter farmer
        and oxen,
    with you I shatter governors
        and officials.

²⁴"Before your eyes I will repay
Babylon and all who live in Babylonia[a] for all the wrong they have
done in Zion," declares the Lord.

²⁵"I am against you,
        O destroying mountain,
    you who destroy the whole
        earth,"
                    declares the Lord.

---

[a] 24 Or *Chaldea*; also in verse 35

"I will stretch out my hand
against you,
roll you off the cliffs,
and make you a burned-out
mountain.   Zec 4:7
²⁶No rock will be taken from
you for a cornerstone,
nor any stone for a
foundation,
for you will be desolate
forever,"
declares the LORD.

²⁷"Lift up a banner in the land!
Blow the trumpet among the
nations!
Prepare the nations for battle
against her;
summon against her these
kingdoms: Jer 25:14
Ararat, Minni and Ashkenaz.
Appoint a commander against
her;
send up horses like a swarm
of locusts.
²⁸Prepare the nations for battle
against her—
the kings of the Medes,   ver 11
their governors and all their
officials,
and all the countries they
rule.
²⁹The land trembles and writhes,
for the LORD's purposes
against Babylon stand—
to lay waste the land of
Babylon   Jer 48:9
so that no one will live
there.   Isa 13:20
³⁰Babylon's warriors have
stopped fighting;   Jer 50:36

they remain in their
strongholds.
Their strength is exhausted;
they have become like
women.   Isa 19:16
Her dwellings are set on
fire;
the bars of her gates are
broken.   La 2:9; Na 3:13
³¹One courier follows another
and messenger follows
messenger
to announce to the king of
Babylon
that his entire city is
captured,   Jer 50:2
³²the river crossings seized,
the marshes set on fire,
and the soldiers terrified."

³³This is what the LORD Almighty, the God of Israel, says:

"The Daughter of Babylon is
like a threshing floor
at the time it is trampled;
the time to harvest her will
soon come."   Isa 17:5

³⁴"Nebuchadnezzar king of
Babylon has devoured
us,   Jer 50:17; Hos 8:8
he has thrown us into
confusion,
he has made us an empty
jar.
Like a serpent he has
swallowed us
and filled his stomach with
our delicacies,
and then has spewed us out.

35May the violence done to our
flesh*a* be upon
Babylon,"   Hab 2:17
say the inhabitants of Zion.
"May our blood be on those
who live in Babylonia,"
says Jerusalem.   Ps 137:8

36Therefore, this is what the
LORD says:

"See, I will defend your cause
and avenge you;   Ro 12:19
I will dry up her sea   Jer 50:38
and make her springs dry.
37Babylon will be a heap of
ruins,
a haunt of jackals,   Isa 13:22
an object of horror and scorn,
a place where no one lives.
38Her people all roar like young
lions,
they growl like lion cubs.
39But while they are aroused,
I will set out a feast for them
and make them drunk,
so that they shout with
laughter —
then sleep forever and not
awake,"   Ps 13:3
declares the LORD.
40"I will bring them down
like lambs to the slaughter,
like rams and goats.   Eze 39:18

41"How Sheshach*b* will be
captured,   Isa 13:19; Jer 25:26
the boast of the whole earth
seized!
What a horror Babylon will be

among the nations!
42The sea will rise over Babylon;
its roaring waves will cover
her.   Isa 8:7
43Her towns will be desolate,
a dry and desert land,
a land where no one lives,
through which no man
travels.   Isa 13:20; Jer 2:6
44I will punish Bel in Babylon
and make him spew out
what he has swallowed.
The nations will no longer
stream to him.
And the wall of Babylon will
fall.   Jer 50:15
45"Come out of her, my people!
Run for your lives!   Jer 50:8
Run from the fierce anger of
the LORD.   Ps 76:10
46Do not lose heart or be afraid
when rumors are heard in
the land;   2Ki 19:7
one rumor comes this year,
another the next,
rumors of violence in the
land
and of ruler against ruler.
47For the time will surely come
when I will punish the idols
of Babylon;   Isa 46:1-2
her whole land will be
disgraced   Jer 50:12
and her slain will all lie
fallen within her.
48Then heaven and earth and all
that is in them
will shout for joy over
Babylon,   Isa 44:23; Rev 18:20

---

a 35 Or *done to us and to our children*   *b 41* Sheshach is a cryptogram for Babylon.

for out of the north   Isa 41:25
destroyers will attack her,"
     declares the LORD.

⁴⁹"Babylon must fall because of
     Israel's slain,
just as the slain in all the
     earth
have fallen because of
     Babylon.   Jer 50:29
⁵⁰You who have escaped the
     sword,
leave and do not linger!
Remember the LORD in a
     distant land,   Ps 137:6
and think on Jerusalem."

⁵¹"We are disgraced,   Ps 44:13-16; 79:4
for we have been insulted
and shame covers our faces,
because foreigners have
     entered
the holy places of the LORD's
     house."   La 1:10

⁵²"But days are coming,"
     declares the LORD,
"when I will punish her
     idols,
and throughout her land
the wounded will groan.
⁵³Even if Babylon reaches the
     sky   Isa 14:13-14
and fortifies her lofty
     stronghold,
I will send destroyers against
     her,"   Jer 49:16
     declares the LORD.

⁵⁴"The sound of a cry comes
     from Babylon,

the sound of great
     destruction   Jer 50:22
from the land of the
     Babylonians.^a
⁵⁵The LORD will destroy Babylon;
     he will silence her noisy din.
Waves ⸤of enemies⸥ will rage
     like great waters;   Ps 18:4
the roar of their voices will
     resound.
⁵⁶A destroyer will come against
     Babylon;
her warriors will be
     captured,
and their bows will be
     broken.   Ps 46:9
For the LORD is a God of
     retribution;
he will repay in full.   Ps 94:1-2
⁵⁷I will make her officials and
     wise men drunk,
her governors, officers and
     warriors as well;
they will sleep forever and not
     awake,"   Ps 76:5; Jer 25:27
     declares the King, whose
     name is the LORD
     Almighty.   Jer 46:18; 48:15

⁵⁸This is what the LORD Al-
mighty says:

"Babylon's thick wall will be
     leveled   Isa 15:1
and her high gates set on
     fire;   Isa 13:2
the peoples exhaust themselves
     for nothing,   Isa 47:13
the nations' labor is only
     fuel for the flames."

---

^a 54 Or *Chaldeans*

⁵⁹This is the message Jeremiah gave to the staff officer Seraiah son of Neriah, the son of Mahseiah, when he went to Babylon with Zedekiah king of Judah in the fourth year of his reign. ⁶⁰Jeremiah had written on a scroll about all the disasters that would come upon Babylon—all that had been recorded concerning Babylon. ⁶¹He said to Seraiah, "When you get to Babylon, see that you read all these words aloud. ⁶²Then say, 'O LORD, you have said you will destroy this place, so that neither man nor animal will live in it; it will be desolate forever.' ⁶³When you finish reading this scroll, tie a stone to it and throw it into the Euphrates. ⁶⁴Then say, 'So will Babylon sink to rise no more because of the disaster I will bring upon her. And her people will fall.'" Rev 18:21; Jer 50:13,39

The words of Jeremiah end here.

The Fall of Jerusalem

52 Zedekiah was twenty-one years old when he became king, and he reigned in Jerusalem eleven years. His mother's name was Hamutal daughter of Jeremiah; she was from Libnah. ²He did evil in the eyes of the LORD, just as Jehoiakim had done. ³It was because of the LORD's anger that all this happened to Jerusalem and Judah, and in the end he thrust them from his presence. 2Ki 24:17

Now Zedekiah rebelled against the king of Babylon. 2Ki 24:18-20

⁴So in the ninth year of Zedekiah's reign, on the tenth day of the tenth month, Nebuchadnezzar king of Babylon marched against Jerusalem with his whole army. They camped outside the city and built siege works all around it. ⁵The city was kept under siege until the eleventh year of King Zedekiah. 2Ki 25:1-7; Jer 39:1

⁶By the ninth day of the fourth month the famine in the city had become so severe that there was no food for the people to eat. ⁷Then the city wall was broken through, and the whole army fled. They left the city at night through the gate between the two walls near the king's garden, though the Babylonians*ᵃ* were surrounding the city. They fled toward the Arabah,*ᵇ* ⁸but the Babylonian*ᶜ* army pursued King Zedekiah and overtook him in the plains of Jericho. All his soldiers were separated from him and scattered, ⁹and he was captured. Jer 32:4

He was taken to the king of Babylon at Riblah in the land of Hamath, where he pronounced sentence on him. ¹⁰There at Riblah the king of Babylon slaughtered the sons of Zedekiah before his eyes; he also killed all the officials of Judah. ¹¹Then he put out Zedekiah's

---

ᵃ7 Or *Chaldeans*; also in verse 17   *ᵇ7* Or *the Jordan Valley*   *ᶜ8* Or *Chaldean*; also in verse 14

eyes, bound him with bronze shackles and took him to Babylon, where he put him in prison till the day of his death. _{Jer 22:30; Eze 12:13}

¹²On the tenth day of the fifth month, in the nineteenth year of Nebuchadnezzar king of Babylon, Nebuzaradan commander of the imperial guard, who served the king of Babylon, came to Jerusalem. ¹³He set fire to the temple of the Lord, the royal palace and all the houses of Jerusalem. Every important building he burned down. ¹⁴The whole Babylonian army under the commander of the imperial guard broke down all the walls around Jerusalem. ¹⁵Nebuzaradan the commander of the guard carried into exile some of the poorest people and those who remained in the city, along with the rest of the craftsmen*a* and those who had gone over to the king of Babylon. ¹⁶But Nebuzaradan left behind the rest of the poorest people of the land to work the vineyards and fields. _{Jer 39:1-10}

¹⁷The Babylonians broke up the bronze pillars, the movable stands and the bronze Sea that were at the temple of the Lord and they carried all the bronze to Babylon. ¹⁸They also took away the pots, shovels, wick trimmers, sprinkling bowls, dishes and all the bronze articles used in the temple service. ¹⁹The commander of the imperial guard took away the basins, censers, sprinkling bowls, pots, lampstands, dishes and bowls used for drink offerings—all that were made of pure gold or silver.

²⁰The bronze from the two pillars, the Sea and the twelve bronze bulls under it, and the movable stands, which King Solomon had made for the temple of the Lord, was more than could be weighed. ²¹Each of the pillars was eighteen cubits high and twelve cubits in circumference*b*; each was four fingers thick, and hollow. ²²The bronze capital on top of the one pillar was five cubits*c* high and was decorated with a network and pomegranates of bronze all around. The other pillar, with its pomegranates, was similar. ²³There were ninety-six pomegranates on the sides; the total number of pomegranates above the surrounding network was a hundred. _{2Ki 25:1-21; 2Ch 36:17-20}

²⁴The commander of the guard took as prisoners Seraiah the chief priest, Zephaniah the priest next in rank and the three doorkeepers. ²⁵Of those still in the city, he took the officer in charge of the fighting men, and seven royal advisers. He also took the secretary who was chief officer in charge of conscripting the people of the land and sixty of his men who were found in the city. ²⁶Nebuzaradan the com-

---

a15 Or *populace*   *b21* That is, about 27 feet (about 8.1 meters) high and 18 feet (about 5.4 meters) in circumference   *c22* That is, about 7 1/2 feet (about 2.3 meters)

nander took them all and brought
hem to the king of Babylon at Rib-
ah. 27There at Riblah, in the land
of Hamath, the king had them exe-
cuted.   2Ki 25:18; Jer 21:1; 37:3

So Judah went into captivity,
away from her land. 28This is the
number of the people Nebuchadnezzar carried into exile:

> in the seventh year, 3,023
> Jews;
> 29in Nebuchadnezzar's eigh-
> teenth year,
> 832 people from Jerusalem;
> 30in his twenty-third year,
> 745 Jews taken into exile by
> Nebuzaradan the com-
> mander of the imperial
> guard.   Jer 43:3
> There were 4,600 people in
> all.   Jer 13:19

Jehoiachin Released

31In the thirty-seventh year of
the exile of Jehoiachin king of Judah, in the year Evil-Merodach[a]
became king of Babylon, he released Jehoiachin king of Judah
and freed him from prison on the
twenty-fifth day of the twelfth
month. 32He spoke kindly to him
and gave him a seat of honor
higher than those of the other
kings who were with him in
Babylon. 33So Jehoiachin put
aside his prison clothes and for
the rest of his life ate regularly
at the king's table. 34Day by day
the king of Babylon gave Jehoiachin a regular allowance as
long as he lived, till the day of his
death.   2Ki 25:27-30

a31 Also called Amel-Marduk

Lamentations

1 *a* How deserted lies the city,
    once so full of people!   Jer 42:2
How like a widow is she,
    who once was great among
        the nations!   1Ki 4:21
She who was queen among the
        provinces
    has now become a slave.

²Bitterly she weeps at night,
    tears are upon her cheeks.
Among all her lovers   Jer 3:1
    there is none to comfort
        her.
All her friends have betrayed
        her;   Jer 4:30; Mic 7:5
    they have become her
        enemies.   Jer 30:14

³After affliction and harsh labor,
    Judah has gone into exile.
She dwells among the nations;
    she finds no resting place.
All who pursue her have
        overtaken her
    in the midst of her
        distress.

⁴The roads to Zion mourn,
    for no one comes to her
        appointed feasts.
All her gateways are desolate,
    her priests groan,
her maidens grieve,
    and she is in bitter anguish.

⁵Her foes have become her
        masters;
    her enemies are at ease.
The LORD has brought her grief
    because of her many sins.
Her children have gone into
        exile,   Jer 52:28-30
    captive before the foe.   Ps 137:3

⁶All the splendor has departed
    from the Daughter of Zion.
Her princes are like deer
    that find no pasture;
in weakness they have fled
    before the pursuer.

⁷In the days of her affliction
        and wandering
    Jerusalem remembers all the
        treasures
    that were hers in days of
        old.
When her people fell into
        enemy hands,
    there was no one to help
        her.   Jer 37:7; La 4:17
Her enemies looked at her
    and laughed at her
        destruction.

⁸Jerusalem has sinned greatly
    and so has become unclean.
All who honored her despise
        her,

---

*a*This chapter is an acrostic poem, the verses of which begin with the successive letters of the Hebrew alphabet.

for they have seen her
nakedness;   Jer 13:22,26
she herself groans   Ps 6:6
and turns away.

9Her filthiness clung to her
skirts;
she did not consider her
future.   Dt 32:28-29; Isa 47:7
Her fall was astounding;
there was none to comfort
her.   Ecc 4:1; Jer 16:7
"Look, O LORD, on my
affliction,   Ps 25:18
for the enemy has
triumphed."

10The enemy laid hands
on all her treasures;   Isa 64:11
she saw pagan nations
enter her sanctuary—   Ps 74:7-8
those you had forbidden   Dt 23:3
to enter your assembly.

11All her people groan   Ps 38:8
as they search for bread;
they barter their treasures for
food
to keep themselves alive.
"Look, O LORD, and consider,
for I am despised."

12"Is it nothing to you, all you
who pass by?   Jer 18:16
Look around and see.
Is any suffering like my
suffering
that was inflicted on me,
that the LORD brought on me

in the day of his fierce
anger?   Jer 30:24

13"From on high he sent fire,
sent it down into my bones.
He spread a net for my feet
and turned me back.
He made me desolate,   Jer 44:6
faint all the day long.   Hab 3:16

14"My sins have been bound into
a yoke[a];   Dt 28:48; Isa 47:6
by his hands they were
woven together.
They have come upon my neck
and the Lord has sapped my
strength.
He has handed me over   Jer 32:5
to those I cannot withstand.

15"The Lord has rejected
all the warriors in my midst;
he has summoned an army
against me   Isa 41:2
to[b] crush my young men.
In his winepress the Lord has
trampled   Jdg 6:11
the Virgin Daughter of
Judah.   Jer 14:17

16"This is why I weep
and my eyes overflow with
tears.   La 2:11,18; 3:48-49
No one is near to comfort me,
no one to restore my spirit.
My children are destitute
because the enemy has
prevailed."   Jer 13:17; 14:17

17Zion stretches out her hands,

---

a 14 Most Hebrew manuscripts; Septuagint *He kept watch over my sins*   b 15 Or *has set a time for me /
when he will*

but there is no one to
comfort her.
The Lord has decreed for
Jacob
that his neighbors become
his foes;   Ex 23:21
Jerusalem has become
an unclean thing among
them.   Lev 18:25-28

18"The Lord is righteous,   Ex 9:27
yet I rebelled against his
command.   1Sa 12:14
Listen, all you peoples;
look upon my suffering.
My young men and maidens
have gone into exile.

19"I called to my allies
but they betrayed me.
My priests and my elders
perished in the city   Jer 14:15
while they searched for food
to keep themselves alive.

20"See, O Lord, how distressed I
am!   Jer 4:19
I am in torment within,
and in my heart I am
disturbed,
for I have been most
rebellious.
Outside, the sword bereaves;
inside, there is only death.

21"People have heard my
groaning,   ver 8; Ps 6:6
but there is no one to
comfort me.   ver 4

All my enemies have heard of
my distress;
they rejoice at what you
have done.   La 2:15
May you bring the day you
have announced   Jer 30:16
so they may become like me.

22"Let all their wickedness come
before you;
deal with them
as you have dealt with me
because of all my sins.   Ne 4:5
My groans are many   Ps 6:6
and my heart is faint."

2 *a* How the Lord has covered
the Daughter of Zion
with the cloud of his anger*b*!
He has hurled down the
splendor of Israel
from heaven to earth;
he has not remembered his
footstool   Ps 99:5; 132:7
in the day of his anger.

2Without pity the Lord has
swallowed up   Ps 21:9
all the dwellings of Jacob;
in his wrath he has torn down
the strongholds of the
Daughter of Judah.
He has brought her kingdom
and its princes
down to the ground in
dishonor.   Isa 25:12

3In fierce anger he has cut off
every horn*c* of Israel.

*a*This chapter is an acrostic poem, the verses of which begin with the successive letters of the Hebrew
alphabet.   *b*1 Or *How the Lord in his anger / has treated the Daughter of Zion with contempt*   *c*3 Or
/ *all the strength*; or *every king*; horn here symbolizes strength.

He has withdrawn his right
      hand   Ps 74:11
   at the approach of the
      enemy.
He has burned in Jacob like a
      flaming fire
   that consumes everything
      around it.   Isa 42:25

⁴Like an enemy he has strung
      his bow;   La 3:12-13
   his right hand is ready.
Like a foe he has slain
   all who were pleasing to the
      eye;   Eze 24:16,25
   he has poured out his wrath
      like fire   Jer 7:20
   on the tent of the Daughter
      of Zion.   Jer 4:20

⁵The Lord is like an enemy;
   he has swallowed up Israel.
He has swallowed up all her
      palaces
   and destroyed her
      strongholds.   ver 2
He has multiplied mourning
      and lamentation
   for the Daughter of Judah.

⁶He has laid waste his dwelling
      like a garden;
   he has destroyed his place of
      meeting.   Jer 52:13
The LORD has made Zion forget
   her appointed feasts and her
      Sabbaths;   Zep 3:18
   in his fierce anger he has
      spurned
   both king and priest.   La 4:16

⁷The Lord has rejected his altar
      and abandoned his
      sanctuary.   Eze 7:24
He has handed over to the
      enemy
   the walls of her palaces;
they have raised a shout in the
      house of the LORD
   as on the day of an
      appointed feast.

⁸The LORD determined to tear
      down
   the wall around the
      Daughter of Zion.
He stretched out a measuring
      line   2Ki 21:13; Isa 34:11
   and did not withhold his
      hand from destroying.
He made ramparts and walls
      lament;   Ps 48:13
   together they wasted away.

⁹Her gates have sunk into the
      ground;   Ne 1:3
   their bars he has broken and
      destroyed.
Her king and her princes are
      exiled among the
      nations,   Dt 28:36
   the law is no more,   2Ch 15:3
and her prophets no longer
      find
   visions from the LORD.

¹⁰The elders of the Daughter of
      Zion
   sit on the ground in silence;
they have sprinkled dust on
      their heads   Job 2:12
   and put on sackcloth.   Isa 15:3
The young women of
      Jerusalem

have bowed their heads to
 the ground.   Job 2:13; Isa 3:26

¹¹My eyes fail from weeping,
 I am in torment within,
my heart is poured out on the
 ground   ver 19; Ps 22:14
because my people are
 destroyed,
because children and infants
 faint   La 4:4
 in the streets of the city.

¹²They say to their mothers,
 "Where is bread and wine?"
as they faint like wounded
 men
 in the streets of the city,
as their lives ebb away
 in their mothers' arms.   La 4:4

¹³What can I say for you?
 With what can I compare
 you,
 O Daughter of Jerusalem?
To what can I liken you,
 that I may comfort you,
 O Virgin Daughter of Zion?
Your wound is as deep as the
 sea.   Jer 14:17; La 1:12
 Who can heal you?

¹⁴The visions of your prophets
 were false and worthless;
they did not expose your sin
 to ward off your captivity.
The oracles they gave you
 were false and misleading.

¹⁵All who pass your way
 clap their hands at you;

they scoff and shake their
 heads   Jer 19:8
 at the Daughter of
 Jerusalem: La 1:21
"Is this the city that was
 called
 the perfection of beauty,
 the joy of the whole earth?"

¹⁶All your enemies open their
 mouths
 wide against you;   Ps 56:2; La 3:46
they scoff and gnash their
 teeth   Job 16:9
and say, "We have
 swallowed her up.
This is the day we have waited
 for;
 we have lived to see it."

¹⁷The LORD has done what he
 planned;
 he has fulfilled his word,
 which he decreed long ago.
He has overthrown you
 without pity,   ver 2; Eze 5:11
he has let the enemy gloat
 over you,   Ps 22:17
he has exalted the horn^a of
 your foes.   Ps 89:42

¹⁸The hearts of the people
 cry out to the Lord.   Ps 119:145
O wall of the Daughter of Zion,
 let your tears flow like a
 river   La 1:16
 day and night;   Jer 9:1
give yourself no relief,
 your eyes no rest.   La 3:49

---

^a 17 Horn here symbolizes strength.

¹⁹Arise, cry out in the night,
    as the watches of the night
        begin;
pour out your heart like water
    in the presence of the Lord.
Lift up your hands to him
    for the lives of your children,
who faint from hunger   Isa 51:20
    at the head of every street.

²⁰"Look, O Lᴏʀᴅ, and consider:
    Whom have you ever treated
        like this?
Should women eat their
        offspring,   Jer 19:9
    the children they have cared
        for?   La 4:10
Should priest and prophet be
        killed   Ps 78:64; Jer 14:15
    in the sanctuary of the
        Lord?

²¹"Young and old lie together
    in the dust of the streets;
my young men and maidens
    have fallen by the sword.
You have slain them in the day
    of your anger;
you have slaughtered them
    without pity.   Jer 13:14

²²"As you summon to a feast
    day,
so you summoned against
    me terrors on every
        side.   Ps 31:13; Jer 6:25
In the day of the Lᴏʀᴅ's anger
    no one escaped or survived;
those I cared for and reared,
    my enemy has destroyed."

3 ᵃ I am the man who has seen
    affliction
        by the rod of his wrath.
²He has driven me away and
        made me walk
    in darkness rather than light;
³indeed, he has turned his hand
        against me   Isa 5:25
    again and again, all day long.

⁴He has made my skin and my
        flesh grow old
    and has broken my bones.
⁵He has besieged me and
        surrounded me
    with bitterness and hardship.
⁶He has made me dwell in
        darkness
    like those long dead.   Ps 88:5-6

⁷He has walled me in so I
        cannot escape;   Job 3:23
    he has weighed me down
        with chains.   Jer 40:4
⁸Even when I call out or cry for
        help,
    he shuts out my prayer.
⁹He has barred my way with
        blocks of stone;
    he has made my paths
        crooked.   Isa 63:17; Hos 2:6

¹⁰Like a bear lying in wait,
    like a lion in hiding,   Hos 13:8
¹¹he dragged me from the path
        and mangled me   Hos 6:1
    and left me without help.
¹²He drew his bow   La 2:4
        and made me the target for
        his arrows.   Job 7:20

ᵃThis chapter is an acrostic poem; the verses of each stanza begin with the successive letters of the
Hebrew alphabet, and the verses within each stanza begin with the same letter.

¹³He pierced my heart
   with arrows from his quiver.
¹⁴I became the laughingstock of
   all my people;   Jer 20:7
   they mock me in song all
   day long.   Job 30:9
¹⁵He has filled me with bitter
   herbs
   and sated me with gall.

¹⁶He has broken my teeth with
   gravel;   Pr 20:17
   he has trampled me in the
   dust.   Ps 7:5
¹⁷I have been deprived of peace;
   I have forgotten what
   prosperity is.
¹⁸So I say, "My splendor is gone
   and all that I had hoped
   from the LORD."   Job 17:15

¹⁹I remember my affliction and
   my wandering,
   the bitterness and the gall.
²⁰I well remember them,
   and my soul is downcast
   within me.   Ps 42:5,11
²¹Yet this I call to mind
   and therefore I have hope:

²²Because of the LORD's great
   love we are not
   consumed,   Ps 103:11
   for his compassions never
   fail.   Ps 78:38; Mal 3:6
²³They are new every morning;
   great is your faithfulness.
²⁴I say to myself, "The LORD is
   my portion;   Ps 16:5
   therefore I will wait for
   him."

²⁵The LORD is good to those
   whose hope is in him,
   to the one who seeks him;
²⁶it is good to wait quietly
   for the salvation of the LORD.
²⁷It is good for a man to bear the
   yoke
   while he is young.

²⁸Let him sit alone in silence,
   for the LORD has laid it on
   him.
²⁹Let him bury his face in the
   dust—
   there may yet be hope.
³⁰Let him offer his cheek to one
   who would strike him,
   and let him be filled with
   disgrace.

³¹For men are not cast off
   by the Lord forever.   Ps 94:14
³²Though he brings grief, he will
   show compassion,
   so great is his unfailing love.
³³For he does not willingly bring
   affliction
   or grief to the children of
   men.   Eze 33:11

³⁴To crush underfoot
   all prisoners in the land,
³⁵to deny a man his rights
   before the Most High,
³⁶to deprive a man of justice—
   would not the Lord see such
   things?   Jer 22:3; Hab 1:13

³⁷Who can speak and have it
   happen
   if the Lord has not decreed
   it?   Ps 33:9-11

38Is it not from the mouth of the
Most High
that both calamities and
good things come?
39Why should any living man
complain
when punished for his sins?

40Let us examine our ways and
test them,   2Co 13:5
and let us return to the
LORD.   Ps 119:59; 139:23-24
41Let us lift up our hearts and
our hands
to God in heaven, and say:
42"We have sinned and rebelled
and you have not forgiven.

43"You have covered yourself
with anger and pursued
us;
you have slain without pity.
44You have covered yourself with
a cloud   Ps 97:2
so that no prayer can get
through.   Zec 7:13
45You have made us scum and
refuse   1Co 4:13
among the nations.

46"All our enemies have opened
their mouths
wide against us.   La 2:16
47We have suffered terror and
pitfalls,   Jer 48:43
ruin and destruction."
48Streams of tears flow from my
eyes   La 1:16
because my people are
destroyed.   La 2:11

49My eyes will flow unceasingly,
without relief,   Jer 14:17

50until the LORD looks down
from heaven and sees.
51What I see brings grief to my
soul
because of all the women of
my city.
52Those who were my enemies
without cause
hunted me like a bird.   Ps 35:7
53They tried to end my life in a
pit   Jer 37:16
and threw stones at me;
54the waters closed over my
head,   Ps 69:2; Jnh 2:3-5
and I thought I was about to
be cut off.   Ps 88:5

55I called on your name, O LORD,
from the depths of the pit.
56You heard my plea: "Do not
close your ears   Ps 55:1
to my cry for relief."
57You came near when I called
you,   Ps 46:1
and you said, "Do not fear."

58O Lord, you took up my case;
you redeemed my life.
59You have seen, O LORD, the
wrong done to me.
Uphold my cause!
60You have seen the depth of
their vengeance,
all their plots against me.

61O LORD, you have heard their
insults,   Ps 89:50
all their plots against me—
62what my enemies whisper and
mutter
against me all day long.

63Look at them! Sitting or
    standing,
  they mock me in their songs.

64Pay them back what they
    deserve, O LORD,
  for what their hands have
    done.   Ps 28:4
65Put a veil over their hearts,
  and may your curse be on
    them!
66Pursue them in anger and
    destroy them
  from under the heavens of
    the LORD.

4 a How the gold has lost its
    luster,
  the fine gold become dull!
The sacred gems are scattered
  at the head of every street.

2How the precious sons of Zion,
  once worth their weight in
    gold,
are now considered as pots of
    clay,
  the work of a potter's hands!

3Even jackals offer their breasts
  to nurse their young,
but my people have become
    heartless
  like ostriches in the desert.

4Because of thirst the infant's
    tongue
  sticks to the roof of its
    mouth;   Ps 22:15
the children beg for bread,

but no one gives it to them.
5Those who once ate delicacies
  are destitute in the streets.
Those nurtured in purple   Jer 6:2
  now lie on ash heaps.   Am 6:3-7
6The punishment of my people
  is greater than that of
    Sodom,   Ge 19:25
which was overthrown in a
    moment
  without a hand turned to
    help her.

7Their princes were brighter
    than snow
  and whiter than milk,
their bodies more ruddy than
    rubies,
  their appearance like
    sapphires.b

8But now they are blacker than
    soot;   Job 30:28
  they are not recognized in
    the streets.
Their skin has shriveled on
    their bones;   Ps 102:3-5
  it has become as dry as a
    stick.

9Those killed by the sword are
    better off
  than those who die of
    famine;
racked with hunger, they waste
    away
  for lack of food from the
    field.   Jer 15:2; 16:4

---

aThis chapter is an acrostic poem, the verses of which begin with the successive letters of the Hebrew
alphabet.   b7 Or lapis lazuli

¹⁰With their own hands
    compassionate women
have cooked their own
    children,   Dt 28:53-57; La 2:20
who became their food
    when my people were
    destroyed.

¹¹The LORD has given full vent to
    his wrath;   Job 20:23
he has poured out his fierce
    anger.   Zep 2:2; 3:8
He kindled a fire in Zion
    that consumed her
    foundations.   Dt 32:22

¹²The kings of the earth did not
    believe,
    nor did any of the world's
    people,
that enemies and foes could
    enter
    the gates of Jerusalem.   1Ki 9:9

¹³But it happened because of the
    sins of her prophets
and the iniquities of her
    priests,   Jer 6:13; Eze 22:28
who shed within her
    the blood of the righteous.

¹⁴Now they grope through the
    streets
    like men who are blind.
They are so defiled with blood
    that no one dares to touch
    their garments.

¹⁵"Go away! You are unclean!"
    men cry to them.
    "Away! Away! Don't touch
    us!"

When they flee and wander
    about,
    people among the nations
    say,
    "They can stay here no
    longer."   Lev 13:46

¹⁶The LORD himself has scattered
    them;
he no longer watches over
    them.   Isa 9:14-16
The priests are shown no
    honor,
    the elders no favor.   La 5:12

¹⁷Moreover, our eyes failed,
    looking in vain for help;
from our towers we watched
    for a nation that could not
    save us.   Jer 37:7

¹⁸Men stalked us at every step,
    so we could not walk in our
    streets.
Our end was near, our days
    were numbered,
    for our end had come.

¹⁹Our pursuers were swifter
    than eagles in the sky;
they chased us over the
    mountains   Isa 5:26-28
and lay in wait for us in the
    desert.   Jer 52:7

²⁰The LORD's anointed, our very
    life breath,   2Sa 19:21
    was caught in their traps.
We thought that under his
    shadow
    we would live among the
    nations.

²¹Rejoice and be glad,
  O Daughter of Edom,
you who live in the land of
  Uz.
But to you also the cup will be
  passed;   Jer 25:15
you will be drunk and
  stripped naked. Am 1:11-12

²²O Daughter of Zion, your
  punishment will
  end;
he will not prolong your
  exile.
But, O Daughter of Edom, he
  will punish your sin
and expose your wickedness.

5 Remember, O Lord, what
  has happened to us;
 look, and see our disgrace.
²Our inheritance has been
  turned over to aliens,
 our homes to foreigners.
³We have become orphans and
  fatherless,
 our mothers like widows.
⁴We must buy the water we
  drink;
 our wood can be had only at
  a price.   Isa 3:1
⁵Those who pursue us are at
  our heels;
 we are weary and find no
  rest.   Jos 1:13; Ne 9:37
⁶We submitted to Egypt and
  Assyria   Hos 9:3
 to get enough bread.
⁷Our fathers sinned and are no
  more,

and we bear their
  punishment. Jer 14:20; 16:12
⁸Slaves rule over us, Ne 5:15
 and there is none to free us
  from their hands. Zec 11:6
⁹We get our bread at the risk of
  our lives
 because of the sword in the
  desert.
¹⁰Our skin is hot as an oven,
  feverish from hunger. La 4:8-9
¹¹Women have been ravished in
  Zion,   Zec 14:2
 and virgins in the towns of
  Judah.
¹²Princes have been hung up by
  their hands;
 elders are shown no respect.
¹³Young men toil at the
  millstones;
 boys stagger under loads of
  wood.
¹⁴The elders are gone from the
  city gate;
 the young men have stopped
  their music. Jer 7:34
¹⁵Joy is gone from our hearts;
 our dancing has turned to
  mourning. Jer 25:10
¹⁶The crown has fallen from our
  head.   Ps 89:39
 Woe to us, for we have
  sinned!   Isa 3:11
¹⁷Because of this our hearts are
  faint,   Isa 1:5
 because of these things our
  eyes grow dim Ps 6:7
¹⁸for Mount Zion, which lies
  desolate, Mic 3:12
 with jackals prowling over
  it.

¹⁹You, O LORD, reign forever;
　　your throne endures from
　　　　generation to generation.
²⁰Why do you always forget
　　us?
　　Why do you forsake us so
　　long?

²¹Restore us to yourself, O LORD,
　　that we may return;
　　renew our days as of old
²²unless you have utterly
　　rejected us　　　　Ps 53:5; 60:1-2
　　and are angry with us
　　beyond measure.　　　Isa 64:9

²²You, O LORD, reign forever;
your throne endures
generation to
²⁰Why do you always forget

²¹Restore us to yourself, O LORD,
that we may return;
out days as of old
²²unless you have utterly
rejected us   Psa 93; 102:2

Ezekiel

The Living Creatures and the Glory of the LORD

1 In the[a] thirtieth year, in the fourth month on the fifth day, while I was among the exiles by the Kebar River, the heavens were opened and I saw visions of God.

²On the fifth of the month—it was the fifth year of the exile of King Jehoiachin— ³the word of the LORD came to Ezekiel the priest, the son of Buzi,[b] by the Kebar River in the land of the Babylonians.[c] There the hand of the LORD was upon him.   2Ki 3:15; Eze 3:14,22

⁴I looked, and I saw a windstorm coming out of the north—an immense cloud with flashing lightning and surrounded by brilliant light. The center of the fire looked like glowing metal, ⁵and in the fire was what looked like four living creatures. In appearance their form was that of a man, ⁶but each of them had four faces and four wings. ⁷Their legs were straight; their feet were like those of a calf and gleamed like burnished bronze. ⁸Under their wings on their four sides they had the hands of a man. All four of them had faces and wings, ⁹and their wings touched one another. Each one went straight ahead; they did not turn as they moved.   Rev 4:6; Eze 10:8

¹⁰Their faces looked like this: Each of the four had the face of a man, and on the right side each had the face of a lion, and on the left the face of an ox; each also had the face of an eagle. ¹¹Such were their faces. Their wings were spread out upward; each had two wings, one touching the wing of another creature on either side, and two wings covering its body. ¹²Each one went straight ahead. Wherever the spirit would go, they would go, without turning as they went. ¹³The appearance of the living creatures was like burning coals of fire or like torches. Fire moved back and forth among the creatures; it was bright, and lightning flashed out of it. ¹⁴The creatures sped back and forth like flashes of lightning.   Isa 6:2; Rev 4:5,7

¹⁵As I looked at the living creatures, I saw a wheel on the ground beside each creature with its four faces. ¹⁶This was the appearance and structure of the wheels: They sparkled like chrysolite, and all four looked alike. Each appeared to be made like a wheel intersecting a wheel. ¹⁷As they moved, they would go in any one of the four

---

[a]1 Or *my*,   [b]3 Or *Ezekiel son of Buzi the priest*   [c]3 Or *Chaldeans*

directions the creatures faced; the wheels did not turn about[a] as the creatures went. [18]Their rims were high and awesome, and all four rims were full of eyes all around.

[19]When the living creatures moved, the wheels beside them moved; and when the living creatures rose from the ground, the wheels also rose. [20]Wherever the spirit would go, they would go, and the wheels would rise along with them, because the spirit of the living creatures was in the wheels. [21]When the creatures moved, they also moved; when the creatures stood still, they also stood still; and when the creatures rose from the ground, the wheels rose along with them, because the spirit of the living creatures was in the wheels.   ver 12; Eze 10:17

[22]Spread out above the heads of the living creatures was what looked like an expanse, sparkling like ice, and awesome. [23]Under the expanse their wings were stretched out one toward the other, and each had two wings covering its body. [24]When the creatures moved, I heard the sound of their wings, like the roar of rushing waters, like the voice of the Almighty,[b] like the tumult of an army. When they stood still, they lowered their wings.   Eze 10:5

[25]Then there came a voice from above the expanse over their heads as they stood with lowered wings. [26]Above the expanse over their heads was what looked like a throne of sapphire,[c] and high above on the throne was a figure like that of a man. [27]I saw that from what appeared to be his waist up he looked like glowing metal, as if full of fire, and that from there down he looked like fire; and brilliant light surrounded him. [28]Like the appearance of a rainbow in the clouds on a rainy day, so was the radiance around him.   Rev 4:2; 10:1

This was the appearance of the likeness of the glory of the Lord. When I saw it, I fell facedown, and I heard the voice of one speaking.

Ezekiel's Call

2 He said to me, "Son of man, stand up on your feet and I will speak to you." [2]As he spoke, the Spirit came into me and raised me to my feet, and I heard him speaking to me.   Eze 3:24; Da 8:18

[3]He said: "Son of man, I am sending you to the Israelites, to a rebellious nation that has rebelled against me; they and their fathers have been in revolt against me to this very day. [4]The people to whom I am sending you are obstinate and stubborn. Say to them, 'This is what the Sovereign Lord says.' [5]And whether they listen or fail to listen—for they are a rebellious house—they will know that a prophet has been among them.

---

[a]17 Or aside   [b]24 Hebrew Shaddai   [c]26 Or lapis lazuli

⁶And you, son of man, do not be afraid of them or their words. Do not be afraid, though briers and thorns are all around you and you live among scorpions. Do not be afraid of what they say or terrified by them, though they are a rebellious house. ⁷You must speak my words to them, whether they listen or fail to listen, for they are rebellious. ⁸But you, son of man, listen to what I say to you. Do not rebel like that rebellious house; open your mouth and eat what I give you." Jer 3:25; Rev 10:9

⁹Then I looked, and I saw a hand stretched out to me. In it was a scroll, ¹⁰which he unrolled before me. On both sides of it were written words of lament and mourning and woe. Eze 8:3; Rev 8:13

3 And he said to me, "Son of man, eat what is before you, eat this scroll; then go and speak to the house of Israel." ²So I opened my mouth, and he gave me the scroll to eat.

³Then he said to me, "Son of man, eat this scroll I am giving you and fill your stomach with it." So I ate it, and it tasted as sweet as honey in my mouth. Ps 19:10

⁴He then said to me: "Son of man, go now to the house of Israel and speak my words to them. ⁵You are not being sent to a people of obscure speech and difficult language, but to the house of Israel— ⁶not to many peoples of obscure speech and difficult language, whose words you cannot under-stand. Surely if I had sent you to them, they would have listened to you. ⁷But the house of Israel is not willing to listen to you because they are not willing to listen to me, for the whole house of Israel is hardened and obstinate. ⁸But I will make you as unyielding and hardened as they are. ⁹I will make your forehead like the hardest stone, harder than flint. Do not be afraid of them or terrified by them, though they are a rebellious house." Isa 50:7; Eze 2:6; Mic 3:8

¹⁰And he said to me, "Son of man, listen carefully and take to heart all the words I speak to you. ¹¹Go now to your countrymen in exile and speak to them. Say to them, 'This is what the Sovereign Lord says,' whether they listen or fail to listen." Eze 2:4-5,7

¹²Then the Spirit lifted me up, and I heard behind me a loud rumbling sound—May the glory of the Lord be praised in his dwelling place!— ¹³the sound of the wings of the living creatures brushing against each other and the sound of the wheels beside them, a loud rumbling sound. ¹⁴The Spirit then lifted me up and took me away, and I went in bitterness and in the anger of my spirit, with the strong hand of the Lord upon me. ¹⁵I came to the exiles who lived at Tel Abib near the Kebar River. And there, where they were living, I sat among them for seven days—overwhelmed. Eze 8:3; 1Ki 18:12; Ac 8:39

Warning to Israel

16At the end of seven days the word of the LORD came to me: **17**"Son of man, I have made you a watchman for the house of Israel; so hear the word I speak and give them warning from me. **18**When I say to a wicked man, 'You will surely die,' and you do not warn him or speak out to dissuade him from his evil ways in order to save his life, that wicked man will die for*a* his sin, and I will hold you accountable for his blood. **19**But if you do warn the wicked man and he does not turn from his wickedness or from his evil ways, he will die for his sin; but you will have saved yourself.   Isa 52:8; Jer 6:17

20"Again, when a righteous man turns from his righteousness and does evil, and I put a stumbling block before him, he will die. Since you did not warn him, he will die for his sin. The righteous things he did will not be remembered, and I will hold you accountable for his blood. **21**But if you do warn the righteous man not to sin and he does not sin, he will surely live because he took warning, and you will have saved yourself."   Eze 18:24

22The hand of the LORD was upon me there, and he said to me, "Get up and go out to the plain, and there I will speak to you." **23**So I got up and went out to the plain. And the glory of the LORD was standing there, like the glory I had seen by the Kebar River, and I fell facedown.   Eze 1:1; 8:4; Ac 9:6

24Then the Spirit came into me and raised me to my feet. He spoke to me and said: "Go, shut yourself inside your house. **25**And you, son of man, they will tie with ropes; you will be bound so that you cannot go out among the people. **26**I will make your tongue stick to the roof of your mouth so that you will be silent and unable to rebuke them, though they are a rebellious house. **27**But when I speak to you, I will open your mouth and you shall say to them, 'This is what the Sovereign LORD says.' Whoever will listen let him listen, and whoever will refuse let him refuse; for they are a rebellious house.

Siege of Jerusalem Symbolized

4 "Now, son of man, take a clay tablet, put it in front of you and draw the city of Jerusalem on it. **2**Then lay siege to it: Erect siege works against it, build a ramp up to it, set up camps against it and put battering rams around it. **3**Then take an iron pan, place it as an iron wall between you and the city and turn your face toward it. It will be under siege, and you shall besiege it. This will be a sign to the house of Israel.   Eze 12:3-6; 24:24,27

4"Then lie on your left side and put the sin of the house of Israel upon yourself.*b* You are to bear their sin for the number of days

---

a 18 Or *in;* also in verses 19 and 20   *b 4* Or *your side*

you lie on your side. [5]I have assigned you the same number of days as the years of their sin. So for 390 days you will bear the sin of the house of Israel.

[6]"After you have finished this, lie down again, this time on your right side, and bear the sin of the house of Judah. I have assigned you 40 days, a day for each year. [7]Turn your face toward the siege of Jerusalem and with bared arm prophesy against her. [8]I will tie you up with ropes so that you cannot turn from one side to the other until you have finished the days of your siege.   Nu 14:34; Eze 3:25

[9]"Take wheat and barley, beans and lentils, millet and spelt; put them in a storage jar and use them to make bread for yourself. You are to eat it during the 390 days you lie on your side. [10]Weigh out twenty shekels[a] of food to eat each day and eat it at set times. [11]Also measure out a sixth of a hin[b] of water and drink it at set times. [12]Eat the food as you would a barley cake; bake it in the sight of the people, using human excrement for fuel." [13]The LORD said, "In this way the people of Israel will eat defiled food among the nations where I will drive them."   Hos 9:3

[14]Then I said, "Not so, Sovereign LORD! I have never defiled myself. From my youth until now I have never eaten anything found dead or torn by wild animals. No unclean meat has ever entered my mouth."   Ex 22:31; Ac 10:14

[15]"Very well," he said, "I will let you bake your bread over cow manure instead of human excrement."

[16]He then said to me: "Son of man, I will cut off the supply of food in Jerusalem. The people will eat rationed food in anxiety and drink rationed water in despair, [17]for food and water will be scarce. They will be appalled at the sight of each other and will waste away because of[c] their sin.   Lev 26:39

5 "Now, son of man, take a sharp sword and use it as a barber's razor to shave your head and your beard. Then take a set of scales and divide up the hair. [2]When the days of your siege come to an end, burn a third of the hair with fire inside the city. Take a third and strike it with the sword all around the city. And scatter a third to the wind. For I will pursue them with drawn sword. [3]But take a few strands of hair and tuck them away in the folds of your garment. [4]Again, take a few of these and throw them into the fire and burn them up. A fire will spread from there to the whole house of Israel.

[5]"This is what the Sovereign LORD says: This is Jerusalem, which I have set in the center of the nations, with countries all

---

[a]10 That is, about 8 ounces (about 0.2 kilogram)   [b]11 That is, about 2/3 quart (about 0.6 liter)
[c]17 Or *away in*

around her. ⁶Yet in her wickedness she has rebelled against my laws and decrees more than the nations and countries around her. She has rejected my laws and has not followed my decrees.   Jer 11:10; Zec 7:11

⁷"Therefore this is what the Sovereign LORD says: You have been more unruly than the nations around you and have not followed my decrees or kept my laws. You have not even*a* conformed to the standards of the nations around you.   2Ch 33:9; Eze 16:47

⁸"Therefore this is what the Sovereign LORD says: I myself am against you, Jerusalem, and I will inflict punishment on you in the sight of the nations. ⁹Because of all your detestable idols, I will do to you what I have never done before and will never do again. ¹⁰Therefore in your midst fathers will eat their children, and children will eat their fathers. I will inflict punishment on you and will scatter all your survivors to the winds. ¹¹Therefore as surely as I live, declares the Sovereign LORD, because you have defiled my sanctuary with all your vile images and detestable practices, I myself will withdraw my favor; I will not look on you with pity or spare you. ¹²A third of your people will die of the plague or perish by famine inside you; a third will fall by the sword outside your walls; and a third I will scatter to the winds and pursue with drawn sword.   Da 9:12

¹³"Then my anger will cease and my wrath against them will subside, and I will be avenged. And when I have spent my wrath upon them, they will know that I the LORD have spoken in my zeal.

¹⁴"I will make you a ruin and a reproach among the nations around you, in the sight of all who pass by. ¹⁵You will be a reproach and a taunt, a warning and an object of horror to the nations around you when I inflict punishment on you in anger and in wrath and with stinging rebuke. I the LORD have spoken. ¹⁶When I shoot at you with my deadly and destructive arrows of famine, I will shoot to destroy you. I will bring more and more famine upon you and cut off your supply of food. ¹⁷I will send famine and wild beasts against you, and they will leave you childless. Plague and bloodshed will sweep through you, and I will bring the sword against you. I the LORD have spoken."   Ne 2:17; Eze 25:17

A Prophecy Against the Mountains of Israel

6 The word of the LORD came to me: ²"Son of man, set your face against the mountains of Israel; prophesy against them ³and say: 'O mountains of Israel, hear the word of the Sovereign LORD. This is what the Sovereign LORD

---

a 7 Most Hebrew manuscripts; some Hebrew manuscripts and Syriac You have

says to the mountains and hills, to the ravines and valleys: I am about to bring a sword against you, and I will destroy your high places. ⁴Your altars will be demolished and your incense altars will be smashed; and I will slay your people in front of your idols. ⁵I will lay the dead bodies of the Israelites in front of their idols, and I will scatter your bones around your altars. ⁶Wherever you live, the towns will be laid waste and the high places demolished, so that your altars will be laid waste and devastated, your idols smashed and ruined, your incense altars broken down, and what you have made wiped out. ⁷Your people will fall slain among you, and you will know that I am the Lord.   Lev 26:30; Eze 36:1

⁸" 'But I will spare some, for some of you will escape the sword when you are scattered among the lands and nations. ⁹Then in the nations where they have been carried captive, those who escape will remember me—how I have been grieved by their adulterous hearts, which have turned away from me, and by their eyes, which have lusted after their idols. They will loathe themselves for the evil they have done and for all their detestable practices. ¹⁰And they will know that I am the Lord; I did not threaten in vain to bring this calamity on them.   Isa 7:13; Jer 44:28

¹¹" 'This is what the Sovereign Lord says: Strike your hands together and stamp your feet and cry out "Alas!" because of all the wicked and detestable practices of the house of Israel, for they will fall by the sword, famine and plague. ¹²He that is far away will die of the plague, and he that is near will fall by the sword, and he that survives and is spared will die of famine. So will I spend my wrath upon them. ¹³And they will know that I am the Lord, when their people lie slain among their idols around their altars, on every high hill and on all the mountaintops, under every spreading tree and every leafy oak—places where they offered fragrant incense to all their idols. ¹⁴And I will stretch out my hand against them and make the land a desolate waste from the desert to Diblah[a]—wherever they live. Then they will know that I am the Lord.' "   Eze 21:14,17; Jer 2:20; Hos 4:13

The End Has Come

7 The word of the Lord came to me: ²"Son of man, this is what the Sovereign Lord says to the land of Israel: The end! The end has come upon the four corners of the land. ³The end is now upon you and I will unleash my anger against you. I will judge you according to your conduct and repay you for all your detestable practices. ⁴I will not look on you with pity or spare you; I will surely re-

---

a 14 Most Hebrew manuscripts; a few Hebrew manuscripts *Riblah*

pay you for your conduct and the detestable practices among you. Then you will know that I am the Lord. Eze 5:11; Am 8:2,10

⁵"This is what the Sovereign Lord says: Disaster! An unheard-of^a disaster is coming. ⁶The end has come! The end has come! It has roused itself against you. It has come! ⁷Doom has come upon you —you who dwell in the land. The time has come, the day is near; there is panic, not joy, upon the mountains. ⁸I am about to pour out my wrath on you and spend my anger against you; I will judge you according to your conduct and repay you for all your detestable practices. ⁹I will not look on you with pity or spare you; I will repay you in accordance with your conduct and the detestable practices among you. Then you will know that it is I the Lord who strikes the blow. 2Ki 21:12; Eze 20:8,21

¹⁰"The day is here! It has come! Doom has burst forth, the rod has budded, arrogance has blossomed! ¹¹Violence has grown into^b a rod to punish wickedness; none of the people will be left, none of that crowd—no wealth, nothing of value. ¹²The time has come, the day has arrived. Let not the buyer rejoice nor the seller grieve, for wrath is upon the whole crowd. ¹³The seller will not recover the land he has sold as long as both of them live, for the vision concerning the whole crowd will not be reversed. Because of their sins, not one of them will preserve his life. ¹⁴Though they blow the trumpet and get everything ready, no one will go into battle, for my wrath is upon the whole crowd.

¹⁵"Outside is the sword, inside are plague and famine; those in the country will die by the sword, and those in the city will be devoured by famine and plague. ¹⁶All who survive and escape will be in the mountains, moaning like doves of the valleys, each because of his sins. ¹⁷Every hand will go limp, and every knee will become as weak as water. ¹⁸They will put on sackcloth and be clothed with terror. Their faces will be covered with shame and their heads will be shaved. ¹⁹They will throw their silver into the streets, and their gold will be an unclean thing. Their silver and gold will not be able to save them in the day of the Lord's wrath. They will not satisfy their hunger or fill their stomachs with it, for it has made them stumble into sin. ²⁰They were proud of their beautiful jewelry and used it to make their detestable idols and vile images. Therefore I will turn these into an unclean thing for them. ²¹I will hand it all over as plunder to foreigners and as loot to the wicked of the earth, and they

---

^a5 Most Hebrew manuscripts; some Hebrew manuscripts and Syriac *Disaster after* one *has become*   ^b11 Or *The violent*

will defile it. ²²I will turn my face away from them, and they will desecrate my treasured place; robbers will enter it and desecrate it.

²³"Prepare chains, because the land is full of bloodshed and the city is full of violence. ²⁴I will bring the most wicked of the nations to take possession of their houses; I will put an end to the pride of the mighty, and their sanctuaries will be desecrated. ²⁵When terror comes, they will seek peace, but there will be none. ²⁶Calamity upon calamity will come, and rumor upon rumor. They will try to get a vision from the prophet; the teaching of the law by the priest will be lost, as will the counsel of the elders. ²⁷The king will mourn, the prince will be clothed with despair, and the hands of the people of the land will tremble. I will deal with them according to their conduct, and by their own standards I will judge them. Then they will know that I am the Lord."

Idolatry in the Temple

8 In the sixth year, in the sixth month on the fifth day, while I was sitting in my house and the elders of Judah were sitting before me, the hand of the Sovereign Lord came upon me there. ²I looked, and I saw a figure like that of a man.ᵃ From what appeared to be his waist down he was like fire, and from there up his appearance was as bright as glowing metal. ³He stretched out what looked like a hand and took me by the hair of my head. The Spirit lifted me up between earth and heaven and in visions of God he took me to Jerusalem, to the entrance to the north gate of the inner court, where the idol that provokes to jealousy stood. ⁴And there before me was the glory of the God of Israel, as in the vision I had seen in the plain.

⁵Then he said to me, "Son of man, look toward the north." So I looked, and in the entrance north of the gate of the altar I saw this idol of jealousy.   Jer 32:34

⁶And he said to me, "Son of man, do you see what they are doing—the utterly detestable things the house of Israel is doing here, things that will drive me far from my sanctuary? But you will see things that are even more detestable."   Eze 5:11; Hos 5:6

⁷Then he brought me to the entrance to the court. I looked, and I saw a hole in the wall. ⁸He said to me, "Son of man, now dig into the wall." So I dug into the wall and saw a doorway there.

⁹And he said to me, "Go in and see the wicked and detestable things they are doing here." ¹⁰So I went in and looked, and I saw portrayed all over the walls all kinds of crawling things and detestable animals and all the idols of the house of Israel. ¹¹In front of them

ᵃ2 Or saw a fiery figure

stood seventy elders of the house of Israel, and Jaazaniah son of Shaphan was standing among them. Each had a censer in his hand, and a fragrant cloud of incense was rising.   Ex 3:16; 20:4

¹²He said to me, "Son of man, have you seen what the elders of the house of Israel are doing in the darkness, each at the shrine of his own idol? They say, 'The LORD does not see us; the LORD has forsaken the land.' " ¹³Again, he said, "You will see them doing things that are even more detestable."

¹⁴Then he brought me to the entrance to the north gate of the house of the LORD, and I saw women sitting there, mourning for Tammuz. ¹⁵He said to me, "Do you see this, son of man? You will see things that are even more detestable than this."   Eze 11:12

¹⁶He then brought me into the inner court of the house of the LORD, and there at the entrance to the temple, between the portico and the altar, were about twenty-five men. With their backs toward the temple of the LORD and their faces toward the east, they were bowing down to the sun in the east.   Dt 4:19; Jer 2:27

¹⁷He said to me, "Have you seen this, son of man? Is it a trivial matter for the house of Judah to do the detestable things they are doing here? Must they also fill the land with violence and continually provoke me to anger? Look at them putting the branch to their nose!

¹⁸Therefore I will deal with them in anger; I will not look on them with pity or spare them. Although they shout in my ears, I will not listen to them."   Isa 1:15; Jer 11:11; Mic 3:4

Idolaters Killed

9 Then I heard him call out in a loud voice, "Bring the guards of the city here, each with a weapon in his hand." ²And I saw six men coming from the direction of the upper gate, which faces north, each with a deadly weapon in his hand. With them was a man clothed in linen who had a writing kit at his side. They came in and stood beside the bronze altar.

³Now the glory of the God of Israel went up from above the cherubim, where it had been, and moved to the threshold of the temple. Then the LORD called to the man clothed in linen who had the writing kit at his side ⁴and said to him, "Go throughout the city of Jerusalem and put a mark on the foreheads of those who grieve and lament over all the detestable things that are done in it."   Ex 12:7

⁵As I listened, he said to the others, "Follow him through the city and kill, without showing pity or compassion. ⁶Slaughter old men, young men and maidens, women and children, but do not touch anyone who has the mark. Begin at my sanctuary." So they began with the elders who were in front of the temple.   2Ch 36:17; 1Pe 4:17

⁷Then he said to them, "Defile

the temple and fill the courts with the slain. Go!" So they went out and began killing throughout the city. **8**While they were killing and I was left alone, I fell facedown, crying out, "Ah, Sovereign LORD! Are you going to destroy the entire remnant of Israel in this outpouring of your wrath on Jerusalem?"

9He answered me, "The sin of the house of Israel and Judah is exceedingly great; the land is full of bloodshed and the city is full of injustice. They say, 'The LORD has forsaken the land; the LORD does not see.' **10**So I will not look on them with pity or spare them, but I will bring down on their own heads what they have done."

11Then the man in linen with the writing kit at his side brought back word, saying, "I have done as you commanded."

The Glory Departs From the Temple

10 I looked, and I saw the likeness of a throne of sapphire*a* above the expanse that was over the heads of the cherubim. **2**The LORD said to the man clothed in linen, "Go in among the wheels beneath the cherubim. Fill your hands with burning coals from among the cherubim and scatter them over the city." And as I watched, he went in.   Eze 1:22; Rev 8:5

3Now the cherubim were standing on the south side of the temple

when the man went in, and a cloud filled the inner court. **4**Then the glory of the LORD rose from above the cherubim and moved to the threshold of the temple. The cloud filled the temple, and the court was full of the radiance of the glory of the LORD. **5**The sound of the wings of the cherubim could be heard as far away as the outer court, like the voice of God Almighty*b* when he speaks.

6When the LORD commanded the man in linen, "Take fire from among the wheels, from among the cherubim," the man went in and stood beside a wheel. **7**Then one of the cherubim reached out his hand to the fire that was among them. He took up some of it and put it into the hands of the man in linen, who took it and went out. **8**(Under the wings of the cherubim could be seen what looked like the hands of a man.)   Eze 1:8

9I looked, and I saw beside the cherubim four wheels, one beside each of the cherubim; the wheels sparkled like chrysolite. **10**As for their appearance, the four of them looked alike; each was like a wheel intersecting a wheel. **11**As they moved, they would go in any one of the four directions the cherubim faced; the wheels did not turn about*c* as the cherubim went. The cherubim went in whatever direction the head faced, without turning as they went. **12**Their entire

---

*a*1 Or *lapis lazuli*   *b*5 Hebrew *El-Shaddai*   *c*11 Or *aside*

bodies, including their backs, their hands and their wings, were completely full of eyes, as were their four wheels. ¹³I heard the wheels being called "the whirling wheels." ¹⁴Each of the cherubim had four faces: One face was that of a cherub, the second the face of a man, the third the face of a lion, and the fourth the face of an eagle.

¹⁵Then the cherubim rose upward. These were the living creatures I had seen by the Kebar River. ¹⁶When the cherubim moved, the wheels beside them moved; and when the cherubim spread their wings to rise from the ground, the wheels did not leave their side. ¹⁷When the cherubim stood still, they also stood still; and when the cherubim rose, they rose with them, because the spirit of the living creatures was in them.

¹⁸Then the glory of the Lord departed from over the threshold of the temple and stopped above the cherubim. ¹⁹While I watched, the cherubim spread their wings and rose from the ground, and as they went, the wheels went with them. They stopped at the entrance to the east gate of the Lord's house, and the glory of the God of Israel was above them.   Ps 18:10; Eze 11:1,22

²⁰These were the living creatures I had seen beneath the God of Israel by the Kebar River, and I realized that they were cherubim. ²¹Each had four faces and four wings, and under their wings was what looked like the hands of a man. ²²Their faces had the same appearance as those I had seen by the Kebar River. Each one went straight ahead.   Eze 1:6

Judgment on Israel's Leaders

11 Then the Spirit lifted me up and brought me to the gate of the house of the Lord that faces east. There at the entrance to the gate were twenty-five men, and I saw among them Jaazaniah son of Azzur and Pelatiah son of Benaiah, leaders of the people. ²The Lord said to me, "Son of man, these are the men who are plotting evil and giving wicked advice in this city. ³They say, 'Will it not soon be time to build houses?[a] This city is a cooking pot, and we are the meat.' ⁴Therefore prophesy against them; prophesy, son of man."   Eze 3:4,17; 8:16

⁵Then the Spirit of the Lord came upon me, and he told me to say: "This is what the Lord says: That is what you are saying, O house of Israel, but I know what is going through your mind. ⁶You have killed many people in this city and filled its streets with the dead.   Jer 17:10; Eze 7:23

⁷"Therefore this is what the Sovereign Lord says: The bodies you have thrown there are the meat and this city is the pot, but I will drive you out of it. ⁸You fear the

---

a 3 Or *This is not the time to build houses.*

sword, and the sword is what I will bring against you, declares the Sovereign LORD. ⁹I will drive you out of the city and hand you over to foreigners and inflict punishment on you. ¹⁰You will fall by the sword, and I will execute judgment on you at the borders of Israel. Then you will know that I am the LORD. ¹¹This city will not be a pot for you, nor will you be the meat in it; I will execute judgment on you at the borders of Israel. ¹²And you will know that I am the LORD, for you have not followed my decrees or kept my laws but have conformed to the standards of the nations around you."

¹³Now as I was prophesying, Pelatiah son of Benaiah died. Then I fell facedown and cried out in a loud voice, "Ah, Sovereign LORD! Will you completely destroy the remnant of Israel?"   Eze 9:8; Am 7:2

¹⁴The word of the LORD came to me: ¹⁵"Son of man, your brothers —your brothers who are your blood relatives*a* and the whole house of Israel—are those of whom the people of Jerusalem have said, 'They are*b* far away from the LORD; this land was given to us as our possession.'   Eze 33:24

Promised Return of Israel

¹⁶"Therefore say: 'This is what the Sovereign LORD says: Although I sent them far away among the nations and scattered them among the countries, yet for a little while I have been a sanctuary for them in the countries where they have gone.'   Ps 90:1; Isa 8:14

¹⁷"Therefore say: 'This is what the Sovereign LORD says: I will gather you from the nations and bring you back from the countries where you have been scattered, and I will give you back the land of Israel again.'   Jer 24:5-6; Eze 28:25

¹⁸"They will return to it and remove all its vile images and detestable idols. ¹⁹I will give them an undivided heart and put a new spirit in them; I will remove from them their heart of stone and give them a heart of flesh. ²⁰Then they will follow my decrees and be careful to keep my laws. They will be my people, and I will be their God. ²¹But as for those whose hearts are devoted to their vile images and detestable idols, I will bring down on their own heads what they have done, declares the Sovereign LORD."   Jer 32:39; Eze 18:31; 36:26

²²Then the cherubim, with the wheels beside them, spread their wings, and the glory of the God of Israel was above them. ²³The glory of the LORD went up from within the city and stopped above the mountain east of it. ²⁴The Spirit lifted me up and brought me to the exiles in Babylonia*c* in the vision given by the Spirit of God.

a 15 Or are in exile with you (see Septuagint and Syriac) Jerusalem have said, 'Stay   *c 24 Or Chaldea*   *b 15 Or those to whom the people of*

Then the vision I had seen went up from me, ²⁵and I told the exiles everything the Lord had shown me.   Eze 3:4,11

The Exile Symbolized

12 The word of the Lord came to me: ²"Son of man, you are living among a rebellious people. They have eyes to see but do not see and ears to hear but do not hear, for they are a rebellious people.

³"Therefore, son of man, pack your belongings for exile and in the daytime, as they watch, set out and go from where you are to another place. Perhaps they will understand, though they are a rebellious house. ⁴During the daytime, while they watch, bring out your belongings packed for exile. Then in the evening, while they are watching, go out like those who go into exile. ⁵While they watch, dig through the wall and take your belongings out through it. ⁶Put them on your shoulder as they are watching and carry them out at dusk. Cover your face so that you cannot see the land, for I have made you a sign to the house of Israel."   Isa 8:18; Eze 4:3; 24:24

⁷So I did as I was commanded. During the day I brought out my things packed for exile. Then in the evening I dug through the wall with my hands. I took my belongings out at dusk, carrying them on my shoulders while they watched.

⁸In the morning the word of the Lord came to me: ⁹"Son of man, did not that rebellious house of Israel ask you, 'What are you doing?'

¹⁰"Say to them, 'This is what the Sovereign Lord says: This oracle concerns the prince in Jerusalem and the whole house of Israel who are there.' ¹¹Say to them, 'I am a sign to you.'   Zec 3:8

"As I have done, so it will be done to them. They will go into exile as captives.   Jer 15:2; 52:15

¹²"The prince among them will put his things on his shoulder at dusk and leave, and a hole will be dug in the wall for him to go through. He will cover his face so that he cannot see the land. ¹³I will spread my net for him, and he will be caught in my snare; I will bring him to Babylonia, the land of the Chaldeans, but he will not see it, and there he will die. ¹⁴I will scatter to the winds all those around him—his staff and all his troops—and I will pursue them with drawn sword.   2Ki 25:5; Eze 5:10,12

¹⁵"They will know that I am the Lord, when I disperse them among the nations and scatter them through the countries. ¹⁶But I will spare a few of them from the sword, famine and plague, so that in the nations where they go they may acknowledge all their detestable practices. Then they will know that I am the Lord."

¹⁷The word of the Lord came to me: ¹⁸"Son of man, tremble as you eat your food, and shudder in fear as you drink your water. ¹⁹Say to

the people of the land: 'This is what the Sovereign LORD says about those living in Jerusalem and in the land of Israel: They will eat their food in anxiety and drink their water in despair, for their land will be stripped of everything in it because of the violence of all who live there. **20**The inhabited towns will be laid waste and the land will be desolate. Then you will know that I am the LORD.' "

21The word of the LORD came to me: **22**"Son of man, what is this proverb you have in the land of Israel: 'The days go by and every vision comes to nothing'? **23**Say to them, 'This is what the Sovereign LORD says: I am going to put an end to this proverb, and they will no longer quote it in Israel.' Say to them, 'The days are near when every vision will be fulfilled. **24**For there will be no more false visions or flattering divinations among the people of Israel. **25**But I the LORD will speak what I will, and it shall be fulfilled without delay. For in your days, you rebellious house, I will fulfill whatever I say, declares the Sovereign LORD.' "   Eze 13:23

26The word of the LORD came to me: **27**"Son of man, the house of Israel is saying, 'The vision he sees is for many years from now, and he prophesies about the distant future.'   Da 10:14

28"Therefore say to them, 'This is what the Sovereign LORD says:

None of my words will be delayed any longer; whatever I say will be fulfilled, declares the Sovereign LORD.' "

False Prophets Condemned

13 The word of the LORD came to me: **2**"Son of man, prophesy against the prophets of Israel who are now prophesying. Say to those who prophesy out of their own imagination: 'Hear the word of the LORD! **3**This is what the Sovereign LORD says: Woe to the foolish*a* prophets who follow their own spirit and have seen nothing! **4**Your prophets, O Israel, are like jackals among ruins. **5**You have not gone up to the breaks in the wall to repair it for the house of Israel so that it will stand firm in the battle on the day of the LORD. **6**Their visions are false and their divinations a lie. They say, "The LORD declares," when the LORD has not sent them; yet they expect their words to be fulfilled. **7**Have you not seen false visions and uttered lying divinations when you say, "The LORD declares," though I have not spoken?   Eze 22:28,30

8" 'Therefore this is what the Sovereign LORD says: Because of your false words and lying visions, I am against you, declares the Sovereign LORD. **9**My hand will be against the prophets who see false visions and utter lying divinations. They will not belong to the council

---

a 3 Or *wicked*

of my people or be listed in the records of the house of Israel, nor will they enter the land of Israel. Then you will know that I am the Sovereign LORD.   Jer 17:13; Eze 20:38

¹⁰" 'Because they lead my people astray, saying, "Peace," when there is no peace, and because, when a flimsy wall is built, they cover it with whitewash, ¹¹therefore tell those who cover it with whitewash that it is going to fall. Rain will come in torrents, and I will send hailstones hurtling down, and violent winds will burst forth. ¹²When the wall collapses, will people not ask you, "Where is the whitewash you covered it with?"   Eze 22:28; 38:22

¹³" 'Therefore this is what the Sovereign LORD says: In my wrath I will unleash a violent wind, and in my anger hailstones and torrents of rain will fall with destructive fury. ¹⁴I will tear down the wall you have covered with whitewash and will level it to the ground so that its foundation will be laid bare. When it[a] falls, you will be destroyed in it; and you will know that I am the LORD. ¹⁵So I will spend my wrath against the wall and against those who covered it with whitewash. I will say to you, "The wall is gone and so are those who whitewashed it, ¹⁶those prophets of Israel who prophesied to Jerusalem and saw visions of peace for her when there was no

peace, declares the Sovereign LORD." '   Isa 57:21; Jer 6:14

¹⁷"Now, son of man, set your face against the daughters of your people who prophesy out of their own imagination. Prophesy against them ¹⁸and say, 'This is what the Sovereign LORD says: Woe to the women who sew magic charms on all their wrists and make veils of various lengths for their heads in order to ensnare people. Will you ensnare the lives of my people but preserve your own? ¹⁹You have profaned me among my people for a few handfuls of barley and scraps of bread. By lying to my people, who listen to lies, you have killed those who should not have died and have spared those who should not live.

²⁰" 'Therefore this is what the Sovereign LORD says: I am against your magic charms with which you ensnare people like birds and I will tear them from your arms; I will set free the people that you ensnare like birds. ²¹I will tear off your veils and save my people from your hands, and they will no longer fall prey to your power. Then you will know that I am the LORD. ²²Because you disheartened the righteous with your lies, when I had brought them no grief, and because you encouraged the wicked not to turn from their evil ways and so save their lives, ²³therefore you will no longer see false visions

a 14 Or the city

or practice divination. I will save my people from your hands. And then you will know that I am the Lord.' " Eze 12:24; Mic 3:6

Idolaters Condemned

14 Some of the elders of Israel came to me and sat down in front of me. ²Then the word of the Lord came to me: ³"Son of man, these men have set up idols in their hearts and put wicked stumbling blocks before their faces. Should I let them inquire of me at all? ⁴Therefore speak to them and tell them, 'This is what the Sovereign Lord says: When any Israelite sets up idols in his heart and puts a wicked stumbling block before his face and then goes to a prophet, I the Lord will answer him myself in keeping with his great idolatry. ⁵I will do this to recapture the hearts of the people of Israel, who have all deserted me for their idols.' Eze 7:19; Zec 11:8

⁶"Therefore say to the house of Israel, 'This is what the Sovereign Lord says: Repent! Turn from your idols and renounce all your detestable practices! Isa 2:20; 30:22

⁷" 'When any Israelite or any alien living in Israel separates himself from me and sets up idols in his heart and puts a wicked stumbling block before his face and then goes to a prophet to inquire of me, I the Lord will answer him myself. ⁸I will set my face against that man and make him an example and a byword. I will cut him off from my people. Then you will know that I am the Lord. Eze 5:15

⁹" 'And if the prophet is enticed to utter a prophecy, I the Lord have enticed that prophet, and I will stretch out my hand against him and destroy him from among my people Israel. ¹⁰They will bear their guilt—the prophet will be as guilty as the one who consults him. ¹¹Then the people of Israel will no longer stray from me, nor will they defile themselves anymore with all their sins. They will be my people, and I will be their God, declares the Sovereign Lord.' " Eze 11:19-20; 48:11

Judgment Inescapable

¹²The word of the Lord came to me: ¹³"Son of man, if a country sins against me by being unfaithful and I stretch out my hand against it to cut off its food supply and send famine upon it and kill its men and their animals, ¹⁴even if these three men—Noah, Daniel[a] and Job—were in it, they could save only themselves by their righteousness, declares the Sovereign Lord. Jer 15:1; Eze 18:20

¹⁵"Or if I send wild beasts through that country and they leave it childless and it becomes

---

[a] 14 Or *Danel*; the Hebrew spelling may suggest a person other than the prophet Daniel; also in verse 20.

desolate so that no one can pass through it because of the beasts, ¹⁶as surely as I live, declares the Sovereign Lord, even if these three men were in it, they could not save their own sons or daughters. They alone would be saved, but the land would be desolate.   Eze 5:17; 18:20

¹⁷"Or if I bring a sword against that country and say, 'Let the sword pass throughout the land,' and I kill its men and their animals, ¹⁸as surely as I live, declares the Sovereign Lord, even if these three men were in it, they could not save their own sons or daughters. They alone would be saved.

¹⁹"Or if I send a plague into that land and pour out my wrath upon it through bloodshed, killing its men and their animals, ²⁰as surely as I live, declares the Sovereign Lord, even if Noah, Daniel and Job were in it, they could save neither son nor daughter. They would save only themselves by their righteousness.   ver 14; Eze 38:22

²¹"For this is what the Sovereign Lord says: How much worse will it be when I send against Jerusalem my four dreadful judgments—sword and famine and wild beasts and plague—to kill its men and their animals! ²²Yet there will be some survivors—sons and daughters who will be brought out of it. They will come to you, and when you see their conduct and their actions, you will be consoled regarding the disaster I have brought

upon Jerusalem—every disaster I have brought upon it. ²³You will be consoled when you see their conduct and their actions, for you will know that I have done nothing in it without cause, declares the Sovereign Lord."   Jer 22:8-9

Jerusalem, A Useless Vine

15 The word of the Lord came to me: ²"Son of man, how is the wood of a vine better than that of a branch on any of the trees in the forest? ³Is wood ever taken from it to make anything useful? Do they make pegs from it to hang things on? ⁴And after it is thrown on the fire as fuel and the fire burns both ends and chars the middle, is it then useful for anything? ⁵If it was not useful for anything when it was whole, how much less can it be made into something useful when the fire has burned it and it is charred?

⁶"Therefore this is what the Sovereign Lord says: As I have given the wood of the vine among the trees of the forest as fuel for the fire, so will I treat the people living in Jerusalem. ⁷I will set my face against them. Although they have come out of the fire, the fire will yet consume them. And when I set my face against them, you will know that I am the Lord. ⁸I will make the land desolate because they have been unfaithful, declares the Sovereign Lord."

An Allegory of Unfaithful Jerusalem

16 The word of the LORD came to me: ²"Son of man, confront Jerusalem with her detestable practices ³and say, 'This is what the Sovereign LORD says to Jerusalem: Your ancestry and birth were in the land of the Canaanites; your father was an Amorite and your mother a Hittite. ⁴On the day you were born your cord was not cut, nor were you washed with water to make you clean, nor were you rubbed with salt or wrapped in cloths. ⁵No one looked on you with pity or had compassion enough to do any of these things for you. Rather, you were thrown out into the open field, for on the day you were born you were despised.   Eze 20:4; 22:2; Hos 2:3

⁶" 'Then I passed by and saw you kicking about in your blood, and as you lay there in your blood I said to you, "Live!"ᵃ ⁷I made you grow like a plant of the field. You grew up and developed and became the most beautiful of jewels.ᵇ Your breasts were formed and your hair grew, you who were naked and bare.   Ex 19:4; Dt 1:10

⁸" 'Later I passed by, and when I looked at you and saw that you were old enough for love, I spread the corner of my garment over you and covered your nakedness. I gave you my solemn oath and entered into a covenant with you, declares the Sovereign LORD, and you became mine.   Jer 2:2; Hos 2:7,19-20

⁹" 'I bathedᶜ you with water and washed the blood from you and put ointments on you. ¹⁰I clothed you with an embroidered dress and put leather sandals on you. I dressed you in fine linen and covered you with costly garments. ¹¹I adorned you with jewelry: I put bracelets on your arms and a necklace around your neck, ¹²and I put a ring on your nose, earrings on your ears and a beautiful crown on your head. ¹³So you were adorned with gold and silver; your clothes were of fine linen and costly fabric and embroidered cloth. Your food was fine flour, honey and olive oil. You became very beautiful and rose to be a queen. ¹⁴And your fame spread among the nations on account of your beauty, because the splendor I had given you made your beauty perfect, declares the Sovereign LORD.   1Ki 10:24; La 2:15

¹⁵" 'But you trusted in your beauty and used your fame to become a prostitute. You lavished your favors on anyone who passed by and your beauty became his.ᵈ ¹⁶You took some of your garments to make gaudy high places, where you carried on your prostitution. Such things should not happen,

---

ᵃ6 A few Hebrew manuscripts, Septuagint and Syriac; most Hebrew manuscripts *"Live!" And as you lay there in your blood I said to you, "Live!"*   ᵇ7 Or *became mature*   ᶜ9 Or *I had bathed*   ᵈ15 Most Hebrew manuscripts; one Hebrew manuscript (see some Septuagint manuscripts) *by. Such a thing should not happen*

nor should they ever occur. ¹⁷You also took the fine jewelry I gave you, the jewelry made of my gold and silver, and you made for yourself male idols and engaged in prostitution with them. ¹⁸And you took your embroidered clothes to put on them, and you offered my oil and incense before them. ¹⁹Also the food I provided for you—the fine flour, olive oil and honey I gave you to eat—you offered as fragrant incense before them. That is what happened, declares the Sovereign LORD.   Isa 57:8; Jer 2:20

²⁰" 'And you took your sons and daughters whom you bore to me and sacrificed them as food to the idols. Was your prostitution not enough? ²¹You slaughtered my children and sacrificed them*a* to the idols. ²²In all your detestable practices and your prostitution you did not remember the days of your youth, when you were naked and bare, kicking about in your blood.   Ps 106:37-38; Jer 2:2; Hos 11:1

²³" 'Woe! Woe to you, declares the Sovereign LORD. In addition to all your other wickedness, ²⁴you built a mound for yourself and made a lofty shrine in every public square. ²⁵At the head of every street you built your lofty shrines and degraded your beauty, offering your body with increasing promiscuity to anyone who passed by. ²⁶You engaged in prostitution with the Egyptians, your lustful neighbors, and provoked me to anger with your increasing promiscuity. ²⁷So I stretched out my hand against you and reduced your territory; I gave you over to the greed of your enemies, the daughters of the Philistines, who were shocked by your lewd conduct. ²⁸You engaged in prostitution with the Assyrians too, because you were insatiable; and even after that, you still were not satisfied. ²⁹Then you increased your promiscuity to include Babylonia,*b* a land of merchants, but even with this you were not satisfied.   Isa 57:7; Jer 2:20

³⁰" 'How weak-willed you are, declares the Sovereign LORD, when you do all these things, acting like a brazen prostitute! ³¹When you built your mounds at the head of every street and made your lofty shrines in every public square, you were unlike a prostitute, because you scorned payment.   Jer 3:3

³²" 'You adulterous wife! You prefer strangers to your own husband! ³³Every prostitute receives a fee, but you give gifts to all your lovers, bribing them to come to you from everywhere for your illicit favors. ³⁴So in your prostitution you are the opposite of others; no one runs after you for your favors. You are the very opposite, for you give payment and none is given to you.   Hos 8:9-10

³⁵" 'Therefore, you prostitute, hear the word of the LORD! ³⁶This

---

a 21 Or *and made them pass through the fire*   *b 29* Or *Chaldea*

is what the Sovereign Lord says: Because you poured out your wealth[a] and exposed your nakedness in your promiscuity with your lovers, and because of all your detestable idols, and because you gave them your children's blood, [37]therefore I am going to gather all your lovers, with whom you found pleasure, those you loved as well as those you hated. I will gather them against you from all around and will strip you in front of them, and they will see all your nakedness. [38]I will sentence you to the punishment of women who commit adultery and who shed blood; I will bring upon you the blood vengeance of my wrath and jealous anger. [39]Then I will hand you over to your lovers, and they will tear down your mounds and destroy your lofty shrines. They will strip you of your clothes and take your fine jewelry and leave you naked and bare. [40]They will bring a mob against you, who will stone you and hack you to pieces with their swords. [41]They will burn down your houses and inflict punishment on you in the sight of many women. I will put a stop to your prostitution, and you will no longer pay your lovers. [42]Then my wrath against you will subside and my jealous anger will turn away from you; I will be calm and no longer angry.   Eze 5:13; 39:29

[43]" 'Because you did not remember the days of your youth but enraged me with all these things, I will surely bring down on your head what you have done, declares the Sovereign Lord. Did you not add lewdness to all your other detestable practices?   Ps 78:42; Eze 11:21

[44]" 'Everyone who quotes proverbs will quote this proverb about you: "Like mother, like daughter." [45]You are a true daughter of your mother, who despised her husband and her children; and you are a true sister of your sisters, who despised their husbands and their children. Your mother was a Hittite and your father an Amorite. [46]Your older sister was Samaria, who lived to the north of you with her daughters; and your younger sister, who lived to the south of you with her daughters, was Sodom. [47]You not only walked in their ways and copied their detestable practices, but in all your ways you soon became more depraved than they. [48]As surely as I live, declares the Sovereign Lord, your sister Sodom and her daughters never did what you and your daughters have done.   Mt 10:15; 11:23-24

[49]" 'Now this was the sin of your sister Sodom: She and her daughters were arrogant, overfed and unconcerned; they did not help the poor and needy. [50]They were haughty and did detestable things before me. Therefore I did away with them as you have seen. [51]Sa-

maria did not commit half the sins you did. You have done more detestable things than they, and have made your sisters seem righteous by all these things you have done. ⁵²Bear your disgrace, for you have furnished some justification for your sisters. Because your sins were more vile than theirs, they appear more righteous than you. So then, be ashamed and bear your disgrace, for you have made your sisters appear righteous.　Ge 13:13

⁵³" 'However, I will restore the fortunes of Sodom and her daughters and of Samaria and her daughters, and your fortunes along with them, ⁵⁴so that you may bear your disgrace and be ashamed of all you have done in giving them comfort. ⁵⁵And your sisters, Sodom with her daughters and Samaria with her daughters, will return to what they were before; and you and your daughters will return to what you were before. ⁵⁶You would not even mention your sister Sodom in the day of your pride, ⁵⁷before your wickedness was uncovered. Even so, you are now scorned by the daughters of Edom^a and all her neighbors and the daughters of the Philistines—all those around you who despise you. ⁵⁸You will bear the consequences of your lewdness and your detestable practices, declares the Lord.　2Ki 16:6; Eze 23:49

⁵⁹" 'This is what the Sovereign Lord says: I will deal with you as you deserve, because you have despised my oath by breaking the covenant. ⁶⁰Yet I will remember the covenant I made with you in the days of your youth, and I will establish an everlasting covenant with you. ⁶¹Then you will remember your ways and be ashamed when you receive your sisters, both those who are older than you and those who are younger. I will give them to you as daughters, but not on the basis of my covenant with you. ⁶²So I will establish my covenant with you, and you will know that I am the Lord. ⁶³Then, when I make atonement for you for all you have done, you will remember and be ashamed and never again open your mouth because of your humiliation, declares the Sovereign Lord.' "　Jer 32:40; Ro 3:19

Two Eagles and a Vine

17 The word of the Lord came to me: ²"Son of man, set forth an allegory and tell the house of Israel a parable. ³Say to them, 'This is what the Sovereign Lord says: A great eagle with powerful wings, long feathers and full plumage of varied colors came to Lebanon. Taking hold of the top of a cedar, ⁴he broke off its topmost shoot and carried it away to a land of merchants, where he planted it in a city of traders.　Jer 22:23; Eze 20:49

⁵" 'He took some of the seed of your land and put it in fertile soil.

---

^a57 Many Hebrew manuscripts and Syriac; most Hebrew manuscripts, Septuagint and Vulgate *Aram*

He planted it like a willow by abundant water, ⁶and it sprouted and became a low, spreading vine. Its branches turned toward him, but its roots remained under it. So it became a vine and produced branches and put out leafy boughs.   Dt 8:7-9; Isa 44:4

⁷" 'But there was another great eagle with powerful wings and full plumage. The vine now sent out its roots toward him from the plot where it was planted and stretched out its branches to him for water. ⁸It had been planted in good soil by abundant water so that it would produce branches, bear fruit and become a splendid vine.'   Eze 31:4

⁹"Say to them, 'This is what the Sovereign LORD says: Will it thrive? Will it not be uprooted and stripped of its fruit so that it withers? All its new growth will wither. It will not take a strong arm or many people to pull it up by the roots. ¹⁰Even if it is transplanted, will it thrive? Will it not wither completely when the east wind strikes it—wither away in the plot where it grew?' "   Hos 13:15

¹¹Then the word of the LORD came to me: ¹²"Say to this rebellious house, 'Do you not know what these things mean?' Say to them: 'The king of Babylon went to Jerusalem and carried off her king and her nobles, bringing them back with him to Babylon. ¹³Then he took a member of the royal family and made a treaty with him, putting him under oath.

He also carried away the leading men of the land, ¹⁴so that the kingdom would be brought low, unable to rise again, surviving only by keeping his treaty. ¹⁵But the king rebelled against him by sending his envoys to Egypt to get horses and a large army. Will he succeed? Will he who does such things escape? Will he break the treaty and yet escape?   2Ch 36:13

¹⁶" 'As surely as I live, declares the Sovereign LORD, he shall die in Babylon, in the land of the king who put him on the throne, whose oath he despised and whose treaty he broke. ¹⁷Pharaoh with his mighty army and great horde will be of no help to him in war, when ramps are built and siege works erected to destroy many lives. ¹⁸He despised the oath by breaking the covenant. Because he had given his hand in pledge and yet did all these things, he shall not escape.

¹⁹" 'Therefore this is what the Sovereign LORD says: As surely as I live, I will bring down on his head my oath that he despised and my covenant that he broke. ²⁰I will spread my net for him, and he will be caught in my snare. I will bring him to Babylon and execute judgment upon him there because he was unfaithful to me. ²¹All his fleeing troops will fall by the sword, and the survivors will be scattered to the winds. Then you will know that I the LORD have spoken.

²²" 'This is what the Sovereign LORD says: I myself will take a

shoot from the very top of a cedar and plant it; I will break off a tender sprig from its topmost shoots and plant it on a high and lofty mountain. ²³On the mountain heights of Israel I will plant it; it will produce branches and bear fruit and become a splendid cedar. Birds of every kind will nest in it; they will find shelter in the shade of its branches. ²⁴All the trees of the field will know that I the LORD bring down the tall tree and make the low tree grow tall. I dry up the green tree and make the dry tree flourish.   Ps 96:12; Jer 23:5

" 'I the LORD have spoken, and I will do it.' "   Eze 19:12; Am 9:11

The Soul Who Sins Will Die

18 The word of the LORD came to me: ²"What do you people mean by quoting this proverb about the land of Israel:

" 'The fathers eat sour grapes,
   and the children's teeth are
      set on edge'?   Isa 3:15

³"As surely as I live, declares the Sovereign LORD, you will no longer quote this proverb in Israel. ⁴For every living soul belongs to me, the father as well as the son—both alike belong to me. The soul who sins is the one who will die.

⁵"Suppose there is a righteous man

who does what is just and
   right.
⁶He does not eat at the
   mountain shrines   Eze 22:9
or look to the idols of the
   house of Israel.   Dt 4:19
He does not defile his
   neighbor's wife
or lie with a woman during
   her period.   Lev 12:2
⁷He does not oppress anyone,
   but returns what he took in
      pledge for a loan.   Dt 24:12
He does not commit robbery
   but gives his food to the
      hungry   Job 22:7
and provides clothing for the
   naked.   Dt 15:11; Mt 25:36
⁸He does not lend at usury
   or take excessive interest.ᵃ
He withholds his hand from
   doing wrong
and judges fairly between
   man and man.   Zec 8:16
⁹He follows my decrees   Lev 19:37
   and faithfully keeps my laws.
That man is righteous;   Hab 2:4
   he will surely live,   Lev 18:5
      declares the Sovereign
         LORD.

¹⁰"Suppose he has a violent son, who sheds blood or does any of these other thingsᵇ ¹¹(though the father has done none of them):

"He eats at the mountain
   shrines.
He defiles his neighbor's
   wife.

ᵃ8 Or take interest; similarly in verses 13 and 17   ᵇ10 Or things to a brother

¹²He oppresses the poor and
  needy.   Am 4:1
He commits robbery.
He does not return what he
  took in pledge.
He looks to the idols.
He does detestable things.
¹³He lends at usury and takes
  excessive interest.

Will such a man live? He will not!
Because he has done all these detestable things, he will surely be
put to death and his blood will be
on his own head.   Eze 33:4-5
¹⁴"But suppose this son has a
son who sees all the sins his father
commits, and though he sees
them, he does not do such things:

¹⁵"He does not eat at the
  mountain shrines
or look to the idols of the
  house of Israel.
He does not defile his
  neighbor's wife.
¹⁶He does not oppress anyone
  or require a pledge for a
  loan.
He does not commit robbery
  but gives his food to the
  hungry
  and provides clothing for the
  naked.   Ps 41:1; Isa 58:10
¹⁷He withholds his hand from
  sin[a]
and takes no usury or
  excessive interest.
He keeps my laws and follows
  my decrees.

He will not die for his father's sin;
he will surely live. ¹⁸But his father
will die for his own sin, because he
practiced extortion, robbed his
brother and did what was wrong
among his people.

¹⁹"Yet you ask, 'Why does the
son not share the guilt of his father?' Since the son has done what
is just and right and has been careful to keep all my decrees, he will
surely live. ²⁰The soul who sins is
the one who will die. The son will
not share the guilt of the father,
nor will the father share the guilt
of the son. The righteousness of
the righteous man will be credited
to him, and the wickedness of the
wicked will be charged against
him.   Dt 24:16; Isa 3:11; Ro 2:9
²¹"But if a wicked man turns
away from all the sins he has committed and keeps all my decrees
and does what is just and right, he
will surely live; he will not die.
²²None of the offenses he has committed will be remembered against
him. Because of the righteous
things he has done, he will live.
²³Do I take any pleasure in the
death of the wicked? declares the
Sovereign Lord. Rather, am I not
pleased when they turn from their
ways and live?   Eze 33:11; 1Ti 2:4

²⁴"But if a righteous man turns
from his righteousness and commits sin and does the same detestable things the wicked man does,
will he live? None of the righteous

---

[a] 17 Septuagint (see also verse 8); Hebrew *from the poor*

things he has done will be remembered. Because of the unfaithfulness he is guilty of and because of the sins he has committed, he will die. ^{Eze 3:20; 20:27; 2Pe 2:20-22}

²⁵"Yet you say, 'The way of the Lord is not just.' Hear, O house of Israel: Is my way unjust? Is it not your ways that are unjust? ²⁶If a righteous man turns from his righteousness and commits sin, he will die for it; because of the sin he has committed he will die. ²⁷But if a wicked man turns away from the wickedness he has committed and does what is just and right, he will save his life. ²⁸Because he considers all the offenses he has committed and turns away from them, he will surely live; he will not die. ²⁹Yet the house of Israel says, 'The way of the Lord is not just.' Are my ways unjust, O house of Israel? Is it not your ways that are unjust?

³⁰"Therefore, O house of Israel, I will judge you, each one according to his ways, declares the Sovereign LORD. Repent! Turn away from all your offenses; then sin will not be your downfall. ³¹Rid yourselves of all the offenses you have committed, and get a new heart and a new spirit. Why will you die, O house of Israel? ³²For I take no pleasure in the death of anyone, declares the Sovereign LORD. Repent and live! ^{Eze 7:3; 11:19}

A Lament for Israel's Princes

19 "Take up a lament concerning the princes of Israel ²and say: ^{2Ki 24:6; Eze 26:17}

" 'What a lioness was your
    mother
    among the lions!
She lay down among the
    young lions
    and reared her cubs.
³She brought up one of her
    cubs,
    and he became a strong lion.
He learned to tear the prey
    and he devoured men.
⁴The nations heard about him,
    and he was trapped in their
    pit.
They led him with hooks
    to the land of Egypt.

⁵" 'When she saw her hope
    unfulfilled,
    her expectation gone,
she took another of her cubs
    and made him a strong lion.
⁶He prowled among the lions,
    for he was now a strong
    lion.
He learned to tear the prey
    and he devoured men. ^{2Ki 24:9}
⁷He broke down^a their
    strongholds
    and devastated their towns.
The land and all who were in
    it
    were terrified by his roaring.
⁸Then the nations came against
    him, ^{2Ki 24:2}

^a 7 Targum (see Septuagint); Hebrew *He knew*

those from regions round
    about.
They spread their net for him,
    and he was trapped in their
    pit.   2Ki 24:11
⁹With hooks they pulled him
    into a cage
    and brought him to the king
    of Babylon.   2Ch 36:6
They put him in prison,
    so his roar was heard no
    longer
    on the mountains of Israel.

¹⁰" 'Your mother was like a vine
    in your vineyard*a*
    planted by the water;
it was fruitful and full of
    branches
    because of abundant water.
¹¹Its branches were strong,
    fit for a ruler's scepter.
It towered high
    above the thick foliage,
conspicuous for its height
    and for its many branches.
¹²But it was uprooted in fury
    and thrown to the ground.
The east wind made it shrivel,
    it was stripped of its fruit;
its strong branches withered
    and fire consumed them.
¹³Now it is planted in the desert,
    in a dry and thirsty land.
¹⁴Fire spread from one of its
    main*b* branches
    and consumed its fruit.
No strong branch is left on it
    fit for a ruler's scepter.'

This is a lament and is to be used
as a lament."

Rebellious Israel

20 In the seventh year, in the fifth month on the tenth day, some of the elders of Israel came to inquire of the LORD, and they sat down in front of me.

²Then the word of the LORD came to me: ³"Son of man, speak to the elders of Israel and say to them, 'This is what the Sovereign LORD says: Have you come to inquire of me? As surely as I live, I will not let you inquire of me, declares the Sovereign LORD.'

⁴"Will you judge them? Will you judge them, son of man? Then confront them with the detestable practices of their fathers ⁵and say to them: 'This is what the Sovereign LORD says: On the day I chose Israel, I swore with uplifted hand to the descendants of the house of Jacob and revealed myself to them in Egypt. With uplifted hand I said to them, "I am the LORD your God." ⁶On that day I swore to them that I would bring them out of Egypt into a land I had searched out for them, a land flowing with milk and honey, the most beautiful of all lands. ⁷And I said to them, "Each of you, get rid of the vile images you have set your eyes on, and do not defile yourselves with the idols of Egypt. I am the LORD your God."

⁸" 'But they rebelled against me

---

a 10 Two Hebrew manuscripts; most Hebrew manuscripts *your blood*   *b 14* Or *from under its* and would not listen to me; they did not get rid of the vile images they had set their eyes on, nor did they forsake the idols of Egypt. So I said I would pour out my wrath on them and spend my anger against them in Egypt. ⁹But for the sake of my name I did what would keep it from being profaned in the eyes of the nations they lived among and in whose sight I had revealed myself to the Israelites by bringing them out of Egypt. ¹⁰Therefore I led them out of Egypt and brought them into the desert. ¹¹I gave them my decrees and made known to them my laws, for the man who obeys them will live by them. ¹²Also I gave them my Sabbaths as a sign between us, so they would know that I the LORD made them holy.   Lev 18:5; Dt 4:7-8

¹³" 'Yet the people of Israel rebelled against me in the desert. They did not follow my decrees but rejected my laws—although the man who obeys them will live by them—and they utterly desecrated my Sabbaths. So I said I would pour out my wrath on them and destroy them in the desert. ¹⁴But for the sake of my name I did what would keep it from being profaned in the eyes of the nations in whose sight I had brought them out. ¹⁵Also with uplifted hand I swore to them in the desert that I would not bring them into the land I had given them—a land flowing with milk and honey, most beautiful of all lands— ¹⁶because they

rejected my laws and did not follow my decrees and desecrated my Sabbaths. For their hearts were devoted to their idols. ¹⁷Yet I looked on them with pity and did not destroy them or put an end to them in the desert. ¹⁸I said to their children in the desert, "Do not follow the statutes of your fathers or keep their laws or defile yourselves with their idols. ¹⁹I am the LORD your God; follow my decrees and be careful to keep my laws. ²⁰Keep my Sabbaths holy, that they may be a sign between us. Then you will know that I am the LORD your God."   Dt 5:32-33; Am 5:26

²¹" 'But the children rebelled against me: They did not follow my decrees, they were not careful to keep my laws—although the man who obeys them will live by them—and they desecrated my Sabbaths. So I said I would pour out my wrath on them and spend my anger against them in the desert. ²²But I withheld my hand, and for the sake of my name I did what would keep it from being profaned in the eyes of the nations in whose sight I had brought them out. ²³Also with uplifted hand I swore to them in the desert that I would disperse them among the nations and scatter them through the countries, ²⁴because they had not obeyed my laws but had rejected my decrees and desecrated my Sabbaths, and their eyes lusted after their fathers' idols. ²⁵I also gave them over to statutes that were not

good and laws they could not live by; ²⁶I let them become defiled through their gifts—the sacrifice of every firstborn*ᵃ*—that I might fill them with horror so they would know that I am the Lord.'

²⁷"Therefore, son of man, speak to the people of Israel and say to them, 'This is what the Sovereign Lord says: In this also your fathers blasphemed me by forsaking me: ²⁸When I brought them into the land I had sworn to give them and they saw any high hill or any leafy tree, there they offered their sacrifices, made offerings that provoked me to anger, presented their fragrant incense and poured out their drink offerings. ²⁹Then I said to them: What is this high place you go to?' " (It is called Bamah*ᵇ* to this day.)   Eze 6:13; Ro 2:24

Judgment and Restoration

³⁰"Therefore say to the house of Israel: 'This is what the Sovereign Lord says: Will you defile yourselves the way your fathers did and lust after their vile images? ³¹When you offer your gifts—the sacrifice of your sons in*ᶜ* the fire—you continue to defile yourselves with all your idols to this day. Am I to let you inquire of me, O house of Israel? As surely as I live, declares the Sovereign Lord, I will not let you inquire of me.

³²" 'You say, "We want to be like the nations, like the peoples of the world, who serve wood and stone." But what you have in mind will never happen. ³³As surely as I live, declares the Sovereign Lord, I will rule over you with a mighty hand and an outstretched arm and with outpoured wrath. ³⁴I will bring you from the nations and gather you from the countries where you have been scattered—with a mighty hand and an outstretched arm and with outpoured wrath. ³⁵I will bring you into the desert of the nations and there, face to face, I will execute judgment upon you. ³⁶As I judged your fathers in the desert of the land of Egypt, so I will judge you, declares the Sovereign Lord. ³⁷I will take note of you as you pass under my rod, and I will bring you into the bond of the covenant. ³⁸I will purge you of those who revolt and rebel against me. Although I will bring them out of the land where they are living, yet they will not enter the land of Israel. Then you will know that I am the Lord.

³⁹" 'As for you, O house of Israel, this is what the Sovereign Lord says: Go and serve your idols, every one of you! But afterward you will surely listen to me and no longer profane my holy name with your gifts and idols. ⁴⁰For on my holy mountain, the high mountain of Israel, declares the Sovereign

---

ᵃ26 Or —*making every firstborn pass through the fire,*   *ᵇ29* Bamah *means* high place.   *ᶜ31* Or —*making your sons pass through*

LORD, there in the land the entire house of Israel will serve me, and there I will accept them. There I will require your offerings and your choice gifts,*a* along with all your holy sacrifices. **41**I will accept you as fragrant incense when I bring you out from the nations and gather you from the countries where you have been scattered, and I will show myself holy among you in the sight of the nations. **42**Then you will know that I am the LORD, when I bring you into the land of Israel, the land I had sworn with uplifted hand to give to your fathers. **43**There you will remember your conduct and all the actions by which you have defiled yourselves, and you will loathe yourselves for all the evil you have done. **44**You will know that I am the LORD, when I deal with you for my name's sake and not according to your evil ways and your corrupt practices, O house of Israel, declares the Sovereign LORD.' "

Prophecy Against the South

45The word of the LORD came to me: **46**"Son of man, set your face toward the south; preach against the south and prophesy against the forest of the southland. **47**Say to the southern forest: 'Hear the word of the LORD. This is what the Sovereign LORD says: I am about to set fire to you, and it will consume all your trees, both green and dry.

The blazing flame will not be quenched, and every face from south to north will be scorched by it. **48**Everyone will see that I the LORD have kindled it; it will not be quenched.' "   Jer 7:20; 21:14

49Then I said, "Ah, Sovereign LORD! They are saying of me, 'Isn't he just telling parables?' "   Mt 13:13

Babylon, God's Sword of Judgment

21 The word of the LORD came to me: **2**"Son of man, set your face against Jerusalem and preach against the sanctuary. Prophesy against the land of Israel **3**and say to her: 'This is what the LORD says: I am against you. I will draw my sword from its scabbard and cut off from you both the righteous and the wicked. **4**Because I am going to cut off the righteous and the wicked, my sword will be unsheathed against everyone from south to north. **5**Then all people will know that I the LORD have drawn my sword from its scabbard; it will not return again.'

6"Therefore groan, son of man! Groan before them with broken heart and bitter grief. **7**And when they ask you, 'Why are you groaning?' you shall say, 'Because of the news that is coming. Every heart will melt and every hand go limp; every spirit will become faint and every knee become as weak as water.' It is coming! It will surely take

---

a 40 Or and the gifts of your firstfruits

place, declares the Sovereign
LORD."   <small>Isa 22:4; Eze 7:17</small>

⁸The word of the LORD came to
me: ⁹"Son of man, prophesy and
say, 'This is what the Lord says:

" 'A sword, a sword,
    sharpened and polished—
¹⁰sharpened for the slaughter,
    polished to flash like
        lightning!

" 'Shall we rejoice in the scepter
of my son ˌJudahˌ? The sword despises every such stick.

¹¹" 'The sword is appointed to be
        polished,   <small>Jer 46:4</small>
    to be grasped with the hand;
it is sharpened and polished,
    made ready for the hand of
        the slayer.
¹²Cry out and wail, son of man,
    for it is against my people;
    it is against all the princes of
        Israel.
They are thrown to the sword
    along with my people.
Therefore beat your breast.

¹³" 'Testing will surely come.
And what if the scepter ˌof Judahˌ,
which the sword despises, does
not continue? declares the Sovereign LORD.'

¹⁴"So then, son of man,
        prophesy
    and strike your hands
        together.   <small>Nu 24:10</small>

Let the sword strike twice,
    even three times.
It is a sword for slaughter—
    a sword for great slaughter,
    closing in on them from
        every side.   <small>Eze 6:11; 30:24</small>
¹⁵So that hearts may melt
    and the fallen be many,
I have stationed the sword for
        slaughterᵃ   <small>Ps 22:14</small>
    at all their gates.
Oh! It is made to flash like
        lightning,
    it is grasped for slaughter.
¹⁶O sword, slash to the right,
        then to the left,
    wherever your blade is
        turned.
¹⁷I too will strike my hands
        together,   <small>Eze 22:13</small>
    and my wrath will subside.
I the LORD have spoken."

¹⁸The word of the LORD came to
me: ¹⁹"Son of man, mark out two
roads for the sword of the king of
Babylon to take, both starting from
the same country. Make a signpost
where the road branches off to the
city. ²⁰Mark out one road for the
sword to come against Rabbah of
the Ammonites and another
against Judah and fortified Jerusalem. ²¹For the king of Babylon will
stop at the fork in the road, at the
junction of the two roads, to seek
an omen: He will cast lots with arrows, he will consult his idols, he
will examine the liver. ²²Into his
right hand will come the lot for Je-

ᵃ 15 Septuagint; the meaning of the Hebrew for this word is uncertain.

rusalem, where he is to set up battering rams, to give the command to slaughter, to sound the battle cry, to set battering rams against the gates, to build a ramp and to erect siege works. ²³It will seem like a false omen to those who have sworn allegiance to him, but he will remind them of their guilt and take them captive.   Nu 23:23

²⁴"Therefore this is what the Sovereign Lord says: 'Because you people have brought to mind your guilt by your open rebellion, revealing your sins in all that you do—because you have done this, you will be taken captive.

²⁵" 'O profane and wicked prince of Israel, whose day has come, whose time of punishment has reached its climax, ²⁶this is what the Sovereign Lord says: Take off the turban, remove the crown. It will not be as it was: The lowly will be exalted and the exalted will be brought low. ²⁷A ruin! A ruin! I will make it a ruin! It will not be restored until he comes to whom it rightfully belongs; to him I will give it.'   Ps 2:6; Eze 37:24

²⁸"And you, son of man, prophesy and say, 'This is what the Sovereign Lord says about the Ammonites and their insults: Zep 2:8

" 'A sword, a sword,   Jer 12:12
      drawn for the slaughter,
   polished to consume
      and to flash like lightning!
²⁹Despite false visions
         concerning you

and lying divinations about
      you,
it will be laid on the necks
      of the wicked who are to be
      slain,
whose day has come,
   whose time of punishment
      has reached its climax.
³⁰Return the sword to its
      scabbard.   Jer 47:6
   In the place where you were
      created,
in the land of your ancestry,
   I will judge you.
³¹I will pour out my wrath upon
      you
   and breathe out my fiery
      anger against you;
I will hand you over to brutal
      men,
   men skilled in destruction.
³²You will be fuel for the
      fire,
   your blood will be shed in
      your land,
you will be remembered no
      more;   Eze 25:10
   for I the Lord have
      spoken.' "

Jerusalem's Sins

22 The word of the Lord came to me: ²"Son of man, will you judge her? Will you judge this city of bloodshed? Then confront her with all her detestable practices ³and say: 'This is what the Sovereign Lord says: O city that brings on herself doom by shedding blood in her midst and defiles herself by making idols, ⁴you

have become guilty because of the blood you have shed and have become defiled by the idols you have made. You have brought your days to a close, and the end of your years has come. Therefore I will make you an object of scorn to the nations and a laughingstock to all the countries. ⁵Those who are near and those who are far away will mock you, O infamous city, full of turmoil. 2Ki 21:16; Eze 5:14; Na 3:1

⁶" "See how each of the princes of Israel who are in you uses his power to shed blood. ⁷In you they have treated father and mother with contempt; in you they have oppressed the alien and mistreated the fatherless and the widow. ⁸You have despised my holy things and desecrated my Sabbaths. ⁹In you are slanderous men bent on shedding blood; in you are those who eat at the mountain shrines and commit lewd acts. ¹⁰In you are those who dishonor their fathers' bed; in you are those who violate women during their period, when they are ceremonially unclean. ¹¹In you one man commits a detestable offense with his neighbor's wife, another shamefully defiles his daughter-in-law, and another violates his sister, his own father's daughter. ¹²In you men accept bribes to shed blood; you take usury and excessive interest*a* and make unjust gain from your neighbors by extortion. And you have

forgotten me, declares the Sovereign LORD. Lev 18:15; Dt 27:25; Mic 7:3

¹³" 'I will surely strike my hands together at the unjust gain you have made and at the blood you have shed in your midst. ¹⁴Will your courage endure or your hands be strong in the day I deal with you? I the LORD have spoken, and I will do it. ¹⁵I will disperse you among the nations and scatter you through the countries; and I will put an end to your uncleanness. ¹⁶When you have been defiled*b* in the eyes of the nations, you will know that I am the LORD.' " Dt 4:27; Eze 21:7; 23:27

¹⁷Then the word of the LORD came to me: ¹⁸"Son of man, the house of Israel has become dross to me; all of them are the copper, tin, iron and lead left inside a furnace. They are but the dross of silver. ¹⁹Therefore this is what the Sovereign LORD says: 'Because you have all become dross, I will gather you into Jerusalem. ²⁰As men gather silver, copper, iron, lead and tin into a furnace to melt it with a fiery blast, so will I gather you in my anger and my wrath and put you inside the city and melt you. ²¹I will gather you and I will blow on you with my fiery wrath, and you will be melted inside her. ²²As silver is melted in a furnace, so you will be melted inside her, and you will know that I the LORD have poured out my wrath upon you.' "

---

a12 Or usury and interest   *b16* Or When I have allotted you your inheritance

²³Again the word of the LORD came to me: ²⁴"Son of man, say to the land, 'You are a land that has had no rain or showers*a* in the day of wrath.' ²⁵There is a conspiracy of her princes*b* within her like a roaring lion tearing its prey; they devour people, take treasures and precious things and make many widows within her. ²⁶Her priests do violence to my law and profane my holy things; they do not distinguish between the holy and the common; they teach that there is no difference between the unclean and the clean; and they shut their eyes to the keeping of my Sabbaths, so that I am profaned among them. ²⁷Her officials within her are like wolves tearing their prey; they shed blood and kill people to make unjust gain. ²⁸Her prophets whitewash these deeds for them by false visions and lying divinations. They say, 'This is what the Sovereign LORD says' — when the LORD has not spoken. ²⁹The people of the land practice extortion and commit robbery; they oppress the poor and needy and mistreat the alien, denying them justice.   Ex 23:9; Eze 13:2,6-7

³⁰"I looked for a man among them who would build up the wall and stand before me in the gap on behalf of the land so I would not have to destroy it, but I found none. ³¹So I will pour out my wrath on them and consume them with my fiery anger, bringing down on their own heads all they have done, declares the Sovereign LORD."   Jer 5:1; Eze 13:5

Two Adulterous Sisters

23 The word of the LORD came to me: ²"Son of man, there were two women, daughters of the same mother. ³They became prostitutes in Egypt, engaging in prostitution from their youth. In that land their breasts were fondled and their virgin bosoms caressed. ⁴The older was named Oholah, and her sister was Oholibah. They were mine and gave birth to sons and daughters. Oholah is Samaria, and Oholibah is Jerusalem.   Jer 3:7

⁵"Oholah engaged in prostitution while she was still mine; and she lusted after her lovers, the Assyrians—warriors ⁶clothed in blue, governors and commanders, all of them handsome young men, and mounted horsemen. ⁷She gave herself as a prostitute to all the elite of the Assyrians and defiled herself with all the idols of everyone she lusted after. ⁸She did not give up the prostitution she began in Egypt, when during her youth men slept with her, caressed her virgin bosom and poured out their lust upon her.   2Ki 16:7; Hos 8:9

⁹"Therefore I handed her over to her lovers, the Assyrians, for whom she lusted. ¹⁰They stripped her naked, took away her sons and

---

a 24 Septuagint; Hebrew *has not been cleansed or rained on*   *b 25* Septuagint; Hebrew *prophets*

daughters and killed her with the sword. She became a byword among women, and punishment was inflicted on her.   Eze 16:36

[11]"Her sister Oholibah saw this, yet in her lust and prostitution she was more depraved than her sister. [12]She too lusted after the Assyrians —governors and commanders, warriors in full dress, mounted horsemen, all handsome young men. [13]I saw that she too defiled herself; both of them went the same way.   2Ki 16:7-15; Jer 3:8-11

[14]"But she carried her prostitution still further. She saw men portrayed on a wall, figures of Chaldeans[a] portrayed in red, [15]with belts around their waists and flowing turbans on their heads; all of them looked like Babylonian chariot officers, natives of Chaldea.[b] [16]As soon as she saw them, she lusted after them and sent messengers to them in Chaldea. [17]Then the Babylonians came to her, to the bed of love, and in their lust they defiled her. After she had been defiled by them, she turned away from them in disgust. [18]When she carried on her prostitution openly and exposed her nakedness, I turned away from her in disgust, just as I had turned away from her sister. [19]Yet she became more and more promiscuous as she recalled the days of her youth, when she was a prostitute in Egypt. [20]There she lusted after her lovers, whose genitals were like those of donkeys and whose emission was like that of horses. [21]So you longed for the lewdness of your youth, when in Egypt your bosom was caressed and your young breasts fondled.[c]

[22]"Therefore, Oholibah, this is what the Sovereign LORD says: I will stir up your lovers against you, those you turned away from in disgust, and I will bring them against you from every side— [23]the Babylonians and all the Chaldeans, the men of Pekod and Shoa and Koa, and all the Assyrians with them, handsome young men, all of them governors and commanders, chariot officers and men of high rank, all mounted on horses. [24]They will come against you with weapons,[d] chariots and wagons and with a throng of people; they will take up positions against you on every side with large and small shields and with helmets. I will turn you over to them for punishment, and they will punish you according to their standards. [25]I will direct my jealous anger against you, and they will deal with you in fury. They will cut off your noses and your ears, and those of you who are left will fall by the sword. They will take away your sons and daughters, and those of you who are left will be consumed by fire. [26]They will also strip you of your clothes

---

[a]14 Or Babylonians   [b]15 Or Babylonia; also in verse 16   [c]21 Syriac (see also verse 3); Hebrew caressed because of your young breasts   [d]24 The meaning of the Hebrew for this word is uncertain.

and take your fine jewelry. **27**So I will put a stop to the lewdness and prostitution you began in Egypt. You will not look on these things with longing or remember Egypt anymore.   Eze 16:37,39,41

28"For this is what the Sovereign LORD says: I am about to hand you over to those you hate, to those you turned away from in disgust. **29**They will deal with you in hatred and take away everything you have worked for. They will leave you naked and bare, and the shame of your prostitution will be exposed. Your lewdness and promiscuity **30**have brought this upon you, because you lusted after the nations and defiled yourself with their idols. **31**You have gone the way of your sister; so I will put her cup into your hand.   Jer 34:20; Eze 6:9

32"This is what the Sovereign LORD says:

"You will drink your sister's
   cup,
   a cup large and deep;
it will bring scorn and derision,
   for it holds so much.   Ps 60:3
33You will be filled with
      drunkenness and
      sorrow,
   the cup of ruin and
      desolation,
   the cup of your sister
      Samaria.   Jer 25:15-16
34You will drink it and drain it
   dry;   Ps 75:8; Isa 51:17

you will dash it to pieces
   and tear your breasts.

I have spoken, declares the Sovereign LORD.

35"Therefore this is what the Sovereign LORD says: Since you have forgotten me and thrust me behind your back, you must bear the consequences of your lewdness and prostitution."   1Ki 14:9

36The LORD said to me: "Son of man, will you judge Oholah and Oholibah? Then confront them with their detestable practices, **37**for they have committed adultery and blood is on their hands. They committed adultery with their idols; they even sacrificed their children, whom they bore to me,*a* as food for them. **38**They have also done this to me: At that same time they defiled my sanctuary and desecrated my Sabbaths. **39**On the very day they sacrificed their children to their idols, they entered my sanctuary and desecrated it. That is what they did in my house.   2Ki 21:4; Jer 7:10

40"They even sent messengers for men who came from far away, and when they arrived you bathed yourself for them, painted your eyes and put on your jewelry. **41**You sat on an elegant couch, with a table spread before it on which you had placed the incense and oil that belonged to me.

42"The noise of a carefree crowd

---

a 37 Or even made the children they bore to me pass through the fire.

was around her; Sabeans[a] were brought from the desert along with men from the rabble, and they put bracelets on the arms of the woman and her sister and beautiful crowns on their heads. ⁴³Then I said about the one worn out by adultery, 'Now let them use her as a prostitute, for that is all she is.' ⁴⁴And they slept with her. As men sleep with a prostitute, so they slept with those lewd women, Oholah and Oholibah. ⁴⁵But righteous men will sentence them to the punishment of women who commit adultery and shed blood, because they are adulterous and blood is on their hands.   Eze 16:38

⁴⁶"This is what the Sovereign Lord says: Bring a mob against them and give them over to terror and plunder. ⁴⁷The mob will stone them and cut them down with their swords; they will kill their sons and daughters and burn down their houses.   2Ch 36:19

⁴⁸"So I will put an end to lewdness in the land, that all women may take warning and not imitate you. ⁴⁹You will suffer the penalty for your lewdness and bear the consequences of your sins of idolatry. Then you will know that I am the Sovereign Lord."   Eze 7:4; 2Pe 2:6

The Cooking Pot

24 In the ninth year, in the tenth month on the tenth day, the word of the Lord came to me: ²"Son of man, record this date, this very date, because the king of Babylon has laid siege to Jerusalem this very day. ³Tell this rebellious house a parable and say to them: 'This is what the Sovereign Lord says: Jer 39:1; Eze 17:2

" 'Put on the cooking pot; put
    it on
and pour water into it.   Jer 1:13
⁴Put into it the pieces of meat,
    all the choice pieces—the leg
      and the shoulder.
Fill it with the best of these
    bones;
⁵ take the pick of the flock.
Pile wood beneath it for the
    bones;
    bring it to a boil
    and cook the bones in it.

⁶" 'For this is what the Sovereign Lord says:

" 'Woe to the city of
    bloodshed,   Eze 22:2
to the pot now encrusted,
whose deposit will not go
    away!
Empty it piece by piece
    without casting lots for
      them.   Ob 1:11; Na 3:10

⁷" 'For the blood she shed is in
    her midst:
She poured it on the bare
    rock;
she did not pour it on the
    ground,

---

[a] 42 Or *drunkards*

where the dust would cover
it.   Lev 17:13
⁸To stir up wrath and take
    revenge
  I put her blood on the bare
      rock,
  so that it would not be
      covered.

⁹" 'Therefore this is what the Sovereign LORD says:

  " 'Woe to the city of
      bloodshed!
  I, too, will pile the wood
      high.
¹⁰So heap on the wood
    and kindle the fire.
  Cook the meat well,
    mixing in the spices;
    and let the bones be charred.
¹¹Then set the empty pot on the
      coals
    till it becomes hot and its
        copper glows
  so its impurities may be melted
    and its deposit burned away.
¹²It has frustrated all efforts;
    its heavy deposit has not
        been removed,
    not even by fire.

¹³" 'Now your impurity is lewdness. Because I tried to cleanse you but you would not be cleansed from your impurity, you will not be clean again until my wrath against you has subsided.

¹⁴" 'I the LORD have spoken. The time has come for me to act. I will not hold back; I will not have pity, nor will I relent. You will be judged

according to your conduct and your actions, declares the Sovereign LORD.' "   Eze 18:30; 36:19

Ezekiel's Wife Dies

¹⁵The word of the LORD came to me: ¹⁶"Son of man, with one blow I am about to take away from you the delight of your eyes. Yet do not lament or weep or shed any tears. ¹⁷Groan quietly; do not mourn for the dead. Keep your turban fastened and your sandals on your feet; do not cover the lower part of your face or eat the customary food ˌof mourners˒."   Jer 13:17; 16:7

¹⁸So I spoke to the people in the morning, and in the evening my wife died. The next morning I did as I had been commanded.

¹⁹Then the people asked me, "Won't you tell us what these things have to do with us?"

²⁰So I said to them, "The word of the LORD came to me: ²¹Say to the house of Israel, 'This is what the Sovereign LORD says: I am about to desecrate my sanctuary—the stronghold in which you take pride, the delight of your eyes, the object of your affection. The sons and daughters you left behind will fall by the sword. ²²And you will do as I have done. You will not cover the lower part of your face or eat the customary food ˌof mourners˒. ²³You will keep your turbans on your heads and your sandals on your feet. You will not mourn or weep but will waste away because

of[a] your sins and groan among yourselves. **24**Ezekiel will be a sign to you; you will do just as he has done. When this happens, you will know that I am the Sovereign Lord.'   Eze 4:3; 12:11

25"And you, son of man, on the day I take away their stronghold, their joy and glory, the delight of their eyes, their heart's desire, and their sons and daughters as well— **26**on that day a fugitive will come to tell you the news. **27**At that time your mouth will be opened; you will speak with him and will no longer be silent. So you will be a sign to them, and they will know that I am the Lord."   Jer 11:22

A Prophecy Against Ammon

25 The word of the Lord came to me: **2**"Son of man, set your face against the Ammonites and prophesy against them. **3**Say to them, 'Hear the word of the Sovereign Lord. This is what the Sovereign Lord says: Because you said "Aha!" over my sanctuary when it was desecrated and over the land of Israel when it was laid waste and over the people of Judah when they went into exile, **4**therefore I am going to give you to the people of the East as a possession. They will set up their camps and pitch their tents among you; they will eat your fruit and drink your milk. **5**I will turn Rabbah into a pasture for camels and Ammon into a rest-

ing place for sheep. Then you will know that I am the Lord. **6**For this is what the Sovereign Lord says: Because you have clapped your hands and stamped your feet, rejoicing with all the malice of your heart against the land of Israel, **7**therefore I will stretch out my hand against you and give you as plunder to the nations. I will cut you off from the nations and exterminate you from the countries. I will destroy you, and you will know that I am the Lord.'"

A Prophecy Against Moab

8"This is what the Sovereign Lord says: 'Because Moab and Seir said, "Look, the house of Judah has become like all the other nations," **9**therefore I will expose the flank of Moab, beginning at its frontier towns—Beth Jeshimoth, Baal Meon and Kiriathaim—the glory of that land. **10**I will give Moab along with the Ammonites to the people of the East as a possession, so that the Ammonites will not be remembered among the nations; **11**and I will inflict punishment on Moab. Then they will know that I am the Lord.'"

A Prophecy Against Edom

12"This is what the Sovereign Lord says: 'Because Edom took revenge on the house of Judah and became very guilty by doing so, **13**therefore this is what the Sover-

---

[a] 23 Or *away in*

eign Lord says: I will stretch out my hand against Edom and kill its men and their animals. I will lay it waste, and from Teman to Dedan they will fall by the sword. [14]I will take vengeance on Edom by the hand of my people Israel, and they will deal with Edom in accordance with my anger and my wrath; they will know my vengeance, declares the Sovereign Lord.'"   2Ch 28:17

A Prophecy Against Philistia

[15]"This is what the Sovereign Lord says: 'Because the Philistines acted in vengeance and took revenge with malice in their hearts, and with ancient hostility sought to destroy Judah, [16]therefore this is what the Sovereign Lord says: I am about to stretch out my hand against the Philistines, and I will cut off the Kerethites and destroy those remaining along the coast. [17]I will carry out great vengeance on them and punish them in my wrath. Then they will know that I am the Lord, when I take vengeance on them.'"   2Ch 28:18

A Prophecy Against Tyre

26 In the eleventh year, on the first day of the month, the word of the Lord came to me: [2]"Son of man, because Tyre has said of Jerusalem, 'Aha! The gate to the nations is broken, and its doors have swung open to me;

now that she lies in ruins I will prosper,' [3]therefore this is what the Sovereign Lord says: I am against you, O Tyre, and I will bring many nations against you, like the sea casting up its waves. [4]They will destroy the walls of Tyre and pull down her towers; I will scrape away her rubble and make her a bare rock. [5]Out in the sea she will become a place to spread fishnets, for I have spoken, declares the Sovereign Lord. She will become plunder for the nations, [6]and her settlements on the mainland will be ravaged by the sword. Then they will know that I am the Lord.   Isa 23; Eze 27:32

[7]"For this is what the Sovereign Lord says: From the north I am going to bring against Tyre Nebuchadnezzar[a] king of Babylon, king of kings, with horses and chariots, with horsemen and a great army. [8]He will ravage your settlements on the mainland with the sword; he will set up siege works against you, build a ramp up to your walls and raise his shields against you. [9]He will direct the blows of his battering rams against your walls and demolish your towers with his weapons. [10]His horses will be so many that they will cover you with dust. Your walls will tremble at the noise of the war horses, wagons and chariots when he enters your gates as men enter a city whose

---

[a] 7 Hebrew *Nebuchadrezzar,* of which *Nebuchadnezzar* is a variant; here and often in Ezekiel and Jeremiah

walls have been broken through. ¹¹The hoofs of his horses will trample all your streets; he will kill your people with the sword, and your strong pillars will fall to the ground. ¹²They will plunder your wealth and loot your merchandise; they will break down your walls and demolish your fine houses and throw your stones, timber and rubble into the sea. ¹³I will put an end to your noisy songs, and the music of your harps will be heard no more. ¹⁴I will make you a bare rock, and you will become a place to spread fishnets. You will never be rebuilt, for I the LORD have spoken, declares the Sovereign LORD.

¹⁵"This is what the Sovereign LORD says to Tyre: Will not the coastlands tremble at the sound of your fall, when the wounded groan and the slaughter takes place in you? ¹⁶Then all the princes of the coast will step down from their thrones and lay aside their robes and take off their embroidered garments. Clothed with terror, they will sit on the ground, trembling every moment, appalled at you. ¹⁷Then they will take up a lament concerning you and say to you: Eze 27:32

" 'How you are destroyed,
    O city of renown,
  peopled by men of the sea!
You were a power on the seas,
    you and your citizens;

you put your terror
    on all who lived there.
¹⁸Now the coastlands tremble
    on the day of your fall;
the islands in the sea
    are terrified at your collapse.'

¹⁹"This is what the Sovereign LORD says: When I make you a desolate city, like cities no longer inhabited, and when I bring the ocean depths over you and its vast waters cover you, ²⁰then I will bring you down with those who go down to the pit, to the people of long ago. I will make you dwell in the earth below, as in ancient ruins, with those who go down to the pit, and you will not return or take your place*a* in the land of the living. ²¹I will bring you to a horrible end and you will be no more. You will be sought, but you will never again be found, declares the Sovereign LORD."   Eze 27:36; 28:19; Rev 18:21

A Lament for Tyre

27 The word of the LORD came to me: ²"Son of man, take up a lament concerning Tyre. ³Say to Tyre, situated at the gateway to the sea, merchant of peoples on many coasts, 'This is what the Sovereign LORD says: Eze 19:1; Hos 9:13

" 'You say, O Tyre,
    "I am perfect in beauty."
⁴Your domain was on the high
    seas;

---

*a 20 Septuagint; Hebrew return, and I will give glory

your builders brought your
 beauty to perfection.
⁵They made all your timbers
 of pine trees from Senirᵃ;
they took a cedar from
 Lebanon   Isa 2:13
to make a mast for you.
⁶Of oaks from Bashan   Nu 21:33
 they made your oars;
of cypress woodᵇ from the
 coasts of Cyprusᶜ   Ge 10:4
they made your deck, inlaid
 with ivory.
⁷Fine embroidered linen from
 Egypt was your sail
 and served as your banner;
your awnings were of blue and
 purple   Ex 25:4; Jer 10:9
 from the coasts of Elishah.
⁸Men of Sidon and Arvad were
 your oarsmen;   Ge 10:18
your skilled men, O Tyre,
 were aboard as your
 seamen.   1Ki 9:27
⁹Veteran craftsmen of Gebalᵈ
 were on board   Jos 13:5
 as shipwrights to caulk your
 seams.
All the ships of the sea and
 their sailors
 came alongside to trade for
 your wares.

¹⁰" 'Men of Persia, Lydia and Put
 served as soldiers in your
 army.
They hung their shields and
 helmets on your walls,

bringing you splendor.
¹¹Men of Arvad and Helech
 manned your walls on every
 side;
men of Gammad
 were in your towers.
They hung their shields around
 your walls;
 they brought your beauty to
 perfection.

¹²" 'Tarshish did business with
you because of your great wealth
of goods; they exchanged silver,
iron, tin and lead for your merchandise.   Ge 10:4
¹³" 'Greece, Tubal and Meshech
traded with you; they exchanged
slaves and articles of bronze for
your wares.   Ge 10:2 Rev 18:13
¹⁴" 'Men of Beth Togarmah exchanged work horses, war horses
and mules for your merchandise.
¹⁵" 'The men of Rhodesᵉ traded
with you, and many coastlands
were your customers; they paid
you with ivory tusks and ebony.
¹⁶" 'Aramᶠ did business with
you because of your many products; they exchanged turquoise,
purple fabric, embroidered work,
fine linen, coral and rubies for
your merchandise.   Jdg 10:6; Eze 28:13
¹⁷" 'Judah and Israel traded with
you; they exchanged wheat from
Minnith and confections,ᵍ honey,
oil and balm for your wares.
¹⁸" 'Damascus, because of your

ᵃ5 That is, Hermon   ᵇ6 Targum; the Masoretic Text has a different division of the consonants.
ᶜ6 Hebrew *Kittim*   ᵈ9 That is, Byblos   ᵉ15 Septuagint; Hebrew *Dedan*   ᶠ16 Most Hebrew
manuscripts; some Hebrew manuscripts and Syriac *Edom*   ᵍ17 The meaning of the Hebrew for this
word is uncertain.

many products and great wealth of goods, did business with you in wine from Helbon and wool from Zahar. _{Ge 14:15; Eze 47:16-18}

¹⁹" 'Danites and Greeks from Uzal bought your merchandise; they exchanged wrought iron, cassia and calamus for your wares.

²⁰" 'Dedan traded in saddle blankets with you.

²¹" 'Arabia and all the princes of Kedar were your customers; they did business with you in lambs, rams and goats. _{Ge 25:13; Isa 60:7}

²²" 'The merchants of Sheba and Raamah traded with you; for your merchandise they exchanged the finest of all kinds of spices and precious stones, and gold. _{Ge 10:7,28}

²³" 'Haran, Canneh and Eden and merchants of Sheba, Asshur and Kilmad traded with you. ²⁴In your marketplace they traded with you beautiful garments, blue fabric, embroidered work and multicolored rugs with cords twisted and tightly knotted. _{2Ki 19:12}

²⁵" 'The ships of Tarshish serve as carriers for your wares. You are filled with heavy cargo in the heart of the sea.
²⁶Your oarsmen take you out to the high seas. But the east wind will break you to pieces _{Ps 48:7} in the heart of the sea.
²⁷Your wealth, merchandise and wares, _{Pr 11:4} your mariners, seamen and shipwrights,

your merchants and all your soldiers, and everyone else on board will sink into the heart of the sea _{Eze 28:8} on the day of your shipwreck.
²⁸The shorelands will quake when your seamen cry out.
²⁹All who handle the oars will abandon their ships; the mariners and all the seamen will stand on the shore.
³⁰They will raise their voice and cry bitterly over you; they will sprinkle dust on their heads _{2Sa 1:2} and roll in ashes. _{Jer 6:26}
³¹They will shave their heads because of you and will put on sackcloth. They will weep over you with anguish of soul _{Isa 16:9} and with bitter mourning.
³²As they wail and mourn over you, they will take up a lament concerning you: _{Eze 26:17} "Who was ever silenced like Tyre, surrounded by the sea?"
³³When your merchandise went out on the seas, you satisfied many nations; with your great wealth and your wares _{ver 12; Eze 28:4-5} you enriched the kings of the earth.
³⁴Now you are shattered by the sea

in the depths of the waters;
your wares and all your
    company
have gone down with you.
35All who live in the coastlands
    are appalled at you;   Lev 26:32
their kings shudder with horror
and their faces are distorted
    with fear.   Eze 26:17-18
36The merchants among the
    nations hiss at you;
you have come to a horrible
    end
and will be no more.' "

A Prophecy Against the King of Tyre

28 The word of the LORD came
to me: 2"Son of man, say to
the ruler of Tyre, 'This is what the
Sovereign LORD says: Isa 13:11

" 'In the pride of your heart
    you say, "I am a god;
I sit on the throne of a god
    in the heart of the seas."
But you are a man and not a
    god,
though you think you are as
    wise as a god.   Ps 9:20
3Are you wiser than Daniel*a*?
    Is no secret hidden from
    you?
4By your wisdom and
    understanding
you have gained wealth for
    yourself
and amassed gold and silver
    in your treasuries.   Zec 9:3

5By your great skill in trading
    you have increased your
    wealth,   Eze 27:33
and because of your wealth
    your heart has grown
    proud.

6" 'Therefore this is what the
Sovereign LORD says:

" 'Because you think you are
    wise,
    as wise as a god,
7I am going to bring foreigners
    against you,
    the most ruthless of nations;
they will draw their swords
    against your beauty and
    wisdom   Jer 9:23
and pierce your shining
    splendor.
8They will bring you down to
    the pit,   Eze 32:30
and you will die a violent
    death
in the heart of the seas.
9Will you then say, "I am a
    god,"
    in the presence of those who
    kill you?
You will be but a man, not a
    god,   Isa 31:3
in the hands of those who
    slay you.   Eze 16:49
10You will die the death of the
    uncircumcised   Eze 31:18
    at the hands of foreigners.

I have spoken, declares the Sovereign LORD.' "

---

a 3 Or *Daniel*; the Hebrew spelling may suggest a person other than the prophet Daniel.

¹¹The word of the LORD came to me: ¹²"Son of man, take up a lament concerning the king of Tyre and say to him: 'This is what the Sovereign LORD says: Eze 19:1

" 'You were the model of
        perfection,
    full of wisdom and perfect in
        beauty.   Eze 27:2-4
¹³You were in Eden,   Ge 2:8
    the garden of God;   Eze 31:8-9
every precious stone adorned
        you:
    ruby, topaz and emerald,
    chrysolite, onyx and jasper,
    sapphire,ᵃ turquoise and
        beryl.ᵇ   Eze 27:16
Your settings and mountingsᶜ
        were made of gold;
    on the day you were created
        they were prepared.
¹⁴You were anointed as a
        guardian cherub,
    for so I ordained you.
You were on the holy mount
        of God;
    you walked among the fiery
        stones.
¹⁵You were blameless in your
        ways
    from the day you were
        created
    till wickedness was found in
        you.
¹⁶Through your widespread trade
    you were filled with
        violence,   Hab 2:17
    and you sinned.

So I drove you in disgrace
        from the mount of God,
    and I expelled you,
        O guardian cherub,
    from among the fiery stones.
¹⁷Your heart became proud
    on account of your beauty,
    and you corrupted your
        wisdom
    because of your splendor.
So I threw you to the earth;
    I made a spectacle of you
        before kings.   Eze 19:12
¹⁸By your many sins and
        dishonest trade
    you have desecrated your
        sanctuaries.
So I made a fire come out from
        you,
    and it consumed you,
    and I reduced you to ashes on
        the ground   Mal 4:3
    in the sight of all who were
        watching.
¹⁹All the nations who knew you
    are appalled at you;
    you have come to a horrible
        end
    and will be no more.' "

A Prophecy Against Sidon

²⁰The word of the LORD came to me: ²¹"Son of man, set your face against Sidon; prophesy against her ²²and say: 'This is what the Sovereign LORD says: Jer 25:22

" 'I am against you, O Sidon,

ᵃ13 Or *lapis lazuli*   ᵇ13 The precise identification of some of these precious stones is uncertain.
ᶜ13 The meaning of the Hebrew for this phrase is uncertain.

and I will gain glory within
    you.   Eze 39:13
They will know that I am the
    LORD,
    when I inflict punishment on
        her   Eze 30:19
    and show myself holy within
        her.   Lev 10:3
²³I will send a plague upon her
    and make blood flow in her
        streets.
The slain will fall within her,
    with the sword against her
        on every side.
Then they will know that I am
        the LORD.   Eze 38:22

²⁴" 'No longer will the people of Israel have malicious neighbors who are painful briers and sharp thorns. Then they will know that I am the Sovereign LORD.   Nu 33:55

²⁵" 'This is what the Sovereign LORD says: When I gather the people of Israel from the nations where they have been scattered, I will show myself holy among them in the sight of the nations. Then they will live in their own land, which I gave to my servant Jacob. ²⁶They will live there in safety and will build houses and plant vineyards; they will live in safety when I inflict punishment on all their neighbors who maligned them. Then they will know that I am the LORD their God.' "   Isa 11:12; Jer 23:6

A Prophecy Against Egypt

29 In the tenth year, in the tenth month on the twelfth day, the word of the LORD came to me: ²"Son of man, set your face against Pharaoh king of Egypt and prophesy against him and against all Egypt. ³Speak to him and say: 'This is what the Sovereign LORD says: Isa 19:1-17; Jer 46:2

" 'I am against you, Pharaoh
    king of Egypt,   Jer 44:30
    you great monster lying
        among your streams.
You say, "The Nile is mine;
    I made it for myself."
⁴But I will put hooks in your
    jaws   2Ki 19:28
    and make the fish of your
        streams stick to your
        scales.
I will pull you out from among
    your streams,
    with all the fish sticking to
        your scales.   Eze 38:4
⁵I will leave you in the desert,
    you and all the fish of your
        streams.
You will fall on the open field
    and not be gathered or
        picked up.
I will give you as food
    to the beasts of the earth
        and the birds of the air.

⁶Then all who live in Egypt will know that I am the LORD.

" 'You have been a staff of reed for the house of Israel. ⁷When they grasped you with their hands, you splintered and you tore open their shoulders; when they leaned on you, you broke and their backs were wrenched. [a]   Isa 36:6; Eze 17:15-17

8" 'Therefore this is what the Sovereign Lord says: I will bring a sword against you and kill your men and their animals. 9Egypt will become a desolate wasteland. Then they will know that I am the Lord.   Eze 14:17; 32:11-13

" 'Because you said, "The Nile is mine; I made it," 10therefore I am against you and against your streams, and I will make the land of Egypt a ruin and a desolate waste from Migdol to Aswan, as far as the border of Cush. [b] 11No foot of man or animal will pass through it; no one will live there for forty years. 12I will make the land of Egypt desolate among devastated lands, and her cities will lie desolate forty years among ruined cities. And I will disperse the Egyptians among the nations and scatter them through the countries.

13" 'Yet this is what the Sovereign Lord says: At the end of forty years I will gather the Egyptians from the nations where they were scattered. 14I will bring them back from captivity and return them to Upper Egypt, [c] the land of their ancestry. There they will be a lowly kingdom. 15It will be the lowliest of kingdoms and will never again exalt itself above the other nations. I will make it so weak that it will never again rule over the nations.

16Egypt will no longer be a source of confidence for the people of Israel but will be a reminder of their sin in turning to her for help. Then they will know that I am the Sovereign Lord.' "   Isa 30:2; Hos 8:13

17In the twenty-seventh year, in the first month on the first day, the word of the Lord came to me: 18"Son of man, Nebuchadnezzar king of Babylon drove his army in a hard campaign against Tyre; every head was rubbed bare and every shoulder made raw. Yet he and his army got no reward from the campaign he led against Tyre. 19Therefore this is what the Sovereign Lord says: I am going to give Egypt to Nebuchadnezzar king of Babylon, and he will carry off its wealth. He will loot and plunder the land as pay for his army. 20I have given him Egypt as a reward for his efforts because he and his army did it for me, declares the Sovereign Lord.   Isa 10:6-7; Jer 25:9

21"On that day I will make a horn [d] grow for the house of Israel, and I will open your mouth among them. Then they will know that I am the Lord."   Ps 132:17; Eze 24:27

A Lament for Egypt

30 The word of the Lord came to me: 2"Son of man, prophesy and say: 'This is what the Sovereign Lord says:

---

[a]7 Syriac (see also Septuagint and Vulgate); Hebrew *and you caused their backs to stand*   [b]10 That is, the upper Nile region   [c]14 Hebrew *to Pathros*   [d]21 *Horn* here symbolizes strength.

" 'Wail and say,   Isa 13:6
    "Alas for that day!"
³For the day is near,   Joel 2:1,11
    the day of the LORD is
    near—   Eze 7:12,19
a day of clouds,
    a time of doom for the
    nations.
⁴A sword will come against
    Egypt,   Da 11:43
    and anguish will come upon
    Cush.ᵃ   Eze 29:10
When the slain fall in Egypt,
    her wealth will be carried
    away
    and her foundations torn
    down.   Eze 29:19

⁵Cush and Put, Lydia and all Arabia, Libyaᵇ and the people of the
covenant land will fall by the
sword along with Egypt.   Jer 25:20
    ⁶" 'This is what the LORD says:

" 'The allies of Egypt will fall
    and her proud strength will
    fail.
From Migdol to Aswan   Eze 29:10
    they will fall by the sword
    within her,
              declares the Sovereign
                                 LORD.
⁷" 'They will be desolate
    among desolate lands,
    and their cities will lie
    among ruined cities.   Eze 29:12
⁸Then they will know that I am
    the LORD,
    when I set fire to Egypt

and all her helpers are
    crushed.   Eze 29:9

⁹" 'On that day messengers will
go out from me in ships to frighten
Cush out of her complacency. Anguish will take hold of them on the
day of Egypt's doom, for it is sure
to come.   Isa 18:1-2; Eze 32:9-10

¹⁰" 'This is what the Sovereign
LORD says:

" 'I will put an end to the
        hordes of Egypt
    by the hand of
        Nebuchadnezzar king of
        Babylon.   Eze 29:19
¹¹He and his army—the most
        ruthless of nations—
    will be brought in to destroy
        the land.
They will draw their swords
        against Egypt
    and fill the land with the
        slain.
¹²I will dry up the streams of the
        Nile   Isa 19:6; Eze 29:9
    and sell the land to evil
        men;
by the hand of foreigners
    I will lay waste the land and
        everything in it.   Eze 19:7

I the LORD have spoken.

¹³" 'This is what the Sovereign
LORD says:

" 'I will destroy the idols

ᵃ4 That is, the upper Nile region; also in verses 5 and 9   ᵇ5 Hebrew Cub

and put an end to the
  images in Memphis.[a]
No longer will there be a
  prince in Egypt,   Zec 10:11
and I will spread fear
  throughout the land.
[14]I will lay waste Upper
  Egypt,[b]
  set fire to Zoan   Ps 78:12,43
  and inflict punishment on
  Thebes.[c]   Jer 46:25
[15]I will pour out my wrath on
  Pelusium,[d]
  the stronghold of Egypt,
  and cut off the hordes of
  Thebes.
[16]I will set fire to Egypt;   Jos 7:15
  Pelusium will writhe in
  agony.
  Thebes will be taken by
  storm;
  Memphis will be in constant
  distress.   Isa 19:13
[17]The young men of Heliopolis[e]
  and Bubastis[f]   Ge 41:45
  will fall by the sword,
  and the cities themselves
  will go into captivity.
[18]Dark will be the day at
  Tahpanhes
  when I break the yoke of
  Egypt;   Lev 26:13; Isa 9:4
  there her proud strength will
  come to an end.
She will be covered with
  clouds,
  and her villages will go into
  captivity.

[19]So I will inflict punishment on
  Egypt,   Eze 28:22
  and they will know that I am
  the Lord.' "

[20]In the eleventh year, in the first month on the seventh day, the word of the Lord came to me: [21]"Son of man, I have broken the arm of Pharaoh king of Egypt. It has not been bound up for healing or put in a splint so as to become strong enough to hold a sword. [22]Therefore this is what the Sovereign Lord says: I am against Pharaoh king of Egypt. I will break both his arms, the good arm as well as the broken one, and make the sword fall from his hand. [23]I will disperse the Egyptians among the nations and scatter them through the countries. [24]I will strengthen the arms of the king of Babylon and put my sword in his hand, but I will break the arms of Pharaoh, and he will groan before him like a mortally wounded man. [25]I will strengthen the arms of the king of Babylon, but the arms of Pharaoh will fall limp. Then they will know that I am the Lord, when I put my sword into the hand of the king of Babylon and he brandishes it against Egypt. [26]I will disperse the Egyptians among the nations and scatter them through the countries. Then they will know that I am the Lord."   Zep 2:12; Zec 10:6,12

---

[a]13 Hebrew Noph; also in verse 16   [b]14 Hebrew waste Pathros   [c]14 Hebrew No; also in verses 15 and 16   [d]15 Hebrew Sin; also in verse 16   [e]17 Hebrew Awen (or On)   [f]17 Hebrew Pi Beseth

A Cedar in Lebanon

31 In the eleventh year, in the third month on the first day, the word of the Lord came to me: ²"Son of man, say to Pharaoh king of Egypt and to his hordes:

" 'Who can be compared with
    you in majesty?
³Consider Assyria, once a cedar
    in Lebanon,   Jer 50:18
  with beautiful branches
    overshadowing the
    forest;
  it towered on high,
    its top above the thick
    foliage.   Isa 10:34
⁴The waters nourished it,   Eze 17:7
  deep springs made it grow
    tall;
  their streams flowed
    all around its base
  and sent their channels
    to all the trees of the field.
⁵So it towered higher
    than all the trees of the field;
  its boughs increased
    and its branches grew long,
    spreading because of
    abundant waters.   Eze 17:5
⁶All the birds of the air
    nested in its boughs,
  all the beasts of the field
    gave birth under its
    branches;
  all the great nations
    lived in its shade.   Eze 17:23
⁷It was majestic in beauty,
    with its spreading boughs,
  for its roots went down
    to abundant waters.

⁸The cedars in the garden of
    God   Ps 80:10
    could not rival it,
  nor could the pine trees
    equal its boughs,
  nor could the plane trees
    compare with its branches—
  no tree in the garden of God
    could match its beauty.
⁹I made it beautiful
    with abundant branches,
  the envy of all the trees of
    Eden   Ge 2:8
  in the garden of God.   Ge 13:10

¹⁰" 'Therefore this is what the Sovereign Lord says: Because it towered on high, lifting its top above the thick foliage, and because it was proud of its height, ¹¹I handed it over to the ruler of the nations, for him to deal with according to its wickedness. I cast it aside, ¹²and the most ruthless of foreign nations cut it down and left it. Its boughs fell on the mountains and in all the valleys; its branches lay broken in all the ravines of the land. All the nations of the earth came out from under its shade and left it. ¹³All the birds of the air settled on the fallen tree, and all the beasts of the field were among its branches. ¹⁴Therefore no other trees by the waters are ever to tower proudly on high, lifting their tops above the thick foliage. No other trees so well-watered are ever to reach such a height; they are all destined for death, for the earth below, among mortal men,

with those who go down to the pit.

15" 'This is what the Sovereign LORD says: On the day it was brought down to the grave[a] I covered the deep springs with mourning for it; I held back its streams, and its abundant waters were restrained. Because of it I clothed Lebanon with gloom, and all the trees of the field withered away. 16I made the nations tremble at the sound of its fall when I brought it down to the grave with those who go down to the pit. Then all the trees of Eden, the choicest and best of Lebanon, all the trees that were well-watered, were consoled in the earth below. 17Those who lived in its shade, its allies among the nations, had also gone down to the grave with it, joining those killed by the sword.   Ps 9:17; Isa 14:15

18" 'Which of the trees of Eden can be compared with you in splendor and majesty? Yet you, too, will be brought down with the trees of Eden to the earth below; you will lie among the uncircumcised, with those killed by the sword.   Eze 32:19,21

" 'This is Pharaoh and all his hordes, declares the Sovereign LORD.' "

A Lament for Pharaoh

32 In the twelfth year, in the twelfth month on the first day, the word of the LORD came to me: 2"Son of man, take up a lament

concerning Pharaoh king of Egypt and say to him: Eze 27:2; 31:1

" 'You are like a lion among
   the nations;   Eze 19:3,6
you are like a monster in the
   seas
thrashing about in your
   streams,
churning the water with
   your feet
and muddying the streams.

3" 'This is what the Sovereign LORD says:

" 'With a great throng of
   people
I will cast my net over you,
and they will haul you up in
   my net.   Eze 12:13
4I will throw you on the land
   and hurl you on the open
   field.
I will let all the birds of the air
   settle on you
and all the beasts of the
   earth gorge themselves
   on you.   Isa 18:6; Eze 31:12-13
5I will spread your flesh on the
   mountains
and fill the valleys with your
   remains.   Eze 31:12
6I will drench the land with
   your flowing blood
all the way to the
   mountains,
and the ravines will be filled
   with your flesh.

---

[a] 15 Hebrew *Sheol*; also in verses 16 and 17

⁷When I snuff you out, I will
    cover the heavens
    and darken their stars;
I will cover the sun with a
    cloud,
    and the moon will not give
    its light.   Joel 2:2,31; 3:15
⁸All the shining lights in the
    heavens
    I will darken over you;
    I will bring darkness over
    your land,   Joel 2:10
        declares the Sovereign
        Lord.
⁹I will trouble the hearts of
    many peoples
    when I bring about your
    destruction among the
    nations,
    amongᵃ lands you have not
    known.
¹⁰I will cause many peoples to
    be appalled at you,
    and their kings will shudder
    with horror because of
    you
    when I brandish my sword
    before them.
On the day of your downfall
    each of them will tremble
    every moment for his life.

¹¹" 'For this is what the Sovereign Lord says:

" 'The sword of the king of
    Babylon   Jer 46:26
    will come against you.
¹²I will cause your hordes to
    fall

by the swords of mighty
    men—
    the most ruthless of all
    nations.   Eze 28:7
They will shatter the pride of
    Egypt,
    and all her hordes will be
    overthrown.   Eze 31:11-12
¹³I will destroy all her cattle
    from beside abundant waters
no longer to be stirred by the
    foot of man
    or muddied by the hoofs of
    cattle.   Eze 29:8,11
¹⁴Then I will let her waters settle
    and make her streams flow
    like oil,
        declares the Sovereign
        Lord.
¹⁵When I make Egypt desolate
    and strip the land of
    everything in it,
when I strike down all who
    live there,
    then they will know that I
    am the Lord.'   Ex 7:5; Eze 6:7

¹⁶"This is the lament they will
chant for her. The daughters of the
nations will chant it; for Egypt and
all her hordes they will chant it,
declares the Sovereign Lord."

¹⁷In the twelfth year, on the fifteenth day of the month, the word
of the Lord came to me: ¹⁸"Son of
man, wail for the hordes of Egypt
and consign to the earth below
both her and the daughters of
mighty nations, with those who go

ᵃ9 Hebrew; Septuagint *bring you into captivity among the nations, / to*

down to the pit. ¹⁹Say to them, 'Are you more favored than others? Go down and be laid among the uncircumcised.' ²⁰They will fall among those killed by the sword. The sword is drawn; let her be dragged off with all her hordes. ²¹From within the grave*ᵃ* the mighty leaders will say of Egypt and her allies, 'They have come down and they lie with the uncircumcised, with those killed by the sword.'   Isa 14:9

²²"Assyria is there with her whole army; she is surrounded by the graves of all her slain, all who have fallen by the sword. ²³Their graves are in the depths of the pit and her army lies around her grave. All who had spread terror in the land of the living are slain, fallen by the sword.   Isa 14:15

²⁴"Elam is there, with all her hordes around her grave. All of them are slain, fallen by the sword. All who had spread terror in the land of the living went down uncircumcised to the earth below. They bear their shame with those who go down to the pit. ²⁵A bed is made for her among the slain, with all her hordes around her grave. All of them are uncircumcised, killed by the sword. Because their terror had spread in the land of the living, they bear their shame with those who go down to the pit; they are laid among the slain.   Jer 49:37

²⁶"Meshech and Tubal are there, with all their hordes around their graves. All of them are uncircumcised, killed by the sword because they spread their terror in the land of the living. ²⁷Do they not lie with the other uncircumcised warriors who have fallen, who went down to the grave with their weapons of war, whose swords were placed under their heads? The punishment for their sins rested on their bones, though the terror of these warriors had stalked through the land of the living.   Eze 27:13

²⁸"You too, O Pharaoh, will be broken and will lie among the uncircumcised, with those killed by the sword.

²⁹"Edom is there, her kings and all her princes; despite their power, they are laid with those killed by the sword. They lie with the uncircumcised, with those who go down to the pit.   Isa 34:5-15

³⁰"All the princes of the north and all the Sidonians are there; they went down with the slain in disgrace despite the terror caused by their power. They lie uncircumcised with those killed by the sword and bear their shame with those who go down to the pit.

³¹"Pharaoh—he and all his army—will see them and he will be consoled for all his hordes that were killed by the sword, declares the Sovereign Lᴏʀᴅ. ³²Although I had him spread terror in the land of the living, Pharaoh and all his hordes will be laid among the uncircum-

---

ᵃ 21 Hebrew Sheol; also in verse 27

cised, with those killed by the sword, declares the Sovereign LORD." *Eze 31:16*

Ezekiel a Watchman

33 The word of the LORD came to me: ²"Son of man, speak to your countrymen and say to them: 'When I bring the sword against a land, and the people of the land choose one of their men and make him their watchman, ³and he sees the sword coming against the land and blows the trumpet to warn the people, ⁴then if anyone hears the trumpet but does not take warning and the sword comes and takes his life, his blood will be on his own head. ⁵Since he heard the sound of the trumpet but did not take warning, his blood will be on his own head. If he had taken warning, he would have saved himself. ⁶But if the watchman sees the sword coming and does not blow the trumpet to warn the people and the sword comes and takes the life of one of them, that man will be taken away because of his sin, but I will hold the watchman accountable for his blood.' *Eze 3:11,18*

⁷"Son of man, I have made you a watchman for the house of Israel; so hear the word I speak and give them warning from me. ⁸When I say to the wicked, 'O wicked man, you will surely die,' and you do not speak out to dissuade him from his ways, that wicked man will die for*ᵃ* his sin, and I will hold you accountable for his blood. ⁹But if you do warn the wicked man to turn from his ways and he does not do so, he will die for his sin, but you will have saved yourself.

¹⁰"Son of man, say to the house of Israel, 'This is what you are saying: "Our offenses and sins weigh us down, and we are wasting away because of*ᵇ* them. How then can we live?" ' ¹¹Say to them, 'As surely as I live, declares the Sovereign LORD, I take no pleasure in the death of the wicked, but rather that they turn from their ways and live. Turn! Turn from your evil ways! Why will you die, O house of Israel?' *Eze 18:32; 2Pe 3:9*

¹²"Therefore, son of man, say to your countrymen, 'The righteousness of the righteous man will not save him when he disobeys, and the wickedness of the wicked man will not cause him to fall when he turns from it. The righteous man, if he sins, will not be allowed to live because of his former righteousness.' ¹³If I tell the righteous man that he will surely live, but then he trusts in his righteousness and does evil, none of the righteous things he has done will be remembered; he will die for the evil he has done. ¹⁴And if I say to the wicked man, 'You will surely die,' but he then turns away from his sin and does what is just and

---

ᵃ8 Or in; also in verse 9   *ᵇ10 Or away in*

right— [15]if he gives back what he took in pledge for a loan, returns what he has stolen, follows the decrees that give life, and does no evil, he will surely live; he will not die. [16]None of the sins he has committed will be remembered against him. He has done what is just and right; he will surely live.   Eze 18:22

[17]"Yet your countrymen say, 'The way of the Lord is not just.' But it is their way that is not just. [18]If a righteous man turns from his righteousness and does evil, he will die for it. [19]And if a wicked man turns away from his wickedness and does what is just and right, he will live by doing so. [20]Yet, O house of Israel, you say, 'The way of the Lord is not just.' But I will judge each of you according to his own ways."   Eze 3:20; 18:26

Jerusalem's Fall Explained

[21]In the twelfth year of our exile, in the tenth month on the fifth day, a man who had escaped from Jerusalem came to me and said, "The city has fallen!" [22]Now the evening before the man arrived, the hand of the Lord was upon me, and he opened my mouth before the man came to me in the morning. So my mouth was opened and I was no longer silent.   Eze 24:27

[23]Then the word of the Lord came to me: [24]"Son of man, the people living in those ruins in the land of Israel are saying, 'Abraham was only one man, yet he possessed the land. But we are many; surely the land has been given to us as our possession.' [25]Therefore say to them, 'This is what the Sovereign Lord says: Since you eat meat with the blood still in it and look to your idols and shed blood, should you then possess the land? [26]You rely on your sword, you do detestable things, and each of you defiles his neighbor's wife. Should you then possess the land?'

[27]"Say this to them: 'This is what the Sovereign Lord says: As surely as I live, those who are left in the ruins will fall by the sword, those out in the country I will give to the wild animals to be devoured, and those in strongholds and caves will die of a plague. [28]I will make the land a desolate waste, and her proud strength will come to an end, and the mountains of Israel will become desolate so that no one will cross them. [29]Then they will know that I am the Lord, when I have made the land a desolate waste because of all the detestable things they have done.'   1Sa 13:6

[30]"As for you, son of man, your countrymen are talking together about you by the walls and at the doors of the houses, saying to each other, 'Come and hear the message that has come from the Lord.' [31]My people come to you, as they usually do, and sit before you to listen to your words, but they do not put them into practice. With their mouths they express devotion, but their hearts are greedy for unjust gain. [32]Indeed, to them you

are nothing more than one who sings love songs with a beautiful voice and plays an instrument well, for they hear your words but do not put them into practice.

³³"When all this comes true— and it surely will—then they will know that a prophet has been among them." 1Sa 3:20; Eze 2:5

Shepherds and Sheep

34 The word of the LORD came to me: ²"Son of man, prophesy against the shepherds of Israel; prophesy and say to them: 'This is what the Sovereign LORD says: Woe to the shepherds of Israel who only take care of themselves! Should not shepherds take care of the flock? ³You eat the curds, clothe yourselves with the wool and slaughter the choice animals, but you do not take care of the flock. ⁴You have not strengthened the weak or healed the sick or bound up the injured. You have not brought back the strays or searched for the lost. You have ruled them harshly and brutally. ⁵So they were scattered because there was no shepherd, and when they were scattered they became food for all the wild animals. ⁶My sheep wandered over all the mountains and on every high hill. They were scattered over the whole earth, and no one searched or looked for them. Jer 23:1; Jn 10:11

⁷"'Therefore, you shepherds, hear the word of the LORD: ⁸As surely as I live, declares the Sover-

eign LORD, because my flock lacks a shepherd and so has been plundered and has become food for all the wild animals, and because my shepherds did not search for my flock but cared for themselves rather than for my flock, ⁹therefore, O shepherds, hear the word of the LORD: ¹⁰This is what the Sovereign LORD says: I am against the shepherds and will hold them accountable for my flock. I will remove them from tending the flock so that the shepherds can no longer feed themselves. I will rescue my flock from their mouths, and it will no longer be food for them.

¹¹"'For this is what the Sovereign LORD says: I myself will search for my sheep and look after them. ¹²As a shepherd looks after his scattered flock when he is with them, so will I look after my sheep. I will rescue them from all the places where they were scattered on a day of clouds and darkness. ¹³I will bring them out from the nations and gather them from the countries, and I will bring them into their own land. I will pasture them on the mountains of Israel, in the ravines and in all the settlements in the land. ¹⁴I will tend them in a good pasture, and the mountain heights of Israel will be their grazing land. There they will lie down in good grazing land, and there they will feed in a rich pasture on the mountains of Israel. ¹⁵I myself will tend my sheep and have them lie down, declares the

Sovereign LORD. ¹⁶I will search for the lost and bring back the strays. I will bind up the injured and strengthen the weak, but the sleek and the strong I will destroy. I will shepherd the flock with justice.

¹⁷" 'As for you, my flock, this is what the Sovereign LORD says: I will judge between one sheep and another, and between rams and goats. ¹⁸Is it not enough for you to feed on the good pasture? Must you also trample the rest of your pasture with your feet? Is it not enough for you to drink clear water? Must you also muddy the rest with your feet? ¹⁹Must my flock feed on what you have trampled and drink what you have muddied with your feet?   Mt 25:32-33

²⁰" 'Therefore this is what the Sovereign LORD says to them: See, I myself will judge between the fat sheep and the lean sheep. ²¹Because you shove with flank and shoulder, butting all the weak sheep with your horns until you have driven them away, ²²I will save my flock, and they will no longer be plundered. I will judge between one sheep and another. ²³I will place over them one shepherd, my servant David, and he will tend them; he will tend them and be their shepherd. ²⁴I the LORD will be their God, and my servant David will be prince among them. I the LORD have spoken.   Isa 40:11

²⁵" 'I will make a covenant of peace with them and rid the land of wild beasts so that they may live in the desert and sleep in the forests in safety. ²⁶I will bless them and the places surrounding my hill.ᵃ I will send down showers in season; there will be showers of blessing. ²⁷The trees of the field will yield their fruit and the ground will yield its crops; the people will be secure in their land. They will know that I am the LORD, when I break the bars of their yoke and rescue them from the hands of those who enslaved them. ²⁸They will no longer be plundered by the nations, nor will wild animals devour them. They will live in safety, and no one will make them afraid. ²⁹I will provide for them a land renowned for its crops, and they will no longer be victims of famine in the land or bear the scorn of the nations. ³⁰Then they will know that I, the LORD their God, am with them and that they, the house of Israel, are my people, declares the Sovereign LORD. ³¹You my sheep, the sheep of my pasture, are people, and I am your God, declares the Sovereign LORD.' "   Ps 100:3

A Prophecy Against Edom

35 The word of the LORD came to me: ²"Son of man, set your face against Mount Seir; prophesy against it ³and say: 'This is what the Sovereign LORD says: I am against you, Mount Seir, and I

ᵃ26 Or I will make them and the places surrounding my hill a blessing will stretch out my hand against you and make you a desolate waste. ⁴I will turn your towns into ruins and you will be desolate. Then you will know that I am the Lord. Jer 6:12; Eze 25:12-14

⁵" 'Because you harbored an ancient hostility and delivered the Israelites over to the sword at the time of their calamity, the time their punishment reached its climax, ⁶therefore as surely as I live, declares the Sovereign Lord, I will give you over to bloodshed and it will pursue you. Since you did not hate bloodshed, bloodshed will pursue you. ⁷I will make Mount Seir a desolate waste and cut off from it all who come and go. ⁸I will fill your mountains with the slain; those killed by the sword will fall on your hills and in your valleys and in all your ravines. ⁹I will make you desolate forever; your towns will not be inhabited. Then you will know that I am the Lord.

¹⁰" 'Because you have said, "These two nations and countries will be ours and we will take possession of them," even though I the Lord was there, ¹¹therefore as surely as I live, declares the Sovereign Lord, I will treat you in accordance with the anger and jealousy you showed in your hatred of them and I will make myself known among them when I judge you. ¹²Then you will know that I the Lord have heard all the contemptible things you have said against the mountains of Israel.

You said, "They have been laid waste and have been given over to us to devour." ¹³You boasted against me and spoke against me without restraint, and I heard it. ¹⁴This is what the Sovereign Lord says: While the whole earth rejoices, I will make you desolate. ¹⁵Because you rejoiced when the inheritance of the house of Israel became desolate, that is how I will treat you. You will be desolate, O Mount Seir, you and all of Edom. Then they will know that I am the Lord.' " Jer 50:11-13; La 4:21; Ob 1:12

A Prophecy to the Mountains of Israel

36 "Son of man, prophesy to the mountains of Israel and say, 'O mountains of Israel, hear the word of the Lord. ²This is what the Sovereign Lord says: The enemy said of you, "Aha! The ancient heights have become our possession." ' ³Therefore prophesy and say, 'This is what the Sovereign Lord says: Because they ravaged and hounded you from every side so that you became the possession of the rest of the nations and the object of people's malicious talk and slander, ⁴therefore, O mountains of Israel, hear the word of the Sovereign Lord: This is what the Sovereign Lord says to the mountains and hills, to the ravines and valleys, to the desolate ruins and the deserted towns that have been plundered and ridiculed by the rest of the nations around you— ⁵this is what the Sovereign LORD says: In my burning zeal I have spoken against the rest of the nations, and against all Edom, for with glee and with malice in their hearts they made my land their own possession so that they might plunder its pastureland.' ⁶Therefore prophesy concerning the land of Israel and say to the mountains and hills, to the ravines and valleys: 'This is what the Sovereign LORD says: I speak in my jealous wrath because you have suffered the scorn of the nations. ⁷Therefore this is what the Sovereign LORD says: I swear with uplifted hand that the nations around you will also suffer scorn.   Ps 123:3-4

⁸" 'But you, O mountains of Israel, will produce branches and fruit for my people Israel, for they will soon come home. ⁹I am concerned for you and will look on you with favor; you will be plowed and sown, ¹⁰and I will multiply the number of people upon you, even the whole house of Israel. The towns will be inhabited and the ruins rebuilt. ¹¹I will increase the number of men and animals upon you, and they will be fruitful and become numerous. I will settle people on you as in the past and will make you prosper more than before. Then you will know that I am the LORD. ¹²I will cause people, my people Israel, to walk upon you. They will possess you, and you will be their inheritance; you

will never again deprive them of their children.   Eze 47:14,22

¹³" 'This is what the Sovereign LORD says: Because people say to you, "You devour men and deprive your nation of its children," ¹⁴therefore you will no longer devour men or make your nation childless, declares the Sovereign LORD. ¹⁵No longer will I make you hear the taunts of the nations, and no longer will you suffer the scorn of the peoples or cause your nation to fall, declares the Sovereign LORD.' "   Nu 13:32; Eze 34:29

¹⁶Again the word of the LORD came to me: ¹⁷"Son of man, when the people of Israel were living in their own land, they defiled it by their conduct and their actions. Their conduct was like a woman's monthly uncleanness in my sight. ¹⁸So I poured out my wrath on them because they had shed blood in the land and because they had defiled it with their idols. ¹⁹I dispersed them among the nations, and they were scattered through the countries; I judged them according to their conduct and their actions. ²⁰And wherever they went among the nations they profaned my holy name, for it was said of them, 'These are the LORD's people, and yet they had to leave his land.' ²¹I had concern for my holy name, which the house of Israel profaned among the nations where they had gone.   Ps 74:18

²²"Therefore say to the house of Israel, 'This is what the Sovereign

Lord says: It is not for your sake, O house of Israel, that I am going to do these things, but for the sake of my holy name, which you have profaned among the nations where you have gone. **23**I will show the holiness of my great name, which has been profaned among the nations, the name you have profaned among them. Then the nations will know that I am the Lord, declares the Sovereign Lord, when I show myself holy through you before their eyes.   Ps 126:2

24" 'For I will take you out of the nations; I will gather you from all the countries and bring you back into your own land. **25**I will sprinkle clean water on you, and you will be clean; I will cleanse you from all your impurities and from all your idols. **26**I will give you a new heart and put a new spirit in you; I will remove from you your heart of stone and give you a heart of flesh. **27**And I will put my Spirit in you and move you to follow my decrees and be careful to keep my laws. **28**You will live in the land I gave your forefathers; you will be my people, and I will be your God. **29**I will save you from all your uncleanness. I will call for the grain and make it plentiful and will not bring famine upon you. **30**I will increase the fruit of the trees and the crops of the field, so that you will no longer suffer disgrace among the nations because of famine. **31**Then you will remember your evil ways and wicked deeds, and

you will loathe yourselves for your sins and detestable practices. **32**I want you to know that I am not doing this for your sake, declares the Sovereign Lord. Be ashamed and disgraced for your conduct, O house of Israel!   Jer 24:7; Eze 11:19

33" 'This is what the Sovereign Lord says: On the day I cleanse you from all your sins, I will resettle your towns, and the ruins will be rebuilt. **34**The desolate land will be cultivated instead of lying desolate in the sight of all who pass through it. **35**They will say, "This land that was laid waste has become like the garden of Eden; the cities that were lying in ruins, desolate and destroyed, are now fortified and inhabited." **36**Then the nations around you that remain will know that I the Lord have rebuilt what was destroyed and have replanted what was desolate. I the Lord have spoken, and I will do it.'

37"This is what the Sovereign Lord says: Once again I will yield to the plea of the house of Israel and do this for them: I will make their people as numerous as sheep, **38**as numerous as the flocks for offerings at Jerusalem during her appointed feasts. So will the ruined cities be filled with flocks of people. Then they will know that I am the Lord."   1Ki 8:63; 2Ch 35:7-9

The Valley of Dry Bones

37 The hand of the Lord was upon me, and he brought

me out by the Spirit of the LORD and set me in the middle of a valley; it was full of bones. ²He led me back and forth among them, and I saw a great many bones on the floor of the valley, bones that were very dry. ³He asked me, "Son of man, can these bones live?"

I said, "O Sovereign LORD, you alone know." Dt 32:39; 1Sa 2:6

⁴Then he said to me, "Prophesy to these bones and say to them, 'Dry bones, hear the word of the LORD! ⁵This is what the Sovereign LORD says to these bones: I will make breath*ᵃ* enter you, and you will come to life. ⁶I will attach tendons to you and make flesh come upon you and cover you with skin; I will put breath in you, and you will come to life. Then you will know that I am the LORD.' "

⁷So I prophesied as I was commanded. And as I was prophesying, there was a noise, a rattling sound, and the bones came together, bone to bone. ⁸I looked, and tendons and flesh appeared on them and skin covered them, but there was no breath in them.

⁹Then he said to me, "Prophesy to the breath; prophesy, son of man, and say to it, 'This is what the Sovereign LORD says: Come from the four winds, O breath, and breathe into these slain, that they may live.' " ¹⁰So I prophesied as he commanded me, and breath entered them; they came to life and

stood up on their feet—a vast army. Ps 104:30; Rev 11:11

¹¹Then he said to me: "Son of man, these bones are the whole house of Israel. They say, 'Our bones are dried up and our hope is gone; we are cut off.' ¹²Therefore prophesy and say to them: 'This is what the Sovereign LORD says: O my people, I am going to open your graves and bring you up from them; I will bring you back to the land of Israel. ¹³Then you, my people, will know that I am the LORD, when I open your graves and bring you up from them. ¹⁴I will put my Spirit in you and you will live, and I will settle you in your own land. Then you will know that I the LORD have spoken, and I have done it, declares the LORD.' " Hos 13:14

One Nation Under One King

¹⁵The word of the LORD came to me: ¹⁶"Son of man, take a stick of wood and write on it, 'Belonging to Judah and the Israelites associated with him.' Then take another stick of wood, and write on it, 'Ephraim's stick, belonging to Joseph and all the house of Israel associated with him.' ¹⁷Join them together into one stick so that they will become one in your hand. Nu 17:2-3

¹⁸"When your countrymen ask you, 'Won't you tell us what you mean by this?' ¹⁹say to them, 'This is what the Sovereign LORD says: I am going to take the stick of Jo-

ᵃ5 The Hebrew for this word can also mean *wind* or *spirit* (see verses 6-14).

seph—which is in Ephraim's hand
—and of the Israelite tribes associated with him, and join it to Judah's stick, making them a single
stick of wood, and they will become one in my hand.' ²⁰Hold before their eyes the sticks you have
written on ²¹and say to them, 'This
is what the Sovereign Lord says: I
will take the Israelites out of the
nations where they have gone. I
will gather them from all around
and bring them back into their
own land. ²²I will make them one
nation in the land, on the mountains of Israel. There will be one
king over all of them and they will
never again be two nations or be
divided into two kingdoms. ²³They
will no longer defile themselves
with their idols and vile images or
with any of their offenses, for I will
save them from all their sinful
backsliding,^a and I will cleanse
them. They will be my people, and
I will be their God.　　　Eze 36:25,28

²⁴" 'My servant David will be
king over them, and they will all
have one shepherd. They will follow my laws and be careful to keep
my decrees. ²⁵They will live in the
land I gave to my servant Jacob,
the land where your fathers lived.
They and their children and their
children's children will live there
forever, and David my servant will
be their prince forever. ²⁶I will
make a covenant of peace with

them; it will be an everlasting covenant. I will establish them and increase their numbers, and I will
put my sanctuary among them for-
ever. ²⁷My dwelling place will be
with them; I will be their God, and
they will be my people. ²⁸Then the
nations will know that I the Lord
make Israel holy, when my sanctuary is among them forever.' "

A Prophecy Against Gog

38 The word of the Lord came
to me: ²"Son of man, set
your face against Gog, of the land
of Magog, the chief prince of^b Meshech and Tubal; prophesy against
him ³and say: 'This is what the
Sovereign Lord says: I am against
you, O Gog, chief prince of^c Meshech and Tubal. ⁴I will turn you
around, put hooks in your jaws
and bring you out with your whole
army—your horses, your horsemen fully armed, and a great horde
with large and small shields, all of
them brandishing their swords.
⁵Persia, Cush^d and Put will be with
them, all with shields and helmets,
⁶also Gomer with all its troops, and
Beth Togarmah from the far north
with all its troops—the many nations with you.　　　Ge 10:2; Eze 39:11

⁷" 'Get ready; be prepared, you
and all the hordes gathered about
you, and take command of them.
⁸After many days you will be
called to arms. In future years you

---

^a23 Many Hebrew manuscripts (see also Septuagint); most Hebrew manuscripts *all their dwelling places
where they sinned*　　^b2 Or *the prince of Rosh,*　　^c3 Or *Gog, prince of Rosh,*　　^d5 That is, the upper
Nile region

will invade a land that has recovered from war, whose people were gathered from many nations to the mountains of Israel, which had long been desolate. They had been brought out from the nations, and now all of them live in safety. ⁹You and all your troops and the many nations with you will go up, advancing like a storm; you will be like a cloud covering the land.

¹⁰" 'This is what the Sovereign LORD says: On that day thoughts will come into your mind and you will devise an evil scheme. ¹¹You will say, "I will invade a land of unwalled villages; I will attack a peaceful and unsuspecting people —all of them living without walls and without gates and bars. ¹²I will plunder and loot and turn my hand against the resettled ruins and the people gathered from the nations, rich in livestock and goods, living at the center of the land." ¹³Sheba and Dedan and the merchants of Tarshish and all her villages*a* will say to you, "Have you come to plunder? Have you gathered your hordes to loot, to carry off silver and gold, to take away livestock and goods and to seize much plunder?" '   Eze 27:22

¹⁴"Therefore, son of man, prophesy and say to Gog: 'This is what the Sovereign LORD says: In that day, when my people Israel are living in safety, will you not take notice of it? ¹⁵You will come from your place in the far north, you and many nations with you, all of them riding on horses, a great horde, a mighty army. ¹⁶You will advance against my people Israel like a cloud that covers the land. In days to come, O Gog, I will bring you against my land, so that the nations may know me when I show myself holy through you before their eyes.   Isa 29:23; Eze 39:21

¹⁷" 'This is what the Sovereign LORD says: Are you not the one I spoke of in former days by my servants the prophets of Israel? At that time they prophesied for years that I would bring you against them. ¹⁸This is what will happen in that day: When Gog attacks the land of Israel, my hot anger will be aroused, declares the Sovereign LORD. ¹⁹In my zeal and fiery wrath I declare that at that time there shall be a great earthquake in the land of Israel. ²⁰The fish of the sea, the birds of the air, the beasts of the field, every creature that moves along the ground, and all the people on the face of the earth will tremble at my presence. The mountains will be overturned, the cliffs will crumble and every wall will fall to the ground. ²¹I will summon a sword against Gog on all my mountains, declares the Sovereign LORD. Every man's sword will be against his brother. ²²I will execute judgment upon him with plague and bloodshed; I will pour down

---

a 13 Or her strong lions

torrents of rain, hailstones and burning sulfur on him and on his troops and on the many nations with him. 23And so I will show my greatness and my holiness, and I will make myself known in the sight of many nations. Then they will know that I am the LORD.'

39 "Son of man, prophesy against Gog and say: 'This is what the Sovereign LORD says: I am against you, O Gog, chief prince of*a* Meshech and Tubal. 2I will turn you around and drag you along. I will bring you from the far north and send you against the mountains of Israel. 3Then I will strike your bow from your left hand and make your arrows drop from your right hand. 4On the mountains of Israel you will fall, you and all your troops and the nations with you. I will give you as food to all kinds of carrion birds and to the wild animals. 5You will fall in the open field, for I have spoken, declares the Sovereign LORD. 6I will send fire on Magog and on those who live in safety in the coastlands, and they will know that I am the LORD.   Jer 25:22; Am 1:4

7" 'I will make known my holy name among my people Israel. I will no longer let my holy name be profaned, and the nations will know that I the LORD am the Holy One in Israel. 8It is coming! It will surely take place, declares the Sov-

ereign LORD. This is the day I have spoken of.   Ex 20:7; Eze 36:16,23

9" 'Then those who live in the towns of Israel will go out and use the weapons for fuel and burn them up—the small and large shields, the bows and arrows, the war clubs and spears. For seven years they will use them for fuel. 10They will not need to gather wood from the fields or cut it from the forests, because they will use the weapons for fuel. And they will plunder those who plundered them and loot those who looted them, declares the Sovereign LORD.

11" 'On that day I will give Gog a burial place in Israel, in the valley of those who travel east toward*b* the Sea.*c* It will block the way of travelers, because Gog and all his hordes will be buried there. So it will be called the Valley of Hamon Gog.*d*   Eze 38:2

12" 'For seven months the house of Israel will be burying them in order to cleanse the land. 13All the people of the land will bury them, and the day I am glorified will be a memorable day for them, declares the Sovereign LORD.   Dt 21:23

14" 'Men will be regularly employed to cleanse the land. Some will go throughout the land and, in addition to them, others will bury those that remain on the ground. At the end of the seven months they will begin their search. 15As

---

*a*1 Or *Gog, prince of Rosh,* *b*11 Or *of* *c*11 That is, the Dead Sea *d*11 *Hamon Gog* means *hordes* of Gog.

they go through the land and one of them sees a human bone, he will set up a marker beside it until the gravediggers have buried it in the Valley of Hamon Gog. ¹⁶(Also a town called Hamonah*ᵃ* will be there.) And so they will cleanse the land.'

¹⁷"Son of man, this is what the Sovereign Lᴏʀᴅ says: Call out to every kind of bird and all the wild animals: 'Assemble and come together from all around to the sacrifice I am preparing for you, the great sacrifice on the mountains of Israel. There you will eat flesh and drink blood. ¹⁸You will eat the flesh of mighty men and drink the blood of the princes of the earth as if they were rams and lambs, goats and bulls—all of them fattened animals from Bashan. ¹⁹At the sacrifice I am preparing for you, you will eat fat till you are glutted and drink blood till you are drunk. ²⁰At my table you will eat your fill of horses and riders, mighty men and soldiers of every kind,' declares the Sovereign Lᴏʀᴅ.   Ps 22:12

²¹"I will display my glory among the nations, and all the nations will see the punishment I inflict and the hand I lay upon them. ²²From that day forward the house of Israel will know that I am the Lᴏʀᴅ their God. ²³And the nations will know that the people of Israel went into exile for their sin, because they were unfaithful to me.

So I hid my face from them and handed them over to their enemies, and they all fell by the sword. ²⁴I dealt with them according to their uncleanness and their offenses, and I hid my face from them.   Eze 36:19

²⁵"Therefore this is what the Sovereign Lᴏʀᴅ says: I will now bring Jacob back from captivity*ᵇ* and will have compassion on all the people of Israel, and I will be zealous for my holy name. ²⁶They will forget their shame and all the unfaithfulness they showed toward me when they lived in safety in their land with no one to make them afraid. ²⁷When I have brought them back from the nations and have gathered them from the countries of their enemies, I will show myself holy through them in the sight of many nations. ²⁸Then they will know that I am the Lᴏʀᴅ their God, for though I sent them into exile among the nations, I will gather them to their own land, not leaving any behind. ²⁹I will no longer hide my face from them, for I will pour out my Spirit on the house of Israel, declares the Sovereign Lᴏʀᴅ."

The New Temple Area

40 In the twenty-fifth year of our exile, at the beginning of the year, on the tenth of the month, in the fourteenth year after the fall of the city—on that very

---

ᵃ16 Hamonah means *horde.*   *ᵇ25* Or *now restore the fortunes of Jacob*

day the hand of the LORD was upon me and he took me there. ²In visions of God he took me to the land of Israel and set me on a very high mountain, on whose south side were some buildings that looked like a city. ³He took me there, and I saw a man whose appearance was like bronze; he was standing in the gateway with a linen cord and a measuring rod in his hand. ⁴The man said to me, "Son of man, look with your eyes and hear with your ears and pay attention to everything I am going to show you, for that is why you have been brought here. Tell the house of Israel everything you see."

The East Gate to the Outer Court

⁵I saw a wall completely surrounding the temple area. The length of the measuring rod in the man's hand was six long cubits, each of which was a cubit[a] and a handbreadth.[b] He measured the wall; it was one measuring rod thick and one rod high.   Eze 42:20

⁶Then he went to the gate facing east. He climbed its steps and measured the threshold of the gate; it was one rod deep.[c] ⁷The alcoves for the guards were one rod long and one rod wide, and the projecting walls between the alcoves

were five cubits thick. And the threshold of the gate next to the portico facing the temple was one rod deep.   ver 36; Eze 8:16

⁸Then he measured the portico of the gateway; ⁹it[d] was eight cubits deep and its jambs were two cubits thick. The portico of the gateway faced the temple.

¹⁰Inside the east gate were three alcoves on each side; the three had the same measurements, and the faces of the projecting walls on each side had the same measurements. ¹¹Then he measured the width of the entrance to the gateway; it was ten cubits and its length was thirteen cubits. ¹²In front of each alcove was a wall one cubit high, and the alcoves were six cubits square. ¹³Then he measured the gateway from the top of the rear wall of one alcove to the top of the opposite one; the distance was twenty-five cubits from one parapet opening to the opposite one. ¹⁴He measured along the faces of the projecting walls all around the inside of the gateway — sixty cubits. The measurement was up to the portico[e] facing the courtyard.[f] ¹⁵The distance from the entrance of the gateway to the far end of its portico was fifty cubits. ¹⁶The alcoves and the projecting walls inside the gateway were

---

a 5 The common cubit was about 1 1/2 feet (about 0.5 meter).   *b* 5 That is, about 3 inches (about 8 centimeters)   *c* 6 Septuagint; Hebrew *deep, the first threshold, one rod deep*   *d* 8,9 Many Hebrew manuscripts, Septuagint, Vulgate and Syriac; most Hebrew manuscripts *gateway facing the temple; it was one rod deep.* *9Then he measured the portico of the gateway; it*   *e* 14 Septuagint; Hebrew *projecting wall*   *f* 14 The meaning of the Hebrew for this verse is uncertain.

surmounted by narrow parapet openings all around, as was the portico; the openings all around faced inward. The faces of the projecting walls were decorated with palm trees.　　　Ex 27:9; 2Ch 3:5

The Outer Court

17Then he brought me into the outer court. There I saw some rooms and a pavement that had been constructed all around the court; there were thirty rooms along the pavement. 18It abutted the sides of the gateways and was as wide as they were long; this was the lower pavement. 19Then he measured the distance from the inside of the lower gateway to the outside of the inner court; it was a hundred cubits on the east side as well as on the north.　　　Eze 41:6; 46:1

The North Gate

20Then he measured the length and width of the gate facing north, leading into the outer court. 21Its alcoves—three on each side—its projecting walls and its portico had the same measurements as those of the first gateway. It was fifty cubits long and twenty-five cubits wide. 22Its openings, its portico and its palm tree decorations had the same measurements as those of the gate facing east. Seven steps led up to it, with its portico opposite them. 23There was a gate to the inner court facing the north gate, just as there was on the east. He measured from one gate to the opposite one; it was a hundred cubits.　　　ver 49

The South Gate

24Then he led me to the south side and I saw a gate facing south. He measured its jambs and its portico, and they had the same measurements as the others. 25The gateway and its portico had narrow openings all around, like the openings of the others. It was fifty cubits long and twenty-five cubits wide. 26Seven steps led up to it, with its portico opposite them; it had palm tree decorations on the faces of the projecting walls on each side. 27The inner court also had a gate facing south, and he measured from this gate to the outer gate on the south side; it was a hundred cubits.　　　ver 22,32

Gates to the Inner Court

28Then he brought me into the inner court through the south gate, and he measured the south gate; it had the same measurements as the others. 29Its alcoves, its projecting walls and its portico had the same measurements as the others. The gateway and its portico had openings all around. It was fifty cubits long and twenty-five cubits wide. 30(The porticoes of the gateways around the inner court were twenty-five cubits wide and five cubits deep.) 31Its portico faced the outer court; palm trees decorated its jambs, and eight steps led up to it.

³²Then he brought me to the inner court on the east side, and he measured the gateway; it had the same measurements as the others. ³³Its alcoves, its projecting walls and its portico had the same measurements as the others. The gateway and its portico had openings all around. It was fifty cubits long and twenty-five cubits wide. ³⁴Its portico faced the outer court; palm trees decorated the jambs on either side, and eight steps led up to it.   ver 22

³⁵Then he brought me to the north gate and measured it. It had the same measurements as the others, ³⁶as did its alcoves, its projecting walls and its portico, and it had openings all around. It was fifty cubits long and twenty-five cubits wide. ³⁷Its portico*a* faced the outer court; palm trees decorated the jambs on either side, and eight steps led up to it.   Eze 44:4; 47:2

The Rooms for Preparing Sacrifices

³⁸A room with a doorway was by the portico in each of the inner gateways, where the burnt offerings were washed. ³⁹In the portico of the gateway were two tables on each side, on which the burnt offerings, sin offerings and guilt offerings were slaughtered. ⁴⁰By the outside wall of the portico of the gateway, near the steps at the entrance to the north gateway were two tables, and on the other side of the steps were two tables. ⁴¹So there were four tables on one side of the gateway and four on the other—eight tables in all—on which the sacrifices were slaughtered. ⁴²There were also four tables of dressed stone for the burnt offerings, each a cubit and a half long, a cubit and a half wide and a cubit high. On them were placed the utensils for slaughtering the burnt offerings and the other sacrifices. ⁴³And double-pronged hooks, each a handbreadth long, were attached to the wall all around. The tables were for the flesh of the offerings.   Lev 4:3,28; 7:1

Rooms for the Priests

⁴⁴Outside the inner gate, within the inner court, were two rooms, one*b* at the side of the north gate and facing south, and another at the side of the south*c* gate and facing north. ⁴⁵He said to me, "The room facing south is for the priests who have charge of the temple, ⁴⁶and the room facing north is for the priests who have charge of the altar. These are the sons of Zadok, who are the only Levites who may draw near to the LORD to minister before him."   1Ki 2:35; Eze 43:19; 44:15

⁴⁷Then he measured the court: It was square—a hundred cubits long and a hundred cubits wide.

---

a 37 Septuagint (see also verses 31 and 34); Hebrew *jambs*   *b* 44 Septuagint; Hebrew *were rooms for singers, which were*   *c* 44 Septuagint; Hebrew *east*

And the altar was in front of the temple. Eze 41:13-14

The Temple

⁴⁸He brought me to the portico of the temple and measured the jambs of the portico; they were five cubits wide on either side. The width of the entrance was fourteen cubits and its projecting walls were*a* three cubits wide on either side. ⁴⁹The portico was twenty cubits wide, and twelve*b* cubits from front to back. It was reached by a flight of stairs,*c* and there were pillars on each side of the jambs.

41 Then the man brought me to the outer sanctuary and measured the jambs; the width of the jambs was six cubits*d* on each side.*e* ²The entrance was ten cubits wide, and the projecting walls on each side of it were five cubits wide. He also measured the outer sanctuary; it was forty cubits long and twenty cubits wide. ver 23
³Then he went into the inner sanctuary and measured the jambs of the entrance; each was two cubits wide. The entrance was six cubits wide, and the projecting walls on each side of it were seven cubits wide. ⁴And he measured the length of the inner sanctuary; it was twenty cubits, and its width was twenty cubits across the end of the outer sanctuary. He said to me, "This is the Most Holy Place."

⁵Then he measured the wall of the temple; it was six cubits thick, and each side room around the temple was four cubits wide. ⁶The side rooms were on three levels, one above another, thirty on each level. There were ledges all around the wall of the temple to serve as supports for the side rooms, so that the supports were not inserted into the wall of the temple. ⁷The side rooms all around the temple were wider at each successive level. The structure surrounding the temple was built in ascending stages, so that the rooms widened as one went upward. A stairway went up from the lowest floor to the top floor through the middle floor. 1Ki 6:5,8; Eze 40:17

⁸I saw that the temple had a raised base all around it, forming the foundation of the side rooms. It was the length of the rod, six long cubits. ⁹The outer wall of the side rooms was five cubits thick. The open area between the side rooms of the temple ¹⁰and the ᴌpriests'᷄ rooms was twenty cubits wide all around the temple. ¹¹There were entrances to the side rooms from the open area, one on the north and another on the south; and the base adjoining the open area was five cubits wide all around.

¹²The building facing the temple courtyard on the west side was

---

*a*48 Septuagint; Hebrew *entrance was*   *b*49 Septuagint; Hebrew *eleven*   *c*49 Hebrew; Septuagint *Ten steps led up to it*   *d*1 The common cubit was about 1 1/2 feet (about 0.5 meter).   *e*1 One Hebrew manuscript and Septuagint; most Hebrew manuscripts *side, the width of the tent* seventy cubits wide. The wall of the building was five cubits thick all around, and its length was ninety cubits.

[13]Then he measured the temple; it was a hundred cubits long, and the temple courtyard and the building with its walls were also a hundred cubits long. [14]The width of the temple courtyard on the east, including the front of the temple, was a hundred cubits.

[15]Then he measured the length of the building facing the courtyard at the rear of the temple, including its galleries on each side; it was a hundred cubits.   Eze 42:3

The outer sanctuary, the inner sanctuary and the portico facing the court, [16]as well as the thresholds and the narrow windows and galleries around the three of them — everything beyond and including the threshold was covered with wood. The floor, the wall up to the windows, and the windows were covered. [17]In the space above the outside of the entrance to the inner sanctuary and on the walls at regular intervals all around the inner and outer sanctuary [18]were carved cherubim and palm trees. Palm trees alternated with cherubim. Each cherub had two faces: [19]the face of a man toward the palm tree on one side and the face of a lion toward the palm tree on the other. They were carved all around the whole temple. [20]From the floor to the area above the entrance, cherubim and palm trees were carved on the wall of the outer sanctuary.

[21]The outer sanctuary had a rectangular doorframe, and the one at the front of the Most Holy Place was similar. [22]There was a wooden altar three cubits high and two cubits square[a]; its corners, its base[b] and its sides were of wood. The man said to me, "This is the table that is before the Lord." [23]Both the outer sanctuary and the Most Holy Place had double doors. [24]Each door had two leaves — two hinged leaves for each door. [25]And on the doors of the outer sanctuary were carved cherubim and palm trees like those carved on the walls, and there was a wooden overhang on the front of the portico. [26]On the sidewalls of the portico were narrow windows with palm trees carved on each side. The side rooms of the temple also had overhangs.   Eze 44:16; Mal 1:7,12

Rooms for the Priests

42 Then the man led me northward into the outer court and brought me to the rooms opposite the temple courtyard and opposite the outer wall on the north side. [2]The building whose door faced north was a hundred cubits[c] long and fifty cubits wide. [3]Both in the section twenty cubits

---

[a]22 Septuagint; Hebrew long   [b]22 Septuagint; Hebrew length   [c]2 The common cubit was about 1 1/2 feet (about 0.5 meter).

from the inner court and in the section opposite the pavement of the outer court, gallery faced gallery at the three levels. ⁴In front of the rooms was an inner passageway ten cubits wide and a hundred cubits*a* long. Their doors were on the north. ⁵Now the upper rooms were narrower, for the galleries took more space from them than from the rooms on the lower and middle floors of the building. ⁶The rooms on the third floor had no pillars, as the courts had; so they were smaller in floor space than those on the lower and middle floors. ⁷There was an outer wall parallel to the rooms and the outer court; it extended in front of the rooms for fifty cubits. ⁸While the row of rooms on the side next to the outer court was fifty cubits long, the row on the side nearest the sanctuary was a hundred cubits long. ⁹The lower rooms had an entrance on the east side as one enters them from the outer court.

¹⁰On the south side*b* along the length of the wall of the outer court, adjoining the temple courtyard and opposite the outer wall, were rooms ¹¹with a passageway in front of them. These were like the rooms on the north; they had the same length and width, with similar exits and dimensions. Similar to the doorways on the north ¹²were the doorways of the rooms on the south. There was a doorway at the beginning of the passageway that was parallel to the corresponding wall extending eastward, by which one enters the rooms.

¹³Then he said to me, "The north and south rooms facing the temple courtyard are the priests' rooms, where the priests who approach the LORD will eat the most holy offerings. There they will put the most holy offerings—the grain offerings, the sin offerings and the guilt offerings—for the place is holy. ¹⁴Once the priests enter the holy precincts, they are not to go into the outer court until they leave behind the garments in which they minister, for these are holy. They are to put on other clothes before they go near the places that are for the people."

¹⁵When he had finished measuring what was inside the temple area, he led me out by the east gate and measured the area all around: ¹⁶He measured the east side with the measuring rod; it was five hundred cubits.*c* ¹⁷He measured the north side; it was five hundred cubits*d* by the measuring rod. ¹⁸He measured the south side; it was five hundred cubits by the measuring rod. ¹⁹Then he turned to the west side and measured; it was five hundred cubits by the measuring rod. ²⁰So he measured the area

---

a 4 Septuagint and Syriac; Hebrew *and one cubit*   *b 10* Septuagint; Hebrew *Eastward*   *c 16* See Septuagint of verse 17; Hebrew *rods*; also in verses 18 and 19.   *d 17* Septuagint; Hebrew *rods*

on all four sides. It had a wall around it, five hundred cubits long and five hundred cubits wide, to separate the holy from the common.   Eze 45:2; Rev 21:16

The Glory Returns to the Temple

43 Then the man brought me to the gate facing east, [2]and I saw the glory of the God of Israel coming from the east. His voice was like the roar of rushing waters, and the land was radiant with his glory. [3]The vision I saw was like the vision I had seen when he[a] came to destroy the city and like the visions I had seen by the Kebar River, and I fell facedown. [4]The glory of the Lord entered the temple through the gate facing east. [5]Then the Spirit lifted me up and brought me into the inner court, and the glory of the Lord filled the temple.   Eze 11:24; 8:3

[6]While the man was standing beside me, I heard someone speaking to me from inside the temple. [7]He said: "Son of man, this is the place of my throne and the place for the soles of my feet. This is where I will live among the Israelites forever. The house of Israel will never again defile my holy name—neither they nor their kings—by their prostitution[b] and the lifeless idols[c] of their kings at their high places. [8]When they placed their threshold next to my threshold and their doorposts beside my doorposts, with only a wall between me and them, they defiled my holy name by their detestable practices. So I destroyed them in my anger. [9]Now let them put away from me their prostitution and the lifeless idols of their kings, and I will live among them forever.   Eze 37:26-28

[10]"Son of man, describe the temple to the people of Israel, that they may be ashamed of their sins. Let them consider the plan, [11]and if they are ashamed of all they have done, make known to them the design of the temple—its arrangement, its exits and entrances—its whole design and all its regulations[d] and laws. Write these down before them so that they may be faithful to its design and follow all its regulations.   Eze 16:61; 44:5

[12]"This is the law of the temple: All the surrounding area on top of the mountain will be most holy. Such is the law of the temple.

The Altar

[13]"These are the measurements of the altar in long cubits, that cubit being a cubit[e] and a handbreadth[f]: Its gutter is a cubit deep and a cubit wide, with a rim of one

---

[a]3 Some Hebrew manuscripts and Vulgate; most Hebrew manuscripts *I*   [b]7 Or *their spiritual adultery*; also in verse 9   [c]7 Or *the corpses*; also in verse 9   [d]11 Some Hebrew manuscripts and Septuagint; most Hebrew manuscripts *regulations and its whole design*   [e]13 The common cubit was about 1 1/2 feet (about 0.5 meter).   [f]13 That is, about 3 inches (about 8 centimeters)

span*a* around the edge. And this is the height of the altar: **14**From the gutter on the ground up to the lower ledge it is two cubits high and a cubit wide, and from the smaller ledge up to the larger ledge it is four cubits high and a cubit wide. **15**The altar hearth is four cubits high, and four horns project upward from the hearth. **16**The altar hearth is square, twelve cubits long and twelve cubits wide. **17**The upper ledge also is square, fourteen cubits long and fourteen cubits wide, with a rim of half a cubit and a gutter of a cubit all around. The steps of the altar face east."

18Then he said to me, "Son of man, this is what the Sovereign Lord says: These will be the regulations for sacrificing burnt offerings and sprinkling blood upon the altar when it is built: **19**You are to give a young bull as a sin offering to the priests, who are Levites, of the family of Zadok, who come near to minister before me, declares the Sovereign Lord. **20**You are to take some of its blood and put it on the four horns of the altar and on the four corners of the upper ledge and all around the rim, and so purify the altar and make atonement for it. **21**You are to take the bull for the sin offering and burn it in the designated part of the temple area outside the sanctuary.   Ex 29:14; Heb 13:11

22"On the second day you are to offer a male goat without defect for a sin offering, and the altar is to be purified as it was purified with the bull. **23**When you have finished purifying it, you are to offer a young bull and a ram from the flock, both without defect. **24**You are to offer them before the Lord, and the priests are to sprinkle salt on them and sacrifice them as a burnt offering to the Lord.   Lev 2:13; Mk 9:49-50

25"For seven days you are to provide a male goat daily for a sin offering; you are also to provide a young bull and a ram from the flock, both without defect. **26**For seven days they are to make atonement for the altar and cleanse it; thus they will dedicate it. **27**At the end of these days, from the eighth day on, the priests are to present your burnt offerings and fellowship offerings*b* on the altar. Then I will accept you, declares the Sovereign Lord."   Lev 8:33; 17:5

The Prince, the Levites, the Priests

44 Then the man brought me back to the outer gate of the sanctuary, the one facing east, and it was shut. **2**The Lord said to me, "This gate is to remain shut. It must not be opened; no one may enter through it. It is to remain shut because the Lord, the God of Israel, has entered through it. **3**The prince himself is the only one who may sit inside the gateway to eat in

---

*a*13 That is, about 9 inches (about 22 centimeters)   *b*27 Traditionally *peace offerings*

the presence of the LORD. He is to enter by way of the portico of the gateway and go out the same way." Eze 46:2,8

⁴Then the man brought me by way of the north gate to the front of the temple. I looked and saw the glory of the LORD filling the temple of the LORD, and I fell facedown.

⁵The LORD said to me, "Son of man, look carefully, listen closely and give attention to everything I tell you concerning all the regulations regarding the temple of the LORD. Give attention to the entrance of the temple and all the exits of the sanctuary. ⁶Say to the rebellious house of Israel, 'This is what the Sovereign LORD says: Enough of your detestable practices, O house of Israel! ⁷In addition to all your other detestable practices, you brought foreigners uncircumcised in heart and flesh into my sanctuary, desecrating my temple while you offered me food, fat and blood, and you broke my covenant. ⁸Instead of carrying out your duty in regard to my holy things, you put others in charge of my sanctuary. ⁹This is what the Sovereign LORD says: No foreigner uncircumcised in heart and flesh is to enter my sanctuary, not even the foreigners who live among the Israelites. Lev 26:41; Joel 3:17

¹⁰" 'The Levites who went far from me when Israel went astray and who wandered from me after their idols must bear the consequences of their sin. ¹¹They may serve in my sanctuary, having charge of the gates of the temple and serving in it; they may slaughter the burnt offerings and sacrifices for the people and stand before the people and serve them. ¹²But because they served them in the presence of their idols and made the house of Israel fall into sin, therefore I have sworn with uplifted hand that they must bear the consequences of their sin, declares the Sovereign LORD. ¹³They are not to come near to serve me as priests or come near any of my holy things or my most holy offerings; they must bear the shame of their detestable practices. ¹⁴Yet I will put them in charge of the duties of the temple and all the work that is to be done in it. 2Ki 23:8

¹⁵" 'But the priests, who are Levites and descendants of Zadok and who faithfully carried out the duties of my sanctuary when the Israelites went astray from me, are to come near to minister before me; they are to stand before me to offer sacrifices of fat and blood, declares the Sovereign LORD. ¹⁶They alone are to enter my sanctuary; they alone are to come near my table to minister before me and perform my service. Nu 18:5; Eze 40:46

¹⁷" 'When they enter the gates of the inner court, they are to wear linen clothes; they must not wear any woolen garment while ministering at the gates of the inner court or inside the temple. ¹⁸They are to wear linen turbans on their

heads and linen undergarments around their waists. They must not wear anything that makes them perspire. ¹⁹When they go out into the outer court where the people are, they are to take off the clothes they have been ministering in and are to leave them in the sacred rooms, and put on other clothes, so that they do not consecrate the people by means of their garments. Eze 42:14; 46:20

²⁰"'They must not shave their heads or let their hair grow long, but they are to keep the hair of their heads trimmed. ²¹No priest is to drink wine when he enters the inner court. ²²They must not marry widows or divorced women; they may marry only virgins of Israelite descent or widows of priests. ²³They are to teach my people the difference between the holy and the common and show them how to distinguish between the unclean and the clean.

²⁴"'In any dispute, the priests are to serve as judges and decide it according to my ordinances. They are to keep my laws and my decrees for all my appointed feasts, and they are to keep my Sabbaths holy. Dt 17:8-9; 2Ch 19:8

²⁵"'A priest must not defile himself by going near a dead person; however, if the dead person was his father or mother, son or daughter, brother or unmarried sister,

then he may defile himself. ²⁶After he is cleansed, he must wait seven days. ²⁷On the day he goes into the inner court of the sanctuary to minister in the sanctuary, he is to offer a sin offering for himself, declares the Sovereign Lord.

²⁸"'I am to be the only inheritance the priests have. You are to give them no possession in Israel; I will be their possession. ²⁹They will eat the grain offerings, the sin offerings and the guilt offerings; and everything in Israel devoted^a to the Lord will belong to them. ³⁰The best of all the firstfruits and of all your special gifts will belong to the priests. You are to give them the first portion of your ground meal so that a blessing may rest on your household. ³¹The priests must not eat anything, bird or animal, found dead or torn by wild animals. Nu 18:20; Dt 10:9; 18:1-2

Division of the Land

45 "'When you allot the land as an inheritance, you are to present to the Lord a portion of the land as a sacred district, 25,000 cubits long and 20,000^b cubits wide; the entire area will be holy. ²Of this, a section 500 cubits square is to be for the sanctuary, with 50 cubits around it for open land. ³In the sacred district, measure off a section 25,000 cubits^c long and 10,000 cubits^d wide. In it

---

^a29 The Hebrew term refers to the irrevocable giving over of things or persons to the Lord.
^b1 Septuagint (see also verses 3 and 5 and 48:9); Hebrew *10,000*   ^c3 That is, about 7 miles (about 12 kilometers)   ^d3 That is, about 3 miles (about 5 kilometers)

will be the sanctuary, the Most Holy Place. ⁴It will be the sacred portion of the land for the priests, who minister in the sanctuary and who draw near to minister before the Lord. It will be a place for their houses as well as a holy place for the sanctuary. ⁵An area 25,000 cubits long and 10,000 cubits wide will belong to the Levites, who serve in the temple, as their possession for towns to live in.ᵃ

⁶" 'You are to give the city as its property an area 5,000 cubits wide and 25,000 cubits long, adjoining the sacred portion; it will belong to the whole house of Israel.

⁷" 'The prince will have the land bordering each side of the area formed by the sacred district and the property of the city. It will extend westward from the west side and eastward from the east side, running lengthwise from the western to the eastern border parallel to one of the tribal portions. ⁸This land will be his possession in Israel. And my princes will no longer oppress my people but will allow the house of Israel to possess the land according to their tribes.

⁹" 'This is what the Sovereign Lord says: You have gone far enough, O princes of Israel! Give up your violence and oppression and do what is just and right. Stop dispossessing my people, declares the Sovereign Lord. ¹⁰You are to use accurate scales, an accurate ephahᵇ and an accurate bath.ᶜ ¹¹The ephah and the bath are to be the same size, the bath containing a tenth of a homerᵈ and the ephah a tenth of a homer; the homer is to be the standard measure for both. ¹²The shekelᵉ is to consist of twenty gerahs. Twenty shekels plus twenty-five shekels plus fifteen shekels equal one mina.ᶠ   Jer 22:3

Offerings and Holy Days

¹³" 'This is the special gift you are to offer: a sixth of an ephah from each homer of wheat and a sixth of an ephah from each homer of barley. ¹⁴The prescribed portion of oil, measured by the bath, is a tenth of a bath from each cor (which consists of ten baths or one homer, for ten baths are equivalent to a homer). ¹⁵Also one sheep is to be taken from every flock of two hundred from the well-watered pastures of Israel. These will be used for the grain offerings, burnt offerings and fellowship offeringsᵍ to make atonement for the people, declares the Sovereign Lord. ¹⁶All the people of the land will participate in this special gift for the use of the prince in Israel. ¹⁷It will be the duty of the prince to provide the burnt offerings, grain offerings and drink offerings at the

---

ᵃ5 Septuagint; Hebrew temple; they will have as their possession 20 rooms   ᵇ10 An ephah was a dry measure.   ᶜ10 A bath was a liquid measure.   ᵈ11 A homer was a dry measure.   ᵉ12 A shekel weighed about 2/5 ounce (about 11.5 grams).   ᶠ12 That is, 60 shekels; the common mina was 50 shekels.   ᵍ15 Traditionally peace offerings; also in verse 17

festivals, the New Moons and the Sabbaths—at all the appointed feasts of the house of Israel. He will provide the sin offerings, grain offerings, burnt offerings and fellowship offerings to make atonement for the house of Israel.

18" 'This is what the Sovereign LORD says: In the first month on the first day you are to take a young bull without defect and purify the sanctuary. 19The priest is to take some of the blood of the sin offering and put it on the doorposts of the temple, on the four corners of the upper ledge of the altar and on the gateposts of the inner court. 20You are to do the same on the seventh day of the month for anyone who sins unintentionally or through ignorance; so you are to make atonement for the temple.   Lev 4:27; Eze 43:20

21" 'In the first month on the fourteenth day you are to observe the Passover, a feast lasting seven days, during which you shall eat bread made without yeast. 22On that day the prince is to provide a bull as a sin offering for himself and for all the people of the land. 23Every day during the seven days of the Feast he is to provide seven bulls and seven rams without defect as a burnt offering to the LORD, and a male goat for a sin offering. 24He is to provide as a grain offering an ephah for each bull

and an ephah for each ram, along with a hin*a* of oil for each ephah.

25" 'During the seven days of the Feast, which begins in the seventh month on the fifteenth day, he is to make the same provision for sin offerings, burnt offerings, grain offerings and oil.   Lev 23:34-43; Nu 29:12-38

46 " 'This is what the Sovereign LORD says: The gate of the inner court facing east is to be shut on the six working days, but on the Sabbath day and on the day of the New Moon it is to be opened. 2The prince is to enter from the outside through the portico of the gateway and stand by the gatepost. The priests are to sacrifice his burnt offering and his fellowship offerings.*b* He is to worship at the threshold of the gateway and then go out, but the gate will not be shut until evening. 3On the Sabbaths and New Moons the people of the land are to worship in the presence of the LORD at the entrance to that gateway. 4The burnt offering the prince brings to the LORD on the Sabbath day is to be six male lambs and a ram, all without defect. 5The grain offering given with the ram is to be an ephah,*c* and the grain offering with the lambs is to be as much as he pleases, along with a hin*a* of oil for each ephah. 6On the day of the New Moon he is to offer a young bull, six lambs and a ram, all with-

*a*24,5 That is, probably about 4 quarts (about 4 liters)   *b*2 Traditionally *peace offerings*; also in verse 12   *c*5 That is, probably about 3/5 bushel (about 22 liters)

out defect. ⁷He is to provide as a grain offering one ephah with the bull, one ephah with the ram, and with the lambs as much as he wants to give, along with a hin of oil with each ephah. ⁸When the prince enters, he is to go in through the portico of the gateway, and he is to come out the same way.   Eze 40:19; 44:3

⁹" 'When the people of the land come before the Lᴏʀᴅ at the appointed feasts, whoever enters by the north gate to worship is to go out the south gate; and whoever enters by the south gate is to go out the north gate. No one is to return through the gate by which he entered, but each is to go out the opposite gate. ¹⁰The prince is to be among them, going in when they go in and going out when they go out.   Ex 23:14; Ps 42:4

¹¹" 'At the festivals and the appointed feasts, the grain offering is to be an ephah with a bull, an ephah with a ram, and with the lambs as much as one pleases, along with a hin of oil for each ephah. ¹²When the prince provides a freewill offering to the Lᴏʀᴅ —whether a burnt offering or fellowship offerings—the gate facing east is to be opened for him. He shall offer his burnt offering or his fellowship offerings as he does on the Sabbath day. Then he shall go out, and after he has gone out, the gate will be shut.   Eze 45:17

¹³" 'Every day you are to provide a year-old lamb without defect for a burnt offering to the Lᴏʀᴅ; morning by morning you shall provide it. ¹⁴You are also to provide with it morning by morning a grain offering, consisting of a sixth of an ephah with a third of a hin of oil to moisten the flour. The presenting of this grain offering to the Lᴏʀᴅ is a lasting ordinance. ¹⁵So the lamb and the grain offering and the oil shall be provided morning by morning for a regular burnt offering.   Nu 28:5-6; Ex 29:38,42

¹⁶" 'This is what the Sovereign Lᴏʀᴅ says: If the prince makes a gift from his inheritance to one of his sons, it will also belong to his descendants; it is to be their property by inheritance. ¹⁷If, however, he makes a gift from his inheritance to one of his servants, the servant may keep it until the year of freedom; then it will revert to the prince. His inheritance belongs to his sons only; it is theirs. ¹⁸The prince must not take any of the inheritance of the people, driving them off their property. He is to give his sons their inheritance out of his own property, so that none of my people will be separated from his property.' "   Eze 45:8

¹⁹Then the man brought me through the entrance at the side of the gate to the sacred rooms facing north, which belonged to the priests, and showed me a place at the western end. ²⁰He said to me, "This is the place where the priests will cook the guilt offering and the sin offering and bake the grain of-

fering, to avoid bringing them into the outer court and consecrating the people." Zec 14:20

²¹He then brought me to the outer court and led me around to its four corners, and I saw in each corner another court. ²²In the four corners of the outer court were enclosed^a courts, forty cubits long and thirty cubits wide; each of the courts in the four corners was the same size. ²³Around the inside of each of the four courts was a ledge of stone, with places for fire built all around under the ledge. ²⁴He said to me, "These are the kitchens where those who minister at the temple will cook the sacrifices of the people."

The River From the Temple

47 The man brought me back to the entrance of the temple, and I saw water coming out from under the threshold of the temple toward the east (for the temple faced east). The water was coming down from under the south side of the temple, south of the altar. ²He then brought me out through the north gate and led me around the outside to the outer gate facing east, and the water was flowing from the south side.

³As the man went eastward with a measuring line in his hand, he measured off a thousand cubits^b and then led me through water that was ankle-deep. ⁴He measured off another thousand cubits and led me through water that was knee-deep. He measured off another thousand and led me through water that was up to the waist. ⁵He measured off another thousand, but now it was a river that I could not cross, because the water had risen and was deep enough to swim in—a river that no one could cross. ⁶He asked me, "Son of man, do you see this?"

Then he led me back to the bank of the river. ⁷When I arrived there, I saw a great number of trees on each side of the river. ⁸He said to me, "This water flows toward the eastern region and goes down into the Arabah,^c where it enters the Sea.^d When it empties into the Sea,^d the water there becomes fresh. ⁹Swarms of living creatures will live wherever the river flows. There will be large numbers of fish, because this water flows there and makes the salt water fresh; so where the river flows everything will live. ¹⁰Fishermen will stand along the shore; from En Gedi to En Eglaim there will be places for spreading nets. The fish will be of many kinds—like the fish of the Great Sea.^e ¹¹But the swamps and marshes will not become fresh; they will be left for salt. ¹²Fruit trees of all kinds will grow on both banks of the river.

---

^a22 The meaning of the Hebrew for this word is uncertain.   ^b3 That is, about 1,500 feet (about 450 meters)   ^c8 Or *the Jordan Valley*   ^d8 That is, the Dead Sea   ^e10 That is, the Mediterranean; also in verses 15, 19 and 20

Their leaves will not wither, nor will their fruit fail. Every month they will bear, because the water from the sanctuary flows to them. Their fruit will serve for food and their leaves for healing." Ps 1:3

The Boundaries of the Land

¹³This is what the Sovereign LORD says: "These are the boundaries by which you are to divide the land for an inheritance among the twelve tribes of Israel, with two portions for Joseph. ¹⁴You are to divide it equally among them. Because I swore with uplifted hand to give it to your forefathers, this land will become your inheritance.

¹⁵"This is to be the boundary of the land:

"On the north side it will run from the Great Sea by the Hethlon road past Lebo[a] Hamath to Zedad, ¹⁶Berothah[b] and Sibraim (which lies on the border between Damascus and Hamath), as far as Hazer Hatticon, which is on the border of Hauran. ¹⁷The boundary will extend from the sea to Hazar Enan,[c] along the northern border of Damascus, with the border of Hamath to the north. This will be the north boundary. ¹⁸"On the east side the boundary

will run between Hauran and Damascus, along the Jordan between Gilead and the land of Israel, to the eastern sea and as far as Tamar.[d] This will be the east boundary. ¹⁹"On the south side it will run from Tamar as far as the waters of Meribah Kadesh, then along the Wadi ⌊of Egypt⌋ to the Great Sea. This will be the south boundary. Eze 48:28 ²⁰"On the west side, the Great Sea will be the boundary to a point opposite Lebo[e] Hamath. This will be the west boundary. Nu 34:6; Eze 48:1

²¹"You are to distribute this land among yourselves according to the tribes of Israel. ²²You are to allot it as an inheritance for yourselves and for the aliens who have settled among you and who have children. You are to consider them as native-born Israelites; along with you they are to be allotted an inheritance among the tribes of Israel. ²³In whatever tribe the alien settles, there you are to give him his inheritance," declares the Sovereign LORD. Eph 3:6; Col 3:11

The Division of the Land

48 "These are the tribes, listed by name: At the northern frontier, Dan will have one por-

---

a 15 Or *past the entrance to*   b 15,16 See Septuagint and Ezekiel 48:1; Hebrew *road to go into Zedad,*
16*Hamath, Berothah*   c 17 Hebrew *Enon,* a variant of *Enan*   d 18 Septuagint and Syriac; Hebrew
Israel. You will measure to the eastern sea   e 20 Or *opposite the entrance to*

tion; it will follow the Hethlon road to Lebo[a] Hamath; Hazar Enan and the northern border of Damascus next to Hamath will be part of its border from the east side to the west side.   Ge 30:6; Eze 47:20

²"Asher will have one portion; it will border the territory of Dan from east to west.   Jos 19:24-31

³"Naphtali will have one portion; it will border the territory of Asher from east to west.

⁴"Manasseh will have one portion; it will border the territory of Naphtali from east to west.

⁵"Ephraim will have one portion; it will border the territory of Manasseh from east to west.

⁶"Reuben will have one portion; it will border the territory of Ephraim from east to west.

⁷"Judah will have one portion; it will border the territory of Reuben from east to west.   Jos 15:1-63

⁸"Bordering the territory of Judah from east to west will be the portion you are to present as a special gift. It will be 25,000 cubits[b] wide, and its length from east to west will equal one of the tribal portions; the sanctuary will be in the center of it.   ver 21

⁹"The special portion you are to offer to the LORD will be 25,000 cubits long and 10,000 cubits[c] wide. ¹⁰This will be the sacred portion for the priests. It will be 25,000 cubits long on the north side, 10,000 cubits wide on the west side, 10,000 cubits wide on the east side and 25,000 cubits long on the south side. In the center of it will be the sanctuary of the LORD. ¹¹This will be for the consecrated priests, the Zadokites, who were faithful in serving me and did not go astray as the Levites did when the Israelites went astray. ¹²It will be a special gift to them from the sacred portion of the land, a most holy portion, bordering the territory of the Levites.   Eze 44:15

¹³"Alongside the territory of the priests, the Levites will have an allotment 25,000 cubits long and 10,000 cubits wide. Its total length will be 25,000 cubits and its width 10,000 cubits. ¹⁴They must not sell or exchange any of it. This is the best of the land and must not pass into other hands, because it is holy to the LORD.   Lev 25:34; 27:10,28

¹⁵"The remaining area, 5,000 cubits wide and 25,000 cubits long, will be for the common use of the city, for houses and for pastureland. The city will be in the center of it ¹⁶and will have these measurements: the north side 4,500 cubits, the south side 4,500 cubits, the east side 4,500 cubits, and the west side 4,500 cubits. ¹⁷The pastureland for the city will be 250 cubits on the north, 250 cubits on the south, 250 cubits on the east, and 250

---

[a]1 Or *to the entrance to*   [b]8 That is, about 7 miles (about 12 kilometers)   [c]9 That is, about 3 miles (about 5 kilometers)

cubits on the west. ¹⁸What remains of the area, bordering on the sacred portion and running the length of it, will be 10,000 cubits on the east side and 10,000 cubits on the west side. Its produce will supply food for the workers of the city. ¹⁹The workers from the city who farm it will come from all the tribes of Israel. ²⁰The entire portion will be a square, 25,000 cubits on each side. As a special gift you will set aside the sacred portion, along with the property of the city.

²¹"What remains on both sides of the area formed by the sacred portion and the city property will belong to the prince. It will extend eastward from the 25,000 cubits of the sacred portion to the eastern border, and westward from the 25,000 cubits to the western border. Both these areas running the length of the tribal portions will belong to the prince, and the sacred portion with the temple sanctuary will be in the center of them. ²²So the property of the Levites and the property of the city will lie in the center of the area that belongs to the prince. The area belonging to the prince will lie between the border of Judah and the border of Benjamin.   Eze 45:7

²³"As for the rest of the tribes: Benjamin will have one portion; it will extend from the east side to the west side.   Jos 18:11-28

²⁴"Simeon will have one portion; it will border the territory of Benjamin from east to west.

²⁵"Issachar will have one portion; it will border the territory of Simeon from east to west.

²⁶"Zebulun will have one portion; it will border the territory of Issachar from east to west.

²⁷"Gad will have one portion; it will border the territory of Zebulun from east to west.   Jos 13:24-28

²⁸"The southern boundary of Gad will run south from Tamar to the waters of Meribah Kadesh, then along the Wadi ˌof Egyptˌ to the Great Sea.ᵃ   Eze 47:19

²⁹"This is the land you are to allot as an inheritance to the tribes of Israel, and these will be their portions," declares the Sovereign LORD.   Eze 45:1

The Gates of the City

³⁰"These will be the exits of the city: Beginning on the north side, which is 4,500 cubits long, ³¹the gates of the city will be named after the tribes of Israel. The three gates on the north side will be the gate of Reuben, the gate of Judah and the gate of Levi.

³²"On the east side, which is 4,500 cubits long, will be three gates: the gate of Joseph, the gate of Benjamin and the gate of Dan.

³³"On the south side, which measures 4,500 cubits, will be

ᵃ28 That is, the Mediterranean

three gates: the gate of Simeon, the gate of Issachar and the gate of Zebulun.

³⁴"On the west side, which is 4,500 cubits long, will be three gates: the gate of Gad, the gate of Asher and the gate of Naphtali.

³⁵"The distance all around will be 18,000 cubits.

"And the name of the city from that time on will be:

THE LORD IS THERE."

Daniel

Daniel's Training in Babylon

1 In the third year of the reign of Jehoiakim king of Judah, Nebuchadnezzar king of Babylon came to Jerusalem and besieged it. ²And the Lord delivered Jehoiakim king of Judah into his hand, along with some of the articles from the temple of God. These he carried off to the temple of his god in Babylonia*a* and put in the treasure house of his god. 2Ch 36:6; Jer 27:19-20

³Then the king ordered Ashpenaz, chief of his court officials, to bring in some of the Israelites from the royal family and the nobility— ⁴young men without any physical defect, handsome, showing aptitude for every kind of learning, well informed, quick to understand, and qualified to serve in the king's palace. He was to teach them the language and literature of the Babylonians.*b* ⁵The king assigned them a daily amount of food and wine from the king's table. They were to be trained for three years, and after that they were to enter the king's service.

⁶Among these were some from Judah: Daniel, Hananiah, Mishael and Azariah. ⁷The chief official gave them new names: to Daniel, the name Belteshazzar; to Hananiah, Shadrach; to Mishael, Meshach; and to Azariah, Abednego.

⁸But Daniel resolved not to defile himself with the royal food and wine, and he asked the chief official for permission not to defile himself this way. ⁹Now God had caused the official to show favor and sympathy to Daniel, ¹⁰but the official told Daniel, "I am afraid of my lord the king, who has assigned your*c* food and drink. Why should he see you looking worse than the other young men your age? The king would then have my head because of you." Ge 39:21

¹¹Daniel then said to the guard whom the chief official had appointed over Daniel, Hananiah, Mishael and Azariah, ¹²"Please test your servants for ten days: Give us nothing but vegetables to eat and water to drink. ¹³Then compare our appearance with that of the young men who eat the royal food, and treat your servants in accordance with what you see." ¹⁴So he agreed to this and tested them for ten days. Rev 2:10

¹⁵At the end of the ten days they looked healthier and better nourished than any of the young men who ate the royal food. ¹⁶So the guard took away their choice food

---

*a*2 Hebrew *Shinar*   *b*4 Or *Chaldeans*   *c*10 The Hebrew for *your* and *you* in this verse is plural.

and the wine they were to drink and gave them vegetables instead.

¹⁷To these four young men God gave knowledge and understanding of all kinds of literature and learning. And Daniel could understand visions and dreams of all kinds. Da 2:19,30; 7:1; 8:1

¹⁸At the end of the time set by the king to bring them in, the chief official presented them to Nebuchadnezzar. ¹⁹The king talked with them, and he found none equal to Daniel, Hananiah, Mishael and Azariah; so they entered the king's service. ²⁰In every matter of wisdom and understanding about which the king questioned them, he found them ten times better than all the magicians and enchanters in his whole kingdom.

²¹And Daniel remained there until the first year of King Cyrus.

Nebuchadnezzar's Dream

2 In the second year of his reign, Nebuchadnezzar had dreams; his mind was troubled and he could not sleep. ²So the king summoned the magicians, enchanters, sorcerers and astrologersᵃ to tell him what he had dreamed. When they came in and stood before the king, ³he said to them, "I have had a dream that troubles me and I want to know what it means.ᵇ"

⁴Then the astrologers answered the king in Aramaic,ᶜ "O king, live forever! Tell your servants the dream, and we will interpret it."

⁵The king replied to the astrologers, "This is what I have firmly decided: If you do not tell me what my dream was and interpret it, I will have you cut into pieces and your houses turned into piles of rubble. ⁶But if you tell me the dream and explain it, you will receive from me gifts and rewards and great honor. So tell me the dream and interpret it for me."

⁷Once more they replied, "Let the king tell his servants the dream, and we will interpret it."

⁸Then the king answered, "I am certain that you are trying to gain time, because you realize that this is what I have firmly decided: ⁹If you do not tell me the dream, there is just one penalty for you. You have conspired to tell me misleading and wicked things, hoping the situation will change. So then, tell me the dream, and I will know that you can interpret it for me."

¹⁰The astrologers answered the king, "There is not a man on earth who can do what the king asks! No king, however great and mighty, has ever asked such a thing of any magician or enchanter or astrologer. ¹¹What the king asks is too difficult. No one can reveal it to the king except the gods, and they do not live among men." Da 5:8,11

¹²This made the king so angry

ᵃ2 Or *Chaldeans*; also in verses 4, 5 and 10   ᵇ3 Or *was*   ᶜ4 The text from here through chapter 7 is in Aramaic.

and furious that he ordered the execution of all the wise men of Babylon. [13]So the decree was issued to put the wise men to death, and men were sent to look for Daniel and his friends to put them to death. Da 1:20; 3:13,19

[14]When Arioch, the commander of the king's guard, had gone out to put to death the wise men of Babylon, Daniel spoke to him with wisdom and tact. [15]He asked the king's officer, "Why did the king issue such a harsh decree?" Arioch then explained the matter to Daniel. [16]At this, Daniel went in to the king and asked for time, so that he might interpret the dream for him.

[17]Then Daniel returned to his house and explained the matter to his friends Hananiah, Mishael and Azariah. [18]He urged them to plead for mercy from the God of heaven concerning this mystery, so that he and his friends might not be executed with the rest of the wise men of Babylon. [19]During the night the mystery was revealed to Daniel in a vision. Then Daniel praised the God of heaven [20]and said: Job 33:15; Da 1:17

"Praise be to the name of God
　　for ever and ever; Ps 113:2
　wisdom and power are his.
[21]He changes times and seasons;
　　he sets up kings and deposes
　　them. Ps 75:6-7
He gives wisdom to the wise
　and knowledge to the
　　discerning. 2Sa 14:17

[22]He reveals deep and hidden
　　things; Da 5:11
　he knows what lies in
　　darkness, Ps 139:11-12
　and light dwells with him.
[23]I thank and praise you, O God
　　of my fathers: Ex 3:15
　You have given me wisdom
　　and power, Da 1:17
　you have made known to me
　　what we asked of you,
　you have made known to us
　　the dream of the king."

Daniel Interprets the Dream

[24]Then Daniel went to Arioch, whom the king had appointed to execute the wise men of Babylon, and said to him, "Do not execute the wise men of Babylon. Take me to the king, and I will interpret his dream for him." ver 14

[25]Arioch took Daniel to the king at once and said, "I have found a man among the exiles from Judah who can tell the king what his dream means." Da 1:6; 5:13; 6:13

[26]The king asked Daniel (also called Belteshazzar), "Are you able to tell me what I saw in my dream and interpret it?" Da 1:7

[27]Daniel replied, "No wise man, enchanter, magician or diviner can explain to the king the mystery he has asked about, [28]but there is a God in heaven who reveals mysteries. He has shown King Nebuchadnezzar what will happen in days to come. Your dream and the visions that passed through your

mind as you lay on your bed are these: Da 4:5; Am 4:13

²⁹"As you were lying there, O king, your mind turned to things to come, and the revealer of mysteries showed you what is going to happen. ³⁰As for me, this mystery has been revealed to me, not because I have greater wisdom than other living men, but so that you, O king, may know the interpretation and that you may understand what went through your mind.

³¹"You looked, O king, and there before you stood a large statue— an enormous, dazzling statue, awesome in appearance. ³²The head of the statue was made of pure gold, its chest and arms of silver, its belly and thighs of bronze, ³³its legs of iron, its feet partly of iron and partly of baked clay. ³⁴While you were watching, a rock was cut out, but not by human hands. It struck the statue on its feet of iron and clay and smashed them. ³⁵Then the iron, the clay, the bronze, the silver and the gold were broken to pieces at the same time and became like chaff on a threshing floor in the summer. The wind swept them away without leaving a trace. But the rock that struck the statue became a huge mountain and filled the whole earth. Hab 1:7; Zec 4:6

³⁶"This was the dream, and now we will interpret it to the king. ³⁷You, O king, are the king of kings. The God of heaven has giv-

en you dominion and power and might and glory; ³⁸in your hands he has placed mankind and the beasts of the field and the birds of the air. Wherever they live, he has made you ruler over them all. You are that head of gold. Da 4:21-22

³⁹"After you, another kingdom will rise, inferior to yours. Next, a third kingdom, one of bronze, will rule over the whole earth. ⁴⁰Finally, there will be a fourth kingdom, strong as iron—for iron breaks and smashes everything—and as iron breaks things to pieces, so it will crush and break all the others. ⁴¹Just as you saw that the feet and toes were partly of baked clay and partly of iron, so this will be a divided kingdom; yet it will have some of the strength of iron in it, even as you saw iron mixed with clay. ⁴²As the toes were partly iron and partly clay, so this kingdom will be partly strong and partly brittle. ⁴³And just as you saw the iron mixed with baked clay, so the people will be a mixture and will not remain united, any more than iron mixes with clay. Da 7:7,23

⁴⁴"In the time of those kings, the God of heaven will set up a kingdom that will never be destroyed, nor will it be left to another people. It will crush all those kingdoms and bring them to an end, but it will itself endure forever. ⁴⁵This is the meaning of the vision of the rock cut out of a mountain, but not by human hands—a rock that broke the iron, the bronze, the

clay, the silver and the gold to pieces.   Isa 9:7; Lk 1:33

"The great God has shown the king what will take place in the future. The dream is true and the interpretation is trustworthy."

⁴⁶Then King Nebuchadnezzar fell prostrate before Daniel and paid him honor and ordered that an offering and incense be presented to him. ⁴⁷The king said to Daniel, "Surely your God is the God of gods and the Lord of kings and a revealer of mysteries, for you were able to reveal this mystery."

⁴⁸Then the king placed Daniel in a high position and lavished many gifts on him. He made him ruler over the entire province of Babylon and placed him in charge of all its wise men. ⁴⁹Moreover, at Daniel's request the king appointed Shadrach, Meshach and Abednego administrators over the province of Babylon, while Daniel himself remained at the royal court.

The Image of Gold and the Fiery Furnace

3 King Nebuchadnezzar made an image of gold, ninety feet high and nine feet ᵃ wide, and set it up on the plain of Dura in the province of Babylon. ²He then summoned the satraps, prefects, governors, advisers, treasurers, judges, magistrates and all the other provincial officials to come to the dedication of the image he had set up. ³So the satraps, prefects, governors, advisers, treasurers, judges, magistrates and all the other provincial officials assembled for the dedication of the image that King Nebuchadnezzar had set up, and they stood before it.   Isa 46:6

⁴Then the herald loudly proclaimed, "This is what you are commanded to do, O peoples, nations and men of every language: ⁵As soon as you hear the sound of the horn, flute, zither, lyre, harp, pipes and all kinds of music, you must fall down and worship the image of gold that King Nebuchadnezzar has set up. ⁶Whoever does not fall down and worship will immediately be thrown into a blazing furnace."   Jer 29:22; Da 6:7

⁷Therefore, as soon as they heard the sound of the horn, flute, zither, lyre, harp and all kinds of music, all the peoples, nations and men of every language fell down and worshiped the image of gold that King Nebuchadnezzar had set up.

⁸At this time some astrologers ᵇ came forward and denounced the Jews. ⁹They said to King Nebuchadnezzar, "O king, live forever! ¹⁰You have issued a decree, O king, that everyone who hears the sound of the horn, flute, zither, lyre, harp, pipes and all kinds of music must fall down and worship

---

ᵃ1 Aramaic *sixty cubits high and six cubits wide* (about 27 meters high and 2.7 meters wide)   ᵇ8 Or *Chaldeans*

the image of gold, [11]and that whoever does not fall down and worship will be thrown into a blazing furnace. [12]But there are some Jews whom you have set over the affairs of the province of Babylon—Shadrach, Meshach and Abednego—who pay no attention to you, O king. They neither serve your gods nor worship the image of gold you have set up."   Da 2:49; 6:13

[13]Furious with rage, Nebuchadnezzar summoned Shadrach, Meshach and Abednego. So these men were brought before the king, [14]and Nebuchadnezzar said to them, "Is it true, Shadrach, Meshach and Abednego, that you do not serve my gods or worship the image of gold I have set up? [15]Now when you hear the sound of the horn, flute, zither, lyre, harp, pipes and all kinds of music, if you are ready to fall down and worship the image I made, very good. But if you do not worship it, you will be thrown immediately into a blazing furnace. Then what god will be able to rescue you from my hand?"

[16]Shadrach, Meshach and Abednego replied to the king, "O Nebuchadnezzar, we do not need to defend ourselves before you in this matter. [17]If we are thrown into the blazing furnace, the God we serve is able to save us from it, and he will rescue us from your hand, O king. [18]But even if he does not, we want you to know, O king, that we will not serve your gods or wor-ship the image of gold you have set up."   Ps 27:1-2

[19]Then Nebuchadnezzar was furious with Shadrach, Meshach and Abednego, and his attitude toward them changed. He ordered the furnace heated seven times hotter than usual [20]and commanded some of the strongest soldiers in his army to tie up Shadrach, Meshach and Abednego and throw them into the blazing furnace. [21]So these men, wearing their robes, trousers, turbans and other clothes, were bound and thrown into the blazing furnace. [22]The king's command was so urgent and the furnace so hot that the flames of the fire killed the soldiers who took up Shadrach, Meshach and Abednego, [23]and these three men, firmly tied, fell into the blazing furnace.   Lev 26:18-28; Da 1:7

[24]Then King Nebuchadnezzar leaped to his feet in amazement and asked his advisers, "Weren't there three men that we tied up and threw into the fire?"

They replied, "Certainly, O king."

[25]He said, "Look! I see four men walking around in the fire, unbound and unharmed, and the fourth looks like a son of the gods."

[26]Nebuchadnezzar then approached the opening of the blazing furnace and shouted, "Shadrach, Meshach and Abednego, servants of the Most High God, come out! Come here!"   Da 4:2,34

So Shadrach, Meshach and Abednego came out of the fire, [27]and the satraps, prefects, governors and royal advisers crowded around them. They saw that the fire had not harmed their bodies, nor was a hair of their heads singed; their robes were not scorched, and there was no smell of fire on them.   Heb 11:32-34

[28]Then Nebuchadnezzar said, "Praise be to the God of Shadrach, Meshach and Abednego, who has sent his angel and rescued his servants! They trusted in him and defied the king's command and were willing to give up their lives rather than serve or worship any god except their own God. [29]Therefore I decree that the people of any nation or language who say anything against the God of Shadrach, Meshach and Abednego be cut into pieces and their houses be turned into piles of rubble, for no other god can save in this way."   Da 6:27

[30]Then the king promoted Shadrach, Meshach and Abednego in the province of Babylon.   Da 2:49

Nebuchadnezzar's Dream of a Tree

4 King Nebuchadnezzar,

To the peoples, nations and men of every language, who live in all the world:

May you prosper greatly!

[2]It is my pleasure to tell you about the miraculous signs and wonders that the Most High God has performed for me.   Ps 74:9; Da 3:26

[3]How great are his signs,
   how mighty his
      wonders!   Da 6:27
His kingdom is an eternal
      kingdom;
   his dominion endures
      from generation to
      generation.   Da 2:44

[4]I, Nebuchadnezzar, was at home in my palace, contented and prosperous. [5]I had a dream that made me afraid. As I was lying in my bed, the images and visions that passed through my mind terrified me. [6]So I commanded that all the wise men of Babylon be brought before me to interpret the dream for me. [7]When the magicians, enchanters, astrologers[a] and diviners came, I told them the dream, but they could not interpret it for me. [8]Finally, Daniel came into my presence and I told him the dream. (He is called Belteshazzar, after the name of my god, and the spirit of the holy gods is in him.)   Da 2:1; 5:11,14

[9]I said, "Belteshazzar, chief of the magicians, I know that the spirit of the holy gods is in

a 7 Or Chaldeans

you, and no mystery is too difficult for you. Here is my dream; interpret it for me. ¹⁰These are the visions I saw while lying in my bed: I looked, and there before me stood a tree in the middle of the land. Its height was enormous. ¹¹The tree grew large and strong and its top touched the sky; it was visible to the ends of the earth. ¹²Its leaves were beautiful, its fruit abundant, and on it was food for all. Under it the beasts of the field found shelter, and the birds of the air lived in its branches; from it every creature was fed.   Da 2:48; 5:11-12

¹³"In the visions I saw while lying in my bed, I looked, and there before me was a messenger,ᵃ a holy one, coming down from heaven. ¹⁴He called in a loud voice: 'Cut down the tree and trim off its branches; strip off its leaves and scatter its fruit. Let the animals flee from under it and the birds from its branches. ¹⁵But let the stump and its roots, bound with iron and bronze, remain in the ground, in the grass of the field.

" 'Let him be drenched with the dew of heaven, and let him live with the animals among the plants of the earth. ¹⁶Let his mind be changed from that of a man and let him be given the mind of an animal, till seven timesᵇ pass by for him.   ver 23,32

¹⁷" 'The decision is announced by messengers, the holy ones declare the verdict, so that the living may know that the Most High is sovereign over the kingdoms of men and gives them to anyone he wishes and sets over them the lowliest of men.'

¹⁸"This is the dream that I, King Nebuchadnezzar, had. Now, Belteshazzar, tell me what it means, for none of the wise men in my kingdom can interpret it for me. But you can, because the spirit of the holy gods is in you."   Ge 41:8

Daniel Interprets the Dream

¹⁹Then Daniel (also called Belteshazzar) was greatly perplexed for a time, and his thoughts terrified him. So the king said, "Belteshazzar, do not let the dream or its meaning alarm you."   Da 7:15,28

Belteshazzar answered, "My lord, if only the dream applied to your enemies and its meaning to your adversaries! ²⁰The tree you saw, which grew large and strong, with its top touching the sky, visible to the whole earth, ²¹with

---

ᵃ 13 Or watchman; also in verses 17 and 23   ᵇ 16 Or years; also in verses 23, 25 and 32

beautiful leaves and abundant fruit, providing food for all, giving shelter to the beasts of the field, and having nesting places in its branches for the birds of the air — ²²you, O king, are that tree! You have become great and strong; your greatness has grown until it reaches the sky, and your dominion extends to distant parts of the earth.   Jer 27:7

²³"You, O king, saw a messenger, a holy one, coming down from heaven and saying, 'Cut down the tree and destroy it, but leave the stump, bound with iron and bronze, in the grass of the field, while its roots remain in the ground. Let him be drenched with the dew of heaven; let him live like the wild animals, until seven times pass by for him.'

²⁴"This is the interpretation, O king, and this is the decree the Most High has issued against my lord the king: ²⁵You will be driven away from people and will live with the wild animals; you will eat grass like cattle and be drenched with the dew of heaven. Seven times will pass by for you until you acknowledge that the Most High is sovereign over the kingdoms of men and gives them to anyone he wishes. ²⁶The command to leave the stump of

the tree with its roots means that your kingdom will be restored to you when you acknowledge that Heaven rules. ²⁷Therefore, O king, be pleased to accept my advice: Renounce your sins by doing what is right, and your wickedness by being kind to the oppressed. It may be that then your prosperity will continue."   Isa 55:6-7; Eze 18:22

The Dream Is Fulfilled

²⁸All this happened to King Nebuchadnezzar. ²⁹Twelve months later, as the king was walking on the roof of the royal palace of Babylon, ³⁰he said, "Is not this the great Babylon I have built as the royal residence, by my mighty power and for the glory of my majesty?"   Da 5:20; Hab 2:4

³¹The words were still on his lips when a voice came from heaven, "This is what is decreed for you, King Nebuchadnezzar: Your royal authority has been taken from you. ³²You will be driven away from people and will live with the wild animals; you will eat grass like cattle. Seven times will pass by for you until you acknowledge that the Most High is sovereign over the kingdoms of men and gives them to anyone he wishes."   2Sa 22:28

³³Immediately what had

been said about Nebuchadnezzar was fulfilled. He was driven away from people and ate grass like cattle. His body was drenched with the dew of heaven until his hair grew like the feathers of an eagle and his nails like the claws of a bird. Da 5:20-21

³⁴At the end of that time, I, Nebuchadnezzar, raised my eyes toward heaven, and my sanity was restored. Then I praised the Most High; I honored and glorified him who lives forever. Da 12:7; Rev 4:10

His dominion is an eternal
    dominion;
his kingdom endures from
    generation to generation.
³⁵All the peoples of the earth
are regarded as nothing.
He does as he pleases Ps 115:3
    with the powers of heaven
    and the peoples of the earth.
No one can hold back his hand
    or say to him: "What have
    you done?"

³⁶At the same time that my sanity was restored, my honor and splendor were returned to me for the glory of my kingdom. My advisers and nobles sought me out, and I was restored to my throne and became even greater than before. ³⁷Now I, Nebuchadnez-

zar, praise and exalt and glorify the King of heaven, because everything he does is right and all his ways are just. And those who walk in pride he is able to humble.

The Writing on the Wall

5 King Belshazzar gave a great banquet for a thousand of his nobles and drank wine with them. ²While Belshazzar was drinking his wine, he gave orders to bring in the gold and silver goblets that Nebuchadnezzar his father[a] had taken from the temple in Jerusalem, so that the king and his nobles, his wives and his concubines might drink from them. ³So they brought in the gold goblets that had been taken from the temple of God in Jerusalem, and the king and his nobles, his wives and his concubines drank from them. ⁴As they drank the wine, they praised the gods of gold and silver, of bronze, iron, wood and stone.

⁵Suddenly the fingers of a human hand appeared and wrote on the plaster of the wall, near the lampstand in the royal palace. The king watched the hand as it wrote. ⁶His face turned pale and he was so frightened that his knees knocked together and his legs gave way. Eze 7:17; Da 4:5

⁷The king called out for the enchanters, astrologers[b] and diviners to be brought and said to these

---

a2 Or ancestor; or predecessor; also in verses 11, 13 and 18   b7 Or Chaldeans; also in verse 11

wise men of Babylon, "Whoever reads this writing and tells me what it means will be clothed in purple and have a gold chain placed around his neck, and he will be made the third highest ruler in the kingdom." Da 2:5-6,48

8Then all the king's wise men came in, but they could not read the writing or tell the king what it meant. **9**So King Belshazzar became even more terrified and his face grew more pale. His nobles were baffled. Isa 21:4

10The queen,[a] hearing the voices of the king and his nobles, came into the banquet hall. "O king, live forever!" she said. "Don't be alarmed! Don't look so pale! **11**There is a man in your kingdom who has the spirit of the holy gods in him. In the time of your father he was found to have insight and intelligence and wisdom like that of the gods. King Nebuchadnezzar your father—your father the king, I say—appointed him chief of the magicians, enchanters, astrologers and diviners. **12**This man Daniel, whom the king called Belteshazzar, was found to have a keen mind and knowledge and understanding, and also the ability to interpret dreams, explain riddles and solve difficult problems. Call for Daniel, and he will tell you what the writing means." Da 1:7

13So Daniel was brought before the king, and the king said to him,

"Are you Daniel, one of the exiles my father the king brought from Judah? **14**I have heard that the spirit of the gods is in you and that you have insight, intelligence and outstanding wisdom. **15**The wise men and enchanters were brought before me to read this writing and tell me what it means, but they could not explain it. **16**Now I have heard that you are able to give interpretations and to solve difficult problems. If you can read this writing and tell me what it means, you will be clothed in purple and have a gold chain placed around your neck, and you will be made the third highest ruler in the kingdom." Da 6:13

17Then Daniel answered the king, "You may keep your gifts for yourself and give your rewards to someone else. Nevertheless, I will read the writing for the king and tell him what it means. 2Ki 5:16

18"O king, the Most High God gave your father Nebuchadnezzar sovereignty and greatness and glory and splendor. **19**Because of the high position he gave him, all the peoples and nations and men of every language dreaded and feared him. Those the king wanted to put to death, he put to death; those he wanted to spare, he spared; those he wanted to promote, he promoted; and those he wanted to humble, he humbled. **20**But when his heart became arrogant and hard-

---

[a] 10 Or *queen mother*

ened with pride, he was deposed from his royal throne and stripped of his glory. ²¹He was driven away from people and given the mind of an animal; he lived with the wild donkeys and ate grass like cattle; and his body was drenched with the dew of heaven, until he acknowledged that the Most High God is sovereign over the kingdoms of men and sets over them anyone he wishes. Da 4:16-17,35

²²"But you his son,ª O Belshazzar, have not humbled yourself, though you knew all this. ²³Instead, you have set yourself up against the Lord of heaven. You had the goblets from his temple brought to you, and you and your nobles, your wives and your concubines drank wine from them. You praised the gods of silver and gold, of bronze, iron, wood and stone, which cannot see or hear or understand. But you did not honor the God who holds in his hand your life and all your ways. ²⁴Therefore he sent the hand that wrote the inscription. Ps 115:4-8

²⁵"This is the inscription that was written:

MENE, MENE, TEKEL, PARSIN ᵇ

²⁶"This is what these words mean:

Mene ᶜ: God has numbered the days of

your reign and brought it to an end.
²⁷*Tekel* ᵈ: You have been weighed on the scales and found wanting. Ps 62:9
²⁸*Peres* ᵉ: Your kingdom is divided and given to the Medes and Persians." Da 6:28

²⁹Then at Belshazzar's command, Daniel was clothed in purple, a gold chain was placed around his neck, and he was proclaimed the third highest ruler in the kingdom. Da 2:6

³⁰That very night Belshazzar, king of the Babylonians,ᶠ was slain, ³¹and Darius the Mede took over the kingdom, at the age of sixty-two. Da 6:1; 9:1

Daniel in the Den of Lions

6 It pleased Darius to appoint 120 satraps to rule throughout the kingdom, ²with three administrators over them, one of whom was Daniel. The satraps were made accountable to them so that the king might not suffer loss. ³Now Daniel so distinguished himself among the administrators and the satraps by his exceptional qualities that the king planned to set him over the whole kingdom. ⁴At this, the administrators and the satraps tried to find grounds for

---

ª22 Or *descendant*; or *successor*   ᵇ25 Aramaic UPARSIN (that is, AND PARSIN)   ᶜ26 *Mene* can mean *numbered* or *mina* (a unit of money).   ᵈ27 *Tekel* can mean *weighed* or *shekel.*   ᵉ28 *Peres* (the singular of *Parsin*) can mean *divided* or *Persia* or *a half mina* or *a half shekel.*   ᶠ30 Or *Chaldeans*

charges against Daniel in his conduct of government affairs, but they were unable to do so. They could find no corruption in him, because he was trustworthy and neither corrupt nor negligent. [5]Finally these men said, "We will never find any basis for charges against this man Daniel unless it has something to do with the law of his God." Est 10:3; Da 5:12-14

[6]So the administrators and the satraps went as a group to the king and said: "O King Darius, live forever! [7]The royal administrators, prefects, satraps, advisers and governors have all agreed that the king should issue an edict and enforce the decree that anyone who prays to any god or man during the next thirty days, except to you, O king, shall be thrown into the lions' den. [8]Now, O king, issue the decree and put it in writing so that it cannot be altered—in accordance with the laws of the Medes and Persians, which cannot be repealed." [9]So King Darius put the decree in writing. Ps 59:3; Da 3:6

[10]Now when Daniel learned that the decree had been published, he went home to his upstairs room where the windows opened toward Jerusalem. Three times a day he got down on his knees and prayed, giving thanks to his God, just as he had done before. [11]Then these men went as a group and found Daniel praying and asking God for help. [12]So they went to the king and spoke to him about his royal decree: "Did you not publish a decree that during the next thirty days anyone who prays to any god or man except to you, O king, would be thrown into the lions' den?" Ps 95:6; Ac 5:29

The king answered, "The decree stands—in accordance with the laws of the Medes and Persians, which cannot be repealed."

[13]Then they said to the king, "Daniel, who is one of the exiles from Judah, pays no attention to you, O king, or to the decree you put in writing. He still prays three times a day." [14]When the king heard this, he was greatly distressed; he was determined to rescue Daniel and made every effort until sundown to save him. Est 3:8

[15]Then the men went as a group to the king and said to him, "Remember, O king, that according to the law of the Medes and Persians no decree or edict that the king issues can be changed." Est 8:8

[16]So the king gave the order, and they brought Daniel and threw him into the lions' den. The king said to Daniel, "May your God, whom you serve continually, rescue you!" Ps 37:39-40

[17]A stone was brought and placed over the mouth of the den, and the king sealed it with his own signet ring and with the rings of his nobles, so that Daniel's situation might not be changed. [18]Then the king returned to his palace and spent the night without eating and without any entertainment being

brought to him. And he could not sleep.   Mt 27:66

¹⁹At the first light of dawn, the king got up and hurried to the lions' den. ²⁰When he came near the den, he called to Daniel in an anguished voice, "Daniel, servant of the living God, has your God, whom you serve continually, been able to rescue you from the lions?"

²¹Daniel answered, "O king, live forever! ²²My God sent his angel, and he shut the mouths of the lions. They have not hurt me, because I was found innocent in his sight. Nor have I ever done any wrong before you, O king."

²³The king was overjoyed and gave orders to lift Daniel out of the den. And when Daniel was lifted from the den, no wound was found on him, because he had trusted in his God.   1Ch 5:20; Da 3:27

²⁴At the king's command, the men who had falsely accused Daniel were brought in and thrown into the lions' den, along with their wives and children. And before they reached the floor of the den, the lions overpowered them and crushed all their bones.   Dt 24:16

²⁵Then King Darius wrote to all the peoples, nations and men of every language throughout the land:

"May you prosper greatly!

²⁶"I issue a decree that in every part of my kingdom

people must fear and reverence the God of Daniel.

"For he is the living God
and he endures forever;
his kingdom will not be
    destroyed,
his dominion will never end.
²⁷He rescues and he saves;
he performs signs and
    wonders   Da 4:3
in the heavens and on the
    earth.
He has rescued Daniel
from the power of the lions."

²⁸So Daniel prospered during the reign of Darius and the reign of Cyrus*a* the Persian.   Da 1:21

Daniel's Dream of Four Beasts

7 In the first year of Belshazzar king of Babylon, Daniel had a dream, and visions passed through his mind as he was lying on his bed. He wrote down the substance of his dream.   Da 1:17; 5:1

²Daniel said: "In my vision at night I looked, and there before me were the four winds of heaven churning up the great sea. ³Four great beasts, each different from the others, came up out of the sea.

⁴"The first was like a lion, and it had the wings of an eagle. I watched until its wings were torn off and it was lifted from the ground so that it stood on two feet like a man, and the heart of a man was given to it.   Jer 4:7; Eze 17:3

a 28 Or *Darius, that is, the reign of Cyrus*

⁵"And there before me was a second beast, which looked like a bear. It was raised up on one of its sides, and it had three ribs in its mouth between its teeth. It was told, 'Get up and eat your fill of flesh!'   Da 2:39

⁶"After that, I looked, and there before me was another beast, one that looked like a leopard. And on its back it had four wings like those of a bird. This beast had four heads, and it was given authority to rule.   Rev 13:2

⁷"After that, in my vision at night I looked, and there before me was a fourth beast—terrifying and frightening and very powerful. It had large iron teeth; it crushed and devoured its victims and trampled underfoot whatever was left. It was different from all the former beasts, and it had ten horns.

⁸"While I was thinking about the horns, there before me was another horn, a little one, which came up among them; and three of the first horns were uprooted before it. This horn had eyes like the eyes of a man and a mouth that spoke boastfully.   Rev 13:5-6

⁹"As I looked,

"thrones were set in place,
    and the Ancient of Days took
      his seat.   Mt 19:28
His clothing was as white as
      snow;   Mt 28:3
    the hair of his head was
      white like wool.   Rev 1:14

His throne was flaming with
      fire,
    and its wheels were all
      ablaze.   Eze 1:15
¹⁰A river of fire was flowing,
    coming out from before him.
Thousands upon thousands
      attended him;
    ten thousand times ten
      thousand stood before
      him.
The court was seated,
    and the books were opened.

¹¹"Then I continued to watch because of the boastful words the horn was speaking. I kept looking until the beast was slain and its body destroyed and thrown into the blazing fire. ¹²(The other beasts had been stripped of their authority, but were allowed to live for a period of time.)   Rev 19:20

¹³"In my vision at night I looked, and there before me was one like a son of man, coming with the clouds of heaven. He approached the Ancient of Days and was led into his presence. ¹⁴He was given authority, glory and sovereign power; all peoples, nations and men of every language worshiped him. His dominion is an everlasting dominion that will not pass away, and his kingdom is one that will never be destroyed.   Heb 12:28

The Interpretation of the Dream

¹⁵"I, Daniel, was troubled in spirit, and the visions that passed

through my mind disturbed me. [16]I approached one of those standing there and asked him the true meaning of all this. Da 4:19

"So he told me and gave me the interpretation of these things: [17]'The four great beasts are four kingdoms that will rise from the earth. [18]But the saints of the Most High will receive the kingdom and will possess it forever—yes, for ever and ever.' Isa 60:12-14; Rev 2:26

[19]"Then I wanted to know the true meaning of the fourth beast, which was different from all the others and most terrifying, with its iron teeth and bronze claws—the beast that crushed and devoured its victims and trampled underfoot whatever was left. [20]I also wanted to know about the ten horns on its head and about the other horn that came up, before which three of them fell—the horn that looked more imposing than the others and that had eyes and a mouth that spoke boastfully. [21]As I watched, this horn was waging war against the saints and defeating them, [22]until the Ancient of Days came and pronounced judgment in favor of the saints of the Most High, and the time came when they possessed the kingdom. Rev 13:7

[23]"He gave me this explanation: 'The fourth beast is a fourth kingdom that will appear on earth. It will be different from all the other kingdoms and will devour the whole earth, trampling it down and crushing it. [24]The ten horns are ten kings who will come from this kingdom. After them another king will arise, different from the earlier ones; he will subdue three kings. [25]He will speak against the Most High and oppress his saints and try to change the set times and the laws. The saints will be handed over to him for a time, times and half a time.[a] Da 2:21; Rev 17:12

[26]" 'But the court will sit, and his power will be taken away and completely destroyed forever [27]Then the sovereignty, power and greatness of the kingdoms under the whole heaven will be handed over to the saints, the people of the Most High. His kingdom will be an everlasting kingdom, and all rulers will worship and obey him.'

[28]"This is the end of the matter I, Daniel, was deeply troubled by my thoughts, and my face turned pale, but I kept the matter to myself." Da 4:19

Daniel's Vision of a Ram and a Goat

8 In the third year of King Belshazzar's reign, I, Daniel, had a vision, after the one that had already appeared to me. [2]In my vision I saw myself in the citadel of Susa in the province of Elam; in the vision I was beside the Ulai Canal. [3]I looked up, and there before me was a ram with two horns,

---

[a] 25 Or for a year, two years and half a year

standing beside the canal, and the horns were long. One of the horns was longer than the other but grew up later. [4]I watched the ram as he charged toward the west and the north and the south. No animal could stand against him, and none could rescue from his power. He did as he pleased and became great.   Da 11:3,16

[5]As I was thinking about this, suddenly a goat with a prominent horn between his eyes came from the west, crossing the whole earth without touching the ground. [6]He came toward the two-horned ram I had seen standing beside the canal and charged at him in great rage. [7]I saw him attack the ram furiously, striking the ram and shattering his two horns. The ram was powerless to stand against him; the goat knocked him to the ground and trampled on him, and none could rescue the ram from his power. [8]The goat became very great, but at the height of his power his large horn was broken off, and in its place four prominent horns grew up toward the four winds of heaven.   2Ch 26:16-21; Rev 7:1

[9]Out of one of them came another horn, which started small but grew in power to the south and to the east and toward the Beautiful Land. [10]It grew until it reached the host of the heavens, and it threw some of the starry host down to the earth and trampled on them.

[11]It set itself up to be as great as the Prince of the host; it took away the daily sacrifice from him, and the place of his sanctuary was brought low. [12]Because of rebellion, the host of the saints[a] and the daily sacrifice were given over to it. It prospered in everything it did, and truth was thrown to the ground.

[13]Then I heard a holy one speaking, and another holy one said to him, "How long will it take for the vision to be fulfilled—the vision concerning the daily sacrifice, the rebellion that causes desolation, and the surrender of the sanctuary and of the host that will be trampled underfoot?"   Da 4:23; 12:6

[14]He said to me, "It will take 2,300 evenings and mornings; then the sanctuary will be reconsecrated."   Da 12:11-12

The Interpretation of the Vision

[15]While I, Daniel, was watching the vision and trying to understand it, there before me stood one who looked like a man. [16]And I heard a man's voice from the Ulai calling, "Gabriel, tell this man the meaning of the vision."   Da 10:16-18

[17]As he came near the place where I was standing, I was terrified and fell prostrate. "Son of man," he said to me, "understand that the vision concerns the time of the end."   Eze 1:28; Rev 1:17

[18]While he was speaking to me,

---

[a] 12 Or rebellion, the armies

I was in a deep sleep, with my face to the ground. Then he touched me and raised me to my feet.

¹⁹He said: "I am going to tell you what will happen later in the time of wrath, because the vision concerns the appointed time of the end.ᵃ ²⁰The two-horned ram that you saw represents the kings of Media and Persia. ²¹The shaggy goat is the king of Greece, and the large horn between his eyes is the first king. ²²The four horns that replaced the one that was broken off represent four kingdoms that will emerge from his nation but will not have the same power.   Hab 2:3

²³"In the latter part of their reign, when rebels have become completely wicked, a stern-faced king, a master of intrigue, will arise. ²⁴He will become very strong, but not by his own power. He will cause astounding devastation and will succeed in whatever he does. He will destroy the mighty men and the holy people. ²⁵He will cause deceit to prosper, and he will consider himself superior. When they feel secure, he will destroy many and take his stand against the Prince of princes. Yet he will be destroyed, but not by human power.   Da 2:34; 11:21,36

²⁶"The vision of the evenings and mornings that has been given you is true, but seal up the vision, for it concerns the distant future."

²⁷I, Daniel, was exhausted and lay ill for several days. Then I got up and went about the king's business. I was appalled by the vision; it was beyond understanding.

Daniel's Prayer

9 In the first year of Darius son of Xerxesᵇ (a Mede by descent), who was made ruler over the Babylonianᶜ kingdom— ²in the first year of his reign, I, Daniel, understood from the Scriptures, according to the word of the Lord given to Jeremiah the prophet, that the desolation of Jerusalem would last seventy years. ³So I turned to the Lord God and pleaded with him in prayer and petition, in fasting, and in sackcloth and ashes.

⁴I prayed to the Lord my God and confessed:

"O Lord, the great and awesome God, who keeps his covenant of love with all who love him and obey his commands, ⁵we have sinned and done wrong. We have been wicked and have rebelled; we have turned away from your commands and laws. ⁶We have not listened to your servants the prophets, who spoke in your name to our kings, our princes and our fathers, and to all the people of the land.   2Ch 36:16; Ps 106:6

⁷"Lord, you are righteous, but this day we are covered

ᵃ19 Or *because the end will be at the appointed time*   ᵇ1 Hebrew *Ahasuerus*   ᶜ1 Or *Chaldean*

with shame—the men of Judah and people of Jerusalem and all Israel, both near and far, in all the countries where you have scattered us because of our unfaithfulness to you. [8]O LORD, we and our kings, our princes and our fathers are covered with shame because we have sinned against you. [9]The Lord our God is merciful and forgiving, even though we have rebelled against him; [10]we have not obeyed the LORD our God or kept the laws he gave us through his servants the prophets. [11]All Israel has transgressed your law and turned away, refusing to obey you.   2Ki 17:13-15; Ne 9:17

"Therefore the curses and sworn judgments written in the Law of Moses, the servant of God, have been poured out on us, because we have sinned against you. [12]You have fulfilled the words spoken against us and against our rulers by bringing upon us great disaster. Under the whole heaven nothing has ever been done like what has been done to Jerusalem. [13]Just as it is written in the Law of Moses, all this disaster has come upon us, yet we have not sought the favor of the LORD our God by turning from our sins and giving attention to your truth. [14]The

LORD did not hesitate to bring the disaster upon us, for the LORD our God is righteous in everything he does; yet we have not obeyed him.   Isa 1:4-6

[15]"Now, O Lord our God, who brought your people out of Egypt with a mighty hand and who made for yourself a name that endures to this day, we have sinned, we have done wrong. [16]O Lord, in keeping with all your righteous acts, turn away your anger and your wrath from Jerusalem, your city, your holy hill. Our sins and the iniquities of our fathers have made Jerusalem and your people an object of scorn to all those around us.   Ps 31:1; Zec 8:3

[17]"Now, our God, hear the prayers and petitions of your servant. For your sake, O Lord, look with favor on your desolate sanctuary. [18]Give ear, O God, and hear; open your eyes and see the desolation of the city that bears your Name. We do not make requests of you because we are righteous, but because of your great mercy. [19]O Lord, listen! O Lord, forgive! O Lord, hear and act! For your sake, O my God, do not delay, because your city and your people bear your Name."

The Seventy "Sevens"

[20]While I was speaking and

praying, confessing my sin and the sin of my people Israel and making my request to the LORD my God for his holy hill— [21]while I was still in prayer, Gabriel, the man I had seen in the earlier vision, came to me in swift flight about the time of the evening sacrifice. [22]He instructed me and said to me, "Daniel, I have now come to give you insight and understanding. [23]As soon as you began to pray, an answer was given, which I have come to tell you, for you are highly esteemed. Therefore, consider the message and understand the vision:

[24]"Seventy 'sevens'[a] are decreed for your people and your holy city to finish[b] transgression, to put an end to sin, to atone for wickedness, to bring in everlasting righteousness, to seal up vision and prophecy and to anoint the most holy.[c]   Isa 53:10; 56:1

[25]"Know and understand this: From the issuing of the decree[d] to restore and rebuild Jerusalem until the Anointed One,[e] the ruler, comes, there will be seven 'sevens,' and sixty-two 'sevens.' It will be rebuilt with streets and a trench, but in times of trouble. [26]After the sixty-two 'sevens,' the Anointed One will be cut off and will have nothing.[f] The people of the ruler who will come will de-stroy the city and the sanctuary. The end will come like a flood: War will continue until the end, and desolations have been decreed. [27]He will confirm a covenant with many for one 'seven.'[g] In the middle of the 'seven'[g] he will put an end to sacrifice and offering. And on a wing ˌof the templeˌ he will set up an abomination that causes desolation, until the end that is decreed is poured out on him.[h]"[i]   Isa 10:22; 53:8

Daniel's Vision of a Man

10 In the third year of Cyrus king of Persia, a revelation was given to Daniel (who was called Belteshazzar). Its message was true and it concerned a great war.[j] The understanding of the message came to him in a vision.

[2]At that time I, Daniel, mourned for three weeks. [3]I ate no choice food; no meat or wine touched my lips; and I used no lotions at all until the three weeks were over.

[4]On the twenty-fourth day of the first month, as I was standing on the bank of the great river, the Tigris, [5]I looked up and there before me was a man dressed in linen, with a belt of the finest gold around his waist. [6]His body was like chrysolite, his face like lightning, his eyes like flaming torches,

---

[a]24 Or 'weeks'; also in verses 25 and 26   [b]24 Or restrain   [c]24 Or Most Holy Place; or most holy One   [d]25 Or word   [e]25 Or an anointed one; also in verse 26   [f]26 Or off and will have no one; or off, but not for himself   [g]27 Or 'week'   [h]27 Or it   [i]27 Or And one who causes desolation will come upon the pinnacle of the abominable ˌtemple,ˌ until the end that is decreed is poured out on the desolated ˌcity,ˌ   [j]1 Or true and burdensome

his arms and legs like the gleam of burnished bronze, and his voice like the sound of a multitude. ⁷I, Daniel, was the only one who saw the vision; the men with me did not see it, but such terror overwhelmed them that they fled and hid themselves. ⁸So I was left alone, gazing at this great vision; I had no strength left, my face turned deathly pale and I was helpless. ⁹Then I heard him speaking, and as I listened to him, I fell into a deep sleep, my face to the ground. 2Ki 6:17-20; Da 8:18,27

¹⁰A hand touched me and set me trembling on my hands and knees. ¹¹He said, "Daniel, you who are highly esteemed, consider carefully the words I am about to speak to you, and stand up, for I have now been sent to you." And when he said this to me, I stood up trembling. Da 9:23; Eze 2:1 ¹²Then he continued, "Do not be afraid, Daniel. Since the first day that you set your mind to gain understanding and to humble yourself before your God, your words were heard, and I have come in response to them. ¹³But the prince of the Persian kingdom resisted me twenty-one days. Then Michael, one of the chief princes, came to help me, because I was detained there with the king of Persia. ¹⁴Now I have come to explain to you what will happen to your people in the future, for the vision concerns a time yet to come."

¹⁵While he was saying this to me, I bowed with my face toward the ground and was speechless. ¹⁶Then one who looked like a man*a* touched my lips, and I opened my mouth and began to speak. I said to the one standing before me, "I am overcome with anguish because of the vision, my lord, and I am helpless. ¹⁷How can I, your servant, talk with you, my lord? My strength is gone and I can hardly breathe." Jer 1:9; Da 4:19

¹⁸Again the one who looked like a man touched me and gave me strength. ¹⁹"Do not be afraid, O man highly esteemed," he said. "Peace! Be strong now; be strong."

When he spoke to me, I was strengthened and said, "Speak, my lord, since you have given me strength." Isa 6:1-8

²⁰So he said, "Do you know why I have come to you? Soon I will return to fight against the prince of Persia, and when I go, the prince of Greece will come; ²¹but first I will tell you what is written in the Book of Truth. (No one supports me against them except Michael, your prince. ¹And in the first year of Darius the Mede, I took my stand to support and protect him.) Da 11:2; Jude 1:9

11

---

a 16 Most manuscripts of the Masoretic Text; one manuscript of the Masoretic Text, Dead Sea Scrolls and Septuagint *Then something that looked like a man's hand*

The Kings of the South and the North

2"Now then, I tell you the truth: Three more kings will appear in Persia, and then a fourth, who will be far richer than all the others. When he has gained power by his wealth, he will stir up everyone against the kingdom of Greece. 3Then a mighty king will appear, who will rule with great power and do as he pleases. 4After he has appeared, his empire will be broken up and parceled out toward the four winds of heaven. It will not go to his descendants, nor will it have the power he exercised, because his empire will be uprooted and given to others.   Da 8:4,21-22

5"The king of the South will become strong, but one of his commanders will become even stronger than he and will rule his own kingdom with great power. 6After some years, they will become allies. The daughter of the king of the South will go to the king of the North to make an alliance, but she will not retain her power, and he and his power*a* will not last. In those days she will be handed over, together with her royal escort and her father*b* and the one who supported her.

7"One from her family line will arise to take her place. He will attack the forces of the king of the North and enter his fortress; he will fight against them and be victorious. 8He will also seize their gods, their metal images and their valuable articles of silver and gold and carry them off to Egypt. For some years he will leave the king of the North alone. 9Then the king of the North will invade the realm of the king of the South but will retreat to his own country. 10His sons will prepare for war and assemble a great army, which will sweep on like an irresistible flood and carry the battle as far as his fortress.   Isa 8:8; Da 9:26

11"Then the king of the South will march out in a rage and fight against the king of the North, who will raise a large army, but it will be defeated. 12When the army is carried off, the king of the South will be filled with pride and will slaughter many thousands, yet he will not remain triumphant. 13For the king of the North will muster another army, larger than the first; and after several years, he will advance with a huge army fully equipped.   Da 8:7-8

14"In those times many will rise against the king of the South. The violent men among your own people will rebel in fulfillment of the vision, but without success. 15Then the king of the North will come and build up siege ramps and will capture a fortified city. The forces of the South will be powerless to resist; even their best

---

*a*6 Or *offspring*   *b*6 Or *child* (see Vulgate and Syriac)

troops will not have the strength to stand. ¹⁶The invader will do as he pleases; no one will be able to stand against him. He will establish himself in the Beautiful Land and will have the power to destroy it. ¹⁷He will determine to come with the might of his entire kingdom and will make an alliance with the king of the South. And he will give him a daughter in marriage in order to overthrow the kingdom, but his plans*a* will not succeed or help him. ¹⁸Then he will turn his attention to the coastlands and will take many of them, but a commander will put an end to his insolence and will turn his insolence back upon him. ¹⁹After this, he will turn back toward the fortresses of his own country but will stumble and fall, to be seen no more.   Ps 27:2; Eze 26:21

²⁰"His successor will send out a tax collector to maintain the royal splendor. In a few years, however, he will be destroyed, yet not in anger or in battle.   Isa 60:17

²¹"He will be succeeded by a contemptible person who has not been given the honor of royalty. He will invade the kingdom when its people feel secure, and he will seize it through intrigue. ²²Then an overwhelming army will be swept away before him; both it and a prince of the covenant will be destroyed. ²³After coming to an agreement with him, he will act deceitfully, and with only a few people he will rise to power. ²⁴When the richest provinces feel secure, he will invade them and will achieve what neither his fathers nor his forefathers did. He will distribute plunder, loot and wealth among his followers. He will plot the overthrow of fortresses—but only for a time.

²⁵"With a large army he will stir up his strength and courage against the king of the South. The king of the South will wage war with a large and very powerful army, but he will not be able to stand because of the plots devised against him. ²⁶Those who eat from the king's provisions will try to destroy him; his army will be swept away, and many will fall in battle. ²⁷The two kings, with their hearts bent on evil, will sit at the same table and lie to each other, but to no avail, because an end will still come at the appointed time. ²⁸The king of the North will return to his own country with great wealth, but his heart will be set against the holy covenant. He will take action against it and then return to his own country.   Ps 64:6; Hab 2:3

²⁹"At the appointed time he will invade the South again, but this time the outcome will be different from what it was before. ³⁰Ships of the western coastlands*b* will oppose him, and he will lose heart. Then he will turn back and vent

---

a 17 Or *but she*   *b* 30 Hebrew *of Kittim*

his fury against the holy covenant. He will return and show favor to those who forsake the holy covenant.   Ge 10:4

31"His armed forces will rise up to desecrate the temple fortress and will abolish the daily sacrifice. Then they will set up the abomination that causes desolation. 32With flattery he will corrupt those who have violated the covenant, but the people who know their God will firmly resist him.   Mt 24:15*; Mic 5:7-9

33"Those who are wise will instruct many, though for a time they will fall by the sword or be burned or captured or plundered. 34When they fall, they will receive a little help, and many who are not sincere will join them. 35Some of the wise will stumble, so that they may be refined, purified and made spotless until the time of the end, for it will still come at the appointed time.   Da 12:10; Zec 13:9; Jn 15:2

The King Who Exalts Himself

36"The king will do as he pleases. He will exalt and magnify himself above every god and will say unheard-of things against the God of gods. He will be successful until the time of wrath is completed, for what has been determined must take place. 37He will show no regard for the gods of his fathers or for the one desired by women, nor will he regard any god, but will exalt himself above them all. 38In-stead of them, he will honor a god of fortresses; a god unknown to his fathers he will honor with gold and silver, with precious stones and costly gifts. 39He will attack the mightiest fortresses with the help of a foreign god and will greatly honor those who acknowledge him. He will make them rulers over many people and will distribute the land at a price.ᵃ   Da 7:25

40"At the time of the end the king of the South will engage him in battle, and the king of the North will storm out against him with chariots and cavalry and a great fleet of ships. He will invade many countries and sweep through them like a flood. 41He will also invade the Beautiful Land. Many countries will fall, but Edom, Moab and the leaders of Ammon will be delivered from his hand. 42He will extend his power over many countries; Egypt will not escape. 43He will gain control of the treasures of gold and silver and all the riches of Egypt, with the Libyans and Nubians in submission. 44But reports from the east and the north will alarm him, and he will set out in a great rage to destroy and annihilate many. 45He will pitch his royal tents between the seas atᵇ the beautiful holy mountain. Yet he will come to his end, and no one will help him.   Isa 5:28; 21:1; Eze 38:4

ᵃ39 Or land for a reward   ᵇ45 Or the sea and

The End Times

12 "At that time Michael, the great prince who protects your people, will arise. There will be a time of distress such as has not happened from the beginning of nations until then. But at that time your people—everyone whose name is found written in the book—will be delivered. ²Multitudes who sleep in the dust of the earth will awake: some to everlasting life, others to shame and everlasting contempt. ³Those who are wise*a* will shine like the brightness of the heavens, and those who lead many to righteousness, like the stars for ever and ever. ⁴But you, Daniel, close up and seal the words of the scroll until the time of the end. Many will go here and there to increase knowledge."

⁵Then I, Daniel, looked, and there before me stood two others, one on this bank of the river and one on the opposite bank. ⁶One of them said to the man clothed in linen, who was above the waters of the river, "How long will it be before these astonishing things are fulfilled?"   Da 8:13; 10:4

⁷The man clothed in linen, who was above the waters of the river, lifted his right hand and his left hand toward heaven, and I heard him swear by him who lives forever, saying, "It will be for a time, times and half a time.*b* When the power of the holy people has been finally broken, all these things will be completed."   Lk 21:24; Rev 10:7

⁸I heard, but I did not understand. So I asked, "My lord, what will the outcome of all this be?"

⁹He replied, "Go your way, Daniel, because the words are closed up and sealed until the time of the end. ¹⁰Many will be purified, made spotless and refined, but the wicked will continue to be wicked. None of the wicked will understand, but those who are wise will understand.   Isa 32:7; Rev 22:11

¹¹"From the time that the daily sacrifice is abolished and the abomination that causes desolation is set up, there will be 1,290 days. ¹²Blessed is the one who waits for and reaches the end of the 1,335 days.   Isa 30:18; Da 8:14

¹³"As for you, go your way till the end. You will rest, and then at the end of the days you will rise to receive your allotted inheritance."

---

a3 Or *who impart wisdom*   *b7* Or *a year, two years and half a year*

Hosea

1

1 The word of the LORD that came to Hosea son of Beeri during the reigns of Uzziah, Jotham, Ahaz and Hezekiah, kings of Judah, and during the reign of Jeroboam son of Jehoash[a] king of Israel: Jer 1:2; 2Ki 13:13

Hosea's Wife and Children

2 When the LORD began to speak through Hosea, the LORD said to him, "Go, take to yourself an adulterous wife and children of unfaithfulness, because the land is guilty of the vilest adultery in departing from the LORD." 3 So he married Gomer daughter of Diblaim, and she conceived and bore him a son. Dt 31:16; Hos 5:3

4 Then the LORD said to Hosea, "Call him Jezreel, because I will soon punish the house of Jehu for the massacre at Jezreel, and I will put an end to the kingdom of Israel. 5 In that day I will break Israel's bow in the Valley of Jezreel."

6 Gomer conceived again and gave birth to a daughter. Then the LORD said to Hosea, "Call her Lo-Ruhamah,[b] for I will no longer show love to the house of Israel, that I should at all forgive them.

7 Yet I will show love to the house of Judah; and I will save them— not by bow, sword or battle, or by horses and horsemen, but by the LORD their God." Ps 44:6; Zec 4:6

8 After she had weaned Lo-Ruhamah, Gomer had another son. 9 Then the LORD said, "Call him Lo-Ammi,[c] for you are not my people, and I am not your God.

10 "Yet the Israelites will be like the sand on the seashore, which cannot be measured or counted. In the place where it was said to them, 'You are not my people,' they will be called 'sons of the living God.' 11 The people of Judah and the people of Israel will be reunited, and they will appoint one leader and will come up out of the land, for great will be the day of Jezreel. Ro 9:26*; Jos 3:10

2

2 "Say of your brothers, 'My people,' and of your sisters, 'My loved one.' 1Pe 2:10

Israel Punished and Restored

2 "Rebuke your mother, rebuke her, Isa 50:1; Hos 1:2
  for she is not my wife,
  and I am not her husband.
Let her remove the adulterous
  look from her face

---

[a]1 Hebrew *Joash*, a variant of *Jehoash*   [b]6 *Lo-Ruhamah* means *not loved.*   [c]9 *Lo-Ammi* means *not my people.*

and the unfaithfulness from
   between her breasts.
³Otherwise I will strip her
   naked
and make her as bare as on
   the day she was born;
I will make her like a desert,
   turn her into a parched
   land,
and slay her with thirst.
⁴I will not show my love to her
   children,   Eze 8:18
because they are the
   children of adultery.
⁵Their mother has been
   unfaithful
and has conceived them in
   disgrace.
She said, 'I will go after my
   lovers,   Jer 3:6
who give me my food and
   my water,
my wool and my linen, my
   oil and my drink.'
⁶Therefore I will block her path
   with thornbushes;
I will wall her in so that she
   cannot find her way.
⁷She will chase after her lovers
   but not catch them;
she will look for them but
   not find them.   Hos 5:13
Then she will say,
'I will go back to my
   husband as at first,
for then I was better off than
   now.'   Eze 16:8
⁸She has not acknowledged that
   I was the one   Isa 1:3
who gave her the grain, the
   new wine and oil,

who lavished on her the silver
   and gold—
which they used for Baal.

⁹"Therefore I will take away my
   grain when it ripens,
and my new wine when it is
   ready.   Hos 9:2
I will take back my wool and
   my linen,
intended to cover her
   nakedness.
¹⁰So now I will expose her
   lewdness
before the eyes of her lovers;
no one will take her out of
   my hands.   Eze 16:37
¹¹I will stop all her celebrations:
her yearly festivals, her New
   Moons,
her Sabbath days—all her
   appointed feasts.   Isa 1:14
¹²I will ruin her vines and her fig
   trees,   Isa 7:23; Jer 8:13
which she said were her pay
   from her lovers;
I will make them a thicket,
and wild animals will devour
   them.   Hos 13:8
¹³I will punish her for the days
   she burned incense to the
   Baals;   Hos 11:2
she decked herself with rings
   and jewelry,   Eze 16:17
and went after her lovers,
but me she forgot,"   Hos 4:6
   declares the LORD.

¹⁴"Therefore I am now going to
   allure her;
I will lead her into the desert
   and speak tenderly to her.

¹⁵There I will give her back her
vineyards,
and will make the Valley of
Achor*a* a door of hope.
There she will sing*b* as in the
days of her youth,   Jer 2:2
as in the day she came up
out of Egypt.   Hos 12:9
¹⁶"In that day," declares the
LORD,
"you will call me 'my
husband';
you will no longer call me   Isa 54:5
'my master.*c*'
¹⁷I will remove the names of the
Baals from her lips;
no longer will their names
be invoked.   Jos 23:7
¹⁸In that day I will make a
covenant for them
with the beasts of the field
and the birds of the air
and the creatures that move
along the ground.   Job 5:22
Bow and sword and battle
I will abolish from the
land,
so that all may lie down in
safety.   Eze 34:25
¹⁹I will betroth you to me
forever;   Isa 62:4
I will betroth you in*d*
righteousness and
justice,   Isa 1:27
in*e* love and compassion.
²⁰I will betroth you in
faithfulness,

and you will acknowledge
the LORD.   Jer 31:34; Hos 6:6
²¹"In that day I will respond,"
declares the LORD —
"I will respond to the skies,
and they will respond to the
earth;
²²and the earth will respond to
the grain,
the new wine and oil,   Jer 31:12
and they will respond to
Jezreel.*f*   Hos 1:4
²³I will plant her for myself in
the land;   Jer 31:27
I will show my love to the
one I called 'Not my
loved one.*g*'   Hos 1:6
I will say to those called 'Not
my people,*h*' 'You are
my people';   Hos 1:10
and they will say, 'You are
my God.' "   Ro 9:25*; 1Pe 2:10

Hosea's Reconciliation With His Wife

3 The LORD said to me, "Go,
show your love to your wife
again, though she is loved by another and is an adulteress. Love
her as the LORD loves the Israelites,
though they turn to other gods and
love the sacred raisin cakes."

²So I bought her for fifteen shekels*i* of silver and about a homer
and a lethek*j* of barley. ³Then I
told her, "You are to live with*k*

---

*a*15 *Achor* means *trouble.*   *b*15 Or *respond*   *c*16 Hebrew *baal*   *d*19 Or *with*; also in verse 20
*e*19 Or *with*   *f*22 *Jezreel* means *God plants.*   *g*23 Hebrew *Lo-Ruhamah*   *h*23 Hebrew *Lo-Ammi*
*i*2 That is, about 6 ounces (about 170 grams)   *j*2 That is, probably about 10 bushels (about 330 liters)
*k*3 Or *wait for*

me many days; you must not be a prostitute or be intimate with any man, and I will live with[a] you."

⁴For the Israelites will live many days without king or prince, without sacrifice or sacred stones, without ephod or idol. ⁵Afterward the Israelites will return and seek the Lord their God and David their king. They will come trembling to the Lord and to his blessings in the last days.   Jer 50:4-5; Eze 34:23-24

The Charge Against Israel

4 Hear the word of the Lord,
    you Israelites,
  because the Lord has a
    charge to bring   Jer 2:9
  against you who live in the
    land: Joel 1:2,14
  "There is no faithfulness, no
    love,   Pr 24:2
  no acknowledgment of God
    in the land.   Jer 7:28
²There is only cursing,[b] lying
    and murder,   Hos 6:9; 7:3
  stealing and adultery;   Hos 7:1
they break all bounds,
  and bloodshed follows
    bloodshed.   2Ki 21:16; Hos 5:2
³Because of this the land
    mourns,[c]   Jer 4:28
  and all who live in it waste
    away;   Isa 33:9
the beasts of the field and the
  birds of the air

and the fish of the sea are
  dying.   Jer 4:25; Zep 1:3

⁴"But let no man bring a
    charge,
  let no man accuse another,
for your people are like those
  who bring charges against a
    priest.   Dt 17:12; Eze 3:26
⁵You stumble day and night,
  and the prophets stumble
    with you.
So I will destroy your
    mother—   Hos 2:2
6   my people are destroyed
      from lack of knowledge.

"Because you have rejected
    knowledge,
  I also reject you as my
    priests;
because you have ignored the
    law of your God,
  I also will ignore your
    children.
⁷The more the priests increased,
  the more they sinned against
    me;
  they exchanged[d] their[e]
    Glory for something
    disgraceful.   Hos 10:1,6; 13:6
⁸They feed on the sins of my
    people
  and relish their wickedness.
⁹And it will be: Like people, like
    priests.   Isa 24:2
  I will punish both of them
    for their ways

---

[a]3 Or wait for   [b]2 That is, to pronounce a curse upon   Hebrew scribal tradition; Masoretic Text I will exchange   tradition my   [c]3 Or dries up   [d]7 Syriac and an ancient   [e]7 Masoretic Text; an ancient Hebrew scribal

and repay them for their
 deeds. Jer 5:31; Hos 9:9,15

10"They will eat but not have
 enough; Lev 26:26; Mic 6:14
they will engage in
 prostitution but not
 increase,
because they have deserted the
 LORD Hos 7:14; 9:17
to give themselves 11to
 prostitution, Hos 5:4
to old wine and new,
which take away the
 understanding 12of my
 people. Pr 20:1
They consult a wooden idol
 and are answered by a stick
 of wood. Hab 2:19
A spirit of prostitution leads
 them astray; Isa 44:20
they are unfaithful to their
 God. Ps 73:27
13They sacrifice on the
 mountaintops
and burn offerings on the
 hills,
under oak, poplar and
 terebinth, Isa 1:29
where the shade is pleasant.
Therefore your daughters turn
 to prostitution Jer 2:20
and your daughters-in-law to
 adultery. Hos 2:13

14"I will not punish your
 daughters
when they turn to
 prostitution,
nor your daughters-in-law

when they commit adultery,
because the men themselves
 consort with harlots
and sacrifice with shrine
 prostitutes— Hos 9:10
a people without
 understanding will come
 to ruin! Pr 10:21

15"Though you commit adultery,
 O Israel,
let not Judah become guilty.

"Do not go to Gilgal; Hos 9:15
do not go up to Beth Aven.[a]
And do not swear, 'As surely
 as the LORD lives!' Jer 4:2
16The Israelites are stubborn,
like a stubborn heifer.
How then can the LORD pasture
 them
like lambs in a meadow?
17Ephraim is joined to idols;
leave him alone!
18Even when their drinks are
 gone,
they continue their
 prostitution;
their rulers dearly love
 shameful ways.
19A whirlwind will sweep them
 away, Hos 12:1; 13:15
and their sacrifices will bring
 them shame. Isa 1:29

Judgment Against Israel

5 "Hear this, you priests!
Pay attention, you Israelites!
Listen, O royal house!

---

a 15 Beth Aven means house of wickedness (a name for Bethel, which means house of God).

This judgment is against
    you: Job 10:2
You have been a snare at
    Mizpah,   Hos 6:9; 9:8
    a net spread out on Tabor.
²The rebels are deep in
    slaughter.   Hos 4:2
    I will discipline all of them.
³I know all about Ephraim;
    Israel is not hidden from
    me.
Ephraim, you have now turned
    to prostitution;
    Israel is corrupt.   Hos 6:10

⁴"Their deeds do not permit
    them
    to return to their God.
A spirit of prostitution is in
    their heart;   Hos 4:11
    they do not acknowledge the
    LORD.   Hos 4:6
⁵Israel's arrogance testifies
    against them;   Hos 7:10
    the Israelites, even Ephraim,
    stumble in their sin;
    Judah also stumbles with
    them.   Hos 14:1
⁶When they go with their flocks
    and herds
    to seek the LORD,   Mic 6:6-7
    they will not find him;
    he has withdrawn himself
    from them.   Pr 1:28; Isa 1:15
⁷They are unfaithful to the
    LORD;   Hos 6:7
    they give birth to illegitimate
    children.   Hos 2:4
Now their New Moon festivals

will devour them and their
    fields.   Hos 2:11-12

⁸"Sound the trumpet in Gibeah,
    the horn in Ramah.   Isa 10:29
Raise the battle cry in Beth
    Aven[a];   Hos 4:15
    lead on, O Benjamin.
⁹Ephraim will be laid waste
    on the day of reckoning.
Among the tribes of Israel
    I proclaim what is certain.
¹⁰Judah's leaders are like those
    who move boundary stones.
I will pour out my wrath on
    them
    like a flood of water. Eze 7:8
¹¹Ephraim is oppressed,
    trampled in judgment,
    intent on pursuing idols.[b]
¹²I am like a moth to Ephraim,
    like rot to the people of
    Judah.

¹³"When Ephraim saw his
    sickness,   Isa 7:16
    and Judah his sores,
    then Ephraim turned to
    Assyria,   Hos 7:11; 8:9
    and sent to the great king for
    help.   Hos 10:6
But he is not able to cure
    you,
    not able to heal your sores.
¹⁴For I will be like a lion to
    Ephraim,   Am 3:4
    like a great lion to Judah.
I will tear them to pieces and
    go away;   Hos 6:1

---

[a] 8 Beth Aven means house of wickedness (a name for Bethel, which means house of God).   [b] 11 The
meaning of the Hebrew for this word is uncertain.

I will carry them off, with no
    one to rescue them.
¹⁵Then I will go back to my
    place
until they admit their guilt.
And they will seek my face;
    in their misery they will
    earnestly seek me."

Israel Unrepentant

6 "Come, let us return to the
    LORD.   Isa 10:20
He has torn us to pieces   Hos 5:14
    but he will heal us;   Jer 3:22
he has injured us
    but he will bind up our
    wounds.   Dt 32:39; Jer 30:17
²After two days he will revive
    us;   Ps 30:5
on the third day he will
    restore us,   Ps 71:20
that we may live in his
    presence.
³Let us acknowledge the LORD;
    let us press on to
    acknowledge him.
As surely as the sun rises,
    he will appear;
he will come to us like the
    winter rains,   Joel 2:23
like the spring rains that
    water the earth."   Ps 72:6

⁴"What can I do with you,
    Ephraim?   Hos 11:8
What can I do with you,
    Judah?
Your love is like the morning
    mist,

like the early dew that
    disappears.   Hos 7:1; 13:3
⁵Therefore I cut you in pieces
    with my prophets,
I killed you with the words
    of my mouth;   Jer 1:9-10
my judgments flashed like
    lightning upon you.
⁶For I desire mercy, not
    sacrifice,   Isa 1:11; Mt 9:13*
and acknowledgment of God
    rather than burnt
    offerings.   Hos 2:20
⁷Like Adam,^a they have broken
    the covenant—   Hos 8:1
they were unfaithful to me
    there.   Hos 5:7
⁸Gilead is a city of wicked men,
    stained with footprints of
    blood.
⁹As marauders lie in ambush
    for a man,   Ps 10:8
so do bands of priests;
they murder on the road to
    Shechem,
    committing shameful crimes.
¹⁰I have seen a horrible thing
    in the house of Israel.
There Ephraim is given to
    prostitution
and Israel is defiled.   Hos 5:3

¹¹"Also for you, Judah,
    a harvest is appointed.

"Whenever I would restore the
    fortunes of my people,

7 ¹whenever I would heal
    Israel,

---

^a7 Or *As at Adam;* or *Like men*

the sins of Ephraim are
    exposed
and the crimes of Samaria
    revealed.   Hos 6:4
They practice deceit,
    thieves break into houses,
    bandits rob in the streets;
²but they do not realize
    that I remember all their evil
    deeds.   Jer 14:10; Hos 8:13
Their sins engulf them;   Jer 2:19
    they are always before me.

³"They delight the king with
    their wickedness,
    the princes with their lies.
⁴They are all adulterers,   Jer 9:2
    burning like an oven
whose fire the baker need not
    stir
    from the kneading of the
    dough till it rises.
⁵On the day of the festival of
    our king
    the princes become inflamed
    with wine,   Isa 28:1,7
and he joins hands with the
    mockers.   Ps 1:1
⁶Their hearts are like an oven;
    they approach him with
    intrigue.
Their passion smolders all
    night;
    in the morning it blazes like
    a flaming fire.
⁷All of them are hot as an
    oven;
    they devour their rulers.
All their kings fall,   Hos 13:10
    and none of them calls on
    me.   Ps 14:4

⁸"Ephraim mixes with the
    nations;   Ps 106:35; Hos 5:13
    Ephraim is a flat cake not
    turned over.
⁹Foreigners sap his strength,
    but he does not realize it.
His hair is sprinkled with
    gray,
    but he does not notice.
¹⁰Israel's arrogance testifies
    against him,   Hos 5:5
but despite all this
he does not return to the LORD
    his God
    or search for him.   Isa 9:13

¹¹"Ephraim is like a dove,
    easily deceived and
    senseless—
now calling to Egypt,   Hos 9:6
    now turning to Assyria.
¹²When they go, I will throw my
    net over them;   Eze 12:13
I will pull them down like
    birds of the air.
When I hear them flocking
    together,
I will catch them.
¹³Woe to them,   Hos 9:12
    because they have strayed
    from me!   Jer 14:10; Eze 34:4-6
Destruction to them,
    because they have rebelled
    against me!
I long to redeem them
    but they speak lies against
    me.   Mt 23:37
¹⁴They do not cry out to me
    from their hearts   Jer 3:10
    but wail upon their
    beds.

They gather together[a] for grain
   and new wine   Am 2:8
but turn away from me.
¹⁵I trained them and
   strengthened them,
but they plot evil against me.
¹⁶They do not turn to the Most
   High;
   they are like a faulty bow.
Their leaders will fall by the
   sword
   because of their insolent
    words.
For this they will be ridiculed
   in the land of Egypt.   Hos 9:3

Israel to Reap the Whirlwind

8 "Put the trumpet to your
   lips!
An eagle is over the house of
   the LORD   Jer 4:13
because the people have
   broken my covenant
and rebelled against my law.
²Israel cries out to me,
   'O our God, we acknowledge
    you!'
³But Israel has rejected what is
   good;
   an enemy will pursue
    him.
⁴They set up kings without my
   consent;
   they choose princes without
    my approval.   Hos 13:10
With their silver and gold
   they make idols for
    themselves   Hos 2:8
to their own destruction.

⁵Throw out your calf-idol,
   O Samaria!   Hos 10:5
My anger burns against
   them.
How long will they be
   incapable of purity?
⁶   They are from Israel!
This calf—a craftsman has
   made it;
   it is not God.   Hos 14:3
It will be broken in pieces,
   that calf of Samaria.   Ex 32:4

⁷"They sow the wind
   and reap the whirlwind.
The stalk has no head;
   it will produce no flour.
Were it to yield grain,
   foreigners would swallow it
    up.   Hos 2:9
⁸Israel is swallowed up;   Jer 51:34
   now she is among the
    nations
   like a worthless thing.
⁹For they have gone up to
   Assyria
   like a wild donkey
    wandering alone.
Ephraim has sold herself to
   lovers.   Eze 23:5; Hos 5:13
¹⁰Although they have sold
   themselves among the
    nations,
I will now gather them
   together.   Eze 16:37; 22:20
They will begin to waste
   away
   under the oppression of the
    mighty king.

---

[a] 14 Most Hebrew manuscripts; some Hebrew manuscripts and Septuagint *They slash themselves*

[11]"Though Ephraim built many
    altars for sin offerings,
these have become altars for
    sinning.   Hos 10:1; 12:11
[12]I wrote for them the many
    things of my law,
but they regarded them as
    something alien.
[13]They offer sacrifices given to
    me
and they eat the meat,   Jer 7:21
but the LORD is not pleased
    with them.
Now he will remember their
    wickedness   Hos 7:2
and punish their sins: Hos 4:9
They will return to Egypt.
[14]Israel has forgotten his Maker
and built palaces;
Judah has fortified many
    towns.
But I will send fire upon their
    cities
that will consume their
    fortresses."   Jer 17:27

Punishment for Israel

9 Do not rejoice, O Israel;
    do not be jubilant like the
        other nations.   Isa 22:12-13
For you have been unfaithful
    to your God;   Hos 10:5
you love the wages of a
    prostitute   Ge 30:15
at every threshing floor.
[2]Threshing floors and
    winepresses will not
        feed the people;
the new wine will fail them.

[3]They will not remain in the
    LORD's land;   Lev 25:23
Ephraim will return to Egypt
and eat unclean[a] food in
    Assyria.   Eze 4:13; Hos 7:11
[4]They will not pour out wine
    offerings to the LORD,
nor will their sacrifices
    please him.   Hos 8:13
Such sacrifices will be to them
    like the bread of
        mourners;   Jer 16:7
all who eat them will be
    unclean.   Hag 2:13-14
This food will be for
    themselves;
it will not come into the
    temple of the LORD.

[5]What will you do on the day of
    your appointed feasts,
on the festival days of the
    LORD?
[6]Even if they escape from
    destruction,
Egypt will gather them,
and Memphis will bury
    them.   Isa 19:13
Their treasures of silver will be
    taken over by briers,
and thorns will overrun their
    tents.   Isa 5:6; Hos 10:8
[7]The days of punishment are
    coming,   Isa 34:8; Jer 10:15
the days of reckoning are at
    hand.
Let Israel know this.
Because your sins are so many
    and your hostility so great,

---

[a] 3 That is, ceremonially unclean

the prophet is considered a
    fool,   Isa 44:25; La 2:14
the inspired man a maniac.
⁸The prophet, along with my
    God,
is the watchman over
    Ephraim,ᵃ
yet snares await him on all his
    paths,   Hos 5:1
and hostility in the house of
    his God.
⁹They have sunk deep into
    corruption,
as in the days of Gibeah.
God will remember their
    wickedness   Hos 8:13
and punish them for their
    sins.   Hos 4:9

¹⁰"When I found Israel,
    it was like finding grapes in
    the desert;
when I saw your fathers,
    it was like seeing the early
    fruit on the fig tree.
But when they came to Baal
    Peor,   Nu 25:1-5; Ps 106:28-29
they consecrated themselves
    to that shameful idol
and became as vile as the
    thing they loved.
¹¹Ephraim's glory will fly away
    like a bird—   Hos 4:7; 10:5
no birth, no pregnancy, no
    conception.
¹²Even if they rear children,
    I will bereave them of every
    one.   Eze 24:21
Woe to them   Hos 7:13

when I turn away from
    them!   Dt 31:17
¹³I have seen Ephraim, like Tyre,
    planted in a pleasant place.
But Ephraim will bring out
    their children to the slayer."

¹⁴Give them, O Lord—
    what will you give them?
Give them wombs that
    miscarry
and breasts that are dry.

¹⁵"Because of all their
    wickedness in Gilgal,
I hated them there.
Because of their sinful deeds,
    I will drive them out of my
    house.
I will no longer love them;
    all their leaders are
    rebellious.   Isa 1:23; Hos 4:9
¹⁶Ephraim is blighted,   Hos 5:11
    their root is withered,
they yield no fruit.   Hos 8:7
Even if they bear children,
    I will slay their cherished
    offspring."   ver 12

¹⁷My God will reject them
    because they have not
    obeyed him;   Hos 4:10
they will be wanderers
    among the nations.

10 Israel was a spreading
    vine;   Eze 15:2
he brought forth fruit for
    himself.
As his fruit increased,
    he built more altars;   1Ki 14:23

ᵃ 8 Or *The prophet is the watchman over Ephraim, / the people of my God*

as his land prospered,
   he adorned his sacred
      stones.   *Hos 8:11; 12:11*
²Their heart is deceitful,   *1Ki 18:21*
   and now they must bear
      their guilt.   *Hos 13:16*
The LORD will demolish their
   altars   *ver 8*
   and destroy their sacred
      stones.   *Mic 5:13*

³Then they will say, "We have
   no king
   because we did not revere
      the LORD.
   But even if we had a king,
      what could he do for
      us?"
⁴They make many promises,
   take false oaths   *Hos 4:2*
   and make agreements;
therefore lawsuits spring up
   like poisonous weeds in a
      plowed field.   *Am 6:12*
⁵The people who live in
      Samaria fear
   for the calf-idol of Beth
      Aven.ᵃ   *Hos 5:8*
Its people will mourn over it,
   and so will its idolatrous
      priests,   *2Ki 23:5*
those who had rejoiced over its
      splendor,
   because it is taken from
      them into exile.   *Hos 8:5*
⁶It will be carried to Assyria
   as tribute for the great
      king.

Ephraim will be disgraced;
   Israel will be ashamed of its
      wooden idols.ᵇ   *Jer 48:13*
⁷Samaria and its king will float
      away   *Hos 13:11*
   like a twig on the surface of
      the waters.
⁸The high places of
      wickednessᶜ will be
      destroyed—   *1Ki 12:28-30*
   it is the sin of Israel.
Thorns and thistles will grow
      up
   and cover their altars.   *Isa 32:13*
Then they will say to the
      mountains, "Cover us!"
   and to the hills, "Fall on
      us!"
⁹"Since the days of Gibeah, you
      have sinned, O Israel,
   and there you have
      remained.ᵈ
Did not war overtake
   the evildoers in Gibeah?
¹⁰When I please, I will punish
      them;   *Eze 5:13; Hos 4:9*
   nations will be gathered
      against them
   to put them in bonds for
      their double sin.
¹¹Ephraim is a trained
      heifer
   that loves to thresh;
so I will put a yoke
   on her fair neck.
I will drive Ephraim,
   Judah must plow,

and Jacob must break up the
ground.
¹²Sow for yourselves
righteousness,   Pr 11:18
reap the fruit of unfailing
love,
and break up your unplowed
ground;   Jer 4:3
for it is time to seek the
LORD,
until he comes   Hos 12:6
and showers righteousness
on you.   Isa 45:8
¹³But you have planted
wickedness,
you have reaped evil,   Job 4:8
you have eaten the fruit of
deception.
Because you have depended on
your own strength
and on your many
warriors,
¹⁴the roar of battle will rise
against your people,
so that all your fortresses
will be devastated—
as Shalman devastated Beth
Arbel on the day of
battle,   2Ki 17:3
when mothers were dashed
to the ground with their
children.   Hos 13:16
¹⁵Thus will it happen to you,
O Bethel,
because your wickedness is
great.
When that day dawns,
the king of Israel will be
completely destroyed.

God's Love for Israel

11 "When Israel was a child,
I loved him,   Jer 2:2
and out of Egypt I called my
son.   Hos 12:9,13; Mt 2:15*
²But the more Iᵃ called Israel,
the further they went from
me.ᵇ
They sacrificed to the Baals
and they burned incense to
images.   2Ki 17:15; Jer 18:15
³It was I who taught Ephraim to
walk,
taking them by the arms;
but they did not realize
it was I who healed them.
⁴I led them with cords of
human kindness,
with ties of love;   Jer 31:2-3
I lifted the yoke from their
neck   Lev 26:13
and bent down to feed them.

⁵"Will they not return to Egypt
and will not Assyria rule
over them   Hos 10:6
because they refuse to
repent?
⁶Swords will flash in their cities,
will destroy the bars of their
gates
and put an end to their
plans.
⁷My people are determined to
turn from me.   Jer 3:6-7; 8:5
Even if they call to the Most
High,
he will by no means exalt
them.

8"How can I give you up,
  Ephraim?   Hos 6:4
How can I hand you over,
  Israel?
How can I treat you like
  Admah?
How can I make you like
  Zeboiim?   Ge 14:8
My heart is changed within
  me;
  all my compassion is
    aroused.   1Ki 3:26; Ps 25:6
9I will not carry out my fierce
  anger,   Dt 13:17; Jer 30:11
nor will I turn and devastate
  Ephraim.   Mal 3:6
For I am God, and not man—
  the Holy One among you.
I will not come in wrath.a
10They will follow the LORD;
  he will roar like a lion.
When he roars,
  his children will come
    trembling from the
    west.
11They will come trembling
  like birds from Egypt,
  like doves from Assyria.
I will settle them in their
  homes,"   Eze 28:26
declares the LORD.

Israel's Sin

12Ephraim has surrounded me
  with lies,   Hos 4:2
  the house of Israel with
    deceit.
And Judah is unruly against
  God,

even against the faithful
  Holy One.   Hos 10:13

12 1Ephraim feeds on the
  wind;   Eze 17:10
he pursues the east wind all
  day
and multiplies lies and
  violence.   Hos 4:19
He makes a treaty with Assyria
  and sends olive oil to
    Egypt.
2The LORD has a charge to bring
  against Judah;   Mic 6:2
he will punish Jacobb
  according to his ways
and repay him according to
  his deeds.   Hos 4:9
3In the womb he grasped his
  brother's heel;   Ge 25:26
as a man he struggled with
  God.   Ge 32:24-29
4He struggled with the angel
  and overcame him;
he wept and begged for his
  favor.
He found him at Bethel
  and talked with him there—
5the LORD God Almighty,
  the LORD is his name of
    renown!   Ex 3:15
6But you must return to your
  God;   Isa 19:22
maintain love and justice,
  and wait for your God
    always.   Hos 6:1-3; 10:12; Mic 7:7

7The merchant uses dishonest
  scales;   Am 8:5
he loves to defraud.

---

a9 Or *come against any city*   b2 *Jacob* means *he grasps the heel* (figuratively, *he deceives*).

⁸Ephraim boasts,
  "I am very rich; I have
    become wealthy.   Ps 62:10
With all my wealth they will
  not find in me
  any iniquity or sin."

⁹"I am the LORD your God,
  ⌊who brought you⌋ out ofᵃ
    Egypt;   Lev 23:43; Hos 11:1
I will make you live in tents
  again,   Ne 8:17
  as in the days of your
    appointed feasts.
¹⁰I spoke to the prophets,
  gave them many visions
  and told parables through
    them."   2Ki 17:13; Eze 20:49

¹¹Is Gilead wicked?   Hos 6:8
  Its people are worthless!
Do they sacrifice bulls in
    Gilgal?   Hos 4:15
  Their altars will be like piles
    of stones
  on a plowed field.   Hos 8:11
¹²Jacob fled to the country of
    Aramᵇ;   Ge 28:5
  Israel served to get a
    wife,
  and to pay for her he tended
    sheep.   Ge 29:18
¹³The LORD used a prophet to
    bring Israel up from
    Egypt,   Hos 11:1
  by a prophet he cared for
    him.   Isa 63:11-14
¹⁴But Ephraim has bitterly
    provoked him to anger;

his Lord will leave upon him
  the guilt of his
    bloodshed   Eze 18:1⌊
  and will repay him for his
    contempt.   Da 11:18

The LORD's Anger Against Israel

13 When Ephraim spoke,
    men trembled;   Jdg 12:1
he was exalted in Israel.
But he became guilty of Baal
    worship and died.
²Now they sin more and more;
  they make idols for
    themselves from their
    silver,   Isa 46:6; Jer 10:4
cleverly fashioned images,
  all of them the work of
    craftsmen.
It is said of these people,
  "They offer human sacrifice
  and kissᶜ the calf-idols."
³Therefore they will be like the
    morning mist,
  like the early dew that
    disappears,   Hos 6:4
  like chaff swirling from a
    threshing floor,   Isa 17:13
  like smoke escaping through
    a window.   Ps 68:2

⁴"But I am the LORD your God,
  ⌊who brought you⌋ out ofᵃ
    Egypt.   Hos 12:9
You shall acknowledge no God
    but me,   Ex 20:3
  no Savior except me.   Isa 43:11
⁵I cared for you in the desert,

ᵃ9,4 Or God / ever since you were in   ᵇ12 That is, Northwest Mesopotamia   ᶜ2 Or "Men who
sacrifice / kiss

in the land of burning heat.
6When I fed them, they were
    satisfied;
when they were satisfied,
    they became proud;
then they forgot me.
7So I will come upon them like
    a lion,
like a leopard I will lurk by
    the path.
8Like a bear robbed of her cubs,
    I will attack them and rip
    them open.
Like a lion I will devour them;
    a wild animal will tear them
    apart.   Ps 50:22

9"You are destroyed, O Israel,
    because you are against me,
    against your helper.
10Where is your king, that he
    may save you?   2Ki 17:4
Where are your rulers in all
    your towns,
of whom you said,
    'Give me a king and
    princes'?   Hos 8:4
11So in my anger I gave you a
    king,
and in my wrath I took him
    away.   1Ki 14:10; Hos 10:7
12The guilt of Ephraim is stored
    up,
his sins are kept on record.
13Pains as of a woman in
    childbirth come to him,
but he is a child without
    wisdom;
when the time arrives,   2Ki 19:3

he does not come to the
    opening of the womb.

14"I will ransom them from the
    power of the grave[a];
I will redeem them from
    death.   Isa 25:8
Where, O death, are your
    plagues?
Where, O grave,[a] is your
    destruction?   1Co 15:55*

"I will have no compassion,
15   even though he thrives
    among his brothers.
An east wind from the Lord
    will come,   Eze 19:12
blowing in from the desert;
his spring will fail
    and his well dry up.   Jer 51:36
His storehouse will be
    plundered   Jer 20:5
    of all its treasures.
16The people of Samaria must
    bear their guilt,   Hos 10:2
because they have rebelled
    against their God.
They will fall by the sword;
    their little ones will be
    dashed to the ground,
    their pregnant women ripped
    open."   2Ki 15:16

Repentance to Bring Blessing

14 Return, O Israel, to the
    Lord your God.   Jer 3:12
Your sins have been your
    downfall!   Hos 5:5
2Take words with you
    and return to the Lord.

a 14 Hebrew *Sheol*

Say to him:
"Forgive all our sins
and receive us graciously,
　　that we may offer the fruit of
　　　our lips.*a*　　　Heb 13:15
3Assyria cannot save us;
　we will not mount
　　war-horses.　　　Isa 31:1
We will never again say 'Our
　　gods'　　　　　Hos 8:6
to what our own hands have
　　made,
for in you the fatherless find
　　compassion."　　Ps 10:14; 68:5

4"I will heal their waywardness
　　and love them freely,　Zep 3:17
for my anger has turned
　　away from them.　Job 13:16
5I will be like the dew to Israel;
　he will blossom like a lily.
Like a cedar of Lebanon　Isa 35:2
he will send down his roots;
6　his young shoots will grow.
His splendor will be like an
　　olive tree,　　Ps 52:8; Jer 11:16

his fragrance like a cedar of
　　Lebanon.　　　SS 4:11
7Men will dwell again in his
　　shade.　　　Ps 91:1-4
He will flourish like the
　　grain.
He will blossom like a vine,
　and his fame will be like the
　　wine from Lebanon.
8O Ephraim, what more have I*b*
　to do with idols?
　I will answer him and care
　　for him.
I am like a green pine tree;
　your fruitfulness comes from
　　me."

9Who is wise? He will realize
　　these things.　Ps 107:43
Who is discerning? He will
　　understand them.　Pr 10:29
The ways of the LORD are
　　right;
　the righteous walk in them,
but the rebellious stumble in
　　them.

---

a 2 Or offer our lips as sacrifices of bulls　　*b 8 Or What more has Ephraim*

Joel

1
The word of the LORD that came to Joel son of Pethuel.

An Invasion of Locusts

2Hear this, you elders;   Hos 5:1
listen, all who live in the
    land.   Hos 4:1
Has anything like this ever
    happened in your days
or in the days of your
    forefathers?   Joel 2:2
3Tell it to your children,
and let your children tell it
    to their children,
and their children to the
    next generation.
4What the locust swarm has left
the great locusts have eaten;
what the great locusts have left
    the young locusts have
    eaten;
what the young locusts have
    left   Ex 10:5
other locusts[a] have eaten.

5Wake up, you drunkards, and
    weep!
Wail, all you drinkers of
    wine;   Joel 3:3
wail because of the new wine,
    for it has been snatched
    from your lips.
6A nation has invaded my land,

powerful and without
    number;   Joel 2:2,11,25
it has the teeth of a lion,   Rev 9:8
    the fangs of a lioness.
7It has laid waste my vines
    and ruined my fig trees.
It has stripped off their bark
    and thrown it away,
leaving their branches white.

8Mourn like a virgin[b] in
    sackcloth   Isa 22:12; Am 8:10
grieving for the husband[c] of
    her youth.
9Grain offerings and drink
    offerings   Hos 9:4; Joel 2:14,17
are cut off from the house of
    the LORD.
The priests are in mourning,
    those who minister before
    the LORD.
10The fields are ruined,
    the ground is dried up[d];
the grain is destroyed,
    the new wine is dried up,
    the oil fails.
11Despair, you farmers,   Jer 14:3-4
    wail, you vine growers;
grieve for the wheat and the
    barley,
because the harvest of the
    field is destroyed.
12The vine is dried up
    and the fig tree is withered;

---

a4 The precise meaning of the four Hebrew words used here for locusts is uncertain.   b8 Or young
woman   c8 Or betrothed   d10 Or ground mourns

the pomegranate, the palm and
  the apple tree—
all the trees of the field—are
  dried up.   Hag 2:19
Surely the joy of mankind
  is withered away.

A Call to Repentance

13Put on sackcloth, O priests,
  and mourn;   Jer 4:8
  wail, you who minister
    before the altar.   Joel 2:17
Come, spend the night in
    sackcloth,
  you who minister before my
    God;
  for the grain offerings and
    drink offerings
  are withheld from the house
    of your God.
14Declare a holy fast;   2Ch 20:3
  call a sacred assembly.
Summon the elders
  and all who live in the land
to the house of the LORD your
    God,
  and cry out to the LORD.

15Alas for that day!   Jer 30:7
For the day of the LORD is
    near;   Joel 2:1,11,31
  it will come like destruction
    from the Almighty.a

16Has not the food been cut off
  before our very eyes—
joy and gladness
  from the house of our God?
17The seeds are shriveled
  beneath the clods.b   Isa 17:10-11

The storehouses are in ruins,
  the granaries have been
    broken down,
  for the grain has dried up.
18How the cattle moan!
The herds mill about
  because they have no pasture;
  even the flocks of sheep are
    suffering.   Jer 9:10

19To you, O LORD, I call,   Ps 50:15
  for fire has devoured the
    open pastures   Jer 9:10
  and flames have burned up
    all the trees of the field.
20Even the wild animals pant for
    you;   Ps 104:21
  the streams of water have
    dried up   1Ki 17:7
  and fire has devoured the
    open pastures.

An Army of Locusts

2 Blow the trumpet in Zion;
  sound the alarm on my holy
    hill.   Ex 15:17
Let all who live in the land
    tremble,
  for the day of the LORD is
    coming.   Zep 1:14-16
It is close at hand—   Ob 1:15
2 a day of darkness and
    gloom,   Da 9:12; Am 5:18
  a day of clouds and
    blackness.   Rev 9:2
Like dawn spreading across the
    mountains
  a large and mighty army
    comes,   Joel 1:6

---

a15 Hebrew *Shaddai*   b17 The meaning of the Hebrew for this word is uncertain.

such as never was of old Joel 1:2
  nor ever will be in ages to
  come.

3Before them fire devours,
  behind them a flame blazes.
Before them the land is like
  the garden of Eden,
  behind them, a desert
  waste—   Ps 105:34-35
nothing escapes them.
4They have the appearance of
  horses;   Rev 9:7
  they gallop along like
  cavalry.
5With a noise like that of
  chariots   Rev 9:9
  they leap over the
  mountaintops,
  like a crackling fire consuming
  stubble,   Isa 5:24; 30:30
  like a mighty army drawn up
  for battle.

6At the sight of them, nations
  are in anguish;   Isa 13:8
  every face turns pale.   Na 2:10
7They charge like warriors;
  they scale walls like soldiers.
They all march in line,
  not swerving from their
  course.   Isa 5:27
8They do not jostle each other;
  each marches straight ahead.
They plunge through defenses
  without breaking ranks.
9They rush upon the city;
  they run along the wall.
They climb into the houses;
  like thieves they enter
  through the windows.

10Before them the earth shakes,
  the sky trembles,
the sun and moon are
  darkened,   Mt 24:29
and the stars no longer
  shine.   Isa 13:10; Eze 32:8
11The Lord thunders   Joel 1:15
  at the head of his army;
his forces are beyond number,
  and mighty are those who
  obey his command.
The day of the Lord is great;
  it is dreadful.
Who can endure it?   Eze 22:14

Rend Your Heart

12"Even now," declares the Lord,
  "return to me with all your
  heart,   Jer 4:1; Hos 12:6
with fasting and weeping
  and mourning."

13Rend your heart   Isa 57:15
  and not your garments.
Return to the Lord your God,
  for he is gracious and
  compassionate,   Dt 4:31
slow to anger and abounding
  in love,   Ex 34:6
and he relents from sending
  calamity.   Jer 18:8
14Who knows? He may turn and
  have pity   Jer 26:3
and leave behind a
  blessing—   Hag 2:19
grain offerings and drink
  offerings   Joel 1:13
for the Lord your God.

15Blow the trumpet in Zion,
  declare a holy fast,   Jer 36:9

call a sacred assembly.
¹⁶Gather the people,
    consecrate the assembly;
bring together the elders,
    gather the children,
    those nursing at the breast.
Let the bridegroom leave his
        room   Ps 19:5
    and the bride her chamber.
¹⁷Let the priests, who minister
        before the Lord,
    weep between the temple
        porch and the altar.
Let them say, "Spare your
        people, O Lord.
    Do not make your
        inheritance an object of
        scorn,   Ps 44:13
    a byword among the nations.
Why should they say among
        the peoples,
    'Where is their God?' " Ps 42:3

The Lord's Answer

¹⁸Then the Lord will be jealous
        for his land   Zec 1:14
    and take pity on his people.

¹⁹The Lord will reply[a] to them:

"I am sending you grain, new
        wine and oil,   Jer 31:12
    enough to satisfy you fully;
never again will I make you
    an object of scorn to the
        nations.   Eze 34:29

²⁰"I will drive the northern army
        far from you,   Jer 1:14-15

pushing it into a parched
        and barren land,
with its front columns going
        into the eastern sea[b]
    and those in the rear into
        the western sea.[c]
And its stench will go up;
    its smell will rise."

Surely he has done great
        things.[d]
²¹ Be not afraid, O land;   Isa 54:4
    be glad and rejoice.   Ps 9:2
Surely the Lord has done great
        things.   Ps 126:3
²² Be not afraid, O wild
        animals,
    for the open pastures are
        becoming green.   Ps 65:12
The trees are bearing their
        fruit;
    the fig tree and the vine
        yield their riches.
²³Be glad, O people of Zion,
    rejoice in the Lord your God,
for he has given you
    the autumn rains in
        righteousness.[e]
He sends you abundant
        showers,   Eze 34:26
    both autumn and spring
        rains, as before.   Lev 26:4
²⁴The threshing floors will be
        filled with grain;
    the vats will overflow with
        new wine and oil.   Am 9:13

²⁵"I will repay you for the years
        the locusts have eaten—

---

a 18,19 Or Lord *was jealous . . . / and took pity . . . / ¹⁹The* Lord *replied*   *b* 20 That is, the Dead Sea
c 20 That is, the Mediterranean   *d* 20 Or *rise. / Surely it has done great things."*   *e* 23 Or / *the teacher*
for righteousness:

the great locust and the
young locust,
the other locusts and the
locust swarm[a] —
my great army that I sent
among you.   Joel 1:6
²⁶You will have plenty to eat,
until you are full,   Lev 26:5
and you will praise the name
of the LORD your God,
who has worked wonders for
you;   Isa 25:1
never again will my people be
shamed.   Isa 29:22
²⁷Then you will know that I am
in Israel,   Ex 6:7
that I am the LORD your God,
and that there is no other;
never again will my people be
shamed.   Zep 3:11

The Day of the LORD

²⁸"And afterward,
I will pour out my Spirit on
all people.   Eze 39:29
Your sons and daughters will
prophesy,   1Sa 19:20
your old men will dream
dreams,   Jer 23:25
your young men will see
visions.
²⁹Even on my servants, both
men and women,
I will pour out my Spirit in
those days.   Eze 36:27
³⁰I will show wonders in the
heavens   Lk 21:11
and on the earth,   Mk 13:24-25

blood and fire and billows of
smoke.
³¹The sun will be turned to
darkness   Mt 24:29
and the moon to blood
before the coming of the
great and dreadful day
of the LORD.   Isa 13:9-10
³²And everyone who calls
on the name of the LORD will
be saved;   Ro 10:13*
for on Mount Zion and in
Jerusalem   Isa 46:13
there will be deliverance,
as the LORD has said,
among the survivors   Mic 4:7
whom the LORD calls.   Ac 2:39

The Nations Judged

3 "In those days and at that
time,
when I restore the fortunes
of Judah and Jerusalem,
²I will gather all nations   Zep 3:8
and bring them down to the
Valley of Jehoshaphat.[b]
There I will enter into
judgment against them
concerning my inheritance,
my people Israel,
for they scattered my people
among the nations
and divided up my land.
³They cast lots for my people
and traded boys for
prostitutes;
they sold girls for wine   Am 2:6
that they might drink.

---

[a]25 The precise meaning of the four Hebrew words used here for locusts is uncertain.
[b]2 *Jehoshaphat* means *the* LORD *judges;* also in verse 12.

4"Now what have you against me, O Tyre and Sidon and all you regions of Philistia? Are you repaying me for something I have done? If you are paying me back, I will swiftly and speedily return on your own heads what you have done. 5For you took my silver and my gold and carried off my finest treasures to your temples. 6You sold the people of Judah and Jerusalem to the Greeks, that you might send them far from their homeland.   2Ch 21:16-17; Isa 34:8

7"See, I am going to rouse them out of the places to which you sold them, and I will return on your own heads what you have done. 8I will sell your sons and daughters to the people of Judah, and they will sell them to the Sabeans, a nation far away." The LORD has spoken.   Isa 43:5-6; Jer 23:8

9Proclaim this among the
    nations:
Prepare for war!   Isa 8:9
Rouse the warriors!   Jer 46:4
Let all the fighting men draw
    near and attack.
10Beat your plowshares into
    swords
and your pruning hooks into
    spears.   Isa 2:4; Mic 4:3
Let the weakling say,   Zec 12:8
    "I am strong!"   Jos 1:6
11Come quickly, all you nations
    from every side,
and assemble there.

Bring down your warriors,
    O LORD!   Isa 13:3

12"Let the nations be roused;
    let them advance into the
        Valley of Jehoshaphat,
for there I will sit
    to judge all the nations on
        every side.   Isa 2:4
13Swing the sickle,   Mk 4:29
    for the harvest is ripe. Hos 6:11
Come, trample the grapes,
    for the winepress is full
    and the vats overflow—
so great is their wickedness!"

14Multitudes, multitudes
    in the valley of decision!
For the day of the LORD is
        near
    in the valley of decision.
15The sun and moon will be
        darkened,
    and the stars no longer
        shine.   Eze 32:7
16The LORD will roar from Zion
    and thunder from Jerusalem;
the earth and the sky will
        tremble.   Eze 38:19
But the LORD will be a refuge
        for his people,   Ps 46:1
    a stronghold for the people
        of Israel.   Jer 16:19

Blessings for God's People

17"Then you will know that I,
        the LORD your God,
    dwell in Zion, my holy
        hill.
Jerusalem will be holy;   Jer 31:40
    never again will foreigners
        invade her.   Isa 52:1

¹⁸"In that day the mountains will
    drip new wine,
and the hills will flow with
    milk;   Ex 3:8
all the ravines of Judah will
    run with water.   Isa 30:25
A fountain will flow out of the
    Lord's house   Rev 22:1-2
and will water the valley of
    acacias.^a Eze 47:1; Am 9:13
¹⁹But Egypt will be desolate,
   Edom a desert waste, Isa 11:14

because of violence done to
    the people of Judah,
in whose land they shed
    innocent blood.
²⁰Judah will be inhabited forever
   and Jerusalem through all
    generations.
²¹Their bloodguilt, which I have
    not pardoned,   Isa 1:15
   I will pardon." Eze 36:25

The Lord dwells in Zion!

Amos

1 The words of Amos, one of the shepherds of Tekoa—what he saw concerning Israel two years before the earthquake, when Uzziah was king of Judah and Jeroboam son of Jehoash[a] was king of Israel. 2Sa 14:2; 2Ki 14:23; Zec 14:5

2He said:

"The LORD roars from Zion
    and thunders from
        Jerusalem;   Joel 3:16
the pastures of the shepherds
        dry up,[b]
    and the top of Carmel
        withers."   Jer 12:4; Am 9:3

Judgment on Israel's Neighbors

3This is what the LORD says:

"For three sins of Damascus,
    even for four, I will not turn
        back ⌞my wrath⌟.   Am 2:6
Because she threshed Gilead
    with sledges having iron
        teeth,
4I will send fire upon the house
    of Hazael   Jer 49:27
    that will consume the
        fortresses of Ben-Hadad.
5I will break down the gate of
    Damascus;   Jer 51:30
I will destroy the king who
    is in[c] the Valley of
        Aven[d]
and the one who holds the
    scepter in Beth Eden.
The people of Aram will go
    into exile to Kir,"   2Ki 16:9
    says the LORD.

6This is what the LORD says:

"For three sins of Gaza,   1Sa 6:17
    even for four, I will not turn
        back ⌞my wrath⌟.
Because she took captive
    whole communities
    and sold them to Edom,
7I will send fire upon the walls
    of Gaza
    that will consume her
        fortresses.
8I will destroy the king[e] of
    Ashdod   2Ch 26:6
    and the one who holds the
        scepter in Ashkelon.
I will turn my hand against
    Ekron,   Ps 81:14
    till the last of the Philistines
        is dead,"   Eze 25:16
    says the Sovereign LORD.

9This is what the LORD says:

"For three sins of Tyre,

---

a1 Hebrew Joash, a variant of Jehoash   b2 Or shepherds mourn   c5 Or the inhabitants of
d5 Aven means wickedness.   e8 Or inhabitants

even for four, I will not turn
　　back ˻my wrath˼.
Because she sold whole
　　communities of captives
　　to Edom,
disregarding a treaty of
　　brotherhood,　　　　1Ki 5:12
¹⁰I will send fire upon the walls
　　of Tyre
that will consume her
　　fortresses."　　　　Zec 9:1-4

¹¹This is what the LORD says:

"For three sins of Edom,
　　even for four, I will not turn
　　back ˻my wrath˼.
Because he pursued his brother
　　with a sword,
　　stifling all compassion,ᵃ
because his anger raged
　　continually
and his fury flamed
　　unchecked,　　　Eze 25:12-14
¹²I will send fire upon Teman
　　that will consume the
　　fortresses of Bozrah."

¹³This is what the LORD says:

"For three sins of Ammon,
　　even for four, I will not turn
　　back ˻my wrath˼.
Because he ripped open the
　　pregnant women of
　　Gilead　　　　　Hos 13:16
　in order to extend his
　　borders,
¹⁴I will set fire to the walls of
　　Rabbah　　　　　Dt 3:11

that will consume her
　　fortresses
amid war cries on the day of
　　battle,　　　　　　Am 2:2
amid violent winds on a
　　stormy day
¹⁵Her kingᵇ will go into exile,
　　he and his officials together,"
　　　　　　　　says the LORD.

2 This is what the LORD says:

"For three sins of Moab,
　　even for four, I will not turn
　　back ˻my wrath˼.
Because he burned, as if to
　　lime,
　　the bones of Edom's king,
²I will send fire upon Moab
　　that will consume the
　　fortresses of Kerioth.ᶜ
Moab will go down in great
　　tumult
　amid war cries and the blast
　　of the trumpet.　　Jos 6:20
³I will destroy her ruler　Ps 2:10
　and kill all her officials with
　　him,"　　　　　　Isa 40:23
　　　　　　　　says the LORD.

⁴This is what the LORD says:

"For three sins of Judah,
　　even for four, I will not turn
　　back ˻my wrath˼.
Because they have rejected the
　　law of the LORD　　Jer 6:19
　and have not kept his
　　decrees,　　　　Eze 20:24

because they have been led
  astray by false gods,^a
the gods^b their ancestors
  followed,   2Ki 22:13; Jer 16:12
⁵I will send fire upon Judah
  that will consume the
  fortresses of Jerusalem."

Judgment on Israel

⁶This is what the LORD says:

"For three sins of Israel,
  even for four, I will not turn
  back ˻my wrath˼.
They sell the righteous for
  silver,
  and the needy for a pair of
  sandals.   Joel 3:3; Am 8:6
⁷They trample on the heads of
  the poor
  as upon the dust of the
  ground
  and deny justice to the
  oppressed.
Father and son use the same
  girl
  and so profane my holy
  name.   Am 5:11-12; 8:4
⁸They lie down beside every
  altar
  on garments taken in pledge.
In the house of their god
  they drink wine taken as
  fines.   Am 4:1; 6:6

⁹"I destroyed the Amorite before
  them,   Nu 21:23-26; Jos 10:12
  though he was tall as the
  cedars

and strong as the oaks.
I destroyed his fruit above
  and his roots below.   Eze 17:9
¹⁰"I brought you up out of
  Egypt,   Ex 20:2; Am 3:1
  and I led you forty years in
  the desert   Dt 2:7
  to give you the land of the
  Amorites.   Ex 3:8; Am 9:7
¹¹I also raised up prophets from
  among your sons   Dt 18:18
  and Nazirites from among
  your young men.   Nu 6:2-3
Is this not true, people of
  Israel?"
            declares the LORD.
¹²"But you made the Nazirites
  drink wine
  and commanded the
  prophets not to
  prophesy.   Isa 30:10; Jer 11:21

¹³"Now then, I will crush you
  as a cart crushes when
  loaded with grain.
¹⁴The swift will not escape,
  the strong will not muster
  their strength,   Jer 9:23
  and the warrior will not save
  his life.   Ps 33:16; Isa 30:16-17
¹⁵The archer will not stand his
  ground,   Eze 39:3
  the fleet-footed soldier will
  not get away,
  and the horseman will not
  save his life.   Ecc 9:11
¹⁶Even the bravest warriors
  will flee naked on that day,"
            declares the LORD.

ᵃ4 Or by lies   ᵇ4 Or lies

Witnesses Summoned Against Israel

3 Hear this word the LORD has spoken against you, O people of Israel—against the whole family I brought up out of Egypt: Am 2:10

²"You only have I chosen   Dt 7:6
  of all the families of the earth;
therefore I will punish you
  for all your sins."   Jer 14:10

³Do two walk together
  unless they have agreed to do so?
⁴Does a lion roar in the thicket
  when he has no prey?
Does he growl in his den
  when he has caught nothing?
⁵Does a bird fall into a trap on the ground
  where no snare has been set?
Does a trap spring up from the earth
  when there is nothing to catch?
⁶When a trumpet sounds in a city,
  do not the people tremble?
When disaster comes to a city,
  has not the LORD caused it?

⁷Surely the Sovereign LORD does nothing
  without revealing his plan
  to his servants the prophets.

⁸The lion has roared—
  who will not fear?

The Sovereign LORD has spoken—
  who can but prophesy?

⁹Proclaim to the fortresses of Ashdod
  and to the fortresses of Egypt:
"Assemble yourselves on the mountains of Samaria;
see the great unrest within her
  and the oppression among her people."

¹⁰"They do not know how to do right," declares the LORD,   Jer 4:22; Am 5:7; 6:12
"who hoard plunder and loot
  in their fortresses."

¹¹Therefore this is what the Sovereign LORD says:

"An enemy will overrun the land;
  he will pull down your strongholds
  and plunder your fortresses."

¹²This is what the LORD says:

"As a shepherd saves from the lion's mouth   1Sa 17:34
  only two leg bones or a piece of an ear,
so will the Israelites be saved,
those who sit in Samaria
  on the edge of their beds
  and in Damascus on their couches.ᵃ"   Am 6:4

ᵃ 12 The meaning of the Hebrew for this line is uncertain.

¹³"Hear this and testify against the house of Jacob," declares the Lord, the Lᴏʀᴅ God Almighty.

¹⁴"On the day I punish Israel for her sins,
I will destroy the altars of Bethel;   Am 5:5-6
the horns of the altar will be cut off
and fall to the ground.
¹⁵I will tear down the winter house   Jer 36:22
along with the summer house;   Jdg 3:20
the houses adorned with ivory will be destroyed   1Ki 22:39
and the mansions will be demolished,"   Isa 34:5
declares the Lᴏʀᴅ.

Israel Has Not Returned to God

4 Hear this word, you cows of Bashan on Mount Samaria,   Ps 22:12; Am 3:9
you women who oppress the poor and crush the needy   Dt 24:14
and say to your husbands, "Bring us some drinks!"
²The Sovereign Lᴏʀᴅ has sworn by his holiness:
"The time will surely come when you will be taken away with hooks,   Am 6:8
the last of you with fishhooks.

³You will each go straight out through breaks in the wall,
and you will be cast out toward Harmon,ᵃ"
declares the Lᴏʀᴅ.
⁴"Go to Bethel and sin;
go to Gilgal and sin yet more.   Hos 4:15
Bring your sacrifices every morning,   Nu 28:3
your tithes every three years.ᵇ   Dt 14:28; Eze 20:39
⁵Burn leavened bread as a thank offering   Lev 7:13
and brag about your freewill offerings—   Lev 22:18-21
boast about them, you Israelites,
for this is what you love to do,"
declares the Sovereign Lᴏʀᴅ.

⁶"I gave you empty stomachsᶜ in every city
and lack of bread in every town,
yet you have not returned to me,"
declares the Lᴏʀᴅ.
⁷"I also withheld rain from you when the harvest was still three months away.
I sent rain on one town, but withheld it from another.
One field had rain;
another had none and dried up.

ᵃ3 Masoretic Text; with a different word division of the Hebrew (see Septuagint) out, O mountain of oppression   ᵇ4 Or tithes on the third day   ᶜ6 Hebrew you cleanness of teeth

8People staggered from town to
 town for water Eze 4:16-17
but did not get enough to
 drink,
yet you have not returned to
 me,"   Jer 3:7
   declares the LORD.

9"Many times I struck your
 gardens and vineyards,
I struck them with blight
 and mildew.   Dt 28:22
Locusts devoured your fig and
 olive trees,   Joel 1:7
yet you have not returned to
 me,"   Jer 3:10; Hag 2:17
   declares the LORD.

10"I sent plagues among you
 as I did to Egypt. Ex 11:5
I killed your young men with
 the sword,   Isa 9:17
along with your captured
 horses.
I filled your nostrils with the
 stench of your camps,
yet you have not returned to
 me,"   Dt 28:21
   declares the LORD.

11"I overthrew some of you
 as I*a* overthrew Sodom and
 Gomorrah. Ge 19:24; Jer 23:14
You were like a burning stick
 snatched from the fire,
yet you have not returned to
 me,"
   declares the LORD.

12"Therefore this is what I will
 do to you, Israel,

and because I will do this to
 you,
prepare to meet your God,
 O Israel."

13He who forms the mountains,
 creates the wind,
and reveals his thoughts to
 man,   Da 2:28
he who turns dawn to
 darkness,
and treads the high places of
 the earth— Mic 1:3
the LORD God Almighty is his
 name. Isa 47:4; Am 5:8,27; 9:6

A Lament and Call to Repentance

5 Hear this word, O house of Israel, this lament I take up concerning you: Eze 19:1

2"Fallen is Virgin Israel, Jer 14:17
 never to rise again,
deserted in her own land,
 with no one to lift her up."

3This is what the Sovereign LORD
says:

"The city that marches out a
 thousand strong for
 Israel
will have only a hundred
 left;
the town that marches out a
 hundred strong
will have only ten left."

4This is what the LORD says to
the house of Israel:

a 11 Hebrew *God*

"Seek me and live;   Isa 55:3
5 do not seek Bethel,
   do not go to Gilgal,   Am 4:4
   do not journey to Beersheba.
For Gilgal will surely go into
      exile,
   and Bethel will be reduced
      to nothing.*a*"   1Sa 7:16
6Seek the LORD and live,   Isa 55:6
   or he will sweep through the
      house of Joseph like a
      fire;   Dt 4:24
   it will devour,
   and Bethel will have no one
      to quench it.   Am 3:14

7You who turn justice into
      bitterness   Am 6:12
   and cast righteousness to the
      ground   Hos 10:4
8(he who made the Pleiades and
      Orion,   Job 9:9
   who turns blackness into
      dawn   Isa 42:16
   and darkens day into night,
   who calls for the waters of the
      sea
   and pours them out over the
      face of the land—
   the LORD is his name—
9he flashes destruction on the
      stronghold
   and brings the fortified city
      to ruin),   Mic 5:11
10you hate the one who reproves
      in court   Isa 29:21
   and despise him who tells
      the truth.   1Ki 22:8
11You trample on the poor   Am 8:6

and force him to give you
      grain.
Therefore, though you have
      built stone mansions,
   you will not live in them;
   though you have planted lush
      vineyards,
   you will not drink their
      wine.   Mic 6:15
12For I know how many are your
      offenses
   and how great your sins.
   You oppress the righteous and
      take bribes
   and you deprive the poor of
      justice in the courts.
13Therefore the prudent man
      keeps quiet in such
      times,
   for the times are evil.   Mic 2:3
14Seek good, not evil,
   that you may live.   ver 6
   Then the LORD God Almighty
      will be with you,
   just as you say he is.
15Hate evil, love good;   Ro 12:9
   maintain justice in the
      courts.   Isa 1:17
   Perhaps the LORD God
      Almighty will have
      mercy   Joel 2:14
   on the remnant of Joseph.

16Therefore this is what the
Lord, the LORD God Almighty,
says:

"There will be wailing in all
      the streets   Jer 9:17

---
a 5 Or *grief*; or *wickedness*; Hebrew *aven*, a reference to Beth Aven (a derogatory name for Bethel)

and cries of anguish in every
  public square.
The farmers will be summoned
  to weep   Joel 1:11
  and the mourners to wail.
¹⁷There will be wailing in all the
  vineyards,
  for I will pass through your
  midst,"   Ex 12:12
          says the LORD.

The Day of the LORD

¹⁸Woe to you who long
  for the day of the LORD!
Why do you long for the day
  of the LORD?
That day will be darkness,
  not light.   Isa 5:19,30; Joel 2:2
¹⁹It will be as though a man fled
  from a lion
  only to meet a bear,
as though he entered his house
  and rested his hand on the
  wall
  only to have a snake bite
  him.   Job 20:24; Jer 48:44
²⁰Will not the day of the LORD be
  darkness, not light—
  pitch-dark, without a ray of
  brightness?   Isa 13:10; Zep 1:15

²¹"I hate, I despise your religious
  feasts;   Lev 26:31
  I cannot stand your
  assemblies.   Isa 1:11-16
²²Even though you bring me
  burnt offerings and
  grain offerings,
  I will not accept them.   Ps 40:6

Though you bring choice
  fellowship offerings,ᵃ
  I will have no regard for
  them.   Isa 66:3; Mic 6:6-7
²³Away with the noise of your
  songs!
  I will not listen to the music
  of your harps.   Am 6:5
²⁴But let justice roll on like a
  river,   Jer 22:3
  righteousness like a
  never-failing stream!

²⁵"Did you bring me sacrifices
  and offerings   Isa 43:23
  forty years in the desert,
  O house of Israel?
²⁶You have lifted up the shrine
  of your king,
  the pedestal of your idols,
  the star of your godᵇ—
  which you made for
  yourselves.
²⁷Therefore I will send you into
  exile beyond
  Damascus,"
  says the LORD, whose name
  is God Almighty.   Am 4:13

Woe to the Complacent

6 Woe to you who are
  complacent in Zion,
  and to you who feel secure
  on Mount Samaria,
  you notable men of the
  foremost nation,
  to whom the people of Israel
  come!   Isa 32:9-11
²Go to Calneh and look at it;

ᵃ22 Traditionally *peace offerings*   ᵇ26 Or *lifted up Sakkuth your king / and Kaiwan your idols, / your
star-gods*; Septuagint *lifted up the shrine of Molech / and the star of your god Rephan, / their idols*

go from there to great
Hamath,   2Ki 18:34
and then go down to Gath in
Philistia.   2Ch 26:6
Are they better off than your
two kingdoms?   Na 3:8
Is their land larger than
yours?
³You put off the evil day
and bring near a reign of
terror.   Isa 56:12; Am 9:10
⁴You lie on beds inlaid with
ivory
and lounge on your couches.
You dine on choice lambs
and fattened calves.   Eze 34:2-3
⁵You strum away on your harps
like David   Isa 5:12; Am 5:23
and improvise on musical
instruments.   1Ch 15:16
⁶You drink wine by the bowlful
and use the finest lotions,
but you do not grieve over
the ruin of Joseph.
⁷Therefore you will be among
the first to go into exile;
your feasting and lounging
will end.   Jer 16:9

*The Lord Abhors the Pride
of Israel*

⁸The Sovereign Lord has sworn
by himself—the Lord God Almighty declares: Ge 22:16; Heb 6:13

"I abhor the pride of Jacob
and detest his fortresses;
I will deliver up the city   Am 4:2
and everything in it."   Dt 32:19

⁹If ten men are left in one house,
they too will die. ¹⁰And if a relative
who is to burn the bodies comes to
carry them out of the house and
asks anyone still hiding there, "Is
anyone with you?" and he says,
"No," then he will say, "Hush! We
must not mention the name of the
Lord."   Am 5:3; 8:3; 1Sa 31:12

¹¹For the Lord has given the
command,
and he will smash the great
house into pieces   Am 3:15
and the small house into
bits.   Isa 55:11

¹²Do horses run on the rocky
crags?
Does one plow there with
oxen?
But you have turned justice
into poison   Hos 10:4
and the fruit of
righteousness into
bitterness—   Am 5:7
¹³you who rejoice in the
conquest of Lo Debar*ᵃ*
and say, "Did we not take
Karnaim*ᵇ* by our own
strength?"   Job 8:15

¹⁴For the Lord God Almighty
declares,
"I will stir up a nation
against you, O house of
Israel,   Jer 5:15
that will oppress you all the
way

ᵃ 13 Lo Debar means *nothing*.   *ᵇ 13* Karnaim means *horns; horn* here symbolizes strength.

from Lebo[a] Hamath to the
    valley of the Arabah."

Locusts, Fire and a Plumb Line

7 This is what the Sovereign
LORD showed me: He was preparing swarms of locusts after the
king's share had been harvested
and just as the second crop was
coming up. ²When they had
stripped the land clean, I cried out,
"Sovereign LORD, forgive! How can
Jacob survive? He is so small!"

³So the LORD relented.   Dt 32:36

"This will not happen," the LORD
said.   Hos 11:8

⁴This is what the Sovereign LORD
showed me: The Sovereign LORD
was calling for judgment by fire; it
dried up the great deep and devoured the land. ⁵Then I cried out,
"Sovereign LORD, I beg you, stop!
How can Jacob survive? He is so
small!"   Joel 2:17

⁶So the LORD relented.   Jnh 3:10

"This will not happen either,"
the Sovereign LORD said.   Eze 9:8

⁷This is what he showed me:
The Lord was standing by a wall
that had been built true to plumb,
with a plumb line in his hand.
⁸And the LORD asked me, "What do
you see, Amos?"   Am 8:2

"A plumb line," I replied.

Then the Lord said, "Look, I am
setting a plumb line among my
people Israel; I will spare them no
longer.   Jer 15:6; Eze 7:2-9

⁹"The high places of Isaac will
    be destroyed
and the sanctuaries of Israel
    will be ruined;   Lev 26:31
with my sword I will rise
    against the house of
    Jeroboam."   2Ki 15:9; Hos 10:8

Amos and Amaziah

¹⁰Then Amaziah the priest of
Bethel sent a message to Jeroboam
king of Israel: "Amos is raising a
conspiracy against you in the very
heart of Israel. The land cannot
bear all his words. ¹¹For this is
what Amos is saying: 1Ki 12:32

" 'Jeroboam will die by the
    sword,
    and Israel will surely go into
        exile,   Am 5:27
    away from their native
        land.' "   Jer 36:16

¹²Then Amaziah said to Amos,
"Get out, you seer! Go back to the
land of Judah. Earn your bread
there and do your prophesying
there. ¹³Don't prophesy anymore
at Bethel, because this is the king's
sanctuary and the temple of the
kingdom."   Am 2:12; Ac 4:18

¹⁴Amos answered Amaziah, "I
was neither a prophet nor a prophet's son, but I was a shepherd, and
I also took care of sycamore-fig
trees. ¹⁵But the LORD took me from
tending the flock and said to me,
'Go, prophesy to my people Israel.'

a 14 Or from the entrance to

16Now then, hear the word of the Lord. You say, 2Ki 2:5; Eze 2:3-4

" 'Do not prophesy against
      Israel,   Eze 20:46; Mic 2:6
and stop preaching against
      the house of Isaac.'

17"Therefore this is what the Lord says:

" 'Your wife will become a
      prostitute in the city,
and your sons and daughters
      will fall by the sword.
Your land will be measured
      and divided up,
and you yourself will die in
      a pagan*a* country.
And Israel will certainly go into
      exile,
away from their native
      land.' "   Eze 4:13; Hos 9:3

A Basket of Ripe Fruit

8 This is what the Sovereign Lord showed me: a basket of ripe fruit. 2"What do you see, Amos?" he asked.   Am 7:8

"A basket of ripe fruit," I answered.   Ge 40:16

Then the Lord said to me, "The time is ripe for my people Israel; I will spare them no longer.

3"In that day," declares the Sovereign Lord, "the songs in the temple will turn to wailing.*b* Many, many bodies—flung everywhere! Silence!"   Am 5:16; 6:10

4Hear this, you who trample the
      needy
and do away with the poor
      of the land,   Ps 14:4; Pr 30:14

5saying,

"When will the New Moon be
      over
that we may sell grain,
and the Sabbath be ended
that we may market
      wheat?"—
skimping the measure,
      boosting the price
and cheating with dishonest
      scales,   Ne 13:15-16; Mic 6:10-11
6buying the poor with silver
      and the needy for a pair of
      sandals,
selling even the sweepings
      with the wheat.   Am 2:6

7The Lord has sworn by the Pride of Jacob: "I will never forget anything they have done.   Hos 8:13

8"Will not the land tremble for
      this,   Hos 4:3
and all who live in it mourn?
The whole land will rise like
      the Nile;
it will be stirred up and then
      sink
like the river of Egypt.   Jer 46:8

9"In that day," declares the Sovereign Lord,

"I will make the sun go down
      at noon

---

a 17 Hebrew *an unclean*   *b 3* Or *"the temple singers will wail"*

and darken the earth in
    broad daylight.   *Jer 15:9*
¹⁰I will turn your religious feasts
    into mourning
and all your singing into
    weeping.
I will make all of you wear
    sackcloth   *Jer 48:37*
and shave your heads.
I will make that time like
    mourning for an only
    son   *Jer 6:26; Zec 12:10*
and the end of it like a bitter
    day.   *Eze 7:18*

¹¹"The days are coming,"
    declares the Sovereign
    LORD,   *1Sa 3:1; 2Ch 15:3*
"when I will send a famine
    through the land—
not a famine of food or a thirst
    for water,
but a famine of hearing the
    words of the LORD.
¹²Men will stagger from sea to
    sea
and wander from north to
    east,
searching for the word of the
    LORD,
but they will not find it.

¹³"In that day

"the lovely young women and
    strong young men
will faint because of thirst.
¹⁴They who swear by the
    shame*ᵃ* of Samaria,

or say, 'As surely as your
    god lives, O Dan,'
or, 'As surely as the god*ᵇ* of
    Beersheba lives'—   *Am 5:5*
they will fall,
    never to rise again."   *Am 5:2*

Israel to Be Destroyed

9 I saw the Lord standing by the
    altar, and he said:

"Strike the tops of the pillars
    so that the thresholds shake.
Bring them down on the heads
    of all the people;   *Ps 68:21*
those who are left I will kill
    with the sword.
Not one will get away,
    none will escape.
²Though they dig down to the
    depths of the grave,*ᶜ*
from there my hand will
    take them.
Though they climb up to the
    heavens,   *Jer 51:53*
from there I will bring them
    down.   *Ob 1:4*
³Though they hide themselves
    on the top of Carmel,
there I will hunt them down
    and seize them.
Though they hide from me at
    the bottom of the sea,
there I will command the
    serpent to bite them.
⁴Though they are driven into
    exile by their enemies,
there I will command the
    sword to slay them.

ᵃ14 Or *by Ashima; or by the idol*   *ᵇ14* Or *power*   *ᶜ2* Hebrew *to Sheol*

I will fix my eyes upon them
for evil and not for good."

⁵The Lord, the LORD Almighty,
he who touches the earth
and it melts,   Ps 46:2; Mic 1:4
and all who live in it
mourn—
the whole land rises like the
Nile,
then sinks like the river of
Egypt—   Am 8:8
⁶he who builds his lofty palaceᵃ
in the heavens
and sets its foundationᵇ on
the earth,
who calls for the waters of the
sea
and pours them out over the
face of the land—
the LORD is his name.

⁷"Are not you Israelites
the same to me as the
Cushitesᶜ?"   Isa 20:4; 43:3
declares the LORD.
"Did I not bring Israel up from
Egypt,
the Philistines from Caphtorᵈ
and the Arameans from Kir?

⁸"Surely the eyes of the
Sovereign LORD
are on the sinful kingdom.
I will destroy it
from the face of the earth—
yet I will not totally destroy
the house of Jacob,"
declares the LORD.

⁹"For I will give the command,
and I will shake the house of
Israel
among all the nations
as grain is shaken in a sieve,
and not a pebble will reach
the ground.
¹⁰All the sinners among my
people
will die by the sword,
all those who say,
'Disaster will not overtake or
meet us.'   Am 6:3

Israel's Restoration

¹¹"In that day I will restore
David's fallen tent.   Isa 7:2
I will repair its broken places,
restore its ruins,   Ps 53:6
and build it as it used to be,
¹²so that they may possess the
remnant of Edom   Nu 24:18
and all the nations that bear
my name,ᵉ"   Isa 43:7
declares the LORD, who
will do these things.

¹³"The days are coming," declares the LORD,

"when the reaper will be
overtaken by the
plowman   Lev 26:5
and the planter by the one
treading grapes.
New wine will drip from the
mountains
and flow from all the hills.

ᵃ6 The meaning of the Hebrew for this phrase is uncertain.   ᵇ6 The meaning of the Hebrew for this
word is uncertain.   ᶜ7 That is, people from the upper Nile region   ᵈ7 That is, Crete   ᵉ12 Hebrew;
Septuagint so that the remnant of men / and all the nations that bear my name may seek the Lord.

14I will bring back my exiled*a*
    people Israel;   Jer 33:7
  they will rebuild the ruined
    cities and live in them.
They will plant vineyards and
    drink their wine;
  they will make gardens and
    eat their fruit.   Jer 30:18

15I will plant Israel in their own
    land,   Isa 60:21
  never again to be
    uprooted
  from the land I have given
    them,"   Isa 65:9

    says the LORD your God.

---

a 14 Or will restore the fortunes of my

Obadiah

¹The vision of Obadiah.

This is what the Sovereign Lord
says about Edom—   Jer 49:7-22

We have heard a message from
    the Lord:
An envoy was sent to the
    nations to say,   Isa 18:2
"Rise, and let us go against her
    for battle"—   Jer 6:4-5

²"See, I will make you small
    among the nations;
you will be utterly
    despised.
³The pride of your heart has
    deceived you,   Isa 16:6
you who live in the clefts of
    the rocks*ᵃ*
and make your home on the
    heights,
you who say to yourself,
    'Who can bring me down to
    the ground?'   Isa 14:13-15
⁴Though you soar like the
    eagle
and make your nest among
    the stars,   Hab 2:9
from there I will bring you
    down,"   Jer 49:14-16; Isa 14:13
        declares the Lord.

⁵"If thieves came to you,
    if robbers in the night—
Oh, what a disaster awaits
    you—
would they not steal only as
    much as they wanted?
If grape pickers came to
    you,
would they not leave a few
    grapes?   Jer 49:9-10
⁶But how Esau will be
    ransacked,
his hidden treasures
    pillaged!
⁷All your allies will force you to
    the border;   Jer 30:14
your friends will deceive and
    overpower you;
those who eat your bread will
    set a trap for you,*ᵇ*
but you will not detect
    it.

⁸"In that day," declares the
    Lord,
"will I not destroy the wise
    men of Edom,   Job 5:12
men of understanding in the
    mountains of Esau?
⁹Your warriors, O Teman, will
    be terrified,   Ge 36:11,34
and everyone in Esau's
    mountains

ᵃ3 Or *of Sela*   ᵇ7 The meaning of the Hebrew for this clause is uncertain.

will be cut down in the
   slaughter.
¹⁰Because of the violence against
   your brother Jacob,
  you will be covered with
   shame;
  you will be destroyed
   forever.   Eze 35:9
¹¹On the day you stood aloof
  while strangers carried off
   his wealth
 and foreigners entered his
   gates
  and cast lots for Jerusalem,
  you were like one of
   them.
¹²You should not look down on
   your brother   Pr 24:17
  in the day of his misfortune,
 nor rejoice over the people of
   Judah   Eze 35:15
  in the day of their
   destruction,   Pr 17:5
 nor boast so much   Ps 137:7
  in the day of their trouble.
¹³You should not march through
   the gates of my people
  in the day of their disaster,
 nor look down on them in
   their calamity   Eze 35:5
  in the day of their disaster,
 nor seize their wealth
  in the day of their disaster.
¹⁴You should not wait at the
   crossroads
  to cut down their fugitives,
 nor hand over their survivors
  in the day of their trouble.

¹⁵"The day of the LORD is near
  for all nations.

As you have done, it will be
   done to you;
  your deeds will return upon
   your own head.   Jer 50:29
¹⁶Just as you drank on my holy
   hill,
  so all the nations will drink
   continually;   Jer 25:15; 49:12
 they will drink and drink
  and be as if they had never
   been.
¹⁷But on Mount Zion will be
   deliverance;   Am 9:11-15
  it will be holy,   Isa 4:3
 and the house of Jacob
  will possess its inheritance.
¹⁸The house of Jacob will be a
   fire
  and the house of Joseph a
   flame;
 the house of Esau will be
   stubble,
  and they will set it on fire
   and consume it.   Zec 12:6
There will be no survivors
from the house of Esau."
     The LORD has spoken.

¹⁹People from the Negev will
   occupy
  the mountains of Esau,
 and people from the foothills
  will possess
  the land of the Philistines.
They will occupy the fields of
   Ephraim and Samaria,
 and Benjamin will possess
   Gilead.
²⁰This company of Israelite
   exiles who are in
   Canaan

will possess the land, as far
as Zarephath;   1Ki 17:9-10
the exiles from Jerusalem who
are in Sepharad
will possess the towns of the
Negev.   Jer 33:13

21Deliverers will go up on^a
Mount Zion
to govern the mountains of
Esau.
And the kingdom will be the
Lord's.   Zec 14:9,16; Rev 11:15

^a21 Or *from*

Jonah

Jonah Flees From the Lord

1 The word of the Lord came to Jonah son of Amittai: ²"Go to the great city of Nineveh and preach against it, because its wickedness has come up before me."

³But Jonah ran away from the Lord and headed for Tarshish. He went down to Joppa, where he found a ship bound for that port. After paying the fare, he went aboard and sailed for Tarshish to flee from the Lord.   Jos 19:46; Ps 139:7

⁴Then the Lord sent a great wind on the sea, and such a violent storm arose that the ship threatened to break up. ⁵All the sailors were afraid and each cried out to his own god. And they threw the cargo into the sea to lighten the ship.   Ps 107:23-26; Ac 27:18-19

But Jonah had gone below deck, where he lay down and fell into a deep sleep. ⁶The captain went to him and said, "How can you sleep? Get up and call on your god! Maybe he will take notice of us, and we will not perish."   Jnh 3:8; Ps 107:28

⁷Then the sailors said to each other, "Come, let us cast lots to find out who is responsible for this calamity." They cast lots and the lot fell on Jonah.   Jos 7:10-18; 1Sa 14:42

⁸So they asked him, "Tell us, who is responsible for making all this trouble for us? What do you do? Where do you come from? What is your country? From what people are you?"

⁹He answered, "I am a Hebrew and I worship the Lord, the God of heaven, who made the sea and the land."   Ps 146:6; Ac 17:24

¹⁰This terrified them and they asked, "What have you done?" (They knew he was running away from the Lord, because he had already told them so.)

¹¹The sea was getting rougher and rougher. So they asked him, "What should we do to you to make the sea calm down for us?"

¹²"Pick me up and throw me into the sea," he replied, "and it will become calm. I know that it is my fault that this great storm has come upon you."   2Sa 24:17; 1Ch 21:17

¹³Instead, the men did their best to row back to land. But they could not, for the sea grew even wilder than before. ¹⁴Then they cried to the Lord, "O Lord, please do not let us die for taking this man's life. Do not hold us accountable for killing an innocent man, for you, O Lord, have done as you pleased." ¹⁵Then they took Jonah and threw him overboard, and the raging sea grew calm. ¹⁶At this the men greatly feared the Lord, and they of-

fered a sacrifice to the Lord and made vows to him. Lk 8:24; Dt 21:8

¹⁷But the Lord provided a great fish to swallow Jonah, and Jonah was inside the fish three days and three nights. Mt 12:40; 16:4; Lk 11:30

Jonah's Prayer

2 From inside the fish Jonah prayed to the Lord his God. ²He said:

"In my distress I called to the
  Lord, Ps 18:6; 120:1
    and he answered me.
From the depths of the grave^a
    I called for help,
    and you listened to my
      cry.
³You hurled me into the
      deep,
  into the very heart of the
      seas,
  and the currents swirled
      about me;
  all your waves and breakers
    swept over me. Ps 42:7
⁴I said, 'I have been banished
    from your sight; Ps 31:22
  yet I will look again
    toward your holy temple.'
⁵The engulfing waters
      threatened me,^b
  the deep surrounded me;
  seaweed was wrapped
      around my head. Ps 69:1-2
⁶To the roots of the mountains I
    sank down;
  the earth beneath barred me
      in forever.

But you brought my life up
    from the pit, Ps 30:3
  O Lord my God.

⁷"When my life was ebbing
      away,
  I remembered you,
      Lord,
  and my prayer rose to
      you,
  to your holy temple. Ps 18:6

⁸"Those who cling to worthless
      idols 2Ki 17:15; Jer 10:8
  forfeit the grace that could
      be theirs.
⁹But I, with a song of
      thanksgiving,
  will sacrifice to you.
  What I have vowed I will make
      good. Ecc 5:4-5
  Salvation comes from the
      Lord." Ps 3:8

¹⁰And the Lord commanded the fish, and it vomited Jonah onto dry land.

Jonah Goes to Nineveh

3 Then the word of the Lord came to Jonah a second time: ²"Go to the great city of Nineveh and proclaim to it the message I give you." Jnh 1:1

³Jonah obeyed the word of the Lord and went to Nineveh. Now Nineveh was a very important city —a visit required three days. ⁴On the first day, Jonah started into the

---

^a2 Hebrew Sheol   ^b5 Or waters were at my throat

city. He proclaimed: "Forty more days and Nineveh will be overturned." ⁵The Ninevites believed God. They declared a fast, and all of them, from the greatest to the least, put on sackcloth.   Da 9:3

⁶When the news reached the king of Nineveh, he rose from his throne, took off his royal robes, covered himself with sackcloth and sat down in the dust. ⁷Then he issued a proclamation in Nineveh:

"By the decree of the king and his nobles:

Do not let any man or beast, herd or flock, taste anything; do not let them eat or drink. ⁸But let man and beast be covered with sackcloth. Let everyone call urgently on God. Let them give up their evil ways and their violence. ⁹Who knows? God may yet relent and with compassion turn from his fierce anger so that we will not perish."

¹⁰When God saw what they did and how they turned from their evil ways, he had compassion and did not bring upon them the destruction he had threatened.

Jonah's Anger at the Lord's Compassion

4 But Jonah was greatly displeased and became angry.

²He prayed to the Lord, "O Lord, is this not what I said when I was still at home? That is why I was so quick to flee to Tarshish. I knew that you are a gracious and compassionate God, slow to anger and abounding in love, a God who relents from sending calamity. ³Now, O Lord, take away my life, for it is better for me to die than to live."   1Ki 19:4; Ps 86:5,15

⁴But the Lord replied, "Have you any right to be angry?"   Mt 20:11-15

⁵Jonah went out and sat down at a place east of the city. There he made himself a shelter, sat in its shade and waited to see what would happen to the city. ⁶Then the Lord God provided a vine and made it grow up over Jonah to give shade for his head to ease his discomfort, and Jonah was very happy about the vine. ⁷But at dawn the next day God provided a worm, which chewed the vine so that it withered. ⁸When the sun rose, God provided a scorching east wind, and the sun blazed on Jonah's head so that he grew faint. He wanted to die, and said, "It would be better for me to die than to live."   Joel 1:12

⁹But God said to Jonah, "Do you have a right to be angry about the vine?"

"I do," he said. "I am angry enough to die."

¹⁰But the Lord said, "You have been concerned about this vine, though you did not tend it or make

it grow. It sprang up overnight and died overnight. [11]But Nineveh has more than a hundred and twenty thousand people who cannot tell their right hand from their left, and many cattle as well. Should I not be concerned about that great city?"

Jnh 1:2; 3:10

Micah

1 The word of the LORD that came to Micah of Moresheth during the reigns of Jotham, Ahaz and Hezekiah, kings of Judah— the vision he saw concerning Samaria and Jerusalem.   Jer 26:18

²Hear, O peoples, all of you,
    listen, O earth and all who
        are in it,   Jer 6:19
that the Sovereign LORD may
        witness against you,
    the Lord from his holy
        temple.   Ps 11:4

Judgment Against Samaria and Jerusalem

³Look! The LORD is coming
        from his dwelling place;
    he comes down and treads
        the high places of the
        earth.   Am 4:13
⁴The mountains melt beneath
        him   Ps 46:2,6
    and the valleys split apart,
like wax before the fire,
    like water rushing down a
        slope.
⁵All this is because of Jacob's
        transgression,
    because of the sins of the
        house of Israel.
What is Jacob's transgression?
    Is it not Samaria?   Am 8:14
What is Judah's high place?
    Is it not Jerusalem?

⁶"Therefore I will make Samaria
        a heap of rubble,
    a place for planting
        vineyards.
I will pour her stones into the
        valley   Am 5:11
    and lay bare her
        foundations.   Eze 13:14
⁷All her idols will be broken to
        pieces;   Eze 6:6
    all her temple gifts will be
        burned with fire;
    I will destroy all her images.
Since she gathered her gifts
        from the wages of
        prostitutes,   Dt 23:17-18
    as the wages of prostitutes
        they will again be used."

Weeping and Mourning

⁸Because of this I will weep and
        wail;   Isa 15:3
    I will go about barefoot and
        naked.
I will howl like a jackal
    and moan like an owl.
⁹For her wound is incurable;
    it has come to Judah.   2Ki 18:13
It[a] has reached the very gate
        of my people,   Isa 3:26
    even to Jerusalem itself.

¹⁰Tell it not in Gath;
    weep not at all.
In Beth Ophrah
    roll in the dust.
¹¹Pass on in nakedness and

---

[a]9 Or *He*

¹⁰Tell it not in Gath*ᵃ*;
  weep not at all.*ᵇ*
In Beth Ophrah*ᶜ*
  roll in the dust.
¹¹Pass on in nakedness and
    shame,   Eze 23:29
  you who live in Shaphir.*ᵈ*
Those who live in Zaanan*ᵉ*
  will not come out.
Beth Ezel is in mourning;
  its protection is taken from
    you.
¹²Those who live in Maroth*ᶠ*
    writhe in pain,
  waiting for relief,   Jer 14:19
because disaster has come
    from the LORD,   Jer 40:2
  even to the gate of
    Jerusalem.
¹³You who live in Lachish,*ᵍ*
  harness the team to the
    chariot.
You were the beginning of sin
  to the Daughter of Zion,
for the transgressions of Israel
  were found in you.
¹⁴Therefore you will give parting
    gifts   2Ki 16:8
  to Moresheth Gath.
The town of Aczib*ʰ* will prove
    deceptive   Jos 15:44; Jer 15:18
  to the kings of Israel.
¹⁵I will bring a conqueror against
    you
  who live in Mareshah.*ⁱ*
He who is the glory of Israel

will come to Adullam.
¹⁶Shave your heads in mourning
  for the children in whom
    you delight;
make yourselves as bald as the
    vulture,
  for they will go from you
    into exile.   Am 5:27

Man's Plans and God's

2 Woe to those who plan
    iniquity,
  to those who plot evil on
    their beds!   Ps 36:4
At morning's light they carry it
    out
  because it is in their power
    to do it.
²They covet fields and seize
    them,   Isa 5:8
  and houses, and take them.
They defraud a man of his
    home,   Jer 22:17
  a fellowman of his
    inheritance.   Eze 46:18

³Therefore, the LORD says:

"I am planning disaster against
    this people,   Jer 18:11
  from which you cannot save
    yourselves.
You will no longer walk
    proudly,   Isa 2:12
  for it will be a time of
    calamity.

ᵃ10 Gath sounds like the Hebrew for *tell.*   *ᵇ10* Hebrew; Septuagint may suggest *not in Acco.* The
Hebrew for *in Acco* sounds like the Hebrew for *weep.*   *ᶜ10 Beth Ophrah* means *house of dust.*
ᵈ11 Shaphir means *pleasant.*   *ᵉ11 Zaanan* sounds like the Hebrew for *come out.*   *ᶠ12 Maroth*
sounds like the Hebrew for *bitter.*   *ᵍ13 Lachish* sounds like the Hebrew for *team.*   *ʰ14 Aczib* means
deception.   *ⁱ15 Mareshah* sounds like the Hebrew for *conqueror.*

⁴In that day men will ridicule
    you;
    they will taunt you with this
        mournful song:
    'We are utterly ruined;   Jer 4:13
    my people's possession is
        divided up.
He takes it from me!
    He assigns our fields to
        traitors.' "

⁵Therefore you will have no one
        in the assembly of the
        LORD
    to divide the land by lot.

False Prophets

⁶"Do not prophesy," their
        prophets say.
    "Do not prophesy about
        these things;
    disgrace will not overtake
        us."   Am 2:12; Mic 6:16
⁷Should it be said, O house of
        Jacob:
    "Is the Spirit of the LORD
        angry?
    Does he do such things?"

    "Do not my words do good
        to him whose ways are
        upright?   Ps 15:2; 84:11
⁸Lately my people have risen up
        like an enemy.
    You strip off the rich robe
    from those who pass by
        without a care,
    like men returning from
        battle.
⁹You drive the women of my
        people

from their pleasant homes.
    You take away my blessing
    from their children forever.
¹⁰Get up, go away!
    For this is not your resting
        place,   Dt 12:9
    because it is defiled,   Lev 18:25-29
    it is ruined, beyond all
        remedy.
¹¹If a liar and deceiver comes
        and says,   Jer 5:31
    'I will prophesy for you
        plenty of wine and
        beer,'
    he would be just the prophet
        for this people!   Isa 30:10

Deliverance Promised

¹²"I will surely gather all of you,
        O Jacob;
    I will surely bring together
        the remnant of Israel.
    I will bring them together like
        sheep in a pen,
    like a flock in its pasture;
    the place will throng with
        people.
¹³One who breaks open the way
        will go up before them;
    they will break through the
        gate and go out.
    Their king will pass through
        before them,
    the LORD at their head."

Leaders and Prophets Rebuked

3 Then I said,
    "Listen, you leaders of
        Jacob,   Jer 5:5

you rulers of the house of
  Israel.
Should you not know justice,
2 you who hate good and love
  evil;
who tear the skin from my
  people
and the flesh from their
  bones;   Ps 53:4; Eze 22:27
³who eat my people's flesh,
strip off their skin
and break their bones in
  pieces;   Zep 3:3
who chop them up like meat
  for the pan,   Job 24:14
  like flesh for the pot?"   Eze 11:7

⁴Then they will cry out to the
  LORD,
  but he will not answer them.
At that time he will hide his
  face from them   Dt 31:17
  because of the evil they have
  done.   Eze 8:18

⁵This is what the LORD says:

"As for the prophets
  who lead my people astray,
if one feeds them,
  they proclaim 'peace';   Jer 4:10
if he does not,
  they prepare to wage war
  against him.
⁶Therefore night will come over
  you, without visions,
  and darkness, without
  divination.   Isa 8:19-22
The sun will set for the
  prophets,   Isa 29:10
  and the day will go dark for
  them.   Eze 7:26

⁷The seers will be ashamed
  and the diviners disgraced.
They will all cover their
  faces
  because there is no answer
  from God."   Eze 20:3

⁸But as for me, I am filled with
  power,
  with the Spirit of the LORD,
  and with justice and
  might,
to declare to Jacob his
  transgression,
  to Israel his sin.   Isa 58:1
⁹Hear this, you leaders of the
  house of Jacob,
  you rulers of the house of
  Israel,
who despise justice
  and distort all that is right;
¹⁰who build Zion with
  bloodshed,   Jer 22:13; Hab 2:12
  and Jerusalem with
  wickedness.   Eze 22:27
¹¹Her leaders judge for a bribe,
  her priests teach for a price,
  and her prophets tell
  fortunes for money.
Yet they lean upon the LORD
  and say,
"Is not the LORD among us?
  No disaster will come upon
  us."   Jer 7:4
¹²Therefore because of you,
  Zion will be plowed like a
  field,
Jerusalem will become a heap
  of rubble,   Jer 26:18
  the temple hill a mound
  overgrown with thickets.

The Mountain of the LORD

4 In the last days
    the mountain of the LORD's
      temple will be
      established   Zec 8:3
    as chief among the
      mountains;
    it will be raised above the hills,
      and peoples will stream to it.

²Many nations will come and
say,

    "Come, let us go up to the
      mountain of the LORD,
    to the house of the God of
      Jacob.   Zec 2:11; 14:16
    He will teach us his ways,
    so that we may walk in his
      paths."
    The law will go out from Zion,
      the word of the LORD from
      Jerusalem.
³He will judge between many
      peoples
    and will settle disputes for
      strong nations far and
      wide.   Isa 11:4
    They will beat their swords
      into plowshares
    and their spears into pruning
      hooks.   Joel 3:10
    Nation will not take up sword
      against nation,
    nor will they train for war
      anymore.   Isa 2:1-4
⁴Every man will sit under his
      own vine
    and under his own fig tree,
    and no one will make them
      afraid,   Lev 26:6
    for the LORD Almighty has
      spoken.   Isa 1:20; Zec 3:10
⁵All the nations may walk
    in the name of their gods;
    we will walk in the name of
      the LORD
    our God for ever and ever.

The LORD's Plan

⁶"In that day," declares the
LORD,

    "I will gather the lame;
    I will assemble the exiles
    and those I have brought to
      grief.   Eze 34:13,16; 37:21
⁷I will make the lame a
      remnant,   Mic 2:12
    those driven away a strong
      nation.
    The LORD will rule over them
      in Mount Zion
    from that day and forever.
⁸As for you, O watchtower of
      the flock,
    O stronghold*ᵃ* of the
      Daughter of Zion,
    the former dominion will be
      restored to you;   Isa 1:26
    kingship will come to the
      Daughter of Jerusalem."

⁹Why do you now cry aloud—
    have you no king?   Jer 8:19
    Has your counselor perished,
    that pain seizes you like that
      of a woman in labor?

ᵃ8 Or *hill*

¹⁰Writhe in agony, O Daughter
     of Zion,
  like a woman in labor,
for now you must leave the
     city
  to camp in the open
     field.
You will go to Babylon;   2Ki 20:18
  there you will be rescued.
There the LORD will redeem
     you   Isa 48:20
  out of the hand of your
     enemies.

¹¹But now many nations
  are gathered against
     you.
They say, "Let her be defiled,
  let our eyes gloat over
     Zion!"
¹²But they do not know
  the thoughts of the LORD;
they do not understand his
     plan,   Isa 55:8; Ro 11:33-34
he who gathers them like
     sheaves to the threshing
     floor.

¹³"Rise and thresh, O Daughter
     of Zion,
  for I will give you horns of
     iron;
I will give you hoofs of bronze
  and you will break to pieces
     many nations."   Da 2:44

You will devote their ill-gotten
     gains to the LORD,
  their wealth to the Lord of
     all the earth.

A Promised Ruler From Bethlehem

5 Marshal your troops, O city
     of troops,ᵃ
for a siege is laid against us.
They will strike Israel's
     ruler
  on the cheek with a
     rod.

²"But you, Bethlehem
     Ephrathah,   Jn 7:42; Ge 48:7
though you are small among
     the clansᵇ of Judah,
out of you will come for me
  one who will be ruler over
     Israel,   1Sa 13:14
whose originsᶜ are from of
     old,
  from ancient times.ᵈ"   Mt 2:6*

³Therefore Israel will be
     abandoned
until the time when she who
     is in labor gives birth
and the rest of his brothers
     return
  to join the Israelites.

⁴He will stand and shepherd his
     flock   Isa 40:11; Eze 34:11-15,23
in the strength of the LORD,
  in the majesty of the name
     of the LORD his God.
And they will live securely, for
     then his greatness
will reach to the ends of the
     earth.
⁵   And he will be their peace.

ᵃ1 Or *Strengthen your walls, O walled city*   ᵇ2 Or *rulers*   ᶜ2 Hebrew *goings out*   ᵈ2 Or *from days*
of eternity

Deliverance and Destruction

When the Assyrian invades our
    land   Isa 8:7
and marches through our
    fortresses,
we will raise against him seven
    shepherds,
even eight leaders of men.
⁶They will rule*ᵃ* the land of
    Assyria with the sword,
the land of Nimrod with
    drawn sword.*ᵇ*   Ge 10:8
He will deliver us from the
    Assyrian
when he invades our land
and marches into our
    borders.   Na 2:11-13

⁷The remnant of Jacob will be
    in the midst of many
    peoples
like dew from the LORD,   Ps 133:3
    like showers on the grass,
which do not wait for man
    or linger for mankind.
⁸The remnant of Jacob will be
    among the nations,
in the midst of many
    peoples,
like a lion among the beasts of
    the forest,   Ge 49:9
    like a young lion among
    flocks of sheep,
which mauls and mangles as it
    goes,   Mic 4:13; Zec 10:5
    and no one can rescue.
⁹Your hand will be lifted up in
    triumph over your
    enemies,   Ps 10:12

and all your foes will be
    destroyed.

¹⁰"In that day," declares the
LORD,

"I will destroy your horses
    from among you
and demolish your chariots.
¹¹I will destroy the cities of your
    land   Isa 6:11
and tear down all your
    strongholds.   Hos 10:14
¹²I will destroy your witchcraft
and you will no longer cast
    spells.   Dt 18:10-12; Isa 2:6
¹³I will destroy your carved
    images
and your sacred stones from
    among you;
you will no longer bow down
    to the work of your hands.
¹⁴I will uproot from among you
    your Asherah poles*ᶜ*
and demolish your cities.
¹⁵I will take vengeance in anger
    and wrath   Isa 65:12
upon the nations that have
    not obeyed me."

The LORD's Case Against Israel

6 Listen to what the LORD says:
"Stand up, plead your case
    before the mountains;
let the hills hear what you
    have to say.
²Hear, O mountains, the LORD's
    accusation;   Dt 32:1; Hos 12:2

---

*ᵃ*6 Or *crush*   *ᵇ*6 Or *Nimrod in its gates*   *ᶜ*14 That is, symbols of the goddess Asherah

listen, you everlasting
    foundations of the
    earth.
For the LORD has a case against
    his people;
he is lodging a charge
    against Israel.   Ps 50:7

³"My people, what have I done
    to you?
How have I burdened you?
    Answer me.   Jer 2:5
⁴I brought you up out of
    Egypt
and redeemed you from the
    land of slavery.   Dt 7:8
I sent Moses to lead you,   Ex 4:16
    also Aaron and Miriam.
⁵My people, remember
    what Balak king of Moab
        counseled   Nu 22:5-6
and what Balaam son of
    Beor answered.
Remember ˻your journey˼ from
    Shittim to Gilgal,   Nu 25:1
that you may know the
    righteous acts of the
    LORD."   Jdg 5:11; 1Sa 12:7

⁶With what shall I come before
    the LORD
and bow down before the
    exalted God?
Shall I come before him with
    burnt offerings,
with calves a year old?
⁷Will the LORD be pleased with
    thousands of rams,
with ten thousand rivers of
    oil?   Ps 50:8-10

Shall I offer my firstborn for
    my transgression,
the fruit of my body for the
    sin of my soul?   2Ki 16:3
⁸He has showed you, O man,
    what is good.
And what does the LORD
    require of you?
To act justly and to love
    mercy
and to walk humbly with
    your God.   Dt 10:12-13; Hos 6:6

Israel's Guilt and Punishment

⁹Listen! The LORD is calling to
    the city—
and to fear your name is
    wisdom—
"Heed the rod and the One
    who appointed it.ᵃ
¹⁰Am I still to forget, O wicked
    house,
your ill-gotten treasures
and the short ephah,ᵇ which
    is accursed?   Eze 45:9-10
¹¹Shall I acquit a man with
    dishonest scales,   Lev 19:36
with a bag of false weights?
¹²Her rich men are violent;
    her people are liars   Isa 3:8
and their tongues speak
    deceitfully.   Jer 9:3
¹³Therefore, I have begun to
    destroy you,   Isa 1:7; 6:11
to ruin you because of your
    sins.
¹⁴You will eat but not be
    satisfied;   Isa 9:20

ᵃ9 The meaning of the Hebrew for this line is uncertain.   ᵇ10 An ephah was a dry measure.

your stomach will still be
    empty.[a]
You will store up but save
    nothing,   Isa 30:6
because what you save I will
    give to the sword.
15You will plant but not harvest;
    you will press olives but not
        use the oil on
        yourselves,
    you will crush grapes but
        not drink the wine.
16You have observed the statutes
        of Omri   1Ki 16:25
    and all the practices of
        Ahab's house,   1Ki 16:29-33
    and you have followed their
        traditions.   Jer 7:24
Therefore I will give you over
        to ruin   Jer 25:9
    and your people to derision;
    you will bear the scorn of
        the nations.[b]"   Jer 51:51

Israel's Misery

7 What misery is mine!
    I am like one who gathers
        summer fruit
    at the gleaning of the
        vineyard;
    there is no cluster of grapes to
        eat,
    none of the early figs that I
        crave.
2The godly have been swept
        from the land;   Ps 12:1
    not one upright man
        remains.   Jer 2:29

All men lie in wait to shed
    blood;   Mic 3:10
each hunts his brother with
    a net.   Jer 5:26
3Both hands are skilled in doing
    evil;   Pr 4:16
    the ruler demands gifts,
    the judge accepts bribes,
    the powerful dictate what
        they desire—
    they all conspire together.
4The best of them is like a
    brier,   Eze 2:6
    the most upright worse than
        a thorn hedge.   2Sa 23:6
The day of your watchmen has
    come,
    the day God visits you.
Now is the time of their
    confusion.   Isa 22:5; Hos 9:7
5Do not trust a neighbor;
    put no confidence in a
        friend.   Jer 9:4
Even with her who lies in your
        embrace
    be careful of your words.
6For a son dishonors his father,
    a daughter rises up against
        her mother,   Eze 22:7
    a daughter-in-law against her
        mother-in-law—
    a man's enemies are the
        members of his own
        household.   Mt 10:35-36*

7But as for me, I watch in hope
    for the LORD,   Ps 130:5
I wait for God my Savior;
    my God will hear me.   Ps 4:3

---

a 14 The meaning of the Hebrew for this word is uncertain.   b 16 Septuagint; Hebrew scorn due my
people

Israel Will Rise

8Do not gloat over me, my
        enemy!   Pr 24:17
    Though I have fallen, I will
        rise.   Ps 37:24; Am 9:11
    Though I sit in darkness,
        the LORD will be my light.
9Because I have sinned against
        him,
    I will bear the LORD's wrath,
    until he pleads my case
        and establishes my right.
    He will bring me out into the
        light;
    I will see his righteousness.
10Then my enemy will see it
        and will be covered with
        shame,   Ps 35:26
    she who said to me,
        "Where is the LORD your
        God?"
    My eyes will see her downfall;
        even now she will be
        trampled underfoot
    like mire in the streets.

11The day for building your
        walls will come,   Isa 54:11
    the day for extending your
        boundaries.
12In that day people will come to
        you
    from Assyria and the cities
        of Egypt,
    even from Egypt to the
        Euphrates
    and from sea to sea
    and from mountain to
        mountain.   Isa 19:23-25

13The earth will become desolate
        because of its
        inhabitants,
    as the result of their deeds.

Prayer and Praise

14Shepherd your people with
        your staff,   Ps 23:4; Mic 5:4
    the flock of your inheritance,
    which lives by itself in a forest,
    in fertile pasturelands.*a*
    Let them feed in Bashan and
        Gilead   Jer 50:19
    as in days long ago.
15"As in the days when you
        came out of Egypt,
    I will show them my
        wonders."   Ex 3:20; Ps 78:12

16Nations will see and be
        ashamed,   Isa 26:11
    deprived of all their power.
    They will lay their hands on
        their mouths
    and their ears will become
        deaf.
17They will lick dust like a
        snake,
    like creatures that crawl on
        the ground.
    They will come trembling out
        of their dens;
    they will turn in fear to the
        LORD our God   Isa 49:23
    and will be afraid of you.
18Who is a God like you,   Ex 8:10
    who pardons sin and
        forgives the
        transgression   Isa 43:25

---

a 14 Or in the middle of Carmel

of the remnant of his
inheritance?   Ex 34:9; Mic 2:12
You do not stay angry forever
but delight to show
mercy.
[19]You will again have
compassion on us;
you will tread our sins
underfoot

and hurl all our iniquities
into the depths of the
sea.   Isa 43:25; Jer 31:34
[20]You will be true to Jacob,
and show mercy to
Abraham,   Gal 3:16
as you pledged on oath to our
fathers   Dt 7:8; Lk 1:72
in days long ago.   Ps 108:4

Nahum

1 An oracle concerning Nineveh. The book of the vision of Nahum the Elkoshite.   Jnh 1:2

The Lord's Anger Against Nineveh

²The Lord is a jealous and
  avenging God;   Ex 20:5
the Lord takes vengeance
  and is filled with wrath.
The Lord takes vengeance on
  his foes
and maintains his wrath
  against his enemies.
³The Lord is slow to anger and
  great in power;   Ne 9:17
the Lord will not leave the
  guilty unpunished.
His way is in the whirlwind
  and the storm,
and clouds are the dust of
  his feet.   Ps 104:3
⁴He rebukes the sea and dries it
  up;   Ex 14:22
he makes all the rivers run
  dry.
Bashan and Carmel wither
and the blossoms of
  Lebanon fade.
⁵The mountains quake before
  him   Ex 19:18
and the hills melt away.

The earth trembles at his
  presence,
the world and all who live in
  it.   Eze 38:20
⁶Who can withstand his
  indignation?   Ps 130:3
Who can endure his fierce
  anger?   Mal 3:2
His wrath is poured out like
  fire;   Jer 10:10
the rocks are shattered
  before him.   1Ki 19:11

⁷The Lord is good,   Jer 33:11
  a refuge in times of trouble.
He cares for those who trust in
  him,   Ps 1:6
⁸ but with an overwhelming
  flood
he will make an end of
  ˌNinevehˌ;
he will pursue his foes into
  darkness.

⁹Whatever they plot against the
  Lord
he[a] will bring to an end;
trouble will not come a
  second time.
¹⁰They will be entangled among
  thorns   2Sa 23:6
and drunk from their wine;
they will be consumed like
  dry stubble.[b]   Isa 5:24

---

[a] 9 Or *What do you foes plot against the Lord? / He*
uncertain.   [b] 10 The meaning of the Hebrew for this verse is

¹¹From you, ⌊O Nineveh,⌋ has one
        come forth
    who plots evil against the
        LORD
    and counsels wickedness.

¹²This is what the LORD says:

"Although they have allies and
        are numerous,
    they will be cut off and pass
        away.   Isa 10:34
Although I have afflicted you,
        ⌊O Judah,⌋
    I will afflict you no more.
¹³Now I will break their yoke
        from your neck   Isa 9:4
    and tear your shackles
        away."   Ps 107:14

¹⁴The LORD has given a
        command concerning
        you, ⌊Nineveh,⌋:
    "You will have no
        descendants to bear
        your name.   Isa 14:22
    I will destroy the carved
        images and cast idols
    that are in the temple of
        your gods.
    I will prepare your grave,
        for you are vile."

¹⁵Look, there on the mountains,
    the feet of one who brings
        good news,   Ro 10:15
    who proclaims peace!   Isa 52:7
Celebrate your festivals,
        O Judah,
    and fulfill your vows.   Lev 23:2-4

No more will the wicked
        invade you;   Isa 52:1
    they will be completely
        destroyed.

Nineveh to Fall

2 An attacker advances against
        you, ⌊Nineveh,⌋.   Jer 51:20
    Guard the fortress,
    watch the road,
    brace yourselves,
    marshal all your strength!

²The LORD will restore the
        splendor of Jacob
    like the splendor of Israel,
though destroyers have laid
        them waste
    and have ruined their vines.

³The shields of his soldiers are
        red;
    the warriors are clad in
        scarlet.   Eze 23:14-15
The metal on the chariots
        flashes
    on the day they are made
        ready;
    the spears of pine are
        brandished.ᵃ
⁴The chariots storm through the
        streets,   Jer 4:13
    rushing back and forth
        through the squares.
They look like flaming torches;
    they dart about like
        lightning.

⁵He summons his picked troops,

ᵃ 3 Hebrew; Septuagint and Syriac / *the horsemen rush to and fro*

yet they stumble on their
    way.   Jer 46:12
They dash to the city wall;
    the protective shield is put
    in place.
⁶The river gates are thrown
    open   Na 3:13
    and the palace collapses.
⁷It is decreedᵃ that ₜthe cityↆ
    be exiled and carried away.
Its slave girls moan like doves
    and beat upon their breasts.
⁸Nineveh is like a pool,
    and its water is draining
    away.
"Stop! Stop!" they cry,
    but no one turns back.
⁹Plunder the silver!
    Plunder the gold!
The supply is endless,
    the wealth from all its
    treasures!
¹⁰She is pillaged, plundered,
    stripped!
Hearts melt, knees give
    way,
bodies tremble, every face
    grows pale.   Isa 29:22
¹¹Where now is the lions' den,
    the place where they fed
    their young,
where the lion and lioness
    went,
and the cubs, with nothing
    to fear?
¹²The lion killed enough for his
    cubs   Jer 51:34
    and strangled the prey for
    his mate,

filling his lairs with the kill
    and his dens with the prey.
¹³"I am against you,"   Jer 21:13; Na 3:5
    declares the LORD Almighty.
"I will burn up your chariots in
    smoke,   Ps 46:9
and the sword will devour
    your young lions.
I will leave you no prey on
    the earth.
The voices of your messengers
    will no longer be heard."

Woe to Nineveh

3 Woe to the city of blood,
    full of lies,   Ps 12:2
full of plunder,
    never without victims!
²The crack of whips,
    the clatter of wheels,
galloping horses
    and jolting chariots!
³Charging cavalry,
    flashing swords
    and glittering spears!
Many casualties,
    piles of dead,
bodies without number,
    people stumbling over the
    corpses—   2Ki 19:35; Isa 34:3
⁴all because of the wanton lust
    of a harlot,
alluring, the mistress of
    sorceries,   Isa 47:9
who enslaved nations by her
    prostitution   Isa 23:17
and peoples by her
    witchcraft.

ᵃ 7 The meaning of the Hebrew for this word is uncertain.

⁵"I am against you," declares
the LORD Almighty.
"I will lift your skirts over
your face.   Jer 13:22
I will show the nations your
nakedness   Isa 47:3
and the kingdoms your
shame.
⁶I will pelt you with filth,   Job 9:31
I will treat you with
contempt   Jer 51:37
and make you a spectacle.
⁷All who see you will flee from
you and say,   Isa 13:14
'Nineveh is in ruins—who
will mourn for her?'
Where can I find anyone to
comfort you?"   Isa 51:19

⁸Are you better than Thebes,ᵃ
situated on the Nile,   Isa 19:6-9
with water around her?
The river was her defense,
the waters her wall.
⁹Cushᵇ and Egypt were her
boundless strength;
Put and Libya were among
her allies.   Eze 27:10; 30:5
¹⁰Yet she was taken captive
and went into exile.
Her infants were dashed to
pieces   Isa 13:16; Hos 13:16
at the head of every
street.
Lots were cast for her nobles,
and all her great men were
put in chains.   Jer 40:1
¹¹You too will become drunk;
you will go into hiding

and seek refuge from the
enemy.
¹²All your fortresses are like fig
trees
with their first ripe fruit;
when they are shaken,
the figs fall into the mouth
of the eater.   Isa 28:4
¹³Look at your troops—
they are all women!   Isa 19:16
The gates of your land   Na 2:6
are wide open to your
enemies;
fire has consumed their bars.

¹⁴Draw water for the siege,
strengthen your defenses!
Work the clay,
tread the mortar,
repair the brickwork!
¹⁵There the fire will devour you;
the sword will cut you down
and, like grasshoppers,
consume you.
Multiply like grasshoppers,
multiply like locusts!   Joel 1:4
¹⁶You have increased the
number of your
merchants
till they are more than the
stars of the sky,
but like locusts they strip the
land   Ex 10:13
and then fly away.
¹⁷Your guards are like locusts,
your officials like swarms of
locusts
that settle in the walls on a
cold day—

ᵃ8 Hebrew *No Amon*   ᵇ9 That is, the upper Nile region

but when the sun appears they
    fly away,
and no one knows where.

¹⁸O king of Assyria, your
    shepherds*a* slumber;
    your nobles lie down to rest.
Your people are scattered on
    the mountains   1Ki 22:17

with no one to gather them.
¹⁹Nothing can heal your wound;
    your injury is fatal.
Everyone who hears the news
    about you
    claps his hands at your
    fall,
for who has not felt
    your endless cruelty?   Isa 37:18

---

a 18 Or rulers

Habakkuk

1

¹ The oracle that Habakkuk the prophet received.   Na 1:1

Habakkuk's Complaint

²How long, O LORD, must I call
      for help,
   but you do not listen?
Or cry out to you, "Violence!"
   but you do not save?   Jer 14:9
³Why do you make me look at
      injustice?
   Why do you tolerate wrong?
Destruction and violence are
      before me;   Jer 20:8
   there is strife, and conflict
      abounds.   Ps 55:9
⁴Therefore the law is paralyzed,
   and justice never prevails.
The wicked hem in the
      righteous,
   so that justice is perverted.

The LORD's Answer

⁵"Look at the nations and
      watch —
   and be utterly amazed.
For I am going to do
      something in your days
   that you would not
      believe,
   even if you were told.
⁶I am raising up the
   Babylonians,ᵃ   2Ki 24:2

that ruthless and impetuous
      people,
who sweep across the whole
      earth
to seize dwelling places not
      their own.   Jer 13:20
⁷They are a feared and dreaded
      people;   Isa 18:7; Jer 39:5-9
   they are a law to themselves
   and promote their own
      honor.
⁸Their horses are swifter than
      leopards,   Jer 4:13
   fiercer than wolves at
      dusk.
Their cavalry gallops headlong;
   their horsemen come from
      afar.
They fly like a vulture
      swooping to devour;
⁹   they all come bent on
      violence.
Their hordesᵇ advance like a
      desert wind
and gather prisoners like
      sand.   Hab 2:5
¹⁰They deride kings
   and scoff at rulers.   2Ch 36:6
They laugh at all fortified
      cities;
   they build earthen ramps
      and capture them.
¹¹Then they sweep past like the
      wind and go on —

ᵃ6 Or *Chaldeans*   ᵇ9 The meaning of the Hebrew for this word is uncertain.

guilty men, whose own
strength is their god."

Habakkuk's Second Complaint

¹²O Lord, are you not from
everlasting?   Ge 21:33
My God, my Holy One, we
will not die.   Isa 31:1
O Lord, you have appointed
them to execute
judgment;   Isa 10:6
O Rock, you have ordained
them to punish.   Ex 33:22
¹³Your eyes are too pure to look
on evil;   Ps 18:26
you cannot tolerate wrong.
Why then do you tolerate the
treacherous?   Ps 25:3
Why are you silent while the
wicked
swallow up those more
righteous than
themselves?   Job 21:7
¹⁴You have made men like fish
in the sea,
like sea creatures that have
no ruler.
¹⁵The wicked foe pulls all of
them up with hooks,
he catches them in his net,
he gathers them up in his
dragnet;
and so he rejoices and is
glad.
¹⁶Therefore he sacrifices to his
net
and burns incense to his
dragnet,   Jer 44:8

for by his net he lives in
luxury
and enjoys the choicest food.
¹⁷Is he to keep on emptying his
net,
destroying nations without
mercy?   Isa 14:6; 19:8

2 I will stand at my watch
and station myself on the
ramparts;   Ps 48:13
I will look to see what he will
say to me,   Ps 85:8
and what answer I am to
give to this complaint.ᵃ

The Lord's Answer

²Then the Lord replied:

"Write down the revelation
and make it plain on tablets
so that a heraldᵇ may run
with it.
³For the revelation awaits an
appointed time;   Da 11:27
it speaks of the end   Da 8:17
and will not prove false.
Though it linger, wait for it;
itᶜ will certainly come and
will not delay.   Eze 12:25

⁴"See, he is puffed up;
his desires are not upright—
but the righteous will live by
his faithᵈ—   Ro 1:17*
⁵indeed, wine betrays him;
he is arrogant and never at
rest.   Isa 2:11

ᵃ1 Or and what to answer when I am rebuked   ᵇ2 Or so that whoever reads it   ᶜ3 Or Though he
linger, wait for him; / he   ᵈ4 Or faithfulness

Because he is as greedy as the
grave[a]
and like death is never
satisfied,   Pr 27:20; 30:15-16
he gathers to himself all the
nations
and takes captive all the
peoples.   Hab 1:9

6"Will not all of them taunt
him with ridicule and scorn, saying,

"'Woe to him who piles up
stolen goods
and makes himself wealthy
by extortion!   Am 2:8
How long must this go
on?'
7Will not your debtors[b]
suddenly arise?
Will they not wake up and
make you tremble?
Then you will become their
victim.   Pr 29:1
8Because you have plundered
many nations,
the peoples who are left will
plunder you.   Isa 33:1
For you have shed man's
blood;
you have destroyed lands
and cities and everyone
in them.   Eze 39:10

9"Woe to him who builds his
realm by unjust gain
to set his nest on high,
to escape the clutches of
ruin!

10You have plotted the ruin of
many peoples,   Jer 26:19
shaming your own house
and forfeiting your life.
11The stones of the wall will cry
out,   Jos 24:27; Lk 19:40
and the beams of the
woodwork will echo it.
12"Woe to him who builds a city
with bloodshed   Mic 3:10
and establishes a town by
crime!
13Has not the LORD Almighty
determined
that the people's labor is
only fuel for the fire,
that the nations exhaust
themselves for nothing?
14For the earth will be filled with
the knowledge of the
glory of the LORD,
as the waters cover the sea.

15"Woe to him who gives drink
to his neighbors,
pouring it from the wineskin
till they are drunk,
so that he can gaze on their
naked bodies.
16You will be filled with shame
instead of glory.
Now it is your turn! Drink
and be exposed[c]!   La 4:21
The cup from the LORD's right
hand is coming around
to you,   Isa 51:22
and disgrace will cover your
glory.

---

a 5 Hebrew *Sheol*   b 7 Or *creditors*   c 16 Masoretic Text; Dead Sea Scrolls, Aquila, Vulgate and Syriac
(see also Septuagint) *and stagger*

¹⁷The violence you have done to
　　Lebanon will overwhelm
　　you, *Jer 51:35*
　and your destruction of
　　animals will terrify you.
For you have shed man's
　　blood;
　you have destroyed lands
　　and cities and everyone
　　in them.

¹⁸"Of what value is an idol, since
　　a man has carved it?
Or an image that teaches
　　lies?
For he who makes it trusts in
　　his own creation;
　he makes idols that cannot
　　speak. *Ps 115:4-5; Jer 10:14*
¹⁹Woe to him who says to wood,
　　'Come to life!'
Or to lifeless stone, 'Wake
　　up!' *1Ki 18:27*
Can it give guidance?
　It is covered with gold and
　　silver; *Jer 10:4*
　there is no breath in it.
²⁰But the LORD is in his holy
　　temple; *Ps 11:4*
　let all the earth be silent
　　before him." *Isa 41:1*

Habakkuk's Prayer

3 A prayer of Habakkuk the
prophet. On *shigionoth.*ᵃ

²LORD, I have heard of your
　　fame; *Ps 44:1*

I stand in awe of your deeds,
　　O LORD. *Ps 119:120*
Renew them in our day, *Ps 85:6*
　in our time make them
　　known;
　in wrath remember mercy.

³God came from Teman,
　the Holy One from Mount
　　Paran. *Selah*ᵇ
His glory covered the heavens
　and his praise filled the
　　earth. *Ps 48:10*
⁴His splendor was like the
　　sunrise; *Isa 18:4*
　rays flashed from his hand,
　where his power was hidden.
⁵Plague went before him;
　pestilence followed his steps.
⁶He stood, and shook the earth;
　he looked, and made the
　　nations tremble.
The ancient mountains
　　crumbled *Ps 46:2*
　and the age-old hills
　　collapsed. *Ps 114:1-6*
His ways are eternal. *Ge 21:33*
⁷I saw the tents of Cushan in
　　distress,
　the dwellings of Midian in
　　anguish. *Ex 15:14; Jdg 7:24-25*

⁸Were you angry with the
　　rivers, O LORD? *Ex 7:20*
Was your wrath against the
　　streams?
Did you rage against the sea
　when you rode with your
　　horses

ᵃ*1 Probably a literary or musical term* ᵇ*3 A word of uncertain meaning; possibly a musical term;
also in verses 9 and 13*

and your victorious chariots?
⁹You uncovered your bow,
you called for many arrows.

Selah

You split the earth with rivers;
10   the mountains saw you and
writhed.
Torrents of water swept by;
the deep roared   Ps 98:7
and lifted its waves on high.

¹¹Sun and moon stood still in
the heavens   Jos 10:13
at the glint of your flying
arrows,   Ps 18:14
at the lightning of your
flashing spear.   Zec 9:14
¹²In wrath you strode through
the earth
and in anger you threshed
the nations.   Isa 41:15
¹³You came out to deliver your
people,   Ps 20:6; 28:8
to save your anointed one.
You crushed the leader of the
land of wickedness,
you stripped him from head
to foot.   *Selah*
¹⁴With his own spear you
pierced his head
when his warriors stormed
out to scatter us,   Jdg 7:22
gloating as though about to
devour
the wretched who were in
hiding.   Ps 64:2-5

¹⁵You trampled the sea with
your horses,
churning the great waters.

¹⁶I heard and my heart pounded,
my lips quivered at the
sound;
decay crept into my bones,
and my legs trembled.
Yet I will wait patiently for the
day of calamity   Ps 37:7
to come on the nation
invading us.
¹⁷Though the fig tree does not
bud
and there are no grapes on
the vines,
though the olive crop fails
and the fields produce no
food,   Joel 1:10-12,18
though there are no sheep in
the pen
and no cattle in the stalls,
¹⁸yet I will rejoice in the LORD,
I will be joyful in God my
Savior.   Lk 1:47

¹⁹The Sovereign LORD is my
strength;   Dt 33:29; Ps 46:1-5
he makes my feet like the
feet of a deer,
he enables me to go on the
heights.   2Sa 22:34; Ps 18:33

For the director of music. On
my stringed
instruments.

Zephaniah

1 The word of the LORD that came to Zephaniah son of Cushi, the son of Gedaliah, the son of Amariah, the son of Hezekiah, during the reign of Josiah son of Amon king of Judah: 2Ki 22:1

Warning of Coming Destruction

2"I will sweep away everything
from the face of the earth,"
declares the LORD.
3"I will sweep away both men
and animals; Jer 50:3
I will sweep away the birds
of the air Jer 4:25
and the fish of the sea.
The wicked will have only
heaps of rubble[a]
when I cut off man from the
face of the earth," Hos 4:3
declares the LORD.

Against Judah

4"I will stretch out my hand
against Judah Jer 6:12
and against all who live in
Jerusalem.
I will cut off from this place
every remnant of Baal,
the names of the pagan and
the idolatrous priests—

5those who bow down on the
roofs
to worship the starry host,
those who bow down and
swear by the LORD
and who also swear by
Molech,[b] Jer 5:7
6those who turn back from
following the LORD Isa 1:4
and neither seek the LORD
nor inquire of him.
7Be silent before the Sovereign
LORD, Hab 2:20; Zec 2:13
for the day of the LORD is
near. Isa 13:6
The LORD has prepared a
sacrifice; Jer 46:10
he has consecrated those he
has invited.
8On the day of the LORD's
sacrifice
I will punish the princes
and the king's sons Jer 39:6
and all those clad
in foreign clothes.
9On that day I will punish
all who avoid stepping on
the threshold,[c]
who fill the temple of their
gods
with violence and deceit.

10"On that day," declares the
LORD, Isa 22:5

---

[a]3 The meaning of the Hebrew for this line is uncertain.   [b]5 Hebrew Malcam, that is, Milcom
[c]9 See 1 Samuel 5:5.

"a cry will go up from the
    Fish Gate,   2Ch 33:14
wailing from the New
    Quarter,
and a loud crash from the
    hills.
¹¹Wail, you who live in the
    market district*;   Jas 5:1
all your merchants will be
    wiped out,
all who trade with* silver
    will be ruined.   Hos 9:6
¹²At that time I will search
    Jerusalem with lamps
and punish those who are
    complacent,   Am 6:1
who are like wine left on its
    dregs,   Jer 48:11
who think, 'The Lord will do
    nothing,   Eze 8:12
either good or bad.'
¹³Their wealth will be plundered,
    their houses demolished.
They will build houses
    but not live in them;
they will plant vineyards
    but not drink the wine.

The Great Day of the Lord

¹⁴"The great day of the Lord is
    near—   Eze 7:7; Joel 1:15
near and coming quickly.
Listen! The cry on the day of
    the Lord will be bitter,
the shouting of the warrior
    there.
¹⁵That day will be a day of
    wrath,

a day of distress and
    anguish,
a day of trouble and ruin,
a day of darkness and
    gloom,
a day of clouds and
    blackness,   Isa 22:5; Joel 2:2
¹⁶a day of trumpet and battle
    cry
against the fortified cities
and against the corner
    towers.   Isa 2:15
¹⁷I will bring distress on the
    people   Dt 28:52
and they will walk like blind
    men,   Isa 59:10
because they have sinned
    against the Lord.
Their blood will be poured out
    like dust   Ps 79:3
and their entrails like filth.
¹⁸Neither their silver nor their
    gold
will be able to save them
on the day of the Lord's
    wrath.   Eze 7:19
In the fire of his jealousy
    the whole world will be
    consumed,   Zep 3:8
for he will make a sudden end
    of all who live in the earth."

2 Gather together, gather
    together,   Joel 1:14
O shameful nation,   Jer 3:3; 6:15
²before the appointed time
    arrives
and that day sweeps on like
    chaff,   Isa 17:13; Hos 13:3

a 11 Or the Mortar   *b 11 Or in*

before the fierce anger of the
  LORD comes upon you,
before the day of the LORD's
  wrath comes upon you.
³Seek the LORD, all you humble
  of the land,   Am 5:6
you who do what he
  commands.
Seek righteousness, seek
  humility;   Ps 45:4; Am 5:14-15
perhaps you will be
  sheltered   Ps 57:1
on the day of the LORD's
  anger.

Against Philistia

⁴Gaza will be abandoned   Am 1:6-8
  and Ashkelon left in ruins.
At midday Ashdod will be
  emptied
and Ekron uprooted.
⁵Woe to you who live by the
  sea,
  O Kerethite people;   Eze 25:16
the word of the LORD is against
  you,   Am 3:1
  O Canaan, land of the
    Philistines.

"I will destroy you,
  and none will be left."

⁶The land by the sea, where the
  Kerethites ᵃ dwell,
will be a place for shepherds
  and sheep pens.   Isa 5:17
⁷It will belong to the remnant of
  the house of Judah;
there they will find pasture.

In the evening they will lie
  down
  in the houses of Ashkelon.
The LORD their God will care
  for them;
he will restore their
  fortunes.ᵇ   Ps 126:4; Jer 32:44

Against Moab and Ammon

⁸"I have heard the insults of
  Moab   Jer 48:27
and the taunts of the
  Ammonites,   Eze 21:28
who insulted my people   Eze 25:3
and made threats against
  their land.   La 3:61
⁹Therefore, as surely as I live,"
  declares the LORD Almighty,
  the God of Israel,
"surely Moab will become like
  Sodom,   Dt 29:23
the Ammonites like
  Gomorrah—   Jer 49:1-6
a place of weeds and salt pits,
  a wasteland forever.
The remnant of my people will
  plunder them;   Isa 11:14
the survivors of my nation
  will inherit their land."

¹⁰This is what they will get in
  return for their pride,
for insulting and mocking
  the people of the LORD
  Almighty.   Jer 48:27
¹¹The LORD will be awesome to
  them   Joel 2:11
when he destroys all the
  gods of the land.   Zep 1:4

ᵃ6 The meaning of the Hebrew for this word is uncertain.   ᵇ7 Or *will bring back their captives*

The nations on every shore
 will worship him,   Zep 3:9
 every one in its own
 land.

Against Cush

12"You too, O Cushites,*a*   Isa 18:1
 will be slain by my
 sword."

Against Assyria

13He will stretch out his hand
 against the north
 and destroy Assyria,
leaving Nineveh utterly
 desolate
 and dry as the desert.   Na 1:1
14Flocks and herds will lie down
 there,   Isa 5:17
 creatures of every kind.
The desert owl and the screech
 owl   Ps 102:6; Isa 14:23
 will roost on her columns.
Their calls will echo through
 the windows,
 rubble will be in the
 doorways,
 the beams of cedar will be
 exposed.
15This is the carefree city   Isa 32:9
 that lived in safety.   Isa 47:8
 She said to herself,
 "I am, and there is none
 besides me."   Eze 28:2
What a ruin she has become,
 a lair for wild beasts!
All who pass by her scoff
 and shake their fists.

The Future of Jerusalem

3 Woe to the city of
 oppressors,
 rebellious and defiled!   Jer 6:6
2She obeys no one,   Jer 22:21
 she accepts no correction.
She does not trust in the LORD,
 she does not draw near to
 her God.   Ps 73:28; Jer 5:3
3Her officials are roaring lions,
 her rulers are evening
 wolves,   Eze 22:27
who leave nothing for the
 morning.
4Her prophets are arrogant;
 they are treacherous men.
Her priests profane the
 sanctuary
 and do violence to the law.
5The LORD within her is
 righteous;   Ezr 9:15
 he does no wrong.   Dt 32:4
Morning by morning he
 dispenses his justice,
 and every new day he does
 not fail,   La 3:23
 yet the unrighteous know no
 shame.   Eze 18:25

6"I have cut off nations;
 their strongholds are
 demolished.
I have left their streets
 deserted,
 with no one passing through.
Their cities are destroyed;
 no one will be left—no one
 at all.
7I said to the city,

---

a 12 That is, people from the upper Nile region

'Surely you will fear me
and accept correction!'
Then her dwelling would not
be cut off,
nor all my punishments
come upon her.
But they were still eager
to act corruptly in all they
did.   Hos 9:9
⁸Therefore wait for me,"
declares the LORD,
"for the day I will stand up
to testify.ᵃ
I have decided to assemble the
nations,   Joel 3:2
to gather the kingdoms
and to pour out my wrath on
them—
all my fierce anger.   Jer 10:25
The whole world will be
consumed   Zep 1:18
by the fire of my jealous
anger.

⁹"Then will I purify the lips of
the peoples,
that all of them may call on
the name of the LORD
and serve him shoulder to
shoulder.   Isa 19:18
¹⁰From beyond the rivers of
Cushᵇ   Ps 68:31
my worshipers, my scattered
people,
will bring me offerings.
¹¹On that day you will not be
put to shame   Joel 2:26-27
for all the wrongs you have
done to me,   Ge 50:15

because I will remove from
this city
those who rejoice in their
pride.   Ps 59:12
Never again will you be
haughty
on my holy hill.   Ex 15:17
¹²But I will leave within you
the meek and humble,
who trust in the name of the
LORD.   Na 1:7
¹³The remnant of Israel will do
no wrong;   Isa 10:21; Mic 4:7
they will speak no lies,
nor will deceit be found in
their mouths.
They will eat and lie
down
and no one will make them
afraid."   Eze 34:25-28

¹⁴Sing, O Daughter of Zion;
shout aloud, O Israel!   Isa 12:6
Be glad and rejoice with all
your heart,   Isa 51:11
O Daughter of Jerusalem!
¹⁵The LORD has taken away your
punishment,
he has turned back your
enemy.
The LORD, the King of Israel, is
with you;   Eze 37:26-28
never again will you fear any
harm.   Isa 54:14
¹⁶On that day they will say to
Jerusalem,
"Do not fear, O Zion;
do not let your hands hang
limp.   Isa 35:3-4; Heb 12:12

ᵃ 8 Septuagint and Syriac; Hebrew *will rise up to plunder*   ᵇ 10 That is, the upper Nile region

¹⁷The LORD your God is with
    you,
    he is mighty to save. Isa 63:1
He will take great delight in
    you, Isa 62:4
    he will quiet you with his
        love, Hos 14:4
    he will rejoice over you with
        singing." Isa 40:1

¹⁸"The sorrows for the appointed
    feasts
    I will remove from you;
    they are a burden and a
        reproach to you.ᵃ
¹⁹At that time I will deal
    with all who oppressed you;

I will rescue the lame
    and gather those who have
        been scattered. Eze 34:16
I will give them praise and
    honor Isa 60:18
    in every land where they
        were put to shame.
²⁰At that time I will gather you;
    at that time I will bring you
        home. Jer 29:14; Eze 37:12
I will give you honor and
    praise Isa 56:5
    among all the peoples of the
        earth
    when I restore your fortunesᵇ
    before your very eyes,"
                        says the LORD.

ᵃ18 Or "I will gather you who mourn for the appointed feasts; / your reproach is a burden to you
ᵇ20 Or I bring back your captives

Haggai

A Call to Build the House of the Lord

1 In the second year of King Darius, on the first day of the sixth month, the word of the Lord came through the prophet Haggai to Zerubbabel son of Shealtiel, governor of Judah, and to Joshua[a] son of Jehozadak, the high priest:

²This is what the Lord Almighty says: "These people say, 'The time has not yet come for the Lord's house to be built.' "   Ezr 1:2

³Then the word of the Lord came through the prophet Haggai: ⁴"Is it a time for you yourselves to be living in your paneled houses, while this house remains a ruin?"

⁵Now this is what the Lord Almighty says: "Give careful thought to your ways. ⁶You have planted much, but have harvested little. You eat, but never have enough. You drink, but never have your fill. You put on clothes, but are not warm. You earn wages, only to put them in a purse with holes in it."

⁷This is what the Lord Almighty says: "Give careful thought to your ways. ⁸Go up into the mountains and bring down timber and build the house, so that I may take pleasure in it and be honored," says the Lord. ⁹"You expected much, but see, it turned out to be little. What you brought home, I blew away. Why?" declares the Lord Almighty. "Because of my house, which remains a ruin, while each of you is busy with his own house. ¹⁰Therefore, because of you the heavens have withheld their dew and the earth its crops. ¹¹I called for a drought on the fields and the mountains, on the grain, the new wine, the oil and whatever the ground produces, on men and cattle, and on the labor of your hands."   Ps 132:13-14; Hag 2:17

¹²Then Zerubbabel son of Shealtiel, Joshua son of Jehozadak, the high priest, and the whole remnant of the people obeyed the voice of the Lord their God and the message of the prophet Haggai, because the Lord their God had sent him. And the people feared the Lord.   Dt 31:12; Isa 50:10

¹³Then Haggai, the Lord's messenger, gave this message of the Lord to the people: "I am with you," declares the Lord. ¹⁴So the Lord stirred up the spirit of Zerubbabel son of Shealtiel, governor of Judah, and the spirit of Joshua son of Jehozadak, the high priest, and

---

a 1 A variant of *Jeshua*; here and elsewhere in Haggai

the spirit of the whole remnant of the people. They came and began to work on the house of the LORD Almighty, their God, ¹⁵on the twenty-fourth day of the sixth month in the second year of King Darius.   Ezr 5:2; Ro 8:31

The Promised Glory of the New House

2 On the twenty-first day of the seventh month, the word of the LORD came through the prophet Haggai: ²"Speak to Zerubbabel son of Shealtiel, governor of Judah, to Joshua son of Jehozadak, the high priest, and to the remnant of the people. Ask them, ³'Who of you is left who saw this house in its former glory? How does it look to you now? Does it not seem to you like nothing? ⁴But now be strong, O Zerubbabel,' declares the LORD. 'Be strong, O Joshua son of Jehozadak, the high priest. Be strong, all you people of the land,' declares the LORD, 'and work. For I am with you,' declares the LORD Almighty. ⁵'This is what I covenanted with you when you came out of Egypt. And my Spirit remains among you. Do not fear.'

⁶"This is what the LORD Almighty says: 'In a little while I will once more shake the heavens and the earth, the sea and the dry land. ⁷I will shake all nations, and the desired of all nations will come, and I will fill this house with glo-

ry,' says the LORD Almighty. ⁸'The silver is mine and the gold is mine,' declares the LORD Almighty. ⁹'The glory of this present house will be greater than the glory of the former house,' says the LORD Almighty. 'And in this place I will grant peace,' declares the LORD Almighty."   Heb 12:26*

Blessings for a Defiled People

¹⁰On the twenty-fourth day of the ninth month, in the second year of Darius, the word of the LORD came to the prophet Haggai: ¹¹"This is what the LORD Almighty says: 'Ask the priests what the law says: ¹²If a person carries consecrated meat in the fold of his garment, and that fold touches some bread or stew, some wine, oil or other food, does it become consecrated?' "   Lev 10:10-11; Mt 23:19

The priests answered, "No."

¹³Then Haggai said, "If a person defiled by contact with a dead body touches one of these things, does it become defiled?"

"Yes," the priests replied, "it becomes defiled."   Lev 22:4-6

¹⁴Then Haggai said, " 'So it is with this people and this nation in my sight,' declares the LORD. 'Whatever they do and whatever they offer there is defiled.   Isa 1:13

¹⁵" 'Now give careful thought to this from this day on*ᵃ*—consider how things were before one stone was laid on another in the LORD's

ᵃ 15 Or to the days past

temple. ¹⁶When anyone came to a heap of twenty measures, there were only ten. When anyone went to a wine vat to draw fifty measures, there were only twenty. ¹⁷I struck all the work of your hands with blight, mildew and hail, yet you did not turn to me,' declares the LORD. ¹⁸'From this day on, from this twenty-fourth day of the ninth month, give careful thought to the day when the foundation of the LORD's temple was laid. Give careful thought: ¹⁹Is there yet any seed left in the barn? Until now, the vine and the fig tree, the pomegranate and the olive tree have not borne fruit.

Hag 1:5-6; Zec 8:9

" 'From this day on I will bless you.' "

Joel 2:14

Zerubbabel the LORD's Signet Ring

²⁰The word of the LORD came to Haggai a second time on the twenty-fourth day of the month: ²¹"Tell Zerubbabel governor of Judah that I will shake the heavens and the earth. ²²I will overturn royal thrones and shatter the power of the foreign kingdoms. I will overthrow chariots and their drivers; horses and their riders will fall, each by the sword of his brother.

²³" 'On that day,' declares the LORD Almighty, 'I will take you, my servant Zerubbabel son of Shealtiel,' declares the LORD, 'and I will make you like my signet ring, for I have chosen you,' declares the LORD Almighty."

Isa 43:10

Zechariah

A Call to Return to the LORD

1 In the eighth month of the second year of Darius, the word of the LORD came to the prophet Zechariah son of Berekiah, the son of Iddo: _{Ezr 4:24; Ne 12:4}

2"The LORD was very angry with your forefathers. 3Therefore tell the people: This is what the LORD Almighty says: 'Return to me,' declares the LORD Almighty, 'and I will return to you,' says the LORD Almighty. 4Do not be like your forefathers, to whom the earlier prophets proclaimed: This is what the LORD Almighty says: 'Turn from your evil ways and your evil practices.' But they would not listen or pay attention to me, declares the LORD. 5Where are your forefathers now? And the prophets, do they live forever? 6But did not my words and my decrees, which I commanded my servants the prophets, overtake your forefathers? _{Mal 3:7; Jas 4:8}

"Then they repented and said, 'The LORD Almighty has done to us what our ways and practices deserve, just as he determined to do.'" _{Jer 12:14-17; La 2:17}

The Man Among the Myrtle Trees

7On the twenty-fourth day of the eleventh month, the month of Shebat, in the second year of Darius, the word of the LORD came to the prophet Zechariah son of Berekiah, the son of Iddo.

8During the night I had a vision —and there before me was a man riding a red horse! He was standing among the myrtle trees in a ravine. Behind him were red, brown and white horses. _{Zec 6:2-7; Rev 6:4}

9I asked, "What are these, my lord?"

The angel who was talking with me answered, "I will show you what they are." _{Zec 4:1,4-5}

10Then the man standing among the myrtle trees explained, "They are the ones the LORD has sent to go throughout the earth." _{Zec 6:5-8}

11And they reported to the angel of the LORD, who was standing among the myrtle trees, "We have gone throughout the earth and found the whole world at rest and in peace." _{Isa 14:7}

12Then the angel of the LORD said, "LORD Almighty, how long will you withhold mercy from Jerusalem and from the towns of Judah, which you have been angry with these seventy years?" 13So the LORD spoke kind and comforting words to the angel who talked with me. _{Da 9:2; Zec 4:1}

14Then the angel who was

speaking to me said, "Proclaim this word: This is what the Lord Almighty says: 'I am very jealous for Jerusalem and Zion, **15**but I am very angry with the nations that feel secure. I was only a little angry, but they added to the calamity.' Am 1:11; Zec 8:2

16"Therefore, this is what the Lord says: 'I will return to Jerusalem with mercy, and there my house will be rebuilt. And the measuring line will be stretched out over Jerusalem,' declares the Lord Almighty. Zec 2:1-2

17"Proclaim further: This is what the Lord Almighty says: 'My towns will again overflow with prosperity, and the Lord will again comfort Zion and choose Jerusalem.'"

Four Horns and Four Craftsmen

18Then I looked up—and there before me were four horns! **19**I asked the angel who was speaking to me, "What are these?"

He answered me, "These are the horns that scattered Judah, Israel and Jerusalem." Am 6:13

20Then the Lord showed me four craftsmen. **21**I asked, "What are these coming to do?"

He answered, "These are the horns that scattered Judah so that no one could raise his head, but the craftsmen have come to terrify them and throw down these horns of the nations who lifted up their

horns against the land of Judah to scatter its people." Ps 75:4,10

A Man With a Measuring Line

2 Then I looked up—and there before me was a man with a measuring line in his hand! **2**I asked, "Where are you going?"

He answered me, "To measure Jerusalem, to find out how wide and how long it is." Rev 21:15

3Then the angel who was speaking to me left, and another angel came to meet him **4**and said to him: "Run, tell that young man, 'Jerusalem will be a city without walls because of the great number of men and livestock in it. **5**And I myself will be a wall of fire around it,' declares the Lord, 'and I will be its glory within.' Ps 46:5; Rev 21:23

6"Come! Come! Flee from the land of the north," declares the Lord, "for I have scattered you to the four winds of heaven," declares the Lord. Eze 17:21

7"Come, O Zion! Escape, you who live in the Daughter of Babylon!" **8**For this is what the Lord Almighty says: "After he has honored me and has sent me against the nations that have plundered you—for whoever touches you touches the apple of his eye— **9**I will surely raise my hand against them so that their slaves will plunder them.*a* Then you will know that the Lord Almighty has sent me. Dt 32:10; Zec 4:9

a 8,9 Or says after . . . eye: 9"I . . . plunder them."

¹⁰"Shout and be glad, O Daughter of Zion. For I am coming, and I will live among you," declares the LORD. ¹¹"Many nations will be joined with the LORD in that day and will become my people. I will live among you and you will know that the LORD Almighty has sent me to you. ¹²The LORD will inherit Judah as his portion in the holy land and will again choose Jerusalem. ¹³Be still before the LORD, all mankind, because he has roused himself from his holy dwelling."

Clean Garments for the High Priest

3 Then he showed me Joshua*a* the high priest standing before the angel of the LORD, and Satan*b* standing at his right side to accuse him. ²The LORD said to Satan, "The LORD rebuke you, Satan! The LORD, who has chosen Jerusalem, rebuke you! Is not this man a burning stick snatched from the fire?"

³Now Joshua was dressed in filthy clothes as he stood before the angel. ⁴The angel said to those who were standing before him, "Take off his filthy clothes."

Then he said to Joshua, "See, I have taken away your sin, and I will put rich garments on you."

⁵Then I said, "Put a clean turban on his head." So they put a clean turban on his head and clothed him, while the angel of the LORD stood by.　　　　　　Ex 29:6

⁶The angel of the LORD gave this charge to Joshua: ⁷"This is what the LORD Almighty says: 'If you will walk in my ways and keep my requirements, then you will govern my house and have charge of my courts, and I will give you a place among these standing here.

⁸"'Listen, O high priest Joshua and your associates seated before you, who are men symbolic of things to come: I am going to bring my servant, the Branch. ⁹See, the stone I have set in front of Joshua! There are seven eyes*c* on that one stone, and I will engrave an inscription on it,' says the LORD Almighty, 'and I will remove the sin of this land in a single day.

¹⁰"'In that day each of you will invite his neighbor to sit under his vine and fig tree,' declares the LORD Almighty."　　1Ki 4:25; Mic 4:4

The Gold Lampstand and the Two Olive Trees

4 Then the angel who talked with me returned and wakened me, as a man is wakened from his sleep. ²He asked me, "What do you see?"　Jer 1:13; Da 8:18

I answered, "I see a solid gold lampstand with a bowl at the top and seven lights on it, with seven channels to the lights. ³Also there are two olive trees by it, one on the right of the bowl and the other on its left."　　　　Rev 4:5; 11:4

⁴I asked the angel who talked

---

*a*1 A variant of *Jeshua*; here and elsewhere in Zechariah　　*b*1 *Satan* means *accuser*.　　*c*9 Or *facets*

with me, "What are these, my lord?"

⁵He answered, "Do you not know what these are?"

"No, my lord," I replied. Zec 1:9

⁶So he said to me, "This is the word of the LORD to Zerubbabel: 'Not by might nor by power, but by my Spirit,' says the LORD Almighty. Isa 11:2-4; Hos 1:7

⁷"What*a* are you, O mighty mountain? Before Zerubbabel you will become level ground. Then he will bring out the capstone to shouts of 'God bless it! God bless it!' " Ps 118:22; Jer 51:25

⁸Then the word of the LORD came to me: ⁹"The hands of Zerubbabel have laid the foundation of this temple; his hands will also complete it. Then you will know that the LORD Almighty has sent me to you. Zec 2:9; 6:12

¹⁰"Who despises the day of small things? Men will rejoice when they see the plumb line in the hand of Zerubbabel. Hag 2:3

"(These seven are the eyes of the LORD, which range throughout the earth.)" Zec 3:9; Rev 5:6

¹¹Then I asked the angel, "What are these two olive trees on the right and the left of the lampstand?" Rev 11:4

¹²Again I asked him, "What are these two olive branches beside the two gold pipes that pour out golden oil?"

¹³He replied, "Do you not know what these are?"

"No, my lord," I said.

¹⁴So he said, "These are the two who are anointed to*b* serve the Lord of all the earth." Ex 29:7

The Flying Scroll

5 I looked again—and there before me was a flying scroll!

²He asked me, "What do you see?"

I answered, "I see a flying scroll, thirty feet long and fifteen feet wide.*c*"

³And he said to me, "This is the curse that is going out over the whole land; for according to what it says on one side, every thief will be banished, and according to what it says on the other, everyone who swears falsely will be banished. ⁴The LORD Almighty declares, 'I will send it out, and it will enter the house of the thief and the house of him who swears falsely by my name. It will remain in his house and destroy it, both its timbers and its stones.' " Lev 14:34-45

The Woman in a Basket

⁵Then the angel who was speaking to me came forward and said to me, "Look up and see what this is that is appearing."

⁶I asked, "What is it?"

He replied, "It is a measuring basket.*d*" And he added, "This is

---

a 7 Or *Who*   *b* 14 Or *two who bring oil and*   *c* 2 Hebrew *twenty cubits long and ten cubits wide* (about 9 meters long and 4.5 meters wide)   *d* 6 Hebrew *an ephah; also in verses 7-11*

the iniquity*a* of the people throughout the land."

⁷Then the cover of lead was raised, and there in the basket sat a woman! ⁸He said, "This is wickedness," and he pushed her back into the basket and pushed the lead cover down over its mouth.

⁹Then I looked up—and there before me were two women, with the wind in their wings! They had wings like those of a stork, and they lifted up the basket between heaven and earth.   Lev 11:19

¹⁰"Where are they taking the basket?" I asked the angel who was speaking to me.

¹¹He replied, "To the country of Babylonia*b* to build a house for it. When it is ready, the basket will be set there in its place."   Ge 10:10

Four Chariots

6 I looked up again—and there before me were four chariots coming out from between two mountains—mountains of bronze! ²The first chariot had red horses, the second black, ³the third white, and the fourth dappled—all of them powerful. ⁴I asked the angel who was speaking to me, "What are these, my lord?"

⁵The angel answered me, "These are the four spirits*c* of heaven, going out from standing in the presence of the Lord of the whole world. ⁶The one with the black horses is going toward the north country, the one with the white horses toward the west,*d* and the one with the dappled horses toward the south."   Eze 37:9

⁷When the powerful horses went out, they were straining to go throughout the earth. And he said, "Go throughout the earth!" So they went throughout the earth.

⁸Then he called to me, "Look, those going toward the north country have given my Spirit*e* rest in the land of the north."   Eze 5:13

A Crown for Joshua

⁹The word of the LORD came to me: ¹⁰"Take ˌsilver and goldˌ from the exiles Heldai, Tobijah and Jedaiah, who have arrived from Babylon. Go the same day to the house of Josiah son of Zephaniah. ¹¹Take the silver and gold and make a crown, and set it on the head of the high priest, Joshua son of Jehozadak. ¹²Tell him this is what the LORD Almighty says: 'Here is the man whose name is the Branch, and he will branch out from his place and build the temple of the LORD. ¹³It is he who will build the temple of the LORD, and he will be clothed with majesty and will sit and rule on his throne. And he will be a priest on his throne. And there will be harmony between the two.' ¹⁴The crown will be given to Heldai,*f* Tobijah, Jedaiah and Hen*g*

---

*a*6 Or *appearance*   *b*11 Hebrew *Shinar*   *c*5 Or *winds*   *d*6 Or *horses after them*   *e*8 Or *spirit*
*f*14 Syriac; Hebrew *Helem*   *g*14 Or *and the gracious one, the*

son of Zephaniah as a memorial in the temple of the LORD. ¹⁵Those who are far away will come and help to build the temple of the LORD, and you will know that the LORD Almighty has sent me to you. This will happen if you diligently obey the LORD your God." Isa 60:10

Justice and Mercy, Not Fasting

7 In the fourth year of King Darius, the word of the LORD came to Zechariah on the fourth day of the ninth month, the month of Kislev. ²The people of Bethel had sent Sharezer and Regem-Melech, together with their men, to entreat the LORD ³by asking the priests of the house of the LORD Almighty and the prophets, "Should I mourn and fast in the fifth month, as I have done for so many years?"

⁴Then the word of the LORD Almighty came to me: ⁵"Ask all the people of the land and the priests, 'When you fasted and mourned in the fifth and seventh months for the past seventy years, was it really for me that you fasted? ⁶And when you were eating and drinking, were you not just feasting for yourselves? ⁷Are these not the words the LORD proclaimed through the earlier prophets when Jerusalem and its surrounding towns were at rest and prosperous, and the Negev and the western foothills were settled?' " Jer 22:21; Zec 1:4

⁸And the word of the LORD came again to Zechariah: ⁹"This is what the LORD Almighty says: 'Administer true justice; show mercy and compassion to one another. ¹⁰Do not oppress the widow or the fatherless, the alien or the poor. In your hearts do not think evil of each other.' Isa 1:17; Zec 8:16

¹¹"But they refused to pay attention; stubbornly they turned their backs and stopped up their ears. ¹²They made their hearts as hard as flint and would not listen to the law or to the words that the LORD Almighty had sent by his Spirit through the earlier prophets. So the LORD Almighty was very angry.

¹³" 'When I called, they did not listen; so when they called, I would not listen,' says the LORD Almighty. ¹⁴'I scattered them with a whirlwind among all the nations, where they were strangers. The land was left so desolate behind them that no one could come or go. This is how they made the pleasant land desolate.' " Isa 1:15

The LORD Promises to Bless Jerusalem

8 Again the word of the LORD Almighty came to me. ²This is what the LORD Almighty says: "I am very jealous for Zion; I am burning with jealousy for her."

³This is what the LORD says: "I will return to Zion and dwell in Jerusalem. Then Jerusalem will be called the City of Truth, and the mountain of the LORD Almighty will be called the Holy Mountain."

⁴This is what the LORD Almighty

says: "Once again men and women of ripe old age will sit in the streets of Jerusalem, each with cane in hand because of his age. ⁵The city streets will be filled with boys and girls playing there."   Isa 65:20

⁶This is what the LORD Almighty says: "It may seem marvelous to the remnant of this people at that time, but will it seem marvelous to me?" declares the LORD Almighty.

⁷This is what the LORD Almighty says: "I will save my people from the countries of the east and the west. ⁸I will bring them back to live in Jerusalem; they will be my people, and I will be faithful and righteous to them as their God."

⁹This is what the LORD Almighty says: "You who now hear these words spoken by the prophets who were there when the foundation was laid for the house of the LORD Almighty, let your hands be strong so that the temple may be built. ¹⁰Before that time there were no wages for man or beast. No one could go about his business safely because of his enemy, for I had turned every man against his neighbor. ¹¹But now I will not deal with the remnant of this people as I did in the past," declares the LORD Almighty.   Isa 12:1; Hag 2:4

¹²"The seed will grow well, the vine will yield its fruit, the ground will produce its crops, and the heavens will drop their dew. I will give all these things as an inheritance to the remnant of this people. ¹³As you have been an object of cursing among the nations, O Judah and Israel, so will I save you, and you will be a blessing. Do not be afraid, but let your hands be strong."   Ge 12:2; Jer 42:18; Joel 2:22

¹⁴This is what the LORD Almighty says: "Just as I had determined to bring disaster upon you and showed no pity when your fathers angered me," says the LORD Almighty, ¹⁵"so now I have determined to do good again to Jerusalem and Judah. Do not be afraid. ¹⁶These are the things you are to do: Speak the truth to each other, and render true and sound judgment in your courts; ¹⁷do not plot evil against your neighbor, and do not love to swear falsely. I hate all this," declares the LORD.   Pr 3:29

¹⁸Again the word of the LORD Almighty came to me. ¹⁹This is what the LORD Almighty says: "The fasts of the fourth, fifth, seventh and tenth months will become joyful and glad occasions and happy festivals for Judah. Therefore love truth and peace."   Ps 30:11

²⁰This is what the LORD Almighty says: "Many peoples and the inhabitants of many cities will yet come, ²¹and the inhabitants of one city will go to another and say, 'Let us go at once to entreat the LORD and seek the LORD Almighty. I myself am going.' ²²And many peoples and powerful nations will come to Jerusalem to seek the LORD Almighty and to entreat him."   Ps 117:1; Zec 2:11

²³This is what the LORD Al-

mighty says: "In those days ten men from all languages and nations will take firm hold of one Jew by the hem of his robe and say, 'Let us go with you, because we have heard that God is with you.' "

Judgment on Israel's Enemies

An Oracle

9 The word of the LORD is against the land of Hadrach
and will rest upon Damascus—   Isa 17:1
for the eyes of men and all the tribes of Israel
are on the LORD— [a]
²and upon Hamath too, which borders on it,   Jer 49:23
and upon Tyre and Sidon,
though they are very skillful.   Eze 28:1-19
³Tyre has built herself a stronghold;
she has heaped up silver like dust,
and gold like the dirt of the streets.   Job 27:16; Eze 28:4
⁴But the Lord will take away her possessions
and destroy her power on the sea,
and she will be consumed by fire.   Isa 23:1; Eze 26:3-5
⁵Ashkelon will see it and fear;
Gaza will writhe in agony,
and Ekron too, for her hope will wither.

Gaza will lose her king
and Ashkelon will be deserted.
⁶Foreigners will occupy Ashdod,
and I will cut off the pride of the Philistines.   Isa 14:30
⁷I will take the blood from their mouths,
the forbidden food from between their teeth.
Those who are left will belong to our God   Job 25:2
and become leaders in Judah,
and Ekron will be like the Jebusites.   Jer 47:1
⁸But I will defend my house against marauding forces.
Never again will an oppressor overrun my people,
for now I am keeping watch.

The Coming of Zion's King

⁹Rejoice greatly, O Daughter of Zion!   Isa 62:11
Shout, Daughter of Jerusalem!
See, your king[b] comes to you,
righteous and having salvation,   Isa 9:6-7; Zep 3:14-15
gentle and riding on a donkey,
on a colt, the foal of a donkey.   Mt 21:5*; Jn 12:15*
¹⁰I will take away the chariots from Ephraim
and the war-horses from Jerusalem,

---

[a] 1 Or Damascus. / For the eye of the LORD is on all mankind, / as well as on the tribes of Israel,
[b] 9 Or King

and the battle bow will be
  broken.   Hos 1:7; 2:18
He will proclaim peace to the
  nations.   Isa 2:4
His rule will extend from sea
  to sea
and from the River*a* to the
  ends of the earth.*b*
11As for you, because of the
  blood of my covenant
  with you,   Ex 24:8
I will free your prisoners
  from the waterless pit.
12Return to your fortress,
  O prisoners of hope;
even now I announce that I
  will restore twice as
  much to you.   Isa 40:2
13I will bend Judah as I bend my
  bow
  and fill it with Ephraim.
I will rouse your sons,
  O Zion,
against your sons, O Greece,
  and make you like a
  warrior's sword.   Jer 51:20

The Lord Will Appear

14Then the Lord will appear over
  them;   Isa 31:5
his arrow will flash like
  lightning.   Ps 18:14; Hab 3:11
The Sovereign Lord will sound
  the trumpet;
he will march in the storms
  of the south,   Isa 21:1; 66:15
15 and the Lord Almighty will
  shield them.   Isa 37:35
They will destroy

and overcome with
  slingstones.
They will drink and roar as
  with wine;
they will be full like a bowl
  used for sprinkling*c* the
  corners of the altar.
16The Lord their God will save
  them on that day
  as the flock of his people.
They will sparkle in his land
  like jewels in a crown.   Isa 62:3
17How attractive and beautiful
  they will be!
Grain will make the young
  men thrive,
and new wine the young
  women.

The Lord Will Care for Judah

10 Ask the Lord for rain in
  the springtime;
it is the Lord who makes the
  storm clouds.
He gives showers of rain to
  men,   Lev 26:4
and plants of the field to
  everyone.   Job 14:9
2The idols speak deceit,   Eze 21:21
diviners see visions that lie;
they tell dreams that are false,
  they give comfort in vain.
Therefore the people wander
  like sheep
oppressed for lack of a
  shepherd.   Eze 34:5; Hos 3:4

3"My anger burns against the
  shepherds,

---

a 10 That is, the Euphrates   *b 10* Or *the end of the land*   *c 15* Or *bowl, / like*

and I will punish the leaders;
for the LORD Almighty will care
  for his flock, the house of
  Judah,
and make them like a proud
  horse in battle.   Eze 34:8-10
⁴From Judah will come the
  cornerstone,   Ps 118:22
from him the tent peg,
from him the battle bow,
from him every ruler.
⁵Together theyᵃ will be like
  mighty men
trampling the muddy streets
  in battle.   2Sa 22:43
Because the LORD is with them,
they will fight and overthrow
  the horsemen.   Am 2:15

⁶"I will strengthen the house of
  Judah
and save the house of
  Joseph.
I will restore them
because I have compassion
  on them.   Zec 8:7-8
They will be as though
  I had not rejected them,
for I am the LORD their God
and I will answer them.
⁷The Ephraimites will become
  like mighty men,
and their hearts will be glad
  as with wine.   Zec 9:15
Their children will see it and
  be joyful;
their hearts will rejoice in
  the LORD.
⁸I will signal for them   Isa 5:26

and gather them in.
Surely I will redeem them;
  they will be as numerous as
  before.   Eze 36:11
⁹Though I scatter them among
  the peoples,
yet in distant lands they will
  remember me.   Eze 6:9
They and their children will
  survive,
and they will return.
¹⁰I will bring them back from
  Egypt
and gather them from
  Assyria.   Isa 11:11
I will bring them to Gilead and
  Lebanon,   Jer 50:19
and there will not be room
  enough for them.   Isa 49:19
¹¹They will pass through the sea
  of trouble;
the surging sea will be
  subdued
and all the depths of the
  Nile will dry up.   Isa 19:5-7
Assyria's pride will be brought
  down   Zep 2:13
and Egypt's scepter will pass
  away.   Eze 30:13
¹²I will strengthen them in the
  LORD
and in his name they will
  walk,"   Mic 4:5
    declares the LORD.

11 Open your doors,
      O Lebanon,   Eze 31:3
so that fire may devour your
  cedars!   Zec 12:6

ᵃ 4,5 Or *ruler, all of them together.* / ⁵*They*

²Wail, O pine tree, for the cedar
        has fallen;
    the stately trees are ruined!
Wail, oaks of Bashan;   Isa 2:13
    the dense forest has been
        cut down!   Isa 32:19
³Listen to the wail of the
        shepherds;
    their rich pastures are
        destroyed!
Listen to the roar of the lions;
    the lush thicket of the
        Jordan is ruined!   Jer 2:15

Two Shepherds

⁴This is what the LORD my God
says: "Pasture the flock marked for
slaughter. ⁵Their buyers slaughter
them and go unpunished. Those
who sell them say, 'Praise the
LORD, I am rich!' Their own shepherds do not spare them. ⁶For I will
no longer have pity on the people
of the land," declares the LORD. "I
will hand everyone over to his
neighbor and his king. They will
oppress the land, and I will not rescue them from their hands."

⁷So I pastured the flock marked
for slaughter, particularly the oppressed of the flock. Then I took
two staffs and called one Favor
and the other Union, and I pastured the flock. ⁸In one month I got
rid of the three shepherds.

The flock detested me, and I
grew weary of them ⁹and said, "I
will not be your shepherd. Let the
dying die, and the perishing perish. Let those who are left eat one
another's flesh."   Jer 15:2; 43:11

¹⁰Then I took my staff called Favor and broke it, revoking the covenant I had made with all the nations. ¹¹It was revoked on that day,
and so the afflicted of the flock
who were watching me knew it
was the word of the LORD.

¹²I told them, "If you think it
best, give me my pay; but if not,
keep it." So they paid me thirty
pieces of silver.   Ex 21:32; Mt 26:15

¹³And the LORD said to me,
"Throw it to the potter"—the
handsome price at which they
priced me! So I took the thirty
pieces of silver and threw them
into the house of the LORD to the
potter.   Mt 27:9-10*; Ac 1:18-19

¹⁴Then I broke my second staff
called Union, breaking the brotherhood between Judah and Israel.

¹⁵Then the LORD said to me,
"Take again the equipment of a
foolish shepherd. ¹⁶For I am going
to raise up a shepherd over the
land who will not care for the lost,
or seek the young, or heal the injured, or feed the healthy, but will
eat the meat of the choice sheep,
tearing off their hoofs.

¹⁷"Woe to the worthless
        shepherd,   Jer 23:1
    who deserts the flock!
May the sword strike his arm
        and his right eye!
May his arm be completely
        withered,
    his right eye totally
        blinded!"

Jerusalem's Enemies to Be Destroyed

An Oracle

12 This is the word of the LORD concerning Israel. The LORD, who stretches out the heavens, who lays the foundation of the earth, and who forms the spirit of man within him, declares: ²"I am going to make Jerusalem a cup that sends all the surrounding peoples reeling. Judah will be besieged as well as Jerusalem. ³On that day, when all the nations of the earth are gathered against her, I will make Jerusalem an immovable rock for all the nations. All who try to move it will injure themselves. ⁴On that day I will strike every horse with panic and its rider with madness," declares the LORD. "I will keep a watchful eye over the house of Judah, but I will blind all the horses of the nations. ⁵Then the leaders of Judah will say in their hearts, 'The people of Jerusalem are strong, because the LORD Almighty is their God.'

⁶"On that day I will make the leaders of Judah like a firepot in a woodpile, like a flaming torch among sheaves. They will consume right and left all the surrounding peoples, but Jerusalem will remain intact in her place.

⁷"The LORD will save the dwellings of Judah first, so that the honor of the house of David and of Jerusalem's inhabitants may not be greater than that of Judah. ⁸On that day the LORD will shield those who live in Jerusalem, so that the feeblest among them will be like David, and the house of David will be like God, like the Angel of the LORD going before them. ⁹On that day I will set out to destroy all the nations that attack Jerusalem.

Mourning for the One They Pierced

¹⁰"And I will pour out on the house of David and the inhabitants of Jerusalem a spirit^a of grace and supplication. They will look on^b me, the one they have pierced, and they will mourn for him as one mourns for an only child, and grieve bitterly for him as one grieves for a firstborn son. ¹¹On that day the weeping in Jerusalem will be great, like the weeping of Hadad Rimmon in the plain of Megiddo. ¹²The land will mourn, each clan by itself, with their wives by themselves: the clan of the house of David and their wives, the clan of the house of Nathan and their wives, ¹³the clan of the house of Levi and their wives, the clan of Shimei and their wives, ¹⁴and all the rest of the clans and their wives. _{Jn 19:34,37*; Rev 1:7}

Cleansing From Sin

13 "On that day a fountain will be opened to the

^a10 Or *the Spirit*   ^b10 Or *to*

house of David and the inhabitants of Jerusalem, to cleanse them from sin and impurity.   Ps 51:2; Heb 9:14

²"On that day, I will banish the names of the idols from the land, and they will be remembered no more," declares the LORD Almighty. "I will remove both the prophets and the spirit of impurity from the land. ³And if anyone still prophesies, his father and mother, to whom he was born, will say to him, 'You must die, because you have told lies in the LORD's name.' When he prophesies, his own parents will stab him.   Dt 18:20

⁴"On that day every prophet will be ashamed of his prophetic vision. He will not put on a prophet's garment of hair in order to deceive. ⁵He will say, 'I am not a prophet. I am a farmer; the land has been my livelihood since my youth.ᵃ' ⁶If someone asks him, 'What are these wounds on your bodyᵇ?' he will answer, 'The wounds I was given at the house of my friends.'

The Shepherd Struck, the Sheep Scattered

⁷"Awake, O sword, against my shepherd,   Isa 40:11; Jer 47:6
  against the man who is close to me!"
declares the LORD Almighty.
"Strike the shepherd,
  and the sheep will be scattered,   Mt 26:31*

and I will turn my hand
  against the little ones.
⁸In the whole land," declares the LORD,
"two-thirds will be struck
  down and perish;
  yet one-third will be left in
  it.   Eze 5:2-4,12
⁹This third I will bring into the
  fire;   Mal 3:2
I will refine them like silver
  and test them like gold.
They will call on my name
  and I will answer them;
I will say, 'They are my
  people,'   Jer 30:22
and they will say, 'The LORD
  is our God.' "   Jer 29:12

The LORD Comes and Reigns

14 A day of the LORD is coming when your plunder will be divided among you.   Isa 13:9

²I will gather all the nations to Jerusalem to fight against it; the city will be captured, the houses ransacked, and the women raped. Half of the city will go into exile, but the rest of the people will not be taken from the city.   Isa 13:6

³Then the LORD will go out and fight against those nations, as he fights in the day of battle. ⁴On that day his feet will stand on the Mount of Olives, east of Jerusalem, and the Mount of Olives will be split in two from east to west, forming a great valley, with half of the mountain moving north and

---

ᵃ5 Or farmer; a man sold me in my youth   ᵇ6 Or wounds between your hands

half moving south. ⁵You will flee by my mountain valley, for it will extend to Azel. You will flee as you fled from the earthquake*ᵃ* in the days of Uzziah king of Judah. Then the LORD my God will come, and all the holy ones with him.

⁶On that day there will be no light, no cold or frost. ⁷It will be a unique day, without daytime or nighttime—a day known to the LORD. When evening comes, there will be light.   Rev 21:23-25; 22:5

⁸On that day living water will flow out from Jerusalem, half to the eastern sea*ᵇ* and half to the western sea,*ᶜ* in summer and in winter.   Eze 47:1-12; Rev 22:1-2

⁹The LORD will be king over the whole earth. On that day there will be one LORD, and his name the only name.   Eph 4:5-6; Rev 11:15

¹⁰The whole land, from Geba to Rimmon, south of Jerusalem, will become like the Arabah. But Jerusalem will be raised up and remain in its place, from the Benjamin Gate to the site of the First Gate, to the Corner Gate, and from the Tower of Hananel to the royal winepresses. ¹¹It will be inhabited; never again will it be destroyed. Jerusalem will be secure.   Am 9:11

¹²This is the plague with which the LORD will strike all the nations that fought against Jerusalem: Their flesh will rot while they are still standing on their feet, their eyes will rot in their sockets, and their tongues will rot in their mouths. ¹³On that day men will be stricken by the LORD with great panic. Each man will seize the hand of another, and they will attack each other. ¹⁴Judah too will fight at Jerusalem. The wealth of all the surrounding nations will be collected—great quantities of gold and silver and clothing. ¹⁵A similar plague will strike the horses and mules, the camels and donkeys, and all the animals in those camps.

¹⁶Then the survivors from all the nations that have attacked Jerusalem will go up year after year to worship the King, the LORD Almighty, and to celebrate the Feast of Tabernacles. ¹⁷If any of the peoples of the earth do not go up to Jerusalem to worship the King, the LORD Almighty, they will have no rain. ¹⁸If the Egyptian people do not go up and take part, they will have no rain. The LORD*ᵈ* will bring on them the plague he inflicts on the nations that do not go up to celebrate the Feast of Tabernacles. ¹⁹This will be the punishment of Egypt and the punishment of all the nations that do not go up to celebrate the Feast of Tabernacles.

²⁰On that day HOLY TO THE LORD will be inscribed on the bells of the horses, and the cooking pots in the LORD's house will be like the sacred bowls in front of the altar.

ᵃ5 Or ⁵My mountain valley will be blocked and will extend to Azel. It will be blocked as it was blocked because of the earthquake   ᵇ8 That is, the Dead Sea   ᶜ8 That is, the Mediterranean   ᵈ18 Or part, then the LORD

21Every pot in Jerusalem and Judah will be holy to the LORD Almighty, and all who come to sacrifice will take some of the pots and cook in them. And on that day there will no longer be a Canaanite*a* in the house of the LORD Almighty.   1Co 10:31; Eze 44:9

²¹Every pot in Jerusalem and Judah will be holy to the Lord Almighty, and all who come to sacrifice will take some of the pots and

cook in them. And on that day
there will no longer be a Canaanite in the house of the Lord Almighty.   1Co 10:31; Eze 44:9

Malachi

1 An oracle: The word of the Lord to Israel through Mala-chi.*a*   Na 1:1; 1Pe 4:11

Jacob Loved, Esau Hated

²"I have loved you," says the Lord.   Dt 4:37

"But you ask, 'How have you loved us?'   Mal 2:14,17

"Was not Esau Jacob's brother?" the Lord says. "Yet I have loved Jacob, ³but Esau I have hated, and I have turned his mountains into a wasteland and left his inheritance to the desert jackals."   Ro 9:13*

⁴Edom may say, "Though we have been crushed, we will rebuild the ruins."   Isa 9:10

But this is what the Lord Al-mighty says: "They may build, but I will demolish. They will be called the Wicked Land, a people always under the wrath of the Lord. ⁵You will see it with your own eyes and say, 'Great is the Lord—even be-yond the borders of Israel!'

Blemished Sacrifices

⁶"A son honors his father, and a servant his master. If I am a father, where is the honor due me? If I am a master, where is the respect due me?" says the Lord Almighty. "It is you, O priests, who show con-tempt for my name.   Isa 1:2; Mt 15:4

"But you ask, 'How have we shown contempt for your name?'

⁷"You place defiled food on my altar.   Lev 21:6

"But you ask, 'How have we de-filed you?'

"By saying that the Lord's table is contemptible. ⁸When you bring blind animals for sacrifice, is that not wrong? When you sacrifice crippled or diseased animals, is that not wrong? Try offering them to your governor! Would he be pleased with you? Would he ac-cept you?" says the Lord Al-mighty.

⁹"Now implore God to be gra-cious to us. With such offerings from your hands, will he accept you?"—says the Lord Almighty.

¹⁰"Oh, that one of you would shut the temple doors, so that you would not light useless fires on my altar! I am not pleased with you," says the Lord Almighty, "and I will accept no offering from your hands. ¹¹My name will be great among the nations, from the rising to the setting of the sun. In every place incense and pure offerings will be brought to my name, be-cause my name will be great

---

a 1 Malachi means *my messenger*.   *31 Or merchant*

among the nations," says the LORD Almighty. Isa 1:11-14; Hos 5:6

¹²"But you profane it by saying of the Lord's table, 'It is defiled,' and of its food, 'It is contemptible.' ¹³And you say, 'What a burden!' and you sniff at it contemptuously," says the LORD Almighty.

"When you bring injured, crippled or diseased animals and offer them as sacrifices, should I accept them from your hands?" says the LORD. ¹⁴"Cursed is the cheat who has an acceptable male in his flock and vows to give it, but then sacrifices a blemished animal to the Lord. For I am a great king," says the LORD Almighty, "and my name is to be feared among the nations.

Admonition for the Priests

2 "And now this admonition is for you, O priests. ²If you do not listen, and if you do not set your heart to honor my name," says the LORD Almighty, "I will send a curse upon you, and I will curse your blessings. Yes, I have already cursed them, because you have not set your heart to honor me. Dt 28:20

³"Because of you I will rebuke[a] your descendants[b]; I will spread on your faces the offal from your festival sacrifices, and you will be carried off with it. ⁴And you will know that I have sent you this admonition so that my covenant with Levi may continue," says the LORD

Almighty. ⁵"My covenant was with him, a covenant of life and peace, and I gave them to him; this called for reverence and he revered me and stood in awe of my name. ⁶True instruction was in his mouth and nothing false was found on his lips. He walked with me in peace and uprightness, and turned many from sin. Nu 25:12; Jer 23:22

⁷"For the lips of a priest ought to preserve knowledge, and from his mouth men should seek instruction—because he is the messenger of the LORD Almighty. ⁸But you have turned from the way and by your teaching have caused many to stumble; you have violated the covenant with Levi," says the LORD Almighty. ⁹"So I have caused you to be despised and humiliated before all the people, because you have not followed my ways but have shown partiality in matters of the law." 1Sa 2:30; Jer 18:15

Judah Unfaithful

¹⁰Have we not all one Father[c]? Did not one God create us? Why do we profane the covenant of our fathers by breaking faith with one another? Ex 19:5; 1Co 8:6

¹¹Judah has broken faith. A detestable thing has been committed in Israel and in Jerusalem: Judah has desecrated the sanctuary the LORD loves, by marrying the daughter of a foreign god. ¹²As for the man who does this, whoever

---

[a]3 Or cut off (see Septuagint)　　[b]3 Or will blight your grain　　[c]10 Or father

he may be, may the LORD cut him off from the tents of Jacob[a]—even though he brings offerings to the LORD Almighty.   Mal 1:10

[13]Another thing you do: You flood the LORD's altar with tears. You weep and wail because he no longer pays attention to your offerings or accepts them with pleasure from your hands. [14]You ask, "Why?" It is because the LORD is acting as the witness between you and the wife of your youth, because you have broken faith with her, though she is your partner, the wife of your marriage covenant.   Pr 5:18; Heb 13:4

[15]Has not the LORD made them one? In flesh and spirit they are his. And why one? Because he was seeking godly offspring.[b] So guard yourself in your spirit, and do not break faith with the wife of your youth.   Mt 19:4-6; 1Co 7:14

[16]"I hate divorce," says the LORD God of Israel, "and I hate a man's covering himself[c] with violence as well as with his garment," says the LORD Almighty.   Dt 24:1; Mt 5:31-32

So guard yourself in your spirit, and do not break faith.   Ps 51:10

The Day of Judgment

[17]You have wearied the LORD with your words.   Isa 43:24

"How have we wearied him?" you ask.   Mal 1:2

By saying, "All who do evil are good in the eyes of the LORD, and he is pleased with them" or "Where is the God of justice?"

3 "See, I will send my messenger, who will prepare the way before me. Then suddenly the Lord you are seeking will come to his temple; the messenger of the covenant, whom you desire, will come," says the LORD Almighty.

[2]But who can endure the day of his coming? Who can stand when he appears? For he will be like a refiner's fire or a launderer's soap. [3]He will sit as a refiner and purifier of silver; he will purify the Levites and refine them like gold and silver. Then the LORD will have men who will bring offerings in righteousness, [4]and the offerings of Judah and Jerusalem will be acceptable to the LORD, as in days gone by, as in former years.   Rev 6:17

[5]"So I will come near to you for judgment. I will be quick to testify against sorcerers, adulterers and perjurers, against those who defraud laborers of their wages, who oppress the widows and the fatherless, and deprive aliens of justice, but do not fear me," says the LORD Almighty.   Lev 19:13; Jer 7:9; Jas 5:4

Robbing God

[6]"I the LORD do not change. So you, O descendants of Jacob, are not destroyed. [7]Ever since the time of your forefathers you have

---

[a]12 Or [12]May the LORD cut off from the tents of Jacob anyone who gives testimony in behalf of the man who does this   [b]15 Or [15]But the one who is our father, did not do this, not as long as life remained in him. And what was he seeking? An offspring from God   [c]16 Or his wife

turned away from my decrees and have not kept them. Return to me, and I will return to you," says the Lord Almighty.   Ac 7:51; Jas 1:17

"But you ask, 'How are we to return?'

8"Will a man rob God? Yet you rob me.

"But you ask, 'How do we rob you?'

"In tithes and offerings. 9You are under a curse—the whole nation of you—because you are robbing me. 10Bring the whole tithe into the storehouse, that there may be food in my house. Test me in this," says the Lord Almighty, "and see if I will not throw open the floodgates of heaven and pour out so much blessing that you will not have room enough for it. 11I will prevent pests from devouring your crops, and the vines in your fields will not cast their fruit," says the Lord Almighty. 12"Then all the nations will call you blessed, for yours will be a delightful land," says the Lord Almighty.   Ne 13:10-12

13"You have said harsh things against me," says the Lord.

"Yet you ask, 'What have we said against you?'

14"You have said, 'It is futile to serve God. What did we gain by carrying out his requirements and going about like mourners before the Lord Almighty? 15But now we call the arrogant blessed. Certainly the evildoers prosper, and even those who challenge God escape.' "   Isa 58:3; Jer 7:10

16Then those who feared the Lord talked with each other, and the Lord listened and heard. A scroll of remembrance was written in his presence concerning those who feared the Lord and honored his name.   Ps 34:15; 56:8

17"They will be mine," says the Lord Almighty, "in the day when I make up my treasured possession.*a* I will spare them, just as in compassion a man spares his son who serves him. 18And you will again see the distinction between the righteous and the wicked, between those who serve God and those who do not.   Ps 103:13

The Day of the Lord

4 "Surely the day is coming; it will burn like a furnace. All the arrogant and every evildoer will be stubble, and that day that is coming will set them on fire," says the Lord Almighty. "Not a root or a branch will be left to them. 2But for you who revere my name, the sun of righteousness will rise with healing in its wings. And you will go out and leap like calves released from the stall. 3Then you will trample down the wicked; they will be ashes under the soles of your feet on the day when I do these things," says the Lord Almighty.   Lk 1:78

4"Remember the law of my servant Moses, the decrees and

---

a 17 Or Almighty, "my treasured possession, in the day when I act

laws I gave him at Horeb for all Israel.

⁵"See, I will send you the prophet Elijah before that great and dreadful day of the LORD comes. ⁶He will turn the hearts of the fathers to their children, and the hearts of the children to their fathers; or else I will come and strike the land with a curse." Mt 11:14

The New Testament

Matthew

The Genealogy of Jesus

1 A record of the genealogy of Jesus Christ the son of David, the son of Abraham: Ge 22:18

2 Abraham was the father of Isaac, Ge 21:3,12

Isaac the father of Jacob,

Jacob the father of Judah and his brothers, Ge 29:35

3 Judah the father of Perez and Zerah, whose mother was Tamar, Ge 38:27-30

Perez the father of Hezron,

Hezron the father of Ram,

4 Ram the father of Amminadab,

Amminadab the father of Nahshon,

Nahshon the father of Salmon,

5 Salmon the father of Boaz, whose mother was Rahab,

Boaz the father of Obed, whose mother was Ruth,

Obed the father of Jesse,

6 and Jesse the father of King David. Ru 4:18-22; 1Sa 16:1

David was the father of Solomon, whose mother had been Uriah's wife,

7 Solomon the father of Rehoboam,

Rehoboam the father of Abijah,

Abijah the father of Asa,

8 Asa the father of Jehoshaphat,

Jehoshaphat the father of Jehoram,

Jehoram the father of Uzziah,

9 Uzziah the father of Jotham,

Jotham the father of Ahaz,

Ahaz the father of Hezekiah,

10 Hezekiah the father of Manasseh, 2Ki 20:21

Manasseh the father of Amon,

Amon the father of Josiah,

11 and Josiah the father of Jeconiah[a] and his brothers at the time of the exile to Babylon. 1Ch 3:10-17

12 After the exile to Babylon:

Jeconiah was the father of Shealtiel, 1Ch 3:17

Shealtiel the father of Zerubbabel, 1Ch 3:19; Ezr 3:2

13 Zerubbabel the father of Abiud,

Abiud the father of Eliakim,

Eliakim the father of Azor,

14 Azor the father of Zadok,

a 11 That is, Jehoiachin; also in verse 12

Zadok the father of Akim,
Akim the father of Eliud,
¹⁵Eliud the father of Eleazar,
Eleazar the father of Matthan,
Matthan the father of Jacob,
¹⁶and Jacob the father of Joseph, the husband of Mary, of whom was born Jesus, who is called Christ.   Mt 27:17; Lk 1:27

¹⁷Thus there were fourteen generations in all from Abraham to David, fourteen from David to the exile to Babylon, and fourteen from the exile to the Christ.ᵃ

The Birth of Jesus Christ

¹⁸This is how the birth of Jesus Christ came about: His mother Mary was pledged to be married to Joseph, but before they came together, she was found to be with child through the Holy Spirit. ¹⁹Because Joseph her husband was a righteous man and did not want to expose her to public disgrace, he had in mind to divorce her quietly.

²⁰But after he had considered this, an angel of the Lord appeared to him in a dream and said, "Joseph son of David, do not be afraid to take Mary home as your wife, because what is conceived in her is from the Holy Spirit. ²¹She will

give birth to a son, and you are to give him the name Jesus,ᵇ because he will save his people from their sins."   Lk 2:11; Ac 13:23,28

²²All this took place to fulfill what the Lord had said through the prophet: ²³"The virgin will be with child and will give birth to a son, and they will call him Immanuel"ᶜ—which means, "God with us."   Isa 8:8,10

²⁴When Joseph woke up, he did what the angel of the Lord had commanded him and took Mary home as his wife. ²⁵But he had no union with her until she gave birth to a son. And he gave him the name Jesus.   Lk 1:31

The Visit of the Magi

2 After Jesus was born in Bethlehem in Judea, during the time of King Herod, Magiᵈ from the east came to Jerusalem ²and asked, "Where is the one who has been born king of the Jews? We saw his star in the eastᵉ and have come to worship him."   Nu 24:17

³When King Herod heard this he was disturbed, and all Jerusalem with him. ⁴When he had called together all the people's chief priests and teachers of the law, he asked them where the Christᶠ was to be born. ⁵"In Bethlehem in Judea," they replied, "for this is what the prophet has written:

ᵃ17 Or *Messiah*. "The Christ" (Greek) and "the Messiah" (Hebrew) both mean "the Anointed One."
ᵇ21 *Jesus* is the Greek form of *Joshua*, which means *the Lord saves*.   ᶜ23 Isaiah 7:14
ᵈ1 Traditionally *Wise Men*   ᵉ2 Or *star when it rose*   ᶠ4 Or *Messiah*

6" 'But you, Bethlehem, in the
    land of Judah,
are by no means least
    among the rulers of
    Judah;
for out of you will come a
    ruler
who will be the shepherd of
    my people Israel.'*a*"

[7]Then Herod called the Magi secretly and found out from them
the exact time the star had appeared. [8]He sent them to Bethlehem and said, "Go and make a
careful search for the child. As
soon as you find him, report to me,
so that I too may go and worship
him."

[9]After they had heard the king,
they went on their way, and the
star they had seen in the east*b*
went ahead of them until it
stopped over the place where the
child was. [10]When they saw the
star, they were overjoyed. [11]On
coming to the house, they saw the
child with his mother Mary, and
they bowed down and worshiped
him. Then they opened their treasures and presented him with gifts
of gold and of incense and of
myrrh. [12]And having been warned
in a dream not to go back to Herod,
they returned to their country by
another route.   Ps 72:10; Isa 60:3

The Escape to Egypt

[13]When they had gone, an angel
of the Lord appeared to Joseph in
a dream. "Get up," he said, "take
the child and his mother and escape to Egypt. Stay there until I tell
you, for Herod is going to search
for the child to kill him."   Rev 12:4

[14]So he got up, took the child
and his mother during the night
and left for Egypt, [15]where he
stayed until the death of Herod.
And so was fulfilled what the Lord
had said through the prophet:
"Out of Egypt I called my son."*c*

[16]When Herod realized that he
had been outwitted by the Magi,
he was furious, and he gave orders
to kill all the boys in Bethlehem
and its vicinity who were two
years old and under, in accordance
with the time he had learned from
the Magi. [17]Then what was said
through the prophet Jeremiah was
fulfilled: Mt 1:22

[18]"A voice is heard in Ramah,
    weeping and great mourning,
Rachel weeping for her
        children
    and refusing to be
        comforted,
because they are no more."*d*

The Return to Nazareth

[19]After Herod died, an angel of
the Lord appeared in a dream to
Joseph in Egypt [20]and said, "Get
up, take the child and his mother
and go to the land of Israel, for

*a*6 Micah 5:2   *b*9 Or *seen when it rose*   *c*15 Hosea 11:1   *d*18 Jer. 31:15

those who were trying to take the child's life are dead." Ex 4:19

²¹So he got up, took the child and his mother and went to the land of Israel. ²²But when he heard that Archelaus was reigning in Judea in place of his father Herod, he was afraid to go there. Having been warned in a dream, he withdrew to the district of Galilee, ²³and he went and lived in a town called Nazareth. So was fulfilled what was said through the prophets: "He will be called a Nazarene."

John the Baptist Prepares the Way

3 In those days John the Baptist came, preaching in the Desert of Judea ²and saying, "Repent, for the kingdom of heaven is near." ³This is he who was spoken of through the prophet Isaiah:

"A voice of one calling in the
        desert,
'Prepare the way for the Lord,
    make straight paths for
        him.' " ᵃ   Lk 1:76; Jn 1:23

⁴John's clothes were made of camel's hair, and he had a leather belt around his waist. His food was locusts and wild honey. ⁵People went out to him from Jerusalem and all Judea and the whole region of the Jordan. ⁶Confessing their sins, they were baptized by him in the Jordan River.   Lev 11:22; 2Ki 1:8

⁷But when he saw many of the Pharisees and Sadducees coming to where he was baptizing, he said to them: "You brood of vipers! Who warned you to flee from the coming wrath? ⁸Produce fruit in keeping with repentance. ⁹And do not think you can say to yourselves, 'We have Abraham as our father.' I tell you that out of these stones God can raise up children for Abraham. ¹⁰The ax is already at the root of the trees, and every tree that does not produce good fruit will be cut down and thrown into the fire.   Mt 7:19; Ac 26:20

¹¹"I baptize you with ᵇ water for repentance. But after me will come one who is more powerful than I, whose sandals I am not fit to carry. He will baptize you with the Holy Spirit and with fire. ¹²His winnowing fork is in his hand, and he will clear his threshing floor, gathering his wheat into the barn and burning up the chaff with unquenchable fire."   Mk 1:3-8; Lk 3:2-17

The Baptism of Jesus

¹³Then Jesus came from Galilee to the Jordan to be baptized by John. ¹⁴But John tried to deter him, saying, "I need to be baptized by you, and do you come to me?"

¹⁵Jesus replied, "Let it be so now; it is proper for us to do this to fulfill all righteousness." Then John consented.

¹⁶As soon as Jesus was baptized, he went up out of the water. At

ᵃ3 Isaiah 40:3   ᵇ11 Or in

that moment heaven was opened, and he saw the Spirit of God descending like a dove and lighting on him. ¹⁷And a voice from heaven said, "This is my Son, whom I love; with him I am well pleased."

The Temptation of Jesus

4 Then Jesus was led by the Spirit into the desert to be tempted by the devil. ²After fasting forty days and forty nights, he was hungry. ³The tempter came to him and said, "If you are the Son of God, tell these stones to become bread." 1Ki 19:8; 1Th 3:5

⁴Jesus answered, "It is written: 'Man does not live on bread alone, but on every word that comes from the mouth of God.'ᵃ" Jn 4:34

⁵Then the devil took him to the holy city and had him stand on the highest point of the temple. ⁶"If you are the Son of God," he said, "throw yourself down. For it is written: Mt 27:53

" 'He will command his angels
        concerning you,
    and they will lift you up in
        their hands,
so that you will not strike your
    foot against a stone.'ᵇ"

⁷Jesus answered him, "It is also written: 'Do not put the Lord your God to the test.'ᶜ"

⁸Again, the devil took him to a very high mountain and showed him all the kingdoms of the world and their splendor. ⁹"All this I will give you," he said, "if you will bow down and worship me."

¹⁰Jesus said to him, "Away from me, Satan! For it is written: 'Worship the Lord your God, and serve him only.'ᵈ"

¹¹Then the devil left him, and angels came and attended him.

Jesus Begins to Preach

¹²When Jesus heard that John had been put in prison, he returned to Galilee. ¹³Leaving Nazareth, he went and lived in Capernaum, which was by the lake in the area of Zebulun and Naphtali— ¹⁴to fulfill what was said through the prophet Isaiah: Mt 14:3; Mk 1:21

¹⁵"Land of Zebulun and land of
        Naphtali,
    the way to the sea, along the
        Jordan,
    Galilee of the Gentiles—
¹⁶the people living in darkness
    have seen a great light;
on those living in the land of
        the shadow of death
    a light has dawned."ᵉ Lk 2:32

¹⁷From that time on Jesus began to preach, "Repent, for the kingdom of heaven is near." Mt 3:2

The Calling of the First Disciples

¹⁸As Jesus was walking beside the Sea of Galilee, he saw two brothers, Simon called Peter and

ᵃ4 Deut. 8:3   ᵇ6 Psalm 91:11,12   ᶜ7 Deut. 6:16   ᵈ10 Deut. 6:13   ᵉ16 Isaiah 9:1,2 his brother Andrew. They were casting a net into the lake, for they were fishermen. ¹⁹"Come, follow me," Jesus said, "and I will make you fishers of men." ²⁰At once they left their nets and followed him.

²¹Going on from there, he saw two other brothers, James son of Zebedee and his brother John. They were in a boat with their father Zebedee, preparing their nets. Jesus called them, ²²and immediately they left the boat and their father and followed him.

Jesus Heals the Sick

²³Jesus went throughout Galilee, teaching in their synagogues, preaching the good news of the kingdom, and healing every disease and sickness among the people. ²⁴News about him spread all over Syria, and people brought to him all who were ill with various diseases, those suffering severe pain, the demon-possessed, those having seizures, and the paralyzed, and he healed them. ²⁵Large crowds from Galilee, the Decapolis,ᵃ Jerusalem, Judea and the region across the Jordan followed him.   Mk 1:14; Ac 10:38

The Beatitudes

5 Now when he saw the crowds, he went up on a mountainside and sat down. His disciples came to him, ²and he began to teach them, saying:

³"Blessed are the poor in spirit,
  for theirs is the kingdom of
    heaven.   Mt 25:34
⁴Blessed are those who mourn,
  for they will be comforted.
⁵Blessed are the meek,
  for they will inherit the
    earth.   Ps 37:11; Ro 4:13
⁶Blessed are those who hunger
  and thirst for
    righteousness,
  for they will be filled.
⁷Blessed are the merciful,
  for they will be shown
    mercy.   Jas 2:13
⁸Blessed are the pure in heart,
  for they will see God.
⁹Blessed are the peacemakers,
  for they will be called sons
    of God.   Ro 8:14
¹⁰Blessed are those who are
  persecuted because of
    righteousness,   1Pe 3:14
  for theirs is the kingdom of
    heaven.   Mt 25:34

¹¹"Blessed are you when people insult you, persecute you and falsely say all kinds of evil against you because of me. ¹²Rejoice and be glad, because great is your reward in heaven, for in the same way they persecuted the prophets who were before you.   Ac 7:52

Salt and Light

¹³"You are the salt of the earth. But if the salt loses its saltiness,

how can it be made salty again? It is no longer good for anything, except to be thrown out and trampled by men.   Mk 9:50; Lk 14:34-35

14"You are the light of the world. A city on a hill cannot be hidden. 15Neither do people light a lamp and put it under a bowl. Instead they put it on its stand, and it gives light to everyone in the house. 16In the same way, let your light shine before men, that they may see your good deeds and praise your Father in heaven.   Jn 8:12; 1Co 10:31

The Fulfillment of the Law

17"Do not think that I have come to abolish the Law or the Prophets; I have not come to abolish them but to fulfill them. 18I tell you the truth, until heaven and earth disappear, not the smallest letter, not the least stroke of a pen, will by any means disappear from the Law until everything is accomplished. 19Anyone who breaks one of the least of these commandments and teaches others to do the same will be called least in the kingdom of heaven, but whoever practices and teaches these commands will be called great in the kingdom of heaven. 20For I tell you that unless your righteousness surpasses that of the Pharisees and the teachers of the law, you will certainly not enter the kingdom of heaven.

Murder

21"You have heard that it was said to the people long ago, 'Do not murder,*a* and anyone who murders will be subject to judgment.' 22But I tell you that anyone who is angry with his brother*b* will be subject to judgment. Again, anyone who says to his brother, 'Raca,*c*' is answerable to the Sanhedrin. But anyone who says, 'You fool!' will be in danger of the fire of hell.   1Jn 3:15

23"Therefore, if you are offering your gift at the altar and there remember that your brother has something against you, 24leave your gift there in front of the altar. First go and be reconciled to your brother; then come and offer your gift.

25"Settle matters quickly with your adversary who is taking you to court. Do it while you are still with him on the way, or he may hand you over to the judge, and the judge may hand you over to the officer, and you may be thrown into prison. 26I tell you the truth, you will not get out until you have paid the last penny.*d*   Lk 12:58-59

Adultery

27"You have heard that it was said, 'Do not commit adultery.'*e* 28But I tell you that anyone who looks at a woman lustfully has already committed adultery with her

---

a 21 Exodus 20:13   *b 22* Some manuscripts *brother without cause*   *c 22* An Aramaic term of contempt
d 26 Greek *kodrantes*   *e 27* Exodus 20:14

in his heart. ²⁹If your right eye causes you to sin, gouge it out and throw it away. It is better for you to lose one part of your body than for your whole body to be thrown into hell. ³⁰And if your right hand causes you to sin, cut it off and throw it away. It is better for you to lose one part of your body than for your whole body to go into hell.   Mk 9:42-47; Pr 6:25

Divorce

³¹"It has been said, 'Anyone who divorces his wife must give her a certificate of divorce.'ᵃ ³²But I tell you that anyone who divorces his wife, except for marital unfaithfulness, causes her to become an adulteress, and anyone who marries the divorced woman commits adultery.   Lk 16:18

Oaths

³³"Again, you have heard that it was said to the people long ago 'Do not break your oath, but keep the oaths you have made to the Lord.' ³⁴But I tell you, Do not swear at all: either by heaven, for it is God's throne; ³⁵or by the earth, for it is his footstool; or by Jerusalem, for it is the city of the Great King. ³⁶And do not swear by your head, for you cannot make even one hair white or black. ³⁷Simply let your 'Yes' be 'Yes,' and your 'No,' 'No'; any-thing beyond this comes from the evil one.   Nu 30:2

An Eye for an Eye

³⁸"You have heard that it was said, 'Eye for eye, and tooth for tooth.'ᵇ ³⁹But I tell you, Do not re-sist an evil person. If someone strikes you on the right cheek, turn to him the other also. ⁴⁰And if someone wants to sue you and take your tunic, let him have your cloak as well. ⁴¹If someone forces you to go one mile, go with him two miles. ⁴²Give to the one who asks you, and do not turn away from the one who wants to borrow from you.   Lk 6:29-30

Love for Enemies

⁴³"You have heard that it was said, 'Love your neighborᶜ and hate your enemy.' ⁴⁴But I tell you: Love your enemiesᵈ and pray for those who persecute you, ⁴⁵that you may be sons of your Father in heaven. He causes his sun to rise on the evil and the good, and sends rain on the righteous and the un-righteous. ⁴⁶If you love those who love you, what reward will you get? Are not even the tax collectors doing that? ⁴⁷And if you greet only your brothers, what are you doing more than others? Do not even pa-gans do that? ⁴⁸Be perfect, there-fore, as your heavenly Father is perfect.   Lev 19:2; Lk 6:27-28

ᵃ31 Deut. 24:1   ᵇ38 Exodus 21:24; Lev. 24:20; Deut. 19:21   ᶜ43 Lev. 19:18   ᵈ44 Some late manuscripts *enemies, bless those who curse you, do good to those who hate you*

Giving to the Needy

6 "Be careful not to do your 'acts of righteousness' before men, to be seen by them. If you do, you will have no reward from your Father in heaven.   Mt 23:5

²"So when you give to the needy, do not announce it with trumpets, as the hypocrites do in the synagogues and on the streets, to be honored by men. I tell you the truth, they have received their reward in full. ³But when you give to the needy, do not let your left hand know what your right hand is doing, ⁴so that your giving may be in secret. Then your Father, who sees what is done in secret, will reward you.   Col 3:23-24

Prayer

⁵"And when you pray, do not be like the hypocrites, for they love to pray standing in the synagogues and on the street corners to be seen by men. I tell you the truth, they have received their reward in full. ⁶But when you pray, go into your room, close the door and pray to your Father, who is unseen. Then your Father, who sees what is done in secret, will reward you. ⁷And when you pray, do not keep on babbling like pagans, for they think they will be heard because of their many words. ⁸Do not be like them, for your Father knows what you need before you ask him.

⁹"This, then, is how you should pray:

" 'Our Father in heaven,   Mal 2:10
    hallowed be your name,
¹⁰your kingdom come,   Mt 3:2
    your will be done   Mt 26:39
        on earth as it is in heaven.
¹¹Give us today our daily bread.
¹²Forgive us our debts,
    as we also have forgiven our
        debtors.   Mt 18:21-35
¹³And lead us not into
        temptation,   Jas 1:13
    but deliver us from the evil
        one.ᵃ'

¹⁴For if you forgive men when they sin against you, your heavenly Father will also forgive you. ¹⁵But if you do not forgive men their sins, your Father will not forgive your sins.   Mt 18:21-35; Mk 11:25,26; Luke 11:2-4

Fasting

¹⁶"When you fast, do not look somber as the hypocrites do, for they disfigure their faces to show men they are fasting. I tell you the truth, they have received their reward in full. ¹⁷But when you fast, put oil on your head and wash your face, ¹⁸so that it will not be obvious to men that you are fasting, but only to your Father, who is unseen; and your Father, who sees what is done in secret, will reward you.   ver 4,6; Isa 58:5

ᵃ 13 Or *from evil*; some late manuscripts *one, / for yours is the kingdom and the power and the glory forever. Amen.*

Treasures in Heaven

¹⁹"Do not store up for your-selves treasures on earth, where moth and rust destroy, and where thieves break in and steal. ²⁰But store up for yourselves treasures in heaven, where moth and rust do not destroy, and where thieves do not break in and steal. ²¹For where your treasure is, there your heart will be also.   Lk 12:33-34; Heb 13:5

²²"The eye is the lamp of the body. If your eyes are good, your whole body will be full of light. ²³But if your eyes are bad, your whole body will be full of dark-ness. If then the light within you is darkness, how great is that dark-ness!   Lk 11:34-36

²⁴"No one can serve two mas-ters. Either he will hate the one and love the other, or he will be devoted to the one and despise the other. You cannot serve both God and Money.   Lk 16:13

Do Not Worry

²⁵"Therefore I tell you, do not worry about your life, what you will eat or drink; or about your body, what you will wear. Is not life more important than food, and the body more important than clothes? ²⁶Look at the birds of the air; they do not sow or reap or store away in barns, and yet your heavenly Father feeds them. Are you not much more valuable than they? ²⁷Who of you by worrying can add a single hour to his life*a*?

²⁸"And why do you worry about clothes? See how the lilies of the field grow. They do not labor or spin. ²⁹Yet I tell you that not even Solomon in all his splendor was dressed like one of these. ³⁰If that is how God clothes the grass of the field, which is here today and to-morrow is thrown into the fire, will he not much more clothe you, O you of little faith? ³¹So do not wor-ry, saying, 'What shall we eat?' or 'What shall we drink?' or 'What shall we wear?' ³²For the pagans run after all these things, and your heavenly Father knows that you need them. ³³But seek first his kingdom and his righteousness, and all these things will be given to you as well. ³⁴Therefore do not worry about tomorrow, for tomor-row will worry about itself. Each day has enough trouble of its own.

Judging Others

7 "Do not judge, or you too will be judged. ²For in the same way you judge others, you will be judged, and with the measure you use, it will be measured to you.

³"Why do you look at the speck of sawdust in your brother's eye and pay no attention to the plank in your own eye? ⁴How can you say to your brother, 'Let me take the speck out of your eye,' when all the time there is a plank in your own eye? ⁵You hypocrite, first take

---

a 27 Or single cubit to his height

the plank out of your own eye, and then you will see clearly to remove the speck from your brother's eye. 6"Do not give dogs what is sacred; do not throw your pearls to pigs. If you do, they may trample them under their feet, and then turn and tear you to pieces.

Ask, Seek, Knock

7"Ask and it will be given to you; seek and you will find; knock and the door will be opened to you. 8For everyone who asks receives; he who seeks finds; and to him who knocks, the door will be opened.   Jer 29:12-13; Jn 15:7,16 9"Which of you, if his son asks for bread, will give him a stone? 10Or if he asks for a fish, will give him a snake? 11If you, then, though you are evil, know how to give good gifts to your children, how much more will your Father in heaven give good gifts to those who ask him! 12So in everything, do to others what you would have them do to you, for this sums up the Law and the Prophets.

The Narrow and Wide Gates

13"Enter through the narrow gate. For wide is the gate and broad is the road that leads to destruction, and many enter through it. 14But small is the gate and narrow the road that leads to life, and only a few find it.   Lk 13:24; Jn 10:7,9

A Tree and Its Fruit

15"Watch out for false prophets. They come to you in sheep's clothing, but inwardly they are ferocious wolves. 16By their fruit you will recognize them. Do people pick grapes from thornbushes, or figs from thistles? 17Likewise every good tree bears good fruit, but a bad tree bears bad fruit. 18A good tree cannot bear bad fruit, and a bad tree cannot bear good fruit. 19Every tree that does not bear good fruit is cut down and thrown into the fire. 20Thus, by their fruit you will recognize them.   Mk 13:22 21"Not everyone who says to me, 'Lord, Lord,' will enter the kingdom of heaven, but only he who does the will of my Father who is in heaven. 22Many will say to me on that day, 'Lord, Lord, did we not prophesy in your name, and in your name drive out demons and perform many miracles?' 23Then I will tell them plainly, 'I never knew you. Away from me, you evildoers!'   Mt 25:12,41

The Wise and Foolish Builders

24"Therefore everyone who hears these words of mine and puts them into practice is like a wise man who built his house on the rock. 25The rain came down, the streams rose, and the winds blew and beat against that house; yet it did not fall, because it had its foundation on the rock. 26But everyone who hears these words of mine and does not put them into practice is like a foolish man who built his house on sand. 27The rain came down, the streams rose, and the winds blew and beat against that house, and it fell with a great crash." Lk 6:47-49

²⁸When Jesus had finished saying these things, the crowds were amazed at his teaching, ²⁹because he taught as one who had authority, and not as their teachers of the law. Lk 4:32; Jn 7:46

The Man With Leprosy

8 When he came down from the mountainside, large crowds followed him. ²A man with leprosy*a* came and knelt before him and said, "Lord, if you are willing, you can make me clean." Mt 15:25

³Jesus reached out his hand and touched the man. "I am willing," he said. "Be clean!" Immediately he was cured*b* of his leprosy. ⁴Then Jesus said to him, "See that you don't tell anyone. But go, show yourself to the priest and offer the gift Moses commanded, as a testimony to them." Mk 1:40-44

The Faith of the Centurion

⁵When Jesus had entered Capernaum, a centurion came to him, asking for help. ⁶"Lord," he said, "my servant lies at home paralyzed and in terrible suffering."

⁷Jesus said to him, "I will go and heal him."

⁸The centurion replied, "Lord, I do not deserve to have you come under my roof. But just say the word, and my servant will be healed. ⁹For I myself am a man under authority, with soldiers under me. I tell this one, 'Go,' and he goes; and that one, 'Come,' and he comes. I say to my servant, 'Do this,' and he does it." Ps 107:20

¹⁰When Jesus heard this, he was astonished and said to those following him, "I tell you the truth, I have not found anyone in Israel with such great faith. ¹¹I say to you that many will come from the east and the west, and will take their places at the feast with Abraham, Isaac and Jacob in the kingdom of heaven. ¹²But the subjects of the kingdom will be thrown outside, into the darkness, where there will be weeping and gnashing of teeth." Lk 13:28-29

¹³Then Jesus said to the centurion, "Go! It will be done just as you believed it would." And his servant was healed at that very hour.

Jesus Heals Many

¹⁴When Jesus came into Peter's house, he saw Peter's mother-in-law lying in bed with a fever. ¹⁵He touched her hand and the fever left her, and she got up and began to wait on him. Mk 1:29-34; Lk 4:38-41

¹⁶When evening came, many who were demon-possessed were brought to him, and he drove out the spirits with a word and healed

---

a2 The Greek word was used for various diseases affecting the skin—not necessarily leprosy.
b3 Greek *made clean*

all the sick. ¹⁷This was to fulfill what was spoken through the prophet Isaiah: Mt 1:22

"He took up our infirmities
    and carried our diseases."ᵃ

The Cost of Following Jesus

¹⁸When Jesus saw the crowd around him, he gave orders to cross to the other side of the lake. ¹⁹Then a teacher of the law came to him and said, "Teacher, I will follow you wherever you go."

²⁰Jesus replied, "Foxes have holes and birds of the air have nests, but the Son of Man has no place to lay his head."   Mk 8:31

²¹Another disciple said to him, "Lord, first let me go and bury my father."

²²But Jesus told him, "Follow me, and let the dead bury their own dead."   Lk 9:57-60

Jesus Calms the Storm

²³Then he got into the boat and his disciples followed him. ²⁴Without warning, a furious storm came up on the lake, so that the waves swept over the boat. But Jesus was sleeping. ²⁵The disciples went and woke him, saying, "Lord, save us! We're going to drown!"   Mk 4:36-41

²⁶He replied, "You of little faith, why are you so afraid?" Then he got up and rebuked the winds and the waves, and it was completely calm.   Ps 65:7; 107:29

²⁷The men were amazed and asked, "What kind of man is this? Even the winds and the waves obey him!"   Mt 14:22-33

The Healing of Two Demon-possessed Men

²⁸When he arrived at the other side in the region of the Gadarenes,ᵇ two demon-possessed men coming from the tombs met him. They were so violent that no one could pass that way. ²⁹"What do you want with us, Son of God?" they shouted. "Have you come here to torture us before the appointed time?"   Mk 1:24; Jn 2:4

³⁰Some distance from them a large herd of pigs was feeding. ³¹The demons begged Jesus, "If you drive us out, send us into the herd of pigs."

³²He said to them, "Go!" So they came out and went into the pigs, and the whole herd rushed down the steep bank into the lake and died in the water. ³³Those tending the pigs ran off, went into the town and reported all this, including what had happened to the demon-possessed men. ³⁴Then the whole town went out to meet Jesus. And when they saw him, they pleaded with him to leave their region.

Jesus Heals a Paralytic

9 Jesus stepped into a boat, crossed over and came to his own town. ²Some men brought to

---

ᵃ17 Isaiah 53:4   ᵇ28 Some manuscripts Gergesenes; others Gerasenes him a paralytic, lying on a mat. When Jesus saw their faith, he said to the paralytic, "Take heart, son; your sins are forgiven." Lk 7:48

3At this, some of the teachers of the law said to themselves, "This fellow is blaspheming!" Mt 26:65

4Knowing their thoughts, Jesus said, "Why do you entertain evil thoughts in your hearts? **5**Which is easier: to say, 'Your sins are forgiven,' or to say, 'Get up and walk'? **6**But so that you may know that the Son of Man has authority on earth to forgive sins...." Then he said to the paralytic, "Get up, take your mat and go home." **7**And the man got up and went home. **8**When the crowd saw this, they were filled with awe; and they praised God, who had given such authority to men. Mk 2:3-12; Lk 5:18-26

The Calling of Matthew

9As Jesus went on from there, he saw a man named Matthew sitting at the tax collector's booth. "Follow me," he told him, and Matthew got up and followed him.

10While Jesus was having dinner at Matthew's house, many tax collectors and "sinners" came and ate with him and his disciples. **11**When the Pharisees saw this, they asked his disciples, "Why does your teacher eat with tax collectors and 'sinners'?" Mt 11:19; Gal 2:15

12On hearing this, Jesus said, "It is not the healthy who need a doc-tor, but the sick. **13**But go and learn what this means: 'I desire mercy, not sacrifice.' *a* For I have not come to call the righteous, but sinners."

Jesus Questioned About Fasting

14Then John's disciples came and asked him, "How is it that we and the Pharisees fast, but your disciples do not fast?" Lk 18:12

15Jesus answered, "How can the guests of the bridegroom mourn while he is with them? The time will come when the bridegroom will be taken from them; then they will fast. Jn 3:29; Ac 13:2-3

16"No one sews a patch of un-shrunk cloth on an old garment, for the patch will pull away from the garment, making the tear worse. **17**Neither do men pour new wine into old wineskins. If they do, the skins will burst, the wine will run out and the wineskins will be ruined. No, they pour new wine into new wineskins, and both are preserved." Mk 2:18-22; Lk 5:33-39

A Dead Girl and a Sick Woman

18While he was saying this, a ruler came and knelt before him and said, "My daughter has just died. But come and put your hand on her, and she will live." **19**Jesus got up and went with him, and so did his disciples. Mt 8:2

20Just then a woman who had

a 13 Hosea 6:6

been subject to bleeding for twelve years came up behind him and touched the edge of his cloak. **21**She said to herself, "If I only touch his cloak, I will be healed."

22Jesus turned and saw her. "Take heart, daughter," he said, "your faith has healed you." And the woman was healed from that moment.   Lk 7:50; 17:19; 18:42

23When Jesus entered the ruler's house and saw the flute players and the noisy crowd, **24**he said, "Go away. The girl is not dead but asleep." But they laughed at him. **25**After the crowd had been put outside, he went in and took the girl by the hand, and she got up. **26**News of this spread through all that region.   Mk 5:22-43; Lk 8:41-56

Jesus Heals the Blind and Mute

27As Jesus went on from there, two blind men followed him, calling out, "Have mercy on us, Son of David!"   Mt 15:22; Mk 10:47

28When he had gone indoors, the blind men came to him, and he asked them, "Do you believe that I am able to do this?"

"Yes, Lord," they replied.

29Then he touched their eyes and said, "According to your faith will it be done to you"; **30**and their sight was restored. Jesus warned them sternly, "See that no one knows about this." **31**But they went

out and spread the news about him all over that region.   Mt 8:4

32While they were going out, a man who was demon-possessed and could not talk was brought to Jesus. **33**And when the demon was driven out, the man who had been mute spoke. The crowd was amazed and said, "Nothing like this has ever been seen in Israel."

34But the Pharisees said, "It is by the prince of demons that he drives out demons."   Mt 12:24

The Workers Are Few

35Jesus went through all the towns and villages, teaching in their synagogues, preaching the good news of the kingdom and healing every disease and sickness. **36**When he saw the crowds, he had compassion on them, because they were harassed and helpless, like sheep without a shepherd. **37**Then he said to his disciples, "The harvest is plentiful but the workers are few. **38**Ask the Lord of the harvest, therefore, to send out workers into his harvest field."   Lk 10:2; Jn 4:35

Jesus Sends Out the Twelve

10 He called his twelve disciples to him and gave them authority*a* to drive out evil*a* spirits and to heal every disease and sickness.   Mk 3:13-15

2These are the names of the twelve apostles: first, Simon (who

---

a 1 Greek *unclean*

is called Peter) and his brother Andrew; James son of Zebedee, and his brother John; ³Philip and Bartholomew; Thomas and Matthew the tax collector; James son of Alphaeus, and Thaddaeus; ⁴Simon the Zealot and Judas Iscariot, who betrayed him. Mk 3:16-19; Lk 6:14-16

⁵These twelve Jesus sent out with the following instructions: "Do not go among the Gentiles or enter any town of the Samaritans. ⁶Go rather to the lost sheep of Israel. ⁷As you go, preach this message: 'The kingdom of heaven is near.' ⁸Heal the sick, raise the dead, cleanse those who have leprosy,ᵃ drive out demons. Freely you have received, freely give. ⁹Do not take along any gold or silver or copper in your belts; ¹⁰take no bag for the journey, or extra tunic, or sandals or a staff; for the worker is worth his keep. Mt 3:2; 15:24;

¹¹"Whatever town or village you enter, search for some worthy person there and stay at his house until you leave. ¹²As you enter the home, give it your greeting. ¹³If the home is deserving, let your peace rest on it; if it is not, let your peace return to you. ¹⁴If anyone will not welcome you or listen to your words, shake the dust off your feet when you leave that home or town. ¹⁵I tell you the truth, it will be more bearable for Sodom and Gomorrah on the day of judgment than for that town. ¹⁶I am sending you out like sheep among wolves. Therefore be as shrewd as snakes and as innocent as doves.

¹⁷"Be on your guard against men; they will hand you over to the local councils and flog you in their synagogues. ¹⁸On my account you will be brought before governors and kings as witnesses to them and to the Gentiles. ¹⁹But when they arrest you, do not worry about what to say or how to say it. At that time you will be given what to say, ²⁰for it will not be you speaking, but the Spirit of your Father speaking through you.

²¹"Brother will betray brother to death, and a father his child; children will rebel against their parents and have them put to death. ²²All men will hate you because of me, but he who stands firm to the end will be saved. ²³When you are persecuted in one place, flee to another. I tell you the truth, you will not finish going through the cities of Israel before the Son of Man comes. Mk 13:11-13; Lk 21:12-17

²⁴"A student is not above his teacher, nor a servant above his master. ²⁵It is enough for the student to be like his teacher, and the servant like his master. If the head of the house has been called Beelzebub,ᵇ how much more the members of his household!

²⁶"So do not be afraid of them.

ᵃ8 The Greek word was used for various diseases affecting the skin—not necessarily leprosy.
ᵇ25 Greek *Beezeboul* or *Beelzeboul*

There is nothing concealed that will not be disclosed, or hidden that will not be made known. 27What I tell you in the dark, speak in the daylight; what is whispered in your ear, proclaim from the roofs. 28Do not be afraid of those who kill the body but cannot kill the soul. Rather, be afraid of the One who can destroy both soul and body in hell. 29Are not two sparrows sold for a penny*a*? Yet not one of them will fall to the ground apart from the will of your Father. 30And even the very hairs of your head are all numbered. 31So don't be afraid; you are worth more than many sparrows.

32"Whoever acknowledges me before men, I will also acknowledge him before my Father in heaven. 33But whoever disowns me before men, I will disown him before my Father in heaven.

34"Do not suppose that I have come to bring peace to the earth. I did not come to bring peace, but a sword. 35For I have come to turn

" 'a man against his father,
    a daughter against her
        mother,
    a daughter-in-law against her
        mother-in-law—
36   a man's enemies will be the
        members of his own
        household.'*b*   Mic 7:6

37"Anyone who loves his father or mother more than me is not worthy of me; anyone who loves his son or daughter more than me is not worthy of me; 38and anyone who does not take his cross and follow me is not worthy of me. 39Whoever finds his life will lose it, and whoever loses his life for my sake will find it.   Lk 14:26; Jn 12:25

40"He who receives you receives me, and he who receives me receives the one who sent me. 41Anyone who receives a prophet because he is a prophet will receive a prophet's reward, and anyone who receives a righteous man because he is a righteous man will receive a righteous man's reward. 42And if anyone gives even a cup of cold water to one of these little ones because he is my disciple, I tell you the truth, he will certainly not lose his reward."   Lk 9:48; Jn 12:44

Jesus and John the Baptist

11 After Jesus had finished instructing his twelve disciples, he went on from there to teach and preach in the towns of Galilee.*c*   Mt 7:28

2When John heard in prison what Christ was doing, he sent his disciples 3to ask him, "Are you the one who was to come, or should we expect someone else?"   Mt 14:3

4Jesus replied, "Go back and report to John what you hear and see: 5The blind receive sight, the lame walk, those who have lepro-

---

a 29 Greek *an assarion*   *b* 36 Micah 7:6   *c* 1 Greek *in their towns* sy[a] are cured, the deaf hear, the dead are raised, and the good news is preached to the poor. [6]Blessed is the man who does not fall away on account of me." Isa 35:4-6; Lk 4:18-19

[7]As John's disciples were leaving, Jesus began to speak to the crowd about John: "What did you go out into the desert to see? A reed swayed by the wind? [8]If not, what did you go out to see? A man dressed in fine clothes? No, those who wear fine clothes are in kings' palaces. [9]Then what did you go out to see? A prophet? Yes, I tell you, and more than a prophet. [10]This is the one about whom it is written:

" 'I will send my messenger
ahead of you,
who will prepare your way
before you.'[b]

[11]I tell you the truth: Among those born of women there has not risen anyone greater than John the Baptist; yet he who is least in the kingdom of heaven is greater than he. [12]From the days of John the Baptist until now, the kingdom of heaven has been forcefully advancing, and forceful men lay hold of it. [13]For all the Prophets and the Law prophesied until John. [14]And if you are willing to accept it, he is the Elijah who was to come. [15]He who has ears, let him hear.

[16]"To what can I compare this generation? They are like children sitting in the marketplaces and calling out to others:

[17]" 'We played the flute for you,
and you did not dance;
we sang a dirge,
and you did not mourn.'

[18]For John came neither eating nor drinking, and they say, 'He has a demon.' [19]The Son of Man came eating and drinking, and they say, 'Here is a glutton and a drunkard, a friend of tax collectors and "sinners." ' But wisdom is proved right by her actions." Lk 7:18-35

Woe on Unrepentant Cities

[20]Then Jesus began to denounce the cities in which most of his miracles had been performed, because they did not repent. [21]"Woe to you, Korazin! Woe to you, Bethsaida! If the miracles that were performed in you had been performed in Tyre and Sidon, they would have repented long ago in sackcloth and ashes. [22]But I tell you, it will be more bearable for Tyre and Sidon on the day of judgment than for you. [23]And you, Capernaum, will you be lifted up to the skies? No, you will go down to the depths.[c] If the miracles that were performed in you had been performed in Sodom, it would have remained to this day. [24]But I tell you that it will be more bear-

[a]5 The Greek word was used for various diseases affecting the skin—not necessarily leprosy.
[b]10 Mal. 3:1   [c]23 Greek Hades

able for Sodom on the day of judgment than for you." Lk 10:13-15

Rest for the Weary

25At that time Jesus said, "I praise you, Father, Lord of heaven and earth, because you have hidden these things from the wise and learned, and revealed them to little children. 26Yes, Father, for this was your good pleasure. 1Co 1:26-29

27"All things have been committed to me by my Father. No one knows the Son except the Father, and no one knows the Father except the Son and those to whom the Son chooses to reveal him.

28"Come to me, all you who are weary and burdened, and I will give you rest. 29Take my yoke upon you and learn from me, for I am gentle and humble in heart, and you will find rest for your souls. 30For my yoke is easy and my burden is light." Jer 6:16; Jn 13:15

Lord of the Sabbath

12 At that time Jesus went through the grainfields on the Sabbath. His disciples were hungry and began to pick some heads of grain and eat them. 2When the Pharisees saw this, they said to him, "Look! Your disciples are doing what is unlawful on the Sabbath." Ex 20:10; Lk 13:14

3He answered, "Haven't you read what David did when he and his companions were hungry? 4He entered the house of God, and he and his companions ate the consecrated bread—which was not lawful for them to do, but only for the priests. 5Or haven't you read in the Law that on the Sabbath the priests in the temple desecrate the day and yet are innocent? 6I tell you that one*a* greater than the temple is here. 7If you had known what these words mean, 'I desire mercy, not sacrifice,'*b* you would not have condemned the innocent. 8For the Son of Man is Lord of the Sabbath." Mk 2:23-28; Lk 6:1-5

9Going on from that place, he went into their synagogue, 10and a man with a shriveled hand was there. Looking for a reason to accuse Jesus, they asked him, "Is it lawful to heal on the Sabbath?"

11He said to them, "If any of you has a sheep and it falls into a pit on the Sabbath, will you not take hold of it and lift it out? 12How much more valuable is a man than a sheep! Therefore it is lawful to do good on the Sabbath."

13Then he said to the man, "Stretch out your hand." So he stretched it out and it was completely restored, just as sound as the other. 14But the Pharisees went out and plotted how they might kill Jesus. Mk 3:1-6; Lk 6:6-11

God's Chosen Servant

15Aware of this, Jesus withdrew from that place. Many followed

*a6 Or something; also in verses 41 and 42   *b7 Hosea 6:6

him, and he healed all their sick, [16]warning them not to tell who he was. [17]This was to fulfill what was spoken through the prophet Isaiah: Mt 4:23; 8:4

[18]"Here is my servant whom I
    have chosen,
  the one I love, in whom I
    delight;   Mt 3:17
I will put my Spirit on him,
  and he will proclaim justice
    to the nations.
[19]He will not quarrel or cry out;
  no one will hear his voice in
    the streets.
[20]A bruised reed he will not
    break,
  and a smoldering wick he
    will not snuff out,
till he leads justice to victory.
[21] In his name the nations will
    put their hope."[a]

Jesus and Beelzebub

[22]Then they brought him a demon-possessed man who was blind and mute, and Jesus healed him, so that he could both talk and see. [23]All the people were astonished and said, "Could this be the Son of David?"   Mt 4:24; 9:32-33

[24]But when the Pharisees heard this, they said, "It is only by Beelzebub,[b] the prince of demons, that this fellow drives out demons."

[25]Jesus knew their thoughts and said to them, "Every kingdom divided against itself will be ruined, and every city or household divided against itself will not stand. [26]If Satan drives out Satan, he is divided against himself. How then can his kingdom stand? [27]And if I drive out demons by Beelzebub, by whom do your people drive them out? So then, they will be your judges. [28]But if I drive out demons by the Spirit of God, then the kingdom of God has come upon you.

[29]"Or again, how can anyone enter a strong man's house and carry off his possessions unless he first ties up the strong man? Then he can rob his house.   Mk 3:23-27

[30]"He who is not with me is against me, and he who does not gather with me scatters. [31]And so I tell you, every sin and blasphemy will be forgiven men, but the blasphemy against the Spirit will not be forgiven. [32]Anyone who speaks a word against the Son of Man will be forgiven, but anyone who speaks against the Holy Spirit will not be forgiven, either in this age or in the age to come.   Mk 9:40

[33]"Make a tree good and its fruit will be good, or make a tree bad and its fruit will be bad, for a tree is recognized by its fruit. [34]You brood of vipers, how can you who are evil say anything good? For out of the overflow of the heart the mouth speaks. [35]The good man brings good things out of the good stored up in him, and the evil man brings evil things out of the evil

[a]21 Isaiah 42:1-4   [b]24 Greek *Beezeboul* or *Beelzeboul*; also in verse 27

stored up in him. 36But I tell you that men will have to give account on the day of judgment for every careless word they have spoken. 37For by your words you will be acquitted, and by your words you will be condemned."   Mt 15:18; Lk 6:45

The Sign of Jonah

38Then some of the Pharisees and teachers of the law said to him, "Teacher, we want to see a miraculous sign from you."

39He answered, "A wicked and adulterous generation asks for a miraculous sign! But none will be given it except the sign of the prophet Jonah. 40For as Jonah was three days and three nights in the belly of a huge fish, so the Son of Man will be three days and three nights in the heart of the earth. 41The men of Nineveh will stand up at the judgment with this generation and condemn it; for they repented at the preaching of Jonah, and now one*a* greater than Jonah is here. 42The Queen of the South will rise at the judgment with this generation and condemn it; for she came from the ends of the earth to listen to Solomon's wisdom, and now one greater than Solomon is here.   Lk 11:29-32

43"When an evil*b* spirit comes out of a man, it goes through arid places seeking rest and does not find it. 44Then it says, 'I will return

to the house I left.' When it arrives, it finds the house unoccupied, swept clean and put in order. 45Then it goes and takes with it seven other spirits more wicked than itself, and they go in and live there. And the final condition of that man is worse than the first. That is how it will be with this wicked generation."   Lk 11:24-26

Jesus' Mother and Brothers

46While Jesus was still talking to the crowd, his mother and brothers stood outside, wanting to speak to him. 47Someone told him, "Your mother and brothers are standing outside, wanting to speak to you."*c*   Mt 13:55; Jn 2:12

48He replied to him, "Who is my mother, and who are my brothers?" 49Pointing to his disciples, he said, "Here are my mother and my brothers. 50For whoever does the will of my Father in heaven is my brother and sister and mother."

The Parable of the Sower

13 That same day Jesus went out of the house and sat by the lake. 2Such large crowds gathered around him that he got into a boat and sat in it, while all the people stood on the shore. 3Then he told them many things in parables, saying: "A farmer went out to sow his seed. 4As he was scattering the seed, some fell along the path, and

---

a41 Or *something*; also in verse 42   *b43* Greek *unclean*   *c47* Some manuscripts do not have verse 47.

the birds came and ate it up. ⁵Some fell on rocky places, where it did not have much soil. It sprang up quickly, because the soil was shallow. ⁶But when the sun came up, the plants were scorched, and they withered because they had no root. ⁷Other seed fell among thorns, which grew up and choked the plants. ⁸Still other seed fell on good soil, where it produced a crop—a hundred, sixty or thirty times what was sown. ⁹He who has ears, let him hear."　　Ge 26:12; Mt 11:15

¹⁰The disciples came to him and asked, "Why do you speak to the people in parables?"

¹¹He replied, "The knowledge of the secrets of the kingdom of heaven has been given to you, but not to them. ¹²Whoever has will be given more, and he will have an abundance. Whoever does not have, even what he has will be taken from him. ¹³This is why I speak to them in parables:　　Lk 19:26; 1Co 2:10,14

"Though seeing, they do not
　　see;
　　though hearing, they do not
　　　hear or understand.

¹⁴In them is fulfilled the prophecy of Isaiah:

" 'You will be ever hearing but
　　never understanding;
　you will be ever seeing but
　　never perceiving.

¹⁵For this people's heart has
　　become calloused;
　they hardly hear with their
　　ears,
　and they have closed their
　　eyes.
Otherwise they might see with
　　their eyes,
　hear with their ears,
　understand with their hearts
　and turn, and I would heal
　　them.'ᵃ

¹⁶But blessed are your eyes because they see, and your ears because they hear. ¹⁷For I tell you the truth, many prophets and righteous men longed to see what you see but did not see it, and to hear what you hear but did not hear it.

¹⁸"Listen then to what the parable of the sower means: ¹⁹When anyone hears the message about the kingdom and does not understand it, the evil one comes and snatches away what was sown in his heart. This is the seed sown along the path. ²⁰The one who received the seed that fell on rocky places is the man who hears the word and at once receives it with joy. ²¹But since he has no root, he lasts only a short time. When trouble or persecution comes because of the word, he quickly falls away. ²²The one who received the seed that fell among the thorns is the man who hears the word, but the worries of this life and the deceit-

ᵃ 15 Isaiah 6:9,10

fulness of wealth choke it, making it unfruitful. ²³But the one who received the seed that fell on good soil is the man who hears the word and understands it. He produces a crop, yielding a hundred, sixty or thirty times what was sown."

The Parable of the Weeds

²⁴Jesus told them another parable: "The kingdom of heaven is like a man who sowed good seed in his field. ²⁵But while everyone was sleeping, his enemy came and sowed weeds among the wheat, and went away. ²⁶When the wheat sprouted and formed heads, then the weeds also appeared.   Mt 18:23

²⁷"The owner's servants came to him and said, 'Sir, didn't you sow good seed in your field? Where then did the weeds come from?'

²⁸" 'An enemy did this,' he replied.

"The servants asked him, 'Do you want us to go and pull them up?'

²⁹" 'No,' he answered, 'because while you are pulling the weeds, you may root up the wheat with them. ³⁰Let both grow together until the harvest. At that time I will tell the harvesters: First collect the weeds and tie them in bundles to be burned; then gather the wheat and bring it into my barn.' "

The Parables of the Mustard Seed and the Yeast

³¹He told them another parable: "The kingdom of heaven is like a mustard seed, which a man took and planted in his field. ³²Though it is the smallest of all your seeds, yet when it grows, it is the largest of garden plants and becomes a tree, so that the birds of the air come and perch in its branches."

³³He told them still another parable: "The kingdom of heaven is like yeast that a woman took and mixed into a large amount[a] of flour until it worked all through the dough."   Lk 13:18-21

³⁴Jesus spoke all these things to the crowd in parables; he did not say anything to them without using a parable. ³⁵So was fulfilled what was spoken through the prophet: Mk 4:33; Jn 16:25

"I will open my mouth in
    parables,
 I will utter things hidden
        since the creation of the
        world."[b]   Ps 78:2; 1Co 2:7

The Parable of the Weeds Explained

³⁶Then he left the crowd and went into the house. His disciples came to him and said, "Explain to us the parable of the weeds in the field."   Mt 15:15

³⁷He answered, "The one who sowed the good seed is the Son of

---

a 33 Greek *three satas* (probably about 1/2 bushel or 22 liters)   *b 35* Psalm 78:2

Man. 38The field is the world, and the good seed stands for the sons of the kingdom. The weeds are the sons of the evil one, 39and the enemy who sows them is the devil. The harvest is the end of the age, and the harvesters are angels.

40"As the weeds are pulled up and burned in the fire, so it will be at the end of the age. 41The Son of Man will send out his angels, and they will weed out of his kingdom everything that causes sin and all who do evil. 42They will throw them into the fiery furnace, where there will be weeping and gnashing of teeth. 43Then the righteous will shine like the sun in the kingdom of their Father. He who has ears, let him hear.   Da 12:3; Mt 8:12

The Parables of the Hidden Treasure and the Pearl

44"The kingdom of heaven is like treasure hidden in a field. When a man found it, he hid it again, and then in his joy went and sold all he had and bought that field.   Isa 55:1; Php 3:7-8

45"Again, the kingdom of heaven is like a merchant looking for fine pearls. 46When he found one of great value, he went away and sold everything he had and bought it.   ver 24

The Parable of the Net

47"Once again, the kingdom of heaven is like a net that was let down into the lake and caught all kinds of fish. 48When it was full, the fishermen pulled it up on the shore. Then they sat down and collected the good fish in baskets, but threw the bad away. 49This is how it will be at the end of the age. The angels will come and separate the wicked from the righteous 50and throw them into the fiery furnace, where there will be weeping and gnashing of teeth.   Mt 25:32

51"Have you understood all these things?" Jesus asked.

"Yes," they replied.

52He said to them, "Therefore every teacher of the law who has been instructed about the kingdom of heaven is like the owner of a house who brings out of his storeroom new treasures as well as old."

A Prophet Without Honor

53When Jesus had finished these parables, he moved on from there. 54Coming to his hometown, he began teaching the people in their synagogue, and they were amazed. "Where did this man get this wisdom and these miraculous powers?" they asked. 55"Isn't this the carpenter's son? Isn't his mother's name Mary, and aren't his brothers James, Joseph, Simon and Judas? 56Aren't all his sisters with us? Where then did this man get all these things?" 57And they took offense at him.   Mt 7:28; Jn 6:42

But Jesus said to them, "Only in his hometown and in his own house is a prophet without honor."

⁵⁸And he did not do many miracles there because of their lack of faith.   Mk 6:1-6

John the Baptist Beheaded

14 At that time Herod the tetrarch heard the reports about Jesus, ²and he said to his attendants, "This is John the Baptist; he has risen from the dead! That is why miraculous powers are at work in him."   Lk 9:7-9

³Now Herod had arrested John and bound him and put him in prison because of Herodias, his brother Philip's wife, ⁴for John had been saying to him: "It is not lawful for you to have her." ⁵Herod wanted to kill John, but he was afraid of the people, because they considered him a prophet.   Mt 11:9

⁶On Herod's birthday the daughter of Herodias danced for them and pleased Herod so much ⁷that he promised with an oath to give her whatever she asked. ⁸Prompted by her mother, she said, "Give me here on a platter the head of John the Baptist." ⁹The king was distressed, but because of his oaths and his dinner guests, he ordered that her request be granted ¹⁰and had John beheaded in the prison. ¹¹His head was brought in on a platter and given to the girl, who carried it to her mother. ¹²John's disciples came and took his body and buried it. Then they went and told Jesus.   Mk 6:14-29

Jesus Feeds the Five Thousand

¹³When Jesus heard what had happened, he withdrew by boat privately to a solitary place. Hearing of this, the crowds followed him on foot from the towns. ¹⁴When Jesus landed and saw a large crowd, he had compassion on them and healed their sick.

¹⁵As evening approached, the disciples came to him and said, "This is a remote place, and it's already getting late. Send the crowds away, so they can go to the villages and buy themselves some food."

¹⁶Jesus replied, "They do not need to go away. You give them something to eat."

¹⁷"We have here only five loaves of bread and two fish," they answered.

¹⁸"Bring them here to me," he said. ¹⁹And he directed the people to sit down on the grass. Taking the five loaves and the two fish and looking up to heaven, he gave thanks and broke the loaves. Then he gave them to the disciples, and the disciples gave them to the people. ²⁰They all ate and were satisfied, and the disciples picked up twelve basketfuls of broken pieces that were left over. ²¹The number of those who ate was about five thousand men, besides women and children.   Mk 6:32-44; Lk 9:10-17

Jesus Walks on the Water

²²Immediately Jesus made the

disciples get into the boat and go on ahead of him to the other side, while he dismissed the crowd. **23**After he had dismissed them, he went up on a mountainside by himself to pray. When evening came, he was there alone, **24**but the boat was already a considerable distance*a* from land, buffeted by the waves because the wind was against it.   Lk 3:21

25During the fourth watch of the night Jesus went out to them, walking on the lake. **26**When the disciples saw him walking on the lake, they were terrified. "It's a ghost," they said, and cried out in fear.   Lk 24:37

27But Jesus immediately said to them: "Take courage! It is I. Don't be afraid."   Mt 17:7; Rev 1:17

28"Lord, if it's you," Peter replied, "tell me to come to you on the water."

29"Come," he said.

Then Peter got down out of the boat, walked on the water and came toward Jesus. **30**But when he saw the wind, he was afraid and, beginning to sink, cried out, "Lord, save me!"

31Immediately Jesus reached out his hand and caught him. "You of little faith," he said, "why did you doubt?"   Mt 6:30

32And when they climbed into the boat, the wind died down. **33**Then those who were in the boat worshiped him, saying, "Truly you are the Son of God."   Mk 6:45-51

34When they had crossed over, they landed at Gennesaret. **35**And when the men of that place recognized Jesus, they sent word to all the surrounding country. People brought all their sick to him **36**and begged him to let the sick just touch the edge of his cloak, and all who touched him were healed.

Clean and Unclean

15 Then some Pharisees and teachers of the law came to Jesus from Jerusalem and asked, **2**"Why do your disciples break the tradition of the elders? They don't wash their hands before they eat!"

3Jesus replied, "And why do you break the command of God for the sake of your tradition? **4**For God said, 'Honor your father and mother'*b* and 'Anyone who curses his father or mother must be put to death.'*c* **5**But you say that if a man says to his father or mother, 'Whatever help you might otherwise have received from me is a gift devoted to God,' **6**he is not to 'honor his father*d*' with it. Thus you nullify the word of God for the sake of your tradition. **7**You hypocrites! Isaiah was right when he prophesied about you:

8" 'These people honor me with
their lips,

---

a 24 Greek *many stadia*   *b* 4 Exodus 20:12; Deut. 5:16   *c* 4 Exodus 21:17; Lev. 20:9   *d* 6 Some manuscripts *father or his mother*

but their hearts are far from
me.
⁹They worship me in vain;
their teachings are but rules
taught by men.'ᵃ"

¹⁰Jesus called the crowd to him
and said, "Listen and understand.
¹¹What goes into a man's mouth
does not make him 'unclean,' but
what comes out of his mouth, that
is what makes him 'unclean.' "

¹²Then the disciples came to
him and asked, "Do you know that
the Pharisees were offended when
they heard this?"

¹³He replied, "Every plant that
my heavenly Father has not planted will be pulled up by the roots.
¹⁴Leave them; they are blind
guides.ᵇ If a blind man leads a
blind man, both will fall into a
pit."

¹⁵Peter said, "Explain the parable to us."   Mt 13:36

¹⁶"Are you still so dull?" Jesus
asked them. ¹⁷"Don't you see that
whatever enters the mouth goes
into the stomach and then out of
the body? ¹⁸But the things that
come out of the mouth come from
the heart, and these make a man
'unclean.' ¹⁹For out of the heart
come evil thoughts, murder, adultery, sexual immorality, theft, false
testimony, slander. ²⁰These are
what make a man 'unclean'; but
eating with unwashed hands does
not make him 'unclean.' "

The Faith of the Canaanite Woman

²¹Leaving that place, Jesus withdrew to the region of Tyre and Sidon. ²²A Canaanite woman from
that vicinity came to him, crying
out, "Lord, Son of David, have
mercy on me! My daughter is suffering terribly from demon-posses-
sion."   Mt 4:24; 9:27

²³Jesus did not answer a word.
So his disciples came to him and
urged him, "Send her away, for she
keeps crying out after us."

²⁴He answered, "I was sent only
to the lost sheep of Israel."

²⁵The woman came and knelt
before him. "Lord, help me!" she
said.   Mt 8:2

²⁶He replied, "It is not right to
take the children's bread and toss
it to their dogs."

²⁷"Yes, Lord," she said, "but
even the dogs eat the crumbs that
fall from their masters' table."

²⁸Then Jesus answered, "Woman, you have great faith! Your request is granted." And her daughter was healed from that very
hour.

Jesus Feeds the Four Thousand

²⁹Jesus left there and went along
the Sea of Galilee. Then he went
up on a mountainside and sat
down. ³⁰Great crowds came to
him, bringing the lame, the blind,
the crippled, the mute and many

ᵃ9 Isaiah 29:13   ᵇ14 Some manuscripts guides of the blind

others, and laid them at his feet; and he healed them. ³¹The people were amazed when they saw the mute speaking, the crippled made well, the lame walking and the blind seeing. And they praised the God of Israel. Mk 7:31-37

³²Jesus called his disciples to him and said, "I have compassion for these people; they have already been with me three days and have nothing to eat. I do not want to send them away hungry, or they may collapse on the way." Mt 9:36

³³His disciples answered, "Where could we get enough bread in this remote place to feed such a crowd?"

³⁴"How many loaves do you have?" Jesus asked.

"Seven," they replied, "and a few small fish."

³⁵He told the crowd to sit down on the ground. ³⁶Then he took the seven loaves and the fish, and when he had given thanks, he broke them and gave them to the disciples, and they in turn to the people. ³⁷They all ate and were satisfied. Afterward the disciples picked up seven basketfuls of broken pieces that were left over. ³⁸The number of those who ate was four thousand, besides women and children. ³⁹After Jesus had sent the crowd away, he got into the boat and went to the vicinity of Magadan. Mt 14:13-21; Mk 8:1-10

The Demand for a Sign

16 The Pharisees and Sadducees came to Jesus and tested him by asking him to show them a sign from heaven. Mt 12:38

²He replied,ᵃ "When evening comes, you say, 'It will be fair weather, for the sky is red,' ³and in the morning, 'Today it will be stormy, for the sky is red and overcast.' You know how to interpret the appearance of the sky, but you cannot interpret the signs of the times. ⁴A wicked and adulterous generation looks for a miraculous sign, but none will be given it except the sign of Jonah." Jesus then left them and went away. Mt 12:39

The Yeast of the Pharisees and Sadducees

⁵When they went across the lake, the disciples forgot to take bread. ⁶"Be careful," Jesus said to them. "Be on your guard against the yeast of the Pharisees and Sadducees." Lk 12:1

⁷They discussed this among themselves and said, "It is because we didn't bring any bread."

⁸Aware of their discussion, Jesus asked, "You of little faith, why are you talking among yourselves about having no bread? ⁹Do you still not understand? Don't you remember the five loaves for the five thousand, and how many basketfuls you gathered? ¹⁰Or the

---

ᵃ2 Some early manuscripts do not have the rest of verse 2 and all of verse 3.

seven loaves for the four thousand, and how many basketfuls you gathered? [11]How is it you don't understand that I was not talking to you about bread? But be on your guard against the yeast of the Pharisees and Sadducees." [12]Then they understood that he was not telling them to guard against the yeast used in bread, but against the teaching of the Pharisees and Sadducees.

Peter's Confession of Christ

[13]When Jesus came to the region of Caesarea Philippi, he asked his disciples, "Who do people say the Son of Man is?"   Mk 8:27-29

[14]They replied, "Some say John the Baptist; others say Elijah; and still others, Jeremiah or one of the prophets."   Mt 14:2; Mk 6:15

[15]"But what about you?" he asked. "Who do you say I am?"

[16]Simon Peter answered, "You are the Christ,[a] the Son of the living God."   Jn 11:27

[17]Jesus replied, "Blessed are you, Simon son of Jonah, for this was not revealed to you by man, but by my Father in heaven. [18]And I tell you that you are Peter,[b] and on this rock I will build my church, and the gates of Hades[c] will not overcome it.[d] [19]I will give you the keys of the kingdom of heaven; whatever you bind on earth will be[e] bound in heaven, and whatev-

er you loose on earth will be[e] loosed in heaven." [20]Then he warned his disciples not to tell anyone that he was the Christ.

Jesus Predicts His Death

[21]From that time on Jesus began to explain to his disciples that he must go to Jerusalem and suffer many things at the hands of the elders, chief priests and teachers of the law, and that he must be killed and on the third day be raised to life.   Mk 9:31; Lk 17:25

[22]Peter took him aside and began to rebuke him. "Never, Lord!" he said. "This shall never happen to you!"

[23]Jesus turned and said to Peter, "Get behind me, Satan! You are a stumbling block to me; you do not have in mind the things of God, but the things of men."   Mt 4:10

[24]Then Jesus said to his disciples, "If anyone would come after me, he must deny himself and take up his cross and follow me. [25]For whoever wants to save his life[f] will lose it, but whoever loses his life for me will find it. [26]What good will it be for a man if he gains the whole world, yet forfeits his soul? Or what can a man give in exchange for his soul? [27]For the Son of Man is going to come in his Father's glory with his angels, and then he will reward each person according to what he has done. [28]I

---

a 16 Or *Messiah*; also in verse 20   *b 18 Peter* means *rock.*   *c 18* Or *hell*   *d 18* Or *not prove stronger than it*   *e 19* Or *have been*   *f 25* The Greek word means either *life* or *soul*; also in verse 26.

tell you the truth, some who are standing here will not taste death before they see the Son of Man coming in his kingdom."

The Transfiguration

17 After six days Jesus took with him Peter, James and John the brother of James, and led them up a high mountain by themselves. ²There he was transfigured before them. His face shone like the sun, and his clothes became as white as the light. ³Just then there appeared before them Moses and Elijah, talking with Jesus.   Mt 4:21

⁴Peter said to Jesus, "Lord, it is good for us to be here. If you wish, I will put up three shelters—one for you, one for Moses and one for Elijah."

⁵While he was still speaking, a bright cloud enveloped them, and a voice from the cloud said, "This is my Son, whom I love; with him I am well pleased. Listen to him!" ⁶When the disciples heard this, they fell facedown to the ground, terrified. ⁷But Jesus came and touched them. "Get up," he said. "Don't be afraid." ⁸When they looked up, they saw no one except Jesus.   Lk 9:28-36

⁹As they were coming down the mountain, Jesus instructed them, "Don't tell anyone what you have seen, until the Son of Man has been raised from the dead."

¹⁰The disciples asked him, "Why then do the teachers of the law say that Elijah must come first?"

¹¹Jesus replied, "To be sure, Elijah comes and will restore all things. ¹²But I tell you, Elijah has already come, and they did not recognize him, but have done to him everything they wished. In the same way the Son of Man is going to suffer at their hands." ¹³Then the disciples understood that he was talking to them about John the Baptist.   Mk 9:2-13

The Healing of a Boy With a Demon

¹⁴When they came to the crowd, a man approached Jesus and knelt before him. ¹⁵"Lord, have mercy on my son," he said. "He has seizures and is suffering greatly. He often falls into the fire or into the water. ¹⁶I brought him to your disciples, but they could not heal him."   Mt 4:24

¹⁷"O unbelieving and perverse generation," Jesus replied, "how long shall I stay with you? How long shall I put up with you? Bring the boy here to me." ¹⁸Jesus rebuked the demon, and it came out of the boy, and he was healed from that moment.

¹⁹Then the disciples came to Jesus in private and asked, "Why couldn't we drive it out?"

²⁰He replied, "Because you have so little faith. I tell you the truth, if you have faith as small as a

mustard seed, you can say to this mountain, 'Move from here to there' and it will move. Nothing will be impossible for you.*a*"

22When they came together in Galilee, he said to them, "The Son of Man is going to be betrayed into the hands of men. **23**They will kill him, and on the third day he will be raised to life." And the disciples were filled with grief.   Mt 16:21

The Temple Tax

24After Jesus and his disciples arrived in Capernaum, the collectors of the two-drachma tax came to Peter and asked, "Doesn't your teacher pay the temple tax*b*?"

25"Yes, he does," he replied.

When Peter came into the house, Jesus was the first to speak. "What do you think, Simon?" he asked. "From whom do the kings of the earth collect duty and taxes —from their own sons or from others?"   Mt 22:17-21; Ro 13:7

26"From others," Peter answered.

"Then the sons are exempt," Jesus said to him. **27**"But so that we may not offend them, go to the lake and throw out your line. Take the first fish you catch; open its mouth and you will find a four-drachma coin. Take it and give it to them for my tax and yours."

The Greatest in the Kingdom of Heaven

18 At that time the disciples came to Jesus and asked, "Who is the greatest in the kingdom of heaven?"

2He called a little child and had him stand among them. **3**And he said: "I tell you the truth, unless you change and become like little children, you will never enter the kingdom of heaven. **4**Therefore, whoever humbles himself like this child is the greatest in the kingdom of heaven.   Mt 19:14; 1Pe 2:2

5"And whoever welcomes a little child like this in my name welcomes me. **6**But if anyone causes one of these little ones who believe in me to sin, it would be better for him to have a large millstone hung around his neck and to be drowned in the depths of the sea.

7"Woe to the world because of the things that cause people to sin! Such things must come, but woe to the man through whom they come! **8**If your hand or your foot causes you to sin, cut it off and throw it away. It is better for you to enter life maimed or crippled than to have two hands or two feet and be thrown into eternal fire. **9**And if your eye causes you to sin, gouge it out and throw it away. It is better for you to enter life with one eye than to have two eyes and be thrown into the fire of hell.

a20 Some manuscripts you. 21But this kind does not go out except by prayer and fasting.   *b24 Greek the two drachmas*

The Parable of the Lost Sheep

10"See that you do not look down on one of these little ones. For I tell you that their angels in heaven always see the face of my Father in heaven.ᵃ Ge 48:16; Ps 34:7

12"What do you think? If a man owns a hundred sheep, and one of them wanders away, will he not leave the ninety-nine on the hills and go to look for the one that wandered off? 13And if he finds it, I tell you the truth, he is happier about that one sheep than about the ninety-nine that did not wander off. 14In the same way your Father in heaven is not willing that any of these little ones should be lost. Lk 15:4-7

A Brother Who Sins Against You

15"If your brother sins against you,ᵇ go and show him his fault, just between the two of you. If he listens to you, you have won your brother over. 16But if he will not listen, take one or two others along, so that 'every matter may be established by the testimony of two or three witnesses.'ᶜ 17If he refuses to listen to them, tell it to the church; and if he refuses to listen even to the church, treat him as you would a pagan or a tax collector. 1Co 6:1-6; Jas 5:19-20

18"I tell you the truth, whatever you bind on earth will beᵈ bound in heaven, and whatever you loose on earth will beᵈ loosed in heaven. 19"Again, I tell you that if two of you on earth agree about anything you ask for, it will be done for you by my Father in heaven. 20For where two or three come together in my name, there am I with them." Mt 7:7

The Parable of the Unmerciful Servant

21Then Peter came to Jesus and asked, "Lord, how many times shall I forgive my brother when he sins against me? Up to seven times?" Lk 17:4

22Jesus answered, "I tell you, not seven times, but seventy-seven times.ᵉ Ge 4:24

23"Therefore, the kingdom of heaven is like a king who wanted to settle accounts with his servants. 24As he began the settlement, a man who owed him ten thousand talentsᶠ was brought to him. 25Since he was not able to pay, the master ordered that he and his wife and his children and all that he had be sold to repay the debt. 2Ki 4:1; Mt 25:19

26"The servant fell on his knees before him. 'Be patient with me,' he begged, 'and I will pay back everything.' 27The servant's master took pity on him, canceled the debt and let him go. Mt 8:2

ᵃ10 Some manuscripts heaven. 11The Son of Man came to save what was lost. ᵇ15 Some manuscripts do not have against you. ᶜ16 Deut. 19:15 ᵈ18 Or have been ᵉ22 Or seventy times seven ᶠ24 That is, millions of dollars

28"But when that servant went out, he found one of his fellow servants who owed him a hundred denarii.ᵃ He grabbed him and began to choke him. 'Pay back what you owe me!' he demanded.

29"His fellow servant fell to his knees and begged him, 'Be patient with me, and I will pay you back.'

30"But he refused. Instead, he went off and had the man thrown into prison until he could pay the debt. 31When the other servants saw what had happened, they were greatly distressed and went and told their master everything that had happened.

32"Then the master called the servant in. 'You wicked servant,' he said, 'I canceled all that debt of yours because you begged me to. 33Shouldn't you have had mercy on your fellow servant just as I had on you?' 34In anger his master turned him over to the jailers to be tortured, until he should pay back all he owed.

35"This is how my heavenly Father will treat each of you unless you forgive your brother from your heart."   Mt 6:14; Jas 2:13

Divorce

19 When Jesus had finished saying these things, he left Galilee and went into the region of Judea to the other side of the Jordan. 2Large crowds followed him, and he healed them there.   Mt 4:23

3Some Pharisees came to him to test him. They asked, "Is it lawful for a man to divorce his wife for any and every reason?"   Mt 5:31

4"Haven't you read," he replied, "that at the beginning the Creator 'made them male and female,'ᵇ 5and said, 'For this reason a man will leave his father and mother and be united to his wife, and the two will become one flesh'ᶜ? 6So they are no longer two, but one. Therefore what God has joined together, let man not separate."

7"Why then," they asked, "did Moses command that a man give his wife a certificate of divorce and send her away?"   Dt 24:1-4; Mt 5:31

8Jesus replied, "Moses permitted you to divorce your wives because your hearts were hard. But it was not this way from the beginning. 9I tell you that anyone who divorces his wife, except for marital unfaithfulness, and marries another woman commits adultery."

10The disciples said to him, "If this is the situation between a husband and wife, it is better not to marry."

11Jesus replied, "Not everyone can accept this word, but only those to whom it has been given. 12For some are eunuchs because they were born that way; others were made that way by men; and others have renounced marriageᵈ because of the kingdom of heaven.

ᵃ28 That is, a few dollars   ᵇ4 Gen. 1:27   ᶜ5 Gen. 2:24   ᵈ12 Or have made themselves eunuchs

The one who can accept this should accept it." <small>Mt 13:11</small>

The Little Children and Jesus

¹³Then little children were brought to Jesus for him to place his hands on them and pray for them. But the disciples rebuked those who brought them. <small>Mk 5:23</small> ¹⁴Jesus said, "Let the little children come to me, and do not hinder them, for the kingdom of heaven belongs to such as these." ¹⁵When he had placed his hands on them, he went on from there.

The Rich Young Man

¹⁶Now a man came up to Jesus and asked, "Teacher, what good thing must I do to get eternal life?"

¹⁷"Why do you ask me about what is good?" Jesus replied. "There is only One who is good. If you want to enter life, obey the commandments." <small>Lev 18:5</small>

¹⁸"Which ones?" the man inquired.

Jesus replied, " 'Do not murder, do not commit adultery, do not steal, do not give false testimony, ¹⁹honor your father and mother,'ᵃ and 'love your neighbor as yourself.'ᵇ" <small>Lev 19:18; Jas 2:11</small>

²⁰"All these I have kept," the young man said. "What do I still lack?"

²¹Jesus answered, "If you want to be perfect, go, sell your posses-sions and give to the poor, and you will have treasure in heaven. Then come, follow me." <small>Mt 6:20; Lk 12:33</small>

²²When the young man heard this, he went away sad, because he had great wealth.

²³Then Jesus said to his disciples, "I tell you the truth, it is hard for a rich man to enter the kingdom of heaven. ²⁴Again I tell you, it is easier for a camel to go through the eye of a needle than for a rich man to enter the kingdom of God." <small>Mt 13:22; 1Ti 6:9-10</small>

²⁵When the disciples heard this, they were greatly astonished and asked, "Who then can be saved?" ²⁶Jesus looked at them and said, "With man this is impossible, but with God all things are possible."

²⁷Peter answered him, "We have left everything to follow you! What then will there be for us?"

²⁸Jesus said to them, "I tell you the truth, at the renewal of all things, when the Son of Man sits on his glorious throne, you who have followed me will also sit on twelve thrones, judging the twelve tribes of Israel. ²⁹And everyone who has left houses or brothers or sisters or father or motherᶜ or children or fields for my sake will receive a hundred times as much and will inherit eternal life. ³⁰But many who are first will be last, and many who are last will be first.

<small>ᵃ19 Exodus 20:12-16; Deut. 5:16-20   ᵇ19 Lev. 19:18   ᶜ29 Some manuscripts mother or wife</small>

The Parable of the Workers in the Vineyard

20 "For the kingdom of heaven is like a landowner who went out early in the morning to hire men to work in his vineyard. ²He agreed to pay them a denarius for the day and sent them into his vineyard.   Mt 21:28,33

³"About the third hour he went out and saw others standing in the marketplace doing nothing. ⁴He told them, 'You also go and work in my vineyard, and I will pay you whatever is right.' ⁵So they went.

"He went out again about the sixth hour and the ninth hour and did the same thing. ⁶About the eleventh hour he went out and found still others standing around. He asked them, 'Why have you been standing here all day long doing nothing?'

⁷" 'Because no one has hired us,' they answered.

"He said to them, 'You also go and work in my vineyard.'

⁸"When evening came, the owner of the vineyard said to his foreman, 'Call the workers and pay them their wages, beginning with the last ones hired and going on to the first.'   Lev 19:13; Dt 24:15

⁹"The workers who were hired about the eleventh hour came and each received a denarius. ¹⁰So when those came who were hired first, they expected to receive more. But each one of them also received a denarius. ¹¹When they received it, they began to grumble against the landowner. ¹²'These men who were hired last worked only one hour,' they said, 'and you have made them equal to us who have borne the burden of the work and the heat of the day.'   Jnh 4:8

¹³"But he answered one of them, 'Friend, I am not being unfair to you. Didn't you agree to work for a denarius? ¹⁴Take your pay and go. I want to give the man who was hired last the same as I gave you. ¹⁵Don't I have the right to do what I want with my own money? Or are you envious because I am generous?'   Dt 15:9; Mk 7:22

¹⁶"So the last will be first, and the first will be last."   Mt 19:30

Jesus Again Predicts His Death

¹⁷Now as Jesus was going up to Jerusalem, he took the twelve disciples aside and said to them, ¹⁸"We are going up to Jerusalem, and the Son of Man will be betrayed to the chief priests and the teachers of the law. They will condemn him to death ¹⁹and will turn him over to the Gentiles to be mocked and flogged and crucified. On the third day he will be raised to life!"   Mk 10:32-34; Lk 18:31-33

A Mother's Request

²⁰Then the mother of Zebedee's sons came to Jesus with her sons and, kneeling down, asked a favor of him.   Mt 4:21; 8:2

²¹"What is it you want?" he asked.

She said, "Grant that one of these two sons of mine may sit at your right and the other at your left in your kingdom." Mt 19:28

²²"You don't know what you are asking," Jesus said to them. "Can you drink the cup I am going to drink?" Mt 26:39,42; Lk 22:42; Jn 18:11

"We can," they answered.

²³Jesus said to them, "You will indeed drink from my cup, but to sit at my right or left is not for me to grant. These places belong to those for whom they have been prepared by my Father." Ac 12:2

²⁴When the ten heard about this, they were indignant with the two brothers. ²⁵Jesus called them together and said, "You know that the rulers of the Gentiles lord it over them, and their high officials exercise authority over them. ²⁶Not so with you. Instead, whoever wants to become great among you must be your servant, ²⁷and whoever wants to be first must be your slave— ²⁸just as the Son of Man did not come to be served, but to serve, and to give his life as a ransom for many." Mk 10:35-45

Two Blind Men Receive Sight

²⁹As Jesus and his disciples were leaving Jericho, a large crowd followed him. ³⁰Two blind men were sitting by the roadside, and when they heard that Jesus was going by, they shouted, "Lord, Son of David, have mercy on us!"

³¹The crowd rebuked them and told them to be quiet, but they shouted all the louder, "Lord, Son of David, have mercy on us!"

³²Jesus stopped and called them. "What do you want me to do for you?" he asked.

³³"Lord," they answered, "we want our sight."

³⁴Jesus had compassion on them and touched their eyes. Immediately they received their sight and followed him. Mk 10:46-52

The Triumphal Entry

21 As they approached Jerusalem and came to Bethphage on the Mount of Olives, Jesus sent two disciples, ²saying to them, "Go to the village ahead of you, and at once you will find a donkey tied there, with her colt by her. Untie them and bring them to me. ³If anyone says anything to you, tell him that the Lord needs them, and he will send them right away." Mk 11:1-10

⁴This took place to fulfill what was spoken through the prophet:

⁵"Say to the Daughter of Zion,
  'See, your king comes to
       you,
gentle and riding on a donkey,
  on a colt, the foal of a
       donkey.' "ᵃ   Isa 62:11

⁶The disciples went and did as Jesus had instructed them. ⁷They brought the donkey and the colt,

ᵃ 5 Zech. 9:9

placed their cloaks on them, and Jesus sat on them. **8**A very large crowd spread their cloaks on the road, while others cut branches from the trees and spread them on the road. **9**The crowds that went ahead of him and those that followed shouted,   2Ki 9:13

"Hosanna*a* to the Son of
      David!"   Mt 9:27

"Blessed is he who comes in
      the name of the Lord!"*b*

"Hosanna*a* in the highest!"

10When Jesus entered Jerusalem, the whole city was stirred and asked, "Who is this?"

11The crowds answered, "This is Jesus, the prophet from Nazareth in Galilee."   Jn 6:14; 7:40

Jesus at the Temple

12Jesus entered the temple area and drove out all who were buying and selling there. He overturned the tables of the money changers and the benches of those selling doves. **13**"It is written," he said to them, " 'My house will be called a house of prayer,'*c* but you are making it a 'den of robbers.'*d*"

14The blind and the lame came to him at the temple, and he healed them. **15**But when the chief priests and the teachers of the law saw the wonderful things he did and the children shouting in the temple

area, "Hosanna to the Son of David," they were indignant.   Mt 9:27

16"Do you hear what these children are saying?" they asked him.

"Yes," replied Jesus, "have you never read,

" 'From the lips of children and
          infants
      you have ordained praise'*e*?"

17And he left them and went out of the city to Bethany, where he spent the night.   Mt 26:6; Mk 11:1

The Fig Tree Withers

18Early in the morning, as he was on his way back to the city, he was hungry. **19**Seeing a fig tree by the road, he went up to it but found nothing on it except leaves. Then he said to it, "May you never bear fruit again!" Immediately the tree withered.   Isa 34:4; Jer 8:13

20When the disciples saw this, they were amazed. "How did the fig tree wither so quickly?" they asked.

21Jesus replied, "I tell you the truth, if you have faith and do not doubt, not only can you do what was done to the fig tree, but also you can say to this mountain, 'Go, throw yourself into the sea,' and it will be done. **22**If you believe, you will receive whatever you ask for in prayer."   Mk 11:12-14,20-24; Jas 1:6

a9 A Hebrew expression meaning "Save!" which became an exclamation of praise; also in verse 15
b9 Psalm 118:26   *c13* Isaiah 56:7   *d13* Jer. 7:11   *e16* Psalm 8:2

The Authority of Jesus Questioned

23Jesus entered the temple courts, and, while he was teaching, the chief priests and the elders of the people came to him. "By what authority are you doing these things?" they asked. "And who gave you this authority?"   Ac 4:7

24Jesus replied, "I will also ask you one question. If you answer me, I will tell you by what authority I am doing these things. **25**John's baptism—where did it come from? Was it from heaven, or from men?"

They discussed it among themselves and said, "If we say, 'From heaven,' he will ask, 'Then why didn't you believe him?' **26**But if we say, 'From men'—we are afraid of the people, for they all hold that John was a prophet."   Mk 6:20

27So they answered Jesus, "We don't know."

Then he said, "Neither will I tell you by what authority I am doing these things.   Mk 11:27-33; Lk 20:1-8

The Parable of the Two Sons

28"What do you think? There was a man who had two sons. He went to the first and said, 'Son, go and work today in the vineyard.'

29" 'I will not,' he answered, but later he changed his mind and went.

30"Then the father went to the other son and said the same thing. He answered, 'I will, sir,' but he did not go.

31"Which of the two did what his father wanted?"

"The first," they answered.

Jesus said to them, "I tell you the truth, the tax collectors and the prostitutes are entering the kingdom of God ahead of you. **32**For John came to you to show you the way of righteousness, and you did not believe him, but the tax collectors and the prostitutes did. And even after you saw this, you did not repent and believe him.

The Parable of the Tenants

33"Listen to another parable: There was a landowner who planted a vineyard. He put a wall around it, dug a winepress in it and built a watchtower. Then he rented the vineyard to some farmers and went away on a journey. **34**When the harvest time approached, he sent his servants to the tenants to collect his fruit.

35"The tenants seized his servants; they beat one, killed another, and stoned a third. **36**Then he sent other servants to them, more than the first time, and the tenants treated them the same way. **37**Last of all, he sent his son to them. 'They will respect my son,' he said.

38"But when the tenants saw the son, they said to each other, 'This is the heir. Come, let's kill him and take his inheritance.' **39**So they took him and threw him out of the vineyard and killed him.   Ps 2:8

40"Therefore, when the owner of the vineyard comes, what will he do to those tenants?"

41"He will bring those wretches to a wretched end," they replied, "and he will rent the vineyard to other tenants, who will give him his share of the crop at harvest time."　　　　*Ac 13:46; 18:6; 28:28*

42Jesus said to them, "Have you never read in the Scriptures:

" 'The stone the builders
　　　rejected
　has become the capstone*a*;
　the Lord has done this,
　and it is marvelous in our
　　　eyes'*b*?　　　*Ac 4:11; 1Pe 2:7*

43"Therefore I tell you that the kingdom of God will be taken away from you and given to a people who will produce its fruit. **44**He who falls on this stone will be broken to pieces, but he on whom it falls will be crushed."*c*　　*Mt 8:12*

45When the chief priests and the Pharisees heard Jesus' parables, they knew he was talking about them. **46**They looked for a way to arrest him, but they were afraid of the crowd because the people held that he was a prophet.　　*Mk 12:1-12*

The Parable of the Wedding Banquet

22 Jesus spoke to them again in parables, saying: **2**"The kingdom of heaven is like a king who prepared a wedding banquet for his son. **3**He sent his servants to those who had been invited to the banquet to tell them to come, but they refused to come.　　*Mt 21:34*

4"Then he sent some more servants and said, 'Tell those who have been invited that I have prepared my dinner: My oxen and fattened cattle have been butchered, and everything is ready. Come to the wedding banquet.'　　*Mt 21:36*

5"But they paid no attention and went off—one to his field, another to his business. **6**The rest seized his servants, mistreated them and killed them. **7**The king was enraged. He sent his army and destroyed those murderers and burned their city.　　*Lk 19:27*

8"Then he said to his servants, 'The wedding banquet is ready, but those I invited did not deserve to come. **9**Go to the street corners and invite to the banquet anyone you find.' **10**So the servants went out into the streets and gathered all the people they could find, both good and bad, and the wedding hall was filled with guests.

11"But when the king came in to see the guests, he noticed a man there who was not wearing wedding clothes. **12**'Friend,' he asked, 'how did you get in here without wedding clothes?' The man was speechless.　　*Mt 20:13; 26:50*

13"Then the king told the attendants, 'Tie him hand and foot, and throw him outside, into the dark-

---

a42 Or *cornerstone*　　*b42* Psalm 118:22,23　　*c44* Some manuscripts do not have verse 44.

ness, where there will be weeping and gnashing of teeth.'   Mt 8:12

[14]"For many are invited, but few are chosen."   Lk 14:6-24

Paying Taxes to Caesar

[15]Then the Pharisees went out and laid plans to trap him in his words. [16]They sent their disciples to him along with the Herodians. "Teacher," they said, "we know you are a man of integrity and that you teach the way of God in accordance with the truth. You aren't swayed by men, because you pay no attention to who they are. [17]Tell us then, what is your opinion? Is it right to pay taxes to Caesar or not?"   Mt 17:25; Mk 3:6

[18]But Jesus, knowing their evil intent, said, "You hypocrites, why are you trying to trap me? [19]Show me the coin used for paying the tax." They brought him a denarius, [20]and he asked them, "Whose portrait is this? And whose inscription?"

[21]"Caesar's," they replied.

Then he said to them, "Give to Caesar what is Caesar's, and to God what is God's."   Ro 13:7

[22]When they heard this, they were amazed. So they left him and went away.   Mk 12:13-17; Lk 20:20-26

Marriage at the Resurrection

[23]That same day the Sadducees, who say there is no resurrection, came to him with a question.

[24]"Teacher," they said, "Moses told us that if a man dies without having children, his brother must marry the widow and have children for him. [25]Now there were seven brothers among us. The first one married and died, and since he had no children, he left his wife to his brother. [26]The same thing happened to the second and third brother, right on down to the seventh. [27]Finally, the woman died. [28]Now then, at the resurrection, whose wife will she be of the seven, since all of them were married to her?"   Dt 25:5-6; Ac 23:8

[29]Jesus replied, "You are in error because you do not know the Scriptures or the power of God. [30]At the resurrection people will neither marry nor be given in marriage; they will be like the angels in heaven. [31]But about the resurrection of the dead—have you not read what God said to you, [32]'I am the God of Abraham, the God of Isaac, and the God of Jacob'[a]? He is not the God of the dead but of the living."   Ex 3:6; Jn 20:9; Ac 7:32

[33]When the crowds heard this, they were astonished at his teaching.   Mk 12:18-27; Lk 20:27-40

The Greatest Commandment

[34]Hearing that Jesus had silenced the Sadducees, the Pharisees got together. [35]One of them, an expert in the law, tested him with this question: [36]"Teacher,

---

[a] 32 Exodus 3:6

which is the greatest commandment in the Law?" Lk 7:30; 10:25; 11:45

37Jesus replied: " 'Love the Lord your God with all your heart and with all your soul and with all your mind.'ᵃ 38This is the first and greatest commandment. 39And the second is like it: 'Love your neighbor as yourself.'ᵇ 40All the Law and the Prophets hang on these two commandments."   Mk 12:28-31

Whose Son Is the Christ?

41While the Pharisees were gathered together, Jesus asked them, 42"What do you think about the Christᶜ? Whose son is he?"

"The son of David," they replied.

43He said to them, "How is it then that David, speaking by the Spirit, calls him 'Lord'? For he says,

44" 'The Lord said to my Lord:
    "Sit at my right hand
    until I put your enemies
    under your feet." 'ᵈ

45If then David calls him 'Lord,' how can he be his son?" 46No one could say a word in reply, and from that day on no one dared to ask him any more questions.

Seven Woes

23 Then Jesus said to the crowds and to his disciples: 2"The teachers of the law and the Pharisees sit in Moses' seat. 3So you must obey them and do everything they tell you. But do not do what they do, for they do not practice what they preach. 4They tie up heavy loads and put them on men's shoulders, but they themselves are not willing to lift a finger to move them.   Lk 11:46

5"Everything they do is done for men to see: They make their phylacteriesᵉ wide and the tassels on their garments long; 6they love the place of honor at banquets and the most important seats in the synagogues; 7they love to be greeted in the marketplaces and to have men call them 'Rabbi.'   Mk 12:38-39

8"But you are not to be called 'Rabbi,' for you have only one Master and you are all brothers. 9And do not call anyone on earth 'father,' for you have one Father, and he is in heaven. 10Nor are you to be called 'teacher,' for you have one Teacher, the Christ.ᶜ 11The greatest among you will be your servant. 12For whoever exalts himself will be humbled, and whoever humbles himself will be exalted.

13"Woe to you, teachers of the law and Pharisees, you hypocrites! You shut the kingdom of heaven in men's faces. You yourselves do not enter, nor will you let those enter who are trying to.ᶠ   Lk 11:52

15"Woe to you, teachers of the

ᵃ37 Deut. 6:5   ᵇ39 Lev. 19:18   ᶜ42,10 Or Messiah   ᵈ44 Psalm 110:1   ᵉ5 That is, boxes containing Scripture verses, worn on forehead and arm   ᶠ13 Some manuscripts to. ¹⁴Woe to you, teachers of the law and Pharisees, you hypocrites! You devour widows' houses and for a show make lengthy prayers. Therefore you will be punished more severely.

law and Pharisees, you hypocrites! You travel over land and sea to win a single convert, and when he becomes one, you make him twice as much a son of hell as you are.

¹⁶"Woe to you, blind guides! You say, 'If anyone swears by the temple, it means nothing; but if anyone swears by the gold of the temple, he is bound by his oath.' ¹⁷You blind fools! Which is greater: the gold, or the temple that makes the gold sacred? ¹⁸You also say, 'If anyone swears by the altar, it means nothing; but if anyone swears by the gift on it, he is bound by his oath.' ¹⁹You blind men! Which is greater: the gift, or the altar that makes the gift sacred? ²⁰Therefore, he who swears by the altar swears by it and by everything on it. ²¹And he who swears by the temple swears by it and by the one who dwells in it. ²²And he who swears by heaven swears by God's throne and by the one who sits on it.   Ex 29:37; Mt 5:34

²³"Woe to you, teachers of the law and Pharisees, you hypocrites! You give a tenth of your spices — mint, dill and cummin. But you have neglected the more important matters of the law — justice, mercy and faithfulness. You should have practiced the latter, without neglecting the former. ²⁴You blind guides! You strain out a gnat but swallow a camel.

²⁵"Woe to you, teachers of the law and Pharisees, you hypocrites! You clean the outside of the cup and dish, but inside they are full of greed and self-indulgence. ²⁶Blind Pharisee! First clean the inside of the cup and dish, and then the outside also will be clean.   Mk 7:4

²⁷"Woe to you, teachers of the law and Pharisees, you hypocrites! You are like whitewashed tombs, which look beautiful on the outside but on the inside are full of dead men's bones and everything unclean. ²⁸In the same way, on the outside you appear to people as righteous but on the inside you are full of hypocrisy and wickedness.

²⁹"Woe to you, teachers of the law and Pharisees, you hypocrites! You build tombs for the prophets and decorate the graves of the righteous. ³⁰And you say, 'If we had lived in the days of our forefathers, we would not have taken part with them in shedding the blood of the prophets.' ³¹So you testify against yourselves that you are the descendants of those who murdered the prophets. ³²Fill up, then, the measure of the sin of your forefathers!   Lk 11:47-48

³³"You snakes! You brood of vipers! How will you escape being condemned to hell? ³⁴Therefore I am sending you prophets and wise men and teachers. Some of them you will kill and crucify; others you will flog in your synagogues and pursue from town to town. ³⁵And so upon you will come all the righteous blood that has been shed on earth, from the blood of righteous Abel to the blood of

Zechariah son of Berekiah, whom you murdered between the temple and the altar. [36]I tell you the truth, all this will come upon this generation.

Lk 11:49-51

[37]"O Jerusalem, Jerusalem, you who kill the prophets and stone those sent to you, how often I have longed to gather your children together, as a hen gathers her chicks under her wings, but you were not willing. [38]Look, your house is left to you desolate. [39]For I tell you, you will not see me again until you say, 'Blessed is he who comes in the name of the Lord.'[a]"

Signs of the End of the Age

24 Jesus left the temple and was walking away when his disciples came up to him to call his attention to its buildings. [2]"Do you see all these things?" he asked. "I tell you the truth, not one stone here will be left on another; every one will be thrown down."

[3]As Jesus was sitting on the Mount of Olives, the disciples came to him privately. "Tell us," they said, "when will this happen, and what will be the sign of your coming and of the end of the age?"

[4]Jesus answered: "Watch out that no one deceives you. [5]For many will come in my name, claiming, 'I am the Christ,[b]' and will deceive many. [6]You will hear of wars and rumors of wars, but see to it that you are not alarmed.

Such things must happen, but the end is still to come. [7]Nation will rise against nation, and kingdom against kingdom. There will be famines and earthquakes in various places. [8]All these are the beginning of birth pains.

Isa 19:2

[9]"Then you will be handed over to be persecuted and put to death, and you will be hated by all nations because of me. [10]At that time many will turn away from the faith and will betray and hate each other, [11]and many false prophets will appear and deceive many people. [12]Because of the increase of wickedness, the love of most will grow cold, [13]but he who stands firm to the end will be saved. [14]And this gospel of the kingdom will be preached in the whole world as a testimony to all nations, and then the end will come.

Ro 10:18; Col 1:6,23

[15]"So when you see standing in the holy place 'the abomination that causes desolation,'[c] spoken of through the prophet Daniel—let the reader understand— [16]then let those who are in Judea flee to the mountains. [17]Let no one on the roof of his house go down to take anything out of the house. [18]Let no one in the field go back to get his cloak. [19]How dreadful it will be in those days for pregnant women and nursing mothers! [20]Pray that your flight will not take place in winter or on the Sabbath. [21]For then there will be great distress,

---

[a]39 Psalm 118:26   [b]5 Or *Messiah*; also in verse 23   [c]15 Daniel 9:27; 11:31; 12:11

unequaled from the beginning of the world until now—and never to be equaled again. ²²If those days had not been cut short, no one would survive, but for the sake of the elect those days will be shortened. ²³At that time if anyone says to you, 'Look, here is the Christ!' or, 'There he is!' do not believe it. ²⁴For false Christs and false prophets will appear and perform great signs and miracles to deceive even the elect—if that were possible. ²⁵See, I have told you ahead of time.   Lk 17:23; 2Th 2:9-11

²⁶"So if anyone tells you, 'There he is, out in the desert,' do not go out; or, 'Here he is, in the inner rooms,' do not believe it. ²⁷For as lightning that comes from the east is visible even in the west, so will be the coming of the Son of Man. ²⁸Wherever there is a carcass, there the vultures will gather.

²⁹"Immediately after the distress of those days

" 'the sun will be darkened,
    and the moon will not give
        its light;
the stars will fall from the sky,
    and the heavenly bodies will
        be shaken.'ᵃ   Eze 32:7

³⁰"At that time the sign of the Son of Man will appear in the sky, and all the nations of the earth will mourn. They will see the Son of Man coming on the clouds of the sky, with power and great glory.

³¹And he will send his angels with a loud trumpet call, and they will gather his elect from the four winds, from one end of the heavens to the other.   Da 7:13; Isa 27:13

³²"Now learn this lesson from the fig tree: As soon as its twigs get tender and its leaves come out, you know that summer is near. ³³Even so, when you see all these things, you know that itᵇ is near, right at the door. ³⁴I tell you the truth, this generationᶜ will certainly not pass away until all these things have happened. ³⁵Heaven and earth will pass away, but my words will never pass away.

The Day and Hour Unknown

³⁶"No one knows about that day or hour, not even the angels in heaven, nor the Son,ᵈ but only the Father. ³⁷As it was in the days of Noah, so it will be at the coming of the Son of Man. ³⁸For in the days before the flood, people were eating and drinking, marrying and giving in marriage, up to the day Noah entered the ark; ³⁹and they knew nothing about what would happen until the flood came and took them all away. That is how it will be at the coming of the Son of Man. ⁴⁰Two men will be in the field; one will be taken and the other left. ⁴¹Two women will be grinding with a hand mill; one will be taken and the other left.

ᵃ29 Isaiah 13:10; 34:4   ᵇ33 Or he   ᶜ34 Or race   ᵈ36 Some manuscripts do not have nor the Son.

[42]"Therefore keep watch, because you do not know on what day your Lord will come. [43]But understand this: If the owner of the house had known at what time of night the thief was coming, he would have kept watch and would not have let his house be broken into. [44]So you also must be ready, because the Son of Man will come at an hour when you do not expect him.   Mt 25:13; Lk 12:39-40

[45]"Who then is the faithful and wise servant, whom the master has put in charge of the servants in his household to give them their food at the proper time? [46]It will be good for that servant whose master finds him doing so when he returns. [47]I tell you the truth, he will put him in charge of all his possessions. [48]But suppose that servant is wicked and says to himself, 'My master is staying away a long time,' [49]and he then begins to beat his fellow servants and to eat and drink with drunkards. [50]The master of that servant will come on a day when he does not expect him and at an hour he is not aware of. [51]He will cut him to pieces and assign him a place with the hypocrites, where there will be weeping and gnashing of teeth.   Lk 12:42-46

The Parable of the Ten Virgins

25 "At that time the kingdom of heaven will be like ten virgins who took their lamps and went out to meet the bridegroom. [2]Five of them were foolish and five were wise. [3]The foolish ones took their lamps but did not take any oil with them. [4]The wise, however, took oil in jars along with their lamps. [5]The bridegroom was a long time in coming, and they all became drowsy and fell asleep.

[6]"At midnight the cry rang out: 'Here's the bridegroom! Come out to meet him!'

[7]"Then all the virgins woke up and trimmed their lamps. [8]The foolish ones said to the wise, 'Give us some of your oil; our lamps are going out.'   Lk 12:35

[9]"'No,' they replied, 'there may not be enough for both us and you. Instead, go to those who sell oil and buy some for yourselves.'

[10]"But while they were on their way to buy the oil, the bridegroom arrived. The virgins who were ready went in with him to the wedding banquet. And the door was shut.   Rev 19:9

[11]"Later the others also came. 'Sir! Sir!' they said. 'Open the door for us!'

[12]"But he replied, 'I tell you the truth, I don't know you.'   Mt 7:23

[13]"Therefore keep watch, because you do not know the day or the hour.   Mt 24:42,44; Mk 13:35; Lk 12:40

The Parable of the Talents

[14]"Again, it will be like a man going on a journey, who called his servants and entrusted his property to them. [15]To one he gave five

talents*a* of money, to another two talents, and to another one talent, each according to his ability. Then he went on his journey. ¹⁶The man who had received the five talents went at once and put his money to work and gained five more. ¹⁷So also, the one with the two talents gained two more. ¹⁸But the man who had received the one talent went off, dug a hole in the ground and hid his master's money.

¹⁹"After a long time the master of those servants returned and settled accounts with them. ²⁰The man who had received the five talents brought the other five. 'Master,' he said, 'you entrusted me with five talents. See, I have gained five more.'   Mt 18:23

²¹"His master replied, 'Well done, good and faithful servant! You have been faithful with a few things; I will put you in charge of many things. Come and share your master's happiness!'   Mt 24:45,47

²²"The man with the two talents also came. 'Master,' he said, 'you entrusted me with two talents; see, I have gained two more.'

²³"His master replied, 'Well done, good and faithful servant! You have been faithful with a few things; I will put you in charge of many things. Come and share your master's happiness!'   ver 21

²⁴"Then the man who had received the one talent came. 'Master,' he said, 'I knew that you are a hard man, harvesting where you have not sown and gathering where you have not scattered seed. ²⁵So I was afraid and went out and hid your talent in the ground. See, here is what belongs to you.'

²⁶"His master replied, 'You wicked, lazy servant! So you knew that I harvest where I have not sown and gather where I have not scattered seed? ²⁷Well then, you should have put my money on deposit with the bankers, so that when I returned I would have received it back with interest.

²⁸"'Take the talent from him and give it to the one who has the ten talents. ²⁹For everyone who has will be given more, and he will have an abundance. Whoever does not have, even what he has will be taken from him. ³⁰And throw that worthless servant outside, into the darkness, where there will be weeping and gnashing of teeth.'

The Sheep and the Goats

³¹"When the Son of Man comes in his glory, and all the angels with him, he will sit on his throne in heavenly glory. ³²All the nations will be gathered before him, and he will separate the people one from another as a shepherd separates the sheep from the goats. ³³He will put the sheep on his right and the goats on his left.

³⁴"Then the King will say to

a 15 A talent was worth more than a thousand dollars.

those on his right, 'Come, you who are blessed by my Father; take your inheritance, the kingdom prepared for you since the creation of the world. ³⁵For I was hungry and you gave me something to eat, I was thirsty and you gave me something to drink, I was a stranger and you invited me in, ³⁶I needed clothes and you clothed me, I was sick and you looked after me, I was in prison and you came to visit me.'   1Co 15:50; Jas 2:15-16; Rev 13:8

³⁷"Then the righteous will answer him, 'Lord, when did we see you hungry and feed you, or thirsty and give you something to drink? ³⁸When did we see you a stranger and invite you in, or needing clothes and clothe you? ³⁹When did we see you sick or in prison and go to visit you?'

⁴⁰"The King will reply, 'I tell you the truth, whatever you did for one of the least of these brothers of mine, you did for me.'   Pr 19:17

⁴¹"Then he will say to those on his left, 'Depart from me, you who are cursed, into the eternal fire prepared for the devil and his angels. ⁴²For I was hungry and you gave me nothing to eat, I was thirsty and you gave me nothing to drink, ⁴³I was a stranger and you did not invite me in, I needed clothes and you did not clothe me, I was sick and in prison and you did not look after me.'   Mt 7:23

⁴⁴"They also will answer, 'Lord, when did we see you hungry or thirsty or a stranger or needing clothes or sick or in prison, and did not help you?'

⁴⁵"He will reply, 'I tell you the truth, whatever you did not do for one of the least of these, you did not do for me.'   Pr 14:31; 17:5

⁴⁶"Then they will go away to eternal punishment, but the righteous to eternal life."   Da 12:2; Jn 5:29

The Plot Against Jesus

26 When Jesus had finished saying all these things, he said to his disciples, ²"As you know, the Passover is two days away—and the Son of Man will be handed over to be crucified."

³Then the chief priests and the elders of the people assembled in the palace of the high priest, whose name was Caiaphas, ⁴and they plotted to arrest Jesus in some sly way and kill him. ⁵"But not during the Feast," they said, "or there may be a riot among the people."   Mk 14:1-2; Lk 22:1-2

Jesus Anointed at Bethany

⁶While Jesus was in Bethany in the home of a man known as Simon the Leper, ⁷a woman came to him with an alabaster jar of very expensive perfume, which she poured on his head as he was reclining at the table.   Mt 21:17

⁸When the disciples saw this, they were indignant. "Why this waste?" they asked. ⁹"This perfume could have been sold at a high price and the money given to the poor."

¹⁰Aware of this, Jesus said to them, "Why are you bothering this woman? She has done a beautiful thing to me. ¹¹The poor you will always have with you, but you will not always have me. ¹²When she poured this perfume on my body, she did it to prepare me for burial. ¹³I tell you the truth, wherever this gospel is preached throughout the world, what she has done will also be told, in memory of her."

Judas Agrees to Betray Jesus

¹⁴Then one of the Twelve—the one called Judas Iscariot—went to the chief priests ¹⁵and asked, "What are you willing to give me if I hand him over to you?" So they counted out for him thirty silver coins. ¹⁶From then on Judas watched for an opportunity to hand him over.   Mk 14:10-11; Lk 22:3-6

The Lord's Supper

¹⁷On the first day of the Feast of Unleavened Bread, the disciples came to Jesus and asked, "Where do you want us to make preparations for you to eat the Passover?"

¹⁸He replied, "Go into the city to a certain man and tell him, 'The Teacher says: My appointed time is near. I am going to celebrate the Passover with my disciples at your house.' " ¹⁹So the disciples did as Jesus had directed them and prepared the Passover.   Mk 14:12-16

²⁰When evening came, Jesus was reclining at the table with the Twelve. ²¹And while they were eating, he said, "I tell you the truth, one of you will betray me."

²²They were very sad and began to say to him one after the other, "Surely not I, Lord?"

²³Jesus replied, "The one who has dipped his hand into the bowl with me will betray me. ²⁴The Son of Man will go just as it is written about him. But woe to that man who betrays the Son of Man! It would be better for him if he had not been born."   Mk 14:17-21; Jn 13:18

²⁵Then Judas, the one who would betray him, said, "Surely not I, Rabbi?"   Mt 23:7

Jesus answered, "Yes, it is you."ᵃ

²⁶While they were eating, Jesus took bread, gave thanks and broke it, and gave it to his disciples, saying, "Take and eat; this is my body."   1Co 10:16

²⁷Then he took the cup, gave thanks and offered it to them, saying, "Drink from it, all of you. ²⁸This is my blood of theᵇ covenant, which is poured out for many for the forgiveness of sins. ²⁹I tell you, I will not drink of this fruit of the vine from now on until that day when I drink it anew with you in my Father's kingdom."

³⁰When they had sung a hymn, they went out to the Mount of Olives.   Mk 14:22-26

ᵃ 25 Or "You yourself have said it"   ᵇ 28 Some manuscripts the new

Jesus Predicts Peter's Denial

31Then Jesus told them, "This very night you will all fall away on account of me, for it is written:

" 'I will strike the shepherd,
    and the sheep of the flock
        will be scattered.'[a]

32But after I have risen, I will go ahead of you into Galilee."

33Peter replied, "Even if all fall away on account of you, I never will."

34"I tell you the truth," Jesus answered, "this very night, before the rooster crows, you will disown me three times."   Jn 13:37-38

35But Peter declared, "Even if I have to die with you, I will never disown you." And all the other disciples said the same.   Mk 14:27-31

Gethsemane

36Then Jesus went with his disciples to a place called Gethsemane, and he said to them, "Sit here while I go over there and pray." **37**He took Peter and the two sons of Zebedee along with him, and he began to be sorrowful and troubled. **38**Then he said to them, "My soul is overwhelmed with sorrow to the point of death. Stay here and keep watch with me."   Mt 4:21

39Going a little farther, he fell with his face to the ground and prayed, "My Father, if it is possible, may this cup be taken from me. Yet not as I will, but as you will."   Mt 20:22; Jn 6:38

40Then he returned to his disciples and found them sleeping. "Could you men not keep watch with me for one hour?" he asked Peter. **41**"Watch and pray so that you will not fall into temptation. The spirit is willing, but the body is weak."   Mt 6:13

42He went away a second time and prayed, "My Father, if it is not possible for this cup to be taken away unless I drink it, may your will be done."

43When he came back, he again found them sleeping, because their eyes were heavy. **44**So he left them and went away once more and prayed the third time, saying the same thing.

45Then he returned to the disciples and said to them, "Are you still sleeping and resting? Look, the hour is near, and the Son of Man is betrayed into the hands of sinners. **46**Rise, let us go! Here comes my betrayer!"   Mk 14:32-42

Jesus Arrested

47While he was still speaking, Judas, one of the Twelve, arrived. With him was a large crowd armed with swords and clubs, sent from the chief priests and the elders of the people. **48**Now the betrayer had arranged a signal with them: "The one I kiss is the man; arrest him." **49**Going at once to Jesus, Judas

---

a31 Zech. 13:7

said, "Greetings, Rabbi!" and kissed him.   Mt 23:7

⁵⁰Jesus replied, "Friend, do what you came for."ᵃ   Mt 20:13; 22:12

Then the men stepped forward, seized Jesus and arrested him. ⁵¹With that, one of Jesus' companions reached for his sword, drew it out and struck the servant of the high priest, cutting off his ear. ⁵²"Put your sword back in its place," Jesus said to him, "for all who draw the sword will die by the sword. ⁵³Do you think I cannot call on my Father, and he will at once put at my disposal more than twelve legions of angels? ⁵⁴But how then would the Scriptures be fulfilled that say it must happen in this way?"   Ge 9:6; Rev 13:10

⁵⁵At that time Jesus said to the crowd, "Am I leading a rebellion, that you have come out with swords and clubs to capture me? Every day I sat in the temple courts teaching, and you did not arrest me. ⁵⁶But this has all taken place that the writings of the prophets might be fulfilled." Then all the disciples deserted him and fled.

Before the Sanhedrin

⁵⁷Those who had arrested Jesus took him to Caiaphas, the high priest, where the teachers of the law and the elders had assembled. ⁵⁸But Peter followed him at a distance, right up to the courtyard of the high priest. He entered and sat

down with the guards to see the outcome.   Jn 18:15

⁵⁹The chief priests and the whole Sanhedrin were looking for false evidence against Jesus so that they could put him to death. ⁶⁰But they did not find any, though many false witnesses came forward.   Ps 27:12; 35:11; Ac 6:13

Finally two came forward ⁶¹and declared, "This fellow said, 'I am able to destroy the temple of God and rebuild it in three days.'"

⁶²Then the high priest stood up and said to Jesus, "Are you not going to answer? What is this testimony that these men are bringing against you?" ⁶³But Jesus remained silent.   Mt 27:12,14

The high priest said to him, "I charge you under oath by the living God: Tell us if you are the Christ,ᵇ the Son of God."   Lk 22:67

⁶⁴"Yes, it is as you say," Jesus replied. "But I say to all of you: In the future you will see the Son of Man sitting at the right hand of the Mighty One and coming on the clouds of heaven."   Ps 110:1; Da 7:13

⁶⁵Then the high priest tore his clothes and said, "He has spoken blasphemy! Why do we need any more witnesses? Look, now you have heard the blasphemy. ⁶⁶What do you think?"   Mk 14:63

"He is worthy of death," they answered.   Lev 24:16; Jn 19:7

⁶⁷Then they spit in his face and struck him with their fists. Others

---

ᵃ 50 Or "Friend, why have you come?"   ᵇ 63 Or Messiah; also in verse 68 slapped him ⁶⁸and said, "Prophesy to us, Christ. Who hit you?"

Peter Disowns Jesus

⁶⁹Now Peter was sitting out in the courtyard, and a servant girl came to him. "You also were with Jesus of Galilee," she said.

⁷⁰But he denied it before them all. "I don't know what you're talking about," he said.

⁷¹Then he went out to the gateway, where another girl saw him and said to the people there, "This fellow was with Jesus of Nazareth."

⁷²He denied it again, with an oath: "I don't know the man!"

⁷³After a little while, those standing there went up to Peter and said, "Surely you are one of them, for your accent gives you away."

⁷⁴Then he began to call down curses on himself and he swore to them, "I don't know the man!"

Immediately a rooster crowed. ⁷⁵Then Peter remembered the word Jesus had spoken: "Before the rooster crows, you will disown me three times." And he went outside and wept bitterly.   ver 34

Judas Hangs Himself

27 Early in the morning, all the chief priests and the elders of the people came to the decision to put Jesus to death. ²They bound him, led him away and handed him over to Pilate, the governor.   Mt 20:19; Mk 15:1; Ac 3:13

³When Judas, who had betrayed him, saw that Jesus was condemned, he was seized with remorse and returned the thirty silver coins to the chief priests and the elders. ⁴"I have sinned," he said, "for I have betrayed innocent blood."   Mt 26:14-15

"What is that to us?" they replied. "That's your responsibility."

⁵So Judas threw the money into the temple and left. Then he went away and hanged himself.

⁶The chief priests picked up the coins and said, "It is against the law to put this into the treasury, since it is blood money." ⁷So they decided to use the money to buy the potter's field as a burial place for foreigners. ⁸That is why it has been called the Field of Blood to this day. ⁹Then what was spoken by Jeremiah the prophet was fulfilled: "They took the thirty silver coins, the price set on him by the people of Israel, ¹⁰and they used them to buy the potter's field, as the Lord commanded me."[a]

Jesus Before Pilate

¹¹Meanwhile Jesus stood before the governor, and the governor asked him, "Are you the king of the Jews?"   Mt 2:2

"Yes, it is as you say," Jesus replied.

¹²When he was accused by the

---

[a]10 See Zech. 11:12,13; Jer. 19:1-13; 32:6-9.

chief priests and the elders, he gave no answer. ¹³Then Pilate asked him, "Don't you hear the testimony they are bringing against you?" ¹⁴But Jesus made no reply, not even to a single charge —to the great amazement of the governor.   Mt 26:62-63; Jn 19:9

¹⁵Now it was the governor's custom at the Feast to release a prisoner chosen by the crowd. ¹⁶At that time they had a notorious prisoner, called Barabbas. ¹⁷So when the crowd had gathered, Pilate asked them, "Which one do you want me to release to you: Barabbas, or Jesus who is called Christ?" ¹⁸For he knew it was out of envy that they had handed Jesus over to him.   Jn 18:39

¹⁹While Pilate was sitting on the judge's seat, his wife sent him this message: "Don't have anything to do with that innocent man, for I have suffered a great deal today in a dream because of him."   Mt 1:20

²⁰But the chief priests and the elders persuaded the crowd to ask for Barabbas and to have Jesus executed.   Ac 3:14

²¹"Which of the two do you want me to release to you?" asked the governor.

"Barabbas," they answered.

²²"What shall I do, then, with Jesus who is called Christ?" Pilate asked.   Mt 1:16

They all answered, "Crucify him!"

²³"Why? What crime has he committed?" asked Pilate.

But they shouted all the louder, "Crucify him!"

²⁴When Pilate saw that he was getting nowhere, but that instead an uproar was starting, he took water and washed his hands in front of the crowd. "I am innocent of this man's blood," he said. "It is your responsibility!"   Dt 21:6-8

²⁵All the people answered, "Let his blood be on us and on our children!"   Jos 2:19; Ac 5:28

²⁶Then he released Barabbas to them. But he had Jesus flogged, and handed him over to be crucified.   Mk 15:2-15; Lk 23:2-3,18-25

The Soldiers Mock Jesus

²⁷Then the governor's soldiers took Jesus into the Praetorium and gathered the whole company of soldiers around him. ²⁸They stripped him and put a scarlet robe on him, ²⁹and then twisted together a crown of thorns and set it on his head. They put a staff in his right hand and knelt in front of him and mocked him. "Hail, king of the Jews!" they said. ³⁰They spit on him, and took the staff and struck him on the head again and again. ³¹After they had mocked him, they took off the robe and put his own clothes on him. Then they led him away to crucify him.

The Crucifixion

³²As they were going out, they met a man from Cyrene, named Simon, and they forced him to carry the cross. ³³They came to a place

called Golgotha (which means The Place of the Skull). ³⁴There they offered Jesus wine to drink, mixed with gall; but after tasting it, he refused to drink it. ³⁵When they had crucified him, they divided up his clothes by casting lots.ᵃ ³⁶And sitting down, they kept watch over him there. ³⁷Above his head they placed the written charge against him: THIS IS JESUS, THE KING OF THE JEWS. ³⁸Two robbers were crucified with him, one on his right and one on his left. ³⁹Those who passed by hurled insults at him, shaking their heads ⁴⁰and saying, "You who are going to destroy the temple and build it in three days, save yourself! Come down from the cross, if you are the Son of God!"

⁴¹In the same way the chief priests, the teachers of the law and the elders mocked him. ⁴²"He saved others," they said, "but he can't save himself! He's the King of Israel! Let him come down now from the cross, and we will believe in him. ⁴³He trusts in God. Let God rescue him now if he wants him, for he said, 'I am the Son of God.' " ⁴⁴In the same way the robbers who were crucified with him also heaped insults on him.   Mk 15:22-32

The Death of Jesus

⁴⁵From the sixth hour until the ninth hour darkness came over all the land. ⁴⁶About the ninth hour Jesus cried out in a loud voice, *"Eloi, Eloi,ᵇ lama sabachthani?"*— which means, "My God, my God, why have you forsaken me?"ᶜ

⁴⁷When some of those standing there heard this, they said, "He's calling Elijah."

⁴⁸Immediately one of them ran and got a sponge. He filled it with wine vinegar, put it on a stick, and offered it to Jesus to drink. ⁴⁹The rest said, "Now leave him alone. Let's see if Elijah comes to save him."   Ps 69:21

⁵⁰And when Jesus had cried out again in a loud voice, he gave up his spirit.   Jn 19:30

⁵¹At that moment the curtain of the temple was torn in two from top to bottom. The earth shook and the rocks split. ⁵²The tombs broke open and the bodies of many holy people who had died were raised to life. ⁵³They came out of the tombs, and after Jesus' resurrection they went into the holy city and appeared to many people.   Ex 26:31-33; Mt 4:5

⁵⁴When the centurion and those with him who were guarding Jesus saw the earthquake and all that had happened, they were terrified, and exclaimed, "Surely he was the Sonᵈ of God!"   Mt 4:3; 17:5

⁵⁵Many women were there, watching from a distance. They had followed Jesus from Galilee to

---

ᵃ35 A few late manuscripts *lots that the word spoken by the prophet might be fulfilled: "They divided my garments among themselves and cast lots for my clothing"* (Psalm 22:18)   ᵇ46 Some manuscripts *Eli, Eli*   ᶜ46 Psalm 22:1   ᵈ54 Or *a son*

care for his needs. ⁵⁶Among them were Mary Magdalene, Mary the mother of James and Joses, and the mother of Zebedee's sons.

The Burial of Jesus

⁵⁷As evening approached, there came a rich man from Arimathea, named Joseph, who had himself become a disciple of Jesus. ⁵⁸Going to Pilate, he asked for Jesus' body, and Pilate ordered that it be given to him. ⁵⁹Joseph took the body, wrapped it in a clean linen cloth, ⁶⁰and placed it in his own new tomb that he had cut out of the rock. He rolled a big stone in front of the entrance to the tomb and went away. ⁶¹Mary Magdalene and the other Mary were sitting there opposite the tomb.

The Guard at the Tomb

⁶²The next day, the one after Preparation Day, the chief priests and the Pharisees went to Pilate. ⁶³"Sir," they said, "we remember that while he was still alive that deceiver said, 'After three days I will rise again.' ⁶⁴So give the order for the tomb to be made secure until the third day. Otherwise, his disciples may come and steal the body and tell the people that he has been raised from the dead. This last deception will be worse than the first." Mt 16:21; 28:13

⁶⁵"Take a guard," Pilate answered. "Go, make the tomb as secure as you know how." ⁶⁶So they went and made the tomb secure by putting a seal on the stone and posting the guard. Da 6:17; Mt 28:11

The Resurrection

28 After the Sabbath, at dawn on the first day of the week, Mary Magdalene and the other Mary went to look at the tomb. Mt 27:56

²There was a violent earthquake, for an angel of the Lord came down from heaven and, going to the tomb, rolled back the stone and sat on it. ³His appearance was like lightning, and his clothes were white as snow. ⁴The guards were so afraid of him that they shook and became like dead men. Da 10:6; Mk 9:3

⁵The angel said to the women, "Do not be afraid, for I know that you are looking for Jesus, who was crucified. ⁶He is not here; he has risen, just as he said. Come and see the place where he lay. ⁷Then go quickly and tell his disciples: 'He has risen from the dead and is going ahead of you into Galilee. There you will see him.' Now I have told you." Mk 16:1-8; Lk 24:1-10

⁸So the women hurried away from the tomb, afraid yet filled with joy, and ran to tell his disciples. ⁹Suddenly Jesus met them. "Greetings," he said. They came to him, clasped his feet and worshiped him. ¹⁰Then Jesus said to them, "Do not be afraid. Go and

tell my brothers to go to Galilee; there they will see me."   Ro 8:29

The Guards' Report

11While the women were on their way, some of the guards went into the city and reported to the chief priests everything that had happened. **12**When the chief priests had met with the elders and devised a plan, they gave the soldiers a large sum of money, **13**telling them, "You are to say, 'His disciples came during the night and stole him away while we were asleep.' **14**If this report gets to the governor, we will satisfy him and keep you out of trouble." **15**So the soldiers took the money and did as they were instructed. And this story has been widely circulated among the Jews to this very day.

The Great Commission

16Then the eleven disciples went to Galilee, to the mountain where Jesus had told them to go. **17**When they saw him, they worshiped him; but some doubted. **18**Then Jesus came to them and said, "All authority in heaven and on earth has been given to me. **19**Therefore go and make disciples of all nations, baptizing them in*a* the name of the Father and of the Son and of the Holy Spirit, **20**and teaching them to obey everything I have commanded you. And surely I am with you always, to the very end of the age."   Mk 16:15-16; Php 2:9-10

---

a 19 Or *into*; see Acts 8:16; 19:5; Romans 6:3; 1 Cor. 1:13; 10:2 and Gal. 3:27.

Mark

John the Baptist Prepares the Way

1 The beginning of the gospel about Jesus Christ, the Son of God.^a   Mt 4:3

²It is written in Isaiah the prophet:

"I will send my messenger
    ahead of you,
who will prepare your
    way"^b—   Mal 3:1; Mt 11:10
³"a voice of one calling in the
    desert,
'Prepare the way for the Lord,
    make straight paths for
    him.' "^c

⁴And so John came, baptizing in the desert region and preaching a baptism of repentance for the forgiveness of sins. ⁵The whole Judean countryside and all the people of Jerusalem went out to him. Confessing their sins, they were baptized by him in the Jordan River. ⁶John wore clothing made of camel's hair, with a leather belt around his waist, and he ate locusts and wild honey. ⁷And this was his message: "After me will come one more powerful than I, the thongs of whose sandals I am not worthy to stoop down and untie. ⁸I

baptize you with^d water, but he will baptize you with the Holy Spirit."

The Baptism and Temptation of Jesus

⁹At that time Jesus came from Nazareth in Galilee and was baptized by John in the Jordan. ¹⁰As Jesus was coming up out of the water, he saw heaven being torn open and the Spirit descending on him like a dove. ¹¹And a voice came from heaven: "You are my Son, whom I love; with you I am well pleased."   Mt 3:13-17; Lk 3:21-22

¹²At once the Spirit sent him out into the desert, ¹³and he was in the desert forty days, being tempted by Satan. He was with the wild animals, and angels attended him.

The Calling of the First Disciples

¹⁴After John was put in prison, Jesus went into Galilee, proclaiming the good news of God. ¹⁵"The time has come," he said. "The kingdom of God is near. Repent and believe the good news!"

¹⁶As Jesus walked beside the Sea of Galilee, he saw Simon and his brother Andrew casting a net

---

^a1 Some manuscripts do not have *the Son of God.*   ^b2 Mal. 3:1   ^c3 Isaiah 40:3   ^d8 Or *in*

into the lake, for they were fisher-men. ¹⁷"Come, follow me," Jesus said, "and I will make you fishers of men." ¹⁸At once they left their nets and followed him.   Mt 4:19

¹⁹When he had gone a little far-ther, he saw James son of Zebedee and his brother John in a boat, pre-paring their nets. ²⁰Without delay he called them, and they left their father Zebedee in the boat with the hired men and followed him.

Jesus Drives Out an Evil Spirit

²¹They went to Capernaum, and when the Sabbath came, Jesus went into the synagogue and be-gan to teach. ²²The people were amazed at his teaching, because he taught them as one who had authority, not as the teachers of the law. ²³Just then a man in their synagogue who was possessed by an evilᵃ spirit cried out, ²⁴"What do you want with us, Jesus of Naz-areth? Have you come to destroy us? I know who you are—the Holy One of God!"   Mt 7:28-29; 8:29; Lk 1:35

²⁵"Be quiet!" said Jesus sternly. "Come out of him!" ²⁶The evil spir-it shook the man violently and came out of him with a shriek.

²⁷The people were all so amazed that they asked each other, "What is this? A new teaching—and with authority! He even gives orders to evil spirits and they obey him." ²⁸News about him spread quickly over the whole region of Galilee.

Jesus Heals Many

²⁹As soon as they left the syna-gogue, they went with James and John to the home of Simon and Andrew. ³⁰Simon's mother-in-law was in bed with a fever, and they told Jesus about her. ³¹So he went to her, took her hand and helped her up. The fever left her and she began to wait on them.   Mt 8:14-15

³²That evening after sunset the people brought to Jesus all the sick and demon-possessed. ³³The whole town gathered at the door, ³⁴and Jesus healed many who had various diseases. He also drove out many demons, but he would not let the demons speak because they knew who he was.   Mt 8:16-17

Jesus Prays in a Solitary Place

³⁵Very early in the morning, while it was still dark, Jesus got up, left the house and went off to a solitary place, where he prayed. ³⁶Simon and his companions went to look for him, ³⁷and when they found him, they exclaimed: "Ev-eryone is looking for you!"   Lk 3:21

³⁸Jesus replied, "Let us go some-where else—to the nearby villages —so I can preach there also. That is why I have come." ³⁹So he trav-eled throughout Galilee, preaching in their synagogues and driving out demons.   Lk 4:42-43

ᵃ23 Greek unclean; also in verses 26 and 27

A Man With Leprosy

40A man with leprosy[a] came to him and begged him on his knees, "If you are willing, you can make me clean." Mk 10:17

41Filled with compassion, Jesus reached out his hand and touched the man. "I am willing," he said. "Be clean!" **42**Immediately the leprosy left him and he was cured.

43Jesus sent him away at once with a strong warning: **44**"See that you don't tell this to anyone. But go, show yourself to the priest and offer the sacrifices that Moses commanded for your cleansing, as a testimony to them." **45**Instead he went out and began to talk freely, spreading the news. As a result, Jesus could no longer enter a town openly but stayed outside in lonely places. Yet the people still came to him from everywhere. Mt 8:2-4

Jesus Heals a Paralytic

2 A few days later, when Jesus again entered Capernaum, the people heard that he had come home. **2**So many gathered that there was no room left, not even outside the door, and he preached the word to them. **3**Some men came, bringing to him a paralytic, carried by four of them. **4**Since they could not get him to Jesus because of the crowd, they made an opening in the roof above Jesus and, after digging through it, low-ered the mat the paralyzed man was lying on. **5**When Jesus saw their faith, he said to the paralytic, "Son, your sins are forgiven."

6Now some teachers of the law were sitting there, thinking to themselves, **7**"Why does this fellow talk like that? He's blaspheming! Who can forgive sins but God alone?" Isa 43:25

8Immediately Jesus knew in his spirit that this was what they were thinking in their hearts, and he said to them, "Why are you thinking these things? **9**Which is easier: to say to the paralytic, 'Your sins are forgiven,' or to say, 'Get up, take your mat and walk'? **10**But that you may know that the Son of Man has authority on earth to forgive sins . . . ." He said to the paralytic, **11**"I tell you, get up, take your mat and go home." **12**He got up, took his mat and walked out in full view of them all. This amazed everyone and they praised God, saying, "We have never seen anything like this!" Mt 9:2-8; Lk 5:18-26

The Calling of Levi

13Once again Jesus went out beside the lake. A large crowd came to him, and he began to teach them. **14**As he walked along, he saw Levi son of Alphaeus sitting at the tax collector's booth. "Follow me," Jesus told him, and Levi got up and followed him. Mt 4:19

15While Jesus was having dinner

---

a40 The Greek word was used for various diseases affecting the skin—not necessarily leprosy.

at Levi's house, many tax collectors and "sinners" were eating with him and his disciples, for there were many who followed him. [16]When the teachers of the law who were Pharisees saw him eating with the "sinners" and tax collectors, they asked his disciples: "Why does he eat with tax collectors and 'sinners'?" Mt 9:11

[17]On hearing this, Jesus said to them, "It is not the healthy who need a doctor, but the sick. I have not come to call the righteous, but sinners." Mt 9:9-13; Lk 5:27-32

Jesus Questioned About Fasting

[18]Now John's disciples and the Pharisees were fasting. Some people came and asked Jesus, "How is it that John's disciples and the disciples of the Pharisees are fasting, but yours are not?" Mt 6:16-18; Ac 13:2

[19]Jesus answered, "How can the guests of the bridegroom fast while he is with them? They cannot, so long as they have him with them. [20]But the time will come when the bridegroom will be taken from them, and on that day they will fast. Lk 17:22

[21]"No one sews a patch of unshrunk cloth on an old garment. If he does, the new piece will pull away from the old, making the tear worse. [22]And no one pours new wine into old wineskins. If he does, the wine will burst the skins, and both the wine and the wine-

skins will be ruined. No, he pours new wine into new wineskins."

Lord of the Sabbath

[23]One Sabbath Jesus was going through the grainfields, and as his disciples walked along, they began to pick some heads of grain. [24]The Pharisees said to him, "Look, why are they doing what is unlawful on the Sabbath?" Dt 23:25; Mt 12:2

[25]He answered, "Have you never read what David did when he and his companions were hungry and in need? [26]In the days of Abiathar the high priest, he entered the house of God and ate the consecrated bread, which is lawful only for priests to eat. And he also gave some to his companions."

[27]Then he said to them, "The Sabbath was made for man, not man for the Sabbath. [28]So the Son of Man is Lord even of the Sabbath." Mt 12:1-8; Lk 6:1-5

3 Another time he went into the synagogue, and a man with a shriveled hand was there. [2]Some of them were looking for a reason to accuse Jesus, so they watched him closely to see if he would heal him on the Sabbath. [3]Jesus said to the man with the shriveled hand, "Stand up in front of everyone."

[4]Then Jesus asked them, "Which is lawful on the Sabbath: to do good or to do evil, to save life or to kill?" But they remained silent.

[5]He looked around at them in anger and, deeply distressed at

their stubborn hearts, said to the man, "Stretch out your hand." He stretched it out, and his hand was completely restored. ⁶Then the Pharisees went out and began to plot with the Herodians how they might kill Jesus.   Mt 12:9-14; Lk 6:6-11

Crowds Follow Jesus

⁷Jesus withdrew with his disciples to the lake, and a large crowd from Galilee followed. ⁸When they heard all he was doing, many people came to him from Judea, Jerusalem, Idumea, and the regions across the Jordan and around Tyre and Sidon. ⁹Because of the crowd he told his disciples to have a small boat ready for him, to keep the people from crowding him. ¹⁰For he had healed many, so that those with diseases were pushing forward to touch him. ¹¹Whenever the evil[a] spirits saw him, they fell down before him and cried out, "You are the Son of God." ¹²But he gave them strict orders not to tell who he was.   Mt 12:15-16; Lk 6:17-19

The Appointing of the Twelve Apostles

¹³Jesus went up on a mountainside and called to him those he wanted, and they came to him. ¹⁴He appointed twelve—designating them apostles[b]—that they might be with him and that he might send them out to preach

¹⁵and to have authority to drive out demons. ¹⁶These are the twelve he appointed: Simon (to whom he gave the name Peter); ¹⁷James son of Zebedee and his brother John (to them he gave the name Boanerges, which means Sons of Thunder); ¹⁸Andrew, Philip, Bartholomew, Matthew, Thomas, James son of Alphaeus, Thaddaeus, Simon the Zealot ¹⁹and Judas Iscariot, who betrayed him.   Mt 10:2-4

Jesus and Beelzebub

²⁰Then Jesus entered a house, and again a crowd gathered, so that he and his disciples were not even able to eat. ²¹When his family heard about this, they went to take charge of him, for they said, "He is out of his mind."   Jn 10:20; Ac 26:24

²²And the teachers of the law who came down from Jerusalem said, "He is possessed by Beelzebub[c]! By the prince of demons he is driving out demons."   Mt 9:34

²³So Jesus called them and spoke to them in parables: "How can Satan drive out Satan? ²⁴If a kingdom is divided against itself, that kingdom cannot stand. ²⁵If a house is divided against itself, that house cannot stand. ²⁶And if Satan opposes himself and is divided, he cannot stand; his end has come. ²⁷In fact, no one can enter a strong man's house and carry off his possessions unless he first ties up the

---

[a] 11 Greek unclean; also in verse 30   [b] 14 Some manuscripts do not have designating them apostles.
[c] 22 Greek Beezeboul or Beelzeboul

strong man. Then he can rob his house. [28]I tell you the truth, all the sins and blasphemies of men will be forgiven them. [29]But whoever blasphemes against the Holy Spirit will never be forgiven; he is guilty of an eternal sin." Mt 12:25-29

[30]He said this because they were saying, "He has an evil spirit."

Jesus' Mother and Brothers

[31]Then Jesus' mother and brothers arrived. Standing outside, they sent someone in to call him. [32]A crowd was sitting around him, and they told him, "Your mother and brothers are outside looking for you." ver 21

[33]"Who are my mother and my brothers?" he asked.

[34]Then he looked at those seated in a circle around him and said, "Here are my mother and my brothers! [35]Whoever does God's will is my brother and sister and mother." Mt 12:46-50; Lk 8:19-21

The Parable of the Sower

4 Again Jesus began to teach by the lake. The crowd that gathered around him was so large that he got into a boat and sat in it out on the lake, while all the people were along the shore at the water's edge. [2]He taught them many things by parables, and in his teaching said: [3]"Listen! A farmer went out to sow his seed. [4]As he was scattering the seed, some fell along the path, and the birds came and ate it up. [5]Some fell on rocky places, where it did not have much soil. It sprang up quickly, because the soil was shallow. [6]But when the sun came up, the plants were scorched, and they withered because they had no root. [7]Other seed fell among thorns, which grew up and choked the plants, so that they did not bear grain. [8]Still other seed fell on good soil. It came up, grew and produced a crop, multiplying thirty, sixty, or even a hundred times." Mk 3:23

[9]Then Jesus said, "He who has ears to hear, let him hear."

[10]When he was alone, the Twelve and the others around him asked him about the parables. [11]He told them, "The secret of the kingdom of God has been given to you. But to those on the outside everything is said in parables [12]so that,

" 'they may be ever seeing but
        never perceiving,
    and ever hearing but never
        understanding;
    otherwise they might turn and
        be forgiven!'[a]" Mt 13:1-15

[13]Then Jesus said to them, "Don't you understand this parable? How then will you understand any parable? [14]The farmer sows the word. [15]Some people are like seed along the path, where the word is sown. As soon as they hear it, Satan comes and takes away the

a 12 Isaiah 6:9,10

word that was sown in them. [16]Others, like seed sown on rocky places, hear the word and at once receive it with joy. [17]But since they have no root, they last only a short time. When trouble or persecution comes because of the word, they quickly fall away. [18]Still others, like seed sown among thorns, hear the word; [19]but the worries of this life, the deceitfulness of wealth and the desires for other things come in and choke the word, making it unfruitful. [20]Others, like seed sown on good soil, hear the word, accept it, and produce a crop— thirty, sixty or even a hundred times what was sown."   Mt 13:18-23

A Lamp on a Stand

[21]He said to them, "Do you bring in a lamp to put it under a bowl or a bed? Instead, don't you put it on its stand? [22]For whatever is hidden is meant to be disclosed, and whatever is concealed is meant to be brought out into the open. [23]If anyone has ears to hear, let him hear."

[24]"Consider carefully what you hear," he continued. "With the measure you use, it will be measured to you—and even more. [25]Whoever has will be given more; whoever does not have, even what he has will be taken from him."

The Parable of the Growing Seed

[26]He also said, "This is what the kingdom of God is like. A man scatters seed on the ground. [27]Night and day, whether he sleeps or gets up, the seed sprouts and grows, though he does not know how. [28]All by itself the soil produces grain—first the stalk, then the head, then the full kernel in the head. [29]As soon as the grain is ripe, he puts the sickle to it, because the harvest has come."   Mt 13:24; Rev 14:15

The Parable of the Mustard Seed

[30]Again he said, "What shall we say the kingdom of God is like, or what parable shall we use to describe it? [31]It is like a mustard seed, which is the smallest seed you plant in the ground. [32]Yet when planted, it grows and becomes the largest of all garden plants, with such big branches that the birds of the air can perch in its shade."

[33]With many similar parables Jesus spoke the word to them, as much as they could understand. [34]He did not say anything to them without using a parable. But when he was alone with his own disciples, he explained everything.

Jesus Calms the Storm

[35]That day when evening came, he said to his disciples, "Let us go over to the other side." [36]Leaving the crowd behind, they took him along, just as he was, in the boat. There were also other boats with him. [37]A furious squall came up, and the waves broke over the boat,

so that it was nearly swamped. ³⁸Jesus was in the stern, sleeping on a cushion. The disciples woke him and said to him, "Teacher, don't you care if we drown?"

³⁹He got up, rebuked the wind and said to the waves, "Quiet! Be still!" Then the wind died down and it was completely calm.

⁴⁰He said to his disciples, "Why are you so afraid? Do you still have no faith?"   Mt 14:31; Mk 16:14

⁴¹They were terrified and asked each other, "Who is this? Even the wind and the waves obey him!"

The Healing of a Demon-possessed Man

5 They went across the lake to the region of the Gerasenes.ᵃ ²When Jesus got out of the boat, a man with an evilᵇ spirit came from the tombs to meet him. ³This man lived in the tombs, and no one could bind him any more, not even with a chain. ⁴For he had often been chained hand and foot, but he tore the chains apart and broke the irons on his feet. No one was strong enough to subdue him. ⁵Night and day among the tombs and in the hills he would cry out and cut himself with stones.

⁶When he saw Jesus from a distance, he ran and fell on his knees in front of him. ⁷He shouted at the top of his voice, "What do you want with me, Jesus, Son of the Most High God? Swear to God that you won't torture me!" ⁸For Jesus had said to him, "Come out of this man, you evil spirit!"   Mt 8:29

⁹Then Jesus asked him, "What is your name?"

"My name is Legion," he replied, "for we are many." ¹⁰And he begged Jesus again and again not to send them out of the area.

¹¹A large herd of pigs was feeding on the nearby hillside. ¹²The demons begged Jesus, "Send us among the pigs; allow us to go into them." ¹³He gave them permission, and the evil spirits came out and went into the pigs. The herd, about two thousand in number, rushed down the steep bank into the lake and were drowned.

¹⁴Those tending the pigs ran off and reported this in the town and countryside, and the people went out to see what had happened. ¹⁵When they came to Jesus, they saw the man who had been possessed by the legion of demons, sitting there, dressed and in his right mind; and they were afraid. ¹⁶Those who had seen it told the people what had happened to the demon-possessed man—and told about the pigs as well. ¹⁷Then the people began to plead with Jesus to leave their region.   Mt 8:28-34

¹⁸As Jesus was getting into the boat, the man who had been demon-possessed begged to go with

---

ᵃ1 Some manuscripts Gadarenes; other manuscripts Gergesenes   ᵇ2 Greek unclean; also in verses 8 and 13

him. ¹⁹Jesus did not let him, but said, "Go home to your family and tell them how much the Lord has done for you, and how he has had mercy on you." ²⁰So the man went away and began to tell in the Decapolis*a* how much Jesus had done for him. And all the people were amazed.   Lk 8:38-39

A Dead Girl and a Sick Woman

²¹When Jesus had again crossed over by boat to the other side of the lake, a large crowd gathered around him while he was by the lake. ²²Then one of the synagogue rulers, named Jairus, came there. Seeing Jesus, he fell at his feet ²³and pleaded earnestly with him, "My little daughter is dying. Please come and put your hands on her so that she will be healed and live." ²⁴So Jesus went with him.   Mk 6:5

A large crowd followed and pressed around him. ²⁵And a woman was there who had been subject to bleeding for twelve years. ²⁶She had suffered a great deal under the care of many doctors and had spent all she had, yet instead of getting better she grew worse. ²⁷When she heard about Jesus, she came up behind him in the crowd and touched his cloak, ²⁸because she thought, "If I just touch his clothes, I will be healed." ²⁹Immediately her bleeding stopped and she felt in her body that she was freed from her suffering.

³⁰At once Jesus realized that power had gone out from him. He turned around in the crowd and asked, "Who touched my clothes?"

³¹"You see the people crowding against you," his disciples answered, "and yet you can ask, 'Who touched me?' "

³²But Jesus kept looking around to see who had done it. ³³Then the woman, knowing what had happened to her, came and fell at his feet and, trembling with fear, told him the whole truth. ³⁴He said to her, "Daughter, your faith has healed you. Go in peace and be freed from your suffering."   Mt 9:22

³⁵While Jesus was still speaking, some men came from the house of Jairus, the synagogue ruler. "Your daughter is dead," they said. "Why bother the teacher any more?"

³⁶Ignoring what they said, Jesus told the synagogue ruler, "Don't be afraid; just believe."

³⁷He did not let anyone follow him except Peter, James and John the brother of James. ³⁸When they came to the home of the synagogue ruler, Jesus saw a commotion, with people crying and wailing loudly. ³⁹

"Why all this commotion and wailing? The child is not dead but asleep." ⁴⁰But they laughed at him.   Mt 4:21; 9:24

a20 That is, the Ten Cities

After he put them all out, he took the child's father and mother and the disciples who were with him, and went in where the child was. [41]He took her by the hand and said to her, *"Talitha koum!"* (which means, "Little girl, I say to you, get up!"). [42]Immediately the girl stood up and walked around (she was twelve years old). At this they were completely astonished. [43]He gave strict orders not to let anyone know about this, and told them to give her something to eat.

A Prophet Without Honor

6 Jesus left there and went to his hometown, accompanied by his disciples. [2]When the Sabbath came, he began to teach in the synagogue, and many who heard him were amazed. Mt 4:23; 7:28

"Where did this man get these things?" they asked. "What's this wisdom that has been given him, that he even does miracles! [3]Isn't this the carpenter? Isn't this Mary's son and the brother of James, Joseph,[a] Judas and Simon? Aren't his sisters here with us?" And they took offense at him.

[4]Jesus said to them, "Only in his hometown, among his relatives and in his own house is a prophet without honor." [5]He could not do any miracles there, except lay his hands on a few sick people and heal them. [6]And he was amazed at their lack of faith. Mt 13:54-58

Jesus Sends Out the Twelve

Then Jesus went around teaching from village to village. [7]Calling the Twelve to him, he sent them out two by two and gave them authority over evil[b] spirits. Mt 10:1

[8]These were his instructions: "Take nothing for the journey except a staff—no bread, no bag, no money in your belts. [9]Wear sandals but not an extra tunic. [10]Whenever you enter a house, stay there until you leave that town. [11]And if any place will not welcome you or listen to you, shake the dust off your feet when you leave, as a testimony against them." Mt 10:1,9-14; Lk 9:1,3-5

[12]They went out and preached that people should repent. [13]They drove out many demons and anointed many sick people with oil and healed them. Lk 9:6; Jas 5:14

John the Baptist Beheaded

[14]King Herod heard about this, for Jesus' name had become well known. Some were saying,[c] "John the Baptist has been raised from the dead, and that is why miraculous powers are at work in him."

[15]Others said, "He is Elijah."

And still others claimed, "He is a prophet, like one of the prophets of long ago." Mt 16:14; Mk 8:28

[16]But when Herod heard this, he said, "John, the man I beheaded, has been raised from the dead!" [17]For Herod himself had given

---

[a]3 Greek *Joses*, a variant of *Joseph*   [b]7 Greek *unclean*   [c]14 Some early manuscripts *He was saying*

orders to have John arrested, and he had him bound and put in prison. He did this because of Herodias, his brother Philip's wife, whom he had married. [18]For John had been saying to Herod, "It is not lawful for you to have your brother's wife." [19]So Herodias nursed a grudge against John and wanted to kill him. But she was not able to, [20]because Herod feared John and protected him, knowing him to be a righteous and holy man. When Herod heard John, he was greatly puzzled[a]; yet he liked to listen to him.   Lev 18:16; Mt 21:26

[21]Finally the opportune time came. On his birthday Herod gave a banquet for his high officials and military commanders and the leading men of Galilee. [22]When the daughter of Herodias came in and danced, she pleased Herod and his dinner guests.   Est 1:3; Lk 3:1

The king said to the girl, "Ask me for anything you want, and I'll give it to you." [23]And he promised her with an oath, "Whatever you ask I will give you, up to half my kingdom."   Est 5:3,6; 7:2

[24]She went out and said to her mother, "What shall I ask for?"

"The head of John the Baptist," she answered.

[25]At once the girl hurried in to the king with the request: "I want you to give me right now the head of John the Baptist on a platter."

[26]The king was greatly distressed, but because of his oaths and his dinner guests, he did not want to refuse her. [27]So he immediately sent an executioner with orders to bring John's head. The man went, beheaded John in the prison, [28]and brought back his head on a platter. He presented it to the girl, and she gave it to her mother. [29]On hearing of this, John's disciples came and took his body and laid it in a tomb.

Jesus Feeds the Five Thousand

[30]The apostles gathered around Jesus and reported to him all they had done and taught. [31]Then, because so many people were coming and going that they did not even have a chance to eat, he said to them, "Come with me by yourselves to a quiet place and get some rest."   Lk 9:10; Ac 1:2,26

[32]So they went away by themselves in a boat to a solitary place. [33]But many who saw them leaving recognized them and ran on foot from all the towns and got there ahead of them. [34]When Jesus landed and saw a large crowd, he had compassion on them, because they were like sheep without a shepherd. So he began teaching them many things.   Mt 14:13-21

[35]By this time it was late in the day, so his disciples came to him. "This is a remote place," they said, "and it's already very late. [36]Send the people away so they can go to

---

[a] 20 Some early manuscripts *he did many things*

the surrounding countryside and villages and buy themselves something to eat." Mk 8:2-9

37But he answered, "You give them something to eat."

They said to him, "That would take eight months of a man's wages[a]! Are we to go and spend that much on bread and give it to them to eat?" 2Ki 4:42-44

38"How many loaves do you have?" he asked. "Go and see."

When they found out, they said, "Five—and two fish." Lk 9:10-17

39Then Jesus directed them to have all the people sit down in groups on the green grass. **40**So they sat down in groups of hundreds and fifties. **41**Taking the five loaves and the two fish and looking up to heaven, he gave thanks and broke the loaves. Then he gave them to his disciples to set before the people. He also divided the two fish among them all. **42**They all ate and were satisfied, **43**and the disciples picked up twelve basketfuls of broken pieces of bread and fish. **44**The number of the men who had eaten was five thousand. Jn 6:5-13

Jesus Walks on the Water

45Immediately Jesus made his disciples get into the boat and go on ahead of him to Bethsaida, while he dismissed the crowd. **46**After leaving them, he went up on a mountainside to pray.

47When evening came, the boat was in the middle of the lake, and he was alone on land. **48**He saw the disciples straining at the oars, because the wind was against them. About the fourth watch of the night he went out to them, walking on the lake. He was about to pass by them, **49**but when they saw him walking on the lake, they thought he was a ghost. They cried out, **50**because they all saw him and were terrified. Lk 24:37

Immediately he spoke to them and said, "Take courage! It is I. Don't be afraid." **51**Then he climbed into the boat with them, and the wind died down. They were completely amazed, **52**for they had not understood about the loaves; their hearts were hardened. Mt 14:22-32; Jn 6:15-21

53When they had crossed over, they landed at Gennesaret and anchored there. **54**As soon as they got out of the boat, people recognized Jesus. **55**They ran throughout that whole region and carried the sick on mats to wherever they heard he was. **56**And wherever he went—into villages, towns or countryside—they placed the sick in the marketplaces. They begged him to let them touch even the edge of his cloak, and all who touched him were healed. Mt 14:34-36

a 37 Greek *take two hundred denarii*

Clean and Unclean

7 The Pharisees and some of the teachers of the law who had come from Jerusalem gathered around Jesus and ²saw some of his disciples eating food with hands that were "unclean," that is, unwashed. ³(The Pharisees and all the Jews do not eat unless they give their hands a ceremonial washing, holding to the tradition of the elders. ⁴When they come from the marketplace they do not eat unless they wash. And they observe many other traditions, such as the washing of cups, pitchers and kettles.ᵃ)   Mt 23:25; Ac 10:14,28

⁵So the Pharisees and teachers of the law asked Jesus, "Why don't your disciples live according to the tradition of the elders instead of eating their food with 'unclean' hands?"   Gal 1:14; Col 2:8

⁶He replied, "Isaiah was right when he prophesied about you hypocrites; as it is written:

" 'These people honor me with
        their lips,
    but their hearts are far from
        me.
⁷They worship me in vain;
    their teachings are but rules
        taught by men.'ᵇ

⁸You have let go of the commands of God and are holding on to the traditions of men."

⁹And he said to them: "You have a fine way of setting aside the commands of God in order to observeᶜ your own traditions! ¹⁰For Moses said, 'Honor your father and your mother,'ᵈ and, 'Anyone who curses his father or mother must be put to death.'ᵉ ¹¹But you say that if a man says to his father or mother: 'Whatever help you might otherwise have received from me is Corban' (that is, a gift devoted to God), ¹²then you no longer let him do anything for his father or mother. ¹³Thus you nullify the word of God by your tradition that you have handed down. And you do many things like that."   Mt 23:16,18

¹⁴Again Jesus called the crowd to him and said, "Listen to me, everyone, and understand this. ¹⁵Nothing outside a man can make him 'unclean' by going into him. Rather, it is what comes out of a man that makes him 'unclean.'ᶠ"

¹⁷After he had left the crowd and entered the house, his disciples asked him about this parable. ¹⁸"Are you so dull?" he asked. "Don't you see that nothing that enters a man from the outside can make him 'unclean'? ¹⁹For it doesn't go into his heart but into his stomach, and then out of his body." (In saying this, Jesus declared all foods "clean.")   Ac 10:15

ᵃ4 Some early manuscripts *pitchers, kettles and dining couches*   ᵇ6,7 Isaiah 29:13   ᶜ9 Some manuscripts *set up*   ᵈ10 Exodus 20:12; Deut. 5:16   ᵉ10 Exodus 21:17; Lev. 20:9   ᶠ15 Some early manuscripts *'unclean.'* ¹⁶*If anyone has ears to hear, let him hear.*

20He went on: "What comes out of a man is what makes him 'unclean.' **21**For from within, out of men's hearts, come evil thoughts, sexual immorality, theft, murder, adultery, **22**greed, malice, deceit, lewdness, envy, slander, arrogance and folly. **23**All these evils come from inside and make a man 'unclean.' "   Mt 15:1-20

The Faith of a Syrophoenician Woman

24Jesus left that place and went to the vicinity of Tyre.*a* He entered a house and did not want anyone to know it; yet he could not keep his presence secret. **25**In fact, as soon as she heard about him, a woman whose little daughter was possessed by an evil*b* spirit came and fell at his feet. **26**The woman was a Greek, born in Syrian Phoenicia. She begged Jesus to drive the demon out of her daughter.

27"First let the children eat all they want," he told her, "for it is not right to take the children's bread and toss it to their dogs."

28"Yes, Lord," she replied, "but even the dogs under the table eat the children's crumbs."

29Then he told her, "For such a reply, you may go; the demon has left your daughter."

30She went home and found her child lying on the bed, and the demon gone.   Mt 15:21-28

The Healing of a Deaf and Mute Man

31Then Jesus left the vicinity of Tyre and went through Sidon, down to the Sea of Galilee and into the region of the Decapolis.*c* **32**There some people brought to him a man who was deaf and could hardly talk, and they begged him to place his hand on the man.

33After he took him aside, away from the crowd, Jesus put his fingers into the man's ears. Then he spit and touched the man's tongue. **34**He looked up to heaven and with a deep sigh said to him, *"Ephphatha!"* (which means, "Be opened!"). **35**At this, the man's ears were opened, his tongue was loosened and he began to speak plainly.   Isa 35:5-6

36Jesus commanded them not to tell anyone. But the more he did so, the more they kept talking about it. **37**People were overwhelmed with amazement. "He has done everything well," they said. "He even makes the deaf hear and the mute speak."   Mt 15:29-31

Jesus Feeds the Four Thousand

8 During those days another large crowd gathered. Since they had nothing to eat, Jesus called his disciples to him and said, **2**"I have compassion for these

---

a 24 Many early manuscripts *Tyre and Sidon*   *b 25* Greek *unclean*   *c 31* That is, the Ten Cities

people; they have already been with me three days and have nothing to eat. ³If I send them home hungry, they will collapse on the way, because some of them have come a long distance."   Mt 9:36

⁴His disciples answered, "But where in this remote place can anyone get enough bread to feed them?"

⁵"How many loaves do you have?" Jesus asked.

"Seven," they replied.

⁶He told the crowd to sit down on the ground. When he had taken the seven loaves and given thanks, he broke them and gave them to his disciples to set before the people, and they did so. ⁷They had a few small fish as well; he gave thanks for them also and told the disciples to distribute them. ⁸The people ate and were satisfied. Afterward the disciples picked up seven basketfuls of broken pieces that were left over. ⁹About four thousand men were present. And having sent them away, ¹⁰he got into the boat with his disciples and went to the region of Dalmanutha.

¹¹The Pharisees came and began to question Jesus. To test him, they asked him for a sign from heaven. ¹²He sighed deeply and said, "Why does this generation ask for a miraculous sign? I tell you the truth, no sign will be given to it." ¹³Then he left them, got back into the boat and crossed to the other side.   Mt 12:38; Mk 7:34

The Yeast of the Pharisees and Herod

¹⁴The disciples had forgotten to bring bread, except for one loaf they had with them in the boat. ¹⁵"Be careful," Jesus warned them. "Watch out for the yeast of the Pharisees and that of Herod."

¹⁶They discussed this with one another and said, "It is because we have no bread."

¹⁷Aware of their discussion, Jesus asked them: "Why are you talking about having no bread? Do you still not see or understand? Are your hearts hardened? ¹⁸Do you have eyes but fail to see, and ears but fail to hear? And don't you remember? ¹⁹When I broke the five loaves for the five thousand, how many basketfuls of pieces did you pick up?"   Isa 6:9-10; Mk 6:52

"Twelve," they replied.   Mt 14:20

²⁰"And when I broke the seven loaves for the four thousand, how many basketfuls of pieces did you pick up?"

They answered, "Seven."

²¹He said to them, "Do you still not understand?"   Mk 6:52

The Healing of a Blind Man at Bethsaida

²²They came to Bethsaida, and some people brought a blind man and begged Jesus to touch him. ²³He took the blind man by the hand and led him outside the village. When he had spit on the man's eyes and put his hands on

him, Jesus asked, "Do you see anything?"   Mk 5:23; 7:33

[24]He looked up and said, "I see people; they look like trees walking around."

[25]Once more Jesus put his hands on the man's eyes. Then his eyes were opened, his sight was restored, and he saw everything clearly. [26]Jesus sent him home, saying, "Don't go into the village.[a]"

Peter's Confession of Christ

[27]Jesus and his disciples went on to the villages around Caesarea Philippi. On the way he asked them, "Who do people say I am?"

[28]They replied, "Some say John the Baptist; others say Elijah; and still others, one of the prophets."

[29]"But what about you?" he asked. "Who do you say I am?"

Peter answered, "You are the Christ.[b]"   Mt 16:13-16; Lk 9:18-20

[30]Jesus warned them not to tell anyone about him.   Mt 8:4; 16:20; 17:9

Jesus Predicts His Death

[31]He then began to teach them that the Son of Man must suffer many things and be rejected by the elders, chief priests and teachers of the law, and that he must be killed and after three days rise again. [32]He spoke plainly about this, and Peter took him aside and began to rebuke him.   Mt 16:21

[33]But when Jesus turned and looked at his disciples, he rebuked Peter. "Get behind me, Satan!" he said. "You do not have in mind the things of God, but the things of men."   Mt 4:10

[34]Then he called the crowd to him along with his disciples and said: "If anyone would come after me, he must deny himself and take up his cross and follow me. [35]For whoever wants to save his life[c] will lose it, but whoever loses his life for me and for the gospel will save it. [36]What good is it for a man to gain the whole world, yet forfeit his soul? [37]Or what can a man give in exchange for his soul? [38]If anyone is ashamed of me and my words in this adulterous and sinful generation, the Son of Man will be ashamed of him when he comes in his Father's glory with the holy angels."   Mt 10:33; Jn 12:25

9 And he said to them, "I tell you the truth, some who are standing here will not taste death before they see the kingdom of God come with power."   Mt 16:21-28; Lk 9:22-27

The Transfiguration

[2]After six days Jesus took Peter, James and John with him and led them up a high mountain, where they were all alone. There he was transfigured before them. [3]His clothes became dazzling white, whiter than anyone in the world

---

[a] 26 Some manuscripts *Don't go and tell anyone in the village*   [b] 29 Or *Messiah.* "The Christ" (Greek) and "the Messiah" (Hebrew) both mean "the Anointed One."   [c] 35 The Greek word means either *life* or *soul*; also in verse 36.

could bleach them. 4And there appeared before them Elijah and Moses, who were talking with Jesus.

5Peter said to Jesus, "Rabbi, it is good for us to be here. Let us put up three shelters—one for you, one for Moses and one for Elijah." 6(He did not know what to say, they were so frightened.)   Mt 23:7

7Then a cloud appeared and enveloped them, and a voice came from the cloud: "This is my Son, whom I love. Listen to him!"

8Suddenly, when they looked around, they no longer saw anyone with them except Jesus.

9As they were coming down the mountain, Jesus gave them orders not to tell anyone what they had seen until the Son of Man had risen from the dead. 10They kept the matter to themselves, discussing what "rising from the dead" meant.   Mt 8:20; Mk 8:30

11And they asked him, "Why do the teachers of the law say that Elijah must come first?"

12Jesus replied, "To be sure, Elijah does come first, and restores all things. Why then is it written that the Son of Man must suffer much and be rejected? 13But I tell you, Elijah has come, and they have done to him everything they wished, just as it is written about him."   Mt 17:1-13

The Healing of a Boy With an Evil Spirit

14When they came to the other disciples, they saw a large crowd around them and the teachers of the law arguing with them. 15As soon as all the people saw Jesus, they were overwhelmed with wonder and ran to greet him.

16"What are you arguing with them about?" he asked.

17A man in the crowd answered, "Teacher, I brought you my son, who is possessed by a spirit that has robbed him of speech. 18Whenever it seizes him, it throws him to the ground. He foams at the mouth, gnashes his teeth and becomes rigid. I asked your disciples to drive out the spirit, but they could not."

19"O unbelieving generation," Jesus replied, "how long shall I stay with you? How long shall I put up with you? Bring the boy to me."

20So they brought him. When the spirit saw Jesus, it immediately threw the boy into a convulsion. He fell to the ground and rolled around, foaming at the mouth.

21Jesus asked the boy's father, "How long has he been like this?"

"From childhood," he answered. 22"It has often thrown him into fire or water to kill him. But if you can do anything, take pity on us and help us."

23" 'If you can'?" said Jesus. "Everything is possible for him who believes."   Mk 11:23; Jn 11:40

24Immediately the boy's father exclaimed, "I do believe; help me overcome my unbelief!"

25When Jesus saw that a crowd

was running to the scene, he rebuked the evil*a* spirit. "You deaf and mute spirit," he said, "I command you, come out of him and never enter him again."

²⁶The spirit shrieked, convulsed him violently and came out. The boy looked so much like a corpse that many said, "He's dead." ²⁷But Jesus took him by the hand and lifted him to his feet, and he stood up.

²⁸After Jesus had gone indoors, his disciples asked him privately, "Why couldn't we drive it out?"

²⁹He replied, "This kind can come out only by prayer.*b*"

³⁰They left that place and passed through Galilee. Jesus did not want anyone to know where they were, ³¹because he was teaching his disciples. He said to them, "The Son of Man is going to be betrayed into the hands of men. They will kill him, and after three days he will rise." ³²But they did not understand what he meant and were afraid to ask him about it.

Who Is the Greatest?

³³They came to Capernaum. When he was in the house, he asked them, "What were you arguing about on the road?" ³⁴But they kept quiet because on the way they had argued about who was the greatest.   Mt 4:13; Lk 22:24

³⁵Sitting down, Jesus called the Twelve and said, "If anyone wants to be first, he must be the very last, and the servant of all."   Mt 20:26

³⁶He took a little child and had him stand among them. Taking him in his arms, he said to them, ³⁷"Whoever welcomes one of these little children in my name welcomes me; and whoever welcomes me does not welcome me but the one who sent me."

Whoever Is Not Against Us Is for Us

³⁸"Teacher," said John, "we saw a man driving out demons in your name and we told him to stop, because he was not one of us."

³⁹"Do not stop him," Jesus said. "No one who does a miracle in my name can in the next moment say anything bad about me, ⁴⁰for whoever is not against us is for us. ⁴¹I tell you the truth, anyone who gives you a cup of water in my name because you belong to Christ will certainly not lose his reward.   Mt 10:42; Mt 12:30; Lk 11:23

Causing to Sin

⁴²"And if anyone causes one of these little ones who believe in me to sin, it would be better for him to be thrown into the sea with a large millstone tied around his neck. ⁴³If your hand causes you to sin, cut it off. It is better for you to enter life maimed than with two hands to go into hell, where the fire never goes

---

a 25 Greek *unclean*   *b* 29 Some manuscripts *prayer and fasting* out.*a* **45**And if your foot causes you to sin, cut it off. It is better for you to enter life crippled than to have two feet and be thrown into hell.*b* **47**And if your eye causes you to sin, pluck it out. It is better for you to enter the kingdom of God with one eye than to have two eyes and be thrown into hell, **48**where

" 'their worm does not die,
   and the fire is not
      quenched.'*c*

49Everyone will be salted with fire. **50**"Salt is good, but if it loses its saltiness, how can you make it salty again? Have salt in yourselves, and be at peace with each other."   Mt 5:13; Ro 12:18

Divorce

10 Jesus then left that place and went into the region of Judea and across the Jordan. Again crowds of people came to him, and as was his custom, he taught them.   Jn 10:40; 11:7

2Some Pharisees came and tested him by asking, "Is it lawful for a man to divorce his wife?"

3"What did Moses command you?" he replied.

4They said, "Moses permitted a man to write a certificate of divorce and send her away."

5"It was because your hearts were hard that Moses wrote you this law," Jesus replied. **6**"But at the beginning of creation God 'made them male and female.'*d* **7**'For this reason a man will leave his father and mother and be united to his wife,*e* **8**and the two will become one flesh.'*f* So they are no longer two, but one. **9**Therefore what God has joined together, let man not separate."   Ge 5:2; 1Co 6:16

10When they were in the house again, the disciples asked Jesus about this. **11**He answered, "Anyone who divorces his wife and marries another woman commits adultery against her. **12**And if she divorces her husband and marries another man, she commits adultery."   Mt 19:1-9; Lk 16:18; Ro 7:3

The Little Children and Jesus

13People were bringing little children to Jesus to have him touch them, but the disciples rebuked them. **14**When Jesus saw this, he was indignant. He said to them, "Let the little children come to me, and do not hinder them, for the kingdom of God belongs to such as these. **15**I tell you the truth, anyone who will not receive the kingdom of God like a little child will never enter it." **16**And he took the children in his arms, put his hands on them and blessed them.

a 43 Some manuscripts *out,* **44***where* / " *'their worm does not die, / and the fire is not quenched.'*
b 45 Some manuscripts *hell,* **46***where* / " *'their worm does not die, / and the fire is not quenched.'*
c 48 Isaiah 66:24   *d 6* Gen. 1:27   *e 7* Some early manuscripts do not have *and be united to his wife.*
f 8 Gen. 2:24

The Rich Young Man

17As Jesus started on his way, a man ran up to him and fell on his knees before him. "Good teacher," he asked, "what must I do to inherit eternal life?"   Lk 10:25; Ac 20:32

18"Why do you call me good?" Jesus answered. "No one is good —except God alone. **19**You know the commandments: 'Do not murder, do not commit adultery, do not steal, do not give false testimony, do not defraud, honor your father and mother.'[a]"   Ex 20:12-16

20"Teacher," he declared, "all these I have kept since I was a boy."

21Jesus looked at him and loved him. "One thing you lack," he said. "Go, sell everything you have and give to the poor, and you will have treasure in heaven. Then come, follow me."   Mt 6:20; Lk 12:33

22At this the man's face fell. He went away sad, because he had great wealth.

23Jesus looked around and said to his disciples, "How hard it is for the rich to enter the kingdom of God!"   Ps 52:7; 1Ti 6:9-10,17

24The disciples were amazed at his words. But Jesus said again, "Children, how hard it is[b] to enter the kingdom of God! **25**It is easier for a camel to go through the eye of a needle than for a rich man to enter the kingdom of God."

26The disciples were even more amazed, and said to each other, "Who then can be saved?"

27Jesus looked at them and said, "With man this is impossible, but not with God; all things are possible with God."   Mt 19:26

28Peter said to him, "We have left everything to follow you!"

29"I tell you the truth," Jesus replied, "no one who has left home or brothers or sisters or mother or father or children or fields for me and the gospel **30**will fail to receive a hundred times as much in this present age (homes, brothers, sisters, mothers, children and fields —and with them, persecutions) and in the age to come, eternal life. **31**But many who are first will be last, and the last first."   Mt 19:16-30

Jesus Again Predicts His Death

32They were on their way up to Jerusalem, with Jesus leading the way, and the disciples were astonished, while those who followed were afraid. Again he took the Twelve aside and told them what was going to happen to him. **33**"We are going up to Jerusalem," he said, "and the Son of Man will be betrayed to the chief priests and teachers of the law. They will condemn him to death and will hand him over to the Gentiles, **34**who will mock him and spit on him, flog him and kill him. Three days later he will rise."   Mt 20:17-19

---

a 19 Exodus 20:12-16; Deut. 5:16-20   *b* 24 Some manuscripts *is for those who trust in riches*

The Request of James and John

35Then James and John, the sons of Zebedee, came to him. "Teacher," they said, "we want you to do for us whatever we ask."

36"What do you want me to do for you?" he asked.

37They replied, "Let one of us sit at your right and the other at your left in your glory." Mt 19:28

38"You don't know what you are asking," Jesus said. "Can you drink the cup I drink or be baptized with the baptism I am baptized with?" Mt 20:22; Lk 12:50

39"We can," they answered.

Jesus said to them, "You will drink the cup I drink and be baptized with the baptism I am baptized with, **40**but to sit at my right or left is not for me to grant. These places belong to those for whom they have been prepared." Ac 12:2

41When the ten heard about this, they became indignant with James and John. **42**Jesus called them together and said, "You know that those who are regarded as rulers of the Gentiles lord it over them, and their high officials exercise authority over them. **43**Not so with you. Instead, whoever wants to become great among you must be your servant, **44**and whoever wants to be first must be slave of all. **45**For even the Son of Man did not come to be served, but to serve, and to give his life as a ransom for many."

Blind Bartimaeus Receives His Sight

46Then they came to Jericho. As Jesus and his disciples, together with a large crowd, were leaving the city, a blind man, Bartimaeus (that is, the Son of Timaeus), was sitting by the roadside begging. **47**When he heard that it was Jesus of Nazareth, he began to shout, "Jesus, Son of David, have mercy on me!" Mt 9:27; Mk 1:24

48Many rebuked him and told him to be quiet, but he shouted all the more, "Son of David, have mercy on me!"

49Jesus stopped and said, "Call him."

So they called to the blind man, "Cheer up! On your feet! He's calling you." **50**Throwing his cloak aside, he jumped to his feet and came to Jesus.

51"What do you want me to do for you?" Jesus asked him.

The blind man said, "Rabbi, I want to see." Mt 23:7

52"Go," said Jesus, "your faith has healed you." Immediately he received his sight and followed Jesus along the road. Mt 20:29-34

The Triumphal Entry

11 As they approached Jerusalem and came to Bethphage and Bethany at the Mount of Olives, Jesus sent two of his disciples, **2**saying to them, "Go to the village ahead of you, and just as you enter it, you will find a colt tied there, which no one has ever ridden. Untie it and bring it here. ³If anyone asks you, 'Why are you doing this?' tell him, 'The Lord needs it and will send it back here shortly.' "   Nu 19:2; Dt 21:3; Mt 21:1

⁴They went and found a colt outside in the street, tied at a doorway. As they untied it, ⁵some people standing there asked, "What are you doing, untying that colt?" ⁶They answered as Jesus had told them to, and the people let them go. ⁷When they brought the colt to Jesus and threw their cloaks over it, he sat on it. ⁸Many people spread their cloaks on the road, while others spread branches they had cut in the fields. ⁹Those who went ahead and those who followed shouted,   Mt 23:39; Mk 14:16

"Hosanna!ᵃ"

"Blessed is he who comes in
    the name of the Lord!"ᵇ

¹⁰"Blessed is the coming
    kingdom of our father
    David!"

"Hosanna in the highest!"

¹¹Jesus entered Jerusalem and went to the temple. He looked around at everything, but since it was already late, he went out to Bethany with the Twelve.

Jesus Clears the Temple

¹²The next day as they were leaving Bethany, Jesus was hungry. ¹³Seeing in the distance a fig tree in leaf, he went to find out if it had any fruit. When he reached it, he found nothing but leaves, because it was not the season for figs. ¹⁴Then he said to the tree, "May no one ever eat fruit from you again." And his disciples heard him say it.

¹⁵On reaching Jerusalem, Jesus entered the temple area and began driving out those who were buying and selling there. He overturned the tables of the money changers and the benches of those selling doves, ¹⁶and would not allow anyone to carry merchandise through the temple courts. ¹⁷And as he taught them, he said, "Is it not written:

" 'My house will be called
    a house of prayer for all
    nations'ᶜ?

But you have made it 'a den of robbers.'ᵈ"   Mt 21:12-16; Lk 19:45-47

¹⁸The chief priests and the teachers of the law heard this and began looking for a way to kill him, for they feared him, because the whole crowd was amazed at his teaching.   Jn 2:13-16

¹⁹When evening came, theyᵉ went out of the city.   Lk 21:37

The Withered Fig Tree

²⁰In the morning, as they went along, they saw the fig tree with-

---

ᵃ9 A Hebrew expression meaning "Save!" which became an exclamation of praise; also in verse 10
ᵇ9 Psalm 118:25,26   ᶜ17 Isaiah 56:7   ᵈ17 Jer. 7:11   ᵉ19 Some early manuscripts *he*

ered from the roots. ²¹Peter remembered and said to Jesus, "Rabbi, look! The fig tree you cursed has withered!" Mt 23:7

²²"Have*a* faith in God," Jesus answered. ²³"I tell you the truth, if anyone says to this mountain, 'Go, throw yourself into the sea,' and does not doubt in his heart but believes that what he says will happen, it will be done for him. ²⁴Therefore I tell you, whatever you ask for in prayer, believe that you have received it, and it will be yours. ²⁵And when you stand praying, if you hold anything against anyone, forgive him, so that your Father in heaven may forgive you your sins.*b*" Mt 21:19-22

The Authority of Jesus Questioned

²⁷They arrived again in Jerusalem, and while Jesus was walking in the temple courts, the chief priests, the teachers of the law and the elders came to him. ²⁸"By what authority are you doing these things?" they asked. "And who gave you authority to do this?"

²⁹Jesus replied, "I will ask you one question. Answer me, and I will tell you by what authority I am doing these things. ³⁰John's baptism—was it from heaven, or from men? Tell me!"

³¹They discussed it among themselves and said, "If we say, 'From heaven,' he will ask, 'Then why didn't you believe him?' ³²But if we say, 'From men' ...." (They feared the people, for everyone held that John really was a prophet.) Mt 11:9

³³So they answered Jesus, "We don't know."

Jesus said, "Neither will I tell you by what authority I am doing these things." Mt 21:23-27; Lk 20:1-8

The Parable of the Tenants

12 He then began to speak to them in parables: "A man planted a vineyard. He put a wall around it, dug a pit for the winepress and built a watchtower. Then he rented the vineyard to some farmers and went away on a journey. ²At harvest time he sent a servant to the tenants to collect from them some of the fruit of the vineyard. ³But they seized him, beat him and sent him away empty-handed. ⁴Then he sent another servant to them; they struck this man on the head and treated him shamefully. ⁵He sent still another, and that one they killed. He sent many others; some of them they beat, others they killed. Isa 5:1-7

⁶"He had one left to send, a son, whom he loved. He sent him last of all, saying, 'They will respect my son.' Heb 1:1-3

⁷"But the tenants said to one another, 'This is the heir. Come, let's

---

*a*22 Some early manuscripts *If you have*   *b*25 Some manuscripts *sins. 26But if you do not forgive, neither will your Father who is in heaven forgive your sins.*

kill him, and the inheritance will be ours.' ⁸So they took him and killed him, and threw him out of the vineyard.

⁹"What then will the owner of the vineyard do? He will come and kill those tenants and give the vineyard to others. ¹⁰Haven't you read this scripture:

" 'The stone the builders rejected
has become the capstone^a;
¹¹the Lord has done this,
and it is marvelous in our eyes'^b?"   Ac 4:11

¹²Then they looked for a way to arrest him because they knew he had spoken the parable against them. But they were afraid of the crowd; so they left him and went away.   Mt 21:33-46; Lk 20:9-19

Paying Taxes to Caesar

¹³Later they sent some of the Pharisees and Herodians to Jesus to catch him in his words. ¹⁴They came to him and said, "Teacher, we know you are a man of integrity. You aren't swayed by men, because you pay no attention to who they are; but you teach the way of God in accordance with the truth. Is it right to pay taxes to Caesar or not? ¹⁵Should we pay or shouldn't we?"   Mt 12:10; 22:16

But Jesus knew their hypocrisy. "Why are you trying to trap me?"

he asked. "Bring me a denarius and let me look at it." ¹⁶They brought the coin, and he asked them, "Whose portrait is this? And whose inscription?"

"Caesar's," they replied.

¹⁷Then Jesus said to them, "Give to Caesar what is Caesar's and to God what is God's."   Ro 13:7

And they were amazed at him.

Marriage at the Resurrection

¹⁸Then the Sadducees, who say there is no resurrection, came to him with a question. ¹⁹"Teacher," they said, "Moses wrote for us that if a man's brother dies and leaves a wife but no children, the man must marry the widow and have children for his brother. ²⁰Now there were seven brothers. The first one married and died without leaving any children. ²¹The second one married the widow, but he also died, leaving no child. It was the same with the third. ²²In fact, none of the seven left any children. Last of all, the woman died too. ²³At the resurrection^c whose wife will she be, since the seven were married to her?"   Dt 25:5; Ac 23:8

²⁴Jesus replied, "Are you not in error because you do not know the Scriptures or the power of God? ²⁵When the dead rise, they will neither marry nor be given in marriage; they will be like the angels in heaven. ²⁶Now about the dead ris-

---

^a10 Or cornerstone   ^b11 Psalm 118:22,23   ^c23 Some manuscripts resurrection, when men rise from the dead,

ing—have you not read in the book of Moses, in the account of the bush, how God said to him, 'I am the God of Abraham, the God of Isaac, and the God of Jacob'*a*? ²⁷He is not the God of the dead, but of the living. You are badly mistaken!" Mt 22:23-33; Lk 20:27-38

The Greatest Commandment

²⁸One of the teachers of the law came and heard them debating. Noticing that Jesus had given them a good answer, he asked him, "Of all the commandments, which is the most important?"

²⁹"The most important one," answered Jesus, "is this: 'Hear, O Israel, the Lord our God, the Lord is one.*b* ³⁰Love the Lord your God with all your heart and with all your soul and with all your mind and with all your strength.'*c* ³¹The second is this: 'Love your neighbor as yourself.'*d* There is no commandment greater than these."

³²"Well said, teacher," the man replied. "You are right in saying that God is one and there is no other but him. ³³To love him with all your heart, with all your understanding and with all your strength, and to love your neighbor as yourself is more important than all burnt offerings and sacrifices." 1Sa 15:22; Mic 6:6-8

³⁴When Jesus saw that he had answered wisely, he said to him,

"You are not far from the kingdom of God." And from then on no one dared ask him any more questions.

Whose Son Is the Christ?

³⁵While Jesus was teaching in the temple courts, he asked, "How is it that the teachers of the law say that the Christ*e* is the son of David? ³⁶David himself, speaking by the Holy Spirit, declared:

" 'The Lord said to my Lord:
"Sit at my right hand
until I put your enemies
under your feet." '*f*

³⁷David himself calls him 'Lord.' How then can he be his son?"

The large crowd listened to him with delight. Mt 9:27; 22:44

³⁸As he taught, Jesus said, "Watch out for the teachers of the law. They like to walk around in flowing robes and be greeted in the marketplaces, ³⁹and have the most important seats in the synagogues and the places of honor at banquets. ⁴⁰They devour widows' houses and for a show make lengthy prayers. Such men will be punished most severely." Mt 23:1-7

The Widow's Offering

⁴¹Jesus sat down opposite the place where the offerings were put and watched the crowd putting their money into the temple treasury. Many rich people threw in

a 26 Exodus 3:6   *b 29* Or *the Lord our God is one Lord*   *c 30* Deut. 6:4,5   *d 31* Lev. 19:18   *e 35* Or *Messiah*   *f 36* Psalm 110:1

large amounts. **42**But a poor widow came and put in two very small copper coins,*a* worth only a fraction of a penny.*b*   2Ki 12:9; Jn 8:20

43Calling his disciples to him, Jesus said, "I tell you the truth, this poor widow has put more into the treasury than all the others. **44**They all gave out of their wealth; but she, out of her poverty, put in everything—all she had to live on."

Signs of the End of the Age

13 As he was leaving the temple, one of his disciples said to him, "Look, Teacher! What massive stones! What magnificent buildings!"

2"Do you see all these great buildings?" replied Jesus. "Not one stone here will be left on another; every one will be thrown down."

3As Jesus was sitting on the Mount of Olives opposite the temple, Peter, James, John and Andrew asked him privately, **4**"Tell us, when will these things happen? And what will be the sign that they are all about to be fulfilled?"

5Jesus said to them: "Watch out that no one deceives you. **6**Many will come in my name, claiming, 'I am he,' and will deceive many. **7**When you hear of wars and rumors of wars, do not be alarmed. Such things must happen, but the end is still to come. **8**Nation will rise against nation, and kingdom against kingdom. There will be earthquakes in various places, and famines. These are the beginning of birth pains.   Eph 5:6; 2Th 2:3,10-12

9"You must be on your guard. You will be handed over to the local councils and flogged in the synagogues. On account of me you will stand before governors and kings as witnesses to them. **10**And the gospel must first be preached to all nations. **11**Whenever you are arrested and brought to trial, do not worry beforehand about what to say. Just say whatever is given you at the time, for it is not you speaking, but the Holy Spirit.

12"Brother will betray brother to death, and a father his child. Children will rebel against their parents and have them put to death. **13**All men will hate you because of me, but he who stands firm to the end will be saved.   Mic 7:6; Mt 10:21-22

14"When you see 'the abomination that causes desolation'*c* standing where it*d* does not belong—let the reader understand—then let those who are in Judea flee to the mountains. **15**Let no one on the roof of his house go down or enter the house to take anything out. **16**Let no one in the field go back to get his cloak. **17**How dreadful it will be in those days for pregnant women and nursing mothers! **18**Pray that this will not take place in winter, **19**because those will be

---

a 42 Greek *two lepta*   *b* 42 Greek *kodrantes*   *c* 14 Daniel 9:27; 11:31; 12:11   *d* 14 Or *he*; also in verse 29

days of distress unequaled from the beginning, when God created the world, until now—and never to be equaled again. ²⁰If the Lord had not cut short those days, no one would survive. But for the sake of the elect, whom he has chosen, he has shortened them. ²¹At that time if anyone says to you, 'Look, here is the Christ[a]!' or, 'Look, there he is!' do not believe it. ²²For false Christs and false prophets will appear and perform signs and miracles to deceive the elect—if that were possible. ²³So be on your guard; I have told you everything ahead of time.   Jn 4:48

²⁴"But in those days, following that distress,

> " 'the sun will be darkened,
>   and the moon will not give
>   its light;
> ²⁵the stars will fall from the sky,
>   and the heavenly bodies will
>   be shaken.'[b]   Mt 24:29

²⁶"At that time men will see the Son of Man coming in clouds with great power and glory. ²⁷And he will send his angels and gather his elect from the four winds, from the ends of the earth to the ends of the heavens.   Da 7:13; Zec 2:6; Rev 1:7

²⁸"Now learn this lesson from the fig tree: As soon as its twigs get tender and its leaves come out, you know that summer is near. ²⁹Even so, when you see these things happening, you know that it is near, right at the door. ³⁰I tell you the truth, this generation[c] will certainly not pass away until all these things have happened. ³¹Heaven and earth will pass away, but my words will never pass away.   Mt 5:18; Mk 9:1

The Day and Hour Unknown

³²"No one knows about that day or hour, not even the angels in heaven, nor the Son, but only the Father. ³³Be on guard! Be alert[d]! You do not know when that time will come. ³⁴It's like a man going away: He leaves his house and puts his servants in charge, each with his assigned task, and tells the one at the door to keep watch.

³⁵"Therefore keep watch because you do not know when the owner of the house will come back —whether in the evening, or at midnight, or when the rooster crows, or at dawn. ³⁶If he comes suddenly, do not let him find you sleeping. ³⁷What I say to you, I say to everyone: 'Watch!' "   Lk 12:35-40

Jesus Anointed at Bethany

14 Now the Passover and the Feast of Unleavened Bread were only two days away, and the chief priests and the teachers of the law were looking for some sly way to arrest Jesus and kill him. ²"But not during the Feast," they said, "or the people may riot."

³While he was in Bethany, re-

---

[a]21 Or *Messiah*   [b]25 Isaiah 13:10; 34:4   [c]30 Or *race*   [d]33 Some manuscripts *alert and pray*

clining at the table in the home of a man known as Simon the Leper, a woman came with an alabaster jar of very expensive perfume, made of pure nard. She broke the jar and poured the perfume on his head.   Mt 21:17; Lk 7:37-39

⁴Some of those present were saying indignantly to one another, "Why this waste of perfume? ⁵It could have been sold for more than a year's wages*ᵃ* and the money given to the poor." And they rebuked her harshly.

⁶"Leave her alone," said Jesus. "Why are you bothering her? She has done a beautiful thing to me. ⁷The poor you will always have with you, and you can help them any time you want. But you will not always have me. ⁸She did what she could. She poured perfume on my body beforehand to prepare for my burial. ⁹I tell you the truth, wherever the gospel is preached throughout the world, what she has done will also be told, in memory of her."   Jn 12:1-8; Dt 15:11

¹⁰Then Judas Iscariot, one of the Twelve, went to the chief priests to betray Jesus to them. ¹¹They were delighted to hear this and promised to give him money. So he watched for an opportunity to hand him over.   Mt 26:2-16; Lk 22:1-6

The Lord's Supper

¹²On the first day of the Feast of Unleavened Bread, when it was customary to sacrifice the Passover lamb, Jesus' disciples asked him, "Where do you want us to go and make preparations for you to eat the Passover?"   Ex 12:1-11; Dt 16:1-4

¹³So he sent two of his disciples, telling them, "Go into the city, and a man carrying a jar of water will meet you. Follow him. ¹⁴Say to the owner of the house he enters, 'The Teacher asks: Where is my guest room, where I may eat the Passover with my disciples?' ¹⁵He will show you a large upper room, furnished and ready. Make preparations for us there."   Ac 1:13

¹⁶The disciples left, went into the city and found things just as Jesus had told them. So they prepared the Passover.

¹⁷When evening came, Jesus arrived with the Twelve. ¹⁸While they were reclining at the table eating, he said, "I tell you the truth, one of you will betray me—one who is eating with me."

¹⁹They were saddened, and one by one they said to him, "Surely not I?"

²⁰"It is one of the Twelve," he replied, "one who dips bread into the bowl with me. ²¹The Son of Man will go just as it is written about him. But woe to that man who betrays the Son of Man! It would be better for him if he had not been born."   Mt 8:20; Jn 13:18-27

²²While they were eating, Jesus took bread, gave thanks and broke

ᵃ5 Greek *than three hundred denarii*

it, and gave it to his disciples, saying, "Take it; this is my body."

²³Then he took the cup, gave thanks and offered it to them, and they all drank from it.   1Co 10:16

²⁴"This is my blood of the*a* covenant, which is poured out for many," he said to them. ²⁵"I tell you the truth, I will not drink again of the fruit of the vine until that day when I drink it anew in the kingdom of God."   1Co 11:23-25

²⁶When they had sung a hymn, they went out to the Mount of Olives.   Mt 26:17-30; Lk 22:7-23

Jesus Predicts Peter's Denial

²⁷"You will all fall away," Jesus told them, "for it is written:

" 'I will strike the shepherd,
    and the sheep will be
    scattered.'*b*

²⁸But after I have risen, I will go ahead of you into Galilee."

²⁹Peter declared, "Even if all fall away, I will not."

³⁰"I tell you the truth," Jesus answered, "today—yes, tonight—before the rooster crows twice*c* you yourself will disown me three times."   Lk 22:34; Jn 13:38

³¹But Peter insisted emphatically, "Even if I have to die with you, I will never disown you." And all the others said the same.

Gethsemane

³²They went to a place called Gethsemane, and Jesus said to his disciples, "Sit here while I pray." ³³He took Peter, James and John along with him, and he began to be deeply distressed and troubled. ³⁴"My soul is overwhelmed with sorrow to the point of death," he said to them. "Stay here and keep watch."   Jn 12:27

³⁵Going a little farther, he fell to the ground and prayed that if possible the hour might pass from him. ³⁶"Abba,*d* Father," he said, "everything is possible for you. Take this cup from me. Yet not what I will, but what you will."

³⁷Then he returned to his disciples and found them sleeping. "Simon," he said to Peter, "are you asleep? Could you not keep watch for one hour? ³⁸Watch and pray so that you will not fall into temptation. The spirit is willing, but the body is weak."   Mt 6:13; Ro 7:22-23

³⁹Once more he went away and prayed the same thing. ⁴⁰When he came back, he again found them sleeping, because their eyes were heavy. They did not know what to say to him.

⁴¹Returning the third time, he said to them, "Are you still sleeping and resting? Enough! The hour has come. Look, the Son of Man is betrayed into the hands of sinners.

---

a 24 Some manuscripts *the new*   *b 27* Zech. 13:7   *c 30* Some early manuscripts do not have *twice*.
d 36 Aramaic for *Father*

⁴²Rise! Let us go! Here comes my betrayer!"   Mt 26:36-46; Lk 22:40-46

Jesus Arrested

⁴³Just as he was speaking, Judas, one of the Twelve, appeared. With him was a crowd armed with swords and clubs, sent from the chief priests, the teachers of the law, and the elders.   Mt 10:4 ⁴⁴Now the betrayer had arranged a signal with them: "The one I kiss is the man; arrest him and lead him away under guard." ⁴⁵Going at once to Jesus, Judas said, "Rabbi!" and kissed him. ⁴⁶The men seized Jesus and arrested him. ⁴⁷Then one of those standing near drew his sword and struck the servant of the high priest, cutting off his ear.   Mt 23:7

⁴⁸"Am I leading a rebellion," said Jesus, "that you have come out with swords and clubs to capture me? ⁴⁹Every day I was with you, teaching in the temple courts, and you did not arrest me. But the Scriptures must be fulfilled." ⁵⁰Then everyone deserted him and fled.   Mt 26:47-56; Lk 22:47-50; Jn 18:3-11

⁵¹A young man, wearing nothing but a linen garment, was following Jesus. When they seized him, ⁵²he fled naked, leaving his garment behind.

Before the Sanhedrin

⁵³They took Jesus to the high priest, and all the chief priests, elders and teachers of the law came together. ⁵⁴Peter followed him at a distance, right into the courtyard of the high priest. There he sat with the guards and warmed himself at the fire.   Mt 26:3; Jn 18:18

⁵⁵The chief priests and the whole Sanhedrin were looking for evidence against Jesus so that they could put him to death, but they did not find any. ⁵⁶Many testified falsely against him, but their statements did not agree.   Mt 5:22

⁵⁷Then some stood up and gave this false testimony against him: ⁵⁸"We heard him say, 'I will destroy this man-made temple and in three days will build another, not made by man.' " ⁵⁹Yet even then their testimony did not agree.

⁶⁰Then the high priest stood up before them and asked Jesus, "Are you not going to answer? What is this testimony that these men are bringing against you?" ⁶¹But Jesus remained silent and gave no answer.   Isa 53:7; Mt 27:12,14

Again the high priest asked him, "Are you the Christ,ᵃ the Son of the Blessed One?"   Mt 16:16; Jn 4:25-26

⁶²"I am," said Jesus. "And you will see the Son of Man sitting at the right hand of the Mighty One and coming on the clouds of heaven."   Rev 1:7

⁶³The high priest tore his clothes. "Why do we need any more witnesses?" he asked. ⁶⁴"You

ᵃ61 Or Messiah

have heard the blasphemy. What do you think?"   Lk 22:67-71

They all condemned him as worthy of death. ⁶⁵Then some began to spit at him; they blindfolded him, struck him with their fists, and said, "Prophesy!" And the guards took him and beat him.

Peter Disowns Jesus

⁶⁶While Peter was below in the courtyard, one of the servant girls of the high priest came by. ⁶⁷When she saw Peter warming himself, she looked closely at him.   ver 54

"You also were with that Nazarene, Jesus," she said.   Mk 1:24

⁶⁸But he denied it. "I don't know or understand what you're talking about," he said, and went out into the entryway.^a

⁶⁹When the servant girl saw him there, she said again to those standing around, "This fellow is one of them." ⁷⁰Again he denied it.

After a little while, those standing near said to Peter, "Surely you are one of them, for you are a Galilean."   Ac 2:7

⁷¹He began to call down curses on himself, and he swore to them, "I don't know this man you're talking about."

⁷²Immediately the rooster crowed the second time.^b Then Peter remembered the word Jesus had spoken to him: "Before the rooster crows twice^c you will disown me three times." And he broke down and wept.   Mt 26:69-75

Jesus Before Pilate

15 Very early in the morning, the chief priests, with the elders, the teachers of the law and the whole Sanhedrin, reached a decision. They bound Jesus, led him away and handed him over to Pilate.   Mt 27:1-2

²"Are you the king of the Jews?" asked Pilate.   Mt 2:2

"Yes, it is as you say," Jesus replied.

³The chief priests accused him of many things. ⁴So again Pilate asked him, "Aren't you going to answer? See how many things they are accusing you of."

⁵But Jesus still made no reply, and Pilate was amazed.   Mk 14:61

⁶Now it was the custom at the Feast to release a prisoner whom the people requested. ⁷A man called Barabbas was in prison with the insurrectionists who had committed murder in the uprising. ⁸The crowd came up and asked Pilate to do for them what he usually did.

⁹"Do you want me to release to you the king of the Jews?" asked Pilate, ¹⁰knowing it was out of envy that the chief priests had handed Jesus over to him. ¹¹But the chief priests stirred up the

---

^a68 Some early manuscripts *entryway and the rooster crowed*   ^b72 Some early manuscripts do not have *the second time.*   ^c72 Some early manuscripts do not have *twice.*

crowd to have Pilate release Barabbas instead. Ac 3:14

12"What shall I do, then, with the one you call the king of the Jews?" Pilate asked them.

13"Crucify him!" they shouted.

14"Why? What crime has he committed?" asked Pilate.

But they shouted all the louder, "Crucify him!"

15Wanting to satisfy the crowd, Pilate released Barabbas to them. He had Jesus flogged, and handed him over to be crucified.

The Soldiers Mock Jesus

16The soldiers led Jesus away into the palace (that is, the Praetorium) and called together the whole company of soldiers. 17They put a purple robe on him, then twisted together a crown of thorns and set it on him. 18And they began to call out to him, "Hail, king of the Jews!" 19Again and again they struck him on the head with a staff and spit on him. Falling on their knees, they paid homage to him. 20And when they had mocked him, they took off the purple robe and put his own clothes on him. Then they led him out to crucify him. Mt 27:27-31; Heb 13:12

The Crucifixion

21A certain man from Cyrene, Simon, the father of Alexander and Rufus, was passing by on his way in from the country, and they forced him to carry the cross. 22They brought Jesus to the place called Golgotha (which means The Place of the Skull). 23Then they offered him wine mixed with myrrh, but he did not take it. 24And they crucified him. Dividing up his clothes, they cast lots to see what each would get. Ps 22:18; Lk 23:26

25It was the third hour when they crucified him. 26The written notice of the charge against him read: THE KING OF THE JEWS. 27They crucified two robbers with him, one on his right and one on his left.a 29Those who passed by hurled insults at him, shaking their heads and saying, "So! You who are going to destroy the temple and build it in three days, 30come down from the cross and save yourself!" Mk 14:58; Jn 2:19

31In the same way the chief priests and the teachers of the law mocked him among themselves. "He saved others," they said, "but he can't save himself! 32Let this Christ,b this King of Israel, come down now from the cross, that we may see and believe." Those crucified with him also heaped insults on him. Mt 27:33-44; Lk 23:33-43

The Death of Jesus

33At the sixth hour darkness came over the whole land until the ninth hour. 34And at the ninth

---

a 27 Some manuscripts left, 28and the scripture was fulfilled which says, "He was counted with the lawless ones" (Isaiah 53:12)　　b 32 Or Messiah

hour Jesus cried out in a loud voice, *"Eloi, Eloi, lama sabachthani?"*—which means, "My God, my God, why have you forsaken me?"*a*   Am 8:9

35When some of those standing near heard this, they said, "Listen, he's calling Elijah."

36One man ran, filled a sponge with wine vinegar, put it on a stick, and offered it to Jesus to drink. "Now leave him alone. Let's see if Elijah comes to take him down," he said.   Ps 69:21

37With a loud cry, Jesus breathed his last.   Jn 19:30

38The curtain of the temple was torn in two from top to bottom. **39**And when the centurion, who stood there in front of Jesus, heard his cry and*b* saw how he died, he said, "Surely this man was the Son*c* of God!"   Mt 4:3; Heb 10:19-20

40Some women were watching from a distance. Among them were Mary Magdalene, Mary the mother of James the younger and of Joses, and Salome. **41**In Galilee these women had followed him and cared for his needs. Many other women who had come up with him to Jerusalem were also there.

The Burial of Jesus

42It was Preparation Day (that is, the day before the Sabbath). So as evening approached, **43**Joseph of Arimathea, a prominent member of the Council, who was himself waiting for the kingdom of God, went boldly to Pilate and asked for Jesus' body. **44**Pilate was surprised to hear that he was already dead. Summoning the centurion, he asked him if Jesus had already died. **45**When he learned from the centurion that it was so, he gave the body to Joseph. **46**So Joseph bought some linen cloth, took down the body, wrapped it in the linen, and placed it in a tomb cut out of rock. Then he rolled a stone against the entrance of the tomb. **47**Mary Magdalene and Mary the mother of Joses saw where he was laid.   Mt 27:57-61; Lk 23:50-56; Jn 19:38-42

The Resurrection

16 When the Sabbath was over, Mary Magdalene, Mary the mother of James, and Salome bought spices so that they might go to anoint Jesus' body. **2**Very early on the first day of the week, just after sunrise, they were on their way to the tomb **3**and they asked each other, "Who will roll the stone away from the entrance of the tomb?"   Mk 15:46; Lk 23:56

4But when they looked up, they saw that the stone, which was very large, had been rolled away. **5**As they entered the tomb, they saw a young man dressed in a white robe sitting on the right side, and they were alarmed.   Jn 20:12

6"Don't be alarmed," he said.

---

a 34 Psalm 22:1   *b 39* Some manuscripts do not have *heard his cry and*   *c 39* Or *a son*

"You are looking for Jesus the Nazarene, who was crucified. He has risen! He is not here. See the place where they laid him. [7]But go, tell his disciples and Peter, 'He is going ahead of you into Galilee. There you will see him, just as he told you.' "   Mk 1:24; 14:28

[8]Trembling and bewildered, the women went out and fled from the tomb. They said nothing to anyone, because they were afraid.

[The earliest manuscripts and some other ancient witnesses do not have Mark 16:9–20.]

[9]When Jesus rose early on the first day of the week, he appeared first to Mary Magdalene, out of whom he had driven seven demons. [10]She went and told those who had been with him and who were mourning and weeping. [11]When they heard that Jesus was alive and that she had seen him, they did not believe it.   Lk 24:11

[12]Afterward Jesus appeared in a different form to two of them while they were walking in the country. [13]These returned and reported it to the rest; but they did not believe them either.   Lk 24:13-32

[14]Later Jesus appeared to the Eleven as they were eating; he rebuked them for their lack of faith and their stubborn refusal to believe those who had seen him after he had risen.   Lk 24:36-43

[15]He said to them, "Go into all the world and preach the good news to all creation. [16]Whoever believes and is baptized will be saved, but whoever does not believe will be condemned. [17]And these signs will accompany those who believe: In my name they will drive out demons; they will speak in new tongues; [18]they will pick up snakes with their hands; and when they drink deadly poison, it will not hurt them at all; they will place their hands on sick people, and they will get well."   Mt 28:18-20

[19]After the Lord Jesus had spoken to them, he was taken up into heaven and he sat at the right hand of God. [20]Then the disciples went out and preached everywhere, and the Lord worked with them and confirmed his word by the signs that accompanied it.   Lk 24:50-51

Luke

Introduction

1 Many have undertaken to draw up an account of the things that have been fulfilled[a] among us, ²just as they were handed down to us by those who from the first were eyewitnesses and servants of the word. ³Therefore, since I myself have carefully investigated everything from the beginning, it seemed good also to me to write an orderly account for you, most excellent Theophilus, ⁴so that you may know the certainty of the things you have been taught.

The Birth of John the Baptist Foretold

⁵In the time of Herod king of Judea there was a priest named Zechariah, who belonged to the priestly division of Abijah; his wife Elizabeth was also a descendant of Aaron. ⁶Both of them were upright in the sight of God, observing all the Lord's commandments and regulations blamelessly. ⁷But they had no children, because Elizabeth was barren; and they were both well along in years.   Ge 7:1

⁸Once when Zechariah's division was on duty and he was serving as priest before God, ⁹he was chosen by lot, according to the custom of the priesthood, to go into the temple of the Lord and burn incense. ¹⁰And when the time for the burning of incense came, all the assembled worshipers were praying outside.   Ex 30:7-8; Lev 16:17

¹¹Then an angel of the Lord appeared to him, standing at the right side of the altar of incense. ¹²When Zechariah saw him, he was startled and was gripped with fear. ¹³But the angel said to him: "Do not be afraid, Zechariah; your prayer has been heard. Your wife Elizabeth will bear you a son, and you are to give him the name John. ¹⁴He will be a joy and delight to you, and many will rejoice because of his birth, ¹⁵for he will be great in the sight of the Lord. He is never to take wine or other fermented drink, and he will be filled with the Holy Spirit even from birth.[b] ¹⁶Many of the people of Israel will he bring back to the Lord their God. ¹⁷And he will go on before the Lord, in the spirit and power of Elijah, to turn the hearts of the fathers to their children and the disobedient to the wisdom of the righteous—to make ready a people prepared for the Lord."

¹⁸Zechariah asked the angel,

---

a 1 Or *been surely believed*   b 15 Or *from his mother's womb*

"How can I be sure of this? I am an old man and my wife is well along in years." Ge 17:17

¹⁹The angel answered, "I am Gabriel. I stand in the presence of God, and I have been sent to speak to you and to tell you this good news. ²⁰And now you will be silent and not able to speak until the day this happens, because you did not believe my words, which will come true at their proper time."

²¹Meanwhile, the people were waiting for Zechariah and wondering why he stayed so long in the temple. ²²When he came out, he could not speak to them. They realized he had seen a vision in the temple, for he kept making signs to them but remained unable to speak.

²³When his time of service was completed, he returned home. ²⁴After this his wife Elizabeth became pregnant and for five months remained in seclusion. ²⁵"The Lord has done this for me," she said. "In these days he has shown his favor and taken away my disgrace among the people." Ge 30:23

The Birth of Jesus Foretold

²⁶In the sixth month, God sent the angel Gabriel to Nazareth, a town in Galilee, ²⁷to a virgin pledged to be married to a man named Joseph, a descendant of David. The virgin's name was Mary. ²⁸The angel went to her and said, "Greetings, you who are highly favored! The Lord is with you." Mt 1:16,18,20; 2:23

²⁹Mary was greatly troubled at his words and wondered what kind of greeting this might be. ³⁰But the angel said to her, "Do not be afraid, Mary, you have found favor with God. ³¹You will be with child and give birth to a son, and you are to give him the name Jesus. ³²He will be great and will be called the Son of the Most High. The Lord God will give him the throne of his father David, ³³and he will reign over the house of Jacob forever; his kingdom will never end." Da 2:44; 7:14,27; Mic 4:7

³⁴"How will this be," Mary asked the angel, "since I am a virgin?"

³⁵The angel answered, "The Holy Spirit will come upon you, and the power of the Most High will overshadow you. So the holy one to be born will be called[a] the Son of God. ³⁶Even Elizabeth your relative is going to have a child in her old age, and she who was said to be barren is in her sixth month. ³⁷For nothing is impossible with God." Mt 19:26

³⁸"I am the Lord's servant," Mary answered. "May it be to me as you have said." Then the angel left her.

Mary Visits Elizabeth

³⁹At that time Mary got ready and hurried to a town in the hill

a 35 Or So the child to be born will be called holy,

country of Judea, [40]where she entered Zechariah's home and greeted Elizabeth. [41]When Elizabeth heard Mary's greeting, the baby leaped in her womb, and Elizabeth was filled with the Holy Spirit. [42]In a loud voice she exclaimed: "Blessed are you among women, and blessed is the child you will bear! [43]But why am I so favored, that the mother of my Lord should come to me? [44]As soon as the sound of your greeting reached my ears, the baby in my womb leaped for joy. [45]Blessed is she who has believed that what the Lord has said to her will be accomplished!"

Mary's Song

[46]And Mary said:

"My soul glorifies the Lord
[47]   and my spirit rejoices in God
         my Savior,   1Ti 1:1; 2:3
[48]for he has been mindful
    of the humble state of his
         servant.   Ps 138:6
From now on all generations
    will call me blessed,
[49]   for the Mighty One has done
         great things for me—
holy is his name.   Ps 111:9
[50]His mercy extends to those
    who fear him,
    from generation to
         generation.   Ex 20:6; Ps 103:17
[51]He has performed mighty
    deeds with his arm;
    he has scattered those who
    are proud in their
         inmost thoughts.   Ge 11:8

[52]He has brought down rulers
         from their thrones
    but has lifted up the humble.
[53]He has filled the hungry with
         good things   Ps 107:9
    but has sent the rich away
         empty.   1Sa 2:1-10
[54]He has helped his servant
         Israel,
    remembering to be merciful
[55]to Abraham and his
         descendants forever,
    even as he said to our
         fathers."

[56]Mary stayed with Elizabeth for about three months and then returned home.

The Birth of John the Baptist

[57]When it was time for Elizabeth to have her baby, she gave birth to a son. [58]Her neighbors and relatives heard that the Lord had shown her great mercy, and they shared her joy.

[59]On the eighth day they came to circumcise the child, and they were going to name him after his father Zechariah, [60]but his mother spoke up and said, "No! He is to be called John."   Ge 17:12; Lk 2:21

[61]They said to her, "There is no one among your relatives who has that name."

[62]Then they made signs to his father, to find out what he would like to name the child. [63]He asked for a writing tablet, and to everyone's astonishment he wrote, "His name is John." [64]Immediately his

mouth was opened and his tongue was loosed, and he began to speak, praising God. 65The neighbors were all filled with awe, and throughout the hill country of Judea people were talking about all these things. 66Everyone who heard this wondered about it, asking, "What then is this child going to be?" For the Lord's hand was with him.   Ge 39:2; Ac 11:21

Zechariah's Song

67His father Zechariah was filled with the Holy Spirit and prophesied: Joel 2:28

68"Praise be to the Lord, the God
        of Israel,   Ps 72:18
    because he has come and
        has redeemed his
        people.   Ps 111:9; Lk 7:16
69He has raised up a horn[a] of
        salvation for us   Ps 18:2
    in the house of his servant
        David   Mt 1:1
70(as he said through his holy
        prophets of long ago),
71salvation from our enemies
    and from the hand of all
        who hate us—
72to show mercy to our fathers
    and to remember his holy
        covenant,   Ps 105:8-9; 106:45
73   the oath he swore to our
        father Abraham:
74to rescue us from the hand of
        our enemies,
    and to enable us to serve
        him without fear   Heb 9:14
75   in holiness and
        righteousness before
        him all our days.   Eph 4:24

76And you, my child, will be
        called a prophet of the
        Most High;   Mt 11:9
    for you will go on before the
        Lord to prepare the way
        for him,   Mal 3:1
77to give his people the
        knowledge of salvation
    through the forgiveness of
        their sins,   Jer 31:34; Mk 1:4
78because of the tender mercy of
        our God,
    by which the rising sun will
        come to us from heaven
79to shine on those living in
        darkness
    and in the shadow of death,
    to guide our feet into the path
        of peace."   Lk 2:14

80And the child grew and became strong in spirit; and he lived in the desert until he appeared publicly to Israel.   Lk 2:40,52

The Birth of Jesus

2 In those days Caesar Augustus issued a decree that a census should be taken of the entire Roman world. 2(This was the first census that took place while Quirinius was governor of Syria.) 3And everyone went to his own town to register.   Mt 24:14; Lk 3:1

---

a69 Horn here symbolizes strength.

⁴So Joseph also went up from the town of Nazareth in Galilee to Judea, to Bethlehem the town of David, because he belonged to the house and line of David. ⁵He went there to register with Mary, who was pledged to be married to him and was expecting a child. ⁶While they were there, the time came for the baby to be born, ⁷and she gave birth to her firstborn, a son. She wrapped him in cloths and placed him in a manger, because there was no room for them in the inn.

The Shepherds and the Angels

⁸And there were shepherds living out in the fields nearby, keeping watch over their flocks at night. ⁹An angel of the Lord appeared to them, and the glory of the Lord shone around them, and they were terrified. ¹⁰But the angel said to them, "Do not be afraid. I bring you good news of great joy that will be for all the people. ¹¹Today in the town of David a Savior has been born to you; he is Christ[a] the Lord. ¹²This will be a sign to you: You will find a baby wrapped in cloths and lying in a manger."

¹³Suddenly a great company of the heavenly host appeared with the angel, praising God and saying,

¹⁴"Glory to God in the highest,
  and on earth peace to men
    on whom his favor
      rests."   Ro 5:1; Eph 2:14,17

¹⁵When the angels had left them and gone into heaven, the shepherds said to one another, "Let's go to Bethlehem and see this thing that has happened, which the Lord has told us about."

¹⁶So they hurried off and found Mary and Joseph, and the baby, who was lying in the manger. ¹⁷When they had seen him, they spread the word concerning what had been told them about this child, ¹⁸and all who heard it were amazed at what the shepherds said to them. ¹⁹But Mary treasured up all these things and pondered them in her heart. ²⁰The shepherds returned, glorifying and praising God for all the things they had heard and seen, which were just as they had been told.   Mt 9:8

Jesus Presented in the Temple

²¹On the eighth day, when it was time to circumcise him, he was named Jesus, the name the angel had given him before he had been conceived.   Lk 1:31,59

²²When the time of their purification according to the Law of Moses had been completed, Joseph and Mary took him to Jerusalem to present him to the Lord ²³(as it is written in the Law of the Lord, "Every firstborn male is to be consecrated to the Lord"[b]), ²⁴and to offer a sacrifice in keeping with what is said in the Law of the Lord: "a

---

[a] 11 Or *Messiah*. "The Christ" (Greek) and "the Messiah" (Hebrew) both mean "the Anointed One"; also in verse 26.   [b] 23 Exodus 13:2,12

pair of doves or two young pigeons."[a]   Ex 13:2,12,15; Lev 12:8

25Now there was a man in Jerusalem called Simeon, who was righteous and devout. He was waiting for the consolation of Israel, and the Holy Spirit was upon him. 26It had been revealed to him by the Holy Spirit that he would not die before he had seen the Lord's Christ. 27Moved by the Spirit, he went into the temple courts. When the parents brought in the child Jesus to do for him what the custom of the Law required, 28Simeon took him in his arms and praised God, saying: Lk 1:6; 23:51

29"Sovereign Lord, as you have
    promised,   ver 26
  you now dismiss[b] your
    servant in peace.   Ac 2:24
30For my eyes have seen your
    salvation,   Isa 52:10
31 which you have prepared in
    the sight of all people,
32a light for revelation to the
    Gentiles
  and for glory to your people
    Israel."   Isa 42:6; 49:6; Ac 13:47

33The child's father and mother marveled at what was said about him. 34Then Simeon blessed them and said to Mary, his mother: "This child is destined to cause the falling and rising of many in Israel, and to be a sign that will be spoken against, 35so that the thoughts of many hearts will be revealed. And a sword will pierce your own soul too."   Mt 21:44; 1Co 1:23; 1Pe 2:7-8

36There was also a prophetess, Anna, the daughter of Phanuel, of the tribe of Asher. She was very old; she had lived with her husband seven years after her marriage, 37and then was a widow until she was eighty-four.[c] She never left the temple but worshiped night and day, fasting and praying. 38Coming up to them at that very moment, she gave thanks to God and spoke about the child to all who were looking forward to the redemption of Jerusalem.   Lk 1:68

39When Joseph and Mary had done everything required by the Law of the Lord, they returned to Galilee to their own town of Nazareth. 40And the child grew and became strong; he was filled with wisdom, and the grace of God was upon him.   Mt 2:23; Lk 1:80

The Boy Jesus at the Temple

41Every year his parents went to Jerusalem for the Feast of the Passover. 42When he was twelve years old, they went up to the Feast, according to the custom. 43After the Feast was over, while his parents were returning home, the boy Jesus stayed behind in Jerusalem, but they were unaware of it. 44Thinking he was in their company, they traveled on for a day.

a24 Lev. 12:8   b29 Or promised, / now dismiss   c37 Or widow for eighty-four years

Then they began looking for him among their relatives and friends. ⁴⁵When they did not find him, they went back to Jerusalem to look for him. ⁴⁶After three days they found him in the temple courts, sitting among the teachers, listening to them and asking them questions. ⁴⁷Everyone who heard him was amazed at his understanding and his answers. ⁴⁸When his parents saw him, they were astonished. His mother said to him, "Son, why have you treated us like this? Your father and I have been anxiously searching for you."   Ex 23:15; Dt 16:1-8

⁴⁹"Why were you searching for me?" he asked. "Didn't you know I had to be in my Father's house?" ⁵⁰But they did not understand what he was saying to them.

⁵¹Then he went down to Nazareth with them and was obedient to them. But his mother treasured all these things in her heart. ⁵²And Jesus grew in wisdom and stature, and in favor with God and men.

John the Baptist Prepares the Way

3 In the fifteenth year of the reign of Tiberius Caesar— when Pontius Pilate was governor of Judea, Herod tetrarch of Galilee, his brother Philip tetrarch of Iturea and Traconitis, and Lysanias tetrarch of Abilene— ²during the high priesthood of Annas and Caiaphas, the word of God came to John son of Zechariah in the desert. ³He went into all the country around the Jordan, preaching a baptism of repentance for the forgiveness of sins. ⁴As is written in the book of the words of Isaiah the prophet: Mk 1:4; Jn 18:13; Ac 4:6

"A voice of one calling in the
    desert,
'Prepare the way for the Lord,
    make straight paths for him.
⁵Every valley shall be filled in,
    every mountain and hill
        made low.
The crooked roads shall
        become straight,
    the rough ways smooth.
⁶And all mankind will see God's
    salvation.' "ᵃ   Ps 98:2

⁷John said to the crowds coming out to be baptized by him, "You brood of vipers! Who warned you to flee from the coming wrath? ⁸Produce fruit in keeping with repentance. And do not begin to say to yourselves, 'We have Abraham as our father.' For I tell you that out of these stones God can raise up children for Abraham. ⁹The ax is already at the root of the trees, and every tree that does not produce good fruit will be cut down and thrown into the fire."

¹⁰"What should we do then?" the crowd asked.   Mt 3:1-10; Mk 1:3-5

¹¹John answered, "The man with two tunics should share with him who has none, and the one

ᵃ6 Isaiah 40:3-5

who has food should do the same."

¹²Tax collectors also came to be baptized. "Teacher," they asked, "what should we do?"   Lk 7:29

¹³"Don't collect any more than you are required to," he told them. ¹⁴Then some soldiers asked him, "And what should we do?"

He replied, "Don't extort money and don't accuse people falsely— be content with your pay."   Ex 23:1

¹⁵The people were waiting expectantly and were all wondering in their hearts if John might possibly be the Christ.ᵃ ¹⁶John answered them all, "I baptize you withᵇ water. But one more powerful than I will come, the thongs of whose sandals I am not worthy to untie. He will baptize you with the Holy Spirit and with fire. ¹⁷His winnowing fork is in his hand to clear his threshing floor and to gather the wheat into his barn, but he will burn up the chaff with unquenchable fire." ¹⁸And with many other words John exhorted the people and preached the good news to them.   Mt 3:11-12; Mk 1:7-8

¹⁹But when John rebuked Herod the tetrarch because of Herodias, his brother's wife, and all the other evil things he had done, ²⁰Herod added this to them all: He locked John up in prison.   Mt 14:3-4

The Baptism and Genealogy of Jesus

²¹When all the people were being baptized, Jesus was baptized too. And as he was praying, heaven was opened ²²and the Holy Spirit descended on him in bodily form like a dove. And a voice came from heaven: "You are my Son, whom I love; with you I am well pleased."   Mt 3:13-17; Mk 1:9-11

²³Now Jesus himself was about thirty years old when he began his ministry. He was the son, so it was thought, of Joseph,   Mt 4:17; Lk 1:27

the son of Heli, ²⁴the son of Matthat,
the son of Levi, the son of Melki,
the son of Jannai, the son of Joseph,
²⁵the son of Mattathias, the son of Amos,
the son of Nahum, the son of Esli,
the son of Naggai, ²⁶the son of Maath,
the son of Mattathias, the son of Semein,
the son of Josech, the son of Joda,
²⁷the son of Joanan, the son of Rhesa,
the son of Zerubbabel, the son of Shealtiel,   Mt 1:12
the son of Neri, ²⁸the son of Melki,
the son of Addi, the son of Cosam,
the son of Elmadam, the son of Er,

29the son of Joshua, the son of
Eliezer,

the son of Jorim, the son of
Matthat,

the son of Levi, 30the son of
Simeon,

the son of Judah, the son of
Joseph,

the son of Jonam, the son of
Eliakim,

31the son of Melea, the son of
Menna,

the son of Mattatha, the son of
Nathan,   2Sa 5:14; 1Ch 3:5

the son of David, 32the son of
Jesse,

the son of Obed, the son of
Boaz,

the son of Salmon,a the son of
Nahshon,

33the son of Amminadab, the
son of Ram,b

the son of Hezron, the son of
Perez,   Ru 4:18-22; 1Ch 2:10-12

the son of Judah, 34the son of
Jacob,

the son of Isaac, the son of
Abraham,

the son of Terah, the son of
Nahor,   Ge 11:24,26

35the son of Serug, the son of
Reu,

the son of Peleg, the son of
Eber,

the son of Shelah, 36the son of
Cainan,

the son of Arphaxad, the son
of Shem,   Ge 11:12

the son of Noah, the son of
Lamech,   Ge 5:28-32

37the son of Methuselah, the
son of Enoch,

the son of Jared, the son of
Mahalalel,

the son of Kenan, 38the son of
Enosh,   Ge 5:12-25

the son of Seth, the son of
Adam,

the son of God.   Mt 1:1-17

The Temptation of Jesus

4 Jesus, full of the Holy Spirit,
returned from the Jordan and
was led by the Spirit in the desert,
2where for forty days he was
tempted by the devil. He ate nothing during those days, and at the
end of them he was hungry.

3The devil said to him, "If you
are the Son of God, tell this stone
to become bread."   Mt 4:3

4Jesus answered, "It is written:
'Man does not live on bread
alone.'c"   Dt 8:3

5The devil led him up to a high
place and showed him in an instant all the kingdoms of the
world. 6And he said to him, "I will
give you all their authority and
splendor, for it has been given to
me, and I can give it to anyone I
want to. 7So if you worship me, it
will all be yours."   Jn 12:31; 14:30

8Jesus answered, "It is written:
'Worship the Lord your God and
serve him only.'d"   Dt 6:13

---

a32 Some early manuscripts Sala   b33 Some manuscripts Amminadab, the son of Admin, the son of
Arni; other manuscripts vary widely.   c4 Deut. 8:3   d8 Deut. 6:13

⁹The devil led him to Jerusalem and had him stand on the highest point of the temple. "If you are the Son of God," he said, "throw yourself down from here. ¹⁰For it is written:

" 'He will command his angels
        concerning you
    to guard you carefully;
¹¹they will lift you up in their
        hands,
    so that you will not strike
        your foot against a
        stone.'ᵃ"   Ps 91:11-12

¹²Jesus answered, "It says: 'Do not put the Lord your God to the test.'ᵇ"   Dt 6:16
¹³When the devil had finished all this tempting, he left him until an opportune time.   Mt 4:1-11; Mk 1

Jesus Rejected at Nazareth

¹⁴Jesus returned to Galilee in the power of the Spirit, and news about him spread through the whole countryside. ¹⁵He taught in their synagogues, and everyone praised him.   Mt 4:12; 9:26
¹⁶He went to Nazareth, where he had been brought up, and on the Sabbath day he went into the synagogue, as was his custom. And he stood up to read. ¹⁷The scroll of the prophet Isaiah was handed to him. Unrolling it, he found the place where it is written: Mt 13:54

¹⁸"The Spirit of the Lord is on
        me,   Jn 3:34
    because he has anointed me
    to preach good news to the
        poor.   Mk 16:15
He has sent me to proclaim
        freedom for the
        prisoners
    and recovery of sight for the
        blind,
    to release the oppressed,
¹⁹   to proclaim the year of the
        Lord's favor."ᶜ   Lev 25:10

²⁰Then he rolled up the scroll, gave it back to the attendant and sat down. The eyes of everyone in the synagogue were fastened on him, ²¹and he began by saying to them, "Today this scripture is fulfilled in your hearing."   Mt 26:55
²²All spoke well of him and were amazed at the gracious words that came from his lips. "Isn't this Joseph's son?" they asked.
²³Jesus said to them, "Surely you will quote this proverb to me: 'Physician, heal yourself! Do here in your hometown what we have heard that you did in Capernaum.' "   Mk 1:21-28; 2:1-12
²⁴"I tell you the truth," he continued, "no prophet is accepted in his hometown. ²⁵I assure you that there were many widows in Israel in Elijah's time, when the sky was shut for three and a half years and there was a severe famine throughout the land. ²⁶Yet Elijah was not

ᵃ11 Psalm 91:11,12   ᵇ12 Deut. 6:16   ᶜ19 Isaiah 61:1,2

sent to any of them, but to a widow in Zarephath in the region of Sidon. ²⁷And there were many in Israel with leprosy*ᵃ* in the time of Elisha the prophet, yet not one of them was cleansed—only Naaman the Syrian." Mt 13:57; Jn 4:44

²⁸All the people in the synagogue were furious when they heard this. ²⁹They got up, drove him out of the town, and took him to the brow of the hill on which the town was built, in order to throw him down the cliff. ³⁰But he walked right through the crowd and went on his way. Jn 8:59; 10:39

Jesus Drives Out an Evil Spirit

³¹Then he went down to Capernaum, a town in Galilee, and on the Sabbath began to teach the people. ³²They were amazed at his teaching, because his message had authority. Mt 7:28-29

³³In the synagogue there was a man possessed by a demon, an evil*ᵇ* spirit. He cried out at the top of his voice, ³⁴"Ha! What do you want with us, Jesus of Nazareth? Have you come to destroy us? I know who you are—the Holy One of God!" Mk 1:24; Jas 2:19

³⁵"Be quiet!" Jesus said sternly. "Come out of him!" Then the demon threw the man down before them all and came out without injuring him.

³⁶All the people were amazed and said to each other, "What is this teaching? With authority and power he gives orders to evil spirits and they come out!" ³⁷And the news about him spread throughout the surrounding area.

Jesus Heals Many

³⁸Jesus left the synagogue and went to the home of Simon. Now Simon's mother-in-law was suffering from a high fever, and they asked Jesus to help her. ³⁹So he bent over her and rebuked the fever, and it left her. She got up at once and began to wait on them.

⁴⁰When the sun was setting, the people brought to Jesus all who had various kinds of sickness, and laying his hands on each one, he healed them. ⁴¹Moreover, demons came out of many people, shouting, "You are the Son of God!" But he rebuked them and would not allow them to speak, because they knew he was the Christ.*ᶜ*

⁴²At daybreak Jesus went out to a solitary place. The people were looking for him and when they came to where he was, they tried to keep him from leaving them. ⁴³But he said, "I must preach the good news of the kingdom of God to the other towns also, because that is why I was sent." ⁴⁴And he kept on preaching in the synagogues of Judea.*ᵈ* Mt 3:2; 4:23

ᵃ27 The Greek word was used for various diseases affecting the skin—not necessarily leprosy. *ᵇ33* Greek *unclean*; also in verse 36   *ᶜ41* Or *Messiah*   *ᵈ44* Or *the land of the Jews*; some manuscripts *Galilee*

The Calling of the First Disciples

5 One day as Jesus was standing by the Lake of Gennesaret,[a] with the people crowding around him and listening to the word of God, [2]he saw at the water's edge two boats, left there by the fishermen, who were washing their nets. [3]He got into one of the boats, the one belonging to Simon, and asked him to put out a little from shore. Then he sat down and taught the people from the boat. *Mt 13:2*

[4]When he had finished speaking, he said to Simon, "Put out into deep water, and let down[b] the nets for a catch." *Jn 21:6*

[5]Simon answered, "Master, we've worked hard all night and haven't caught anything. But because you say so, I will let down the nets." *Lk 8:24,45; 9:33,49; 17:13*

[6]When they had done so, they caught such a large number of fish that their nets began to break. [7]So they signaled their partners in the other boat to come and help them, and they came and filled both boats so full that they began to sink. *Jn 21:11*

[8]When Simon Peter saw this, he fell at Jesus' knees and said, "Go away from me, Lord; I am a sinful man!" [9]For he and all his companions were astonished at the catch of fish they had taken, [10]and so

were James and John, the sons of Zebedee, Simon's partners.

Then Jesus said to Simon, "Don't be afraid; from now on you will catch men." [11]So they pulled their boats up on shore, left everything and followed him. *Mt 4:18-22*

The Man With Leprosy

[12]While Jesus was in one of the towns, a man came along who was covered with leprosy.[c] When he saw Jesus, he fell with his face to the ground and begged him, "Lord, if you are willing, you can make me clean." *Mt 8:2*

[13]Jesus reached out his hand and touched the man. "I am willing," he said. "Be clean!" And immediately the leprosy left him. [14]Then Jesus ordered him, "Don't tell anyone, but go, show yourself to the priest and offer the sacrifices that Moses commanded for your cleansing, as a testimony to them." *Mt 8:2-4; Mk 1:40-44*

[15]Yet the news about him spread all the more, so that crowds of people came to hear him and to be healed of their sicknesses. [16]But Jesus often withdrew to lonely places and prayed. *Mt 14:23; Lk 3:21*

Jesus Heals a Paralytic

[17]One day as he was teaching, Pharisees and teachers of the law, who had come from every village of Galilee and from Judea and Je-

---

a 1 That is, Sea of Galilee   *b 4* The Greek verb is plural.   *c 12* The Greek word was used for various diseases affecting the skin—not necessarily leprosy.

rusalem, were sitting there. And the power of the Lord was present for him to heal the sick. **18**Some men came carrying a paralytic on a mat and tried to take him into the house to lay him before Jesus. **19**When they could not find a way to do this because of the crowd, they went up on the roof and lowered him on his mat through the tiles into the middle of the crowd, right in front of Jesus.   Mk 5:30

20When Jesus saw their faith, he said, "Friend, your sins are forgiven."   Lk 7:48-49

21The Pharisees and the teachers of the law began thinking to themselves, "Who is this fellow who speaks blasphemy? Who can forgive sins but God alone?"

22Jesus knew what they were thinking and asked, "Why are you thinking these things in your hearts? **23**Which is easier: to say, 'Your sins are forgiven,' or to say, 'Get up and walk'? **24**But that you may know that the Son of Man has authority on earth to forgive sins. . . ." He said to the paralyzed man, "I tell you, get up, take your mat and go home." **25**Immediately he stood up in front of them, took what he had been lying on and went home praising God. **26**Everyone was amazed and gave praise to God. They were filled with awe and said, "We have seen remarkable things today."   Mt 9:2-8; Mk 2:3-12

The Calling of Levi

27After this, Jesus went out and saw a tax collector by the name of Levi sitting at his tax booth. "Follow me," Jesus said to him, **28**and Levi got up, left everything and followed him.   Mt 4:19

29Then Levi held a great banquet for Jesus at his house, and a large crowd of tax collectors and others were eating with them. **30**But the Pharisees and the teachers of the law who belonged to their sect complained to his disciples, "Why do you eat and drink with tax collectors and 'sinners'?"   Lk 15:1

31Jesus answered them, "It is not the healthy who need a doctor, but the sick. **32**I have not come to call the righteous, but sinners to repentance."   Mt 9:9-13; Mk 2:14-17

Jesus Questioned About Fasting

33They said to him, "John's disciples often fast and pray, and so do the disciples of the Pharisees, but yours go on eating and drinking."   Lk 7:18; Jn 1:35; 3:25-26

34Jesus answered, "Can you make the guests of the bridegroom fast while he is with them? **35**But the time will come when the bridegroom will be taken from them; in those days they will fast."   Lk 17:22

36He told them this parable: "No one tears a patch from a new garment and sews it on an old one. If he does, he will have torn the new garment, and the patch from the new will not match the old. **37**And no one pours new wine into old wineskins. If he does, the new wine will burst the skins, the wine will run out and the wineskins will be ruined. ³⁸No, new wine must be poured into new wineskins. ³⁹And no one after drinking old wine wants the new, for he says, 'The old is better.' "   Mt 9:14-17; Mk 2:18-22

Lord of the Sabbath

6 One Sabbath Jesus was going through the grainfields, and his disciples began to pick some heads of grain, rub them in their hands and eat the kernels. ²Some of the Pharisees asked, "Why are you doing what is unlawful on the Sabbath?"   Dt 23:25

³Jesus answered them, "Have you never read what David did when he and his companions were hungry? ⁴He entered the house of God, and taking the consecrated bread, he ate what is lawful only for priests to eat. And he also gave some to his companions." ⁵Then Jesus said to them, "The Son of Man is Lord of the Sabbath."

⁶On another Sabbath he went into the synagogue and was teaching, and a man was there whose right hand was shriveled. ⁷The Pharisees and the teachers of the law were looking for a reason to accuse Jesus, so they watched him closely to see if he would heal on the Sabbath. ⁸But Jesus knew what they were thinking and said to the man with the shriveled hand, "Get

up and stand in front of everyone." So he got up and stood there.

⁹Then Jesus said to them, "I ask you, which is lawful on the Sabbath: to do good or to do evil, to save life or to destroy it?"

¹⁰He looked around at them all, and then said to the man, "Stretch out your hand." He did so, and his hand was completely restored. ¹¹But they were furious and began to discuss with one another what they might do to Jesus.   Mt 12:1-14

The Twelve Apostles

¹²One of those days Jesus went out to a mountainside to pray, and spent the night praying to God. ¹³When morning came, he called his disciples to him and chose twelve of them, whom he also designated apostles: ¹⁴Simon (whom he named Peter), his brother Andrew, James, John, Philip, Bartholomew, ¹⁵Matthew, Thomas, James son of Alphaeus, Simon who was called the Zealot, ¹⁶Judas son of James, and Judas Iscariot, who became a traitor.   Mt 10:2-4; Mk 3:16-19

Blessings and Woes

¹⁷He went down with them and stood on a level place. A large crowd of his disciples was there and a great number of people from all over Judea, from Jerusalem, and from the coast of Tyre and Sidon, ¹⁸who had come to hear him and to be healed of their diseases.

Those troubled by evil*a* spirits were cured, **19**and the people all tried to touch him, because power was coming from him and healing them all. Mt 14:36; Lk 5:17

20Looking at his disciples, he said:

"Blessed are you who are poor,
     for yours is the kingdom of
     God. Mt 25:34
21Blessed are you who hunger
     now,
     for you will be satisfied.
Blessed are you who weep
     now,
     for you will laugh. Isa 61:2-3
22Blessed are you when men
     hate you,
     when they exclude you and
          insult you Jn 9:22; 16:2
     and reject your name as evil,
          because of the Son of
          Man. Jn 15:21

23"Rejoice in that day and leap for joy, because great is your reward in heaven. For that is how their fathers treated the prophets.

24"But woe to you who are rich,
     for you have already
          received your comfort.
25Woe to you who are well fed
     now,
     for you will go hungry.
Woe to you who laugh now,
     for you will mourn and
          weep. Pr 14:13

a 18 Greek unclean

26Woe to you when all men
     speak well of you,
     for that is how their fathers
          treated the false
          prophets. Mt 7:15

Love for Enemies

27"But I tell you who hear me: Love your enemies, do good to those who hate you, **28**bless those who curse you, pray for those who mistreat you. **29**If someone strikes you on one cheek, turn to him the other also. If someone takes your cloak, do not stop him from taking your tunic. **30**Give to everyone who asks you, and if anyone takes what belongs to you, do not demand it back. **31**Do to others as you would have them do to you. Mt 5:39-42

32"If you love those who love you, what credit is that to you? Even 'sinners' love those who love them. **33**And if you do good to those who are good to you, what credit is that to you? Even 'sinners' do that. **34**And if you lend to those from whom you expect repayment, what credit is that to you? Even 'sinners' lend to 'sinners,' expecting to be repaid in full. **35**But love your enemies, do good to them, and lend to them without expecting to get anything back. Then your reward will be great, and you will be sons of the Most High, because he is kind to the ungrateful and wicked. **36**Be merciful, just as your Father is merciful.

Judging Others

37"Do not judge, and you will not be judged. Do not condemn, and you will not be condemned. Forgive, and you will be forgiven. **38**Give, and it will be given to you. A good measure, pressed down, shaken together and running over, will be poured into your lap. For with the measure you use, it will be measured to you." Mt 7:1; Mk 4:24

39He also told them this parable: "Can a blind man lead a blind man? Will they not both fall into a pit? **40**A student is not above his teacher, but everyone who is fully trained will be like his teacher.

41"Why do you look at the speck of sawdust in your brother's eye and pay no attention to the plank in your own eye? **42**How can you say to your brother, 'Brother, let me take the speck out of your eye,' when you yourself fail to see the plank in your own eye? You hypocrite, first take the plank out of your eye, and then you will see clearly to remove the speck from your brother's eye. Mt 7:1-5

A Tree and Its Fruit

43"No good tree bears bad fruit, nor does a bad tree bear good fruit. **44**Each tree is recognized by its own fruit. People do not pick figs from thornbushes, or grapes from briers. **45**The good man brings good things out of the good stored up in his heart, and the evil man brings evil things out of the evil stored up in his heart. For out of the overflow of his heart his mouth speaks. Mt 12:33-35

The Wise and Foolish Builders

46"Why do you call me, 'Lord, Lord,' and do not do what I say? **47**I will show you what he is like who comes to me and hears my words and puts them into practice. **48**He is like a man building a house, who dug down deep and laid the foundation on rock. When a flood came, the torrent struck that house but could not shake it, because it was well built. **49**But the one who hears my words and does not put them into practice is like a man who built a house on the ground without a foundation. The moment the torrent struck that house, it collapsed and its destruction was complete." Mt 7:24-27

The Faith of the Centurion

7 When Jesus had finished saying all this in the hearing of the people, he entered Capernaum. **2**There a centurion's servant, whom his master valued highly, was sick and about to die. **3**The centurion heard of Jesus and sent some elders of the Jews to him, asking him to come and heal his servant. **4**When they came to Jesus, they pleaded earnestly with him, "This man deserves to have you do this, **5**because he loves our nation and has built our synagogue." **6**So Jesus went with them. He was not far from the house when the centurion sent friends to say to him: "Lord, don't trouble yourself, for I do not deserve to have you come under my roof. ⁷That is why I did not even consider myself worthy to come to you. But say the word, and my servant will be healed. ⁸For I myself am a man under authority, with soldiers under me. I tell this one, 'Go,' and he goes; and that one, 'Come,' and he comes. I say to my servant, 'Do this,' and he does it."   Ps 107:20

⁹When Jesus heard this, he was amazed at him, and turning to the crowd following him, he said, "I tell you, I have not found such great faith even in Israel." ¹⁰Then the men who had been sent returned to the house and found the servant well.   Mt 8:5-13

Jesus Raises a Widow's Son

¹¹Soon afterward, Jesus went to a town called Nain, and his disciples and a large crowd went along with him. ¹²As he approached the town gate, a dead person was being carried out—the only son of his mother, and she was a widow. And a large crowd from the town was with her. ¹³When the Lord saw her, his heart went out to her and he said, "Don't cry."   Jn 11:1-44

¹⁴Then he went up and touched the coffin, and those carrying it stood still. He said, "Young man, I say to you, get up!" ¹⁵The dead man sat up and began to talk, and Jesus gave him back to his mother.

¹⁶They were all filled with awe and praised God. "A great prophet has appeared among us," they said. "God has come to help his people." ¹⁷This news about Jesus spread throughout Judea*a* and the surrounding country.

Jesus and John the Baptist

¹⁸John's disciples told him about all these things. Calling two of them, ¹⁹he sent them to the Lord to ask, "Are you the one who was to come, or should we expect someone else?"   Mt 3:1; Lk 5:33

²⁰When the men came to Jesus, they said, "John the Baptist sent us to you to ask, 'Are you the one who was to come, or should we expect someone else?'"

²¹At that very time Jesus cured many who had diseases, sicknesses and evil spirits, and gave sight to many who were blind. ²²So he replied to the messengers, "Go back and report to John what you have seen and heard: The blind receive sight, the lame walk, those who have leprosy*b* are cured, the deaf hear, the dead are raised, and the good news is preached to the poor. ²³Blessed is the man who does not fall away on account of me."   Isa 29:18-19; Lk 4:18

²⁴After John's messengers left, Jesus began to speak to the crowd

---

*a*17 Or *the land of the Jews*   *b*22 The Greek word was used for various diseases affecting the skin—not necessarily leprosy.

about John: "What did you go out into the desert to see? A reed swayed by the wind? 25If not, what did you go out to see? A man dressed in fine clothes? No, those who wear expensive clothes and indulge in luxury are in palaces. 26But what did you go out to see? A prophet? Yes, I tell you, and more than a prophet. 27This is the one about whom it is written:

" 'I will send my messenger
      ahead of you,
   who will prepare your way
      before you.'a

28I tell you, among those born of women there is no one greater than John; yet the one who is least in the kingdom of God is greater than he."   Mt 3:2; 11:10; Mk 1:2

29(All the people, even the tax collectors, when they heard Jesus' words, acknowledged that God's way was right, because they had been baptized by John. 30But the Pharisees and experts in the law rejected God's purpose for themselves, because they had not been baptized by John.)   Mt 22:35; Lk 3:12

31"To what, then, can I compare the people of this generation? What are they like? 32They are like children sitting in the marketplace and calling out to each other:

" 'We played the flute for you,
      and you did not dance;
   we sang a dirge,
      and you did not cry.'

33For John the Baptist came neither eating bread nor drinking wine, and you say, 'He has a demon.' 34The Son of Man came eating and drinking, and you say, 'Here is a glutton and a drunkard, a friend of tax collectors and "sinners." ' 35But wisdom is proved right by all her children."

Jesus Anointed by a Sinful Woman

36Now one of the Pharisees invited Jesus to have dinner with him, so he went to the Pharisee's house and reclined at the table. 37When a woman who had lived a sinful life in that town learned that Jesus was eating at the Pharisee's house, she brought an alabaster jar of perfume, 38and as she stood behind him at his feet weeping, she began to wet his feet with her tears. Then she wiped them with her hair, kissed them and poured perfume on them.

39When the Pharisee who had invited him saw this, he said to himself, "If this man were a prophet, he would know who is touching him and what kind of woman she is—that she is a sinner."   Mt 21:11

40Jesus answered him, "Simon, I have something to tell you."

"Tell me, teacher," he said.

41"Two men owed money to a certain moneylender. One owed

a27 Mal. 3:1

him five hundred denarii,[a] and the other fifty. [42]Neither of them had the money to pay him back, so he canceled the debts of both. Now which of them will love him more?"

[43]Simon replied, "I suppose the one who had the bigger debt canceled."

"You have judged correctly," Jesus said.

[44]Then he turned toward the woman and said to Simon, "Do you see this woman? I came into your house. You did not give me any water for my feet, but she wet my feet with her tears and wiped them with her hair. [45]You did not give me a kiss, but this woman, from the time I entered, has not stopped kissing my feet. [46]You did not put oil on my head, but she has poured perfume on my feet. [47]Therefore, I tell you, her many sins have been forgiven—for she loved much. But he who has been forgiven little loves little."   Ge 18:4

[48]Then Jesus said to her, "Your sins are forgiven."   Mt 9:2

[49]The other guests began to say among themselves, "Who is this who even forgives sins?"

[50]Jesus said to the woman, "Your faith has saved you; go in peace."   Mk 5:34; Lk 8:48; Ac 15:33

The Parable of the Sower

8 After this, Jesus traveled about from one town and village to another, proclaiming the good news of the kingdom of God. The Twelve were with him, [2]and also some women who had been cured of evil spirits and diseases: Mary (called Magdalene) from whom seven demons had come out; [3]Joanna the wife of Cuza, the manager of Herod's household; Susanna; and many others. These women were helping to support them out of their own means.

[4]While a large crowd was gathering and people were coming to Jesus from town after town, he told this parable: [5]"A farmer went out to sow his seed. As he was scattering the seed, some fell along the path; it was trampled on, and the birds of the air ate it up. [6]Some fell on rock, and when it came up, the plants withered because they had no moisture. [7]Other seed fell among thorns, which grew up with it and choked the plants. [8]Still other seed fell on good soil. It came up and yielded a crop, a hundred times more than was sown."

When he said this, he called out, "He who has ears to hear, let him hear."   Mt 11:15

[9]His disciples asked him what this parable meant. [10]He said, "The knowledge of the secrets of the kingdom of God has been given to you, but to others I speak in parables, so that,   Mt 13:11

---

[a]41 A denarius was a coin worth about a day's wages.

" 'though seeing, they may not
see;
though hearing, they may
not understand.' *a*   Isa 6:9

¹¹"This is the meaning of the parable: The seed is the word of God. ¹²Those along the path are the ones who hear, and then the devil comes and takes away the word from their hearts, so that they may not believe and be saved. ¹³Those on the rock are the ones who receive the word with joy when they hear it, but they have no root. They believe for a while, but in the time of testing they fall away. ¹⁴The seed that fell among thorns stands for those who hear, but as they go on their way they are choked by life's worries, riches and pleasures, and they do not mature. ¹⁵But the seed on good soil stands for those with a noble and good heart, who hear the word, retain it, and by persevering produce a crop.   Mt 13:2-23; Mk 4:1-20

A Lamp on a Stand

¹⁶"No one lights a lamp and hides it in a jar or puts it under a bed. Instead, he puts it on a stand, so that those who come in can see the light. ¹⁷For there is nothing hidden that will not be disclosed, and nothing concealed that will not be known or brought out into the open. ¹⁸Therefore consider carefully how you listen. Whoever has will be given more; whoever does not have, even what he thinks he has will be taken from him."

Jesus' Mother and Brothers

¹⁹Now Jesus' mother and brothers came to see him, but they were not able to get near him because of the crowd. ²⁰Someone told him, "Your mother and brothers are standing outside, wanting to see you."   Jn 7:5

²¹He replied, "My mother and brothers are those who hear God's word and put it into practice."

Jesus Calms the Storm

²²One day Jesus said to his disciples, "Let's go over to the other side of the lake." So they got into a boat and set out. ²³As they sailed, he fell asleep. A squall came down on the lake, so that the boat was being swamped, and they were in great danger.

²⁴The disciples went and woke him, saying, "Master, Master, we're going to drown!"   Mk 6:47-52

He got up and rebuked the wind and the raging waters; the storm subsided, and all was calm. ²⁵"Where is your faith?" he asked his disciples.   Mt 8:23-27

In fear and amazement they asked one another, "Who is this? He commands even the winds and the water, and they obey him."

a 10 Isaiah 6:9

The Healing of a Demon-possessed Man

²⁶They sailed to the region of the Gerasenes,ᵃ which is across the lake from Galilee. ²⁷When Jesus stepped ashore, he was met by a demon-possessed man from the town. For a long time this man had not worn clothes or lived in a house, but had lived in the tombs. ²⁸When he saw Jesus, he cried out and fell at his feet, shouting at the top of his voice, "What do you want with me, Jesus, Son of the Most High God? I beg you, don't torture me!" ²⁹For Jesus had commanded the evilᵇ spirit to come out of the man. Many times it had seized him, and though he was chained hand and foot and kept under guard, he had broken his chains and had been driven by the demon into solitary places.   Mt 8:29

³⁰Jesus asked him, "What is your name?"

"Legion," he replied, because many demons had gone into him. ³¹And they begged him repeatedly not to order them to go into the Abyss.   Rev 9:1-2,11; 11:7

³²A large herd of pigs was feeding there on the hillside. The demons begged Jesus to let them go into them, and he gave them permission. ³³When the demons came out of the man, they went into the pigs, and the herd rushed down the steep bank into the lake and was drowned.   ver 22-23

³⁴When those tending the pigs saw what had happened, they ran off and reported this in the town and countryside, ³⁵and the people went out to see what had happened. When they came to Jesus, they found the man from whom the demons had gone out, sitting at Jesus' feet, dressed and in his right mind; and they were afraid. ³⁶Those who had seen it told the people how the demon-possessed man had been cured. ³⁷Then all the people of the region of the Gerasenes asked Jesus to leave them, because they were overcome with fear. So he got into the boat and left.   Mt 8:28-34

³⁸The man from whom the demons had gone out begged to go with him, but Jesus sent him away, saying, ³⁹"Return home and tell how much God has done for you." So the man went away and told all over town how much Jesus had done for him.   Mk 5:1-20

A Dead Girl and a Sick Woman

⁴⁰Now when Jesus returned, a crowd welcomed him, for they were all expecting him. ⁴¹Then a man named Jairus, a ruler of the synagogue, came and fell at Jesus' feet, pleading with him to come to his house ⁴²because his only

---

ᵃ26 Some manuscripts *Gadarenes*; other manuscripts *Gergesenes*; also in verse 37   ᵇ29 Greek *unclean*

daughter, a girl of about twelve, was dying.   Mk 5:22

As Jesus was on his way, the crowds almost crushed him. **43**And a woman was there who had been subject to bleeding for twelve years,*a* but no one could heal her. **44**She came up behind him and touched the edge of his cloak, and immediately her bleeding stopped.

45"Who touched me?" Jesus asked.

When they all denied it, Peter said, "Master, the people are crowding and pressing against you."   Lk 5:5

46But Jesus said, "Someone touched me; I know that power has gone out from me."   Lk 5:17

47Then the woman, seeing that she could not go unnoticed, came trembling and fell at his feet. In the presence of all the people, she told why she had touched him and how she had been instantly healed. **48**Then he said to her, "Daughter, your faith has healed you. Go in peace."   Mt 9:22; Ac 15:33

49While Jesus was still speaking, someone came from the house of Jairus, the synagogue ruler. "Your daughter is dead," he said. "Don't bother the teacher any more."

50Hearing this, Jesus said to Jairus, "Don't be afraid; just believe, and she will be healed."

51When he arrived at the house of Jairus, he did not let anyone go in with him except Peter, John and James, and the child's father and mother. **52**Meanwhile, all the people were wailing and mourning for her. "Stop wailing," Jesus said. "She is not dead but asleep."

53They laughed at him, knowing that she was dead. **54**But he took her by the hand and said, "My child, get up!" **55**Her spirit returned, and at once she stood up. Then Jesus told them to give her something to eat. **56**Her parents were astonished, but he ordered them not to tell anyone what had happened.   Mt 9:18-26; Mk 5:22-43

Jesus Sends Out the Twelve

9 When Jesus had called the Twelve together, he gave them power and authority to drive out all demons and to cure diseases, **2**and he sent them out to preach the kingdom of God and to heal the sick. **3**He told them: "Take nothing for the journey—no staff, no bag, no bread, no money, no extra tunic. **4**Whatever house you enter, stay there until you leave that town. **5**If people do not welcome you, shake the dust off your feet when you leave their town, as a testimony against them." **6**So they set out and went from village to village, preaching the gospel and healing people everywhere.

7Now Herod the tetrarch heard about all that was going on. And he was perplexed, because some were saying that John had been

---

a 43 Many manuscripts *years, and she had spent all she had on doctors* raised from the dead, ⁸others that Elijah had appeared, and still others that one of the prophets of long ago had come back to life. ⁹But Herod said, "I beheaded John. Who, then, is this I hear such things about?" And he tried to see him.   Mt 14:1-2; Mk 6:14-16

Jesus Feeds the Five Thousand

¹⁰When the apostles returned, they reported to Jesus what they had done. Then he took them with him and they withdrew by themselves to a town called Bethsaida, ¹¹but the crowds learned about it and followed him. He welcomed them and spoke to them about the kingdom of God, and healed those who needed healing.   Mt 11:21

¹²Late in the afternoon the Twelve came to him and said, "Send the crowd away so they can go to the surrounding villages and countryside and find food and lodging, because we are in a remote place here."

¹³He replied, "You give them something to eat."   Mt 14:13-21

They answered, "We have only five loaves of bread and two fish—unless we go and buy food for all this crowd." ¹⁴(About five thousand men were there.)   Jn 6:5-13

But he said to his disciples, "Have them sit down in groups of about fifty each." ¹⁵The disciples did so, and everybody sat down. ¹⁶Taking the five loaves and the two fish and looking up to heaven, he gave thanks and broke them. Then he gave them to the disciples to set before the people. ¹⁷They all ate and were satisfied, and the disciples picked up twelve basketfuls of broken pieces that were left over.   2Ki 4:42-44

Peter's Confession of Christ

¹⁸Once when Jesus was praying in private and his disciples were with him, he asked them, "Who do the crowds say I am?"   Lk 3:21

¹⁹They replied, "Some say John the Baptist; others say Elijah; and still others, that one of the prophets of long ago has come back to life."   Mt 3:1

²⁰"But what about you?" he asked. "Who do you say I am?"

Peter answered, "The Christᵃ of God."   Mk 8:27-29; Jn 6:66-69

²¹Jesus strictly warned them not to tell this to anyone. ²²And he said, "The Son of Man must suffer many things and be rejected by the elders, chief priests and teachers of the law, and he must be killed and on the third day be raised to life."   Mt 16:20-21; Mk 8:30

²³Then he said to them all: "If anyone would come after me, he must deny himself and take up his cross daily and follow me. ²⁴For whoever wants to save his life will lose it, but whoever loses his life for me will save it. ²⁵What good is it for a man to gain the whole

ᵃ20 Or Messiah

world, and yet lose or forfeit his very self? ²⁶If anyone is ashamed of me and my words, the Son of Man will be ashamed of him when he comes in his glory and in the glory of the Father and of the holy angels. ²⁷I tell you the truth, some who are standing here will not taste death before they see the kingdom of God."   Mt 16:21-28

The Transfiguration

²⁸About eight days after Jesus said this, he took Peter, John and James with him and went up onto a mountain to pray. ²⁹As he was praying, the appearance of his face changed, and his clothes became as bright as a flash of lightning. ³⁰Two men, Moses and Elijah, ³¹appeared in glorious splendor, talking with Jesus. They spoke about his departure, which he was about to bring to fulfillment at Jerusalem. ³²Peter and his companions were very sleepy, but when they became fully awake, they saw his glory and the two men standing with him. ³³As the men were leaving Jesus, Peter said to him, "Master, it is good for us to be here. Let us put up three shelters —one for you, one for Moses and one for Elijah." (He did not know what he was saying.)   Lk 3:21

³⁴While he was speaking, a cloud appeared and enveloped them, and they were afraid as they entered the cloud. ³⁵A voice came from the cloud, saying, "This is my Son, whom I have chosen; listen to him." ³⁶When the voice had spoken, they found that Jesus was alone. The disciples kept this to themselves, and told no one at that time what they had seen.   Mt 17:1-8

The Healing of a Boy With an Evil Spirit

³⁷The next day, when they came down from the mountain, a large crowd met him. ³⁸A man in the crowd called out, "Teacher, I beg you to look at my son, for he is my only child. ³⁹A spirit seizes him and he suddenly screams; it throws him into convulsions so that he foams at the mouth. It scarcely ever leaves him and is destroying him. ⁴⁰I begged your disciples to drive it out, but they could not."   Mt 17:14-18,22-23

⁴¹"O unbelieving and perverse generation," Jesus replied, "how long shall I stay with you and put up with you? Bring your son here."

⁴²Even while the boy was coming, the demon threw him to the ground in a convulsion. But Jesus rebuked the evilᵃ spirit, healed the boy and gave him back to his father. ⁴³And they were all amazed at the greatness of God.

While everyone was marveling at all that Jesus did, he said to his disciples, ⁴⁴"Listen carefully to what I am about to tell you: The Son of Man is going to be betrayed

ᵃ42 Greek unclean

into the hands of men." **45**But they did not understand what this meant. It was hidden from them, so that they did not grasp it, and they were afraid to ask him about it.   Mk 9:14-27,30-32

Who Will Be the Greatest?

46An argument started among the disciples as to which of them would be the greatest. **47**Jesus, knowing their thoughts, took a little child and had him stand beside him. **48**Then he said to them, "Whoever welcomes this little child in my name welcomes me; and whoever welcomes me welcomes the one who sent me. For he who is least among you all—he is the greatest."   Mt 18:1-5

49"Master," said John, "we saw a man driving out demons in your name and we tried to stop him, because he is not one of us."   Lk 5:5

50"Do not stop him," Jesus said, "for whoever is not against you is for you."   Mt 12:30; Lk 11:23

Samaritan Opposition

51As the time approached for him to be taken up to heaven, Jesus resolutely set out for Jerusalem. **52**And he sent messengers on ahead, who went into a Samaritan village to get things ready for him; **53**but the people there did not welcome him, because he was heading for Jerusalem. **54**When the dis-ciples James and John saw this, they asked, "Lord, do you want us to call fire down from heaven to destroy them*a*?" **55**But Jesus turned and rebuked them, **56**and*b* they went to another village.

The Cost of Following Jesus

57As they were walking along the road, a man said to him, "I will follow you wherever you go."

58Jesus replied, "Foxes have holes and birds of the air have nests, but the Son of Man has no place to lay his head."

59He said to another man, "Follow me."

But the man replied, "Lord, first let me go and bury my father."

60Jesus said to him, "Let the dead bury their own dead, but you go and proclaim the kingdom of God."   Mt 8:19-22

61Still another said, "I will follow you, Lord; but first let me go back and say good-by to my family."

62Jesus replied, "No one who puts his hand to the plow and looks back is fit for service in the kingdom of God."

Jesus Sends Out the Seventy-two

10 After this the Lord appointed seventy-two*c* others and sent them two by two ahead of him to every town and place where he was about to go. **2**He told them,

---

a 54 Some manuscripts *them, even as Elijah did*   *b* 55,56 Some manuscripts *them. And he said, "You do not know what kind of spirit you are of, for the Son of Man did not come to destroy men's lives, but to save them." *56*And*   *c* 1 Some manuscripts *seventy;* also in verse 17

"The harvest is plentiful, but the workers are few. Ask the Lord of the harvest, therefore, to send out workers into his harvest field. ³Go! I am sending you out like lambs among wolves. ⁴Do not take a purse or bag or sandals; and do not greet anyone on the road.

⁵"When you enter a house, first say, 'Peace to this house.' ⁶If a man of peace is there, your peace will rest on him; if not, it will return to you. ⁷Stay in that house, eating and drinking whatever they give you, for the worker deserves his wages. Do not move around from house to house.   Mt 10:10; 1Co 9:14

⁸"When you enter a town and are welcomed, eat what is set before you. ⁹Heal the sick who are there and tell them, 'The kingdom of God is near you.' ¹⁰But when you enter a town and are not welcomed, go into its streets and say, ¹¹'Even the dust of your town that sticks to our feet we wipe off against you. Yet be sure of this: The kingdom of God is near.' ¹²I tell you, it will be more bearable on that day for Sodom than for that town.   Lk 9:3-5; 1Co 10:27

¹³"Woe to you, Korazin! Woe to you, Bethsaida! For if the miracles that were performed in you had been performed in Tyre and Sidon, they would have repented long ago, sitting in sackcloth and ashes. ¹⁴But it will be more bearable for Tyre and Sidon at the judgment than for you. ¹⁵And you, Capernaum, will you be lifted up to the skies? No, you will go down to the depths.ᵃ   Mt 4:13; Rev 11:3

¹⁶"He who listens to you listens to me; he who rejects you rejects me; but he who rejects me rejects him who sent me."   Mt 10:40; Jn 13:20

¹⁷The seventy-two returned with joy and said, "Lord, even the demons submit to us in your name."   Mk 16:17

¹⁸He replied, "I saw Satan fall like lightning from heaven. ¹⁹I have given you authority to trample on snakes and scorpions and to overcome all the power of the enemy; nothing will harm you. ²⁰However, do not rejoice that the spirits submit to you, but rejoice that your names are written in heaven."   Ex 32:32; Heb 12:23; Rev 13:8

²¹At that time Jesus, full of joy through the Holy Spirit, said, "I praise you, Father, Lord of heaven and earth, because you have hidden these things from the wise and learned, and revealed them to little children. Yes, Father, for this was your good pleasure.   1Co 1:26-29

²²"All things have been committed to me by my Father. No one knows who the Son is except the Father, and no one knows who the Father is except the Son and those to whom the Son chooses to reveal him."   Mt 11:21-23,25-27

²³Then he turned to his disciples and said privately, "Blessed are the

---

ᵃ 15 Greek *Hades*

eyes that see what you see. ²⁴For I tell you that many prophets and kings wanted to see what you see but did not see it, and to hear what you hear but did not hear it."

The Parable of the Good Samaritan

²⁵On one occasion an expert in the law stood up to test Jesus. "Teacher," he asked, "what must I do to inherit eternal life?"   Mt 19:16

²⁶"What is written in the Law?" he replied. "How do you read it?"

²⁷He answered: " 'Love the Lord your God with all your heart and with all your soul and with all your strength and with all your mind'^a; and, 'Love your neighbor as yourself.'^b   Lev 19:18; Dt 6:5

²⁸"You have answered correctly," Jesus replied. "Do this and you will live."   Mt 22:34-40; Mk 12:28-31

²⁹But he wanted to justify himself, so he asked Jesus, "And who is my neighbor?"   Lk 16:15

³⁰In reply Jesus said: "A man was going down from Jerusalem to Jericho, when he fell into the hands of robbers. They stripped him of his clothes, beat him and went away, leaving him half dead. ³¹A priest happened to be going down the same road, and when he saw the man, he passed by on the other side. ³²So too, a Levite, when he came to the place and saw him, passed by on the other side. ³³But a Samaritan, as he traveled, came where the man was; and when he saw him, he took pity on him. ³⁴He went to him and bandaged his wounds, pouring on oil and wine. Then he put the man on his own donkey, took him to an inn and took care of him. ³⁵The next day he took out two silver coins^c and gave them to the innkeeper. 'Look after him,' he said, 'and when I return, I will reimburse you for any extra expense you may have.'

³⁶"Which of these three do you think was a neighbor to the man who fell into the hands of robbers?"

³⁷The expert in the law replied, "The one who had mercy on him."

Jesus told him, "Go and do likewise."

At the Home of Martha and Mary

³⁸As Jesus and his disciples were on their way, he came to a village where a woman named Martha opened her home to him. ³⁹She had a sister called Mary, who sat at the Lord's feet listening to what he said. ⁴⁰But Martha was distracted by all the preparations that had to be made. She came to him and asked, "Lord, don't you care that my sister has left me to do the work by myself? Tell her to help me!"   Lk 8:35; Jn 11:1

⁴¹"Martha, Martha," the Lord answered, "you are worried and upset about many things, ⁴²but only

^a27 Deut. 6:5   ^b27 Lev. 19:18   ^c35 Greek *two denarii*

one thing is needed.[a] Mary has chosen what is better, and it will not be taken away from her."

Jesus' Teaching on Prayer

11 One day Jesus was praying in a certain place. When he finished, one of his disciples said to him, "Lord, teach us to pray, just as John taught his disciples."

²He said to them, "When you pray, say:

" 'Father,[b]
hallowed be your name,
your kingdom come.[c] Mt 3:2
³Give us each day our daily
  bread.
⁴Forgive us our sins,
  for we also forgive everyone
  who sins against us.[d]
And lead us not into
  temptation.[e] ' " Mt 6:9-13

⁵Then he said to them, "Suppose one of you has a friend, and he goes to him at midnight and says, 'Friend, lend me three loaves of bread, ⁶because a friend of mine on a journey has come to me, and I have nothing to set before him.'

⁷"Then the one inside answers, 'Don't bother me. The door is already locked, and my children are with me in bed. I can't get up and give you anything.' ⁸I tell you, though he will not get up and give him the bread because he is his friend, yet because of the man's boldness[f] he will get up and give him as much as he needs.

⁹"So I say to you: Ask and it will be given to you; seek and you will find; knock and the door will be opened to you. ¹⁰For everyone who asks receives; he who seeks finds; and to him who knocks, the door will be opened. Mt 7:7

¹¹"Which of you fathers, if your son asks for[g] a fish, will give him a snake instead? ¹²Or if he asks for an egg, will give him a scorpion? ¹³If you then, though you are evil, know how to give good gifts to your children, how much more will your Father in heaven give the Holy Spirit to those who ask him!"

Jesus and Beelzebub

¹⁴Jesus was driving out a demon that was mute. When the demon left, the man who had been mute spoke, and the crowd was amazed. ¹⁵But some of them said, "By Beelzebub,[h] the prince of demons, he is driving out demons." ¹⁶Others tested him by asking for a sign from heaven. Mt 12:22,24

¹⁷Jesus knew their thoughts and said to them: "Any kingdom divided against itself will be ruined, and a house divided against itself will fall. ¹⁸If Satan is divided against

---

[a]42 Some manuscripts *but few things are needed—or only one* [b]2 Some manuscripts *Our Father in heaven* [c]2 Some manuscripts *come. May your will be done on earth as it is in heaven.* [d]4 Greek *everyone who is indebted to us* [e]4 Some manuscripts *temptation but deliver us from the evil one* [f]8 Or *persistence* [g]11 Some manuscripts *for bread, will give him a stone; or if he asks for* [h]15 Greek *Beezeboul* or *Beelzeboul*; also in verses 18 and 19

himself, how can his kingdom stand? I say this because you claim that I drive out demons by Beelzebub. ¹⁹Now if I drive out demons by Beelzebub, by whom do your followers drive them out? So then, they will be your judges. ²⁰But if I drive out demons by the finger of God, then the kingdom of God has come to you. Mt 12:25-28

²¹"When a strong man, fully armed, guards his own house, his possessions are safe. ²²But when someone stronger attacks and overpowers him, he takes away the armor in which the man trusted and divides up the spoils.

²³"He who is not with me is against me, and he who does not gather with me, scatters. Mt 12:30

²⁴"When an evilᵃ spirit comes out of a man, it goes through arid places seeking rest and does not find it. Then it says, 'I will return to the house I left.' ²⁵When it arrives, it finds the house swept clean and put in order. ²⁶Then it goes and takes seven other spirits more wicked than itself, and they go in and live there. And the final condition of that man is worse than the first." Mt 12:43-45

²⁷As Jesus was saying these things, a woman in the crowd called out, "Blessed is the mother who gave you birth and nursed you." Lk 23:29

²⁸He replied, "Blessed rather are those who hear the word of God and obey it." Lk 8:21; Jn 14:21

The Sign of Jonah

²⁹As the crowds increased, Jesus said, "This is a wicked generation. It asks for a miraculous sign, but none will be given it except the sign of Jonah. ³⁰For as Jonah was a sign to the Ninevites, so also will the Son of Man be to this generation. ³¹The Queen of the South will rise at the judgment with the men of this generation and condemn them; for she came from the ends of the earth to listen to Solomon's wisdom, and now oneᵇ greater than Solomon is here. ³²The men of Nineveh will stand up at the judgment with this generation and condemn it; for they repented at the preaching of Jonah, and now one greater than Jonah is here.

The Lamp of the Body

³³"No one lights a lamp and puts it in a place where it will be hidden, or under a bowl. Instead he puts it on its stand, so that those who come in may see the light. ³⁴Your eye is the lamp of your body. When your eyes are good, your whole body also is full of light. But when they are bad, your body also is full of darkness. ³⁵See to it, then, that the light within you is not darkness. ³⁶Therefore, if your whole body is full of light, and no part of it dark, it will be

ᵃ24 Greek unclean   ᵇ31 Or something; also in verse 32

completely lighted, as when the light of a lamp shines on you."

Six Woes

37When Jesus had finished speaking, a Pharisee invited him to eat with him; so he went in and reclined at the table. **38**But the Pharisee, noticing that Jesus did not first wash before the meal, was surprised.   Mk 7:3-4

39Then the Lord said to him, "Now then, you Pharisees clean the outside of the cup and dish, but inside you are full of greed and wickedness. **40**You foolish people! Did not the one who made the outside make the inside also? **41**But give what is inside ˌthe dish,ᵃ to the poor, and everything will be clean for you.   Mt 23:25-26; Lk 12:33

42"Woe to you Pharisees, because you give God a tenth of your mint, rue and all other kinds of garden herbs, but you neglect justice and the love of God. You should have practiced the latter without leaving the former undone.   Mic 6:8; Mt 23:23

43"Woe to you Pharisees, because you love the most important seats in the synagogues and greetings in the marketplaces.   Mt 23:6-7

44"Woe to you, because you are like unmarked graves, which men walk over without knowing it."

45One of the experts in the law answered him, "Teacher, when you say these things, you insult us also."   Mt 22:35

46Jesus replied, "And you experts in the law, woe to you, because you load people down with burdens they can hardly carry, and you yourselves will not lift one finger to help them.   Mt 23:4

47"Woe to you, because you build tombs for the prophets, and it was your forefathers who killed them. **48**So you testify that you approve of what your forefathers did; they killed the prophets, and you build their tombs. **49**Because of this, God in his wisdom said, 'I will send them prophets and apostles, some of whom they will kill and others they will persecute.' **50**Therefore this generation will be held responsible for the blood of all the prophets that has been shed since the beginning of the world, **51**from the blood of Abel to the blood of Zechariah, who was killed between the altar and the sanctuary. Yes, I tell you, this generation will be held responsible for it all.

52"Woe to you experts in the law, because you have taken away the key to knowledge. You yourselves have not entered, and you have hindered those who were entering."   Mt 23:13

53When Jesus left there, the Pharisees and the teachers of the law began to oppose him fiercely and to besiege him with questions,

ᵃ41 Or *what you have*

54waiting to catch him in something he might say.   Mk 12:13

Warnings and Encouragements

12 Meanwhile, when a crowd of many thousands had gathered, so that they were trampling on one another, Jesus began to speak first to his disciples, saying: "Be on your guard against the yeast of the Pharisees, which is hypocrisy. **2**There is nothing concealed that will not be disclosed, or hidden that will not be made known. **3**What you have said in the dark will be heard in the daylight, and what you have whispered in the ear in the inner rooms will be proclaimed from the roofs. Mk 4:22

4"I tell you, my friends, do not be afraid of those who kill the body and after that can do no more. **5**But I will show you whom you should fear: Fear him who, after the killing of the body, has power to throw you into hell. Yes, I tell you, fear him. **6**Are not five sparrows sold for two pennies[a]? Yet not one of them is forgotten by God. **7**Indeed, the very hairs of your head are all numbered. Don't be afraid; you are worth more than many sparrows.   Mt 10:30; Jn 15:14,15

8"I tell you, whoever acknowledges me before men, the Son of Man will also acknowledge him before the angels of God. **9**But he who disowns me before men will be disowned before the angels of God. **10**And everyone who speaks a word against the Son of Man will be forgiven, but anyone who blasphemes against the Holy Spirit will not be forgiven.   Mt 10:26-33; 1Jn 5:16

11"When you are brought before synagogues, rulers and authorities, do not worry about how you will defend yourselves or what you will say, **12**for the Holy Spirit will teach you at that time what you should say."   Mt 10:20; Mk 13:11

The Parable of the Rich Fool

13Someone in the crowd said to him, "Teacher, tell my brother to divide the inheritance with me."

14Jesus replied, "Man, who appointed me a judge or an arbiter between you?" **15**Then he said to them, "Watch out! Be on your guard against all kinds of greed; a man's life does not consist in the abundance of his possessions."

16And he told them this parable: "The ground of a certain rich man produced a good crop. **17**He thought to himself, 'What shall I do? I have no place to store my crops.'

18"Then he said, 'This is what I'll do. I will tear down my barns and build bigger ones, and there I will store all my grain and my goods. **19**And I'll say to myself, "You have plenty of good things laid up for many years. Take life easy; eat, drink and be merry." '

20"But God said to him, 'You fool! This very night your life will be demanded from you. Then who will get what you have prepared for yourself?' Ps 39:6; Jer 17:11 **21**"This is how it will be with anyone who stores up things for himself but is not rich toward God." ver 33

Do Not Worry

22Then Jesus said to his disciples: "Therefore I tell you, do not worry about your life, what you will eat; or about your body, what you will wear. **23**Life is more than food, and the body more than clothes. **24**Consider the ravens: They do not sow or reap, they have no storeroom or barn; yet God feeds them. And how much more valuable you are than birds! **25**Who of you by worrying can add a single hour to his life*a*? **26**Since you cannot do this very little thing, why do you worry about the rest?

27"Consider how the lilies grow. They do not labor or spin. Yet I tell you, not even Solomon in all his splendor was dressed like one of these. **28**If that is how God clothes the grass of the field, which is here today, and tomorrow is thrown into the fire, how much more will he clothe you, O you of little faith! **29**And do not set your heart on what you will eat or drink; do not worry about it. **30**For the pagan world runs after all such things, and your Father knows that you need them. **31**But seek his kingdom, and these things will be given to you as well. Mt 6:25-33

32"Do not be afraid, little flock, for your Father has been pleased to give you the kingdom. **33**Sell your possessions and give to the poor. Provide purses for yourselves that will not wear out, a treasure in heaven that will not be exhausted, where no thief comes near and no moth destroys. **34**For where your treasure is, there your heart will be also. Mt 6:20-21; 14:27

Watchfulness

35"Be dressed ready for service and keep your lamps burning, **36**like men waiting for their master to return from a wedding banquet, so that when he comes and knocks they can immediately open the door for him. **37**It will be good for those servants whose master finds them watching when he comes. I tell you the truth, he will dress himself to serve, will have them recline at the table and will come and wait on them. **38**It will be good for those servants whose master finds them ready, even if he comes in the second or third watch of the night. **39**But understand this: If the owner of the house had known at what hour the thief was coming, he would not have let his house be broken into. **40**You also must be

a 25 Or single cubit to his height

ready, because the Son of Man will come at an hour when you do not expect him." Mt 25:1-13; Mk 13:33-37

⁴¹Peter asked, "Lord, are you telling this parable to us, or to everyone?"

⁴²The Lord answered, "Who then is the faithful and wise manager, whom the master puts in charge of his servants to give them their food allowance at the proper time? ⁴³It will be good for that servant whom the master finds doing so when he returns. ⁴⁴I tell you the truth, he will put him in charge of all his possessions. ⁴⁵But suppose the servant says to himself, 'My master is taking a long time in coming,' and he then begins to beat the menservants and maidservants and to eat and drink and get drunk. ⁴⁶The master of that servant will come on a day when he does not expect him and at an hour he is not aware of. He will cut him to pieces and assign him a place with the unbelievers. Mt 24:43-51

⁴⁷"That servant who knows his master's will and does not get ready or does not do what his master wants will be beaten with many blows. ⁴⁸But the one who does not know and does things deserving punishment will be beaten with few blows. From everyone who has been given much, much will be demanded; and from the one who has been entrusted with much, much more will be asked.

Not Peace but Division

⁴⁹"I have come to bring fire on the earth, and how I wish it were already kindled! ⁵⁰But I have a baptism to undergo, and how distressed I am until it is completed! ⁵¹Do you think I came to bring peace on earth? No, I tell you, but division. ⁵²From now on there will be five in one family divided against each other, three against two and two against three. ⁵³They will be divided, father against son and son against father, mother against daughter and daughter against mother, mother-in-law against daughter-in-law and daughter-in-law against mother-in-law." Mt 10:34-36

Interpreting the Times

⁵⁴He said to the crowd: "When you see a cloud rising in the west, immediately you say, 'It's going to rain,' and it does. ⁵⁵And when the south wind blows, you say, 'It's going to be hot,' and it is. ⁵⁶Hypocrites! You know how to interpret the appearance of the earth and the sky. How is it that you don't know how to interpret this present time? Mt 16:2-3

⁵⁷"Why don't you judge for yourselves what is right? ⁵⁸As you are going with your adversary to the magistrate, try hard to be reconciled to him on the way, or he may drag you off to the judge, and the judge turn you over to the officer, and the officer throw you into

prison. [59]I tell you, you will not get out until you have paid the last penny.[a]"   Mt 5:25-26; Mk 12:42

Repent or Perish

13 Now there were some present at that time who told Jesus about the Galileans whose blood Pilate had mixed with their sacrifices. [2]Jesus answered, "Do you think that these Galileans were worse sinners than all the other Galileans because they suffered this way? [3]I tell you, no! But unless you repent, you too will all perish. [4]Or those eighteen who died when the tower in Siloam fell on them—do you think they were more guilty than all the others living in Jerusalem? [5]I tell you, no! But unless you repent, you too will all perish."   Mt 27:2

[6]Then he told this parable: "A man had a fig tree, planted in his vineyard, and he went to look for fruit on it, but did not find any. [7]So he said to the man who took care of the vineyard, 'For three years now I've been coming to look for fruit on this fig tree and haven't found any. Cut it down! Why should it use up the soil?'   Mt 3:10

[8]" 'Sir,' the man replied, 'leave it alone for one more year, and I'll dig around it and fertilize it. [9]If it bears fruit next year, fine! If not, then cut it down.' "

A Crippled Woman Healed on the Sabbath

[10]On a Sabbath Jesus was teaching in one of the synagogues, [11]and a woman was there who had been crippled by a spirit for eighteen years. She was bent over and could not straighten up at all. [12]When Jesus saw her, he called her forward and said to her, "Woman, you are set free from your infirmity." [13]Then he put his hands on her, and immediately she straightened up and praised God.   Mt 4:23

[14]Indignant because Jesus had healed on the Sabbath, the synagogue ruler said to the people, "There are six days for work. So come and be healed on those days, not on the Sabbath."   Ex 20:9; Mk 5:22

[15]The Lord answered him, "You hypocrites! Doesn't each of you on the Sabbath untie his ox or donkey from the stall and lead it out to give it water? [16]Then should not this woman, a daughter of Abraham, whom Satan has kept bound for eighteen long years, be set free on the Sabbath day from what bound her?"   Lk 14:5; 19:9

[17]When he said this, all his opponents were humiliated, but the people were delighted with all the wonderful things he was doing.

The Parables of the Mustard Seed and the Yeast

[18]Then Jesus asked, "What is

---

[a] 59 Greek lepton

the kingdom of God like? What shall I compare it to? ¹⁹It is like a mustard seed, which a man took and planted in his garden. It grew and became a tree, and the birds of the air perched in its branches."

²⁰Again he asked, "What shall I compare the kingdom of God to? ²¹It is like yeast that a woman took and mixed into a large amount*a* of flour until it worked all through the dough."   Mt 13:31-33

The Narrow Door

²²Then Jesus went through the towns and villages, teaching as he made his way to Jerusalem. ²³Someone asked him, "Lord, are only a few people going to be saved?"   Lk 9:51

He said to them, ²⁴"Make every effort to enter through the narrow door, because many, I tell you, will try to enter and will not be able to. ²⁵Once the owner of the house gets up and closes the door, you will stand outside knocking and pleading, 'Sir, open the door for us.'

"But he will answer, 'I don't know you or where you come from.'   Mt 7:23; 25:10-12

²⁶"Then you will say, 'We ate and drank with you, and you taught in our streets.'

²⁷"But he will reply, 'I don't know you or where you come from. Away from me, all you evildoers!'   Mt 7:23; 25:41

²⁸"There will be weeping there, and gnashing of teeth, when you see Abraham, Isaac and Jacob and all the prophets in the kingdom of God, but you yourselves thrown out. ²⁹People will come from east and west and north and south, and will take their places at the feast in the kingdom of God. ³⁰Indeed there are those who are last who will be first, and first who will be last."   Mt 19:30

Jesus' Sorrow for Jerusalem

³¹At that time some Pharisees came to Jesus and said to him, "Leave this place and go somewhere else. Herod wants to kill you."   Mt 14:1

³²He replied, "Go tell that fox, 'I will drive out demons and heal people today and tomorrow, and on the third day I will reach my goal.' ³³In any case, I must keep going today and tomorrow and the next day—for surely no prophet can die outside Jerusalem!

³⁴"O Jerusalem, Jerusalem, you who kill the prophets and stone those sent to you, how often I have longed to gather your children together, as a hen gathers her chicks under her wings, but you were not willing! ³⁵Look, your house is left to you desolate. I tell you, you will not see me again until you say, 'Blessed is he who comes in the name of the Lord.'*b*"   Mt 23:37-39

---

a 21 Greek *three satas* (probably about 1/2 bushel or 22 liters)   *b 35* Psalm 118:26

Jesus at a Pharisee's House

14 One Sabbath, when Jesus went to eat in the house of a prominent Pharisee, he was being carefully watched. **2**There in front of him was a man suffering from dropsy. **3**Jesus asked the Pharisees and experts in the law, "Is it lawful to heal on the Sabbath or not?" **4**But they remained silent. So taking hold of the man, he healed him and sent him away.

5Then he asked them, "If one of you has a son*a* or an ox that falls into a well on the Sabbath day, will you not immediately pull him out?" **6**And they had nothing to say.

Lk 13:15

7When he noticed how the guests picked the places of honor at the table, he told them this parable: **8**"When someone invites you to a wedding feast, do not take the place of honor, for a person more distinguished than you may have been invited. **9**If so, the host who invited both of you will come and say to you, 'Give this man your seat.' Then, humiliated, you will have to take the least important place. **10**But when you are invited, take the lowest place, so that when your host comes, he will say to you, 'Friend, move up to a better place.' Then you will be honored in the presence of all your fellow guests. **11**For everyone who exalts himself will be humbled, and he who humbles himself will be exalted."

Pr 25:6-7

12Then Jesus said to his host, "When you give a luncheon or dinner, do not invite your friends, your brothers or relatives, or your rich neighbors; if you do, they may invite you back and so you will be repaid. **13**But when you give a banquet, invite the poor, the crippled, the lame, the blind, **14**and you will be blessed. Although they cannot repay you, you will be repaid at the resurrection of the righteous."

The Parable of the Great Banquet

15When one of those at the table with him heard this, he said to Jesus, "Blessed is the man who will eat at the feast in the kingdom of God."

Rev 19:9

16Jesus replied: "A certain man was preparing a great banquet and invited many guests. **17**At the time of the banquet he sent his servant to tell those who had been invited, 'Come, for everything is now ready.'

18"But they all alike began to make excuses. The first said, 'I have just bought a field, and I must go and see it. Please excuse me.'

19"Another said, 'I have just bought five yoke of oxen, and I'm on my way to try them out. Please excuse me.'

20"Still another said, 'I just got married, so I can't come.'

a 5 Some manuscripts *donkey*

21"The servant came back and reported this to his master. Then the owner of the house became angry and ordered his servant, 'Go out quickly into the streets and alleys of the town and bring in the poor, the crippled, the blind and the lame.'   ver 13

22" 'Sir,' the servant said, 'what you ordered has been done, but there is still room.'

23"Then the master told his servant, 'Go out to the roads and country lanes and make them come in, so that my house will be full. **24**I tell you, not one of those men who were invited will get a taste of my banquet.' "   Mt 22:2-14

The Cost of Being a Disciple

25Large crowds were traveling with Jesus, and turning to them he said: **26**"If anyone comes to me and does not hate his father and mother, his wife and children, his brothers and sisters—yes, even his own life—he cannot be my disciple. **27**And anyone who does not carry his cross and follow me cannot be my disciple.   Mt 10:37-38; Lk 9:23

28"Suppose one of you wants to build a tower. Will he not first sit down and estimate the cost to see if he has enough money to complete it? **29**For if he lays the foundation and is not able to finish it, everyone who sees it will ridicule him, **30**saying, 'This fellow began to build and was not able to finish.'

31"Or suppose a king is about to go to war against another king. Will he not first sit down and consider whether he is able with ten thousand men to oppose the one coming against him with twenty thousand? **32**If he is not able, he will send a delegation while the other is still a long way off and will ask for terms of peace. **33**In the same way, any of you who does not give up everything he has cannot be my disciple.   Php 3:7-8

34"Salt is good, but if it loses its saltiness, how can it be made salty again? **35**It is fit neither for the soil nor for the manure pile; it is thrown out.   Mt 5:13; Mk 9:50

"He who has ears to hear, let him hear."   Mt 11:15

The Parable of the Lost Sheep

15 Now the tax collectors and "sinners" were all gathering around to hear him. **2**But the Pharisees and the teachers of the law muttered, "This man welcomes sinners and eats with them."   Mt 9:11; Lk 5:29

3Then Jesus told them this parable: **4**"Suppose one of you has a hundred sheep and loses one of them. Does he not leave the ninety-nine in the open country and go after the lost sheep until he finds it? **5**And when he finds it, he joyfully puts it on his shoulders **6**and goes home. Then he calls his friends and neighbors together and says, 'Rejoice with me; I have found my lost sheep.' **7**I tell you that in the same way there will be more rejoicing in heaven over one sinner who repents than over ninety-nine righteous persons who do not need to repent. Mt 18:12-14

The Parable of the Lost Coin

8"Or suppose a woman has ten silver coins*a* and loses one. Does she not light a lamp, sweep the house and search carefully until she finds it? 9And when she finds it, she calls her friends and neighbors together and says, 'Rejoice with me; I have found my lost coin.' 10In the same way, I tell you, there is rejoicing in the presence of the angels of God over one sinner who repents." ver 6-7

The Parable of the Lost Son

11Jesus continued: "There was a man who had two sons. 12The younger one said to his father, 'Father, give me my share of the estate.' So he divided his property between them. Dt 21:17; Mt 21:28

13"Not long after that, the younger son got together all he had, set off for a distant country and there squandered his wealth in wild living. 14After he had spent everything, there was a severe famine in that whole country, and he began to be in need. 15So he went and hired himself out to a citizen of that country, who sent him to his fields to feed pigs. 16He longed to fill his stomach with the pods that the pigs were eating, but no one gave him anything. Lev 11:7; Lk 16:1

17"When he came to his senses, he said, 'How many of my father's hired men have food to spare, and here I am starving to death! 18I will set out and go back to my father and say to him: Father, I have sinned against heaven and against you. 19I am no longer worthy to be called your son; make me like one of your hired men.' 20So he got up and went to his father. Lev 26:40

"But while he was still a long way off, his father saw him and was filled with compassion for him; he ran to his son, threw his arms around him and kissed him.

21"The son said to him, 'Father, I have sinned against heaven and against you. I am no longer worthy to be called your son.*b*' Ps 51:4

22"But the father said to his servants, 'Quick! Bring the best robe and put it on him. Put a ring on his finger and sandals on his feet. 23Bring the fattened calf and kill it. Let's have a feast and celebrate. 24For this son of mine was dead and is alive again; he was lost and is found.' So they began to celebrate. Eph 2:1,5; 5:14; 1Ti 5:6

25"Meanwhile, the older son was in the field. When he came near the house, he heard music and dancing. 26So he called one of the servants and asked him what was going on. 27'Your brother has

---

a8 Greek ten *drachmas,* each worth about a day's wages   *b21* Some early manuscripts *son. Make me like one of your hired men.*

come,' he replied, 'and your father has killed the fattened calf because he has him back safe and sound.'

28"The older brother became angry and refused to go in. So his father went out and pleaded with him. 29But he answered his father, 'Look! All these years I've been slaving for you and never disobeyed your orders. Yet you never gave me even a young goat so I could celebrate with my friends. 30But when this son of yours who has squandered your property with prostitutes comes home, you kill the fattened calf for him!'

31" 'My son,' the father said, 'you are always with me, and everything I have is yours. 32But we had to celebrate and be glad, because this brother of yours was dead and is alive again; he was lost and is found.' "   Mal 3:17

The Parable of the Shrewd Manager

16 Jesus told his disciples: "There was a rich man whose manager was accused of wasting his possessions. 2So he called him in and asked him, 'What is this I hear about you? Give an account of your management, because you cannot be manager any longer.'   Lk 15:13,30

3"The manager said to himself, 'What shall I do now? My master is taking away my job. I'm not strong

enough to dig, and I'm ashamed to beg— 4I know what I'll do so that, when I lose my job here, people will welcome me into their houses.'

5"So he called in each one of his master's debtors. He asked the first, 'How much do you owe my master?'

6" 'Eight hundred gallonsa of olive oil,' he replied.

"The manager told him, 'Take your bill, sit down quickly, and make it four hundred.'

7"Then he asked the second, 'And how much do you owe?'

" 'A thousand bushelsb of wheat,' he replied.

"He told him, 'Take your bill and make it eight hundred.'

8"The master commended the dishonest manager because he had acted shrewdly. For the people of this world are more shrewd in dealing with their own kind than are the people of the light. 9I tell you, use worldly wealth to gain friends for yourselves, so that when it is gone, you will be welcomed into eternal dwellings.

10"Whoever can be trusted with very little can also be trusted with much, and whoever is dishonest with very little will also be dishonest with much. 11So if you have not been trustworthy in handling worldly wealth, who will trust you with true riches? 12And if you have

---

a6 Greek one hundred batous (probably about 3 kiloliters)   b7 Greek one hundred korous (probably about 35 kiloliters)

not been trustworthy with someone else's property, who will give you property of your own? [13]"No servant can serve two masters. Either he will hate the one and love the other, or he will be devoted to the one and despise the other. You cannot serve both God and Money."   Mt 6:24

[14]The Pharisees, who loved money, heard all this and were sneering at Jesus. [15]He said to them, "You are the ones who justify yourselves in the eyes of men, but God knows your hearts. What is highly valued among men is detestable in God's sight.   1Sa 16:7

Additional Teachings

[16]"The Law and the Prophets were proclaimed until John. Since that time, the good news of the kingdom of God is being preached, and everyone is forcing his way into it. [17]It is easier for heaven and earth to disappear than for the least stroke of a pen to drop out of the Law.   Mt 5:18; 11:12-13

[18]"Anyone who divorces his wife and marries another woman commits adultery, and the man who marries a divorced woman commits adultery.   Mt 5:31-32

The Rich Man and Lazarus

[19]"There was a rich man who was dressed in purple and fine linen and lived in luxury every day. [20]At his gate was laid a beggar named Lazarus, covered with sores [21]and longing to eat what fell from the rich man's table. Even the dogs came and licked his sores.

[22]"The time came when the beggar died and the angels carried him to Abraham's side. The rich man also died and was buried. [23]In hell,[a] where he was in torment, he looked up and saw Abraham far away, with Lazarus by his side. [24]So he called to him, 'Father Abraham, have pity on me and send Lazarus to dip the tip of his finger in water and cool my tongue, because I am in agony in this fire.'

[25]"But Abraham replied, 'Son, remember that in your lifetime you received your good things, while Lazarus received bad things, but now he is comforted here and you are in agony. [26]And besides all this, between us and you a great chasm has been fixed, so that those who want to go from here to you cannot, nor can anyone cross over from there to us.'   Ps 17:14

[27]"He answered, 'Then I beg you, father, send Lazarus to my father's house, [28]for I have five brothers. Let him warn them, so that they will not also come to this place of torment.'   Ac 2:40; 1Th 4:6

[29]"Abraham replied, 'They have Moses and the Prophets; let them listen to them.'   Lk 4:17; Jn 5:45-47

[30]" 'No, father Abraham,' he said, 'but if someone from the

[a]23 Greek *Hades*

dead goes to them, they will repent.'   Lk 3:8

31"He said to him, 'If they do not listen to Moses and the Prophets, they will not be convinced even if someone rises from the dead.' "

Sin, Faith, Duty

17 Jesus said to his disciples: "Things that cause people to sin are bound to come, but woe to that person through whom they come. ²It would be better for him to be thrown into the sea with a millstone tied around his neck than for him to cause one of these little ones to sin. ³So watch yourselves.   Mt 18:7; Mk 10:24; Lk 10:21

"If your brother sins, rebuke him, and if he repents, forgive him. ⁴If he sins against you seven times in a day, and seven times comes back to you and says, 'I repent,' forgive him."   Mt 18:15,21-22

⁵The apostles said to the Lord, "Increase our faith!"   Mk 6:30; Lk 7:13

⁶He replied, "If you have faith as small as a mustard seed, you can say to this mulberry tree, 'Be uprooted and planted in the sea,' and it will obey you.   Mt 17:20; 21:21

⁷"Suppose one of you had a servant plowing or looking after the sheep. Would he say to the servant when he comes in from the field, 'Come along now and sit down to eat'? ⁸Would he not rather say, 'Prepare my supper, get yourself ready and wait on me while I eat

and drink; after that you may eat and drink'? ⁹Would he thank the servant because he did what he was told to do? ¹⁰So you also, when you have done everything you were told to do, should say, 'We are unworthy servants; we have only done our duty.' "   Lk 12:37

Ten Healed of Leprosy

¹¹Now on his way to Jerusalem, Jesus traveled along the border between Samaria and Galilee. ¹²As he was going into a village, ten men who had leprosy*a* met him. They stood at a distance ¹³and called out in a loud voice, "Jesus, Master, have pity on us!"   Lk 5:5; 9:51; Jn 4:3-4

¹⁴When he saw them, he said, "Go, show yourselves to the priests." And as they went, they were cleansed.   Lev 14:2; Mt 8:4

¹⁵One of them, when he saw he was healed, came back, praising God in a loud voice. ¹⁶He threw himself at Jesus' feet and thanked him—and he was a Samaritan.

¹⁷Jesus asked, "Were not all ten cleansed? Where are the other nine? ¹⁸Was no one found to return and give praise to God except this foreigner?" ¹⁹Then he said to him, "Rise and go; your faith has made you well."   Mt 9:22

The Coming of the Kingdom of God

²⁰Once, having been asked by the Pharisees when the kingdom

---

a 12 The Greek word was used for various diseases affecting the skin—not necessarily leprosy.

of God would come, Jesus replied, "The kingdom of God does not come with your careful observation, 21nor will people say, 'Here it is,' or 'There it is,' because the kingdom of God is within*a* you."

22Then he said to his disciples, "The time is coming when you will long to see one of the days of the Son of Man, but you will not see it. 23Men will tell you, 'There he is!' or 'Here he is!' Do not go running off after them. 24For the Son of Man in his day*b* will be like the lightning, which flashes and lights up the sky from one end to the other. 25But first he must suffer many things and be rejected by this generation.   Mt 9:15; Lk 9:22; 21:8

26"Just as it was in the days of Noah, so also will it be in the days of the Son of Man. 27People were eating, drinking, marrying and being given in marriage up to the day Noah entered the ark. Then the flood came and destroyed them all.   Ge 7:6-24; Mt 24:37-39

28"It was the same in the days of Lot. People were eating and drinking, buying and selling, planting and building. 29But the day Lot left Sodom, fire and sulfur rained down from heaven and destroyed them all.   Ge 19:1-28

30"It will be just like this on the day the Son of Man is revealed. 31On that day no one who is on the roof of his house, with his goods

inside, should go down to get them. Likewise, no one in the field should go back for anything. 32Remember Lot's wife! 33Whoever tries to keep his life will lose it, and whoever loses his life will preserve it. 34I tell you, on that night two people will be in one bed; one will be taken and the other left. 35Two women will be grinding grain together; one will be taken and the other left.*c*"   Mt 24:41; Mk 13:15-16

37"Where, Lord?" they asked.

He replied, "Where there is a dead body, there the vultures will gather."   Mt 24:28

The Parable of the Persistent Widow

18 Then Jesus told his disciples a parable to show them that they should always pray and not give up. 2He said: "In a certain town there was a judge who neither feared God nor cared about men. 3And there was a widow in that town who kept coming to him with the plea, 'Grant me justice against my adversary.'

4"For some time he refused. But finally he said to himself, 'Even though I don't fear God or care about men, 5yet because this widow keeps bothering me, I will see that she gets justice, so that she won't eventually wear me out with her coming!' "   Lk 11:8

6And the Lord said, "Listen to

*a*21 Or *among*   *b*24 Some manuscripts do not have *in his day.*   *c*35 Some manuscripts *left.* 36*Two men will be in the field; one will be taken and the other left.*

what the unjust judge says. [7]And will not God bring about justice for his chosen ones, who cry out to him day and night? Will he keep putting them off? [8]I tell you, he will see that they get justice, and quickly. However, when the Son of Man comes, will he find faith on the earth?"   Mt 8:20; Rev 6:10

The Parable of the Pharisee and the Tax Collector

[9]To some who were confident of their own righteousness and looked down on everybody else, Jesus told this parable: [10]"Two men went up to the temple to pray, one a Pharisee and the other a tax collector. [11]The Pharisee stood up and prayed about[a] himself: 'God, I thank you that I am not like other men—robbers, evildoers, adulterers—or even like this tax collector. [12]I fast twice a week and give a tenth of all I get.'   Isa 65:5; Lk 16:15

[13]"But the tax collector stood at a distance. He would not even look up to heaven, but beat his breast and said, 'God, have mercy on me, a sinner.'   Lk 5:32; 23:48

[14]"I tell you that this man, rather than the other, went home justified before God. For everyone who exalts himself will be humbled, and he who humbles himself will be exalted."   Mt 23:12; Lk 14:11

The Little Children and Jesus

[15]People were also bringing babies to Jesus to have him touch them. When the disciples saw this, they rebuked them. [16]But Jesus called the children to him and said, "Let the little children come to me, and do not hinder them, for the kingdom of God belongs to such as these. [17]I tell you the truth, anyone who will not receive the kingdom of God like a little child will never enter it."   Mt 18:3

The Rich Ruler

[18]A certain ruler asked him, "Good teacher, what must I do to inherit eternal life?"   Lk 10:25

[19]"Why do you call me good?" Jesus answered. "No one is good —except God alone. [20]You know the commandments: 'Do not commit adultery, do not murder, do not steal, do not give false testimony, honor your father and mother.'[b]"   Ex 20:12-16; Dt 5:16-20; Ro 13:9

[21]"All these I have kept since I was a boy," he said.

[22]When Jesus heard this, he said to him, "You still lack one thing. Sell everything you have and give to the poor, and you will have treasure in heaven. Then come, follow me."   Mt 6:20; Ac 2:45

[23]When he heard this, he became very sad, because he was a man of great wealth. [24]Jesus looked at him and said, "How hard it is for the rich to enter the kingdom of God! [25]Indeed, it is easier for a camel to go through the eye

---

[a]11 Or to   [b]20 Exodus 20:12-16; Deut. 5:16-20

of a needle than for a rich man to enter the kingdom of God."

²⁶Those who heard this asked, "Who then can be saved?"

²⁷Jesus replied, "What is impossible with men is possible with God."   Mt 19:26

²⁸Peter said to him, "We have left all we had to follow you!"

²⁹"I tell you the truth," Jesus said to them, "no one who has left home or wife or brothers or parents or children for the sake of the kingdom of God ³⁰will fail to receive many times as much in this age and, in the age to come, eternal life."   Mt 19:16-29; Mk 10:17-30

Jesus Again Predicts His Death

³¹Jesus took the Twelve aside and told them, "We are going up to Jerusalem, and everything that is written by the prophets about the Son of Man will be fulfilled. ³²He will be handed over to the Gentiles. They will mock him, insult him, spit on him, flog him and kill him. ³³On the third day he will rise again."   Mt 20:17-19; Mk 10:32-34

³⁴The disciples did not understand any of this. Its meaning was hidden from them, and they did not know what he was talking about.   Mk 9:32; Lk 9:45

A Blind Beggar Receives His Sight

³⁵As Jesus approached Jericho, a blind man was sitting by the roadside begging. ³⁶When he heard the crowd going by, he asked what was happening. ³⁷They told him, "Jesus of Nazareth is passing by."   Lk 19:1,4

³⁸He called out, "Jesus, Son of David, have mercy on me!"

³⁹Those who led the way rebuked him and told him to be quiet, but he shouted all the more, "Son of David, have mercy on me!"

⁴⁰Jesus stopped and ordered the man to be brought to him. When he came near, Jesus asked him, ⁴¹"What do you want me to do for you?"

"Lord, I want to see," he replied.

⁴²Jesus said to him, "Receive your sight; your faith has healed you." ⁴³Immediately he received his sight and followed Jesus, praising God. When all the people saw it, they also praised God.

Zacchaeus the Tax Collector

19 Jesus entered Jericho and was passing through. ²A man was there by the name of Zacchaeus; he was a chief tax collector and was wealthy. ³He wanted to see who Jesus was, but being a short man he could not, because of the crowd. ⁴So he ran ahead and climbed a sycamore-fig tree to see him, since Jesus was coming that way.   1Ki 10:27; 1Ch 27:28

⁵When Jesus reached the spot, he looked up and said to him, "Zacchaeus, come down immediately. I must stay at your house today." ⁶So he came down at once and welcomed him gladly.

⁷All the people saw this and began to mutter, "He has gone to be the guest of a 'sinner.' "   Mt 9:11

⁸But Zacchaeus stood up and said to the Lord, "Look, Lord! Here and now I give half of my possessions to the poor, and if I have cheated anybody out of anything, I will pay back four times the amount."   Ex 22:1; Lk 7:13

⁹Jesus said to him, "Today salvation has come to this house, because this man, too, is a son of Abraham. ¹⁰For the Son of Man came to seek and to save what was lost."   Lk 3:8; Jn 3:17

The Parable of the Ten Minas

¹¹While they were listening to this, he went on to tell them a parable, because he was near Jerusalem and the people thought that the kingdom of God was going to appear at once. ¹²He said: "A man of noble birth went to a distant country to have himself appointed king and then to return. ¹³So he called ten of his servants and gave them ten minas.ᵃ 'Put this money to work,' he said, 'until I come back.'   Mk 13:34; Lk 17:20

¹⁴"But his subjects hated him and sent a delegation after him to say, 'We don't want this man to be our king.'

¹⁵"He was made king, however, and returned home. Then he sent for the servants to whom he had given the money, in order to find out what they had gained with it.

¹⁶"The first one came and said, 'Sir, your mina has earned ten more.'

¹⁷" 'Well done, my good servant!' his master replied. 'Because you have been trustworthy in a very small matter, take charge of ten cities.'   Pr 27:18; Lk 16:10

¹⁸"The second came and said, 'Sir, your mina has earned five more.'

¹⁹"His master answered, 'You take charge of five cities.'

²⁰"Then another servant came and said, 'Sir, here is your mina; I have kept it laid away in a piece of cloth. ²¹I was afraid of you, because you are a hard man. You take out what you did not put in and reap what you did not sow.'

²²"His master replied, 'I will judge you by your own words, you wicked servant! You knew, did you, that I am a hard man, taking out what I did not put in, and reaping what I did not sow? ²³Why then didn't you put my money on deposit, so that when I came back, I could have collected it with interest?'   2Sa 1:16; Mt 25:26

²⁴"Then he said to those standing by, 'Take his mina away from him and give it to the one who has ten minas.'

²⁵" 'Sir,' they said, 'he already has ten!'

²⁶"He replied, 'I tell you that to everyone who has, more will be

ᵃ13 A mina was about three months' wages.

given, but as for the one who has nothing, even what he has will be taken away. ²⁷But those enemies of mine who did not want me to be king over them—bring them here and kill them in front of me.' "

The Triumphal Entry

²⁸After Jesus had said this, he went on ahead, going up to Jerusalem. ²⁹As he approached Bethphage and Bethany at the hill called the Mount of Olives, he sent two of his disciples, saying to them, ³⁰"Go to the village ahead of you, and as you enter it, you will find a colt tied there, which no one has ever ridden. Untie it and bring it here. ³¹If anyone asks you, 'Why are you untying it?' tell him, 'The Lord needs it.' "   Mt 21:1-9; Mk 10:32

³²Those who were sent ahead went and found it just as he had told them. ³³As they were untying the colt, its owners asked them, "Why are you untying the colt?" ³⁴They replied, "The Lord needs it."

³⁵They brought it to Jesus, threw their cloaks on the colt and put Jesus on it. ³⁶As he went along, people spread their cloaks on the road.   Mk 11:1-10; 2Ki 9:13

³⁷When he came near the place where the road goes down the Mount of Olives, the whole crowd of disciples began joyfully to praise God in loud voices for all the miracles they had seen:

³⁸"Blessed is the king who
  comes in the name of
  the Lord!"^a   Ps 118:26

"Peace in heaven and glory in
  the highest!"   Jn 12:12-15

³⁹Some of the Pharisees in the crowd said to Jesus, "Teacher, rebuke your disciples!"   Mt 21:15-16

⁴⁰"I tell you," he replied, "if they keep quiet, the stones will cry out."   Hab 2:11

⁴¹As he approached Jerusalem and saw the city, he wept over it ⁴²and said, "If you, even you, had only known on this day what would bring you peace—but now it is hidden from your eyes. ⁴³The days will come upon you when your enemies will build an embankment against you and encircle you and hem you in on every side. ⁴⁴They will dash you to the ground, you and the children within your walls. They will not leave one stone on another, because you did not recognize the time of God's coming to you."   Lk 21:6; 1Pe 2:12

Jesus at the Temple

⁴⁵Then he entered the temple area and began driving out those who were selling. ⁴⁶"It is written," he said to them, " 'My house will be a house of prayer'^b; but you have made it 'a den of robbers.'^c"

⁴⁷Every day he was teaching at the temple. But the chief priests, the teachers of the law and the

---

^a38 Psalm 118:26   ^b46 Isaiah 56:7   ^c46 Jer. 7:11

leaders among the people were trying to kill him. ⁴⁸Yet they could not find any way to do it, because all the people hung on his words.

The Authority of Jesus Questioned

20 One day as he was teaching the people in the temple courts and preaching the gospel, the chief priests and the teachers of the law, together with the elders, came up to him. ²"Tell us by what authority you are doing these things," they said. "Who gave you this authority?"   Lk 8:1

³He replied, "I will also ask you a question. Tell me, ⁴John's baptism — was it from heaven, or from men?"   Mk 1:4

⁵They discussed it among themselves and said, "If we say, 'From heaven,' he will ask, 'Why didn't you believe him?' ⁶But if we say, 'From men,' all the people will stone us, because they are persuaded that John was a prophet."

⁷So they answered, "We don't know where it was from."

⁸Jesus said, "Neither will I tell you by what authority I am doing these things."   Mt 21:23-27; Mk 11:27-33

The Parable of the Tenants

⁹He went on to tell the people this parable: "A man planted a vineyard, rented it to some farmers and went away for a long time. ¹⁰At harvest time he sent a servant to the tenants so they would give him some of the fruit of the vineyard. But the tenants beat him and sent him away empty-handed. ¹¹He sent another servant, but that one also they beat and treated shamefully and sent away empty-handed. ¹²He sent still a third, and they wounded him and threw him out.

¹³"Then the owner of the vineyard said, 'What shall I do? I will send my son, whom I love; perhaps they will respect him.'

¹⁴"But when the tenants saw him, they talked the matter over. 'This is the heir,' they said. 'Let's kill him, and the inheritance will be ours.' ¹⁵So they threw him out of the vineyard and killed him.

"What then will the owner of the vineyard do to them? ¹⁶He will come and kill those tenants and give the vineyard to others."

When the people heard this, they said, "May this never be!"

¹⁷Jesus looked directly at them and asked, "Then what is the meaning of that which is written:

" 'The stone the builders rejected
has become the capstone[a]'[b]?

¹⁸Everyone who falls on that stone will be broken to pieces, but he on whom it falls will be crushed."

¹⁹The teachers of the law and the chief priests looked for a way to arrest him immediately, because they knew he had spoken

---

ᵃ 17 Or cornerstone   ᵇ 17 Psalm 118:22

this parable against them. But they were afraid of the people.

Paying Taxes to Caesar

20Keeping a close watch on him, they sent spies, who pretended to be honest. They hoped to catch Jesus in something he said so that they might hand him over to the power and authority of the governor. 21So the spies questioned him: "Teacher, we know that you speak and teach what is right, and that you do not show partiality but teach the way of God in accordance with the truth. 22Is it right for us to pay taxes to Caesar or not?" Mt 12:10; Jn 3:2

23He saw through their duplicity and said to them, 24"Show me a denarius. Whose portrait and inscription are on it?"

25"Caesar's," they replied.

He said to them, "Then give to Caesar what is Caesar's, and to God what is God's." Lk 23:2; Ro 13:7

26They were unable to trap him in what he had said there in public. And astonished by his answer, they became silent. Mt 22:15-22

The Resurrection and Marriage

27Some of the Sadducees, who say there is no resurrection, came to Jesus with a question. 28"Teacher," they said, "Moses wrote for us that if a man's brother dies and leaves a wife but no children, the man must marry the widow and have children for his brother. 29Now there were seven brothers. The first one married a woman and died childless. 30The second 31and then the third married her, and in the same way the seven died, leaving no children. 32Finally, the woman died too. 33Now then, at the resurrection whose wife will she be, since the seven were married to her?" Dt 25:5; Ac 23:8

34Jesus replied, "The people of this age marry and are given in marriage. 35But those who are considered worthy of taking part in that age and in the resurrection from the dead will neither marry nor be given in marriage, 36and they can no longer die; for they are like the angels. They are God's children, since they are children of the resurrection. 37But in the account of the bush, even Moses showed that the dead rise, for he calls the Lord 'the God of Abraham, and the God of Isaac, and the God of Jacob.'a 38He is not the God of the dead, but of the living, for to him all are alive." Ex 3:6; 1Jn 3:1-2

39Some of the teachers of the law responded, "Well said, teacher!" 40And no one dared to ask him any more questions. Mt 22:23-33

Whose Son Is the Christ?

41Then Jesus said to them, "How is it that they say the Christb is the Son of David? 42David himself declares in the Book of Psalms:

a37 Exodus 3:6   b41 Or Messiah

" 'The Lord said to my Lord:
  "Sit at my right hand
43until I make your enemies
    a footstool for your feet." ' [a]

44David calls him 'Lord.' How then can he be his son?"

45While all the people were listening, Jesus said to his disciples, 46"Beware of the teachers of the law. They like to walk around in flowing robes and love to be greeted in the marketplaces and have the most important seats in the synagogues and the places of honor at banquets. 47They devour widows' houses and for a show make lengthy prayers. Such men will be punished most severely."

The Widow's Offering

21 As he looked up, Jesus saw the rich putting their gifts into the temple treasury. 2He also saw a poor widow put in two very small copper coins. [b] 3"I tell you the truth," he said, "this poor widow has put in more than all the others. 4All these people gave their gifts out of their wealth; but she out of her poverty put in all she had to live on."   Mk 12:41-44

Signs of the End of the Age

5Some of his disciples were remarking about how the temple was adorned with beautiful stones and with gifts dedicated to God. But Jesus said, 6"As for what you

see here, the time will come when not one stone will be left on another; every one of them will be thrown down."   Lk 19:44

7"Teacher," they asked, "when will these things happen? And what will be the sign that they are about to take place?"

8He replied: "Watch out that you are not deceived. For many will come in my name, claiming, 'I am he,' and, 'The time is near.' Do not follow them. 9When you hear of wars and revolutions, do not be frightened. These things must happen first, but the end will not come right away."   Lk 17:23

10Then he said to them: "Nation will rise against nation, and kingdom against kingdom. 11There will be great earthquakes, famines and pestilences in various places, and fearful events and great signs from heaven.   2Ch 15:6; Isa 29:6

12"But before all this, they will lay hands on you and persecute you. They will deliver you to synagogues and prisons, and you will be brought before kings and governors, and all on account of my name. 13This will result in your being witnesses to them. 14But make up your mind not to worry beforehand how you will defend yourselves. 15For I will give you words and wisdom that none of your adversaries will be able to resist or contradict. 16You will be betrayed even by parents, brothers, rela-

[a]43 Psalm 110:1   [b]2 Greek two lepta

tives and friends, and they will put some of you to death. [17]All men will hate you because of me. [18]But not a hair of your head will perish. [19]By standing firm you will gain life.   Mt 10:17-22

[20]"When you see Jerusalem being surrounded by armies, you will know that its desolation is near. [21]Then let those who are in Judea flee to the mountains, let those in the city get out, and let those in the country not enter the city. [22]For this is the time of punishment in fulfillment of all that has been written. [23]How dreadful it will be in those days for pregnant women and nursing mothers! There will be great distress in the land and wrath against this people. [24]They will fall by the sword and will be taken as prisoners to all the nations. Jerusalem will be trampled on by the Gentiles until the times of the Gentiles are fulfilled.

[25]"There will be signs in the sun, moon and stars. On the earth, nations will be in anguish and perplexity at the roaring and tossing of the sea. [26]Men will faint from terror, apprehensive of what is coming on the world, for the heavenly bodies will be shaken. [27]At that time they will see the Son of Man coming in a cloud with power and great glory. [28]When these things begin to take place, stand up and lift up your heads, because your redemption is drawing near."

[29]He told them this parable: "Look at the fig tree and all the trees. [30]When they sprout leaves, you can see for yourselves and know that summer is near. [31]Even so, when you see these things happening, you know that the kingdom of God is near.   Mt 3:2

[32]"I tell you the truth, this generation[a] will certainly not pass away until all these things have happened. [33]Heaven and earth will pass away, but my words will never pass away.   Mt 5:18; Lk 11:50

[34]"Be careful, or your hearts will be weighed down with dissipation, drunkenness and the anxieties of life, and that day will close on you unexpectedly like a trap. [35]For it will come upon all those who live on the face of the whole earth. [36]Be always on the watch, and pray that you may be able to escape all that is about to happen, and that you may be able to stand before the Son of Man."   Mk 4:19; 1Th 5:2-7

[37]Each day Jesus was teaching at the temple, and each evening he went out to spend the night on the hill called the Mount of Olives, [38]and all the people came early in the morning to hear him at the temple.   Mk 11:19; Jn 8:2

Judas Agrees to Betray Jesus

22 Now the Feast of Unleavened Bread, called the Passover, was approaching, [2]and the chief priests and the teachers of the law were looking for some way to get rid of Jesus, for they were afraid of the people. ³Then Satan entered Judas, called Iscariot, one of the Twelve. ⁴And Judas went to the chief priests and the officers of the temple guard and discussed with them how he might betray Jesus. ⁵They were delighted and agreed to give him money. ⁶He consented, and watched for an opportunity to hand Jesus over to them when no crowd was present.

The Last Supper

⁷Then came the day of Unleavened Bread on which the Passover lamb had to be sacrificed. ⁸Jesus sent Peter and John, saying, "Go and make preparations for us to eat the Passover."   Dt 16:5-8; Ac 3:1,11

⁹"Where do you want us to prepare for it?" they asked.

¹⁰He replied, "As you enter the city, a man carrying a jar of water will meet you. Follow him to the house that he enters, ¹¹and say to the owner of the house, 'The Teacher asks: Where is the guest room, where I may eat the Passover with my disciples?' ¹²He will show you a large upper room, all furnished. Make preparations there."

¹³They left and found things just as Jesus had told them. So they prepared the Passover.   Mt 26:17-19

¹⁴When the hour came, Jesus and his apostles reclined at the table. ¹⁵And he said to them, "I have eagerly desired to eat this Passover with you before I suffer. ¹⁶For I tell you, I will not eat it again until it finds fulfillment in the kingdom of God."   Lk 14:15; Rev 19:9

¹⁷After taking the cup, he gave thanks and said, "Take this and divide it among you. ¹⁸For I tell you I will not drink again of the fruit of the vine until the kingdom of God comes."

¹⁹And he took bread, gave thanks and broke it, and gave it to them, saying, "This is my body given for you; do this in remembrance of me."   Mt 26:26-29; Mk 14:22-25

²⁰In the same way, after the supper he took the cup, saying, "This cup is the new covenant in my blood, which is poured out for you. ²¹But the hand of him who is going to betray me is with mine on the table. ²²The Son of Man will go as it has been decreed, but woe to that man who betrays him." ²³They began to question among themselves which of them it might be who would do this.   Mt 26:21-24

²⁴Also a dispute arose among them as to which of them was considered to be greatest. ²⁵Jesus said to them, "The kings of the Gentiles lord it over them; and those who exercise authority over them call themselves Benefactors. ²⁶But you are not to be like that. Instead, the greatest among you should be like the youngest, and the one who rules like the one who serves. ²⁷For who is greater, the one who is at the table or the one who serves? Is

it not the one who is at the table? But I am among you as one who serves. ²⁸You are those who have stood by me in my trials. ²⁹And I confer on you a kingdom, just as my Father conferred one on me, ³⁰so that you may eat and drink at my table in my kingdom and sit on thrones, judging the twelve tribes of Israel. *Mt 20:25-28; Mk 10:42-45*

³¹"Simon, Simon, Satan has asked to sift you[a] as wheat. ³²But I have prayed for you, Simon, that your faith may not fail. And when you have turned back, strengthen your brothers." *Jn 21:15-17*

³³But he replied, "Lord, I am ready to go with you to prison and to death." *Jn 11:16*

³⁴Jesus answered, "I tell you, Peter, before the rooster crows today, you will deny three times that you know me." *Mt 26:33-35; Mk 14:29-31*

³⁵Then Jesus asked them, "When I sent you without purse, bag or sandals, did you lack anything?" *Mt 10:9-10; Lk 9:3; 10:4*

"Nothing," they answered.

³⁶He said to them, "But now if you have a purse, take it, and also a bag; and if you don't have a sword, sell your cloak and buy one. ³⁷It is written: 'And he was numbered with the transgressors'[b]; and I tell you that this must be fulfilled in me. Yes, what is written about me is reaching its fulfillment." *Isa 53:12*

³⁸The disciples said, "See, Lord, here are two swords."

"That is enough," he replied.

Jesus Prays on the Mount of Olives

³⁹Jesus went out as usual to the Mount of Olives, and his disciples followed him. ⁴⁰On reaching the place, he said to them, "Pray that you will not fall into temptation." ⁴¹He withdrew about a stone's throw beyond them, knelt down and prayed, ⁴²"Father, if you are willing, take this cup from me; yet not my will, but yours be done." ⁴³An angel from heaven appeared to him and strengthened him. ⁴⁴And being in anguish, he prayed more earnestly, and his sweat was like drops of blood falling to the ground.[c] *Mt 4:11; 6:13; Lk 21:37*

⁴⁵When he rose from prayer and went back to the disciples, he found them asleep, exhausted from sorrow. ⁴⁶"Why are you sleeping?" he asked them. "Get up and pray so that you will not fall into temptation." *Mt 26:36-46*

Jesus Arrested

⁴⁷While he was still speaking a crowd came up, and the man who was called Judas, one of the Twelve, was leading them. He approached Jesus to kiss him, ⁴⁸but Jesus asked him, "Judas, are you

---

a 31 The Greek is plural.　*b 37 Isaiah 53:12*　*c 44 Some early manuscripts do not have verses 43 and 44.*

betraying the Son of Man with a kiss?"

49When Jesus' followers saw what was going to happen, they said, "Lord, should we strike with our swords?" **50**And one of them struck the servant of the high priest, cutting off his right ear.

51But Jesus answered, "No more of this!" And he touched the man's ear and healed him.

52Then Jesus said to the chief priests, the officers of the temple guard, and the elders, who had come for him, "Am I leading a rebellion, that you have come with swords and clubs? **53**Every day I was with you in the temple courts, and you did not lay a hand on me. But this is your hour—when darkness reigns."   Mt 26:47-56; Mk 14:43-50

Peter Disowns Jesus

54Then seizing him, they led him away and took him into the house of the high priest. Peter followed at a distance. **55**But when they had kindled a fire in the middle of the courtyard and had sat down together, Peter sat down with them. **56**A servant girl saw him seated there in the firelight. She looked closely at him and said, "This man was with him."

57But he denied it. "Woman, I don't know him," he said.

58A little later someone else saw him and said, "You also are one of them."

"Man, I am not!" Peter replied.

59About an hour later another asserted, "Certainly this fellow was with him, for he is a Galilean."

60Peter replied, "Man, I don't know what you're talking about!" Just as he was speaking, the rooster crowed. **61**The Lord turned and looked straight at Peter. Then Peter remembered the word the Lord had spoken to him: "Before the rooster crows today, you will disown me three times." **62**And he went outside and wept bitterly.

The Guards Mock Jesus

63The men who were guarding Jesus began mocking and beating him. **64**They blindfolded him and demanded, "Prophesy! Who hit you?" **65**And they said many other insulting things to him.   Mt 26:67-68

Jesus Before Pilate and Herod

66At daybreak the council of the elders of the people, both the chief priests and teachers of the law, met together, and Jesus was led before them. **67**"If you are the Christ,*a*" they said, "tell us."

Jesus answered, "If I tell you, you will not believe me, **68**and if I asked you, you would not answer. **69**But from now on, the Son of Man will be seated at the right hand of the mighty God."   Mk 16:19; Lk 20:3-8

70They all asked, "Are you then the Son of God?"   Mt 4:3

a 67 Or *Messiah*

He replied, "You are right in saying I am." Mt 27:11; Lk 23:3

71Then they said, "Why do we need any more testimony? We have heard it from his own lips."

23 Then the whole assembly rose and led him off to Pilate. 2And they began to accuse him, saying, "We have found this man subverting our nation. He opposes payment of taxes to Caesar and claims to be Christ,a a king."

3So Pilate asked Jesus, "Are you the king of the Jews?"

"Yes, it is as you say," Jesus replied.   Mt 27:11-14; Mk 15:2-5; Jn 18:29-37

4Then Pilate announced to the chief priests and the crowd, "I find no basis for a charge against this man." Mt 27:23; 2Co 5:21

5But they insisted, "He stirs up the people all over Judeab by his teaching. He started in Galilee and has come all the way here."

6On hearing this, Pilate asked if the man was a Galilean. 7When he learned that Jesus was under Herod's jurisdiction, he sent him to Herod, who was also in Jerusalem at that time. Mt 14:1; Lk 3:1

8When Herod saw Jesus, he was greatly pleased, because for a long time he had been wanting to see him. From what he had heard about him, he hoped to see him perform some miracle. 9He plied him with many questions, but Jesus gave him no answer. 10The chief priests and the teachers of the law were standing there, vehemently accusing him. 11Then Herod and his soldiers ridiculed and mocked him. Dressing him in an elegant robe, they sent him back to Pilate. 12That day Herod and Pilate became friends—before this they had been enemies. Mk 15:17-19; Lk 9:9

13Pilate called together the chief priests, the rulers and the people, 14and said to them, "You brought me this man as one who was inciting the people to rebellion. I have examined him in your presence and have found no basis for your charges against him. 15Neither has Herod, for he sent him back to us; as you can see, he has done nothing to deserve death. 16Therefore, I will punish him and then release him.c" Mt 27:26; Jn 19:1

18With one voice they cried out, "Away with this man! Release Barabbas to us!" 19(Barabbas had been thrown into prison for an insurrection in the city, and for murder.) Ac 3:13-14

20Wanting to release Jesus, Pilate appealed to them again. 21But they kept shouting, "Crucify him! Crucify him!"

22For the third time he spoke to them: "Why? What crime has this man committed? I have found in him no grounds for the death penalty. Therefore I will have him punished and then release him."

a2 Or Messiah; also in verses 35 and 39   b5 Or over the land of the Jews   c16 Some manuscripts him." 17Now he was obliged to release one man to them at the Feast.

²³But with loud shouts they insistently demanded that he be crucified, and their shouts prevailed. ²⁴So Pilate decided to grant their demand. ²⁵He released the man who had been thrown into prison for insurrection and murder, the one they asked for, and surrendered Jesus to their will.

The Crucifixion

²⁶As they led him away, they seized Simon from Cyrene, who was on his way in from the country, and put the cross on him and made him carry it behind Jesus. ²⁷A large number of people followed him, including women who mourned and wailed for him. ²⁸Jesus turned and said to them, "Daughters of Jerusalem, do not weep for me; weep for yourselves and for your children. ²⁹For the time will come when you will say, 'Blessed are the barren women, the wombs that never bore and the breasts that never nursed!' ³⁰Then

" 'they will say to the
　　　mountains, "Fall on us!"
　and to the hills, "Cover
　　　us!" ' ᵃ

³¹For if men do these things when the tree is green, what will happen when it is dry?"　Eze 20:47; Hos 10:8

³²Two other men, both criminals, were also led out with him to be executed. ³³When they came to the place called the Skull, there they crucified him, along with the criminals—one on his right, the other on his left. ³⁴Jesus said, "Father, forgive them, for they do not know what they are doing." ᵇ And they divided up his clothes by casting lots.　Ps 22:18; Mt 27:38

³⁵The people stood watching, and the rulers even sneered at him. They said, "He saved others; let him save himself if he is the Christ of God, the Chosen One."　Ps 22:17

³⁶The soldiers also came up and mocked him. They offered him wine vinegar ³⁷and said, "If you are the king of the Jews, save yourself."　Mt 27:48; Lk 4:3,9

³⁸There was a written notice above him, which read: THIS IS THE KING OF THE JEWS.　Mt 2:2

³⁹One of the criminals who hung there hurled insults at him: "Aren't you the Christ? Save yourself and us!"　ver 35,37

⁴⁰But the other criminal rebuked him. "Don't you fear God," he said, "since you are under the same sentence? ⁴¹We are punished justly, for we are getting what our deeds deserve. But this man has done nothing wrong."

⁴²Then he said, "Jesus, remember me when you come into your kingdom.ᶜ"　Mt 16:27

⁴³Jesus answered him, "I tell you the truth, today you will be with me in paradise."　Mt 27:33-44

ᵃ30 Hosea 10:8　　ᵇ34 Some early manuscripts do not have this sentence.　ᶜ42 Some manuscripts come with your kingly power

Jesus' Death

44It was now about the sixth hour, and darkness came over the whole land until the ninth hour, **45**for the sun stopped shining. And the curtain of the temple was torn in two. **46**Jesus called out with a loud voice, "Father, into your hands I commit my spirit." When he had said this, he breathed his last. Ps 31:5; Jn 19:30

47The centurion, seeing what had happened, praised God and said, "Surely this was a righteous man." **48**When all the people who had gathered to witness this sight saw what took place, they beat their breasts and went away. **49**But all those who knew him, including the women who had followed him from Galilee, stood at a distance, watching these things. Mt 27:45-56

Jesus' Burial

50Now there was a man named Joseph, a member of the Council, a good and upright man, **51**who had not consented to their decision and action. He came from the Judean town of Arimathea and he was waiting for the kingdom of God. **52**Going to Pilate, he asked for Jesus' body. **53**Then he took it down, wrapped it in linen cloth and placed it in a tomb cut in the rock, one in which no one had yet been laid. **54**It was Preparation Day, and the Sabbath was about to begin. Mt 27:62; Lk 2:25,38

55The women who had come with Jesus from Galilee followed Joseph and saw the tomb and how his body was laid in it. **56**Then they went home and prepared spices and perfumes. But they rested on the Sabbath in obedience to the commandment. Mt 27:57-61

The Resurrection

24 On the first day of the week, very early in the morning, the women took the spices they had prepared and went to the tomb. **2**They found the stone rolled away from the tomb, **3**but when they entered, they did not find the body of the Lord Jesus. **4**While they were wondering about this, suddenly two men in clothes that gleamed like lightning stood beside them. **5**In their fright the women bowed down with their faces to the ground, but the men said to them, "Why do you look for the living among the dead? **6**He is not here; he has risen! Remember how he told you, while he was still with you in Galilee: **7**'The Son of Man must be delivered into the hands of sinful men, be crucified and on the third day be raised again.' " **8**Then they remembered his words. Mt 28:1-8

9When they came back from the tomb, they told all these things to the Eleven and to all the others. **10**It was Mary Magdalene, Joanna, Mary the mother of James, and the others with them who told this to the apostles. **11**But they did not believe the women, because their words seemed to them like nonsense. [12]Peter, however, got up and ran to the tomb. Bending over, he saw the strips of linen lying by themselves, and he went away, wondering to himself what had happened.   Mk 16:1-8; Jn 20:1-8

On the Road to Emmaus

[13]Now that same day two of them were going to a village called Emmaus, about seven miles[a] from Jerusalem. [14]They were talking with each other about everything that had happened. [15]As they talked and discussed these things with each other, Jesus himself came up and walked along with them; [16]but they were kept from recognizing him.   Jn 20:14; 21:4

[17]He asked them, "What are you discussing together as you walk along?"

They stood still, their faces downcast. [18]One of them, named Cleopas, asked him, "Are you only a visitor to Jerusalem and do not know the things that have happened there in these days?"

[19]"What things?" he asked.

"About Jesus of Nazareth," they replied. "He was a prophet, powerful in word and deed before God and all the people. [20]The chief priests and our rulers handed him over to be sentenced to death, and they crucified him; [21]but we had hoped that he was the one who was going to redeem Israel. And

what is more, it is the third day since all this took place. [22]In addition, some of our women amazed us. They went to the tomb early this morning [23]but didn't find his body. They came and told us that they had seen a vision of angels, who said he was alive. [24]Then some of our companions went to the tomb and found it just as the women had said, but him they did not see."   Mt 21:11; Mk 1:24

[25]He said to them, "How foolish you are, and how slow of heart to believe all that the prophets have spoken! [26]Did not the Christ[b] have to suffer these things and then enter his glory?" [27]And beginning with Moses and all the Prophets, he explained to them what was said in all the Scriptures concerning himself.   Jn 1:45

[28]As they approached the village to which they were going, Jesus acted as if he were going farther. [29]But they urged him strongly, "Stay with us, for it is nearly evening; the day is almost over." So he went in to stay with them.

[30]When he was at the table with them, he took bread, gave thanks, broke it and began to give it to them. [31]Then their eyes were opened and they recognized him, and he disappeared from their sight. [32]They asked each other, "Were not our hearts burning within us while he talked with us

---

[a] 13 Greek *sixty stadia* (about 11 kilometers)   [b] 26 Or *Messiah*; also in verse 46

on the road and opened the Scriptures to us?" Ps 39:3; Mt 14:19

33They got up and returned at once to Jerusalem. There they found the Eleven and those with them, assembled together 34and saying, "It is true! The Lord has risen and has appeared to Simon." 35Then the two told what had happened on the way, and how Jesus was recognized by them when he broke the bread. 1Co 15:5

Jesus Appears to the Disciples

36While they were still talking about this, Jesus himself stood among them and said to them, "Peace be with you." Jn 20:19,21,26

37They were startled and frightened, thinking they saw a ghost. 38He said to them, "Why are you troubled, and why do doubts rise in your minds? 39Look at my hands and my feet. It is I myself! Touch me and see; a ghost does not have flesh and bones, as you see I have." Mk 6:49; Jn 20:27

40When he had said this, he showed them his hands and feet. 41And while they still did not believe it because of joy and amazement, he asked them, "Do you have anything here to eat?" 42They gave him a piece of broiled fish,

43and he took it and ate it in their presence. Ac 10:41

44He said to them, "This is what I told you while I was still with you: Everything must be fulfilled that is written about me in the Law of Moses, the Prophets and the Psalms." Mt 18:31-33

45Then he opened their minds so they could understand the Scriptures. 46He told them, "This is what is written: The Christ will suffer and rise from the dead on the third day, 47and repentance and forgiveness of sins will be preached in his name to all nations, beginning at Jerusalem. 48You are witnesses of these things. 49I am going to send you what my Father has promised; but stay in the city until you have been clothed with power from on high."

The Ascension

50When he had led them out to the vicinity of Bethany, he lifted up his hands and blessed them. 51While he was blessing them, he left them and was taken up into heaven. 52Then they worshiped him and returned to Jerusalem with great joy. 53And they stayed continually at the temple, praising God. 2Ki 2:11; Ac 2:46

John

on the road and opened the Scriptures to us?"

³³They got up and returned at
once to Jerusalem. There they
found the Eleven and those with

The Word Became Flesh

1 In the beginning was the Word, and the Word was with God, and the Word was God. ²He was with God in the beginning.

³Through him all things were made; without him nothing was made that has been made. ⁴In him was life, and that life was the light of men. ⁵The light shines in the darkness, but the darkness has not understood[a] it. Jn 3:19; 5:26; Col 1:16

⁶There came a man who was sent from God; his name was John. ⁷He came as a witness to testify concerning that light, so that through him all men might believe. ⁸He himself was not the light; he came only as a witness to the light. ⁹The true light that gives light to every man was coming into the world.[b] Isa 49:6; 1Jn 2:8

¹⁰He was in the world, and though the world was made through him, the world did not recognize him. ¹¹He came to that which was his own, but his own did not receive him. ¹²Yet to all who received him, to those who believed in his name, he gave the right to become children of God— ¹³children born not of natural descent,[c] nor of human decision or a husband's will, but born of God.

¹⁴The Word became flesh and made his dwelling among us. We have seen his glory, the glory of the One and Only,[d] who came from the Father, full of grace and truth. Gal 4:4; 1Ti 3:16

¹⁵John testifies concerning him. He cries out, saying, "This was he of whom I said, 'He who comes after me has surpassed me because he was before me.'" ¹⁶From the fullness of his grace we have all received one blessing after another. ¹⁷For the law was given through Moses; grace and truth came through Jesus Christ. ¹⁸No one has ever seen God, but God the One and Only,[d,e] who is at the Father's side, has made him known.

John the Baptist Denies Being the Christ

¹⁹Now this was John's testimony when the Jews of Jerusalem sent priests and Levites to ask him who he was. ²⁰He did not fail to confess, but confessed freely, "I am not the Christ.[f]" Lk 3:15-16

²¹They asked him, "Then who are you? Are you Elijah?" Mt 11:14

---

[a]5 Or *darkness, and the darkness has not overcome every man who comes into the world* [c]13 Greek *of bloods* [d]14,18 Or *the Only Begotten* [e]18 Some manuscripts *but the only* (or *only begotten*) *Son* [f]20 Or *Messiah.* "The Christ" (Greek) and "the Messiah" (Hebrew) both mean "the Anointed One"; also in verse 25. [b]9 Or *This was the true light that gives light to*

He said, "I am not."

"Are you the Prophet?" Dt 18:15

He answered, "No."

22Finally they said, "Who are you? Give us an answer to take back to those who sent us. What do you say about yourself?"

23John replied in the words of Isaiah the prophet, "I am the voice of one calling in the desert, 'Make straight the way for the Lord.' "*a*

24Now some Pharisees who had been sent 25questioned him, "Why then do you baptize if you are not the Christ, nor Elijah, nor the Prophet?"

26"I baptize with*b* water," John replied, "but among you stands one you do not know. 27He is the one who comes after me, the thongs of whose sandals I am not worthy to untie." Mk 1:4,7

28This all happened at Bethany on the other side of the Jordan, where John was baptizing. Jn 3:26

Jesus the Lamb of God

29The next day John saw Jesus coming toward him and said, "Look, the Lamb of God, who takes away the sin of the world! 30This is the one I meant when I said, 'A man who comes after me has surpassed me because he was before me.' 31I myself did not know him, but the reason I came baptizing with water was that he might be revealed to Israel."

32Then John gave this testimo-ny: "I saw the Spirit come down from heaven as a dove and remain on him. 33I would not have known him, except that the one who sent me to baptize with water told me, 'The man on whom you see the Spirit come down and remain is he who will baptize with the Holy Spirit.' 34I have seen and I testify that this is the Son of God."

Jesus' First Disciples

35The next day John was there again with two of his disciples. 36When he saw Jesus passing by, he said, "Look, the Lamb of God!"

37When the two disciples heard him say this, they followed Jesus. 38Turning around, Jesus saw them following and asked, "What do you want?"

They said, "Rabbi" (which means Teacher), "where are you staying?" Mt 23:7

39"Come," he replied, "and you will see."

So they went and saw where he was staying, and spent that day with him. It was about the tenth hour.

40Andrew, Simon Peter's broth-er, was one of the two who heard what John had said and who had followed Jesus. 41The first thing Andrew did was to find his brother Simon and tell him, "We have found the Messiah" (that is, the Christ). 42And he brought him to Jesus. Jn 4:25

a23 Isaiah 40:3   *b26* Or *in*; also in verses 31 and 33

Jesus looked at him and said, "You are Simon son of John. You will be called Cephas" (which, when translated, is Peter[a]).

Jesus Calls Philip and Nathanael

[43]The next day Jesus decided to leave for Galilee. Finding Philip, he said to him, "Follow me."   Mt 10:3

[44]Philip, like Andrew and Peter, was from the town of Bethsaida. [45]Philip found Nathanael and told him, "We have found the one Moses wrote about in the Law, and about whom the prophets also wrote—Jesus of Nazareth, the son of Joseph."   Mt 2:23; Lk 3:23

[46]"Nazareth! Can anything good come from there?" Nathanael asked.   Jn 7:41-42,52

"Come and see," said Philip.

[47]When Jesus saw Nathanael approaching, he said of him, "Here is a true Israelite, in whom there is nothing false."   Ps 32:2; Ro 9:4,6

[48]"How do you know me?" Nathanael asked.

Jesus answered, "I saw you while you were still under the fig tree before Philip called you."

[49]Then Nathanael declared, "Rabbi, you are the Son of God; you are the King of Israel."   Mt 4:3

[50]Jesus said, "You believe[b] because I told you I saw you under the fig tree. You shall see greater things than that." [51]He then added,

"I tell you[c] the truth, you[c] shall see heaven open, and the angels of God ascending and descending on the Son of Man."   Ge 28:12; Mt 3:16

Jesus Changes Water to Wine

2 On the third day a wedding took place at Cana in Galilee. Jesus' mother was there, [2]and Jesus and his disciples had also been invited to the wedding. [3]When the wine was gone, Jesus' mother said to him, "They have no more wine."   Mt 12:46; Jn 4:46

[4]"Dear woman, why do you involve me?" Jesus replied. "My time has not yet come."   Jn 7:6; 19:26

[5]His mother said to the servants, "Do whatever he tells you."

[6]Nearby stood six stone water jars, the kind used by the Jews for ceremonial washing, each holding from twenty to thirty gallons.[d]

[7]Jesus said to the servants, "Fill the jars with water"; so they filled them to the brim.

[8]Then he told them, "Now draw some out and take it to the master of the banquet."

They did so, [9]and the master of the banquet tasted the water that had been turned into wine. He did not realize where it had come from, though the servants who had drawn the water knew. Then he called the bridegroom aside [10]and said, "Everyone brings out the choice wine first and then the

---

[a]42 Both *Cephas* (Aramaic) and *Peter* (Greek) mean *rock*.   [b]50 Or *Do you believe . . . ?*   [c]51 The Greek is plural.   [d]6 Greek *two to three metretes* (probably about 75 to 115 liters)

cheaper wine after the guests have had too much to drink; but you have saved the best till now."

[11]This, the first of his miraculous signs, Jesus performed at Cana in Galilee. He thus revealed his glory, and his disciples put their faith in him.   Ex 14:31; Jn 1:14

Jesus Clears the Temple

[12]After this he went down to Capernaum with his mother and brothers and his disciples. There they stayed for a few days.

[13]When it was almost time for the Jewish Passover, Jesus went up to Jerusalem. [14]In the temple courts he found men selling cattle, sheep and doves, and others sitting at tables exchanging money. [15]So he made a whip out of cords, and drove all from the temple area, both sheep and cattle; he scattered the coins of the money changers and overturned their tables. [16]To those who sold doves he said, "Get these out of here! How dare you turn my Father's house into a market!"   Dt 16:1-6; Lk 2:49

[17]His disciples remembered that it is written: "Zeal for your house will consume me."[a]   Ps 69:9

[18]Then the Jews demanded of him, "What miraculous sign can you show us to prove your authority to do all this?"   Mt 12:38

[19]Jesus answered them, "Destroy this temple, and I will raise it again in three days."   Mt 26:61; 27:40

[20]The Jews replied, "It has taken forty-six years to build this temple, and you are going to raise it in three days?" [21]But the temple he had spoken of was his body. [22]After he was raised from the dead, his disciples recalled what he had said. Then they believed the Scripture and the words that Jesus had spoken.   Lk 24:5-8; 1Co 6:19

[23]Now while he was in Jerusalem at the Passover Feast, many people saw the miraculous signs he was doing and believed in his name.[b] [24]But Jesus would not entrust himself to them, for he knew all men. [25]He did not need man's testimony about man, for he knew what was in a man.   Jn 6:61,64; 13:11

Jesus Teaches Nicodemus

3 Now there was a man of the Pharisees named Nicodemus, a member of the Jewish ruling council. [2]He came to Jesus at night and said, "Rabbi, we know you are a teacher who has come from God. For no one could perform the miraculous signs you are doing if God were not with him."   Jn 9:16,33

[3]In reply Jesus declared, "I tell you the truth, no one can see the kingdom of God unless he is born again.[c]   Jn 1:13; 1Pe 1:23

[4]"How can a man be born when he is old?" Nicodemus asked. "Surely he cannot enter a second time into his mother's womb to be born!"

---

[a]17 Psalm 69:9   [b]23 Or and believed in him   [c]3 Or born from above; also in verse 7

5Jesus answered, "I tell you the truth, no one can enter the kingdom of God unless he is born of water and the Spirit. 6Flesh gives birth to flesh, but the Spirit*a* gives birth to spirit. 7You should not be surprised at my saying, 'You*b* must be born again.' 8The wind blows wherever it pleases. You hear its sound, but you cannot tell where it comes from or where it is going. So it is with everyone born of the Spirit."

Jn 1:13; Tit 3:5

9"How can this be?" Nicodemus asked.

Jn 6:52,60

10"You are Israel's teacher," said Jesus, "and do you not understand these things? 11I tell you the truth, we speak of what we know, and we testify to what we have seen, but still you people do not accept our testimony. 12I have spoken to you of earthly things and you do not believe; how then will you believe if I speak of heavenly things? 13No one has ever gone into heaven except the one who came from heaven—the Son of Man.*c* 14Just as Moses lifted up the snake in the desert, so the Son of Man must be lifted up, 15that everyone who believes in him may have eternal life.*d*

Nu 21:8-9; Jn 8:28

16"For God so loved the world that he gave his one and only Son,*e* that whoever believes in him shall not perish but have eternal life. 17For God did not send his Son into the world to condemn the world, but to save the world through him. 18Whoever believes in him is not condemned, but whoever does not believe stands condemned already because he has not believed in the name of God's one and only Son.*f* 19This is the verdict: Light has come into the world, but men loved darkness instead of light because their deeds were evil. 20Everyone who does evil hates the light, and will not come into the light for fear that his deeds will be exposed. 21But whoever lives by the truth comes into the light, so that it may be seen plainly that what he has done has been done through God."*g*

Ro 5:8

John the Baptist's Testimony About Jesus

22After this, Jesus and his disciples went out into the Judean countryside, where he spent some time with them, and baptized. 23Now John also was baptizing at Aenon near Salim, because there was plenty of water, and people were constantly coming to be baptized. 24(This was before John was put in prison.) 25An argument developed between some of John's disciples and a certain Jew*h* over the matter of ceremonial washing. 26They came to John and said to him, "Rabbi, that man

*a*6 Or *but spirit*   *b*7 The Greek is plural.   *c*13 Some manuscripts *Man, who is in heaven*   *d*15 Or *believes may have eternal life in him*   *e*16 Or *his only begotten Son*   *f*18 Or *God's only begotten Son*   *g*21 Some interpreters end the quotation after verse 15.   *h*25 Some manuscripts *and certain Jews*

who was with you on the other side of the Jordan—the one you testified about—well, he is baptizing, and everyone is going to him." *Jn 1:7*

27To this John replied, "A man can receive only what is given him from heaven. 28You yourselves can testify that I said, 'I am not the Christ*a* but am sent ahead of him.' 29The bride belongs to the bridegroom. The friend who attends the bridegroom waits and listens for him, and is full of joy when he hears the bridegroom's voice. That joy is mine, and it is now complete. 30He must become greater; I must become less. *Jn 1:20,23; 16:24*

31"The one who comes from above is above all; the one who is from the earth belongs to the earth, and speaks as one from the earth. The one who comes from heaven is above all. 32He testifies to what he has seen and heard, but no one accepts his testimony. 33The man who has accepted it has certified that God is truthful. 34For the one whom God has sent speaks the words of God, for God*b* gives the Spirit without limit. 35The Father loves the Son and has placed everything in his hands. 36Whoever believes in the Son has eternal life, but whoever rejects the Son will not see life, for God's wrath remains on him."*c* *Mt 28:18; Jn 5:20,22*

Jesus Talks With a Samaritan Woman

4 The Pharisees heard that Jesus was gaining and baptizing more disciples than John, 2although in fact it was not Jesus who baptized, but his disciples. 3When the Lord learned of this, he left Judea and went back once more to Galilee. *Jn 3:22,26*

4Now he had to go through Samaria. 5So he came to a town in Samaria called Sychar, near the plot of ground Jacob had given to his son Joseph. 6Jacob's well was there, and Jesus, tired as he was from the journey, sat down by the well. It was about the sixth hour.

7When a Samaritan woman came to draw water, Jesus said to her, "Will you give me a drink?" 8(His disciples had gone into the town to buy food.) *Ge 24:17; 1Ki 17:10*

9The Samaritan woman said to him, "You are a Jew and I am a Samaritan woman. How can you ask me for a drink?" (For Jews do not associate with Samaritans.*d*)

10Jesus answered her, "If you knew the gift of God and who it is that asks you for a drink, you would have asked him and he would have given you living water." *Isa 44:3; Rev 21:6; 22:1,17*

11"Sir," the woman said, "you have nothing to draw with and the well is deep. Where can you get this living water? 12Are you greater

a 28 Or *Messiah*   *b 34* Greek *he*   *c 36* Some interpreters end the quotation after verse 30.   *d 9* Or *do not use dishes Samaritans have used*

than our father Jacob, who gave us the well and drank from it himself, as did also his sons and his flocks and herds?"   ver 6

¹³Jesus answered, "Everyone who drinks this water will be thirsty again, ¹⁴but whoever drinks the water I give him will never thirst. Indeed, the water I give him will become in him a spring of water welling up to eternal life."

¹⁵The woman said to him, "Sir, give me this water so that I won't get thirsty and have to keep coming here to draw water."   Jn 6:34

¹⁶He told her, "Go, call your husband and come back."

¹⁷"I have no husband," she replied.

Jesus said to her, "You are right when you say you have no husband. ¹⁸The fact is, you have had five husbands, and the man you now have is not your husband. What you have just said is quite true."

¹⁹"Sir," the woman said, "I can see that you are a prophet. ²⁰Our fathers worshiped on this mountain, but you Jews claim that the place where we must worship is in Jerusalem."   Dt 11:29; Lk 9:53

²¹Jesus declared, "Believe me, woman, a time is coming when you will worship the Father neither on this mountain nor in Jerusalem. ²²You Samaritans worship what you do not know; we worship what we do know, for salvation is from the Jews. ²³Yet a time is coming and has now come when the true worshipers will worship the Father in spirit and truth, for they are the kind of worshipers the Father seeks. ²⁴God is spirit, and his worshipers must worship in spirit and in truth."   Mal 1:11; Php 3:3

²⁵The woman said, "I know that Messiah" (called Christ) "is coming. When he comes, he will explain everything to us."   Mt 1:16

²⁶Then Jesus declared, "I who speak to you am he."   Jn 8:24; 9:35-37

The Disciples Rejoin Jesus

²⁷Just then his disciples returned and were surprised to find him talking with a woman. But no one asked, "What do you want?" or "Why are you talking with her?"

²⁸Then, leaving her water jar, the woman went back to the town and said to the people, ²⁹"Come, see a man who told me everything I ever did. Could this be the Christ[a]?" ³⁰They came out of the town and made their way toward him.   Jn 7:26,31

³¹Meanwhile his disciples urged him, "Rabbi, eat something."

³²But he said to them, "I have food to eat that you know nothing about."   Job 23:12; Mt 4:4; Jn 6:27

³³Then his disciples said to each other, "Could someone have brought him food?"

³⁴"My food," said Jesus, "is to do the will of him who sent me and to

a 29 Or Messiah

finish his work. ³⁵Do you not say, 'Four months more and then the harvest'? I tell you, open your eyes and look at the fields! They are ripe for harvest. ³⁶Even now the reaper draws his wages, even now he harvests the crop for eternal life, so that the sower and the reaper may be glad together. ³⁷Thus the saying 'One sows and another reaps' is true. ³⁸I sent you to reap what you have not worked for. Others have done the hard work, and you have reaped the benefits of their labor."   Mt 9:37; Jn 6:38; Ro 1:13

Many Samaritans Believe

³⁹Many of the Samaritans from that town believed in him because of the woman's testimony, "He told me everything I ever did." ⁴⁰So when the Samaritans came to him, they urged him to stay with them, and he stayed two days. ⁴¹And because of his words many more became believers.   ver 5,29

⁴²They said to the woman, "We no longer believe just because of what you said; now we have heard for ourselves, and we know that this man really is the Savior of the world."   Lk 2:11; 1Jn 4:14

Jesus Heals the Official's Son

⁴³After the two days he left for Galilee. ⁴⁴(Now Jesus himself had pointed out that a prophet has no honor in his own country.) ⁴⁵When he arrived in Galilee, the Galileans welcomed him. They had seen all that he had done in Jerusalem at the Passover Feast, for they also had been there.

⁴⁶Once more he visited Cana in Galilee, where he had turned the water into wine. And there was a certain royal official whose son lay sick at Capernaum. ⁴⁷When this man heard that Jesus had arrived in Galilee from Judea, he went to him and begged him to come and heal his son, who was close to death.   Jn 2:1-11

⁴⁸"Unless you people see miraculous signs and wonders," Jesus told him, "you will never believe."

⁴⁹The royal official said, "Sir, come down before my child dies."

⁵⁰Jesus replied, "You may go. Your son will live."

The man took Jesus at his word and departed. ⁵¹While he was still on the way, his servants met him with the news that his boy was living. ⁵²When he inquired as to the time when his son got better, they said to him, "The fever left him yesterday at the seventh hour."

⁵³Then the father realized that this was the exact time at which Jesus had said to him, "Your son will live." So he and all his household believed.   Ac 11:14

⁵⁴This was the second miraculous sign that Jesus performed, having come from Judea to Galilee.   Jn 2:11

The Healing at the Pool

5 Some time later, Jesus went up to Jerusalem for a feast of the Jews. ²Now there is in Jerusa-

lem near the Sheep Gate a pool, which in Aramaic is called Bethesda^a and which is surrounded by five covered colonnades. ³Here a great number of disabled people used to lie—the blind, the lame, the paralyzed.^b ⁵One who was there had been an invalid for thirty-eight years. ⁶When Jesus saw him lying there and learned that he had been in this condition for a long time, he asked him, "Do you want to get well?"   Ne 3:1; 12:39

⁷"Sir," the invalid replied, "I have no one to help me into the pool when the water is stirred. While I am trying to get in, someone else goes down ahead of me."

⁸Then Jesus said to him, "Get up! Pick up your mat and walk." ⁹At once the man was cured; he picked up his mat and walked.

The day on which this took place was a Sabbath, ¹⁰and so the Jews said to the man who had been healed, "It is the Sabbath; the law forbids you to carry your mat."

¹¹But he replied, "The man who made me well said to me, 'Pick up your mat and walk.' "

¹²So they asked him, "Who is this fellow who told you to pick it up and walk?"

¹³The man who was healed had no idea who it was, for Jesus had slipped away into the crowd that was there.

¹⁴Later Jesus found him at the temple and said to him, "See, you are well again. Stop sinning or something worse may happen to you." ¹⁵The man went away and told the Jews that it was Jesus who had made him well.   Jn 1:19; 8:11

Life Through the Son

¹⁶So, because Jesus was doing these things on the Sabbath, the Jews persecuted him. ¹⁷Jesus said to them, "My Father is always at his work to this very day, and I, too, am working." ¹⁸For this reason the Jews tried all the harder to kill him; not only was he breaking the Sabbath, but he was even calling God his own Father, making himself equal with God.   Jn 7:1

¹⁹Jesus gave them this answer: "I tell you the truth, the Son can do nothing by himself; he can do only what he sees his Father doing, because whatever the Father does the Son also does. ²⁰For the Father loves the Son and shows him all he does. Yes, to your amazement he will show him even greater things than these. ²¹For just as the Father raises the dead and gives them life, even so the Son gives life to whom he is pleased to give it. ²²Moreover, the Father judges no one, but has entrusted all judgment to the Son, ²³that all may honor the Son just as they honor the Father. He who

---

^a2 Some manuscripts *Bethzatha*; other manuscripts *Bethsaida*   ^b3 Some less important manuscripts *paralyzed—and they waited for the moving of the waters.* ⁴*From time to time an angel of the Lord would come down and stir up the waters. The first one into the pool after each such disturbance would be cured of whatever disease he had.*

does not honor the Son does not honor the Father, who sent him.

²⁴"I tell you the truth, whoever hears my word and believes him who sent me has eternal life and will not be condemned; he has crossed over from death to life. ²⁵I tell you the truth, a time is coming and has now come when the dead will hear the voice of the Son of God and those who hear will live. ²⁶For as the Father has life in himself, so he has granted the Son to have life in himself. ²⁷And he has given him authority to judge because he is the Son of Man.

²⁸"Do not be amazed at this, for a time is coming when all who are in their graves will hear his voice ²⁹and come out—those who have done good will rise to live, and those who have done evil will rise to be condemned. ³⁰By myself I can do nothing; I judge only as I hear, and my judgment is just, for I seek not to please myself but him who sent me.   Da 12:2; Mt 25:46; 26:39

Testimonies About Jesus

³¹"If I testify about myself, my testimony is not valid. ³²There is another who testifies in my favor, and I know that his testimony about me is valid.   Jn 8:14

³³"You have sent to John and he has testified to the truth. ³⁴Not that I accept human testimony; but I mention it that you may be saved.

³⁵John was a lamp that burned and gave light, and you chose for a time to enjoy his light.   Jn 1:7

³⁶"I have testimony weightier than that of John. For the very work that the Father has given me to finish, and which I am doing, testifies that the Father has sent me. ³⁷And the Father who sent me has himself testified concerning me. You have never heard his voice nor seen his form, ³⁸nor does his word dwell in you, for you do not believe the one he sent. ³⁹You diligently studyᵃ the Scriptures because you think that by them you possess eternal life. These are the Scriptures that testify about me, ⁴⁰yet you refuse to come to me to have life.   Jn 8:18; 10:25; Ro 2:17-18

⁴¹"I do not accept praise from men, ⁴²but I know you. I know that you do not have the love of God in your hearts. ⁴³I have come in my Father's name, and you do not accept me; but if someone else comes in his own name, you will accept him. ⁴⁴How can you believe if you accept praise from one another, yet make no effort to obtain the praise that comes from the only Godᵇ?   Ro 2:29

⁴⁵"But do not think I will accuse you before the Father. Your accuser is Moses, on whom your hopes are set. ⁴⁶If you believed Moses, you would believe me, for he wrote about me. ⁴⁷But since you do not believe what he wrote, how

---

ᵃ 39 Or *Study diligently* (the imperative)   ᵇ 44 Some early manuscripts *the Only One*

are you going to believe what I say?" Lk 16:29,31; Jn 9:28; Ro 2:17

Jesus Feeds the Five Thousand

6 Some time after this, Jesus crossed to the far shore of the Sea of Galilee (that is, the Sea of Tiberias), ²and a great crowd of people followed him because they saw the miraculous signs he had performed on the sick. ³Then Jesus went up on a mountainside and sat down with his disciples. ⁴The Jewish Passover Feast was near. Jn 2:11; 11:55

⁵When Jesus looked up and saw a great crowd coming toward him, he said to Philip, "Where shall we buy bread for these people to eat?" ⁶He asked this only to test him, for he already had in mind what he was going to do. Jn 1:43

⁷Philip answered him, "Eight months' wages*a* would not buy enough bread for each one to have a bite!"

⁸Another of his disciples, Andrew, Simon Peter's brother, spoke up, ⁹"Here is a boy with five small barley loaves and two small fish, but how far will they go among so many?" 2Ki 4:43; Jn 1:40

¹⁰Jesus said, "Have the people sit down." There was plenty of grass in that place, and the men sat down, about five thousand of them. ¹¹Jesus then took the loaves, gave thanks, and distributed to those who were seated as much as they wanted. He did the same with the fish. Mt 14:19

¹²When they had all had enough to eat, he said to his disciples, "Gather the pieces that are left over. Let nothing be wasted." ¹³So they gathered them and filled twelve baskets with the pieces of the five barley loaves left over by those who had eaten. Mt 14:13-21

¹⁴After the people saw the miraculous sign that Jesus did, they began to say, "Surely this is the Prophet who is to come into the world." ¹⁵Jesus, knowing that they intended to come and make him king by force, withdrew again to a mountain by himself. Mt 14:23

Jesus Walks on the Water

¹⁶When evening came, his disciples went down to the lake, ¹⁷where they got into a boat and set off across the lake for Capernaum. By now it was dark, and Jesus had not yet joined them. ¹⁸A strong wind was blowing and the waters grew rough. ¹⁹When they had rowed three or three and a half miles,*b* they saw Jesus approaching the boat, walking on the water; and they were terrified. ²⁰But he said to them, "It is I; don't be afraid." ²¹Then they were willing to take him into the boat, and immediately the boat reached the shore where they were heading.

²²The next day the crowd that had stayed on the opposite shore

---

a 7 Greek *two hundred denarii*   *b 19* Greek *rowed twenty-five or thirty stadia* (about 5 or 6 kilometers) of the lake realized that only one boat had been there, and that Jesus had not entered it with his disciples, but that they had gone away alone. 23Then some boats from Tiberias landed near the place where the people had eaten the bread after the Lord had given thanks. 24Once the crowd realized that neither Jesus nor his disciples were there, they got into the boats and went to Capernaum in search of Jesus.

Jesus the Bread of Life

25When they found him on the other side of the lake, they asked him, "Rabbi, when did you get here?" *Mt 23:7*

26Jesus answered, "I tell you the truth, you are looking for me, not because you saw miraculous signs but because you ate the loaves and had your fill. 27Do not work for food that spoils, but for food that endures to eternal life, which the Son of Man will give you. On him God the Father has placed his seal of approval." *Isa 55:2; Jn 4:14; Ro 4:11*

28Then they asked him, "What must we do to do the works God requires?"

29Jesus answered, "The work of God is this: to believe in the one he has sent." *Jn 3:17; 1Jn 3:23*

30So they asked him, "What miraculous sign then will you give that we may see it and believe you? What will you do? 31Our forefa-

thers ate the manna in the desert; as it is written: 'He gave them bread from heaven to eat.'*ᵃ*"

32Jesus said to them, "I tell you the truth, it is not Moses who has given you the bread from heaven, but it is my Father who gives you the true bread from heaven. 33For the bread of God is he who comes down from heaven and gives life to the world." *Jn 3:13,31*

34"Sir," they said, "from now on give us this bread." *Jn 4:15*

35Then Jesus declared, "I am the bread of life. He who comes to me will never go hungry, and he who believes in me will never be thirsty. 36But as I told you, you have seen me and still you do not believe. 37All that the Father gives me will come to me, and whoever comes to me I will never drive away. 38For I have come down from heaven not to do my will but to do the will of him who sent me. 39And this is the will of him who sent me, that I shall lose none of all that he has given me, but raise them up at the last day. 40For my Father's will is that everyone who looks to the Son and believes in him shall have eternal life, and I will raise him up at the last day."

41At this the Jews began to grumble about him because he said, "I am the bread that came down from heaven." 42They said, "Is this not Jesus, the son of Joseph, whose father and mother we

ᵃ31 Exodus 16:4; Neh. 9:15; Psalm 78:24,25

know? How can he now say, 'I came down from heaven'?"

43"Stop grumbling among yourselves," Jesus answered. 44"No one can come to me unless the Father who sent me draws him, and I will raise him up at the last day. 45It is written in the Prophets: 'They will all be taught by God.'*a* Everyone who listens to the Father and learns from him comes to me. 46No one has seen the Father except the one who is from God; only he has seen the Father. 47I tell you the truth, he who believes has everlasting life. 48I am the bread of life. 49Your forefathers ate the manna in the desert, yet they died. 50But here is the bread that comes down from heaven, which a man may eat and not die. 51I am the living bread that came down from heaven. If anyone eats of this bread, he will live forever. This bread is my flesh, which I will give for the life of the world."   Isa 54:13; Jn 1:18; Heb 10:10

52Then the Jews began to argue sharply among themselves, "How can this man give us his flesh to eat?"   Jn 9:16; 10:19

53Jesus said to them, "I tell you the truth, unless you eat the flesh of the Son of Man and drink his blood, you have no life in you. 54Whoever eats my flesh and drinks my blood has eternal life, and I will raise him up at the last day. 55For my flesh is real food and my blood is real drink. 56Whoever eats my flesh and drinks my blood remains in me, and I in him. 57Just as the living Father sent me and I live because of the Father, so the one who feeds on me will live because of me. 58This is the bread that came down from heaven. Your forefathers ate manna and died, but he who feeds on this bread will live forever." 59He said this while teaching in the synagogue in Capernaum.   1Jn 3:24; 4:15

Many Disciples Desert Jesus

60On hearing it, many of his disciples said, "This is a hard teaching. Who can accept it?"

61Aware that his disciples were grumbling about this, Jesus said to them, "Does this offend you? 62What if you see the Son of Man ascend to where he was before! 63The Spirit gives life; the flesh counts for nothing. The words I have spoken to you are spirit*b* and they are life. 64Yet there are some of you who do not believe." For Jesus had known from the beginning which of them did not believe and who would betray him. 65He went on to say, "This is why I told you that no one can come to me unless the Father has enabled him."   Jn 2:25; 3:13; 2Co 3:6

66From this time many of his disciples turned back and no longer followed him.   ver 60

67"You do not want to leave too, do you?" Jesus asked the Twelve.

a 45 Isaiah 54:13   *b* 63 Or *Spirit*

68Simon Peter answered him, "Lord, to whom shall we go? You have the words of eternal life. **69**We believe and know that you are the Holy One of God." Mk 8:29

70Then Jesus replied, "Have I not chosen you, the Twelve? Yet one of you is a devil!" **71**(He meant Judas, the son of Simon Iscariot, who, though one of the Twelve, was later to betray him.) Jn 13:27

Jesus Goes to the Feast of Tabernacles

7 After this, Jesus went around in Galilee, purposely staying away from Judea because the Jews there were waiting to take his life. **2**But when the Jewish Feast of Tabernacles was near, **3**Jesus' brothers said to him, "You ought to leave here and go to Judea, so that your disciples may see the miracles you do. **4**No one who wants to become a public figure acts in secret. Since you are doing these things, show yourself to the world." **5**For even his own brothers did not believe in him. Mt 12:46; Jn 5:18; Lev 23:34

6Therefore Jesus told them, "The right time for me has not yet come; for you any time is right. **7**The world cannot hate you, but it hates me because I testify that what it does is evil. **8**You go to the Feast. I am not yet*a* going up to this Feast, because for me the right time has not yet come." **9**Having said this, he stayed in Galilee.

10However, after his brothers had left for the Feast, he went also, not publicly, but in secret. **11**Now at the Feast the Jews were watching for him and asking, "Where is that man?" Jn 11:56

12Among the crowds there was widespread whispering about him. Some said, "He is a good man."

Others replied, "No, he deceives the people." **13**But no one would say anything publicly about him for fear of the Jews. Jn 9:22; 12:42

Jesus Teaches at the Feast

14Not until halfway through the Feast did Jesus go up to the temple courts and begin to teach. **15**The Jews were amazed and asked, "How did this man get such learning without having studied?"

16Jesus answered, "My teaching is not my own. It comes from him who sent me. **17**If anyone chooses to do God's will, he will find out whether my teaching comes from God or whether I speak on my own. **18**He who speaks on his own does so to gain honor for himself, but he who works for the honor of the one who sent him is a man of truth; there is nothing false about him. **19**Has not Moses given you the law? Yet not one of you keeps the law. Why are you trying to kill me?" Jn 5:41; 8:50,54; 14:24

20"You are demon-possessed," the crowd answered. "Who is trying to kill you?"

a 8 Some early manuscripts do not have *yet*.

21Jesus said to them, "I did one miracle, and you are all astonished. **22**Yet, because Moses gave you circumcision (though actually it did not come from Moses, but from the patriarchs), you circumcise a child on the Sabbath. **23**Now if a child can be circumcised on the Sabbath so that the law of Moses may not be broken, why are you angry with me for healing the whole man on the Sabbath? **24**Stop judging by mere appearances, and make a right judgment."   Jn 8:15,48

Is Jesus the Christ?

25At that point some of the people of Jerusalem began to ask, "Isn't this the man they are trying to kill? **26**Here he is, speaking publicly, and they are not saying a word to him. Have the authorities really concluded that he is the Christ[a]? **27**But we know where this man is from; when the Christ comes, no one will know where he is from."   Mt 13:55; Lk 4:22

28Then Jesus, still teaching in the temple courts, cried out, "Yes, you know me, and you know where I am from. I am not here on my own, but he who sent me is true. You do not know him, **29**but I know him because I am from him and he sent me."   Mt 11:27

30At this they tried to seize him, but no one laid a hand on him, because his time had not yet come.

31Still, many in the crowd put their faith in him. They said, "When the Christ comes, will he do more miraculous signs than this man?"

32The Pharisees heard the crowd whispering such things about him. Then the chief priests and the Pharisees sent temple guards to arrest him.

33Jesus said, "I am with you for only a short time, and then I go to the one who sent me. **34**You will look for me, but you will not find me; and where I am, you cannot come."   Jn 8:21; 13:33

35The Jews said to one another, "Where does this man intend to go that we cannot find him? Will he go where our people live scattered among the Greeks, and teach the Greeks? **36**What did he mean when he said, 'You will look for me, but you will not find me,' and 'Where I am, you cannot come'?"   Jas 1:1

37On the last and greatest day of the Feast, Jesus stood and said in a loud voice, "If anyone is thirsty, let him come to me and drink. **38**Whoever believes in me, as[b] the Scripture has said, streams of living water will flow from within him." **39**By this he meant the Spirit, whom those who believed in him were later to receive. Up to that time the Spirit had not been given, since Jesus had not yet been glorified.   Isa 55:1; Joel 2:28; Jn 12:23

40On hearing his words, some of

---

a 26 Or *Messiah*; also in verses 27, 31, 41 and 42   b 37,38 Or / *If anyone is thirsty, let him come to me.*
/ *And let him drink,* 38*who believes in me. / As*

the people said, "Surely this man is the Prophet." Mt 21:11; Jn 1:21

41Others said, "He is the Christ."

Still others asked, "How can the Christ come from Galilee? **42**Does not the Scripture say that the Christ will come from David's family*a* and from Bethlehem, the town where David lived?" **43**Thus the people were divided because of Jesus. **44**Some wanted to seize him, but no one laid a hand on him.

Unbelief of the Jewish Leaders

45Finally the temple guards went back to the chief priests and Pharisees, who asked them, "Why didn't you bring him in?"

46"No one ever spoke the way this man does," the guards declared. Mt 7:28

47"You mean he has deceived you also?" the Pharisees retorted. **48**"Has any of the rulers or of the Pharisees believed in him? **49**No! But this mob that knows nothing of the law—there is a curse on them." Jn 12:42

50Nicodemus, who had gone to Jesus earlier and who was one of their own number, asked, **51**"Does our law condemn anyone without first hearing him to find out what he is doing?" Jn 3:1; 19:39

52They replied, "Are you from Galilee, too? Look into it, and you will find that a prophet*b* does not come out of Galilee."

[The earliest manuscripts and many other ancient witnesses do not have John 7:53–8:11.]

53Then each went to his own home.

8 But Jesus went to the Mount of Olives. **2**At dawn he appeared again in the temple courts, where all the people gathered around him, and he sat down to teach them. **3**The teachers of the law and the Pharisees brought in a woman caught in adultery. They made her stand before the group **4**and said to Jesus, "Teacher, this woman was caught in the act of adultery. **5**In the Law Moses commanded us to stone such women. Now what do you say?" **6**They were using this question as a trap, in order to have a basis for accusing him. Lev 20:10; Dt 22:22; Mt 12:10

But Jesus bent down and started to write on the ground with his finger. **7**When they kept on questioning him, he straightened up and said to them, "If any one of you is without sin, let him be the first to throw a stone at her." **8**Again he stooped down and wrote on the ground. Dt 17:7; Ro 2:1,22

9At this, those who heard began to go away one at a time, the older ones first, until only Jesus was left, with the woman still standing there. **10**Jesus straightened up and

a42 Greek *seed*　　*b52* Two early manuscripts *the Prophet*

asked her, "Woman, where are they? Has no one condemned you?"

[11]"No one, sir," she said.

"Then neither do I condemn you," Jesus declared. "Go now and leave your life of sin."

The Validity of Jesus' Testimony

[12]When Jesus spoke again to the people, he said, "I am the light of the world. Whoever follows me will never walk in darkness, but will have the light of life." Jn 1:4

[13]The Pharisees challenged him, "Here you are, appearing as your own witness; your testimony is not valid." Jn 5:31

[14]Jesus answered, "Even if I testify on my own behalf, my testimony is valid, for I know where I came from and where I am going. But you have no idea where I come from or where I am going. [15]You judge by human standards; I pass judgment on no one. [16]But if I do judge, my decisions are right, because I am not alone. I stand with the Father, who sent me. [17]In your own Law it is written that the testimony of two men is valid. [18]I am one who testifies for myself; my other witness is the Father, who sent me." Mt 18:16; Jn 5:37; 7:28

[19]Then they asked him, "Where is your father?"

"You do not know me or my Father," Jesus replied. "If you knew me, you would know my Father also." [20]He spoke these words while teaching in the temple area near the place where the offerings were put. Yet no one seized him, because his time had not yet come.

[21]Once more Jesus said to them, "I am going away, and you will look for me, and you will die in your sin. Where I go, you cannot come." Jn 7:34; 13:33

[22]This made the Jews ask, "Will he kill himself? Is that why he says, 'Where I go, you cannot come'?"

[23]But he continued, "You are from below; I am from above. You are of this world; I am not of this world. [24]I told you that you would die in your sins; if you do not believe that I am the one I claim to be,[a] you will indeed die in your sins." Jn 3:31; 4:26

[25]"Who are you?" they asked.

"Just what I have been claiming all along," Jesus replied. [26]"I have much to say in judgment of you. But he who sent me is reliable, and what I have heard from him I tell the world." Jn 3:32; 7:28; 15:15

[27]They did not understand that he was telling them about his Father. [28]So Jesus said, "When you have lifted up the Son of Man, then you will know that I am the one I claim to be, and that I do nothing

---

[a]24 Or I am he; also in verse 28

on my own but speak just what the Father has taught me. ²⁹The one who sent me is with me; he has not left me alone, for I always do what pleases him." ³⁰Even as he spoke, many put their faith in him.

The Children of Abraham

³¹To the Jews who had believed him, Jesus said, "If you hold to my teaching, you are really my disciples. ³²Then you will know the truth, and the truth will set you free."   Jn 15:7; Ro 8:2; Jas 2:12

³³They answered him, "We are Abraham's descendants*ᵃ* and have never been slaves of anyone. How can you say that we shall be set free?"   Mt 3:9

³⁴Jesus replied, "I tell you the truth, everyone who sins is a slave to sin. ³⁵Now a slave has no permanent place in the family, but a son belongs to it forever. ³⁶So if the Son sets you free, you will be free indeed. ³⁷I know you are Abraham's descendants. Yet you are ready to kill me, because you have no room for my word. ³⁸I am telling you what I have seen in the Father's presence, and you do what you have heard from your father.*ᵇ*"   Jn 5:19,30; Ro 6:16; Gal 4:30

³⁹"Abraham is our father," they answered.

"If you were Abraham's children," said Jesus, "then you would*ᶜ* do the things Abraham

did. ⁴⁰As it is, you are determined to kill me, a man who has told you the truth that I heard from God. Abraham did not do such things. ⁴¹You are doing the things your own father does."   Ro 9:7; Gal 3:7

"We are not illegitimate children," they protested. "The only Father we have is God himself."

The Children of the Devil

⁴²Jesus said to them, "If God were your Father, you would love me, for I came from God and now am here. I have not come on my own; but he sent me. ⁴³Why is my language not clear to you? Because you are unable to hear what I say. ⁴⁴You belong to your father, the devil, and you want to carry out your father's desire. He was a murderer from the beginning, not holding to the truth, for there is no truth in him. When he lies, he speaks his native language, for he is a liar and the father of lies. ⁴⁵Yet because I tell the truth, you do not believe me! ⁴⁶Can any of you prove me guilty of sin? If I am telling the truth, why don't you believe me? ⁴⁷He who belongs to God hears what God says. The reason you do not hear is that you do not belong to God."   Jn 18:37; 1Jn 4:6

The Claims of Jesus About Himself

⁴⁸The Jews answered him,

ᵃ33 Greek *seed*; also in verse 37   *ᵇ38* Or *presence. Therefore do what you have heard from the Father.*
ᶜ39 Some early manuscripts *"If you are Abraham's children," said Jesus, "then*

"Aren't we right in saying that you are a Samaritan and demon-possessed?" Mt 10:5; Jn 7:20

⁴⁹"I am not possessed by a demon," said Jesus, "but I honor my Father and you dishonor me. ⁵⁰I am not seeking glory for myself; but there is one who seeks it, and he is the judge. ⁵¹I tell you the truth, if anyone keeps my word, he will never see death." Jn 5:41; 11:26

⁵²At this the Jews exclaimed, "Now we know that you are demon-possessed! Abraham died and so did the prophets, yet you say that if anyone keeps your word, he will never taste death. ⁵³Are you greater than our father Abraham? He died, and so did the prophets. Who do you think you are?" Mk 3:22; Jn 4:12

⁵⁴Jesus replied, "If I glorify myself, my glory means nothing. My Father, whom you claim as your God, is the one who glorifies me. ⁵⁵Though you do not know him, I know him. If I said I did not, I would be a liar like you, but I do know him and keep his word. ⁵⁶Your father Abraham rejoiced at the thought of seeing my day; he saw it and was glad." Jn 7:28-29

⁵⁷"You are not yet fifty years old," the Jews said to him, "and you have seen Abraham!"

⁵⁸"I tell you the truth," Jesus answered, "before Abraham was born, I am!" ⁵⁹At this, they picked up stones to stone him, but Jesus hid himself, slipping away from the temple grounds. Ex 3:14; Jn 10:31

Jesus Heals a Man Born Blind

9 As he went along, he saw a man blind from birth. ²His disciples asked him, "Rabbi, who sinned, this man or his parents, that he was born blind?" Ex 20:5

³"Neither this man nor his parents sinned," said Jesus, "but this happened so that the work of God might be displayed in his life. ⁴As long as it is day, we must do the work of him who sent me. Night is coming, when no one can work. ⁵While I am in the world, I am the light of the world." Jn 8:12; 12:46

⁶Having said this, he spit on the ground, made some mud with the saliva, and put it on the man's eyes. ⁷"Go," he told him, "wash in the Pool of Siloam" (this word means Sent). So the man went and washed, and came home seeing.

⁸His neighbors and those who had formerly seen him begging asked, "Isn't this the same man who used to sit and beg?" ⁹Some claimed that he was. Ac 3:2,10

Others said, "No, he only looks like him."

But he himself insisted, "I am the man."

¹⁰"How then were your eyes opened?" they demanded.

¹¹He replied, "The man they call Jesus made some mud and put it on my eyes. He told me to go to Siloam and wash. So I went and washed, and then I could see."

¹²"Where is this man?" they asked him.

"I don't know," he said.

The Pharisees Investigate the Healing

¹³They brought to the Pharisees the man who had been blind. ¹⁴Now the day on which Jesus had made the mud and opened the man's eyes was a Sabbath. ¹⁵Therefore the Pharisees also asked him how he had received his sight. "He put mud on my eyes," the man replied, "and I washed, and now I see." Jn 5:9

¹⁶Some of the Pharisees said, "This man is not from God, for he does not keep the Sabbath."

But others asked, "How can a sinner do such miraculous signs?" So they were divided. Jn 7:43; 10:19

¹⁷Finally they turned again to the blind man, "What have you to say about him? It was your eyes he opened."

The man replied, "He is a prophet." Mt 21:11

¹⁸The Jews still did not believe that he had been blind and had received his sight until they sent for the man's parents. ¹⁹"Is this your son?" they asked. "Is this the one you say was born blind? How is it that now he can see?" Jn 1:19

²⁰"We know he is our son," the parents answered, "and we know he was born blind. ²¹But how he can see now, or who opened his eyes, we don't know. Ask him. He is of age; he will speak for him-self." ²²His parents said this because they were afraid of the Jews, for already the Jews had decided that anyone who acknowledged that Jesus was the Christ[a] would be put out of the synagogue. ²³That was why his parents said, "He is of age; ask him." Jn 7:13

²⁴A second time they summoned the man who had been blind. "Give glory to God,[b]" they said. "We know this man is a sinner." ver 16; Jos 7:19

²⁵He replied, "Whether he is a sinner or not, I don't know. One thing I do know. I was blind but now I see!"

²⁶Then they asked him, "What did he do to you? How did he open your eyes?"

²⁷He answered, "I have told you already and you did not listen. Why do you want to hear it again? Do you want to become his disciples, too?"

²⁸Then they hurled insults at him and said, "You are this fellow's disciple! We are disciples of Moses! ²⁹We know that God spoke to Moses, but as for this fellow, we don't even know where he comes from." Jn 5:45; 8:14

³⁰The man answered, "Now that is remarkable! You don't know where he comes from, yet he opened my eyes. ³¹We know that God does not listen to sinners. He listens to the godly man who does his will. ³²Nobody has ever heard

a 22 Or Messiah   b 24 A solemn charge to tell the truth (see Joshua 7:19)

of opening the eyes of a man born blind. [33]If this man were not from God, he could do nothing."

[34]To this they replied, "You were steeped in sin at birth; how dare you lecture us!" And they threw him out.   Isa 66:5

Spiritual Blindness

[35]Jesus heard that they had thrown him out, and when he found him, he said, "Do you believe in the Son of Man?"   Mt 8:20

[36]"Who is he, sir?" the man asked. "Tell me so that I may believe in him."   Ro 10:14

[37]Jesus said, "You have now seen him; in fact, he is the one speaking with you."   Jn 4:26

[38]Then the man said, "Lord, I believe," and he worshiped him.

[39]Jesus said, "For judgment I have come into this world, so that the blind will see and those who see will become blind."   Mt 13:13

[40]Some Pharisees who were with him heard him say this and asked, "What? Are we blind too?"

[41]Jesus said, "If you were blind, you would not be guilty of sin; but now that you claim you can see, your guilt remains.   Jn 15:22,24

The Shepherd and His Flock

10 "I tell you the truth, the man who does not enter the sheep pen by the gate, but climbs in by some other way, is a thief and a robber. [2]The man who enters by the gate is the shepherd of his sheep. [3]The watchman opens the gate for him, and the sheep listen to his voice. He calls his own sheep by name and leads them out. [4]When he has brought out all his own, he goes on ahead of them, and his sheep follow him because they know his voice. [5]But they will never follow a stranger; in fact, they will run away from him because they do not recognize a stranger's voice." [6]Jesus used this figure of speech, but they did not understand what he was telling them.   Mk 9:32; Jn 16:25

[7]Therefore Jesus said again, "I tell you the truth, I am the gate for the sheep. [8]All who ever came before me were thieves and robbers, but the sheep did not listen to them. [9]I am the gate; whoever enters through me will be saved. [a] He will come in and go out, and find pasture. [10]The thief comes only to steal and kill and destroy; I have come that they may have life, and have it to the full.   Jn 1:4; Ro 5:17

[11]"I am the good shepherd. The good shepherd lays down his life for the sheep. [12]The hired hand is not the shepherd who owns the sheep. So when he sees the wolf coming, he abandons the sheep and runs away. Then the wolf attacks the flock and scatters it. [13]The man runs away because he is a hired hand and cares nothing for the sheep.   Isa 40:11; Eze 34:11-16,23

[a]9 Or kept safe

¹⁴"I am the good shepherd; I know my sheep and my sheep know me— ¹⁵just as the Father knows me and I know the Father— and I lay down my life for the sheep. ¹⁶I have other sheep that are not of this sheep pen. I must bring them also. They too will listen to my voice, and there shall be one flock and one shepherd. ¹⁷The reason my Father loves me is that I lay down my life—only to take it up again. ¹⁸No one takes it from me, but I lay it down of my own accord. I have authority to lay it down and authority to take it up again. This command I received from my Father."   Mt 11:27; Jn 15:10

¹⁹At these words the Jews were again divided. ²⁰Many of them said, "He is demon-possessed and raving mad. Why listen to him?"

²¹But others said, "These are not the sayings of a man possessed by a demon. Can a demon open the eyes of the blind?"   Ex 4:11; Jn 9:32-33

The Unbelief of the Jews

²²Then came the Feast of Dedication*a* at Jerusalem. It was winter, ²³and Jesus was in the temple area walking in Solomon's Colonnade. ²⁴The Jews gathered around him, saying, "How long will you keep us in suspense? If you are the Christ,*b* tell us plainly."   Jn 16:25,29

²⁵Jesus answered, "I did tell you, but you do not believe. The mira-cles I do in my Father's name speak for me, ²⁶but you do not believe because you are not my sheep. ²⁷My sheep listen to my voice; I know them, and they follow me. ²⁸I give them eternal life, and they shall never perish; no one can snatch them out of my hand. ²⁹My Father, who has given them to me, is greater than all*c*; no one can snatch them out of my Father's hand. ³⁰I and the Father are one."   Jn 17:21-23

³¹Again the Jews picked up stones to stone him, ³²but Jesus said to them, "I have shown you many great miracles from the Father. For which of these do you stone me?"   Jn 8:59

³³"We are not stoning you for any of these," replied the Jews, "but for blasphemy, because you, a mere man, claim to be God."

³⁴Jesus answered them, "Is it not written in your Law, 'I have said you are gods'*d*? ³⁵If he called them 'gods,' to whom the word of God came—and the Scripture cannot be broken— ³⁶what about the one whom the Father set apart as his very own and sent into the world? Why then do you accuse me of blasphemy because I said, 'I am God's Son'? ³⁷Do not believe me unless I do what my Father does. ³⁸But if I do it, even though you do not believe me, believe the mira-cles, that you may know and un-

---

a 22 That is, Hanukkah   *b 24* Or *Messiah*   *c 29* Many early manuscripts *What my Father has given me is greater than all*   *d 34* Psalm 82:6

derstand that the Father is in me, and I in the Father." **39**Again they tried to seize him, but he escaped their grasp. *Jn 14:10-11,20; 15:24*

40Then Jesus went back across the Jordan to the place where John had been baptizing in the early days. Here he stayed **41**and many people came to him. They said, "Though John never performed a miraculous sign, all that John said about this man was true." **42**And in that place many believed in Jesus.

The Death of Lazarus

11 Now a man named Lazarus was sick. He was from Bethany, the village of Mary and her sister Martha. **2**This Mary, whose brother Lazarus now lay sick, was the same one who poured perfume on the Lord and wiped his feet with her hair. **3**So the sisters sent word to Jesus, "Lord, the one you love is sick."

4When he heard this, Jesus said, "This sickness will not end in death. No, it is for God's glory so that God's Son may be glorified through it." **5**Jesus loved Martha and her sister and Lazarus. **6**Yet when he heard that Lazarus was sick, he stayed where he was two more days. *Jn 9:3*

7Then he said to his disciples, "Let us go back to Judea." *Jn 10:40*

8"But Rabbi," they said, "a short while ago the Jews tried to stone you, and yet you are going back there?" *Mt 23:7; Jn 10:31*

9Jesus answered, "Are there not twelve hours of daylight? A man who walks by day will not stumble, for he sees by this world's light. **10**It is when he walks by night that he stumbles, for he has no light." *Jn 9:4; 12:35*

11After he had said this, he went on to tell them, "Our friend Lazarus has fallen asleep; but I am going there to wake him up."

12His disciples replied, "Lord, if he sleeps, he will get better." **13**Jesus had been speaking of his death, but his disciples thought he meant natural sleep. *Mt 9:24*

14So then he told them plainly, "Lazarus is dead, **15**and for your sake I am glad I was not there, so that you may believe. But let us go to him."

16Then Thomas (called Didymus) said to the rest of the disciples, "Let us also go, that we may die with him." *Mt 10:3; Jn 14:5; 20:24-28*

Jesus Comforts the Sisters

17On his arrival, Jesus found that Lazarus had already been in the tomb for four days. **18**Bethany was less than two miles*a* from Jerusalem, **19**and many Jews had come to Martha and Mary to comfort them in the loss of their brother. **20**When Martha heard that Jesus was coming, she went out to

a 18 Greek *fifteen stadia* (about 3 kilometers)

meet him, but Mary stayed at home. Job 2:11; Lk 10:38-42

21"Lord," Martha said to Jesus, "if you had been here, my brother would not have died. 22But I know that even now God will give you whatever you ask." Jn 9:31

23Jesus said to her, "Your brother will rise again."

24Martha answered, "I know he will rise again in the resurrection at the last day." Jn 5:28-29; Ac 24:15

25Jesus said to her, "I am the resurrection and the life. He who believes in me will live, even though he dies; 26and whoever lives and believes in me will never die. Do you believe this?" Jn 1:4; 3:15

27"Yes, Lord," she told him, "I believe that you are the Christ,a the Son of God, who was to come into the world." Mt 16:16; Jn 6:14

28And after she had said this, she went back and called her sister Mary aside. "The Teacher is here," she said, "and is asking for you." 29When Mary heard this, she got up quickly and went to him. 30Now Jesus had not yet entered the village, but was still at the place where Martha had met him. 31When the Jews who had been with Mary in the house, comforting her, noticed how quickly she got up and went out, they followed her, supposing she was going to the tomb to mourn there. Mt 26:18

32When Mary reached the place where Jesus was and saw him, she fell at his feet and said, "Lord, if you had been here, my brother would not have died."

33When Jesus saw her weeping, and the Jews who had come along with her also weeping, he was deeply moved in spirit and troubled. 34"Where have you laid him?" he asked. Jn 12:27

"Come and see, Lord," they replied.

35Jesus wept. Lk 19:41

36Then the Jews said, "See how he loved him!"

37But some of them said, "Could not he who opened the eyes of the blind man have kept this man from dying?" Jn 9:6-7

Jesus Raises Lazarus From the Dead

38Jesus, once more deeply moved, came to the tomb. It was a cave with a stone laid across the entrance. 39"Take away the stone," he said. Mt 27:60; Lk 24:2; Jn 20:1

"But, Lord," said Martha, the sister of the dead man, "by this time there is a bad odor, for he has been there four days."

40Then Jesus said, "Did I not tell you that if you believed, you would see the glory of God?"

41So they took away the stone. Then Jesus looked up and said, "Father, I thank you that you have heard me. 42I knew that you always hear me, but I said this for the benefit of the people standing

a27 Or Messiah

here, that they may believe that you sent me." _{Jn 3:17; 12:30}

⁴³When he had said this, Jesus called in a loud voice, "Lazarus, come out!" ⁴⁴The dead man came out, his hands and feet wrapped with strips of linen, and a cloth around his face. _{Jn 19:40; 20:7}

Jesus said to them, "Take off the grave clothes and let him go."

The Plot to Kill Jesus

⁴⁵Therefore many of the Jews who had come to visit Mary, and had seen what Jesus did, put their faith in him. ⁴⁶But some of them went to the Pharisees and told them what Jesus had done. ⁴⁷Then the chief priests and the Pharisees called a meeting of the Sanhedrin.

"What are we accomplishing?" they asked. "Here is this man performing many miraculous signs. ⁴⁸If we let him go on like this, everyone will believe in him, and then the Romans will come and take away both our place*ᵃ* and our nation." _{Jn 2:11}

⁴⁹Then one of them, named Caiaphas, who was high priest that year, spoke up, "You know nothing at all! ⁵⁰You do not realize that it is better for you that one man die for the people than that the whole nation perish." _{Mt 26:3; Jn 18:13-14}

⁵¹He did not say this on his own, but as high priest that year he prophesied that Jesus would die for the Jewish nation, ⁵²and not only for that nation but also for the scattered children of God, to bring them together and make them one. ⁵³So from that day on they plotted to take his life. _{Isa 49:6; Mt 12:14}

⁵⁴Therefore Jesus no longer moved about publicly among the Jews. Instead he withdrew to a region near the desert, to a village called Ephraim, where he stayed with his disciples. _{Jn 7:1}

⁵⁵When it was almost time for the Jewish Passover, many went up from the country to Jerusalem for their ceremonial cleansing before the Passover. ⁵⁶They kept looking for Jesus, and as they stood in the temple area they asked one another, "What do you think? Isn't he coming to the Feast at all?" ⁵⁷But the chief priests and Pharisees had given orders that if anyone found out where Jesus was, he should report it so that they might arrest him. _{2Ch 30:17-18}

Jesus Anointed at Bethany

12 Six days before the Passover, Jesus arrived at Bethany, where Lazarus lived, whom Jesus had raised from the dead. ²Here a dinner was given in Jesus' honor. Martha served, while Lazarus was among those reclining at the table with him. ³Then Mary took about a pint*ᵇ* of pure nard, an expensive perfume; she poured it on Jesus' feet and wiped his feet with her hair. And the house was

---

*ᵃ*48 Or *temple*   *ᵇ*3 Greek *a litra* (probably about 0.5 liter)

filled with the fragrance of the perfume.   Jn 11:2,55

4But one of his disciples, Judas Iscariot, who was later to betray him, objected, 5"Why wasn't this perfume sold and the money given to the poor? It was worth a year's wages.*a*" 6He did not say this because he cared about the poor but because he was a thief; as keeper of the money bag, he used to help himself to what was put into it.

7"Leave her alone," Jesus replied. "It was intended that she should save this perfume for the day of my burial. 8You will always have the poor among you, but you will not always have me."

9Meanwhile a large crowd of Jews found out that Jesus was there and came, not only because of him but also to see Lazarus, whom he had raised from the dead. 10So the chief priests made plans to kill Lazarus as well, 11for on account of him many of the Jews were going over to Jesus and putting their faith in him.   Jn 7:31

The Triumphal Entry

12The next day the great crowd that had come for the Feast heard that Jesus was on his way to Jerusalem. 13They took palm branches and went out to meet him, shouting,

"Hosanna!*b*"

            Lev 23:40

"Blessed is he who comes in
    the name of the Lord!"*c*

"Blessed is the King of Israel!"

14Jesus found a young donkey and sat upon it, as it is written,

15"Do not be afraid, O Daughter
    of Zion;
    see, your king is coming,
    seated on a donkey's colt."*d*

16At first his disciples did not understand all this. Only after Jesus was glorified did they realize that these things had been written about him and that they had done these things to him.   Jn 7:39; 14:26

17Now the crowd that was with him when he called Lazarus from the tomb and raised him from the dead continued to spread the word. 18Many people, because they had heard that he had given this miraculous sign, went out to meet him. 19So the Pharisees said to one another, "See, this is getting us nowhere. Look how the whole world has gone after him!"

Jesus Predicts His Death

20Now there were some Greeks among those who went up to worship at the Feast. 21They came to Philip, who was from Bethsaida in Galilee, with a request. "Sir," they said, "we would like to see Jesus." 22Philip went to tell Andrew; Andrew and Philip in turn told Jesus.

a 5 Greek *three hundred denarii*   *b* 13 A Hebrew expression meaning "Save!" which became an exclamation of praise   *c* 13 Psalm 118:25, 26   *d* 15 Zech. 9:9

²³Jesus replied, "The hour has come for the Son of Man to be glorified. ²⁴I tell you the truth, unless a kernel of wheat falls to the ground and dies, it remains only a single seed. But if it dies, it produces many seeds. ²⁵The man who loves his life will lose it, while the man who hates his life in this world will keep it for eternal life. ²⁶Whoever serves me must follow me; and where I am, my servant also will be. My Father will honor the one who serves me.   Mt 10:39

²⁷"Now my heart is troubled, and what shall I say? 'Father, save me from this hour'? No, it was for this very reason I came to this hour. ²⁸Father, glorify your name!"

Then a voice came from heaven, "I have glorified it, and will glorify it again." ²⁹The crowd that was there and heard it said it had thundered; others said an angel had spoken to him.   Mt 3:17

³⁰Jesus said, "This voice was for your benefit, not mine. ³¹Now is the time for judgment on this world; now the prince of this world will be driven out. ³²But I, when I am lifted up from the earth, will draw all men to myself." ³³He said this to show the kind of death he was going to die.   Jn 11:42; 14:30

³⁴The crowd spoke up, "We have heard from the Law that the Christ*ᵃ* will remain forever, so how can you say, 'The Son of Man must be lifted up'? Who is this 'Son of Man'?"   Ps 110:4; Eze 37:25

³⁵Then Jesus told them, "You are going to have the light just a little while longer. Walk while you have the light, before darkness overtakes you. The man who walks in the dark does not know where he is going. ³⁶Put your trust in the light while you have it, so that you may become sons of light." When he had finished speaking, Jesus left and hid himself from them.   Jn 8:59; Eph 5:8; 1Jn 2:11

The Jews Continue in Their Unbelief

³⁷Even after Jesus had done all these miraculous signs in their presence, they still would not believe in him. ³⁸This was to fulfill the word of Isaiah the prophet:

"Lord, who has believed our
    message
and to whom has the arm of
    the Lord been
    revealed?"*ᵇ*   Ro 10:16

³⁹For this reason they could not believe, because, as Isaiah says elsewhere:

⁴⁰"He has blinded their eyes
    and deadened their hearts,
so they can neither see with
    their eyes,

ᵃ34 Or *Messiah*   *ᵇ38* Isaiah 53:1

nor understand with their
    hearts,
nor turn—and I would heal
    them."[a]

[41]Isaiah said this because he saw Jesus' glory and spoke about him. [42]Yet at the same time many even among the leaders believed in him. But because of the Pharisees they would not confess their faith for fear they would be put out of the synagogue; [43]for they loved praise from men more than praise from God.   Jn 5:44; 7:13; 9:22

[44]Then Jesus cried out, "When a man believes in me, he does not believe in me only, but in the one who sent me. [45]When he looks at me, he sees the one who sent me. [46]I have come into the world as a light, so that no one who believes in me should stay in darkness.

[47]"As for the person who hears my words but does not keep them, I do not judge him. For I did not come to judge the world, but to save it. [48]There is a judge for the one who rejects me and does not accept my words; that very word which I spoke will condemn him at the last day. [49]For I did not speak of my own accord, but the Father who sent me commanded me what to say and how to say it. [50]I know that his command leads to eternal life. So whatever I say is just what the Father has told me to say."

Jesus Washes His Disciples' Feet

13 It was just before the Passover Feast. Jesus knew that the time had come for him to leave this world and go to the Father. Having loved his own who were in the world, he now showed them the full extent of his love.[b]

[2]The evening meal was being served, and the devil had already prompted Judas Iscariot, son of Simon, to betray Jesus. [3]Jesus knew that the Father had put all things under his power, and that he had come from God and was returning to God; [4]so he got up from the meal, took off his outer clothing, and wrapped a towel around his waist. [5]After that, he poured water into a basin and began to wash his disciples' feet, drying them with the towel that was wrapped around him.   Mt 28:18; Jn 8:42

[6]He came to Simon Peter, who said to him, "Lord, are you going to wash my feet?"

[7]Jesus replied, "You do not realize now what I am doing, but later you will understand."

[8]"No," said Peter, "you shall never wash my feet."

Jesus answered, "Unless I wash you, you have no part with me."

[9]"Then, Lord," Simon Peter replied, "not just my feet but my hands and my head as well!"

[10]Jesus answered, "A person

who has had a bath needs only to wash his feet; his whole body is clean. And you are clean, though not every one of you." **11**For he knew who was going to betray him, and that was why he said not every one was clean.   Jn 15:3

12When he had finished washing their feet, he put on his clothes and returned to his place. "Do you understand what I have done for you?" he asked them. **13**"You call me 'Teacher' and 'Lord,' and rightly so, for that is what I am. **14**Now that I, your Lord and Teacher, have washed your feet, you also should wash one another's feet. **15**I have set you an example that you should do as I have done for you. **16**I tell you the truth, no servant is greater than his master, nor is a messenger greater than the one who sent him. **17**Now that you know these things, you will be blessed if you do them.   Mt 10:24

Jesus Predicts His Betrayal

18"I am not referring to all of you; I know those I have chosen. But this is to fulfill the scripture: 'He who shares my bread has lifted up his heel against me.'ᵃ   Ps 41:9

19"I am telling you now before it happens, so that when it does happen you will believe that I am He. **20**I tell you the truth, whoever accepts anyone I send accepts me; and whoever accepts me accepts the one who sent me."   Lk 10:16

21After he had said this, Jesus was troubled in spirit and testified, "I tell you the truth, one of you is going to betray me."   Mt 26:21

22His disciples stared at one another, at a loss to know which of them he meant. **23**One of them, the disciple whom Jesus loved, was reclining next to him. **24**Simon Peter motioned to this disciple and said, "Ask him which one he means."

25Leaning back against Jesus, he asked him, "Lord, who is it?"

26Jesus answered, "It is the one to whom I will give this piece of bread when I have dipped it in the dish." Then, dipping the piece of bread, he gave it to Judas Iscariot, son of Simon. **27**As soon as Judas took the bread, Satan entered into him.   Lk 22:3

"What you are about to do, do quickly," Jesus told him, **28**but no one at the meal understood why Jesus said this to him. **29**Since Judas had charge of the money, some thought Jesus was telling him to buy what was needed for the Feast, or to give something to the poor. **30**As soon as Judas had taken the bread, he went out. And it was night.   Lk 22:53; Jn 12:6

Jesus Predicts Peter's Denial

31When he was gone, Jesus said, "Now is the Son of Man glorified and God is glorified in him. **32**If God is glorified in him,ᵇ God will

---

ᵃ18 Psalm 41:9   ᵇ32 Many early manuscripts do not have *If God is glorified in him.*

glorify the Son in himself, and will glorify him at once.   Jn 14:13; 1Pe 4:11

33"My children, I will be with you only a little longer. You will look for me, and just as I told the Jews, so I tell you now: Where I am going, you cannot come.   Jn 7:33-34

34"A new command I give you: Love one another. As I have loved you, so you must love one another. **35**By this all men will know that you are my disciples, if you love one another."   Lev 19:18; 1Jn 2:7-11; 4:20

36Simon Peter asked him, "Lord, where are you going?"

Jesus replied, "Where I am going, you cannot follow now, but you will follow later."   Jn 21:18-19

37Peter asked, "Lord, why can't I follow you now? I will lay down my life for you."

38Then Jesus answered, "Will you really lay down your life for me? I tell you the truth, before the rooster crows, you will disown me three times!   Mt 26:33-35; Mk 14:29-31

Jesus Comforts His Disciples

14 "Do not let your hearts be troubled. Trust in God*a*; trust also in me. **2**In my Father's house are many rooms; if it were not so, I would have told you. I am going there to prepare a place for you. **3**And if I go and prepare a place for you, I will come back and take you to be with me that you also may be where I am. **4**You

know the way to the place where I am going."   Jn 12:26; 13:33,36

Jesus the Way to the Father

5Thomas said to him, "Lord, we don't know where you are going, so how can we know the way?"

6Jesus answered, "I am the way and the truth and the life. No one comes to the Father except through me. **7**If you really knew me, you would know*b* my Father as well. From now on, you do know him and have seen him."

8Philip said, "Lord, show us the Father and that will be enough for us."   Jn 1:43

9Jesus answered: "Don't you know me, Philip, even after I have been among you such a long time? Anyone who has seen me has seen the Father. How can you say, 'Show us the Father'? **10**Don't you believe that I am in the Father, and that the Father is in me? The words I say to you are not just my own. Rather, it is the Father, living in me, who is doing his work. **11**Believe me when I say that I am in the Father and the Father is in me; or at least believe on the evidence of the miracles themselves. **12**I tell you the truth, anyone who has faith in me will do what I have been doing. He will do even greater things than these, because I am going to the Father. **13**And I will do whatever you ask in my name, so that the Son may bring glory to the

---

*a*1 Or *You trust in God*   *b*7 Some early manuscripts *If you really have known me, you will know*

Father. [14]You may ask me for anything in my name, and I will do it.

Jesus Promises the Holy Spirit

[15]"If you love me, you will obey what I command. [16]And I will ask the Father, and he will give you another Counselor to be with you forever— [17]the Spirit of truth. The world cannot accept him, because it neither sees him nor knows him. But you know him, for he lives with you and will be[a] in you. [18]I will not leave you as orphans; I will come to you. [19]Before long, the world will not see me anymore, but you will see me. Because I live, you also will live. [20]On that day you will realize that I am in my Father, and you are in me, and I am in you. [21]Whoever has my commands and obeys them, he is the one who loves me. He who loves me will be loved by my Father, and I too will love him and show myself to him." Jn 15:10

[22]Then Judas (not Judas Iscariot) said, "But, Lord, why do you intend to show yourself to us and not to the world?" Lk 6:16; Ac 10:41

[23]Jesus replied, "If anyone loves me, he will obey my teaching. My Father will love him, and we will come to him and make our home with him. [24]He who does not love me will not obey my teaching. These words you hear are not my own; they belong to the Father who sent me. Jn 7:16; 1Jn 2:24

[25]"All this I have spoken while still with you. [26]But the Counselor, the Holy Spirit, whom the Father will send in my name, will teach you all things and will remind you of everything I have said to you. [27]Peace I leave with you; my peace I give you. I do not give to you as the world gives. Do not let your hearts be troubled and do not be afraid. Jn 15:26; Php 4:7; 1Jn 2:20,27

[28]"You heard me say, 'I am going away and I am coming back to you.' If you loved me, you would be glad that I am going to the Father, for the Father is greater than I. [29]I have told you now before it happens, so that when it does happen you will believe. [30]I will not speak with you much longer, for the prince of this world is coming. He has no hold on me, [31]but the world must learn that I love the Father and that I do exactly what my Father has commanded me.

"Come now; let us leave." Mt 26:33-35; Mk 14:29-31

The Vine and the Branches

15 "I am the true vine, and my Father is the gardener. [2]He cuts off every branch in me that bears no fruit, while every branch that does bear fruit he prunes[b] so that it will be even more fruitful. [3]You are already clean because of the word I have spoken to you. [4]Remain in me, and I will remain in you. No branch can bear fruit by itself; it must remain in the vine.

---

[a]17 Some early manuscripts and is   [b]2 The Greek for prunes also means cleans.

Neither can you bear fruit unless you remain in me.   Isa 5:1-7; 1Jn 2:6 ⁵"I am the vine; you are the branches. If a man remains in me and I in him, he will bear much fruit; apart from me you can do nothing. ⁶If anyone does not remain in me, he is like a branch that is thrown away and withers; such branches are picked up, thrown into the fire and burned. ⁷If you remain in me and my words remain in you, ask whatever you wish, and it will be given you. ⁸This is to my Father's glory, that you bear much fruit, showing yourselves to be my disciples.

⁹"As the Father has loved me, so have I loved you. Now remain in my love. ¹⁰If you obey my commands, you will remain in my love, just as I have obeyed my Father's commands and remain in his love. ¹¹I have told you this so that my joy may be in you and that your joy may be complete. ¹²My command is this: Love each other as I have loved you. ¹³Greater love has no one than this, that he lay down his life for his friends. ¹⁴You are my friends if you do what I command. ¹⁵I no longer call you servants, because a servant does not know his master's business. Instead, I have called you friends, for everything that I learned from my Father I have made known to you. ¹⁶You did not choose me, but I chose you and appointed you to go and bear fruit—fruit that will last. Then the Father will give you whatever you ask in my name. ¹⁷This is my command: Love each other.   Jn 13:18,34; 14:15

The World Hates the Disciples

¹⁸"If the world hates you, keep in mind that it hated me first. ¹⁹If you belonged to the world, it would love you as its own. As it is, you do not belong to the world, but I have chosen you out of the world. That is why the world hates you. ²⁰Remember the words I spoke to you: 'No servant is greater than his master.'ᵃ If they persecuted me, they will persecute you also. If they obeyed my teaching, they will obey yours also. ²¹They will treat you this way because of my name, for they do not know the One who sent me. ²²If I had not come and spoken to them, they would not be guilty of sin. Now, however, they have no excuse for their sin. ²³He who hates me hates my Father as well. ²⁴If I had not done among them what no one else did, they would not be guilty of sin. But now they have seen these miracles, and yet they have hated both me and my Father. ²⁵But this is to fulfill what is written in their Law: 'They hated me without reason.'ᵇ   Jn 9:41; 1Jn 3:13

²⁶"When the Counselor comes, whom I will send to you from the Father, the Spirit of truth who goes

---

ᵃ20 John 13:16   ᵇ25 Psalms 35:19; 69:4

out from the Father, he will testify about me. ²⁷And you also must testify, for you have been with me from the beginning.　Jn 14:17; 1Jn 5:7

16 "All this I have told you so that you will not go astray. ²They will put you out of the synagogue; in fact, a time is coming when anyone who kills you will think he is offering a service to God. ³They will do such things because they have not known the Father or me. ⁴I have told you this, so that when the time comes you will remember that I warned you. I did not tell you this at first because I was with you.　Mt 11:6; Jn 9:22; 15:21

The Work of the Holy Spirit

⁵"Now I am going to him who sent me, yet none of you asks me, 'Where are you going?' ⁶Because I have said these things, you are filled with grief. ⁷But I tell you the truth: It is for your good that I am going away. Unless I go away, the Counselor will not come to you; but if I go, I will send him to you. ⁸When he comes, he will convict the world of guilt[a] in regard to sin and righteousness and judgment: ⁹in regard to sin, because men do not believe in me; ¹⁰in regard to righteousness, because I am going to the Father, where you can see me no longer; ¹¹and in regard to judgment, because the prince of this world now stands condemned.　Jn 7:33,39; 14:16,26

¹²"I have much more to say to you, more than you can now bear. ¹³But when he, the Spirit of truth, comes, he will guide you into all truth. He will not speak on his own; he will speak only what he hears, and he will tell you what is yet to come. ¹⁴He will bring glory to me by taking from what is mine and making it known to you. ¹⁵All that belongs to the Father is mine. That is why I said the Spirit will take from what is mine and make it known to you.　Jn 14:17,26; 17:10

¹⁶"In a little while you will see me no more, and then after a little while you will see me."　Jn 14:18-24

The Disciples' Grief Will Turn to Joy

¹⁷Some of his disciples said to one another, "What does he mean by saying, 'In a little while you will see me no more, and then after a little while you will see me,' and 'Because I am going to the Father'?" ¹⁸They kept asking, "What does he mean by 'a little while'? We don't understand what he is saying."

¹⁹Jesus saw that they wanted to ask him about this, so he said to them, "Are you asking one another what I meant when I said, 'In a little while you will see me no more, and then after a little while you will see me'? ²⁰I tell you the truth, you will weep and mourn while the world rejoices. You will grieve,

---

a 8 Or *will expose the guilt of the world*

but your grief will turn to joy. ²¹A woman giving birth to a child has pain because her time has come; but when her baby is born she forgets the anguish because of her joy that a child is born into the world. ²²So with you: Now is your time of grief, but I will see you again and you will rejoice, and no one will take away your joy. ²³In that day you will no longer ask me anything. I tell you the truth, my Father will give you whatever you ask in my name. ²⁴Until now you have not asked for anything in my name. Ask and you will receive, and your joy will be complete.

²⁵"Though I have been speaking figuratively, a time is coming when I will no longer use this kind of language but will tell you plainly about my Father. ²⁶In that day you will ask in my name. I am not saying that I will ask the Father on your behalf. ²⁷No, the Father himself loves you because you have loved me and have believed that I came from God. ²⁸I came from the Father and entered the world; now I am leaving the world and going back to the Father." Jn 10:6; 14:21,23

²⁹Then Jesus' disciples said, "Now you are speaking clearly and without figures of speech. ³⁰Now we can see that you know all things and that you do not even need to have anyone ask you questions. This makes us believe that you came from God." Jn 13:3

³¹"You believe at last!"^a Jesus answered. ³²"But a time is coming, and has come, when you will be scattered, each to his own home. You will leave me all alone. Yet I am not alone, for my Father is with me. Mt 26:31; Jn 8:16,29

³³"I have told you these things, so that in me you may have peace. In this world you will have trouble. But take heart! I have overcome the world." Jn 14:27; Ro 8:37

Jesus Prays for Himself

17 After Jesus said this, he looked toward heaven and prayed:

"Father, the time has come. Glorify your Son, that your Son may glorify you. ²For you granted him authority over all people that he might give eternal life to all those you have given him. ³Now this is eternal life: that they may know you, the only true God, and Jesus Christ, whom you have sent. ⁴I have brought you glory on earth by completing the work you gave me to do. ⁵And now, Father, glorify me in your presence with the glory I had with you before the world began. Jn 1:2

Jesus Prays for His Disciples

⁶"I have revealed you^b to those whom you gave me out

of the world. They were yours; you gave them to me and they have obeyed your word. ⁷Now they know that everything you have given me comes from you. ⁸For I gave them the words you gave me and they accepted them. They knew with certainty that I came from you, and they believed that you sent me. ⁹I pray for them. I am not praying for the world, but for those you have given me, for they are yours. ¹⁰All I have is yours, and all you have is mine. And glory has come to me through them. ¹¹I will remain in the world no longer, but they are still in the world, and I am coming to you. Holy Father, protect them by the power of your name—the name you gave me—so that they may be one as we are one. ¹²While I was with them, I protected them and kept them safe by that name you gave me. None has been lost except the one doomed to destruction so that Scripture would be fulfilled.   Jn 6:39,70

¹³"I am coming to you now, but I say these things while I am still in the world, so that they may have the full measure of my joy within them. ¹⁴I have given them your word and the world has hated them, for they are not of the world any more than I am of the world. ¹⁵My prayer is not that you take them out of the world but that you protect them from the evil one. ¹⁶They are not of the world, even as I am not of it. ¹⁷Sanctifyᵃ them by the truth; your word is truth. ¹⁸As you sent me into the world, I have sent them into the world. ¹⁹For them I sanctify myself, that they too may be truly sanctified.   Jn 8:23; 20:21

Jesus Prays for All Believers

²⁰"My prayer is not for them alone. I pray also for those who will believe in me through their message, ²¹that all of them may be one, Father, just as you are in me and I am in you. May they also be in us so that the world may believe that you have sent me. ²²I have given them the glory that you gave me, that they may be one as we are one: ²³I in them and you in me. May they be brought to complete unity to let the world know that you sent me and have loved them even as you have loved me.   Jn 10:38; 14:20

²⁴"Father, I want those you have given me to be with me where I am, and to see my glory, the glory you have given

ᵃ17 Greek hagiazo (set apart for sacred use or make holy); also in verse 19

me because you loved me before the creation of the world.

25 "Righteous Father, though the world does not know you, I know you, and they know that you have sent me. 26I have made you known to them, and will continue to make you known in order that the love you have for me may be in them and that I myself may be in them."

Jesus Arrested

18 When he had finished praying, Jesus left with his disciples and crossed the Kidron Valley. On the other side there was an olive grove, and he and his disciples went into it.   2Sa 15:23; Mt 21:1

2Now Judas, who betrayed him, knew the place, because Jesus had often met there with his disciples. 3So Judas came to the grove, guiding a detachment of soldiers and some officials from the chief priests and Pharisees. They were carrying torches, lanterns and weapons.   Lk 21:37; 22:39; Ac 1:16

4Jesus, knowing all that was going to happen to him, went out and asked them, "Who is it you want?"

5"Jesus of Nazareth," they replied.   Mk 1:24

"I am he," Jesus said. (And Judas the traitor was standing there with them.) 6When Jesus said, "I am he," they drew back and fell to the ground.

7Again he asked them, "Who is it you want?"

And they said, "Jesus of Nazareth."

8"I told you that I am he," Jesus answered. "If you are looking for me, then let these men go." 9This happened so that the words he had spoken would be fulfilled: "I have not lost one of those you gave me."a   Jn 17:12

10Then Simon Peter, who had a sword, drew it and struck the high priest's servant, cutting off his right ear. (The servant's name was Malchus.)

11Jesus commanded Peter, "Put your sword away! Shall I not drink the cup the Father has given me?"

Jesus Taken to Annas

12Then the detachment of soldiers with its commander and the Jewish officials arrested Jesus. They bound him 13and brought him first to Annas, who was the father-in-law of Caiaphas, the high priest that year. 14Caiaphas was the one who had advised the Jews that it would be good if one man died for the people.   Mt 26:57

Peter's First Denial

15Simon Peter and another disciple were following Jesus. Because this disciple was known to the high priest, he went with Jesus into the high priest's courtyard, 16but Peter had to wait outside at

a9 John 6:39

the door. The other disciple, who was known to the high priest, came back, spoke to the girl on duty there and brought Peter in.

¹⁷"You are not one of his disciples, are you?" the girl at the door asked Peter.

He replied, "I am not."

¹⁸It was cold, and the servants and officials stood around a fire they had made to keep warm. Peter also was standing with them, warming himself.   Mt 26:69-70

The High Priest Questions Jesus

¹⁹Meanwhile, the high priest questioned Jesus about his disciples and his teaching.

²⁰"I have spoken openly to the world," Jesus replied. "I always taught in synagogues or at the temple, where all the Jews come together. I said nothing in secret. ²¹Why question me? Ask those who heard me. Surely they know what I said."   Mt 26:55; Jn 7:26

²²When Jesus said this, one of the officials nearby struck him in the face. "Is this the way you answer the high priest?" he demanded.   Jn 19:3

²³"If I said something wrong," Jesus replied, "testify as to what is wrong. But if I spoke the truth, why did you strike me?" ²⁴Then Annas sent him, still bound, to Caiaphas the high priest.ᵃ   Mt 26:59-68

Peter's Second and Third Denials

²⁵As Simon Peter stood warming himself, he was asked, "You are not one of his disciples, are you?"

He denied it, saying, "I am not."

²⁶One of the high priest's servants, a relative of the man whose ear Peter had cut off, challenged him, "Didn't I see you with him in the olive grove?" ²⁷Again Peter denied it, and at that moment a rooster began to crow.   Mt 26:71-75

Jesus Before Pilate

²⁸Then the Jews led Jesus from Caiaphas to the palace of the Roman governor. By now it was early morning, and to avoid ceremonial uncleanness the Jews did not enter the palace; they wanted to be able to eat the Passover. ²⁹So Pilate came out to them and asked, "What charges are you bringing against this man?"   Mt 27:2; Mk 15:1

³⁰"If he were not a criminal," they replied, "we would not have handed him over to you."

³¹Pilate said, "Take him yourselves and judge him by your own law."

"But we have no right to execute anyone," the Jews objected. ³²This happened so that the words Jesus had spoken indicating the kind of death he was going to die would be fulfilled.   Mt 20:19; Jn 12:32-33

³³Pilate then went back inside

ᵃ 24 Or (Now Annas had sent him, still bound, to Caiaphas the high priest.)

the palace, summoned Jesus and asked him, "Are you the king of the Jews?"   Lk 23:3; Jn 19:9

34"Is that your own idea," Jesus asked, "or did others talk to you about me?"

35"Am I a Jew?" Pilate replied. "It was your people and your chief priests who handed you over to me. What is it you have done?"

36Jesus said, "My kingdom is not of this world. If it were, my servants would fight to prevent my arrest by the Jews. But now my kingdom is from another place."

37"You are a king, then!" said Pilate.

Jesus answered, "You are right in saying I am a king. In fact, for this reason I was born, and for this I came into the world, to testify to the truth. Everyone on the side of truth listens to me."   Jn 8:47; 1Jn 4:6

38"What is truth?" Pilate asked. With this he went out again to the Jews and said, "I find no basis for a charge against him. **39**But it is your custom for me to release to you one prisoner at the time of the Passover. Do you want me to release 'the king of the Jews'?"

40They shouted back, "No, not him! Give us Barabbas!" Now Barabbas had taken part in a rebellion.

Jesus Sentenced to be Crucified

19 Then Pilate took Jesus and had him flogged. **2**The soldiers twisted together a crown of thorns and put it on his head. They clothed him in a purple robe **3**and

went up to him again and again, saying, "Hail, king of the Jews!" And they struck him in the face.

4Once more Pilate came out and said to the Jews, "Look, I am bringing him out to you to let you know that I find no basis for a charge against him." **5**When Jesus came out wearing the crown of thorns and the purple robe, Pilate said to them, "Here is the man!"   Lk 23:4

6As soon as the chief priests and their officials saw him, they shouted, "Crucify! Crucify!"

But Pilate answered, "You take him and crucify him. As for me, I find no basis for a charge against him."   Lk 23:4; Ac 3:13

7The Jews insisted, "We have a law, and according to that law he must die, because he claimed to be the Son of God."   Lev 24:16; Mt 26:63-66

8When Pilate heard this, he was even more afraid, **9**and he went back inside the palace. "Where do you come from?" he asked Jesus, but Jesus gave him no answer. **10**"Do you refuse to speak to me?" Pilate said. "Don't you realize I have power either to free you or to crucify you?"   Mk 14:61; Jn 18:33

11Jesus answered, "You would have no power over me if it were not given to you from above. Therefore the one who handed me over to you is guilty of a greater sin."   Jn 18:28-30; Ac 3:13; Ro 13:1

12From then on, Pilate tried to set Jesus free, but the Jews kept shouting, "If you let this man go, you are no friend of Caesar. Anyone who claims to be a king opposes Caesar." Lk 23:2

¹³When Pilate heard this, he brought Jesus out and sat down on the judge's seat at a place known as the Stone Pavement (which in Aramaic is Gabbatha). ¹⁴It was the day of Preparation of Passover Week, about the sixth hour.

"Here is your king," Pilate said to the Jews.

¹⁵But they shouted, "Take him away! Take him away! Crucify him!"

"Shall I crucify your king?" Pilate asked.

"We have no king but Caesar," the chief priests answered.

¹⁶Finally Pilate handed him over to them to be crucified. Mt 27:27-31

The Crucifixion

So the soldiers took charge of Jesus. ¹⁷Carrying his own cross, he went out to the place of the Skull (which in Aramaic is called Golgotha). ¹⁸Here they crucified him, and with him two others—one on each side and Jesus in the middle.

¹⁹Pilate had a notice prepared and fastened to the cross. It read: JESUS OF NAZARETH, THE KING OF THE JEWS. ²⁰Many of the Jews read this sign, for the place where Jesus was crucified was near the city, and the sign was written in Aramaic, Latin and Greek. ²¹The chief priests of the Jews protested to Pilate, "Do not write 'The King of the Jews,'

ᵃ 24 Psalm 22:18

but that this man claimed to be king of the Jews." Mk 1:24; Heb 13:12

²²Pilate answered, "What I have written, I have written."

²³When the soldiers crucified Jesus, they took his clothes, dividing them into four shares, one for each of them, with the undergarment remaining. This garment was seamless, woven in one piece from top to bottom.

²⁴"Let's not tear it," they said to one another. "Let's decide by lot who will get it."

This happened that the scripture might be fulfilled which said,

"They divided my garments
  among them
and cast lots for my
  clothing."ᵃ Ps 22:18

So this is what the soldiers did. ²⁵Near the cross of Jesus stood his mother, his mother's sister, Mary the wife of Clopas, and Mary Magdalene. ²⁶When Jesus saw his mother there, and the disciple whom he loved standing nearby, he said to his mother, "Dear woman, here is your son," ²⁷and to the disciple, "Here is your mother." From that time on, this disciple took her into his home. Mk 15:40-41

The Death of Jesus

²⁸Later, knowing that all was now completed, and so that the Scripture would be fulfilled, Jesus said, "I am thirsty." ²⁹A jar of wine

vinegar was there, so they soaked a sponge in it, put the sponge on a stalk of the hyssop plant, and lifted it to Jesus' lips. ³⁰When he had received the drink, Jesus said, "It is finished." With that, he bowed his head and gave up his spirit.

³¹Now it was the day of Preparation, and the next day was to be a special Sabbath. Because the Jews did not want the bodies left on the crosses during the Sabbath, they asked Pilate to have the legs broken and the bodies taken down. ³²The soldiers therefore came and broke the legs of the first man who had been crucified with Jesus, and then those of the other. ³³But when they came to Jesus and found that he was already dead, they did not break his legs. ³⁴Instead, one of the soldiers pierced Jesus' side with a spear, bringing a sudden flow of blood and water. ³⁵The man who saw it has given testimony, and his testimony is true. He knows that he tells the truth, and he testifies so that you also may believe. ³⁶These things happened so that the scripture would be fulfilled: "Not one of his bones will be broken,"ᵃ ³⁷and, as another scripture says, "They will look on the one they have pierced."ᵇ   1Jn 5:6,8

The Burial of Jesus

³⁸Later, Joseph of Arimathea asked Pilate for the body of Jesus.

Now Joseph was a disciple of Jesus, but secretly because he feared the Jews. With Pilate's permission, he came and took the body away. ³⁹He was accompanied by Nicodemus, the man who earlier had visited Jesus at night. Nicodemus brought a mixture of myrrh and aloes, about seventy-five pounds.ᶜ ⁴⁰Taking Jesus' body, the two of them wrapped it, with the spices, in strips of linen. This was in accordance with Jewish burial customs. ⁴¹At the place where Jesus was crucified, there was a garden, and in the garden a new tomb, in which no one had ever been laid. ⁴²Because it was the Jewish day of Preparation and since the tomb was nearby, they laid Jesus there.   Mt 27:57-61

The Empty Tomb

20 Early on the first day of the week, while it was still dark, Mary Magdalene went to the tomb and saw that the stone had been removed from the entrance. ²So she came running to Simon Peter and the other disciple, the one Jesus loved, and said, "They have taken the Lord out of the tomb, and we don't know where they have put him!"

³So Peter and the other disciple started for the tomb. ⁴Both were running, but the other disciple outran Peter and reached the tomb

---

ᵃ36 Exodus 12:46; Num. 9:12; Psalm 34:20   ᵇ37 Zech. 12:10   ᶜ39 Greek *a hundred litrai* (about 34 kilograms)

first. ⁵He bent over and looked in at the strips of linen lying there but did not go in. ⁶Then Simon Peter, who was behind him, arrived and went into the tomb. He saw the strips of linen lying there, ⁷as well as the burial cloth that had been around Jesus' head. The cloth was folded up by itself, separate from the linen. ⁸Finally the other disciple, who had reached the tomb first, also went inside. He saw and believed. ⁹(They still did not understand from Scripture that Jesus had to rise from the dead.)

Jesus Appears to Mary Magdalene

¹⁰Then the disciples went back to their homes, ¹¹but Mary stood outside the tomb crying. As she wept, she bent over to look into the tomb ¹²and saw two angels in white, seated where Jesus' body had been, one at the head and the other at the foot.   Mk 16:5; Lk 24:4

¹³They asked her, "Woman, why are you crying?"

"They have taken my Lord away," she said, "and I don't know where they have put him." ¹⁴At this, she turned around and saw Jesus standing there, but she did not realize that it was Jesus.

¹⁵"Woman," he said, "why are you crying? Who is it you are looking for?"

Thinking he was the gardener, she said, "Sir, if you have carried him away, tell me where you have put him, and I will get him."

¹⁶Jesus said to her, "Mary."

She turned toward him and cried out in Aramaic, "Rabboni!" (which means Teacher).   Mt 23:7

¹⁷Jesus said, "Do not hold on to me, for I have not yet returned to the Father. Go instead to my brothers and tell them, 'I am returning to my Father and your Father, to my God and your God.' "   Mt 28:10

¹⁸Mary Magdalene went to the disciples with the news: "I have seen the Lord!" And she told them that he had said these things to her.   Lk 24:10,22-23

Jesus Appears to His Disciples

¹⁹On the evening of that first day of the week, when the disciples were together, with the doors locked for fear of the Jews, Jesus came and stood among them and said, "Peace be with you!" ²⁰After he said this, he showed them his hands and side. The disciples were overjoyed when they saw the Lord.   Lk 24:36-39; Jn 16:20,22

²¹Again Jesus said, "Peace be with you! As the Father has sent me, I am sending you." ²²And with that he breathed on them and said, "Receive the Holy Spirit. ²³If you forgive anyone his sins, they are forgiven; if you do not forgive them, they are not forgiven."

Jesus Appears to Thomas

²⁴Now Thomas (called Didymus), one of the Twelve, was not

with the disciples when Jesus came. ²⁵So the other disciples told him, "We have seen the Lord!"

But he said to them, "Unless I see the nail marks in his hands and put my finger where the nails were, and put my hand into his side, I will not believe it." Mk 16:11

²⁶A week later his disciples were in the house again, and Thomas was with them. Though the doors were locked, Jesus came and stood among them and said, "Peace be with you!" ²⁷Then he said to Thomas, "Put your finger here; see my hands. Reach out your hand and put it into my side. Stop doubting and believe." Lk 24:40

²⁸Thomas said to him, "My Lord and my God!"

²⁹Then Jesus told him, "Because you have seen me, you have believed; blessed are those who have not seen and yet have believed."

³⁰Jesus did many other miraculous signs in the presence of his disciples, which are not recorded in this book. ³¹But these are written that you may*a* believe that Jesus is the Christ, the Son of God, and that by believing you may have life in his name. Jn 3:15; 21:25

Jesus and the Miraculous Catch of Fish

21 Afterward Jesus appeared again to his disciples, by the Sea of Tiberias.*b* It happened this way: ²Simon Peter, Thomas (called Didymus), Nathanael from Cana in Galilee, the sons of Zebedee, and two other disciples were together. ³"I'm going out to fish," Simon Peter told them, and they said, "We'll go with you." So they went out and got into the boat, but that night they caught nothing.

⁴Early in the morning, Jesus stood on the shore, but the disciples did not realize that it was Jesus. Lk 24:16; Jn 20:14

⁵He called out to them, "Friends, haven't you any fish?"

"No," they answered.

⁶He said, "Throw your net on the right side of the boat and you will find some." When they did, they were unable to haul the net in because of the large number of fish. Lk 5:4-7

⁷Then the disciple whom Jesus loved said to Peter, "It is the Lord!" As soon as Simon Peter heard him say, "It is the Lord," he wrapped his outer garment around him (for he had taken it off) and jumped into the water. ⁸The other disciples followed in the boat, towing the net full of fish, for they were not far from shore, about a hundred yards.*c* ⁹When they landed, they saw a fire of burning coals there with fish on it, and some bread.

¹⁰Jesus said to them, "Bring some of the fish you have just caught."

a31 Some manuscripts *may continue to* cubits (about 90 meters)   *b1* That is, Sea of Galilee   *c8* Greek *about two hundred*

¹¹Simon Peter climbed aboard and dragged the net ashore. It was full of large fish, 153, but even with so many the net was not torn. ¹²Jesus said to them, "Come and have breakfast." None of the disciples dared ask him, "Who are you?" They knew it was the Lord. ¹³Jesus came, took the bread and gave it to them, and did the same with the fish. ¹⁴This was now the third time Jesus appeared to his disciples after he was raised from the dead.   Jn 20:19,26

Jesus Reinstates Peter

¹⁵When they had finished eating, Jesus said to Simon Peter, "Simon son of John, do you truly love me more than these?"

"Yes, Lord," he said, "you know that I love you."   Mt 26:33,35; Jn 13:37

Jesus said, "Feed my lambs."

¹⁶Again Jesus said, "Simon son of John, do you truly love me?"

He answered, "Yes, Lord, you know that I love you."

Jesus said, "Take care of my sheep."   Ac 20:28; 1Pe 5:2-3

¹⁷The third time he said to him, "Simon son of John, do you love me?"

Peter was hurt because Jesus asked him the third time, "Do you love me?" He said, "Lord, you know all things; you know that I love you."   Jn 16:30

Jesus said, "Feed my sheep. ¹⁸I

tell you the truth, when you were younger you dressed yourself and went where you wanted; but when you are old you will stretch out your hands, and someone else will dress you and lead you where you do not want to go." ¹⁹Jesus said this to indicate the kind of death by which Peter would glorify God. Then he said to him, "Follow me!"

²⁰Peter turned and saw that the disciple whom Jesus loved was following them. (This was the one who had leaned back against Jesus at the supper and had said, "Lord, who is going to betray you?") ²¹When Peter saw him, he asked, "Lord, what about him?"

²²Jesus answered, "If I want him to remain alive until I return, what is that to you? You must follow me." ²³Because of this, the rumor spread among the brothers that this disciple would not die. But Jesus did not say that he would not die; he only said, "If I want him to remain alive until I return, what is that to you?"   Mt 16:27; Ac 1:16

²⁴This is the disciple who testifies to these things and who wrote them down. We know that his testimony is true.   Jn 19:35

²⁵Jesus did many other things as well. If every one of them were written down, I suppose that even the whole world would not have room for the books that would be written.   Jn 20:30

Acts

Jesus Taken Up Into Heaven

1 In my former book, Theophilus, I wrote about all that Jesus began to do and to teach ²until the day he was taken up to heaven, after giving instructions through the Holy Spirit to the apostles he had chosen. ³After his suffering, he showed himself to these men and gave many convincing proofs that he was alive. He appeared to them over a period of forty days and spoke about the kingdom of God. ⁴On one occasion, while he was eating with them, he gave them this command: "Do not leave Jerusalem, but wait for the gift my Father promised, which you have heard me speak about. ⁵For John baptized with*a* water, but in a few days you will be baptized with the Holy Spirit." Lk 1:1-4; Jn 14:16

⁶So when they met together, they asked him, "Lord, are you at this time going to restore the kingdom to Israel?" Mt 17:11

⁷He said to them: "It is not for you to know the times or dates the Father has set by his own authority. ⁸But you will receive power when the Holy Spirit comes on you; and you will be my witnesses in Jerusalem, and in all Judea and Samaria, and to the ends of the earth." Mt 24:36; Lk 24:48

⁹After he said this, he was taken up before their very eyes, and a cloud hid him from their sight. ¹⁰They were looking intently up into the sky as he was going, when suddenly two men dressed in white stood beside them. ¹¹"Men of Galilee," they said, "why do you stand here looking into the sky? This same Jesus, who has been taken from you into heaven, will come back in the same way you have seen him go into heaven."

Matthias Chosen to Replace Judas

¹²Then they returned to Jerusalem from the hill called the Mount of Olives, a Sabbath day's walk*b* from the city. ¹³When they arrived, they went upstairs to the room where they were staying. Those present were Peter, John, James and Andrew; Philip and Thomas, Bartholomew and Matthew; James son of Alphaeus and Simon the Zealot, and Judas son of James. ¹⁴They all joined together constantly in prayer, along with the women and Mary the mother of Jesus, and with his brothers.

¹⁵In those days Peter stood up

a 5 Or *in*   *b 12* That is, about 3/4 mile (about 1,100 meters)

among the believers[a] (a group numbering about a hundred and twenty) [16]and said, "Brothers, the Scripture had to be fulfilled which the Holy Spirit spoke long ago through the mouth of David concerning Judas, who served as guide for those who arrested Jesus— [17]he was one of our number and shared in this ministry." Jn 6:70-71

[18](With the reward he got for his wickedness, Judas bought a field; there he fell headlong, his body burst open and all his intestines spilled out. [19]Everyone in Jerusalem heard about this, so they called that field in their language Akeldama, that is, Field of Blood.)

[20]"For," said Peter, "it is written in the book of Psalms,

" 'May his place be deserted;
     let there be no one to dwell
        in it,'[b]   Ps 69:25

and,

" 'May another take his place
        of leadership.'[c]

[21]Therefore it is necessary to choose one of the men who have been with us the whole time the Lord Jesus went in and out among us, [22]beginning from John's baptism to the time when Jesus was taken up from us. For one of these must become a witness with us of his resurrection." Mk 1:4; Lk 24:48

[23]So they proposed two men: Joseph called Barsabbas (also known as Justus) and Matthias. [24]Then they prayed, "Lord, you know everyone's heart. Show us which of these two you have chosen [25]to take over this apostolic ministry, which Judas left to go where he belongs." [26]Then they cast lots, and the lot fell to Matthias; so he was added to the eleven apostles. 1Sa 16:7; Jer 17:10; Rev 2:23

The Holy Spirit Comes at Pentecost

2 When the day of Pentecost came, they were all together in one place. [2]Suddenly a sound like the blowing of a violent wind came from heaven and filled the whole house where they were sitting. [3]They saw what seemed to be tongues of fire that separated and came to rest on each of them. [4]All of them were filled with the Holy Spirit and began to speak in other tongues[d] as the Spirit enabled them. Mk 16:17; 1Co 12:10

[5]Now there were staying in Jerusalem God-fearing Jews from every nation under heaven. [6]When they heard this sound, a crowd came together in bewilderment, because each one heard them speaking in his own language. [7]Utterly amazed, they asked: "Are not all these men who are speaking Galileans? [8]Then how is it that each of us hears them in his own native language? [9]Parthians,

---

[a]15 Greek brothers   [b]20 Psalm 69:25   [c]20 Psalm 109:8   [d]4 Or languages; also in verse 11

Medes and Elamites; residents of Mesopotamia, Judea and Cappadocia, Pontus and Asia, ¹⁰Phrygia and Pamphylia, Egypt and the parts of Libya near Cyrene; visitors from Rome ¹¹(both Jews and converts to Judaism); Cretans and Arabs—we hear them declaring the wonders of God in our own tongues!" ¹²Amazed and perplexed, they asked one another, "What does this mean?"   Ac 1:11

¹³Some, however, made fun of them and said, "They have had too much wine.^a"   1Co 14:23

Peter Addresses the Crowd

¹⁴Then Peter stood up with the Eleven, raised his voice and addressed the crowd: "Fellow Jews and all of you who live in Jerusalem, let me explain this to you; listen carefully to what I say. ¹⁵These men are not drunk, as you suppose. It's only nine in the morning! ¹⁶No, this is what was spoken by the prophet Joel: 1Th 5:7

¹⁷" 'In the last days, God says,
    I will pour out my Spirit on
        all people.   Jn 7:37-39
Your sons and daughters will
        prophesy,   Ac 21:9
    your young men will see
        visions,
    your old men will dream
        dreams.
¹⁸Even on my servants, both
        men and women,

I will pour out my Spirit in
        those days,
    and they will prophesy.
¹⁹I will show wonders in the
        heaven above
    and signs on the earth
        below,
    blood and fire and billows of
        smoke.
²⁰The sun will be turned to
        darkness
    and the moon to blood
    before the coming of the
        great and glorious day
        of the Lord.
²¹And everyone who calls
    on the name of the Lord will
        be saved.'^b   Ro 10:13; 2Ti 2:22

²²"Men of Israel, listen to this: Jesus of Nazareth was a man accredited by God to you by miracles, wonders and signs, which God did among you through him, as you yourselves know. ²³This man was handed over to you by God's set purpose and foreknowledge; and you, with the help of wicked men,^c put him to death by nailing him to the cross. ²⁴But God raised him from the dead, freeing him from the agony of death, because it was impossible for death to keep its hold on him. ²⁵David said about him: Jn 4:48; 2Co 4:14

" 'I saw the Lord always before
        me.
    Because he is at my right
        hand,

a 13 Or sweet wine   b 21 Joel 2:28-32   c 23 Or of those not having the law (that is, Gentiles)

I will not be shaken.
26Therefore my heart is glad and
    my tongue rejoices;
    my body also will live in
    hope,
27because you will not abandon
    me to the grave,
    nor will you let your Holy
    One see decay.   Ac 13:35
28You have made known to me
    the paths of life;
    you will fill me with joy in
    your presence.'a   Ps 16:8-11

29"Brothers, I can tell you confidently that the patriarch David died and was buried, and his tomb is here to this day. 30But he was a prophet and knew that God had promised him on oath that he would place one of his descendants on his throne. 31Seeing what was ahead, he spoke of the resurrection of the Christ,b that he was not abandoned to the grave, nor did his body see decay. 32God has raised this Jesus to life, and we are all witnesses of the fact. 33Exalted to the right hand of God, he has received from the Father the promised Holy Spirit and has poured out what you now see and hear. 34For David did not ascend to heaven, and yet he said,   Ac 10:45

" 'The Lord said to my Lord:
    "Sit at my right hand
35until I make your enemies
    a footstool for your feet." 'c

36"Therefore let all Israel be assured of this: God has made this Jesus, whom you crucified, both Lord and Christ."   Lk 2:11

37When the people heard this, they were cut to the heart and said to Peter and the other apostles, "Brothers, what shall we do?"

38Peter replied, "Repent and be baptized, every one of you, in the name of Jesus Christ for the forgiveness of your sins. And you will receive the gift of the Holy Spirit. 39The promise is for you and your children and for all who are far off—for all whom the Lord our God will call."   Lk 24:47; Ac 3:19; Eph 2:13

40With many other words he warned them; and he pleaded with them, "Save yourselves from this corrupt generation." 41Those who accepted his message were baptized, and about three thousand were added to their number that day.   Dt 32:5; Php 2:15

The Fellowship of the Believers

42They devoted themselves to the apostles' teaching and to the fellowship, to the breaking of bread and to prayer. 43Everyone was filled with awe, and many wonders and miraculous signs were done by the apostles. 44All the believers were together and had everything in common. 45Selling their possessions and goods, they gave to anyone as he had

---

a28 Psalm 16:8-11   b31 Or Messiah. "The Christ" (Greek) and "the Messiah" (Hebrew) both mean "the Anointed One"; also in verse 36.   c35 Psalm 110:1

need. ⁴⁶Every day they continued to meet together in the temple courts. They broke bread in their homes and ate together with glad and sincere hearts, ⁴⁷praising God and enjoying the favor of all the people. And the Lord added to their number daily those who were being saved.   Ac 5:14; Ro 14:18

Peter Heals the Crippled Beggar

3 One day Peter and John were going up to the temple at the time of prayer—at three in the afternoon. ²Now a man crippled from birth was being carried to the temple gate called Beautiful, where he was put every day to beg from those going into the temple courts. ³When he saw Peter and John about to enter, he asked them for money. ⁴Peter looked straight at him, as did John. Then Peter said, "Look at us!" ⁵So the man gave them his attention, expecting to get something from them.

⁶Then Peter said, "Silver or gold I do not have, but what I have I give you. In the name of Jesus Christ of Nazareth, walk." ⁷Taking him by the right hand, he helped him up, and instantly the man's feet and ankles became strong. ⁸He jumped to his feet and began to walk. Then he went with them into the temple courts, walking and jumping, and praising God. ⁹When all the people saw him walking and praising God, ¹⁰they

recognized him as the same man who used to sit begging at the temple gate called Beautiful, and they were filled with wonder and amazement at what had happened to him.   Ac 4:10,16,21

Peter Speaks to the Onlookers

¹¹While the beggar held on to Peter and John, all the people were astonished and came running to them in the place called Solomon's Colonnade. ¹²When Peter saw this, he said to them: "Men of Israel, why does this surprise you? Why do you stare at us as if by our own power or godliness we had made this man walk? ¹³The God of Abraham, Isaac and Jacob, the God of our fathers, has glorified his servant Jesus. You handed him over to be killed, and you disowned him before Pilate, though he had decided to let him go. ¹⁴You disowned the Holy and Righteous One and asked that a murderer be released to you. ¹⁵You killed the author of life, but God raised him from the dead. We are witnesses of this. ¹⁶By faith in the name of Jesus, this man whom you see and know was made strong. It is Jesus' name and the faith that comes through him that has given this complete healing to him, as you can all see.   Mk 1:24; Jn 10:23; Ac 2:24

¹⁷"Now, brothers, I know that you acted in ignorance, as did your leaders. ¹⁸But this is how God fulfilled what he had foretold through all the prophets, saying that his

Christ[a] would suffer. [19]Repent, then, and turn to God, so that your sins may be wiped out, that times of refreshing may come from the Lord, [20]and that he may send the Christ, who has been appointed for you—even Jesus. [21]He must remain in heaven until the time comes for God to restore everything, as he promised long ago through his holy prophets. [22]For Moses said, 'The Lord your God will raise up for you a prophet like me from among your own people; you must listen to everything he tells you. [23]Anyone who does not listen to him will be completely cut off from among his people.'[b]

[24]"Indeed, all the prophets from Samuel on, as many as have spoken, have foretold these days. [25]And you are heirs of the prophets and of the covenant God made with your fathers. He said to Abraham, 'Through your offspring all peoples on earth will be blessed.'[c] [26]When God raised up his servant, he sent him first to you to bless you by turning each of you from your wicked ways."   Ac 13:46; Ro 1:16

Peter and John Before the Sanhedrin

4 The priests and the captain of the temple guard and the Sadducees came up to Peter and John while they were speaking to the people. [2]They were greatly disturbed because the apostles were teaching the people and proclaiming in Jesus the resurrection of the dead. [3]They seized Peter and John, and because it was evening, they put them in jail until the next day. [4]But many who heard the message believed, and the number of men grew to about five thousand.

[5]The next day the rulers, elders and teachers of the law met in Jerusalem. [6]Annas the high priest was there, and so were Caiaphas, John, Alexander and the other men of the high priest's family. [7]They had Peter and John brought before them and began to question them: "By what power or what name did you do this?"   Mt 26:3

[8]Then Peter, filled with the Holy Spirit, said to them: "Rulers and elders of the people! [9]If we are being called to account today for an act of kindness shown to a cripple and are asked how he was healed, [10]then know this, you and all the people of Israel: It is by the name of Jesus Christ of Nazareth, whom you crucified but whom God raised from the dead, that this man stands before you healed. [11]He is

" 'the stone you builders rejected,
which has become the capstone.'[d][e]

[12]Salvation is found in no one else, for there is no other name under

---

[a]18 Or *Messiah*; also in verse 20   [b]23 Deut. 18:15,18,19   [c]25 Gen. 22:18; 26:4   [d]11 Or *cornerstone*   [e]11 Psalm 118:22

heaven given to men by which we must be saved." Mt 1:21; Ac 10:43

¹³When they saw the courage of Peter and John and realized that they were unschooled, ordinary men, they were astonished and they took note that these men had been with Jesus. ¹⁴But since they could see the man who had been healed standing there with them, there was nothing they could say. ¹⁵So they ordered them to withdraw from the Sanhedrin and then conferred together. ¹⁶"What are we going to do with these men?" they asked. "Everybody living in Jerusalem knows they have done an outstanding miracle, and we cannot deny it. ¹⁷But to stop this thing from spreading any further among the people, we must warn these men to speak no longer to anyone in this name." Mt 11:25

¹⁸Then they called them in again and commanded them not to speak or teach at all in the name of Jesus. ¹⁹But Peter and John replied, "Judge for yourselves whether it is right in God's sight to obey you rather than God. ²⁰For we cannot help speaking about what we have seen and heard."

²¹After further threats they let them go. They could not decide how to punish them, because all the people were praising God for what had happened. ²²For the man who was miraculously healed was over forty years old. Ac 5:26

The Believers' Prayer

²³On their release, Peter and John went back to their own people and reported all that the chief priests and elders had said to them. ²⁴When they heard this, they raised their voices together in prayer to God. "Sovereign Lord," they said, "you made the heaven and the earth and the sea, and everything in them. ²⁵You spoke by the Holy Spirit through the mouth of your servant, our father David:

" 'Why do the nations rage
    and the peoples plot in vain?
²⁶The kings of the earth take
        their stand
    and the rulers gather
        together
  against the Lord
    and against his Anointed
        One.ᵃ·ᵇ

²⁷Indeed Herod and Pontius Pilate met together with the Gentiles and the peopleᶜ of Israel in this city to conspire against your holy servant Jesus, whom you anointed. ²⁸They did what your power and will had decided beforehand should happen. ²⁹Now, Lord, consider their threats and enable your servants to speak your word with great boldness. ³⁰Stretch out your hand to heal and perform miraculous signs and wonders through the name of your holy servant Jesus."

³¹After they prayed, the place where they were meeting was

ᵃ26 That is, Christ or Messiah   ᵇ26 Psalm 2:1,2   ᶜ27 The Greek is plural.

shaken. And they were all filled with the Holy Spirit and spoke the word of God boldly.   Ac 2:2; Heb 4:12

The Believers Share Their Possessions

³²All the believers were one in heart and mind. No one claimed that any of his possessions was his own, but they shared everything they had. ³³With great power the apostles continued to testify to the resurrection of the Lord Jesus, and much grace was upon them all. ³⁴There were no needy persons among them. For from time to time those who owned lands or houses sold them, brought the money from the sales ³⁵and put it at the apostles' feet, and it was distributed to anyone as he had need.

³⁶Joseph, a Levite from Cyprus, whom the apostles called Barnabas (which means Son of Encouragement), ³⁷sold a field he owned and brought the money and put it at the apostles' feet.   Ac 5:2; 9:27

Ananias and Sapphira

5 Now a man named Ananias, together with his wife Sapphira, also sold a piece of property. ²With his wife's full knowledge he kept back part of the money for himself, but brought the rest and put it at the apostles' feet.

³Then Peter said, "Ananias, how is it that Satan has so filled your heart that you have lied to the Holy Spirit and have kept for yourself some of the money you received for the land? ⁴Didn't it belong to you before it was sold? And after it was sold, wasn't the money at your disposal? What made you think of doing such a thing? You have not lied to men but to God."

⁵When Ananias heard this, he fell down and died. And great fear seized all who heard what had happened. ⁶Then the young men came forward, wrapped up his body, and carried him out and buried him.   Jn 19:40

⁷About three hours later his wife came in, not knowing what had happened. ⁸Peter asked her, "Tell me, is this the price you and Ananias got for the land?"

"Yes," she said, "that is the price."

⁹Peter said to her, "How could you agree to test the Spirit of the Lord? Look! The feet of the men who buried your husband are at the door, and they will carry you out also."

¹⁰At that moment she fell down at his feet and died. Then the young men came in and, finding her dead, carried her out and buried her beside her husband. ¹¹Great fear seized the whole church and all who heard about these events.   Ac 19:17

The Apostles Heal Many

¹²The apostles performed many miraculous signs and wonders among the people. And all the believers used to meet together in

Solomon's Colonnade. ¹³No one else dared join them, even though they were highly regarded by the people. ¹⁴Nevertheless, more and more men and women believed in the Lord and were added to their number. ¹⁵As a result, people brought the sick into the streets and laid them on beds and mats so that at least Peter's shadow might fall on some of them as he passed by. ¹⁶Crowds gathered also from the towns around Jerusalem, bringing their sick and those tormented by evil^a spirits, and all of them were healed.   Ac 2:47; 3:11; 19:12

The Apostles Persecuted

¹⁷Then the high priest and all his associates, who were members of the party of the Sadducees, were filled with jealousy. ¹⁸They arrested the apostles and put them in the public jail. ¹⁹But during the night an angel of the Lord opened the doors of the jail and brought them out. ²⁰"Go, stand in the temple courts," he said, "and tell the people the full message of this new life."   Jn 6:63,68; Ac 4:1

²¹At daybreak they entered the temple courts, as they had been told, and began to teach the people.

When the high priest and his associates arrived, they called together the Sanhedrin—the full assembly of the elders of Israel—and sent to the jail for the apostles.

²²But on arriving at the jail, the officers did not find them there. So they went back and reported, ²³"We found the jail securely locked, with the guards standing at the doors; but when we opened them, we found no one inside." ²⁴On hearing this report, the captain of the temple guard and the chief priests were puzzled, wondering what would come of this.

²⁵Then someone came and said, "Look! The men you put in jail are standing in the temple courts teaching the people." ²⁶At that, the captain went with his officers and brought the apostles. They did not use force, because they feared that the people would stone them.

²⁷Having brought the apostles, they made them appear before the Sanhedrin to be questioned by the high priest. ²⁸"We gave you strict orders not to teach in this name," he said. "Yet you have filled Jerusalem with your teaching and are determined to make us guilty of this man's blood."   Mt 23:35; Ac 2:23,36

²⁹Peter and the other apostles replied: "We must obey God rather than men! ³⁰The God of our fathers raised Jesus from the dead—whom you had killed by hanging him on a tree. ³¹God exalted him to his own right hand as Prince and Savior that he might give repentance and forgiveness of sins to Israel. ³²We are witnesses of these

---

^a16 Greek *unclean*

things, and so is the Holy Spirit, whom God has given to those who obey him." _{Jn 15:26; Ac 3:13; 4:19}

³³When they heard this, they were furious and wanted to put them to death. ³⁴But a Pharisee named Gamaliel, a teacher of the law, who was honored by all the people, stood up in the Sanhedrin and ordered that the men be put outside for a little while. ³⁵Then he addressed them: "Men of Israel, consider carefully what you intend to do to these men. ³⁶Some time ago Theudas appeared, claiming to be somebody, and about four hundred men rallied to him. He was killed, all his followers were dispersed, and it all came to nothing. ³⁷After him, Judas the Galilean appeared in the days of the census and led a band of people in revolt. He too was killed, and all his followers were scattered. ³⁸Therefore, in the present case I advise you: Leave these men alone! Let them go! For if their purpose or activity is of human origin, it will fail. ³⁹But if it is from God, you will not be able to stop these men; you will only find yourselves fighting against God." _{Ac 7:51; 11:17}

⁴⁰His speech persuaded them. They called the apostles in and had them flogged. Then they ordered them not to speak in the name of Jesus, and let them go.

⁴¹The apostles left the Sanhedrin, rejoicing because they had been counted worthy of suffering disgrace for the Name. ⁴²Day after day, in the temple courts and from house to house, they never stopped teaching and proclaiming the good news that Jesus is the Christ.ᵃ _{Jn 15:21; Ac 2:46}

The Choosing of the Seven

6 In those days when the number of disciples was increasing, the Grecian Jews among them complained against the Hebraic Jews because their widows were being overlooked in the daily distribution of food. ²So the Twelve gathered all the disciples together and said, "It would not be right for us to neglect the ministry of the word of God in order to wait on tables. ³Brothers, choose seven men from among you who are known to be full of the Spirit and wisdom. We will turn this responsibility over to them ⁴and will give our attention to prayer and the ministry of the word." _{Ac 4:35; 9:29}

⁵This proposal pleased the whole group. They chose Stephen, a man full of faith and of the Holy Spirit; also Philip, Procorus, Nicanor, Timon, Parmenas, and Nicolas from Antioch, a convert to Judaism. ⁶They presented these men to the apostles, who prayed and laid their hands on them. _{Ac 1:24}

⁷So the word of God spread. The number of disciples in Jerusalem increased rapidly, and a large

ᵃ42 Or Messiah

number of priests became obedient to the faith.   Ac 12:24; 19:20

Stephen Seized

8Now Stephen, a man full of God's grace and power, did great wonders and miraculous signs among the people. **9**Opposition arose, however, from members of the Synagogue of the Freedmen (as it was called) — Jews of Cyrene and Alexandria as well as the provinces of Cilicia and Asia. These men began to argue with Stephen, **10**but they could not stand up against his wisdom or the Spirit by whom he spoke.   Lk 21:15; Jn 4:48

11Then they secretly persuaded some men to say, "We have heard Stephen speak words of blasphemy against Moses and against God."   Mt 26:59-61; 1Ki 21:10

12So they stirred up the people and the elders and the teachers of the law. They seized Stephen and brought him before the Sanhedrin. **13**They produced false witnesses, who testified, "This fellow never stops speaking against this holy place and against the law. **14**For we have heard him say that this Jesus of Nazareth will destroy this place and change the customs Moses handed down to us."   Mt 5:22; Ac 15:1

15All who were sitting in the Sanhedrin looked intently at Stephen, and they saw that his face was like the face of an angel.

Stephen's Speech to the Sanhedrin

7 Then the high priest asked him, "Are these charges true?" **2**To this he replied: "Brothers and fathers, listen to me! The God of glory appeared to our father Abraham while he was still in Mesopotamia, before he lived in Haran. **3**'Leave your country and your people,' God said, 'and go to the land I will show you.'*a*   Ac 22:1

4"So he left the land of the Chaldeans and settled in Haran. After the death of his father, God sent him to this land where you are now living. **5**He gave him no inheritance here, not even a foot of ground. But God promised him that he and his descendants after him would possess the land, even though at that time Abraham had no child. **6**God spoke to him in this way: 'Your descendants will be strangers in a country not their own, and they will be enslaved and mistreated four hundred years. **7**But I will punish the nation they serve as slaves,' God said, 'and afterward they will come out of that country and worship me in this place.'*b* **8**Then he gave Abraham the covenant of circumcision. And Abraham became the father of Isaac and circumcised him eight days after his birth. Later Isaac became the father of Jacob, and Ja-

a3 Gen. 12:1   *b7* Gen. 15:13,14

cob became the father of the twelve patriarchs. _{Ge 29:31-35; Ex 3:12}

9"Because the patriarchs were jealous of Joseph, they sold him as a slave into Egypt. But God was with him 10and rescued him from all his troubles. He gave Joseph wisdom and enabled him to gain the goodwill of Pharaoh king of Egypt; so he made him ruler over Egypt and all his palace.

11"Then a famine struck all Egypt and Canaan, bringing great suffering, and our fathers could not find food. 12When Jacob heard that there was grain in Egypt, he sent our fathers on their first visit. 13On their second visit, Joseph told his brothers who he was, and Pharaoh learned about Joseph's family. 14After this, Joseph sent for his father Jacob and his whole family, seventy-five in all. 15Then Jacob went down to Egypt, where he and our fathers died. 16Their bodies were brought back to Shechem and placed in the tomb that Abraham had bought from the sons of Hamor at Shechem for a certain sum of money. _{Ge 45:1-4; Dt 10:22}

17"As the time drew near for God to fulfill his promise to Abraham, the number of our people in Egypt greatly increased. 18Then another king, who knew nothing about Joseph, became ruler of Egypt. 19He dealt treacherously with our people and oppressed our forefathers by forcing them to throw out their newborn babies so that they would die. _{Ex 1:10-22}

20"At that time Moses was born, and he was no ordinary child.*a* For three months he was cared for in his father's house. 21When he was placed outside, Pharaoh's daughter took him and brought him up as her own son. 22Moses was educated in all the wisdom of the Egyptians and was powerful in speech and action. _{1Ki 4:30; Isa 19:11}

23"When Moses was forty years old, he decided to visit his fellow Israelites. 24He saw one of them being mistreated by an Egyptian, so he went to his defense and avenged him by killing the Egyptian. 25Moses thought that his own people would realize that God was using him to rescue them, but they did not. 26The next day Moses came upon two Israelites who were fighting. He tried to reconcile them by saying, 'Men, you are brothers; why do you want to hurt each other?'

27"But the man who was mistreating the other pushed Moses aside and said, 'Who made you ruler and judge over us? 28Do you want to kill me as you killed the Egyptian yesterday?'*b* 29When Moses heard this, he fled to Midian, where he settled as a foreigner and had two sons. _{Ex 2:11-15}

30"After forty years had passed, an angel appeared to Moses in the flames of a burning bush in the

---

a 20 Or *was fair in the sight of God*   *b 28* Exodus 2:14

desert near Mount Sinai. ³¹When he saw this, he was amazed at the sight. As he went over to look more closely, he heard the Lord's voice: ³²'I am the God of your fathers, the God of Abraham, Isaac and Jacob.'ᵃ Moses trembled with fear and did not dare to look.

³³"Then the Lord said to him, 'Take off your sandals; the place where you are standing is holy ground. ³⁴I have indeed seen the oppression of my people in Egypt. I have heard their groaning and have come down to set them free. Now come, I will send you back to Egypt.'ᵇ   Ex 3:5,7-10

³⁵"This is the same Moses whom they had rejected with the words, 'Who made you ruler and judge?' He was sent to be their ruler and deliverer by God himself, through the angel who appeared to him in the bush. ³⁶He led them out of Egypt and did wonders and miraculous signs in Egypt, at the Red Seaᶜ and for forty years in the desert.   Ex 12:41; 14:21

³⁷"This is that Moses who told the Israelites, 'God will send you a prophet like me from your own people.'ᵈ ³⁸He was in the assembly in the desert, with the angel who spoke to him on Mount Sinai, and with our fathers; and he received living words to pass on to us.

³⁹"But our fathers refused to obey him. Instead, they rejected him and in their hearts turned back to Egypt. ⁴⁰They told Aaron, 'Make us gods who will go before us. As for this fellow Moses who led us out of Egypt—we don't know what has happened to him!'ᵉ ⁴¹That was the time they made an idol in the form of a calf. They brought sacrifices to it and held a celebration in honor of what their hands had made. ⁴²But God turned away and gave them over to the worship of the heavenly bodies. This agrees with what is written in the book of the prophets:

" 'Did you bring me sacrifices
    and offerings
forty years in the desert,
    O house of Israel?
⁴³You have lifted up the shrine
    of Molech
and the star of your god
    Rephan,
the idols you made to
    worship.
Therefore I will send you into
    exile'ᶠ beyond Babylon.

⁴⁴"Our forefathers had the tabernacle of the Testimony with them in the desert. It had been made as God directed Moses, according to the pattern he had seen. ⁴⁵Having received the tabernacle, our fathers under Joshua brought it with them when they took the land from the nations God drove out before them. It remained in the land

until the time of David, **46**who enjoyed God's favor and asked that he might provide a dwelling place for the God of Jacob.*a* **47**But it was Solomon who built the house for him.   Jos 3:14-17; 2Sa 7:8-16

48"However, the Most High does not live in houses made by men. As the prophet says: 1Ki 8:27; 2Ch 2:6

49" 'Heaven is my throne,
    and the earth is my
        footstool.   Mt 5:34-35
What kind of house will you
        build for me?
                    says the Lord.
Or where will my resting
        place be?
50Has not my hand made all
        these things?'*b*   Isa 66:1-2

51"You stiff-necked people, with uncircumcised hearts and ears! You are just like your fathers: You always resist the Holy Spirit! **52**Was there ever a prophet your fathers did not persecute? They even killed those who predicted the coming of the Righteous One. And now you have betrayed and murdered him— **53**you who have received the law that was put into effect through angels but have not obeyed it."   Ac 3:14; Gal 3:19

The Stoning of Stephen

54When they heard this, they were furious and gnashed their teeth at him. **55**But Stephen, full of the Holy Spirit, looked up to heaven and saw the glory of God, and Jesus standing at the right hand of God. **56**"Look," he said, "I see heaven open and the Son of Man standing at the right hand of God."

57At this they covered their ears and, yelling at the top of their voices, they all rushed at him, **58**dragged him out of the city and began to stone him. Meanwhile, the witnesses laid their clothes at the feet of a young man named Saul.   Lev 24:14,16; Dt 13:9

59While they were stoning him, Stephen prayed, "Lord Jesus, receive my spirit." **60**Then he fell on his knees and cried out, "Lord, do not hold this sin against them." When he had said this, he fell asleep.   Ps 31:5; Ac 9:40

8 And Saul was there, giving approval to his death.   Ac 7:58

The Church Persecuted and Scattered

On that day a great persecution broke out against the church at Jerusalem, and all except the apostles were scattered throughout Judea and Samaria. **2**Godly men buried Stephen and mourned deeply for him. **3**But Saul began to destroy the church. Going from house to house, he dragged off men and women and put them in prison.

Philip in Samaria

4Those who had been scattered

---

a 46 Some early manuscripts *the house of Jacob*   *b* 50 Isaiah 66:1,2

preached the word wherever they went. [5]Philip went down to a city in Samaria and proclaimed the Christ[a] there. [6]When the crowds heard Philip and saw the miraculous signs he did, they all paid close attention to what he said. [7]With shrieks, evil[b] spirits came out of many, and many paralytics and cripples were healed. [8]So there was great joy in that city.

Simon the Sorcerer

[9]Now for some time a man named Simon had practiced sorcery in the city and amazed all the people of Samaria. He boasted that he was someone great, [10]and all the people, both high and low, gave him their attention and exclaimed, "This man is the divine power known as the Great Power." [11]They followed him because he had amazed them for a long time with his magic. [12]But when they believed Philip as he preached the good news of the kingdom of God and the name of Jesus Christ, they were baptized, both men and women. [13]Simon himself believed and was baptized. And he followed Philip everywhere, astonished by the great signs and miracles he saw.   Ac 13:6; 19:11

[14]When the apostles in Jerusalem heard that Samaria had accepted the word of God, they sent Peter and John to them. [15]When they arrived, they prayed for them that they might receive the Holy Spirit, [16]because the Holy Spirit had not yet come upon any of them; they had simply been baptized into[c] the name of the Lord Jesus. [17]Then Peter and John placed their hands on them, and they received the Holy Spirit.

[18]When Simon saw that the Spirit was given at the laying on of the apostles' hands, he offered them money [19]and said, "Give me also this ability so that everyone on whom I lay my hands may receive the Holy Spirit."

[20]Peter answered: "May your money perish with you, because you thought you could buy the gift of God with money! [21]You have no part or share in this ministry, because your heart is not right before God. [22]Repent of this wickedness and pray to the Lord. Perhaps he will forgive you for having such a thought in your heart. [23]For I see that you are full of bitterness and captive to sin."   2Ki 5:16; Mt 10:8; Ac 2:38

[24]Then Simon answered, "Pray to the Lord for me so that nothing you have said may happen to me."

[25]When they had testified and proclaimed the word of the Lord, Peter and John returned to Jerusalem, preaching the gospel in many Samaritan villages.   Ac 13:48

Philip and the Ethiopian

[26]Now an angel of the Lord said to Philip, "Go south to the road—

---

a 5 Or *Messiah*   b 7 Greek *unclean*   c 16 Or *in*

the desert road—that goes down from Jerusalem to Gaza." ²⁷So he started out, and on his way he met an Ethiopian*a* eunuch, an important official in charge of all the treasury of Candace, queen of the Ethiopians. This man had gone to Jerusalem to worship, ²⁸and on his way home was sitting in his chariot reading the book of Isaiah the prophet. ²⁹The Spirit told Philip, "Go to that chariot and stay near it."   Jn 12:20; Ac 5:19

³⁰Then Philip ran up to the chariot and heard the man reading Isaiah the prophet. "Do you understand what you are reading?" Philip asked.

³¹"How can I," he said, "unless someone explains it to me?" So he invited Philip to come up and sit with him.

³²The eunuch was reading this passage of Scripture:

"He was led like a sheep to the
        slaughter,
  and as a lamb before the
        shearer is silent,
  so he did not open his
        mouth.
³³In his humiliation he was
        deprived of justice.
  Who can speak of his
        descendants?
  For his life was taken from
        the earth."*b*   Isa 53:7-8

³⁴The eunuch asked Philip, "Tell me, please, who is the prophet talking about, himself or someone else?" ³⁵Then Philip began with that very passage of Scripture and told him the good news about Jesus.   Lk 24:27; Ac 18:28

³⁶As they traveled along the road, they came to some water and the eunuch said, "Look, here is water. Why shouldn't I be baptized?"*c* ³⁸And he gave orders to stop the chariot. Then both Philip and the eunuch went down into the water and Philip baptized him. ³⁹When they came up out of the water, the Spirit of the Lord suddenly took Philip away, and the eunuch did not see him again, but went on his way rejoicing. ⁴⁰Philip, however, appeared at Azotus and traveled about, preaching the gospel in all the towns until he reached Caesarea.   1Ki 18:12; 2Ki 2:16

Saul's Conversion

9 Meanwhile, Saul was still breathing out murderous threats against the Lord's disciples. He went to the high priest ²and asked him for letters to the synagogues in Damascus, so that if he found any there who belonged to the Way, whether men or women, he might take them as prisoners to Jerusalem. ³As he neared Damascus on his journey, suddenly a light from heaven flashed around him. ⁴He fell to the ground

a27 That is, from the upper Nile region   b33 Isaiah 53:7,8   c36 Some late manuscripts baptized?"
37Philip said, "If you believe with all your heart, you may." The eunuch answered, "I believe that Jesus Christ is the Son of God."

and heard a voice say to him, "Saul, Saul, why do you persecute me?"   Ac 8:3; 19:9,23; 1Co 15:8

⁵"Who are you, Lord?" Saul asked.

"I am Jesus, whom you are persecuting," he replied. ⁶"Now get up and go into the city, and you will be told what you must do."

⁷The men traveling with Saul stood there speechless; they heard the sound but did not see anyone. ⁸Saul got up from the ground, but when he opened his eyes he could see nothing. So they led him by the hand into Damascus. ⁹For three days he was blind, and did not eat or drink anything.   Da 10:7; Ac 22:9

¹⁰In Damascus there was a disciple named Ananias. The Lord called to him in a vision, "Ananias!"   Ac 10:3,17,19

"Yes, Lord," he answered.

¹¹The Lord told him, "Go to the house of Judas on Straight Street and ask for a man from Tarsus named Saul, for he is praying. ¹²In a vision he has seen a man named Ananias come and place his hands on him to restore his sight."

¹³"Lord," Ananias answered, "I have heard many reports about this man and all the harm he has done to your saints in Jerusalem. ¹⁴And he has come here with authority from the chief priests to arrest all who call on your name."

¹⁵But the Lord said to Ananias, "Go! This man is my chosen instrument to carry my name before the Gentiles and their kings and before the people of Israel. ¹⁶I will show him how much he must suffer for my name."   Ac 13:2; 20:23

¹⁷Then Ananias went to the house and entered it. Placing his hands on Saul, he said, "Brother Saul, the Lord—Jesus, who appeared to you on the road as you were coming here—has sent me so that you may see again and be filled with the Holy Spirit." ¹⁸Immediately, something like scales fell from Saul's eyes, and he could see again. He got up and was baptized, ¹⁹and after taking some food, he regained his strength.

Saul in Damascus and Jerusalem

Saul spent several days with the disciples in Damascus. ²⁰At once he began to preach in the synagogues that Jesus is the Son of God. ²¹All those who heard him were astonished and asked, "Isn't he the man who raised havoc in Jerusalem among those who call on this name? And hasn't he come here to take them as prisoners to the chief priests?" ²²Yet Saul grew more and more powerful and baffled the Jews living in Damascus by proving that Jesus is the Christ.ᵃ   Ac 8:3; 18:5,28

²³After many days had gone by, the Jews conspired to kill him, ²⁴but Saul learned of their plan.

ᵃ22 Or Messiah

Day and night they kept close watch on the city gates in order to kill him. ²⁵But his followers took him by night and lowered him in a basket through an opening in the wall.   1Sa 19:12; Ac 20:3,19

²⁶When he came to Jerusalem, he tried to join the disciples, but they were all afraid of him, not believing that he really was a disciple. ²⁷But Barnabas took him and brought him to the apostles. He told them how Saul on his journey had seen the Lord and that the Lord had spoken to him, and how in Damascus he had preached fearlessly in the name of Jesus. ²⁸So Saul stayed with them and moved about freely in Jerusalem, speaking boldly in the name of the Lord. ²⁹He talked and debated with the Grecian Jews, but they tried to kill him. ³⁰When the brothers learned of this, they took him down to Caesarea and sent him off to Tarsus.   Ac 6:1; 22:17

³¹Then the church throughout Judea, Galilee and Samaria enjoyed a time of peace. It was strengthened; and encouraged by the Holy Spirit, it grew in numbers, living in the fear of the Lord.

Aeneas and Dorcas

³²As Peter traveled about the country, he went to visit the saints in Lydda. ³³There he found a man named Aeneas, a paralytic who had been bedridden for eight years. ³⁴"Aeneas," Peter said to him, "Jesus Christ heals you. Get up and take care of your mat." Immediately Aeneas got up. ³⁵All those who lived in Lydda and Sharon saw him and turned to the Lord.   Ac 3:6,16; 11:21

³⁶In Joppa there was a disciple named Tabitha (which, when translated, is Dorcas[a]), who was always doing good and helping the poor. ³⁷About that time she became sick and died, and her body was washed and placed in an upstairs room. ³⁸Lydda was near Joppa; so when the disciples heard that Peter was in Lydda, they sent two men to him and urged him, "Please come at once!"   1Ti 2:10

³⁹Peter went with them, and when he arrived he was taken upstairs to the room. All the widows stood around him, crying and showing him the robes and other clothing that Dorcas had made while she was still with them.

⁴⁰Peter sent them all out of the room; then he got down on his knees and prayed. Turning toward the dead woman, he said, "Tabitha, get up." She opened her eyes, and seeing Peter she sat up. ⁴¹He took her by the hand and helped her to her feet. Then he called the believers and the widows and presented her to them alive. ⁴²This became known all over Joppa, and many people believed in the Lord. ⁴³Peter stayed in Joppa for some

---

ᵃ 36 Both *Tabitha* (Aramaic) and *Dorcas* (Greek) mean *gazelle*.

time with a tanner named Simon.

Cornelius Calls for Peter

10 At Caesarea there was a man named Cornelius, a centurion in what was known as the Italian Regiment. ²He and all his family were devout and God-fearing; he gave generously to those in need and prayed to God regularly. ³One day at about three in the afternoon he had a vision. He distinctly saw an angel of God, who came to him and said, "Cornelius!"   Ac 3:1; 5:19

⁴Cornelius stared at him in fear. "What is it, Lord?" he asked.

The angel answered, "Your prayers and gifts to the poor have come up as a memorial offering before God. ⁵Now send men to Joppa to bring back a man named Simon who is called Peter. ⁶He is staying with Simon the tanner, whose house is by the sea."

⁷When the angel who spoke to him had gone, Cornelius called two of his servants and a devout soldier who was one of his attendants. ⁸He told them everything that had happened and sent them to Joppa.   Ac 9:36

Peter's Vision

⁹About noon the following day as they were on their journey and approaching the city, Peter went up on the roof to pray. ¹⁰He became hungry and wanted some-thing to eat, and while the meal was being prepared, he fell into a trance. ¹¹He saw heaven opened and something like a large sheet being let down to earth by its four corners. ¹²It contained all kinds of four-footed animals, as well as reptiles of the earth and birds of the air. ¹³Then a voice told him, "Get up, Peter. Kill and eat."   Mt 24:17

¹⁴"Surely not, Lord!" Peter replied. "I have never eaten anything impure or unclean."   Dt 14:3-20

¹⁵The voice spoke to him a second time, "Do not call anything impure that God has made clean."

¹⁶This happened three times, and immediately the sheet was taken back to heaven.

¹⁷While Peter was wondering about the meaning of the vision, the men sent by Cornelius found out where Simon's house was and stopped at the gate. ¹⁸They called out, asking if Simon who was known as Peter was staying there.

¹⁹While Peter was still thinking about the vision, the Spirit said to him, "Simon, three[a] men are looking for you. ²⁰So get up and go downstairs. Do not hesitate to go with them, for I have sent them."

²¹Peter went down and said to the men, "I'm the one you're looking for. Why have you come?"

²²The men replied, "We have come from Cornelius the centurion. He is a righteous and God-fearing man, who is respected by all

the Jewish people. A holy angel told him to have you come to his house so that he could hear what you have to say." ²³Then Peter invited the men into the house to be his guests.   Ac 11:14

Peter at Cornelius' House

The next day Peter started out with them, and some of the brothers from Joppa went along. ²⁴The following day he arrived in Caesarea. Cornelius was expecting them and had called together his relatives and close friends. ²⁵As Peter entered the house, Cornelius met him and fell at his feet in reverence. ²⁶But Peter made him get up. "Stand up," he said, "I am only a man myself."   Rev 19:10

²⁷Talking with him, Peter went inside and found a large gathering of people. ²⁸He said to them: "You are well aware that it is against our law for a Jew to associate with a Gentile or visit him. But God has shown me that I should not call any man impure or unclean. ²⁹So when I was sent for, I came without raising any objection. May I ask why you sent for me?"   Jn 4:9

³⁰Cornelius answered: "Four days ago I was in my house praying at this hour, at three in the afternoon. Suddenly a man in shining clothes stood before me ³¹and said, 'Cornelius, God has heard your prayer and remembered your gifts to the poor. ³²Send to Joppa for Simon who is called Peter. He is a guest in the home of Simon the tanner, who lives by the sea.' ³³So I sent for you immediately, and it was good of you to come. Now we are all here in the presence of God to listen to everything the Lord has commanded you to tell us."

³⁴Then Peter began to speak: "I now realize how true it is that God does not show favoritism ³⁵but accepts men from every nation who fear him and do what is right. ³⁶You know the message God sent to the people of Israel, telling the good news of peace through Jesus Christ, who is Lord of all. ³⁷You know what has happened throughout Judea, beginning in Galilee after the baptism that John preached — ³⁸how God anointed Jesus of Nazareth with the Holy Spirit and power, and how he went around doing good and healing all who were under the power of the devil, because God was with him.

³⁹"We are witnesses of everything he did in the country of the Jews and in Jerusalem. They killed him by hanging him on a tree, ⁴⁰but God raised him from the dead on the third day and caused him to be seen. ⁴¹He was not seen by all the people, but by witnesses whom God had already chosen—by us who ate and drank with him after he rose from the dead. ⁴²He commanded us to preach to the people and to testify that he is the one whom God appointed as judge of the living and the dead. ⁴³All the prophets testify about him that everyone who believes in him re-

ceives forgiveness of sins through his name."   Isa 53:11; Ac 2:24; 5:30

44While Peter was still speaking these words, the Holy Spirit came on all who heard the message. **45**The circumcised believers who had come with Peter were astonished that the gift of the Holy Spirit had been poured out even on the Gentiles. **46**For they heard them speaking in tongues*a* and praising God.   Mk 16:17; Ac 11:18

Then Peter said, **47**"Can anyone keep these people from being baptized with water? They have received the Holy Spirit just as we have." **48**So he ordered that they be baptized in the name of Jesus Christ. Then they asked Peter to stay with them for a few days.

Peter Explains His Actions

11 The apostles and the brothers throughout Judea heard that the Gentiles also had received the word of God. **2**So when Peter went up to Jerusalem, the circumcised believers criticized him **3**and said, "You went into the house of uncircumcised men and ate with them."   Ac 10:25,28; Gal 2:12

4Peter began and explained everything to them precisely as it had happened: **5**"I was in the city of Joppa praying, and in a trance I saw a vision. I saw something like a large sheet being let down from heaven by its four corners, and it came down to where I was. **6**I

looked into it and saw four-footed animals of the earth, wild beasts, reptiles, and birds of the air. **7**Then I heard a voice telling me, 'Get up, Peter. Kill and eat.'   Ac 10:9-32

8"I replied, 'Surely not, Lord! Nothing impure or unclean has ever entered my mouth.'

9"The voice spoke from heaven a second time, 'Do not call anything impure that God has made clean.' **10**This happened three times, and then it was all pulled up to heaven again.   Ac 10:15

11"Right then three men who had been sent to me from Caesarea stopped at the house where I was staying. **12**The Spirit told me to have no hesitation about going with them. These six brothers also went with me, and we entered the man's house. **13**He told us how he had seen an angel appear in his house and say, 'Send to Joppa for Simon who is called Peter. **14**He will bring you a message through which you and all your household will be saved.'   Ac 8:29; 15:9

15"As I began to speak, the Holy Spirit came on them as he had come on us at the beginning. **16**Then I remembered what the Lord had said: 'John baptized with*b* water, but you will be baptized with the Holy Spirit.' **17**So if God gave them the same gift as he gave us, who believed in the Lord Jesus Christ, who was I to think that I could oppose God?"   Ac 2:4

a 46 Or *other languages*   *b 16* Or *in*

[18]When they heard this, they had no further objections and praised God, saying, "So then, God has granted even the Gentiles repentance unto life." Ro 10:12-13

The Church in Antioch

[19]Now those who had been scattered by the persecution in connection with Stephen traveled as far as Phoenicia, Cyprus and Antioch, telling the message only to Jews. [20]Some of them, however, men from Cyprus and Cyrene, went to Antioch and began to speak to Greeks also, telling them the good news about the Lord Jesus. [21]The Lord's hand was with them, and a great number of people believed and turned to the Lord. Lk 1:66; Ac 2:47

[22]News of this reached the ears of the church at Jerusalem, and they sent Barnabas to Antioch. [23]When he arrived and saw the evidence of the grace of God, he was glad and encouraged them all to remain true to the Lord with all their hearts. [24]He was a good man, full of the Holy Spirit and faith, and a great number of people were brought to the Lord. Ac 5:14; 13:43

[25]Then Barnabas went to Tarsus to look for Saul, [26]and when he found him, he brought him to Antioch. So for a whole year Barnabas and Saul met with the church and taught great numbers of people. The disciples were called Christians first at Antioch. Ac 9:11; 26:28

[27]During this time some prophets came down from Jerusalem to Antioch. [28]One of them, named Agabus, stood up and through the Spirit predicted that a severe famine would spread over the entire Roman world. (This happened during the reign of Claudius.) [29]The disciples, each according to his ability, decided to provide help for the brothers living in Judea. [30]This they did, sending their gift to the elders by Barnabas and Saul.

Peter's Miraculous Escape From Prison

12 It was about this time that King Herod arrested some who belonged to the church, intending to persecute them. [2]He had James, the brother of John, put to death with the sword. [3]When he saw that this pleased the Jews, he proceeded to seize Peter also. This happened during the Feast of Unleavened Bread. [4]After arresting him, he put him in prison, handing him over to be guarded by four squads of four soldiers each. Herod intended to bring him out for public trial after the Passover. Ex 12:15; 23:15; Mt 4:21

[5]So Peter was kept in prison, but the church was earnestly praying to God for him. Eph 6:18

[6]The night before Herod was to bring him to trial, Peter was sleeping between two soldiers, bound with two chains, and sentries stood guard at the entrance. [7]Suddenly an angel of the Lord ap-

peared and a light shone in the cell. He struck Peter on the side and woke him up. "Quick, get up!" he said, and the chains fell off Peter's wrists.   Ac 5:19; 16:26

[8]Then the angel said to him, "Put on your clothes and sandals." And Peter did so. "Wrap your cloak around you and follow me," the angel told him. [9]Peter followed him out of the prison, but he had no idea that what the angel was doing was really happening; he thought he was seeing a vision. [10]They passed the first and second guards and came to the iron gate leading to the city. It opened for them by itself, and they went through it. When they had walked the length of one street, suddenly the angel left him.   Ac 16:26

[11]Then Peter came to himself and said, "Now I know without a doubt that the Lord sent his angel and rescued me from Herod's clutches and from everything the Jewish people were anticipating."

[12]When this had dawned on him, he went to the house of Mary the mother of John, also called Mark, where many people had gathered and were praying. [13]Peter knocked at the outer entrance, and a servant girl named Rhoda came to answer the door. [14]When she recognized Peter's voice, she was so overjoyed she ran back without opening it and exclaimed, "Peter is at the door!"   Lk 24:41; Jn 18:16-17

[15]"You're out of your mind," they told her. When she kept insisting that it was so, they said, "It must be his angel."   Mt 18:10

[16]But Peter kept on knocking, and when they opened the door and saw him, they were astonished. [17]Peter motioned with his hand for them to be quiet and described how the Lord had brought him out of prison. "Tell James and the brothers about this," he said, and then he left for another place.

[18]In the morning, there was no small commotion among the soldiers as to what had become of Peter. [19]After Herod had a thorough search made for him and did not find him, he cross-examined the guards and ordered that they be executed.   Ac 16:27

Herod's Death

Then Herod went from Judea to Caesarea and stayed there a while. [20]He had been quarreling with the people of Tyre and Sidon; they now joined together and sought an audience with him. Having secured the support of Blastus, a trusted personal servant of the king, they asked for peace, because they depended on the king's country for their food supply.

[21]On the appointed day Herod, wearing his royal robes, sat on his throne and delivered a public address to the people. [22]They shouted, "This is the voice of a god, not of a man." [23]Immediately, because Herod did not give praise to God, an angel of the Lord struck him

down, and he was eaten by worms and died.   1Sa 25:38; 2Sa 24:16-17

²⁴But the word of God continued to increase and spread.   Ac 6:7

²⁵When Barnabas and Saul had finished their mission, they returned from^a Jerusalem, taking with them John, also called Mark.

Barnabas and Saul Sent Off

13 In the church at Antioch there were prophets and teachers: Barnabas, Simeon called Niger, Lucius of Cyrene, Manaen (who had been brought up with Herod the tetrarch) and Saul. ²While they were worshiping the Lord and fasting, the Holy Spirit said, "Set apart for me Barnabas and Saul for the work to which I have called them." ³So after they had fasted and prayed, they placed their hands on them and sent them off.   Ac 14:26; 22:21

On Cyprus

⁴The two of them, sent on their way by the Holy Spirit, went down to Seleucia and sailed from there to Cyprus. ⁵When they arrived at Salamis, they proclaimed the word of God in the Jewish synagogues. John was with them as their helper.   Ac 12:12; Heb 4:12

⁶They traveled through the whole island until they came to Paphos. There they met a Jewish sorcerer and false prophet named Bar-Jesus, ⁷who was an attendant

^a25 Some manuscripts to

of the proconsul, Sergius Paulus. The proconsul, an intelligent man, sent for Barnabas and Saul because he wanted to hear the word of God. ⁸But Elymas the sorcerer (for that is what his name means) opposed them and tried to turn the proconsul from the faith. ⁹Then Saul, who was also called Paul, filled with the Holy Spirit, looked straight at Elymas and said, ¹⁰"You are a child of the devil and an enemy of everything that is right! You are full of all kinds of deceit and trickery. Will you never stop perverting the right ways of the Lord? ¹¹Now the hand of the Lord is against you. You are going to be blind, and for a time you will be unable to see the light of the sun."

Immediately mist and darkness came over him, and he groped about, seeking someone to lead him by the hand. ¹²When the proconsul saw what had happened, he believed, for he was amazed at the teaching about the Lord.

In Pisidian Antioch

¹³From Paphos, Paul and his companions sailed to Perga in Pamphylia, where John left them to return to Jerusalem. ¹⁴From Perga they went on to Pisidian Antioch. On the Sabbath they entered the synagogue and sat down. ¹⁵After the reading from the Law and the Prophets, the synagogue rulers

sent word to them, saying, "Brothers, if you have a message of encouragement for the people, please speak." Ac 14:19,21; 16:13

¹⁶Standing up, Paul motioned with his hand and said: "Men of Israel and you Gentiles who worship God, listen to me! ¹⁷The God of the people of Israel chose our fathers; he made the people prosper during their stay in Egypt, with mighty power he led them out of that country, ¹⁸he endured their conduct[a] for about forty years in the desert, ¹⁹he overthrew seven nations in Canaan and gave their land to his people as their inheritance. ²⁰All this took about 450 years. Dt 1:31; 7:6-8; Jos 19:51

"After this, God gave them judges until the time of Samuel the prophet. ²¹Then the people asked for a king, and he gave them Saul son of Kish, of the tribe of Benjamin, who ruled forty years. ²²After removing Saul, he made David their king. He testified concerning him: 'I have found David son of Jesse a man after my own heart; he will do everything I want him to do.' 1Sa 13:14; 15:23,26

²³"From this man's descendants God has brought to Israel the Savior Jesus, as he promised. ²⁴Before the coming of Jesus, John preached repentance and baptism to all the people of Israel. ²⁵As John was completing his work, he said: 'Who do you think I am? I am not that one. No, but he is coming after me, whose sandals I am not worthy to untie.' Mt 1:21; 3:11; Jn 1:27

²⁶"Brothers, children of Abraham, and you God-fearing Gentiles, it is to us that this message of salvation has been sent. ²⁷The people of Jerusalem and their rulers did not recognize Jesus, yet in condemning him they fulfilled the words of the prophets that are read every Sabbath. ²⁸Though they found no proper ground for a death sentence, they asked Pilate to have him executed. ²⁹When they had carried out all that was written about him, they took him down from the tree and laid him in a tomb. ³⁰But God raised him from the dead, ³¹and for many days he was seen by those who had traveled with him from Galilee to Jerusalem. They are now his witnesses to our people. Mt 28:16; Lk 24:48; Ac 3:17

³²"We tell you the good news: What God promised our fathers ³³he has fulfilled for us, their children, by raising up Jesus. As it is written in the second Psalm:

" 'You are my Son;
    today I have become your
    Father.'[b][c]

³⁴The fact that God raised him from the dead, never to decay, is stated in these words:

---

a 18 Some manuscripts *and cared for them*   b 33 Or *have begotten you*   c 33 Psalm 2:7

" 'I will give you the holy and
sure blessings promised
to David.' *a*

³⁵So it is stated elsewhere:

" 'You will not let your Holy
One see decay.' *b*   Ps 16:10

³⁶"For when David had served
God's purpose in his own generation, he fell asleep; he was buried
with his fathers and his body decayed. ³⁷But the one whom God
raised from the dead did not see
decay.   Ac 2:24,29; 1Ki 2:10

³⁸"Therefore, my brothers, I
want you to know that through
Jesus the forgiveness of sins is proclaimed to you. ³⁹Through him everyone who believes is justified
from everything you could not be
justified from by the law of Moses.
⁴⁰Take care that what the prophets
have said does not happen to you:

⁴¹" 'Look, you scoffers,
wonder and perish,
for I am going to do something
in your days
that you would never
believe,
even if someone told you.' *c*"

⁴²As Paul and Barnabas were
leaving the synagogue, the people
invited them to speak further
about these things on the next Sabbath. ⁴³When the congregation
was dismissed, many of the Jews
and devout converts to Judaism
followed Paul and Barnabas, who
talked with them and urged them
to continue in the grace of God.
⁴⁴On the next Sabbath almost
the whole city gathered to hear the
word of the Lord. ⁴⁵When the Jews
saw the crowds, they were filled
with jealousy and talked abusively
against what Paul was saying.
⁴⁶Then Paul and Barnabas answered them boldly: "We had to
speak the word of God to you first.
Since you reject it and do not consider yourselves worthy of eternal
life, we now turn to the Gentiles.
⁴⁷For this is what the Lord has
commanded us: Ac 3:26; 18:6; 28:28

" 'I have made you *d* a light for
the Gentiles,
that you *d* may bring
salvation to the ends of
the earth.' *e*"   Lk 2:32; Isa 49:6

⁴⁸When the Gentiles heard this,
they were glad and honored the
word of the Lord; and all who were
appointed for eternal life believed.
⁴⁹The word of the Lord spread
through the whole region. ⁵⁰But
the Jews incited the God-fearing
women of high standing and
the leading men of the city. They
stirred up persecution against Paul
and Barnabas, and expelled them
from their region. ⁵¹So they shook
the dust from their feet in protest
against them and went to Iconium.
⁵²And the disciples were filled with
joy and with the Holy Spirit.

*a*34 Isaiah 55:3   *b*35 Psalm 16:10   *c*41 Hab. 1:5   *d*47 The Greek is singular.   *e*47 Isaiah 49:6

In Iconium

14 At Iconium Paul and Barnabas went as usual into the Jewish synagogue. There they spoke so effectively that a great number of Jews and Gentiles believed. ²But the Jews who refused to believe stirred up the Gentiles and poisoned their minds against the brothers. ³So Paul and Barnabas spent considerable time there, speaking boldly for the Lord, who confirmed the message of his grace by enabling them to do miraculous signs and wonders. ⁴The people of the city were divided; some sided with the Jews, others with the apostles. ⁵There was a plot afoot among the Gentiles and Jews, together with their leaders, to mistreat them and stone them. ⁶But they found out about it and fled to the Lycaonian cities of Lystra and Derbe and to the surrounding country, ⁷where they continued to preach the good news.

In Lystra and Derbe

⁸In Lystra there sat a man crippled in his feet, who was lame from birth and had never walked. ⁹He listened to Paul as he was speaking. Paul looked directly at him, saw that he had faith to be healed ¹⁰and called out, "Stand up on your feet!" At that, the man jumped up and began to walk.

¹¹When the crowd saw what Paul had done, they shouted in the Lycaonian language, "The gods have come down to us in human form!" ¹²Barnabas they called Zeus, and Paul they called Hermes because he was the chief speaker. ¹³The priest of Zeus, whose temple was just outside the city, brought bulls and wreaths to the city gates because he and the crowd wanted to offer sacrifices to them.   Ac 8:10

¹⁴But when the apostles Barnabas and Paul heard of this, they tore their clothes and rushed out into the crowd, shouting: ¹⁵"Men, why are you doing this? We too are only men, human like you. We are bringing you good news, telling you to turn from these worthless things to the living God, who made heaven and earth and sea and everything in them. ¹⁶In the past, he let all nations go their own way. ¹⁷Yet he has not left himself without testimony: He has shown kindness by giving you rain from heaven and crops in their seasons; he provides you with plenty of food and fills your hearts with joy." ¹⁸Even with these words, they had difficulty keeping the crowd from sacrificing to them.   Ac 10:26; Jas 5:17

¹⁹Then some Jews came from Antioch and Iconium and won the crowd over. They stoned Paul and dragged him outside the city, thinking he was dead. ²⁰But after the disciples had gathered around him, he got up and went back into the city. The next day he and Barnabas left for Derbe.   Ac 13:45

The Return to Antioch in Syria

21They preached the good news in that city and won a large number of disciples. Then they returned to Lystra, Iconium and Antioch, **22**strengthening the disciples and encouraging them to remain true to the faith. "We must go through many hardships to enter the kingdom of God," they said. **23**Paul and Barnabas appointed elders*a* for them in each church and, with prayer and fasting, committed them to the Lord, in whom they had put their trust. **24**After going through Pisidia, they came into Pamphylia, **25**and when they had preached the word in Perga, they went down to Attalia.   2Ti 3:12; Tit 1:5

26From Attalia they sailed back to Antioch, where they had been committed to the grace of God for the work they had now completed. **27**On arriving there, they gathered the church together and reported all that God had done through them and how he had opened the door of faith to the Gentiles. **28**And they stayed there a long time with the disciples.   Ac 13:1,3; 1Co 16:9

The Council at Jerusalem

15 Some men came down from Judea to Antioch and were teaching the brothers: "Unless you are circumcised, according to the custom taught by Moses, you cannot be saved." **2**This brought Paul and Barnabas into sharp dispute and debate with them. So Paul and Barnabas were appointed, along with some other believers, to go up to Jerusalem to see the apostles and elders about this question. **3**The church sent them on their way, and as they traveled through Phoenicia and Samaria, they told how the Gentiles had been converted. This news made all the brothers very glad. **4**When they came to Jerusalem, they were welcomed by the church and the apostles and elders, to whom they reported everything God had done through them.   Ac 14:27; Gal 5:2-3

5Then some of the believers who belonged to the party of the Pharisees stood up and said, "The Gentiles must be circumcised and required to obey the law of Moses."   Ac 5:17

6The apostles and elders met to consider this question. **7**After much discussion, Peter got up and addressed them: "Brothers, you know that some time ago God made a choice among you that the Gentiles might hear from my lips the message of the gospel and believe. **8**God, who knows the heart, showed that he accepted them by giving the Holy Spirit to them, just as he did to us. **9**He made no distinction between us and them, for he purified their hearts by faith. **10**Now then, why do you try to test God by putting on the necks of the

---

a 23 Or Barnabas ordained elders; or Barnabas had elders elected

disciples a yoke that neither we nor our fathers have been able to bear? [11]No! We believe it is through the grace of our Lord Jesus that we are saved, just as they are."   Mt 23:4; Ac 10:44,47; Ro 3:24

[12]The whole assembly became silent as they listened to Barnabas and Paul telling about the miraculous signs and wonders God had done among the Gentiles through them. [13]When they finished, James spoke up: "Brothers, listen to me. [14]Simon[a] has described to us how God at first showed his concern by taking from the Gentiles a people for himself. [15]The words of the prophets are in agreement with this, as it is written:

[16]" 'After this I will return
    and rebuild David's fallen
        tent.
  Its ruins I will rebuild,
    and I will restore it,
[17]that the remnant of men may
        seek the Lord,
    and all the Gentiles who
        bear my name,
  says the Lord, who does these
        things'[b]   Am 9:11-12
[18] that have been known for
        ages.[c]   Isa 45:21

[19]"It is my judgment, therefore, that we should not make it difficult for the Gentiles who are turning to God. [20]Instead we should write to them, telling them to abstain from food polluted by idols, from sexual immorality, from the meat of strangled animals and from blood. [21]For Moses has been preached in every city from the earliest times and is read in the synagogues on every Sabbath."   Ac 13:15; 1Co 10:14-28

The Council's Letter to Gentile Believers

[22]Then the apostles and elders, with the whole church, decided to choose some of their own men and send them to Antioch with Paul and Barnabas. They chose Judas (called Barsabbas) and Silas, two men who were leaders among the brothers. [23]With them they sent the following letter:

The apostles and elders, your brothers,

To the Gentile believers in Antioch, Syria and Cilicia:

Greetings.   Jas 1:1

[24]We have heard that some went out from us without our authorization and disturbed you, troubling your minds by what they said. [25]So we all agreed to choose some men and send them to you with our dear friends Barnabas and Paul— [26]men who have risked their lives for the name of our Lord Jesus Christ.

---

[a]14 Greek *Simeon*, a variant of *Simon*; that is, Peter   [b]17 Amos 9:11,12   [c]17,18 Some manuscripts
things'— / [18]*known to the Lord for ages is his work*

²⁷Therefore we are sending Judas and Silas to confirm by word of mouth what we are writing. ²⁸It seemed good to the Holy Spirit and to us not to burden you with anything beyond the following requirements: ²⁹You are to abstain from food sacrificed to idols, from blood, from the meat of strangled animals and from sexual immorality. You will do well to avoid these things.

Farewell.

³⁰The men were sent off and went down to Antioch, where they gathered the church together and delivered the letter. ³¹The people read it and were glad for its encouraging message. ³²Judas and Silas, who themselves were prophets, said much to encourage and strengthen the brothers. ³³After spending some time there, they were sent off by the brothers with the blessing of peace to return to those who had sent them.ᵃ ³⁵But Paul and Barnabas remained in Antioch, where they and many others taught and preached the word of the Lord.   Ac 8:4; 1Co 16:11

Disagreement Between Paul and Barnabas

³⁶Some time later Paul said to Barnabas, "Let us go back and visit the brothers in all the towns where we preached the word of the Lord and see how they are doing." ³⁷Barnabas wanted to take John, also called Mark, with them, ³⁸but Paul did not think it wise to take him, because he had deserted them in Pamphylia and had not continued with them in the work. ³⁹They had such a sharp disagreement that they parted company. Barnabas took Mark and sailed for Cyprus, ⁴⁰but Paul chose Silas and left, commended by the brothers to the grace of the Lord. ⁴¹He went through Syria and Cilicia, strengthening the churches.   Ac 12:12; 13:13

Timothy Joins Paul and Silas

16 He came to Derbe and then to Lystra, where a disciple named Timothy lived, whose mother was a Jewess and a believer, but whose father was a Greek. ²The brothers at Lystra and Iconium spoke well of him. ³Paul wanted to take him along on the journey, so he circumcised him because of the Jews who lived in that area, for they all knew that his father was a Greek. ⁴As they traveled from town to town, they delivered the decisions reached by the apostles and elders in Jerusalem for the people to obey. ⁵So the churches were strengthened in the faith and grew daily in numbers.   Ac 9:31

Paul's Vision of the Man of Macedonia

⁶Paul and his companions trav-

ᵃ 33 Some manuscripts them, ³⁴but Silas decided to remain there

eled throughout the region of Phrygia and Galatia, having been kept by the Holy Spirit from preaching the word in the province of Asia. [7]When they came to the border of Mysia, they tried to enter Bithynia, but the Spirit of Jesus would not allow them to. [8]So they passed by Mysia and went down to Troas. [9]During the night Paul had a vision of a man of Macedonia standing and begging him, "Come over to Macedonia and help us." [10]After Paul had seen the vision, we got ready at once to leave for Macedonia, concluding that God had called us to preach the gospel to them.   Ac 9:10; Ro 8:9

Lydia's Conversion in Philippi

[11]From Troas we put out to sea and sailed straight for Samothrace, and the next day on to Neapolis. [12]From there we traveled to Philippi, a Roman colony and the leading city of that district of Macedonia. And we stayed there several days.   Php 1:1; 1Th 2:2

[13]On the Sabbath we went outside the city gate to the river, where we expected to find a place of prayer. We sat down and began to speak to the women who had gathered there. [14]One of those listening was a woman named Lydia, a dealer in purple cloth from the city of Thyatira, who was a worshiper of God. The Lord opened her heart to respond to Paul's message. [15]When she and the members of her household were bap-

tized, she invited us to her home. "If you consider me a believer in the Lord," she said, "come and stay at my house." And she persuaded us.   Lk 24:45; Ac 13:14

Paul and Silas in Prison

[16]Once when we were going to the place of prayer, we were met by a slave girl who had a spirit by which she predicted the future. She earned a great deal of money for her owners by fortune-telling. [17]This girl followed Paul and the rest of us, shouting, "These men are servants of the Most High God, who are telling you the way to be saved." [18]She kept this up for many days. Finally Paul became so troubled that he turned around and said to the spirit, "In the name of Jesus Christ I command you to come out of her!" At that moment the spirit left her.   Mk 16:17; 1Sa 28:3,7

[19]When the owners of the slave girl realized that their hope of making money was gone, they seized Paul and Silas and dragged them into the marketplace to face the authorities. [20]They brought them before the magistrates and said, "These men are Jews, and are throwing our city into an uproar [21]by advocating customs unlawful for us Romans to accept or practice."   Ac 17:6; 19:25-26

[22]The crowd joined in the attack against Paul and Silas, and the magistrates ordered them to be stripped and beaten. [23]After they had been severely flogged, they

were thrown into prison, and the jailer was commanded to guard them carefully. 24Upon receiving such orders, he put them in the inner cell and fastened their feet in the stocks.   Jer 20:2-3; 2Co 11:25; 1Th 2:2

25About midnight Paul and Silas were praying and singing hymns to God, and the other prisoners were listening to them. 26Suddenly there was such a violent earthquake that the foundations of the prison were shaken. At once all the prison doors flew open, and everybody's chains came loose. 27The jailer woke up, and when he saw the prison doors open, he drew his sword and was about to kill himself because he thought the prisoners had escaped. 28But Paul shouted, "Don't harm yourself! We are all here!"   Ac 4:31; 12:19; Eph 5:19

29The jailer called for lights, rushed in and fell trembling before Paul and Silas. 30He then brought them out and asked, "Sirs, what must I do to be saved?"   Ac 2:37

31They replied, "Believe in the Lord Jesus, and you will be saved—you and your household." 32Then they spoke the word of the Lord to him and to all the others in his house. 33At that hour of the night the jailer took them and washed their wounds; then immediately he and all his family were baptized. 34The jailer brought them into his house and set a meal before them; he was filled with joy because he had come to believe in God—he and his whole family.

35When it was daylight, the magistrates sent their officers to the jailer with the order: "Release those men." 36The jailer told Paul, "The magistrates have ordered that you and Silas be released. Now you can leave. Go in peace."

37But Paul said to the officers: "They beat us publicly without a trial, even though we are Roman citizens, and threw us into prison. And now do they want to get rid of us quietly? No! Let them come themselves and escort us out."

38The officers reported this to the magistrates, and when they heard that Paul and Silas were Roman citizens, they were alarmed. 39They came to appease them and escorted them from the prison, requesting them to leave the city. 40After Paul and Silas came out of the prison, they went to Lydia's house, where they met with the brothers and encouraged them. Then they left.   Mt 8:34; Ac 1:16

In Thessalonica

17 When they had passed through Amphipolis and Apollonia, they came to Thessalonica, where there was a Jewish synagogue. 2As his custom was, Paul went into the synagogue, and on three Sabbath days he reasoned with them from the Scriptures, 3explaining and proving that the

Christ^a had to suffer and rise from the dead. "This Jesus I am proclaiming to you is the Christ,^a" he said. ⁴Some of the Jews were persuaded and joined Paul and Silas, as did a large number of God-fearing Greeks and not a few prominent women.   Ac 15:22; 18:28

⁵But the Jews were jealous; so they rounded up some bad characters from the marketplace, formed a mob and started a riot in the city. They rushed to Jason's house in search of Paul and Silas in order to bring them out to the crowd.^b ⁶But when they did not find them, they dragged Jason and some other brothers before the city officials, shouting: "These men who have caused trouble all over the world have now come here, ⁷and Jason has welcomed them into his house. They are all defying Caesar's decrees, saying that there is another king, one called Jesus." ⁸When they heard this, the crowd and the city officials were thrown into turmoil. ⁹Then they made Jason and the others post bond and let them go.   Lk 23:2; Ro 16:21

In Berea

¹⁰As soon as it was night, the brothers sent Paul and Silas away to Berea. On arriving there, they went to the Jewish synagogue. ¹¹Now the Bereans were of more noble character than the Thessalonians, for they received the message with great eagerness and examined the Scriptures every day to see if what Paul said was true. ¹²Many of the Jews believed, as did also a number of prominent Greek women and many Greek men.

¹³When the Jews in Thessalonica learned that Paul was preaching the word of God at Berea, they went there too, agitating the crowds and stirring them up. ¹⁴The brothers immediately sent Paul to the coast, but Silas and Timothy stayed at Berea. ¹⁵The men who escorted Paul brought him to Athens and then left with instructions for Silas and Timothy to join him as soon as possible.   Ac 16:1; 18:5

In Athens

¹⁶While Paul was waiting for them in Athens, he was greatly distressed to see that the city was full of idols. ¹⁷So he reasoned in the synagogue with the Jews and the God-fearing Greeks, as well as in the marketplace day by day with those who happened to be there. ¹⁸A group of Epicurean and Stoic philosophers began to dispute with him. Some of them asked, "What is this babbler trying to say?" Others remarked, "He seems to be advocating foreign gods." They said this because Paul was preaching the good news about Jesus and the resurrection. ¹⁹Then they took him and brought him to a meeting of the Areopagus, where

^a3 Or Messiah   ^b5 Or the assembly of the people

they said to him, "May we know what this new teaching is that you are presenting? ²⁰You are bringing some strange ideas to our ears, and we want to know what they mean." ²¹(All the Athenians and the foreigners who lived there spent their time doing nothing but talking about and listening to the latest ideas.) Ac 4:2; 9:20

²²Paul then stood up in the meeting of the Areopagus and said: "Men of Athens! I see that in every way you are very religious. ²³For as I walked around and looked carefully at your objects of worship, I even found an altar with this inscription: TO AN UNKNOWN GOD. Now what you worship as something unknown I am going to proclaim to you. Jn 4:22

²⁴"The God who made the world and everything in it is the Lord of heaven and earth and does not live in temples built by hands. ²⁵And he is not served by human hands, as if he needed anything, because he himself gives all men life and breath and everything else. ²⁶From one man he made every nation of men, that they should inhabit the whole earth; and he determined the times set for them and the exact places where they should live. ²⁷God did this so that men would seek him and perhaps reach out for him and find him, though he is not far from each one of us. ²⁸'For in him we live and move and have our being.' As some of your own poets have said, 'We are his offspring.' Dt 32:8; Ac 14:17

²⁹"Therefore since we are God's offspring, we should not think that the divine being is like gold or silver or stone—an image made by man's design and skill. ³⁰In the past God overlooked such ignorance, but now he commands all people everywhere to repent. ³¹For he has set a day when he will judge the world with justice by the man he has appointed. He has given proof of this to all men by raising him from the dead." Lk 24:47

³²When they heard about the resurrection of the dead, some of them sneered, but others said, "We want to hear you again on this subject." ³³At that, Paul left the Council. ³⁴A few men became followers of Paul and believed. Among them was Dionysius, a member of the Areopagus, also a woman named Damaris, and a number of others. ver 19,22

In Corinth

18 After this, Paul left Athens and went to Corinth. ²There he met a Jew named Aquila, a native of Pontus, who had recently come from Italy with his wife Priscilla, because Claudius had ordered all the Jews to leave Rome. Paul went to see them, ³and because he was a tentmaker as they were, he stayed and worked with them. ⁴Every Sabbath he reasoned in the synagogue, trying to persuade Jews and Greeks.

5When Silas and Timothy came from Macedonia, Paul devoted himself exclusively to preaching, testifying to the Jews that Jesus was the Christ.*a* 6But when the Jews opposed Paul and became abusive, he shook out his clothes in protest and said to them, "Your blood be on your own heads! I am clear of my responsibility. From now on I will go to the Gentiles."

7Then Paul left the synagogue and went next door to the house of Titius Justus, a worshiper of God. 8Crispus, the synagogue ruler, and his entire household believed in the Lord; and many of the Corinthians who heard him believed and were baptized.   Mk 5:22; 1Co 1:14

9One night the Lord spoke to Paul in a vision: "Do not be afraid; keep on speaking, do not be silent. 10For I am with you, and no one is going to attack and harm you, because I have many people in this city." 11So Paul stayed for a year and a half, teaching them the word of God.   Mt 28:20

12While Gallio was proconsul of Achaia, the Jews made a united attack on Paul and brought him into court. 13"This man," they charged, "is persuading the people to worship God in ways contrary to the law."   Ro 15:26; 1Co 16:15

14Just as Paul was about to speak, Gallio said to the Jews, "If you Jews were making a complaint about some misdemeanor or seri-ous crime, it would be reasonable for me to listen to you. 15But since it involves questions about words and names and your own law— settle the matter yourselves. I will not be a judge of such things." 16So he had them ejected from the court. 17Then they all turned on Sosthenes the synagogue ruler and beat him in front of the court. But Gallio showed no concern what-ever.   Ac 23:29; 1Co 1:1

Priscilla, Aquila and Apollos

18Paul stayed on in Corinth for some time. Then he left the brothers and sailed for Syria, accompanied by Priscilla and Aquila. Before he sailed, he had his hair cut off at Cenchrea because of a vow he had taken. 19They arrived at Ephesus, where Paul left Priscilla and Aquila. He himself went into the synagogue and reasoned with the Jews. 20When they asked him to spend more time with them, he declined. 21But as he left, he promised, "I will come back if it is God's will." Then he set sail from Ephesus. 22When he landed at Caesarea, he went up and greeted the church and then went down to Antioch.   Ac 11:19; 1Co 4:19

23After spending some time in Antioch, Paul set out from there and traveled from place to place throughout the region of Galatia and Phrygia, strengthening all the disciples.   Ac 14:22; 16:6

²⁴Meanwhile a Jew named Apollos, a native of Alexandria, came to Ephesus. He was a learned man, with a thorough knowledge of the Scriptures. ²⁵He had been instructed in the way of the Lord, and he spoke with great fervor*a* and taught about Jesus accurately, though he knew only the baptism of John. ²⁶He began to speak boldly in the synagogue. When Priscilla and Aquila heard him, they invited him to their home and explained to him the way of God more adequately.   Ac 19:3; 1Co 1:12

²⁷When Apollos wanted to go to Achaia, the brothers encouraged him and wrote to the disciples there to welcome him. On arriving, he was a great help to those who by grace had believed. ²⁸For he vigorously refuted the Jews in public debate, proving from the Scriptures that Jesus was the Christ.

Paul in Ephesus

19 While Apollos was at Corinth, Paul took the road through the interior and arrived at Ephesus. There he found some disciples ²and asked them, "Did you receive the Holy Spirit when*b* you believed?"   Ac 18:1,19

They answered, "No, we have not even heard that there is a Holy Spirit."

³So Paul asked, "Then what baptism did you receive?"

"John's baptism," they replied.

⁴Paul said, "John's baptism was a baptism of repentance. He told the people to believe in the one coming after him, that is, in Jesus." ⁵On hearing this, they were baptized into*c* the name of the Lord Jesus. ⁶When Paul placed his hands on them, the Holy Spirit came on them, and they spoke in tongues*d* and prophesied. ⁷There were about twelve men in all.

⁸Paul entered the synagogue and spoke boldly there for three months, arguing persuasively about the kingdom of God. ⁹But some of them became obstinate; they refused to believe and publicly maligned the Way. So Paul left them. He took the disciples with him and had discussions daily in the lecture hall of Tyrannus. ¹⁰This went on for two years, so that all the Jews and Greeks who lived in the province of Asia heard the word of the Lord.   Ac 1:3; 9:2; 20:31

¹¹God did extraordinary miracles through Paul, ¹²so that even handkerchiefs and aprons that had touched him were taken to the sick, and their illnesses were cured and the evil spirits left them.

¹³Some Jews who went around driving out evil spirits tried to invoke the name of the Lord Jesus over those who were demon-possessed. They would say, "In the name of Jesus, whom Paul preaches, I command you to come out." ¹⁴Seven sons of Sceva, a Jew-

---

a 25 Or *with fervor in the Spirit*   *b 2* Or *after*   *c 5* Or *in*   *d 6* Or *other languages* ish chief priest, were doing this. ¹⁵One day, the evil spirit answered them, "Jesus I know, and I know about Paul, but who are you?" ¹⁶Then the man who had the evil spirit jumped on them and overpowered them all. He gave them such a beating that they ran out of the house naked and bleeding.

¹⁷When this became known to the Jews and Greeks living in Ephesus, they were all seized with fear, and the name of the Lord Jesus was held in high honor. ¹⁸Many of those who believed now came and openly confessed their evil deeds. ¹⁹A number who had practiced sorcery brought their scrolls together and burned them publicly. When they calculated the value of the scrolls, the total came to fifty thousand drachmas.ᵃ ²⁰In this way the word of the Lord spread widely and grew in power.

²¹After all this had happened, Paul decided to go to Jerusalem, passing through Macedonia and Achaia. "After I have been there," he said, "I must visit Rome also." ²²He sent two of his helpers, Timothy and Erastus, to Macedonia, while he stayed in the province of Asia a little longer.   Ro 15:25; 16:23

The Riot in Ephesus

²³About that time there arose a great disturbance about the Way. ²⁴A silversmith named Demetrius, who made silver shrines of Artemis, brought in no little business for the craftsmen. ²⁵He called them together, along with the workmen in related trades, and said: "Men, you know we receive a good income from this business. ²⁶And you see and hear how this fellow Paul has convinced and led astray large numbers of people here in Ephesus and in practically the whole province of Asia. He says that man-made gods are no gods at all. ²⁷There is danger not only that our trade will lose its good name, but also that the temple of the great goddess Artemis will be discredited, and the goddess herself, who is worshiped throughout the province of Asia and the world, will be robbed of her divine majesty."   Ps 115:4; Isa 44:10-20; Jer 10:3-5

²⁸When they heard this, they were furious and began shouting: "Great is Artemis of the Ephesians!" ²⁹Soon the whole city was in an uproar. The people seized Gaius and Aristarchus, Paul's traveling companions from Macedonia, and rushed as one man into the theater. ³⁰Paul wanted to appear before the crowd, but the disciples would not let him. ³¹Even some of the officials of the province, friends of Paul, sent him a message begging him not to venture into the theater.   Ac 20:4; 27:2; Col 4:10

³²The assembly was in confusion: Some were shouting one

ᵃ19 A drachma was a silver coin worth about a day's wages.

thing, some another. Most of the people did not even know why they were there. ³³The Jews pushed Alexander to the front, and some of the crowd shouted instructions to him. He motioned for silence in order to make a defense before the people. ³⁴But when they realized he was a Jew, they all shouted in unison for about two hours: "Great is Artemis of the Ephesians!"   Ac 12:17; 21:34

³⁵The city clerk quieted the crowd and said: "Men of Ephesus, doesn't all the world know that the city of Ephesus is the guardian of the temple of the great Artemis and of her image, which fell from heaven? ³⁶Therefore, since these facts are undeniable, you ought to be quiet and not do anything rash. ³⁷You have brought these men here, though they have neither robbed temples nor blasphemed our goddess. ³⁸If, then, Demetrius and his fellow craftsmen have a grievance against anybody, the courts are open and there are proconsuls. They can press charges. ³⁹If there is anything further you want to bring up, it must be settled in a legal assembly. ⁴⁰As it is, we are in danger of being charged with rioting because of today's events. In that case we would not be able to account for this commotion, since there is no reason for it." ⁴¹After he had said this, he dismissed the assembly.   Ac 18:19

Through Macedonia and Greece

20 When the uproar had ended, Paul sent for the disciples and, after encouraging them, said good-by and set out for Macedonia. ²He traveled through that area, speaking many words of encouragement to the people, and finally arrived in Greece, ³where he stayed three months. Because the Jews made a plot against him just as he was about to sail for Syria, he decided to go back through Macedonia. ⁴He was accompanied by Sopater son of Pyrrhus from Berea, Aristarchus and Secundus from Thessalonica, Gaius from Derbe, Timothy also, and Tychicus and Trophimus from the province of Asia. ⁵These men went on ahead and waited for us at Troas. ⁶But we sailed from Philippi after the Feast of Unleavened Bread, and five days later joined the others at Troas, where we stayed seven days.

Eutychus Raised From the Dead at Troas

⁷On the first day of the week we came together to break bread. Paul spoke to the people and, because he intended to leave the next day, kept on talking until midnight. ⁸There were many lamps in the upstairs room where we were meeting. ⁹Seated in a window was a young man named Eutychus, who was sinking into a deep sleep as Paul talked on and on. When he

was sound asleep, he fell to the ground from the third story and was picked up dead. ¹⁰Paul went down, threw himself on the young man and put his arms around him. "Don't be alarmed," he said. "He's alive!" ¹¹Then he went upstairs again and broke bread and ate. After talking until daylight, he left. ¹²The people took the young man home alive and were greatly comforted.   Mt 9:23-24; Ac 1:13; 1Co 16:2

Paul's Farewell to the Ephesian Elders

¹³We went on ahead to the ship and sailed for Assos, where we were going to take Paul aboard. He had made this arrangement because he was going there on foot. ¹⁴When he met us at Assos, we took him aboard and went on to Mitylene. ¹⁵The next day we set sail from there and arrived off Kios. The day after that we crossed over to Samos, and on the following day arrived at Miletus. ¹⁶Paul had decided to sail past Ephesus to avoid spending time in the province of Asia, for he was in a hurry to reach Jerusalem, if possible, by the day of Pentecost.   Ac 2:1; 19:21

¹⁷From Miletus, Paul sent to Ephesus for the elders of the church. ¹⁸When they arrived, he said to them: "You know how I lived the whole time I was with you, from the first day I came into the province of Asia. ¹⁹I served the

Lord with great humility and with tears, although I was severely tested by the plots of the Jews. ²⁰You know that I have not hesitated to preach anything that would be helpful to you but have taught you publicly and from house to house. ²¹I have declared to both Jews and Greeks that they must turn to God in repentance and have faith in our Lord Jesus.   Ac 2:38; 18:5

²²"And now, compelled by the Spirit, I am going to Jerusalem, not knowing what will happen to me there. ²³I only know that in every city the Holy Spirit warns me that prison and hardships are facing me. ²⁴However, I consider my life worth nothing to me, if only I may finish the race and complete the task the Lord Jesus has given me—the task of testifying to the gospel of God's grace.   Ac 21:13; Gal 1:1

²⁵"Now I know that none of you among whom I have gone about preaching the kingdom will ever see me again. ²⁶Therefore, I declare to you today that I am innocent of the blood of all men. ²⁷For I have not hesitated to proclaim to you the whole will of God. ²⁸Keep watch over yourselves and all the flock of which the Holy Spirit has made you overseers.ᵃ Be shepherds of the church of God,ᵇ which he bought with his own blood. ²⁹I know that after I leave, savage wolves will come in among you and will not spare the flock.

ᵃ28 Traditionally bishops   ᵇ28 Many manuscripts of the Lord

[30]Even from your own number men will arise and distort the truth in order to draw away disciples after them. [31]So be on your guard! Remember that for three years I never stopped warning each of you night and day with tears.

[32]"Now I commit you to God and to the word of his grace, which can build you up and give you an inheritance among all those who are sanctified. [33]I have not coveted anyone's silver or gold or clothing. [34]You yourselves know that these hands of mine have supplied my own needs and the needs of my companions. [35]In everything I did, I showed you that by this kind of hard work we must help the weak, remembering the words the Lord Jesus himself said: 'It is more blessed to give than to receive.'"

[36]When he had said this, he knelt down with all of them and prayed. [37]They all wept as they embraced him and kissed him. [38]What grieved them most was his statement that they would never see his face again. Then they accompanied him to the ship.

On to Jerusalem

21 After we had torn ourselves away from them, we put out to sea and sailed straight to Cos. The next day we went to Rhodes and from there to Patara. [2]We found a ship crossing over to Phoenicia, went on board and set sail. [3]After sighting Cyprus and passing to the south of it, we sailed on to Syria. We landed at Tyre, where our ship was to unload its cargo. [4]Finding the disciples there, we stayed with them seven days. Through the Spirit they urged Paul not to go on to Jerusalem. [5]But when our time was up, we left and continued on our way. All the disciples and their wives and children accompanied us out of the city, and there on the beach we knelt to pray. [6]After saying good-by to each other, we went aboard the ship, and they returned home.

[7]We continued our voyage from Tyre and landed at Ptolemais, where we greeted the brothers and stayed with them for a day. [8]Leaving the next day, we reached Caesarea and stayed at the house of Philip the evangelist, one of the Seven. [9]He had four unmarried daughters who prophesied.   Ac 6:5

[10]After we had been there a number of days, a prophet named Agabus came down from Judea. [11]Coming over to us, he took Paul's belt, tied his own hands and feet with it and said, "The Holy Spirit says, 'In this way the Jews of Jerusalem will bind the owner of this belt and will hand him over to the Gentiles.'"   1Ki 22:11; Ac 11:28

[12]When we heard this, we and the people there pleaded with Paul not to go up to Jerusalem. [13]Then Paul answered, "Why are you weeping and breaking my heart? I am ready not only to be bound, but also to die in Jerusalem for the name of the Lord Jesus." [14]When

he would not be dissuaded, we gave up and said, "The Lord's will be done." Ac 9:16; 20:24

15After this, we got ready and went up to Jerusalem. 16Some of the disciples from Caesarea accompanied us and brought us to the home of Mnason, where we were to stay. He was a man from Cyprus and one of the early disciples. Ac 8:40; 19:21

Paul's Arrival at Jerusalem

17When we arrived at Jerusalem, the brothers received us warmly. 18The next day Paul and the rest of us went to see James, and all the elders were present. 19Paul greeted them and reported in detail what God had done among the Gentiles through his ministry. Ac 1:17; 15:4

20When they heard this, they praised God. Then they said to Paul: "You see, brother, how many thousands of Jews have believed, and all of them are zealous for the law. 21They have been informed that you teach all the Jews who live among the Gentiles to turn away from Moses, telling them not to circumcise their children or live according to our customs. 22What shall we do? They will certainly hear that you have come, 23so do what we tell you. There are four men with us who have made a vow. 24Take these men, join in their purification rites and pay their expenses, so that they can have their heads shaved. Then everybody will know there is no

truth in these reports about you, but that you yourself are living in obedience to the law. 25As for the Gentile believers, we have written to them our decision that they should abstain from food sacrificed to idols, from blood, from the meat of strangled animals and from sexual immorality." Ac 18:18

26The next day Paul took the men and purified himself along with them. Then he went to the temple to give notice of the date when the days of purification would end and the offering would be made for each of them.

Paul Arrested

27When the seven days were nearly over, some Jews from the province of Asia saw Paul at the temple. They stirred up the whole crowd and seized him, 28shouting, "Men of Israel, help us! This is the man who teaches all men everywhere against our people and our law and this place. And besides, he has brought Greeks into the temple area and defiled this holy place." 29(They had previously seen Trophimus the Ephesian in the city with Paul and assumed that Paul had brought him into the temple area.) Ac 20:4; 24:18

30The whole city was aroused, and the people came running from all directions. Seizing Paul, they dragged him from the temple, and immediately the gates were shut. 31While they were trying to kill him, news reached the commander of the Roman troops that the whole city of Jerusalem was in an uproar. **32**He at once took some officers and soldiers and ran down to the crowd. When the rioters saw the commander and his soldiers, they stopped beating Paul.

33The commander came up and arrested him and ordered him to be bound with two chains. Then he asked who he was and what he had done. **34**Some in the crowd shouted one thing and some another, and since the commander could not get at the truth because of the uproar, he ordered that Paul be taken into the barracks. **35**When Paul reached the steps, the violence of the mob was so great he had to be carried by the soldiers. **36**The crowd that followed kept shouting, "Away with him!"

Paul Speaks to the Crowd

37As the soldiers were about to take Paul into the barracks, he asked the commander, "May I say something to you?"

"Do you speak Greek?" he replied. **38**"Aren't you the Egyptian who started a revolt and led four thousand terrorists out into the desert some time ago?" Mt 24:26

39Paul answered, "I am a Jew, from Tarsus in Cilicia, a citizen of no ordinary city. Please let me speak to the people." Ac 9:11; 22:3

40Having received the commander's permission, Paul stood on the steps and motioned to the crowd. When they were all silent, he said to them in Aramaic*a*:

22 **1**"Brothers and fathers, listen now to my defense."

2When they heard him speak to them in Aramaic, they became very quiet. Jn 5:2; Ac 21:40

Then Paul said: **3**"I am a Jew, born in Tarsus of Cilicia, but brought up in this city. Under Gamaliel I was thoroughly trained in the law of our fathers and was just as zealous for God as any of you are today. **4**I persecuted the followers of this Way to their death, arresting both men and women and throwing them into prison, **5**as also the high priest and all the Council can testify. I even obtained letters from them to their brothers in Damascus, and went there to bring these people as prisoners to Jerusalem to be punished. Ac 21:20; 26:5

6"About noon as I came near Damascus, suddenly a bright light from heaven flashed around me. **7**I fell to the ground and heard a voice say to me, 'Saul! Saul! Why do you persecute me?' Ac 9:3

8" 'Who are you, Lord?' I asked.

" 'I am Jesus of Nazareth, whom you are persecuting,' he replied. **9**My companions saw the light, but they did not understand the voice of him who was speaking to me.

10" 'What shall I do, Lord?' I asked.

" 'Get up,' the Lord said, 'and go

a 40 Or possibly *Hebrew*; also in 22:2

into Damascus. There you will be told all that you have been assigned to do.' **11**My companions led me by the hand into Damascus, because the brilliance of the light had blinded me.   Ac 9:8; 16:30

12"A man named Ananias came to see me. He was a devout observer of the law and highly respected by all the Jews living there. **13**He stood beside me and said, 'Brother Saul, receive your sight!' And at that very moment I was able to see him.   Ac 9:17; 10:22

14"Then he said: 'The God of our fathers has chosen you to know his will and to see the Righteous One and to hear words from his mouth. **15**You will be his witness to all men of what you have seen and heard. **16**And now what are you waiting for? Get up, be baptized and wash your sins away, calling on his name.'   Ac 9:1-22; 26:9-18

17"When I returned to Jerusalem and was praying at the temple, I fell into a trance **18**and saw the Lord speaking. 'Quick!' he said to me. 'Leave Jerusalem immediately, because they will not accept your testimony about me.'   Ac 9:26

19" 'Lord,' I replied, 'these men know that I went from one synagogue to another to imprison and beat those who believe in you. **20**And when the blood of your martyr[a] Stephen was shed, I stood there giving my approval and

guarding the clothes of those who were killing him.'   Ac 8:1,3

21"Then the Lord said to me, 'Go; I will send you far away to the Gentiles.' "   Ac 9:15; 13:46

Paul the Roman Citizen

22The crowd listened to Paul until he said this. Then they raised their voices and shouted, "Rid the earth of him! He's not fit to live!"

23As they were shouting and throwing off their cloaks and flinging dust into the air, **24**the commander ordered Paul to be taken into the barracks. He directed that he be flogged and questioned in order to find out why the people were shouting at him like this. **25**As they stretched him out to flog him, Paul said to the centurion standing there, "Is it legal for you to flog a Roman citizen who hasn't even been found guilty?"   2Sa 16:13

26When the centurion heard this, he went to the commander and reported it. "What are you going to do?" he asked. "This man is a Roman citizen."

27The commander went to Paul and asked, "Tell me, are you a Roman citizen?"

"Yes, I am," he answered.

28Then the commander said, "I had to pay a big price for my citizenship."

"But I was born a citizen," Paul replied.

29Those who were about to

---

a20 Or *witness*

question him withdrew immediately. The commander himself was alarmed when he realized that he had put Paul, a Roman citizen, in chains. Ac 16:38

Before the Sanhedrin

³⁰The next day, since the commander wanted to find out exactly why Paul was being accused by the Jews, he released him and ordered the chief priests and all the Sanhedrin to assemble. Then he brought Paul and had him stand before them. Mt 5:22; Ac 23:28

23 Paul looked straight at the Sanhedrin and said, "My brothers, I have fulfilled my duty to God in all good conscience to this day." ²At this the high priest Ananias ordered those standing near Paul to strike him on the mouth. ³Then Paul said to him, "God will strike you, you whitewashed wall! You sit there to judge me according to the law, yet you yourself violate the law by commanding that I be struck!"

⁴Those who were standing near Paul said, "You dare to insult God's high priest?"

⁵Paul replied, "Brothers, I did not realize that he was the high priest; for it is written: 'Do not speak evil about the ruler of your people.'ᵃ" Ex 22:28

⁶Then Paul, knowing that some of them were Sadducees and the others Pharisees, called out in the Sanhedrin, "My brothers, I am a Pharisee, the son of a Pharisee. I stand on trial because of my hope in the resurrection of the dead." ⁷When he said this, a dispute broke out between the Pharisees and the Sadducees, and the assembly was divided. ⁸(The Sadducees say that there is no resurrection, and that there are neither angels nor spirits, but the Pharisees acknowledge them all.) Mt 22:23

⁹There was a great uproar, and some of the teachers of the law who were Pharisees stood up and argued vigorously. "We find nothing wrong with this man," they said. "What if a spirit or an angel has spoken to him?" ¹⁰The dispute became so violent that the commander was afraid Paul would be torn to pieces by them. He ordered the troops to go down and take him away from them by force and bring him into the barracks.

¹¹The following night the Lord stood near Paul and said, "Take courage! As you have testified about me in Jerusalem, so you must also testify in Rome."

The Plot to Kill Paul

¹²The next morning the Jews formed a conspiracy and bound themselves with an oath not to eat or drink until they had killed Paul. ¹³More than forty men were involved in this plot. ¹⁴They went to the chief priests and elders and

ᵃ5 Exodus 22:28

said, "We have taken a solemn oath not to eat anything until we have killed Paul. ¹⁵Now then, you and the Sanhedrin petition the commander to bring him before you on the pretext of wanting more accurate information about his case. We are ready to kill him before he gets here." Ac 22:30

¹⁶But when the son of Paul's sister heard of this plot, he went into the barracks and told Paul.

¹⁷Then Paul called one of the centurions and said, "Take this young man to the commander; he has something to tell him." ¹⁸So he took him to the commander.

The centurion said, "Paul, the prisoner, sent for me and asked me to bring this young man to you because he has something to tell you." Eph 3:1

¹⁹The commander took the young man by the hand, drew him aside and asked, "What is it you want to tell me?"

²⁰He said: "The Jews have agreed to ask you to bring Paul before the Sanhedrin tomorrow on the pretext of wanting more accurate information about him. ²¹Don't give in to them, because more than forty of them are waiting in ambush for him. They have taken an oath not to eat or drink until they have killed him. They are ready now, waiting for your consent to their request." ver 14-15

²²The commander dismissed the young man and cautioned him, "Don't tell anyone that you have reported this to me."

Paul Transferred to Caesarea

²³Then he called two of his centurions and ordered them, "Get ready a detachment of two hundred soldiers, seventy horsemen and two hundred spearmenᵃ to go to Caesarea at nine tonight. ²⁴Provide mounts for Paul so that he may be taken safely to Governor Felix." Ac 24:1-3,10

²⁵He wrote a letter as follows:

²⁶Claudius Lysias,

To His Excellency, Governor Felix: Ac 24:3

Greetings. Ac 15:23

²⁷This man was seized by the Jews and they were about to kill him, but I came with my troops and rescued him, for I had learned that he is a Roman citizen. ²⁸I wanted to know why they were accusing him, so I brought him to their Sanhedrin. ²⁹I found that the accusation had to do with questions about their law, but there was no charge against him that deserved death or imprisonment. ³⁰When I was informed of a plot to be carried out against the man, I sent him to you at once. I also

---

ᵃ23 The meaning of the Greek for this word is uncertain.

ordered his accusers to present to you their case against him. Ac 24:19; 26:31

³¹So the soldiers, carrying out their orders, took Paul with them during the night and brought him as far as Antipatris. ³²The next day they let the cavalry go on with him, while they returned to the barracks. ³³When the cavalry arrived in Caesarea, they delivered the letter to the governor and handed Paul over to him. ³⁴The governor read the letter and asked what province he was from. Learning that he was from Cilicia, ³⁵he said, "I will hear your case when your accusers get here." Then he ordered that Paul be kept under guard in Herod's palace. Ac 21:39

The Trial Before Felix

24 Five days later the high priest Ananias went down to Caesarea with some of the elders and a lawyer named Tertullus, and they brought their charges against Paul before the governor. ²When Paul was called in, Tertullus presented his case before Felix: "We have enjoyed a long period of peace under you, and your foresight has brought about reforms in this nation. ³Everywhere and in every way, most excellent Felix, we acknowledge this with profound gratitude. ⁴But in order not to wea-

ry you further, I would request that you be kind enough to hear us briefly. Ac 23:2,24

⁵"We have found this man to be a troublemaker, stirring up riots among the Jews all over the world. He is a ringleader of the Nazarene sect ⁶and even tried to desecrate the temple; so we seized him. ⁸Byᵃ examining him yourself you will be able to learn the truth about all these charges we are bringing against him." Ac 16:20; 21:28

⁹The Jews joined in the accusation, asserting that these things were true. 1Th 2:16

¹⁰When the governor motioned for him to speak, Paul replied: "I know that for a number of years you have been a judge over this nation; so I gladly make my defense. ¹¹You can easily verify that no more than twelve days ago I went up to Jerusalem to worship. ¹²My accusers did not find me arguing with anyone at the temple, or stirring up a crowd in the synagogues or anywhere else in the city. ¹³And they cannot prove to you the charges they are now making against me. ¹⁴However, I admit that I worship the God of our fathers as a follower of the Way, which they call a sect. I believe everything that agrees with the Law and that is written in the Prophets, ¹⁵and I have the same hope in God as these men, that there will be a

---

ᵃ 6-8 Some manuscripts *him and wanted to judge him according to our law. ⁷But the commander, Lysias, came and with the use of much force snatched him from our hands ⁸and ordered his accusers to come before you.* By

resurrection of both the righteous and the wicked. [16]So I strive always to keep my conscience clear before God and man.   Ac 9:2; 23:1

[17]"After an absence of several years, I came to Jerusalem to bring my people gifts for the poor and to present offerings. [18]I was ceremonially clean when they found me in the temple courts doing this. There was no crowd with me, nor was I involved in any disturbance. [19]But there are some Jews from the province of Asia, who ought to be here before you and bring charges if they have anything against me. [20]Or these who are here should state what crime they found in me when I stood before the Sanhedrin— [21]unless it was this one thing I shouted as I stood in their presence: 'It is concerning the resurrection of the dead that I am on trial before you today.'"

[22]Then Felix, who was well acquainted with the Way, adjourned the proceedings. "When Lysias the commander comes," he said, "I will decide your case." [23]He ordered the centurion to keep Paul under guard but to give him some freedom and permit his friends to take care of his needs.   Ac 27:3; 28:16

[24]Several days later Felix came with his wife Drusilla, who was a Jewess. He sent for Paul and listened to him as he spoke about faith in Christ Jesus. [25]As Paul discoursed on righteousness, self-control and the judgment to come, Felix was afraid and said, "That's enough for now! You may leave. When I find it convenient, I will send for you." [26]At the same time he was hoping that Paul would offer him a bribe, so he sent for him frequently and talked with him.

[27]When two years had passed, Felix was succeeded by Porcius Festus, but because Felix wanted to grant a favor to the Jews, he left Paul in prison.   Ac 12:3; 25:1,4,9,14

The Trial Before Festus

25 Three days after arriving in the province, Festus went up from Caesarea to Jerusalem, [2]where the chief priests and Jewish leaders appeared before him and presented the charges against Paul. [3]They urgently requested Festus, as a favor to them, to have Paul transferred to Jerusalem, for they were preparing an ambush to kill him along the way. [4]Festus answered, "Paul is being held at Caesarea, and I myself am going there soon. [5]Let some of your leaders come with me and press charges against the man there, if he has done anything wrong."

[6]After spending eight or ten days with them, he went down to Caesarea, and the next day he convened the court and ordered that Paul be brought before him. [7]When Paul appeared, the Jews who had come down from Jerusalem stood around him, bringing many serious charges against him, which they could not prove.

[8]Then Paul made his defense: "I

have done nothing wrong against the law of the Jews or against the temple or against Caesar." Ac 6:13

⁹Festus, wishing to do the Jews a favor, said to Paul, "Are you willing to go up to Jerusalem and stand trial before me there on these charges?" Ac 12:3; 24:27

¹⁰Paul answered: "I am now standing before Caesar's court, where I ought to be tried. I have not done any wrong to the Jews, as you yourself know very well. ¹¹If, however, I am guilty of doing anything deserving death, I do not refuse to die. But if the charges brought against me by these Jews are not true, no one has the right to hand me over to them. I appeal to Caesar!" Ac 26:32; 28:19

¹²After Festus had conferred with his council, he declared: "You have appealed to Caesar. To Caesar you will go!"

Festus Consults King Agrippa

¹³A few days later King Agrippa and Bernice arrived at Caesarea to pay their respects to Festus. ¹⁴Since they were spending many days there, Festus discussed Paul's case with the king. He said: "There is a man here whom Felix left as a prisoner. ¹⁵When I went to Jerusalem, the chief priests and elders of the Jews brought charges against him and asked that he be condemned. Ac 24:1,27

¹⁶"I told them that it is not the Roman custom to hand over any man before he has faced his accusers and has had an opportunity to defend himself against their charges. ¹⁷When they came here with me, I did not delay the case, but convened the court the next day and ordered the man to be brought in. ¹⁸When his accusers got up to speak, they did not charge him with any of the crimes I had expected. ¹⁹Instead, they had some points of dispute with him about their own religion and about a dead man named Jesus who Paul claimed was alive. ²⁰I was at a loss how to investigate such matters; so I asked if he would be willing to go to Jerusalem and stand trial there on these charges. ²¹When Paul made his appeal to be held over for the Emperor's decision, I ordered him held until I could send him to Caesar." Ac 18:15; 23:29

²²Then Agrippa said to Festus, "I would like to hear this man myself."

He replied, "Tomorrow you will hear him." Ac 9:15

Paul Before Agrippa

²³The next day Agrippa and Bernice came with great pomp and entered the audience room with the high ranking officers and the leading men of the city. At the command of Festus, Paul was brought in. ²⁴Festus said: "King Agrippa, and all who are present with us, you see this man! The whole Jewish community has petitioned me about him in Jerusalem and here in Caesarea, shouting that he

ought not to live any longer. 25I found he had done nothing deserving of death, but because he made his appeal to the Emperor I decided to send him to Rome. 26But I have nothing definite to write to His Majesty about him. Therefore I have brought him before all of you, and especially before you, King Agrippa, so that as a result of this investigation I may have something to write. 27For I think it is unreasonable to send on a prisoner without specifying the charges against him." Ac 22:22; 23:9

26 Then Agrippa said to Paul, "You have permission to speak for yourself." Ac 9:15; 25:22

So Paul motioned with his hand and began his defense: 2"King Agrippa, I consider myself fortunate to stand before you today as I make my defense against all the accusations of the Jews, 3and especially so because you are well acquainted with all the Jewish customs and controversies. Therefore, I beg you to listen to me patiently. Ac 6:14; 25:19

4"The Jews all know the way I have lived ever since I was a child, from the beginning of my life in my own country, and also in Jerusalem. 5They have known me for a long time and can testify, if they are willing, that according to the strictest sect of our religion, I lived as a Pharisee. 6And now it is because of my hope in what God has promised our fathers that I am on trial today. 7This is the promise our twelve tribes are hoping to see fulfilled as they earnestly serve God day and night. O king, it is because of this hope that the Jews are accusing me. 8Why should any of you consider it incredible that God raises the dead? 1Th 3:10; 1Ti 5:5

9"I too was convinced that I ought to do all that was possible to oppose the name of Jesus of Nazareth. 10And that is just what I did in Jerusalem. On the authority of the chief priests I put many of the saints in prison, and when they were put to death, I cast my vote against them. 11Many a time I went from one synagogue to another to have them punished, and I tried to force them to blaspheme. In my obsession against them, I even went to foreign cities to persecute them. Ac 8:3; 1Ti 1:13

12"On one of these journeys I was going to Damascus with the authority and commission of the chief priests. 13About noon, O king, as I was on the road, I saw a light from heaven, brighter than the sun, blazing around me and my companions. 14We all fell to the ground, and I heard a voice saying to me in Aramaic,a 'Saul, Saul, why do you persecute me? It is hard for you to kick against the goads.' Ac 9:7

15"Then I asked, 'Who are you, Lord?'

a 14 Or Hebrew

" 'I am Jesus, whom you are persecuting,' the Lord replied. 16'Now get up and stand on your feet. I have appeared to you to appoint you as a servant and as a witness of what you have seen of me and what I will show you. 17I will rescue you from your own people and from the Gentiles. I am sending you to them 18to open their eyes and turn them from darkness to light, and from the power of Satan to God, so that they may receive forgiveness of sins and a place among those who are sanctified by faith in me.' Isa 35:5; 42:7,16; 1Pe 2:9

19"So then, King Agrippa, I was not disobedient to the vision from heaven. 20First to those in Damascus, then to those in Jerusalem and in all Judea, and to the Gentiles also, I preached that they should repent and turn to God and prove their repentance by their deeds. 21That is why the Jews seized me in the temple courts and tried to kill me. 22But I have had God's help to this very day, and so I stand here and testify to small and great alike. I am saying nothing beyond what the prophets and Moses said would happen— 23that the Christ[a] would suffer and, as the first to rise from the dead, would proclaim light to his own people and to the Gentiles."

24At this point Festus interrupted Paul's defense. "You are out of your mind, Paul!" he shouted.

"Your great learning is driving you insane." Jn 10:20; 1Co 4:10

25"I am not insane, most excellent Festus," Paul replied. "What I am saying is true and reasonable. 26The king is familiar with these things, and I can speak freely to him. I am convinced that none of this has escaped his notice, because it was not done in a corner. 27King Agrippa, do you believe the prophets? I know you do."

28Then Agrippa said to Paul, "Do you think that in such a short time you can persuade me to be a Christian?" Ac 11:26

29Paul replied, "Short time or long—I pray God that not only you but all who are listening to me today may become what I am, except for these chains." Ac 21:33

30The king rose, and with him the governor and Bernice and those sitting with them. 31They left the room, and while talking with one another, they said, "This man is not doing anything that deserves death or imprisonment." Ac 23:9

32Agrippa said to Festus, "This man could have been set free if he had not appealed to Caesar."

Paul Sails for Rome

27 When it was decided that we would sail for Italy, Paul and some other prisoners were handed over to a centurion named Julius, who belonged to the Imperial Regiment. 2We boarded a

---

[a] 23 Or *Messiah*

ship from Adramyttium about to sail for ports along the coast of the province of Asia, and we put out to sea. Aristarchus, a Macedonian from Thessalonica, was with us.

³The next day we landed at Sidon; and Julius, in kindness to Paul, allowed him to go to his friends so they might provide for his needs. ⁴From there we put out to sea again and passed to the lee of Cyprus because the winds were against us. ⁵When we had sailed across the open sea off the coast of Cilicia and Pamphylia, we landed at Myra in Lycia. ⁶There the centurion found an Alexandrian ship sailing for Italy and put us on board. ⁷We made slow headway for many days and had difficulty arriving off Cnidus. When the wind did not allow us to hold our course, we sailed to the lee of Crete, opposite Salmone. ⁸We moved along the coast with difficulty and came to a place called Fair Havens, near the town of Lasea.   Ac 24:23; 28:11

⁹Much time had been lost, and sailing had already become dangerous because by now it was after the Fast.ᵃ So Paul warned them, ¹⁰"Men, I can see that our voyage is going to be disastrous and bring great loss to ship and cargo, and to our own lives also." ¹¹But the centurion, instead of listening to what Paul said, followed the advice of the pilot and of the owner of the ship. ¹²Since the harbor was unsuitable to winter in, the majority decided that we should sail on, hoping to reach Phoenix and winter there. This was a harbor in Crete, facing both southwest and northwest.   Lev 23:27-29; Nu 29:7

The Storm

¹³When a gentle south wind began to blow, they thought they had obtained what they wanted; so they weighed anchor and sailed along the shore of Crete. ¹⁴Before very long, a wind of hurricane force, called the "northeaster," swept down from the island. ¹⁵The ship was caught by the storm and could not head into the wind; so we gave way to it and were driven along. ¹⁶As we passed to the lee of a small island called Cauda, we were hardly able to make the lifeboat secure. ¹⁷When the men had hoisted it aboard, they passed ropes under the ship itself to hold it together. Fearing that they would run aground on the sandbars of Syrtis, they lowered the sea anchor and let the ship be driven along. ¹⁸We took such a violent battering from the storm that the next day they began to throw the cargo overboard. ¹⁹On the third day, they threw the ship's tackle overboard with their own hands. ²⁰When neither sun nor stars appeared for many days and the storm continued raging, we finally

---

ᵃ9 That is, the Day of Atonement (Yom Kippur)

gave up all hope of being saved. ²¹After the men had gone a long time without food, Paul stood up before them and said: "Men, you should have taken my advice not to sail from Crete; then you would have spared yourselves this damage and loss. ²²But now I urge you to keep up your courage, because not one of you will be lost; only the ship will be destroyed. ²³Last night an angel of the God whose I am and whom I serve stood beside me ²⁴and said, 'Do not be afraid, Paul. You must stand trial before Caesar; and God has graciously given you the lives of all who sail with you.' ²⁵So keep up your courage, men, for I have faith in God that it will happen just as he told me. ²⁶Nevertheless, we must run aground on some island."   Ac 23:11

The Shipwreck

²⁷On the fourteenth night we were still being driven across the Adriatic*a* Sea, when about midnight the sailors sensed they were approaching land. ²⁸They took soundings and found that the water was a hundred and twenty feet*b* deep. A short time later they took soundings again and found it was ninety feet*c* deep. ²⁹Fearing that we would be dashed against the rocks, they dropped four anchors from the stern and prayed for daylight. ³⁰In an attempt to escape from the ship, the sailors let the lifeboat down into the sea, pretending they were going to lower some anchors from the bow. ³¹Then Paul said to the centurion and the soldiers, "Unless these men stay with the ship, you cannot be saved." ³²So the soldiers cut the ropes that held the lifeboat and let it fall away.   ver 16,24

³³Just before dawn Paul urged them all to eat. "For the last fourteen days," he said, "you have been in constant suspense and have gone without food—you haven't eaten anything. ³⁴Now I urge you to take some food. You need it to survive. Not one of you will lose a single hair from his head." ³⁵After he said this, he took some bread and gave thanks to God in front of them all. Then he broke it and began to eat. ³⁶They were all encouraged and ate some food themselves. ³⁷Altogether there were 276 of us on board. ³⁸When they had eaten as much as they wanted, they lightened the ship by throwing the grain into the sea.   Mt 10:30; 14:19

³⁹When daylight came, they did not recognize the land, but they saw a bay with a sandy beach, where they decided to run the ship aground if they could. ⁴⁰Cutting loose the anchors, they left them in the sea and at the same time untied the ropes that held the rud-

*a*27 In ancient times the name referred to an area extending well south of Italy.   *b*28 Greek *twenty orguias* (about 37 meters)   *c*28 Greek *fifteen orguias* (about 27 meters)

ders. Then they hoisted the foresail to the wind and made for the beach. **41**But the ship struck a sandbar and ran aground. The bow stuck fast and would not move, and the stern was broken to pieces by the pounding of the surf.

42The soldiers planned to kill the prisoners to prevent any of them from swimming away and escaping. **43**But the centurion wanted to spare Paul's life and kept them from carrying out their plan. He ordered those who could swim to jump overboard first and get to land. **44**The rest were to get there on planks or on pieces of the ship. In this way everyone reached land in safety.   ver 22,31

Ashore on Malta

28 Once safely on shore, we found out that the island was called Malta. **2**The islanders showed us unusual kindness. They built a fire and welcomed us all because it was raining and cold. **3**Paul gathered a pile of brushwood and, as he put it on the fire, a viper, driven out by the heat, fastened itself on his hand. **4**When the islanders saw the snake hanging from his hand, they said to each other, "This man must be a murderer; for though he escaped from the sea, Justice has not allowed him to live." **5**But Paul shook the snake off into the fire and suffered no ill effects. **6**The people expected him to swell up or suddenly fall dead, but after waiting a long time and see-

ing nothing unusual happen to him, they changed their minds and said he was a god.   Lk 10:19; Ac 14:11

7There was an estate nearby that belonged to Publius, the chief official of the island. He welcomed us to his home and for three days entertained us hospitably. **8**His father was sick in bed, suffering from fever and dysentery. Paul went in to see him and, after prayer, placed his hands on him and healed him. **9**When this had happened, the rest of the sick on the island came and were cured. **10**They honored us in many ways and when we were ready to sail, they furnished us with the supplies we needed.

Arrival at Rome

11After three months we put out to sea in a ship that had wintered in the island. It was an Alexandrian ship with the figurehead of the twin gods Castor and Pollux. **12**We put in at Syracuse and stayed there three days. **13**From there we set sail and arrived at Rhegium. The next day the south wind came up, and on the following day we reached Puteoli. **14**There we found some brothers who invited us to spend a week with them. And so we came to Rome. **15**The brothers there had heard that we were coming, and they traveled as far as the Forum of Appius and the Three Taverns to meet us. At the sight of these men Paul thanked God and was encouraged. **16**When we got to Rome, Paul was allowed to live by himself, with a soldier to guard him. Ac 1:16; 24:23; 27:6

Paul Preaches at Rome Under Guard

¹⁷Three days later he called together the leaders of the Jews. When they had assembled, Paul said to them: "My brothers, although I have done nothing against our people or against the customs of our ancestors, I was arrested in Jerusalem and handed over to the Romans. ¹⁸They examined me and wanted to release me, because I was not guilty of any crime deserving death. ¹⁹But when the Jews objected, I was compelled to appeal to Caesar—not that I had any charge to bring against my own people. ²⁰For this reason I have asked to see you and talk with you. It is because of the hope of Israel that I am bound with this chain." Ac 25:11; 26:6-7

²¹They replied, "We have not received any letters from Judea concerning you, and none of the brothers who have come from there has reported or said anything bad about you. ²²But we want to hear what your views are, for we know that people everywhere are talking against this sect." Ac 22:5

²³They arranged to meet Paul on a certain day, and came in even larger numbers to the place where he was staying. From morning till evening he explained and declared to them the kingdom of God and tried to convince them about Jesus from the Law of Moses and from the Prophets. ²⁴Some were convinced by what he said, but others would not believe. ²⁵They disagreed among themselves and began to leave after Paul had made this final statement: "The Holy Spirit spoke the truth to your forefathers when he said through Isaiah the prophet: Ac 14:4; 19:8

²⁶" 'Go to this people and say,
  "You will be ever hearing but
        never understanding;
  you will be ever seeing but
        never perceiving."
²⁷For this people's heart has
        become calloused;
  they hardly hear with their
        ears,
  and they have closed their
        eyes.
  Otherwise they might see with
        their eyes,
  hear with their ears,
  understand with their hearts
  and turn, and I would heal
        them.'ᵃ Mt 13:15

²⁸"Therefore I want you to know that God's salvation has been sent to the Gentiles, and they will listen!"ᵇ Ac 13:46

³⁰For two whole years Paul

ᵃ 27 Isaiah 6:9,10   ᵇ 28 Some manuscripts listen!" ²⁹After he said this, the Jews left, arguing vigorously among themselves.

stayed there in his own rented house and welcomed all who came to see him. ³¹Boldly and without hindrance he preached the kingdom of God and taught about the Lord Jesus Christ.   Ac 4:29

stayed there in his own rented house and welcomed all who came to see him. ³¹Boldly a

hindrance he preached the king- and and taught about the Christ.

Romans

1 Paul, a servant of Christ Jesus, called to be an apostle and set apart for the gospel of God— ²the gospel he promised beforehand through his prophets in the Holy Scriptures ³regarding his Son, who as to his human nature was a descendant of David, ⁴and who through the Spirit*a* of holiness was declared with power to be the Son of God*b* by his resurrection from the dead: Jesus Christ our Lord. ⁵Through him and for his name's sake, we received grace and apostleship to call people from among all the Gentiles to the obedience that comes from faith. ⁶And you also are among those who are called to belong to Jesus Christ.

⁷To all in Rome who are loved by God and called to be saints:

Grace and peace to you from God our Father and from the Lord Jesus Christ.　　　1Co 1:3; 1Pe 1:2

Paul's Longing to Visit Rome

⁸First, I thank my God through Jesus Christ for all of you, because your faith is being reported all over the world. ⁹God, whom I serve with my whole heart in preaching the gospel of his Son, is my witness how constantly I remember you ¹⁰in my prayers at all times; and I pray that now at last by God's will the way may be opened for me to come to you.　　　Ro 15:32; 2Ti 1:3

¹¹I long to see you so that I may impart to you some spiritual gift to make you strong— ¹²that is, that you and I may be mutually encouraged by each other's faith. ¹³I do not want you to be unaware, brothers, that I planned many times to come to you (but have been prevented from doing so until now) in order that I might have a harvest among you, just as I have had among the other Gentiles.

¹⁴I am obligated both to Greeks and non-Greeks, both to the wise and the foolish. ¹⁵That is why I am so eager to preach the gospel also to you who are at Rome.　　　Ro 15:20

¹⁶I am not ashamed of the gospel, because it is the power of God for the salvation of everyone who believes: first for the Jew, then for the Gentile. ¹⁷For in the gospel a righteousness from God is revealed, a righteousness that is by faith from first to last,*c* just as it is written: "The righteous will live by faith."*d*　　　Ro 3:21; 1Co 1:18; Gal 3:11

---

a 4 Or *who as to his spirit*　　　*b* 4 Or *was appointed to be the Son of God with power*　　　*c* 17 Or *is from faith to faith*　　　*d* 17 Hab. 2:4

God's Wrath Against Mankind

18The wrath of God is being revealed from heaven against all the godlessness and wickedness of men who suppress the truth by their wickedness, **19**since what may be known about God is plain to them, because God has made it plain to them. **20**For since the creation of the world God's invisible qualities—his eternal power and divine nature—have been clearly seen, being understood from what has been made, so that men are without excuse.   Ps 19:1-6; Ac 14:17

21For although they knew God, they neither glorified him as God nor gave thanks to him, but their thinking became futile and their foolish hearts were darkened. **22**Although they claimed to be wise, they became fools **23**and exchanged the glory of the immortal God for images made to look like mortal man and birds and animals and reptiles.   Ps 106:20; Jer 2:5

24Therefore God gave them over in the sinful desires of their hearts to sexual impurity for the degrading of their bodies with one another. **25**They exchanged the truth of God for a lie, and worshiped and served created things rather than the Creator—who is forever praised. Amen.   Jer 10:14; Eph 4:19

26Because of this, God gave them over to shameful lusts. Even their women exchanged natural relations for unnatural ones. **27**In the same way the men also abandoned natural relations with women and were inflamed with lust for one another. Men committed indecent acts with other men, and received in themselves the due penalty for their perversion.   Lev 18:22

28Furthermore, since they did not think it worthwhile to retain the knowledge of God, he gave them over to a depraved mind, to do what ought not to be done. **29**They have become filled with every kind of wickedness, evil, greed and depravity. They are full of envy, murder, strife, deceit and malice. They are gossips, **30**slanderers, God-haters, insolent, arrogant and boastful; they invent ways of doing evil; they disobey their parents; **31**they are senseless, faithless, heartless, ruthless. **32**Although they know God's righteous decree that those who do such things deserve death, they not only continue to do these very things but also approve of those who practice them.   Ro 6:23; 2Ti 3:2

God's Righteous Judgment

2 You, therefore, have no excuse, you who pass judgment on someone else, for at whatever point you judge the other, you are condemning yourself, because you who pass judgment do the same things. **2**Now we know that God's judgment against those who do such things is based on truth. **3**So when you, a mere man, pass judgment on them and yet do the same things, do you think you will escape God's judgment? [4]Or do you show contempt for the riches of his kindness, tolerance and patience, not realizing that God's kindness leads you toward repentance? Ex 34:6; Ro 3:25; 2Pe 3:9

[5]But because of your stubbornness and your unrepentant heart, you are storing up wrath against yourself for the day of God's wrath, when his righteous judgment will be revealed. [6]God "will give to each person according to what he has done."[a] [7]To those who by persistence in doing good seek glory, honor and immortality, he will give eternal life. [8]But for those who are self-seeking and who reject the truth and follow evil, there will be wrath and anger. [9]There will be trouble and distress for every human being who does evil: first for the Jew, then for the Gentile; [10]but glory, honor and peace for everyone who does good: first for the Jew, then for the Gentile. [11]For God does not show favoritism. Ac 10:34; 2Th 2:12

[12]All who sin apart from the law will also perish apart from the law, and all who sin under the law will be judged by the law. [13]For it is not those who hear the law who are righteous in God's sight, but it is those who obey the law who will be declared righteous. [14](Indeed, when Gentiles, who do not have the law, do by nature things required by the law, they are a law for themselves, even though they do not have the law, [15]since they show that the requirements of the law are written on their hearts, their consciences also bearing witness, and their thoughts now accusing, now even defending them.) [16]This will take place on the day when God will judge men's secrets through Jesus Christ, as my gospel declares. Ac 10:42; Jas 1:22-23,25

The Jews and the Law

[17]Now you, if you call yourself a Jew; if you rely on the law and brag about your relationship to God; [18]if you know his will and approve of what is superior because you are instructed by the law; [19]if you are convinced that you are a guide for the blind, a light for those who are in the dark, [20]an instructor of the foolish, a teacher of infants, because you have in the law the embodiment of knowledge and truth— [21]you, then, who teach others, do you not teach yourself? You who preach against stealing, do you steal? [22]You who say that people should not commit adultery, do you commit adultery? You who abhor idols, do you rob temples? [23]You who brag about the law, do you dishonor God by breaking the law? [24]As it is written: "God's name is blasphemed among the Gentiles because of you."[b] Isa 52:5; Mic 3:11

[25]Circumcision has value if you

a 6 Psalm 62:12; Prov. 24:12   b 24 Isaiah 52:5; Ezek. 36:22

observe the law, but if you break the law, you have become as though you had not been circumcised. 26If those who are not circumcised keep the law's requirements, will they not be regarded as though they were circumcised? 27The one who is not circumcised physically and yet obeys the law will condemn you who, even though you have the[a] written code and circumcision, are a lawbreaker.   Mt 12:41-42; Gal 5:3

28A man is not a Jew if he is only one outwardly, nor is circumcision merely outward and physical. 29No, a man is a Jew if he is one inwardly; and circumcision is circumcision of the heart, by the Spirit, not by the written code. Such a man's praise is not from men, but from God.   2Co 10:18; Gal 6:15

God's Faithfulness

3 What advantage, then, is there in being a Jew, or what value is there in circumcision? 2Much in every way! First of all, they have been entrusted with the very words of God.   Dt 4:8; Ps 147:19

3What if some did not have faith? Will their lack of faith nullify God's faithfulness? 4Not at all! Let God be true, and every man a liar. As it is written: Ps 116:11; Heb 4:2

"So that you may be proved
    right when you speak

and prevail when you
    judge."[b]   Ps 51:4

5But if our unrighteousness brings out God's righteousness more clearly, what shall we say? That God is unjust in bringing his wrath on us? (I am using a human argument.) 6Certainly not! If that were so, how could God judge the world? 7Someone might argue, "If my falsehood enhances God's truthfulness and so increases his glory, why am I still condemned as a sinner?" 8Why not say—as we are being slanderously reported as saying and as some claim that we say—"Let us do evil that good may result"? Their condemnation is deserved.   Ge 18:25; Gal 3:15

No One Is Righteous

9What shall we conclude then? Are we any better[c]? Not at all! We have already made the charge that Jews and Gentiles alike are all under sin. 10As it is written: Gal 3:22

"There is no one righteous, not
    even one;
11   there is no one who
        understands,
    no one who seeks God.
12All have turned away,
    they have together become
        worthless;
    there is no one who does good,
        not even one."[d]   Ps 14:1-3
13"Their throats are open graves;

their tongues practice
 deceit."[a]   Ps 5:9
"The poison of vipers is on
 their lips."[b]   Ps 140:3
[14] "Their mouths are full of
 cursing and bitterness."[c]
[15]"Their feet are swift to shed
 blood;
[16] ruin and misery mark their
 ways,
[17]and the way of peace they do
 not know."[d]   Isa 59:7-8
[18] "There is no fear of God
 before their eyes."[e]

[19]Now we know that whatever
the law says, it says to those who
are under the law, so that every
mouth may be silenced and the
whole world held accountable to
God. [20]Therefore no one will be declared righteous in his sight by observing the law; rather, through
the law we become conscious of
sin.   Ac 13:39; Ro 7:7

Righteousness Through Faith

[21]But now a righteousness from
God, apart from law, has been
made known, to which the Law
and the Prophets testify. [22]This
righteousness from God comes
through faith in Jesus Christ to all
who believe. There is no difference, [23]for all have sinned and fall
short of the glory of God, [24]and
are justified freely by his grace
through the redemption that came
by Christ Jesus. [25]God presented

him as a sacrifice of atonement,[f]
through faith in his blood. He did
this to demonstrate his justice, because in his forbearance he had
left the sins committed beforehand unpunished— [26]he did it to
demonstrate his justice at the
present time, so as to be just and
the one who justifies those who
have faith in Jesus.   Ro 1:17; 4:16

[27]Where, then, is boasting? It is
excluded. On what principle? On
that of observing the law? No, but
on that of faith. [28]For we maintain
that a man is justified by faith
apart from observing the law. [29]Is
God the God of Jews only? Is he
not the God of Gentiles too? Yes, of
Gentiles too, [30]since there is only
one God, who will justify the circumcised by faith and the uncircumcised through that same faith.
[31]Do we, then, nullify the law by
this faith? Not at all! Rather, we
uphold the law.   1Co 1:29-31; Gal 3:8

Abraham Justified by Faith

4 What then shall we say that
Abraham, our forefather, discovered in this matter? [2]If, in fact,
Abraham was justified by works,
he had something to boast about
—but not before God. [3]What does
the Scripture say? "Abraham believed God, and it was credited to
him as righteousness."[g]   Ge 15:6

[4]Now when a man works, his
wages are not credited to him as a

---

[a]13 Psalm 5:9   [b]13 Psalm 140:3   [c]14 Psalm 10:7   [d]17 Isaiah 59:7,8   [e]18 Psalm 36:1   [f]25 Or
as the one who would turn aside his wrath, taking away sin   [g]3 Gen. 15:6; also in verse 22

gift, but as an obligation. ⁵However-er, to the man who does not work but trusts God who justifies the wicked, his faith is credited as righteousness. ⁶David says the same thing when he speaks of the blessedness of the man to whom God credits righteousness apart from works: Ro 11:6

⁷"Blessed are they
   whose transgressions are
      forgiven,
   whose sins are covered.
⁸Blessed is the man
   whose sin the Lord will
      never count against
      him."ᵃ   Ps 32:1-2; 2Co 5:19

⁹Is this blessedness only for the circumcised, or also for the uncir-cumcised? We have been saying that Abraham's faith was credited to him as righteousness. ¹⁰Under what circumstances was it credit-ed? Was it after he was circum-cised, or before? It was not after, but before! ¹¹And he received the sign of circumcision, a seal of the righteousness that he had by faith while he was still uncircumcised. So then, he is the father of all who believe but have not been circum-cised, in order that righteousness might be credited to them. ¹²And he is also the father of the circum-cised who not only are circum-cised but who also walk in the footsteps of the faith that our fa-ther Abraham had before he was circumcised.   Ge 17:10-11; Lk 19:9

¹³It was not through law that Abraham and his offspring re-ceived the promise that he would be heir of the world, but through the righteousness that comes by faith. ¹⁴For if those who live by law are heirs, faith has no value and the promise is worthless, ¹⁵be-cause law brings wrath. And where there is no law there is no transgression.   Ro 3:20; 7:7-25; Gal 3:18

¹⁶Therefore, the promise comes by faith, so that it may be by grace and may be guaranteed to all Abra-ham's offspring—not only to those who are of the law but also to those who are of the faith of Abra-ham. He is the father of us all. ¹⁷As it is written: "I have made you a father of many nations."ᵇ He is our father in the sight of God, in whom he believed—the God who gives life to the dead and calls things that are not as though they were.

¹⁸Against all hope, Abraham in hope believed and so became the father of many nations, just as it had been said to him, "So shall your offspring be."ᶜ ¹⁹Without weakening in his faith, he faced the fact that his body was as good as dead—since he was about a hundred years old—and that Sar-ah's womb was also dead. ²⁰Yet he did not waver through unbelief re-garding the promise of God, but was strengthened in his faith and

---

ᵃ8 Psalm 32:1,2   ᵇ17 Gen. 17:5   ᶜ18 Gen. 15:5

gave glory to God, [21]being fully persuaded that God had power to do what he had promised. [22]This is why "it was credited to him as righteousness." [23]The words "it was credited to him" were written not for him alone, [24]but also for us, to whom God will credit righteousness—for us who believe in him who raised Jesus our Lord from the dead. [25]He was delivered over to death for our sins and was raised to life for our justification.

Peace and Joy

5 Therefore, since we have been justified through faith, we[a] have peace with God through our Lord Jesus Christ, [2]through whom we have gained access by faith into this grace in which we now stand. And we[a] rejoice in the hope of the glory of God. [3]Not only so, but we[a] also rejoice in our sufferings, because we know that suffering produces perseverance; [4]perseverance, character; and character, hope. [5]And hope does not disappoint us, because God has poured out his love into our hearts by the Holy Spirit, whom he has given us.

[6]You see, at just the right time, when we were still powerless, Christ died for the ungodly. [7]Very rarely will anyone die for a righteous man, though for a good man someone might possibly dare to die. [8]But God demonstrates his own love for us in this: While we were still sinners, Christ died for us.   Jn 15:13; 1Pe 3:18

[9]Since we have now been justified by his blood, how much more shall we be saved from God's wrath through him! [10]For if, when we were God's enemies, we were reconciled to him through the death of his Son, how much more, having been reconciled, shall we be saved through his life! [11]Not only is this so, but we also rejoice in God through our Lord Jesus Christ, through whom we have now received reconciliation.

Death Through Adam, Life Through Christ

[12]Therefore, just as sin entered the world through one man, and death through sin, and in this way death came to all men, because all sinned— [13]for before the law was given, sin was in the world. But sin is not taken into account when there is no law. [14]Nevertheless, death reigned from the time of Adam to the time of Moses, even over those who did not sin by breaking a command, as did Adam, who was a pattern of the one to come.   Ge 2:17; 1Co 15:22,45

[15]But the gift is not like the trespass. For if the many died by the trespass of the one man, how much more did God's grace and the gift that came by the grace of the one man, Jesus Christ, overflow to the many! [16]Again, the gift

of God is not like the result of the one man's sin: The judgment followed one sin and brought condemnation, but the gift followed many trespasses and brought justification. [17]For if, by the trespass of the one man, death reigned through that one man, how much more will those who receive God's abundant provision of grace and of the gift of righteousness reign in life through the one man, Jesus Christ.   Ac 15:11

[18]Consequently, just as the result of one trespass was condemnation for all men, so also the result of one act of righteousness was justification that brings life for all men. [19]For just as through the disobedience of the one man the many were made sinners, so also through the obedience of the one man the many will be made righteous.   Ro 4:25; Php 2:8

[20]The law was added so that the trespass might increase. But where sin increased, grace increased all the more, [21]so that, just as sin reigned in death, so also grace might reign through righteousness to bring eternal life through Jesus Christ our Lord.   Gal 3:19; 1Ti 1:13-14

Dead to Sin, Alive in Christ

6 What shall we say, then? Shall we go on sinning so that grace may increase? [2]By no means! We died to sin; how can we live in it any longer? [3]Or don't you know that all of us who were baptized into Christ Jesus were baptized into his death? [4]We were therefore buried with him through baptism into death in order that, just as Christ was raised from the dead through the glory of the Father, we too may live a new life.   Col 2:12

[5]If we have been united with him like this in his death, we will certainly also be united with him in his resurrection. [6]For we know that our old self was crucified with him so that the body of sin might be done away with,[a] that we should no longer be slaves to sin— [7]because anyone who has died has been freed from sin.   Ro 7:24; Gal 2:20

[8]Now if we died with Christ, we believe that we will also live with him. [9]For we know that since Christ was raised from the dead, he cannot die again; death no longer has mastery over him. [10]The death he died, he died to sin once for all; but the life he lives, he lives to God.   Ac 2:24; Rev 1:18

[11]In the same way, count yourselves dead to sin but alive to God in Christ Jesus. [12]Therefore do not let sin reign in your mortal body so that you obey its evil desires. [13]Do not offer the parts of your body to sin, as instruments of wickedness, but rather offer yourselves to God, as those who have been brought from death to life; and offer the parts of your body to him as instruments of righteousness. [14]For sin

---

[a]6 Or be rendered powerless

shall not be your master, because you are not under law, but under grace. Ro 3:24; Gal 5:18

Slaves to Righteousness

¹⁵What then? Shall we sin because we are not under law but under grace? By no means! ¹⁶Don't you know that when you offer yourselves to someone to obey him as slaves, you are slaves to the one whom you obey—whether you are slaves to sin, which leads to death, or to obedience, which leads to righteousness? ¹⁷But thanks be to God that, though you used to be slaves to sin, you wholeheartedly obeyed the form of teaching to which you were entrusted. ¹⁸You have been set free from sin and have become slaves to righteousness. Jn 8:34; Ro 8:2

¹⁹I put this in human terms because you are weak in your natural selves. Just as you used to offer the parts of your body in slavery to impurity and to ever-increasing wickedness, so now offer them in slavery to righteousness leading to holiness. ²⁰When you were slaves to sin, you were free from the control of righteousness. ²¹What benefit did you reap at that time from the things you are now ashamed of? Those things result in death! ²²But now that you have been set free from sin and have become slaves to God, the benefit you reap leads to holiness, and the result is eternal life. ²³For the wages of sin is death, but the gift of God is eternal life inᵃ Christ Jesus our Lord.

An Illustration From Marriage

7 Do you not know, brothers— for I am speaking to men who know the law—that the law has authority over a man only as long as he lives? ²For example, by law a married woman is bound to her husband as long as he is alive, but if her husband dies, she is released from the law of marriage. ³So then, if she marries another man while her husband is still alive, she is called an adulteress. But if her husband dies, she is released from that law and is not an adulteress, even though she marries another man. Ro 1:13; 1Co 7:39

⁴So, my brothers, you also died to the law through the body of Christ, that you might belong to another, to him who was raised from the dead, in order that we might bear fruit to God. ⁵For when we were controlled by the sinful nature,ᵇ the sinful passions aroused by the law were at work in our bodies, so that we bore fruit for death. ⁶But now, by dying to what once bound us, we have been released from the law so that we serve in the new way of the Spirit, and not in the old way of the written code. Ro 2:29; 6:13

ᵃ23 Or through   ᵇ5 Or the flesh; also in verse 25

Struggling With Sin

7What shall we say, then? Is the law sin? Certainly not! Indeed I would not have known what sin was except through the law. For I would not have known what coveting really was if the law had not said, "Do not covet."*a* **8**But sin, seizing the opportunity afforded by the commandment, produced in me every kind of covetous desire. For apart from law, sin is dead. **9**Once I was alive apart from law; but when the commandment came, sin sprang to life and I died. **10**I found that the very commandment that was intended to bring life actually brought death. **11**For sin, seizing the opportunity afforded by the commandment, deceived me, and through the commandment put me to death. **12**So then, the law is holy, and the commandment is holy, righteous and good.

Lev 18:5; 1Ti 1:8

13Did that which is good, then, become death to me? By no means! But in order that sin might be recognized as sin, it produced death in me through what was good, so that through the commandment sin might become utterly sinful.

Ro 6:23

14We know that the law is spiritual; but I am unspiritual, sold as a slave to sin. **15**I do not understand what I do. For what I want to do I do not do, but what I hate I do.

16And if I do what I do not want to do, I agree that the law is good. **17**As it is, it is no longer I myself who do it, but it is sin living in me. **18**I know that nothing good lives in me, that is, in my sinful nature.*b* For I have the desire to do what is good, but I cannot carry it out. **19**For what I do is not the good I want to do; no, the evil I do not want to do—this I keep on doing. **20**Now if I do what I do not want to do, it is no longer I who do it, but it is sin living in me that does it.

21So I find this law at work: When I want to do good, evil is right there with me. **22**For in my inner being I delight in God's law; **23**but I see another law at work in the members of my body, waging war against the law of my mind and making me a prisoner of the law of sin at work within my members. **24**What a wretched man I am! Who will rescue me from this body of death? **25**Thanks be to God— through Jesus Christ our Lord!

So then, I myself in my mind am a slave to God's law, but in the sinful nature a slave to the law of sin.

Life Through the Spirit

8 Therefore, there is now no condemnation for those who are in Christ Jesus,*c* **2**because through Christ Jesus the law of the Spirit of life set me free from the law of sin and death. **3**For what the

---

a7 Exodus 20:17; Deut. 5:21   *b18* Or *my flesh*   *c1* Some later manuscripts *Jesus, who do not live according to the sinful nature but according to the Spirit,*

law was powerless to do in that it was weakened by the sinful nature,[a] God did by sending his own Son in the likeness of sinful man to be a sin offering.[b] And so he condemned sin in sinful man,[c] [4]in order that the righteous requirements of the law might be fully met in us, who do not live according to the sinful nature but according to the Spirit.   1Co 15:45; Gal 5:16

[5]Those who live according to the sinful nature have their minds set on what that nature desires; but those who live in accordance with the Spirit have their minds set on what the Spirit desires. [6]The mind of sinful man[d] is death, but the mind controlled by the Spirit is life and peace; [7]the sinful mind[e] is hostile to God. It does not submit to God's law, nor can it do so. [8]Those controlled by the sinful nature cannot please God.   Gal 6:8

[9]You, however, are controlled not by the sinful nature but by the Spirit, if the Spirit of God lives in you. And if anyone does not have the Spirit of Christ, he does not belong to Christ. [10]But if Christ is in you, your body is dead because of sin, yet your spirit is alive because of righteousness. [11]And if the Spirit of him who raised Jesus from the dead is living in you, he who raised Christ from the dead will also give life to your mortal bodies through his Spirit, who lives in you.

[12]Therefore, brothers, we have an obligation—but it is not to the sinful nature, to live according to it. [13]For if you live according to the sinful nature, you will die; but if by the Spirit you put to death the misdeeds of the body, you will live, [14]because those who are led by the Spirit of God are sons of God. [15]For you did not receive a spirit that makes you a slave again to fear, but you received the Spirit of sonship.[f] And by him we cry, "Abba,[g] Father." [16]The Spirit himself testifies with our spirit that we are God's children. [17]Now if we are children, then we are heirs—heirs of God and co-heirs with Christ, if indeed we share in his sufferings in order that we may also share in his glory.   Gal 4:7; 1Pe 4:13

Future Glory

[18]I consider that our present sufferings are not worth comparing with the glory that will be revealed in us. [19]The creation waits in eager expectation for the sons of God to be revealed. [20]For the creation was subjected to frustration, not by its own choice, but by the will of the one who subjected it, in hope [21]that[h] the creation itself will be liberated from its bondage to decay and brought into the glorious freedom of the children of God.

[22]We know that the whole creation has been groaning as in the

---

[a]3 Or the flesh; also in verses 4, 5, 8, 9, 12 and 13   [b]3 Or man, for sin   [c]3 Or in the flesh   [d]6 Or mind set on the flesh   [e]7 Or the mind set on the flesh   [f]15 Or adoption   [g]15 Aramaic for Father [h]20,21 Or subjected it in hope. [21]For

pains of childbirth right up to the present time. ²³Not only so, but we ourselves, who have the firstfruits of the Spirit, groan inwardly as we wait eagerly for our adoption as sons, the redemption of our bodies. ²⁴For in this hope we were saved. But hope that is seen is no hope at all. Who hopes for what he already has? ²⁵But if we hope for what we do not yet have, we wait for it patiently.   2Co 5:2,4; Gal 5:5

²⁶In the same way, the Spirit helps us in our weakness. We do not know what we ought to pray for, but the Spirit himself intercedes for us with groans that words cannot express. ²⁷And he who searches our hearts knows the mind of the Spirit, because the Spirit intercedes for the saints in accordance with God's will.

More Than Conquerors

²⁸And we know that in all things God works for the good of those who love him,ᵃ whoᵇ have been called according to his purpose. ²⁹For those God foreknew he also predestined to be conformed to the likeness of his Son, that he might be the firstborn among many brothers. ³⁰And those he predestined, he also called; those he called, he also justified; those he justified, he also glorified.

³¹What, then, shall we say in response to this? If God is for us, who can be against us? ³²He who did not spare his own Son, but gave him up for us all—how will he not also, along with him, graciously give us all things? ³³Who will bring any charge against those whom God has chosen? It is God who justifies. ³⁴Who is he that condemns? Christ Jesus, who died—more than that, who was raised to life—is at the right hand of God and is also interceding for us. ³⁵Who shall separate us from the love of Christ? Shall trouble or hardship or persecution or famine or nakedness or danger or sword? ³⁶As it is written: Ps 118:6; Jn 3:16

"For your sake we face death
    all day long;
we are considered as sheep
    to be slaughtered."ᶜ

³⁷No, in all these things we are more than conquerors through him who loved us. ³⁸For I am convinced that neither death nor life, neither angels nor demons,ᵈ neither the present nor the future, nor any powers, ³⁹neither height nor depth, nor anything else in all creation, will be able to separate us from the love of God that is in Christ Jesus our Lord.   Ps 44:22

God's Sovereign Choice

9 I speak the truth in Christ—I am not lying, my conscience confirms it in the Holy Spirit— ²I

ᵃ28 Some manuscripts *And we know that all things work together for good to those who love God*
ᵇ28 Or *works together with those who love him to bring about what is good—with those who*
ᶜ36 Psalm 44:22   ᵈ38 Or *nor heavenly rulers*

have great sorrow and unceasing anguish in my heart. ³For I could wish that I myself were cursed and cut off from Christ for the sake of my brothers, those of my own race, ⁴the people of Israel. Theirs is the adoption as sons; theirs the divine glory, the covenants, the receiving of the law, the temple worship and the promises. ⁵Theirs are the patriarchs, and from them is traced the human ancestry of Christ, who is God over all, forever praised!ᵃ Amen.   Jn 1:1; Heb 9:1

⁶It is not as though God's word had failed. For not all who are descended from Israel are Israel. ⁷Nor because they are his descendants are they all Abraham's children. On the contrary, "It is through Isaac that your offspring will be reckoned."ᵇ ⁸In other words, it is not the natural children who are God's children, but it is the children of the promise who are regarded as Abraham's offspring. ⁹For this was how the promise was stated: "At the appointed time I will return, and Sarah will have a son."ᶜ   Ge 18:10,14

¹⁰Not only that, but Rebekah's children had one and the same father, our father Isaac. ¹¹Yet, before the twins were born or had done anything good or bad—in order that God's purpose in election might stand: ¹²not by works but by him who calls—she was told, "The older will serve the younger."ᵈ ¹³Just as it is written: "Jacob I loved, but Esau I hated."ᵉ

¹⁴What then shall we say? Is God unjust? Not at all! ¹⁵For he says to Moses,   2Ch 19:7

"I will have mercy on whom I
   have mercy,
and I will have compassion
   on whom I have
   compassion."ᶠ

¹⁶It does not, therefore, depend on man's desire or effort, but on God's mercy. ¹⁷For the Scripture says to Pharaoh: "I raised you up for this very purpose, that I might display my power in you and that my name might be proclaimed in all the earth."ᵍ ¹⁸Therefore God has mercy on whom he wants to have mercy, and he hardens whom he wants to harden.   Ex 4:21; 9:16

¹⁹One of you will say to me: "Then why does God still blame us? For who resists his will?" ²⁰But who are you, O man, to talk back to God? "Shall what is formed say to him who formed it, 'Why did you make me like this?'"ʰ ²¹Does not the potter have the right to make out of the same lump of clay some pottery for noble purposes and some for common use?

²²What if God, choosing to show his wrath and make his power known, bore with great patience the objects of his wrath—prepared

---

ᵃ5 Or Christ, who is over all. God be forever praised! Or Christ. God who is over all be forever praised!
ᵇ7 Gen. 21:12   ᶜ9 Gen. 18:10,14   ᵈ12 Gen. 25:23   ᵉ13 Mal. 1:2,3   ᶠ15 Exodus 33:19
ᵍ17 Exodus 9:16   ʰ20 Isaiah 29:16; 45:9

for destruction? ²³What if he did this to make the riches of his glory known to the objects of his mercy, whom he prepared in advance for glory— ²⁴even us, whom he also called, not only from the Jews but also from the Gentiles? ²⁵As he says in Hosea: Ro 3:29; 8:30

> "I will call them 'my people'
>   who are not my people;
> and I will call her 'my loved
>   one' who is not my
>   loved one,"[a]

²⁶and,

> "It will happen that in the very
>   place where it was said
>   to them,
> 'You are not my people,'
> they will be called 'sons of the
>   living God.' "[b]   Mt 16:16

²⁷Isaiah cries out concerning Israel:

> "Though the number of the
>   Israelites be like the
>   sand by the sea,   Ge 22:17
> only the remnant will be
>   saved.   Ro 11:5

²⁸For the Lord will carry out
>   his sentence on earth with
>   speed and finality."[c]

²⁹It is just as Isaiah said previously:

> "Unless the Lord Almighty
>   had left us descendants,
> we would have become like
>   Sodom,

we would have been like Gomorrah."[d]   Isa 13:19

Israel's Unbelief

³⁰What then shall we say? That the Gentiles, who did not pursue righteousness, have obtained it, a righteousness that is by faith; ³¹but Israel, who pursued a law of righteousness, has not attained it. ³²Why not? Because they pursued it not by faith but as if it were by works. They stumbled over the "stumbling stone." ³³As it is written: Ro 1:17; 10:2-3; Gal 5:4

> "See, I lay in Zion a stone that
>   causes men to stumble
>   and a rock that makes them
>   fall,
> and the one who trusts in him
>   will never be put to
>   shame."[e]   Isa 28:16; Ro 10:11

10 Brothers, my heart's desire and prayer to God for the Israelites is that they may be saved. ²For I can testify about them that they are zealous for God, but their zeal is not based on knowledge. ³Since they did not know the righteousness that comes from God and sought to establish their own, they did not submit to God's righteousness. ⁴Christ is the end of the law so that there may be righteousness for everyone who believes.   Ac 21:20; Ro 1:17; Gal 3:24

⁵Moses describes in this way the righteousness that is by the law:

a25 Hosea 2:23   b26 Hosea 1:10   c28 Isaiah 10:22,23   d29 Isaiah 1:9   e33 Isaiah 8:14; 28:16

"The man who does these things will live by them."[a] [6]But the righteousness that is by faith says: "Do not say in your heart, 'Who will ascend into heaven?'[b]" (that is, to bring Christ down) [7]"or 'Who will descend into the deep?'[c]" (that is, to bring Christ up from the dead). [8]But what does it say? "The word is near you; it is in your mouth and in your heart,"[d] that is, the word of faith we are proclaiming: [9]That if you confess with your mouth, "Jesus is Lord," and believe in your heart that God raised him from the dead, you will be saved. [10]For it is with your heart that you believe and are justified, and it is with your mouth that you confess and are saved. [11]As the Scripture says, "Anyone who trusts in him will never be put to shame."[e] [12]For there is no difference between Jew and Gentile—the same Lord is Lord of all and richly blesses all who call on him, [13]for, "Everyone who calls on the name of the Lord will be saved."[f]

Ac 2:21

[14]How, then, can they call on the one they have not believed in? And how can they believe in the one of whom they have not heard? And how can they hear without someone preaching to them? [15]And how can they preach unless they are sent? As it is written, "How beautiful are the feet of those who bring good news!"[g]

Isa 52:7; Na 1:15

[16]But not all the Israelites accepted the good news. For Isaiah says, "Lord, who has believed our message?"[h] [17]Consequently, faith comes from hearing the message, and the message is heard through the word of Christ. [18]But I ask: Did they not hear? Of course they did:

"Their voice has gone out into
    all the earth,
their words to the ends of
    the world."[i]

[19]Again I ask: Did Israel not understand? First, Moses says,

"I will make you envious by
    those who are not a
    nation;   Ro 11:11,14
I will make you angry by a
    nation that has no
    understanding."[j]

[20]And Isaiah boldly says,

"I was found by those who did
    not seek me;
I revealed myself to those
    who did not ask for
    me."[k]

[21]But concerning Israel he says,

"All day long I have held out
    my hands
to a disobedient and
    obstinate people."[l]

---

[a]5 Lev. 18:5   [b]6 Deut. 30:12   [c]7 Deut. 30:13   [d]8 Deut. 30:14   [e]11 Isaiah 28:16   [f]13 Joel 2:32
[g]15 Isaiah 52:7   [h]16 Isaiah 53:1   [i]18 Psalm 19:4   [j]19 Deut. 32:21   [k]20 Isaiah 65:1
[l]21 Isaiah 65:2

The Remnant of Israel

11 I ask then: Did God reject his people? By no means! I am an Israelite myself, a descendant of Abraham, from the tribe of Benjamin. ²God did not reject his people, whom he foreknew. Don't you know what the Scripture says in the passage about Elijah—how he appealed to God against Israel: ³"Lord, they have killed your prophets and torn down your altars; I am the only one left, and they are trying to kill me"[a]? ⁴And what was God's answer to him? "I have reserved for myself seven thousand who have not bowed the knee to Baal."[b] ⁵So too, at the present time there is a remnant chosen by grace. ⁶And if by grace, then it is no longer by works; if it were, grace would no longer be grace.[c]   Ro 4:4; 9:27

⁷What then? What Israel sought so earnestly it did not obtain, but the elect did. The others were hardened, ⁸as it is written:

"God gave them a spirit of
     stupor,
   eyes so that they could not
       see
   and ears so that they could
       not hear,   Mt 13:13-15
 to this very day."[d]

⁹And David says:

"May their table become a
     snare and a trap,
 a stumbling block and a
       retribution for them.
¹⁰May their eyes be darkened so
     they cannot see,
 and their backs be bent
       forever."[e]   Ps 69:22-23

Ingrafted Branches

¹¹Again I ask: Did they stumble so as to fall beyond recovery? Not at all! Rather, because of their transgression, salvation has come to the Gentiles to make Israel envious. ¹²But if their transgression means riches for the world, and their loss means riches for the Gentiles, how much greater riches will their fullness bring!   Ac 13:46

¹³I am talking to you Gentiles. Inasmuch as I am the apostle to the Gentiles, I make much of my ministry ¹⁴in the hope that I may somehow arouse my own people to envy and save some of them. ¹⁵For if their rejection is the reconciliation of the world, what will their acceptance be but life from the dead? ¹⁶If the part of the dough offered as firstfruits is holy, then the whole batch is holy; if the root is holy, so are the branches.

¹⁷If some of the branches have been broken off, and you, though a wild olive shoot, have been grafted in among the others and now

---

*a*3 1 Kings 19:10,14   *b*4 1 Kings 19:18   *c*6 Some manuscripts *by grace. But if by works, then it is no longer grace; if it were, work would no longer be work.*   *d*8 Deut. 29:4; Isaiah 29:10
*e*10 Psalm 69:22,23

share in the nourishing sap from the olive root, [18]do not boast over those branches. If you do, consider this: You do not support the root, but the root supports you. [19]You will say then, "Branches were broken off so that I could be grafted in." [20]Granted. But they were broken off because of unbelief, and you stand by faith. Do not be arrogant, but be afraid. [21]For if God did not spare the natural branches, he will not spare you either.   1Co 10:12

[22]Consider therefore the kindness and sternness of God: sternness to those who fell, but kindness to you, provided that you continue in his kindness. Otherwise, you also will be cut off. [23]And if they do not persist in unbelief, they will be grafted in, for God is able to graft them in again. [24]After all, if you were cut out of an olive tree that is wild by nature, and contrary to nature were grafted into a cultivated olive tree, how much more readily will these, the natural branches, be grafted into their own olive tree!   Jn 15:2; 1Co 15:2

All Israel Will Be Saved

[25]I do not want you to be ignorant of this mystery, brothers, so that you may not be conceited: Israel has experienced a hardening in part until the full number of the Gentiles has come in. [26]And so all Israel will be saved, as it is written:

"The deliverer will come from Zion;
> he will turn godlessness
> > away from Jacob.
[27]And this is[a] my covenant with them
> when I take away their
> > sins."[b]   Heb 8:10,12

[28]As far as the gospel is concerned, they are enemies on your account; but as far as election is concerned, they are loved on account of the patriarchs, [29]for God's gifts and his call are irrevocable. [30]Just as you who were at one time disobedient to God have now received mercy as a result of their disobedience, [31]so they too have now become disobedient in order that they too may now[c] receive mercy as a result of God's mercy to you. [32]For God has bound all men over to disobedience so that he may have mercy on them all.

Doxology

[33]Oh, the depth of the riches of
> the wisdom and[d]
> > knowledge of God!
How unsearchable his
> judgments,
and his paths beyond tracing
> out!   Job 11:7
[34]"Who has known the mind of
> the Lord?
Or who has been his
> counselor?"[e]   Isa 40:13-14
[35]"Who has ever given to God,

---

[a]27 Or *will be*   [b]27 Isaiah 59:20,21; 27:9; Jer. 31:33,34   [c]31 Some manuscripts do not have *now*.
[d]33 Or *riches and the wisdom and the*   [e]34 Isaiah 40:13

that God should repay
him?"*a*   Job 35:7
36For from him and through him
and to him are all
things.   1Co 8:6; Col 1:16
To him be the glory forever!
Amen.   Ro 16:27

Living Sacrifices

12 Therefore, I urge you,
brothers, in view of God's
mercy, to offer your bodies as living sacrifices, holy and pleasing to
God—this is your spiritual*b* act of
worship. 2Do not conform any
longer to the pattern of this world,
but be transformed by the renew-
ing of your mind. Then you will be
able to test and approve what
God's will is—his good, pleasing
and perfect will. Eph 4:23; 5:17; 1Pe 1:14

3For by the grace given me I say
to every one of you: Do not think
of yourself more highly than you
ought, but rather think of yourself
with sober judgment, in accordance with the measure of faith
God has given you. 4Just as each of
us has one body with many members, and these members do not all
have the same function, 5so in
Christ we who are many form one
body, and each member belongs to
all the others. 6We have different
gifts, according to the grace given
us. If a man's gift is prophesying,
let him use it in proportion to his*c*
faith. 7If it is serving, let him serve;

if it is teaching, let him teach; 8if it
is encouraging, let him encourage;
if it is contributing to the needs of
others, let him give generously; if
it is leadership, let him govern diligently; if it is showing mercy, let
him do it cheerfully.   Ac 15:32

Love

9Love must be sincere. Hate
what is evil; cling to what is good.
10Be devoted to one another in
brotherly love. Honor one another
above yourselves. 11Never be lacking in zeal, but keep your spiritual
fervor, serving the Lord. 12Be joyful in hope, patient in affliction,
faithful in prayer. 13Share with
God's people who are in need.
Practice hospitality.   1Ti 3:2

14Bless those who persecute
you; bless and do not curse. 15Re-
joice with those who rejoice;
mourn with those who mourn.
16Live in harmony with one another. Do not be proud, but be willing
to associate with people of low position.*d* Do not be conceited.

17Do not repay anyone evil for
evil. Be careful to do what is right
in the eyes of everybody. 18If it is
possible, as far as it depends on
you, live at peace with everyone.
19Do not take revenge, my friends,
but leave room for God's wrath, for
it is written: "It is mine to avenge;
I will repay,"*e* says the Lord. 20On
the contrary: Lev 19:18; Ro 14:19; 2Co 8:21

---

*a*35 Job 41:11   *b*1 Or reasonable   *c*6 Or in agreement with the   *d*16 Or willing to do menial work
*e*19 Deut. 32:35

"If your enemy is hungry, feed
    him;
if he is thirsty, give him
    something to drink.
In doing this, you will heap
    burning coals on his
    head."[a]   Mt 5:44; Lk 6:27

21Do not be overcome by evil, but
overcome evil with good.

Submission to the Authorities

13 Everyone must submit
himself to the governing
authorities, for there is no authority except that which God has established. The authorities that exist have been established by God.
2Consequently, he who rebels
against the authority is rebelling
against what God has instituted,
and those who do so will bring
judgment on themselves. 3For rulers hold no terror for those who do
right, but for those who do wrong.
Do you want to be free from fear of
the one in authority? Then do what
is right and he will commend you.
4For he is God's servant to do you
good. But if you do wrong, be
afraid, for he does not bear the
sword for nothing. He is God's servant, an agent of wrath to bring
punishment on the wrongdoer.
5Therefore, it is necessary to submit to the authorities, not only because of possible punishment but
also because of conscience.
    6This is also why you pay taxes,

for the authorities are God's servants, who give their full time to
governing. 7Give everyone what
you owe him: If you owe taxes, pay
taxes; if revenue, then revenue; if
respect, then respect; if honor,
then honor.   Mt 22:17,21; Lk 23:2

Love, for the Day Is Near

8Let no debt remain outstanding, except the continuing debt to
love one another, for he who loves
his fellowman has fulfilled the law.
9The commandments, "Do not
commit adultery," "Do not murder," "Do not steal," "Do not covet,"[b] and whatever other commandment there may be, are
summed up in this one rule: "Love
your neighbor as yourself."[c]
10Love does no harm to its neighbor. Therefore love is the fulfillment of the law.   Mt 19:19; 22:39-40

11And do this, understanding
the present time. The hour has
come for you to wake up from
your slumber, because our salvation is nearer now than when we
first believed. 12The night is nearly
over; the day is almost here. So let
us put aside the deeds of darkness
and put on the armor of light. 13Let
us behave decently, as in the daytime, not in orgies and drunkenness, not in sexual immorality and
debauchery, not in dissension and
jealousy. 14Rather, clothe yourselves with the Lord Jesus Christ,
and do not think about how to

---

a20 Prov. 25:21,22   b9 Exodus 20:13-15,17; Deut. 5:17-19,21   c9 Lev. 19:18

gratify the desires of the sinful nature.[a]

Gal 3:27; 5:19-21

The Weak and the Strong

14 Accept him whose faith is weak, without passing judgment on disputable matters. ²One man's faith allows him to eat everything, but another man, whose faith is weak, eats only vegetables. ³The man who eats everything must not look down on him who does not, and the man who does not eat everything must not condemn the man who does, for God has accepted him. ⁴Who are you to judge someone else's servant? To his own master he stands or falls. And he will stand, for the Lord is able to make him stand.

⁵One man considers one day more sacred than another; another man considers every day alike. Each one should be fully convinced in his own mind. ⁶He who regards one day as special, does so to the Lord. He who eats meat, eats to the Lord, for he gives thanks to God; and he who abstains, does so to the Lord and gives thanks to God. ⁷For none of us lives to himself alone and none of us dies to himself alone. ⁸If we live, we live to the Lord; and if we die, we die to the Lord. So, whether we live or die, we belong to the Lord.

⁹For this very reason, Christ died and returned to life so that he might be the Lord of both the dead and the living. ¹⁰You, then, why do you judge your brother? Or why do you look down on your brother? For we will all stand before God's judgment seat. ¹¹It is written:

" 'As surely as I live,' says the
Lord,

Isa 49:18

'every knee will bow before
me;
every tongue will confess to
God.' "[b]

¹²So then, each of us will give an account of himself to God.

¹³Therefore let us stop passing judgment on one another. Instead, make up your mind not to put any stumbling block or obstacle in your brother's way. ¹⁴As one who is in the Lord Jesus, I am fully convinced that no food[c] is unclean in itself. But if anyone regards something as unclean, then for him it is unclean. ¹⁵If your brother is distressed because of what you eat, you are no longer acting in love. Do not by your eating destroy your brother for whom Christ died. ¹⁶Do not allow what you consider good to be spoken of as evil. ¹⁷For the kingdom of God is not a matter of eating and drinking, but of righteousness, peace and joy in the Holy Spirit, ¹⁸because anyone who serves Christ in this way is pleasing to God and approved by men.

¹⁹Let us therefore make every effort to do what leads to peace and to mutual edification. ²⁰Do not de-

a 14 Or the flesh   b 11 Isaiah 45:23   c 14 Or that nothing stroy the work of God for the sake of food. All food is clean, but it is wrong for a man to eat anything that causes someone else to stumble. 21It is better not to eat meat or drink wine or to do anything else that will cause your brother to fall.

22So whatever you believe about these things keep between yourself and God. Blessed is the man who does not condemn himself by what he approves. 23But the man who has doubts is condemned if he eats, because his eating is not from faith; and everything that does not come from faith is sin.

15 We who are strong ought to bear with the failings of the weak and not to please ourselves. 2Each of us should please his neighbor for his good, to build him up. 3For even Christ did not please himself but, as it is written: "The insults of those who insult you have fallen on me."a 4For everything that was written in the past was written to teach us, so that through endurance and the encouragement of the Scriptures we might have hope.   Ro 14:1,19

5May the God who gives endurance and encouragement give you a spirit of unity among yourselves as you follow Christ Jesus, 6so that with one heart and mouth you may glorify the God and Father of our Lord Jesus Christ.   Ps 34:3

7Accept one another, then, just as Christ accepted you, in order to bring praise to God. 8For I tell you that Christ has become a servant of the Jewsb on behalf of God's truth, to confirm the promises made to the patriarchs 9so that the Gentiles may glorify God for his mercy, as it is written: Mt 15:24; Ro 14:1; 2Co 1:20

"Therefore I will praise you
    among the Gentiles;
  I will sing hymns to your
    name."c

10Again, it says,

"Rejoice, O Gentiles, with his
    people."d

11And again,

"Praise the Lord, all you
    Gentiles,
  and sing praises to him, all
    you peoples."e

12And again, Isaiah says,

"The Root of Jesse will spring
    up,   Rev 5:5
  one who will arise to rule
    over the nations;
  the Gentiles will hope in
    him."f   Dt 32:43; 2Sa 22:50

13May the God of hope fill you with all joy and peace as you trust in him, so that you may overflow with hope by the power of the Holy Spirit.   Ro 14:17; 1Th 1:5

a3 Psalm 69:9   b8 Greek circumcision   c9 2 Samuel 22:50; Psalm 18:49   d10 Deut. 32:43
e11 Psalm 117:1   f12 Isaiah 11:10

Paul the Minister to the Gentiles

14I myself am convinced, my brothers, that you yourselves are full of goodness, complete in knowledge and competent to instruct one another. **15**I have written you quite boldly on some points, as if to remind you of them again, because of the grace God gave me **16**to be a minister of Christ Jesus to the Gentiles with the priestly duty of proclaiming the gospel of God, so that the Gentiles might become an offering acceptable to God, sanctified by the Holy Spirit.

17Therefore I glory in Christ Jesus in my service to God. **18**I will not venture to speak of anything except what Christ has accomplished through me in leading the Gentiles to obey God by what I have said and done— **19**by the power of signs and miracles, through the power of the Spirit. So from Jerusalem all the way around to Illyricum, I have fully proclaimed the gospel of Christ. **20**It has always been my ambition to preach the gospel where Christ was not known, so that I would not be building on someone else's foundation. **21**Rather, as it is written: Ac 21:19; 2Co 10:15-16

"Those who were not told
    about him will see,
and those who have not
    heard will understand."[a]

22This is why I have often been hindered from coming to you.

Paul's Plan to Visit Rome

23But now that there is no more place for me to work in these regions, and since I have been longing for many years to see you, **24**I plan to do so when I go to Spain. I hope to visit you while passing through and to have you assist me on my journey there, after I have enjoyed your company for a while. **25**Now, however, I am on my way to Jerusalem in the service of the saints there. **26**For Macedonia and Achaia were pleased to make a contribution for the poor among the saints in Jerusalem. **27**They were pleased to do it, and indeed they owe it to them. For if the Gentiles have shared in the Jews' spiritual blessings, they owe it to the Jews to share with them their material blessings. **28**So after I have completed this task and have made sure that they have received this fruit, I will go to Spain and visit you on the way. **29**I know that when I come to you, I will come in the full measure of the blessing of Christ.   Ro 1:10-11; 1Co 9:11

30I urge you, brothers, by our Lord Jesus Christ and by the love of the Spirit, to join me in my struggle by praying to God for me. **31**Pray that I may be rescued from the unbelievers in Judea and that my service in Jerusalem may be

---

[a] 21 Isaiah 52:15

acceptable to the saints there, [32]so that by God's will I may come to you with joy and together with you be refreshed. [33]The God of peace be with you all. Amen.   Ro 16:20

Personal Greetings

16 I commend to you our sister Phoebe, a servant[a] of the church in Cenchrea. [2]I ask you to receive her in the Lord in a way worthy of the saints and to give her any help she may need from you, for she has been a great help to many people, including me.

[3]Greet Priscilla[b] and Aquila, my fellow workers in Christ Jesus. [4]They risked their lives for me. Not only I but all the churches of the Gentiles are grateful to them.   Ac 18:2
[5]Greet also the church that meets at their house.   1Co 16:19; Col 4:15
Greet my dear friend Epenetus, who was the first convert to Christ in the province of Asia.
[6]Greet Mary, who worked very hard for you.
[7]Greet Andronicus and Junias, my relatives who have been in prison with me. They are outstanding among the apostles, and they were in Christ before I was.   ver 11,21
[8]Greet Ampliatus, whom I love in the Lord.

[9]Greet Urbanus, our fellow worker in Christ, and my dear friend Stachys.   ver 3
[10]Greet Apelles, tested and approved in Christ.   ver 3
Greet those who belong to the household of Aristobulus.
[11]Greet Herodion, my relative.
Greet those in the household of Narcissus who are in the Lord.   Ac 11:14
[12]Greet Tryphena and Tryphosa, those women who work hard in the Lord.
Greet my dear friend Persis, another woman who has worked very hard in the Lord.
[13]Greet Rufus, chosen in the Lord, and his mother, who has been a mother to me, too.   Mk 15:21
[14]Greet Asyncritus, Phlegon, Hermes, Patrobas, Hermas and the brothers with them.
[15]Greet Philologus, Julia, Nereus and his sister, and Olympas and all the saints with them.
[16]Greet one another with a holy kiss.
All the churches of Christ send greetings.   1Co 16:20; 2Co 13:12

[17]I urge you, brothers, to watch out for those who cause divisions and put obstacles in your way that are contrary to the teaching you have learned. Keep away from them. [18]For such people are not serving our Lord Christ, but their own appetites. By smooth talk and

---

a 1 Or deaconess   b 3 Greek Prisca, a variant of Priscilla

flattery they deceive the minds of naive people. ¹⁹Everyone has heard about your obedience, so I am full of joy over you; but I want you to be wise about what is good, and innocent about what is evil.

²⁰The God of peace will soon crush Satan under your feet.

The grace of our Lord Jesus be with you. 1Th 5:28

²¹Timothy, my fellow worker, sends his greetings to you, as do Lucius, Jason and Sosipater, my relatives. Ac 13:1; 16:1; 17:5

²²I, Tertius, who wrote down this letter, greet you in the Lord.

²³Gaius, whose hospitality I and the whole church here enjoy, sends you his greetings. Ac 19:29

Erastus, who is the city's director of public works, and our brother Quartus send you their greetings.ᵃ Ac 19:22; 2Ti 4:20

²⁵Now to him who is able to establish you by my gospel and the proclamation of Jesus Christ, according to the revelation of the mystery hidden for long ages past, ²⁶but now revealed and made known through the prophetic writings by the command of the eternal God, so that all nations might believe and obey him— ²⁷to the only wise God be glory forever through Jesus Christ! Amen.

ᵃ23 Some manuscripts *their greetings.* ²⁴*May the grace of our Lord Jesus Christ be with all of you. Amen.*

1 Corinthians

1 Paul, called to be an apostle of Christ Jesus by the will of God, and our brother Sosthenes, Ro 1:1

²To the church of God in Corinth, to those sanctified in Christ Jesus and called to be holy, together with all those everywhere who call on the name of our Lord Jesus Christ—their Lord and ours:

³Grace and peace to you from God our Father and the Lord Jesus Christ. Ro 1:7

Thanksgiving

⁴I always thank God for you because of his grace given you in Christ Jesus. ⁵For in him you have been enriched in every way—in all your speaking and in all your knowledge— ⁶because our testimony about Christ was confirmed in you. ⁷Therefore you do not lack any spiritual gift as you eagerly wait for our Lord Jesus Christ to be revealed. ⁸He will keep you strong to the end, so that you will be blameless on the day of our Lord Jesus Christ. ⁹God, who has called you into fellowship with his Son Jesus Christ our Lord, is faithful.

Divisions in the Church

¹⁰I appeal to you, brothers, in the name of our Lord Jesus Christ, that all of you agree with one another so that there may be no divisions among you and that you may be perfectly united in mind and thought. ¹¹My brothers, some from Chloe's household have informed me that there are quarrels among you. ¹²What I mean is this: One of you says, "I follow Paul"; another, "I follow Apollos"; another, "I follow Cephas*a*"; still another, "I follow Christ." Jn 1:42; 1Co 3:4,22

¹³Is Christ divided? Was Paul crucified for you? Were you baptized into*b* the name of Paul? ¹⁴I am thankful that I did not baptize any of you except Crispus and Gaius, ¹⁵so no one can say that you were baptized into my name. ¹⁶(Yes, I also baptized the household of Stephanas; beyond that, I don't remember if I baptized anyone else.) ¹⁷For Christ did not send me to baptize, but to preach the gospel—not with words of human wisdom, lest the cross of Christ be emptied of its power. Jn 4:2

Christ the Wisdom and Power of God

¹⁸For the message of the cross is foolishness to those who are perishing, but to us who are being

---

a 12 That is, Peter   *b 13* Or *in*; also in verse 15

saved it is the power of God. ¹⁹For it is written: Ro 1:16; 2Co 2:15

"I will destroy the wisdom of
     the wise;
  the intelligence of the
     intelligent I will
     frustrate."ᵃ   Isa 29:14

²⁰Where is the wise man? Where is the scholar? Where is the philosopher of this age? Has not God made foolish the wisdom of the world? ²¹For since in the wisdom of God the world through its wisdom did not know him, God was pleased through the foolishness of what was preached to save those who believe. ²²Jews demand miraculous signs and Greeks look for wisdom, ²³but we preach Christ crucified: a stumbling block to Jews and foolishness to Gentiles, ²⁴but to those whom God has called, both Jews and Greeks, Christ the power of God and the wisdom of God. ²⁵For the foolishness of God is wiser than man's wisdom, and the weakness of God is stronger than man's strength.

²⁶Brothers, think of what you were when you were called. Not many of you were wise by human standards; not many were influential; not many were of noble birth. ²⁷But God chose the foolish things of the world to shame the wise; God chose the weak things of the world to shame the strong. ²⁸He chose the lowly things of this world and the despised things— and the things that are not—to nullify the things that are, ²⁹so that no one may boast before him. ³⁰It is because of him that you are in Christ Jesus, who has become for us wisdom from God—that is, our righteousness, holiness and redemption. ³¹Therefore, as it is written: "Let him who boasts boast in the Lord."ᵇ   2Co 10:17; Eph 1:7,14; 2:9

2 When I came to you, brothers, I did not come with eloquence or superior wisdom as I proclaimed to you the testimony about God.ᶜ ²For I resolved to know nothing while I was with you except Jesus Christ and him crucified. ³I came to you in weakness and fear, and with much trembling. ⁴My message and my preaching were not with wise and persuasive words, but with a demonstration of the Spirit's power, ⁵so that your faith might not rest on men's wisdom, but on God's power.   Ro 15:19; 2Co 4:7; 6:7

Wisdom From the Spirit

⁶We do, however, speak a message of wisdom among the mature, but not the wisdom of this age or of the rulers of this age, who are coming to nothing. ⁷No, we speak of God's secret wisdom, a wisdom that has been hidden and that God destined for our glory before time

---

ᵃ19 Isaiah 29:14   ᵇ31 Jer. 9:24   ᶜ1 Some manuscripts *as I proclaimed to you God's mystery*

began. **8**None of the rulers of this age understood it, for if they had, they would not have crucified the Lord of glory. **9**However, as it is written:

Ac 7:2; 1Co 1:20; Eph 4:13

"No eye has seen,
no ear has heard,
no mind has conceived
what God has prepared for
those who love him"[a]—

10but God has revealed it to us by his Spirit.

Isa 65:17; Jn 14:26

The Spirit searches all things, even the deep things of God. **11**For who among men knows the thoughts of a man except the man's spirit within him? In the same way no one knows the thoughts of God except the Spirit of God. **12**We have not received the spirit of the world but the Spirit who is from God, that we may understand what God has freely given us. **13**This is what we speak, not in words taught us by human wisdom but in words taught by the Spirit, expressing spiritual truths in spiritual words.[b] **14**The man without the Spirit does not accept the things that come from the Spirit of God, for they are foolishness to him, and he cannot understand them, because they are spiritually discerned. **15**The spiritual man makes judgments about all things, but he himself is not subject to any man's judgment:

1Co 1:17-18

16"For who has known the mind
of the Lord
that he may instruct him?"[c]

But we have the mind of Christ.

On Divisions in the Church

3 Brothers, I could not address you as spiritual but as worldly—mere infants in Christ. **2**I gave you milk, not solid food, for you were not yet ready for it. Indeed, you are still not ready. **3**You are still worldly. For since there is jealousy and quarreling among you, are you not worldly? Are you not acting like mere men? **4**For when one says, "I follow Paul," and another, "I follow Apollos," are you not mere men?

Gal 5:20; Heb 5:13

5What, after all, is Apollos? And what is Paul? Only servants, through whom you came to believe—as the Lord has assigned to each his task. **6**I planted the seed, Apollos watered it, but God made it grow. **7**So neither he who plants nor he who waters is anything, but only God, who makes things grow. **8**The man who plants and the man who waters have one purpose, and each will be rewarded according to his own labor. **9**For we are God's fellow workers; you are God's field, God's building.

2Co 6:1

10By the grace God has given me, I laid a foundation as an expert builder, and someone else is building on it. But each one should be

---

a 9 Isaiah 64:4   *b* 13 Or *Spirit, interpreting spiritual truths to spiritual men*   *c* 16 Isaiah 40:13

careful how he builds. ¹¹For no one can lay any foundation other than the one already laid, which is Jesus Christ. ¹²If any man builds on this foundation using gold, silver, costly stones, wood, hay or straw, ¹³his work will be shown for what it is, because the Day will bring it to light. It will be revealed with fire, and the fire will test the quality of each man's work. ¹⁴If what he has built survives, he will receive his reward. ¹⁵If it is burned up, he will suffer loss; he himself will be saved, but only as one escaping through the flames.

¹⁶Don't you know that you yourselves are God's temple and that God's Spirit lives in you? ¹⁷If anyone destroys God's temple, God will destroy him; for God's temple is sacred, and you are that temple.

¹⁸Do not deceive yourselves. If any one of you thinks he is wise by the standards of this age, he should become a "fool" so that he may become wise. ¹⁹For the wisdom of this world is foolishness in God's sight. As it is written: "He catches the wise in their craftiness"ᵃ; ²⁰and again, "The Lord knows that the thoughts of the wise are futile."ᵇ ²¹So then, no more boasting about men! All things are yours, ²²whether Paul or Apollos or Cephasᶜ or the world or life or death or the present or the future—all are yours, ²³and you are of Christ, and Christ is of God.

Apostles of Christ

4 So then, men ought to regard us as servants of Christ and as those entrusted with the secret things of God. ²Now it is required that those who have been given a trust must prove faithful. ³I care very little if I am judged by you or by any human court; indeed, I do not even judge myself. ⁴My conscience is clear, but that does not make me innocent. It is the Lord who judges me. ⁵Therefore judge nothing before the appointed time; wait till the Lord comes. He will bring to light what is hidden in darkness and will expose the motives of men's hearts. At that time each will receive his praise from God.   Ro 2:1,29

⁶Now, brothers, I have applied these things to myself and Apollos for your benefit, so that you may learn from us the meaning of the saying, "Do not go beyond what is written." Then you will not take pride in one man over against another. ⁷For who makes you different from anyone else? What do you have that you did not receive? And if you did receive it, why do you boast as though you did not?

⁸Already you have all you want! Already you have become rich! You have become kings—and that without us! How I wish that you really had become kings so that we might be kings with you! ⁹For it seems to me that God has put us

---

ᵃ19 Job 5:13   ᵇ20 Psalm 94:11   ᶜ22 That is, Peter

apostles on display at the end of the procession, like men condemned to die in the arena. We have been made a spectacle to the whole universe, to angels as well as to men. [10]We are fools for Christ, but you are so wise in Christ! We are weak, but you are strong! You are honored, we are dishonored! [11]To this very hour we go hungry and thirsty, we are in rags, we are brutally treated, we are homeless. [12]We work hard with our own hands. When we are cursed, we bless; when we are persecuted, we endure it; [13]when we are slandered, we answer kindly. Up to this moment we have become the scum of the earth, the refuse of the world.   Ac 17:18; Ro 8:35

[14]I am not writing this to shame you, but to warn you, as my dear children. [15]Even though you have ten thousand guardians in Christ, you do not have many fathers, for in Christ Jesus I became your father through the gospel. [16]Therefore I urge you to imitate me. [17]For this reason I am sending to you Timothy, my son whom I love, who is faithful in the Lord. He will remind you of my way of life in Christ Jesus, which agrees with what I teach everywhere in every church.   1Co 7:17; 1Th 1:6; 2:11

[18]Some of you have become arrogant, as if I were not coming to you. [19]But I will come to you very soon, if the Lord is willing, and then I will find out not only how these arrogant people are talking, but what power they have. [20]For the kingdom of God is not a matter of talk but of power. [21]What do you prefer? Shall I come to you with a whip, or in love and with a gentle spirit?   Ro 15:13; 2Co 1:15-16

Expel the Immoral Brother!

5 It is actually reported that there is sexual immorality among you, and of a kind that does not occur even among pagans: A man has his father's wife. [2]And you are proud! Shouldn't you rather have been filled with grief and have put out of your fellowship the man who did this? [3]Even though I am not physically present, I am with you in spirit. And I have already passed judgment on the one who did this, just as if I were present. [4]When you are assembled in the name of our Lord Jesus and I am with you in spirit, and the power of our Lord Jesus is present, [5]hand this man over to Satan, so that the sinful nature[a] may be destroyed and his spirit saved on the day of the Lord.   1Ti 1:20; 2Th 3:6

[6]Your boasting is not good. Don't you know that a little yeast works through the whole batch of dough? [7]Get rid of the old yeast that you may be a new batch without yeast—as you really are. For Christ, our Passover lamb, has been sacrificed. [8]Therefore let us

[a] 5 Or that his body; or that the flesh

keep the Festival, not with the old yeast, the yeast of malice and wickedness, but with bread without yeast, the bread of sincerity and truth. Gal 5:9; 1Pe 1:19

⁹I have written you in my letter not to associate with sexually immoral people— ¹⁰not at all meaning the people of this world who are immoral, or the greedy and swindlers, or idolaters. In that case you would have to leave this world. ¹¹But now I am writing you that you must not associate with anyone who calls himself a brother but is sexually immoral or greedy, an idolater or a slanderer, a drunkard or a swindler. With such a man do not even eat.

¹²What business is it of mine to judge those outside the church? Are you not to judge those inside? ¹³God will judge those outside. "Expel the wicked man from among you."ᵃ Mk 4:11; 1Co 6:1-4

Lawsuits Among Believers

6 If any of you has a dispute with another, dare he take it before the ungodly for judgment instead of before the saints? ²Do you not know that the saints will judge the world? And if you are to judge the world, are you not competent to judge trivial cases? ³Do you not know that we will judge angels? How much more the things of this life! ⁴Therefore, if you have disputes about such matters, appoint as judges even men of little account in the church!ᵇ ⁵I say this to shame you. Is it possible that there is nobody among you wise enough to judge a dispute between believers? ⁶But instead, one brother goes to law against another—and this in front of unbelievers! Mt 19:28; 2Co 6:14-15

⁷The very fact that you have lawsuits among you means you have been completely defeated already. Why not rather be wronged? Why not rather be cheated? ⁸Instead, you yourselves cheat and do wrong, and you do this to your brothers. Mt 5:39-40; 1Th 4:6

⁹Do you not know that the wicked will not inherit the kingdom of God? Do not be deceived: Neither the sexually immoral nor idolaters nor adulterers nor male prostitutes nor homosexual offenders ¹⁰nor thieves nor the greedy nor drunkards nor slanderers nor swindlers will inherit the kingdom of God. ¹¹And that is what some of you were. But you were washed, you were sanctified, you were justified in the name of the Lord Jesus Christ and by the Spirit of our God.

Sexual Immorality

¹²"Everything is permissible for me"—but not everything is beneficial. "Everything is permissible for me"—but I will not be mastered by

---

ᵃ13 Deut. 17:7; 19:19; 21:21; 22:21,24; 24:7   ᵇ4 Or matters, do you appoint as judges men of little account in the church?

anything. [13]"Food for the stomach and the stomach for food"—but God will destroy them both. The body is not meant for sexual immorality, but for the Lord, and the Lord for the body. [14]By his power God raised the Lord from the dead, and he will raise us also. [15]Do you not know that your bodies are members of Christ himself? Shall I then take the members of Christ and unite them with a prostitute? Never! [16]Do you not know that he who unites himself with a prostitute is one with her in body? For it is said, "The two will become one flesh."[a] [17]But he who unites himself with the Lord is one with him in spirit.   Jn 17:21-23; Gal 2:20

[18]Flee from sexual immorality. All other sins a man commits are outside his body, but he who sins sexually sins against his own body. [19]Do you not know that your body is a temple of the Holy Spirit, who is in you, whom you have received from God? You are not your own; [20]you were bought at a price. Therefore honor God with your body.   Ro 6:12; Heb 13:4; Rev 5:9

Marriage

7 Now for the matters you wrote about: It is good for a man not to marry.[b] [2]But since there is so much immorality, each man should have his own wife, and each woman her own husband. [3]The husband should fulfill his marital duty to his wife, and likewise the wife to her husband. [4]The wife's body does not belong to her alone but also to her husband. In the same way, the husband's body does not belong to him alone but also to his wife. [5]Do not deprive each other except by mutual consent and for a time, so that you may devote yourselves to prayer. Then come together again so that Satan will not tempt you because of your lack of self-control. [6]I say this as a concession, not as a command. [7]I wish that all men were as I am. But each man has his own gift from God; one has this gift, another has that.   1Co 9:5; 12:4,11

[8]Now to the unmarried and the widows I say: It is good for them to stay unmarried, as I am. [9]But if they cannot control themselves, they should marry, for it is better to marry than to burn with passion.   1Ti 5:14

[10]To the married I give this command (not I, but the Lord): A wife must not separate from her husband. [11]But if she does, she must remain unmarried or else be reconciled to her husband. And a husband must not divorce his wife.

[12]To the rest I say this (I, not the Lord): If any brother has a wife who is not a believer and she is willing to live with him, he must not divorce her. [13]And if a woman has a husband who is not a believer and he is willing to live with her,

_____
[a] 16 Gen. 2:24   [b] 1 Or "It is good for a man not to have sexual relations with a woman."

she must not divorce him. ¹⁴For the unbelieving husband has been sanctified through his wife, and the unbelieving wife has been sanctified through her believing husband. Otherwise your children would be unclean, but as it is, they are holy.   Mal 2:15

¹⁵But if the unbeliever leaves, let him do so. A believing man or woman is not bound in such circumstances; God has called us to live in peace. ¹⁶How do you know, wife, whether you will save your husband? Or, how do you know, husband, whether you will save your wife?   Ro 14:19; 1Pe 3:1

¹⁷Nevertheless, each one should retain the place in life that the Lord assigned to him and to which God has called him. This is the rule I lay down in all the churches. ¹⁸Was a man already circumcised when he was called? He should not become uncircumcised. Was a man uncircumcised when he was called? He should not be circumcised. ¹⁹Circumcision is nothing and uncircumcision is nothing. Keeping God's commands is what counts. ²⁰Each one should remain in the situation which he was in when God called him. ²¹Were you a slave when you were called? Don't let it trouble you—although if you can gain your freedom, do so. ²²For he who was a slave when he was called by the Lord is the Lord's freedman; similarly, he who was a free man when he was called is Christ's slave. ²³You were bought at a price; do not become slaves of men. ²⁴Brothers, each man, as responsible to God, should remain in the situation God called him to.

²⁵Now about virgins: I have no command from the Lord, but I give a judgment as one who by the Lord's mercy is trustworthy. ²⁶Because of the present crisis, I think that it is good for you to remain as you are. ²⁷Are you married? Do not seek a divorce. Are you unmarried? Do not look for a wife. ²⁸But if you do marry, you have not sinned; and if a virgin marries, she has not sinned. But those who marry will face many troubles in this life, and I want to spare you this.   1Ti 1:13,16

²⁹What I mean, brothers, is that the time is short. From now on those who have wives should live as if they had none; ³⁰those who mourn, as if they did not; those who are happy, as if they were not; those who buy something, as if it were not theirs to keep; ³¹those who use the things of the world, as if not engrossed in them. For this world in its present form is passing away.   Ro 13:11-12; 1Jn 2:17

³²I would like you to be free from concern. An unmarried man is concerned about the Lord's affairs—how he can please the Lord. ³³But a married man is concerned about the affairs of this world—how he can please his wife— ³⁴and his interests are divided. An unmarried woman or virgin is con-

cerned about the Lord's affairs: Her aim is to be devoted to the Lord in both body and spirit. But a married woman is concerned about the affairs of this world—how she can please her husband. **35**I am saying this for your own good, not to restrict you, but that you may live in a right way in undivided devotion to the Lord.

36If anyone thinks he is acting improperly toward the virgin he is engaged to, and if she is getting along in years and he feels he ought to marry, he should do as he wants. He is not sinning. They should get married. **37**But the man who has settled the matter in his own mind, who is under no compulsion but has control over his own will, and who has made up his mind not to marry the virgin—this man also does the right thing. **38**So then, he who marries the virgin does right, but he who does not marry her does even better.*a*

39A woman is bound to her husband as long as he lives. But if her husband dies, she is free to marry anyone she wishes, but he must belong to the Lord. **40**In my judgment, she is happier if she stays as she is—and I think that I too have the Spirit of God.   Ro 7:2-3; 2Co 6:14

Food Sacrificed to Idols

8 Now about food sacrificed to idols: We know that we all possess knowledge.*b* Knowledge puffs up, but love builds up. **2**The man who thinks he knows something does not yet know as he ought to know. **3**But the man who loves God is known by God.

4So then, about eating food sacrificed to idols: We know that an idol is nothing at all in the world and that there is no God but one. **5**For even if there are so-called gods, whether in heaven or on earth (as indeed there are many "gods" and many "lords"), **6**yet for us there is but one God, the Father, from whom all things came and for whom we live; and there is but one Lord, Jesus Christ, through whom all things came and through whom we live.   Ro 11:36; Mal 2:10

7But not everyone knows this. Some people are still so accustomed to idols that when they eat such food they think of it as having been sacrificed to an idol, and since their conscience is weak, it is defiled. **8**But food does not bring us near to God; we are no worse if we do not eat, and no better if we do.   Ro 14:14,17

9Be careful, however, that the exercise of your freedom does not

---

a 36-38 Or 36If anyone thinks he is not treating his daughter properly, and if she is getting along in years, and he feels she ought to marry, he should do as he wants. He is not sinning. He should let her get married. 37But the man who has settled the matter in his own mind, who is under no compulsion but has control over his own will, and who has made up his mind to keep the virgin unmarried—this man also does the right thing. 38So then, he who gives his virgin in marriage does right, but he who does not give her in marriage does even better.   *b 1 Or "We all possess knowledge," as you say*

become a stumbling block to the weak. [10]For if anyone with a weak conscience sees you who have this knowledge eating in an idol's temple, won't he be emboldened to eat what has been sacrificed to idols? [11]So this weak brother, for whom Christ died, is destroyed by your knowledge. [12]When you sin against your brothers in this way and wound their weak conscience, you sin against Christ. [13]Therefore, if what I eat causes my brother to fall into sin, I will never eat meat again, so that I will not cause him to fall. Mt 18:6; Ro 14:21; Gal 5:13

The Rights of an Apostle

9 Am I not free? Am I not an apostle? Have I not seen Jesus our Lord? Are you not the result of my work in the Lord? [2]Even though I may not be an apostle to others, surely I am to you! For you are the seal of my apostleship in the Lord. 1Co 3:6; 2Co 3:2-3

[3]This is my defense to those who sit in judgment on me. [4]Don't we have the right to food and drink? [5]Don't we have the right to take a believing wife along with us, as do the other apostles and the Lord's brothers and Cephas[a]? [6]Or is it only I and Barnabas who must work for a living? Ac 4:36; 1Th 2:6

[7]Who serves as a soldier at his own expense? Who plants a vineyard and does not eat of its grapes? Who tends a flock and does not drink of the milk? [8]Do I say this merely from a human point of view? Doesn't the Law say the same thing? [9]For it is written in the Law of Moses: "Do not muzzle an ox while it is treading out the grain."[b] Is it about oxen that God is concerned? [10]Surely he says this for us, doesn't he? Yes, this was written for us, because when the plowman plows and the thresher threshes, they ought to do so in the hope of sharing in the harvest. [11]If we have sown spiritual seed among you, is it too much if we reap a material harvest from you? [12]If others have this right of support from you, shouldn't we have it all the more? Ro 15:27; 2Ti 2:6

But we did not use this right. On the contrary, we put up with anything rather than hinder the gospel of Christ. [13]Don't you know that those who work in the temple get their food from the temple, and those who serve at the altar share in what is offered on the altar? [14]In the same way, the Lord has commanded that those who preach the gospel should receive their living from the gospel. Mt 10:10; 1Ti 5:18

[15]But I have not used any of these rights. And I am not writing this in the hope that you will do such things for me. I would rather die than have anyone deprive me of this boast. [16]Yet when I preach the gospel, I cannot boast, for I am compelled to preach. Woe to me if

---

[a]5 That is, Peter   [b]9 Deut. 25:4

I do not preach the gospel! ¹⁷If I preach voluntarily, I have a reward; if not voluntarily, I am simply discharging the trust committed to me. ¹⁸What then is my reward? Just this: that in preaching the gospel I may offer it free of charge, and so not make use of my rights in preaching it.   1Co 3:8,14

¹⁹Though I am free and belong to no man, I make myself a slave to everyone, to win as many as possible. ²⁰To the Jews I became like a Jew, to win the Jews. To those under the law I became like one under the law (though I myself am not under the law), so as to win those under the law. ²¹To those not having the law I became like one not having the law (though I am not free from God's law but am under Christ's law), so as to win those not having the law. ²²To the weak I became weak, to win the weak. I have become all things to all men so that by all possible means I might save some. ²³I do all this for the sake of the gospel, that I may share in its blessings.   Ro 2:12,14; 1Co 10:33

²⁴Do you not know that in a race all the runners run, but only one gets the prize? Run in such a way as to get the prize. ²⁵Everyone who competes in the games goes into strict training. They do it to get a crown that will not last; but we do it to get a crown that will last forever. ²⁶Therefore I do not run like a man running aimlessly; I do not fight like a man beating the air. ²⁷No, I beat my body and make it my slave so that after I have preached to others, I myself will not be disqualified for the prize.

Warnings From Israel's History

10 For I do not want you to be ignorant of the fact, brothers, that our forefathers were all under the cloud and that they all passed through the sea. ²They were all baptized into Moses in the cloud and in the sea. ³They all ate the same spiritual food ⁴and drank the same spiritual drink; for they drank from the spiritual rock that accompanied them, and that rock was Christ. ⁵Nevertheless, God was not pleased with most of them; their bodies were scattered over the desert.   Nu 14:29; Heb 3:17

⁶Now these things occurred as examples*ᵃ* to keep us from setting our hearts on evil things as they did. ⁷Do not be idolaters, as some of them were; as it is written: "The people sat down to eat and drink and got up to indulge in pagan revelry."*ᵇ* ⁸We should not commit sexual immorality, as some of them did—and in one day twenty-three thousand of them died. ⁹We should not test the Lord, as some of them did—and were killed by snakes. ¹⁰And do not grumble, as some of them did—and were killed by the destroying angel.

---

*ᵃ*6 Or *types*; also in verse 11   *ᵇ*7 Exodus 32:6

[11]These things happened to them as examples and were written down as warnings for us, on whom the fulfillment of the ages has come. [12]So, if you think you are standing firm, be careful that you don't fall! [13]No temptation has seized you except what is common to man. And God is faithful; he will not let you be tempted beyond what you can bear. But when you are tempted, he will also provide a way out so that you can stand up under it. Ro 11:20; 2Pe 2:9

Idol Feasts and the Lord's Supper

[14]Therefore, my dear friends, flee from idolatry. [15]I speak to sensible people; judge for yourselves what I say. [16]Is not the cup of thanksgiving for which we give thanks a participation in the blood of Christ? And is not the bread that we break a participation in the body of Christ? [17]Because there is one loaf, we, who are many, are one body, for we all partake of the one loaf. Mt 26:26-28; 1Co 12:27

[18]Consider the people of Israel: Do not those who eat the sacrifices participate in the altar? [19]Do I mean then that a sacrifice offered to an idol is anything, or that an idol is anything? [20]No, but the sacrifices of pagans are offered to demons, not to God, and I do not want you to be participants with demons. [21]You cannot drink the cup of the Lord and the cup of demons too; you cannot have a part in both the Lord's table and the table of demons. [22]Are we trying to arouse the Lord's jealousy? Are we stronger than he? Dt 32:16,21; Isa 45:9

The Believer's Freedom

[23]"Everything is permissible"— but not everything is beneficial. "Everything is permissible"—but not everything is constructive. [24]Nobody should seek his own good, but the good of others.

[25]Eat anything sold in the meat market without raising questions of conscience, [26]for, "The earth is the Lord's, and everything in it."[a]

[27]If some unbeliever invites you to a meal and you want to go, eat whatever is put before you without raising questions of conscience. [28]But if anyone says to you, "This has been offered in sacrifice," then do not eat it, both for the sake of the man who told you and for conscience' sake[b]— [29]the other man's conscience, I mean, not yours. For why should my freedom be judged by another's conscience? [30]If I take part in the meal with thankfulness, why am I denounced because of something I thank God for?

[31]So whether you eat or drink or whatever you do, do it all for the glory of God. [32]Do not cause anyone to stumble, whether Jews,

---

[a]26 Psalm 24:1 [b]28 Some manuscripts conscience' sake, for "the earth is the Lord's and everything in it"

Greeks or the church of God— ³³even as I try to please everybody in every way. For I am not seeking my own good but the good of many, so that they may be saved.

11

¹Follow my example, as I follow the example of Christ.

Ro 11:14; 15:2

Propriety in Worship

²I praise you for remembering me in everything and for holding to the teachings,ᵃ just as I passed them on to you.

1Co 4:17; 15:2-3

³Now I want you to realize that the head of every man is Christ, and the head of the woman is man, and the head of Christ is God. ⁴Every man who prays or prophesies with his head covered dishonors his head. ⁵And every woman who prays or prophesies with her head uncovered dishonors her head—it is just as though her head were shaved. ⁶If a woman does not cover her head, she should have her hair cut off; and if it is a disgrace for a woman to have her hair cut or shaved off, she should cover her head. ⁷A man ought not to cover his head,ᵇ since he is the image and glory of God; but the woman is the glory of man. ⁸For man did not come from woman, but woman from man; ⁹neither was man created for woman, but woman for man. ¹⁰For this reason, and because of the angels, the woman ought to have a sign of authority on her head.

Ge 2:21-23; Jas 3:9

¹¹In the Lord, however, woman is not independent of man, nor is man independent of woman. ¹²For as woman came from man, so also man is born of woman. But everything comes from God. ¹³Judge for yourselves: Is it proper for a woman to pray to God with her head uncovered? ¹⁴Does not the very nature of things teach you that if a man has long hair, it is a disgrace to him, ¹⁵but that if a woman has long hair, it is her glory? For long hair is given to her as a covering. ¹⁶If anyone wants to be contentious about this, we have no other practice—nor do the churches of God.

Ro 11:36; 1Co 7:17

The Lord's Supper

¹⁷In the following directives I have no praise for you, for your meetings do more harm than good. ¹⁸In the first place, I hear that when you come together as a church, there are divisions among you, and to some extent I believe it. ¹⁹No doubt there have to be differences among you to show which of you have God's approval. ²⁰When you come together, it is not the Lord's Supper you eat,

---

ᵃ2 Or traditions   ᵇ4-7 Or ⁴Every man who prays or prophesies with long hair dishonors his head. ⁵And every woman who prays or prophesies with no covering of hair on her head dishonors her head—she is just like one of the "shorn women." ⁶If a woman has no covering, let her be for now with short hair, but since it is a disgrace for a woman to have her hair shorn or shaved, she should grow it again. ⁷A man ought not to have long hair

²¹for as you eat, each of you goes ahead without waiting for anybody else. One remains hungry, another gets drunk. ²²Don't you have homes to eat and drink in? Or do you despise the church of God and humiliate those who have nothing? What shall I say to you? Shall I praise you for this? Certainly not!   1Co 1:10-12; 1Jn 2:19

²³For I received from the Lord what I also passed on to you: The Lord Jesus, on the night he was betrayed, took bread, ²⁴and when he had given thanks, he broke it and said, "This is my body, which is for you; do this in remembrance of me." ²⁵In the same way, after supper he took the cup, saying, "This cup is the new covenant in my blood; do this, whenever you drink it, in remembrance of me." ²⁶For whenever you eat this bread and drink this cup, you proclaim the Lord's death until he comes.

²⁷Therefore, whoever eats the bread or drinks the cup of the Lord in an unworthy manner will be guilty of sinning against the body and blood of the Lord. ²⁸A man ought to examine himself before he eats of the bread and drinks of the cup. ²⁹For anyone who eats and drinks without recognizing the body of the Lord eats and drinks judgment on himself. ³⁰That is why many among you are weak and sick, and a number of you have fallen asleep. ³¹But if we judged ourselves, we would not come under judgment. ³²When we are judged by the Lord, we are being disciplined so that we will not be condemned with the world.

³³So then, my brothers, when you come together to eat, wait for each other. ³⁴If anyone is hungry, he should eat at home, so that when you meet together it may not result in judgment.   ver 21-22

And when I come I will give further directions.   1Co 4:19

Spiritual Gifts

12 Now about spiritual gifts, brothers, I do not want you to be ignorant. ²You know that when you were pagans, somehow or other you were influenced and led astray to mute idols. ³Therefore I tell you that no one who is speaking by the Spirit of God says, "Jesus be cursed," and no one can say, "Jesus is Lord," except by the Holy Spirit.   Ro 1:11; 1Th 1:9; 1Jn 4:2-3

⁴There are different kinds of gifts, but the same Spirit. ⁵There are different kinds of service, but the same Lord. ⁶There are different kinds of working, but the same God works all of them in all men.

⁷Now to each one the manifestation of the Spirit is given for the common good. ⁸To one there is given through the Spirit the message of wisdom, to another the message of knowledge by means of the same Spirit, ⁹to another faith by the same Spirit, to another gifts of healing by that one Spirit, ¹⁰to

another miraculous powers, to another prophecy, to another distinguishing between spirits, to another speaking in different kinds of tongues,[a] and to still another the interpretation of tongues.[a] [11]All these are the work of one and the same Spirit, and he gives them to each one, just as he determines.

One Body, Many Parts

[12]The body is a unit, though it is made up of many parts; and though all its parts are many, they form one body. So it is with Christ. [13]For we were all baptized by[b] one Spirit into one body—whether Jews or Greeks, slave or free—and we were all given the one Spirit to drink. Gal 3:28; Col 3:11

[14]Now the body is not made up of one part but of many. [15]If the foot should say, "Because I am not a hand, I do not belong to the body," it would not for that reason cease to be part of the body. [16]And if the ear should say, "Because I am not an eye, I do not belong to the body," it would not for that reason cease to be part of the body. [17]If the whole body were an eye, where would the sense of hearing be? If the whole body were an ear, where would the sense of smell be? [18]But in fact God has arranged the parts in the body, every one of them, just as he wanted them to be. [19]If they were all one part, where would the body be? [20]As it is, there are many parts, but one body. Ro 12:5

[21]The eye cannot say to the hand, "I don't need you!" And the head cannot say to the feet, "I don't need you!" [22]On the contrary, those parts of the body that seem to be weaker are indispensable, [23]and the parts that we think are less honorable we treat with special honor. And the parts that are unpresentable are treated with special modesty, [24]while our presentable parts need no special treatment. But God has combined the members of the body and has given greater honor to the parts that lacked it, [25]so that there should be no division in the body, but that its parts should have equal concern for each other. [26]If one part suffers, every part suffers with it; if one part is honored, every part rejoices with it.

[27]Now you are the body of Christ, and each one of you is a part of it. [28]And in the church God has appointed first of all apostles, second prophets, third teachers, then workers of miracles, also those having gifts of healing, those able to help others, those with gifts of administration, and those speaking in different kinds of tongues. [29]Are all apostles? Are all prophets? Are all teachers? Do all work miracles? [30]Do all have gifts of healing? Do all speak in

[a] 10 Or *languages*; also in verse 28   [b] 13 Or *with*; or *in*

tongues*a*? Do all interpret? **31**But eagerly desire*b* the greater gifts.

Love

And now I will show you the most excellent way.

13 If I speak in the tongues*c* of men and of angels, but have not love, I am only a resounding gong or a clanging cymbal. **2**If I have the gift of prophecy and can fathom all mysteries and all knowledge, and if I have a faith that can move mountains, but have not love, I am nothing. **3**If I give all I possess to the poor and surrender my body to the flames,*d* but have not love, I gain nothing.

4Love is patient, love is kind. It does not envy, it does not boast, it is not proud. **5**It is not rude, it is not self-seeking, it is not easily angered, it keeps no record of wrongs. **6**Love does not delight in evil but rejoices with the truth. **7**It always protects, always trusts, always hopes, always perseveres.

8Love never fails. But where there are prophecies, they will cease; where there are tongues, they will be stilled; where there is knowledge, it will pass away. **9**For we know in part and we prophesy in part, **10**but when perfection comes, the imperfect disappears. **11**When I was a child, I talked like a child, I thought like a child, I reasoned like a child. When I became a man, I put childish ways behind me. **12**Now we see but a poor reflection as in a mirror; then we shall see face to face. Now I know in part; then I shall know fully, even as I am fully known. 1Co 8:3

13And now these three remain: faith, hope and love. But the greatest of these is love. 1Co 16:14

Gifts of Prophecy and Tongues

14 Follow the way of love and eagerly desire spiritual gifts, especially the gift of prophecy. **2**For anyone who speaks in a tongue*e* does not speak to men but to God. Indeed, no one understands him; he utters mysteries with his spirit.*f* **3**But everyone who prophesies speaks to men for their strengthening, encouragement and comfort. **4**He who speaks in a tongue edifies himself, but he who prophesies edifies the church. **5**I would like every one of you to speak in tongues,*g* but I would rather have you prophesy. He who prophesies is greater than one who speaks in tongues,*g* unless he interprets, so that the church may be edified. Nu 11:29; 1Co 12:31

6Now, brothers, if I come to you and speak in tongues, what good will I be to you, unless I bring you some revelation or knowledge or prophecy or word of instruction? **7**Even in the case of lifeless things that make sounds, such as the

---

a 30 Or *other languages*   *b 31* Or *But you are eagerly desiring*   *c 1* Or *languages*   *d 3* Some early manuscripts *body that I may boast*   *e 2* Or *another language*; also in verses 4, 13, 14, 19, 26 and 27   *f 2* Or *by the Spirit*   *g 5* Or *other languages*; also in verses 6, 18, 22, 23 and 39

flute or harp, how will anyone know what tune is being played unless there is a distinction in the notes? ⁸Again, if the trumpet does not sound a clear call, who will get ready for battle? ⁹So it is with you. Unless you speak intelligible words with your tongue, how will anyone know what you are saying? You will just be speaking into the air. ¹⁰Undoubtedly there are all sorts of languages in the world, yet none of them is without meaning. ¹¹If then I do not grasp the meaning of what someone is saying, I am a foreigner to the speaker, and he is a foreigner to me. ¹²So it is with you. Since you are eager to have spiritual gifts, try to excel in gifts that build up the church.

¹³For this reason anyone who speaks in a tongue should pray that he may interpret what he says. ¹⁴For if I pray in a tongue, my spirit prays, but my mind is unfruitful. ¹⁵So what shall I do? I will pray with my spirit, but I will also pray with my mind; I will sing with my spirit, but I will also sing with my mind. ¹⁶If you are praising God with your spirit, how can one who finds himself among those who do not understand*ᵃ* say "Amen" to your thanksgiving, since he does not know what you are saying? ¹⁷You may be giving thanks well enough, but the other man is not edified.   1Ch 16:36; 1Co 11:24

¹⁸I thank God that I speak in tongues more than all of you. ¹⁹But in the church I would rather speak five intelligible words to instruct others than ten thousand words in a tongue.   ver 6

²⁰Brothers, stop thinking like children. In regard to evil be infants, but in your thinking be adults. ²¹In the Law it is written:

"Through men of strange
        tongues
and through the lips of
        foreigners
I will speak to this people,
but even then they will not
        listen to me,"*ᵇ*   Isa 28:11-12

says the Lord.

²²Tongues, then, are a sign, not for believers but for unbelievers; prophecy, however, is for believers, not for unbelievers. ²³So if the whole church comes together and everyone speaks in tongues, and some who do not understand*ᶜ* or some unbelievers come in, will they not say that you are out of your mind? ²⁴But if an unbeliever or someone who does not understand*ᵈ* comes in while everybody is prophesying, he will be convinced by all that he is a sinner and will be judged by all, ²⁵and the secrets of his heart will be laid bare. So he will fall down and worship God, exclaiming, "God is really among you!"   Isa 45:14; Zec 8:23; Ac 2:13

ᵃ16 Or among the inquirers   ᵇ21 Isaiah 28:11,12   ᶜ23 Or some inquirers   ᵈ24 Or or some inquirer

Orderly Worship

26What then shall we say, brothers? When you come together, everyone has a hymn, or a word of instruction, a revelation, a tongue or an interpretation. All of these must be done for the strengthening of the church. 27If anyone speaks in a tongue, two—or at the most three—should speak, one at a time, and someone must interpret. 28If there is no interpreter, the speaker should keep quiet in the church and speak to himself and God.   Ro 14:19; 1Co 12:7-10

29Two or three prophets should speak, and the others should weigh carefully what is said. 30And if a revelation comes to someone who is sitting down, the first speaker should stop. 31For you can all prophesy in turn so that everyone may be instructed and encouraged. 32The spirits of prophets are subject to the control of prophets. 33For God is not a God of disorder but of peace.   1Co 12:10; 1Jn 4:1

As in all the congregations of the saints, 34women should remain silent in the churches. They are not allowed to speak, but must be in submission, as the Law says. 35If they want to inquire about something, they should ask their own husbands at home; for it is disgraceful for a woman to speak in the church.   1Ti 2:11-12

36Did the word of God originate with you? Or are you the only people it has reached? 37If anybody thinks he is a prophet or spiritually gifted, let him acknowledge that what I am writing to you is the Lord's command. 38If he ignores this, he himself will be ignored.a

39Therefore, my brothers, be eager to prophesy, and do not forbid speaking in tongues. 40But everything should be done in a fitting and orderly way.   1Co 12:31

The Resurrection of Christ

15 Now, brothers, I want to remind you of the gospel I preached to you, which you received and on which you have taken your stand. 2By this gospel you are saved, if you hold firmly to the word I preached to you. Otherwise, you have believed in vain.

3For what I received I passed on to you as of first importanceb: that Christ died for our sins according to the Scriptures, 4that he was buried, that he was raised on the third day according to the Scriptures, 5and that he appeared to Peter,c and then to the Twelve. 6After that, he appeared to more than five hundred of the brothers at the same time, most of whom are still living, though some have fallen asleep. 7Then he appeared to James, then to all the apostles, 8and last of all he appeared to me also, as to one abnormally born.   Ac 1:3-4; 9:3-6,17

---

a38 Some manuscripts If he is ignorant of this, let him be ignorant   b3 Or you at the first   c5 Greek Cephas

⁹For I am the least of the apostles and do not even deserve to be called an apostle, because I persecuted the church of God. ¹⁰But by the grace of God I am what I am, and his grace to me was not without effect. No, I worked harder than all of them—yet not I, but the grace of God that was with me. ¹¹Whether, then, it was I or they, this is what we preach, and this is what you believed.   2Co 11:23; Php 2:13

The Resurrection of the Dead

¹²But if it is preached that Christ has been raised from the dead, how can some of you say that there is no resurrection of the dead? ¹³If there is no resurrection of the dead, then not even Christ has been raised. ¹⁴And if Christ has not been raised, our preaching is useless and so is your faith. ¹⁵More than that, we are then found to be false witnesses about God, for we have testified about God that he raised Christ from the dead. But he did not raise him if in fact the dead are not raised. ¹⁶For if the dead are not raised, then Christ has not been raised either. ¹⁷And if Christ has not been raised, your faith is futile; you are still in your sins. ¹⁸Then those also who have fallen asleep in Christ are lost. ¹⁹If only for this life we have hope in Christ, we are to be pitied more than all men.   Ac 2:24; Ro 4:25

²⁰But Christ has indeed been raised from the dead, the firstfruits of those who have fallen asleep. ²¹For since death came through a man, the resurrection of the dead comes also through a man. ²²For as in Adam all die, so in Christ all will be made alive. ²³But each in his own turn: Christ, the firstfruits; then, when he comes, those who belong to him. ²⁴Then the end will come, when he hands over the kingdom to God the Father after he has destroyed all dominion, authority and power. ²⁵For he must reign until he has put all his enemies under his feet. ²⁶The last enemy to be destroyed is death. ²⁷For he "has put everything under his feet."[a] Now when it says that "everything" has been put under him, it is clear that this does not include God himself, who put everything under Christ. ²⁸When he has done this, then the Son himself will be made subject to him who put everything under him, so that God may be all in all.   1Co 3:23; Php 3:21

²⁹Now if there is no resurrection, what will those do who are baptized for the dead? If the dead are not raised at all, why are people baptized for them? ³⁰And as for us, why do we endanger ourselves every hour? ³¹I die every day—I mean that, brothers—just as surely as I glory over you in Christ Jesus our Lord. ³²If I fought wild beasts in Ephesus for merely hu-

a 27 Psalm 8:6

man reasons, what have I gained? If the dead are not raised,   2Co 1:8

"Let us eat and drink,
    for tomorrow we die."[a]

33Do not be misled: "Bad company corrupts good character." 34Come back to your senses as you ought, and stop sinning; for there are some who are ignorant of God—I say this to your shame.   Isa 22:13

The Resurrection Body

35But someone may ask, "How are the dead raised? With what kind of body will they come?" 36How foolish! What you sow does not come to life unless it dies. 37When you sow, you do not plant the body that will be, but just a seed, perhaps of wheat or of something else. 38But God gives it a body as he has determined, and to each kind of seed he gives its own body. 39All flesh is not the same: Men have one kind of flesh, animals have another, birds another and fish another. 40There are also heavenly bodies and there are earthly bodies; but the splendor of the heavenly bodies is one kind, and the splendor of the earthly bodies is another. 41The sun has one kind of splendor, the moon another and the stars another; and star differs from star in splendor.

42So will it be with the resurrection of the dead. The body that is sown is perishable, it is raised imperishable; 43it is sown in dishonor, it is raised in glory; it is sown in weakness, it is raised in power; 44it is sown a natural body, it is raised a spiritual body.   Mt 13:43

If there is a natural body, there is also a spiritual body. 45So it is written: "The first man Adam became a living being"[b]; the last Adam, a life-giving spirit. 46The spiritual did not come first, but the natural, and after that the spiritual. 47The first man was of the dust of the earth, the second man from heaven. 48As was the earthly man, so are those who are of the earth; and as is the man from heaven, so also are those who are of heaven. 49And just as we have borne the likeness of the earthly man, so shall we[c] bear the likeness of the man from heaven.   Ge 5:3; Ro 8:29

50I declare to you, brothers, that flesh and blood cannot inherit the kingdom of God, nor does the perishable inherit the imperishable. 51Listen, I tell you a mystery: We will not all sleep, but we will all be changed— 52in a flash, in the twinkling of an eye, at the last trumpet. For the trumpet will sound, the dead will be raised imperishable, and we will be changed. 53For the perishable must clothe itself with the imperishable, and the mortal with immortality. 54When the perishable has been clothed with the imperishable, and the mortal with immortality, then the saying that is

a32 Isaiah 22:13   b45 Gen. 2:7   c49 Some early manuscripts so let us written will come true: "Death has been swallowed up in victory."[a]

55"Where, O death, is your
      victory?
   Where, O death, is your
      sting?"[b]

56The sting of death is sin, and the power of sin is the law. 57But thanks be to God! He gives us the victory through our Lord Jesus Christ. Hos 13:14; Ro 4:15; 8:37

58Therefore, my dear brothers, stand firm. Let nothing move you. Always give yourselves fully to the work of the Lord, because you know that your labor in the Lord is not in vain. 1Co 16:10

The Collection for God's People

16 Now about the collection for God's people: Do what I told the Galatian churches to do. 2On the first day of every week, each one of you should set aside a sum of money in keeping with his income, saving it up, so that when I come no collections will have to be made. 3Then, when I arrive, I will give letters of introduction to the men you approve and send them with your gift to Jerusalem. 4If it seems advisable for me to go also, they will accompany me.

Personal Requests

5After I go through Macedonia, I will come to you—for I will be going through Macedonia. 6Perhaps I will stay with you awhile, or even spend the winter, so that you can help me on my journey, wherever I go. 7I do not want to see you now and make only a passing visit; I hope to spend some time with you, if the Lord permits. 8But I will stay on at Ephesus until Pentecost, 9because a great door for effective work has opened to me, and there are many who oppose me.

10If Timothy comes, see to it that he has nothing to fear while he is with you, for he is carrying on the work of the Lord, just as I am. 11No one, then, should refuse to accept him. Send him on his way in peace so that he may return to me. I am expecting him along with the brothers. 1Co 15:58; 1Ti 4:12

12Now about our brother Apollos: I strongly urged him to go to you with the brothers. He was quite unwilling to go now, but he will go when he has the opportunity. Ac 18:24; 1Co 1:12

13Be on your guard; stand firm in the faith; be men of courage; be strong. 14Do everything in love.

15You know that the household of Stephanas were the first converts in Achaia, and they have devoted themselves to the service of the saints. I urge you, brothers, 16to submit to such as these and to everyone who joins in the work, and labors at it. 17I was glad when Stephanas, Fortunatus and Achaicus arrived, because they have supplied what was lacking from you. [18]For they refreshed my spirit and yours also. Such men deserve recognition.   2Co 11:9; Php 2:29

Final Greetings

[19]The churches in the province of Asia send you greetings. Aquila and Priscilla[a] greet you warmly in the Lord, and so does the church that meets at their house. [20]All the brothers here send you greetings. Greet one another with a holy kiss.

[21]I, Paul, write this greeting in my own hand.   Gal 6:11; Col 4:18

[22]If anyone does not love the Lord—a curse be on him. Come, O Lord[b]!   Ro 9:3; Eph 6:24

[23]The grace of the Lord Jesus be with you.   Ro 16:20

[24]My love to all of you in Christ Jesus. Amen.[c]

---

[a]19 Greek Prisca, a variant of Priscilla   [b]22 In Aramaic the expression Come, O Lord is Marana tha.
[c]24 Some manuscripts do not have Amen.

2 Corinthians

1 Paul, an apostle of Christ Jesus by the will of God, and Timothy our brother,   Col 1:1; 2Ti 1:1

To the church of God in Corinth, together with all the saints throughout Achaia: Ac 18:12

[2]Grace and peace to you from God our Father and the Lord Jesus Christ.   Ro 1:7

The God of All Comfort

[3]Praise be to the God and Father of our Lord Jesus Christ, the Father of compassion and the God of all comfort, [4]who comforts us in all our troubles, so that we can comfort those in any trouble with the comfort we ourselves have received from God. [5]For just as the sufferings of Christ flow over into our lives, so also through Christ our comfort overflows. [6]If we are distressed, it is for your comfort and salvation; if we are comforted, it is for your comfort, which produces in you patient endurance of the same sufferings we suffer. [7]And our hope for you is firm, because we know that just as you share in our sufferings, so also you share in our comfort.   2Co 4:10,15

[8]We do not want you to be uninformed, brothers, about the hardships we suffered in the province of Asia. We were under great pressure, far beyond our ability to endure, so that we despaired even of life. [9]Indeed, in our hearts we felt the sentence of death. But this happened that we might not rely on ourselves but on God, who raises the dead. [10]He has delivered us from such a deadly peril, and he will deliver us. On him we have set our hope that he will continue to deliver us, [11]as you help us by your prayers. Then many will give thanks on our[a] behalf for the gracious favor granted us in answer to the prayers of many.   Ro 15:30

Paul's Change of Plans

[12]Now this is our boast: Our conscience testifies that we have conducted ourselves in the world, and especially in our relations with you, in the holiness and sincerity that are from God. We have done so not according to worldly wisdom but according to God's grace. [13]For we do not write you anything you cannot read or understand. And I hope that, [14]as you have understood us in part, you will come to understand fully that you can boast of us just as we will boast of you in the day of the Lord Jesus.

[a]11 Many manuscripts your

¹⁵Because I was confident of this, I planned to visit you first so that you might benefit twice. ¹⁶I planned to visit you on my way to Macedonia and to come back to you from Macedonia, and then to have you send me on my way to Judea. ¹⁷When I planned this, did I do it lightly? Or do I make my plans in a worldly manner so that in the same breath I say, "Yes, yes" and "No, no"?   1Co 16:5-7; 2Co 10:2-3

¹⁸But as surely as God is faithful, our message to you is not "Yes" and "No." ¹⁹For the Son of God, Jesus Christ, who was preached among you by me and Silas[a] and Timothy, was not "Yes" and "No," but in him it has always been "Yes." ²⁰For no matter how many promises God has made, they are "Yes" in Christ. And so through him the "Amen" is spoken by us to the glory of God. ²¹Now it is God who makes both us and you stand firm in Christ. He anointed us, ²²set his seal of ownership on us, and put his Spirit in our hearts as a deposit, guaranteeing what is to come.   2Co 5:5; 1Jn 2:20,27

²³I call God as my witness that it was in order to spare you that I did not return to Corinth. ²⁴Not that we lord it over your faith, but we work with you for your joy, because it is by faith you stand firm.

2 ¹So I made up my mind that I would not make another painful visit to you. ²For if I grieve you, who is left to make me glad but you whom I have grieved? ³I wrote as I did so that when I came I should not be distressed by those who ought to make me rejoice. I had confidence in all of you, that you would all share my joy. ⁴For I wrote you out of great distress and anguish of heart and with many tears, not to grieve you but to let you know the depth of my love for you.   2Co 7:8,12; 12:21

Forgiveness for the Sinner

⁵If anyone has caused grief, he has not so much grieved me as he has grieved all of you, to some extent—not to put it too severely. ⁶The punishment inflicted on him by the majority is sufficient for him. ⁷Now instead, you ought to forgive and comfort him, so that he will not be overwhelmed by excessive sorrow. ⁸I urge you, therefore, to reaffirm your love for him. ⁹The reason I wrote you was to see if you would stand the test and be obedient in everything. ¹⁰If you forgive anyone, I also forgive him. And what I have forgiven—if there was anything to forgive—I have forgiven in the sight of Christ for your sake, ¹¹in order that Satan might not outwit us. For we are not unaware of his schemes.   2Co 10:6

Ministers of the New Covenant

¹²Now when I went to Troas to preach the gospel of Christ and

---

a 19 Greek Silvanus, a variant of Silas

found that the Lord had opened a door for me, ¹³I still had no peace of mind, because I did not find my brother Titus there. So I said good-by to them and went on to Macedonia. Ac 16:8; 2Co 7:5-6,13

¹⁴But thanks be to God, who always leads us in triumphal procession in Christ and through us spreads everywhere the fragrance of the knowledge of him. ¹⁵For we are to God the aroma of Christ among those who are being saved and those who are perishing. ¹⁶To the one we are the smell of death; to the other, the fragrance of life. And who is equal to such a task? ¹⁷Unlike so many, we do not peddle the word of God for profit. On the contrary, in Christ we speak before God with sincerity, like men sent from God. Lk 2:34; 2Co 1:12

3 Are we beginning to commend ourselves again? Or do we need, like some people, letters of recommendation to you or from you? ²You yourselves are our letter, written on our hearts, known and read by everybody. ³You show that you are a letter from Christ, the result of our ministry, written not with ink but with the Spirit of the living God, not on tablets of stone but on tablets of human hearts. Jer 31:33; Eze 11:19

⁴Such confidence as this is ours through Christ before God. ⁵Not that we are competent in ourselves to claim anything for ourselves, but our competence comes from God. ⁶He has made us competent as ministers of a new covenant—not of the letter but of the Spirit; for the letter kills, but the Spirit gives life. Jn 6:63; 1Co 15:10

The Glory of the New Covenant

⁷Now if the ministry that brought death, which was engraved in letters on stone, came with glory, so that the Israelites could not look steadily at the face of Moses because of its glory, fading though it was, ⁸will not the ministry of the Spirit be even more glorious? ⁹If the ministry that condemns men is glorious, how much more glorious is the ministry that brings righteousness! ¹⁰For what was glorious has no glory now in comparison with the surpassing glory. ¹¹And if what was fading away came with glory, how much greater is the glory of that which lasts! Ex 34:29-35; Ro 1:17

¹²Therefore, since we have such a hope, we are very bold. ¹³We are not like Moses, who would put a veil over his face to keep the Israelites from gazing at it while the radiance was fading away. ¹⁴But their minds were made dull, for to this day the same veil remains when the old covenant is read. It has not been removed, because only in Christ is it taken away. ¹⁵Even to this day when Moses is read, a veil covers their hearts. ¹⁶But whenever anyone turns to the Lord, the veil is taken away.

[17]Now the Lord is the Spirit, and where the Spirit of the Lord is, there is freedom. [18]And we, who with unveiled faces all reflect[a] the Lord's glory, are being transformed into his likeness with ever-increasing glory, which comes from the Lord, who is the Spirit.

Treasures in Jars of Clay

4 Therefore, since through God's mercy we have this ministry, we do not lose heart. [2]Rather, we have renounced secret and shameful ways; we do not use deception, nor do we distort the word of God. On the contrary, by setting forth the truth plainly we commend ourselves to every man's conscience in the sight of God. [3]And even if our gospel is veiled, it is veiled to those who are perishing. [4]The god of this age has blinded the minds of unbelievers, so that they cannot see the light of the gospel of the glory of Christ, who is the image of God. [5]For we do not preach ourselves, but Jesus Christ as Lord, and ourselves as your servants for Jesus' sake. [6]For God, who said, "Let light shine out of darkness,"[b] made his light shine in our hearts to give us the light of the knowledge of the glory of God in the face of Christ.

[7]But we have this treasure in jars of clay to show that this all-surpassing power is from God and not from us. [8]We are hard pressed on every side, but not crushed; perplexed, but not in despair; [9]persecuted, but not abandoned; struck down, but not destroyed. [10]We always carry around in our body the death of Jesus, so that the life of Jesus may also be revealed in our body. [11]For we who are alive are always being given over to death for Jesus' sake, so that his life may be revealed in our mortal body. [12]So then, death is at work in us, but life is at work in you.   1Co 2:5

[13]It is written: "I believed; therefore I have spoken."[c] With that same spirit of faith we also believe and therefore speak, [14]because we know that the one who raised the Lord Jesus from the dead will also raise us with Jesus and present us with you in his presence. [15]All this is for your benefit, so that the grace that is reaching more and more people may cause thanksgiving to overflow to the glory of God.

[16]Therefore we do not lose heart. Though outwardly we are wasting away, yet inwardly we are being renewed day by day. [17]For our light and momentary troubles are achieving for us an eternal glory that far outweighs them all. [18]So we fix our eyes not on what is seen, but on what is unseen. For what is seen is temporary, but what is unseen is eternal.   Ro 8:24

---

a 18 Or *contemplate*   *b 6* Gen. 1:3   *c 13* Psalm 116:10

Our Heavenly Dwelling

5 Now we know that if the earthly tent we live in is destroyed, we have a building from God, an eternal house in heaven, not built by human hands. ²Meanwhile we groan, longing to be clothed with our heavenly dwelling, ³because when we are clothed, we will not be found naked. ⁴For while we are in this tent, we groan and are burdened, because we do not wish to be unclothed but to be clothed with our heavenly dwelling, so that what is mortal may be swallowed up by life. ⁵Now it is God who has made us for this very purpose and has given us the Spirit as a deposit, guaranteeing what is to come.

⁶Therefore we are always confident and know that as long as we are at home in the body we are away from the Lord. ⁷We live by faith, not by sight. ⁸We are confident, I say, and would prefer to be away from the body and at home with the Lord. ⁹So we make it our goal to please him, whether we are at home in the body or away from it. ¹⁰For we must all appear before the judgment seat of Christ, that each one may receive what is due him for the things done while in the body, whether good or bad.

The Ministry of Reconciliation

¹¹Since, then, we know what it is to fear the Lord, we try to persuade men. What we are is plain to God, and I hope it is also plain to your conscience. ¹²We are not trying to commend ourselves to you again, but are giving you an opportunity to take pride in us, so that you can answer those who take pride in what is seen rather than in what is in the heart. ¹³If we are out of our mind, it is for the sake of God; if we are in our right mind, it is for you. ¹⁴For Christ's love compels us, because we are convinced that one died for all, and therefore all died. ¹⁵And he died for all, that those who live should no longer live for themselves but for him who died for them and was raised again.

¹⁶So from now on we regard no one from a worldly point of view. Though we once regarded Christ in this way, we do so no longer. ¹⁷Therefore, if anyone is in Christ, he is a new creation; the old has gone, the new has come! ¹⁸All this is from God, who reconciled us to himself through Christ and gave us the ministry of reconciliation: ¹⁹that God was reconciling the world to himself in Christ, not counting men's sins against them. And he has committed to us the message of reconciliation. ²⁰We are therefore Christ's ambassadors, as though God were making his appeal through us. We implore you on Christ's behalf: Be reconciled to God. ²¹God made him who had no sin to be sin[a] for us, so that

---

[a] 21 Or *be a sin offering*

in him we might become the righteousness of God.   1Pe 2:22,24; 1Jn 3:5

6 As God's fellow workers we urge you not to receive God's grace in vain. ²For he says,

"In the time of my favor I
          heard you,
and in the day of salvation I
          helped you."ª

I tell you, now is the time of God's favor, now is the day of salvation.

Paul's Hardships

³We put no stumbling block in anyone's path, so that our ministry will not be discredited. ⁴Rather, as servants of God we commend ourselves in every way: in great endurance; in troubles, hardships and distresses; ⁵in beatings, imprisonments and riots; in hard work, sleepless nights and hunger; ⁶in purity, understanding, patience and kindness; in the Holy Spirit and in sincere love; ⁷in truthful speech and in the power of God; with weapons of righteousness in the right hand and in the left; ⁸through glory and dishonor, bad report and good report; genuine, yet regarded as impostors; ⁹known, yet regarded as unknown; dying, and yet we live on; beaten, and yet not killed; ¹⁰sorrowful, yet always rejoicing; poor, yet making many rich; having

nothing, and yet possessing everything.   Ro 8:32; 2Co 1:8-10

¹¹We have spoken freely to you, Corinthians, and opened wide our hearts to you. ¹²We are not withholding our affection from you, but you are withholding yours from us. ¹³As a fair exchange—I speak as to my children—open wide your hearts also.   1Co 4:14

Do Not Be Yoked With Unbelievers

¹⁴Do not be yoked together with unbelievers. For what do righteousness and wickedness have in common? Or what fellowship can light have with darkness? ¹⁵What harmony is there between Christ and Belialᵇ? What does a believer have in common with an unbeliever? ¹⁶What agreement is there between the temple of God and idols? For we are the temple of the living God. As God has said: "I will live with them and walk among them, and I will be their God, and they will be my people."ᶜ   1Co 3:16; 5:9-10

¹⁷"Therefore come out from
          them
and be separate,   Rev 18:4
          says the Lord.
Touch no unclean thing,
          and I will receive you."ᵈ

ª2 Isaiah 49:8   ᵇ15 Greek Beliar, a variant of Belial   ᶜ16 Lev. 26:12; Jer. 32:38; Ezek. 37:27
ᵈ17 Isaiah 52:11; Ezek. 20:34,41

18"I will be a Father to you,
    and you will be my sons and
      daughters,
          says the Lord
          Almighty."*a*

7 Since we have these promises, dear friends, let us purify ourselves from everything that contaminates body and spirit, perfecting holiness out of reverence for God.   2Co 6:17-18

Paul's Joy

2Make room for us in your hearts. We have wronged no one, we have corrupted no one, we have exploited no one. **3**I do not say this to condemn you; I have said before that you have such a place in our hearts that we would live or die with you. **4**I have great confidence in you; I take great pride in you. I am greatly encouraged; in all our troubles my joy knows no bounds.   2Co 6:10-13

5For when we came into Macedonia, this body of ours had no rest, but we were harassed at every turn—conflicts on the outside, fears within. **6**But God, who comforts the downcast, comforted us by the coming of Titus, **7**and not only by his coming but also by the comfort you had given him. He told us about your longing for me, your deep sorrow, your ardent concern for me, so that my joy was greater than ever.   2Co 2:13; 4:8

8Even if I caused you sorrow by my letter, I do not regret it. Though I did regret it—I see that my letter hurt you, but only for a little while — **9**yet now I am happy, not because you were made sorry, but because your sorrow led you to repentance. For you became sorrowful as God intended and so were not harmed in any way by us. **10**Godly sorrow brings repentance that leads to salvation and leaves no regret, but worldly sorrow brings death. **11**See what this godly sorrow has produced in you: what earnestness, what eagerness to clear yourselves, what indignation, what alarm, what longing, what concern, what readiness to see justice done. At every point you have proved yourselves to be innocent in this matter. **12**So even though I wrote to you, it was not on account of the one who did the wrong or of the injured party, but rather that before God you could see for yourselves how devoted to us you are. **13**By all this we are encouraged.   1Co 5:1-2; 2Co 2:2,4

In addition to our own encouragement, we were especially delighted to see how happy Titus was, because his spirit has been refreshed by all of you. **14**I had boasted to him about you, and you have not embarrassed me. But just as everything we said to you was true, so our boasting about you to Titus has proved to be true as well.

a 18 2 Samuel 7:14; 7:8

¹⁵And his affection for you is all the greater when he remembers that you were all obedient, receiving him with fear and trembling. ¹⁶I am glad I can have complete confidence in you.   2Co 2:9; Php 2:12

Generosity Encouraged

8 And now, brothers, we want you to know about the grace that God has given the Macedonian churches. ²Out of the most severe trial, their overflowing joy and their extreme poverty welled up in rich generosity. ³For I testify that they gave as much as they were able, and even beyond their ability. Entirely on their own, ⁴they urgently pleaded with us for the privilege of sharing in this service to the saints. ⁵And they did not do as we expected, but they gave themselves first to the Lord and then to us in keeping with God's will. ⁶So we urged Titus, since he had earlier made a beginning, to bring also to completion this act of grace on your part. ⁷But just as you excel in everything—in faith, in speech, in knowledge, in complete earnestness and in your love for us*ᵃ*—see that you also excel in this grace of giving.   1Co 1:5

⁸I am not commanding you, but I want to test the sincerity of your love by comparing it with the earnestness of others. ⁹For you know the grace of our Lord Jesus Christ, that though he was rich, yet for your sakes he became poor, so that you through his poverty might become rich.   1Co 7:6; Php 2:6-8

¹⁰And here is my advice about what is best for you in this matter: Last year you were the first not only to give but also to have the desire to do so. ¹¹Now finish the work, so that your eager willingness to do it may be matched by your completion of it, according to your means. ¹²For if the willingness is there, the gift is acceptable according to what one has, not according to what he does not have.

¹³Our desire is not that others might be relieved while you are hard pressed, but that there might be equality. ¹⁴At the present time your plenty will supply what they need, so that in turn their plenty will supply what you need. Then there will be equality, ¹⁵as it is written: "He who gathered much did not have too much, and he who gathered little did not have too little."*ᵇ*   Ex 16:18; 2Co 9:12

Titus Sent to Corinth

¹⁶I thank God, who put into the heart of Titus the same concern I have for you. ¹⁷For Titus not only welcomed our appeal, but he is coming to you with much enthusiasm and on his own initiative. ¹⁸And we are sending along with him the brother who is praised by all the churches for his service to the gospel. ¹⁹What is more, he was

*ᵃ7 Some manuscripts in our love for you   *ᵇ15 Exodus 16:18

chosen by the churches to accompany us as we carry the offering, which we administer in order to honor the Lord himself and to show our eagerness to help. **20**We want to avoid any criticism of the way we administer this liberal gift. **21**For we are taking pains to do what is right, not only in the eyes of the Lord but also in the eyes of men.   Ro 12:17; 14:18; 1Co 16:3-4

22In addition, we are sending with them our brother who has often proved to us in many ways that he is zealous, and now even more so because of his great confidence in you. **23**As for Titus, he is my partner and fellow worker among you; as for our brothers, they are representatives of the churches and an honor to Christ. **24**Therefore show these men the proof of your love and the reason for our pride in you, so that the churches can see it.   2Co 9:2; Php 2:25

9 There is no need for me to write to you about this service to the saints. **2**For I know your eagerness to help, and I have been boasting about it to the Macedonians, telling them that since last year you in Achaia were ready to give; and your enthusiasm has stirred most of them to action. **3**But I am sending the brothers in order that our boasting about you in this matter should not prove hollow, but that you may be ready, as I said you would be. **4**For if any Mace-

donians come with me and find you unprepared, we—not to say anything about you—would be ashamed of having been so confident. **5**So I thought it necessary to urge the brothers to visit you in advance and finish the arrangements for the generous gift you had promised. Then it will be ready as a generous gift, not as one grudgingly given.   Php 4:17

Sowing Generously

6Remember this: Whoever sows sparingly will also reap sparingly, and whoever sows generously will also reap generously. **7**Each man should give what he has decided in his heart to give, not reluctantly or under compulsion, for God loves a cheerful giver. **8**And God is able to make all grace abound to you, so that in all things at all times, having all that you need, you will abound in every good work. **9**As it is written: Eph 3:20; Php 4:19

> "He has scattered abroad his
>   gifts to the poor;   Mal 3:10
> his righteousness endures
>   forever."[a]

10Now he who supplies seed to the sower and bread for food will also supply and increase your store of seed and will enlarge the harvest of your righteousness. **11**You will be made rich in every way so that you can be generous on every occasion, and through us your gener-

---

[a] 9 Psalm 112:9

osity will result in thanksgiving to God. Ps 112:9; Isa 55:10; Hos 10:12

¹²This service that you perform is not only supplying the needs of God's people but is also overflowing in many expressions of thanks to God. ¹³Because of the service by which you have proved yourselves, men will praise God for the obedience that accompanies your confession of the gospel of Christ, and for your generosity in sharing with them and with everyone else. ¹⁴And in their prayers for you their hearts will go out to you, because of the surpassing grace God has given you. ¹⁵Thanks be to God for his indescribable gift! Mt 9:8

Paul's Defense of His Ministry

10 By the meekness and gentleness of Christ, I appeal to you—I, Paul, who am "timid" when face to face with you, but "bold" when away! ²I beg you that when I come I may not have to be as bold as I expect to be toward some people who think that we live by the standards of this world. ³For though we live in the world, we do not wage war as the world does. ⁴The weapons we fight with are not the weapons of the world. On the contrary, they have divine power to demolish strongholds. ⁵We demolish arguments and every pretension that sets itself up against the knowledge of God, and we take captive every thought to make it obedient to Christ. ⁶And we will be ready to punish every act of disobedience, once your obedience is complete. Jer 1:10

⁷You are looking only on the surface of things.ᵃ If anyone is confident that he belongs to Christ, he should consider again that we belong to Christ just as much as he. ⁸For even if I boast somewhat freely about the authority the Lord gave us for building you up rather than pulling you down, I will not be ashamed of it. ⁹I do not want to seem to be trying to frighten you with my letters. ¹⁰For some say, "His letters are weighty and forceful, but in person he is unimpressive and his speaking amounts to nothing." ¹¹Such people should realize that what we are in our letters when we are absent, we will be in our actions when we are present.

¹²We do not dare to classify or compare ourselves with some who commend themselves. When they measure themselves by themselves and compare themselves with themselves, they are not wise. ¹³We, however, will not boast beyond proper limits, but will confine our boasting to the field God has assigned to us, a field that reaches even to you. ¹⁴We are not going too far in our boasting, as would be the case if we had not come to you, for we did get as far as you with the gospel of Christ.

ᵃ7 Or Look at the obvious facts

15Neither do we go beyond our limits by boasting of work done by others.*a* Our hope is that, as your faith continues to grow, our area of activity among you will greatly expand, 16so that we can preach the gospel in the regions beyond you. For we do not want to boast about work already done in another man's territory. 17But, "Let him who boasts boast in the Lord."*b* 18For it is not the one who commends himself who is approved, but the one whom the Lord commends.   Ro 2:29; 1Co 4:5

Paul and the False Apostles

11 I hope you will put up with a little of my foolishness; but you are already doing that. 2I am jealous for you with a godly jealousy. I promised you to one husband, to Christ, so that I might present you as a pure virgin to him. 3But I am afraid that just as Eve was deceived by the serpent's cunning, your minds may somehow be led astray from your sincere and pure devotion to Christ. 4For if someone comes to you and preaches a Jesus other than the Jesus we preached, or if you receive a different spirit from the one you received, or a different gospel from the one you accepted, you put up with it easily enough. 5But I do not think I am in the least inferior to those "super-apostles." 6I may not be a trained speaker, but I do have knowledge. We have made this perfectly clear to you in every way.   1Co 1:17; Eph 3:4

7Was it a sin for me to lower myself in order to elevate you by preaching the gospel of God to you free of charge? 8I robbed other churches by receiving support from them so as to serve you. 9And when I was with you and needed something, I was not a burden to anyone, for the brothers who came from Macedonia supplied what I needed. I have kept myself from being a burden to you in any way, and will continue to do so. 10As surely as the truth of Christ is in me, nobody in the regions of Achaia will stop this boasting of mine. 11Why? Because I do not love you? God knows I do! 12And I will keep on doing what I am doing in order to cut the ground from under those who want an opportunity to be considered equal with us in the things they boast about.   1Co 9:18

13For such men are false apostles, deceitful workmen, masquerading as apostles of Christ. 14And no wonder, for Satan himself masquerades as an angel of light. 15It is not surprising, then, if his servants masquerade as servants of righteousness. Their end will be what their actions deserve.   Php 3:19

---

a 13-15 Or 13We, however, will not boast about things that cannot be measured, but we will boast according to the standard of measurement that the God of measure has assigned us—a measurement that relates even to you. 14 .... 15Neither do we boast about things that cannot be measured in regard to the work done by others.   *b* 17 Jer. 9:24

Paul Boasts About His Sufferings

[16]I repeat: Let no one take me for a fool. But if you do, then receive me just as you would a fool, so that I may do a little boasting. [17]In this self-confident boasting I am not talking as the Lord would, but as a fool. [18]Since many are boasting in the way the world does, I too will boast. [19]You gladly put up with fools since you are so wise! [20]In fact, you even put up with anyone who enslaves you or exploits you or takes advantage of you or pushes himself forward or slaps you in the face. [21]To my shame I admit that we were too weak for that!   1Co 4:10; Php 3:3-4

What anyone else dares to boast about—I am speaking as a fool—I also dare to boast about. [22]Are they Hebrews? So am I. Are they Israelites? So am I. Are they Abraham's descendants? So am I. [23]Are they servants of Christ? (I am out of my mind to talk like this.) I am more. I have worked much harder, been in prison more frequently, been flogged more severely, and been exposed to death again and again. [24]Five times I received from the Jews the forty lashes minus one. [25]Three times I was beaten with rods, once I was stoned, three times I was shipwrecked, I spent a night and a day in the open sea, [26]I have been constantly on the move. I have been in danger from rivers, in danger from bandits, in danger from my own countrymen, in danger from Gentiles; in danger in the city, in danger in the country, in danger at sea; and in danger from false brothers. [27]I have labored and toiled and have often gone without sleep; I have known hunger and thirst and have often gone without food; I have been cold and naked. [28]Besides everything else, I face daily the pressure of my concern for all the churches. [29]Who is weak, and I do not feel weak? Who is led into sin, and I do not inwardly burn?   Ro 9:4; 1Co 15:10

[30]If I must boast, I will boast of the things that show my weakness. [31]The God and Father of the Lord Jesus, who is to be praised forever, knows that I am not lying. [32]In Damascus the governor under King Aretas had the city of the Damascenes guarded in order to arrest me. [33]But I was lowered in a basket from a window in the wall and slipped through his hands.

Paul's Vision and His Thorn

12 I must go on boasting. Although there is nothing to be gained, I will go on to visions and revelations from the Lord. [2]I know a man in Christ who fourteen years ago was caught up to the third heaven. Whether it was in the body or out of the body I do not know—God knows. [3]And I know that this man—whether in the body or apart from the body I do not know, but God knows— [4]was caught up to paradise. He

heard inexpressible things, things that man is not permitted to tell. [5]I will boast about a man like that, but I will not boast about myself, except about my weaknesses. [6]Even if I should choose to boast, I would not be a fool, because I would be speaking the truth. But I refrain, so no one will think more of me than is warranted by what I do or say.   Lk 23:43; 2Co 11:16

[7]To keep me from becoming conceited because of these surpassingly great revelations, there was given me a thorn in my flesh, a messenger of Satan, to torment me. [8]Three times I pleaded with the Lord to take it away from me. [9]But he said to me, "My grace is sufficient for you, for my power is made perfect in weakness." Therefore I will boast all the more gladly about my weaknesses, so that Christ's power may rest on me. [10]That is why, for Christ's sake, I delight in weaknesses, in insults, in hardships, in persecutions, in difficulties. For when I am weak, then I am strong.   2Co 13:4; 2Th 1:4

Paul's Concern for the Corinthians

[11]I have made a fool of myself, but you drove me to it. I ought to have been commended by you, for I am not in the least inferior to the "super-apostles," even though I am nothing. [12]The things that mark an apostle—signs, wonders and miracles—were done among you with great perseverance. [13]How were you inferior to the other churches, except that I was never a burden to you? Forgive me this wrong!   1Co 9:12,18; 2Co 11:7

[14]Now I am ready to visit you for the third time, and I will not be a burden to you, because what I want is not your possessions but you. After all, children should not have to save up for their parents, but parents for their children. [15]So I will very gladly spend for you everything I have and expend myself as well. If I love you more, will you love me less? [16]Be that as it may, I have not been a burden to you. Yet, crafty fellow that I am, I caught you by trickery! [17]Did I exploit you through any of the men I sent you? [18]I urged Titus to go to you and I sent our brother with him. Titus did not exploit you, did he? Did we not act in the same spirit and follow the same course?

[19]Have you been thinking all along that we have been defending ourselves to you? We have been speaking in the sight of God as those in Christ; and everything we do, dear friends, is for your strengthening. [20]For I am afraid that when I come I may not find you as I want you to be, and you may not find me as you want me to be. I fear that there may be quarreling, jealousy, outbursts of anger, factions, slander, gossip, arrogance and disorder. [21]I am afraid that when I come again my God will humble me before you, and I

will be grieved over many who have sinned earlier and have not repented of the impurity, sexual sin and debauchery in which they have indulged. 1Co 14:33; 2Co 13:2

Final Warnings

13 This will be my third visit to you. "Every matter must be established by the testimony of two or three witnesses."[a] [2]I already gave you a warning when I was with you the second time. I now repeat it while absent: On my return I will not spare those who sinned earlier or any of the others, [3]since you are demanding proof that Christ is speaking through me. He is not weak in dealing with you, but is powerful among you. [4]For to be sure, he was crucified in weakness, yet he lives by God's power. Likewise, we are weak in him, yet by God's power we will live with him to serve you. Ro 1:4

[5]Examine yourselves to see whether you are in the faith; test yourselves. Do you not realize that Christ Jesus is in you—unless, of course, you fail the test? [6]And I trust that you will discover that we have not failed the test. [7]Now we pray to God that you will not do anything wrong. Not that people will see that we have stood the test but that you will do what is right even though we may seem to have failed. [8]For we cannot do anything against the truth, but only for the truth. [9]We are glad whenever we are weak but you are strong; and our prayer is for your perfection. [10]This is why I write these things when I am absent, that when I come I may not have to be harsh in my use of authority—the authority the Lord gave me for building you up, not for tearing you down.

Final Greetings

[11]Finally, brothers, good-by. Aim for perfection, listen to my appeal, be of one mind, live in peace. And the God of love and peace will be with you. Ro 15:33; Eph 6:23

[12]Greet one another with a holy kiss. [13]All the saints send their greetings. Ro 16:16; Php 4:22

[14]May the grace of the Lord Jesus Christ, and the love of God, and the fellowship of the Holy Spirit be with you all. Ro 16:20

a 1 Deut. 19:15

Galatians

1 Paul, an apostle—sent not from men nor by man, but by Jesus Christ and God the Father, who raised him from the dead—[2] and all the brothers with me,

To the churches in Galatia:

[3] Grace and peace to you from God our Father and the Lord Jesus Christ, [4] who gave himself for our sins to rescue us from the present evil age, according to the will of our God and Father, [5] to whom be glory for ever and ever. Amen.

No Other Gospel

[6] I am astonished that you are so quickly deserting the one who called you by the grace of Christ and are turning to a different gospel— [7] which is really no gospel at all. Evidently some people are throwing you into confusion and are trying to pervert the gospel of Christ. [8] But even if we or an angel from heaven should preach a gospel other than the one we preached to you, let him be eternally condemned! [9] As we have already said, so now I say again: If anybody is preaching to you a gospel other than what you accepted, let him be eternally condemned!

[10] Am I now trying to win the approval of men, or of God? Or am I trying to please men? If I were still trying to please men, I would not be a servant of Christ.   Ro 2:29

Paul Called by God

[11] I want you to know, brothers, that the gospel I preached is not something that man made up. [12] I did not receive it from any man, nor was I taught it; rather, I received it by revelation from Jesus Christ.   1Co 11:23; 15:1

[13] For you have heard of my previous way of life in Judaism, how intensely I persecuted the church of God and tried to destroy it. [14] I was advancing in Judaism beyond many Jews of my own age and was extremely zealous for the traditions of my fathers. [15] But when God, who set me apart from birth[a] and called me by his grace, was pleased [16] to reveal his Son in me so that I might preach him among the Gentiles, I did not consult any man, [17] nor did I go up to Jerusalem to see those who were apostles before I was, but I went immediately into Arabia and later returned to Damascus.   Mt 15:2; 16:17

[18] Then after three years, I went up to Jerusalem to get acquainted with Peter[b] and stayed with him

---

[a] 15 Or *from my mother's womb*   [b] 18 Greek *Cephas*

fifteen days. ¹⁹I saw none of the other apostles—only James, the Lord's brother. ²⁰I assure you before God that what I am writing you is no lie. ²¹Later I went to Syria and Cilicia. ²²I was personally unknown to the churches of Judea that are in Christ. ²³They only heard the report: "The man who formerly persecuted us is now preaching the faith he once tried to destroy." ²⁴And they praised God because of me.   Ro 9:1; 1Th 2:14

Paul Accepted by the Apostles

2 Fourteen years later I went up again to Jerusalem, this time with Barnabas. I took Titus along also. ²I went in response to a revelation and set before them the gospel that I preach among the Gentiles. But I did this privately to those who seemed to be leaders, for fear that I was running or had run my race in vain. ³Yet not even Titus, who was with me, was compelled to be circumcised, even though he was a Greek. ⁴This matter arose, because some false brothers had infiltrated our ranks to spy on the freedom we have in Christ Jesus and to make us slaves. ⁵We did not give in to them for a moment, so that the truth of the gospel might remain with you.

⁶As for those who seemed to be important—whatever they were makes no difference to me; God does not judge by external appearance—those men added nothing to my message. ⁷On the contrary, they saw that I had been entrusted with the task of preaching the gospel to the Gentiles,ᵃ just as Peter had been to the Jews.ᵇ ⁸For God, who was at work in the ministry of Peter as an apostle to the Jews, was also at work in my ministry as an apostle to the Gentiles. ⁹James, Peterᶜ and John, those reputed to be pillars, gave me and Barnabas the right hand of fellowship when they recognized the grace given to me. They agreed that we should go to the Gentiles, and they to the Jews. ¹⁰All they asked was that we should continue to remember the poor, the very thing I was eager to do.   Ac 24:17; Ro 12:3

Paul Opposes Peter

¹¹When Peter came to Antioch, I opposed him to his face, because he was clearly in the wrong. ¹²Before certain men came from James, he used to eat with the Gentiles. But when they arrived, he began to draw back and separate himself from the Gentiles because he was afraid of those who belonged to the circumcision group. ¹³The other Jews joined him in his hypocrisy, so that by their hypocrisy even Barnabas was led astray.   Ac 4:36

¹⁴When I saw that they were not acting in line with the truth of the

---

ᵃ7 Greek uncircumcised   ᵇ7 Greek circumcised; also in verses 8 and 9   ᶜ9 Greek Cephas; also in verses 11 and 14 gospel, I said to Peter in front of them all, "You are a Jew, yet you live like a Gentile and not like a Jew. How is it, then, that you force Gentiles to follow Jewish customs?

[15]"We who are Jews by birth and not 'Gentile sinners' [16]know that a man is not justified by observing the law, but by faith in Jesus Christ. So we, too, have put our faith in Christ Jesus that we may be justified by faith in Christ and not by observing the law, because by observing the law no one will be justified.   Ac 13:39; Ro 9:30

[17]"If, while we seek to be justified in Christ, it becomes evident that we ourselves are sinners, does that mean that Christ promotes sin? Absolutely not! [18]If I rebuild what I destroyed, I prove that I am a lawbreaker. [19]For through the law I died to the law so that I might live for God. [20]I have been crucified with Christ and I no longer live, but Christ lives in me. The life I live in the body, I live by faith in the Son of God, who loved me and gave himself for me. [21]I do not set aside the grace of God, for if righteousness could be gained through the law, Christ died for nothing!"[a]

Faith or Observance of the Law

3 You foolish Galatians! Who has bewitched you? Before your very eyes Jesus Christ was clearly portrayed as crucified. [2]I would like to learn just one thing from you: Did you receive the Spirit by observing the law, or by believing what you heard? [3]Are you so foolish? After beginning with the Spirit, are you now trying to attain your goal by human effort? [4]Have you suffered so much for nothing—if it really was for nothing? [5]Does God give you his Spirit and work miracles among you because you observe the law, or because you believe what you heard?

[6]Consider Abraham: "He believed God, and it was credited to him as righteousness."[b] [7]Understand, then, that those who believe are children of Abraham. [8]The Scripture foresaw that God would justify the Gentiles by faith, and announced the gospel in advance to Abraham: "All nations will be blessed through you."[c] [9]So those who have faith are blessed along with Abraham, the man of faith.

[10]All who rely on observing the law are under a curse, for it is written: "Cursed is everyone who does not continue to do everything written in the Book of the Law."[d] [11]Clearly no one is justified before God by the law, because, "The righteous will live by faith."[e] [12]The law is not based on faith; on the contrary, "The man who does these things will live by them."[f] [13]Christ redeemed us from the

---

[a]21 Some interpreters end the quotation after verse 14.   [b]6 Gen. 15:6   [c]8 Gen. 12:3; 18:18; 22:18
[d]10 Deut. 27:26   [e]11 Hab. 2:4   [f]12 Lev. 18:5

curse of the law by becoming a curse for us, for it is written: "Cursed is everyone who is hung on a tree."*a* 14He redeemed us in order that the blessing given to Abraham might come to the Gentiles through Christ Jesus, so that by faith we might receive the promise of the Spirit.   Ac 2:33

The Law and the Promise

15Brothers, let me take an example from everyday life. Just as no one can set aside or add to a human covenant that has been duly established, so it is in this case. 16The promises were spoken to Abraham and to his seed. The Scripture does not say "and to seeds," meaning many people, but "and to your seed,"*b* meaning one person, who is Christ. 17What I mean is this: The law, introduced 430 years later, does not set aside the covenant previously established by God and thus do away with the promise. 18For if the inheritance depends on the law, then it no longer depends on a promise; but God in his grace gave it to Abraham through a promise.

19What, then, was the purpose of the law? It was added because of transgressions until the Seed to whom the promise referred had come. The law was put into effect through angels by a mediator. 20A mediator, however, does not represent just one party; but God is one.   Ac 7:53; Heb 8:6

21Is the law, therefore, opposed to the promises of God? Absolutely not! For if a law had been given that could impart life, then righteousness would certainly have come by the law. 22But the Scripture declares that the whole world is a prisoner of sin, so that what was promised, being given through faith in Jesus Christ, might be given to those who believe.   Ro 11:32; Gal 2:17

23Before this faith came, we were held prisoners by the law, locked up until faith should be revealed. 24So the law was put in charge to lead us to Christ*c* that we might be justified by faith. 25Now that faith has come, we are no longer under the supervision of the law.   Ro 10:4; 11:32

Sons of God

26You are all sons of God through faith in Christ Jesus, 27for all of you who were baptized into Christ have clothed yourselves with Christ. 28There is neither Jew nor Greek, slave nor free, male nor female, for you are all one in Christ Jesus. 29If you belong to Christ, then you are Abraham's seed, and heirs according to the promise.

4 What I am saying is that as long as the heir is a child, he is no different from a slave, although he owns the whole estate.

---

*a*13 Deut. 21:23   *b*16 Gen. 12:7; 13:15; 24:7   *c*24 Or *charge until Christ came*

²He is subject to guardians and trustees until the time set by his father. ³So also, when we were children, we were in slavery under the basic principles of the world. ⁴But when the time had fully come, God sent his Son, born of a woman, born under law, ⁵to redeem those under law, that we might receive the full rights of sons. ⁶Because you are sons, God sent the Spirit of his Son into our hearts, the Spirit who calls out, "Abba,ᵃ Father." ⁷So you are no longer a slave, but a son; and since you are a son, God has made you also an heir. Ro 5:5; 8:15-17

Paul's Concern for the Galatians

⁸Formerly, when you did not know God, you were slaves to those who by nature are not gods. ⁹But now that you know God—or rather are known by God—how is it that you are turning back to those weak and miserable principles? Do you wish to be enslaved by them all over again? ¹⁰You are observing special days and months and seasons and years! ¹¹I fear for you, that somehow I have wasted my efforts on you. Eph 2:12

¹²I plead with you, brothers, become like me, for I became like you. You have done me no wrong. ¹³As you know, it was because of an illness that I first preached the gospel to you. ¹⁴Even though my illness was a trial to you, you did not treat me with contempt or scorn. Instead, you welcomed me as if I were an angel of God, as if I were Christ Jesus himself. ¹⁵What has happened to all your joy? I can testify that, if you could have done so, you would have torn out your eyes and given them to me. ¹⁶Have I now become your enemy by telling you the truth? 1Co 2:3; Gal 6:18

¹⁷Those people are zealous to win you over, but for no good. What they want is to alienate you ⸢from us⸣, so that you may be zealous for them. ¹⁸It is fine to be zealous, provided the purpose is good, and to be so always and not just when I am with you. ¹⁹My dear children, for whom I am again in the pains of childbirth until Christ is formed in you, ²⁰how I wish I could be with you now and change my tone, because I am perplexed about you! 1Co 4:15; Eph 4:13

Hagar and Sarah

²¹Tell me, you who want to be under the law, are you not aware of what the law says? ²²For it is written that Abraham had two sons, one by the slave woman and the other by the free woman. ²³His son by the slave woman was born in the ordinary way; but his son by the free woman was born as the result of a promise. Ro 9:7-8

²⁴These things may be taken figuratively, for the women represent

---

ᵃ6 Aramaic for *Father*

two covenants. One covenant is from Mount Sinai and bears children who are to be slaves: This is Hagar. ²⁵Now Hagar stands for Mount Sinai in Arabia and corresponds to the present city of Jerusalem, because she is in slavery with her children. ²⁶But the Jerusalem that is above is free, and she is our mother. ²⁷For it is written:

"Be glad, O barren woman,
    who bears no children;
break forth and cry aloud,
    you who have no labor
        pains;
because more are the children
        of the desolate woman
    than of her who has a
        husband."ᵃ   Isa 54:1

²⁸Now you, brothers, like Isaac, are children of promise. ²⁹At that time the son born in the ordinary way persecuted the son born by the power of the Spirit. It is the same now. ³⁰But what does the Scripture say? "Get rid of the slave woman and her son, for the slave woman's son will never share in the inheritance with the free woman's son."ᵇ ³¹Therefore, brothers, we are not children of the slave woman, but of the free woman.

Freedom in Christ

5 It is for freedom that Christ has set us free. Stand firm, then, and do not let yourselves be burdened again by a yoke of slavery.   1Co 16:13; Gal 2:4

²Mark my words! I, Paul, tell you that if you let yourselves be circumcised, Christ will be of no value to you at all. ³Again I declare to every man who lets himself be circumcised that he is obligated to obey the whole law. ⁴You who are trying to be justified by law have been alienated from Christ; you have fallen away from grace. ⁵But by faith we eagerly await through the Spirit the righteousness for which we hope. ⁶For in Christ Jesus neither circumcision nor uncircumcision has any value. The only thing that counts is faith expressing itself through love.

⁷You were running a good race. Who cut in on you and kept you from obeying the truth? ⁸That kind of persuasion does not come from the one who calls you. ⁹"A little yeast works through the whole batch of dough." ¹⁰I am confident in the Lord that you will take no other view. The one who is throwing you into confusion will pay the penalty, whoever he may be. ¹¹Brothers, if I am still preaching circumcision, why am I still being persecuted? In that case the offense of the cross has been abolished. ¹²As for those agitators, I wish they would go the whole way and emasculate themselves!

¹³You, my brothers, were called to be free. But do not use your free-

ᵃ27 Isaiah 54:1   ᵇ30 Gen. 21:10

dom to indulge the sinful nature*a*;
rather, serve one another in love.
14The entire law is summed up in
a single command: "Love your
neighbor as yourself."*b* 15If you
keep on biting and devouring each
other, watch out or you will be destroyed by each other.   Mt 22:39

Life by the Spirit

16So I say, live by the Spirit, and
you will not gratify the desires of
the sinful nature. 17For the sinful
nature desires what is contrary to
the Spirit, and the Spirit what is
contrary to the sinful nature. They
are in conflict with each other, so
that you do not do what you want.
18But if you are led by the Spirit,
you are not under law.   Ro 7:15-23

19The acts of the sinful nature
are obvious: sexual immorality,
impurity and debauchery; 20idola-
try and witchcraft; hatred, discord,
jealousy, fits of rage, selfish ambition, dissensions, factions 21and
envy; drunkenness, orgies, and the
like. I warn you, as I did before,
that those who live like this will
not inherit the kingdom of God.

22But the fruit of the Spirit is
love, joy, peace, patience, kindness, goodness, faithfulness,
23gentleness and self-control.
Against such things there is no
law. 24Those who belong to Christ
Jesus have crucified the sinful nature with its passions and desires.

25Since we live by the Spirit, let us
keep in step with the Spirit. 26Let
us not become conceited, provoking and envying each other.

Doing Good to All

6 Brothers, if someone is caught
in a sin, you who are spiritual
should restore him gently. But
watch yourself, or you also may be
tempted. 2Carry each other's burdens, and in this way you will fulfill the law of Christ. 3If anyone
thinks he is something when he is
nothing, he deceives himself.
4Each one should test his own actions. Then he can take pride
in himself, without comparing
himself to somebody else, 5for
each one should carry his own
load.

6Anyone who receives instruction in the word must share all
good things with his instructor.

7Do not be deceived: God cannot be mocked. A man reaps what
he sows. 8The one who sows to
please his sinful nature, from that
nature*c* will reap destruction; the
one who sows to please the Spirit,
from the Spirit will reap eternal
life. 9Let us not become weary in
doing good, for at the proper time
we will reap a harvest if we do
not give up. 10Therefore, as we
have opportunity, let us do good
to all people, especially to those
who belong to the family of believers.

a 13 Or the flesh; also in verses 16, 17, 19 and 24   *b 14 Lev. 19:18*   *c 8 Or his flesh, from the flesh*

Ephesians

1 Paul, an apostle of Christ Jesus by the will of God,

To the saints in Ephesus,[a] the faithful[b] in Christ Jesus: Col 1:2

[2]Grace and peace to you from God our Father and the Lord Jesus Christ.   Ro 1:7

Spiritual Blessings in Christ

[3]Praise be to the God and Father of our Lord Jesus Christ, who has blessed us in the heavenly realms with every spiritual blessing in Christ. [4]For he chose us in him before the creation of the world to be holy and blameless in his sight. In love [5]he[c] predestined us to be adopted as his sons through Jesus Christ, in accordance with his pleasure and will— [6]to the praise of his glorious grace, which he has freely given us in the One he loves. [7]In him we have redemption through his blood, the forgiveness of sins, in accordance with the riches of God's grace [8]that he lavished on us with all wisdom and understanding. [9]And he[d] made known to us the mystery of his will according to his good pleasure, which he purposed in Christ, [10]to be put into effect when the times will have reached their fulfillment—to bring all things in heaven and on earth together under one head, even Christ.   Ro 8:29-30

[11]In him we were also chosen,[e] having been predestined according to the plan of him who works out everything in conformity with the purpose of his will, [12]in order that we, who were the first to hope in Christ, might be for the praise of his glory. [13]And you also were included in Christ when you heard the word of truth, the gospel of your salvation. Having believed, you were marked in him with a seal, the promised Holy Spirit, [14]who is a deposit guaranteeing our inheritance until the redemption of those who are God's possession—to the praise of his glory.

Thanksgiving and Prayer

[15]For this reason, ever since I heard about your faith in the Lord Jesus and your love for all the saints, [16]I have not stopped giving thanks for you, remembering you in my prayers. [17]I keep asking that the God of our Lord Jesus Christ, the glorious Father, may give you the Spirit[f] of wisdom and revelation, so that you may know him

---

[a]1 Some early manuscripts do not have *in Ephesus*.   [b]1 Or *believers who are*   [c]4,5 Or *sight in love. [5]He*   [d]8,9 Or *us. With all wisdom and understanding, [9]he*   [e]11 Or *were made heirs*   [f]17 Or *a spirit*

Not Circumcision but a New Creation

¹¹See what large letters I use as I write to you with my own hand!

¹²Those who want to make a good impression outwardly are trying to compel you to be circumcised. The only reason they do this is to avoid being persecuted for the cross of Christ. ¹³Not even those who are circumcised obey the law, yet they want you to be circumcised that they may boast about your flesh. ¹⁴May I never boast except in the cross of our Lord Jesus Christ, through which[a] the world has been crucified to me, and I to the world. ¹⁵Neither circumcision nor uncircumcision means anything; what counts is a new creation. ¹⁶Peace and mercy to all who follow this rule, even to the Israel of God. Ro 6:2,6; Gal 5:11

¹⁷Finally, let no one cause me trouble, for I bear on my body the marks of Jesus. Isa 44:5; 2Co 1:5

¹⁸The grace of our Lord Jesus Christ be with your spirit, brothers. Amen. Ro 16:20; 2Ti 4:22

a 14 Or whom

better. [18]I pray also that the eyes of your heart may be enlightened in order that you may know the hope to which he has called you, the riches of his glorious inheritance in the saints, [19]and his incomparably great power for us who believe. That power is like the working of his mighty strength, [20]which he exerted in Christ when he raised him from the dead and seated him at his right hand in the heavenly realms, [21]far above all rule and authority, power and dominion, and every title that can be given, not only in the present age but also in the one to come. [22]And God placed all things under his feet and appointed him to be head over everything for the church, [23]which is his body, the fullness of him who fills everything in every way.	Php 2:9-10

Made Alive in Christ

2 As for you, you were dead in your transgressions and sins, [2]in which you used to live when you followed the ways of this world and of the ruler of the kingdom of the air, the spirit who is now at work in those who are disobedient. [3]All of us also lived among them at one time, gratifying the cravings of our sinful nature[a] and following its desires and thoughts. Like the rest, we were by nature objects of wrath. [4]But because of his great love for us, God, who is rich in mercy, [5]made us

alive with Christ even when we were dead in transgressions—it is by grace you have been saved. [6]And God raised us up with Christ and seated us with him in the heavenly realms in Christ Jesus, [7]in order that in the coming ages he might show the incomparable riches of his grace, expressed in his kindness to us in Christ Jesus. [8]For it is by grace you have been saved, through faith—and this not from yourselves, it is the gift of God— [9]not by works, so that no one can boast. [10]For we are God's workmanship, created in Christ Jesus to do good works, which God prepared in advance for us to do.	Isa 29:23; Eph 4:24; Tit 2:14

One in Christ

[11]Therefore, remember that formerly you who are Gentiles by birth and called "uncircumcised" by those who call themselves "the circumcision" (that done in the body by the hands of men)— [12]remember that at that time you were separate from Christ, excluded from citizenship in Israel and foreigners to the covenants of the promise, without hope and without God in the world. [13]But now in Christ Jesus you who once were far away have been brought near through the blood of Christ.

[14]For he himself is our peace, who has made the two one and has destroyed the barrier, the dividing

a 3 Or our flesh

wall of hostility, ¹⁵by abolishing in his flesh the law with its commandments and regulations. His purpose was to create in himself one new man out of the two, thus making peace, ¹⁶and in this one body to reconcile both of them to God through the cross, by which he put to death their hostility. ¹⁷He came and preached peace to you who were far away and peace to those who were near. ¹⁸For through him we both have access to the Father by one Spirit.

¹⁹Consequently, you are no longer foreigners and aliens, but fellow citizens with God's people and members of God's household, ²⁰built on the foundation of the apostles and prophets, with Christ Jesus himself as the chief cornerstone. ²¹In him the whole building is joined together and rises to become a holy temple in the Lord. ²²And in him you too are being built together to become a dwelling in which God lives by his Spirit.   Mt 16:18; 1Co 3:16-17

Paul the Preacher to the Gentiles

3 For this reason I, Paul, the prisoner of Christ Jesus for the sake of you Gentiles—   Ac 23:18

²Surely you have heard about the administration of God's grace that was given to me for you, ³that is, the mystery made known to me by revelation, as I have already written briefly. ⁴In reading this, then, you will be able to understand my insight into the mystery of Christ, ⁵which was not made known to men in other generations as it has now been revealed by the Spirit to God's holy apostles and prophets. ⁶This mystery is that through the gospel the Gentiles are heirs together with Israel, members together of one body, and sharers together in the promise in Christ Jesus.   Gal 3:29; Eph 2:15-16

⁷I became a servant of this gospel by the gift of God's grace given me through the working of his power. ⁸Although I am less than the least of all God's people, this grace was given me: to preach to the Gentiles the unsearchable riches of Christ, ⁹and to make plain to everyone the administration of this mystery, which for ages past was kept hidden in God, who created all things. ¹⁰His intent was that now, through the church, the manifold wisdom of God should be made known to the rulers and authorities in the heavenly realms, ¹¹according to his eternal purpose which he accomplished in Christ Jesus our Lord. ¹²In him and through faith in him we may approach God with freedom and confidence. ¹³I ask you, therefore, not to be discouraged because of my sufferings for you, which are your glory.   Eph 2:18; Heb 4:16

A Prayer for the Ephesians

¹⁴For this reason I kneel before the Father, ¹⁵from whom his whole

family*a* in heaven and on earth derives its name. ¹⁶I pray that out of his glorious riches he may strengthen you with power through his Spirit in your inner being, ¹⁷so that Christ may dwell in your hearts through faith. And I pray that you, being rooted and established in love, ¹⁸may have power, together with all the saints, to grasp how wide and long and high and deep is the love of Christ, ¹⁹and to know this love that surpasses knowledge — that you may be filled to the measure of all the fullness of God.   Eph 1:23; Col 2:10

²⁰Now to him who is able to do immeasurably more than all we ask or imagine, according to his power that is at work within us, ²¹to him be glory in the church and in Christ Jesus throughout all generations, for ever and ever! Amen.

Unity in the Body of Christ

4 As a prisoner for the Lord, then, I urge you to live a life worthy of the calling you have received. ²Be completely humble and gentle; be patient, bearing with one another in love. ³Make every effort to keep the unity of the Spirit through the bond of peace. ⁴There is one body and one Spirit — just as you were called to one hope when you were called — ⁵one Lord, one faith, one baptism; ⁶one God and Father of all, who is over all and through all and in all.

⁷But to each one of us grace has been given as Christ apportioned it. ⁸This is why it*b* says: Ro 12:3

"When he ascended on high,
he led captives in his train
and gave gifts to men."*c*

⁹(What does "he ascended" mean except that he also descended to the lower, earthly regions*d*? ¹⁰He who descended is the very one who ascended higher than all the heavens, in order to fill the whole universe.) ¹¹It was he who gave some to be apostles, some to be prophets, some to be evangelists, and some to be pastors and teachers, ¹²to prepare God's people for works of service, so that the body of Christ may be built up ¹³until we all reach unity in the faith and in the knowledge of the Son of God and become mature, attaining to the whole measure of the fullness of Christ.   1Co 12:27-28; Col 1:28

¹⁴Then we will no longer be infants, tossed back and forth by the waves, and blown here and there by every wind of teaching and by the cunning and craftiness of men in their deceitful scheming. ¹⁵Instead, speaking the truth in love, we will in all things grow up into him who is the Head, that is, Christ. ¹⁶From him the whole body, joined and held together by every supporting ligament, grows and builds itself up in love, as each part does its work.   1Co 14:20; Eph 1:22

---

a 15 Or *whom all fatherhood*   *b* 8 Or *God*   *c* 8 Psalm 68:18   *d* 9 Or *the depths of the earth*

Living as Children of Light

17So I tell you this, and insist on it in the Lord, that you must no longer live as the Gentiles do, in the futility of their thinking. **18**They are darkened in their understanding and separated from the life of God because of the ignorance that is in them due to the hardening of their hearts. **19**Having lost all sensitivity, they have given themselves over to sensuality so as to indulge in every kind of impurity, with a continual lust for more.

20You, however, did not come to know Christ that way. **21**Surely you heard of him and were taught in him in accordance with the truth that is in Jesus. **22**You were taught, with regard to your former way of life, to put off your old self, which is being corrupted by its deceitful desires; **23**to be made new in the attitude of your minds; **24**and to put on the new self, created to be like God in true righteousness and holiness.   Ro 6:4; Col 3:10

25Therefore each of you must put off falsehood and speak truthfully to his neighbor, for we are all members of one body. **26**"In your anger do not sin"*a*: Do not let the sun go down while you are still angry, **27**and do not give the devil a foothold. **28**He who has been stealing must steal no longer, but must work, doing something useful with his own hands, that he may have something to share with those in need.   Zec 8:16; Lk 3:11

29Do not let any unwholesome talk come out of your mouths, but only what is helpful for building others up according to their needs, that it may benefit those who listen. **30**And do not grieve the Holy Spirit of God, with whom you were sealed for the day of redemption. **31**Get rid of all bitterness, rage and anger, brawling and slander, along with every form of malice. **32**Be kind and compassionate to one another, forgiving each other, just as in Christ God forgave you.   Col 3:8

5 Be imitators of God, therefore, as dearly loved children **2**and live a life of love, just as Christ loved us and gave himself up for us as a fragrant offering and sacrifice to God.   Lk 6:36; 2Co 2:15

3But among you there must not be even a hint of sexual immorality, or of any kind of impurity, or of greed, because these are improper for God's holy people. **4**Nor should there be obscenity, foolish talk or coarse joking, which are out of place, but rather thanksgiving. **5**For of this you can be sure: No immoral, impure or greedy person —such a man is an idolater—has any inheritance in the kingdom of Christ and of God.*b* **6**Let no one deceive you with empty words, for because of such things God's wrath comes on those who are dis-

---

a 26 Psalm 4:4   *b 5* Or *kingdom of the Christ and God* obedient. [7]Therefore do not be partners with them.　　Ro 1:18; 1Co 6:9

[8]For you were once darkness, but now you are light in the Lord. Live as children of light [9](for the fruit of the light consists in all goodness, righteousness and truth) [10]and find out what pleases the Lord. [11]Have nothing to do with the fruitless deeds of darkness, but rather expose them. [12]For it is shameful even to mention what the disobedient do in secret. [13]But everything exposed by the light becomes visible, [14]for it is light that makes everything visible. This is why it is said:　　Lk 16:8

"Wake up, O sleeper,　　Ro 13:11
　　rise from the dead,　　Jn 5:25
and Christ will shine on you."

[15]Be very careful, then, how you live—not as unwise but as wise, [16]making the most of every opportunity, because the days are evil. [17]Therefore do not be foolish, but understand what the Lord's will is. [18]Do not get drunk on wine, which leads to debauchery. Instead, be filled with the Spirit. [19]Speak to one another with psalms, hymns and spiritual songs. Sing and make music in your heart to the Lord, [20]always giving thanks to God the Father for everything, in the name of our Lord Jesus Christ.　　Ps 34:1

[21]Submit to one another out of reverence for Christ.　　Gal 5:13

Wives and Husbands

[22]Wives, submit to your husbands as to the Lord. [23]For the husband is the head of the wife as Christ is the head of the church, his body, of which he is the Savior. [24]Now as the church submits to Christ, so also wives should submit to their husbands in everything.　　1Co 11:3; Eph 6:5

[25]Husbands, love your wives, just as Christ loved the church and gave himself up for her [26]to make her holy, cleansing[a] her by the washing with water through the word, [27]and to present her to himself as a radiant church, without stain or wrinkle or any other blemish, but holy and blameless. [28]In this same way, husbands ought to love their wives as their own bodies. He who loves his wife loves himself. [29]After all, no one ever hated his own body, but he feeds and cares for it, just as Christ does the church— [30]for we are members of his body. [31]"For this reason a man will leave his father and mother and be united to his wife, and the two will become one flesh."[b] [32]This is a profound mystery—but I am talking about Christ and the church. [33]However, each one of you also must love his wife as he loves himself, and the wife must respect her husband.　　Mt 19:5

---

a 26 Or *having cleansed*　　b 31 Gen. 2:24

Children and Parents

6 Children, obey your parents in the Lord, for this is right. [2]"Honor your father and mother" —which is the first commandment with a promise— [3]"that it may go well with you and that you may enjoy long life on the earth."[a]

[4]Fathers, do not exasperate your children; instead, bring them up in the training and instruction of the Lord.   Ge 18:19; Col 3:21

Slaves and Masters

[5]Slaves, obey your earthly masters with respect and fear, and with sincerity of heart, just as you would obey Christ. [6]Obey them not only to win their favor when their eye is on you, but like slaves of Christ, doing the will of God from your heart. [7]Serve wholeheartedly, as if you were serving the Lord, not men, [8]because you know that the Lord will reward everyone for whatever good he does, whether he is slave or free.

[9]And masters, treat your slaves in the same way. Do not threaten them, since you know that he who is both their Master and yours is in heaven, and there is no favoritism with him.   Col 3:18-4:1

The Armor of God

[10]Finally, be strong in the Lord and in his mighty power. [11]Put on the full armor of God so that you can take your stand against the devil's schemes. [12]For our struggle is not against flesh and blood, but against the rulers, against the authorities, against the powers of this dark world and against the spiritual forces of evil in the heavenly realms. [13]Therefore put on the full armor of God, so that when the day of evil comes, you may be able to stand your ground, and after you have done everything, to stand. [14]Stand firm then, with the belt of truth buckled around your waist, with the breastplate of righteousness in place, [15]and with your feet fitted with the readiness that comes from the gospel of peace. [16]In addition to all this, take up the shield of faith, with which you can extinguish all the flaming arrows of the evil one. [17]Take the helmet of salvation and the sword of the Spirit, which is the word of God. [18]And pray in the Spirit on all occasions with all kinds of prayers and requests. With this in mind, be alert and always keep on praying for all the saints.   Lk 18:1; Heb 4:12

[19]Pray also for me, that whenever I open my mouth, words may be given me so that I will fearlessly make known the mystery of the gospel, [20]for which I am an ambassador in chains. Pray that I may declare it fearlessly, as I should.

Final Greetings

[21]Tychicus, the dear brother and

[a]3 Deut. 5:16

faithful servant in the Lord, will tell you everything, so that you also may know how I am and what I am doing. ²²I am sending him to you for this very purpose, that you may know how we are, and that he may encourage you. Ac 20:4; Col 4:7-9

²³Peace to the brothers, and love with faith from God the Father and the Lord Jesus Christ. ²⁴Grace to all who love our Lord Jesus Christ with an undying love. Gal 6:16

Philippians

1 Paul and Timothy, servants of Christ Jesus,   Ac 16:1; 2Co 1:1

To all the saints in Christ Jesus at Philippi, together with the overseers[a] and deacons: 1Ti 3:1,8

2Grace and peace to you from God our Father and the Lord Jesus Christ.   Ro 1:7

Thanksgiving and Prayer

3I thank my God every time I remember you. 4In all my prayers for all of you, I always pray with joy 5because of your partnership in the gospel from the first day until now, 6being confident of this, that he who began a good work in you will carry it on to completion until the day of Christ Jesus.   Ac 16:12-40

7It is right for me to feel this way about all of you, since I have you in my heart; for whether I am in chains or defending and confirming the gospel, all of you share in God's grace with me. 8God can testify how I long for all of you with the affection of Christ Jesus.

9And this is my prayer: that your love may abound more and more in knowledge and depth of insight, 10so that you may be able to discern what is best and may be pure and blameless until the day of Christ, 11filled with the fruit of righteousness that comes through Jesus Christ—to the glory and praise of God.   1Co 1:8; 1Th 3:12

Paul's Chains Advance the Gospel

12Now I want you to know, brothers, that what has happened to me has really served to advance the gospel. 13As a result, it has become clear throughout the whole palace guard[b] and to everyone else that I am in chains for Christ. 14Because of my chains, most of the brothers in the Lord have been encouraged to speak the word of God more courageously and fearlessly.

15It is true that some preach Christ out of envy and rivalry, but others out of goodwill. 16The latter do so in love, knowing that I am put here for the defense of the gospel. 17The former preach Christ out of selfish ambition, not sincerely, supposing that they can stir up trouble for me while I am in chains.[c] 18But what does it matter? The important thing is that in every way, whether from false motives or true, Christ is preached. And because of this I rejoice.

---

a 1 Traditionally *bishops*   b 13 Or *whole palace*   c 16,17 Some late manuscripts have verses 16 and 17 in reverse order.

Yes, and I will continue to rejoice, ¹⁹for I know that through your prayers and the help given by the Spirit of Jesus Christ, what has happened to me will turn out for my deliverance.ᵃ ²⁰I eagerly expect and hope that I will in no way be ashamed, but will have sufficient courage so that now as always Christ will be exalted in my body, whether by life or by death. ²¹For to me, to live is Christ and to die is gain. ²²If I am to go on living in the body, this will mean fruitful labor for me. Yet what shall I choose? I do not know! ²³I am torn between the two: I desire to depart and be with Christ, which is better by far; ²⁴but it is more necessary for you that I remain in the body. ²⁵Convinced of this, I know that I will remain, and I will continue with all of you for your progress and joy in the faith, ²⁶so that through my being with you again your joy in Christ Jesus will overflow on account of me.   2Co 5:8

²⁷Whatever happens, conduct yourselves in a manner worthy of the gospel of Christ. Then, whether I come and see you or only hear about you in my absence, I will know that you stand firm in one spirit, contending as one man for the faith of the gospel ²⁸without being frightened in any way by those who oppose you. This is a sign to them that they will be destroyed, but that you will be saved —and that by God. ²⁹For it has been granted to you on behalf of Christ not only to believe on him, but also to suffer for him, ³⁰since you are going through the same struggle you saw I had, and now hear that I still have.   Ac 16:19-40

Imitating Christ's Humility

2 If you have any encouragement from being united with Christ, if any comfort from his love, if any fellowship with the Spirit, if any tenderness and compassion, ²then make my joy complete by being like-minded, having the same love, being one in spirit and purpose. ³Do nothing out of selfish ambition or vain conceit, but in humility consider others better than yourselves. ⁴Each of you should look not only to your own interests, but also to the interests of others.   Ro 12:10; Gal 5:26

⁵Your attitude should be the same as that of Christ Jesus:

⁶Who, being in very natureᵇ
    God,   Jn 1:1; 14:9
did not consider equality
    with God something to
    be grasped,   Jn 5:18
⁷but made himself nothing,
    taking the very natureᶜ of a
    servant,   Mt 20:28
being made in human
    likeness.   Jn 1:14; Heb 2:17
⁸And being found in appearance
    as a man,

ᵃ19 Or *salvation*   ᵇ6 Or *in the form of*   ᶜ7 Or *the form*

he humbled himself
and became obedient to
death —   Mt 26:39; Heb 5:8
even death on a cross!
[9]Therefore God exalted him to
the highest place   Ac 2:33
and gave him the name that
is above every name,
[10]that at the name of Jesus every
knee should bow,
in heaven and on earth and
under the earth,   Mt 28:18
[11]and every tongue confess that
Jesus Christ is Lord,
to the glory of God the
Father.

Shining as Stars

[12]Therefore, my dear friends, as you have always obeyed — not only in my presence, but now much more in my absence — continue to work out your salvation with fear and trembling, [13]for it is God who works in you to will and to act according to his good purpose.   2Co 7:15; Ezr 1:5

[14]Do everything without complaining or arguing, [15]so that you may become blameless and pure, children of God without fault in a crooked and depraved generation, in which you shine like stars in the universe [16]as you hold out[a] the word of life — in order that I may boast on the day of Christ that I did not run or labor for nothing. [17]But even if I am being poured out like a drink offering on the sacrifice and service coming from your faith, I am glad and rejoice with all of you. [18]So you too should be glad and rejoice with me.   Ro 15:16; 2Ti 4:6

Timothy and Epaphroditus

[19]I hope in the Lord Jesus to send Timothy to you soon, that I also may be cheered when I receive news about you. [20]I have no one else like him, who takes a genuine interest in your welfare. [21]For everyone looks out for his own interests, not those of Jesus Christ. [22]But you know that Timothy has proved himself, because as a son with his father he has served with me in the work of the gospel. [23]I hope, therefore, to send him as soon as I see how things go with me. [24]And I am confident in the Lord that I myself will come soon.

[25]But I think it is necessary to send back to you Epaphroditus, my brother, fellow worker and fellow soldier, who is also your messenger, whom you sent to take care of my needs. [26]For he longs for all of you and is distressed because you heard he was ill. [27]Indeed he was ill, and almost died. But God had mercy on him, and not on him only but also on me, to spare me sorrow upon sorrow. [28]Therefore I am all the more eager to send him, so that when you see him again you may be glad and I may have less anxiety. [29]Welcome him in the Lord with great joy, and

[a] 16 Or hold on to

honor men like him, [30]because he almost died for the work of Christ, risking his life to make up for the help you could not give me.

No Confidence in the Flesh

3 Finally, my brothers, rejoice in the Lord! It is no trouble for me to write the same things to you again, and it is a safeguard for you. [2]Watch out for those dogs, those men who do evil, those mutilators of the flesh. [3]For it is we who are the circumcision, we who worship by the Spirit of God, who glory in Christ Jesus, and who put no confidence in the flesh— [4]though I myself have reasons for such confidence.   Ps 22:16,20; Gal 6:15

If anyone else thinks he has reasons to put confidence in the flesh, I have more: [5]circumcised on the eighth day, of the people of Israel, of the tribe of Benjamin, a Hebrew of Hebrews; in regard to the law, a Pharisee; [6]as for zeal, persecuting the church; as for legalistic righteousness, faultless.   Ro 11:1; 2Co 11:22

[7]But whatever was to my profit I now consider loss for the sake of Christ. [8]What is more, I consider everything a loss compared to the surpassing greatness of knowing Christ Jesus my Lord, for whose sake I have lost all things. I consider them rubbish, that I may gain Christ [9]and be found in him, not having a righteousness of my own that comes from the law, but that which is through faith in Christ— the righteousness that comes from God and is by faith. [10]I want to know Christ and the power of his resurrection and the fellowship of sharing in his sufferings, becoming like him in his death, [11]and so, somehow, to attain to the resurrection from the dead.   Ro 6:3-5; 8:17

Pressing on Toward the Goal

[12]Not that I have already obtained all this, or have already been made perfect, but I press on to take hold of that for which Christ Jesus took hold of me. [13]Brothers, I do not consider myself yet to have taken hold of it. But one thing I do: Forgetting what is behind and straining toward what is ahead, [14]I press on toward the goal to win the prize for which God has called me heavenward in Christ Jesus.   Lk 9:62; Heb 6:1

[15]All of us who are mature should take such a view of things. And if on some point you think differently, that too God will make clear to you. [16]Only let us live up to what we have already attained.

[17]Join with others in following my example, brothers, and take note of those who live according to the pattern we gave you. [18]For, as I have often told you before and now say again even with tears, many live as enemies of the cross of Christ. [19]Their destiny is destruction, their god is their stomach, and their glory is in their shame. Their mind is on earthly things. [20]But our citizenship is in heaven. And we eagerly await a

Savior from there, the Lord Jesus Christ, [21]who, by the power that enables him to bring everything under his control, will transform our lowly bodies so that they will be like his glorious body.

4 Therefore, my brothers, you whom I love and long for, my joy and crown, that is how you should stand firm in the Lord, dear friends!   Php 1:8,27

Exhortations

[2]I plead with Euodia and I plead with Syntyche to agree with each other in the Lord. [3]Yes, and I ask you, loyal yokefellow,[a] help these women who have contended at my side in the cause of the gospel, along with Clement and the rest of my fellow workers, whose names are in the book of life.   Php 2:2,25

[4]Rejoice in the Lord always. I will say it again: Rejoice! [5]Let your gentleness be evident to all. The Lord is near. [6]Do not be anxious about anything, but in everything, by prayer and petition, with thanksgiving, present your requests to God. [7]And the peace of God, which transcends all understanding, will guard your hearts and your minds in Christ Jesus.

[8]Finally, brothers, whatever is true, whatever is noble, whatever is right, whatever is pure, whatever is lovely, whatever is admirable —if anything is excellent or praiseworthy—think about such things.

[9]Whatever you have learned or received or heard from me, or seen in me—put it into practice. And the God of peace will be with you.

Thanks for Their Gifts

[10]I rejoice greatly in the Lord that at last you have renewed your concern for me. Indeed, you have been concerned, but you had no opportunity to show it. [11]I am not saying this because I am in need, for I have learned to be content whatever the circumstances. [12]I know what it is to be in need, and I know what it is to have plenty. I have learned the secret of being content in any and every situation, whether well fed or hungry, whether living in plenty or in want. [13]I can do everything through him who gives me strength.   2Co 12:9; 1Ti 6:6,8

[14]Yet it was good of you to share in my troubles. [15]Moreover, as you Philippians know, in the early days of your acquaintance with the gospel, when I set out from Macedonia, not one church shared with me in the matter of giving and receiving, except you only; [16]for even when I was in Thessalonica, you sent me aid again and again when I was in need. [17]Not that I am looking for a gift, but I am looking for what may be credited to your account. [18]I have received full payment and even more; I am amply

supplied, now that I have received from Epaphroditus the gifts you sent. They are a fragrant offering, an acceptable sacrifice, pleasing to God. [19]And my God will meet all your needs according to his glorious riches in Christ Jesus.   Ps 23:1

[20]To our God and Father be glory for ever and ever. Amen.

Final Greetings

[21]Greet all the saints in Christ Jesus. The brothers who are with me send greetings. [22]All the saints send you greetings, especially those who belong to Caesar's household.   Ac 9:13; Gal 1:2

[23]The grace of the Lord Jesus Christ be with your spirit. Amen.[a]

---

a[23] Some manuscripts do not have *Amen*.

Colossians

1

1 Paul, an apostle of Christ Jesus by the will of God, and Timothy our brother, 1Co 1:1; 2Co 1:1

2To the holy and faithful[a] brothers in Christ at Colosse:

Grace and peace to you from God our Father.[b]   Ro 1:7; Col 4:18

Thanksgiving and Prayer

3We always thank God, the Father of our Lord Jesus Christ, when we pray for you, **4**because we have heard of your faith in Christ Jesus and of the love you have for all the saints— **5**the faith and love that spring from the hope that is stored up for you in heaven and that you have already heard about in the word of truth, the gospel **6**that has come to you. All over the world this gospel is bearing fruit and growing, just as it has been doing among you since the day you heard it and understood God's grace in all its truth. **7**You learned it from Epaphras, our dear fellow servant, who is a faithful minister of Christ on our[c] behalf, **8**and who also told us of your love in the Spirit.   Ro 15:30; 1Th 5:8

9For this reason, since the day we heard about you, we have not stopped praying for you and asking God to fill you with the knowledge of his will through all spiritual wisdom and understanding. **10**And we pray this in order that you may live a life worthy of the Lord and may please him in every way: bearing fruit in every good work, growing in the knowledge of God, **11**being strengthened with all power according to his glorious might so that you may have great endurance and patience, and joyfully **12**giving thanks to the Father, who has qualified you[d] to share in the inheritance of the saints in the kingdom of light. **13**For he has rescued us from the dominion of darkness and brought us into the kingdom of the Son he loves, **14**in whom we have redemption,[e] the forgiveness of sins.   Eph 1:7; 6:12

The Supremacy of Christ

15He is the image of the invisible God, the firstborn over all creation. **16**For by him all things were created: things in heaven and on earth, visible and invisible, whether thrones or powers or rulers or authorities; all things were created by him and for him. **17**He is before all things, and in him all things

---

a2 Or believing   b2 Some manuscripts Father and the Lord Jesus Christ   c7 Some manuscripts your   d12 Some manuscripts us   e14 A few late manuscripts redemption through his blood

hold together. [18]And he is the head of the body, the church; he is the beginning and the firstborn from among the dead, so that in everything he might have the supremacy. [19]For God was pleased to have all his fullness dwell in him, [20]and through him to reconcile to himself all things, whether things on earth or things in heaven, by making peace through his blood, shed on the cross.   2Co 5:18; Eph 2:13

[21]Once you were alienated from God and were enemies in your minds because of[a] your evil behavior. [22]But now he has reconciled you by Christ's physical body through death to present you holy in his sight, without blemish and free from accusation— [23]if you continue in your faith, established and firm, not moved from the hope held out in the gospel. This is the gospel that you heard and that has been proclaimed to every creature under heaven, and of which I, Paul, have become a servant.

Paul's Labor for the Church

[24]Now I rejoice in what was suffered for you, and I fill up in my flesh what is still lacking in regard to Christ's afflictions, for the sake of his body, which is the church. [25]I have become its servant by the commission God gave me to present to you the word of God in its fullness— [26]the mystery that has been kept hidden for ages and generations, but is now disclosed to the saints. [27]To them God has chosen to make known among the Gentiles the glorious riches of this mystery, which is Christ in you, the hope of glory.   Ro 8:10; Eph 3:2

[28]We proclaim him, admonishing and teaching everyone with all wisdom, so that we may present everyone perfect in Christ. [29]To this end I labor, struggling with all his energy, which so powerfully works in me.   1Co 15:10; Eph 1:19; Col 2:1

2 I want you to know how much I am struggling for you and for those at Laodicea, and for all who have not met me personally. [2]My purpose is that they may be encouraged in heart and united in love, so that they may have the full riches of complete understanding, in order that they may know the mystery of God, namely, Christ, [3]in whom are hidden all the treasures of wisdom and knowledge. [4]I tell you this so that no one may deceive you by fine-sounding arguments. [5]For though I am absent from you in body, I am present with you in spirit and delight to see how orderly you are and how firm your faith in Christ is.   1Co 14:40

Freedom From Human Regulations Through Life With Christ

[6]So then, just as you received Christ Jesus as Lord, continue to live in him, [7]rooted and built up in

a 21 Or minds, as shown by

him, strengthened in the faith as you were taught, and overflowing with thankfulness.   Eph 3:17; Col 1:10

⁸See to it that no one takes you captive through hollow and deceptive philosophy, which depends on human tradition and the basic principles of this world rather than on Christ.   Gal 4:3; 1Ti 6:20

⁹For in Christ all the fullness of the Deity lives in bodily form, ¹⁰and you have been given fullness in Christ, who is the head over every power and authority. ¹¹In him you were also circumcised, in the putting off of the sinful nature,ᵃ not with a circumcision done by the hands of men but with the circumcision done by Christ, ¹²having been buried with him in baptism and raised with him through your faith in the power of God, who raised him from the dead.

¹³When you were dead in your sins and in the uncircumcision of your sinful nature,ᵇ God made youᶜ alive with Christ. He forgave us all our sins, ¹⁴having canceled the written code, with its regulations, that was against us and that stood opposed to us; he took it away, nailing it to the cross. ¹⁵And having disarmed the powers and authorities, he made a public spectacle of them, triumphing over them by the cross.ᵈ   Eph 2:15; 6:12

¹⁶Therefore do not let anyone judge you by what you eat or drink, or with regard to a religious festival, a New Moon celebration or a Sabbath day. ¹⁷These are a shadow of the things that were to come; the reality, however, is found in Christ. ¹⁸Do not let anyone who delights in false humility and the worship of angels disqualify you for the prize. Such a person goes into great detail about what he has seen, and his unspiritual mind puffs him up with idle notions. ¹⁹He has lost connection with the Head, from whom the whole body, supported and held together by its ligaments and sinews, grows as God causes it to grow.   Eph 1:22; 4:16

²⁰Since you died with Christ to the basic principles of this world, why, as though you still belonged to it, do you submit to its rules: ²¹"Do not handle! Do not taste! Do not touch!"? ²²These are all destined to perish with use, because they are based on human commands and teachings. ²³Such regulations indeed have an appearance of wisdom, with their self-imposed worship, their false humility and their harsh treatment of the body, but they lack any value in restraining sensual indulgence.   Mt 15:9

Rules for Holy Living

3 Since, then, you have been raised with Christ, set your hearts on things above, where Christ is seated at the right hand of God. ²Set your minds on things

ᵃ 11 Or *the flesh*   ᵇ 13 Or *your flesh*   ᶜ 13 Some manuscripts *us*   ᵈ 15 Or *them in him*

above, not on earthly things. ³For you died, and your life is now hidden with Christ in God. ⁴When Christ, who is your*a* life, appears, then you also will appear with him in glory.   Ro 6:2; 1Jn 3:2

⁵Put to death, therefore, whatever belongs to your earthly nature: sexual immorality, impurity, lust, evil desires and greed, which is idolatry. ⁶Because of these, the wrath of God is coming.*b* ⁷You used to walk in these ways, in the life you once lived. ⁸But now you must rid yourselves of all such things as these: anger, rage, malice, slander, and filthy language from your lips. ⁹Do not lie to each other, since you have taken off your old self with its practices ¹⁰and have put on the new self, which is being renewed in knowledge in the image of its Creator. ¹¹Here there is no Greek or Jew, circumcised or uncircumcised, barbarian, Scythian, slave or free, but Christ is all, and is in all.

¹²Therefore, as God's chosen people, holy and dearly loved, clothe yourselves with compassion, kindness, humility, gentleness and patience. ¹³Bear with each other and forgive whatever grievances you may have against one another. Forgive as the Lord forgave you. ¹⁴And over all these virtues put on love, which binds them all together in perfect unity. ¹⁵Let the peace of Christ rule in

your hearts, since as members of one body you were called to peace. And be thankful. ¹⁶Let the word of Christ dwell in you richly as you teach and admonish one another with all wisdom, and as you sing psalms, hymns and spiritual songs with gratitude in your hearts to God. ¹⁷And whatever you do, whether in word or deed, do it all in the name of the Lord Jesus, giving thanks to God the Father through him.   1Co 10:31; Eph 5:19

Rules for Christian Households

¹⁸Wives, submit to your husbands, as is fitting in the Lord.

¹⁹Husbands, love your wives and do not be harsh with them.

²⁰Children, obey your parents in everything, for this pleases the Lord.

²¹Fathers, do not embitter your children, or they will become discouraged.

²²Slaves, obey your earthly masters in everything; and do it, not only when their eye is on you and to win their favor, but with sincerity of heart and reverence for the Lord. ²³Whatever you do, work at it with all your heart, as working for the Lord, not for men, ²⁴since you know that you will receive an inheritance from the Lord as a reward. It is the Lord Christ you are serving. ²⁵Anyone who does wrong will be repaid for his wrong, and there is no favoritism.

a4 Some manuscripts our   b6 Some early manuscripts coming on those who are disobedient

4 Masters, provide your slaves with what is right and fair, because you know that you also have a Master in heaven.   Eph 5:22-6:9

Further Instructions

²Devote yourselves to prayer, being watchful and thankful. ³And pray for us, too, that God may open a door for our message, so that we may proclaim the mystery of Christ, for which I am in chains. ⁴Pray that I may proclaim it clearly, as I should. ⁵Be wise in the way you act toward outsiders; make the most of every opportunity. ⁶Let your conversation be always full of grace, seasoned with salt, so that you may know how to answer everyone.   Mk 9:50; Eph 5:16; 1Pe 3:15

Final Greetings

⁷Tychicus will tell you all the news about me. He is a dear brother, a faithful minister and fellow servant in the Lord. ⁸I am sending him to you for the express purpose that you may know about our[a] circumstances and that he may encourage your hearts. ⁹He is coming with Onesimus, our faithful and dear brother, who is one of you. They will tell you everything that is happening here.   Eph 6:21-22

¹⁰My fellow prisoner Aristarchus sends you his greetings, as does Mark, the cousin of Barnabas. (You have received instructions about him; if he comes to you, welcome him.) ¹¹Jesus, who is called Justus, also sends greetings. These are the only Jews among my fellow workers for the kingdom of God, and they have proved a comfort to me. ¹²Epaphras, who is one of you and a servant of Christ Jesus, sends greetings. He is always wrestling in prayer for you, that you may stand firm in all the will of God, mature and fully assured. ¹³I vouch for him that he is working hard for you and for those at Laodicea and Hierapolis. ¹⁴Our dear friend Luke, the doctor, and Demas send greetings. ¹⁵Give my greetings to the brothers at Laodicea, and to Nympha and the church in her house.   Ac 4:36

¹⁶After this letter has been read to you, see that it is also read in the church of the Laodiceans and that you in turn read the letter from Laodicea.   2Th 3:14

¹⁷Tell Archippus: "See to it that you complete the work you have received in the Lord."   2Ti 4:5; Phm 2

¹⁸I, Paul, write this greeting in my own hand. Remember my chains. Grace be with you.

---

a 8 Some manuscripts *that he may know about your*

1 Thessalonians

1 Paul, Silas[a] and Timothy,

To the church of the Thessalonians in God the Father and the Lord Jesus Christ: Ac 17:1

Grace and peace to you.[b]

Thanksgiving for the Thessalonians' Faith

2We always thank God for all of you, mentioning you in our prayers. 3We continually remember before our God and Father your work produced by faith, your labor prompted by love, and your endurance inspired by hope in our Lord Jesus Christ.   Ro 1:8; 8:25

4For we know, brothers loved by God, that he has chosen you, 5because our gospel came to you not simply with words, but also with power, with the Holy Spirit and with deep conviction. You know how we lived among you for your sake. 6You became imitators of us and of the Lord; in spite of severe suffering, you welcomed the message with the joy given by the Holy Spirit. 7And so you became a model to all the believers in Macedonia and Achaia. 8The Lord's message rang out from you not only in Mac-edonia and Achaia—your faith in God has become known everywhere. Therefore we do not need to say anything about it, 9for they themselves report what kind of reception you gave us. They tell how you turned to God from idols to serve the living and true God, 10and to wait for his Son from heaven, whom he raised from the dead—Jesus, who rescues us from the coming wrath.   Ac 2:24; Ro 5:9

Paul's Ministry in Thessalonica

2 You know, brothers, that our visit to you was not a failure. 2We had previously suffered and been insulted in Philippi, as you know, but with the help of our God we dared to tell you his gospel in spite of strong opposition. 3For the appeal we make does not spring from error or impure motives, nor are we trying to trick you. 4On the contrary, we speak as men approved by God to be entrusted with the gospel. We are not trying to please men but God, who tests our hearts. 5You know we never used flattery, nor did we put on a mask to cover up greed—God is our witness. 6We were not looking

---

a 1 Greek Silvanus, a variant of Silas   b 1 Some early manuscripts you from God our Father and the Lord Jesus Christ

for praise from men, not from you or anyone else.   Gal 1:10; 1Th 1:5,9

As apostles of Christ we could have been a burden to you, **7**but we were gentle among you, like a mother caring for her little children. **8**We loved you so much that we were delighted to share with you not only the gospel of God but our lives as well, because you had become so dear to us. **9**Surely you remember, brothers, our toil and hardship; we worked night and day in order not to be a burden to anyone while we preached the gospel of God to you.   2Co 12:15

10You are witnesses, and so is God, of how holy, righteous and blameless we were among you who believed. **11**For you know that we dealt with each of you as a father deals with his own children, **12**encouraging, comforting and urging you to live lives worthy of God, who calls you into his kingdom and glory.   Eph 4:1; 1Th 1:5

13And we also thank God continually because, when you received the word of God, which you heard from us, you accepted it not as the word of men, but as it actually is, the word of God, which is at work in you who believe. **14**For you, brothers, became imitators of God's churches in Judea, which are in Christ Jesus: You suffered from your own countrymen the same things those churches suf-

fered from the Jews, **15**who killed the Lord Jesus and the prophets and also drove us out. They displease God and are hostile to all men **16**in their effort to keep us from speaking to the Gentiles so that they may be saved. In this way they always heap up their sins to the limit. The wrath of God has come upon them at last.*a*   Mt 23:32

Paul's Longing to See the Thessalonians

17But, brothers, when we were torn away from you for a short time (in person, not in thought), out of our intense longing we made every effort to see you. **18**For we wanted to come to you—certainly I, Paul, did, again and again—but Satan stopped us. **19**For what is our hope, our joy, or the crown in which we will glory in the presence of our Lord Jesus when he comes? Is it not you? **20**Indeed, you are our glory and joy.

3 So when we could stand it no longer, we thought it best to be left by ourselves in Athens. **2**We sent Timothy, who is our brother and God's fellow worker*b* in spreading the gospel of Christ, to strengthen and encourage you in your faith, **3**so that no one would be unsettled by these trials. You know quite well that we were destined for them. **4**In fact, when we were with you, we kept telling you

---

a 16 Or *them fully*   *b* 2 Some manuscripts *brother and fellow worker*; other manuscripts *brother and God's servant*

that we would be persecuted. And it turned out that way, as you well know. [5]For this reason, when I could stand it no longer, I sent to find out about your faith. I was afraid that in some way the tempter might have tempted you and our efforts might have been useless. Ac 9:16; Gal 2:2

Timothy's Encouraging Report

[6]But Timothy has just now come to us from you and has brought good news about your faith and love. He has told us that you always have pleasant memories of us and that you long to see us, just as we also long to see you. [7]Therefore, brothers, in all our distress and persecution we were encouraged about you because of your faith. [8]For now we really live, since you are standing firm in the Lord. [9]How can we thank God enough for you in return for all the joy we have in the presence of our God because of you? [10]Night and day we pray most earnestly that we may see you again and supply what is lacking in your faith.

[11]Now may our God and Father himself and our Lord Jesus clear the way for us to come to you. [12]May the Lord make your love increase and overflow for each other and for everyone else, just as ours does for you. [13]May he strengthen your hearts so that you will be blameless and holy in the presence of our God and Father when our Lord Jesus comes with all his holy ones. 1Co 1:8; 1Th 4:9-10

Living to Please God

4 Finally, brothers, we instructed you how to live in order to please God, as in fact you are living. Now we ask you and urge you in the Lord Jesus to do this more and more. [2]For you know what instructions we gave you by the authority of the Lord Jesus. 2Co 5:9

[3]It is God's will that you should be sanctified: that you should avoid sexual immorality; [4]that each of you should learn to control his own body[a] in a way that is holy and honorable, [5]not in passionate lust like the heathen, who do not know God; [6]and that in this matter no one should wrong his brother or take advantage of him. The Lord will punish men for all such sins, as we have already told you and warned you. [7]For God did not call us to be impure, but to live a holy life. [8]Therefore, he who rejects this instruction does not reject man but God, who gives you his Holy Spirit. Ro 5:5; Gal 4:6

[9]Now about brotherly love we do not need to write to you, for you yourselves have been taught by God to love each other. [10]And in fact, you do love all the brothers throughout Macedonia. Yet we urge you, brothers, to do so more and more. 1Th 1:7; 3:12

a4 Or learn to live with his own wife; or learn to acquire a wife

[11]Make it your ambition to lead a quiet life, to mind your own business and to work with your hands, just as we told you, [12]so that your daily life may win the respect of outsiders and so that you will not be dependent on anybody.

The Coming of the Lord

[13]Brothers, we do not want you to be ignorant about those who fall asleep, or to grieve like the rest of men, who have no hope. [14]We believe that Jesus died and rose again and so we believe that God will bring with Jesus those who have fallen asleep in him. [15]According to the Lord's own word, we tell you that we who are still alive, who are left till the coming of the Lord, will certainly not precede those who have fallen asleep. [16]For the Lord himself will come down from heaven, with a loud command, with the voice of the archangel and with the trumpet call of God, and the dead in Christ will rise first. [17]After that, we who are still alive and are left will be caught up together with them in the clouds to meet the Lord in the air. And so we will be with the Lord forever. [18]Therefore encourage each other with these words.

5 Now, brothers, about times and dates we do not need to write to you, [2]for you know very well that the day of the Lord will come like a thief in the night. [3]While people are saying, "Peace and safety," destruction will come on them suddenly, as labor pains on a pregnant woman, and they will not escape. <small>1Th 4:9; 2Pe 3:10</small>

[4]But you, brothers, are not in darkness so that this day should surprise you like a thief. [5]You are all sons of the light and sons of the day. We do not belong to the night or to the darkness. [6]So then, let us not be like others, who are asleep, but let us be alert and self-controlled. [7]For those who sleep, sleep at night, and those who get drunk, get drunk at night. [8]But since we belong to the day, let us be self-controlled, putting on faith and love as a breastplate, and the hope of salvation as a helmet. [9]For God did not appoint us to suffer wrath but to receive salvation through our Lord Jesus Christ. [10]He died for us so that, whether we are awake or asleep, we may live together with him. [11]Therefore encourage one another and build each other up, just as in fact you are doing. <small>1Th 4:18; Eph 4:29</small>

Final Instructions

[12]Now we ask you, brothers, to respect those who work hard among you, who are over you in the Lord and who admonish you. [13]Hold them in the highest regard in love because of their work. Live in peace with each other. [14]And we urge you, brothers, warn those who are idle, encourage the timid, help the weak, be patient with everyone. [15]Make sure that nobody pays back wrong for wrong, but al-

ways try to be kind to each other and to everyone else.   Eph 4:32

[16]Be joyful always; [17]pray continually; [18]give thanks in all circumstances, for this is God's will for you in Christ Jesus.   Php 4:4

[19]Do not put out the Spirit's fire; [20]do not treat prophecies with contempt. [21]Test everything. Hold on to the good. [22]Avoid every kind of evil.   1Co 14:29; Eph 4:30

[23]May God himself, the God of peace, sanctify you through and through. May your whole spirit, soul and body be kept blameless at the coming of our Lord Jesus Christ. [24]The one who calls you is faithful and he will do it.   1Co 1:9

[25]Brothers, pray for us. [26]Greet all the brothers with a holy kiss. [27]I charge you before the Lord to have this letter read to all the brothers.

[28]The grace of our Lord Jesus Christ be with you.   Ro 16:20

2 Thessalonians

1

Paul, Silas[a] and Timothy,

To the church of the Thessalonians in God our Father and the Lord Jesus Christ: Ac 17:1

[2]Grace and peace to you from God the Father and the Lord Jesus Christ.   Ro 1:7

Thanksgiving and Prayer

[3]We ought always to thank God for you, brothers, and rightly so, because your faith is growing more and more, and the love every one of you has for each other is increasing. [4]Therefore, among God's churches we boast about your perseverance and faith in all the persecutions and trials you are enduring.   1Th 3:12; 2:14

[5]All this is evidence that God's judgment is right, and as a result you will be counted worthy of the kingdom of God, for which you are suffering. [6]God is just: He will pay back trouble to those who trouble you [7]and give relief to you who are troubled, and to us as well. This will happen when the Lord Jesus is revealed from heaven in blazing fire with his powerful angels. [8]He will punish those who do not know God and do not obey the gospel of our Lord Jesus. [9]They

will be punished with everlasting destruction and shut out from the presence of the Lord and from the majesty of his power [10]on the day he comes to be glorified in his holy people and to be marveled at among all those who have believed. This includes you, because you believed our testimony to you.

[11]With this in mind, we constantly pray for you, that our God may count you worthy of his calling, and that by his power he may fulfill every good purpose of yours and every act prompted by your faith. [12]We pray this so that the name of our Lord Jesus may be glorified in you, and you in him, according to the grace of our God and the Lord Jesus Christ.[b]

The Man of Lawlessness

2

Concerning the coming of our Lord Jesus Christ and our being gathered to him, we ask you, brothers, [2]not to become easily unsettled or alarmed by some prophecy, report or letter supposed to have come from us, saying that the day of the Lord has already come. [3]Don't let anyone deceive you in any way, for ˌthat day will not comeˌ until the rebellion occurs and the man of lawlessness[c] is re-

---

a 1 Greek *Silvanus*, a variant of *Silas*   b 12 Or *God and Lord, Jesus Christ*   c 3 Some manuscripts *sin*

vealed, the man doomed to destruction. [4]He will oppose and will exalt himself over everything that is called God or is worshiped, so that he sets himself up in God's temple, proclaiming himself to be God. Isa 14:13-14; 1Co 8:5

[5]Don't you remember that when I was with you I used to tell you these things? [6]And now you know what is holding him back, so that he may be revealed at the proper time. [7]For the secret power of lawlessness is already at work; but the one who now holds it back will continue to do so till he is taken out of the way. [8]And then the lawless one will be revealed, whom the Lord Jesus will overthrow with the breath of his mouth and destroy by the splendor of his coming. [9]The coming of the lawless one will be in accordance with the work of Satan displayed in all kinds of counterfeit miracles, signs and wonders, [10]and in every sort of evil that deceives those who are perishing. They perish because they refused to love the truth and so be saved. [11]For this reason God sends them a powerful delusion so that they will believe the lie [12]and so that all will be condemned who have not believed the truth but have delighted in wickedness.

Stand Firm

[13]But we ought always to thank God for you, brothers loved by the Lord, because from the beginning God chose you[a] to be saved through the sanctifying work of the Spirit and through belief in the truth. [14]He called you to this through our gospel, that you might share in the glory of our Lord Jesus Christ. [15]So then, brothers, stand firm and hold to the teachings[b] we passed on to you, whether by word of mouth or by letter. 1Co 11:2; 16:13

[16]May our Lord Jesus Christ himself and God our Father, who loved us and by his grace gave us eternal encouragement and good hope, [17]encourage your hearts and strengthen you in every good deed and word. Jn 3:16; 1Th 3:2

Request for Prayer

3 Finally, brothers, pray for us that the message of the Lord may spread rapidly and be honored, just as it was with you. [2]And pray that we may be delivered from wicked and evil men, for not everyone has faith. [3]But the Lord is faithful, and he will strengthen and protect you from the evil one. [4]We have confidence in the Lord that you are doing and will continue to do the things we command. [5]May the Lord direct your hearts into God's love and Christ's perseverance. 1Ch 29:18; 1 Co 1:9

Warning Against Idleness

[6]In the name of the Lord Jesus Christ, we command you, broth-

---

[a] 13 Some manuscripts *because God chose you as his firstfruits*   [b] 15 Or *traditions*

ers, to keep away from every brother who is idle and does not live according to the teaching*a* you received from us. [7]For you yourselves know how you ought to follow our example. We were not idle when we were with you, [8]nor did we eat anyone's food without paying for it. On the contrary, we worked night and day, laboring and toiling so that we would not be a burden to any of you. [9]We did this, not because we do not have the right to such help, but in order to make ourselves a model for you to follow. [10]For even when we were with you, we gave you this rule: "If a man will not work, he shall not eat."   1Co 9:4-14; 1Th 4:11

[11]We hear that some among you are idle. They are not busy; they are busybodies. [12]Such people we command and urge in the Lord Jesus Christ to settle down and earn the bread they eat. [13]And as for you, brothers, never tire of doing what is right.   Gal 6:9; 1Ti 5:13

[14]If anyone does not obey our instruction in this letter, take special note of him. Do not associate with him, in order that he may feel ashamed. [15]Yet do not regard him as an enemy, but warn him as a brother.   Gal 6:1; 1Th 5:14

Final Greetings

[16]Now may the Lord of peace himself give you peace at all times and in every way. The Lord be with all of you.   Ro 15:33

[17]I, Paul, write this greeting in my own hand, which is the distinguishing mark in all my letters. This is how I write.   1Co 16:21

[18]The grace of our Lord Jesus Christ be with you all.   Ro 16:20

a 6 Or tradition

1 Timothy

1 Paul, an apostle of Christ Jesus by the command of God our Savior and of Christ Jesus our hope, Col 1:27; Tit 1:3

²To Timothy my true son in the faith: Ac 16:1; 2Ti 1:2

Grace, mercy and peace from God the Father and Christ Jesus our Lord. Ro 1:7

Warning Against False Teachers of the Law

³As I urged you when I went into Macedonia, stay there in Ephesus so that you may command certain men not to teach false doctrines any longer ⁴nor to devote themselves to myths and endless genealogies. These promote controversies rather than God's work—which is by faith. ⁵The goal of this command is love, which comes from a pure heart and a good conscience and a sincere faith. ⁶Some have wandered away from these and turned to meaningless talk. ⁷They want to be teachers of the law, but they do not know what they are talking about or what they so confidently affirm. 2Ti 2:22

⁸We know that the law is good if one uses it properly. ⁹We also know that law*ᵃ* is made not for the righteous but for lawbreakers and rebels, the ungodly and sinful, the unholy and irreligious; for those who kill their fathers or mothers, for murderers, ¹⁰for adulterers and perverts, for slave traders and liars and perjurers—and for whatever else is contrary to the sound doctrine ¹¹that conforms to the glorious gospel of the blessed God, which he entrusted to me. Gal 2:7

The Lord's Grace to Paul

¹²I thank Christ Jesus our Lord, who has given me strength, that he considered me faithful, appointing me to his service. ¹³Even though I was once a blasphemer and a persecutor and a violent man, I was shown mercy because I acted in ignorance and unbelief. ¹⁴The grace of our Lord was poured out on me abundantly, along with the faith and love that are in Christ Jesus. Ac 8:3; 2Ti 1:13

¹⁵Here is a trustworthy saying that deserves full acceptance: Christ Jesus came into the world to save sinners—of whom I am the worst. ¹⁶But for that very reason I was shown mercy so that in me, the worst of sinners, Christ Jesus might display his unlimited patience as an example for those who

---

ᵃ9 Or *that the law*

would believe on him and receive eternal life. [17]Now to the King eternal, immortal, invisible, the only God, be honor and glory for ever and ever. Amen.   Ro 11:36; Col 1:15

[18]Timothy, my son, I give you this instruction in keeping with the prophecies once made about you, so that by following them you may fight the good fight, [19]holding on to faith and a good conscience. Some have rejected these and so have shipwrecked their faith. [20]Among them are Hymenaeus and Alexander, whom I have handed over to Satan to be taught not to blaspheme.   1Ti 4:14; 2Ti 2:3

Instructions on Worship

2 I urge, then, first of all, that requests, prayers, intercession and thanksgiving be made for everyone— [2]for kings and all those in authority, that we may live peaceful and quiet lives in all godliness and holiness. [3]This is good, and pleases God our Savior, [4]who wants all men to be saved and to come to a knowledge of the truth. [5]For there is one God and one mediator between God and men, the man Christ Jesus, [6]who gave himself as a ransom for all men—the testimony given in its proper time. [7]And for this purpose I was appointed a herald and an apostle— I am telling the truth, I am not lying—and a teacher of the true faith to the Gentiles.   1Co 1:6; Gal 3:20

[8]I want men everywhere to lift up holy hands in prayer, without anger or disputing.   Ps 134:2; Lk 24:50

[9]I also want women to dress modestly, with decency and propriety, not with braided hair or gold or pearls or expensive clothes, [10]but with good deeds, appropriate for women who profess to worship God.   Pr 31:13; 1Pe 3:3

[11]A woman should learn in quietness and full submission. [12]I do not permit a woman to teach or to have authority over a man; she must be silent. [13]For Adam was formed first, then Eve. [14]And Adam was not the one deceived; it was the woman who was deceived and became a sinner. [15]But women[a] will be saved[b] through childbearing—if they continue in faith, love and holiness with propriety.

Overseers and Deacons

3 Here is a trustworthy saying: If anyone sets his heart on being an overseer,[c] he desires a noble task. [2]Now the overseer must be above reproach, the husband of but one wife, temperate, self-controlled, respectable, hospitable, able to teach, [3]not given to drunkenness, not violent but gentle, not quarrelsome, not a lover of money. [4]He must manage his own family well and see that his children obey him with proper respect. [5](If anyone does not know how to manage

---

[a]15 Greek she   [b]15 Or restored   [c]1 Traditionally bishop; also in verse 2

his own family, how can he take care of God's church?) **6**He must not be a recent convert, or he may become conceited and fall under the same judgment as the devil. **7**He must also have a good reputation with outsiders, so that he will not fall into disgrace and into the devil's trap.   1Ti 6:4; 2Ti 2:26

8Deacons, likewise, are to be men worthy of respect, sincere, not indulging in much wine, and not pursuing dishonest gain. **9**They must keep hold of the deep truths of the faith with a clear conscience. **10**They must first be tested; and then if there is nothing against them, let them serve as deacons.   1Ti 1:19; Tit 2:3

11In the same way, their wives[a] are to be women worthy of respect, not malicious talkers but temperate and trustworthy in everything.   Tit 2:3

12A deacon must be the husband of but one wife and must manage his children and his household well. **13**Those who have served well gain an excellent standing and great assurance in their faith in Christ Jesus.

14Although I hope to come to you soon, I am writing you these instructions so that, **15**if I am delayed, you will know how people ought to conduct themselves in God's household, which is the church of the living God, the pillar and foundation of the truth. **16**Be-

yond all question, the mystery of godliness is great: Ro 16:25; Eph 2:21

He[b] appeared in a body,[c]
  was vindicated by the Spirit,
  was seen by angels,
  was preached among the
    nations,   Col 1:23
  was believed on in the world,
  was taken up in glory.

Instructions to Timothy

4 The Spirit clearly says that in later times some will abandon the faith and follow deceiving spirits and things taught by demons. **2**Such teachings come through hypocritical liars, whose consciences have been seared as with a hot iron. **3**They forbid people to marry and order them to abstain from certain foods, which God created to be received with thanksgiving by those who believe and who know the truth. **4**For everything God created is good, and nothing is to be rejected if it is received with thanksgiving, **5**because it is consecrated by the word of God and prayer.   Ro 14:14-18

6If you point these things out to the brothers, you will be a good minister of Christ Jesus, brought up in the truths of the faith and of the good teaching that you have followed. **7**Have nothing to do with godless myths and old wives' tales; rather, train yourself to be godly. **8**For physical training is of some

---

a 11 Or *way, deaconesses*   *b 16* Some manuscripts *God*   *c 16* Or *in the flesh*

value, but godliness has value for all things, holding promise for both the present life and the life to come. 1Ti 6:6; Ps 37:9,11; Mk 10:29-30

⁹This is a trustworthy saying that deserves full acceptance ¹⁰(and for this we labor and strive), that we have put our hope in the living God, who is the Savior of all men, and especially of those who believe. 1Ti 1:15

¹¹Command and teach these things. ¹²Don't let anyone look down on you because you are young, but set an example for the believers in speech, in life, in love, in faith and in purity. ¹³Until I come, devote yourself to the public reading of Scripture, to preaching and to teaching. ¹⁴Do not neglect your gift, which was given you through a prophetic message when the body of elders laid their hands on you. 1Ti 1:14,18; Tit 2:7

¹⁵Be diligent in these matters; give yourself wholly to them, so that everyone may see your progress. ¹⁶Watch your life and doctrine closely. Persevere in them, because if you do, you will save both yourself and your hearers.

Advice About Widows, Elders and Slaves

5 Do not rebuke an older man harshly, but exhort him as if he were your father. Treat younger men as brothers, ²older women as mothers, and younger women as sisters, with absolute purity.

³Give proper recognition to those widows who are really in need. ⁴But if a widow has children or grandchildren, these should learn first of all to put their religion into practice by caring for their own family and so repaying their parents and grandparents, for this is pleasing to God. ⁵The widow who is really in need and left all alone puts her hope in God and continues night and day to pray and to ask God for help. ⁶But the widow who lives for pleasure is dead even while she lives. ⁷Give the people these instructions, too, so that no one may be open to blame. ⁸If anyone does not provide for his relatives, and especially for his immediate family, he has denied the faith and is worse than an unbeliever. 1Ti 4:11; Tit 1:16

⁹No widow may be put on the list of widows unless she is over sixty, has been faithful to her husband,ᵃ ¹⁰and is well known for her good deeds, such as bringing up children, showing hospitality, washing the feet of the saints, helping those in trouble and devoting herself to all kinds of good deeds. Lk 7:44; 1Pe 2:12

¹¹As for younger widows, do not put them on such a list. For when their sensual desires overcome their dedication to Christ, they want to marry. ¹²Thus they bring

---

ᵃ9 Or has had but one husband

judgment on themselves, because they have broken their first pledge. [13]Besides, they get into the habit of being idle and going about from house to house. And not only do they become idlers, but also gossips and busybodies, saying things they ought not to. [14]So I counsel younger widows to marry, to have children, to manage their homes and to give the enemy no opportunity for slander. [15]Some have in fact already turned away to follow Satan.   1Co 7:9; 2Th 3:11

[16]If any woman who is a believer has widows in her family, she should help them and not let the church be burdened with them, so that the church can help those widows who are really in need.

[17]The elders who direct the affairs of the church well are worthy of double honor, especially those whose work is preaching and teaching. [18]For the Scripture says, "Do not muzzle the ox while it is treading out the grain,"[a] and "The worker deserves his wages."[b] [19]Do not entertain an accusation against an elder unless it is brought by two or three witnesses. [20]Those who sin are to be rebuked publicly, so that the others may take warning.

[21]I charge you, in the sight of God and Christ Jesus and the elect angels, to keep these instructions without partiality, and to do nothing out of favoritism.   1Ti 6:13; 2Ti 4:1

[22]Do not be hasty in the laying on of hands, and do not share in the sins of others. Keep yourself pure.   Ac 6:6; Eph 5:11

[23]Stop drinking only water, and use a little wine because of your stomach and your frequent illnesses.   1Ti 3:8

[24]The sins of some men are obvious, reaching the place of judgment ahead of them; the sins of others trail behind them. [25]In the same way, good deeds are obvious, and even those that are not cannot be hidden.

6 All who are under the yoke of slavery should consider their masters worthy of full respect, so that God's name and our teaching may not be slandered. [2]Those who have believing masters are not to show less respect for them because they are brothers. Instead, they are to serve them even better, because those who benefit from their service are believers, and dear to them. These are the things you are to teach and urge on them.

Love of Money

[3]If anyone teaches false doctrines and does not agree to the sound instruction of our Lord Jesus Christ and to godly teaching, [4]he is conceited and understands nothing. He has an unhealthy interest in controversies and quarrels about words that result in envy, strife, malicious talk, evil suspicions [5]and constant friction

[a]18 Deut. 25:4   [b]18 Luke 10:7

between men of corrupt mind, who have been robbed of the truth and who think that godliness is a means to financial gain. 1Ti 1:10

[6]But godliness with contentment is great gain. [7]For we brought nothing into the world, and we can take nothing out of it. [8]But if we have food and clothing, we will be content with that. [9]People who want to get rich fall into temptation and a trap and into many foolish and harmful desires that plunge men into ruin and destruction. [10]For the love of money is a root of all kinds of evil. Some people, eager for money, have wandered from the faith and pierced themselves with many griefs.

Paul's Charge to Timothy

[11]But you, man of God, flee from all this, and pursue righteousness, godliness, faith, love, endurance and gentleness. [12]Fight the good fight of the faith. Take hold of the eternal life to which you were called when you made your good confession in the presence of many witnesses. [13]In the sight of God, who gives life to everything, and of Christ Jesus, who while testifying before Pontius Pilate made the good confession, I charge you

[14]to keep this command without spot or blame until the appearing of our Lord Jesus Christ, [15]which God will bring about in his own time—God, the blessed and only Ruler, the King of kings and Lord of lords, [16]who alone is immortal and who lives in unapproachable light, whom no one has seen or can see. To him be honor and might forever. Amen. Jn 18:33-37

[17]Command those who are rich in this present world not to be arrogant nor to put their hope in wealth, which is so uncertain, but to put their hope in God, who richly provides us with everything for our enjoyment. [18]Command them to do good, to be rich in good deeds, and to be generous and willing to share. [19]In this way they will lay up treasure for themselves as a firm foundation for the coming age, so that they may take hold of the life that is truly life.

[20]Timothy, guard what has been entrusted to your care. Turn away from godless chatter and the opposing ideas of what is falsely called knowledge, [21]which some have professed and in so doing have wandered from the faith.

Grace be with you. Col 4:18

2 Timothy

1 Paul, an apostle of Christ Jesus by the will of God, according to the promise of life that is in Christ Jesus, *2Co 1:1*

²To Timothy, my dear son:

Grace, mercy and peace from God the Father and Christ Jesus our Lord. *Ro 1:7*

Encouragement to Be Faithful

³I thank God, whom I serve, as my forefathers did, with a clear conscience, as night and day I constantly remember you in my prayers. ⁴Recalling your tears, I long to see you, so that I may be filled with joy. ⁵I have been reminded of your sincere faith, which first lived in your grandmother Lois and in your mother Eunice and, I am persuaded, now lives in you also. ⁶For this reason I remind you to fan into flame the gift of God, which is in you through the laying on of my hands. ⁷For God did not give us a spirit of timidity, but a spirit of power, of love and of self-discipline. *Ro 8:15*

⁸So do not be ashamed to testify about our Lord, or ashamed of me his prisoner. But join with me in suffering for the gospel, by the power of God, ⁹who has saved us and called us to a holy life—not because of anything we have done but because of his own purpose and grace. This grace was given us in Christ Jesus before the beginning of time, ¹⁰but it has now been revealed through the appearing of our Savior, Christ Jesus, who has destroyed death and has brought life and immortality to light through the gospel. ¹¹And of this gospel I was appointed a herald and an apostle and a teacher. ¹²That is why I am suffering as I am. Yet I am not ashamed, because I know whom I have believed, and am convinced that he is able to guard what I have entrusted to him for that day. *1Ti 2:7; 6:20*

¹³What you heard from me, keep as the pattern of sound teaching, with faith and love in Christ Jesus. ¹⁴Guard the good deposit that was entrusted to you—guard it with the help of the Holy Spirit who lives in us. *1Ti 1:14; Tit 1:9*

¹⁵You know that everyone in the province of Asia has deserted me, including Phygelus and Hermogenes. *2Ti 4:10-11,16*

¹⁶May the Lord show mercy to the household of Onesiphorus, because he often refreshed me and was not ashamed of my chains. ¹⁷On the contrary, when he was in Rome, he searched hard for me until he found me. ¹⁸May the Lord grant that he will find mercy from

the Lord on that day! You know very well in how many ways he helped me in Ephesus. ^{2Ti 4:19}

2 You then, my son, be strong in the grace that is in Christ Jesus. ²And the things you have heard me say in the presence of many witnesses entrust to reliable men who will also be qualified to teach others. ³Endure hardship with us like a good soldier of Christ Jesus. ⁴No one serving as a soldier gets involved in civilian affairs—he wants to please his commanding officer. ⁵Similarly, if anyone competes as an athlete, he does not receive the victor's crown unless he competes according to the rules. ⁶The hardworking farmer should be the first to receive a share of the crops. ⁷Reflect on what I am saying, for the Lord will give you insight into all this.

⁸Remember Jesus Christ, raised from the dead, descended from David. This is my gospel, ⁹for which I am suffering even to the point of being chained like a criminal. But God's word is not chained. ¹⁰Therefore I endure everything for the sake of the elect, that they too may obtain the salvation that is in Christ Jesus, with eternal glory. ¹¹Here is a trustworthy saying:

If we died with him,
     we will also live with him;
¹²if we endure,
     we will also reign with him.

If we disown him,
     he will also disown us;
¹³if we are faithless,
     he will remain faithful,
     for he cannot disown
          himself.

A Workman Approved by God

¹⁴Keep reminding them of these things. Warn them before God against quarreling about words; it is of no value, and only ruins those who listen. ¹⁵Do your best to present yourself to God as one approved, a workman who does not need to be ashamed and who correctly handles the word of truth. ¹⁶Avoid godless chatter, because those who indulge in it will become more and more ungodly. ¹⁷Their teaching will spread like gangrene. Among them are Hymenaeus and Philetus, ¹⁸who have wandered away from the truth. They say that the resurrection has already taken place, and they destroy the faith of some. ¹⁹Nevertheless, God's solid foundation stands firm, sealed with this inscription: "The Lord knows those who are his,"ᵃ and, "Everyone who confesses the name of the Lord must turn away from wickedness." ^{Jn 10:14; 1Co 1:2}

²⁰In a large house there are articles not only of gold and silver, but also of wood and clay; some are for noble purposes and some for ignoble. ²¹If a man cleanses himself

---

ᵃ 19 Num. 16:5 (see Septuagint)

from the latter, he will be an instrument for noble purposes, made holy, useful to the Master and prepared to do any good work. ²²Flee the evil desires of youth, and pursue righteousness, faith, love and peace, along with those who call on the Lord out of a pure heart. ²³Don't have anything to do with foolish and stupid arguments, because you know they produce quarrels. ²⁴And the Lord's servant must not quarrel; instead, he must be kind to everyone, able to teach, not resentful. ²⁵Those who oppose him he must gently instruct, in the hope that God will grant them repentance leading them to a knowledge of the truth, ²⁶and that they will come to their senses and escape from the trap of the devil, who has taken them captive to do his will.   1Ti 1:5; 3:7

Godlessness in the Last Days

3 But mark this: There will be terrible times in the last days. ²People will be lovers of themselves, lovers of money, boastful, proud, abusive, disobedient to their parents, ungrateful, unholy, ³without love, unforgiving, slanderous, without self-control, brutal, not lovers of the good, ⁴treacherous, rash, conceited, lovers of pleasure rather than lovers of God— ⁵having a form of godliness but denying its power. Have nothing to do with them.   Ro 1:30

⁶They are the kind who worm their way into homes and gain control over weak-willed women, who are loaded down with sins and are swayed by all kinds of evil desires, ⁷always learning but never able to acknowledge the truth. ⁸Just as Jannes and Jambres opposed Moses, so also these men oppose the truth—men of depraved minds, who, as far as the faith is concerned, are rejected. ⁹But they will not get very far because, as in the case of those men, their folly will be clear to everyone.   Ex 7:12; 1Ti 6:5

Paul's Charge to Timothy

¹⁰You, however, know all about my teaching, my way of life, my purpose, faith, patience, love, endurance, ¹¹persecutions, sufferings—what kinds of things happened to me in Antioch, Iconium and Lystra, the persecutions I endured. Yet the Lord rescued me from all of them. ¹²In fact, everyone who wants to live a godly life in Christ Jesus will be persecuted, ¹³while evil men and impostors will go from bad to worse, deceiving and being deceived. ¹⁴But as for you, continue in what you have learned and have become convinced of, because you know those from whom you learned it, ¹⁵and how from infancy you have known the holy Scriptures, which are able to make you wise for salvation through faith in Christ Jesus. ¹⁶All Scripture is God-breathed and is useful for teaching, rebuking, correcting and training in righteous-

ness, [17]so that the man of God may be thoroughly equipped for every good work.   2Pe 1:20-21

4 In the presence of God and of Christ Jesus, who will judge the living and the dead, and in view of his appearing and his kingdom, I give you this charge: [2]Preach the Word; be prepared in season and out of season; correct, rebuke and encourage—with great patience and careful instruction. [3]For the time will come when men will not put up with sound doctrine. Instead, to suit their own desires, they will gather around them a great number of teachers to say what their itching ears want to hear. [4]They will turn their ears away from the truth and turn aside to myths. [5]But you, keep your head in all situations, endure hardship, do the work of an evangelist, discharge all the duties of your ministry.   Ac 21:8; 1Ti 1:10

[6]For I am already being poured out like a drink offering, and the time has come for my departure. [7]I have fought the good fight, I have finished the race, I have kept the faith. [8]Now there is in store for me the crown of righteousness, which the Lord, the righteous Judge, will award to me on that day—and not only to me, but also to all who have longed for his appearing.

Personal Remarks

[9]Do your best to come to me quickly, [10]for Demas, because he loved this world, has deserted me and has gone to Thessalonica. Crescens has gone to Galatia, and Titus to Dalmatia. [11]Only Luke is with me. Get Mark and bring him with you, because he is helpful to me in my ministry. [12]I sent Tychicus to Ephesus. [13]When you come, bring the cloak that I left with Carpus at Troas, and my scrolls, especially the parchments.   Col 4:14

[14]Alexander the metalworker did me a great deal of harm. The Lord will repay him for what he has done. [15]You too should be on your guard against him, because he strongly opposed our message.

[16]At my first defense, no one came to my support, but everyone deserted me. May it not be held against them. [17]But the Lord stood at my side and gave me strength, so that through me the message might be fully proclaimed and all the Gentiles might hear it. And I was delivered from the lion's mouth. [18]The Lord will rescue me from every evil attack and will bring me safely to his heavenly kingdom. To him be glory for ever and ever. Amen.   Ps 121:7; Ro 11:36

Final Greetings

[19]Greet Priscilla[a] and Aquila and the household of Onesipho-

---

[a] 19 Greek Prisca, a variant of Priscilla

rus. ²⁰Erastus stayed in Corinth, and I left Trophimus sick in Miletus. ²¹Do your best to get here before winter. Eubulus greets you, and so do Pudens, Linus, Claudia and all the brothers. Ac 19:22; 20:4

²²The Lord be with your spirit. Grace be with you. Gal 6:18; Col 4:18

Titus

1 Paul, a servant of God and an apostle of Jesus Christ for the faith of God's elect and the knowledge of the truth that leads to godliness— ²a faith and knowledge resting on the hope of eternal life, which God, who does not lie, promised before the beginning of time, ³and at his appointed season he brought his word to light through the preaching entrusted to me by the command of God our Savior,   2Ti 1:1,10

⁴To Titus, my true son in our common faith: 2Co 2:13

Grace and peace from God the Father and Christ Jesus our Savior.

Titus' Task on Crete

⁵The reason I left you in Crete was that you might straighten out what was left unfinished and appoint*ᵃ* elders in every town, as I directed you. ⁶An elder must be blameless, the husband of but one wife, a man whose children believe and are not open to the charge of being wild and disobedient. ⁷Since an overseerᵇ is entrusted with God's work, he must be blameless—not overbearing, not quick-tempered, not given to drunkenness, not violent, not pursuing dishonest gain. ⁸Rather he must be hospitable, one who loves what is good, who is self-controlled, upright, holy and disciplined. ⁹He must hold firmly to the trustworthy message as it has been taught, so that he can encourage others by sound doctrine and refute those who oppose it.   1Ti 3:2-4

¹⁰For there are many rebellious people, mere talkers and deceivers, especially those of the circumcision group. ¹¹They must be silenced, because they are ruining whole households by teaching things they ought not to teach— and that for the sake of dishonest gain. ¹²Even one of their own prophets has said, "Cretans are always liars, evil brutes, lazy gluttons." ¹³This testimony is true. Therefore, rebuke them sharply, so that they will be sound in the faith ¹⁴and will pay no attention to Jewish myths or to the commands of those who reject the truth. ¹⁵To the pure, all things are pure, but to those who are corrupted and do not believe, nothing is pure. In fact, both their minds and consciences are corrupted. ¹⁶They claim to know God, but by their actions they deny him. They are

---

ᵃ5 Or *ordain*   ᵇ7 Traditionally *bishop*

detestable, disobedient and unfit for doing anything good.   1Ti 1:4

What Must Be Taught to Various Groups

2 You must teach what is in accord with sound doctrine. [2]Teach the older men to be temperate, worthy of respect, self-controlled, and sound in faith, in love and in endurance.   1Ti 1:10; Tit 1:13

[3]Likewise, teach the older women to be reverent in the way they live, not to be slanderers or addicted to much wine, but to teach what is good. [4]Then they can train the younger women to love their husbands and children, [5]to be self-controlled and pure, to be busy at home, to be kind, and to be subject to their husbands, so that no one will malign the word of God.

[6]Similarly, encourage the young men to be self-controlled. [7]In everything set them an example by doing what is good. In your teaching show integrity, seriousness [8]and soundness of speech that cannot be condemned, so that those who oppose you may be ashamed because they have nothing bad to say about us.   1Ti 4:12

[9]Teach slaves to be subject to their masters in everything, to try to please them, not to talk back to them, [10]and not to steal from them, but to show that they can be fully trusted, so that in every way they will make the teaching about God our Savior attractive.   Mt 5:16; Eph 6:5

[11]For the grace of God that brings salvation has appeared to all men. [12]It teaches us to say "No" to ungodliness and worldly passions, and to live self-controlled, upright and godly lives in this present age, [13]while we wait for the blessed hope—the glorious appearing of our great God and Savior, Jesus Christ, [14]who gave himself for us to redeem us from all wickedness and to purify for himself a people that are his very own, eager to do what is good.   2Ti 3:12

[15]These, then, are the things you should teach. Encourage and rebuke with all authority. Do not let anyone despise you.

Doing What Is Good

3 Remind the people to be subject to rulers and authorities, to be obedient, to be ready to do whatever is good, [2]to slander no one, to be peaceable and considerate, and to show true humility toward all men.   Eph 4:31; 2Ti 2:24

[3]At one time we too were foolish, disobedient, deceived and enslaved by all kinds of passions and pleasures. We lived in malice and envy, being hated and hating one another. [4]But when the kindness and love of God our Savior appeared, [5]he saved us, not because of righteous things we had done, but because of his mercy. He saved us through the washing of rebirth and renewal by the Holy Spirit,

⁶whom he poured out on us generously through Jesus Christ our Savior, ⁷so that, having been justified by his grace, we might become heirs having the hope of eternal life. ⁸This is a trustworthy saying. And I want you to stress these things, so that those who have trusted in God may be careful to devote themselves to doing what is good. These things are excellent and profitable for everyone.   1Ti 1:15; Tit 2:14

⁹But avoid foolish controversies and genealogies and arguments and quarrels about the law, because these are unprofitable and useless. ¹⁰Warn a divisive person once, and then warn him a second time. After that, have nothing to do with him. ¹¹You may be sure that such a man is warped and sinful; he is self-condemned.   1Ti 1:4

Final Remarks

¹²As soon as I send Artemas or Tychicus to you, do your best to come to me at Nicopolis, because I have decided to winter there. ¹³Do everything you can to help Zenas the lawyer and Apollos on their way and see that they have everything they need. ¹⁴Our people must learn to devote themselves to doing what is good, in order that they may provide for daily necessities and not live unproductive lives.   Ac 18:24; 20:4

¹⁵Everyone with me sends you greetings. Greet those who love us in the faith.   1Ti 1:2

Grace be with you all.   Col 4:18

Philemon

1 Paul, a prisoner of Christ Jesus, and Timothy our brother,   Eph 3:1

To Philemon our dear friend and fellow worker, **2** to Apphia our sister, to Archippus our fellow soldier and to the church that meets in your home: Ro 16:5; Php 2:25; Col 4:17

3 Grace to you and peace from God our Father and the Lord Jesus Christ.   Ro 1:7

Thanksgiving and Prayer

4 I always thank my God as I remember you in my prayers, **5** because I hear about your faith in the Lord Jesus and your love for all the saints. **6** I pray that you may be active in sharing your faith, so that you will have a full understanding of every good thing we have in Christ. **7** Your love has given me great joy and encouragement, because you, brother, have refreshed the hearts of the saints.   2Co 7:4,13

Paul's Plea for Onesimus

8 Therefore, although in Christ I could be bold and order you to do what you ought to do, **9** yet I appeal to you on the basis of love. I then, as Paul—an old man and now also a prisoner of Christ Jesus—

10 I appeal to you for my son Onesimus, [a] who became my son while I was in chains. **11** Formerly he was useless to you, but now he has become useful both to you and to me.

12 I am sending him—who is my very heart—back to you. **13** I would have liked to keep him with me so that he could take your place in helping me while I am in chains for the gospel. **14** But I did not want to do anything without your consent, so that any favor you do will be spontaneous and not forced. **15** Perhaps the reason he was separated from you for a little while was that you might have him back for good — **16** no longer as a slave, but better than a slave, as a dear brother. He is very dear to me but even dearer to you, both as a man and as a brother in the Lord.   2Co 9:7; 1Ti 6:2

17 So if you consider me a partner, welcome him as you would welcome me. **18** If he has done you any wrong or owes you anything, charge it to me. **19** I, Paul, am writing this with my own hand. I will pay it back—not to mention that you owe me your very self. **20** I do wish, brother, that I may have some benefit from you in the Lord; refresh my heart in Christ. **21** Confi-

---

_a 10_ Onesimus means _useful._

dent of your obedience, I write to you, knowing that you will do even more than I ask.   2Co 2:3; 8:23

²²And one thing more: Prepare a guest room for me, because I hope to be restored to you in answer to your prayers.   2Co 1:11; Php 1:25

²³Epaphras, my fellow prisoner in Christ Jesus, sends you greetings. ²⁴And so do Mark, Aristarchus, Demas and Luke, my fellow workers.   Ac 12:12; Col 1:7

²⁵The grace of the Lord Jesus Christ be with your spirit.   2Ti 4:22

Hebrews

The Son Superior to Angels

1 In the past God spoke to our forefathers through the prophets at many times and in various ways, ²but in these last days he has spoken to us by his Son, whom he appointed heir of all things, and through whom he made the universe. ³The Son is the radiance of God's glory and the exact representation of his being, sustaining all things by his powerful word. After he had provided purification for sins, he sat down at the right hand of the Majesty in heaven. ⁴So he became as much superior to the angels as the name he has inherited is superior to theirs.   Php 2:9-10

⁵For to which of the angels did God ever say,

"You are my Son;
    today I have become your
        Father*a*"*b*?   Ps 2:7

Or again,

"I will be his Father,
    and he will be my Son"*c*?

⁶And again, when God brings his firstborn into the world, he says,

"Let all God's angels worship
    him."*d*   Ps 97:7

⁷In speaking of the angels he says,

"He makes his angels winds,
    his servants flames of fire."*e*

⁸But about the Son he says,

"Your throne, O God, will last
        for ever and ever,   Lk 1:33
    and righteousness will be the
        scepter of your
        kingdom.
⁹You have loved righteousness
        and hated wickedness;
    therefore God, your God, has
        set you above your
        companions   Php 2:9
    by anointing you with the oil
        of joy."*f*   Isa 61:1,3

¹⁰He also says,

"In the beginning, O Lord, you
        laid the foundations of
        the earth,
    and the heavens are the
        work of your hands.
¹¹They will perish, but you
        remain;
    they will all wear out like a
        garment.   Isa 34:4; Heb 12:27
¹²You will roll them up like a
        robe;
    like a garment they will be
        changed.
    But you remain the same,

---

a 5 Or *have begotten you*   *b 5* Psalm 2:7   *c 5* 2 Samuel 7:14; 1 Chron. 17:13   *d 6* Deut. 32:43 (see
Dead Sea Scrolls and Septuagint)   *e 7* Psalm 104:4   *f 9* Psalm 45:6,7

and your years will never
    end."[a]   Ps 102:25-27

[13]To which of the angels did God
ever say,

"Sit at my right hand   Mk 16:19
until I make your enemies
    a footstool for your feet"[b]?

[14]Are not all angels ministering
spirits sent to serve those who will
inherit salvation?   Jos 10:24; Ps 103:20

Warning to Pay Attention

2 We must pay more careful attention, therefore, to what we
have heard, so that we do not drift
away. [2]For if the message spoken
by angels was binding, and every
violation and disobedience received its just punishment, [3]how
shall we escape if we ignore such
a great salvation? This salvation,
which was first announced by the
Lord, was confirmed to us by those
who heard him. [4]God also testified
to it by signs, wonders and various
miracles, and gifts of the Holy Spirit distributed according to his will.

Jesus Made Like His Brothers

[5]It is not to angels that he has
subjected the world to come,
about which we are speaking. [6]But
there is a place where someone
has testified: Heb 4:4

"What is man that you are
    mindful of him,

the son of man that you care
    for him?   Job 7:17; Ps 144:3
[7]You made him a little[c] lower
    than the angels;
you crowned him with glory
    and honor
[8] and put everything under his
    feet."[d]
                                1Co 15:25

In putting everything under him,
God left nothing that is not subject
to him. Yet at present we do not
see everything subject to him. [9]But
we see Jesus, who was made a little lower than the angels, now
crowned with glory and honor because he suffered death, so that by
the grace of God he might taste
death for everyone.   Jn 3:16; Ac 2:33

[10]In bringing many sons to glory, it was fitting that God, for
whom and through whom everything exists, should make the author of their salvation perfect
through suffering. [11]Both the one
who makes men holy and those
who are made holy are of the same
family. So Jesus is not ashamed to
call them brothers. [12]He says,

"I will declare your name to
    my brothers;
in the presence of the
    congregation I will sing
    your praises."[e]

[13]And again,

"I will put my trust in him."[f]

And again he says,

---

[a]12 Psalm 102:25-27   [b]13 Psalm 110:1   [c]7 Or *him for a little while*; also in verse 9
[d]8 Psalm 8:4-6   [e]12 Psalm 22:22   [f]13 Isaiah 8:17

"Here am I, and the children
    God has given me."[a]

[14]Since the children have flesh and blood, he too shared in their humanity so that by his death he might destroy him who holds the power of death—that is, the devil —[15]and free those who all their lives were held in slavery by their fear of death. [16]For surely it is not angels he helps, but Abraham's descendants. [17]For this reason he had to be made like his brothers in every way, in order that he might become a merciful and faithful high priest in service to God, and that he might make atonement for[b] the sins of the people. [18]Because he himself suffered when he was tempted, he is able to help those who are being tempted.

Jesus Greater Than Moses

3 Therefore, holy brothers, who share in the heavenly calling, fix your thoughts on Jesus, the apostle and high priest whom we confess. [2]He was faithful to the one who appointed him, just as Moses was faithful in all God's house. [3]Jesus has been found worthy of greater honor than Moses, just as the builder of a house has greater honor than the house itself. [4]For every house is built by someone, but God is the builder of everything. [5]Moses was faithful as a servant in all God's house, testi-

fying to what would be said in the future. [6]But Christ is faithful as a son over God's house. And we are his house, if we hold on to our courage and the hope of which we boast.   Heb 2:11,17

Warning Against Unbelief

[7]So, as the Holy Spirit says:

"Today, if you hear his voice,
[8]   do not harden your hearts
  as you did in the rebellion,
    during the time of testing in
      the desert,
[9]where your fathers tested and
      tried me
    and for forty years saw what
      I did.   Ac 7:36
[10]That is why I was angry with
      that generation,
    and I said, 'Their hearts are
      always going astray,
    and they have not known
      my ways.'
[11]So I declared on oath in my
      anger,   Dt 1:34-35
    'They shall never enter my
      rest.' "[c]   Ps 95:7-11; Heb 4:3,5

[12]See to it, brothers, that none of you has a sinful, unbelieving heart that turns away from the living God. [13]But encourage one another daily, as long as it is called Today, so that none of you may be hardened by sin's deceitfulness. [14]We have come to share in Christ if we hold firmly till the end the confi-

---

[a]13 Isaiah 8:18   [b]17 Or and that he might turn aside God's wrath, taking away   [c]11 Psalm 95:7-11

dence we had at first. [15]As has just been said: Eph 4:22; Heb 10:24-25

"Today, if you hear his voice,
    do not harden your hearts
    as you did in the rebellion."[a]

[16]Who were they who heard and rebelled? Were they not all those Moses led out of Egypt? [17]And with whom was he angry for forty years? Was it not with those who sinned, whose bodies fell in the desert? [18]And to whom did God swear that they would never enter his rest if not to those who disobeyed[b]? [19]So we see that they were not able to enter, because of their unbelief.   Jn 3:36; Nu 14:20-23

A Sabbath-Rest for the People of God

4 Therefore, since the promise of entering his rest still stands, let us be careful that none of you be found to have fallen short of it. [2]For we also have had the gospel preached to us, just as they did; but the message they heard was of no value to them, because those who heard did not combine it with faith.[c] [3]Now we who have believed enter that rest, just as God has said,   1Th 2:13; Heb 12:15

"So I declared on oath in my
    anger,
'They shall never enter my
    rest.' "[d]   Ps 95:11; Heb 3:11

And yet his work has been finished since the creation of the world. [4]For somewhere he has spoken about the seventh day in these words: "And on the seventh day God rested from all his work."[e] [5]And again in the passage above he says, "They shall never enter my rest."   Ex 20:11; Ps 95:11

[6]It still remains that some will enter that rest, and those who formerly had the gospel preached to them did not go in, because of their disobedience. [7]Therefore God again set a certain day, calling it Today, when a long time later he spoke through David, as was said before: Heb 3:18

"Today, if you hear his voice,
    do not harden your hearts."[a]

[8]For if Joshua had given them rest, God would not have spoken later about another day. [9]There remains, then, a Sabbath-rest for the people of God; [10]for anyone who enters God's rest also rests from his own work, just as God did from his. [11]Let us, therefore, make every effort to enter that rest, so that no one will fall by following their example of disobedience.   Heb 1:1; 3:18

[12]For the word of God is living and active. Sharper than any double-edged sword, it penetrates even to dividing soul and spirit, joints and marrow; it judges the thoughts and attitudes of the

---

[a]15,7 Psalm 95:7,8   [b]18 Or disbelieved   [c]2 Many manuscripts because they did not share in the faith of those who obeyed   [d]3 Psalm 95:11; also in verse 5   [e]4 Gen. 2:2

heart. ¹³Nothing in all creation is hidden from God's sight. Everything is uncovered and laid bare before the eyes of him to whom we must give account.   Ps 33:13-15

Jesus the Great High Priest

¹⁴Therefore, since we have a great high priest who has gone through the heavens,ᵃ Jesus the Son of God, let us hold firmly to the faith we profess. ¹⁵For we do not have a high priest who is unable to sympathize with our weaknesses, but we have one who has been tempted in every way, just as we are—yet was without sin. ¹⁶Let us then approach the throne of grace with confidence, so that we may receive mercy and find grace to help us in our time of need.

5 Every high priest is selected from among men and is appointed to represent them in matters related to God, to offer gifts and sacrifices for sins. ²He is able to deal gently with those who are ignorant and are going astray, since he himself is subject to weakness. ³This is why he has to offer sacrifices for his own sins, as well as for the sins of the people. ⁴No one takes this honor upon himself; he must be called by God, just as Aaron was. ⁵So Christ also did not take upon himself the glory of becoming a high priest. But God said to him,   Jn 8:54; Heb 1:1

"You are my Son;
    today I have become your
    Father.ᵇ"ᶜ

⁶And he says in another place,

"You are a priest forever,
    in the order of
    Melchizedek."ᵈ   Ps 110:4

⁷During the days of Jesus' life on earth, he offered up prayers and petitions with loud cries and tears to the one who could save him from death, and he was heard because of his reverent submission. ⁸Although he was a son, he learned obedience from what he suffered ⁹and, once made perfect, he became the source of eternal salvation for all who obey him ¹⁰and was designated by God to be high priest in the order of Melchizedek.   Mk 14:36; Heb 2:10

Warning Against Falling Away

¹¹We have much to say about this, but it is hard to explain because you are slow to learn. ¹²In fact, though by this time you ought to be teachers, you need someone to teach you the elementary truths of God's word all over again. You need milk, not solid food! ¹³Anyone who lives on milk, being still an infant, is not acquainted with the teaching about righteousness. ¹⁴But solid food is for the mature,

---

ᵃ 14 Or *gone into heaven*   ᵇ 5 Or *have begotten you*   ᶜ 5 Psalm 2:7   ᵈ 6 Psalm 110:4

who by constant use have trained themselves to distinguish good from evil.   1Co 2:6; 3:2

6 Therefore let us leave the elementary teachings about Christ and go on to maturity, not laying again the foundation of repentance from acts that lead to death,[a] and of faith in God, [2]instruction about baptisms, the laying on of hands, the resurrection of the dead, and eternal judgment. [3]And God permitting, we will do so.   Php 3:12-14; Heb 5:12

[4]It is impossible for those who have once been enlightened, who have tasted the heavenly gift, who have shared in the Holy Spirit, [5]who have tasted the goodness of the word of God and the powers of the coming age, [6]if they fall away, to be brought back to repentance, because[b] to their loss they are crucifying the Son of God all over again and subjecting him to public disgrace.   Heb 10:26-31

[7]Land that drinks in the rain often falling on it and that produces a crop useful to those for whom it is farmed receives the blessing of God. [8]But land that produces thorns and thistles is worthless and is in danger of being cursed. In the end it will be burned.

[9]Even though we speak like this, dear friends, we are confident of better things in your case—things that accompany salvation. [10]God is not unjust; he will not forget your work and the love you have shown him as you have helped his people and continue to help them. [11]We want each of you to show this same diligence to the very end, in order to make your hope sure. [12]We do not want you to become lazy, but to imitate those who through faith and patience inherit what has been promised.   1Th 1:3

The Certainty of God's Promise

[13]When God made his promise to Abraham, since there was no one greater for him to swear by, he swore by himself, [14]saying, "I will surely bless you and give you many descendants."[c] [15]And so after waiting patiently, Abraham received what was promised.

[16]Men swear by someone greater than themselves, and the oath confirms what is said and puts an end to all argument. [17]Because God wanted to make the unchanging nature of his purpose very clear to the heirs of what was promised, he confirmed it with an oath. [18]God did this so that, by two unchangeable things in which it is impossible for God to lie, we who have fled to take hold of the hope offered to us may be greatly encouraged. [19]We have this hope as an anchor for the soul, firm and secure. It enters the inner sanctuary behind the curtain, [20]where Jesus, who went before us, has entered on our behalf. He has be-

---

a 1 Or *from* useless rituals   *b* 6 Or *repentance while*   *c* 14 Gen. 22:17

come a high priest forever, in the order of Melchizedek. Heb 2:17; 4:14

Melchizedek the Priest

7 This Melchizedek was king of Salem and priest of God Most High. He met Abraham returning from the defeat of the kings and blessed him, ²and Abraham gave him a tenth of everything. First, his name means "king of righteousness"; then also, "king of Salem" means "king of peace." ³Without father or mother, without genealogy, without beginning of days or end of life, like the Son of God he remains a priest forever.

⁴Just think how great he was: Even the patriarch Abraham gave him a tenth of the plunder! ⁵Now the law requires the descendants of Levi who become priests to collect a tenth from the people—that is, their brothers—even though their brothers are descended from Abraham. ⁶This man, however, did not trace his descent from Levi, yet he collected a tenth from Abraham and blessed him who had the promises. ⁷And without doubt the lesser person is blessed by the greater. ⁸In the one case, the tenth is collected by men who die; but in the other case, by him who is declared to be living. ⁹One might even say that Levi, who collects the tenth, paid the tenth through Abraham, ¹⁰because when Melchizedek met Abraham, Levi was still in the body of his ancestor.

Jesus Like Melchizedek

¹¹If perfection could have been attained through the Levitical priesthood (for on the basis of it the law was given to the people), why was there still need for another priest to come—one in the order of Melchizedek, not in the order of Aaron? ¹²For when there is a change of the priesthood, there must also be a change of the law. ¹³He of whom these things are said belonged to a different tribe, and no one from that tribe has ever served at the altar. ¹⁴For it is clear that our Lord descended from Judah, and in regard to that tribe Moses said nothing about priests. ¹⁵And what we have said is even more clear if another priest like Melchizedek appears, ¹⁶one who has become a priest not on the basis of a regulation as to his ancestry but on the basis of the power of an indestructible life. ¹⁷For it is declared: Isa 11:1; Lk 3:33

"You are a priest forever,
     in the order of
          Melchizedek."ᵃ   Ps 110:4

¹⁸The former regulation is set aside because it was weak and useless ¹⁹(for the law made nothing perfect), and a better hope is introduced, by which we draw near to God.   Ro 3:20; Heb 4:16

ᵃ17 Psalm 110:4

²⁰And it was not without an oath! Others became priests without any oath, ²¹but he became a priest with an oath when God said to him:

"The Lord has sworn
and will not change his
mind: 1Sa 15:29; Ro 11:29
'You are a priest forever.'"ᵃ

²²Because of this oath, Jesus has become the guarantee of a better covenant.   Heb 5:6; 8:6

²³Now there have been many of those priests, since death prevented them from continuing in office; ²⁴but because Jesus lives forever, he has a permanent priesthood. ²⁵Therefore he is able to save completelyᵇ those who come to God through him, because he always lives to intercede for them.

²⁶Such a high priest meets our need—one who is holy, blameless, pure, set apart from sinners, exalted above the heavens. ²⁷Unlike the other high priests, he does not need to offer sacrifices day after day, first for his own sins, and then for the sins of the people. He sacrificed for their sins once for all when he offered himself. ²⁸For the law appoints as high priests men who are weak; but the oath, which came after the law, appointed the Son, who has been made perfect forever.   Heb 2:10; 5:2

The High Priest of a New Covenant

8 The point of what we are saying is this: We do have such a high priest, who sat down at the right hand of the throne of the Majesty in heaven, ²and who serves in the sanctuary, the true tabernacle set up by the Lord, not by man.

³Every high priest is appointed to offer both gifts and sacrifices, and so it was necessary for this one also to have something to offer. ⁴If he were on earth, he would not be a priest, for there are already men who offer the gifts prescribed by the law. ⁵They serve at a sanctuary that is a copy and shadow of what is in heaven. This is why Moses was warned when he was about to build the tabernacle: "See to it that you make everything according to the pattern shown you on the mountain."ᶜ ⁶But the ministry Jesus has received is as superior to theirs as the covenant of which he is mediator is superior to the old one, and it is founded on better promises.   Ex 25:40; Lk 22:20

⁷For if there had been nothing wrong with that first covenant, no place would have been sought for another. ⁸But God found fault with the people and saidᵈ: Heb 7:11,18

"The time is coming, declares
the Lord,
when I will make a new
covenant   Jer 31:31

ᵃ21 Psalm 110:4   ᵇ25 Or forever   ᶜ5 Exodus 25:40   ᵈ8 Some manuscripts may be translated fault and said to the people.

with the house of Israel
and with the house of Judah.
⁹It will not be like the covenant
I made with their forefathers
when I took them by the hand
to lead them out of Egypt,
because they did not remain
faithful to my covenant,
and I turned away from
them,
                    declares the Lord.
¹⁰This is the covenant I will
make with the house of
Israel   Ro 11:27
after that time, declares the
Lord.
I will put my laws in their
minds
and write them on their
hearts.   Heb 10:16
I will be their God,
and they will be my people.
¹¹No longer will a man teach his
neighbor,
or a man his brother, saying,
'Know the Lord,'
because they will all know me,
from the least of them to the
greatest.   Isa 54:13; Jn 6:45
¹²For I will forgive their
wickedness
and will remember their sins
no more."ᵃ   Jer 31:31-34

¹³By calling this covenant
"new," he has made the first one
obsolete; and what is obsolete and
aging will soon disappear. 2Co 5:17

Worship in the Earthly Tabernacle

9 Now the first covenant had regulations for worship and also an earthly sanctuary. ²A tabernacle was set up. In its first room were the lampstand, the table and the consecrated bread; this was called the Holy Place. ³Behind the second curtain was a room called the Most Holy Place, ⁴which had the golden altar of incense and the gold-covered ark of the covenant. This ark contained the gold jar of manna, Aaron's staff that had budded, and the stone tablets of the covenant. ⁵Above the ark were the cherubim of the Glory, overshadowing the atonement cover.ᵇ But we cannot discuss these things in detail now.   Ex 25:8,23-29

⁶When everything had been arranged like this, the priests entered regularly into the outer room to carry on their ministry. ⁷But only the high priest entered the inner room, and that only once a year, and never without blood, which he offered for himself and for the sins the people had committed in ignorance. ⁸The Holy Spirit was showing by this that the way into the Most Holy Place had not yet been disclosed as long as the first tabernacle was still standing. ⁹This is an illustration for the present time, indicating that the gifts and sacrifices being offered were not able to clear the con-

---

ᵃ 12 Jer. 31:31-34   ᵇ 5 Traditionally *the mercy seat*

science of the worshiper. ¹⁰They are only a matter of food and drink and various ceremonial washings—external regulations applying until the time of the new order.

The Blood of Christ

¹¹When Christ came as high priest of the good things that are already here,ᵃ he went through the greater and more perfect tabernacle that is not man-made, that is to say, not a part of this creation. ¹²He did not enter by means of the blood of goats and calves; but he entered the Most Holy Place once for all by his own blood, having obtained eternal redemption. ¹³The blood of goats and bulls and the ashes of a heifer sprinkled on those who are ceremonially unclean sanctify them so that they are outwardly clean. ¹⁴How much more, then, will the blood of Christ, who through the eternal Spirit offered himself unblemished to God, cleanse our consciences from acts that lead to death,ᵇ so that we may serve the living God!

¹⁵For this reason Christ is the mediator of a new covenant, that those who are called may receive the promised eternal inheritance—now that he has died as a ransom to set them free from the sins committed under the first covenant.

1Ti 2:5; Heb 7:22

¹⁶In the case of a will,ᶜ it is necessary to prove the death of the one who made it, ¹⁷because a will is in force only when somebody has died; it never takes effect while the one who made it is living. ¹⁸This is why even the first covenant was not put into effect without blood. ¹⁹When Moses had proclaimed every commandment of the law to all the people, he took the blood of calves, together with water, scarlet wool and branches of hyssop, and sprinkled the scroll and all the people. ²⁰He said, "This is the blood of the covenant, which God has commanded you to keep."ᵈ ²¹In the same way, he sprinkled with the blood both the tabernacle and everything used in its ceremonies. ²²In fact, the law requires that nearly everything be cleansed with blood, and without the shedding of blood there is no forgiveness.

Ex 24:8; Mt 26:28

²³It was necessary, then, for the copies of the heavenly things to be purified with these sacrifices, but the heavenly things themselves with better sacrifices than these. ²⁴For Christ did not enter a man-made sanctuary that was only a copy of the true one; he entered heaven itself, now to appear for us in God's presence. ²⁵Nor did he enter heaven to offer himself again

---

ᵃ11 Some early manuscripts *are to come*   ᵇ14 Or *from useless rituals*   ᶜ16 Same Greek word as *covenant*; also in verse 17   ᵈ20 Exodus 24:8

and again, the way the high priest enters the Most Holy Place every year with blood that is not his own. ²⁶Then Christ would have had to suffer many times since the creation of the world. But now he has appeared once for all at the end of the ages to do away with sin by the sacrifice of himself. ²⁷Just as man is destined to die once, and after that to face judgment, ²⁸so Christ was sacrificed once to take away the sins of many people; and he will appear a second time, not to bear sin, but to bring salvation to those who are waiting for him.

Christ's Sacrifice Once for All

10 The law is only a shadow of the good things that are coming—not the realities themselves. For this reason it can never, by the same sacrifices repeated endlessly year after year, make perfect those who draw near to worship. ²If it could, would they not have stopped being offered? For the worshipers would have been cleansed once for all, and would no longer have felt guilty for their sins. ³But those sacrifices are an annual reminder of sins, ⁴because it is impossible for the blood of bulls and goats to take away sins.   Heb 9:7,11,23

⁵Therefore, when Christ came into the world, he said: Heb 1:6

"Sacrifice and offering you did
    not desire,
but a body you prepared for
    me;   1Pe 2:24
⁶with burnt offerings and sin
    offerings
you were not pleased.
⁷Then I said, 'Here I am—it is
    written about me in the
    scroll—   Jer 36:2
I have come to do your will,
    O God.' "ᵃ

⁸First he said, "Sacrifices and offerings, burnt offerings and sin offerings you did not desire, nor were you pleased with them" (although the law required them to be made). ⁹Then he said, "Here I am, I have come to do your will." He sets aside the first to establish the second. ¹⁰And by that will, we have been made holy through the sacrifice of the body of Jesus Christ once for all.   Jn 17:19; Heb 7:27

¹¹Day after day every priest stands and performs his religious duties; again and again he offers the same sacrifices, which can never take away sins. ¹²But when this priest had offered for all time one sacrifice for sins, he sat down at the right hand of God. ¹³Since that time he waits for his enemies to be made his footstool, ¹⁴because by one sacrifice he has made perfect forever those who are being made holy.   Eph 5:26; Heb 1:13

ᵃ7 Psalm 40:6-8 (see Septuagint)

¹⁵The Holy Spirit also testifies to us about this. First he says:

¹⁶"This is the covenant I will
        make with them
    after that time, says the
        Lord.
I will put my laws in their
        hearts,
    and I will write them on
        their minds."ᵃ

¹⁷Then he adds:

"Their sins and lawless acts
    I will remember no more."ᵇ

¹⁸And where these have been forgiven, there is no longer any sacrifice for sin.

A Call to Persevere

¹⁹Therefore, brothers, since we have confidence to enter the Most Holy Place by the blood of Jesus, ²⁰by a new and living way opened for us through the curtain, that is, his body, ²¹and since we have a great priest over the house of God, ²²let us draw near to God with a sincere heart in full assurance of faith, having our hearts sprinkled to cleanse us from a guilty conscience and having our bodies washed with pure water. ²³Let us hold unswervingly to the hope we profess, for he who promised is faithful. ²⁴And let us consider how we may spur one another on toward love and good deeds. ²⁵Let us not give up meeting together, as some are in the habit of doing, but let us encourage one another—and all the more as you see the Day approaching. *Ac 2:42; 1Co 1:9*

²⁶If we deliberately keep on sinning after we have received the knowledge of the truth, no sacrifice for sins is left, ²⁷but only a fearful expectation of judgment and of raging fire that will consume the enemies of God. ²⁸Anyone who rejected the law of Moses died without mercy on the testimony of two or three witnesses. ²⁹How much more severely do you think a man deserves to be punished who has trampled the Son of God under foot, who has treated as an unholy thing the blood of the covenant that sanctified him, and who has insulted the Spirit of grace? ³⁰For we know him who said, "It is mine to avenge; I will repay,"ᶜ and again, "The Lord will judge his people."ᵈ ³¹It is a dreadful thing to fall into the hands of the living God. *Eph 4:30; Heb 6:6*

³²Remember those earlier days after you had received the light, when you stood your ground in a great contest in the face of suffering. ³³Sometimes you were publicly exposed to insult and persecution; at other times you stood side by side with those who were so treated. ³⁴You sympathized with those in prison and joyfully accepted the confiscation of your property, because you knew that

---

ᵃ 16 Jer. 31:33   ᵇ 17 Jer. 31:34   ᶜ 30 Deut. 32:35   ᵈ 30 Deut. 32:36; Psalm 135:14

you yourselves had better and lasting possessions.   1Co 4:9; Php 1:29-30

³⁵So do not throw away your confidence; it will be richly rewarded. ³⁶You need to persevere so that when you have done the will of God, you will receive what he has promised. ³⁷For in just a very little while,   Lk 21:19; Heb 12:1

"He who is coming will come
        and will not delay.
³⁸   But my righteous one*a* will
        live by faith.   Ro 1:17
And if he shrinks back,
    I will not be pleased with
        him."*b*

³⁹But we are not of those who shrink back and are destroyed, but of those who believe and are saved.   Hab 2:3-4

By Faith

11 Now faith is being sure of what we hope for and certain of what we do not see. ²This is what the ancients were commended for.   Ro 8:24; 2Co 4:18

³By faith we understand that the universe was formed at God's command, so that what is seen was not made out of what was visible.   Ge 1; 2Pe 3:5

⁴By faith Abel offered God a better sacrifice than Cain did. By faith he was commended as a righteous man, when God spoke well of his offerings. And by faith he still speaks, even though he is dead.

⁵By faith Enoch was taken from this life, so that he did not experience death; he could not be found, because God had taken him away. For before he was taken, he was commended as one who pleased God. ⁶And without faith it is impossible to please God, because anyone who comes to him must believe that he exists and that he rewards those who earnestly seek him.   Ge 5:21-24; Heb 7:19

⁷By faith Noah, when warned about things not yet seen, in holy fear built an ark to save his family. By his faith he condemned the world and became heir of the righteousness that comes by faith.

⁸By faith Abraham, when called to go to a place he would later receive as his inheritance, obeyed and went, even though he did not know where he was going. ⁹By faith he made his home in the promised land like a stranger in a foreign country; he lived in tents, as did Isaac and Jacob, who were heirs with him of the same promise. ¹⁰For he was looking forward to the city with foundations, whose architect and builder is God.   Heb 6:17; 12:22

¹¹By faith Abraham, even though he was past age—and Sarah herself was barren—was enabled to become a father because

---

a 38 One early manuscript *But the righteous*   *b 38* Hab. 2:3,4

he*a* considered him faithful who had made the promise. ¹²And so from this one man, and he as good as dead, came descendants as numerous as the stars in the sky and as countless as the sand on the seashore.   Ge 22:17; Ro 4:19

¹³All these people were still living by faith when they died. They did not receive the things promised; they only saw them and welcomed them from a distance. And they admitted that they were aliens and strangers on earth. ¹⁴People who say such things show that they are looking for a country of their own. ¹⁵If they had been thinking of the country they had left, they would have had opportunity to return. ¹⁶Instead, they were longing for a better country—a heavenly one. Therefore God is not ashamed to be called their God, for he has prepared a city for them.   Ex 3:6,15; Heb 13:14

¹⁷By faith Abraham, when God tested him, offered Isaac as a sacrifice. He who had received the promises was about to sacrifice his one and only son, ¹⁸even though God had said to him, "It is through Isaac that your offspring*b* will be reckoned."*c* ¹⁹Abraham reasoned that God could raise the dead, and figuratively speaking, he did receive Isaac back from death.

²⁰By faith Isaac blessed Jacob and Esau in regard to their future.

²¹By faith Jacob, when he was dying, blessed each of Joseph's sons, and worshiped as he leaned on the top of his staff.   Ge 48:1,8-22

²²By faith Joseph, when his end was near, spoke about the exodus of the Israelites from Egypt and gave instructions about his bones.

²³By faith Moses' parents hid him for three months after he was born, because they saw he was no ordinary child, and they were not afraid of the king's edict.   Ex 1:16,22

²⁴By faith Moses, when he had grown up, refused to be known as the son of Pharaoh's daughter. ²⁵He chose to be mistreated along with the people of God rather than to enjoy the pleasures of sin for a short time. ²⁶He regarded disgrace for the sake of Christ as of greater value than the treasures of Egypt, because he was looking ahead to his reward. ²⁷By faith he left Egypt, not fearing the king's anger; he persevered because he saw him who is invisible. ²⁸By faith he kept the Passover and the sprinkling of blood, so that the destroyer of the firstborn would not touch the firstborn of Israel.   Ex 12:21-23; Heb 13:13

²⁹By faith the people passed through the Red Sea*d* as on dry land; but when the Egyptians tried to do so, they were drowned.

³⁰By faith the walls of Jericho fell, after the people had marched around them for seven days.

---

a 11 Or *By faith even Sarah, who was past age, was enabled to bear children because she*   *b 18* Greek *seed*   *c 18* Gen. 21:12   *d 29* That is, Sea of Reeds

³¹By faith the prostitute Rahab, because she welcomed the spies, was not killed with those who were disobedient.ᵃ   Jos 6:22-25

³²And what more shall I say? I do not have time to tell about Gideon, Barak, Samson, Jephthah, David, Samuel and the prophets, ³³who through faith conquered kingdoms, administered justice, and gained what was promised; who shut the mouths of lions, ³⁴quenched the fury of the flames, and escaped the edge of the sword; whose weakness was turned to strength; and who became powerful in battle and routed foreign armies. ³⁵Women received back their dead, raised to life again. Others were tortured and refused to be released, so that they might gain a better resurrection. ³⁶Some faced jeers and flogging, while still others were chained and put in prison. ³⁷They were stonedᵇ; they were sawed in two; they were put to death by the sword. They went about in sheepskins and goatskins, destitute, persecuted and mistreated— ³⁸the world was not worthy of them. They wandered in deserts and mountains, and in caves and holes in the ground.   1Ki 18:4; 2Ki 1:8

³⁹These were all commended for their faith, yet none of them received what had been promised. ⁴⁰God had planned something better for us so that only together with us would they be made perfect.

God Disciplines His Sons

12 Therefore, since we are surrounded by such a great cloud of witnesses, let us throw off everything that hinders and the sin that so easily entangles, and let us run with perseverance the race marked out for us. ²Let us fix our eyes on Jesus, the author and perfecter of our faith, who for the joy set before him endured the cross, scorning its shame, and sat down at the right hand of the throne of God. ³Consider him who endured such opposition from sinful men, so that you will not grow weary and lose heart.   Gal 6:9; Php 2:8-9

⁴In your struggle against sin, you have not yet resisted to the point of shedding your blood. ⁵And you have forgotten that word of encouragement that addresses you as sons: Heb 10:32-34

"My son, do not make light of
    the Lord's discipline,
and do not lose heart when
    he rebukes you,
⁶because the Lord disciplines
    those he loves,   Ps 94:12
and he punishes everyone he
    accepts as a son."ᶜ

⁷Endure hardship as discipline; God is treating you as sons. For what son is not disciplined by his father? ⁸If you are not disciplined (and everyone undergoes discipline), then you are illegitimate children and not true sons. ⁹More-

---

ᵃ31 Or *unbelieving*   ᵇ37 Some early manuscripts *stoned; they were put to the test;*   ᶜ6 Prov. 3:11,12 over, we have all had human fathers who disciplined us and we respected them for it. How much more should we submit to the Father of our spirits and live! [10]Our fathers disciplined us for a little while as they thought best; but God disciplines us for our good, that we may share in his holiness. [11]No discipline seems pleasant at the time, but painful. Later on, however, it produces a harvest of righteousness and peace for those who have been trained by it.

[12]Therefore, strengthen your feeble arms and weak knees. [13]"Make level paths for your feet,"[a] so that the lame may not be disabled, but rather healed.

Warning Against Refusing God

[14]Make every effort to live in peace with all men and to be holy; without holiness no one will see the Lord. [15]See to it that no one misses the grace of God and that no bitter root grows up to cause trouble and defile many. [16]See that no one is sexually immoral, or is godless like Esau, who for a single meal sold his inheritance rights as the oldest son. [17]Afterward, as you know, when he wanted to inherit this blessing, he was rejected. He could bring about no change of mind, though he sought the blessing with tears.   Ge 25:29-34; 27:30-40

[18]You have not come to a mountain that can be touched and that is burning with fire; to darkness, gloom and storm; [19]to a trumpet blast or to such a voice speaking words that those who heard it begged that no further word be spoken to them, [20]because they could not bear what was commanded: "If even an animal touches the mountain, it must be stoned."[b] [21]The sight was so terrifying that Moses said, "I am trembling with fear."[c]   Ex 20:19; Dt 5:5,25

[22]But you have come to Mount Zion, to the heavenly Jerusalem, the city of the living God. You have come to thousands upon thousands of angels in joyful assembly, [23]to the church of the firstborn, whose names are written in heaven. You have come to God, the judge of all men, to the spirits of righteous men made perfect, [24]to Jesus the mediator of a new covenant, and to the sprinkled blood that speaks a better word than the blood of Abel.   Php 3:12; Heb 11:4

[25]See to it that you do not refuse him who speaks. If they did not escape when they refused him who warned them on earth, how much less will we, if we turn away from him who warns us from heaven? [26]At that time his voice shook the earth, but now he has promised, "Once more I will shake not only the earth but also the heavens."[d] [27]The words "once more" indicate the removing of what can be shaken—that is, cre-

---

[a]13 Prov. 4:26   [b]20 Exodus 19:12,13   [c]21 Deut. 9:19   [d]26 Haggai 2:6

ated things—so that what cannot be shaken may remain.   1Co 7:31

²⁸Therefore, since we are receiving a kingdom that cannot be shaken, let us be thankful, and so worship God acceptably with reverence and awe, ²⁹for our "God is a consuming fire."*a*   Dt 4:24; Heb 13:15

Concluding Exhortations

13 Keep on loving each other as brothers. ²Do not forget to entertain strangers, for by so doing some people have entertained angels without knowing it. ³Remember those in prison as if you were their fellow prisoners, and those who are mistreated as if you yourselves were suffering.

⁴Marriage should be honored by all, and the marriage bed kept pure, for God will judge the adulterer and all the sexually immoral. ⁵Keep your lives free from the love of money and be content with what you have, because God has said,   1Co 6:9; Php 4:11

"Never will I leave you;
   never will I forsake you."*b*

⁶So we say with confidence,

"The Lord is my helper; I will
      not be afraid.
   What can man do to me?"*c*

⁷Remember your leaders, who spoke the word of God to you. Consider the outcome of their way of life and imitate their faith. ⁸Jesus Christ is the same yesterday and today and forever.   Heb 1:12

⁹Do not be carried away by all kinds of strange teachings. It is good for our hearts to be strengthened by grace, not by ceremonial foods, which are of no value to those who eat them. ¹⁰We have an altar from which those who minister at the tabernacle have no right to eat.   1Co 9:13; Eph 4:14

¹¹The high priest carries the blood of animals into the Most Holy Place as a sin offering, but the bodies are burned outside the camp. ¹²And so Jesus also suffered outside the city gate to make the people holy through his own blood. ¹³Let us, then, go to him outside the camp, bearing the disgrace he bore. ¹⁴For here we do not have an enduring city, but we are looking for the city that is to come.

¹⁵Through Jesus, therefore, let us continually offer to God a sacrifice of praise—the fruit of lips that confess his name. ¹⁶And do not forget to do good and to share with others, for with such sacrifices God is pleased.   Php 4:18; Hos 14:2

¹⁷Obey your leaders and submit to their authority. They keep watch over you as men who must give an account. Obey them so that their work will be a joy, not a burden, for that would be of no advantage to you.   Isa 62:6; Ac 20:28

a 29 Deut. 4:24   *b 5* Deut. 31:6   *c 6* Psalm 118:6,7

[18]Pray for us. We are sure that we have a clear conscience and desire to live honorably in every way. [19]I particularly urge you to pray so that I may be restored to you soon.

[20]May the God of peace, who through the blood of the eternal covenant brought back from the dead our Lord Jesus, that great Shepherd of the sheep, [21]equip you with everything good for doing his will, and may he work in us what is pleasing to him, through Jesus Christ, to whom be glory for ever and ever. Amen.   Php 2:13

[22]Brothers, I urge you to bear with my word of exhortation, for I have written you only a short letter.   1Pe 5:12

[23]I want you to know that our brother Timothy has been released. If he arrives soon, I will come with him to see you.   Ac 16:1

[24]Greet all your leaders and all God's people. Those from Italy send you their greetings.   Ac 18:2

[25]Grace be with you all.   Col 4:18

James

1 James, a servant of God and of the Lord Jesus Christ,

To the twelve tribes scattered among the nations:

Greetings. Ac 15:23

Trials and Temptations

²Consider it pure joy, my brothers, whenever you face trials of many kinds, ³because you know that the testing of your faith develops perseverance. ⁴Perseverance must finish its work so that you may be mature and complete, not lacking anything. ⁵If any of you lacks wisdom, he should ask God, who gives generously to all without finding fault, and it will be given to him. ⁶But when he asks, he must believe and not doubt, because he who doubts is like a wave of the sea, blown and tossed by the wind. ⁷That man should not think he will receive anything from the Lord; ⁸he is a double-minded man, unstable in all he does. 1Ki 3:9-10

⁹The brother in humble circumstances ought to take pride in his high position. ¹⁰But the one who is rich should take pride in his low position, because he will pass away like a wild flower. ¹¹For the sun rises with scorching heat and withers the plant; its blossom falls and its beauty is destroyed. In the same way, the rich man will fade away even while he goes about his business. Ps 102:4,11; Isa 40:6-8

¹²Blessed is the man who perseveres under trial, because when he has stood the test, he will receive the crown of life that God has promised to those who love him. ¹³When tempted, no one should say, "God is tempting me." For God cannot be tempted by evil, nor does he tempt anyone; ¹⁴but each one is tempted when, by his own evil desire, he is dragged away and enticed. ¹⁵Then, after desire has conceived, it gives birth to sin; and sin, when it is full-grown, gives birth to death. Job 15:35; Ps 7:14

¹⁶Don't be deceived, my dear brothers. ¹⁷Every good and perfect gift is from above, coming down from the Father of the heavenly lights, who does not change like shifting shadows. ¹⁸He chose to give us birth through the word of truth, that we might be a kind of firstfruits of all he created. Jn 1:13

Listening and Doing

¹⁹My dear brothers, take note of this: Everyone should be quick to listen, slow to speak and slow to become angry, ²⁰for man's anger does not bring about the righteous life that God desires. ²¹Therefore, get rid of all moral filth and the evil

that is so prevalent and humbly accept the word planted in you, which can save you.   Eph 1:13; 4:22

²²Do not merely listen to the word, and so deceive yourselves. Do what it says. ²³Anyone who listens to the word but does not do what it says is like a man who looks at his face in a mirror ²⁴and, after looking at himself, goes away and immediately forgets what he looks like. ²⁵But the man who looks intently into the perfect law that gives freedom, and continues to do this, not forgetting what he has heard, but doing it—he will be blessed in what he does.   Jn 13:17

²⁶If anyone considers himself religious and yet does not keep a tight rein on his tongue, he deceives himself and his religion is worthless. ²⁷Religion that God our Father accepts as pure and faultless is this: to look after orphans and widows in their distress and to keep oneself from being polluted by the world.   Isa 1:17,23; 1Pe 3:10

Favoritism Forbidden

2 My brothers, as believers in our glorious Lord Jesus Christ, don't show favoritism. ²Suppose a man comes into your meeting wearing a gold ring and fine clothes, and a poor man in shabby clothes also comes in. ³If you show special attention to the man wearing fine clothes and say, "Here's a good seat for you," but say to the poor man, "You stand there" or "Sit on the floor by my feet," ⁴have you not discriminated among yourselves and become judges with evil thoughts?   Jn 7:24; 1Co 2:8

⁵Listen, my dear brothers: Has not God chosen those who are poor in the eyes of the world to be rich in faith and to inherit the kingdom he promised those who love him? ⁶But you have insulted the poor. Is it not the rich who are exploiting you? Are they not the ones who are dragging you into court? ⁷Are they not the ones who are slandering the noble name of him to whom you belong?   Lk 12:21

⁸If you really keep the royal law found in Scripture, "Love your neighbor as yourself,"ᵃ you are doing right. ⁹But if you show favoritism, you sin and are convicted by the law as lawbreakers. ¹⁰For whoever keeps the whole law and yet stumbles at just one point is guilty of breaking all of it. ¹¹For he who said, "Do not commit adultery,"ᵇ also said, "Do not murder."ᶜ If you do not commit adultery but do commit murder, you have become a lawbreaker.   Mt 5:19; Gal 3:10

¹²Speak and act as those who are going to be judged by the law that gives freedom, ¹³because judgment without mercy will be shown to anyone who has not been merciful. Mercy triumphs over judgment!   Mt 5:7; Jas 1:25

ᵃ8 Lev. 19:18   ᵇ11 Exodus 20:14; Deut. 5:18   ᶜ11 Exodus 20:13; Deut. 5:17

Faith and Deeds

14What good is it, my brothers, if a man claims to have faith but has no deeds? Can such faith save him? **15**Suppose a brother or sister is without clothes and daily food. **16**If one of you says to him, "Go, I wish you well; keep warm and well fed," but does nothing about his physical needs, what good is it? **17**In the same way, faith by itself, if it is not accompanied by action, is dead.　　　　　Mt 7:26; 1Jn 3:17-18

18But someone will say, "You have faith; I have deeds."

Show me your faith without deeds, and I will show you my faith by what I do. **19**You believe that there is one God. Good! Even the demons believe that—and shudder.　　　　　Mt 8:29; Jas 3:13

20You foolish man, do you want evidence that faith without deeds is useless*a*? **21**Was not our ancestor Abraham considered righteous for what he did when he offered his son Isaac on the altar? **22**You see that his faith and his actions were working together, and his faith was made complete by what he did. **23**And the scripture was fulfilled that says, "Abraham believed God, and it was credited to him as righteousness,"*b* and he was called God's friend. **24**You see that a person is justified by what he does and not by faith alone.

25In the same way, was not even Rahab the prostitute considered righteous for what she did when she gave lodging to the spies and sent them off in a different direction? **26**As the body without the spirit is dead, so faith without deeds is dead.　　　　Heb 11:31

Taming the Tongue

3 Not many of you should presume to be teachers, my brothers, because you know that we who teach will be judged more strictly. **2**We all stumble in many ways. If anyone is never at fault in what he says, he is a perfect man, able to keep his whole body in check.　　　　Mt 12:37; Jas 1:26

3When we put bits into the mouths of horses to make them obey us, we can turn the whole animal. **4**Or take ships as an example. Although they are so large and are driven by strong winds, they are steered by a very small rudder wherever the pilot wants to go. **5**Likewise the tongue is a small part of the body, but it makes great boasts. Consider what a great forest is set on fire by a small spark. **6**The tongue also is a fire, a world of evil among the parts of the body. It corrupts the whole person, sets the whole course of his life on fire, and is itself set on fire by hell.　　　　Pr 16:27; Mt 15:11,18-19

7All kinds of animals, birds, reptiles and creatures of the sea are being tamed and have been tamed

a 20 Some early manuscripts *dead*　　*b 23* Gen. 15:6

by man, **8**but no man can tame the tongue. It is a restless evil, full of deadly poison.   Ps 140:3; Ro 3:13

9With the tongue we praise our Lord and Father, and with it we curse men, who have been made in God's likeness. **10**Out of the same mouth come praise and cursing. My brothers, this should not be. **11**Can both fresh water and salt*a* water flow from the same spring? **12**My brothers, can a fig tree bear olives, or a grapevine bear figs? Neither can a salt spring produce fresh water.   Ge 1:26-27

Two Kinds of Wisdom

13Who is wise and understanding among you? Let him show it by his good life, by deeds done in the humility that comes from wisdom. **14**But if you harbor bitter envy and selfish ambition in your hearts, do not boast about it or deny the truth. **15**Such "wisdom" does not come down from heaven but is earthly, unspiritual, of the devil. **16**For where you have envy and selfish ambition, there you find disorder and every evil practice.

17But the wisdom that comes from heaven is first of all pure; then peace-loving, considerate, submissive, full of mercy and good fruit, impartial and sincere. **18**Peacemakers who sow in peace raise a harvest of righteousness.

Submit Yourselves to God

4 What causes fights and quarrels among you? Don't they come from your desires that battle within you? **2**You want something but don't get it. You kill and covet, but you cannot have what you want. You quarrel and fight. You do not have, because you do not ask God. **3**When you ask, you do not receive, because you ask with wrong motives, that you may spend what you get on your pleasures.   Ro 7:23; 1Jn 3:22

4You adulterous people, don't you know that friendship with the world is hatred toward God? Anyone who chooses to be a friend of the world becomes an enemy of God. **5**Or do you think Scripture says without reason that the spirit he caused to live in us envies intensely?*b* **6**But he gives us more grace. That is why Scripture says:

"God opposes the proud
   but gives grace to the
      humble."*c*   Pr 3:34; Mt 23:12

7Submit yourselves, then, to God. Resist the devil, and he will flee from you. **8**Come near to God and he will come near to you. Wash your hands, you sinners, and purify your hearts, you double-minded. **9**Grieve, mourn and wail. Change your laughter to mourning and your joy to gloom.

a 11 Greek bitter (see also verse 14)   *b* 5 Or that God jealously longs for the spirit that he made to live in us; or that the Spirit he caused to live in us longs jealously   *c* 6 Prov. 3:34

¹⁰Humble yourselves before the Lord, and he will lift you up. ¹¹Brothers, do not slander one another. Anyone who speaks against his brother or judges him speaks against the law and judges it. When you judge the law, you are not keeping it, but sitting in judgment on it. ¹²There is only one Lawgiver and Judge, the one who is able to save and destroy. But you—who are you to judge your neighbor?   Mt 10:28; Ro 14:4

Boasting About Tomorrow

¹³Now listen, you who say, "Today or tomorrow we will go to this or that city, spend a year there, carry on business and make money." ¹⁴Why, you do not even know what will happen tomorrow. What is your life? You are a mist that appears for a little while and then vanishes. ¹⁵Instead, you ought to say, "If it is the Lord's will, we will live and do this or that." ¹⁶As it is, you boast and brag. All such boasting is evil. ¹⁷Anyone, then, who knows the good he ought to do and doesn't do it, sins.   Lk 12:47; 1Co 5:6

Warning to Rich Oppressors

5 Now listen, you rich people, weep and wail because of the misery that is coming upon you. ²Your wealth has rotted, and moths have eaten your clothes. ³Your gold and silver are corroded. Their corrosion will testify against you and eat your flesh like fire. You have hoarded wealth in the last days. ⁴Look! The wages you failed to pay the workmen who mowed your fields are crying out against you. The cries of the harvesters have reached the ears of the Lord Almighty. ⁵You have lived on earth in luxury and self-indulgence. You have fattened yourselves in the day of slaughter.ᵃ ⁶You have condemned and murdered innocent men, who were not opposing you.   Heb 10:38

Patience in Suffering

⁷Be patient, then, brothers, until the Lord's coming. See how the farmer waits for the land to yield its valuable crop and how patient he is for the autumn and spring rains. ⁸You too, be patient and stand firm, because the Lord's coming is near. ⁹Don't grumble against each other, brothers, or you will be judged. The Judge is standing at the door!   Mt 24:33

¹⁰Brothers, as an example of patience in the face of suffering, take the prophets who spoke in the name of the Lord. ¹¹As you know, we consider blessed those who have persevered. You have heard of Job's perseverance and have seen what the Lord finally brought about. The Lord is full of compassion and mercy.   Job 42:10,12-17

¹²Above all, my brothers, do not swear—not by heaven or by earth

ᵃ5 Or yourselves as in a day of feasting

or by anything else. Let your "Yes" be yes, and your "No," no, or you will be condemned.   Mt 5:34-37

The Prayer of Faith

[13]Is any one of you in trouble? He should pray. Is anyone happy? Let him sing songs of praise. [14]Is any one of you sick? He should call the elders of the church to pray over him and anoint him with oil in the name of the Lord. [15]And the prayer offered in faith will make the sick person well; the Lord will raise him up. If he has sinned, he will be forgiven. [16]Therefore confess your sins to each other and pray for each other so that you

may be healed. The prayer of a righteous man is powerful and effective.   Jn 9:31; 1Pe 2:24

[17]Elijah was a man just like us. He prayed earnestly that it would not rain, and it did not rain on the land for three and a half years. [18]Again he prayed, and the heavens gave rain, and the earth produced its crops.   1Ki 18:41-45; Ac 14:15

[19]My brothers, if one of you should wander from the truth and someone should bring him back, [20]remember this: Whoever turns a sinner from the error of his way will save him from death and cover over a multitude of sins.   Mt 18:15

1 Peter

1 Peter, an apostle of Jesus Christ,   2Pe 1:1

To God's elect, strangers in the world, scattered throughout Pontus, Galatia, Cappadocia, Asia and Bithynia, ²who have been chosen according to the foreknowledge of God the Father, through the sanctifying work of the Spirit, for obedience to Jesus Christ and sprinkling by his blood: 2Th 2:13; Heb 10:22

Grace and peace be yours in abundance.   Ro 1:7

Praise to God for a Living Hope

³Praise be to the God and Father of our Lord Jesus Christ! In his great mercy he has given us new birth into a living hope through the resurrection of Jesus Christ from the dead, ⁴and into an inheritance that can never perish, spoil or fade —kept in heaven for you, ⁵who through faith are shielded by God's power until the coming of the salvation that is ready to be revealed in the last time. ⁶In this you greatly rejoice, though now for a little while you may have had to suffer grief in all kinds of trials. ⁷These have come so that your faith—of greater worth than gold, which perishes even though refined by fire—may be proved genuine and may result in praise, glory and honor when Jesus Christ is revealed. ⁸Though you have not seen him, you love him; and even though you do not see him now, you believe in him and are filled with an inexpressible and glorious joy, ⁹for you are receiving the goal of your faith, the salvation of your souls.   Jn 20:29; Ro 6:22

¹⁰Concerning this salvation, the prophets, who spoke of the grace that was to come to you, searched intently and with the greatest care, ¹¹trying to find out the time and circumstances to which the Spirit of Christ in them was pointing when he predicted the sufferings of Christ and the glories that would follow. ¹²It was revealed to them that they were not serving themselves but you, when they spoke of the things that have now been told you by those who have preached the gospel to you by the Holy Spirit sent from heaven. Even angels long to look into these things.   Lk 24:49; 2Pe 1:21

Be Holy

¹³Therefore, prepare your minds for action; be self-controlled; set your hope fully on the grace to be given you when Jesus Christ is revealed. ¹⁴As obedient children, do

not conform to the evil desires you had when you lived in ignorance. ¹⁵But just as he who called you is holy, so be holy in all you do; ¹⁶for it is written: "Be holy, because I am holy."ᵃ   Ro 12:2; Eph 4:18

¹⁷Since you call on a Father who judges each man's work impartially, live your lives as strangers here in reverent fear. ¹⁸For you know that it was not with perishable things such as silver or gold that you were redeemed from the empty way of life handed down to you from your forefathers, ¹⁹but with the precious blood of Christ, a lamb without blemish or defect. ²⁰He was chosen before the creation of the world, but was revealed in these last times for your sake. ²¹Through him you believe in God, who raised him from the dead and glorified him, and so your faith and hope are in God.

²²Now that you have purified yourselves by obeying the truth so that you have sincere love for your brothers, love one another deeply, from the heart.ᵇ ²³For you have been born again, not of perishable seed, but of imperishable, through the living and enduring word of God. ²⁴For,   Jn 1:13; Heb 13:1

"All men are like grass,
    and all their glory is like the
        flowers of the field;
the grass withers and the
    flowers fall,

²⁵ but the word of the Lord
    stands forever."ᶜ

And this is the word that was preached to you.

2 Therefore, rid yourselves of all malice and all deceit, hypocrisy, envy, and slander of every kind. ²Like newborn babies, crave pure spiritual milk, so that by it you may grow up in your salvation, ³now that you have tasted that the Lord is good.   1Co 3:2

The Living Stone and a Chosen People

⁴As you come to him, the living Stone—rejected by men but chosen by God and precious to him— ⁵you also, like living stones, are being built into a spiritual house to be a holy priesthood, offering spiritual sacrifices acceptable to God through Jesus Christ. ⁶For in Scripture it says: Php 4:18; Heb 13:15

"See, I lay a stone in Zion,
    a chosen and precious
        cornerstone,   Eph 2:20
and the one who trusts in him
    will never be put to shame."ᵈ

⁷Now to you who believe, this stone is precious. But to those who do not believe,   2Co 2:16

"The stone the builders
    rejected
        has become the capstone,ᵉ"ᶠ

⁸and,

ᵃ16 Lev. 11:44,45; 19:2; 20:7   ᵇ22 Some early manuscripts *from a pure heart*   ᶜ25 Isaiah 40:6-8
ᵈ6 Isaiah 28:16   ᵉ7 Or *cornerstone*   ᶠ7 Psalm 118:22

"A stone that causes men to
    stumble
and a rock that makes them
    fall."[a]

They stumble because they disobey the message—which is also what they were destined for.

⁹But you are a chosen people, a royal priesthood, a holy nation, a people belonging to God, that you may declare the praises of him who called you out of darkness into his wonderful light. ¹⁰Once you were not a people, but now you are the people of God; once you had not received mercy, but now you have received mercy.

¹¹Dear friends, I urge you, as aliens and strangers in the world, to abstain from sinful desires, which war against your soul. ¹²Live such good lives among the pagans that, though they accuse you of doing wrong, they may see your good deeds and glorify God on the day he visits us.   Mt 5:16

Submission to Rulers and Masters

¹³Submit yourselves for the Lord's sake to every authority instituted among men: whether to the king, as the supreme authority, ¹⁴or to governors, who are sent by him to punish those who do wrong and to commend those who do right. ¹⁵For it is God's will that by doing good you should silence the ignorant talk of foolish men. ¹⁶Live as free men, but do not use your freedom as a cover-up for evil; live as servants of God. ¹⁷Show proper respect to everyone: Love the brotherhood of believers, fear God, honor the king.   Ro 12:10; 13:7

¹⁸Slaves, submit yourselves to your masters with all respect, not only to those who are good and considerate, but also to those who are harsh. ¹⁹For it is commendable if a man bears up under the pain of unjust suffering because he is conscious of God. ²⁰But how is it to your credit if you receive a beating for doing wrong and endure it? But if you suffer for doing good and you endure it, this is commendable before God. ²¹To this you were called, because Christ suffered for you, leaving you an example, that you should follow in his steps.   Mt 16:24; Eph 6:5; 1Pe 3:14,17

²²"He committed no sin,
    and no deceit was found in
      his mouth."[b]   Isa 53:9

²³When they hurled their insults at him, he did not retaliate; when he suffered, he made no threats. Instead, he entrusted himself to him who judges justly. ²⁴He himself bore our sins in his body on the tree, so that we might die to sins and live for righteousness; by his wounds you have been healed. ²⁵For you were like sheep going

---

[a] 8 Isaiah 8:14   [b] 22 Isaiah 53:9

astray, but now you have returned to the Shepherd and Overseer of your souls.   Isa 53:6; Jn 10:11

Wives and Husbands

3 Wives, in the same way be submissive to your husbands so that, if any of them do not believe the word, they may be won over without words by the behavior of their wives, ²when they see the purity and reverence of your lives. ³Your beauty should not come from outward adornment, such as braided hair and the wearing of gold jewelry and fine clothes. ⁴Instead, it should be that of your inner self, the unfading beauty of a gentle and quiet spirit, which is of great worth in God's sight. ⁵For this is the way the holy women of the past who put their hope in God used to make themselves beautiful. They were submissive to their own husbands, ⁶like Sarah, who obeyed Abraham and called him her master. You are her daughters if you do what is right and do not give way to fear.

⁷Husbands, in the same way be considerate as you live with your wives, and treat them with respect as the weaker partner and as heirs with you of the gracious gift of life, so that nothing will hinder your prayers.   Eph 5:25-33

Suffering for Doing Good

⁸Finally, all of you, live in harmony with one another; be sympathetic, love as brothers, be compassionate and humble. ⁹Do not repay evil with evil or insult with insult, but with blessing, because to this you were called so that you may inherit a blessing. ¹⁰For,

"Whoever would love life
  and see good days
must keep his tongue from evil
  and his lips from deceitful
    speech.
¹¹He must turn from evil and do
    good;
  he must seek peace and
    pursue it.
¹²For the eyes of the Lord are on
    the righteous
  and his ears are attentive to
    their prayer,
but the face of the Lord is
    against those who do
    evil."ᵃ   Ps 34:12-16

¹³Who is going to harm you if you are eager to do good? ¹⁴But even if you should suffer for what is right, you are blessed. "Do not fear what they fearᵇ; do not be frightened."ᶜ ¹⁵But in your hearts set apart Christ as Lord. Always be prepared to give an answer to everyone who asks you to give the reason for the hope that you have. But do this with gentleness and respect, ¹⁶keeping a clear conscience, so that those who speak maliciously against your good behavior in Christ may be ashamed

---

ᵃ12 Psalm 34:12-16   ᵇ14 Or *not fear their threats*   ᶜ14 Isaiah 8:12

of their slander. [17]It is better, if it is God's will, to suffer for doing good than for doing evil. [18]For Christ died for sins once for all, the righteous for the unrighteous, to bring you to God. He was put to death in the body but made alive by the Spirit, [19]through whom[a] also he went and preached to the spirits in prison [20]who disobeyed long ago when God waited patiently in the days of Noah while the ark was being built. In it only a few people, eight in all, were saved through water, [21]and this water symbolizes baptism that now saves you also—not the removal of dirt from the body but the pledge[b] of a good conscience toward God. It saves you by the resurrection of Jesus Christ, [22]who has gone into heaven and is at God's right hand—with angels, authorities and powers in submission to him. Ro 8:38; 1Pe 1:3

Living for God

4 Therefore, since Christ suffered in his body, arm yourselves also with the same attitude, because he who has suffered in his body is done with sin. [2]As a result, he does not live the rest of his earthly life for evil human desires, but rather for the will of God. [3]For you have spent enough time in the past doing what pagans choose to do—living in debauchery, lust, drunkenness, orgies, carousing and detestable idolatry. [4]They think it strange that you do not plunge with them into the same flood of dissipation, and they heap abuse on you. [5]But they will have to give account to him who is ready to judge the living and the dead. [6]For this is the reason the gospel was preached even to those who are now dead, so that they might be judged according to men in regard to the body, but live according to God in regard to the spirit. Ac 10:42; 1Pe 3:19

[7]The end of all things is near. Therefore be clear minded and self-controlled so that you can pray. [8]Above all, love each other deeply, because love covers over a multitude of sins. [9]Offer hospitality to one another without grumbling. [10]Each one should use whatever gift he has received to serve others, faithfully administering God's grace in its various forms. [11]If anyone speaks, he should do it as one speaking the very words of God. If anyone serves, he should do it with the strength God provides, so that in all things God may be praised through Jesus Christ. To him be the glory and the power for ever and ever. Amen. Pr 10:12

Suffering for Being a Christian

[12]Dear friends, do not be surprised at the painful trial you are suffering, as though something strange were happening to you.

---

[a] 18,19 Or *alive in the spirit,* [19]*through which*   [b] 21 Or *response*

[13]But rejoice that you participate in the sufferings of Christ, so that you may be overjoyed when his glory is revealed. [14]If you are insulted because of the name of Christ, you are blessed, for the Spirit of glory and of God rests on you. [15]If you suffer, it should not be as a murderer or thief or any other kind of criminal, or even as a meddler. [16]However, if you suffer as a Christian, do not be ashamed, but praise God that you bear that name. [17]For it is time for judgment to begin with the family of God; and if it begins with us, what will the outcome be for those who do not obey the gospel of God? [18]And,   Ac 5:41; Ro 8:17

"If it is hard for the righteous
    to be saved,
what will become of the
    ungodly and the
    sinner?"[a]   Pr 11:31; Lk 23:31

[19]So then, those who suffer according to God's will should commit themselves to their faithful Creator and continue to do good.

To Elders and Young Men

5 To the elders among you, I appeal as a fellow elder, a witness of Christ's sufferings and one who also will share in the glory to be revealed: [2]Be shepherds of God's flock that is under your care, serving as overseers—not because you must, but because you are willing, as God wants you to be; not greedy for money, but eager to serve; [3]not lording it over those entrusted to you, but being examples to the flock. [4]And when the Chief Shepherd appears, you will receive the crown of glory that will never fade away.   1Co 9:25; 1Ti 3:3; Rev 1:9

[5]Young men, in the same way be submissive to those who are older. All of you, clothe yourselves with humility toward one another, because,   Eph 5:21

"God opposes the proud
    but gives grace to the
      humble."[b]

[6]Humble yourselves, therefore, under God's mighty hand, that he may lift you up in due time. [7]Cast all your anxiety on him because he cares for you.   Heb 13:5; Jas 4:6,10

[8]Be self-controlled and alert. Your enemy the devil prowls around like a roaring lion looking for someone to devour. [9]Resist him, standing firm in the faith, because you know that your brothers throughout the world are undergoing the same kind of sufferings.

[10]And the God of all grace, who called you to his eternal glory in Christ, after you have suffered a little while, will himself restore you and make you strong, firm and steadfast. [11]To him be the power for ever and ever. Amen.   Ro 11:36

Final Greetings

¹²With the help of Silas,ᵃ whom I regard as a faithful brother, I have written to you briefly, encouraging you and testifying that this is the true grace of God. Stand fast in it.

¹³She who is in Babylon, chosen together with you, sends you her greetings, and so does my son Mark. ¹⁴Greet one another with a kiss of love. Ac 12:12; Ro 16:16

Peace to all of you who are in Christ. Eph 6:23

ᵃ 12 Greek *Silvanus*, a variant of *Silas*

2 Peter

1 Simon Peter, a servant and apostle of Jesus Christ, _{Ro 1:1}

To those who through the righteousness of our God and Savior Jesus Christ have received a faith as precious as ours: Ro 3:21-26

²Grace and peace be yours in abundance through the knowledge of God and of Jesus our Lord.

Making One's Calling and Election Sure

³His divine power has given us everything we need for life and godliness through our knowledge of him who called us by his own glory and goodness. ⁴Through these he has given us his very great and precious promises, so that through them you may participate in the divine nature and escape the corruption in the world caused by evil desires. 2Co 7:1; 1Pe 1:5

⁵For this very reason, make every effort to add to your faith goodness; and to goodness, knowledge; ⁶and to knowledge, self-control; and to self-control, perseverance; and to perseverance, godliness; ⁷and to godliness, brotherly kindness; and to brotherly kindness, love. ⁸For if you possess these qualities in increasing measure, they will keep you from being inef-

fective and unproductive in your knowledge of our Lord Jesus Christ. ⁹But if anyone does not have them, he is nearsighted and blind, and has forgotten that he has been cleansed from his past sins. 1Jn 2:11; Eph 5:26

¹⁰Therefore, my brothers, be all the more eager to make your calling and election sure. For if you do these things, you will never fall, ¹¹and you will receive a rich welcome into the eternal kingdom of our Lord and Savior Jesus Christ.

Prophecy of Scripture

¹²So I will always remind you of these things, even though you know them and are firmly established in the truth you now have. ¹³I think it is right to refresh your memory as long as I live in the tent of this body, ¹⁴because I know that I will soon put it aside, as our Lord Jesus Christ has made clear to me. ¹⁵And I will make every effort to see that after my departure you will always be able to remember these things. 2Co 5:1,4; 1Jn 2:21

¹⁶We did not follow cleverly invented stories when we told you about the power and coming of our Lord Jesus Christ, but we were eyewitnesses of his majesty. ¹⁷For he received honor and glory from God the Father when the voice

came to him from the Majestic Glory, saying, "This is my Son, whom I love; with him I am well pleased."[a] [18]We ourselves heard this voice that came from heaven when we were with him on the sacred mountain.   Mt 3:17; 17:1-8

[19]And we have the word of the prophets made more certain, and you will do well to pay attention to it, as to a light shining in a dark place, until the day dawns and the morning star rises in your hearts. [20]Above all, you must understand that no prophecy of Scripture came about by the prophet's own interpretation. [21]For prophecy never had its origin in the will of man, but men spoke from God as they were carried along by the Holy Spirit.   Ac 1:16; 2Ti 3:16

False Teachers and Their Destruction

2 But there were also false prophets among the people, just as there will be false teachers among you. They will secretly introduce destructive heresies, even denying the sovereign Lord who bought them—bringing swift destruction on themselves. [2]Many will follow their shameful ways and will bring the way of truth into disrepute. [3]In their greed these teachers will exploit you with stories they have made up. Their condemnation has long been hanging over them, and their destruction has not been sleeping.   2Co 2:17

[4]For if God did not spare angels when they sinned, but sent them to hell,[b] putting them into gloomy dungeons[c] to be held for judgment; [5]if he did not spare the ancient world when he brought the flood on its ungodly people, but protected Noah, a preacher of righteousness, and seven others; [6]if he condemned the cities of Sodom and Gomorrah by burning them to ashes, and made them an example of what is going to happen to the ungodly; [7]and if he rescued Lot, a righteous man, who was distressed by the filthy lives of lawless men [8](for that righteous man, living among them day after day, was tormented in his righteous soul by the lawless deeds he saw and heard) — [9]if this is so, then the Lord knows how to rescue godly men from trials and to hold the unrighteous for the day of judgment, while continuing their punishment.[d] [10]This is especially true of those who follow the corrupt desire of the sinful nature[e] and despise authority.   1Co 10:13; 2Pe 3:3

Bold and arrogant, these men are not afraid to slander celestial beings; [11]yet even angels, although they are stronger and more powerful, do not bring slanderous accusations against such beings in the presence of the Lord. [12]But these

---

[a]17 Matt. 17:5; Mark 9:7; Luke 9:35   [b]4 Greek Tartarus   [c]4 Some manuscripts into chains of darkness   [d]9 Or unrighteous for punishment until the day of judgment   [e]10 Or the flesh

men blaspheme in matters they do not understand. They are like brute beasts, creatures of instinct, born only to be caught and destroyed, and like beasts they too will perish.   Jude 8-10

¹³They will be paid back with harm for the harm they have done. Their idea of pleasure is to carouse in broad daylight. They are blots and blemishes, reveling in their pleasures while they feast with you.^a ¹⁴With eyes full of adultery, they never stop sinning; they seduce the unstable; they are experts in greed—an accursed brood! ¹⁵They have left the straight way and wandered off to follow the way of Balaam son of Beor, who loved the wages of wickedness. ¹⁶But he was rebuked for his wrongdoing by a donkey—a beast without speech—who spoke with a man's voice and restrained the prophet's madness.   Nu 22:21-30

¹⁷These men are springs without water and mists driven by a storm. Blackest darkness is reserved for them. ¹⁸For they mouth empty, boastful words and, by appealing to the lustful desires of sinful human nature, they entice people who are just escaping from those who live in error. ¹⁹They promise them freedom, while they themselves are slaves of depravity—for a man is a slave to whatever has mastered him. ²⁰If they have escaped the corruption of the world by knowing our Lord and Savior Jesus Christ and are again entangled in it and overcome, they are worse off at the end than they were at the beginning. ²¹It would have been better for them not to have known the way of righteousness, than to have known it and then to turn their backs on the sacred command that was passed on to them. ²²Of them the proverbs are true: "A dog returns to its vomit,"^b and, "A sow that is washed goes back to her wallowing in the mud."

The Day of the Lord

3 Dear friends, this is now my second letter to you. I have written both of them as reminders to stimulate you to wholesome thinking. ²I want you to recall the words spoken in the past by the holy prophets and the command given by our Lord and Savior through your apostles.   2Pe 1:13

³First of all, you must understand that in the last days scoffers will come, scoffing and following their own evil desires. ⁴They will say, "Where is this 'coming' he promised? Ever since our fathers died, everything goes on as it has since the beginning of creation." ⁵But they deliberately forget that long ago by God's word the heavens existed and the earth was formed out of water and by water. ⁶By these waters also the world of that time was deluged and de-

^a13 Some manuscripts *in their love feasts*   ^b22 Prov. 26:11

stroyed. [7]By the same word the present heavens and earth are reserved for fire, being kept for the day of judgment and destruction of ungodly men.   Eze 12:22; 2Pe 2:10

[8]But do not forget this one thing, dear friends: With the Lord a day is like a thousand years, and a thousand years are like a day. [9]The Lord is not slow in keeping his promise, as some understand slowness. He is patient with you, not wanting anyone to perish, but everyone to come to repentance.

[10]But the day of the Lord will come like a thief. The heavens will disappear with a roar; the elements will be destroyed by fire, and the earth and everything in it will be laid bare.[a]   Mt 24:35; Rev 21:1

[11]Since everything will be destroyed in this way, what kind of people ought you to be? You ought to live holy and godly lives [12]as you look forward to the day of God and speed its coming.[b] That day will bring about the destruction of the heavens by fire, and the elements will melt in the heat. [13]But

in keeping with his promise we are looking forward to a new heaven and a new earth, the home of righteousness.   Isa 65:17; 1Co 1:7

[14]So then, dear friends, since you are looking forward to this, make every effort to be found spotless, blameless and at peace with him. [15]Bear in mind that our Lord's patience means salvation, just as our dear brother Paul also wrote you with the wisdom that God gave him. [16]He writes the same way in all his letters, speaking in them of these matters. His letters contain some things that are hard to understand, which ignorant and unstable people distort, as they do the other Scriptures, to their own destruction.   Eph 3:3; 2Pe 2:14

[17]Therefore, dear friends, since you already know this, be on your guard so that you may not be carried away by the error of lawless men and fall from your secure position. [18]But grow in the grace and knowledge of our Lord and Savior Jesus Christ. To him be glory both now and forever! Amen.   2Pe 1:11

---

[a]10 Some manuscripts *be burned up*   [b]12 Or *as you wait eagerly for the day of God to come*

1 John

The Word of Life

1 That which was from the beginning, which we have heard, which we have seen with our eyes, which we have looked at and our hands have touched—this we proclaim concerning the Word of life. ²The life appeared; we have seen it and testify to it, and we proclaim to you the eternal life, which was with the Father and has appeared to us. ³We proclaim to you what we have seen and heard, so that you also may have fellowship with us. And our fellowship is with the Father and with his Son, Jesus Christ. ⁴We write this to make our*ᵃ* joy complete.   Jn 3:29; 1Jn 2:1

Walking in the Light

⁵This is the message we have heard from him and declare to you: God is light; in him there is no darkness at all. ⁶If we claim to have fellowship with him yet walk in the darkness, we lie and do not live by the truth. ⁷But if we walk in the light, as he is in the light, we have fellowship with one another, and the blood of Jesus, his Son, purifies us from all*ᵇ* sin.   Heb 9:14; Rev 1:5

⁸If we claim to be without sin, we deceive ourselves and the truth is not in us. ⁹If we confess our sins, he is faithful and just and will forgive us our sins and purify us from all unrighteousness. ¹⁰If we claim we have not sinned, we make him out to be a liar and his word has no place in our lives.   1Jn 2:14; 5:10

2 My dear children, I write this to you so that you will not sin. But if anybody does sin, we have one who speaks to the Father in our defense—Jesus Christ, the Righteous One. ²He is the atoning sacrifice for our sins, and not only for ours but also for*ᶜ* the sins of the whole world.   Ro 3:25; Heb 7:25

³We know that we have come to know him if we obey his commands. ⁴The man who says, "I know him," but does not do what he commands is a liar, and the truth is not in him. ⁵But if anyone obeys his word, God's love*ᵈ* is truly made complete in him. This is how we know we are in him: ⁶Whoever claims to live in him must walk as Jesus did.   1Pe 2:21

⁷Dear friends, I am not writing you a new command but an old one, which you have had since the beginning. This old command is the message you have heard. ⁸Yet

---

ᵃ4 Some manuscripts *your*   *ᵇ7* Or *every away our sins, and not only ours but also*   *ᶜ2* Or *He is the one who turns aside God's wrath, taking*   *ᵈ5* Or *word, love for God*

I am writing you a new command; its truth is seen in him and you, because the darkness is passing and the true light is already shining. Jn 1:9; 13:34 ⁹Anyone who claims to be in the light but hates his brother is still in the darkness. ¹⁰Whoever loves his brother lives in the light, and there is nothing in him[a] to make him stumble. ¹¹But whoever hates his brother is in the darkness and walks around in the darkness; he does not know where he is going, because the darkness has blinded him. Jn 12:35; 1Jn 3:14

¹²I write to you, dear children,
    because your sins have been
        forgiven on account of
            his name. 1Jn 3:23
¹³I write to you, fathers,
    because you have known
        him who is from the
            beginning. Jn 1:1
  I write to you, young men,
    because you have overcome
        the evil one. Mt 5:37
  I write to you, dear children,
    because you have known the
        Father.
¹⁴I write to you, fathers,
    because you have known
        him who is from the
            beginning. Jn 1:1
  I write to you, young men,
    because you are strong,
      and the word of God lives in
        you, Jn 5:38; 1Jn 1:10

and you have overcome the
    evil one. ver 13

Do Not Love the World

¹⁵Do not love the world or anything in the world. If anyone loves the world, the love of the Father is not in him. ¹⁶For everything in the world—the cravings of sinful man, the lust of his eyes and the boasting of what he has and does—comes not from the Father but from the world. ¹⁷The world and its desires pass away, but the man who does the will of God lives forever. Pr 27:20; Ro 12:2; 1Co 7:31

Warning Against Antichrists

¹⁸Dear children, this is the last hour; and as you have heard that the antichrist is coming, even now many antichrists have come. This is how we know it is the last hour. ¹⁹They went out from us, but they did not really belong to us. For if they had belonged to us, they would have remained with us; but their going showed that none of them belonged to us. 1Co 11:19 ²⁰But you have an anointing from the Holy One, and all of you know the truth.[b] ²¹I do not write to you because you do not know the truth, but because you do know it and because no lie comes from the truth. ²²Who is the liar? It is the man who denies that Jesus is the Christ. Such a man is the antichrist —he denies the Father and the

---

a 10 Or it   b 20 Some manuscripts and you know all things

Son. ²³No one who denies the Son has the Father; whoever acknowledges the Son has the Father also.

²⁴See that what you have heard from the beginning remains in you. If it does, you also will remain in the Son and in the Father. ²⁵And this is what he promised us—even eternal life.   Jn 14:23; 1Jn 1:3

²⁶I am writing these things to you about those who are trying to lead you astray. ²⁷As for you, the anointing you received from him remains in you, and you do not need anyone to teach you. But as his anointing teaches you about all things and as that anointing is real, not counterfeit—just as it has taught you, remain in him.   2Jn 7

Children of God

²⁸And now, dear children, continue in him, so that when he appears we may be confident and unashamed before him at his coming.

²⁹If you know that he is righteous, you know that everyone who does what is right has been born of him.

3 How great is the love the Father has lavished on us, that we should be called children of God! And that is what we are! The reason the world does not know us is that it did not know him. ²Dear friends, now we are children of God, and what we will be has not yet been made known. But we know that when he appears,ᵃ we

shall be like him, for we shall see him as he is. ³Everyone who has this hope in him purifies himself, just as he is pure.   Jn 1:12; 16:3

⁴Everyone who sins breaks the law; in fact, sin is lawlessness. ⁵But you know that he appeared so that he might take away our sins. And in him is no sin. ⁶No one who lives in him keeps on sinning. No one who continues to sin has either seen him or known him.   2Co 5:21

⁷Dear children, do not let anyone lead you astray. He who does what is right is righteous, just as he is righteous. ⁸He who does what is sinful is of the devil, because the devil has been sinning from the beginning. The reason the Son of God appeared was to destroy the devil's work. ⁹No one who is born of God will continue to sin, because God's seed remains in him; he cannot go on sinning, because he has been born of God. ¹⁰This is how we know who the children of God are and who the children of the devil are: Anyone who does not do what is right is not a child of God; nor is anyone who does not love his brother.   1Jn 4:8; 5:18

Love One Another

¹¹This is the message you heard from the beginning: We should love one another. ¹²Do not be like Cain, who belonged to the evil one and murdered his brother. And why did he murder him? Because

---

ᵃ2 Or *when it is made known*

his own actions were evil and his brother's were righteous. ¹³Do not be surprised, my brothers, if the world hates you. ¹⁴We know that we have passed from death to life, because we love our brothers. Anyone who does not love remains in death. ¹⁵Anyone who hates his brother is a murderer, and you know that no murderer has eternal life in him.   Mt 5:21-22

¹⁶This is how we know what love is: Jesus Christ laid down his life for us. And we ought to lay down our lives for our brothers. ¹⁷If anyone has material possessions and sees his brother in need but has no pity on him, how can the love of God be in him? ¹⁸Dear children, let us not love with words or tongue but with actions and in truth. ¹⁹This then is how we know that we belong to the truth, and how we set our hearts at rest in his presence ²⁰whenever our hearts condemn us. For God is greater than our hearts, and he knows everything.   Ro 12:9; 1Jn 2:1

²¹Dear friends, if our hearts do not condemn us, we have confidence before God ²²and receive from him anything we ask, because we obey his commands and do what pleases him. ²³And this is his command: to believe in the name of his Son, Jesus Christ, and to love one another as he commanded us. ²⁴Those who obey his commands live in him, and he in

them. And this is how we know that he lives in us: We know it by the Spirit he gave us.   1Jn 2:6; 4:13

Test the Spirits

4 Dear friends, do not believe every spirit, but test the spirits to see whether they are from God, because many false prophets have gone out into the world. ²This is how you can recognize the Spirit of God: Every spirit that acknowledges that Jesus Christ has come in the flesh is from God, ³but every spirit that does not acknowledge Jesus is not from God. This is the spirit of the antichrist, which you have heard is coming and even now is already in the world.

⁴You, dear children, are from God and have overcome them, because the one who is in you is greater than the one who is in the world. ⁵They are from the world and therefore speak from the viewpoint of the world, and the world listens to them. ⁶We are from God, and whoever knows God listens to us; but whoever is not from God does not listen to us. This is how we recognize the Spirit*a* of truth and the spirit of falsehood.   Jn 8:47

God's Love and Ours

⁷Dear friends, let us love one another, for love comes from God. Everyone who loves has been born of God and knows God. ⁸Whoever does not love does not know God,

a6 Or spirit

because God is love. ⁹This is how God showed his love among us: He sent his one and only Son*a* into the world that we might live through him. ¹⁰This is love: not that we loved God, but that he loved us and sent his Son as an atoning sacrifice for*b* our sins. ¹¹Dear friends, since God so loved us, we also ought to love one another. ¹²No one has ever seen God; but if we love one another, God lives in us and his love is made complete in us.   1Jn 2:2,5

¹³We know that we live in him and he in us, because he has given us of his Spirit. ¹⁴And we have seen and testify that the Father has sent his Son to be the Savior of the world. ¹⁵If anyone acknowledges that Jesus is the Son of God, God lives in him and he in God. ¹⁶And so we know and rely on the love God has for us.   Ro 10:9

God is love. Whoever lives in love lives in God, and God in him. ¹⁷In this way, love is made complete among us so that we will have confidence on the day of judgment, because in this world we are like him. ¹⁸There is no fear in love. But perfect love drives out fear, because fear has to do with punishment. The one who fears is not made perfect in love.   Ro 8:15

¹⁹We love because he first loved us. ²⁰If anyone says, "I love God,"

yet hates his brother, he is a liar. For anyone who does not love his brother, whom he has seen, cannot love God, whom he has not seen. ²¹And he has given us this command: Whoever loves God must also love his brother.   Mt 5:43

Faith in the Son of God

5 Everyone who believes that Jesus is the Christ is born of God, and everyone who loves the father loves his child as well. ²This is how we know that we love the children of God: by loving God and carrying out his commands. ³This is love for God: to obey his commands. And his commands are not burdensome, ⁴for everyone born of God overcomes the world. This is the victory that has overcome the world, even our faith. ⁵Who is it that overcomes the world? Only he who believes that Jesus is the Son of God.   Jn 14:15; 16:33

⁶This is the one who came by water and blood—Jesus Christ. He did not come by water only, but by water and blood. And it is the Spirit who testifies, because the Spirit is the truth. ⁷For there are three that testify: ⁸the*c* Spirit, the water and the blood; and the three are in agreement. ⁹We accept man's testimony, but God's testimony is greater because it is the testimony of God, which he has given about

---

a 9 Or *his only begotten Son*   *b* 10 Or *as the one who would turn aside his wrath, taking away*
c 7,8 Late manuscripts of the Vulgate *testify in heaven: the Father, the Word and the Holy Spirit, and these three are one.* ⁸*And there are three that testify on earth: the* (not found in any Greek manuscript before the sixteenth century)

his Son. [10]Anyone who believes in the Son of God has this testimony in his heart. Anyone who does not believe God has made him out to be a liar, because he has not believed the testimony God has given about his Son. [11]And this is the testimony: God has given us eternal life, and this life is in his Son. [12]He who has the Son has life; he who does not have the Son of God does not have life.   Jn 3:15-16,36; 1Jn 2:25

Concluding Remarks

[13]I write these things to you who believe in the name of the Son of God so that you may know that you have eternal life. [14]This is the confidence we have in approaching God: that if we ask anything according to his will, he hears us. [15]And if we know that he hears us—whatever we ask—we know that we have what we asked of him.   Jn 20:31; 1Jn 3:21

[16]If anyone sees his brother commit a sin that does not lead to death, he should pray and God will give him life. I refer to those whose sin does not lead to death. There is a sin that leads to death. I am not saying that he should pray about that. [17]All wrongdoing is sin, and there is sin that does not lead to death.   Jas 5:15; 1Jn 3:4

[18]We know that anyone born of God does not continue to sin; the one who was born of God keeps him safe, and the evil one cannot harm him. [19]We know that we are children of God, and that the whole world is under the control of the evil one. [20]We know also that the Son of God has come and has given us understanding, so that we may know him who is true. And we are in him who is true— even in his Son Jesus Christ. He is the true God and eternal life.

[21]Dear children, keep yourselves from idols.   1Co 10:14; 1Th 1:9

2 John

¹The elder,   3Jn 1

To the chosen lady and her children, whom I love in the truth—and not I only, but also all who know the truth— ²because of the truth, which lives in us and will be with us forever: Jn 8:32; 1Jn 1:8

³Grace, mercy and peace from God the Father and from Jesus Christ, the Father's Son, will be with us in truth and love.   Ro 1:7

⁴It has given me great joy to find some of your children walking in the truth, just as the Father commanded us. ⁵And now, dear lady, I am not writing you a new command but one we have had from the beginning. I ask that we love one another. ⁶And this is love: that we walk in obedience to his commands. As you have heard from the beginning, his command is that you walk in love.   1Jn 2:5; 3:11

⁷Many deceivers, who do not acknowledge Jesus Christ as coming in the flesh, have gone out into the world. Any such person is the deceiver and the antichrist. ⁸Watch out that you do not lose what you have worked for, but that you may be rewarded fully. ⁹Anyone who runs ahead and does not continue in the teaching of Christ does not have God; whoever continues in the teaching has both the Father and the Son. ¹⁰If anyone comes to you and does not bring this teaching, do not take him into your house or welcome him. ¹¹Anyone who welcomes him shares in his wicked work.   Ro 16:17; 1Jn 2:23

¹²I have much to write to you, but I do not want to use paper and ink. Instead, I hope to visit you and talk with you face to face, so that our joy may be complete.

¹³The children of your chosen sister send their greetings.   ver 1

3 John

¹The elder, 2Jn 1

To my dear friend Gaius, whom I love in the truth.

²Dear friend, I pray that you may enjoy good health and that all may go well with you, even as your soul is getting along well. ³It gave me great joy to have some brothers come and tell about your faithfulness to the truth and how you continue to walk in the truth. ⁴I have no greater joy than to hear that my children are walking in the truth.

⁵Dear friend, you are faithful in what you are doing for the brothers, even though they are strangers to you. ⁶They have told the church about your love. You will do well to send them on their way in a manner worthy of God. ⁷It was for the sake of the Name that they went out, receiving no help from the pagans. ⁸We ought therefore to show hospitality to such men so that we may work together for the truth. Ac 20:33,35; Ro 12:13

⁹I wrote to the church, but Diotrephes, who loves to be first, will have nothing to do with us. ¹⁰So if I come, I will call attention to what he is doing, gossiping maliciously about us. Not satisfied with that, he refuses to welcome the brothers. He also stops those who want to do so and puts them out of the church. Jn 9:22,34; 2Jn 12

¹¹Dear friend, do not imitate what is evil but what is good. Anyone who does what is good is from God. Anyone who does what is evil has not seen God. ¹²Demetrius is well spoken of by everyone—and even by the truth itself. We also speak well of him, and you know that our testimony is true. Jn 21:24

¹³I have much to write you, but I do not want to do so with pen and ink. ¹⁴I hope to see you soon, and we will talk face to face. 2Jn 12

Peace to you. The friends here send their greetings. Greet the friends there by name. Jn 10:3

Jude

¹Jude, a servant of Jesus Christ and a brother of James,   Ac 1:13

To those who have been called, who are loved by God the Father and kept by[a] Jesus Christ:

²Mercy, peace and love be yours in abundance.   2Pe 1:2

The Sin and Doom of Godless Men

³Dear friends, although I was very eager to write to you about the salvation we share, I felt I had to write and urge you to contend for the faith that was once for all entrusted to the saints. ⁴For certain men whose condemnation was written about[b] long ago have secretly slipped in among you. They are godless men, who change the grace of our God into a license for immorality and deny Jesus Christ our only Sovereign and Lord.   Gal 2:4; 2Pe 2:1

⁵Though you already know all this, I want to remind you that the Lord[c] delivered his people out of Egypt, but later destroyed those who did not believe. ⁶And the angels who did not keep their positions of authority but abandoned their own home—these he has kept in darkness, bound with everlasting chains for judgment on the great Day. ⁷In a similar way, Sodom and Gomorrah and the surrounding towns gave themselves up to sexual immorality and perversion. They serve as an example of those who suffer the punishment of eternal fire.   Dt 29:23; 2Pe 2:6

⁸In the very same way, these dreamers pollute their own bodies, reject authority and slander celestial beings. ⁹But even the archangel Michael, when he was disputing with the devil about the body of Moses, did not dare to bring a slanderous accusation against him, but said, "The Lord rebuke you!" ¹⁰Yet these men speak abusively against whatever they do not understand; and what things they do understand by instinct, like unreasoning animals—these are the very things that destroy them.   2Pe 2:10,12

¹¹Woe to them! They have taken the way of Cain; they have rushed for profit into Balaam's error; they have been destroyed in Korah's rebellion.   Nu 16:1-3,31-35; 1Jn 3:12

¹²These men are blemishes at your love feasts, eating with you without the slightest qualm—

---

[a] 1 Or for; or in   [b] 4 Or men who were marked out for condemnation   [c] 5 Some early manuscripts Jesus

shepherds who feed only themselves. They are clouds without rain, blown along by the wind; autumn trees, without fruit and uprooted—twice dead. ¹³They are wild waves of the sea, foaming up their shame; wandering stars, for whom blackest darkness has been reserved forever.   Isa 57:20; Php 3:19

¹⁴Enoch, the seventh from Adam, prophesied about these men: "See, the Lord is coming with thousands upon thousands of his holy ones ¹⁵to judge everyone, and to convict all the ungodly of all the ungodly acts they have done in the ungodly way, and of all the harsh words ungodly sinners have spoken against him." ¹⁶These men are grumblers and faultfinders; they follow their own evil desires; they boast about themselves and flatter others for their own advantage.

A Call to Persevere

¹⁷But, dear friends, remember what the apostles of our Lord Jesus Christ foretold. ¹⁸They said to you, "In the last times there will be scoffers who will follow their own ungodly desires." ¹⁹These are the men who divide you, who follow mere natural instincts and do not have the Spirit.   1Ti 4:1; 2Pe 2:1

²⁰But you, dear friends, build yourselves up in your most holy faith and pray in the Holy Spirit. ²¹Keep yourselves in God's love as you wait for the mercy of our Lord Jesus Christ to bring you to eternal life.   Tit 2:13; 2Pe 3:12

²²Be merciful to those who doubt; ²³snatch others from the fire and save them; to others show mercy, mixed with fear—hating even the clothing stained by corrupted flesh.   Am 4:11; Zec 3:2-5

Doxology

²⁴To him who is able to keep you from falling and to present you before his glorious presence without fault and with great joy— ²⁵to the only God our Savior be glory, majesty, power and authority, through Jesus Christ our Lord, before all ages, now and forevermore! Amen.   Ro 11:36; Col 1:22

Revelation

Prologue

1 The revelation of Jesus Christ, which God gave him to show his servants what must soon take place. He made it known by sending his angel to his servant John, ²who testifies to everything he saw —that is, the word of God and the testimony of Jesus Christ. ³Blessed is the one who reads the words of this prophecy, and blessed are those who hear it and take to heart what is written in it, because the time is near.   Lk 11:28; 1Co 1:6

Greetings and Doxology

⁴John,

To the seven churches in the province of Asia: ver 11,20

Grace and peace to you from him who is, and who was, and who is to come, and from the seven spirits*a* before his throne, ⁵and from Jesus Christ, who is the faithful witness, the firstborn from the dead, and the ruler of the kings of the earth.   Col 1:18; Rev 17:14

To him who loves us and has freed us from our sins by his blood, ⁶and has made us to be a kingdom and priests to serve his God and Father—to him be glory and power for ever and ever! Amen.   Ro 11:36; 1Pe 2:5

⁷Look, he is coming with the
    clouds,   Da 7:13
and every eye will see him,
  even those who pierced him;
  and all the peoples of the
    earth will mourn
    because of him.
      So shall it be! Amen.

⁸"I am the Alpha and the Omega," says the Lord God, "who is, and who was, and who is to come, the Almighty."   Rev 4:8; 21:6

One Like a Son of Man

⁹I, John, your brother and companion in the suffering and kingdom and patient endurance that are ours in Jesus, was on the island of Patmos because of the word of God and the testimony of Jesus. ¹⁰On the Lord's Day I was in the Spirit, and I heard behind me a loud voice like a trumpet, ¹¹which said: "Write on a scroll what you see and send it to the seven churches: to Ephesus, Smyrna, Pergamum, Thyatira, Sardis, Philadelphia and Laodicea."   2Ti 2:12

¹²I turned around to see the voice that was speaking to me.

a4 Or the sevenfold Spirit

And when I turned I saw seven golden lampstands, [13]and among the lampstands was someone "like a son of man,"[a] dressed in a robe reaching down to his feet and with a golden sash around his chest. [14]His head and hair were white like wool, as white as snow, and his eyes were like blazing fire. [15]His feet were like bronze glowing in a furnace, and his voice was like the sound of rushing waters. [16]In his right hand he held seven stars, and out of his mouth came a sharp double-edged sword. His face was like the sun shining in all its brilliance.   Heb 4:12; Rev 2:12,16

[17]When I saw him, I fell at his feet as though dead. Then he placed his right hand on me and said: "Do not be afraid. I am the First and the Last. [18]I am the Living One; I was dead, and behold I am alive for ever and ever! And I hold the keys of death and Hades.

[19]"Write, therefore, what you have seen, what is now and what will take place later. [20]The mystery of the seven stars that you saw in my right hand and of the seven golden lampstands is this: The seven stars are the angels[b] of the seven churches, and the seven lampstands are the seven churches.

To the Church in Ephesus

2 "To the angel[c] of the church in Ephesus write:

These are the words of him who holds the seven stars in his right hand and walks among the seven golden lampstands: [2]I know your deeds, your hard work and your perseverance. I know that you cannot tolerate wicked men, that you have tested those who claim to be apostles but are not, and have found them false. [3]You have persevered and have endured hardships for my name, and have not grown weary.

[4]Yet I hold this against you: You have forsaken your first love. [5]Remember the height from which you have fallen! Repent and do the things you did at first. If you do not repent, I will come to you and remove your lampstand from its place. [6]But you have this in your favor: You hate the practices of the Nicolaitans, which I also hate.   Mt 24:12; Rev 1:20

[7]He who has an ear, let him hear what the Spirit says to the churches. To him who overcomes, I will give the right to eat from the tree of life, which is in the paradise of God.

To the Church in Smyrna

[8]"To the angel of the church in Smyrna write:

---

[a] 13 Daniel 7:13   [b] 20 Or messengers   [c] 1 Or messenger; also in verses 8, 12 and 18

These are the words of him who is the First and the Last, who died and came to life again. ⁹I know your afflictions and your poverty—yet you are rich! I know the slander of those who say they are Jews and are not, but are a synagogue of Satan. ¹⁰Do not be afraid of what you are about to suffer. I tell you, the devil will put some of you in prison to test you, and you will suffer persecution for ten days. Be faithful, even to the point of death, and I will give you the crown of life.   Da 1:12,14; Jas 2:5

¹¹He who has an ear, let him hear what the Spirit says to the churches. He who overcomes will not be hurt at all by the second death.

To the Church in Pergamum

¹²"To the angel of the church in Pergamum write:

These are the words of him who has the sharp, double-edged sword. ¹³I know where you live—where Satan has his throne. Yet you remain true to my name. You did not renounce your faith in me, even in the days of Antipas, my faithful witness, who was put to death in your city—where Satan lives.   Rev 1:16; 14:12

¹⁴Nevertheless, I have a few things against you: You have people there who hold to the teaching of Balaam, who taught Balak to entice the Israelites to sin by eating food sacrificed to idols and by committing sexual immorality. ¹⁵Likewise you also have those who hold to the teaching of the Nicolaitans. ¹⁶Repent therefore! Otherwise, I will soon come to you and will fight against them with the sword of my mouth.

¹⁷He who has an ear, let him hear what the Spirit says to the churches. To him who overcomes, I will give some of the hidden manna. I will also give him a white stone with a new name written on it, known only to him who receives it.

To the Church in Thyatira

¹⁸"To the angel of the church in Thyatira write:

These are the words of the Son of God, whose eyes are like blazing fire and whose feet are like burnished bronze. ¹⁹I know your deeds, your love and faith, your service and perseverance, and that you are now doing more than you did at first.

²⁰Nevertheless, I have this against you: You tolerate that woman Jezebel, who calls herself a prophetess. By her teaching she misleads my servants into sexual immorality

and the eating of food sacrificed to idols. [21]I have given her time to repent of her immorality, but she is unwilling. [22]So I will cast her on a bed of suffering, and I will make those who commit adultery with her suffer intensely, unless they repent of her ways. [23]I will strike her children dead. Then all the churches will know that I am he who searches hearts and minds, and I will repay each of you according to your deeds. [24]Now I say to the rest of you in Thyatira, to you who do not hold to her teaching and have not learned Satan's so-called deep secrets (I will not impose any other burden on you): [25]Only hold on to what you have until I come.

[26]To him who overcomes and does my will to the end, I will give authority over the nations—   Ps 2:8; Rev 3:21

[27]'He will rule them with an
        iron scepter;   Rev 12:5
    he will dash them to
        pieces like
        pottery'[a]—   Isa 30:14

just as I have received authority from my Father. [28]I will also give him the morning star. [29]He who has an ear, let him hear what the Spirit says to the churches.

To the Church in Sardis

3 "To the angel[b] of the church in Sardis write:

These are the words of him who holds the seven spirits[c] of God and the seven stars. I know your deeds; you have a reputation of being alive, but you are dead. [2]Wake up! Strengthen what remains and is about to die, for I have not found your deeds complete in the sight of my God. [3]Remember, therefore, what you have received and heard; obey it, and repent. But if you do not wake up, I will come like a thief, and you will not know at what time I will come to you.   2Pe 3:10; Rev 1:4,16

[4]Yet you have a few people in Sardis who have not soiled their clothes. They will walk with me, dressed in white, for they are worthy. [5]He who overcomes will, like them, be dressed in white. I will never blot out his name from the book of life, but will acknowledge his name before my Father and his angels. [6]He who has an ear, let him hear what the Spirit says to the churches.

To the Church in Philadelphia

[7]"To the angel of the church in Philadelphia write:

---

[a]27 Psalm 2:9   [b]1 Or *messenger*; also in verses 7 and 14   [c]1 Or *the sevenfold Spirit*

These are the words of him who is holy and true, who holds the key of David. What he opens no one can shut, and what he shuts no one can open. ⁸I know your deeds. See, I have placed before you an open door that no one can shut. I know that you have little strength, yet you have kept my word and have not denied my name. ⁹I will make those who are of the synagogue of Satan, who claim to be Jews though they are not, but are liars—I will make them come and fall down at your feet and acknowledge that I have loved you. ¹⁰Since you have kept my command to endure patiently, I will also keep you from the hour of trial that is going to come upon the whole world to test those who live on the earth.   Rev 6:10; 17:8

¹¹I am coming soon. Hold on to what you have, so that no one will take your crown. ¹²Him who overcomes I will make a pillar in the temple of my God. Never again will he leave it. I will write on him the name of my God and the name of the city of my God, the new Jerusalem, which is coming down out of heaven from my God; and I will also write on him my new name. ¹³He who has an ear, let him hear what the Spirit says to the churches.

To the Church in Laodicea

¹⁴"To the angel of the church in Laodicea write:

These are the words of the Amen, the faithful and true witness, the ruler of God's creation. ¹⁵I know your deeds, that you are neither cold nor hot. I wish you were either one or the other! ¹⁶So, because you are lukewarm—neither hot nor cold—I am about to spit you out of my mouth. ¹⁷You say, 'I am rich; I have acquired wealth and do not need a thing.' But you do not realize that you are wretched, pitiful, poor, blind and naked. ¹⁸I counsel you to buy from me gold refined in the fire, so you can become rich; and white clothes to wear, so you can cover your shameful nakedness; and salve to put on your eyes, so you can see.   Hos 12:8; 1Co 4:8

¹⁹Those whom I love I rebuke and discipline. So be earnest, and repent. ²⁰Here I am! I stand at the door and knock. If anyone hears my voice and opens the door, I will come in and eat with him, and he with me.   Lk 12:36

²¹To him who overcomes, I will give the right to sit with me on my throne, just as I overcame and sat down with my Father on his throne. ²²He who has an ear, let him hear

what the Spirit says to the churches."

The Throne in Heaven

4 After this I looked, and there before me was a door standing open in heaven. And the voice I had first heard speaking to me like a trumpet said, "Come up here, and I will show you what must take place after this." ²At once I was in the Spirit, and there before me was a throne in heaven with someone sitting on it. ³And the one who sat there had the appearance of jasper and carnelian. A rainbow, resembling an emerald, encircled the throne. ⁴Surrounding the throne were twenty-four other thrones, and seated on them were twenty-four elders. They were dressed in white and had crowns of gold on their heads. ⁵From the throne came flashes of lightning, rumblings and peals of thunder. Before the throne, seven lamps were blazing. These are the seven spirits*ᵃ* of God. ⁶Also before the throne there was what looked like a sea of glass, clear as crystal.

In the center, around the throne, were four living creatures, and they were covered with eyes, in front and in back. ⁷The first living creature was like a lion, the second was like an ox, the third had a face like a man, the fourth was like a flying eagle. ⁸Each of the four living creatures had six wings and

was covered with eyes all around, even under his wings. Day and night they never stop saying:

"Holy, holy, holy
is the Lord God Almighty,
who was, and is, and is to
come."

⁹Whenever the living creatures give glory, honor and thanks to him who sits on the throne and who lives for ever and ever, ¹⁰the twenty-four elders fall down before him who sits on the throne, and worship him who lives for ever and ever. They lay their crowns before the throne and say:

¹¹"You are worthy, our Lord and
God,
to receive glory and honor
and power,   Rev 5:12
for you created all things,
and by your will they were
created
and have their being."   Rev 10:6

The Scroll and the Lamb

5 Then I saw in the right hand of him who sat on the throne a scroll with writing on both sides and sealed with seven seals. ²And I saw a mighty angel proclaiming in a loud voice, "Who is worthy to break the seals and open the scroll?" ³But no one in heaven or on earth or under the earth could open the scroll or even look inside

---

ᵃ 5 Or *the sevenfold Spirit*

it. [4]I wept and wept because no one was found who was worthy to open the scroll or look inside. [5]Then one of the elders said to me, "Do not weep! See, the Lion of the tribe of Judah, the Root of David, has triumphed. He is able to open the scroll and its seven seals."

[6]Then I saw a Lamb, looking as if it had been slain, standing in the center of the throne, encircled by the four living creatures and the elders. He had seven horns and seven eyes, which are the seven spirits[a] of God sent out into all the earth. [7]He came and took the scroll from the right hand of him who sat on the throne. [8]And when he had taken it, the four living creatures and the twenty-four elders fell down before the Lamb. Each one had a harp and they were holding golden bowls full of incense, which are the prayers of the saints. [9]And they sang a new song:

"You are worthy to take the
         scroll   Rev 4:11
   and to open its seals,
because you were slain,
   and with your blood you
         purchased men for God
   from every tribe and
         language and people
         and nation.   Rev 13:7
[10]You have made them to be a
         kingdom and priests to
         serve our God,   1Pe 2:5

and they will reign on the
         earth."

[11]Then I looked and heard the voice of many angels, numbering thousands upon thousands, and ten thousand times ten thousand. They encircled the throne and the living creatures and the elders. [12]In a loud voice they sang: Da 7:10

"Worthy is the Lamb, who was
         slain,   ver 9,13
to receive power and wealth
         and wisdom and
         strength
and honor and glory and
         praise!"   Rev 4:11

[13]Then I heard every creature in heaven and on earth and under the earth and on the sea, and all that is in them, singing: Php 2:10

"To him who sits on the
         throne and to the Lamb
be praise and honor and glory
         and power,
   for ever and ever!"

[14]The four living creatures said, "Amen," and the elders fell down and worshiped.   1Ch 29:11; Rev 4:10

The Seals

6 I watched as the Lamb opened the first of the seven seals. Then I heard one of the four living creatures say in a voice like thunder, "Come!" [2]I looked, and there before me was a white horse! Its

---

[a]6 Or *the sevenfold Spirit*

rider held a bow, and he was given a crown, and he rode out as a conqueror bent on conquest.   Zec 6:11

³When the Lamb opened the second seal, I heard the second living creature say, "Come!" ⁴Then another horse came out, a fiery red one. Its rider was given power to take peace from the earth and to make men slay each other. To him was given a large sword.   Rev 4:7

⁵When the Lamb opened the third seal, I heard the third living creature say, "Come!" I looked, and there before me was a black horse! Its rider was holding a pair of scales in his hand. ⁶Then I heard what sounded like a voice among the four living creatures, saying, "A quart*a* of wheat for a day's wages,*b* and three quarts of barley for a day's wages,*b* and do not damage the oil and the wine!"

⁷When the Lamb opened the fourth seal, I heard the voice of the fourth living creature say, "Come!" ⁸I looked, and there before me was a pale horse! Its rider was named Death, and Hades was following close behind him. They were given power over a fourth of the earth to kill by sword, famine and plague, and by the wild beasts of the earth.

⁹When he opened the fifth seal, I saw under the altar the souls of those who had been slain because of the word of God and the testimony they had maintained. ¹⁰They called out in a loud voice, "How

long, Sovereign Lord, holy and true, until you judge the inhabitants of the earth and avenge our blood?" ¹¹Then each of them was given a white robe, and they were told to wait a little longer, until the number of their fellow servants and brothers who were to be killed as they had been was completed.

¹²I watched as he opened the sixth seal. There was a great earthquake. The sun turned black like sackcloth made of goat hair, the whole moon turned blood red, ¹³and the stars in the sky fell to earth, as late figs drop from a fig tree when shaken by a strong wind. ¹⁴The sky receded like a scroll, rolling up, and every mountain and island was removed from its place.   Jer 4:24; Rev 8:10

¹⁵Then the kings of the earth, the princes, the generals, the rich, the mighty, and every slave and every free man hid in caves and among the rocks of the mountains. ¹⁶They called to the mountains and the rocks, "Fall on us and hide us from the face of him who sits on the throne and from the wrath of the Lamb! ¹⁷For the great day of their wrath has come, and who can stand?"   Ps 76:7; Zep 1:14-15

144,000 Sealed

7 After this I saw four angels standing at the four corners of the earth, holding back the four winds of the earth to prevent any

---

*a*6 Greek *a choinix* (probably about a liter)   *b*6 Greek *a denarius*

wind from blowing on the land or on the sea or on any tree. ²Then I saw another angel coming up from the east, having the seal of the living God. He called out in a loud voice to the four angels who had been given power to harm the land and the sea: ³"Do not harm the land or the sea or the trees until we put a seal on the foreheads of the servants of our God." ⁴Then I heard the number of those who were sealed: 144,000 from all the tribes of Israel. Rev 9:16; 14:1,3

⁵From the tribe of Judah
    12,000 were sealed,
from the tribe of Reuben
    12,000,
from the tribe of Gad 12,000,
⁶from the tribe of Asher
    12,000,
from the tribe of Naphtali
    12,000,
from the tribe of Manasseh
    12,000,
⁷from the tribe of Simeon
    12,000,
from the tribe of Levi 12,000,
from the tribe of Issachar
    12,000,
⁸from the tribe of Zebulun
    12,000,
from the tribe of Joseph
    12,000,
from the tribe of Benjamin
    12,000.

The Great Multitude in White Robes

⁹After this I looked and there before me was a great multitude that no one could count, from every nation, tribe, people and language, standing before the throne and in front of the Lamb. They were wearing white robes and were holding palm branches in their hands. ¹⁰And they cried out in a loud voice: Rev 5:9

"Salvation belongs to our God,
    who sits on the throne,   Rev 5:1
and to the Lamb."

¹¹All the angels were standing around the throne and around the elders and the four living creatures. They fell down on their faces before the throne and worshiped God, ¹²saying: Rev 4:4,6,10

"Amen!
Praise and glory
    and wisdom and thanks and
        honor
and power and strength
    be to our God for ever and
        ever.
Amen!"   Rev 5:12-14

¹³Then one of the elders asked me, "These in white robes—who are they, and where did they come from?" Rev 3:4

¹⁴I answered, "Sir, you know."

And he said, "These are they who have come out of the great tribulation; they have washed their robes and made them white in the blood of the Lamb. ¹⁵Therefore, Heb 9:14; 1Jn 1:7

"they are before the throne of
God   ver 9
and serve him day and night
in his temple;   Rev 11:19
and he who sits on the throne
will spread his tent over
them.   Rev 21:3
16Never again will they hunger;
never again will they thirst.
The sun will not beat upon
them,
nor any scorching heat.
17For the Lamb at the center of
the throne will be their
shepherd;   Ps 23:1; Jn 10:11
he will lead them to springs
of living water.   Jn 4:10
And God will wipe away every
tear from their eyes."

The Seventh Seal and the Golden Censer

8 When he opened the seventh
seal, there was silence in heav-
en for about half an hour. Rev 6:1
2And I saw the seven angels who
stand before God, and to them
were given seven trumpets.
3Another angel, who had a gold-
en censer, came and stood at the
altar. He was given much incense
to offer, with the prayers of all the
saints, on the golden altar before
the throne. 4The smoke of the incense, together with the prayers of
the saints, went up before God
from the angel's hand. 5Then the
angel took the censer, filled it with
fire from the altar, and hurled it on

the earth; and there came peals of
thunder, rumblings, flashes of
lightning and an earthquake.

The Trumpets

6Then the seven angels who had
the seven trumpets prepared to
sound them.   ver 2
7The first angel sounded his
trumpet, and there came hail and
fire mixed with blood, and it was
hurled down upon the earth. A
third of the earth was burned up,
a third of the trees were burned
up, and all the green grass was
burned up.   Eze 38:22; Rev 9:4
8The second angel sounded his
trumpet, and something like a
huge mountain, all ablaze, was
thrown into the sea. A third of the
sea turned into blood, 9a third of
the living creatures in the sea died,
and a third of the ships were destroyed.   Jer 51:25; Rev 16:3
10The third angel sounded his
trumpet, and a great star, blazing
like a torch, fell from the sky on a
third of the rivers and on the
springs of water— 11the name of
the star is Wormwood.a A third of
the waters turned bitter, and many
people died from the waters that
had become bitter.   Isa 14:12; Rev 16:4
12The fourth angel sounded his
trumpet, and a third of the sun was
struck, a third of the moon, and a
third of the stars, so that a third of
them turned dark. A third of the

a 11 That is, Bitterness

day was without light, and also a third of the night.　　　Ex 10:21-23

[13]As I watched, I heard an eagle that was flying in midair call out in a loud voice: "Woe! Woe! Woe to the inhabitants of the earth, because of the trumpet blasts about to be sounded by the other three angels!"　　　Rev 9:12; 14:6

9 The fifth angel sounded his trumpet, and I saw a star that had fallen from the sky to the earth. The star was given the key to the shaft of the Abyss. [2]When he opened the Abyss, smoke rose from it like the smoke from a gigantic furnace. The sun and sky were darkened by the smoke from the Abyss. [3]And out of the smoke locusts came down upon the earth and were given power like that of scorpions of the earth. [4]They were told not to harm the grass of the earth or any plant or tree, but only those people who did not have the seal of God on their foreheads. [5]They were not given power to kill them, but only to torture them for five months. And the agony they suffered was like that of the sting of a scorpion when it strikes a man. [6]During those days men will seek death, but will not find it; they will long to die, but death will elude them.　　　Jer 8:3; Rev 8:7

[7]The locusts looked like horses prepared for battle. On their heads they wore something like crowns of gold, and their faces resembled human faces. [8]Their hair was like women's hair, and their teeth were like lions' teeth. [9]They had breastplates like breastplates of iron, and the sound of their wings was like the thundering of many horses and chariots rushing into battle. [10]They had tails and stings like scorpions, and in their tails they had power to torment people for five months. [11]They had as king over them the angel of the Abyss, whose name in Hebrew is Abaddon, and in Greek, Apollyon.[a]

[12]The first woe is past; two other woes are yet to come.　　　Rev 8:13

[13]The sixth angel sounded his trumpet, and I heard a voice coming from the horns[b] of the golden altar that is before God. [14]It said to the sixth angel who had the trumpet, "Release the four angels who are bound at the great river Euphrates." [15]And the four angels who had been kept ready for this very hour and day and month and year were released to kill a third of mankind. [16]The number of the mounted troops was two hundred million. I heard their number.

[17]The horses and riders I saw in my vision looked like this: Their breastplates were fiery red, dark blue, and yellow as sulfur. The heads of the horses resembled the heads of lions, and out of their mouths came fire, smoke and sulfur. [18]A third of mankind was killed by the three plagues of fire,

smoke and sulfur that came out of their mouths. ¹⁹The power of the horses was in their mouths and in their tails; for their tails were like snakes, having heads with which they inflict injury. _{Rev 11:5}

²⁰The rest of mankind that were not killed by these plagues still did not repent of the work of their hands; they did not stop worshiping demons, and idols of gold, silver, bronze, stone and wood—idols that cannot see or hear or walk. ²¹Nor did they repent of their murders, their magic arts, their sexual immorality or their thefts.

The Angel and the Little Scroll

10 Then I saw another mighty angel coming down from heaven. He was robed in a cloud, with a rainbow above his head; his face was like the sun, and his legs were like fiery pillars. ²He was holding a little scroll, which lay open in his hand. He planted his right foot on the sea and his left foot on the land, ³and he gave a loud shout like the roar of a lion. When he shouted, the voices of the seven thunders spoke. ⁴And when the seven thunders spoke, I was about to write; but I heard a voice from heaven say, "Seal up what the seven thunders have said and do not write it down." _{Da 8:26}

⁵Then the angel I had seen standing on the sea and on the land raised his right hand to heaven. ⁶And he swore by him who lives for ever and ever, who creat-

ed the heavens and all that is in them, the earth and all that is in it, and the sea and all that is in it, and said, "There will be no more delay! ⁷But in the days when the seventh angel is about to sound his trumpet, the mystery of God will be accomplished, just as he announced to his servants the prophets."

⁸Then the voice that I had heard from heaven spoke to me once more: "Go, take the scroll that lies open in the hand of the angel who is standing on the sea and on the land." _{ver 2,4}

⁹So I went to the angel and asked him to give me the little scroll. He said to me, "Take it and eat it. It will turn your stomach sour, but in your mouth it will be as sweet as honey." ¹⁰I took the little scroll from the angel's hand and ate it. It tasted as sweet as honey in my mouth, but when I had eaten it, my stomach turned sour. ¹¹Then I was told, "You must prophesy again about many peoples, nations, languages and kings." _{Jer 15:16; Eze 2:8-3:3}

The Two Witnesses

11 I was given a reed like a measuring rod and was told, "Go and measure the temple of God and the altar, and count the worshipers there. ²But exclude the outer court; do not measure it, because it has been given to the Gentiles. They will trample on the holy city for 42 months. ³And I will give power to my two witnesses, and they will prophesy for 1,260 days, clothed in sackcloth." [4]These are the two olive trees and the two lampstands that stand before the Lord of the earth. [5]If anyone tries to harm them, fire comes from their mouths and devours their enemies. This is how anyone who wants to harm them must die. [6]These men have power to shut up the sky so that it will not rain during the time they are prophesying; and they have power to turn the waters into blood and to strike the earth with every kind of plague as often as they want. Rev 13:5; Zec 4:14 [7]Now when they have finished their testimony, the beast that comes up from the Abyss will attack them, and overpower and kill them. [8]Their bodies will lie in the street of the great city, which is figuratively called Sodom and Egypt, where also their Lord was crucified. [9]For three and a half days men from every people, tribe, language and nation will gaze on their bodies and refuse them burial. [10]The inhabitants of the earth will gloat over them and will celebrate by sending each other gifts, because these two prophets had tormented those who live on the earth. Est 9:19,22; Da 7:21 [11]But after the three and a half days a breath of life from God entered them, and they stood on their feet, and terror struck those who saw them. [12]Then they heard a loud voice from heaven saying to them, "Come up here." And they went up to heaven in a cloud, while their enemies looked on. [13]At that very hour there was a severe earthquake and a tenth of the city collapsed. Seven thousand people were killed in the earthquake, and the survivors were terrified and gave glory to the God of heaven. Rev 6:12; 16:11 [14]The second woe has passed; the third woe is coming soon.

The Seventh Trumpet

[15]The seventh angel sounded his trumpet, and there were loud voices in heaven, which said:

"The kingdom of the world has
    become the kingdom of
    our Lord and of his
    Christ,   Rev 12:10
    and he will reign for ever
        and ever."

[16]And the twenty-four elders, who were seated on their thrones before God, fell on their faces and worshiped God, [17]saying: Rev 4:4

"We give thanks to you, Lord
    God Almighty,   Rev 1:8
    the One who is and who
        was,   Rev 1:4
    because you have taken your
        great power
    and have begun to reign.
[18]The nations were angry;   Ps 2:1
    and your wrath has come.
The time has come for judging
        the dead,
    and for rewarding your
        servants the prophets

and your saints and those who
reverence your name,
both small and great—
and for destroying those who
destroy the earth."

¹⁹Then God's temple in heaven
was opened, and within his temple
was seen the ark of his covenant.
And there came flashes of lightning, rumblings, peals of thunder,
an earthquake and a great hail-
storm.   Rev 15:5,8; 16:21

The Woman and the Dragon

12 A great and wondrous sign
appeared in heaven: a
woman clothed with the sun, with
the moon under her feet and a
crown of twelve stars on her head.
²She was pregnant and cried out in
pain as she was about to give birth.
³Then another sign appeared in
heaven: an enormous red dragon
with seven heads and ten horns
and seven crowns on his heads.
⁴His tail swept a third of the stars
out of the sky and flung them to
the earth. The dragon stood in
front of the woman who was about
to give birth, so that he might devour her child the moment it was
born. ⁵She gave birth to a son, a
male child, who will rule all the
nations with an iron scepter. And
her child was snatched up to God
and to his throne. ⁶The woman
fled into the desert to a place prepared for her by God, where she
might be taken care of for 1,260
days.   Da 8:10; Rev 11:2

⁷And there was war in heaven.
Michael and his angels fought
against the dragon, and the dragon
and his angels fought back. ⁸But
he was not strong enough, and
they lost their place in heaven.
⁹The great dragon was hurled
down—that ancient serpent called
the devil, or Satan, who leads the
whole world astray. He was hurled
to the earth, and his angels with
him.   Jn 12:31; Rev 20:3,8,10
¹⁰Then I heard a loud voice in
heaven say: Rev 11:15

"Now have come the salvation
and the power and the
kingdom of our God,
and the authority of his
Christ.
For the accuser of our
brothers,   Job 1:9-11; Zec 3:1
who accuses them before
our God day and night,
has been hurled down.
¹¹They overcame him   Jn 16:33
by the blood of the Lamb
and by the word of their
testimony;   Rev 6:9
they did not love their lives so
much
as to shrink from death.
¹²Therefore rejoice, you heavens
and you who dwell in them!
But woe to the earth and the
sea,   Rev 10:6
because the devil has gone
down to you!
He is filled with fury,
because he knows that his
time is short."

¹³When the dragon saw that he had been hurled to the earth, he pursued the woman who had given birth to the male child. ¹⁴The woman was given the two wings of a great eagle, so that she might fly to the place prepared for her in the desert, where she would be taken care of for a time, times and half a time, out of the serpent's reach. ¹⁵Then from his mouth the serpent spewed water like a river, to overtake the woman and sweep her away with the torrent. ¹⁶But the earth helped the woman by opening its mouth and swallowing the river that the dragon had spewed out of his mouth. ¹⁷Then the dragon was enraged at the woman and went off to make war against the rest of her offspring—those who obey God's commandments and hold to the testimony of Jesus.

13 ¹And the dragon*ᵃ* stood on the shore of the sea.

The Beast out of the Sea

And I saw a beast coming out of the sea. He had ten horns and seven heads, with ten crowns on his horns, and on each head a blasphemous name. ²The beast I saw resembled a leopard, but had feet like those of a bear and a mouth like that of a lion. The dragon gave the beast his power and his throne and great authority. ³One of the heads of the beast seemed to have had a fatal wound, but the fatal wound had been healed. The whole world was astonished and followed the beast. ⁴Men worshiped the dragon because he had given authority to the beast, and they also worshiped the beast and asked, "Who is like the beast? Who can make war against him?"

⁵The beast was given a mouth to utter proud words and blasphemies and to exercise his authority for forty-two months. ⁶He opened his mouth to blaspheme God, and to slander his name and his dwelling place and those who live in heaven. ⁷He was given power to make war against the saints and to conquer them. And he was given authority over every tribe, people, language and nation. ⁸All inhabitants of the earth will worship the beast—all whose names have not been written in the book of life belonging to the Lamb that was slain from the creation of the world.*ᵇ*

⁹He who has an ear, let him hear.

Rev 2:7

¹⁰If anyone is to go into
    captivity,
  into captivity he will go.
If anyone is to be killed*ᶜ* with
    the sword,
  with the sword he will be
    killed.

This calls for patient endurance

---

*ᵃ*1 Some late manuscripts *And I* *ᵇ*8 Or *written from the creation of the world in the book of life belonging to the Lamb that was slain* *ᶜ*10 Some manuscripts *anyone kills*

and faithfulness on the part of the saints. Heb 6:12; Rev 14:12

The Beast out of the Earth

¹¹Then I saw another beast, coming out of the earth. He had two horns like a lamb, but he spoke like a dragon. ¹²He exercised all the authority of the first beast on his behalf, and made the earth and its inhabitants worship the first beast, whose fatal wound had been healed. ¹³And he performed great and miraculous signs, even causing fire to come down from heaven to earth in full view of men. ¹⁴Because of the signs he was given power to do on behalf of the first beast, he deceived the inhabitants of the earth. He ordered them to set up an image in honor of the beast who was wounded by the sword and yet lived. ¹⁵He was given power to give breath to the image of the first beast, so that it could speak and cause all who refused to worship the image to be killed. ¹⁶He also forced everyone, small and great, rich and poor, free and slave, to receive a mark on his right hand or on his forehead, ¹⁷so that no one could buy or sell unless he had the mark, which is the name of the beast or the number of his name.

¹⁸This calls for wisdom. If anyone has insight, let him calculate the number of the beast, for it is man's number. His number is 666.

The Lamb and the 144,000

14 Then I looked, and there before me was the Lamb, standing on Mount Zion, and with him 144,000 who had his name and his Father's name written on their foreheads. ²And I heard a sound from heaven like the roar of rushing waters and like a loud peal of thunder. The sound I heard was like that of harpists playing their harps. ³And they sang a new song before the throne and before the four living creatures and the elders. No one could learn the song except the 144,000 who had been redeemed from the earth. ⁴These are those who did not defile themselves with women, for they kept themselves pure. They follow the Lamb wherever he goes. They were purchased from among men and offered as firstfruits to God and the Lamb. ⁵No lie was found in their mouths; they are blameless.

The Three Angels

⁶Then I saw another angel flying in midair, and he had the eternal gospel to proclaim to those who live on the earth—to every nation, tribe, language and people. ⁷He said in a loud voice, "Fear God and give him glory, because the hour of his judgment has come. Worship him who made the heavens, the earth, the sea and the springs of water." Rev 8:10; 15:4

⁸A second angel followed and said, "Fallen! Fallen is Babylon the

Great, which made all the nations drink the maddening wine of her adulteries."   Isa 21:9; Jer 51:8

9A third angel followed them and said in a loud voice: "If anyone worships the beast and his image and receives his mark on the forehead or on the hand, 10he, too, will drink of the wine of God's fury, which has been poured full strength into the cup of his wrath. He will be tormented with burning sulfur in the presence of the holy angels and of the Lamb. 11And the smoke of their torment rises for ever and ever. There is no rest day or night for those who worship the beast and his image, or for anyone who receives the mark of his name." 12This calls for patient endurance on the part of the saints who obey God's commandments and remain faithful to Jesus.

13Then I heard a voice from heaven say, "Write: Blessed are the dead who die in the Lord from now on."   1Co 15:18; 1Th 4:16

"Yes," says the Spirit, "they will rest from their labor, for their deeds will follow them."   Rev 2:7

The Harvest of the Earth

14I looked, and there before me was a white cloud, and seated on the cloud was one "like a son of man"a with a crown of gold on his head and a sharp sickle in his hand. 15Then another angel came out of the temple and called in a loud voice to him who was sitting on the cloud, "Take your sickle and reap, because the time to reap has come, for the harvest of the earth is ripe." 16So he who was seated on the cloud swung his sickle over the earth, and the earth was harvested.   Jer 51:33; Joel 3:13

17Another angel came out of the temple in heaven, and he too had a sharp sickle. 18Still another angel, who had charge of the fire, came from the altar and called in a loud voice to him who had the sharp sickle, "Take your sharp sickle and gather the clusters of grapes from the earth's vine, because its grapes are ripe." 19The angel swung his sickle on the earth, gathered its grapes and threw them into the great winepress of God's wrath. 20They were trampled in the winepress outside the city, and blood flowed out of the press, rising as high as the horses' bridles for a distance of 1,600 stadia.b   Heb 13:12; Rev 19:15

Seven Angels With Seven Plagues

15 I saw in heaven another great and marvelous sign: seven angels with the seven last plagues—last, because with them God's wrath is completed. 2And I saw what looked like a sea of glass mixed with fire and, standing be-

a 14 Daniel 7:13   b 20 That is, about 180 miles (about 300 kilometers)

side the sea, those who had been victorious over the beast and his image and over the number of his name. They held harps given them by God ³and sang the song of Moses the servant of God and the song of the Lamb: Rev 4:6; 13:14

"Great and marvelous are your
        deeds, Ps 111:2
    Lord God Almighty. Rev 1:8
Just and true are your
        ways,
    King of the ages.
⁴Who will not fear you,
        O Lord,
    and bring glory to your
        name? Ps 86:9
For you alone are holy.
All nations will come
    and worship before you,
for your righteous acts have
        been revealed." Rev 19:8

⁵After this I looked and in heaven the temple, that is, the tabernacle of the Testimony, was opened. ⁶Out of the temple came the seven angels with the seven plagues. They were dressed in clean, shining linen and wore golden sashes around their chests. ⁷Then one of the four living creatures gave to the seven angels seven golden bowls filled with the wrath of God, who lives for ever and ever. ⁸And the temple was filled with smoke from the glory of God and from his power, and no one could enter the temple until the seven plagues of the seven angels were completed.

The Seven Bowls of God's Wrath

16 Then I heard a loud voice from the temple saying to the seven angels, "Go, pour out the seven bowls of God's wrath on the earth." Rev 15:1

²The first angel went and poured out his bowl on the land, and ugly and painful sores broke out on the people who had the mark of the beast and worshiped his image. Rev 8:7; 13:15-17

³The second angel poured out his bowl on the sea, and it turned into blood like that of a dead man, and every living thing in the sea died. Ex 7:17-21; Rev 8:8-9

⁴The third angel poured out his bowl on the rivers and springs of water, and they became blood. ⁵Then I heard the angel in charge of the waters say: Ex 7:17-21; Rev 8:10

"You are just in these
        judgments, Rev 15:3
    you who are and who were,
        the Holy One, Rev 1:4; 15:4
because you have so judged;
⁶for they have shed the blood of
        your saints and
        prophets, Lk 11:49-51
and you have given them
        blood to drink as they
        deserve."

⁷And I heard the altar respond:

"Yes, Lord God Almighty,
    true and just are your
        judgments." Isa 49:26

⁸The fourth angel poured out his bowl on the sun, and the sun was given power to scorch people with fire. ⁹They were seared by the intense heat and they cursed the name of God, who had control over these plagues, but they refused to repent and glorify him.

¹⁰The fifth angel poured out his bowl on the throne of the beast, and his kingdom was plunged into darkness. Men gnawed their tongues in agony ¹¹and cursed the God of heaven because of their pains and their sores, but they refused to repent of what they had done.   Rev 9:2; 13:2

¹²The sixth angel poured out his bowl on the great river Euphrates, and its water was dried up to prepare the way for the kings from the East. ¹³Then I saw three evil*a* spirits that looked like frogs; they came out of the mouth of the dragon, out of the mouth of the beast and out of the mouth of the false prophet. ¹⁴They are spirits of demons performing miraculous signs, and they go out to the kings of the whole world, to gather them for the battle on the great day of God Almighty.   1Ti 4:1; Rev 17:14

¹⁵"Behold, I come like a thief! Blessed is he who stays awake and keeps his clothes with him, so that he may not go naked and be shamefully exposed."   Lk 12:37

¹⁶Then they gathered the kings together to the place that in Hebrew is called Armageddon.

¹⁷The seventh angel poured out his bowl into the air, and out of the temple came a loud voice from the throne, saying, "It is done!" ¹⁸Then there came flashes of lightning, rumblings, peals of thunder and a severe earthquake. No earthquake like it has ever occurred since man has been on earth, so tremendous was the quake. ¹⁹The great city split into three parts, and the cities of the nations collapsed. God remembered Babylon the Great and gave her the cup filled with the wine of the fury of his wrath. ²⁰Every island fled away and the mountains could not be found. ²¹From the sky huge hailstones of about a hundred pounds each fell upon men. And they cursed God on account of the plague of hail, because the plague was so terrible.

The Woman on the Beast

17 One of the seven angels who had the seven bowls came and said to me, "Come, I will show you the punishment of the great prostitute, who sits on many waters. ²With her the kings of the earth committed adultery and the inhabitants of the earth were intoxicated with the wine of her adulteries."   Jer 51:13; Rev 16:19

³Then the angel carried me away in the Spirit into a desert. There I saw a woman sitting on a

a 13 Greek *unclean*

scarlet beast that was covered with blasphemous names and had seven heads and ten horns. ⁴The woman was dressed in purple and scarlet, and was glittering with gold, precious stones and pearls. She held a golden cup in her hand, filled with abominable things and the filth of her adulteries. ⁵This title was written on her forehead:

MYSTERY

BABYLON THE GREAT

THE MOTHER OF PROSTITUTES

AND OF THE ABOMINATIONS OF THE

EARTH.

⁶I saw that the woman was drunk with the blood of the saints, the blood of those who bore testimony to Jesus.   Rev 18:24

When I saw her, I was greatly astonished. ⁷Then the angel said to me: "Why are you astonished? I will explain to you the mystery of the woman and of the beast she rides, which has the seven heads and ten horns. ⁸The beast, which you saw, once was, now is not, and will come up out of the Abyss and go to his destruction. The inhabitants of the earth whose names have not been written in the book of life from the creation of the world will be astonished when they see the beast, because he once was, now is not, and yet will come.   Rev 13:3,10

⁹"This calls for a mind with wisdom. The seven heads are seven hills on which the woman sits. ¹⁰They are also seven kings. Five have fallen, one is, the other has not yet come; but when he does come, he must remain for a little while. ¹¹The beast who once was, and now is not, is an eighth king. He belongs to the seven and is going to his destruction.   Rev 13:18

¹²"The ten horns you saw are ten kings who have not yet received a kingdom, but who for one hour will receive authority as kings along with the beast. ¹³They have one purpose and will give their power and authority to the beast. ¹⁴They will make war against the Lamb, but the Lamb will overcome them because he is Lord of lords and King of kings— and with him will be his called, chosen and faithful followers."

¹⁵Then the angel said to me, "The waters you saw, where the prostitute sits, are peoples, multitudes, nations and languages. ¹⁶The beast and the ten horns you saw will hate the prostitute. They will bring her to ruin and leave her naked; they will eat her flesh and burn her with fire. ¹⁷For God has put it into their hearts to accomplish his purpose by agreeing to give the beast their power to rule, until God's words are fulfilled. ¹⁸The woman you saw is the great city that rules over the kings of the earth."   Rev 10:7; 16:19

The Fall of Babylon

18 After this I saw another angel coming down from heaven. He had great authority, and the earth was illuminated by his splendor. ²With a mighty voice he shouted: Eze 43:2; Rev 17:1

"Fallen! Fallen is Babylon the
    Great!   Rev 14:8
She has become a home for
    demons
and a haunt for every evil[a]
    spirit,   Rev 16:13
a haunt for every unclean
    and detestable bird.
³For all the nations have drunk
    the maddening wine of her
    adulteries.   Rev 14:8
The kings of the earth
    committed adultery with
    her,   Rev 17:2
and the merchants of the
    earth grew rich from her
    excessive luxuries."

⁴Then I heard another voice from heaven say:

"Come out of her, my people,
    so that you will not share in
    her sins,
    so that you will not receive
    any of her plagues;
⁵for her sins are piled up to
    heaven,   Jer 51:9
and God has remembered
    her crimes.   Rev 16:19
⁶Give back to her as she has
    given;
pay her back double for
    what she has done.
Mix her a double portion
    from her own cup.

⁷Give her as much torture and
    grief
    as the glory and luxury she
    gave herself.   Eze 28:2-8
In her heart she boasts,
    'I sit as queen; I am not a
    widow,
    and I will never mourn.'
⁸Therefore in one day her
    plagues will overtake
    her: Isa 47:9
death, mourning and famine.
She will be consumed by fire,
    for mighty is the Lord God
    who judges her.

⁹"When the kings of the earth who committed adultery with her and shared her luxury see the smoke of her burning, they will weep and mourn over her. ¹⁰Terrified at her torment, they will stand far off and cry: Eze 26:17-18; Rev 19:3

" 'Woe! Woe, O great city,
    O Babylon, city of power!
In one hour your doom has
    come!'   Rev 17:12

¹¹"The merchants of the earth will weep and mourn over her because no one buys their cargoes any more— ¹²cargoes of gold, silver, precious stones and pearls; fine linen, purple, silk and scarlet cloth; every sort of citron wood, and articles of every kind made of ivory, costly wood, bronze, iron and marble; ¹³cargoes of cinnamon and spice, of incense, myrrh

_____
a 2 Greek *unclean*

and frankincense, of wine and olive oil, of fine flour and wheat; cattle and sheep; horses and carriages; and bodies and souls of men.   Eze 27:13; Rev 17:4

¹⁴"They will say, 'The fruit you longed for is gone from you. All your riches and splendor have vanished, never to be recovered.' ¹⁵The merchants who sold these things and gained their wealth from her will stand far off, terrified at her torment. They will weep and mourn ¹⁶and cry out: Eze 27:31

" 'Woe! Woe, O great city,
    dressed in fine linen, purple
        and scarlet,
    and glittering with gold,
        precious stones and
        pearls!   Rev 17:4
¹⁷In one hour such great wealth
    has been brought to
    ruin!'   Rev 17:12,16

"Every sea captain, and all who travel by ship, the sailors, and all who earn their living from the sea, will stand far off. ¹⁸When they see the smoke of her burning, they will exclaim, 'Was there ever a city like this great city?' ¹⁹They will throw dust on their heads, and with weeping and mourning cry out:

" 'Woe! Woe, O great city,
    where all who had ships on
        the sea
    became rich through her
        wealth!
In one hour she has been
    brought to ruin!   Rev 17:16

²⁰Rejoice over her, O heaven!
    Rejoice, saints and apostles
        and prophets!
    God has judged her for the
        way she treated you.' "

²¹Then a mighty angel picked up a boulder the size of a large millstone and threw it into the sea, and said: Jer 51:63; Rev 5:2

"With such violence
    the great city of Babylon will
        be thrown down,
    never to be found again.
²²The music of harpists and
        musicians, flute players
        and trumpeters,
    will never be heard in you
        again.   Eze 26:13
No workman of any trade
    will ever be found in you
        again.
The sound of a millstone
    will never be heard in you
        again.   Jer 25:10
²³The light of a lamp
    will never shine in you
        again.
The voice of bridegroom and
        bride
    will never be heard in you
        again.   Jer 7:34
Your merchants were the
        world's great men.
    By your magic spell all the
        nations were led astray.
²⁴In her was found the blood of
        prophets and of the
        saints,   Rev 17:6
    and of all who have been
        killed on the earth."

Hallelujah!

19 After this I heard what sounded like the roar of a great multitude in heaven shouting: Rev 11:15

"Hallelujah!
Salvation and glory and power
       belong to our God,
2   for true and just are his
       judgments.   Rev 16:7
He has condemned the great
       prostitute   Rev 17:1
who corrupted the earth by
       her adulteries.
He has avenged on her the
       blood of his servants."

3And again they shouted:

"Hallelujah!
The smoke from her goes up
       for ever and ever."

4The twenty-four elders and the four living creatures fell down and worshiped God, who was seated on the throne. And they cried:

"Amen, Hallelujah!"

5Then a voice came from the throne, saying:

"Praise our God,
     all you his servants,   Ps 134:1
you who fear him,
     both small and great!"

6Then I heard what sounded like a great multitude, like the roar of rushing waters and like loud peals of thunder, shouting: Rev 11:15

"Hallelujah!

For our Lord God Almighty
       reigns.   Rev 1:8
7Let us rejoice and be glad
     and give him glory!   Rev 11:13
For the wedding of the Lamb
     has come,   Mt 22:2; Eph 5:32
and his bride has made
     herself ready.   Rev 21:2,9
8Fine linen, bright and clean,
     was given her to wear."
(Fine linen stands for the righteous acts of the saints.)   Rev 15:4

9Then the angel said to me, "Write: 'Blessed are those who are invited to the wedding supper of the Lamb!' " And he added, "These are the true words of God."

10At this I fell at his feet to worship him. But he said to me, "Do not do it! I am a fellow servant with you and with your brothers who hold to the testimony of Jesus. Worship God! For the testimony of Jesus is the spirit of prophecy."   Rev 22:8-9

The Rider on the White Horse

11I saw heaven standing open and there before me was a white horse, whose rider is called Faithful and True. With justice he judges and makes war. 12His eyes are like blazing fire, and on his head are many crowns. He has a name written on him that no one knows but he himself. 13He is dressed in a robe dipped in blood, and his name is the Word of God. 14The armies of heaven were following him, riding on white horses and dressed in fine linen, white and clean. ¹⁵Out of his mouth comes a sharp sword with which to strike down the nations. "He will rule them with an iron scepter."ᵃ He treads the winepress of the fury of the wrath of God Almighty. ¹⁶On his robe and on his thigh he has this name written:

KING OF KINGS AND LORD OF LORDS.

¹⁷And I saw an angel standing in the sun, who cried in a loud voice to all the birds flying in midair, "Come, gather together for the great supper of God, ¹⁸so that you may eat the flesh of kings, generals, and mighty men, of horses and their riders, and the flesh of all people, free and slave, small and great."   Eze 39:17-20

¹⁹Then I saw the beast and the kings of the earth and their armies gathered together to make war against the rider on the horse and his army. ²⁰But the beast was captured, and with him the false prophet who had performed the miraculous signs on his behalf. With these signs he had deluded those who had received the mark of the beast and worshiped his image. The two of them were thrown alive into the fiery lake of burning sulfur. ²¹The rest of them were killed with the sword that came out of the mouth of the rider on the horse, and all the birds gorged themselves on their flesh.   Da 7:11

The Thousand Years

20 And I saw an angel coming down out of heaven, having the key to the Abyss and holding in his hand a great chain. ²He seized the dragon, that ancient serpent, who is the devil, or Satan, and bound him for a thousand years. ³He threw him into the Abyss, and locked and sealed it over him, to keep him from deceiving the nations anymore until the thousand years were ended. After that, he must be set free for a short time.   Da 6:17; Rev 12:9

⁴I saw thrones on which were seated those who had been given authority to judge. And I saw the souls of those who had been beheaded because of their testimony for Jesus and because of the word of God. They had not worshiped the beast or his image and had not received his mark on their foreheads or their hands. They came to life and reigned with Christ a thousand years. ⁵(The rest of the dead did not come to life until the thousand years were ended.) This is the first resurrection. ⁶Blessed and holy are those who have part in the first resurrection. The second death has no power over them, but they will be priests of God and of Christ and will reign with him for a thousand years.   Rev 1:6; 2:11

Satan's Doom

⁷When the thousand years are

ᵃ *15* Psalm 2:9

over, Satan will be released from his prison ⁸and will go out to deceive the nations in the four corners of the earth—Gog and Magog—to gather them for battle. In number they are like the sand on the seashore. ⁹They marched across the breadth of the earth and surrounded the camp of God's people, the city he loves. But fire came down from heaven and devoured them. ¹⁰And the devil, who deceived them, was thrown into the lake of burning sulfur, where the beast and the false prophet had been thrown. They will be tormented day and night for ever and ever.   Eze 38:9,16; Rev 14:10-11

The Dead Are Judged

¹¹Then I saw a great white throne and him who was seated on it. Earth and sky fled from his presence, and there was no place for them. ¹²And I saw the dead, great and small, standing before the throne, and books were opened. Another book was opened, which is the book of life. The dead were judged according to what they had done as recorded in the books. ¹³The sea gave up the dead that were in it, and death and Hades gave up the dead that were in them, and each person was judged according to what he had done. ¹⁴Then death and Hades were thrown into the lake of fire. The lake of fire is the second death. ¹⁵If anyone's name was not found written in the book of life, he was thrown into the lake of fire.

The New Jerusalem

21 Then I saw a new heaven and a new earth, for the first heaven and the first earth had passed away, and there was no longer any sea. ²I saw the Holy City, the new Jerusalem, coming down out of heaven from God, prepared as a bride beautifully dressed for her husband. ³And I heard a loud voice from the throne saying, "Now the dwelling of God is with men, and he will live with them. They will be his people, and God himself will be with them and be their God. ⁴He will wipe every tear from their eyes. There will be no more death or mourning or crying or pain, for the old order of things has passed away."   Isa 35:10

⁵He who was seated on the throne said, "I am making everything new!" Then he said, "Write this down, for these words are trustworthy and true."   Rev 4:9; 19:9

⁶He said to me: "It is done. I am the Alpha and the Omega, the Beginning and the End. To him who is thirsty I will give to drink without cost from the spring of the water of life. ⁷He who overcomes will inherit all this, and I will be his God and he will be my son. ⁸But the cowardly, the unbelieving, the vile, the murderers, the sexually immoral, those who practice mag-

ic arts, the idolaters and all liars—their place will be in the fiery lake of burning sulfur. This is the second death." Rev 1:8; 16:17

⁹One of the seven angels who had the seven bowls full of the seven last plagues came and said to me, "Come, I will show you the bride, the wife of the Lamb." ¹⁰And he carried me away in the Spirit to a mountain great and high, and showed me the Holy City, Jerusalem, coming down out of heaven from God. ¹¹It shone with the glory of God, and its brilliance was like that of a very precious jewel, like a jasper, clear as crystal. ¹²It had a great, high wall with twelve gates, and with twelve angels at the gates. On the gates were written the names of the twelve tribes of Israel. ¹³There were three gates on the east, three on the north, three on the south and three on the west. ¹⁴The wall of the city had twelve foundations, and on them were the names of the twelve apostles of the Lamb. Eze 48:30-34; Rev 15:1,6-7

¹⁵The angel who talked with me had a measuring rod of gold to measure the city, its gates and its walls. ¹⁶The city was laid out like a square, as long as it was wide. He measured the city with the rod and found it to be 12,000 stadia[a] in length, and as wide and high as it is long. ¹⁷He measured its wall and it was 144 cubits[b] thick,[c] by man's measurement, which the angel was using. ¹⁸The wall was made of jasper, and the city of pure gold, as pure as glass. ¹⁹The foundations of the city walls were decorated with every kind of precious stone. The first foundation was jasper, the second sapphire, the third chalcedony, the fourth emerald, ²⁰the fifth sardonyx, the sixth carnelian, the seventh chrysolite, the eighth beryl, the ninth topaz, the tenth chrysoprase, the eleventh jacinth, and the twelfth amethyst.[d] ²¹The twelve gates were twelve pearls, each gate made of a single pearl. The great street of the city was of pure gold, like transparent glass.

²²I did not see a temple in the city, because the Lord God Almighty and the Lamb are its temple. ²³The city does not need the sun or the moon to shine on it, for the glory of God gives it light, and the Lamb is its lamp. ²⁴The nations will walk by its light, and the kings of the earth will bring their splendor into it. ²⁵On no day will its gates ever be shut, for there will be no night there. ²⁶The glory and honor of the nations will be brought into it. ²⁷Nothing impure will ever enter it, nor will anyone who does what is shameful or deceitful, but only those whose names are written in the Lamb's book of life. Isa 24:23; 52:1; Rev 22:14-15

a 16 That is, about 1,400 miles (about 2,200 kilometers)   b 17 That is, about 200 feet (about 65 meters)   c 17 Or high   d 20 The precise identification of some of these precious stones is uncertain.

The River of Life

22 Then the angel showed me the river of the water of life, as clear as crystal, flowing from the throne of God and of the Lamb ²down the middle of the great street of the city. On each side of the river stood the tree of life, bearing twelve crops of fruit, yielding its fruit every month. And the leaves of the tree are for the healing of the nations. ³No longer will there be any curse. The throne of God and of the Lamb will be in the city, and his servants will serve him. ⁴They will see his face, and his name will be on their foreheads. ⁵There will be no more night. They will not need the light of a lamp or the light of the sun, for the Lord God will give them light. And they will reign for ever and ever.   Eze 47:1; Zec 14:11; Rev 21:23

⁶The angel said to me, "These words are trustworthy and true. The Lord, the God of the spirits of the prophets, sent his angel to show his servants the things that must soon take place."   Rev 1:1; 19:9

Jesus Is Coming

⁷"Behold, I am coming soon! Blessed is he who keeps the words of the prophecy in this book."

⁸I, John, am the one who heard and saw these things. And when I had heard and seen them, I fell down to worship at the feet of the angel who had been showing them to me. ⁹But he said to me, "Do not do it! I am a fellow servant with you and with your brothers the prophets and of all who keep the words of this book. Worship God!"

¹⁰Then he told me, "Do not seal up the words of the prophecy of this book, because the time is near. ¹¹Let him who does wrong continue to do wrong; let him who is vile continue to be vile; let him who does right continue to do right; and let him who is holy continue to be holy."   Eze 3:27; Da 8:26

¹²"Behold, I am coming soon! My reward is with me, and I will give to everyone according to what he has done. ¹³I am the Alpha and the Omega, the First and the Last, the Beginning and the End.

¹⁴"Blessed are those who wash their robes, that they may have the right to the tree of life and may go through the gates into the city. ¹⁵Outside are the dogs, those who practice magic arts, the sexually immoral, the murderers, the idolaters and everyone who loves and practices falsehood.   Gal 5:19-21

¹⁶"I, Jesus, have sent my angel to give you*a* this testimony for the churches. I am the Root and the Offspring of David, and the bright Morning Star."   2Pe 1:19; Rev 1:1

¹⁷The Spirit and the bride say, "Come!" And let him who hears

---

a 16 The Greek is plural.

say, "Come!" Whoever is thirsty, let him come; and whoever wishes, let him take the free gift of the water of life.   Rev 2:7

¹⁸I warn everyone who hears the words of the prophecy of this book: If anyone adds anything to them, God will add to him the plagues described in this book. ¹⁹And if anyone takes words away from this book of prophecy, God will take away from him his share in the tree of life and in the holy city, which are described in this book.   Dt 4:2; Pr 30:6

²⁰He who testifies to these things says, "Yes, I am coming soon."   Rev 1:2

Amen. Come, Lord Jesus.

²¹The grace of the Lord Jesus be with God's people. Amen.   Ro 16:20

Table
of Weights
and
Measures

Table of Weights and Measures

BIBLICAL UNIT		APPROXIMATE AMERICAN EQUIVALENT	APPROXIMATE METRIC EQUIVALENT
WEIGHTS			
talent	*(60 minas)*	75 pounds	34 kilograms
mina	*(50 shekels)*	1 1/4 pounds	0.6 kilogram
shekel	*(2 bekas)*	2/5 ounce	11.5 grams
pim	*(2/3 shekel)*	1/3 ounce	7.6 grams
beka	*(10 gerahs)*	1/5 ounce	5.5 grams
gerah		1/50 ounce	0.6 gram
LENGTH			
cubit		18 inches	0.5 meter
span		9 inches	23 centimeters
handbreadth		3 inches	8 centimeters
CAPACITY			
Dry Measure			
cor [homer]	*(10 ephahs)*	6 bushels	220 liters
lethek	*(5 ephahs)*	3 bushels	110 liters
ephah	*(10 omers)*	3/5 bushel	22 liters
seah	*(1/3 ephah)*	7 quarts	7.3 liters
omer	*(1/10 ephah)*	2 quarts	2 liters
cab	*(1/18 ephah)*	1 quart	1 liter
Liquid Measure			
bath	*(1 ephah)*	6 gallons	22 liters
hin	*(1/6 bath)*	4 quarts	4 liters
log	*(1/72 bath)*	1/3 quart	0.3 liter

The figures of the table are calculated on the basis of a shekel equaling 11.5 grams, a cubit equaling 18 inches and an ephah equaling 22 liters. The quart referred to is either a dry quart (slightly larger than a liter) or a liquid quart (slightly smaller than a liter), whichever is applicable. The ton referred to in the footnotes is the American ton of 2,000 pounds.

This table is based upon the best available information, but it is not intended to be mathematically precise; like the measurement equivalents in the footnotes, it merely gives approximate amounts and distances. Weights and measures differed somewhat at various times and places in the ancient world. There is uncertainty particularly about the ephah and the bath; further discoveries may give more light on these units of capacity.

Bible Study Helps

Introductions to the Books of the Bible

Pentateuch

The first five books of the Bible are called the Pentateuch—a word that means "five books." They are also known as the books of the law because they contain the laws and instruction God gave Moses for the people of Israel. These books were most likely written by Moses, except for the last chapter of Deuteronomy which tells about Moses' death.

Genesis. The word Genesis means "beginning." The book of Genesis is about many beginnings—the beginning of the universe, the beginning of man and woman, the beginning of human sin, and the beginning of God's promises of salvation. Genesis tells us about God's special people and his plan for their lives. We learn about Adam and Eve, Noah, Abraham, Isaac, Jacob, and Joseph and his brothers.

Exodus. The word Exodus means "going out." Exodus continues the story of God's chosen people, the nation of Israel. It tells how God called Moses to lead the people out of slavery in Egypt to the promised land of Canaan. Through the miracles of the ten plagues and the crossing of the Red Sea, God showed his people that he was more powerful than any Egyptian Pharaoh.

While the people of Israel were traveling in the desert, God gave them a set of rules to follow, including the Ten Commandments. God continually reminded his people that they would be a great nation if they loved and worshiped only him and obeyed his laws.

Leviticus means "about the Levites." The Levites were God's priests, and the book of Leviticus contains many of the rules they needed to do their work—rules for worshiping God and for making sacrifices. In Leviticus 11:45 God says, "Be holy, because I am holy." The rules God gave Israel in the book of Leviticus helped the people live holy lives.

Numbers gets its name from the two accounts in chapters 1 and 26 of the numberings or countings of the people of Israel.

The rest of the book tells about the 38 years of wandering in the desert. God's continual care for his people is shown throughout the book of Numbers. He miraculously supplied them with water, manna, and quails. He continued to love and forgive the people even when they complained, grumbled, and rebelled against him.

Deuteronomy means "second law." After forty years the Israelites were about to enter the promised land of Canaan. Before they did, Moses wanted to remind them about all that God had done for them and about the laws they must continue to obey as God's chosen people. He also emphasized that they must also teach their children to love and obey God. Deuteronomy ends with the renewal of God's covenant with Israel (chapter 29), Joshua's appointment to be the new leader (chapter 31), and Moses' death (chapter 34).

History

The books from Joshua through Esther, cover about 800 years of Israel's history. They tell about the Israelites conquering Canaan, the reigns of the kings, the division of Israel into northern and southern kingdoms, the fall of the northern kingdom to Assyria, the exile of the southern kingdom into Babylon, and the return to Jerusalem and Judah.

Joshua is named after its key character, Joshua, whom God named as the new leader of Israel. The people miraculously crossed the Jordan River and conquered the town of Jericho. Then, with God's help, they quickly took possession of the main areas of Canaan. Before Joshua died, he reminded the people of God's covenant promises to them and challenged them to keep on loving and obeying God.

Judges. After Joshua died, Israel was without a leader. The people often forgot about God and his laws and worshiped idols. Then God would punish them by sending a neighboring nation to fight them. When the people turned to God and asked for forgiveness, he would send them a special leader to help conquer their enemy. These special leaders were called judges. The best-known judges are Deborah, Gideon, and Samson.

Ruth tells the story of an Israelite couple who moved to Moab during a time of famine. The husband and his two sons died, leaving the mother (Naomi) alone with her two daughters-in-law (Orpah and Ruth). Naomi decided to move back to Israel and Ruth insisted on going with her. Back in Israel, they looked to their relative Boaz for help. Ruth finally married Boaz. From their family came the royal family of David and the Messiah—Jesus Christ. The book of Ruth shows how God cares for all our needs. It also shows how God was working to carry out his plan of salvation.

1 Samuel begins with the birth of Samuel and his training in the temple. It describes how he led Israel as prophet, priest, and judge. When the people of Israel demanded a king, Samuel anointed Saul to be the first king. But God rejected Saul for being disobedient, and Samuel secretly anointed David to take Saul's place. The rest of the book describes the struggles between Saul and David.

2 Samuel continues the story of the beginning of Israel's kingdom. It starts with Saul's death. Then it describes David's forty-year reign. Some of the best-known stories are the capture of Jerusalem, David's sin with Bathsheba, and Absalom's rebellion.

1 Kings. After David's death, his son Solomon became king. Chapters 1-11 describe Solomon's reign, including the building of the temple and the palace in Jerusalem. The next king was Rehoboam, who lost the northern part of the kingdom. After this the northern kingdom was known as Israel, and the southern kingdom was called Judah. The last chapters of 1 Kings tell about the evil King Ahab and God's prophet Elijah, who condemned Ahab's wickedness and Israel's disobedience.

2 Kings continues the stories of Elijah and Elisha. It also tells the history of the northern kingdom of Israel and the southern kingdom of Judah until they are finally conquered. Israel fell to Assyria in 722 B.C. and Judah fell to the Babylonians in 586 B.C. In both kingdoms prophets continually

warned the people that God would punish them if they did not repent.

1 Chronicles begins with an outline of history from Adam through the death of King Saul. The rest of the book is about the reign of King David. The books of Chronicles seem like a repeat of Samuel and Kings. But they were written for the returned exiles to remind them that they came from the royal line of David and that they were God's chosen people. The main theme is that God is faithful to his covenant.

2 Chronicles continues the history of David's line. Chapters 1-9 describe the building of the temple during Solomon's reign. Chapters 10-36 trace the history of the southern kingdom of Judah to the final destruction of Jerusalem and the exile of the people to Babylon.

Ezra tells about the return of the Jews from exile in Babylon. It begins with the decree of Cyrus, king of Persia, allowing the people to go back. The people enthusiastically began rebuilding the temple. But for 18 years they were delayed by enemies from the north. Finally a decree from Darius let them finish (see Ezra 1-6). Chapters 7-10 tell about the return of the priest Ezra. He taught the people the law and reformed their religious life. Ezra probably is the author of the books of Ezra and Nehemiah.

Nehemiah continues the history of the Jews who returned from exile. Nehemiah gave up his job as cupbearer to Artaxerxes, the Persian king, to become governor of Jerusalem. He led the people in repairing the city walls. This book shows how important prayer was in Nehemiah's life.

Esther tells the story of a beautiful Jewish girl whom King Xerxes of Persia chose to be his queen. When Haman plotted to murder all the Jews, Queen Esther's cousin Mordecai persuaded Esther to try to save her people. Risking her own life, she appealed to the king and rescued the Jews. Although the name of God does not appear in this book, his care for his chosen people is clearly shown.

Poetry

The next five books of the Old Testament are books of poetry and wisdom. Hebrew poetry often uses pairs of lines. The second line either repeats the thought of the first or gives an opposite. Look for these pairs of lines as you read, especially in the book of Psalms.

Job is named for its chief character, a "blameless and upright" man who was very rich. Even after losing everything he owned and suffering from a terrible sickness, Job still was devoted to God. The book of Job questions the reasons for suffering, especially the suffering of good people. Job's friends insisted he was suffering as punishment for his sin. He defended his innocence and expressed his trust in God. Then God spoke and showed his mighty power. Job finally admitted that God is too great and wonderful for us to understand.

Psalms is one of the most beautiful books of the Bible. The psalms are poems of praise, worship, thankfulness, and repentance. Many of them were written by King David. The rest were written by the sons of Korah, Solomon, Moses, and other people.

Proverbs is a collection of wise sayings and good advice for daily living. The book begins by reminding us that "The fear of the Lord is the beginning of knowledge" (Proverbs 1:7). Many of these proverbs came from King Solomon. Others were copied by the men of Hezekiah. Agur and Lemuel wrote the last two chapters.

Ecclesiastes studies the meaning of life. The "Teacher" looks at wisdom, pleasure, work, power, riches, religion, and other things. He decides that all of life is meaningless and empty without God.

Song of Songs is a collection of love poems between a lover and his beloved. It is a beautiful picture of ideal human love and marriage.

Prophecy

The last 17 books of the Old Testament are books of prophecy. Except for Lamentations, each book is named for its author. God sent these prophets at different times in Israel's and Judah's history. They called the people back to God and warned them that God would punish their disobedience.

Isaiah prophesied in Judah during the reigns of Kings Uzziah, Jotham, Ahaz, and Hezekiah. He repeatedly warned the people that Jerusalem and Judah would be judged because of their wickedness. In chapter 39 he predicted the Babylonian exile. But he

also held out hope that the kingdom would be restored. Beginning in chapter 40 Isaiah offered comfort with these promises from God: 1) the Babylonian exiles would be allowed to return to Jerusalem; 2) a righteous, suffering servant would bring salvation; 3) God would set up a new, righteous kingdom.

Jeremiah, like Isaiah, was a young man called by God to warn Judah about its wickedness. Jeremiah spent the first 20 years of his ministry under Josiah, a good king who tried to bring the people of Judah back to God. But after this, Jeremiah was often in danger from political and religious leaders who were angry about his messages. God protected Jeremiah so he could continue to warn the wicked and to comfort those who trusted in God. After Jerusalem was destroyed, Jeremiah chose to remain with the people, and he went with them to Egypt.

Lamentations. The title of this book means "funeral songs." The author was probably Jeremiah, and he was grieving about the destruction of Jerusalem. He confessed the people's sin and prayed to God for mercy.

Ezekiel is named after the prophet, Ezekiel, who was a priest in Jerusalem. He was taken to Babylon with other Jewish exiles in 598 B.C. Chapters 1-24 are prophecies about Jerusalem's destruction. Then, after Jerusalem was destroyed, Ezekiel preached a new message of hope that the people of Israel would return to Palestine.

Daniel tells the well-known story of Daniel and his three friends who were taken to captivity. These four men continued to obey and worship God, even though it sometimes put their lives in danger. In the last six chapters of this book, Daniel described his visions of the rise and fall of earthly kingdoms and finally the rise of an everlasting kingdom.

Hosea was a prophet in the northern kingdom of Israel during the reign of King Jeroboam II. Chapters 1-3 tell about Hosea's love for his unfaithful wife. In the rest of the book Hosea used his marriage as a picture of God's love for unfaithful Israel.

Joel prophesied at the time of King Joash. He described a terrible plague of locusts that invaded Palestine. Then Joel warned the people to turn to God in repentance. He announced that "the day of the LORD" would come and bring even greater judgment.

Amos was a shepherd called by God to be a prophet in the northern cities of Israel. He announced God's judgment on the people for turning away from God, for being cruel to the poor, and for living selfishly.

Obadiah, the shortest book in the Bible, is a book of prophecy against the nation of Edom. Obadiah announced God's judgment against them and prophesied that their kingdom would be destroyed.

Jonah was a prophet whom God called to preach in the foreign city of Nineveh. Jonah tried to run away from God and was swallowed by a great fish. When the fish returned him to land, Jonah went to Nineveh and warned the people about God's judgment. Jonah learned that God would forgive even a heathen city if the people were sorry for their sins.

Micah contains the writings of a prophet who lived in the countryside of Judah during the reigns of Ahaz and Hezekiah. Micah warned about God's judgment against Jerusalem and Samaria because of the sinfulness of their leaders. But he promised the restoration of Zion and a kingdom of peace for those who trust in God. He prophesied that a ruler born in Bethlehem would set up a kingdom that will last forever.

Nahum is a book of prophecy against Nineveh, the capital of Assyria. The prophet describes the cruelty of the Assyrians as they conquered nation after nation. He predicted the destruction of Nineveh and the end of the kingdom of Assyria.

Habakkuk was written as a dialogue or conversation between God and the prophet. Habakkuk first asked why God let wickedness and violence continue. When God told him he would send the Babylonians to punish Judah, Habakkuk became more concerned. He did not understand how God could use the Babylonians, who were even more wicked than the Jews. God answered that "the righteous will live by his faith" and that the Babylonians would also be judged. Habakkuk ended his book with a psalm of praise.

Zephaniah prophesied during the reign of King Josiah. He warned that the day of the Lord would bring judgment on Judah and Jerusalem, and he called the Jews to turn back to God. Zephaniah then predicted that Judah's neighboring nations would be destroyed, and he promised that God would bring his people home.

Haggai. Eighteen years had passed since Cyrus's decree had allowed the Jews to return from exile. But they still had not finished building God's temple. Haggai's message was that the time had come to build the house of the Lord. He promised that God would fill this house with his glory.

Zechariah. Zechariah's prophecies began two months after Haggai's first message. God sent Zechariah eight visions to encourage the builders of the temple. In chapters 7 and 8 Zechariah called the people to obey God by acting fairly and mercifully to one another. Chapters 9-14 predict the coming of Zion's King, "the LORD Almighty."

Malachi prophesied to the Jews who had returned from exile. He warned them that they were neglecting and disobeying God and that God would judge them for their wickedness. He also promised that God would save the righteous.

New Testament History

The first five books of the New Testament tell the story of Jesus' life and of the beginning of the Christian church. The four Gospels tell us almost everything we know about Jesus Christ. The word gospel means "good news." These four books tell us the Good News that Jesus is the Son of God and that he came to earth and died for our sins. The book of Acts continues the story from Jesus' return to heaven to Paul's imprisonment in Rome.

Matthew. The first Gospel was written by Matthew, one of Jesus' twelve disciples, sometime before the Romans destroyed Jerusalem in the year A.D. 70. Matthew wrote his Gospel for the Jews, to show them that Jesus was the Messiah who had been promised in the Old Testament. He quoted many Old Testament prophecies and showed how they came true in Jesus' life. He also included many of Jesus' teachings about the kingdom of heaven, since the Jews were looking for a king. One of the best-known parts of Matthew's Gospel is the Sermon on the Mount, which shows Jesus as a great teacher.

Mark, the author of this Gospel, may

have been the first to write down the events of Jesus' life. He is probably the same person who worked for many years as a missionary with Paul and Barnabas. Mark wrote his Gospel so the early Christians would know what Jesus was like and why he had to die. He shows Jesus as a man of action and authority. One-third of his book tells the events of Jesus' last week on earth, ending with his death and resurrection.

Luke, the doctor who traveled with Paul, wrote the third Gospel. Luke tells us in the first four verses of his book that he wrote this Gospel so we would have the true story of Jesus' life. He wrote the fullest, most orderly story of Jesus' life and showed Jesus' love for all kinds of people — not just the rich and important, but also the poor or unpopular.

John. The fourth Gospel was also written by one of Jesus' twelve disciples — John, "the disciple whom Jesus loved." John wrote this Gospel so that "you may believe that Jesus is the Christ, the Son of God, and that by believing you may have life in his name" (John 20:31). John wanted to show that the things Jesus said and the miracles he did prove that he is God. He chose stories that show Jesus' godly powers at times when men were powerless. But he also showed that Jesus was human and could become tired or hungry or sad, just like us.

Acts is the second part of Luke's history. It was written so we would have the true story of how the Christian church began and grew. This book is sometimes called "The Acts of the Apostles." It especially tells about the work of two of the apostles — Peter and Paul. Acts can also be called "The Acts of the Holy Spirit" because it teaches about the coming and work of the Spirit. The book of Acts teaches three things about the early church: 1) what the message of the early church was; 2) how the Jews rejected this message and how God sent the apostles to the Gentiles, who accepted the gospel; and 3) how the early church was treated by the local and Roman governments.

Letters

Except for the last book, Revelation, the rest of the New Testament is made up of letters written by leaders in the early church to local churches and individuals. There are twenty-one letters — thirteen were written by Paul, one (Hebrews) is anonymous, one is by James, two by Peter, three by John, and one by Jude.

Romans. Paul probably wrote this letter to the Romans at the end of his third missionary journey. He was returning to Jerusalem, and then he planned to visit Rome and go on to Spain (Romans 15:23-25). The theme of this letter is righteousness. Paul taught that: 1) no human being is righteous; 2) Jesus Christ is perfectly righteous; 3) if we have faith in Jesus, we are freed from the power of sin, given a new life, and returned to a right relationship with God; 4) we should live Christian lives that are "holy and pleasing to God."

1 Corinthians was written by Paul from Ephesus, where he had heard disturbing news about the church at Corinth. The Christians there were not getting along with one another — they were taking sides. And some of them were living sinful lives. Paul wrote this letter to scold them and teach them how Christians should act. Corinth was a wicked city. It was hard for the Christians there not to act like their neighbors. In this letter Paul was trying to teach practical lessons about the Christian life so they would know right from wrong.

2 Corinthians. When the Corinthians got Paul's first letter, some of the people became angry. But most of them knew that what they were doing was wrong. They sent news to Paul that they would change their behavior. The first part of this letter tells how happy and thankful Paul was when he heard that the Corinthians were sorry for the way they had acted and were now trying to live the way God wanted them to. In the second part of the letter, Paul defended himself against the people who were angry with him and who were saying untrue things about him.

Galatians. Paul wrote this letter to the Christian churches in the Roman province of Galatia. These churches were being confused by false teachers called Judaizers. These men were teaching the Gentile Christians that they were not really saved unless they obeyed all the Jewish laws — such as being circumcised, eating special foods, and celebrating Jewish feast days. Paul wrote that we cannot be saved from our sins by obeying the law; we are saved only by believing in Jesus Christ. He also taught that Christians are free to live by the law of love, not the Law of Moses.

Ephesians was written by Paul while he was in prison in Rome. Probably this letter was sent not just to the church at Ephesus but to all the Christian churches near Ephesus. Ephesus was a large, important city at that time, so it was a natural center for the Christian churches. In this letter Paul wrote about the church—not a church building in a certain place but the church that is made up of all Christians who have ever lived. We call this "the church universal." Paul wrote that because all Christians are one family in Jesus, they should act with love toward each other.

Philippians was also written while Paul was in prison in Rome. The Philippians had sent Epaphroditus to Paul with a gift. While he was in Rome, Epaphroditus became sick, and the Philippian Christians were worried about him. After Epaphroditus was better, Paul sent him back to Philippi with this letter. Even though Paul was writing from prison, this letter is full of joy. Paul was thankful for the love and helpfulness of the Philippians.

Colossians is a third letter written from prison in Rome. Epaphras had come to Rome and told Paul that there were false teachers in Colosse who were telling the people that the Christian faith was incomplete. They were teaching the Colossians to worship angels and to follow special rules and ceremonies. Paul wrote to the Colossians to oppose these false teachers. He reminded them that Jesus is supreme over everything, that his death is all we need to save us from our sins, and that through him we are free from man-made rules.

1 Thessalonians. Paul started the church at Thessalonica on his second missionary journey. He taught there for about three weeks, but then he had to leave because the Jews were opposing him so strongly. Paul wrote this letter from Corinth to encourage the Thessalonians and to teach them more about Christianity. He praised them for being brave and not giving up their faith "in spite of severe suffering." He instructed them "how to live in order to please God." And he taught them about Jesus' second coming. He explained that the time of Jesus' coming was secret, so they should keep on working hard till he came.

2 Thessalonians was sent from Corinth a little while after the first letter. Some people had misunderstood Paul and were sure Jesus was coming very soon. They had stopped working and were just waiting for Jesus. Paul told the Thessalonians again what Jesus' second coming would be like. He reminded them to keep working hard till Jesus came.

1 Timothy. Timothy was a young friend of Paul who became a Christian on Paul's first missionary journey. He went with Paul on his second missionary journey and from then on he helped Paul in his work. At the time Paul wrote this letter, Timothy was working as the teacher and leader of the church at Ephesus. Timothy was young to have the important job of leading a church. Paul wrote to give him help and advice for his work. This letter teaches how people in the church should act and what kind of leaders a church should have.

2 Timothy. When Paul wrote this second letter to Timothy, he was a prisoner in Rome again. He knew that there was no chance of getting out and that he would be killed soon. He wanted to encourage Timothy because Timothy would have to continue Paul's missionary work after Paul's death. Paul gave Timothy more instructions on how to lead a church. He told him to resist false teachers and to be faithful to true Christian teachings.

Titus was another friend and helper of Paul. He had traveled with Paul on some of his missionary journeys. Now he was working as the leader of the church on Crete. This letter is much like the two letters to Timothy. Paul wanted to teach Titus how to be a good leader of the church. He told him how God's people should behave and what his own responsibilities were.

Philemon was a leader of the church at Colosse and a friend of Paul. Philemon's slave, Onesimus, had stolen money from Philemon and had run away to Rome. While he was there he met Paul and became a Christian. Paul sent Onesimus back to Philemon with this letter. He begged Philemon to forgive Onesimus and to treat him as a brother in Christ instead of a runaway slave.

Hebrews. At the time this letter was written, Christians were being hurt and killed because they believed in Jesus. Some of the Jewish Christians were thinking about giving up their Christianity and going back to the Jewish faith. The book of Hebrews was written to teach Jewish Christians that the Christian faith is better in every way than the Jewish faith. It shows how Jesus completed the Jewish faith by making the final sacrifice for sin. After his death, none of the Old Testament sacrifices were needed. Chapter 11—the famous chapter on men of faith in Old Testament times—gives Christians examples to follow of faith and trust in God.

James. The seven books of the New Testament from James through Jude are called the General Letters. This first one was written by James, the brother of Jesus. He was one of the leaders of the church in Jerusalem. James wrote this letter to teach Christians the practice of Christianity. He insisted that if we have real faith, we will show it by acting like Christians. He gave practical advice on things like anger and quarreling, showing favoritism, taming the tongue, boasting, patience, and prayer.

1 Peter was written by Peter, one of Jesus' twelve disciples, to the Christians who lived in the northern provinces of Asia Minor. These Christians were being persecuted for their faith, so Peter wrote to encourage them. Peter told these Christians to remember how much Jesus had suffered for them and to follow his example by being brave and trusting God. He said that because God chose them to be his people and because Jesus suffered and died for them, they should live the way God wanted them to.

2 Peter was written to the same group of Christians as Peter's first letter. These Christians were now in danger of being led astray by false teachers. Peter reminded them that the best way to resist false teachers was to grow in the knowledge and practice of the Christian faith. He warned them that God would destroy the false teachers. Peter also reminded these Christians to live "holy and godly lives," because Jesus would certainly keep his promise to come again.

1 John. John, the beloved disciple, who wrote the fourth Gospel, also wrote these next three letters. The first letter was written to warn Christians about dangerous false teachers who were trying to mislead them. They were teaching that the man Jesus was not the Christ, the Son of God. They said that God did not become a man. John wrote about how important it is to know and believe that Jesus Christ is both God and man. He said Christians can know they are God's children if they love one another and if they obey God's commands.

2 John. John wrote this letter to "the chosen lady and her children." He might have meant either a Christian woman and her family or a church and its members. In this letter John wrote how important it is for Christians to love one another. He said that to love means to obey God's commandments, and God's commandments tell us to live lives of love. John also warned about the dangers of false teachers.

3 John was written to Gaius, a friend of John and a leader in the church. There was a man named Diotrephes in Gaius's church who was refusing to welcome messengers sent by John. He would not recognize John's leadership. John wrote this letter to praise and thank Gaius for his help and to scold Diotrephes for not cooperating. John promised to come to this church soon to deal with this matter personally.

Jude, like James, was a brother of Jesus. He wrote to warn Christians about the same false teachers Peter wrote about in his second letter. These false teachers were not only teaching that Jesus was not the Son of God; they were also leading the people to live sinfully. Jude warned that God would punish and destroy these false teachers just as he had punished sinners in the Old Testament.

Revelation

Revelation is the only book of its kind in the New Testament. It is a book about the end of this present world and the beginning of "a new heaven and a new earth." The book of Revelation was written by the apostle John during his exile on the island of Patmos. While John was there, Jesus gave him a vision of what would happen in the future. John wrote this book so Christians who were being persecuted would trust that God controls whatever happens here on earth. John's vision shows that Jesus is the ruler over everyone and everything — even powerful human governments — and he will judge and punish whatever is evil. It also gives Christians a picture of heaven, where we will be with Jesus.

Bible Verses for Daily Life

"Your word," writes the psalmist, "is a lamp to my feet and a light for my path" (Ps. 119:105). Throughout history God has continued to direct and illumine humankind through his written Word, the Bible. It presents a lifelong challenge: to learn to know God, to love him, to obey him.

The following selected verses help to highlight the Biblical message. If you find a particular topic or verse helpful, you may wish to locate the reference in the Bible and read its context. As you incorporate the Word of God into your life, he will bless you with direction and meaning.

Our Relationship to God

Guilt (Sin)

Isaiah 64:6   All of us have become like one who is unclean, and all our righteous acts are like filthy rags.

Jeremiah 17:9   The heart is deceitful above all things and beyond cure. Who can understand it?

Romans 3:10   There is no one righteous, not even one.

Forgiveness (Repentance)

Psalm 32:5   Then I acknowledged my sin to you and did not cover up my iniquity. I said, "I will confess my transgressions to the LORD" — and you forgave the guilt of my sin.

1 John 1:9   If we confess our sins, he is faithful and just and will forgive us our sins and purify us from all unrighteousness.

God's Love

1 John 4:9   This is how God showed his love among us: He sent his one and only Son into the world that we might live through him.

John 3:16   For God so loved the world that he gave his one and only Son, that whoever believes in him shall not perish but have eternal life.

Salvation

Romans 10:9   If you confess with your mouth, "Jesus is Lord," and believe in your heart that God raised him from the dead, you will be saved.

Acts 4:12   Salvation is found in no one else, for there is no other name under heaven given to men by which we must be saved.

Ephesians 2:8,9   It is by grace you have been saved, through faith — and this not from yourselves, it is the gift of God — not by works, so that no one can boast.

Worship (Praise)

Hebrews 13:15   Through Jesus let us continually offer to God a sacrifice of praise — the fruit of lips that confess his name.

Psalm 29:2   Ascribe to the LORD the glory due his name; worship the LORD in the splendor of his holiness.

John 4:23,24   ... true worshipers will worship the Father in spirit and truth, for they are the kind of worshipers the Father seeks. God is spirit, and his worshipers must worship in spirit and in truth.

Guidance

Psalm 143:10   Teach me to do your will, for you are my God; may your good Spirit lead me on level ground.

John 16:13   When he, the Spirit of truth, comes, he will guide you into all truth.

Obedience

Matthew 12:50   Whoever does the will of my Father in heaven is my brother and sister and mother.

Luke 11:28   Blessed are those who hear the word of God and obey it.

John 14:15   If you love me, you will obey what I command.

Our Relationships With Others

Love

John 13:34,35   Love one another. As I have loved you, so you must love one another. All men will know that you are my disciples if you love one another.

John 15:13   Greater love has no one than this, that he lay down his life for his friends.

Ephesians 5:1,2   Be imitators of God as dearly loved children and live a life of love, just as Christ loved us and gave himself up for us ...

1 Peter 4:8   Above all, love each other

deeply, because love covers over a multitude of sins.

1 John 3:18 Dear children, let us not love with words or tongue but with actions and in truth.

Compassion (Kindness)

Colossians 3:12 Clothe yourselves with compassion, kindness, humility, gentleness and patience.

Philippians 2:4 Each of you should look not only to your own interests, but also to the interests of others.

Romans 12:15 Rejoice with those who rejoice; mourn with those who mourn.

Matthew 25:40 The King will reply, "I tell you the truth, whatever you did for one of the least of these brothers of mine, you did for me."

Galatians 6:2 Carry each other's burdens, and in this way you will fulfill the law of Christ.

Ephesians 4:32 Be kind and compassionate to one another, forgiving each other, just as in Christ God forgave you.

Forgiveness

Colossians 3:13 Bear with each other and forgive whatever grievances you may have against one another. Forgive as the Lord forgave you.

Mark 11:25 And when you stand praying, if you hold anything against anyone, forgive him, so that your Father in heaven may forgive you your sins.

Proverbs 19:11 A man's wisdom gives him patience; it is to his glory to overlook an offense.

Proverbs 24:17 Do not gloat when your enemy falls; when he stumbles, do not let your heart rejoice.

Revenge

Romans 12:19-21 Do not take revenge, my friends, but leave room for God's wrath, for it is written: "It is mine to avenge; I will repay," says the Lord. On the contrary: "If your enemy is hungry, feed him; if he is thirsty, give him something to drink. In doing this, you will heap burning coals on his head." Do not be overcome by evil, but overcome evil with good.

Romans 12:14 Bless those who persecute you; bless and do not curse.

Matthew 5:43,44 You have heard that it was said, "Love your neighbor and hate your enemy." But I tell you: Love your enemies and pray for those who persecute you.

Luke 6:31 Do to others as you would have them do to you.

Anger

1 Timothy 2:8 I want men everywhere to lift up holy hands in prayer, without anger or disputing.

James 1:19,20 My dear brothers, take note of this: Everyone should be quick to listen, slow to speak and slow to become angry, for man's anger does not bring about the righteous life that God desires.

Psalm 37:8 Refrain from anger and turn from wrath; do not fret—it leads only to evil.

Proverbs 15:1 A gentle answer turns away wrath, but a harsh word stirs up anger.

Ephesians 4:26 Do not let the sun go down while you are still angry.

Galatians 5:19,20 The acts of the sinful nature are . . . hatred, discord, jealousy, fits of rage . . .

Hatred (Strife)

1 John 4:20 If anyone says, "I love God," yet hates his brother, he is a liar. For anyone who does not love his brother, whom he has seen, cannot love God, whom he has not seen.

Proverbs 10:12 Hatred stirs up dissension, but love covers over all wrongs.

Peace

Romans 12:18 If it is possible, as far as it depends on you, live at peace with everyone.

Romans 14:19 Let us therefore make every effort to do what leads to peace and to mutual edification.

The Church

Romans 12:5 In Christ we who are many form one body, and each member belongs to all the others.

Ephesians 4:4-6 There is one body and one Spirit—just as you were called to one hope when you were called—one Lord, one faith, one baptism; one God and Father of all, who is over all and through all and in all.

1 Peter 4:10 Each one should use whatever gift he has received to serve others,

faithfully administering God's grace in its various forms.

Ephesians 4:11–13 It was [Christ] who gave [gifts], to prepare God's people for works of service, so that the body of Christ may be built up until we all reach unity in the faith and in the knowledge of the Son of God.

Unity

Romans 15:5,6 May the God who gives endurance and encouragement give you a spirit of unity among yourselves as you follow Christ Jesus, so that with one heart and mouth you may glorify the God and Father of our Lord Jesus Christ.

Ephesians 4:2,3 Be completely humble and gentle; be patient, bearing with one another in love. Make every effort to keep the unity of the Spirit through the bond of peace.

Psalm 133:1 How good and pleasant it is when brothers live together in unity!

Honesty (Truthfulness)

Ephesians 4:25 Each of you must put off falsehood and speak truthfully to his neighbor, for we are all members of one body.

Psalm 15:1–3 LORD, who may dwell in your sanctuary? Who may live on your holy hill? He whose walk is blameless and who does what is righteous, who speaks the truth from his heart and has no slander on his tongue, who does his neighbor no wrong and casts no slur on his fellow man.

Acceptance (Judging)

Romans 15:7 Accept one another, then, just as Christ accepted you, in order to bring praise to God.

Matthew 7:1,2 Do not judge, or you too will be judged. For in the same way you judge others, you will be judged, and with the measure you use, it will be measured to you.

Ephesians 5:21 Submit to one another out of reverence for Christ.

The Family

Ephesians 5:22 Wives, submit to your husbands as to the Lord.

Ephesians 5:25 Husbands, love your wives, just as Christ loved the church and gave himself up for her.

Hebrews 13:4 Marriage should be honored by all, and the marriage bed kept pure, for God will judge the adulterer and all the sexually immoral.

Matthew 5:32 Anyone who divorces his wife, except for marital unfaithfulness, causes her to commit adultery, and anyone who marries a woman so divorced commits adultery.

Ephesians 6:1 Children, obey your parents in the Lord, for this is right.

Proverbs 22:6 Train a child in the way he should go, and when he is old he will not turn from it.

Deuteronomy 11:19 Teach [God's commandments] to your children, talking about them when you sit at home and when you walk along the road, when you lie down and when you get up.

Society

1 Peter 2:11,12 Dear friends, I urge you, as aliens and strangers in the world, to abstain from sinful desires, which war against your soul. Live such good lives among the pagans that, though they accuse you of doing wrong, they may see your good deeds and glorify God on the day he visits us.

Romans 13:7 Give everyone what you owe him: If you owe taxes, pay taxes; if revenue, then revenue; if respect, then respect; if honor, then honor.

1 Peter 2:17 Show proper respect to everyone: Love the brotherhood of believers, fear God, honor the king.

Personal Guidelines

Correct Values

Philippians 4:8 Finally, brothers, whatever is true, whatever is noble, whatever is right, whatever is pure, whatever is lovely, whatever is admirable—if anything is excellent or praiseworthy—think about such things.

Jeremiah 9:23,24 This is what the LORD says: "Let not the wise man boast of his wisdom or the strong man boast of his strength or the rich man boast of his riches, but let him who boasts boast about this: that he understands and knows me, that I am the LORD, who exercises kindness, justice and righteousness on earth, for in these I delight," declares the LORD.

Proverbs 4:7 Wisdom is supreme; therefore get wisdom. Though it cost all you have, get understanding.

Matthew 22:37–40 Jesus replied: " 'Love the Lord your God with all your heart and with all your soul and with all your mind.' This is the first and greatest commandment. And the second is like it: 'Love your neighbor as yourself.' All the Law and the Prophets hang on these two commandments."

Humility (Pride)

Micah 6:8 He has showed you, O man, what is good. And what does the LORD require of you? To act justly and to love mercy and to walk humbly with your God.

Psalm 25:9 He guides the humble in what is right and teaches them his way.

1 Peter 5:5,6 Clothe yourselves with humility toward one another, because, "God opposes the proud but gives grace to the humble." Humble yourselves, therefore, under God's mighty hand, that he may lift you up in due time.

Luke 18:14 Everyone who exalts himself will be humbled, and he who humbles himself will be exalted.

Worldliness

1 John 2:15,16 Do not love the world or anything in the world. If anyone loves the world, the love of the Father is not in him. For everything in the world—the cravings of sinful man, the lust of his eyes and the boasting of what he has and does—comes not from the Father but from the world.

Colossians 3:5,8,9 Put to death whatever belongs to your earthly nature: sexual immorality, impurity, lust, evil desires and greed, which is idolatry.... Rid yourselves of all such things as these: anger, rage, malice, slander, and filthy language from your lips. Do not lie to each other, since you have taken off your old self with its practices.

Galatians 5:24 Those who belong to Christ Jesus have crucified the sinful nature with its passions and desires.

Godliness (Righteousness)

Galatians 5:22,23 But the fruit of the Spirit is love, joy, peace, patience, kindness, goodness, faithfulness, gentleness and self-control.

Ephesians 4:22–24 You were taught ... to be made new in the attitude of your minds; and to put on the new self, created to be like God in true righteousness and holiness.

1 Peter 1:15 But just as he who called you is holy, so be holy in all you do.

Contentment (Greed)

1 Timothy 6:6,10 Godliness with contentment is great gain.... For the love of money is a root of all kinds of evil.

Hebrews 13:5 Keep your lives free from the love of money and be content with what you have.

Luke 12:15 Watch out! Be on your guard against all kinds of greed; a man's life does not consist in the abundance of his possessions.

Matthew 6:19–21 Do not store up for yourselves treasures on earth, where moth and rust destroy, and where thieves break in and steal. But store up for yourselves treasures in heaven, where moth and rust do not destroy, and where thieves do not break in and steal. For where your treasure is, there your heart will be also.

Peace

Proverbs 14:30 A heart at peace gives life to the body, but envy rots the bones.

Philippians 4:7 And the peace of God, which transcends all understanding, will guard your hearts and your minds in Christ Jesus.

Isaiah 26:3 You will keep in perfect peace him whose mind is steadfast, because he trusts in you.

John 14:27 Peace I leave with you; my peace I give you. I do not give to you as the world gives. Do not let your hearts be troubled and do not be afraid.

Fear

Psalm 27:1 The LORD is my light and my salvation—whom shall I fear? The LORD is the stronghold of my life—of whom shall I be afraid?

Hebrews 13:5,6 God has said, "Never will I leave you; never will I forsake you." So we say with confidence, "The Lord is my helper; I will not be afraid. What can man do to me?"

Anxiety (Worry)

Psalm 55:22 Cast your cares on the LORD and he will sustain you; he will never let the righteous fall.

Matthew 6:25 Do not worry about your life, what you will eat or drink; or about your body, what you will wear. Is not life more important than food, and the body more important than clothes?

Philippians 4:6   Do not be anxious about anything, but in everything, by prayer and petition, with thanksgiving, present your requests to God.

Depression

Psalm 42:5,6   Why are you downcast, O my soul? Why so disturbed within me? Put your hope in God, for I will yet praise him, my Savior and my God.

Suffering (Trials)

Matthew 11:28   Come to me, all you who are weary and burdened, and I will give you rest.

2 Corinthians 12:9   My grace is sufficient for you, for my power is made perfect in weakness.

Hebrews 12:2,3   Let us fix our eyes on Jesus, the author and perfecter of our faith, who for the joy set before him endured the cross, scorning its shame, and sat down at the right hand of the throne of God. Consider him who endured such opposition from sinful men, so that you will not grow weary and lose heart.

John 16:33   In this world you will have trouble. But take heart! I have overcome the world.

2 Corinthians 4:8,9   We are hard pressed on every side, but not crushed; perplexed, but not in despair; persecuted, but not abandoned; struck down, but not destroyed.

Hebrews 4:16   Let us approach the throne of grace with confidence, so that we may receive mercy and find grace to help us in our time of need.

Faith (Doubt)

John 20:29   Jesus told him, "Because you have seen me, you have believed; blessed are those who have not seen and yet have believed."

Hebrews 11:1,6   Now faith is being sure of what we hope for and certain of what we do not see. . . . And without faith it is impossible to please God, because anyone who comes to him must believe that he exists and that he rewards those who earnestly seek him.

Matthew 21:22   If you believe, you will receive whatever you ask for in prayer.

James 1:6,7   When he asks, he must believe and not doubt, because he who doubts is like a wave of the sea, blown and tossed by the wind. That man should not think he will receive anything from the Lord.

Prayer

Matthew 7:7,8   Ask and it will be given to you; seek and you will find; knock and the door will be opened to you. For everyone who asks receives; he who seeks finds; and to him who knocks, the door will be opened.

Psalm 37:7   Be still before the Lord and wait patiently for him.

James 4:8   Come near to God and he will come near to you.

Psalm 61:1,2   Hear my cry, O God; listen to my prayer. From the ends of the earth I call to you, I call as my heart grows faint; lead me to the rock that is higher than I.

Luke 18:1   [Disciples] should always pray and not give up.

Perseverance

2 Thessalonians 3:13   And as for you, brothers, never tire of doing what is right.

Galatians 6:9   Let us not become weary in doing good, for at the proper time we will reap a harvest if we do not give up.

Hebrews 10:36   You need to persevere so that when you have done the will of God, you will receive what he has promised.

Happiness (Joy)

Psalm 16:11   You have made known to me the path of life; you will fill me with joy in your presence, with eternal pleasures at your right hand.

1 Peter 1:8   Though you have not seen him, you love him; and even though you do not see him now, you believe in him and are filled with an inexpressible and glorious joy.

Psalm 37:4   Delight yourself in the Lord and he will give you the desires of your heart.

Psalm 97:1   The Lord reigns, let the earth be glad; let the distant shores rejoice.

Philippians 4:4   Rejoice in the Lord always. I will say it again: Rejoice!

Psalm 28:7   The Lord is my strength and my shield; my heart trusts in him, and I am helped. My heart leaps for joy and I will give thanks to him in song.

Thankfulness (Gratitude)

Psalm 136:1   Give thanks to the Lord, for he is good.

Isaiah 63:7   I will tell of the kindnesses of the LORD, the deeds for which he is to be praised, according to all the LORD has done for us—yes, the many good things he has done for the house of Israel, according to his compassion and many kindnesses.

Ephesians 5:20   Always [give] thanks to God the Father for everything, in the name of our Lord Jesus Christ.

Psalm 68:19   Praise be to the Lord, to God our Savior, who daily bears our burdens.

Temptation

2 Thessalonians 3:3   The Lord is faithful, and he will strengthen and protect you from the evil one.

Hebrews 2:18   Because he himself suffered when he was tempted, he is able to help those who are being tempted.

1 Corinthians 10:13   No temptation has seized you except what is common to man. And God is faithful; he will not let you be tempted beyond what you can bear. But when you are tempted, he will also provide a way out so that you can stand up under it.

Grief (Loss)

Matthew 5:4   Blessed are those who mourn, for they will be comforted.

John 11:25,26   Jesus said to her, "I am the resurrection and the life. He who believes in me will live, even though he dies; and whoever lives and believes in me will never die."

John 16:22   Now is your time of grief, but I will see you again and you will rejoice, and no one will take away your joy.

Psalm 23:1   The LORD is my shepherd, I shall lack nothing.

Loneliness

Psalm 25:1,16   To you, O LORD, I lift up my soul. . . . Turn to me and be gracious to me, for I am lonely and afflicted.

Matthew 28:20   [Jesus said,] "Surely I will be with you always, to the very end of the age."

PROMISES
from the Bible

GOD'S PROMISE OF:
  Love — Matthew 10:30-31; John 3:16: John 15:9, 13; 1 John 4:9
  Forgiveness — Luke 15:3-7; Acts 10:43; Ephesians 1:7; 1 John 1:9
  Salvation — Matthew 1:21; Acts 16:31; Ephesians 2:8; Hebrews 7:25
  the Holy Spirit — Luke 11:13; John 14:16-17; Acts 2:38; Romans 8:11
  Everlasting Life — John 6:40; John 10:28; 1 Corinthians 15:51-52; 1 Thessalonians 4:17
  Peace — John 14:27; Romans 5:1-2; Ephesians 2:14; 2 Thessalonians 3:16
  Joy — John 15:10-11; John 16:22; Romans 16:13; 1 Peter 1:8
  Freedom — John 8:34-36; Romans 6:6, 14, 20-22; 2 Corinthians 3:17; Revelation 1:5
  Growth — Philippians 1:6; 2 Corinthians 3:18; Ephesians 4:14-15; 2 Peter 1:3-4
  Encouragement — 1 Thessalonians 5:23; 2 Thessalonians 2:16-17; Hebrews 6:10;
    1 Peter 2:9
  Excellence — Matthew 20:26-28; John 14:12; John 15:15-16; 2 Corinthians 3:5-6
  Strength — 1 Corinthians 1:8; Ephesians 3:20; 2 Thessalonians 3:3; 1 Peter 5:10
  Blessing — John 1:16; John 10:10; Romans 8:28; Ephesians 1:3
  His Presence — Matthew 18:20; Matthew 28:20; John 6:37; Romans 8:38-39
  Answered Prayer — Matthew 7:7-11; Matthew 21:22, 1 Peter 3:12; 1 John 5:14-15
  Christ's Return — John 14:2-3; Acts 1:11; 1 Thessalonians 4:16-17; Revelation 1:7

GOD'S PROMISE WHEN YOU:
  Feel Guilty — Romans 8:1-2; 1 Corinthians 6:11; Ephesians 3:12; Hebrews 10:22-23
  Feel Dejected — Matthew 11:28-30; Romans 8:26-27; Hebrews 4:16; James 4:8, 10
  Are Disappointed — Matthew 19:25-26; Mark 9:21-24; John 15:7; Ephesians 3:20
  Are Persecuted — Matthew 5:10-12; 2 Corinthians 4:8-12; 2 Timothy 1:11-12; 1 Peter
    3:13-14
  Are Anxious — Matthew 6:25; Matthew 11:28-29; Philippians 4:6-7; 1 Peter 5:7
  Are Sick — Matthew 8:16-17; John 16:33; Romans 8:37-39; James 5:14-15
  Are Impatient — Romans 2:7; 1 Timothy 1:16; Hebrews 6:12; 1 Peter 3:9
  Are Confused — John 8:12; John 14:27; 1 Corinthians 2:15-16; James 1:5
  Are Tempted — 1 Corinthians 10:13; Hebrews 2:18; Hebrews 4:15-16; 1 Peter 5:8-10
  Are Weak — Romans 8:26; 1 Corinthians 1:7-9; 2 Corinthians 4:7-9; 2 Corinthians
    12:9-10
  Are Afraid — Romans 8:37-39; 2 Corinthians 1:10; 2 Timothy 1:7; Hebrews 13:6
  Obey — Matthew 16:27; John 8:31-32; John 14:21, 23; James 1:25
  Are In Need — John 6:35; 2 Corinthians 9:10-11; Ephesians 3:20-21; Philippians 4:19
  Grieve — Matthew 5:4; John 16:20-22; 1 Thessalonians 4:13-14; Revelation 21:3-4
  Suffer — John 16:33; Romans 8:16-17; 1 Peter 2:20-21; 1 Peter 4:12-13
  Fail — Romans 3:23-24; Romans 5:8; Hebrews 10:36; 1 John 1:8-9
  Doubt — John 3:18; John 11:25-26; Romans 4:5; 1 John 4:15-16

PERSPECTIVES
from the Bible

WHAT TO READ WHEN:

The Future Seems Hopeless—1 Corinthians 15:20-28; 1 Peter 1:1-9; 1 Peter 5:10-11; Revelation 11:15-19

Seeking God's Direction—Romans 12:1-3; Ephesians 5:15-17; Colossians 1:9-14; James 1:5-8

You Need Comfort—2 Corinthians 1:3-7; 2 Corinthians 7:6-13

Others Disagree With You—Matthew 7:1-5; Romans 12:9-21; Romans 14:1-15:7; 2 Corinthians 5:11-21

The World Seems Enticing—2 Corinthians 6:14-7:1; James 1:26-27; James 4:4-10; 1 John 2:15-17

You Need Assurance of Salvation—John 3:14-21; John 11:25-26; Acts 16:31-34; 1 John 5:9-13

Others Have Sinned Against You—Matthew 6:14-15; Matthew 18:21-35; Colossians 3:12-14; James 2:12-13

You Are Tempted to be Bitter—1 Corinthians 13; Ephesians 4:29-5:2; Hebrews 12:14-15

You Are Tempted to Neglect Public Worship—Acts 2:42-47; Hebrews 10:19-25

Your Faith Needs Strengthening—Romans 5:1-11; 1 Corinthians 9:24-27; Hebrews 10:19-25, 35-39; Hebrews 11:1-12:13

You Need to Control Your Tongue—Matthew 15:1-20; James 3:1-12

You Are Prone to Judge Others—Matthew 7:1-5; 1 Corinthians 4:1-5; James 2:1-13; James 4:11-12

You Have Been Cheated—Matthew 18:15-17; 1 Corinthians 6:1-8; James 5:1-8

Things Are Going Well—Luke 12:13-21; 1 Timothy 6:3-19; Hebrews 13:5; James 2:1-17

You Wonder About Your Spiritual Gifts—Romans 8; 1 Corinthians 1:4-9; 1 Corinthians 12:1-14:25; 1 Peter 4:7-11

You Are Starting a New Job—Matthew 5:13-16; Romans 12:1-2; Galatians 5:13-26; Ephesians 1:3-14

You Are in a Position of Responsibility—Mark 10:35-45; Luke 7:1-10; 1 Corinthians 16:13-14; Galatians 6:9-10

You Are Establishing a New Home—Ephesians 5:22-6:4; Colossians 3:18-21; 1 Peter 3:1-7

You Have Been Quarreling—1 Corinthians 3; Ephesians 4:1-6, 4:15-5:2; 2 Timothy 2:14-26; James 4:1-12

You Are Challenged by Dark Forces—Romans 8:38-39; 2 Corinthians 4:7-18; Ephesians 6:10-18; 2 Timothy 4:6-7

You Are Jealous—Galatians 5:13-15, 19-21; James 3:13-18

You Struggle With Laziness—Ephesians 5:15-16; Philippians 2:12-13; 1 Thessalonians 4:1-12; 2 Thessalonians 3:6-15

You Struggle With Lust—Matthew 5:27-30; Romans 7:7-25; Romans 13:8-14; James 1:13-18

You Are Angry—Matthew 5:21-22; Matthew 18:21-35; Ephesians 4:25-5:2; James 1:19-21

You Desire Revenge—Matthew 5:38-42; Romans 12:17-21; 1 Thessalonians 5:12-15; 1 Peter 3:8-14

You Are Proud—Matthew 25:34-40; Mark 10:35-45; Romans 12:3; Philippians 2:1-11

You Struggle With Addiction—Romans 6:1-23; Romans 12:1-2; 1 Corinthians 6:12-20; Philippians 3:17-4:1

You Are Greedy—Luke 12:13-21; 2 Corinthians 9:6-15; Ephesians 5:3-7; 1 John 3:16-18

You Desire to Learn How to Pray—Matthew 6:5-15; Mark 11:22-25; Luke 18:9-14; Philippians 4:4-7

You Struggle With Apathy—Matthew 25:1-13; Luke 12:35-48; 1 Thessalonians 5:1-11; Revelation 3:1-6, 14-22

WHAT THE BIBLE SAYS ABOUT:

Adultery—Matthew 5:27-32; Galatians 5:13-26; Ephesians 4:17–5:3

Ambition—Matthew 16:21-27; Mark 9:33-37; Mark 10:35-45; Philippians 2:1-4

Anger—Matthew 5:21-26; Ephesians 4:25–5:2; James 1:19-27

Anxiety—Luke 12:22-34; Philippians 4:4-9; Hebrews 13:5-6

Atonement—Romans 3:21-26; 2 Corinthians 5:14-21; Hebrews 9; 1 Peter 2:22-25

Baptism—Matthew 3:1-12; Matthew 28:16-20; Romans 6:1-5

Bible Reading—2 Timothy 3:14-17; Hebrews 4:12; James 1:19-27

Blood of Christ—Matthew 26:27-29; Hebrews 28

Body of Christ—Mark 14:22-24; 1 Corinthians 12:12-31; Hebrews 2:14-18

Celibacy—Matthew 19:4-12; 1 Corinthians 7:32-40; 1 Timothy 4:1-5

Children—Matthew 18:1-9; Mark 10:13-16; Ephesians 6:1-4

Compassion—John 11:17-44; 2 Corinthians 1:3-7; 1 John 3:11-24

Conversion—John 3:1-21; 2 Corinthians 5:17-19; Ephesians 2:1-10

Creation—Romans 1:18-23; Romans 8:18-27; Colossians 1:15-17

Cross—Mark 8:31–9:1; Luke 23:26-49

Death—John 12:23-26; Romans 6:1-23; 1 Corinthians 15

Discipleship—Luke 14:25-34; John 15:1-17; John 21:15-19

Discipline—1 Corinthians 11:27-32; Hebrews 12:1-13; Revelation 3:19

Divorce—Matthew 19:1-12; Mark 10:2-12; 1 Corinthians 7:10-16

Eternal Life—Matthew 19:16-30; John 3:1-21; Romans 6:15-23

Faith—Matthew 6:25-34; Romans 3:21–5:11; Hebrews 11

Freedom—John 8:31-41; Romans 8:1-17; Galatians 4:21–5:26

Friendship—John 14:23–15:17; Colossians 3:12-17; 1 John 1:1-7

Giving—Matthew 6:1-4; 2 Corinthians 8–9

Grace—Luke 15:11-31; Romans 5; Ephesians 2

Greed—Luke 12:13-21; 1 Timothy 6:3-10; James 5:1-6

Happiness—Matthew 5:1-12; John 13:1-17; Philippians 4:4-9

Heaven—Matthew 6:19-24; Matthew 25:31-46; Philippians 3:12–4:1

Holy Spirit—John 14:15-31; John 16:5-16; Acts 2; Romans 8:1-17

Homosexuality—Romans 1:18-32; 1 Corinthians 6:9-11; 1 Timothy 1:9-11

Hope—Romans 5:1-11; Colossians 1:3-27; 1 Peter 1:3-9

Hospitality—Luke 14:12-14; Romans 12:13; 1 Peter 4:9

Hypocrisy—Matthew 6:1-24; Matthew 23; James 1:22-27

Joy—Luke 15; James 1:2-18; 1 Peter 4:12-19

Justification—Romans 3:21-31; Romans 4:1–5:11; Galatians 2:15-21

Loneliness—Matthew 26:36-46; 2 Timothy 4:16-18

Lord's Supper—Luke 22:7-23; John 13; 1 Corinthians 11:17-34

Love—Mark 12:28-34; 1 Corinthians 13; 1 John 4:7-21

Marriage—Matthew 19:1-12; 1 Corinthians 7; Ephesians 5:22-33

Peace—John 14:25-27; Romans 5:1-11; Ephesians 2:14-18; Philippians 4:4-9

Poor—Matthew 25:31-46; Luke 1:39-56; James 2:1-13

Profanity—Ephesians 4:29-32; James 3:1-12

Reconciliation—Matthew 5:23-26; 2 Corinthians 5:11–6:2; Ephesians 2:11-22

Repentance—Matthew 4:12-17; Luke 18:9-14; Acts 2:38-41

Resurrection — Matthew 27:57–28:20; 1 Corinthians 15
Revenge — Matthew 5:38-47; Romans 12:17-21
Reward — Matthew 5:3-12; Mark 10:29-31; 1 Corinthians 3:10-15
Salvation — Luke 19:1-10; Acts 16:16-34; Ephesians 2:1-10
Sanctification — 2 Corinthians 7:1; 1 Thessalonians 5:23; 2 Peter 1:3-11
Second Coming — Matthew 24; John 14:1-4; 1 Corinthians 15:12-28; 1 Thessalonians 4:13–5:11
Stewardship — Matthew 25:14-30; Luke 12:35-48
Suffering — Romans 8:12-17; 1 Peter 3:8-22; 1 Peter 4:12-19
Unity — John 17; Ephesians 4:1-16

Dictionary-Concordance

Aaron — the brother of Moses; he served as Moses' spokesman before Pharaoh (Ex 4:14-16,27-31; 7:1-2); Israel's first high priest (Ex 28:1; Nu 17; Heb 5:1-4).

Abba — the word for *father* in Aramaic, one of the three languages Jesus spoke.
> Ro 8:15 And by him we cry "*A*, Father."
> Gal 4:6 the Spirit who calls out, "*A*, Father"

Abel — the second son of Adam (Ge 4:2); he offered the proper sacrifice to God (Ge 4:4; Heb 11:4), but was murdered by his brother Cain (Ge 4:8; Mt 23:35; 1Jn 3:12).

abhor — to hate or to turn away from.

Abigail — the wife of Nabal; she helped save David's life (1Sa 25:14-35) and later became his wife (1Sa 25:36-42).

abolish — to destroy completely; to put an end to.

abomination — a thing to be hated.

abound — to be more than enough; to overflow.

Abraham — the father of the Jewish nation. God established a covenant with him in which God promised that he would make a mighty nation of Abraham's children and would give them the land of Canaan (Ge 15; 17; 22; Ro 4; Heb 6:13-15). A son, Isaac, was born to Sarah and Abraham in their old age (Ge 17:16; 18:9-15; 21:1-7; Heb 11:11-12). Later, as a test, God told him to offer Isaac as a sacrifice (Ge 22; Heb 11:17-19) but withdrew this command when Abraham showed that he would trust the Lord even in this matter.

Absalom — a son of David (2Sa 3:3); he fled from Israel after murdering his half-brother Amnon (2Sa 13). Upon his return, he plotted to take David's throne. He met death when his long hair became entangled in an oak tree and Joab, David's commander, thrust javelins into his heart (2Sa 14-18).

abstain — to keep yourself from doing something.

accordance — agreement.

accredited — officially approved.

accursed — to be condemned or doomed by a curse.

Achan — an Israelite who kept spoil from the conquest of Jericho for himself; as a result of Achan's stealing what belonged to God, the Israelites were defeated at Ai and he and his family were stoned to death (Jos 7; 22:20).

acknowledge — to know and to say that something is true.

acquit — to free from punishment or blame.

acts — deeds.
> Ps 150:2 Praise him for his *a* of power
> Isa 64:6 all our righteous *a* are like filthy

Adam — the first man God created (Ge 1:26-2:25); he sinned by disobeying God (Ge 3) thereby bringing all people under the curse of sin (Ro 5:12-21).

admonish — to give warning or advice in a caring way.

adorn — to make more beautiful.

adultery — having sexual relations with someone other than one's husband or wife.
> Ex 20:14 You shall not commit *a*
> Mt 5:28 lustfully has already committed *a*

adversary — enemy; opponent.

advocate — 1. (*v.*) to speak in favor of. 2. (*n.*) someone who speaks in another person's defense. Jesus is our advocate.

affliction — trouble or pain that lasts a long time.
> Ro 12:12 patient in *a*, faithful in prayer.

aforethought — thought about or planned ahead of time.

Ahab — a wicked king of Israel; the husband of Jezebel (1Ki 16:31). He caused Israel to worship Baal rather than God (1Ki 16:31-33) and was opposed by God's prophet Elijah (1Ki 17:1; 18; 21).

alabaster — a hard marblelike material that can be made into jars, vases or sculptures.

alien — a foreigner or stranger.
> Ex 22:21 "Do not mistreat an *a*
> Eph 2:19 no longer foreigners and *a*, but fellow citizens
> 1Pe 2:11 as *a* and strangers in the world

alienate — to make unfriendly; to turn a person's interest or affection away from another person or thing.

allot — to divide and give away in parts. In Old Testament times the land of Canaan was allotted to the twelve tribes of Israel.

Almighty — a name used to show how strong and powerful God is.

Ge 17:1 "I am God *A;* walk before me
Isa 6:3 "Holy, holy, holy is the LORD *A*

altar — a raised platform, made of stones, metal, dirt or wood, on which sacrifices were made.

Amen — So be it; Let it become true.

Ananias — 1. the husband of Sapphira; he was struck dead for lying to God (Ac 5:1-11); 2. the disciple who baptized Saul (Ac 9:10-19); 3. the high priest before whom Paul was tried in Jerusalem (Ac 22:30-24:1).

Ancient of Days — a name for God that was often used to tell of his wisdom and dignity.

Andrew — one of the twelve apostles; the brother of Peter (Mt 4:18; 10:2; Ac 1:13).

angel — a heavenly being.

Ps 34:7 The *a* of the LORD encamps
Heb 1:14 Are not all *a* ministering spirits
Heb 2:7 made him a little lower than the *a*
1Pe 1:12 Even *a* long to look

annals — historical writings.

annihilate — to destroy completely.

anoint — to pour oil on a person's head.

antichrist — a person who is against Christ.
1Jn 2:18 have heard that the *a* is coming
1Jn 2:22 a man is the *a* — he denies

anxiety — worry.
1Pe 5:7 Cast all your *a* on him

Apollos — a Christian from Alexandria who knew the Scriptures well (Ac 18:24-28) and helped Paul to minister in Corinth (Ac 19:1; 1Co 1:12).

apostle — 1. the twelve men Jesus chose to work with him during his earthly ministry; after being equipped by the Holy Spirit, they were sent out to preach about Jesus; The twelve are: Andrew, James the son of Alphaeus, James the son of Zebedee, John, Judas Iscariot, Matthew, Nathanael (Bartholomew), Peter, Philip, Simon, Thaddaeus (Judas), and Thomas. 2. later, someone who had been with Jesus, had seen his miracles and then taught others about him.

Mk 3:14 twelve — designating them *a* —

1Co 12:28 God has appointed first of all *a*
1Co 15:9 For I am the least of the *a*

aqueduct — a channel for bringing water from one place to another.

Aquila — the husband of Priscilla; Aquila and Priscilla were co-workers with Paul in Corinth (Ac 18; Ro 16:3).

Aramaic — the main language used in the countries east of the Mediterranean Sea during Jesus' earthly ministry.

archangel — an angel of high rank; a leader of other angels.

archives — the official records of a government.

ark of the Testimony — a large gold-covered box housed in the Tabernacle, with two gold cherubim on its lid. It contained the Ten Commandments (Tablets of Testimony), a jar of manna and Aaron's staff, and was kept inside the Most Holy Place in the Tent of Meeting. It was a sign to the Israelites of God's presence with them, and was also the place where God revealed to his people, through the priests, what was his will for them.

Armageddon — the site of the final battle between God and Satan.

Rev 16:16 that in Hebrew is called *A*.

armor — protective clothing worn in battle, usually made of metal

Eph 6:11 Put on the full *a* of God.

arrogant — proud; conceited.

ascend — to go up. Jesus ascended to heaven to return to God the Father.

ascribe — to think of as caused by, coming from or belonging to.

1Ch 16:28 *a* to the LORD glory and strength

assert — to say positively.

astray — mistaken; not on the right path; lost.

atone — to make right, by paying the penalty, the relationship between God and humans that we broke through sin. In the Old Testament people atoned symbolically for their sins by offering sacrifices to God. In the New Testament Jesus corrected the relationship between God and people once and for all by dying for our sins.

atonement — the payment that corrects the relationship between God and humans that we broke through sin.

Lev 17:11 it is the blood that makes *a*
Lev 23:27 this seventh month is the Day of *A*.
Ro 3:25 presented him as a sacrifice of *a*,
Heb 2:17 that he might make *a* for the sins

authority — the right and power to give orders.
Mt 9:6 the Son of Man has *a* on earth
Mt 28:18 "All *a* in heaven and on earth has
Ro 13:1 for there is no *a* except that which
Heb 13:17 your leaders and submit to their *a*.

avenge — to get back at or punish someone who has done wrong.
Dt 32:35 It is mine to *a; I will repay.

awe — respect and wonder; a holy fear of God because of his great power.
Ecc 5:7 Therefore stand in *a* of God.
Ac 2:43 Everyone was filled with *a*
Heb 12:28 acceptably with reverence and *a*

Baal — the name of many false gods in Canaan. Each section of Canaan had its own Baal, for example, Baal of Peor, Baal of Hermon, Baal-Berith.
1Ki 18:25 Elijah said to the prophets of *B*

Babylon — the beautiful capital of Babylonia; it was a powerful and influential city in the Near East from the eighteenth to the sixth centuries B.C. The Babylonians destroyed Jerusalem in 602 B.C. and took many Israelites, such as Daniel and his friends, to Babylon. These captives lived there for about seventy years. In the New Testament, Babylon represents the godless city.
Ps 137:1 By the rivers of *B* we sat and wept

Balaam — a seer who tried to curse Israel during their journey to the promised land, but God would not allow it (Nu 22-24).

balm — a skin cream used to heal sores and relieve pain.

banish — to force a person away from a place.

baptize — a religious ceremony in which water is used as a symbol of cleansing from sin. Churches today baptize by sprinkling or pouring or immersing in water. Baptism is a sign that our sins are washed away and that Jesus has taken us to be his own.
Mk 1:9 and was *b* by John in the Jordan.
Mk 16:16 believes and is *b* will be saved,
Ac 1:5 but in a few days you will be *b*
Ac 2:38 Repent and be *b*, every one of you,
Ac 16:33 he and all his family were *b*.
Ac 18:8 heard him believed and were *b*.

Barabbas — the Jews chose this criminal, rather than Jesus, to be released by Pilate (Mt 27:26).

Barnabas — an apostle; he was a co-worker with Paul on his first missionary journey (Ac 9:27; chs 13-15).

barren — 1. unable to have children. 2. unable to produce crops.

Bartholomew — one of the twelve apostles (Mt 10:3; Ac 1:13). He was also probably known as Nathanael (Jn 1:45-49; 21:2).

Bathsheba — the wife of Uriah; she committed adultery with David and later became his wife (2Sa 11); the mother of Solomon (2Sa 12:24).

Beelzebub — the prince of demons; Satan.
Lk 11:15, "By *B*, the prince of demons,

believe — to accept as true; to trust; to have faith.
Mk 1:15 Repent and *b* the good news!"
Mk 9:24 "I do *b*; help me overcome my
Jn 1:7 that through him all men might *b*.
Jn 3:18 does not *b* stands condemned
Jn 20:27 Stop doubting and *b*."
Ac 16:31 They replied, "*B* in the Lord Jesus,
Ro 3:22 faith in Jesus Christ to all who *b*.
1Th 4:14 We *b* that Jesus died and rose again

Benjamin — the twelfth son of Jacob. Rachel was his mother and he was the younger brother of Joseph (Ge 35:16-24; chs. 42-45).

bereaved — left alone, especially because of the death of a close friend or relative.

besiege — to surround a city or town completely with an army, so that nothing can go in or out.

bestow — to give.

Bethlehem — the city in Judea where Jesus was born (Mt 2:1).

betray — to turn a friend over to his or her enemies; to be unfaithful to.

betroth — to promise to marry.

bewildered — confused; puzzled.

bier — a platform on which a coffin or dead body is carried.

birthright — the special rights of the first-born son. In the Old Testament, after the father died the oldest son received the father's power and right to make decisions for the entire family. He also got twice as much money and property as each of his brothers.

Ge 25:34 So Esau despised his *b.*

blameless — without fault.

Ge 17:1 walk before me and be *b.*

1Co 1:8 so that you will be *b* on the day

Php 2:15 so that you may become *b* and pure

blaspheme — to speak carelessly, falsely or insultingly about God or holy things.

Mk 3:29 whoever *b* against the Holy Spirit

blemish — a spot or mark that makes something imperfect.

bless — 1. to make holy; 2. to show favor to; 3. to ask God to show favor to.

Ge 2:3 And God *b* the seventh day

Ge 12:3 I will *b* those who *b* you,

Mt 5:3 saying "*B* are the poor in spirit

Ro 12:14 *b* those who persecute you; *b*

blight — a disease in plants that makes them shrivel up and die.

blood —

Ex 12:13 and when I see the *b,* I will pass

Mt 26:28 This is my *b* of the covenant

Ro 5:9 have now been justified by his *b*

Eph 1:7 we have redemption through his *b*

Heb 9:12 once for all by his own *b*

Rev 5:9 with your *b* you purchased men

Rev 7:14 white in the *b* of the Lamb.

boast — to brag.

Ps 34:2 My soul will *b* in the Lord

Gal 6:14 May I never *b* except in the cross

Boaz — a wealthy man who lived in Bethlehem in the days of the judges; he married Ruth (Ru 2; 4).

body —

Ro 6:13 Do not offer the parts of your *b*

Ro 12:1 to offer your *b* as living sacrifices,

1Co 6:19 not know that your *b* is a temple

1Co 12:12 The *b* is a unit, though it is made up

Eph 5:30 for we are members of his *b.*

bondage — slavery.

Ezr 9:9 God has not deserted us in our *b.*

booty — valuables taken from a conquered people.

branch —

Isa 4:2 In that day the *B* of the Lord will

Jer 33:15 I will make a righteous *B* sprout

Jn 15:5 "I am the vine; you are the *b.*

bread —

Dt 8:3 that man does not live on *b* alone

Pr 30:8 but give me only my daily *b.*

Isa 55:2 Why spend money on what is not *b*

Mt 6:11 Give us today our daily *b.*

Jn 6:35 Jesus declared, "I am the *b* of life.

breastpiece — a decorated square of linen cloth worn by the high priest when he entered the Holy Place. The breastpiece was worn chest-high and over a robe. On it were twelve gems, one for each of the twelve tribes of Israel.

Ex 28:15 "Fashion a *b* for making decisions

breastplate — a chest-covering made of metal or leather, worn by soldiers for protection.

brother —

Ge 4:9 "Am I my *b* keeper?"

Ps 133:1 is when *b* live together in unity!

Mt 18:15 'If your *b* sins against you

burden — a heavy load.

Mt 11:30 my yoke is easy and my *b* is light.

Gal 6:2 Carry each other's *b*

Caesar — the title of many Roman emperors.

Lk 2:1 In those days *C* Augustus

Mt 22:21 "Give to *C* what is Caesar's

Cain — Adam and Eve's firstborn son; he murdered his brother Abel (Ge 4:1-16).

calamity — a disaster, usually causing great loss and suffering.

caldron — a large clay or metal pot.

Caleb — one of the twelve men who spied out Canaan. He came back with a positive report and encouraged the Israelites to take possession of Canaan. His faith allowed him to enter Canaan (Nu 13:6-14:38; Dt 1:36) whereas those Israelites who believed the report of the other ten spies died during Israel's forty years of wandering in the desert.

call (*v.*) —
  2Ch 7:14 if my people, who are *c*
  Ps 145:18 near to all who *c* on him
  Isa 65:24 Before they *c* I will answer
  Mt 9:13 come to *c* the righteous
  Jn 10:3 He *c* his own sheep by name
  Ro 8:30 And those he predestined, he also *c*
  Ro 10:12 and richly blesses all who *c* on
  1Pe 2:9 of him who *c* you out of darkness

call, calling (*n.*) —
  Ro 11:29 gifts and his *c* are irrevocable
  Eph 4:1 worthy of the *c* you have received
  2Pe 1:10 all the more eager to make your *c*

Canaan — 1. the land God promised to the nation of Israel; 2. the promised land.
  1Ch 16:18 "To you I will give the land of *C*

capstone — the stone that holds two walls together; the stone that finishes a wall.
  1Pe 2:7 has become the *c,*

censer — a bowl or dish used for carrying hot coals or for burning incense.

centurion — a Roman army officer in charge of one hundred soldiers.

chaff — the seed covering of a grain such as wheat. In Bible times the grain and chaff were separated by tossing the grain into the air so the wind could blow the chaff away.
  Ps 1:4 they are like *c*
  Mt 3:12 up the *c* with unquenchable fire

chariot — a two-wheeled vehicle pulled by horses.
  2Ki 6:17 and *c* of fire all around Elisha

chasten — to correct or improve by punishment or suffering.

cheerful —
  Pr 15:13 A happy heart makes the face *c*
  2Co 9:7 for God loves a *c* giver.

cherub — an angel, with an appearance something like a human being. The word for more than one cherub is *cherubim.*

children —
  Ps 8:2 from the lips of *c* and infants
  Pr 17:6 Children's *c* are a crown
  Mt 19:14 "Let the little *c* come to me
  Ro 8:16 with our spirit that we are God's *c.*
  Eph 6:1 *C,* obey your parents in the Lord,
  Eph 6:4 do not exasperate your *c;* instead
  1Jn 3:1 that we should be called *c* of God

choose —
  Jos 24:15 then *c* for yourselves this day
  Jn 15:16 You did not *c* me,
  Jn 15:16 But I *c* you to go and bear fruit
  Eph 1:4 he *c* us in him before the creation
  2Th 2:13 from the beginning God *c* you

chosen —
  Mt 22:14 For many are invited, but few are *c*
  Jn 15:19 but I have *c* you out of the world
  1Pe 2:9 But you are a *c* people, a royal

Christ — the official title of Jesus, meaning "the Anointed One." It is a Greek word, and it means the same as the Hebrew word *Messiah.*
  Mt 1:16 was born Jesus, who is called *C.*
  Mt 16:16 Peter answered, "You are the *C*
  Jn 1:41 found the Messiah" (that is, the *C*).
  Jn 20:31 you may believe that Jesus is the *C*
  Ro 5:8 While we were still sinners, *C* died
  1Co 1:23 but we preached *C* crucified
  1Co 12:27 Now you are the body of *C*
  Eph 5:2 as *C* loved us and gave himself up
  Eph 5:23 as *C* is the head of the church
  Php 1:21 to live is *C* and to die is gain.
  2Th 2:1 the coming of our Lord Jesus *C*

Christian — a believer in or follower of Christ.
  Ac 11:26 The disciples were first called *C*
  1Pe 4:16 as a *C,* do not be ashamed,

chronicles — a history of events in the order in which they took place.

church —
  Mt 16:18 and on this rock I will build my *c*
  Eph 5:23 as Christ is the head of the *c*
  Col 1:24 the sake of his body, which is the *c.*

circumcise — to cut off the loose fold of skin at the end of the penis.
  Ge 17:10 Every male among you shall be *c.*

cistern — a pit dug into the ground for storing rainwater.

citadel — a tower or building equipped for war, especially one in a city.

city of refuge — one of six cities set aside by Moses and Joshua for those who had accidentally killed someone. Such people would be safe there until a fair trial could be held.

clean animals — animals God allowed the Israelites to sacrifice and eat.

cleanse — to make clean; to wash.

cloak — a loose-fitting coat without sleeves.

co-heir — one of two persons who receive an inheritance. Because of Christ's death and resurrection, we are co-heirs with him of our inheritance in God.

Ro 8:17 heirs of God and *c* with Christ

comfort —

Ps 23:4 rod and your staff, they *c* me.
Zec 1:17 and the Lord will again *c* Zion
2Co 1:4 so that we can *c* those

commandment — an order given by God. God gave the Ten Commandments to the Israelites while they were encamped in the area of Mount Sinai.

Ex 20:6 who love me and keep my *c*.
Mt 22:38 This is the first and greatest *c*.
Jn 13:34 "A new *c* I give you: Love one

commemorate — to remember an event with a special celebration or ceremony.

commend — 1. to praise; 2. to hand over to someone for safekeeping.

compassion — sympathy; pity.

Ps 103:4 and crowns me with love and *c*.
Mt 9:36 When he saw the crowds, he had *c*
Ro 9:15 and I will have *c* on whom I have *c*.
Col 3:12 clothe yourselves with *c*, kindness,

compassionate —

Ne 9:17 gracious and *c*, slow to anger

complacent — contented; unconcerned.

conceive — 1. to become pregnant; 2. to think up or imagine.

Mt 1:20 what is *c* in her is from the Holy
1Co 2:9 no mind has *c*

concubine — in Bible times, a woman who belonged to a man but did not have the rights of a wife. She was often one of the spoils of war, and her primary purpose was to bear children for the man.

condemn — to give out punishment to; to pronounce guilty.

Jn 3:17 Son into the world to *c* the world,
Ro 8:34 Who is he that *c*? Christ Jesus

condemnation —

Ro 8:1 there is now no *c* for those who are

confess — 1. to say what you believe; 2. to tell your sins to someone.

Lev 26:40 "But if they will *c* their sins
Ro 10:9 That if you *c* with your mouth
Php 2:11 every tongue *c* that Jesus Christ
1Jn 1:9 If we *c* our sins, he is faithful

conform — to agree with and try to be like someone; to do what others say to do.

Ro 8:29 predestined to be *c* to the likeness
1Pe 1:14 do not *c* to the evil desires you had

conscience — the sense of knowing if something is good or bad; a sense of right and wrong.

Ro 2:15 their *c* also bearing witness
Tit 1:15 their minds and *c* are corrupted.
Heb 9:14 cleanse our *c* from acts that lead

conscript — 1. to take for government use; 2. to force to serve in an army.

consecrate — to set aside or dedicate for God's use.

Ex 13:2 "*C* to me every firstborn male
Lev 20:7 "*C* yourselves and be holy

console — to comfort.

conspire — to plan together to do evil.

consume — 1. to use up or eat up; 2. to destroy completely.

Jn 2:17 "Zeal for your house will *c* me."
Heb 12:29 for our God is a *c* fire.

contempt — lack of respect; looking down on someone or something as being worthless.

Pr 14:31 He who oppresses the poor shows *c*
1Th 5:20 do not treat prophecies with *c*.

content —

Php 4:11 to be *c* whatever the circumstances,
Heb 13:5 and be *c* with what you have

contrite — to feel sorry for one's sins; to feel repentant.

Ps 51:17 a broken and *c* heart
Isa 66:2 he who is humble and *c* in spirit

convert — a person who has changed from one belief to another.

1Ti 3:6 He must not be a recent *c*

convict — 1. to prove one wrong; 2. to make a person feel sorrow.

Jn 16:8 he will *c* the world of guilt in regard

convulsion — a wild shaking of the body; violent contraction and expansion of one's muscles.

Cornelius — a Roman to whom Peter preached the gospel; he became the first Gentile Christian (Ac 10).

cornerstone — the first or most important stone laid when constructing a building.
Eph 2:20 with Christ Jesus himself as the chief *c*.

corrupt — 1. (*v.*) to change from good to bad; 2. (*adj.*) wicked.
Ge 6:11 Now the earth was *c* in God's sight
1Co 15:33 "Bad company *c* good character."

counsel — to give advice to.

Counselor — another name for the Holy Spirit.
Jn 14:26 But the *C*, the Holy Spirit,
Jn 15:26 "When the *C* comes, whom I will

covenant — 1. an agreement between two people or two groups of people, in which usually both make specific promises. 2. the promises of God for salvation.
Ge 9:9 "I now establish my *c* with you
Ge 17:2 I will confirm my *c* between me
Ex 19:5 if you obey me fully and keep my *c*
Jer 31:31 "when I will make a new *c*
Eze 37:26 I will make a *c* of peace with them
1Co 11:25 "This cup is the new *c* in my blood
Heb 9:15 Christ is the mediator of a new *c*

covet — to want for yourself something that belongs to another person.
Ex 20:17 You shall not *c* your neighbor's

create — to make; to bring into being. God created the world; the world is God's creation; God is the Creator.
Ge 1:1 In the beginning God *c* the heavens
Ps 51:10 *C* in me a pure heart, O God
Col 1:16 For by him all things were *c*
Rev 10:6 who *c* the heavens and all that

cross —
Mt 10:38 and anyone who does not take his *c*
Gal 6:14 in the *c* of our Lord Jesus Christ

Php 2:8 even death on a *c*!
Col 2:14 he took it away, nailing it to the *c*
Heb 12:2 set before him endured the *c*

crown —
Pr 4:9 present you with a *c* of splendor."
Isa 61:3 to bestow on them a *c* of beauty
1Co 9:25 it to get a *c* that will last forever.
2Ti 4:8 store for me the *c* of righteousness
Rev 2:10 and I will give you the *c* of life.

crucify — to put to death by nailing or tying a person's body to a cross.
Mt 27:22 They all answered,"*C* him!"
Jn 19:18 Here they *c* him, and with him two
1Co 1:23 but we preach Christ *c*: a stumbling
Gal 2:20 I have been *c* with Christ

curse — (*v.*) to ask God to bring evil or injury to; (*n.*) a prayer or desire that evil or injury come upon someone.
Lev 20:9 "If anyone *c* his father or mother
Dt 21:23 hung on a tree is under God's *c*.
Lk 6:28 bless those who *c* you, pray
Gal 3:13 *C* is everyone who is hung on a tree
Jas 3:9 with it we *c* men, who have been

Daniel — a young Jewish exile; he lived in Babylon during the reign of several kings, including Nebuchadnezzar. He was found praying to God, contrary to an edict prohibiting for thirty days subjects from praying to anyone except the king. For this he was thrown into a lion's den (Da 1-6).

David — the son of Jesse; in early life: anointed by Samuel to become king of Israel (1Sa 16:1-13); killed the giant Goliath (1Sa 17); and was pursued by Saul. After Saul's death (2Sa 1) he was made king (2Sa 5:1-4), and it was during his reign that Israel's place in the land of Canaan was made secure.

day —
Ge 1:5 God called the light "*d*"
Ps 118:24 This is the *d* the Lord has made;
Ecc 12:1 Creator in the *d* of your youth,
Joel 2:31 and dreadful *d* of the Lord.
Mic 4:1 in the last *d*
Lk 11:3 Give us each *d* our daily bread.
Heb 1:2 in these last *d* he has spoken to
2Pe 3:8 With the Lord a *d* is like

deacon — a church leader chosen to take

care of money matters and to give money to the widows and the poor.

1Ti 3:8 *D*, likewise, are to be men worthy

death —
Ps 23:4 the valley of the shadow of *d*,
Ecc 7:2 for *d* is the destiny of every man;
Isa 25:8 he will swallow up *d* forever.
Ro 6:23 For the wages of sin is *d*,
1Co 15:21 For since *d* came through a man,
1Co 15:55 Where, O *d*, is your sting?"
Rev 1:18 And I hold the keys of *d* and Hades
Rev 21:4 There will be no more *d*

debauchery — living an immoral life or a life without religion; living to please only yourself.

Deborah — a prophetess who led Israel to victory over the Canaanites (Jdg 4-5).

debt — something that one person owes another. (Also, debtor.)
Mt 6:12 Forgive us our *d*,

deceive — (*v.*) to fool or trick; to lie (*n.* deceit, deception; *adj.* deceitful).
Ge 3:13 "The serpent *d* me, and I ate."
1Co 3:18 Do not *d* yourselves.
Gal 6:7 Do not be *d*: God cannot be
1Jn 1:8 we *d* ourselves and the truth is

decree — an order or law given by someone with power and authority.

dedicate — to set apart for a special purpose, often for God's use.

defect — imperfection; fault.

defile — to make something that is good and pure impure or unclean.

defraud — to cheat someone by trickery.

Deity — God.
Col 2:9 of the *D* lives in bodily form,

deliver — to rescue; to set free.

demon — evil spirit. A demon-possessed person is one who is controlled by evil spirits.
Mk 5:15 possessed by the legion of *d*
Ro 8:38 neither angels not *d*, neither
1Co 10:20 of pagans are offered to *d*,
1Ti 4:1 spirits and things taught by *d*.
Jas 2:19 Good! Even the *d* believe that
Rev 16:14 of *d* performing miraculous signs

denarius — a small Roman coin made of silver. During Jesus' earthly ministry, one de-

narius was the payment for about one day's work.

denounce — to say a person or thing is evil.

depraved — evil or sinful.
Php 2:15 fault in a crooked and *d* generation

depravity —
Ro 1:29 of wickedness, evil, greed and *d*.
2Pe 2:19 they themselves are slaves of *d*

desecrate — to treat without respect or reverence.

desolate — not lived in; lonely; deserted.

destine — (*v.*) to decide ahead of time (*n.* destiny).

destitute — not having necessary things such as money and food.

detest — to hate.

devil —
Lk 4:2 forty days he was tempted by the *d*.
Eph 4:27 and do not give the *d* a foothold.
Eph 6:11 stand against the *d* schemes.
2Ti 2:26 and escape from the trap of the *d*,
Jas 4:7 Resist the *d*, and he will flee
1Pe 5:8 Your enemy the *d* prowls
1Jn 3:8 was to destroy the *d* work.
Rev 12:9 that ancient serpent called the *d*

devote — to set apart for a special person or for a special reason; to set apart for God's use.

devout — religious; giving much time to prayer and worship.

die —
Ge 2:17 when you eat of it you will surely *d*
2Ki 14:6 each is to *d* for his own sins."
Ecc 3:2 a time to be born and a time to *d*
Eze 3:18 that wicked man will *d* for his sin
Eze 18:4 soul who sins is the one who will *d*.
Jn 11:26 and believes in me will never *d*.
Ro 14:8 and if we *d*, we *d* to the Lord.
1Co 15:22 in Adam all *d*, so in Christ all
Php 1:21 to live is Christ and to *d* is gain.
Rev 14:13 Blessed are the dead who *d*

dirge — a song of deep sadness, usually sung at funerals.

discern — to understand; to come to know the difference between two or more things.

Php 1:10 you may be able to *d* what is best

disciple—a follower or student, especially one who believes what the leader teaches. Anyone who believes in Jesus is his disciple.

Lk 14:27 and follow me cannot be my *d*.
Jn 13:35 men will know that you are my *d*

discipline—(*v*.) to correct; to teach what is right; (*n*.) training that corrects, molds or perfects moral character.

Ps 39:11 You rebuke and *d* men for their sin
Pr 15:5 A fool spurns his father's *d*
Pr 29:17 *D* your son, and he will give you
Heb 12:6 the Lord *d* those he loves
Rev 3:19 Those whom I love I rebuke and *d*.

disclose—to show or reveal.

discourse—1. (*v*.) to talk together; 2. (*n*.) a conversation or speech.

discriminate—to make a difference where no such difference should or does exist; to treat two persons or things differently because one seems better than the other.

Jas 2:4 have you not *d* among yourselves

disgrace—to bring shame to.

disown—to reject someone or something so completely that it no longer belongs to you.

Mt 26:35 to die with you, I will never *d* you."
2Ti 2:12 if we *d* him,

disperse—to scatter; to spread around.

dissension—disagreement; quarreling.

dissipation—living only for your own pleasure; wasting your life on foolish or evil pleasures.

divination—seeing into the future by magic.

Lev 19:26 " 'Do not practice *d* or sorcery.

divine—given by God; belonging to God.

Ro 1:20 his eternal power and *d* nature
2Co 10:4 they have *d* power

divorce—

Mal 2:16 "I hate *d*," says the LORD God
Mt 19:3 for a man to *d* his wife for any
1Co 7:11 And a husband must not *d* his wife.

doctrine—teachings or beliefs about God.

1Ti 4:16 Watch your life and *d* closely.
Tit 2:1 is in accord with sound *d*.

dominion—power; rule.

Ps 22:28 for *d* belongs to the LORD
Eph 1:21 far above all rule and authority, power and *d*

doom—1. (*v*.) to make certain something will fail or be destroyed; 2. (*n*.) fate; condemnation; ruin.

door—

Mt 7:7 and the *d* will be opened to you.
Rev 3:20 I stand at the *d* and knock.

doubt—

Mt 21:21 if you have faith and do not *d*
Mk 11:23 and does not *d* in his heart
Jas 1:6 he must believe and not *d*

dropsy—puffiness or swelling of the body caused by a disease of the kidneys, liver or heart.

earth—

Ge 1:1 God created the heavens and the *e*.
Ps 24:1 *e* is the LORD's and everything
Mt 6:10 done on *e* as it is in heaven.
Mt 24:35 Heaven and *e* will pass away
Lk 2:14 on *e* peace to men
Php 2:10 in heaven and on *e* and under the *e*
2Pe 3:13 to a new heaven and a new *e*

edict—an order or law made by a person who has the power to enforce it.

edify—to teach someone to live a godly life, or to help someone to live in such a way.

1Co 14:4 but he who prophesies *e* the church

elders—1. the older men of a town or nation. They were the leaders of their community and made all the important decisions. Each town had its own groups of elders. After the Jews returned from exile in Babylon, the elders made up the Sanhedrin, the ruling council of the Jews. 2. the leaders of the church.

1Ti 5:17 The *e* who direct the affairs
Tit 1:5 and appoint *e* in every town

election—

Ro 9:11 God's purpose in *e* might stand
2Pe 1:10 to make your calling and *e* sure.

Eli—the high priest with whom Samuel spent the early years of his life (1Sa 2:11-26).

Elijah—a prophet of the Lord during the reign of Ahab. He predicted a famine in Israel (1Ki 17:1), and defeated the prophets of Baal at Carmel in the test of whose God would set fire to the altar (1Ki 18:16-46). He was taken to heaven in a whirlwind (2Ki 2:11-12) and later appeared with Moses at the transfiguration of Jesus (Mk 9:1-8).

Elisha — the prophet who succeeded Elijah. He was present when God took Elijah to heaven, and he took his place as prophet to Israel (2Ki 2:1-18).

Elizabeth — the mother of John the Baptist. She became pregnant when she was very old; Mary went to visit her when she found out she, too, was pregnant (Lk 1:5-58).

enchanter — a magician or snake charmer.

endure — to continue; to keep on going; to bear something that is difficult or painful.
  Ps 136:1 His love e forever.
  Mal 3:2 who can e the day of his coming
  2Ti 2:3 E hardship with us like a good

enmity — hatred or bad feelings that make two people or two groups enemies.
  Ge 3:15 And I will put e

Enoch — a man who "walked with God." Later in life, God "took him away" (Ge 5:18-24).

envy — to want for yourself something that belongs to another person.
  1Co 13:4 It does not e, it does not boast

ephod — a linen apron worn by a priest over his robe. It was decorated with gold, blue, purple and scarlet yarns.

Ephraim — 1. one of Joseph's sons; 2. one of the tribes of Israel. Its members were descendants of Ephraim. 3. a name for the northern kingdom of Israel after the ten tribes of Israel and the two tribes of Judah separated from each other.
  Ge 41:52 The second son he named E
  Isa 7:17 unlike any since E broke away
    from Judah

epileptic — a person afflicted with a disorder of the brain that makes one lose control of his or her muscles and sometimes causes unconsciousness. In Bible times epilepsy was a dreaded disease; but today it can be controlled by medicine.

equity — fairness.

Esau — the firstborn son of Isaac and twin of Jacob (Ge 25:21-26). He sold his birthright to Jacob for a pot of stew (Ge 25:29-34) and was tricked out of his blessing by this same brother (Ge 27). Later in his life

he and Jacob met and were reconciled (Ge 33).

esteem — 1. (v.) to value; to consider important; 2. (n.) high regard or respect.

Esther — a Jewish woman who lived in Persia (Est 2:7). Xerxes chose her to be queen (Est 2:8-18). Upon being told of a plot by Haman to kill the Jews, she went to the king and pleaded for the Jewish people and thus saved them (Est 3-4; 7-9).

eternal — without beginning or end; forever; timeless. God is eternal.
  Dt 33:27 The e God is your refuge,
  Jn 3:16 him shall not perish but have e
    life.
  Ro 6:23 but the gift of God is e life
  1Jn 5:13 you may know that you have e
    life.

eunuch — 1. the most important official after the king or queen; 2. a man whose sex organs have been removed so that he cannot produce children.

evangelist — a person who preaches the good news about Jesus.
  Ac 21:8 stayed at the house of Philip the e
  Eph 4:11 some to be prophets, some to
    be e

Eve — the first woman God created (Ge 2:20-24). Her name means, Mother of all the living (Ge 3:20).

everlasting — forever; without end.
  Ps 90:2 from e to e you are God.
  Isa 9:6 E Father, Prince of Peace
  Isa 55:3 I will make an e covenant with
    you
  Jn 6:47 the truth, he who believes has e
    life.
  2Th 1:9 punished with e destruction

evil — wicked; doing things against God's will.
  Ge 2:9 of the knowledge of good and e
  Ps 23:4 I will fear no e
  Isa 13:11 I will punish the world for its e
  Isa 55:7 and the e man his thoughts.
  Mt 6:13 but deliver us from the e one."
  Ro 12:9 Hate what is e; cling
  Ro 12:17 Do not repay anyone e for e.
  Eph 6:16 all the flaming arrows of the e
    one.
  Jas 1:13 For God cannot be tempted by e

exalt — to praise; to raise to an important position.

Ps 118:28 you are my God, and I will *e* you.

Ps 148:13 for his name alone is *e*

Pr 14:34 Righteousness *e* a nation

Mt 23:12 For whoever *e* himself will be

exile — (*v.*) to force someone to leave his or her country or home; (*n.*) forced removal from one's country or home.

2Ch 36:20 He carried into *e* to Babylon

exodus — the departure of a large group of people from one place to go to another. The book of Exodus is the story of the Israelites' journey from Egypt to Canaan.

exploit — to take unfair advantage of.

extol — to praise.

Ps 34:1 I will *e* the Lord at all times

Ps 95:2 and *e* him with music and song.

extortion — something gotten from a person by force or by using other illegal means.

Ezekiel — a priest who was called to be a prophet to the Jewish people when they were in exile in Babylon (Eze 1-3). He had many visions from the Lord (Eze 37; 40).

Ezra — a priest and teacher of the Law; he led a group of Jewish exiles back to Israel and helped them reestablish the temple of God and restore proper worship (Ezr 7-8).

faction — a group of people trying to get its own way or promote its own interests.

faith — belief and trust in God; knowing that God is real, even though we can't see him.

Hab 2:4 but the righteous will live by his *f*

Mt 17:20 if you have *f* as small as a

Lk 7:9 I have not found such great *f*

Ro 1:17 "The righteous will live by *f*."

Ro 3:22 comes through *f* in Jesus Christ

1Co 13:2 and if I have a *f* that can move

2Co 5:7 We live by *f*, not by sight.

Eph 6:16 to all this, take up the shield of *f*,

1Ti 6:12 Fight the good fight of the *f*.

Heb 11:1 *f* is being sure of what we hope

Heb 11:8 By *f* Abraham, when called to

Heb 12:2 the author and perfecter of our *f*

Jas 2:26 so *f* without deeds is dead.

faithful — trustworthy; loyal. God is faithful.

Ps 145:13 the Lord is *f* to all his promises

Mt 25:21 "Well done, good and *f* servant!

Ro 12:12 patient in affliction, *f* in prayer.

1Co 10:13 And God is *f*; he will not let you be

1Jn 1:9 he is *f* and just and will forgive

Rev 1:5 who is the *f* witness, the firstborn

faithfulness —

Ps 86:15 to anger, abounding in love and *f*.

La 3:23 great is your *f*.

Gal 5:22 patience, kindness, goodness, *f*

falsehood — a lie.

family —

Ps 68:6 God sets the lonely in *f*

Lk 9:61 go back and say good-by to my *f*."

Lk 12:52 in one *f* divided against each other

1Ti 3:4 He must manage his own *f* well

1Ti 5:4 practice by caring for their own *f*

father —

Ge 2:24 this reason a man will leave his *f*

Ge 17:4 You will be the *f* of many nations.

Ex 20:12 "Honor your *f* and your mother

Pr 23:22 Listen to your *f*, who gave you life

Mt 6:9 "Our *F* in heaven

Lk 11:11 "Which of you *f*, if your son asks

Lk 23:34 Jesus said, "*F*, forgive them

Jn 10:30 I and the *F* are one."

Jn 14:2 In my *F* house are many rooms

Jn 14:6 No one comes to the *F*

fear — (*v.*) 1. to respect highly; to feel reverence and awe for; 2. to be afraid of. (*n.*) profound reverence toward God; anticipation or awareness of danger.

Dt 6:13 *F* the Lord your God, serve him

Job 1:8 a man who *f* God and shuns evil."

Ps 91:5 You will not *f* the terror of night

Ps 111:10 *f* of the Lord is the beginning

Isa 41:10 So do not *f*, for I am with you

Php 2:12 to work out your salvation with *f*

fellowship — companionship or friendship.

1Jn 1:6 claim to have *f* with him yet walk

1Jn 1:7 we have *f* with one another,

fig — 1. a brownish pear-shaped fruit that grows in countries near the Mediterranean Sea; 2. the tree that grows this fruit.

firstborn — a family's first male child. The firstborn son became the head of the family when his father died. He also received twice as much money and property as each of his brothers.

Ex 11:5 Every *f* son in Eygpt will die

firstfruits — the first vegetables, fruits and grains harvested from the field.

Ex 23:19 "Bring the best of the *f* of your soil

flawless—without fault or defect; perfect.

flog—to beat with a stick or a whip.

forbearance—patience; tolerance.

forefather—a male ancestor.

foreknow—to know ahead of time.

   Ro 8:29 For those God *f* he

   Ro 11:2 not reject his people, whom he *f*

forgive—to pardon or excuse; no longer to blame or be angry with someone who had done you wrong.

   Mt 6:14 For if you *f* men when they sin

   Lk 23:34 Jesus said, "Father, *f* them

   Col 3:13 *F* as the Lord forgave you.

   1Jn 1:9 and just and will *f* us our sins

forsake—to leave another completely alone, with no hope that you will ever return.

   Jos 1:5 I will never leave you or *f* you.

   Isa 55:7 Let the wicked *f* his way

   Mt 27:46 my God, why have you *f* me?

frankincense—an incense burned for its sweet smell.

free—

   Jn 8:32 and the truth will set you *f*."

   Ro 6:18 You have been set *f* from sin

freedom—

   2Co 3:17 the Spirit of the Lord is, there is *f*.

   Gal 5:13 But do not use your *f* to indulge

friend—

   Pr 18:24 there is a *f* who sticks closer

   Jn 15:13 that one lay down his life for his *f*.

   Jas 4:4 Anyone who chooses to be a *f*

fruitful—productive; yielding much fruit.

   Ge 1:22 "Be *f* and increase in number

   Jn 15:2 clean so that it will be even more *f*.

fulfill—to complete a promise or project.

   Ps 116:14 I will *f* my vows to the Lord

   Mk 14:49 But the Scriptures must be *f*."

   Lk 24:44 Everything must be *f* that is

fulfillment—

   Ro 13:10 Therefore love is the *f* of the law.

Gabriel—the angel who announced the births of John the Baptist and Jesus (Lk 1:11-20, 26-38).

Galilee—the northern part of Palestine. Palestine had three main parts: Galilee, Samaria and Judea. Jesus grew up, preached and did most of his miracles in Galilee. Today this area is in northern Israel.

gall—1. a plant with an extremely bitter-tasting fruit; 2. the liquid made by the liver.

   Mt 27:34 mixed with *g*; but after tasting

genealogy—a list of a person's ancestors or descendants; a family tree.

generation—the entire number of people born and living at about the same time. Grandparents, parents and children are three different generations.

   Ps 102:12 your renown endures through all *g*.

   Lk 1:48 now on all *g* will call me blessed

Gentile—anyone who is not a Jew.

   Ro 3:9 and *G* alike are all under sin

   Ro 11:13 as I am the apostle to the *G*

   Eph 3:6 the gospel the *G* are heirs together

Gideon—a judge who freed Israel from the rule and terror of the Midianites (Jdg 6-8). He asked for a sign from God, and God showed him his will by means of dew and a fleece (Jdg 6:36-40).

gift—

   Ro 6:23 but the *g* of God is eternal life

   1Co 12:4 There are different kinds of *g*,

   2Co 9:15 be to God for his indescribable *g*!

gleanings—the grain or fruit left behind after harvesting. Poor people were allowed to pick up and use these leftovers.

glory—1. honor; praise; 2. a source of pride or worthiness.

   Ps 8:5 and crowned him with *g* and honor.

   Ps 19:1 The heavens declare the *g* of God

   Lk 2:14 saying, "*G* to God in the highest

   Jn 1:14 We have seen his *g*, the *g* of the one

   1Co 10:31 whatever you do, do it all for the *g*

   Rev 4:11 to receive *g* and honor and power

glutton—a person who eats too much.

gnash—to grind (one's teeth) together.

God—

   Ge 1:1 In the beginning *G* created

   Ge 17:1 "I am *G* Almighty; walk before me

   Ge 50:20 but *G* intended it for good

   Ex 8:10 is no one like the Lord our *G*.

Ex 20:5 the Lord your G, am a jealous G
Nu 23:19 G is not a man, that he should lie
Dt 4:31 the Lord your G is a merciful G
Dt 6:4 Lord our G, the Lord is one.
Dt 6:5 Love the Lord your G
Dt 32:4 A faithful G who does no wrong
Ne 9:17 But you are a forgiving G
Ps 46:1 G is our refuge and strength
Ps 71:22 harp for your faithfulness, O my G
Jn 1:18 ever seen G, but G the only Son
Jn 3:16 "For G so loved the world that he
Jn 4:24 G is spirit, and his worshipers must
1Co 10:13 G is faithful; he will not let you
1Co 14:33 For G is not a G of disorder
Heb 12:10 but G disciplines us for our good
Jas 1:13 For G cannot be tempted by evil
1Jn 4:16 G is love.
Rev 4:8 holy is the Lord G Almighty

Golgotha — the hill outside Jerusalem where Jesus was hung on a cross.
Jn 19:17 (which in Aramaic is called G).

Goliath — the Philistine giant who was killed by David (1Sa 17; 21:9).

gospel — 1. the good news that Jesus died for our sins and rose again; 2. Gospel, any of the first four books of the New Testament.
Ro 1:16 I am not ashamed of the g
Ro 15:16 duty of proclaiming the g of God
1Co 9:16 Woe to me if I do not preach the g!
1Co 15:2 By this g you are saved
2Co 9:13 your confession of the g
1Th 2:4 by God to be entrusted with the g

grace — an undeserved favor or gift; the undeserved forgiveness, kindness and mercy that God gives us.
Ro 3:24 and are justified freely by his g
Ro 5:20 where sin increased, g increased
2Co 12:9 "My g is sufficient for you
Eph 2:5 it is by g you have been saved.
Tit 3:7 having been justified by his g

guilty — having broken a law or commandment; deserving punishment.
Ex 34:7 does not leave the g unpunished
1Co 11:27 in an unworthy manner will be g
Heb 10:22 to cleanse us from a g conscience

Jas 2:10 at just one point is g of breaking

Hades — hell; the place where the spirits of the dead live.
Mt 16:18 the gates of H will not overcome

Hagar — a servant of Sarah and one of Abraham's wives; the mother of Ishmael (Ge 16:1-6; 25:12). After giving birth to Isaac, Sarah drove Hagar away (Ge 21:9-21).

Haggai — a prophet who encouraged the Israelites who returned from exile in Babylon to rebuild the temple (Ezr 5:1; Hag 1-2).

hallelujah — praise the Lord; a song of praise.
Rev 19:1 "H! Salvation and glory and power

hallow — to make holy; to set apart as special.

Hannah — the wife of Elkanah; she prayed for a son and God gave her Samuel. She dedicated him to God and he lived in the temple as a boy and became a prophet and judge (1Sa 1-2).

harlot — a woman who lets a man use her body for sex in exchange for money.

haughty — proud.
Pr 16:18 a h spirit before a fall.

heart —
Dt 6:5 Lord your God with all your h
1Sa 16:7 but the Lord looks at the h."
1Ch 28:9 for the Lord searches every h
Ps 51:10 Create in me a pure h, O God
Ps 119:11 I have hidden your word in my h
Ps 139:23 Search me, O God, and know my h
Jer 29:13 when you seek me with all your h.
Eze 36:26 I will give you a new h
Mt 5:8 Blessed are the pure in h
Mt 22:37 the Lord your God with all your h
Ro 10:10 is with your h that you believe

heaven —
Ge 14:19 Creator of h and earth.
Mt 19:23 man to enter the kingdom of h.
Mk 16:19 he was taken up into h
Php 3:20 But our citizenship is in h.
Rev 21:1 Then I saw a new h and a new earth

Hebrew — 1. another name for an Israelite; a descendant of Abraham; 2. the language spoken by the Jews. The Old Testament was written in Hebrew.

heir — someone who receives the property or blessings of a person who has died. In Bible times an heir was usually male.

Ro 8:17 then we are *h—h* of God

Eph 3:6 gospel the Gentiles are *h* together

heresy — false teaching about God.

Herod — the family name of five kings who ruled Palestine under the Roman emperor: Herod the Great (Mt 2:16); Herod Antipas (Mk 6:14-29); Herod Philip (Mt 14:3; Mk 6:17); Herod Agrippa I (Ac 12:1-4,19-23); Herod Agrippa II (Ac 23:35; 25:13-26:32).

Herodias — the wife of Herod Antipas; she persuaded her daughter to ask Antipas for the head of John the Baptist (Mk 6:17).

Hezekiah — a king of Judah; he restored the temple, reinstituted proper worship and sought the Lord's help against the Assyrians. He showed his faith when, suffering from a serious illness, he prayed to God and was healed; yet he also showed the Babylonians his treasures and God punished him and the Israelites for this (2Ch 29-31; 2Ki 18-20).

high priest — the chief religious official in the Jewish religion. In the Old Testament he offered the most important sacrifices to God in behalf of the people. In Jesus' time he was also the head of the Sanhedrin (the highest Jewish court), and a powerful political leader — even having a small army.

hinder — to hold back; to prevent; to delay.

holy — (*v.*) set apart for God; (*adj.*) belonging to God; pure; godly.

Ex 20:8 the Sabbath day by keeping it *h.*

Lev 11:44 and be *h,* because I am *h.*

Isa 6:3 "*H, h, h* is the Lord Almighty;

Ro 12:1 as living sacrifices, *h* and pleasing

Rev 4:8 "*H, h, h* is the LORD Almighty

Holy Spirit — the third person of the Trinity; the Spirit lives and works in our hearts and minds. Jesus promised his disciples that he would send his Spirit (Jn 14:16-26), and it came at Pentecost in a powerful way (Ac 2). Other names are: the Spirit, Counselor and Comforter.

homage — honor; respect.

homosexual — someone who has sexual relations with a person of the same sex.

1Co 6:9 male prostitutes nor *h* offenders

hope (*v.; n.*) —

Ps 42:5 Put your *h* in God

Isa 40:31 but those who *h* in the LORD

Ro 8:24 But *h* that is seen is no *h* at all.

1Co 15:19 for this life we have *h* in Christ

Heb 11:1 faith is being sure of what we *h* for

hosanna — a Hebrew word of praise meaning "save."

Mt 21:9 "*H* in the highest!"

hospitality — welcoming people into one's home; sharing one's home and food with others.

Ro 12:13 Practice *h.*

1Pe 4:9 Offer *h* to one another

humble — (*v.*) to make humble in spirit or manner; (*adj.*) not proud; not pretending to be important.

Ps 147:6 The LORD sustains the *h*

Mt 23:12 whoever exalts himself will be *h*

Jas 4:10 *H* yourselves before the Lord

humiliate — to make humble; to reduce to a lower position; to make ashamed.

1Co 11:22 and *h* those who have nothing?

hymn — a song of praise to God.

hypocrite — a person who pretends to love God.

Mt 6:5 when you pray, do not be like the *h*

Mt 7:5 you *h,* first take the plank out

hyssop — a plant used to sprinkle water or blood for religious cleansing.

Ps 51:7 with *h,* and I will be clean

idol — a statue made by people and worshiped as if it had the power of a god; anything that takes the place of God in a person's life. Worshiping idols is called idolatry.

1Co 8:4 We know that an *i* is nothing at

Col 3:5 evil desires and greed, which is *i.*

Immanuel — a name for Jesus meaning "God with us."

Isa 7:14 birth to a son, and will call him *I.*

Mt 1:23 and they will call him *I*"

immortal — free from death; not able to die.

1Ti 1:17 Now to the King eternal, *i*

immortality —

1Co 15:53 and the mortal with *i.*

imperishable — not able to die or to be destroyed.

1Pe 1:23 not of perishable seed, but of *i*

impure — not pure; not clean.
1Th 4:7 For God did not call us to be *i*

incense — 1. spices burned to make a sweet-smelling smoke, as a way of worshiping God; 2. the sweet smell or the smoke of burning spices.
Ps 141:2 my prayer be set before you like *i*
Mt 2:11 him with gifts of gold and of *i*

incensed — very angry; filled with rage.

indignation — anger.

infirmity — physical weakness; disease.
Isa 53:4 Surely he took up our *i*

inherit — to receive money, property or keepsakes from a person after his or her death.
Mt 5:5 for they will *i* the earth.
Mk 10:17 "what must I do to *i* eternal life?"

inheritance — money, property or keepsakes received from a person after his or her death.
Dt 4:20 to be the people of his *i*
1Pe 1:4 and into an *i* that can never perish

iniquity — sin; wickedness.
Ps 51:2 Wash away all my *i*
Ps 103:10 or repay us according to our *i.*
Isa 53:6 the *i* of us all.
Mic 7:19 and hurl all our *i* into the depths.

injustice — unfairness.

inscription — 1. the writing on a coin; 2. a written title or message.

insolent — proud, in an insulting way.

institute — to establish; to begin.

insurrection — revolt or rebellion against a government.

integrity — complete honesty.

intercede — to beg or plead for another person.
Ro 8:26 but the Spirit himself *i* for us

intercession —
Isa 53:12 and made *i* for the transgressors.

intermarry — to marry someone from a different race or religion.
Dt 7:3 Do not *i* with them.

irrevocable — not able to be taken back or changed.

Isaac — the promised son of Abraham and Sarah (Ge 17:19; 21:1-7); offered as a sacrifice by Abraham (Ge 22); married Rebekah (Ge 24) and was the father of Esau and Jacob (Ge 25). Rebekah and Jacob plotted together to trick Isaac into blessing Jacob instead of Esau (Ge 27).

Isaiah — prophet called by God (Isa 6) to prophesy to Judah (Isa 1:1). Some of his prophesies are about the coming Messiah (Isa 53).

Ishmael — the son of Abraham and Hagar (Ge 16); he was not to be the son of the covenant (Ge 17:18-21). Sarah and Abraham sent both Hagar and Ishmael away from them (Ge 21:8-21).

Israel — 1. the nation made up of descendants of the twelve sons of Jacob. Israel became a nation when God took his people out of Egypt (Ex 1-14); 2. the new name God gave to Jacob (Ge 32:28); 3. the northern ten tribes after they separated from Judah and Benjamin.
Dt 6:4 Hear, O *I;* The LORD our God
Eze 39:23 of *I* went into exile for their sin
Lk 22:30 judging the twelve tribes of *I.*
Eph 3:6 Gentiles are heirs together with *I*

Israelites — the people of Israel.
Ex 14:22 and the *I* went through the sea
Ro 9:27 the number of the *I* be like the sand

Jacob — the second son of Isaac and Rebekah; he was the twin brother of Esau (Ge 25:21-26). He bought Esau's birthright for a pot of stew (Ge 25:29-34) and later tricked Isaac into giving him the blessing that belonged to Esau (Ge 27:1-37). After running away from Esau, he wrestled with God, and his name was changed to Israel (Ge 32:22-32). He had twelve sons and all of them eventually went to Egypt during a famine (Ge 42-43). He settled in Egypt, but was buried by his son Joseph in Canaan, the promised land (Ge 46; 50).

James — 1. one of the twelve apostles; the brother of John (Mt 4:21-22). He was present at the transfiguration (Mt 17:1-13); he was later killed by Herod (Ac 12:2); 2. one of the twelve apostles; the son of Alphaeus (Mt 10:3); 3. the brother of Jesus (Mk 6:30); he waited with the believers for the promised Holy Spirit after Christ's ascension (Ac 2:1-3); became a leader in the church in Jerusalem (Ac 12:17; 15; 21:18; Gal 2:9); author of the letter of James (Jas 1:1).

Japheth — one of the sons of Noah (Ge 5:32); he was blessed because he covered his father's nakedness (Ge 9:18-28).

jealous — 1. afraid of losing someone's love or affection; 2. angry or unhappy because of what someone else has; 3. careful to guard or keep what one has.

Joel 2:18 the LORD will be *j* for his land

2Co 11:2 I am *j* for you with a godly jealousy

jealousy —

Gal 5:20 hatred, discord, *j*, fits of rage

Jeremiah — a prophet called by God (Jer 1) to prophesy to Judah (Jer 1:1-3). His life was in danger because of what he prophesied (Jer 11:18-23:26), and he was subsequently put in stocks (Jer 20:1-2), imprisoned (Jer 37), and thrown in a cistern (Jer 38). He was forced to flee to Egypt from the Babylonians (Jer 43). He is often referred to as the prophet of gloom, because he prophesied about the destruction of Judah.

Jeroboam — an official in Solomon's court; he rebelled and became the first king of Israel (the northern ten tribes) (1Ki 11:26-40; 12:1-20).

Jerusalem — the political and religious center of Judah.

2Ki 23:27 and I will reject *J*, the city I chose

Ne 2:17 Come, let us rebuild the wall of *J*

Ps 137:5 If I forget you, O *J*

Jn 4:20 where we must worship is in *J*."

Rev 21:2 I saw the Holy City, the new *J*

Jeshua — see Joshua (2).

Jew — an Israelite; one of the chosen people of God; a descendant of Abraham through Jacob.

Mt 2:2 who has been born king of the *J*?

Ro 3:29 Is God the God of *J* only?

Gal 3:28 There is neither *J* nor Greek

Jezebel — the Sidonian wife of King Ahab (1Ki 16:31). She promoted Baal worship in Israel (1Ki 16:32-33); had many prophets of God killed (1Ki 18:4,13); and opposed the prophet Elijah (1Ki 19:1-2). Elijah prophesied her death (1Ki 21:17-24).

Joash — the boy-king of Judah; he repaired the temple (2Ki 12).

Job — a wealthy man from the land of Uz who feared God (Job 1:1-5). His righteousness was tested by disaster (Job 1:6-22) and personal affliction (Job 2), but, in the end, God restored wealth and honor to him (Job 42).

John — 1. John the Baptist (Mk 1:2-8); the son of Zechariah and Elizabeth (Lk 1). He preached in the desert, preparing the people for Jesus (Mt 3:11-12); baptized Jesus in the Jordan River (Mt 3:13-17); was arrested (Mk 1:14) and executed by Herod (Mk 6:14-29); 2. one of the twelve apostles; brother of the apostle James (Lk 5:1-10). He was present at Jesus' transfiguration (Lk 9:28-36); became one of the leaders of the church at Jerusalem (Ac 4:1-3); wrote the Gospel of John, the letters of John (2Jn 1; 3Jn 1) and the book of Revelation (Rev 1:1; 22:8).

John, Mark (see Mark, John).

Jonah — a prophet in the days of Jeroboam II of Israel (2Ki 14:25). He was called to preach to Nineveh but instead fled to Tarshish (Jnh 1:1-3). While at sea a great storm arose because of his disobedience; he was thrown into the sea and was swallowed by a large fish (Jnh 1:4-17). He then repented and went to Nineveh and preached, telling the people to repent (Jnh 3).

Jonathan — a son of King Saul (1Sa 13:16). He had a special friendship with David (1Sa 18:1-4); 19-20; 23:16-18). When he was killed (1Sa 31) David mourned greatly for him (2Sa 1).

Jordan — a river in Palestine that flows between the Sea of Galilee and the Dead Sea.

Jos 4:22 Israel crossed the *J* on dry ground."

Mt 3:6 baptized by him in the *J* River.

Joseph — 1. the son of Jacob and Rachel (Ge 30:24). He was favored by his father, but hated by his brothers (Ge 37:3-4). He was sold into slavery by his brothers (Ge 37:12-36), taken to Egypt and there served Potiphar until put in prison on a false charge (Ge 39). While in prison he interpreted the dreams of Pharaoh's servants (Ge 40), and then interpreted Pharaoh's dreams (Ge 41:4-40). For this, he was given a high position under Pharaoh (Ge 41:41-57). During a famine his brothers came to Egypt to buy grain, and so Joseph was reunited with his aged father and with his brothers (Ge 42-47); 2. the husband of Mary and childhood father of Jesus (Mt 1:16-24; 2:13-19); 3. a disciple of Jesus from Arimathea; he gave his tomb for Jesus' burial (Mt 27:57-61); 4. the original name of Barnabas (Ac 4:36).

Joshua — 1. the son of Nun (Nu 13:8); Moses' aide on Mount Sinai, when God revealed how Israel was to live as his chosen people (Ex 24:13); spied out the land of Canaan (Nu 13); and he and Caleb, though members of the generation of Israelites who had showed a lack of faith forty years earlier, were allowed to enter the promised land (Nu 14:6,30). As the successor of Moses (Dt 31:1-18), he led the Israelites across the Jordan River into Canaan (Jos 3-4); was the commander in the conquest of Jericho (Jos 6), Ai (Jos 7-8), and a large part of Canaan (Jos 10-12); oversaw the dividing up of the promised land among the twelve tribes of Israel (Jos 13-22); 2. the high priest in Israel during the rebuilding of both the temple (Hag 1-2) and the altar (Ezr 3:2,8); also called Jeshua.

Judah — 1. Jacob's fourth son; 2. the tribe of Israel whose members were descendants of Judah; 3. a name for the southern kingdom after Judah and Benjamin separated from the northern ten tribes.

Ge 29:35 So she named him J.
Jer 13:19 All J will be carried into exile,
Zec 10:4 From J will come the cornerstone

Judaism — the teachings of the Jewish religion.

Judas — 1. one of the twelve apostles (Lk 6:16; Ac 1:13); was probably also called Thaddaeus (Mt 10:3); 2. one of the brothers of Jesus (Mt 13:55); author of the last letter in the New Testament (Jude 1); 3. one of the twelve apostles, also called Iscariot; he betrayed Jesus (Mk 3:19; 14:10-50) and then hung himself (Mt 27:3-5).

judge — to decide if something is good or bad; to condemn.

Ps 9:8 He will j the world in righteousness
Mt 7:1 Do not j, or you too will be judged.
2Ti 4:1 who will j the living and the dead.

judgment — 1. a decision or opinion; 2. a decision of guilt or innocence made by a judge in a court of law; punishment decided on

by a court; 3. a decision from God, especially the final judgment when God will reward those who believe in him and condemn all others to hell.

Dt 1:17 of any man, for j belongs to God.
Ps 119:66 Teach me knowledge and good j
Isa 66:16 the Lord will execute j
Mt 5:21 who murders will be subject to j.
Mt 12:36 have to give account on the day of j
Jn 5:22 but has entrusted all j to the Son
Ro 14:10 stand before God's j seat.
2Co 5:10 appear before the j seat of Christ

jurisdiction — one's power and right to rule.

justice — fairness.

Isa 30:18 For the Lord is a God of j.
Isa 61:8 "For I, the Lord, love j
Zec 7:9 'Administer true j; show mercy
Lk 11:42 you neglect j and the love of God.

justification — God's action in treating us as if we had never sinned.

Ro 4:25 and was raised to life for our j.
Ro 5:18 of righteousness was j that brings

justify — to erase someone's sins; to declare righteous.

Ac 13:39 him everyone who believes is j
Ro 3:24 and are j freely by his grace
Ro 5:1 since we have been j through faith
Gal 3:24 to Christ that we might be j by faith

kingdom —

Ex 19:6 you will be for me a k of priests
Mt 6:33 But seek first his k and his
Mt 16:19 the keys of the k of heaven
Jn 18:36 "My k is not of this world.
1Co 15:24 hand over the k to God the Father
Rev 11:15 of the world has become the k

kingdom of heaven (also called, kingdom of God) — God's rule in the lives of his chosen people and in his creation. Anyone who is born again by believing in Jesus enters this kingdom.

Mt 3:2 "Repent, for the k of heaven is near,"
Mt 5:3 for theirs is the k of heaven.

kinsman-redeemer — a close male relative who had the right to marry a widow and buy ("redeem") her husband's property.

Ruth 3:9 over me, since you are a k."

mediator—one who makes peace between two people or two groups who are displeased and/or angry with each other. Jesus is the mediator between us and God.

1Ti 2:5 and one *m* between God and men
Heb 9:15 For this reason Christ is the *m*

meditate—to think seriously and carefully.

Ps 1:2 and on his law he *m* day and night.
Ps 119:15 I *m* on your precepts

medium—a person who can supposedly talk with the spirits of people who have died.

meek—patient; mild; gentle.

Mt 5:5 Blessed are the *m*

mercy—kindness and forgiveness, especially when given to a person who doesn't deserve it.

Mic 6:8 To act justly and to love *m*
Ro 9:15 "I will have *m* on whom I have *m*
1Pe 1:3 In his great *m* he has given us

Messiah—the "Anointed One"; Christ; the one the Jews expected to come and be their king.

Jn 1:41 "We have found the *M*" (that is

Methuselah—a man in early Bible times who lived 969 years (Ge 5:27).

midwife—a woman who helped with the birth of a baby.

millstone—one of a pair of stones used to crush grain for flour.

Lk 17:2 sea with a *m* tied around his neck

minister—(*v.*) to serve; to give care or attention to; (*n.*) one who serves; one who gives care or attention to.

1Sa 3:1 The boy Samuel *m*
2Co 3:6 as *m* of a new covenant
1Ti 4:6 you will be a good *m*

miracle—an unusual happening, one that goes against the normal laws of nature. Miracles are done by the power of God.

Ps 77:14 You are the God who performs *m*
Jn 14:11 the evidence of the *m* themselves.
Ac 2:22 accredited by God to you by *m*
Heb 2:4 it by signs, wonders and various *m*

Miriam—the sister of Moses and Aaron (Nu 26:59); led the Israelites in praising God in dance and song after he had parted the waters of the Red Sea (Ex 15:20-21); later tem-porarily struck with leprosy because she criticized Moses (Nu 12).

money—

Ecc 5:10 Whoever loves *m* never has *m*
Mt 6:24 You cannot serve both God and *M.*
1Co 16:2 set aside a sum of *m* in keeping
1Ti 6:10 For the love of *m* is a root

mortal—human; able to die.

1Co 15:53 and the *m* with immortality.

Moses—the leader of Israel from the flight out of Egypt to their arrival outside the promised land. As a baby, his mother and sister placed him in a basket in the Nile River to save his life; he was discovered here by Pharaoh's daughter (Ex 2:1-10), who raised him at the royal court. After killing an Egyptian he fled to Midian (Ex 2:11-15), where he was called by the Lord to deliver Israel (Ex 3-4). Pharaoh refused to listen to God's warnings (Ex 5), and God punished him and his people with ten plagues (Ex 7-11). Moses instructed the people in their initial observance of the Passover and led them in the exodus out of Egypt, culminating in their passing through the Red Sea (Ex 12-14). He received the law of God at Sinai (Ex 19-23) and gave it to the people of Israel. He supervised the building of the tabernacle (Ex 36-40), set apart Aaron and priests to lead the Israelites in worshiping God (Ex 8-9), and, under his supervision, twelve spies were sent into Canaan (Nu 13). When ten of the spies returned with a pessimistic report, the Israelites believed this account, thereby showing a lack of faith in God. God in turn punished them with forty years of wandering outside the promised land (Nu 14). Moses was allowed to view the land of Canaan from the top of Mount Nebo, but died without entering it (Nu 20:1-13; Dt 34:5-12).

muster—to gather together, especially to gather soldiers for war.

mute—unable to speak.

myrrh—the sweet-smelling sap of the myrrh bush. It was used to make the sacred anointing oil.

Mt 2:11 of gold and of incense and of *m.*

Naomi—the mother-in-law of Ruth (Ru 1); she advised Ruth to seek marriage with Boaz (Ru 2-4).

nard—a pleasant-smelling oil from the spikenard, a plant that grew in India. Since this oil had to be brought from India to Israel, it was very expensive.

Nathanael—one of the twelve apostles (Jn 1:45-49); was probably also called Bartholomew (Mt 10:3).

Nazarene—1. a person who lived in or came from the town of Nazareth in Galilee. 2. a member of an early sect of Jewish converts to Christianity who retained the Mosaic ritual.

Mk 16:6 looking for Jesus the *N*

Nazirite—a person who separated himself or herself by taking a vow to do special work for God. This included a promise not to cut one's hair and not to drink wine.

Jdg 13:5 because the boy is to be a *N*

Nehemiah—the Jewish "cupbearer" of King Artaxerxes of Persia (Ne 2:1); a trusted and highly placed official in the court of Artaxerxes; temporarily appointed governor of Judah; while in Jerusalem rebuilt the walls of the city (Ne 2-6) and with Ezra reestablished the worship of God there after the Babylonian exile (Ne 8).

Nicodemus—a Pharisee who visited Jesus at night (Jn 3) and learned about being born again. With Joseph of Arimathea, he prepared Jesus' body for burial (Jn 19:38-42).

Noah—"a righteous man" in early Bible times; he built an ark, as God commanded him (Ge 6-8). God made a covenant with him never again to cover the entire earth with a flood (Ge 9).

nullify—to make of no value; to make unimportant.

oath—a promise in which one asks God to witness that something is true.

obey—to do as asked; to yield to someone's commands or wishes.

Dt 6:3 careful to *o* so that it may go well
Dt 13:4 Keep his commands and *o* him
1Sa 15:22 To *o* is better than sacrifice
Jn 14:23 loves me, he will *o* my teaching.
Ac 5:29 "We must *o* God rather than men!
Eph 6:1 *o* your parents in the Lord

offend—to make someone angry by what you do.

offering—1. something given to God as an act of worship; 2. the killing of an animal to make the relationship between God and

man right again. In the Old Testament, animals and grains were regularly used as offerings, in an attempt to bring the people closer to God.

Ge 22:8 provide the lamb for the burnt *o*
Isa 53:10 the Lord makes his life a guilt *o*
Mk 12:33 is more important than all burnt *o*
Eph 5:2 as a fragrant *o* and sacrifice to God.

offshoot—a branch off the main stem of a tree or plant.

offspring—children.

Ge 3:15 and between your *o* and hers
Ge 12:7 "To your *o* I will give this land."

omen—an event or sign believed to foretell the future.

oppress—to control people unfairly and cruelly by the use of one's power.

Isa 53:7 He was *o* and afflicted
Zec 7:10 Do not *o* the widow

oracle—1. a saying or answer; 2. the word of the Lord.

ordain—1. to set apart for a specific office or duty; 2. to order or command.

ordinance—1. an official law; 2. a law made or commanded by God.

overseer—a person who watches over and takes care of others. *Overseer* was one of the terms used for leaders in the early church.

Ac 20:28 the Holy Spirit has made you *o*.
1Ti 3:2 Now the *o* must be above reproach

pagan—a person who does not worship God, especially someone who worships idols.

1Pe 2:12 such good lives among the *p* that

papyrus—1. a large water plant, similar to the reed, that grows in marshes and lakes. Moses' mother put him in a basket made from papyrus (Ex 2:3); 2. a paper made from this plant.

parable—a story that tells a special lesson or truth. Jesus told many parables.

paradise—a perfect place; heaven.

Lk 23:43 today you will be with me in *p*."

paralytic—a person who is unable to move certain parts of his or her body.

Mk 2:3 bringing to him a *p*, carried by

parents—
Pr 17:6 and *p* are the pride of their
Eph 6:1 Children, obey your *p* in the Lord
Col 3:20 obey your *p* in everything

Passover—an annual Jewish holiday that yet today reminds the Jewish people of how God freed them from slavery in Egypt. At the Passover feast, the Jews eat bread made without yeast (unleavened bread), bitter herbs and lamb. With the unleavened bread they remember that they left Egypt hastily. There was no time to wait for yeast bread to rise. Bitter herbs remind them of their suffering in Egypt. The lamb reminds them of the lamb they killed at the first Passover and how they put its blood on their doorframes. The Lord "passed over" the homes so marked, but he killed all the other firstborn in Egypt.
Ex 12:11 Eat it in haste; it is the LORD's *P.*

Passover Lamb—the lamb killed on the Passover as a sacrifice. Jesus is our Passover Lamb. He was sacrificed for our deliverance from sin, in the same way a lamb was sacrificed to show deliverance from Egypt.
1Co 5:7 our *P* lamb, has been sacrificed.

patience—
Gal 5:22 joy, peace, *p*, kindness, goodness

patient—able to put up with problems or pain without complaining or becoming angry.
Ro 12:12 Be joyful in hope, *p* in affliction
1Co 13:4 Love is *p*, love is kind.

patriarch—the father and ruler of a family; the head of a tribe.

Paul—a Pharisee from Tarsus (Ac 9:11); named Saul at birth (Ac 13:9). Jesus appeared to him on the road to Damascus, and in this way God turned one of the fiercest persecutors of the Christian church into one of its mightiest servants (Ac 9:4-9; 26:12-18). Paul became an apostle (Gal 1), and preached the Good News to the Gentiles. His first missionary journey was to Cyprus and Galatia (Ac 13-14); his second journey, with Silas, took him to Macedonia (Ac 16:6-10). After his return to Jerusalem, he was arrested (Ac 21), but continued to preach (Ac 23:1-11). He was then transferred to Caesarea (Ac 23:12-35), where he was tried before Felix (Ac 24). After being imprisoned for two years Paul was tried further, first

before Festus and then before King Agrippa (Ac 25; 26). Despite shipwreck on the voyage to Rome (Ac 27), he arrived safely and was put under house arrest (Ac 28). It seems evident from Paul's writings that he was released from this first Roman imprisonment and that he ministered further to the growing Christian church. He died, perhaps beheaded, in Rome. Paul's writings make up a significant portion of the New Testament, and range from intricate theology to passionate letters to struggling churches.

peace—freedom from disturbance; calm.
Isa 9:6 Everlasting Father, Prince of *P*
Lk 2:14 on earth *p* to men on whom his
Jn 14:27 *P* I leave with you; my *p*
Ro 5:1 we have *p* with God
Gal 5:22 joy, *p*, patience, kindness
1Pe 3:11 he must seek *p* and pursue it.

Pentecost—a Jewish feast celebrated fifty days after the Passover. Today the Christian church celebrates Pentecost because it was the day the Holy Spirit came to dwell with Christ's followers.
Ac 2:1-4

people—
Jer 24:7 They will be my *p*
Ac 15:14 from the Gentiles a *p*
2Co 6:16 and they will be my *p.*"
1Pe 2:9 you are a chosen *p*

perishable—able to spoil; able to be destroyed.
1Co 15:42 the body that is sown is *p*

perjurer—a person who lies under oath.

persecute—to continually treat someone cruelly and unfairly, even though that person has done nothing wrong. The early Christians were persecuted for believing in Jesus as the Son of God.
Jn 15:20 they *p* me, they will *p* you
Ro 12:14 Bless those who *p* you; bless

persecution—
Ro 8:35 or hardship or *p* or famine

perseverance—
Ro 5:3 we know that suffering produces *p*
Ro 5:4 *p*, character; and character, hope.
Heb 12:1 run with *p* the race marked out

persevere—to refuse to give up; to keep on trying; to continue in one's actions or beliefs in spite of problems.
Heb 10:36 You need to *p* so that

pervert — to use wrongly; to turn from what is right.

pestilence — a plague; a disease that spreads quickly and kills many people.

Peter — one of the twelve apostles; the brother of Andrew, also called Simon (Lk 6:14) and Cephas (Jn 1:42). Although Jesus predicted that Peter would deny him (Mk 14:27-31), and though he did deny Jesus three times (Mk 14:66-72), after his resurrection Jesus commissioned Peter to shepherd his flock (Jn 21:15-23). At Pentecost he becomes bold and preaches a sermon (Ac 2), and he continues to heal (Ac 3:1-10) and preach (Ac 3:11-26), even though challenged by the Sanhedrin (Ac 4:1-22). Later God speaks to him in a vision and Peter goes to the Gentile Cornelius to tell him about Jesus (Ac 10).

Pharisees — a group of Jews who obeyed very strictly both God's laws and all their own rules about God's laws.

Mt 5:20 surpasses that of the P

Philip — 1. one of the twelve apostles (Mt 10:3); 2. a deacon (Ac 6:1-7) and evangelist in Samaria; he witnessed to an Ethiopian (Ac 8:4-40).

phylactery — a small leather box containing verses from the Old Testament; male Jews wore these boxes on their foreheads and left arms when they prayed.

Mt 23:5 They make their p wide

piety — love and reverence for God; devotion to God.

Pilate — the governor of Judea who questioned Jesus (Lk 22:66-23:25) and then sent him to Herod (Lk 23:6-12). Pilate finally consented to Jesus' crucifixion when the crowds chose Barabbas rather than Jesus to be released (Lk 23:13-25).

plague — 1. a disease that kills many people, such as the plague of boils; 2. an event that causes much suffering or loss, especially a trouble in which there is a great number of offending agents, such as the plague of locusts.

plowshare — the pointed part of the plow; it cuts into the soil to make rows.

Isa 2:4 They will beat their swords into p

plunder — 1. (v.) to loot or rob during a war; 2. (n.) property taken by plundering.

pomegranate — a reddish fruit about the size of an orange. It has many seeds and a juicy pulp.

poor —
Dt 15:4 there should be no p among you
Ps 82:3 maintain the rights of the p
Pr 14:31 oppresses the p shows contempt
Isa 61:1 me to preach good news to the p.
Mt 5:3 "Blessed are the p in spirit
Mt 26:11 the p you will always have
1Co 13:3 If I give all I possess to the p
2Co 8:9 yet for your sakes he became p

praise — (v.) to glorify; to say good things about someone or something; (n.) approval; worship.

Ex 15:2 He is my God, and I will p him
Ps 119:175 Let me live that I may p you
Eph 1:12 might be for the p of his glory

pray —
2Ch 7:14 will humble themselves and p
Mt 6:5 "But when you p, do not be like
Ro 8:26 do not know what we ought to p.
1Th 5:16,17 Be joyful always; p continually

precept — command; law; rule.
Ps 19:8 the p of the Lord are right
Ps 119:69 I keep your p with all my heart.

predestine — to decide or decree ahead of time.
Ro 8:30 And those he p, he also called
Eph 1:5 In love he p us to be adopted

prevail — to triumph or succeed.

pride —
Pr 8:13 I hate p and arrogance
Pr 16:18 P goes before destruction
Gal 6:4 Then he can take p in himself

priest — a Levite who offered sacrifices and prayers to God for the people.
Heb 4:14 have a great high p who has gone
Heb 7:26 Such a high p meets our need

proclaim — to announce or declare.
1Ch 16:23 p his salvation day after day
Ps 19:1 the skies p the work of his hands.
1Co 11:26 you p the Lord's death

profane — to make a holy thing impure by treating it with disrespect or irreverence.
Lev 22:32 Do no p my holy name.

prone — naturally inclined; having a tendency toward or liking for.

prophecy — a message from God that a prophet brings to the people.

1Co 13:8 where there are *p*, they will cease

2Pe 1:20 you must understand that no *p*

prophesy — to give the message of God to the people.

Joel 2:28 Your sons and daughters will *p*

1Co 14:39 my brothers, be eager to *p*

prophet — a person who receives messages from God to tell to his people. A prophet is called by God to speak for him.

Dt 18:18 up for them a *p* like you

Lk 24:25 believe all that the *p* have spoken!

Ac 10:43 All the *p* testify about him that

2Pe 1:19 word of the *p* made more certain

prostitute — a person who lets someone use his or her body for sexual relations, in exchange for money.

Lk 15:30 property with *p* comes home

1Co 6:9 male *p* nor homosexual offenders

prostrate — lying facedown on the ground.

provoke — to make angry; to cause trouble.

psalm — poetry written to praise God.

Eph 5:19 Speak to one another with *p*

purify — to make pure or clean.

1Jn 1:7 of Jesus, his Son, *p* us from all sin.

1Jn 1:9 and *p* us from all unrighteousness

Purim — an annual Jewish holiday for celebrating Queen Esther's rescue of the Jews when Haman plotted to destroy them.

Rachel — the daughter of Laban (Ge 29:16); she became Jacob's wife (Ge 29:28) and bore him two sons, Joseph and Benjamin (Ge 30:22-24; 35:16-24).

ransom — the price paid to get back a person who is held as a slave. Because we were slaves of sin, a ransom had to be paid for us. That ransom was the death of a sinless person. Jesus, the perfect one, paid our ransom when he died on the cross for us.

Mt 20:28 and to give his life as a *r* for many."

Heb 9:15 as a *r* to set them free

reap — 1. to cut down grain at harvest time; to gather a crop together; 2. to get as a result or reward.

Gal 6:7 A man *r* what he sows.

Rebekah — the sister of Laban and Isaac's wife (Ge 24); the mother of Esau and Jacob (Ge 25:19-26). With her encouragement Ja-cob tricked his father into giving him the blessing that belonged to Esau (Ge 27:1-17).

rebel — 1. (*v.*) to disobey and turn against those in authority; 2. (*n.*) a person who disobeys and flaunts authority.

rebuke — to scold sharply.

2Ti 4:2 correct, *r* and encourage

Rev 3:19 Those whom I love I *r*

recompense — to pay or repay; to make up for.

reconcile — to return to friendship after a quarrel.

Mt 5:24 First go and be *r* to your brother

Ro 5:10 we were *r* to him through death

reconciliation —

Ro 5:11 whom we have now received *r*.

2Co 5:18 and gave us the ministry of *r*

2Co 5:19 committed to us the message of *r*

redeem — 1. to free from evil by paying a price (Gal 3:13); 2. to buy back.

Ex 6:6 slaves to them and will *r* you

Gal 3:13 Christ *r* us from the curse

redemption — the act of being bought back.

Eph 1:7 In him we have *r* through his blood

Col 1:14 in whom we have *r*, the forgiveness

Rehoboam — the son of Solomon; he became king after his father's death (1Ki 11:43). Because of his harsh treatment of the people, Israel was divided into two kingdoms (1Ki 12:1-24; 14:21-31).

rejoice — to express joy or gladness.

Ps 118:24 let us *r* and be glad in it.

Lk 1:47 and my spirit *r* in God my Savior

Php 4:4 *R* in the Lord always.

repent — to turn away from sin; to be sorry for what you have done and to promise not to do it again.

Mt 4:17 "*R*, for the kingdom of heaven is

Lk 13:3 unless you *r*, you too will all perish.

Ac 2:38 Peter replied, "*R* and be baptized,

repentance —

Lk 3:8 Produce fruit in keeping with *r*.

2Co 7:10 Godly sorrow brings *r* that leads

reproach — 1. (*v.*) to blame or accuse; 2. (*n.*) something for which one can be blamed or criticized; blame, criticism.

restore — to bring back; to return something to its former condition.

  Ps 23:3 he *r* my soul.

  Ps 51:12 *R* to me the joy of your salvation

resurrection — the act of coming back to life after being dead.

  Jn 11:25 Jesus said to her, "I am the *r*

  Ro 1:4 Son of God by his *r* from the dead

  1Co 15:12 some of you say that there is no *r*

retribution — punishment for doing wrong.

  Jer 51:56 For the Lord is a God of *r*

revelation — the act of making known or telling about.

  Gal 1:12 I received it by *r* from Jesus Christ.

  Rev 1:1 *r* of Jesus Christ, which God gave

revenge — to hurt or punish a person who has wronged you; to get back at someone who has hurt you.

  Lev 19:18 "Do not seek *r* or bear a grudge

  Ro 12:19 Do not take *r*, my friends

revere — to feel respect for.

reverence — a feeling of respect and honor.

  Ps 5:7 in *r* will I bow down

  Col 3:22 of heart and *r* for the Lord.

revile — to call someone a bad name; to scold in an insulting way.

reward (*v*.; *n*.) —

  Ps 127:3 children a *r* from him.

  Jer 17:10 to *r* a man according to his conduct

  Mt 5:12 because great is your *r* in heaven

  Mt 6:5 they have received their *r* in full.

  Rev 22:12 I am coming soon! My *r* is with

righteous — without sin; doing what is right.

  Isa 64:6 and all our *r* acts are like filthy rags

  Mt 13:49 and separate the wicked from the *r*

  Ro 1:17 as it is written: "The *r* will live

  Ro 3:10 "There is no one *r*, not even one

  1Jn 3:7 does what is right is *r*, just as he is *r*

righteousness —

  Ge 15:6 and he credited it to him as *r*.

  Ps 23:3 He guides me in paths of *r*

  Mt 5:6 those who hunger and thirst for *r*

  Mt 6:33 But seek first his kingdom and his *r*

  Ro 4:3 and it was credited to him as *r*."

  2Ti 3:16 correcting and training in *r*

Ruth — a Moabite widow who went with her mother-in-law Naomi to Bethlehem (Ru 1). There she gathered the gleanings from the field of Boaz (Ru 2), whom she later married (Ru 3-4:12). She was an ancestor of David (Ru 4:13-22) and of Jesus (Mt 1:5).

Sabbath — the seventh day of the week; the Jewish day of rest and worship. It extended from Friday sunset until Saturday sunset.

  Ex 20:8 "remember the *S* day

sackcloth — a rough cloth, usually woven from goats' hair. Clothing made of sackcloth was worn as a sign of mourning for the dead or as a sign that a person was sorry for his or her sins.

sacred — holy; set apart for God in a special way.

sacrifice — (*v*.) to offer as a sacrifice, (*n*.) an offering given to God for the sins of the people. In the Old Testament God commanded the people to pay for their sins by sacrificing cattle, lambs, goats, doves or pigeons. The animals were killed, their blood splattered against the altar and their bodies burned on the altar. People who were very poor could bring flour to be burned on the altar. These sacrifices were pictures of Jesus' coming as a once-for-all sacrifice for sinners.

  Ge 22:2 *S* him there as a burnt offering

  Ex 12:27 "It is the Passover *s* to the Lord

  1Sa 15:22 To obey is better than *s*

  Ro 12:1 to offer your bodies as living *s*

  Heb 9:28 so Christ was *s* once

  1Jn 2:2 He is the atoning *s* for our sins

Sadducees — a group of Jewish leaders, many of them priests, who accepted only the written law of God. They opposed the Pharisees, who had many additional laws that had been passed down to them by their religious teachers. Unlike the Pharisees, the Sadducees did not believe in a resurrection of the dead, but they agreed with the Pharisees in their hatred of Jesus.

  Mk 12:18 *S*, who say there is no resurrection

saints — Christians; people whom God has made holy. A saint can be either a Christian who is alive on earth or one who is already in heaven.

  Ro 8:27 intercedes for the *s* in accordance

  Eph 1:1 To the *s* in Ephesus,

salvation — deliverance from the guilt and

power of sin. By his death and resurrection, Jesus brings salvation to people who believe in him.

Ps 27:1 The Lord is my light and my *s*
Lk 2:30 For my eyes have seen your *s*
Ac 4:12 *S* is found in no one else,
2Co 7:10 brings repentance that leads to *s*
Php 2:12 to work out your *s* with fear
Heb 2:3 escape if we ignore such a great *s*?

Samaritan—a person of late Old Testament or New Testament times who lived in or came from Samaria. The Samaritans were only partly Jewish, and they worshiped God differently than Jews in Israel. Jews from Judea and Galilee hated the Samaritans. They would go out of their way to travel around Samaria (Lk 10:30-37).

Samson—an Israelite judge whose birth was foretold by an angel (Jdg 13). He married a Philistine woman (Jdg 14) and later took vengeance on the Philistines for forcing his wife to tell the answer to the riddle with which he had challenged them (Jdg 15). He was again betrayed by a woman, Delilah, but in the end became obedient to God and was used by God to punish the Philistines (Jdg 16).

Samuel—often called the last of Israel's judges and the first of her prophets (see also Heb 11:32). His birth was earnestly prayed for by his mother Hannah (1Sa 1:10-18), and when he was old enough she brought him to the temple and he was dedicated to the Lord (1Sa 1:21-28). There he was raised by Eli (1Sa 2:11; 18-26) and was called to be a prophet (1Sa 3). He anointed Saul as king (1Sa 9-10), but later announced God's rejection of Saul (1Sa 15). He anointed David as king (1Sa 16) and protected him from Saul (1Sa 19:18-24).

sanctify—to make holy. Our sanctification begins when we become Christians. It is continued by the ongoing work of the Holy Spirit in our hearts.

Ro 15:16 to God, *s* by the Holy Spirit.
1Th 5:23 *s* you through and through.
2Th 2:13 through the *s* work of the Spirit

sanctuary—a place where God is worshiped; a holy place.

Sanhedrin—the ruling council of the Jews in Jesus' time. It was made up of seventy men, and the leader was the high priest. Even though the Romans had conquered Palestine and a Roman governor ruled the country, the Jews were allowed to judge many of their own matters. The Sanhedrin could decide whether someone was innocent or guilty of breaking a Jewish law, but it could not put anyone to death without the permission of the Roman governor.

Mk 14:55 and the whole *S* were looking for evidence

Sarah—the wife of Abraham and mother of Isaac; first called Sarai (Ge 11:29-31). God promised her that, though she had been barren throughout her life, she would give birth to a son in her old age (Ge 17:15-21; 18:10-15).

Satan—the devil; the leader of the fallen spirits; the most powerful enemy of God and humans.

Mk 4:15 *S* comes and takes away the word
2Co 11:14 for *S* himself masquerades
Rev 12:9 serpent called the devil or *S*

Saul—1. the first king of Israel (1Sa 9-10). He was anointed by Samuel but was later rejected by God because he failed to destroy all of the Amalekites (1Sa 15). When David killed Goliath (1Sa 17), Saul attempted to kill him (1Sa 18; 19). Although pursued by Saul, David spared the king's life twice (1Sa 24; 26). Saul was wounded by the Philistines in battle and took his own life (1Sa 31). 2. See Paul.

Savior—a name for Jesus that means he saves his people from sin.

Isa 43:11 and apart from me there is no *s*.
Lk 1:47 and my spirit rejoices in God my *S*
1Ti 4:10 who is the *S* of all men
1Jn 4:14 Son to be the *S* of the world

scabbard—the case that a knife, dagger or sword is carried in.

scepter—a rod or stick held by a king or queen as a sign of royal power and authority.

scorpion—a spider-like animal with a poisonous stinger at the end of its tail.

scribe—a person with the important task of copying letters, books and legal papers.

Scripture—all or part of the Bible. When the Bible uses this word it means the Old

Testament, since the New Testament had not yet been written. Today we call the Old and New Testaments the Bible or Scripture.

Jn 10:35 and the *S* cannot be broken
2Ti 3:16 All *S* is God-breathed
2Pe 1:20 that no prophecy of *S* came about

scroll — a book made of a long piece of leather or paper that was rolled around a stick at both ends.

Eze 3:1 eat what is before you, eat this *s*

seal — 1. a tool with a design raised on it or cut into it; 2. the mark made by pressing this tool onto wax, paper or other soft material. A seal was used to close a letter or legal paper or to prove the authority of the paper.

2Co 1:22 set his *s* of ownership on us
Rev 5:2 "Who is worthy to break the *s*

sect — a group of people who hold one or more beliefs in common; especially, a small religious group that has separated from a larger group.

seer — a prophet; a person who, with God's help, can see what will happen in the future.

1Sa 9:9 of today used to be called a *s*.

self-control — the ability to control your own actions and feelings.

Gal 5:23 faithfulness, gentleness and *s*.
2Pe 1:6 and to knowledge, *s*; and to *s*

self-indulgence — doing whatever you feel like doing. Self-indulgence is the opposite of self-control.

sensual — appealing to the body's senses; caring too much for physical pleasures.

sexual immorality — using sex in ways God says are wrong.

1Co 6:13 body is not meant for *s* immorality
1Th 4:3 that you should avoid *s* immorality

shekel — a specific weight of silver, used as money.

Shem — one of the three sons of Noah (Ge 5:32). He, along with his brother Japheth, covered his father when he was naked (Ge 9:21-31). Abraham was one of his descendants (Ge 11:10-32).

shepherd —

Ps 23:1 Lord is my *s*, I shall lack nothing.
Jer 31:10 watch over his flock like a *s*.'
Jn 10:11 The good *s* lays down his life

Ac 20:28 Be *s* of the church of God

sickle — a tool with a long, curved blade and a short handle, used for cutting grain.

signet — a ring with a design on it. The design was stamped in wax to seal a letter or legal paper. Signet rings were usually worn by people in authority.

Simon — 1. see Peter; 2. one of the twelve apostles; also called the Zealot (Mt 10:4; Ac 1:13); 3. a sorcerer in Samaria who had great influence on the Samaritan people during the early days of the church; he was severely rebuked by Peter (Ac 8:9-24) for attempting to buy the power of the Holy Spirit.

sin — (*v.*) to break the law of God; (*n.*) the act of not doing what God wants.

Nu 32:23 be sure that your *s* will find you
1Ki 8:46 for there is no one who does not *s*
Ps 51:2 and cleanse me from my *s*.
Ps 119:11 that I might not *s* against you.
Jn 1:29 who takes away the *s* of the world!
Ro 3:23 for all have *s* and fall short
Ro 6:23 For the wages of *s* is death
2Co 5:21 God made him who had no *s* to be *s*
1Jn 3:6 No one who lives in him keeps on *s*

sinner —

Ps 1:1 or stand in the way of *s*
Ps 51:5 Surely I have been a *s* from birth
Mt 9:13 come to call the righteous, but *s*."
Lk 15:7 in heaven over one *s* who repents
Lk 18:13 'God, have mercy on me, a *s*.'
Ro 5:8 While we were still *s*, Christ died

sins —

Isa 1:18 "Though your *s* are like scarlet
Mt 1:21 he will save his people from their *s*."
Mt 18:15 "If your brother *s* against you
Lk 11:4 Forgive us our *s*
Ac 22:16 be baptized and wash your *s* away
Eph 2:1 dead in your transgressions and *s*
Heb 7:27 He sacrificed for their *s* once for all
1Pe 2:24 He himself bore our *s* in his body
1Jn 1:9 If we confess our *s*, he is faithful

Rev 1:5 has freed us from our *s* by his blood

slander — (*v.*) saying untrue things about another person in order to hurt him or her; (*n.*) false charges or misrepresentations about another person.

Lev 19:16 " 'Do not go about spreading *s*
Tit 3:2 to *s* no one, to be peaceable

Sodom and Gomorrah — the two cities destroyed by God because the people were so wicked.

Ge 19:24 rained down burning sulfur on *S*

Solomon — the son of David and Bathsheba (2Sa 12:24). He became king of Israel after David died (1Ki 1). He asked God for wisdom and was given it (1Ki 3), and he built the temple (1Ki 5-7) and dedicated it to God with prayer (1Ki 8). His many foreign wives turned his heart away from God (1Ki 11:1-13). Jeroboam, one of his officials, rebelled against him (1Ki 11:26-40).

son —

Pr 10:1 A wise *s* brings joy to his father
Joel 2:28 Your *s* and daughters will prophesy
Jn 12:36 so that you may become *s* of light."
Ro 8:14 by the Spirit of God are *s* of God
1Jn 4:9 only *S* into the world that we might

Son of Man — a name for Jesus. Jesus used this name to show he was the Messiah prophesied about in Daniel 7:13.

Mt 20:18 and the *S* of Man will be betrayed
Mk 14:62 you will see the *S* of Man sitting
Lk 19:10 For the *S* of Man came to seek
Jn 3:14 so the *S* of Man must be lifted up

soothsayer — a person who could foretell the future.

sorcerer — a magician.

soul — the spiritual part of a person; the part of a person that does not die.

Dt 6:5 with all your *s* and with all your
Ps 23:3 he restores my *s.*
Mt 10:28 kill the body but cannot kill the *s.*
Mt 11:29 and you will find rest for your *s.*
Mt 16:26 yet forfeits his *s*? Or what can
Mt 22:37 with all your *s* and with all your

sovereign — having authority over everything.

sow — to plant seeds. In Jesus' time seeds were sown by scattering them by hand over the ground.

Job 4:8 and those who *s* trouble reap it
Gal 6:7 A man reaps what he *s.*

spirit — 1. the part of a person that is not the body; the soul; 2. beings who do not have bodies; 3. another name for Holy Spirit.

1. spirit
Ps 31:5 Into your hands I commit my *s*
Eze 36:26 you a new heart and put a new *s*
Mt 5:3 saying: "Blessed are the poor in *s*
Mt 26:41 *s* is willing, but the body is weak."

2. spirit
1Jn 4:1 Dear friends, do not believe every *s*

3. Spirit
Ge 1:2 and the *S* of God was hovering
Ps 51:11 or take your Holy *S* from me.
Mt 1:18 to be with child through the Holy *S.*
Mt 3:11 will baptize you with the Holy *S*
Mt 3:16 he saw the *S* of God descending
Mt 28:19 and of the Son and of the Holy *S*
Jn 14:26 But the Counselor, the Holy *S*
Jn 20:22 and said, "Receive the Holy *S.*
Ac 1:5 will be baptized with the Holy *S.*"
Ac 2:4 of them were filled with the Holy *S*
Ac 2:38 will receive the gift of the Holy *S.*
Ro 8:26 the *S* helps us in our weakness.
1Co 2:10 God has revealed it to us by his *S.*
1Co 6:19 body is a temple of the Holy *S,*
Gal 5:22 But the fruit of the *S* is love,
Eph 5:18 Instead, be filled with the *S.*

squall — a sudden, strong wind often accompanied by rain or snow.

staff — a stick used to lean on; a rod used by a shepherd.

Ps 23:4 your rod and your *s*

stature — height; normal growth or development.

Lk 2:52 And Jesus grew in wisdom and *s*

stiff-necked — stubborn.

stone — to kill or to try to kill someone by throwing rocks or stones at him or her.

strength —

Ex 15:2 The LORD is my *s* and my song

Dt 6:5 all your soul and with all your *s.*
Ps 46:1 God is our refuge and *s*
Isa 40:31 will renew their *s.*
Php 4:13 through him who gives me *s*

subdue—to bring under control; to conquer.

submission—humbleness; obedience.
1Co 14:34 but must be in *s,* as the Law says.
1Ti 2:11 learn in quietness and full *s.*

submit—
Ro 13:1 Everyone must *s* himself
Eph 5:21 *S* to one another out of reverence
Col 3:18 Wives, *s* to your husbands
Jas 4:7 *S* yourselves, then, to God.

suffer—
Mk 8:31 the Son of Man must *s* many things
Lk 24:26 the Christ have to *s* these things
1Co 12:26 If one part *s,* every part *s* with

suffering—
Isa 53:3 of sorrows, and familiar with *s.*
Ac 5:41 worthy of *s* disgrace for the Name.
Ro 8:17 share in his *s* in order that we may
2Ti 1:8 But join with me in *s* for the gospel

supplication—a humble prayer to God; pleading or begging.

sustain—to give support; to help; to comfort.
Ps 18:35 and your right hand *s* me;
Ps 146:9 and *s* the fatherless and the widow,

symbol—an object or action that stands for or suggests something else. The cross is a symbol of Jesus' death.

synagogue—the Jewish place of worship and religious teaching.
Lk 4:16 the Sabbath day he went into the *s*
Ac 17:2 custom was, Paul went into the *s*

tabernacle—the tent used by the Israelites for meeting with God; the place where God chose to show his presence. The tabernacle was made by God's command and according to his plans. It is described in detail in Exodus 26.
Ex 40:34 the glory of the Lord filled the *t.*

talent—a large amount of silver or gold, worth very much money.
Mt 25:15 to another one *t,* each according

teach—
Ex 33:13 *t* me your ways so I may know
Ps 90:12 *T* us to number our days aright
Lk 11:1 said to him, "Lord, *t* us to pray
Jn 14:26 will *t* you all things and will remind

temperate—moderate; having self-control.

tempest—a violent storm.

temple—1. the place where the Jewish people worshiped and sacrificed in Jerusalem. The first temple was built by King Solomon as a house for God. 2. the human body.
1Ki 8:27 How much less this *t* I have built!
Ac 17:24 does not live in *t* built by hands.
1Co 6:19 you not know that your body is a *t*
2Co 6:16 For we are the *t* of the living God.

tempt—to try to get someone to do wrong.
Mt 4:1 into the desert to be *t* by the devil.
1Co 7:5 again so that Satan will not *t* you.

temptation—
Mt 6:13 And lead us not into *t*
1Co 10:13 No *t* has seized you except

testimony—a statement made by a witness to prove that something is true.
Lk 18:20 not give false *t,* honor your father

tetrarch—a ruler over one-fourth of a kingdom.

Thaddaeus—one of the twelve apostles (Mk 3:18); son of James and probably also known as Judas (Lk 6:16; Ac 1:13).

thanks—
1Ch 16:8 give *t* to the Lord, call
Ps 100:4 give *t* to him and praise his name.
1Co 15:57 *t* be to God! He gives us the victory
2Co 9:15 *T* be to God for his indescribable
1Th 5:18 give *t* in all circumstances

thanksgiving—
Ps 100:4 Enter his gates with *t*
Php 4:6 by prayer and petition, with *t*

Thomas—one of the twelve apostles (Lk 6:15; Ac 1:13); he doubted Jesus' resurrection but upon seeing Jesus believed (Jn 20:24-28).

threshing floor — the place where grain was trampled by oxen or beaten with a stick to separate it from the stalk.

Timothy — fellow-traveler and official representative of the apostle Paul. He and his mother and grandmother were led by Paul to see Christ as the fulfillment of the Old Testament law (2Ti 1:5). He joined Paul on his second missionary journey (Ac 16-20), and at one point in this journey Paul sent him to minister to the church at Corinth (1Co 4:17; 16:10). He was the leader of the church at Ephesus (1Ti 1:3) and a co-writer with Paul (1Th 1:1; 2Th 1:1; Phm 1).

tithe — the giving to God of one-tenth of what you earn.

Lev 27:30 " 'A *t* of everything from the land

Mal 3:8 the whole *t* into the storehouse

Titus — a Gentile co-worker with Paul (Gal 2:1-3; 2Ti 4:10). Paul sent him to Corinth to aid in solving some of the problems there (2Co 2:13; 7-8; 12:18).

tomb — a burial place. In Bible times, tombs often were either caves or were dug into stone cliffs.

Mt 27:65 make the *t* as secure as you know

Lk 24:2 the stone rolled away from the *t*

tongue —

Ps 39:1 and keep my *t* from sin

Ac 2:4 and began to speak in other *t*

Php 2:11 every *t* confess that Jesus Christ

Jas 1:26 does not keep a tight rein on his *t*

tradition of the elders — the rules that the Jewish religious leaders gave to the people and which they in turn passed on to their children; laws added to the Old Testament by the Jewish leaders.

Mt 15:2 break the *t* of the elders?

trance — a condition of being partly awake and partly in a dream-like state.

transfigure — to change the appearance of; to make bright and glorious.

Mt 17:2 There he was *t* before them.

transgression — sin; disobeying the law of God.

Ps 32:1 whose *t* are forgiven,

Isa 53:5 But he was pierced for our *t*

Eph 2:1 you were dead in your *t* and sins

treaty — an agreement between two people or groups or nations.

trespass — sin; wrongdoing.

Ro 5:17 For if, by the *t* of the one man

true —

Ps 119:160 All your words are *t*

Jn 17:3 the only *t* God, and Jesus Christ

Ro 3:4 Let God be *t*, and every man a liar.

Php 4:8 whatever is *t*, whatever is noble

trust (*v.*); (*n.*) —

Ps 37:3 *T* in the LORD and do good

Pr 3:5 *T* in the LORD with all your heart

Isa 30:15 in quietness and *t* is your strength

Jn 14:1 *T* in God; *t* also in me.

1Co 4:2 been given a *t* must prove faithful.

truth —

Ps 51:6 Surely you desire *t*

Zec 8:16 are to do: Speak the *t* to each other

Jn 8:32 Then you will know the *t*

Jn 8:32 and the *t* will set you free."

Jn 14:6 I am the way and the *t* and the life.

Ro 1:25 They exchanged the *t* of God.

1Co 13:6 in evil but rejoices with the *t*.

Eph 4:15 Instead, speaking the *t* in love

Heb 10:26 received the knowledge of the *t*

1Jn 1:6 we lie and do not live by the *t*.

1Jn 1:8 deceive ourselves and the *t* is not

tunic — a long shirt worn by men in Bible times.

Lk 6:29 do not stop him from taking your *t*.

turban — a head-covering made by winding a cloth around the head.

unbelief — doubt.

Mk 9:24 help me overcome my *u*!

unbeliever — one who does not believe in Jesus.

2Co 6:14 Do not be yoked together with *u*.

unclean animals — animals the Israelites were not allowed to sacrifice or to eat.

unity — being one.

Ps 133:1 when brothers live together in *u*!

Col 3:14 them all together in perfect *u*.

unleavened bread — bread made without yeast. It is usually flat, like a pancake or cracker.

Ex 12:17 "Celebrate the Feast of *U* Bread

unrepentant — not sorry for one's sins.

upright — honest; doing what is right and good.

usury — very high and unfair interest charged on a loan.

    Ne 5:10 But let the exacting of *u* stop!

vain — worthless; unsuccessful; foolish. "In vain" means without success or result.

vassal — 1. a servant or slave; 2. someone who is under another person's protection. The vassal received land and protection from a lord. In return, he owed the lord his loyalty and obedience, part of his crops, and, in case of war, help in fighting.

vengeance — hurt or punishment done to another person who has done something wrong to you.

    Isa 34:8 For the LORD has a day of *v*,

vile — disgusting, evil.

vindicate — to defend; to provide justice for; to set free.

violate — 1. to rape; 2. to make something unholy; 3. to fail to obey.

virgin — a woman or girl who has never had sexual intercourse.

    Isa 7:14 The *v* will be with child
    Mt 1:23 "The *v* will be with child

vision — a dream from God.

    Nu 12:6 I reveal myself to him in *v*
    Joel 2:28 your young men will see *v*.
    Ac 26:19 disobedient to the *v* from heaven.

vow — a solemn promise made before God or to God.

    Jdg 11:30 Jephthah made a *v* to the LORD
    Ps 116:14 I will fulfill my *v* to the LORD

wail — to cry loudly.

walk —

    Ps 1:1 who does not *w* in the counsel
    Isa 2:5 let us *w* in the light of the LORD.
    Mic 6:8 and to *w* humbly with your God.
    2Jn 6 his command is that you *w* in love.

wash —

    Ps 51:7 *w* me and I will be whiter
    Ac 22:16 be baptized and *w* your sins away

watch —

    Jer 31:10 will *w* over his flock like a shepherd.'
    Mt 26:41 "*W* and pray so that you will not fall

way —

    2Sa 22:31 "As for God, his *w* is perfect
    Ps 1:1 or stand in the *w* of sinners
    Ps 37:5 Commit your *w* to the LORD
    Isa 53:6 each of us has turned to his own *w*
    Jn 14:6 "I am the *w* and the truth
    2Co 12:31 will show you the most excellent *w*.

wicked — sinful.

    Ps 1:1 walk in the counsel of the *w*
    Isa 55:7 Let the *w* forsake his way

will (*v.*; *n.*) —

    Ps 143:10 Teach me to do your *w*
    Isa 53:10 Yet it was the LORD's *w*
    Mt 6:10 your *w* be done
    Mt 26:39 Yet not as I *w*, but as you *w*."
    Ro 12:2 and approve what God's *w* is
    Eph 5:17 understand what the Lord's *w*
    1Jn 5:14 we ask anything according to his *w*
    Rev 4:11 and by your *w* they were created

work — (*v.*; *n.*) —

    Ex 23:12 "Six days do your *w*
    Jn 9:4 we must do the *w* of him who sent
    Php 2:12 continue to *w* out your salvation
    2Ti 3:17 equipped for every good *w*.

world —

    Mt 5:14 "You are the light of the *w*.
    Mk 16:15 into all the *w* and preach the good
    Jn 1:29 who takes away the sin of the *w*!
    Jn 3:16 so loved the *w* that he gave his one
    Jn 8:12 he said, "I am the light of the *w*.
    1Jn 2:15 not love the *w* or anything in the *w*.

worldly — loving the things of the world more than the things of God.

    Tit 2:12 to ungodliness and *w* passions

worship — (*v.*) to give praise, honor and respect to God; (*n.*) reverence given to God.

    Ps 95:6 Come, let us bow down in *w*
    Jn 4:24 and his worshipers must *w* in spirit

worthy — having value; honorable; deserving.

    1Ch 16:25 For great is the LORD and most *w*
    Eph 4:1 to live a life *w* of the calling you
    Rev 5:2 "Who is *w* to break the seals

wrath — great anger; the strong anger of God.

Pr 15:1 A gentle answer turns away *w*
Ro 5:9 saved from God's *w* through him!

wretch — 1. a very unhappy person; someone who has had many bad or difficult things happen to him or her; 2. an evil person.

yearn — to long for; to want very much.

yoke — 1. (*v.*) to join together; 2. (*n.*) a wooden bar that goes over the necks of two animals, usually oxen. The yoke holds the animals together as they pull an object, such as a plow or a cart.

Mt 11:29 Take my *y* upon you and learn
2Co 6:14 Do not be *y* together

zeal — eagerness; strong desire.

Ro 12:11 Never be lacking in *z*

Zealot — a member of the Jewish group that wanted to fight against and overthrow the Roman government.

Zechariah — a prophet and priest who returned to Jerusalem from the Babylonian captivity; he encouraged the Jews to rebuild the temple (Ezr 5:1; 6:14; Zec 1:1).

Zerubbabel — a descendant of David (1Ch 3:19) and heir to the throne of Judah (1Ch 3:17-19); he led the return from the Babylonian captivity and was appointed governor of Judah by Cyrus, king of Persia (Ezr 1-3; Ne 7:7; Hag 1-2; Zec 4).

Zion — 1. the hill on which the city of Jerusalem first stood; David's royal palace and the temple were both built on Mount Zion; 2. the entire city of Jerusalem.

Jer 50:5 They will ask the way to *Z*
Ro 11:26 "The deliverer will come from *Z*

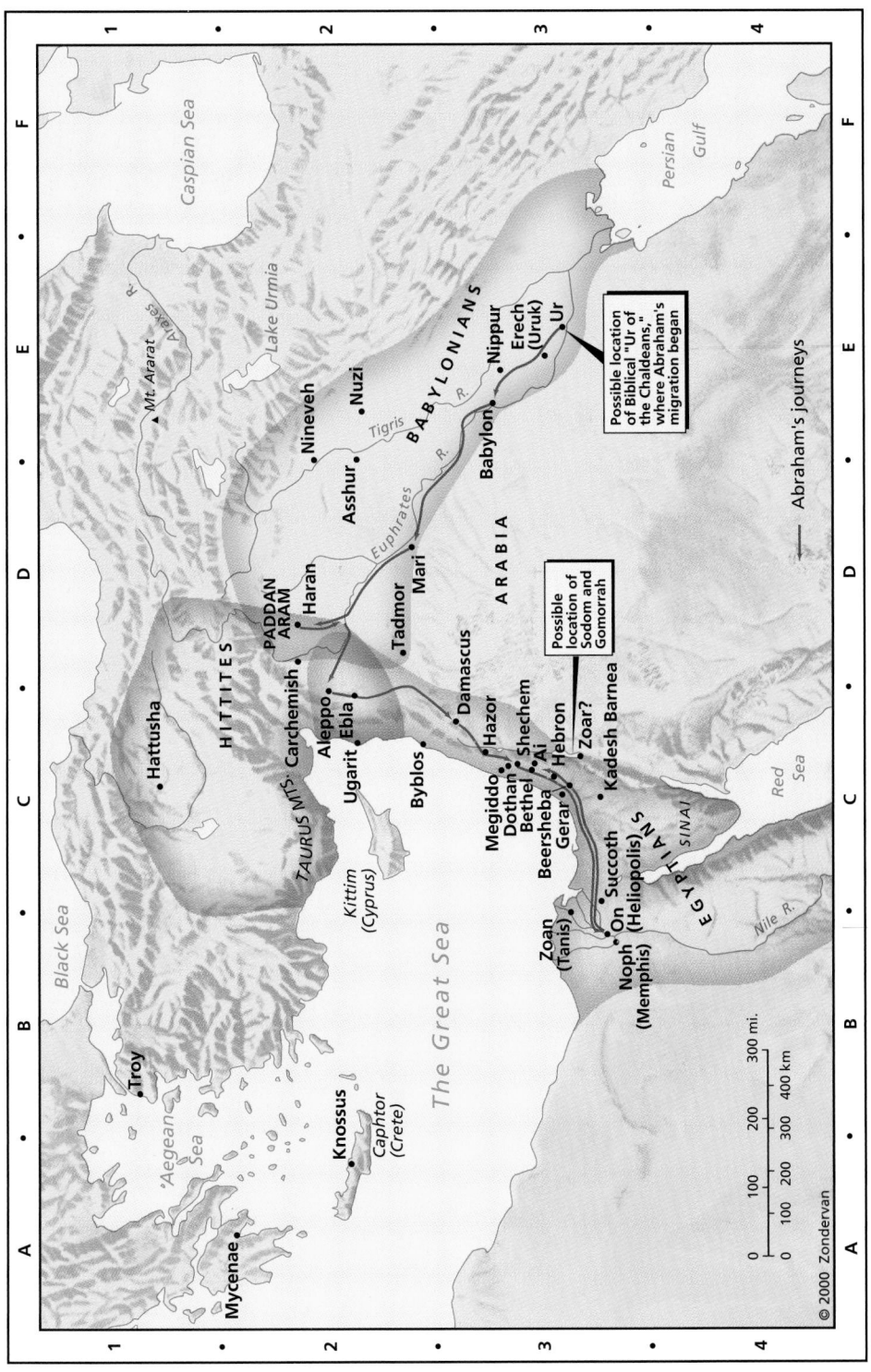

© 2000 Zondervan

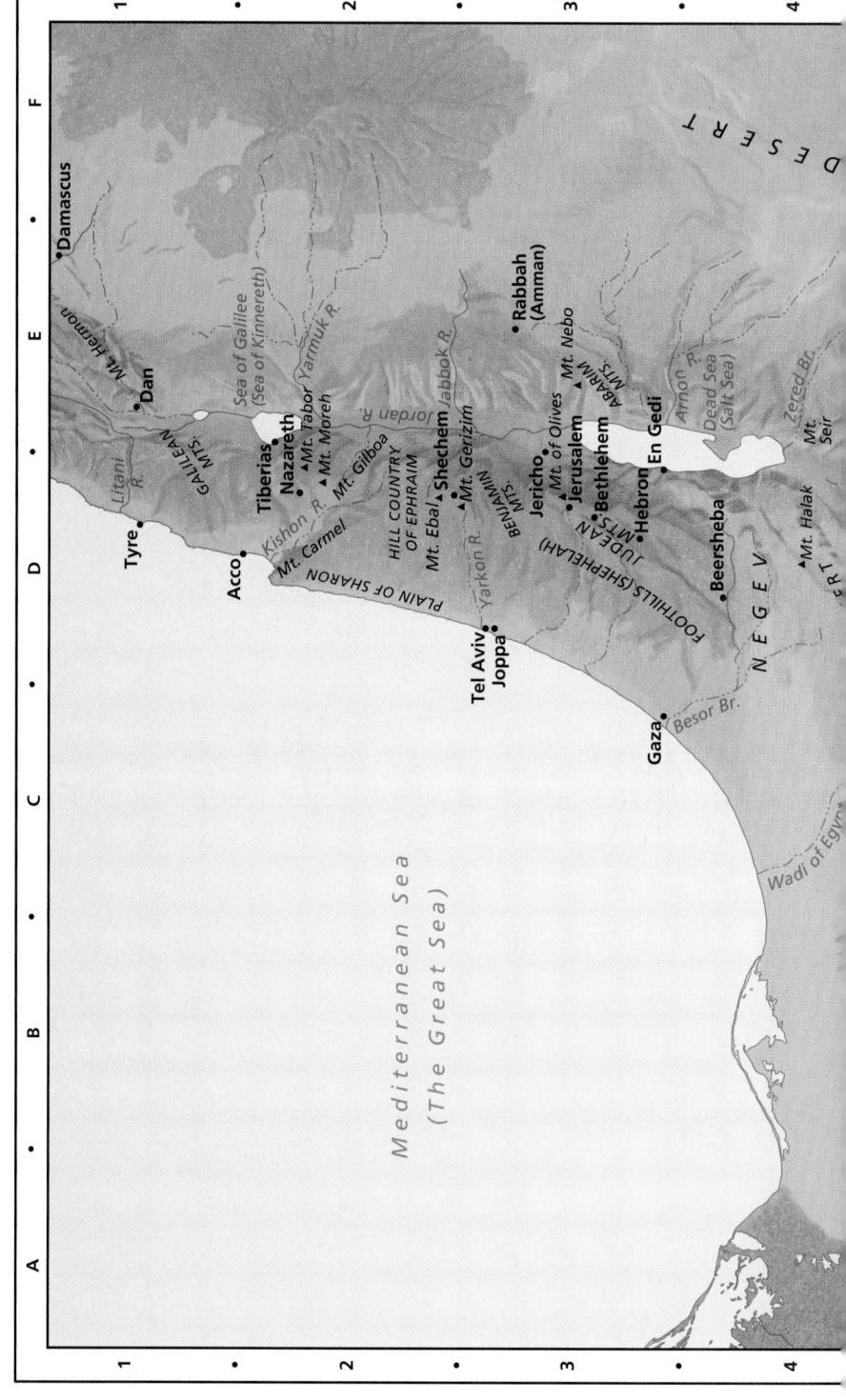

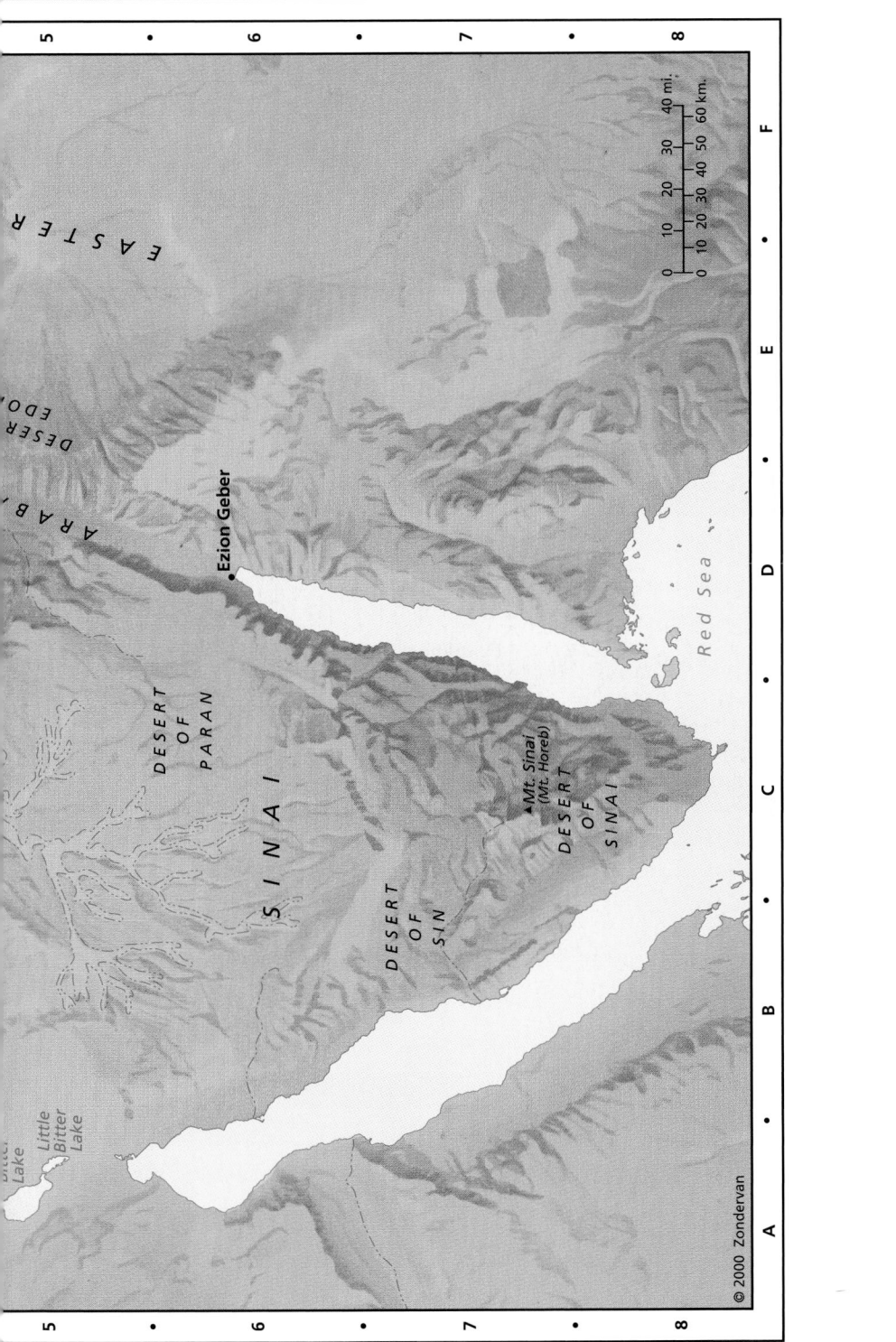

© 2000 Zondervan

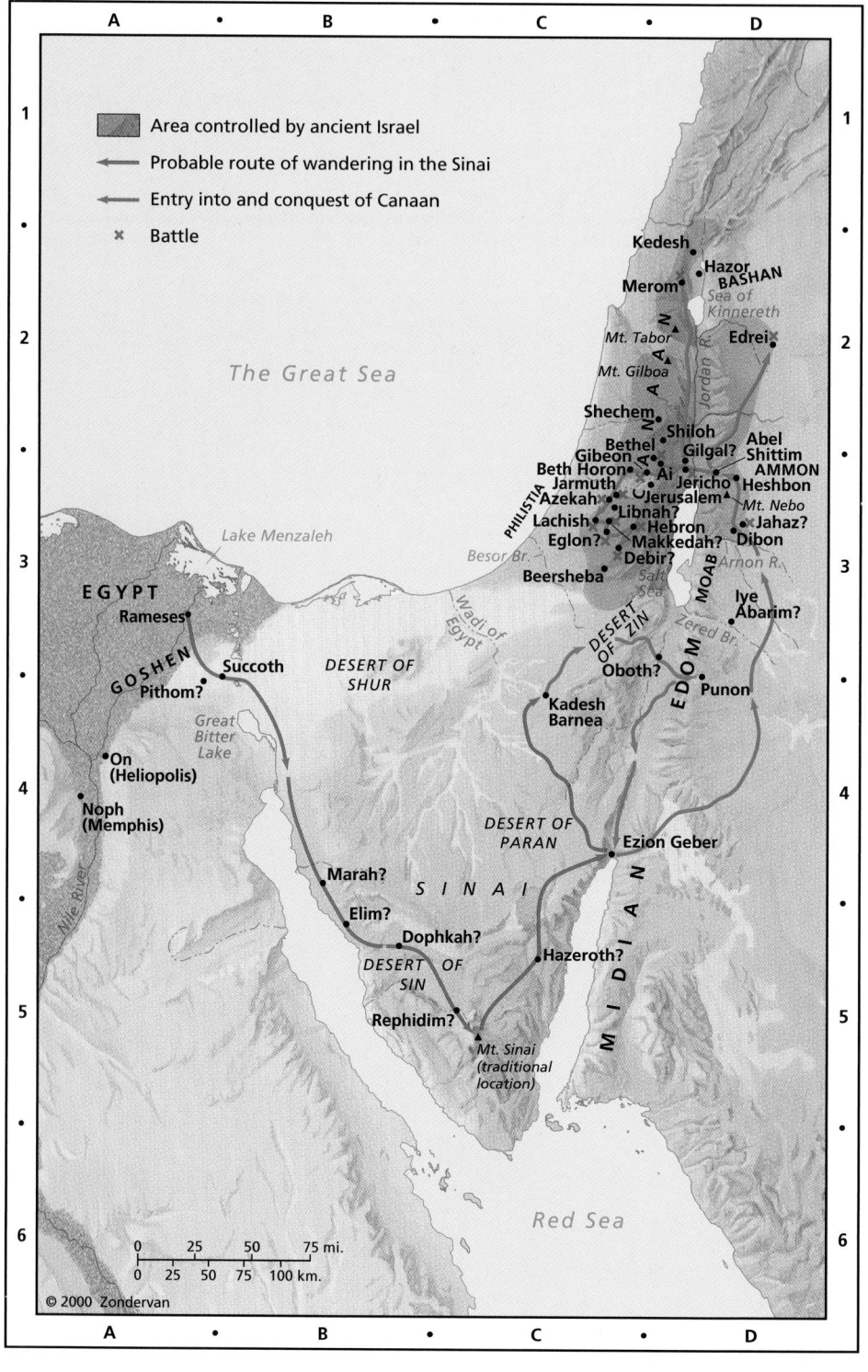

Map 3: **EXODUS AND CONQUEST OF CANAAN**

Area controlled by ancient Israel

Probable route of wandering in the Sinai

Entry into and conquest of Canaan

× Battle

The Great Sea

EGYPT

Rameses

GOSHEN

Pithom?

Succoth

On
(Heliopolis)

Noph
(Memphis)

Lake Menzaleh

DESERT OF
SHUR

Great
Bitter
Lake

Marah?

Elim?

Dophkah?

DESERT OF
SIN

Rephidim?

Mt. Sinai
(traditional
location)

Besor Br.

Wadi of
Egypt

Beersheba

DESERT OF
ZIN

Kadesh
Barnea

DESERT OF
PARAN

SINAI

Hazeroth?

Ezion Geber

MIDIAN

Kedesh

Hazor BASHAN

Merom

Sea of
Kinnereth

Mt. Tabor

Edrei

Mt. Gilboa

Shechem

CANAAN

Bethel

Gibeon

Beth Horon

Jarmuth

Azekah

Lachish

Eglon?

Shiloh

Gilgal?

Ai

Jericho

Jerusalem

Libnah?

Hebron

Makkedah?

Debir?

Abel

Shittim

AMMON

Heshbon

Mt. Nebo

Jahaz?

Dibon

PHILISTIA

Jordan R.

Salt
Sea

MOAB

Arnon R.

Zered Br.

EDOM

Iye
Abarim?

Oboth?

Punon

Red Sea

0   25   50   75 mi.

0 25 50 75 100 km.

© 2000 Zondervan

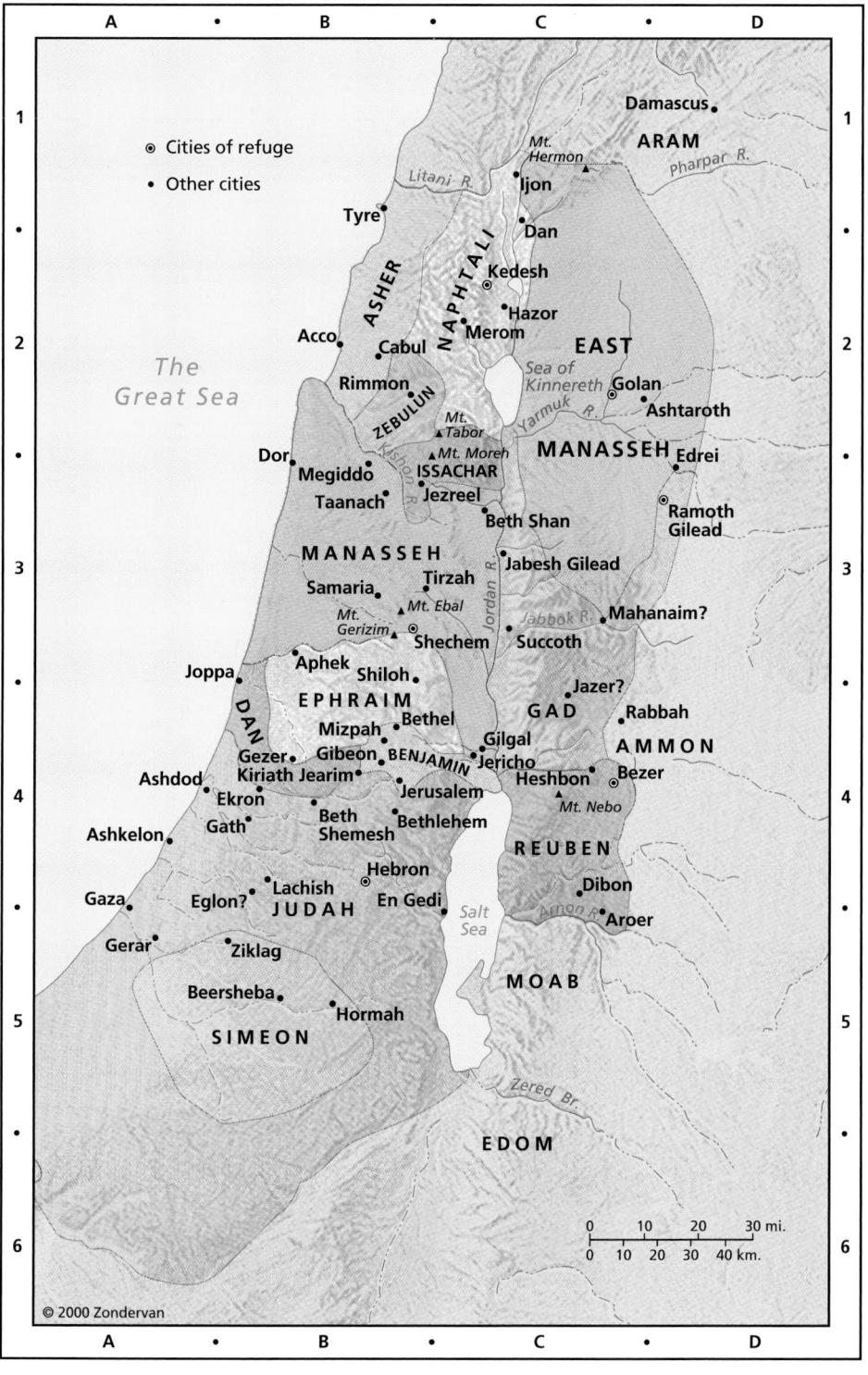

Map 4: LAND OF THE TWELVE TRIBES

A • **B** • **C** • **D**

⊙ Cities of refuge

• Other cities

Damascus

ARAM

Mt. Hermon

Pharpar R.

Litani R.

Ijon

Tyre

Dan

ASHER

NAPHTALI

Kedesh ⊙

Hazor

Acco

Merom

Cabul

EAST

Rimmon

Sea of Kinnereth

Golan ⊙

ZEBULUN

Yarmuk R.

Ashtaroth

Mt. Tabor

MANASSEH

Edrei

Dor

Mt. Moreh

Megiddo

ISSACHAR

Kishon R.

Jezreel

Ramoth Gilead ⊙

Taanach

Beth Shan

MANASSEH

Jabesh Gilead

Jordan R.

Samaria

Tirzah

Mt. Ebal

Mt. Gerizim ⊙

Shechem

Succoth

Jabbok R.

Mahanaim?

Joppa

Aphek

Shiloh

Jazer?

GAD

DAN

EPHRAIM

Bethel

Rabbah

Mizpah

Gilgal

Gezer

Gibeon

BENJAMIN

Jericho

AMMON

Ashdod

Kiriath Jearim

Heshbon

Bezer ⊙

Ekron

Jerusalem

Mt. Nebo

Gath

Beth Shemesh

Bethlehem

Ashkelon

REUBEN

Hebron ⊙

Gaza

Lachish

En Gedi

Dibon

Eglon?

JUDAH

Salt Sea

Aroer

Gerar

Arnon R.

Ziklag

Beersheba

MOAB

Hormah

SIMEON

Zered Br.

EDOM

The Great Sea

0	10	20	30 mi.
0	10	20	30	40 km.

© 2000 Zondervan

A • **B** • **C** • **D**

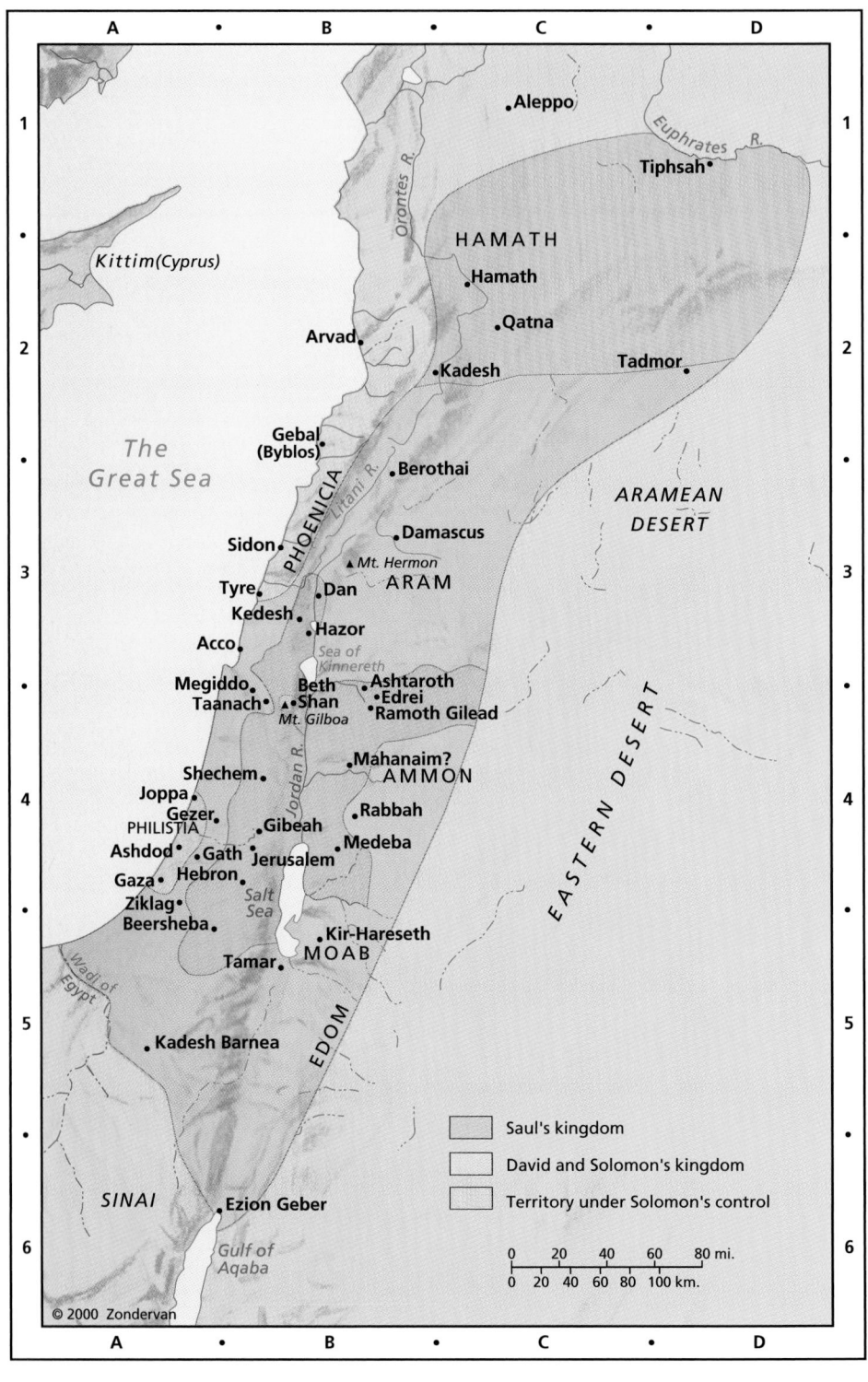

Aleppo

Euphrates R.

Tiphsah

Kittim(Cyprus)

Orontes R.

HAMATH

Hamath

Qatna

Arvad

Tadmor

Kadesh

Gebal
(Byblos)

Berothai

The
Great Sea

PHOENICIA

Litani R.

ARAMEAN
DESERT

Damascus

Sidon

▲ Mt. Hermon

ARAM

Tyre

Dan

Kedesh

Acco

Hazor

Sea of
Kinnereth

Megiddo

Beth

Ashtaroth

Taanach

▲ Shan

Edrei

Mt. Gilboa

Ramoth Gilead

Jordan R.

Mahanaim?

Shechem

AMMON

Joppa

Gezer

Rabbah

PHILISTIA

Gibeah

Ashdod

Gath

Medeba

Jerusalem

Gaza

Hebron

Ziklag

Salt
Sea

Beersheba

EASTERN DESERT

Kir-Hareseth

Tamar

MOAB

Wadi of
Egypt

EDOM

Kadesh Barnea

Saul's kingdom

David and Solomon's kingdom

Territory under Solomon's control

SINAI

Ezion Geber

0   20   40   60   80 mi.

0 20 40 60 80 100 km.

Gulf of
Aqaba

© 2000 Zondervan

A • B • C • D

1

0   10   20   30 mi.

0 10 20 30 40 km.

Beirut

PHOENICIA

Abana R.

Sidon

•Damascus

Litani R.

▲ Mt. Hermon

Pharpar R.

Tyre

•Dan

ARAM

2

Kedesh

•Hazor

J. Jarmuk ▲

Acco

Sea of
Kinnereth

Mt. Carmel ▲

Kishon R.

Mt.
Tabor ▲

•Ashtaroth

Yarmuk R.

The Great
Sea

Megiddo

Mt. Moreh ▲

•Edrei

Taanach

Beth Shan

•Ramoth Gilead

3

Ibleam

Mt.
Gilboa ▲

•Jabesh Gilead?

Tirzah

Jordan R.

Samaria

Succoth? Penuel? •Mahanaim?

Mt. Ebal ▲

Shechem

Jabbok R.

Mt. Gerizim ▲

Yarkon R.

Joppa

•Aphek

Shiloh

ISRAEL

•Rabbah (Amman)

Bethel

AMMON

Gezer

Jericho

4

Ashdod

Aijalon

Jerusalem

Mt. Nebo ▲

•Heshbon

Gath

Bethlehem

•Medeba

Ashkelon

Mareshah

Gaza

•Hebron

•Dibon

Gerar

JUDAH

Salt
Sea

Arnon R.

Raphia

Beersheba

MOAB

5

PHILISTIA

•Kir Hareseth

Zered Br.

WILDERNESS

W. el-Arish

Region
periodically
contested
by Judah
and Edom

•Bozrah

EDOM

Kadesh
Barnea

6

WILDERNESS

© 2000 Zondervan

A • B • C • D

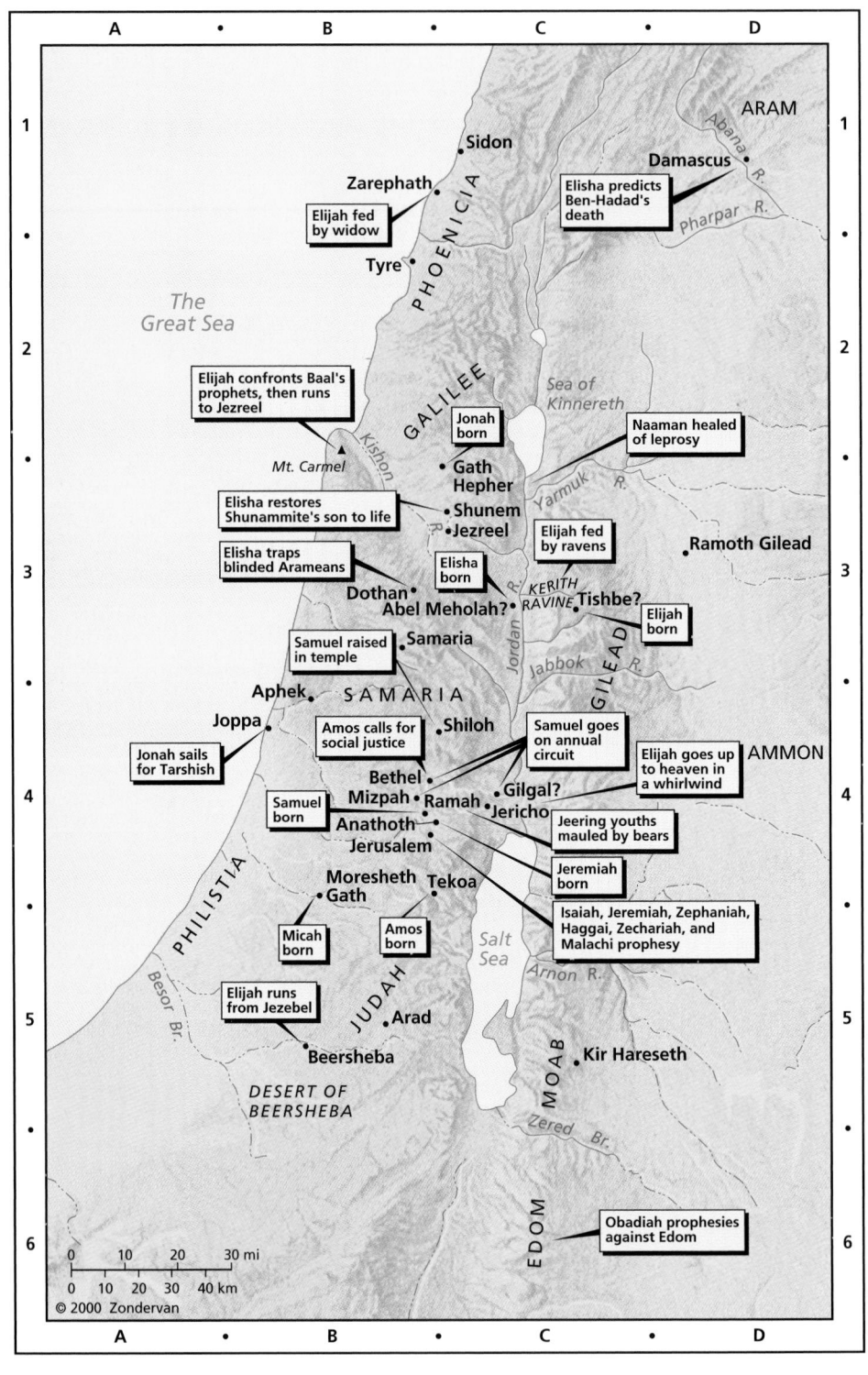

ARAM

Sidon

Zarephath

Elijah fed by widow

Elisha predicts Ben-Hadad's death

Damascus

Abana R.

Pharpar R.

Tyre

PHOENICIA

The Great Sea

Elijah confronts Baal's prophets, then runs to Jezreel

GALILEE

Kishon

Mt. Carmel

Sea of Kinnereth

Jonah born

Naaman healed of leprosy

Gath Hepher

Yarmuk R.

Elisha restores Shunammite's son to life

Shunem

Jezreel

Elijah fed by ravens

Ramoth Gilead

Elisha traps blinded Arameans

Elisha born

Dothan

Abel Meholah?

KERITH RAVINE

Tishbe?

Elijah born

Jordan R.

Jabbok R.

GILEAD

Samuel raised in temple

Samaria

Aphek

SAMARIA

Joppa

Amos calls for social justice

Shiloh

Samuel goes on annual circuit

Elijah goes up to heaven in a whirlwind

AMMON

Jonah sails for Tarshish

Bethel

Mizpah

Ramah

Gilgal?

Jericho

Samuel born

Anathoth

Jerusalem

Jeering youths mauled by bears

Jeremiah born

Moresheth Gath

Tekoa

Isaiah, Jeremiah, Zephaniah, Haggai, Zechariah, and Malachi prophesy

Micah born

Amos born

Salt Sea

Arnon R.

PHILISTIA

Elijah runs from Jezebel

Arad

JUDAH

MOAB

Kir Hareseth

Beersheba

DESERT OF BEERSHEBA

Besor Br.

Zered Br.

EDOM

Obadiah prophesies against Edom

| 0 | 10 | 20 | 30 mi |
| 0 | 10 | 20 | 30 | 40 km |

© 2000 Zondervan

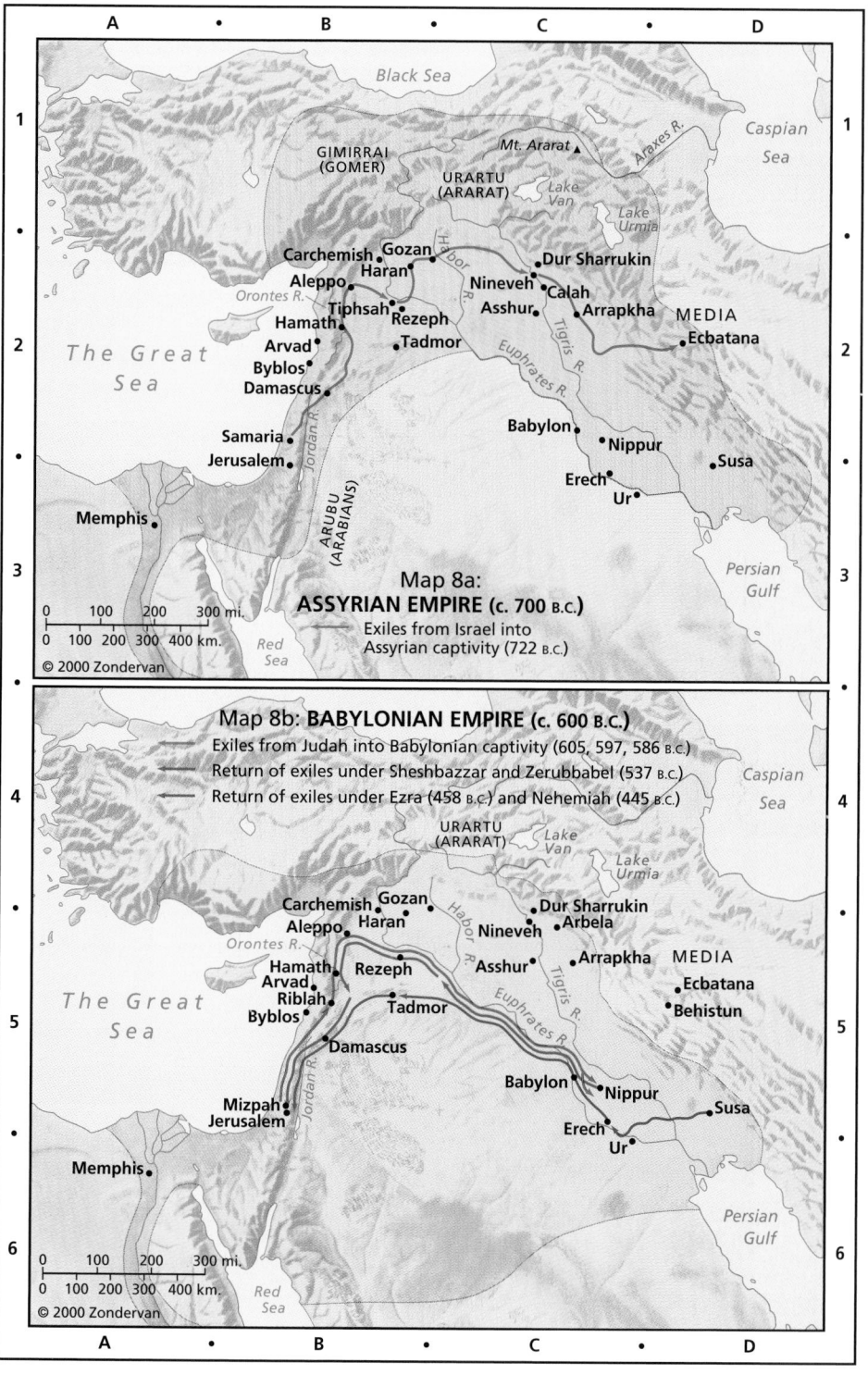

Map 8a:
ASSYRIAN EMPIRE (c. 700 B.C.)
Exiles from Israel into
Assyrian captivity (722 B.C.)

© 2000 Zondervan

Map 8b: **BABYLONIAN EMPIRE (c. 600 B.C.)**
Exiles from Judah into Babylonian captivity (605, 597, 586 B.C.)
Return of exiles under Sheshbazzar and Zerubbabel (537 B.C.)
Return of exiles under Ezra (458 B.C.) and Nehemiah (445 B.C.)

© 2000 Zondervan

Map 9: HOLY LAND IN THE TIME OF JESUS

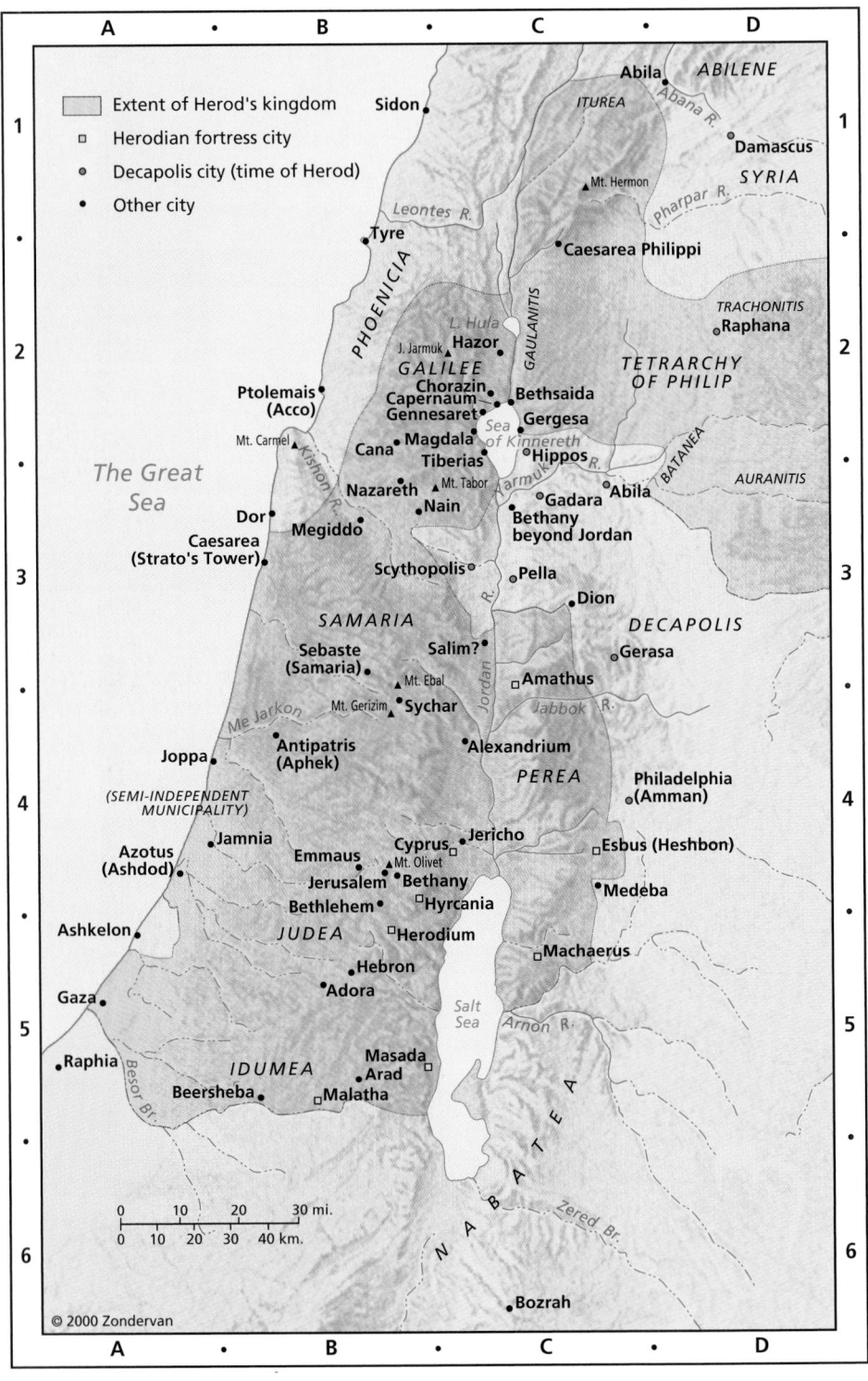

Extent of Herod's kingdom
□ Herodian fortress city
◉ Decapolis city (time of Herod)
• Other city

ABILENE
Abila
ITUREA
Sidon
Damascus
SYRIA
Mt. Hermon
Leontes R.
Pharpar R.
Tyre
Caesarea Philippi
PHOENICIA
TRACHONITIS
Raphana
L. Hula
GAULANITIS
J. Jarmuk Hazor
TETRARCHY
OF PHILIP
GALILEE
Chorazin
Ptolemais
(Acco)
Capernaum Bethsaida
Gennesaret Gergesa
Mt. Carmel
Kishon R.
Cana Magdala
Sea of Kinnereth
Hippos
BATANEA
Tiberias
AURANITIS
The Great
Sea
Nazareth Mt. Tabor
Gadara Abila
Dor
Nain
Bethany
beyond Jordan
Caesarea
(Strato's Tower)
Megiddo
Scythopolis
Pella
Dion
SAMARIA
DECAPOLIS
Sebaste
(Samaria)
Salim?
Gerasa
Mt. Ebal
Amathus
Me Jarkon
Mt. Gerizim Sychar
Jabbok R.
Antipatris
(Aphek)
Alexandrium
Joppa
PEREA
Philadelphia
(Amman)
(SEMI-INDEPENDENT
MUNICIPALITY)
Jamnia
Cyprus Jericho
Esbus (Heshbon)
Azotus
(Ashdod)
Emmaus
Mt. Olivet
Jerusalem Bethany
Medeba
Bethlehem Hyrcania
Ashkelon
JUDEA
Herodium
Machaerus
Hebron
Gaza
Adora
Salt
Sea
Arnon R.
Raphia
Masada
IDUMEA
Arad
Beersheba
Malatha
Besor Br.
N
A
B
A
T
E
A
Zered Br.
0   10   20   30 mi.
0   10   20   30   40 km.
Bozrah

© 2000 Zondervan

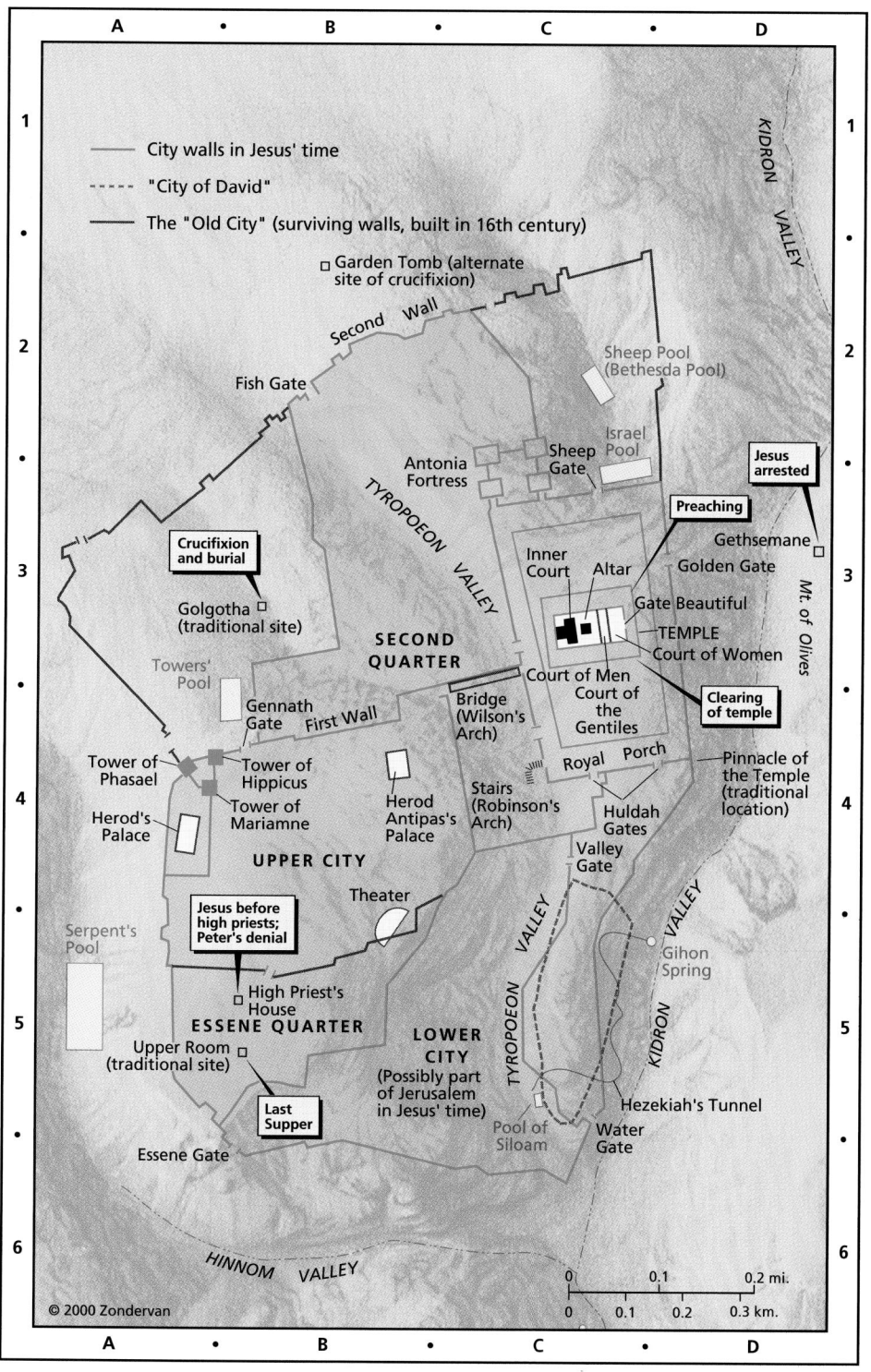

- City walls in Jesus' time
- - - - "City of David"
— The "Old City" (surviving walls, built in 16th century)

KIDRON VALLEY

☐ Garden Tomb (alternate site of crucifixion)

Second Wall

Fish Gate

Sheep Pool (Bethesda Pool)

Israel Pool

Sheep Gate

Antonia Fortress

TYROPOEON VALLEY

Jesus arrested

Gethsemane ☐

Preaching

Inner Court   Altar   Golden Gate

Crucifixion and burial

Golgotha ☐ (traditional site)

Gate Beautiful

TEMPLE
Court of Women

Mt. of Olives

Towers' Pool

SECOND QUARTER

Gennath Gate   First Wall

Bridge (Wilson's Arch)

Court of Men   Court of the Gentiles

Clearing of temple

Pinnacle of the Temple (traditional location)

Tower of Phasael
Tower of Hippicus
Tower of Mariamne

Herod's Palace

Herod Antipas's Palace

Stairs (Robinson's Arch)

Royal   Porch

Huldah Gates

Valley Gate

UPPER CITY

Theater

Jesus before high priests; Peter's denial

Serpent's Pool

TYROPOEON VALLEY

KIDRON VALLEY

Gihon Spring

☐ High Priest's House

ESSENE QUARTER

Upper Room ☐ (traditional site)

LOWER CITY
(Possibly part of Jerusalem in Jesus' time)

Hezekiah's Tunnel

Last Supper

Pool of Siloam

Water Gate

Essene Gate

HINNOM VALLEY

0   0.1   0.2 mi.

0   0.1   0.2   0.3 km.

© 2000 Zondervan

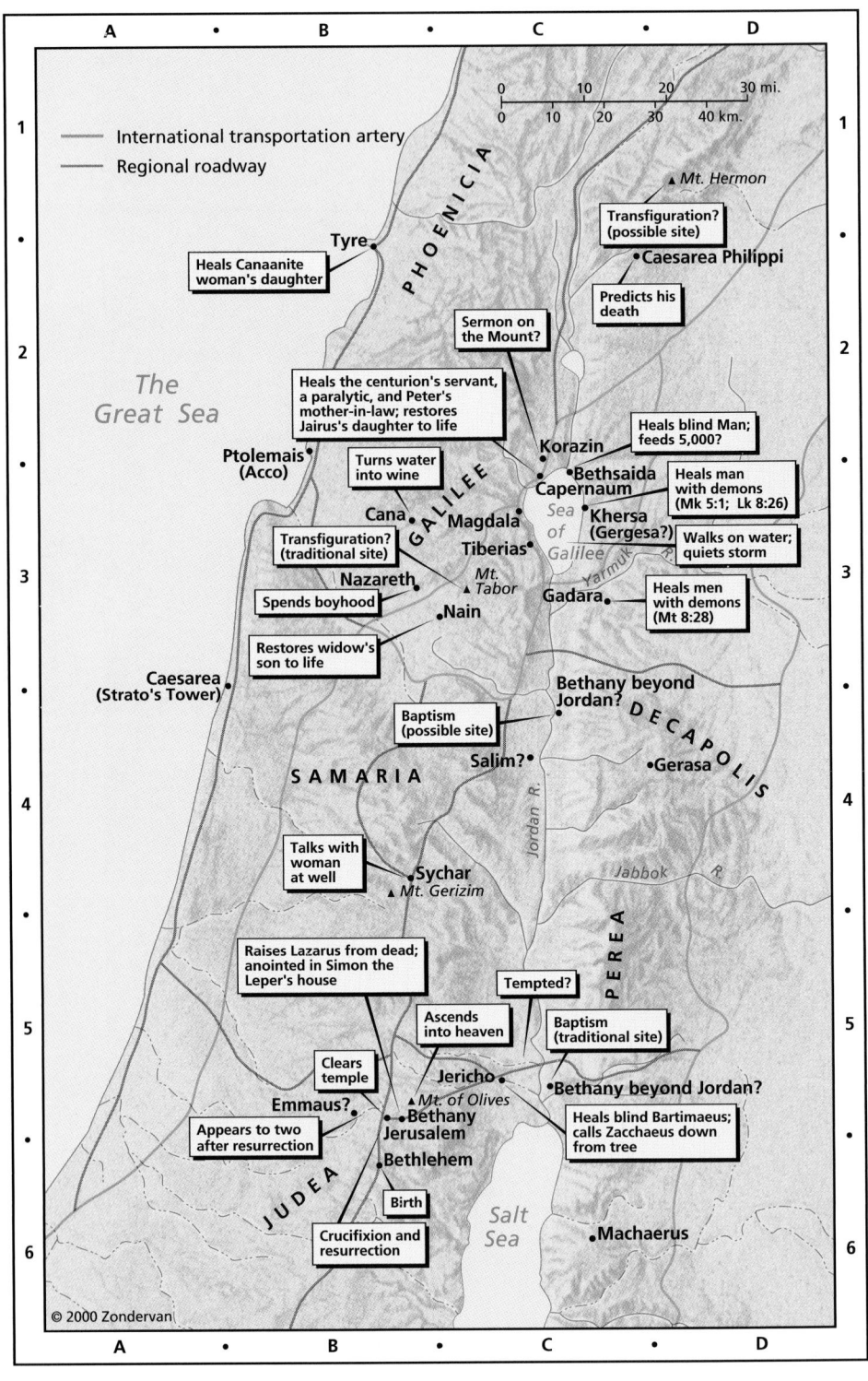

International transportation artery
Regional roadway

0 — 10 — 20 — 30 mi.
0 — 10 — 20 — 30 — 40 km.

PHOENICIA

▲ Mt. Hermon

Transfiguration?
(possible site)

• Caesarea Philippi

Tyre •

Heals Canaanite
woman's daughter

Predicts his
death

Sermon on
the Mount?

The
Great Sea

Heals the centurion's servant,
a paralytic, and Peter's
mother-in-law; restores
Jairus's daughter to life

GALILEE

• Korazin

Heals blind Man;
feeds 5,000?

Ptolemais •
(Acco)

Turns water
into wine

• Bethsaida
Capernaum

Heals man
with demons
(Mk 5:1; Lk 8:26)

Cana •

Magdala

Sea
of
Galilee

• Khersa
(Gergesa?)

Transfiguration?
(traditional site)

Tiberias •

Walks on water;
quiets storm

Nazareth

Mt.
▲ Tabor

Yarmuk

Gadara •

Heals men
with demons
(Mt 8:28)

Spends boyhood

• Nain

Restores widow's
son to life

Caesarea •
(Strato's Tower)

Bethany beyond
Jordan?

DECAPOLIS

Baptism
(possible site)

Salim? •

• Gerasa

SAMARIA

Jordan R.

Talks with
woman
at well

• Sychar
▲ Mt. Gerizim

Jabbok R.

PEREA

Raises Lazarus from dead;
anointed in Simon the
Leper's house

Tempted?

Ascends
into heaven

Baptism
(traditional site)

Clears
temple

Jericho •

• Bethany beyond Jordan?

Emmaus? •

▲ Mt. of Olives
• Bethany

Heals blind Bartimaeus;
calls Zacchaeus down
from tree

Appears to two
after resurrection

Jerusalem

• Bethlehem

JUDEA

Birth

Salt
Sea

Crucifixion and
resurrection

• Machaerus

© 2000 Zondervan

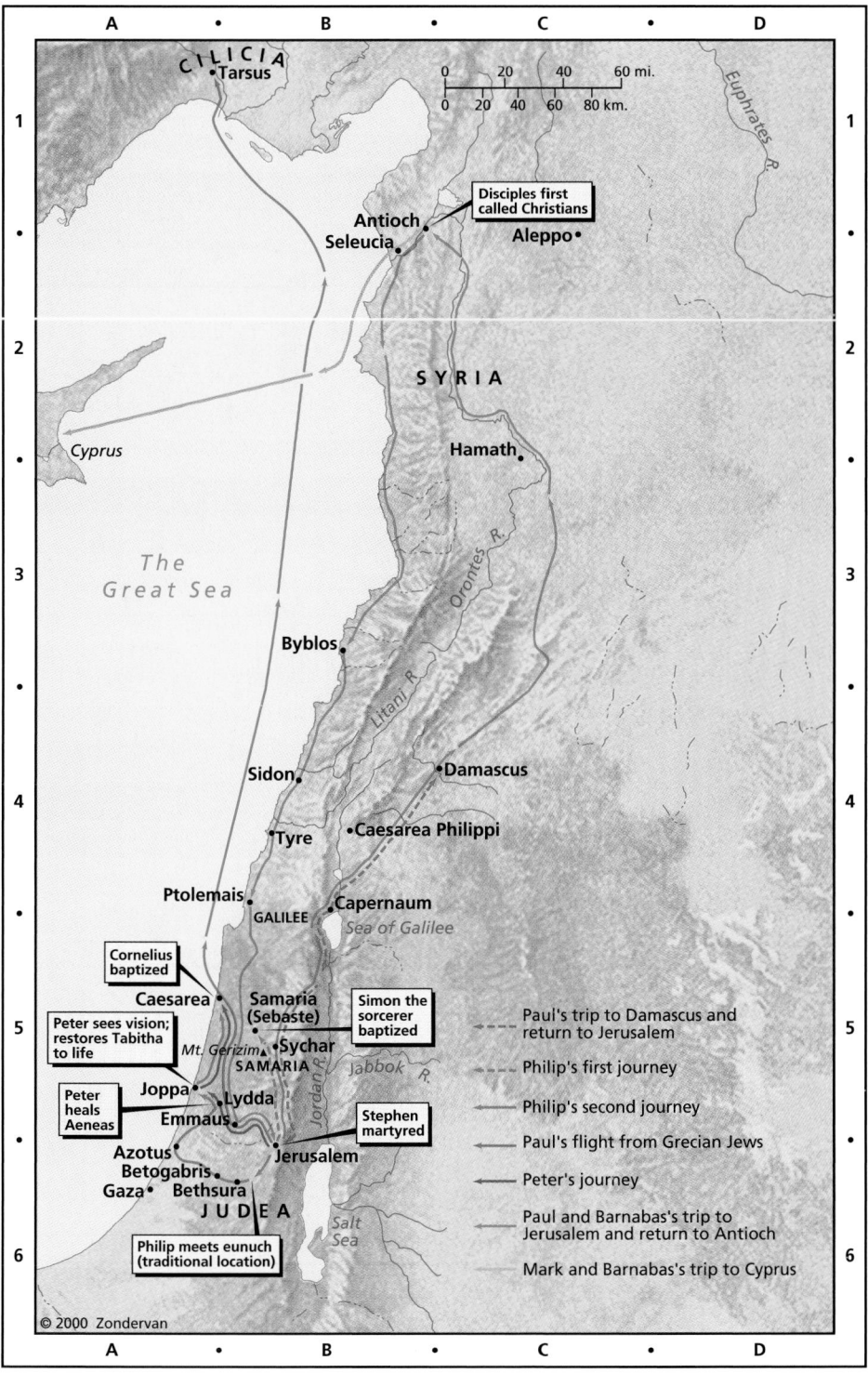

A • B • C • D

CILICIA
•Tarsus

0   20   40   60 mi.
0   20   40   60   80 km.

Euphrates R.

1

Disciples first
called Christians

Antioch
Seleucia.   Aleppo•

•

S Y R I A

2

Cyprus

Hamath•

•

The
Great Sea

3

Orontes R.

Byblos•

•

Litani R.

Sidon.   •Damascus

4

•Tyre   •Caesarea Philippi

Ptolemais.
          GALILEE   •Capernaum
                    Sea of Galilee   •

Cornelius
baptized

Caesarea •   **Samaria**   Simon the
                    (Sebaste)   sorcerer
Peter sees vision;   baptized
restores Tabitha   *Mt. Gerizim*▲•**Sychar**
to life   **SAMARIA**   *Jabbok R.*   Paul's trip to Damascus and
                                                              return to Jerusalem
Peter   **Joppa**•   Philip's first journey
heals   •**Lydda**
Aeneas   **Emmaus.**   **Stephen**   Philip's second journey
                              martyred
Azotus•   •**Jerusalem**   Paul's flight from Grecian Jews
Betogabris.
Gaza• **Bethsura**   Peter's journey
          J U D E A   *Salt*
                              Sea   Paul and Barnabas's trip to
Philip meets eunuch   Jerusalem and return to Antioch
(traditional location)   Mark and Barnabas's trip to Cyprus

6

© 2000 Zondervan

A • B • C • D

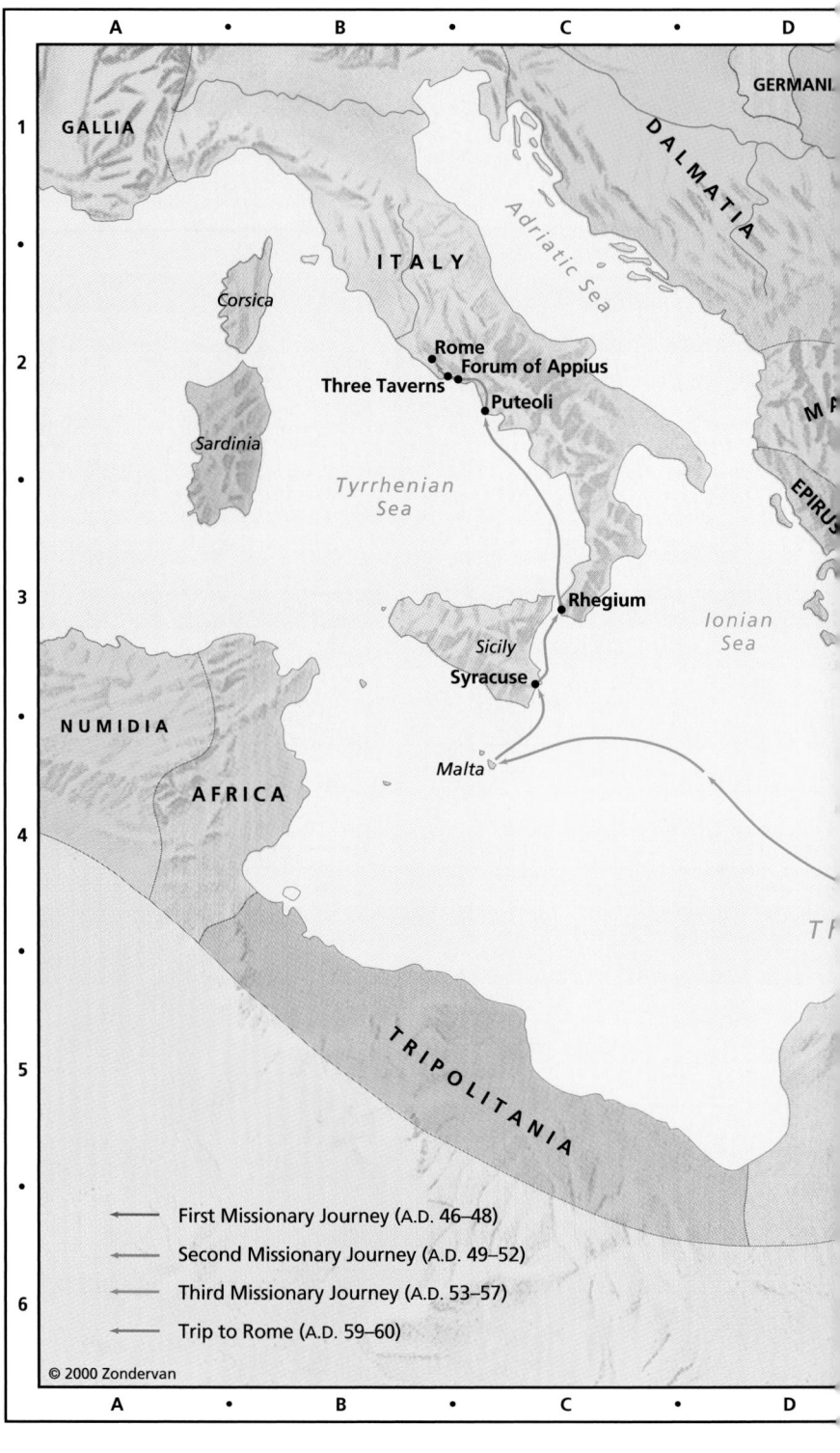

GERMANI

GALLIA

DALMATIA

ITALY

Adriatic Sea

Corsica

Rome
Forum of Appius
Three Taverns
Puteoli

EPIRUS

Sardinia

Tyrrhenian Sea

Rhegium

Ionian Sea

Sicily

Syracuse

NUMIDIA

AFRICA

Malta

TH

TRIPOLITANIA

⟵ First Missionary Journey (A.D. 46–48)

⟵ Second Missionary Journey (A.D. 49–52)

⟵ Third Missionary Journey (A.D. 53–57)

⟵ Trip to Rome (A.D. 59–60)

© 2000 Zondervan

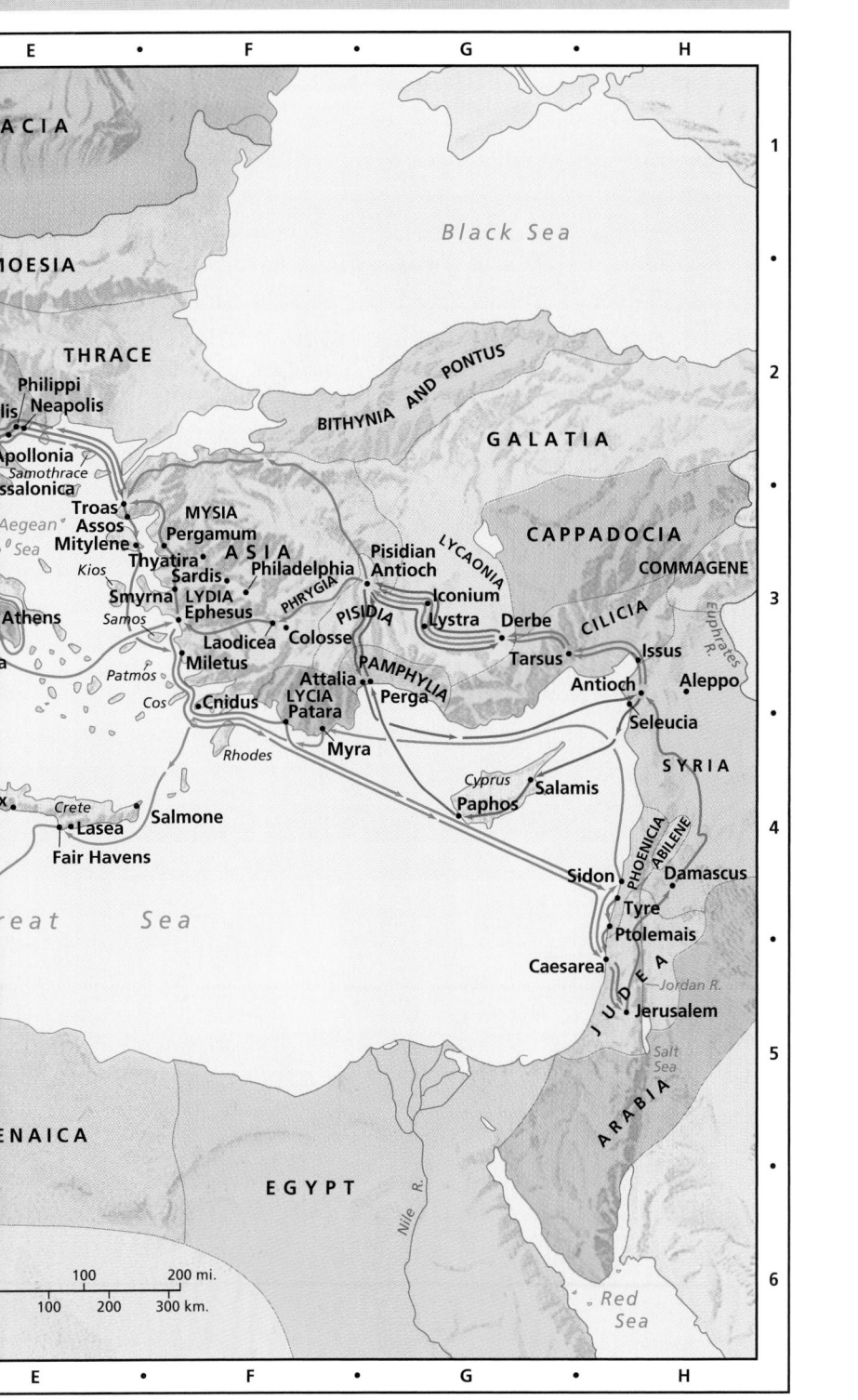

E • F • G • H

1

Black Sea

MOESIA

THRACE

2

Philippi
Neapolis
olis
Apollonia   Samothrace
ssalonica

BITHYNIA AND PONTUS

GALATIA

CAPPADOCIA

COMMAGENE

Troas   MYSIA
Assos   Pergamum
Aegean   Mitylene
Sea   Kios   Thyatira   ASIA   Philadelphia   Pisidian
Sardis   PHRYGIA   Antioch
Smyrna   LYDIA   Iconium   LYCAONIA
Athens   Samos   Ephesus   PISIDIA   Lystra   Derbe   CILICIA
Laodicea   Colosse   Tarsus   Issus
Miletus   PAMPHYLIA   Antioch   Aleppo
a   Patmos   Attalia   Seleucia
Cos   Cnidus   LYCIA   Perga
Patara   SYRIA
Rhodes   Myra
Cyprus   Salamis
Paphos

Euphrates R.

3

x   Crete   Salmone
Lasea
Fair Havens

reat   Sea

Sidon   PHOENICIA   Damascus
ABILENE
Tyre
Ptolemais
Caesarea   Jordan R.
JUDEA   Jerusalem

Salt
Sea

4

ENAICA

EGYPT

Nile R.

ARABIA

5

100   200 mi.
100   200   300 km.

Red
Sea

6

E • F • G • H

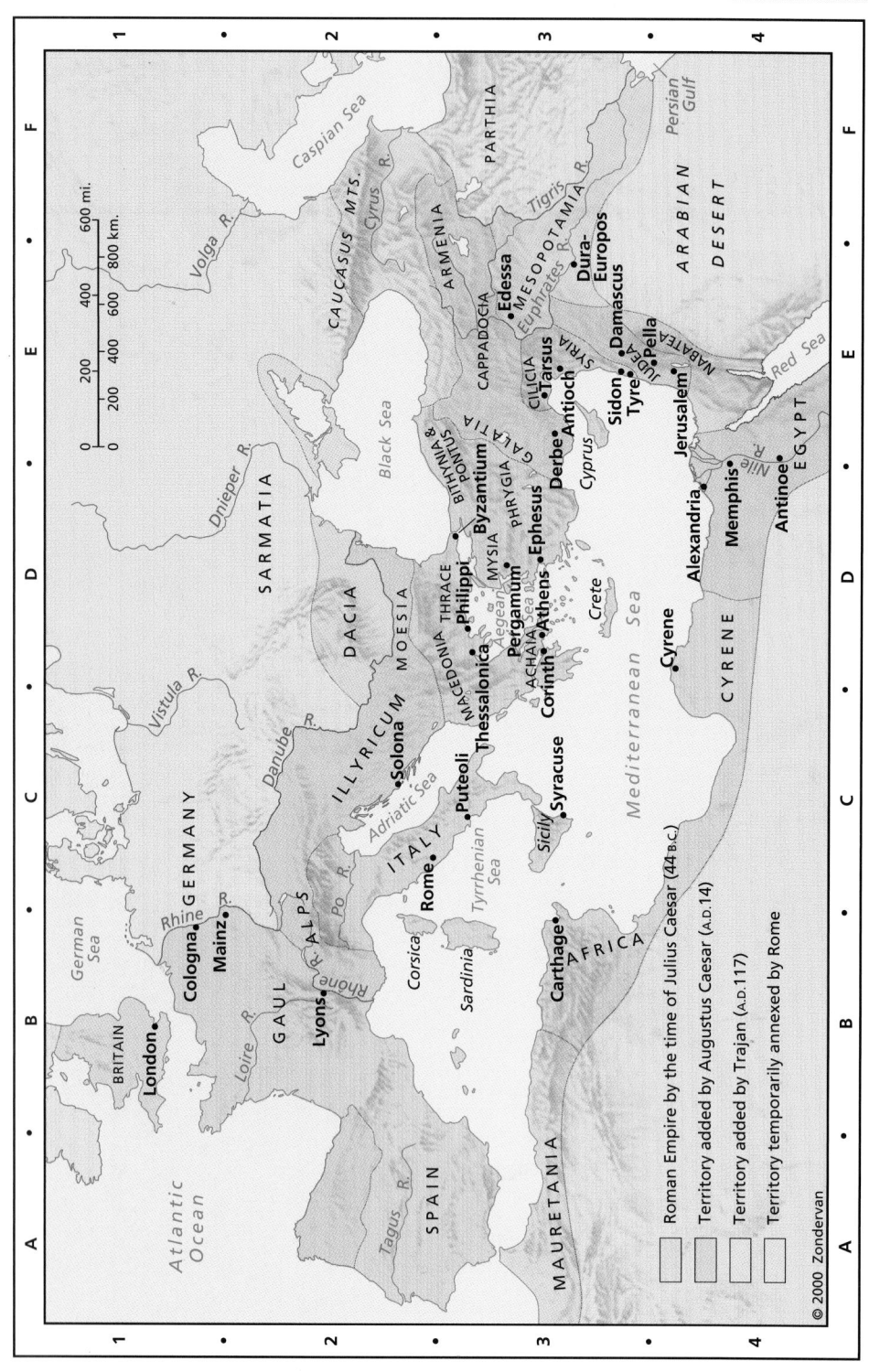

Roman Empire by the time of Julius Caesar (44 B.C.)

Territory added by Augustus Caesar (A.D.14)

Territory added by Trajan (A.D.117)

Territory temporarily annexed by Rome

© 2000 Zondervan

BRITAIN
London

GERMANY
Cologna
Mainz

GAUL
Lyons

Rhine R.
Rhone R.
Loire R.

ALPS
Po R.

SPAIN
Tagus R.

Atlantic
Ocean

German
Sea

Corsica

Sardinia

MAURETANIA

AFRICA
Carthage

ITALY
Rome
Puteoli

Tyrrhenian
Sea

Sicily
Syracuse

ILLYRICUM
Solona

Adriatic Sea

Danube R.

Vistula R.

SARMATIA

DACIA

MOESIA

THRACE
MACEDONIA
Philippi
Thessalonica

Byzantium
BITHYNIA &
PONTUS

PHRYGIA
MYSIA
Pergamum
Ephesus

ACHAIA
Corinth
Athens

Aegean
Sea

Crete

GALATIA

Mediterranean Sea

Cyrene
CYRENE

Dnieper R.

Black Sea

Caspian Sea

Volga R.

CAUCASUS MTS.

Cyrus

ARMENIA

PARTHIA

CAPPADOCIA

CILICIA
Tarsus
Derbe

Antioch
SYRIA

Cyprus

Edessa
MESOPOTAMIA
Euphrates R.

Tigris R.

Dura-
Europos
Damascus
Sidon
Tyre
Pella
JUDEA
Jerusalem
NABATEA

Alexandria
Memphis
Antinoe

EGYPT
Nile R.

ARABIAN
DESERT

Persian
Gulf

Red Sea

600 mi.
800 km.

0 200 400 600
0 200 400 600